Fodor's 28th Edition

USA

he Guide
or All Budgets

Completely
Updated

Where to Stay,
at, and Explore

On and Off
e Beaten Path

When to Go,
What to Pack

Maps, Travel Tips,
nd Web Sites

dor's Travel Publications • New York, Toronto, London, Sydney, Auckland
www.fodors.com

Fodor's USA

EDITOR: Paul Eisenberg

Editorial Contributors: Nuha Ansari, Carissa Bluestone, Mary Bet Bohman, Linda Cabasin, Melisse Gelula, Satu Hummasti, Constanc Jones, Shannon Kelly, Laura Kidder, Melissa Klurman, Christin Knight, Matthew Lombardi, Diane Mehta, Emmanuelle Morgen, Joh Rambow, Douglas Stallings, Mark Sullivan, Christine Swiac, Willian Travis

Maps: David Lindroth, *cartographer*; Rebecca Baer and Bob Blake, *ma editors*

Design: Fabrizio La Rocca, *creative director*; Guido Caroti, *art direc tor*; Jolie Novak, *senior picture editor*; Melanie Marin, *photo edito*

Cover Design: Pentagram

Production/Manufacturing: Robert B. Shields

Cover Photograph: Richard Nowitz

Copyright

Twenty-Eighth Edition

ISBN 1–4000–1088–8

ISSN 1043–0253

Important Tip

Although all prices, opening times, and other details in this book a based on information supplied to us at press time, changes occur the time in the travel world, and Fodor's cannot accept responsibil for facts that become outdated or for inadvertent errors or omissio So **always confirm information when it matters,** especially if you're ma ing a detour to visit a specific place.

Special Sales

Fodor's Travel Publications are available at special discounts for b purchases for sales promotions or premiums. Special editions, incl ing personalized covers, excerpts of existing guides, and corporate i prints, can be created in large quantities for special needs. For m information, contact your local bookseller or write to Special Mark Fodor's Travel Publications, 1745 Broadway, New York, NY 100 Inquiries from Canada should be directed to your local Canad bookseller or sent to Random House of Canada, Ltd., Marketing I partment, 2775 Matheson Boulevard East, Mississauga, Ontario L 4P7. Inquiries from the United Kingdom should be sent to Fodor's Tra Publications, 20 Vauxhall Bridge Road, London SW1V 2SA, Engla

PRINTED IN THE UNITED STATES OF AMERICA

10 9 8 7 6 5 4 3 2 1

CONTENTS

🌐 *Italic entries are maps.*

ON THE ROAD WITH FODOR'S

A **TRIP TAKES YOU OUT OF YOURSELF.** Concerns of life at home completely disappear, driven away by nore immediate thoughts—about, say, vhat marvels will beguile the next day, or vhere you'll have dinner. That's where 'odor's comes in. We make sure that you :now all your options, so that you don't niss something that's around the next end just because you didn't know it was here. Mindful that the best memories of 'our trip might have nothing to do with vhat you came to a particular state to see, ve guide you to sights large and small all ver the USA. With Fodor's at your side, erendipitous discoveries are never far way, whether you're visiting the major ities or the small towns covered in this ;uide.

łow to Use This Book

Jp front is Smart Travel Tips A to Z, aranged alphabetically by topic and loaded vith tips, Web sites, and contact infor-nation. The region-by-region chapter elps you frame your trip; subsequent hapters in Fodor's USA are arranged al-habetically by state. Each chapter beins with exploring information, and the ssentials at the end of every section or hapter include additional resources.

cons and Symbols

★ Our special recommendations
✕ Restaurant
▣ Lodging establishment
✕▣ Lodging establishment whose restaurant warrants a special trip
⛺ Campgrounds
Good for kids (rubber duck)
☞ Sends you to another section of the guide for more information
✉ Address
☎ Telephone number
⏲ Opening and closing times
🎟 Admission prices (those we give apply to adults; substantially reduced fees are almost always available for children, students, and senior citizens)

For hotels, you can assume that all rooms have private baths, phones, TVs, and air-conditioning unless otherwise noted and that all hotels operate on the European Plan (with no meals) if we don't specify another meal plan. We always list a property's facilities but not whether you'll be charged extra to use them, so when pricing accommodations, do ask what's included. For restaurants, it's always a good idea to book ahead; we mention reservations only when they're essential or are not accepted. All restaurants we list are open daily for lunch and dinner unless stated otherwise; dress is mentioned only when men are required to wear a jacket or a jacket and tie.

Don't Forget to Write

Your experiences—positive and negative—matter to us. If we have missed or misstated something, we want to hear about it. We follow up on all suggestions. Contact the USA editor at editors@fodors.com or c/o Fodor's at 1745 Broadway, New York, New York 10019. And have a fabulous trip!

Karen Cure

Karen Cure
Editorial Director

The United States

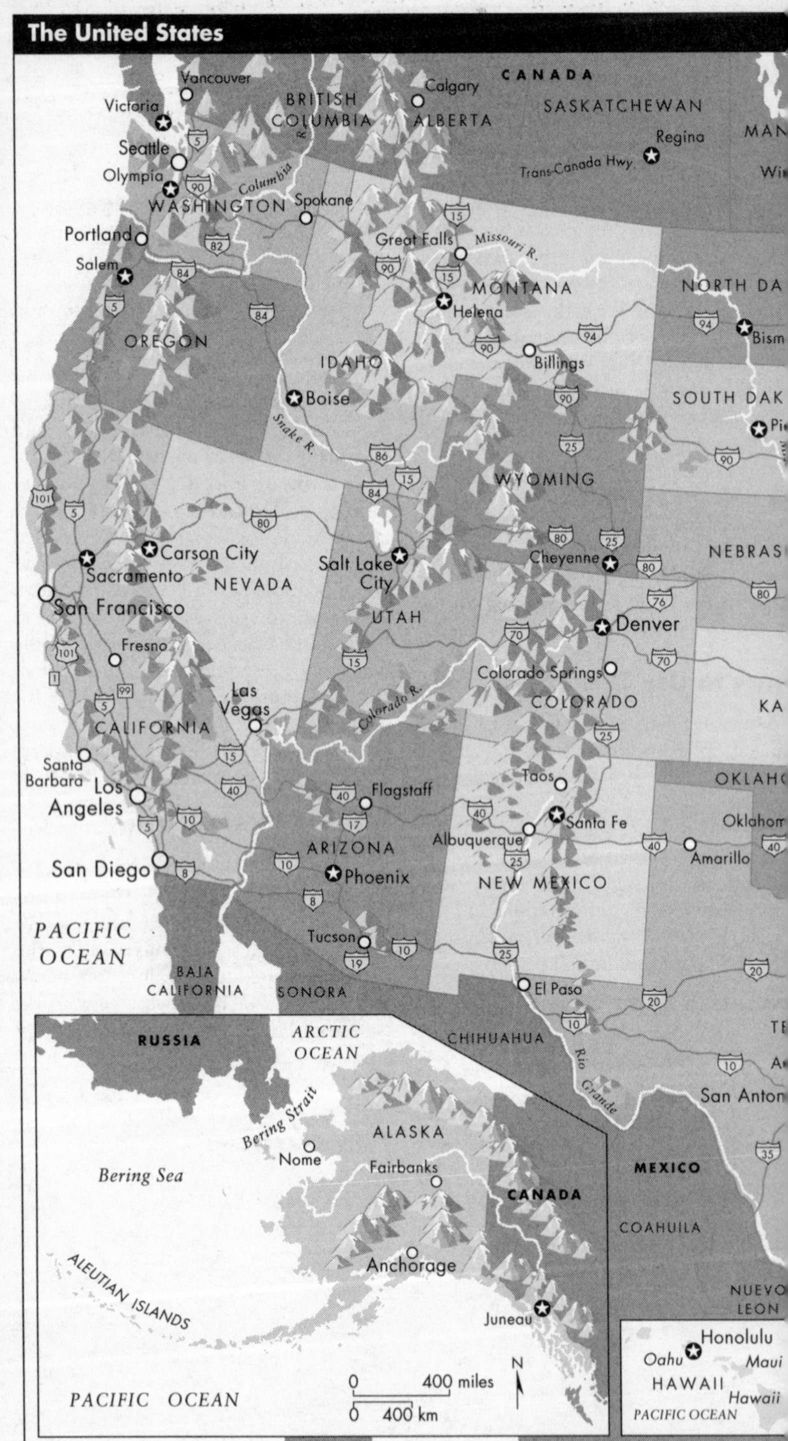

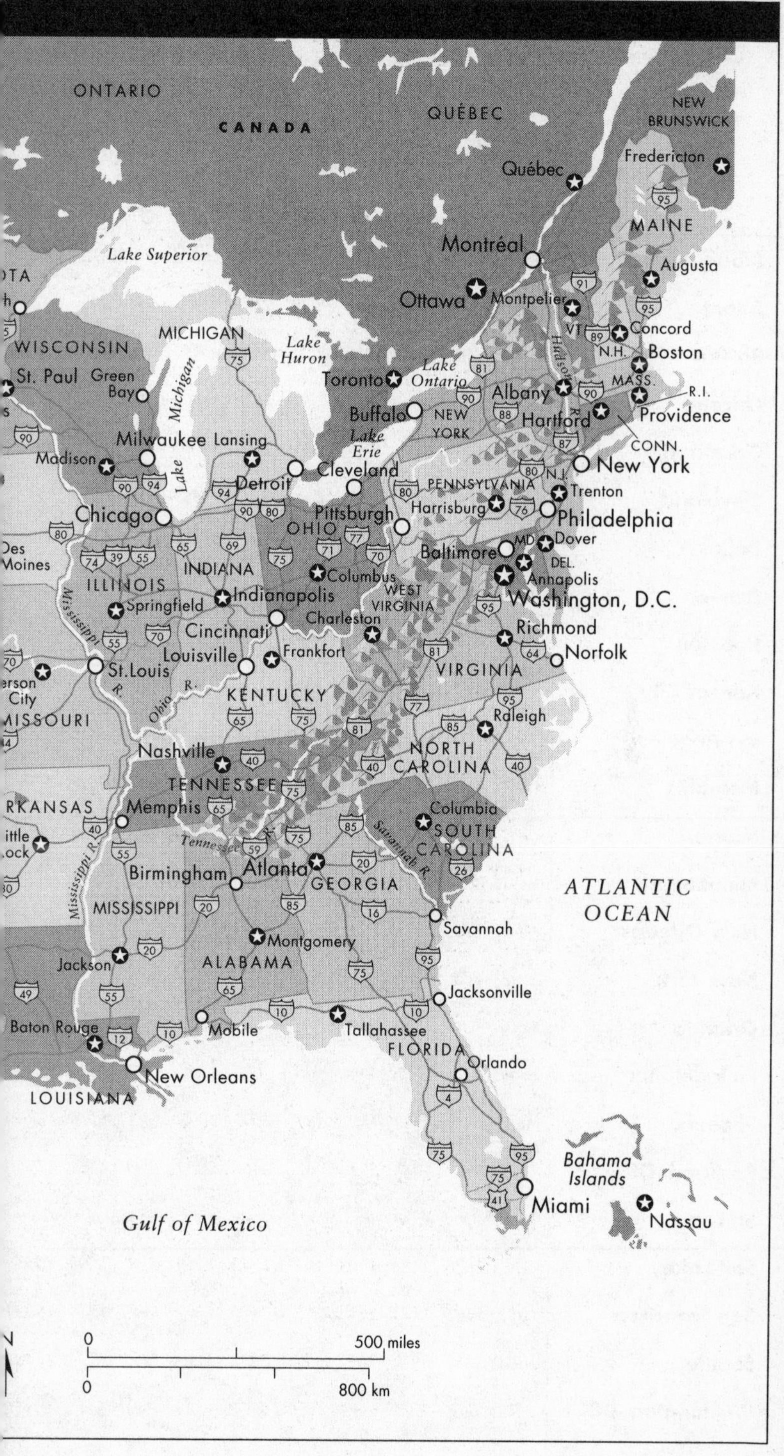
ONTARIO
CANADA
QUÉBEC
NEW BRUNSWICK
Fredericton
Québec
MAINE
Augusta
Montréal
Ottawa
Montpelier
VT
Concord
N.H.
Boston
MASS.
R.I.
Providence
Hartford
CONN.
Albany
Hudson R.
New York
N.J.
Trenton
Philadelphia
Dover
MD
DEL.
Annapolis
Washington, D.C.
Baltimore
Harrisburg
PENNSYLVANIA
NEW YORK
Buffalo
Lake Ontario
Toronto
Lake Erie
Lake Huron
Lake Superior
Lake Michigan
MICHIGAN
WISCONSIN
St. Paul
Green Bay
Milwaukee
Madison
Lansing
Detroit
Cleveland
Pittsburgh
Chicago
OHIO
Columbus
INDIANA
Indianapolis
ILLINOIS
Springfield
Des Moines
Cincinnati
Louisville
Frankfort
St. Louis
Mississippi R.
Ohio R.
KENTUCKY
MISSOURI
WEST VIRGINIA
Charleston
VIRGINIA
Richmond
Norfolk
Raleigh
NORTH CAROLINA
Nashville
TENNESSEE
Tennessee R.
Memphis
ARKANSAS
Little Rock
Columbia
SOUTH CAROLINA
Savannah R.
Atlanta
GEORGIA
Birmingham
MISSISSIPPI
Montgomery
ALABAMA
Jackson
Savannah
Jacksonville
Tallahassee
Mobile
Baton Rouge
New Orleans
LOUISIANA
FLORIDA
Orlando
Miami
ATLANTIC OCEAN
Bahama Islands
Nassau
Gulf of Mexico
0
500 miles
0
800 km

Mileages Between Major U.S. Cities

	Albuquerque	Atlanta	Boston	Chicago	Cincinnati	Cleveland	Dallas	Denver	Houston	Kansas
Albuquerque	—	1409	2225	1343	1402	1608	666	446	876	818
Atlanta	1409	—	1105	703	466	715	791	1404	800	801
Boston	2225	1105	—	1018	861	657	1765	2006	1857	1414
Chicago	1343	703	1018	—	296	365	940	1013	1107	511
Cincinnati	1402	466	861	296	—	249	943	1195	1079	592
Cleveland	1608	715	657	365	249	—	1193	1354	1328	797
Dallas	666	791	1765	940	943	1193	—	825	241	523
Denver	446	1404	2006	1013	1195	1354	825	—	1075	606
Houston	876	800	1857	1107	1079	1328	241	1075	—	764
Kansas City	818	801	1414	511	592	797	523	606	764	—
Los Angeles	790	2199	3007	2014	2192	2355	1440	1004	1545	1610
Memphis	1004	401	1309	533	487	736	456	1113	592	474
Miami	2009	695	1524	1388	1149	1251	1342	2088	1215	1485
Minneapolis	1255	1121	1435	417	713	782	962	916	1202	437
New Orleans	1178	473	1529	928	818	1067	511	1273	350	842
New York	2002	878	226	814	634	463	1538	1802	1630	1192
Orlando	1770	446	1314	1149	912	1041	1104	1850	976	1247
Philadelphia	1949	779	326	798	581	437	1462	1742	1554	1139
Phoenix	463	1859	2687	1805	1865	2071	1068	832	1173	1280
Portland, OR	1411	2599	3046	2126	2370	2466	2009	1241	2205	1796
St. Louis	1050	555	1175	293	352	558	647	852	819	249
Salt Lake	646	1876	2396	1403	1647	1743	1290	518	1500	1073
San Francisco	1095	2505	3125	2132	2376	2472	1761	1247	1923	1802
Seattle	1463	2651	3085	2067	2328	2432	2117	1293	2274	1848
Washington, DC	1875	641	462	733	488	377	1323	1649	1415	1045

Miami	Minneapolis	New Orleans	New York	Orlando	Philadelphia	Phoenix	Portland, OR	St. Louis	Salt Lake	San Francisco	Seattle	Washington, DC
2009	1255	1178	2002	1770	1949	463	1411	1050	646	1095	1463	1875
685	1121	473	878	446	779	1859	2599	555	1876	2505	2651	641
1524	1435	1529	226	1314	326	2687	3046	1175	2396	3125	3085	462
1388	417	928	814	1149	798	1805	2126	293	1403	2132	2067	733
1149	713	818	634	912	581	1865	2370	352	1647	2376	2328	488
1251	782	1067	453	1041	437	2071	2466	558	1743	2472	2432	377
1342	962	511	1538	1104	1462	1068	2009	647	1290	1761	2177	1323
2088	916	1273	1802	1850	1742	832	1241	852	518	1247	1293	1649
1215	1202	350	1630	976	1554	1173	2205	819	1500	1923	2274	1415
1485	437	842	1192	1247	1139	1280	1796	249	1073	1802	1848	1045
2759	1889	1894	2803	2521	2738	372	963	1840	689	381	1136	2665
1045	848	398	1082	807	1006	1471	2276	286	1553	2104	2328	867
—	1805	887	1298	245	1203	2387	3284	1239	2561	3137	3336	1066
1805	—	1243	1231	1567	1215	1718	1737	575	1264	1994	1651	1150
887	1243	—	1302	649	1226	1512	2505	681	1802	2272	2574	1087
1298	1231	1302	—	1088	95	2465	2915	952	2192	2921	2881	237
245	1567	649	1088	—	994	2149	3046	1061	2322	2899	3098	856
1203	1215	1226	95	994	—	2412	2899	899	2176	2905	2751	142
2387	1718	1512	2465	2149	2412	—	1333	1513	673	750	1489	2337
3284	1737	2505	2915	3046	2899	1333	—	2048	765	634	173	2835
1239	575	681	952	1061	899	1513	2048	—	1324	2054	2100	806
2561	1264	1802	2192	2322	2176	673	765	1324	—	735	817	2111
3137	1994	2272	2921	2899	2905	750	634	2054	735	—	807	2841
3336	1651	2574	2881	3098	2751	1489	173	2100	817	807	—	2800
1066	1150	1087	237	856	142	2337	2835	806	2111	2841	2800	—

ESSENTIAL INFORMATION

AIR TRAVEL

BOOKING

Price is just one factor to consider when booking a flight: frequency of service and even a carrier's safety record are often just as important. Major airlines offer the greatest number of departures. Smaller airlines—including regional and no-frills airlines—usually have a limited number of flights daily. On the other hand, so-called low-cost airlines usually are cheaper, and their fares impose fewer restrictions, such as advance-purchase requirements. Safety-wise, low-cost carriers as a group have a good history—about equal to that of major carriers.

When you book **look for nonstop flights** and **remember that "direct" flights stop at least once.** Try to avoid connecting flights, which require a change of plane. Two airlines may operate a connecting flight jointly, so ask if your airline operates every segment of the trip; you may find that the carrier you prefer flies you only part of the way. To find more booking tips and to check prices and make on-line flight reservations, log on to www.fodors.com.

CARRIERS

➤ MAJOR AIRLINES: **Air Canada** (☎ 888/247–2262, WEB www.aircanada.ca). **Alaska Airlines** (☎ 800/426–0333, WEB www.alaskaair.com). **American Airlines** (☎ 800/433–7300, WEB www.aa.com). **America West** (☎ 800/235–9292, WEB www.americawest.com). **Continental** (☎ 800/525–0280, WEB www.continental.com). **Delta** (☎ 800/221–1212, WEB www.delta.com). **Northwest** (☎ 800/225–2525, WEB www.nwa.com). **United** (☎ 800/241–6522, WEB www.united.com). **US Airways** (☎ 800/428–4322, WEB www.usairways.com).

➤ SMALLER AIRLINES: **Aloha** (☎ 800/367–5250, WEB www.alohaairlines.com). **Hawaiian** (☎ 800/367–5320, WEB www.hawaiianair.com). **IslandAir** (☎ 800/323–3345, WEB www.islandai[r.]com). **Mesa Airlines** (☎ 800/637–2247, WEB www.mesa-air.com). **SkyWest** (☎ 800/453–9417, WEB www.skywest.com/custmain.html). **Southwest Airlines** (☎ 800/435–9792, WEB www.southwest.com).

➤ FROM THE U.K.: **American** (☎ 0208/572–5555). **British Airways** (☎ 0845/773–3377, WEB www.britishairways.com). **Continental** (☎ 01293/776–464, 0800/776–464 toll-free). **Delta** (☎ 0800/414–767). **Northwest** (☎ 0870/507–4074). **United** (☎ 0845/844–4777). **Virgin Atlantic** (☎ 01293/747–747, WEB www.virgin-atlantic.com). Most serv[e] at least the New York area plus their own U.S. hubs. British Airways serve[s] the largest number of U.S. cities—an impressive 23 destinations, including Atlanta, Boston, Charlotte, Chicago, Dallas, Detroit, Houston, Los Angeles, Miami, New York, Orlando, Philadelphia, San Francisco, Seattle, and Washington, D.C. A few cities not served by British Airways can be reached by connections with other major carriers.

➤ FROM AUSTRALIA: **Air New Zealan[d]** (☎ 132476, WEB www.airnewzealand.com). **Qantas** (☎ 131313, WEB www.quantas.com).

CHECK-IN AND BOARDING

Always **ask your carrier about its check-in policy.** Plan to arrive at the airport about 2 hours before your scheduled departure time for domest[ic] flights and 2½ to 3 hours before international flights.

Assuming that not everyone with a ticket will show up, airlines routinely overbook planes. When everyone do[es] show up, airlines ask for volunteers t[o] give up their seats. In return, these volunteers usually get a certificate for a free flight and are rebooked on the next flight out. If there are not enough volunteers, the airline must choose who will be denied boarding. The first to get bumped are passengers who checked in late and those flying on discounted tickets, so **get to the gate and check in as early as possible,** especially during peak periods. Always **bring a government-issued photo ID to the airport;** even when it's not required, a passport is best.

CUTTING COSTS

The least expensive airfares to the United States are priced for round-trip travel and must usually be purchased in advance. Airlines generally allow you to change your return date for a fee; most low-fare tickets, however, are nonrefundable. **Call a number of airlines and check the Internet;** when you are quoted a good price, **book it on the spot**—the same fare may not be available the next day. Always **check different routings** and look into using alternate airports. Price off-peak flights, which may be significantly less expensive than others. Travel agents, especially low-fare specialists (☞ Discounts and Deals, *below*), are helpful.

Consolidators are another good source. They buy tickets for scheduled international flights at reduced rates from the airlines, then sell them at prices that beat the best fare available directly from the airlines. Sometimes you can even get your money back if you need to return the ticket. Carefully read the fine print detailing penalties for changes and cancellations, purchase the ticket with a credit card, and **confirm your consolidator reservation with the airline.**

When you **fly as a courier,** you trade your checked-luggage space for a ticket deeply subsidized by a courier service. There are restrictions on when you can book and how long you can stay. Some courier companies list with membership organizations, such as the Air Courier Association and the International Association of Air Travel Couriers; these require you to become a member before you can book a flight.

Many airlines, singly or in collaboration, offer discount air passes that allow foreigners to travel economically in a particular country or region. These visitor passes usually must be reserved and purchased before you leave home. Information about passes can be difficult to find on airline Web sites, which tend to be geared to travelers departing from a given carrier's country rather than to those intending to visit that country. Try typing the name of the pass into a search engine, or search for "pass" within the carrier's Web site.

➤ CONSOLIDATORS: **Cheap Tickets** (☎ 800/377–1000 or 888/922–8849, WEB www.cheaptickets.com). **Discount Airline Ticket Service** (☎ 800/576–1600). **Unitravel** (☎ 800/325–2222, WEB www.unitravel.com). **Up & Away Travel** (☎ 212/889–2345, WEB www.upandaway.com). **World Travel Network** (☎ 800/409–6753).

➤ COURIER RESOURCES: **Air Courier Association** (☎ 800/282–1202, WEB www.aircourier.org). **International Association of Air Travel Couriers** (☎ 352/475–1584, WEB www.courier.org). **Now Voyager Travel** (☎ 212/431–1616).

➤ DISCOUNT PASSES: **All Asia Pass,** Cathay Pacific (☎ 800/233–2742, WEB www.cathay-usa.com). **Boomerang Pass,** Qantas (☎ 800/227–4500; 0845/774–7767 in the U.K.; 131–313 in Australia; 0800/808–767 in New Zealand; WEB www.qantas.com). **FlightPass,** EuropebyAir (☎ 888/387–2479, WEB www.europebyair.com). **Pacific Explorer Airpass,** Hideaway Holidays (☎ 61–2/9743–0253 in Australia; FAX 530/325–4069 in the U.S.; WEB www.hideawayholidays.com.au). **Polypass,** Polynesian Airlines (☎ 800/264–0823 or 808/842–7659; 020/8846–0519 in the U.K.; 1300/653737 in Australia; 0800/800–993 in New Zealand; WEB www.polynesianairlines.co.nz). **SAS Air Passes,** Scandinavian Airlines (☎ 800/221–2350; 0845/6072–7727 in the U.K.; 1300/727707 in Australia; WEB www.scandinavian.net).

ENJOYING THE FLIGHT

State your seat preference when purchasing your ticket, and then repeat it when you confirm and when you check in. For more legroom, you can request one of the few emergency-aisle seats at check-in, if you are capable of lifting at least 50 pounds—a Federal Aviation Administration requirement of passengers in these seats. Seats behind a bulkhead also offer more legroom, but they don't have under-seat storage. Don't sit in the row in front of the emergency aisle or in front of a bulkhead, where seats may not recline.

Ask the airline whether a snack or meal is served on the flight. If you have dietary concerns, **request special meals when booking.** These can be vegetarian, low-cholesterol, or kosher, for example. It's a good idea to pack some healthy snacks and a small (plastic) bottle of water in your carry-on bag. On long flights, try to maintain a normal routine, to help fight jet lag. At night, **get some sleep.** By day, **eat light meals, drink water** (not alcohol), and **move around the cabin** to stretch your legs. For additional jet-lag tips consult *Fodor's FYI: Travel Fit & Healthy* (available at bookstores everywhere). Smoking policies vary from carrier to carrier. Many airlines prohibit smoking on all of their international flights; others allow smoking only on certain routes or certain departures. Ask your carrier about its policy.

FLYING TIMES

Flying time from London is 7 hours, 55 minutes to New York; 8 hours, 45 minutes to Chicago; 9 hours, 45 minutes to Miami; and 11 hours, 20 minutes to Los Angeles. Flying time from Sydney is 22–23 hours to New York and 13 hours, 25 minutes to Los Angeles on a direct flight. Flying time from Toronto is 1½ hours to New York and 5¼ hours to Los Angeles. Flying time from Vancouver is 3 hours to Los Angeles, 4 hours to Chicago.

HOW TO COMPLAIN

If your baggage goes astray or your flight goes awry, complain right away. Most carriers require that you **file a claim immediately.** The Aviation Consumer Protection Division of the Department of Transportation publishes *Fly-Rights,* which discusses airlines and consumer issues and is available on-line. At PassengerRights.com, a Web site, you can compose a letter of complaint and distribute it electronically.

➤ AIRLINE COMPLAINTS: **Aviation Consumer Protection Division** (✉ U.S. Department of Transportation, Room 4107, C-75, Washington, DC 20590, ☎ 202/366–2220, WEB www.dot.gov/airconsumer). **Federal Aviation Administration Consumer Hotline** (☎ 800/322–7873).

RECONFIRMING

Check the status of your flight before you leave for the airport. You can do this on your carrier's Web site, by linking to a flight-status checker (many Web booking services offer these), or by calling your carrier or travel agent.

AIRPORTS

Major gateways to the United States include New York, Miami, Chicago, and Los Angeles.

➤ AIRPORT INFORMATION: *See* Arriving and Departing by Plane *in* New York City, Miami, Chicago, and Los Angeles for specific information about airports in these cities, or the appropriate Arriving and Departing by Plane section under whatever city or region you are planning to fly into.

BIKE TRAVEL

Biking the nation's byways, you'll discover farms, forests and strip malls, antique mansions and trailer parks. Stick to roads and bike paths or go mountain biking on the designated trail systems in city, county, and state parks. **Check the area's policy on mountain bikes before you hop on the trail,** as many parks have banned them to protect the terrain. If you ignore the ban, you could be issued a fine or have your bicycle impounded. Many ski resorts open their slopes, trails, and chairlifts to mountain bikers during the off-season.

➤ RESOURCES: **Adventure Cycling** (✉ 150 E. Pine St. [Box 8308, Missoula, MT 59807], ☎ 406/721–1776 or 800/721–8719, FAX 406/721–8754, WEB www.adventurecycling.org). **Rails to Trails Conservancy** (✉ 1100 17th St. NW, 10th floor, Washington, DC 20036, ☎ 202/331–9696, FAX 202/

31–9680, WEB www.railtrails.org) has nformation on the more than 10,000 ni of abandoned railroad beds that ave been turned into bike trails.

IKES IN FLIGHT

Most airlines accommodate bikes as ıggage, provided they are dismantled nd boxed; check with individual irlines about packing requirements. Airlines sell bike boxes, which are often free at bike shops, for about 15 (bike bags start at $100). International travelers often can substitute a ike for a piece of checked luggage at o charge; otherwise, the cost is bout $100. Domestic and Canadian irlines charge $40–$80 each way.

BUSINESS HOURS

Banks are generally open weekdays 9 AM–3 PM, post offices weekdays 8 AM–5 PM; many branches operate aturday morning hours. Business ours tend to be weekdays 9–5, a ittle later on the East Coast and arlier the farther west you go. Many tores may not open until 10 or 11, out they remain open until 6 or 7; nost carry on brisk business on aturday as well. Large suburban hopping malls, the focus of most Americans' shopping activity, are enerally open seven days a week, vith evening hours every day except unday. Large all-purpose stores like Wal-Mart are often open 24 hours a lay, seven days a week, even in small owns. All across the country, socalled convenience stores sell food nd sundries until about 11 PM. Along the highways and in major ities you can usually find all-night liners, supermarkets, drugstores, and onvenience stores.

BUS TRAVEL

Aside from the two coasts and the najor cities, long-distance buses motor coaches) serve more of the Jnited States than trains do. Various egional bus companies serve their reas of the country; the most extenive long-haul service is provided by Greyhound Lines. Generally no eservations are needed—**buy your ickets before boarding** (allow 15 ninutes in advance in small towns, up o 45 minutes in larger cities). Longlistance buses often have reclining seats, individually controlled reading lights, rest rooms, and air-conditioning and heating.

CUTTING COSTS

Visitors from overseas can sometimes receive substantial savings on Greyhound by purchasing an Ameripass through their travel agent prior to arriving in the United States. Student discount cards are available at local bus stations.

Students age 15 and over can buy a Student Advantage Card for $22.50, which gives the user a 15% discount on all Greyhound bus tickets. The cards are valid for one academic year (August to August) and also entitle the holder to discounts at participating hotels, restaurants, car rental agencies, and retail stores.

➤ DISCOUNT PASSES: **Greyhound International** (✉ Port Authority, 625 8th Ave., New York, NY 10018, ☎ 212/971–0492 or 800/246–8572). **Greyhound** (☎ 888/454–7277, WEB www.greyhound.com). **Student Advantage** (☎ 800/333–2920, WEB www.studentadvantage.com).

➤ BUS INFORMATION: **Greyhound** (☎ 800/231–2222, 800/345–3109 TDD).

CAMERAS AND PHOTOGRAPHY

The *Kodak Guide to Shooting Great Travel Pictures* (available at bookstores everywhere) is loaded with tips.

➤ PHOTO HELP: **Kodak Information Center** (☎ 800/242–2424, WEB www.kodak.com).

EQUIPMENT PRECAUTIONS

Don't pack film and equipment in checked luggage, where it is much more susceptible to damage. X-ray machines used to view checked luggage are becoming much more powerful and therefore are much more likely to ruin your film. Try to **ask for hand inspection of film,** which becomes clouded after repeated exposure to airport X-ray machines, and **keep videotapes and computer disks away from metal detectors.** Always **keep film, tape, and computer disks out of the sun.** Carry an extra supply of batteries, and **be prepared to turn on your camera, camcorder, or laptop**

to prove to airport security personnel that the device is real.

CAR RENTAL

➤ MAJOR AGENCIES: **Alamo** (☎ 800/327–9633; WEB www.alamo.com). **Avis** (☎ 800/331–1212; 800/879–2847 in Canada; 0870/606–0100 in the U.K.; 02/9353–9000 in Australia; 09/526–2847 in New Zealand; WEB www.avis.com). **Budget** (☎ 800/527–0700; 0870/156–5656 in the U.K.; WEB www.budget.com). **Dollar** (☎ 800/800–4000; 0124/622–0111 in the U.K.; where it's affiliated with Sixt; 02/9223–1444 in Australia; WEB www.dollar.com). **Hertz** (☎ 800/654–3131; 800/263–0600 in Canada; 020/8897–2072 in the U.K.; 02/9669–2444 in Australia; 09/256–8690 in New Zealand; WEB www.hertz.com). **National Car Rental** (☎ 800/227–7368; 020/8680–4800 in the U.K.; WEB www.nationalcar.com).

CUTTING COSTS

For a good deal, **book through a travel agent who will shop around.** Also, **price local car-rental companies**—whose prices may be lower still, although their service and maintenance may not be as good as those of major rental agencies—and **research rates on-line.** Ask about required deposits, cancellation penalties, and drop-off charges if you're planning to pick up the car in one city and leave it in another. If you're traveling during a holiday period, also make sure that a confirmed reservation guarantees you a car. Do **look into wholesalers,** companies that do not own fleets but rent in bulk from those that do and often offer better rates than traditional car-rental operations. Prices are best during off-peak periods. Rentals booked through wholesalers often must be paid for before you leave home.

➤ WHOLESALERS: **Auto Europe** (☎ 207/842–2000 or 800/223–5555, FAX 207/842–2222, WEB www.autoeurope.com).

INSURANCE

When driving a rented car, you are generally responsible for any damage to or loss of the vehicle. You may also be liable for any property damage or personal injury that you may cause while driving. Before you rent, see what coverage you already have under the terms of your personal auto-insurance policy and credit cards. For about $15 to $20 a day, rental companies sell protection, known as a collision- or loss-damage waiver (CDW or LDW), that eliminates your liability for damage to the car; it's always optional and should never be automatically added to your bill. In most states you don't need a CDW if you have personal auto insurance or other liability insurance. Some states, including California, Nevada, and Illinois, have capped the price of the CDW and LDW. In New York State, which has outlawed the sale of the CDW and LDW altogether, you pay for only the first $100 of damage to the rental car. In Arizona, Maryland, and Massachusetts, the car-rental agency's insurance is primary; therefore, the company must pay for damage to third parties up to a preset legal limit, beyond which your own liability insurance kicks in. However, **make sure you have enough coverage to pay for the car.** If you do not have auto insurance or an umbrella policy that covers damage to third parties, purchasing liability insurance and a CDW or LDW is recommended.

REQUIREMENTS AND RESTRICTIONS

In the United States you must be 21 to rent a car, and rates may be higher if you're under 25. In New York you must be 18 to rent a car. You'll pay extra for child seats (about $5 per day), which are compulsory for children under five, and for additional drivers (about $5 per day). Non-U.S. residents will need a reservation voucher, a passport, a driver's license, and a travel policy that cover each driver, when picking up a car.

SURCHARGES

Before you pick up a car in one city and leave it in another, **ask about drop-off charges or one-way service fees,** which can be substantial. Note, too, that some rental agencies charge extra if you return the car before the time specified in your contract. To avoid a hefty refueling fee, **fill the tank just before you turn in the car,** but be aware that gas stations near the rental outlet may overcharge. It's almost never a deal to buy the tank of gas in the car when you rent it; the understanding is that you'll return it empty, but some fuel usually remains. Surcharges may apply if you're under 25. You'll pay extra for child seats (about $6 a day), which are compulsory for children under five, and for additional drivers (about $5 per day).

CAR TRAVEL

AUTO CLUBS

Consider joining the American Automobile Association (AAA), a federation of state auto clubs that offers maps, route planning, and emergency road service to its members; members of Britain's Automobile Association (AA) are granted reciprocal privileges. Check local phone directories under AAA for the nearest club or contact the national organization.

➤ IN AUSTRALIA: **Australian Automobile Association** (☏ 02/6247–7311, WEB www.aaa.asn.au).

➤ IN CANADA: **Canadian Automobile Association** (CAA; ☏ 613/247–0117, WEB www.caa.ca).

➤ IN NEW ZEALAND: **New Zealand Automobile Association** (☏ 09/377–4660, WEB www.nzaa.co.nz).

➤ IN THE U.K.: **Automobile Association** (AA; ☏ 0870/600–0371, WEB www.theaa.com). **Royal Automobile Club** (RAC; ☏ 0800/092–2222 membership; 08457/121–345 insurance; WEB www.rac.co.uk).

➤ IN THE U.S.: **American Automobile Association** (☏ 800/564–6222, WEB www.aaa.com).

EMERGENCY SERVICES

From any phone, **dial 911** in an emergency to reach the police, fire, or ambulance services. If your car breaks down on an interstate highway, try to pull over onto the shoulder of the road and either wait for the state police to find you or, if you have other passengers who can wait in the car, walk to the nearest emergency roadside phone and call the state police. When calling for help, note your location according to the small green mileage markers posted along the highway. Other highways are also patrolled but may not have emergency phones or mileage markers.

GASOLINE

Gasoline is relatively inexpensive in the United States, though of course the price varies from region to region and fluctuates over time. In many parts of the United States, long stretches of road present challenges to unwary drivers. Be sure to stock up on gasoline whenever you have the chance. Most gas stations are open late, and many large highways and big cities have 24-hour stations. However, many stations close early on Sunday night.

HIGHWAYS

The fastest routes are usually the interstate highways, each numbered with a prefix "I." Even numbers (I–80, I–40, and so on) are east–west roads; odd numbers (I–91, I–55, and so on) run north–south. These are fully signposted, limited-access highways, with at least two lanes in each direction. In some cases they are toll roads (the Pennsylvania Turnpike is I–76; the Massachusetts Turnpike is I–90). Near large cities, interstates usually intersect with a circumferential loop highway (I–295, and so on) that carries traffic around the city. Another highway system is the U.S. highway (designated U.S. 1, and so on); they are not necessarily limited access but well paved and usually multilane. State highways are also well paved and often have more than one lane in each direction. Large cities usually have a number of limited-access expressways, freeways, and parkways, referred to by names rather than numbers (the Merritt Parkway, the Kennedy Expressway, the Santa Monica Freeway).

ROAD CONDITIONS

Road and highway conditions vary from state to state, depending on the climate and budget allocations of a given area. In general, interstates and parkways are well maintained through revenue generated from tolls charged to all motorists. These can be collected at periodic tollbooths along the road or where you exit, depending on the distance traveled. Large highways also have the advantage of well-spaced roadside stops with public rest rooms and stores selling fast food, maps, and other sundries. Major interstates are frequented by state police and tow trucks, whose drivers can lend assistance in the event of an accident or breakdown.

ROAD MAPS

Maps can usually be purchased at gas stations, convenience stores, and rest stops for about $3. If you plan to cover an entire region within the United States, consider a detailed road atlas; these generally cost about $10 and can be purchased in the same locations mentioned above, as well as in bookstores.

RULES OF THE ROAD

Driving in the United States is done on the right side of the road. Speed limits vary and are signposted along roads and highways. **Adhere to speed limits.** Recent federal legislation allows each state to set individual speed limits; they may range from 55 or 65 mph to 75 mph west of the Mississippi. Watch for lower speed limits on back roads. Except for limited-access roads, highways usually post a lower speed limit in towns, so slow down when houses and buildings start to appear. Most states require front-seat occupants to wear seat belts, and in all states **children under age four must ride in approved child-safety seats.**

In most communities, it is permissible to make a right turn at a red light once the car has come to a full stop and there is no oncoming traffic. When in doubt about local laws, however, wait for the green light. In New York City, making a right on red is strictly prohibited.

Beware of weekday rush-hour traffic—anywhere from 6 AM to 10 AM and 4 PM to 7 PM—around major cities. To encourage car sharing, some crowded expressways may reserve an express lane for cars carrying more than one passenger. In downtown areas, watch signs carefully—there are lots of one-way streets, "no-left-turn" intersections, and blocks closed to car traffic, all in the name of easing congestion.

➤ PUBLICATIONS: *Great American Drives of the East* and *Great American Drives of the West*; both are available in bookstores or from **Fodor's Travel Publications** (☎ 800/533–6478; $16.95).

CHILDREN AND TRAVEL

Be sure to plan ahead and **involve your youngsters** as you outline your trip. When packing, include things to keep them busy en route. On sightseeing days try to schedule activities of special interest to your children. If you are renting a car, don't forget to **arrange for a car seat** when you reserve. For general advice about traveling with children, consult *Fodor's FYI: Travel with Your Baby* (available in bookstores everywhere).

FLYING

If your children are two or older, **ask about children's airfares.** As a general rule, infants under two not occupying a seat fly at greatly reduced fares or even for free. Many carriers require children two and older to pay full fare, but again, it pays to ask.Experts agree that it's a good idea to use safety seats aloft for children weighing less than 40 pounds. Airlines set their own policies: U.S. carriers usually require that the child be ticketed, even if he or she is young enough to ride free, since the seats must be strapped into regular seats. Do **check your airline's policy about using safety seats during takeoff and landing.** And since safety seats are not allowed just anywhere, get your seat assignments early; many airlines do not allow safety seats in emergency exit rows and do require that the seats be strapped into window seats. When reserving, **request children's meals or a freestanding bassinet** (not available at all airlines) if you need them. But note that bulkhead seats, where you must sit to use the bassinet, may lack an overhead bin or storage space on the floor.

LODGING

Most hotels in the United States allow children under a certain age to stay in their parents' room at no extra charge, but others may add a surcharge or charge for them as extra adults; be sure to **find out the cutoff age for children's discounts.**

SIGHTS AND ATTRACTIONS

Places that are especially appealing to children are indicated by a rubber-duckie icon (☺) in the margin.

COMPUTERS ON THE ROAD

Checking your e-mail or surfing the World Wide Web can sometimes be done in the business centers of major hotels, which usually charge an hourly rate. Web access is also available at many fax and copy centers, many of which are open 24 hours and on weekends. In major cities look for cybercafés, where tabletop computers allow you to log on while sipping coffee or listening to live jazz. Do check out the World Wide Web when you're planning. You'll find everything from up-to-date weather forecasts to virtual tours of famous cities. Fodor's Web site (www.fodors.com) is a great place to start your on-line travels.

CONCIERGES

Concierges, found in many hotels, can help you with theater tickets and dinner reservations: a good one with connections may be able to get you seats for a hot show or prime-time dinner reservations at the restaurant of the moment. You can also turn to your hotel's concierge for help with travel arrangements, sightseeing plans, services ranging from aromatherapy to zipper repair, and emergencies. Always **always tip** a concierge who has been of assistance (☞ Tipping, *below*).

CONSUMER PROTECTION

Whether you're shopping for gifts or purchasing travel services, **pay with a major credit card** whenever possible, so you can cancel payment or get reimbursed if there's a problem (and you can provide documentation). If you're doing business with a particular company for the first time, **contact your local Better Business Bureau and the attorney general's offices** in your state and (for U.S. businesses) the company's home state as well. Have any complaints been filed? Finally, if you're buying a package or tour, always **consider travel insurance** that includes default coverage (☞ Insurance, *below*).

➤ BBBs: **Council of Better Business Bureaus** (✉ 4200 Wilson Blvd., Suite 800, Arlington, VA 22203, ☎ 703/276–0100, FAX 703/525–8277, WEB www.bbb.org).

CRUISE TRAVEL

To learn how to plan, choose, and book a cruise-ship voyage, consult *Fodor's FYI: Plan & Enjoy Your Cruise* (available in bookstores everywhere).

CUSTOMS AND DUTIES

When shopping abroad, **keep receipts** for all purchases. Upon reentering the country, **be ready to show customs officials what you've bought.** If you feel a duty is incorrect, appeal the assessment. If you object to the way your clearance was handled, note the inspector's badge number. In either case, first ask to see a supervisor. If the problem isn't resolved, write to the appropriate authorities, beginning with the port director at your point of entry.

IN AUSTRALIA

Australian residents who are 18 or older may bring home A$400 worth of souvenirs and gifts (including jewelry), 250 cigarettes or 250 grams of tobacco, and 1,125 ml of alcohol (including wine, beer, and spirits). Residents under 18 may bring back A$200 worth of goods. Prohibited items include meat products. Seeds, plants, and fruits need to be declared upon arrival.

➤ INFORMATION: **Australian Customs Service** (Regional Director, ✉ Box 8, Sydney, NSW 2001; ☎ 02/9213–2000 or 1300/363263; 1800/020504 quarantine-inquiry line; FAX 02/9213–4043; WEB www.customs.gov.au).

IN CANADA

Canadian residents who have been out of Canada for at least seven days may bring in C$750 worth of goods duty-free. If you've been away fewer than seven days but more than 48 hours, the duty-free allowance drops to C$200. If your trip lasts 24 to 48 hours, the allowance is C$50. You may not pool allowances with family members. Goods claimed under the C$750 exemption may follow you by mail; those claimed under the lesser exemptions must accompany you. Alcohol and tobacco products may be included in the seven-day and 48-hour exemptions but not in the 24-hour exemption. If you meet the age requirements of the province or territory through which you reenter Canada, you may bring in, duty-free, 1.5 liters of wine *or* 1.14 liters (40 imperial ounces) of liquor *or* 24 12-ounce cans or bottles of beer or ale. If you are 19 or older you may bring in, duty-free, 200 cigarettes and 50 cigars. Check ahead of time with the Canada Customs and Revenue Agency or the Department of Agriculture for policies regarding meat products, seeds, plants, and fruits. You may send an unlimited number of gifts (only one gift per recipient, however) worth up to C$60 each duty-free to Canada. Label the package UNSOLICITED GIFT—VALUE UNDER $60. Alcohol and tobacco are excluded.

➤ INFORMATION: **Canada Customs and Revenue Agency** (✉ 2265 St. Laurent Blvd. S, Ottawa, Ontario K1G 4K3, ☎ 204/983–3500, 506/636–5064, 800/461–9999, WEB www.ccra-adrc.gc.ca/).

IN NEW ZEALAND

All homeward-bound residents may bring back NZ$700 worth of souvenirs and gifts; passengers may not pool their allowances, and children can claim only the concession on goods intended for their own use. For those 17 or older, the duty-free allowance also includes 4.5 liters of wine or beer; one 1,125-ml bottle of spirits; and either 200 cigarettes, 250 grams of tobacco, 50 cigars, *or* a combination of the three up to 250 grams. Meat products, seeds, plants, and fruits must be declared upon arrival to the Agricultural Services Department.

➤ INFORMATION: **New Zealand Customs** (Custom House, ✉ 50 Anzac Ave. [Box 29, Auckland, New Zealand], ☎ 0800/428–726 or 09/359–6655, FAX 09/359–6732).

IN THE U.K.

If you are a U.K. resident and your journey was wholly within the European Union, you probably won't have to pass through customs when you return to the United Kingdom. If you plan to bring back large quantities of alcohol or tobacco, check EU limits beforehand. In most cases, if you bring back more than 200 cigars, 800 cigarettes, 10 liters of spirits, and/or 90 liters of wine, you have to declare the goods upon return.From countries outside the European Union, including the United States, you may bring home, duty-free, 200 cigarettes or 50 cigars; 1 liter of spirits or 2 liters of fortified or sparkling wine or liqueurs; 2 liters of still table wine; 60 ml of perfume; 250 ml of toilet water; plus £145 worth of other goods, including gifts and souvenirs. Prohibited items include meat products, seeds, plants, and fruits.

➤ INFORMATION: **HM Customs and Excise** (✉ Portcullis House, 21 Cowbridge Rd. E, Cardiff CF11 9SS, ☎ 029/2038–6423 or 0845/010–9000, WEB www.hmce.gov.uk).

IN THE U.S.

U.S. residents who have been out of the country for at least 48 hours may bring home, for personal use, $400 worth of foreign goods duty-free, as long as they haven't used the $400 allowance or any part of it in the past 30 days. This exemption may include 1 liter of alcohol (for travelers 21 and older), 200 cigarettes, and 100 non-Cuban cigars. Family members from the same household who are traveling together may pool their $400 personal exemptions. For fewer than 48 hours, the duty-free allowance drops to $200, which may include 50 cigarettes, 10 non-Cuban cigars, and 150 ml of alcohol (or perfume containing alcohol). The $200 allowance cannot be combined with other individuals' exemptions, and if you exceed it, the full value of all the goods will be taxed. Antiques, which the U.S. Customs Service defines as objects more than 100 years old, enter duty-free, as do original works of art done entirely by hand, including paintings, drawings, and sculptures. You may also send packages home duty-free, with a limit of one parcel per addressee per day (except alcohol or tobacco products or perfume worth more than $5). You can mail up to $200 worth of goods for personal use; label the package PERSONAL USE and attach a list of its contents and their retail value. If the package contains your used personal belongings, mark it PERSONAL GOODS RETURNED to avoid paying duties. You may send up to $100 worth of goods as a gift; mark the package UNSOLICITED GIFT. Mailed items do not affect your duty-free allowance on your return.

➤ INFORMATION: **U.S. Customs Service** (for inquiries, ✉ 1300 Pennsylvania Ave. NW, Washington, DC 20229, WEB www.customs.gov, ☎ 202/354–1000; for complaints, ✉ Customer Satisfaction Unit, 1300 Pennsylvania Ave. NW, Room 5.5A, Washington, DC 20229; for registration of equipment, ✉ Office of Passenger Programs, 1300 Pennsylvania Ave. NW, Room 5.4D, Washington, DC 20229, ☎ 202/927–0530).

DINING

The restaurants we list are the cream of the crop in each price category. Properties indicated by an ✕🏨 are lodging establishments whose restaurant warrants a special trip. Price categories are as follows:

CATEGORY	COST*
$$$$	over $32
$$$	$22–$32
$$	$12–$22
$	under $12

**per person for a dinner entrée, or a lunch entrée if no dinner is served*

DISABILITIES AND ACCESSIBILITY

LODGING RESERVATIONS

Despite the Americans with Disabilities Act, the definition of accessibility seems to differ from hotel to hotel. Some properties may be accessible by ADA standards for people with mobility problems but not for people with hearing or vision impairments, for example. If you have mobility problems, ask for the lowest floor on which accessible services are offered. If you have a hearing impairment, check whether the hotel has devices to alert you visually to the ring of the telephone, knock at the door, and a fire/emergency alarm. Some hotels provide these devices without charge. Discuss your needs with hotel personnel if this equipment isn't available, so that a staff member can personally alert you in the event of an emergency. If you're bringing a guide dog, get authorization ahead of time and write down the name of the person you spoke with.

RESERVATIONS

When discussing accessibility with an operator or reservations agent, **ask hard questions.** Are there any stairs, inside *or* out? Are there grab bars next to the toilet *and* in the shower/tub? How wide is the doorway to the room? To the bathroom? For the most extensive facilities meeting the latest legal specifications, **opt for newer accommodations.** If you reserve through a toll-free number, also call the hotel's local number to confirm the information from the central reservations office. Get confirmation in writing when you can.

➤ COMPLAINTS: **Aviation Consumer Protection Division** (☞ Air Travel, *above*) for airline-related problems. **Departmental Office of Civil Rights** (for general inquiries, ✉ U.S. Department of Transportation, S-30, 400 7th St. SW, Room 10215, Washington, DC 20590, ☎ 202/366–4648, FAX 202/366–3571, WEB www.dot.gov/ost/docr/index.htm). **Disability Rights Section** (✉ NYAV, U.S. Department of Justice, Civil Rights Division, 950 Pennsylvania Ave. NW, Washington, DC 20530; ☎ 202/514–0301 or 800/514–0301 ADA information; 202/514–0383 or 800/514–0383 TTY; WEB www.usdoj.gov/crt/ada).

TRAVEL AGENCIES

In the United States, the Americans with Disabilities Act requires that travel firms serve the needs of all travelers. Some agencies specialize in working with people with disabilities.

➤ TRAVELERS WITH MOBILITY PROBLEMS: **Access Adventures** (✉ 206 Chestnut Ridge Rd., Scottsville, NY 14624, ☎ 716/889–9096, dltravel@prodigy.net), run by a former physical-rehabilitation counselor. **Accessible Vans of America** (✉ 9 Spielman Rd., Fairfield, NJ 07004, ☎ 877/282–8267; 888/282–8267 reservations; FAX 973/808–9713; WEB www.accessiblevans.com). **CareVacations** (✉ No. 5, 5110–50 Ave., Leduc, Alberta T9E 6V4, Canada, ☎ 780/

986–6404 or 877/478–7827, FAX 780/986–8332, WEB www.carevacations.com), for group tours and cruise vacations. **Flying Wheels Travel** (✉ 143 W. Bridge St. [Box 382, Owatonna, MN 55060], ☎ 507/451–5005, FAX 507/451–1685, WEB www.flyingwheelstravel.com).

➤ TRAVELERS WITH DEVELOPMENTAL DISABILITIES: **New Directions** (✉ 5276 Hollister Ave., Suite 207, Santa Barbara, CA 93111, ☎ 805/967–2841 or 888/967–2841, FAX 805/964–7344, WEB www.newdirectionstravel.com). **Sprout** (✉ 893 Amsterdam Ave., New York, NY 10025, ☎ 212/222–9575 or 888/222–9575, FAX 212/222–9768, WEB www.gosprout.org).

DISCOUNTS AND DEALS

Be a smart shopper and **compare all your options** before making decisions. A plane ticket bought with a promotional coupon from travel clubs, coupon books, and direct-mail offers or purchased on-line may not be cheaper than the least expensive fare from a discount ticket agency. Bear in mind that what you get is just as important as what you save.

DISCOUNT RESERVATIONS

To save money, **look into discount reservations services** with Web sites and toll-free numbers, which use their buying power to get a better price on hotels, airline tickets, even car rentals. When booking a room, always **call the hotel's local toll-free number** (if one is available) rather than the central reservations number—you'll often get a better price. Always ask about special packages or corporate rates.

➤ AIRLINE TICKETS: ☎ **800/AIR–4LESS.**

➤ HOTEL ROOMS: **Accommodations Express** (☎ 800/444–7666, WEB www.accommodationsexpress.com). **Central Reservation Service** (CRS; ☎ 800/548–3311, WEB www.roomconnection.net). **Hotel Reservations Network** (☎ 800/964–6835, WEB www.hoteldiscount.com). **Quikbook** (☎ 800/789–9887, WEB www.quikbook.com). **RMC Travel** (☎ 800/245–5738, WEB www.rmcwebtravel.com). **Steigenberger Reservation Service** (☎ 800/223–5652, WEB www.srs-worldhotels.com). **Turbotrip.com** (☎ 800/473–7829, WEB www.turbotrip.com).

PACKAGE DEALS

Don't confuse packages and guided tours. When you buy a package, you travel on your own, just as though you had planned the trip yourself. Fly-drive packages, which combine airfare and car rental, are often a good deal.

EMBASSIES

In addition to their principal headquarters, most embassies have offices in Washington, D.C.

➤ AUSTRALIA: **Australian Embassy** (✉ 1601 Massachusetts Ave. NW, Washington, DC 20036, ☎ 202/797–3000, FAX 202/797–3040, WEB www.austemb.org).

➤ CANADA: **Canadian Embassy** (✉ 501 Pennsylvania Ave. NW, Washington, DC 20001, ☎ 202/682–1740, FAX 202/682–7726, WEB www.canadianembassy.org).

➤ NEW ZEALAND: **New Zealand Embassy** (✉ 37 Observatory Cir. NW, Washington, DC 20008, ☎ 202/328–4800, FAX 202/667–5227, WEB www.nzemb.org).

➤ UNITED KINGDOM: **British Embassy** (✉ 19 Observatory Cir. NW, Washington, DC 20008, ☎ 202/588–7800, FAX 202/588–7850, WEB www.britainusa.com).

GAY AND LESBIAN TRAVEL

For details about the gay and lesbian scene, consult *Fodor's Gay Guide to the USA* (available in bookstores everywhere).

➤ GAY- AND LESBIAN-FRIENDLY TOUR OPERATORS: **R.S.V.P. Travel Productions** (✉ 2800 University Ave. SE, Minneapolis, MN 55414, ☎ 612/379–4697 or 800/328–7787, FAX 612/379–0484), for cruises and resort vacations. **Hanns Ebensten Travel** (✉ 513 Fleming St., Key West, FL 33040, ☎ 305/294–8174 or 866/294–8174, FAX 305/292–9665, WEB wwwhetravel.com), one of the oldest operators in the gay market. **Toto Tours** (✉ 1326 W. Albion Ave., Suite 3W, Chicago, IL 60626, ☎ 773/274–8686 or 800/565–1241, FAX 773/274–8695, WEB www.tototours.com), for groups.

➤ GAY- AND LESBIAN-FRIENDLY TRAVEL AGENCIES: **Different Roads Travel** (✉ 8383 Wilshire Blvd., Suite 902, Beverly Hills, CA 90211, ☎ 323/651–5557 or 800/429–8747, FAX 323/651–3678, lgernert@tzell.com). **Kennedy Travel** (✉ 314 Jericho Turnpike, Floral Park, NY 11001, ☎ 516/352–4888 or 800/237–7433, FAX 516/354–8849, WEB www.kennedytravel.com). **Now, Voyager** (✉ 4406 18th St., San Francisco, CA 94114, ☎ 415/626–1169 or 800/255–6951, FAX 415/626–8626, WEB www.nowvoyager.com). **Skylink Travel and Tour** (✉ 1006 Mendocino Ave., Santa Rosa, CA 95401, ☎ 707/546–9888 or 800/225–5759, FAX 707/546–9891, WEB www.skylinktravel.com), serving lesbian travelers.

➤ GAY TRAVEL ASSOCIATIONS: **International Gay and Lesbian Travel Association** (✉ 4331 N. Federal Hwy., Suite 304, Ft. Lauderdale, FL 33308, ☎ 800/448–8550, WEB www.iglta.com) has more than 1,500 travel-industry members. Upon request they will provide, at no charge, a listing of gay-friendly travel agents and tour operators for any specified region.

HOLIDAYS

Major national holidays include New Year's Day; Martin Luther King Jr. Day (3rd Mon. in Jan.); Presidents' Day (3rd Mon. in Feb.); Memorial Day (last Mon. in May); Independence Day; Labor Day (1st Mon. in Sept.); Thanksgiving Day (4th Thurs. in Nov.); Christmas Eve and Christmas Day; and New Year's Eve.

INSURANCE

The most useful travel insurance plan is a comprehensive policy that includes coverage for trip cancellation and interruption, default, trip delay, and medical expenses (with a waiver for preexisting conditions). Without insurance you will lose all or most of your money if you cancel your trip, regardless of the reason. Default insurance covers you if your tour operator, airline, or cruise line goes out of business. Trip-delay covers expenses that arise because of bad weather or mechanical delays. Study the fine print when comparing policies.

Always **buy travel policies directly from the insurance company**; if you buy them from a cruise line, airline, or tour operator that goes out of business you probably will not be covered for the agency or operator's default. Before making any purchase, **review your existing health and homeowner's policies** to see what they cover away from home.

➤ TRAVEL INSURERS: In the U.S.: **Access America** (✉ 6600 W. Broad St., Richmond, VA 23230, ☎ 800/284–8300, FAX 804/673–1491 or 800/346–9265, WEB www.accessamerica.com). **Travel Guard International** (✉ 1145 Clark St., Stevens Point, WI 54481, ☎ 715/345–0505 or 800/826–1300, FAX 800/955–8785, WEB www.travelguard.com).

FOR INTERNATIONAL TRAVELERS

For information on customs restrictions, *see* Customs and Duties, *above*.

CAR RENTAL

When picking up a rental car, non-U.S. residents need a reservation voucher for any prepaid reservations that were made in the traveler's home country, a passport, a driver's license, and a travel policy that covers each driver. Also *see* Car Travel, *above*.

CURRENCY

The dollar is the basic unit of U.S. currency. It has 100 cents. Coins include the copper penny (1¢); the silvery nickel (5¢), dime (10¢), quarter (25¢), and half-dollar (50¢); and the golden $1 coin, replacing a now-rare silver dollar. Bills are denominated $1, $5, $10, $20, $50, and $100, all green and identical in size; designs vary.

ELECTRICITY

The U.S. standard is AC, 110 volts/60 cycles. Plugs have two flat pins set parallel to each other.

EMERGENCIES

For police, fire, or ambulance, **dial 911** (0 in rural areas).

INSURANCE

Britons and Australians need extra medical coverage when traveling overseas.

➤ INSURANCE INFORMATION: In the U.K.: **Association of British Insurers** (✉ 51 Gresham St., London EC2V 7HQ, ☎ 020/7600–3333, FAX 020/7696–8999, WEB www.abi.org.uk). In Australia: **Insurance Council of Australia** (✉ Level 3, 56 Pitt St., Sydney, NSW 2000, ☎ 02/9253–5100, FAX 02/9253–5111, WEB www.ica.com.au). In Canada: **RBC Insurance** (✉ 6880 Financial Dr., Mississauga, Ontario L5N 7Y5, ☎ 905/816–2400 or 800/668–4342, FAX 905/813–4704, WEB www.rbcinsurance.com). In New Zealand: **Insurance Council of New Zealand** (✉ Level 7, 111–115 Customhouse Quay [Box 474, Wellington], ☎ 04/472–5230, FAX 04/473–3011, WEB www.icnz.org.nz).

MAIL AND SHIPPING

You can buy stamps and aerograms and send letters and parcels in post offices. Stamp-dispensing machines can occasionally be found in airports, bus and train stations, office buildings, drugstores, and the like. You can also deposit mail in the stout, dark blue, steel bins at strategic locations everywhere and in the mail chutes of large buildings; pickup schedules are posted. For mail sent within the United States, you need a 37¢ stamp for first-class letters weighing up to 1 ounce (23¢ for each additional ounce) and 23¢ for postcards. You pay 80¢ for 1-ounce airmail letters and 70¢ for airmail postcards to most other countries; to Canada and Mexico, you need a 60¢ stamp for a 1-ounce letter and 50¢ for a postcard. An aerogram—a single sheet of lightweight blue paper that folds into its own envelope, stamped for overseas airmail—costs 70¢. To receive mail on the road, have it sent c/o General Delivery at your destination's main post office (use the correct five-digit ZIP code). You must pick up mail in person within 30 days and show a driver's license or passport.

PASSPORTS AND VISAS

When traveling internationally, **carry your passport** even if you don't need one (it's always the best form of I.D.) and **make two photocopies of the data page** (one for someone at home and another for you, carried separately from your passport). If you lose your passport, promptly call the nearest embassy or consulate and the local police. Visitor visas are not necessary for Canadian citizens, or for citizens of Australia and the United Kingdom who are staying fewer than 90 days.

➤ AUSTRALIAN CITIZENS: **Australian State Passport Office** (☎ 131–232, WEB www.passports.gov.au). **United States Consulate General** (✉ MLC Centre, 19–29 Martin Pl., 59th floor, Sydney, NSW 2000, ☎ 02/9373–9200; 1902/941–641 fee-based visa-inquiry line; WEB www.usis-australia.gov/index.html).

➤ CANADIAN CITIZENS: **Passport Office** (to mail in applications: ✉ Department of Foreign Affairs and International Trade, Ottawa, Ontario K1A 0G3, ☎ 819/994–3500 or 800/567–6868, WEB www.dfait-maeci.gc.ca/passport).

➤ NEW ZEALAND CITIZENS: **New Zealand Passport Office** (☎ 04/474–8100 or 0800/22–5050, WEB www.passports.govt.nz). **Embassy of the United States** (✉ 29 Fitzherbert Terr., Thorndon, Wellington, ☎ 04/462–6000 WEB usembassy.org.nz). **U.S. Consulate General** (✉ Citibank Bldg., 3rd floor, 23 Customs St. E, Auckland, ☎ 09/303–2724, WEB usembassy.org.nz).

➤ U.K. CITIZENS: **London Passport Office** (☎ 0870/521–0410, WEB www.passport.gov.uk). **U.S. Consulate General** (✉ Queen's House, 14 Queen St., Belfast, Northern Ireland BT1 6EQ, ☎ 028/9032–8239, WEB www.usembassy.org.uk). **U.S. Embassy** (enclose an SASE to: ✉ Consular Information Unit, 24 Grosvenor Sq., London W1 1AE, for general information; ✉ Visa Branch, 5 Upper Grosvenor St., London W1A 2JB, to submit an application via mail; ☎ 09068/200–290 recorded visa information; 09055/444–546 operator service [both with per-minute charges]; WEB www.usembassy.org.uk).

TELEPHONES

All U.S. telephone numbers consist of a three-digit area code and a seven-digit local number. Within most local calling areas, you dial only the seven-digit number. Within the same area code, dial "1" first. To call between area-code regions, dial "1" then all 10 digits; the same goes for calls to numbers prefixed by "800," "888," and "877"—all toll-free. For calls to numbers preceded by "900" you must pay—usually dearly. For international calls, dial "011" followed by the country code and the local number. For help, dial "0" and ask for an overseas operator. The country code is 61 for Australia, 64 for New Zealand, 44 for the United Kingdom. Calling Canada is the same as calling within the United States. Most local phone books list country codes and U.S. area codes. The country code for the United States is 1.

For operator assistance, dial "0". To obtain someone's phone number, call directory assistance, 555–1212 or occasionally 411 (free at public phones). To have the person you're calling foot the bill, phone collect; dial "0" instead of "1" before the 10-digit number.

At pay phones, instructions are usually posted. Usually you insert coins in a slot (10¢–50¢ for local calls) and wait for a steady tone before dialing. When you call long-distance, the operator tells you how much to insert; prepaid phone cards, widely available in various denominations, are easier. Call the number on the back, punch in the card's personal identification number when prompted, then dial your number.

LIQUOR LAWS

Liquor laws vary from state to state, affecting such matters as bar and liquor-store opening times and whether restaurants can sell liquor by the glass or only by the bottle. A few states—mostly in the South or Midwest—allow each county to choose its own policy, resulting in so-called dry counties, where no alcoholic beverages are sold, next to counties where the bars do a roaring business. The drinking age is 21 in all states, and you should **be prepared to show identification** in order to be served. Restaurants must obtain a license to sell alcoholic beverages on the premises, so some inexpensive establishments, or places that have recently opened, may not sell drinks at all or may sell only beer or wine. In many of these restaurants, however, you can bring your own beer or wine to drink with your meal. Local laws against driving while intoxicated are growing stricter. Many bars now serve nonalcoholic drinks for the "designated driver," so at least one person in a group is sober enough to drive everyone else safely home.

LODGING

A wide variety of lodging facilities is available in the United States, from gilded suites with marble bathrooms and sweeping views to bare-bones rooms with concrete walls and plastic furniture. An ultralavish hotel or resort room can easily run $500-plus a night, while a spartan roadside motel in a small town could cost $20–$30 per night. Prices vary dramatically depending on location and level of luxury.

Motels are close to highways, with convenient parking. At **Airport hotels** noise may be a problem, although the best ones are soundproofed. **Convention hotels** have hundreds of guest rooms, many meeting rooms, and big ballrooms used for exhibits and banquets. Other **downtown hotels** cater more to individual guests and may offer more in the way of health facilities and à la carte restaurants. **Suburban hotels** in many cities attract travelers who want to be close to the circumferential highway and to suburban office parks, shopping malls, or theme parks; they may be larger and more upscale than motels, offering more restaurants, health facilities, and other amenities. **Resorts** tend to be destinations in and of themselves, with golf courses, tennis courts, beaches, several restaurants, and on-site entertainment. One resort variation is the **dude ranch,** where paying guests sample horseback riding, hiking, lake fishing, cookouts, and such western-style activities as rodeos. **Country inns and bed-and-breakfasts** are generally charming older properties that, unlike European B&Bs, tend to be pricey and upscale. They may not have private bathrooms, an in-room phone, or TVs, and as they are frequently furnished with antiques, they may not be the best place to take young children. There is often an inviting common room where guests can gather for quiet conversation. Breakfast is usually included in the room rate, but verify this when you make a reservation.

The lodgings we list are the cream of the crop in each price category. We list facilities that are available—but we don't specify whether they cost extra: when pricing accommodations, always ask what's included and what's extra. Properties indicated by an ✕🏨 are lodging establishments whose restaurant warrants a special trip.

CATEGORY	COST*
$$$$	over $225
$$$	$150–$225
$$	$100–$150
$	under $100

**cost of a double room for two during peak season, excluding tax and service charges*

Assume that hotels operate on the **European Plan** (EP, with no meals) unless we specify that they use the **Continental Plan** (CP, with a Continental breakfast), **Breakfast Plan** (BP, with a full breakfast), **Modified American Plan** (MAP, with breakfast and dinner), or the **Full American Plan** (FAP, with all meals).

APARTMENT AND VILLA RENTALS

For a home base that's roomy enough for a family and comes with cooking facilities, **consider a furnished rental.** These can save you money, especially if you're with a group. Home-exchange directories sometimes list rentals as well as exchanges.

➤ INTERNATIONAL AGENTS: **Hideaways International** (✉ 767 Islington St., Portsmouth, NH 03801, ☎ 603/430–4433 or 800/843–4433, FAX 603/430–4444, WEB www.hideaways.com; membership $129). **Hometours International** (✉ Box 11503, Knoxville, TN 37939, ☎ 865/690–8484 or 800/367–4668, WEB thor.he.net/~hometour). **Interhome** (✉ 1990 N.E. 163rd St., Suite 110, N. Miami Beach, FL 33162, ☎ 305/940–2299 or 800/882–6864, FAX 305/940–2911, WEB www.interhome.com). **Vacation Home Rentals Worldwide** (✉ 235 Kensington Ave., Norwood, NJ 07648, ☎ 201/767–9393 or 800/633–3284, FAX 201/767–5510, WEB www.vhrww.com).

BED-AND-BREAKFASTS

A quaint and sometimes inexpensive option for those interested in getting to know the people as well as the local flavor of a town is to check into a bed-and-breakfast inn (also referred to as B&Bs). These are often run by individuals or families who open up their homes to paying visitors. Accommodations range from modest to museum-like but often entail shared bathrooms and a limited number of bedrooms. The fastest way to learn about current availability in a specific town or city is to call the local chamber of commerce for a list of the names and phone numbers of B&Bs in the area.

CAMPING

Some of the most reasonably priced campgrounds with the most compelling sites operate under the auspices of the national park system (☞ National Parks, *below*). If, however, you opt for private commercial operations, your best source for nationwide information on both public and private parks is the National Association of RV Parks and Campgrounds. You can also look for annually updated directories published by the American Automobile Association for camping assessments.

An overnight stay at a commercial campground can cost from $15 to $30, depending on three factors: the amenities, location, and time of year. Tent camping, of course, is the least expensive form of accommodation; if you want water, electric, and sewage hookups, you move into the higher end of the price range. Many private campgrounds are not open year-round, so it's important to **call ahead.** You can make reservations over the phone, and, customarily, a one-night deposit is required. The peak summer months of June, July, and August are very busy at the more desirable locations; the sooner you book, the more you can count on being awarded an attractive site.

➤ INFORMATION: **National Association of RV Parks and Campgrounds** (✉ 113 Park Ave., Fall Church, VA 22046, ☎ 703/241–8801, WEB www.gocampingamerica.com).

HOME EXCHANGES

If you would like to exchange your home for someone else's, **join a home-exchange organization,** which will send you its updated listings of available exchanges for a year and will include your own listing in at least one of them. It's up to you to make specific arrangements.

➤ EXCHANGE CLUBS: **HomeLink International** (✉ Box 47747, Tampa, FL 33647, ☎ 813/975–9825 or 800/638–3841, FAX 813/910–8144, WEB www.homelink.org; $106 per year). **Intervac U.S.** (✉ 30 Corte San Fernando, Tiburon, CA 94920, ☎ 800/756–4663, FAX 415/435–7440, WEB www.intervacus.com; $90 yearly fee for a listing, on-line access, and a catalog; $50 without catalog).

HOSTELS

No matter what your age, you can **save on lodging costs by staying at hostels.**In some 4,500 locations in more than 70 countries around the world, Hostelling International (HI), the umbrella group for a number of national youth-hostel associations, offers single-sex, dorm-style beds and, at many hostels, rooms for couples and family accommodations. Membership in any HI national hostel association, open to travelers of all ages, allows you to stay in HI-affiliated hostels at member rates; one-year membership is about $25 for adults (C$35 for a two-year minimum membership in Canada, £13 in the U.K., A$52 in Australia, and NZ$40 in New Zealand); hostels run about $10–$30 per night. Members have priority if the hostel is full; they're also eligible for discounts around the world, even on rail and bus travel in some countries.

➤ ORGANIZATIONS: **Hostelling International—American Youth Hostels** (✉ 733 15th St. NW, Suite 840, Washington, DC 20005, ☎ 202/783–6161, FAX 202/783–6171, WEB www.hiayh.org). **Hostelling International—Canada** (✉ 400–205 Catherine St., Ottawa, Ontario K2P 1C3, ☎ 613/237–7884 or 800/663–5777, FAX 613/237–7868, WEB www.hihostels.ca). **Youth Hostel Association of England and Wales** (✉ Trevelyan House, Dimple Rd., Matlock, Derbyshire DE4 3YH, U.K., ☎ 0870/870–8808, FAX 0169/592–702, WEB www.yha.org.uk). **Australian Youth Hostel Association** (✉ 10 Mallett St., Camperdown, NSW 2050, ☎ 02/9565–1699, FAX 02/9565–1325, WEB www.yha.com.au). **Youth Hostels Association of New Zealand** (✉ Box 436, Christchurch, ☎ 03/379–9970, FAX 03/365–4476, WEB www.yha.org.nz).

HOTELS

Hotel chains dominate the lodging landscape in the United States. Some of the large chains, such as Holiday Inn, Hilton, Hyatt, Marriott, and Ramada, are even further subdivided into chains of budget properties, all-suite properties, downtown hotels, or luxury resorts, each with a different name. Though some chain hotels may have a standardized look to them, this "cookie-cutter" approach also means that you can rely on the same level of comfort and efficiency at all properties in a well-managed chain, and at a chain's premier properties—its so-called flagship hotels—decor and services may be outstanding.

Most hotels will hold your reservation until 6 PM; **call ahead if you plan to arrive late.** Hotels will be more willing to hold a late reservation for you if you reserve with a credit-card number. When you call to make a reservation, **ask all the necessary questions up front.** If you are arriving with a car, ask if the hotel has a parking lot or covered garage and whether there is an extra fee for parking. If you like to eat your meals in, ask if the hotel has a restaurant or whether it has room service (most do, but not necessarily 24 hours a day—and be forewarned that it can be expensive). Most hotels have in-room telephones, but double-check this at inexpensive properties and bed-and-breakfasts. Most hotels and motels have in-room TVs, often with cable movies (usually pay-per-view), and many properties also have in-room data ports; verify all of these amenities if they're important to you. If you want an in-room crib or cot for your child, there will probably be an additional charge. All hotels listed have private bath unless noted.

➤ TOLL-FREE NUMBERS: **Adam's Mark** (☎ 800/444–2326, WEB www.adamsmark.com). **Baymont Inns** (☎ 800/428–3438, WEB www.baymontinns.com). **Best Western** (☎ 800/528–1234, WEB www.bestwestern.com). **Choice** (☎ 800/424–6423, WEB www.choicehotels.com). **Clarion** (☎ 800/424–6423, WEB www.choicehotels.com). **Colony Resorts** (☎ 800/777–1700). **Comfort Inn** (☎ 800/424–6423, WEB www.choicehotels.com). **Days Inn** (☎ 800/325–2525, WEB www.daysinn.com). **Doubletree and Red Lion Hotels** (☎ 800/222–8733, WEB www.hilton.com). **Embassy Suites** (☎ 800/362–2779, WEB www.embassysuites.com). **Fairfield Inn** (☎ 800/228–2800, WEB www.marriott.com). **Four Seasons** (☎ 800/332–3442, WEB www.fourseasons.com). **Hilton** (☎ 800/445–8667, WEB www.hilton.com). **Holiday Inn** (☎ 800/465–4329, WEB www.sixcontinentshotels.com). **Howard Johnson** (☎ 800/654–4656, WEB www.hojo.com). **Hyatt Hotels & Resorts** (☎ 800/233–1234, WEB www.hyatt.com). **Inter-Continental** (☎ 800/327–0200, WEB www.intercontinental.com). **La Quinta** (☎ 800/531–5900, WEB www.laquinta.com). **Marriott** (☎ 800/228–9290, WEB www.marriott.com). **Le Meridien** (☎ 800/543–4300, WEB www.lemeridien-hotels.com). **Nikko Hotels International** (☎ 800/645–5687, WEB www.nikkohotels.com). **Omni** (☎ 800/843–6664, WEB www.omnihotels.com). **Quality Inn** (☎ 800/424–6423, WEB www.choicehotels.com). **Radisson** (☎ 800/333–3333, WEB www.radisson.com). **Ramada** (☎ 800/228–2828; 800/854–7854 international reservations; WEB www.ramada.com or www.ramadahotels.com). **Renaissance Hotels & Resorts** (☎ 800/468–3571, WEB www.renaissancehotels.com). **Ritz-Carlton** (☎ 800/241–3333, WEB www.ritzcarlton.com). **Sheraton** (☎ 800/325–3535, WEB www.starwood.com/sheraton). **Sleep Inn** (☎ 800/424–6423, WEB www.choicehotels.com). **Westin Hotels & Resorts** (☎ 800/228–3000, WEB www.starwood.com/westin). **Wyndham Hotels & Resorts** (☎ 800/822–4200, WEB www.wyndham.com).

MOTELS

➤ TOLL-FREE NUMBERS: **Budget Hosts Inns** (☎ 800/283–4678, WEB www.budgethost.com). **Econo Lodge** (☎ 800/553–2666, WEB www.econolodge.com). **Friendship Inns** (☎ 800/453–4511, WEB www.hotelchoice.com). **Motel 6** (☎ 800/466–8356, WEB www.motel6.com). **Rodeway** (☎ 800/228–2000, WEB www.choicehotels.com). **Super 8** (☎ 800/848–8888, WEB www.super8.com).

MONEY MATTERS

Prices throughout this guide are given for adults. Substantially reduced fees are almost always available for children, students, and senior citizens. For information on taxes, *see* Taxes, *below.*

ATMS

A debit card, also known as a check card, deducts funds directly from your checking account and helps you stay within your budget. When you want to rent a car, though, you may still need an old-fashioned credit card. Although you can always *pay* for your car with a debit card, some agencies will not allow you to *reserve* a car with a debit card. Otherwise, the two types of plastic are virtually the same. Both will get you cash advances at ATMs worldwide if your card is properly programmed with your personal identification number (PIN). Both offer excellent, wholesale exchange rates. And both protect you against unauthorized use if the card is lost or stolen. Your liability is limited to $50, as long as you report the card missing.

CREDIT CARDS

Should you use a credit card or a debit card when traveling? Both have benefits. A credit card allows you to delay payment and gives you certain rights as a consumer (☞ Consumer Protection, *above*). Throughout this guide, the following abbreviations are used: **AE,** American Express; **D,** Discover; **DC,** Diners Club; **MC,** MasterCard; and **V,** Visa.

➤ REPORTING LOST CARDS: **American Express** (☎ 800/441–0519). **Discover**

(☎ 800/347–2683). **Diners Club** (☎ 800/234–6377). **MasterCard** (☎ 800/622–7747). **Visa** (☎ 800/ 847–2911).

BANKS

In general, U.S. banks will not cash a personal check for you unless you have an account at that bank (it doesn't have to be at that branch). Only in major cities are large bank branches equipped to exchange foreign currencies. Therefore, it's best to rely on credit cards, cash machines, and traveler's checks to handle expenses while you're traveling.

EXCHANGING MONEY

In the United States, it is not as easy to find places to exchange currency as it is in European cities. In major international cities, such as New York and Los Angeles, currency may be exchanged at some bank branches, as well as at currency-exchange booths in airports and at foreign-currency offices such as American Express Travel Service and Thomas Cook (check local directories for addresses and phone numbers). The best strategy is to **buy traveler's checks in U.S. dollars** before you come to the United States; although the rates may not be as good abroad, the time saved by not having to search constantly for exchange facilities far outweighs any financial loss. For the most favorable rates, **change money through banks.** Although fees charged for ATM transactions may be higher abroad than at home, Cirrus and Plus exchange rates are excellent, because they are based on wholesale rates offered only by major banks. You won't do as well at exchange booths in airports or rail and bus stations, in hotels, in restaurants, or in stores, although you may find their hours more convenient. To avoid lines at airport exchange booths, **get a bit of local currency before you leave home.**

► EXCHANGE SERVICES: **Chase Foreign Currency** (☎ 888/242–7384). **Capital Foreign Exchange** (☎ 888/842–0880 on the East Coast, 888/278–6628 on the West Coast). **Thomas Cook Currency Services** (☎ 800/287–7362 telephone orders and retail locations, WEB www.travelex.com).

MONEY ORDERS, FUNDS TRANSFERS

Any U.S. bank is equipped to accept transfers of funds from foreign banks. It helps if you can plan dates to pick up money at specific bank branches. Your home bank can supply you with a list of its correspondent banks in the United States. If you have more time, and you have a U.S. address where you can receive mail, you can have someone send you a certified check, which you can cash at any bank, or a postal money order (for as much as $700, obtained for a fee of up to 85¢ at any U.S. post office and redeemable at any other post office). From overseas, you can have someone go to a bank to send you an international money order (also called a bank draft), which will cost a $15–$20 commission plus airmail postage. Always bring two valid pieces of identification, preferably with photos, to claim your money.

TRAVELER'S CHECKS

Do you need traveler's checks? It depends on where you're headed. If you're going to rural areas and small towns, go with cash; traveler's checks are best used in cities. Lost or stolen checks can usually be replaced within 24 hours. To ensure a speedy refund, buy your own traveler's checks—don't let someone else pay for them, as this can cause delays. The person who bought the checks should make the call to request a refund.

NATIONAL PARKS

Look into discount passes to save money on park entrance fees. For $50, the National Parks Pass admits you (and any passengers in your private vehicle) to all national parks, monuments, and recreation areas, as well as other sites run by the National Park Service, for a year. (In parks that charge per person, the pass admits you, your spouse and children, and your parents, when you arrive together.) Camping and parking are extra. The $15 Golden Eagle Pass, a hologram you affix to your National Parks Pass, functions as an upgrade, granting entry to all sites run by the NPS, the U.S. Fish and Wildlife Service, the U.S. Forest Service, and the Bureau of Land Management (BLM).

The upgrade, which expires with the parks pass, is sold by most national-park, Fish and Wildlife, and BLM fee stations. A percentage of the proceeds from pass sales funds National Parks projects.

Both the Golden Age Passport ($10), for U.S. citizens or permanent residents who are 62 and older, and the Golden Access Passport (free), for those with disabilities, entitle holders (and any passengers in their private vehicles) to lifetime free entry to all national parks, plus 50% off fees for the use of many park facilities and services. (The discount doesn't always apply to companions.) To obtain them, you must show proof of age and of U.S. citizenship or permanent residency—such as a U.S. passport, driver's license, or birth certificate—and, if requesting Golden Access, proof of disability. The Golden Age and Golden Access passes, as well as the National Parks Pass, are available at any NPS-run site that charges an entrance fee. The National Parks Pass is also available by mail and via the Internet.

➤ INFORMATION: **National Park Foundation** (✉ 1101 17th St. NW, Suite 1102, Washington, DC 20036, ☎ 202/785–4500, WEB www.nationalparks.org). **National Park Service** (✉ National Park Service/ Department of Interior, 1849 C St. NW, Washington, DC 20240, ☎ 202/208–4747, WEB www.nps.gov). **National Parks Conservation Association** (✉ 1300 19th St. NW, Suite 300, Washington, DC 20036, ☎ 202/223–6722, WEB www.npca.org.)

➤ PASSES BY MAIL AND ON-LINE: **National Park Foundation** (WEB www.nationalparks.org). **National Parks Pass** (✉ 27540 Ave. Mentry, Valencia, CA 91355, ☎ 888/GO–PARKS or 888/467–2757, WEB www.nationalparks.org); include a check or money order payable to the National Park Service for the pass, plus $3.95 for shipping and handling.

PACKING

The American lifestyle is generally casual: women may wear slacks and men may go without a jacket and tie virtually anywhere, except expensive restaurants in larger cities. If you prefer to dress up for dinner or the theater, though, go right ahead. As a rule, people in the Northeast dress more formally, while people in such places as Florida, Texas, and southern California are relatively informal. In beach towns, many hotels and restaurants post signs announcing that they will not serve customers who are shoeless, shirtless, or dressed in bathing suits or other skimpy attire, so tote along some shoes and cover-ups.

The United States has a wide range of climates. When deciding what weather to dress for, **read the "When to Go" sections in chapter introductions** for each region you'll be visiting. One caveat: even in warm destinations, you may want an extra layer of clothing to compensate for overactive air-conditioning or to protect against brisk ocean breezes. Although you can count on all modern buildings being well heated in winter, historic inns and hunting lodges in rugged climates—New England, the Great Lakes states, the Rockies, or the Pacific Northwest—may be poorly insulated, drafty, or heated only by wood-burning fireplaces. Pack accordingly.

If you'll be sightseeing in historic cities, you'll spend a lot of time walking, so **bring sturdy, well-fitting, flat-heeled shoes.** Don't forget deck shoes if you want to go sailing and sandals for walking across the burning-hot sand of sunny beaches. If you plan to hike in the country, pack shoes or boots with strong flexible soles and wear long pants to protect your legs from brambles and insect bites.

Bring sunscreen lotion if you expect to be out in the sun, because prices may be high at beachside stores. These days most upscale hotels provide a basket of toiletries—soaps, shampoo, conditioner, bath gel—but if you prefer using a certain brand, bring your own. Hand-held hair dryers are sometimes provided, but don't rely on this. You can generally request an iron and ironing board from the front desk.

In your carry-on luggage, **pack an extra pair of eyeglasses or contact lenses and enough of any medication** you take to last a few days longer than the entire trip. You may also ask your doctor to write a spare prescription using the drug's generic name, since brand names may vary from country to country. In luggage to be checked, **never pack prescription drugs or valuables.** And don't forget to carry with you the addresses of offices that handle refunds of lost traveler's checks. Check *Fodor's How to Pack* (available in bookstores everywhere) for more tips.

To avoid customs and security delays, carry medications in their original packaging. Don't pack any sharp objects in your carry-on luggage, including knives of any size or material, scissors, manicure tools, and corkscrews, or anything else that might arouse suspicion.

CHECKING LUGGAGE

You are allowed one carry-on bag and one personal article, such as a purse or a laptop computer. Make sure that everything you carry aboard will fit under your seat or in the overhead bin. Get to the gate early, so you can board as soon as possible, before the overhead bins fill up. If you are flying internationally, note that baggage allowances may be determined not by piece but by weight—generally 88 pounds (40 kilograms) in first class, 66 pounds (30 kilograms) in business class, and 44 pounds (20 kilograms) in economy.

Airline liability for baggage is limited to $2,500 per person on flights within the United States. On international flights it amounts to $9.07 per pound or $20 per kilogram for checked baggage (roughly $640 per 70-pound bag) and $400 per passenger for unchecked baggage. You can buy additional coverage at check-in for about $10 per $1,000 of coverage, but it excludes a rather extensive list of items, shown on your airline ticket.

Before departure, **itemize your bags' contents** and their worth, and label the bags with your name, address, and phone number. (If you use your home address, cover it so potential thieves can't see it readily.) Inside each bag, **pack a copy of your itinerary.** At check-in, **make sure that each bag is correctly tagged** with the destination airport's three-letter code. If your bags arrive damaged or fail to arrive at all, file a written report with the airline before leaving the airport.

SENIOR-CITIZEN TRAVEL

To qualify for age-related discounts, **mention your senior-citizen status up front** when booking hotel reservations (not when checking out) and before you're seated in restaurants (not when paying the bill). Be sure to have identification on hand. When renting a car, ask about promotional car-rental discounts, which can be cheaper than senior-citizen rates.

➤ EDUCATIONAL PROGRAMS: **Elderhostel** (✉ 75 Federal St., 3rd floor, Boston, MA 02110, ☎ 877/426–8056, FAX 877/426–2166, WEB www.elderhostel.org). **Interhostel** (✉ University of New Hampshire, 6 Garrison Ave., Durham, NH 03824, ☎ 603/862–1147 or 800/733–9753, FAX 603/862–1113, WEB www.learn.unh.edu).

STUDENTS IN THE UNITED STATES

➤ IDS AND SERVICES: **Council Travel** (✉ 205 E. 42nd St., 15th floor, New York, NY 10017, ☎ 212/822–2700 or 888/226–8624, FAX 212/822–2719, WEB www.counciltravel.com). **Travel Cuts** (✉ 187 College St., Toronto, Ontario M5T 1P7, Canada, ☎ 416/979–2406 or 888/838–2887, FAX 416/979–8167, WEB www.travelcuts.com).

TAXES

HOTEL

Many states and cities levy hotel taxes, usually as a percentage of the room rate. For example, in New York City, there is a 13.25% progressive hotel tax and an additional $2 per-room, per-night occupancy tax. When you make room reservations **ask how much tax will be added to the basic rate.**

SALES TAX

There is no U.S. value-added tax, but sales taxes are set by most individual states, and they can range anywhere from 3% to 8¼%. In some states, localities are permitted to add their own sales taxes as well. Exactly what is taxable, however, varies from place to place. In some areas, food and other essentials are not taxable, although you might pay tax for restaurant food. Luxury items such as cigarettes and alcohol are sometimes subject to an extra tax (known colloquially as a "sin tax"), as is gasoline, on the theory that car users should provide funds used to improve local roads.

TIPPING

At restaurants, a 15% tip is standard for waiters; up to 20% may be expected at more expensive establishments. The same goes for taxi drivers, bartenders, and hairdressers. Coat-check operators usually expect $1; bellhops and porters should get $1 per bag; hotel maids in upscale hotels should get about $1 per day of your stay. A concierge typically receives a tip of $5 to $10, with an additional gratuity for special services or favors. On package tours, conductors and drivers usually get $10 per day from the group as a whole; check whether this has already been figured into your cost. For local sightseeing tours, you may individually tip the driver-guide $2–$5 if he or she has been helpful or informative. Ushers in theaters do not expect tips.

TOURS AND PACKAGES

Because everything is prearranged on a prepackaged tour or independent vacation, you spend less time planning—and often get it all at a good price.

BOOKING WITH AN AGENT

Travel agents are excellent resources. But it's a good idea to collect brochures from several agencies, as some agents' suggestions may be influenced by relationships with tour and package firms that reward them for volume sales. If you have a special interest, **find an agent with expertise in that area**; the American Society of Travel Agents (ASTA; ☞ Travel Agencies, *below*) has a database of specialists worldwide. Make sure your travel agent knows the accommodations and other services of the place being recommended. Ask about the hotel's location, room size, beds, and whether it has a pool, room service, or programs for children, if you care about these. Has your agent been there in person or sent others whom you can contact? Do some homework on your own, too: local tourism boards can provide information about lesser-known and small-niche operators, some of which may sell only direct.

BUYER BEWARE

Each year consumers are stranded or lose their money when tour operators—even large ones with excellent reputations—go out of business. So **check out the operator.** Ask several travel agents about its reputation, and try to **book with a company that has a consumer-protection program.** (Look for information in the company's brochure.) In the United States, members of the National Tour Association and the United States Tour Operators Association are required to set aside funds to cover your payments and travel arrangements in the event that the company defaults. It's also a good idea to choose a company that participates in the American Society of Travel Agents' Tour Operator Program (TOP); ASTA will act as mediator in any disputes between you and your tour operator.

Remember that the more your package or tour includes the better you can predict the ultimate cost of your vacation. Make sure you know exactly what is covered, and **beware of hidden costs.** Are taxes, tips, and transfers included? Entertainment and excursions? These can add up.

➤ TOUR-OPERATOR RECOMMENDATIONS: **American Society of Travel Agents** (☞ Travel Agencies, *below*). **National Tour Association** (NTA; ✉ 546 E. Main St., Lexington, KY 40508, ☎ 859/226–4444 or 800/682–8886, WEB www.ntaonline.com). **United States Tour Operators Association** (USTOA; ✉ 275 Madison Ave. Suite 2014, New York, NY 10016, ☎ 212/599–6599 or 800/468–7862, FAX 212/599–6744, WEB www.ustoa.com).

TRAIN TRAVEL

Amtrak is the national passenger rail service. It runs a limited number of routes; the northeast coast from Boston down to Washington, D.C., i generally well served. Chicago is a major rail terminus as well. Some trains travel overnight, and you can sleep in your seat or book a sleeping car at additional cost. Most trains have diner cars with acceptable food, but you may prefer to bring your own. Excursion fares, when available, may save you nearly half the round-trip fare.

FARES AND SCHEDULES

Train schedules can be obtained at ticket counters or special displays in train terminals. Automated schedule and fare information is often available 24 hours a day on local or toll-free numbers.

➤ TRAIN INFORMATION: **Amtrak** (☎ 800/872–7245, 800/523–6590 TDD, WEB www.amtrak.com).

CHILDREN

Children under 2 ride free (one child per adult) if they don't occupy a seat; children 2–15 accompanied by a fare-paying adult pay half-price (two children per adult); children 16 and over pay the full adult fare.

CUTTING COSTS

The USA Rail Pass allows overseas visitors 15 or 30 days of unlimited nationwide travel for $440 or $550 (peak season, June–September 4) and $295–$385 (off peak, September 5–May), respectively. Fifteen- and 30-day regional rail passes can be purchased by non-U.S. citizens for the Far West ($245/$320, peak season; $190/$250, off-peak), Western ($325/$405, peak; $200/$270, off-peak), Eastern ($260/$320, peak; $210/$265, off-peak), and Northeast ($205/$240, peak; $185/$225, off-peak) areas of the United States; 30-day passes are also offered for rail travel along the East Coast and West Coast (each is $285, peak; $235, off-peak) regions of the country. You can purchase these rail passes in the United States at any Amtrak station, but to qualify you must show a valid non-U.S. passport. If you're a student, ask about student discounts that may apply to certain passes.

SENIOR CITIZENS

Senior citizens (over 62) are entitled to a 15% discount on the lowest available fares.

TRAVELERS WITH DISABILITIES

Amtrak requests 48 hours' advance notice to provide redcap service, special seats, or wheelchair assistance at stations equipped to provide these services. Passengers with disabilities receive 15% off an adult one-way fare.

TRAVEL AGENCIES

A good travel agent puts your needs first. Look for an agency that has been in business at least five years, emphasizes customer service, and has someone on staff who specializes in your destination. In addition, **make sure the agency belongs to a professional trade organization.** The American Society of Travel Agents (ASTA)—the largest and most influential in the field, with more than 24,000 members in some 140 countries—maintains and enforces a strict code of ethics and will step in to help mediate any agent-client disputes involving ASTA members if necessary. ASTA (whose motto is "Without a travel agent, you're on your own") also maintains a Web site that includes a directory of agents. (If a travel agency is also acting as your tour operator, *see* Buyer Beware *in* Tours and Packages, *above.*)

➤ LOCAL AGENT REFERRALS: **American Society of Travel Agents** (ASTA; ✉ 1101 King St., Suite 200, Alexandria, VA 22314, ☎ 800/965–2782 24-hr hot line, FAX 703/739–3268, WEB www.astanet.com). **Association of British Travel Agents** (✉ 68–71 Newman St., London W1T 3AH, ☎ 020/7637–2444, FAX 020/7637–0713, WEB www.abtanet.com). **Association of Canadian Travel Agents** (✉ 130 Albert St., Suite 1705, Ottawa, Ontario K1P 5G4, ☎ 613/237–3657, FAX 613/237–7052, WEB www.acta.ca). **Australian Federation of Travel Agents** (✉ Level 3, 309 Pitt St., Sydney, NSW 2000, ☎ 02/9264–3299, FAX 02/9264–1085, WEB www.afta.com.au). **Travel Agents' Association of New Zealand** (✉ Level 5, Tourism and Travel House, 79 Boulcott St. [Box 1888, Wellington 6001], ☎ 04/499–0104, FAX 04/499–0827, WEB www.taanz.org.nz).

VISITOR INFORMATION

State tourism offices, city tourist bureaus, and local chambers of commerce, which are usually the best sources of information about their communities, are listed throughout this book at the beginning of each state, city, or regional section. Government agencies can be an excellent source of inexpensive travel information. When planning your trip, **find out what government materials are available.**

➤ IN THE U.K.: There is no single tourist organization for the United States; U.S. states have their own agencies. Call **Visit USA** (☎ 0891/600–530) for contact addresses and telephone numbers; calls cost 50p per minute peak times, 45p per minute all other times.

➤ U.S. GOVERNMENT RESOURCES: Contact the **Consumer Information Center** (✉ Consumer Information Catalogue, Pueblo, CO 81009, ☎ 888/878–3256, FAX 719/948–9724, WEB www.pueblo.gsa.gov) for a free catalog that includes travel titles.

WEB SITES

Do check out the World Wide Web when planning your trip. You'll find everything from weather forecasts to virtual tours of famous cities. Be sure to **visit Fodors.com** (www.fodors.com), a complete travel-planning site. You can research prices and book plane tickets, hotel rooms, rental cars, vacation packages, and more. In addition, you can post your pressing questions in the "Travel Talk" section. Other planning tools include a currency converter and weather reports, and there are loads of links to travel resources.

WHEN TO GO

Although there is no country-wide tourist season, various regions may have high and low seasons that are reflected in airfares and hotel rates. Unless the weather is a real drawback (as in Alaska in the winter or Miami in August), **visit areas during their off season to save money and avoid crowds.**

CLIMATE

For climate information in specific regions of the country, **read the "When to Go" sections in United States Region by Region chapter.**

➤ FORECASTS: **Weather Channel Connection** (☎ 900/932–8437), 95¢ per minute from a Touch-Tone phone.

THE UNITED STATES REGION BY REGION

From mountains and oceans to deserts and meadows, from sprawling cities of towering skyscrapers to villages with roots still firmly planted in the past, the U.S.A. cannot be summed up easily. This chapter attempts to make sense of it all by dividing the country into 10 regions.

THE NORTHEAST

Connecticut, Maine, Massachusetts, New Hampshire, New York, Rhode Island, Vermont

The Northeast fans out in waves of increasingly soothing vistas, from the placid charms of the Connecticut River valley and Rhode Island's Narragansett Bay, through the forests of Vermont and New Hampshire, to the pristine hinterland of northern Maine.

The region was historically defined by the coastline, where the Pilgrims first established a toehold in the New World. Until it veers inland north of Yarmouth, Maine, I–95 skirts the inlets and harbors that sheltered the whaling and trading vessels of 17th- to 19th-century settlers. Every season brings its own recreations—fishing in New York, skiing in Vermont, biking along Maine's rocky coast.

When to Go

Spring blooms start in April along the southern coastal regions and begin later the farther north you go. This tends to be the quietest period throughout the region. **Summer,** which ranges from an average monthly high of 85°F in the southern region to an average monthly low of 59°F in the north, attracts beach lovers to the islands and coastal regions; those preferring cooler climes head to the lakes in New York State, the mists of Maine, or the mountains. **Autumn** is a kaleidoscope of colors as leaves change from green to burning gold. Temperatures remain around 55°F into October in many places. **Winter** brings snow and skiers to the mountain slopes of most states in the region.

Festivals and Seasonal Events

Winter

➤ MID-JAN.: Vermont's **Stowe Winter Carnival** (☎ 802/253–7321 or 800/247–8693) is among the country's oldest such celebrations.

Spring

➤ MAR. 17: All of Boston turns out for the **St. Patrick's Day Parade** (☎ 888/733–2678).

➤ MID-APR.: On Patriot's Day in Boston, celebrants reenact **Paul Revere's ride** (☎ 888/733–2678). The **Boston Marathon** (☎ 617/236–1652) fills the streets from Hopkinton to Back Bay.

Summer

➤ LATE JUNE: **Lesbian and Gay Pride Week** (☎ 212/807–7433, WEB www.nycpride.org) in New York City, includes the world's biggest annual gay pride parade. New York's **JVC Jazz Festival** (☎ 212/501–1390, WEB www.festivalproductions.net/jvc/ny) brings giants of jazz and new faces alike to theaters and clubs about town.

➤ LATE JUNE–EARLY JULY: Boston's weeklong Fourth of July celebration, **Harborfest** (☎ 617/227–1528), includes a concert synchronized to fireworks over the harbor.

➤ EARLY JULY: The **North Atlantic Blues Festival** showcase top blues singers in a Rockland, Maine, harbor-front park (☎ 207/596–0376).

➤ JULY–AUG.: The **Tanglewood Music Festival** (☎ 413/637–1600 or 617/638–9235), in Lenox, Massachusetts, the summer home of the Boston Symphony Orchestra, schedules top performers.

➤ LATE JULY: Forty wineries take part in the **Finger Lakes Wine Festival** (☎ 607/535–2481) in Watkins Glen, New York.

➤ EARLY AUG.: The **Maine Lobster Festival** (☎ 207/596–0376) is a public feast held on the first weekend of the month in Rockland. **Ben & Jerry's Folk Festival** (☎ 401/847–3700), held in Newport, Rhode Island, books top names like the Indigo Girls and Joan Baez.

➤ MID-AUG.: Newport, Rhode Island's Fort Adams State Park is host to the **JVC Jazz Festival** (☎ 401/847–3700), formerly the Newport Jazz Festival, one of the nation's premier jazz events.

➤ LATE AUG.–EARLY SEPT.: The **U.S. Open Tennis Tournament** (☎ 718/760–6200), in Flushing Meadows–Corona Park, Queens, is one of New York City's premier sport events.

Autumn

➤ OCT.: College crew teams and spectators bearing blankets and beer come from all over for the **Head of the Charles Regatta** (☎ 617/868–6200, WEB www.hocr.org) in Boston.

➤ EARLY NOV.: The **New York City Marathon** (☎ 212/860–4455) is the world's largest; it winds through all boroughs of the city.

'HE MIDDLE ATLANTIC STATES

)elaware, Maryland, New Jersey, Pennsylvania, /irginia, West Virginia, Vashington, D.C.

n the closing decades of the 18th century, he major action in the New World was ere: George Washington's audacious rossing of the Delaware River made posible the colonists' victory in the Battle of 'renton; Virginia saw the war's final battles and surrender; the Constitution was ammered out in Philadelphia; and)elaware ratified the Constitution and ecame the first state.

'he Middle Atlantic countryside is a land nuch walked through and fought over. Beond the New Jersey Turnpike are long eaches, casino-filled Atlantic City, and /ictorian Cape May to the east; horse ountry, ski resorts, and Philadelphia to he west. The Eastern Shore's Delaware nd Maryland beaches are sedate or swingng; Virginia Beach is both. Baltimore ombines historic buildings with new estaurants and shops; Annapolis and Oxord are ports for boaters tooling around he Chesapeake. Washington, D.C., the naion's seat of government, has myriad reasures set off by cherry trees. In Williamsburg you'll hear echoes of the Revolution and sample 18th-century life.

Vhen to Go

n the cool early **spring** Washington's pink herry blossoms are at their peak for a few pectacular days. **Summer** is swampy in Washington, Baltimore, and Philadelphia, vith temperatures in the 80s, yet thouands flock to all three for monuments or aseball. The dazzling **autumn** foliage in /irginia's Shenandoah Valley and West /irginia's Potomac Highlands draws ordes. In **winter,** when temperatures average in the 40s, Maryland, Pennsylvania, 'irginia, and West Virginia offer downill and cross-country skiing.

Festivals and Seasonal Events

Winter

➤ JAN. 1: The **Mummers Parade** (☎ 215/735–6430; 215/336–3050 Mummers Museum), in **Philadelphia,** ushers in the year with some 20,000 sequined and feathered marchers.

➤ MID-FEB.: **George Washington's Birthday** (☎ 703/838–4200) is celebrated in **Alexandria, Virginia,** with a parade and reenactment of a Revolutionary War skirmish at nearby Fort Ward.

Spring

➤ LATE MAR.–EARLY APR.: The two-week-long **National Cherry Blossom Festival** (☎ 202/728–1137, 202/547–1500, or 202/619–7275) takes place in **Washington, D.C.,** with a parade, a marathon, and a Japanese lantern-lighting ceremony.

➤ LATE APR.–EARLY MAY: The **Philadelphia Festival of World Cinema** (☎ 800/969–7392) presents films from more than 30 countries.

➤ MID-MAY: The **Preakness** (☎ 410/837–3030), held in **Baltimore, Maryland,** is the second event of horse-racing's Triple Crown.

Summer

➤ JUNE: **Philadelphia's First Union U.S. Pro Cycling Championship** (☎ 610/676–0390) is the country's premier bicycle race.

➤ LATE JUNE: The **Hampton Jazz Festival** (☎ 757/838–4203), in **Hampton, Virginia,** brings together top performers in various styles of jazz.

➤ LATE AUG.: The **Philadelphia Folk Festival** (☎ 215/242–0150) is America's oldest (1962) continuous folk festival.

Autumn

➤ MID-OCT.: The **Taste of DC Festival** (☎ 202/724–5430) presents dishes from a variety of **Washington, D.C.,** eateries.

➤ LATE OCT.–EARLY NOV.: New Hollywood and independent movies are screened at the **Virginia Film Festival** (☎ 434/982–5277) in **Charlottesville, Virginia.**

The Northeast

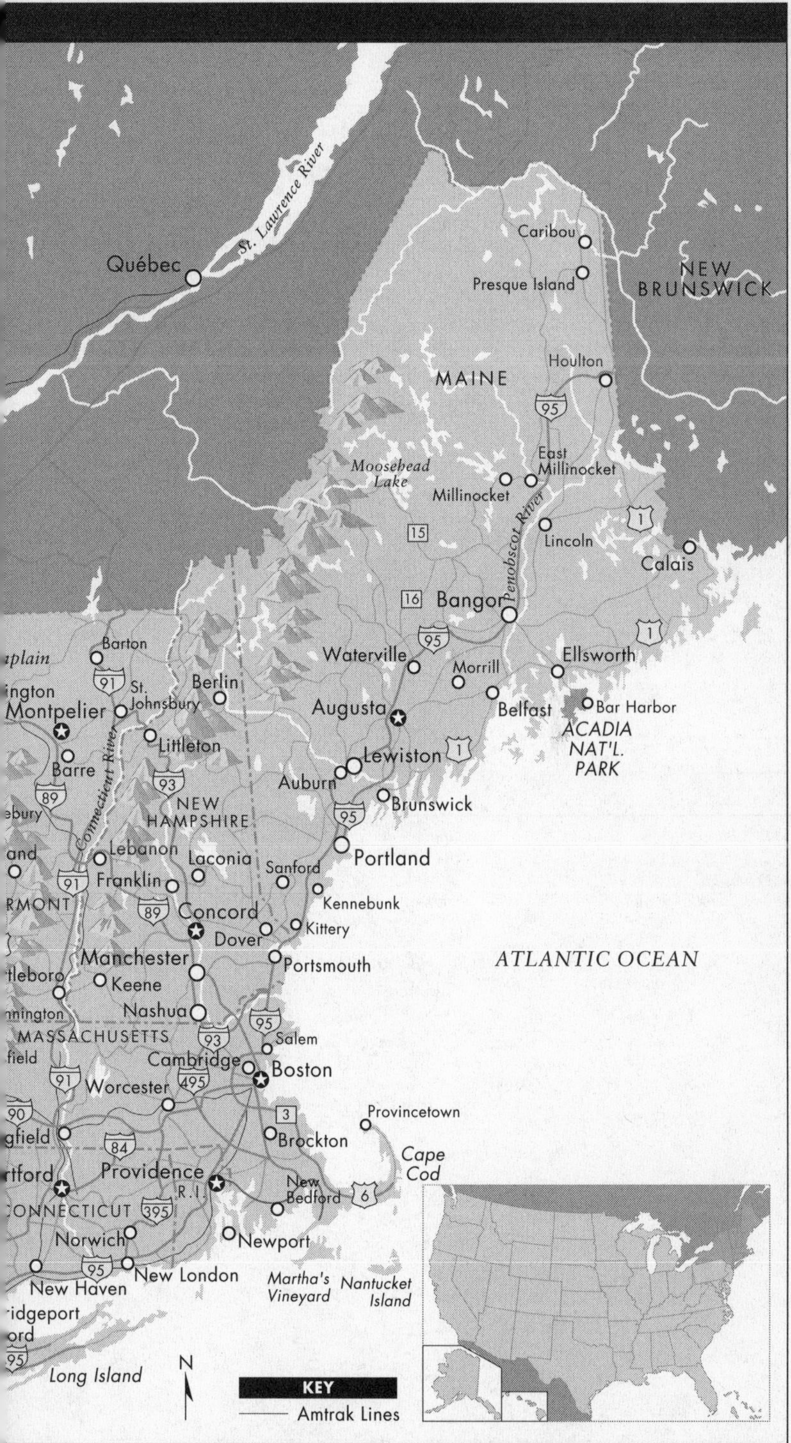
St. Lawrence River
Québec
Caribou
Presque Island
NEW BRUNSWICK
Houlton
MAINE
95
Moosehead Lake
East Millinocket
Millinocket
Penobscot River
1
15
Lincoln
Calais
16
Bangor
1
Barton
95
Waterville
Morrill
Ellsworth
91
St. Johnsbury
Berlin
Augusta
Belfast
Bar Harbor
Montpelier
Littleton
ACADIA NAT'L. PARK
Lewiston
1
Barre
Connecticut River
93
Auburn
Brunswick
89
NEW HAMPSHIRE
95
Lebanon
Laconia
Sanford
Portland
91
Franklin
Kennebunk
89
Concord
Kittery
Dover
Manchester
Portsmouth
ATLANTIC OCEAN
Keene
Nashua
95
MASSACHUSETTS
93
Salem
Cambridge
Boston
91
Worcester
495
3
Provincetown
Brockton
84
Cape Cod
Providence
R.I.
New Bedford
6
CONNECTICUT
395
Norwich
Newport
95
New London
New Haven
Martha's Vineyard
Nantucket Island
Long Island
N
KEY
Amtrak Lines

The Middle Atlantic States

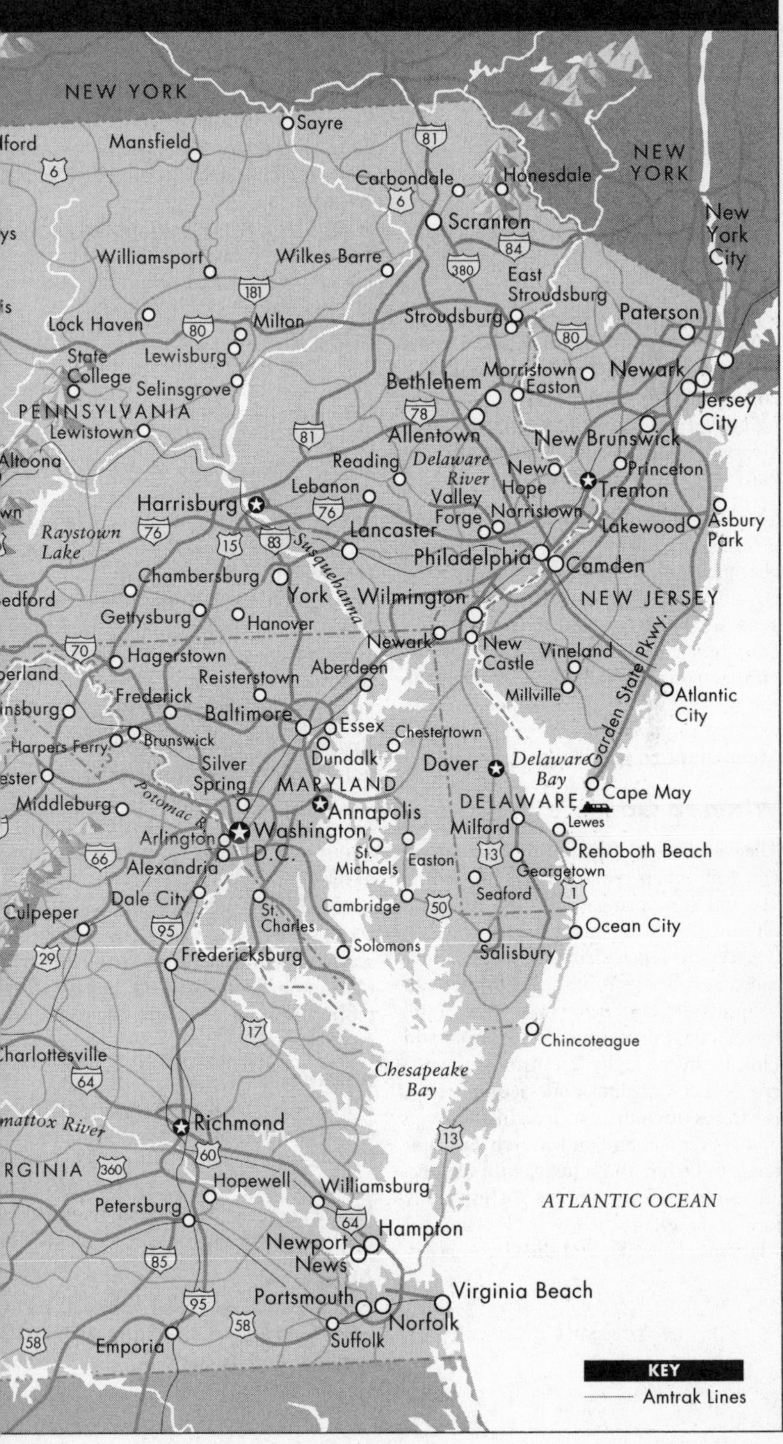

NEW YORK
Sayre
Mansfield
Carbondale
Honesdale
NEW YORK
Scranton
New York City
Williamsport
Wilkes Barre
East Stroudsburg
Stroudsburg
Paterson
Lock Haven
Milton
Lewisburg
State College
Selinsgrove
Bethlehem
Morristown
Easton
Newark
Jersey City
PENNSYLVANIA
Lewistown
Allentown
New Brunswick
Altoona
Reading
Delaware River
New Hope
Princeton
Trenton
Lebanon
Valley Forge
Norristown
Harrisburg
Lakewood
Asbury Park
Raystown Lake
Lancaster
Susquehanna
Philadelphia
Camden
Chambersburg
York
Wilmington
NEW JERSEY
Gettysburg
Hanover
Newark
New Castle
Vineland
Hagerstown
Reisterstown
Aberdeen
Millville
Atlantic City
Garden State Pkwy.
Frederick
Baltimore
Essex
Chestertown
Harpers Ferry
Brunswick
Dundalk
Dover
Delaware Bay
Silver Spring
MARYLAND
Cape May
Potomac R.
Middleburg
Annapolis
DELAWARE
Lewes
Washington D.C.
Milford
Rehoboth Beach
Arlington
St. Michaels
Easton
Alexandria
Georgetown
Seaford
Dale City
Culpeper
Cambridge
St. Charles
Ocean City
Solomons
Salisbury
Fredericksburg
Chincoteague
Charlottesville
Chesapeake Bay
Richmond
RGINIA
Hopewell
Williamsburg
Petersburg
ATLANTIC OCEAN
Hampton
Newport News
Virginia Beach
Portsmouth
Norfolk
Suffolk
Emporia
KEY
Amtrak Lines

THE SOUTHEAST

Alabama, Florida, Georgia, North Carolina, South Carolina

The Southeast stretches from pine to palm, lapped by the Atlantic Ocean and the Gulf of Mexico. With the exception of Florida, all of these states have both mountains and seashore. Wealthy southerners often sought refuge from the region's legendary heat in the highlands and piney woods of the Carolinas and northern Georgia. Today these areas are highly regarded resort destinations.

Some of the region's cities—Savannah, Charleston, Edenton, and Mobile—are charmingly old-fashioned. There are modern cities, too: the dynamic, high-tech Research Triangle region of Raleigh–Durham–Chapel Hill; the booming transportation hub that is Atlanta; Birmingham, the city that grew up on steelmaking and is today a major medical center; and hip Miami, infused with Cuban culture.

When to Go

The best times to visit the South are **spring** and **fall,** when temperatures are in the 70s and 80s. Spring also brings the magnificent azaleas and magnolias to life. Fall, when colors reach their peak in the mountains, also draws thousands. **Winter** can be quite pleasant in the more temperate, lower coastal regions of Georgia and Florida. In the higher elevations of western North Carolina and Georgia, temperatures often drop to freezing between mid-November and mid-March. **Summer** tends to be hot and muggy, with temperatures often soaring into the 90s, especially in Florida and at the lower elevations of Alabama, Georgia, and the Carolinas.

Festivals and Seasonal Events

Winter

➤ EARLY DEC.: The **Atlanta Festival of Trees** (☎ 404/264–9348) celebrates the Christmas season with a parade and exhibit of elaborately decorated trees and wreaths.

➤ MID-JAN.: **Art Deco Weekend** (☎ 305/539–3000) spotlights Miami Beach's historic district with a street fair, a gala, and live entertainment.

➤ LATE JAN.–EARLY FEB.: The **Cloister Food and Wine Classic** (☎ 912/638–3611 or 800/732–4752), on Sea Island, Georgia, has enjoyed an international reputation for quality classes and tastings.

➤ FEB.: **Black History Month** is observed throughout the South, with special events at many bookstores, universities, and other cultural venues, including Tuskegee University (☎ 334/727–8837), in Tuskegee, Alabama; Southern University (☎ 225/771–4500), in Baton Rouge, Louisiana; and in Atlanta, Georgia, at the Martin Luther King Jr. Center for Nonviolent Social Change (☎ 404/526–8900).

Spring

➤ LATE MAY: Over Memorial Day weekend Anderson, South Carolina, celebrates **Freedom Weekend Aloft** (☎ 864/232–3700), one of the largest balloon rallies in the country.

➤ LATE MAY–EARLY JUNE: **Spoleto Festival USA** (☎ 843/722–2764), which draws world-renowned performers and artists to Charleston, South Carolina, gets global attention (advance tickets necessary for most events).

Summer

➤ MID-JULY: The **Annual Highland Games and Gathering of the Scottish Clans** (☎ 828/733–1333 or 800/468–7325), held in the high meadows of Grandfather Mountain in North Carolina, is one of the largest Scottish celebrations in the world.

Autumn

➤ MID-OCT.: The second full week in October, Gulf Shores celebrates **Alabama's National Shrimp Festival** (☎ 251/968–6904).

THE MISSISSIPPI VALLEY

Arkansas, Kentucky, Louisiana, Mississippi, Tennessee

The waters of the Mississippi River feed the imagination of the South. The five states that constitute the Mississippi Valley all have Civil War battlefields and citizens with long, long memories. You can find the New South here, of course, but the Old South—of Cotton Is King, of Christ Is Coming, of aristocracy and its flip side, poverty—is never far away.

The folk culture that sprouted among the poor people of these states took root and spread its branches far out into the world. Nashville calls itself the capital of country music; Memphis will always mean rhythm and blues; New Orleans is the cradle of jazz. Graceland, the Memphis mansion where Elvis lived and died in tacky majesty, stands now as an unofficial monument to the best American art and the worst American taste.

When to Go

The best times to visit the Mississippi Valley states are **April** and **October,** when temperatures and humidity are comfortable: in Louisiana and Mississippi, the mid-70s; in the mountains of Arkansas, Kentucky, and Tennessee, the 60s, cooling off to the mid-40s at night. In **spring** everything is in glorious bloom; in the **fall** the trees, especially in the mountains, are bright with turning leaves. If you dislike crowds, avoid New Orleans during Mardi Gras (February or March, depending on when Easter falls) and Louisville during the Kentucky Derby (the first Saturday in May).

Festivals and Seasonal Events

Winter

➤ FEB. OR EARLY MAR.: **Mardi Gras** (☎ 504/523–5652) in **New Orleans, Louisiana,** caps several weeks of madness: street festivals, parades with fantastic floats, marching bands, and eye-popping costumes.

Spring

➤ MAR.–APR.: In **Mississippi, spring pilgrimages** to elegant antebellum mansions are held throughout the state, with **Natchez** (☎ 800/647–6724 or 800/647–6742) claiming grande-dame status, followed by **Columbus** (☎ 800/327–2686) and **Vicksburg** (☎ 800/221–3536).

➤ LATE APR.–EARLY MAY: The **New Orleans Jazz & Heritage Festival** (☎ 504/522–4786) draws hundreds of thousands of musicians, fans, and artisans for a 10-day all-out jam session.

➤ MAY 6: In **Louisville** the **Kentucky Derby,** one of horse racing's premier events, is preceded by a two-week festival (☎ 502/584–6383 or 502/636–4402) with parades, riverboat races, and many a mint julep.

Summer

➤ MID-JUNE: The **International Country Music Fan Fair** (☎ 866/326–3247), in **Nashville, Tennessee,** lets country music fans mix with their favorite stars in a weeklong celebration.

➤ AUG.: **Memphis, Tennessee,** pulls out all the stops for the **Elvis International Tribute Week** (☎ 901/543–5333 or 901/332–3322).

The Southeast
KENTUCKY
VIRGINIA
TENNESSEE
NORTH CAROLINA
SOUTH CAROLINA
GEORGIA
ALABAMA
MISSISSIPPI
ATLANTIC OCEAN
Nashville
Knoxville
GREAT SMOKY MTS. NAT'L PARK
Winston-Salem
Greensboro
Durham
Elizabeth City
Edenton
Manteo
High Point
Chapel Hill
Raleigh
Goldsboro
Cape Hatteras Nat'l Seashore
Hickory
Asheville
Concord
Shelby
Charlotte
Fayetteville
Warsaw
New Bern
Spartanburg
Rock Hill
Greenville
Bennettsville
Black River
Lumberton
Cape Lookout Nat'l Seashore
Wilmington
Florence
Huntsville
Dalton
Decatur
Anderson
Congaree River
Florence
Rome
Gainesville
Columbia
Gadsden
Athens
Batesburg
Savannah River
Conway
Myrtle Beach
Decatur
Atlanta
Birmingham
Anniston
Aiken
Augusta
Orangeburg
Lake Moultrie
Georgetown
Bessemer
Griffin
Tuscaloosa
Milledgeville
Waynesboro
Walterboro
LaGrange
Charleston
Eutaw
Auburn
Macon
Selma
Phenix City
Columbus
Warner Robins
Statesboro
Beaufort
Hilton Head Island
Montgomery
Vidalia
Savannah
Alabama River
Eufaula
Hazlehurst
Monroeville
Albany
Jesup

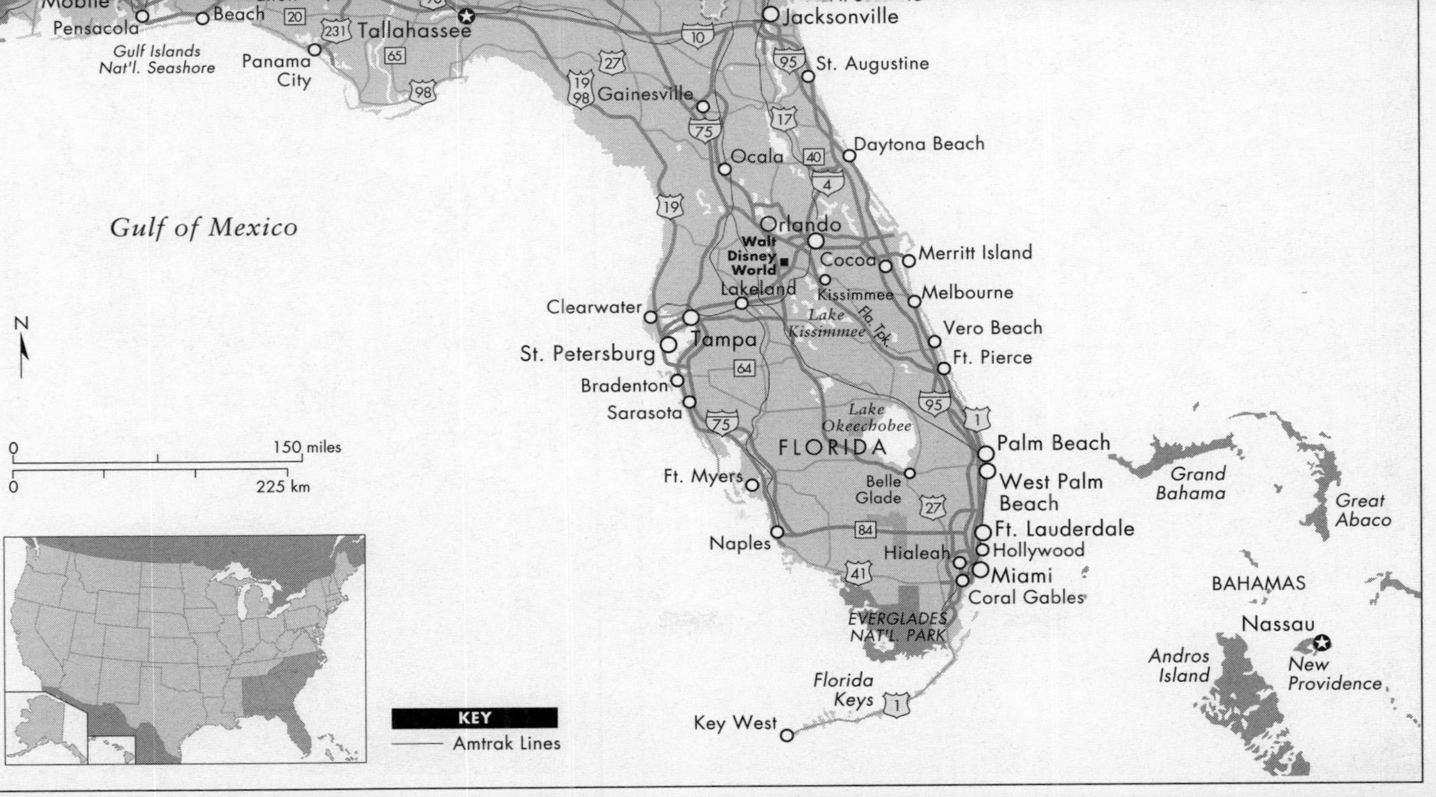

Pensacola
Beach
Gulf Islands Nat'l. Seashore
Panama City
Tallahassee
Jacksonville
St. Augustine
Gainesville
Daytona Beach
Ocala
Gulf of Mexico
Orlando
Walt Disney World
Cocoa
Merritt Island
Lakeland
Kissimmee
Melbourne
Clearwater
Lake Kissimmee
Fla. Tpk.
Vero Beach
Tampa
St. Petersburg
Ft. Pierce
Bradenton
Sarasota
Lake Okeechobee
FLORIDA
Palm Beach
West Palm Beach
Ft. Myers
Belle Glade
Grand Bahama
Great Abaco
Ft. Lauderdale
Naples
Hialeah
Hollywood
Miami
Coral Gables
BAHAMAS
EVERGLADES NAT'L PARK
Nassau
Andros Island
New Providence
Florida Keys
Key West
N
0 150 miles
0 225 km
KEY
Amtrak Lines

The Mississippi Valley

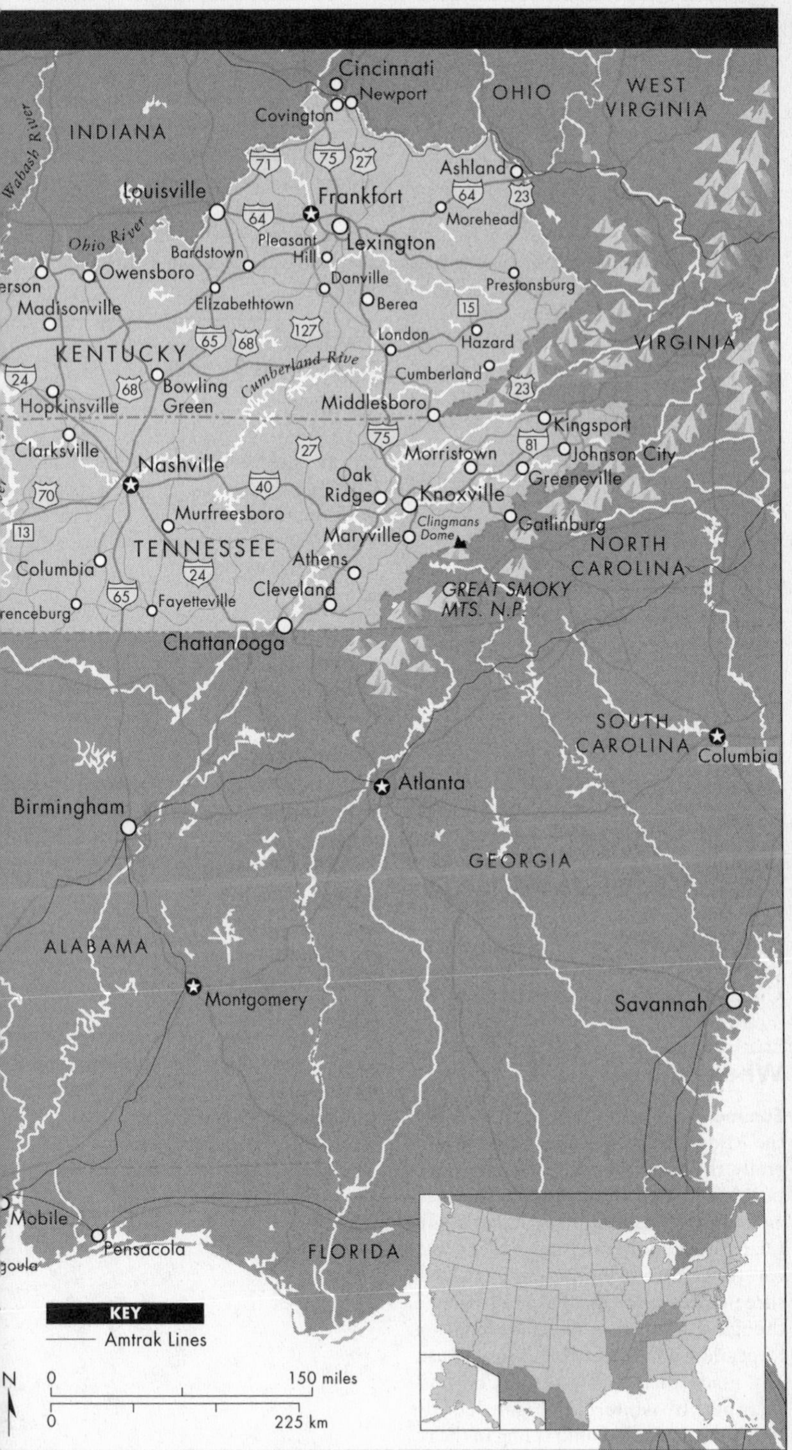
Cincinnati
Newport
Covington
OHIO
WEST VIRGINIA
INDIANA
Wabash River
Ohio River
Louisville
Frankfort
Lexington
Ashland
Morehead
Pleasant Hill
Bardstown
Owensboro
Madisonville
Elizabethtown
Danville
Berea
Prestonsburg
KENTUCKY
London
Hazard
VIRGINIA
Cumberland River
Cumberland
Bowling Green
Hopkinsville
Middlesboro
Kingsport
Clarksville
Nashville
Morristown
Johnson City
Greeneville
Oak Ridge
Knoxville
Murfreesboro
Clingmans Dome
Maryville
Gatlinburg
TENNESSEE
NORTH CAROLINA
Columbia
Athens
Cleveland
GREAT SMOKY MTS. N.P.
Fayetteville
Chattanooga
SOUTH CAROLINA
Columbia
Atlanta
Birmingham
GEORGIA
ALABAMA
Montgomery
Savannah
Mobile
Pensacola
FLORIDA
KEY
Amtrak Lines
N
0
150 miles
0
225 km

THE MIDWEST AND GREAT LAKES

Illinois, Indiana, Michigan, Minnesota, Ohio, Wisconsin

The midwest is America, that prototypical vision of neat farmland, affluent suburbs, and compact, skyscrapered downtowns strung together along purposefully straight silver highways. Unlike the stark Great Plains to the west, this is gently rolling landscape, defined by great geological features: to the east, the Appalachian Mountains; to the north, the Great Lakes; to the south, the Ohio River; to the west, the majestic Mississippi.

Smarting from years of being labeled the sticks, midwestern cities are always trying to prove themselves. Ohio has no fewer than five important cities (Cleveland, Cincinnati, Columbus, Dayton, and Toledo). Minnesota's major population center comprises two cities, Minneapolis and St. Paul. Indiana's capital, Indianapolis, is the amateur-sports capital of the country. In Michigan, Detroit is the home of America's auto industry. Surprisingly, it also has the greatest number of theater seats outside of New York City. Milwaukee, Wisconsin, poised on the western shore of Lake Michigan, is a rich melting pot of immigrant cultures, as is Chicago, Illinois, the region's great metropolis.

When to Go

Summer is the most popular time to visit the Midwest and the Great Lakes. Generally, the farther north you go, the fewer people you'll find. Daily temperatures average in the 80s in Illinois, Indiana, and Ohio, though July and August heat waves can push them high into the 90s. These three states have the best **fall** foliage, though you can see good color in all six. Depending on the weather, the leaves usually reach their most colorful by mid-October. In **winter** Michigan has the only significant downhill skiing in the region, but cross-country is all the rage in Wisconsin and Minnesota. The Midwest usually gets at least one subzero cold snap every year. For the rest of winter expect temperatures in the 20s and 30s and about 10°F colder in northern Michigan, Wisconsin, and Minnesota. Sudden snowstorms can make winter driving unpredictable and treacherous. **Spring** is damp and clammy, with erratic weather and temperatures ranging from the 30s to the 60s.

Festivals and Seasonal Events

Winter

➤ LATE JAN.–EARLY FEB.: Minnesota's 10-day **St. Paul Winter Carnival** (☏ 800/488–4023) celebrates winter with a sleigh and cutter parade, an ice palace, car races on the ice, and ice sculptures by artists from around the world.

Spring

➤ MAY: The monthlong **Indianapolis 500 Festival** (☏ 317/927–3378) culminates in the most famous car race in the United States.

Summer

➤ LATE JULY: The **Pro Football Hall of Fame Game** (☏ 330/456–8207) and induction ceremonies, in Canton, Ohio, kick off the season.

Autumn

➤ EARLY SEPT.: On Labor Day weekend, the **Detroit Jazz Festival** (☏ 313/963–7622) attracts more than 700,000 jazz fans.

➤ OCT.: On the third weekend of the month, the **LaSalle Bank Chicago Marathon** (☏ 312/904–9800) draws runners from all over the world.

THE GREAT PLAINS

Iowa, Kansas, Missouri, Nebraska, North Dakota, Oklahoma, South Dakota

The name Great Plains evokes an image of flat farmland stretching to the horizon, unbroken save for the occasional cluster of buildings marking a town or farmstead. Those who go there, however, know this limitless terrain destroys as many preconceived images as it confirms. The seemingly uniform landscape actually encompasses geography as diverse as the towering buttes that loom over the horizons of northwestern South Dakota and the fertile river valleys that crisscross the eastern boundaries of Missouri and Kansas.

Countless historical theme parks and Old West towns dot the region, along with abundant archaeological and Civil War battle sites, U.S. Army forts, pioneer trail markers, and museums of Native American and pioneer lore. But alongside these landmarks lies another Great Plains. To know it, you must drive its hundreds of miles of roads bisecting fields of grain or leave the highway for one of its small towns, just to walk the Main Street and see the serene old houses. Here, somewhere between myth and reality, the true spirit of this region is revealed.

When to Go

Tourist season for most of the Great Plains is **summer,** despite the soaring temperatures and high humidity. Many attractions are open during June, July, and August. Northern states, such as the Dakotas and Nebraska, are generally cooler, but you should be prepared for anything in this variable region. **Winter** weather can be equally extreme, especially in Nebraska and the Dakotas, where subzero temperatures and snowy conditions are common. In Oklahoma, winter is generally mild and may be more pleasant than during the summer heat. **Spring** and **fall** can be excellent times to visit, with moderate temperatures and crowds at a minimum. Fall in the Ozarks or in the eastern border of Iowa has the added attraction of colorful foliage.

Festivals and Seasonal Events

Summer

➤ JUNE: **Nebraskaland Days** (☎ 308/532–7939) is a western hootenanny in North Platte that's highlighted by the Buffalo Bill Rodeo. The **Red Earth Native American Cultural Festival** (☎ 405/427–5228), in Oklahoma City, attracts hundreds of Native American dancers from the United States and Canada.

➤ JULY: **Kansas City Blues & Jazz Festival** (☎ 816/753–3378 or 800/530–5266) features performances by nationally known blues and jazz artists on three stages.

➤ JULY–AUG.: In Kansas, the **Dodge City Roundup Rodeo** (☎ 866/327–6336) takes place during the Dodge City Days festival.

➤ AUG.: **Days of '76** (☎ 605/578–1876), in Deadwood, South Dakota, celebrates the town's wild and woolly gold-rush days.

Autumn

➤ SEPT.: The **United Tribes International Powwow** (☎ 701/255–3285) brings Native Americans from around the country to Bismarck, North Dakota, to hold dance competitions and celebrate cultural ties.

➤ OCT.: **Octoberfest** (☎ 573/486–2744) in Hermann, Missouri, draws thousands of people to celebrate this Missouri River town's German heritage. **Buffalo Roundup** (☎ 605/255–4515) in Custer State Park, South Dakota, allows visitors to witness one of the great remaining roundups in the West.

The Midwest and Great Lakes

CANADA
Lake Superior
PICTURED ROCKS NAT'L LAKESHORE
Sault Sainte Marie
Marquette
MICHIGAN
Sudbury
Mackinac Island
Mackinaw City
Manitoulin Island
Georgian Bay
Beaver Island
Escanaba
Petoskey
Alpena
Northport
Grand Traverse Bay
SLEEPING BEAR DUNES NAT'L LAKESHORE
Traverse City
Lake Huron
MICHIGAN
Toronto
Lake Ontario
Manitowoc
Cadillac
Bay City
Lake Michigan
Sheboygan
Saginaw
Buffalo
NEW YORK
Cedarburg
Grand Rapids
Flint
Port Huron
Muskegon
Lansing
Milwaukee
Battle Creek
Jackson
Detroit
Lake Erie
Kenosha
Waukegan
Woodstock
Evanston
Kalamazoo
Ann Arbor
South Bass Island
Kelleys Island
Marblehead
Ashtabula
PENNSYLVANIA
Chicago
Toledo
Catawba Point
Cleveland
Gary
South Bend
Angola
Port Clinton
Sandusky
Michigan City
La Porte
Auburn
Akron
Youngstown
Ft. Wayne
Mansfield
Huntington
Lima
Canton
Logansport
Marion
OHIO
INDIANA
Wapakoneta
Muncie
Lafayette
Anderson
Zanesville
Wheeling
Noblesville
Zionsville
Centerville
Columbus
Crawfordsville
Richmond
Dayton
Marietta
Rockville
Indianapolis
Chillicothe
Terre Haute
Columbus
Dillsboro
Cincinnati
Bloomington
Madison
Aurora
WEST VIRGINIA
Vincennes
Wabash River
New Albany
Corydon
Gentryville
Louisville
KENTUCKY
Ohio R.
Evansville
VIRGINIA
75
23
25
131
31
75
69
96
23
94
196
94
69
90
80 90
80 90
80
75
7
65
24
69
71
77
70
70
71
40
75
74
7
41
46
50
36
65
275

The Great Plains

Ogallala
Kearney
Grand Island
Lincoln
Burlington
Keokuk
ILLINOIS
Platte River
McCook
Hastings
Nebraska City
Auburn
Rock Port
Beatrice
Kirksville
Red Cloud
Denver
Macon
Hannibal
St. Joseph
Waconda Lake
Mankato
Atchison
Goodland
Manhattan
MISSOURI
Independence
St. Charles
Alton
COLORADO
Russell
Oakley
Topeka
Kansas City
Sedalia
Columbia
Abilene
Lawrence
St. Louis
KANSAS
Scott City
Jefferson City
Garden City
Great Bend
Emporia
Clinton
Lake of the Ozarks
St. Genevieve
Hutchinson
Florence
Waynesville
Dodge City
El Dorado
Fort Scott
Cape Girardeau
Wichita
Medicine Lodge
Joplin
Springfield
Van Buren
Liberal
Coffeyville
Poplar Bluff
West Plains
Guymon
OSAGE INDIAN RES.
Ponca City
Branson
THE OZARKS
Bartlesville
Table Rock Lake
Enid
Woodward
Tulsa
ARKANSAS
NEW MEXICO
TENNESSEE
OKLAHOMA
Guthrie
Clinton
Muskogee
Amarillo
Oklahoma City
Elk City
Shawnee
KEY
TEXAS
McAlester
Amtrak Lines
Altus
Duncan
Lawton
Atoka
Ardmore
Hugo
N
0
150 miles
0
225 km
Marietta

THE SOUTHWEST

Arizona, Nevada, New Mexico, Texas

A region that demands superlatives, the Southwest is the ruggedly beautiful, wide-open land out of which America's myths continue to emerge. Cowboys and Indians, old-world conquistadors and new religions, rising and falling fortunes in gold—all feed into the vision of an untamed territory with limitless horizons.

Of course, Phoenix and Dallas are sophisticated metropolises, and Santa Fe is becoming a rival Los Angeles in wealth and number of art galleries per square foot. Las Vegas is sui generis, an unbridled, peculiarly American phenomenon.

But other, more ancient cultures vie here with contemporary ones. The country's largest Native American reservation, that of the Navajo Nation, occupies millions of acres and traverses state boundaries, and dozens of other tribes—among them Hopi, Zuni, and Apache—live in the region as well. It is their vanishing civilization and, above all, the area's natural phenomena—spectacular canyons, eerily towering rock formations, and clear, lambent light—that continue to capture the imagination of all who visit the area.

When to Go

In the semiarid climate of most of the Southwest, **spring** is the season of choice, with cool, fresh, clear weather. In March and April, when temperatures average in the 70s, short-lived wildflowers produce carpets of extravagant color in many parts of the region. **Summer** is dry and often very hot, sometimes unpleasantly so, across the Southwest. Summer thunderstorms are typical in most areas. After spring, **fall**—from September to November, in general—is the preferred time to visit, with temperatures falling back into the 70s and 80s and gorgeous foliage to be seen in many areas. Skiers flock to slopes across the Southwest in **winter.** In general, temperatures vary tremendously even within the same state and season.

Festivals and Seasonal Events

Winter

➤ MAR.: Find high-quality artwork at the **Heard Museum Guild Indian Fair and Market** (☎ 602/252–8848), a juried invitational for Native American artists held in **Phoenix, Arizona.** Hundreds of rock bands, along with filmmakers and Internet artists, descend on **Austin, Texas,** during the 10-day **South by Southwest** (☎ 512/467–7979) conference.

Spring

➤ EARLY APR.: **The Houston International Festival** (☎ 713/654–8808) in **Texas** features a different country each year for a 10-day celebration ending with the hilarious Art Car parade.

➤ APR.: In **Dallas,** film buffs rub elbows with professional filmmakers from around the world at the **USA Film Festival** (☎ 214/821–3456).

➤ LATE APR.: Native Americans celebrate **American Indian Week** (☎ 505/843–7270) in **Albuquerque, New Mexico,** with dance, arts and crafts, and the Gathering of Nations Pow Wow.

Summer

➤ LATE JUNE: New Mexico's craftspeople are world famous, and some of the best display and sell their work at the **New Mexico Arts & Crafts Fair** (☎ 505/884–9043) in **Albuquerque, New Mexico.**

➤ LATE JULY: The **Fiesta de Santiago y Santa Ana** (☎ 505/758–3873 or 800/732–8267) is a colorful street party and fair in **Taos, New Mexico.**

Autumn

➤ MID-SEPT.: On the first weekend after Labor Day, Zozobra, or Old Man Gloom, is burned to open the annual **Fiestas de Santa Fe** (☎ 505/984–6760 or 800/777–2489), in **Santa Fe, New Mexico.**

➤ MID-OCT.: The **Albuquerque International Balloon Fiesta** (☎ 505/821–1000), has more than 850 colorful hot-air balloons rising in spectacular unison with the dawn.

THE ROCKIES

Colorado, Idaho, Montana, Wyoming, Utah

To many minds, the term Rocky Mountains conjures up images of wolves and outlaws, the click of cowboy spurs and the rustling of leather chaps. Indeed, the unpredictable charms and crimes of nature and human action that thrived in the Old West have marked the Rocky Mountains with a crude but poetic beauty.

The westernmost state, Idaho, has terrain encompassing everything from fruit orchards to the tallest sand dunes in the United States. Utah has a vast salt lake, mountain peaks, and improbable red-rock canyons in the southern reaches. Montana's Glacier National Park is home to the grizzly bear, wolf, mountain goat, and moose. Wyoming is dotted with thermal pools, bubbling hot springs, and, within a square-mile area in Yellowstone National Park, a quarter of the earth's geysers. In Colorado, the ski capital of the United States, high-country lakes, meadows frosted with blue columbine, and treeless alpine tundra assemble in one sweeping vista.

When to Go

For those willing to risk sometimes capricious weather, fall and spring are the Rockies' best-kept secrets. **Spring** is a good time for fishing, rafting the runoff, or birding and viewing wildlife. **Fall** may be the prettiest season of all, with golden splashes of aspen on the mountainsides, more wildlife at lower elevations, and excellent fishing during spawning. Driving in the **winter** can be chancy, and although the interstates are usually kept open even in fearsome weather, highway passes can be blocked from late October to June. Winter visitors should prepare for the possibility of temperatures below zero. Wilderness snowbanks can linger through June, so backcountry hikers generally crowd in from July through Labor Day. **Summer** temperatures rarely rise into the 90s (except in southern Utah, where the mercury may top 100°F).

Festivals and Seasonal Events

Winter

➤ JAN.: Utah's **Sundance Film Festival** (☎ 801/328–3456), founded by Robert Redford, brings independent filmmakers to Park City and Salt Lake City for one of the country's premier film screening events. During **Ullr Fest** (☎ 970/453–6018), the town of Breckenridge, Colorado, declares itself an independent kingdom and pays homage to the Norse god of snow in a weeklong wild revel.

➤ FEB.: **Race to the Sky** (☎ 406/442–4008), near Helena, Montana, is a 500-mi dogsled race that crisscrosses the Continental Divide at elevations up to 7,000 ft.

Spring

➤ LATE MAY: Memorial Day brings the annual **Bolder Boulder** run (☎ 303/444–7223) to Boulder, Colorado, where a top international field and 40,000 ordinary citizens race through the closed streets of town.

Summer

➤ JUNE–AUG.: At the **Aspen Music Festival and School** (☎ 970/925–3254) students from around the world perform with faculty, and world-class soloists and conductors are also featured.

➤ JULY: Wyoming's **Cheyenne Frontier Days** (☎ 307/778–7222 or 800/227–6336) includes evening shows featuring the biggest names in country music, as well as parades, and Native American dancing.

➤ LATE JULY–EARLY AUG.: In Colorado, the **Vail International Dance Festival** (☎ 970/949–1999) is set amid wildflowers.

➤ AUG.: The **Crow Fair and Rodeo** (☎ 406/638–2601) celebrates native culture and customs in Crow Agency, Montana, tepee capital of the world.

Autumn

➤ EARLY OCT.: In Denver, the **Great American Beer Festival** (☎ 303/447–0126) is the country's largest and longest-running beer fest, with samples of about 2,000 brews.

➤ OCT.–LATE DEC.: Join the **Eagle Watch** (☎ 406/475–3128) to see hundreds of bald eagles gather annually near Helena, Montana.

The Southwest

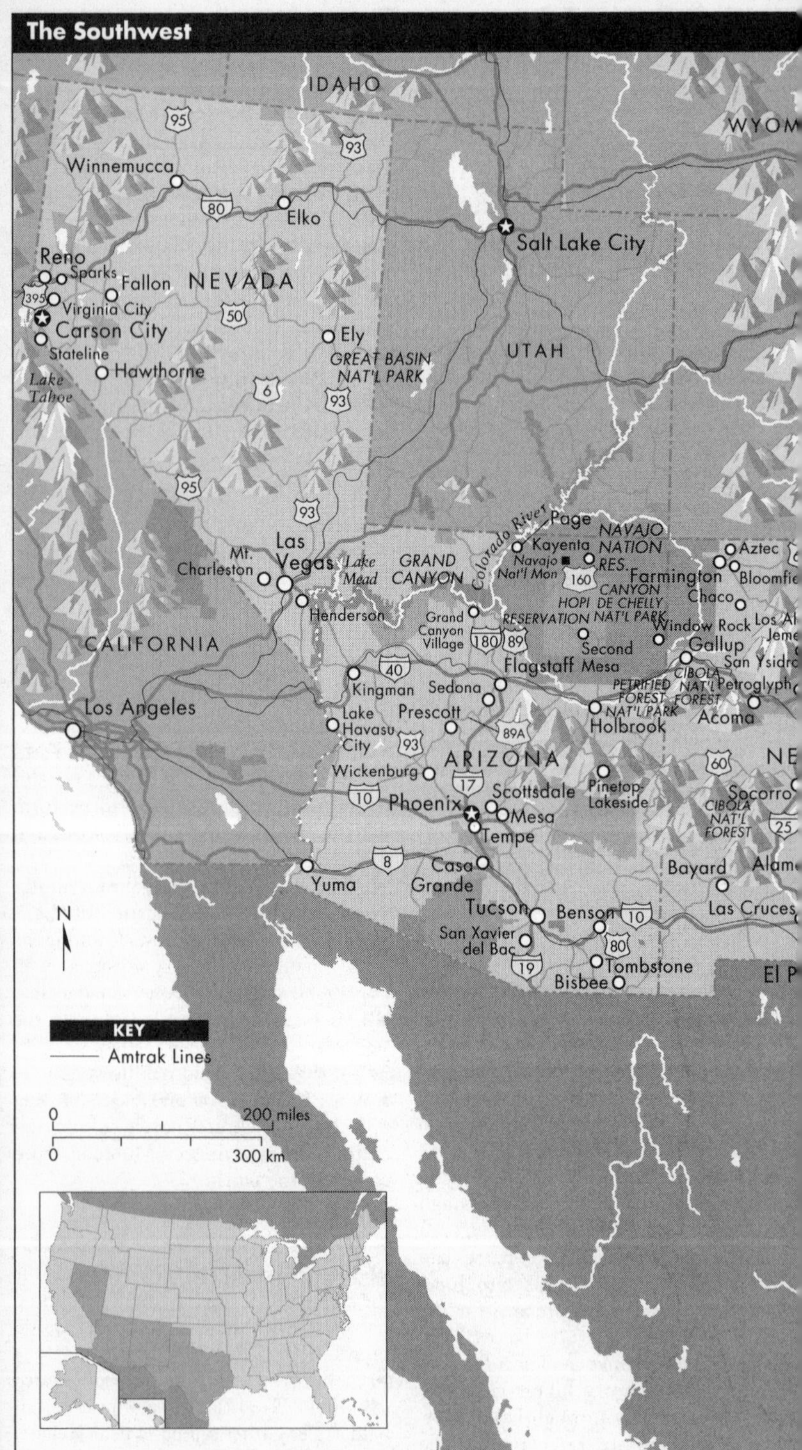

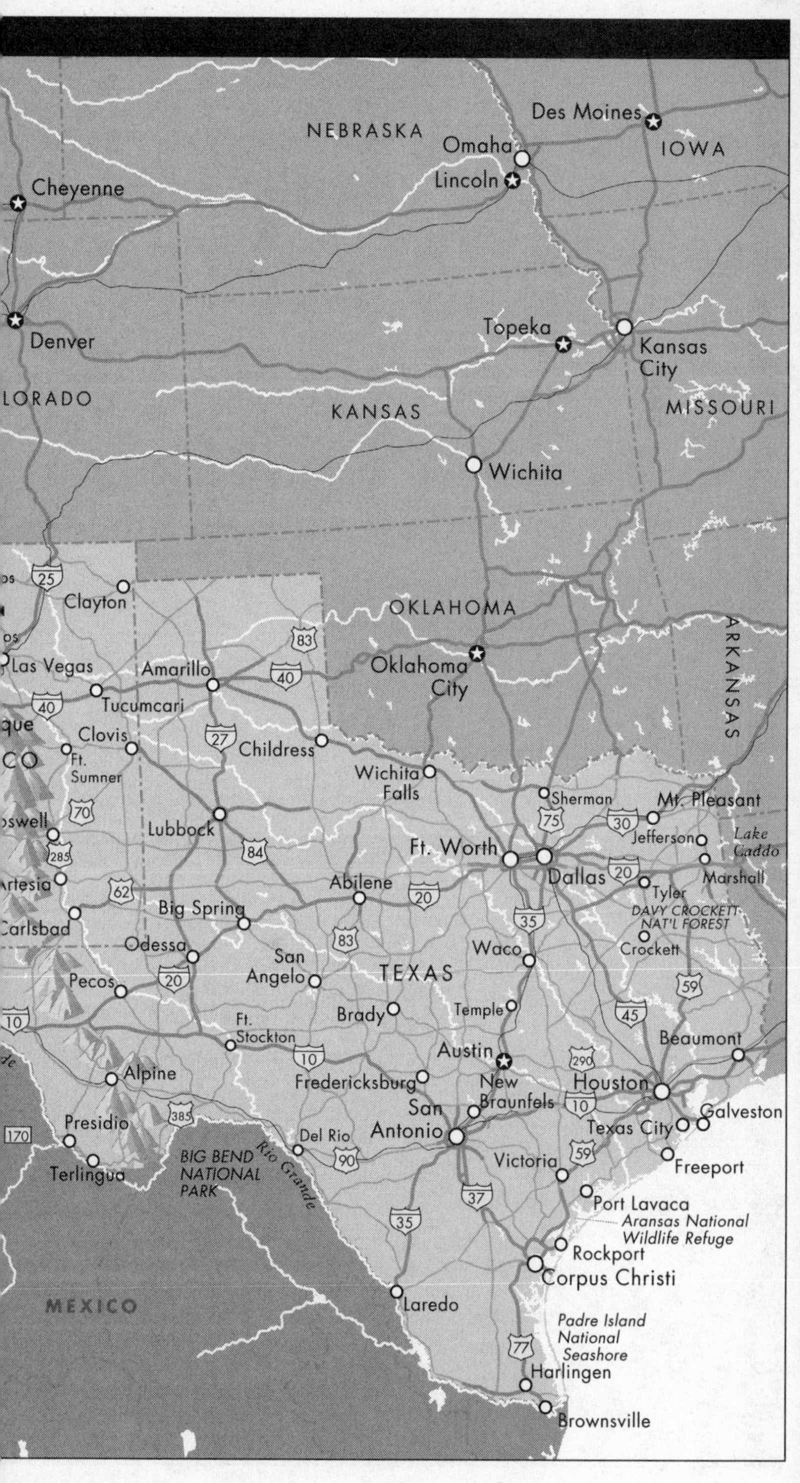

NEBRASKA
Des Moines
IOWA
Omaha
Lincoln
Cheyenne
Denver
Topeka
Kansas City
LORADO
KANSAS
MISSOURI
Wichita
OKLAHOMA
ARKANSAS
Clayton
Las Vegas
Amarillo
Oklahoma City
Tucumcari
Clovis
Ft. Sumner
Childress
Wichita Falls
Sherman
Mt. Pleasant
Lubbock
Ft. Worth
Dallas
Jefferson
Lake Caddo
Marshall
Tyler
Artesia
Abilene
DAVY CROCKETT NAT'L FOREST
Carlsbad
Big Spring
Crockett
Odessa
Waco
San Angelo
TEXAS
Pecos
Ft. Stockton
Brady
Temple
Beaumont
Austin
Alpine
Fredericksburg
New Braunfels
Houston
San Antonio
Galveston
Presidio
Del Rio
Texas City
Terlingua
BIG BEND NATIONAL PARK
Rio Grande
Victoria
Freeport
Port Lavaca
Aransas National Wildlife Refuge
Rockport
Corpus Christi
MEXICO
Laredo
Padre Island National Seashore
Harlingen
Brownsville

The Rockies

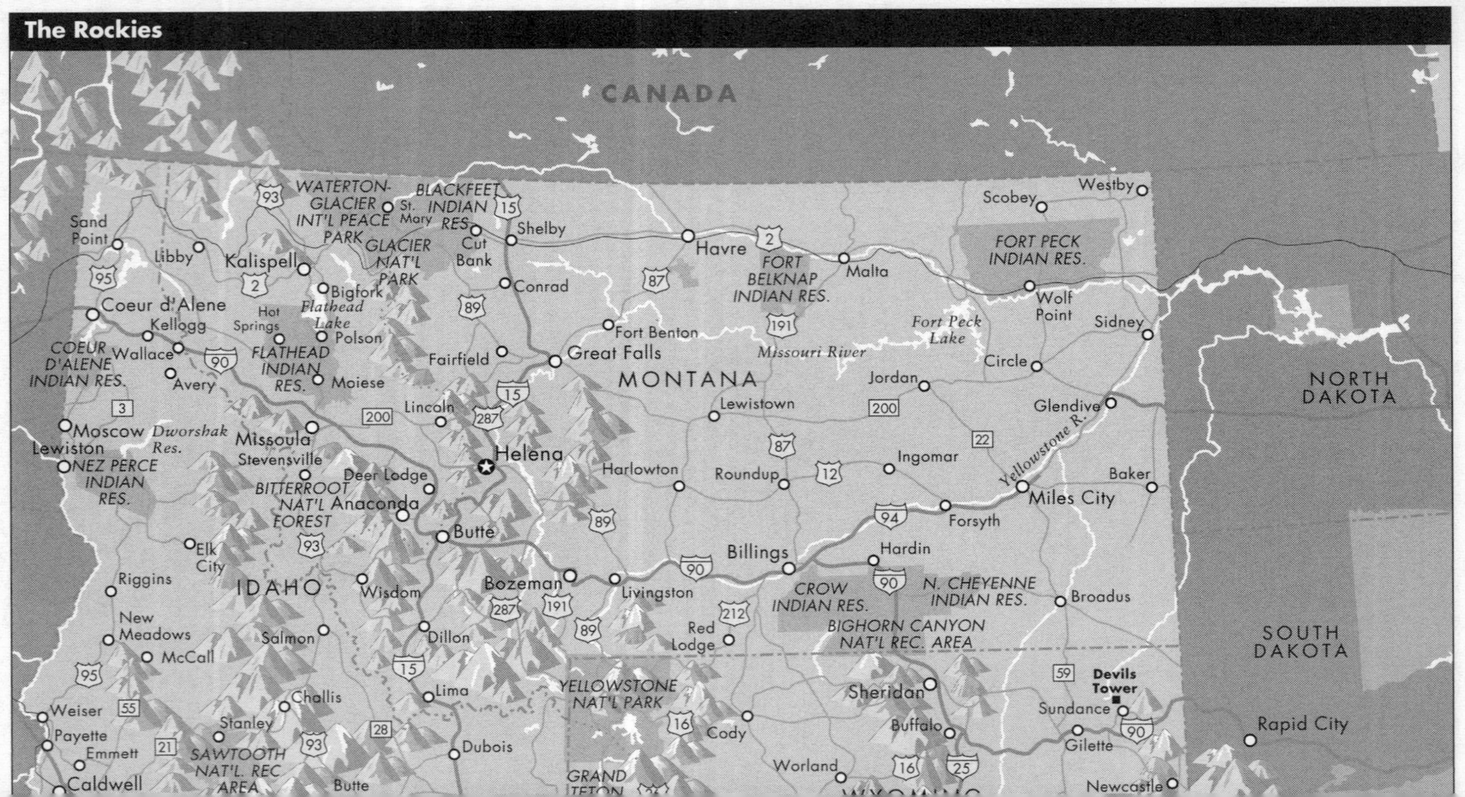
CANADA
MONTANA
IDAHO
NORTH DAKOTA
SOUTH DAKOTA
WATERTON-GLACIER INT'L PEACE PARK
BLACKFEET INDIAN RES.
GLACIER NAT'L PARK
St. Mary
Shelby
Cut Bank
Conrad
Havre
FORT BELKNAP INDIAN RES.
Malta
FORT PECK INDIAN RES.
Scobey
Westby
Wolf Point
Sidney
Sand Point
Libby
Kalispell
Bigfork
Flathead Lake
Hot Springs
Polson
FLATHEAD INDIAN RES.
Moiese
Coeur d'Alene
Kellogg
Wallace
Avery
COEUR D'ALENE INDIAN RES.
Fairfield
Great Falls
Fort Benton
Missouri River
Fort Peck Lake
Circle
Jordan
Glendive
Lewistown
Lincoln
Helena
Moscow
Dworshak Res.
Lewiston
NEZ PERCE INDIAN RES.
Missoula
Stevensville
BITTERROOT NAT'L FOREST
Deer Lodge
Anaconda
Butte
Harlowton
Roundup
Ingomar
Yellowstone R.
Miles City
Baker
Forsyth
Hardin
Billings
Elk City
Riggins
Wisdom
Bozeman
Livingston
CROW INDIAN RES.
N. CHEYENNE INDIAN RES.
Broadus
BIGHORN CANYON NAT'L REC. AREA
Red Lodge
New Meadows
McCall
Salmon
Dillon
YELLOWSTONE NAT'L PARK
Sheridan
Devils Tower
Sundance
Rapid City
Lima
Challis
Stanley
Weiser
Payette
Emmett
Caldwell
SAWTOOTH NAT'L REC AREA
Butte
Dubois
Cody
Buffalo
Gilette
Worland
Newcastle
GRAND TETON

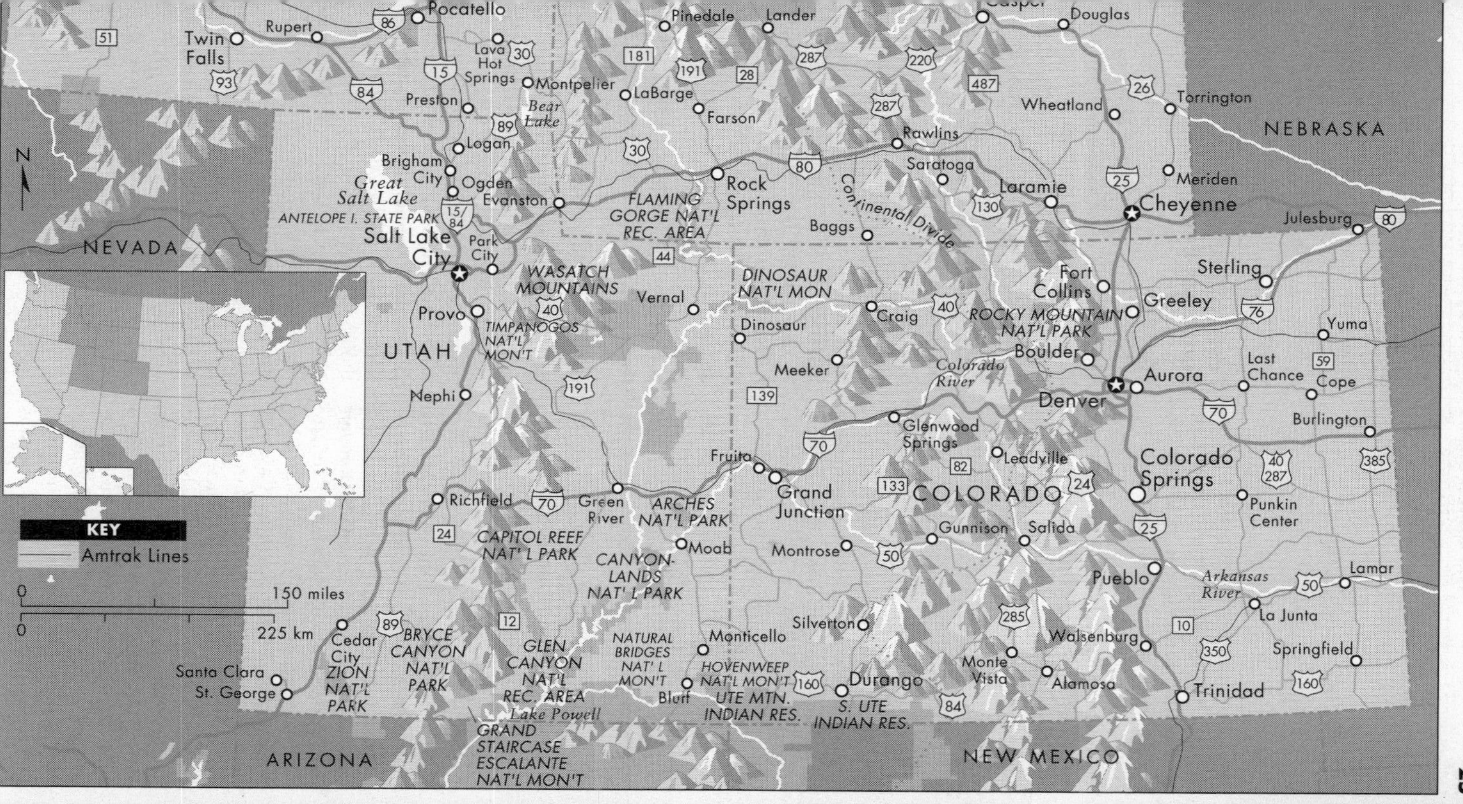

NEBRASKA
COLORADO
UTAH
NEVADA
ARIZONA
NEW MEXICO
Pocatello
Twin Falls
Rupert
Lava Hot Springs
Montpelier
Preston
Bear Lake
Logan
Brigham City
Ogden
Great Salt Lake
ANTELOPE I. STATE PARK
Salt Lake City
Park City
Evanston
Pinedale
Lander
LaBarge
Farson
Rock Springs
FLAMING GORGE NAT'L REC. AREA
Rawlins
Saratoga
Continental Divide
Baggs
Douglas
Wheatland
Torrington
Laramie
Meriden
Cheyenne
Julesburg
WASATCH MOUNTAINS
Provo
TIMPANOGOS NAT'L MON'T
Vernal
DINOSAUR NAT'L MON
Dinosaur
Craig
Meeker
Fort Collins
ROCKY MOUNTAIN NAT'L PARK
Boulder
Greeley
Sterling
Yuma
Colorado River
Denver
Aurora
Last Chance
Cope
Burlington
Nephi
Glenwood Springs
Leadville
Fruita
Grand Junction
COLORADO
Colorado Springs
Punkin Center
Richfield
Green River
ARCHES NAT'L PARK
CAPITOL REEF NAT' L PARK
Moab
CANYON-LANDS NAT' L PARK
Montrose
Gunnison
Salida
Pueblo
Arkansas River
Lamar
La Junta
Springfield
Cedar City
ZION NAT'L PARK
BRYCE CANYON NAT'L PARK
GLEN CANYON NAT'L REC. AREA
Lake Powell
GRAND STAIRCASE ESCALANTE NAT'L MON'T
NATURAL BRIDGES NAT' L MON'T
Bluff
Monticello
HOVENWEEP NAT'L MON'T
UTE MTN. INDIAN RES.
Silverton
Durango
S. UTE INDIAN RES.
Monte Vista
Alamosa
Walsenburg
Trinidad
Santa Clara
St. George
KEY
Amtrak Lines
0
150 miles
0
225 km
N

THE WEST COAST

California, Oregon, Washington

Throughout its history the West Coast has been a destination for trendsetters and fortune seekers. The gold-seeking Spanish built missions and huge ranchos in what is now California, long before modern empire builders headed for Silicon Valley in a race to lead the nation's communications, information, and technology revolution.

The great West Coast cities—Seattle, Portland, San Francisco, Los Angeles, and San Diego—continue to attract a hopeful mix of immigrants in search of personal freedom and economic opportunity. In contrast to the urban areas, the extraordinary rural landscapes of these states feature wild climatic changes and altitudes—deserts, forests, a 1,500-mi seashore, mountains, and rich agricultural valleys. In addition to rock climbing, deep-sea fishing, wilderness camping, surfing, skiing, and snowboarding, tourists and residents enjoy five-star resorts, historic western towns, Disneyland, Hollywood studios, world-class museums, and top-notch art and entertainment from grunge to opera.

When to Go

You can take a West Coast vacation any time of the year. Weather in coastal areas is generally mild year-round, with the rainy season running from **late fall through early spring**—though rain may occur any time of year, especially in Washington. Ski season in the High Sierra and Cascades runs from November through March, occasionally into April and May. These same months are also ideal for those who want to enjoy the sun-drenched delights of the desert; wildflowers are at their peak in April. **Summer** is the busiest tourist season. It's also a time of heavy fog in the coastal areas (Mark Twain once remarked that the coldest winter he ever spent was a summer in San Francisco). Inland areas such as Napa Valley, the Columbia Gorge, and the High Sierra can be hot in summer, with temperatures reaching up to 90°F in the plains and mountains; in California's Central Valley and desert regions, summer temperatures can soar to 110°F. Whenever you visit the West Coast, expect temperatures to vary widely from night to day, sometimes by as much as 40°F.

Festivals and Seasonal Events

Winter

➤ JAN. 1: The **Tournament of Roses** (☏ 626/449–4100), in **Pasadena, California,** features a parade of more than 50 floral floats, equestrian units, and marching bands and is followed by the Rose Bowl football game.

➤ FEB.: **Chinese New Year** celebrations are held in **San Francisco** (☏ 415/982–3000) and **Los Angeles** (☏ 213/617–0396), complete with dragon parades, fireworks, and feasts.

Spring

➤ EARLY MAR.: The **Mendocino Whale Festival** (☏ 707/961–6300), in **Mendocino, California,** combines whale-watching with art viewing, wine tasting, lighthouse tours, music, and merriment.

➤ LATE MAY: The **Northwest Folklife Festival** (☏ 206/684–7300) lures musicians to **Seattle** for one of the largest folk festivals in the United States.

Summer

➤ JUNE: The **Portland Rose Festival** (☏ 503/227–2681) includes a rose show, a hot-air balloon race, an air show, and an auto show. The sand becomes an art form at Oregon's **Cannon Beach Sandcastle Contest** (☏ 503/436–2623), attended by thousands each year.

➤ EARLY AUG.: In California, **Old Spanish Days Fiesta** (☏ 805/962–8101) is **Santa Barbara**'s biggest event, with parades, a carnival, a rodeo, and dancers in the Spanish marketplace.

➤ LATE AUG.–EARLY SEPT.: **Bumbershoot** (☏ 206/281–7788), a **Seattle** festival of the arts, presents more than 450 performers in music, dance, theater, comedy, and the visual and literary arts.

THE PACIFIC STATES

Alaska, Hawai'i

The two youngest states in the union, Alaska and Hawai'i, have more in common than their images might suggest. Both are thousands of miles from the U.S. mainland, both have dramatic landscapes, and both have significant populations of indigenous people. Humpback whales also forge a link, summering in Alaska, then swimming 4,000 mi to Hawai'i to mate, calve, and nurse their young.

Alaska, with its vast, austere wilderness and extreme weather, is demanding, but it rewards exploration with temperate summers, a frontier atmosphere, and flora and fauna rarely accessible elsewhere.

Each of Hawai'i's eight major volcanic islands has its own character—from stunning white beaches to towering cliffs and volcanic terrain. You can surf on O'ahu, explore volcanoes on Maui and the Big Island, hike around Waimea Canyon on Kaua'i , and experience true seclusion on Moloka'i and Lāna'i.

When to Go

Alaska

Most visitors come to Alaska in **summer,** when milder temperatures and the midnight sun prevail. The farther north you go in summer, the longer the days; in Fairbanks in June the sun sets for a couple of hours. In the interior temperatures can easily reach the 80s and 90s in June and July. The rest of the state is cooler, and rain is common in coastal areas. **Fall** in Alaska is an abbreviated three weeks, when trees and bushes blaze with color and daytime temperatures are still pleasant. **Winters** are extremely cold in the interior (daytime temperatures of 0°F or lower). In the southeast's temperate maritime climate, though, temperatures rarely dip below freezing. **Spring** is often a monthlong foggy period of thawing, starting at the beginning of April.

Hawai'i

Hawai'i's long days of sunshine and fairly mild year-round temperatures allow for 12 months of pleasurable island travel. In resort areas near sea level the average afternoon temperature during the coldest months of December and January is 80°F; during the hottest months of August through October, temperatures can reach the low 90s. The northern shores of each island usually receive more rain than those in the south. Mid-December through mid-April and July through August are peak travel times.

Festivals and Seasonal Events

Alaska

➤ MID-FEB.: The **Anchorage Fur Rendezvous** (☎ 907/277–1172) brings a three-day world-championship dogsled race through city streets.

➤ EARLY JULY: The **July 4th Mount Marathon Race and Celebration** in Seward (☎ 907/224–8051) is a grueling race up a 3,022-ft mountain, followed by a parade and festival of crafts, games, and food booths.

Hawai'i

➤ LATE MAR.–EARLY APR.: Reserve tickets months in advance for the **Merrie Monarch Festival** (☎ 808/935–9168) in Hilo on the Big Island—a full week of hula competitions beginning Easter Sunday.

➤ MAY 1: The statewide **Lei Day** (☎ 808/547–7393) is an annual flower-filled celebration with lei-making competitions.

➤ NOV.: The **Hawai'i International Film Festival** (☎ 808/528–3456), on O'ahu and Neighbor Islands, showcases films from the United States, Asia, and the Pacific.

➤ DEC.: The **Triple Crown of Surfing** (☎ 808/638–7266) on O'ahu draws the world's top pro surfers to the famed North Shore for big winter waves.

West Coast (Northern)

West Coast (Southern)

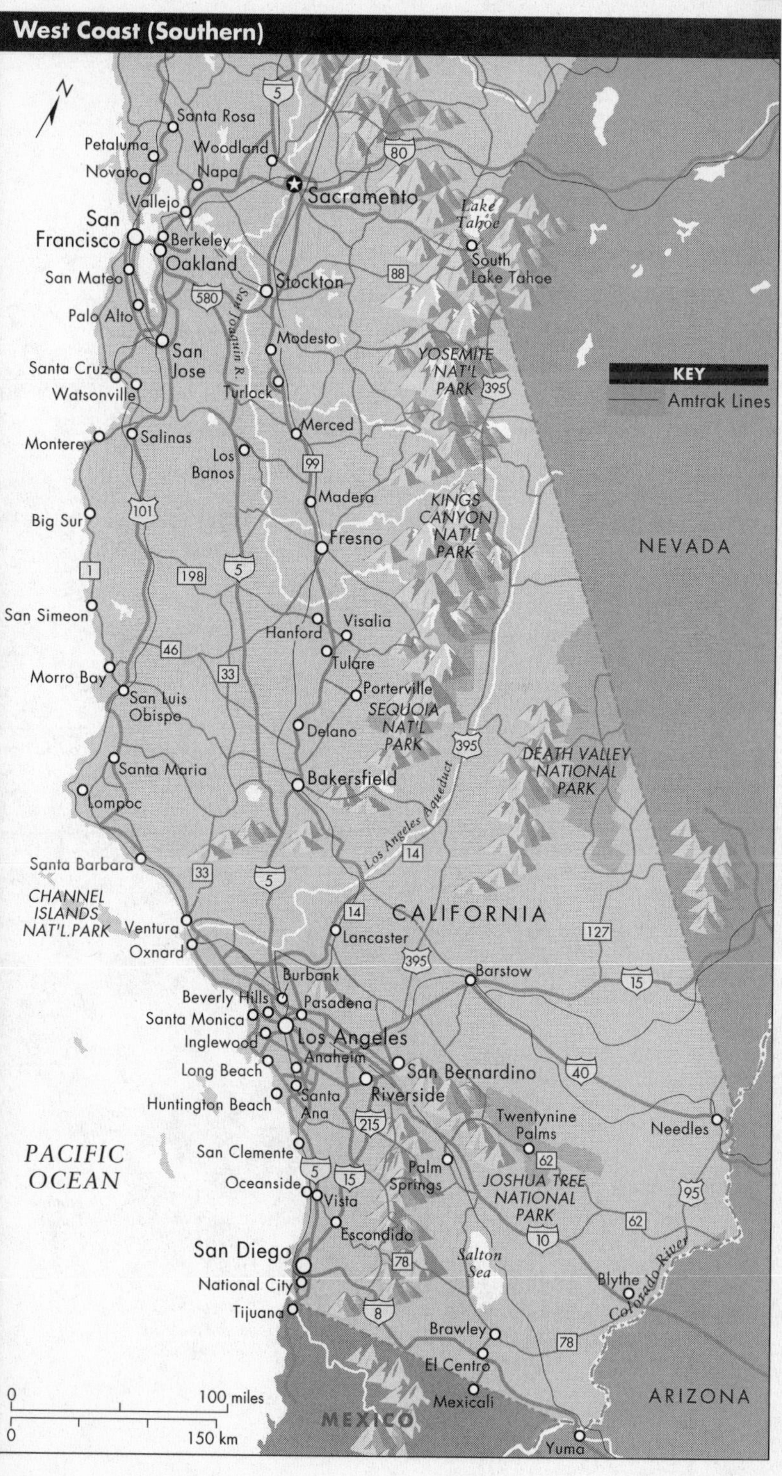

Alaska and Hawai`i

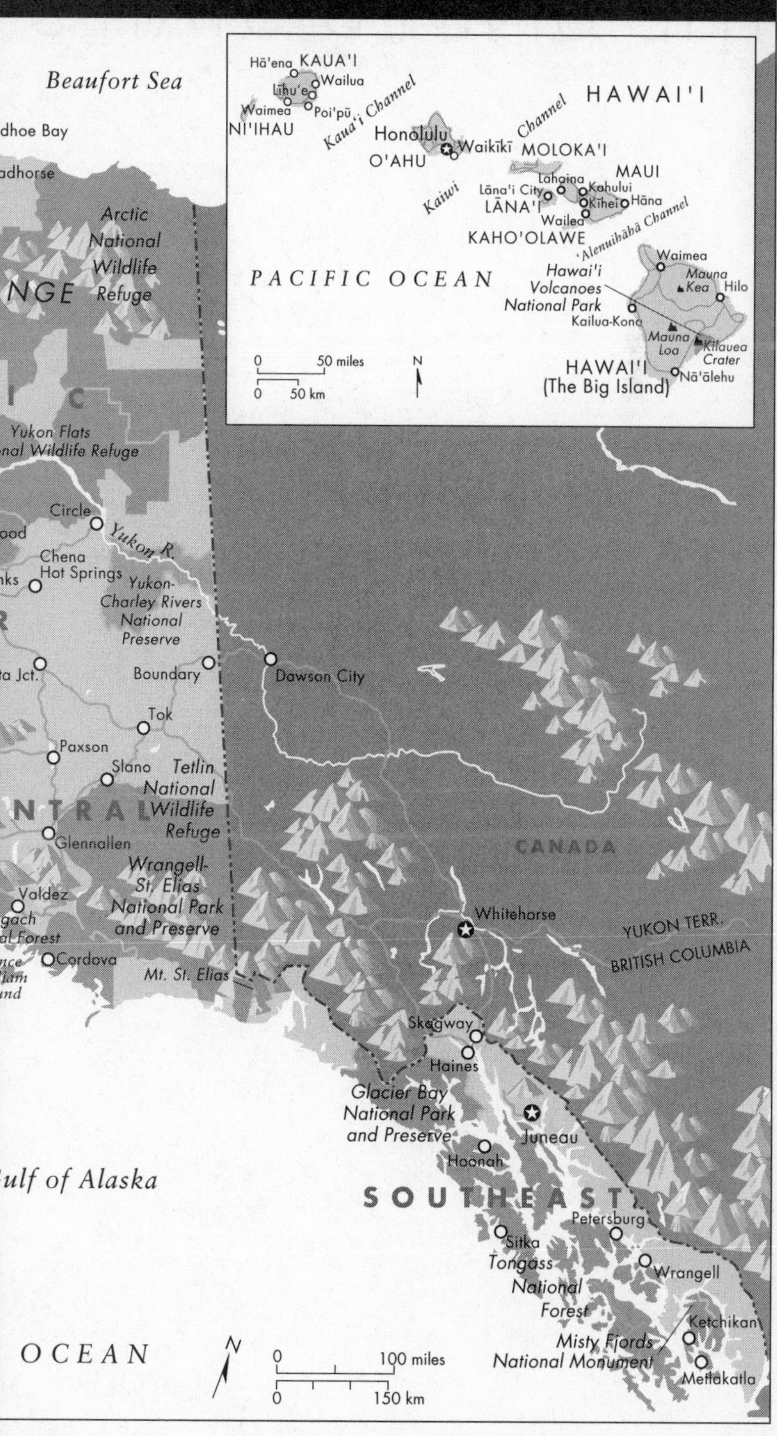

Beaufort Sea
Arctic National Wildlife Refuge
Yukon Flats
Circle
Yukon R.
Chena Hot Springs
Yukon-Charley Rivers National Preserve
Boundary
Dawson City
Tok
Paxson
Slana
Tetlin National Wildlife Refuge
Glennallen
Wrangell-St. Elias National Park and Preserve
Valdez
Cordova
Mt. St. Elias
CANADA
Whitehorse
YUKON TERR.
BRITISH COLUMBIA
Skagway
Haines
Glacier Bay National Park and Preserve
Juneau
Hoonah
Gulf of Alaska
SOUTHEAST
Petersburg
Sitka
Tongass National Forest
Wrangell
Ketchikan
Misty Fjords National Monument
Metlakatla
OCEAN
N
0 100 miles
0 150 km
Hā'ena
KAUA'I
Wailua
Līhu'e
Waimea
Poi'pū
NI'IHAU
Kaua'i Channel
HAWAI'I
Honolulu
Waikīkī
O'AHU
Channel
MOLOKA'I
MAUI
Kaiwi
Lahaina
Kahului
Lāna'i City
LĀNA'I
Kīhei
Hāna
Wailea
KAHO'OLAWE
'Alenuihāhā Channel
PACIFIC OCEAN
Waimea
Mauna Kea
Hawai'i Volcanoes National Park
Hilo
Kailua-Kona
Mauna Loa
Kīlauea Crater
HAWAI'I (The Big Island)
Nā'ālehu
0 50 miles
0 50 km

THE UNITED STATES

Each state is a unique entity with its own character. (In the case of some of the larger states, you'll find multiple personalities.) Each chapter contains sections on major cities, the most popular sights, and worthwhile but lesser-known destinations, along with good suggestions on where to stay, eat, and explore.

ALABAMA

Updated by Michelle Roberts Matthews

Capital	Montgomery
Population	4,447,100
Motto	We Dare Defend Our Rights
State Bird	Yellowhammer
State Flower	Camellia
Postal Abbreviation	AL

Statewide Visitor Information

Alabama Bureau of Tourism and Travel (✉ 401 Adams Ave., Box 4927, Montgomery 36103, ☎ 334/242–4169 or 800/252–2262, WEB www.touralabama.org). **Welcome centers:** I–59 near Valley Head, I–20/59 at Cuba, I–65 at Elkmont, I–10 north of Seminole, I–10 at Grand Bay, I–20 east of Heflin, I–85 at Lanett, U.S. 231 south of Dothan.

Scenic Drives

Talladega Scenic Drive begins at U.S. 78 near Heflin and winds through Talladega National Forest to Adams Gap, southwest of Cheaha State Park. The 25-mi drive has scenic views, especially in March and April and mid-October–mid-November. In and around Mobile, the **Azalea Trail** twines for 27 mi; flowering time is February and March.

State Parks

Alabama's 24 state parks include many recreational activities and lodgings. You have the choice of resort lodges, hotels, campgrounds, chalets, and cabins, both modern and rustic. Several parks have marinas, golf courses, and tennis facilities. Contact **Alabama State Parks** (✉ 64 N. Union St., Folsom Administrative Bldg., Suite 547, Montgomery 36130, ☎ 800/252–7275, WEB www.dcnr.state.al.us) for reservations or information. **DeSoto State Park** (✉ 13883 CR 89, Fort Payne, ☎ 256/845–5380 or 800/568–8840), in northern Alabama, has the spectacular Little River Canyon and falls. **Lake Guntersville State Park** (✉ 1155 Lodge Dr., Guntersville, ☎ 256/571–5440 or 800/548–5455), also in the northern part of the state, is home of the annual Eagle Awareness programs. **Gulf State Park** (✉ 20115 Rte. 135, Gulf Shores, ☎ 251/948–4853 or 800/544–4853), near Gulf Shores, has 2½ mi of powdery white dunes and beaches.

CENTRAL ALABAMA

This region encompasses the hilly Highlands around Birmingham, the state's largest city, and the state capital, Montgomery, which is in the heart of the "black belt region," named for its rich, dark soil.

Exploring Central Alabama

Birmingham is a relatively new Alabama city, having blossomed with the development of the iron industry and coal mines in the early 1900s. Today its primary employer is the University of Alabama at Birmingham, which has one of the country's largest medical centers. The city has restored many of its early 20th-century buildings and is an attractive, welcoming metropolis.

The **Birmingham Museum of Art,** the Southeast's largest municipal museum, has some 18,000 works, from Italian Early Renaissance to contemporary American. The museum houses the region's largest collection of Asian art and has the finest collection of Wedgwood outside England. ✉ *2000 8th Ave. N,* ☎ *205/254–2565,* WEB *www.artsbma.org.* 🎟 *Free. Closed Mon.*

The **Alabama Sports Hall of Fame and Museum** (✉ 2150 Civic Center Blvd., ☎ 205/323–6665, WEB www.alasports.org; 🎟 $5), adjacent to the Civic Center, displays memorabilia of such Alabama athletic heroes as coach Bear Bryant, Jesse Owens, Willie Mays, and Hank Aaron.

In the Kelly Ingram Park area, southwest of the Civic Center, is the **16th Street Baptist Church,** a civil rights landmark where numerous protests were staged in the 1960s. A bomb planted by white supremacists exploded here in 1963, killing four black children. There is a plaque in their memory. On Saturday, tours are by appointment only. ✉ *1530 16th St.,* ☎ *205/251–9402.* 🎟 *$2.*

★ The **Birmingham Civil Rights Institute** documents the civil rights movement from the 1920s to the present using exhibits, multimedia presentations, music, and oral histories. ✉ *520 16th St. N,* ☎ *205/328–9696,* WEB *www.bcri.bham.al.us.* 🎟 *$5. Closed Mon.*

The **Alabama Jazz Hall of Fame,** two blocks from the Civil Rights Institute, has photos and memorabilia of the state's jazz legends, including Nat "King" Cole, Duke Ellington, and Lionel Hampton. ✉ *1631 4th Ave. N,* ☎ *205/254–2720,* WEB *www.jazzhall.com/jazz.* 🎟 *Free. Closed Mon.*

The **Sloss Furnaces,** a massive ironworks, used ore from the hills around Birmingham when it was in operation between 1882 and 1971. Now it's a monument to Birmingham's industrial past and home to metal artwork by local sculptors. Guided tours of this National Historic Landmark are given weekends. In October, the site is transformed into a scary Halloween phenomenon known as **Sloss Fright Furnace** (☎ 205/324–6881). ✉ *20 32nd St.,* ☎ *205/324–1911.* 🎟 *Free. Closed Mon.*

With 900 animals, the **Birmingham Zoo** (✉ 2630 Cahaba Rd., ☎ 205/879–0408, WEB www.birminghamzoo.com; 🎟 $5) is one of the Southeast's largest zoos. The **McWane Center** (✉ 200 19th St. N, ☎ 205/714–8300, WEB www.mcwane.org; 🎟 museum $7.50, IMAX $7.50, both $11) is a hands-on science museum with an IMAX theater.

VisionLand Theme Park (✉ VisionLand Pkwy., Bessemer, ☎ 205/481-4750, WEB www.visionlandpark.com; 🎟 $24.99) is 16 mi southwest of Birmingham on I–20/59 near I–459. It has more than 20 rides including Rampage, a giant wooden roller coaster; the white-water rapids of Wild River Gorge; and the StratosFear Screamer.

DeSoto Caverns Park, 40 mi from Birmingham (head southeast on U.S. 280 to Childersburg, then east on Route 76), is a network of caves that were used as a Native American burial ground 2,000 years ago. Rediscovered by Spanish explorer Hernando De Soto in 1540, the caverns later served as a Confederate gunpowder mining center and a Prohibition speakeasy. Tours begin with a sound, water, and laser-light show in the 12-story Great Onyx Cathedral. The park is open Monday–Saturday 9–5:30 and Sunday 1–5:30. ✉ *DeSoto Caverns Pkwy., Childersburg,* ☎ *256/378–7252 or 800/933–2283,* WEB *www.desotocavernspark.com.* 🎟 *1-hr guided tour $9.99.*

More than 300 Confederate veterans and their wives are buried in **Confederate Memorial Park** (✉ 437 CR 63, Marbury, ☎ 205/755–1990 free), southwest of Childersburg off U.S. 31 near Mountain Creek. Here you also can see Civil War uniforms, weapons, and equipment.

Montgomery, 90 mi south of Birmingham via I–65, is a city steeped in antebellum history. Today, many of its old houses are restored and occupy charming, well-kept neighborhoods. Downtown, new buildings and developments are changing the skyline and riverfront. The **visitor center** (✉ 300 Water St. 36104, ☎ 334/261–1100 or 800/240–9452, WEB www.visitingmontgomery.com) shows a brief video covering the city's history and things to do. Park your car at the center and you can walk to many attractions.

The handsome **state capitol** (✉ Bainbridge St. at Dexter Ave., ☎ 334/242–3935, WEB www.preserveala.org), built in 1851, served as the first capitol for the Confederate States of America. Dr. Martin Luther King Jr. began his career as a minister in 1954 at the **Dexter Avenue King Memorial Baptist Church** (✉ 454 Dexter Ave., ☎ 334/263–3970, WEB www.dexterkingmemorial.org). A basement mural depicts people and events associated with the civil rights movement. The first **White House of the Confederacy** (✉ Washington Ave. at Union St., ☎ 334/242–1861; free), built in 1835 in the Italianate style, has Civil War artifacts and items that belonged to Jefferson Davis, the Confederate president.

A tribute to Montgomery's role in the civil rights movement, Troy State University Montgomery's **Rosa Parks Library and Museum** (✉ 251 Montgomery St., ☎ 334/241–8661, WEB www.tsum.edu/museum; $5) was built on the site where Parks refused to give up her seat on a city bus, sparking the Montgomery bus boycott. The museum holds artifacts and documents from that period.

★ At the **Civil Rights Memorial** (✉ 400 Washington Ave., ☎ 334/264–0286, WEB www.splcenter.org), a circular black granite table records the names of 40 people who lost their lives in the civil rights movement and chronicles its history in lines radiating like clock hands. Water emerges from the table's center and flows evenly across the top. On a curved black granite wall behind the table are engraved the words from the bible that Dr. Martin Luther King Jr. often quoted, "Until justice rolls down like waters and righteousness like a mighty stream."

Dining and Lodging

Throughout Alabama, Old South dishes—fried chicken and catfish, barbecue, fatback, seasoned vegetables, and corn bread—weigh down the tables. But since the early '90s, Birmingham has become known among southerners—and, increasingly, outside of the region—for its sophisticated dining scene, attracting some of the South's finest chefs. Football games in Auburn and legislative sessions can book up Montgomery hotels, so it's best to reserve ahead.

Birmingham

$$–$$$$ ★ ✕ **Highlands Bar and Grill.** Owner-chef Frank Stitt, a James Beard Award winner, opened this restaurant in 1982 and has been making waves in the culinary world ever since. His creative dishes express his love of the "two souths"—his native Alabama and the south of France—and are served in a romantic, candlelit atmosphere so coveted that reservations are accepted a month in advance. ✉ *2011 11th Ave. S,* ☎ *205/939–1400. Reservations essential. AE, MC, V. Closed Sun.–Mon.*

$–$$ ✕ **Nabeel's Café & Market.** Greek-born John Krontiras, his Italian-born wife, Ottavia, and family prepare gyros, hummus, spinach pie, and other Mediterranean delicacies with artistry in this neighborhood restaurant. The market sells hard-to-find international foods, and the adjacent Café

Capri serves pastries and coffee. ✉ *1706 Oxmoor Rd., Homewood,* ☎ *205/879–9292. AE, MC, V. Closed Sun.*

$–$$ ✕ **Silvertron Cafe.** This lively, popular hangout keeps regulars coming back for more pasta, chicken fingers, and giant salads. The spectacular Sunday brunch also draws crowds, so arrive early. ✉ *3813 Clairmont Ave.,* ☎ *205/591–3707. AE, DC, MC, V.*

$ ✕ **Irondale Café.** Mary Jo and Bill McMichael's homey little restaurant was the inspiration for the café in Fannie Flagg's *Fried Green Tomatoes at the Whistle Stop Café.* And, yes, fried green tomatoes are on the menu, as well as a dozen other fresh vegetables, at least six entrées, and an array of desserts—all served cafeteria style. ✉ *1906 1st Ave. N, Irondale (7 mi east of Birmingham),* ☎ *205/956–5258. No credit cards. Closed Sat. No dinner.*

$$$ ★ **The Tutwiler.** This 13-story, redbrick National Historic Landmark was built in 1913 as a luxury apartment building and was converted into a hotel in 1986. The lobby has marble floors, chandeliers, and lots of flowers. ✉ *2021 Park Pl., at 21st St. N 35203,* ☎ *205/322–2100 or 800/996–3426,* FAX *205/325–1183,* WEB *www.wyndham.com. 147 rooms. Restaurant. AE, D, DC, MC, V.*

$$–$$$ **Wynfrey Hotel.** Rising 15 stories above the Riverchase Galleria mall, this deluxe hotel has a beautiful European-style lobby complete with Italian marble and enormous chandeliers. There is a 24-hour business center, and the Robert Trent Jones Golf Trail is 20 minutes away. ✉ *1000 Riverchase Galleria (U.S. 31 S), 35244,* ☎ *205/987–1600 or 800/996–3739,* FAX *205/987–9552,* WEB *www.wynfrey.com. 329 rooms. Restaurant, pool, health club. AE, D, DC, MC, V.*

$–$$ **Mountain Brook Inn.** This hotel at the foot of Red Mountain has an eight-story glass exterior, a marble-floor lobby, and bi-level suites with spiral staircases. ✉ *2800 U.S. 280, 35223,* ☎ *205/870–3100 or 800/523–7771,* FAX *205/414–2128,* WEB *www.mountainbrookinn.com. 170 rooms. Restaurant, pool. AE, D, DC, MC, V.*

Montgomery

$–$$$ ✕ **Jubilee Seafood Company.** In this small café you'll find some of the finest and freshest seafood in town, from Greek-style snapper to soft-shell crab and crab claws. ✉ *1057 Woodley Rd., Cloverdale Plaza,* ☎ *334/262–6224. AE, MC, V. Closed Sun.–Mon. No lunch.*

$–$$$ ★ ✕ **Sahara Restaurant.** Proprietors Joe and Mike Deep carry on a family tradition, serving perfectly prepared broiled snapper, shrimp scampi, and certified Angus beef. ✉ *511 E. Edgemont Ave.,* ☎ *334/262–1215. AE, D, DC, MC, V. Closed Sun.*

$ ✕ **Chris' Hot Dog Stand.** A Montgomery tradition for more than 80 years, this small eatery is always busy at lunchtime. Chris's famous sauce contains chili peppers, onions, and a variety of herbs that give his hot dogs a one-of-a-kind flavor. ✉ *138 Dexter Ave.,* ☎ *334/265–6850. Reservations not accepted. No credit cards. Closed Sun.*

$$$ ★ **Embassy Suites Hotel.** Adjacent to the Montgomery Conference Center and within walking distance of the state capitol, this high-rise hotel centers on a spectacular atrium lobby that resembles a tropical rain forest. Glass elevators provide a bird's-eye view. ✉ *300 Tallapoosa St. 36104,* ☎ *334/269–5055,* FAX *334/269–0360. 237 suites. Restaurant, pool, gym. AE, D, DC, MC, V.*

$$ **Red Bluff Cottage.** In this delightful cottage in the heart of downtown, you can relax on a veranda overlooking the Alabama River plain and the state capitol. Rooms have ceiling fans and antiques. The sitting room with a fireplace and the music room–library are good places to relax. ✉ *551 Clay St. 36104,* ☎ *334/264–0056 or 888/551–2529,* WEB *www.bbonline.com/al/redbluff. 4 rooms. AE, D, MC, V. BP.*

Motels

Deluxe Inns and Suites (✉ 7905 Crestwood Blvd., Birmingham 35210, ☎ 205/956–4440 or 800/338–9275, FAX 205/956–3011), 108 rooms; pool; $. **Hampton Inn** (✉ 1401 East Blvd., Montgomery 36117, ☎ 334/277–2400), 105 rooms; pool; $.

The Arts

In Montgomery at the world-class **Alabama Shakespeare Festival** (✉ 1 Festival Dr.; Eastern Bypass exit off I–85, ☎ 334/271–5353 or 800/841–4273, WEB www.asf.net), Shakespearean plays, contemporary dramas and comedies, and musicals are performed on two stages year-round.

Shopping

Birmingham's **Riverchase Galleria** (✉ U.S. 31 S at I–459, ☎ 205/985–3039), with more than 200 stores, is one of the Southeast's largest malls. The **Summit** (✉ U.S. 280 at I–459, ☎ 205/967–0111), one of Birmingham's most upscale malls, is a pedestrian-friendly, one-level shopping center. **Boaz Fashion Outlets** (✉ 501 Elizabeth St., Boaz, about 60 mi north of Birmingham, ☎ 256/593–1199) has more than 100 outlet and specialty stores.

Central Alabama Essentials

AIRPORTS

➤ AIRPORT INFORMATION: **Birmingham International Airport** (✉ 5900 Airport Hwy., ☎ 205/599–0500). **Dannelly Field** (✉ 4445 Selma Hwy., ☎ 334/281–5040).

BUS TRAVEL

➤ BUS INFORMATION: **Greyhound** (✉ 618 N. 19th St., Birmingham; ✉ 950 W. South Blvd., Montgomery; ☎ 800/231–2222).

CAR TRAVEL

I–59 runs northeast from Birmingham into Georgia and Tennessee and southwest into Mississippi. I–20 runs east–west through Birmingham. I–65 is the north–south route connecting Birmingham with Montgomery. I–85 leads southwest from Atlanta to Montgomery.

TRAIN TRAVEL

➤ TRAIN INFORMATION: **Amtrak** (✉ 1819 Morris Ave., Birmingham; ✉ 950 W. South Blvd., Montgomery, ☎ 800/872–7245, WEB www.amtrak.com).

VISITOR INFORMATION

➤ TOURIST INFORMATION: **Birmingham Convention and Visitors Bureau** (✉ 2200 9th Ave. N, Birmingham 35203-1100, ☎ 205/458–8000 or 800/458–8085, WEB www.birminghamal.org). **Montgomery Area Visitor Center** (✉ 300 Water St., Montgomery 36104, ☎ 334/261–1100 or 800/240–9452, WEB www.visitingmontgomery.com).

MOBILE AND THE GULF COAST

In Mobile, a busy port and one of Alabama's oldest cities (the old gal celebrated her 300th birthday in 2002), many antebellum buildings survive as a bridge to the past despite the "urban renewal" development of the 1960s. A springtime explosion of azaleas beneath Spanish moss–draped oak canopies shows why Mobile is known as the Azalea City. The country's first Mardi Gras was held here (not in New Orleans, as native Mobilians love to explain), and today the city still exults in two

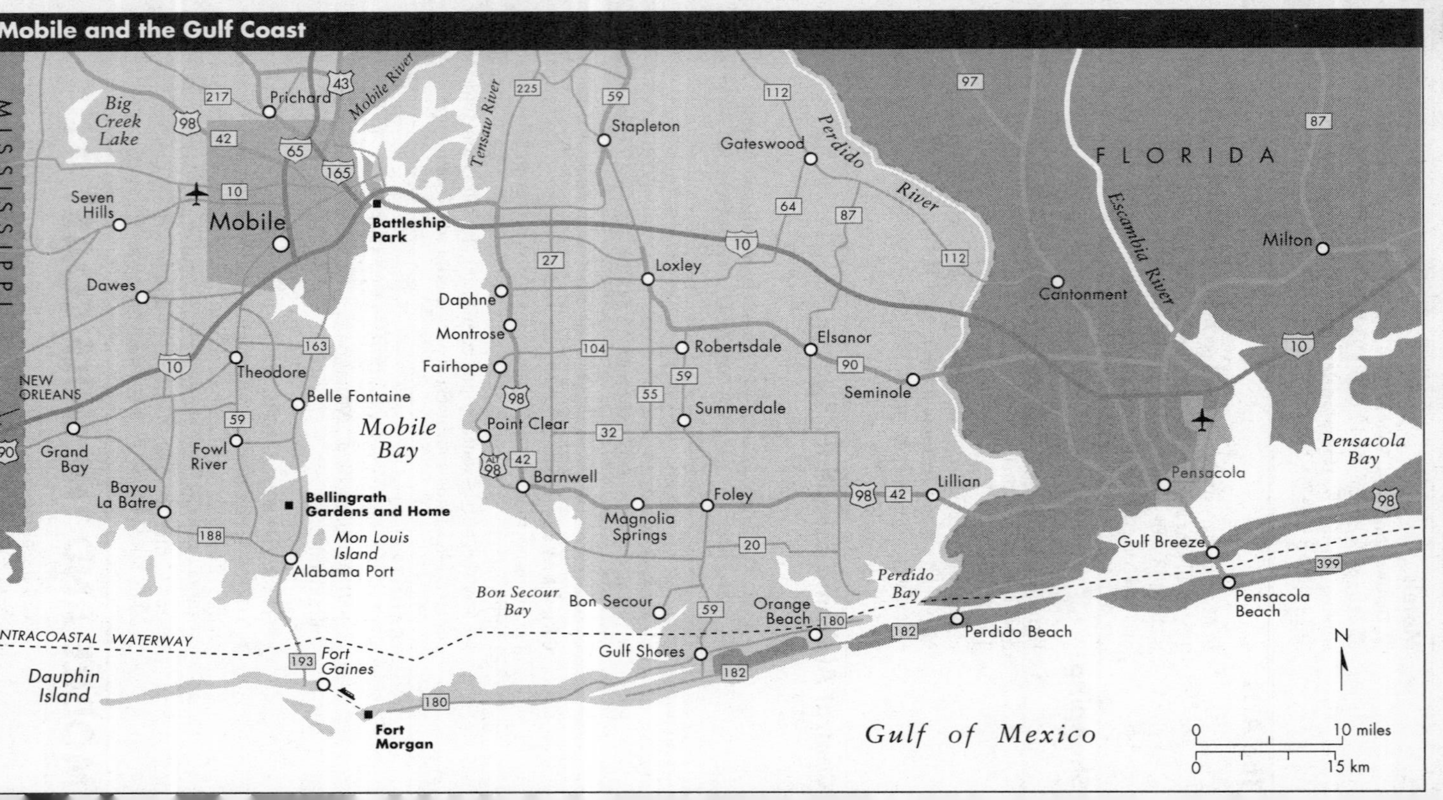
Mobile and the Gulf Coast
MISSISSIPPI
Big Creek Lake
Prichard
Mobile River
Tensaw River
Stapleton
Gateswood
Perdido River
FLORIDA
Escambia River
Milton
Seven Hills
Mobile
Battleship Park
Loxley
Cantonment
Dawes
Daphne
Montrose
Fairhope
Robertsdale
Elsanor
Seminole
Theodore
Belle Fontaine
NEW ORLEANS
Summerdale
Point Clear
Mobile Bay
Grand Bay
Fowl River
Barnwell
Lillian
Pensacola
Pensacola Bay
Bayou La Batre
Bellingrath Gardens and Home
Magnolia Springs
Foley
Mon Louis Island
Alabama Port
Gulf Breeze
Perdido Bay
Pensacola Beach
Bon Secour Bay
Bon Secour
Orange Beach
Perdido Beach
INTRACOASTAL WATERWAY
Gulf Shores
Fort Gaines
Dauphin Island
Fort Morgan
N
Gulf of Mexico
0 10 miles
0 15 km

weeks of pre-Lenten parades, balls, and merrymaking. South of Mobile, across Mobile Bay, the area around Gulf Shores has 32 mi of white-sand beaches, including 2½ mi protected in Gulf State Park. On the eastern shore of Mobile Bay in Fairhope and Point Clear, incredible sunsets are not-to-be-missed events.

Exploring Mobile and the Gulf Coast

In 1711 **Fort Condé** (✉ 150 S. Royal St., Mobile, ☎ 251/208–7304; 🎫 free) was the name the French gave to the colonial outpost that would one day expand and become Mobile. Today, the city's French origins endure in its creole cuisine. One hundred fifty years after the fort was destroyed, its remains were discovered during construction of the I–10 interchange. A reconstructed portion houses the city's **visitor center**, as well as a museum. Costumed guides conduct tours.

The visitor center has information on major events in Mobile, the biggest of which is **Mardi Gras,** with balls, parties, and parades. The **Azalea Trail Festival** in March showcases the annual Azalea Trail Run and the fabulous Festival of Flowers. The two-day **Historic Mobile Homes Tour,** also in March, opens private houses for viewing.

Near Fort Condé, the **Gulf Coast Exploreum Science Center** (✉ 65 Government St., Mobile, ☎ 251/208–6883 or 877/625–4386, WEB www.exploreum.net; 🎫 museum $11, IMAX $7, both $15) is a children's museum that hosts traveling exhibits and an IMAX dome theater. The **Museum of Mobile** (✉ 111 S. Royal St., Mobile, ☎ 251/208–7569, WEB www.museumofmobile.com; 🎫 $5) opened in 2001 in the renovated circa-1857 Southern Market/Old City Hall building next to the Exploreum. Interactive exhibits and special collections of antique silver, weapons, and more tell the 300-year history of Mobile.

Oakleigh (✉ 350 Oakleigh Pl., Mobile, ☎ 251/432–1281; 🎫 $5), 1½ mi from Fort Condé, in the heart of the historic Oakleigh Garden District, is an antebellum Greek Revival–style mansion, built between 1833 and 1838. Costumed guides give tours of the home, which has fine period furniture, portraits, silver, jewelry, kitchen implements, toys, and more. Tickets include a tour of neighboring **Cox-Deasy House,** an 1850s cottage furnished with simple 19th-century pieces.

★ Mobile Bay, east of downtown, is the site of the 155-acre **Battleship Memorial Park** (✉ 2703 Battleship Pkwy., Mobile, ☎ 251/433–2703 or 800/426–4929, WEB www.ussalabama.com; 🎫 $10), where the battleship USS *Alabama* is anchored. A self-guided tour gives a fascinating glimpse into the World War II vessel, which had a crew of 2,500. Anchored next to it is the USS *Drum,* a World War II submarine. Other exhibits include the B-52 bomber *Calamity Jane.*

★ **Bellingrath Gardens and Home,** 20 mi south of Mobile, is the site of one of the world's most magnificent azalea gardens. Here, amid a 905-acre semitropical landscape, 65 acres of gardens bloom in all seasons: 200 species of azaleas in spring, 3,000 rosebushes in summer, 60,000 chrysanthemum plants in autumn, and fields of poinsettias in winter. Built by Coca-Cola bottling pioneer Walter D. Bellingrath, who started the gardens with his wife in 1917, the house has a fine collection of antiques, including Boehm porcelain. Sightseeing cruises along Fowl River are available aboard the *Southern Belle.* ✉ *12401 Bellingrath Gardens Rd., Theodore,* ☎ *251/973–2217,* WEB *www.bellingrath.org.* 🎫 *Gardens $8.50, gardens and home $15.75.*

Fairhope, on the eastern shore of Mobile Bay, resembles an art colony with its quaint shops and potteries, flower-filled streets (even the trash cans are adorned with blooms year-round), and annual arts-and-crafts festival in March. Its public pier and bay-side park provide ample opportunities for fishing and boating. **Point Clear,** down the road from Fairhope, has long been a favorite summert destination for wealthy Mobilians and is best known for Marriott's Grand Hotel Resort and Golf Club.

The family-operated **Punta Clara Kitchen** (✉ 17111 Scenic Hwy. 98, Point Clear, ☎ 251/928–8477) sells exquisite confections, preserves, and other treats from an 1897 Victorian home.

From Mobile take I–10 and Route 59 south to **Gulf Shores.** There's ample free parking along the white-as-snow beach, though the traffic can be bumper to bumper at peak times (Memorial Day–Labor Day). Star-shape **Fort Morgan** (✉ Mobile Point, end of Rte. 180, 20 mi west of Gulf Shores, ☎ 251/540–7125) sits at the western tip of Pleasure Island and is rumored to be haunted. The fort was built in the early 1800s to guard the entrance to Mobile Bay. In 1864, after Confederate torpedoes sank the ironclad *Tecumseh* in the Battle of Mobile Bay, Union admiral David Farragut shouted, "Damn the torpedoes! Full speed ahead!" The rest of Farragut's fleet pushed its way to the bay, forcing the Confederates' surrender. The museum on-site tells the story. Wednesday–Sunday, actors in period dress present plays of the events that occurred inside the fort.

Dining and Lodging

In Mobile and throughout the Gulf Coast area, fresh seafood abounds. Shrimp, crab claws, and oysters (fried, stewed, or nude) as well as gumbo, West Indies salad, and po'boy sandwiches are staples on many menus.

Gulf Shores

$–$$ ★ ✕ **Original Oyster House.** Dining at this nautically themed restaurant on the bayou is a local tradition. Oysters, plucked fresh from nearby Perdido Bay, are the house specialty. Don't miss the homemade gumbo—brimming with crab claws, shrimp, okra, and a secret combination of spices. ✉ *Bayou Village Shopping Center, Rte. 59,* ☎ *251/948–2445. Reservations not accepted. AE, D, DC, MC, V.*

$$–$$$ **Gulf Shores Plantation.** Perfect for large groups or families needing more space than a hotel room provides, this 320-acre family resort, 8 mi east of Fort Morgan on the Gulf, has condominiums with fully equipped kitchens as well as duplexes that house as many as 15 people. ✉ *Rte. 180 W (Box 1299, 36547),* ☎ *251/540–5000 or 800/554–0344,* FAX *334/540–6055,* WEB *www.gulfshoresplantation.com. 524 units. 2 restaurants, 8 pools, tennis. AE, MC, V.*

Mobile

$$$–$$$$ ★ ✕ **Justine's Courtyard and Carriageway.** Just blocks from the Mobile River in the heart of the city, Justine's has two beautiful settings for outdoor dining—in the courtyard or the carriageway—as well as two elegant inside dining rooms. Owner-chef Matt Shipp concocts creative dishes from southern staples. Try the butter-bean cakes with feta cheese, leeks, and red peppers. ✉ *80 St. Michael St.,* ☎ *251/438–4535. AE, D, DC, MC, V. Closed Tues. No lunch Mon. or Sat.*

$$–$$$ ✕ **Gus's Azalea Manor Restaurant and Courtyard.** The airy bar has a colorful mural and a view of equally colorful Dauphin Street, and the lush rear courtyard is a great place to dine alfresco. Greek chef Gus Ravanos's menu includes pastas, seafood, steaks, and chicken. ✉ *751 Dauphin St.,* ☎ *251/433–4877. AE, D, DC, MC, V. Closed Sun.*

$ ✕ **Roussos.** This family-owned restaurant next door to Fort Condé has become an institution in Mobile. The outstanding service and excellent seafood—fried, broiled, or Greek style—keep people coming back. ✉ *166 S. Royal St.,* ☎ *251/433–3322. AE, D, DC, MC, V. Closed Sun.*

$$ 🏨 **Radisson Admiral Semmes Hotel.** This downtown hotel, next to Mobile Government Plaza, is popular with local politicians. Revelers appreciate its excellent location on the Mardi Gras parade route. Rooms are furnished in Queen Anne and Chippendale styles. ✉ *251 Government St., 36602,* ☎ *251/432–8000,* FAX *334/405–5942. 170 rooms. Restaurant, pool. AE, D, DC, MC, V.*

$–$$ 🏨 **Malaga Inn.** At the center of this delightful, historic inn is a lush, gaslit courtyard with a fountain. The large rooms are furnished with period antiques, and many have original hardwood floors. ✉ *359 Church St., 36602,* ☎ *251/438–4701 or 800/235–1586. 38 rooms. Pool. AE, D, MC, V.*

Orange Beach

$$–$$$ ✕ **The Outrigger.** Perched at the tip of Alabama Point on Perdido Pass, this contemporary restaurant has panoramic views of the water. The fried seafood, served with hush puppies, is hard to pass up, but you can also order fish broiled or blackened. Shrimp Perdido and veal are specialties. ✉ *27500 Perdido Beach Blvd.,* ☎ *251/981–6700. Reservations not accepted. AE, D, DC, MC, V.*

$–$$$ ✕ **Bayside Grill.** The nautical decorations blend smartly with the marina view. Fresh seafood is the specialty; steak, chicken, pasta, and salads also are served. A New Orleans–born chef creates such down-home fare as coconut shrimp, black bean soup, Cajun-style gumbo, and bananas Foster strudel. Sunday brunch is bountiful. The early dinner menu, served 4–6 PM November 1–March 15, is a bargain. ✉ *27842 Canal Rd.,* ☎ *251/981–4899. AE, D, DC, MC, V.*

$–$$ ✕ **Franco's.** This comfortable, casual Italian restaurant specializes in stuffed mushrooms, seafood fettuccine, veal, and steak—all prepared with the freshest ingredients. ✉ *26651 Perdido Beach Blvd.,* ☎ *251/981–9800. Reservations not accepted. AE, D, DC, MC, V.*

$$–$$$ 🏨 **Original Romar House.** This unassuming beach cottage is full of surprises—from the Purple Parrot Bar to the Caribbean-style upstairs sitting area to the luxurious art deco–style guest rooms. Eat breakfast on the covered deck overlooking the Gulf, and enjoy wine and cheese every evening. ✉ *23500 Perdido Beach Blvd., 36561,* ☎ *334/974–1625 or 800/487–6627,* FAX *334/974–1163. 6 rooms, 1 cottage. AE, MC, V. BP.*

$$–$$$ ★ 🏨 **Perdido Beach Resort.** The exteriors of these Mediterranean-style eight- and nine-story hotel towers are stucco and red tile, and the lobby is tiled in terra-cotta and has mosaics by Venetian artists. Luxurious rooms have beach views and balconies. ✉ *27200 Perdido Beach Blvd., 36561,* ☎ *334/981–9811 or 800/634–8001,* FAX *334/981–5670,* WEB *www.perdidobeachresort.com. 345 rooms. 3 restaurants, pool, tennis, gym. AE, D, DC, MC, V.*

Point Clear

$$–$$$$ ★ ✕🏨 **Marriott's Grand Hotel Resort and Golf Club.** One of the Gulf Coast's true treasures since 1847, the Grand became even grander in 2002 with a complete renovation and expansion. Cottages were replaced with contemporary suites and a European-style spa. An incredible pool area with a water park, fountains, geysers, and waterfalls awaits children, while a more serene adults-only pool lies under the oaks beside the bay. You can rent sailboats or kayaks at the new man-made beach. ✉ *1 Grand Blvd., Point Clear 36564,* ☎ *334/928–9201 or 800/544–9933,* FAX *334/928–1149,* WEB *www.marriotthotels.com/PTLAL. 400 rooms. 4 restaurants, 2 pools, golf, tennis. AE, D, DC, MC, V.*

The Arts

The **Mobile Museum of Art** (✉ 4850 Museum Dr., Mobile, ☎ 251/208–5200, WEB www.mobilemuseumofart.com; 🎫 free), slated to reopen in late 2002 after a $15 million renovation, has a collection that includes contemporary American art as well as works from Europe, Asia, and Africa. A dramatic lobby overlooks the lake in Langan Park.

Across the bay in Fairhope, the **Eastern Shore Art Center** hosts monthly exhibits of oils, watercolors, graphics, mixed media, photography, sculpture, and ceramics. ✉ *401 Oak St., Fairhope,* ☎ *251/928–2228.* 🎫 *Free. Closed Sun.–Mon.*

Outdoor Activities and Sports

Canoeing

Sunshine Canoe Rentals (✉ 5460 Old Shell Rd., Mobile, ☎ 251/344–8664) runs canoe trips at Mississippi's Escatawpa River, 15 mi west of Mobile. The river has no rapids, so you travel at a leisurely pace past lots of white sandbars.

Fishing

Fishing here is excellent. You can obtain a fishing license from most bait shops. For information contact the **Department of Conservation and Natural Resources** (☎ 334/242–3829). In Gulf Shores, **Gulf State Park** (✉ 20115 Rte. 135, Gulf Shores, ☎ 251/948–4853) has fishing from an 825-ft pier; you can also rent flat-bottom boats for lake fishing. Deep-sea fishing from charter boats is very popular. Orange Beach has more than 100 charter boats, including the ***Moreno Queen*** (☎ 251/981–8499), which offers four- and six-hour fishing trips.

Golf

In recent years, coastal Alabama has developed into one of the most popular golfing destinations in the Southeast. With winter temperatures averaging 60°F, the area has become a true year-round spot. Prices range from about $32 to $70 for greens fees and cart rental. The **Robert Trent Jones Golf Trail** (☎ 800/949–4444 reservations and information, WEB www.rtjgolf.com) includes challenging, scenic courses in eight locations around the state, including Mobile.

The spectacular **Kiva Dunes** course, adjacent to Gulf Shores Plantation Resort (✉ Rte. 180, 12 mi west of Gulf Shores, ☎ 251/540–7000), designed by Jerry Pate, combines oceanfront-dunes golf with Scottish-style links golf. The **Craft Farms** complex (✉ Rte. 59, north of Gulf Shores, ☎ 251/968–7500) has 36 holes on two Arnold Palmer–designed courses at Cotton Creek and another 18 on the Woodlands course designed by Larry Nelson. About 12 mi north of Gulf Shores in Foley, the **Glenlakes Golf Club** (✉ 9530 Clubhouse Dr., ☎ 251/955–1220 or 800/435–5253), a course designed by Bruce Devlin, has 18 challenging holes that play over 7,000 yards and another 9 holes stretching 3,100 yards. The course at **Gulf State Park** (✉ 20115 Rte. 135, ☎ 251/948–7275) sits on 3,600 resort acres. The Earl Stone–designed course (☎ 251/948–4653), built in 1972, is challenging and well bunkered.

Water Sports

Fun Marina (✉ 29531 Perdido Beach Blvd., Orange Beach, ☎ 251/980–5122) rents Jet Skis, pontoon boats, and 16-ft fishing boats. **Island Recreation Services** (✉ 360 E. Beach Blvd., Gulf Shores, ☎ 251/948–7334) rents Jet Skis, body boards, surfboards, and sailboats.

Mobile and the Gulf Coast Essentials

AIRPORTS

Mobile Regional Airport and Florida's Pensacola Regional Airport (about 40 mi east of Gulf Shores/Orange Beach) are served by major domestic carriers.

➤ AIRPORT INFORMATION: **Mobile Regional Airport** (✉ 8400 Airport Blvd., ☎ 251/633–0313). **Pensacola Regional Airport** (✉ 2430 Airport Blvd., ☎ 850/435–1746).

BUS TRAVEL

➤ BUS INFORMATION: **Greyhound** (✉ 2545 Government Blvd., Mobile, ☎ 251/478–9793; ✉ 505 W. Burgess Rd., Pensacola, FL, ☎ 800/231–2222, WEB www.greyhound.com).

CAR TRAVEL

I–10 leads west from Florida to Mobile and continues into Mississippi. I–65 leads south from Birmingham and Montgomery and ends at Mobile. Along Baldwin County's eastern shore of Mobile Bay, 20 mi east of Mobile, the communities of Fairhope and Point Clear are accessible via U.S. 98 and U.S. 98A. Gulf Shores is connected with Mobile via I–10 and Route 59; Routes 180 and 182 are the main beach routes.

TRAIN TRAVEL

➤ TRAIN INFORMATION: **Amtrak** (✉ 11 Government St., Mobile, ☎ 800/872–7245; WEB www.amtrak.com).

VISITOR INFORMATION

➤ TOURIST INFORMATION: **Alabama Gulf Coast Convention and Visitors Bureau** (✉ Drawer 457, Gulf Shores 36542; ✉ 3150 Gulf Shores Pkwy., Gulf Shores 36547; ✉ 23685 Perdido Beach Blvd., Orange Beach 36561; ☎ 800/745–7263; WEB www.gulfshores.com). **Eastern Shore Chamber of Commerce** (✉ 327 Fairhope Ave., Fairhope 36532, ☎ 251/928–6387;✉ 29750 L. D. Cawyer Dr., Daphne 36527, ☎ 251/621–8222; WEB www.eschamber.com). **Mobile Convention and Visitors Corp.** (✉ 1 Water St., 36602, ☎ 800/566–2453, WEB www.mobile.org).

ELSEWHERE IN ALABAMA

Huntsville

What to See and Do

The **U.S. Space and Rocket Center** (✉ 1 Tranquility Base, ☎ 256/837–3400 or 800/637–7223, WEB www.spacecamp.com/museum; 🎟 $16.95) is home to the **U.S. Space Camp, Space Academy, and Aviation Challenge.** The center runs a bus tour of the NASA labs and shuttle test sites, hands-on exhibits in the museum, and an outdoor park filled with spacecraft; the **Spacedome Theater** shows IMAX movies.

EarlyWorks is a hands-on history center comprising four properties. **Alabama Constitution Village** is the site of Alabama's Constitutional Convention of 1819. Craftspeople in period dress demonstrate skills such as woodworking, printing, and weaving. At the **EarlyWorks Museum,** you can hear stories from a talking tree, build a house at an interactive architectural exhibit, and examine a 46-ft keelboat. The **Decorative Arts Center** houses exhibits in a restored 1848 home. A few blocks from the village, the **Historic Huntsville Depot** gives a glimpse of railroad life in the early 1800s. ✉ *404 Madison St.,* ☎ *256/564–8100 or 800/678–1819,* WEB *www.earlyworks.com.* 🎟 *$14. Closed Sun.*

Dining and Lodging

$–$$ ✕ **Cafe Berlin.** One of Huntsville's most popular restaurants showcases the city's German heritage and culinary delights, serving schnitzel, wurst, hot German potato salad, and other specialties. You can't go wrong with your dessert choice, so save room. ✉ *505 Airport Rd.,* ☎ *256/880–9920. AE, D, MC, V.*

$–$$ 🏨 **Huntsville Hilton.** The Hilton is within walking distance of the historic district, museums, and the civic center. ✉ *401 Williams Ave., 35801,* ☎ *256/533–1400,* FAX *256/534–7787,* WEB *www.hilton.com. 277 rooms. Restaurant, pool, gym. AE, D, DC, MC, V.*

Huntsville Essentials

CAR TRAVEL

Huntsville is 100 mi north of Birmingham via I–65 and U.S. 72 E.

VISITOR INFORMATION

➤ TOURIST INFORMATION: **Huntsville Convention and Visitors Bureau** (✉ 700 Monroe St., Huntsville 35801, ☎ 256/533–5723 or 800/772–2348, WEB www.huntsville.org).

Tuscumbia

What to See and Do

Tuscumbia and the adjoining towns of Florence, Sheffield, and Muscle Shoals form a quad-city area known throughout Alabama simply as **the Shoals.** Spreading out on both sides of the Tennessee River basin, this area is rich in culture and history.

Ivy Green (✉ 300 W. North Commons, ☎ 256/383–4066 or 888/329–2124; 🎟 $5) is the birthplace of author and lecturer Helen Keller, who after an illness, was left unable to hear or see at the age of 19 months. With the help of her teacher, Anne Sullivan, she graduated from Radcliffe with honors in 1904 and became a champion for all those with similar disabilities. Tours are year-round. *The Miracle Worker,* the play about Keller's childhood, is performed outdoors mid-June–late July.

The **Alabama Music Hall of Fame** (✉ U.S. 72, ☎ 256/381–4417 or 800/239–2643, WEB www.alamhof.org; 🎟 $6) celebrates the history of Alabama's musical heritage and holds the original contracts of Elvis Presley's deal with Sun Records; the touring bus of the band Alabama; and exhibits on the likes of Hank Williams, Lionel Richie, and Nat "King" Cole. The outdoor **Concert Series** draws performers and fans from across the country.

Lodging

$–$$ 🏨 **Sharlotte's House Bed and Breakfast.** Two blocks from Helen Keller's birthplace in Tuscumbia's historic district, this antiques-filled, stately Victorian home has served as an inn since 1993. ✉ *105 E. North Commons, Tuscumbia 35674,* ☎ *256/386–7269 or 877/215–8720. 3 rooms. AE, D, MC, V. BP.*

Tuscumbia Essentials

CAR TRAVEL

Tuscumbia is 120 mi northwest of Birmingham via I–65 and U.S. Alternate 72. Take Exit 310 off I–65 at Cullman.

VISITOR INFORMATION

➤ TOURIST INFORMATION: **Colbert County Tourism and Convention Bureau** (✉ U.S. 72, Tuscumbia 35674, ☎ 256/383–0783 or 800/344–0783, WEB www.colbertcountytourism.org).

ALASKA

Updated by Bill Sherwonit

Capital	Juneau
Population	627,000
Motto	North to the Future
State Bird	Willow ptarmigan
State Flower	Forget-me-not
Postal Abbreviation	AK

Statewide Visitor Information

The **Alaska Public Lands Information Center** (✉ 605 W. 4th Ave., Suite 105, Anchorage 99501, ☎ 907/271–2737, WEB www.nps.gov/aplic/center) is a clearinghouse of information on state and federal lands, including hiking trails, cabins, and campgrounds. The **Alaska Travel Industry Association** (✉ 2600 Cordova St., Suite 201, Anchorage 99503, ☎ 907/929–2200; 800/667–8489 for a vacation planner; FAX 907/561–5727; WEB www.TravelAlaska.com) provides general visitor information. The **Department of Fish and Game** (✉ Box 25526, Juneau 99802, ☎ 907/465–4180 seasons and regulations; 907/465–2376 licenses; WEB www.state.ak.us) can answer questions about sportfishing. For bed-and-breakfast reservations throughout Alaska, call **Alaska Private Lodging: Stay with a Friend** (✉ Box 200047, Anchorage 99520, ☎ 907/258–1717, FAX 907/258–6613, WEB www.alaskabandb.com).

Cruising

More than a third of Alaska's visitors arrive by cruise ship. Most cruises leave from Vancouver, British Columbia, on a weeklong itinerary up the Inside Passage of Alaska's Southeast Panhandle. All cruise lines stop at Ketchikan, Juneau, and Skagway, while some also visit Sitka, Haines, and Petersburg. Many include a day in Glacier Bay National Park, but call ahead to be sure. Some cruises also continue across the Gulf of Alaska, to the south-central towns of Seward and Valdez. One of the largest cruise fleets to sail Alaskan waters is operated by **Princess Cruises** (✉ 24844 Ave. Rockefeller, Santa Clarita, CA 91355, ☎ 800/774–6237 or 800/568–3262, WEB www.princess.com). A naturalist and Native-in-residence are aboard every cruise run by **Holland America Line/Westours** (✉ 300 Elliott Ave. W, Seattle, WA 98119, ☎ 206/281–3535 or 877/724–5425, WEB www.hollandamerica.com). For a small-ship tour, contact **Cruise West** (✉ 2401 4th Ave., Suite 700, Seattle, WA 98121, ☎ 206/441–8687 or 800/888–9378, WEB www.cruisewest.com). State ferries provide year-round budget service for passengers and vehicles (☞ Boat and Ferry Travel *in* Southeast Essentials) on similar routes.

National and State Parks

Alaska has more land in national parks, wilderness areas, and national wildlife refuges than all the other states combined.

National Parks

Denali National Park and Preserve (✉ Box 9, Denali Park 99755, ☎ 907/683–2294, WEB www.nps.gov/dena) is home to North America's tallest peak, Mt. McKinley; admission to the park is $5 per person, or $10 per family. **Glacier Bay National Park and Preserve** (✉ Box 140, Gustavus 99826, ☎ 907/697–2230, WEB www.nps.gov/glba) is a marine preserve where 17 spectacular glaciers meet tidewater and seals float on icebergs. Huge coastal brown bears fish for salmon in the Brooks River and other wild, remote, clear-water streams at **Katmai National Park**

and Preserve (✉ Box 7, King Salmon 99613, ☎ 907/246–3305, WEB www.nps.gov/katm), a mixture of volcanic moonscape, rugged coast, large lake systems, mountains, and forested lowlands on the Alaska Peninsula. On the Kenai Peninsula south of Anchorage is **Kenai Fjords National Park** (✉ 1212 4th Ave., at the small-boat harbor [Box 1727, Seward 99664], ☎ 907/224–3175, WEB www.nps.gov/kefj), known for its tidewater glaciers, rugged fjords, and abundant marine wildlife. The country's largest national park, **Wrangell–St. Elias** (✉ Box 439, Copper Center 99573, ☎ 907/822–5234, WEB www.nps.gov/wrst), east of Anchorage along the Canadian border, is six times the size of Yellowstone.

The nation's largest national forest, the **Tongass** (✉ Southeast Alaska Discovery Center, 50 Main St., Ketchikan 99901, ☎ 907/228–6237, WEB www.fs.fed.us/r10/tongass) stretches the length of the Panhandle. **Chugach National Forest** (✉ 3301 C St., Suite 300, Anchorage 99503, ☎ 907/271–2500, WEB www.fs.fed.us/r10/chugach) encompasses much of the Kenai Peninsula and Prince William Sound.

State Parks

Chugach State Park (✉ HC 52, Box 8999, Indian 99540, ☎ 907/345–5014, WEB www.dnr.state.ak.us/parks/units/chugach), near Anchorage, has more than 100 mi of hiking trails, wildlife viewing, and easily accessible wilderness. **Denali State Park** (✉ HC 32, Box 6706, Wasilla 99654, ☎ 907/745–3975, WEB www.dnr.state.ak.us/parks/units/denali) has a ridge-top trail with views of the Alaska Range, and public-use cabins.

SOUTHEAST

Southeast Alaska is a maritime region of thousands of islands blanketed by old-growth spruce forest and mountainous areas with rugged snow-covered peaks, huge ice fields, and tidewater glaciers. The waters abound in Pacific salmon (five species) and sea mammals, and the shore is home to deer, bears, and coastal communities that cling to the mountainsides. The villages of Tlingit, Haida, and Tsimshian Indians, as well as museums and cultural centers in the region's larger communities, give insights into Native American cultures.

Exploring the Southeast

Ketchikan

Ketchikan is a fishing and logging town at the southern end of the Panhandle. Its centerpiece is **Creek Street,** the historic red-light district, now home to quaint shops built on stilts over Ketchikan Creek. Ten miles ★ north of town, **Totem Bight State Historic Park** (✉ 9883 N. Tongass Hwy., ☎ 907/247–8574, WEB www.dnr.ak.us) displays 14 beautiful, historic totem poles from the Tlingit-Haida cultures and a replica of a clan house. The village of **Saxman** (☎ 907/225–4846, WEB www.capefoxtours.com), 2½ mi south of Ketchikan, exhibits many colorful totem poles. Original, unrestored totem poles, some 200 years old, can be seen at the **Totem Heritage Center** (✉ 601 Deermont St., ☎ 907/225–5900, WEB www.city.ketchikan.ak.us; 🎫 $4 May–Sept.). The city, in fact, contains the world's largest collection of totem poles.

Sitka

This historic town was the capital of Russian America before Alaska was sold to the United States in 1867. Russian cannons still crown **Castle Hill,** and the flagpole where the Stars and Stripes replaced the czarist Russian standard still stands. **St. Michael's Cathedral** (✉ 240 Lincoln St., ☎ 907/747–8120; 🎫 $2) is a 1976 replica of the 1848 church. During the 1966 fire that destroyed the original, townspeople entered

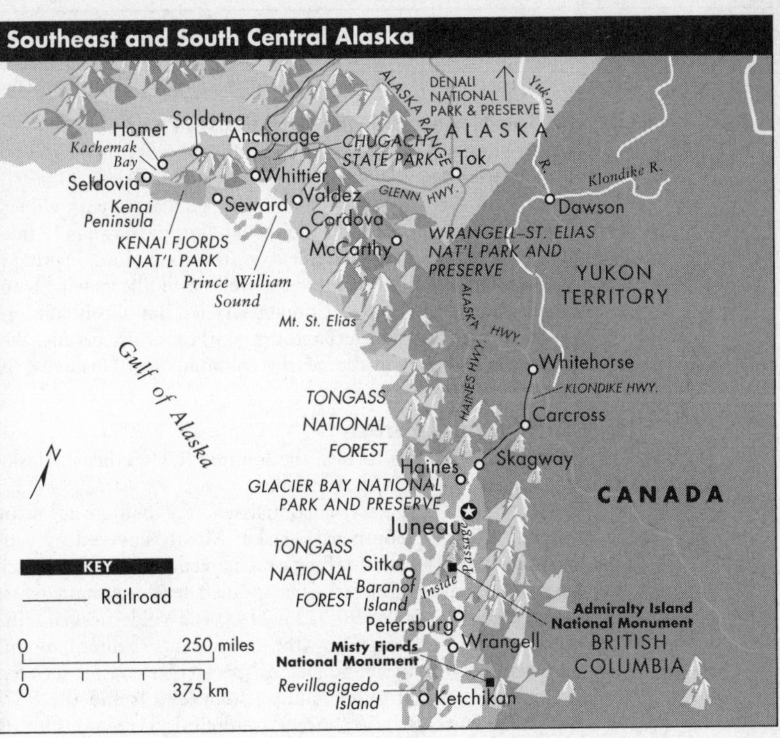

the burning building to rescue precious icons and other religious objects, which are now on display.

Open daily May–September and by appointment October–April, the **Russian Bishop's House** (✉ Monastery and Lincoln Sts., ☎ 907/747–6281, WEB www.nps.gov/sitk; 🎫 $3) is a restored log structure, originally built in 1842. The **Sheldon Jackson Museum** (✉ 104 College Dr., ☎ 907/747–8981, WEB www.museums.state.ak.us; 🎫 $4) has a fine collection of priceless Tlingit, Haida, Tsimshian, Athabascan, Aleut, and Eskimo artwork and crafts. In **Sitka National Historical Park** (✉ 106 Metlakatla St., 99835, ☎ 907/747–6281, WEB www.nps.gov/sitk), Tlingit carvers still work at the venerable craft of carving totems and also do weaving and silversmithing; a trail through old-growth coastal forest winds among 15 totems, both old and new.

Juneau

The state capital clings to the mountainside along a narrow saltwater channel. It was born as a gold-rush town in 1880 and remained an active gold-mining center until World War II. Today its number one employer is the state government, with transportation and tourism important runners-up.

Although Juneau's hills are steep, you can still explore the charming town on foot. Houses downtown date from the gold rush. On South Franklin Street, the **Red Dog Saloon** (☎ 907/463–3777, WEB www.reddogsaloon.com) preserves the rough-and-tumble spirit of 1898. The Victorian **Alaskan Hotel** (☞ Dining and Lodging) is a more genteel relic of the gold-rush era. The tiny, onion-domed **St. Nicholas Russian Orthodox Church** (✉ 5th and Gold Sts., ☎ 907/586–1023; 🎫 $2 requested donation), constructed in 1894, is the oldest original Russian church in Alaska. The **Alaska State Museum** (✉ 395 Whittier St., ☎ 907/465–2901, WEB www.museums.state.ak.us; 🎫 $5 mid-May–mid-

Sept., $3 mid-Sept.–mid-May), near the waterfront, highlights the state's rich Russian-American cultural heritage, along with Native American artifacts, gold rush memorabilia, and natural history displays.

Glacier Bay National Park and Preserve

Whales, porpoises, sea otters, sea lions, seals, and seabirds inhabit the ★ 62-mi-long **Glacier Bay** (✉ Box 140, Gustavus 99826, ☎ 907/697–2230, WEB www.nps.gov/glba), a remote and wild marine-park wilderness accessible only by boat. In addition to wildlife, the bay has 17 tidewater glaciers and about a dozen inlets or arms to explore, making it a favorite destination for sea-kayaking as well as wildlife viewing from charter boats and cruise ships. Contact **Glacier Bay Cruiseline** (☎ 800/451–5952, WEB www.glacierbaytours.com) for cruise details. Visitor services are available in the nearby community of Gustavus, 30 minutes by plane from Juneau.

Tongass National Forest

The largest of the nation's forests, the **Tongass** (✉ Southeast Alaska Discovery Center, 50 Main St., Ketchikan 99901, ☎ 907/228–6237, WEB www.fs.fed.us/r10/tongass) encompasses 16.8 million acres, or nearly three-fourths of Southeast Alaska. Mostly covered by old-growth temperate rain forest, the Tongass is a breeding ground for black and brown bears, bald eagles, Sitka black-tailed deer, mountain goats, and wolves. **Misty Fiords** (☎ 907/225–2148) is a wilderness of cliff-faced fjords (or fiords, if you follow the monument's spelling), mountains, and islands with an abundance of spectacular coastal scenery, wildlife, and recreational opportunities. **Admiralty Island** (☎ 907/586–8800, WEB www.fs.fed.us/r10/tongass/admiralty) is famous for its lush rain forests and abundant wildlife, including one of the largest concentrations of brown bears anywhere on the planet.

Dining and Lodging

Juneau

$$–$$$ ✕ **Summit Restaurant.** Housed in a converted turn-of-the-20th-century brothel, this restaurant serves its meals in a small, candlelit room. You have a choice of nearly 15 local fish and shellfish dishes or steaks. ✉ *455 S. Franklin St.,* ☎ *907/586–2050. AE, D, DC, MC, V.*

$$ ✕ **The Fiddlehead.** Downstairs, you'll find healthy, eclectic dishes such as black beans with rice served in a cozy room with stained glass, historic photos, and a view of Mt. Juneau. Upstairs, you can dine in a more elegant setting with Tuscan-Italian decor; pastas and fresh fish are featured dishes. The homemade bread is delectable, and the restaurant has one of Alaska's finest wine lists. ✉ *429 Willoughby Ave.,* ☎ *907/586–3150,* WEB *www.alaska.net/~fiddle. AE, D, MC, V.*

$$ ✕🏨 **Silverbow Inn.** Remodeled from a bakery dating from the 1890s, this is a B&B built in European style and adorned with antiques and personal memorabilia. Each guest room is individually decorated in a specific style that blends history with contemporary art and design. The Backroom restaurant ($–$$) has settings, chairs, and tables (no two are alike) from the turn of the 20th century. Meals include sandwiches with an international flavor. ✉ *120 2nd St., 99801,* ☎ *907/586–4146,* WEB *www.silverbowinn.com. 6 rooms. Restaurant. D, MC, V. BP.*

$$–$$$ 🏨 **Baranof Hotel.** This grande dame of Juneau hotels still reflects its 1930s origins. The lobby is art deco style, but guest rooms are contemporary. Some rooms look out on Juneau's harbor and across it to forested Douglas Island. ✉ *127 N. Franklin St., 99801,* ☎ *907/586–2660 or 800/544–0970,* FAX *907/586–8315,* WEB *www.westmarkhotels.com. 196 rooms. Restaurant. AE, D, DC, MC, V.*

$$–$$$ 🏨 **The Prospector.** A short walk west of downtown, this small, modern hotel has spacious rooms with bright watercolors and views of the channel, mountains, or city; most rooms have kitchenettes. Outstanding prime rib, steak, and seafood is served in T. K. McGuires' dining room and lounge. ✉ *375 Whittier St., 99801,* ☎ *907/586–3737 or 800/331–2711,* FAX *907/586–1204,* WEB *www.prospectorhotel.com. 58 rooms. Restaurant. AE, D, DC, MC, V.*

$ ★ 🏨 **Alaskan Hotel.** This historic 1913 hotel is 15 mi from the ferry terminal and 9 mi from the airport (city bus service is available). Rooms are on three floors and have turn-of-the-20th-century antiques and room designs that are reminiscent of the gold-rush era. Some rooms have a shared bath. ✉ *167 S. Franklin St., 99801,* ☎ *907/586–1000 or 800/327–9347,* FAX *907/463–3775. 44 rooms. D, DC, MC, V.*

Ketchikan

$$–$$$$ ✕ **Salmon Falls Resort.** It's a half-hour drive from town, but the fresh seafood and steaks served in the huge, octagonal dining room make the trip more than worthwhile. The pine-log restaurant overlooks the waters of Clover Passage, where sunsets glow in vivid red. This is a convenient stop after a visit to Totem Bight Park. ✉ *Mile 17, N. Tongass Hwy.,* ☎ *907/225–2752; 800/247–9059 outside Alaska;* WEB *www.salmonfallsresort.net. AE, MC, V. Closed Oct.–Apr.*

Sitka

$$–$$$$ ✕ **Channel Club.** Fine steaks, seafood, and a salad bar with dozens of salad choices are served in nautical surroundings, including glass and fishnet floats and whalebone carvings. ✉ *2906 Halibut Point Rd.,* ☎ *907/747–9916. AE, D, DC, MC, V.*

$$–$$$ 🏨 **Westmark Shee Atika.** Southeast Alaskan Native artwork illustrates the history, legends, and exploits of the Tlingit people at this rustic Westmark chain outpost. Many rooms overlook Crescent Harbor and the islands beyond; others have mountain and forest views. Fried halibut nuggets in the Raven Room restaurant are not to be missed. ✉ *330 Seward St., 99835,* ☎ *907/747–6241 or 800/544–0970,* FAX *907/747–5486,* WEB *www.westmarkhotels.com. 101 rooms. Restaurant. AE, D, DC, MC, V. EP.*

Campgrounds

State and national forest campgrounds are available near all southeast communities (☞ Alaska Public Lands Information Center *in* Statewide Visitor Information). *The Milepost,* available in most Alaska and Washington bookstores, lists campgrounds throughout the state.

Outdoor Activities and Sports

Fishing

Southeast Alaskans are blessed with great salmon fishing off city docks and on beaches where creeks meet saltwater. You can also take an air taxi to a remote spot for a day's fishing or an extended stay. Fishing licenses are available in most grocery and sporting-goods stores.

Kayaking and Rafting

You can bring your own kayak aboard state ferries or hire a local outfitter—such as **Alaska Discovery Wilderness Adventures** (✉ 5310 Glacier Hwy., Juneau 99801, ☎ 907/780–6226 or 800/586–1911, WEB www.akdiscovery.com)—for a guided Inside Passage or Glacier Bay excursion. The company also guides kayak trips on Admiralty Island and at Icy Bay, near Yakutat, and float trips on the Tatshenshini and Alsek rivers. For rafting on the Mendenhall River as well as glacial travel, canoe and kayak trips, and hiking, contact **Alaska Travel Adventures** (✉ 9085 Glacier Hwy., Suite 301, Juneau 99801, ☎ 907/789–0052;

800/478–0052 in Alaska; WEB www.alaskaadventures.com). Guided sea-kayaking tours of nearby Misty Fjords National Monument in Tongass National Forest are available from **Southeast Exposure** (✉ 515 Water St. [Box 9143, Ketchikan 99901], ☎ 907/225–8829 in summer, WEB www.southeastexposure.com); the company also leads day trips in the Ketchikan area and rents both kayaks and canoes.

Wildlife Viewing

Southeast Alaska is renowned for its whales, eagles, and brown bears (the coastal cousins of grizzlies). **Glacier Bay National Park** is a prime viewing area for several species of whales, including humpbacks and orcas. **Alaska Discovery Wilderness Adventures** (☞ Kayaking and Rafting) leads whale-watching tours at Icy Strait, near Chichagof Island. A popular brown bear–viewing area near Juneau is **Pack Creek,** within Admiralty Island National Monument (☞ Tongass National Forest). Both black and brown bears may be seen at **Anan Creek** in the Tongass Forest near Wrangell (contact U.S. Forest Service in Wrangell, ☎ 907/874–2323, WEB www.fs.fed.us/r10/tongass). The **Alaska Chilkat Bald Eagle Preserve** (☎ 907/766–2292, WEB www.dnr.state.ak.us), near Haines, hosts the world's largest gathering of bald eagles: between 1,000 and 4,000 eagles congregate here each November and December.

Ski Areas

Check with local visitor centers for **cross-country ski trails** groomed for either diagonal or skate skiing.The **Eaglecrest** ski area, across the channel from Juneau on Douglas Island, has 31 trails, three lifts, a ski school, tubing hill, cross-country ski trails, a cafeteria, and equipment rental. ✉ *155 S. Seward St., Juneau 99801,* ☎ *907/586–5284; 907/586–5330 recorded ski conditions;* WEB *www.juneau.org/eaglecrest. Closed May–Nov.*

Shopping

Silver Lining Seafoods (✉ 1705 Tongass Ave., ☎ 907/225–9865, WEB www.norquest.com), north of Ketchikan's city dock, has locally smoked seafood and fish-motif postcards and T-shirts by local artist Ray Troll.

In Juneau the **Alaska Steam Laundry Building,** on South Franklin Street, has shops and a good coffeehouse downstairs. The **Senate Building Mall,** also on South Franklin, houses a Christmas store and other import shops. In the Senate Building Mall, **Taku Smokeries** has two retail outlets selling locally smoked seafood.

Southeast Essentials

AIR TRAVEL

The Southeast is served year-round by Alaska Airlines. Flight service to the villages is available from the region's larger communities.

➤ AIRLINES: **Alaska Airlines** (☎ 800/426–0333, WEB www.alaskaair.com).

AIRPORTS

Regular jet service is available from Pacific Coast and southwestern U.S. cities to Ketchikan, Wrangell, Petersburg, Sitka, and Juneau International Airport.

➤ AIRPORT INFORMATION: **Juneau International Airport** (☎ 907/789–7821, WEB www.juneau.lib.ak.us/airport).

BOAT AND FERRY TRAVEL

The Alaska Marine Highway System is an extensive network of large and small vessels that link most southeast communities. All ferries take cars (reservations necessary in summer) and have cafeterias or restaurants; most also have staterooms, but many Alaskans camp on deck in tents—or on the lounges' floors. The system makes connections with BC Ferries in Prince Rupert, British Columbia.

➤ BOAT AND FERRY INFORMATION: **Alaska Marine Highway System** (✉ 1591 Glacier Ave., Juneau 99801, ☎ 907/465–3941 or 800/642–0066, FAX 907/465–2476, WEB www.dot.state.ak.us/ferry).

CAR TRAVEL

Ferries that will transport vehicles to southeast Alaska leave from Bellingham, Washington, and from Prince Rupert, British Columbia. From the north, the Alaska and Haines or Klondike Highway lead to Skagway and Haines, and ferries continue south through the region.

TRANSPORTATION AROUND THE SOUTHEAST

Southeast Alaska is accessible mainly by air or water. The mainland road system (from Anchorage, through the Canadian Yukon) connects only with tiny northern communities after hundreds of miles of wilderness road. Cruise ships (☞ Cruising) and state ferries are the most common means of visitor transportation.

VISITOR INFORMATION

For general information on the Southeast, contact the Tourism Council in Juneau.

➤ TOURIST INFORMATION: **Juneau Convention and Visitors Bureau Log Cabin Information Center** (✉ 134 3rd St., Juneau 99801, ☎ 907/586–2201 or 888/581–2201, FAX 907/586–6304, WEB www.traveljuneau.com). **Ketchikan Visitors Bureau** (✉ 131 Front St., Ketchikan 99901, ☎ 907/225–6166; 800/770–3300; 800/770–2200 for brochures; FAX 907/225–4250; WEB www.visit-ketchikan.com). **Sitka Convention and Visitors Bureau** (✉ 303 Lincoln St., Suite 4 [Box 1226, Sitka 99835], ☎ 907/747–5940, FAX 907/747–3739, WEB www.sitka.org) provides brochures and advice. **Southeast Alaska Tourism Council** (✉ Box 20710, Juneau 99802, ☎ 907/586–4777, FAX 907/463–4961, WEB www.alaskainfo.org).

SOUTH CENTRAL

South Central Alaska is home to most of the state's population and many of its most sought-out attractions. Many visitors start their trips in Anchorage, then continue south to the fishing and artists' communities of the Kenai Peninsula.

Exploring South Central

Anchorage

Anchorage is a young, spirited city in a spectacular setting between mountains and sea. Nearly half the state's population resides here, which may explain why you can find everything from oil industry high-rises to backwoods cabins with resident sled-dog teams.

The **Anchorage Museum of History and Art** (✉ W. 7th Ave. and A St., ☎ 907/343–6173, WEB www.anchoragemuseum.org; 🎫 $6.50) has an outstanding exhibit on Native Alaskan life and a permanent display of artwork depicting Alaska as seen by explorers, resident painters, and latter-day visitors. It also hosts many world-class traveling exhibits. The **Imaginarium** (✉ 737 W. 5th Ave., Suite G, ☎ 907/276–3179, WEB www.imaginarium.org; 🎫 $5) is an interactive science museum with a shop selling educational toys. At **Ship Creek,** north of downtown, you can see salmon jump in summer as they head upstream to spawn; a platform enables easy viewing.

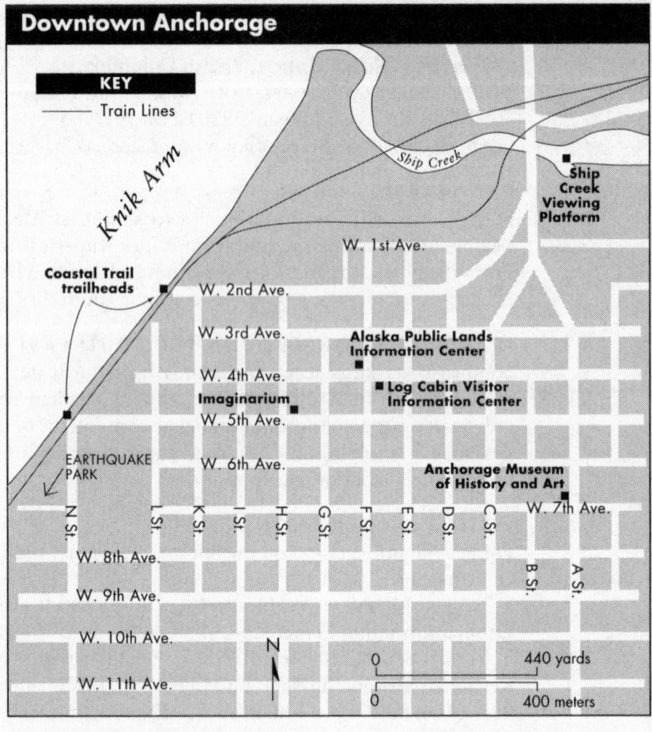

A display at **Earthquake Park,** at the west end of Northern Lights Boulevard, shows the damage wrought by the 1964 quake, when houses tumbled into the ocean. Trees have claimed the earth mounds and ponds created by the quake's force. The **floatplane base at Lake Hood,** near the Anchorage International Airport, is the world's largest and busiest. Plan a sunset stroll by the scenic **Coastal Trail,** which runs along Cook Inlet, with several trailhead access points in mid- and downtown.

The Kenai Peninsula

Thrusting into the Gulf of Alaska south of Anchorage, the Kenai Peninsula is a glacier-hewn landscape with magnificent wildlife viewing and fishing from its spectacular coastline. In summer the Alaska Railroad runs a passenger train daily to **Seward,** a small fishing and tourist town on Resurrection Bay, but most people drive the three hours from Anchorage. Tour boats leave Seward's busy downtown harbor for excursions that include visits to sea lion and bird rookeries and close-up views of tidewater glaciers.

Seward is the jumping-off point for **Kenai Fjords National Park. Mariah Tours** (☎ 907/224–4560 in summer; 800/270–1238 year-round; WEB www.kenaifjords.com) run out of Seward, leads wildlife and glacier tours of the park.

At the southern terminus of the Seward Highway, 225 mi from Anchorage, lies **Homer,** in a breathtaking setting that includes a sand spit jutting into Kachemak Bay. The town's buildings are picturesque, and you can comb the beach, fish off the docks, or charter a boat for halibut fishing (☞ Outdoor Activities and Sports). Wildlife abounds in the bay, and fishing charters may give you a close-up view of seals, porpoises, birds, and, more rarely, whales. If you walk along the docks at the end of the day, you can see fishermen unloading their catch. Across from the end of the Homer spit is **Halibut Cove,** one of the prettiest spots in south-central Alaska and reachable by water taxi. **Seldovia,** on the other side of Kachemak Bay from Homer, has an onion-dome Russian church, lots of shops, and fishing.

Kenai Fjords National Park

★ One of only three national parks connected to Alaska's highway system, the 670,000-acre **Kenai Fjords** (✉ 1212 4th Ave., at the small-boat harbor [Box 1727, Seward 99664], ☎ 907/224–3175, WEB www.nps.gov/kefj) is known for its abundant marine wildlife, deep-blue tidewater glaciers, waterfalls, and coastal fjords (long and steep-sided glacially carved valleys now filled with seawater). People come here by boat to see whales, porpoises, seals, and seabirds; fish for salmon; and hear the booming echoes of calving tidewater glaciers. Yet the park's most popular visitor attraction is on land: the pale-blue icy snout of **Exit Glacier** is a short walk from the one gravel road that leads into the park.

Wrangell–St. Elias National Park and Preserve

Bridging the Canadian border, 13-million-acre **Wrangell–St. Elias** (✉ Box 439, Copper Center 99573, ☎ 907/822–5234, WEB www.nps.gov/wrst) could fit six Yellowstones within its borders. Known to some as Alaska's Mountain Kingdom, the park encompasses four major mountain ranges and six of the continent's 10 highest peaks, including the 18,008-ft **Mt. St. Elias.** Here, too, is North America's largest subpolar ice field, the Bagley, which calved several gigantic glaciers; one of them, the **Malaspina,** is larger than Rhode Island. The park has two main entryways: on the north side is Nabesna Road; on the east is 60-mi-long McCarthy Road, which leads to the historic town of **McCarthy** and neighboring **Kennecott Mine** (now closed), two of the park's key attractions if you don't want to venture far from the road system.

Chugach National Forest

Second only to the Tongass in size, **Chugach National Forest** (✉ 3301 C St., Suite 300, Anchorage 99503, ☎ 907/271–2500, WEB www.fs.fed.us/r10/chugach) encompasses much of Prince William Sound, the Kenai Peninsula, and the Copper River delta region. Its 5.8 million acres include forested hills and valleys, rugged coastal mountains, one of the world's largest tidewater glaciers, and wetlands that support migrating waterfowl and shorebirds. About an hour's drive south of Anchorage, **Portage Glacier** and the **Begich-Boggs Visitor Center** are two of Alaska's premier visitor attractions.

Dining and Lodging

For bed-and-breakfast reservations, call **Alaska Private Lodging: Stay with a Friend** (✉ Box 200047, Anchorage 99520, ☎ 907/258–1717, FAX 907/258–6613, WEB www.alaskabandb.com).

Anchorage

$$$–$$$$ ✕ **Seven Glaciers Restaurant.** A high-speed tram transports you to this alpine restaurant, perched on the side of Mt. Alyeska at 2,300 ft. You are assured a culinary adventure that emphasizes Alaska fish and grilled meats. ✉ *Westin Alyeska Prince Hotel, 1000 Arlberg, Girdwood,* ☎ *907/754–2237,* WEB *www.alyeskaresort.com. Reservations essential. AE, D, DC, MC, V. Closed Sun.–Thurs. Nov.–Apr. No lunch.*

$$–$$$$ ★ ✕ **Double Musky.** It's worth the 40-mi trip south of town and the wait once you arrive. The little building set among spruce trees is casually decorated with Mardi Gras memorabilia, the better to prepare you for the fine Cajun dishes and huge, tender steaks to come. ✉ *Crow Creek Rd., Girdwood,* ☎ *907/783–2822,* WEB *www.muskyx2.com. Reservations not accepted. AE, D, DC, MC, V. Closed Mon. No lunch.*

$$–$$$$ ★ ✕ **Marx Brothers Cafe.** The second-oldest house in Anchorage was originally constructed for the engineers who built the Alaska Railroad; now it's a restaurant serving sophisticated fare such as macadamia-crusted halibut and, for dessert, wild-berry crisp with Alaskan birch syrup. The restaurant is also known for its Caesar salads and its wine list, with more than 500 selections. ✉ *627 W. 3rd Ave.,* ☎ *907/278–2133,* WEB *www.marxcafe.com. AE, DC, MC, V. Closed Sun. Labor Day–Memorial Day. No lunch.*

$$–$$$$ ✕ **Simon and Seafort's Saloon and Grill.** A bustling place, especially in summer, this longtime local favorite is known for its fresh local seafood, salt-rock-roasted prime rib, and the large windows that look out across Cook Inlet and afford views of the Alaska Range. ✉ *420 L St.,* ☎ *907/274–3502,* WEB *www.rui.com. AE, DC, MC, V. No lunch Sun.*

$$–$$$ ✕ **Sacks Cafe.** A favorite before- or after-show dining option for those attending concerts and plays at Anchorage's Performing Arts Center, this downtown restaurant serves fresh seafood, pasta, and dinner salads. Brunch is served weekends 11–3. ✉ *328 G St.,* ☎ *907/276–3546,* WEB *www.sackscafe.com. AE, DC, MC, V.*

$–$$ ✕ **Downtown Deli.** Alaska's governor owns this classic delicatessen, where you can get anything from deli classics like chopped-liver sandwiches to local specialties such as reindeer stew. Nestle into a wooden booth inside, or watch the street action from a sidewalk table outside. ✉ *525 W. 4th Ave.,* ☎ *907/276–7116. AE, D, DC, MC, V.*

$$$$ **The Westin Alyeska Prince Hotel.** Seven glaciers and lush forests surround this château-style luxury hotel at the base of Mt. Alyeska. Rooms have refrigerators, safes, heated towel racks, ski-boot storage, bathrobes, and slippers, and all have views of the Chugach Mountains. A tram taking you to Seven Glaciers Restaurant leaves from the hotel. ✉ *1000 Arlberg (Box 249, Girdwood 99587),* ☎ *907/754–1111; 800/880–3880 reservations;* FAX *907/754–2200;* WEB *www.alyeskaresort.com. 307 rooms. 4 restaurants, pool, gym. AE, D, DC, MC, V.*

$$$ **Anchorage Hotel.** Built in 1916, this charming hotel has its original sinks and tubs, and the hallways upstairs are lined with old photos of the city. You can warm up by the fireplace in the lobby. ✉ *330 E St., 99501,* ☎ *907/272–4553 or 800/544–0988,* FAX *907/277–4483,* WEB *www.historicanchoragehotel.com. 26 rooms. AE, D, DC, MC, V. CP.*

$$$ **Hotel Captain Cook.** This three-tower hotel takes up a full city block. Teak paneling lines most public walls, recalling Captain Cook's voyages in the South Pacific. ✉ *939 W. 5th Ave., 99501,* ☎ *907/276–6000 or 800/843–1950,* FAX *907/343–2298,* WEB *www.captain cook.com. 547 rooms. 3 restaurants, pool, health club. AE, D, DC, MC, V.*

$$$ **Voyager Hotel.** This small four-story hotel caters to both leisure and business travelers. All rooms are no-smoking; they have galley kitchens, coffeemakers, data ports, voice mail, and bathrooms with pedestal sinks and wainscoting. ✉ *501 K St., 99501,* ☎ *907/277–9501 or 800/247–9070,* FAX *907/274–0333,* WEB *www.voyagerhotel.com. 38 rooms. Restaurant. AE, D, DC, MC, V.*

$ **Alaskan Samovar Inn.** This well-worn but clean motel is east of downtown on one of the city's main thoroughfares. Victorian-style rooms are small and dark, but each has a whirlpool tub, cable TV, and refrigerator. ✉ *720 Gambell St., 99501,* ☎ *907/277–1511 or 800/478–1511,* FAX *907/272–5192,* WEB *www.samovar.ci.st. 68 rooms. Restaurant. AE, D, MC, V.*

$ **Hosteling International Anchorage.** At this cinder-block building downtown, most guests share dorm-style rooms, though you can also stay in one of the few private rooms (all with shared bathrooms). There's a 1 AM curfew and a five-night maximum stay in summer. ✉ *700 H St., 99501,* ☎ *907/276–3635,* FAX *907/276–7772,* WEB *www.alaska.net/~hianch. 6 rooms, 95 beds. MC, V.*

The Kenai Peninsula

$$–$$$$ ✕ **Harbor Dinner Club.** Run by the same family since 1958, this eatery serves local halibut and salmon in a dining room with a view of Resurrection Bay and the mountains. There's dancing in the lounge. ✉ *220 5th Ave., Seward,* ☎ *907/224–3012. AE, D, DC, MC, V.*

$$–$$$ ★ ✕ **The Saltry.** A 45-minute ride from Homer Harbor on the Kachemak Bay Ferry takes you to this restaurant with a deck over the water. Once there, sample some of south-central Alaska's best seafood dishes. Arrange for boat and dining reservations through the Central Charter Booking Agency. ✉ *Halibut Cove,* ☎ *907/235–7847; 800/478–7847 in Alaska;* WEB *www.centralcharter.com/tours.html. MC, V. Closed Oct.–May.*

$$$ **Best Western Hotel Seward.** Gold rush–style rooms in this downtown hotel have VCRs and refrigerators, and some have views of Resurrection Bay. The hotel runs a shuttle to the harbor in summer and is close to the ferry. ✉ *221 5th Ave., Seward 99664,* ☎ *907/224–2378 or 800/528–1234,* FAX *907/224–3112,* WEB *www.bestwestern.com. 38 rooms. AE, D, DC, MC, V. CP.*

$$–$$$ **Land's End.** The three wings of this sprawling beachfront hotel at the far end of the Homer Spit have contemporary themes that range from nautical to floral. All rooms facing Kachemak Bay have small balconies or full decks for watching the sunset. ✉ *4786 Homer Spit Rd., Homer 99603,* ☎ *907/235–2500; 800/478–0400 in Alaska (reservations only);* FAX *907/235–0420;* WEB *www.lands-end-resort.com. 83 rooms. Restaurant. AE, D, DC, MC, V.*

Campgrounds

In Anchorage, the city-operated **Centennial and Lions Campground** (✉ Box 196650, 99519, ☎ 907/333–9711) has 88 spaces for tent camping, showers, and a dump station; it's closed mid-October–April. Near Anchorage, **Chugach State Park** (✉ HC52, Box 8999, Indian 99540, ☎ 907/345–5014, WEB www.dnr.state.ak.us/parks/units/chugach) has three public campgrounds. For **Kenai Peninsula** and other area campgrounds, contact the Alaska Public Lands Information Center (☞ Statewide Visitor Information).

Nightlife and the Arts

The **Alaska Center for the Performing Arts** (✉ 621 W. 6th Ave., ☎ 907/263–2900, WEB www.alaskapac.org) is home to a local symphony orchestra and theater companies and also presents operas, symphonies, concerts, and plays by national and international touring companies. The **Fly-by-Night Club** (✉ 3300 Spenard Rd., ☎ 907/279–7726; closed Jan.–Mar.) hosts everything from pop rock and blues to poetry readings and stage revues with tacky jokes. The *Anchorage Daily News* publishes a weekend activity guide every Friday, and the *Anchorage Press* includes a calender of events in its weekly editions.

Outdoor Activities and Sports

Biking

Most south-central highways are suitable for biking on the shoulder. Anchorage has more than 125 mi of bike trails. The **Matanuska Valley** is an increasingly popular place for farm-road rides. **Downtown Bicycle Rental** (✉ 5th Ave. and C St., Anchorage, ☎ 907/279–5293, WEB www.alaska-bike-rentals.com) rents mountain bikes and suggests trails.

Fishing

All south-central coastal communities have fishing charters, outfitters, and guides. Although Anchorage does not have good saltwater fishing—glacial runoff makes the water too murky—the freshwater lakes are stocked, and hatchery-enhanced runs of salmon return to Ship and

Campbell creeks each summer. Licenses are sold in most grocery and other retail stores. In Homer, **Central Charter Booking Agency** (✉ 4241 Homer Spit, 99603, ☎ 907-235-7847 or 800-478-7847 WEB www.centralcharter.com) arranges salmon and halibut charters. **Alaska Wildland Adventures** (✉ Box 389, Girdwood 99587, ☎ 800/334–8730; 800/478–4100 in Alaska; WEB www.alaskarivertrips.com or www.alaskasportfish.com) sells float and fish packages on the Kenai River, world famous for its huge salmon runs, and conducts guided fishing trips on other south-central waters.

Hiking and Backpacking

You can rent public cabins along many hiking trails in south-central Alaska (☞ Alaska Public Lands Information Center *in* Statewide Visitor Information). **Chugach State Park** (☎ 907/345–5014, WEB www.dnr.state.ak.us.parks/units/chugach), east of Anchorage, has approximately 30 trails totaling more than 150 mi. Trails are also maintained within **Chugach National Forest,** on the Kenai Peninsula.

Kayaking and Rafting

Floating is available on hundreds of rivers within a small area. **Nova River Runners** (✉ Box 1129, Chickaloon 99674, ☎ 907/745–5753 or 800/746–5753, WEB www.novaalaska.com) leads guided day trips on the Chickaloon, Matanuska, and Six-Mile rivers and overnighters on the Matanuska, Talkeetna, and Copper rivers. **Ketchum Air Service** (✉ Box 190588, Anchorage 99519, ☎ 907/243–5525 or 800/433–9114) provides drop-off and pickup service and gear for wilderness float trips.

Sled-Dog Racing

On winter weekends the **Alaska Sled Dog and Racing Association** (☎ 907/562–2235, WEB www.asdra.com) hosts races at the Tudor Track in mid-Anchorage. The three-day **Fur Rendezvous World-Championship Sled Dog Race** is staged in downtown Anchorage in mid-February. March brings the famous, 1,049-mi **Iditarod,** which begins in Anchorage and ends in Nome.

Wildlife Viewing

Some of Alaska's best wildlife viewing is possible right outside Anchorage in **Chugach State Park:** look for moose, Dall sheep, bears, and many smaller mammals and bird life in this accessible wilderness. Along the coastline of the **Kenai Peninsula,** you'll often see whales, sea lions, sea otters, seals, and seabirds.

Ski Areas

The **Alyeska Resort** (✉ Box 249, Girdwood 99587, ☎ 907/754–1111 800/880–3880; 907/754–7669 recorded ski conditions; WEB www alyeskaresort.com), about 40 mi south of Anchorage, is the largest in the state, with 1,000 acres of skiable terrain, a 2,600-ft vertical drop 68 trails, six chairlifts, two cable tows, a 60-passenger tram, a terrain park, and a halfpipe course for snowboarders. It also has a 307-room hotel, a ski school, and two mountaintop restaurants (☞ Seven Glaciers *in* Dining and Lodging). **Hilltop Ski Area** (✉ 7015 Abbott Rd., Anchorage 99516, ☎ 907/346–1446; 907/346–2167 recorded ski conditions; WEB www.hilltopskiarea.org), 10 mi from downtown Anchorage has one lift, one surface lift, nine trails, a vertical drop of 300 ft, ski instruction, cross-country trails, and a national-grade halfpipe for snowboarders.

Anchorage also has a vast and diverse Nordic ski-trail system, with more than 100 mi of groomed trails for both diagonal skiers and skate-skiers. The **Nordic Skiing Association of Anchorage** (☎ 907/276–7609, WEB www.alaska.net/~nsaa) has a **ski hot line** (☎ 907/248–6667) that gives grooming and trail-condition updates.

Shopping

In summer, Anchorage's **Saturday Market,** at 3rd Avenue and E. Street, is filled with vendors selling fresh produce from Matanuska-Susitna farms and Alaska-made crafts.The shops along 4th and 5th avenues sell T-shirts, trinkets, and Alaskan arts and crafts. The **Cook Inlet Book Company** (✉ 415 W. 5th Ave., ☎ 907/258–4544, WEB www.cookinlet.com) has the largest collection of books on Alaska.

South Central Essentials

AIRPORTS

Anchorage International Airport, about 6 mi from downtown, is served by Alaska Airlines, American, American West, Continental, Northwest, Delta Airlines, and United. Commuter plane service is available to Denali National Park, Homer, Kenai, and other destinations within the region. A cab from the Anchorage airport to downtown costs about $15 plus tip. Some hotels have shuttles.

➤ AIRPORT INFORMATION: **Ted Stevens Anchorage International Airport** (☎ 907/266–2529, WEB www.anchorageairport.com).

BOAT AND FERRY TRAVEL

The south-central section of the Alaska Marine Highway ferry system (☞ Southeast Essentials) links communities on Prince William Sound, the Gulf of Alaska, and Cook Inlet. Road connections to and from Anchorage can be made in Whittier and Seward. No regular ferry service runs between the south-central and southeast regions.

BUS TRAVEL

Gray Line of Alaska serves Anchorage, Denali, and Fairbanks and also makes runs to Seward, Valdez, Skagway, and Whitehorse.

➤ BUS INFORMATION: **Gray Line of Alaska** (☎ 907/277–5581 in Anchorage; 907/456–7741 in Fairbanks; WEB www.graylineofalaska.com).

CAR TRAVEL

To get to Anchorage from Tok, on the Alaska Highway near the Canadian border, head southwest on the Glenn Highway. From Fairbanks travel south on the George Parks Highway. South of Anchorage, the Seward and Sterling highways connect with communities on the Kenai Peninsula.

TRAIN TRAVEL

The Alaska Railroad has mainline service between Seward, Anchorage, Denali National Park, and Fairbanks and secondary service between Portage and Whittier.

➤ TRAIN INFORMATION: **Alaska Railroad** (☎ 800/544–0552; 907/265–2494 in Anchorage; 907/458–6025; 800/895–7245 in Fairbanks; FAX 907/265–2323; WEB www.alaskarailroad.com).

VISITOR INFORMATION

➤ TOURIST INFORMATION: **Anchorage Convention and Visitors Bureau** (✉ 524 W. 4th Ave., Anchorage 99501, ☎ 907/276–4118; 907/276–3200 events hot line; FAX 907/278–5559; WEB www.anchorage.net). **Anchorage Log Cabin Visitor Information Center** (✉ W. 4th Ave. and F St., Anchorage, ☎ 907/274–3531). **Homer Chamber of Commerce Visitor Center** (✉ 201 Sterling Hwy. [Box 541, Homer 99603], ☎ 907/235–7740, FAX 907/235–8766, WEB www.homeralaska.org). **Kenai Peninsula Tourism Marketing Council** (✉ 14896 Kenai Spur Hwy., Suite

106A, Kenai 99611, ☎ 907/283–3850; 800/535–3624 to order a vacation planner; FAX 907/283–3913; WEB www.kenaipeninsula.org). **Seward Chamber of Commerce Visitor Information Center** (✉ 2001 Seward Hwy. [Box 749, Seward 99664], ☎ 907/224–8051, FAX 907/224–5353, WEB www.sewardak.org). **Soldotna Chamber of Commerce Visitor Information Center** (✉ 44790 Sterling Hwy., Soldotna 99669, ☎ 907/262–1337, FAX 907/262–3566, WEB www.soldotnachamber.com).

THE INTERIOR

The Alaska and George Parks highways give access to this diverse area, a vast wilderness of birch and spruce forest, high mountains, tundra valleys, and abundant wildlife. Its crown jewel is Denali National Park, whose entrance area is 240 highway mi north of Anchorage. En route here from Anchorage, you'll travel through green Matanuska Valley farm country. North of Fairbanks, two hot-springs retreats are open year-round.

Exploring the Interior

Denali National Park

Denali (✉ Box 9, Denali National Park 99755, ☎ 907/683–2294, WEB www.nps.gov/dena) encompasses 6 million acres of wilderness, including the majestic ★ **Mt. McKinley**—at 20,320 ft the highest peak in North America. Along with panoramic vistas of unspoiled taiga and tundra, the park is the natural habitat of bears, wolves, moose, Dall sheep, caribou and many other mammals, birds, and fish. The only road through the park is closed to private vehicles beyond Mile 15. You can, however, take a **shuttle bus** (☎ 800/622–7275), which costs $12–$30 depending on turn-around point, on an 11-hour round-trip excursion to Wonder Lake, famous for its views of wading moose and Mt. McKinley. If you tire of the ride, you can get out and walk, then catch another bus (they leave from the park entrance every half hour starting at 5 AM) in either direction. Check with the **visitor center,** near the park entrance, for the day's schedule of naturalist walks and sled-dog demonstrations. Denali is open year-round, but services and accommodations are minimal from September to May. For information on camping *see* Campgrounds *in* Dining and Lodging.

Fairbanks

Built on the banks of the Chena River, Fairbanks was founded by gold miners early in the 20th century and later became a transportation hub for all the Interior. Today it's the state's second-largest city, although its atmosphere is more that of a frontier town. Its residents cope with incredible winter temperatures (lows reach –50°F) and only three to four hours of daylight in the dead of winter. Summer brings the midnight sun and temperatures that occasionally reach into the 90s.

One of Fairbanks's main attractions is the **University of Alaska** (✉ 501 Yukon Dr., ☎ 907/474–7211, WEB www.uaf.edu). On its grounds are the **Large Animal Research Station** (☎ 907/474–7207; 🎫 $5), where live musk ox and caribou can be seen on one-hour tours in summer and the **University of Alaska Museum** (☎ 907/474–7505, WEB www.uaf.edu/museum; 🎫 $5), whose ethnographic, historic, and fine arts collection includes a 38,000-year-old mummified steppe bison, a whale skull, dinosaur fossils, ivory carvings, and a 5,500-pound copper nugget. In summer, daily programs focus on Alaska's northern Native peoples and the aurora borealis (a.k.a. the northern lights); you are welcome to explore and touch such items as Native masks and tools, wolf pelts, and historic artifacts. The **Geophysical Institute** (☎ 907

474–7558, WEB www.gi.alaska.edu) presents programs and tours during the summer months. The west ridge of the campus has a view of the Alaska Range to the south.

Another big draw in Fairbanks is **Alaskaland Park** (✉ Airport Way and Peger Rd., ☎ 907/459–1087, WEB www.co.fairbanks.ak.us), on the Chena River near downtown. Among its numerous free attractions are museums, a theater, an art gallery, a Native village, and a reconstructed gold-rush town. The park's visitor attractions are closed between Labor Day and Memorial Day.

Hot Springs Retreats

The discovery of natural hot springs in the frozen wilderness north of Fairbanks sent early miners scrambling to build communities around this heaven-sent phenomenon. Today, Fairbanks residents come to soak in pools filled with hot-springs water and to enjoy excellent fishing, hiking, and cross-country skiing. The springs are also a favorite viewing point for the famed northern lights.

Dining and Lodging

Denali

$–$$ ✕ **Lynx Creek Pizza & Pub.** Sit alongside park workers and other park visitors to enjoy beer, pizza, salads, sandwiches, ice cream, and Mexican dishes while dining on picnic tables in this funky frame building just outside Denali. Try the reindeer-sausage pizza topping. ✉ *Parks Hwy., 1½ mi north of park entrance,* ☎ *907/683–2548. Reservations not accepted. AE, D, MC, V. Closed Sept.–May.*

$$$ **Denali Princess Lodge.** This large log complex above the Nenana River has suites with whirlpools, landscaped walkways, and a lounge with fireplace. ✉ *Parks Hwy., 1 mi north of park entrance (reservations: 2815 2nd Ave., Suite 400, Seattle, WA 98121),* ☎ *907/683–2282 in summer; 800/426–0500 for reservations;* FAX *907/683–2545 in summer; 206/336–6100 for reservations;* WEB *www.princessalaskalodges.com. 352 rooms. 3 restaurants. AE, D, DC, MC, V. Closed mid-Sept.–mid-May.*

$ **Denali Morning Hostel and Lodge.** A log building with two dormitory-style bunkhouses, this independent hostel provides bus service to and from the park. You can rent a family-style apartment if you want privacy. The hostel is 10 mi north of the park entrance, near Healy. ✉ *Box 801, Denali National Park 99755,* ☎ *907/683–1295,* FAX *907/683–2106,* WEB *www.hostelalaska.com. 15 beds, 2 rooms, 2 cabins No credit cards. Bunkhouses closed mid-Sept.–mid-May.*

WILDERNESS CAMPS AND LODGES

$$$$ ★ **Camp Denali.** This rustic yet comfortable compound in the heart of the park has cabins lighted by gas light and communal buildings with electricity, running water, and showers. Its authentic charm, delicious home cooking, and views of Mt. McKinley make it a favorite place to stay in Denali. A knowledgeable staff and naturalist programs will acquaint you with the surrounding wilderness. Visits are arranged according to a fixed schedule, with a three-night minimum stay (Friday–Monday only). You can also stay four days or a week (or more). ✉ *Wonder Lake, Box 67, Denali National Park 99755,* ☎ *907/683–2290,* FAX *907/683–1568,* WEB *www.campdenali.com. 17 cabins. No credit cards. Closed early Sept.–early June. FAP.*

$$$$ **Denali Wilderness Lodge.** Built as a hunting camp to supply gold rush–era miners, this complex of more than two dozen log buildings is reachable only by bush plane. Activities include horseback riding, hiking, bird-watching, and nature walking. ✉ *30 mi east of Denali Park entrance (Box 810, Girdwood, AK 99587);* ☎ *907/683–1287 in summer; 800/541–9779 year-round;* FAX *907/683–1286 in summer; 907/*

783–5201 in winter; WEB *www.denaliwildernesslodge.com. 22 cabins. Closed mid-Sept.–late May. FAP.*

CAMPGROUNDS

You have seven campgrounds in Denali from which to choose. Three are open to private vehicles for tent and RV camping; three others are reached by shuttle bus and are restricted to tent camping; and one is for backpackers only. For reservations call **Denali Park Resorts** (☎ 907/272–7275 or 800/622–7275, WEB www.denaliparkresorts.com). For more information contact the park superintendent (☞ Visitor Information). Several private campgrounds are outside the park along the highway; try **McKinley RV Park and Campground** (✉ Mile 248.5, Parks Hwy., Healy 99743, ☎ 907/683–2379 or 800/478–2562). For general campsite information and availability, contact the **Alaska Public Lands Information Center** (☞ Statewide Visitor Information).

Fairbanks

$$–$$$$ ✕ **Two Rivers Lodge.** Once a wilderness homestead, this rustic log building is now a full-service restaurant with acclaimed cuisine. In summer you can sit on a deck that overlooks a pond and sample *tapas,* appetizer-size portions of Mediterranean dishes cooked in a wood-fired oven. The wine list is one of Alaska's largest. ✉ *Mile 16, Chena Hot Springs Rd., Fairbanks,* ☎ *907/488–6815,* WEB *www.tworiverslodge.com. AE, D, DC, MC, V. No lunch.*

$$$ **Sophie Station.** Every room has a full-size kitchen and refrigerator at this all-suite hotel near Fairbanks International Airport. ✉ *1717 University Ave., Fairbanks 99709,* ☎ *907/479–3650 or 800/528–4916,* FAX *907/479–7951,* WEB *www.fountainheadhotels.com. 147 suites. Restaurant. AE, D, DC, MC, V.*

$$$ **Westmark Fairbanks.** This full-service member of Alaska's biggest chain is built around a courtyard on a quiet street in downtown Fairbanks. Some rooms have exercise equipment. ✉ *813 Noble St., Fairbanks 99701,* ☎ *907/456–7722; 800/544–0970 reservations;* FAX *907/451–7478;* WEB *www.westmarkhotels.com. 244 rooms. Restaurant. AE, D, DC, MC, V.*

Hot Springs

$$ **Chena Hot Springs Resort.** This resort, 60 mi from Fairbanks on Chena Hot Springs Road, is the local favorite. You can stay in the campground, in one of the antiques-filled hotel rooms, or rustic cabins with electricity but no water. Nonguests can pay to use the heated pool and eat in the restaurant. ✉ *Box 58740, Fairbanks 99711,* ☎ *907/452–7867, 800/478–4681 in Alaska;* FAX *907/456–3122;* WEB *www.chenahotsprings.com. 80 rooms, 6 cabins. Restaurant, pool. AE, D, DC, MC, V.*

$–$$ **Arctic Circle Hot Springs Resort.** A three-hour drive from Fairbanks on the Steese Highway, this four-story spa-hotel dates from 1930 and includes everything from hostel-style rooms (for your sleeping bags and pads) to luxury suites. There are also one- and two-bedroom cabins with whirlpool baths and kitchenettes. The entire complex is naturally heated by hot springs. ✉ *Box 30069, Central 99730,* ☎ *907/520–5113,* FAX *907/520–5116,* WEB *www.indiana.edu/~kurichtc/achshome.html. 24 rooms, 14 cabins. Restaurant, pool. MC, V.*

Outdoor Activities and Sports

Canoeing

The Chena River attracts canoeists, both in Fairbanks and out in the wilderness. Entry points are marked along Chena Hot Springs Road. Avoid the Tanana River, with its hidden sandbars and swift current.

Fishing

Char, grayling, and pike are abundant in the lakes and rivers of the Interior. The Chena River between Fairbanks and Chena Hot Springs is known for its grayling fishing.

Hiking and Backpacking

Skilled outdoorspeople can hike virtually anywhere in Denali National Park's northern foothills and tundra, though they should be prepared for the park's trailless wilderness. Well-marked beginner trails are near the park entrance.

Ice Hockey

The **University of Alaska Nanooks** (☎ 907/474–7205, WEB www.uaf.edu) draws big crowds of ice hockey fans.

Rafting

Several companies run white-water trips on the thrilling Nenana River, which parallels the George Parks Highway near the Denali entrance. **Denali Raft Adventures** (✉ Drawer 190, Denali National Park 99755, ☎ 907/683–2234, WEB www.denaliraft.com) leads raft trips ranging from two hours to overnight. The **Denali Outdoor Center** (✉ Mile 238.5, Parks Hwy. [Box 170, Denali National Park 99755], ☎ 907/683–1925 or 888/303–1925, WEB www.denalioutdoorcenter.com) guides adventuresome people through the Nenana River rapids in inflatable kayaks.

Sled-Dog Racing

The **North American Open Sled Dog Championship** is held in downtown Fairbanks in March. Check with the visitor center (☞ Visitor Information) for details.

Wildlife Viewing

Few places in North America can equal the wildlife-viewing opportunities at Denali National Park, where you can most likely see grizzly bears, caribou, moose, and Dall sheep. Wolves and golden eagles can also sometimes be spied, as well as many other subarctic mammals and birds.

Shopping

In Fairbanks, **Beads and Things** (✉ 537 2nd Ave., ☎ 907/456–2323) sells Native handicrafts from around the state. On College Road, near the University of Alaska Fairbanks campus, **Apocalypse Design** (✉ 101 College Rd., ☎ 907/451–7555, WEB www.akgear.com) makes its own specialized cold-weather clothing for mushers and cyclists, as well as miscellaneous outdoor-gear accessories. In Ester, outside Fairbanks, **Judie Gumm Designs** (✉ 3600 Main St., Ester, ☎ 907/479–4568, WEB www.judiegumm.com) sells silver and gold jewelry patterned after Alaska's best-known wildlife and plants. In North Pole, about 15 mi southeast of Fairbanks, the **Santa Claus House Gift Shop** (✉ Mile 349, Richardson Hwy., 101 St. Nicholas Dr., ☎ 907/488–2200) has a variety of toys and Alaskan handicrafts.

The Interior Essentials

AIR TRAVEL

Year-round, Alaska Airlines and Delta have daily nonstop jet service between Anchorage and the Fairbanks International Airport. Alaska Airlines also flies nonstop between Seattle and Fairbanks. Also in summer Northwest flies to Fairbanks from Minneapolis. A number of bush carriers originate in Fairbanks and will take you to otherwise inaccessible destinations in the region.

AIRPORTS

➤ AIRPORT INFORMATION: **Fairbanks International Airport** (☎ 907/474–2500, WEB www.dot.state.ak.us).

CAR TRAVEL

Much of the Interior is inaccessible by road, but some major roadways do pass through the region. Fairbanks is connected to Anchorage in south-central Alaska by the George Parks Highway. The Steese, Elliot, and Dalton highways provide access north of Fairbanks. Hardy RVers and campers drive the Alaska Highway through British Columbia and the Yukon to Fairbanks; the drive takes at least a week.

TRAIN TRAVEL

The Alaska Railroad runs between Anchorage and Fairbanks via Denali.

➤ TRAIN INFORMATION: **Alaska Railroad** (☎ 800/544–0552; 907/265–2494 in Anchorage; 907/458–6025; 800/895–7245 in Fairbanks; FAX 907/265–2323; WEB www.alaskarailroad.com).

VISITOR INFORMATION

➤ TOURIST INFORMATION: **Denali National Park and Preserve** (✉ Superintendent, Box 9, Denali National Park 99755, ☎ 907/683–2294 year-round; 907/683–1266 in summer; FAX 907/683–9612 year-round; WEB www.nps.gov/dena). **Fairbanks Convention and Visitors Bureau Information Cabin** (✉ 550 1st Ave., Fairbanks 99701, ☎ 907/456–5774; 800/327–5774 visitors guide to Fairbanks and interior Alaska; 907/456–4636 events hot line; FAX 907/452–2867; WEB www.explorefairbanks.com).

SOUTHWEST

Exploring the Southwest

Kodiak

The largest island in the United States, Kodiak is home to the brown bear, one of North America's largest land mammals. Before the seat of colonial government was moved to Sitka, Kodiak was the original capital of Russian Alaska. Today the town is a commercial fishing center: you can go halibut fishing, sea-kayaking, or flightseeing for bears. Much of the rain forest–covered island lies within 1.6-million-acre **Kodiak National Wildlife Refuge** (☎ 907/487–2600, WEB www.fws.gov).

Katmai National Park and Preserve

Katmai National Park and Preserve (✉ Box 7, King Salmon 99613, ☎ 907/246–3305, WEB www.nps.gov/katm) is a more remote and less developed park than Denali, but therein lies its appeal. A lush valley within what is now the park became a land of steaming fumaroles after the 1912 eruption of Mt. Novarupta and the collapse of nearby Mt. Katmai's peak. The eruption forced residents to flee surrounding areas and produced the Valley of Ten Thousand Smokes. These days the area is known for its trophy rainbow trout and salmon, as well as brown bears, which congregate along the **Brooks River** and other wilderness streams. Hiking, boat touring, and coastal kayaking are other Katmai attractions. **Katmailand Inc.** (✉ 4125 Aircraft Dr., Suite 2, Anchorage 99502, ☎ 907/243–5448 or 800/544–0551, WEB www.katmailand.com) arranges tours and backcountry lodging.

The Aleutian and Pribilof Islands

For most people package tours are the only practical way to see these areas. Schedules are changeable, depending on the weather.

The **Aleutian Islands,** a volcanic, treeless archipelago of 20 large and several hundred smaller islands, stretch 1,000 mi from the Alaska Peninsula toward Japan. The Aleuts who live in the tiny settlements here work in canneries or as commercial fishermen and guides; many continue to lead subsistence lifestyles. Out here, where the wind blows constantly and fog is common, bird-watching opportunities are limitless: look for terns, guillemots, murres, and puffins. The Japanese invaded the Aleutian Islands during World War II, and at Dutch Harbor on Unalaska Island you can still see concrete bunkers, gun batteries, and a partially sunken ship. The **Grand Aleutian Hotel** (✉ 498 Salmon Way, Box 921169, Dutch Harbor 99692, ☎ 800/891–1194, FAX 907/581–7150, WEB www.grandaleutian.com), in Dutch Harbor, arranges guided activities and tours as well as lodging.

Every spring the largest herd of northern fur seals in the world—nearly 1 million seals—comes to the tiny, volcanic **Pribilof Islands,** in the Bering Sea about 200 mi northwest of Cold Bay. Tours fly to **St. Paul Island,** largest of the Pribilofs and home to the world's largest Aleut community (about 600 of the island's 750 year-round residents are Aleuts). The island is also the summer home of legions of birds. Contact the **TDX Village Corporation** (✉ 4300 B St., Anchorage 99503, ☎ 877/424–5637, WEB www.alaskabirding.com) for St. Paul Island tour information. Next to St. Paul, **St. George Island** is the only other island in the Pribilof chain to be inhabited by humans. It is also a birder's paradise; more than 1½ million seabirds nest here each summer.

Southwest Essentials

AIR TRAVEL

Alaska Airlines runs daily nonstop jet service to Kodiak Island from Anchorage. Commuter planes serve the town of King Salmon, which is a short floatplane ride from Katmai National Park and Preserve, 290 mi southwest of Anchorage. Airlines serving King Salmon include Alaska Airlines and PenAir; PenAir also flies to communities in the Aleutians and Pribilof Islands.

➤ AIRLINES AND CONTACTS: **Alaska Airlines** (☎ 800/426–0333, WEB www.alaskaair.com). **PenAir** (☎ 907/243–2323 or 800/448–4226, WEB www.penair.com).

BOAT AND FERRY TRAVEL

The Alaska Marine Highway System (☞ Southeast Essentials) serves some Alaska Peninsula and Aleutian Islands communities in summer.

TRANSPORTATION AROUND THE SOUTHWEST

For packages to Kodiak contact Alaska Airlines Vacations.

➤ CONTACT: **Alaska Airlines Vacations** (✉ SEARV, Box 68900, Seattle, WA 98168, ☎ 800/468–2248, WEB www.alaskaair.com).

VISITOR INFORMATION

➤ TOURIST INFORMATION: **Southwest Alaska Municipal Conference** (✉ 3300 Arctic Blvd., Suite 203, Anchorage 99503, ☎ 907/562–7380, FAX 907/562–0438, WEB www.southwestalaska.com).

THE ARCTIC

Exploring the Arctic

Gold was discovered in 1898 in **Nome,** below the Arctic Circle. Colorful saloons and low-slung, ramshackle buildings help perpetuate its vintage gold-camp aura. **Kotzebue** is a proud Eskimo community north of Nome where salmon dries on wooden racks and Eskimo boats rest in yards. The **Living Museum of the Arctic** (☎ 907/442–3301, WEB www.nana.com; free) preserves Nome's Eskimo heritage, as does a cultural camp where elders pass on traditions to the next generation. The museum is open for tour groups or upon request; in summer, daily cultural shows are performed for visitors. The cost to attend the shows is $20.

At the top of the state, tours of the **Prudhoe Bay** area explore the oil industry life here, as well as the wildlife and tundra surrounding it. Fees range from $25 for a 1-hour tour to $50 for a 2½-hour tour; call **NANA Development Corporation** (☎ 800/478–3301, WEB www.nana.com) for information. In **Barrow,** the northernmost community in the United States, the sun rises on May 10 and doesn't set for nearly three months.

In the northernmost portion of the Brooks Range, the 18-million-acre ★ **Arctic National Wildlife Refuge** (☎ 907/456–0250, WEB www.fws.gov) contains the United States' only protected Arctic coastal lands as well as millions of acres of mountains and alpine tundra. The refuge is home to one of the world's largest groups of caribou, the 130,000-member Porcupine Caribou Herd. Other residents are grizzly and polar bears, Dall sheep, wolves, musk ox, and myriad bird species. Accessible only by boat, plane, or foot, the refuge can be explored by backpacking or river running.

The Arctic Essentials

TRANSPORTATION AROUND THE ARCTIC

Nearly all destinations in the Arctic are accessible only by plane. The only public highway that leads to the Arctic—the Dalton Highway—is open to traffic all the way to Deadhorse, on the North Slope, but is impassable in winter due to snow conditions. Alaska Airlines Vacations runs air tours of the Arctic from Anchorage and Fairbanks.

➤ CONTACT: **Alaska Airlines Vacations** (✉ SEARV, Box 68900, Seattle, WA 98168, ☎ 800/468–2248, WEB www.alaskaair.com).

VISITOR INFORMATION

For information on Barrow and Kotzebue, contact the Alaska Travel Industry Association (☞ Statewide Visitor Information). For information on Nome, contact the Convention and Visitors Bureau listed below.

➤ TOURIST INFORMATION: **Nome Convention and Visitors Bureau** (✉ Box 240, Nome 99762, ☎ 907/443–5535 or 800/478–1901, FAX 907/443–5832, WEB www.nomealaska.org).

ARIZONA

Updated by
Satu Hummasti,
Mara Levin,
Kim Westerman,
Bob Willis,
Gloria Willis

Capital	Phoenix
Population	5,307,331
Motto	God Enriches
State Bird	Cactus wren
State Flower	Saguaro cactus
Postal Abbreviation	AZ

Statewide Visitor Information

Arizona Office of Tourism (✉ 2702 N. 3rd St., Suite 4015, Phoenix 85004, ☎ 602/230–7733 or 800/842–8257, FAX 602/240–5475, WEB www.arizonaguide.com).

Scenic Drives

The drive from the South Rim to the North Rim of the Grand Canyon follows U.S. 89 through the **Arizona Strip,** a starkly beautiful, largely uninhabited part of the state. Almost all the Grand Canyon drives are breathtaking, especially West Rim Drive on the South Rim and the dirt road to Point Sublime on the North Rim. Fall foliage is spectacular on AZ 89A from Flagstaff to Sedona via **Oak Creek Canyon.** From Tucson, I–10 east of Benson passes through the startling rock formations of **Texas Canyon.**

National and State Parks

National Parks

Arizona has three national parks: Grand Canyon in the north, Petrified Forest in the northeast, and Saguaro in greater Tucson. The state has 15 national monuments, including Canyon de Chelly, Navajo, Sunset Crater Volcano, Walnut Canyon, and Wupatki. There are also two national historic sites, one national memorial, one national historic park, and two national recreation areas. For information on any National Park Service units in Arizona, contact the National Park Service's **Intermountain Region Support Office** (✉ Box 728, Santa Fe, NM 87504-0728, ☎ 505/988–6011; WEB www.nps.gov).

State Parks

Arizona has 28 state parks, which run the gamut from historic sites to red-rock plateaus to the 13,000-acre Lake Havasu. Among the most popular are Slide Rock and Red Rock state parks near Sedona, Jerome State Historic Park in the mining town of Jerome, Riordan Mansion State Park in Flagstaff, and the Tombstone Courthouse State Historic Park in Tombstone. Most parks charge day-use fees of $2 to $10, and 15 offer inexpensive campsites, most with utility hook-ups available. For extensive information on all the parks, contact the **Arizona State Parks Department** (✉ 1300 W. Washington St., Phoenix 85007, ☎ 602/542–4174, WEB www.pr.state.az.us).

GRAND CANYON NATIONAL PARK

Not even the finest photographs convey a fraction of the impact of a personal encounter with the Grand Canyon. This awesome, vastly silent, ancient erosion of the surface of our planet is 277 mi long, 17 mi across at its widest spot, and more than 1 mi deep at its lowest point. Its twisted and contorted layers of rock reveal a fascinating geological profile of the earth. All around you, otherworldly stone monuments change colors with the hours.

Exploring Grand Canyon National Park

Large crowds converge on the South Rim every summer, but shuttle buses during the busiest season help ease the congestion by ferrying visitors around. You'll pay a $20 per vehicle fee, which is good for one week's stay, if you arrive by car; if you arrive on foot or other conveyance the fee is $10 per person, also good for one week's stay.

South Rim

Grand Canyon Village, the commercial heart of the South Rim, is where you'll find most visitor services as well as all the dining and lodging in this part of the park. The paved Village Rim Trail (about 1 mi round-trip) starts at **Hopi House,** one of the canyon's first curio stores. The **El Tovar Hotel** is the jewel in the crown of the country's national park system. **Lookout Studio** is a combination lookout point, museum, and gift shop. **Bright Angel Trailhead** is the starting point for the best-known trail to the bottom of the canyon. **Bright Angel Lodge** is another historic lodge in the park, with a fireplace made of regional rocks arranged in layers that match those of the canyon. From **Mather Point,** at the outskirts of Grand Canyon Village, you'll get your first glimpse of the canyon from one of the most impressive and accessible overlooks on the rim.

There are many scenic overlooks on the 25-mi-long **Desert View Drive.** Yaki Point is where the much-traveled Kaibab Trail starts the canyon descent to the inner gorge. Grandview Point supports large stands of ponderosa and piñon pine, oak, and juniper. Moran Point is a favorite of photographers. At the **Tusayan Ruins and Museum** (✉ Desert View Dr., ☎ 928/638–2305; 🎫 free after $20 per-vehicle park admission), 3 mi east of Moran Point, partially intact rock dwellings are evidence of early habitation in the gorge. **Lipan Point** looks out over the widest part of the canyon. The highest point at the South Rim is the glass-enclosed observatory at the **Watchtower** (✉ Desert View Dr., ☎ 928/638–2736; 928/638–2360 trading post; 🎫 25¢ to climb Watchtower), which has a panoramic view of the Grand Canyon, as well as a trading post selling Native American art.

On **Hermit Road,** formerly West Rim Drive, you can get an unobstructed view from Trailview Overlook of the distant San Francisco Peaks, Arizona's highest mountains. At Maricopa Point you'll see the remnants of an early Grand Canyon mining operation. The Abyss reveals a sheer canyon drop of 3,000 ft. Pima Point provides a bird's-eye view of the Tonto Plateau and the Tonto Trail, which winds for more than 90 mi through the canyon. At Hermits Rest, the westernmost viewpoint on the road, you'll find the trailhead for the **Hermit Trail,** named for Louis Boucher, a 19th-century prospector and recluse who had a roughly built home in the canyon. The trail into the canyon is suitable only for experienced hikers. Hermit Road is closed to auto traffic in summer; from early May through September free shuttle buses leave daily from Grand Canyon Village for Hermits Rest.

North Rim

The relative solitude of the North Rim, set in deep forest near the 9,000-ft crest of Kaibab Plateau in the isolated Arizona Strip, is well worth the extra miles. From central Arizona, the only route into this area is more than 200 mi of lonely U.S. 89 to the north from Flagstaff. From late fall through early spring the North Rim and its facilities are closed because heavy snows cut off highway access to the area.

The trail to **Bright Angel Point,** one of the most awe-inspiring overlooks on either rim, starts on the grounds of the Grand Canyon Lodge, a massive stone structure built in 1928 by the Union Pacific Railroad. At 8,803 ft, **Point Imperial,** 11 mi northeast of the Grand Canyon Lodge, is the canyon's highest viewpoint. **Cape Royal,** 23 mi southeast of Grand Canyon Lodge, is the southernmost viewpoint on the North Rim.

Dining and Lodging

The North Rim is less crowded than the South Rim, but it has limited lodging facilities. In summer you should make reservations as far in advance as practical. The Grand Canyon National Park Lodges on the South Rim—Bright Angel Lodge, El Tovar, Maswik Lodge, Yavapai Lodge, Kachina Lodge, and Thunderbird Lodge—are comfortable but not luxurious, so come for the setting, not for the amenities. If you can't find accommodations in the park or in Tusayan, just outside its boundaries, try the nearby communities of Williams, an hour away by car, or Flagstaff.

South Rim

$$–$$$$ ✕ 🏨 **El Tovar Hotel.** Built in 1905 of native stone and heavy pine logs and renovated in 1998, the hotel and its once excellent reputation for service have suffered slightly, and the rooms don't seem to be as elegant as they once were. Some rooms are small, but all are well appointed. Only four suites have canyon views. For decades the hotel's restaurant has served fine seasonal southwestern cuisine in a hunting lodge–style dining room. ✉ *West Rim Dr. (Box 699, Grand Canyon 86023),* ☎ *303/297–2757 reservations only; 928/638–2631 ext. 6384 direct to hotel (no reservations),* FAX *303/297–3175 reservations only; 928/638–2855 direct to hotel (no reservations);* WEB *www.grandcanyonlodges.com. 78 rooms. Restaurant. AE, D, DC, MC, V.*

$–$$ ✕ 🏨 **Bright Angel Lodge.** Built in 1935, this log-and-stone structure a few yards from the canyon rim has rooms in the main lodge and cabins (some with fireplaces) scattered among the pines. All were remodeled in 2000. The cheapest rooms have shared baths. The informal steak house overlooks the canyon. You'll find moderately priced, good-quality beef on the menu. ✉ *West Rim Dr. (Box 699, Grand Canyon 86023),* ☎ *303/297–2757 reservations only; 928/638–2631 ext. 6284 direct to hotel (no reservations),* FAX *303/297–3175 reservations only; 928/638–2876 direct to hotel (no reservations);* WEB *www.grandcanyonlodges.com. 32 rooms, 42 cabins. Restaurant. AE, D, MC, V.*

$$–$$$$ 🏨 **Sheridan House Inn.** This bed-and-breakfast in Williams provides a good alternative to crowded park lodgings. Nicely appointed large rooms in the pines, just a few blocks from Route 66, are quiet, and hearty breakfasts will ready you for the hour's drive to the Grand Canyon. ✉ *460 E. Sheridan Ave., Williams 86046,* ☎ *520/635–9441 or 888/635–9345.* WEB *www.thegrandcanyon.com/sheridan. 8 rooms. AE, D, MC, V. BP.*

North Rim

$–$$ 🏨 **Grand Canyon Lodge.** The lounge area of the historic stone lodge, built in 1928, with hardwood floors and high-beamed ceilings, has a spectacular view of the canyon through massive plate-glass windows. Accommodations are in rustic cabins or motel-style rooms. ✉ *AZ 67,* ☎ *303/297–2757 reservations only; 928/638–2611 direct to hotel (no reservations);* FAX *303/297–3175 reservations only;* WEB *www.grandcanyonlodges.com. 44 rooms, 157 cabins. Restaurant. AE, D, MC, V.*

Outdoor Activities and Sports

Hiking

Detailed area maps of the many canyon trails are available at ranger stations and visitor centers. Overnight hikes in the Grand Canyon require a permit that can be obtained in advance only by written or faxed request to the **Backcountry Reservations Office** (✉ Box 129, Grand Canyon 86023, ☎ 520/638–7875, FAX 520/638–2125). Get one in advance if possible; otherwise, pick one up at the Backcountry Reservations Office, either near the entrance to Maswik Lodge, on the South Rim, or at the North Rim's ranger station. Allow five days to hike the gorge from rim to rim.

The **Bright Angel Trail,** which begins in Grand Canyon Village, a steep (4,460-ft), demanding ascent, connects the bottom of the canyon to the South Rim (8 mi). The 9-mi **Hermit Trail,** which begins on Hermit Road, provides inspiring views of Hermit Gorge and the Redwall and Supai formations. The steep, 7-mi **South Kaibab Trail** begins near Yaki Point, on Desert View Drive near Grand Canyon Village. The 14-mi **North Kaibab Trail,** the only maintained trail into the canyon from the North Rim, connects at the bottom of the canyon with the South Kaibab Trail.

Mule Trips

Mule trips down the precipitous trails to the inner gorge are nearly as well known as the canyon itself and usually sell out months in advance. Inquire via **Xanterra Parks & Resorts** (✉ 14001 E. Iliff, Suite 600, Aurora, CO 80014, ☎ 303/297–2757, FAX 303/297–3175, WEB www.grandcanyonlodges.com) about prices and restrictions for riders. Book as far in advance as possible.

Rafting

Reservations for white-water rafting trips, which last from 3 to 18 days, must often be made more than six months ahead of time. For a complete list of park service–approved concessionaires, contact the park at **River Permits Office** (✉ Grand Canyon National Park, Box 129, Grand Canyon 86023, ☎ 928/638–7888, WEB www.nps.gov/grca). **Fred Harvey Transportation Company** (☎ 928/638–2822) specializes in smooth-water rafting day trips. **Wilderness River Adventures** (☎ 928/645–3279 or 800/992–8022, WEB www.riveradventures.com) specializes in white-water trips leaving from Lees Ferry.

Shopping

Native American items sold at most of the lodges and at major gift shops are authentic. The **Desert View Trading Post** (✉ Desert View Dr., ☎ 928/638–2360) sells Southwest souvenirs and Native American crafts. The **El Tovar Hotel Gift Shop** (✉ West Rim Dr., ☎ 928/638–2631) features silver jewelry. **Hopi House** (✉ West Rim Dr., ☎ 928/638–2631), east of El Tovar Hotel, has some museum-quality Native American artifacts.

Grand Canyon National Park Essentials

AIR TRAVEL

➤ AIRLINES AND CONTACTS: **Air Vegas** (☎ 702/736–3599, WEB www.airvegas.com). **Scenic Airlines** (☎ 702/ 638–3300 or 800/634–6801, WEB www.scenic.com).

AIRPORTS

McCarran International Airport, in Las Vegas, Nevada, is the primary hub for flights to Grand Canyon National Park Airport. The Canyon

Airport Shuttle Services, Inc., operates between Grand Canyon airport and the nearby towns of Tusayan and Grand Canyon Village. The Fred Harvey Transportation Company provides taxi service.

➤ CONTACTS: **Fred Harvey Transportation Company** (☎ 928/638–2822). **Grand Canyon National Park Airport** (☎ 928/638–2446). **McCarran International Airport** (☎ 702/261–5743). **Tusayan/Canyon Airport Shuttle** (☎ 928/638–0821).

BUS TRAVEL

Greyhound stops at Flagstaff and Williams.

➤ BUS INFORMATION: **Greyhound** (☎ 800/231–2222, WEB www.greyhound.com).

CAR TRAVEL

From the east, west, or south, the fastest route to the Grand Canyon is via Flagstaff, either northwest on U.S. 180 (81 mi) to Grand Canyon Village on the South Rim or, for a more scenic route, north on U.S. 89 to Route 64 west; from Utah, take U.S. 89 south. To visit the North Rim, some 210 mi from Flagstaff, follow U.S. 89 north to Bitter Springs, and then take U.S. 89A to the junction of Route 67. Travel south on AZ 67 for approximately 40 mi to the North Rim. From the west on I–40, the most direct route to the South Rim is via Route 64 to U.S. 180. Summer traffic approaching the South Rim is very congested around Grand Canyon Village. Facilities at the more remote North Rim open May 15. From October 15 through December 1 or until heavy snows close the road, the North Rim remains open for day use only. The quickest route from Los Angeles is U.S. 93, which intersects with I–40 in Kingman, Arizona.

LODGING

CAMPING

Reservations for Grand Canyon campgrounds can be made either online or by a phone line. You can usually make campground reservations several months in advance.

➤ CONTACTS: **National Park Reservation Service** (☎ 800/365–2267 or 301/722–1257, WEB reservations.nps.gov).

RESERVING A ROOM

For information on accommodations in the park, and for reservations, contact Xanterra Parks and Resorts.

➤ CONTACTS: **Xanterra Parks and Resorts** (✉ 14001 E. Iliff, Suite 600, Aurora, CO 80014, ☎ 303/297–2757; 520/638–2631 same-day reservations; WEB www.grandcanyonlodges.com).

TRAIN TRAVEL

Flagstaff is the town closest to the Grand Canyon that is served by Amtrak. From Williams you can take the historic Grand Canyon Railway to the South Rim.

➤ TRAIN INFORMATION: **Amtrak** (☎ 928/774–8679 or 800/872–7245). **Grand Canyon Railway** (☎ 800/843–8724, WEB www.thetrain.com).

VISITOR INFORMATION

Before you go, write to Grand Canyon National Park for a complimentary *Trip Planner.* A free newspaper, the *Guide,* which contains a detailed area map, is available at both rims. The national park Web site is also extremely useful.

➤ TOURIST INFORMATION: **Grand Canyon National Park** (✉ Box 129, Grand Canyon 86023, ☎ 928/638–7888, WEB www.nps.gov/grca).

NORTHEAST ARIZONA

A vast and magnificent landscape of lofty buttes and towering cliffs, northeast Arizona is the home of the Navajo and Hopi peoples, who call the area "the rez." The mysterious ruins of ancient tribes can be found within the stunning landscapes of Navajo National Monument, Monument Valley, and Canyon de Chelly. All of these areas lie within the northeastern portion of the Navajo reservation. Homolovi Ruins State Historical Park, an ancient Hopi settlement and active archaeological dig, is 5 mi northeast of Winslow on I–40. Just below the southeastern boundary of the Navajo reservation, straddling I–40, the Petrified Forest National Park is an intriguing geologic open book of Earth's distant past. Above the far northwest corner of the Navajo reservation on U.S. 80 lies Glen Canyon Dam. Behind it more than 120 mi of Lake Powell's emerald waters are held in precipitous canyons of erosion-carved stone.

Throughout both reservations, excellent traditional Native American arts and crafts may be found for sale in shops, galleries, and trading posts. Visitors are sometimes invited to watch ancient cultural traditions such as Hopi ceremonial dances; however, the privacy, customs, and laws of the tribes should be respected.

Exploring Northeast Arizona

Some 115 mi east of Flagstaff off I–40, **Petrified Forest National Park** (✉ North entrance, I–40, Milepost 311, Petrified Forest; South Entrance, U.S. 180, 18 mi southeast of Holbrook, Petrified Forest (Box 2217, 86028), ☎ 928/524–6228, WEB www.nps.gov/pefo; 🎫 $10 per vehicle) is strewn with ancient ruins and fossilized tree trunks whose wood cells were replaced over the centuries by brightly hued mineral deposits. The park's 94,000 acres include portions of the **Painted Desert**, a colorful but essentially barren and waterless series of windswept plains, hills, and mesas. Also look for Native American petroglyphs.

Window Rock, northeast of Petrified Forest, is the capital of the Navajo Nation and the business and social center for families from the surrounding rural areas.The **Navajo Nation Museum,** north of the Navajo Nation Inn, has exhibits on Navajo art, culture, and history. ✉ *Rte. 264, at Indian Hwy. 12,* ☎ *928/871–6673.* 🎫 *$1.* ⏲ *Weekdays 1–5.*

The **Navajo Arts and Crafts Enterprise** (✉ Rte. 264 at Indian Hwy. 12), next to the Navajo Nation Inn, displays and sells local authentic Navajo arts and crafts.

Northwest of Window Rock, occupying nearly 84,000 acres, **Canyon de Chelly** (pronounced "Canyon de *Shay*") (✉ Indian Hwy. 7, Chinle 86503–0588, ☎ 928/674–5500, WEB www.nps.gov/cach; 🎫 free) is one of the Southwest's most extraordinary national monuments. Gigantic sandstone cliffs rise hundreds of feet above small streams, hogans (Navajo huts made of logs and mud), tilled fields, peach orchards, and grazing lands; thousand-year-old cliff dwellings, petroglyphs, and pictographs made by precursors of the Pueblo people are carved into some of its sheer cliff walls. Paved rim drives afford marvelous views. There are also horseback and jeep tours of the canyon.

At the approximate center of the Navajo reservation lies the 4,000-square-mi **Hopi reservation,** a series of stone-and-adobe villages built on high mesas. On First Mesa (✉ Ponsi Hall Visitor Center, Sichomovi, ☎ 928/737–2262; 🎫 guided tours $8) is the town of Walpi, built on solid rock and surrounded by steep cliffs. Its 30 residents defy modernity and live without electricity and running water. In Second Mesa's oldest and largest village, Shungopavi, the famous Hopi snake dances take place in August of even-numbered years. Currently, the village closes to the public during the dances, and permission for a tour must be obtained at the visitor center. On Second Mesa, the **Hopi Cultural Center** has a pueblo-style museum, shops, and a good restaurant and motel. ✉ *AZ 264, west of AZ 87, Second Mesa,* ☎ *928/734–6650.* WEB *www.psv.com/hopi.html.* 🎫 *museum $3. Museum closed weekends Oct.–mid-March.*

Homolovi Ruins State Historic Park (✉ AZ 87, Winslow, ☎ 928/289–4106, WEB www.pr.state.az.us/parkhtml/homolovi.html; 🎫 $4 per vehicle) south of Second Mesa, offers visitors a close look at an active archaeological dig of an ancient Hopi settlement. Extensive information is available about the Hopi people and their lands. Kykotsmovi, at the eastern base of **Third Mesa,** is known for its greenery and peach orchards. It is the site of the Hopi Tribal headquarters. Atop Third Mesa, Oraibi, established around AD 1150, is widely believed to be the oldest continuously inhabited community in the United States. The Hopi people are much more strict about privacy rules than the Navajo; avoid taking pictures or notes, making sketches, or scanning through binoculars. Permission is required to visit the villages. ✉ *Cultural Preservation Office, AZ 264, Kykotsmovi (Box 123, 86039),* ☎ *928/734–2441,* WEB *www.hopi.nsn.us.* ⏲ *Weekdays 8–5.*

Monument Valley Navajo Tribal Park (✉ off U.S. 163, Monument Valley, ☎ 435/727–3353, WEB www.navajonationparks.org; 🎫 $3), near the Utah border 24 mi north of Kayenta, may look familiar to those who have seen it in westerns and commercials. This sprawling expanse of soaring red buttes, eroded mesas, deep canyons, and naturally sculpted rock formations was populated by the ancestors of the Pueblo people and has been home to generations of Navajo. You can take a 17-mi self-guided driving tour of the park.

At **Navajo National Monument** (✉ AZ 564, Black Mesa, ☎ 928/672–2700, WEB www.nps.gov/nava; 🎫 free), southwest of Monument Valley off U.S. 160, two unoccupied 13th-century cliff pueblos, **Keet Seel** and **Betatakin,** stand under the overhang of soaring orange and ocher cliffs. The largest Native American ruins in Arizona, these pueblos, too, were built by the ancestors of the Pueblo people, whose reasons for suddenly abandoning them prior to AD 1300 are still disputed by scholars.

Glen Canyon National Recreation Area (✉ Carl Hayden Visitor Center, U.S. 89, Page, ☎ 928/608–6404, WEB www.nps.gov/glca; 🎫 $5 per vehicle) and Lake Powell, 136 mi north of Flagstaff on U.S. 89, were created when the massive Glen Canyon Dam was finished in 1962. The best way to see eerie, man-made lake as it twists through rugged canyon country is by boat. Popular half-day excursions go to Rainbow Bridge, a 290-ft red-sandstone arch that straddles one of the lake's coves.

Dining and Lodging

Northeast Arizona is vast and spacious land. Good dining is available at Page, Window Rock, Fort Defiance, Ganado, Chinle, Holbrook, Hopi Second Mesa, Keams Canyon, Tuba City, Kayenta, Goulding's Trading Post/Monument Valley, and Cameron. No alcoholic beverages are sold on the Navajo and Hopi reservations, and possession or consumption of alcohol is against the law in these areas. In summer, lodging reservations are highly advised.

Cameron

$ ✕ 🏨 **Cameron Trading Post and Motel.** This is a good place to fuel up along the drive from the Hopi mesas to the Grand Canyon. Motel rooms and RV sites are available; there's also a wood-beamed dining room serving hearty Navajo fare such as their popular Navajo tacos, green chili, and mutton stew. ✉ *U.S. 89 (Box 339, Cameron 86020),* ☎ *928/679–2231,* FAX *928/679–2350. 66 rooms. Restaurant. AE, DC, MC, V.*

Chinle/Canyon de Chelly

$–$$ ✕ 🏨 **Best Western Canyon de Chelly.** This rustic motel about 2 mi south of Canyon de Chelly has cheerful, modern rooms. There's also an indoor pool. The on-site Junction Restaurant offers a wide variety of standard American and Navajo fare. Lunch features the Navajo taco, fry bread heaped with homemade chili beans, lettuce, tomatoes, olives, and onions. Dinner specials include beef stew and thick broiled T-bone steaks. ✉ *Indian Hwy. 7 (Box 295, 86503),* ☎ *928/674–5875, 928/674–5288, or 800/327–0354.* FAX *928/674–3715,* WEB *www.bestwestern.com. 102 rooms. Restaurant, pool. AE, D, DC, MC, V.*

$–$$ ✕ 🏨 **Holiday Inn Canyon de Chelly.** This Navajo-staffed motel stands on the site of a former trading post and incorporates part of the historic structure. Rooms are predictable, but the lobby restaurant serves Navajo specialties like fresh mountain trout dusted in blue cornmeal. A gift shop on the premises features authentic local Indian crafts and arts. ✉ *Indian Hwy. 7 (Box 1889, 86503),* ☎ *928/674–5000,* FAX *928/674–8264,* WEB *www.sixcontinentshotels.com/holiday-inn. 108 rooms. Restaurant. AE, D, DC, MC, V.*

$–$$ ✕ 🏨 **Thunderbird Lodge.** At the mouth of Canyon de Chelly is this lodge, with stone-and-adobe units spread over manicured lawns among cottonwood trees. Some rooms have hewn-beam ceilings and rustic furniture. An all-Navajo staff prepares inexpensive meals in the cafeteria. Navajo tacos and mutton stew are tasty highlights on the menu. The lodge also offers drives into the canyon in open jeeps. ✉ *Indian Hwy. 7 (Box 548, 86503),* ☎ *928/674–5841 or 800/679–2473,* WEB *www.tbirdlodge.com. 72 rooms. Restaurant. AE, D, DC, V.*

Kayenta

$$ 🏨 **Holiday Inn Monument Valley.** This typical chain motel near Monument Valley has one of the best swimming pools in the area. The gift shop offers authentic native arts and crafts, and the on-site restaurant offers standard American and Southwest fare. ✉ *U.S. 160 at U.S. 163 (Box 307, 86033),* ☎ *928/697–3221 or 800/465–4329,* FAX *928/697–3349,* WEB *www.sixcontinentshotels.com. 164 rooms. Restaurant, pool. AE, D, DC, MC, V.*

$–$$ 🏨 **Best Western Wetherill Inn.** This clean, cheerful, two-story motel was named for frontier explorer and trader John Wetherill. A gift shop on site offers excellent local Indian arts and crafts. ✉ *U.S. 163 (Box 175, 86033),* ☎ *928/697–3231 or 800/528–1234,* WEB *www.bestwestern.com. 54 rooms. Pool. AE, D, DC, MC, V.*

Keams Canyon

$ ✕ **Keams Canyon Restaurant.** At this typical rural roadside café you'll find a few American dishes and Native American standards such as Hopi tacos, which are much like Navajo tacos with slightly spicier seasoning. Closing time on weekends is 3 PM. ✉ *Keams Canyon Shopping Center, AZ 264,* ☎ *520/738–2296. D, MC, V.*

Page/Lake Powell

$$–$$$ ✕ **Butterfield Stage Co.** This is the best place in town to watch the sunset. Steak is the main menu item, but the chef features at least one fresh fish dish every evening. ✉ *704 Rimview Dr.,* ☎ *928/645–2467. AE, MC, V. No lunch.*

$$$ ★ ✕🏨 **Wahweap Lodge.** On a promontory above Lake Powell, the rustic Wahweap Lodge serves as a base for boating, fishing, and other outdoor pursuits. All rooms have balconies or patios, and many have lake views. The circular Rainbow Room, with a panoramic lake view, has a seasonal menu of southwestern and Continental fare. ✉ *100 Lake Shore Dr., 7 mi north of Page off of U.S. 89 (Box 1597, 86040),* ☎ *928/645–2433 or 800/528–6154,* WEB *www.visitlakepowell.com. 350 rooms. Restaurant, bar, gym. AE, D, DC, MC, V.*

$$ 🏨 **Courtyard by Marriott.** This hotel, located at the foot of the mesa, is adjacent to Lake Powell National Golf Course. Rooms are spartan but spacious. ✉ *600 Clubhouse Dr. (Box 4150, 86040),* ☎ *928/645–5000,* WEB *www.marriott.com. 153 rooms. Restaurant, pool, golf, gym. AE, D, DC, MC, V. BP.*

$–$$ 🏨 **Best Western at Lake Powell.** On the main street of Page, overlooking Glen Canyon Dam, this friendly motel has a fitness room, pool and hot tub, and complimentary breakfast. Many good restaurants are nearby. ✉ *208 N. Lake Powell Blvd., 86040,* ☎ *928/645–5988 or 888/794–2888,* WEB *www.bestwestern.com/atlakepowell. 132 rooms. Pool, gym. AE, D, DC, MC, V. BP.*

Monument Valley, Utah

$$–$$$ ✕🏨 **Goulding's Lodge.** Built near the base of an immense red-sandstone butte, the lodge has private balconied rooms with spectacular views of Monument Valley. The on-premises Stagecoach Restaurant serves tasty fare such as its New York–cut Fiesta steak with fry bread, chili, and southwestern salsa, or the always-popular Navajo taco. A landing strip for Scenic Airlines is just across the street. ✉ *Off U.S. 163, 24 mi north of Kayenta (Box 360001, Monument Valley, UT 84536),* ☎ *435/727–3231,* WEB *www.gouldings.com. 62 rooms. Restaurant, pool. AE, D, DC, MC, V.*

Second Mesa

$ ★ ✕🏨 **Hopi Cultural Center Restaurant and Motel.** High atop Second Mesa is this pueblo-style lodging with immaculate rooms. An inexpensive restaurant serves traditional dishes such as Hopi blue-corn pancakes and *nok qui vi* (lamb stew). ✉ *5 mi west of Hwy 87 on AZ 264, Second Mesa 86403, 5 mi west of AZ 87,* ☎ *928/734–2401,* WEB *www.psv.com/hopi.html. 33 units. Restaurant. AE, D, DC, MC, V.*

Tuba City

$–$$ ✕ **Kate's Cafe.** A local favorite, this all-American café serves a great breakfast, lunch, and dinner at reasonable prices. The dinner house specialty is fettuccine Alfredo. ✉ *264 Main St.,* ☎ *435/283–6773. No credit cards.*

$ ✕🏨 **Quality Inn Tuba City.** This motel has 56 spacious rooms, each with queen beds and cable TV. The facility also has a trading post for gifts, art, and crafts that dates back to 1870. On-site Hogan Restaurant offers standard southwestern fare at reasonable prices. ✉ *AZ 264/Main St. at U.S. 160 (Box 247, 86045),* ☎ *928/283–4545 or 800/644–8383,* FAX *928/283–4144,* WEB *www.qualityinn.com. Restaurant. AE, D, DC, MC, V.*

Outdoor Activities and Sports

Boating

Houseboats, water-sports equipment, and excursion boats on the Arizona side of Lake Powell can be rented at **Wahweap Marina** (✉ Wahweap Resort, 100 Lake Shore Dr., off U.S. 89, Page, ☎ 928/645–2433 or 800/528–6154, WEB www.lakepowell.com).

Hiking

There's excellent hiking in **Canyon de Chelly.** Guides are required for all but the White House Ruin Trail; contact the visitor center. Hike on your own along the rim areas at **Navajo National Monument,** or sign up for guided hikes to Betatakin from early May to mid-October. A permit is needed for the unsupervised longer hike to Keet Seel (open only from Memorial Day to Labor Day). **Monument Valley Navajo Tribal Park** also has superb hiking trails. Permits are available at the visitor center.

Horseback Riding

Homeland Horseback Tours (✉ Monument Valley Tribal Park Visitor Center, off U.S. 163, 24 mi north of Kayenta, ☎ 435/727–3227), at the Monument Valley visitor center, offers hourly, half-day, full-day, and overnight tours into Monument Valley. **Justin's Horse Rental** (✉ Indian Hwy. 7, near the South Rim Drive entrance [Box 881, Chinle 86503], ☎ 928/674–5678) conducts horseback rides into Canyon de Chelly for $10 per hour for each horse plus another $15 per hour for a guide (two-hour minimum, but a typical ride is six to eight hours). Longer and overnight rides can also be arranged.

Shopping

You may find exactly what you want at a good price from one of the many roadside vendors in the area, but the following have dependable selections of Native American wares. **Cameron Trading Post** (✉ U.S. 89, Cameron, ☎ 928/679–2231) sells Navajo, Hopi, Zuni, and New Mexico Pueblo jewelry, rugs, baskets, and pottery. **Hubbell Trading Post** (✉ AZ 264, Ganado, ☎ 928/755–3254, WEB navajorugs.spma.org) is famous for its "Ganado red" Navajo rugs; it also has a good collection of Native American pottery. Fine authentic Navajo products are sold at **Navajo Arts and Crafts Enterprises** (✉ U.S. 89 at AZ 64, Cameron, ☎ 928/679–2244), which is adjacent to the Cameron Trading Post.

Northeast Arizona Essentials

AIR TRAVEL

No major airlines fly directly to this area. Great Lakes Air flies from Phoenix with a stop in Page Municipal Airport, near Lake Powell. Scenic Airlines conducts scenic flights over Monument Valley and Lake Powell from Las Vegas, with options for overnight stays.

➤ AIRLINES AND CONTACTS: **Great Lakes Air** (☎ 800/241–6522, WEB www.greatlakesav.com). **Page Municipal Airport** (☎ 800/245–8668). **Scenic Airlines** (☎ 800/634–6801 or 602/225–9135, WEB www.scenic.com).

BUS TRAVEL

Inexpensive but slow and erratic, the Navajo Transit System provides the only bus service on the vast Navajo reservation.

➤ BUS INFORMATION: **Navajo Transit System** (☎ 928/729–4002).

CAR TRAVEL

From the east or west I–40 passes through Flagstaff, a good entry point to the region. From the north or northwest U.S. 89 brings you to Page. From the northeast U.S. 64 leads west from Farmington, New Mexico. From the northwest out of Page, U.S. 89 and U.S. 98 head respectively south and southeast into the Navajo and Hopi nations. Touring Navajo and Hopi country involves driving long distances among widely scattered communities, so a detailed road map is essential.

In this sparsely populated area, service stations are rare, so fuel up wherever you can. Never drive into dips or low-lying road areas during a heavy rainstorm; dangerous flash floods are common. Tune to the following radio stations for news and weather on the Navajo and Hopi reservations: 660 AM, 770 AM, 97.9 FM, and 107.3 FM.

TRAIN TRAVEL

Amtrak stops in Flagstaff, a good jumping-off point for a car trip into the area.

➤ TRAIN INFORMATION: **Amtrak** (☎ 928/774–8679 or 800/872–7245).

VISITOR INFORMATION

➤ TOURIST INFORMATION: **Glen Canyon Recreation Area** (✉ National Park Service, Box 1507, Page 86040–1507, ☎ 928/608–6200 or 928/608–6404, WEB www.nps.govþglca). **Hopi Tribe Office of Public Relations** (✉ Box 123, Kykotsmovi 86039, ☎ 928/734–2441, WEB www.hopi.nsn.us). **Navajo Nation Tourism Office** (✉ Box 663, Window Rock 86515, ☎ 928/871–7371, WEB www.navajoland.com). **Page/Lake Powell Chamber of Commerce** (✉ 644 N. Navajo Dr. [Box 727, Page 86040], ☎ 928/645–2741, WEB www.powellguide.com).

FLAGSTAFF

Few visitors slow down long enough to explore Flagstaff, a town of 58,000. Still, set against a backdrop of pine forests and the snow-capped San Francisco Peaks, "Flag" (as it's known locally) makes a good base for exploring the Grand Canyon and Navajo-Hopi country. Downtown retains a frontier flavor, and motels and restaurants abound.

Exploring Flagstaff

The **Historic Downtown District,** where many interesting shops and buildings are concentrated, is near the Santa Fe railroad station. To view an architectural masterpiece built by two lumber-baron brothers, visit the **Riordan State Historic Park** (✉ 1300 Riordan Ranch St., ☎ 928/779–4395, WEB www.pr.state.az.us; 🎫 $4). The **Lowell Observatory** (✉ 1400 W. Mars Hill, ☎ 928/774–2096, WEB www.lowell.edu; 🎫 $3) has educational displays on astronomy and allows visitors to peer through its 24-inch telescope on some evenings (schedules vary seasonally). In a striking native-stone building, the **Museum of Northern Arizona** (✉ 3101 N. Fort Valley Rd., ☎ 928/774–5213, WEB www.musnaz.org; 🎫 $5) traces the natural and cultural history of the Colorado Plateau.

The **Arizona Snowbowl** (✉ Snowbowl Rd., ☎ 928/779–1951, WEB www.arizonasnowbowl.com; 🎫 Skyride $9) has fine skiing in winter and excellent views from the ski-lift skyride in summer; you'll see the exit 5 mi north of town on U.S. 180. In a pine forest about 10 mi southeast of Flagstaff, off I–40, is **Walnut Canyon National Monument** (✉ Walnut Canyon Rd., Winona, ☎ 928/526–3367, WEB www.nps.gov/waca; 🎫 $3), the site of 14th-century cliff dwellings. The 2,000-square-mi San Francisco Volcanic Field, about 14 mi north of Flagstaff via U.S. 89, is home to **Sunset Crater Volcano National Monument** (Sunset Crater–Wupatki Loop Rd., ☎ 928/556–7042, WEB www.nps.gov/sucr; 🎫 $3, including admission to Wupatki National Monument). You can take a 20-mi loop road from Sunset Crater to **Wupatki National Monument** (✉ Sunset Crater–Wupatki Loop Rd., 19 mi north of Sunset Crater visitor center, ☎ 928/556–7040, WEB www.nps.gov/wupa; 🎫 $3 per person, including Sunset Crater), rich in Indian history.

Dining and Lodging

$$–$$$ ✕ **Cottage Place.** Unexpectedly elegant in a town known for hearty food and drive-through service, this restaurant in a 50-year-old cottage serves Continental cuisine in a series of intimate dining rooms. Try the artichoke chicken breast or chateaubriand for two, carved table-side. ✉ *126 W. Cottage Ave.,* ☎ *928/774–8431. AE, MC, V. Closed Mon. No lunch.*

$$–$$$ ★ ✕ **Down Under New Zealand Restaurant.** This charming restaurant serves wonderful lamb chops and other regional specialties, including kangaroo. The small wine list features impressive bottlings from both Australia and New Zealand. ✉ *6 E. Aspen St.,* ☎ *928/773–7771. AE, MC, V. Closed Sun. No lunch weekends.*

$ ✕ **Café Espress.** The menu is largely vegetarian at this wholesome, all-day natural-foods restaurant, whose walls are covered with works by local artists. The baked goods are heavenly. ✉ *16 N. San Francisco St.,* ☎ *928/774–0541. MC, V.*

$$–$$$ **Inn at Four Ten.** This quiet and convenient downtown bed-and-breakfast, in a beautifully restored 1907 building, has spacious two-room suites. Fresh-baked cookies are served in the afternoon. ✉ *410 N. Leroux St., 86001,* ☎ *928/774–0088 or 800/774–2008,* FAX *928/774–6354,* WEB *www.inn410.com. 9 rooms. MC, V. BP.*

$–$$ **Little America of Flagstaff.** The biggest motel in town is deservedly popular: it's surrounded by evergreen forest, and it's one of the few places in Flagstaff with room service. Plush rooms have brass chandeliers and French provincial–style furniture. A courtesy van gives complimentary rides to the airport and bus and train stations. ✉ *2515 E. Butler Ave., 86004,* ☎ *928/779–2741 or 800/352–4386,* FAX *928/779–7983,* WEB *www.flagstaff.littleamerica.com. 248 rooms. Restaurant, pool, gym. AE, D, DC, MC, V.*

Nightlife and the Arts

Nightlife

Charly's (✉ Weatherford Hotel, 23 N. Leroux St., ☎ 928/779–1919) attracts a loyal local following to its late-night jazz and blues bands. **Main Street Bar and Grill** (✉ 14 S. San Francisco St., ☎ 928/774–1519) features bluegrass, jazz, and rock. **Monsoons** (✉ 22 E. Rte. 66, ☎ 928/774–7929) books an eclectic array of live music, from alternative to world beat. There's usually a country-and-western band at the **Museum Club** (✉ 3404 E. Rte. 66, ☎ 928/526–9434), a lively cowboy honky-tonk.

The Arts

A Celebration of Native American Art, featuring exhibits of work by Zuni, Hopi, and Navajo artists, is held at the Museum of Northern Arizona (✉ 3101 N. Fort Valley Rd., ☎ 928/774–5211) from late May through September. During the month of August, the **Flagstaff Festival of the Arts** (☎ 928/774–7750 or 800/266–7740) fills the air with the sounds of classical music and pops performances, many by world-renowned artists. The **Flagstaff Symphony Orchestra** (☎ 928/774–5107, WEB www.flagstaffsymphony.org) offers year-round musical events.

Flagstaff Essentials

AIR TRAVEL

America West flies frequently from Phoenix into Flagstaff Pullium Airport.

➤ CONTACTS: America West (☎ 800/235–9292, WEB www.americawest.com). Flagstaff Pullium Airport (☎ 928/556–1234).

CAR TRAVEL

Flagstaff lies at the intersection of I–40 (east–west) and I–17 (running south from Flagstaff), 134 mi north of Phoenix via I–17. It's 80 mi south of the Grand Canyon.

VISITOR INFORMATION

➤ CONTACTS: **Flagstaff Visitors Center** (✉ 1 E. Rte. 66, 86001, ☎ 928/774–9541 or 800/842–7293, WEB www.flagstaffarizona.org).

SEDONA AND ENVIRONS

Sedona is perhaps the most attractive stopover en route north from Phoenix to the Grand Canyon. Startling formations of deep-red rocks reach up into an almost always clear blue sky, both colors intensified by dark-green pine forests. Filmmakers in the 1940s and '50s saw this as a quintessential Wild West landscape and shot more than 80 films in the area. Now an upscale art colony, Sedona is also a center of interest to New Age enthusiasts, who believe the area contains important vortices (energy centers).

Exploring Sedona and Environs

The **Chapel of the Holy Cross** (✉ Chapel Rd., off AZ 179, ☎ 928/282–4069; 🎫 free) is worth a visit for its striking architecture and stunning vistas. **Tlaquepaque Arts & Crafts Village** (✉ AZ 179, just south of the "Y," ☎ 928/282–4838) has the largest concentration of shops and galleries.

Scenic hiking areas close to town include Long Canyon, Devil's Kitchen, and Boynton Canyon, and there are almost limitless other opportunities for hikes and walks; contact the rangers of the **Coconino National Forest** (✉ Sedona Ranger District, 250 Brewer Rd., ☎ 928/282–4119, WEB www.fs.fed.us/r3/coconino). Five miles southwest of Sedona, **Red Rock State Park** (4050 Red Rock Loop Rd., ☎ 928/282–6907, WEB www.pr.state.az.us; 🎫 $5 per car) has incredible rock formations. Visit **Slide Rock State Park** (6871 N. AZ 89A, ☎ 928/282–3034, WEB www.pr.state.az.us; 🎫 $5 per vehicle), 8 mi north of Sedona in Oak Creek Canyon, for a picnic and a plunge into a natural swimming hole.

On Cleopatra Hill, **Jerome** is about 37 mi southwest of Sedona on U.S. 89A. Once known as the Billion Dollar Copper Camp, it had a booming population of 15,000 that dwindled to 50 determined souls after the last mines closed in 1953, earning Jerome the "ghost town" designation it still holds, even though the population has risen to almost 450. Today, with many artsy boutiques, Jerome is a shopper's haven. **Jerome State Historic Park** (✉ State Park Rd., ☎ 928/634–5381, WEB www.pr.state.az.us; 🎫 $2) is housed in former mine owner's mansion.

The town's mining history is chronicled at the **Mine Museum** (✉ 200 Main St., ☎ 928/634–5477; 🎫 $1).

Dining and Lodging

$$–$$$ ✕ **Heartline Café.** This plant-filled café west of Sedona serves tasty southwestern-style food, such as grilled salmon marinated in tequila and lime. On nice days you can eat on the rose-planted terrace. ✉ *1610 W. AZ 89A,* ☎ *928/282–0785. AE, D, MC, V. No lunch Sun.*

$$–$$$ ✕ **Pietro's.** Good northern Italian cuisine is served by a friendly, attentive staff in a lively (often noisy) room. Creative pastas might include fettuccine with duck, cabbage, and figs; the veal piccata is excellent. ✉ *2445 W. AZ 89A,* ☎ *928/282–2525. AE, D, DC, MC, V. No lunch.*

$$$$ ★ **Enchantment Resort.** Designed as a tennis resort, Enchantment has excellent sports facilities (including a putting green), but it's the setting of Boynton Canyon that makes it unique. Rooms are in pueblo-style casitas, many with beehive fireplaces and kitchenettes, and all have dazzling views. ✉ *525 Boynton Canyon Rd., 86336,* ☎ *928/282–2900 or 800/826–4180,* FAX *928/282–9249,* WEB *www.enchantmentresort.com. 122 rooms. Restaurants, pools, tennis, health club. AE, D, MC, V.*

$$ ★ **The Canyon Wren.** The best value in the Oak Creek Canyon area, this small B&B has free-standing cabins with views of the canyon walls. Milena and Mike (she's Slovenian, he's Floridian) are consummate hosts, regarding guests' privacy first and foremost. Cabins have private decks, fireplaces, and whirlpool tubs. Breakfast is a selection of delicious baked goods from Milena's kitchen. ✉ *6425 N. AZ 89A, 86336,* ☎ *928/282–6900 or 800/437–9736,* FAX *928/282–6978.* WEB *www.canyonwrencabins.com. 4 cabins. AE, D, MC, V. CP.*

Sedona and Environs Essentials

CAR TRAVEL

Sedona is 125 mi north of downtown Phoenix and 27 mi south of Flagstaff, at the south end of Oak Creek Canyon on AZ 89A.

VISITOR INFORMATION

➤ CONTACTS: **Sedona–Oak Creek Canyon Chamber of Commerce** (✉ 331 Forest Rd., at N. AZ 89A, ☎ 928/282–7722 or 800/288–7336, WEB www.sedona.net/chamber.html).

PRESCOTT

In a forested bowl among the Mingus Mountains, Prescott was Arizona's first territorial capital and remains the Southwest's richest repository of late-19th-century New England–style architecture. Because of its temperate climate, in summer the town draws escapees from the Phoenix heat—as well as retirees year-round. The town's two institutions of higher learning, Yavapai and Prescott colleges, ensure a younger scene, too. Many visitors come to buy reasonably priced antiques and collectibles on the stretch of Cortez Street east of Courthouse Plaza.

Exploring Prescott

Courthouse Plaza (✉ bounded by Gurley and Goodwin Sts. to the north and south and by Cortez and Montezuma Sts. to the west and east) is the heart of downtown Prescott. **Whiskey Row** (✉ Montezuma St., along the west side of Courthouse Plaza), named for a string of brawling pioneer taverns, was once lined with 20 saloons and houses of pleasure. Social activity is more subdued these days, and the historic bars provide an escape from the street's many boutiques.

Two blocks west of Courthouse Plaza, the **Sharlot Hall Museum** (✉ 415 W. Gurley St., 2 blocks west of Courthouse Plaza, ☎ 928/445–3122, WEB www.sharlot.org; 🎫 $5 donation requested per family), devoted to the area's history, includes the log cabin that housed the territorial governor and three restored late-19th-century houses. The **Phippen Museum of Western Art** (✉ 4701 AZ 89 N, ☎ 928/778–1385, WEB www.phippenartmuseum.org; 🎫 $3), about 5 mi north of downtown, displays work by many prominent artists of the West, along with the painting and bronze sculptures of George Phippen.

Dining and Lodging

$–$$ ✕ **Prescott Brewing Company.** In addition to the pub fare you'd expect, including fish-and-chips, you'll also find a surprising range of vegetarian selections. Four good beers are brewed on the premises. ✉ *130 W. Gurley St.,* ☎ *928/771–2795. AE, D, DC, MC, V.*

$$–$$$ ★ **Hassayampa Inn.** Built in 1927 for early automobile travelers, the Hassayampa Inn oozes character. Rooms are individually decorated, some with original furnishings such as oak headboards inset with tiles. A cocktail in the elegant lounge and a full breakfast are included in the reasonable rates. The Peacock Room, the hotel's art-nouveau-style dining room, serves impressive Continental cuisine. ✉ *122 E. Gurley St., 86301,* ☎ *928/778–9434; 800/322–1927 in AZ;* FAX *928/445–8590;* WEB *www.hassayampainn.com. 68 rooms. Restaurant. AE, D, DC, MC, V. BP.*

Prescott Essentials

AIRPORTS

America West flies frequently from Phoenix into Prescott Municipal Airport.

➤ CONTACTS: **America West** (☎ 800/235–9292). **Prescott Municipal Airport** (☎ 928/445–7860).

BUS TRAVEL

Buses run between Prescott and Phoenix Sky Harbor International Airport.

➤ BUS INFORMATION: **Greyhound** (✉ 820 E. Sheldon St., ☎ 928/445–5470 or 800/231–2222).

CAR TRAVEL

Prescott is 34 mi southwest of Jerome via U.S. 89A. From Phoenix take I–17 north for 60 mi to Cordes Junction, and then drive northwest on Highway 69 for 36 mi into town.

VISITOR INFORMATION

➤ TOURIST INFORMATION: **Prescott Chamber of Commerce** (✉ 117 W. Goodwin St., 86303, ☎ 928/445–2000 or 800/266–7534, WEB www.prescott.org).

METROPOLITAN PHOENIX

One of America's newest, fastest-growing major urban centers, metropolitan Phoenix lies at the northern tip of the Sonoran Desert, in the Valley of the Sun, named for its 330-plus days of sunshine each year. Now-chic Scottsdale began in 1901 as fewer than a dozen adobe houses and 30-odd tents put up by seekers of healthful desert air. Glendale and Peoria on the west side and Tempe, Mesa, Gilbert, and Chandler on the east constitute the nation's third-largest Silicon Valley. Excellent hiking, golf, shopping, and dining and some of the best luxury resorts in the country make the valley one of the country's leading business and vacation destinations.

Exploring Metropolitan Phoenix

★ The **Heard Museum** (✉ 2301 N. Central Ave., ☎ 602/252–8848 or 602/252–8840, WEB www.heard.org; 🎟 $7), with a stunning expansion, reaffirms its position as the world's foremost showcase of Native American art and culture. The exceptional collection of fine art, basketry, and pottery, including first-class contemporary work, is supplemented by interactive exhibits, a multimedia show, and live demon-

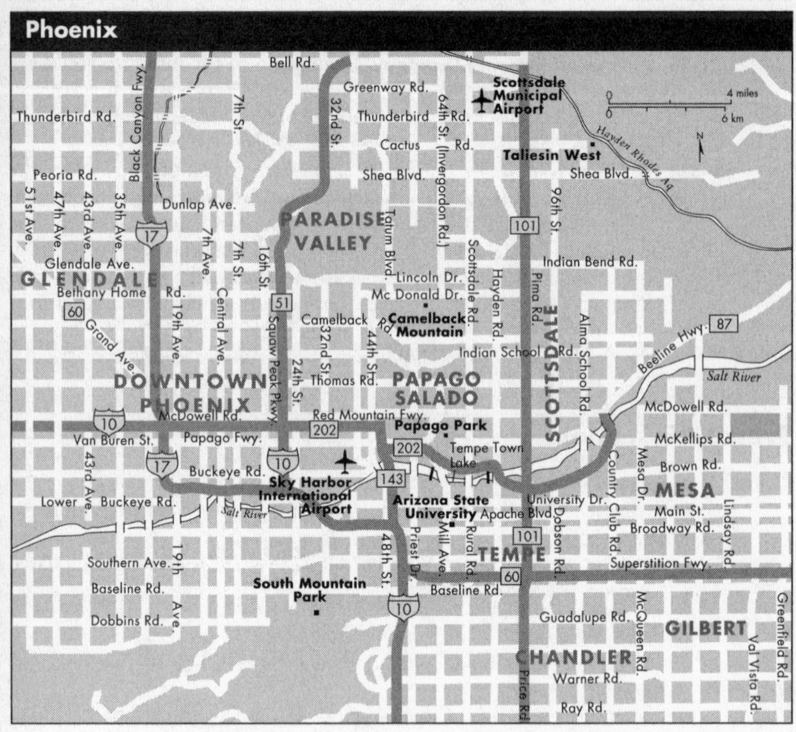

strations by artisans and performers. Western painting is a primary focus of the galleries at the **Phoenix Art Museum** (✉ 1625 N. Central Ave., ☎ 602/257–1880, WEB www.phxart.org; 🎫 $7).

A piece of the city as it was at the turn of the 20th century still stands in parklike **Heritage Square** (✉ 5th to 7th Sts. between Monroe and Adams Sts.), at the east end of downtown.

Within Heritage Square is the **Arizona Science Center** (✉ 600 E. Washington St., ☎ 602/716–2000, WEB www.azscience.org; 🎫 $8; combination museum, theater, and planetarium, $11), where lively hands-on exhibits let kids discover the science of making gigantic soap bubbles, the technology of satellite weather systems, and more. Within the science center are the **Dorrance Planetarium** and the **Irene P. Flinn Theater,** with a 50-ft screen.

Scottsdale, no suburb anymore but a booming city in its own right, has a downtown rich in historic sites, nationally known art galleries, and smart boutiques. Historic **Old Town** (✉ Main St. from Scottsdale Rd. to Brown Ave.), with its rustic storefronts and wooden sidewalks, has the look of the Old West and souvenirs galore.Gallery after gallery in the **Main Street Arts District** (✉ bounded by Main St. and 1st Ave., Scottsdale Rd. and 69th St.) displays artwork of myriad styles. Several antiques shops are also here; specialties include elegant porcelains and china, jewelry, and Oriental rugs. In the **Marshall Way Arts District** (✉ Marshall Way, from Indian School Rd. to 5th Ave.) galleries exhibit and sell predominantly contemporary art. Upscale gift and jewelry stores can be found here, too. Across 3rd Avenue, the galleries and stores have a more southwestern flair.The **Scottsdale Museum of Contemporary Art** (✉ 7380 E. 2nd St., ☎ 480/994–2787, WEB www.scottsdalearts.org; 🎫 $5), with a stunning design by architect Will Bruder and constantly changing exhibits of dynamic work, solidifies Scottsdale's reputation as a top-notch arts destination.

Now the western campus of the Frank Lloyd Wright School of Architecture, **Taliesin West** (✉ 12621 Frank Lloyd Wright Blvd., Scottsdale, ☎ 480/860–8810 or 480/860–2700, WEB www.franklloydwright.org; 🎫 $16–$35) was originally Wright's desert retreat, built after his visit to Phoenix in 1927 to consult on the Arizona Biltmore project. Guided tours are conducted year-round, but times vary by season.

An hour's drive south of Phoenix, **Casa Grande Ruins National Monument** (✉ AZ 87, Coolidge, ☎ 520/723–3172, WEB www.nps.gov/cagr; 🎫 $3) is the site of the 35-ft-tall house, built in the early 13th century by the Hohokam Indians. These early inhabitants farmed the area from more than 1,500 years ago until they vanished around 1450. A small museum displays artifacts and archaeological exhibits.

Parks, Gardens, and Zoos

★ The **Desert Botanical Garden** (✉ 1201 N. Galvin Pkwy., ☎ 480/941–1225, WEB www.dbg.org; 🎫 $7.50) is an urban oasis with the world's largest collection of desert plants in a natural setting.

Five trails wind through the 125-acre **Phoenix Zoo** (✉ 455 N. Galvin Pkwy., ☎ 602/273–1341, WEB www.phoenixzoo.org; 🎫 $10), where the habitats of an African savanna and a tropical rain forest are expertly replicated. Children can help groom goats and sheep at the zoo's big red barn.

Dining

$$$–$$$$ ✕ **Rancho Pinot Grill.** The attention to quality paid by the husband-and-wife proprietors—he manages, she cooks—has made this tiny, southwestern-style Scottsdale spot one of the town's top restaurants. The inventive menu changes weekly, but you'll usually find favorites like "Nonni's Sunday Chicken" (braised with white wine and mushrooms) or bay-marinated pork tenderloin with balsamic-bacon potatoes. ✉ *6208 N. Scottsdale Rd., Scottsdale,* ☎ *480/367–8030. Reservations essential. AE, D, MC, V. Closed Sun.–Mon. and mid-Aug.–mid-Sept. No lunch.*

$$$–$$$$ ✕ **RoxSand.** Chef RoxSand Scocos doesn't follow trends; she sets them. Who else would think to stuff tamales with curried lamb moistened in a Thai-style peanut sauce? The air-dried duck entrée, served with a trio of sauces (Szechuan Black Bean, Evil Jungle Prince, Elephant Plum), is a house specialty. ✉ *Biltmore Fashion Park, 2594 E. Camelback Rd.,* ☎ *602/381–0444. Reservations essential. AE, DC, MC, V.*

$$–$$$$ ★ ✕ **Michael's at the Citadel.** If you're celebrating a special occasion, Michael's is the spot. Entrées are the real stars here, including pan-seared duck paired with foie gras and pearl couscous, venison with a dried-cherry demiglace, and grilled lamb with a goat-cheese potato tart. ✉ *8700 E. Pinnacle Peak Rd., Scottsdale,* ☎ *480/515–2575. AE, DC, MC, V.*

$$–$$$ ✕ **Restaurant Hapa.** "Hapa" is Hawaiian slang for "half," which describes the half-Japanese, half-American background of the chef here. But there's nothing halfway about Hapa's flavorful, Asian-inspired cuisine. Appetizers include skillet-roasted mussels coated in a Thai-inspired broth, and the signature entrée is beef tenderloin, lined with hot Chinese mustard and caramelized brown sugar. ✉ *6204 N. Scottsdale Rd., Scottsdale,* ☎ *480/998–8220. AE, MC, V. Closed Sun. No lunch.*

$$–$$$ ✕ **Tarbell's.** Sleek modern ambience meets down-home friendliness at Mark Tarbell's popular restaurant. Menus rotate often, but count on such new American specialties as vibrant smoked rock shrimp starter, or aromatic mussels steamed in a heady broth of white wine and shallots. ✉ *3213 E. Camelback Rd.,* ☎ *602/955–8100. Reservations essential. AE, D, DC, MC, V. No lunch.*

$$ ✕ **Malee's on Main.** This fashionable eatery serves up sophisticated, Thai-inspired fare. The recommended *ahoi phannee* is a medley of seafood in a bamboo-leaf bowl moistened with red curry sauce redolent of coconut, lime leaf, and Thai basil. The Thai barbecued chicken, grilled to a sizzle and coated with rum, is outstanding. Beware: take Malee's spices seriously—even the "mild" dishes have a bite. ✉ *7131 E. Main St., Scottsdale,* ☎ *480/947–6042. AE, DC, MC, V. No lunch Sun.*

$–$$ ✕ **Los Dos Molinos.** A hanging Arizona license plate with the word "HHHHOT" should clue you in that the food's a touch spicy at this beloved Mexican restaurant. Adobada ribs, a specialty, feature fall-off-the-bone meat marinated in red chilies, and the green chili enchilada and beef taco are potentially lethal. This restaurant is a riot of color, sound, and (best of all) taste. ✉ *8646 S. Central Ave.,* ☎ *602/243–9113. Reservations not accepted. AE, D, MC, V. Closed Sun.–Mon.*

$ ✕ **Pizzeria Bianco.** Bronx native Chris Bianco is a craftsman of pizza. His wood-fired crust is a work of art, not too bready, not too light. Toppings include imported cheeses, homemade fennel sausage, wood-roasted mushrooms or onions, and the freshest herbs and spices. ✉ *623 E. Adams St.,* ☎ *602/258–8300. MC, V. Reservations not accepted. Closed Mon. No lunch weekends.*

Lodging

Off-season rates in Phoenix can be a great savings—sometimes more than 50% off winter prices, even at the top resorts.

$$$$ ★ **Arizona Biltmore.** Designed by Frank Lloyd Wright's colleague Albert Chase McArthur, the Biltmore has remained Phoenix's premier resort since it opened in 1929. Every president since Herbert Hoover has stayed here: the landscaped grounds and low-key, southwestern-style elegance might explain why. Rooms have marble bathrooms and are decorated in earth tones and accented with southwestern-patterned accessories. ✉ *24th St. and Missouri Ave., 85016,* ☎ *602/955–6600 or 800/950–0086,* FAX *602/381–7600,* WEB *www.arizonabiltmore.com. 720 rooms, 50 villas. 4 restaurants, pools, tennis, health club. AE, D, DC, MC, V.*

$$$$ ★ **The Boulders.** The desert setting of the valley's most serene luxury resort is its most spectacular feature; buildings nestle among hill-size granite boulders in Carefree (just over the border from Scottsdale). Accommodations have wood-beam ceilings, kiva fireplaces, and huge bath-dressing areas. The golf course is one of the valley's most famous. ✉ *34631 N. Tom Darlington Dr., Carefree 85377,* ☎ *480/488–9009 or 800/553–1717,* FAX *480/488–4118,* WEB *www.grandbay.com. 160 casitas, 46 patio homes. 5 restaurants, pools, golf, tennis, gym. AE, D, DC, MC, V.*

$$$$ **Fairmont Scottsdale Princess.** Built around a series of outdoor plazas, the Princess has a Mexican-colonial feel, with spacious rooms in soothing desert tones, beautifully landscaped grounds, and dining that makes you never want to leave the property. ✉ *7575 E. Princess Dr., Scottsdale 85255,* ☎ *480/585–4848 or 800/344–4758,* FAX *480/585–0091,* WEB *www.fairmont.com. 671 rooms, 125 casitas, 75 villas. 5 restaurants, pools, golf, tennis, health club. AE, D, DC, MC, V.*

$$$$ **Hermosa Inn.** Once the home and studio of cowboy artist Lon Megargee, the Hermosa lives up to its name (Spanish for "beautiful"), providing a restful alternative to the megaresorts. Individually decorated casitas and villas as big as private homes are hung with an enviable collection of museum-quality art. ✉ *5532 N. Palo Cristi Rd., Paradise Valley 85253,* ☎ *602/955–8614 or 800/241–1210,* FAX *602/*

955–8299, WEB www.hermosainn.com. 4 villas, 3 haciendas, 22 casitas, 17 ranchos. Restaurant, pool, tennis. AE, D, DC, MC, V. BP.

$$$$ ★ **Marriott's Camelback Inn.** Desert landscaping, large rooms (some with private swimming pools), and a world-class spa make this a perennial favorite for those wanting to be pampered in a dramatic setting between the Camelback and Mummy mountains. ✉ *5402 E. Lincoln Dr., Paradise Valley 85253,* ☎ *480/948–1700 or 800/242–2635,* FAX *480/951–8469,* WEB *www.camelbackinn.com. 481 rooms. 5 restaurants, pools, golf, tennis, spa. AE, D, DC, MC, V.*

$$$$ ★ **Royal Palms.** A luxurious Mediterranean look prevails, from the titular palms at the entrance to the manicured gardens dotted with antique fountains. Casitas are given individually themed treatment by well-known designers. ✉ *5200 E. Camelback Rd. 85018,* ☎ *602/840–3610 or 800/672–6011,* FAX *602/840–6927,* WEB *www.royalpalmshotel.com. 120 rooms. Restaurant, pool, tennis, gym. AE, D, DC, MC, V.*

$$$ **Hotel San Carlos.** Built in 1927, this downtown landmark retains historic touches such as pedestal sinks in the rooms and crystal chandeliers in the lobby. The 3-inch concrete walls in the rooms ensure quiet, and though the rooms aren't huge, the staff is among the valley's friendliest. ✉ *202 N. Central Ave. 85004,* ☎ *602/253–4121 or 800/678–8946,* FAX *602/253–6668,* WEB *www.hotelsancarlos.com. 133 rooms. 3 restaurants, pool, gym. AE, D, DC, MC, V. CP.*

$$ **Quality Hotel & Resort.** With a 1½-acre Getaway Lagoon complete with rock waterfalls pouring into a free-form pool, and plenty of facilities (a putting green, playground, and business center), the Quality is central Phoenix's best bargain oasis. Cabana suites on the VIP floor have private rooftop pools with great views of the Phoenix skyline. ✉ *3600 N. 2nd Ave. 85013,* ☎ *602/248–0222,* FAX *602/265–6331,* WEB *www.getawayresort.com. 280 rooms. Restaurant, pools, gym. AE, D, DC, MC, V.*

Nightlife and the Arts

Cultural and entertainment events are listed in the free weekly *New Times* newspaper, distributed Wednesday. The *Rep Entertainment Guide* and Sunday "Arts" section of the *Arizona Republic* also detail the current goings-on.

Nightlife

There are plenty of nightclubs, restaurants, and bars in downtown's **Arizona Center,** but there's no lack of nightlife elsewhere, particularly in Scottsdale and Tempe. On Camelback Road, restaurants abound in the **Biltmore Fashion Park.** Scottsdale's Main Street comes alive for **Art Walk,** held Thursday evenings from 7 to 9. **Mill Avenue,** near the Arizona State University campus, is the center of action in Tempe.

The Arts

Facing the Herberger Theater, **Symphony Hall** (✉ 225 E. Adams St., ☎ 602/534–5600) is the home of the Phoenix Symphony and Arizona Opera as well as a venue for pop concerts by top-name performers. The permanent home of the Arizona Theatre Company, Actors Theatre of Phoenix, and Ballet Arizona, the **Herberger Theater Center** (✉ 222 E. Monroe St., ☎ 602/534–5600, WEB www.herbergertheater.org) also hosts performances of visiting dance troupes and orchestras.

Outdoor Activities and Sports

Golf

The Valley of the Sun has more than 100 courses, from par-3 to PGA-championship links. For a detailed listing of the state's courses, contact the **Arizona Golf Association** (✉ 7226 N. 16th St., 85020, ☎ 602/944–3035 or 800/458–8484, WEB www.azgolf.org).

Hiking

Camelback Mountain (✉ 48th St., north of Camelback Rd., ☎ 602/256–3220 Phoenix Parks & Recreation Dept., Eastern and Central District), the city's most prominent landmark, presents a challenging climb that will take one to three hours. **South Mountain Park** (✉ 10919 S. Central Ave., ☎ 602/261–8457), the world's largest city park, contains more than 40 mi of multiuse trails. Rangers can help you plan hikes to see some of the 200 Native American petroglyph sites in the park. Phoenix has some of the best-trod hiking trails in the world, and the area favorite is in **Squaw Peak Summit Trail** (✉ 2701 E. Squaw Peak Dr., Paradise Valley, ☎ 602/262–7901 North Mountain Preserves Ranger Station). The 1¼-mi trail to the top is steep; plan for 1½ hours in each direction.

Spectator Sports

Baseball: Arizona Diamondbacks (✉ Bank One Ballpark, 401 E. Jefferson St., between S. 4th and S. 7th Sts., ☎ 602/462–6000 team offices; 602/514–8400 Bank One Ballpark Ticket Office; WEB www.azdiamondbacks.com) is the Phoenix Major League Baseball team. Several major-league baseball teams train in the Phoenix area during March. Contact the **Cactus League Baseball Association** (✉ Mesa Convention and Visitor's Bureau, 120 N. Center St., Mesa 85201, ☎ 602/827–4700 or 800/283–6372) for information. **Basketball: Phoenix Suns** (✉ America West Arena, 201 E. Jefferson St., at 2nd St., Phoenix, ☎ 602/379–7867 team offices; 602/379–2000 America West Arena Ticket Office; WEB www.suns.com) is the local NBA team. **Football:** The **Arizona Cardinals** (✉ Sun Devil Stadium, Stadium Dr., Tempe, ☎ 602/379–0102, WEB www.azcardinals.com), the area's professional football team, plays at ASU's outdoor Sun Devil Stadium in Tempe. **Golf:** The **Phoenix Open** (✉ ☎ 602/870–0163, WEB www.phoenixopen.com) is held each January at the Tournament Players Club of Scottsdale. **Hockey: Phoenix Coyotes** (✉ America West Arena, 201 E. Jefferson St., at 2nd St., Phoenix, ☎ 602/379–7825 team offices; 602/379–2000 American West Arena Ticket Office; WEB www.phoenixcoyotes.com) are the NHL team in Phoenix.

Shopping

The valley is a shopper's delight, with everything from glitzy malls in Phoenix and Mesa to charming boutiques and galleries in downtown Scottsdale. Souvenir shops and stores selling Native American jewelry and crafts are found along Scottsdale's **5th Avenue,** between Goldwater Boulevard and Scottsdale Road, and in **Old Town,** bordered by Brown Avenue, Scottsdale Road, Indian School Road, and 2nd Street. Head to **Main Street** and **Marshall Way,** just west of Scottsdale Road, for the fine art for which Scottsdale is known.

Arizona Mills (✉ 5000 Arizona Mills Cir., Tempe, ☎ 480/491–9700) is a mammoth outlet mall with almost 200 stores, a food court, cinemas, and a faux rain forest.

Anchored by Saks Fifth Avenue and Macy's, **Biltmore Fashion Park** (✉ 24th St. and Camelback Rd., Phoenix, ☎ 602/955–8400) has posh shops as well as some of the city's most popular restaurants.

Scottsdale Fashion Square (✉ Scottsdale and Camelback Rds., Scottsdale, ☎ 480/941–2140) sprawls across Camelback Road, with a Nordstrom and several other stores, including Neiman-Marcus, Robinson's-May, and Dillard's. The ritzy **Borgata of Scottsdale** (✉ 6166

N. Scottsdale Rd., Scottsdale, ☏ 480/998–1822) has more than 50 boutiques in an Italian village–style complex.

Metropolitan Phoenix Essentials

AIRPORTS AND TRANSFERS

Sky Harbor International Airport, 3 mi east of downtown Phoenix, is home base for America West and a hub for the Southwest. It is also served by other major airlines. By car, downtown Phoenix is 10 minutes from the airport; Scottsdale, about 30 minutes; Tempe, 10 minutes; Glendale and Mesa, 25 minutes; and Sun City, 30–45 minutes.

➤ AIRPORT INFORMATION: **Sky Harbor International Airport** (☏ 602/273–3300, WEB www.phxskyharbor.com).

BUS TRAVEL

➤ BUS INFORMATION: **Greyhound** (✉ 2115 E. Buckeye Rd., ☏ 602/389–4200 or 800/231–2222).

CAR TRAVEL

From the west you'll probably come to Phoenix on I–10. Interstate 40 enters Arizona in the northwest; U.S. 93 continues to Phoenix. From the east I–10 brings you from El Paso into Tucson, then north to Phoenix. The northeastern route, I–40 from Albuquerque, leads to Flagstaff, where I–17 goes south to Phoenix. If you plan to see anything beyond the pedestrian-friendly downtowns of Phoenix, Scottsdale, or Tempe, you will need a car.

TRAIN TRAVEL

➤ TRAIN INFORMATION: **Amtrak** (✉ 401 W. Harrison St., ☏ 602/253–0121 or 800/872–7245).

VISITOR INFORMATION

➤ TOURIST INFORMATION: **Arizona Office of Tourism** (✉ 2702 N. 3rd St., Suite 4015, 85004, ☏ 602/230–7733 or 888/520–3444, WEB www.arizonaguide.com). **Greater Phoenix Convention and Visitors Bureau** (✉ Arizona Center, 2nd and Adams Sts., ☏ 602/254–6500, WEB www.phoenixcvb.com). **Phoenix Chamber of Commerce** (✉ Bank One Plaza, 201 N. Central Ave., Suite 2700, ☏ 602/254–5521, WEB www.phoenixchamber.com). **Scottsdale Convention and Vistors Bureau** (✉ 7343 Scottsdale Mall, Scottsdale, ☏ 480/945–8481 or 800/877–1117, WEB www.scottsdalecvb.com).

TUCSON

Tucson, Arizona's second-largest city, has a small-town atmosphere enriched by its deep Hispanic and Old West roots. Because of its large university, myriad resorts, and desirable climate—the sun shines more than 340 days a year, on the average—Tucson hosts all kinds of recreational and cultural activities, including historical tours, year-round.

Exploring Tucson

Tucson covers more than 500 square mi in a valley ringed by mountains, so a car is necessary. The downtown area, east of I–10 off the Broadway-Congress exit, is easy to navigate on foot.

In the El Presidio neighborhood, the **Tucson Museum of Art and Historic Block** includes a group of five buildings listed in the National Register of Historic Places, plus a museum whose permanent collection of pre-Columbian art is often supplemented by traveling shows, mostly of contemporary art. The **Edward Nye Fish House** holds the art mu-

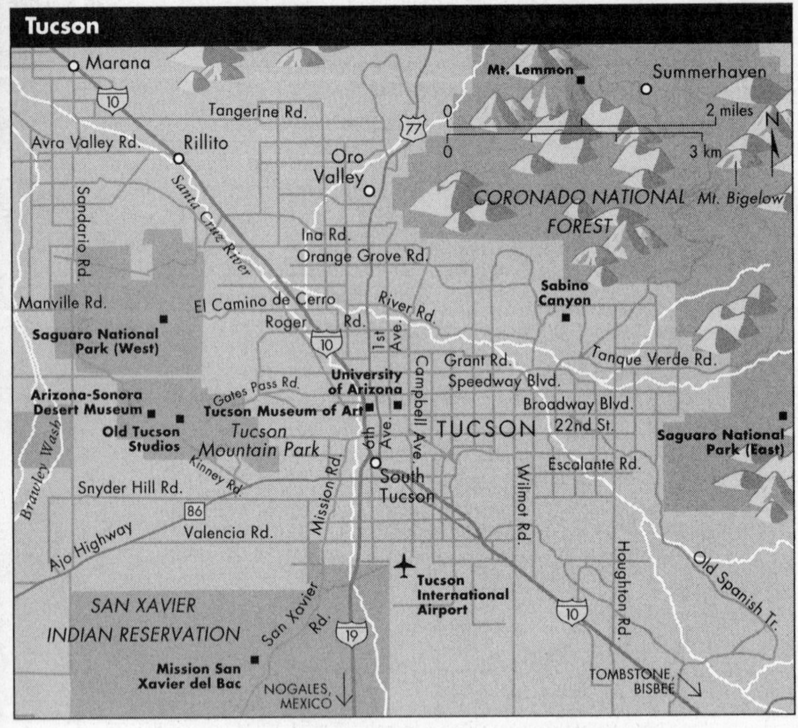

seum's western collection. **La Casa Cordova** (✉ 175 N. Meyer Ave.) is one of the best examples of the simple but elegant Sonoran row house. The **J. Knox Corbett House** (✉ 180 N. Main Ave.) is a two-story, Mission Revival–style residence. The **Stevens House** (✉ 150 N. Main Ave.) was the home of a wealthy politician and cattle rancher. ✉ *140 N. Main Ave.,* ☎ *520/624–2333,* WEB *www.tucsonarts.com.* *$5; Sun. free (includes historic buildings).* ⏲ *Mon.–Sat. 10–4, Sun. noon–4. Closed Mon. late May–early Sept.*

The city divides **Saguaro National Park** into two sections; the part west of town is the most heavily visited, in part because of its **Red Hills Visitor Center.** Both parks are forested by the huge saguaro cactus, a native of the Sonoran Desert that is known for its towering height (often 50 ft) and for arms that reach out in strange configurations. ✉ *3693 S. Old Spanish Trail,* ☎ *520/733–5153; 2700 N. Kinney Rd.;* ☎ *520/733–5158;* WEB *www.nps.gov/sagu.* *$6 per vehicle.*

★ Near Saguaro National Park West is the **Arizona–Sonora Desert Museum** (2021 N. Kinney Rd., ☎ 520/883–2702, WEB www.desertmuseum.org; $8.95), where birds and animals busy themselves in a desert microcosm. **Old Tucson Studios** (✉ Tucson Mountain Park, 201 S. Kinney Rd., ☎ 520/883–0100, WEB www.oldtucson.com; $14.95) is a western theme park that's been used as a location for 350 movie and television productions over the past 50 years.

A university might not seem to be the most likely spot for a vacation visit, but the **University of Arizona** (✉ Park Ave. at Speedway Blvd., ☎ 520/621–5130 university visitor center, WEB www.arizona.edu; museums free–$3) is unusual. Not only is the institution itself of historical importance, but it also supports several museums with exhibitions ranging from astronomy to photography. Among the museums are the **Center for Creative Photography,** the **Arizona Historical Soci-**

ety's Museum, the **Arizona State Museum**, and the **Flandrau Science Center and Planetarium.**

The 1692 **Mission San Xavier del Bac** (✉ San Xavier Rd., ☎ 520/294–2624; 🎫 free), 9 mi southwest of Tucson on I–19, is the oldest Catholic church in the United States still serving the community for which it was built: the Tohonó O'odham Indian tribe. Painted statues, carvings, and frescoes make this beautiful Spanish-Moorish–style structure a sight to behold.

Dining

$$$–$$$$ ★ ✕ **Janos.** Chef Janos Wilder brings his Southwest hacienda-style cuisine to the grounds of the Westin La Paloma hotel. Roasted quail stuffed with chihuacle spoon bread on prickly-pear compote tastes magical as you survey stunning views of the city and desert. J Bar next door is a casual Latin alternative. ✉ *3770 E. Sunrise Dr.,* ☎ *520/615–6100. AE, DC, MC, V. Closed Sun. No lunch.*

$$–$$$ ✕ **Cafe Terra Cotta.** Everything about this restaurant says Southwest. Specialties here include duck two ways (grilled breast and duck carnitas spring roll), chilies relleno, and pork chop with black beans. This is the ultimate casual yet classy place to dine, for natives and their out-of-town guests. ✉ *3500 E. Sunrise Dr.,* ☎ *520/577–8100. AE, D, DC, MC, V.*

$$ ★ ✕ **Café Poca Cosa.** Chef-owner Susan Davila pays homage to different regions of her native Mexico in what is arguably Tucson's best Mexican restaurant. The chalkboard menu changes daily; ingredients are always fresh. Order the daily "Plato Poca Cosa," and the chef will select one beef, one chicken, and one vegetarian entrée for you to sample. ✉ *Park Inn, 88 E. Broadway,* ☎ *520/622–6400. MC, V. Closed Sun.*

$$ ✕ **Kingfisher Bar and Grill.** Brick walls and black banquettes create a chic setting for Kingfisher's innovative cuisine. You might find stuffed grilled trout with a pecan-cilantro pesto sauce or braised shank of Colorado lamb on the seasonally changing menu. Added bonuses include an extensive bourbon selection and late hours (food is served until midnight). ✉ *2564 E. Grant Rd.,* ☎ *520/323–7739. AE, D, DC, MC, V. No lunch weekends.*

$–$$ ★ ✕ **Feast.** Local celeb chef Doug Levy offers two menus here: food prepared to order (like grilled salmon with balsamic syrup and long-stemmed artichoke hearts) and a beautiful display case of take-out (which might include gingered carrot soup with coconut milk and lemongrass). Either menu can be enjoyed in the cozy restaurant with wine from an eclectic list, and each changes monthly. ✉ *4122 E. Speedway Blvd.,* ☎ *520/326–9363. AE, MC, V. Closed Sun.*

$–$$ ✕ **Pinnacle Peak Steakhouse.** No nouvelle-cuisine fans welcome here: it's a cowboy steak house all the way. Excellent mesquite-broiled steak comes with salad and pinto beans; for dessert, there's a heavenly hot apple cobbler. The restaurant is part of Trail Dust Town, a re-created turn-of-the-20th-century town where gunfights take place Tuesday through Saturday at 7 and 8 PM. ✉ *6541 E. Tanque Verde Rd.,* ☎ *520/296–0911. Reservations not accepted. AE, D, DC, MC, V. No lunch.*

Lodging

$$$$ ★ 🏨 **Canyon Ranch.** Since 1979, this health spa has drawn an international crowd of glitterati. Set on 70 acres in the desert foothills northeast of Tucson, the resort has a full-time staff of dieticians, exercise physiologists, and medical professionals who attend to body and soul. There's a four-night minimum stay. ✉ *8600 E. Rockcliff Rd., 85750,*

☎ *520/749–9000 or 800/742–9000,* FAX *520/749–1646,* WEB *www.canyonranch.com. 240 rooms. Restaurant, pool, tennis, health club. AE, D, MC, V. FAP.*

$$$$ ★ 🏨 **Sheraton Tucson El Conquistador.** In the rugged Santa Catalina Mountains, this golf and tennis resort has a truly southwestern feel. A mural in the cathedral-ceiling lobby illustrates cowboys and cacti; rooms, either in private casitas or the main hotel building, have balconies or patios, and some suites have kiva-shape fireplaces. ✉ *10000 N. Oracle Rd., 85737,* ☎ *520/544–5000 or 800/325–7832,* FAX *520/544–1224,* WEB *www.sheratonelconquistador.com. 385 rooms, 43 casitas. 4 restaurants, pools, golf, tennis, gym. AE, D, DC, MC, V.*

$$$$ 🏨 **Tanque Verde Ranch.** One of the oldest guest ranches in the country, Tanque Verde sits on more than 600 acres in the Rincon Mountains between Coronado National Forest and Saguaro National Park. Rooms are in the main ranch house or in private casitas; many have patios and fireplaces. ✉ *14301 E. Speedway Blvd., 85748,* ☎ *520/296–6275 or 800/234–3833,* FAX *520/721–9426,* WEB *www.tanqueverderanch.com. 72 rooms, 2 houses. Restaurant, pools, tennis, gym. AE, D, MC, V. FAP.*

$$$$ 🏨 **Westin La Paloma.** Vying with the Sheraton for convention business, this sprawling pink resort has top-notch golf, fitness, and beauty centers; there's also a huge pool with Tucson's only swim-up bar and Arizona's longest resort water slide. Child-care programs help parents relax. ✉ *3800 E. Sunrise Dr., 85718,* ☎ *520/742–6000,* FAX *520/577–5878,* WEB *www.westin.com. 487 rooms. 5 restaurants, pools, golf, tennis, gym. AE, D, DC, MC, V.*

$$$–$$$$ ★ 🏨 **Arizona Inn.** Though it's close to the university and downtown, this landmark 1930s-era inn is secluded on 14 acres of lushly landscaped grounds. The spacious rooms are spread out in pink stucco houses; all have patios and some have fireplaces. Groups can rent a guest house. ✉ *2200 E. Elm St., 85719,* ☎ *520/325–1541 or 800/933–1093,* FAX *520/881–5830,* WEB *www.arizonainn.com. 86 rooms, 3 houses. 2 restaurants, pool, tennis. AE, DC, MC, V.*

$$–$$$ 🏨 **Windmill Inn at St. Philip's Plaza.** In a shopping plaza, this modern inn has 122 suites with microwave, wet bar, two TVs, and three phones. Complimentary coffee, muffins, and a newspaper are delivered to your door. ✉ *4250 N. Campbell Ave., 85718,* ☎ *520/577–0007 or 800/547–4747,* FAX *520/577–0045,* WEB *www.windmillinns.com. 122 suites. Pool. AE, D, DC, MC, V. CP.*

$ 🏨 **Ghost Ranch Lodge.** The logo of this hotel was designed by Georgia O'Keeffe, a friend of the original owner. The units have Spanish-tile roofs and are spread over 8 acres amid an orange grove and garden with 400 types of cacti. The cottages are a bargain, with separate kitchens and carports. ✉ *801 W. Miracle Mile, 85705,* ☎ *520/791–7565 or 800/456–7565,* FAX *520/791–3898,* WEB *www.ghostranchlodge.com. 72 rooms, 11 cottages. Restaurant, pool. AE, D, DC, MC, V. CP.*

$ 🏨 **Hotel Congress.** This downtown hotel, built in 1919 in Art Deco style, has a convenient location, low rates, and a hip young crowd that frequents the popular Club Congress. Rooms have original iron beds. ✉ *311 E. Congress St., 85701,* ☎ *520/622–8848 or 800/722–8848,* FAX *520/792–6366,* WEB *www.hotcong.com. 40 rooms. Restaurant. AE, D, MC, V.*

Nightlife and the Arts

Nightlife

The **Cactus Moon Café** (✉ 5470 E. Broadway, ☎ 520/748–0049) offers an eclectic mix from Top 40 and hip-hop to country line dancing, often with free appetizer buffets during happy hour. **Club Congress** (✉

311 E. Congress St., ☎ 520/622–8848) is Tucson's best alternative-music venue.

The Arts

The **Arizona Opera Company** (☎ 520/293–4336, WEB www.azopera.com) puts on five major productions each year. The season of the **Arizona Theatre Company** (☎ 520/884–8210 company office; 520/622–2823 box office; WEB www.aztheatreco.org) runs from September through May.

The **Tucson Convention Center Music Hall** (✉ 260 S. Church St., ☎ 520/791–4266 box office, WEB www.ci.tucson.az.us/tcc) hosts both the Tucson Symphony Orchestra and the Arizona Opera Company. The **Tucson Symphony Orchestra** (☎ 520/882–8585 box office; 520/792–9155 main office; WEB www.tucsonsymphony.org) has been a part of Tucson's cultural scene since 1929.

Outdoor Activities and Sports

Golf

Tucson has five good municipal golf courses. Contact the **Tucson Parks and Recreation Department** (☎ 520/791–4873 general information; 520/791–4336 tee time reservations; WEB www.ci.tucson.az.us/parksandrec/golf.html) for information. Tucson has many fine resort courses. Get a free copy of *Arizona: The Golf State,* a free publication with information on the state's courses, from **Madden Publishing** (✉ Box 42915, Tucson 85733, ☎ 520/322–0895, WEB www.maddenpublishing.com). A complete list with links is on the company's Web site.

Hiking

For great hiking opportunities around Tucson, head for **Tucson Mountain Park, Mt. Lemmon, Sabino Canyon,** or **Kitt Peak.** A little-visited treasure, **Chiricahua National Monument,** about two hours east of Tucson off I–10, south of Bowie, has spectacular rugged rock vistas. Directly south of Tucson, the Huachuca Mountains, home of **Ramsey Canyon,** are a bird-watcher's paradise. The Santa Ritas, just south of Tucson, host another bird lover's haven, **Madera Canyon.** The Tucson chapter of the **Sierra Club** (☎ 520/620–6401) welcomes out-of-town visitors on its weekend hikes.

Horseback Riding

Tucson stables include **Pusch Ridge Stables** (✉ 13700 N. Oracle Rd., ☎ 520/825–1664). Many resorts and dude ranches have horseback riding.

Shopping

Old Town Artisans Complex (✉ 186 N. Meyer Ave., ☎ 520/623–6024) houses a variety of local arts and crafts. **Plaza Palomino** (✉ 2970 N. Swan, ☎ 520/795–1177), an outdoor mall, has restaurants, movies, and everyday shopping. **St. Philip's Plaza** (✉ 4380 N. Campbell Ave., ☎ 520/886–7485) arranges its chic shops around a series of Spanish-style outdoor patios.

Hard-core bargain hunters head for **Nogales,** the Mexican border town 63 mi south of Tucson on I–19.

Tucson Essentials

AIRPORTS AND TRANSFERS

Tucson International Airport, 8½ mi south of downtown, is served by 10 carriers, some of which serve Mexico as well as domestic destinations.

➤ AIRPORT INFORMATION: Tucson International Airport (☎ 520/573–8000, WEB www.tucsonairport.org).

BUS TRAVEL

➤ BUS INFORMATION: **Greyhound** (✉ 2 S. 4th Ave., ☎ 520/792–3475 or 800/231–2222).

CAR TRAVEL

From Phoenix, 111 mi to the northwest, or from the east, take I–10 to Tucson. From the south take I–19.

TRAIN TRAVEL

➤ TRAIN INFORMATION: **Amtrak** (✉ 400 E. Toole Ave., ☎ 520/623–4442 or 800/872–7245).

VISITOR INFORMATION

➤ TOURIST INFORMATION: **Metropolitan Tucson Convention and Visitors Bureau** (✉ 110 S. Church Ave., 85701, ☎ 520/624–1817 or 800/638–8350, WEB www.visittucson.org).

SOUTHERN ARIZONA

Southeastern Arizona is a relatively undiscovered treasure of mountains, deserts, canyons, and dusty little cowboy towns. Of particular interest are Bisbee and Tombstone, which recall Arizona during its Wild West heyday.

Exploring Southern Arizona

Tombstone

Born on the site of a wildly successful silver mine, this town 67 mi southeast of Tucson on U.S. 80 was headquarters of many of the West's rowdies in the late 1800s. The famous shoot-out at the OK Corral and other gunfights are replayed on Sunday on the town's main drag, **Allen Street.** As you enter Tombstone from the northwest, you'll pass **Boot Hill Graveyard** (✉ Hwy. 80), where the victims of the OK Corral shoot-out are buried. The **Tombstone Courthouse State Historic Park** (✉ Toughnut and 3rd Sts., ☎ 520/457–3311, WEB www.pr.state.az.us; 🎟 $2.50) has a reconstruction of the town's original 1882 courthouse, plus area artifacts and old photographs.

Bisbee

Once a mining boomtown, Bisbee, set on a mountainside 24 mi south of Tombstone, is now an artists' colony. Behind the Mining and Historical Museum is the venerable **Copper Queen Hotel** (✉ 11 Howell Ave., ☎ 520/432–2216; 🎟 free), home away from home to such guests as "Black Jack" Pershing, John Wayne, and Teddy Roosevelt. The **Copper Queen mine tour** (✉ 478 N. Dart Rd., ☎ 520/432–2071; 🎟 $10.75), led by retired miners, is an entertaining way to learn about the town's history. Arizona's largest pit mine yielded some 94 million tons of copper ore before mining activity halted in the early 1970s; at the **Lavender Pit Mine** (✉ U.S. 80) you can still see the huge crater left by the process. The **Mining and Historical Museum** (✉ 5 Copper Queen Plaza, ☎ 520/432–7071; 🎟 $4) is filled with old photos and artifacts from the town's heyday.

Dining and Lodging

Bisbee

$$ ★ ✕ **Café Roka.** One of the best bargains in southern Arizona, this chic northern Italian restaurant is in a historic building with exposed brick walls and an original 1906 tinwork ceiling. Generous portions of pasta are served with soup, salad, and sorbet. ✉ *35 Main St.,* ☎ *520/432–5153. MC, V. Closed Sun.–Tues. No lunch.*

$–$$ **Copper Queen Hotel.** This turn-of-the-20th-century hotel in the heart of downtown has thin walls but a lot of Victorian charm. The boom-days memorabilia throughout is fascinating. ✉ *11 Howell Ave. (Drawer CQ, 85603),* ☎ *520/432–2216 or 800/247–5829,* FAX *520/432–4298,* WEB *www.copperqueen.com. 47 rooms. Restaurant, pool. AE, D, DC, MC, V.*

Tombstone

$–$$ ✕ **Nellie Cashman's.** Named for the Tombstone pioneer who opened it in 1882, Nellie Cashman's is known for its juicy pork chops, chicken-fried steaks, and country breakfasts complete with biscuits and gravy. ✉ *5th and Toughnut Sts.,* ☎ *520/457–2212. AE, D, MC, V.*

$ **Tombstone Boarding House Bed & Breakfast.** Two meticulously restored 1880s adobes sit side by side in a quiet residential neighborhood. In one of the buildings, a dining room serves a limited but daily-changing menu. Typical selections are chicken breast in a sherry-mushroom sauce and beef Wellington. Next door, spotless rooms with hardwood floors contain period furnishings from surrounding Cochise County. ✉ *108 N. 4th St. (Box 906, 85638),* ☎ *520/457–3716 or 877/225–1313,* FAX *520/457–3038.* WEB *www.tombstoneboardinghouse.com. 8 rooms. Restaurant. AE, D, MC, V. BP.*

$ **Best Western Look-Out Lodge.** Western-print bedspreads and hewn-wood clocks give this motel off U.S. 80 a lot of character. Rooms have views of the Dragoon Mountains and desert valley and come with Continental breakfast. ✉ *U.S. 80 W (Box 787, 85638),* ☎ *520/457–2223 or 877/652–6772,* FAX *520/457–3870,* WEB *www.tombstone1880.com. 40 rooms. Pool. AE, D, DC, MC, V. CP.*

Southern Arizona Essentials

CAR TRAVEL

East of Tucson, U.S. 80 cuts south from I–10 to Tombstone and Bisbee.

VISITOR INFORMATION

➤ TOURIST INFORMATION: **Bisbee Chamber of Commerce** (✉ 31 Subway St. [Box BA, Bisbee 85603], ☎ 520/432–5421, FAX 520/432–3308, WEB www.bisbeearizona.com). **Tombstone Chamber of Commerce and Visitor Center** (✉ 4th and Allen Sts., Tombstone 85638, ☎ 520/457–3929 or 888/457–3929, WEB www.cityoftombstone.com).

ARKANSAS

By Ruth Mitchell

Capital	Little Rock
Population	2,673,4000
Motto	The Natural State
State Bird	Mockingbird
State Flower	Apple blossom
Postal Abbreviation	AR

Statewide Visitor Information

Arkansas Department of Parks and Tourism (✉ 1 Capitol Mall, Little Rock 72201, ☎ 501/682–7777 or 800/628–8725, WEB www.arkansas.com). There are 13 state tourist information centers on major highways near the state borders and one in Little Rock.

Scenic Drives

Arkansas's billing as the Natural State is appropriate: The state has more than 17 million acres of public and private forests, 600,000 acres of lakes, and 9,700 mi of rivers and streams. Its **Ozark** and **Ouachita mountains** rival New England for scenic vistas and fall colors seen along meandering roadways, including nine state and national scenic byways. **Route 7** between Arkadelphia and Harrison winds over both ranges and through two national forests. The **Talimena Scenic Byway** stretches across mountain crests from Mena to Talihina, Oklahoma, passing through **Queen Wilhelmina State Park.** The **St. Francis Scenic Byway**—part of the **Great River Road** that follows the Mississippi River—leads through wild terrain between Marianna and Helena/West Helena.

National and State Parks

Arkansas has 351 public and private campgrounds with some 9,800 campsites and has more than 300 trails stretching over 1,622 mi. The *Camper's and Hiker's Guide* and *Arkansas State Parks* booklet, both available from the state tourism department, provide locations, fees, and other useful information. Arkansas is prime territory for fly-fishing and warm-water angling. Contact the **Arkansas Game and Fish Commission** (☎ 501/223–6346 or 800/364–6300, WEB www.agfc.com).

National Parks

★ The **Buffalo National River** (✉ 402 N. Walnut St., Suite 136, Harrison 72601, ☎ 870/741–5443, WEB www.nps.gov/buff) became the first federally protected river in 1972. Its 132 mi of pristine waters are good for canoeing, white-water rafting, and fishing and wind through wilderness areas and historic sites. The **Ouachita National Forest** (✉ USFS, Box 1270, Hot Springs 71902, ☎ 501/321–5202, WEB www.fs.fed.us/oonf/ouachita), dotted by crystal lakes, is the oldest and largest in the South. The **Ozark National Forest** (✉ 605 W. Main St., Russellville 72801, ☎ 501/968–2354, WEB www.fs.fed.us/oonf/ozark) encompasses wild hills, hollows, rivers, and streams, as well as Arkansas's highest peak—the 2,753-ft Mt. Magazine. **Hot Springs National Park** (✉ Box 1860, Hot Springs 71902, ☎ 501/624–3383, WEB www.nps.gov/hosp) is centered on Bathhouse Row—eight turn-of-the-20th-century spa buildings—plus a campground and hiking trails in mountains and gorges surrounding the town. **Felsenthal National Wildlife Refuge** (✉ Box 1157, Crossett 71635, ☎ 870/364–3167, WEB felsenthal.fws.gov) is a mosaic of wetlands providing some of the best duck hunting in the world; it's also a habitat for endangered species like the red-cockaded woodpecker, American alligator, and bald eagle.

State Parks

Arkansas has 51 state parks, some with museums and monuments; 28 have campgrounds, and 21 have lodges or cabins. Contact the **Arkansas Department of Parks and Tourism** for more information (☎ 501/682–7777, WEB www.arkansasstateparks.com). **Devil's Den** (✉ 11333 W. Ark. 74, West Fork 72774, ☎ 501/761–3325) encompasses an Ozark valley full of caves, crevices, bluffs, and Civilian Conservation Corps structures from the 1930s. **Lake Chicot** (✉ 2542 Ark. 257, Lake Village 71653, ☎ 870/265–5480) sits on a 20-mi-long oxbow lake edged by cypress and noted for fishing and bird-watching. Volunteers participate in seasonal excavations in **Parkin Archaeological State Park** (✉ Box 1110, Parkin 72373-1110, ☎ 870/755–2500) to uncover the remains of a Native American village chronicled by Hernando de Soto's Spanish expedition of 1541. **Petit Jean** (✉ 1285 Petit Jean Mountain Rd., Morrilton 72110, ☎ 501/727–5441) is a scenic mountaintop with canyon trails, waterfalls, a lake, a lodge, and cabins, plus the Museum of Automobiles. **Village Creek** (✉ 201 CR 754, Wynne 72396, ☎ 870/238–9406) lies atop Crowley's Ridge, an unusual forested highland that slices through the Mississippi Delta.

LITTLE ROCK

Little Rock, on the south bank of the Arkansas River, is Arkansas's geographical, governmental, and financial center. As the state capital, it's where you'll find the Arkansas State Capitol building, a scaled replica of the Nation's Capitol building. The city gets its name from French explorers who identified a river landmark as "La Petite Roche." In 1821 Little Rock became the territorial capital, when settlers found it more suitable and centrally located than Arkansas Post, which was the first European settlement in the lower Mississippi Valley. Little Rock also lies at the point where the Mississippi Delta gives way to the Ouachita Mountain foothills. Today, this vibrant city of just under 200,000 is the largest city in the state. Some of the best duck hunting in the world is just an hour's journey to the east, in the rich rice-growing region of the Delta. To the north and west are forested mountains, streams, and scenic trails.

Exploring Little Rock

A series of free walking-driving tours lead through several historic areas in and near downtown. The **MacArthur Park Historic District** has several examples of antebellum architecture, as well as some fine Victorian buildings. A highlight is the 1843 Trapnall Hall (✉ 423 E. Capitol Ave.). The birthplace of General Douglas MacArthur, in the eponymous park, is part of an 1838 arsenal. The **Arkansas Arts Center** (✉ 9th and Commerce Sts., ☎ 501/372–4000, WEB www.arkarts.com; 🎟 free), which was remodeled in 2001, has revolving exhibits plus an outstanding permanent collection, an above-average children's theater program, a museum school, a gift shop, and an excellent restaurant. Changing crafts and furniture exhibits are at the Decorative Arts Museum (✉ 7th and Rock Sts., ☎ 501/396–0357; 🎟 free), in an 1840 mansion.

The area surrounding the **governor's mansion** (✉ 1800 Center St., ☎ 501/324–9805; 🎟 free) encompasses elegant post–Civil War and turn-of-the-20th-century churches and homes; tours of the mansion are by appointment. The 1881 Italianate **Villa Marre,** whose facade was featured in the TV series *Designing Women,* is now open by appointment to the public, complete with period furnishings. ✉ *1321 S. Scott St.,* ☎ *501/371–0075.* 🎫 *$3. Closed Sat.*

You can tour the **Empress of Little Rock** (✉ 2120 S. Louisiana, ☎ 501/374–7966, WEB www.theempress.com; 🎫 $5), a beautifully restored 1888 Gothic Queen Anne house that is described in the National Register of Historic Places as the best example of ornate Victorian architecture in Arkansas. Tours are offered Monday–Thursday at 11:30 and 3.

★ Historic public buildings in the riverfront district include the **Old State House** (✉ 300 W. Markham St., ☎ 501/324–9685; 🎫 free), built between 1833 and 1842 and recently restored as a museum devoted to Arkansas history. Bill Clinton used this building as his backdrop for victory speeches on gubernatorial election nights. The six galleries of the **Historic Arkansas Museum** (✉ 200 E. 3rd St., ☎ 501/324–9351; 🎫 $2.50) include a contemporary art gallery, restored and furnished frontier buildings with living-history tours, hands-on children's exhibit, local crafts, and one of the best knife exhibits in the United States.

The neoclassical **state capitol** (✉ Capitol Ave. and Woodlane, ☎ 501/682–5080; 🎫 free), built between 1899 and 1915 on a hilltop west of downtown, has an imposing rotunda, grand marble staircases and columns, stained-glass skylights, murals, and six intricately crafted 4-inch-thick brass doors from Tiffany & Co. It's a good idea to phone ahead to make a tour reservation.

The **Central High School Museum Visitor Center** (✉ 2125 W. 14th St., Suite 200, ☎ 501/374–1957, WEB home.swbell.net/chmuseum; 🎫 free), a National Historic Site, has exhibits and audiovisual programs commemorating the school's integration in 1957, when nine black students were enrolled under the protection of federal troops. In historic Union Train Station, the interactive **Children's Museum of Arkansas** (✉ 1400 W. Markham St., ☎ 501/374–6655, WEB www.cmuseum.org; 🎫 $4) lets kids make stationery in the post office, shop at the farmers' market, or contribute to the Kids Gallery of collectibles.

The **Aerospace Education Center** (✉ 3301 E. Roosevelt Rd., ☎ 501/376–4629, WEB www.aerospaced.org) has an IMAX theater (🎫 $6.75), a small free museum, and a library, which houses the Jay Miller Aviation History Collection, one of the world's most significant aviation and aerospace reference libraries. The **Arkansas Museum of Discovery** (✉ 500 E. Markham St., ☎ 501/396–7050 or 800/880–6475, WEB www.amod.org; 🎫 $5.95), a large, bright hands-on museum, explores science and culture with exhibits to interest all ages.

Outside Little Rock

Just 15 mi west of downtown is **Pinnacle Mountain State Park** (✉ 11901 Pinnacle Valley Rd., Roland, ☎ 501/868–5806; 🎫 free), an educational park for day use with habitats ranging from high peaks to river bottomlands lined with hardwoods and ancient cypress.

Less than 30 minutes east of downtown on U.S. 165 is the state park–operated **Plantation Agriculture Museum,** which has displays on the history of cotton agriculture. ✉ *4815 Hwy. 161, Scott,* ☎ *501/961-1409.* 🎫 *Free. Closed Mon. except Mon. holidays.*

Several miles beyond Scott off U.S. 165 sits **Toltec Mounds Archaeological State Park,** the remains of a large Native American ceremonial and governmental complex inhabited from AD 600 to AD 950. ✉ *49[illegible] Toltec Mounds Rd., Scott,* ☎ *501/961–9442.* 🎫 *$2.25. Closed Mon*

Parks, Gardens, and Zoos

War Memorial Park (✉ north off I–630 at Fair Park Ave. and W. Markham St., ☎ 501/371–4770), one of Little Rock's oldest and most popular parks, contains a public golf course, tennis courts, a football stadium, and the baseball park of the minor-league Arkansas Travelers. It also has a fitness center (open to the public) and a zoo.

Riverfront Park edges both sides of the Arkansas River. On the Little Rock side it lies behind the Old State House and Convention Center, with playgrounds, a history pavilion, and an amphitheater. The site of the future **Bill Clinton Presidential Library** is east of I–30 adjacent to the park. In North Little Rock, across the river from Riverfront Park, the **ALLTEL Arena** (✉ 1 ALLTEL Arena Way, North Little Rock, ☎ 501/340–5660, WEB www.alltelarena.com) is an 18,000-capacity arena, home of the River Blades minor-league hockey team and the Arkansas Twisters, an indoor football team, as well as the site of many other sports and entertainment events. The **Little Rock Zoo** (✉ 1 Jonesboro Dr., ☎ 501/663–4733, WEB www.littlerockzoo.com; $5) has gorillas, a big cat exhibit, a rare black rhino, a red panda exhibit, giant anteaters, and many other species.

Dining and Lodging

Note: Some of the counties outside the city are dry, which means you won't be able to buy alcohol.

$$$–$$$$ ★ ✕ **Alouette's.** Enjoy fine French cuisine in a formal setting. Seasonal menus might include fillet of tilapia Provençale with artichoke hearts, tomatoes, olives, peppers, onions, and capers in a lemon and wine sauce. The lobster bisque and made-to-order soufflés are unforgettable. Wine connoisseurs will not be disappointed. ✉ *11401 N. Rodney Parham Rd.,* ☎ *501/225–4152,* WEB *www.alouettes.com. AE, D, DC, MC, V. Closed Sun.–Mon.*

$$–$$$ ✕ **Vermillion Bistro.** From entrées like truffled pork tenderloin Napoleon to honey chipotle roasted quail, the fine cuisine is presented with flair in a very attractive dining room complete with a trendy exhibition kitchen and colorful artworks on the walls. ✉ *17200 Chenal Pkwy., Suite 100,* ☎ *501/448–7400. AE, D, DC, MC, V. Closed Sun.*

$–$$ ✕ **Trio's.** Artful cuisine with a global perspective is served up by pleasant, professional staff in a stylish, smoke-free dining room with bright artwork. Choose from selections like lamb chops Athena (buttery tender and stuffed with feta cheese and fresh basil in a pomegranate demiglace) or Chilean sea bass encrusted in macadamia nuts. Desserts such as the raspberry pie are sumptuous. A full espresso bar and extensive wine selection complete the mix. ✉ *8201 Cantrell Rd.,* ☎ *501/221–3330. AE, D, DC, MC, V. Closed Sun.*

$–$$ ✕ **Whole Hog Cafe.** One of the best barbecue joints in the South is run by three men who love to compete in barbecue competitions—the restaurant is decorated with their trophies—and who settled down in this strip mall to serve up their delicious ribs and pulled pork. ✉ *2516 Cantrell Rd.,* ☎ *501/664–5025. AE, D, DC, MC, V. Closed Sun.*

$$–$$$$ **Capital Hotel.** This 1872 National Historic Landmark gem is in the heart of the business district. A beautiful lobby has mosaic floors, a lead-glass skylight, and handsome columns. Let the staff pamper you. For fine dining, Ashley's at the Capital has fine food and a nationally acclaimed wine list. Or enjoy a casual lunch in the Capital Bar & Grill. ✉ *Markham and Louisiana Sts., 72201,* ☎ *501/374–7474 or 800/766–7666,* FAX *501/370–7091,* WEB *www.thecapitalhotel.com. 126 rooms. 2 restaurants. AE, D, DC, MC, V. BP.*

$$–$$$$ **Peabody Little Rock.** This hotel—formerly the Excelsior, renovated and redecorated in 2001—is on the banks of the Arkansas River and atop the Statehouse Convention Center. The daily duck parade of live mallards through the lobby is part of the charm. The Capriccio restaurant presents northern Italian cuisine for breakfast, lunch, and dinner. ⊠ *3 Statehouse Plaza, 72201,* ☎ *501/375–5000 or 800/527–1745,* FAX *501/375–4721,* WEB *www.peabodylittlerock.com. 440 rooms. Restaurant, gym. AE, D, DC, MC, V.*

$$–$$$$ **Embassy Suites.** This all-suite hotel lies in West Little Rock, 10 to 15 minutes from downtown. The two-room suites have sofa beds and kitchenettes. ⊠ *11301 Financial Centre Pkwy., 72211,* ☎ *501/312–9000,* FAX *501/312–9455,* WEB *www.embassy-suites.com. 251 suites. Restaurant, pool, gym. AE, D, DC, MC, V. BP.*

$–$$ **Holiday Inn–Select.** This West Little Rock hotel is convenient to downtown as well as nearby restaurants and businesses. Business facilities and an airport shuttle are provided. ⊠ *201 S. Shackleford Rd., 72211,* ☎ *501/223–3000,* FAX *501/223–2833,* WEB *www.holiday-inn.com. 269 rooms. 2 restaurants, pool, gym. AE, D, DC, MC, V.*

Motels

Hampton Inn North Little Rock–McCain Mall (⊠ 4801 W. Commercial Dr., North Little Rock 72116, ☎ 501/753–8660, FAX 501/753–3433, WEB www.hamptoninn.com), 62 rooms; gym, pool; CP; *$*. **Springhill Suites by Marriott** (⊠ 306 Markham Centre Dr., 72205, ☎ 501/978–6000 or 888/287–9400, FAX 501/978–6000, WEB www.springhillsuites.com), 78 rooms; pool, gym; CP; *$*.

Nightlife and the Arts

The "Weekend" section of Friday's *Arkansas Democrat-Gazette* and the weekly *Arkansas Times* list nightlife and arts events. You can call a recorded "What's Happening" line (☎ 501/372–3399).

Nightlife

After Thought (⊠ 2721 Kavanaugh Blvd., ☎ 501/663–1196) has live music nightly, with Jazz & Heritage Foundation performances on Monday night. **Cajuns Wharf** (⊠ 2400 Cantrell Rd., ☎ 501/375–5351) is back. After closing for a few years, this seminal nightspot has new ownership, fantastic cuisine, and all ages coming out to enjoy live blues, rock and oldies nightly. **Juanita's Cantina** (⊠ 1300 S. Main St., ☎ 501/372–1228) serves up Mexican fare daily along with an eclectic mix of evening entertainment—rock, blues, reggae, and other touring groups Tuesday to Saturday nights. A microbrewery serving good pizza too, **Vino's** (⊠ 923 W. 7th St., ☎ 501/375–8466) dishes up avant-garde Red Octopus theater productions and is the home of the Little Rock Folk Club. Poetry readings are on the first Thursday of every month.

The Performing Arts

The **Robinson Center** (⊠ Markham St. and Broadway, ☎ 501/376–1500) is the city's major venue for the performing arts. The **Arkansas Repertory Theater** (⊠ 601 Main St., ☎ 501/378–0405, WEB www.therep.org) stages popular and avant-garde works. The **Arkansas Symphony Orchestra** (☎ 501/666–1761), at various locations, performs both classical and pop concerts. **Celebrity Attractions** (☎ 501/224–8800, WEB www.celebrityattractions.com) brings in national touring companies of Broadway shows. At **Murry's Dinner Playhouse** (⊠ 6323 Asher Ave., ☎ 501/562–3131) a buffet accompanies Broadway comedies and musicals or solo performances. The **UALR Fine Arts Galleries & Theatre** (⊠ 2801 S. University Ave., ☎ 501/569–3291 for theater; 501/569–3183 for galleries) sponsors concerts and theater as well as art exhibits. For theater with a conscience, the **Weekend Theatre–Off Broadway** (⊠

1001 W. 7th St., ☎ 501/374–3761, WEB www.weekendtheater.org) offers Broadway and off-Broadway musicals, comedy, and drama in a small, intimate space. **Wildwood Park for the Performing Arts** (✉ 20919 Denny Rd., ☎ 501/821–7275, WEB www.wildwoodpark.org) offers opera, jazz, cabaret, chamber music, and festivals.

Outdoor Activities

For a cooling experience bring your bathing suit and enjoy a plethora of water activities at **Wild River Country,** the state's largest water park. Enjoy the rush of the Accelerator, the Pipeline, the Lily Pad Walk, or the Tidal Wave. ✉ *Crystal Hill exit off I-40, North Little Rock,* ☎ *501/753–8600,* WEB *www.wildrivercountry.com.* *$21.99. Closed Labor Day–Memorial Day.*

Shopping

Major department stores are at **Park Plaza** and **University Mall,** on either side of Markham Street at University Avenue in Little Rock, and at **McCain Mall** at Arkansas 67/U.S. 167 and McCain Boulevard in North Little Rock. Galleries, specialty shops, and boutiques lie along winding **Kavanaugh Boulevard** and **Rodney Parham Road.** A growing shopping area has developed in and around **West Little Rock,** particularly along **Bowman and Kanis roads** out into **Chenal Parkway.** In a restored warehouse alongside Riverfront Park, the **River Market** (✉ 400 E. Markham St., ☎ 501/375–2552) has blossomed into a lively center of gourmet shops, boutiques, cafés, and ethnic-food stalls, with an outdoor farmers' market spring through late fall. It has become the anchor for a revitalized neighborhood that now has the Museum of Discovery, galleries, restaurants, and year-round special events.

Little Rock Essentials

AIRPORTS AND TRANSFERS

American, ComAir, Continental, Delta, Northwest, Southwest, and US Airways fly into Little Rock National Airport, 5 mi east of downtown off I–440. Most major Little Rock hotels provide airport shuttles. Cab fare to downtown is about $17. The Greater Little Rock Transportation company operates black-and-white and yellow cabs.

➤ AIRPORT AND TRANSFER INFORMATION: **Greater Little Rock Transportation** (☎ 501/374–0333 or 501/568–0462). **Little Rock National Airport** (✉ 1 Airport Dr., ☎ 501/372–3439).

BUS TRAVEL WITHIN LITTLE ROCK

Central Arkansas Transit serves Little Rock and North Little Rock.

➤ BUS INFORMATION: **Central Arkansas Transit** (☎ 501/375–1163).

CAR TRAVEL

I–40 and I–30 lead to Little Rock, as do U.S. 65 and U.S. 67. Little Rock is easily negotiated by interstate highways and major streets. There are plenty of parking facilities and taxis.

VISITOR INFORMATION

➤ TOURIST INFORMATION: **Little Rock Convention & Visitors Bureau** (✉ Box 3232, Little Rock 72203, ☎ 501/376–4781 or 800/844–4781, WEB www.littlerock.com).

THE ARKANSAS OZARKS

The forested mountains and hollows, sparkling waters, and calcite caverns of the Arkansas highlands provide a breathtaking backdrop for gatherings of self-taught folk musicians in town squares, for the display of handicrafts from pioneer days, and for tiny towns barely changed in the last century. Yet the Ozarks also encompass upscale shopping malls, fine-arts centers, and sophisticated restaurants. The area's rivers offer superb fishing and canoeing, the lakes boating and water sports. Networks of trails lace the mountains, from easygoing, accessible paths to the rugged, 178-mi-long Ozark Highlands trail. Dozens of scenic byways lead past exquisite vistas. Civil War battlefields at Pea Ridge and Prairie Grove, ecotours exploring natural and human history, railway excursions, antiques, outdoor theater, great golfing, and lively festivals and fairs round out the appeal of this scenic playground.

Exploring the Arkansas Ozarks

Fayetteville, Springdale, Rogers, and Bentonville—together Arkansas's fastest-growing metropolitan area—offer walking-driving tours of each of their fascinating historic districts.

The **Headquarters House** (✉ 118 E. Dickson St., ☎ 479/521–2970; 🎫 $3) served as both Union and Confederate headquarters during the Civil War. Living-history tours of the house and the historic district are by appointment only.

The **Peel Mansion Museum & Gardens** belonged to a pioneer businessman and U.S. Congressman. Its shop is in a restored log cabin. ✉ *400 S. Walton Blvd., Bentonville,* ☎ *479/273–9664,* WEB *www.peelmansion.org.* 🎫 *$3. Closed Sun.–Mon.* The **Rogers Historical Museum** is in the 1895 Hawkins House. ✉ *322 S. 2nd St., Rogers,* ☎ *479/621–1154,* ★ WEB *www.rogersarkansas.com/museum.* 🎫 *Free. Closed Sun.* The **Shiloh Museum of Ozark History** contains the Howard collection of Native American artifacts and a photographic archive of the area with more than 120,000 images. ✉ *118 W. Johnson Ave., Springdale,* ☎ *479/750–8165,* WEB *www.springdaleark.org/shiloh.* 🎫 *Free. Closed Sun.*

The **Pea Ridge National Military Park** (✉ U.S. 62, ☎ 479/451–8122, WEB www.nps.gov; 🎫 $2), 10 mi northeast of Rogers, is composed of 4,300 acres in and around the site of the Battle of Pea Ridge, the first major Civil War encounter in Arkansas. **Prairie Grove Battlefield Park** (✉ U.S. 62, ☎ 479/846–2990, WEB www.nps.gov; 🎫 $2.25; museum and interpreter-led tour $4), 10 mi southwest of Fayetteville, commemorates the last Civil War battle in northwest Arkansas. The **University of Arkansas** (✉ Fayetteville, ☎ 479/575–2000), home of the hallowed Razorback teams, has museums and a lively arts calendar. Former president Bill Clinton and Hillary Rodham Clinton taught law here. Vintage railroad cars on the **Arkansas and Missouri Railroad** make daylong round-trips through the Ozarks to Van Buren and two-hour excursions from Van Buren. ✉ *306 E. Emma St., Springdale,* ☎ *479/751–8600 or 800/687–8600,* WEB *www.arkansasmissouri-rr.com.* 🎫 *$20–$48. Closed Nov.–Mar.*

★ The **Ozark Folk Center** (✉ Mountain View, ☎ 870/269–3851, WEB arkansasstateparks.com; 🎫 $8–$13.50) is a unique state park devoted to the perpetuation and lively demonstration of traditional Ozark Mountain crafts, acoustic music, and dance. The park has a lodge, a gift shop, and the Iron Skillet Restaurant. In **Mountain View,** the music continues in informal sessions on the courthouse square, surrounded by crafts, antiques, and other shops in old stone buildings.

★ The U.S. Forest Service leads year-round tours of **Blanchard Springs Caverns,** 15 mi northwest of Mountain View, providing the state's premier underground experience. ✉ *AK 14,* ☎ *870/757–2211.* 🎫 *$9. Closed Mon.–Tues. winter months.*

Eureka Springs is a bed-and-breakfast center with more than 125 B&Bs and is considered one of the best-preserved communities in the United States. Nestled in the Ozark Mountains with scenic rivers, beautiful lakes, and camping nearby, Eureka Springs also has some 100 specialty shops including fine-arts and crafts galleries in a delightful downtown. In the tradition of the origination of the town, spas are plentiful for relaxation. The town and its many attractions host a packed schedule of music and crafts festivals year-round. A system of easily accessible trolley buses is available for transport, but six scenic walking tours you can follow with a brochure will get you a more thorough view of this unique destination.

The stunning **Thorncrown Chapel** (✉ U.S. 62 W, ☎ 479/253–7401, WEB www.thorncrown.com; 🎟 free), designed by architect E. Fay Jones, was honored as fourth on the AIA's list of top buildings for the 20th century. It is the site of many weddings due to its natural beauty and the surrounding woodlands. **Turpentine Creek** (✉ Hwy. 23, ☎ 479/253–5841, WEB www.turpentinecreek.org; 🎟 $10), 7 mi south of Eureka Springs, is one of the very few USDA-licensed refuges for large carnivores. Several hundred rescued lions, tigers, and other exotic animals can be seen up close in a natural setting.

The 33-acre **Eureka Springs Gardens** has the spectacular "Blue Spring" at its center as well as many beautiful species of plants. *✉ U.S. 62 W, ☎ 479/253–9256, WEB www.eurekagardens.com. 🎟 $6.45. Closed Dec.–Feb.* The ***Belle of the Ozarks*** makes 12-mi trips along the beautiful Beaver Lake shoreline. *✉ Starkey Marina, off U.S. 62 W, ☎ 479/253–6200 or 800/552–3803. 🎟 $14. Closed Nov.–Feb.* Enjoy the excitement and nostalgia of the vintage steam locomotives of the **Eureka Springs & North Arkansas Railway** that chug into the Ozarks from a historic depot. Some trips allow you to dine in an antique dining car. *✉ 299 N. Main St., ☎ 479/253–9623, WEB www.esnarailway.com. 🎟 $9. Closed Nov.–Feb. and most Suns.*

Dining and Lodging

Eureka Springs

$$–$$$$ ★ ✕ **Chez Charles.** This fine-dining spot in the Grand Hotel presents American staples with high style, using imaginative spices and sauces. The luncheon menu is à la carte. Dinner is a five-course menu that changes monthly. Dinner seatings are at 6 and 9 PM, 6 PM only December–March. *✉ 37 N. Main St., Eureka Springs, ☎ 479/253–9509 or 888/253–1003. Reservations essential. AE, D, MC, V. Closed Tues.– Wed. Apr.–Dec., Mon.–Wed. Jan.–Mar.*

$$ ✕ **Ermilio's.** This cozy spot, popular with locals and visitors alike, serves sumptuous Italian favorites created with pungent spices, fresh ingredients, and plenty of cheese that will sate the heartiest appetite. There's easy, free parking. *✉ 26 White St., ☎ 479/253–8806. Reservations not accepted. MC, V. Closed Thurs. No lunch Sun.–Wed.*

$–$$ ✕ **Forest Hill.** Up the hill from the historic district, this casual restaurant can handle crowds with a buffet for breakfast, lunch, or dinner. The menu has custom omelets, steaks, and seafood as well as a large selection of wood-fired pizzas. *✉ Hwy 62 E, ☎ 479/253–2422. Reservations not accepted. MC, V.*

$–$$ ✕ **Local Flavor.** In the heart of town, this bright, friendly restaurant has reasonably priced yet delicious and inventive fare. The Sunday brunch is outstanding. Try the stuffed French toast or eggs Benedict; be sure to indulge in the bacon. The dinner menu includes pan-seared tilapia, grilled salmon with a raspberry barbecue sauce, and tortellini. *✉ 71 S. Main, ☎ 479/253–9522. MC, V.*

$$–$$$ **All Seasons Inn.** This cozy Victorian B&B in the heart of the historic district has plenty of free parking. The suites have king and queen beds and minikitchens. Each suite opens out to the veranda where you can enjoy the breeze from the comfort of a wicker chair. ✉ *156 Spring St., 72632,* ☎ *479/253–2001,* WEB *www.estc.net/allseasonsinn. 10 suites. D, MC, V. BP.*

$$–$$$ **Palace Hotel & Bath House.** Built in 1901, this elegant little hotel has suites for two with all the comforts of home, including well-stocked refrigerators, whirlpool tubs, antique furnishings, and a luscious Continental breakfast brought to your room each morning. The bathhouse offers mineral baths, eucalyptus steam, massages, and facial mask treatments. ✉ *135 Spring St., 72632,* ☎ *479/253–7474,* WEB *www.palacehotelbathhouse.com. 8 suites. D, MC, V. CP.*

$$–$$$ ✕ **Rogue's Manor.** Suites based on the art of Maxfield Parrish are loaded with amenities such as spacious beds, luxury linens, spa tubs, and sound systems. The well-appointed restaurant serves fine cuisine that has been featured in food magazines. Try the potted Montrachet for a starter, a dreamy, creamy goat cheese mixed with sun-dried tomatoes, artichoke hearts, and herbs. The curried seafood chowder with a creamy tomato base is a specialty of the house. The prime rib is also good. ✉ *124 Spring St., 72632,* ☎ *479/253–4911 or 800/250–5827,* WEB *www.roguesmanor.com. 4 suites. Restaurant. MC, V. Restaurant closed Mon.–Tues.*

$–$$$ ✕ **Crescent Hotel.** To stay at the Crescent Hotel is to experience some of the history of this Victorian village. Renovations have kept this grande dame in shape while not altering its historical nature. The location high atop a mountain affords spectacular views. Ride a horse-drawn carriage into town, or spend the afternoon in the New Moon Spa. The restaurant has a young and resourceful chef. If you don't stay here, be sure to have at least one meal in the large Crystal Dining Room. ✉ *75 Prospect, 72632,* ☎ *800/342–9760,* FAX *479/253–5296,* WEB *www.crescent-hotel.com. 68 rooms. Restaurant. AE, DC, MC, V.*

Fayetteville

$$ ✕ **Ozark Brewing Co.** In the heart of the activity on Dickson Street, this attractive microbrewery, in a beautifully restored historic building, offers a lively menu and more than a dozen beers brewed on the premises. Order up the pecan-crusted pork loin with apple brandy cream sauce and pair it with a Friesian Black lager. ✉ *430 W. Dickson St.,* ☎ *479/521–2739. AE, D, MC, V.*

$–$$ ✕ **Uncle Gaylord's.** This cozy restaurant, just off the square, offers breakfast and lunch every day and an outstanding dinner menu most nights. The scrumptious Sicilian shrimp is sautéed in olive oil with basil, artichoke hearts, olives, and crushed chilies and served on angel hair pasta. Or try the salmon fillet with Gorgonzola cream sauce, rice, and fresh vegetables. ✉ *315 Mountain St.,* ☎ *479/444–0605. AE, D, MC, V. No dinner Sun.–Mon.*

$–$$$ **Radisson Hotel Fayetteville.** Under new ownership since 2001, this is the former Hilton, just off the square, with a face-lift. Keep your car parked in the garage and enjoy. ✉ *70 N. East St., 72701,* ☎ *479/442–5555 or 800/333–3333,* FAX *479/442–2105,* WEB *www.radisson.com. 235 rooms. Restaurant, pool, gym. AE, D, DC, MC, V.*

$–$$ **Fayetteville Clarion.** Remodeled in 2000, this standard-fare hotel is near the University of Arkansas and historic districts. ✉ *1255 S. Shiloh Dr., 72701,* ☎ *479/521–1166 or 800/223–7275,* FAX *501/521–1204. 197 rooms. Restaurant, pool, gym. AE, D, DC, MC, V.*

Johnson

$$$–$$$$ ★ ✕ **James at the Mill.** This restaurant is a feast for the eyes as well as the palate. The inventive menu serves up Ozark Plateau cuisine. Traditional southern dishes divinely reinvented include game, dry-aged rib-

eye steaks, and fresh local produce. ✉ *3906 Greathouse Springs Rd., Johnson,* ☎ *479/443–1400,* FAX *479/575–0295. AE, D, DC, MC, V. Closed Sun. No lunch Sat.*

$–$$$ **Inn at the Mill.** Adjacent to James at the Mill, this comfortable, stylish country inn, built around a restored 1835 mill and pond, is convenient to all points in northwest Arkansas. Enjoy sumptuous baked goods for breakfast as part of the package. ✉ *3906 Greathouse Springs Rd., Johnson 72741,* ☎ *479/443–1800,* WEB *www.innatthemill.com. 48 rooms. Gym. AE, D, DC, MC, V. CP.*

Lakeview

$$–$$$ ★ ✕ **Gaston's White River Resort.** This lodge draws serious anglers and families with cottages, a marina, fishing guides, an outstanding restaurant serving steak and seafood, and lovely scenery. ✉ *1777 River Rd., Lakeview 72642,* ☎ *870/431–5202,* FAX *870/431–5216,* WEB *www.gastons.com. 79 cottages. Restaurant, pool, tennis. MC, V.*

Rogers

$ ✕ **The Market at Pinnacle Point.** This is the perfect place for people who like to sample lots of different tastes from around the world. You can dine inside or out, and it's also a marketplace, so you can buy delicacies to take back to your hotel. Order a coffee from the espresso bar or sample something from the bakery. ✉ *5415 Pinnacle Point Dr.,* ☎ *479/464–8615. AE, D, DC, MC, V.*

Silver Hill

$–$$$ **Buffalo River Outfitters.** Ten log cabins above the Buffalo National River have full kitchens, fireplaces, and barbecue grills. The extensive nearby possibilities for outdoor activities include hiking trails, canoe and raft floats, kayaking, fishing, hunting, mountain biking, and horseback riding. ✉ *U.S. 65 at Silver Hill, St. Joe (Rte. 1, Box 56, 72675),* ☎ *479/439–2244 or 800/582–2244,* FAX *870/439–2211,* WEB *www.buffalorivercabins.com. 10 cabins. D, MC, V.*

Springdale

$$–$$$$ **Holiday Inn Northwest Arkansas.** Convenient to interstates, this hotel has an eight-story atrium and five-story waterfall along with a sports bar and grill. ✉ *1500 S. 48th St., Springdale 72762,* ☎ *479/751–8300,* FAX *479/751–4640,* WEB *www.holiday-inn.com. 206 rooms. Restaurant, pool, golf privileges, gym. AE, D, DC, MC, V.*

Nightlife and the Arts

Friday's "Northwest Arkansas Weekend" section in the *Arkansas Democrat-Gazette* lists nightlife and arts events. Northwest Arkansas's major club and café scene is along Fayetteville's **Dickson Street.** There is a lively representation of national-caliber bands who stop over in this college town to perform.

The **Arts Center of the Ozarks** (✉ 214 S. Main St., Springdale, ☎ 479/751–5441) has an active schedule of visual and performing arts. The **Walton Arts Center** (✉ 495 Dickson St., Fayetteville, ☎ 479/443–5600, WEB www.waltonartscenter.org) presents fine- and performing-arts events atypical of what you would expect in a small town, including such notable entertainers as Bill Cosby.

The Arkansas Ozarks Essentials

AIRPORTS

American Eagle, Atlantic Southeast Airline, Northwest Airlink, and US Airways Express all have scheduled flights into Northwest Arkansas Airport (XNA), west of U.S. 71 Bypass and Bentonville.

➤ AIRPORT INFORMATION: **Northwest Arkansas Airport** (✉ 1 Airport Blvd., Bentonville, ☎ 479/205–1000, WEB www.nwara.com).

CAR TRAVEL

To reach northwest Arkansas from Little Rock, take I–40 west, and then turn north on I–540. The fastest route to other parts of the Ozarks from Little Rock is U.S. 65 north from I–40 at Conway and then the appropriate highway to your destination. At Harrison, U.S. 62 leads from U.S. 65 to Eureka Springs, Pea Ridge National Military Park, and U.S. 71 at Rogers.

VISITOR INFORMATION

Ozark Gateway Tourist Council handles the eastern Ozarks. Ozark Mountain Region covers the central Ozarks.

➤ TOURIST INFORMATION: **Eureka Springs Visitor Bureau** (✉ Box 522, Eureka Springs 72632, ☎ 479/253–7333, WEB www.eurekasprings.org). **Northwest Arkansas Tourism Association** (✉ Box 5176, Bella Vista 72714, ☎ 888/398–3444, WEB www.nwatourism.org). **Ozark Gateway Tourist Council** (✉ Box 4049, Batesville 72503, ☎ 870/793–9316 or 800/264–0316, WEB www.ozarkgateway.com). **Ozark Mountain Region** (✉ Box 137, Yellville 72687, ☎ 800/544–6867, WEB www.ozarkmountainregion.com).

WESTERN ARKANSAS

Western Arkansas reaches south from Fort Smith and Van Buren—which preserve the region's wild and woolly frontier heritage as well as its Victorian era—through the ancient forests and rivers of the Ouachita (pronounced *wash*-i-taw) Mountains. The quartz-rich mountains cradle Hot Springs (nicknamed Spa City), the boyhood home of former president Bill Clinton. The five crystal-clear Diamond Lakes also lure vacationers who love water and beautiful scenery. The region's rivers offer white-water rafting trips and scenic canoeing and fishing, and the Ouachitas are laced with top-notch trail systems and campsites.

Exploring Western Arkansas

When Spanish explorer Hernando de Soto came upon the "Valley of the Vapors" in 1541, he learned of the healing properties of the thermal springs from Native Americans, who revered the valley known today as **Hot Springs.** Even warring tribes would lay down their arms to bathe peacefully in the pure water that comes bubbling up out of fissures on a route that takes more than 4,000 years. In 1832, U.S. Congress created the first federal reservation around the 47 springs, and in 1921 the area became a national park. President Harry S. Truman was known to enjoy reading the newspaper on the front porch of the landmark Arlington Hotel. From the 1920s to the early 1960s, the town of Hot Springs became a gathering spot for the elite as well as for infamous gangsters like Al Capone, who were drawn by two disparate elements: gambling and the therapeutic waters.

Today, Hot Springs offers a host of activities and events, including a wax museum; country-music, magic, and comedy shows; a Christian musical drama; and land-and-lake tours on amphibious World War II "ducks." The downtown historic district is filled with shops and galleries and has become home in recent years to a vibrant art community.

The 400-passenger ***Belle of Hot Springs*** (✉ 5200 Central Ave./Ark. 7 S, ☎ 501/525–4438, WEB www.belleriverboat.com; 🎫 excursion $9.99, $20.99–$27.99 for dinner cruise) sails Lake Hamilton daily on sightseeing, lunch, and dinner-dance cruises. Only a handful of spas providing min-

Hot Springs and the Ozarks

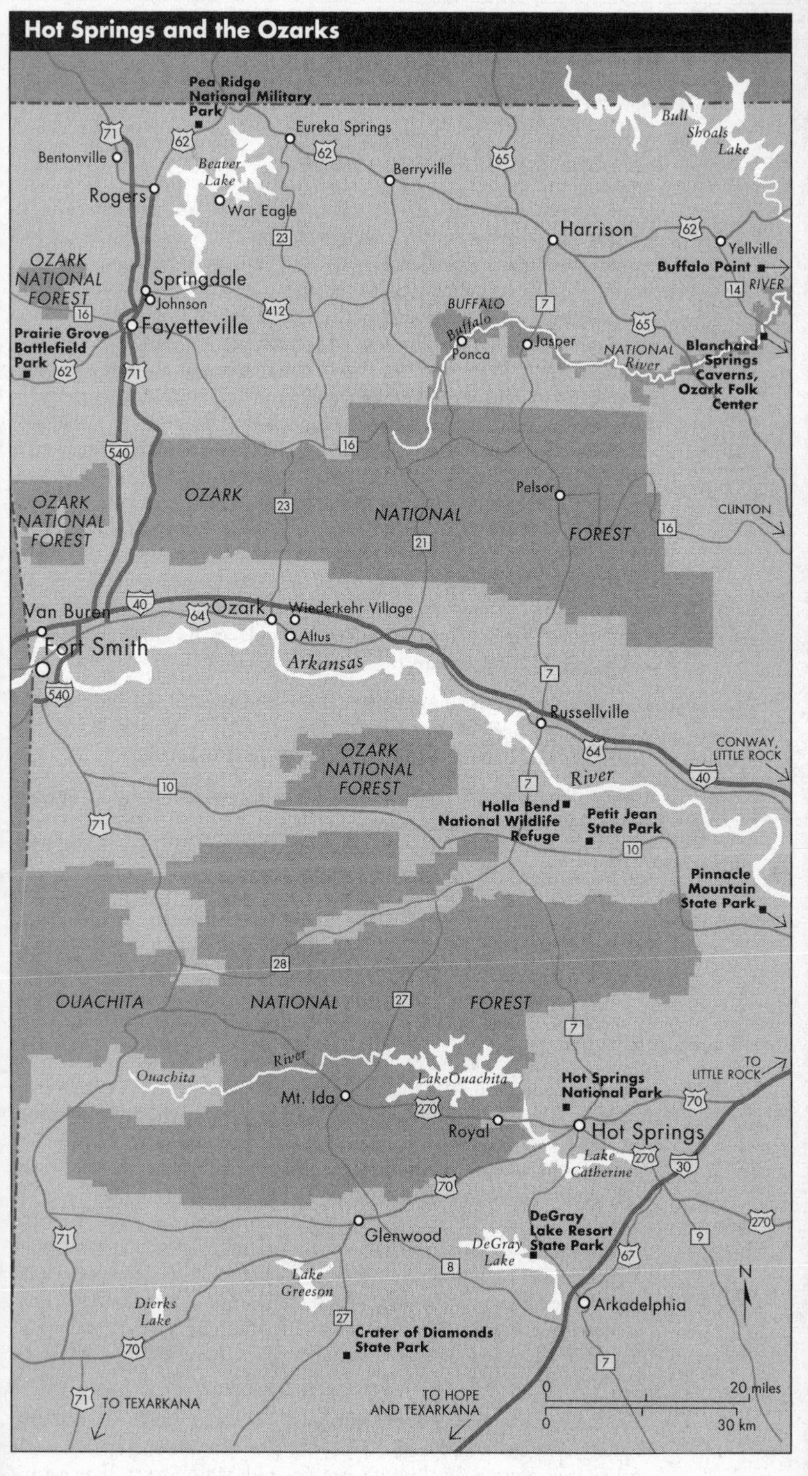

eral baths remain, including the old-fashioned **Buckstaff,** a 1912 National Historic Landmark. ✉ *509 Central Ave.,* ☎ *501/623–2308,* WEB *www.buckstaffbaths.com.* 🎫 *$16.50–$38.25. Closed Sun.* Get a feel for this ★ opulent era on Bathhouse Row at the **Fordyce Bathhouse,** now the Hot Springs National Park Visitor Center (✉ 369 Central Ave. [Box 1860, 71902], ☎ 501/624–3383, WEB www.nps.gov; 🎫 free). On 210 acres of wooded land on the edge of Lake Hamilton and accessible by car or boat, **Garvan Woodland Gardens**—once destined to be timber—offers an inspirational and educational experience. You can walk the trails of this world-class botanical garden. Of particular interest is the wood-and-glass pavilion designed by renowned architect E. Fay Jones, a secret garden, a swinging bridge, and moon bridge. ✉ *550 Arkridge Rd.,* ☎ *800/366–4664 or 501/262–9300,* WEB *www.garvangardens.org.* 🎫 *$7. Closed Tues.* There's a great view from the top of the 216-ft **Hot Springs Mountain Tower** (✉ Hot Springs Mountain Dr. off Fountain St., ☎ 501/623–6035, WEB www.hotsprings.org; 🎫 $4).At the restored headquarters of **Mountain Valley Spring Company** you can try samples of natural spring water. ✉ *150 Central Ave.,* ☎ *501/623–6671.* 🎫 *Free. Closed Sun.* The **Mid-America Science Museum** explores science and nature in interactive exhibits. ✉ *500 Mid-America Blvd., off U.S. 270 W,* ☎ *501/767–3461 or 800/632–0583,* WEB *www.hotsprings.org.* 🎫 *$6. Closed Mon.* **President Bill Clinton's boyhood homes,** at 1011 Park Avenue and 213 Scully Street—along with his schools, church, and favorite teenage hangouts—are detailed in a brochure and map available at the Hot Springs Convention & Visitors Bureau.

Dig for crystals or browse among those already cleaned and polished at **Coleman's Crystal Mine & Rock Shop** (✉ AR 7, Jessieville, ☎ 501/624–7280; 🎫 digging $20), 14 mi north of Hot Springs.

Fort Smith was established in 1817 on the Indian frontier. The **Clayton House,** built in the 1850s and extensively renovated after 1870, has some beautiful hand-carved woodwork. Many of its period furnishings belonged to the Clayton family. ✉ *514 N. 6th St.,* ☎ *479/783–3000.* 🎫 *$2. Closed Mon.–Tues.* The **Darby House** was the boyhood home of General William O. Darby, who organized and commanded Darby's Rangers in World War II. ✉ *311 N. 8th St.,* ☎ *479/782–3388.* 🎫 *Free. Closed weekends.* The **Fort Smith Museum of History** covers regional history ✉ *320 Rogers Ave.,* ☎ *479/783–7841.* 🎫 *$5. Closed Mon.* The **Fort Smith National Historic Site** (✉ 3rd St. and Rogers Ave., ☎ 479/783–3961; 🎫 $3) includes the remains of two successive frontier forts and a reproduction of Hanging Judge Isaac Parker's 1870s gallows—big enough to hang 12 outlaws at once. The **Fort Smith Trolley Museum** (✉ 100 S. 4th St., ☎ 479/783–0205; 🎫 free) displays a 1926 streetcar and other transportation memorabilia. The Fort Smith visitor center is in **Miss Laura's** (✉ 2 N. B St., ☎ 479/783–8888 or 800/637–1477, WEB fortsmith.org; 🎫 free), a stylishly decorated former brothel on the National Register of Historic Places. From the visitor center a **trolley** carries visitors to museums, historic homes, and other sights, except on winter weekdays, when it doesn't run. 🎫 *$1. Closed weekdays in winter.* **Vaughn-Schaap House** is now the Fort Smith Arts Center; this 1857 Victorian Second Empire–style home displays changing art exhibits. ✉ *423 N. 6th St.,* ☎ *479/784–2787.* 🎫 *Free. Closed Mon.*

Van Buren, just north of Fort Smith over the Arkansas River, was also settled in the early 1800s as a riverboat stop and prospered as a trade and supply center. Van Buren's century-old **Main Street,** which runs six blocks from the Old Frisco Depot to the county courthouse, is an architectural and historic delight, with shops filled with antiques and country crafts, as well as cafés, restaurants, and a theater.

Dining and Lodging

Fort Smith

$$–$$$ ✕ **Folie à Deux.** This fine restaurant has distinctive Continental cuisine and an extensive wine list. For starters try roasted garlic cloves baked in a Gorgonzola cream or the lobster custard, an herbed cheese and lobster baked with a cornmeal crust. Entrées include a shiitake mushroom–crusted sea bass sautéed with wild mushroom ragout and polenta medallions. ✉ *2909 Old Greenwood Rd.,* ☎ *479/648–0041. AE, D, DC, MC, V. Closed Sun. No lunch.*

$$ 🏨 **Holiday Inn Fort Smith Civic Center.** Many historic sites are within walking distance of this hotel, as is the convention center. ✉ *700 Rogers Ave., 72901,* ☎ *479/783–1000,* FAX *479/783–0312,* WEB *www.holiday-inn.com. 263 rooms. Restaurant, pool, gym. AE, D, DC, MC, V. BP.*

$–$$ 🏨 **Hampton Inn.** This motel is convenient to I–540, restaurants, and shopping. ✉ *6201-D Rogers Ave., 72901,* ☎ *479/452–2000,* FAX *479/452–6668,* WEB *www.hamptoninn.com. 143 rooms. Pool, tennis, gym. AE, D, DC, MC, V. CP.*

Hot Springs

$–$$$$ ✕ **Belle Arti.** Transplanted New Yorkers have uplifted the classic Italian fare at this spot in the historic district to cosmopolitan heights. You can choose from more than a dozen inventive salads, feast on entrées such as *filetto al Barolo* (grilled medallions of beef in Barolo); or saltimbocca *alla Romana* (medallions of thin, tender veal smothered in Marsala wine and mushroom sauce with prosciutto and mozzarella cheese). ✉ *719 Central Ave.,* ☎ *501/624–7772. AE, MC, V.*

$ ✕ **Cafe 1217.** Named for its address on Malvern Avenue, this fancy-food-to-go and sit-down eatery is popular with the locals, so get there early. Choose from some inventive sandwiches like the Bombay Turkey Salad with ginger cream cheese on raisin bread or the pork tamales with avocado sauce. Save room for dessert. ✉ *1217 Malvern Ave.,* ☎ *501/318–01094. AE, MC, V. Closed Sun.*

$ ✕ **McClard's.** Bill Clinton loved this old-fashioned barbecue spot as a teenager—and for good cause. Try the tamales. ✉ *505 Albert Pike,* ☎ *501/624–9586. No credit cards. Closed Sun.–Mon., mid-Dec.–mid-Jan., and 1 wk in July.*

$–$$$ 🏨 **Arlington.** To stay at the Arlington, the grande dame of spa hotels in Hot Springs, is to experience the true flavor of this town. Enjoy a luxurious old-fashioned bathhouse-spa experience. Ask for a room with the mineral water on tap. ✉ *239 Central Ave., 71901,* ☎ *501/623–7771 or 800/643–1502,* FAX *501/623–2243,* WEB *www.arlingtonhotel.com. 481 rooms. 2 restaurants, 2 pools, golf, tennis, gym. AE, D, DC, MC, V.*

$ 🏨 **1884 Wildwood Bed & Breakfast.** A beautifully restored 1884 Queen Anne Victorian mansion has luxury period suites just a few blocks from downtown. ✉ *808 Park Ave., 71901,* ☎ *501/624–4267 or 888/763–3707,* WEB *www.wildwood1884.com. 5 suites. AE, MC, V.*

Outdoor Activities and Sports

For information on trails, scenic drives, and campsites, contact **Ouachita National Forest** (✉ USFS, Box 1270, Hot Springs 71902, ☎ 501/321–5202, WEB www.fs.fed.us/oonf/ouachita.htm). Close to the national forest is the **DeGray Lake Resort State Park** (✉ 2027 State Park Entrance Rd., Bismarck 71929–8194, ☎ 501/865–2801 or 800/737–8355, WEB www.arkansasstateparks.com), with a newly renovated lodge on the edge of a 13,800-acre lake, with a golf course, marina, campsites, horseback riding, tennis, biking, and interpretive activities such as eagle watches.

Spectator Sports

Thoroughbred racing: Hot Springs's **Oaklawn Jockey Club** (✉ 2705 Central Ave., ☎ 800/625–5296; 🎫 live racing $2, simulcasts $1) has racing from late January through mid-April and simulcasts the rest of year.

Shopping

Dozens of artists and gallery owners have transformed Hot Springs's Victorian downtown into a vibrant, cosmopolitan arts district. There's a self-guided **gallery walk** the first Friday of each month. Shop for finer things at the Villa shops or visit Tillman's Antiques. Several **malls** lie south of downtown on Arkansas 7/Central Avenue.

Western Arkansas Essentials

AIRPORTS

Big Sky Airlines flies from Dallas–Fort Worth to the Hot Springs municipal airport daily. The Hot Springs–Little Rock Airport Shuttle service provides transportation between Hot Springs and Little Rock National Airport. American Eagle and Northwest Airlink fly into Fort Smith Regional Airport.

➤ AIRPORT INFORMATION: **Big Sky Airlines** (☎ 800/237–7788, WEB www.bigskyair.com). **Hot Springs–Little Rock Airport Shuttle Service** (☎ 800/643–1505).

CAR TRAVEL

The easiest way to arrive and get around is by car. From Little Rock, I–30 and U.S. 70 lead to Hot Springs. I–40 reaches Fort Smith and Van Buren.

VISITOR INFORMATION

➤ TOURIST INFORMATION: **Fort Smith Convention and Visitors Bureau** (✉ 2 N. B St., 72901, ☎ 479/783–8888 or 800/637–1477, WEB www.fortsmith.org). **Hot Springs Convention & Visitors Bureau** (✉ 629 Central Ave. [Box K, 71902], ☎ 800/922–6478, WEB www.hotsprings.org).

ELSEWHERE IN ARKANSAS

Texarkana

What to See and Do

The **Post Office** and **Photographer's Island** (✉ 500 State Line Ave.) are half in Arkansas, half in Texas. Winnings from a poker game built the 1885 **Ace of Clubs House,** designed, fittingly, in the shape of a playing card. ✉ *5th and Pine Sts.,* ☎ *903/793–4831.* 🎫 *$5. Closed Sun.–Mon.* The **Texarkana Historical Museum** is in the city's oldest brick building. ✉ *219 State Line Ave.,* ☎ *903/793–4831.* 🎫 *$2. Closed Sun.–Mon.* Opened in 1924, the elaborate **Perot Theater** (✉ 219 Main St., ☎ 903/792–4992) was restored thanks to a major donation by native son and presidential hopeful H. Ross Perot. Across the street, a mural pays tribute to another native son, ragtime composer Scott Joplin.

Dining and Lodging

$–$$ ✕ **Cattleman's Steak House.** The specialty of prime rib, plus T-bones, rib eyes, and other choice cuts, will make you think you're deep in the heart of Texas. The menu also includes shrimp, fish, and sandwiches. ✉ *4018 N. State Line Ave.,* ☎ *870/774–4481. AE, D, MC, V. Closed Sun.*

$$ ✕ **Lake Country.** Market-fresh Continental specialties with Mediterranean touches are on the menu here. The wine list is extensive. ✉ *3920 N. State Line Rd.,* ☎ *870/773–1550. AE, D, MC, V. Closed Sun.–Mon.*

$–$$ **Four Points by Sheraton.** This conveniently located and service-oriented hotel has a concierge floor with business services. Airport-shuttle service is also available. ✉ *5301 N. State Line Ave., 75503,* ☎ *800/563–4464 or 888/563–4464,* FAX *903/793–3930,* WEB *www.fourpoints.com. 147 rooms. Restaurant, pool, gym. AE, D, DC, MC, V. CP.*

$ **Hampton Inn.** Convenient to the interstate as well as the downtown historic district, this hotel offers free access to a nearby health club. ✉ *5300 N. State Line Ave., at I–30, 71854,* ☎ *870/774–4444,* FAX *870/779–1303,* WEB *www.hampton-inn.com. 60 rooms. Pool. AE, D, DC, MC, V. CP.*

Texarkana Essentials

CAR TRAVEL

From Little Rock take I–30 to Texarkana, which straddles the Arkansas–Texas border.

VISITOR INFORMATION

➤ TOURIST INFORMATION: **Texarkana Chamber of Commerce** (✉ Box 1468, Texarkana, TX 75504, ☎ 903/792–7191, WEB www.texarkana.org).

Hope

What to See and Do

Hope is Arkansas's watermelon capital, growing some of the nation's largest and tastiest melons. It's also the birthplace of Bill Clinton, who lived here until he was six. The **Clinton Center,** where the president was born and lived with his grandparents until age four, is now a restored home and gardens open to the public. ✉ *117 S. Hervey St., at 2nd St.,* ☎ *870/777–4455.* *$5 (purchase tickets at Clinton Center on 2nd St.). Closed Mon., also Sun. in winter.*

★ Near Hope is **Old Washington Historic State Park** (✉ Washington, ☎ 870/983–2684; $6.50 tours). Established in 1824 on the Southwest Trail, this was the Confederate state capital after Little Rock's capture. Some 40 buildings remain from the 1820s–70s. **Crater of Diamonds State Park** (✉ 209 State Park Rd., Murfreesboro, ☎ 870/285–3113; $5), near Murfreesboro, is North America's only public diamond mine where you can keep what you find.

Dining and Lodging

$–$$ ✕ **Loco Gringos.** This casual steak house serves all the usual cuts as well as Mexican dishes. ✉ *2406 N. Hervey St. (Hwy. 4),* ☎ *870/777–3377. AE, D, MC, V.*

$ ✕ **Williams Tavern.** This tavern was built in 1832 on a plantation northeast of town. Before it was moved to its present location in Old Washington Historic State Park, it served as a residence, post office, and stagecoach stop. Enjoy a simple, southern-style lunch. ✉ *Morrison and Carroll Sts., Washington,* ☎ *870/983–2890. AE, D, MC, V.*

$ **Best Western of Hope.** This chain motel is convenient to major highways and the local Clinton sites. ✉ *I–30 and Hwy. 4 (Box 6611, 71801),* ☎ *870/777–9222,* FAX *870/777–9077,* WEB *www.bestwestern.com. 74 rooms. Restaurant, pool. AE, D, DC, MC, V. CP.*

$ **Holiday Inn Express.** This hotel is convenient to highways and Clinton sites. Hotel guests have privileges at a nearby health club. ✉ *2600 N. Hervey St., 71801,* ☎ *870/722–6262,* FAX *870/722–1922,* WEB *www.holiday-inn.com. 61 rooms. Pool. AE, D, DC, MC, V. CP.*

Hope Essentials

CAR TRAVEL

I–30 leads from Little Rock to Hope.

VISITOR INFORMATION

The Hope Visitor Center is in the restored 1912 railroad depot; it provides a map showing Clinton sites.

➤ TOURIST INFORMATION: **Hope Visitor Center** (✉ S. Main and Division Sts., ☎ 870/722–2580).

Helena

What to See and Do

One of the oldest Mississippi River settlements and a Civil War battle site, Helena is where you'll find the **Delta Cultural Center** (✉ 141 Cherry St., ☎ 870/338–4350; 🎫 free), which documents the roots of the Delta blues, pioneer days, and the river life described by Mark Twain. Helena shows off numerous antebellum and postwar mansions, several of which are now B&Bs. The 1896 **Pillow-Thompson House** is one of the South's finest examples of Queen Anne architecture. ✉ *718 Perry St.,* ☎ *870/338–8535.* 🎫 *Free. Closed Mon.–Wed.*

Each October Helena hosts the **King Biscuit Blues Festival** (✉ Box 118, 72342, ☎ 870/338–8798), which has gained international acclaim.

Dining and Lodging

$ ✕ **Pasquale's Tamales.** This casual eatery, in a historic building, serves up dynamite tamales, chili with trimmings, New Orleans muffalettas, roast beef po'boys, and meatball sandwiches among other dishes. It's open 9 AM–5 PM Monday–Thursday but serves until 9 PM Friday. ✉ *201 Missouri St.,* ☎ *870/338–6722 or 800/390–3992. MC, V. Closed weekends. No dinner except Fri.*

$ 🏨 **Best Western Inn.** All rooms at this motel have microwaves and refrigerators. It's convenient to the Isle of Capris casinos. ✉ *1053 Hwy. 49 W, West Helena 72390,* ☎ *870/572–2592,* FAX *870/572–7561,* WEB *www.bestwestern.com. 64 rooms. Pool. AE, D, MC, V. CP.*

$ 🏨 **Edwardian Inn.** Elegantly restored and decorated, this 1904 Colonial Revival–style house has some rooms with 14-ft ceilings and fireplaces; all have televisions. You'll also find a common room, a garden room, decks, and a wide front porch. ✉ *317 Biscoe St., 72342,* ☎ *870/338–9155 or 800/597–4749,* WEB *www.edwardianinn.com. 12 rooms. AE, D, DC, MC, V. BP.*

Helena Essentials

CAR TRAVEL

From Little Rock take I–40, turning south on U.S. 49.

VISITOR INFORMATION

➤ TOURIST INFORMATION: **Helena Tourism Commission** (✉ 226 Perry St., 72342, ☎ 870/338–9831).

CALIFORNIA

Capital	Sacramento
Population	34,336,000
Motto	Eureka
State Bird	Valley quail
State Flower	Golden poppy
Postal Abbreviation	CA

Statewide Visitor Information

California Division of Tourism (✉ 801 K St., Suite 1600, Sacramento 95814, ☎ 916/322–2881 or 800/862–2543, FAX 916/322–3402 or 916/322–0501, WEB www.visitcalifornia.com).

Scenic Drives

The land- and seascapes along the nearly 400 mi of coastline between San Francisco Bay and the Oregon border are beautiful and rugged; switchbacking **Route 1** is punctuated by groves of giant redwood trees, tiny coastal towns, and secluded coves and beaches. **U.S. 395** north from San Bernardino rises in elevation gradually from the Mojave Desert to the Sierra foothills and on past the east entrance to Yosemite National Park. **Route 49** winds 325 mi through the historic towns and dry forests of northern California's Gold Country.

National and State Parks

National Parks

California has eight national parks: Death Valley, Joshua Tree, Lassen Volcanic, Redwood, Sequoia, Kings Canyon, Yosemite, and the Channel Islands. National monuments include Cabrillo, in San Diego, and Muir Woods, north of San Francisco. For information contact the western regional office of the **National Park Service** (✉ Fort Mason Center, Bldg. 201, San Francisco 94123, ☎ 415/561–4700, WEB www.nps.gov).

State Parks

The **California State Park System** (✉ Box 942896, Sacramento 94296, ☎ 916/653–6995, WEB cal-parks.ca.gov) includes more than 200 sites; many are recreational and scenic, others historic or scientific. In an effort to make the park system more accessible for everyone, the state has capped camping fees at $12 or less and eliminated all weekend, premium, and seasonal rates as well as boating fees. *For more information on any of the state parks mentioned in this chapter, visit the California State Park System Web site.*

THE NORTH COAST

The 400 mi of shoreline between San Francisco and the Oregon border is a surprise to those who think of California as a land of sunny, sandy beaches. Such places exist on the North Coast, but more common are craggy cliffs, hills that tumble into the ocean, and rocky flats covered in tide pools—a constantly changing landscape that offers view after breathtaking view.

Exploring the North Coast

Over the Golden Gate Bridge from San Francisco in southern Marin County, the spectacular outdoors of the North Coast begins.

Marin Headlands (✉ U.S. 101 at Alexander Ave., Sausalito, ☎ 415/331–1540) offers well-biked paths through eucalyptus groves and gentle hills and on to rocky beaches. **Muir Woods National Monument** (✉ Muir Woods Rd., Mill Valley, ☎ 415/388–2595, WEB www.visitmuirwoods.com) protects some of the oldest (and most accessible) giant redwoods in the world.Roughly an hour north of San Francisco, ★ **Point Reyes National Seashore** (✉ Point Reyes, ☎ 415/663–1092, WEB www.nps.gov/pore) is a hidden jewel: 110 square mi of pristine beaches, emerald pastures, and delicate marshes that attract birds and mammals, but curiously few visitors.

The first and biggest town north of the Sonoma County line is **Bodega Bay,** one of the busiest harbors on this stretch of coast and the setting of Alfred Hitchcock's film *The Birds*.Watch big sea creatures at **Sonoma Coast State Beach** (✉ Rte. 1, 10 mi north of Bodega Bay, ☎ 707/875–3483), particularly at windy Goat Rock, where a colony of sea lions resides most of the year.The North Coast's history is well documented in the museum at **Fort Ross State Historic Park** (✉ Rte. 1, 9 mi north of Jenner, ☎ 707/847–3286), a reconstructed group of buildings from the 1800s which includes a Russian Orthodox chapel and officers' barracks. For a dramatic view of the surf and, in winter, migrating whales, visit **Point Arena Lighthouse** (✉ off Rte. 1, Point Arena, ☎ 707/882–2777, WEB www.mcn.org/1/palight/; 🎫 $4), a towering structure that was rebuilt in 1907 after being destroyed by the earthquake that rocked San Francisco.

Seaside **Mendocino** is the most visited town on the North Coast, and for good reason. The main activity here is strolling along quiet streets lined with colorful gardens and homes, shops, restaurants, and art galleries, often in view of the crashing ocean below.The town's cultural core is **Mendocino Art Center** (✉ 45200 Little Lake St., ☎ 707/937–5818 or 800/653–3328, WEB www.mendocinoartcenter.org), a community-run gallery and theater. Up the coast from town, the ★ **Mendocino Coast Botanical Gardens** (✉ 18220 N. Rte. 1, ☎ 707/964–4352, WEB www.gardenbythesea.org; 🎫 $6) offer 2 mi of coastal trails, with ocean views and observation points for whale-watching, and a profusion of flowers year-round.

South of the Humboldt County line, Route 1 ducks inland and enters **Redwood Country.** The best place to see the giant redwoods is at **Humboldt Redwoods State Park** (✉ Ave. of the Giants, 2 mi south of Weott, ☎ 707/946–2409 or 707/946–2263), where short and long trails offer easy access to dark, ancient groves like nowhere else.The best redwood driving tour is the crowded but impressive **Avenue of the Giants** (✉ Rte. 254), which begins about 7 mi north of Garberville.

Dining and Lodging

Marin and Sonoma Counties

$$$–$$$$ ★ ✕🏨 **Manka's.** Rustic wood-paneled dining rooms glowing with candlelight are the backdrop for an evening of creative American cuisine. Two of the four smallish guest rooms above the restaurant have private decks overlooking Tomales Bay. Rooms in the redwood annex and two cabins are also available. If you can get a reservation to dine at the restaurant, prepare for one of the best and richest meals in northern California. ✉ *30 Callendar Way, Inverness, 94937,* ☎ *415/669–1034,* WEB *www.mankas.com. 14 rooms. Restaurant. MC, V. BP.*

$$$–$$$$ ★ ✕🏨 **Pelican Inn.** A five-minute walk from Muir Beach, this Tudor-style B&B is well appointed with Oriental rugs, English prints, and hanging tapestries. Locals and tourists compete at darts in the ground-floor pub, which has a wide selection of brews, sherries, and ports. The Pelican's restaurant serves sturdy English fare. ✉ *10 Pacific Way, at Rte. 1, Muir Beach, 94965,* ☎ *415/383–6000,* FAX *415/383–3424,* WEB *www.pelicaninn.com. 7 rooms. Restaurant. MC, V. BP.*

$$$$ **Sonoma Coast Villa.** Founded as an Arabian horse ranch in 1976, this 60-acre property in the coastal hills between Valley Ford and Bodega Bay has two single-story rows of accommodations beside a swimming pool. Behind the Mediterranean-looking exteriors of stucco and red tile lie rooms with slate floors, French doors, beam ceilings, and wood-burning fireplaces. ✉ *16702 Rte. 1, Bodega 94922,* ☎ *707/876–9818 or 888/404–2255,* FAX *707/876–9856,* WEB *www.scvilla.com. 16 rooms. Pool. AE, MC, V. BP.*

Mendocino County

$$–$$$ ★ ✕ **Cafe Beaujolais.** This famous restaurant is housed in a charming cottage that makes it all the more appealing. The ever-evolving menu is cross-cultural, with duck, seafood, and free-range, hormone-free meats. Try the Yucetecan-Thai crab cakes. The restaurant typically closes for a month or more in winter. ✉ *961 Ukiah St., Mendocino,* ☎ *707/937–5614. D, MC, V.*

$$–$$$ ✕ **MacCallum House.** With the most meticulously restored Victorian exterior in Mendocino, this 1882 inn, complete with gingerbread trim, transports patrons back to another era—but without sacrificing comfort. In addition to the main house, there are individual cottages and barn suites around a garden. The menu at the redwood-paneled restaurant changes quarterly, but the focus is always on local seafood and organic and free-range meats. ✉ *45020 Albion St. (Box 206, Mendocino 95460),* ☎ *707/937–0289 or 800/609–0492,* WEB *www.maccallumhouse.com. 22 rooms. Restaurant. AE, MC, V.*

$$–$$$$ ★ **Elk Cove Inn.** Perched on a bluff above the surf that pounds on a virtually private beach, Elk Cove offers priceless views from most of its rooms. The plushest suites are in a stone-and-cedar-shingle Arts and Crafts–style building separate from the main house. The full bar is open daily. ✉ *6300 S. Rte. 1 (Box 367, Elk 95432),* ☎ *707/877–3321 or 800/275–2967,* FAX *707/877–1808,* WEB *www.elkcoveinn.com. 16 rooms. AE, D, DC, MC, V. BP.*

North Coast Essentials

AIR TRAVEL

Arcata/Eureka Airport receives United Express flights from San Francisco.

➤ AIRPORT INFORMATION: **Arcata/Eureka Airport** (✉ off U.S. 101, McKinleyville, ☎ 707/839–5401). **United Airlines** (☎ 800/241–6522, WEB www.ual.com).

BUS TRAVEL

Greyhound buses travel along U.S. 101 from San Francisco to Seattle, with regular stops in Eureka and Crescent City. Bus drivers will stop in other towns along the route if you specify your destination when you board.

➤ BUS INFORMATION: **Greyhound** (☎ 800/231–2222, WEB www.greyhound.com).

CAR TRAVEL

Route 1 and U.S. 101 are the main north–south coastal routes. Route 1 is often curvy and difficult all along the coast. Driving directly to Mendocino from San Francisco is quicker if instead of driving up the coast on Route 1 you take U.S. 101 north to Route 128 west (from Cloverdale) to Route 1 north.

VISITOR INFORMATION

Fort Bragg–Mendocino Coast Chamber of Commerce (✉ Box 1141, Fort Bragg 95437, ☎ 707/961–6300 or 800/726–2780, WEB www.mendocinocoast.com). **Redwood Empire Association** (✉ Cannery, 2801 Leavenworth St., San Francisco 94133, ☎ 415/543–8334, WEB www.redwoodempire.com). **Sonoma County Tourism Program** (✉ 2300 County Center Dr., Room B260, Santa Rosa 95405, ☎ 707/565–5383, WEB www.sonomacounty.com). **West Marin Chamber of Commerce** (✉ Box 1045, Point Reyes Station 94956, ☎ 415/663–9232, WEB www.pointreyes.org).

THE WINE COUNTRY

Napa and Sonoma counties produce some of the world's finest wines. Napa Valley becomes crowded on weekends, when visitors jam the gift shops and restaurants. The pace is less frenetic in Sonoma County. Admission is free to the wineries listed below, but many have nominal tasting fees.

Exploring the Wine Country

The Napa Valley

Along Route 29 north of the town of Napa and parallel to the highway on the Silverado Trail are some of California's most important wineries. **Domaine Chandon** (✉ 1 California Dr., Yountville, ☎ 707/944–8844, WEB www.dchandon.com) is owned by Moët-Hennessey and Louis Vuitton. **Stag's Leap** (✉ 5766 Silverado Trail, Napa, ☎ 707/944–2020, WEB www.cask23.com) produces a superb chardonnay.

The **Napa Valley Museum** (✉ 55 Presidents Cir., Yountville, ☎ 707/944–0500, WEB www.napavalleymuseum.org; 🎫 $4.50) has an innovative, permanent exhibit devoted to regional wine making as well as changing art shows. Some of the largest wine caves in America are below **Rutherford Hill Winery** (✉ 200 Rutherford Hill Rd., Rutherford, ☎ 707/963–1871, WEB www.rutherfordhill.com). **Beaulieu Vineyard** (✉ 1960 St. Helena Hwy., Rutherford, ☎ 707/963–2411, WEB www.bvwine.com) utilizes the same wine-making process it did in the early 20th century. At **Robert Mondavi** (✉ Rte. 29, Oakville, ☎ 707/259–9463, WEB www.robertmondavi.com), the 60-minute tour is encouraged before imbibing. Visitors ride up the side of a hill in a gondola to reach **Sterling Vineyards** (✉ 1111 Dunaweal La., Calistoga, ☎ 707/942–3300, WEB www.sterlingvineyards.com).

Calistoga, at the Napa Valley's north end, was founded as a spa and remains notable for its mineral water, hot mineral springs, mud baths, steam baths, and massages.**Indian Springs Resort and Spa** (✉ 1712 Lincoln Ave., ☎ 707/942–4913, WEB www.indianspringscalistoga.com) has full spa amenities.

The Sonoma Valley

East of U.S. 101 and west of the Napa Valley, Route 12 runs through the hills of Sonoma County. The historic central plaza in the town of Sonoma is the site of **Mission San Francisco de Solano** (✉ 114 Spain St. E, ☎ 707/938–9560; 🎫 $3), which is a re-creation of the original early 19th-century structure.

California's wine-making industry got its start at the **Buena Vista Carneros Winery** (✉ 18000 Old Winery Rd., Sonoma, ☎ 707/938–1266, WEB www.buenavistawinery.com) in 1857. The **Benziger Family Winery** (✉ 1883 London Ranch Rd., Glen Ellen, ☎ 707/935–3000, WEB www.benziger.com) specializes in premium estate and Sonoma County wines.

The rustic grounds at **Kenwood Vineyards** (✉ 9592 Sonoma Hwy., Kenwood, ☎ 707/833–5891, WEB www.kenwoodvineyards.com) complement the attractive tasting room. The charred but evocative ruins of the author's dream home and the House of Happy Walls museum are among the highlights at **Jack London State Historic Park** (✉ 2400 London Ranch Rd., Glen Ellen, ☎ 707/938–5216, WEB www.parks.sonoma.net/JLPark.html; $3 per vehicle).

Dining and Lodging

Napa County

$$$$ ★ ✕ **French Laundry.** This intimate, cottage-style restaurant, surrounded by gardens, offers exquisite prix-fixe French menus of five courses. Call exactly two months in advance for reservations. ✉ *6640 Washington St.,* ☎ *707/944–2380. Reservations essential. AE, MC, V. Closed 1st 2 wks in Jan.; lunch hrs and days vary.*

$$–$$$ ✕ **Catahoula Restaurant and Saloon.** Chef Jan Birnbaum employs a large wood-burning oven to churn out such California-Cajun dishes as andouille sausage pizza and oven-braised lamb shank with red beans. ✉ *Mount View Hotel, 1457 Lincoln Ave.,* ☎ *707/942–2275. Reservations essential. MC, V. No lunch weekdays.*

$$$$ ★ ✕ **Auberge du Soleil.** The dining terrace of this hilltop inn, looking down across groves of olive trees to the Napa Valley vineyards, is the closest you can get to the charm and cuisine of southern France without a passport. The inn itself is a luxurious retreat with full spa facilities. ✉ *180 Rutherford Hill Rd., off Silverado Trail north of Rte. 128, 94573,* ☎ *707/963–1211 or 800/348–5406,* FAX *707/963–8764,* WEB *www.aubergedusoleil.com. 50 rooms. Restaurant, pool, gym. AE, D, DC, MC, V. CP.*

$$$$ **Meadowood Resort.** Croquet lawns, a 9-hole golf course, tennis courts, and gorgeous hiking trails add to the glamour of this sprawling 256-acre resort with a rambling country lodge and bungalow suites. ✉ *900 Meadowood La., 94574,* ☎ *707/963–3646 or 800/458–8080,* FAX *707/963–3532,* WEB *www.meadowood.com. 85 rooms. 2 restaurants, pools. AE, D, DC, MC, V.*

$$–$$$ **Mount View Hotel.** This hotel has a small but full-service European spa offering state-of-the-art pampering. Three cottages are equipped with private redwood decks, hot tubs, and wet bars. ✉ *1457 Lincoln Ave., 94515,* ☎ *707/942–6877,* FAX *707/942–6904,* WEB *www.mountviewhotel.com. 32 rooms. Restaurant, pool. AE, D, MC, V.*

Sonoma County

$$–$$$ ★ ✕ **John Ash & Co.** The chef emphasizes presentation, innovation, and freshness and uses mainly seasonal foods grown in Sonoma County. This is a favorite spot for Sunday brunch. ✉ *4430 Barnes Rd.,* ☎ *707/527–7687. Reservations essential. AE, DC, MC, V. No lunch Mon.*

$$$–$$$$ **Thistle Dew Inn.** Half a block from Sonoma Plaza is this Victorian inn with Arts and Crafts furnishings and antique quilts. Welcome bonuses include a hot tub and free use of the inn's bicycles. ✉ *171 W. Spain St., 95476,* ☎ *707/938–2909; 800/382–7895 in California;* WEB *www.thistledew.com. 6 rooms. AE, MC, V. BP.*

Outdoor Activities and Sports

Many hotels arrange excursions, or contact **Napa Valley Balloons** (☎ 707/944–0228; 800/253–2224 in California). For Sonoma trips try **Above the Wine Country Balloons and Tours** (☎ 707/538–7359 or 800/759–5638).

The Wine Country Essentials

BUS TRAVEL

Greyhound runs buses from San Francisco to the cities of Sonoma and Santa Rosa in Sonoma County; the line's buses stop along U.S. 101 in inland Mendocino County. Sonoma County Area Transit and Napa Valley Transit provide local transportation.

➤ Bus Information: **Greyhound** (☎ 800/231–2222, WEB www.greyhound.com). **Napa Valley Transit** (☎ 800/696–6443, WEB www.mtc.ca.gov/publications/sonoma/napa.html). **Sonoma County Transit** (☎ 707/576–7433, WEB www.sctransit.com).

CAR TRAVEL

The best way to get around the Wine Country is by car. From San Francisco cross the Golden Gate Bridge and follow U.S. 101 north to Route 37 east to Route 121 north and east. Take Route 12 north from Route 121 for Sonoma wineries; continue east on Route 121 to Route 29 north for Napa wineries. From the East Bay take I–80 north to Route 37 east to Route 29 north for Napa; Route 12 heads west from Route 29 toward Sonoma.

TRAIN TRAVEL

The Napa Valley Wine Train serves lunch ($70), dinner ($79), and a weekend brunch ($60) on restored Pullman cars that run between Napa and St. Helena.

➤ Train Information: **Napa Valley Wine Train** (☎ 707/253–2111 or 800/427–4124, WEB www.winetrain.com).

VISITOR INFORMATION

➤ Tourist Information: **Napa Valley Conference and Visitors Bureau** (✉ 1310 Napa Town Center, 94559, ☎ 707/226–7459, WEB www.napavalley.com). **Sonoma Valley Visitors Bureau** (✉ 453 1st St. E, Sonoma 95476, ☎ 707/996–1090, WEB www.sonomavalley.com).

ELSEWHERE IN NORTHERN CALIFORNIA

The Gold Country

What to See and Do

When gold was discovered at Coloma in 1848, people came from all over the world to search for the treasure. Today, clustered along Route 49 are restored villages and ghost towns, antiques shops, crafts stores, and vineyards. The heart of the Gold Country lies on Route 49 between Nevada City and Mariposa.

★ **Empire Mine State Historic Park** (✉ 10791 E. Empire St., Grass Valley, ☎ 530/273–8522; ★ $1) has exhibits on gold mining. The **Marshall Gold Discovery State Historical Park** (✉ 310 Back St., Coloma, ☎ 530/622–3470; $2) has a replica of Sutter's Mill, where the gold ★ rush started. In **Columbia State Historic Park** (✉ 22708 Broadway, Columbia, ☎ 209/532–0150; free) you can ride a stagecoach, pan for gold, or watch a blacksmith working at his anvil.

At the **California State Mining and Mineral Museum** (✉ Mariposa County Fairgrounds, Rte. 49, Mariposa, ☎ 209/742–7625; $2) a glittering 13-pound crystallized gold nugget vividly illustrates what the gold rush was all about. The museum is closed on Tuesday between October and April.

Sacramento, the California state capital, is also the largest Gold Country city. The **Discovery Museum** (✉ 101 I St., ☎ 916/264–7057, WEB www.

thediscovery.org; 🎫 $5) presents a streamlined introduction to Sacramento's history. ★ The **California State Railroad Museum** (✉ 125 I St., ☎ 916/445–6645, WEB www.csrmf.org; 🎫 $3) displays restored locomotives and railroad cars.

Dining and Lodging

SACRAMENTO

$$–$$$ ★ ✕ **Biba.** The capitol crowd flocks here for delicate pasta dishes, veal specials, and homemade ravioli, as well as specialties from the Emilia-Romagna region of Italy. ✉ *2801 Capitol Ave.,* ☎ *916/455–2422. AE, DC, MC, V. Closed Sun. No lunch Sat.*

$$–$$$ ✕🏨 **Delta King.** This grand old riverboat, now permanently moored on Old Sacramento's waterfront, has retained its mahogany paneling and brass fittings but has been transformed into a fun hotel with 44 delightful staterooms. ✉ *1000 Front St., 95814,* ☎ *916/444–5464 or 800/825–5464,* FAX *916/447–5959,* WEB *www.deltaking.com. 44 rooms. Restaurant. AE, D, DC, MC, V. CP.*

The Gold Country Essentials

AIRPORTS

Sacramento International Airport, off I–5, is served by major domestic airlines.

➤ AIRPORT INFORMATION: **Sacramento International Airport** (✉ 6900 Airport Blvd., ☎ 916/874–0719, WEB airports.co.sacramento.ca.us).

BUS TRAVEL

Greyhound serves Sacramento, Auburn, Grass Valley, and Placerville from San Francisco.

➤ BUS INFORMATION: **Greyhound** (☎ 800/231–2222, WEB www.greyhound.com).

CAR TRAVEL

The most convenient way to see the area is by car. I–80 intersects with Route 49, the main route through the region, at Auburn; U.S. 50 intersects with Route 49 at Placerville.

VISITOR INFORMATION

➤ TOURIST INFORMATION: **Grass Valley/Nevada County Chamber of Commerce** (✉ 248 Mill St., Grass Valley 95945, ☎ 530/273–4667 or 800/655–4667, WEB www.ncgold.com/chamber). **Mariposa County Visitors Bureau** (✉ 5158 Rte. 140, Mariposa 95338, ☎ 209/966–7081 or 800/208–2434, WEB mariposa.yosemite.net/visitor). **Sacramento Convention and Visitors Bureau** (✉ 1303 J St., Suite 600, Sacramento 95814, ☎ 916/264–7777, WEB www.sacramentocvb.org).

Lake Tahoe

What to See and Do

★ In South Lake Tahoe, ride the **Heavenly Gondola** (✉ north on Ski Run Blvd. off U.S. 50 and follow signs, ☎ 775/586–7000, WEB www.skiheavenly.com; 🎫 $12) for a view of Lake Tahoe from 8,200 ft.The ***Hornblower's Tahoe Queen*** (✉ Ski Run Marina, off U.S. 50, South Lake Tahoe, ☎ 530/541–3364, WEB www.hornblower.com; 🎫 $22–$87), a glass-bottom stern-wheeler, cruises on the lake and swings by famous Emerald Bay year-round.

California's Lake Tahoe shoreline is best seen along **Route 89,** which leads through wooded flatlands and past beaches, climbing to vistas on the rugged west side of the lake. The 30-mi stretch northwest from South Lake Tahoe to Tahoe City should take about an hour to drive, but the going can be slow in summer and on holiday weekends. West of South Lake Tahoe is the **Pope-Baldwin Recreation Area** (☎ 530/542–4166; free), where three grand century-old mansions (fees to enter ★ vary) are open to the public. Tahoe's **Emerald Bay** (✉ Rte. 89, 5 mi north of Camp Richardson) is famed for its shape and color. At Tahoe City, Route 89 turns north to **Squaw Valley** (✉ 1960 Squaw Valley Rd., Olympic Valley, ☎ 530/583–6955, WEB www.squaw.com), site of the 1960 Winter Olympics.

Dining and Lodging

$$–$$$ ★ ✕ **Nepheles.** A chalet on the road to Heavenly Ski Resort houses this cozy restaurant, which has been serving creative contemporary cuisine since 1977. Entrées range from Chilean sea bass with a hot mustard glaze to broiled tenderloin of elk with a sauce made from black currants and merlot. Appetizers include escargots, swordfish egg rolls, and Cajun calamari. You can also soak in private-room hot tubs here. ✉ *1169 Ski Run Blvd., South Lake Tahoe,* ☎ *530/544–8130. AE, D, DC, MC, V. No lunch.*

$$–$$$$ **Best Western Station House Inn.** This inn has won design awards for its exterior and interior. The rooms have king- and queen-size beds and double-vanity bathrooms. The location is ideal, one block from a private beach, two blocks from the casinos, and three blocks from the Heavenly Gondola. ✉ *901 Park Ave., South Lake Tahoe 96150,* ☎ *530/542–1101 or 800/822–5953,* FAX *530/542–1714,* WEB *www.stationhouseinn.com. 102 rooms. Restaurant, pool. AE, D, DC, MC, V.*

$$–$$$$ **Inn by the Lake.** Across the road from a beach, this luxury motel has spacious rooms, all with balconies. You can summon a casino shuttle from a direct-dial phone in the lobby. ✉ *3300 Lake Tahoe Blvd., South Lake Tahoe 96150,* ☎ *530/542–0330 or 800/877–1466,* FAX *530/541–6596,* WEB *www.innbythelake.com. 100 rooms. Pool. AE, D, DC, MC, V. CP.*

Lake Tahoe Essentials

AIRPORTS

Reno–Tahoe International Airport, about 40 mi from Lake Tahoe, is served by several domestic airlines.

➤ AIRPORT INFORMATION: **Reno–Tahoe International Airport** (✉ U.S. 395, Exit 65B, Reno, NV, ☎ 775/328–6400, WEB www.renoairport.com).

BUS TRAVEL

Greyhound serves the Tahoe area. South Tahoe Area Ground Express and Tahoe Area Regional Transit are the local bus companies.

➤ BUS INFORMATION: **Greyhound** (☎ 800/231–2222, WEB www.greyhound.com). **South Tahoe Area Ground Express** (☎ 530/542–6077). **Tahoe Area Regional Transit** (☎ 530/550–1212, 800/736–6365, WEB www.placer.ca.gov/works/tart.htm).

CAR TRAVEL

Lake Tahoe is 198 mi northeast of San Francisco. The drive takes about four hours. The major route is I–80 through the Sierra Nevadas; U.S. 50 from Sacramento is the direct route to the south shore. Tire chains are regularly necessary in winter.

TRAIN TRAVEL

Amtrak serves the Lake Tahoe area.

➤ TRAIN INFORMATION: **Amtrak** (☎ 800/872–7245, WEB www.amtrak.com).

VISITOR INFORMATION

➤ TOURIST INFORMATION: **Lake Tahoe Visitors Authority** (☎ 530/544–5050 or 800/288–2463, WEB www.virtualtahoe.com). **Lake Tahoe Vis-**

itors Center (✉ Hwy. 89, ☎ 530/573–2674 in season, WEB www.tahoechamber.org).

SAN FRANCISCO

San Francisco's 800,000 residents nest on a 46½-square-mi tip of land between San Francisco Bay and the Pacific Ocean. Experiencing San Francisco means visiting its neighborhoods: the eclectic Mission District, the gay-friendly Castro, countercultural Haight Street, upscale Pacific Heights, bustling Chinatown, and still-bohemian North Beach.

Exploring San Francisco

Touring San Francisco is best done on foot—although the hills are a challenge. Dependable walking shoes are essential. You'll need a jacket for the dramatic temperature swings, especially in summer, when fog rolls in during the afternoon.

Union Square

The landmark of Union Square is the **Westin St. Francis Hotel** (✉ 335 Powell St., ☎ 415/397–7000, WEB www.westin.com). The hotel's Art Deco **Compass Rose** lounge is a stylish place to sip afternoon tea. Boutiques line two-block **Maiden Lane,** across Union Square from the St. Francis. The building that holds **Folk Art International/Boretti Amber/Xanadu** (✉ 140 Maiden La., ☎ 415/392–9999, WEB www.folkartintl.com) galleries is the only Frank Lloyd Wright building in the city. It's said to have been the architect's model for the Guggenheim Museum in New York City.

Chinatown

The dragon-crowned **Chinatown Gate** (✉ Bush St. and Grant Ave.) is the main entrance to colorful, bustling Chinatown. Among the many interesting architectural examples here is the **Chinese Six Companies** building (✉ 843 Stockton St.). The **Old Chinese Telephone Exchange** (✉ 743 Washington St.), a three-tier pagoda that's now the Bank of Canton, was built after the 1906 earthquake. To learn about the area's history, visit the **Chinese Culture Center** (✉ Holiday Inn, 750 Kearny St., 3rd floor, ☎ 415/986–1822, WEB www.c-c-c.org; 🎫 free); it is closed on Monday.

Nob Hill

The 1906 earthquake destroyed the mansions of railroad barons and gold- and silver-rush millionaires, with the exception of the shell of James Flood's brownstone, now the **Pacific Union Club** (✉ 1000 California St.). The Episcopal **Grace Cathedral** (✉ 1100 California St.) has bronze doors cast from Ghiberti's *Gates of Paradise* in Florence. The **Mark Hopkins Inter-Continental Hotel** (✉ 1 Nob Hill, ☎ 415/392–3434, WEB hotels.san-francisco.interconti.com) is known for the view from its **Top of the Mark** lounge.

Civic Center

City Hall (✉ between Van Ness Ave. and Polk, Grove, and McAllister Sts.), a granite-and-marble masterpiece, faces **Civic Center Plaza,** which has a lawn, walkways, and flower beds. Many transients frequent the plaza, and caution is advised after dark. Weekday tours are available of City Hall, which positively gleams after a long renovation. Inside is the small **Museum of the City of San Francisco** (☎ 415/928–0289, WEB www.sfmuseum.org; 🎫 free), where you can view artifacts related to the city's history. The **Performing Arts Center** complex, on Van Ness Avenue between McAllister and Hayes streets, includes the **War Memorial Opera House** and the **Louise M. Davies Symphony Hall.** The

San Francisco

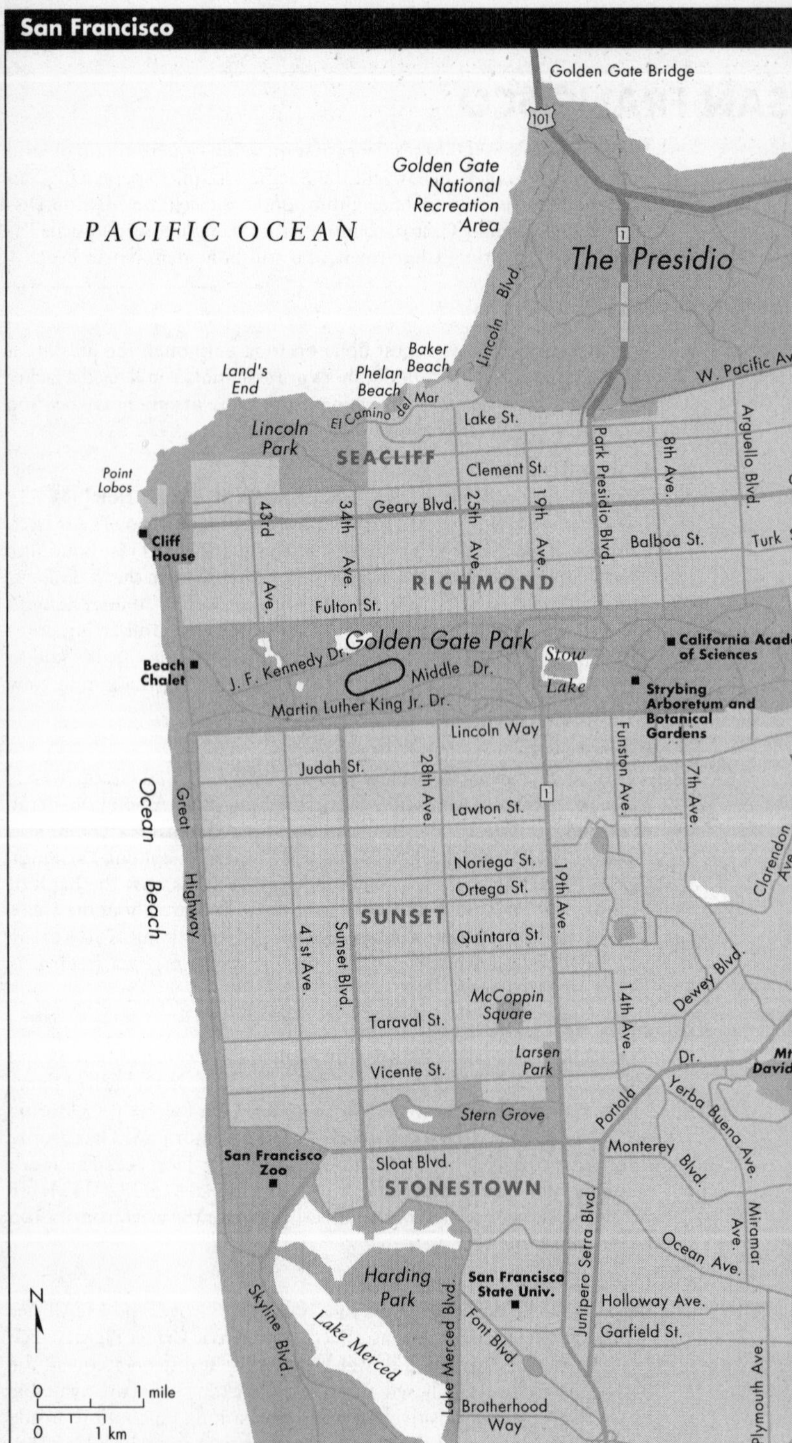

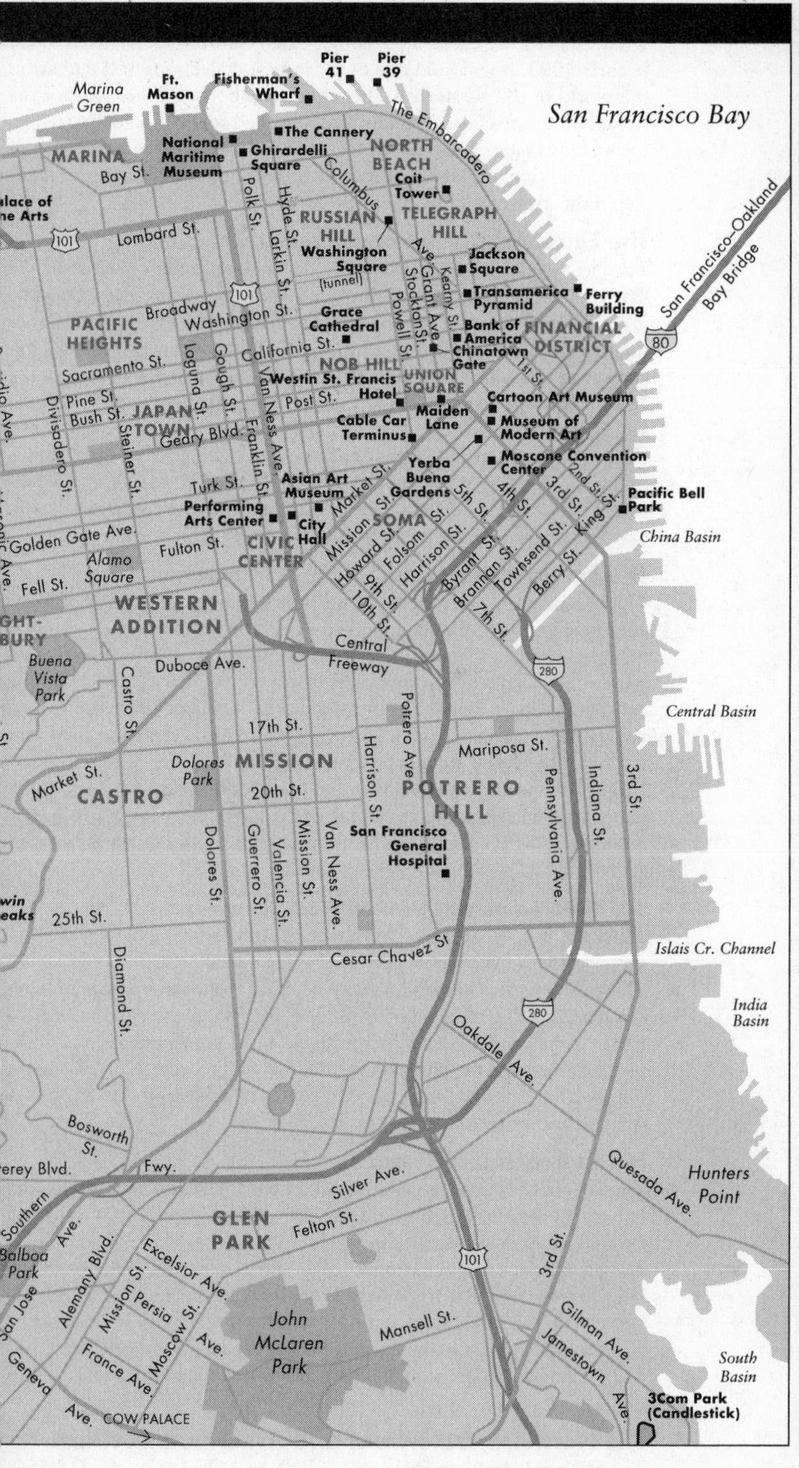

San Francisco Bay
Pier 41
Pier 39
Ft. Mason
Fisherman's Wharf
Marina Green
The Embarcadero
The Cannery
National Maritime Museum
Ghirardelli Square
MARINA
NORTH BEACH
Bay St.
Coit Tower
Columbus
Polk St.
Hyde St.
RUSSIAN HILL
TELEGRAPH HILL
Lombard St.
Larkin St.
Washington Square
(tunnel)
Ave
Jackson Square
Grant Ave.
Kearny St.
Stockton St.
Transamerica Pyramid
Ferry Building
San Francisco–Oakland Bay Bridge
Broadway
Washington St.
Powell St.
Grace Cathedral
PACIFIC HEIGHTS
Bank of America
FINANCIAL DISTRICT
California St.
Chinatown Gate
80
Laguna St.
Gough St.
Van Ness Ave.
NOB HILL
Sacramento St.
1st St.
Westin St. Francis Hotel
UNION SQUARE
Pine St.
Post St.
Cartoon Art Museum
Bush St.
JAPAN TOWN
Maiden Lane
Cable Car Terminus
Museum of Modern Art
Divisadero St.
Steiner St.
Geary Blvd.
Franklin St.
Yerba Buena Gardens
Moscone Convention Center
Market St.
2nd St.
Turk St.
Asian Art Museum
3rd St.
Performing Arts Center
Mission St.
5th St.
4th St.
King St.
Pacific Bell Park
City Hall
SOMA
Golden Gate Ave.
CIVIC CENTER
Howard St.
Folsom St.
Harrison St.
Townsend St.
China Basin
Alamo Square
Fulton St.
Bryant St.
Brannan St.
Berry St.
Fell St.
9th St.
10th St.
7th St.
WESTERN ADDITION
Central Freeway
Buena Vista Park
Duboce Ave.
Castro St.
280
Central Basin
17th St.
Potrero Ave
Mariposa St.
Harrison St.
Dolores Park
MISSION
Market St.
CASTRO
20th St.
POTRERO HILL
Pennsylvania Ave.
Indiana St.
3rd St.
Dolores St.
Guerrero St.
Valencia St.
Mission St.
Van Ness Ave.
San Francisco General Hospital
25th St.
Cesar Chavez St
Islais Cr. Channel
Diamond St.
India Basin
Oakdale Ave.
Bosworth St.
Fwy.
Quesada Ave.
Hunters Point
Silver Ave.
Southern
GLEN PARK
Felton St.
Balboa Park
Ave.
Alemany Blvd.
Excelsior Ave.
101
3rd St.
Mission St.
Persia Ave.
Moscow St.
John McLaren Park
Mansell St.
Gilman Ave.
Jamestown Ave.
San Jose
France Ave.
Geneva Ave.
COW PALACE
South Basin
3Com Park (Candlestick)

new **Asian Art Museum** (✉ 200 Larkin St., ☎ 415/668–8921, WEB www.asianart.org), relocated from Golden Gate Park, is slated to open in early 2003. It will hold one of the largest collections of Asian art in the world.In the Western Addition, a neighborhood due west of the Civic Center area, is the much-photographed row of six identical Victorian houses along **Steiner Street,** at the east end of Alamo Square. If you're walking, the safest route is up Fulton Street to Steiner Street. Avoid the area at night.

The Financial District and the Barbary Coast

The city's signature high-rise is the 853-ft **Transamerica Pyramid** (✉ Clay and Montgomery Sts.). Dominating the Financial District skyline is the 52-story **Bank of America** (✉ California and Kearny Sts.).Other notable structures in the Financial District include the **Pacific Stock Exchange** (✉ 301 Pine St.). The ceiling and entry are black marble in the **Stock Exchange Tower** (✉ 155 Sansome St.), an Art Deco gem. **Jackson Square** is at the heart of what used to be called the Barbary Coast, a late-19th-century haven for brawling and boozing. The brick buildings and narrow alleys in the area bordered by Pacific Avenue and Washington, Sansome, and Montgomery streets recall the romance of early San Francisco; many have been turned into genteel antiques shops.

The Embarcadero and South of Market (SoMa)

The beacon of the port area is the **Ferry Building,** at the foot of Market Street on the Embarcadero. The clock tower is 230 ft high and was modeled after the campanile of Seville's cathedral. A **waterfront promenade** that extends from the piers north of the Ferry Building to the San Francisco–Oakland Bay Bridge is great for watching sailboats on the bay or enjoying a picnic.Across the Embarcadero from the Ferry Building, the **Hyatt Regency Hotel** (✉ 5 Embarcadero, ☎ 415/788–1234, WEB www.hyatt.com) is noted for its lobby and 17-story hanging garden. On the waterfront side of the Hyatt Regency is **Justin Herman Plaza,** often the site of arts-and-crafts shows and rallies for various social causes.

The **Center for the Arts at Yerba Buena Gardens** (✉ 701 Mission St., ☎ 415/978–2787, WEB www.yerbabuenaarts.org; 🎫 galleries $6) presents dance, music, performance, theater, visual arts, film, and video. ★ The galleries are closed on Monday. The **San Francisco Museum of Modern Art** (✉ 151 3rd St., ☎ 415/357–4000, WEB www.sfmoma.org; 🎫 $10), which is closed on Wednesday, has a fine permanent collection.The **Cartoon Art Museum** (✉ 655 Mission St., ☎ 415/227–8666, WEB www.cartoonart.org; 🎫 $5), which is closed on Monday, is a worthwhile stop.

North Beach and Telegraph Hill

★ The streets of **North Beach** are packed with Italian delicatessens and bakeries, coffeehouses, and, increasingly, Chinese markets. Grant and Columbus avenues contain shops selling upscale fashions, often by local designers, and intriguing housewares and other items. **Telegraph Hill** rises to the east of North Beach. From Filbert Street above Grant Avenue, the Greenwich Stairs climb to **Coit Tower** (☎ 415/362–0808; 🎫 $3.75), a monument to the city's volunteer firemen. Inside are the works of 25 muralists. From the top there's a panoramic view of the bay, bridges, and islands.

The Northern Waterfront and Fisherman's Wharf

The **National Maritime Museum** (✉ Polk St. at Beach St., ☎ 415/556–3002, WEB www.maritime.org; 🎫 donation suggested) and Ghirardelli Square are west of the Hyde Street cable-car turnaround; Fisherman's Wharf and Pier 39 are east of it. The historic vessels at the **Hyde Street**

Pier (✉ Hyde St. at Jefferson St., ☎ 415/556–3002, WEB www.maritime.org; 🎫 $6) are a delight to explore. **Bay cruises** (☎ 415/773–1188 Blue and Gold ferries; 415/673–2900 Red and White line) leave from Piers 39, 41, and 43½. The renovated factory buildings of **Ghirardelli Square** (✉ 900 N. Point St., between Polk and Larkin Sts.) are filled with shops, restaurants, and galleries. East of the Hyde Street Pier is the **Cannery** (✉ 2801 Leavenworth St., at Beach St.), a former fruit and vegetable cannery that houses shops and restaurants and is often the site of impromptu performances by local musicians and street artists.The shopping and entertainment options at the popular **Pier 39** include **Aquarium of the Bay** (☎ 415/623–5300 or 888/732–3483, WEB www.aquariumofthebay.com), which surveys Bay Area marine life. Aboveground are a carousel, food stalls, and some noisy sea lions that bask on the pier's north side.

★ **Lombard Street,** better known as "the crookedest street in the world," is south of the waterfront area between Hyde and Leavenworth streets.To the west of the waterfront area, at the edge of the Marina District, is the **Palace of Fine Arts** (✉ Baker and Beach Sts.), with massive columns, an imposing rotunda, and a swan-filled lagoon. Built for the 1915 Panama-Pacific International Exposition, the palace is a cherished San Francisco landmark. ★ The **Exploratorium** (✉ Palace of Fine Arts, ☎ 415/561–0360, WEB www.exploratorium.edu; 🎫 $10) contains imaginative interactive science exhibits.

To reach the **Golden Gate Bridge,** walk along the bay from the Marina District or take Muni Bus 28 to the toll plaza. Conditions are sometimes gusty and misty, but a walk across the nearly 2-mi-long bridge offers unparalleled views of the skyline, the bay, the Marin Headlands, and the Pacific Ocean. Check the bridge's Web site, WEB www.goldengatebridge.org, for information about hours of access to the sidewalks, which are sometimes restricted because of security concerns.

Golden Gate Park and the Western Shore

★ **Golden Gate Park,** in the northwestern part of town, is ideal for strolling. On Sunday many of its streets are closed to car traffic. Inside the **California Academy of Sciences** (✉ 55 Concourse Dr., ☎ 415/750–7145, WEB www.calacademy.org; 🎫 $8.50), a fine natural history museum, are the **Steinhart Aquarium** and the **Morrison Planetarium.** The **Strybing Arboretum and Botanical Gardens** (✉ 9th Ave. at Lincoln Way, ☎ 415/661–1316, WEB www.strybing.org; 🎫 free) shelters Californian, Australian, Mediterranean, and South African plants.The **Beach Chalet,** at the park's west end, contains a visitor center and a brewpub restaurant with views of Ocean Beach. At the north end of Ocean Beach is the **Cliff House** (✉ 1090 Point Lobos Ave., ☎ 415/386–3330), a restaurant where you can dine to the sound of crashing surf. The restaurant will stay open during renovations slated for September 2002 to March 2004. The **San Francisco Zoo** (✉ Sloat Blvd. at 45th Ave., ☎ 415/753–7080; 🎫 $10), at the south end of Ocean Beach, also has a children's zoo where kids can interact with the animals.

Dining

$$$ ★ ✕ **Hawthorne Lane.** On a quiet alley a block or so from the Museum of Modern Art, patrons in the somewhat formal, light-flooded dining room find contemporary fare all turned out with Mediterranean and Asian touches. ✉ *22 Hawthorne St.,* ☎ *415/777–9779. Reservations essential. D, DC, MC, V. No lunch weekends.*

$$$ ★ ✕ **Jardinière.** This is *the* place to dine before a performance at the nearby Opera House and Symphony Hall. The sophisticated interior, with its eye-catching oval atrium, plays host to a contemporary menu with memorable first courses of ahi tartare, duck confit, and foie gras. A three-

course "staccato menu" puts music-loving diners in their seats before the curtain goes up. ✉ *300 Grove St.,* ☎ *415/861–5555. Reservations essential. AE, DC, MC, V. No lunch.*

$$–$$$ ✕ **Jianna.** This stylish newcomer bucks the North Beach Italian tradition to serve gutsy California cuisine. Gracious service and reasonable prices make the dishes like oregano-crusted lamb loin and goat cheese fondue taste even better. ✉ *1548 Stockton St.,* ☎ *415/398–0442. AE, D, MC, V. No lunch.*

$–$$$ ★ ✕ **Rose Pistola.** Chef-owner Reed Hearon celebrates North Beach's Ligurian roots with a wide assortment of small antipasti plates, such as roasted peppers and house-cured fish, in addition to pizzas from a wood-burning oven and cioppino, the classic San Francisco Italian seafood stew. ✉ *532 Columbus Ave.,* ☎ *415/399–0499. Reservations essential. AE, D, DC, MC, V.*

$$ ★ ✕ **B44.** With its spare, modern design and open kitchen, B44 draws locals who love the menu of authentic Catalan tapas and paellas. ✉ *44 Belden Pl.,* ☎ *415/986–6287. AE, MC, V. Closed Sun. No lunch Sat.*

$$ ✕ **Scala's Bistro.** Smart leather-and-wood booths, an extravagant mural along one wall, and an appealing menu of Italian plates make this one of downtown's most attractive destinations. ✉ *432 Powell St.,* ☎ *415/395–8555. AE, DC, MC, V.*

$–$$ ✕ **Café Claude.** Order a salade niçoise or simple roast chicken from the French-speaking staff at this café in a Financial District alley, and you might forget what country you're in. On weekends the boisterous crowds regularly spill out into the alleyway. ✉ *7 Claude La.,* ☎ *415/392–3505. AE, DC, MC, V. Closed Sun.*

$–$$ ★ ✕ **Delfina.** This clean, modern, and very popular spot attracts a loyal crowd with chef-owner Craig Stoll's simple yet exquisite Italian fare. ✉ *3621 18th St.,* ☎ *415/552–4055. MC, V. No lunch.*

$–$$ ★ ✕ **Ton Kiang.** The lightly seasoned Hakka cuisine of southern China, rarely found in this country, was introduced to San Francisco at this restaurant. Most come for the fabulous dim sum, served until 10 PM daily. ✉ *5821 Geary Blvd.,* ☎ *415/387–8273. AE, D, DC, MC, V.*

$ ✕ **La Taqueria.** This attractive taqueria in the Mission is one of the finest among many. The tacos—with a spoonful of perfectly fresh salsa—are superb. ✉ *2889 Mission St.,* ☎ *415/285–7117. Reservations not accepted. No credit cards.*

$ ★ ✕ **Thep Phanom.** The fine Thai food and the lovely interior at this Lower Haight institution keep local food critics and restaurant goers singing its praises. ✉ *400 Waller St.,* ☎ *415/431–2526. AE, D, DC, MC, V. No lunch.*

$ ✕ **Mifune.** Bowls of thin brown *soba* (buckwheat) and thick white *udon* (wheat) noodles are the traditional Japanese specialties served at this outpost of an Osaka-based noodle empire. ✉ *Japan Center, Kintetsu Bldg., 1737 Post St.,* ☎ *415/922–0337. Reservations not accepted. AE, D, DC, MC, V.*

Lodging

$$$$ ★ **Mandarin Oriental.** Since the Mandarin comprises the top 11 floors (38 to 48) of the California Center, all rooms provide sweeping panoramic vistas of the city and beyond; those facing west fill up quickly because of their views of the Golden Gate Bridge and the Pacific Ocean. Touches like silk slippers, plush robes, binoculars, and fresh fruit pamper guests. ✉ *222 Sansome St., 94104,* ☎ *415/276–9888 or 800/622–0404,* FAX *415/433–0289,* WEB *www.mandarinoriental.com. 158 rooms. Restaurant, gym. AE, D, DC, MC, V.*

$$$–$$$$ **Hotel Milano.** Adjacent to the San Francisco Shopping Centre and near all the museums and attractions south of Market Street, the eight-story hotel has spacious and handsomely decorated Italian-inspired guest rooms. Enjoy a soak, steam, or sauna in the split-level fitness center. ✉ *55 5th St., 94103,* ☎ *415/543–8555 or 800/398–7555,* FAX *415/543–5885,* WEB *hotelmilano.citysearch.com. 108 rooms. Restaurant, gym. AE, D, DC, MC, V.*

$$$–$$$$ ★ **Hotel Monaco.** This very hip hotel with a yellow Beaux-Arts facade has small but comfortable and inviting guest rooms. In the evening, there's a complimentary wine and cheese hour featuring a tarot reader and massage therapist. ✉ *501 Geary St., 94102,* ☎ *415/292–0100 or 866/622–5284,* FAX *415/292–0111,* WEB *www.monaco-sf.com. 201 rooms. Restaurant, health club. AE, D, DC, MC, V.*

$$$ **Maxwell Hotel.** This handsome, stylish hotel is a block from Union Square. Rooms have a clubby, retro feel, with classic Edward Hopper prints on the walls. ✉ *386 Geary St., 94102,* ☎ *415/986–2000 or 888/734–6299,* FAX *415/397–2447,* WEB *www.maxwellhotel.com. 153 rooms. Restaurant. AE, D, DC, MC, V.*

$$$ **Sir Francis Drake Hotel.** A Beefeater-costumed doorman welcomes you into the regal lobby of this 1928 landmark property. The guest rooms look neoclassical, with boldly striped fabrics and mahogany and cherry-wood furniture. On the top floor, Harry Denton's Starlight Room is one of the city's plushest skyline bars. ✉ *450 Powell St., 94102,* ☎ *415/392–7755 or 800/227–5480,* FAX *415/391–8719,* WEB *www.sirfrancisdrake.com. 417 rooms. 2 restaurants, gym. AE, D, DC, MC, V.*

$$–$$$ **Clarion Bedford Hotel.** Pass under Art Nouveau arches to enter the bright lobby of this handsome 1929 building. Most of the light and airy rooms with white furniture and canopied beds have gorgeous bay and city views. Frequent package deals make this hotel, always a good buy, an even better bargain. ✉ *761 Post St., 94109,* ☎ *415/673–6040 or 800/252–7466,* FAX *415/563–6739,* WEB *www.hotelbedford.com. 144 rooms. Restaurant. AE, D, DC, MC, V.*

$$–$$$ ★ **Hotel Del Sol.** Once a typical '50s-style motor court, the Hotel Del Sol has a sunny courtyard and yellow-and-blue three-story building that are candy for the eyes. Rooms evoke a beach-house feeling with plantation shutters and rattan chairs. Some have brick fireplaces. ✉ *3100 Webster St., 94123,* ☎ *415/921–5520 or 877/433–5765,* FAX *415/931–4137,* WEB *www.thehoteldelsol.com. 57 rooms. Pool. AE, D, DC, MC, V.*

$–$$ **Golden Gate Hotel.** This homey, family-run B&B is set in a four-story Edwardian with bay windows. The original "birdcage" elevator takes you to the rooms, which are individually decorated with antiques, wicker pieces, and floral bedding and curtains. The least expensive rooms share a bath. ✉ *775 Bush St., 94108,* ☎ *415/392–3702 or 800/835–1118,* FAX *415/392–6202,* WEB *www.goldengatehotel.com. 23 rooms, 14 with bath. AE, DC, MC, V. CP.*

$ **Adelaide Hostel.** The bedspreads don't match the curtains, but the rooms are clean and cheap at this friendly small hostel popular with Europeans. There are sinks in every room, but the baths down the hall are shared. Private rooms are available for one to four, and dorm rooms have a maximum of four beds. ✉ *5 Isadora Duncan La., at Taylor St. between Geary and Post Sts., 94102,* ☎ *415/441–2474 or 877/359–1915,* FAX *415/441–0161,* WEB *www.adelaidehostel.com. 18 rooms. AE, D, DC, MC, V.*

Nightlife and the Arts

For club and events listings, see the pink "Datebook" section of the Sunday *Examiner-Chronicle* or pick up the weekly *Bay Guardian* or

S.F. Weekly, available throughout the city. You can charge tickets from **Tickets.com** (☎ 415/776–1999 or 510/762–2277) by phone. Half-price same-day tickets to many stage shows go on sale at 11 AM Tuesday–Saturday at the **TIX Bay Area** (☎ 415/433–7827) ticket booth, inside the Geary Street entrance of the Union Square Garage, between Stockton and Powell streets. Cash only is accepted.

Nightlife

DANCE CLUBS

El Rio (✉ 3158 Mission St., ☎ 415/282–3325) hosts a mix of salsa, Arab, and world dance events. **Metronome Ballroom** (✉ 1830 17th St., ☎ 415/252–9000), a dance instruction venue by day, attracts serious salsa, swing, and ballroom dancers on weekends, when it throws six different dance parties.

MUSIC CLUBS

Bimbo's 365 Club (✉ 1025 Columbus Ave., ☎ 415/474–0365) is a plush place with a retro feel for a variety of rock acts. **Bottom of the Hill** (✉ 1233 17th St., ☎ 415/621–4455) showcases some of the city's best alternative rock. **Cafe Du Nord** (✉ 2170 Market St., ☎ 415/861–5016) presents live jazz, blues, and rock, as well as occasional DJ events. The **Great American Music Hall** (✉ 859 O'Farrell St., ☎ 415/885–0750) hosts top blues, folk, jazz, and rock entertainers. Count on **Slim's** (✉ 333 11th St., ☎ 415/522–0333) for high-quality rock, jazz, and blues.

SAN FRANCISCO'S FAVORITE BARS

The outrageously hip **Redwood Room** (✉ 495 Geary St., ☎ 415/929–2372), reopened after a redesign by Philippe Starck, is an expensive and glamorous spot for people-watching. The draws at the famously kitschy **Tonga Room** (✉ Fairmont Hotel, 950 Mason St., ☎ 415/772–5278) are the over-the-top Polynesian theme and the faux rainstorm, complete with simulated thunder, that takes place every half hour. **Vesuvio Cafe** (✉ 255 Columbus Ave., ☎ 415/362–3370) recalls the heyday of the beat poets, with memorabilia from the era covering nearly every surface.

GAY AND LESBIAN NIGHTLIFE

At the **Lexington Club** (✉ 3464 19th St., ☎ 415/863–2052), where "Every night is ladies' night," you'll find a younger lesbian crowd. The **Stud** (✉ 399 9th St., ☎ 415/252–7883) attracts mostly gay men for different dance events six nights a week. Friday nights are lesbian events.

The Arts

The **American Conservatory Theater** (✉ Geary Theater, 415 Geary St., ☎ 415/749–2228), the city's main nonprofit theater company, specializes in classics and contemporary dramas. The **San Francisco Ballet** (✉ War Memorial Opera House, 301 Van Ness Ave., ☎ 415/865–2000) performs from February to May. The **San Francisco Opera** (✉ War Memorial Opera House, 301 Van Ness Ave., ☎ 415/864–3330) performs September to January and June to July. The **San Francisco Symphony** (✉ Louise M. Davies Symphony Hall, 201 Van Ness Ave., ☎ 415/864–6000) plays from September to May.

Shopping

Shopping Districts

In **Chinatown** you can find gift items, foodstuffs, home furnishings, and clothing imported from Asia. The **Embarcadero Center,** occupying four blocks of Clay Street on the waterfront, houses 125 retailers and a multiplex movie theater, as well as a number of restaurants. **Fisherman's**

Wharf is the place to buy San Francisco souvenirs. **Haight-Ashbury** has some interesting shops, particularly on the 1500 block of Haight Street. **Union Square** is surrounded by Macy's, Saks Fifth Avenue, and Neiman Marcus. On or near the square are Tiffany & Co., Disney, Border's Books and Music, Niketown, and Virgin Megastore.

Side Trip to Berkeley and Oakland

Arriving and Departing

By car, follow I–80 across the Bay Bridge; exit at University Avenue for Berkeley or pick up I–580 and exit at Grand Avenue for Oakland. By BART, Berkeley is 30 to 45 minutes from the city; exit at the downtown Berkeley stop, and then take the shuttle or walk about 15 minutes to campus. Oakland is a 15- to 30-minute BART ride from San Francisco; exit at the Lake Merritt station for the museum.

What to See and Do

Berkeley is the home of the **University of California at Berkeley.** Along Telegraph Avenue south of the campus is a student-oriented business district with a dog-eared counterculture ambience.

Oakland has the second-largest port in California. **Jack London Square** (✉ Embarcadero at Broadway, ☎ 510/814–6000), along the waterfront, holds shops, restaurants, small museums, and historic sites. The **Oakland Museum of California** (✉ 1000 Oak St., ☎ 510/238–2200 or 888/625–6873, WEB www.museumca.org; $6) displays California art, history, and natural sciences through engaging exhibits and films.

Dining

$$–$$$$ ★ ✕ **Chez Panisse.** This culinary institution was one of the birthplaces of California cuisine. Meals at the formal downstairs restaurant are pricey; things are less expensive upstairs in the informal café. ✉ *1517 Shattuck Ave., north of University Ave.,* ☎ *510/548–5525 restaurant; 510/548–5049 café. Reservations essential for restaurant. AE, D, DC, MC, V. Closed Sun.*

San Francisco Essentials

AIRPORTS AND TRANSFERS

San Francisco International Airport (SFO), 30 minutes south of the city off U.S. 101, is served by most major airlines. Several domestic airlines serve Oakland Airport (OAK), across the bay.

➤ AIRPORT INFORMATION: **San Francisco International Airport** (☎ 650/875–8575, WEB www.flysfo.com). **Oakland Airport** (☎ 510/577–4000, WEB www.flyoakland.com).

AIRPORT TRANSFER

SuperShuttle will take you from SFO to anywhere within the city limits ($12.50–$17). Taxis between downtown and either airport take 20–30 minutes and cost about $35.

➤ TAXIS AND SHUTTLES: **SuperShuttle** (☎ 415/558–8500, WEB www.supershuttle.com/htm/cities/sfo.htm).

BOAT AND FERRY TRAVEL

Golden Gate Ferry, which departs from the south wing of the Ferry Building at Market Street and the Embarcadero, and Blue and Gold Fleet ferries, at Pier 41 near Fisherman's Wharf, offer trips to outlying cities and attractions around the bay.

➤ BOAT AND FERRY INFORMATION: **Blue and Gold Fleet** (☎ 415/705–5555, WEB www.blueandgoldfleet.com). **Golden Gate Ferry** (☎ 415/923–2000, WEB www.goldengateferry.org).

BUS TRAVEL TO AND FROM SAN FRANCISCO

Greyhound serves San Francisco's Transbay Terminal.

➤ Bus Information: **Greyhound** (☎ 800/231–2222, WEB www.greyhound.com). **Transbay Terminal** (✉ 1st and Mission Sts.).

CAR TRAVEL

I–80 comes into San Francisco from the east, crossing the Bay Bridge from Oakland. U.S. 101 runs north–south through the city and across the Golden Gate Bridge.

PARKING

Public parking garages (look for the city seal) tend to be less expensive than private lots. Hotel garages charge as much as $35 per day.

RULES OF THE ROAD

Watch out for one-way streets, curb your wheels when parking on hills, and check street signs for parking restrictions. Except at a few marked intersections, a right turn at a red light is legal, as is a left turn on red at two intersecting one-way streets.

TAXIS

Rates are high—$2.50 to get in and about $2 a mile after that. It's difficult to hail a cab in most neighborhoods. Call Yellow Cab Co., but expect long waits during peak periods. When possible, book in advance.

➤ Taxi Companies: **Yellow Cab Co.** (☎ 415/626–2345, WEB www.yellowcabsf.com).

TOURS

BUS TOURS

Gray Line offers tours on buses and double-deckers ranging in price from $25 to $55. The Great Pacific Tour, a minivan tour of the city, lasts 3½ hours at a cost of $37; multilingual guides are available, and the company will pick you up at most downtown hotels.

➤ Fees and Schedules: **Gray Line** (✉ 350 8th St., ☎ 415/558–9400 or 800/826–0202, WEB www.grayline.com). **Great Pacific Tour** (✉ 518 Octavia St., ☎ 415/626–4499, WEB www.greatpacifictour.com).

WALKING TOURS

The Chinese Culture Center offers a Heritage Walk and a Culinary Walk through Chinatown. The Precita Eyes Mural Arts and Visitors Center leads walking and biking tours of the vibrant murals of the Mission District.

➤ Fees and Schedules: **Chinese Culture Center** (☎ 415/986–1822, WEB www.c-c-c.org). **Precita Eyes Mural Arts and Visitors Center** (☎ 415/285–2287, WEB www.precitaeyes.org).

TRAIN TRAVEL

Amtrak trains stop in Oakland and Emeryville; shuttle buses connect the Emeryville station and San Francisco's Ferry Building, on the Embarcadero. CalTrain travels from the city to San Jose, with stops in most communities along the way.

➤ Train Information: **Amtrak** (✉ 5885 Landregan St., Emeryville; ✉ Jack London Sq., 245 2nd St., Oakland, ☎ 800/872–7245, WEB www.amtrak.com). **CalTrain** (✉ 4th and Townsend Sts., ☎ 800/660–4287 or 650/817–1717, WEB www.caltrain.com).

TRANSPORTATION AROUND SAN FRANCISCO

Most of the light-rail and bus lines of the Municipal Railway System, called Muni, operate continuously; standard fare is $1, and exact change (coins or a dollar bill) is required. If you'll be changing buses, get a transfer (good for 90 minutes) when you board. Three cable car lines crisscross downtown; information and tickets ($2) are available on board.

Multiday tourist passes can be obtained at the lower level of Hallidie Plaza, at Powell and Market streets. BART (Bay Area Rapid Transit) trains service Berkeley, Oakland, and beyond to Daly City, Concord, Dublin, and Richmond; wall maps list destinations and fares.

➤ CONTACTS: **BART** (☎ 650/992–2278, WEB www.bart.gov). **Muni** (☎ 415/673–6864, WEB www.sfmuni.com).

VISITOR INFORMATION

Contact the San Francisco Convention and Visitors Bureau by phone or visit its Web site for an information kit or pick one up at the lower level of Hallidie Plaza, at the corner of Market and Powell streets.

➤ TOURIST INFORMATION: **San Francisco Convention and Visitors Bureau** (✉ 900 Market St., 94102, ☎ 415/974–6900, WEB www.sfvisitor.org).

SAN JOSE

In 1777, El Pueblo de San Jose de Guadalupe became California's first civil settlement under Spanish rule. Today, strikingly modern architecture contrasts with restored 19th-century and Mission-style buildings. San Jose is a great city to explore on foot.

Exploring San Jose

The **Children's Discovery Museum** (✉ 180 Woz Way, at Auzerais St., ☎ 408/298–5437, WEB www.cdm.org; 🎫 $7) contains interactive installations on science, the humanities, and the arts. At the northeast corner of the Plaza de Cesar Chavez is the **San Jose Museum of Art** (✉ 110 S. Market St., ☎ 408/294–2787, WEB www.sjmusart.org; 🎫 free), a well-rounded modern museum with specialties in tech-inspired and Latino art. The multidome **Cathedral Basilica of St. Joseph** (✉ 80 S. Market St., ☎ 408/283–8100, WEB www.stjosephcathedral.org), built in 1877, has extraordinary stained-glass windows and murals. On the western edge of Plaza de Cesar Chavez, at Park Avenue, is the dazzling ★ **Tech Museum of Innovation** (✉ 201 S. Market St., ☎ 408/294–8324, WEB www.thetech.org; 🎫 $9), which has many hands-on exhibits about technology and an IMAX dome theater.

Fallon House and Peralta Adobe (✉ 175 and 184 W. St. John St., ☎ 408/993–8182, WEB www.historysanjose.org; 🎫 $6 for both), across the street from each other, date far back in California's history. The circa-1797 Peralta Adobe is the last remaining structure from the pueblo that was once San Jose. Fallon House was built in 1855 by the city's seventh mayor. ★ The **Rosicrucian Egyptian Museum** (✉ 1342 Naglee Ave., ☎ 408/947–3635, WEB www.rosicrucian.org; 🎫 museum $9) exhibits Egyptian and Babylonian antiquities, including mummies.

Dining and Lodging

$$$–$$$$ ★ ✕ **Emile's.** The cuisine of Swiss chef and owner Emile Mooser has classical and contemporary Californian influences. Specialties include house-cured gravlax, rack of lamb, fresh game, and a Grand Marnier soufflé. *✉ 545 S. 2nd St., ☎ 408/289–1960. AE, D, DC, MC, V. Closed Sun.–Mon. No lunch.*

$–$$ ✕ **Gordon Biersch Brewery Restaurant.** San Jose's younger set feasts on the kitchen's legendary garlic fries, ahi tuna, and burgers, both in the bustling dining room and outside in the four-season courtyard. *✉ 33 E. San Fernando St., ☎ 408/294–6785. AE, D, DC, MC, V.*

$$–$$$$ 🏨 **Hotel De Anza.** This lushly appointed 1931 Art Deco hotel, listed on the National Register of Historic Places, has been carefully restored. Hand-painted ceilings, a warm color scheme, and an enclosed

terrace with towering palms and dramatic fountains set a refined mood. The elegant lounge is a great place to hear live jazz or just pretend you're a movie star. ✉ *233 W. Santa Clara St., 95113,* ☎ *408/286–1000 or 800/843–3700,* FAX *408/286–0500,* WEB *www.hoteldeanza.com. 100 rooms. Restaurant, gym. AE, D, DC, MC, V.*

Nightlife and the Arts

Agenda (✉ 399 N. 1st St., ☎ 408/287–3991) consists of a restaurant, lounge, and nightclub with live music most nights. The **Center for Performing Arts** (✉ 225 Almaden Blvd., ☎ 408/277–3900; 408/998–2277 BASS tickets) is a venue for drama, musical-theater, symphony, opera, and ballet performances. **San Jose Repertory Theatre** (✉ 101 Paseo de San Antonio, ☎ 408/367–7255) is a well-regarded company.

San Jose Essentials

AIRPORTS AND TRANSFERS

San Jose International Airport is served by many major airlines.

➤ AIRPORT INFORMATION: **San Jose International Airport** (✉ 1661 Airport Blvd., off Rte. 87, ☎ 408/225–4444, WEB www.sjc.org).

AIRPORT TRANSFER

South & East Bay Airport Shuttle transports travelers to and from the airport.

➤ TAXIS AND SHUTTLES: **South & East Bay Airport Shuttle** (☎ 408/559–9477).

CAR TRAVEL

San Jose is 44 mi south of San Francisco; the easiest route to downtown is I–280 south to the Guadalupe Parkway (also known as Route 87) north to the Santa Clara Street exit east.

TRAIN TRAVEL

CalTrain runs from 4th and Townsend streets in San Francisco to San Jose's Rod Diridon station ($5.25 one-way). The Santa Clara Valley Transportation Authority (VTA) operates a shuttle bus between downtown San Jose and the CalTrain station during morning and evening commute hours.

➤ TRAIN INFORMATION: **CalTrain** (☎ 800/660–4287, WEB www.caltrain.com). **Santa Clara Valley Transportation Authority** (☎ 408/321–2300, 800/894–9908, WEB www.vta.org).

TRANSPORTATION AROUND SAN JOSE

Light-rail trains pass near most major attractions and historic sites downtown. Tickets cost $1.25 one-way or $3 for a day pass. The Downtown Customer Service Center has information about local bus routes.

➤ CONTACTS: **Downtown Customer Service Center** (✉ 2 N. 1st St., ☎ 408/321–2300).

VISITOR INFORMATION

➤ TOURIST INFORMATION: **San Jose Convention and Visitors Bureau** (✉ 150 W. San Carlos St., 95110, ☎ 408/977–0900 or 408/295–2265, WEB www.sjcc.com).

SOUTHERN SIERRA AND DEATH VALLEY

The quintessential image of California's spectacular wilderness is Yosemite's U-shape valleys, formed by the action of glaciers during recent ice ages and immortalized in the photographs of Ansel Adams. South of Yosemite are Sequoia and Kings Canyon National parks, spectacular for their giant trees and deep canyons.

Exploring the Southern Sierra and Death Valley

★ The highlights of **Yosemite National Park** lie in Yosemite Valley and include **Yosemite Fall,** the highest waterfall in North America; the famous **El Capitan** and **Half Dome** granite peaks; misty **Bridalveil Fall;** and **Glacier Point,** which affords a phenomenal bird's-eye view of the entire valley. Near **Wawona** at the park's south entrance are the historic **Wawona Hotel** and the **Mariposa Grove of Big Trees.** A free **shuttle bus** runs around the east end of Yosemite Valley year-round. A summer shuttle runs from Wawona to the Mariposa Grove of Big Trees.

As you exit Yosemite via Route 41 south and enter **Kings Canyon National Park** via Route 180 east, your first stop is **Grant Grove Village.** Nearby is the **General Grant Tree,** which has been standing for nearly 2,000 years. A drive through the **Sequoia National Forest** leads along the scenic **Kings River Canyon,** which in places is deeper than the Grand Canyon.

Route 198 will take you south into **Sequoia National Park.** Follow Generals Highway south to reach **General Sherman Tree,** the world's largest living tree, and take a stroll down **Congress Trail,** a 2-mi loop through the heart of the sequoia forest. About 2 mi farther south, stop at **Giant Forest** to walk the **Big Trees Trail,** which passes through forest and meadow in an easy loop. At the **Giant Forest Museum** you can learn about the giant sequoia.

East of the Southern Sierra, **Death Valley National Park** is a desert wonderland of sand dunes, crusty salt flats, 11,000-ft mountains, and hills and canyons of many hues. To reach the park from the west side of the Sierra, drive Route 99 south to Bakersfield, then Route 58 east to Mojave, where you can pick up U.S. 395 north. At Olancha, turn onto Route 190 east into Death Valley. In the northwestern section of the park is **Scotty's Castle,** a Moorish-style mansion built by a onetime performer in Buffalo Bill's Wild West Show. **Harmony Borax Works** illustrates the mining history of Death Valley, from which 20-mule teams hauled borax to the railroad at Mojave. **Dante's View,** 5,000 ft up in the Black Mountains, has views of the lowest (Badwater) and highest (Mt. Whitney) points in the contiguous United States.

Dining and Lodging

$–$$ ✕ **Grant Grove Restaurant.** Simple family-style dining is available at this Kings Canyon spot year-round. The restaurant serves full breakfasts and hot entrées and sandwiches for lunch and dinner. Counter service is available. ✉ *Grant Grove Village, Kings Canyon National Park,* ☎ *559/335–5500. D, MC, V.*

$$$$ ✕ **Inn Dining Room.** This beautiful Mission-style restaurant on the grounds of the Furnace Creek Inn in Death Valley National Park has views of the Panamint Mountains. The seasonally changing main courses could include seared ahi tuna, fire-roasted corn chowder, chilled lobster salad, and a rack of lamb. There's a brunch on Sunday. ✉ *Furnace Creek, Death Valley National Park,* ☎ *760/786–2345. Reservations essential. AE, D, DC, MC, V.*

$$$$ ★ ✕🏨 **Ahwahnee Hotel & Dining Room.** Yosemite's grand 1920s-era mountain lodge, designated a National Historical Landmark, is constructed of rocks and sugar-pine logs. In the Ahwahnee's comfortable rooms, you'll enjoy some of the amenities found in a luxury hotel, including turn-down service and guest bathrobes. The Ahwahnee Dining Room, with its 34-ft-tall trestle-beam ceiling, serves poached salmon, roasted duckling, and prime rib. Jackets are required, and reservations are essential. ✉ *Ahwahnee Rd. north of Northside Dr., Yosemite*

National Park, ☎ *559/252–4848,* WEB *www.yosemitepark.com. 103 rooms, 24 cottages. Restaurant, pool, tennis. AE, D, DC, MC, V.*

$$ ✕🏨 **Wuksachi Village & Lodge.** Three wood, stone, and cedar buildings make up this facility in Sequoia National Park. Rooms are comfortable, with a rustic edge, and have space to store your skis. The huge windows of the dining room look out on the trees at Sequoia's only white-tablecloth restaurant. The menu features southwestern cuisine and borrows elements from Asian cooking. Reservations are essential for dinner. ✉ *Generals Hwy., 2 mi east of Lodgepole visitor center, Sequoia National Park,* ☎ *559/253–2199 or 888/252–5757,* WEB *www. visitsequoia.com. 102 rooms. Restaurant. AE, D, DC, MC, V.*

$$ 🏨 **Furnace Creek Ranch.** What was once crew headquarters for the Pacific Coast Borax Company is now the family-oriented, less-expensive sister motel to the Furnace Creek Inn. Though it exudes a sense of the rustic life, facilities are thoroughly modern. The rooms all have views of an 18-hole golf course, and some have balconies. ✉ *Furnace Creek, Death Valley National Park,* ☎ *760/786–2345 or 800/528–6367,* FAX *760/786–2423,* WEB *www.furnacecreekresort.com. 224 rooms. Restaurant, pool, golf, tennis. AE, D, DC, MC, V.*

$$–$$$ 🏨 **John Muir Lodge.** In a wooded area of Kings Canyon National Park, this modern lodge has rooms with queen-size beds and private baths. The lobby has a stone fireplace. ✉ *Grant Grove Village, Kings Canyon National Park,* ☎ *559/335–5500,* FAX *559/335–5507,* WEB *www.sequoia-kingscanyon.com. 30 rooms. AE, D, DC, MC, V.*

Southern Sierra and Death Valley Essentials

AIRPORTS

Fresno Yosemite International Airport, the nearest major airport to the Sierra national parks, is served by national and regional carriers. McCarran International Airport in Las Vegas, Nevada, is the closest major airport to Death Valley National Park.

➤ AIRPORT INFORMATION: **Fresno Yosemite International Airport** (✉ 4995 E. Clinton Ave., ☎ 559/498–4700, WEB www.flyfresno.org). **McCarran International Airport** (☎ 702/261–5733).

BUS TRAVEL

Yosemite VIA runs four daily buses from Merced to Yosemite Valley. Greyhound serves Merced from the California coast. There is no scheduled bus service to Death Valley National Park.

➤ BUS INFORMATION: **Greyhound** (☎ 800/231–2222, WEB www. greyhound.com). **Yosemite VIA** (☎ 209/384–1315 or 800/369–7275, WEB www.via-adventures.com).

CAR TRAVEL

Route 99, which runs north–south through California's Central Valley, intersects all of the routes into the southern Sierra and the Death Valley area. To reach Yosemite, take Route 120 east from Manteca, Route 140 east from Merced, or Route 41 north from Fresno. To reach Kings Canyon, take Route 180 east from Fresno or Route 63 north from Tulare and Visalia to Route 180 east. To reach Sequoia, take Route 180 east from Fresno to Route 198 south, or take Route 198 north from Visalia. To reach Death Valley, take Route 58 from Bakersfield to U.S. 395 north, then Route 190 east. In this land of weather extremes (record snowfall in the mountains and record high temperatures in the desert) and sparse population, reliable maps are a must.

VISITOR INFORMATION

➤ TOURIST INFORMATION: **Death Valley National Park** (✉ Furnace Creek, Rte. 190, ☎ 760/786–2331, WEB www.nps.gov/deva). **Sequoia** and Kings Canyon National Parks (✉ 47050 Generals Hwy. Three Rivers, CA 93271–9651, ☎ 559/565–3341 or 559/565–3134, WEB www.nps.gov/seki). **Yosemite National Park** (✉ Box 577, Yosemite National Park 95389, ☎ 209/372–0264; 209/372–0200 24-hr information; WEB www.nps.gov/yose).

THE CENTRAL COAST

Raging surf, rugged rocks, hidden tidal pools, and wind-warped trees mark the coastline south from San Francisco. Several towns provide entertainment, but the Pacific Ocean is the main attraction. Coast-hugging Route 1, sometimes precariously narrow, is the route of choice. It's slow and winding, but the views are worth the extra time.

Exploring the Central Coast

About 125 mi south of San Francisco, the city of **Monterey** is rich in California history.The Path of History is a 2-mi self-guided tour through ★ **Monterey State Historic Park** (✉ 20 Custom House Plaza, ☎ 831/649–7118), a neighborhood of well-preserved adobe buildings dating from the first half of the 19th century. Two museums document the Monterey Bay area's history. Monterey's barking sea lions are best seen along **Fisherman's Wharf** (✉ Custom House Plaza, ☎ 831/649–6544, WEB www.montereywharf.com), a touristy pier. A footpath leads from Fisherman's Wharf to **Cannery Row** (✉ between Reeside and David Sts., ☎ 831/649–6690, WEB www.canneryrow.com), where the old tin-roof canneries made famous by John Steinbeck's eponymous book have been converted into restaurants, art galleries, and kayak outfitters offering ★ tours of the local waters. The outstanding **Monterey Bay Aquarium** (✉ 886 Cannery Row, ☎ 831/648–4888; 800/756–3737 in California for tickets; WEB www.mbayaq.com; 🎫 $17.95) is a window on the sea waters beyond.

Pacific Grove recalls its Victorian heritage in tiny board-and-batten cottages and in stately mansions.For years migrating monarch butterflies from Canada and the Pacific Northwest have made Pacific Grove their winter home. Between October and March, the **Monarch Grove Sanctuary** (✉ 1073 Lighthouse Ave., WEB www.93950.com/monarchs.htm) is a good viewing spot.

★ **17-Mile Drive** (✉ Rte. 68 at Pebble Beach or Pacific Grove, ☎ 800/654–9300, WEB www.pebblebeach.com, 🎫 $8 at any of the guarded posts entering Pebble beach) offers a chance to explore an 8,400-acre microcosm of the Monterey Peninsula's coastal landscape. You'll find the weather-sculpted **Lone Cypress** tree here. At **Seal Rock** and **Bird Rock,** just offshore, you can watch the creatures sunning themselves en masse. Also along the drive is the famous **Pebble Beach Golf Link.**

Carmel was an important religious center for Spanish California. At the center of town is the 1770 **Carmel Mission** (✉ Rio Rd. and Lasuen Dr., ☎ 831/624–3600, www.carmelmission.org; 🎫 $2), whose stone buildings and tower dome have been beautifully restored. The diversity of Carmel's architectural heritage is apparent in the late poet Robinson Jeffers's **Tor House** (✉ 26304 Ocean View Ave., ☎ 831/624–1813 or 831/624–3696, WEB www.torhouse.org; 🎫 $7). The house is open on Friday and Saturday; reservations are recommended to view it.

Point Lobos State Reserve (☎ 831/624–4909 for both) is a 350-acre headland south of Carmel. It is the location of the **Sea Lion Point Trail,** a good spot to observe sea lions, otters, harbor seals, and seasonally migrating whales. Perched atop a sandstone cliff to the south, the

Point Sur Light Station marks the beginning of Big Sur. At **Pfeiffer Big Sur State Park** (✉ Rte. 1, 26 mi south of Carmel, ☎ 831/667–2315) a trail leads up a small valley to a waterfall. One of the few places in the area where you can actually reach the waters of the Pacific is Pfeiffer Beach (follow the road past the Big Sur Ranger Station for 2 mi).

★ **Hearst Castle** (✉ 750 Hearst Castle Rd., San Simeon, ☎ 805/927–2020 or 800/444–4445, WEB www.hearstcastle.org; 🎫 day tour $10) reigns in solitary splendor a few miles north of Cambria. William Randolph Hearst's grandiose mansion contains extravagant marble halls, ornate swimming pools, and an extensive European art and antiquities collection. Tour reservations are necessary. The coastal ribbon of Route 1 ends at the town of **Morro Bay,** 14 mi northwest of San Luis Obispo. In the bay Morro Rock, with the sheltered harbor on one side and the Pacific surf on the other, is a preserve for peregrine falcons.

At San Luis Obispo, south of Morro Bay, halfway between San Francisco and Los Angeles, are such historic sites as the 1772 **Mission San Luis Obispo de Tolosa** (✉ Mission Plaza, ☎ 805/543–6850) downtown. Drop by the garish but fabulous **Madonna Inn** (✉ 100 Madonna Rd., off U.S. 101, ☎ 805/543–3000 or 800/543–9666, WEB www.madonnainn.com) if only for a drink and a look at the kitschy accoutrements.

Temperate **Santa Barbara** retains its Spanish character with wide tree-shaded streets, red-tile-roof arcades downtown, and courtyards filled with upscale boutiques and restaurants.Well worth a visit is the Spanish-Moorish style ★ **Santa Barbara County Courthouse** (✉ 1100 Anacapa St., ☎ 805/962–6464, WEB www.sbcourts.org), where scenic murals adorn the interior walls. The Spanish built what is now **El Presidio State Historic Park** (✉ 123 E. Cañon Perdido St., ☎ 805/965–0093) as a military stronghold in 1782. Along the Santa Barbara waterfront, not far from downtown, is **Stearns Wharf** (✉ Cabrillo Blvd. at State St., WEB www.stearnswharf.org), a pier holding shops and eateries. The landmark ★ **Mission Santa Barbara** (✉ 2201 Laguna St., ☎ 805/682–4149, WEB www.sbmission.org; 🎫 $4) lies a bit north of Stearns Wharf. Offshore, in the Santa Barbara Channel, **Channel Islands National Park** protects plant and animal species found nowhere else on Earth as well as more familiar creatures such as sea lions, pelicans, and whales. Outdoors Santa Barbara Visitor Center (✉ 113 Harbor Dr., ☎ 805/884–1475) provides maps and other information about the park. In the Santa Ynez foothills, the **Santa Barbara Botanic Garden** (✉ 1212 Mission Canyon Rd., ☎ 805/682–4726, WEB www.sbbg.org; 🎫 $5) has 5 mi of trails through 65 acres of native plants.

Dining and Lodging

Big Sur

$$–$$$ ✕ **Nepenthe.** On an 800-ft cliff overlooking lush meadows and the ocean, the house now occupied by this restaurant was once owned by Orson Welles. The food—from roast chicken to sandwiches and hamburgers—is only adequate; it's the location that warrants a stop. ✉ *Rte. 1 at south end of town,* ☎ *831/667–2345. AE, MC, V.*

$$$$ ★ ✕🏨 **Post Ranch Inn.** Each unit at this cliff-top resort has its own spa tub, stereo, private deck, fireplace, and massage table. The inn's restaurant, serving a prix-fixe menu of cutting-edge American fare, is the best in the area. ✉ *Rte. 1 (Box 219, 93920),* ☎ *831/667–2200 or 800/527–2200,* FAX *831/687–2824,* WEB *www.postranchinn.com. 30 rooms. Restaurant, pool, gym. AE, MC, V. CP.*

$$$$ ★ ✕🏨 **Ventana.** The activities at this quintessential California getaway with lodge-style rooms are purposely limited to sunning at poolside—there is a clothing-optional deck—and walks in the hills nearby. The hotel's stone-and-wood restaurant serves California cuisine with Continental influences. ✉ *Rte. 1, 93920,* ☎ *831/667–2331 or 800/628–6500,* FAX *831/667–2419,* WEB *www.ventanainn.com. 59 rooms, 3 houses. Restaurant, pools, gym. AE, D, DC, MC, V. CP.*

Carmel

$$$–$$$$ ★ ✕ **Casanova.** Southern French and northern Italian cuisine come together at Casanova, one of the most romantic restaurants in Carmel. A heated outdoor garden and the more than 1,000 domestic and imported wines enhance the dining experience. The menu changes monthly. All entrées come with an antipasto plate and choice of appetizers. ✉ *5th Ave. between San Carlos and Mission Sts.,* ☎ *831/625–0501. MC, V.*

$$–$$$ ✕ **Caffé Napoli.** Redolent of garlic and olive oil, this small Italian restaurant is a favorite of locals, who come for the crisp-crusted pizzas, house-made pastas, and fresh seafood. Reservations are essential on weekends. ✉ *Ocean Ave. at Lincoln,* ☎ *831/625–4033. MC, V.*

$$–$$$$ ★ 🏨 **Cypress Inn.** When Doris Day became part owner of this inn, she added her own touches, such as posters from her many movies and photo albums of her favorite canines. (Pets are welcome in all rooms here.) In nice weather, enjoy your Continental breakfast in a garden courtyard surrounded by bougainvillea. ✉ *Lincoln St. and 7th Ave. (Box Y, 93921),* ☎ *831/624–3871 or 800/443–7443,* FAX *831/624–8216,* WEB *www.cypress-inn.com. 33 rooms. AE, MC, V. CP.*

$–$$$ 🏨 **Carmel River Inn.** This motel-cabins complex is away from the crowds of downtown. Some cabins have kitchenettes. ✉ *Rte. 1, at the Carmel River Bridge (Box 221609, 93922),* ☎ *831/624–1575 or 800/882–8142,* FAX *831/624–0290,* WEB *www.carmelriverinn.com. 43 rooms. Pool. AE, D, DC, MC, V.*

Monterey

$$$–$$$$ ✕ **Fresh Cream.** The cuisine at this harbor-view restaurant is French, with imaginative Californian accents. Typical dishes on the menu (which changes weekly) are rack of lamb Dijonnaise and roast boned duck in black-currant sauce. ✉ *99 Pacific St., Suite 100C,* ☎ *831/375–9798. AE, D, DC, MC, V. No lunch.*

$$–$$$$ ✕ **Tarpy's Roadhouse.** Fun, dressed-down roadhouse lunch and dinner are served in a renovated farmhouse built in the early 1900s. The kitchen cooks everything Mom used to make, only better. ✉ *2999 Monterey–Salinas Rte./Rte. 68, at Canyon Del Rey Rd.,* ☎ *831/647–1444. AE, D, MC, V.*

$$–$$$$ ★ 🏨 **Spindrift Inn.** This Cannery Row hotel has beach access and a rooftop garden. Rooms are spacious, with hardwood floors, fireplaces, canopied beds, sitting areas, down comforters, and other luxuries. ✉ *652 Cannery Row, 93940,* ☎ *831/646–8900 or 800/841–1879,* FAX *831/646–5342,* WEB *www.coastalinn.com. 42 rooms. AE, D, DC, MC, V. CP.*

$–$$$ 🏨 **Quality Inn Monterey.** Some rooms at this friendly property have fireplaces; all have refrigerators, microwaves, and VCRs. ✉ *1058 Munras Ave., 93940,* ☎ *831/372–3381, 800/361–3835,* FAX *831/372–4687,* WEB *www.qualityinnmonterey.com. 55 rooms. Pool. AE, D, DC, MC, V. CP.*

Morro Bay

$–$$$ 🏨 **Embarcadero Inn.** A drab metallic exterior hides a more welcoming interior of sparkling clean rooms, all of them with balconies that face the sea. The two hot tubs are a plus. ✉ *456 Embarcadero, 93442,* ☎ *805/772–2700 or 800/292–7625,* FAX *805/772–1060,* WEB *www.embarcaderoinn.com. 32 rooms. AE, D, DC, MC, V.*

Pacific Grove

$$$–$$$$ ★ ✕ **Old Bath House.** This romantic converted bathhouse overlooks the water at Lovers Point. The menu makes the most of local seafood and produce. ✉ *620 Ocean View Blvd.,* ☎ *831/375–5195. AE, D, DC, MC, V. No lunch.*

Santa Barbara

$$$–$$$$ ★ ✕ **Citronelle.** The accent at this offspring of Citron in Los Angeles is on French Riviera–style dishes: light and delicate but loaded with intriguing good tastes. Sweeping harbor views can be had from the dining room. ✉ *901 E. Cabrillo Blvd.,* ☎ *805/963–0111. AE, D, DC, MC, V.*

$$ ✕ **Brophy Bros.** The seafood salads at this boisterous harborfront restaurant are excellent, as are the daytime ocean views. Arrive hungry—the straightforward fish and seafood entrées are huge. ✉ *119 Harbor Way,* ☎ *805/966–2535. Reservations not accepted. AE, MC, V.*

$ ★ ✕ **La Super-Rica.** Fans of this food stand with a patio drive for miles to fill up on soft tacos and incredible beans. ✉ *622 N. Milpas St., at Alphonse St.,* ☎ *805/963–4940. No credit cards.*

$$$$ ★ 🏨 **Four Seasons Biltmore.** This grande dame of Santa Barbara hostelries is more formal than other city accommodations, with lush gardens and palm trees galore. ✉ *1260 Channel Dr., Montecito 93108,* ☎ *805/969–2261 or 800/332–3442,* FAX *805/565–8329,* WEB *www.fourseasons.com. 230 rooms. 2 restaurants, pool, health club. AE, DC, MC, V.*

$$–$$$$ ★ 🏨 **Glenborough Inn.** One of the best B&Bs in Santa Barbara County, this inn is composed of four buildings constructed around the dawn of the 20th century. ✉ *1327 Bath St., 93101,* ☎ *805/966–0589 or 800/962–0589,* FAX *805/564–8610,* WEB *www.glenboroughinn.com. 16 rooms. AE, D, DC, MC, V. BP.*

Nightlife and the Arts

The Carmel-Monterey area's top performing arts venue is the **Sunset Community Cultural Center** (✉ San Carlos St. between 8th and 10th Aves., Carmel, ☎ 831/624–3996), which presents concerts, lectures, and headline performers. The **Arlington Theater** (✉ 1317 State St., Santa Barbara, ☎ 805/963–4408) is where the Santa Barbara Symphony performs.

Outdoor Activities and Sports

Biking

Santa Barbara offers great city bicycling, especially along the **Cabrillo Bike Lane,** which passes the city zoo, a bird refuge, beaches, and the harbor.Rent bicycles at **Bay Bikes** (✉ 640 Wave St., Monterey, ☎ 831/646–9090). You can get two-wheelers, quadricycles, and skates from **Wheel Fun Rentals** (✉ 22 State St., Santa Barbara, ☎ 805/966–6733).

Fishing

Charter boats leave from Monterey, Morro Bay, and Santa Barbara. Most trips include equipment rental, bait, fish cleaning, and a license. **Monterey Sport Fishing and Whale Watching** (✉ 96 Fisherman's Wharf, Monterey, ☎ 831/372–2203, 800/200–2203) will take you out to fish or just to admire the wildlife.Deep-sea fishing charters from **Sea Landing Aquatic Center** (✉ Cabrillo Blvd. at Bath, Santa Barbara, ☎ 805/963–3564) are popular with sportsmen.

Golf

Pebble Beach Golf Links (✉ 17-Mile Dr., Pebble Beach, ☎ 831/624–3811, 800/654–9300), with its sweeping ocean views, is one of the world's most famous courses; reservations are essential. At **Spyglass Hill** (✉ Spyglass Hill Rd., Pebble Beach, ☎ 831/625–8563), the holes are unforgiving, but the views offer consolation.

Whale-Watching

On their annual migration between the Bering Sea and Baja California, 45-ft gray whales can be spotted at many points not far off the coast. The migration south takes place December– February; the journey north, March–mid-May. Other species of whales can be seen in the summer and autumn.

Beaches

In general, the shoreline north of San Luis Obispo is rocky and backed by cliffs, the water rough and often cold, and sunbathing limited to only the warmest hours of the early afternoon. Still, the beaches are more than worthwhile. The beaches of **Big Sur** are highly photogenic. At **Morro Bay** there is unparalleled tide-pooling and beachcombing.

Farther south, from Point Concepción down through Santa Barbara and into Ventura County are some fine and relatively uncrowded beaches with good swimming. **Pismo Beach** is the northernmost of the classic southern California beaches, with long, low stretches of sand. The state beaches near Santa Barbara—**El Capitan, Refugio,** and **Gaviota**—have campsites, picnic tables, and fire pits.

Central Coast Essentials

AIRPORTS

Airlines serving Monterey Peninsula Airport and Santa Barbara Municipal Airport include America West, American Eagle, United, United Express, and Skywest/Delta.

➤ AIRPORT INFORMATION: **Monterey Peninsula Airport** (✉ 200 Fred Kane Dr., ☎ 831/648–7000, WEB www.montereyairport.com). **Santa Barbara Municipal Airport** (✉ 500 Fowler Rd., ☎ 805/683–4011, WEB www.flysba.com).

CAR TRAVEL

Route 1 heads south from San Francisco through the region. The quickest but markedly less scenic route to Monterey from San Francisco or San Jose is I–280 south to Route 17 west to Route 1 south. U.S. 101 is the quickest route to Santa Barbara from Los Angeles or San Francisco. To get to Monterey from Los Angeles, take U.S. 101 to Salinas and head west on Route 68.

TRAIN TRAVEL

Amtrak's *Coast Starlight* makes stops in Santa Barbara, San Luis Obispo, and Salinas on its run from Los Angeles to Seattle.

➤ TRAIN INFORMATION: **Amtrak** (☎ 800/872–7245, WEB www.amtrak.com).

VISITOR INFORMATION

➤ TOURIST INFORMATION: **Monterey Peninsula Visitors and Convention Bureau** (✉ 380 Alvarado St., Monterey 93942, ☎ 831/649–1770, WEB www.montereyinfo.org). **Santa Barbara Conference and Visitors Bureau** (✉ 12 E. Carrillo St., 93101, ☎ 805/966–9222 or 800/549–5133, WEB www.santabarbaraca.com).

LOS ANGELES

Los Angeles is a wholly modern city, created, defined, dependent on, and thrust into prominence by the advances of the modern age: automobiles, airplanes, and the movies. It is among the nation's most ethnically diverse cities, with thriving Hispanic, Korean, Chinese, Japanese, and Middle Eastern communities.

Exploring Los Angeles

Downtown

★ Pyramidal skylights mark the **Museum of Contemporary Art (MOCA)** (✉ 250 S. Grand Ave., at California Plaza, ☎ 213/626–6222, WEB www.moca.org; 🎫 $8; free Thurs. 5–8), which was designed by renowned Japanese architect Arata Isozaki. The 5,000-piece permanent collection is split between the **Geffen Contemporary** (✉ 152 Central Ave., ☎ 213/626–6222) and the galleries at this site. The collection includes works from the 1940s to the present; artists represented include Mark Rothko, Franz Kline, Susan Rothenberg, Diane Arbus, and Robert Frank.

On weekends especially, the colorful shops, exotic markets, and restaurants of **Chinatown** (✉ bordered by Yale, Bernard, Ord, and Alameda Sts.) attract crowds of shoppers. Fiestas are held nearly every weekend on **Olvera Street**, a Mexican-style marketplace with shops, stalls, restaurants, and one of L.A.'s oldest buildings (1818). Olvera Street is part of the 44-acre **El Pueblo de Los Angeles Historical Monument** (✉ Sepulveda House visitor center, 622 N. Main St., ☎ 213/628–1274, WEB www.olvera-street.com), which celebrates the birthplace of Los Angeles (no one knows exactly where the original 1781 settlement was). **Little Tokyo** (✉ bordered by 1st, San Pedro, 3rd, and Central Sts.) was the original neighborhood of L.A.'s Japanese community, though most of those immigrants have moved elsewhere. Sushi bars and trinket shops
★ abound. The **Japanese American National Museum** (✉ 369 E. 1st St., ☎ 213/625–0414, WEB www.janm.org; 🎫 $6) chronicles the Japanese-American experience.

A few miles south of the Civic Center is 114-acre **Exposition Park** (✉ Figueroa St. at Exposition Blvd.), site of 1932 and 1984 Olympics events and home to a lovely sunken rose garden and three fascinating museums: the impressive **California Science Center** (☎ 323/724–3623; 🎫 free, IMAX prices vary, parking $5), the **California African-American Museum** (☎ 213/744–7432; 🎫 free, parking $5), and the **Natural History Museum of Los Angeles County** (☎ 213/763–3466, WEB www.nhm.org; 🎫 $8, free 1st Tues. of month).

Hollywood and Griffith Park

The cradle of the movie industry is rife with landmarks of its glamorous past, such as the 50-ft-tall **HOLLYWOOD** sign in the hills above the movie colony.From the famous intersection of Hollywood and Vine, you can't miss the **Capitol Records Tower** (✉ 1750 N. Vine St.), built in 1956 to resemble a stack of records. The multi-million-dollar hotel-
★ retail-entertainment complex **Hollywood & Highland** (✉ Hollywood Blvd. and Highland Ave., WEB www.hollywoodandhighland.com.) opened to much fanfare in 2001 and is the site of the glitzy **Kodak Theater,** home of the Academy Awards since March 2002; and **Babylon Court,** where there is no end to the diversion among the shops, restaurants, nightclubs, and movie theaters.

★ **Mann's Chinese Theatre** (✉ 6925 Hollywood Blvd., ☎ 323/461–3331), originally Grauman's Chinese, invented the gala movie premiere; its courtyard bears the footprints of more than 160 celebrities.

Frederick's of Hollywood (✉ 6608 Hollywood Blvd., ☎ 323/466–8506), the famous name in risqué lingerie, has a bra museum that includes one of Madonna's bustiers.The ★ **Hollywood Entertainment Museum** (✉ 7021 Hollywood Blvd., ☎ 323/465–7900; 🎫 $7.50) tracks the evolution of Hollywood through multimedia exhibits. The **Hollywood Walk of Fame** immortalizes the names of movie and other entertainment greats on brass plaques embedded in pink stars along the city's sidewalks. Marlon Brando is at 1765 Vine Street, Clark Gable at 1608 Vine, John Wayne at 1541 Vine, and Marilyn Monroe at 6774 Hollywood Boulevard.

★ **Griffith Park** (✉ Ventura and Golden State Fwys., ☎ 213/665–5188) has acres of picnic areas, hiking and bridle trails, a carousel, and pony rides. Also in the park are the **Los Angeles Zoo** (☎ 323/644–6400; 🎫 $8.25); the **Autry Museum of Western Heritage** (☎ 323/667–2000, WEB www.autry-museum.org; 🎫 $7.50); **Travel Town** (☎ 323/662–5874; 🎫 free), where kids can explore old railcars; and the **Planetarium and Observatory** (☎ 323/664–1191), though it is closed for renovation until August 2004.

Miracle Mile and Farmers' Market

On its grand, 16-mi sweep to the sea, **Wilshire Boulevard** runs from downtown Los Angeles through formerly grand but now run-down neighborhoods near MacArthur Park and the elegant old-money enclave of Hancock Park before reaching Miracle Mile, a stretch of museums and cultural institutions. At **La Brea Tar Pits** (✉ Hancock Park, WEB www.tarpits.org; 🎫 free) more than 100 tons of fossils have been removed from the sludge. Many fossils are on view at the **Page Museum** (✉ 5801 Wilshire Blvd., ☎ 323/934–7243; 🎫 $6, free 1st Tues. of month). The ★ **Los Angeles County Museum of Art** (✉ 5905 Wilshire Blvd., ☎ 323/857–6000, 🎫 $7, free 2nd Tues. of month) contains fine collections of American and Asian art, and a small sculpture garden. The **Petersen Automotive Museum** (✉ 6060 Wilshire Blvd., ☎ 323/930–2277; 🎫 $7) traces the history of the automobile with exhibits of unique cars, cars used in movies, and lifelike dioramas and street scenes. North of Museum Row and close to CBS Television Studios is **Farmers Market** (✉ 6333 W. 3rd St., ☎ 323/933–9211), a partly covered marketplace with food stalls, produce vendors, and a few boutiques.On the northern and eastern flanks of the farmers market is the **Grove,** an open-air dining, shopping, and entertainment mall that opened in 2002.

Beverly Hills

Beverly Hills lures people on the lookout for famous faces and a glimpse of opulence—especially in the ritzy **Rodeo Drive** (WEB www.rodeodrive.com) shopping district. The Pink Palace, the **Beverly Hills Hotel** (✉ 9641 Sunset Blvd., ☎ 310/276–2251, WEB www.beverlyhillshotel.com), is a landmark of the Hollywood high life. The ★ **Museum of Television & Radio** (✉ 465 N. Beverly Dr., ☎ 310/786–1000, WEB www.mtr.org; 🎫 $6) has a collection of 100,000 radio and TV programs spanning eight decades.

The Westside

★ The **Museum of Tolerance** (✉ 9786 W. Pico Blvd., ☎ 310/553–8403, WEB www.wiesenthal.com/mot; 🎫 $9) uses state-of-the-art technology in exhibits that challenge visitors to confront bigotry and racism. The **University of California at Los Angeles** (✉ 405 Hilgard Ave.) has sculpture and botanical gardens, and the **Fowler Museum of Cultural History** (☎ 310/825–4361). Call for walking tours of the campus (☎ 310/825–8764). The university operates the nearby **UCLA Hammer Museum** (✉ 10899 Wilshire Blvd., ☎ 310/443–7000; 🎫 $4.50, free Thurs. 11–

Los Angeles

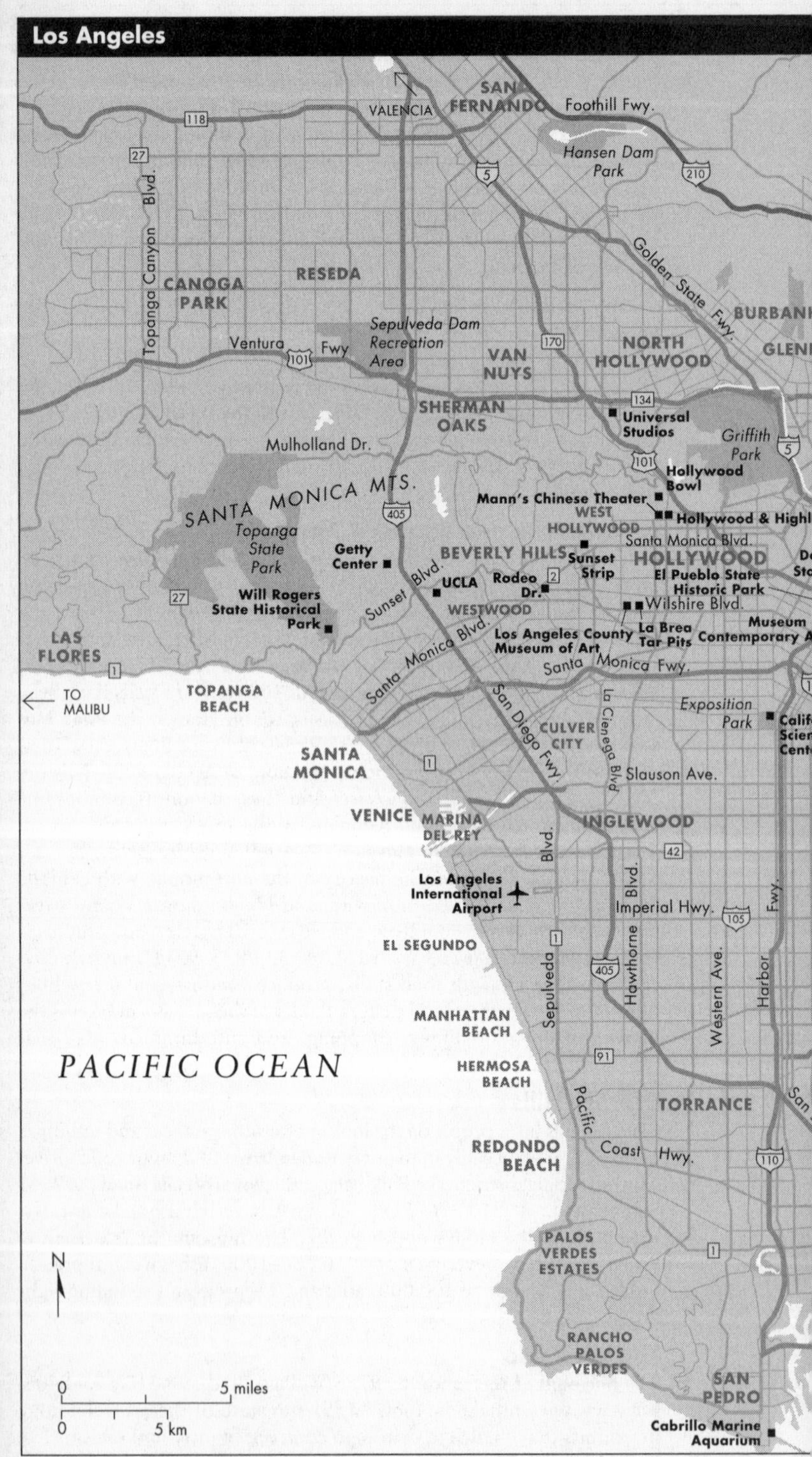

VALENCIA
SAN FERNANDO
Foothill Fwy.
Hansen Dam Park
118
27
5
210
Topanga Canyon Blvd.
CANOGA PARK
RESEDA
Golden State Fwy.
BURBANK
GLENDALE
Sepulveda Dam Recreation Area
Ventura
101
Fwy
VAN NUYS
170
NORTH HOLLYWOOD
SHERMAN OAKS
134
Universal Studios
Griffith Park
Mulholland Dr.
Hollywood Bowl
SANTA MONICA MTS.
Mann's Chinese Theater
WEST HOLLYWOOD
Hollywood & Highland
405
Topanga State Park
Getty Center
BEVERLY HILLS
Sunset Strip
Santa Monica Blvd.
HOLLYWOOD
El Pueblo State Historic Park
Will Rogers State Historical Park
Sunset Blvd.
UCLA
Rodeo Dr.
2
WESTWOOD
Wilshire Blvd.
Los Angeles County Museum of Art
La Brea Tar Pits
Museum of Contemporary Art
LAS FLORES
1
Santa Monica Blvd.
Santa Monica Fwy.
TO MALIBU
TOPANGA BEACH
San Diego Fwy.
La Cienega Blvd.
Exposition Park
California Science Center
SANTA MONICA
CULVER CITY
Slauson Ave.
VENICE
MARINA DEL REY
INGLEWOOD
42
Los Angeles International Airport
Imperial Hwy.
105
EL SEGUNDO
Sepulveda Blvd.
Hawthorne Blvd.
Western Ave.
Harbor Fwy.
MANHATTAN BEACH
PACIFIC OCEAN
HERMOSA BEACH
91
TORRANCE
Pacific Coast Hwy.
REDONDO BEACH
110
PALOS VERDES ESTATES
N
RANCHO PALOS VERDES
SAN PEDRO
0
5 miles
0
5 km
Cabrillo Marine Aquarium

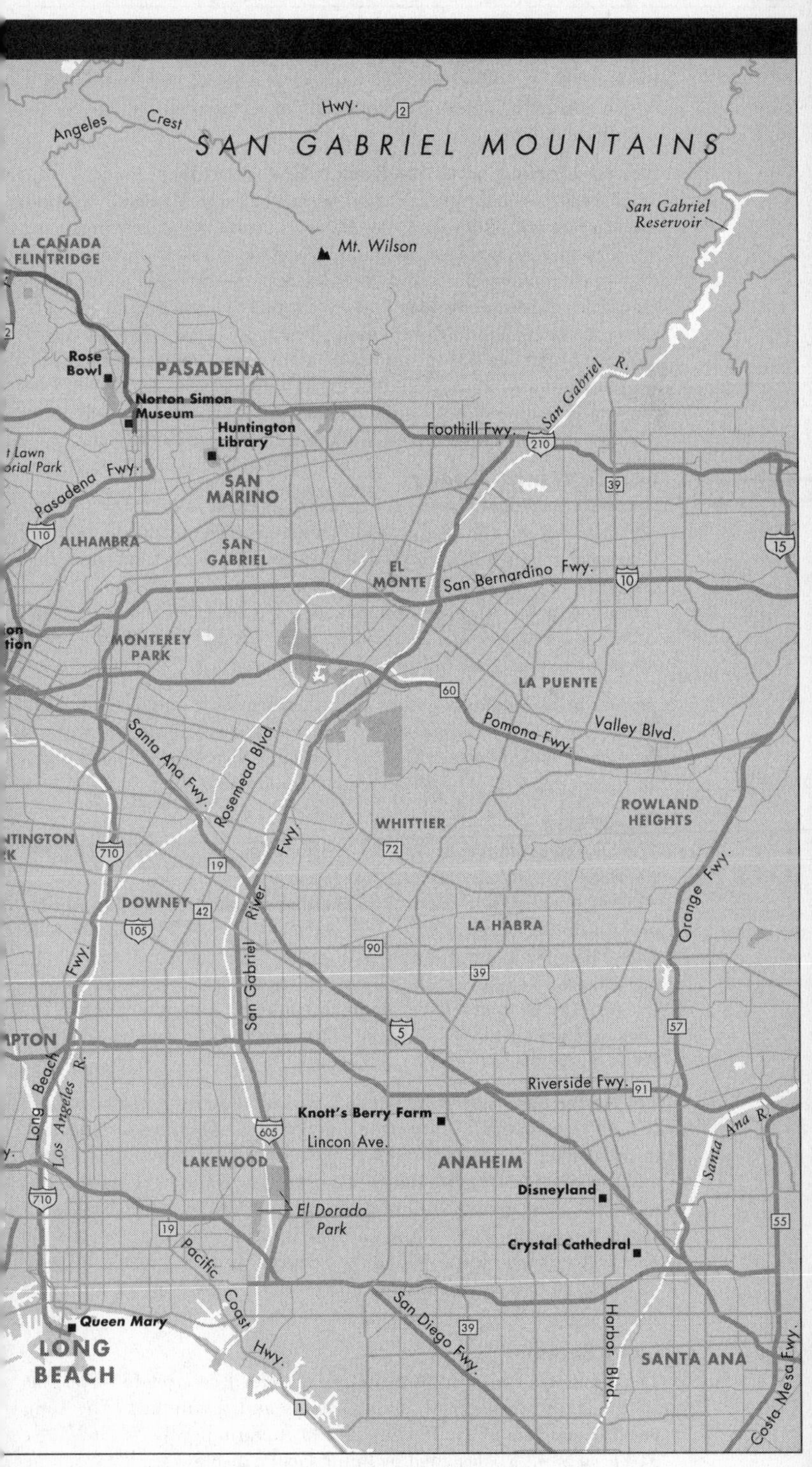

SAN GABRIEL MOUNTAINS
Angeles Crest Hwy.
Mt. Wilson
San Gabriel Reservoir
LA CAÑADA FLINTRIDGE
Rose Bowl
PASADENA
Norton Simon Museum
Huntington Library
Foothill Fwy.
San Gabriel R.
Pasadena Fwy.
SAN MARINO
ALHAMBRA
SAN GABRIEL
EL MONTE
San Bernardino Fwy.
MONTEREY PARK
LA PUENTE
Pomona Fwy.
Valley Blvd.
Santa Ana Fwy.
Rosemead Blvd.
WHITTIER
ROWLAND HEIGHTS
San Gabriel River Fwy.
DOWNEY
Orange Fwy.
LA HABRA
Long Beach Fwy.
Los Angeles R.
Riverside Fwy.
Knott's Berry Farm
Lincon Ave.
LAKEWOOD
ANAHEIM
Santa Ana R.
Disneyland
El Dorado Park
Crystal Cathedral
Pacific Coast Hwy.
San Diego Fwy.
Harbor Blvd.
Queen Mary
LONG BEACH
SANTA ANA
Costa Mesa Fwy.

9, parking $2.75). Northwest of Beverly Hills in the Santa Monica Mountains is the Richard Meier–designed **Getty Center** (✉ 1200 Getty Center Dr., ☎ 310/440–7300, WEB www.getty.edu; 🎫 free, parking $5), which houses the famous art collection of oil billionaire J. Paul Getty. It's closed Monday.

Santa Monica and the Beach Communities

Wilshire Boulevard ends at Ocean Avenue in **Santa Monica.** The **Santa Monica Pier** (☎ 310/458–8900, WEB www.santamonicapier.org) has a 46-horse antique carousel, an amusement park, gift shops, arcade, cafés, and a psychic adviser. A sandy beach stretches north and south of the pier. Palm-shaded **Palisades Park** overlooks the beach from the cliffs above. North of Santa Monica along the Pacific Coast Highway is **Malibu,** site of the beachfront homes of many stars. **Venice,** immediately south of Santa Monica, is known for its active scenes—street vendors, musicians, in-line skaters, guys and gals pumping iron, and folks simply tanning—on **Ocean Front Walk** and the **Venice Boardwalk.**

San Fernando Valley

★ **Universal Studios Hollywood,** 5 mi north of Hollywood in the San Fernando Valley via the Hollywood Freeway, is a tremendously popular theme park, with stage shows and five- to seven-hour tram tours that feature plenty of special effects. Aside from the park, **CityWalk** is a promenade with a slew of shops, restaurants, nightclubs, and movie theaters, including an IMAX-3D. ✉ *100 Universal City Pl.,* ☎ *818/508–9600,* WEB *www.universalstudios.com.* 🎫 *$45, parking $7. AE, MC, V*

Warner Bros. Studios provides an authentic behind-the-scenes tour of its television and film operations. Reserve tickets at least one week in advance. ✉ *4000 Warner Blvd., Burbank,* ☎ *818/954–1744,* WEB *www.wbsf.com.* 🎫 *$32. AE, MC, V. No children under 8.*

Pasadena

The **Southwest Museum** (✉ 234 Museum Dr., ☎ 323/221–2163, WEB www.southwestmuseum.org; 🎫 $6) houses a collection of Native American art and artifacts. The **Huntington Library, Art Collections, and Botanical Gardens** (✉ 1151 Oxford Rd., San Marino, ☎ 626/405–2100, WEB www.huntington.org; 🎫 $10, free 1st Thurs. of the month) are spread over 207 hilly acres. The complex's collections consist of more than 4 million items, including a Gutenberg Bible, the Ellesmere manuscript of Chaucer's *Canterbury Tales,* and first editions by Shakespeare.

The **Norton Simon Museum** (✉ 411 W. Colorado Blvd., Pasadena, ☎ 626/449–6840, WEB www.nortonsimon.org; 🎫 $6) houses important Impressionist paintings, as well as masterpieces by Rembrandt, Goya, and Picasso. The **Gamble House** (✉ 4 Westmoreland Pl., Pasadena, ☎ 626/793–3334, WEB www.gamblehous.org; 🎫 $8), built by Charles and Henry Greene in 1908, is the ultimate in California Craftsman–style architecture. It's closed Monday–Wednesday. The restored historic buildings of **Old Town Pasadena** now house many popular cafés and shops.

Long Beach

The famous ocean liner ***Queen Mary*** (✉ Pier J, ☎ 562/435–3511) is now a stylish hotel, with several shops and restaurants. The **Long Beach Aquarium of the Pacific** (✉ 100 Aquarium Way, ☎ 562/590–3100; 🎫 $14.95), designed by Frank Gehry, displays sea life from the Artic to the tropics. The small Gehry-designed **Cabrillo Marine Aquarium** (✉ 3720 Stephen White Dr., San Pedro, ☎ 310/548–7562; 🎫 $2 donation requested, parking $6.50), offers intimate, instructive exhibits, including a touch pool.

Dining

$$$–$$$$ ★ ✕ **Campanile.** This restaurant in Charlie Chaplin's former office complex serves dishes that include celery-root soup with pesto, lobster risotto, and loin of venison with quince puree. ✉ *624 S. La Brea Ave.,* ☎ *323/938–1447. Reservations essential. AE, D, DC, MC, V. No dinner Sun.*

$$$–$$$$ ★ ✕ **L'Orangerie.** French Mediterranean dishes, like John Dory with roasted figs, duck with coffee beans, and rack of lamb with fall vegetables, are served in this rococo dining room, complete with white flower arrangements and oil paintings of European castles. The apple tart accompanied by a jug of double cream is sublime. ✉ *903 N. La Cienega Blvd., West Hollywood,* ☎ *310/652–9770. Reservations essential. AE, D, DC, MC, V. Closed Mon. No lunch.*

$$$–$$$$ ✕ **Spago Beverly Hills.** Wolfgang Puck wows celebrity and business circles with a menu that changes daily, offering appetizers like white-bean and duck-confit soup and entrées like wild striped bass with celery-root puree. Also worth trying are Puck's renowned pizzas, with or without smoked salmon. ✉ *176 N. Canon Dr., Beverly Hills,* ☎ *310/385–0880. Reservations essential. AE, D, DC, MC, V. No lunch Sun.*

$$–$$$$ ★ ✕ **Matsuhisa.** Cutting-edge Pacific Rim cuisine is pushed to new limits at this modest-looking yet high-profile Japanese bistro. Tempuras are light, and the sushi is ultra-fresh. Regulars ask the chef to prepare whatever's best that day—usually a seven-course meal—and then steel themselves for a daunting tab. ✉ *129 N. La Cienega Blvd., Beverly Hills,* ☎ *310/659–9639. Reservations essential. AE, DC, MC, V.*

$$–$$$ ✕ **Gladstone's 4 Fish.** Gladstone's is notable mostly for its Brobdingnagian portions: giant bowls of crab chowder, mounds of steamed clams, heaps of barbecued ribs, and the famous mile-high chocolate cake. The real reason to visit Gladstone's is the glorious vista of sea, sky, and beach. ✉ *17300 Pacific Coast Hwy., at Sunset Blvd.,* ☎ *310/454–3474. AE, D, DC, MC, V.*

$$–$$$ ★ ✕ **Granita.** Wolfgang Puck's famed Granita is a glamourous fantasy world of handmade tiles embedded with seashells, blown-glass lighting fixtures, and an exotic koi pond and waterfall. With a beachside location, it's fitting that the menu favors seafood, including polenta crepes with Maine lobster and bigeye with spicy miso glaze. There's brunch on weekends. ✉ *23725 W. Malibu Rd., Malibu,* ☎ *310/456–0488. Reservations essential. AE, D, DC, MC, V. Closed Mon. No lunch.*

$$–$$$ ★ ✕ **La Cachette.** Owner-chef Jean-François Meteigner's modern French cuisine manages to be both light and appealing. Entrées include rack of lamb with garlic-tarragon *jus* and Alaskan butterfish with Cajun spices. ✉ *10506 Little Santa Monica Blvd., West Los Angeles,* ☎ *310/470–4992. Reservations essential. AE, MC, V. No lunch weekends.*

$$–$$$ ★ ✕ **Valentino.** The light, modern Italian dishes at this top-notch restaurant include carpaccio with arugula and shaved Parmesan and lamb shank with saffron risotto. Order from the lengthy list of daily specials. The wine list is considered one of the best in the nation. ✉ *3115 Pico Blvd., Santa Monica,* ☎ *310/829–4313. Reservations essential. AE, DC, MC, V. Closed Sun. No lunch Sat.–Thurs.*

$–$$ ★ ✕ **Broadway Deli.** Whatever you feel like eating at this brasserie–cum–upscale diner, you will probably find it on the menu, from Caesar salad to shepherd's pie, carpaccio, steak, and grilled swordfish. ✉ *1457 3rd St. Promenade, Santa Monica,* ☎ *310/451–0616. Reservations not accepted. AE, DC, MC, V.*

$–$$ ✕ **Chan Dara.** Try any of the Thai noodle dishes, especially those with crab and shrimp, the *satay* (skewered meat with peanut sauce), the barbecued chicken, or the deep-fried whole catfish. ✉ *310 N. Larchmont Blvd.,* ☎ *323/467–1052. AE, D, DC, MC, V. No lunch weekends.*

$–$$ ★ ✕ **El Cholo.** Zesty margaritas, green corn tamales, enchiladas Suizas, and tacos are served in large portions at this progenitor of the chain that keeps generations of Angelenos coming back. ✉ *1121 S. Western Ave.,* ☎ *323/734–2773. AE, D, DC, MC, V.*

$–$$ ★ ✕ **Yujean Kang's Gourmet Chinese Cuisine.** Start with the tender slices of veal on a bed of enoki mushrooms, or the sea bass with kumquats and passion-fruit sauce; then finish with poached plums or watermelon ice under a mantle of white chocolate. ✉ *67 N. Raymond Ave.,* ☎ *626/585–0855. AE, D, DC, MC, V.*

Lodging

$$$$ ★ **Mondrian.** Mod apartment-size accommodations at this ultrahip Ian Schrager–run property have floor-to-ceiling windows, slipcovered sofas, and marble coffee tables; many have kitchens. ✉ *8440 Sunset Blvd., West Hollywood 90069,* ☎ *323/650–8999 or 800/525–8029,* FAX *323/650–9241,* WEB *www.mondrianhotel.com. 238 rooms. 2 restaurants, pool, health club. AE, D, DC, MC, V.*

$$$$ ★ **Regent Beverly Wilshire.** Known as the *Pretty Woman* hotel (a presidential suite was showcased in the film), the Regent is a longtime classic. Accommodations have appropriate period furnishings and glorious marble bathrooms with deep tubs. ✉ *9500 Wilshire Blvd., Beverly Hills 90212,* ☎ *310/275–5200; 800/427–4354 in California; 800/421–4354 outside California;* FAX *310/274–2851,* WEB *www.regenthotels.com 415 rooms. 2 restaurants, pool, health club. AE, DC, MC, V.*

$$$–$$$$ ★ **Beverly Hills Inn.** This European-style inn is a nice alternative to the town's more mammoth (and more expensive) luxury hotels. The address is trendy, the service is excellent, and a complimentary breakfast is delivered to your door each morning. ✉ *125 S. Spalding Dr., Beverly Hills, 90212,* ☎ *310/278–0303 or 800/463–4466,* FAX *310/278–1728,* WEB *www.innatbeverlyhills.com. 50 rooms. Pool, gym. AE, DC, MC, V. CP.*

$$$–$$$$ **Millennium Biltmore Hotel.** A Beaux-Arts masterpiece with a storied past, the Biltmore retains its historic flavor even after a $70 million renovation in 2001. The spectacular lobby and ballrooms shine with Spanish-style marble and gilded columns, and the rooms are appointed with elegant, 1920s-inspired furnishings. ✉ *506 S. Grand Ave., 90071,* ☎ *213/624–1011 or 800/245–8673,* FAX *213/612–1545. 683 rooms. 5 restaurants, pool, health club. AE, D, DC, MC, V.*

$$–$$$$ **Beverly Crescent Hotel.** A rare value in its swank zip code, this small-European-style hotel has small rooms but provides little extras such as complimentary fresh fruit and afternoon tea. ✉ *403 N. Crescent Dr., Beverly Hills, 90210,* ☎ *310/247–0505 or 800/451–1566,* FAX *310/247–9053,* WEB *www.beverlycrescenthotel.com. 38 rooms. AE, D, DC, MC, V. CP.*

$$–$$$ ★ **Channel Road Inn.** One of a handful of B&Bs in L.A., Channel Road is a charming country retreat just steps from the beach. Rooms in the historic shingle-clad mansion are beautifully old-fashioned (canopy beds, balloon shades), and some have refrigerators. ✉ *219 W. Channel Rd. 90402,* ☎ *310/459–1920,* FAX *310/454–9920,* WEB *www.channelroadinn.com. 14 rooms. AE, MC, V. BP.*

$$–$$$ **Sportsmen's Lodge.** The English country–style, five-story structure is surrounded by waterfalls, a swan-filled lagoon, and a gazebo, all of which make you forget you're in a city. Studio suites with private patios are available. ✉ *12825 Ventura Blvd. 91604,* ☎ *818/769–4700 or 800/821–8511,* FAX *818/769–4798,* WEB *www.slhotel.com. 191 rooms. 3 restaurants, pool, gym. AE, D, DC, MC, V.*

$$ **Carlyle Inn.** It's niceties like wine and cheese on weekday afternoons, a breakfast buffet, a sundeck, and bathrobes that make this small, four-

story inn a good choice. Despite somewhat nondescript furniture and decor, the rooms are comfy. ✉ *1119 S. Robertson Blvd., 90035,* ☎ *310/275–4445 or 800/322–7595,* FAX *310/859–0496,* WEB *www.carlyle-inn.com. 32 rooms. Gym. AE, D, DC, MC, V. BP.*

$$ **Figueroa Hotel.** On the outside, it's Spanish Revival; on the inside, this 1926, 12-story hotel is a mix of Southwest, Mexican, and Mediterranean styles, with earth tones, hand-painted furniture, wrought-iron beds, and, in many rooms, ceiling fans. ✉ *939 S. Figueroa St., 90015,* ☎ *213/627–8971 or 800/421–9092,* FAX *213/689–0305,* WEB *www.figueroahotel.com. 287 rooms. 2 restaurants, pool. AE, DC, MC, V.*

Nightlife and the Arts

For the most complete listing of weekly events, consult the current issue of *Los Angeles* magazine. The "Calendar" section of the *Los Angeles Times* also lists a wide survey of Los Angeles arts events, as do the more alternative publications, the *L.A. Weekly* and the *New Times Los Angeles* (both free). Most event tickets can be purchased by phone from **Ticketmaster** (☎ 213/480–3232). For an additional charge, buy tickets from **Good Time Tickets** (☎ 323/464–7383). **Tickets L.A.** (☎ 323/655–8587) brokers shows and cultural events, primarily at museums and smaller theaters.

Nightlife

COMEDY

Three stages supply the yuks, sometimes from famous comedians, at the **Comedy Store** (✉ 8433 Sunset Blvd., West Hollywood, ☎ 323/656–6225). Look for top stand-ups and unannounced celebrity drop-ins, like Roger Dangerfield, at the **Laugh Factory** (✉ 8001 Sunset Blvd., West Hollywood, ☎ 323/656–1336).

DANCE CLUBS

A dressed-to-impress, upscale crowd frequents the **Century Club** (✉ 10131 Constellation Blvd., ☎ 310/553–6000), where dance grooves range from Latin to hip hop to electronic. **Sugar** (✉ 814 Broadway, Santa Monica, ☎ 310/899–1989) is one of the most popular Westside dance clubs, with DJs spinning house, drum and bass, and techno Friday and Saturday.

LIVE MUSIC

At the **Atlas Bar and Grill** (✉ 3760 Wilshire Blvd., Los Angeles, ☎ 213/380–8400) you'll hear jazz and torch in a classy, historic Art Deco supper club. The **Roxy** (✉ 9009 Sunset Blvd., West Hollywood, ☎ 310/276–2222), classy and comfortable, is L.A.'s premier rock club, though it presents stage productions as well. The **Viper Room** (✉ 8852 Sunset Blvd., West Hollywood, ☎ 310/358–1880) is a notorious hangout for musicians and movie stars. The live music is loud, with an alternative bent. **Whiskey A Go Go** (✉ 8901 Sunset Blvd., West Hollywood, ☎ 310/652–4202) is the most famous rock-and-roll club on the Sunset Strip, with up-and-coming alternative, hard rock, and punk bands.

The Arts

MUSIC

The **Dorothy Chandler Pavilion** (✉ 135 N. Grand Ave., ☎ 213/972–7211) is home to the Los Angeles Philharmonic Orchestra. The **Hollywood Bowl** (✉ 2301 Highland Ave., ☎ 323/850–2000) offers an outdoor summer season of classical jazz, international, and pop music. The outdoor **Greek Theater** (✉ 2700 N. Vermont Ave., ☎ 323/665–1927) presents big-name performers in its mainly pop-rock-jazz schedule from June through October. The jewel in the crown of Hollywood & Highland, the **Kodak Theatre** (✉ 6801 Hollywood Blvd., ☎ 323/

308–6363, WEB www.kodaktheater.com) hosts music concerts and ballets, as well as the Academy Awards.

THEATER

Plays are presented at two of the three theaters at the **Performing Arts Center of Los Angeles County** (✉ 135 N. Grand Ave.). The **James A. Doolittle Theatre** (✉ 1615 N. Vine St., ☎ 323/462–6666) presents dramas, comedies, and musicals. The **Geffen Playhouse** (✉ 10886 Le Conte Ave., ☎ 310/208–6500 or 310/208–5454) presents musicals and comedies year-round. Many of the productions here are on their way to or from Broadway.

Beaches

Malibu is beach after glorious beach. **Leo Carrillo State Beach** (✉ 35000 Pacific Coast Hwy., Malibu, ☎ 818/880–0350) is fun at low tide, when tide pools emerge. There are hiking trails, sea caves and tunnels, and you can often see dolphins and sea lions. **Zuma Beach Park** (✉ 30050 Pacific Coast Hwy., Malibu, ☎ 310/457–9891), Malibu's largest and sandiest beach, is a favorite surfing spot and teen hangout, although the surf can be rough and inconsistent. **Surfrider Beach/Malibu Lagoon State Beach** (✉ 23200 Pacific Coast Hwy., Malibu, ☎ 818/880–0350), north of Malibu Pier, has steady 3- to 5-ft waves that make it great for long-board surfing. The International Surfing Contest is held here each September. The lagoon is a sanctuary for 250 species of birds. **Topanga County Beach** (✉ 18700 Pacific Coast Hwy., Malibu, ☎ 310/394–3260), rocky but a favorite with surfers, stretches from the mouth of Topanga Canyon down to Coastline Drive.

There are plenty of great L.A. beaches beyond Malibu. **Will Rogers State Beach** (✉ 15100 Pacific Coast Hwy., ☎ 310/394–3266) is a wide, sandy beach with a steady, even surf. There's plenty of beach, volleyball, and bodysurfing action parallel to the pedestrian bridge. Parking is limited. **Santa Monica State Beach** (✉ 1642 Promenade [Pacific Coast Hwy. at California Incline], Santa Monica, ☎ 310/394–3266), the widest stretch of beach on the Pacific coast, is also one of the most popular, with bike paths, facilities for people with disabilities, playgrounds, and volleyball. **Manhattan Beach** (✉ Manhattan Beach Blvd. and North Ocean Dr., Manhattan Beach, ☎ 310/372–2166) is a sandy beach with swimming, diving, surfing, fishing, and picnicking. **Redondo Beach** (✉ Torrance Blvd. and Catalina Ave., Redondo Beach, ☎ 310/372–2166) is wide and sandy, but usually packed in summer. Parking is limited.

Shopping

Shopping Districts

Rodeo Drive is the world-famous street where pricey shops sell designer fashions. You'll find more boutiques plus the department stores Robinsons-May, Neiman Marcus, Saks Fifth Avenue, and Barneys on **Wilshire Boulevard,** which intersects with Rodeo Drive. In downtown L.A., the **Citadel Factory Stores** (✉ 5675 E. Telegraph Rd., Commerce, ☎ 323/888–1220) has Benetton, Betsey Johnson, and other outlets. For vintage styles or the just plain weird, go to **Melrose Avenue** between La Brea and Crescent Heights. The **Beverly Center** (✉ 8500 Beverly Blvd., between and, ☎ 310/854–0070) holds more than 200 upscale stores and boutiques and is anchored by Bloomingdale's and Macy's. The **3rd Street Promenade** in Santa Monica is a pedestrian-only street lined with boutiques and chain stores, movie theaters, clubs, pubs, and restaurants. **Montana Avenue** in Santa Monica has boutique after boutique of quality goods.

Los Angeles Essentials

AIRPORTS AND TRANSFERS

Los Angeles International Airport (LAX), about 25 mi west of downtown and 10 mi from Beverly Hills, is served by more than 85 major airlines. Four smaller regional airports—in Burbank, Long Beach, Orange County, and Ontario—also serve the greater L.A. area.

➤ AIRPORT INFORMATION: **Los Angeles International Airport** (1 World Way, Los Angeles, ☎ 310/646–5252).

AIRPORT TRANSFERS

Taxis to downtown cost $27–$30 (request a flat fee—metered fares are more) and take 20–60 minutes, depending on traffic. SuperShuttle services downtown hotels for about $13 ($14 to Disneyland hotels); fares to private residences vary. Airport Bus provides service from LAX to Anaheim ($16 and $25).

➤ TAXIS AND SHUTTLES: **Airport Bus** (☎ 714/938–8900 or 800/772–5299). **SuperShuttle** (☎ 310/782–6600, WEB www.supershuttle.com).

BUS TRAVEL TO AND FROM LOS ANGELES

➤ BUS INFORMATION: **Greyhound** (✉ 1716 E. 7th St., at Alameda St., ☎ 800/231–2222 or 213/629–8405).

CAR TRAVEL

Freeways, whose names can change along the route, are the most efficient way to get from one end of the city to another. The main north–south route into Los Angeles is I–5 (called the Golden State or Santa Ana Freeway). U.S. 101 (called the Hollywood Freeway) travels south through Los Angeles to San Diego and the Mexican border. I–10 (called the Santa Monica Freeway) runs east–west across the United States; its western terminus is Santa Monica. I–15 travels north from San Diego to about 60 mi east of Los Angeles, then heads northeast toward California's border with Nevada.

TAXIS

All cabs must be ordered by phone; companies include Independent Cab. Co. and United Independent Taxi. The metered rate is $1.90 at the flag drop and $1.80 per mile thereafter. A flat fee is available in the downtown area.

➤ TAXI COMPANIES: **Independent Cab Co.** (☎ 323/666–0040). **United Independent Taxi** (☎ 323/462–1088).

TOURS

Starline Tours of Hollywood offers tours of movie stars' homes, Disneyland, Universal Studios, Sea World of California, the J. Paul Getty Museum, and other attractions.

➤ FEES AND SCHEDULES: **Starline Tours of Hollywood** (☎ 323/463–3333 or 800/959–3131, WEB www.starlinetours.com).

TRAIN TRAVEL

Amtrak serves Los Angeles's Union Station.

➤ TRAIN INFORMATION: **Amtrak** (☎ 800/872–7245). **Metrolink** (☎ 800/371–LINK)provides commuter train service into L.A. from Oxnard, Lancaster, San Bernardino, Riverside, San Juan Capistrano, and Oceanside. **Union Station** (✉ 800 N. Alameda St.).

TRANSPORTATION AROUND LOS ANGELES

The Southern California Metropolitan Transit Authority (MTA) provides bus and light-rail service. Bus fare is $1.35 plus 25¢ for a transfer. DASH (Downtown Area Short Hop) is a system of minibuses serving the downtown area. DASH runs weekdays 6 AM–7 PM, Saturday 10–5. Stops are every two blocks or so, and you pay 25¢ every time you get on, no matter how far you go. L.A.'s subway, the Metro Red Line, is run by the L.A. MTA and serves Union Station, Hollywood, Beverly Hills, Santa Monica, Universal City, and North Hollywood, stopping at most major tourist attractions. Fares are $1.35 plus 25¢ to transfer.

➤ CONTACTS: **DASH** (☎ 213/808–2273, WEB www.ladottransit.com). **Los Angeles County Metropolitan Transit Authority** (☎ 800/266–6883, WEB www.mta.net). **Southern California Metropolitan Transit Authority** (☎ 213/626–4455).

VISITOR INFORMATION

➤ TOURIST INFORMATION: **Convention and Visitors Bureau** (✉ 633 W. 5th St., Suite 6000, 90071, ☎ 213/624–7300).

ORANGE COUNTY

Orange County lies between Los Angeles to the north and San Diego to the south. Though primarily suburban, it is one of the top tourist destinations in California, with attractions such as Disneyland Resort, pro sports, and miles of beaches.

Exploring Orange County

Inland Orange County

★ Anaheim is the home of **Disneyland.** You enter the Magic Kingdom on Main Street, a romanticized image of an American street circa 1900. Inside the park you'll find thrill rides and high-tech wizardry, Disney characters strolling about, a daily parade, the nighttime "Fantasmic" show, and fireworks in summer. Each land within the Big D has a different theme. In **Fantasyland,** rides are based on children's stories. **Frontierland** lets you explore the Wild West on the Mark Twain Riverboat, Big Thunder Railroad, and more. The Indiana Jones thrill ride is the highlight of **Adventureland.** And **Tomorrowland** has a Buck Rogers–ish feel, with the Space Mountain roller coaster and the *Honey I Shrunk the Audience* and *Innoventions* shows. Favorite attractions include **Pirates of the Caribbean**—a boat ride through scenes of plundering pirates; the **Haunted Mansion,** full of holographic ghosts; **Splash Mountain,** a flume ride that drops 52 ft at 40 mph; and **Mickey's Toontown,** a child-size interactive community that gives kids the feeling of being inside a cartoon with Mickey and other characters. ✉ *1313 Harbor Blvd., Anaheim,* ☎ *714/781–4565.* WEB *www.disneyland.com.* *$43.*

Disney's California Adventure, next to Disneyland, has three theme areas: the beach-side boardwalks of **Paradise Pier; Hollywood Pictures Backlot,** which glorifies the movie industry; and **Golden State,** with miniature versions of each of California's regions. Among the highlights are the **Grizzly River Run** raft ride, **California Screamin'** roller coaster, an elaborate ferris wheel, and **Soarin' Over California,** a simulated hang-glider ride over the California landscape. The film *Golden Dreams* is a sentimental run through California history with Whoopi Goldberg, and *It's Tough to Be a Bug!* is an amusing 3-D film. There's also a working 1-acre farm and winery, an animation exhibit, Broadway-style theater, nature trail and tortilla factory, a daily parade, shops, and restaurants. ✉ *1313 Harbor Blvd., Anaheim,* ☎ *714/781–4565,* WEB *www.disneyland.com.* *$43.*

Downtown Disney, a 20-acre, non-gated promenade of dining, shopping, and entertainment, connects the Disneyland Resort hotels and theme parks. Restaurant-nightclubs here include **Y Arriba! Y Arriba!,**

with Latin dishes, dancing, and entertainment; **House of Blues,** with Delta-inspired ribs, seafood, and music; **Ralph Brennan's Jazz Kitchen,** with New Orleans–style food and music; and **Rainforest Café,** Latin American and Caribbean food in a room full of animated jungle animals. Sports fans gravitate to the **ESPN Zone,** a sports bar–restaurant–entertainment center with American grill food. Shops include **World of Disney,** which sells everything from souvenirs to home decor; and **Tin Pan Alley,** with magnets, lunch boxes, and other metal items. ✉ *Disneyland Dr., between Ball Rd. and Katella Ave., Anaheim,* ☎ *714/300–7800,* WEB *www.disneyland.com.* 🎫 *Free.*

★ **Knott's Berry Farm,** a 150-acre complex of food, shops, rides, and other attractions, is near Disneyland, in Buena Park. **Ghost Town** re-creates an 1880s mining town; the **Gold Mine** ride descends into a replica of a working gold mine. **Camp Snoopy** is a kid-size High Sierra wonderland where the *Peanuts* gang hangs out. At **Wild Water Wilderness** riders can brave white water in an inner tube. Thrill-seekers who don't mind traveling in a roller coaster upside down will like rides like the **Boomerang** and **Montezooma's Revenge.** The **Boardwalk** includes dolphin and sea lion shows at the Pacific Pavilion, more rides, and the Good Time and 3-D Nu Wave theaters. And don't forget what made Knott's famous: the fried chicken dinners and boysenberry pies at **Mrs. Knott's Chicken Dinner Restaurant,** outside the park gates in Knott's California MarketPlace. ✉ *8039 Beach Blvd., Buena Park,* ☎ *714/220–5200.* WEB *www.knotts.com* 🎫 *$40.*

The Coast

The **Pacific Coast Highway** (a.k.a. PCH or Route 1) connects all the beach towns along the Orange County coast.**Huntington Beach** is a popular surfer hangout; you can watch the action from the Huntington Pier. South of Huntington Beach is **Newport Beach,** a Beverly-Hills-by-the-sea. Nearly 10,000 boats bob in the U-shape Newport Harbor, which arcs around eight small islands. **Balboa Peninsula,** with its Victorian Balboa Pavilion and active Fun Zone, is a popular visitor area.
★ Farther south is **Corona del Mar,** a small jewel of a town with exceptional beaches. You can walk clear out over the bay on a rough-and-tumble rock jetty, or you can wander about tide pools and hidden caves. In **Laguna Beach** art galleries in town coexist with volleyball games and sun worship on nearby Main Beach; in July and August the **Pageant of the Masters** (☎ 949/494–1145) features living models re-creating famous paintings. The **Laguna Art Museum** (✉ 307 Cliff Dr., ☎ 949/494–6531; 🎫 $5) displays American art with an emphasis on California artists. Below Laguna the small harbor town of **Dana Point** is reminiscent of northern California's beaches. In March migrating swallows and spectacle-loving tourists flock to **Mission San Juan Capistrano** (✉ Camino Capistrano and Ortega Hwy., ☎ 949/488–7825).

Dining and Lodging

Anaheim

$$–$$$ ✕ **Mr. Stox.** Prime rib, mesquite-grilled rack of lamb, and fresh fish specials are accompanied by a stellar wine list. Pastas, breads, and pastries are made on the premises. ✉ *1105 E. Katella Ave., Anaheim,* ☎ *714/634–2994. AE, D, DC, MC, V. No lunch weekends.*

$–$$ ✕ **Luigi's D'Italia.** Though the surroundings are simple, the classic Italian cuisine, from huge portions of spaghetti marinara to cioppino, is outstanding. ✉ *801 S. State College Blvd., Anaheim,* ☎ *714/490–0990. AE, MC, V.*

$$$$ ★ **Disneyland Hotel.** Not surprisingly, Disney's first hotel is the most Disney-themed of the resort's three hotels. Check out the Peter Pan theme pool and Goofy's Kitchen, where kids dine with Disney characters. Rooms are 1950-style and spacious. Room-and-ticket packages are available. ✉ *1150 W. Cerritos Ave. 92802,* ☎ *714/778–6600,* FAX *714/956–6582,* WEB *www.disneyland.com. 990 rooms. 5 restaurants, pools, health club. AE, D, DC, MC, V.*

$$$$ ★ **Disney's Grand Californian.** This Craftsman-style luxury hotel, adjacent to Disney's California Adventure, has beautifully furnished rooms and lush, landscaped grounds. Disney characters entertain children at breakfast, there's an evening child activity center, and one of the swimming pools is in the shape of Mickey Mouse. Room-and-ticket packages are available. ✉ *1600 S. Disneyland Dr., 92803,* ☎ *714/635–2300,* FAX *714/300–7701,* WEB *www.disneyland.com. 750 rooms. 4 restaurants, 3 pools, health club AE, D, DC, MC, V.*

$–$$ **Candy Cane Inn.** The name of this motel speaks volumes about the fanciful, family-friendly feel inside. Rooms are basic but spacious. Free Disneyland shuttles run every 30 minutes. ✉ *1747 S. Harbor Blvd., Anaheim 92802,* ☎ *714/774–5284 or 800/345–7057,* FAX *714/772–5462 or 714/772–1305,* WEB *www.candycaneinn.net. 172 rooms. Pool. AE, D, DC, MC, V.*

Dana Point

$–$$$ ✕ **Luciana's.** Linguine with clams, prawns, calamari, and green-lip mussels in a light tomato sauce is one of the many creative specials you'll find at this intimate Italian restaurant. ✉ *24312 Del Prado Ave., Dana Point,* ☎ *949/661–6500. AE, DC, MC, V. No lunch.*

$$$$ ★ ✕ **Ritz-Carlton, Laguna Niguel.** An unrivaled setting on the edge of the Pacific and a top-notch restaurant, combined with the hallmark Ritz-Carlton service, have made this hotel justifiably famous. Rooms have marble bathrooms and private balconies. ✉ *1 Ritz-Carlton Dr., Dana Point 92629,* ☎ *949/240–2000 or 800/241–3333,* FAX *949/240–0829,* WEB *www.ritzcarlton.com. 362 rooms. 3 restaurants, pools, tennis, health club. AE, D, DC, MC, V.*

Laguna Beach

$$–$$$$ ★ ✕ **Five Feet.** Delicate potstickers, and mussels and clams sautéed in spicy black-bean sauce are two of the scrumptious dishes here. The setting is pure Laguna: exposed ceiling, open kitchen, high noise level, and brick walls hung with works by local artists. ✉ *328 Gleneyre St., Laguna Beach,* ☎ *949/497–4955. AE, D, DC, MC, V. No lunch.*

$$ ✕ **Ti Amo.** A romantic setting and creative Mediterranean cuisine have earned this place acclaim. Try the sesame-crusted ahi or farfalle with smoked chicken and tomato brandy cream sauce. To maximize romance, request a table in the enclosed garden in back. ✉ *31727 S. Coast Hwy., Laguna Beach,* ☎ *949/499–5350. AE, D, DC, MC, V. No lunch.*

$$$$ ★ **Surf and Sand Hotel.** Laguna's largest hotel is right on the beach. Tastefully decorated rooms have a beachlike feel, with soft sand colors, bleached-wood shutters, and private balconies that hover over the waves. ✉ *1555 S. Coast Hwy., Laguna Beach 92651,* ☎ *949/497–4477 or 800/524–8621,* FAX *949/497–1092,* WEB *www.surfandsandresort.com. 181 rooms. Restaurant, pool, health club. AE, D, DC, MC, V.*

Newport Beach

$$$$ ★ ✕ **Aubergine.** A husband-and-wife team runs this restaurant. He heads up the kitchen and she handles the dining room. The prix-fixe French menus offer an unforgettable gastronomical experience. ✉ *508 29th St., Newport Beach,* ☎ *949/723–4150. Reservations essential. AE, MC, V. Closed Sun.–Mon. No lunch.*

$–$$ ★ ✕ **El Torito Grill.** The tortilla soup is to die for, as is the carne asada. Just-baked tortillas with fresh salsa replace the usual chip basket. The bar serves hand-shaken margaritas and 80 brands of tequila. ✉ *Fashion Island, 951 Newport Center Dr., Newport Beach,* ☎ *949/640–2875. AE, D, DC, MC, V.*

$$$$ ★ **Four Seasons Hotel.** A suitably stylish hotel in an ultrachic neighborhood (it's across the street from Fashion Island mall), the 20-story Four Seasons caters to luxury seekers by offering weekend golf packages and extensive fitness facilities. Guest rooms have spectacular views and private bars. ✉ *690 Newport Center Dr., Newport Beach 92660,* ☎ *949/759–0808 or 800/332–3442,* FAX *949/759–0568,* WEB *www.fourseasons.com. 378 rooms. 3 restaurants, pool, tennis, health club. AE, D, DC, MC, V.*

$$$–$$$$ **Sutton Place Hotel.** An eye-catching ziggurat design is the trademark of this ultramodern hotel in Koll Center. Despite its futuristic exterior, the inside remains traditional with comfortable, understated rooms. ✉ *4500 MacArthur Blvd., Newport Beach 92660,* ☎ *949/476–2001 or 800/243–4141,* FAX *949/476–0153,* WEB *www.suttonplace.com. 464 rooms. 2 restaurants, pool, tennis, health club. AE, D, DC, MC, V.*

Nightlife and the Arts

The **Orange County Performing Arts Center** (✉ 600 Town Center Dr., Costa Mesa, ☎ 714/556–2787) presents symphony orchestras, opera companies, and musicals. Next door to the center is the **South Coast Repertory Theater** (✉ 655 Town Center Dr., Costa Mesa, ☎ 714/708–5555), which presents traditional and contemporary works.

Outdoor Activities and Sports

Biking

A **bike path** runs from Marina del Rey down to San Diego with only minor breaks. For rentals try **Rainbow Bicycles** (✉ Laguna Beach, ☎ 949/494–5806).

Water Sports

Hobie Sports (☎ 949/4976–3304 at Dana Point; ☎ 949/497–3304 in Laguna Beach) rents sailboats. **Balboa Boat Rentals** (☎ 949/673–7200) rents sail and powerboats in Newport Harbor. **Embarcadero Marina** (☎ 949/496–6177) rents boats at Dana Point.

Beaches

The beaches along Route 1 in Orange County are among the finest and most varied in southern California, with good swimming, great surfing, and many services. Take posted warnings about undertow seriously.

Huntington State Beach is a long stretch of flat, sandy beach with changing rooms, concessions, fire pits, and lifeguards. **Lower Newport Bay** is a sheltered 740-acre preserve for ducks and geese. **Newport Dunes Resort** offers picnic facilities, changing rooms, and a boat launch. **Corona del Mar State Beach** has sandy beaches backed by rocky bluffs and tide pools and caves. **Laguna** has the county's best spot for scuba diving—the Marine Life Refuge, which runs from Seal Rock to Diver's Cove. **Main Beach,** a sandy arc steps from downtown Laguna, is a popular picnic and sand volleyball venue. In South Laguna **Aliso County Park** has recreational facilities and a playground. **Doheny State Park,** near Dana Point Harbor, has food stands, camping, and a fishing pier. **San Clemente State Beach** has camping facilities and food stands and is renowned for its surf.

Orange County Essentials

AIRPORTS

John Wayne Airport Orange County is served by a number of major carriers.

➤ AIRPORT INFORMATION: **John Wayne Airport Orange County** (✉ MacArthur Blvd. at I–405, Santa Ana, ☎ 949/252–5252).

BUS TRAVEL

Greyhound serves Santa Ana and Anaheim.

➤ BUS INFORMATION: **Greyhound** (☎ 714/999–1256).

CAR TRAVEL

I–405 (San Diego Freeway) and I–5 (Santa Ana Freeway) run north–south through Orange County. I–405 merges into I–5 at Irvine.

TRAIN TRAVEL

Amtrak trains stop in Fullerton, Anaheim, Santa Ana, Irvine, San Juan Capistrano, and San Clemente.

➤ TRAIN INFORMATION: **Amtrak** (☎ 800/872–7245).

VISITOR INFORMATION

➤ TOURIST INFORMATION: **Convention and Visitors Bureau** (✉ Anaheim Convention Center, 800 W. Katella Ave., Anaheim 92802, ☎ 714/765–8888).

PALM SPRINGS

A desert playground for Hollywood celebrities since the 1930s, Palm Springs has plenty of attractions: luxurious resorts, nearly year-round golf and tennis, and fine upscale and outlet shopping.

Exploring Palm Springs

★ For a panoramic view of the Palm Springs area, ride up the **Palm Springs Aerial Tramway** (✉ 1 Tramway Rd., ☎ 760/325–1391 or 888/515–8726, WEB www.pstramway.com; 🎫 $20.80). The desert's natural attractions include ★ **Joshua Tree National Park** (✉ Rte. 62 northeast from Rte. 111, ☎ 760/367–7511, WEB www.nps.gov/jotr). Its oddly shaped shrubs, with their branches raised like arms, and its weather-sculpted rocks are entrancing.Come eyeball to eyeball with coyotes, mountain lions, cheetahs, and golden eagles at the **Living Desert Zoo and Gardens** (✉ 47-900 Portola Ave., Palm Desert, ☎ 760/346–5694, WEB www.livingdesert.org; 🎫 $8.50). Easy to challenging trails traverse desert gardens populated with plants of the Mojave, Colorado, and Sonoran deserts.

The **Palm Springs Desert Museum** (✉ 101 Museum Dr., ☎ 760/325–7186, WEB www.psmuseum.org; 🎫 $7.50) has a fine collection that emphasizes natural science and 20th-century art. The museum's Annenberg Theater presents plays, concerts, lectures, operas, and other cultural events. The hottest ticket in the desert is the ★ **Fabulous Palm Springs Follies** (✉ Plaza Theater, 128 S. Palm Canyon Dr., ☎ 760/327–0225, WEB www.palmspringsfollies.com; 🎫 $35–$70), a vaudeville-style revue that stars extravagantly costumed retired (but still buff) showgirls, singers, and dancers.

Dining and Lodging

$$$–$$$$ ✕ **Cuistot.** ★ Signature dishes at chef-owner Bernard Dervieux's French restaurant include grilled shrimp with spinach linguine, Chinese-style duck in a mango-Madeira-ginger sauce, and rack of lamb with rosemary. ✉ *73-111 El Paseo, Palm Desert,* ☎ *760/340–1000. Reservations essential. AE, DC, MC, V. Closed Mon. No lunch Sun.*

$$–$$$ ✕ **Shame on the Moon.** The kitchen here turns out consistently delicious Continental fare like roasted salmon with horseradish crust and calves' liver and onions with a bourbon glaze. The desserts are alluringly decadent. ✉ *69-950 Frank Sinatra Dr., Rancho Mirage,* ☎ *760/324–5515. Reservations essential. AE, MC, V. No lunch.*

$–$$$ ✕ **Palomino Euro Bistro.** The cuisine at this ultrapopular restaurant ranges from pizza and snacking items to grilled and roasted entrées with Mediterranean influences. ✉ *73–101 Rte. 111, Palm Desert,* ☎ *760/773–9091. AE, D, DC, MC, V. No lunch.*

$$$$ **Merv Griffin's Resort Hotel and Givenchy Spa.** Indulgence is the word for this French-style resort with opulent rooms, perfectly manicured gardens, and fine restaurants. Personalized spa services include everything from facials to marine mud wraps to aromatherapy. ✉ *4200 E. Palm Canyon Dr., Palm Springs 92264,* ☎ *760/770–5000 or 800/276–5000,* FAX *760/324–6104,* WEB *www.merv.com. 104 rooms. Restaurant, pool, health club. AE, D, DC, MC, V.*

$$–$$$$ **Ingleside Inn.** Many rooms at this 1920s hacienda-style inn have antiques, fireplaces, and private patios; many have two-person whirlpool tubs and steam showers. ✉ *200 W. Ramon Rd., Palm Springs 92264,* ☎ *760/325–0046 or 800/772–6655,* FAX *760/325–0710,* WEB *www.inglesideinn.com. 30 rooms. Restaurant, pool. AE, D, DC, MC, V. CP.*

$–$$ **Park Inn and Suites.** Just a block from the antiques district, this inn offers comfortable rooms and a delightfully sunny patio. ✉ *2000 N. Palm Canyon Dr., Palm Springs 92262,* ☎ *760/320–0555 or 800/732–7755,* FAX *760/320–2261,* WEB *www.parkhtls.com. 96 rooms. Pool. AE, D, DC, MC, V. CP.*

Palm Springs Essentials

AIRPORTS

Palm Springs International Airport is served by national and regional airlines.

➤ AIRPORT INFORMATION: **Palm Springs International Airport** (✉ 3400 E. Tahquitz Canyon Way, ☎ 760/318–3800, WEB www.palmspringsairport.com).

CAR TRAVEL

Palm Springs is about a two-hour drive east of Los Angeles and a three-hour drive northeast of San Diego. From L.A. take I–10 east to Route 111. From San Diego take I–15 north to Route 60, then I–10 east to Route 111.

VISITOR INFORMATION

Both of Palm Springs' information centers can make reservations for accommodations in the area and have lists of golf courses that are open to the public.

➤ TOURIST INFORMATION: **Palm Springs Desert Resorts Conventions and Visitors Authority** (✉ 69–930 Rte. 111, Suite 201, Rancho Mirage 92270, ☎ 760/770–9000 or 800/967–3767, WEB www.desert-resorts.com). **Palm Springs Visitor Information Center** (✉ 2781 N. Palm Canyon, Palm Springs 92262, ☎ 800/347–7746, WEB www.palm-springs.org).

SAN DIEGO

San Diego is the birthplace of Spanish California—a visit to Old Town and a meal at one of the city's numerous Mexican restaurants will confirm that. For museums, botanical gardens, and San Diego's world-class zoo, head for Balboa Park. Downtown, you'll find excellent shops and restaurants, a lively waterfront, and the quaint and walkable historic Gaslamp Quarter. And almost every day, a perfect climate and gorgeous beaches encourage plenty of outdoor activities.

Exploring San Diego

Central San Diego

★ **Balboa Park** (WEB www.balboapark.org) encompasses 1,200 acres of cultural, recreational, and environmental delights, including a theater complex and gardens. Among the park's several museums are the **Mingei International Museum** (☎ 619/239–0003; $5), devoted to folk art; the **Museum of Photographic Arts** (☎ 619/238–7559; $6), with works by Ansel Adams and Henri Cartier-Bresson; the **San Diego Museum of Art** (☎ 619/232–7931; $8), which hosts major traveling shows; and the **San Diego Aerospace Museum and International Aerospace Hall of Fame** (☎ 619/234–8291; $8). Wide-format films are shown on the Omnimax screen of the **Reuben H. Fleet Space Theater and Science Center** (☎ 619/238–1233; $6.50).

★ The park's most famous attraction is the **San Diego Zoo** (⊠ 2920 Zoo Dr., ☎ 619/234–3153, WEB www.sandiegozoo.org; $19.50), where more than 4,000 animals of 800 species roam in habitats like the Gorilla Tropics, Tiger River, and Polar Bear Plunge. The young giant panda Hua Mei is the zoo's darling. Call 888/697–2632 to learn about viewing times.

★ The **Embarcadero,** at the foot of Ash Street on Harbor Drive, is a waterfront walkway lined with restaurants and cruise-ship piers. The **Maritime Museum** (⊠ 1306 N. Harbor Dr., ☎ 619/234–9153; $5) has a collection of restored ships, including the windjammer *Star of India.* **Seaport Village,** bustling with specialty shops, snack bars, and restaurants, spreads out across 14 acres and connects the harbor with the San Diego Convention Center.

The **Gaslamp Quarter** is a 16-block National Historic District containing most of San Diego's Victorian-era commercial buildings and many restaurants. At the fringe of the quarter, the **William Heath Davis House** (⊠ 410 Island Ave., at 4th Ave., ☎ 619/233–4692), one of the first residences in town, serves as the information center.

San Diego's Spanish and Mexican history and heritage are most evident in **Old Town San Diego State Historic Park** (☎ 619/220–5422), a six-block district north of downtown. The **Robinson-Rose House,** once the commercial center of San Diego, is the park headquarters. **Old Town Plaza** contains 20 historic buildings, restored or re-created. **Bazaar del Mundo** resembles a colonial Mexican square, bordered by shops with Latin American crafts. Ballet Folklorico and flamenco dancers perform here on weekend afternoons.

Mission Bay, with ocean and bay-shore beaches, is a 4,600-acre aquatic park dedicated to action and leisure. On land are joggers, skaters, and bikers. The traditional favorite at **SeaWorld of California** (⊠ 1720 S. Shores Rd., ☎ 619/226–3901, WEB www.seaworld.com; $42.95) theme park is the Shamu show, with giant killer whales entertaining the crowds, but performing dolphins, sea lions, and otters at other shows also delight. There are wet amusement rides, too.

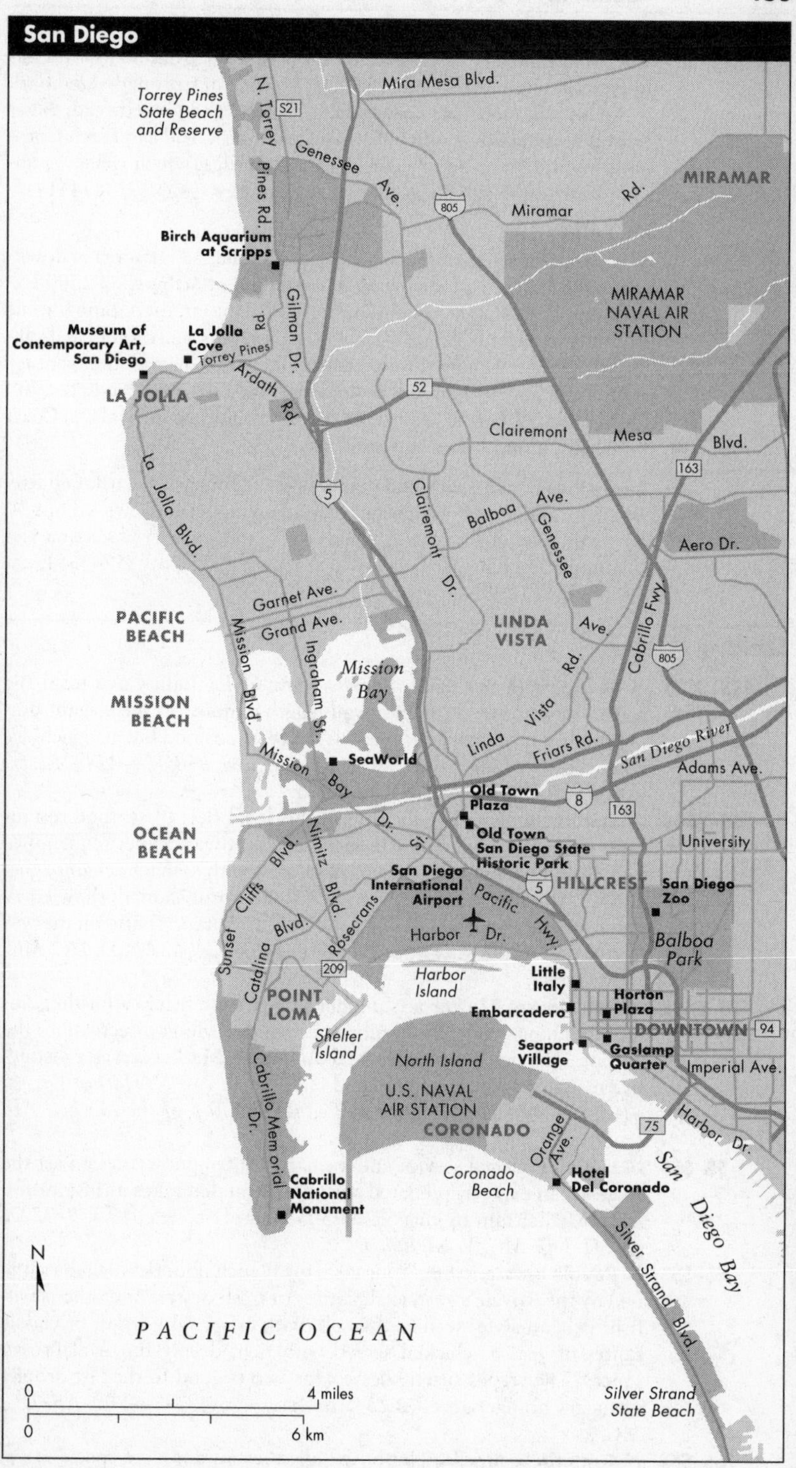
San Diego
Mira Mesa Blvd.
Torrey Pines State Beach and Reserve
N. Torrey Pines Rd.
S21
Genessee Ave.
805
Miramar Rd.
MIRAMAR
Birch Aquarium at Scripps
MIRAMAR NAVAL AIR STATION
Gilman Dr.
Museum of Contemporary Art, San Diego
La Jolla Cove
Torrey Pines Rd.
Ardath Rd.
52
LA JOLLA
Clairemont Mesa Blvd.
163
La Jolla Blvd.
5
Clairemont Dr.
Balboa Ave.
Genessee Ave.
Aero Dr.
Garnet Ave.
PACIFIC BEACH
Grand Ave.
LINDA VISTA
Cabrillo Fwy.
805
Mission Blvd.
Ingraham St.
Mission Bay
Linda Vista Rd.
MISSION BEACH
Friars Rd.
San Diego River
Adams Ave.
Mission Bay Dr.
SeaWorld
Old Town Plaza
8
163
OCEAN BEACH
Nimitz Blvd.
St.
Old Town San Diego State Historic Park
University
Sunset Cliffs Blvd.
San Diego International Airport
HILLCREST
San Diego Zoo
Pacific Hwy.
Rosecrans
Harbor Dr.
Balboa Park
Catalina Blvd.
209
Harbor Island
Little Italy
Horton Plaza
POINT LOMA
Embarcadero
DOWNTOWN
94
Shelter Island
Seaport Village
Gaslamp Quarter
North Island
Imperial Ave.
U.S. NAVAL AIR STATION
CORONADO
75
Harbor Dr.
Cabrillo Memorial Dr.
Orange Ave.
San Diego Bay
Coronado Beach
Hotel Del Coronado
Cabrillo National Monument
Silver Strand Blvd.
N
PACIFIC OCEAN
0
4 miles
0
6 km
Silver Strand State Beach

Coronado

The villagelike city of **Coronado** across the bay from San Diego has numerous Victorian houses.The most prominent Coronado landmark is the historic **Hotel Del Coronado,** all turrets and gingerbread. **Silver Strand State Beach** is one of San Diego's nicest. You can reach Coronado via the 2¼-mi San Diego–Coronado Bridge, which yields a stunning view of the San Diego skyline, or by **ferry** (☎ 619/234–4111).

La Jolla

The attractions in the upscale village of La Jolla, 13 mi north of downtown San Diego, include the **Birch Aquarium at Scripps** (✉ 2300 Expedition Way, ☎ 858/534–3474; 🎫 $8.50), the largest oceanographic exhibit in the United States. A 70,000-gallon tank and a simulated submarine ride are among the attractions. Works of the past half-century are featured at the **Museum of Contemporary Art, San Diego** (✉ 700 Prospect St., ☎ 858/454–3541; 🎫 $4). Palms line the sidewalk on Coast ★ Boulevard along scenic **La Jolla Cove.**

Torrey Pines State Beach and Reserve (✉ N. Torrey Pines Rd./Old Rte. 101, ☎ 858/755–2063) has hiking trails with ocean views. About 30 mi north, Route 76 east of I–5 leads to the well-preserved **Mission San Luis Rey** (✉ 4050 Mission Ave., Oceanside, ☎ 760/757–3651; 🎫 $4), built in 1798.

Dining

$$$–$$$$ ★ ✕ **George's at the Cove.** Enjoy a view of La Jolla Cove from the rooftop terrace or through a wall-length window in the elegant dining room. The imaginative menu is heavy on seafood but also includes pasta, beef, and lamb. ✉ *1250 Prospect St.,* ☎ *858/454–4244. Reservations essential. AE, D, DC, MC, V.*

$$$–$$$$ ★ ✕ **Star of the Sea.** The flagship of this local fleet of seafood restaurants has a changing menu, though you can always expect contemporary preparations such as roasted salmon with spinach, champagne, and sorrel sauce; and macadamia-crusted swordfish in a yellow curry sauce. There's a formal dining room and an outdoor patio on the waterfront. ✉ *1360 N. Harbor Dr.,* ☎ *619/232–7408. AE, D, DC, MC, V. No lunch.*

$$–$$$$ ✕ **Fish Market.** Downstairs, families enjoy fresh fish in a bustling, informal dining room whose enormous windows look directly onto the harbor. Upstairs, the more formal Top of the Market serves a distinctive menu of exquisitely prepared seafood. ✉ *750 N. Harbor Dr.,* ☎ *619/232–3474 Fish Market; 619/234–4867 Top of the Market. AE, D, DC, MC, V.*

$$–$$$ ✕ **Laurel.** Polished service and a smart, contemporary design set the stage for an expertly prepared seasonal menu that takes its inspiration from Mediterranean cuisine. ✉ *505 Laurel St.,* ☎ *619/239–2222. AE, D, DC, MC, V. No lunch.*

$$–$$$ ★ ✕ **Royale Brasserie Bar.** Your taste for French doubtless will be satisfied by the Royale's vast, iced platters of fresh oysters and other shellfish; Belgian-style steamed mussels, with crisp, salty frites; or classic sautés of veal or chicken served with rich, deeply flavorful brown sauces. The crepes suzette dessert for two is good to the last droplet of sugary orange sauce. ✉ *224 5th Ave.,* ☎ *619/237–4900. AE, DC, MC, V.*

$$–$$$ ✕ **Trattoria La Strada.** This busy Italian restaurant has a spacious terrace and an airy dining room with good views of the bustle outside. Carpaccio appetizers are a house specialty. Moving on, try the polenta dressed with rich, melted Fontina cheese and wild mushrooms, or any one of the excellent pastas. The second-course selection stars grilled lamb chops with herb sauce and filet mignon in Chianti sauce. ✉ *702 5th Ave.,* ☎ *619/239–3400. AE, DC, MC.*

$$ ✕ **Bayou Bar and Grill.** Seafood gumbo and fresh Louisiana Gulf seafood dishes are among the Cajun and creole specialties served here. Sunday brunches are hearty. ✉ *329 Market St.,* ☎ *619/696–8747. AE, D, DC, MC, V.*

$–$$ ★ ✕ **Panda Inn.** This dining room at the top of Horton Plaza serves Mandarin and Szechuan dishes in an elegant room that feels far removed from the rush of commerce below. Try the honey walnut shrimp, the Peking duck, the spicy bean curd, or the Panda beef. ✉ *506 Horton Plaza,* ☎ *619/233–7800. AE, D, DC, MC, V.*

$–$$ ✕ **Berta's Latin American Restaurant.** Berta's serves wonderful Latin American dishes that manage to be tasty and health-conscious at the same time. The simple dining room is small, but there's also a little patio. ✉ *3928 Twiggs St.,* ☎ *619/295–2343. AE, MC, V.*

$–$$ ★ ✕ **Sushi Ota.** San Diego's best sushi restaurant is wedged into a minimall, but you won't mind the cramped quarters once you taste the mouthwatering seafood, which is served cooked as well as raw. Besides the usual California roll, tuna, and shrimp sushi, sample the sea urchin or surf clam, and the soft-shell crab roll. ✉ *4529 Mission Bay Dr.,* ☎ *619/270–5670. Reservations essential. AE, D, MC, V. No lunch Sat.–Mon.*

$–$$ ✕ **Hob Nob Hill.** The French toast, corned beef, and fried chicken taste truly homemade at this restaurant, whose dark-wood booths lend a vintage feel. ✉ *2271 1st Ave.,* ☎ *619/239–8176. AE, D, MC, V.*

Lodging

$$$$ **Hotel Del Coronado.** Preserving the memory of seaside vacations long gone by, "The Del" stands as a social and historic landmark, its whimsical red turrets, balconied walkways, and Victorian-decorated rooms and suites taking you as far back as 1888, the year it was built. The hotel's oceanfront cottages, seven-story towers, and cabanas are more modern and quieter than the main building. ✉ *1500 Orange Ave., Coronado 92118,* ☎ *619/435–6611 or 800/468–3533,* FAX *619/522–8262,* WEB *www.hoteldel.com. 676 rooms. 2 restaurants, pools, tennis, gym. AE, D, DC, MC, V.*

$$$ ★ **Ramada Limited–Old Town.** Already an excellent value for Old Town, this cheerful property throws in such perks as garage parking, Continental breakfast, and afternoon snacks. Rooms have a European look, and you'll find modern appliances, including a coffeemaker. ✉ *3900 Old Town Ave., 92110,* ☎ *619/299–7400 or 800/451–9846,* FAX *619/299–1619,* WEB *www.ramada.com 125 rooms. Pool. AE, D, DC, MC, V. CP.*

$$$$ ★ **La Valencia.** This pink-stucco Spanish-Mediterranean confection is a La Jolla landmark. It has a courtyard for patio dining, tiered gardens, and an elegant lobby where guests congregate to enjoy the ocean view. Rooms have a romantic European look, with antique pieces and colorful rugs. ✉ *1132 Prospect St. 92037,* ☎ *858/454–0771 or 800/451–0772,* FAX *858/456–3921,* WEB *www.lavalencia.com. 100 rooms. 3 restaurants, pool, gym. AE, D, DC, MC, V.*

$$$$ ★ **Westgate Hotel.** Antiques, Italian marble counters, and bath fixtures with 24-karat-gold overlays typify the opulent furnishings inside this modern high-rise. High tea, breathtaking views from the ninth floor up, and nearby Horton Plaza are other highlights. ✉ *1055 2nd Ave., 92101,* ☎ *619/238–1818 or 800/221–3802, 800/522–1564 in California;* FAX *619/557–3737;* WEB *www.westgatehotel.com. 223 rooms. 2 restaurants, gym. AE, D, DC, MC, V.*

$$–$$$ 🏨 **Gaslamp Plaza Suites.** Listed on the National Register of Historic Places, this 11-story structure built in 1913 was San Diego's first "skyscraper." Although most rooms are rather small, they are well decorated with dark wood furnishings that give the hotel an elegant flair. You can enjoy the view and breakfast on the rooftop terrace. ✉ *520 E St., 92101,* ☎ *619/232–9500 or 800/874–8770,* FAX *619/238–9945,* WEB *www.gaslampplaza.com. 52 suites. Restaurant. AE, D, DC, MC, V. CP.*

$$–$$$ 🏨 **Heritage Park Inn.** This romantic 1889 Queen Anne mansion is full of 19th-century antiques. Rooms range from small to ample, and some share a bath. ✉ *2470 Heritage Park Row, 92110,* ☎ *619/299–6832 or 800/995–2470,* FAX *619/299–9465.* WEB *www.heritageparkinn.com. 12 rooms. AE, MC, V. BP.*

$ 🏨 **Point Loma Travelodge.** You'll get the same view here as at the higher-priced hotels—for far less money. Of course, there are fewer amenities and the neighborhood isn't as serene, but the rooms are adequate and clean. ✉ *5102 N. Harbor Dr., 92106,* ☎ *619/223–8171; 800/578–7878 central reservations;* FAX *619/222–7330;* WEB *www.travelodge.com. 45 rooms. Pool. AE, D, DC, MC, V.*

Nightlife and the Arts

The daily *San Diego Union-Tribune* and weekly *Reader* have nightlife and cultural-event listings. Half-price tickets to most theater, music, and dance events can be bought on the day of performance at **Times Arts Tix** (✉ Horton Plaza, ☎ 619/497–5000). Only cash is accepted. Advance full-price tickets are also sold. **Ticketmaster** (☎ 619/220–8497) sells tickets to many cultural and entertainment events. Service charges vary, and most tickets are nonrefundable.

Nightlife

San Diego's nightlife ranges from quiet piano bars to cutting-edge rock. Both the Gaslamp Quarter and Pacific Beach have a large concentration of trendy nightspots and hangouts.The **Casbah** (✉ 2501 Kettner Blvd., ☎ 619/232–4355) is a small club with a national reputation for showcasing promising rock bands. The **Comedy Store La Jolla** (✉ 916 Pearl St., ☎ 619/454–9176) books local and national talent. **Humphrey's by the Bay** (✉ 2241 Shelter Island Dr., ☎ 619/523–1010) presents outdoor concerts by national acts every summer. For cowgirls, cowboys, and city slickers alike, **In Cahoots** (✉ 5373 Mission Center Rd., ☎ 619/291–8635) gives free dance lessons every day except Wednesday, when seasoned two-steppers strut their stuff on the large dance floor. The best local Latin, jazz, and blues artists can be found playing the two clubs at **Croce's** (✉ 802 5th Ave., ☎ 619/233–4355).

The Arts

Lamb's Players Theatre (✉ 1142 Orange Ave., Coronado, ☎ 619/437–0600) has a season of five productions from February through November and stages a period musical, "Festival of Christmas." **Lyceum Theatre** (✉ 79 Horton Plaza, ☎ 619/544–1000) is the permanent home of the San Diego Repertory Theatre and also presents productions from visiting theater companies. The **Old Globe Theatres** (✉, ☎ 619/239–2255) present classics, experimental works, and a summer Shakespeare festival. **San Diego Symphony Orchestra** (✉ 750 B St., ☎ 619/235–0804) presents year-round special events including classics, summer and winter pops, and various special events. All events are held at Copley Symphony Hall with the exception of the Summer Pops series at the Navy Pier, on North Harbor Drive downtown. **Spreckels Organ Pavilion** (✉, ☎ 619/702–8138) holds a giant outdoor pipe organ.

Civic organist Carol Williams gives concerts on most Sunday afternoons and on most Monday evenings in summer.

Beaches

San Diego, of course, is known world-wide for its beaches. The northernmost, **La Jolla Cove,** is one of the prettiest spots in the world. A palm-lined park sits on top of the cliffs. Rough-water swimmers like the cove, and divers and snorkelers can explore the underwater delights of the San Diego–La Jolla Underwater Ecological Reserve. The Children's Pool, a shallow lagoon at the south end, is a good place to watch seals and sea lions.

Pacific Beach runs roughly from Crystal Pier to the north end of Mission Beach. A sidewalk and a bike path border the shoreline, and there are picnic tables along the way. There are designated surfing areas, and fire rings are available.

Mission Beach, San Diego's most popular, draws huge crowds on hot summer days. A wide boardwalk is busy with strollers, roller skaters, and cyclists year-round. The 2-mi-long continuous stretch extends from the north entrance of Mission Bay to Pacific Beach.

Ocean Beach is a haven for volleyball players, sunbathers, and swimmers (beware of unusually vicious rip currents). You can fish off the pier without a license or just have your fish in the restaurant at the middle.

Coronado Beach is perfect for sunbathing or Frisbee throwing. There are rest rooms and fire rings; parking can be difficult on busy days.

Silver Strand State Beach, in Coronado, has relatively calm water, an RV campground ($12–$16 per night), and places to rollerblade or ride bikes.

Shopping

The **Gaslamp Quarter** is studded with art galleries, antiques shops, and other specialty stores. **Horton Plaza** (✉ Broadway and G St. from 1st to 4th Ave., ☏ 619/238–1596) is a uniquely festive, postmodern mall. **Old Town** has the Bazaar del Mundo, La Esplanade, and the Old Town Mercado, with international goods, toys, souvenirs, and arts and crafts.Gay and funky **Hillcrest** has many gift, book, and music stores and coffeehouses. **Coronado**'s shops are at the ferry landing and along upscale Orange Avenue.The western end of Garnet Avenue in **Pacific Beach** has trendy shops catering to the beach and evening party crowd.Trendy boutiques and galleries line Girard Avenue and Prospect Street in **La Jolla.** Major department stores anchor the huge **Fashion Valley Center** (✉ 452 Fashion Valley Dr., ☏ 619/297–3386).

San Diego Essentials

AIRPORTS AND TRANSFERS

San Diego International Airport is 3 mi northwest of downtown and is served by most domestic and many international air carriers.

➤ AIRPORT INFORMATION: **San Diego International Airport** (✉ N. Harbor Dr., ☏ 619/231–2100, WEB www.san.org).

AIRPORT TRANSFERS

The Cloud 9 Shuttle has door-to-door service to anywhere in San Diego County, often for less than the cost of a taxi. San Diego Transit buses leave the airport every 10–15 minutes and cost $2.25. Taxi fare is $7–$9 plus tip to most center-city hotels.

➤ TAXIS AND SHUTTLES: **Cloud 9 Shuttle** (☏ 858/278–8877, WEB www.cloud9shuttle.com). **San Diego Transit** (☏ 619/233–3004, WEB www.sdcommute.com).

BOAT AND FERRY TRAVEL

The San Diego–Coronado Ferry provides service from the Broadway Pier to Coronado.

➤ BOAT AND FERRY INFORMATION: **San Diego–Coronado Ferry** (☎ 619/234–4111).

BUS TRAVEL TO AND FROM SAN DIEGO

➤ BUS INFORMATION: **Greyhound** (✉ 120 W. Broadway, ☎ 800/231–2222, WEB www.greyhound.com).

CAR TRAVEL

I–5 runs north–south. I–8 comes into San Diego from the east, I–15 from the northeast.

TRAIN TRAVEL

Amtrak trains arrive at the Santa Fe Depot.

➤ TRAIN INFORMATION: **Amtrak** (☎ 800/872–7245, WEB www.amtrak.com). **Santa Fe Depot** (✉ 1050 Kettner Blvd. at Broadway, ☎ 619/239–9021).

TRANSPORTATION AROUND SAN DIEGO

It's best to have a car, but avoid the freeways during rush hours. The San Diego Trolley travels the 20 mi from downtown to within 100 ft of the Mexican border; other trolleys on the line serve Seaport Village, the Convention Center, Qualcomm Stadium, and inland areas.

➤ CONTACTS: **San Diego Trolley** (☎ 619/233–3004, WEB www.sdcommute.com).

VISITOR INFORMATION

➤ TOURIST INFORMATION: **International Visitor Information Center** (✉ 11 Horton Plaza 92101, ☎ 619/236–1212). **San Diego Visitor Information Center** (✉ 2688 E. Mission Bay Dr., off I–5, 92109, ☎ 858/276–8200, WEB www.sandiego.org).

COLORADO

Updated by Eric Peterson

Capital	Denver
Population	4,488,000
Motto	Nothing Without Providence
State Bird	Lark bunting
State Flower	Columbine
Postal Abbreviation	CO

Statewide Visitor Information

Colorado Tourism Office (✉ 1625 Broadway, Suite 1700, Denver 80202, ☎ 800/265–6723, WEB www.colorado.com).

Scenic Drives

Colorado has 17 designated scenic routes, marked by signs with blue columbines. The 232-mi **San Juan Skyway** traverses historic ranching and mining towns such as Durango, Silverton, Ouray, Telluride, and Cortez. The **Peak-to-Peak Highway** follows Routes 119, 72, and 7 through gold-mining towns to Rocky Mountain National Park.

National and State Parks

National Parks

Black Canyon of the Gunnison National Park (✉ 15 mi northeast of Montrose on U.S. 50 and Colo. 347, Gunnison 81230, ☎ 970/641–2337; 💵 $7 per vehicle) is a small but striking park centered on a uniquely narrow and deep canyon. **Great Sand Dunes National Monument and Preserve** (✉ 35 mi northeast of Alamosa off Rte. 150, Mosca 81146, ☎ 719/378–2312; 💵 $3), with sand dunes almost 750 ft high, has a year-round campground and a nature trail. **Mesa Verde National Park** (✉ U.S. 160, 9 mi east of Cortez, Mesa Verde National Park, 81330, ☎ 970/529–4465; 💵 $10 per vehicle, tour $2) has well-preserved cliff dwellings of the ancestral Puebloan peoples. **Rocky Mountain National Park** (✉ 5 mi west of Estes Park on U.S. 36, Estes Park 80517, ☎ 970/586–1206; 💵 $15 per vehicle) is a 265,000-acre picture-book vision of craggy mountains, abundant wildlife, and deep-blue mountain lakes, with camping, hiking, and scenic drives.

State Parks

Contact the **Colorado State Parks** office (✉ 1313 Sherman St., Room 618, Denver 80203, ☎ 303/866–3437, WEB www.colroadoparks.org) for information on the state's 40 parks.

DENVER

Colorado's capital city lies nearly smack in the middle of the state and is a reasonable drive from the major ski areas. Denver's sharp-edged skyscrapers, clean streets, and dozens of well-used parks evoke the image of a young, progressive city, but much of the essence of Denver lies in its western past. Areas like LoDo, a historic part of lower downtown, buzz with jazz clubs, restaurants, and art galleries in century-old buildings. The Platte River valley between LoDo and I–25 is full of attractions such as aquariums, amusement parks, and sport stadiums.

Exploring Denver

Several of Denver's major attractions border the **Civic Center** (✉ Bannock St. to Broadway south of Colfax Ave. and north of 14th Ave.), a three-block park with lawns, gardens, and a Greek amphitheater. East of the Civic Center is the 1886 **state capitol,** which as a reminder of the state's mining heritage periodically re-covers its dome with hammered gold leaf. The balcony affords a panoramic view of the Rockies. ✉ *200 E. Colfax Ave.,* ☎ *303/866–2604. Closed weekends.*

Just south of the Civic Center park is the **Colorado History Museum** (✉ 1300 Broadway, ☎ 303/866–3682, WEB www.coloradohistory.org; 🎟 $5), with Colorado and western memorabilia and dioramas, plus special exhibits. ★ The **Denver Art Museum** has an excellent collection of Native American art, as well as superlative holdings in pre-Columbian and Spanish colonial art. ✉ *100 W. 14th Ave. Pkwy.,* ☎ *720/865–5000,* WEB *www.denverartmuseum.org.* 🎟 *$6. Closed Mon.*

Connected to the Denver Art Museum by an underground walkway is the **Denver Public Library** (✉ 10 W. 14th Ave. Pkwy., ☎ 720/865–1111). This Michael Graves–designed building houses a world-renowned collection of books, photographs, and newspapers that chronicle the American West. Adjacent to the Denver Art Museum, the elaborate redbrick Victorian **Byers-Evans House** (✉ 1310 Bannock St., ☎ 303/620–4933; 🎟 $3), built in 1883, is an elegantly restored house-museum. An average of 10 billion coins are stamped yearly at the **U.S. Mint,** which has several exhibits on the history of money and a restored version of Denver's original mint. ✉ *320 W. Colfax Ave.,* ☎ *303/405–4761,* WEB *www.usmint.gov.* 🎟 *Free. Closed weekends.*

Free shuttle buses are the only vehicles allowed on the **16th Street Mall,** which has shade trees, outdoor cafés, historic buildings, and shops. Be ★ sure to peek inside the **Brown Palace Hotel** (✉ 321 17th St., ☎ 303/297–3111, WEB www.brownpalace.com), the grande dame of Denver hotels, built in 1892 and still proud of her antique charms. The 330-ft **D&F Tower** (✉ 16th St. at Arapahoe St.) emulates the campanile of St. Mark's Cathedral in Venice.

Denver's most charming shopping area is historic **Larimer Square** (✉ Larimer and 15th Sts.), which has some of the city's oldest retail buildings and finest specialty shops. **LoDo,** north of Larimer Street between Speer Boulevard and 22nd Street, is a quirky historic area. East of downtown, the **Molly Brown House Museum** (✉ 1340 Pennsylvania St., ☎ 303/832–4092, WEB www.mollybrown.org; 🎟 $6.50), a Victorian confection, celebrates the life and times of the scandalous Ms. Brown, whose story was made into the film *The Unsinkable Molly Brown.*

The interactive exhibits at the **Children's Museum of Denver** include a maze, a child-size grocery store, and a hands-on art studio. ✉ *2121 Crescent Dr.,* ☎ *303/433–7444,* WEB *www.cmdenver.org.* 🎟 *$6.50. Closed Mon. Sept.–May.*

Colorado's Ocean Journey (✉ 700 Water St., ☎ 303/561–4450, WEB www.oceanjourney.org; 🎟 $14.95), the largest aquarium between Chicago and Monterrey, features river ecosystems replicated via state-of-the-art technology. Across the Platte River from Colorado's Ocean Journey sits **Six Flags Elitch Gardens,** the nation's only downtown amusement park and a popular destination for roller coaster fanatics. ✉ *Speer Blvd. and I–25,* ☎ *303/595–4386,* WEB *www.sixflags.com/elitchgardens.* 🎟 *$33; children under 48" $20. Closed Nov.–late Apr.*

★ The **Denver Museum of Nature and Science** (✉ 2001 Colorado Blvd., ☎ 303/322–7009, WEB www.dmns.org; 🎟 $8) has traditional collec-

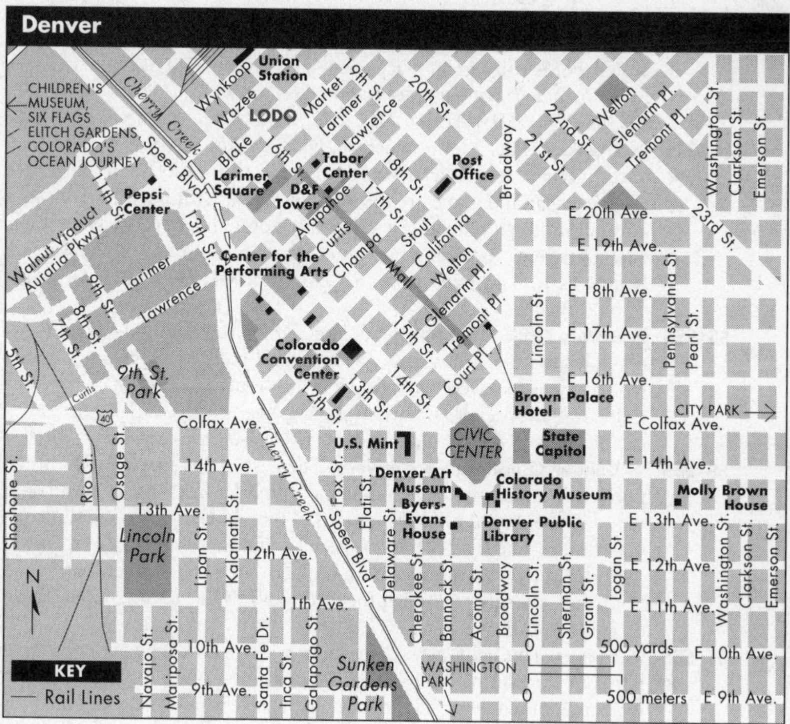

tions and hands-on exhibits, plus an IMAX movie theater with a four-story screen. The museum's planetarium is being expanded and renovated and will be closed until mid-year 2003. The Prehistoric Journey exhibit invites you to walk through the seven stages of the earth's development, beginning 3½ billion years ago.

Parks, Gardens, and Zoos

Denver has one of the largest city **park systems** (☎ 303/698–4900 for park headquarters office) in the country, with more than 360 parks and 14,000 acres of outlying mountain lands. Flower gardens and lakes abound in **Washington Park,** east of Downing Street between Virginia and Louisiana avenues. The **Denver Zoo** (✉ E. 23rd St. between York St. and Colorado Blvd., ☎ 303/376–4800, WEB www.denverzoo.org; 🎫 $9) has a nursery for baby animals and the Primate Panorama, where you can view 29 primate species in simulated natural habitats.

★ Southeast of downtown are the **Denver Botanic Gardens** (✉ 1005 York St., ☎ 720/865–3500, WEB www.botanicgardens.com; 🎫 $6.50). The conservatory houses a rain forest; outside are a Japanese garden, an alpine rock garden that blooms with brilliant wildflowers in spring, and other horticulture displays. **Platte River Greenway** includes more than 20 mi of biking and jogging paths that follow Cherry Creek and the Platte River, much of it through downtown Denver.

Dining

Beef, buffalo, and burritos are prominent on Denver's menus. Cruise LoDo or 17th Avenue East for inventive kitchens, and check out Federal Street for cheap ethnic eats.

$$–$$$$ ✕ **Buckhorn Exchange.** In proud possession of the city's first liquor license (issued in 1893), this Denver landmark with handsome men's-club decor is still a great place to eat elk, buffalo, and beef and to gawk at the menagerie of trophies mounted on the walls. ✉ *1000 Osage St.,* ☎ *303/534–9505. AE, D, DC, MC, V. No lunch weekends.*

$$–$$$$ ★ ✕ **The Fort.** This adobe structure, with a piñon bonfire in the courtyard, is a perfect replica of Bent's Fort, a Colorado fur trade center. Buffalo meat and game are the specialties; elk with huckleberry sauce and balsamic-glazed yak are especially good. There is occasional live entertainment, including costumed "mountain men" and mariachi bands. ✉ *U.S. 285 and Colo. 8,* ☎ *303/697–4771. AE, D, DC, MC, V. No lunch.*

$$–$$$ ✕ **Barolo Grill.** This spot looks like a chichi farmhouse—dried flowers in brass urns, straw baskets, and hand-painted porcelain. Choose from duckling stewed with red wine, house-made gnocchi, or other rotating Italian specialties. ✉ *3030 E. 6th Ave.,* ☎ *303/393–1040. Reservations essential. AE, D, DC, MC, V. Closed Sun.–Mon. No lunch.*

$$–$$$ ✕ **Denver Chophouse & Brewery.** The best of the many LoDo brewpubs and restaurants surrounding the ballpark, the Chophouse, all dark wood and exposed brick, is housed in the old Union Pacific Railroad warehouse. The food is basic American and there's plenty of it: steak, seafood, and chicken served with hot corn bread and honey-butter and "bottomless" salad tossed at the table. ✉ *1735 19th St., Suite 100,* ☎ *303/296–0800. AE, DC, MC, V.*

$$–$$$ ★ ✕ **Strings.** This light, airy spot with its wide-open kitchen is a preferred hangout for visiting celebs, whose autographs are mounted. The food is casual-contemporary. One specialty is the cashew-encrusted sea bass with vanilla butter sauce. ✉ *1700 Humboldt St.,* ☎ *303/831–7310. Reservations essential. AE, D, DC, MC, V. No lunch Sun.*

$–$$ ✕ **Bayou Bob's.** In the Paramount Theatre Building downtown, Bayou Bob's whips up Cajun classics—gumbo, jambalaya, étouffée—in a casual atmosphere. Try the panfried alligator tail. ✉ *1635 Glenarm St.,* ☎ *303/573–6828. Reservations not accepted. AE, D, DC, MC, V.*

$–$$ ✕ **Nicois.** Chef Kevin Taylor has created a simple, sublime menu full of inventive variations on Mediterranean dishes. The column-laden space, in the former Guaranty National Bank building, also features an outstanding tapas bar—four or five delectable appetizers (about $3.50 apiece) make a good substitute for an entrée. ✉ *815 17th St.,* ☎ *303/293–2322. AE, DC, MC, V. Closed Sun. No lunch weekends.*

$–$$ ✕ **T-WA Inn.** This South Asian hole-in-the-wall serves a broad range of great food, including delicate Vietnamese spring rolls and daily specials. ✉ *555 S. Federal Blvd.,* ☎ *303/922–4584. AE, D, MC, V.*

$–$$ ★ ✕ **Wynkoop Brewing Company.** The beer is brewed on the premises, and the pub fare is hearty. Try the shepherd's pie or charbroiled elk medallions with brandy peppercorn sauce; then check out the pool hall and cabaret for a full night's entertainment. ✉ *1634 18th St.,* ☎ *303/297–2700. AE, D, DC, MC, V.*

$ ✕ **Blue Bonnet Café.** Its location in a fairly seedy neighborhood southeast of downtown doesn't stop the crowds from lining up early. The western decor, Naugahyde, and jukebox set an upbeat mood for killer margaritas and great burritos. ✉ *457 S. Broadway,* ☎ *303/778–0147. Reservations not accepted. MC, V.*

$ ✕ **Hotcakes.** This jumping Capitol Hill spot is a breakfast and lunch hangout. Weekend brunch draws crowds of bicyclists and newspaper readers in search of the croissant French toast, "health nut" pancakes, colossal omelets, and scrumptious skillets. ✉ *1400 E. 18th Ave.,* ☎ *303/830–1909. MC, V. No dinner.*

Lodging

Denver's lodging choices range from the stately Brown Palace to budget chain motels, with bed-and-breakfasts in between. **Bed & Breakfast Innkeepers of Colorado** (✉ Box 38416, Dept. W, Colorado Springs 80937-8416, ☎ 800/265–7696, WEB www.innsofcolorado.org) handles B&Bs throughout the state. **Hostelling International–Rocky Mountain Council** (✉ Box 2370, Boulder 80306, ☎ 303/442–1166, WEB www.hiayh.org) covers hostels in eight Colorado locations.

$$$$ ★ **Brown Palace Hotel.** This downtown grande-dame hotel has hosted President Eisenhower, the Beatles, and other illustrious guests. The eight-story lobby is topped by a glorious stained-glass ceiling. Rooms are Victorian in style and have modern conveniences such as high-speed Web access and cordless telephones. ✉ *321 17th St., 80202,* ☎ *303/297–3111 or 800/321–2599,* FAX *303/312–5900,* WEB *www.brownpalace.com. 241 rooms. 4 restaurants, gym. AE, D, DC, MC, V.*

$$$$ **Westin Tabor Center.** Oversize rooms at this high-rise overlooking the 16th Street Mall are done in gray and taupe and have paisley duvets. A view of the Denver skyline from the indoor-pool room makes swimming laps a pleasure. One of the hotel restaurants is a branch of the Palm, the Manhattan-based steak house. ✉ *1672 Lawrence St., 80202,* ☎ *303/572–9100 or 888/627–8435,* FAX *303/572–7288,* WEB *www.westin.com. 430 rooms. 2 restaurants, pool, health club. AE, D, DC, MC, V.*

$$–$$$$ **Castle Marne.** This B&B with balconies, a four-story turret, and intricate stone- and woodwork is east of downtown and near several fine restaurants. Most rooms have brass or mahogany beds, throw rugs, tile fireplaces (nonworking), a profusion of dried and fresh flowers, and claw-foot tubs; a few have hot tubs or whirlpool baths. ✉ *1572 Race St., 80206,* ☎ *303/331–0621 or 800/926–2763,* FAX *303/331–0623,* WEB *www.castlemarne.com. 10 rooms. AE, D, DC, MC, V. BP.*

$$$ **Adam's Mark.** In the mid-1990s the I. M. Pei–designed Radisson and the old May D&F department store across the street from it were converted into a convention-oriented property—one of the 25 largest hotels in the country. The location, at the south end of the 16th Street Mall, is ideal. ✉ *1550 Court Pl., 80202,* ☎ *303/893–3333 or 800/444–2326,* FAX *303/626–2543,* WEB *www.adamsmark.com. 1,225 rooms. 3 restaurants, pool, gym. AE, D, DC, MC, V.*

$$$ ★ **Loews Denver.** A 12-story steel-and-black glass facade conceals the delightful Italian Baroque motif within. Rooms are spacious and elegant, with Continental touches. The hotel is halfway between downtown and the Denver Tech Center, a local business hub. ✉ *4150 E. Mississippi Ave., 80246,* ☎ *303/782–9300 or 800/235–6397,* FAX *303/758–6542,* WEB *www.loewsdenver.com. 183 rooms. Restaurant, gym. AE, D, DC, MC, V.*

$$$ ★ **Oxford.** The city's most charming small hotel was a Denver fixture in the Victorian era. Guest rooms have antiques and reproductions. Complimentary shoe shines, afternoon sherry, and morning coffee are among the civilized touches here. ✉ *1600 17th St., 80202,* ☎ *303/628–5400 or 800/228–5838,* FAX *303/628–5413,* WEB *www.theoxfordhotel.com. 80 rooms. 2 restaurants, health club. AE, D, DC, MC, V.*

$$–$$$ **Comfort Inn/Downtown.** The advantages to this hotel are its reasonable rates and its location, right across from—and connected to via a skywalk—the Brown Palace. Rooms higher up have panoramic views. ✉ *401 17th St., 80202,* ☎ *303/296–0400 or 800/221–2222,* FAX *303/297–0774. 229 rooms. Restaurant. AE, D, DC, MC, V.*

$–$$$ **Holiday Chalet.** This B&B is in the heart of Capitol Hill, immediately east of downtown. It's full of charm, with stained-glass windows and family heirlooms. Many of the rooms are furnished with overstuffed Victorian armchairs and such historic touches as furniture once owned by Baby Doe Tabor. Some units have tile fireplaces, others have small sitting rooms, and each has a full kitchen. ✉ *1820 E. Colfax Ave., 80218,* ☎ *303/321–9975 or 800/626–4497,* FAX *303/377–6556,* WEB *www.bbonline.com/co/holiday. 10 rooms. AE, D, DC, MC, V. CP.*

$–$$$ ★ **Queen Anne Inn.** North of downtown in a reclaimed historic area, this B&B (composed of two adjacent Victorian houses) makes a romantic getaway, with fresh flowers and antiques. An afternoon Colorado-wine tasting is free. ✉ *2147 Tremont Pl., 80205,* ☎ *303/296–6666 or 800/432–4667,* FAX *303/296–2151,* WEB *www.queenannebnb.com. 14 rooms. AE, D, DC, MC, V. BP.*

Nightlife and the Arts

Friday's *Denver Post* and *Rocky Mountain News* list entertainment events, as does the weekly *Westword.* **TicketMan** (☎ 303/430–1111) sells tickets to major events. The **Ticket Bus** (✉ 16th St. Mall at Curtis St.) is open weekdays 10–6 and sells same-day half-price tickets.

Nightlife

Downtown is where you'll find mainstream entertainment. LoDo is home to nightclubs and small theaters. Remember that Denver's high altitude makes you react more quickly to alcohol.

Comedy Works (✉ 1226 15th St., ☎ 303/595–3637) has local and nationally known stand-up comics. The **Grizzly Rose** (✉ I–25 Exit 215, ☎ 303/295–1330), with its miles of dance floor, hosts national bands. **El Chapultepec** (✉ 1962 Market St., ☎ 303/295–9126) is a smoky dive where visiting jazz musicians often jam after hours. **Bluebird Theatre** (✉ 3317 E. Colfax Ave., ☎ 303/322–2308), one of Denver's oldest theaters (1912), has edgy entertainment—live rock music and cult movies—every night. The smoky, grungy **Cricket on the Hill** (✉ 1209 E. 13th Ave., ☎ 303/777–5840) is the top venue for local music, with everything from country and folk to punk and metal. The **Mercury Café** (✉ 2199 California St., ☎ 303/294–9281) triples as a health-food restaurant, fringe theater, and music venue for rock and world-music artists.

The Arts

The modern **Denver Center for the Performing Arts** (✉ 14th and Curtis Sts., ☎ 303/893–3272) houses most of the city's large concert halls and theaters. The **Colorado Ballet** (☎ 303/837–8888) presents classics in the performing arts center. The **Colorado Symphony Orchestra** (✉ 13th and Curtis Sts., ☎ 303/893–4100) performs at Boettcher Concert Hall. The **Denver Center Theater Company** (☎ 303/893–4100) presents fine repertory theater. **Hunger Artists** (☎ 303/620–4933) presents smaller works at a variety of venues, ranging from children's plays to dark adaptations.

Spectator Sports

Baseball: The Colorado Rockies (✉ Coors Field, 2001 Blake St., ☎ 303/762–5437) play at one of the country's best retro ballparks. **Basketball: The Denver Nuggets** (✉ Pepsi Center, 1000 Chopper Cir., at Auraria Pkwy. and Speer Blvd., ☎ 303/405–1100) have floundered in recent years and are something of an ugly stepchild in Denver's sports scene. **Football: The Denver Broncos** (✉ Invesco Field at Mile High, 1900 Eliot St., ☎ 720/258–3333) play at a sparkling new venue to sellout crowds. **Hockey: The Colorado Avalanche** (✉ Pepsi Center, 1000 Chopper Cir., at Auraria Pkwy. and Speer Blvd., ☎ 303/405–1100) are perennial contenders in the National Hockey League.

Shopping

Denver is one of the top places to buy recreational equipment and clothing. Pick up a pair of cowboy boots and other western apparel at any western store.

Shopping Districts

The Cherry Creek shopping district, 2 mi from downtown, is Denver's best. On one side of 1st Avenue at Milwaukee Street is the **Cherry Creek Shopping Mall,** a granite-and-glass behemoth containing some of the nation's finest retailers. On the other side is **Cherry Creek North,** with art galleries and specialty shops. On the pedestrian-only **16th Street Mall** are Tabor Center, a light-filled atrium with specialty shops and restaurants, and other large downtown retailers. **South Broadway** between 1st Avenue and Evans Street has blocks of antiques stores; prices are sometimes lower than those elsewhere. **LoDo** has the trendiest galleries, many in restored warehouses.

Books

Tattered Cover (✉ 2995 E. 1st Ave., ☎ 303/322–7727; ✉ 1628 16th St., ☎ 303/436–1070) has overstuffed armchairs, four floors of books (more than 250,000 titles), afternoon lectures and musical presentations, and a knowledgeable staff. The original location, at 1st Avenue and Milwaukee Street, is more active and bigger.

Sporting Goods

Gart Brothers Sports Castle (✉ 1000 Broadway, ☎ 303/861–1122) is a huge, multistory shrine to the Colorado sporting lifestyle.The new **REI Flagship Store** (✉ 1416 Platte St., ☎ 303/756–3100) has a climbing wall, a "cold room" for testing outerwear and sleeping bags, and an outdoor bike track.

Western Wear

At Larimer Square, **Cry Baby Ranch** (✉ 1422 Larimer St., ☎ 303/623–3979) has a rambunctious assortment of 1940s and '50s cowboy kitsch. **Denver Buffalo Company Trading Post** (✉ 1109 Lincoln St., ☎ 303/832–0884) carries top-of-the-line western clothing and souvenirs.

Side Trip to Boulder

Arriving and Departing

From Denver take I–25 north to the Boulder Turnpike (U.S. 36). Denver's RTD buses make the 27-mi commute regularly. The turnpike is notorious for traffic, especially during rush hour.

What to See and Do

Home of the University of Colorado, Boulder is a quintessential college town, but it's also the headquarters of a hard-core group of professional athletes who live to bike and run. The atmosphere is peaceful, new age, and cultural, with a gorgeous backdrop of mountains. **Pearl Street Mall** is a see-and-be-seen pedestrian street with benches, grassy spots, great shopping, and outdoor cafés. Weekdays from 10 to 3, the **Celestial Seasonings Plant** (✉ 4600 Sleepytime Dr., ☎ 303/581–1202) conducts free tours; you'll see raw tea ingredients (the Mint Room is off-limits because of its potent scent), then watch them being blended. Rich in lectures, theater, and music year-round, Boulder celebrates classical music each summer at its **Colorado Music Festival** (✉ Chautauqua Park, ☎ 303/449–1397). Colorado University's Mary Rippon outdoor theater is the **Colorado Shakespeare Festival**'s (☎ 303/492–0554, WEB www.coloradoshakes.org) annual venue for the bard's comedies and tragedies from mid-June to mid-August.

Side Trip to Georgetown

Arriving and Departing

Take I–70 west to the Georgetown exit, 46 mi from Denver.

What to See and Do

With gingerbread-Victorian houses on quiet streets, Georgetown provides a tantalizing glimpse of Colorado's heady mining past. The dramatic alpine scenery also makes this a worthy expedition. This National Historic District has restaurants, small shops, and the **Georgetown Loop Railroad** (☎ 303/569–2403), a 3-mi narrow-gauge line that travels into the mountains and back during the summer.

Side Trip to Golden

Arriving and Departing

From I–70 take Colo. 58 to Golden, 12 mi west of Denver.

What to See and Do

Coors (✉ 13th and Ford Sts., ☎ 303/277–2337) operates the world's largest brewery. Daily tours (except on Sundays) cover the basics of brewing beer and end with a trip to the tasting rooms. The drive up Lookout Mountain to the **Buffalo Bill Grave and Museum** (✉ Rte. 5 off I–70 Exit 256, or 19th Ave. out of Golden, ☎ 303/526–0747; 🎫 $3) affords a sensational panoramic view of Denver. Contrary to popular belief, Bill Cody never expressed a burning desire to be buried here: The *Denver Post* bought the corpse from Bill's sister and bribed her to concoct a teary story about his dying wish. Apparently, rival towns were so outraged that the National Guard had to be called in to protect the grave from robbers—and many still claim that Cody's final resting place is elsewhere.

Denver Essentials

AIRPORTS AND TRANSFERS

Denver International Airport (DIA), 23 mi from downtown Denver, is served by most major carriers.

➤ AIRPORT INFORMATION: **Denver International Airport** (✉ 8500 Peña Blvd., ☎ 303/342–2000 or 800/247–2336, WEB www.flydenver.com).

AIRPORT TRANSFER

Cab fare downtown averages $50; RTD, the local bus service (☞ Transportation Around Denver, *below*), can also get you there. The Denver Super Shuttle provides express bus service from the airport to locations in Denver and surrounding areas; a trip downtown costs about $20 depending on your destination. Reservations are essential.

➤ SHUTTLE: **Denver Super Shuttle** (☎ 800/525–3177, WEB www.supershuttledenver.com).

BUS TRAVEL TO AND FROM DENVER

➤ BUS INFORMATION: **Greyhound** (✉ 1055 19th St., ☎ 800/231–2222, WEB www.greyhound.com).

CAR TRAVEL

I–70 (east–west) and I–25 (north–south) intersect just north of downtown and both can be congested during rush hours. Despite many one-way streets, driving in Denver is not difficult. Numbered streets intersect numbered avenues at a right angle at Broadway. When you're looking for a particular road, know whether it's a street or avenue.

TAXIS

Yellow Cab and Metro Taxi are two 24-hour taxi services.

➤ TAXI COMPANIES: **Metro Taxi** (☎ 303/333–3333). **Yellow Cab** (☎ 303/777–7777).

TOURS

BUS TOURS

Gray Line conducts a 3½-hour city tour and a mountain-parks tour.

➤ FEES AND SCHEDULES: **Gray Line** (☎ 303/289–2841, WEB www.coloradograyline.com).

TRAIN TRAVEL

Amtrak serves Union Station.

➤ TRAIN INFORMATION: **Amtrak** (☎ 800/872–7245, WEB www.amtrak.com). **Union Station** (✉ 17th St. at Wynkoop St., ☎ 303/534–6333).

TRANSPORTATION AROUND DENVER

A free shuttle bus operates frequently down the length of the 16th Street Mall. The region's public bus service, RTD, has routes throughout Denver and to towns such as Boulder, Longmont, and Nederland. RTD's light-rail system serves the downtown and southwestern regions. Buy bus tokens, which cost $1 to $3.50, depending on the distance of your trip, at grocery stores or pay on board; rail tickets are available from machines in the train stations. Tickets ($3) for the Cultural Connection Trolley, operated by the RTD, are sold at outlets downtown, from the trolley driver, or from most hotel concierges. The trolley operates daily, every half hour 9–6, linking 18 attractions from the Denver Performing Arts Complex downtown to the Denver Museum of Nature and Science in City Park. Tickets are good for the entire day.

➤ CONTACT: **RTD** (☎ 303/299–6000, WEB www.rtd-denver.com).

VISITOR INFORMATION

➤ TOURIST INFORMATION: **Denver Metro Convention and Visitors Bureau** (✉ 1555 California St., Suite 300, 80202, ☎ 303/892–1112, WEB www.denver.org).

COLORADO SPRINGS AND ENVIRONS

Colorado Springs is the state's second-largest city after Denver, which is 65 mi north of it. The region abounds in natural and man-made wonders, from the eerie sandstone formations of the Garden of the Gods to the space-age architecture of the U.S. Air Force Academy. However, the most indelible landmark is unquestionably Pikes Peak, from whose vantage point Katharine Lee Bates penned "America the Beautiful."

Exploring Colorado Springs and Environs

A mix of attractions surrounding Colorado Springs complements the city's Victorian houses and wide, tree-lined streets. Tours at the **U.S. Olympic Training Center** (✉ 1 Olympic Plaza, ☎ 719/578–4888; 🎫 free) include a stirring half-hour movie and a half-hour walk around the facilities. A highlight is the flume—a kind of water treadmill, where swimmers can have every aspect of their stroke analyzed. The **Broadmoor** (✉ 1 Lake Ave.) is a rambling ensemble of pink-stucco Italian Renaissance–style hotel buildings, gardens, and a lake skimmed by black swans. The **Carriage House Museum** (✉ Lake Circle, ☎ 719/634–7711; 🎫 free), on the Broadmoor's grounds, displays an old stagecoach, vintage cars, and carriages used at presidential inaugurals.

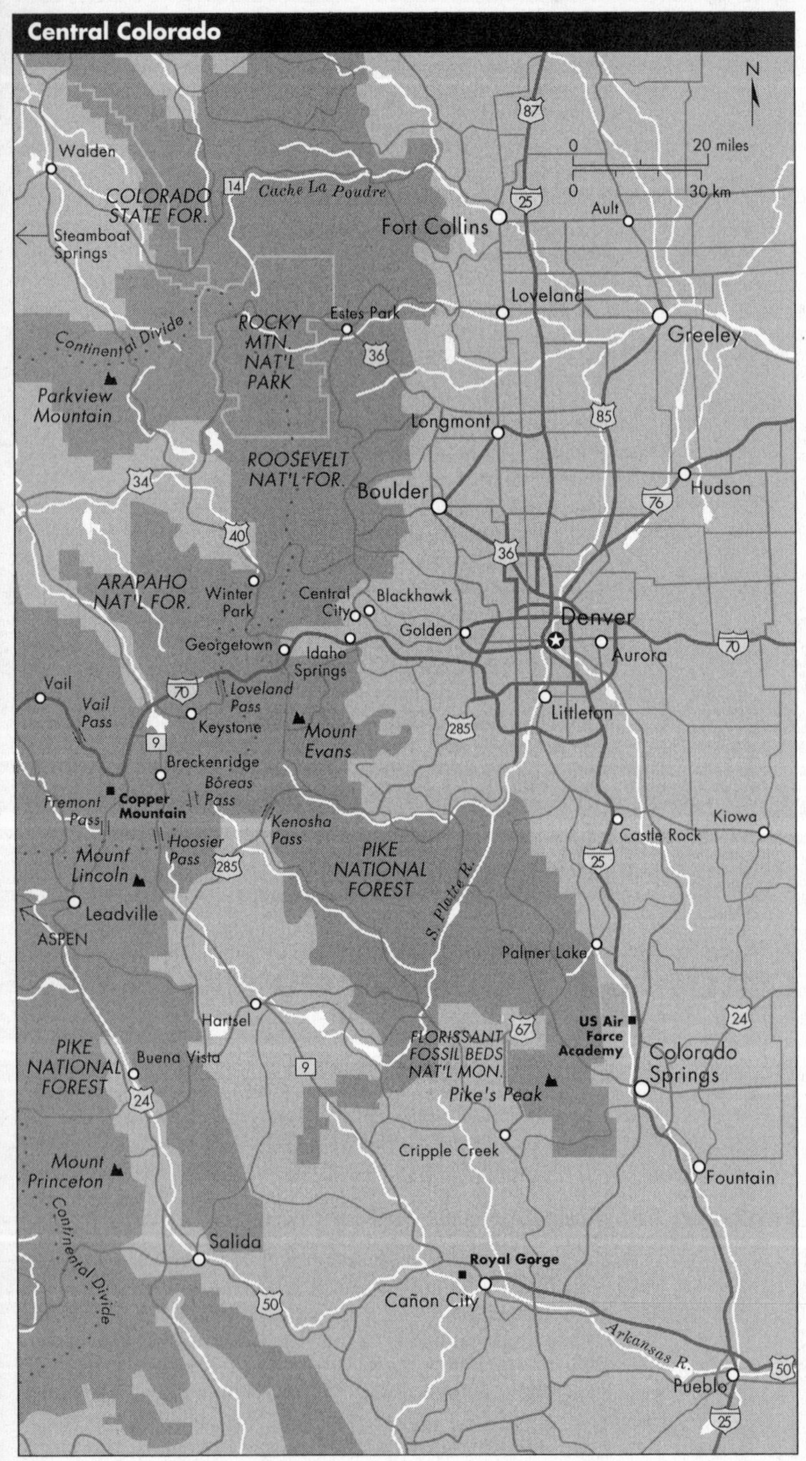
Central Colorado
N
0
20 miles
0
30 km
Walden
COLORADO STATE FOR.
Cache La Poudre
Steamboat Springs
Fort Collins
Ault
Loveland
Greeley
Estes Park
Continental Divide
ROCKY MTN. NAT'L PARK
Parkview Mountain
Longmont
ROOSEVELT NAT'L FOR.
Boulder
Hudson
ARAPAHO NAT'L FOR.
Winter Park
Central City
Blackhawk
Denver
Golden
Aurora
Georgetown
Idaho Springs
Vail
Vail Pass
Loveland Pass
Keystone
Mount Evans
Littleton
Breckenridge
Boreas Pass
Fremont Pass
Copper Mountain
Kenosha Pass
Kiowa
Castle Rock
Hoosier Pass
Mount Lincoln
PIKE NATIONAL FOREST
S. Platte R.
Leadville
ASPEN
Palmer Lake
Hartsel
US Air Force Academy
PIKE NATIONAL FOREST
Buena Vista
FLORISSANT FOSSIL BEDS NAT'L MON.
Colorado Springs
Pike's Peak
Cripple Creek
Mount Princeton
Fountain
Salida
Royal Gorge
Cañon City
Arkansas R.
Pueblo

Two routes— a **cog railway** (✉ 515 Ruxton Ave., Manitou Springs, ☎ 719/685–5401, WEB www.cograilway.com) and a **toll road** (✉ 10 mi west on U.S. 24, left at marked exit at Cascade)—lead to breathtaking views atop **Pikes Peak,** the summit Zebulon Pike claimed could never be scaled. The railway is $26.50 round-trip; the toll road, $10 per adult to a maximum of $35 per vehicle. The **U.S. Air Force Academy** (✉ 10 mi north on I–25, Exits 156B and 150B, ☎ 719/333–2025) has a futuristic **Cadet Chapel,** with 17 spires, each rising 150 ft. The academy sometimes gives guided tours in summer. The **Garden of the Gods** (✉ off Ridge Rd., north of U.S. 24, ☎ 719/634–6666, WEB www.gardenofgods.com) has picnic spots and hikes among 1,350 acres of weird, windswept red-rock formations and unusual plant life. The visitor center has geologic, historic, and hands-on displays. Follow the road as it loops past such oddities as the Siamese Twins and the Kissing Camels. High Point, near the south entrance, provides camera hounds with the ultimate photo-op: the jagged formations framing Pikes Peak.

Parks, Gardens, and Zoos

The **Cheyenne Mountain Zoo** (✉ 4250 Cheyenne Mountain Zoo Rd., ☎ 719/633–9925, WEB www.cmzoo.org; $10) is a haven for more than 50 endangered species. Highlights include feeding the giraffes or viewing the primates, wolves, or big cats of Asia. You can hike 224 steep steps or take an elevator to the top of **Seven Falls** (✉ Cheyenne Blvd., ☎ 719/632–0765; $8.50), a series of falls plunging into a tiny pool, set in a breathtaking red-rock canyon.

Dining and Lodging

$$$–$$$$ ✕ **Briarhurst Manor.** An 1876 stone mansion provides the setting for fine cuisine. Dishes such as blackberry salmon and braised rabbit Dijonnaise are prepared with Colorado ingredients and a European touch. *✉ 404 Manitou Ave., Manitou Springs, ☎ 719/685–1864. AE, D, DC, MC, V. No lunch.*

$–$$$ ★ ✕ **The Ritz Grill.** This hip and lively downtown restaurant is centered on a horseshoe-shape marble bar and features an art deco style. It is known for its Cajun food and chicken and shrimp pasta, and it transforms into a nightclub after 9:30 PM. *✉ 15 S. Tejon St., ☎ 719/635–8484. AE, MC, V.*

$–$$ ★ ✕ **El Tesoro.** This historic site doubles as a restaurant and art gallery; exposed brick walls, colorful rugs, and *ristras* (strings) of chilies complement the northern New Mexican food, a savory blend of Native American, Spanish, and Anglo influences. The *posole* (hominy with pork and red chili), green chili, and originals like mango quesadillas are heavenly. *✉ 10 N. Sierra Madre St., ☎ 719/471–0106. AE, D, MC, V. Closed Sun.*

$$$–$$$$ ★ ✕ **The Broadmoor.** This resort is a Colorado legend. The 1918 buildings house plush, traditional rooms; the restaurants serve everything from formal French food to Sunday brunch. The parklike grounds have golf, tennis, horseback riding, and paddle-boating facilities. The spa provides such treatments as the Broadmoor Falls water massage, which uses 17 jets of water. Substantially lower rates are available in fall and spring. *✉ 1 Lake Ave., 80906, ☎ 719/634–7711 or 800/634–7711, FAX 719/577–5700, WEB www.broadmoor.com. 700 rooms. 9 restaurants, 2 pools, golf, tennis, health club. AE, D, DC, MC, V.*

$–$$$ **Victoria's Keep.** The parlor in this turreted 1891 Queen Anne B&B verges on the Dickensian, with its slightly fussy, Victorian clutter. There are carved tile ceilings and intricate tracery. Each Victorian-style room has its own fireplace and some distinguishing feature—a Jacuzzi or a claw-foot tub, stained-glass windows, or views of Miramont Castle. Relax with afternoon tea. ✉ *202 Ruxton Ave., 80829,* ☎ *719/685–5354 or 800/905–5337,* FAX *719/685–5913,* WEB *www.victoriaskeep.com. 6 rooms. AE, D, MC, V. BP.*

$–$$ ★ **The Crescent Lily.** This elegant 1898 Victorian home just north of downtown serves gourmet breakfasts. Rooms may have whirlpools, fireplaces, or balconies. ✉ *6 Boulder Crescent, 80903,* ☎ *719/442–2331 or 800/869–2721,* FAX *719/442–6947,* WEB *www.crescentlilyinn.com. 5 rooms. AE, MC, V. BP.*

Motels

Palmer House Best Western (✉ I–25 near Exit 145, 3010 N. Chestnut St., Colorado Springs 80907, ☎ 719/636–5201 or 800/223–9127, FAX 719/636–3108), 150 rooms; restaurant, pool; *$–$$.* **Red Lion Inn** (✉ 314 W. Bijou, Colorado Springs 80905, ☎ 719/471–8680 or 800/477–8610, FAX 719/471–0894), 202 rooms; restaurant, pool, gym; *$.*

Colorado Springs and Environs Essentials

AIRPORTS

➤ AIRPORT INFORMATION: **Colorado Springs Airport** (✉ 7770 Drennan Rd., 14 mi southeast of the city, ☎ 719/550–1900).

BUS TRAVEL

Greyhound serves national routes, and Springs Transit Scheduling serves local ones.

➤ BUS INFORMATION: **Greyhound** (✉ 120 S. Weber St., ☎ 800/231–2222, WEB www.greyhound.com). **Springs Transit Scheduling** (✉ 1210 S. Hancock Expressway, ☎ 719/385–5974).

VISITOR INFORMATION

➤ TOURIST INFORMATION: **Convention and Visitors Bureau** (✉ 515 S. Cascade Ave., Colorado Springs 80903, ☎ 719/635–7506 or 800/745–3773, WEB www.coloradosprings-travel.com).

THE HIGH ROCKIES

As you climb west from Denver, the mountains rear up, pine forests line the road, and the legendary Colorado of powder skiing and alpine scenery. Old mining towns have attracted skiers and scenery buffs, and sophisticated dining and lodging have followed.

Exploring the High Rockies

Estes Park is a bustling tourist town that serves as the gateway to **Rocky Mountain National Park.** Through the park, **Trail Ridge Road** (closed in winter) provides a spectacular ride on one of the highest auto routes in the world. On the west side of Rocky Mountain National Park is **Grand Lake,** the largest natural lake in Colorado, with the world's highest yacht club. The turn-of-the-20th-century town of the same name is also a snowmobiling mecca in winter.

The resort skiing closest to Denver is off I–70 at **Winter Park,** a family-oriented resort with more challenging terrain on the Mary Jane side of the mountain. Denverites often come here via the Ski Train (☎ 303/296–4754, WEB www.skitrain.com; 🎫 $45 round-trip) on weekends. The mountains of **Summit County,** 70 mi from Denver off I–70, attract climbers, hikers, and skiers. County residents accurately sum up their ski resorts this way: Copper for skiing, Breck for lodging, and Keystone for food. **Copper Mountain,** the first Club Med in North America, has terrain for most abilities, with an emphasis on intermediate and advanced skiers. **Keystone Resort** encompasses the peaks of Keystone, for beginning and intermediate skiers, and the Outback and North Peak for more serious skiers. Pretty **Breckenridge** is an old mining town that comprises one of Colorado's largest National Historic Districts. For a change from resort atmosphere and prices, head to **Lake Dillon,** a large reservoir popular with boaters and anglers. Up U.S. 40 (northwest from I–70), **Steamboat Springs** has great skiing for all abilities, shorter lift lines, and a decidedly western feel.

West of Summit County is **Vail,** celebrated home of the largest ski mountain in North America. Constructed from the ground up to look like a European ski village, the town is huge, varied in its attractions, and pricey. It tends to be more conservative and family-oriented than Aspen. **Beaver Creek** was created for those seeking an even more exclusive atmosphere than that of Vail; everything here lives up to its billing, from the billeting to the bill of fare. The ski area is geared to intermediate and advanced skiers.

At the turnoff for Aspen on I–70 is **Glenwood Springs,** a jumping-off point for outdoor enthusiasts of all stripes. The main attraction here (besides the glorious scenery) is **Yampah Hot Springs** (✉ 709 E. 6th St., ☎ 970/945–0667, WEB www.yampahhotsprings.com; 🎫 $8.75), which is heated by the world's largest outdoor mineral hot springs.

Between galleries, museums, international conferences, and events, there's so much going on year-round in **Aspen** that even in winter many people come to "do the scene" and don't even ski. Aspen is as much a national icon as it is a town—forever in the news as a litmus test of the American public's tolerance of radical-chic politics, conspicuous consumption, and conspicuous love affairs.

Many prefer the warmer seasons, though, for the beauty of the setting or for the summer **Aspen Music Festival** (☎ 970/925–3254, WEB www.aspenmusicfestival.org), a renowned classical series.

Within Aspen's orbit are several ski areas, each geared to a different level of ability. Skiers can get a multiday ticket to all four mountains: **Buttermilk,** serving primarily beginners and low-intermediate skiers; **Aspen Highlands,** for intermediate skiers, with some of the highest vertical drops and best views; **Snowmass,** a perfect intermediate hill; and, for experts, **Aspen Mountain,** which hosts international competitions.

Dining and Lodging

The celebrity atmosphere of towns like Aspen and Vail attracts celebrity chefs, and hot restaurants come and go quickly. If you don't want to spend the money to eat with stars, consider heading to nearby towns, where the atmosphere and prices are more down-home western. Condos are the most common lodging option. The ski resorts make booking accommodations easy. Calling the following for a variety of lodgings: **Aspen** (☎ 800/262–7736), **Beaver Creek** (☎ 800/622–3131), **Breckenridge** (☎ 800/221–1091), **Copper Mountain** (☎ 800/458–8386), **Keystone** (☎ 800/222–0188), **Steamboat Springs** (☎ 800/922–2722), **Vail** (☎ 800/525–3875), and **Winter Park** (☎ 800/729–5813).

Aspen

$$$$ ★ ✕ **Renaissance.** This stunner is a seductive, abstract rendition of a sultan's tent—one that has a knockout view of Aspen Mountain. Opt for one of owner-chef Charles Dale's two tasting menus, which changes

seasonally. Among standouts are crispy Chilean sea bass and rack of lamb. Upstairs, the Bistro grants a taste of the kitchen's splendors at down-to-earth prices. Across the street, Dale's new venture, Rustique, is less expensive. ✉ *304 E. Hopkins St., Aspen,* ☎ *970/925–2402. Reservations essential. AE, DC, MC, V. Closed mid-Apr.–mid-June and Oct.–Thanksgiving. No lunch.*

$$$–$$$$ ✕ **Syzygy.** Upstairs and unmarked, this restaurant is for those who like sleek modern design and sophisticated food that blends flavors from French to Asian to southwestern. Follow starters such as Szechuan tempura lobster and Asian vegetable salad with main courses such as elk tenderloin with sun-dried fig chutney and ancho-chili aioli. Enjoy a glass of wine while listening to Aspen's best live jazz. ✉ *520 E. Hyman,* ☎ *970/925–3700. Reservations essential. AE, D, DC, MC, V. Closed mid-Apr.–May and mid-Oct.–late Nov. No lunch.*

$$$ ✕ **Ajax Tavern.** This is a bright, bustling restaurant with mahogany paneling, leather banquettes, and an open kitchen. The menu emphasizes northern Italian flavors prepared with classic French techniques, using regional ingredients whenever possible. The wine list, showcasing Napa Valley's best, is almost matched by the fine selection of microbrews. ✉ *685 E. Durant Ave.,* ☎ *970/920–9333. Reservations essential. AE, D, DC, MC, V.*

$$$$ ★ **Hotel Jerome.** This redbrick property is a treasure trove of Victoriana and froufrou. The public rooms have five kinds of wallpaper, antler sconces, rose damask curtains, intricate woodwork, and gold-laced floor tiling. Rooms in the original hotel face Aspen Mountain; those in the new portion face Independence Pass or the Red Mountains. All rooms are large, with high ceilings, oversize beds, antique armoires and chests, and huge bathtubs. The J-Bar is a lively local's hangout. ✉ *330 E. Main St., 81611,* ☎ *970/920–1000 or 800/331–7213,* FAX *970/925–2784,* WEB *www.hoteljerome.com. 93 rooms. 2 restaurants, pool. AE, D, DC, MC, V.*

$$$$ **St. Regis at Aspen.** The august reception area is comfortably furnished with overstuffed leather chairs, leather-topped tables, and rawhide lamp shades. The rooms follow suit with dark-wood furniture, muted colors, and Aspen photos, plus fruit bowls, bottled water, and Bijan toiletries. The house restaurant is Olives, a venture of celebrity chef Todd English; Whiskey Rocks, a cousin to L.A.'s Sky Bar, is the chic place to imbibe. ✉ *315 E. Dean St., 81611,* ☎ *970/920–3300 or 888/454–9005,* FAX *970/925–8998,* WEB *www.stregisaspen.com. 257 rooms. Restaurant, pool, health club. AE, D, DC, MC, V.*

$–$$$ **Snowflake Inn.** This motel has a prime downtown location, but the guest rooms, with rough-wood paneling, are in need of a face-lift. Nevertheless, it could be an ideal choice for a family on a budget, as many of the rooms are actually suites. The rustic lobby with its stone fireplace and wood beams is a convivial gathering place for the complimentary Continental breakfast and afternoon tea. ✉ *221 E. Hyman Ave., 81611,* ☎ *970/925–3221 or 800/247–2069,* FAX *970/925–8740,* WEB *www.snowflakeinn.com. 38 rooms. Pool. AE, D, DC, MC, V. CP.*

Beaver Creek

$$$$ ★ **Park Hyatt Beaver Creek Resort & Spa.** An antler chandelier, huge stone fireplaces, and upholstered comfort characterize the public rooms here. Guests exiting the hotel step into their warmed and waiting ski boots and skis. There's also a full spa and health club, as well as a top-notch children's program. Watch for much lower rates off-season. ✉ *136 E. Thomas Pl. (Box 1595, Avon 81620),* ☎ *970/949–1234 or 800/554–9288,* FAX *970/949–4164,* WEB *www.beavercreek.hyatt.com. 275 rooms. 3 restaurants, pool, health club. AE, D, DC, MC, V.*

Breckenridge

$$–$$$ ✕ **Café Alpine.** This bright, cheerful place serves terrific soups, salads, and sandwiches at lunch (summer only) and more substantial regional American cuisine on a menu that changes daily at dinner. At the tapas bar (served after 5 PM) you can sample global cuisine. ✉ *106 E. Adams Ave., ☎ 970/453–8218. AE, D, MC, V.*

$–$$$ ★ **B&Bs on North Main St.** Two picture-perfect five-room inns date from the 1880s; a rustic timber-frame barn is a more modern addition. ✉ *303 N. Main St., 80424, ☎ 970/453–2975 or 800/795—2975, FAX 970/453–5258, WEB www.breckenridge-inn.com. 11 rooms, 1 cottage. AE, D, MC, V. BP.*

Estes Park

$–$$$ ✕ **Dunraven Inn.** This casual establishment in a canyon just outside town specializes in Italian cuisine, good steaks, and fresh seafood. The dark wood paneling is embellished with many copies of da Vinci's *Mona Lisa,* all nicely visible in the low light. The bar at the inn is "wallpapered" with more than 12,000 $1 bills autographed by diners. ✉ *2470 Colo. 66, ☎ 970/586–6409. AE, D, MC, V. No lunch.*

$$$$ ★ **C Lazy U Ranch.** Near Rocky Mountain National Park, this rambling southwestern-style wooden lodge has fireplaces and Navajo rugs in its rooms and cabins. Activities include horseback riding, ice-skating, and sledding; the minimum stay in the summertime is one week. The fare ranges from ranch food to contemporary cuisine. ✉ *3640 Colo. 125 (Box 379, Granby 80446), ☎ 970/887–3344, FAX 970/887–3917, WEB www.clazyu.com. 3 rooms, 37 cabins. Restaurant, pool, gym. No credit cards. Closed mid-Jan.–early June and late Sept.–mid-Dec. FAP.*

$$$ ★ **Stanley Hotel.** This is one of Colorado's great old hotels, though the sunny rooms, with antiques and period reproductions, are not as sumptuous as they once were. Still, there is an incomparable air of history to this 1909 hotel, along with all the modern conveniences; it inspired Stephen King's *The Shining.* ✉ *333 Wonderview Ave., 80517, ☎ 970/586–3371 or 800/976–1377, FAX 970/586–3673, WEB www.stanleyhotel.com. 135 rooms. Restaurant, pool. AE, D, DC, MC, V.*

$–$$$ **Boulder Brook.** Luxury suites at this secluded spot on the river are tucked in the pines yet close to town. All feature full kitchen or kitchenette, private deck, gas fireplace, double-headed showers, cable TV, and VCR. All of the units have whirlpool tubs. ✉ *1900 Fall River Rd., 80517, ☎ 970/586–0910 or 800/238–0910, WEB www.estes-par.com/boulderbrook. 16 suites. AE, D, MC, V.*

Glenwood Springs

$$ **Hotel Colorado.** Teddy Roosevelt stayed at this hotel, now listed in the National Historic Register, to take advantage of the adjacent hot springs. The imposing sandstone structure has a grand marble lobby. Bedrooms are huge and sparsely furnished. ✉ *526 Pine St., 81601, ☎ 970/945–6511 or 800/544–3998, FAX 970/945–7030, WEB www.hotelcolorado.com. 128 rooms. Restaurant, gym. AE, D, DC, MC, V.*

Grand Lake

$ **Grand Lake Lodge.** Set majestically above Grand Lake and bordering Rocky Mountain National Park, the lodge is actually a collection of rustic cabins. Some have wood-burning stoves for heat, and all are comfortable and well worn. ✉ *15500 U.S. 34 (Box 569, 80447), ☎ 970/627–3967, FAX 970/627–9495, WEB www.grandlakelodge.com. 56 cabins. Restaurant, pool. AE, D, DC, MC, V. Closed mid-Sept.–May.*

Keystone

$$–$$$ ★ ✕🏨 **Ski Tip Lodge.** This premium B&B reflects its 1880s origins with four-poster beds, handmade quilts, and log-cabin decor. In the main room, huge picture windows overlook a forest. The American regional cuisine, served prix-fixe, is exceptional. The lodge is ½ mi from the slopes. ✉ *758 Montezuma Rd., Box 38, Keystone 80435,* ☎ *970/496–4950 or 800/222–0188. 10 rooms. Restaurant. AE, D, DC, MC, V.*

Steamboat Springs

$$–$$$ ★ ✕ **Antares.** In a splendid Victorian building, you'll find fieldstone walls, pressed-tin ceilings, stained glass, and exciting cuisine inspired by America's rich ethnic stew. The menu features dishes such as elk medallions with a Bing cherry–merlot sauce and cashew-breaded ruby trout with pineapple pico de gallo. ✉ *57½ 8th St.,* ☎ *970/879–9939. Reservations essential. MC, V. No lunch.*

$$–$$$ ★ ✕ **La Montaña.** Among the standouts at this southwestern establishment are polenta lasagna with a New Mexican chili sauce; interwoven strands of mesquite-grilled chorizo, lamb, and elk sausages; and cilantro- and pesto-crusted elk loin with smoked chili mashed potatoes. ✉ *2500 Village Dr.,* ☎ *970/879–5800. AE, D, MC, V. No lunch.*

$$$$ ★ 🏨 **Home Ranch.** This rustic yet luxurious western lodge in the Steamboat Springs area is a member of the prestigious Relais & Châteaux group. Each log cabin has a wood-burning stove and hot tub. Hiking, fishing, and horseback riding are the main summer activities, and the minimum stay is one week. ✉ *54880 CR 129 (Box 822, Clark 80428),* ☎ *970/879–1780,* FAX *970/879–1795,* WEB *www.homeranch.com. 6 lodge rooms, 8 cabins. Restaurant, pool. AE, MC, V. Closed Apr.–May and Oct.–Nov.*

$$ 🏨 **Sky Valley Lodge.** Glorious scenery surrounds this homey property a few miles from downtown. Rooms are English country style. ✉ *31490 E. U.S. 40, 80477,* ☎ *970/879–7749 or 800/499–4759,* FAX *970/879–7752,* WEB *www.steamboat-lodging.com. 24 rooms. AE, D, DC, MC, V. CP.*

Vail

$$–$$$$ ★ ✕ **Sweet Basil.** A meal here will wake up your taste buds. The creative menu includes linguine with lobster and bay scallops and double-cut pork chops with smoked bacon and endive stuffing. ✉ *193 E. Gore Creek Dr.,* ☎ *970/476–0125. Reservations essential. AE, MC, V.*

$$–$$$ ★ ✕ **Terra Bistro.** In the Vail Mountain Lodge & Spa, where a warm fireplace contrasts with black-iron chairs and black-and-white photographs, this soaring space has an innovative menu that caters to both meat-and-potatoes diners and vegans. Everything is crisply textured and pungently seasoned. Organic produce and free-range meat and poultry are used whenever possible. ✉ *352 E. Meadow Dr.,* ☎ *970/476–6836. Reservations essential. AE, D, DC, MC, V. No lunch.*

$$$$ ★ 🏨 **Sonnenalp Resort of Vail.** A German family runs this central Bavarian-style hotel, where small but luxurious suites have a European alpine feel. It features a full-service spa and an 18-hole golf course. ✉ *20 Vail Rd., 81657,* ☎ *970/476–5656 or 800/654–8312,* FAX *970/476–1639,* WEB *www.sonnenalp.com. 90 suites. 2 restaurants, pool, golf, health club. AE, DC, MC, V.*

Winter Park

$–$$ ★ ✕🏨 **Gasthaus Eichler.** This romantic dining room has quaint Bavarian decor, antler chandeliers, and stained-glass windows. Veal and grilled items round out the menu of German classics. The Eichler also has cozy rooms, with down comforters, lace curtains, armoires, and whirlpool tubs. ✉ *78786 U.S. 40, 80482,* ☎ *970/726–5133 or 800/*

543–3899, FAX 970/726–5175, WEB www.gasthauseichler.com. 15 rooms. Restaurant. AE, D, MC, V.

Campgrounds

You can reserve **camping spaces** at many of the national forest campgrounds by calling ☎ 800/280–2267 or visiting WEB www.reserveamerica.com. ⛺ **Tiger Run Resort** (✉ 3 mi north of Breckenridge on Colo. 9, 80424, ☎ 970/453–9690) is a retreat for RVs, with tennis courts, a pool, and a recreation room. ⛺ **Winding River Resort Village** (✉ 1447 CR 491 [Box 629, Grand Lake 80447], ☎ 970/627–3215, WEB www.windingriverresort.com) is a combination campground and low-cost dude ranch in a beautiful forest.

Outdoor Activities and Sports

Boating

Grand Lake and Lake Granby are the premier boating and fishing centers. Contact the **Grand Lake Recreation District** (✉ Box 590, 80447, ☎ 970/627–8872) for information. **Beacon Landing** (✉ 1 mi off U.S. 34 on CR 64, ☎ 970/627–3671) arranges boat rentals. Call the **Trail Ridge Marina** (✉ Shadow Mountain Lake, ☎ 970/627–3586) for information on renting pontoon boats.

Fishing

Grand Lake and the connected reservoirs Shadow Mountain Lake and Lake Granby are known for their trout fishing. Dillon Reservoir is stocked with salmon and trout. The Lower Blue River, below Dillon Reservoir, is a Gold Medal catch-and-release area, as is the Fryingpan River near Aspen. **Roaring Fork Anglers** (✉ Glenwood Springs, ☎ 800/781–8120) is a good source for guides, gear, and advice.

Golf

Reservations are essential at the Jack Nicklaus–designed **Breckenridge Golf Club** (✉ 200 Clubhouse Dr., ☎ 970/453–9104). The difficult **Eagle-Vail Golf Course** (✉ 0431 Eagle Dr., Avon, ☎ 970/949–5267 or 800/341–8051) has reduced fees in fall and spring. **Sheraton Steamboat Golf Club** (✉ 2000 Clubhouse Dr., ☎ 970/879–1391) was designed by Robert Trent Jones Jr.

Hiking and Backpacking

Hikers (as well as cross-country skiers and mountain bikers) might want to take a trek through the **10th Mountain Hut and Trail System** (✉ 1280 Ute Ave., Aspen, ☎ 970/925–5775) and sleep in a comfortable backcountry hut in the Elk Mountains at night. To find out about parks and wilderness areas with hiking and backpacking trails, contact the **Holy Cross Ranger District Office** (✉ 24747 U.S. 24, Minturn, ☎ 970/827–5715) for Vail area information. The **Aspen Ranger District Office** (✉ 806 W. Hallam St., ☎ 970/925–3445) can provide advice for the mountains around Aspen. The **Dillon Ranger District Office** (✉ 680 W. Blue River Pkwy., Silverthorne, ☎ 970/468–5400) can point you in the right direction from Dillon.

Ski Areas

For **snow conditions** at Colorado resorts, call ☎ 303/825–7669 or surf to WEB www.coloradoski.com.

Cross-Country

Aspen Cross-Country Center (☎ 970/544–9246) contains 40 mi of trails through the Roaring Fork Valley. **Breckenridge Nordic Ski Center** (☎ 970/453–6855) maintains 19 mi of trails. **Devil's Thumb Ranch** (✉ Devil's Thumb, 7 mi north of Winter Park, ☎ 970/726–5632) is a full-service resort with 63 mi of groomed trails. **Frisco Nordic Center** (✉ 18454 Colo. 9, ☎ 970/668–0866) has nearly 27 mi of one-way loops. **Snowmass Cross-Country Training Center** (☎ 970/923–3148) offers solitude in about 20 mi of trails in the backcountry. **Steamboat Ski Touring Center** (☎ 970/879–8180) has trails emanating from the golf course. **Vail Cross-Country Ski Centers** (☎ 970/479–3210) has information on Vail Valley trails.

Downhill

Aspen Highlands (✉ 1498 Maroon Creek Rd., Aspen 81611, ☎ 970/925–1220) has 680 skiable acres, 4 lifts, and a 3,635-ft vertical drop. **Aspen Mountain** (✉ Box 1248, Aspen 81612, ☎ 970/925–1220) has 675 acres of runs, a gondola, 7 lifts, and a 3,267-ft drop. **Beaver Creek** (✉ Box 7, Vail 81658, ☎ 970/845–9090) has 1,625 acres of runs, 13 lifts, and a 4,040-ft drop. **Breckenridge** (✉ Box 1058, Breckenridge 80424, ☎ 970/453–5000) has 2,043 acres of runs, 23 lifts, and a 3,398-ft drop. **Buttermilk** (✉ Box 1248, Aspen 81612, ☎ 970/925–1220) has 420 acres of runs, 7 lifts, and a 2,030-ft drop. **Copper Mountain** (✉ Box 3001, Copper Mountain 80443, ☎ 970/968–2882) has 2,433 acres of runs, 21 lifts, and a 2,601-ft drop. **Keystone** (✉ Box 38, Keystone 80435, ☎ 970/468–2316) has 1,861 acres of runs, 23 lifts, and a 2,900-ft drop. **Snowmass** (✉ Box 5566, Snowmass Village 80446, ☎ 970/925–1220) has 3,010 acres of runs, 20 lifts, and a 4,406-ft drop. **Steamboat** (✉ 2305 Mt. Werner Circle, Steamboat Springs 80487, ☎ 970/879–6111) has 2,939 acres of runs, a gondola, 21 lifts, and a 3,668-ft drop. **Vail** (✉ Box 7, Vail 81658, ☎ 970/845–2500 or 800/525–2257) has 5,289 acres of runs, a gondola, 32 lifts, and a 3,450-ft drop. **Winter Park** (✉ Box 36, Winter Park 80482, ☎ 970/726–5514) has 2,886 acres of runs, 22 lifts, and a 3,060-ft drop.

Shopping

Dillon Factory Stores Complex (✉ 765 Anemone Terr., Exit 205 off I–70, Silverthorne, ☎ 970/468–6765) features shops like Nautica, Reebok, Coach, and Donna Karan. **Silverthorne Factory Stores Complex** (✉ 145 Stevens Way, Exit 205 off I–70, Silverthorne, ☎ 970/468–5780) includes discount wares from J. Crew, Tommy Hilfiger, Liz Claiborne, Eddie Bauer, Bass Shoe, Nike, and many others.

High Rockies Essentials

AIRPORTS

Eagle County Airport, 35 mi west of Vail, serves Vail Valley. Pitkin County Airport is 7 mi east of Aspen; most flights connect from Denver. Steamboat Springs Airport is 3 mi northwest of town.

➤ AIRPORT INFORMATION: **Eagle County Airport** (✉ 0219 Eldon Wilson Rd., Gypsum 81637, ☎ 970/524–9490). **Pitkin County Airport** (✉ 0233 E. Airport Rd., Aspen, ☎ 970/920–5385, WEB www.aspenairport.org). **Steamboat Springs Airport** (✉ 3495 Airport Cir., ☎ 970/879–1204).

BUS TRAVEL

➤ BUS INFORMATION: **Greyhound** (☎ 800/231–2222, WEB www.greyhound.com).

CAR TRAVEL

I–70 is the major artery that fearlessly slices the Continental Divide, passing through or near many of Colorado's most fabled resorts and towns: Vail, Breckenridge, Keystone, Copper Mountain, Beaver Creek, Winter Park. From Glenwood Springs on I–70, Colo. 82 heads to Aspen and Snowmass. From Empire, U.S. 40 heads to Steamboat

Springs. From Denver, U.S. 36 leads to Rocky Mountain National Park and Estes Park.

TRAIN TRAVEL

Amtrak stops in Glenwood Springs, Granby, and Winter Park.

VISITOR INFORMATION

➤ TOURIST INFORMATION: **Aspen Chamber Resort Association** (✉ 425 Rio Grande Pl., 81611, ☎ 970/925–1940 or 800/262–7736, WEB www.aspenchamber.org). **Breckenridge Resort Chamber** (✉ 309 N. Main St., 80424, ☎ 970/453–6018, WEB gobreck.com). **Copper Mountain Resort** (✉ Box 3001, Copper Mountain 80443, ☎ 800/458–8386 or 970/968–2882, WEB ski-copper.com). **Glenwood Springs Chamber Resort Association** (✉ 1102 Grand Ave., 81601, ☎ 970/945–6589 or 800/221–0098, WEB www.glenwoodchamber.org). **Keystone Resort** (✉ Box 38, Keystone 80435, ☎ 970/468–2316, WEB keystoneresort.com). **Steamboat Springs Chamber Resort Association** (✉ 1255 S. Lincoln Ave., 80477, ☎ 970/879–0880 or 800/922–2722, WEB www.steamboatchamber.com). **Summit County Chamber of Commerce** (✉ 916 N. Summit Blvd., Frisco 80443, ☎ 800/530–3099, WEB www.summitchamber.org). **Vail Valley Tourism and Convention Bureau** (✉ 100 E. Meadow Dr., Suite 34, 81657, ☎ 970/476–1000 or 800/525–3875, WEB www.visitvailvalley.com). **Winter Park/Fraser Valley Chamber of Commerce** (✉ Box 3236, Winter Park 80482, ☎ 970/726–4118 or 800/903–7275, WEB winterpark-info.com).

SOUTHWESTERN COLORADO

Southwestern Colorado offers such diversity that you can have radically different experiences even during the same season. You can spiral from the towering peaks of the San Juan range to the plunging Black Canyon of the Gunnison, taking in alpine scenery along the way, as well as the eerie remains of old mining camps, before winding through striking desert landscapes, the superlative ancestral Puebloan ruins, and the Old West railroad town of Durango. Most of the mining towns are National Historic Landmark Districts, and the resorts of Crested Butte, Purgatory, and Telluride offer world-class skiing and golfing.

Exploring Southwestern Colorado

Telluride is another old mining town turned ski resort but with a difference: its relative isolation in a box canyon makes it more laid-back than many other Colorado resorts, and its beauty is legendary. Skiers of all abilities will find suitable terrain.The summer brings nationally known **festivals** of **film** (☎ 603/433–9202, WEB www.telluridefilmfestival.com), **bluegrass** (☎ 800/624–2422), and **jazz** (☎ 970/728–7009, WEB www.telluridejazz.com). South of Telluride is a complete change of scene. At **Mesa Verde National Park,** forests give way to dramatic red-rock cliff dwellings. The structures were fashioned more than 700 years ago by the ancestral Puebloan peoples.

East of Mesa Verde is the old railroad town of **Durango,** with dramatic views of the San Juan Mountains, and strong frontier traditions. A trip on the **Durango and Silverton Narrow-Gauge Railroad** (✉ 479 Main Ave., ☎ 970/247–2733, WEB www.durangotrain.com; 🎫 $60 round-trip) is worth the trouble of reserving well in advance. The nine-hour round-trip takes you over tracks laid between the two towns in 1881, past unspoiled scenery, dramatic gorge crossings, and rails dug into the mountainside. The entire town of **Silverton,** 45 mi north of Durango, is a National Historic District. Glorious peaks ring the unspoiled old mining community. **Ouray,** about 25 mi up the twisty, breathtaking Million-Dollar Highway from Silverton, is a sleepy western town surrounded by the magnificent red San Juan Mountains. Dive into the million-gallon **Ouray Hot Springs Pool** (☎ 970/325–4638; $7.50) on the north end of town. **Orvis Hot Springs** (☎ 970/626–5324; $10) has a large outdoor pool and four smaller indoor pools 9 mi north of Ouray. **Crested Butte** is literally just over the mountain from Aspen, but a 15-minute scenic flight or one-hour drive (or five-hour walk) in summer turns into a four-hour trek by car in winter, when Kebler Pass (on Route 135) is closed. The town of Crested Butte was once a mining center, and its exquisite Victorian gingerbread-trim houses remain. The excellent Crested Butte Mountain Resort ski area is best suited for high-intermediate and expert skiers.

Dining and Lodging

Note that many restaurants and hotels in Crested Butte close between mid-April and Memorial Day, and again in the fall, between October and the start of ski season around mid-December.

Crested Butte

$$–$$$$ ★ ✕ **Soupçon.** Among the innovative variations on classic bistro cuisine, duck and fish are sublime, as is the intimate dining room inside a log cabin. ✉ *Just off 2nd St. behind the Forest Queen,* ☎ *970/349–5448. Reservations essential. AE, D, MC, V. Closed late Apr.–mid-June and Oct.–Nov. No lunch.*

$$–$$$ ★ ✕ **Slogar.** A soul-satisfying prix-fixe meal of plump fried chicken, flaky buttermilk biscuits, coleslaw, mashed potatoes, and ice cream costs just $13.50 inside this Victorian tavern with a lace and stained-glass motif. ✉ *2nd and Whiterock Sts.,* ☎ *970/349–5765. MC, V. Closed mid-Apr.–early June and Oct.–mid-Nov. No lunch.*

$$$–$$$$ ★ **Crested Butte Club.** This quaint, stylish inn has cherrywood antiques and claw-foot brass tubs. The bar is a convivial gathering spot, and the full-scale health club is a great place to relax after skiing or biking. ✉ *512 2nd St., 81224,* ☎ *970/349–6655 or 800/815–2582,* FAX *970/349–7580,* WEB *www.crestedbutteclub.com. 8 rooms. Pool, health club. D, MC, V. CP.*

$ **Pioneer Guest Cabins.** Only 10 minutes out of town, on 7 acres of the Gunnison National Forest, this is a dream getaway. Log cabins are equipped with kitchens and new appliances, down comforters, and antique furnishings. Cement Creek, ½ mi away, is a world-class fishing stream. A resident guide leads mountain-bike tours. ✉ *Cement Creek Rd., 81224,* ☎ *970/349–5517,* FAX *970/349–9697. 8 cabins. MC, V.*

Durango

$–$$$ ✕ **Ariano's.** Pasta made fresh daily and a sure touch with meats make this northern Italian restaurant one of Durango's most popular. The veal scallopini is excellent. ✉ *150 E. College Dr.,* ☎ *970/247–8146. Reservations not accepted. AE, MC, V. No lunch.*

$–$$$ ✕ **Carver's Bakery and Brew Pub.** This microbrewery pours about eight tap beers at any given time and there's a patio out back. From breakfast to the wee hours, the place is always hopping. Try the bread bowls filled with either soup or salad. ✉ *1022 Main Ave.,* ☎ *970/259–2545. Reservations not accepted. AE, D, MC, V. No lunch or dinner on Sun.*

$$–$$$ **Rochester Hotel.** This former flophouse was built in 1892 and beautifully renovated nearly a century later. Its spacious rooms are full of western artifacts and are named for the many movies shot in the area, such as *Butch Cassidy and the Sundance Kid.* ✉ *726 E. 2nd Ave., 81301,* ☎ *970/385–1920 or 800/664–1920,* FAX *970/385–1967,* WEB *www.rochesterhotel.com. 14 rooms. AE, D, DC, MC, V. BP.*

Ouray

$–$$$ **China Clipper Inn.** A welcome relief from the area's western- and Victorian-style inns, the China Clipper has tasteful Oriental and nautical antiques. Innkeeper Earl Yarbrough is warm and interesting. ✉ *525 2nd St., 81427,* ☎ *970/325–0565 or 800/315–0565,* FAX *970/325–4190,* WEB *www.chinaclipperinn.com. 12 rooms. AE, D, MC, V. BP.*

Telluride

$$–$$$$ ✕ **Campagna.** Oak and terra-cotta floors and vintage photos of the Italian countryside give this place the feel of a Tuscan farmhouse; its assured, classically simple cuisine comes as no surprise. Wild boar chops are among the enticing possibilities. Finish off your meal with a perfect tiramisu and a shot of fiery grappa. ✉ *435 W. Pacific Ave.,* ☎ *970/728–6190. Reservations essential. MC, V. Closed mid-Apr.–mid-June and mid-Oct.–Thanksgiving. No lunch.*

$$–$$$$ ★ ✕ **La Marmotte.** At this rustic restaurant decorated like a French country cottage, the Gallic owners and chefs change the menu seasonally, serving such dishes as loin of venison with juniper-berry sauce or rack of lamb with tomato marmalade sauce. ✉ *150 W. San Juan Ave.,* ☎ *970/728–6232. Reservations essential. AE, MC, V. Closed mid-Apr.–mid-June and early Oct.–Thanksgiving. No lunch.*

$$$$ ★ **The Wyndham Peaks Resort and Golden Door Spa.** The prisonlike exterior can be excused at this ski-in, ski-out luxury resort, thanks to its invigorating spa treatments. But the biggest kick is the two-story water slide, which deposits you into the glorious pool, with Mt. Wilson looming in the background. ✉ *136 Country Club Dr., 81435,* ☎ *970/728–6800 or 800/789–2220,* FAX *970/728–6567,* WEB *www.thepeaksresort.com. 174 rooms. 2 restaurants, 3 pools, tennis, health club. AE, D, DC, MC, V.*

$$$–$$$$ **New Sheridan Hotel.** William Jennings Bryan delivered his rousing "Cross of Gold" speech here in 1896, garnering a presidential nomination in the process. Victoriana abounds, with exposed brick walls, brass beds, red-velour love seats, and wicker rocking chairs. Complimentary breakfast and afternoon wine service complete the experience of fin de siècle gracious living. The bar is a local institution. ✉ *231 W. Colorado Ave., 81435,* ☎ *970/728–4351 or 800/200–1891,* FAX *970/728–5024,* WEB *www.newsheridan.com. 32 rooms. Restaurant, gym. AE, MC, V. BP.*

$$$–$$$$ ★ **San Sophia Inn.** If you eschew Victorian frills, this is the inn for you: There's no trace of Laura Ashley here, except for the brass beds and handmade quilts. Rooms, although smallish, are luxurious, and there is a complimentary cocktail hour every afternoon. ✉ *330 W. Pacific St., 81435,* ☎ *970/728–3001 or 800/537–4781,* FAX *970/728–6226,* WEB *www.sansophia.com. 16 rooms. AE, MC, V. BP.*

Campgrounds

Ranger district offices have information on campgrounds in the state and national forests. Near Durango is a **KOA** campground (✉ east on U.S. 160, ☎ 970/247–0783), which is closed mid-October–April.

Outdoor Activities and Sports

Biking

Crested Butte is a mountain-biking destination; Durango is home to many world-class road cyclists because of its great riding terrain. Bike-rental locations abound in both towns.

Fishing

The Dolores River, in the San Juan National Forest, and the Animas River, near Durango, are good for trout. The Vallecito Reservoir, also near Durango, has pike, trout, and salmon. At **Ridgeway State Park** (☎ 970/626–5822), 15 mi north of Ouray, you can catch rainbow trout.

Golf

The **Crested Butte Country Club** (✉ 385 Country Club Dr., outside Crested Butte, ☎ 970/349–6127), designed by Robert Trent Jones Jr., converts into cross-country ski trails. Overlooking town from a mesa, the **Hillcrest Golf Course** (✉ 2300 Rim Dr., Durango, ☎ 970/247–1499) is cheaper than most other courses in the region. **Tamarron** (✉ 40292 U.S. 550 N, north of Durango, ☎ 970/259–2000) has been named one of the country's 50 best courses by *Golf Digest*. The par-71 **Telluride Golf Club** (✉ Telluride Mountain Village, ☎ 970/728–3856) has an idyllic location at the base of the ski mountain.

Hiking and Backpacking

The 460-mi **Colorado Trail,** from Durango to Denver, is a major route. The **San Juan National Forest Supervisor's Office** (✉ 15 Burnett Ct., Durango, ☎ 970/247–4874) has information on trails in the area.

Rafting

Rafting is popular on the San Miguel, Dolores, Gunnison, and Animas rivers. Arrange trips through the **Colorado River Outfitters Association** (✉ Box 1662, Buena Vista 81211, ☎ 303/280–2554, WEB www.croa.org).

Ski Areas

For **snow conditions** at Colorado resorts, call ☎ 303/825–7669 or visit WEB www.coloradoski.com.

Cross-Country

Trails abound; check with local tourist offices for details. **Purgatory Ski Touring Center** (✉ Purgatory Ski Area, 1 Skier Pl., Durango 81301, ☎ 970/247–9000) manages 26 mi of trails. **Telluride Nordic Center** (✉ Box 1784, Telluride 81435, ☎ 970/728–1144) has 15 mi of trails and a free shuttle from the alpine ski area.

Downhill

Crested Butte (✉ off Rte. 135 [Box A, 81225], ☎ 970/349–2333) has 1,160 acres of runs, 13 lifts, and a 2,775-ft vertical drop. **Purgatory** (✉ U.S. 550, 81301, ☎ 970/247–9000) has 1,200 acres of runs, 11 lifts, and a 2,029-ft drop. **Telluride** (✉ 565 Mountain Village Blvd. [Box 11155, 81435], ☎ 970/728–3856) has 1,700 acres of runs, 16 lifts, and a 3,535-ft drop.

Shopping

Western Goods

Buckskin Booksellers (✉ Beaumont Hotel, 505 Main St., Ouray, ☎ 970/325–4044) has an array of titles in stock, but the emphasis is on the western-book selection. **North Moon** (✉ Beaumont Hotel, 505 Main St., Ouray, ☎ 970/325–4885) carries irresistible jewelry and art. **Toh-Atin Gallery** (✉ 145 W. 9th St., Durango, ☎ 970/247–8277) has perhaps the best western, Native American, and southwestern art gallery in Colorado, and also sells CDs and jewelry.

Southwestern Colorado Essentials

AIRPORTS

Durango–La Plata Airport is 14 mi east of Durango, and Gunnison County Airport is 23 mi south of Crested Butte.

➤ AIRPORT INFORMATION: **Durango–La Plata Airport** (✉ 1000 Airport Rd., ☎ 970/247–8143). **Gunnison County Airport** (✉ 711 W. Rio

Grande Rd., ☎ 970/641–2304). **Montrose Regional Airport** (✉ 2100 Airport Rd., ☎ 970/249–3203, WEB www.montroseairport.com). **Telluride Regional Airport** (✉ 1500 Last Dollar Rd., ☎ 970/728–5051).

BUS TRAVEL

Greyhound serves Durango and major mountain towns such as Purgatory, Silverton, Ouray, Ridgeway, and Montrose.

CAR TRAVEL

Colo. 141 from Grand Junction to Colo. 145 leads to Telluride; U.S. 550 is the route from Durango to Silverton and Ouray.

TRAIN TRAVEL

Amtrak stops in Glenwood Springs, Granby, and Winter Park.

VISITOR INFORMATION

➤ Tourist Information: **Durango Chamber of Commerce** (✉ 111 S. Camino del Rio [Box 2587, Durango 81302], ☎ 970/247–0312 or 800/525–8855, WEB www.durango.org). **Southwest Colorado Travel Region** (✉ 295-A Girard St., Durango 81301, ☎ 800/933–4340, WEB www.swcolotravel.org). **Telluride Chamber of Commerce** (✉ 666 W. Colorado Ave., Telluride 81435, ☎ 970/728–3041 or 800/525–3455, WEB www.telluride.com).

SOUTH-CENTRAL COLORADO

This territory scouted and explored by the likes of Kit Carson and Zebulon Pike has plenty to offer history buffs. The haunting remains of the Santa Fe Trail, which guided pioneers westward, weave through the southeastern section of the region. Towns such as Cripple Creek and Trinidad are living history. Favorite fishing spots for pike, bass, and trout include Trinidad Lake, Spinney Mountain Reservoir (between Florissant and Buena Vista), and the Arkansas and South Platte rivers.

Exploring South-Central Colorado

Cripple Creek—24 mi west from Colorado Springs to Divide, then 20 mi south on Colo. 67—was once known for vast deposits of gold and has gone upscale with the legalization of low-stakes gambling. The **Cripple Creek and Victor Narrow-Gauge Railroad** (☎ 719/689–2640, WEB www.cripplecreekrailroad.com; 🎫 $9 round-trip), on the north end of town, runs a 4-mi route (May–October) past old mines and older mountains.

Southwest of Colorado Springs on U.S. 50 is **Cañon City,** gateway to one of the Rockies' most powerful sights.The 1,053-ft-deep **Royal Gorge** (☎ 719/275–7507, WEB www.royalgorgebridge.com; 🎫 toll including aerial tram $16), often called the Grand Canyon of Colorado, was carved by the Arkansas River more than 3 million years ago. It's spanned by the world's highest suspension bridge. Other activities include riding the 2,200-ft long aerial tram and traveling aboard the **Scenic Railway,** the world's steepest incline rail. For kids, there's a miniature train trolley and a carousel. A theater presents a 25-minute multimedia show, and there's outdoor musical entertainment in summer.

Famous films such as *True Grit* and *Cat Ballou* were shot in **Buckskin Joe Frontier Town and Railway** (✉ off U.S. 50, Cañon City, ☎ 719/275–5149, WEB www.buckskinjoe.com; 🎫 $13), which vividly evokes the Old West. Children love the horse-drawn trolley rides, horseback rides, and gold-panning. Adults enjoy the live entertainment in the Crystal Palace and Saloon.

Hiking, biking, and climbing are king in **Buena Vista,** where the Collegiate Peaks Wilderness Area has 14,000-ft peaks. After a full day of activities, head to the **Mt. Princeton Hot Springs** (✉ 5 mi west of Nathrop, CR 162, ☎ 719/395–2447 or 888/395–7799, WEB www.mtprinceton.com; 🎟 $6) for a restorative soak. Within the 1882 Chaffee County Courthouse, the **Buena Vista Heritage Museum** contains artifacts from the life and times of the regional pioneers. It is open during the summer only. ✉ *E. Main St.,* ☎ *719/395–8458.* 🎟 *$2. Closed early Sept.–late May.*

Pueblo, a multiethnic working-class steel town, has some glorious historical neighborhoods. Pick up walking tours of the **Union Avenue Historic District** at the Chamber of Commerce (✉ 302 N. Santa Fe Ave., 81003, ☎ 719/542–1704 or 800/233–3446, WEB www.pueblochamber.org).The **Sangre de Cristo Arts Center** (✉ 210 N. Santa Fe Ave., ☎ 719/543–0130, WEB www.sdc-arts.org; 🎟 $4) celebrates regional arts and crafts. The **Rosemount Victorian Museum** is an opulent 37-room mansion, showplace of the wealthy Thatcher family's Italian marble fireplaces, Tiffany-glass fixtures, and frescoed ceilings. ✉ *419 W. 14th St.,* ☎ *719/545–5290,* WEB *www.rosemount.org.* 🎟 *$6. Closed Sun.–Mon.*

U.S. 50 roughly follows the faded tracks of the **Santa Fe Trail** from the Kansas border through La Junta, where U.S. 350 picks up the scent, traveling southwest to Trinidad. If you detour onto the quiet county roads, you can still discern the faint outline of the trail. Here, amid the magpies and prairie dogs, it takes little imagination to conjure visions of the pioneers struggling to travel just 10 mi a day by oxcart over vast stretches of territory. Just east of La Junta, **Bent's Fort** (✉ 35110 Colo. 194 E, ☎ 719/383–5010; 🎟 $3), now a living-history museum, was the most important stop along the route.

The **Trinidad History Museum,** occupying a historic city block, has old homes and exhibits chronicling the area's past and the effect of the Santa Fe Trail on the community. ✉ *300 E. Main St.,* ☎ *719/846–7217.* 🎟 *$5. Closed Oct.–Apr.*

Dining and Lodging

Pueblo

$–$$ ★ ✕ **Irish Brew Pub & Grille.** Pub grub is elevated to an art form here. The grilled smoked-duck sausage with goat cheese is a standout, as are beaver (yes, beaver) sandwiches. Seven varieties of beer are brewed on the premises. ✉ *108 W. 3rd St., Pueblo,* ☎ *719/542–9974. AE, D, DC, MC, V. Closed Sun. No lunch.*

$–$$ ★ 🏨 **Abriendo Inn.** With original parquet floors, stained glass, and Minnequa oak wainscoting, this 1906 home is on the National Register of Historic Places. Cookies and snacks are available around the clock. ✉ *300 W. Abriendo Ave., Pueblo 81004,* ☎ *719/544–2703,* FAX *719/542–6544,* WEB *www.abriendoinn.com. 10 rooms. AE, DC, MC, V. BP.*

Salida

$ 🏨 **River Run Inn.** On the Arkansas River, this historic Victorian structure (it was built in 1892 as the Chaffee County Poor Farm) has breathtaking mountain prospects. There's a large room available that sleeps from 5 to 13 people. ✉ *8495 CR 160, east off U.S. 285, Salida 81201,* ☎ *719/539–3818 or 800/385–6925,* WEB *www.riverruninn.com. 8 rooms. AE, MC, V. BP.*

Outdoor Activities and Sports

During the summer on the Arkansas River, Buena Vista also bills itself as the White-Water Rafting Capital of the World. Contact rafting firms through the **Colorado River Outfitters Association** (✉ Box 1662, Buena Vista 81211, ☎ 303/280–2554, WEB www.croa.org). **Dvorak Kayak & Rafting Expeditions** (✉ Nathrop, ☎ 800/824–3795) and **Wilderness Aware** (✉ Buena Vista, ☎ 800/462–7238) also have trip information.

South-Central Colorado Essentials

CAR TRAVEL

Buena Vista is 90 mi west of Colorado Springs on U.S. 24; the only way to get there is by car. Pueblo is a half hour south of Colorado Springs on I–25 south; Trinidad is just over an hour farther.

THE SAN LUIS VALLEY

Nestled between the San Juan Mountains and the Sangre de Cristo range and watered by the mighty Rio Grande and its tributaries, the 8,000-square-mi San Luis Valley is the world's largest alpine valley.

Exploring the San Luis Valley

The terrain of the San Luis Valley ranges from the stark moonscape of the Wheeler Geologic Area to the tawny, undulating **Great Sand Dunes National Monument and Preserve** (✉ 35 mi from Alamosa, east on U.S. 160 and north on Rte. 150, ☎ 719/378–2312). Created by windswept grains from the Rio Grande floor, the sand dunes—which rise up to 750 ft and stretch for 55 square mi—are an improbable, unforgettable sight, as curvaceous as Rubens's nudes.

The **Alamosa–Monte Vista National Wildlife Refuge** (✉ 9383 El Rancho La., Alamosa, ☎ 719/589–4021) is an important migratory stopover for the nearly extinct whooping crane and its cousin, the sandhill. **San Luis,** founded in 1851, is the oldest incorporated town in Colorado.Its Hispanic heritage is celebrated in the **San Luis Museum and Cultural Center** (✉ 401 Church Pl., ☎ 719/672–3611; $2). Murals depicting famous stories and legends of the area adorn the town's tree-lined streets.

Dining and Lodging

Alamosa

$–$$$ ✕ **True Grit Steakhouse.** This popular steak house serves outstanding chicken-fried steaks, hand-cut steaks, and prime rib accompanied by huge salads and baked potatoes. If you're a John Wayne fan, you'll be pleased. Everything here is named for the Duke. *✉ 100 Santa Fe Ave., Alamosa, ☎ 719/589–9954. D, MC, V. No lunch weekdays.*

$–$$ **Conejos River Guest Ranch.** This peaceful, family-friendly retreat 14 mi south of Alamosa offers private fishing and horseback riding. The cabins—all fully equipped—and guest rooms are pleasantly outfitted with ranch-style decor, including lodgepole pine furnishings. The lodge rooms include breakfast; the cabins do not. *✉ 25390 Colo. 17, Antonito 81120, ☎ 719/376–2464, WEB www.conejosranch.com. 8 rooms, 6 cabins. Restaurant. D, MC, V. Closed Dec.–Apr. BP.*

$–$$ ★ **Cottonwood Inn B&B.** This cranberry-and-azure house, built in 1908, has Stickley furniture and regional photographs and watercolors. It's also a gathering place for cooking and writing workshops, and the walls are a gallery for local artists. Rooms are sunny, with country-French washed walls; some have claw-foot tubs. ✉ *123 San Juan Ave., Alamosa 81101,* ☎ *719/589–3882 or 800/955–2623,* FAX *719/589–6437,* WEB *www.cottonwoodinn.com. 10 rooms. AE, D, MC, V. BP.*

The San Luis Valley Essentials

AIRPORTS

The Durango–La Plata Airport receives daily commuter flights.

➤ AIRPORT INFORMATION: **Durango–La Plata Airport** (✉ 1000 Airport Rd., ☎ 970/247–8143).

CAR TRAVEL

Alamosa is 150 mi east of Durango on U.S. 160 or 115 mi from Pueblo on I–25 and U.S. 160. San Luis is on Route 159 south of U.S. 160.

CONNECTICUT

Updated by Michelle Bodak Acri

Capital	Hartford
Population	3,405,565
Motto	He Who Transplanted Still Sustains
State Bird	American robin
State Flower	Mountain laurel
Postal Abbreviation	CT

Statewide Visitor Information

Office of Tourism (✉ 505 Hudson St., Hartford 06106, ☎ 800/282–6863 for brochure).

Scenic Drives

Scenic delights unfold on the narrow roads that wind through the **Litchfield Hills** in northwestern Connecticut, especially in the spring and autumn. Each road bridge crossing the beautiful and historic **Merritt Parkway** (Route 15) between Greenwich and Stratford has its own architecturally significant design. **Route 57 to 53 to 107 to 302,** which connect Exit 42 of the Merritt Parkway in Westport to Exit 10 of I–84 in Newtown, take you by Colonial homesteads, over steep ridges, and alongside the **Saugatuck Reservoir.** In northeastern Connecticut, **Route 169** from Norwich to North Woodstock has been designated a National Scenic Byway.

National and State Parks

National Park

Dapper, wooded Wilton is home to **Weir Farm National Historic Site,** former home of celebrated impressionist painter J. Alden Weir. The 60 acres here include hiking paths, picnic areas, and restored rose and perennial gardens. Tours of Weir's studio and sculptor Mahonri Young's studio are conducted, and you can take a self-guided tour of Weir's painting sites. ✉ *735 Nod Hill Rd.,* ☎ *203/834–1896,* WEB *www.nps.go/wefa.* 🎫 *Free. Visitor center closed Mon.–Tues.*

State Parks

For information on the state's nearly 100 parks, contact the **State Parks Division, Bureau of Parks and Forests** (✉ 79 Elm St., Hartford 06106, ☎ 860/424–3200).

COASTAL CONNECTICUT

The state's 253-mi coastline contains a series of bedroom communities serving New York City with smaller towns linked to Connecticut's major cities of Stamford, Bridgeport, New Haven, and New London. Along with its colonial heritage and 21st-century urban sprawl, the region has nature centers and wilderness preserves for hiking and bird-watching, as well as restored 18th- and 19th-century townships and museums dedicated to bringing Connecticut's past alive.

Exploring Coastal Connecticut

Greenwich, which borders New York State, epitomizes affluent Fairfield County, with gourmet restaurants and chic boutiques. The **Bruce Museum** (✉ 1 Museum Dr., ☎ 203/869–0376, WEB www.brucemuseum.com; 🎫 $4), closed Monday, has a mineral collection, a small but worth-

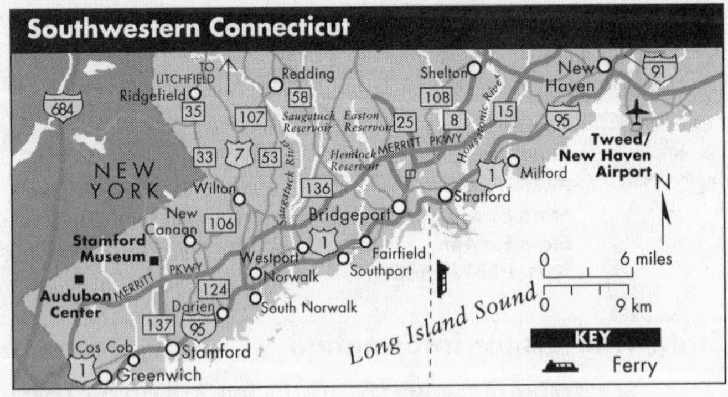

while collection of American Impressionist paintings, and a 16th-century-era woodland diorama. The 522-acre **Audubon Center** (✉ 613 Riversville Rd., ☎ 203/869–5272, WEB www.greenwich.center.audubon.org; 🎫 $3) has exhibits on the local environment and 15 mi of secluded hiking trails. The small barn-red **Putnam Cottage,** built about 1690, was operated as Knapp's Tavern during the Revolutionary War. Inside are colonial-era furnishings; outside is a lush herb garden. ✉ *243 E. Putnam Ave./Rte. 1,* ☎ *203/869–9697.* 🎫 *$4.*

Cos Cob is a village within the township of Greenwich. The **Bush-Holley Historic Site,** built circa 1732, exhibits paintings by Childe Hassam and John Twachtman, sculptures by John Rogers, and pottery by Leon Volkmar. ✉ *39 Strickland Rd.,* ☎ *203/869–6899.* 🎫 *$6. Closed weekends Jan.–Feb. and Mon. Mar.–Dec.*

Stamford's shoreline is given over primarily to industry and commerce, but to the north some beautiful nature areas remain. The 118-acre **Stamford Museum and Nature Center** (✉ 39 Scofieldtown Rd., ☎ 203/322–1646, WEB www.stamfordmuseum.org; 🎫 $6) has five galleries with changing exhibits on natural history, art, and Americana; a working New England farm; and a permanent exhibit on local Native American history. Shows are presented at the center's observatory and planetarium.

★ Affectionately dubbed SoNo, **South Norwalk,** off I–95's Exit 15, has restored art galleries, restaurants, and boutiques. The **Maritime Aquarium at Norwalk** (✉ 10 N. Water St., ☎ 203/852–0700, WEB www.maritimeaquarium.org; 🎫 aquarium $8.75, IMAX $6.75) includes a huge aquarium, marine vessels, and an IMAX theater.

Wilton, a brief detour from the coast, up Routes 7 and 33 from Norwalk, is a well-preserved community with a wooded countryside and good antiques shopping. Wilton has Connecticut's first national park, **Weir Farm National Historical Site** (☞ National and State Parks). **Ridgefield,** with its sweeping lawns and stately mansions, is where you'll find northwestern Connecticut atmosphere within an hour of Manhattan. Ridgefield is home to the **Aldrich Museum of Contemporary Art,** which has changing exhibits of cutting-edge works and one of the finest sculpture gardens in the Northeast. ✉ *258 Main St.,* ☎ *203/438–4519,* WEB *www.aldrichart.org.* 🎫 *$5. Closed Mon.*

★ **Westport** has long been an artistic and literary community and now is also a trendy hub of shops and eateries. In summer visitors flock to **Sherwood Island State Park** (✉ I–95 Exit 18, ☎ 203/226–6983; 🎫 $5–$12) for its 1½-mi sweep of sandy beach.

The exclusive colonial village of **Southport** is on the Pequot River. To get there from Sherwood Island, head east along Greens Farms Road.

Fairfield was almost destroyed in a raid by the British in 1779—four houses survived the attack and still stand on Beach Road. In the northern part of town, the **Connecticut Audubon Center at Fairfield** (✉ 2325 Burr St., ☎ 203/259–6305, WEB www.ct.audubon.org/centers/fairfield/fairfield.htm; 🎟 $2), America's oldest nature center, maintains a 160-acre wildlife sanctuary.

Despite a poor reputation because of economic difficulties, **Bridgeport** is improving thanks to the hard work of city leaders. This fact, and a handful of unique attractions, makes it a worthwhile stop. **Beardsley Park and Zoological Gardens** (✉ 1875 Noble Ave., ☎ 203/394–6565, WEB www.beardsleyzoo.org; 🎟 $6) is Connecticut's only zoo. Here you'll find more than 350 animals as well as a South American rain forest and a carousel. The **Barnum Museum,** associated with onetime mayor P. T. Barnum, houses exhibits depicting the great showman's career and a scaled-down model of his famous creation, the five-ring circus. ✉ *820 Main St.,* ☎ *203/331–1104.* 🎟 *$5. Closed Mon.*

At the **Discovery Museum and Wonder Workshop** (✉ 4450 Park Ave., ☎ 203/372–3521, WEB www.discoverymuseum.org; 🎟 $7) you can visit a planetarium, hands-on science exhibits, a computer art exhibit, and the *Challenger* learning center (which has a simulated space flight).

★ **New Haven** is a city of extremes: although it's prosperous in the area around the green—encompassing the Yale University campus and the numerous shops, museums, and restaurants of Chapel Street—20% of the city's residents live below the poverty level. Stay near the campus and city common, especially at night, and get a good street map. Knowledgeable guides give one-hour walking tours of the **Yale University campus** (✉ 149 Elm St., ☎ 203/432–2300, WEB www.yale.edu; 🎟 free). Part of Yale University, the **Beinecke Rare Book and Manuscript Library** (✉ 121 Wall St., ☎ 203/432–2977, WEB www.library.yale.edu/beinecke; 🎟 free), closed Sunday, houses a world-class collection of rare books and manuscripts—including a Gutenberg Bible and original Audubon bird prints—in a stunning building made from panels of translucent marble. The **Yale University Art Gallery** (✉ 1111 Chapel St., ☎ 203/432–0600, WEB www.yale.edu/artgallery; 🎟 free), closed Monday, has a collection that spans the centuries and the continents. The **Yale Center for British Art** (✉ 1080 Chapel St., ☎ 203/432–2800, WEB www.yale.edu/ycba; 🎟 free), closed Monday, houses the most extensive collection of British artwork and rare books outside the United Kingdom. The **Peabody Museum of Natural History** (✉ 170 Whitney Ave., ☎ 203/432–5050, WEB www.peabody.yale.edu; 🎟 $5), part of Yale University, is the largest of its kind in New England.

The urban buildup that characterizes the Connecticut coast west of New Haven dissipates as you drive east on I–95 toward New London. **Old Saybrook** was once a lively shipbuilding and fishing town; today the bustle comes mostly from its many summer vacationers. **Old Lyme,** on the other side of the Connecticut River from Old Saybrook, has a rich artistic history. The **Florence Griswold Museum** (✉ 96 Lyme St., ☎ 860/434–5542, WEB www.flogris.org; 🎟 $5) once housed an art colony that included Childe Hassam. The museum displays the artists' works, along with 19th-century furnishings and decorative items. The **Lyme Academy of Fine Arts** (✉ 84 Lyme St., ☎ 860/434–5232, WEB www.lymeacademy.com; 🎟 donation suggested) shows works by students and other contemporary artists.

The seagoing community of New London is the home of the **U.S. Coast Guard Academy** (✉ 15 Mohegan Ave., ☎ 860/444–8270, WEB www.cga.com; 🎟 free), whose 100-acre cluster of traditional redbrick

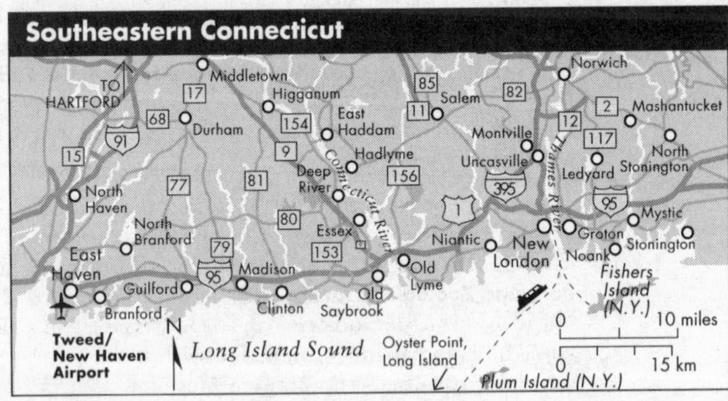

buildings includes a museum. The three-masted training bark *Eagle* may be boarded when in port.

In **Groton,** across the Thames River from New London, is a U.S. submarine base. The world's first nuclear-powered submarine, the *Historic Ship Nautilus,* was launched here in 1954 and is now permanently berthed here and is open to visitors. The **Submarine Force Museum,** next to the base, contains memorabilia, artifacts, and displays, including working periscopes and controls. ✉ *Crystal Lake Rd.,* ☎ *860/694–3174 or 800/343–0079,* WEB *www.ussnautilus.org.* *Free. Closed Tues. late Oct.–early May.*

★ **Mystic** is a celebrated whaling seaport. At **Mystic Seaport** (✉ 75 Greenmanville Ave., ☎ 860/572–0711, WEB www.mysticseaport.org; $17)—the nation's largest maritime museum, on 17 riverfront acres—you can board 19th-century sailing vessels, including the *Charles W. Morgan,* the last wooden whaling ship afloat. You can also stroll around the maritime village, which has historic homes, a spectacular collection of sailing-related artifacts, and craftspeople who give demonstrations. At the **Mystic Marinelife Aquarium and Institute for Exploration** (✉ off I–95 on Coogan Blvd., ☎ 860/572–5955, WEB www.mysticaquarium.org; $16) you can see more than 6,000 specimens and 50 live exhibits of sea life and take a simulated dive 3,000 ft below the surface of the ocean with world-renowned ocean explorer Dr. Robert Ballard.

Stonington is a quiet fishing community clustered around white-spired churches. Past the historic buildings that surround the town green is the **Old Lighthouse Museum,** where you'll find displays about shipping, whaling, and other subjects. You can climb to the top of the granite tower for a view of Long Island Sound and three states. ✉ *7 Water St.,* ☎ *860/535–1440,* WEB *www.stoningtonhistory.org/light.htm.* *$4. Closed Nov.–Apr. and Mon. May–June and Sept.–Oct.*

Ledyard was a quiet town that has been transformed by the local Native American tribe, the Pequots, into a major tourist center. The **Mashantucket Pequot Museum and Research Center** (✉ 110 Pequot Trail, ☎ 800/411–9671, WEB www.mashantucket.com; $12), a vast, innovative museum, uses state-of-the-art technology to explore more than 18,000 years of Northeastern Woodland tribes' history. The gambling and entertainment complex **Foxwoods** (✉ 39 Norwich Westerly Rd., ☎ 860/312–3000, WEB www.foxwoods.com) is the world's largest casino, with more than 5,500 slot machines, a high-stakes bingo parlor, poker rooms, a smoke-free gaming area, and more.

The **Mohegan Sun** casino (✉ Mohegan Sun Blvd., ☎ 888/226–7711, WEB www.mohegansun.com), in **Uncasville,** is similar to Foxwoods and was substantially expanded in April 2002.

Dining and Lodging

B&B, Ltd. (☏ 203/469–3260) is a service for small B&Bs, inns, and rooms rented in private homes. Rooms are costliest in summer and autumn. The **Covered Bridge B&B Reservation Service** (☏ 860/542–5944) provides listings for inns all around the state. The **Nutmeg B&B Agency** (☏ 860/236–6698) is a reliable statewide service for B&Bs and small inns.

Greenwich

$$$$ ★ ✕ **Restaurant Jean-Louis.** Roses, Limoges china, and crisp white tablecloths with lace underskirts complement extraordinary food, carefully served. The fixed-price menu might include diced vegetables cooked in saffron bouillon with mussels and scallops served with parsley coulis or roast breast of duck on a bed of spinach. ✉ *61 Lewis St.,* ☏ *203/622–8450. Jacket required. AE, D, DC, MC, V. Closed Sun. No lunch Sat.*

$$$$ ✕🏨 **Homestead Inn.** Each bedroom in this Italianate mansion is decorated with antiques and reproductions. The restaurant ($$$$; jacket required) serves up-to-the-minute French cuisine. ✉ *420 Field Point Rd., 06830,* ☏ *203/869–7500,* FAX *203/869–7502,* WEB *www.homesteadinn.com. 26 rooms. Restaurant. AE, MC, V.*

Mystic

$–$$$$ ✕🏨 **Inn at Mystic.** The highlight of this inn, which sprawls over 15 hilltop acres and overlooks Pequotsepos Cove, is the five-bedroom Georgian Colonial mansion. Almost as impressive is the four-bedroom gatehouse in which Lauren Bacall and Humphrey Bogart honeymooned and the unusually attractive motor lodge. The sun-filled Floodtide Restaurant ($$$–$$$$) serves traditional New England fare. ✉ *Rtes. 1 and 27, 06355,* ☏ *860/536–9604 or 800/237–2415,* FAX *860/572–1635,* WEB *www.innatmystic.com. 67 rooms. Restaurant, pool. AE, D, DC, MC, V.*

$$ 🏨 **Whaler's Inn and Motor Court.** A perfect compromise between a chain motel and a country inn, this complex is one block from the Mystic River and downtown. The rooms are decorated in a Victorian style with quilts and reproduction four-poster beds. ✉ *20 E. Main St., 06355,* ☏ *860/536–1506; 800/243–2588 outside Connecticut;* FAX *860/572–1250;* WEB *whalersinnmystic.com. 41 rooms. 3 restaurants. AE, MC, V.*

New Haven

$–$$ ★ ✕ **Frank Pepe's.** The big ovens on the back wall of this New Haven institution bake pizzas that are revered throughout the country. On weekend evenings the wait for a table can be more than an hour, but the pizza—the sole item on the menu—is worth it. ✉ *157 Wooster St.,* ☏ *203/865–5762. Reservations not accepted. No credit cards. Closed Tues. No lunch Mon. or Wed.–Thurs.*

$$$ ★ 🏨 **Three Chimneys Inn.** This 1870 Victorian mansion is one of the most polished small inns in the state. Rooms have posh Georgian-style furnishings: mahogany four-poster beds, oversize armoires, and Chippendale desks. The sitting room and library have working fireplaces. ✉ *1201 Chapel St., 06511,* ☏ *203/789–1201,* FAX *203/776–7363,* WEB *www.threechimneysinn.com. 11 rooms. AE, D, DC, MC, V. BP.*

North Stonington

$$$$ ✕🏨 **Randall's Ordinary.** Famed for its open-hearth cooking of authentic colonial dishes, the Ordinary creates tasty lunches and three-course fixed-price dinners ($$$; reservations essential), served by staff in period costume. Accommodations are available in the 17th-century John Randall House, where rooms are simply furnished with antiques, or in the converted barn. ✉ *Rte. 2 (Box 243, 06359),* ☏ *860/599–4540,* FAX *860/*

599–3308, WEB *www.randallsordinary.com. 15 rooms. Restaurant. AE, MC, V.*

Norwalk

$$ ✕ **Habana.** Ceiling fans, banana trees, and a high energy level characterize Habana, which serves contemporary Cuban cuisine with some Argentinian, Peruvian, Mexican, Puerto Rican, and Brazilian dishes thrown in for spice. Some favorites are roasted sea bass with a crispy plantain crust, empanadas stuffed with minced duck or chorizo, ceviche, and baby-back ribs with guava sauce. ✉ *70 N. Main St.,* ☎ *203/852–9790. AE, D, MC, V. No lunch.*

Norwich

$$$$ ✕🏨 **The Spa at Norwich Inn.** This luxurious Georgian-style inn is on 42 acres high on a bluff a few hundred yards from the Thames River. Top-notch treatments and fitness classes are held in the spa facility. Kensington's restaurant ($$–$$$$) serves Continental delicacies as well as lighter spa cuisine. ✉ *607 W. Thames St./Rte. 32, 06360,* ☎ *860/886–2401 or 800/275–4772,* FAX *860/886–4492,* WEB *www.thespaatnorwichinn.com. 145 rooms. Restaurant, pool, health club. AE, DC, MC, V.*

Old Lyme

$$–$$$ ★ ✕🏨 **Bee & Thistle Inn.** This three-story 1756 colonial contains period antiques, sunlit porches, and a formal garden. Most rooms have canopy or four-poster beds. Fireplaces and candlelight create a romantic atmosphere in the restaurant ($$$; closed Tues. and 1st 3 wks in Jan.), where classic American cuisine is served with style. ✉ *100 Lyme St., 06371,* ☎ *860/434–1667; 800/622–4946 outside Connecticut;* FAX *860/434–3402;* WEB *www.beeandthistleinn.com. 12 rooms. Restaurant. AE, DC, MC, V.*

Old Saybrook

$$–$$$ ✕ **Aleia's.** Light, bright, and bountiful as the Italian countryside, this restaurant has raffia, silk flowers, and hand-painted plates from Capri on the walls. Trompe l'oeil fruits, vegetables, and herbs adorn the tabletops. Chef-owner Kimberly Snow takes a contemporary approach to Italian cuisine by applying nouvelle touches to her mother's tried-and-true recipes. ✉ *1687 Boston Post Rd.,* ☎ *860/399–5050. AE, MC, V. Closed Sun.–Mon. No lunch.*

Stamford

$$–$$$ ★ ✕ **Beacon.** Wraparound harbor views and a brick exterior highlight this stylish waterfront restaurant. Its open kitchen prepares shared platters—try the one with lamb, chicken, and crisp braised pork shank—and standout entrées such as grass-fed rib-eye steak and herb-roasted salmon. If you want to linger before or after dinner, head to the bar upstairs for some lively chatter. ✉ *183 Harbor Dr.,* ☎ *203/327–4600. AE, DC, MC, V.*

Westbrook

$$$$ 🏨 **Water's Edge Inn & Resort.** With a spectacular setting on Long Island Sound and its own beach, this weathered gray-shingle compound is one of the Connecticut shore's premier resorts. Rooms in the main building, though not as large as the suites in surrounding outbuildings, have better views and nicer furnishings. ✉ *1525 Boston Post Rd., 06498,* ☎ *860/399–5901 or 800/222–5901,* FAX *860/399–6172,* WEB *www.watersedge-resort.com. 167 rooms. Restaurant, pools, health club. AE, D, DC, MC, V.*

Westport

$$$ ✕ **Da Pietro's.** This romantic storefront café serves a savory mix of Italian and French specialties. Roasted monkfish with curry-coconut sauce,

lasagna filled with snails and spinach, and sautéed veal tenderloins are possible choices. ✉ *36 Riverside Ave.,* ☎ *203/454–1213. AE, DC, MC, V. Closed Sun. No lunch.*

$$$$ ★ ✕🏨 **Inn at National Hall.** The inn's redbrick building on the downtown banks of the Saugatuck River belies its whimsical, exotic interior. Each room is a study in innovative restoration. Chef Todd English, a Boston superstar, prepares such dishes ($$$$) as grilled sirloin over Tuscan bruschetta and tortellini of butternut squash with brown butter and sage. ✉ *2 Post Rd. W, 06880,* ☎ *203/221–1351 or 800/628–4255,* FAX *203/221–0276,* WEB *www.innatnationalhall.com. 15 rooms. Restaurant. AE, DC, MC, V. CP.*

Campgrounds

⛺ **Riverdale Farm Campsite** (✉ 111 River Rd., Clinton, ☎ 860/669–5388). ⛺ **Hammonasset Beach State Park** (✉ I–95, Exit 62, Madison, ☎ 203/245–1817).

Nightlife and the Arts

Nightlife

Bars and clubs are sprinkled throughout southern Connecticut. The best of them are concentrated in Westport, South Norwalk, New Haven's Chapel West area, and along New London's Bank Street.

With two dance floors, the **Art Bar** (✉ 84 W. Park Pl., Stamford, ☎ 203/973–0300) spins dance music from 1980s pop and New Wave to Gothic and Industrial. The crowd is sometimes on the young side. The **El 'n' Gee Club** (✉ 86 Golden St., ☎ 860/437–3800) presents heavy metal, reggae, and local and national bands. Alternative and traditional rock bands play at **Toad's Place** (✉ 300 York St., New Haven, ☎ 203/624–8623).

The Arts

The Connecticut coast's wealth of successful repertory and Broadway-style theaters includes the **Long Wharf Theatre** (✉ 222 Sargent Dr., New Haven, ☎ 203/787–4282), known for its revivals of neglected classics and imaginative productions of new work. The **Shubert Performing Arts Center** (✉ 247 College St., New Haven, ☎ 203/562–5666) presents an array of full-scale productions. **Stamford Center for the Arts** (✉ 307 Atlantic St., ☎ 203/325–4466) stages everything from one-act plays to musicals to film festivals. In summer the **Westport Country Playhouse** (✉ 25 Powers Ct., ☎ 203/227–4177) presents first-rate plays. The **Yale Repertory Theatre** (✉ 222 York St., New Haven, ☎ 203/432–1234) is known for its fresh interpretations of classics.

Most coastal towns have outdoor summer concerts and music festivals, and some have smaller regional theaters. Call tourist offices for details (☞ Visitor Information).

Outdoor Activities and Sports

Fishing

Saltwater fishing is best June–October; bass, bluefish, and flounder are popular catches. Striped bass and blues are the catch of the day on ***Hel-Cat II*** (✉ Groton, ☎ 860/445–5991), a 144-ft party fishing boat, from June to October. **Sunbeam Fleet** (✉ Waterford, ☎ 860/443–7259) is a top choice for sportfishing.

Golf

Danbury's 18-hole **Richter Park Golf Course** (✉ 100 Aunt Hack Rd., ☎ 203/792–2550) is one of the top public courses in the nation. A top 18-hole course in the area is the **H. Smith Richardson Golf Course** (✉

2425 Morehouse Hwy., Fairfield, ☎ 203/255–7300). The 18-hole courses designed by Robert Trent Jones and Gary Player at the **Lyman Orchards Golf Club** (✉ Rte. 147, Middlefield, ☎ 860/349–8055) are popular choices.

Shopping

Southwestern Connecticut

Main Street in **Westport** is like an outdoor mall, with J. Crew, Ann Taylor, Coach, and dozens of other fashionable shops. **New Canaan, Darien,** and **Greenwich** are renowned for their swank stores and boutiques. **Route 7,** which runs through Wilton and Ridgefield, has dozens of antiques sheds and boutiques. **Cannondale Village** (✉ off Rte. 7, Wilton, ☎ 203/762–2233) is a pre–Civil War farm village turned shopping complex. Washington Street in **South Norwalk** (SoNo) has galleries and crafts dealers. The **Stamford Town Center** (✉ 100 Greyrock Pl., ☎ 203/356–9700) houses 130 mostly upscale shops.

Southeastern Connecticut

You'll find shopping centers throughout New Haven and New London areas. **Clinton Crossing Premium Outlets** (✉ I–95, Exit 63, Clinton, ☎ 860/664–0700) has 70 upscale shops. **Westbrook Factory Stores** (✉ I–95, Exit 65, Westbrook, ☎ 860/399–8656) has more than 60 outlets. You'll find a collection of boutiques and galleries in downtown **Mystic. Olde Mistick Village** (✉ I–95, Exit 90, Mystic, ☎ 860/536–1641), a re-created colonial village, has crafts and souvenir shops. The **Tradewinds Gallery** (✉ 42 W. Main St., Mystic, ☎ 860/536–0119) specializes in antique prints and maps. The **Essex–Saybrook Antiques Village** (✉ 345 Middlesex Turnpike, Old Saybrook, ☎ 860/388–0689) has more than 120 dealers. **Old Lyme, Guilford,** and **Stonington** are good sources for antiques.

Coastal Connecticut Essentials

AIRPORTS

The state's chief airport is Bradley International Airport, 12 mi north of Hartford, with daily flights by most major U.S. airlines. US Airways Express flies into Tweed/New Haven Airport, 5 mi southeast of New Haven.

➤ AIRPORT INFORMATION: **Bradley International Airport** (✉ Rte. 20, Exit 40 off I–91, ☎ 860/292–2000). **Tweed/New Haven Airport** (✉ Burr St. off I–95, ☎ 203/466–8833).

BOAT AND FERRY TRAVEL

The Bridgeport and Port Jefferson Steamboat Company has ferries connecting Bridgeport with the north shore of New York's Long Island. Cross Sound Ferry connects New London with northeastern Long Island's Orient Point.

➤ BOAT AND FERRY INFORMATION: **Bridgeport and Port Jefferson Steamboat Company** (☎ 888/443–3779). **Cross Sound Ferry** (☎ 860/443–5281).

BUS TRAVEL

Greyhound provides bus service from throughout the United States. Bonanza provides service from various points in New England. Connecticut Transit has bus service in the Stamford, Hartford, and New Haven areas. Southeast Area Transit serves Norwich, New London, and Mystic.

➤ BUS INFORMATION: **Bonanza** (☎ 800/556–3815). **Connecticut Transit** (☎ 203/327–7433). **Greyhound** (☎ 800/231–2222). **Southeast Area Transit** (☎ 860/886–2631).

CAR TRAVEL

The Merritt Parkway and I–95, both known for severe traffic jams during rush hour, are the principal coastal highways between New York and New Haven. I–95 continues beyond New Haven into Rhode Island. From Hartford, I–91 goes south to New Haven.

TRAIN TRAVEL

Amtrak stops at Stamford, Bridgeport, New Haven, Hartford, New London, and Mystic. Metro North runs between New York City and New Haven, with stops at a few inland stations and many towns along the coast.

➤ TRAIN INFORMATION: **Amtrak** (☎ 800/872–7245). **Metro North** (☎ 212/532–4900 or 800/638–7646).

VISITOR INFORMATION

➤ TOURIST INFORMATION: **Coastal Fairfield County Convention and Visitor Bureau** (✉ 297 West Ave., The Gate Lodge–Mathews Park, Norwalk 06850, ☎ 203/899–2799 or 800/866–7925, WEB www.coastalct.com). **Connecticut's Mystic and More** (✉ Box 89, New London 06320, ☎ 860/444–2206 or 800/863–6569, WEB www.mysticmore.com). **Greater New Haven Convention and Visitors Bureau** (✉ 59 Elm St., New Haven 06510, ☎ 203/777–8550 or 800/332–7829, WEB www.newhavencvb.com).

THE LITCHFIELD HILLS

Here, in the foothills of the Berkshires, is some of the most unspoiled scenery in the state. Grand old inns are plentiful, as are surprisingly sophisticated eateries. Rolling farmlands abut thick forests, and engaging trails traverse state parks. Two rivers, the Housatonic and Farmington, attract anglers and canoeing enthusiasts, and there are three sizable lakes—Waramaug, Bantam, and Twin lakes. Most towns are anchored by sweeping greens and stately homes and provide a glimpse of New England life as it existed two centuries ago.

Exploring the Litchfield Hills

The mountainous northern towns of **Sharon, Lakeville, Salisbury,** and **Norfolk** are crisscrossed by scenic winding roads. From late April to mid-October auto-racing fans come to **Lime Rock Park** (✉ Rte. 112, Lakeville, ☎ 860/435–5000, WEB www.limerockpark.com), home to the Northeast's best road racing.

The crossroads village of **New Preston** is packed with antiques shops. North of downtown is Lake Waramaug. Route 478, a scenic drive around the lake (8 mi), will take you past stately homes and beautiful old inns, many of which serve outstanding Continental cuisine. **Kent,** to the northwest of New Preston, has the area's greatest concentration of art galleries, some of them nationally recognized. **Bull's Bridge** (✉ off Rte. 7), in Kent, is one of the state's three remaining covered bridges. Within **Kent Falls State Park** (✉ Rte. 7, ☎ 860/927–3238) is one of the state's most impressive waterfalls.

Everything seems on a larger scale in **Litchfield** than in neighboring towns: great white colonials line broad streets shaded by majestic elms, and serene Litchfield Green is surrounded by lovely shops and restaurants. Near the green is the **Tapping Reeve House and Law School** (✉ 82 South St., ☎ 860/567–4501, WEB www.litchfieldhistoricalsociety.org; 🎟 $5), America's first law school, which was founded in 1773. The **Litchfield History Museum** (✉ Rtes. 63 and 118, ☎ 860/567–4501, WEB www.litchfieldhistoricalsociety.org; 🎟 $5) has galleries, a reference library, and information on the town's historic buildings. **White Flower Farm**

(✉ Rte. 63, ☎ 860/567–8789), where much of America shops in person or by mail for perennials and bulbs, is a restful stop.

A gentle landscape with pastoral rolling hills unfolds in and around the villages of **Washington, Roxbury,** and **Bridgewater,** where numerous actors and writers seek refuge from the din of Manhattan and Hollywood. You can buy the ingredients for a gourmet picnic lunch—try the **Pantry** (✉ Titus Rd., Washington, ☎ 860/868–0258)—and laze on the shores of sparkling Lake Waramaug or enjoy a leisurely drive along precipitous ridges, passing gracious farmsteads and meadows alive with wildflowers.

In Bristol are two amusements for the child in everyone. The **Carousel Museum of New England** (✉ 95 Riverside Ave., ☎ 860/585–5411, WEB www.thecarouselmuseum.com; $4) displays carousel art. **Lake Compounce** (✉ Rte. 229 N, I–84, Exit 31, ☎ 860/583–3631, WEB www.lakecompounce.com; $28.95 with rides) is the country's oldest continually operating amusement park. Highlights of the 325-acre park include an antique carousel, a classic wooden roller coaster, a new water playground, and a lake with a beach.

Dining and Lodging

Litchfield

$$–$$$ ✕ **West Street Grill.** This stylish dining room on Litchfield's historic green is the favorite of local glitterati, but all are warmly welcomed. Imaginative grilled fish, steak, poultry, and lamb dishes are served with fresh vegetables and pasta or risotto. The desserts are superb. ✉ *43 West St./Rte. 202,* ☎ *860/567–3885. AE, MC, V.*

New Preston

$$–$$$$ ★ ✕ **Birches Inn.** One of the area's poshest inns, the Birches is something of a Lake Waramaug institution. Antiques and reproductions decorate the rooms; three on the waterfront have private decks. Executive chef Frederic Faveau presides over the lake-view dining room ($$; closed Tues.–Wed.; no lunch). Among his signature dishes are grilled marinated leg of lamb with herb risotto cake, sautéed mustard greens, and a roasted garlic sauce. ✉ *233 W. Shore Rd., 06777,* ☎ *860/868–1735,* FAX *860/868–1815,* WEB *www.thebirchesinn.com. 8 rooms. Restaurant. AE, MC, V. CP.*

Norfolk

$$–$$$$ ★ **Manor House.** Among the highlights of this 1898 Bavarian Tudor are its bibelots, mirrors, carpets, antique beds, and prints—not to mention the 20 stained-glass windows designed by Louis Tiffany. The vast Spofford Room has windows on three sides, a king-size canopy bed with a cheery fireplace opposite, and a balcony. The Morgan Room has a private wood-panel elevator (added in 1939); it also has a private deck. ✉ *69 Maple Ave. (Box 447, 06058),* ☎ FAX *860/542–5690,* WEB *www.manorhouse-norfolk.com. 8 rooms. AE, MC, V. BP.*

Washington

$$$$ ★ ✕ **Mayflower Inn.** Though some suites at this inn will set you back $1,000 a night, the place is always booked well ahead—with good reason. The Mayflower is impeccably decorated: guest rooms have fine 18th- and 19th-century antiques and four-poster canopy beds; oversize baths have mahogany wainscoting and marble throughout. Streams and trails crisscross the 28-acre grounds. The mouthwatering cuisine ($$$–$$$$) might include roast Muscovy duck breast. ✉ *118 Woodbury Rd./Rte. 47, 06793,* ☎ *860/868–9466,* FAX *860/868–1497,* WEB *www.mayflowerinn.com. 25 rooms. Restaurant, pool, health club. AE, MC, V.*

Woodbury

$$–$$$$ ★ ✕ **Good News Café.** The emphasis is on healthful, innovative fare: braised veal shanks on pearl couscous with fiddlehead ferns and roasted tomatoes is a tasty example. Or you can bounce in for cappuccino and munchies, served in a separate room just for this purpose, decorated with a fascinating collection of vintage radios. ✉ *694 Main St. S,* ☎ *203/266–4663. AE, MC, V. Closed Tues.*

Nightlife and the Arts

World-renowned artists and ensembles perform Friday and Saturday evening June–August at the **Norfolk Chamber Music Festival** (☎ 860/542–3000), at the Music Shed on the Ellen Battell Stoeckel Estate at the northwest corner of the Norfolk green. Yale School of Music students perform at the festival Thursday evening and Saturday morning.

Outdoor Activities and Sports

Canoeing

Clarke Outdoors (✉ 163 Rte. 7, West Cornwall, ☎ 860/672–6365) has canoe and kayak rentals and conducts 10-mi trips from Falls Village to Housatonic Meadows State Park.

Hiking

The Litchfield Hills area has terrific hiking terrain with **Haystack Mountain and Dennis Hill** (✉ Rte. 272, Norfolk, ☎ 860/482–1817). The 758-acre **Sharon Audubon Center** (✉ 325 Cornwall Bridge Rd., ☎ 860/364–0520) provides some of the region's best hiking opportunities.

Ski Areas

Mohawk Mountain (✉ 46 Great Hollow Rd., Cornwall, ☎ 860/672–6100). **Ski Sundown** (✉ 126 Ratlum Rd., New Hartford, ☎ 860/379–7669). **Woodbury Ski Area** (✉ 785 Washington Rd., Woodbury, ☎ 203/263–2203).

Shopping

The best antiques and crafts shopping is along Route 6 in **Woodbury** and **Southbury,** Route 45 in **New Preston,** U.S. 7 in **Kent,** Route 128 in **West Cornwall,** and U.S. 202 in **Bantam.**

The Litchfield Hills Essentials

VISITOR INFORMATION

➤ TOURIST INFORMATION: Litchfield Hills Visitors Council (✉ Box 968, Litchfield 06759, ☎ 860/567–4506, WEB www.litchfieldhills.com).

THE CONNECTICUT RIVER VALLEY AND HARTFORD

What to See and Do

The Connecticut River valley meanders through rolling hills, providing a taste of Colonial history as well as sophisticated inns. **Essex,** on the west bank of the Connecticut River, is where the first submarine, the *American Turtle,* was built. A full-size reproduction of the *Turtle* is at the **Connecticut River Museum** (✉ Steamboat Dock, ☎ 860/767–8269, WEB www.ctrivermuseum.org; 🎫 $4). In East Haddam is the region's leading oddity: a 24-room oak-and-fieldstone hilltop castle that is part of **Gillette Castle State Park** (✉ 67 River Rd., off Rte. 82, ☎ 860/526–2336; 🎫 grounds free, castle $5).East Haddam is the home of the **Goodspeed Opera House** (✉ Rte. 82, ☎ 860/873–8668, WEB www.goodspeed.org). The upper floors of this elaborate structure have served as a venue for theatrical performances since 1877.

Hartford, known as the "insurance capital of America," is also the state capital. The Federal **Old State House** (✉ 800 Main St., ☎ 860/522–6766; 🎫 free) was designed by Charles Bulfinch, architect of the U.S. Capitol. The **Mark Twain House** (✉ 351 Farmington Ave., ☎ 860/247–0998, WEB www.marktwainhouse.org; 🎫 $9) is named after the author who made his home here in this extravagant Victorian mansion. The ★ 50,000 artworks and artifacts at the **Wadsworth Atheneum Museum of Art** (✉ 600 Main St., ☎ 860/278–2670, WEB www.wadsworthatheneum.org; 🎫 $7), the nation's first public art museum, span 5,000 years and include paintings from the Hudson River School, the Impressionists, and other 20th-century painters.

Dining and Lodging

$$$ ✕ **Restaurant du Village.** A black wrought-iron gate beckons you away from the tony antiques shops of Chester's quaint Main Street to this colonial storefront, painted in Newport blue and adorned with flower boxes. Sample classic French cuisine—escargots in puff pastry, filet mignon—while recapping the day's shopping coups. ✉ *59 Main St., Chester,* ☎ *860/526–5301. AE, MC, V. Closed Mon.–Tues. No lunch.*

$$–$$$ ✕ **Max Downtown.** One of restaurateur Richard Rosenthal's culinary creations, upscale Max Downtown serves cuisine from around the world—everything from smoked Chilean sea bass to porcini-mushroom ravioli to fire-roasted pork tenderloin. A separate cigar bar serves classic port and single-malt liquor. ✉ *185 Asylum St., CityPlace, Hartford,* ☎ *860/522–2530. Reservations essential. AE, DC, MC, V. No lunch weekends.*

$$–$$$ ✕🏨 **Copper Beech Inn.** A magnificent copper beech tree shades the imposing main building of this Victorian inn, which is furnished in period pieces. Each of the main house's four guest rooms has an old-fashioned tub; the nine rooms in the carriage house are more modern and have decks. Seven acres of wooded grounds and terraced gardens create an atmosphere of privileged seclusion. The country French menu in the romantic dining room ($$$; reservations essential; jacket and tie) changes seasonally. ✉ *46 Main St., Ivoryton 06442,* ☎ *860/767–0330 or 888/809–2056,* WEB *www.copperbeechinn.com. 13 rooms. Restaurant. AE, DC, MC, V. CP.*

$–$$$ ✕🏨 **Griswold Inn.** The decor at what's billed as America's oldest inn is kaleidoscopic—some colonial, a touch of Federal, a little Victorian, and just as much modern (air-conditioning, phones, but no in-room TVs) as is necessary to meet present-day expectations. The chefs at the restaurant ($$$–$$$$) prepare country-style and gourmet dishes—try the famous 1776 sausages, which come with sauerkraut and German potato salad, or the risotto croquettes. ✉ *36 Main St., Essex 06426,* ☎ *860/767–1776,* FAX *860/767–0481,* WEB *www.griswoldinn.com. 30 rooms. Restaurant. AE, MC, V. CP.*

$$–$$$ ★ 🏨 **Goodwin Hotel.** Connecticut's only truly grand city hotel looks a little odd in the downtown business district—the Civic Center dwarfs the ornate dark red structure, a registered historic landmark built in 1881. Its rooms are large and tastefully done in colonial style and have Italian marble baths. The clubby, mahogany-panel Pierpont's Restaurant serves popular new American fare. ✉ *1 Haynes St., Hartford 06103,* ☎ *860/246–7500 or 800/922–5006,* FAX *860/247–4576,* WEB *www.goodwinhotel.com. 124 rooms. Restaurant, gym. AE, D, DC, MC, V.*

The Connecticut River Valley and Hartford Essentials

BUS TRAVEL

Greyhound and Bonanza provide service to the Hartford area (☞ Coastal Connecticut Essentials).

CAR TRAVEL

By car take I–91 north from New Haven or I–84, which cuts diagonally southwest–northeast through the state. Head north along Route 9 from Old Saybrook for a scenic drive through this historic area.

TRAIN TRAVEL

Amtrak also provides service to the Hartford area.

➤ TRAIN INFORMATION: **Amtrak** (☏ 800/872–7245).

VISITOR INFORMATION

➤ TOURIST INFORMATION: **Connecticut River Valley and Shoreline Visitors Council** (✉ 393 Main St., Middletown 06457, ☏ 860/347–0028 or 800/486–3346, WEB www.ctrivershore.org). **Greater Hartford Tourism District** (✉ 234 Murphy Rd., Hartford 06114, ☏ 860/244–8181 or 800/793–4480, WEB www.enjoyhartford.com).

DELAWARE

Updated by Anne Dubuisson Anderson

Capital	Dover
Population	796,000
Motto	Liberty and Independence
State Bird	Blue hen
State Flower	Peach blossom
Postal Abbreviation	DE

Statewide Visitor Information

Delaware State Visitor Center (✉ 406 Federal St., Dover 19901, ☎ 302/739–4266, WEB www.destatemuseums.org/vc). **Delaware Tourism Office** (✉ 99 Kings Hwy., Dover 19901, ☎ 866/284–7483, WEB www.state.de.us/tourism). **Visitor centers:** I–95, between Exits 1 and 3 (☎ 302/737–4059); at Delaware Memorial Bridge (☎ 302/571–6340); and north of Smyrna, on U.S. 13 north (☎ 302/653–8910).

Scenic Drives

From Wilmington's western edge, a **30-mi loop** follows winding Route 100 past well-screened estates, a state park, and the meandering Brandywine Creek; then into Pennsylvania on a busy section of U.S. 1 W, which takes you past several historical attractions; and finally back into Delaware, where you'll travel on Route 52 (locally called Château Country) to villages lined with antiques shops, to horse farms, and to Winterthur, a du Pont estate turned museum.

A drive south along **Route 9** from New Castle to Dover across creeks on one-lane bridges and onto side roads follows the **Coastal Heritage Greenway,** with site markings for tidal marshes, bird sanctuaries, and the nearby historic villages of **Odessa, Port Penn,** and **Delaware City.**

National and State Parks

National Parks

Bombay Hook National Wildlife Refuge (✉ 2591 Whitehall Neck Rd., Smyrna 19977, ☎ 302/653–6872), more than 15,000 acres of ponds and fields, is filled between April and November with both resident and migrating waterfowl. Smaller than Bombay Hook, **Prime Hook National Wildlife Refuge** (✉ Rte. 236, just off Rte. 16 [R.D. 3, Box 195, Milton 19968], ☎ 302/684–8419) is a well-developed preserve with boat ramps, canoe trails, and a boardwalk trail through marshes.

State Parks

Fourteen parks run by the **Delaware Division of Parks and Recreation** (✉ 89 Kings Hwy., Richardson and Robbins Bldg., Dover 19901, ☎ 302/739–4702, WEB www.destateparks.com) are set up for hiking, fishing, and picnicking. The chief inland parks, with freshwater ponds, add seasonal boat rentals to basic amenities. All parks are free from October through April; they charge $2.50 per Delaware car or $5 per out-of-state car on weekends and holidays in October and daily from May through September.

Brandywine Creek State Park (✉ Rtes. 92 and 100 [Box 3782, Wilmington 19807], ☎ 302/577–3534), about 5 mi from Wilmington, is the state's best picnic park. It has more than 1,000 acres of open fields and wooded grounds, a nature center, 12 mi of hiking trails, and perfect sledding slopes in winter. **Cape Henlopen** (✉ 42 Cape Henlopen Dr., Lewes 19958, ☎ 302/645–8983) contains more than 150 pinelands campsites. Its Seaside Nature Center has marine tanks and sea-life displays. **Bellevue State Park** (✉ 800 Carr Rd., Wilmington 19809, ☎ 302/577–3390), once a du Pont family estate, offers summer concerts, horseback riding, and tennis. **Delaware Seashore State Park** (✉ 850 Inlet, Rehoboth Beach 19971, ☎ 302/227–2800; 302/227–3071 for marina) has both ocean surf and calm bay waters, large bathhouses with showers, and nearly 400 campsites with hookups. More than 70 campsites are at **Lums Pond State Park** (✉ U.S. 301 and Rte. 71 south of Newark; 1068 Howell School Rd., Bear 19701, ☎ 302/368–6989), site of Delaware's largest freshwater pond. **Trap Pond State Park** (✉ off Rte. 24 east of Laurel [R.D. 2, Box 331, Laurel 19956], ☎ 302/875–5153) includes part of the Great Cypress Swamp and has rowboats, kayaks, and canoes for rent. **Killens Pond State Park** (✉ 5025 Kellens Pond Rd., Felton 19943, ☎ 302/284–4526) has a 66-acre millpond for boating and fishing, plus a water park, campground, and 11 rustic cabins, which are available for overnight rental.

WILMINGTON

Wilmington, the state's commercial hub and largest city, was founded in 1638 as a Swedish settlement and successively taken over by the Dutch and the English. More recently it has been populated by employees of du Pont's company headquarters, credit-card banks, and nearby poultry ranches. The city has handsome buildings done in such styles as Federal, Greek Revival, Queen Anne, and Art Deco, as well as abundant cultural attractions. Outside the compact city center are several outstanding museums, including some that are legacies of the du Ponts.

Two nearby towns—Newark, home of the University of Delaware, and New Castle, the state's beautifully restored colonial capital—are linked to Wilmington by a few miles of neighborhoods and strip malls. The wide ribbon of I–95, which crosses the state, connects Wilmington at the eastern edge to Newark at the western border. It's unfortunate that this nondescript 20-minute drive is all many travelers ever see of the First State (so named because it was the first state to ratify the Constitution).

Exploring Wilmington

The four-block **Market Street Mall** marks the city center. The **Grand Opera House** (✉ 818 N. Market St. Mall, ☎ 302/658–7897, WEB www.grandopera.org) is a working theater that also hosts jazz, classical, and pop performances. Built by the Masonic Order in 1871 and restored a hundred years later, the four-story Grand's facade is cast iron painted white in French Second Empire style to mimic the old Paris Opéra. The adjoining Giacco Building houses a smaller theater and art galleries.

The **Delaware History Museum,** in a restored 1940s Woolworth's building, has three galleries and changing historical exhibits. The museum is also headquarters for the **Historical Society of Delaware.** ✉ *504 Market St.,* ☎ *302/656–0637.* *$4. Closed Sun.–Mon.*

The **Hercules Building** (✉ 1313 N. Market St., ☎ 302/594–5000), north of the mall, was built in the 1980s with ziggurat walls and a 20-ft-diameter clock. The core of the building is a 14-story atrium, with ground-level shops and a jungle of plants.

East of the mall and surrounded by some of the city's poorest neighborhoods is a monument to the 1638 landing of a Swedish expedition; it marks the first permanent settlement in the Delaware Valley. Two

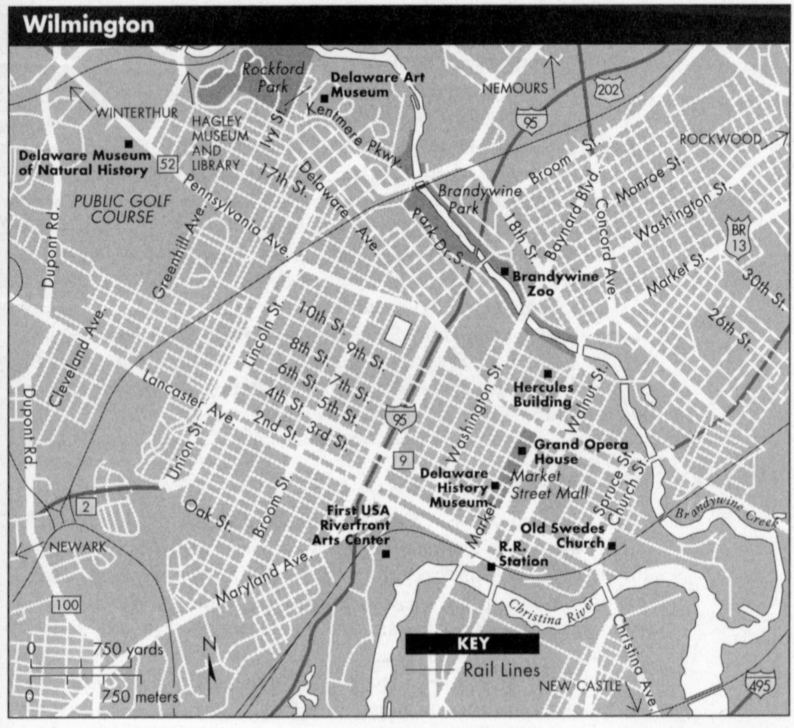

nearby 17th-century structures are worth a visit. **Old Swedes Church,** built in 1698, retains its original hipped roof and high wooden pulpit and is still used regularly for religious services. The **Hendrickson House Museum,** a farmhouse built in 1690 by Swedish settlers and now used for church offices and as a museum, is furnished with period pieces. ✉ *606 Church St.,* ☎ *302/652–5629.* 🎫 *Free.*

★ Children who visit the **Delaware Museum of Natural History** (✉ 4840 Kennett Pike, ☎ 302/658–9111, WEB www.delmnh.org; 🎫 $5), 5 mi northwest of Wilmington, can explore the mysteries of Australia's Great Barrier Reef and examine an African water hole, dinosaur replicas, and a 500-pound clam. The museum's hands-on, interactive discovery room encourages children to use all their senses.

The **Delaware Art Museum,** a few miles west of the city center and I–95, houses a major collection of post-1840 American paintings and illustrations, including works by major figures such as Homer, Eakins, Hopper, N. C. Wyeth, John Sloan, and illustrator Howard Pyle, as well as the foremost assemblage of English Pre-Raphaelite paintings and decorative arts in the United States. Children create their own masterpieces in the children's gallery. ✉ *2301 Kentmere Pkwy.,* ☎ *302/571–9590,* WEB *www.delart.mus.de.us.* 🎫 *$7. Closed Mon.*

Nemours Mansion and Gardens, on the grounds of the Alfred I. du Pont Hospital for Children, gives evidences of the Alfred du Pont family's preference for fine automobiles, European antiques, Louis XVI–style architecture, and formal French gardens. The estate, a 102-room mansion on 300 acres, is open only to those 12 and over. ✉ *1600 Rockland Rd.,* ☎ *302/651–6912,* WEB *www.nemours.org.* 🎫 *$10. Reservations essential. Closed Mon. and Dec.–Apr.*

The **Hagley Museum and Library,** where the first du Pont gunpowder mills still stand, offers a glimpse of the du Ponts at work and an enlightening look at the development of early industrial America. You can tour the mills, a 19th-century machine shop, and the family home and gardens, all set on 240 acres. ✉ *Rte. 141,* ☎ *302/658–2400,* WEB *www.hagley.lib.de.us.* 🎫 *$8. Hrs vary seasonally.*

The **First USA Riverfront Arts Center** (✉ 800 S. Madison St., ☎ 302/425–3929 or 888/862–2787, WEB www.riverfrontwilmington.com/arts; 🎫 varies with exhibition), which hosts major touring art and artifact exhibitions, was constructed in 1998 as the first step in the revitalization of Wilmington's waterfront. It has no permanent displays. Tickets must be purchased in advance for a specific date and entry time.

Outside Wilmington

New Castle, 5 mi south of Wilmington on Route 9, is a barely commercialized gem of a town with restored colonial houses, cobblestone streets, and historic sites along the Delaware River. William Penn's first landing in North America is memorialized in **Battery Park.** Two blocks west of the waterfront, the **New Castle Courthouse,** Delaware's colonial capital until 1777, is a pristine museum of state history, with three brick wings and a white cupola and spire. ✉ *211 Delaware St.,* ☎ *302/322–4453.* 🎫 *Free. Closed Mon.*

New Castle's **George Read II House and Gardens** and formal gardens was built in 1801 in Federal style by a signer of both the Declaration of Independence and the Constitution. Twelve rooms of the big brick house are open, including three furnished in period style. ✉ *42 The Strand,* ☎ *302/322–8411.* 🎫 *$4. Closed Mon., and weekdays Jan.–Feb.*

★ **Winterthur Museum, Garden, and Library** (✉ Rte. 52, Winterthur, ☎ 302/888–4600 or 800/448–3883, WEB www.winterthur.org; 🎫 varies depending on tour and season) focuses on Henry Francis du Pont's passion for collecting furniture and decorative arts made or used in America from 1640 to 1860. The nine-story, 175-room hillside stucco mansion and museum wing contain one of the nation's finest collections of decorative arts, with furniture, silver, paintings, and textiles in period settings. There are three exhibition galleries and an elegant pavilion that houses the museum shop and glass-enclosed restaurant. The 966 acres of naturalistic gardens showcase native and exotic plants. The 3-acre Enchanted Woods is a fantasy-theme children's garden.

Parks, Gardens, and Zoos

In **Brandywine Park** (✉ 1021 W. 18th St.), shady paths pass colonial stone walls and a tiny brick church that was built in 1740 and used for British wounded during the Revolutionary War. Lush Brandywine Creek and a millrace attract fishermen and splash-happy children. Wilmington's Brandywine Zoo tucks outdoor exhibits into cliffs along Brandywine Creek. ✉ *1001 N. Park Dr.,* ☎ *302/571–7747.* 🎫 *$3 Apr.–Oct., free Nov.–Mar. Exotic-animal house closed Nov.–Mar.*

Rockwood Museum (✉ 610 Shipley Rd., ☎ 302/761–4340; 🎫 free), inside a Gothic manor house, displays 19th-century decorative arts and furnishings. The museum is on a 19th-century country estate with 6 acres of landscaped grounds and 62 acres of woodlands.

Dining

$$$–$$$$ ★ ✕ **Green Room.** At the Hotel du Pont, French cuisine is served in Edwardian splendor under massive chandeliers and a gold-encrusted ceiling. Seafood entrées such as sautéed sea scallops over tomato fettuccine and crab cakes with chive oil and deep-fried leeks are especially fine. Harp music accompanies formal dinners. The hotel's dark-paneled, smaller **Brandywine Room,** with original N. .C, Andrew, and Jamie Wyeth paintings on the wall, has a similar menu. Men are required to wear a jacket and tie for dinner. ✉ *Hotel du Pont, 11th and Market Sts.,* ☎ *302/594–3154. Reservations essential. AE, D, DC, MC, V.*

$$$–$$$$ ✕ **Restaurant 821.** This popular and stylish restaurant is furnished in warm colors with leather banquettes and slate floors. The changing menu, which makes use of the room's wood-burning oven, is Mediterranean-influenced and may include salmon chowder with oyster frites and braised short rib with roasted garlic polenta. ✉ *821 Market St.,* ☎ *302/652–8821. AE, D, DC, MC, V. Closed Sun.*

$$–$$$ ✕ **Deep Blue.** Ultramodern, airy, and convivial, this bar and bistro has eclectic offerings that include imaginatively prepared seafood, which may mean Atlantic salmon in a truffle crust or rockfish with pesto mashed potatoes and red peppers. The bar has an extensive microbrew selection on tap. ✉ *111 W. 11 St.,* ☎ *302/777–2040. AE, D, DC, MC, V. Closed Sun.*

$$–$$$ ✕ **Eclipse.** The innovative seasonal menu at this intimate bistro (a Wilmington favorite) has included grilled ostrich loin with fennel and Vidalia onion as well as lamb chops in a lingonberry and green peppercorn demiglace. ✉ *1020-B N. Union St.,* ☎ *302/658–1588. AE, MC, V.*

$–$$$ ★ ✕ **Jessop's Tavern & Colonial Restaurant.** In a tiny space near the waterfront that brings to mind an old-world pub, chef Tim Bell presents a comfort-food menu inspired by the region's English, Dutch, and Swedish founders. The rich oyster chowder, double-crusted chicken potpie, and crusty flat bread can be followed by an English bread pudding. ✉ *114 Delaware St., New Castle,* ☎ *302/322–6111. AE, MC, V. Closed Mon.*

$–$$$ ★ ✕ **Saigon Vietnam.** This authentic, well-run Vietnamese eatery is spacious and beautifully decorated. It's in a revived shopping center at the end of Main Street. Don't miss the crispy spring rolls, sweet yet spicy lemongrass chicken, or clay-cooked specialties. ✉ *207 Main St., Newark,* ☎ *302/737–1590. AE, D, DC, MC, V. Closed Mon.*

$$ ★ ✕ **Harry's Savoy Grill.** Residents come for the friendly service, great food, and warm feelings. The slow-roasted prime rib is a top seller, and in season (May–October) nobody does soft-shell crab better. ✉ *2020 Naamans Rd.,* ☎ *302/475–3000. AE, DC, MC, V.*

$$ ✕ **Iron Hill Brewery & Restaurant.** Good burgers, beer brewed on the premises, and a satisfying selection of regional American entrées make this place perfect for a casual meal. Don't miss the Louisiana barbecue shrimp and Jamaican jerk pork chop. ✉ *147 E. Main St., Newark,* ☎ *302/266–9000. AE, D, MC, V.*

Lodging

Most Wilmington-area hotels are geared toward business. For variety there are restored colonial inns (not modern adaptations) and a few bed-and-breakfasts. **Bed & Breakfast of Delaware, Inc.** (✉ 2701 Landon Dr., Suite 200, Wilmington 19810, ☎ 302/479–9500), a reservation service, can help you locate moderately priced lodgings.

$$$–$$$$ **Hotel du Pont.** A Wilmington mainstay, this 12-story downtown hotel, owned by du Pont, has formal guest rooms decorated in earth tones with high ceilings, 18th-century reproduction furnishings, and original art. ✉ *11th and Market Sts., 19801,* ☎ *302/594–3100 or 800/441–9019,* FAX *302/594–3108,* WEB *www.dupont.com/hotel. 217 rooms. 3 restaurants, health club. AE, D, DC, MC, V.*

$$$–$$$$ ★ **Inn at Montchanin Village.** Eleven painstakingly restored 19th-century buildings that once housed du Pont gunpowder-mill workers make up this small luxury hotel. Each unique guest unit makes elegant use of antique reproduction furniture and luxurious linens. The village is only five minutes from the Winterthur Museum and Gardens, in the heart of Château Country. A full breakfast at Krazy Kat's, the inn's excellent four-star restaurant, is part of the room rates. ✉ *Rte. 100 and Kirk Rd., Montchanin 19710,* ☎ *302/888–2133 or 800/269–2473,* FAX *302/888–0389,* WEB *www.montchanin.com. 37 rooms. Restaurant. AE, D, DC, MC, V. BP.*

$–$$$ **Wyndham Hotel Wilmington.** Centrally located in downtown Wilmington, this modern hotel has rooms that are clean, comfortable, and reliable, making it a favorite of business travelers. ✉ *700 King St., 19801,* ☎ *302/655–0400 or 888/996–3426,* FAX *302/655–0430,* WEB *www.wyndham.com/Wilmington. 225 rooms. Restaurant, pool, health club. AE, D, DC, MC, V.*

$$ ★ **Brandywine Suites.** This former store, on a nondescript downtown block, has dramatic contemporary architecture, suites with rich traditional furnishings, and a popular lounge. ✉ *707 King St., 19801,* ☎ *302/656–9300,* FAX *302/656–2459. 49 suites. Restaurant. AE, DC, MC, V.*

$–$$ **Darley Manor Inn.** Once the home of Felix Darley, the mid-Victorian illustrator of titles including *The Scarlet Letter* and *Rip Van Winkle,* this inn now caters to business travelers and weekend visitors to the nearby Longwood Gardens and Brandywine Valley. Rooms have modern amenities, including data ports. ✉ *3701 Philadelphia Pike (U.S. 13), Claymont 19703,* ☎ *302/792–2127,* WEB *www.dca.net/darley. 6 rooms. AE, DC, MC, V. BP.*

$ **Fairfield Inn.** Close to the University of Delaware and about 9 mi west of Wilmington, this Marriott-owned inn is spartan but convenient. ✉ *65 Geoffrey Dr., Newark 19713,* ☎ *302/292–1500. 135 rooms. Pool. AE, D, DC, MC, V.*

$ **Terry House Bed and Breakfast.** In a Federal town house amid the other historic buildings of New Castle, this comfortable B&B has rooms with four-poster beds and an enormous garden overlooking the river. ✉ *130 Delaware St., New Castle 19720,* ☎ *302/322–2505,* WEB *www.terryhouse.com. 6 rooms. AE, D, MC, V. BP.*

Shopping

Newark's **Christiana Mall** (✉ Rte. 7 at I–95 Exit 4 south, ☎ 302/731–9815) has 130 stores, including Macy's, Lord and Taylor, and Strawbridge's. At **Concord Mall** (✉ 4737 Concord Pike, ☎ 302/478–9271) you'll find 95 stores and 3 department-store biggies: Strawbridge's, Sears, and Boscov's.

Wilmington Essentials

AIRPORTS AND TRANSFERS

Philadelphia International Airport, about 30 mi north of downtown Wilmington, is served by all major U.S. and international airlines.

➤ AIRPORT INFORMATION: **Philadelphia International Airport** (PHL; ✉ 8000 Essington Ave., ☎ 217/937–6937).

AIRPORT TRANSFER

Taxi fare is about $25 to Wilmington.

BUS TRAVEL TO AND FROM WILMINGTON

➤ BUS INFORMATION: **Greyhound** (✉ 101 N. French St., ☎ 302/655–6111 or 800/231–2222).

CAR TRAVEL

Situated between Baltimore and Philadelphia, Wilmington is bisected by I–95 north–south and linked to small-town Pennsylvania by U.S. 202 and Routes 52 and 41.

PARKING

Downtown parking is moderately priced in garages and impossible to find on the streets in the jam-packed office district.

TRAIN TRAVEL

Wilmington Train Station has Amtrak service, as well as SEPTA commuter service to Philadelphia.

➤ TRAIN INFORMATION: **Amtrak** (☎ 800/872–7245). **SEPTA** (☎ 215/580–7800). **Wilmington Train Station** (✉ Martin Luther King Blvd. and French St., ☎ 302/429–6523).

TRANSPORTATION AROUND WILMINGTON

Downtown is compact enough to stroll, but visits to New Castle, Newark, or the museums and parks ringing Wilmington require a car. Buses are geared to commuters, not explorers.

VISITOR INFORMATION

➤ TOURIST INFORMATION: **Convention and Visitors Bureau** (✉ 100 W. 10th St., 19801-1661, ☎ 302/652–4088 or 800/422–1181, WEB www.wilmcvb.org). **New Castle Historical Society** (✉ 2 E. 4th St., New Castle 19720, ☎ 302/322–8932, WEB www.newcastlecity.net).

THE ATLANTIC COAST

Whether you have a day, a weekend, or the whole summer, a visit to Delaware's beaches will likely be a highlight of a trip to the First State. From Cape Henlopen State Park, at the northern end, to Fenwick Island, at the southern border, are 23 mi of Atlantic shoreline. The main route south gets you to shore points the fastest, but if you have time, drive scenic Route 9 (it runs from New Castle to Dover) between farm fields and stands of 10-ft-high grasses. The prettiest stretch of shoreline is south of Dewey Beach, where sand dunes and wide, white-sand Atlantic beaches are just an arm's reach from Route 1.

Exploring the Atlantic Coast

There is ample public access to the Atlantic surf and to the 23 mi of sand, though crowds pour in from Washington, D.C., and points west on holidays and summer weekends. The Broadkill River, Rehoboth Bay, Indian River Bay, and Little Assawoman Bay have sheltered coves.

Just west of the beaches are some of the state's historic villages and scenic bay-side parks. **Milton,** at the head of the Broadkill River, was once a major shipbuilding center: the whole downtown area is now a historic district of 18th- and 19th-century architecture, including old cypress-shingle houses. **Lewes,** a 1631 Dutch settlement at the mouth of Delaware Bay, cherishes its seafaring past with a marine museum and draws visitors with good restaurants, shops, and lodging away from the hectic beach resorts.

Coastal towns include **Rehoboth Beach,** the largest, with a busy boardwalk for strolling and shopping. Rehoboth is the main gay getaway destination for the Middle Atlantic region. Next door is **Dewey Beach,** popular with young singles. **Bethany Beach, South Bethany,** and **Fenwick Island** (founded as a church camp and known for its fishing), south of the Indian River inlet, are quieter resorts.

Dining and Lodging

Once upon a time this sleepy resort area was full of basic motels and guest houses with kitchens that served generic fried seafood and burgers. Today, the coast is lined with swank hotels and restaurants run by talented young chefs. Rehoboth Beach is the center of the culinary boom, which has spread as far north as Milford and southward to the state line at Fenwick Island.

Bethany Beach

$$$ ✕ **Sedona.** Among the restaurant's creative dishes are grilled ahi tuna, spicy almond-encrusted salmon, and West Texas crab cakes with Santa Fe salsa. The casual interior makes use of tan walls and soft light. ✉ *26 Pennsylvania Ave.,* ☎ *302/539–1200. AE, DC, MC, V. Closed Nov.–Jan., Mon. and Wed.*

Dewey Beach

$$–$$$ ✕ **Rusty Rudder.** In this barnlike, nautical-theme space overlooking Rehoboth Bay, the specialties are down-home service and local seafood, such as crab imperial. A land-and-sea buffet of seafood and chicken specialties is served every Friday year-round and several times weekly during summer months. There's also a Sunday brunch. ✉ *113 Dickinson St., on the bay,* ☎ *302/227–3888. AE, D, DC, MC, V.*

$$$–$$$$ **Best Western Gold Leaf.** A half block from the beach and across the street from the bay, the rooms here are traditionally styled; some have water views. ✉ *1400 Rte. 1, 19971,* ☎ *302/226–1100 or 800/422–8566,* FAX *302/226–9785,* WEB *www.bestwesterngoldleaf.com. 75 rooms. Pool. AE, D, DC, MC, V.*

Lewes

$–$$$ ✕ **Lazy Susan's.** For the fattest, sweetest steamed blue-shell crabs, this simple roadside eatery is the place. Eating inside can be stifling, and the outside deck overlooks the highway, so takeout may be your best bet. Call ahead to make sure the crabs are fresh. ✉ *Rte. 1 at Tenley Ct., Lewes,* ☎ *302/645–5115. MC, V.*

$–$$$$ **Inn at Canal Square.** Valued for its waterfront location, this modern B&B was built to fit in with its older neighbors. Most rooms have balconies overlooking the harbor. ✉ *122 Market St., 19958,* ☎ *302/644–3377 or 888/644–1911,* FAX *302/645–7083,* WEB *www.beachnet.com/canalsquare. 19 rooms. AE, MC, V. CP.*

$$ ★ **Zwaanendael Inn.** The former New Devon Inn, built in 1926 and listed in the National Register of Historic Places, has been refurbished and updated with a restaurant. There are now data ports and two phone lines in every room. The lobby and parlor hold many fine Early American pieces. ✉ *142 2nd St. (Box 516, 19958),* ☎ *302/645–6466 or 800/824–8754,* FAX *302/645–7196,* WEB *www.zwaanendaelinn.com. 23 rooms. Restaurant, health club. AE, D, MC, V.*

Milford

$–$$ ★ **Inns on the Mispillion.** The Marshall House, a restored Victorian bank building, and the Towers, on the National Register of Historic Places, make up this hotel. Both have traditionally decorated guest rooms, some with fireplaces. ✉ *112 N.W. Front St., 19963,* ☎ *800/366–3814,* WEB *www.mispillion.com. 9 rooms. Restaurant. DC, MC, V. BP.*

$ **Traveler's Inn Motel.** Rooms in this two-story, balconied motel are plain, with two double beds and minimal furnishings (a hanging rack, no closet). ✉ *1036 N. Walnut St., 19963,* ☎ *302/422–8089. 38 rooms. AE, MC, V.*

Rehoboth Beach

$$$–$$$$ ★ ✕ **La La Land.** In a tiny beach house, this magic-theme restaurant serves eclectic French–cum–Southwest–meets–Pacific Rim cuisine. Try lobster-claw risotto or the homemade corn–and–ricotta ravioli. ✉ *22 Wilmington Ave.,* ☎ *302/227–3887. AE, DC, MC, V. Closed Mon.–Wed.*

$$–$$$ ★ ✕ **Dogfish Head Brewing and Eats.** Delaware's first brewpub, Dogfish Head is owned by two young entrepreneurs who keep everyone happy with a changing menu of in-house brews, pizzas, and musical performers. ✉ *320 Rehoboth Ave.,* ☎ *302/226–2739. AE, MC, V. Closed Tues.–Wed.*

$$–$$$ ✕ **Sydney's Blues and Jazz.** New Orleans–influenced American cooking issues from the kitchen, including such specialties as oysters Rockefeller and authentic gumbo and jambalaya. Wine-flight tastings—samples of three wines served in small portions—are also offered. The innovative "grazing" menu is great for light eaters; the bar menu features po'boys. There's live blues and jazz music on Wednesday, Friday, and Saturday. ✉ *25 Christian St.,* ☎ *302/227–1339 or 800/808–1924. AE, D, DC, MC, V. Closed Mon.–Tues.*

$ ✕ **Nicola's Pizza.** Home of the original Nic-O-Boli, this family-run pizzeria ships its trademarked neo-stromboli all over the world to demanding fans. The bustling shop is packed until the wee hours of the morning. ✉ *8 N. 1st St.,* ☎ *302/227–6211. MC, V.*

$$$–$$$$ 🏨 **Brighton Suites.** Each spacious suite has a living room and fully equipped kitchen; the bedrooms have either a king bed or two doubles. ✉ *34 Wilmington Ave., 19971,* ☎ *302/227–5780 or 800/227–5788,* WEB *www.brightonsuites.com. 66 suites. Pool. AE, D, DC, MC, V.*

$–$$$$ 🏨 **Boardwalk Plaza Hotel.** The most deluxe hotel on the boardwalk has grand Victorian trappings. You can breakfast on a terrace right on the boardwalk, and those staying on the fourth floor have the use of a rooftop pool. ✉ *2 Olive Ave., 19971,* ☎ *302/227–7169 or 800/332–3224,* WEB *www.boardwalkplaza.com. 84 rooms. Restaurant, pool, gym. AE, D, MC, V.*

Outdoor Activities and Sports

Fishing

Charter boats for either deep-sea or bay (trout, bluefish) fishing can be booked for either day or half-day trips, which include all the gear. Book through your hotel or try **Fisherman's Wharf** (✉ Lewes, ☎ 302/645–8862). The **Delaware Division of Fish and Wildlife** (☎ 302/739–5296, WEB www.dnrec.state.de.us) has information on boating and fishing access areas.

Water Sports

Marinas on Rehoboth Bay and Delaware Bay (at Lewes) rent sailboards, sailboats, and motorboats. Catamarans are for rent at **Fenwick Island State Park** (✉ ½ mi north of Fenwick Island on Rte. 1, ☎ 302/539–9060).

Shopping

On the Atlantic coast bargain hunters scour the shops at **Rehoboth Outlets** (✉ Rte. 1, Rehoboth Beach, ☎ 302/226–9223), a manufacturers' outlet center where the 140 stores sprawl along both sides of the busy, four-lane highway. Farther north, on the southbound side of the highway, the same owner operates a 35-unit outlet mall that is anchored by an L. L. Bean factory store. Just north of Lewes is the **Lighthouse Outlet** (✉ 753 Rte. 1, Lewes, ☎ 302/645–1207), which sells discounted fixtures and ceiling fans.

The Atlantic Coast Essentials

BOAT AND FERRY TRAVEL

Cape May–Lewes Ferry makes a 70-minute ride from Cape May, New Jersey, to Lewes, Delaware. Passage for a car and driver is $18 November–April and $20 May–October. Pedestrian travelers and additional car passengers both cost $6.50 November–April and $4.50 May–October.

➤ BOAT AND FERRY INFORMATION: **Cape May–Lewes Ferry** (☎ 302/644–6030).

BUS TRAVEL

Greyhound links Rehoboth Beach with Wilmington, New Castle, and Dover.

➤ BUS INFORMATION: **Greyhound** (☎ 800/231–2222).

CAR TRAVEL

From the north take I–95 S to U.S. 13 S (in Wilmington). Then pick up U.S. 113 at Dover and take it to Route 1 (in Milford). From the south the scenic route to Delaware's northern shores crosses Chesapeake Bay at Annapolis and continues east via U.S. 301/50; follows U.S. 50 to Route 404 at Wye Mills, Maryland; then crosses Delaware on Routes 404, 18, and 9 to Route 1 at Lewes.

MEDIA

NEWSPAPERS AND MAGAZINES

Delaware Today magazine, published monthly, covers events and restaurants throughout the state.

➤ CONTACT: ***Delaware Today*** (☎ 302/656–1809 or 800/285–0400, WEB www.delawaretoday.com).

VISITOR INFORMATION

➤ TOURIST INFORMATION: **Bethany-Fenwick Chamber of Commerce** (✉ Rte. 1 N, Fenwick Island [Box 1450, Bethany Beach 19930], ☎ 302/539–2100 or 800/962–7873, WEB www.bethany-fenwick.org).

Lewes Chamber of Commerce (✉ Savannah Rd. and Kings Hwy. [Box 1, Lewes 19958], ☎ 302/645–8073, WEB www.leweschamber.com). **Milton Chamber of Commerce** (✉ 104 Federal St., Milton 19968, ☎ 302/684–1101, WEB www.historicmilton.com).

Rehoboth Beach–Dewey Beach Chamber of Commerce (✉ 501 Rehoboth Ave. [Box 216, Rehoboth Beach 19971], ☎ 302/227–2233 or 800/441–1329, WEB www.beach-fun.com).

ELSEWHERE IN DELAWARE

Dover

What to See and Do

An oasis of colonial preservation in a busy government center, the **capitol complex** historic area is on a square laid out in 1722 according to William Penn's 1683 plan. Information about Delaware's historic sites and attractions is available at the **Delaware State Visitor Center** (✉ 406 Federal St., 19901, ☎ 302/739–4266); the **Sewell C. Biggs Museum of American Art** (WEB www.biggsmuseum.org; 🎫 free), in the building's upper floors, houses an impressive collection of 20th-century decorative art and paintings, as well as art from earlier eras.

The **John Dickinson Plantation** (✉ 340 Kitts Hummock Rd., ☎ 302/739–3277) gives visitors a glimpse of 18th-century plantation life in Kent County, Delaware. A horse-drawn wagon, a crop duster, threshers, a corn house, and a privy are some tools and structures exhibited at the **Delaware Agricultural Museum and Village** (✉ 866 N. du Pont Hwy., ☎ 302/734–1618). A re-created 1890s village and farmstead, the operation is devoted to Delaware's rich agrarian past and present (agriculture is still the state's number one industry).

Had enough culture? Then head straight for **Dover Downs International Speedway** (✉ north of Dover on U.S. 13, ☎ 302/674–4600), where the grandstands can handle up to 5,000 spectators for NASCAR and harness racing; there's also a casino.

Dining and Lodging

$–$$$ ✕ **Where Pigs Fly.** With family-style food that's a notch above most, this is a kid-friendly place that's easy on the wallet. Try the "pulled pig" (tender hickory smoked pork pulled from the bone) or the baby back ribs. ✉ *617 E. Loockerman St., at U.S. 13,* ☎ *302/678–0586. AE, D, DC, MC, V.*

$$–$$$ 🏨 **Sheraton Dover Hotel.** Convenient, comfortable, and well appointed, the Sheraton also has spacious meeting rooms and a conference center. ✉ *1570 N. du Pont Hwy., 19901,* ☎ *302/678–8500 or 800/325–3535,* FAX *302/678–9073,* WEB *www.sheratondover.com. 153 rooms. Restaurant, pool, health club. AE, D, DC, MC, V.*

Dover Essentials

BUS TRAVEL

DART, a statewide public bus system, serves Wilmington, Newark, Middletown, Dover, and the Atlantic beaches, with various intermediate points.

➤ BUS INFORMATION: DART (☎ 800/652–3278).

CAR TRAVEL

The north and south approaches to Dover are on U.S. 13; Route 10 links it with Goldsboro, Maryland; Route 1 bypasses Dover and heads toward Dover from the coastal towns.

FLORIDA

Updated by Jennie Hess, Diane Marshall, Rowland Stiteler

Capital	Tallahassee
Population	15, 982, 378
Motto	In God We Trust
State Bird	Mockingbird
State Flower	Orange blossom
Postal Abbreviation	FL

Statewide Visitor Information

Florida Division of Tourism (✉ 661 E. Jefferson St., Suite 300, Tallahassee 32301, ☎ 850/488–5607 or 888/735–2872, WEB www.flausa.com). **Information centers:** on U.S. 231 in Campbellton–Graceville, I–75 near Jennings, I–10 at Pensacola, I–95 near Yulee, and in the lobby of the capitol in Tallahassee.

Scenic Drives

In **Everglades National Park** the 38-mi drive from the Main Visitor Center to Flamingo reveals a patchwork of ecosystems, including mangrove and cypress forests and saw-grass marshes. Although traffic jams abound during the winter, the **Overseas Highway** (U.S. 1) from Key Largo to Key West has spectacular views of the Atlantic, Florida Bay, the Gulf of Mexico, and the myriad islands of the Keys. **Route 789,** along the Gulf Coast south from Holmes Beach in Bradenton to Lido Beach in Sarasota and from Casey Key south of Osprey to Nokomis Beach, passes over several picturesque barrier islands. Along the Atlantic coast, north of Jacksonville, the **Buccaneer Trail** (Route A1A) from Mayport to the old seaport town of Fernandina Beach passes through marshlands and along pristine beaches. **U.S. 98** winds east from historic Pensacola through the lush coastal landscape of the Panhandle.

National and State Parks

National Parks

Everglades National Park (✉ Main Visitor Center, 40001 Rte. 9336, Homestead 33034, ☎ 305/242–7700) is in Homestead, south of Miami. **Biscayne National Park** (✉ 9700 S.W. 328th St. [Box 1369, Homestead 33090], ☎ 305/230–7275) is near Everglades National Park, south of Miami. In southwestern Florida **Big Cypress National Preserve** (✉ 20 mi east of Ochopee on U.S. 41 [HCR 61, Box 110, Ochopee 33943], ☎ 941/695–2000 or 941/262–1066), noted for the bald and dwarf cypress trees that line its marshlands, is a sanctuary for alligators, bald eagles, and the endangered Florida panther.

Florida has three national forests. The 556,500-acre **Apalachicola National Forest** (✉ north of Apalachicola and west of Tallahassee and U.S. 319, [Apalachicola Ranger District, Box 579, Bristol 32321], ☎ 850/643–2282) is great for canoeing and hiking and has a recreational facility designed for people with disabilities. **Ocala National Forest** (✉ Forest Visitor Center, 10863 E. Rte. 40, Silver Springs 34488, ☎ 904/625–7470) has lakes, springs, hiking trails, campgrounds, and historic sites. **Osceola National Forest** (✉ Osceola Ranger District, 10090 Rte. 90 [Box 70, Olustee 32072], ☎ 904/752–2577) is dotted with cypress swamps and offers good fishing and hunting. In addition, the state has five national monuments, two national seashores, and eight national wildlife refuges.

State Parks

The state administers hundreds of parks, nature preserves, and historic sites. Among these are **Blackwater River State Park** (✉ Rte. 1 [Box 57C, Holt 32564], ☎ 850/623–2363), 40 mi northeast of Pensacola on I–10, popular with canoeists; **Delnor-Wiggins Pass State Recreation Area** (✉ 1100 Gulfshore Dr. N, Naples 33963, ☎ 941/597–6196), with miles of beaches, picnic areas, and fishing spots; **Florida Caverns State Park** (✉ 3345 Caverns Rd., Mariana 32446, ☎ 850/482–9598), two hours north of Panama City on Route 167, comprising 1,783 acres of caves and nature trails; **Ft. Clinch State Park** (☞ Elsewhere in Florida, *below*); **St. Andrews State Recreation Area** (✉ 4415 Thomas Dr., Panama City Beach 32408, ☎ 850/233–5140), in the Panhandle, encompassing 1,038 acres of beaches, pinewoods, and marshes for swimming, pier fishing, and dune hiking; and the **John Pennekamp Coral Reef State Park** (✉ U.S. Hwy. 1, MM 102.5 [Box 487, Key Largo 33037], ☎ 305/451–1202), with the only coral reef in the continental United States. For more information contact the **Florida Department of Natural Resources** (✉ Marjory Stoneman Douglas Bldg., MS 525, 3900 Commonwealth Blvd., Tallahassee 32399, ☎ 904/488–9872) or go to WEB www.funandsun.com/parks.

MIAMI

Running with the energy and passion of Rio, Monte Carlo, and Hemingway's Paris, Miami is arguably the most exotic city that you can visit without a passport. More than half of its population is Hispanic in origin, and Miami is sometimes called the capital of Latin America. Indeed, Miami is a city of superlatives. This ever-growing metropolis has one of the busiest airports and cruise-ship ports in the world; more than 150 companies base their international operations here; four professional sports teams attract the faithful; and fashion models are photographed for a worldwide audience. Add Miami's architectural treasures, exotic foods, and outdoor recreation, and you have America's favorite sun-drenched tropical playground.

Exploring Miami

Downtown

★ Begin your tour of downtown Miami at the **Miami-Dade Cultural Center** (✉ 101 W. Flagler St.), a 3.3-acre postmodern Mediterranean-style complex. You may recognize it from the movie *There's Something About Mary.* The elevated plaza provides a serene haven from the city's commotion, and within the complex are several arts venues, including the **Miami Art Museum** (MAM; ☎ 305/375–3000, WEB www.miamiartmuseum.org; 🎟 $5, with Historical Museum $6), which has both a permanent collection and major touring exhibitions focusing on work completed since 1945. The **Historical Museum of Southern Florida** (☎ 305/375–1492, WEB www.historical-museum.org; 🎟 $5), also in the cultural center, has artifacts including Tequesta and Seminole ceramics, a 1920s streetcar, cigar and citrus labels, and a railroad exhibit—pure Floridiana. Another cultural-center tenant, the **Main Public Library** (☎ 305/375–2665; 🎟 free) has nearly 4 million holdings and art exhibits in its auditorium and second-floor lobby.

Bayside Marketplace (☎ 305/577–3344; 🎟 free), between Bayfront Park and the entrance to the Port of Miami, is a massive waterside entertainment and shopping center that includes shops, outdoor cafés, and a food court. Street performers entertain throughout the day and evening, and free concerts take place every day of the year. Scenic boat tours and disco cruises also depart from here.

Mildred and Claude Pepper Bayfront Park (✉ Biscayne Blvd. between 2nd and 3rd Sts.) was an urban landfill in the 1920s; it now includes a memorial to the *Challenger* astronauts, two amphitheaters, and a fountain honoring the late Florida congressman Claude Pepper and his wife.

★ The beauty of the **Gusman Center for the Performing Arts** (✉ 174 E. Flagler St., ☎ 305/374–2444 information; 305/372–0925 box office), a former movie palace, is startling. The inside, with its cool, vivid colors, resembles a Moorish courtyard with twinkling stars. The Florida Philharmonic performs here year-round, except when the Miami Film Festival takes over in late January–early February. If the hall is closed, call the office and ask to take a look around.

Miami Beach

Made up of 17 islands in Biscayne Bay, Miami Beach is a separate city from Miami. In recent years this "American Riviera" has revived the ★ carefree spirit of the early 1920s by renewing its **South Beach** area. Today South Beach revels in world glory as a lure for models and millionaires. The hub of South Beach is the 1-square-mi **Art Deco District,** which stretches along Ocean Drive and is the most talked-about beachfront in America. About 800 significant buildings in the district are listed on the National Register of Historic Places—it's the nation's first 20th-century district to be honored as such.

Begin your tour of the Art Deco District at the **Art Deco District Welcome Center** (✉ 1001 Ocean Dr., ☎ 305/531–3484). Proceed north past pastel-hue Art Deco hotels (outlined in brilliant neon at night) on your left and the palm-fringed beach on your right. You'll also pass the magnificently restored **Casa Casuarina** (✉ 1114 Ocean Dr.), home of the late fashion designer Gianni Versace. The neighborhood's two main commercial streets are **Collins Avenue,** one block west of Ocean Drive, and, one block farther west, **Washington Avenue.** The latter is a colorful mix of Jewish, Cuban, Haitian, and more familiar American cultures, containing delicatessens, avant-garde stores, produce markets, shops selling religious artifacts, and many of the city's best restaurants and nightclubs. **Espanola Way,** off Washington, is a quaint avenue with a youth hostel, clubs, restaurants, and ethnic shops—a late-afternoon flea market is held here each Sunday. Three blocks north is the **Lincoln Road Mall,** a lively pedestrian shopping street with upscale restaurants, eclectic shops, and great people-watching.

The **Holocaust Memorial** (✉ 1933–1945 Meridian Ave., ☎ 305/538–1663, WEB www.holocaustmmb.org; 🎟 free), across from the Miami Beach Convention Center, is a chilling sculpture and a graphic record in memory of 6 million Jewish victims. The **Bass Museum of Art** (✉ 2121 Park Ave., ☎ 305/673–7530, WEB www.bassmuseum.org; 🎟 $5), four blocks north of South Beach proper, has a diverse collection of European works including pieces by Albrecht Dürer and Henri de Toulouse-Lautrec. A new expansion has doubled the museum's size to nearly 40,000 square ft. A 70,000-plus-item collection of modern de-★ sign and "propaganda arts" lies within the **Wolfsonian—Florida International University** (✉ 1001 Washington Ave., ☎ 305/531–1001, WEB www.wolfsonian.fiu.edu; 🎟 $5, free Thurs. 6–9), an elegantly renovated 1927 storage facility. The gallery is closed Wednesday.

The striking triumphal archway that looms on Collins Avenue is a mural of illusionary art by Richard Haas that depicts the **Fontainebleau Hilton Resort and Towers** (✉ 4441 Collins Ave., ☎ 305/538–2000), which actually sits behind it.

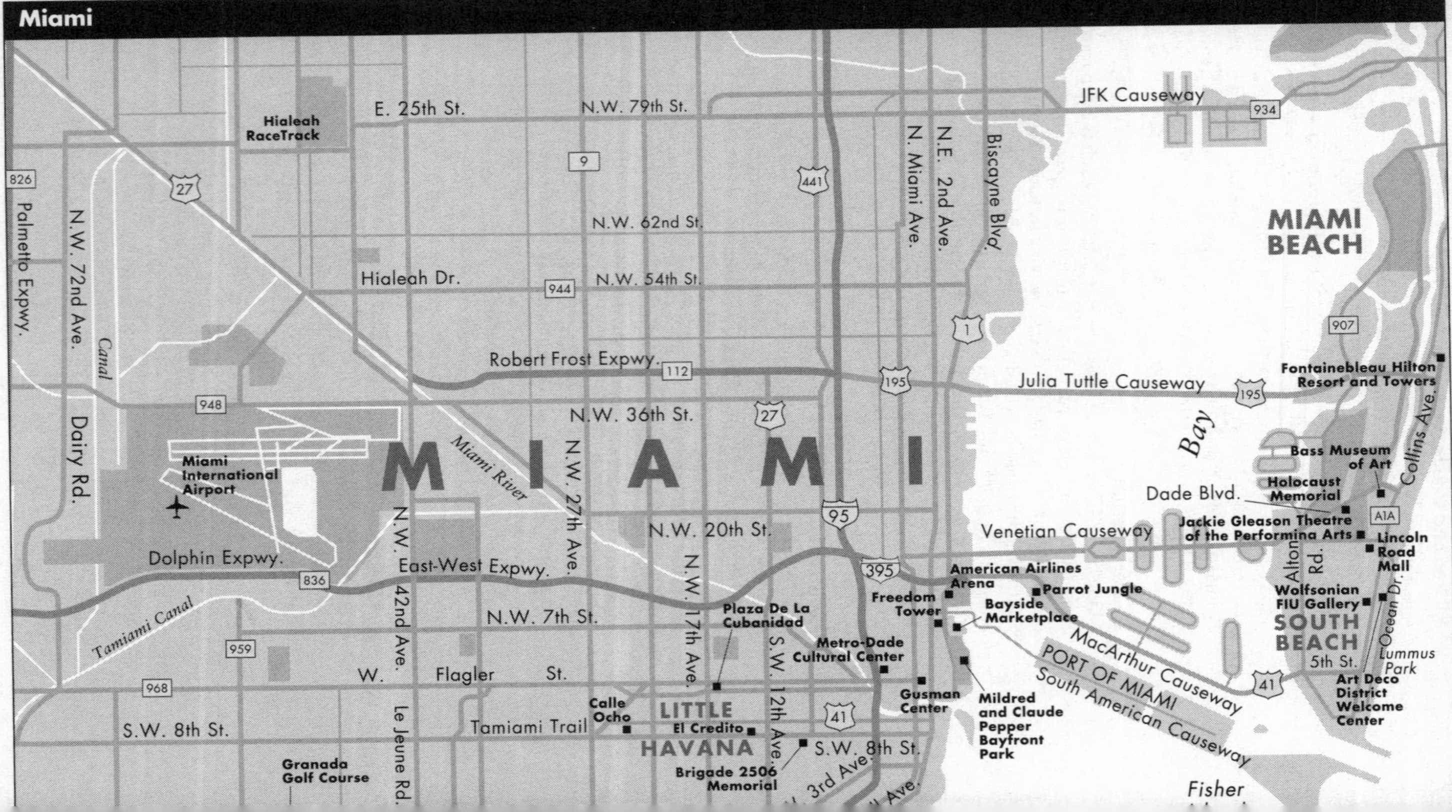

Miami
Hialeah RaceTrack
E. 25th St.
N.W. 79th St.
JFK Causeway
934
826
27
9
441
N.W. 62nd St.
MIAMI BEACH
Palmetto Expwy.
N.W. 72nd Ave.
Canal
Hialeah Dr.
944
N.W. 54th St.
N. Miami Ave.
N.E. 2nd Ave.
Biscayne Blvd.
1
907
Robert Frost Expwy.
112
195
Julia Tuttle Causeway
Fontainebleau Hilton Resort and Towers
948
N.W. 36th St.
Collins Ave.
Bay
Dairy Rd.
Miami International Airport
MIAMI
Miami River
N.W. 27th Ave.
Bass Museum of Art
Holocaust Memorial
Dade Blvd.
95
N.W. 20th St.
Jackie Gleason Theatre of the Performina Arts
A1A
Venetian Causeway
Lincoln Road Mall
Dolphin Expwy.
East-West Expwy.
836
395
American Airlines Arena
Parrot Jungle
Alton Rd.
Wolfsonian FIU Gallery
Freedom Tower
Bayside Marketplace
Ocean Dr.
Tamiami Canal
N.W. 42nd Ave.
N.W. 7th St.
Plaza De La Cubanidad
SOUTH BEACH
959
N.W. 17th Ave.
S.W. 12th Ave.
Metro-Dade Cultural Center
MacArthur Causeway
PORT OF MIAMI
5th St.
Lummus Park
W. Flagler St.
968
Gusman Center
Mildred and Claude Pepper Bayfront Park
South American Causeway
41
Art Deco District Welcome Center
Calle Ocho
LITTLE HAVANA
El Credito
S.W. 8th St.
Tamiami Trail
Le Jeune Rd.
S.W. 8th St.
Granada Golf Course
Brigade 2506 Memorial
3rd Ave.
Fisher

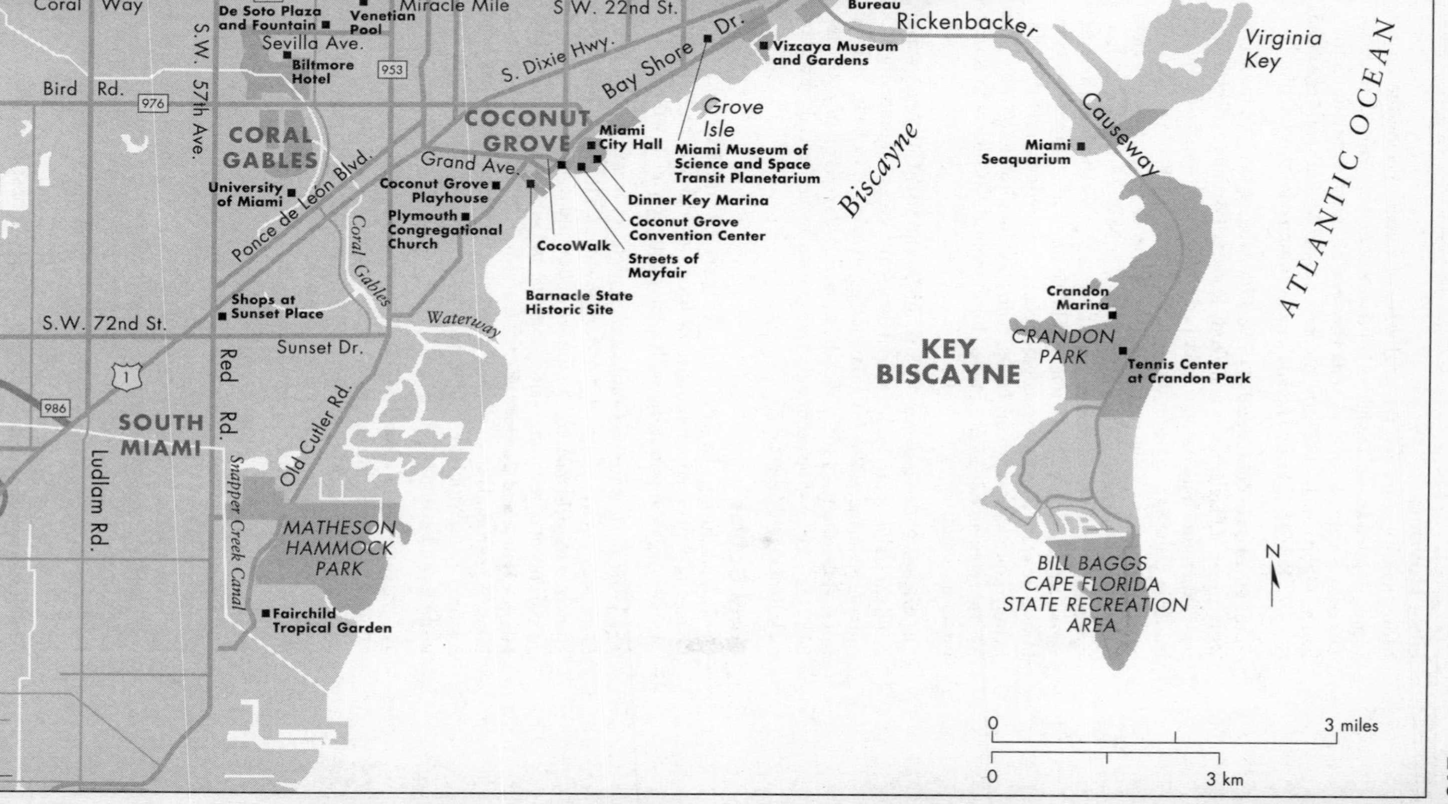
Coral Way
Miracle Mile
S.W. 22nd St.
De Soto Plaza and Fountain
Venetian Pool
Sevilla Ave.
Biltmore Hotel
Bird Rd.
976
953
S.W. 57th Ave.
S. Dixie Hwy.
Bay Shore Dr.
Bureau
Rickenbacker Causeway
Vizcaya Museum and Gardens
Virginia Key
ATLANTIC OCEAN
CORAL GABLES
COCONUT GROVE
Grove Isle
Miami City Hall
Miami Museum of Science and Space Transit Planetarium
Biscayne
Miami Seaquarium
Grand Ave.
University of Miami
Ponce de León Blvd.
Coconut Grove Playhouse
Plymouth Congregational Church
Dinner Key Marina
Coconut Grove Convention Center
CocoWalk
Streets of Mayfair
Barnacle State Historic Site
Coral Gables Waterway
Shops at Sunset Place
S.W. 72nd St.
Sunset Dr.
Crandon Marina
CRANDON PARK
KEY BISCAYNE
Tennis Center at Crandon Park
Red Rd.
1
986
SOUTH MIAMI
Old Cutler Rd.
Ludlam Rd.
Snapper Creek Canal
MATHESON HAMMOCK PARK
Fairchild Tropical Garden
BILL BAGGS CAPE FLORIDA STATE RECREATION AREA
N
0
3 miles
0
3 km

Little Havana

More than 40 years ago the tidal wave of Cubans fleeing the Castro regime flooded an older neighborhood west of downtown with refugees. The area became known as **Little Havana,** although today more than half a million Cubans live throughout the greater Miami area. **Calle Ocho** (✉ S.W. 8th St.) is Little Havana's main commercial thoroughfare.

At the **Plaza de la Cubanidad** (✉ S.W. 17th Ave.; 🎟 free), on the southwest corner of Flagler Street and Teddy Roosevelt Avenue, redbrick sidewalks surround a monument inscribed with words from José Martí, a leader in Cuba's struggle for independence from Spain: LAS PALMAS SON NOVIAS QUE ESPÉRAN (the palm trees are girlfriends who will wait). **Elián González's House** (✉ 2319 N.W. 2nd St., at N.W 23rd Ave.; 🎟 free) is where 6-year-old Gonzalez stayed for nearly six months after surviving a raft journey from Cuba that killed his mother. From this same house, he was removed by federal agents in a predawn raid that ultimately united him with his father, who took him home to Cuba. The Miami relatives have since moved but bought the property to turn it into a museum.

The **Brigade 2506 Memorial** (✉ S.W. 8th St. and S.W. 13th Ave.), which stands at Calle Ocho and Memorial Boulevard, commemorates the victims of the unsuccessful 1961 Bay of Pigs invasion of Cuba by an exile force. **El Credito** (✉ 1106 S.W. 8th St., ☎ 305/858–4162 or 800/726–9481) is a cigar shop seemingly transported from the Cuban capital lock, stock, and stogie.

Coral Gables

Developed during the 1920s by visionary George Merrick, Coral Gables is a planned community of broad boulevards and Spanish-Mediterranean architecture, with a busy commercial downtown.

The heart of downtown Coral Gables stretches from Douglas Road (37th Avenue) to LeJeune Road (42nd Avenue). This four-block area, known as **Miracle Mile,** has a mixture of boutiques, bridal salons, and an assortment of restaurants along the Mile and side streets. **Coral Gables Merrick House and Gardens** (✉ 907 Coral Way, ☎ 305/460–5361; 🎟 house $5, grounds free), George Merrick's boyhood home, has been restored to its original 1920s appearance and contains family furnishings and artifacts.

The dazzling **Biltmore Hotel** (✉ 1200 Anastasia Ave., ☎ 305/445–1926, WEB www.biltmorehotel.com), a replica of Seville's Giralda Tower, has a charming lobby, richly ornamented Beaux-Arts architecture, and the largest hotel swimming pool in the continental United States. On Sunday, free tours are offered at 1:30, 2:30, and 3:30 PM.

At Granada Boulevard and Sevilla Avenue you'll find the **De Soto Plaza and Fountain,** a classical column on a pedestal, with water flowing from ★ 👶 the mouths of four sculpted faces. This and the stunning **Venetian Pool** (✉ 2701 De Soto Blvd., ☎ 305/460–5356, WEB www.venetianpool.com; 🎟 $8, free parking across De Soto Blvd.) were designed by Merrick's artist-uncle, Denman Fink. The pool, on northeast-bound De Soto Boulevard, is a fantastic, fantasy-theme municipal pool created from a rock quarry.

The **University of Miami** (✉ off U.S. 1), with almost 14,000 students, is the largest private research university in the Southeast. On its 260-acre main campus is the **Lowe Art Museum** (✉ 1301 Stanford Dr., ☎ 305/284–3535; 🎟 $5; closed Mon.), which has a permanent collection of 8,000 works.

Coconut Grove

Coconut Grove is the oldest section of Miami, begun during the 1870s and annexed to the city in 1925. Its earliest settlers included New England intellectuals, bohemians, Bahamians, and—later—artists, writers, and scientists who established winter homes here. The Grove still reflects the pioneers' eclectic origins, with posh estates next to rustic cottages and starkly modern dwellings, all amid lush subtropical foliage. The tone of Coconut Grove today is upscale and urban.

Before exploring the restaurants and shops of the Grove, you may want to visit the **Plymouth Congregational Church** (✉ 3400 Devon Rd., ☎ 305/444–6521; 🎟 free), a handsome coral-rock Mexican mission–style structure dating from 1917. Also on the 11-acre grounds are natural sunken gardens; the first schoolhouse in Dade County (one room), which was moved to this property; and the site of the original Coconut Grove water and electric works. Main Highway returns you to the historic ★ **Village of Coconut Grove,** a trendy commercial district with redbrick sidewalks and more than 300 restaurants, stores, and art galleries. Parking is often a problem at night, so be prepared to walk several blocks to the heart of the district.

In Coconut Grove's village center is **CocoWalk** (✉ 3015 Grand Ave., ☎ 305/444–0777), a multilevel open mall of Mediterranean-style brick courtyards and terraces overflowing with restaurants, bars, movie theaters, and shops. The **Streets of Mayfair** (✉ 2911 Grand Ave., Coconut Grove, ☎ 305/448–1700), next to CocoWalk, is another entertainment and retail center. The Spanish rococo–style **Coconut Grove Playhouse** (✉ 3500 Main Hwy., ☎ 305/442–4000) opened in 1926 as a movie theater and now presents Broadway-bound plays, musical revues, and experimental productions. The **Barnacle State Historic Site** (✉ 3485 Main Hwy., ☎ 305/448–9445, WEB www.barnacle.cjb.net; 🎟 $1, concerts $5), a 19th-century pioneer residence, was built by Commodore Ralph Munroe in 1891. The house, which is open Friday and weekends, is the oldest in Miami still on its original site. If your timing is right, you may catch one of the monthly Moonlight Concerts.

North on Bayshore Drive is **Dinner Key Marina** (✉ 3400 Pan American Dr., ☎ 305/579–6980), Greater Miami's largest marina. Antiques, boat, and home furnishings shows are held annually at the 105,000-square-ft **Coconut Grove Convention Center** (✉ 2700 S. Bayshore Dr., ☎ 305/579–3310). **Miami City Hall** (✉ 3500 Pan American Dr., ☎ 305/250–5400; 🎟 free) is known for its nautical-motif Art Deco trim. It was built in 1934 as the terminal for the Pan American Airways seaplane base at Dinner Key. Sadly, the interior is now generic government design.

You can manipulate and marvel at the many hands-on sound, gravity, and electricity exhibits at the **Miami Museum of Science and Space Transit Planetarium** (✉ 3280 S. Miami Ave., ☎ 305/854–4247 or 305/854–2222, WEB www.miamisci.org; 🎟 $9, laser concerts $6), there are also virtual reality exhibits, life science demonstrations, and Internet technology. ★ Overlooking Biscayne Bay on South Miami Avenue is **Vizcaya Museum and Gardens** (✉ 3251 S. Miami Ave., ☎ 305/250–9133, WEB www.vizcayamuseum.com; 🎟 $10), an estate with an Italian Renaissance–style villa that was built in the early 20th century as the winter residence of Chicago industrialist James Deering.

South Miami

South Miami is a former pioneer farming community that has managed to retain its small-town charm, while growing into a major suburb. Contrary to what its name implies, South Miami is a city, not just a geographical moniker.

Fine old homes and mature trees line **Sunset Drive,** the city-designated "historic and scenic road" to and through downtown South Miami. At the **Parrot Jungle and Garden** (✉ Watson Island, ☎ 305/666–7834, WEB www.parrotjungle.com; 🎟 $14.95), you can marvel at postcard-perfect flamingos, watch a trained-bird show, or stroll among orchids.

Not far from Parrot Jungle is the 83-acre **Fairchild Tropical Garden** (✉ 10901 Old Cutler Rd., ☎ 305/667–1651, WEB www.fairchildgarden.org; 🎟 $8), the largest tropical botanical garden in the continental United States. Old Cutler Road traverses Miami–Dade County's oldest and most scenic park, **Matheson Hammock Park** (✉ 9610 Old Cutler Rd., ☎ 305/665–5475; 🎟 free, $3.50 parking), which dates from the days of the Civilian Conservation Corps in the 1930s. The park has a bathing beach, sailing school, marina, restaurant, and changing facilities.

A few miles south on Old Cutler Road, the **Deering Estate at Cutler** (✉ 16701 S.W. 72nd Ave., ☎ 305/235–1668; 🎟 $6) contains the 1913 Mediterranean Revival stone house of Charles Deering on a site rich in archaeological, historical, and natural treasures. A huge Environmental Education and Visitor's Center presents programs for children and adults. Nature tours and canoe trips are available.

Virginia Key and Key Biscayne

The waters of Government Cut and the Port of Miami separate densely populated Miami Beach from two of Greater Miami's playground islands, Virginia Key and Key Biscayne—the latter no longer the laid-back village where Richard Nixon set up his presidential vacation compound. Parks and stretches of dense mangrove swamp occupy much of both keys. To reach the keys, take the **Rickenbacker Causeway** across Biscayne Bay at Brickell Avenue and Southwest 26th Road, about 2 mi south of downtown Miami. The causeway links several islands in the bay.

★ On Virginia Key, the **Miami Seaquarium** (✉ 4400 Rickenbacker Causeway, ☎ 305/361–5705, WEB www.miamiseaquarium.com; 🎟 $24.45, parking $4) spotlights sea lion, dolphin, and killer whale performances and a 235,000-gallon tropical-reef aquarium. Many educated beach enthusiasts rate **Crandon Park** (✉ 4000 Crandon Blvd., ☎ 305/361–5421; 🎟 free; parking $4 per vehicle) among the top 10 beaches in North America.

The commercial center of Key Biscayne is a mix of shops and stores catering to neighborhood needs. At the key's south end is the **Bill Baggs Cape Florida State Recreation Area** (✉ 1200 S. Crandon Blvd., ☎ 305/361–5811; 🎟 $4 per vehicle; $1 per person on foot, bicycle, or bus), with a 1¼-mi expanse of palm-topped white-sand beach, several boardwalks, fishing piers, picnic shelters, a café, and the **Cape Florida Lighthouse,** South Florida's oldest structure.

Dining

Dining in Miami is an essential part of nightlife, whether in the Cuban restaurants on Calle Ocho or in the exclusive eateries of South Beach. Here you can taste New World cuisine—fresh, inventive dishes that make ample use of indigenous ingredients such as mango, local seafood, and peppers, while drawing on influences from the Caribbean, Mexico, and South America. The sizzle in Miami's food scene means fierce competition among restaurateurs, such that hopefuls open and failures close almost every week. Restaurants listed here have passed the test of time, but double-check by phone before you set out for the evening.

$$$–$$$$ ★ ✕ **Blue Door at Delano.** The flavors of classic French cuisine are combined with South American influences to create dishes like "The Big Ravioli," filled with crab-and-scallop mousseline, and osso buco in Thai curry sauce with caramelized pineapple and bananas. Equally pleasing is dining with the crème de la crème of Miami (and New York and Paris) society. ✉ *1685 Collins Ave.,* ☎ *305/674–6400. Reservations essential. AE, D, DC, MC, V.*

$$$–$$$$ ✕ **The Forge.** Often compared to a museum, this landmark bills itself as "the Versailles of steak." Each intimate dining salon has historical artifacts, including a chandelier that hung in James Madison's White House. The wine cellar contains 380,000 bottles—including more than 500 dating from 1822 (and costing as much as $35,000). In addition to steak, specialties include salmon with spinach vinaigrette and free-range duck roasted with black currants. ✉ *432 Arthur Godfrey Rd.,* ☎ *305/538–8533. Reservations essential. AE, DC, MC, V. No lunch.*

$$$–$$$$ ★ ✕ **Norman's.** At this elegantly casual restaurant, the art of New-World cuisine has been perfected—a combination rooted in Latin, North American, Caribbean, and Asian influences. Bold tastes are delivered in every dish, from a simple black-and-white-bean soup to a rum-and-pepper-painted grouper on a mango-*habañero* sauce. Service here is stellar. ✉ *21 Almeria Ave.,* ☎ *305/446–6767. AE, DC, MC, V. Closed Sun. No lunch.*

$$$–$$$$ ★ ✕ **Chef Allen's.** You'll find innovative New-World cuisine like no other, with such creations as rock-shrimp hash with roasted corn, and swordfish with conch-citrus couscous, macadamia nuts, and lemon. Finish off your meal with a mouthwatering soufflé. ✉ *19088 N.E. 29th Ave.,* ☎ *305/935–2900. AE, DC, MC, V.*

$$$–$$$$ ✕ **Nemo.** The open-air environment, bright colors, copper fixtures, and tree-shaded courtyard lend casual comfort. The menu, which blends Caribbean, Japanese, and Southeast Asian influences, includes garlic-cured salmon rolls with *tobiko* caviar and a grilled Indian-spiced pork loin. ✉ *100 Collins Ave.,* ☎ *305/532–4550. AE, MC, V.*

$$–$$$$ ✕ **China Grill.** This crowded, noisy ever-vaunted celebrity haunt turns out not Chinese food but rather "world cuisine" in large portions meant for sharing. Crispy duck with scallion pancakes and caramelized black-vinegar sauce is a nice surprise, as is pork and beans with green apple and balsamic mojo (a garlicky Cuban marinade). ✉ *404 Washington Ave.,* ☎ *305/534–2211. AE, DC, MC, V. No lunch weekends.*

$$–$$$$ ✕ **Joe's Stone Crab Restaurant.** The centerpiece of the ample à la carte menu is, of course, stone crab, with a piquant mustard sauce. Side orders include creamed garlic spinach, french-fried onions, fried green tomatoes, and hash browns. Desserts include a justifiably famous key lime pie. If you can't stand loitering hungrily (there's a several-*hour* wait at peak times), come for lunch or go next door for Joe's takeout. ✉ *227 Biscayne St.,* ☎ *305/673–0365. Reservations not accepted. AE, D, DC, MC, V. Closed mid-May–mid-Oct. No lunch Mon.*

$$–$$$ ★ ✕ **Pacific Time.** Packed nearly every night, chef-proprietor Jonathan Eismann's superb eatery has a high blue ceiling, banquettes, plank floors, and an open kitchen. The brilliant American-Asian cuisine includes such entrées as cedar-roasted salmon, rosemary-roasted chicken, and dry-aged Colorado beef grilled with shiitake mushrooms. The cuttlefish appetizer and the Florida pompano entrée are masterpieces. Desserts include a fresh pear-pecan spring roll. ✉ *915 Lincoln Rd.,* ☎ *305/534–5979. Reservations essential. AE, DC, MC, V.*

$$–$$$ ★ ✕ **Osteria del Teatro.** Orchids grace the tables in the intimate gray-on-gray room with a low, laced-canvas ceiling and deco lamps. Start with an appetizer of poached asparagus served over polenta triangles with a Gorgonzola sauce. Stuffed pastas, including spinach crepes overflowing with ricotta, can seem heavy but taste light; fish dishes yield a rosemary-marinated tuna in a pink peppercorn–citrus sauce. ✉ *1443 Washington Ave.,* ☎ *305/538–7850. AE, DC, MC, V. Closed Sun. No lunch.*

$–$$$ ★ ✕ **Café Prima Pasta.** Consistently intense flavors, high-quality ingredients, and plain good cooking are the hallmarks of this cozy Argentinian-Italian spot in the emerging North Beach neighborhood. After fresh-made bread and a dipping oil with garlic, parsley, and crushed red pepper arrives at the table, you can choose from such favorites as penne *alla vodka* and black linguine with seafood and creamy lobster sauce. ✉ *414 71st St.,* ☎ *305/867–0106. MC, V.*

$–$$$ ✕ **Versailles.** This Cuban restaurant is possibly the most ornate budget restaurant you'll ever see, all mirrors and candelabras; and the royal treatment isn't limited to the decor in this veritable institution. The food is terrific, especially such classics as ropa vieja, *arroz con pollo* (chicken and rice), *palomilla* (thin, boneless) steak, *sopa de platanos* (plantain soup), ham shank, and roast pork. ✉ *3555 S.W. 8th St.,* ☎ *305/444–0240. AE, D, DC, MC, V.*

$–$$ ★ ✕ **News Café.** An Ocean Drive landmark, this 24-hour café attracts a big crowd around the clock with snacks, light meals, drinks, and the sidewalk people parade. There's a bar in back, but most diners prefer sitting outside to watch the action on Ocean Drive. ✉ *800 Ocean Dr.,* ☎ *305/538–6397. AE, DC, MC, V.*

$ ✕ **Arnie and Richie's.** Take a deep whiff when you walk in, and you'll know what you're in for: onion rolls, smoked whitefish salad, half-sour pickles, herring in sour cream sauce, chopped liver, corned beef, pastrami. Deli doesn't get more delicious than in this family-run operation. Service can be brusque, but it sure is quick. ✉ *525 41st St.,* ☎ *305/531–7691. AE, MC, V.*

Lodging

Lodgings are concentrated in Miami Beach and downtown Miami, around the airport, and in Coral Gables, Coconut Grove, and Key Biscayne. For historic bed-and-breakfast accommodations contact **Miami Area Bed-and-Breakfast Inns and Boutique Hotels** (✉ Box 331891, Miami 33233–1891, ☎ 305/665–2274 or 800/339–9430, FAX 305/666–1186). Winter is peak season; summer is also busy but rates are much lower.

$$$$ 🏨 **Delano Hotel.** Fashion models and men of independent means gather beneath cabanas, pose by the infinity pool, and sniff the heady aromas from the Blue Door restaurant. There are comprehensive business services and a rooftop bathhouse and solarium. Although the standard rooms are of average size, their stark whiteness makes them appear larger. The real appeal here is the *Alice in Wonderland*–like surrealism. ✉ *1685 Collins Ave., Miami Beach 33139,* ☎ *305/672–2000 or 800/555–5001,* FAX *305/532–0099,* WEB *www.delano-hotel-miami-beach.com. 208 rooms. Restaurant, pool, health club. AE, D, DC, MC, V.*

$$$$ 🏨 **National Hotel.** The most spectacular part of this resurrected 1939 shorefront hotel is its tropical pool—it's also Miami Beach's longest (205 ft). In daylight it's a perfect backdrop for the film crews that often work here. With curtains closed, poolside rooms could be generic Holiday Inn, displaying little of the creativity of other recently arrived hotels. Rooms in the main building are far more appealing, however. ✉ *1677 Collins Ave., Miami Beach 33139,* ☎ *305/532–2311 or 800/327–*

8370, FAX 305/534–1426, WEB *www.nationalhotel.com. 120 rooms. Restaurant, pool, gym. AE, DC, MC, V.*

$$$$ ★ **Sonesta Beach Resort Key Biscayne.** With its 750-ft beach, this hotel has always been one of Miami's best. Some rooms are in villas with full kitchens and screened-in pools. Facilities include parasailing, catamaran rental, and children's programs. The grand size of the property, Olympic pool, and a multitude of activities make this a good family getaway. ✉ *350 Ocean Dr. 33149,* ☎ *305/361–2021 or 800/766–3782,* FAX *305/361–3096,* WEB *www.sonesta.com. 303 rooms, 4 villas. 3 restaurants, pool, tennis, health club. AE, D, DC, MC, V.*

$$$$ ★ **Turnberry Isle Resort & Club.** Finest of the grand resorts, even more so with the addition of a stellar spa, Turnberry is a tapestry of islands and waterways on 300 superbly landscaped acres by the bay. You'll stay at the 1920s Addison Mizner–designed Country Club Hotel on the Intracoastal Waterway where oversize rooms in light woods and earth tones have large curving terraces and hot tubs. There are not one but two Robert Trent Jones golf courses. ✉ *19999 W. Country Club Dr. 33180,* ☎ *305/932–6200 or 800/327–7028,* FAX *305/933–6560,* WEB *www.turnberryisle.com. 340 rooms. 3 restaurants, pools, golf, tennis, health club. AE, D, DC, MC, V.*

$$$–$$$$ ✕ **Alexander Hotel.** Amid the high-rises of the Mid-Beach district, this 16-story hotel exemplifies the elegance of Miami Beach. It has immense suites furnished with antiques and reproductions, each with a terrace that has ocean or bay views and each with a living and dining room, kitchen, and two baths. With the Aveda salon and Shula's Steak House on the second floor, you can pamper your body and appetite without leaving the property. ✉ *5225 Collins Ave., Miami Beach 33140,* ☎ *305/865–6500 or 800/327–6121,* FAX *305/341–6554,* WEB *www.alexanderhotel.com. 141 suites. 3 restaurants, pools, health club. AE, D, DC, MC, V.*

$$$–$$$$ ★ **Biltmore Hotel.** The 1926 Biltmore rises like a sienna-color wedding cake in the heart of a residential district. The vaulted lobby has hand-painted rafters on a twinkling sky-blue background. The huge swimming pool is breathtaking. Large guest rooms are done in a restrained Moorish style. For a slightly higher nightly rate ($2,650) you can book the Everglades (a.k.a. Al Capone) Suite. ✉ *1200 Anastasia Ave. 33134,* ☎ *305/445–1926 or 800/727–1926,* FAX *305/913–3159,* WEB *www.biltmorehotel.com. 280 rooms. Restaurant, pool, golf, tennis, health club. AE, DC, MC, V.*

$$–$$$$ **Fontainebleau Hilton Resort.** This big, busy, and ornate grande dame has completed an overhaul of its original building, but even more grandiose plans are in the works. All public areas and guest rooms have been renovated, but rooms still vary wildly, ranging from 1950s to very contemporary furnishings. Adults enjoy free admission to the hotel's *Club Tropigala* Vegas-style floor show. The most popular spot for kids is Cookie's World, a water playground. ✉ *4441 Collins Ave. 33140,* ☎ *305/538–2000 or 800/548–8886,* FAX *305/673–5351,* WEB *www.hilton.com. 1,206 rooms. 12 restaurants, pools, tennis. AE, D, DC, MC, V.*

$$$–$$$$ ★ **Loews Miami Beach Hotel.** Unlike other South Beach properties, this 18-story gem was built from the blueprints up. Not only did Loews manage to snag 99 ft of beach, it also took over the vacant St. Moritz next door and restored it to its original 1939 Art Deco splendor. The resort has comprehensive kids' programs, tons of meeting space, and an enormous ocean-view grand ballroom. Dining, too, is a pleasure, courtesy of the Argentinian-inspired Gaucho Room. ✉ *1601 Collins Ave., Miami Beach 33139,* ☎ *305/604–1601,* FAX *305/531–8677,* WEB *www.loewshotels.com. 790 rooms. 4 restaurants, health club. AE, D, DC, MC, V.*

$$-$$$$ **Nassau Suite Hotel.** For a boutique hotel one block from the beach, this airy retreat almost qualifies as a steal (by South Beach standards). The original 1937 floor plan of 50 rooms gave way to 22 spacious and smart-looking suites with king beds, fully equipped kitchens, hardwood floors, white wood blinds, and free local calls. The Nassau is in the heart of the action yet quiet enough to give you the rest you need. Note: this three-floor hotel has no elevator and no bellman. There's also very limited parking. ✉ *1414 Collins Ave., Miami Beach 33139,* ☎ *305/534–2354,* FAX *305/534–3133,* WEB *www.nassausuite.com. 22 suites. AE, D, DC, MC, V.*

$$$ ★ **Hotel Place St. Michel.** The finest boutique hotel in metropolitan Miami is in the heart of downtown Coral Gables. Art nouveau chandeliers are suspended from vaulted lobby ceilings, and the scent of fresh flowers is circulated through the public spaces by paddle fans. Each room is unique, and count on English, French, and Scottish antiques. Dinner at the superb Restaurant St. Michel is a must. ✉ *162 Alcazar Ave. 33134,* ☎ *305/444–1666 or 800/848–4683,* FAX *305/529–0074,* WEB *www.hotelplacestmichel.com. 27 rooms. Restaurant. AE, DC, MC, V, CP.*

$$-$$$ ★ **Indian Creek Hotel.** This 1936 pueblo-inspired deco jewel may be Miami's most charming accommodation. Owner Marc Levin rescued the inn and was fortunate enough to find original deco furniture in the basement (which no doubt helped him win the Miami Design Preservation League's award for outstanding restoration). The restaurant has an eclectic and appetizing menu that you can also enjoy outdoors by the lush pool and garden. ✉ *2727 Indian Creek Dr. 33140,* ☎ *305/531–2727 or 800/491–2772,* FAX *305/531–5651,* WEB *www.indiancreekhotelmb.com. 61 rooms. Restaurant, pool. AE, D, DC, MC, V.*

$-$$ **Bayliss.** Rooms are abnormally large, surprisingly inexpensive, and clean. An easy three blocks west of the ocean, this place is in a residential neighborhood that's comfortably close to—but far enough away from—the din of the Deco District. You can't do much better than this for the price. ✉ *500 14th Ave., Miami Beach 33139,* ☎ *305/531–3755 or 888/305–4683,* FAX *305/673–8609,* WEB *www.thebayliss.com. 19 rooms. AE, DC, MC, V.*

Nightlife and the Arts

The best sources for events are the widely distributed free weeklies *New Times, Miami Today,* and *Street.* The *Miami Herald* publishes a "Weekend" section on Friday and a "Lively Arts" section on Sunday. If you read Spanish, rely on *El Nuevo Herald* (the Spanish-language version of the *Miami Herald*).

Nightlife

The liveliest scenes are in South Beach (Miami Beach's Art Deco District—especially on Washington Avenue) and Coconut Grove, but clubs can be found in the suburbs, downtown, Little Havana, and Little Haiti.

BARS WITH MUSIC

At the **Clevelander** (✉ 1020 Ocean Dr., ☎ 305/531–3485), a giant pool-bar area attracts a young crowd of revelers for happy-hour drink specials and live music. At the Streets of Mayfair, the **Iguana Cantina and Babalu Bar** (✉ 3390 Mary St., ☎ 305/443–3300) serves up salsa, merengue, and Latin music on weekends. **Tobacco Road** (✉ 626 S. Miami Ave., ☎ 305/374–1198) holds Miami's oldest liquor license (Number 0001) and is one of the city's oldest bars, with excellent blues nightly.

DANCE CLUBS

Nightclubs are the lifeblood of Miami. Although many clubs fall out of favor quickly, these seem to have withstood the test of time: **Club-**

Space (✉ 142 N.E. 11th St., ☎ 305/375–0001), created from four warehouses downtown, has three dance rooms, an outdoor patio, and a 24-hour liquor license. It's open weekends only. Hot spot **crobar**'s(✉ 1445 Washington Ave., ☎ 305/531–5027) exterior is the historic Cameo Theater, while the interior is a *Blade Runner*–esque blend of high-tech marvels with some performance art thrown in. **Honey** (✉ 645 Washington Ave., Miami Beach, ☎ 305/ 604–8222) has soft lighting, cozy couches and chaise longues, and vibey music. **Level** (✉ 1235 Washington Ave., ☎ 305/532–1525) has an impressive four dance floors, and—as its name suggests—lots of levels to search out fun.

The Arts

To order tickets for performing arts events by telephone, call **Ticketmaster** (☎ 305/358–5885).

BALLET

Miami City Ballet (✉ 2200 Liberty Ave., ☎ 305/929–7000) is an acclaimed troupe under the direction of Edward Villella. You can catch a performance between September and March at the **Jackie Gleason Theater of the Performing Arts.**

MUSIC

New World Symphony (✉ 541 Lincoln Rd., ☎ 305/673–3331), conducted by Michael Tilson Thomas, is also a national orchestral academy for young music-school graduates. **Concert Association of Florida** (✉ 555 Hank Meyer Blvd., at 17th St., ☎ 305/532–3491) is the Southeast's largest presenter of classical artists, dance, and music—concerts are held at a variety of venues. Past performers have included Itzhak Perlman, Mikhail Baryshnikov, and Luciano Pavarotti.

OPERA

Florida Grand Opera (✉ 1200 Coral Way, Miami, ☎ 305/854–1643) presents five operas a year at the Dade County Auditorium. Operas are sung in the original language, with English subtitles projected above the stage.

THEATER

The **Coconut Grove Playhouse** (✉ 3500 Main Hwy., ☎ 305/442–4000) stages Broadway-bound plays and musical revues as well as experimental productions. **Colony Theater** (✉ 1040 Lincoln Rd., Miami Beach, ☎ 305/674–1026), once a movie theater, is now a city-owned 465-seat performing arts center featuring dance, drama, music, and experimental cinema. **Jackie Gleason Theater of the Performing Arts** (✉ 1700 Washington Ave., ☎ 305/673–7300) is home of the Broadway Series and other stage events. The **Miami–Dade County Auditorium** (✉ 2901 W. Flagler St., ☎ 305/545–3395) hosts opera, concerts, and touring musicals. **Teatro de Bellas Artes** (✉ 2173 S.W. 8th St., ☎ 305/ 325–0515), a 255-seat theater on Little Havana's Calle Ocho, presents Spanish plays and musicals year-round.

Outdoor Activities and Sports

Beaches

Millions visit the beaches in Miami–Dade County each year. **Miami Beach** extends continuously for 10 mi. A boardwalk runs from 23rd to 44th Street, and along this stretch various groups congregate in specific areas. **Lummus Park,** the stretch of beach opposite the Art Deco District, between 5th and 15th streets, attracts all ages, with volleyball courts, inline skating along a paved upland path, and children's playgrounds. Gays frequent the beach between 11th and 13th streets. Sidewalk cafés parallel the entire beach area. **North Beach,** along Ocean Terrace between 72nd and 75th streets, is more serene.

Two of metropolitan Miami's best beaches are on Key Biscayne. Nearest the causeway is the 3½-mi county beach in **Crandon Park** (✉ 4000 Crandon Blvd., ☎ 305/361–5421). **Bill Baggs Cape Florida State Recreation Area** (✉ 1200 S. Crandon Blvd., ☎ 305/361–5811) has beaches, boardwalks, bicycle paths, and nature trails.

Diving

Summer diving conditions in Greater Miami have been compared with those in the Caribbean. Winter can bring rough, cold waters. Fowey, Triumph, Long, and Emerald reefs are good for snorkelers and beginning divers. For charters, rentals, and instruction, try **Divers Paradise of Key Biscayne** (✉ 4000 Crandon Blvd., ☎ 305/361–3483). The **Diving Locker** (✉ 223 Sunny Isles Blvd., ☎ 305/947–6025) has rentals and instructions. **Bubbles Dive Center** (✉ 2671 S.W. 27th Ave., ☎ 305/856–0565) is an all-purpose dive shop. Most dive shops host night and wreck dives.

Fishing

Smaller charter boats can cost $350–$400 for a half day and provide everything but food and drinks. If you're on a budget, book a passage on a larger fishing boat for around $25. Charter boats depart from **Crandon Marina** (✉ 4000 Crandon Blvd., ☎ 305/361–1281 for marina office). **Haulover Park** (✉ 10800 Collins Ave., ☎ 305/947–3525) also has charter boats. Fishing charters are available at **Miami Beach Marina** (✉ 300 Alton Rd., MacArthur Causeway, ☎ 305/673–6000).

Golf

Miami–Dade County has more than 30 private and public golf courses (☎ 305/857–3350 for Miami–Dade County; 305/673–7730 for Miami Beach). Call ahead for discount afternoon-twilight rates. A few of Miami's more notable courses include the **Biltmore Golf Course** (✉ 1210 Anastasia Ave., ☎ 305/460–5364); **Don Shula's Hotel & Golf Club** (✉ 7601 Miami Lakes Dr., Miami Lakes, ☎ 305/820–8106); the "Blue Monster" at the **Doral Golf Resort and Spa** (✉ 4400 N.W. 87th Ave., ☎ 305/592–2000 or 800/713–6725); and the **Granada Golf Course** (✉ 2001 Granada Blvd., ☎ 305/460–5367) is one of Coral Gables's two public courses.

Sailing

The center of sailing in Greater Miami remains at the **Dinner Key** and the **Coconut Grove** waterfronts, although moorings and rentals are found elsewhere up the bay and up the Miami River.

Tennis

Greater Miami has more than 60 private and public tennis centers. All public courts charge nonresidents an hourly fee. If you're on a schedule, call in advance; some courts take reservations on weekdays. **Biltmore Tennis Center** (✉ 1150 Anastasia Ave., ☎ 305/460–5360) has 10 hard courts. **Flamingo Tennis Center** (✉ 11th St. and Alton Rd., ☎ 305/673–7761) has 19 clay courts. **Tennis Center at Crandon Park** (✉ 7300 Crandon Blvd., ☎ 305/365–2300), which hosts the annual Ericsson Championships in March, has 2 grass, 8 clay, and 17 hard courts.

Windsurfing

You can rent windsurfing equipment and take lessons at **Sailboards Miami** (✉, ☎ 305/361–7245), on Hobie Island just past the tollbooth for the Rickenbacker Causeway to Key Biscayne.

Spectator Sports

In addition to the usual spectator sports, in Miami you can watch and bet on jai alai, known as the fastest game on earth. Pelotas (hard balls) are thrown from handheld baskets called cestas, traveling at speeds of more than 170 mph.

Baseball: The 1997 World Series champion **Florida Marlins** play at Pro Player Stadium (⊠ 2269 N.W. 199th St., Miami, ☎ 305/626–7400). **Basketball:** The NBA's **Miami Heat** and the WNBA's **Miami Sol** play at American Airlines Arena (⊠ Biscayne Blvd. between N.E. 8th and 9th Sts., Miami, ☎ 305/577–4328). **Football:** Miami's favorite team, the **Miami Dolphins,** play at Pro Player Stadium (⊠ 2269 N.W. 199th St., ☎ 305/620–2578). **Jai Alai: Miami Jai Alai** (⊠ 3500 N.W. 37th Ave., ☎ 305/633–6400).

Shopping

Shopping Districts

The shopping is great on a two-block stretch of **Collins Avenue** (⊠ between 6th and 8th Aves.). Club Monaco, Polo Sport, Nicole Miller, Nike, Kenneth Cole, Guess, Armani Exchange, and Banana Republic are among the high-profile tenants, and a parking garage is a block away. The busy **Lincoln Road Mall** is a few blocks from the beach and convention center, making it popular with locals and tourists. There's an energy to shopping here, especially on weekends, when the pedestrian mall is filled with locals. Creative merchandise, galleries, and a Sunday-morning antiques market can be found among the art galleries and cool cafés. The **Miami Design District** (⊠ between N.E. 36th and N.E. 41st Sts. and between N.E. 2nd Ave. and N. Miami Ave.) contains some 225 designer showrooms and galleries specializing in interior furnishings, decorative arts, antiques, and a rich mix of exclusive and unusual merchandise. **Miracle Mile** (⊠ Coral Way between 37th and 42nd Aves.) consists of some 160 shops along a wide, tree-lined boulevard. Shops range from posh bridal boutiques to bargain basements, from beauty salons to chain restaurants. As you go west, the quality improves.

Miami Essentials

AIRPORTS

Miami International Airport (MIA), 6 mi west of downtown via Route 836, is served by most major carriers and many minor ones.

➤ AIRPORT INFORMATION: **Miami International Airport** (⊠ N.W. 21 St. and 45 Ave., ☎ 305/876–7000).

BUS TRAVEL TO AND FROM MIAMI

Greyhound stops at five terminals in Greater Miami, including a terminal at the airport.

➤ BUS INFORMATION: **Greyhound** (☎ 800/231–2222).

CAR TRAVEL

I–95, which runs north–south along Florida's east coast, flows into the heart of Miami. From the northwest I–75 leads to the city. Route 836 (also called East–West Expressway or Dolphin Expressway), connecting the airport to downtown (toll eastbound only, 50¢), continues across I–395 and the MacArthur Causeway to lower Miami Beach and the Art Deco District. Route 112 (Airport Expressway) connects the airport with midtown (toll eastbound only, 50¢) and continues across I–195 and the Julia Tuttle Causeway to mid–Miami Beach.

RULES OF THE ROAD

Miami is laid out in quadrants: northwest, northeast, southwest, southeast. These meet at Miami Avenue, which separates east from west, and Flagler Street, which separates north from south. Avenues and courts run north–south; streets, terraces, and ways run east–west. Roads run diagonally, northwest–southeast. In Miami Beach avenues run north–south; streets, east–west. Streets in Coral Gables have names, not numbers. In other words, be prepared to ask directions early and often.

TAXIS

One cab "company" stands out immeasurably above the rest. It's actually a consortium of drivers who have banded together to provide good service, in marked contrast to some Miami cabbies, who are rude, unhelpful, or dishonest. To plug into this consortium—they don't have a name, simply a number—call the dispatch service, although they can be hard to understand over the phone. If you have to use another company, try to be familiar with your route and destination.

➤ TAXI COMPANIES: **Dispatch service** (☎ 305/888–4444).

VISITOR INFORMATION

➤ TOURIST INFORMATION: **Greater Miami Convention & Visitors Bureau** (✉ 701 Brickell Ave., Suite 2700 33131, ☎ 305/539–3063 or 800/283–2707, WEB www.tropicoolmiami.com). Satellite tourist information centers are at **Bayside Marketplace** (✉ 401 Biscayne Blvd. Miami 33132, ☎ 305/539–2980) and **Surfside Tourist Board** (✉ 9301 Collins Ave., Surfside 33154, ☎ 305/864–0722 or 800/327–4557, FAX 305/861–1302).

WALT DISNEY WORLD™ AND THE ORLANDO AREA

Once upon a time about the only things to see in Orlando were at the Walt Disney World Resort. Today, however, cosmopolitan Orlando is an international business center and tourist mecca. Universal Orlando and SeaWorld have their own smaller but burgeoning theme park empires, and many other attractions, shopping areas, and nightspots make the area an exciting, if sometimes frenetic and crowded, vacation destination. Away from the tourist areas, hundreds of spring-fed lakes surrounded by oak trees recall Orlando's bucolic past. About an hour's drive on the Atlantic coast are the Cocoa Beach area and the Kennedy Space Center.

Exploring Walt Disney World and the Orlando Area

Walt Disney World Resort

★ The focal point of an Orlando vacation is **Walt Disney World Resort** (✉ Box 10040, Lake Buena Vista 32830, ☎ 407/824–4321, WEB disneyworld.disney.go.com), a collection of theme parks and attractions connected by an extensive bus, monorail, motor-launch, and tram network (access is included in the price of a multiday pass or available for a small fee). Admission is not cheap: a one-day adult ticket (including tax) costs $50.88; a child's ticket ages 3–9 is $40.28 (as of press time) and admits you to only one of the parks: Magic Kingdom, Epcot, Disney–MGM Studios, or Disney's Animal Kingdom. Depending on how many parks you want to visit in what amount of time, it may pay to purchase a Park Hopper (four days $203.52 adults, $161.12 children; five days $230.02 adults, $182.32 children) or an all-in-one Park Hopper Plus (five days $261.84 adults, $208.83 children; six days $293.64 adults, $235.34 children; seven days $325.44 adults, $261.84 children). All admit you to the four major parks, but only the Plus passes include admission to Disney's water parks, Downtown Disney Pleasure Island, and Disney's Wide World of Sports. A major innovation in all four Disney theme parks is the FASTPASS, which allows you to avoid lengthy lines at 24 of the highest-demand attractions by making appointments to return later at a specified time.

THE MAGIC KINGDOM

The Magic Kingdom is divided into seven lands. To do the Kingdom justice, try to visit all (or at least most) of them.

For an overview, or a rest on a hot afternoon, hop aboard the **Walt Disney World Railroad** and take a 1½-mi ride around the perimeter of the park. You can board at the Victorian-style station by the park entrance, in Frontierland, or at Mickey's Toontown Fair.

Main Street, U.S.A. is a shop-filled boulevard with Victorian-style stores and restaurants. Stop at **City Hall** (on your left as you enter) to get general information, including a map and entertainment schedule, and character meet-and-greet locations. At the **Main Street Exposition Hall** you can learn more about the man behind the Mouse, Walt Disney, and catch some vintage Disney short cartoons in the theater. If you walk two blocks along Main Street, you'll enter **Central Plaza,** with **Cinderella Castle**rising directly in front of you. The plaza is the hub of the Kingdom; all the lands radiate from it. Disney characters appear in daily shows on the outdoor castle stage and in parades that pass through the hub and down Main Street.

Adventureland is a mishmash of tropical and swashbuckling attractions that are among the most crowded in the Magic Kingdom. Visit first thing in the morning, late in the afternoon, or in the evening. The **Swiss Family Treehouse** is a good way to get both exercise and a view of the park. You walk single file up the many-staired tree and past the imaginatively furnished "rooms," a trip that can take up to a half hour. The **Jungle Cruise** takes you along the Nile, the Mekong, the Congo, and the Amazon rivers. The tour guide's narration is corny but worth a few chuckles. **Pirates of the Caribbean** is a journey through a world of pirate strongholds and treasure-filled dungeons. On your way out of Adventureland, hop a "magic carpet" at the **Magic Carpets of Aladdin,** a family-friendly ride where the only danger is an Audio-Animatronic spitting camel.

Frontierland's major draw is **Splash Mountain,** an elaborate flume ride based on Disney's 1946 film *Song of the South,* with characters and some songs from the movie. An eight-person hollowed-out log takes a meandering journey through Brer Rabbit's habitat before plummeting down a long, sharp flume drop. **Big Thunder Mountain Railroad,** the "runaway train," takes twists and turns through a mountain but has none of the huge drops serious roller-coaster fans adore. The lines here are often shorter than they are for Splash Mountain or Space Mountain, and this is the perfect ride for children who are ready to graduate from "kiddie" coasters. Families shouldn't miss the comical serenading bears of **Country Bear Jamboree.**

Liberty Square is a journey back to colonial America. The **Hall of Presidents** is a 30-minute multimedia tribute to the Constitution and the nation's 43 presidents. The star attraction here is the **Haunted Mansion.** Scary but not terrifying, this "doom buggie" ride takes you past a plethora of dust, cobwebs, tombstones, and creepy characters.

Fantasyland is, as the map says, "where storybook dreams come true." Gingerbread houses, gleaming gold turrets, and streams sparkling with shiny pennies dot the landscape, and its rides are based on Disney's animated movies. Unlike many other Magic Kingdom stage shows, *Legend of the Lion King* does not draw on human talent. Simba, Mufasa, Scar, and the rest are played by "humanimals," larger-than-life figures that are manipulated by hidden human "animateers." Other attractions include the rides **Dumbo the Flying Elephant, Peter Pan's Flight, Snow White's Scary Adventures,** and the **Mad Tea Party.** Kids of all ages love the antique **Cinderella's Golden Carrousel.**Small children adore **It's A Small World,** a boat ride accompanied by the now-famous theme song of international brotherhood and the **Many Adventures of Winnie the Pooh.**

Mickey's Toontown Fair is filled with all manner of things child size. Kids can visit **Mickey and Minnie's country houses;** the **Barnstormer at Goofy's Wiseacres Farm,** a kid-size roller coaster; and the **Toontown Hall of Fame Tent** and the **Judge's Tent** for visits with Mickey and the most other popular Disney characters. At **Toon Park,** a spongy green meadow filled with foam topiary in the shapes of goats, cows, pigs, and horses, weary parents can rest while their children scramble around and climb on **Donald's Boat.**

Tomorrowland had a face-lift in the mid-'90s. **Space Mountain** is still here, however, and the needlelike spires of this space-age roller coaster are a Magic Kingdom landmark. Although the ride's speed never exceeds 28 mph, the experience in the dark, with everyone yelling, is thrilling. Prepare to scream at **ExtraTERRORestrial Alien Encounter,** where you'll have a very close encounter with an "extraTERRORestrial" creature. Those less into raising their heart rate can opt for **Timekeeper,** a time-traveling movie adventure for older kids and adults (small children won't be able to see unless held up), or **Buzz Lightyear's Space Ranger Spin,** a great interactive laser shoot-em-up ride for kids and adults.

EPCOT

Epcot is that rare paradox—an educational theme park—and a very successful one at that. Although rides have been added, the thrills are mostly for the mind. As such, older children and adults get the most out of Epcot, though the park has adapted to provide more entertainment fun for families with younger kids.

Epcot comprises two distinct parts separated by the 40-acre World Showcase Lagoon. The northern half, **Future World,** itself consists of two concentric circles of pavilions. In the inner core are the **Spaceship Earth** geosphere—the giant, golf-ball-shape Epcot icon with a ride that explores the development of human communication—and beyond it, the **Innoventions** buildings, where exhibits highlight new technology that affects daily living. Making up the circle's outer ring are six corporate-sponsored pavilions with rides and interactive displays on such topics as energy, the human body, the earth, and imagination. **Test Track,** which takes you through the paces of a General Motors automobile proving ground, is the park's big-thrill ride, with its close-call Barrier Test and its high-speed finale. A new pavilion called **Mission: Space** is expected to blast off in 2003.

The southern half of the park, **World Showcase,** stretches 1⅓ mi around the lagoon; in this space you can circumnavigate the globe—or at least explore it. Eleven pavilions present a Disney version of life in various countries with food, entertainment, and wares. Models of some of the world's best-known monuments, such as the Eiffel Tower, a Maya temple, and a majestic Japanese pagoda, are painstakingly re-created. Except for the boat rides in **Mexico** and **Norway,** World Showcase has no amusement-park-type rides. Instead, it has breathtaking films, ethnic art, cultural entertainment, Audio-Animatronics presentations, and dozens of fine shops and highly rated restaurants featuring national specialties. Throughout the day there are live street shows spotlighting comedy, song, or dance; demonstrations of folk arts and crafts; and Kidcot Fun Stop activities for children. The park's evening parade around the World Showcase Lagoon, **Tapestry of Dreams,** and its nightly fireworks, laser, and light show, **IllumiNations,** are first-rate spectacles.

DISNEY–MGM STUDIOS

At this combination theme park and fully functioning movie and television production center, exhilarating rides are blended with instructional tours, nostalgia with high-tech wonders.

Sunset Boulevard is a destination for thrill seekers. At the **Rock 'n' Roller Coaster,** rock music booms as a high-speed launch sets you off for a ride with multiple complete inversions. Board the giant elevator in the **Twilight Zone Tower of Terror** and head upward 13 stories past seemingly deserted hallways. Suddenly, the creaking vehicle will plunge in a terrifying 130-ft free-fall drop—and then go back up to do it again! The ride is for older children and adults.

Hollywood Boulevard oozes Tinseltown of the 1930s and '40s, though the park's giant new Sorcerer Mickey hat icon blocks the avenue's previously wonderful view of its Chinese Theater replica, which houses the **Great Movie Ride.** Take the ride's nostalgia trip past famous recreated movie sets and get a load of the life-like Audio-Animatronic Wicked Witch of the West.

At **Animation Courtyard,** the **Magic of Disney Animation** reveals the secrets of animation filmmaking in a humorous film tailor-made for the attraction and a 30-minute self-guided tour through the Disney animation process, complete with views of actual artists at work. **Walt Disney: One Man's Dream** is a colorful archive of Walt Disney's life that culminates in a film about the entertainment icon. Both **Playhouse Disney—Live on Stage!** and **Voyage of the Little Mermaid** are among the park's greatest hits for families with young children.

On **Mickey Avenue,** the **Studios Backlot Tour** and **Backstage Pass!** take you behind the scenes on a tram ride and walking tour exploring the set design, costumes, props, lighting, and special effects of movies—including a close call with an earthquake, fire, and flash flood at Catastrophe Canyon. Then it's time for your "fastest-finger" test at **Who Wants to Be a Millionaire—Play It!,** the park's popular audience-participation game show on Soundstages 2 and 3.

Kids can unwind in the **New York Street** area at ***Honey, I Shrunk the Kids* Movie Set Adventure,** a larger-than-life playground straight from the film. **Jim Henson's MuppetVision 3-D** is a special-effects hoot, and **Disney's *The Hunchback of Notre Dame*—A Musical Adventure** is worth a stop if it's showtime.

The **Echo Lake** area packs several popular attractions. The 30-minute **Indiana Jones Epic Stunt Spectacular!,** presented in a 2,200-seat amphitheater, highlights the stunt choreography of veteran coordinator Glenn Randall (*Raiders of the Lost Ark, E.T.,* and *Jewel of the Nile* are among his credits). **Star Tours** is a flight-simulator thrill ride. Created under the direction of George Lucas, the five 40-seat theaters become spaceships, and you're off to the moon of Endor.

DISNEY'S ANIMAL KINGDOM

At Walt Disney World's fourth major theme park, lifelike experiences with fictional animals and dinosaurs combine with high-adventure encounters including real exotic animals. Sprawling over 500 acres, much of the park resembles the animal reserves of Africa and Asia and is a habitat for more than 1,000 animals, including endangered species.

Enter at the **Oasis,** a cool green grotto filled with waterfalls and gardens alive with exotic birds, reptiles, and animals. **Discovery Island,** the centerpoint of the park, is home to the **Tree of Life,** which serves as the park's great icon. Beneath the tree roots is a theater for **"It's Tough to be a Bug!,"** a humorous 3-D film and special-effects show modeled after the animated film *A Bug's Life*. From Discovery Island, bridges connect to the other lands.

The park's largest land is **Africa.** It starts in the village of **Harambe,** featuring the architecture of an East African port city on the northern banks of the Discovery River. Board a safari vehicle for the exciting **Kilmanjaro Safaris,** where herds of wild animals roam among the trees, lakes, and grasslands of Disney's realistic African savanna. The safari also includes a race to save elephants from ivory poachers. At the end of the trip, you can follow the **Pangani Forest Exploration Trail** to see lowland gorillas, hippos, meerkats, and colorful birds. By **Wildlife Express** steam train, you can journey to **Conservation Station** at **Rafiki's Planet Watch** to investigate the worldwide efforts to save endangered animals and preserve wild habitats. Here you can experience interactive displays and take a backstage look at how the park's animals are kept happy and healthy. At the **Affection Station,** you can observe and touch small animals.

Another major land, **Asia,** has **Kali River Rapids,** a thrilling white-water rafting journey, and **Maharajah Jungle Trek,** a hike with an up-close view of jungle animals including fascinating fruit bats and magnificent tigers. Pause at the outdoor **Caravan Stage** to catch Flights of Wonders, spectacular demonstrations by falcons, hawks, and other fascinating birds.

In **DinoLand U.S.A.,** youngsters can climb, crawl, and slide in a simulated paleontological dig at the **Boneyard,** which is complete with scaffolding, excavations, dinosaur skeletons, and fascinating "fossils." **TriceraTop Spin** is a ride for young dino-philes, and **Primeval Whirl** is a coaster-like time machine. Nearby is a primeval forest, **Cretaceous Trail,** which gives walkers a visit with some of the plant and animal survivors of the dinosaur age. Dinosaurs are brought back to life in the thrilling **DINOSAUR.** You're whisked back 65 million years on a journey to save the last dinosaur from extinction when the crash of a fiery asteroid threatens everything in sight. At the 1,500-seat outdoor **Theater in the Wild,** *Tarzan Rocks!* is a hip song–dance–extreme stunt version of the classic film.

Part of **Camp Minnie-Mickey** is a character meet-and-greet location. Stars from many Disney favorites sign autographs and pose for pictures. If you have time for only one show, don't miss *Festival of the Lion King,* a high-energy tribal celebration of song, dance, acrobatics, and character performances. In *Pocahontas and Her Forest Friends,* Pocahontas introduces live animal performers.

WATER PARKS

Blizzard Beach (🎫 $31.75 adults, $25.44 children) promises the seemingly impossible—a seaside playground with an alpine theme. **River Country** (🎫 $16.91 adults, $13.25 children), the first of Walt Disney World Resort's water parks, is a rustic and rugged swimming hole; call ahead though, as there's a chance that Disney may be closing this. **Typhoon Lagoon** (🎫 $31.75 adults, $25.44 children), four times the size of River Country, contains everything from a giant wave pool and rafting adventures to a lazy river that circles the entire park.

Universal Orlando

Universal Studios has a movie theme and many rides and attractions based on popular films of the past few decades such as *Men in Black, E.T., Jaws, Twister,* and *Back to the Future.* A theme park *and* working film studio, it includes the special-effects magic of creative consultant Steven Spielberg as well as the animation wizardry of Hanna-Barbera. Here you can view live Nickelodeon shows, participate in movie-themed attractions, tour back-lot sets, and frolic in play areas with *Barney* and *Woody Woodpecker* themes. Jimmy Neutron and Shrek attractions are both set to open soon, too.

Islands of Adventure is hip, cool, modern, and fun for teenagers and other thrill seekers as well as the young-at-heart. Small children will delight in **Seuss Landing,** where the magical world of Dr. Seuss's books come to life. The Orlando area's highest-tech thrill rides are here as well. Don't miss the **Amazing Adventures of Spider Man,** a 3-D simulator thrill ride unlike anything you've ever tried before. If you're a roller coaster fan you'll want to head straight for the **Incredible Hulk Coaster** and then to **Dueling Dragons** for can't-catch-your-breath-because-you're-still-screaming zigs, zags, and drops. Islands is also the permanent home of some of the world's most beloved characters, including Popeye and the dinosaurs of *Jurassic Park.* ✉ *1000 Universal Studios Plaza,* ☎ *407/363–8000 or 800/407–4275,* WEB *www.universalstudios.com.* 🎫 *$50.88 adults, $41.34 children 3–9; 2-day combination with Islands of Adventure $95.35 adults, $81.57 children.*

The Orlando Area

Performing dolphins, killer whales, and a walk-through Plexiglas tunnel that lets you view sharks and barracudas capture your attention at **SeaWorld Orlando.** The park also has penguins, tropical fish, manatees, seals and sea lions, and other educational diversions. **Discovery Cove** (☎ 877/434–7268 reservations line [daily 9–8], WEB www.discoverycove.com), across the street from SeaWorld, is a reservations only, daylong experience where you can swim with dolphins and interact with tropical sea creatures and birds in an exotic setting. There's a 1,000 person per day maximum, so be sure to reserve well in advance. Take Exit 27A or 28 off I–4. ✉ *7007 Sea World Dr.,* ☎ *407/351–3600 or 800/327–2424,* WEB *www.seaworld.com.* 🎫 *SeaWorld $52.95 adults, $43.41 children 3–9, 10% discount for on-line purchase; with "2nd Day Fun" promotion receive a complimentary pass that you can use to return within seven days. Discovery Cove $219 ages 6 and up.*

The **Orlando Science Center** has 12 themed display halls housing exciting hands-on exhibits as well as an eight-story theater for Cinedome films, planetarium programs, and laser light shows. ✉ *777 E. Princeton St.,* ☎ *407/514–2000.* 🎫 *$9.50 adults, $6.75 children 3–11; films and planetarium shows $6 adults and $4.50 children.*

Cypress Gardens is a land of exotic gardens, with bird and animal exhibits and shows, a famous waterskiing revue, and a small-scale water park for kids. Take I–4 to the U.S. 27 S exit and follow signs. It's about an hour southwest of Orlando. ✉ *Off Rte. 540 east of Winter Haven,* ☎ *863/324–2111; 800/237–4826; 800/282–2123 in FL;* WEB *www.cypressgardens.com.* 🎫 *$34.95 plus tax adults, $19.95 children 6–12.*

A big hit with children, **Gatorland** is a campy attraction with thousands of alligators, crocodiles, and other Florida wildlife. The "gator wrestlin" show is a highlight, and there are a train ride and a small kids' water play area. ✉ *14501 S. Orange Blossom Trail, between Orlando and*

Orlando Area

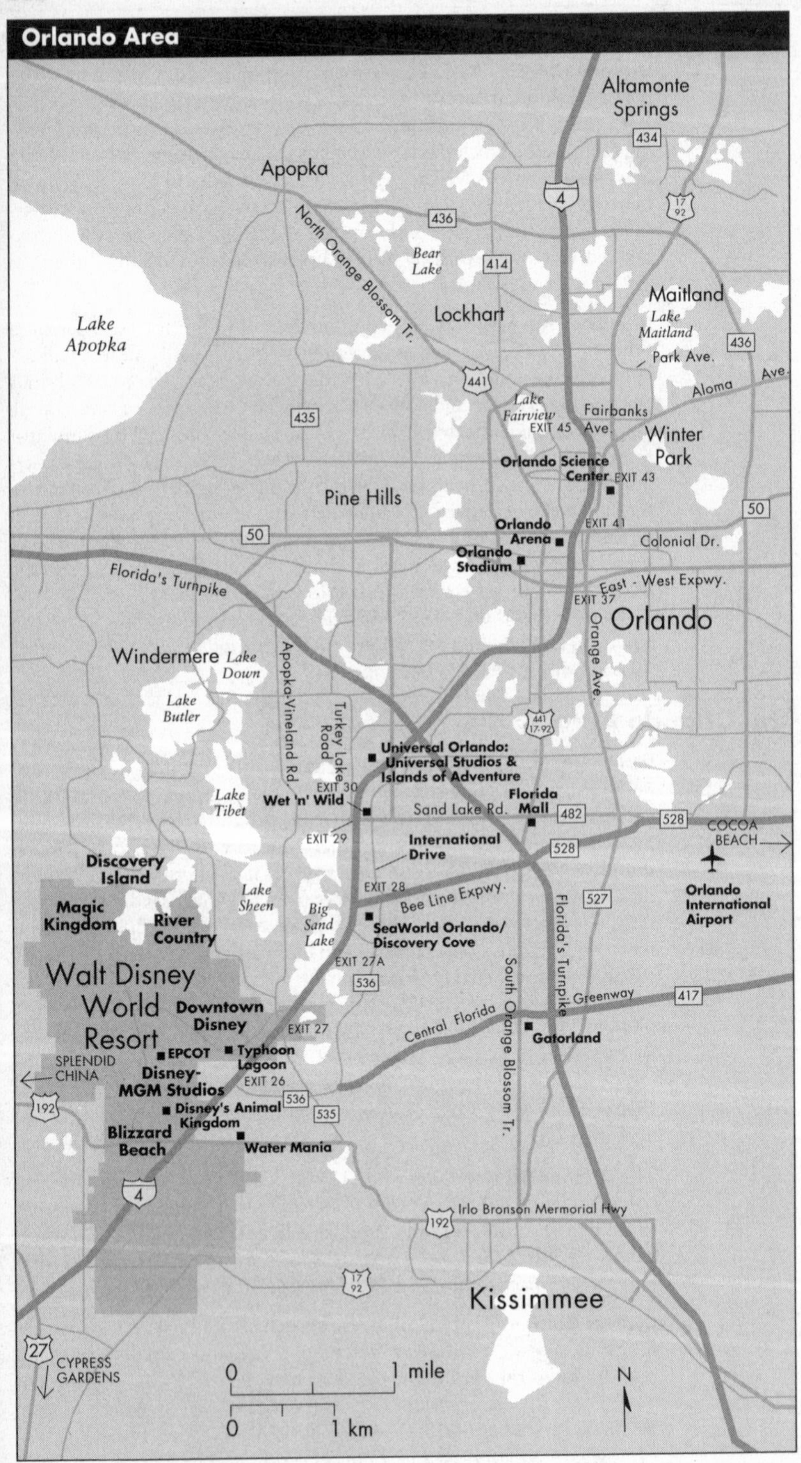

Kissimmee, ☎ *407/855–5496 or 800/393–5297,* WEB *www.gatorland.com.* 🎫 *$17.93 adults, $8.48 children 3–12.*

Splendid China—12 mi southwest of Orlando—has more than 60 scaled-down replicas of China's greatest landmarks, including the Great Wall, the Imperial Palace of Beijing's Forbidden City, and the Dalai Lama's Potala Palace. ✉ *3000 Splendid China Blvd., Kissimmee,* ☎ *407/396–7111; 800/244–6226; 407/397–8800 recording;* WEB *www.floridasplendidchina.com.* 🎫 *$28.88 adults, $18.18 children 5-12.*

★ **Kennedy Space Center Visitor Complex.** Get there early and begin with a bus tour past the Vehicle Assembly Building and on to the historical Apollo/Saturn V Center and the shuttle-launch-pad observation gantry. Don't miss the International Space Station center stop, where pieces of the station are readied for launch. Back at the main complex, see the IMAX film *The Dream Is Alive,* take a virtual visit to Mars in the *Mad Mission to Mars* show, and meet a real astronaut at a scheduled Astronaut Encounter. The center is one hour east of Orlando. ✉ *Rte. 405, Kennedy Space Center, Cocoa Beach,* ☎ *321/449–4444,* WEB *www.kennedyspacecenter.com.* 🎫 *$25 adults, $15 children 3–11.*

Dining and Lodging

Even dining is an adventure in the Orlando area, where international cuisines, fresh fish and seafood, and such exotic local dishes as grilled alligator tail are all on hand. Besides hotels in Walt Disney World Resort, you'll find accommodations in Orlando; Kissimmee, east of Walt Disney World; and other outlying towns.

Cocoa Beach

$$–$$$$ ✕ **Mango Tree Restaurant.** Dine in elegance amid orchid gardens, with piano music playing in the background. Broiled grouper topped with scallops, shrimp, and hollandaise sauce is a favorite. ✉ *118 N. Atlantic Ave.,* ☎ *321/799–0513. AE, MC, V. Closed Mon. No lunch.*

$–$$$ **Inn at Cocoa Beach.** The spacious rooms in this charming oceanfront inn are each decorated differently, but all have some combination of reproduction 18th- and 19th-century armoires and four-poster beds, plus balconies or patios with ocean views. ✉ *4300 Ocean Beach Blvd., 32931,* ☎ *321/799–3460; 800/343–5307 outside Florida;* FAX *321/784–8632,* WEB *www.theinnatcocoabeach.com. 50 rooms. Pool. AE, D, MC, V. CP.*

Kissimmee

$$$–$$$$ ★ **Gaylord Palms Resort.** A 3-acre atrium enclosed in the hotel includes indoor versions of the Everglades, old St. Augustine, and Key West, plus a 60-ft sailboat-restaurant on an indoor lagoon—just the interior view from your balcony is worth the price of a room. The Gaylord has a children's program and one of the biggest spas in the state. This luxurious property is a strong contender for most spectacular hotel in Florida. ✉ *6000 W. Osceola Pkwy., 34746,* ☎ *407/586–0000,* FAX *407/586–1999,* WEB *www.gaylordpalms.com. 1,406 rooms. 6 restaurants, pools, health club. AE, D, MC, V.*

Orlando

$$–$$$$ ★ ✕ **Emeril's.** At this shrine to New Orleans-based Emeril Lagasse, the ubiquitous TV chef who occasionally appears here, it's understandably the Louisiana treats that stand out: smoked chicken and andouille sausage, gumbo, and shrimp remoulade. The desserts, which might include a traditional New Orleans bread pudding, are great. The cellar stocks 12,000 bottles. ✉ *6000 Universal Blvd., at Universal Studios Escape's CityWalk,* ☎ *407/224–2424. Reservations essential. AE, D, MC, V.*

$$–$$$ ★ ✕ **Le Coq au Vin.** The traditional French fare served at this modest, charming little house in south Orlando is as expertly prepared as any you'll find in town. Fresh rainbow trout with champagne sauce or an excellent version of the house namesake dish are topped off with crème brûlée or the venerable Grand Marnier soufflé for dessert. Take I–4 to Exit 34 or 35. ✉ *4800 S. Orange Ave.,* ☎ *407/851–6980. AE, DC, MC, V. Closed Mon.*

$–$$$ ✕ **Wolfgang Puck Café.** Lots of choices are on offer here, from wood-oven pizza at the informal Puck Express to five-course meals at the upstairs, formal dining room. Must-tries at Express include the pizzas, with toppings such as grilled chicken or salmon. The dining room always offers a worthy fresh ravioli and a Puck trademark—Wiener schnitzel. ✉ *Downtown Disney West Side,* ☎ *407/938–9653. AE, MC, V.*

$$$–$$$$ **Hard Rock Hotel.** Universal Orlando's super-cool California mission–style hotel has lots of stucco and palm trees and rock music playing in the lobby and hallways; it should be your first choice if you're traveling with teens. Stylish and spacious guest rooms have artwork from the extensive Hard Rock pop art collection. The pool is surrounded by a sand beach and has an underwater sound system. ✉ *1000 Universal Studios Plaza, Orlando 32819,* ☎ *407/224–7117,* WEB *www.loewshotels.com. 650 rooms. 3 restaurants, pool, gym room. AE, D, DC, MC, V.*

$$$–$$$$ ★ **Peabody Orlando.** The bland facade gives no hint of this 27-story hotel's beautifully decorated interior, with marble floors, fountains, and modern art. Many rooms have views of Walt Disney World Resort, but the real show is watching the Peabody's ducks waddle their way to the marble fountain, where they pass the day. ✉ *9801 International Dr., 32819,* ☎ *407/352–4000 or 800/732–2639,* FAX *407/351–9177,* WEB *www.peabodyorlando.com. 891 rooms. 3 restaurants, pools, golf, tennis. AE, D, DC, MC, V.*

$$$–$$$$ **Wyndham Palace Resort and Spa in the WDW Resort.** Don't be fooled by the corporate-looking sand-color tower; this resort—the largest at Lake Buena Vista—is a very elegant establishment featuring the largest health and beauty spa in the area. The best rooms look out toward Epcot's Spaceship Earth. ✉ *1900 Buena Vista Dr., 32830,* ☎ *407/827–2727 or 800/327–2990,* FAX *407/827–6034,* WEB *www.wyndhampalace.com. 1,014 rooms. 4 restaurants, pools, tennis, health club. AE, D, DC, MC, V.*

$–$$ **Travelodge Orlando South.** If you don't want a room with just the bare essentials yet don't have the budget for luxury, this two-story motel is a find. The rooms are comfy if not spectacular; most have two double beds. The hotel is ¼ mi from SeaWorld. ✉ *6263 Westwood Blvd., 32821,* ☎ *407/345–8000 or 800/346–1551,* FAX *407/345–1508,* WEB *www.travelodge.com. 144 rooms. Restaurant, pools. AE, D, DC, MC, V.*

Walt Disney World

Thanks to the park's **central reservations line** (☎ 407/939–3463), reservations for restaurants within Walt Disney World are especially easy to make. For the very popular Epcot restaurants, you can make reservations at any of the WorldKey Information System terminals in the park. Although hotels and resorts on Disney property cost more than comparable facilities elsewhere, their convenience is a significant advantage, and you don't have to drive or pay for parking when visiting Disney parks. Book all Disney hotels through **Walt Disney World Central Reservations** (☎ 407/934–7639, WEB www.disneyworld.com).

World Showcase, in Epcot, offers some of the best dining in the Orlando area, with specialties from various nations that will appeal to every taste. Bistro de Paris ($$$–$$$$) is the great secret at the France pavilion with a sophisticated menu that reflects the cutting edge of French cooking. L'Originale Alfredo di Roma Ristorante ($$–$$$$), in Italy of course, is known for its namesake dish, fettuccine Alfredo, served by singing waiters. **Marrakesh** ($$–$$$) delights the palate with such Moroccan fare as couscous with vegetables, exotic to some Americans. The **Rose and Crown** pub ($–$$), in the United Kingdom, serves hearty portions of fish-and-chips with a Guinness stout.

$$–$$$$ ✕ **California Grill.** The view from this rooftop restaurant matches the food—both are stunning. Start with the brick-oven flatbread with grilled duck sausage and move onto the charcoal-roasted venison or the roasted red snapper with butternut-squash risotto. Good dessert choices include the lemon meringue-pie soufflé and the apple upside-down cake. You can watch the nightly Magic Kingdom fireworks from the restaurant's patio. ✉ *Contemporary Resort,* ☎ *407/939–3463. Reservations essential. AE, MC, V.*

$–$$$ ✕ **Rainforest Café.** People start lining up half an hour before the 11 AM opening of this 30,000-square-ft jungle fantasy. A pump system creates periodic "rain storms," and a 3½-story man-made volcano, forming the roof, erupts frequently, shaking the tables. Top choices include "Eyes of the Ocelot," a nice meat loaf topped with sautéed mushrooms, and "Mojo Bones," tender ribs with barbecue sauce. ✉ *Downtown Disney Marketplace,* ☎ *407/827–8500;* ✉ *Disney's Animal Kingdom,* ☎ *407/938–9100. AE, D, DC, MC, V.*

$$$$ ★ 🏨 **Grand Floridian.** With its brick chimneys, gabled roof, sweeping verandas, and stained-glass domes, this resort exudes Victorian charm but has all the 21st-century conveniences—it's Disney's most expensive hotel. Water sports are a focal point at the marina; there's a children's pool with a giant waterslide. ☎ *407/824–3000,* FAX *407/824–3186. 990 rooms. 6 restaurants, pool, tennis, health club. AE, MC, V.*

$$$–$$$$ ★ 🏨 **Animal Kingdom Lodge.** Giraffes, zebras, and other African wildlife roam three 11-acre savannas separated by wings of this grand hotel. Inside, the atrium lobby exudes African style, from the inlaid carvings on the hardwood floors to the massive faux-thatched roof almost 100 ft above. All of the rooms are somewhat tentlike, with drapes descending from the ceiling, and have a bit of African art; most rooms looks out on one of the savannas. ☎ *407/934–7629,* FAX *407/938–4799. 1,293 rooms. 3 restaurants, pools, health club. AE, D, DC MC, V.*

$$$–$$$$ 🏨 **Contemporary Resort.** Even though this 15-story, flat-topped pyramid is old enough for some parents to have dreamed of riding into it on the monorail when they were kids (it was built in 1971), it remains current. Looking like an intergalactic docking bay, the ideally located resort bustles from dawn to after midnight. Upper floors of the main tower (where rooms are most expensive) offer a great view of the Magic Kingdom. ☎ *407/824–1000,* FAX *407/824–3539. 1,044 rooms. 3 restaurants, pools, tennis, health club. AE, D, DC, MC, V.*

$$–$$$ 🏨 **Caribbean Beach Resort.** On a 42-acre lake, this resort has several villages named after Caribbean islands, each with a pool, but all share a beach. There's a promenade around the lake, and Parrot Cay, an island in the lagoon with bike paths, trails, and a play area. ☎ *407/934–3400,* FAX *407/934–3288. 2,112 rooms. Restaurant, pools, health club. AE, MC, V.*

Motels

U.S. 192 is crammed with motels convenient to Walt Disney World Resort. Rates range from inexpensive to moderate, and most have a pool but few other extras. Among these are **Best Western, Quality Suites,** and **Residence Inn** (☞ Toll-Free Numbers *in* Smart Travel Tips A to Z).

Campgrounds

$–$$$ ⛺ **Fort Wilderness Resort and Campground** (✉ Walt Disney World Central Reservations) encompasses 700 acres of scrubby pine and tiny streams within Walt Disney World Resort. You can rent a trailer or bring your own tent or RV to campsites equipped with electrical outlets, outdoor grills, running water, and waste disposal. Tent sites with water and electricity are also available. Facilities include a cafeteria, 2 pools, 2 tennis courts, basketball, horseback riding, shuffleboard, volleyball, beach, boating, bicycles, playground, and coin laundry.

Nightlife and the Arts

Nightlife

Inside Walt Disney World Resort most every hotel has bars and lounges. Nightly shows include Epcot's **IllumiNations,** with fireworks, lasers, and special effects; the long-running **Hoop-Dee-Doo Musical Revue** (☎ 407/939–3463), at Fort Wilderness; and the **Polynesian Luau** (☎ 407/939–3463 in advance; 407/824–1593 day of show), at the Polynesian Resort. **Downtown Disney** is a huge complex of shops, nightclubs, restaurants, and themed eateries, movie theaters with stadium seating, and live entertainment. (☒ off Buena Vista Dr., I–4 Exit 27, ☎ 407/934–7781 or 407/824–2222). **Cirque du Soleil** (☒ off Buena Vista Dr., ☎ 407/939–7600) in Downtown Disney West Side combines live music, extraordinary acrobatics, theatrics, avant-garde stagings, costumes, and choreography. **CityWalk** next to Universal Studios (☎ 888/331–9108) lights up the night with themed restaurants and nightclubs, shops, and a 20-screen multiplex with stadium seating. **Pointe Orlando** (☒ 9101 International Dr., Orlando, ☎ 407/248–2838) is the site of the XS Orlando virtual playground for teens and adult, plus restaurants, shops, and movie theaters. **Arabian Nights** (☒ 6225 W. Irlo Bronson Memorial Hwy., Kissimmee, ☎ 407/396–7400 or 800/553–6116) is a dinner show featuring 13 breeds of horses and costumed performers in a fairy-tale setting. **Medieval Times** (☒ 4510 W. Irlo Bronson Memorial Hwy., Kissimmee, ☎ 407/239–0214 or 800/229–8300) has a dinner show with knights, nobles, and maidens.

The Arts

Carr Performing Arts Centre (☒ 401 W. Livingston St., Orlando, ☎ 407/849–2577) routinely showcases dance, music, and theater performances. The **UCF Civic Theater** (☒ 1001 E. Princeton St., Orlando, ☎ 407/896–7365) presents a variety of shows. **TD Waterhouse Centre** (☒ 600 W. Amelia St., Orlando, ☎ 407/839–3900) presents big-name performers.

Outdoor Activities and Sports

Biking

The most scenic biking in Orlando is on Walt Disney World Resort property. Two good bike trails were created from former railroad lines: the **West Orange Trail,** running through western Orlando and Apopka, and the **Cady Way Trail,** connecting east Orlando with the suburb of Winter Park. Serious cyclists head to the rolling hills of nearby Lake County.

Golf

The **Celebration Golf Club** (☒ 700 Golf Park Dr., Celebration, ☎ 407/566–4653) was designed by Robert Trent Jones Jr. and Sr. and is 1 mi off the U.S. 192 strip. The course at **Falcon's Fire Golf Club** (☒ 3200 Seralago Blvd., Kissimmee, ☎ 407/239–5445) was designed by Rees Jones. **Grand Cypress Resort** (☒ 1 N. Jacaranda Dr., Orlando, ☎ 407/239–1909 or 800/297–7377) has 45 holes. **Timacuan Golf and Country Club** (☒ 550 Timacuan Blvd., Lake Mary, ☎ 407/321–0010) has a front 9 that's open, with lots of sand, and a back 9 that's heavily wooded. There are five championship courses within **Walt Disney World** (☎ 407/824–4321).

Horseback Riding

Fort Wilderness Campground (✉ Walt Disney World Resort, ☎ 407/824–2832) offers tame trail rides through backwoods. **Horse World** (✉ 3705 S. Poinciana Blvd., Kissimmee, ☎ 407/847–4343) leads trail rides for beginners and advanced riders.

Spectator Sports

The NBA **Orlando Magic** and the WNBA's **Orlando Miracle** play in the **TD Waterhouse Arena** (✉ 600 W. Amelia St., ☎ 407/839–3900), two blocks west of the I–4 Amelia Street exit. At **Disney's Wide World of Sports** (☎ 407/363–6600), the Atlanta Braves play spring training baseball in March, the Orlando Rays play in the summer, and other sporting events take place year-round.

Beaches and Water Sports

A plethora of water sports is available in the Orlando area. Marinas at resorts in **Walt Disney World** rent all types of boats, from pontoon boats and pedal boats to catamarans and outrigger canoes. North of the Kennedy Space Center, the **Canaveral National Seashore** (✉ 7611 S. Atlantic Ave., between New Smyrna Beach and Titusville, ☎ 321/267–1110 or 321/861–0667) has 24 mi of unspoiled, uncrowded beaches.

Shopping

Much of the Walt Disney World Resort shopping that isn't in the theme parks is concentrated in the area known as **Downtown Disney,** comprising the Marketplace, Pleasure Island, and West Side. Universal has answered the shopping-entertainment challenge with its own complex, **Universal Studios CityWalk. Florida Mall** (✉ 8001 S. Orange Blossom Terr., Orlando) is the largest mall in central Florida, with department stores, 200 specialty shops, seven theaters, and one of the area's better food courts. The festive **Mercado Mediterranean Village** (✉ 8445 International Dr., Orlando) has specialty shops and a large food court with cuisines from around the world. **Renninger's Twin Markets,** near the charming village of Mount Dora (30 mi northwest of Orlando on U.S. 441), hosts hundreds of flea market and antiques dealers every weekend. The really big shows take place the third weekend of November, January, and February, when some 1,400 antiques dealers converge. **Belz Factory Outlet World** (✉ 5401 W. Oak Ridge Rd., northern tip of International Dr., Orlando) is the area's largest collection of outlet stores—more than 180, in two malls and four nearby annexes. **Pointe*Orlando** (✉ 9101 International Dr., Orlando) has 70 specialty shops.

Walt Disney World and the Orlando Area Essentials

AIRPORTS

Orlando International Airport, off the Bee Line Expressway, is served by major airlines.

➤ AIRPORT INFORMATION: **Orlando International Airport** (✉ 6086 McCoy Rd., ☎ 407/825–2001, WEB fcn.state.fl.us/goaa).

BUS TRAVEL

Greyhound provides service from major Florida cities and from outside the state.

➤ BUS INFORMATION: **Greyhound** (☎ 800/231–2222).

CAR TRAVEL

From Jacksonville take I–95 south, then I–4 from Port Orange. From Tampa/St. Petersburg take I–4 east. From Miami take I–95 north and connect with Florida's Turnpike going northbound at White City. From Atlanta take I–75 south and connect with Florida's Turnpike.

TRAIN TRAVEL

Amtrak operates the *Silver Star* and the *Silver Meteor,* which stop at Winter Park, Orlando, and Kissimmee. Amtrak's Auto Train runs between Sanford and Lorton, Virginia.

➤ TRAIN INFORMATION: **Amtrak** (☎ 800/872–7245).

VISITOR INFORMATION

➤ TOURIST INFORMATION: **Kissimmee/St. Cloud Convention and Visitors Bureau** (✉ 1925 E. Irlo Bronson Memorial Hwy., Kissimmee 34744, ☎ 407/847–5000 or 800/327–9159, WEB www.floridakiss.com). **Orlando/Orange County Convention & Visitors Bureau** (✉ 6700 Forum Dr., Suite 100, Orlando 32821-8087, ☎ 407/363–5800, WEB www.orlandoinfo.com).

THE FLORIDA KEYS

The string of 41 islands—or keys—placed like a comma between the Atlantic Ocean and the Gulf of Mexico, at the southern tip of Florida, presents a paradox. On the one hand, the Keys are natural wonders of lush vegetation, tropical birds, and wildlife, washed by waters teeming with more than 600 kinds of fish; a place where swimming, fishing, diving, and boating are a way of life. On the other hand, the Keys are a highly commercialized tourist attraction that have brought a clutter of unsightly billboards, motels, and shopping malls to U.S. 1 (also known as the Overseas Highway), which links the islands to the mainland. Although the 110-mi drive from Key Largo to Key West is often clogged with traffic on weekends and holidays, it is still a mesmerizing journey into expanses of blue water and blue sky, especially where the road is the only thing separating the ocean from the Gulf. A note about addresses, which are listed by island or mile marker (MM) number: Residents use the abbreviation BS for the Bay Side of the Overseas Highway (U.S. 1) and OS for the Atlantic Ocean side of the highway.

Exploring the Florida Keys

The Keys are divided into the Upper Keys (from Key Largo to Long Key Channel), the Middle Keys (from Long Key Channel to Seven Mile Bridge), and the Lower Keys (from Seven Mile Bridge to Key West). Pause to explore the flora and fauna of the backcountry and the fragile reefs and aquatic life of the surrounding waters as you weave your way south to historically rich Key West.

Upper Keys

The Upper Keys are dominated by **Key Largo,** with its wildlife refuges, offshore coral reefs, and nature parks.Bikers, walkers, and rollerbladers can cruise along the 1¼-mi paved road (one way) through the 2,400-acre **Dagny Johnson Key Largo Hammocks State Botanical Site** (✉ 1 mi north of U.S. 1 on Rte. 905, OS, ☎ 305/451–1202; 🎫 free), the largest remaining stand of West Indian tropical hardwood hammock and mangrove wetland in the Keys. It has rest rooms, information kiosks, picnic tables, and interpretive signs. ★ **John Pennekamp Coral Reef State Park** (✉ 102601 Overseas Hwy., MM 102.5, OS, ☎ 305/451–1202, 🎫 $4 per vehicle, plus 50¢ per passenger, $2 for walk-ins and cyclists) encompasses 78 square mi of coral reefs, which contain 40 species of coral and more than 650 varieties of fish. Diving and snorkeling here are exceptional. A concessionaire rents watercraft and offers boat trips to the reef. The visitor center–aquarium has a floor-to-ceiling aquarium surrounded by numerous smaller tanks, a video room, and exhibits.

Get a close-up look at bird life at the **Florida Keys Wild Bird Rehabilitation Center** (✉ MM 93.6, BS, 93600 Overseas Hwy., Tavernier, ☎ 305/852–4486; 🎫 free), where at any time the resident population can include ospreys, hawks, pelicans, cormorants, terns, and herons. When the Florida East Coast Railway drilled, dynamited, and carved Windley Key's limestone bed, it exposed the once-living fossilized coral reef that was laid down about 125,000 years ago. Explore the five trails and Alison Fahrer Environmental Education Center on a tour or on your own Thursday–Monday at the **Windley Key Geological State Park** (✉ MM 85.5, BS, ☎ 305/664–2540; 🎫 free, trail access $1.50).

Theater of the Sea (✉ MM 84.5, OS, Islamorada, ☎ 305/664–2431; 🎫 $17.25) has dolphin and sea lion shows, a touch tank, a pool where sharks are fed by a trainer, and several small aquariums. For $125, you can swim with the dolphins (reservations recommended). At **Robbie's Marina** (✉ MM 77.5, BS, Islamorada, ☎ 305/664–9814; 🎫 dock access $1), 50 or so tarpon—some as long as 5 ft—gather below the docks, waiting to be fed. The following two sites are accessible only by boat; you can take a ferry ($15 for one site, $25 for both) or rent a boat or kayak from the official state concessionaire, **Robbie's Marina. Indian Key State Historic Site** (✉ MM 78.5, OS, Islamorada, ☎ 305/664–4815; 🎫 tour $1, free if you arrive by ferry), inhabited by Indians for several thousand years before Europeans arrived, was also a base for early 19th-century shipwreck salvagers until an Indian attack wiped out the settlement in 1840. A virgin hardwood forest still cloaks **Lignumvitae Key State Botanical Site** (✉ MM 78.5, BS, Islamorada; 🎫 tour $1, free if you arrive by ferry), punctuated only by the house and gardens built by chemical magnate William Matheson in 1919. For information and reservations contact **Long Key State Recreation Area** (✉ MM 67.5, OS [Box 776, Long Key], ☎ 305/664–4815; 🎫 $3.75, plus 50¢ per each additional person; canoe rental $4 per hr).

The Middle Keys

Once you cross **Long Key Viaduct** (MM 65), one of 42 bridges in the island chain, the Keys become more rustic. The second-longest bridge on the former rail line (known informally as the Overseas Railroad), this 2-mi-long structure has 222 reinforced-concrete arches. The nonprofit **Dolphin Research Center** (✉ MM 59, BS, ☎ 305/289–1121; 🎫 $15 tour, Dolphin Encounter $125) runs educational tours and dolphin interaction programs.

The Florida Keys Land Trust owns the **Museums and Nature Center of Crane Point Hammock** (✉ MM 50, BS, 5550 Overseas Hwy., Marathon, ☎ 305/743–9100; 🎫 $7.50), which houses the **Museum of Natural History of the Florida Keys** and the **Florida Keys Children's Museum** and includes a 1-mi loop trail, the remnants of a Bahamian village, and the **George Adderly House,** the oldest surviving example of Conch-style architecture outside Key West. From November to Easter, weekly docent-led hammock tours may be available; call for times. Bring good walking shoes and bug repellent. At the end of Marathon are the Old Seven Mile Bridge and the new Seven Mile Bridge.You can walk 2.2 mi or take a shuttle (from Knight's Key, MM 47, OS) across the old bridge to tour ★ **Pigeon Key** (✉ MM 45, OS [Box 500130, Pigeon Key 33050], ☎ 305/289–0025 general information; 305/743–7655 eco-tour information; 🎫 $8.50), a former work camp for the Overseas Railroad, and visit a museum that recalls the history of the railroad, the Keys, and railroad baron Henry M. Flagler.

The Lower Keys

South of Marathon, the **Seven Mile Bridge,** believed to be the world's longest segmented bridge, is the gateway to the Lower Keys. The delicate, dog-size Key deer can be viewed at **National Key Deer Refuge** (✉ Headquarters, MM 30.5, BS, Big Pine Shopping Center, ☎ 305/872–0774; 🎟 free; headquarters closed weekends), on Big Pine Key.

The final key is **Key West,** famous for its climate, laid-back lifestyle, sizable gay population, colorful heritage, and 19th-century architecture. Key West's rich ethnic past comes alive through vintage photographs and memorabilia at the **Lofton B. Sands African-Bahamian Museum** (✉ 324 Truman Ave., ☎ 305/295–7337 or 305/293–9692; 🎟 donation suggested) in the **Bahama Village** area (✉ Thomas and Petronia Sts.), easily recognized by the peach, yellow, and pink homes of early Bahamian settlers. The **San Carlos Institute** (✉ 516 Duval St., ☎ 305/294–3887; 🎟 $3; closed Mon.) is a Cuban-American heritage center, with a museum and research library focusing on the history of Key West and 19th- and 20th-century Cuban exiles. **Fort Zachary Taylor State Historic Site** (✉ Southard St., ☎ 305/292–6713; 🎟 $2.50 per vehicle, $1.50 per pedestrian or bicyclist) was an important fort during the Civil and Spanish-American wars. It's 88 steps to the top of the 92-ft lighthouse at the **Lighthouse Museum** (✉ 938 Whitehead St., ☎ 305/294–0012; 🎟 $8). The adjacent keeper's cottage displays ship models and lighthouse artifacts. The **Audubon House and Gardens** (✉ 205 Whitehead St., ☎ 305/294–2116; 🎟 $8.50) has beautiful tropical gardens ★ and a large collection of Audubon engravings. The **Hemingway House** (✉ 907 Whitehead St., ☎ 305/294–1575, 🎟 $9) is dedicated to the life and work of the author who wrote 70% of his works in Key West, including *For Whom the Bell Tolls.* **Harry S. Truman Little White House Museum** (✉ 111 Front St., ☎ 305/294–9911; 🎟 $10), a winter White House for Presidents Truman, Eisenhower, and Kennedy, includes a photographic review of visiting dignitaries and exhibits. It's on the grounds of **Truman Annex,** a 103-acre former military parade grounds and barracks. The island's newest attraction is the **Key West Museum of Art & History** (✉ 281 Front St., ☎ 305/295–6616; 🎟 $6), a former U.S. Customs House. The impressive redbrick and terra-cotta Richardsonian Romanesque–style building houses permanent and rotating exhibits about the history of Key West.

Nancy Forrester's Secret Garden (✉ 1 Free School La., ☎ 305/294–0015; 🎟 $6) is one of the prettiest spots in Key West. It has rare palms and cycads, trails lined with ferns, bromeliads, bright gingers, heliconias, and towering native gumbo-limbos strewn with hanging orchids and twining vines.

At the **Key West Aquarium** (✉ 1 Whitehead St., ☎ 305/296–2051; 🎟 $9) kids learn about the marine life found around the Keys in an up-close-and-personal experience with turtles, rays, sharks, parrot fish, eels, and tarpon swimming in glass tanks, coral pools, a pond, and touch tanks.

Dining and Lodging

Local specialties include conch chowder, Florida lobster, and key lime pie. Accommodations, from historic hotels and guest houses to large resorts and run-of-the-mill motels, are more expensive here than elsewhere in southern Florida.

Islamorada

$$–$$$$ ★ ✕ **Morada Bay.** This bayfront restaurant has a spectacular water view, traditional wooden Key West architecture, and a contemporary menu with tapas and innovative dishes, mostly from the sea. There's frequently live entertainment, especially on weekends. ✉ *MM 81, BS, 81590 Overseas Hwy.,* ☎ *305/664–0604. AE, MC, V.*

$$–$$$ ✕ **Squid Row.** Along with local fish, either grilled, divinely flaky, or in bread crumbs and sautéed, this affable seafood eatery offers a nightly special of bouillabaisse ($27.95) thick with fish and shellfish—even stone crab claws–that is simply wonderful. Finish it by yourself and they'll serve you a free slice of key lime pie. ✉ *MM 81.9, OS,* ☎ *305/664–9865. AE, D, DC, MC, V.*

$–$$$ ✕ **Manny & Isa's.** This Keys institution has no frills, fancy decor, or pretense, but it does have delicious Cuban and Spanish dishes, local seafood, and daily fish, chicken, and pork chop specials. Manny's key lime pies are heavenly. To avoid the wait for dinner on weekends and in high season, call for takeout. ✉ *MM 81.6, OS, 81610 Old Hwy.,* ☎ *305/664–5019. AE, D, MC, V. Closed Tues. and mid-Oct.–mid-Nov.*

$$$$ 🏨 **Cheeca Lodge.** This classy, 27-acre, low-rise resort combines a sense of luxury with a sense of familiarity. Suites have kitchens and screened balconies; fourth-floor rooms in the main lodge have ocean or bay views. The resort, which has a full-service spa and a children's program, is the local leader in green activism, with everything from recycling to ecotours. ✉ *MM 82, OS (Box 527, 33036),* ☎ *305/664–4651 or 800/327–2888,* FAX *305/664–2893,* WEB *www.cheeca.com. 203 rooms. 2 restaurants, pools, golf, tennis, health club. AE, D, DC, MC, V.*

Key Largo

$–$$$$ ★ ✕ **Fish House.** Expect nautical, Keys-y casual decor and friendly, diligent servers at this perennial favorite. Nightly specials like shrimp and lobster creole in a spicy tomato sauce served over rice are another reason why diners return. The next-door annex, the Gift House, has coffees, fabulous desserts, and souvenirs. ✉ *MM 102.4, OS,* ☎ *305/451–4665. AE, D, MC, V. Closed early Sept.–early Oct.*

$–$$ ✕ **Cafe Largo.** This bistro-style eatery prepares seafood and traditional Italian dishes quite well. The penne with shrimp and broccoli has tender shrimp, al dente broccoli, and garlic. There's lobster and shrimp scampi, too. The dessert list is short but sweet. ✉ *MM 99.5, BS, Overseas Hwy.,* ☎ *305/451–4885. AE, MC, V. No lunch.*

$–$$ ✕ **Mrs. Mac's Kitchen.** The architecture, decorations, and vibe of this rustic screened, open-air restaurant hark back to the 1950s, when the Keys had more fishermen than well-heeled visitors. Mrs. Mac's still prepares traditional American foods like sandwiches, burgers, barbecue, and seafood. ✉ *MM 99.4, BS, 99336 Overseas Hwy.,* ☎ *305/451–3722. No credit cards. Closed Sun.*

$ ✕ **Chad's Deli & Bakery.** Each morning the namesake owner bakes eight kinds of fresh breads, which he uses to make sandwiches large enough to feed two hungry adults. The menu also includes salads, sides, soft drinks, and cookies. ✉ *MM 92.3, BS, Overseas Hwy.,* ☎ *305/853–5566. No credit cards. Closed Sun.*

$$$–$$$$ 🏨 **Westin Beach Resort, Key Largo.** This large resort with lush landscaping is tucked away among the trees of a hardwood hammock. The spacious, comfortable rooms have tropical touches. Lighted nature trails and boardwalks wind through the woods to a small beach. Both restaurants overlook the water. ✉ *MM 96.9, BS, 97000 Overseas Hwy., 33037,* ☎ *305/852–5553 or 800/826–1006,* FAX *305/852–8669,* WEB *www.keylargoresort.com. 200 rooms. 2 restaurants, pools, tennis, health club. AE, D, DC, MC, V.*

$$$–$$$$ ★ **Kona Kai Resort.** A sidewalk links landscaped cottages to a sandy beach at this stylish, laid-back resort. There are no room phones, and maid service is every third morning. Studios and one- and two-bedroom suites—with full kitchens—are spacious and light-filled. Beachfront hammocks and a cozy pool make it easy to while away the day. Smoking is not permitted; neither are children under 16. ✉ *MM 97.8, BS, 97802 Overseas Hwy., 33037,* ☎ *305/852–7200 or 800/365–7829* WEB *www.konakairesort.com. 11 units. Pool, tennis. AE, D, MC, V.*

$$ **Largo Lodge.** A palpable calm hangs over the 1950s-vintage adults-only cottages hidden in a garden of palms, sea grapes, and orchids. Cozy accommodations are fully equipped with kitchens and screened porches but no phones. There's 200 ft of bay frontage. ✉ *MM 101.5, BS, 101740 Overseas Hwy., 33037,* ☎ *305/451–0424 or 800/468–4378,* WEB *www.largolodge.com. 7 units. MC, V.*

Key West

$$$–$$$$ ★ ✕ **Louie's Backyard.** This oceanfront contemporary restaurant with a steal-your-breath view consistently offers an enticing menu that changes seasonally. Dine outside under a mahoe tree. Come for lunch if you're on a budget; the menu is less expensive and there's that view. For night owls, the Afterdeck Bar serves cocktails on the water until the wee hours. ✉ *700 Waddell Ave.,* ☎ *305/294–1061. MC, V.*

$$–$$$ ★ ✕ **Alice's at LaTeDa.** Chef-owner Alice Weingarten, a popular local chef, serves breakfast, brunch, lunch, and dinner poolside with live evening entertainment. It's right in the middle of LaTeDa Hotel, an in-vogue, very gay-friendly hotel/bar complex. Her talent shows in her exemplary selection of wines that complement the creative mix of seafood, game, beef, pork, and poultry dishes. ✉ *1125 Duval St.,* ☎ *305/296–6706. AE, D, MC, V. Closed Mon.*

$–$$ ✕ **Mangia Mangia.** Select a fresh pasta from the daily selection and match it with one of Mangia Mangia's freshly made Italian sauces: alfredo, marinara, meat, or with pesto. Tables are arranged in a brick patio and in a nicely dressed-up old-house dining room. It's one of the best restaurants in Key West, and one of its best values. The wine list of more than 350 selections contains many under $20. ✉ *900 Southard St.,* ☎ *305/294–2469. AE, MC, V. No lunch.*

$$$$ ★ **Marquesa Hotel.** This coolly elegant restored 1884 home is Key West's finest lodging. You can relax among richly landscaped pools and gardens against a backdrop of brick steps rising to the villa-like suites on the property's perimeter. Elegant rooms contain eclectic antique and reproduction furnishings and botanical print fabrics. Although the clientele is mostly straight, the hotel is very gay-friendly. ✉ *600 Fleming St., 33040,* ☎ *305/292–1919 or 800/869–4631,* FAX *305/294–2121,* WEB *www.marquesa.com. 27 rooms. Restaurant, pools. AE, DC, MC, V.*

$$$$ ★ **Paradise Inn.** Gloriously chic best describes this romantic palm-shaded inn composed of renovated cigar makers' cottages and authentically reproduced Bahamian-style houses with sundecks and balconies. The lush tropical garden with a heated pool and lily pond are light-years away from the bustle of Key West. ✉ *819 Simonton St., 33040,* ☎ *305/293–8007 or 800/888–9648,* FAX *305/293–0807,* WEB *www.theparadiseinn.com. 18 units. Pool. AE, D, DC, MC, V. CP.*

$$$ **Ambrosia House.** Relax in a casual environment with a dollop of style at these twin inns comprising pool-view rooms, suites, town houses, and cottages spread out on nearly 2 acres. Rooms are distinctly decorated with original artwork by Keys artists, wicker or wood furniture, and spacious bathrooms. They all have a private entrance and a deck, patio, or porch. ✉ *615, 618, 622 Fleming St., 33040,* ☎ *305/296–9838 or 800/535–9838,* FAX *305/296–2425. 31 rooms, 1 cottage. 3 pools. AE, D, MC, V. BP.*

$–$$$$ ★ **Popular House/Key West Bed & Breakfast.** Local art—large, splashy canvases; a mural in the style of Gauguin—hangs on the walls, and tropical gardens and music set the mood. You'll find both inexpensive rooms with shared bath (whose rates haven't been raised in more than 10 years) and luxury rooms. ✉ *415 William St., 33040,* ☎ *305/296–7274 or 800/438–6155,* FAX *305/293–0306,* WEB *www.keywestbandb.com. 8 rooms. AE, D, DC, MC, V. CP.*

Marathon

$–$$$$ **Barracuda Grill.** If you think Keys food is limited to grilled dolphinfish and coconut shrimp, this contemporary eatery will be a revelation. An eclectic menu capitalizes on the local bounty—fresh fish—but is equally represented by tender, aged Angus beef; rack of lamb; and even a meat loaf that defies the stereotype. ✉ *MM 49.5, BS,* ☎ *305/743–3314. AE, MC, V. Closed Sun. No lunch.*

$ ★ **7 Mile Grill.** This nearly 50-year-old weatherworn, open-air seafood restaurant could serve as a set for a 1950s movie. At the Marathon end of the Seven Mile Bridge, it serves up friendly service and casual food. Favorites on the mostly seafood menu include creamy shrimp bisque, and fresh grouper and dolphinfish grilled, broiled, or fried. ✉ *MM 47, BS, 1240 Overseas Hwy.,* ☎ *305/743–4481. MC, V. Closed Wed.; Thurs. mid-Apr.–mid-Nov.; and at owner's discretion Aug.–Sept.*

$$$$ ★ **Hawk's Cay Resort.** This rambling Caribbean-style retreat, which opened in 1959, is popular with vacationing families and people looking for a little piece of a tropical paradise. Two-bedroom villas and upgrades improved the tony resort, which has spacious rooms decorated in a light, casual style of wicker and earthy colors. Sports and recreational facilities are extensive, as are supervised programs for kids and teens. The Dolphin Connection provides three educational experiences with dolphins. ✉ *MM 61, OS, 33050,* ☎ *305/743–7000 or 800/432–2242,* FAX *305/743–5215,* WEB *www.hawkscay.com. 176 rooms, 170 villas. 4 restaurants, pools, tennis, health club. AE, D, DC, MC, V.*

$$$ ★ **Seascape Ocean Resort.** The charming lobby filled with soothing sea colors and original artwork gives way to pastel-color guest rooms decorated with more artwork, hand-painted headboards, and fresh flowers and fruit. The 5-acre oceanfront property with a large, two-story house is an exclusive yet unsnobbish retreat. You can swim in the pool or ocean, paddle a kayak, or relax under a shade tree. Continental breakfast and afternoon cocktails and hors d'oeuvres are served. Rooms are no-smoking and have no phones. ✉ *MM 50.5, OS, 1075 75th St., 33050,* ☎ *305/743–6455 or 800/332–7327,* FAX *305/743–8469,* WEB *www.floridakeys.net/seascape. 9 rooms. Pool. AE, MC, V. CP.*

$–$$ **Coral Lagoon.** This little resort has cheerfully painted duplex cottages with kitchens, private sundecks with lazy hammocks, views of a deep-water canal, and pretty landscaping. Extras not usually found at this price include videocassette players, safes, hair dryers, morning coffee, tennis rackets, fishing equipment, dockage, and barbecues. ✉ *MM 53.5, OS, 12399 Overseas Hwy., Marathon 33050,* ☎ *305/289–0121,* FAX *305/289–0195. 18 cottages. Pool, tennis. AE, D, MC, V.*

Nightlife and the Arts

Key West is the Keys' hub for artistic performances and nightlife. This city alone claims among its current residents 55 full-time writers and 500 painters and craftspeople.The most popular entertainment is the nightly gathering of street vendors, performers, and onlookers at **Mallory Square Dock** who come to celebrate the sunset. The **Tennessee Williams Fine Arts Center** (✉ Florida Keys Community College, 5901 College Rd., ☎ 305/296–9081 ext. 5) offers dance, music, plays, and star performers from December to April. You can pick your entertainment at the **Bourbon Street Complex** (✉ 724–801 Duval St., ☎ 305/293–9600), a gay-oriented complex with facilities featuring a nightly drag show, 10 video screens, and male dancers grooving to the latest DJ spins. **Capt. Tony's Saloon** (✉ 428 Greene St., ☎ 305/294–1838), a landmark bar noted for its connection with Ernest Hemingway, has nightly entertainment. Hemingway liked to gamble in the club room at **Sloppy Joe's** (✉ 201 Duval St., ☎ 305/294–5717), a popular, noisy bar.

Outdoor Activities and Sports

Biking

Cyclists are now able to ride all but a tiny portion of the bike path that runs along the Overseas Highway from Mile Marker 106 south to MM 73, then picks up again at MM 70 to MM 66, then again from MM 53 to the Seven Mile Bridge. Trails crisscross the Marathon area; most popular is the 2.2-mi section of the old **Seven Mile Bridge** leading to Pigeon Key. In the Upper Keys, **Tavernier Bicycle & Hobbies** (✉ MM 91.9, BS, 91958 Overseas Hwy, Tavernier, ☎ 305/852–2859) rents single-speed adult and children's bikes.In the Middle Keys **Bike Marathon Bike Rentals** (✉ ☎ 305/743–3204) delivers beach cruisers to your hotel door. **Equipment Locker Sport & Cycle** (✉ MM 53, BS, ☎ 305/289–1670) rents cruisers and mountain bikes for adults and children.For moped rentals, contact **Keys Moped & Scooter** (✉ 523 Truman Ave., Key West, ☎ 305/294–0399) or **Moped Hospital** (✉ 601 Truman Ave., Key West, ☎ 305/296–3344).

Diving and Snorkeling

Miles of living coral reefs are populated with 650 species of tropical fish, as well as four centuries of explorable shipwrecks. Outstanding diving areas include **John Pennekamp Coral Reef State Park** (✉ MM 102.5, OS, Key Largo, ☎ 305/451–1621) and **Looe Key Reef,** 5 mi off Ramrod Key (✉ MM 27.5, OS). **American Diving Headquarters** (✉ MM 105.5, BS, 10550 Overseas Hwy., Key Largo, ☎ 305/451–0037) and **Looe Key Reef Resort and Dive Center** (✉ MM 27.5, OS, Ramrod Key, ☎ 305/872–2215 or 800/942–5397) lead dives in the area.

Fishing and Boating

Anglers can enjoy deep-sea fishing on the ocean or Gulf and flat-water fishing in the backcountry shallows. Numerous marinas rent all types of boats and water-sports equipment. Particularly popular are the glass-bottom-boat tours to the coral reefs. Check with chambers of commerce for information on charter- and party-boat operators.Sandy Moret is one of the most recognizable names in Keys fly-fishing. He operates **Florida Keys Outfitters** (✉ MM 82, BS, ☎ 305/664–5423), where there's a store and the Florida Keys Fly Fishing School, which attracts anglers from around the world. There are classes, fishing trips, and fishing and accommodations packages (at Cheeca Lodge). Try **Hubba Hubba** for backcountry fishing (✉ MM 79.8, OS, Islamorada, ☎ 305/664–9281). In Key West, Captain Steven Impallomeni works as a flats-fishing guide, specializing in ultralight and fly-fishing for tarpon, permit, and bonefish, as well as near-shore and light-tackle fishing on the *Gallopin' Ghost*, which leaves from **Murray's Marina** (✉ MM 5, Stock Island, ☎ 305/292–9837).

Golf

Key Colony Beach Par 3 (✉ MM 53.5, OS, 8th St., Key Colony Beach near Marathon, ☎ 305/289–1533) is a 9-hole public course. **Key West Resort Golf Club** (✉ 6450 E. College Rd., Stock Island, ☎ 305/294–5232) is an 18-hole public course.

Beaches

Keys beaches, particularly in Key West, have been closed periodically to swimming because of sewage contamination. Observe signs about the water's health conditions. Since the natural shorelines of the Keys are a combination of marshes, rocky outcroppings, and grassy wetlands, most beaches for sunbathing and swimming are man-made from imported sand.The exception is **Bahia Honda State Park** (⊠ MM 37, OS, Bahia Honda Key, ☏ 305/872–2353), which has a naturally sandy beach, plus a nature trail, campground and waterfront cabins (reserve up to 11 months in advance), marina, and dive shop. **Anne's Beach** (⊠ MM 73.5, OS, Islamorada, ☏ 305/852–2381) has a ½-mi elevated wooden boardwalk that crosses a wetlands hammock at the edge of the shore. Information on **Curry Hammock State Park** (⊠ MM 57, OS) is provided by Long Key State Recreation Area (☞ Long Key *in* Exploring, *above*). It comprises upland hammock, wetlands, mangroves, and a long sandy beach with a bathhouse and picnic tables. **Sombrero Beach** (⊠ MM 50, OS, Sombrero Rd., Marathon, ☏ 305/743–0033) has areas for swimmers, jet boats, and windsurfers. Behind the narrow, sandy beach is a large, grassy park with grills, picnic kiosks, showers, and a playground. **Ft. Zachary Taylor State Historic Site** (⊠ end of Southard St., through Truman Annex, ☏ 305/292–6713) is the best of the several Key West beaches. It's uncrowded and has picnic areas, grills, and a historic fort.

Shopping

The Keys are a thriving artists' community, so art is in good supply here. Original works by major international artists—including American Everglades photographer Clyde Butcher, French painter Jalinepol W, and French sculptor Polles—are shown at the **Gallery at Kona Kai** (⊠ MM 97.8, BS, 97802 Overseas Hwy, ☏ 305/852–7200). **Rain Barrel** (⊠ MM 86.7, BS, 86700 Overseas Hwy., Islamorada, ☏ 305/852–3084) is a 3-acre crafts village with eight resident artists and works by scores of others, plus a delightful restaurant serving primarily vegetarian dishes. Across the street, an enormous fabricated lobster by artist Richard Blaes stands in front of **Treasure Village** (⊠ MM 86.7, OS, 86729 Old Hwy., Islamorada, ☏ 305/852–0511), which has a dozen crafts and specialty shops. **Redbone Gallery** (⊠ MM 81, OS, 200 Industrial Dr., Islamorada, ☏ 305/664–2002) specializes in art with a fishing and marine theme. The **Gallery at Morada Bay** (⊠ MM 81.6, BS, Overseas Hwy., Islamorada, ☏ 305/664–3650) carries fine arts and crafts, including blown glass, jewelry, and paintings by top South Florida artists. **World Wide Sportsman** (⊠ MM 82.5, BS, Overseas Hwy., Islamorada, ☏ 305/664–4615) is a two-level attraction–retail center–lounge, selling upscale fishing equipment. Key West has numerous fine art galleries and unique specialty shops, such as **Fast Buck Freddie's** (⊠ 500 Duval St., ☏ 305/294–2007), which sells housewares, clothing, and furnishings with a tropical theme. The **Gallery on Greene** (⊠ 606 Greene St., ☏ 305/294–1669) showcases politically incorrect art by Jeff McNally and three-dimensional paintings by local artist Mario Sanchez, among others, in Key West's largest gallery.

The Florida Keys Essentials

AIR TRAVEL

Service to Key West is provided by American Eagle, Cape Air, Comair/Delta Connection, Gulfstream/Continental Connection, and US Airways/US Airways Express. Direct service between Miami and Marathon is provided by American Eagle.

➤ AIRLINES AND CONTACTS: **American Eagle** (☎ 800/433–7300). **Cape Air** (☎ 800/352–0714). **Comair/Delta Connection** (☎ 800/354–9822). **Gulfstream/Continental Connection** (☎ 800/525–0280). **US Airways/US Airways Express** (☎ 800/428–4322).

AIRPORTS

Continuous improvements in service now link airports in Miami, Fort Lauderdale/Hollywood, Naples, Orlando, and Tampa directly with Key West International Airport.

➤ AIRPORT INFORMATION: **Key West International Airport** (✉ 3491 S. Roosevelt Blvd., ☎ 305/296–5439).

BOAT AND FERRY TRAVEL

You can travel to Key West via the Intracoastal Waterway through Florida Bay or in Hawk Channel along the Atlantic coast. Marinas abound in the Keys, but be sure to make docking reservations in advance. For more information contact the Florida Marine Patrol.

➤ BOAT AND FERRY INFORMATION: **Florida Marine Patrol** (✉ MM 48, BS, 2796 Overseas Hwy., Suite 100, State Regional Service Center, Marathon 33050, ☎ 305/289–2320; 800/342–5367 after 5 PM).

BUS TRAVEL

Greyhound runs a Keys shuttle three or four times a day between Miami International Airport's Concourse E (lower level) and the Keys. Fares run about $13 one-way and $25 round-trip to Key Largo (MM 102) and about $31 one-way and $61 round-trip to Key West (MM1).

➤ BUS INFORMATION: **Greyhound** (☎ 800/231–2222).

CAR TRAVEL

From Miami take Florida's Turnpike (toll road) or State Highway 826/874 to the Homestead Extension of Florida's Turnpike south until it links with U.S. 1 in Florida City. South of here U.S. 1 becomes the Overseas Highway.

VISITOR INFORMATION

➤ TOURIST INFORMATION: **Florida Keys & Key West Visitors Bureau** (✉ 402 Wall St., 33040, ☎ 800/352–5397, WEB florida-keys.fl.us/chamber.htm). **Greater Key West Chamber of Commerce** (✉ 402 Wall St., 33040, ☎ 305/294–2587 or 800/527–8539, FAX 305/294–7806). **Islamorada Chamber of Commerce** (✉ MM 82.5, BS [Box 915, 33036], ☎ 305/664–4503 or 800/322–5397). **Key Largo Chamber of Commerce** (✉ MM 106, BS, 106000 Overseas Hwy., 33037, ☎ 305/451–1414 or 800/822–1088). **Key West Business Guild** (oriented toward gays and lesbians; ✉ 728 Duval St. [Box 1208, 33041], ☎ 305/294–4603 or 800/535–7797). **Lower Keys Chamber of Commerce** (✉ MM 31, OS [Box 430511, Big Pine Key 33043], ☎ 305/872–2411 or 800/872–3722, FAX 305/872–0752). **Marathon Chamber of Commerce & Visitor Center** (✉ MM 53.5, BS, 12222 Overseas Hwy., 33050, ☎ 305/743–5417 or 800/262–7284).

SOUTHWEST FLORIDA

Swimming, sunbathing, sailing, and shelling are the draws of the 200-mi coastal stretch between the Tampa Bay area and the Everglades. Venturing inland from the miles of sun-splashed beaches along the Gulf of Mexico, you'll discover culturally rich and ethnically diverse towns, interesting historic sites, and stellar attractions, such as Busch Gardens. This area also tends to be more affordable than other parts of Florida. The region is divided into three areas: Tampa Bay (including Tampa,

St. Petersburg, Clearwater, and Tarpon Springs), Sarasota (including Bradenton and Venice), and Fort Myers/Naples.

Exploring Southwest Florida

The Tampa Bay Area

Tampa Bay is the commercial center of southwestern Florida, with a bustling international port and the largest shrimp fleet in the state. Known as the City by the Bay, Tampa pays homage to its waterfront location ★ with the **Florida Aquarium** (⊠ 701 Channelside Dr., ☎ 813/273–4000, WEB www.flaquarium.net; $15), whose 83-ft-high glass dome is already a landmark. More than 4,300 specimens of fish, other animals, and plants represent 550 species native to Florida. Half-day Dolphin-Quest eco-tours on a catamaran are also available ($18). The 35,000-square-ft **Tampa Museum of Art** (⊠ 600 N. Ashley Dr., ☎ 813/274–8130, WEB www.tampamuseum.com; $5) has a permanent collection of more than 7,000 works, including the most comprehensive collection of Greek, Roman, and Etruscan antiquities in the southeastern United States, and an excellent collection of 20th-century American art. Reserve a day in Tampa for a journey through **Busch Gardens** (⊠ 3000 E. Busch Blvd., ☎ 813/987–5082, WEB www.buschgardens.com; $50 adults; $41 children 3–9), a 335-acre African-inspired theme park with rides, live shows, and a monorail "safari."

Busch Gardens' water-park cousin, 25-acre **Adventure Island** (⊠ 10001 Malcolm McKinley Dr., ☎ 813/987–5600; $26 adults, $24 children 3–9) has water slides and man-made waves. It's closed late October–mid-March.

★ With cobblestone streets and wrought-iron balconies, Tampa's **Ybor City** (pronounced *Ee*-bor) is one of only three National Historic Landmark districts in Florida. Cubans expanded their cigar-making industry to this city in 1866. The ornately tiled **Columbia Restaurant** and the stores lining 7th Avenue are representative of this enclave's ethnic history and vitality. Today once-empty cigar factories, like the one at **Ybor Square** (⊠ 1901 13th St.), house boutiques, shops, restaurants, and nightclubs. To get here, take I–4 west to Exit 1 (22nd Street) and go south five blocks to 7th Avenue.

Tarpon Springs. Famous for its sponge divers, the town reflects the heritage of its predominantly Greek population. At **Weeki Wachee Spring** (⊠ 45 mi north of Tampa on U.S. 19 and Rte. 50, Weeki Wachee, ☎ 352/596–2062; $13), 27 mi north of Tarpon Springs, "mermaids" have been presenting shows in an underwater theater for more than 50 years.

You can watch manatees up close at **Homosassa Springs State Wildlife Park** (⊠ 1 mi west of U.S. 19 on Fish Bowl Dr., Homosassa Springs, ☎ 352/628–2311, WEB www.citruscounty-fl.com; $7.95). Here you can also see reptile and alligator shows, take a 20-minute pontoon-boat cruise on the Homosassa River, and view sea life in a floating observatory.

Head south from Tampa and cross Old Tampa Bay on I–275 to get to the heart of **St. Petersburg.** Set on a peninsula whose three sides border bays and the Gulf of Mexico, this city has beautiful beaches. With more than 1,500 pieces, the **Salvador Dali Museum** (⊠ 1000 3rd St. S, ☎ 727/823–3767, WEB www.salvadordalimuseum.org; $10) has the world's largest collection of originals by the Spanish surrealist. An affiliate of the Smithsonian Institution, the **Florida International Museum** (⊠ 100 2nd St. N, ☎ 800/777–9882, WEB www.floridamuseum.org; $12) has the world's largest collection of John F. Kennedy memorabilia on public display—about 600 items. **Great Explorations!** (✉ 800 2nd Ave. NE, ☎ 727/821–8992, WEB www.greatexplorations.org; 🎫 $4) is a hands-on museum with mind-stretching puzzles and games and a 90-ft-long pitch-black maze you crawl through.

The Sarasota Area

Known for its plentiful, clean beaches and profusion of golf courses, the Sarasota area, south of Tampa Bay via U.S. 41 or U.S. 301, is also a growing cultural center and winter home of the Ringling Brothers Barnum & Bailey Circus. Midway between Tampa and Sarasota, the low-key beach city of Bradenton is the site of **De Soto National Memorial** (✉ 75th St. NW, ☎ 941/792–0458; 🎫 free), where costumed guides recount Spanish conquistador Hernando de Soto's 16th-century landing and expedition and present live shows December to April. Near Bradenton is **Gamble Plantation and Confederate Memorial State Historical Site** (✉ 3708 Patten Ave., Ellenton, ☎ 941/723–4536, WEB www.dep.state.fl.us/parks; 🎫 $3), the only surviving pre–Civil War plantation house in South Florida.

★ In the smart resort city of Sarasota you'll find the **Ringling Museums** (✉ ½ mi south of Sarasota-Bradenton Airport on U.S. 41, ☎ 941/359–5700, WEB www.ringling.org; 🎫 $10), which includes the Venetian-style mansion of circus magnate John Ringling, his art museum with its collection of Rubens paintings, and a circus museum. The **Marie Selby Botanical Gardens** (✉ 811 S. Palm Ave., ☎ 941/366–5730, WEB www.selby.org; 🎫 $10) has world-class orchid displays as well as a small museum of botany and art, all contained in a restored mansion on the grounds. Kids enjoy the bird and reptile shows at **Sarasota Jungle Gardens** (✉ 3701 Bayshore Rd., ☎ 941/355–5305, WEB www.sarasotajunglegardens.com; 🎫 $10). A petting zoo and a museum displaying seashells and butterflies are also here. For a good beach escape head for the barrier island of **Siesta Key,** across the water from Sarasota. To reach Siesta Key, take U.S. 41 south from southern Sarasota to either Siesta Drive or Stickney Point Road, both of which lead west to the island.

The Fort Myers/Naples Area

The bustle of commercially oriented Fort Myers gives way to the relaxed atmosphere of the Gulf communities elsewhere in growing Lee County. Beach lovers head for the resort islands of Estero (popular with young singles); Captiva and Sanibel; and the Lover's Key State Recreation Area—all of which are known for superb shelling and fishing. Most of the beautiful residences here are hidden by Australian pines, but the beaches and tranquil Gulf waters are readily accessible.

Fort Myers is a small inland city; although it's a half hour from the nearest beach, its downtown business district overlooks the broad, flat Caloosahatchee River. One of the most scenic stretches of highway in southeastern Florida, **McGregor Boulevard** is framed by hundreds of towering palms. Fort Myers's premier attraction, **Thomas A. Edison's Winter Home** (✉ 2350 McGregor Blvd., ☎ 941/334–3614, WEB www.edison-ford-estate.com; 🎫 $12, including Mangoes), on a 14-acre estate, houses Edison's laboratory and a museum devoted to his inventions. Next door is **Mangoes,** the winter house of the inventor's longtime friend, automaker Henry Ford.

The refined city of **Naples** is fast becoming Florida's west-coast version of Palm Beach, with excellent beaches and golf courses, luxury high-rise condos, and several upscale shopping and dining districts. The ★ cool, contemporary **Naples Museum of Art** (✉ 5833 Pelican Bay Blvd., ☎ 239/597–1900, WEB www.naplesphilcenter.org; 🎫 $6) displays a provocative collection of innovative pieces including dazzling installations by glass artist Dale Chihuly.

About 30 mi northeast of Naples you can return to Florida's unspoiled past at the **Corkscrew Swamp Sanctuary** (✉ 16 mi east of I–75 on Rte. 846, ☎ 941/348–9151; 🎟 $8), an 11,000-acre tract that the National Audubon Society set aside to protect 500-year-old trees and endangered birds.

Dining and Lodging

Around **Tampa** the ethnic diversity of the region makes for some adventurous dining, from honey-soaked Greek baklava to Cuban saffron rice casserole. A generous mix of roadside motels, historic hotels, and sprawling resorts can be found here.

Raw bars and seafood restaurants are everywhere in and around **Sarasota.** Tamiami Trail (U.S. 41), which traverses the region, is lined with inexpensive motels, while the islands have more expensive resort complexes and high-rise hotels.

In **Fort Myers** and **Naples,** seafood reigns supreme. It's hard to find restaurants on Sanibel and Captiva islands that aren't expensive. For budget options (both dining and lodging) you'll have better luck in Fort Myers and Naples along the Tamiami Trail.

Bradenton

$$–$$$ 🏨 **BridgeWalk.** This all-in-one beachfront resort has one- and two-bedroom suites with fireplaces, whirlpool baths, and terra-cotta tile floors. Minimum stays may be required during high season (February through April). ✉ *100 Bridge St., Bradenton Beach 34217,* ☎ *941/779–2545,* FAX *941/746–4289,* WEB *www.silverresorts.com. 28 suites. Restaurant, pool, health club. AE, DC, MC, V.*

Naples

$$–$$$ ✕ **Bistro 821.** The look for this trendy restaurant is spare and sophisticated. Entrées include marinated leg of lamb with basil mashed potatoes, snapper baked in parchment, wild mushroom pasta, vodka penne, risotto, and a seasonal vegetable plate. ✉ *821 5th Ave. S,* ☎ *941/261–5821. Reservations essential. AE, DC, MC, V. No lunch.*

$$$$ ★ 🏨 **Ritz-Carlton, Naples.** This is a classic Ritz-Carlton, awash in marble, antiques, and 19th-century European oil paintings. In the rooms, the comforts of home prevail—assuming your home is a palace. Outside, steps away, the beach is soft, white, and dense with seashells. There's an extensive spa, children's programs, and golf privileges at the nearby Ritz-Carlton Golf Resort. ✉ *280 Vanderbilt Beach Rd., 34108,* ☎ *239/598–3300 or 800/241–3333,* FAX *239/598–6691,* WEB *www.ritzcarlton.com. 463 rooms. 7 restaurants, pool, tennis, health club. AE, D, DC, MC, V.*

St. Pete Beach

$$$$ ★ 🏨 **Don CeSar Beach Resort.** Still echoing with the ghosts of Scott and Zelda Fitzgerald, this sprawling beachfront "Pink Palace" has long been a Gulf Coast landmark. Turn-of-the-20th-century elegance abounds, and service is first-rate. You can indulge in various treatments and sea scrubs at the beach spa. ✉ *3400 Gulf Blvd., 33706,* ☎ *727/360–1881,* FAX *813/367–3609,* WEB *www.doncesar.com. 295 rooms. 3 restaurants, pools, tennis, gym. AE, DC, MC, V.*

Sanibel and Captiva Islands

$$–$$$ ✕ **Bubble Room.** At this lively, kitschy favorite, a basket loaded with cheesy Bubble Bread and sweet, yeasty sticky buns starts you off; then go for aged prime rib or the Eddie Fisherman (poached fresh grouper steamed in a brown paper bag). The triple-layer homemade cakes come in quarter-of-a-cake slices; the buttermilk-based red velvet cake is legendary. Arrive early or be prepared to wait for a table. ✉ *15001 Captiva Dr., Captiva,* ☎ *239/472–5558. Reservations not accepted. AE, D, DC, MC, V.*

$$$–$$$$ ★ **Sanibel Harbour Resort & Spa.** This high-rise resort complex is not on Sanibel proper but instead towers over the last mainland exit before the causeway. Laid-back, beachy Sanibel style is not the draw; instead, come for the sweeping views of island-studded San Carlos Bay as well as the racquet club, the exceptional spa, the large free-form pool, and children's program. ✉ *17260 Harbour Pointe Dr., Fort Myers 33908,* ☎ *239/466–4000 or 800/767–7777,* FAX *239/466–6050,* WEB *www.sanibel-resort.com. 347 rooms, 70 condos. 4 restaurants, pools, tennis, health club. AE, D, DC, MC, V.*

Sarasota

$$–$$$$ ✕ **Cafe L'Europe.** This art-filled café is on fashionable St. Armand's Circle, on Lido Key. The menu may include such dishes as Wiener schnitzel sautéed in butter and topped with anchovies, olives, and capers, or Dover sole served with fruit. ✉ *431 St. Armand's Cir.,* ☎ *941/388–4415. AE, DC, MC, V.*

$$$–$$$$ **Colony Beach and Tennis Resort.** If tennis is your game, this is the place to stay—such tennis greats as Björn Borg make the Colony their home court, and for good reason. Suites sleep up to eight. Private beach houses that open onto sand and sea are available. ✉ *1620 Gulf of Mexico Dr., Longboat Key 34228,* ☎ *941/383–6464; 800/237–9443; 800/282–1138 in FL,* FAX *941/383–7549,* WEB *www.colonybeachresort.com. 235 suites. 3 restaurants, pool, tennis, health club. AE, D, MC, V.*

Tampa

$$–$$$$ ★ ✕ **Bern's Steak House.** This nationally known steak house has more than just steak. Organically grown vegetables from the owner's farm are the specialty here, and scrumptious desserts are served upstairs in intimate glass-enclosed rooms. ✉ *1208 S. Howard Ave.,* ☎ *813/251–2421. AE, DC, MC, V. No lunch.*

$$ ★ ✕ **Columbia.** An institution in Ybor City since 1905, this light and spacious Spanish restaurant serves excellent paella, with some flamenco dancing on the side. ✉ *2117 E. 7th Ave.,* ☎ *813/248–4961. AE, DC, MC, V.*

$$–$$$$ **Don Vicente de Ybor Inn** In a carefully restored building originally constructed in 1895 by Vicente Martinez Ybor, this historic charmer is a boutique hotel at its best. Rooms have antique furnishings, Persian rugs, and four-poster canopied beds. Most rooms have wrought-iron balconies. ✉ *1915 Republica de Cuba, 33605,* ☎ *813/241–4545,* FAX *813/367–2917,* WEB *www.donvicenteinn.com. 16 suites. Restaurant. AE, D, DC, MC, V.*

$ **Holiday Inn Busch Gardens.** This well-maintained motor lodge is 1 mi west of Busch Gardens. Rooms are bright and spacious; some look out on a central courtyard. ✉ *2701 E. Fowler Ave., 33612,* ☎ *813/971–4710 or 800/206–2747,* FAX *813/977–0155,* WEB *www.holiday-inn.com. 402 rooms. Restaurant, pool, gym. AE, DC, MC, V.*

Tarpon Springs

$–$$$ ✕ **Louis Pappas' Riverside Restaurant.** This waterfront landmark is always crowded with diners savoring the fine Greek fare, including moussaka, Greek meatballs, and *spanakopita* (white cheese and spinach baked into phyllo pastry). ✉ *10 W. Dodecanese Blvd.,* ☎ *727/937–5101. AE, DC, MC, V. No lunch Sun.*

Nightlife and the Arts

The region between Tampa and Sarasota hums with cultural activities. Professional theater, dance, and music events are presented at **Tampa Bay Performing Arts Center** (✉ 1010 W. C. MacInnes Pl., Tampa, ☎ 813/229–7827 or 800/955–1045) and **Ruth Eckerd Hall** (✉ 1111 McMullen Booth Rd., Clearwater, ☎ 727/791–7400). Broadway touring companies of plays, concerts, dance, ice-skating, and other shows are held at Sarasota's **Van Wezel Performing Arts Hall** (✉ 777 N. Tamiami Terr., Sarasota, ☎ 941/953–3366). Other major venues in the city are the **Florida West Coast Symphony Center** (✉ 709 N. Tamiami Terr., ☎ 941/953–4252), the **Sarasota Opera** (✉ Opera House, 61 N. Pineapple Ave., ☎ 941/953–7030), and the **Asolo Center for the Performing Arts** (✉ 5555 N. Tamiami Terr., ☎ 941/351–8000).

The **Naples Philharmonic Center for the Arts** (✉ 5833 Pelican Bay Blvd., ☎ 941/597–1111) presents plays, concerts, and art exhibits.

Outdoor Activities and Sports

Biking

Sanibel Island has the best biking in the region, with extensive paths along the waterways and through wildlife refuges. On Sanibel you can rent bicycles by the hour at **Bike Route** (✉ 2330 Palm Ridge Rd., ☎ 941/472–1955).

Boating and Sailing

Sailing is popular on the calm bays and Gulf waters. Sailing schools include **Seacoast Yacht Charters** (✉ Port Sanibel Yacht Club, South Fort Myers, ☎ 941/540–8050). For powerboat rentals contact **Boat House of Sanibel** (✉ Sanibel Marina, 634 N. Yachtman Dr., ☎ 941/472–2531). **Jensen's Marina** (✉ Captiva, ☎ 941/472–5800) rents little powerboats perfect for fishing and shelling.

Canoeing

Canoeists can explore many waterways here, including those at **Myakka River State Park** (✉ Rte. 72, 15 mi south of Sarasota, ☎ 941/365–0100). **Tarpon Bay Marina** (✉ 900 Tarpon Bay Rd., Sanibel, ☎ 941/472–8900) has canoes and equipment for exploring the waters of the J. N. "Ding" Darling National Wildlife Refuge. With several locations throughout Florida, **Canoe Outpost** offers canoe and camping trips on the Little Manatee River (✉ 18001 U.S. 301 S, Wimauma, 20 mi southeast of Tampa, ☎ 813/634–2228) and the Peace River (✉ Rte. 7, Arcadia, ☎ 941/494–1215).

Fishing

The Tampa Bay area and Fort Myers are major fishing centers. Speckled trout and kingfish are often caught in the Tampa Bay inlets. Deep-sea fishing enthusiasts can charter boats or join a party boat to catch tarpon, marlin, grouper, redfish, and shark. Charter outfitters include **Florida Deep Sea Fishing** (✉ 60 Corey Ave., St. Pete Beach, ☎ 727/360–2082). Fishing is popular in Sanibel. Call **Captain Pat Lovetro** (✉ Sanibel Marina, 634 N. Yachtman Dr., ☎ 941/472–2723) for half-day, six-hour, and full-day trips.

Golf

Championship and other courses abound here. All of these have 18 holes: **Babe Zaharias Golf Course** (✉ 11412 Forest Hills Dr., Tampa, ☎ 813/932–8932); **Ironwood Golf Club** (✉ 4710 Lakewood Blvd., Naples, ☎ 239/775–2584); **Lely Flamingo Island Club** (✉ 8004 Lely Resort Blvd., Naples, ☎ 941/793–2223); the **Fort Myers Country Club** (✉ 3591 McGregor Blvd., Fort Myers, ☎ 941/936–2457); **Resort at**

Longboat Key Club (✉ 301 Gulf of Mexico Dr., Longboat Key, ☎ 941/383–8821); **Pelican's Nest Golf Course** (✉ 4450 Pelican's Nest Dr. SW, Bonita Springs, ☎ 941/947–4600); and the **Dunes** (✉ 949 Sandcastle Rd., Sanibel, ☎ 941/472–2535).

Spectator Sports

Baseball: Tampa Bay Devil Rays (✉ Tropicana Field, 1 Tropicana Dr., St. Petersburg, ☎ 727/825–3120). **Football: Tampa Bay Buccaneers** (✉ Raymond James Stadium, 4201 N. Dale Mabry Hwy., Tampa, ☎ 813/870–2700 or 800/282–0683), August–December. **Hockey: Tampa Bay Lightning** (✉ Ice Palace, 401 Channelside Dr., Tampa, ☎ 813/229–2658). **Horse Racing: Tampa Bay Downs** (✉ Race Track Rd., off Rte. 580, Oldsmar, ☎ 813/855–4401), Thoroughbred races from mid-December to early May.

Beaches

The waters of the Gulf of Mexico tend to be cloudy, so snorkeling and diving are best on the Atlantic side of the state. The southwestern beaches are good for shelling and sunbathing on quiet stretches of sand. Sunsets are spectacular here.

In the Bradenton area the **Manatee County Beach,** on Anna Maria Island, has picnic facilities, a snack bar, showers, lifeguards, and rest rooms. **Estero Island (Fort Myers Beach),** 18 mi from downtown Fort Myers, attracts families and young singles; hotels, restaurants, and condominiums run its length. The island's shores slope gradually into the usually tranquil and warm Gulf waters. Along Gulf Shore Boulevard in Naples, **Lowdermilk Park** has 1,000 ft of beach, picnic tables, showers, rest rooms, and a pavilion with vending machines.

In the St. Petersburg area the 900-acre **Fort De Soto Park** encompasses six islands. Its 7 mi of beaches include two fishing piers, picnic sites, and a waterskiing and boating area. **Old Lighthouse Beach,** at the southern end of Sanibel Island, attracts a mix of singles, families, and shellers. Beautiful **Siesta Beach,** on Siesta Key near Sarasota, has a concession stand, picnic areas, nature trails, and facilities for soccer, softball, volleyball, and tennis. **Caspersen Beach,** on Beach Drive in South Venice, is one of the county's largest parks. Beachcombers find lots of shells and sharks' teeth here.

Shopping

Seven blocks of fine shops and restaurants line Tampa's Swan Avenue in **Old Hyde Park Village** (☎ 813/251–3500). If you're looking for Cuban cigars, try **Ybor City** on Tampa's east side. In Pinellas Park **Wagonwheel** (✉ 7801 Park Blvd., ☎ 727/544–5319) is a weekend flea market with about 2,000 vendors. For unique gifts, shop for natural sponges on **Dodecanese Boulevard** in Tarpon Springs.

Art lovers can browse through the art galleries on **Main Street** and **Palm Avenue** in downtown Sarasota. A British telephone booth or an Australian boomerang is available for a price at the unique shops of Harding Circle on fashionable **St. Armand's Circle,** west of downtown Sarasota across the Ringling Causeway.

For a great display of shells, coral, and jewelry, visit the **Shell Factory** (✉ 2787 N. Tamiami Trail, North Fort Myers, ☎ 888/995–2141). For boutiques selling resort wear, designer fashions, and jewelry, try the **Royal Palm Square** area (✉ Colonial Blvd., between McGregor Blvd. and U.S. 41) in Fort Myers. The largest shopping area in Naples is **Old Naples,** an eight-block area bordered by Broad Avenue on the north and 4th Street South on the east. The classy **Village on Venetian Bay** (✉ 4200 Gulf Shore Blvd., Naples) has more than 60 shops and restaurants built over the bay. The **Waterside Shops** (✉ Seagate Dr. and U.S. 41, Naples), known by locals as Bell Tower because of its landmark bell tower, are anchored by a Saks Fifth Avenue and a Jacobson's department store and and several noteworthy eating spots.

Southwest Florida Essentials

AIRPORTS

Most major U.S. airlines serve at least one of the region's airports. Tampa International, 6 mi from downtown, is also served by international airlines. Sarasota-Bradenton Airport is 5 mi north of downtown Sarasota off U.S. 41. Southwest Florida International Airport, served by regional and some international carriers, is about 12 mi south of Fort Myers and 25 mi north of Naples.

➤ AIRPORT INFORMATION: **Sarasota-Bradenton Airport** (✉ 6000 Airport Cir., ☎ 941/359–5200). **Southwest Florida International Airport** (✉ 16000 Chamberlin Pkwy., ☎ 941/768–1000). **Tampa International** (✉ 5507 Spruce St., ☎ 813/870–8700).

BUS TRAVEL

Greyhound provides statewide service, including stops at Tampa, St. Petersburg, Sarasota, Fort Myers, and Naples. For local bus service contact Hillsborough Area Regional Transit for the Tampa area, Sarasota County Area Transit for Sarasota, and Lee County Transit System for the Fort Myers area.

➤ BUS INFORMATION: **Greyhound** (☎ 800/231–2222). **Hillsborough Area Regional Transit** (☎ 813/254–4278). **Lee County Transit System** (☎ 941/275–8726). **Sarasota County Area Transit** (☎ 941/951–5850).

CAR TRAVEL

From the Georgia-Florida border, it's a three-hour drive via I–75 south to Tampa, four hours to Sarasota, five to Fort Myers, and six to Naples. U.S. 41 (the Tamiami Trail) also traverses the region, but because it pierces many towns' business districts, traffic can be extremely heavy, particularly from Tampa south. Naples is linked to Fort Lauderdale, on the eastern side of the state, via Alligator Alley (I–75).

VISITOR INFORMATION

➤ TOURIST INFORMATION: **Greater Naples Area Chamber of Commerce** (✉ 3620 Tamiami Terr. N, 33940, ☎ 941/262–6141, WEB www.napleschamber.org). **Greater Tampa Chamber of Commerce** (✉ Box 420, 33601, ☎ 813/228–7777, WEB www.tampachamber.com). **St. Petersburg Chamber of Commerce** (✉ 100 2nd Ave. N, 33701, ☎ 727/821–4069, WEB www.stpete.com). **Sanibel-Captiva Chamber of Commerce** (✉ Causeway Rd., Sanibel 33957, ☎ 941/472–1080, WEB www.sanibel-captiva.org). **Sarasota Convention and Visitors Bureau** (✉ 655 N. Tamiami Terr., 34236, ☎ 941/957–1877 or 800/522–9799, WEB www.sarasotafl.org).

THE GOLD AND TREASURE COASTS

The Gold Coast exudes wealth and opulence, but it's also steeped in natural beauty. Once famous as a spring-break haven for the college crowd, Fort Lauderdale now attracts families by offering recreational, sports, cultural, and historical activities. Farther north is the international high-society resort of Palm Beach, with its elegant mansions and world-class shopping. Long considered Palm Beach's less privileged relative, sprawling West Palm has evolved into an economically vibrant destination of its own, ranking as the cultural, entertainment, and business center of the entire county and territory to the north. Inland about 50 mi is 448,000-acre Lake Okeechobee, noted for catfish, bass, and perch fishing. As you head north from West Palm Beach to Sebastian Inlet, the Treasure Coast offers barrier islands, beaches, and sea-turtle havens to the east and citrus groves and cattle ranches to the west.

Exploring the Gold and Treasure Coasts

Fort Lauderdale and Palm Beach dazzle with their fabulous homes and pricey shops, shimmering beaches, plentiful sports activities, first-class museums, and cultural events. North of Palm Beach are the Treasure Coast's 70 mi of soothing sand, sea, and nature refuges.

Don't miss a visit to the splendidly redesigned **Fort Lauderdale beachfront,** along Route A1A. The beach side remains open and uncluttered, and trendy shops and restaurants (plus a mix of new and dated hotels) line the opposite side of the street. From the beach, picturesque **Las Olas Boulevard** takes you inland through the Isles, where expensive homes line canals dotted with yachts. After this the boulevard becomes an upscale shopping street, with Spanish colonial buildings housing boutiques and galleries. The **Museum of Art** (✉ 1 E. Las Olas Blvd., ☎ 954/763–6464, WEB www.museumofart.org; 🎟 $10), closed Monday, has an extensive early 20th-century European and American art collection.

Palm-lined **Riverwalk,** which begins around U.S. 1 south of Broward Boulevard, is a lovely paved promenade with fine shops, restaurants, popular nightspots, and views of New River. Riverwalk leads into the city's newly burgeoning **Arts and Science District,** which has spawned a slew of new shops, restaurants, and entertainment venues in the heart of downtown. The top attraction in the Arts and Science District is the ★ 👶 **Museum of Discovery and Science/Blockbuster IMAX Theater** (✉ 401 S.W. 2nd St., ☎ 954/467–6637 museum; 954/463–4629 IMAX; WEB www.mods.org; 🎟 museum $13, includes one IMAX show), with an IMAX theater and interactive exhibits on ecology, health, and outer space. For an interesting side trip, head south a few miles to the **Seminole Native Village** (✉ 3551 N. State Rd. 7, Hollywood, ☎ 954/961–4519; 🎟 self-guided tour $5, guided tour including alligator wrestling and snake demonstrations $10), a reservation where you can pet a cougar, hold a baby alligator, and watch other wildlife demonstrations.

As you travel north from Fort Lauderdale along U.S. 1, pause to admire the 1920s Spanish-style architecture in affluent **Boca Raton.** In the posh island community of **Palm Beach,** you can rub shoulders with the rich and famous as you stroll along the 12-mi-long island's **Worth Avenue,** one of the world's premier shopping streets. To recapture the glitter and flamboyance of Florida's boom years, when railroad magnate Henry M. Flagler first established Palm Beach as a playground for the wealthy, visit his ornate hotel, the **Breakers,** a legendary bastion of wealth and privilege. Henry Flagler's palatial 73-room Whitehall Mansion, known as the **Henry Morrison Flagler Museum** (✉ 1 Whitehall Way, ☎ 561/655–2833, WEB www.flagler.org; 🎟 $8), closed Monday, contains original furnishings and an art collection.

After visiting Palm Beach, take a drive past the secluded mansions along **County Road** and around the northern tip of the island. Directly across the Fort Worth inlet from Palm Beach is the rapidly gentrifying mainland city of **West Palm Beach.** Long considered Palm Beach's impoverished cousin, West Palm is now economically vibrant in its own right—it's become the cultural, entertainment, and business center of

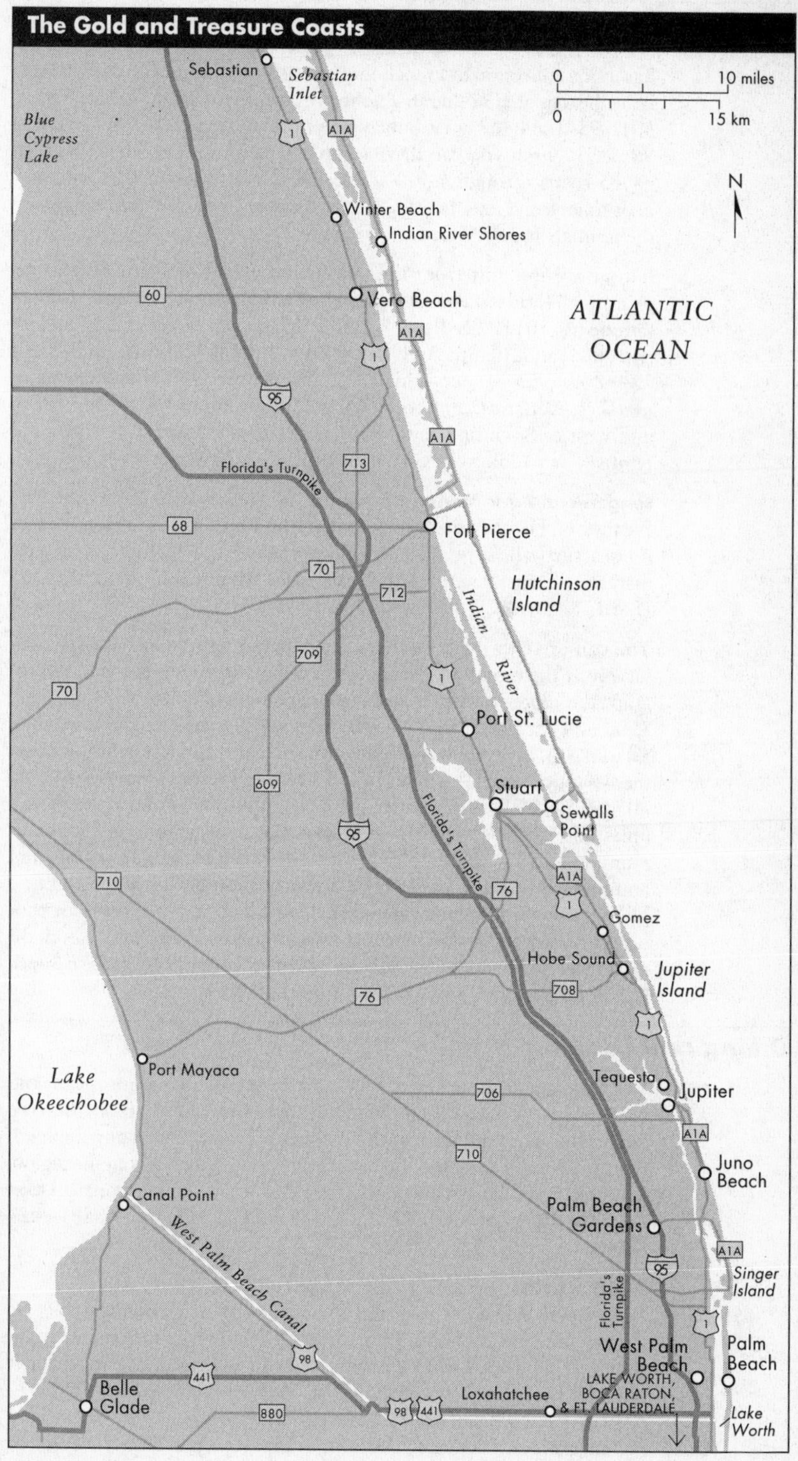
The Gold and Treasure Coasts
Sebastian
Sebastian Inlet
0 10 miles
0 15 km
N
Blue Cypress Lake
Winter Beach
Indian River Shores
Vero Beach
ATLANTIC OCEAN
Florida's Turnpike
Fort Pierce
Hutchinson Island
Indian River
Port St. Lucie
Stuart
Sewalls Point
Gomez
Hobe Sound
Jupiter Island
Lake Okeechobee
Port Mayaca
Tequesta
Jupiter
Juno Beach
Canal Point
Palm Beach Gardens
West Palm Beach Canal
Singer Island
West Palm Beach
Palm Beach
Belle Glade
Loxahatchee
LAKE WORTH, BOCA RATON, & FT. LAUDERDALE
Lake Worth

the county and of the region to the north. The **Norton Museum of Art** (✉ 1451 S. Olive St., ☎ 561/832–5194, WEB www.norton.org; 🎟 $6) has a fine collection of French Impressionist works. Southwest of West Palm Beach, at **Lion Country Safari** (✉ Southern Blvd. W/U.S. 98, ☎ 561/793–1084, WEB www.lioncountrysafari.com; 🎟 $16.95, van rental $8 per 1½ hrs), you can drive (with car windows closed) on 8 mi of paved roads through a 500-acre cageless zoo where 1,000 wild animals roam free. Lions, giraffes, zebras, ostriches, and elephants are among the animals in residence.

It's an abrupt shift from the man-made world of Palm Beach into primitive Florida at **Arthur R. Marshall Loxahatchee National Wildlife Refuge** (✉ 10119 Lee Rd., off U.S. 441 between Boynton Beach Blvd. [Rte. 804] and Atlantic Ave. [Rte. 806], west of Boynton Beach, ☎ 561/734–8303; 🎟 $5 per vehicle, $1 per pedestrian), a wilderness of marshes, wetlands, and bountiful wildlife south of West Palm Beach and west of Boynton Beach. Stroll the nature trails, fish for bass and panfish, or paddle your own canoe through the waterways.

Loggerhead Park Marine Life Center of Juno Beach. Established by Eleanor N. Fletcher, the "turtle lady of Juno Beach," the center focuses on sea turtle history, including loggerheads and leatherbacks, with displays of coastal natural history, sharks, whales, and shells. ✉ *1200 U.S. 1,* ☎ *561/627–8280.* 🎟 *Free. Closed Mon.*

You can drive through sand dunes at **Jupiter,** on the Intracoastal Waterway at the mouth of the scenic Loxahatchee River. Pause to photograph the impressive 105-ft **Jupiter Inlet Lighthouse** (✉ Rte. 707 to Captain Armour's Way, ☎ 561/747–8380, WEB www.jupiterinletlighthouse.com; 🎟 tour $6), open Sunday–Wednesday, one of the oldest lighthouses on the Atlantic coast. At Jupiter Island's **Blowing Rocks Preserve** (✉ Rte. 707, ☎ 561/575–2297), water sprays burst through holes in the shore's limestone facade at high tide. The preserve is home to large bird communities and a wealth of plants native to beachfront dune, marsh, and hammock. The revival of historic downtown **Stuart** (✉ at the St. Lucie Inlet) is transforming this onetime fishing village into a magnet for people who want to live and work in a small-town atmosphere. About 30 mi farther north along the coast, the affluent community of **Vero Beach** has elegant houses, many dating from the 1920s.

Dining and Lodging

The Gold and Treasure coasts have a mix of American, European, and Caribbean cuisines, all emphasizing local fish and seafood. Accommodations are expensive in the Palm Beach area, but many inexpensive motels line U.S. 1 and the major exits of I–95 throughout the region. B&B accommodations are popular in Palm Beach County; contact **Open House Bed & Breakfast** (✉ Box 3025, Palm Beach 33480, ☎ 561/842–5190).

Boca Raton

$$$–$$$$ ★ ✕ **La Vieille Maison.** Closets transformed into private dining nooks are part of the charm of this 1920s home turned elegant French restaurant serving such dishes as venison chop with red currant–pepper sauce and roasted chestnuts. ✉ *770 E. Palmetto Park Rd.,* ☎ *561/391–6701. AE, D, DC, MC, V. Closed early July–Aug.*

$–$$ ✕ **Tom's Place.** It's worth the wait in line for mouthwatering ribs or chicken in homemade barbecue sauce and the sweet-potato pie in this casual, family-run eatery. ✉ *7251 N. Federal Hwy.,* ☎ *561/997–0920. Reservations not accepted. MC, V. Closed Sun.*

Fort Lauderdale

$$–$$$$ ✕ **Burt & Jack's.** This local favorite—operated by veteran restaurateur Jack Jackson and actor Burt Reynolds since 1984—offers seafood, steaks, and chops, and scenic views of Port Everglades. ✉ *Berth 23, Port Everglades,* ☎ *954/522–2878 or 954/525–5225. AE, D, DC, MC, V. No lunch.*

$$–$$$$ ★ ✕ **Mark's Las Olas.** The Florida-style cuisine here blends flavors from Caribbean, southwestern, and Mediterranean traditions and includes entrées that highlight gulf shrimp, dolphinfish, and yellowtail snapper, often paired with combinations of callaloo (a West Indian spinach), chayote, ginger, jícama, and plantain. ✉ *1032 E. Las Olas Blvd.,* ☎ *954/463–1000. AE, D, DC, MC, V. Reservations required. No lunch weekends.*

$$–$$$ 🏨 **Riverside Hotel.** This 1936 hotel amid the upscale shops on Las Olas Boulevard has an attentive staff, murals by well-known artist Bob Jenny (one of which stretches across 725 square ft of the building's facade), and antique oak furnishings in the guest rooms. ✉ *620 E. Las Olas Blvd., 33301,* ☎ *954/467–0671 or 800/325–3280,* FAX *954/462–2148,* WEB *www.riversidehotel.com. 110 rooms. 2 restaurants, pool. AE, DC, MC, V.*

Hutchinson Island

$$–$$$$ 🏨 **Hutchinson Island Marriott Beach Resort & Marina.** With golf, tennis, a 77-slip marina, and a full watersports program, plus many restaurants and bars, this 200-acre self-contained resort is excellent for families. Reception, some restaurants, and many rooms are in a trio of yellow four-story buildings that form an open courtyard with a large pool. Additional rooms and apartments with kitchens are spread over the property. ✉ *555 N.E. Ocean Blvd., Hutchinson Island, Stuart 34996,* ☎ *561/225–3700 or 800/775–5936,* FAX *561/225–0033,* WEB *www.marriotthotels.com. 317 rooms, 150 condos. 5 restaurants, pools, tennis, health club. AE, DC, MC, V.*

Palm Beach

$$–$$$ ★ ✕ **Ta-boo.** The spaces of this Worth Avenue landmark are divided into discreet salons: one resembles a courtyard, another an elegant living room with a fireplace, and a third a skylighted gazebo. Expect eclectic fare including chicken and arugula from the grill, prime rib, steaks, frogs' legs, main-course salads, and pizzas. ✉ *221 Worth Ave.,* ☎ *561/835–3500. AE, DC, MC, V.*

$$$$ ★ 🏨 **The Breakers.** Dating from 1896, and on the National Register of Historic Places, this opulent Italian Renaissance–style resort sprawls over 140 ocean-front acres. Cupids frolic at the main Florentine fountain, while majestic frescoes grace ceilings leading to restaurants. A $120 million guest-room renovation also brought the addition of a spa and beach club. Elegance thus enhanced, a relaxed atmosphere replaces old-world formality, with jackets and ties no longer *required* after 7 PM. ✉ *1 S. County Rd., 33480,* ☎ *561/655–6611 or 800/833–3141,* FAX *561/659–8403,* WEB *www.thebreakers.com. 620 rooms. 5 restaurants, pool, tennis, health club. AE, D, DC, MC, V.*

$$$$ 🏨 **PGA National Resort & Spa.** At this sybaritic getaway where golf and tennis pros exercise during tournaments, the spa facilities include the signature mineral pools with salts from around the world. Choose from large guest rooms with tropical details or cottage units with two bedrooms and a kitchen. ✉ *400 Ave. of the Champions, Palm Beach Gardens 33418,* ☎ *561/627–2000 or 800/633–9150,* FAX *561/622–0261,* WEB *www.pga-resorts.com. 419 units. 4 restaurants, pools, tennis, gym. AE, D, DC, MC, V.*

$–$$$ 🏨 **Palm Beach Hawaiian Ocean Inn.** Families gravitate to this casual, two-story resort, which is reasonably priced and right on the beach. Large rooms and spacious suites face tropical gardens or look out to the ocean and are simply but adequately furnished and have bedspreads and draperies in colorful striped pastels. ✉ *3550 S. Ocean Blvd., 33480,* ☎ FAX *561/582–5631,* WEB *www.palmbeachhawaiian.com. 58 rooms. Restaurant, pool. D, MC, V.*

Nightlife and the Arts

Fort Lauderdale and the Palm Beach area offer a full roster of performing arts events. Major venues include **Broward Center for the Performing Arts** (✉ 201 S.W. 5th Ave., Fort Lauderdale, ☎ 954/462–0222) and the magnificent **Raymond F. Kravis Center for the Performing Arts** (✉ 701 Okeechobee Blvd., West Palm Beach, ☎ 561/832–7469), the cultural center of Palm Beach. Many of the cultural events in Vero Beach take place at the **Center for the Arts** (✉ 3001 Riverside Park Dr., ☎ 561/231–6990). Fort Lauderdale has the liveliest nightlife, with comedy clubs, discos, and clubs featuring music for all ages and tastes; popular ones include **Howl at the Moon** (✉ Beach Place, 17 S. Fort Lauderdale Beach Blvd., ☎ 954/522–5054), with dueling piano players and sing-alongs nightly, and **O'Hara's Pub & Sidewalk Cafe** (✉ 722 E. Las Olas Blvd., ☎ 954/524–1764), which has nightly live jazz and blues.

Outdoor Activities and Sports

Biking

The beautiful **Palm Beach Bicycle Trail** runs for 10 mi along the shoreline of Lake Worth. For bike rentals try **Palm Beach Bicycle Trail Shop** (✉ 223 Sunrise Ave., ☎ 561/659–4583). In Fort Lauderdale, some of the most popular routes are along A1A—the beach road. For bike rentals, contact the **International Bicycle and Skate Shop** (✉ 1900 E. Sunrise Blvd., ☎ 954/792–2298).

Diving

A popular place to dive is the 23-mi-long, 2-mi-wide **Fort Lauderdale Reef,** one of 80 dive sites in Broward County. Palm Beach County offers excellent drift diving and anchor diving off the Atlantic coast. Try **Pro Dive** (✉ Radisson Bahia Mar Beach Resort, 801 Seabreeze Blvd., Fort Lauderdale, ☎ 954/761–3413 or 800/772–3483) for diving equipment and packages.

Fishing

Anglers can deep-sea or freshwater fish year-round. Pompano, amberjack, and snapper are caught off the numerous piers and bridges, while Lake Okeechobee yields bass and perch. Sailfish are a popular catch on deep-sea charters, offered at **Hillsboro Inlet Marina** (✉ 2629 N. Riverside Dr., Pompano Beach, ☎ 954/943–8222) and **B-Love Fleet** (✉ 314 E. Ocean Ave., Lantana, ☎ 561/588–7612).

Golf

Among the 50-plus golf courses in Greater Fort Lauderdale is **Colony West Country Club** (✉ 6800 N.W. 88th Ave., Tamarac, ☎ 954/726–8430). The **Breakers Hotel Golf Club** (✉ 1 S. County Rd., ☎ 561/655–6611 or 800/833–3141) has 36 holes. **Palm Beach Par 3** (✉ 2345 S. Ocean Blvd., ☎ 561/547–0598) has 18 holes, including 4 on the Atlantic and 3 on the inland waterway.

Spectator Sports

Horse Racing: Gulfstream Park Race Track (✉ 901 S. Federal Hwy., Hallandale, ☎ 954/454–7000), January–mid-March. **Pompano Harness Track** (✉ 1800 Race Track Rd., Pompano Beach, ☎ 954/972–2000), Monday and Wednesday–Saturday, October–August.

Polo: Palm Beach Polo and Country Club (✉ 13198 Forest Hill Blvd., West Palm Beach, ☎ 561/793–1440) has games on Sunday, January–April.

Beaches

Crystal-clear warm waters are the main draw of the miles of beaches along the Atlantic coast. Each coastal town has a public beach area; many, like **Pompano Beach** and **Deerfield Beach,** have fishing piers. The area is popular with snorkelers and divers.

The **beachfront,** along Route A1A between Las Olas Boulevard and Sunrise Boulevard in Fort Lauderdale, is a very popular beach; shops, restaurants, and hotels line the road. In Dania the **John U. Lloyd Beach State Recreation Area** (✉ 6503 N. Ocean Dr., ☎ 954/923–2833), the locals' favorite, is a fine beach with picnicking, fishing, and canoeing facilities and 251 acres of mangroves to explore. **Bathtub Beach,** on Hutchinson Island north of Jupiter, has placid waters and a gentle sea slope, making it ideal for children.

Shopping

Both Palm Beach and Fort Lauderdale have shopping districts that cater to an upscale clientele. In Fort Lauderdale expensive boutiques are clustered along tree-lined **Las Olas Boulevard.** In Palm Beach more than 250 specialty shops and pricey boutiques, with such famous names as Gucci and Cartier, beckon to well-heeled shoppers along **Worth Avenue.** A few miles west of Fort Lauderdale, bargain shoppers flock to **Sawgrass Mills Mall** (✉ 12801 W. Sunrise Blvd., at Flamingo Rd., Sunrise), which has 270 stores.

The Gold and Treasure Coasts Essentials

AIRPORTS

Major foreign and domestic carriers serve the Fort Lauderdale–Hollywood International Airport and Palm Beach International Airport.

➤ AIRPORT INFORMATION: **Fort Lauderdale–Hollywood International Airport** (✉ 4 mi south of downtown Fort Lauderdale off U.S. 1, ☎ 954/359–6100). **Palm Beach International Airport** (✉ Congress Ave. and Belvedere Rd., West Palm Beach, ☎ 561/471–7400).

BUS TRAVEL

Greyhound stops in Fort Lauderdale and West Palm Beach, and Broward Transit serves the surrounding county. CoTran buses ply the Greater Palm Beach area.

➤ BUS INFORMATION: **Broward Transit** (☎ 954/357–8400). **CoTran** (☎ 561/233–1111). **Greyhound** (☎ 800/231–2222).

CAR TRAVEL

Two major north–south routes, I–95 and U.S. 1, connect the region with Miami to the south and Jacksonville to the north. Alligator Alley (I–75) runs east–west from Fort Lauderdale to Naples. Florida's Turnpike is a less congested and less direct route from Orlando to the Gold and Treasure coasts.

The four-lane route Okeechobee Boulevard (Route 704) carries traffic from west of downtown West Palm Beach, near the Amtrak station in the airport district, directly into Palm Beach. Plans are under way to turn Flagler Drive pedestrian-only in the next several years.

VISITOR INFORMATION

➤ TOURIST INFORMATION: **Chamber of Commerce of the Palm Beaches** (✉ 401 N. Flagler Dr., West Palm Beach 33401, ☎ 561/833–3711, WEB www.palmbeaches.com). **Greater Fort Lauderdale Convention & Visitors Bureau** (✉ 1850 Eller Dr., Suite 303, 33301, ☎ 954/765–4466, WEB www.ftlchamber.com).

ELSEWHERE IN FLORIDA

Everglades and Biscayne National Parks

What to See and Do

★ **Everglades National Park** (✉ Main Visitor Center, 40001 Rte. 9336, Homestead 33034, ☎ 305/242–7700), the country's largest remaining subtropical wilderness, contains more than 1.4 million acres—half land, half water—that can be explored by boat, by bike, on foot, and partly by car. This slow-moving "river of grass" is a maze of saw-grass marshes, mangrove swamps, salt prairies, and pinelands that shelter a variety of plants and animals, even though increased pollution by pesticide runoff from local farms has reduced the number of birds and brought the Florida panther to near extinction. The visitor center is superb; the three park entrances are in Homestead, along U.S. 41 (Tamiami Trail), and, on the west coast of Florida, in Everglades City.

Biscayne National Park (✉ 9700 S.W. 328th St. [Box 1369, Homestead 33090], ☎ 305/230–7275) is the nation's largest marine park and the largest national park with a living coral reef in the continental United States. It covers about 274 square mi, mostly underwater, and has several ecosystems. Shallow Biscayne Bay is home to the manatee, the upper Florida Keys harbor moray eels, and brilliantly colored parrot fish in a 150-mi coral reef, and bald eagles and other large birds inhabit the mainland mangrove forests. A visitor center with interactive exhibits, a glass-bottom-boat tour, canoeing, snorkeling, and scuba diving are popular ways to experience the park.

Everglades and Biscayne National Parks Essentials

AIRPORTS

Miami International Airport (☞ Miami Essentials, *above*) is about 35 mi from Homestead and Florida City, gateways to the national parks.

CAR TRAVEL

Traveling south by car, use Florida's Turnpike or Routes 826 and 874 and the Florida's Turnpike Extension to reach the gateway towns.

The Panhandle: Northwestern Florida

What to See and Do

The Panhandle, in Florida's northwest corner, stretches between the Gulf of Mexico and the Alabama and Georgia state lines. This area is lush with thick pine forests, magnolias, live oaks draped in Spanish moss, and pristine rivers and lakes more common to the Deep South than Florida. Dubbed the Emerald Coast due to the color of the Gulf's blue-green emerald water and the snow-white beaches, the region draws visitors with its historical and archaeological sites, golf, hiking, water sports, and outstanding fishing.

Stroll through the historic districts of **Pensacola** and absorb some of the city's colorful Spanish, French, British, and Civil War past. **Fort Walton Beach** is a family vacation playground famous for its beaches and spectacular sand dunes. **Eglin Air Force Base** (✉ Rte. 85, ☎ 850/882–3931, WEB www.eglin.af.mil), in Fort Walton Beach, includes 10 auxiliary fields and a total of 21 runways. You can tour the base and the **Airforce Armament Museum,** which contains vintage aircraft, guns, and other weapons. Kids especially enjoy the **Indian Temple Mound Museum** (✉ 139 Miracle Strip Pkwy. [U.S. 98], Fort Walton Beach, ☎ 850/833–9595; $2), where they can learn all about the prehistoric peoples who lived in the region during the past 10,000 years.

Destin, Fort Walton Beach's neighbor, a once-quiet fishing village, has developed into a bustling seaside vacation spot popular with anglers, sun worshipers, and foodies, and offers some of the area's finest restaurants. East of Destin are the quiet, family-friendly **Beaches of South** ★ **Walton,** including **Grayton Beach State Recreation Area** (✉ Rte. 30A, ☎ 850/231–4210; $3.25 per vehicle with up to 8 people), near the quaint, Victorian-style community of **Seaside,** which has one of the most scenic beaches along the Gulf Coast, if not the country.

For sun-up until sun-down action, head for the snow-white beaches, miles of waterways, and amusement parks of **Panama City Beach,** a prime vacation area and *the* spot for students on spring break.

The Panhandle: Northwestern Florida Essentials

AIRPORTS

Pensacola Regional Airport serves the region.

➤ Airport Information: **Pensacola Regional Airport** (☎ 850/435–1746).

CAR TRAVEL

I–10 and U.S. 90 are the main east–west highways across the top of the state, U.S. 98 runs along the coast, and U.S. 231, 331, and 29 and Route 85 traverse the Panhandle north–south.

VISITOR INFORMATION

➤ Tourist Information: **Destin Chamber of Commerce** (✉ 1021 U.S. 98 E, Destin 32541, ☎ 850/837–6241 or 850/837–0087, WEB www.destinchamber.com). **Emerald Coast Convention & Visitors Bureau** (✉ 1540 Miracle Strip Pkwy. SE, Fort Walton Beach 32549, ☎ 850/651–7122 or 800/322–3319, WEB www.destin-fwb.com). **Panama City Beach Convention & Visitors Bureau** (✉ 12015 W. Front Beach Rd., Panama City Beach 32407, ☎ 850/233–6503 or 800/722–3224, WEB www.800pcbeach.org). **Pensacola Visitor Information Center** (✉ 1401 E. Gregory St., Pensacola 32501, ☎ 850/434–1234 or 800/874–1234, WEB www.visitpensacola.com).

Northeastern Florida

What to See and Do

Variety is the key word for northeastern Florida: you can see live-oak-framed roads and plantations that recall the Old South all along St. Johns River; Thoroughbred horse farms in Ocala; impressive savannas in Gainesville; and the cosmopolitan city of Jacksonville. The beaches range from rocky shorelines to the glistening sand beaches of Jacksonville and the famous hard-packed, drivable beach at Daytona. The **Daytona 500** auto race is held annually in February at Daytona International Speedway (✉ U.S. 92, ☎ 904/254–2700). Jacksonville is the host of collegiate football's New Year's Day **Gator Bowl** (☎ 904/396–1800).

St. Augustine, the oldest permanent settlement in the United States, dates to 1565. Explore the 300-year-old Spanish fortress of **Castillo de San Marcos National Monument** (✉ 1 Castillo Dr., ☎ 904/829–6506; $5), which guards Matanzas Bay. Stroll down St. George Street through St. Augustine's restored **Spanish Quarter** for a glimpse of life in the

1700s. Drink from the spring reputed to be the fountain of youth discovered by Ponce de León in 1513 at the **Fountain of Youth Archaeological Park** (✉ 155 Magnolia Ave., ☎ 904/829–3168, WEB www.fountainofyouthflorida.com; 🎫 $4.75).

Silver Springs (✉ Rte. 40, 1 mi east of Ocala, ☎ 352/236–2121, WEB www.wildwaterspark.com; 🎫 $31.95), the state's oldest attraction and the world's largest formation of clear artesian springs, has glass-bottom-boat tours and a jungle cruise.

Amelia Island, north of Jacksonville, contains the historic town of Fernandina Beach, with its 19th-century mansions and many posh resorts. North of Fernandina Beach lies 1,086-acre **Fort Clinch State Park** (✉ N. 14th St., ☎ 904/277–7274; 🎫 $3.25 per vehicle), with a brick fort, nature trails, swimming, and living-history reenactments.

Northeastern Florida Essentials

AIRPORTS

Jacksonville International Airport and Daytona Beach International Airport serve the region.

➤ AIRPORT INFORMATION: **Daytona Beach International Airport** (☎ 904/248–8069). **Jacksonville International Airport** (☎ 904/741–4902).

CAR TRAVEL

I–10 is the major east–west artery through the north, and I–4 from Tampa and Orlando enters the region to the south, near Daytona Beach. The primary north–south routes are I–95 along the east coast and I–75 through the center of the state.

VISITOR INFORMATION

➤ TOURIST INFORMATION: **Amelia Island–Fernandina Beach Chamber of Commerce** (✉ 102 Centre St., Fernandina Beach 32034, ☎ 904/261–3248, WEB www.aifby.com). **Destination Daytona!** (✉ 126 E. Orange Ave., 32120, ☎ 904/255–0415 or 800/854–1234, WEB www.daytonabeach.com). **Jacksonville Convention and Visitors Bureau** (✉ 6 E. Bay St., Suite 200, 32202, ☎ 904/798–9111, WEB www.jaxcvb.com). **St. Augustine Visitor Information Center** (✉ 10 Castillo Dr., 32084, ☎ 800/653–2489, WEB www.visitoldcity.com).

GEORGIA

Updated by Hollis Gillespie

Capital	Atlanta
Population	8,186,453
Motto	Wisdom, Justice, and Moderation
State Bird	Brown thrasher
State Flower	Cherokee rose
Postal Abbreviation	GA

Statewide Visitor Information

Georgia Department of Industry, Trade and Tourism (✉ Box 1776, Atlanta 30301, ☎ 404/656–3590 or 800/847–4842, WEB www.georgia.org). There are 11 **visitor centers** at various border points and 45 locally operated **welcome centers** in Atlanta, Savannah, and throughout the state.

Scenic Drives

Along the coast Jekyll Island's **North Riverview Drive** passes scenery ranging from historic homes in the Jekyll Island Historic District to glimpses of marshland. **Route 157** north from Cloudland Canyon State Park to the Tennessee border at Lookout Mountain has views of northwestern Georgia's mountains. **U.S. 76** east from Dalton to the Chattooga River traverses the north Georgia mountains.

National and State Parks

National Parks

The **Andersonville National Historic Site** (✉ Georgia Hwy. 49 N [Rte. 1, Box 800, Andersonville 31711], ☎ 229/924–0343, WEB www.mcaoncountaga.org; 🎫 free), formerly a Confederate prison camp, is now the site of the National Prisoner of War Museum. **Chattahoochee River National Recreation Area** (✉ 1978 Island Ford Pkwy., Dunwoody 30350, ☎ 770/399–8070, WEB www.nps.gov/chat; 🎫 parking $2) has picnic areas, hiking trails, and rivers with swimming areas. **Kennesaw Mountain National Battlefield** (✉ 900 Kennesaw Mountain Dr., Kennesaw 30152, ☎ 770/427–4686, WEB http://ngeorgia.com; 🎫 free), a 2,884-acre park outside Atlanta, commemorates one of the Civil War's most decisive battles and has 16 mi of hiking trails.

State Parks

Georgia's state parks charge $2 per day per vehicle for all-day parking passes. **Cloudland Canyon State Park** (✉ 122 Cloudland Canyon Park Rd., Rising Fawn 30738, ☎ 706/657–4050, WEB www.georgiastateparks.org), on the west side of Lookout Mountain in the state's northwest corner, has cabin facilities, camping, and dramatic scenery. **Vogel State Park** (✉ 7485 Vogel State Park Rd., Blairsville 30512, ☎ 706/745–2628, WEB www.georgiastateparks.org), a 280-acre park surrounded by the Chattahoochee National Forest, includes a 22-acre lake. The park has cottages and campsites. **Providence Canyon** (✉ Rte. 1, Box 158, Lumpkin 31815, ☎ 229/838–6202 or 800/864–7275, WEB www.georgiastateparks.org), known as Georgia's Grand Canyon, is a day park for picnicking, exploring, and hiking.

ATLANTA

Atlanta is one of the fastest-growing cities in the United States, with a skyline that is constantly changing. Initially founded as a railroad cen-

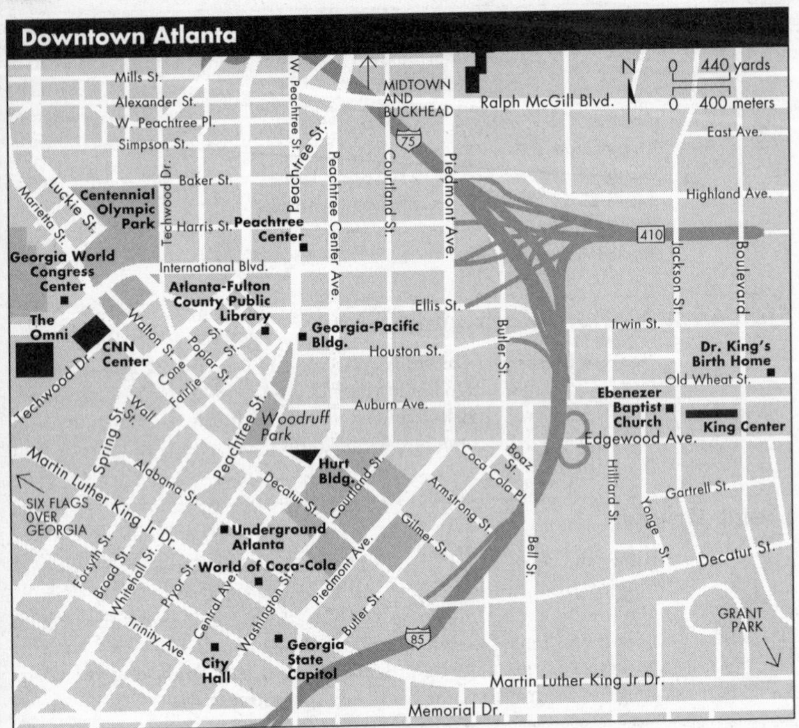

ter, the city has blossomed into a major metropolis with a population of nearly half a million citizens and a surrounding metro area that includes more than 3 million people. It is an aviation hub and a regional leader in commerce and industry. But for all its modernity, the city's winning character is defined by its southern hospitality and its near-picture-perfect residential neighborhoods.

Exploring Atlanta

Because Atlanta is a sprawling city, a car is a necessity, though there are a number of walkable neighborhoods and districts with interesting architecture and attractions. Beginning downtown, you can move north past an eclectic mix of Renaissance Revival towers and contemporary skyscrapers; through Midtown's genteel, garden-filled neighborhoods punctuated by parks and museums; and into upscale Buckhead, lined with mansions and glitzy shopping centers.

Downtown

Atlanta had its inauspicious beginning as a 19th-century settlement and later became a railway hub; a few sites from the earliest days are preserved downtown. A three-level, six-block entertainment and shopping center called **Underground Atlanta** (✉ 50 Upper Alabama St., ☎ 404/523–2311) encompasses some of the original city center's 19th-century storefronts and streets. The **World of Coca-Cola** (✉ 55 Martin Luther King Jr. Dr., ☎ 404/676–5151; 🎫 $6) gives free samples and has three floors of memorabilia from the two-centuries-old soft drink company.

At the corner of Marietta Street and Techwood Drive is the **CNN Center** (✉ 1 CNN Center, ☎ 404/827–2300; 🎫 $8), headquarters of Cable News Network. There are daily guided behind-the-scenes tours, including newscasters in action. Call in advance to make a reservation. Children under six are not admitted on the tours.

Thrusting into the sky a block north of Woodruff Park are the striking angles of the red-marble **Georgia-Pacific Building** (✉ 133 Peachtree St., at John Wesley Dobbs Ave.). Built between 1979 and 1982 on the site of Loew's Grand Theatre, where *Gone With the Wind* premiered in 1939, the 50-story corporate flagship building houses the **High Museum of Folk Art and Photography Galleries** (✉ 30 John Wesley Dobbs Ave., ☎ 404/577–6940; 🎫 free), a branch of the High Museum of Art.

★ Walking tours of the **Martin Luther King Jr. National Historic District** start from the **King Center** (✉ 449 Auburn Ave., ☎ 404/526–8900; 🎫 free), established by King's widow, Coretta Scott King. Inside the center there's a museum, a library, and a gift shop; King's tomb is marked by an eternal flame.

The Queen Anne–style clapboard house that was **Dr. King's Birth Home** (✉ 501 Auburn Ave., ☎ 404/331–3920; 🎫 free) is open for tours. Three generations of the King family have preached at **Ebenezer Baptist Church** (✉ 407 Auburn Ave., ☎ 404/688–7263; 🎫 free).

The **Georgia State Capitol** (✉ Washington St. at Martin Luther King Jr. Dr., ☎ 404/656–2844; 🎫 free) houses government offices and a museum. Built in 1889, it has a dome gilded with gold leaf from ore mined in nearby Dahlonega. The capitol building is undergoing extensive renovation. The **Georgia Capitol Museum** (404/651–6996) houses exhibits on the history of the Capitol Building and the historical events that took place inside it.

Atlantan John Portman designed the **Peachtree Center** (☎ 404/524–3787), built between 1960 and 1992. The climate-controlled complex, filled with shops, restaurants, hotels, and offices, is on the city's main thoroughfare, **Peachtree Street.** In the lobby of the center's Marriott Marquis Two Tower is the **Atlanta International Museum of Art, Design and Culture** (✉ 285 Peachtree Center Ave., ☎ 404/688–2467; 🎫 free), which specializes in international art and design.

★ In Grant Park, 2 mi southeast of downtown, is the unique **Atlanta Cyclorama** (✉ Grant Park, 800 Cherokee Ave., ☎ 404/624–1071 tickets; 404/658–7625 information; 🎫 $5), designed in 1921 by John Francis Downing. Within its walls hangs a huge circular painting that depicts the Battle of Atlanta (1864), when the city was burned by General William T. Sherman.

Six Flags Over Georgia a large theme park 10 mi west of downtown, has dozens of rides (including roller coasters and water rides), musical revues, and concerts. ✉ *I–20 at 7561 Six Flags Rd., Austell,* ☎ *770/739–3400;* 🎫 *$40, $25 if under 48" tall; closed Nov.–Feb.*

Midtown

Midtown, north of downtown, was the heart of Atlanta's hippie scene during the 1960s and early '70s and now is the city's primary art and theater district and the home of a large segment of Atlanta's gay population, as well as young families, young professionals, artists, and musicians. The area is popular for its bars, restaurants, and specialty shops. Like downtown, it has a distinctive skyline created by the many modern office towers.

SciTrek (✉ 395 Piedmont Ave., ☎ 404/522–5500; 🎫 $7.50) is among the top science museums in the country, with hands-on exhibits and Kidspace, a special area for two- to seven-year-olds. The Egyptian-style **Fox Theatre** (✉ 660 Peachtree St., ☎ 404/881–2100), the city's oldest movie palace, was designed by Marye, Alger, and Vinour and opened in 1929. It hosts splashy events ranging from touring companies of Broadway plays to rock concerts; tours are offered year-round.

In Midtown, the **Margaret Mitchell House** (✉ 990 Peachtree St., ☎ 404/249–7012; 💰 $12), the thrice-renovated (having been torched twice by arsonists) apartment building in which Margaret Mitchell wrote her famous novel *Gone With the Wind,* pays tribute to the famous Georgia author.

Designed by Richard Meier, the **High Museum of Art** showcases a major collection of American contemporary and decorative art as well as sub-Saharan African art. ✉ *1280 Peachtree St.,* ☎ *404/733–4444.* 💰 *$8. closed Mon.* The **Center for Puppetry Arts** displays puppets from around the world, holds puppet-making workshops, and stages original productions for children and adults. ✉ *1404 Spring St.,* ☎ *404/873–3391.* 💰 *$9. closed Sun.* Atlanta architect Willis Denny's impressive Romanesque Victorian mansion, **Rhodes Memorial Hall** (✉ 1516 Peachtree St., ☎ 404/881–9980; 💰 $5), is the headquarters for the **Georgia Trust for Historic Preservation,** which presents occasional traveling exhibits on Georgia architecture. The **Fernbank Science Center** (✉ 156 Heaton Park Dr., ☎ 404/378–4311; 💰 free, planetarium shows $2), with an *Apollo* spacecraft and a planetarium, is in Druid Hills, a tree-lined neighborhood north of Ponce de Leon Avenue.

Buckhead

Buckhead, 5 mi north of Midtown on Peachtree Street, is to Atlanta what Beverly Hills is to Los Angeles. This residential and shopping area has plenty of fine restaurants, designer boutiques, and expensive homes. To see the manicured lawns and mansions of Atlanta's elite, take a scenic drive along Tuxedo, Valley, and Habersham roads.

The white-columned, neoclassical **Georgia Governor's Mansion** (✉ 391 W. Paces Ferry Rd., ☎ 404/261–1776; 💰 free) has many Federal-period antiques; it's open for tours Tuesday–Thursday. The **Atlanta History Center** (✉ 130 W. Paces Ferry Rd., ☎ 404/814–4000; 💰 $12)—comprising the **Atlanta History Museum,** the **Tullie Smith Farm,** the neoclassic **Swan House** mansion, and **McElreath Hall**—is a 33-acre forested and garden-filled site.

Parks, Gardens, and Zoos

Zoo Atlanta (✉ 800 Cherokee Ave., ☎ 404/624–5600; 💰 $16) is southeast of downtown. Nearly 1,000 animals live here in naturalistic habitats, including the main attraction—two giant pandas.

Near the CNN Center, **Centennial Olympic Park** (✉ Marietta St. and Techwood Dr.), a legacy of the 1996 Centennial Olympic Games, enhances the streetscape with green space and sculpture. The fountains are especially popular for cooling off during the late-summer heat. **Piedmont Park,** in Midtown between 10th Street and the Prado, is the city's premier urban green space, with paved paths for biking, running, and roller skating. You can rent bikes and in-line skates from **Skate Escape** (✉ 1086 Piedmont Ave., ☎ 404/892–1292), across the street.

Adjoining Piedmont Park is the 30-acre **Atlanta Botanical Garden,** with landscaped gardens and the climate-controlled Fuqua Conservatory. ✉ *1345 Piedmont Ave., ½ mi north of 14th St.,* ☎ *404/876–5859.* 💰 *$7, free Thurs. after 3* PM. *exhibits closed Mon.*

Stone Mountain Park (✉ U.S. 78, ☎ 770/498–5690; 💰 $7 parking, additional fees for individual attractions and special events), 7 mi northeast of the city, contains the world's largest sculpture, a memorial to Confederate heroes Jefferson Davis, Robert E. Lee, and Stonewall Jackson (a cable car takes you 825 ft up the mountain face for a closer look). The 3,200-acre park contains an antebellum plantation and museums, plus a railroad, a riverboat, and nightly laser shows in summer.

Dining

Atlanta prides itself on a wide selection of international restaurants but has plenty of places to sample the traditional and new-style fare of the Deep South.

$$$$ ★ ✕ **Bacchanalia.** The best ingredients from America's farms are used to craft dishes such as foie gras with nectarines, dates with cheese, and salmon with green lentils. The imaginative vegetable tasting menu is outstanding. ✉ *1198 Howell Mill Rd.,* ☎ *404/365–0410. Reservations essential. AE, DC, MC, V. Closed Sun.–Mon. No lunch.*

$$$$ ★ ✕ **The Dining Room, the Ritz-Carlton, Buckhead.** French basics are deftly blended with Asian techniques and ingredients. Thai soup with crab roll and fresh coriander appears on the table next to a plate of fromage blanc with cucumber gelée. The fare changes daily, but the best deal is the tasting menu ($82). ✉ *3434 Peachtree Rd.,* ☎ *404/237–2700. Reservations essential. Jacket and tie. AE, D, DC, MC, V. Closed Sun. No lunch.*

$$$$ ★ ✕ **Seeger's.** The roulade of foie gras with onion marmalade and puree of red wine, apple, and quince is characteristic of the restaurant. Local ingredients also appear, as in grilled lamb chops with Vidalia onions. Fixed-price menus (including a vegetable menu) may be paired with selected wines for an additional charge. ✉ *111 W. Paces Ferry Rd.,* ☎ *404/846–9779. Reservations essential. Jacket and tie. AE, D, DC, MC, V. Closed Sun. No lunch.*

$$$–$$$$ ✕ **The Atlanta Fish Market.** It's busy and it's noisy, but there is no better seafood in the area. An intimidating menu is made simple by the quick and knowledgeable waitstaff, but many still choose the simpler favorites like the clam and cod chowder or the shrimp and scallops en brochette. ✉ *265 Pharr Rd.,* ☎ *404/262–3165. AE, D, DC, MC, V. No lunch Sun.*

$$–$$$$ ✕ **City Grill.** The setting of this restaurant in the historic Hurt Building includes high ceilings and romantic table lamps. The menu is American with a southern flair as seen in such dishes as creole barbecued shrimp and hickory-grilled pork fillet with Tennessee whiskey sauce. Save room for the chocolate pecan soufflé. ✉ *50 Hurt Plaza,* ☎ *404/524–2489. AE, D, DC, MC, V. Closed Sun. No lunch Sat.*

$$–$$$$ ✕ **South City Kitchen.** The cuisine at this popular restaurant is the traditional Low Country style of coastal South Carolina and Georgia. The she-crab soup, crab hash with poached eggs, buttermilk fried chicken, and chocolate pecan pie are all superb. ✉ *1144 Crescent Ave.,* ☎ *404/873–7358. AE, DC, MC, V.*

$$$ ✕ **Babette's Feast.** The flavors of Provence make a strong gastronomic statement at this restaurant in a freestanding house in Virginia Highland. What could be more transporting than a succulent white-bean soup with pancetta, or sweetbreads smoothly complemented with wild mushrooms and hazelnut sauce? ✉ *573 N. Highland Ave.,* ☎ *404/523–9121. Reservations essential. AE, D, MC, V. Closed Mon. No lunch.*

$$–$$$ ✕ **Meritage.** This is a jazzy establishment that offers a serious menu with a vast selection of meals prepared with intricate care. Of note is the crab-stuffed salmon wrapped in rice paper, and the roasted quail stuffed with white truffles. The long dessert list is equally elaborate. ✉ *3125 Piedmont Rd.,* ☎ *404/231–6700. AE, MC, V. Closed Sun. No lunch.*

$–$$$ ★ ✕ **Colonnade Restaurant.** For traditional southern cuisine, such as oyster stew, Parker House rolls, crab cakes, and ham steak, insiders head for the Colonnade, an Atlanta institution since 1927. ✉ *1879 Cheshire Bridge Rd.,* ☎ *404/874–5642. Reservations not accepted. No credit cards.*

$ ✕ **Thelma's Kitchen.** Thelma Grundy's down-home self-service restaurant on the street level of a somewhat renovated Roxy Hotel has some of the best southern food in town. The okra pancakes are not to be missed. Fried catfish, "cold" slaw, macaroni and cheese, and pecan pie are all special. ✉ *768 Marietta St. NW,* ☎ *404/688–5855. Reservations not accepted. No credit cards. Closed weekends. No dinner.*

Lodging

The city's booming convention business means hotel and motel options in all price ranges. The downtown, Buckhead, and north I–285 areas have the greatest concentration of accommodations.

$$$$ **Four Seasons Hotel.** A sweeping staircase at the entrance leads up to a welcoming bar with cozy seating and Park 75, the hotel's fine restaurant. Rooms have marble bathrooms, brass chandeliers, and data ports. ✉ *75 14th St., 30309,* ☎ *404/881–9898,* FAX *404/873–4692,* WEB *www.fourseasons.com. 244 rooms. Restaurant, pool, health club. AE, D, DC, MC, V.*

$$$$ ★ **Ritz-Carlton, Buckhead.** The elegant lobby with fine art, a fireplace, and comfortable, antique furniture is perfect for lingering over afternoon tea before returning to rooms with luxury linens, marble baths, and reproduction period furnishings. The hotel's restaurant, the Dining Room, is among the finest the southeast has to offer, and don't pass up the Wine Bar, a lounge that hosts informative wine tastings for everyone from the novice to the aficionado. ✉ *3434 Peachtree Rd., 30326,* ☎ *404/237–2700,* FAX *404/239–0078,* WEB *www.ritzcarlton.com. 553 rooms. 2 restaurants, pool, health club. AE, D, DC, MC, V.*

$$$–$$$$ **Atlanta Marriott Marquis.** The lobby of this convention hotel stretches to the skylighted roof 50 stories above. Traditionally furnished guest rooms open onto this central atrium. A skywalk connects the hotel to the Peachtree Center and its shops. ✉ *265 Peachtree Center Ave., 30303,* ☎ *404/521–0000,* FAX *404/586–6299,* WEB *www.marriott.com. 1,674 rooms. 4 restaurants, pools, health club. AE, D, DC, MC, V.*

$$$–$$$$ **JW Marriott.** Handsome Chippendale-style furniture graces the lobby and the guest rooms of this 25-story hotel, which connects with Lenox Square mall. Some rooms also have spacious marble baths with separate shower stalls. ✉ *3300 Lenox Rd., 30326,* ☎ *404/262–3344,* FAX *404/262–8689,* WEB *www.marriott.com. 371 rooms. Restaurant, pool, health club. AE, D, DC, MC, V.*

$$$–$$$$ **Swissôtel.** An international clientele frequents this European-style luxury hotel, with its chic, modern glass exterior; sophisticated Biedermeier-style interiors; and fabulous art on view in the public spaces. Palm, an outpost of the popular Manhattan restaurant of the same name, is famous for its steaks. ✉ *3391 Peachtree Rd., 30326,* ☎ *404/365–0065 or 800/253–1397,* FAX *404/365–8787,* WEB *www.swissotel.com. 365 rooms. Restaurant, pool, health club. AE, D, DC, MC, V.*

$$$ **Embassy Suites.** This Buckhead high-rise is blocks from two of the city's top shopping centers, Phipps Plaza and Lenox Square. Suites range from basic bedroom and sitting-room combinations to luxurious rooms with wet bars. All units have microwaves and refrigerators. ✉ *3285 Peachtree Rd., 30305,* ☎ *404/261–7733,* FAX *404/261–6857,* WEB *www.embassy-suites.com. 317 suites. Restaurant, pool. AE, D, DC, MC, V. BP.*

$$–$$$ ⊡ **Sierra Suites Atlanta Brookhaven.** Studio-style suites with kitchens are decorated in earth tones and forest green. Light wood modern-style furniture with an oak finish is standard. Continental breakfast and 24-hour coffee and tea bar is included in room rate. ✉ *3967 Peachtree Rd., 30319,* ☎ *404/237–9100,* FAX *404/237–0055,* WEB *www.sierrasuites.com. 91 suites. Pool. AE, D, DC, MC, V. CP.*

$$ ⊡ **Quality Hotel Downtown.** Rooms in this quiet hotel have views of downtown; some have balconies. The marble lobby is lit by crystal chandeliers, and modest-size rooms are done in teal and navy. ✉ *89 Luckie St., 30303,* ☎ *404/524–7991,* FAX *404/524–0672,* WEB *www.qualityhotel.com. 89 rooms. Pool. AE, DC, MC, V. BP.*

Nightlife and the Arts

Arts and nightlife events are listed in the *Atlanta Journal Constitution* and *Creative Loafing* newspapers, as well as *Symbol,* the *Season, WHERE ATLANTA,* and *KNOW ATLANTA* magazines, available at visitor information centers and in hotels. Ticket brokers include **Ticketmaster** (☎ 404/249–6400 or 800/326–4000) and **Ticket-X-Press** (☎ 404/231–5888).

Nightlife

Buckhead, Virginia Highland, East Atlanta, and **Little Five Points** neighborhoods are Atlanta's nightlife centers. **Atkins Park Bar & Grill** (✉ 794 N. Highland Ave., ☎ 404/876–7249), one of the city's oldest neighborhood bars, attracts a thirty-something crowd. **Backstreet** (✉ 845 Peachtree St., ☎ 404/873–1986), drawing both men and women, has been Midtown's mainstay gay club for nearly two decades. But nongay couples often enjoy the all-hours club as well. The venerable **Blind Willie's** (✉ 828 N. Highland Ave., ☎ 404/873–2583) offers New Orleans– and Chicago-style blues. At **Churchill Arms** (✉ 3223 Cain Hill Pl., ☎ 404/233–5633) folks of all ages gather to shoot pool, sing old-time songs, and listen to live piano music. The **EARL** (✉ 488 Flat Shoals Ave., ☎ 404/522–3950) is a restaurant and lounge that puts on rock and hip-hop shows. For contemporary rock try **Echo Lounge** (✉ 551 Flat Shoals Ave., ☎ 404/681–3600).

Eddie's Attic (✉ 515-B N. McDonough St., ☎ 404/377–4976), next to the MARTA station, is the best venue for local acoustic acts. **Havana Club** (✉ East Village Square, 247 Buckhead Ave., ☎ 404/869–8484) has Latin music and dancing every night. **Sambuca Jazz Cafe** (✉ 3102 Piedmont Rd., ☎ 404/237–5299) attracts a chic young set to its decent table dining, lively bar, and good live jazz. Latin music invites dancing Thursday to Saturday night at **Sanctuary** (✉ 128 E. Andrews Dr., ☎ 404/262–1377). **Tongue & Groove** (✉ 3055 Peachtree Rd., ☎ 404/261–2325) is Buckhead's see-and-be-seen nightspot.

The Arts

Most touring Broadway productions make their way to Atlanta's **Fox Theatre** (☞ Midtown *in* Exploring Atlanta, *above*). The **Civic Center** (✉ 395 Piedmont Ave., ☎ 404/523–6275) puts on popular Broadway musicals. The **Alliance Theater Company** (✉ 1280 Peachtree St., ☎ 404/733–5000) is one of the city's leading theatrical groups. Woodruff Arts Center's Symphony Hall (✉ 1280 Peachtree St., ☎ 404/733–5000) is the home of the **Atlanta Symphony Orchestra.** The **Atlanta Ballet Company** (☎ 404/892–3303) performs at the Fox Theatre. In summer the **Atlanta Opera** (☎ 404/881–8801) usually presents four operas at the Fox Theatre.

Outdoor Activities and Sports

Golf

The **Alfred Tup Holmes Club** (✉ 2300 Wilson Dr., ☎ 404/753–6158), with 18 par-72 holes, is known for doglegs and blind shots. The only public course near downtown, **Bobby Jones Golf Course** (✉ 384 Woodward Way, ☎ 404/355–1009) has some of the city's worst fairways and greens; still, the 18-hole, par-71 course is always crowded. With 18 holes, the par-71 **North Fulton Golf Course** (✉ 216 W. Wieuca Rd., ☎ 404/255–0723) in Chastain Park has one of the best layouts in the city. Outside I–285, in the suburbs, **Stone Mountain Park** (✉ U.S. 78, ☎ 770/498–5715) offers two courses: Stonemont, an 18-hole, par-71 course; and par-70 Lakemont, with 18 holes.

Tennis

Bitsy Grant Tennis Center (✉ 2125 Northside Dr., ☎ 404/609–7193) has 13 clay courts, 6 of which are lighted, and 10 lighted hard courts; it's the area's best public facility. **Piedmont Park** (✉ Piedmont Ave. between 10th St. and the Prado, ☎ 404/853–3461) has 12 hard courts with lights. Access the tennis center from Park Drive off Monroe Drive; even though the sign reads DO NOT ENTER, the security guard will show you the parking lot.

Spectator Sports

Tickets for the teams listed below are available through **Ticketmaster** (☎ 800/326–4000).

Baseball: Atlanta Braves (✉ Turner Field, 755 Hank Aaron Dr., ☎ 404/522–7630). **Basketball: Atlanta Hawks** (✉ Philips Arena, 1 Philips Dr., ☎ 404/827–3865). **Football: Atlanta Falcons** (✉ Georgia Dome, 1 Georgia Dome Dr., ☎ 404/223–8000). **Hockey: Atlanta Thrashers** (✉ Philips Arena, 1 Philips Dr., ☎ 404/584–7825).

Shopping

Antiques Stores

Shops selling antique pine pieces, collectibles, and crafts line **Bennett Street** in Buckhead. European furnishings and fine art are sold in more than 25 shops in Buckhead's **2300 Peachtree Road** complex. **Miami Circle,** a street on the northern edge of Buckhead off Piedmont Road, is a hot spot for lovers of antiques, with such stores as Gables Antiques (✉ 711 Miami Cir., ☎ 404/231–0734) and Williams Antiques (✉ 699 Miami Cir., ☎ 404/231–9818). **Chamblee Antique Row** (✉ turn east at the intersection of Broad St. and Peachtree Industrial Blvd., Chamblee, ☎ 770/458–1614) has more than 200 dealers in its numerous antiques stores and malls.

Shopping Districts

Atlanta's shopping centers are generally open Monday–Saturday 10–6 and Sunday noon–5; many stay open until 9 or 9:30 several weeknights and most weekends. The primary downtown shopping areas are **Underground Atlanta,** where specialty boutiques, chain stores, and pushcarts mix with restaurants and nightclubs; and the stretch of Peachtree between **Macy's** and **Peachtree Center Mall.** North of downtown, **Lenox Square** (✉ 3393 Peachtree St.) has more than 250 stores on its second level. **Phipps Plaza** (✉ 3500 Peachtree Rd.) attracts shoppers from throughout the Southeast. It has more than 100 stores. **Perimeter Mall** (✉ 4400 Ashford-Dunwoody Rd., Dunwoody) serves the Dunwoody area with many big-name retailers like Macy's and Nordstrom. **Cumberland Mall** (✉ I–285 at Cobb Pkwy.) is easily accessible from I–75 and I–285. **Galleria** (✉ 1 Galleria Pkwy.) is directly across from the Cumberland Mall and is also convenient to I–75 and I–285.

Atlanta Essentials

AIRPORTS AND TRANSFERS

Hartsfield Atlanta International Airport has scheduled flights by most major domestic and foreign carriers.

➤ AIRPORT INFORMATION: **Hartsfield Atlanta International Airport** (✉ 6000 N. Terminal Pkwy., 30320, ☎ 404/530–6600).

AIRPORT TRANSFER

Cab fare to downtown Atlanta, 13 mi north of the airport via I–75 and I–85, is about $18 for one person, $20 for two people, and $8 each additional for three or more. From the airport, the MARTA rapid-rail subway system is one of the quickest and easiest ways to reach many areas including downtown.

➤ SHUTTLE: **MARTA** (☎ 404/848–4711).

BUS TRAVEL TO AND FROM ATLANTA

Greyhound provides transportation to downtown Atlanta, Decatur, Hapeville, Marietta, Conyers, Douglasville, and Norcross.

➤ BUS INFORMATION: **Greyhound** (✉ 232 Forsyth St., ☎ 404/584–1731 or 800/231–2222, WEB www.greyhound.com).

CAR TRAVEL

Atlanta is called the Crossroads of the South for good reason. Between South Carolina and Alabama, I–85 runs northeast–southwest through Atlanta and I–20 runs east–west; I–75 runs north–south through the state. I–285 makes a 65-mi loop around the metro area. If driving from I–75 north to Decatur, use I–675 to connect to I–285 on the east side of the metro Atlanta area.

PARKING

Major public parking lots downtown are at the CNN Center, the Georgia World Congress Center, Peachtree Center, Macy's, and Underground Atlanta. Buckhead and Midtown have on-street parking and more lots.

➤ CONTACTS: **CNN Center** (✉ entrance off Techwood Dr.). **Georgia World Congress Center** (✉ off International Blvd.). **Macy's** (✉ Carnegie Way, 1 block off Peachtree St.). **Peachtree Center** (✉ Peachtree St.). **Underground Atlanta** (✉ 65 Upper Alabama St.).

TAXIS

You can hail a cab fairly easily at hotels in the downtown or Buckhead districts. Buckhead Safety Cab and Checker Cab have 24-hour service. With advance reservations, Carey Executive Limousine also provides 24-hour service.

➤ TAXI COMPANIES: **Buckhead Safety Cab** (☎ 404/233–1152 or 404/233–1153). **Carey Executive Limousine** (☎ 404/223–2000 or 800/241–3943). **Checker Cab** (☎ 404/351–1111).

TOURS

BUS AND VAN TOURS

Atlanta Discovery Tours and American Sightseeing Atlanta arrange customized sightseeing tours. Gray Line of Atlanta offers tours of downtown, Midtown, Buckhead, and the King Center.

➤ FEES AND SCHEDULES: **American Sightseeing Atlanta** (☎ 404/233–9140 or 800/572–3050). **Atlanta Discovery Tours** (☎ 770/667–1414). **Gray Line of Atlanta** (✉ 705 Lively Ave., Norcross 30071, ☎ 770/449–1806 or 800/593–1818, FAX 770/246–9397).

WALKING TOURS

Atlanta Preservation Center has guided tours of 10 historic neighborhoods, from March through November, and a tour of the Fox Theatre that's available year-round.

➤ FEES AND SCHEDULES: **Atlanta Preservation Center** (✉ 156 7th St., Suite 3, ☎ 404/876–2041; 404/876–2040 tour hot line; 🎫 $5).

TRAIN TRAVEL

Amtrak serves Brookwood Station.

➤ TRAIN INFORMATION: **Amtrak** (☎ 404/881–3060 or 800/872–7245, WEB www.amtrak.com). **Brookwood Station** (✉ 1688 Peachtree St.).

TRANSPORTATION AROUND ATLANTA

MARTA operates buses and a modern rapid-rail subway system. Fare for either is $1.75; exact change or a token is required. The rapid-rail trains operate every 8–10 minutes, weekdays 5 AM–1 AM and weekends 6 AM–12:30 AM. Bus schedules depend on the route. Information is available in five languages.

➤ CONTACT: **MARTA** (☎ 404/848–4711, WEB www.itsmarta.com).

VISITOR INFORMATION

➤ TOURIST INFORMATION: **Atlanta Chamber of Commerce** (✉ 235 International Blvd., 30303, ☎ 404/880–9000, WEB www.metroatlantachamber.com). **Convention and Visitors Bureau visitor centers** (✉ Peachtree Center Mall, 233 Peachtree St., 30303, ☎ 404/222–6688 or 800/285–2682; ✉ Underground Atlanta, 65 Upper Alabama St., ☎ 404/577–2148; ✉ Georgia World Congress Center, 285 International Blvd., 30313, ☎ 404/233–4017; ✉ Hartsfield International Airport, North Terminal at West Crossover, 30320, ☎ 404/305–8426; ✉ Lenox Square, 3393 Peachtree Rd., 30324, ☎ 404/266–1398).

SAVANNAH

Four hours southeast of Atlanta, but a world away from the bustling, modern metropolis, lies Savannah, wrapped in a mantle of old-world grace. Established in 1733, the city preserves its heritage in a 2½-square-mi historic district, the nation's largest urban landmark. Here 1,000 structures have been restored, and families still live in the 19th-century mansions and town houses. Known as the City of Festivals, Savannah rarely lets a weekend pass without some sort of celebration, from the St. Patrick's Day bash in March and the Riverfront Seafood Festival in April to the spring azalea and dogwood festivals to the house tours and concerts at Christmas.

Exploring Savannah

A good way to start a tour is by picking up information at the **Visitors Center** in the old Central Georgia railway station. For entertainment of every sort, visit the restored **City Market** (✉ W. St. Julian St. between Ellis and Franklin Sqs.), a four-block area of shops, art galleries, restaurants, and music venues. Near the riverfront, narrow cobblestone streets wind from Bay Street down to Factors Walk and, below, to River Street and the **River Front** district, a nine-block area with shops, restaurants, taverns, and some wonderfully restored old buildings. The **Ships of the Sea Museum** (✉ 41 Martin Luther King Jr. Blvd., ☎ 912/232–1511, WEB www.shipsofthesea.org; 🎫 $5) displays memorabilia ranging from models of the earliest ships and nuclear submarines to nautical folk art. This William Jay–designed building dates to 1819.

Savannah

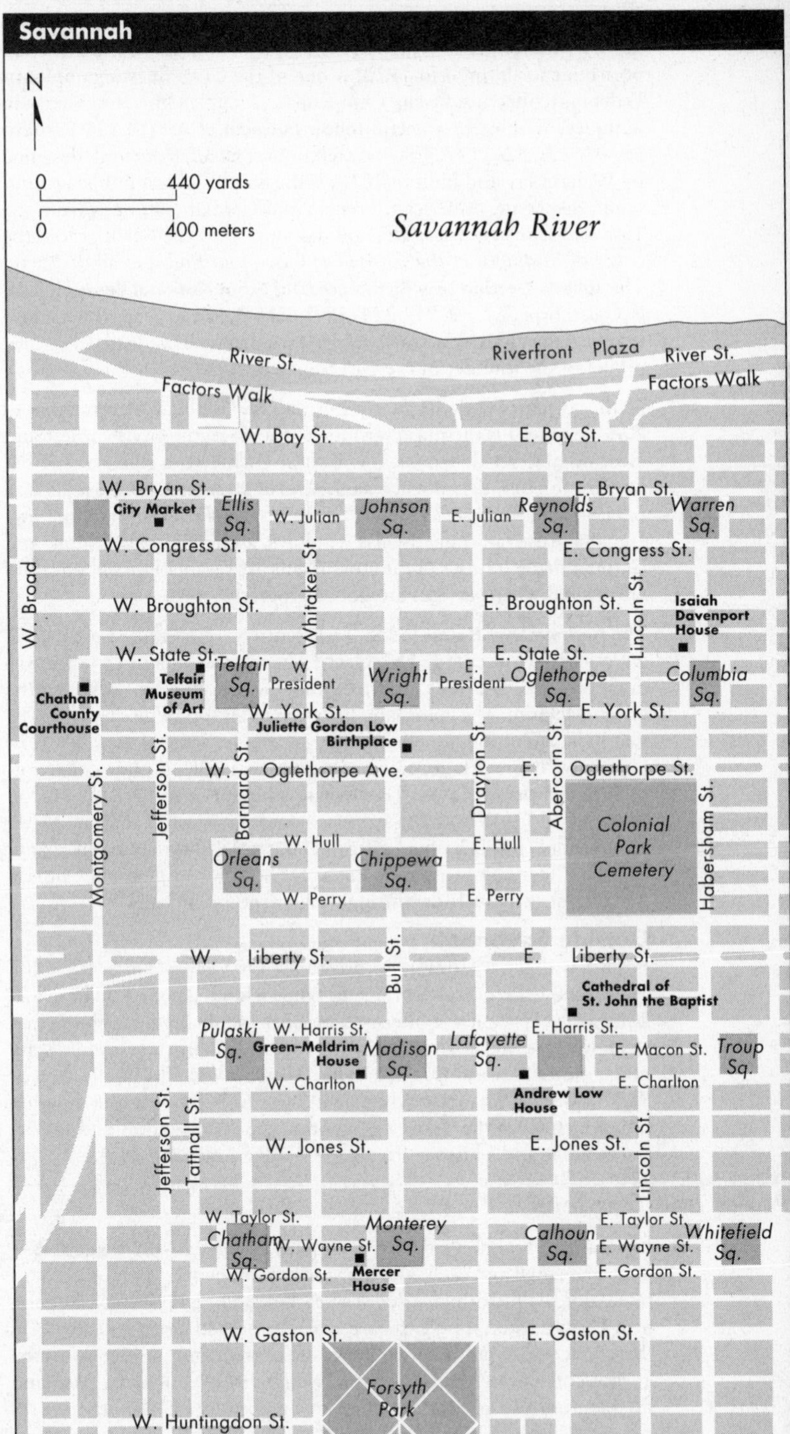
N
0
440 yards
0
400 meters
Savannah River
River St.
Riverfront Plaza
River St.
Factors Walk
Factors Walk
W. Bay St.
E. Bay St.
W. Bryan St.
E. Bryan St.
City Market
Ellis Sq.
W. Julian
Johnson Sq.
E. Julian
Reynolds Sq.
Warren Sq.
W. Congress St.
E. Congress St.
W. Broad
Whitaker St.
W. Broughton St.
E. Broughton St.
Lincoln St.
Isaiah Davenport House
W. State St.
E. State St.
Telfair Sq.
W. President
Wright Sq.
E. President
Oglethorpe Sq.
Columbia Sq.
Chatham County Courthouse
Telfair Museum of Art
W. York St.
E. York St.
Juliette Gordon Low Birthplace
Drayton St.
Abercorn St.
W. Oglethorpe Ave.
E. Oglethorpe St.
Montgomery St.
Jefferson St.
Barnard St.
Colonial Park Cemetery
Habersham St.
W. Hull
E. Hull
Orleans Sq.
Chippewa Sq.
W. Perry
E. Perry
W. Liberty St.
E. Liberty St.
Bull St.
Cathedral of St. John the Baptist
Pulaski Sq.
W. Harris St.
E. Harris St.
Green-Meldrim House
Madison Sq.
Lafayette Sq.
E. Macon St.
Troup Sq.
W. Charlton
E. Charlton
Andrew Low House
Jefferson St.
Tattnall St.
W. Jones St.
E. Jones St.
Lincoln St.
W. Taylor St.
Monterey Sq.
E. Taylor St.
Chatham Sq.
W. Wayne St.
Calhoun Sq.
E. Wayne St.
Whitefield Sq.
W. Gordon St.
Mercer House
E. Gordon St.
W. Gaston St.
E. Gaston St.
Forsyth Park
W. Huntingdon St.

★ The **Isaiah Davenport House** (✉ 324 E. State St., ☎ 912/236–8097, WEB www.davenportsavga.com; 🎟 $6), which master builder Davenport built for himself in 1820, is one of the city's finest examples of Federal architecture. It has Chippendale, Hepplewhite, and Sheraton antiques. Within the graceful **Telfair Museum of Art** (✉ 121 Barnard St., ☎ 912/232–1177, WEB www.telfair.org; 🎟 $8, free Sun.), designed by William Jay and built in 1818, is the South's oldest public art museum, displaying American, French, and German paintings from the 18th and 19th centuries. The now-famous "Bird Girl" that graced the cover of *Midnight in the Garden of Good and Evil* is exhibited here. The **Juliette Gordon Low Birthplace/Girl Scout National Center** (✉ 10 E. Oglethorpe Ave., ☎ 912/233–4501; 🎟 $6), in a Regency town house that was the city's first National Historic Landmark, displays memorabilia of the founder of the Girl Scouts of America.

At the corner of Oglethorpe Avenue and McDonough Street, **Colonial Park Cemetery** is the burial ground for some of the city's earliest and most notable residents, such as Button Gwinnett, a signatory of the Declaration of Independence. **Cathedral of St. John the Baptist** (✉ 222 E. Harris St., ☎ 912/233–4709; 🎟 free), a late-19th-century structure, contains Austrian stained-glass windows, an Italian marble altar, and German-made stations of the cross. Tours are by appointment only and are offered when services are not in progress.

The **Andrew Low House** (✉ 329 Abercorn St., ☎ 912/233–6854, WEB www.andrewlow.com; 🎟 $7; closed Thurs.) was built in 1848 for Andrew Low by New York architect John Norris, who also designed the Green-Meldrim. The home later belonged to his son, William, who married Juliette Gordon, founder of the Girl Scouts. Some of the city's most impressive ironwork decorates the exterior; inside is a fine collection
★ of 19th-century antiques. The **Green-Meldrim House** (✉ 1 W. Macon St., ☎ 912/233–3845; 🎟 $5 suggested donation; closed Mon. and Wed.) is a splendid Gothic Revival mansion built in 1852 for cotton merchant Charles Green. Now a parish house for St. John's Episcopal Church, it is furnished with 16th- through 19th-century antiques.

Outside Savannah

From Savannah a 30-minute drive east on Victory Drive (U.S. 80/Tybee Rd.) leads across a bridge to **Tybee Island.** About 5 mi long and 2 mi wide, Tybee has white-sand beaches for shelling, crabbing, and swimming, as well as covered picnic facilities, a marina, seafood restaurants, motels, and shops. The **Tybee Museum** (✉ 30 Meddin Dr., ☎ 912/786–5801, WEB www.tybeeisland.com; 🎟 lighthouse and museum $4), which faces the **Tybee Lighthouse,** the state's oldest and tallest, traces the island's history from early Native American days.

Parks and Gardens

★ Integral to Savannah's design is its park system: 22 **town squares**—large and small and each with a historic monument or a graceful fountain—dot the historic district. The earliest square is Johnson Square, near City Market; food carts are typically parked along its edges. On West Macon Street is **Forsyth Park,** site of frequent outdoor concerts; at the center of its shady 20 acres, which include a jogging path and the Fragrant Garden for the Blind, is a graceful white fountain.

Dining

$$$–$$$$ ★ ✕ **Elizabeth on 37th.** This restaurant in a turn-of-the-20th-century mansion has earned a national reputation for its fine seafood and delicate sauces. Regional foods such as stone-ground grits, black-eyed peas, country ham, and succulent white Georgia shrimp grace the seasonal menu. Finish with Savannah Cream Cake. ✉ *105 E. 37th St.,* ☎ *912/236–5547. Reservations essential. AE, D, DC, MC, V. No lunch.*

$$–$$$$ ★ ✕ **Sapphire Grill.** Squab, grits, Georgia white shrimp, and fried green tomatoes are expertly used in contemporary Low Country dishes. The chocolate flan is delicious. ✉ *110 W. Congress St.,* ☎ *912/443–9962. Reservations essential. AE, D, DC, MC, V. No lunch.*

$$–$$$ ★ ✕ **Bistro Savannah.** This establishment, housed in a circa-1878 building, specializes in fresh regional fare that uses both farmed and wild ingredients. Try the crab cakes with lemon-caper aioli and chowchow and the shrimp and tasso ham with stone ground grits. ✉ *309 W. Congress St.,* ☎ *912/233–6266. AE, MC, V. No lunch.*

$–$$ ✕ **Johnny Harris.** What started as a small roadside stand in 1924 is now one of the city's culinary mainstays. The menu includes steaks, fried chicken, seafood, and barbecued meats smothered in the restaurant's famous sauce. There's live piano or guitar music on Friday night and dancing on Saturday night. ✉ *1651 E. Victory Dr.,* ☎ *912/354–7810. AE, DC, MC, V. Closed Sun.*

$–$$ ✕ **The Lady & Sons.** Yes, it is run by a mother and her sons. Visitors and locals stand in line patiently waiting to attack the buffet ($12.95 at dinner). They come for moist and crispy fried chicken, great baked spaghetti, crab stew, and fresh lemonade. An à la carte menu and a decent wine list are also available. ✉ *311 W. Congress St.,* ☎ *912/233–2600. AE, D, MC, V.*

$ ★ ✕ **Mrs. Wilkes Dining Room.** Come to this unassuming basement restaurant for comfort food served family style. Folks line up at breakfast and lunch for such quintessentially southern dishes as biscuits, grits, collard greens, mashed potatoes, and fried chicken. ✉ *107 W. Jones St.,* ☎ *912/232–5997. Reservations not accepted. No credit cards. Closed weekends. No dinner.*

$ ★ ✕ **Nita's Place.** A half block from the Colonial Cemetery, this little steam-table operation offers nothing by way of interior design. But Juanita Dixon has established a reputation for down-home southern cooking with her salmon patties, baked chicken, perfectly cooked okra, outstanding squash casserole, and homemade desserts. ✉ *140 Abercorn St.,* ☎ *912/238–8233. Reservations not accepted. D, MC, V. No dinner.*

Lodging

$$$–$$$$ ★ **Ballastone Inn.** This sumptuous inn occupies a mansion dating from 1838 that once served as a bordello. Each room is decorated differently. On the garden level, rooms are small and cozy, with exposed-brick walls and beamed ceilings. Afternoon tea, hors d'oeuvres, robes, movies, and bicycles are among the amenities. ✉ *14 E. Oglethorpe Ave., 31401,* ☎ *912/236–1484 or 800/822–4553,* FAX *912/236–4626,* WEB *www.ballastone.com. 16 rooms. AE, MC, V. BP.*

$$$–$$$$ **Hamilton-Turner Inn.** Experience *Midnight in the Garden of Good and Evil* with a stay in this 1873 Second Empire mansion built by wealthy Savannah jeweler Samuel Hamilton. Until recently, the house belonged to Mandy Nichols, one of the principal figures in the John Berendt book. It is furnished with fine antiques. Complimentary afternoon tea, robes, and a film library are among the amenities. All rooms have desks and data ports. ✉ *330 Abercorn St., 31401,* ☎ *912/233–1833 or 888/448–8849,* FAX *912/233–0291,* WEB *www.hamilton-turnerinn.com. 17 rooms. AE, D, DC, MC, V. BP.*

$$$–$$$$ ★ **Kehoe House.** A fabulously appointed bed-and-breakfast inn, the Victorian Kehoe House has brass-and-marble chandeliers, a courtyard garden, and a music room. On the main floor, a double parlor with a 14-ft ceiling holds two fireplaces. Here, you can enjoy sump-

tuous breakfasts, wine with hors d'oeuvres, and lavish afternoon tea. Guests have access to the Downtown Athletic Club. ✉ *123 Habersham St., 31401,* ☎ *912/232–1020 or 800/820–1020,* FAX *912/231–0208,* WEB *www.williamkehoehouse.com. 18 rooms. AE, D, DC, MC, V. BP.*

$$$–$$$$ ★ **The President's Quarters.** At this inn composed of two 19th-century town houses, you are greeted with wine and fruit, and afternoon tea comes with sumptuous cakes. A renovated house across the street contains two suites and a guest room, each with fireplaces and whirlpool tubs. ✉ *225 E. President St., 31401,* ☎ *912/233–1600 or 800/592–1812,* FAX *912/238–0849,* WEB *www.presidentsquarters.com. 19 rooms. AE, D, DC, MC, V. CP.*

$$$ ★ **Gaston Gallery.** Some of the city's most deluxe accommodations are found at this 1868 inn two blocks from Forsyth Park. All rooms have working fireplaces and antiques from the Georgian and Regency periods. Breakfast might include ginger pancakes, and pralines await you at turndown. ✉ *220 E. Gaston St., 31401,* ☎ *912/232–2869 or 800/671–0716,* FAX *912/232–0710,* WEB *www.gastongallery.com. 15 rooms. AE, D, MC, V. BP.*

Nightlife

Savannah's nightlife is a reflection of the city's laid-back, easygoing personality. Some clubs have live reggae, hard rock, and other contemporary music, but most stay with traditional blues, jazz, and piano-bar vocalists. At **Hard Hearted Hannah's East** (✉ Pirate's House, 20 E. Broad St., ☎ 912/233–2225) Emma Kelly, the famed Lady of 6,000 Songs, performs Tuesday–Saturday. Irish music fills the air Wednesday–Saturday at **Kevin Barry's Irish Pub** (✉ 117 W. River St., ☎ 912/233–9626). If you're in the mood for a low-key evening, drop in for coffee at **Gallery Espresso** (✉ 6 E. Liberty St., ☎ 912/233–5348).

Shopping

Savannah's many specialty shops sell such merchandise as English antiques, antiquarian books, and Low Country handmade quilts. Stores in the historic district are housed in ground floors of mansions and town houses or in renovated warehouses along the waterfront. The **River Front** and **City Market** areas have a variety of shops, and downtown is becoming a draw for antiques and collectibles hunters.

Savannah Essentials

AIRPORTS AND TRANSFERS

Savannah International Airport, served by major airlines, is 18 mi west of town on I–16.

➤ AIRPORT INFORMATION: **Savannah International Airport** (✉ 400 Airways Ave., 31408, ☎ 912/964–0514).

TRANSFER

There is no bus service into town, but McCall's Shuttle runs a van between the airport and the city for $16 per person one-way.

➤ SHUTTLE: **McCall's Shuttle** (☎ 912/966–5364).

BUS TRAVEL TO AND FROM SAVANNAH

➤ BUS INFORMATION: **Greyhound** (✉ 610 W. Oglethorpe Ave., ☎ 912/232–2135 or 800/231–2222, WEB www.greyhound.com).

CAR TRAVEL

I–95, running north–south along the coast, and I–16, leading east from Macon, intersect west of Savannah; I–16 dead-ends downtown.

The Coastal Highway (U.S. 17) runs north–south through town, and U.S. 80 runs east–west.

TRAIN TRAVEL

The Amtrak station is 4 mi southwest of downtown.
Train InformationAmtrak (✉ 2611 Seaboard Coastline Dr., ☎ 912/234–2611 or 800/872–7245, WEB www.amtrak.com).

TRANSPORTATION AROUND SAVANNAH

Savannah's historic district is best seen on foot as you can better observe the intricate architectural details. It's laid out in a grid pattern, and strategically placed benches allow for frequent rests. If you bring a car, park it in one of the metered and off-street pay lots.

VISITOR INFORMATION

➤ Tourist Information: **Convention and Visitors Bureau** (✉ 101 E. Bay St., 31402, ☎ 877/728–2662, WEB www.savcvb.com). **Visitors Center** (✉ 301 Martin Luther King Jr. Blvd., 31401, ☎ 912/944–0455, WEB www.savannah-visit.com).

THE GOLDEN ISLES

An hour south of Savannah lie the Golden Isles, a chain of barrier islands stretching along Georgia's coast to the Florida state line. The three most developed—Jekyll Island, Sea Island, and St. Simons Island—are the only ones accessible by car; they are connected to the mainland near Brunswick by a network of causeways. A ferry from St. Marys connects Cumberland Island National Seashore with the mainland, and a launch transports visitors from St. Simons to Little St. Simons, a private vacation retreat. Spring, when temperatures are mild, is the ideal time for a visit; the superb beaches attract large crowds in summer.

Exploring the Golden Isles

Little St. Simons Island

Accessible by private boat, Little St. Simons is a Robinson Crusoe–style getaway 6 mi long and less than 3 mi wide. The island's only development is a rustic but comfortable guest compound. The island's forests and marshes are inhabited by wildlife and more than 200 species of birds. There's a 7-mi stretch of beach for swimming and water sports.

Sea Island

Five-mile-long Sea Island's main attraction is the Cloister, a Spanish Mediterranean–style resort. This luxurious, low-key property has a beach club with a health spa, formal and casual restaurants, and many outdoor activities. Outside the resort, beautiful mansions line Sea Island Drive.

St. Simons Island

The contrasting beauties of white-sand beaches and salt marshes characterize St. Simons, north of Jekyll and Cumberland islands. As large as Manhattan and with more than 14,000 residents, it's the Golden Isles' most complete and commercial resort destination.

At the island's south end, the **Village** is dotted with T-shirt and souvenir shops, boutiques, restaurants, and a public pier for fishing and crabbing. Overlooking the ocean is **Neptune Park,** with a playground, a miniature golf course, and picnic tables shaded by live oaks. Also in the park are the **St. Simons Lighthouse** and the **Museum of Coastal History** (✉ 101 12th St., ☎ 912/638–4666; 🎫 lighthouse and museum $4) in the former lightkeeper's cottage.

Fort Frederica National Monument, on the island's north end, contains the foundation ruins of a fort and buildings inhabited by English soldiers and civilians in the mid-18th century. Tours begin at the **National Park Service visitor center** (✉ off Frederica Rd., ☎ 912/638–3639; 🎫 $4 per vehicle). Visit the Gothic-style, cruciform **Christ Church** (✉ 6329 Frederica Rd., ☎ 912/638–8683), where the stained-glass windows illustrate local history and religious themes. One of the windows is by Louis Tiffany. The church was rebuilt in 1886.

Jekyll Island

The golf courses and system of bike paths here can be enjoyed year-round. Jekyll Island was once the favored retreat of the Vanderbilts, Rockefellers, Morgans, and other American aristocrats. Many of these millionaires' mansions are part of the **Jekyll Island Historic District.** Stop for maps and information at the **visitor center** (✉ 45 S. Beachview Dr., ☎ 877/453–5955; 912/635–3636 locally; WEB www.jekyllisland.com). An 11-acre water park, **Summer Waves,** ranks as a top summer attraction. *✉ 210 S. Riverview Dr., ☎ 912/635–2074, WEB www.summerwaves.com. 🎫 $14.95. closed Oct.–Apr..*

Cumberland Island National Seashore

The largest and most remote of the Golden Isles, **Cumberland Island** (🎫 $4 day-use fee) is a 200-square-mi sanctuary of marshes, dunes, beaches, forests, ponds, estuaries, and inlets. You can tour the unspoiled ★ terrain and the ruins of Thomas Carnegie's **Dungeness** estate on your own or join history and nature walks led by park rangers. You must bring along whatever food, beverages, sunscreen, and insect repellent you may need; the island has no shops.

Dining and Lodging

Cumberland Island

$$$$ ✕🏨 **Greyfield Inn.** This turn-of-the-20th-century house, built by the Carnegie family, is the island's only lodging; its wide, colonnaded porches beckon invitingly. The inn is furnished with Asian and English antiques; burnished hardwood floors are warmed by Persian rugs. *✉ Box 900, Fernandina Beach, FL 32035, ☎ 904/261–6408, WEB www.greyfieldinn.com. 17 rooms. Restaurant. AE, D, MC, V. FAP.*

Jekyll Island

$$–$$$ ★ ✕🏨 **Jekyll Island Club Hotel.** Built in 1886, the four-story clubhouse with wraparound verandas and Queen Anne–style towers and turrets once served as the winter hunting retreat for wealthy financiers. Rooms are custom-decorated with mahogany beds, armoires, and plush sofas and chairs. The nearby Sans Souci Apartments, built in 1896 by a group of club members, have been converted into spacious guest rooms. Two lovingly restored former "millionaires' cottages"—the Crane Cottage and the Cherokee Cottage—add 23 guest rooms to the manicured grounds. The Grand Dining Room serves southern cuisine, such as famed Georgia white shrimp and fried green tomatoes with black-eyed-pea relish; meal plans are available. *✉ 371 Riverview Dr., 31527, ☎ 912/635–2600; 800/535–9547; 912/635–2400 dining room; FAX 912/635–2818; WEB www.jekyllclub.com. 154 rooms. 2 restaurants, pool, tennis. AE, D, DC, MC, V.*

Little St. Simons Island

$$$$ ★ 🏨 **Lodge on Little St. Simons Island.** This lodge is an exclusive little treasure. Guests stay in spacious rooms in one of four buildings: a two-bedroom cottage; the 1917 Hunting Lodge, with two antiques-filled guest rooms; or one of two houses with four guest rooms each. All buildings have screened porches or decks. Meals are served family-style in the main dining room; platters are heaped with fresh fish, home-baked breads, and pies. ✉ *Box 21078, 31522,* ☎ *912/638–7472 or 888/733–5774,* FAX *912/634–1811,* WEB *www.littlestsimonsisland.com. 15 rooms. Pool. AE, D, MC, V. FAP.*

St. Simons Island

$–$$ ✕ **P. G. Archibald's.** In the village, this lively restaurant and nightclub has a "Bayou Victorian" style, with lots of antiques and memorabilia. The menu has seafood as well as basic steak and chicken dishes, plus oysters prepared 15 ways. Blue crab soup is a local favorite, and the huge seafood platter could easily feed two. Open seven days a week until late, the restaurant showcases a variety of live entertainment Thursday–Saturday. ✉ *440 King's Way,* ☎ *912/638–3030. AE, DC, MC, V.*

$$–$$$ **King and Prince Beach and Golf Resort.** This beachfront hotel-and-condominium complex has spacious guest rooms and two- and three-bedroom villas. Villas are privately owned, so the total number available for rent varies from time to time. ✉ *201 Arnold Rd. (Box 20798, 31522),* ☎ *912/638–3631 or 800/342–0212,* FAX *912/634–1720,* WEB *www.kingandprince.com. 140 rooms, 43 villas. 2 restaurants, pools, golf, tennis. AE, D, DC, MC, V.*

$$–$$$ **Sea Palms Golf and Tennis Resort.** A contemporary resort complex with fully furnished villas, most with kitchens, nestles on an 800-acre site. ✉ *5445 Frederica Rd., St. Simons Island 31522,* ☎ *912/638–3351 or 800/841–6268,* FAX *912/634–8029,* WEB *www.seapalms.com. 175 rooms. 2 restaurants, pools, golf, tennis, health club. AE, DC, MC, V.*

Sea Island

$$$$ ✕ **The Cloister.** At this classic resort, modern ocean-side villas, condos, and rental homes have grown up around a 1920s Spanish Mediterranean–style hotel. Formal dining, casual grill lunches, and seafood and breakfast buffets are included in the rate. The Cloister's Ocean Houses are the resort's oceanfront accommodations, with a total of 56 suites complete with luxurious house parlors, fireplaces, and staffed service bars. The spa at the Cloister is in a beautiful building of its own. ✉ *The Cloister, Sea Island 31561,* ☎ *912/638–3611 or 800/732–4752,* FAX *912/638–5159,* WEB *www.cloister.com. 286 rooms. 4 restaurants, pools, golf, tennis. AE, MC, V. FAP.*

Campgrounds

Cumberland Island National Seashore (☞ Visitor Information, *below*) maintains a tent campground with rest rooms, showers, and freshwater sources (bring your own container). Known as Seacamp, this area costs $4 per person, per night. Hikers may want to explore the backcountry, where there are no amenities. The fee for camping in the backcountry is $2 per person per night. Reserve well in advance.

Outdoor Activities and Sports

Biking

Sea Island, Jekyll Island, and St. Simons have paved bike paths. **Barry's Beach Service** (✉ 1300 Ocean Blvd., ☎ 912/638–8053), on St. Simon's, has bikes for rent as well as other recreational equipment. You can rent bikes from **Benjy's Bike Shop** (✉ 130 Retreat Pl., ☎ 912/638–6766), on St. Simons.

Fishing

The Intracoastal Waterway and the Atlantic Ocean are teeming with trout, barracuda, snapper, amberjack, and other fish. On St. Simons, **Ducky II Charter Boat Service** (✉ 402 Kelsall Ave., ☎ 912/634–0312) organizes deep-sea and inshore fishing. **Capt. Martin Noble Charter Fish-**

ing (☎ 912/634–1219) handles both offshore and inshore fishing for St. Simons. **St. Simons Transit Company** (✉ 105 Marina Dr., ☎ 912/638–5678) organizes river and deep-sea fishing expeditions, dolphin tours, and land tours and operates a water-taxi service between the coastal islands. **Taylor Fish Camp** (✉ Lawrence Rd., ☎ 912/638–7690) gives guided fishing trips.

Golf

St. Simons Island has three courses: **Hampton Club** (✉ 100 Tabbystone, ☎ 912/634–0255), with 18 holes at par 72; **St. Simons Island Club** (✉ 100 King's Way, ☎ 912/638–5130), with 18 holes at par 72; and **Sea Palms Golf and Tennis Resort** (✉ 5445 Frederica Rd., ☎ 912/638–3351), with 27 holes, par 72 on any two nines. Though it has several courses, Jekyll Island is known for two in particular: **Oceanside** (✉ N. Beachview Dr., ☎ 912/635–2170), with 9 holes, par 36; and **Jekyll Island Golf Club** (✉ 322 Captain Wylly Rd., ☎ 912/635–2368 or 912/635–3464), with three 18-hole courses—Indian Mound, Oleander, and Pine Lake—all par 72.

Tennis

Jekyll Island Tennis Center (✉ 400 Captain Wylly Rd., ☎ 912/635–3154) has 13 clay courts, 7 of which are lighted. The center hosts USTA-sanctioned tournaments and offers tennis camps. **Sea Palms Golf and Tennis Resort** (✉ 5445 Frederica Rd., ☎ 912/638–3351, WEB www.seapalms.com) has 12 Rubico courts, 3 of which are lighted.

Beaches

Wide expanses of clean, sandy beaches skirt all the islands. St. Simons's **East Beach** attracts large groups and families and has sailboat rentals. The beaches rimming **Jekyll Island** are usually not too busy during the week but become crowded on weekends. On **Sea Island** you can rent sailboats, sea kayaks, and boogie boards. The dunes and beaches of **Cumberland Island National Seashore** offer peaceful isolation.

The Golden Isles Essentials

AIR TRAVEL

Glynco Jetport, is served by Delta affiliate Atlantic Southeast Airlines.
➤ AIRLINE: Atlantic Southeast Airlines (☎ 800/282–3424, WEB www.asa-air.com).

AIRPORTS

Glynco Jetport is on the mainland, 6 mi outside Brunswick. International airports are in Savannah, an hour's drive north, and in Jacksonville, Florida, an hour's drive south, but there are no scheduled international flights operating at either airport. Jekyll and St. Simons islands maintain small airstrips for private planes.
➤ AIRPORT INFORMATION: Glynco Jetport (✉ 500 Connole St., 31525, ☎ 912/265–2070, WEB glynncountyairports.com).

BOAT AND FERRY TRAVEL

To reach Cumberland Island, you must reserve passage on the *Cumberland Queen* ferry, which leaves from St. Marys for the 45-minute journey. For a schedule, reservations, and fare information, contact Cumberland Island National Seashore (☞ Visitor Information, *below*).

BUS TRAVEL

Greyhound connects Brunswick with surrounding towns and cities, including Savannah and Jacksonville, Florida.

➤ Bus Information: **Greyhound** (☎ 800/231–2222, WEB www.greyhound.com).

CAR TRAVEL

From Brunswick take the Jekyll Island Causeway ($2 per car) to Jekyll Island or the F. J. Torras Causeway (35¢) to St. Simons. From St. Simons you can reach Sea Island via the Sea Island Causeway. Only residents and park service personnel are allowed to drive cars on Cumberland Island.

VISITOR INFORMATION

➤ Tourist Information: **Brunswick/Golden Isles Visitors Bureau** (✉ 4 Glynn Ave., 31520, ☎ 912/265–0620 or 800/933–2627). **Cumberland Island National Seashore** (✉ National Park Service, Box 806, St. Marys 31558, ☎ 912/882–4335). **Jekyll Island Welcome Center** (✉ 45 S. Beachview Dr., 31527, ☎ 912/635–3636 or 800/841–6586, WEB www.jekyllisland.com).

ELSEWHERE IN GEORGIA

Historic Sites Along I–75

What to See and Do

New Echota State Historic Site (✉ Rte. 225, 1 mi east of I–75, Exit 317, near Calhoun, ☎ 706/624–1321, WEB http://ngeorgia.com/parks/; 🎫 $3) is the location of the 1825–38 capital of the Cherokee Nation, whose constitution was patterned after that of the United States. Some buildings have been reconstructed. Native Americans frequently hold special events at the site.

The **Chief Vann House,** a three-story brick edifice, was built in 1804 by Moravian artisans hired by Chief James Vann, a leader of the Cherokee Nation. To get here, take Exit 317 from I–75 to Route 52A going west. *✉ 82 Rte. 225, 17 mi east of New Echota, Chatsworth, ☎ 706/695–2598. WEB http://ngeorgia.com/parks/. 🎫 $3. Closed Mon..*

The **Chickamauga and Chattanooga National Military Park** (✉ U.S. 27 off I–75, Exit 350, south of Chattanooga, TN, ☎ 706/866–9241, WEB http://ngeorgia.com/site/; 🎫 free), established in 1890, was the nation's first military park. In 1863, this was the site of one of the Civil War's bloodiest battles (30,000 casualties), which ended in the Union Capture of Chattanooga. Monuments, battlements, and weapons adorn the road that traverses the 8,000-acre park, with markers explaining the action. An excellent visitor center offers reproduction memorabilia, superb books, and a film on the battle.

Dining and Lodging

$–$$ ✕ **La Scala.** Piero Barba from Capri, Italy, established this outpost of Italian cooking in 1996. The menu is dominated by classic dishes such as osso buco, braciola, and seafood and pasta. The wine list, which Barba claims is the largest in north Georgia, includes French, American, and Italian wines. The lunch buffet is a bargain. *✉ 413 Broad St., Rome, ☎ 706/238–9000. AE, D, DC, MC, V. Closed Sun. No lunch.*

$$ 🏨 **Claremont House.** This beautifully restored 1890s Victorian inn has huge rooms furnished with period antiques. Breakfast is sumptuous, with stuffed French toast and the like. *✉ 906 E. 2nd Ave., Rome 30161, ☎ 706/291–0900 or 800/254–4797, FAX 706/802–0551, WEB www.theclaremonthouse.com. 6 rooms. AE, D, MC, V. BP.*

Historic Sites Essentials

CAR TRAVEL

Take I–75 north to the Tennessee state line and look for the brown state historic markers that indicate historic sites.

Callaway Gardens

What to See and Do

★ **Callaway Gardens** is a 14,000-acre, year-round horticultural fantasyland and family-style golf and tennis resort, best known for its impressive gardens developed in the 1930s by a couple determined to breathe new life into the area's dormant cotton fields. On the grounds are 10 tennis courts, bicycling trails, a lakefront beach, and four nationally recognized golf courses. The **Cecil B. Day Butterfly Center,** the largest glass-enclosed tropical conservatory of living butterflies in North America, and the **John A. Sibley Horticultural Center** (both: ✉ U.S. 27, Pine Mountain, ☎ 706/663–2281 or 800/282–8181, FAX 706/663–5049; 🎫 $12), one of the most advanced garden greenhouse complexes in the world, are part of the gardens. Trails and paved paths traverse the world's largest collection of hollies and more than 700 varieties of azaleas and wildflowers.

Just 15 mi east of Callaway Gardens on Route 85 is the **Little White House Historic Site** (✉ 401 Little White House Rd., Warm Springs, ☎ 706/655–5870; 🎫 $5), where in 1932 President Franklin Delano Roosevelt built the "Little White House," the simple, three-bedroom cottage in which he died in 1945.

Callaway Gardens Essentials

CAR TRAVEL

Callaway Gardens is on U.S. 27 in Pine Mountain, 70 mi southwest of Atlanta. From Atlanta drive south on I–85, I–185, and U.S. 27.

Macon

What to See and Do

Founded in 1823, Macon lies at the state's geographic center. Its rich architecture includes both antebellum and Victorian residences and commercial buildings. The Italianate **Hay House** (✉ 934 Georgia Ave., ☎ 478/742–8155; 🎫 $6) is worth a visit for its marvelous stained-glass windows and marble mantels. Famous artists who have called Macon home include flutist and pre–Civil War poet laureate of the United States Sidney Lanier, Little Richard, the Allman Brothers, and Otis Redding. Experience the state's contribution to American music at the **Georgia Music Hall of Fame.** ✉ *200 Martin Luther King Jr. Blvd.,* ☎ *478/750–8555.* 🎫 *$8. Closed Sun..* Directly across the street from the Georgia Music Hall of Fame, the **Georgia Sports Hall of Fame** (✉ 301 Cherry St., ☎ 478/752–1585; 🎫 $6) has the look of an old ballpark. The **Tubman African American Museum** (✉ 340 Walnut St., ☎ 478/743–8544; 🎫 $3) salutes the former slave who led more than 300 people to freedom and displays African artifacts and African-American art.

Dining and Lodging

$ ✕ **The Cherry Corner.** This taste of Italy is the perfect spot for lunch, a quick snack of pizza or soup, or coffee and a pastry. Dine at one of the sidewalk tables when it's warm. ✉ *502 Cherry St.,* ☎ *478/741–9525. MC, V. Closed Sun.*

$$$ 🏨 **1842 Inn.** With its grand, white-pillared front porch and period antiques, this inn offers a taste of antebellum Macon. From here, it's an easy walk to downtown. ✉ *353 College St., 31201,* ☎ *877/452–6599,* WEB *www.1842inn.com. 21 rooms. AE, MC, V.*

Macon Essentials

CAR TRAVEL

Take I–75 south from Atlanta 90 mi. There are several exits into Macon from I–75; get off at Exit 2, Martin Luther King Jr. Blvd., to get to downtown and the attractions listed below.

Andersonville

What to See and Do

The tiny town of Andersonville grew up around a railway stop. The depot is the **Andersonville Welcome Center** (✉ 114 Church St., 31711, ☎ 229/924–2558). Antiques and memorabilia fill the restored storefront shops that form the town center. Two Civil War festivals, both with crafts and collectibles, take place here: the Andersonville Historic Fair (first weekend in October) and the smaller Memorial Day weekend fair.

★ The **Andersonville National Historic Site** (☞ National and State Parks, *above*) marks the Civil War's most notorious prisoner-of-war camp, which opened in 1864: 13,000 Union prisoners died here. Today it is the site of the National Prisoner of War Museum and serves as a final resting place for U.S. veterans and their spouses. The site's living-history event takes place in spring.

Dining and Lodging

$$ ✕🏨 **Windsor Hotel.** Americus, 10 mi southwest of Andersonville via Route 49, has one of America's most intriguing historic hotels. This Romanesque structure dominates downtown, and its lobby, rich in Moorish detail, is breathtaking. In the dining room, the menu focuses on fine southern fare, with such dishes as barbecued shrimp on linguine, crab cakes, and pecan-crusted salmon. ✉ *125 W. Lamar St., Americus 31709,* ☎ *229/924–1555 or 888/297–9567,* FAX *229/928–0533,* WEB *www.windsor-americus.com. 53 rooms. Restaurant. AE, D, MC, V. No dinner Sun.*

Andersonville Essentials

CAR TRAVEL

Take I–75 south from Macon to Route 49 and follow the signs that read THE ANDERSONVILLE TRAIL to Andersonville.

Okefenokee National Wildlife Refuge

What to See and Do

★ **Okefenokee National Wildlife Refuge** (✉ Folkston, ☎ 912/496–3331 canoe rental and reservations; 912/496–7836 information; 🎫 $5 per vehicle), covering about 730 square mi, is a vast peat bog once part of the ocean floor and now 100 ft above sea level. Its thick vegetation is inhabited by at least 54 reptile species (including alligators), 49 mammal species, and 234 types of birds.

The **Okefenokee Swamp Park** (✉ 8 mi south of Waycross, ☎ 912/283–0583; 🎫 $5 per car) offers guided tours ($10.50 for 1 hr, $19 for 2 hrs, per person) of the refuge. Boardwalks lead to an observation tower; guided boat tours are available, or you can rent a canoe ($16 per person). A 1½-mi train tour passes by a Seminole village and stops at Pioneer Island for a 30-minute walking tour. There's an eastern entrance at the Suwanee Canal Recreation Area (✉ near Folkston, ☎ 912/496–7156 or 800/792–6796); the 11-mi waterway was built more than two centuries ago. Wilderness canoeing and camping in the Okefenokee's interior are by reserved fee permit only. Permits are tough to get, especially in cool weather. Call **refuge headquarters** (☎ 912/496–3331) *exactly 60 days* in advance of the desired starting date. There's also a western entrance at **Stephen C. Foster State Park** (✉ Rte. 177, off U.S. 441, Fargo, ☎ 912/637–5274), an 80-acre park with boat rides through a swamp, a ½-mi nature trail, restored homesteads, and cypress and black gum trees.

Lodging

$$ **Inn at Folkston.** This restored 1920s bungalow is right in the center of town. Two of the guest rooms have a front veranda and gas-log fireplaces, and all of them are individually decorated. *✉ 509 W. Main St., Folkston 31537, ☎ 912/496–6256 or 888/509–6246, WEB www.innatfolkston.com. 4 rooms. AE, MC, V. BP.*

Okefenokee National Wildlife Refuge Essentials

CAR TRAVEL

The refuge is near the Georgia-Florida border, 40 minutes northwest of Jacksonville, Florida, and 40 minutes southwest of the Golden Isles. From Atlanta take I–75 south to U.S. 82 into Waycross. From the Golden Isles take U.S. 84 to U.S. 301.

HAWAI'I

Updated by Maggie Wunsch

Capital	Honolulu
Population	1,193,001
Motto	"Ua mau ke ea o ka aina i ka pono" (The Life of the Land Is Perpetuated in Righteousness)
State Bird	Nēnē (Hawaiian goose)
State Flower	Yellow Hibiscus
Postal Abbreviation	HI

Statewide Visitor Information

Hawai'i Visitors and Convention Bureau (✉ Waikīkī Business Plaza, 2270 Kalākaua Ave., Suite 801, Honolulu 96815, ☎ 808/923–1811; 800/464–2924 brochures; WEB www.gohawaii.com).

Scenic Drives

On the eastern tip of O'ahu the 10-mi stretch of **Kalaniana'ole Highway** from Hanauma Bay to Waimānalo is a cliff-side road resembling Highway 1 up the California coast. On the Big Island **Highway 19** north out of Hilo runs along the lush and rugged Hāmākua Coast to Waipi'o Valley, past sugarcane fields and spectacular ocean views. From Pā'ia to Hāna, Maui's **Hāna Highway** (Highway 36) is a winding 55-mi coastal route that spans rivers and passes tropical waterfalls. From the town of Waimea, Kaua'i's **Waimea Canyon Drive** meanders upward past panoramas of Waimea Canyon, culminating at the 4,120-ft Kalalau Lookout.

National and State Parks

National Parks

On the Big Island of Hawai'i, **Hawai'i Volcanoes National Park** (✉ National Park Service, Box 52, 96718, ☎ 808/985–6000, WEB www.nps.gov/havo; 🎫 $10 per car, $5 on foot or by bike), 30 mi southeast of Hilo on Highway 11, has the only rain forest and the only active volcano in the U.S. National Park system. Call ahead for eruption updates. **Pu'uhonua o Hōnaunau National Historic Park** (✉ Box 129, Hōnaunau 96726, ☎ 808/328–2288, WEB www.nps.gov/puho; 🎫 $2), 20 mi south of Kailua-Kona on Highway 160, is famous for harboring those who have broken the *kapu* (laws) of ancient Hawai'i. **Pu'ukōholā Heiau National Historic Site** (✉ Hwy. 270, Kawaihae, ☎ 808/882–7218, WEB www.nps.gov/puhe; 🎫 free) at Kawaihae Harbor has two impressive *heiaus* (temples) built by King Kamehameha. The largest of these, Pu'ukōholā, at 224 ft by 100 ft, is one of the biggest heiaus in the islands.

Haleakalā National Park (☞ Maui, *below*) has some of the island's most spectacular sunrises, hiking trails, and camping. **Kalaupapa National Historic Park** (☞ Elsewhere in Hawai'i, *below*) on Moloka'i's unspoiled Kalaupapa peninsula houses a former leprosy colony. To reach the park, you must either hike in or make the pilgrimage by mule ride. The **USS *Arizona* Memorial at Pearl Harbor** (✉ 1 Arizona Memorial Pl., Honolulu 96818-3145, ☎ 808/422–0561, WEB www.nps.gov/usar; 🎫 free) pays tribute to the more than 1,100 sailors who lost their lives aboard the battleship when it was attacked by the Japanese on December 7, 1941, sending the United States into World War II. The memorial bridges the hulk of the USS *Arizona,* which is forever laid to rest on the ocean floor below it.

State Parks

For information and trail maps contact the **Hawai'i State Department of Land and Natural Resources** Division of State Parks (✉ Box 621, Honolulu 96809, ☎ 808/587–0300, WEB www.hawaii.gov).

Hawai'i's state parks enjoy some of the best recreational locations on each of the islands. **Hāpuna State Recreation Area** (☞ The Big Island of Hawai'i, *below*) has one of the Big Island's best beaches for swimming, snorkeling, and body-surfing during the summer months. **Kōke'e State Park** (☞ Kaua'i, *below*) above Waimea Canyon offers more than 4,000 acres for campers, hikers, and eco-travelers interested in Kaua'i's magnificent tropical wilderness. **Wailua River State Park** (✉ Wailua Marina, Kapa'a, Kaua'i 96746, ☎ 808/822–5065) has the remains of ancient Hawaiian temples and 'Ōpaeka'a Falls. Navigate the river itself via boat or kayak tour.

HONOLULU AND WAIKĪKĪ

Honolulu, on the island of O'ahu, is the urban metropolis of the Aloha State. Here, differing cultures blend harmoniously, yet each retains its distinct character. Downtown, royal history contrasts with the modern-day action of a major government and business capital. Just 3½ mi from downtown is the tourist mecca of Waikīkī. Set on the sunny, dry side of O'ahu, Waikīkī provides a stunning setting along with the buzz of international hotel and shopping destinations.

Exploring Honolulu and Waikīkī

In Hawai'i directions are often given as *mauka* (toward the mountains) and *makai* (toward the ocean), or they may refer to Diamond Head (east, toward the famous volcanic landmark) and *'ewa* (west).

Downtown Honolulu

Aloha Tower Marketplace (✉ 1 Aloha Tower Dr., at Piers 8–10, ☎ 808/528–5700) has two stories of shops, kiosks, and indoor and outdoor restaurants—some with live entertainment—right next to Honolulu Harbor. The landmark 10-story Aloha Tower is its anchor; to view the harbor take the free ride up to the observation deck. A trolley runs regularly between the marketplace and Waikīkī.

The **Hawai'i Maritime Center** (✉ Ala Moana Blvd. at Pier 7, ☎ 808/536–6373; 🎫 $7.50) is on the Diamond Head side of the marketplace. Look for the century-old sailing vessel ***Falls of Clyde,*** a four-masted, square-rigged tall ship moored out front. Lively, informative exhibits trace the history of Hawai'i's love affair with the sea.

'Iolani Palace (✉ King St. at Richards St., ☎ 808/522–0832; 🎫 $15; Closed Sun.–Mon.; reservations essential; no children under 5), built in 1882 on the site of an earlier palace and beautifully restored today, is America's only royal palace built with the assistance of American Masons. It contains the thrones of King Kalākaua and his successor (and sister), Queen Lili'uokalani.

Honolulu Hale (✉ 530 S. King St., at Punchbowl St., ☎ 808/527–5666 concert information; 🎫 free), the city hall, is a Mediterranean Renaissance–style building constructed in 1929. Free live concerts take place here in the evenings. Built in 1842 of massive blocks of solid coral, **Kawaiaha'o Church** (✉ 957 Punchbowl St., ☎ 808/522–1333; 🎫 free)

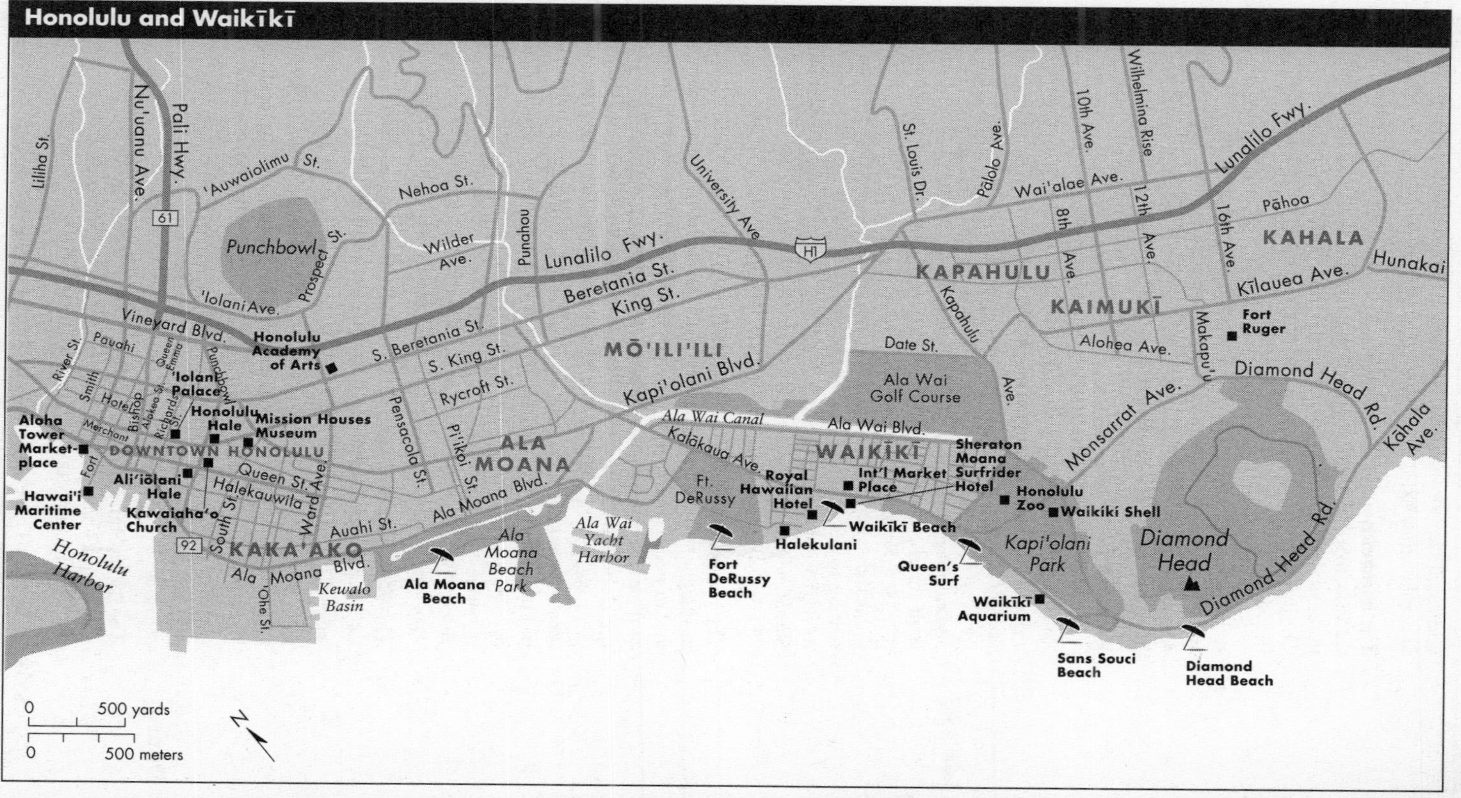
Honolulu and Waikīkī
Līliha St.
Nu'uanu Ave.
Pali Hwy.
61
'Auwaiolimu St.
Nehoa St.
Punchbowl
Prospect St.
Wilder Ave.
Punahou
Lunalilo Fwy.
University Ave.
St. Louis Dr.
Pālolo Ave.
10th Ave.
Wilhelmina Rise
Wai'alae Ave.
Lunalilo Fwy.
12th Ave.
8th Ave.
Pāhoa
16th Ave.
KAHALA
Hunakai
H1
Beretania St.
King St.
KAPAHULU
Kapahulu Ave.
KAIMUKĪ
Kīlauea Ave.
Fort Ruger
Makapu'u
Alohea Ave.
'Iolani Ave.
Vineyard Blvd.
Honolulu Academy of Arts
S. Beretania St.
S. King St.
MŌ'ILI'ILI
Date St.
Ala Wai Golf Course
Diamond Head Rd.
Kāhala Ave.
Monsarrat Ave.
River St.
Pauahi
Smith
Hotel
Bishop
Alakea St.
Richards St.
Queen Emma
Punchbowl
'Iolani Palace
Honolulu Hale
Mission Houses Museum
Rycroft St.
Kapi'olani Blvd.
Ala Wai Canal
Ala Wai Blvd.
Aloha Tower Market-place
Merchant
Fort
DOWNTOWN HONOLULU
Pensacola St.
Pi'ikoi St.
ALA MOANA
Kalākaua Ave.
WAIKĪKĪ
Sheraton Moana Surfrider Hotel
Int'l Market Place
Royal Hawaiian Hotel
Ft. DeRussy
Honolulu Zoo
Waikīkī Shell
Ali'iōlani Hale
Queen St.
Halekauwila
Ward Ave.
Ala Moana Blvd.
Hawai'i Maritime Center
Kawaiaha'o Church
South St.
Auahi St.
Waikīkī Beach
Halekulani
Kapi'olani Park
Diamond Head
Diamond Head Rd.
92
KAKA'AKO
Ala Moana Blvd.
Honolulu Harbor
'Ohe St.
Kewalo Basin
Ala Moana Beach
Ala Moana Beach Park
Ala Wai Yacht Harbor
Fort DeRussy Beach
Queen's Surf
Waikīkī Aquarium
Sans Souci Beach
Diamond Head Beach
0 500 yards
0 500 meters
N

witnessed the coronations, weddings, and funerals of generations of Hawaiian royalty.

The **Mission Houses Museum** (✉ 553 S. King St., ☎ 808/531–0481; 🎫 $8; Closed Sun.–Mon.), next door to Kawaiaha'o Church, was the home of the first U.S. missionaries to Hawai'i after their arrival in 1820. The mission's three main structures are among the oldest buildings on the islands.

From here it's three long blocks toward Diamond Head to Ward Avenue and one block mauka to Beretania Street, where the **Honolulu Academy of Arts** (✉ 900 S. Beretania St., ☎ 808/532–8700; 🎫 $7; Closed Mon.) houses a world-class collection of Western and Asian art.

Waikīkī

A paved ocean walk leads up to the pink **Royal Hawaiian Hotel** (✉ 2259 Kalākaua Ave., ☎ 808/923–7311), built in 1921 when Waikīkī was still a sleepy paradise. **International Market Place** (✉ 2330 Kalākaua Ave., ☎ 808/923–9871) is on the mauka side of Kalākaua Avenue, about 100 yards east of the Royal Hawaiian. With its spreading banyan tree, the outdoor bazaar retains a little authentic flavor among the dozens of souvenir stands. The oldest hotel in Waikīkī, the **Sheraton Moana Surfrider** (✉ 2365 Kalākaua Ave., ☎ 808/922–3111) is on the makai side of Kalākaua Avenue. The beautifully restored Beaux Arts building is worth visiting to get a sense of what Hawai'i was like before the days of jet travel. East of the hotel about a block away stands the **Duke Kahanamoku Statue,** where free walking tours of the Waikīkī Historical Trail (☎ 808/841–6462) begin weekdays at 9 AM and Saturday at 4:30 PM.

The **Honolulu Zoo** (✉ 151 Kapahulu Ave., ☎ 808/971–7171; 🎫 $6), at the Diamond Head end of Waikīkī, is home to thousands of furry and finned creatures. It's not the biggest zoo in the country, but its one of the prettiest. **Kapi'olani Park** is a vast green playing field adjoining the Honolulu Zoo. Here you'll find the **Waikīkī Shell** (✉ 2805 Monsarrat Ave., ☎ 808/924–8934), Honolulu's outdoor concert arena, where locals spread out on "grass seats" (the lawn) with picnics to hear some of Hawai'i's best musicians and visiting pop stars. Most concerts are held between May 1 and Labor Day. Check the newspapers to see what's playing. Next door to the Waikīkī Shell, the **Pleasant Hawaiian Hula Show** (✉ 2805 Monsarrat Ave., ☎ 808/945–1851; 🎫 free) has been wowing crowds (Tuesday–Thursday at 10 AM) for more than 50 years.

The **Waikīkī Aquarium** (✉ 2777 Kalākaua Ave., ☎ 808/923–9741; 🎫 $7) harbors more than 300 species of marine life.

The steep hike to the summit of **Diamond Head** (✉ Monsarrat Ave. near 18th Ave., ☎ 808/971–2525; 🎫 $1) gives you a marvelous view of O'ahu's southern coastline. The entrance is about 1 mi above Kapi'olani Park. Drive through the tunnel to the inside of the crater, and then park and start walking up the paved trail to the summit.

Dining

The Aloha State is known for fine ethnic food—especially Chinese, Japanese, and Thai—and the spectacular Hawai'i Regional cuisine, based on fresh local produce and seafood.

$$$$ ★ ✕ **La Mer.** This exotic, oceanfront Mandalay mansion serves some of Hawai'i's best contemporary cuisine. A standout entrée is *onaga* (red snapper) fillet accompanied by a lobster mosaic with fresh hearts of palm and caviar. ✉ *Halekūlani, 2199 Kālia Rd., Waikīkī,* ☎ *808/923–2311. Reservations essential. Jacket required. AE, MC, V. No lunch.*

$$$–$$$$ ★ ✕ **Alan Wong's.** In his fabulous, low-key restaurant, Wong relies on Hawaiian-grown products to keep the flavors super-fresh, and he's utterly creative, turning local "grinds" into gourmet treats. Garlic-mashed potatoes come with a black-bean salsa; salmon is grilled with a wasabi potato crust. Finding the restaurant can be difficult: look for a white apartment building and a small sign after a parking garage, where your car can be valet parked. ✉ *McCully Court, 1857 S. King St., 3rd floor,* ☎ *808/949–2526. AE, MC, V. No lunch.*

$$$–$$$$ ★ ✕ **Sam Choy's at Diamond Head.** His motto is "Never trust a skinny chef," and indeed, Choy's broad girth and even broader smile let you know you'll be well taken care of. The theme is upscale local, as the Hawai'i-born chef modernizes the foods he grew up with. The result? Brie-stuffed wontons with pineapple marmalade, seared ahi seasoned with ginger, and roasted duck with orange sauce. Portions are huge. ✉ *449 Kapahulu Ave., 2nd level, Honolulu,* ☎ *808/732–8645. AE, MC, V. No lunch.*

$$–$$$ ★ ✕ **Golden Dragon.** Chef Steve Chiang is known for his unconventional Cantonese and nouvelle-Chinese cuisine; signature dishes include stir-fried lobster with curry sauce and Szechuan beef. ✉ *Hilton Hawaiian Village, 2005 Kālia Rd., Waikīkī,* ☎ *808/946–5336. Reservations essential. AE, D, DC, MC, V. No lunch.*

$$–$$$ ★ ✕ **3660 on the Rise.** Ten minutes from Waikīkī, in the up-and-coming culinary center of Kaimukī, this stellar restaurant is known for home-grown ingredients combined with European flavors: Dungeness crab cakes served atop angel-hair pasta with a ginger-cilantro aioli, crispy fried oyster salad, and the sumptuous Wai'alae pie are just a sampling of what keeps this restaurant on the rise to culinary success. ✉ *3660 Wai'alae Ave., Honolulu,* ☎ *808/737–1177. AE, DC, MC, V.*

$–$$ ★ ✕ **Keo's in Waikīkī.** Hollywood celebrities have discovered this orchid-filled nook, where the Evil Jungle Prince (chicken, shrimp, or vegetables in a sauce of fresh basil, coconut milk, and red chili) is tops. ✉ *2028 Kūhiō Ave., Waikīkī,* ☎ *808/951–9355. Reservations essential. AE, D, DC, MC, V. No lunch.*

$ ✕ **'Ono Hawaiian Foods.** There's usually a line outside after about 5 PM at this no-frills storefront restaurant. Locals come for Island innovations such as poi, *lomilomi* salmon (salmon massaged until tender and served with minced onions and tomatoes), and *laulau* (steamed bundle of ti leaves containing pork, butterfish, and taro tops). ✉ *726 Kapahulu Ave., Honolulu,* ☎ *808/737–2275. Reservations not accepted. No credit cards. Closed Sun.*

Lodging

O'ahu's best accommodations are in or near Waikīkī, with a few places of note in the rest of Honolulu. Except for Christmas week and the peak months of January, February, and August, you'll have no trouble getting a room if you call first. For bed-and-breakfasts contact **Bed and Breakfast Hawai'i** (✉ Box 449, Kapa'a 96746, ☎ 808/822–7771 or 800/733–1632, FAX 808/822–2723).

$$$$ ★ **Halekūlani.** The sleek, modern, and luxurious ocean-side Halekūlani exemplifies the translation of its name—the "house befitting heaven." Guest rooms are spacious and artfully appointed in marble and wood; most have ocean views, and each has its own lānai. ✉ *2199 Kālia Rd., Waikīkī 96815,* ☎ *808/923–2311 or 800/367–2343,* FAX *808/926–8004,* WEB *www.halekulani.com. 456 rooms. 3 restaurants, pool, gym. AE, DC, MC, V.*

$$$$ **Hilton Hawaiian Village Beach Resort and Spa.** Waikīkī's largest resort includes five towers, a botanical garden, and a pond with penguins. Rooms are done in a variety of styles of tropical woods, rattan, and bamboo furnishings. ✉ *2005 Kālia Rd., Waikīkī 96815,* ☎ *808/949–4321 or 800/445–8667,* FAX *808/947–7898,* WEB *www.hawaiianvillage.hilton.com. 2,545 rooms. 6 restaurants, pools, health club. AE, D, DC, MC, V.*

$$$$ **Kāhala Mandarin Oriental Hawai'i.** Minutes away from Waikīkī, on the quiet side of Diamond Head, this oceanfront hotel is an oasis of peace and comfort. Guest rooms are in off-white hues, with touches of Asia and old Hawai'i in the art and furnishings. ✉ *5000 Kāhala Ave., Honolulu 96816,* ☎ *808/739–8888 or 800/367–2525,* FAX *808/739–8800,* WEB *www.mohnl.com. 370 rooms. 3 restaurants, pool, gym. AE, D, DC, MC, V.*

$$$$ **Outrigger Waikīkī on the Beach.** At this beachfront property in the heart of the best shopping and dining action, rooms have a Polynesian motif, and each has a lānai. The popular Duke's Canoe Club offers beachfront dining along with Hawaiian music concerts on the beach on weekend evenings. ✉ *2335 Kalākaua Ave., Waikīkī 96815,* ☎ *808/923–0711 or 800/688–7444,* FAX *800/622–4852,* WEB *www.outrigger.com. 530 rooms. 6 restaurants, pool. AE, D, DC, MC, V.*

$$$–$$$$ ★ **J. W. Marriott 'Ihilani Resort & Spa.** Tucked away on the west side of the island, the 'Ihilani is a 15-minute drive from Honolulu International Airport. The guest rooms have marble bathrooms with deep soaking tubs, and private lānai, many with ocean views. The 35,000-square-ft 'Ihilani Spa presents everything from seaweed baths to stair-climbers. ✉ *92–1001 'Ōlani St., Kapolei 96707,* ☎ *808/679–0079 or 800/626–4446,* FAX *808/679–0295. 387 rooms. 4 restaurants, pools, golf, tennis, health club. AE, DC, MC, V.*

$$–$$$$ ★ **New Otani Kaimana Beach Hotel.** Polished to a shine, this hotel is open to the trade winds—right on the beach at the quiet end of Waikīkī, practically at the foot of Diamond Head. Get a room with an ocean view, if possible, and dine at least once at the Hau Tree Lānai. ✉ *2863 Kalākaua Ave., Honolulu 96815,* ☎ *808/923–1555 or 800/356–8264,* FAX *808/922–9404,* WEB *www.kaimana.com. 125 rooms. 2 restaurants. AE, D, DC, MC, V.*

$–$$ **Waikīkī Hāna.** One block from the beach in Waikīkī, this eight-story hotel is convenient and clean; many rooms have private lānai. For a little extra you can rent a refrigerator for your room. ✉ *2424 Koa Ave., Honolulu 96815,* ☎ *808/926–8841 or 800/367–5004,* FAX *808/586–0158. 72 rooms. Restaurant. AE, DC, MC, V.*

$ **Royal Grove Hotel.** This small flamingo-pink hotel has rooms with kitchenettes. Go for the high-end rooms if possible, because the economy rooms have no air-conditioning and more street noise. The hotel is about two blocks from the beach. ✉ *15 Uluniu Ave., Waikīkī 96815,* ☎ *808/923–7691,* FAX *808/922–7508. 85 rooms. Pool. AE, D, DC, MC, V.*

Nightlife and the Arts

Cocktail and Dinner Shows

Waikīkī's old pro, **Don Ho** (✉ Waikīkī Beachcomber Hotel, 2300 Kalākaua Ave., ☎ 808/923–3981) still packs them in to his Polynesian revue with its cast of attractive Hawaiian performers. There's a cocktail and dinner show Sunday–Thursday at 7. Magician John Hirokawa displays mystifying sleight-of-hand in **Magic of Polynesia** (✉ Waikīkī Beachcomber Hotel, 2300 Kalākaua Ave., ☎ 808/971–4321), with hula dancers and island music. Shows are nightly at 6:30 and 8:45.

Lū'au

Royal Hawaiian Lū'au (✉ 2259 Kalākaua Ave., Waikīkī, ☎ 808/923–7311) takes place at the venerable Royal Hawaiian and is a notch above many other commercial lū'au presentations on the island.

Nightclubs

At **Lewers Lounge** (✉ Halekūlani, 2199 Kālia Rd., ☎ 808/923–2311), Bruce Hamada and friends perform contemporary jazz and standards Tuesday–Saturday 10:30–midnight. A vocalist-pianist sits in Sunday and Monday. The **Paradise Lounge,** at Hilton Hawaiian Village (✉ 2005 Kālia Rd., ☎ 808/949–4321), has all kinds of acts, such as island band Olomana (Friday–Saturday 8–midnight). **Rumours** (✉ Ala Moana Hotel, 410 Atkinson St., ☎ 808/955–4811) is where the after-work crowd gathers to unwind. You can chill out with music from the '60s during the week or dance on Saturdays 9 PM –4 AM. **Zanabar** (✉ Waikīkī Trade Center, 2255 Kuhio Ave., ☎ 808/924–3939) is Waikīkī's newest high-energy hot spot featuring DJs who spin hits from hip hop to soul nightly 9 PM–4 AM.

Theater

The **Hawaii Theater** (✉ 1130 Bethel St., ☎ 808/528–0506) opened in Hawaii in the 1920s and has been restored to its original neoclassic Beaux Arts style. Throughout the year, it hosts unique international theatrical performances in all art forms.

The **Diamond Head Theater** (✉ 520 Makapu'u Ave., ☎ 808/734–0274) is five minutes away from Waikīkī, right next to Diamond Head. Its repertoire includes a little of everything: musical comedies and experimental, contemporary, and classical dramas. The **John F. Kennedy Theater** (✉ 1770 East–West Rd., ☎ 808/956–7655) at the University of Hawai'i's Mānoa campus is the setting for eclectic dramatic offerings—everything from Kabuki, Nō, and Chinese opera to contemporary musical comedy.

Outdoor Activities and Sports

Golf

Ala Wai Golf Course (✉ 404 Kapahulu Ave., ☎ 808/733–7387), on Waikīkī's mauka end, is quite popular; call ahead. Advance reservations are also recommended at the 6,222-yard **Hawai'i Kai Championship Course** (✉ 8902 Kalaniana'ole Hwy., Honolulu, ☎ 808/395–2358, WEB www.hawaiikaigolf.com) along the East O'ahu shoreline. The 2,386-yard **Hawai'i Kai Executive Course** (✉ 8902 Kalaniana'ole Hwy., Honolulu, ☎ 808/395–2358) gives golfers who want a quick game some skill challenges along with an ocean view.

Tennis

In the Waikīkī area there are six free public courts at **Kapi'olani Tennis Courts** (✉ 2748 Kalākaua Ave., ☎ 808/971–2525) situated on the Diamond Head side of Kapi'olani Park. The **Diamond Head Tennis Center** (✉ 3908 Pākī Ave., ☎ 808/971–7150) on the mauka side of Kapi'olani Park at the base of Diamond Head has nine courts. Ten courts are available for public play at the 'ewa end of Waikīkī across from Ala Moana Shopping Center at **Ala Moana Park** (✉ makai side of Ala Moana Blvd., ☎ 808/522–7031).

Water Sports

Seemingly endless ocean options—from sailing to surfing—can be arranged through any hotel travel desk or beach concession. Try the **Waikīkī Beach Center** next to the Sheraton Moana Surfrider (✉ 2365 Kalākaua Ave., ☎ no phone), to rent surfboards, take a surfing lesson, or catch a ride on an outrigger canoe. At the west end of Waikīkī Beach, try the **C&K Beach Service,** by the Hilton Hawaiian Village (✉ 2005 Kālia Rd., ☎ no phone), for equipment rental and group and individual surfing lessons.

Sailing lessons may be arranged through **Honolulu Sailing Company** (☎ 808/239–3900). For scuba diving, **South Seas Aquatics** (☎ 808/922–0852) offers two-tank boat dives for $75. **Captain Bruce's Scuba Charters** (☎ 808/373–3590) leads intimate dive trips off O'ahu's west coast.

Hanauma Bay is famous for snorkeling; **Hanauma Bay Snorkeling Excursions** (☎ 808/373–5060) runs to and from Waikīkī.

Beaches

Honolulu

Ala Moana Beach Park, across from Ala Moana Shopping Center, has a protective reef that keeps waters calm. Facilities include bathhouses, indoor and outdoor showers, lifeguards, concession stands, and tennis courts. **Hanauma Bay,** a 30-minute drive (or a $1 bus ride) east of Waikīkī, is a designated marine preserve with coral reefs and turquoise waters. Food and snorkel-equipment rental concessions, changing rooms, and showers are among the facilities.

Waikīkī

★ **Kahaloa and Ulukou Beaches.** Possibly the best swimming and lots of activities are available along this little stretch of Waikīkī Beach in front of Royal Hawaiian Hotel and Sheraton Moana Surfrider. Take a catamaran or outrigger canoe ride out into the bay, unless you're ready to try your skill at surfing. **Queen's Surf,** across from the Honolulu Zoo, is named for Queen Lili'uokalani's beach house, which once stood here. The sand is soft, and there are plenty of shade trees and picnic tables; there's also a changing house with showers. The beach attracts a mixture of families and gays and lesbians.

Shopping

Just outside Waikīkī is the **Ala Moana Shopping Center** (✉ 1450 Ala Moana Blvd., ☎ 808/946–2811), a 50-acre open-air mall with a host of major department stores, including Macy's West and Neiman Marcus. **Ward Centre** (✉ 1200 Ala Moana Blvd., ☎ 808/591–8451) has upscale boutiques and eateries. **Ward Warehouse** (✉ 1050 Ala Moana Blvd.) is a two-story mall with 65 shops and restaurants.

In Waikīkī shopping options include the **International Market Place** (☞ Exploring Honolulu and Waikīkī, *above*). The **DFS Galleria Waikīkī** (✉ 330 Royal Hawaiian Ave., ☎ 808/931–2655) features a walk-through aquarium, nightly entertainment, and a three-story shopping emporium, of which one floor is restricted to international travelers eligible for duty-free shopping. The **Royal Hawaiian Shopping Center** (✉ 2201 Kalākaua Ave., ☎ 808/922–0588) is three stories high and three blocks long, with 150 stores.

Side Trip to the North Shore

Arriving and Departing

From the Diamond Head end of Waikīkī go toward the mountains on Kapahulu Avenue and follow the signs to the Lunalilo Freeway (H–1). Take H–1 northwest to H–2 through Wahiawa. Then follow the signs to Hale'iwa, which marks the official beginning of the North Shore.

What to See and Do

The **North Shore** of O'ahu is the flip side of Honolulu. Instead of high-rises there are old homes and stores, some converted into businesses catering to tourists, surfers, and beach bums. The area's wide and uncrowded beaches, rural countryside, and slower pace are reminiscent of Hawai'i's other islands.

Hale'iwa is a sleepy plantation town that has come of age with contemporary boutiques and galleries. Northeast of Hale'iwa the road continues past such beaches as **Waimea Bay,** where winter waves can crest at 30 ft. **Waimea Falls Park** (✉ 59–864 Kamehameha Hwy., Hale'iwa, ☎ 808/638–8511), once an ancient Hawaiian community, is a lush garden setting with wildlife, walks, and cliff-diving shows. You can have a free hula lesson here.

East of Hale'iwa is the **Polynesian Cultural Center** (✉ 55–370 Kamehameha Hwy., Lā'ie, ☎ 808/293–3333 or 808/923–1861; general admission $35, lū'au and entertainment packages $125), 40 acres containing lagoons and seven re-created South Pacific villages, with daily interactive cultural demonstrations, an IMAX theater, and a spectacular evening lū'au and revue. The center is closed on Sunday.

Honolulu and Waikīkī Essentials

AIRPORTS AND TRANSFERS

Honolulu International Airport is only 20 minutes from Waikīkī. U.S. carriers serving Honolulu include Aloha, American, Continental, Delta, Hawaiian, Northwest, and United.

➤ AIRPORT INFORMATION: **Honolulu International Airport** (✉ 300 Rodgers Blvd., ☎ 808/836–6413).

AIRPORT TRANSFER

A cab from the airport to downtown or to Waikīkī costs about $24 plus tip. TransHawaiian Services runs a shuttle service to Waikīkī ($8 one-way, $13 round-trip). Some hotels also provide pickup and shuttle service; ask when you make reservations.

➤ SHUTTLE INFORMATION: **TransHawaiian Services** (☎ 808/566–7333 or 800/533–8760, WEB www.transhawaiian.com).

CAR RENTAL

Don't bother renting a car unless you're planning to travel outside Waikīkī. When making hotel or plane reservations, ask if there's a car tie-in. At peak times—summer, Christmas vacation, and February—reservations are a must. Avis, Hertz, and Budget are among the many national agencies with locations in Honolulu.

➤ MAJOR AGENCIES: **Avis** (☎ 800/333–1212, WEB www.avis.com). **Budget** (☎ 800/935–6878, WEB www.budget.com). **Hertz** (☎ 800/654–3011, WEB www.hertz.com).

TAXIS

You can usually get a cab outside your hotel. Meter rates are $1.50–$2 at the drop of the flag, plus $1.50 for each additional mile. The two biggest cab companies are Charley's and SIDA of Hawai'i.

➤ TAXI COMPANIES: **Charley's** (☎ 808/531–1333). **SIDA of Hawai'i** (☎ 808/836–0011).

TOURS

BOAT TOURS

View wild dolphins at play off O'ahu's leeward coastline during a unique eco-cruise boat tour offered by Dream Cruises.

➤ FEES AND SCHEDULES: **Dream Cruises, Inc.** (☎ 800/400–7300 or 808/592–5216).

WALKING TOURS

Chinatown Walking Tour in downtown Honolulu provides a look at O'ahu's oldest neighborhood.

➤ FEES AND SCHEDULES: **Chinatown Walking Tour** (☎ 808/533–3181).

TRANSPORTATION AROUND HONOLULU AND WAIKĪKĪ

You can go anywhere on the island for $1.50 on Honolulu's municipal transportation system, affectionately known as The Bus; *and* you'll receive a free transfer if you ask for it when boarding. Exact change is required, and dollar bills are accepted. A four-day pass for visitors costs $10 and is sold at the more than 30 ABC stores in Waikīkī.

➤ CONTACT: **Oahu Transit Services Inc. (TheBus)** (☎ 808/848–5555).

VISITOR INFORMATION

➤ TOURIST INFORMATION: **Oahu Visitors Bureau** (✉ 733 Bishop St., Honolulu 96813, ☎ 808/524–0722 or 877/525–6248, WEB www.visit-oahu.com).

THE BIG ISLAND OF HAWAI'I

Nearly twice as large as all the other Hawaiian Islands combined, this youngest of the chain is still growing: since 1983 lava flowing from Kīlauea, the world's most active volcano, has added more than 70 acres to the island. In a land of South Seas superlatives, the Big Island is also the Aloha State's most diverse region. You can hike into volcanic craters, catch marlin, visit *paniolo* (cowboy) country, tour orchid farms and waterfalls, or simply sunbathe along 266 mi of coastline.

Exploring the Big Island

The Big Island is so large and varied that it's best to split up your exploring itinerary. You might spend a night in the county seat of Hilo, visit the paniolo town of Waimea, head to Volcanoes National Park for some hiking, then wind up on the west coast, home of the best beaches, weather, and nightlife.

Hilo and the Hāmākua Coast

Hilo is nicknamed the City of Rainbows because of its frequent showers, but rain or shine, this east-coast town is truly beautiful. You can take a self-guided walking tour of downtown Hilo and its historic buildings with the help of a map from the **Lyman Museum and Mission House** (✉ 276 Haili St., Hilo, ☎ 808/935–5021; 🎫 $7 includes guided tour of Museum and Mission House, map $1.50).

Banyan Drive, in Hilo, is lined with huge, leafy banyan trees with dangling aerial roots. They were planted along here in the 1930s by visiting luminaries such as Amelia Earhart and Franklin Delano Roosevelt; look for their names on plaques on the trees.

'Akaka Falls State Park (☎ 808/974–6200), where two waterfalls provide dramatic photo opportunities, is about 10 mi north of Hilo and 5 mi inland off Highway 19. **Honoka'a,** one of the sleepy little towns along Highway 19 north of Hilo, is where the first macadamia trees were planted in Hawai'i in 1881.

Waipi'o lies 8 mi west of Honoka'a on Highway 240. Arrange here for a four-wheel-drive tour of **Waipi'o Valley** (☎ 808/775–7121)—the least strenuous way to visit the valley's dramatic 2,000-ft cliffs and 1,200-ft waterfalls. The view from an overlook at the end of the highway is spectacular.

If you drive cross-island over to the west coast from here, stop at Waimea (also known by its older name, Kamuela), home to the **Parker Ranch Visitor Center and Museum** (✉ Parker Ranch Shopping Center, Hwy. 19, Waimea, ☎ 808/885–7655, WEB www.parkerranch.com). Several residences are open on the property, and a prestigious art collection is on display. It's a 90-minute drive from Hilo.

Hawai'i Volcanoes National Park

Hawai'i Volcanoes National Park, a 359-square-mi park established in 1916, features an abundance of attractions inspired by Kīlauea. Just beyond the park entrance, 30 mi southwest of Hilo on Highway 11, is **Kīlauea Visitor Center** (☎ 808/985–6011, WEB www.nps.gov/havo), open daily 6:45–5, where displays and a movie focus on past eruptions. **Volcano House** (☎ 808/967–7321), dating from 1941, is a charming lodge with a huge stone fireplace. Windows in the restaurant and bar provide picture-perfect views of Kīlauea Caldera and its steaming fire pit, Halema'uma'u Crater. Drive around the caldera to see the **Thomas A. Jaggar Museum** (☎ 808/985–6049), with seismographs and film-strips of current and previous eruptions. *Park Headquarters:* ✉ *Highway Belt Rd./Hwy. 11, Hawai'i Volcanoes National Park 96718,* ☎ *808/985–6000.* 🎟 *$10 per vehicle, $5 on foot or bike, $20 annual pass.*

Kailua-Kona

Kailua Pier is the center of much of the action in this seaside village on the west coast. During the sportfishing tournaments each summer, daily catches are weighed in here. A short walk from Kailua Pier, **Hulihe'e Palace** (✉ 75-5718 Ali'i Dr., ☎ 808/329–1877; 🎟 $5) is one of only three royal palaces in America. Tour guides can fill you in on the royal lifestyle here, but the oversize doors and koa-wood furniture will more graphically illustrate how huge some of the early Hawaiian people were. During weekday afternoons hula *hālau* (schools) rehearse on the grounds.

A boat shuttles passengers from Kailua Pier to the 65-ft ***Atlantis IV* submarine** (✉ 75–5669 Ali'i Dr., ☎ 800/548–6262 or 808/329–6626; 🎟 $84), which feels more like an amusement park ride than the real thing. A large glass dome in the bow and 13 viewing ports on the sides give up to 48 passengers clear views of the watery world outside.

Kohala Coast

Tour the Kohala Coast by driving north from Kailua-Kona on Highway 19 along the base of Mt. Hualālai, past sweeping stretches of old lava flows. When you get to the split in the road 33 mi from Kailua-Kona, turn left on Highway 270 toward Kawaihae and stop at the **Pu'ukōholā Heiau National Historic Site** (☎ 808/882–7218, WEB www.nps.gov/puhe). The visitor center tells the story of the three stone *heiau* (temples), one of them submerged offshore, built here by King Kamehameha's men in 1791.

Dining and Lodging

With so many good restaurants on the scene, choosing a place to eat in the western part of the Big Island is difficult. The Kohala Coast is somewhat pricey, although Hilo dining has remained fairly inexpensive and family oriented. You can find good deals on charming accommodations by contacting **Hawai'i's Best Bed and Breakfasts** (✉ Box 563, Kamuela 96743, ☎ 808/885–4550 or 800/262–9912, FAX 808/885–0559, WEB www.bestbnb.com).

Hilo

$–$$ ✕ **Café Pesto.** This is not your ordinary pizza place: sample pizza *al pesto,* with sun-dried tomatoes, eggplant, and fresh basil pesto. Not in the mood for a pie? Order seafood risotto made with sweet Thai chili, Hawaiian spiny lobster, jumbo scallops, and tiger prawns. ✉ *308 Kamehameha Ave.,* ☎ *808/969–6640. AE, D, DC, MC, V.*

$-$$ ✕ **Harrington's.** A popular and reliable steak-and-seafood restaurant, Harrington's has a dining lānai that extends out over the water. The mahimahi meunière and the Slavic steak (thinly sliced and slathered with garlic butter) are outstanding. ✉ *135 Kalaniana'ole Ave.,* ☎ *808/961–4966. MC, V.*

$ ✕ **Royal Siam.** A downtown Hilo fixture, this authentic Thai eatery offers little ambiance—but you don't need a view when you can choose from a menu that includes five curries and plenty of stir-fry. ✉ *70 Mamo St.,* ☎ *808/961–6100. AE, D, DC, MC, V. Closed Sun.*

$$$ ★ **Shipman House Bed & Breakfast Inn.** You'll have a choice between one of the three rooms in the main house—a 100-year-old turreted "castle"—or one of two rooms in a separate cottage unit. The B&B is on 5½ verdant acres on Reed's Island. ✉ *131 Ka'iulani St., 96720,* ☎ *808/934–8002 or 800/627–8447,* FAX *808/934–8002,* WEB *www.hilo-hawaii.com. 3 rooms, 2 cottage units. AE, MC, V.*

$$-$$$ **Hawai'i Naniloa Hotel.** This is probably the most contemporary hotel in downtown Hilo and is ideal for those who seek a touch of the luxury resort. Be sure to ask for an ocean view. The Paradise Spa specializes in Hawaiian treatments. ✉ *93 Banyan Dr., 96720,* ☎ *808/969–3333 or 800/367–5360,* FAX *808/969–6622. 325 rooms. 2 restaurants, pools, golf, health club. AE, DC, MC, V.*

$ **Dolphin Bay Hotel.** True, the units are modest, but they are clean and inexpensive, and the staff has plenty of aloha. Four blocks from Hilo Bay, the private hotel borders a 2-acre Hawaiian garden with jungle trails and shady places to rest. ✉ *333 'Iliahi St., Hilo 96720,* ☎ *808/935–1466,* FAX *808/935–1523,* WEB *www.dolphinbayhilo.com. 13 rooms, four 1-bedroom units, one 2-bedroom unit. MC, V.*

Kailua-Kona

$$$-$$$$ ✕ **Jameson's by the Sea.** Sit outside next to the ocean or inside by the picture windows for glorious sunset views over Magic Sands Beach. Choose from three or four daily Island fish specials, or try stir-fried ocean scallops or Jameson's creamy clam chowder. ✉ *77-6452 Ali'i Dr.,* ☎ *808/329–3195. AE, D, DC, MC, V. No lunch weekends.*

$$-$$$ ✕ **La Bourgogne.** A genial husband-and-wife team owns this country-style restaurant with dark-wood walls and private, romantic booths. The traditional-French menu has classics such as rack of lamb with roasted garlic and rosemary, and less traditional meals like venison with a pomegranate glaze. ✉ *Kuakini Plaza S on Hwy. 11, 77-6400 Nālani, Kailua-Kona,* ☎ *808/329–6711. Reservations essential. AE, D, DC, MC, V. Closed Sun.–Mon. No lunch.*

$ ✕ **Ocean View Inn.** To those on a tight budget, this local hangout facing the pier at Kailua Bay has been a lifesaver since the 1920s. Chinese and American food are on the plate-lunch menu, and you can get Hawaiian specialties à la carte. ✉ *75-5683 Ali'i Dr., Kailua-Kona,* ☎ *808/329–9998. No credit cards. Closed Mon.*

$$$-$$$$ ★ **Ohana Keauhou Beach Resort.** This oceanfront hotel is 5 mi south of Kailua-Kona. Its 10-acre grounds include a *heiau,* a sacred fishpond, and a replica of the summer home of King David Kalākaua. The hotel is adjacent to Kahalu'u, one of the Big Island's best snorkeling beaches. ✉ *78-6740 Ali'i Dr., Kailua-Kona 96740,* ☎ *808/322–3441 or 800/922–7866,* FAX *808/322–3117,* WEB *www.aston-hotels.com. 317 rooms. Restaurant, pool, tennis, health club. AE, D, DC, MC, V.*

$ **Uncle Billy's Kona Bay Hotel.** These two- and four-story motel-type units are right in the center of town, across the street from the ocean. The atmosphere is friendly and fun-loving. Open-air dining around the pool is casual. Some rooms have kitchenettes. ✉ *75-5739 Ali'i Dr., Kailua-Kona 96740,* ☎ *808/329–1393 or 800/367–5102,* FAX *808/*

329–9210, WEB *www.unclebilly.com. 146 rooms. Restaurant, pool. AE, D, DC, MC, V.*

Kohala Coast and Waimea

$$$–$$$$ ★ ✕ **CanoeHouse at the Mauna Lani Bay Hotel and Bungalows.** This open-air beachfront restaurant, surrounded by fishponds, serves Pacific Rim cuisine the way it used to be: a matching of pure Asian and Western flavors with imaginative entrées such as grilled lemon-pepper scallops with Chinese-mustard soy sauce. ✉ *68-1400 Mauna Lani Dr., Kohala Coast,* ☎ *808/885–6622. AE, D, DC, MC, V.*

$$–$$$ ★ ✕ **Merriman's.** This is the signature restaurant of Peter Merriman, one of the pioneers of Hawai'i regional cuisine including the original wok-charred ahi. If you prefer meat opt for the prime "Kansas City Cut" steak, grilled to order. The wine list includes 22 selections poured by the glass. ✉ *'Opelo Plaza, Hwy. 19 and 'Opelo Rd.,* ☎ *808/885–6822. Reservations essential. AE, MC, V.*

$–$$ ✕ **Harbor Grill.** The view of Kawaihae Harbor's docks may not be exciting, but this little restaurant is always packed. You may have to wait for one of the lānai tables, or you can dine inside in a funky area full of beachcombing treasures. ✉ *Kawaihae Harbor, Hwy. 270, Kawaihae,* ☎ *808/882–1368. MC, V.*

$$$$ ★ 🏨 **Four Seasons Resort Hualālai.** Slate floors, Hawaiian artwork, warm earth and cool white tones, and spacious bathrooms create peaceful retreats, tucked into four clusters of oceanfront bungalows. Ground-level rooms have outdoor garden showers. Natural ponds dot the property. ✉ *100 Ka'ūpūlehu Dr., Ka'ūpūlehu/Kona,* ☎ *808/325–8000, 800/332–3442, or 888/340–5662,* FAX *808/325–8200,* WEB *www.fourseasons.com. 274 rooms. 3 restaurants, pools, tennis, golf. AE, DC, MC, V.*

$$$$ 🏨 **Outrigger Waikoloa Beach.** The most affordable of the Kohala resorts, this hotel covers 15 acres bordering the white-sand beach of 'Anaeho'omalu Bay and encompasses ancient royal fishponds, historic trails, and petroglyph fields. The oversize cabana rooms overlook the lagoon. ✉ *69-275 Waikoloa Beach Dr., Waikoloa 96738,* ☎ *808/886–6789 or 800/922–5533,* FAX *808/886–7852,* WEB *www.outrigger.com. 545 rooms. Restaurant, pool, tennis, golf, health club. AE, D, DC, MC, V.*

$ 🏨 **Waimea Country Lodge.** Rooms, all with kitchenettes, look out on the green pastures of the island's cool Upcountry. ✉ *65-1210 Lindsey Rd., Kamuela 96743,* ☎ *808/885–4100,* FAX *808/885–6711. 21 rooms. AE, D, DC, MC, V.*

Nightlife

Lulu's (✉ 75-5819 Ali'i Dr., Kailua-Kona, ☎ 808/331–2633). A crowd dances every evening here to hot contemporary music. From Tuesday through Saturday you might be able to find some easy-listening jazz at the **Honu Bar,** in the Mauna Lani Bay Hotel and Bungalows (✉ 68-1400 Mauna Lani Dr., Kohala Coast, ☎ 808/885–6622).

Jazz, country, and even rock bands perform at **Huggo's** (✉ 75-5828 Kahakai Rd., at Ali'i Dr., Kailua-Kona, ☎ 808/329–1493), so call ahead of time to find out what's on. Outside, people often dance in the sand to Hawaiian songs.

Outdoor Activities and Sports

Camping and Hiking

Popular areas are the 13,796-ft **Mauna Kea,** in the northeast, and **Hawai'i Volcanoes National Park.** For more information contact the **Department of Parks and Recreation** (✉ 25 Aupuni St., Hilo 96720, ☎ 808/961–8311).

Fishing

More than 50 charter boats are available for hire, most of them out of Honokōhau Harbor, north of Kailua. For bookings call the **Kona Activities Center** (☎ 808/329–3171 or 800/367–5288).

Golf

On the Kohala Coast the **Mauna Kea Beach Resort** (✉ 1 Mauna Kea Beach Dr., ☎ 808/882–5400) has an extremely challenging 18-hole course designed by Robert Trent Jones, Sr. The North and South courses of the stunning **Francis I'i Brown Golf Course** (✉ Mauna Lani Resort, ☎ 808/885–6655) have 18 holes each.

Sailing/Snorkeling

Captain Zodiac Raft Expedition (☎ 808/329–3199) offers a four-hour snorkel cruise off the Kona Coast. From January through April you may see humpback whales.

Scuba Diving

A reputable scuba charter in Kailua-Kona is **Big Island Divers** (✉ 75-5467 Kaiwi St., Kailua-Kona, ☎ 808/329–6068 or 800/488–6068, WEB www.bigislanddivers.com). **Ocean Eco Tours** (✉ 79-7539 Hawai'i Belt Rd., south of mile marker 113, Kealakekua, ☎ 808/324–7873, WEB www.oceanecotours.com) is an eco-friendly, full-service outfit eager to share a wealth of knowledge.

Beaches

Onekahakaha Beach Park, a protected white-sand beach 3 mi south of Hilo, is a favorite of local families. Close to Kailua-Kona the most popular beach is **Kahalu'u Beach Park,** where the swimming, snorkeling, and fine facilities attract weekend crowds. Currents can pull swimmers away from the beach when the surf is high. On the Kohala Coast **'Anaeho'omalu Bay Beach** (✉ Royal Waikoloan Resort) is an expanse perfect for water sports. Instruction and equipment rentals are available at the north end. The long, white-sand **Kauna'oa Beach** (✉ Mauna Kea Beach Resort) is one of the most beautiful on the island, but beware of the high surf that pounds the shore in winter. Between the Mauna Kea Beach and Mauna Lani resorts, **Hāpuna State Recreation Area** is a ½-mi crescent of sand flanked by rocky points. The surf can be hazardous in winter, but calmer summer water makes it ideal for swimming, snorkeling, and scuba diving.

Shopping

Hilo's **Prince Kūhiō Shopping Plaza** (✉ 111 E. Puainako St., Hilo, ☎ 808/959–8451) has specialty boutiques and larger stores; it stays open until 9 Monday–Friday. In Kona, most of the stores at the **Kona Coast Shopping Center** (✉ Palani Rd.) are open daily 9–9, though the KTA Super Stores (☎ 808/329–1677) outlet (a supermarket) is open 6 AM–midnight. Ali'i Drive is lined with small shopping malls. On the makai side, extending an entire block, is **Kona Inn Shopping Village** (☎ 808/329–6573). Much of this shopping arcade was once Kona Inn, a hotel built in 1929 that was a longtime landmark. Broad lawns on the ocean side are lovely for afternoon picnics.

The Big Island of Hawai'i Essentials

AIRPORTS

Visitors to the west side of the island fly into Kona International Airport. Those staying on the east side fly into Hilo International Airport. United has direct flights from the mainland to Keāhole Kona International.

➤ AIRPORT INFORMATION: **Hilo International Airport** (☎ 808/934–5801). **Kona International Airport** (☎ 808/329–2484).

VISITOR INFORMATION

Information and brochures are dispensed at the Big Island Visitors Center (HVCB) booths at Big Island airports and at HVCB offices in Hilo and Kailua-Kona.

➤ TOURIST INFORMATION: **Big Island Visitors Bureau** (✉ 250 Keawe St., Hilo, ☎ 808/961–5797, FAX 808/961–2126; ✉ 250 Waikoloa Beach Dr., B12, King's Shops, Waikoloa 96738, ☎ 808/886–1655, WEB www.bigisland.org).

MAUI

Maui is known for its perfect beaches, lively nightlife, and sophisticated resorts. Presiding over everything—from the sunny, active western Maui Gold Coast to laid-back Hāna, on the east side—is Haleakalā, the 10,023-ft dormant volcano whose peak is among the finest sunrise-viewing vantage points in the world.

Exploring Maui

West Maui

The condo-filled beach towns of Nāpili, Kahana, and Honokōwai are arrayed between the stunning resorts of Kapalua and Kā'anapali. West Maui is anchored by the amusing old whaling town of **Lahaina.** On the ocean side of Lahaina's **Front Street** is a **banyan tree** planted in 1873 and the largest of its kind in Hawai'i. Docked at Lahaina Harbor is the brig ***Carthaginian II*** (☎ 808/661–3262; 🎫 $3), a replica of a whaler now open as a museum. Also worth a visit is the **Baldwin Home** (✉ 696 Front St., ☎ 808/661–3262; 🎫 $3), an attractive thick-walled house of coral and stone where missionary doctor Dwight Baldwin lived in the 1830s. The **Wo Hing Museum** (✉ 858 Front St., Lahaina, ☎ 808/661–5553; 🎫 donation requested) was built in 1912 as a mutual-aid-society headquarters for Chinese immigrants.

Central Maui

Kahului, an industrial and commercial town in the center of the island, is home to many of Maui's permanent residents but offers little in the way of tourist attractions.The **Alexander & Baldwin Sugar Museum** (✉ 3957 Hansen Rd., Pu'unēnē, ☎ 808/871–8058; 🎫 $4), which details the rise of sugarcane in the Islands, is about 2 mi from Ka'ahumanu Avenue (Highway 32), Kahului's main street. A right onto Pu'unēnē Avenue (Highway 350) from Highway 32 will take you there. The museum is closed on Sunday.

West of Kahului, **Wailuku** is certainly the most charming town in Central Maui. The county seat since 1950, Wailuku was a politically important town until the sugar industry began to decline in the 1960s and tourism took hold. **Wailuku's Historical District** centers on Main Street—drive out of Kahului on Ka'humanu Avenue. You can pick up a free brochure that describes a self-guided walking tour at **Wailuku Main Street Association** (✉ 2062 Main St., ☎ 808/244–3888). One of Wailuku's most-photographed landmarks is the **'Īao Theater** (✉ 68 N. Market St., ☎ 808/242–6969), a charming movie house that went up in 1927 and served as a community gathering spot. The Art Deco building is now the showpiece of Main Street.

Mark Twain dubbed **'Īao Valley State Park** (☎ 808/984–8100) the Yosemite of the Pacific. Yosemite it's not, but it is a lovely deep valley with the curious **'Īao Needle,** a spire that rises more than 2,000 ft from the valley floor. Drive toward the mountains on Wailuku's Main Street to reach the park.

Haleakalā and Upcountry

Haleakalā, a 10,023-ft dormant volcano, is the font from which all of East Maui flowed and the centerpiece of a 27,284-acre national park—the terrain and views are unmatched anywhere in the world. Bring a sweater or jacket, since it's chilly at the top. From Kahului, drive on Haleakalā Highway (Highway 37) toward the volcano's slopes. Turn left on Highway 377. After about 6 mi make a left onto Haleakalā Crater Road, where the switchback ascent begins. You can stop and learn something of the volcano's origins and eruption history at the **Park Headquarters/Visitor Center,** at 7,000-ft elevation on Haleakalā Highway. Maps, posters, and other memorabilia are available at the gift shop here. **Haleakalā Visitor Center,** at 9,740-ft elevation, has exhibits inside and a trail that leads to a small crater nearby. The road ends at **Pu'u 'Ula'ula Overlook,** the highest point on Maui, where you'll find a glass-enclosed lookout. On a clear day you can see the islands of Moloka'i, Lāna'i, Kaho'olawe, and Hawai'i. Before you head up Haleakalā, call for the latest park weather conditions. ✉ *Haleakalā Crater Rd./Hwy. 378, Makawao,* ☎ *808/572–4400.* 🎫 *$10 per vehicle. Park headquarters and visitor center close at 4; Haleakalā visitor center closes at 3.*

Upcountry, as the western slopes of Haleakalā are known, encompasses the fertile land responsible for much of Hawai'i's produce and flowers. Heading down from the volcano's summit on Highway 377, stop at **Kula Botanical Gardens** (✉ Upper Kula Rd., Kula, ☎ 808/878–1715; 🎫 $5) to admire the tropical flora. At **Tedeschi Vineyards and Winery** (✉ Kula Hwy., 'Ulupalakua Ranch, ☎ 808/878–6058, WEB www.mauiwine.com; 🎫 free) you can take a tour of the winery and its historic grounds, the former Rose Ranch, and sample the island's only wines: a pleasant Maui Blush, the Maui Brut-Blanc de Noirs Hawaiian Champagne, and Tedeschi's annual Maui Nouveau.

East Maui

The **Road to Hāna** is 55 mi of hairpin turns, one-lane bridges, and spectacular scenery. It begins in **Pā'ia** on the north coast and passes **Ho'okipa Beach.** At mile marker 11 stop at the bridge over **Puohokamoa Stream,** where there are pools, waterfalls, and picnic tables. Another mile takes you to **Kaumahina State Wayside Park,** which has a picnic area and a lovely overlook to the Keanae Peninsula. Past **Honomanū Valley,** with its 3,000-ft cliffs and a 1,000-ft waterfall, is the **Ke'anae Arboretum** (✉ Hāna Hwy., Mile Marker 17, Ke'anae; 🎫 free), devoted to native plants and trees. Nearby is the **Ke'anae Overlook,** with views of taro farms and the ocean; it's an excellent spot for photos. As you continue on toward Hāna, you'll pass **Wai'ānapanapa State Park** (✉ Hāna Hwy. near Mile Marker 32, Hāna, ☎ 808/248–8061; 🎫 free), which has state-run cabins and picnic areas.

The town of **Hāna** is down the road from Wai'ānapanapa State Park. **'Ohe'o Gulch** and its famous pools are about 10 mi past Hāna on a bumpy stretch of road called Pi'ilani Highway; swimming is hazardous here, but it's a great place to sit in the sun or take pictures.

Dining and Lodging

Some of Maui's best restaurants are at resort hotels, which are mainly in West Maui and South Maui.

For B&B accommodations contact **Affordable Accommodations Maui** (✉ 2825 Kauhale St., Kīhei 96753, ☎ 808/879–7865).

West Maui

$$$–$$$$ ★ ✕ **Gerard's.** One of Hawai'i's most talented chefs, owner Gerard Reversade changes the French menu daily: you might find confit of duck or shiitake and oyster mushrooms in puff pastry. Prepare to do some stargazing, as this is a celebrity favorite. ✉ *Plantation Inn, 174 Lahainaluna Rd., Lahaina,* ☎ *808/661–8939. AE, D, DC, MC, V. No lunch.*

$$$–$$$$ ★ ✕ **Pacific'O.** You can sit outdoors at umbrella-shaded tables near the water's edge, or find a spot in the breezy, marble-floor interior. The menu is exciting, with the likes of fresh ahi-and-*ono* tempura (ono is a mackerel-like fish) and a great lamb dish—a whole rack of sweet New Zealand lamb, sesame-crusted and served with roasted macadamia sauce. ✉ *505 Front St., Lahaina,* ☎ *808/667–4341. AE, D, DC, MC, V.*

$–$$ ★ ✕ **Lahaina Coolers.** This breezy little café with a surfboard hanging from its ceiling serves up such tantalizing fare as shrimp-pesto linguine with prawns, basil, garlic, and cream, as well as pizzas, steaks, and burgers. For dessert, try a chocolate taco filled with tropical fruit and berry "salsa." ✉ *180 Dickenson St., Lahaina,* ☎ *808/661–7082. AE, MC, V.*

$$$$ ★ 🏨 **Ritz-Carlton Kapalua.** This quietly luxurious Kapalua resort has spacious, comfortable rooms with oversize marble bathrooms and individual lānai, most with panoramic ocean views. Service and business facilities are first rate. ✉ *1 Ritz-Carlton Dr., Kapalua 96761,* ☎ *808/669–6200 or 800/262–8440,* FAX *808/665–0026,* WEB *www.ritzcarlton.com. 550 rooms. 3 restaurants, pool, golf, tennis, health club. AE, D, DC, MC, V.*

$$$ 🏨 **Nāpili Kai Beach Club.** The beach here is one of the best on the west side for swimming and snorkeling, and the hotel draws a loyal following. Shoji doors open onto your lānai, with the beach and ocean right outside. The rooms closest to the beach have no air-conditioning, but ceiling fans usually suffice. ✉ *5900 Lower Honoapi'ilani Hwy., Nāpili Bay 96761,* ☎ *808/669–6271 or 800/367–5030,* FAX *808/669–5740,* WEB *www.napilikai.com. 162 rooms. Pools. AE, MC, V.*

$$–$$$ ★ 🏨 **Plantation Inn.** Charm and luxury set apart this inn reminiscent of a southern plantation home. Filled with Victorian and Asian furnishings, it's on a quiet street in the heart of Lahaina. Secluded lānai draped with hanging plants face a central courtyard, pool, and garden pavilion perfect for morning coffee. ✉ *174 Lahainaluna Rd., Lahaina 96761,* ☎ *808/667–9225 or 800/433–6815,* FAX *808/667–9293,* WEB *www.theplantationinn.com. 18 rooms. Restaurant, pool. AE, MC, V.*

East Maui

$$$–$$$$ ★ ✕ **Mama's Fish House.** As you enjoy the views at this cliff-top restaurant done in a Hawaiian nautical theme, check out the stone path engraved with whimsical Hawaiian geckos. But the real treat here is the fish, prepared seven ways—grilled with spicy wasabi butter, for example. ✉ *799 Poho Pl., Kū'au,* ☎ *808/579–8488. Reservations essential. AE, D, DC, MC, V.*

$$–$$$ ★ ✕ **Hali'imaile General Store.** This lofty wooden building in the middle of sugarcane and pineapple fields used to be a camp store in the 1920s. The Szechuan barbecued salmon and rack of lamb Hunan style are classics; the pineapple upside-down cake is worth a stop alone. ✉ *900 Hali'imaile Rd., 2 mi north of Pukalani,* ☎ *808/572–2666. MC, V.*

$ ★ ✕ **Pauwela Café.** Casual and ultrafriendly, this spot off Hāna Highway is worth the detour. Order a kālua-pork sandwich and a piece of coffee cake and pass the afternoon. The large breakfast burritos and homemade soups are also good. ✉ *375 W. Kuiaha Rd., off Hāna Hwy. past Ha'ikū Rd., Ha'ikū,* ☎ *808/575–9242. No credit cards. No dinner.*

$$$$ ★ 🏨 **Hotel Hāna-Maui.** One of the best places to stay in Hawai'i is this small, secluded Hāna hotel surrounded by a 7,000-acre ranch. Rooms have bleached-wood floors, overstuffed furniture in natural fabrics, and local art. ✉ *Hāna Hwy. (Box 9, Hāna 96713),* ☎ *808/248–8211 or 800/321–4262,* FAX *808/248–7202. 96 rooms. Restaurant, pool, tennis, health club. AE, D, DC, MC, V.*

$$$–$$$$ 🏨 **Heavenly Hāna Inn.** An impressive Japanese gate marks the entrance to this small upscale inn. The three suites, one a two-bedroom unit, all have TVs. Decor is spare, with Japanese overtones. ✉ *Near mile marker 32 on Hāna Hwy., Hāna, Box 790, Hāna 96713,* ☎ *808/248–8442. 3 suites. AE, D, MC, V.*

$–$$ ★ 🏨 **Silver Cloud Guest Ranch.** Silver Cloud is in cowboy country, on the high mountainside beyond Kula. The noble Plantation House, with six rooms, surveys pasturelands and a spellbinding panorama of islands and sea. In addition to the main house, the ranch has the separate Lānai Cottage and five studios with kitchenettes (good for families). ✉ *R.R. 2 (Box 201, Kula 96790),* ☎ *808/878–6101 or 800/532–1111,* FAX *808/878–2132,* WEB *www.maui.net/~slvrcld. 11 rooms, 1 cottage. AE, D, DC, MC, V.*

Nightlife

The best options are in resort areas and Lahaina. **Moose McGillycuddy's** (✉ 844 Front St., Lahaina, ☎ 808/667–7758) has live music Tuesday and Thursday evenings for a young crowd. **Molokini Lounge** (✉ Maui Prince Hotel, Mākena Resort, ☎ 808/874–1111) is a pleasant bar with live Hawaiian music, a dance floor, and an ocean view. **Tropica** (✉ Westin Maui, 2365 Kā'anapali Pkwy., Lahaina, ☎ 808/667–2525), the restaurant at the Westin Kā'anapali, is the latest and hottest, more for its Thursday-night dance mix than its food.

Outdoor Activities and Sports

Golf

Maui's major resorts all have golf courses, and all are open to the public. Most lower their greens fees after 2:30 on weekday afternoons. **Kapalua Golf Club** (✉ 300 Kapalua Dr., Kapalua, ☎ 808/669–8044) has three 18-holers. **Kā'anapali Golf Courses** (✉ Kā'anapali Beach Resort, Kā'anapali, ☎ 808/661–3691) contains two of Maui's most famous. The **Wailea Golf Club** (✉ 100 Wailea Golf Club Dr., Wailea, ☎ 808/875–7450) has three courses.

Fees are lower at Maui's municipal courses such as **Waiehu Municipal Golf Course** (✉ off Hwy. 340 in West Maui, ☎ 808/244–5934), on the northeast coast, a few miles past Wailuku.

Water Sports

Fishing. You can fish year-round in Maui for such catch as Pacific blue marlin and wahoo. Plenty of fishing boats run out of Lahaina and Mā'alaea harbors, including those from **Luckey Strike Charters** (✉ Box 1502, Lahaina 96767, ☎ 808/661–4606).

Sailing, Snorkeling, and Scuba Diving. Many outfitters provide combination sailing and snorkeling cruises or scuba expeditions; some also have whale-watching expeditions and sunset cruises. For "one-stop" booking and information on various water activities, call the **Ocean Activities Center** (✉ 1847 S. Kīhei Rd., Suite 203, Kīhei, ☎ 808/879–4485 or 800/798–0652). **Trilogy Excursions** (✉ 180 Lahainaluna Rd., Lahaina, ☎ 808/661–4743 or 800/874–2666) offers snorkeling and diving tours that leave from Lahaina and drop anchor in the waters off Lāna'i. **Maui-Moloka'i Sea Cruises** (✉ 831 Eha St., Wailuku, ☎

808/242–8777) has scuba and snorkeling excursions to Moloka'i's prime diving spots.

Surfing. Although on land it may not look as if there are seasons on Maui, the tides tell another story. In winter the surf is up on the northern shores of the Hawaiian Islands, while summer brings big swells to the southern side. You can rent surfboards and boogie boards at many surf shops, such as **Second Wind Sail Surf & Kite Company** (✉ 111 Hāna Hwy., Kahului, ☎ 808/877–7467), which offers both equipment rental and lessons for surfers, windsurfers, and kite-surfers. **Lightning Bolt Maui** (✉ 55 Ka'ahumanu Ave., Kahului, ☎ 808/877–3484) is Maui's oldest surf shop.

Whale-Watching. Quite a few operations run whale-watching excursions off the coast of Maui, with many boats departing from the wharves at Lahaina and Ma'alaea each day. **Pacific Whale Foundation** (✉ Kealia Beach Plaza, 101 N. Kīhei Rd., Kīhei 96753, ☎ 808/879–8811) pioneered whale-watching back in 1979 and now runs four boats, plus sea-kayak excursions and special trips to encounter turtles and dolphins.

Windsurfing. Ho'okipa Bay, 10 mi east of Kahului, is the windsurfing capital of the world. Rent a board or take lessons from **Maui Ocean Activities** (✉ 104 Wahikuli Rd., Lahaina, ☎ 808/667–1964).

Beaches

West Maui's **Nāpili Beach** is a sparkling white crescent—a perfect cove for strolling and sunbathing. It's right outside the Nāpili Kai Beach Club, a popular little resort for honeymooners. If you want lots of action, lay out your towel on **Kā'anapali Beach.** The beach fronts the big hotels at Kā'anapali and is one of Maui's best people-watching spots: cruises, windsurfers, and parasailers head out from here while the beautiful people take in the scenery.

South of Wailea is the state park at **Mākena,** with two good beaches. The water off Big Beach is fine for swimming and snorkeling, and you'll find showers, rest rooms, and paved parking here. Walk to the northern end of Big Beach toward the cinder cliffs and you'll hit Little Beach, as popular for nude sunbathing (officially illegal here) as it is for its viewing Molokini islet and Lāna'i.

Baldwin Beach, west of Pā'ia town, is a local favorite. There's not much wave action for bodysurfing, but this is a good place to stretch out and swim or jog. If you want to see some of the world's finest windsurfers, stop at **Ho'okipa Beach** along Hāna Highway. It's also one of Maui's hottest surfing spots, with waves as high as 15 ft. This is not a good swimming beach.

Shopping

You can browse through the stores of Front Street in Lahaina or the boutiques in the major hotels. Maui also has several major shopping malls. **Ka'ahumanu Center** (✉ 275 Ka'ahumanu Ave., Kahului, ☎ 808/877–3369) has nearly 100 shops and restaurants. Also in Kahului is the **Maui Mall Shopping Center** (✉ corner of Ka'ahumanu and Pu'unēnē Aves., ☎ 808/877–7559), with 33 stores and a 12-screen megaplex. **Whalers Village** (✉ 2435 Kā'anapali Pkwy., Kā'anapali, ☎ 808/661–4567) in the Kā'anapali resort area has good restaurants and upscale boutiques such as Tiffany & Co. and Louis Vuitton.

Maui Essentials

AIRPORTS

Maui's major airport, Kahului Airport, at the center of the island, is served by United, American, Delta, ATA, Hawaiian, and Aloha airlines. If you're staying in West Maui, you might be better off flying into Kapalua–West Maui Airport, served by Aloha Airlines. The landing strip at Hāna Airport is served by Aloha Airlines.

➤ AIRPORT INFORMATION: **Hāna Airport** (☎ 808/248–8208). **Kahului Airport** (☎ 808/872–3893). **Kapalua Airport** (☎ 808/669–0623).

VISITOR INFORMATION

➤ TOURIST INFORMATION: **Maui Visitors Bureau** (✉ 1727 Wili Pa Loop, Wailuku 96793, ☎ 808/244–3530, FAX 808/244–1337, WEB www.visitmaui.com).

KAUA'I

Kaua'i's natural beauty is amazingly diverse. The cooler, damper north shore has lush landscaping, mist-shrouded peaks, and world-class golf courses; the southern shore has the sunshine; and the west coast is home to two geologic wonders: Waimea Canyon—the Grand Canyon of the Pacific—and the Nā Pali Coast.

Exploring Kaua'i

A coastal road runs around the rim of Kaua'i and dead-ends on either side of the rugged Nā Pali Coast. If you're looking for sunshine, head to the southern resort of Po'ipū; for greener scenery and a wetter climate, try Hanalei and Princeville to the north. For a bird's-eye view of the whole island, consider a helicopter excursion.

The Road North

Kīlauea Lighthouse (☎ 808/828–1413; 🎟 $2), built in 1913, is now part of a wildlife refuge near the former plantation town of Kīlauea, north of Wailua on Highway 56. The **Hanalei Valley Overlook** encompasses a view of more than ½ mi of taro, the staple plant of the Hawaiian diet, plus a 900-acre endangered-waterfowl refuge. Hanalei is the site of the **Waioli Mission** (✉ Kūhiō Hwy., ☎ 808/245–3202; 🎟 suggested donation $5; Closed Mon., Wed., Fri., and Sun.), founded by Christian missionaries in 1837.

Smith's Tropical Paradise (✉ 174 Wailua Rd., Kapa'a, ☎ 808/821–6895; 🎟 $5) is a 30-acre expanse of jungle, exotic foliage, tropical birds, and lagoons. From Wailua Marina, on the east coast, boats cruise up Wailua River to **Fern Grotto** (✉ Smith's Motor Boat Service, 174 Wailua Rd., Kapa'a, ☎ 808/821–6892; 🎟 $15), a yawning lava tube with enormous fishtail ferns.

To the South and West

Kilohana (✉ 3–2087 Kaumuali'i Hwy., ☎ 808/245–5608; 🎟 free), a historic sugar plantation, is now a 35-acre visitor attraction with upscale shops. **Po'ipū** is the premier resort town of Kaua'i's south shore and a mecca for bodysurfers. **Spouting Horn,** a waterspout that shoots up through an ancient lava tube, lies west of Po'ipū along Highway 52.

Waimea, a sleepy little town, marks the first landfall of British captain James Cook to the Sandwich Islands in 1778. **Waimea Canyon,** created by an ancient fault in the earth's crust, stretches inland from Waimea. Spectacular views of the ever-changing reds, greens, and golden browns of the canyon—3,600 ft deep, 2 mi wide, and 10 mi long—can be seen from Pu'uka-pele and Pu'uhinahina lookouts. Waimea Canyon Drive passes through **Kōke'e State Park** (☎ 808/335–5871; free), a 4,345-acre wilderness. The drive ends 4 mi above the park at the 4,120-ft **Kalalau Lookout**, the best viewpoint in Kaua'i.

For a flightseeing adventure you won't easily forget—the rugged splendor of the Nā Pali Coast or the hidden waterfalls of Waimea Canyon—call the **South Sea Tour Company** (✉ Main Terminal, Līhu'e Airport, ☎ 808/245–2222 or 800/367–9214). The spectacular Nā Pali Coast is not accessible by land, so this may be your best way to have a good look.

Dining and Lodging

For an insider's look at Kaua'i, book with **Bed and Breakfast Hawai'i** (✉ Box 449, Kapa'a 96746, ☎ 808/822–7771 or 800/733–1632, WEB www.bandb-hawaii.com).

East and North Kaua'i

$$–$$$ ★ ✕ **A Pacific Cafe.** The daily-changing menu at this cutting-edge café might include grilled moonfish with black-olive polenta, sun-dried tomatoes, pancetta, and shiitake mushrooms. The macadamia-nut torte sprinkled with toasted coconut is tops. ✉ *Kaua'i Village Shopping Center, 4-831 Kuhio Hwy., Kapa'a,* ☎ *808/822–0013. AE, D, DC, MC, V. No lunch.*

$$–$$$ ★ ✕ **Postcards Cafe.** This great little place is quietly known as one of the best restaurants on Kaua'i, and with good reason. The menu is geared toward the healthy eater and features mostly organic, additive-free foods. But don't get the wrong idea—this isn't simple cooking: specials might include macadamia-crusted opah, a marine fish, in a banana papaya relish mashed potatoes. ✉ *5-5075A Kūhiō Hwy., Hanalei,* ☎ *808/826–1191. AE, MC, V. No lunch.*

$–$$ ✕ **Kīlauea Bakery and Pau Hana Pizza.** The bakery has garnered tons of press for their Hawaiian sourdough loaf made with guava starter, and such pizzas as the Billie Holiday (smoked fish, roasted onions, Gorgonzola rosemary sauce, and mozzarella). ✉ *Kong Lung Center, 2490 Keneke St., Kīlauea,* ☎ *808/828–2020. MC, V.*

$$$$ ★ **Princeville Resort.** This splendid cliff-side property has breathtaking views of Hanalei Bay. Bathrooms have gold-plated fixtures and picture windows that cloud up for privacy at the flick of a switch. The setting and service are unmatched. ✉ *5520 Ka Haku Rd., Princeville 96722,* ☎ *808/826–9644 or 800/826–4400,* FAX *808/826–1166,* WEB *www.princeville.com. 252 rooms. 3 restaurants, pool, golf, tennis. AE, D, DC, MC, V.*

$–$$ **Kapa'a Sands.** Furnishings in this intimate condominium are bungalow style, with rustic wood and ceiling fans. Ask for an oceanfront room with open-air lānai and Pacific views. ✉ *380 Papaloa Rd., Kapa'a 96746,* ☎ *808/822–4901 or 800/222–4901. 20 units. Pool. MC, V.*

South and West

$$$ ★ ✕ **Beach House.** This may be the best ocean view from any restaurant on the south shore. The cuisine is equally superlative: the menu changes often, but you might find grilled salmon with spinach wonton and shrimp-tomato broth. ✉ *5022 Lawai Rd., Kōloa,* ☎ *808/742–1424. AE, D, DC, MC, V. No lunch.*

$$–$$$ ★ ✕ **Roy's Po'ipū Bar & Grill.** Hawai'i's culinary superstar Roy Yamaguchi serves first-rate Euro-Asian-Pacific cuisine. Who but Roy could team fresh seared 'ōpakapaka with orange shrimp butter and Chinese black-bean sauce? ✉ *Po'ipū Shopping Village, 2360 Kiahuna Plantation Dr., Po'ipū Beach,* ☎ *808/742–5000. AE, D, DC, MC, V. No lunch.*

$–$$ ✕ **Green Garden.** In business since 1948, this family-run no-frills restaurant is brightened by an assortment of hanging and standing plants. Local fare includes breaded mahimahi fillet and passion-fruit chiffon pie. ✉ *Hwy. 50, Hanapēpē,* ☎ *808/335–5422. AE, MC, V. Closed Tues.*

$$$$ ★ **Gloria's Spouting Horn Bed & Breakfast.** This cedar home is the most oceanfront B&B on Kaua'i. Waves dash the black rocks below, while just above the ocean's edge, the beach invites sunbathers. All three bedrooms have four-poster beds with canopies and private bathrooms with deep soaking tubs. ✉ *4464 Lawai Rd., Po'ipū,* ☎ *808/742–6995,* WEB *www.gloriasbedandbreakfast.com. 3 rooms. Pool. No credit cards.*

$$$$ ★ **Hyatt Regency Kaua'i Resort and Spa.** Low-rise, plantation-style architecture with dramatic open-air courtyards, lush tropical landscaping, and spectacular rock-enclosed swimming lagoons make this the most Hawaiian of Hyatts—and one of the most striking hotel resorts anywhere. ✉ *1571 Po'ipū Rd., Koloa 96756,* ☎ *808/742–1234 or 800/233–1234,* FAX *808/742–1557,* WEB *www.hyatt.com. 607 rooms. 5 restaurants, pools, golf, tennis, health club. AE, D, DC, MC, V.*

$$ **Garden Isle Cottages.** Tropical flower gardens surround these spacious ocean-side cottages five minutes from the restaurants of Po'ipū. One of the cottages, Hale Waipahu, sits on the highest point in Po'ipū, with a 360-degree ocean vista that takes in Brennecke's Beach. ✉ *2666 Pu'uholo Rd., Kōloa 96756,* ☎ *808/742–6717 or 800/742–6711,* WEB *www.oceancottages.com. 7 cottages. No credit cards.*

Nightlife

Weekends, people gather at **Duke's Barefoot Bar** (✉ Kalapaki Beach, Lihu'e, ☎ 808/246–9599) to hear contemporary Hawaiian tunes. Of Kaua'i's lū'au options, **Kaua'i Coconut Beach Resort Lū'au** (✉ Coconut Plantation, Kapa'a, ☎ 808/822–3455 or 800/760–8555) is regarded by many as the best on the island.

Outdoor Activities and Sports

Fishing

For deep-sea fishing, **Sportfishing Kaua'i** (☎ 808/639–0013) has a 28-ft and a 38-ft six-passenger custom sportfisher.

Golf

Best known are the Makai and Prince courses at **Princeville Resort** (✉ Princeville, ☎ 808/826–2726 or 800/826–1105).

Hiking

Kōke'e State Park (✉ Kōke'e Rd., Kōke'e, ☎ 808/335–5871) has 45 mi of hiking trails. The **Department of Land and Natural Resources** (✉ Līhu'e, ☎ 808/241–3446) provides hiking information.

Snorkeling and Scuba Diving

Explore spectacular underwater reefs with **Dive Kaua'i** (✉ 4–976 Kūhiō Hwy., Suite 4, Kapa'a, ☎ 808/822–0452). **Hanalei Sea Tours** (☎ 808/826–7254) has a four-hour snorkeling cruise off the Nā Pali coast.

Beaches

The waters that hug Kaua'i are clean, clear, and inviting, but be careful where you go in: the south shore sees higher surf in the summer, and north-shore waters are treacherous in winter.

North Shore

On the winding section of Highway 56 west of Hanalei is **Lumahai Beach,** flanked by high mountains and lava rocks. There are no lifeguards here, so swim only in summer. **Hanalei Beach Park** has views of the Nā Pali coast and shaded picnic tables, but swimming here can be treacherous. Near the end of Highway 56, **Ha'ēna State Park** is good for swimming when the surf is down in summer. Highway 56 dead-ends at **Kē'ē Beach,** a fine swimming beach in summer.

South and West Shores

Kalapak'i Beach, a sheltered bay ideal for water sports, fronts the Marriott in Līhu'e. Small- to medium-size waves make **Brennecke's Beach** in Po'ipū a bodysurfer's heaven, and there are showers, rest rooms, and lifeguards. At the end of Highway 50 is **Polihale Beach Park,** a long, wide strand flanked by huge cliffs. Swim here only when the surf is low; there are no lifeguards.

Shopping

In Līhu'e is **Kukui Grove Center** (✉ 3–2600 Kaumuali'i Hwy., ☎ 808/245–7742), Kaua'i's largest mall. **Coconut Marketplace** (✉ 4–484 Kūhiō Hwy., Kapa'a, ☎ 808/822–0744) is a standout among east-coast malls. **Kaua'i Village Shopping Center** (✉ 4–831 Kūhiō Hwy., Kapa'a, ☎ 808/822–4904) has 19th-century plantation-style architecture and 25 shops. **Princeville Shopping Center** (✉ 5–4280 Kūhiō Hwy., Kapa'a, ☎ 808/826–3040), in the north end of the island, has interesting shops.

Kaua'i Essentials

AIRPORTS

Līhu'e Airport, 3 mi east of the county seat of Līhu'e, handles most of Kaua'i's air traffic; it is served by United, Aloha and Hawaiian airlines.
➤ AIRPORT INFORMATION: **Līhu'e Airport** (☎ 808/246–1400).

VISITOR INFORMATION

Po'ipū Beach Resort Association is the central source of information about the south shore.
➤ TOURIST INFORMATION: **Kaua'i Visitors Bureau** (✉ 4334 Rice St., Suite 101, Līhu'e 96766, ☎ 808/245–3971 or 800/262–1400, FAX 808/246–9235, WEB www.kauaivisitorsbureau.org). **Po'ipū Beach Resort Association** (✉ Box 730, Kōloa 96756, ☎ 808/742–7444 or 888/744–0888, FAX 808/742–7887, WEB poipu-beach.org).

ELSEWHERE IN HAWAI'I

Moloka'i

With its slow pace and emphasis on Hawaiiana, Moloka'i drowses in another era. There are no high-rises, no traffic jams, and no stoplights on the 10- by 38-mi island. The fanciest hotels are bungalow style, and there's plenty of undeveloped countryside.

What to See and Do

Kalaupapa National Historic Park (✉ Box 2222, Moloka'i 96742, ☎ 808/567–6802) was a leper colony until 1888. The pretty little town is now a National Historic Landmark. It's *only* accessible via **Damien Tours** (☎ 808/567–6171) or **Moloka'i Mule Rides** (✉ 100 Kala'e Hwy., Kualapu'u 96757, ☎ 808/567–6088).

Tucked away on the slopes of Mt. Kamakou, Moloka'i's highest peak, ★ the 2,774-acre **Kamakou Preserve** (✉ The Nature Conservancy, 23 Pueo Pl., Kualapu'u, ☎ 808/553–5236, WEB www.tnc-hawaii.org; 🎫 free; donation suggested for guided hike) is a dazzling wonderland full of forests, rare bogs, and native wildlife. Reservations for guided hikes are required well in advance.

One of the most sensational beaches in Hawai'i is **Pāpōhaku Beach** (✉ Kaluako'i Rd.; 2 mi beyondKaluako'i Hotel and Golf Club), a 3-mi-long strip of white sand, the longest of its kind on the island. Some places are too rocky for swimming; look carefully before entering the water.

Moloka'i Essentials

AIRPORT

Ho'olehua Airport, a tiny strip west of central Moloka'i, is served by Hawaiian, Island, and Pacific Wings airlines.

➤ AIRPORT INFORMATION: **Ho'olehua Airport** (☎ 808/567–6140).

VISITOR INFORMATION

➤ TOURIST INFORMATION: **Maui Visitors Bureau** (✉ 1727 Wili Pa Loop, Wailuku, Maui 96793, ☎ 808/245–3971, WEB www.visitmaui.com). **Moloka'i Visitors Association** (✉ Box 960, Kaunakakai 96748, ☎ 808/553–3876 or 800/800–6367, WEB www.molokai-hawaii.com).

Lāna'i

For decades Lāna'i was known as the Pineapple Island, with hundreds of acres devoted to growing the golden fruit. Today this 140-square-mi island has been called Hawai'i's most secluded island, and the pineapple industry has given way to tourism. There are two upscale hotels and two championship golf courses, but despite these additions, Lāna'i—the third smallest of the islands—remains remote and intimate.

What to See and Do

★ **Garden of the Gods** is a preternatural plateau scattered with boulders of different sizes, shapes, and colors, the products of a million years of wind erosion.The 9-mi **Munro Trail** follows a pine-covered ridge up to **Lāna'ihale** (House of Lāna'i), which, at 3,370 ft, is the island's highest point.

Hulopo'e Beach is one of the best beaches in all of Hawai'i. This sparkling crescent beckons with clear waters that are safe for swimming; great snorkeling reefs; tide pools; and, often, spinner dolphins. The rusting World War II tanker may be a clue that the waters off of **Shipwreck Beach** aren't friendly. Strong trade winds have propelled innocent vessels onto the reef ever since 1824.

Lāna'i Essentials

AIRPORTS

Hawaiian Airlines and Island Air serve this tiny island, whose airport is a 10-minute drive from Lāna'i City.

➤ AIRPORT INFORMATION: **Lāna'i Airport** (☎ 808/565–6757).

VISITOR INFORMATION

➤ TOURIST INFORMATION: **Destination Lāna'i** (✉ 730 Lāna'i Ave., Suite 102, Lāna'i City 96763, ☎ 808/565–7600 or 800/947–4774).

IDAHO

Updated by
Kristin Rodine

Capital	Boise
Population	1,293,953
Motto	Esto Perpetua (It Is Perpetual)
State Bird	Mountain bluebird
State Flower	Syringa
Postal Abbreviation	ID

Statewide Visitor Information

Idaho Travel Council (✉ Dept. of Commerce, 700 W. State St. [Box 83720, Boise 83720-0093], ☎ 208/334–2470 or 800/847–4843, WEB www.visitid.org).

Outdoor Activities and Sports

Idaho Travel Council has information about private campgrounds. For camping on federal and state lands, phone national recreation areas and state parks directly. For information about hiking, backpacking, and rafting, contact the regional travel associations and local chambers of commerce or **Idaho Outfitters and Guides Association** (✉ Box 95, Boise 83701, ☎ 208/342–1919 or 800/494–3246).

The fishing season generally runs from the Saturday before Memorial Day through November. The **Idaho Department of Fish & Game** (✉ 600 S. Walnut St. [Box 25, Boise 83707], ☎ 208/334–3717 or 800/554–8685) provides licenses and information, including the excellent "Official Guide to Fishing in Idaho." A visitor's fishing permit costs $10.50 for the first day and $4 for each additional consecutive day. The department also publishes a wildlife viewing guide that lists the best and most easily accessible viewing sites in the state.

Scenic Drives

Twenty historic or scenic byways and segments of 10 historic trails are shown on the Official Idaho Highway Map, available from the Idaho Travel Council. The 39-mi **Lewis and Clark Back Country Byway,** 20 mi south of Salmon off Route 28 at Tendoy, traces the passage of explorers Meriwether Lewis and William Clark through the Continental Divide, along the pine-studded crest of the Bitterroot and Beaverhead mountains near the Montana state line. The **Lake Coeur d'Alene Scenic Byway** follows Route 97 S to Route 3, shadowing the lake's crooked eastern shore for 35 mi.

National and State Parks

Idaho has no national parks, but it is full of national monuments and recreation areas. With 40% of its acreage in trees, Idaho is the most heavily forested of the Rocky Mountain states. For information on all of Idaho's forests, contact **Boise National Forest** (✉ 1387 Vinnell Way, Boise 83709, ☎ 208/373–4007). Federal land in Idaho is under the jurisdiction of the **Bureau of Land Management Idaho State Office** (✉ 1387 Vinnell Way, Boise 83709, ☎ 208/373–4000).

National Parks

The Salmon River and its Middle Fork, an acclaimed stretch of white water, are surrounded by the 2-million-acre **Frank Church–River of No Return Wilderness Area** (✉ Rte. 2, Grangeville 83530, ☎ 208/983–1950). Once used as a training site for U.S. astronauts because of its

Idaho

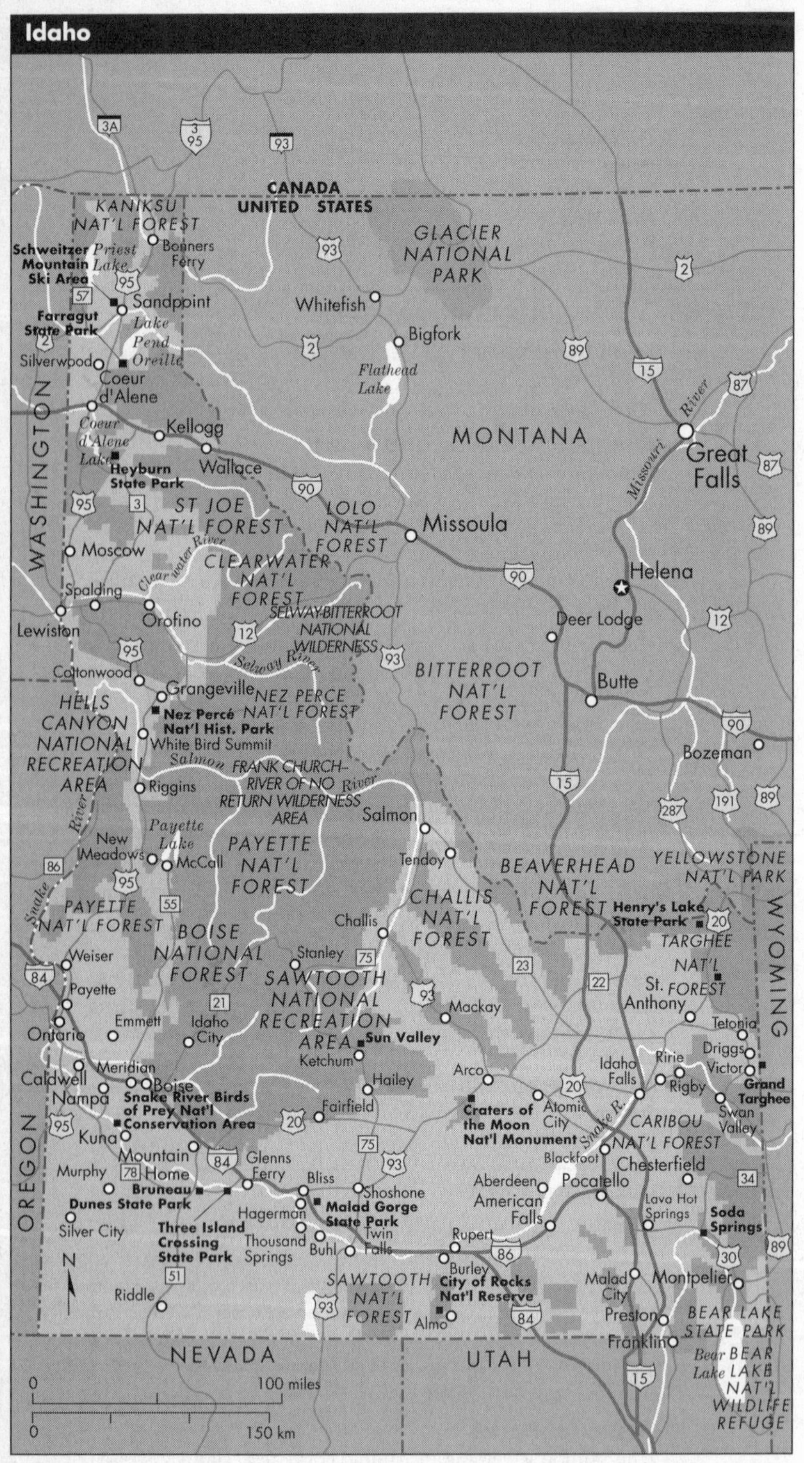

CANADA
UNITED STATES
KANIKSU NAT'L FOREST
Schweitzer Mountain Ski Area
Priest Lake
Bonners Ferry
Sandpoint
Farragut State Park
Lake Pend Oreille
Silverwood
Coeur d'Alene
Coeur d'Alene Lake
Kellogg
Wallace
Heyburn State Park
ST JOE NAT'L FOREST
LOLO NAT'L FOREST
GLACIER NATIONAL PARK
Whitefish
Bigfork
Flathead Lake
MONTANA
Great Falls
Missouri River
Missoula
Helena
Deer Lodge
Butte
Bozeman
WASHINGTON
Moscow
Clearwater River
CLEARWATER NAT'L FOREST
SELWAY-BITTERROOT NATIONAL WILDERNESS
Spalding
Orofino
Lewiston
Selway River
Cottonwood
Grangeville
NEZ PERCE NAT'L FOREST
BITTERROOT NAT'L FOREST
HELLS CANYON NATIONAL RECREATION AREA
Nez Percé Nat'l Hist. Park
White Bird Summit
Salmon River
FRANK CHURCH–RIVER OF NO RETURN WILDERNESS AREA
Riggins
Salmon
Snake River
Payette Lake
New Meadows
McCall
PAYETTE NAT'L FOREST
Tendoy
BEAVERHEAD NAT'L FOREST
YELLOWSTONE NAT'L PARK
CHALLIS NAT'L FOREST
Henry's Lake State Park
TARGHEE NAT'L FOREST
WYOMING
Challis
BOISE NATIONAL FOREST
Weiser
Stanley
SAWTOOTH NATIONAL RECREATION AREA
Payette
St. Anthony
Mackay
Tetonia
Emmett
Idaho City
Ontario
Sun Valley
Ketchum
Driggs
Victor
Meridian
Caldwell
Boise
Nampa
Hailey
Arco
Idaho Falls
Ririe
Rigby
Grand Targhee
Snake River Birds of Prey Nat'l Conservation Area
Fairfield
Craters of the Moon Nat'l Monument
Atomic City
Snake R.
Swan Valley
CARIBOU NAT'L FOREST
OREGON
Kuna
Mountain Home
Glenns Ferry
Blackfoot
Chesterfield
Murphy
Bruneau
Bliss
Aberdeen
Pocatello
Dunes State Park
Shoshone
Malad Gorge State Park
American Falls
Lava Hot Springs
Soda Springs
Silver City
Hagerman
Three Island Crossing State Park
Thousand Springs
Buhl
Twin Falls
Rupert
Burley
SAWTOOTH NAT'L FOREST
City of Rocks Nat'l Reserve
Malad City
Montpelier
Riddle
Almo
Preston
BEAR LAKE STATE PARK
Franklin
Bear Lake
BEAR LAKE NAT'L WILDLIFE REFUGE
NEVADA
UTAH
N
0
100 miles
0
150 km

strikingly lunar appearance, the **Craters of the Moon National Monument** (✉ Box 29, Arco 83213, ☎ 208/527–3257; 🎫 $4 per vehicle) covers 83 square mi, with spatter cones, lava caves, and other eerie volcanic-formed features. **Hagerman Fossil Beds National Monument** (✉ Box 570, Hagerman 83332, ☎ 208/837–4793) has yielded remains of tiny horses, early camels, and other prehistoric residents of the area. **Nez Percé National Historical Park** (✉ Hwy. 95 [Box 93, Spalding 83551], ☎ 208/843–2261; 🎫 $4 per vehicle) features detailed exhibits of the tribal culture and history. **City of Rocks National Reserve** (✉ Box 169, Almo 83312, ☎ 208/824–5519) is a popular rock-climbing spot and offers inspiring vistas for the less energetic.

State Parks

The **Idaho Department of Parks & Recreation** (✉ 5657 Warm Springs Ave. [Box 83720, Boise 83720], ☎ 208/334–4199 or 800/247–6332) maintains 24 state parks. **Heyburn State Park** (✉ 1291 Chatcolet Rd., Plummer 83851, ☎ 208/686–1308), at the southern tip of Lake Coeur d'Alene on Route 5, encompasses nearly 8,000 acres of land and water and is known for its migratory herons, eagles, and osprey as well as an annual fall harvest of wild rice. Rising 470 ft, North America's tallest single-structured sand dunes are the centerpiece of **Bruneau Dunes State Park** (✉ HC 85, Box 41, Mountain Home 83647, ☎ 208/366–7919; 🎫 $3), just a stone's throw from the Snake River and roughly 60 mi southeast of Boise on Route 78. Fly fishers and a third of the Rocky Mountain trumpeter swan population flock to Henry's Fork of the Snake River, which winds through **Harriman State Park** (✉ HC 66, Box 500, Island Park 83429, ☎ 208/558–7368; 🎫 $3), on U.S. 20, 33 mi southwest of West Yellowstone, Montana.

SOUTHERN IDAHO

Idaho's longest river, the Snake, carves a steely-blue course of nearly 1,000 mi through southern Idaho, linking a diverse mix of terrain. Vast stretches of fertile farmland give way to desert plateaus blanketed in jet-black lava. Sweeps of sand dunes anchor the southwestern and eastern portions of the state. In between, waterfalls and springs spill into deep, rugged canyons. Pine-and-sage-clad mountains along the upper fringe of the Snake River plain hint of the taller Northern Rockies that rise within the state's borders.

Exploring Southern Idaho

Boise

The name Boise, French for "wooded," is traced to French-Canadian trappers who found a tree-laced greenway on the Boise River, a sight for sore eyes after trekking across the area's semiarid plain. Boise and surrounding Ada County now form a modern center of government, business, and the arts.

Next to the Boise River, the grassy expanse of **Julia Davis Park** is home to two museums and **Zoo Boise** (✉ 355 N. Julia Davis Dr., ☎ 208/384–4260; 🎫 $4), where zebras and Amur tigers roam. An Old West saloon and relics from Idaho's early days as an Oregon Trail outpost fill the **Idaho State Historical Museum** (✉ 610 N. Julia Davis Dr., ☎ 208/334–2120, WEB www2.state.id.us.ishs/museum; 🎫 free). The **Boise Art Museum** (✉ 670 S. Julia Davis Dr., ☎ 208/345–8330, WEB www.boiseartmuseum.org; 🎫 $5) focuses on American realism and a lovely collection of ceramics, but visiting exhibits showcase a wide range of artists and media.

★ **Discovery Center of Idaho,** a hands-on science learning center, has more than 120 displays on the northern edge of Julia Davis Park. ✉ *131 W. Myrtle St.,* ☎ *208/343–9895,* WEB *www.scidaho.org.* 🎫 *$4. Closed Mon.*

Lady Bluebeard and Diamondfield Jack were among the felons who did time at the **Old Idaho Penitentiary** (✉ 2445 N. Penitentiary Rd., ☎ 208/368–6080; 🎫 $4). The jail was in operation from 1870 until 1973; today it welcomes visitors for shorter stays. You can tour a garden of Idaho native plants, a garden for children, a garden for butterflies and hummingbirds, and other theme plots within the penitentiary confines at the **Idaho Botanical Garden** (✉ 2355 N. Penitentiary Rd., ☎ 208/343–8649; 🎫 $3.50). At Christmastime, the gardens are festooned with colorful lights and open at night as "Gardens Aglow."

The **Morrison-Knudsen Nature Center** (✉ 600 S. Walnut Ave., ☎ 208/334–2225; 🎫 donations accepted) has walk-through ecosystem exhibits of wetlands, plains, high-desert terrain, and mountain streams where fish can be viewed from above and below the surface. Its visitor center is closed Monday.

Eight miles south of downtown Boise (take South Cole Road from I–84 Exit 50 and follow signs), the ★ **World Center for Birds of Prey** (✉ 5666 Flying Hawk La., ☎ 208/362–8687; 🎫 $4) has live falcons, eagles, condors, and other birds of prey. Guided tours leave from the visitor center; special float tours through the nearby Snake River Birds of Prey Conservation Area are offered in summer. The largest concentration of Basque people in the United States has called Idaho's Snake River plain home since the late 1800s. You can visit a restored 1864 former boardinghouse, then go next door to the **Basque Museum and Cultural Center** to see colorful costumes, relics, and exhibits on Basque culture. ✉ *611 Grove St.,* ☎ *208/343–2671,* WEB *www.basquemuseum.com.* 🎫 *Donations accepted. Closed Sun.–Mon.*

The Owyhee Uplands and the South-Central Region

South of Boise, from the Owyhee Mountains and arid Uplands east along the verdant Snake River canyon to Twin Falls, you'll find Oregon Trail wagon ruts, rocky gorges, hushed waterfalls, and springs trickling from canyon walls behind a veil of moss and ferns.South of Murphy a 25-mi dirt road off Route 78 leads to the onetime queen of Idaho's mining region, **Silver City** (☎ 208/495–2319), now a ghost town with 70 rustic buildings. **Three Island Crossing State Park** (✉ Rte. 78 off I–84 near Glenns Ferry, ☎ 208/366–2394; 🎫 $3) marks an important Oregon Trail wagon-train fording site on the Snake River. At **Malad Gorge State Park** (✉ off U.S. 30 north of Hagerman, ☎ 208/837–4505; 🎫 $2) a suspension footbridge spans a 250-ft chasm as a 60-ft waterfall gushes into the Devil's Washbowl below. Warmed by geothermal springs, the Hagerman Valley—a patchwork of melon fields, orchards, and trout farms off U.S. 30—is the gateway to the **Thousand Springs Scenic Byway,** where springs gush from the north canyon wall. Five miles north of the town of Twin Falls (take Falls Avenue east from U.S. 30 and head north on 3300 East Road), **Shoshone Falls** (☎ 208/733–3974 or 800/255–8946; 🎫 $3 per vehicle) cascade 21 ft–52 ft farther than Niagara Falls. They are most dramatic in spring.

Blackfoot, Bear Lake, and Lava Hot Springs

Billionaire J. R. Simplot made Idaho famous for its potatoes beginning in the 1940s. Today much of southeastern Idaho's fertile Snake River crescent, from Burley to Idaho Falls, is devoted to agriculture.

★ A must-see is the **Idaho Potato Exposition.** Exhibits explain potato production and display spud oddities from the world's largest potato chip to a spud signed by Dan Quayle. The gift shop sells potato cookbooks and fudge and hands out "free 'taters for out-of-staters." ✉ *130 N. Main St., Blackfoot,* ☎ *208/785–2517.* 🎫 *$3. Closed Nov.–Apr. and Sun.–Mon.*

Bear Lake State Park (☎ 208/847–1045; 🎫 $3), south of Montpelier off U.S. 89 at St. Charles, is known for its dip-net fishing. Light reflecting off limestone particles suspended in the 80,000-acre lake (roughly half of which is in Utah) give it a stunning turquoise color that has earned it the moniker Caribbean of the Rockies. **Bear Lake National Wildlife Refuge** (☎ 208/847–1757; 🎫 free), on the north shore of the lake, has one of the largest Canada geese populations in the western United States. The **National Oregon/California Trail Center** (☎ 800/448–2327, WEB www.oregontrailcenter.org), at the junction of U.S. 89 and 30 in Montpelier, depicts life on a wagon train and in frontier settlements. A continuous flow of warm spring water at the base of lava cliffs has spawned the charming resort community of **Lava Hot Springs** (☎ 208/776–5221), 21 mi west of Soda Springs on U.S. 30.

Yellowstone/Teton Territory

Sixty miles of interconnecting scenic byways yield breathtaking views of the back sides of the Grand Tetons and Yellowstone Park. The Mesa Falls Scenic Byway (Route 47) travels through a 23-mi-wide caldera (volcanic crater) before traversing the Idaho portions of the **Targhee National Forest** (☎ 208/624–3151), which shelters pristine Upper and Lower Mesa falls. The **Teton Scenic Byway** (Routes 32, 33, and 31 as the byway heads south from Ashton) passes through the small farming communities of Tetonia, Driggs, and Victor, all dwarfed by the Tetons to the east. In winter hundreds of inches of dry, powdery snow draw skiers to the resort of **Grand Targhee** (✉ Box SKI, Alta, WY 83422, ☎ 800/827–4433), over the state line near Driggs.

Dining and Lodging

Boise

$$–$$$ ★ ✕ **Mortimer's.** In downtown's historic, turreted Belgravia Building, this casually elegant spot veers close to perfection. From the complimentary savory appetizer to the creative desserts, food preparation and presentation are superb, and the service is as good as it gets. The menu changes weekly, but offerings include braised duck crepes with sweet-and-sour blackberry sauce and, for dessert, poached pear with frozen honey mousse. For $35 per person, a seven-course tasting menu skillfully transports your palate from start to finish. ✉ *110 S. 5th St.,* ☎ *208/338–6550. AE, MC, V. Closed Sun.–Mon. No lunch.*

$$ ✕ **Saffron.** This stylish place in the historic Basque Block downtown offers pan-Asian cuisine that ranges from hoisin lamb to curry. For spicy items, the chef will customize the heat to your comfort level. Standouts include spicy hummus and delectable crispy snapper with a Thai tomato Sambal sauce. Rich mahogany and gleaming chrome combine to pleasing affect, and unobtrusive live guitar music enhances the experience. ✉ *612 Grove St.,* ☎ *208/426–9990. AE, MC, V.*

$–$$ ✕ **Bardenay.** This spacious, wood-rich restaurant-bar on Boise's Basque Block makes its own gin, vodka, and rum. From sandwiches to salmon, Bardenay has well-prepared meals with creative touches and a variety of spirits to accompany them. The place is noisy and vibrant on weekday evenings. ✉ *610 Grove St.,* ☎ *208/426–0538. AE, MC, V.*

$–$$ ✕ **Berryhill and Co. Wine Bar–Cafe.** This tiny café tucked into the 8th Street Marketplace is thriving. The fare could be described as gourmet comfort food—chicken fricassee with potatoes and veggies under a delectable puff pastry crust, roasted butternut-squash ravioli, penne pasta baked with four cheeses. There's even an elegant take on a meatloaf sandwich, fashioned of ground pork and veal with raisins, walnuts, Chartreuse, and smoked Gouda. The list of by-the-glass wines is outstanding. ✉ *370 S. 8th St.,* ☎ *208/387–3553. AE, MC, V. Closed Sun. No dinner Mon.*

$–$$ ✕ **Table Rock Brew Pub & Grill.** This microbrewery across from Julia Davis Park makes some of the best beer in Idaho, and it has parlayed that skill into a happening restaurant with long, high tables, an energetic staff; and loud pop music. The menu has hearty portions of varied fare—from fiery Cajun dishes to British bangers and mashers. At least six varieties of beer are offered nightly, including the popular Nut Brown Ale. ✉ *705 Fulton St.,* ☎ *208/342–0944. AE, D, DC, MC, V.*

$–$$ ✕🏨 **Owyhee Plaza.** Giant light fixtures and rich oak paneling remain from 1910, when this three-story downtown hotel was built. The Gamekeeper restaurant specializes in flaming presentations. ✉ *1109 Main St., 83702,* ☎ *208/343–4611 or 800/233–4611,* FAX *208/381–0695,* WEB *www.owyheeplaza.com. 100 rooms. 2 restaurants, pool. AE, MC, V.*

$ 🏨 **Doubletree Hotel Riverside.** Nestled along the river, this hotel has airy public areas; spacious, well-equipped rooms; a spa and sauna; and complimentary fresh-baked chocolate chip cookies. ✉ *2900 Chinden Blvd., 83714,* ☎ *208/343–1871,* FAX *208/344–1079,* WEB *www.doubletree.com. 304 rooms. Restaurant, pool. AE, D, DC, MC, V.*

$ ★ 🏨 **Idaho Heritage Inn.** Each room has its own personality and politically themed name at this B&B in a former governor's residence, about a mile east of downtown. Antiques, wallpaper, and old-style bed frames capture an early 1900s mood. Breakfasts feature such fare as apple skillet cakes and French toast stuffed with apricot cream cheese. ✉ *109 W. Idaho St., 83702,* ☎ *208/342–8066,* FAX *208/343–2325,* WEB *www.idheritageinn.com. 6 rooms. AE, D, MC, V. BP.*

Idaho Falls

$ ✕ **Mama Inez.** Five homemade salsas head the menu at this friendly Mexican restaurant two blocks from the scenic Snake River Falls. Try the braised-pork burritos heaped with green-chili sauce. ✉ *344 Park Ave.,* ☎ *208/525–8968. MC, V. Closed Sun.*

$–$$ 🏨 **Best Western Driftwood.** Rooms in this two-story motel have refrigerators or kitchenettes, with coffeemakers. Picture windows gaze across the lawn to the falls of the Snake River, a short walk away. On the grounds are a rose garden and landscaped niches with benches and chairs. ✉ *575 River Pkwy., 83402,* ☎ *208/523–2242 or 800/528–1234,* WEB *www.bestwestern.com. 74 rooms. Pool. AE, D, DC, MC, V.*

Lava Hot Springs

$–$$ 🏨 **Lava Hot Springs Inn.** This grand old building began as a hospital and is now a B&B with an ample buffet breakfast. The interior is done in pinks and purples, and the rooms are neat and well appointed. Five suites have whirlpool tubs; a hot mineral pool, steps away from the back door, overlooks the Portneuf River. ✉ *94 E. Portneuf Ave. (Box 670, 83246),* ☎ *208/776–5830 or 800/527–5830,* WEB *www.lavahotspringsinn.com. 24 rooms. AE, D, MC, V. BP.*

Twin Falls

$–$$$ ✕ **Rock Creek.** There's a massive salad bar to accompany your steak, prime rib, or seafood—plus many wines, vintage ports, and single-malt whiskeys. The thick booths and dark-red interior go well with red meat. ✉ *200 Addison Ave. W,* ☎ *208/734–4154. AE, MC, V. No lunch.*

$ ★ ✕ **Buffalo Café.** Ask anybody in town where to go for breakfast, and you'll get the same answer: this tiny café. The house specialty is the Buffalo Chip, a plate-filling concoction of eggs, fried potatoes, cheese, bacon, peppers, and onion. ✉ *218 4th Ave. W,* ☎ *208/734–0271. MC, V. Closed Mon. No dinner.*

$ **Ameritel Inn–Twin Falls.** This motel has large rooms with dark wood furnishings. Some units have whirlpool tubs. Fresh-baked cookies are served in the evening, and a generous Continental breakfast helps start your day. ✉ *1377 Blue Lakes Blvd. N, 83301,* ☎ *208/736–8000 or 800/822–8946,* FAX *208/734–7777. 118 rooms. Pool, gym. AE, D, DC, MC, V. CP.*

Nightlife and the Arts

The **Idaho Shakespeare Festival** (✉ 5657 Warm Springs Ave., ☎ 208/336–9221) puts on first-rate performances in its open-air theater on Boise's eastern edge from June through September. The **Boise River Festival** (☎ 208/344–7777 or 800/635–5240), held the last Thursday through Sunday in June, includes more than 300 events, colorful hot-air balloons, a huge nighttime parade, and entertainment on six stages.

Outdoor Activities and Sports

Fishing

The **Silver Creek Preserve** (✉ Box 165, Sun Valley, ☎ 208/788–2203; admission free), northeast of Shoshone in south-central Idaho, offers catch-and-release fishing for rainbow, brown, and brook trout. In eastern Idaho, Henry's Fork of the Snake River and Henry's Lake in **Henry's Lake State Park** (☎ 208/558–7532) are renowned fly-fishing waters, with enormous rainbow and cutthroat trout. The **Targhee National Forest** (✉ 420 N. Bridge St., St. Anthony 83445, ☎ 208/624–3151) watershed is home to Big Springs, spawning grounds for rainbow trout, which can be viewed from a bridge. **Bear Lake,** in the southeast corner of the state, is the only place where fishing for sardinelike ciscoes with dip nets is allowed. Fishing licenses are required.

Ski Areas

DOWNHILL

Bogus Basin (✉ 2405 Bogus Basin Rd., Boise, ☎ 208/332–515 or 800/367–4397) has 53 runs, eight lifts, and a 1,800-ft drop. **Grand Targhee** (✉ Driggs, ☎ 208/443–8146 or 800/827–4433) has 63 runs, four lifts, and a 2,200-ft drop. **Kelly Canyon** (✉ Box 367, Idaho Falls, ☎ 208/538–7700) has 23 runs, four lifts, and a 1,000-ft drop.

Shopping

The **8th Street Marketplace** (✉ Capitol Blvd. and Front St., Boise), a brick warehouse converted into more than 30 stores, sits on the east side of 8th Street, catercorner from the convention center. Near the marketplace, **Capitol Terrace** (✉ Idaho and Main Sts., Boise) resembles a New Orleans French Quarter building, with a balcony level of shops. **Boise Factory Outlets** (✉ Gowen Rd. off I–84, Exit 57, ☎ 208/331–5500) stretches along the freeway in southeast Boise with outlets from London Fog to Corning Revere. Power shoppers find bliss at **Boise Towne Square Mall** (✉ Franklin Rd. exit off I–84, ☎ 208/378–4400), a sprawling indoor mall with 185 stores and a wide array of surrounding shopping plazas and restaurants.

Southern Idaho Essentials

AIRPORTS

Boise Airport, 3 mi from downtown, is served by America West, Delta, Horizon, Northwest, Sky West, Southwest, and United.

➤ AIRPORT INFORMATION: **Boise Airport** (✉ 3201 Airport Way, ☎ 208/383–3110).

BUS TRAVEL

Greyhound serves Boise, Twin Falls, Pocatello, and Idaho Falls. Sun Valley Express runs several daily round-trip van shuttles between Boise and Sun Valley.

➤ BUS INFORMATION: **Greyhound** (✉ 1212 W. Bannock St., Boise, ☎ 800/231–2222). **Sun Valley Express** (✉ Boise Municipal Airport, ☎ 800/634–6539).

CAR TRAVEL

Boise is reached by I–84 from the east and the west. Route 55 heads south.

TOURS

The Boise Tour Train provides a one-hour introduction to the city from May through October; tours depart from the depot across from the rose garden in Julia Davis Park.

➤ FEES AND SCHEDULES: **Boise Tour Train** (✉ Capitol Blvd., ☎ 208/342–4796; $6.50).

VISITOR INFORMATION

➤ TOURIST INFORMATION: **South Central Idaho Travel Committee** (✉ 858 Blue Lakes Blvd., Twin Falls 83301, ☎ 208/733–3974 or 800/255–8946, WEB www.rideidaho.com). **Southeastern Idaho Travel Association** (✉ Box 498, Lava Hot Springs 83246, ☎ 208/776–5273 or 800/423–8597, WEB www.seidaho.org). **Southwest Idaho Travel Association** (✉ 312 S. 9th St., Suite 100 [Box 2106, Boise 83702], ☎ 208/344–7777 or 800/635–5240). **Yellowstone/Teton Territory Travel Association** (✉ 505 Lindsay Blvd., Idaho Falls 83402, ☎ 208/523–1010 or 800/634–3246).

CENTRAL IDAHO

Idaho's midsection is a dense, rugged wilderness terrain so impenetrable that even cartographers are hard-pressed to sketch roadways across the northern part of this region. A teeming waterway system fed by the **Snake** and **Salmon rivers** spins a lacy web across the bumpy landscape and has been the favored mode of transportation since the days of Lewis and Clark. The 420-mi Salmon is the longest undammed river in the lower 48 states.

Exploring Central Idaho

Sun Valley–Ketchum

At the point where alpine and desert climes converge, the legendary **Sun Valley** resort opened in 1935. Its signature pedestrian mall is patterned after an Austrian village. **Ketchum,** a mile away, is an old mining town with an array of shops and restaurants. Outside Ketchum, beside Trail Creek, the **Ernest Hemingway Memorial** commemorates the writer's last years there. He is buried in the town cemetery.

McCall

The 108-mi drive north from Boise on Route 55 to the resort town of McCall runs along the shore of the Payette River as it rushes over boulders and through forests. The arid plains give way to higher and higher mountains covered by tremendous stands of pines. McCall lies at the southern end of lovely **Payette Lake.**

Hells Canyon and Lewiston-Clarkston

The ragged Seven Devils Range stands at 9,000 ft, rimming the southeastern lip of the Snake River Canyon, a deep, dark basalt abyss within the **Hells Canyon National Recreation Area** (✉ 2535 Riverside Dr., Clarkston, WA 99403, ☎ 509/758–0616 or 800/523–1235), the deepest river gorge in the nation. Route 71 traces a portion of the gorge, but the best way to take in the scenery is by jet boat or raft. North of Hells Canyon, Lewiston and its sister city, Clarkston, Oregon, owe their lifeblood to the confluence of the Clearwater and Snake rivers. Ships ply the waters 470 mi from the ocean via the Columbia River to Lewiston's inland seaport. Lovely Route 12, among the few east–west motor routes in this part of the state, travels from Lewiston to **Lolo Pass** on the Montana border, following the route that Sacagawea, Lewis and Clark's Native American guide, traced through the rugged wilderness. The **Nez Percé National Historical Park** displays Nez Percé artifacts and outlines the history and culture of the Native American nation and its famous leader, Chief Joseph.

Dining and Lodging

McCall

$–$$$$ ✕ **The Mill Supper Club.** This antiques-laden place with heavy wooden beams is entering its fourth decade as a local institution. The Mill is a carnivore's dream, dishing out huge portions of steak and prime rib, with seafood options for those who want to go against the flow. The place even has two signature cocktails, the Tall Tamarack and the Green Spruce. ✉ *324 N. 3rd St., 83638,* ☎ *208/634–7683. AE, D, MC, V.*

$–$$$ 🏨 **Hotel McCall.** This hybrid between a hotel and a B&B is in the center of town. Rooms (and prices) vary widely; six are small and share a bath, while others are almost grand and have lots of light and antique furnishings. Some have views of Payette Lake. ✉ *1101 N. 3rd St. (Box 1778, 83638),* ☎ *208/634–8105,* FAX *208/634–8755. 22 rooms. AE, MC, V. CP.*

Sun Valley–Ketchum

$$–$$$ ✕ **Michel's Christiania.** Among the highlights at this Sun Valley classic are roast lamb in a parsley crust, sautéed ruby Idaho trout with hazelnuts and cream, and similarly elegant treatments of elk, duckling, and fresh seafood. The atmosphere blends white-linen elegance with rustic timbers and gigantic wrought-iron chandeliers. ✉ *Sun Valley Rd. and Walnut St., Ketchum,* ☎ *208/726–3388. AE, D, MC, V.*

$–$$ ✕ **Desperado's.** Huge fish burritos and four kinds of salsa headline the menu at this popular Mexican restaurant in the heart of Ketchum. ✉ *4th St. and Washington Ave.,* ☎ *208/726–3068. AE, D, MC, V.*

$$$–$$$$ ✕🏨 **Knob Hill Inn.** Rooms at this modern luxury hotel with an alpine motif have large tubs, wet bars, and balconies with mountain views. Intermediate rooms, suites, and penthouses have fireplaces. ✉ *960 N. Main St. (Box 800, Ketchum 83340),* ☎ *208/726–8010 or 800/526–8010,* FAX *208/726–2712,* WEB *www.knobhillinn.com. 24 rooms. 2 restaurants, pool, gym. AE, MC, V. BP.*

$$–$$$$ ✕🏨 **Sun Valley Resort.** The area's biggest resort includes a family-oriented inn, lodge-style accommodations, and condominiums. Within the lodge complex, the Lodge Dining Room is the area's signature restaurant, known for its Sunday brunch. The resort is surrounded by towering pines; some rooms on the back side overlook the property's ice-skating rink and the ski-run carved face of ski mecca Baldy Mountain, 1 mi away. ✉ *Sun Valley Resort, Sun Valley 83353,* ☎ *208/622–4111 or 800/786–8259; 208/622–2150 for dining room,* FAX *208/622–3700,* WEB *www.sunvalley.com. 260 rooms, 280 condos. 5 restaurants, 3 pools, 18 tennis courts. AE, D, DC, MC, V.*

$ 🏨 **Lift Tower Lodge.** Look for the lift tower and chair (Western-style lawn art) in front of this basic motel. Half of the rooms face the ski mountain; the rest front Route 75, Ketchum's heavily traveled main drag. Ski lifts and restaurants are about three blocks away. ✉ *703 S. Main St. (Box 185, Ketchum 83340),* ☎ *208/726–5163 or 800/462–8646,* FAX *208/726–2614. 14 rooms. AE, D, DC, MC, V.*

Wilderness Camps and Lodges

$$$–$$$$ ✕🏨 **The Lodge at Riggins Hot Springs.** About 10 mi north of Riggins, this massive wood A-frame is nestled among pine trees overlooking the banks of the Salmon River. Rafting, jet boating, and fishing trips can be arranged, and the huge outdoor pool is fed by hot springs. Meals are outstanding. ✉ *9 mi up Big Salmon River Rd., off Hwy. 95,* ☎ *208/628–3785,* WEB *www.rhslodge.com. 10 rooms. Pool. MC, V. FAP.*

$$$$ 🏨 **Twin Peaks Ranch.** One of America's first dude ranches is nestled in a mile-high valley between the Salmon River and the Frank Church–River of No Return Wilderness Area. The 2,900-acre property, 2 mi off U.S. 93, contains cabins, the original 1923 ranch house, and an apple orchard. Experienced wranglers teach horsemanship in the full-size rodeo arena; guided day rides and overnight pack trips are also available. Stocked trout ponds attract anglers, and guided fishing and white-water rafting trips can be arranged. ✉ *Box 774, Salmon 83467,* ☎ *208/894–2290 or 800/659–4899,* FAX *208/894–2429,* WEB *www.twinpeaksranch.com. 13 cabins. Pool. MC, V. Closed Jan.–Apr. FAP.*

$$–$$$ 🏨 **Idaho Rocky Mountain Ranch.** The ranch's 8,000-square-ft lodgepole-pine lodge remains much the same as when it was constructed in the 1930s. Period photographs hang on the walls, and animal trophies, rustic artifacts, and a massive rock fireplace immediately catch the eye. Lodge rooms and most of the duplex cabins have Oakley stone showers and handcrafted log furniture. Activities on the ranch's 1,000 acres range from hot-springs swimming to volleyball to horseback riding. ✉ *HC 64, off Rte. 75 (Box 9934, Stanley 83278),* ☎ *208/774–3544,* FAX *208/774–3477,* WEB *www.idahorocky.com. 2 lodge rooms, 8 cabins. Pool. D, MC, V. Closed May and Oct. FAP.*

Outdoor Activities and Sports

Fishing

Steelhead fishing is a major attraction in the **Frank Church–River of No Return Wilderness Area.** The 20-pound fish swim 1,800 mi to the ocean and back again to spawn in the Salmon River.

Hiking and Backpacking

Extensive trail systems run through the **Selway Bitterroot** and **Frank Church–River of No Return** wilderness areas. In the **Sawtooth National Recreation Area** (✉ Star Rte., Ketchum 83340, ☎ 208/727–5013 or 800/260–5970; 🎫 $5 per vehicle), the jagged Sawtooth Mountains (often called America's Alps, with 42 peaks reaching at least 10,000 ft) join the Boulder and White Cloud ranges to stretch across 1,180 square mi, beginning north of Ketchum on Route 75. In winter, yurts (tents made of skins) in the Boulder, Smoky, and Sawtooth mountains are accessible for day ski trips or backcountry multiday trips.

Rafting

Salmon and Stanley are launching points for trips on the **Salmon River,** including the famous **Middle Fork,** which runs 100 mi with 100 rapids. Reserve well ahead for summer. Riggins and White Bird are the take-off points for trips down the northern portion of the Salmon and **Snake** rivers. The **Selway** and **Clearwater** rivers are other prime rafting waterways.

Ski Areas

Cross-Country

The central Idaho mountain valleys and backcountry are ideal for Nordic skiing. The **Wood River Trails** (✉ Blaine County Recreation District, 308 N. Main St., Hailey, ☎ 208/788–2117) system in the Ketchum–Sun Valley area grooms nearly 20 mi of trails. The **Sun Valley Nordic Center** (✉ Box 10, Sun Valley, ☎ 208/622–2251 or 800/786–8259) includes almost 25 mi of groomed trails spread across the Sun Valley Golf Course, north of the Sun Valley Resort.

Downhill

Brundage (✉ Box 1062, McCall, ☎ 208/634–4151 or 800/888–7544) has 38 runs, five lifts, and a 1,800-ft drop. **Sun Valley** (✉ Sun Valley 83353, ☎ 800/635–8261 or 800/786–8259) has 78 runs, 19 lifts, and a 3,400-ft drop. **Soldier Mountain** (✉ Box 465, Fairfield, ☎ 208/764–2526) has 35 runs, two lifts, and a 1,400-ft drop.

Central Idaho Essentials

CAR TRAVEL

From Montana, take U.S. 93. From Oregon, take U.S. 12 to U.S. 95. From Boise, take I–84 to U.S. 20/26.

VISITOR INFORMATION

For information on Hells Canyon and the Lewiston-Clarkston area, contact the North Central Idaho Travel Association. For information on the Sawtooth Mountains, visit the Stanley/Sawtooth Chamber of Commerce in Stanley.

➤ TOURIST INFORMATION: **McCall Chamber of Commerce** (✉ Box D, McCall 83638, ☎ 208/634–7631, WEB www.mccall-idchamber.org). **North Central Idaho Travel Association** (✉ 2207 E. Main St., Suite G, Lewiston 83501, ☎ 208/743–3531 or 800/473–3543, WEB www.idahonwp.org). **Stanley/Sawtooth Chamber of Commerce** (✉ Hwy. 75 [Box 8, Stanley 83278], ☎ 208/774–3411 or 800/878–7950, WEB www.stanleycc.org). **Sun Valley/Ketchum Chamber of Commerce** (✉ Box 2420, Sun Valley 83353, ☎ 208/726–3423 or 800/634–3347, WEB www.visitsunvalley.com).

NORTHERN IDAHO

Water reigns supreme in wooded northern Idaho, which claims more than 140 lakes (the highest concentration in the western United States) and 2,000 mi of streams and rivers. Six major lakes, including **Coeur d'Alene** and the state's largest, **Pend Oreille,** dominate the Panhandle.

Exploring Northern Idaho

Coeur d'Alene and the Silver Valley

Nestled in a pine-green mantle beside a gem of a lake, **Coeur d'Alene** has perhaps the most idyllic setting of any Idaho town. Restaurants with waterfront dining, a 3,300-ft floating boardwalk, and resort hotels cluster along the water's edge. American bald eagles and the largest population of osprey in the western United States make their homes here; the watery playground attracts sailors and water-skiers as well. There are more than 29 golf courses within an hour's drive of Coeur d'Alene; sightseeing cruises pass by the floating 14th hole of the golf course at the Coeur d'Alene Resort. **Plaza Shops at the Coeur d'Alene** (☒ 210 Sherman Ave., at 2nd St., Coeur d'Alene) is an enclosed minimall with 22 small shops, many with a Northwest emphasis.

About 14 mi north of Coeur d'Alene, **Silverwood Amusement Park** (☒ U.S. 95, ☎ 208/683–3400; 🎟 $22) features a perfectly reconstructed turn-of-the-20th-century mining town. Rides range from a vintage biplane to an eight-story roller coaster called Tremors.

Silver Valley, the world's largest silver-mining district, is centered in the towns of Kellogg and Wallace along I–90. The entire town of **Wallace** is listed on the National Register of Historic Places. Throughout July and August, the **Sixth Street Melodrama** (☎ 208/556–1592; 🎟 $8) recalls Wallace's colorful past. The **Wallace District Mining Museum** (509 Banks St., ☎ 208/753–7151; 🎟 $1.50) contains a mother lode of mining history. From May to mid-October, the Sierra Silver Mine Tour (420 5th St., ☎ 208/752–5151; 🎟 $8) provides a peek into an old mine.

The Northern Lakes

The resort town of **Sandpoint,** on the northwestern shores of Lake Pend Oreille, is completely surrounded by mountains; it has been a railroad depot and a mining town but now survives on tourism and lumber. At the southern end of Lake Pend Oreille, 4,000-acre **Farragut State Park** (Rte. 54, 4 mi east of Athol, ☎ 208/683–2425; 🎟 $3) supports a diverse wildlife population and has camping. Its roads close in winter, but there are cross-country ski trails.Route 57 provides access to remote **Priest Lake,** with 70 mi of densely wooded shoreline, and the **Upper Priest Lake Scenic Area,** just a jump from the Canadian border. The **Grove of Ancient Cedars,** on the west side of Priest Lake, is a virgin forest with trees up to 12 ft across and 150 ft high.

Dining and Lodging

Coeur d'Alene

$$–$$$ ✕ **Cedars Floating Restaurant.** This restaurant is actually *on* the lake, giving it wonderful views. Beer-marinated charbroiled steak is a specialty. *☒ U.S. 95, ¼ mi south of I–90, ☎ 208/664–2922. AE, DC, MC, V. No lunch.*

$ ✕ **Hudson's Hamburgers.** These folks have been in business since 1907 with a six-item menu of tasty, inexpensive eats until 6 PM nightly. Even rivals admit that Hudson's serves the town's favorite burgers. *☒ 207 Sherman Ave., ☎ 208/664–5444. No credit cards. Closed Sun.*

$$–$$$$ ✕🏨 **Coeur d'Alene Resort.** The plush rooms at this lakeside high-rise resort have either fireplaces or balconies with terrific views of the water. The lower-priced rooms are standard motel fare. Its top-of-the-line restaurant, Beverly's, is known for its fine Northwest cuisine, superb wine cellar, and incomparable views. *☒ 2nd and Front Sts., 83814, ☎ 208/765–4000 or 800/688–5253,* FAX *208/667–2707,* WEB *www.cdaresort.com. 336 rooms. 4 restaurants, pool, golf, gym. AE, D, DC, MC, V.*

$$ 🏨 **Berry Patch Inn Bed and Breakfast.** On landscaped grounds atop a hill west of Lake Coeur d'Alene, this 4,500-square-ft cedar chalet has wonderful views of Mt. Spokane and the Cabinet Mountains to the north. Paths through an adjacent forest are perfect for summer strolls. Inside, the spacious living room has a large stone fireplace and a TV, VCR, and stereo. Decor throughout is country elegant. Breakfasts include an abundance of fresh fruit and such entrées as stuffed griddle cakes topped with huckleberries. ✉ *1150 N. Four Winds Rd., 83814,* ☎ *208/775–4994,* FAX *800/667–7336,* WEB *www.bbhost.com/berrypatchinn. 3 rooms. MC, V. BP.*

Priest Lake

$–$$$$ ✕🏨 **Hill's Resort.** Cabins and condos all have kitchen areas, and many have fireplaces. The acclaimed restaurant, open daily in summer and on weekends throughout the year, features cream of morel soup, barbecued baby-back ribs, margarita shrimp, and huckleberry pie. Nearby are hiking trails, a golf course, tennis courts, and a boat launch. In winter, snowmobiling and cross-country skiing are popular pursuits. ✉ *HCR 5, Box 162A, 83856,* ☎ *208/443–2551,* FAX *208/443–2363,* WEB *www.hillsresort.com. 52 units. Restaurant. D, MC, V.*

Outdoor Activities and Sports

Fishing

Lake Pend Oreille is famous for kamloops (large rainbow trout), Priest Lake for mackinaw, and Lake Coeur d'Alene for cutthroat trout and chinook salmon. The St. Joe and Coeur d'Alene rivers are good for stream angling.

Ski Areas

DOWNHILL

Schweitzer Mountain (✉ 10,000 Schweitzer Mountain Rd., Sandpoint, ☎ 208/263–9555 or 800/831–8810) has 55 runs, six lifts, and a 2,400-ft vertical drop. **Silver Mountain** (✉ 610 Bunker Ave., Kellogg, ☎ 208/783–1111 or 800/204–6428) has 51 runs, a gondola, five lifts, and a 2,200-ft drop.

Northern Idaho Essentials

AIRPORTS

The nearest airport is Spokane International, 20 mi from Coeur d'Alene in eastern Washington. Alaska, Delta, Northwest, Southwest, and United fly into Spokane.

➤ AIRPORT INFORMATION: **Spokane International Airport** (☎ 509/455–6455).

BUS TRAVEL

➤ BUS INFORMATION: **Greyhound** (✉ 1923½ N. 4th St., Coeur d'Alene, ☎ 208/667–3343 or 800/231–2222).

CAR TRAVEL

The major highways serving northern Idaho are I–90 (east–west) and U.S. 95 (north–south).

TRAIN TRAVEL

Amtrak's *Empire Builder* stops at the Sandpoint Amtrak Depot, bound for Seattle or Chicago. Sandpoint is about 40 mi north of Coeur d'Alene.

➤ Train Information: *Empire Builder* (✉ 409 Railroad Ave., Sandpoint, ☏ 800/872–7245).

VISITOR INFORMATION

For information on Silver Valley, contact the Wallace Chamber of Commerce.

➤ Tourist Information: **Coeur d'Alene Chamber of Commerce** (✉ 1621 N. 3rd St., Suite 100, 83814, ☏ 208/664–3194 or 877/782–9232, WEB www.coeurdalene.org). **North Idaho Tourism Alliance** (✉ Box 877, Coeur d'Alene 83814, ☏ 208/664–3194 or 888/333–3737, WEB www.visitnorthidaho.com). **Wallace Chamber of Commerce** (✉ 10 River St., Wallace 83873, ☏ 208/753–7151, WEB www.historic-wallace.org).

ILLINOIS

Updated by Joanne Cleaver

Capital	Springfield
Population	12,419,293
Motto	State Sovereignty—National Union
State Bird	Cardinal
State Flower	Purple violet
Postal Abbreviation	IL

Statewide Visitor Information

Illinois Bureau of Tourism (✉ James R. Thompson Center, 100 W. Randolph St., Suite 3-400, Chicago 60601, ☎ 800/226-6632, WEB www.enjoyillinois.com).

Scenic Drives

The Illinois part of the **Lake Michigan Circle Tour** follows the shoreline along Lake Shore Drive through Chicago and passes through the elegant suburbs of the North Shore: Evanston, Wilmette, Kenilworth, Winnetka, Glencoe, Highland Park, and Lake Forest. **Great River Road** follows the Mississippi River, stretching the length of Illinois (more than 500 mi) from East Dubuque to Cairo (pronounced *kay*-ro).

National and State Parks

National Park

Shawnee National Forest (✉ 50 Hwy. 145 S, Harrisburg 62946, ☎ 618/253–7114 or 800/699–6637, WEB www.fs.fed.us) blankets the southern tip of Illinois with 275,000 acres.

State Parks

Illinois has more than 260 state parks, conservation areas, fish and wildlife areas, and recreation areas. For a magazine on state parks, including descriptions of state-owned resorts and lodges, contact the **Illinois Department of Natural Resources** (✉ 524 S. 2nd St., Springfield 62701-1787, ☎ 217/782–7454, WEB dnr.state.il.us). **Illinois Beach State Park** (✉ Lake Front, Zion 60099, ☎ 847/662–4828, WEB www.ilresorts.com), on Lake Michigan near the Wisconsin border, has sandy beaches along 6½ mi of shoreline. **Rend Lake/Wayne Fitzgerald State Park** (✉ 11094 Ranger Rd., Whittington 62897, ☎ 618/629–2320, WEB dnr.state.il.us) has the state's second-largest inland lake, where you can fish, sail, and swim. **Starved Rock State Park** (✉ Box 509, Utica 61373, ☎ 815/667–4726, WEB dnr.state.il.us), on the Illinois River between LaSalle and Ottawa, has 18 canyons formed during the melting of the glaciers. The park is about a two-hour drive from downtown Chicago.

CHICAGO

From the elegance of Michigan Avenue's shops to the stunning sweep of the lakefront skyline, Chicago has much to offer. The Loop, the city's central business district, is a living museum of 19th- and 20th-century architecture, and many outlying neighborhoods retain the grace and homey qualities of pre–World War II America. Chicago's arts community is world class, and lively ethnic communities embrace immigrants from countries as disparate as Croatia and Cambodia, all of whom leave their cultural stamp on the region.

Exploring Chicago

The Loop and Magnificent Mile epitomize the city's practical, savvy style. The patchwork of ethnic neighborhoods composing the rest of the city reflects the waves of immigrants who contribute to Chicago's cultural wealth.

The Loop

Walking through Chicago's central business district (defined by and named for the loop of the elevated train that circles it) is like taking a course in the history of American commercial architecture. From the Monadnock Building, the tallest load-bearing masonry structure in the world, to the Sears Tower, technically the tallest building of any kind in North America, Chicago's skyscrapers have unique personalities. Adorning the plazas of many buildings are sculptures by Picasso, Calder, Miró, and other artists.

The **Chicago Cultural Center** (☒ 78 E. Washington St., at Michigan Ave., ☎ 312/346–3278, WEB www.ci.chi.il.us/tourism/culturalcenter; free) used to be the city's main library; now it's used primarily for free art and history exhibits, lectures, and performances. Two splendid, back-lit interior Tiffany-glass domes are among its treasures.

The terra-cotta **Reliance Building** (☒ 32 N. State St., at Washington St.), designed by John Root and Charles Atwood in 1894, has the distinctive Chicago window, an innovation in early skyscrapers: two small panes of glass, which open to catch the Lake Michigan breezes, flanking a large center panel. The **Richard J. Daley Center** (☒ Dearborn and Washington Sts.), named for the late mayor, father of the current mayor Richard Daley, is headquarters for the Cook County court system; in the plaza is a 52-ft Cor-Ten steel sculpture by Picasso.

Spacious halls, high ceilings, and plenty of marble define the handsome neoclassical **Chicago City Hall** (☒ 121 N. La Salle St.). Replete with neoclassical detail and bustling with local political honchos, the **Cook County Building** (☒ 118 N. Clark St.) was designed by the influential turn-of-the-20th-century architectural firm Holabird & Roche in 1911. If you're lucky, you may catch the city council in session—usually a good show, with plenty of hot air. Helmut Jahn's 1985 **James R. Thompson Center** (☒ Clark and Randolph Sts.), which houses state offices, has a jarring futuristic design in striking contrast to the city's classically styled civic structures.

A softly curving building emphasizing the bend in the Chicago River, **333 West Wacker Drive** was constructed in an irregular shape dictated by the triangular parcel on which it sits. The building, designed by Kohn Pedersen Fox in 1983 and set in a spacious plaza, has forest-green marble columns and a shimmering green-glass skin resembling the color of the river.

The graceful 1969 **First National Bank** (☒ Dearborn and Madison Sts.) was one of the first skyscrapers to slope upward from its base like the capital letter *A*. The adjoining plaza is a summer lunchtime hangout. A Chagall mosaic, *The Four Seasons,* is at the northeast corner.

Chicago has some handsome examples of very early skyscrapers. The 1894 **Marquette Building** (☒ 140 S. Dearborn St.), by Holabird & Roche, has an exterior terra-cotta bas-relief and interior reliefs and mosaics depicting scenes from early Chicago history. The darkly handsome **Monadnock Building** (☒ 53 W. Jackson Blvd., at Dearborn St.) has walls 6 ft thick at the base. Groundbreaking architects Burnham & Root and Holabird & Roche worked out their structural engineering concepts on the building, erecting the north half of the building by 1891 and the south half in 1893.

The Gothic-style **Fisher Building** (✉ 343 S. Dearborn St.), designed by D. H. Burnham & Co. in 1895, is exquisitely ornamented with carved terra-cotta cherubs and fish. The **Chicago Board of Trade** (✉ 141 W. Jackson Blvd., at La Salle St.), a 1930 design by Holabird & Root, is one of the few important art deco buildings in Chicago. At the top is a gilded statue of Ceres, the Roman goddess of agriculture—an apt overseer of the frenetic commodities trading within.

★ The **Sears Tower** (✉ 233 S. Wacker Dr., at Jackson Blvd., ☎ 312/875–9696, WEB www.sears-tower.com; 🎫 $9.50) has 110 stories and reaches to 1,454 ft. A Skidmore, Owings & Merrill design of 1974, the tower affords unbeatable views from the sky deck, but there are long lines on weekends. The Wacker Drive lobby has a jolly mobile by Alexander Calder. The imposing red-stone **Rookery Building** (✉ 209 S. La Salle St., ☎ 312/553–6150), east of the Sears Tower, was designed in 1888 by Burnham & Root; Frank Lloyd Wright remodeled the magnificent lobby in 1905.

The Chicago Symphony Orchestra performs in Orchestra Hall, part of **Symphony Center** (✉ 220 S. Michigan Ave.), known for its excellent acoustics and elegant 1904 design.

★ 👋 The **Museum of the Art Institute of Chicago** (✉ 111 S. Michigan Ave., ☎ 312/443–3600, WEB www.artic.edu; 🎫 $8), across the street from the Symphony Center, is one of the finest art museums in the world. In addition to its renowned collections of Impressionist and Postimpressionist paintings and medieval and Renaissance works, the museum contains the Thorne Miniature Rooms, faithfully crafted interiors that reflect every historical genre of decoration and furniture; a renowned collection of Chinese, Japanese, and Korean art spanning five millennia; and a meticulous reconstruction of the trading room of the old Chicago Stock Exchange. The Kraft Education Center educates kids on artistic traditions and has an ever-changing gallery of original illustrations from well-known children's books. Reserve tickets for special museum exhibits as early as you can; only a few same-day tickets are available, and the line is usually long.

Largely unchanged since 1898, the **Fine Arts Building** (✉ 410 S. Michigan Ave.) contains movie theaters showing foreign and art films. The handsome detailing on the exterior previews the marble and woodwork in the lobby. Around the corner from the Fine Arts Building, the 4,000-seat **Auditorium Theatre** (✉ 50 E. Congress Pkwy., ☎ 312/922–2110, WEB www.auditoriumtheatre.org), built in 1889 by Adler and Sullivan, has unobstructed sight lines and near-perfect acoustics. From May to September the mammoth Buckingham Fountain bubbles and gushes in **Grant Park,** two blocks east of the Auditorium Theatre. It's worth a detour to see the profusion of nymphs, cherubs, and fish.

The **Harold Washington Library Center** (✉ 400 S. State St., ☎ 312/747–4999, WEB www.chipublib.org), a postmodern homage to classical-style public buildings, was completed in 1991. Said to be the largest municipal library in the nation, it includes a performing arts auditorium, rooftop winter garden, and nearly 71 mi of shelves.

The museum campus north of Soldier Field and east of Lake Shore Drive contains three venues, with free trolleys running among the sites. At 👋 the **John G. Shedd Aquarium** (✉ 1200 S. Lake Shore Dr., ☎ 312/939–2438, WEB www.sheddnet.org; 🎫 $15) the dazzling oceanarium is the

Chicago

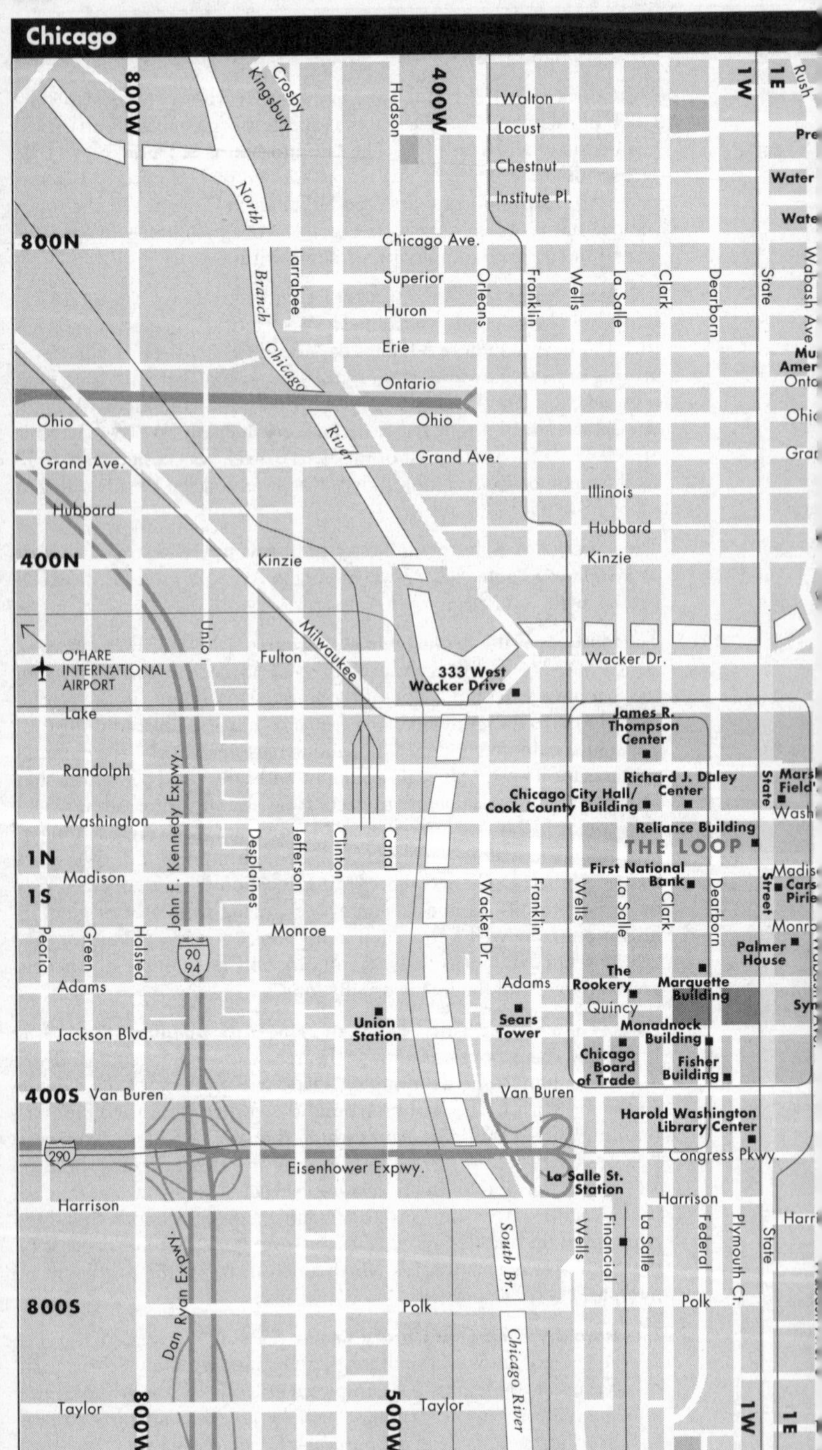

800W
400W
1W
1E
500W
800N
400N
1N
1S
400S
800S
Crosby
Kingsbury
Hudson
Walton
Locust
Chestnut
Institute Pl.
North
Branch
Chicago
River
Larrabee
Chicago Ave.
Superior
Huron
Erie
Ontario
Ohio
Grand Ave.
Orleans
Franklin
Wells
La Salle
Clark
Dearborn
State
Wabash Ave.
Rush
Illinois
Hubbard
Kinzie
Milwaukee
Fulton
O'HARE INTERNATIONAL AIRPORT
Wacker Dr.
333 West Wacker Drive
Lake
Randolph
Washington
Madison
Monroe
Adams
Jackson Blvd.
Van Buren
Harrison
Polk
Taylor
James R. Thompson Center
Richard J. Daley Center
Chicago City Hall/ Cook County Building
Reliance Building
THE LOOP
First National Bank
State Street
The Rookery
Quincy
Marquette Building
Palmer House
Monadnock Building
Chicago Board of Trade
Fisher Building
Union Station
Sears Tower
John F. Kennedy Expwy.
Desplaines
Jefferson
Clinton
Canal
Peoria
Green
Halsted
90
94
290
Eisenhower Expwy.
Harold Washington Library Center
Congress Pkwy.
La Salle St. Station
Financial
Federal
Plymouth Ct.
South Br.
Chicago River
Dan Ryan Expwy.

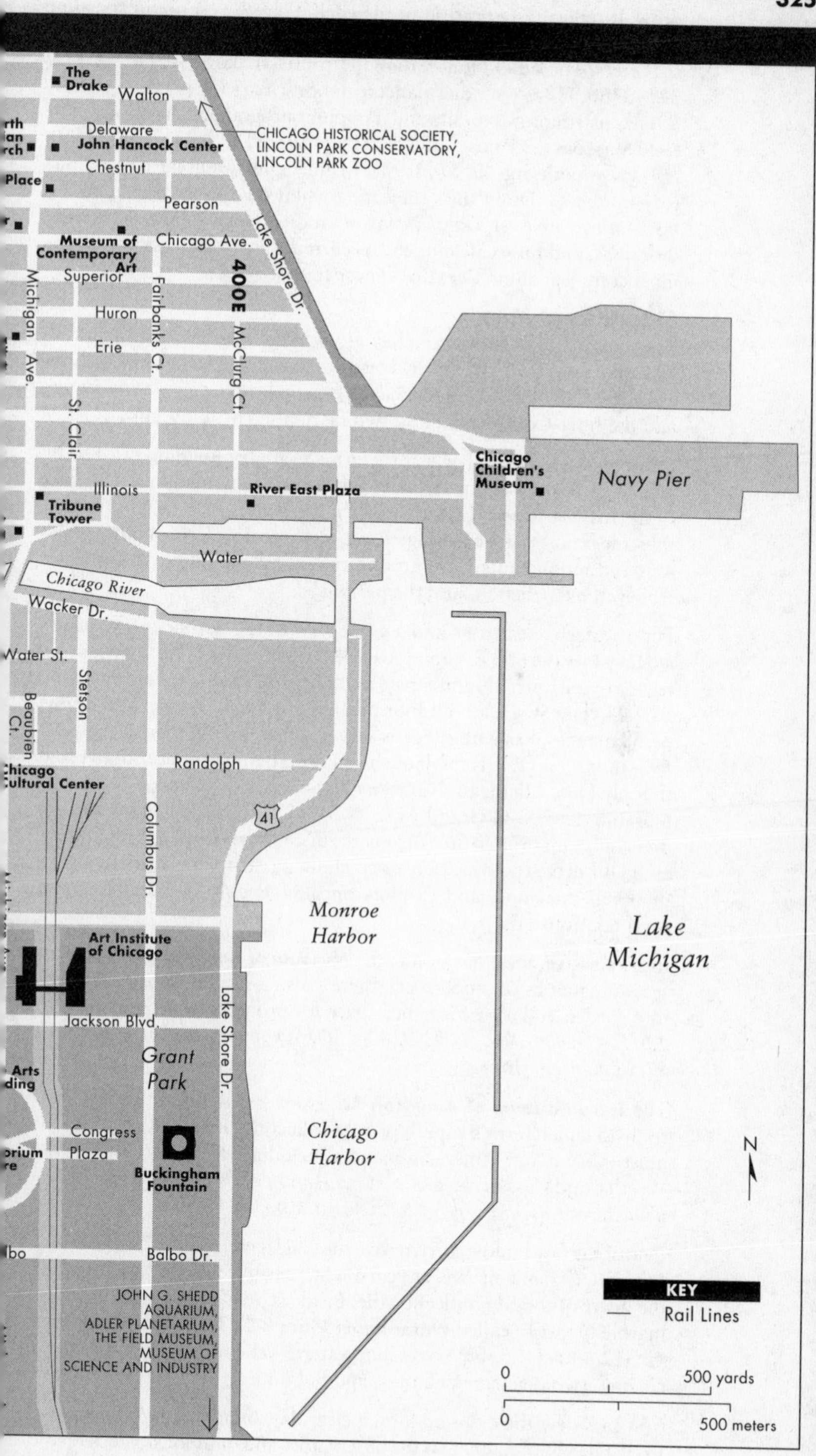
The Drake
Walton
Delaware
John Hancock Center
CHICAGO HISTORICAL SOCIETY, LINCOLN PARK CONSERVATORY, LINCOLN PARK ZOO
Chestnut
Pearson
Museum of Contemporary Art
Chicago Ave.
Lake Shore Dr.
Superior
400E
Huron
Erie
Michigan Ave.
Fairbanks Ct.
McClurg Ct.
St. Clair
Chicago Children's Museum
Navy Pier
Illinois
River East Plaza
Tribune Tower
Water
Chicago River
Wacker Dr.
Water St.
Stetson
Beaubien Ct.
Randolph
Chicago Cultural Center
41
Columbus Dr.
Monroe Harbor
Lake Michigan
Art Institute of Chicago
Jackson Blvd.
Grant Park
Lake Shore Dr.
Chicago Harbor
Congress Plaza
Buckingham Fountain
N
Balbo Dr.
JOHN G. SHEDD AQUARIUM, ADLER PLANETARIUM, THE FIELD MUSEUM, MUSEUM OF SCIENCE AND INDUSTRY
KEY
Rail Lines
0
500 yards
0
500 meters

draw. It replicates a portion of the Pacific Northwest ocean coastline complete with beluga whales, Pacific dolphins, and a lively family of sea otters. The **Adler Planetarium** (⊠ 1300 S. Lake Shore Dr., ☎ 312/322–0300, WEB www.adlerplanetarium.org; $5 general, sky show $3) has astronomy exhibits and a popular program of sky shows. The ★ **Field Museum** (⊠ Roosevelt Rd. at Lake Shore Dr., ☎ 312/922–9410, WEB www.fmnh.org; $8) is one of the country's great natural history museums. Don't miss the eerie exhibit on ancient Egypt, or the fascinating Life over Time display, with its extensive dinosaur fossils, dioramas, and full-scale models. Its current showstopper is "Sue," the most complete adult T-rex fossil ever found.

Magnificent Mile

The Magnificent Mile stretches along Michigan Avenue from the Chicago River to Oak Street. Here you'll find such high-price shops as Gucci, Tiffany & Co., and Chanel; venerable hotels such as the Drake and the Inter-Continental; and two fascinating art museums.

Fronting the Chicago River is the ornate **Wrigley Building** (⊠ 410 N. Michigan Ave.), headquarters of the chewing-gum empire. The base of the **Tribune Tower** (⊠ 435 N. Michigan Ave.), a 1930s Gothic-style skyscraper north of the Chicago River, incorporates pieces of other buildings and monuments from around the world, including Westminster Abbey, the Parthenon, and the pyramids.

For a waterfront detour and a great view of the skyline, make a stop ★ at **Navy Pier** (⊠ 600 E. Grand Ave., ☎ 312/595–7437, WEB www.navypier.com), a former shipping pier that now has shops, restaurants, and bars. **Skyline Stage**, an outdoor pavilion for music, dance, and drama performances, has a huge Ferris wheel and an **IMAX theater** (☎ 312/595–0090). Skyline is the launch site for a number of cruising vessels that ply Lake Michigan. Navy Pier also houses the **Chicago Children's Museum** (⊠ 700 E. Grand Ave., ☎ 312/527–1000, WEB www.chichildrensmuseum.org; $6.50), where educational hands-on exhibits include an arts studio, a two-story climbing structure, an "invention-making" machine, and exhibits on intergenerational and intercultural relationships.

In its massive, modular home, the **Museum of Contemporary Art** has several galleries of modern art; there's also a terraced outdoor sculpture garden and a performance space for progressive productions. ⊠ *220 E. Chicago Ave.,* ☎ *312/280–2660,* WEB *www.mcachicago.org. $7.50. Closed Mon.*

The **Terra Museum of American Art** a small museum housing industrialist Daniel Terra's superb private collection, includes works by almost every major American painter, including Whistler, Sargent, the Wyeths, and Cassatt. ⊠ *664 N. Michigan Ave.,* ☎ *312/664–3939,* WEB *www.terramuseum.org. $7. Closed Mon.*

One of the few buildings to survive the Chicago Fire of 1871, the **Water Tower** (⊠ Michigan Ave. at Pearson St.) sits like a giant sand castle at the heart of the Magnificent Mile. Inside is a visitor center. The gray-marble high-rise called **Water Tower Place** (⊠ 835 N. Michigan Ave., ☎ 312/440–3165, WEB www.shopwatertower.com) has restaurants, a cinema, two department stores, and boutiques.

You can view the city—and, on a clear day, Indiana and Wisconsin—from a height of 1,000 ft at the **observatory and outdoor skydeck** on the 94th floor of the 100-story **John Hancock Center** (⊠ 875 N. Michigan Ave., ☎ 312/751–3681, WEB www.hancock-observatory.com; $8.75); or enjoy the same view while you have a drink in the bar on the 96th floor. A change of pace from the North Michigan Avenue shops, the **Fourth Presbyterian Church** (✉ 126 E. Chestnut St., ☎ 312/787–4570, WEB www.fourthchurch.org) is a Gothic-style jewel with a quiet courtyard. On Friday, the sanctuary often holds organ recitals and concerts.

Lincoln Park

The Lincoln Park neighborhood stretches from North Avenue to Diversey Parkway and from the lakefront on the east to about Racine Avenue on the west. The adjoining lakefront park is also called Lincoln Park (causing occasional confusion), though it stretches several miles farther north than the neighborhood.

The **Chicago Historical Society** (✉ 1601 N. Clark St., ☎ 312/642–4600, WEB www.chicagohs.org; $5) contains an extensive collection of historic costumes as well as history galleries where you can view Lincoln's deathbed and artifacts and first-hand testimonials from the great Chicago Fire of 1871. Children love to climb aboard the *Pioneer* locomotive, Chicago's first train.

You'll find elegant town houses and small apartment buildings from ★ the late 1800s and early 1900s in the **Lincoln Park neighborhood,** the heart of which is the intersection of Fullerton Avenue, Lincoln Avenue, and Halsted Street. The area declined after World War II as residents moved to the suburbs, but it was rediscovered in the 1970s; now it's full of million-dollar homes, coffeehouses, and funky boutiques.

Other Attractions

River North—a former warehouse neighborhood west of Michigan Avenue, bounded roughly by Clark Street, Chicago Avenue, Orleans Street, and the Chicago River—bloomed during the mid-1980s gentrification craze and now is home to a number of art galleries and trendy restaurants. The **Visitor Welcome Center** in the historic Water Tower (✉ Michigan Ave. at Pearson St., ☎ 877/244–2246 WEB www.cityofchicago.org/Tourism) carries the *Chicago Gallery News,* which lists addresses, hours, and current exhibits.

The **Museum of Science and Industry** (✉ E. 57th St. and S. Lake Shore Dr., ☎ 773/684–1414, WEB www.msichicago.org; $8), on the lake in Hyde Park about 7 mi south of the Loop, offers historic and high-tech engineering marvels, applied science, and hands-on exhibits. There's a genuine German U-boat, a reproduction coal mine, Colleen Moore's Fairy Castle (a dollhouse to end all dollhouses), actual spacecraft from early NASA missions, and a giant-screen Omnimax theater.

Parks, Gardens, and Zoos

Most of Chicago's more than 20 mi of shoreline is parkland or beach reserved for public use. A 19-mi path stretches along the lakefront, snaking through **Lincoln Park, Grant Park** (east of the Loop), and **Jackson Park** (south of the Museum of Science and Industry, with a wooded island and the Osaka Japanese garden) and winding past half a dozen harbors, two golf courses, Navy Pier, Buckingham Fountain, the lakefront museum campus, McCormick Place, and all the city's popular beaches. Bikes are the best way to cover maximum territory; they can be rented in summer at the concession near the Lincoln Park entrance at Fullerton Avenue and Cannon Drive. Beware of bicycle thieves along the comparatively deserted stretch south of McCormick Place, especially on weekdays and at night.

★ The 35-acre **Lincoln Park Zoo** (✉ 2200 N. Cannon Dr., ☎ 312/742–2000, WEB www.lpzoo.com; free), the nation's oldest, houses all the requisite zoo denizens, including koalas, reptiles, great apes, and lowland gorillas. Bring the kids to the extensive, indoor **Children's Zoo,** which features plenty of small furry animals to pet, as well as hands-on activities for older children. In Lincoln Park's **South Pond,** south of the Lincoln Park Zoo, you can rent paddleboats May–October. The **Lincoln Park Conservatory** (✉ 2400 N. Stockton Dr., ☎ 312/742–7736, WEB www.chicagoparkdistrict.com; 🎟 free), which borders the Lincoln Park Zoo, has a palm house, a fernery, special exhibits, and large outdoor gardens.

There are hundreds of parks in neighborhoods throughout the city and suburbs. The **Garfield Park Conservatory** (✉ 300 N. Central Park Blvd., ☎ 312/746–5100, WEB www.chicagoparkdistrict.com; 🎟 free) maintains 5 acres of plants and flowers under glass and holds four shows a year. The **Chicago Botanic Garden** (✉ 1000 Lake Cook Rd., Glencoe, ☎ 847/835–5440, WEB www.chicago-botanic.org; 🎟 $7.75 per car), north of the city in Glencoe, covers 385 acres and has 15 separate gardens, including a sensory garden for the disabled and a children's demonstration garden, and three biodomes. The **Morton Arboretum** (✉ Rte. 53 north of I–88, Lisle, ☎ 630/719–2465, WEB www.mortonarb.org; 🎟 $7 per car), in the western suburbs, has 1,700 acres of woody plants, woodlands, and outdoor gardens, plus 13 mi of walking trails.

Dining

Most places listed below are in the Near North, River North, and Loop areas, within walking distance of the major hotel districts. For clusters of ethnic restaurants too numerous to mention here, try Greektown, at Halsted and Madison streets; Chinatown, at Wentworth Avenue and 23rd Street; Little Italy, on Taylor Street between Racine and Ashland avenues; Argyle Street, between Broadway and Sheridan Road (for Chinese and Vietnamese); Devon Avenue, between Leavitt Street and Sacramento Avenue (Indian); and Clark Street, from Belmont Avenue to Addison Street (Thai, Japanese, Chinese, Korean, Ethiopian, Italian, and Mexican).

$$$$ ✕ **Arun's.** Long considered the city's best—and most expensive—Thai restaurant, Arun's is also known for its congenial staff, its elegant dining room with Thai art, and, most importantly, the degustation dinner menu, made with fresh ingredients. ✉ *4156 N. Kedzie Ave.,* ☎ *773/539–1909. AE, D, DC, MC, V. Closed Mon. No lunch.*

$$$$ ★ ✕ **Charlie Trotter's.** This top-of-the-line Lincoln Park town house accommodates 28 tables. Chef-owner Charlie Trotter prepares stellar, innovative American cuisine with French and Asian overtones. Dishes are presented in a multicourse degustation format with a wine chosen for each mini-course. ✉ *816 W. Armitage Ave.,* ☎ *773/248–6228. Reservations essential. AE, D, DC, MC, V. Closed Sun.–Mon. No lunch.*

$$$$ ★ ✕ **Everest.** On the 40th floor of a postmodern skyscraper in the heart of the financial district, Everest continues to scale heights by reinventing regional French cuisine with a contemporary twist. ✉ *440 S. La Salle St.,* ☎ *312/663–8920. Reservations essential. AE, D, DC, MC, V. Closed Sun.–Mon. No lunch.*

$$$$ ✕ **Le Français.** In a country-French setting, this restaurant in the northwestern suburbs turns out contemporary French creations that are visual masterpieces. ✉ *269 S. Milwaukee Ave., Wheeling,* ☎ *847/541–7470. Reservations essential. Jacket required. AE, D, DC, MC, V. Closed Sun. No lunch Mon. or Sat.*

$$$$ ★ ✕ **Trio.** Creative touches distinguish Trio's elaborate contemporary cuisine; dishes may be served on such unique objects as painters' palettes. A prix-fixe $35 three-course lunch is offered Friday at noon. ✉ *1625*

Hinman Ave., Evanston, ☎ 847/733–8746. AE, D, DC, MC, V. Closed Mon. No lunch Sat.–Thurs.

$$$–$$$$ ✕ **Ambria.** In an art nouveau building in Lincoln Park, Ambria has a seasonal, contemporary French menu that complements entrées with natural juices and vegetable reductions. Finish with the sensational dessert soufflé. ✉ *2300 N. Lincoln Park W, ☎ 773/472–5959. Reservations essential. Jacket required. AE, D, DC, MC, V. Closed Sun. No lunch.*

$$$–$$$$ ✕ **Morton's of Chicago.** Chicago's best steak house serves beautiful, hefty steaks cooked to perfection. Excellent service, a classy ambience, and a very good wine list add to the appeal. Vegetarians should look elsewhere. ✉ *1050 N. State St., ☎ 312/266–4820. AE, D, DC, MC, V. No lunch.*

$$$–$$$$ ✕ **Signature Room at the 95th.** The main draw here is the view—it's at the top of the John Hancock Center—though the elegant restaurant also has good food. At $10, the weekday sandwich lunch is a good bargain. Dinner is a very formal affair; the expensive Sunday brunch is splendid. ✉ *John Hancock Center, 875 N. Michigan Ave., ☎ 312/787–9596. AE, D, DC, MC, V.*

$$$–$$$$ ✕ **Spago.** At this Wolfgang Puck spin-off, diners go for the stir-fry lamb and house-smoked salmon in the beautiful, modern dining room. The service is excellent. ✉ *520 N. Dearborn St., ☎ 312/527–3700. Reservations essential. AE, D, DC, MC, V. No lunch weekends.*

$$$–$$$$ ★ ✕ **Spiaggia.** In elegant pink-and-teal quarters overlooking the lake, Spiaggia is the most opulent Italian restaurant in town, with elaborate stuffed pastas, veal chops in a vodka-cream sauce, and other inventive dishes. Sample the kitchen's talents next door at Café Spiaggia, with lower prices but equally excellent meals. ✉ *980 N. Michigan Ave., ☎ 312/280–2750. Reservations essential. Jacket required. AE, D, DC, MC, V. No lunch Sun.*

$$–$$$$ ✕ **Marché.** This hip restaurant west of the Loop draws a see-and-be-seen crowd that includes many celebs. Standouts on the bistro menu are spit-roasted chicken and tempting desserts such as crème brûlée and chocolate truffle cake. ✉ *833 W. Randolph St., ☎ 312/226–8399. AE, D, DC, MC, V. No lunch weekends.*

$$–$$$$ ✕ **Rosebud Cafe.** Specializing in good, old-fashioned southern Italian cuisine, Rosebud serves a superior red sauce, and the roasted peppers, homemade sausage, chicken Vesuvio, and exquisitely prepared pastas are not to be missed. ✉ *1500 W. Taylor St., ☎ 312/942–1117. AE, D, DC, MC, V. No lunch weekends.*

$–$$$$ ★ ✕ **Frontera Grill/Topolobampo.** In Frontera Grill's cozy, colorful storefront, genuine regional Mexican cooking goes way beyond burritos and chips. At Topolobampo, next door, slightly higher prices give the chef an opportunity to experiment with more expensive ingredients. ✉ *445 N. Clark St., ☎ 312/661–1434. Reservations essential at Topolobampo. AE, D, DC, MC, V. Closed Sun.–Mon. No lunch Sat. at Topolobampo.*

$–$$$$ ✕ **Yoshi's Cafe.** Chef Yoshi Katsumura's restaurant specializes in Asian-influenced French bistro cuisine. Dishes are gorgeously presented; try the fresh seafood, such as tuna tartare with homemade guacamole. ✉ *3257 N. Halsted St., ☎ 773/248–6160. AE, DC, MC, V. Closed Mon. No lunch.*

$$–$$$ ★ ✕ **Brasserie Jo.** Discerning diners come here to sample Everest chef Jean Joho's food at relatively moderate prices. Don't miss the shrimp in a phyllo-dough bag or classic coq au vin. ✉ *59 W. Hubbard St., ☎ 312/595–0800. AE, D, DC, MC, V. No lunch weekends.*

$$–$$$ ✕ **Le Bouchon.** Chef-owner Jean-Claude Poilevey serves reasonably priced bistro fare at this intimate 45-seat French restaurant in Bucktown. The onion tart is a signature appetizer. Typical entrées include duck for two and sautéed rabbit with shallots and mustard. ✉ *1958*

N. Damen Ave., ☎ 773/862–6600. AE, D, DC, MC, V. Closed Sun. No lunch.

$$–$$$ ✕ **Maggiano's Little Italy.** This convivial restaurant serves up enormous portions of red-sauce Italian food in a wide-open dining room. Lunchtime sandwiches are especially good. ✉ *516 N. Clark St., ☎ 312/644–7700. AE, D, DC, MC, V.*

$$–$$$ ✕ **Printer's Row.** Named after its chic loft neighborhood in the South Loop, this warm and attractive restaurant specializes in game meats and seafood, with notable venison and bison preparations. ✉ *550 S. Dearborn St., ☎ 312/461–0780. AE, D, DC, MC, V. Closed Sun. No lunch Sat.*

$$ ★ ✕ **Pizzeria Uno/Pizzeria Due.** This is where Chicago deep-dish pizza got its start. There's usually a shorter wait for a table at Pizzeria Due (same ownership and menu, different decor and longer hours), a block away. ✉ *Uno: 29 E. Ohio St., ☎ 312/321–1000;* ✉ *Due: 619 N. Wabash Ave., ☎ 312/943–2400. Reservations not accepted. AE, D, DC, MC, V.*

$–$$ ✕ **The Berghoff.** This Loop institution has two huge, oak-paneled dining rooms and a splendid bar with Berghoff beer on tap. Expect a wait of 15 minutes or so at midday. American favorites augment the menu of German classics (Wiener schnitzel, sauerbraten). ✉ *17 W. Adams St., ☎ 312/427–3170. AE, MC, V. Closed Sun.*

$–$$ ✕ **Heaven on Seven.** Enter at Rush and Ontario streets to sample authentic cajun and creole specialties—shrimp étouffée, jambalaya, gumbo, and the like—served in lively surroundings. ✉ *600 N. Michigan Ave., ☎ 312/280–7774. AE, D, DC, MC, V.*

$–$$ ✕ **Mia Francesca.** Why is this tiny restaurant so insanely popular? Principally because of its very good, authentic Italian cooking; its moderate prices don't hurt. Try the classic bruschetta or full-flavored pasta and chicken dishes. ✉ *3311 N. Clark St., ☎ 773/281–3310. Reservations not accepted. AE, MC, V. No lunch.*

$ ✕ **Ann Sather.** The line often stretches down the street for home-style breakfasts at this large Swedish restaurant. Specialties include omelets, Swedish pancakes, homemade cinnamon rolls, potato sausage, chicken croquettes, and sandwiches. ✉ *929 W. Belmont Ave., ☎ 773/348–2378;* ✉ *3416 N. Southport, ☎ 773/404–4475;* ✉ *5207 N. Clark St., ☎ 773/271–6677. AE, DC, MC, V.*

Lodging

Chicago is the country's biggest convention town, and accommodations can be tight when major events are scheduled. Most hotels run weekend specials when no big shows are on. Accommodations are concentrated in the Loop, North Michigan Avenue, and River North. **Bed and Breakfast Chicago** (✉ Box 14088, 60614, ☎ 773/394–2000, FAX 773/394–2002, WEB www.chicago-bed-breakfast.com) handles more than 50 B&Bs in the downtown area.

$$$$ ★ **The Drake.** The grandest of Chicago's traditional hotels was built in 1920 in the style of an Italian Renaissance palace. The Palm Court, with its fountain and harpist, is lovely for afternoon tea. Asian art and lamps bring a touch of class to the rooms, many of which have splendid lake views. ✉ *140 E. Walton Pl., 60611, ☎ 312/787–2200 or 800/553–7253, FAX 312/787–1431, WEB www.hilton.com/hotels/CHIDHVI. 535 rooms. 3 restaurants, gym. AE, D, DC, MC, V.*

$$$$ ★ **Four Seasons.** Though it feels more like a grand English manor house than an urban skyscraper, the Four Seasons has spectacular lake and city views. Rooms have handcrafted armoires and beds piled with throw pillows. The sumptuous afternoon tea is the perfect pick-me-up for weary shoppers. ✉ *120 E. Delaware Pl., 60611, ☎ 312/280–*

8800, FAX *312/280–9184,* WEB *www.fourseasons.com. 343 rooms. 2 restaurants, pool, health club. AE, D, DC, MC, V.*

$$$$ **Hotel Inter-Continental Chicago.** A grand architectural gem, the Inter-Continental has a dramatic lobby, ornately painted ceilings, marble steps, and a second-floor terra-cotta fountain. The Italianate junior-Olympic-size pool helped earn the hotel a spot on the National Register of Historic Places. The hotel's fabulous art deco interior is being completely renovated; construction is likely to continue through 2003. ✉ *505 N. Michigan Ave., 60611,* ☎ *312/944–4100 or 800/628–2112,* FAX *312/944–1320,* WEB *www.chicago.interconti.com. 844 rooms. Restaurant, pool, health club. AE, D, DC, MC, V.*

$$$$ **Le Meridien.** Spacious rooms, understated decor, and an unbeatable location make this a top hotel choice for business and leisure travelers. Super-comfortable rooms have European-style down comforters. The hotel is linked by skybridge to the Shops at North Bridge mall. A smallish terrace at the fifth-floor lobby level rounds out the intimate dining and lobby space. ✉ *520 N. Michigan Ave., 60611,* ☎ *312/645–1500,* FAX *312/645–1550,* WEB *www.lemeridien-chicago.com. 311 rooms. Restaurant, health club. AE, D, DC, MC, V.*

$$$$ **The Peninsula.** The latest branch of the Hong Kong–based luxury chain, the Peninsula opened in mid 2001. Moderately sized but luxe rooms have well-appointed dressing areas and luxury bathrooms. The spa offers a complete menu of services, a full-scale gym, and an indoor pool overlooking Michigan Avenue—all rare commodities in downtown Chicago. ✉ *108 E. Superior St., 60611,* ☎ *312/337–2888,* FAX *312/932–9529,* WEB *www.peninsula.com. 339 rooms. 3 restaurants, pool, health club. AE, D, DC, MC, V.*

$$$$ ★ **Renaissance Chicago Hotel.** The modern stone-and-glass exterior houses a tidy '90s interpretation of turn-of-the-20th-century splendor. Lavish floral carpets, crystal-beaded chandeliers, and French-provincial furniture create rich-looking public areas. Rooms have separate sitting areas. ✉ *1 W. Wacker Dr., 60601,* ☎ *312/372–7200 or 800/468–3571,* FAX *312/372–0093,* WEB *www.renaissancehotels.com. 553 rooms. 2 restaurants, pool, gym. AE, D, DC, MC, V.*

$$$$ ★ **Ritz-Carlton.** The Ritz-Carlton, run by Four Seasons Hotels and Resorts, sits atop the Water Tower Place shopping mall. Magnificent flower arrangements adorn the public areas, and the two-story greenhouse lobby serves afternoon tea. The luxurious, spacious rooms are a tasteful blend of European styles. ✉ *160 E. Pearson St., 60611,* ☎ *312/266–1000 or 800/621–6906,* FAX *312/266–1194,* WEB *www.fourseasons.com. 430 rooms. 3 restaurants, pool, health club. AE, D, DC, MC, V.*

$$$$ **Sutton Place Hotel.** This ultramodern hotel has a sleek Art Deco lobby and similarly stylish guest rooms, with black leather headboards and photographs by Robert Mapplethorpe (not to worry, the subjects are floral). ✉ *21 E. Bellevue Pl., 60611,* ☎ *312/266–2100 or 800/606–8188,* FAX *312/266–2103,* WEB *www.suttonplace.com. 246 rooms. Restaurant, gym. AE, D, DC, MC, V.*

$$$$ **W Chicago Lakeshore.** This formerly undistinguished hotel has been utterly transformed from dowdy to hip. The decor is techno-cool and the lobbies and restaurants jammed with black-clad twentysomethings. Whiskey River, the penthouse bar, is routinely packed. Many rooms overlook Lake Michigan and Navy Pier. ✉ *644 N. Lakeshore Dr., 60611,* ☎ *312/943–9200 or 877/946–8357,* FAX *312/255–4411,* WEB *www.starwoodhotels.com. 556 rooms. Restaurant, pool, health club. AE, D, DC, MC, V.*

$$$–$$$$ **Claridge Hotel.** Nestled among Victorian houses on a tree-lined Near North street, this simply outfitted 1930s building is intimate and homey. ✉ *1244 N. Dearborn Pkwy., 60610,* ☎ *312/787–4980 or 800/*

245–1258, FAX *312/787–4069,* WEB *www.claridge-hotel.com. 163 rooms. Restaurant. AE, D, DC, MC, V.*

$$$–$$$$ **Embassy Suites Downtown Chicago.** These family-friendly digs are close to the attractions of Navy Pier, North Michigan Avenue, and the piers. There is no restaurant on-site, but a finger-food buffet in the evening and hot breakfast buffet are included in the room rate. ✉ *511 N. Columbus Dr., 60611,* ☎ *312/836–5900,* FAX *312/836–5901,* WEB *www.embassysuites.com. 456 rooms. Pool, gym. AE, D, DC, MC, V.*

$$$–$$$$ **The Fairmont.** This 37-story neoclassical structure of Spanish pink granite is next to the Illinois Center complex (where guests have access to a huge athletic facility). Many of the sizable rooms have views of the lake and Grant Park. ✉ *200 N. Columbus Dr., 60601,* ☎ *312/565–8000,* FAX *312/856–1032,* WEB *www.fairmont.com. 692 rooms. 2 restaurants. AE, D, DC, MC, V.*

$$$–$$$$ **Lenox Suites.** Conveniently located near North Michigan Avenue, the hotel has one-room "suites" with a Murphy bed, sofa bed, and kitchenette, in addition to one-bedroom suites with a separate living room and kitchen. ✉ *616 N. Rush St., 60611,* ☎ *312/337–1000 or 800/445–3669,* FAX *312/337–7217,* WEB *www.lenoxsuites.com. 324 suites. 2 restaurants, gym. AE, D, DC, MC, V.*

$$$–$$$$ **Palmer House Hilton.** Built in 1871 by the Chicago merchant Potter Palmer, this hotel has public areas that reflect the opulence of that era, including a frescoed rococo lobby. Its modern guest rooms are more ordinary. The high-tech golf simulator will tell you where your ball would land on a real course. ✉ *17 E. Monroe St., 60603,* ☎ *312/726–7500,* FAX *312/917–1707,* WEB *www.hilton.com/hotels/CHIPHHH. 1,639 rooms. 3 restaurants, pool, gym. AE, D, DC, MC, V.*

$$$–$$$$ **The Raphael.** This charming hotel is on a quiet, pretty street off the Magnificent Mile. Some of the guest rooms have quirky touches such as chaise lounges and arched entries. ✉ *201 E. Delaware Pl., 60611,* ☎ *312/943–5000,* FAX *312/943–9483. 172 rooms. Restaurant. AE, D, DC, MC, V.*

$$–$$$ **City Suites Hotel.** A small, European-style hotel with a fireplace in the lobby has cozy guest rooms with chic black-and-white tile baths. The location—10 minutes north of the Loop—is unbeatable. ✉ *933 W. Belmont Ave., 60657,* ☎ *773/404–3400 or 800/248–9108,* FAX *773/404–3405,* WEB *www.cityinns.com. 45 rooms. AE, D, DC, MC, V.*

$–$$$ **Best Western River North** This former warehouse in the thriving River North entertainment district has an undistinguished exterior, but inside are large, reasonably priced guest rooms with pinstriped duvets, buffalo-plaid blankets, and black-and-white tiled bathrooms. Sofa sleepers in the suites and an indoor pool make it a family favorite. ✉ *125 W. Ohio St., 60610,* ☎ *312/467–0800 or 800/727–0800,* FAX *312/467–1665,* WEB *www.bestwestern.com. 150 rooms. Pool, gym. AE, D, DC, MC, V.*

Motels

Comfort Inn of Lincoln Park (✉ 601 W. Diversey Pkwy., 60614, ☎ 773/348–2810, FAX 773/348–1912, WEB www.comfortinn.com), 74 rooms; CP; *$$.*

Hojo Inn (✉ 720 N. La Salle St., 60610, ☎ 312/664–8100, FAX 312/664–2365, WEB www.hojo.com), 71 rooms; restaurant; *$$.*

Ohio House (✉ 600 N. La Salle St., 60610, ☎ 312/943–6000, FAX 312/943–6063), 50 rooms; restaurant; *$$.*

Nightlife and the Arts

For listings of arts and entertainment events, check the monthly *Chicago* magazine (on newsstands) or the Friday edition of the *Chicago Tribune* or the *Chicago Sun-Times.* Two free weeklies, the *Reader* (available Friday) and *New City* (available Thursday), which can be found at bookstores, restaurants, and bars, are the best sources for what's happening in clubs and small theaters and for showings of noncommercial films.

Nightlife

Chicago comes alive at night. Shows usually begin at 9 PM; cover charges generally range from $4 to $10, depending on the day of the week. Most bars are open until 2 AM, and some larger dance clubs don't close until 4 AM.

BLUES CLUBS

In the years following World War II, Chicago-style blues grew into its own musical form. After fading in the 1960s, Chicago blues is coming back, although more strongly on the trendy North Side than on the South Side, where it all began. **Kingston Mines** (✉ 2548 N. Halsted St., ☎ 773/477–4646) has been king of Chicago blues clubs for more than 30 years, with bands on two stages weekends. The intimate **B.L.U.E.S.** (✉ 2519 N. Halsted St., ☎ 773/528–1012) pulses with music in a rather small space. At the elaborate **House of Blues** (✉ 329 N. Dearborn, ☎ 312/527–2583), top-notch groups play in an ornate, theater-like setting with unconventional art adorning the walls. **Buddy Guy's Legends** (✉ 754 S. Wabash Ave., ☎ 312/427–0333), owned by the famous blues man, sits in a spacious former storefront. The **Checkerboard Lounge** (✉ 423 E. 43rd St., ☎ 773/624–3240) is in a rough neighborhood but has a long pedigree.

COMEDY CLUBS

Many comedy clubs have a drink minimum instead of or in addition to a cover charge. The granddaddy of all comedy clubs is **Second City** (✉ 1616 N. Wells St., ☎ 312/337–3992), which usually has two different revues playing at once. The best stand-up comedy in town is found at **Zanies** (✉ 1548 N. Wells St., ☎ 312/337–4027). **Improv Olympic** (✉ 3541 N. Clark St., ☎ 773/880–0199) presents improv troupes as well as staged shows.

DANCE CLUBS

Kustom (✉ 1997 N. Clybourn Ave., ☎ 773/528–3400) hosts high-energy dance nightly. **Mad Bar** (✉ 1640 N. Damen Ave., ☎ 773/227–2277), a see-and-be-seen bar, has bands, DJs, and dancing.

FOLK CLUBS

No Exit Cafe/Gallery (✉ 6970 N. Glenwood Ave., ☎ 773/743–3355), a coffeehouse right out of the 1960s, has folk, jazz, and poetry readings. **Old Town School of Folk Music** (✉ 4544 N. Lincoln Ave., ☎ 773/525–7793) mixes local talent and outstanding nationally known performers.

JAZZ CLUBS

Jazz Showcase (✉ 59 W. Grand Ave., ☎ 312/670–2473) books nationally known groups in its classy River North home. **Pops for Champagne** (✉ 2934 N. Sheffield Ave., ☎ 773/472–1000) has jazz combos and a champagne bar. The **Green Mill** (✉ 4802 N. Broadway, ☎ 773/878–5552), a Chicago institution off the beaten track, books solid, sizzling local acts in an ornate 1940s space. **Green Dolphin Street** (✉ 2200 N. Ashland Ave., ☎ 773/395–0066) offers bossa, bebop, Latin, and world jazz in a large, open club.

ROCK CLUBS

Metro (✉ 3730 N. Clark St., ☎ 773/549–4140) presents progressive nationally known and local artists. Downstairs from Metro, **Smart Bar** (☎ 773/549–4140) throbs with punk and funk dance tunes. The **Cubby**

Bear (✉ 1059 W. Addison St., ☎ 773/327–1662), across from Wrigley Field, plays rock, fusion, and country-tinged acts. In the hip Wicker Park neighborhood, the **Double Door** (✉ 1572 N. Milwaukee Ave., ☎ 773/489–3160) books top and up-and-coming local artists. **Wild Hare** (✉ 3530 N. Clark St., ☎ 773/327–4273) is the city's premier reggae club.

FOR SINGLES

Chicago's legendary swinging singles scene moved years ago from Rush Street to Lincoln Park, primarily on Division Street between Clark and State. **Original Mother's** (✉ 26 W. Division St., ☎ 312/642–7251) was featured in the movie *. . . About Last Night.* **Butch McGuire's** (✉ 20 W. Division St., ☎ 312/337–9080) is jammed with out-of-towners on the make. Trendy bars also open and close frequently in the Halsted and Armitage area of Lincoln Park. River East Plaza (✉ 435 E. Illinois St. and McClurg Crescent) has several popular singles spots, including rough-around-the-edges **Dick's Last Resort** (☎ 312/836–7870).

GAY BARS

The area around Halsted Street—approximately between Belmont and Waveland avenues—has the city's highest concentration of gay bars, including the yuppified **Roscoe's Tavern & Cafe** (✉ 3356 N. Halsted St., ☎ 773/281–3355). **Berlin** (✉ 954 W. Belmont Ave., ☎ 773/348–4975) attracts a mixed crowd to its dance floor, video bar, and theme nights. **Gentry** (✉ 440 N. State St., ☎ 312/836–0933), a prime meeting spot downtown, has a piano bar and video bar.

The Arts

Chicago is a splendid city for the arts, with more than 50 theater groups, world-class orchestra and opera companies, and dozens of smaller musical ensembles.

DANCE

Ballet Chicago (☎ 312/251–8838, WEB www.balletchicago.org) is the city's oldest resident classical ballet company. You can also enjoy the **Joffrey Ballet of Chicago** (☎ 312/739–0120, WEB www.joffrey.com), which relocated from New York in the mid-1990s. **Hubbard Street Dance Chicago** (☎ 312/850–9744, WEB www.hubbardstreetdance.com) is known for its contemporary, jazzy vitality.

FILM

In addition to the usual commercial theaters, Chicago has several venues for the avant-garde, vintage, or merely offbeat. The **Gene Siskel Film Center of the Art Institute of Chicago** (✉ Columbus Dr. at Jackson Blvd., ☎ 312/846–2800, WEB www.artic.edu) sometimes presents lectures in conjunction with its films. The ornate **Music Box Theatre** (✉ 3733 N. Southport Ave., ☎ 773/871–6604), a 1920s movie palace, shows many independent films. The Northwestern University Film Society holds weekend film fests, often augmented by theme-related live performances, at the **Block Museum of Art** (✉ 1967 S. Campus Dr., Evanston, ☎ 847/491–5209).

MUSIC

The **Chicago Symphony Orchestra** performs September–May at the Orchestra Hall (✉ 220 S. Michigan Ave., ☎ 312/294–3000 or 800/223–7114, WEB www.chicagosymphony.org) under the direction of Daniel Barenboim. In summer the Chicago Symphony moves outdoors to take part in the **Ravinia Festival** (☎ 847/266–5100, WEB www.ravinia.org), in north suburban Highland Park.

OPERA

From September to March the **Lyric Opera of Chicago** (✉ 20 N. Wacker Dr., ☎ 312/332–2244, WEB www.lyricopera.org) performs grand opera with international stars; tickets are difficult to come by. The **Chicago Opera Theater** (☎ 312/704–8414, WEB www.chicagooperatheater.org) presents innovative versions of traditional favorites and contemporary American pieces, all sung in English.

THEATER

Half-price theater tickets are available for many productions on the day of performance, and on Friday afternoon for many weekend performances, at **Hot Tix** booths (✉ 108 N. State St., ☎ 312/977–1755 for both; WEB www.hottix.org). With excellent acoustics, the **Auditorium Theatre** (✉ 50 E. Congress Pkwy., ☎ 312/922–2110) shows popular Broadway musicals. The grand **Shubert Theatre** (✉ 22 W. Monroe St., ☎ 312/977–1700), built in 1906, offers touring Broadway plays, musicals, and dance companies. The **Chicago Theatre** (✉ 175 N. State St., ☎ 312/443–1130), a restored 1920s-era movie palace, presents musicals, concerts, and special events. The **Athenaeum Theatre** (✉ 2936 N. Southport Ave., ☎ 773/935–6860) hosts thought provoking music, opera, dance, and drama performances.

Several local ensembles have made the big jump into national prominence, most notably the successful **Steppenwolf** (✉ 1650 N. Halsted St., ☎ 312/335–1650, WEB www.steppenwolf.org). **Victory Gardens** (✉ 2257 N. Lincoln Ave., ☎ 773/871–3000, WEB www.victorygardens.org) presents plays by local playwrights on its four stages. The city's oldest repertory theater, the **Goodman Theatre** (✉ 170 N. Dearborn, ☎ 312/443–3800, WEB www.goodman-theatre.org), features contemporary works and classics.

Spectator Sports

Chicago's long and tortuous history with its local sports teams—whose track records are essentially long stretches of mediocrity occasionally punctuated by heartbreaking championship losses—has done nothing to erode the loyalty of local fans. The primary exception is the early 1990s golden streak of the Chicago Bulls pro basketball team, whose star, Michael Jordan, enjoys enormous affection from hometown fans even in retirement.

Baseball: Chicago Cubs (✉ Wrigley Field, 1060 W. Addison St., ☎ 773/404–2827, WEB www.cubs.com); **Chicago White Sox** (✉ Comiskey Park, 333 W. 35th St., ☎ 312/674–1000, WEB www.chisox.com). **Basketball: Chicago Bulls** (✉ United Center, 1901 W. Madison St., ☎ 312/455–4000, WEB www.nba.com/bulls). **Football:** The **Chicago Bears** (✉ Soldier Field, 425 E. McFetridge Dr., ☎ 847/295–6600, WEB www.chicagobears.com) play at Soldier Field, which, at press time, was under renovation to reorient its 67,000 seats for improved sightlines. If the project goes as planned, the Bears will resume playing at Soldier Field in midseason 2003. **Hockey: Chicago Blackhawks** (✉ United Center, 1901 W. Madison St., ☎ 312/455–7000, WEB www.chicagoblackhawks.com). **Horse racing: Hawthorne Race Course** (✉ 3501 S. Laramie Ave., Stickney, ☎ 708/780–3700, WEB www.hawthorneracecourse.com) has Thoroughbred racing July–November. **Sportsman's Park** (✉ 3301 S. Laramie Ave., Cicero, ☎ 708/652–2812, WEB www.sportsmanspark.com) has Thoroughbred racing March–May. **Maywood Park** (✉ North and 5th Aves., Maywood, ☎ 708/343–4800, WEB www.maywoodpark.com) has harness racing year-round.

Shopping

Shopping Districts

The **Loop** and the **Magnificent Mile** (☞ Exploring Chicago, *above,* for both) are filled with major department and upscale specialty stores.

Oak Street, between Michigan Avenue and State Street, has such top-of-the-line stores as **Barneys New York** (✉ 25 E. Oak St., ☎ 312/587–1700), **Ultimo** (✉ 114 E. Oak St., ☎ 312/787–1171), and **Giorgio Armani** (✉ 800 N. Michigan Ave., ☎ 312/427–6264). Four vertical (multiple-story) malls combine department stores and specialty shops along the Magnificent Mile, providing plenty of weather-protected window-shopping and inexpensive food-court dining: **Water Tower Place** (☞ Exploring Chicago, *above*); the **900 North Michigan Shops** (☎ 312/915–3916); **Chicago Place** (✉ 700 N. Michigan Ave., ☎ 312/642–4811). The latest Mag Mile Mall is the **Shops at North Bridge** (✉ 520 N. Michigan Ave., ☎ 312/327–2300). The **Lincoln Park neighborhood** has several worthwhile shopping strips. Clark Street between Armitage and Diversey avenues has clothing boutiques and specialty stores. From Diversey north to Addison Street are several large antiques stores, more boutiques, and some bookstores.

Department Stores

Marshall Field's (✉ 111 N. State St., ☎ 312/781–1000), the city's biggest department store, takes up an entire city block. With 500 departments, it's the second-largest retail store in the country and is revered for its extravagant window displays and signature Frango mints. **Carson Pirie Scott** (✉ 1 S. State St., ☎ 312/641–7000) doesn't have the style or selection of its North Michigan Avenue competitors, but it does have spectacular turn-of-the-20th-century art nouveau ornamental ironwork around the main entrance. To keep up with the latest fashion trends, visit **Bloomingdale's** (✉ 900 N. Michigan Ave., ☎ 312/440–4460). For couture clothing don't miss **Neiman Marcus** (✉ 737 N. Michigan Ave., ☎ 312/642–5900). **Saks Fifth Avenue** (✉ Chicago Place, 700 N. Michigan Ave., ☎ 312/944–6500) is a must for those in search of classy high style.

Specialty Stores

Crate & Barrel (✉ 646 N. Michigan Ave., ☎ 312/787–5900) sells its own stylish brand of home accessories, cookware, and furniture. **Nike-Town** (✉ 669 N. Michigan Ave., ☎ 312/642–6363) draws tourists with its displays of sports memorabilia and merchandise. Girls flock to **American Girl Place** (✉ 111 E. Chicago Ave., ☎ 877/247–5223), the only retail outlet in the country for the Pleasant Company's popular brand of dolls, accessories, and clothing. Reservations are required for its live **revue show** (🎫 $26) and for lunch or tea at the **AG Restaurant.** In the Loop, **Illinois Artisans Shop** (✉ James R. Thompson Center, 100 W. Randolph St., ☎ 312/814–5321) showcases the best work from artists and craftspeople from around the state. For clever souvenirs, browse in the shops at major museums and at the quirky stalls of **Navy Pier** (☞ Magnificent Mile *in* Exploring Chicago, *above*).

Side Trip to Oak Park

Arriving and Departing

Take I–290 west to Harlem Avenue and exit from the left lane. Turn right at the top of the ramp, head north on Harlem Avenue to Lake Street, turn right, and proceed to Oak Park Avenue.

What to See and Do

Founded in the 1850s, west of the Chicago border, is Oak Park, one of Chicago's oldest suburbs and a living museum of Prairie School residential architecture. The **Frank Lloyd Wright Home and Studio** (✉ 951 Chicago Ave., corner of Forest Ave., ☎ 708/848–1976, WEB www.wrightplus.org; 🎫 $8) looks as it did in 1889, when it was built for Wright, who lived and worked here until 1909. The poured-concrete **Unity Temple** (✉ 875

Lake St., ☎ 708/383–8873, WEB www.oprf.com/unity; 🎫 $6), which Frank Lloyd Wright designed in 1905, was the architect's first public building.

Learn about Ernest Hemingway's first 20 years at the **Ernest Hemingway Museum** (✉ 200 N. Oak Park Ave., ☎ 708/848–2222, WEB www.hemingway.org), closed Monday–Wednesday. The **Ernest Hemingway Birthplace** (✉ 339 N. Oak Park Ave., ☎ 708/848–2222, WEB www.hemingway.org), closed Monday–Wednesday, is the Victorian home where the Nobel prize-winning author was born in 1899. Combined admission to the Hemingway museum and birthplace costs $6. The **Oak Park Visitors Center** (✉ 158 N. Forest Ave., ☎ 708/848–1500 or 888/625–7275, WEB www.visitoakpark.com) sells tour tickets and provides information.

Side Trip to Baha'i House of Worship

Arriving and Departing

Take Lake Shore Drive north until it ends at Hollywood; then turn right onto Sheridan Road and follow it about 10 mi.

What to See and Do

Baha'i House of Worship (✉ 100 Linden Ave., Wilmette, ☎ 847/853–2300; 🎫 free) is a lovely nine-sided building whose architectural styles and icons from the world's religions symbolize unity. The symmetry and harmony of the building are paralleled in the surrounding formal gardens.

Side Trip to Woodstock

Arriving and Departing

Take I–90 west and exit on Route 47 going north. Make a left on Calhoun Street and then a right on Dean Street.

What to See and Do

Woodstock, 65 mi north of Chicago, is a Victorian oasis set in rolling countryside. The city square, lined with antiques stores and restaurants, hosts summer band concerts and ice cream socials. Most of *Groundhog Day,* starring Bill Murray, was filmed here. Orson Welles and Paul Newman cut their teeth at the **Woodstock Opera House** (✉ 121 Van Buren St., ☎ 815/338–4212, WEB www.woodstock-il.com), which was built in 1890 and still houses musical and theatrical productions. The **Old Court House Arts Center** (✉ 101 N. Johnson St., ☎ 815/338–4525; 🎫 free), built in 1857, showcases local artists' works. In the basement is the former jail, now the **Tavern on the Square** restaurant (☎ 815/334–9540), where meals are served Tuesday–Sunday in the old cell blocks. The center is closed from Monday–Wednesday. The **Chester Gould–Dick Tracy Museum** (☎ 815/338–8281, WEB www.dicktracymuseum.org; 🎫 $1), in the Old Court House Arts Center (☞ *above*), displays the artwork of Chester Gould, the creator of the *Dick Tracy* comic strip, who lived and worked in Woodstock. It, too, is closed Monday–Wednesday. Contact the **Woodstock Chamber of Commerce** (✉ 136 Cass St., 60098, ☎ 815/338–2436) for more information.

Side Trip to Naperville

Arriving and Departing

Naperville is about 35 mi west of the Loop. Take I–290 west to I–88 west, and exit south on Naperville Road. Proceed south to Diehl Street, take Diehl west to Washington Street, and Washington south to downtown Naperville.

What to See and Do

A living history museum, the 19th-century **Naper Settlement** (✉ 523 S. Webster St., Naperville, ☎ 630/420–6010, WEB www.napersettlement.org; 🎫 $6.50) has many buildings with hands-on activities and demonstrations. Start at the visitor center, and then visit the 1864 American Gothic Revival chapel, the Victorian Martin-Mitchell Mansion, and the Greek Revival Murray Mansion House. Children enjoy the re-created log-picket Fort Payne and the rough-hewn, one-room Paw Paw post office.

Downtown Naperville, a block north of Naper Settlement, is a charming area bordered to the west by the DuPage River. Stroll along the river walk, stopping to enjoy its shrubbery-shaded nooks, playgrounds, and even a covered bridge. Specialty clothing stores, home accessory shops, and antiques stores abound here. For more information on the area, call the **Naperville Chamber of Commerce** (✉ 131 N. Jefferson St., 60540, ☎ 630/355–4141, WEB www.visitnaperville.com).

Chicago Essentials

AIRPORTS AND TRANSFERS

Every national airline, most international airlines, and a number of regional carriers fly into O'Hare International Airport (ORD), some 20 mi northwest of downtown Chicago. One of the world's busiest airports, it is a hub for United and American airlines. Many major carriers also use Midway Airport (MDW) on the city's southwest side, close to downtown.

➤ AIRPORT INFORMATION: **Midway Airport** (✉ 5700 S. Cicero, ☎ 773/838–0600, WEB www.chicago-mdw.com). **O'Hare International Airport** (✉ I–90 W, ☎ 773/686–2200, WEB www.ohare.com).

AIRPORT TRANSFER

At O' Hare, the Chicago Transit Authority subway station is in the underground concourse between terminals; for $1.50, trains will take you into the Loop. Airport Express provides express coach service from O'Hare to major downtown and Near North hotels for a fare of $16 one-way. Metered taxicab service is available at O'Hare; expect to pay $35–$40 (plus tip) to Near North and downtown locations.

The Chicago Transit Authority's Orange Line train runs from Midway to the Loop, where you can transfer to other lines. Or for $13 you can take an Airport Express bus from Midway to hotels in the Loop and Near North. Cabs from Midway cost $19–$22, plus tip.

➤ TAXIS AND SHUTTLES: **Airport Express** (☎ 312/454–7799 or 800/654–7871). **Chicago Transit Authority** (☎ 312/836–7000, WEB www.transitchicago.com).

BUS TRAVEL TO AND FROM CHICAGO

➤ BUS INFORMATION: **Greyhound** (✉ 630 W. Harrison St., ☎ 312/408–5980 or 800/231–2222, WEB www.greyhound.com).

CAR TRAVEL

From the east the Indiana Toll Road (I–80/90) leads to the Chicago Skyway (also a toll road), which runs into the Dan Ryan Expressway (I–90/94); take the Dan Ryan west to any downtown exit. From the south, take I–57 to the Dan Ryan. From the west follow I–80 to I–55, which is the major artery from the southwest and leads into Lake Shore Drive. From the north I–94 and I–90 eastbound merge about 10 mi north of downtown to form the John F. Kennedy Expressway (I–90/94).

Leave your car behind if you're visiting the Loop, the Near North Side, or Lincoln Park. You'll need a car to go to the suburbs or outlying city neighborhoods.

PARKING

Downtown parking lots charge $12–$32 a day.

TAXIS

Taxis are metered. The base fare is $1.60, plus $1.40 for each additional mile or minute of waiting time. Taxi drivers expect a 15% tip.

➤ TAXI COMPANIES: **American United Cab** (☎ 773/248–7600). **Checker Taxi Association** (☎ 312/243–2537). **Yellow Cab** (☎ 312/829–4222).

TOURS

BOAT TOURS

Wendella Sightseeing Boats and Mercury Chicago Skyline Cruiseline run guided tours of the Chicago River and Lake Michigan throughout the spring, summer, and early fall.

➤ FEES AND SCHEDULES: **Mercury Chicago Skyline Cruiseline** (✉ Michigan Ave. at Wacker Dr., ☎ 312/332–1353). **Wendella Sightseeing Boats** (✉ Lower Michigan Ave. at the Wrigley Bldg., ☎ 312/337–1446, WEB www.wendellaboats.com).

SPECIAL-INTEREST TOURS

The Chicago Architecture Foundation operates downtown walking tours; bus tours; a river cruise; neighborhood tours; and, during summer, tours of two historical Prairie Avenue house museums—the Glessner House and the Henry B. Clarke House.

➤ FEES AND SCHEDULES: **Chicago Architecture Foundation** (✉ 224 S. Michigan Ave., ☎ 312/922–3432, WEB www.architecture.org).

TRAIN TRAVEL

Amtrak serves Chicago's Union Station.

➤ TRAIN INFORMATION: **Amtrak** (✉ 225 S. Canal St., ☎ 800/872–7245, WEB www.amtrak.com).

TRANSPORTATION AROUND CHICAGO

The best way to see Chicago is on foot, supplemented by public transportation or taxi. Streets are laid out in a grid, the center of which is the intersection of Madison Street, which runs east–west, and State Street, which runs north–south.

The Chicago Transit Authority and the Regional Transportation Authority provide information on how to get around on city rapid-transit and bus lines, suburban bus lines, and commuter trains; the base fare is $1.50. On the subway and the El, you must use a fare card, which can be purchased at the station. Buses accept either cash (exact change only) or fare cards.

➤ CONTACTS: **Chicago Transit Authority/ Regional Transportation Authority** (☎ 312/836–7000, WEB www.transitchicago.com).

VISITOR INFORMATION

➤ TOURIST INFORMATION: **Chicago Office of Tourism** (Visitor Information Center: ✉ Chicago Cultural Center, 77 E. Randolph St., 60602, ☎ 312/744–2400 or 800/226–6632, WEB www.ci.chi.il.us/tourism; walk-in center: historic Water Tower, 806 N. Michigan Ave.). **Mayor's Office of Special Events** (✉ 121 N. La Salle St., Room 703, 60602, ☎ 312/744–3315; 312/744–3370 recordings on events and festivals; WEB www.ci.chi.il.us/specialevents).

GALENA AND NORTHWESTERN ILLINOIS

The tiny town of Galena (population: 3,600) has beautifully preserved pre–Civil War architecture, with houses in Federal, Italianate, and Gothic Revival styles; a large concentration of specialty shops; and (rare in the Midwest) hilly terrain. There's good biking, cross-country skiing, fishing, hunting, and camping in the region.

Lead mining took off here in the 1820s, and Galena had a near-monopoly on the shipping of ore down the Mississippi until the railroad came through in 1854. A depression later that decade and then the Civil War disrupted the lead trade and sent the city into an economic decline from which it never recovered. As a result, Galena today looks much as it did in the 1850s; 85% of the town is on the National Register of Historic Places. This was once the home of Ulysses S. Grant, commander of the Union Army in the Civil War and later the 18th president of the United States. The region surrounding Galena is dotted with tiny towns that have been similarly bypassed by modern life.

Exploring Galena and Northwestern Illinois

In Galena the **Ulysses S. Grant Home** (✉ 500 Bouthillier St., ☎ 815/777–3310, WEB www.granthome.com; 🎫 $2), built in 1860 in the Italianate bracketed style, was presented to Grant in 1865 by Galena residents in honor of his service to the Union. The Grant family lived there until Grant's victory in the 1868 presidential election. In 1904 Grant's children gave the house to the city of Galena. Now a state historic site, the house has been meticulously restored to its 1868 appearance.

The heart of the **Belvedere Mansion and Gardens** is the 1857 Italianate mansion built for a steamboat magnate. Some might consider its lavishness gaudy; accoutrements include the famous green drapes from the movie *Gone With the Wind* and furnishings from Liberace's estate. ✉ *1008 Park Ave.,* ☎ *815/777–0747,* WEB *www.belvederemansion.com.* 🎫 *$10. Closed Nov.–May.*

The **Galena/Jo Daviess County History Museum** (✉ 211 S. Bench St., ☎ 815/777–9129, WEB www.galena.org; 🎫 $4) provides interesting background on the area. A large Civil War exhibit shows the effect of the war on Galena's development. Display cases house period dolls, toys, clothing, and household artifacts.

Galena's oldest house is the 1826 **Dowling House** (✉ 220 Diagonal St., ☎ 815/777–1250; 🎫 $3.50), which is open daily in summer and only on weekends in winter. **Galena Trolley Tours** (✉ 314 S. Main St., ☎ 815/777–1248, WEB www.galenatrolley.com; 🎫 $10) offers tours of the town.

A huge swath of rolling countryside east of town, the **Galena Territory** started as a vacation-home development in the early 1980s but has taken on a life of its own as a recreation area with hunting, fishing, and golf. Watch out for deer and turkey on the back roads; they're everywhere.

Mallards outnumber people 200 to 1 in **Hanover,** southeast of Galena, off Route 20 on Route 84. The **Whistling Wings Hatchery** (✉ 113 Washington St., ☎ 815/591–3512) hatches 200,000 mallards a year; a viewing window lets you see the baby ducks in incubators. **Savanna,** on Route 84 along the Mississippi, has many large, well-preserved 19th-century houses. In **Mount Carroll,** east of Savanna on Route 52, rolling hills and gracious 19th-century frame and masonry buildings recall a small New England town, complete with a town square.

Stockton, about 30 mi east of Galena on Route 20, is the highest town in Illinois, at 1,000 ft; the business district preserves many lacy, cupola-topped Victorian structures. **Arlo's Tractor Collection and Museum** (⊠ 7871 S. Ridge Rd., ☎ 815/947–2593; free) contains 60 restored antique tractors, all in working order. The museum is closed November–April; tours are by appointment only.

Dining and Lodging

Restaurant fare here tends toward hearty steaks, burgers, and ribs. Several bakeries along Galena's Main Street sell tempting cookies and pastries. A stay in one of the area's 40-plus B&Bs is almost de rigueur; some are right in town, and others are in the Galena Territory or other rustic outlying areas. The Convention and Visitors Bureau (☞ Galena and Northwestern Illinois Essentials, *below*) has a complete list of B&Bs and other types of lodging.

East Dubuque

$$ ✕ **Timmerman's Supper Club.** This swanky restaurant across the parking lot from Timmerman's Motor Lodge (but under separate ownership) has spectacular views, rib-eye steaks, and DJs on weekends. ⊠ *7777 Timmerman Dr.,* ☎ *815/747–3316. AE, D, MC, V.*

$–$$ 🏨 **Timmerman's Motor Lodge.** Perched on a bluff near the Mississippi River, this modern complex is frequented by riverboat gamblers in neighboring Dubuque, Iowa. Most of the rooms are 1980s Holiday Inn style. ⊠ *7777 Timmerman Dr., 61025,* ☎ *815/747–3181 or 800/336–3181,* FAX *815/747–6556. 74 rooms. Restaurant, pool. AE, D, MC, V.*

Galena

$$–$$$ ★ ✕ **El Dorado.** Wild game specials include a mixed grill of locally raised venison, Texas antelope, and wild boar sausage. A Southwest motif prevails in the lofted space with exposed brick walls. ⊠ *219 N. Main St.,* ☎ *815/777–1224. AE, D, MC, V. Closed Tues.–Wed. No lunch.*

$$ ✕ **Café Italia and Twisted Taco Café.** Featured in the movie *Field of Dreams,* this cozy wood-and tile restaurant serves minestrone, lasagna, veal parmigiana, and other Italian standards, in addition to a full Mexican menu. ⊠ *301 N. Main St.,* ☎ *815/777–0033. AE, D, DC, MC, V. Closed Mon.–Tues.*

$$–$$$ ✕🏨 **DeSoto House Hotel.** Opened in 1855, the DeSoto House served as presidential campaign headquarters for Ulysses S. Grant, and Lincoln really did sleep here. The spacious rooms recall the 1860s. The stately Generals' Restaurant serves straightforward steaks, chops, and seafood; the Courtyard Restaurant is open for breakfast and lunch. ⊠ *230 S. Main St., 61036,* ☎ *815/777–0090 or 800/343–6562,* FAX *815/777–9529,* WEB *desotohouse.com. 55 rooms. 2 restaurants. AE, D, DC, MC, V.*

$$–$$$ 🏨 **Chestnut Mountain Resort.** Looking like a Swiss chalet, the resort sits atop a bluff above the Mississippi, 8 mi southeast of downtown Galena; bedrooms overlook the ski slopes. There are mountain bikes for rent and ski packages that include lodging and meals. ⊠ *8700 W. Chestnut Rd., 61036,* ☎ *815/777–1320 or 800/397–1320,* FAX *815/777–1068,* WEB *www.chestnutmtn.com. 119 rooms. Restaurant, pool, tennis. AE, D, DC, MC, V.*

Galena Territory

$$$–$$$$ ✕🏨 **Eagle Ridge Inn and Resort.** This rustic yet elegant "inn resort for golf" is set on 6,800 acres; horseback riding, boating, and cross-country skiing abound. Guest rooms have views of lake or woodland. The formal Woodlands restaurant serves excellent American cuisine. ⊠ *444 Eagle Ridge Dr., Galena 61036,* ☎ *815/777–2444 or 800/892–2269,*

FAX 815/777–4502, WEB www.eagleridge.com. 80 rooms; 320 condos, town houses, and homes. 2 restaurants, pool, gym. AE, D, DC, MC, V.

Motels

Best Western Quiet House Suites (✉ 9923 Rte. 20 W, Galena 61036, ☎ 815/777–2577, FAX 815/777–0584, WEB www.quiethouse.com), 42 suites; pool, gym; *$$*.

Allen's Victorian Pines Lodging (✉ 11383 Rte. 20 W, Galena 61036, ☎ 815/777–2043, FAX 815/777–2625, WEB www.victorianpineslodging.com), 64 rooms; *$–$$*.

Grant Hills Motel (✉ 9372 Rte. 20 E, Galena 61036, ☎ 815/777–2116, WEB www.granthills.com), 35 rooms; pool; *$*.

Nightlife

The **Depot Theater** (✉ 314 S. Main St., ☎ 815/777–1248), at the Galena Trolley Depot, presents cabaret-style theater in a candlelit space. Shows tend to be historical, such as Jim Post's *Mark Twain and the Laughing River.*

Outdoor Activities and Sports

Biking

Bicyclists will find plenty of hilly back roads around Galena. The **Old Stagecoach Trail** runs parallel to Route 20, winding from Lena through Apple River and Warren to Galena. **Chestnut Mountain Resort** (☞ Dining and Lodging, *above*) rents mountain bikes. The Visitor Information Center (☞ Galena and Northwestern Illinois Essentials, *below*) has maps.

Fishing

Licenses can be purchased at marinas, bait shops, hardware stores, and other outlets, or contact the **Illinois Bureau of Tourism** (☞ Statewide Visitor Information, *above*) or the **Illinois Department of Natural Resources** (✉ 2612 Locust St., Sterling 61081, ☎ 815/625–2968, WEB www.dnr.state.il.us).

Golf

Eagle Ridge Inn and Resort (☞ Dining and Lodging, *above*), in Galena Territory, has three championship 18-hole courses and one 9-hole course. **Galena Golf Club** (✉ Hwy. 20 W, Galena, ☎ 815/777–3599) has one 18-hole course and a driving range. **Lacoma Golf Course** (✉ 8080 Timmerman Dr., East Dubuque, ☎ 815/747–3874) has one 18-hole course, two regulation 9-hole courses, and one 9-hole par-three course.

Hiking and Backpacking

Mississippi Palisades State Park (✉ 16327A Rte. 84 N, Savanna, ☎ 815/273–2731, WEB www.dnr.state.il.us), about 30 mi south of Galena, has hiking trails with river views and nature preserves with accessible lookouts. More cliffs and canyons, in addition to camping, fishing, and five 1-mi-long hiking trails, can be found at **Apple River Canyon State Park** (✉ 8763 E. Canyon Rd., north of Rte. 20 between Stockton and Warren, ☎ 815/745–3302, WEB www.dnr.state.il.us).

Horseback Riding

Shenandoah Riding Center (✉ Galena Territory, 200 N. Brodrecht Rd., off Rte. 20 E, Galena, ☎ 815/777–2373, WEB www.shenandoahridingcenter.com) offers riding lessons and hay and sleigh rides.

Ski Areas

Cross-Country

Eagle Ridge Inn and Resort (☞ Dining and Lodging, *above*) maintains more than 35 mi of groomed trails. **Lacoma Golf Course** (☞ Golf *in* Outdoor Activities and Sports, *above*) opens its 260-acre course to skiers, but you have to break your own trails. **Mississippi Palisades State Park** (☞ Hiking and Backpacking *in* Outdoor Activities and Sports, *above*) also has marked trails.

Downhill

It's not the Alps, or even the Catskills, but if you want downhill skiing in Illinois, try **Chestnut Mountain Resort** (☞ Dining and Lodging, *above*), with 19 runs that overlook the Mississippi, plus a 7-acre snowboard park and a children's learn-to-ski program.

Shopping

Galena's Main Street is lined with more than 30 shops selling antiques, folk art, contemporary collectibles, and locally produced wine and foodstuffs. **Stockton, Warren,** and **Elizabeth** have antiques stores and artists' studios.

Galena and Northwestern Illinois Essentials

CAR TRAVEL

From Chicago take I–90 86 mi to Rockford, then Route 20 west 81 mi to Galena. From Iowa pick up Route 20 at Dubuque and continue 16 mi east across the Mississippi.

VISITOR INFORMATION

➤ TOURIST INFORMATION: **Galena Area Chamber of Commerce Visitor Information Center** (Walk-In Center: ✉ 101 Bouthillier St., Galena 61036). **Galena/Jo Daviess County Convention and Visitors Bureau** (☎ 815/777–3557 or 800/747–9377, WEB www.galena.org).

ELSEWHERE IN ILLINOIS

Springfield

What to See and Do

A surprisingly generous slice of Abraham Lincoln's life is preserved and re-created in Springfield, Illinois's capital. The importance of preserving artifacts from the president's life was recognized even as his funeral plans were being made, and so the historic sites here offer an extensive collection of personal and family artifacts. In the summer, you might want to visit New Salem, which is about a 45-minute drive northwest of Springfield. The Illinois State Fair held there in mid-August is a two-week extravaganza of midwestern farming and domestic triumphs. If you want to go, though, make your hotel reservations long in advance—rooms are impossible to find then.

In Springfield, start early in the day and pick up a free admission ticket at the visitor center of the **Lincoln Home National Historic Site** (✉ 426 S. 7th St., ☎ 217/492–4150, WEB www.nps.gov/liho). The two blocks surrounding the Lincoln House are being restored to their mid-19th-century state, and biographies of the neighbors who befriended Mary Lincoln and baby-sat the Lincoln boys are being pieced together in exhibits in those neighbors' restored homes. Springfield's Oak Ridge Cemetery contains the **Lincoln Tomb State Historic Site** (✉ 1500 N. Monument Ave., ☎ 217/782–2717; 🎫 free), the final resting place for Lincoln, Mary Todd, and three of their four sons. On Tuesday nights in summer, catch the Civil War Retreat Ceremony held at the tomb. The **Lincoln-Herndon Law Offices** (✉ 6th and Adams Sts., ☎ 217/785–7960; 🎫 $2) provide glimpses into Lincoln's life and career before he became president. Exceptionally well versed guides provide intimate details of the Lincolns' family life in Springfield. The **Old State Capitol** (✉ 5th and Adams Sts., ☎ 217/785–7961; 🎫 $2), where Lincoln delivered his "House Divided" speech and where he lay in state before burial, has been restored to the way it looked during Lincoln's legislative years. **Lincoln's New Salem State Historic Site** (✉ Rte. 97 near Petersburg, ☎ 217/632–4000, WEB www.lincolnsnewsalem.com; 🎫 free), which lies about 20 mi northwest of Springfield, is a reconstructed village where Lincoln spent his early adulthood; in summer volunteers in period dress re-create village life. In summer, the site hosts a corny but touching musical of Lincoln's young adulthood in its outdoor amphitheater.

Aside from Lincolniana, Springfield is also home to the **Dana-Thomas House,** built by Frank Lloyd Wright from 1902 to 1904 for a local socialite and now a state historic site. Elaborately restored in the late 1980s, it's among the most perfectly preserved examples of early Wright architecture, art glass, and furniture. ✉ *301 E. Lawrence Ave.,* ☎ *217/782–6776,* WEB *www.dana-thomas.org.* 🎫 *$3. Closed Mon.–Tues.*

Next to the Executive Mansion, home of the current governor of Illinois, is the **Vachel Lindsay Home,** the historic homestead of early 20th-century "prairie poet" Vachel Lindsay. ✉ *603 S. 5th St.,* ☎ *217/524–0901.* 🎫 *$2. Closed Sun.–Mon.*

The **Museum of Funeral Customs** opened in late 2001 next door to Springfield's Oak Ridge Cemetery. The brainchild of the Illinois Funeral Directors Association, the museum aims to demystify cultural death rites from Egyptian times through the present. Highlights include a scale model of Lincoln's funeral procession; replicas of other presidential caskets; and a thorough exploration of embalming. Be sure to pick up a few chocolate caskets at the gift shop on your way out. ✉ *1440 Monument Ave.,* ☎ *217/544–3480,* WEB *www.funeralmuseum.org.* 🎫 *$3. Closed Mon.*

Dining and Lodging

$$ ✕ **Café Brio.** Colorful and lively, Brio serves aromatic Mexican, Caribbean, and Mediterranean cuisine. Margaritas are made with fresh lime juice. ✉ *524 E. Monroe St.,* ☎ *217/544–0574. AE, MC, V. No dinner Sun.*

$$ ✕ **Maldener's.** This hangout for local politicians still has its original turn-of-the-20th-century decor, right up to the pressed-tin ceiling. Lunches are classic midwestern fare—especially the hot sandwiches smothered in gravy. ✉ *222 S. 6th St.,* ☎ *217/522–4313. AE, D, MC, V. Closed Sun.*

$$–$$$ 🏨 **Springfield Hilton.** The 30-story hotel has good city views and spacious rooms. In the heart of downtown, it's within walking distance of Lincoln historical sites. ✉ *700 E. Adams St., 62701,* ☎ *217/789–1530,* FAX *217/522–5346,* WEB *www.hilton.com. 366 rooms. 3 restaurants, pool, health club. AE, D, DC, MC, V.*

$$ 🏨 **The Inn at 835 Bed & Breakfast.** Just around the corner from the Dana-Thomas House, this stately late-19th-century inn has a Classical Revival exterior and is filled with oak detailing and large fireplaces. Rooms are spacious and decorated in authentic midwestern Victorian—fancy, but not fussy. ✉ *835 S. 2nd St., 62704,* ☎ *217/523–4466,* FAX *217/523–4468,* WEB *www.innat835.com. 10 rooms. MC, V.*

Springfield Essentials

CAR TRAVEL

Loop I–55 runs north–south through the city. I–72 comes from Champaign and Decatur to the east.

TRAIN TRAVEL

The Amtrak route from Chicago to St. Louis stops in Springfield.

➤ TRAIN INFORMATION: **Amtrak** (☎ 800/872–7245, WEB www.amtrak.com).

VISITOR INFORMATION

➤ TOURIST INFORMATION: **Springfield Convention and Visitors Bureau** (✉ 109 N. 7th St., 62701, ☎ 217/789–2360 or 800/545–7300, WEB www.visit-springfieldillinois.com).

INDIANA

Updated by
Peggy Sailors

Capital	Indianapolis
Population	6,080,485
Motto	The Crossroads of America
State Bird	Cardinal
State Flower	Peony
Postal Abbreviation	IN

Statewide Visitor Information

Indiana Department of Commerce, Tourism Division (✉ 1 N. Capitol Ave., Suite 700, Indianapolis 46204, ☎ 317/232–8860 or 800/289–6646, WEB www.enjoyindiana.com).

Scenic Drives

Charming 19th-century river towns front the **Ohio River Scenic Route** from Madison to Aurora on Routes 56 and 156. Trace Indiana's early frontier history along the **Chief White Eyes Trail** from Madison to Dillsboro on Route 62. The 50-mi **Lincoln Heritage Trail–George Rogers Clark Trail,** on Routes 462, 62, and 162 from Corydon to Gentryville, takes a gentle ride across southern hill country. From Newburgh to Sulphur the **Hoosier Heritage Trail Scenic Route** follows the Ohio River's squiggly course, then cuts north through state forests on Route 66. Indiana's 40-mi portion of the 1,100-mi **Lake Michigan Circle Tour** around the second largest of the Great Lakes follows U.S. 12 from Illinois to Michigan.

National and State Parks

National Parks

The murals and statue of George Rogers Clark in the columned, circular-stone memorial at **George Rogers Clark National Historical Park** (✉ 401 S. 2nd St., Vincennes 47591, ☎ 812/882–1776, WEB www.nps.gov/gero) commemorate Clark's capture of Britain's Fort Sackville in 1779 and the subsequent acquisition of the Northwest Territory, the ★ largest land conquest of the Revolutionary War. The 13,400-acre **Indiana Dunes National Lakeshore** (✉ 1100 N. Mineral Springs Rd., Porter 46304, ☎ 219/926–7561, WEB www.nps.gov/indu) encompasses dune grasses, arctic bearberries, and prickly pear cacti. A living-history farm and a replica of Abraham Lincoln's boyhood home are the lures at the **Lincoln Boyhood National Memorial** (✉ Box 1816, Lincoln City 47552, ☎ 812/937–4541, WEB www.nps.gov/libo). Ridge-top trails at the 197,000-acre **Hoosier National Forest** (✉ 811 Constitution Ave., Bedford 47421, ☎ 812/275–5987 for Brownstown Ranger District; ✉ 248 15th St., Tell City 47586, ☎ 812/547–7051, WEB www.fs.fed.us/r9/hoosier for Tell City Ranger District) border quiet lakes and pass through dense woodlands in the state's south-central corridor, which stretches to the banks of the Ohio River.

State Parks

Indiana's 24 state parks are operated by the **Department of Natural Resources** (✉ 402 W. Washington St., Room W256, Indianapolis 46204, ☎ 317/232–4124; 800/622–4931 in Indiana, WEB www.state.in.us/dnr/parklake/parks) and are open daily year-round. **Falls of the Ohio** (✉ Box 1327, Jeffersonville 47131, ☎ 812/280–9970, WEB www.state.in.us/dnr/parklake/parks/fallsofohio) has 220 acres of 386-million-year-old exposed Devonian fossil beds in the Ohio River. At **Spring**

Mill (✉ Rte. 60, Box 376, Mitchell 47446, ☎ 812/849–4129, WEB www.state.in.us/dnr/parklake/parks/springmill) you can tour a reconstructed 1800s pioneer village and gristmill on its original site, hike an 80-acre tract of virgin hardwood forest, then explore two caves on foot or by boat. Lacy hemlocks line 15 mi of trails that wind through deep sandstone canyons and woodlands bordering Sugar Creek at **Turkey Run** (✉ Rte. 47, Box 37, Marshall 47859, ☎ 765/597–2635, WEB www.state.in.us/dnr/parklake/parks/turkeyrun). Moss and ferns carpet deep ravines at **Shades** (✉ Rte. 1, Box 72, Waveland 47989, ☎ 765/435–2810, WEB www.state.in.us/dnr/parklake/parks/shades), a quiet, woodsy preserve that is lesser developed than Turkey Run, 15 mi away. Central Indiana's largest unbroken forest canopy comprises 1,700-acre **Fort Harrison** (✉ 5753 Glenn Rd., Indianapolis 46216, ☎ 317/591–0904, WEB www.state.in.us/dnr/parklake/parks/ftharrison), which is minutes from downtown Indianapolis and has hiking trails and a hilly, challenging golf course. Climb to the top of 123-ft Mt. Baldy at the **Indiana Dunes** (✉ 1600 N. 25 E., Chesterton 46304, ☎ 219/926–1952, WEB www.state.in.us/dnr/parklake/parks/indianadunes.html) for a view of Lake Michigan's sweeping dune-studded shoreline and, on a clear day, the Chicago skyline.

INDIANAPOLIS

For a city of its size, Indianapolis has a surprising assortment of museums and performance halls, sports and recreation facilities, plus plenty of green space. One welcome addition to the IndyParks system is the Indy Greenways, 175 mi of marked pedestrian trails, some of which are paved, as well as conservation corridors along creeks and even canoe trails on waterways throughout the metropolitan area. Downtown, there's an abundance of Olympic-class amateur and professional sports facilities including the newer Conseco Fieldhouse where the Indiana Pacers play. Finally, there's Circle Centre, a swanky, villagelike enclosed complex of shops and entertainment attractions that has helped transform a formerly sleepy downtown into a revitalized urban center.

Exploring Indianapolis

Attractions extend into a wider metropolitan area than the square-mile downtown area. Many of the museums, arts and entertainment venues, and shopping areas, all generally within a 45-minute drive, are scattered around, both downtown and beyond in the contiguous counties. It's easy to get around Indianapolis, and the center is perfectly walkable. Street numbers are based on a rectangular coordinate system, with each block roughly equal to 100. The intersection of Washington and Meridian streets, south of Monument Circle, is the zero point for numbering in all directions.

Downtown

Monument Circle is Indianapolis's centerpiece. Avenues radiate from it across the grid of streets, as in Washington, D.C. (Indianapolis architect Alexander Ralston was a protégé of Pierre L'Enfant). At the center is the 1902 **Soldiers' and Sailors' Monument,** a 284-ft limestone spire that pays homage to those who served in the Civil War. It's decorated with carved stone statuary and crowned by the 30-ft bronze statue *Victory,* better known as *Miss Indiana.* There's also a Civil War museum and an **observation area** (☎ 317/232–7615, WEB www.state.in.us/iwm; 💵 free) with a panoramic view. Also on Monument Circle is the city's oldest church, the Episcopalian **Christ Church Cathedral** (✉ 55 Monument Cir., ☎ 317/636–4577, WEB www.cccindy.org; 💵 free),

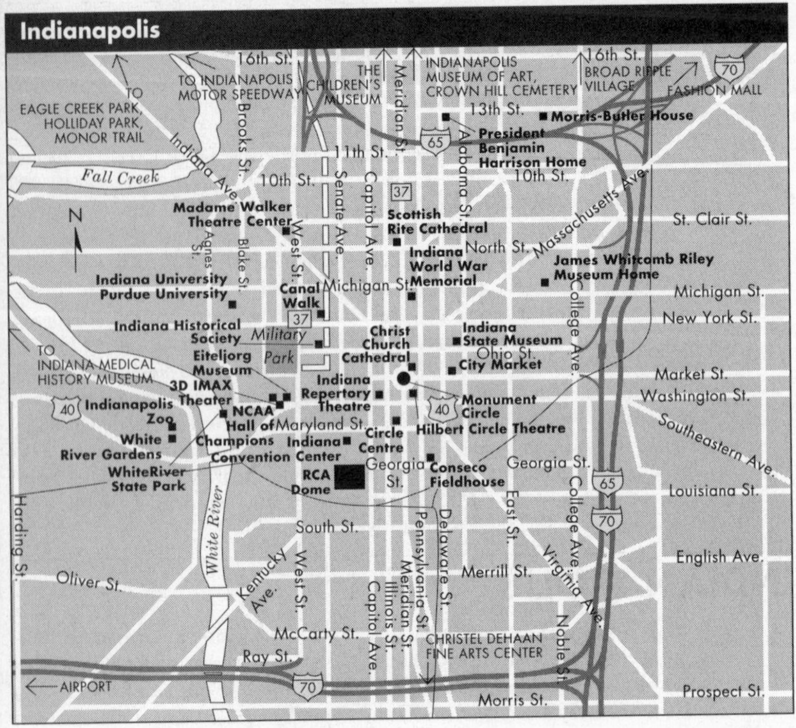

an 1857 Gothic country–style masterpiece, with a spire, steep gables, bell tower, and arched Tiffany windows. Tours are Sunday at noon or by appointment.

The **Indiana State Museum** (✉ 202 N. Alabama St., ☎ 317/232–1637, WEB www.in.gov/ism/museum; 🎫 free), in the Old City Hall, chronicles the state's history and culture. The massive limestone-and-marble **Indiana World War Memorial** (✉ 431 N. Meridian, ☎ 317/232–7615, WEB www.state.in.us/iwm; 🎫 free) pays tribute to fallen Hoosier veterans of World War I, World War II, the Korean War, and the Vietnam War. The circa-1929 Gothic Tudor–style Masonic **Scottish Rite Cathedral** (✉ 650 N. Meridian St., ☎ 800/489–3579, WEB www.aasr-indy.org; 🎫 free) contains a 54-bell carillon and a 7,000-pipe organ.

There's lunchtime entertainment most Fridays at the historic 1886 **Indianapolis City Market** (✉ 222 E. Market St., ☎ 317/634–9266, WEB www.indianapoliscitymarket.com; 🎫 free), where shops sell ethnic and deli fare.

In a contemporary adobe building, the **Eiteljorg Museum of American Indians and Western Art** (✉ 500 W. Washington St., ☎ 317/636–9378, WEB www.eiteljorg.org; 🎫 $5) displays works by Frederic Remington and Georgia O'Keeffe, among others. Next door is an **IMAX 3D Theater** (☎ 317/233–4629, WEB www.in.gov/whiteriver/imax; 🎫 $8).

The **NCAA Hall of Champions** (✉ 700 W. Washington St., ☎ 317/917–6222 or 800/735–6222, WEB www.ncaa.org) is in White River State Park. Visitors to the 40,000-square-ft museum can see college games on a 144-ft video monitor, watch championship games in one of four theaters, and tour the multimedia exhibits to learn about past NCAA champs. Across from White River State Park, the Indiana Historical Society has erected a stunning neoclassical-style building, the **Indiana**

Historical Society Headquarters (✉ 450 W. Ohio St., ☎ 317/232–1882, WEB www.ncaa.org; 🎟 free). The complex includes a museum of Indiana history, a 30,000-square-ft library, and the Cole Porter Room, where you can listen to music by such Hoosiers as Porter, Hoagy Carmichael, and John Mellencamp.

The **Indiana Convention Center & RCA Dome** (✉ 100 S. Capitol Ave., ☎ 317/262–3389; 317/262–3452 for entertainment line, WEB www.iccrd.com; 🎟 free), home to the NFL's Indianapolis Colts, is 19 stories and is one of six major air-supported domed stadiums in the world.

Ornate Victorian furnishings, political mementos, and period ball gowns of the nation's 23rd president and first lady fill the 1875 **President Benjamin Harrison Home** (✉ 1230 N. Delaware St., ☎ 317/631–1888, WEB www.surf-ici.com/harrison; 🎟 $5.50). The **Morris-Butler House** (✉ 1204 N. Park Ave., ☎ 317/636–5409, WEB www.historiclandmarks.org; 🎟 $5), a restored 1865 Second Empire–style gem, is filled with fancy furnishings, dazzling chandeliers, and rich woodwork.

In the historic Lockerbie Square neighborhood, the **James Whitcomb Riley Museum Home** (✉ 528 Lockerbie St., ☎ 317/631–5885; 🎟 $3), acclaimed as one of the nation's finest examples of Victoriana, remains almost as the noted poet left it.

Midtown/Crosstown

Named for the country's first black female self-made millionaire and once frequented by jazz legends Ella Fitzgerald and Wes Montgomery, the 1927 **Madame Walker Theatre Center** (✉ 617 Indiana Ave., ☎ 317/236–2099; 🎟 free, tours by appointment) today presents "Jazz on the Avenue" on Friday night.

The world's largest water clock, a planetarium, the nation's first Cine-Dome Theater, a science center, Playscape, and nine other major galleries make up the **Children's Museum of Indianapolis** (✉ 3000 N. Meridian St., ☎ 317/924–5437 or 800/208–5437, WEB www.childrensmuseum.org; 🎟 $8). With 11,000 artifacts on five floors, the museum ranks as one of the nation's 20 most-visited museums. Take a spin on the turn-of-the-20th-century carousel and explore the replica limestone cave.

The **Indianapolis Museum of Art** (✉ 1200 W. 38th St., ☎ 317/920–2660, WEB www.ima-art.org; 🎟 free), a five-pavilion complex and botanical gardens on 152 acres of manicured lawns, has works by J. M. W. Turner, the old masters, and the neo-impressionists, along with major Asian, African, and decorative arts collections. **Crown Hill Cemetery** (✉ 700 W. 38th St., ☎ 317/920–2726, WEB www.crownhill.org; 🎟 free), the nation's third largest, is the final resting place of notorious criminal John Dillinger, President Benjamin Harrison, and a host of American authors.

South Side

The stunning **Christel DeHaan Fine Arts Center** (✉ 1400 E. Hanna Ave., ☎ 317/788–3211, WEB www.uindy.edu; 🎟 free) at the University of Indianapolis has exhibition space and a 500-seat concert hall renowned for its acoustics.

West Side

The **Indianapolis Motor Speedway Hall of Fame Museum** (✉ 4790 W. 16th St., ☎ 317/484–6747, WEB www.indy500.com/museum; 🎟 $3) displays winning cars of the Indianapolis 500, as well as classic and antique autos. The **Indiana Medical History Museum** (✉ 3045 W. Vermont St., ☎ 317/635–7329, WEB www.imhm.org; 🎟 $5), a turn-of-the-20th-century pathology laboratory, exhibits 15,000 medical treatment and health-care artifacts.

Parks, Gardens, and Zoos

There are jogging, biking, hiking, golfing, and swimming facilities at the rustic 4,200-acre **Eagle Creek Park** (✉ 7840 W. 56th St., ☎ 317/327–7110, WEB www.indygov.org/indyparks; 💵 $2 per car). A nature center, huge playground, and a network of trails and riverfront boardwalks fill woodsy **Holliday Park** (✉ 6363 Spring Mill Rd., ☎ 317/327–7180, WEB www.indygov.org/indyparks; 💵 free).

White River State Park (✉ 801 W. Washington St., ☎ 317/665–9056, WEB www.state.in.us/dnr/parklake/parks/whiteriver.html; 💵 free) is a 250-acre greenbelt straddling White River with sculptures dotting grassy areas, a waterfall, paved walkways, and a ½-mi walled gardenlike riverside trail, the River Promenade. Within the park is the **Indianapolis Zoo** (✉ 1200 W. Washington St., ☎ 317/630–2001, WEB www.indyzoo.com; 💵 $10.75). Next door is the **White River Gardens** (✉ 1200 W. Washington St., ☎ 317/630–2001, WEB www.whiterivergardens.com; 💵 $6.50), a 3⅓-acre complex with a 5,000-square-ft glass conservatory, a gift shop, more than 1,000 species of plants, and 1½ mi of pathways.

The downtown **Canal Walk,** a 10½-block vestige of the historic 400-mi canal system linking the Great Lakes and the Ohio River, is an urban haven, with benches, fountains, and wide walkways lining both sides of the canal. The 7½-mi paved **Monon Trail** (☎ 317/327–7431, WEB www.indygov.org/indyparks) connects northern suburbs and Broad Ripple Village to the Indiana State Fairgrounds on East 38th Street.

Dining

$$$–$$$$ ✕ **St. Elmo Steak House.** Since 1902 this has been the place for big steaks, large martinis, and eye-watering shrimp cocktail sauce. Visiting celebrities often book a table here or stop by the cigar room. *✉ 127 S. Illinois St., ☎ 317/635–0636 or 800/637–1811. AE, MC, V. No lunch.*

$$–$$$$ ✕ **Peter's A Restaurant & Bar.** The seasonal menu here may include pomegranate-glazed Indiana duckling with sweet-potato custard and mustard greens. Chilean sea bass is seared and basted with a spicy orange-chili marinade. *✉ 8505 Keystone Crossing Blvd., ☎ 317/465–1155 or 800/479–0909. AE, D, DC, MC, V. Closed Sun. No lunch.*

$$–$$$$ ✕ **The Restaurant at the Canterbury.** Inside the Canterbury Hotel, this is one of the city's best restaurants. The clubby dining room has wood paneling and crisp white linens. The traditional dishes—Dover sole, pepper-crusted rack of lamb—are expertly prepared. *✉ 123 S. Illinois St., ☎ 317/634–3000 Ext. 7230. AE, D, DC, MC, V.*

$$–$$$$ ✕ **Something Different/SNAX.** Tapas at SNAX are just enough to whet your appetite for dinner next door. Sister restaurant Something Different serves dinners that consistently push the envelope with inspired, well-prepared fare. The setting is chic, the menu innovative American. *✉ 4939 E. 82nd St., ☎ 317/570–7700. AE, D, MC, V. Closed Sun. No lunch.*

$–$$$ ✕ **Palomino.** Fine contemporary food is the hallmark of this upscale and popular European bistro. The oven-roasted mussels in rosemary-lemon butter and authentic paella casserole are not to be missed. *✉ 49 W. Maryland St., ☎ 317/974–0400. AE, D, DC, MC, V.*

$ ✕ **Shapiro's Delicatessen Cafeteria.** The strawberry cheesecake and huge corned-beef sandwiches on rye are signature items at this nationally known deli, an Indianapolis institution since 1904. *✉ 808 S. Meridian St., ☎ 317/631–4041; ✉ 2370 W. 86th St., ☎ 317/872–7255. Reservations not accepted. No credit cards.*

Lodging

$$$–$$$$ **University Place–IUPUI, Doubletree Hotel.** Rooms in this hotel on the shared campus of Indiana and Purdue universities are handsomely appointed, with desks, easy chairs, and 18th-century reproduction furnishings. ✉ *850 W. Michigan St., 46202,* ☎ *317/269–9000 or 800/627–2700,* FAX *317/231–5168,* WEB *www.universityplace.iupui.edu. 278 rooms. 2 restaurants, pool, health club. AE, D, DC, MC, V. BP.*

$$$ ★ **Canterbury Hotel.** The luxurious guest rooms at this 60-year-old hostelry have armoires, queen-size four-poster beds, and elegant baths. A covered skywalk leads to Circle Centre. ✉ *123 S. Illinois St., 46225,* ☎ *317/634–3000 or 800/538–8186,* FAX *317/685–2519. 99 rooms. Restaurant, health club. AE, D, DC, MC, V. CP.*

$$$ **Sheraton Indianapolis Hotel & Suites.** The upscale high-rise hotel is at the Fashion Mall, Keystone at the Crossing shopping and entertainment complex, a 40-minute drive from downtown or the airport. A covered skywalk connects to 100 shops and restaurants. ✉ *8787 Keystone Crossing, 46240,* ☎ *317/846–2700,* FAX *317/574–6775,* WEB *www.starwood.com/sheraton. 560 rooms. Restaurant, pool, health club. AE, D, DC, MC, V. CP.*

$$–$$$ **Omni Severin Hotel.** Across from historic Union Station, this hotel has crystal chandeliers, a marble staircase, and cast-iron balustrades recalling its 1913 origins. Guest rooms are a blend of traditional and Mediterranean styles. ✉ *40 W. Jackson Pl., 46225,* ☎ *317/634–6664 or 800/843–6664,* FAX *317/687–3619,* WEB *www.omnihotels.com. 424 rooms. 2 restaurants, pool, health club. AE, D, DC, MC, V. CP.*

Nightlife and the Arts

Nightlife

Pub crawling is best in out-of-the-way neighborhoods such as **Broad Ripple Village.** Explore the offbeat **Massachusetts Avenue Arts District** for interesting art galleries, unusual shops, and neighborhood eateries and taverns. There are Christmas lights and checkered flags year-round at the **Chatterbox** (✉ 435 Massachusetts Ave., ☎ 317/636–0584), where a varied clientele stops by for late-night jazz. On Level 4 of **Circle Centre,** there are nightclubs, nine cinemas, and virtual-reality and arcade games.

The Arts

NUVO Newsweekly, Indianapolis Monthly magazine, and the Friday and Sunday editions of the *Indianapolis Star* list events. **Tickets: Court Side Tickets, Inc.** (✉ 6100 N. Keystone Ave., Suite 103, ☎ 317/254–9500 or 800/627–1334) is a good source for sporting events. **Front Row Tickets** (✉ 1001 Broad Ripple Ave., Suite C, ☎ 317/255–3220 or 800/695–9676) sells tickets for sporting events and concerts. You can snag tickets for Colts games at **Premium Tickets, Inc.** (✉ 2113 Broad Ripple Ave., ☎ 317/255–3220 or 800/695–9676). You can buy tickets for several venues at **Ticketmaster** (✉ 2 W. Washington St., ☎ 317/239–5151).

MUSIC

Indianapolis Symphony Orchestra (✉ 45 Monument Cir., ☎ 317/262–1100 for tickets, WEB www.indyorch.org) performs at the Hilbert Circle Theatre from September through May and outdoors at Conner Prairie in summer. The **Indianapolis Opera** (✉ 250 E. 38th St., ☎ 317/283–3531 or 317/239–1000, WEB www.indyopera.org) stages productions from its grand opera repertoire and new works each season.

About 20 mi northeast of downtown Indianapolis, **Verizon Wireless Music Center** (✉ 12880 E. 146th St., Noblesville, ☎ 317/776–3337 or 317/841–8900) brings top-name performers to its outdoor facility.

THEATER

Indiana's only resident professional theater, the **Indiana Repertory Theatre** (✉ 140 W. Washington St., ☎ 317/635–5277 or 317/635–5252, WEB www.indianarep.com) presents major works in a restored 1927 movie palace downtown. The resident troupe at **Beef & Boards Dinner Theatre** (✉ 9301 N. Michigan Rd., ☎ 317/872–9664, WEB www.beefandboards.com), on the northwest side, stages Broadway shows with a dinner buffet. Original musical revues play at **American Cabaret Theatre** (✉ 401 E. Michigan St., ☎ 317/631–0334, WEB www.americancabarettheatre.com). Avant-garde plays take the stage at the **Phoenix Theatre** (✉ 749 N. Park Ave., ☎ 317/635–7529, WEB www.phoenixtheatre.org).

Spectator Sports

Baseball: The city's Minor League team is the **Indianapolis Indians** (✉ Victory Field, 501 W. Maryland St., ☎ 317/269–3545). **Basketball:** If you catch the **Indiana Pacers** (✉ Conseco Fieldhouse, 125 S. Pennsylvania St., ☎ 317/917–2500; 317/239–5151 for tickets) take note that the field house was constructed with the help of the world's largest crane. **Football:** The RCA Dome is the home of the **Indianapolis Colts** (✉ 7001 W. 56th St., ☎ 317/297–7000). **Ice hockey:** The **Indianapolis Ice** (✉ 1202 E. 38th St., ☎ 317/925–4423 or 317/239–5151) roost at the Pepsi Coliseum and also play some games at the Pacers' Conseco Fieldhouse. **Soccer:** Indiana's pro soccer and women's soccer teams are respectively the **Indiana Blast/Indiana Blaze** (✉ Kuntz Memorial Soccer Stadium, 1502 W. 16th St., ☎ 317/585–9203).

Shopping

Downtown, the **Circle Centre** (✉ 1 W. Washington St., ☎ 317/681–8000) is home to Nordstrom (☎ 317/636–2121) and Parisian (☎ 317/971–6200), which headline a roster of 120 retailers at the swanky mall. On the north side of town, the **Fashion Mall, Keystone at the Crossing** (✉ 9000 Keystone Crossing, ☎ 317/574–4002) is anchored by the upscale Jacobson's (☎ 317/574–0088) and Parisian (☎ 317/581–8200) department stores. About 6 mi north of downtown, **Broad Ripple Village** (✉ 62nd St. at Broad Ripple and College Aves., ☎ 317/251–2782) has art galleries, gift shops, and boutiques.

Side Trips from Indianapolis

Bloomington, Brown County, and Columbus

About an hour's drive south of the capital city on Route 46, the flat expanse of farmland dominating the upper two-thirds of the state gives way to hilly terrain. In **Bloomington,** home of Indiana University, ethnic restaurants, boutiques, galleries, and shops surround the courthouse square and fill **Fountain Square** (✉ 308 Fountain Sq., Kirkwood and College Aves., ☎ 812/336–3681), a block-long mall distinguished by historic storefront facades. For information contact the **Monroe County Convention & Visitors Bureau** (✉ 2855 N. Walnut St., Bloomington 47404, ☎ 812/334–8900 or 800/800–0037, WEB www.visitbloomington.com).

Columbus is a forward-thinking city with more than 50 contemporary-style structures by world-renowned architects. Contact the **Columbus**

Area Visitors Center (✉ Box 1589, 506 5th St., 47202, ☎ 812/378–2622 or 800/468–6564, WEB www.columbus.in.us) for information.

In picturesque Brown County, the quaint village of **Nashville** was a gathering place for artists in the early 1900s. Today, country-cooking eateries and shops nestle in alongside artists' studios and galleries throughout town.

Contact the **Nashville/Brown County Convention &Visitors Bureau** (✉ Main and Van Buren Sts. [Box 840, Nashville 47448], ☎ 812/988–7303 or 800/753–3255, WEB www.browncounty.com) for information.

Centerville and Richmond

Beginning in the 1820s, historic **Centerville** and **Richmond,** on the Ohio state line, saw as many as 200 wagons pass daily on the National Road, a western immigration trail and America's first federally funded highway (now U.S. Highway 40). Today, a 30-mi stretch of road from Richmond to Knightstown is known as Antique Alley, with more than 800 dealers. The **Richmond/Wayne County Convention & Visitors Bureau** (✉ 5701 National Rd. E, Richmond 47374, ☎ 765/935–8687 or 800/828–8414, WEB www.visitrichmond.org) has information on the area.

Hamilton County

Towns in this county northeast of downtown were once simply bedroom communities for Indianapolis. But restoration of the stately county courthouse in Noblesville coincided with a renaissance of museums, shops, and restaurants. It's always 1836 at **Conner Prairie** (✉ 13400 Allisonville Rd., Fishers 46038, ☎ 317/776–6000 or 800/966–1836, WEB www.connerprairie.org), a re-created pioneer village complex in Fishers with costumed interpreters. For information contact the **Hamilton County Convention & Visitors Bureau** (✉ 11601 Municipal Dr., Fishers 46038, ☎ 317/598–4444 or 800/776–8687, WEB www.hccvb.com).

Parke County

Dubbed the Covered-Bridge Capital of the World, Parke County has 32 covered bridges scattered within an hour's drive west of Indianapolis (take Route 136). Every October Rockville and seven nearby towns welcome 1 million visitors to the 10-day **Covered Bridge Festival,** with crafts fairs, quilts and antiques shows, and barbecue beef and bean-soup dinners. During the **Maple Syrup Festival** in early spring, sugar shacks open their doors to let visitors peek inside and taste the sweet treats. The **Covered Bridge Capital Convention & Visitors Bureau** (✉ 401 E. Ohio St. [Box 165, Rockville 47872], ☎ 765/569–5226, WEB www.coveredbridges.com) provides details about the area.

Zionsville

Brick streets and Stick-style early 19th-century wood cottages create a fairy-tale setting for the town's quaint shops and intimate restaurants. Though a 30-minute drive from downtown's domed stadium and shiny new high-rises, Zionsville seems to be perfectly preserved. Contact the **Greater Zionsville Chamber of Commerce** (✉ 135 S. Elm St. [Box 148, 46077], ☎ 317/873–3836).

Indianapolis Essentials

AIRPORTS AND TRANSFERS

The Indianapolis International Airport is served by major and commuter airlines.

➤ Airport Information: **Indianapolis International Airport** (✉ 1500 S. High School Rd., ☎ 317/487–9594, WEB www.indianapolisairport.com).

AIRPORT TRANSFER

The trip from the airport to downtown or to the west side of town is about 20–25 minutes. To the other parts of town it's a 30- to 45-minute drive. By taxi or limo, the cost is $10–$46 to downtown, $35–$71 to most other destinations. Carey Indiana charges $10 per passenger for shared rides from the airport to downtown and provides shared-ride limousine service from the airport to outlying parts of the city for $30 per passenger.

➤ TAXIS AND SHUTTLES: **Carey Indiana** (☎ 317/241–7100).

BUS TRAVEL TO AND FROM INDIANAPOLIS

➤ BUS INFORMATION: **Greyhound Bus Terminal** (✉ 350 S. Illinois St., ☎ 317/267–3071 or 800/231–2222).

BUS TRAVEL WITHIN INDIANAPOLIS

IndyGo buses run from 4:45 AM to 11:45 PM on heavily traveled routes, with shorter schedules in the suburbs. Fares ($1) are payable upon boarding.

➤ BUS INFORMATION: **IndyGo** (☎ 317/635–3344).

CAR TRAVEL

With more segments of interstate highway (I–65, I–69, I–70, I–74, and I–465) intersecting here than anywhere else in the country, Indianapolis is indisputably a driving city. Car rentals are available at major hotels and at the airport.

TAXIS

Yellow Cab taxis are radio dispatched; call ahead to be sure of getting a cab, unless you're at the airport or downtown. The fare includes a pick-up fare of $1.25, then $2 for each mile.

➤ TAXI COMPANY: **Indianapolis Yellow Cab** (☎ 317/487–7777).

TRAIN TRAVEL

Amtrak offers limited service.

➤ TRAIN INFORMATION: **Amtrak** (✉ Union Station, 350 S. Illinois St., ☎ 317/263–0550 or 800/872–7245).

TRANSPORTATION AROUND INDIANAPOLIS

VISITOR INFORMATION

➤ TOURIST INFORMATION: **Indianapolis City Center** (✉ 201 S. Capitol Ave., Pan American Plaza, Suite 200, 46225, ☎ 317/237–5200 or 800/824–4639, WEB www.indy.org). **Indianapolis Convention & Visitors Association** (✉ 1 RCA Dome, Suite 100, 46225, ☎ 317/639–4282).

SOUTHERN INDIANA

Dense stands of oak, hickory, and maple crown the rolling terrain that dominates southern Indiana. Tucked among the hills and valleys are 19th-century riverfront towns, caves that beg to be explored, and vast stretches of clear blue water.

Exploring Southern Indiana

Three-hundred-year-old **Vincennes** brims with history. **Grouseland** (✉ 3 W. Scott St., ☎ 812/882–2096, WEB www.accessknoxcounty.com; 🎫 $3) was the home of the ninth U.S. president, William Henry Harrison. The log-and-mud **Old French House and Indian Museum** (✉ 509 N. 1st St., ☎ 812/882–7886 or 800/886–6443, WEB www.accessknoxcounty.com; 🎫 $1) is a French-Creole cottage constructed by a French fur trader in 1806.

In the southwesternmost corner of Indiana, quaint **New Harmony** was the site of two 19th-century utopian communities; contact Historic New Harmony, Inc. (✉ Box 579, New Harmony 47631, ☎ 812/682–4488 or 800/231–2168, WEB www.newharmony.org; 🎫 $8) for information. Special tours are held at Christmas.

In the historic Riverside District of **Evansville,** columned mansions such as the **Historic Reitz Home** (✉ 224 S.E. 1st St., ☎ 812/426–1871, www.reitzhome.evansville.net, WEB www.evansvillecvb.org; 🎫 $2) overlook the Ohio River. The **Evansville Museum of Arts and Science** (✉ 411 S.E. Riverside Dr., ☎ 812/425–2406, WEB www.emuseum.org; 🎫 free) has American and European art from the 1700s to the present, a planetarium, and a reconstructed turn-of-the-20th-century village.

In **Corydon,** Indiana's first capital, you can browse through 10,000 square ft of antiques in two downtown malls. Corydon's Federal-style **Corydon Capitol State Historic Site** (✉ 202 E. Walnut St., ☎ 812/738–4890, www.ai.org/ism/sites/corydon, WEB www.tourindiana.com; 🎫 free) is where the state's first constitution was drafted. The **Corydon 1883 Scenic Railroad** (✉ 210 Walnut St., ☎ 812/738–8000, WEB www.tourindiana.com; 🎫 $9) makes a 16-mi (90-minute) trip through the countryside in the summer and fall.

Dubbed the Williamsburg of the Midwest, **Madison** is an antebellum-era town whose entire main street and 100 additional blocks are listed on the National Register of Historic Places. See the gleaming white Greek Revival **Lanier Mansion State Historic Site** (✉ 511 W. 1st St., ☎ 812/265–3526, WEB www.ai.org/ism/sites/lanier; 🎫 free), whose portico overlooks the Ohio River. Exhibits trace the heydays of steamboating and trains in southeastern Indiana at the **Jefferson County Historical Society Museum and 1895 Madison Railroad Station** (✉ 615 W. 1st St., ☎ 812/265–2335; 🎫 $2).

Dining and Lodging

For a directory of inns, contact the **Indiana Bed & Breakfast Association** (✉ Box 1127, Goshen 46526, ☎ no phone, WEB www.BedandBreakfast.org).

Corydon

$ 🏨 **Kintner House Inn.** Once the headquarters of Confederate general John Hunt Morgan, the inn dates from the mid-1800s. The large rooms have Victorian furnishings and antique light fixtures. ✉ *101 S. Capitol St., at Chestnut St., 47112,* ☎ *812/738–2020,* WEB *www.kintnerhouse.com. 15 rooms. AE, D, DC, MC, V. BP.*

New Harmony

$ ✕🏨 **New Harmony Inn.** On spacious grounds overlooking a small lake, this contemporary-style inn has two fine restaurants, the Red Geranium and the Bayou Grill. Rooms are furnished sparsely, with Shaker-style furniture, original artwork, and antiques. ✉ *506 North St. (Box 581, 47631),* ☎ *812/682–4724 or 800/782–8605,* WEB *www.redg.com. 90 rooms. 2 restaurants, pool, tennis, gym. AE, D, DC, MC, V. CP.*

Outdoor Activities and Sports

Biking

Six routes on the **Hoosier Bikeway System** managed by the Outdoor Recreation Division of the Indiana Department of Natural Resources (✉ 402 W. Washington St., Room W271, Indianapolis 46204, ☎ 317/232–4070) run through this area.

Fishing

Anglers at **Patoka Lake** (✉ 3084 N. Dillard Rd., Birdseye, ☎ 812/685–2464, WEB www.state.in.us/dnr/parklake/reservoirs/patoka) haul in record catches of bass, carp, and catfish. The **Markland Dam,** on the Ohio River off Route 156 near Vevay (☎ 812/358–4110) is a prime fishing spot for carp, catfish, sauger, and striped bass. Contact the **Indiana Department of Natural Resources, Division of Fish and Wildlife** (✉ 402 W. Washington St., Room W273, Indianapolis 46204, ☎ 317/232–4080, WEB www.state.in.us/dnr/fishwild) for permits and information.

Southern Indiana Essentials

AIRPORTS

Evansville Regional Airport is served by commuter and regional airlines.

➤ AIRPORT INFORMATION: **Evansville Regional Airport** (✉ 7801 Bussing Dr., ☎ 812/421–4401, WEB www.evvairport.com).

BUS TRAVEL

Service between Indianapolis, Evansville, and Vincennes is available on Greyhound.

➤ BUS INFORMATION: **Greyhound** (☎ 812/425–8274 or 800/231–2222).

CAR TRAVEL

The major road through this region is I–64. From Indianapolis take I–70 and U.S. 41 to Vincennes and Evansville, I–65 and Route 7 to Madison, and I–65 to Clarksville and Jeffersonville. From Louisville, Kentucky, take I–65; from Cincinnati, Ohio, take I–74.

VISITOR INFORMATION

For general information on southern Indiana, contact the Clark/Floyd Counties Convention & Tourism Bureau. For information on New Harmony, contact the Evansville Convention & Visitors Bureau.

➤ TOURIST INFORMATION: **Clark/Floyd Counties Convention & Tourism Bureau** (✉ 305 Southern Indiana Ave., Jeffersonville 47130, ☎ 812/280–5566 or 800/552–3842, WEB www.sunnysideoflouisville.org). **Evansville Convention & Visitors Bureau** (✉ 401 S.E. Riverside Dr., Evansville 47713, ☎ 812/421–2200 or 800/433–3025, WEB www.evansvillecvb.org). **Lincoln Hills/Patoka Lake Recreation Region** (✉ 125 S. 8th St., Courthouse Annex, Cannelton 47520, ☎ 812/547–7028, WEB www.explore-si.com). **Madison Area Convention & Visitors Bureau** (✉ 301 E. Main St., Madison 47250, ☎ 812/265–2956 or 800/559–2956, WEB www.visitmadison.org). **Vincennes/Knox County Convention & Visitors Bureau** (✉ 102 N. 3rd St., Box 602, Vincennes 47591, ☎ 812/886–0400 or 800/886–6443, WEB www.accessknoxcounty.com).

NORTHERN INDIANA

Stretches of dunes and inviting beaches along Lake Michigan give way to a neat grid of lush farmland dotted with Amish communities in northeastern Indiana. The state's second-largest city, Fort Wayne, has lake country to the west and charming Amish towns like Grabill to the northwest and east.

Exploring Northern Indiana

In one of the nation's earliest conservation efforts, the poet Carl Sandburg fought to save the land that is now the 2,200-acre **Indiana Dunes State Park** in the northwestern corner of the state. Visitors can reach 40 mph on twin ¼-mi refrigerated toboggan tracks at **Pokagan State**

Park (✉ 450 Lane 100, Lake James, Angola, ☎ 219/833–2012, WEB www.state.in.us/dnr/parklake/parks/pokagon; 🎟 park $2 per car residents, $5 nonresidents; toboggan $4 per hr).

In Michigan City, the 1905 **Barker Mansion & Civic Center** (✉ 631 Washington St., ☎ 219/873–1520, WEB www.harborcountry-in.org/Pages/attract; 🎟 $3) showcases the opulent lifestyle of freight car magnate John H. Barker with its lavish interior and marble fireplaces. **Old Lighthouse Museum** (✉ Heisman Harbor Rd., ☎ 219/872–6133, WEB www.harborcountry-in.org/Pages/attract; 🎟 $2) is the only Indiana lighthouse along Lake Michigan. The 1858 lighthouse—which hasn't shone a light since 1904—has city-history exhibits.

Fans flock to South Bend each year to see the **University of Notre Dame**'s Fighting Irish. Be sure to stop by the landmark Golden Dome (✉ U.S. 33 N, ☎ 219/239–7367, WEB www.nd.edu). At the **College Football Hall of Fame,** a "stadium" theater shows rousing videos of gridiron action on a 360-degree screen and interactive exhibits trace legendary players and coaches from the collegiate ranks (✉ 111 S. St. Joseph St., ☎ 219/235–9999 or 800/440–3263, WEB www.collegefootball.org; 🎟 $10). Downtown South Bend's **East Race Waterway** (✉ 321 E. Walter St., ☎ 219/299–4768) attracts tubers, rafters, and Olympic kayakers. The **Studebaker National Museum** (✉ 525 S. Main St., ☎ 219/235–9714, WEB www.studebakermusuem.org; 🎟 $4.50) celebrates the company's 114-year history with exhibits of 75 Studebaker-related vehicles, from Conestoga wagons to automobiles, including the last Studebaker built in South Bend, a red 1964 hardtop.

The 75-mi corridor from South Bend southeast to Fort Wayne goes through Indiana's **Amish Country. Amish Acres** (✉ 1600 W. Market St., U.S. 6, Nappanee, ☎ 219/773–4188 or 800/800–4942, WEB www.amishacres.com; 🎟 $6.95) is an 80-acre restored Amish farm with a dinner theater in the round and a restaurant and inn with Amish furnishings. **Riegsecker Marketplace** (✉ 105 E. Middlebury St., Shipshewana, ☎ 219/768–4725, WEB www.riegsecker.com) is composed of shops and the Blue Gate Restaurant & Bakery at the four-way stop in the tiny Amish farm town of Shipshewana. More than 1,000 vendors crowd the 40-acre open-air **Shipshewana Auction & Flea Market** (✉ Rte. 5 S, Shipshewana, ☎ 219/768–4129, WEB www.tradingplaceamerica.com) every Tuesday and Wednesday from May to October, drawing 35,000 visitors daily. The **Old Bag Factory** (✉ 1100 Chicago Ave., Goshen, ☎ 219/534–2502, WEB www.oldbagfactory.com; 🎟 free), a massive redbrick structure dating from 1895, has 18 shops, including a custom hardwood-furniture maker and potter. Outside Fort Wayne, **Grabill** (✉ Chamber of Commerce, Box 7, Grabill 46741, ☎ 219/627–522 or 800/939–3216, WEB www.grabill.org) seems caught in a time warp, with Amish buggies hitched up all around town. West of Fort Wayne, hundreds of kettle lakes, as well as **Lake Wawasee and Lake Maxinkuckee,** attract summer vacationers in the Lake County of Kosciusko County.

Dining and Lodging

For a directory of inns, contact the **Indiana Bed & Breakfast Association** (✉ Box 1127, Goshen 46526, ☎ no phone, WEB www.bedandbreakfast.org). For Amish Country inn bookings contact the **Four Seasons Bed & Breakfast Group** (✉ Box 1458, Middlebury 46540, ☎ 800/262–8161).

Amish Country

$$–$$$ ✕🏨 **Checkerberry Inn.** On 100 acres, this elegant hostelry has the state's only professional croquet course, a walking lane, and woodlands. A cup of tea in the solarium is a must. The restaurant features sumptuous French-accented three-course dinners. (✉ *62644 CR 37, Goshen 46526,* ☎ FAX *219/642–4445,* WEB *www.checkerberryinn.com. 14 rooms. Restaurant, tennis. AE, MC, V. CP.*

$ **Das Dutchman Essenhaus.** The three-story, softly lit atrium with a potbellied stove is the centerpiece of this inn. Locally handcrafted Amish quilts and furniture make guest rooms simple but inviting. Within the Essenhaus complex is a huge restaurant and bakery with more than 20 kinds of pie, shops, a petting farm, and miniature golf. ✉ *240 U.S. 20, Middlebury 46540,* ☎ *800/455–9471,* ☎ FAX *219/825–9447,* WEB *www.essenhaus.com. 33 rooms. Restaurant. AE, D, MC, V.*

$ **Farmstead Inn.** The styling of this inn is inspired by the white Amish farmhouses that dot the surrounding countryside. There are a basketball court and recreation facilities in the adjoining Red Barn building. The inn is across from the famous Shipshewana Flea Market & Auction and a two-block walk from 70 shops in the tiny downtown area. ✉ *370 S. Van Buren St., at Rte. 5 S, 46565,* ☎ *219/768–4595,* FAX *219/768–7319,* WEB *www.tradingplaceamerica.com. 85 rooms. Pool, exercise equipment. AE, D, MC, V.*

Indiana's North Coast

$$–$$$ ✕ **Miller Bakery Cafe.** A cozy bakery turned eatery, this spot has received rave reviews for its inventive fare. Start dinner with savory bread pudding with cilantro pesto or wild mushroom ragout. Then, move on to New Zealand rack of lamb with coarse whole-grain mustard sauce or sautéed veal medallions with caramelized mushrooms. ✉ *555 S. Lake St., Gary,* ☎ *219/938–2229. MC, V.*

$–$$ **Hutchinson Mansion Inn.** The 1876 mansion spanning almost a city block is accented with stained-glass windows and marble fireplaces. Antiques and fresh flowers fill the guest rooms and public spaces. ✉ *220 W. 10th St., Michigan City 46360,* ☎ *219/879–1700,* WEB *www.bbonline.com/in/hutchinson. 10 rooms. AE, MC, V. BP.*

South Bend/Mishawaka

$$–$$$ **Book Inn.** High ceilings, original woodwork, and a homemade breakfast served with silver and Waterford crystal make this downtown South Bend inn a favorite. The decor in the Charlotte Brontë, Louisa May Alcott, and Jane Austen guest rooms reflects the era of its respective namesakes; amenities, such as data ports, reflect this one. ✉ *508 W. Washington St., South Bend 46601,* ☎ *219/288–1990 or 877/288–1990,* FAX *219/234–2338,* WEB *www.book-inn.co. 5 rooms. AE, MC, V. BP.*

Northern Indiana Essentials

AIRPORTS

The South Bend Regional Airport is served by national and regional carriers.

➤ AIRPORT INFORMATION: **South Bend Regional Airport** (✉ 4477 Terminal Dr., South Bend, ☎ 219/233–2185, WEB www.sbnair.com).

BUS TRAVEL

United Limo in Osceola provides daily service to and from Chicago. Other service is available on Greyhound.

➤ BUS INFORMATION: **Greyhound** (✉ 4671 Terminal Dr., South Bend, ☎ 800/231–2222 or 219/287–6541). **United Limo** (☎ 219/234–6600 or 800/833–5555).

CAR TRAVEL

Major east–west roads are I–80/90 and U.S. 12 and 20. Traversing the region north–south are I–65, I–69, and U.S. 31 and 41.

TRAIN TRAVEL

The South Shore Line connects South Bend, northwestern Indiana, and Chicago with regular service daily.

➤ TRAIN INFORMATION: **Amtrak** (✉ 2702 Washington Ave., South Bend, ☎ 800/872–7245). **South Shore Line** (✉ 2702 W. Washington St., South Bend, ☎ 219/233–3111 or 800/356–2079).

VISITOR INFORMATION

For Amish Country information, contact the Amish Country/ Elkhart County Convention & Visitors Bureau and the LaGrange County Convention & Visitors Bureau. Kosciusko County Convention & Visitors Bureau has information on the Lake Country. The convention and visitors bureaus in Lake County, Porter County, LaPorte County, and South Bend/Mishawaka all have information on the Lake Michigan North Coast and South Bend areas.

➤ TOURIST INFORMATION: **Amish Country/Elkhart County Convention & Visitors Bureau** (✉ 219 Caravan Dr., Elkhart 46514, ☎ 219/262–8161 or 800/262–8161, WEB www.amishcountry.org). **Fort Wayne/Allen County Convention & Visitors Bureau** (✉ 1021 S. Calhoun St., 46802, ☎ 219/424–3700 or 800/767–7752, WEB www.fwcvb.org). **Kosciusko County Convention & Visitors Bureau** (✉ 111 Capital Dr., Warsaw 46580, ☎ 219/269–6090 or 800/800–6090, WEB koscvb.org). **LaGrange County Convention & Visitors Bureau** (✉ 440½ S. Van Buren St., Route 5 S, Shipshewana 46565, ☎ 219/768–4008 or 800/254–8090, WEB www.backroads.org). **Lake County Convention & Visitors Bureau** (✉ 7770 Corinne Dr., Hammond 46323, ☎ 219/989–7770 or 800/255–5253, WEB alllake.org). **Northern Indiana Harbor Country/LaPorte County Convention & Visitors Bureau** (✉ 1503 S. Meer Rd., LaPorte 46360, ☎ 219/872–5055 or 800/685–7174, WEB www.harborcountry-in.org). **Porter County Convention, Recreation & Visitors Bureau** (✉ 800 Indian Boundary Rd., Chesterton 46304, ☎ 219/926–2255 or 800/283–8687, WEB www.casualcoast.com). **South Bend/Mishawaka Convention & Visitors Bureau** (✉ 401 E. Colfax Ave., South Bend 46617, ☎ 219/234–0051 or 800/282–2230, WEB www.livethelegends.org).

Updated by Diana Lambdin Meyer

Capital	Des Moines
Population	2,926,324
Motto	Our Liberties We Prize and Our Rights We Will Maintain
State Bird	Eastern goldfinch
State Flower	Wild rose
Postal Abbreviation	IA

Statewide Visitor Information

The **Tourism Office** (✉ Iowa Dept. of Economic Development, 200 E. Grand Ave., Des Moines 50309, ☎ 515/242–4705 or 800/345–4692, WEB www.traveliowa.com) has 21 welcome centers along I–35 and I–80 and in towns throughout the state. For regional visitor information call or write **Eastern Iowa Tourism Association** (✉ Box 189, Dyersville 52040, ☎ 319/875–7269 or 800/875–2358), **Central Iowa Tourism Region** (✉ Box 454, Webster City 50595–0454, ☎ 515/832–4808 or 800/285–5842), or **Western Iowa Tourism Region** (✉ 103 N. 3rd St., Red Oak 51566, ☎ 712/623–4232 or 888/623–4232).

Scenic Drives

Iowa's most beautiful scenic drive may be the series of roads that take you south along the high bluffs and verdant banks of the Mississippi River on the state's eastern border. In western Iowa, the **Loess Hills Scenic Byway** crisscrosses the Missouri River valley, featuring ancient soil gathered by ice-age winds. Follow Route 12 N from Sioux City. In southeast Iowa **Route 5** from Des Moines to Lake Rathbun, near Centerville, makes a nice detour from I–35; to return to the interstate, take **Route 2 west** from Centerville for about 50 mi.

National and State Parks

National Parks

Effigy Mounds National Monument has hiking trails along prehistoric burial mounds. Iowa has four federal reservoir areas around large man-made lakes: **Coralville Lake** (✉ 2850 Prairie du Chien Rd. NE, Iowa City 52240, ☎ 319/338–3543), **Rathbun Lake** (✉ 20112 Hwy. J5T, Centerville 52544, ☎ 641/647–2464), **Lake Red Rock** (✉ 1105 Hwy. T15, Knoxville 50138-9522, ☎ 641/828–7522), and **Saylorville Lake** (✉ 5600 N.W. 78th Ave., Johnston 50131, ☎ 515/276–4656).

The **Neal Smith National Wildlife Refuge** (✉ 9981 Pacific St., Prairie City 50228, ☎ 515/994–3400), 20 mi east of Des Moines on I–80, has 8,600 acres of reconstructed tallgrass prairie, 5 mi of hiking trails accessible to travelers with disabilities, a prairie education center, and an elk and bison viewing area.

State Parks

Iowa's 69 state parks include 5,306 campsites, many with showers and electrical hookups. Some well-developed parks with campsites, cabins, lodge rentals, and boat rentals are **Clear Lake** (☎ 641/357–4212), near Mason City; **George Wyth Memorial** (☎ 319/232–5505), near Waterloo; **Lacey-Keosauqua** (☎ 319/293–3502), near Keosauqua; and **Lake of Three Fires** (☎ 712/523–2700), near Bedford. Virgin prairie areas, state parks without facilities, include **Cayler Prairie,** near the Great Lakes area in northwestern Iowa; **Hayden Prairie,** near the Minnesota border in the northeastern corner of the state; **Kalsow Prairie,** about 90 mi northwest of Des Moines; and **Sheeder Prairie,** about 50 mi west of Des Moines. Contact the **Iowa Department of Natural Resources** (☎ 515/281–5918) for more information.

DES MOINES

If you were to peer down from an airplane or the top of a hill, the capital of Iowa would look like a cluster of office towers popping out of a green corduroy landscape. Downtown straddles the confluence of two rivers—the Raccoon and the Des Moines. The skyline of historic buildings and modern structures faces granite government buildings and a classic gold-domed capitol across four bridges. Although hardly a glittering metropolis, Des Moines is a relatively hassle-free city with a number of museums, historic districts, and parks, as well as Drake University.

Exploring Des Moines

Downtown

Start a walking tour of downtown Des Moines at the **capitol complex** (✉ E. 9th St. and Grand Ave., ☎ 515/281–5591; free), on the east bank of the Des Moines River. There you can see the elaborate murals in the rotunda of the capitol and climb into the dome, covered in 22-karat gold leaf. Near the capitol, the **Botanical Center** (✉ 909 E. River Dr., ☎ 515/323–8900, WEB www.botanicalcenter.com; $1.50) has flower displays and a three-story, dome-topped jungle. The **Iowa Historical Building** (✉ 600 E. Locust St., ☎ 515/281–5111, WEB www.culturalaffairs.org; free), one block west of the capitol, shakes off any dusty-old-stuff image with its postmodern design, abstract sculpture of neon and glass, and striking fountain display. The building houses the state archives, library, and museum.

Just west of downtown in Greenwood Park, the **Des Moines Art Center** (✉ 4700 Grand Ave., ☎ 515/277–4405, WEB www.desmoinesartcenter.og; free) has a permanent collection of contemporary art. The **Science Center of Iowa** (✉ 4500 Grand Ave., ☎ 515/274–4138, WEB www.sciowa.org; $5.50), in Greenwood–Ashworth Park, has interactive programs that include laser shows, a planetarium, and a space-shuttle simulator appropriate for all ages.

Terrace Hill, an 1866 Victorian mansion known as the "palace of the prairie," is the Iowa governor's mansion. ✉ *2300 Grand Ave.,* ☎ *515/281–3604.* *$5. Closed Sat.–Mon. and Jan.–Feb.*

Some of the city's most interesting buildings are on the west side of the Des Moines River (follow Locust Street from the east side). Get brochures with self-guided walking tours from the **Downtown Community Alliance** (✉ 700 Locust St., Suite 100, ☎ 515/243–6625, WEB www.desmoinesdt.com). The **Sherman Hill Historic District** has impressive Victorian houses. The **Court Avenue District** has restored 19th-century warehouses and other commercial buildings, many of which now have shops, restaurants, and entertainment venues.

Outside the City

Spend a half day exploring **Living History Farms,** a 600-acre open-air museum a few miles northwest of Des Moines. The farms are a trip back in time via the sights, sounds, and smells of an 18th-century Native American village, two working farms from 1850 and 1900, and an 1875 town. ✉ *2600 111th St., Urbandale 50322,* ☎ *515/278–2400,* WEB *www.livinghistoryfarms.org.* *$10. Closed Nov.–Apr. Call for special events in winter.*

Dining

$$–$$$ ✕ **Cafe Su.** Dim sum appetizers are the specialty at this chic restaurant in the Valley Junction shopping area in West Des Moines. ✉ *225 5th St.,* ☎ *515/274–5102. AE, D, DC, MC, V. Closed Sun.–Mon.*

$$–$$$ ✕ **Iowa Room.** In the historic Savery Hotel, the Iowa Room attracts a downtown business crowd for breakfast, lunch, and dinner who enjoy Iowa pork and roast beef served with pastas, soup, and salad. The restaurant has intimate booth seating and is decorated with original art. ✉ *401 Locust St.,* ☎ *515/244–2151. AE, D, MC, V.*

$$–$$$ ✕ **Waterfront Seafood Market.** Fresh- and saltwater fish are flown in daily from around the world to this supercasual seafood market and restaurant. ✉ *2900 University Ave., West Des Moines,* ☎ *515/223–5106. AE, MC, V. Closed Sun.*

$$ ✕ **Jesse's Embers.** Just west of downtown, Jesse's is prized for grilled steaks cooked over a pit in the main dining room. The room is small, plain, and crowded with locals waiting at the bar, but service is swift. ✉ *3301 Ingersoll Ave.,* ☎ *515/255–6011. AE, MC, V. Closed Sun.*

$$ ✕ **Trostel's Greenbriar.** The menu at this restaurant in the northern suburb of Johnston mixes elegant and basic fare; choices include Iowa pork chops, rack of lamb, and seafood. Frosted glass and dark wood accent the three dining rooms and bar. ✉ *5810 Merle Hay Rd., Johnston,* ☎ *515/253–0124. AE, D, MC, V. Closed Sun.*

$$ ✕ **Tursi's Latin King.** Traditional Italian-American food—which might include *chicken spiedini* (breaded chicken on a skewer), filet mignon marsala, and a variety of pastas—has been served at this family-owned restaurant since 1947. ✉ *2200 Hubble Ave.,* ☎ *515/266–4466. AE, D, MC, V. Closed Sun.–Mon.*

$–$$ ★ ✕ **Drake Diner.** Students from nearby Drake University mix with older patrons at this chrome-and-neon spot, with a soup, salad, and sandwich menu. ✉ *1111 25th St.,* ☎ *515/277–1111. AE, D, DC, MC, V.*

$–$$ ✕ **El Patio.** Southwestern artifacts fill this converted bungalow just west of downtown, where diners sit in colorful rooms and on a covered patio. More Tex than Mex, the food is still a cut above the fare found at chains. ✉ *611 37th St.,* ☎ *515/274–2303. AE, MC, V. No lunch.*

$–$$ ★ ✕ **India Cafe.** Classic aromatic dishes range from zingy lamb vindaloo to mild tandoori chicken. The restaurant's peach-color walls have Indian paintings, and seating is at booths and tables with armchairs. ✉ *Parkwood Plaza, 86th and Douglas Sts., Urbandale,* ☎ *515/278–2929. AE, D, MC, V.*

Lodging

Call the **Iowa Bed and Breakfast Innkeepers' Association** (✉ Box 304, Royal 51357, ☎ 800/888–4667, WEB www.iowainns.com) for information on B&Bs.

$$$ **Des Moines Marriott.** The location—downtown on the skywalk, which connects several buildings—is a plus. Rooms on higher floors have unobstructed views of the city. The restaurant, Quenelle's, serves rich Continental fare. ✉ *700 Grand Ave., 50309,* ☎ *515/245–5500 or 800/228–9290,* FAX *515/245–5567,* WEB *www.marriott.com. 415 rooms. 2 restaurants, pool, health club. AE, D, MC, V.*

$$–$$$ ★ **Embassy Suites Hotel on the River.** Across the bridge from the Court Avenue District, this hotel has seven balconies around an atrium with a waterfall. Beyond this, the Embassy Suites lacks flash but dazzles with attentive service. ✉ *101 E. Locust St., 50309,* ☎ *515/244–1700 or 800/362–2779,* FAX *515/244–2537,* WEB *www.embassy-suites.com. 234 suites. Restaurant, pool, health club. AE, D, DC, MC, V.*

$$ **Holiday Inn Downtown.** Expect fresh but ordinary rooms and a few suites with whirlpool baths at this chain motel north of downtown. ✉ *1050 6th Ave., 50314,* ☎ *515/283–0151,* FAX *515/283–0151,* WEB *www.holiday-inn.com. 251 rooms. Restaurant, pool. AE, D, MC, V.*

$$ ★ **Hotel Fort Des Moines.** Some of the greatest names in world history have stayed in this hotel since its opening in 1919. Marble floors and walnut woodwork original to the structure are among the reasons the hotel is on the National Register of Historic Places. ✉ *1000 Walnut St., 50309,* ☎ *515/243–1161 or 800/532–1466,* FAX *515/243–4317,* WEB *www.hotelfortdm.com. 245 rooms. AE, D, DC, MC, V.*

$ **Airport Comfort Inn.** Two blocks from the airport, this three-story hotel has meeting rooms. ✉ *5231 Fleur Dr., 50321,* ☎ *515/287–3434 or 800/517–4000. 55 rooms. Pool. AE, D, DC, MC, V.*

$ ★ **Heartland Inn.** The inn, a rustic three-story building on the northeastern edge of Des Moines, is next to an amusement complex. ✉ *5000 N.E. 56th St., Altoona 50009,* ☎ *515/967–2400 or 800/334–3277,* FAX *515/967–0150. 86 rooms. Pool. AE, D, DC, MC, V.*

$ **Valley West Inn.** The three-story inn next to West Des Moines's big mall has simply furnished rooms done in rosy fabrics and blond woods. ✉ *3535 Westown Pkwy., West Des Moines 50266,* ☎ *515/225–2524 or 800/833–6755,* FAX *515/225–9058,* WEB *www.knapphotels.com. 136 rooms. Restaurant, pool. AE, D, DC, MC, V.*

The Arts

The **Des Moines Art Center** (✉ 4700 Grand Ave., ☎ 515/277–4405, WEB www.desmoinesartcenter.org), just west of downtown in Greenwood-Ashworth Park, hosts poetry readings, lectures, and films. It also has contemporary art. The **Des Moines Symphony** (✉ 221 Walnut St., ☎ 515/243–1160, WEB dmsymphony.org) presents local musicians and guest performers throughout the year.

Spectator Sports

Track and Field: The **Drake Relays** (✉ Drake University, Forest and 27th Sts., ☎ 515/271–3791, WEB www.drakerelays.org), held in late April, draw track-and-field athletes from 744 colleges, universities, and high schools, as well as some big-name Olympians and professional athletes. Call for ticket packages.

Shopping

Valley Junction (☎ 515/222–3642, WEB www.valleyjunction.com), six square blocks 5 mi west of downtown on 5th Street in West Des Moines, has a mix of antiques stores and contemporary shops selling country furnishings, collectibles, and Iowa souvenirs.

Des Moines Essentials

AIRPORTS AND TRANSFERS

Des Moines International Airport is about 3 mi south of downtown.

➤ AIRPORT INFORMATION: **Des Moines International Airport** (✉ 5800 Fleur Dr., ☎ 515/256–5100, WEB www.dsmairport.com).

AIRPORT TRANSFER

The drive from the airport into town takes about 10 minutes in normal traffic. Cab fare, including tip, is less than $10. Hotel shuttles serve the route, and major car-rental companies are in the airport.

BUS TRAVEL TO AND FROM DES MOINES

Greyhound and Jefferson share a terminal at Keosauqua Way and 12th Street.

➤ Bus Information: **Greyhound** (☎ 800/231–2222). **Jefferson** (☎ 515/283–0074).

CAR TRAVEL

I–80, the major east–west thoroughfare through the state, and I–35, Iowa's main north–south route, intersect northwest of Des Moines and link with I–235, which runs through the heart of the city.

TRANSPORTATION AROUND DES MOINES

Streets both in the city and in suburban Urbandale and West Des Moines are laid out in a grid, which makes getting around fairly easy; a car is essential, however, as sights are scattered. Downtown is compact enough to explore in comfortable shoes.

VISITOR INFORMATION

The Des Moines Convention and Visitors Bureau has visitor centers in the airport lobby, the Living History Farms, and in the skywalk above the corner of 6th and Locust streets downtown.

➤ Tourist Information: **Greater Des Moines Convention and Visitors Bureau** (✉ 405 6th Ave., Suite 201, 50309, ☎ 800/451–2625; 515/256–5575 for airport center; 515/334–9625 for the Living History Farms; 515/286–4960 for skywalk center, WEB www.seedesmoines.com).

EAST-CENTRAL IOWA

East of Des Moines, this region is a mix of historic towns, trim farmsteads, and forested river valleys. Cedar Rapids is the largest town in the area. Iowa City, about 25 mi south, is the home of the University of Iowa. The Amana Colonies are the major attraction.

Exploring East-Central Iowa

★ Begin at the **Amana Colonies,** as the seven villages of Amana are known. They were founded in the 19th century as a utopian religious community. Although descendants of the German-Swiss immigrants who founded the community voted to end its communal way of life in 1932, little has visibly changed since then. The 30-square-mi area of the Amana Colonies region encompasses nearly 500 restored buildings, including barns and kitchens now housing museums, and a schoolhouse, which together have been designated a National Historic Landmark. Members of the Amana community still manufacture prized woolen goods, furniture, wine, cheese, and baskets. The original **Amana Appliance Store** (✉ 836 48th Ave., ☎ 319/622–7655), founded after residents abandoned communal life, is still in business, although the appliances are no longer manufactured by the Amanites. The **Museum of Amana History** has historical artifacts and documents relating to the settlement of the area. ✉ *4310 220th Trail,* ☎ *319/622–3567,* WEB *www.amanaheritage.org.* 🎫 *$5. Closed Jan.–Feb., limited hrs until late spring.*

Cedar Rapids is on U.S. 151 in east-central Iowa, just north of the Amana Colonies. In the 19th and early 20th centuries, waves of Czechoslovakian immigrants settled in this manufacturing town. A sampling of Czech heritage is on view at the **National Czech & Slovak Museum & Library.** ✉ *30 16th Ave. SW,* ☎ *319/362–8500,* WEB *www.ncsml.org.* 🎫 *$5. Closed Mon.*

Cedar Rapids has the world's largest permanent collection of paintings by renowned native son Grant Wood, at its **Museum of Art.** ✉

Eastern Iowa

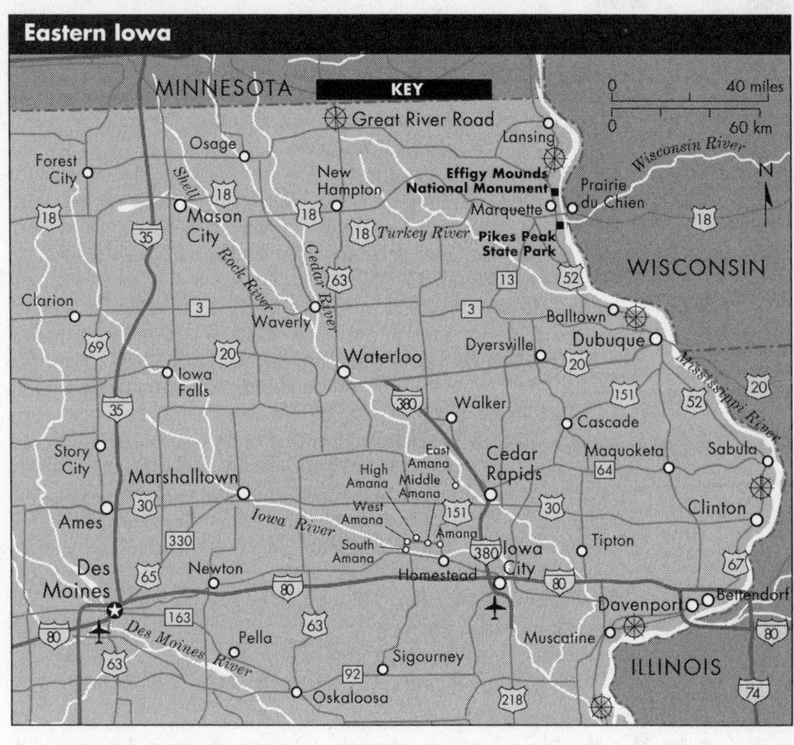

410 3rd Ave. SE, ☎ 319/366–7503, WEB www.crma.org. 🎫 $4. Closed Mon.

Iowa City, in east-central Iowa, served as the seat of state government until the capital moved to Des Moines in the mid-19th century. The golden dome of the **Old Capitol** (✉ 24 Old Capitol Dr., ☎ 319/335–0548, WEB www.uiowa.edu) is now the center of the beautiful, hilly campus of the **University of Iowa** on the banks of the Iowa River. Heavily damaged by fire in 2001, the dome has been painstakingly restored and houses a museum of area artifacts.

West Branch, a community of 2,000 with more than two dozen buildings listed on the National Register of Historic Places, is just west of Iowa City on I–80. The **Herbert Hoover Presidential Library and Birthplace** (✉ Parkside Dr. and Main St., ☎ 319/643–5301, WEB www.hoover.nara.gov; 🎫 $2), the cottage where the future president was born to Quaker parents in 1874, contains period furnishings, many of them original.

Dining and Lodging

Amana kitchens bustle with rich German meals, often served family style. Try the locally made rhubarb wine. Hotels in Cedar Rapids tend to cater to business travelers, but the Amanas, like many other Iowa towns, are home to a growing number of B&Bs (**Iowa Bed and Breakfast Innkeepers' Association**; ✉ Box 304, Royal 51357, ☎ 800/888–4667, WEB www.iowainns.com). Decent chain hotels and motels dominate in Iowa City.

Amana Colonies

$–$$ ✕ **Brick Haus Restaurant.** Large portions of Wiener schnitzel *mit* spaetzle are a specialty at this place in the middle of prime Amana shopping. Food is served at long tables covered in checkered cloths. ✉ *728 47th Ave., Amana,* ☎ *319/622–3278. AE, MC, V.*

$–$$ ★ ✕ **Ox Yoke Inn.** Come for traditional German-American food in an Old Country–inspired setting. ✉ *Main St., Amana,* ☎ *319/622–3441. AE, D, MC, V. Closed Mon. Jan.–Feb.*

$–$$ ✕ **Zuber's Restaurant.** The comfortable surroundings haven't changed much since the 1950s, nor has the menu, a primer on German cuisine: hearty portions of oven-baked steak, country-style chicken, salad, vegetables, and dessert, served family style. ✉ *Main St., Homestead,* ☎ *319/622–3911. AE, D, MC, V.*

$–$$ **Amana Holiday Inn.** The rustic setting of the pool and sauna enlivens this good-size hotel located just off the interstate. ✉ *Exit 225 off I–80 (Box 187, Little Amana 52203),* ☎ *319/668–1175 or 800/633–9244,* FAX *319/668–2853,* WEB *www.amanaholidayinn.com. 155 rooms. Restaurant, pool. AE, D, MC, V.*

$–$$ ★ **Rawson's Bed & Breakfast.** During the days of communal living, this unique B&B was a kitchen workers' dormitory. There are two large, distinctive rooms, with exposed beams and brick walls, and one suite; all have period furnishings and fabrics, and lavish baths. ✉ *4424 V St. (Box 118, Homestead 52236),* ☎ *319/622–6035 or 800/637–6035,* WEB *www.amanacolonies.com/rawson. 6 rooms. MC, V. BP.*

$ **Die Heimat Country Inn.** The two-story B&B is the oldest in the colonies. It has small rooms with locally made, traditional furnishings and deluxe units with canopy beds. ✉ *4430 V St. (Box 160, Homestead 52236),* ☎ *319/622–3937. 19 rooms. D, MC, V. BP.*

Cedar Rapids

$–$$ **Collins Plaza.** In this hotel north of downtown, rooms are large, with traditional furnishings and pastel colors. There's an airport shuttle. ✉ *1200 Collins Rd. NE, 52402,* ☎ *319/393–6600 or 800/541–1067,* FAX *319/393–2308,* WEB *www.collinsplazacedarrapids.com. 221 rooms. Restaurant, pool, gym. AE, D, DC, MC, V.*

Iowa City

$$ ✕ **Iowa River Power Company.** The former power station for much of eastern Iowa, set on the banks of the Iowa River, was turned into a restaurant serving classic American cuisine. ✉ *501 1st Ave., Coralville,* ☎ *319/351–1904. AE, DC, MC, V. No lunch.*

$–$$ ✕ **Givanni's.** Neon lights enhance the exposed-brick walls at this Italian-American-vegetarian restaurant in the downtown mall. ✉ *109 E. College St.,* ☎ *319/338–5967. AE, D, DC, MC, V.*

Walcott

$ ✕ **Iowa 80 Kitchen.** The native stone fireplace, beamed ceiling, and spacious dining room make this one of the most elegantly furnished truck stops in the country. With a 48-ft salad bar, an in-house bakery, laundry facilities, and a warehouse store, it's also a traveler's dream. Walcott is about 55 mi east of Iowa City. ✉ *395 W. Iowa 80 Rd.,* ☎ *563/284–6965. D, MC, V.*

Motel

Heartland Inn (✉ 3315 Southgate Ct. SW, Cedar Rapids 52404, ☎ 319/362–9012 or 800/334–3277, FAX 319/362–9694, WEB www.heartlandinn.com), 114 rooms; pool; *$*.

Shopping

Amana's eight-block center is a shopping hub. The **Woolen Mill Salesroom** (✉ 800 48th Ave., ☎ 319/622–3432) sells many woolens, from clothing to blankets; take a self-guided tour of the mill. On weekdays at the **Furniture and Clock Shop** (✉ 724 48th Ave., ☎ 319/622–

3291) you can watch craftspeople making the products sold here. The fragrant, creaky **Old Fashioned High Amana Store** (✉ 1308 G St., ☎ 319/622–3797), 2 mi west of the visitor center, stocks old-time-type gifts. The **Amana Arts Guild Center** (✉ 1210 G St., ☎ 319/622–3678) sells high-quality quilts and crafts. **Little Amana,** at I–80 and U.S. 151, is more of a quick-stop outlet for woolens, gifts, and souvenirs than a typical Amana village. The **Tanger Factory Outlet Center** (✉ Exit 220 off I–80, Williamsburg, ☎ 800/406–2887) has 70 stores with designer clothing and accessories, housewares, and brand-name shoes.

East-Central Iowa Essentials

AIRPORTS

The Eastern Iowa Regional Airport, 7 mi south of Cedar Rapids and off I–380, is served by American, American Eagle, ComAir, Delta Connection, Northwest/Northwest Airlink, United, and US Airways Express.

➤ AIRPORT INFORMATION: **Eastern Iowa Regional Airport** (✉ 2515 Wright Brothers Blvd. W, ☎ 319/362–3131, WEB eiairport.org).

CAR TRAVEL

I–80, the state's major east–west thoroughfare, runs from Des Moines east to Iowa City. From Iowa City I–380 passes Lake MacBride on the way north to Cedar Rapids. From Cedar Rapids U.S. 151 meanders southwest for about 25 mi through a rural farmscape to Middle Amana, the start of the cluster of Amana colonies.

VISITOR INFORMATION

The Amana Colonies Welcome Center has area information and a lodging reservation service.

➤ TOURIST INFORMATION: **Amana Colonies Welcome Center** (✉ 39 38th Ave., Suite 100, near U.S. 151 and Rte. 220, Amana 52203, ☎ 319/622–7622 or 800/579–2294, WEB www.amanacolonies.com). **Cedar Rapids Convention and Visitors Bureau** (✉ 119 1st Ave. SE, 52401, ☎ 319/398–5009 or 800/735–5557, WEB www.cedar-rapids.com). **Iowa City/Coralville Visitors Bureau** (✉ 408 1st Ave., Coralville 52241, ☎ 319/337–6592 or 800/283–6592, WEB www.icccvb.org).

DUBUQUE AND THE GREAT RIVER ROAD

The mighty Mississippi River forms the eastern border of Iowa; the top third of the border, from the Minnesota line to Dubuque, has the oldest settlements, highest bluffs, and closest river access of the entire stretch. The **Great River Road** is a network of federal, state, and county roads that wind along this magnificent stretch of riverbank, highlighting wildlife refuges and the river's complicated locks and dams system. Routes 26, 52, and 99 make up this road in Iowa.

Exploring Dubuque and the Great River Road

Just 11 mi south of the Minnesota border, the **Municipal Park,** in Lansing, Iowa, provides spectacular views of the Mississippi River. The **Effigy Mounds National Monument** (✉ Rte. 76, ☎ 563/873–3491, WEB www.nps.gov/efmo; 🎟 $2 per person, up to $4 per car, free Nov.–Mar.), 3 mi north of McGregor along the Great River Road, has hiking trails that run alongside eerie, animal-shape prehistoric Native American burial mounds. One-, four-, and six-hour walks lead to cliff-top views of the upper Mississippi River Valley.

Pikes Peak State Park (☎ 563/873–2341), 3 mi south of McGregor, has a view of the Wisconsin River as it links up with the Mississippi. The stretch of road approaching **Balltown,** 7 mi north of Dubuque, reveals green hills rolling down to the river.

Dubuque is full of river merchants' homes, some of them lavish Victorian houses turned B&Bs, snuggled against the limestone cliffs that back this small harbor town. Get out of the car here and explore **Cable Car Square** (☎ 563/583–5000), at 4th and Bluff streets, site of two dozen shops and restaurants. From April through November you can ride the **Fenelon Place Elevator** (☎ 563/582–6496; 🎫 $1.50) to the top of a 200-ft bluff for a sweeping view of the city.

Dyersville, 25 mi west of Dubuque on U.S. 20, found fame as a setting for the 1989 movie *Field of Dreams.* The **Field of Dreams Movie Site** (✉ 28963 Lansing Rd., ☎ 563/875–8404 or 888/875–8404; 🎫 free), about 3 mi north of town, has been preserved as a tourist attraction. Bring your own equipment to play in the continual pickup game; the field is closed November–March. The **National Farm Toy Museum** (✉ 1110 16th Ave. SE, ☎ 563/875–2727, WEB www.nftmonline.com. 🎫 $4) has more than 30,000 old farm toys.

Dining and Lodging

Ethnic and family-style restaurants line Dubuque's 4th Street at Cable Car Square. As in the rest of the state, B&Bs are abundant (**Iowa Bed and Breakfast Innkeepers' Association;** ✉ Box 304, Royal 51357, ☎ 800/888–4667, WEB www.iowainns.com).

Balltown

$ ★ ✕ **Breitbach's Country Dining.** Down-home cooking, including tasty rolls and pies, is the draw of this funky, rambling piece of folk architecture. *✉ 563 Balltown Rd., ☎ 563/552–2220. MC, V.*

Dubuque

$$–$$$ ✕ **Yen Ching.** The café serves dependable Chinese food, with a few spicy Hunan dishes for variety. *✉ 926 Main St., ☎ 563/556–2574. AE, MC, V. Closed Sun.*

$–$$$ ★ **Hancock House.** Perched halfway up a bluff, this meticulously restored Victorian has four-poster beds, lace-covered windows, ornate fireplaces, and a rare Tiffany lamp collection. *✉ 1105 Grove Terr., 52001, ☎ 563/557–8989, FAX 563/583–0813, WEB www.thehancockhouse.com. 9 rooms. AE, D, MC, V. BP.*

$–$$$ **Redstone Inn.** Bedrooms are grand and baths lavish at this British manor–like establishment on the prairie. *✉ 504 Bluff St., 52001, ☎ 563/582–1894, FAX 563/582–1893, WEB www.theredstoneinn.com. 14 rooms. AE, D, MC, V. BP.*

Dubuque and the Great River Road Essentials

BUS TRAVEL

Greyhound links Dubuque to most major cities; its local bus station is on the lower level of the Julien Inn.

➤ Bus Information: **Greyhound** (☎ 800/231–2222). **Julien Inn** (✉ 200 Main St.).

CAR TRAVEL

You can join Iowa's Great River Road from the north on U.S. 18 at Prairie du Chien, Wisconsin, or pick up the scenic route anywhere on Iowa's eastern border. The entire length of the Great River Road is marked by signs with a 12-spoke pilot's wheel symbol.

VISITOR INFORMATION

➤ TOURIST INFORMATION: **Tourist Information Center** (✉ Port of Dubuque Welcome Center, 300 Main St., Dubuque 52001, ☎ 563/556–4372 or 800/798–8844, WEB www.traveldubuque.com).

ELSEWHERE IN IOWA

Iowa's Great Lakes

What to See and Do

The Iowa Great Lakes lie in the northwest corner of the state. The region has six lakes (including West Okoboji—one of only three true blue-water lakes in the world) and dozens of vacation resorts. The ***Queen II*** excursion boat (✉ Arnolds Park, ☎ 712/332–5159, www.arnoldsparkamusement.com) gives tours of West Okoboji.

Dining and Lodging

Lodging rates may drop in this area between late fall and spring.

$$ ✕ **Lighthouse Bar & Grill.** Guests come by boat, bike, or car to dine inside or out. Steak and seafood get top billing on the menu, which has everything from sandwiches to full dinners. ✉ *U.S. 71 at East Oak Mall, Okoboji,* ☎ *712/332–5995. AE, MC, V.*

$$ ✕ **Maxwell's on the Lake.** A lovely view, elegant dining, fine service, and an extensive menu with plenty of seafood and steak make dining here a memorable experience. ✉ *144 Lakeshore Dr., Arnold's Park,* ☎ *712/332–7578. AE, MC, V.* ⊙ *May–Sept.*

$$$ **Village East Resort.** Overlooking Brooks Golf Course and East Lake Okoboji, this resort has indoor and outdoor pools. Additional draws are a pro shop and weight room. ✉ *Box 499, Okoboji 51355-0499,* ☎ *712/332–2161 or 800/727–4561,* FAX *712/332–7727,* WEB *www.villageeastresort.com. 101 rooms. Restaurant, 2 pools, tennis, health club. AE, D, DC, MC, V.*

$–$$$ **Beaches Resort.** On the quiet north end of West Lake Okoboji, these clapboard cottages offer simple but comfortable furnishings at a family-oriented resort. At day's end, you can gather around the fire pit on the sandy beach for complimentary s'mores. ✉ *15109 215th Ave., Spirit Lake 51360,* ☎ *712/336–2230. 6 cottages, 5 apartments, 1 house. Restaurant. D, MC, V.*

Iowa's Great Lakes Essentials

CAR TRAVEL

Take I–80 W from Des Moines and U.S. 71 N to Spirit Lake or take I–35 N from Des Moines to U.S. 18, which leads west to the Great Lakes area.

VISITOR INFORMATION

➤ TOURIST INFORMATION: **Iowa Great Lakes Chamber of Commerce** (✉ 243 W. Broadway [Box 9, Arnolds Park 51331], ☎ 800/270–2574, WEB www.vacationokoboji.com).

The Quad Cities

What to See and Do

Davenport and **Bettendorf** make up Iowa's side of the Quad Cities (the others are Rock Island and Moline in Illinois), which straddle the Mississippi River. The **Rhythm City Casino** (✉ 130 W. River Dr., ☎ 800/262–8711, WEB www.rhythmcitycasinos.com), a National Historic Landmark, is as big as a football field and has five decks decorated in Victorian splendor. Hotels, restaurants, and antiques shops are within walking distance. The **Bix Beiderbecke Jazz Festival** (☎ 563/324–

7170) is held each July in Davenport's riverfront park.The **Village of East Davenport** (☎ 563/322–0546) is Iowa's second-largest historic district, with about 50 specialty shops and restaurants.

Dining and Lodging

$–$$ ✕ **Iowa Machine Shed.** Enjoy Iowa pork chops and beef, homemade desserts, and fresh vegetables served in a farmhouse atmosphere. Drinks are served in mason jars. ✉ *7250 Northwest Blvd., Davenport,* ☎ *563/391–2427. MC, V.*

$–$$$ 🏨 **Jumer's Castle Lodge.** Impressive both inside and out, this lodge is furnished with heavy walnut carvings, rich carpets, and elegant accessories. ✉ *900 Spruce Hill Dr., Bettendorf 52722,* ☎ FAX *563/359–7141 or 800/285–8637,* WEB *www.jumers.com. 210 rooms. Restaurant, 2 pools, gym. AE, D, MC, V.*

The Quad Cities Essentials

CAR TRAVEL

From Des Moines take I–80 E to Davenport.

VISITOR INFORMATION

➤ Tourist Information: **Quad Cities Visitors Bureau** (✉ 102 S. Harrison St., Davenport 52801, ☎ 309/788–7800 or 800/747–7800, WEB www.visitquadcities.com).

The Covered Bridges Region

What to See and Do

Made famous by Robert James Waller's novel *The Bridges of Madison County* and the eponymous 1995 movie, **Madison County,** 50 mi southwest of Des Moines (take I–35 S from Des Moines to U.S. 92), is home to six covered bridges that date from the 1880s. **Bus tours** (☎ 515/462–1185) of the bridges take place all day, or you can take a self-guided one. Maps are available at the chamber office (✉ 73 Jefferson St.). Tours are also available at Francesca's Farmhouse and other buildings used as sites for the movie. The Covered Bridge Festival is held here each October. In Winterset, the **birthplace of John Wayne** (✉ 224 S. 2nd St., ☎ 515/462–1044, WEB www.johnwaynebirthplace.org; 🎫 $2.50) is furnished with family memorabilia and authentic turn-of-the-20th-century pieces; you can watch Wayne's films in the gift shop.

Dining

$–$$ ✕ **Summerset House.** A Victorian mansion two blocks from the courthouse square is now a tearoom. Lunch includes sandwiches and quiche; choices for the five-course dinner are salmon steaks, apricot-glazed game hens, and prime rib. ✉ *204 W. Washington St., Winterset,* ☎ *515/462–9014. Reservations essential. No credit cards.*

$ ✕ **Northside Cafe.** You'll find typical café fare—meat loaf, fried chicken, mashed potatoes, and homemade pie—at this spot, where Clint Eastwood ate in the movie *The Bridges of Madison County.* ✉ *61 W. Jefferson St., Winterset,* ☎ *515/462–1523. No credit cards.*

KANSAS

By Janet Majure

Updated by Diana Lambdin Meyer

Capital	Topeka
Population	2,688,000
Motto	To the Stars Through Difficulties
State Bird	Western meadowlark
State Flower	Wild native sunflower
Postal Abbreviation	KS

Statewide Visitor Information

Kansas Department of Commerce, Travel & Tourism Division (✉ 100 S.W. Jackson St., Suite 100, Topeka 66612-1354, ☎ 785/296–2009 or 800/252–6727, WEB www.travelks.com). **Kansas State Historical Society visitor information center** (✉ Kansas State Capitol, 1st floor, Topeka, ☎ 785/296–3966, WEB www.kshs.org). **Kansas Travel Information Center** (✉ I–70 and 110th St., Kansas City, ☎ 913/299–2253; ✉ 2815 S. Hwy. 27, Goodland, ☎ 785/899–6695; ✉ 770 N. I–35, Belle Plaine, ☎ 620/326–5123).

Scenic Drives

Highway 177 south from I–70 to historic Council Grove provides lovely views of the undulating Flint Hills, especially in late afternoon or early morning.

National and State Parks

National Parks

There are several national-park-service sites in Kansas. Federal sites include the **Fort Larned National Historic Site** (✉ Hwy. 156, 4 mi west of Larned, ☎ 620/285–6911, WEB www.nps.gov/fols; 🎟 $3), a restored prairie fort from the 19th century. The **Fort Scott National Historic Site** (✉ Old Fort Blvd., Fort Scott, ☎ 620/223–0310 or 800/245–3678, WEB www.nps.gov/fosc; 🎟 $3) preserves a fort built in 1842 to keep the peace in Native American territory and includes exhibits on pivotal confrontations of the Civil War. The **Tallgrass Prairie National Preserve** (✉ Strong City, ☎ 620/273–8494, WEB www.nps.gov/tapr; 🎟 free) offers self-guided and ranger-escorted tours of tallgrass prairie that once covered much of the Great Plains. **Cimarron National Grassland** (✉ 242 E. Hwy. 56, Elkhart, ☎ 620/697–4621, WEB www.fs.fed.us/r2/psicc/cim; 🎟 free), less than a mile from central Elkhart, offers a self-guided auto tour of key Santa Fe Trail sites.

State Parks

Kansas has 22 state parks, most associated with recreational lakes. State parks are administered by the **Kansas Department of Wildlife and Parks** (✉ 512 S.E. 25th Ave., Pratt 67124, ☎ 620/672–5911, WEB www.kdwp.state.ks.us). **Scott State Park** (✉ 520 W. Scott Lake Dr., Scott City 67871, ☎ 620/872–2061) contains archaeological evidence of the northernmost Native American pueblo and one of the first white settlements in Kansas. **Milford State Park** (✉ 8811 State Park Rd., Milford 66514, ☎ 785/238–3014) has a 37,000-acre reservoir, a nature center, and a fish hatchery.

EAST-CENTRAL KANSAS

Heading west from Kansas City across east-central Kansas, you'll follow in the footsteps of pioneers who blazed the Oregon and Santa Fe trails, and you'll cross the paths of those who followed the Smoky Hill and Chisholm trails. Native American history, Civil War sites, and the Old West loom large along this 150-mi stretch of prairie.

Exploring East-Central Kansas

Along I–70 you'll encounter an array of historic sites. Kansas City, which straddles the border between Kansas and Missouri, was a major provisioning point for frontier travelers in the 19th century.

Wyandotte County is where you'll find the **Kansas Speedway** a 1½-mi tri-oval race track that hosts several professional racing events, including the NASCAR Winston Cup series. ✉ *400 Speedway Blvd., I–70 Exit 410, Bonner Springs,* ☎ *913/328–3300,* WEB *www.kansasspeedway.com.* 🎫 *Tickets from $50. Closed Nov.–May.*

The **Mahaffie Farmstead & Stagecoach Stop** once served the Santa Fe Trail, one of the routes established in the 19th century for trade and later for westward expansion. There are guided tours of the stone house, one of three farmstead buildings here listed on the National Register of Historic Places. ✉ *1100 Kansas City Rd., Olathe 66061,* ☎ *913/782–6972,* WEB *www.mahaffie.com.* 🎫 *$3. Closed Jan. and weekends Feb.–Apr.*

In Fairway, a Kansas City suburb, the **Shawnee Indian Mission** was created in 1839 as a school to teach English and trade skills to Native Americans. You can tour two of its three buildings. ✉ *3403 W. 53rd St.,* ☎ *913/262–0867,* WEB *www.kshs.org.* 🎫 *Free. Closed Mon.*

About 40 mi west of Kansas City on I–70 is **Lawrence.** The town was rebuilt after being raided and burned by William Quantrill and a band of Confederate sympathizers for the antislavery stance of its citizens during the Civil War; many structures from this time remain. Stroll along Massachusetts Street through the lovely downtown area, where turn-of-the-20th-century buildings and retail shops retain a small-town flavor.

A few blocks away from Massachusetts Street is the scenic main campus of the 29,000-student **University of Kansas.** Lining Jayhawk Boulevard is an assortment of university buildings, including the Romanesque native-limestone building that houses the **University of Kansas Natural History Museum** (✉ Dyche Hall, Jayhawk Blvd., ☎ 785/864–4450, WEB www.nhm.ku.edu; 🎫 free), one of the school's four museums. The Natural History Museum has fossils, mounted animals, and rotating exhibits highlighting the biodiversity of the Great Plains; kids will enjoy the dinosaur bones and live snakes, bees, and fish. **Haskell Indian Nations University** (✉ 155 Indian Ave., ☎ 785/749–8450, WEB www.haskell.edu) has provided higher education for Native Americans since 1884 and includes several **Stan Herd Earth Works** sculptures for viewing on the southwest corner of the campus.

Fifty miles northwest of Kansas City on Route 7, overlooking the Missouri River, is **Atchison,** the birthplace of famed aviator Amelia Earhart. The **Amelia Earhart Birthplace Museum** (✉ 223 N. Terrace St., 66002, ☎ 913/367–4217, WEB www.ameilaearhartmuseum.org; 🎫 $2), owned by the International Ninety-Nines, Inc., a group of women pilots, displays flying memorabilia and childhood treasures of the famed pilot.

Trees from 50 states and 38 countries grow in harmony at the **International Forest of Friendship** (✉ Warnock Lake, 1½ mi southwest of Atchison, ☎ 913/367–1419, WEB www.ninety-nines.org; 🎫 free), a gift to the United States for its bicentennial from the city and International Ninety-Nines, Inc. The forest is accessed through Memory Lane, which is paved with plaques that list the names of more than 600 pilots, astronauts, and manufacturers who have contributed to aviation. A nice view of the Amelia Earhart Earthworks sculpture is available from this walking trail.

About 70 mi west of Kansas City on I–70 is **Topeka,** with its outstanding classical **state capitol building** (✉ 300 W. 10th St., ☎ 785/296–3966), begun in 1866 and completed nearly 40 years later. Lobby murals include a striking depiction of abolitionist John Brown by John Steuart Curry. Be sure to visit the ornate senate chambers, which have magnificent bronze columns and variegated-marble accents. Topeka holds a place in history as the site of the *Brown* v. *Board of Education* lawsuit, the 1954 case that outlawed segregation in public schools. The **Monroe School** (✉ 424 S. Kansas Ave., ☎ 785/354–4273, WEB www.nps.gov/brvb), the focal point of the case, is now part of the national park system. West of downtown Topeka, the **Kansas Museum of History** (✉ 6425 S.W. 6th St., ☎ 785/272–8681, WEB www.kshs.org; 🎫 free), perversely situated in a modernist box of a building, traces Kansas's history from the Native American era to the present. Kids like **Discovery Place,** a hands-on exhibit involving 19th-century tools, clothes, and household items. Outside Topeka, the **Combat Air Museum** (✉ Hangars 602 and 604, Forbes Field, ☎ 785/862–3303, WEB www.combatairmuseum.org; 🎫 $5) has two hangars full of military aircraft dating from World War I. **Historic Ward-Meade Park** (✉ 124 N. Fillmore St., ☎ 785/368–3888) is as lovely as it is historic, with a restored mansion, a cabin, a train depot, a one-room schoolhouse, and botanical gardens. **Gage Park** (✉ 635 Gage Blvd., ☎ 785/368–3700) has a carousel. In Gage Park you'll find the **Topeka Zoo** (☎ 785/272–5821, WEB www.topekazoo.org; 🎫 $4.50). The zoo has a small but impressive domed tropical rain forest.

Tallgrass Prairie National Preserve (✉ Strong City, ☎ 620/273–8494, WEB www.nps.gov/tapr; 🎫 free) contains the last large vestiges of the bluestem—or tallgrass—prairie that once covered much of the Great Plains. Sites include a stone mansion and barn built in 1881. The historic **Grand Central Hotel** (✉ 215 Broadway St., Cottonwood Falls, ☎ 620/273–6763 or 800/951–6763, WEB www.grandcentralhotel.com) in Cottonwood Falls has been welcoming guests since 1884.

The small town of **Abilene,** about 85 mi west of Topeka, is famous for cattle drives and for Dwight D. Eisenhower.

The **Eisenhower Center complex** (✉ 200 S.E. 4th St., ☎ 785/263–4751 or 877/746–4453, WEB www.eisenhower.utexas.edu; 🎫 $3.50) includes the late president's **boyhood home** as well as the **Eisenhower Museum,** the **Eisenhower Presidential Library,** and the **Place of Meditation,** a chapel where the president, his wife, Mamie, and their son, Doud Dwight, are interred. The museum displays memorabilia from Eisenhower's youth in Abilene to his success as a World War II general through his popular presidency.

The **Dickinson County Historical Museum** (✉ 412 S. Campbell St., ☎ 785/263–2681; 🎫 $3) has exhibits on the life of the Plains Indians, cowboys on the Chisholm Trail, as well as a fully restored and functioning 1901 C. W. Parker carousel. The **Greyhound Hall of Fame** (✉ 407 S. Buckeye St., ☎ 785/263–3000, WEB www.greyhoundhalloffame.com; 🎫 free) documents the history of the illustrious canine breed and the sport of racing these dogs.

Dining and Lodging

Typical Kansas roadhouse fare is chicken-fried steak and fried chicken. Restaurants in east-central cities and towns also serve good barbecue and Mexican food. Contact the **Kansas Bed & Breakfast Association** (✉ Box 71, Enterprise 67441–0071, ☎ 888/854–4667, WEB www.kbba.com) for information on Kansas B&Bs.

Abilene

$$ ✕ **Kirby House.** The traditional midwestern fare is nothing special, but the modestly elegant setting in a restored Victorian mansion makes this place worthwhile. ✉ *205 N.E. 3rd St.,* ☎ *785/263–7336. AE, D, MC, V.*

$ ✕ **Mr. K's Farmhouse.** Once a favorite of Dwight and Mamie Eisenhower, the "house on the hill" serves fried chicken and homemade desserts. ✉ *407 S. Van Buren,* ☎ *785/263–7995. D, MC, V. Closed Mon.*

Kansas City Area

$ ✕ **Dick Clark's American Bandstand Grill.** Rock-and-roll history comes alive in this diner, owned by America's perpetual teenager. Vintage posters, gold albums, and artists' contracts on the walls complement a varied menu. Clark and other music celebrities often stop in. ✉ *10975 Metcalf Ave., Overland Park,* ☎ *913/451–1600. AE, D, MC, V.*

$ ★ ✕ **Hayward's Pit Bar-B-Que.** Locals flock to this hillside restaurant for piles of succulent smoked beef, ribs, chicken, pork, and sausage. ✉ *11051 Antioch Rd., Overland Park,* ☎ *913/451–8080. AE, D, DC, MC, V.*

$ ✕ **Kansas Machine Shed.** Kansas farm cooking—including ham, homemade cottage cheese, and apple dumplings the size of a dinner plate—along with antique farm machinery and a gift shop make this stop off the interstate an attraction in its own right. ✉ *12080 Strang Line Rd., Olathe,* ☎ *913/780–2697. AE, D, DC, MC, V.*

$$$ **Double Tree Hotel.** Adjacent to two major highways, a business park, and a scenic public jogging trail, this 18-story hotel is also convenient to shops, restaurants, and a bowling alley. ✉ *10100 College Blvd., Overland Park 66210,* ☎ *913/451–6100,* FAX *913/451–0386,* WEB *www.doubletreehotels.com. 357 rooms. Restaurant, pool, gym. AE, D, DC, MC, V.*

$$$ **Overland Park Marriott Hotel.** This upscale hotel in a suburban business area has a marble-floor lobby and traditionally styled rooms. ✉ *10800 Metcalf Ave., Overland Park 66210,* ☎ *913/451–8000,* FAX *913/451–5914,* WEB *www.marriott.com. 390 rooms. 2 restaurants, pool, gym. AE, D, DC, MC, V.*

Lawrence

$ ✕ **Free State Brewing Co.** Kansas's first legal brewpub, opened in 1989, serves dishes like fish-and-chips and a Burgundy beef sandwich (shredded beef brisket on a baguette, smothered with gravy) to complement the selection of beers. ✉ *636 Massachusetts St.,* ☎ *785/843–4555. AE, D, DC, MC, V.*

$ ★ ✕ **Stone Canyon Pizza.** The stone landscaping, eclectic decor, and outdoor dining area are as interesting as the gourmet pizza and pastas served at this popular hangout for watching KU basketball. ✉ *3801 W. 6th St.,* ☎ *785/830–8500. AE, MC, V.*

$$ ★ **Eldridge Hotel.** Listed on the National Register of Historic Places, this downtown hotel has attractive suites with parlors and wet bars. Rooms on the top (fifth) floor have great views. The downtown location means some traffic noise but great convenience. ✉ *701 Massachusetts St., 66044,* ☎ *785/749–5011 or 800/527–0909,* FAX *785/749–4512,* WEB *www.eldridgehotel.com. 48 suites. Restaurant. AE, D, DC, MC, V.*

Topeka

$ **Club House Inn.** In western Topeka near the Kansas Museum of History, this modern white-stucco hotel has spacious rooms, many overlooking a landscaped courtyard; suites have kitchenettes. ✉ *924 S.W. Henderson St., 66615,* ☎ *785/273–8888,* FAX *785/273–5809,* WEB *www.clubhouseinn.com. 121 rooms. Pool. AE, D, DC, MC, V.*

Motels

Best Western Inn (✉ 2210 N. Buckeye St., Abilene 67410, ☎ 785/263–2050, FAX 785/263–7230), 64 rooms; restaurant, pool; *$*.

Nightlife

The **New Theatre Restaurant** (✉ 9229 Foster St., Overland Park 66212, ☎ 913/649–7469, WEB www.newtheatre.com), an Equity theater and restaurant, stages first-run and recent musicals and comedies that often feature nationally recognized actors.

Outdoor Activities and Sports

Fishing

Most of east-central Kansas follows the Kansas River (called the Kaw River locally), where a series of large-scale flood-control reservoirs yield good fishing for walleye, bass, and crappie. Licenses, which are required, can be purchased at county clerks' offices, state parks offices, some retail outlets, and on-line. The **Kansas Department of Fish and Game** (☎ 620/672–5911, WEB www.kdwp.st.ks.us) governs fishing in the state. **Clinton State Park** (✉ 798 N. 1415 Rd., Lawrence 66049) is south of Lawrence. **Milford State Park** (✉ 8811 State Park Rd., Milford 66514, ☎ 785/238–3014) is on a large lake west of Manhattan. **Perry State Park** (✉ 5441 West Lake Rd., Ozawkie 66070, ☎ 785/246–3449) is near Topeka. **Tuttle Creek State Park** (✉ 5800-A River Pond Rd., Manhattan 66502, ☎ 785/539–7941) is northeast of Manhattan.

Hiking

Kansas's reservoirs are bordered by state parks with marked nature trails. The **Konza Prairie** (✉ McDowell Creek Rd., 5 mi off I–70 at Exit 307, southeast of Manhattan, ☎ 785/587–0441, WEB www.konza.ksu.edu), an 8,600-acre section of tallgrass prairie set aside for research and preservation, has a self-guided nature trail.

Spectator Sports

The **University of Kansas Jayhawks** (✉ Memorial Stadium, 11th and Mississippi Sts., Lawrence, ☎ 785/864–3141 or 800/344–2957, WEB www.kustore.com) are often ranked among the best college basketball teams in the country.

Shopping

Johnson County, which incorporates the Kansas City suburbs of Overland Park, Lenexa, and Olathe, has abundant shopping in several fashionable centers and strip malls. There are also a number of unique shops along Metcalf Avenue at I–435, at 95th and I–35 in the Kansas City area. You'll find 150 stores at the **Great Mall of the Great Plains** (✉ 20700 W. 151st St., at I–35, Olathe, ☎ 913/829–6277) outlet mall. For products homegrown or handcrafted by Kansas artists, visit the shops of the **Amazing 100 Miles** (WEB www.amazing100miles.com), a stretch of communities that line I–70 between Salina and Hays. Watch for interstate exit signs and brochures at rest stops that will direct you to more than 50 small towns no more than about 20 mi off the interstate with unique galleries and shops.

East-Central Kansas Essentials

AIRPORTS

The biggest airport serving east-central Kansas is Kansas City International Airport. US Airways Express serves Topeka's Forbes Field.

➤ AIRPORT INFORMATION: **Forbes Field** (✉ J St. and 1st N St., ☎ 785/862–2362).

BUS TRAVEL

Greyhound connects Kansas City, Lawrence, Topeka, and Abilene en route to Denver, Colorado. Jefferson Lines serves Kansas City, Overland Park, Ottawa, and Lawrence.

➤ BUS INFORMATION: **Greyhound** (☎ 800/231–2222, www.greyhound.com). **Jefferson Lines** (☎ 800/451–5333, WEB www.jeffersonlines.com).

CAR TRAVEL

I–70 west enters Kansas from Kansas City, Missouri; I–70 east, from Colorado. Most attractions are off the interstate. Note: Kansas weather is extremely variable. Listen to the radio for forecasts, as ice storms, heavy snowfalls, flash floods, and high winds can make driving treacherous. Road conditions are also posted at toll booths along I–70.

TRAIN TRAVEL

Amtrak serves Lawrence, Topeka, and Kansas City.

➤ TRAIN INFORMATION: **Amtrak** (☎ 800/872–7245, WEB www.amtrak.com).

VISITOR INFORMATION

➤ TOURIST INFORMATION: **Abilene Convention & Visitors Bureau** (✉ 201 N.W. 2nd St., Abilene 67410, ☎ 785/263–2231 or 800/569–5915, WEB www.abileneks.com). **Atchison Visitor Information Center** (✉ 200 S. 10th St., Atchison 66002, ☎ 913/367–2427 or 800/234–1854, WEB www.atchison.org). **Kansas City Convention & Visitors Bureau** (✉ 727 Minnesota Ave., Kansas City 66101, ☎ 913/321–5800 or 800/264–1563, WEB www.kckcvb.org). **Lawrence Convention & Visitors Bureau** (✉ 734 Vermont St., Suite 101, Lawrence 66044, ☎ 785/865–4411, WEB www.visitlawrence.com). **Manhattan Convention & Visitors Bureau** (✉ 501 Poyntz Ave., Manhattan 66502, ☎ 785/776–8829, WEB www.manhattan.org). **Overland Park Convention & Visitors Bureau** (✉ 9001 W. 110th St., Overland Park 66210, ☎ 913/491–0123 or 800/262–7275, WEB www.opcvb.org). **Topeka Convention & Visitors Bureau** (✉ 1275 S.W. Topeka Blvd., Topeka 66612, ☎ 785/234–1030 or 800/235–1030, WEB www.topekacvb.org).

THE SANTA FE TRAIL REGION

Although the Santa Fe Trail spans the entire state, the towns in western Kansas are most closely associated with its lore and history. This is the Kansas we know from film and myth: remote, flat, treeless, littered with tumbleweeds, and windy, but imbued with a romance identified with such names as Wyatt Earp and Dodge City. Towns sprang up here first along the trail, then near the railroad lines that followed. Today the mainstay is agriculture and natural gas. Tourism is growing, but don't expect resorts.

Exploring the Santa Fe Trail Region

Central Kansas has several interesting historic sites near and along the Arkansas River between Hutchinson and Larned, a well-preserved Old West town. Hutchinson is home to the state fairgrounds and some

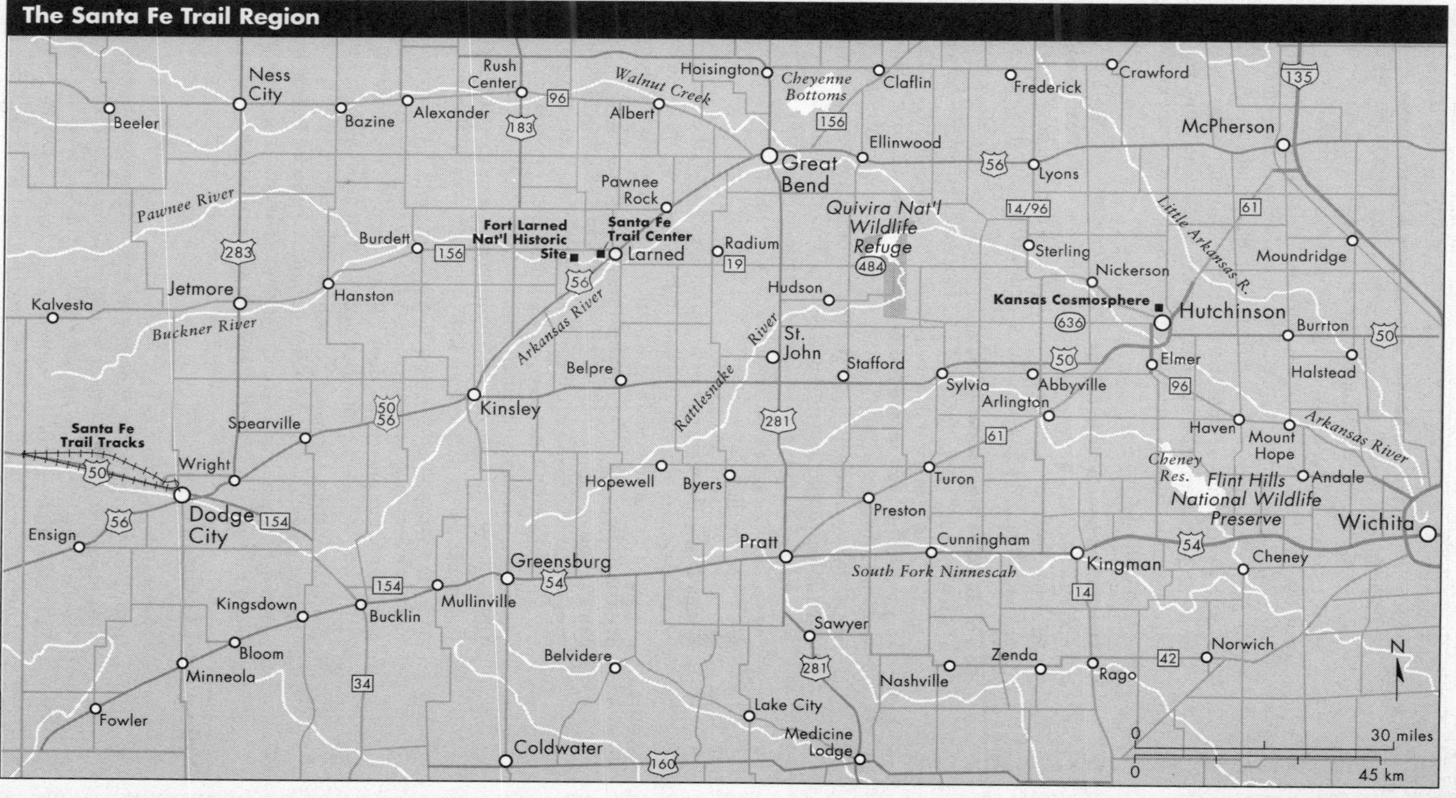
The Santa Fe Trail Region
Ness City
Beeler
Bazine
Alexander
Rush Center
Walnut Creek
Hoisington
Cheyenne Bottoms
Claflin
Frederick
Crawford
McPherson
Albert
Great Bend
Ellinwood
Lyons
Pawnee River
Pawnee Rock
Fort Larned Nat'l Historic Site
Santa Fe Trail Center
Larned
Burdett
Radium
Quivira Nat'l Wildlife Refuge
Sterling
Little Arkansas R.
Moundridge
Nickerson
Jetmore
Hanston
Kalvesta
Hudson
Kansas Cosmosphere
Hutchinson
Burrton
Buckner River
Arkansas River
Rattlesnake River
St. John
Stafford
Elmer
Halstead
Belpre
Sylvia
Abbyville
Arlington
Kinsley
Spearville
Santa Fe Trail Tracks
Haven
Mount Hope
Arkansas River
Wright
Hopewell
Byers
Turon
Cheney Res.
Flint Hills National Wildlife Preserve
Andale
Dodge City
Preston
Wichita
Ensign
Pratt
Cunningham
Kingman
Cheney
Greensburg
South Fork Ninnescah
Kingsdown
Bucklin
Mullinville
Sawyer
Norwich
Bloom
Belvidere
Zenda
Rago
Minneola
Nashville
Lake City
Fowler
Medicine Lodge
Coldwater
N
0
30 miles
45 km

of the world's largest grain elevators, but what really makes this small ★ town worth a visit is the **Kansas Cosmosphere & Space Center** (✉ 1100 N. Plum St., Hutchinson, ☎ 620/662–2305 or 800/397–0330, WEB www.cosmo.org; $5.50). Housing more than $100 million worth of space exhibits, the center's museum has the largest such collection outside the Smithsonian Institution. Various displays, including interactive exhibits, trace the history of space exploration and solutions to the many challenges of human flight. Exhibits include the *Apollo 13 Odyssey* command module and the world's largest display of Soviet space artifacts; the center also has a planetarium and an Omnimax theater. Omnimax tickets are an additional fee and advance purchase is recommended.

Quivira National Wildlife Refuge (✉ Stafford, ☎ 620/486–2393, WEB quivira.fws.gov; free), between Hutchinson and Great Bend, is a 22,000-acre preserve, where more than 250 bird species have been spotted, including bald eagles, pelicans, and whooping cranes.

The **Santa Fe Trail Center** (✉ Hwy. 156, Larned, ☎ 620/285–2054, WEB www.larned.net/trailsctr; $4), 2 mi west of the town center, details the history of the trail and displays artifacts from early 20th-century prairie life. **Fort Larned National Historic Site** (✉ Hwy. 156, 4 mi west of Larned, ☎ 620/285–6911, WEB www.nps.gov/fols; $3) is a meticulous restoration of an 1868 prairie fort that protected travelers and railroad workers on the Santa Fe Trail. Buffalo Soldiers (post–Civil War regiments of black soldiers) were stationed here. The nine-building site includes a museum, restored barracks, and a nature trail; a slide show depicts the fort's history.

Dodge City, in the western part of the state, still capitalizes on its 19th-century reputation as the "wickedest little city in America." Founded 5 mi west of Fort Dodge in anticipation of the arrival of the Santa Fe Railroad, the town thrived on the drinking and gambling of buffalo hunters and cowboys until it burned down in 1885. It was here that lawmen Bat Masterson and Wyatt Earp earned their fame. Front Street, a reconstruction of the town's original houses, saloons, and other businesses, is the tourist center. There's also a re-creation of the Boot Hill cemetery (the remains of those buried here were moved years ago). In summer, gunfights, medicine shows, and stagecoach rides are staged daily. A wholesome chuck-wagon dinner is available in Miss Kitty's Saloon, where you can learn to play the spoons while you enjoy the Old West atmosphere. The **Boot Hill Museum** (✉ Front St., ☎ 620/227–8188, WEB www.boothill.org; $7) includes exhibits on Native American history, the Santa Fe Trail, and the town's early life. From Dodge City, follow U.S. 50 west for 9 mi to the **Santa Fe Trail tracks,** a 140-acre preserve where ruts from wagons on the trail are still visible in the sandy prairie earth more than 130 years later.

Dining and Lodging

Motels hold sway in this part of the state, and you'll find few fancy restaurants. If you're traveling in summer, make reservations early for lodging, and try to make reservations for dinner on weekends. Note: The term "red beer" on menus means beer mixed with tomato juice (it's better than it sounds). Kansas liquor laws vary from county to county; in dry counties alcohol is served only in private clubs, to which many hotels offer courtesy memberships (ask when you call to reserve).

Dodge City

$$ ✕ **Casey's Cowtown Steakhouse.** A little more elegant than the name implies, Casey's is known for steak dinners served in a fine dining atmo-

sphere and features an extensive wine list. ✉ *503 East Trail,* ☎ *620/227–5225. AE, D, MC, V. Closed Sun.*

$ ✕ **El Charro.** Mexican dishes such as Enchilada Delights, topped with cheese, lettuce, tomato, and sour cream, make this a favorite. ✉ *1209 W. Wyatt Earp Blvd.,* ☎ *620/225–0371. MC, V. Closed Sun.*

$$ 🏨 **Boot Hill Bed & Breakfast.** In a colonial Dutch home, the owners incorporate a Wild West theme into the elegance of fine linens, homemade pastries, and beautiful gardens. ✉ *603 W. Spruce St., 67801,* ☎ *620/225–7600 or 888/225–7655,* FAX *620/225–3343,* WEB *www.bbonline.com/ks/boothill. 6 rooms. AE, D, DC, MC, V.*

$ 🏨 **Best Western Silver Spur Lodge.** You'll find pleasant but undistinguished rooms at this sprawling complex, five minutes from Front Street. ✉ *1510 W. Wyatt Earp Blvd., 67801,* ☎ *620/227–2125,* FAX *620/227–2030,* WEB *www.bestwestern.com. 121 rooms. 2 restaurants, pool. AE, D, DC, MC, V.*

Motels

EconoLodge (✉ 1610 W. Wyatt Earp Blvd, Dodge City 67801, ☎ 620/225–0231, FAX 620/225–8036), 100 rooms; *$.*

Super 8 (✉ 1708 W. Wyatt Earp Blvd., Dodge City 67801, ☎ 620/225–3924, FAX 620/225–5793), 64 rooms; pool; *$.*

Hutchinson

$ ★ ✕ **Anchor Inn.** Two large brick-walled rooms in these older downtown buildings are the setting for Mexican dishes that use the restaurant's distinctive homemade flour tortillas. Portions are bounteous. ✉ *126–128 S. Main St.,* ☎ *620/669–0311. Reservations not accepted. AE, D, MC, V.*

$ ✕ **Roy's Hickory Pit BBQ.** This tiny restaurant seating 36 serves barbecued pork spareribs, beef brisket, sausage, ham, and turkey. There's nothing else on the menu except beans, salad, and bread—but what more do you want? ✉ *1018 W. 5th St.,* ☎ *620/663–7421. Reservations not accepted. No credit cards. Closed Sun.–Mon.*

$ ★ 🏨 **Ramada Inn Hutchinson.** Rooms in the "minidome" section of this busy convention hotel look onto a quiet, landscaped courtyard. "Maindome" rooms open onto a recreation area with a putting green and swimming pool. ✉ *1400 N. Lorraine St., 67501,* ☎ *620/669–9311 or 800/362–5018,* FAX *620/669–9830,* WEB *www.ramada.com. 220 rooms. Restaurant, pool, gym. AE, D, DC, MC, V.*

Larned

$ ✕ **Harvest Inn.** Chicken, steaks, and seafood are on the menu at this family restaurant; pub grub is served in the accompanying bar, the Grain Club. ✉ *718 Ft. Larned Ave.,* ☎ *620/285–3870. AE, MC, V.*

Motels

🏨 **Best Western Townsman Inn** (✉ 123 E. 14th St., Larned 67550, ☎ 620/285–3114, FAX 620/285–7139), 44 rooms; pool; *$.*

🏨 **EconoLodge** (✉ 15 W. 4th St., Hutchinson 67501, ☎ 620/663–1211, FAX 620/669–3710), 98 rooms; pool; *$.*

🏨 **Scotsman Inn** (✉ 322 E. 4th Ave., Hutchinson 67501, ☎ 620/669–8281 or 888/864–7268, FAX 620/669–8282), 48 rooms; *$.*

Nightlife

In Dodge City, the Boot Hill Museum puts on the 19th-century-style Long Branch Variety Show at the Longbranch Saloon on Front Street each evening from Memorial Day through Labor Day. The **Longhorn Saloon** (✉ 706 N. 2nd St., ☎ 620/225–3546) has a restaurant and a 1,350-square-ft wooden dance floor for western stomping.

Outdoor Activities and Sports

Hiking

At **Dillon Nature Center** (✉ 3002 E. 30th Ave., Hutchinson, ☎ 620/663–7411, WEB www.hutchrec.com), a 2-mi National Recreation Trail takes in woods, prairie, wetlands, and a prairie-dog town. Inside the Discovery Center, both kids and adults can use hands-on exhibits to learn about the Kansas outdoors.

Spectator Sports

The biggest Professional Rodeo Cowboys Association–affiliated rodeo in Kansas is the **Dodge City Roundup Rodeo** (☎ 620/225–2244, WEB www.dodgecityroundup.com), held for five days each summer during the Dodge City Days festival.

The Santa Fe Trail Region Essentials

AIR TRAVEL

US Airways Express and Frontier Airlines from Denver and United Airlines Express from Kansas City serve the Dodge City Regional Airport.
➤ AIRLINES AND CONTACTS: **Frontier Airlines** (☎ 620/225–5065). **United Airlines Express** (☎ 620/225–5065). **US Airways Express** (☎ 620/227–8679).

AIRPORTS

Dodge City Regional Airport is about 2 mi east of downtown.
➤ AIRPORT INFORMATION: **Dodge City Regional Airport** (✉ 100 Airport Rd., ☎ No phone).

BUS TRAVEL

Greyhound connects with TNM&O Coaches to provide service to Dodge City and Garden City from Wichita. Salt City Shuttle connects several small towns throughout the state.
➤ BUS INFORMATION: **Greyhound** (☎ 800/231–2222). **Salt City Shuttle** (☎ 316/664–6117). **TNM&O Coaches** (☎ 620/276–3731).

CAR TRAVEL

From Kansas City or Topeka take I–70 west and I–135 south, then Route 61 to Hutchinson. Eastbound travelers enter Dodge City via U.S. 50 or U.S. 56.

TRAIN TRAVEL

Amtrak serves Hutchinson, Newton, Garden City, and Dodge City.
➤ TRAIN INFORMATION: **Amtrak** (☎ 800/872–7245, WEB www.amtrak.com).

VISITOR INFORMATION

➤ TOURIST INFORMATION: **Dodge City Convention & Visitors Bureau** (✉ 400 W. Wyatt Earp Blvd., Dodge City [Box 1474, 67801], ☎ 620/225–8186, WEB www.dodgecity.org). **Hutchinson Convention & Visitors Bureau** (✉ 117 N. Walnut St., Hutchinson 67501, ☎ 620/662–3391, WEB www.hutchchamber.com). **Larned Area Chamber of Commerce** (✉ 502 Broadway, Larned 67550, ☎ 620/285–6916 or 800/747–6919, WEB www.larned.org).

SOUTHEAST KANSAS

Wichita

What to See and Do

Originally a frontier town, **Wichita** is known today as one of the world's capitals of airplane production—Beech, Cessna, and Learjet are based here, and Boeing has a major installation. The city is also home to such corporate giants as Coleman, makers of camping equipment, and Pizza Hut.

The **Indian Center Museum** displays artifacts from numerous tribes, including the Crow and the Sioux. The center is a great place for lunch on Tuesday, when Indian tacos are served. ✉ *650 N. Seneca St.,* ☎ *316/262–5221,* WEB *www.theindiancenter.com.* *$3. Closed Mon.*

The **Old Cowtown Museum** is a re-created 19th-century town. ✉ *1871 Sim Park Dr.,* ☎ *316/264–0671.* WEB *www.old-cowtown.org.* *$7. Closed Nov.–Mar.*

At **Botanica, the Wichita Gardens** (✉ 701 N. Amidon, ☎ 316/264–0448, WEB www.botanica.org; $6; free Jan.–Mar.), more than 9 acres of perennials and woody plants are displayed among dozens of fountains and pools. A highlight is the 2,800-square-ft free-flight butterfly enclosure that is home to more than 5,000 butterflies in various stages of development. The **Wichita Greyhound Park** (✉ I–335, 10 mi north of downtown, ☎ 316/755–4000 or 800/872–2894, WEB www.wgpi.com) offers live horse and greyhound racing, as well as simulcast races from around the country, year-round. There is no live racing on Monday or Tuesday.

Just 15 minutes north of Wichita on I–35 is El Dorado, where you'll find the **Coutts Museum of Art** (✉ 110 N. Main St., El Dorado, ☎ 316/321–1212; free), with an impressive collection of Renoirs, Remingtons, and works by local artists.

Dining and Lodging

$$ ✕ **Scotch & Sirloin.** Hearty comfort food is served amid red carpets and brass candelabras. Prime rib is the specialty, but you can opt for seafood or poultry. ✉ *5325 E. Kellogg,* ☎ *316/685–8701. AE, D, MC, V.*

$ ✕ **River City Brewery.** This rustic pub lives up to its slogan: "Fresh ales, flavorful food, and fair prices." Venison is a regular favorite. ✉ *150 N. Mosely,* ☎ *316/263–2739. AE, D, MC, V.*

$$$ 🏨 **Hyatt Regency.** Located on the east bank of the Arkansas River, the Hyatt is connected to the Century II Convention Center. ✉ *400 W. Waterman St., 67202,* ☎ *316/293–1234 or 800/233–1234,* FAX *316/293–1200,* WEB *www.hyatt.com. 303 rooms. Restaurant, pool, gym. AE, D, DC, MC, V. CP.*

$$ 🏨 **Hotel at Old Town.** In the center of the city's renovated historic district, this all-suites hotel is furnished with 19th-century antiques while supporting modern amenities. ✉ *830 E. 1st St., 67202,* ☎ *316/267–4800 or 877/265–3869,* FAX *316/267–4840,* WEB *www.hotelatoldtown.com. 115 rooms. Gym. AE, D, DC, MC, V.*

Nightlife

Old Town Wichita, between 1st and 3rd in downtown Wichita, is an entertainment district of 60 restored buildings with raised boardwalks and antique lighting and a wide array of dance clubs, restaurants, art galleries, and cigar bars. The **Crown Uptown Dinner Theatre** (✉ 3207 E. Douglas, ☎ 316/681–1566, WEB www.newtheatre.com) is one of the 10 largest dinner theaters in the country, serving American cuisine buffet-style prior to performances of Broadway-style shows.

Wichita Essentials

AIRPORTS

Most visitors arrive by car or fly into Wichita Mid-Continent Airport, served by most major domestic carriers.

➤ AIRPORT INFORMATION: **Wichita Mid-Continent Airport** (✉ 2299 Airport Rd., ☎ 316/946–4700).

BUS TRAVEL

Greyhound Lines stops in Wichita en route between Kansas City and Dallas.

➤ BUS INFORMATION: **Greyhound** (☎ 800/231–2222, WEB www.greyhound.com).

CAR TRAVEL

Wichita lies about 190 mi southwest of Kansas City on the Kansas Turnpike (I–35).

VISITOR INFORMATION

➤ TOURIST INFORMATION: **Wichita Convention and Visitors Bureau** (✉ 100 S. Main St., Suite 100, 67202, ☎ 316/265–2800 or 800/288–9424, WEB www.wichita-cvb.org).

Fort Scott

What to See and Do

Some historians argue that the violence and bloodshed that plagued this part of the Kansas-Missouri border in the years leading up to the Civil War had a greater impact on the start of the war than the shots ★ fired at Fort Sumter. Today, nine of the original buildings at the **Fort Scott National Historic Site** (✉ Old Fort Blvd., Fort Scott, ☎ 620/223–0310, WEB www.nps.gov/fosc; 🎫 $3; free Dec.–Feb.) are fully restored, and frequent reenactments demonstrate life in this frontier post. Summer and fall bring numerous festivals and activities.

Dining and Lodging

$ ✕ **Papa Don's.** Feast on excellent pizza and pasta; then finish up with ice cream and cookies at this charming stop on historic Main Street. *✉ 22 N. Main St., ☎ 620/223–4171. D, MC, V.*

$ 🏨 **The Lyons Victorian Mansion Bed & Breakfast and Spa.** One of two identical homes built side-by-side in the 1860s for daughters of a wealthy banker, this three-story Victorian is completely restored in rich velvets, tapestries, and detailed walnut carvings. *✉ 742 S. National, 66701, ☎ 620/223–3644 or 800/784–8378, FAX 620/223–0062, WEB www.lyonsmansion.com. 6 rooms. AE, MC, V.*

Fort Scott Essentials

CAR TRAVEL

Fort Scott is an easy 100-mi drive south of Kansas City on Route 69. Designated a National Military Highway, the route is sparsely populated but dotted with several historical markers describing the Indian and Civil War battles that took place around here.

VISITOR INFORMATION

The Fort Scott Visitor Center runs an hourly trolley tour (April–December only) of town highlights.

➤ VISITOR INFORMATION: **Fort Scott Visitor Center** (✉ 231 E. Wall St., ☎ 800/245–3678, WEB www.fortscott.com).

KENTUCKY

Updated by Susan Reigler

Capital	Frankfort
Population	4,041,769
Motto	United We Stand, Divided We Fall
State Bird	Cardinal
State Flower	Goldenrod
Postal Abbreviation	KY

Statewide Visitor Information

Kentucky Department of Travel Development (✉ 2200 Capital Plaza Tower, Frankfort 40601, ☎ 502/564–4930 or 800/225–8747, WEB www.kentuckytourism.com). **Welcome centers:** I–75 S at Florence, I–65 N at Franklin, I–64 W at Grayson, I–24 E at Paducah, I–75 N at Williamsburg, and U.S. 68 at Maysville.

Scenic Drives

The loop around rugged **Red River Gorge** in the eastern Kentucky mountains starts near Natural Bridge State Park, on **Route 77** near Slade. **Forest Development Road 918** is a 9-mi National Scenic Byway in the Daniel Boone National Forest, near Morehead. In the fall, the oak hickory maples along the 35-mi stretch of **Little Shepherd Trail** (U.S. 119), between Harlan and Whitesburg, have brilliant foliage. **Old Frankfort Pike** between Lexington and Frankfort passes through classic bluegrass countryside.

National and State Parks

National Parks

Daniel Boone National Forest (✉ U.S. 27, Whitley City [100 Vaught Rd., Winchester 40391], ☎ 859/745–3100, WEB www.southernregion.fs.fed.us/boone) has spectacular mountain scenery, especially in the Red River Gorge Geological Area, known for its natural arches, native plants, and 300-ft cliffs. **Land Between the Lakes** (✉ 100 Van Morgan Dr., Golden Pond 42211, ☎ 502/924–2000, WEB www.lbl.org), a demonstration project in environmental education and resource management, occupies an uninhabited 40-mi-long peninsula between Kentucky and Barkley lakes. ★ **Mammoth Cave National Park** (✉ entrances on Rte. 70, 10 mi west of Cave City, and on Rte. 255, 8 mi northwest of Park City, Mammoth Cave 42259, ☎ 270/758–2328, WEB www.nps.gov/maca) is a 350-mi-long system of twisting underground passages full of colorful mineral formations.

State Parks

Kentucky's 50 state parks are ideal for hiking or simply enjoying the countryside; most also have facilities for picnicking, camping, horseback riding, and enjoying water sports. Sixteen resort parks have rustic but comfortable lodges and/or cottages; 16 have tent and trailer sites, available April–October; 14 have year-round campgrounds. For information contact the **Kentucky Department of Parks** (✉ Capital Plaza Tower, Frankfort 40601, ☎ 502/564–2172 or 800/255–7275, WEB www.kystateparks.com).

LOUISVILLE

Louisville (locally pronounced *loo*-uh-vul) was founded in 1778 by Revolutionary War hero General George Rogers Clark and named for King Louis XVI as gratitude for France's help during the war. The city's charter was signed in 1780 by Thomas Jefferson, then the governor of Virginia, of which Kentucky was the westernmost district. Louisville's location—on a bend of the mighty Ohio River and smack in the center of the eastern half of the nation—has molded its culture and history. During the first half of the 19th century the city was a bustling river port. Then, with the invention of the train, it became a railroad hub. Waves of European immigrants settled into colorful neighborhoods that still retain their character. Today, the city is an international air hub for United Parcel Service. Every May crowds of visitors come to Louisville for the nation's premier horse race: the Kentucky Derby.

Exploring Louisville

Downtown

Historic sites abound in the heart of Louisville. **West Main Street** has more examples of 19th-century cast-iron architecture than anyplace else in the country except New York City's SoHo. The facade of the **Hart Block** (✉ 728 W. Main St.), a five-story building designed in 1884 at the height of Louisville's Victorian era, is a jigsaw puzzle of cast-iron pieces bolted together. The tiny **St. Charles Hotel** (✉ 634 W. Main St.) was constructed before 1832. The Roman Catholic **Cathedral of the Assumption** (✉ 443 S. 5th St.), a Gothic Revival structure built between 1849 and 1852, was restored between 1985 and 1994. The **Jefferson County Courthouse** (✉ 531 W. Jefferson St.), a Greek Revival landmark designed by Gideon Shyrock, was built in 1835 with the intent of luring the state government to Louisville.

The 35-story **Aegon Center** (✉ 400 W. Market St.) dominates Louisville's skyline and holds court as the tallest building in Kentucky. A dramatic geodesic dome tops the 1992 art deco–style structure, designed by New York architect John Burgee. Another contemporary work, the grand **Humana Building** (✉ 500 W. Main St.) of 1985, is the eclectic creation of architect Michael Graves. The **American Life and Accident Building** (✉ 3 Riverfront Plaza), designed by Mies van der Rohe and completed in 1973, is called the Rusty Building, after its oxidized Cor-Ten steel covering. The **Kentucky Center for the Arts,** on Riverfront Plaza, has a distinguished collection of 20th-century sculpture by artists such as Louise Nevelson, Alexander Calder, and Jean Dubuffet. The **Louisville Science Center/IMAX Theatre** (✉ 727 W. Main St., ☎ 502/561–6103, WEB www.louisvillescience.org; 🎟 center and IMAX $9, each $6.50), a 19th-century warehouse full of science arcades and demonstrations, has an Egyptian mummy's tomb, a Foucault pendulum, and plenty of hands-on displays that pack appeal for kids, including exhibits on space exploration and the human body.

★ Look for the giant baseball bat in front of the **Louisville Slugger Museum** (✉ 800 W. Main St., ☎ 502/588–7228, WEB www.sluggermuseum.org; 🎟 $6), and the giant baseball seemingly lodged in a pane of the plate-glass factory next door. Try interactive exhibits such as a "virtual pitch," in which a computerized baseball comes hurtling at you at 90 mph. A tour of the adjoining Hillerich & Bradsby factory, where the famous baseball bats are made, is included.

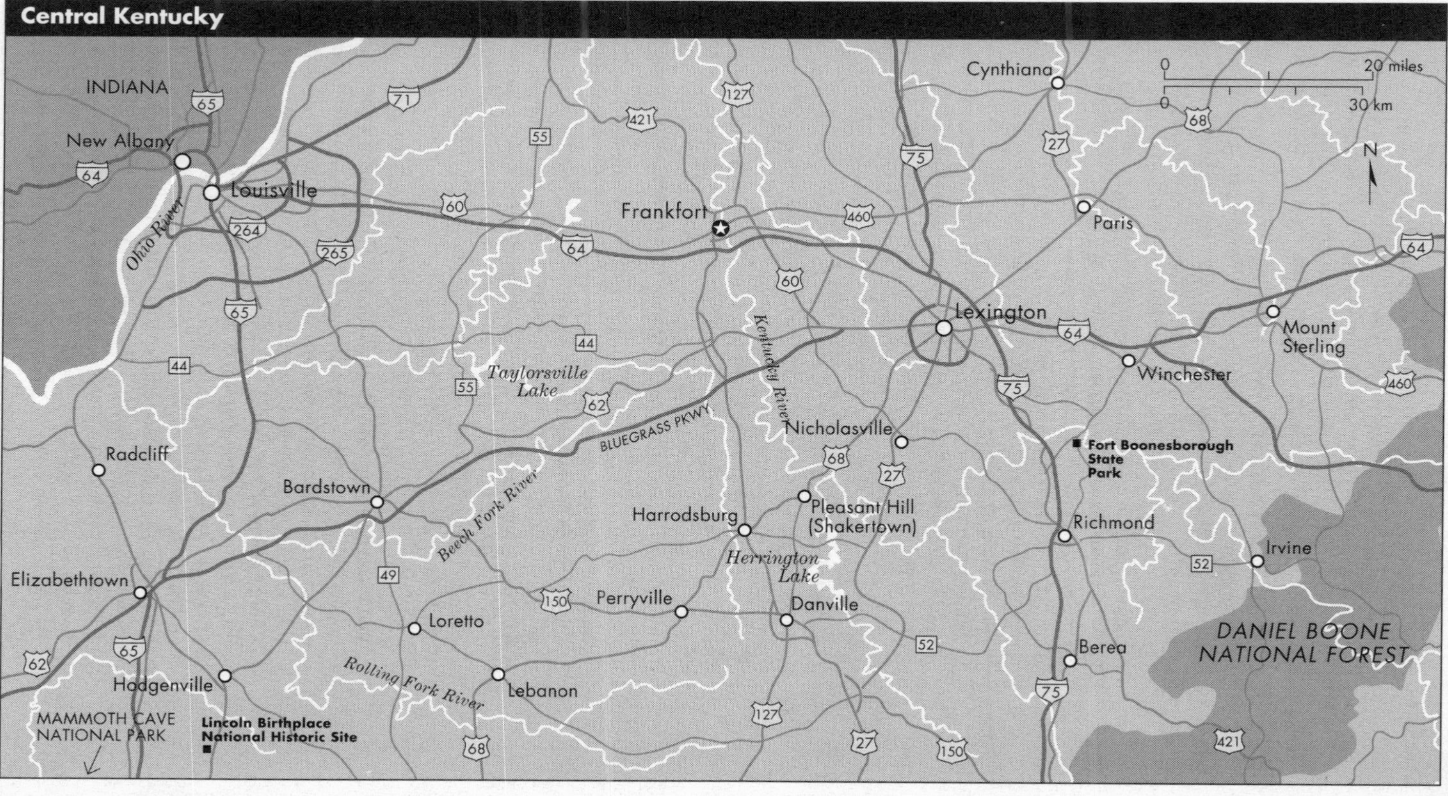
Central Kentucky
INDIANA
New Albany
Louisville
Ohio River
Frankfort
Cynthiana
Paris
Lexington
Mount Sterling
Winchester
0
20 miles
0
30 km
N
Taylorsville Lake
BLUEGRASS PKWY.
Kentucky River
Nicholasville
Fort Boonesborough State Park
Radcliff
Bardstown
Beech Fork River
Harrodsburg
Pleasant Hill (Shakertown)
Herrington Lake
Richmond
Irvine
Elizabethtown
Perryville
Danville
Loretto
Berea
DANIEL BOONE NATIONAL FOREST
Rolling Fork River
Hodgenville
Lebanon
MAMMOTH CAVE NATIONAL PARK
Lincoln Birthplace National Historic Site
65
71
127
421
55
75
27
68
64
60
460
264
265
44
62
49
150
52
127
150

Ten blocks east of the bat museum is a place where the home runs are real, not virtual. **Louisville Slugger Field** (✉ 401 E. Main St., ☎ 502/367–9121, WEB www.batsbaseball.com/slugger; $7) is a 12,000-seat jewel box of a baseball stadium that incorporates architectural elements from a 19th-century redbrick warehouse. It's home to the Louisville RiverBats, the AAA affiliate team to the Cincinnati Reds.

Scenic 6.9-mi **RiverWalk** stretches from downtown's 4th Street Wharf westward to Chickasaw Park. The path parallels the Ohio shore and has a variety of views, from the locks and dam on the shipping channel to quiet, wooded portions where the occasional deer roams. Parking is available at 4th, 8th Street, 10th Street, and 31st streets and at Lannan, Shawnee, and Chickasaw parks. One-quarter mile east of River Walk, **Linear Park** has a playground with attractions for all age groups. Between the playground and the wharf is the **Great Lawn,** an outdoor concert and recreation area where visitors can stroll to the river's edge.At the river, check out the ***Belle of Louisville*** (☎ 502/574–2355, WEB www.belleoflouisville.org; $9). It's usually moored at City Wharf at 4th and River streets. The gingerbread-trim steamboat, built in 1914, is the oldest Mississippi-style stern-wheeler still afloat. If you grow tired, hire a horse-drawn carriage from **River City Horse Carriage** (☎ 502/895–7268) or **Louisville Horse Trams** (☎ 502/581–0100).

Other Attractions

Butchertown was settled in the 1830s, mostly by Germans who worked in meatpacking plants and lived in "shotgun" and "camelback" houses under the shadow of the **Bourbon Stock Yards,** demolished in 2001. In 1814 French immigrants settled in **Portland,** where goods came ashore to be portaged past the falls of the Ohio River. Today barges carry 5 million tons of cargo per month through the **McAlpine Locks and Dam** (✉ 27th St.).

Bound by Cave Hill Cemetery, Cherokee Park, and Bardstown Road, the **Cherokee Triangle,** a classic Victorian village of grand homes on broad, tree-lined streets, was built between 1870 and 1910. Northeast of Bardstown Road and I–264 is **Farmington** (✉ 3033 Bardstown Rd., ☎ 502/452–9920; $4), a Federal-style mansion built in 1810 from a design by Thomas Jefferson. The president's special touches include two octagonal rooms and an adventurously steep hidden staircase.

★ **Old Louisville** is the most elegant of Louisville's neighborhoods. Its architectural styles include Victorian Gothic, Richardsonian Romanesque, Queen Anne, Italianate, Châteauesque, and Beaux Arts. Look for lead- and stained-glass windows, turrets, and gargoyles as you explore. The **Conrad-Caldwell House** (✉ 1402 St. James Ct., ☎ 502/636–5023; $4), a Victorian Romanesque Revival building, has an intricately carved stone exterior and elaborate interior woodwork. It's open for tours Saturday 10–4, Sunday and Wednesday noon–4. On the southern edge of ★ Old Louisville is the **University of Louisville** campus. Its **J. B. Speed Art Museum** innovatively displays masterworks by artists such as Rembrandt, Rubens, Picasso, and Caravaggio and has frequent contemporary exhibits. ✉ *2035 S. 3rd St.,* ☎ *502/636–2893,* WEB *www.speedmuseum.org.* *Free. Closed Mon.*

South of the university is **Churchill Downs** (✉ 700 Central Ave., ☎ 502/636–4400, WEB www.kentuckyderby.org), the world-famous home of the Kentucky Derby. Since the track's opening in 1875, scores of heroic three-year-old Thoroughbreds have thundered past its famous twin spires into legend. During the regular racing season don't miss **"Dawn at the**

Downs" (☎ 502/636–3351; 🎫 $10.95), when the track opens shortly after daybreak on Saturday, allowing visitors to watch the horses exercise and see the infield grass and flower beds peaceful and still covered in dew. The **Kentucky Derby Museum** (☎ 502/637–1111, WEB www.derbymuseum.org; 🎫 $8) documents the careers of champions. During the annual Kentucky Derby Festival—the two weeks leading up to and including Derby Day (the first Saturday in May)—be prepared to pay more for everything in Louisville, from lodging to transportation.

East of downtown is peaceful **Locust Grove** (✉ 561 Blankenbaker La., ☎ 502/897–9845, WEB www.locustgrove.org; 🎫 $4), the former home of Louisville's founder. Three presidents—James Monroe, Andrew Jackson, and Zachary Taylor—slept here.

Six Flags Kentucky Kingdom, near Louisville International Airport, has rides and games, including three roller coasters, a water park, and a playground for young children. *✉ 937 Phillips La., ☎ 502/366–2231, WEB www.sixflags.com. 🎫 $34.99, children under 48" $19.99, children 3 or younger free. Closed Nov.–Mar.*

Outside Louisville

Bernheim Forest (✉ Rte. 245 off I–65, Clermont, ☎ 502/543–2451, WEB www.bernheim.org) is about 25 mi south of the city, in bourbon country. The 14,000-acre preserve has 1,800 species of plants, a nature center, a museum, picnic areas, hiking trails, and lakes; in spring it gives the state's best show of rhododendrons and azaleas. The forest is free on weekdays; weekends and holidays it's $5 per vehicle. In Clermont, ½ mi southeast of Bernheim Forest on scenic Route 245, is the **Jim Beam American Outpost Museum** (☎ 502/543–9877, WEB www.jimbeam.com; 🎫 free), which has a collection of the famous Jim Beam bourbon decanters and a film about making bourbon.

Farther southeast on Route 245 is **Bardstown,** a historic city in a rural setting, best known as the site of **My Old Kentucky Home State Park** (✉ 501 E. Stephen Foster Ave., ☎ 502/348–3502, WEB www.kystateparks.com/agencies/parks/kyhome.htm. It's closed January–February. Stephen Foster visited **Federal Hill** (🎫 $4), the Georgian Colonial mansion that is the park's centerpiece, in 1852 shortly before he wrote the state song, "My Old Kentucky Home," sung at every Kentucky Derby.

Southeast of Bardstown, in Loretto, is the **Maker's Mark Distillery** (✉ 3350 Burks Spring Rd., ☎ 270/865–2881, WEB www.markersmark.com; 🎫 free), a National Historic Landmark and a working distillery. Southwest of Bardstown is the **Abraham Lincoln Birthplace National Historic Site** (✉ 3 mi south of Hodgenville on U.S. 31 E/Rte. 61, ☎ 270/358–3137, WEB www.nps.gov/abli; 🎫 free), where Lincoln was born February 12, 1809. The 116-acre park includes about 110 acres of the original Thomas Lincoln farm.

Parks, Gardens, and Zoos

In 1891 Louisville's Board of Parks hired Frederick Law Olmsted, designer of New York's Central Park, to design a system of public lands that would be "free to all forever." Among his creations were **Shawnee Park** in the west, a plain of river bottomland; **Cherokee Park** in the east, where Beargrass Creek wanders among woods and meadows; and **Iroquois Park** in the south, a tall, rugged escarpment offering views of the city. Another Olmsted jewel, little **Tyler Park,** on Baxter Avenue, is a spot of solitude in the city bustle. The **Louisville Zoo** (✉ 1100 Trevilian Way, ☎ 502/459–2181, WEB www.louisvillezoo.org; 🎫 $8.95) has more than 1,600 animals in naturalistic environments.

Dining

The two major Restaurant Rows are east of downtown on Bardstown Road and on Frankfort Avenue. Many of Louisville's finer restaurants put a new twist on regional products such as country ham, grits, and bourbon.

$$–$$$$ ★ ✕ **The Oakroom.** Specialties include bluegrass free-range chicken with country ham-pesto stuffing, Kentucky beef Wellington, and a bananas Foster with bourbon instead of rum. The formal dining room radiates southern hospitality, and the award-winning wine list is one of the best in the Ohio Valley. ✉ *500 S. 4th St., in the Seelbach Hilton,* ☎ *502/585–3200. AE, D, DC, MC, V.*

$$–$$$$ ✕ **Pat's Steak House.** Traditional southern cooking and scents of bourbon and tobacco fill this cozy, old-fashioned restaurant and bar. Waiters wear white coats and call most customers by name as they serve plates of marvelous fried chicken livers, country ham, fried chicken, and tender aged steaks. ✉ *2437 Brownsboro Rd.,* ☎ *502/893–2062. No credit cards. Closed Sun.*

$$–$$$ ★ ✕ **English Grill.** An oak-paneled dining room evokes a 19th-century London gentlemen's club. The menu, a blend of Continental and Kentucky specialties, changes with the seasons; typical choices are pork tenderloin marinated with apple butter, grenadine of beef tenderloin with oxtail vol-au-vent, and a bourbon dessert soufflé. ✉ *335 W. Broadway, in the Camberly Brown Hotel,* ☎ *502/583–1234. AE, D, DC, MC, V.*

$$–$$$ ★ ✕ **Lilly's.** Innovative "haute Kentucky" fare centers on farm-fresh produce and meats. Dishes such as sweetbreads and morels cooked with country ham, and slow-roasted rabbit with lamb sausage fill the seasonal menu. The stylish dining room is green, black, and purple. ✉ *1147 Bardstown Rd.,* ☎ *502/451–0447. AE, MC, V. Closed Sun.*

$$–$$$ ✕ **Vincenzo's.** Deep leather chairs, 17th-century paintings, and crisp tablecloths complement impeccable service and Italian meals such as *vitello alla Sinatra* (spinach-stuffed veal scallopini with wine sauce). The much-honored wine list has many Italian and California vintages. ✉ *Humana Bldg., 150 S. 5th St.,* ☎ *502/580–1350. AE, D, DC, MC, V. Closed Sun.*

$$–$$$ ✕ **Zephyr Cove.** From vegetarian entrées to game, there's something for everyone at this California-style bistro. Dishes include rabbit loin, Portobello duck breast, and vegetable moussaka. The outstanding wine list was chosen to match the fare. ✉ *2330 Frankfort Ave.,* ☎ *502/893–0106. AE, MC, V.*

$$ ✕ **Asiatique.** Euro-Asian preparations and modern art prevail in this casual suburban eatery. Try the wok-seared salmon, roasted quail on a noodle pancake, or lemongrass beef medallions. Dessert specialties include ginger ice cream. ✉ *106 Sears Ave.,* ☎ *502/899–3578. AE, DC, MC, V.*

$$ ✕ **Cafe Metro.** Come for the Art Deco and the creative Continental cuisine. All entrées have a set price; they include Jaeger Schnitzel in a spicy brown cream sauce and duck-confit crepes. Decadent desserts are de rigueur. ✉ *1700 Bardstown Rd.,* ☎ *502/458–4830. AE, DC, MC, V. Closed Sun.*

$$ ✕ **Mayan Gypsy.** Bold colors define the funky furnishings, just as bold flavors shape the menu. Look for such Yucatecan specialties as chicken in mole sauce, roasted squash, and panfried lima beans. ✉ *624 E. Market St.,* ☎ *502/583–3300. AE, MC, V. Closed Sun.*

$–$$ ★ ✕ **Lynn's Paradise Cafe.** There's a giant red coffeepot and cup-and-saucer fountain out front; inside, portions are enormous. Best bets are the breakfast burrito and Dagwood-size sandwiches. Dinner includes a famous meat loaf and pecan-crusted rainbow trout. ✉ *984 Barret Ave., ☎ 502/583–3447. MC, V. Closed Mon.*

$–$$ ★ ✕ **Uptown Café.** A remarkable Caesar salad, shrimp bisque, and such entrées as duck ravioli and salmon croquettes make this a local favorite for fine food at moderate prices. Like its sister bistro, the upscale Cafe Metro, the Uptown specializes in imaginative combinations. Ask for a booth in the cozy back room. ✉ *1624 Bardstown Rd., ☎ 502/458–4212. AE, DC, MC, V. Closed Sun.*

$ ✕ **Check's Cafe.** The food at this Germantown eatery—like the atmosphere and service—is down-home. Bratwurst sandwiches, chili, and fish are some favorites. ✉ *1101 E. Burnett Ave., ☎ 502/637–9515. No credit cards.*

$ ✕ **Come Back Inn.** South Side Chicago Italian cuisine is the specialty of this neighborhood hangout. Beef sandwiches, pastas with homemade marinara, and traditional pizzas are highlights. ✉ *909 Swan St., ☎ 502/627–1777. AE, MC, V. No dinner Mon.*

$ ✕ **Kitty O'Kirwans.** Country furniture and etched glass accentuate this beautiful pub, which serves such favorites as corned beef and cabbage and lavender roast pork loin. Guinness is on tap. ✉ *102 Bauer Ave., ☎ 502/894–8030. AE, MC, V. No dinner Sun.*

Lodging

Louisville has a long tradition of hospitality. Choose either a lovingly restored, pricey downtown hotel or a budget room in a place that feels like home. Bed-and-breakfast accommodations can be found through **Kentucky Homes B&B** (✉ 1219 S. 4th Ave., Louisville 40203, ☎ 502/635–7341, WEB bbonline.com/ky/index.html).

$$–$$$ 🏨 **Camberly Brown Hotel.** Built in 1923, this 16-story historic hotel has been fully restored with Old English–style furnishings. The artwork, atmosphere, and service are impeccable. The English Grill is one of the city's finest restaurants. ✉ *335 W. Broadway, 40202, ☎ 502/583–1234 or 800/866–7666, FAX 502/587–7006, WEB www.camberleyhotels.com. 294 rooms. 2 restaurants, gym. AE, D, DC, MC, V.*

$$–$$$ ★ 🏨 **The Seelbach Hilton.** The refurbished guest rooms in this 11-story landmark have four-poster beds, armoires, and marble baths with gold fixtures. ✉ *500 4th Ave., 40202, ☎ 502/585–3200 or 800/333–3399, FAX 502/585–9239, WEB www.hilton.com. 322 rooms. 2 restaurants. AE, D, DC, MC, V.*

$–$$$ 🏨 **Breckinridge Inn.** Most rooms have art deco designs in this clean, plain, and comfortable two-story hotel. ✉ *2800 Breckinridge La., at I–264, 40220, ☎ 502/456–5050, FAX 502/451–1577. 123 rooms. Restaurant, pool, tennis. AE, D, DC, MC, V.*

$–$$$ 🏨 **Hyatt Regency Louisville.** Hyatt's familiar plant-filled atrium and glass-and-brass lobby are the focus of this 18-story hotel. The rooms have a back-to-nature theme, with redwood and pastels. ✉ *320 W. Jefferson St., 40202, ☎ 502/587–3434, FAX 502/581–0133, WEB www.hyatt.com. 388 rooms. Restaurant, pool, gym. AE, D, DC, MC, V.*

$–$$$ 🏨 **Old Louisville Inn Bed & Breakfast.** The guest rooms in this 1901 brick house have elaborately carved mahogany woodwork and antiques. The atmosphere and service make it feel just like old times. ✉ *1359 S. 3rd St., 40208, ☎ 502/635–1574, FAX 502/637–5892, WEB www.bbonline.com/ky/oldlouisville. 10 rooms. AE, D, MC, V. BP.*

$$ 🏨 **Galt House East.** Overlooking the river, this downtown hotel has an elaborately landscaped, modern 18-story atrium, but the room furnishings emphasize old-fashioned comfort. ✉ *141 N. 4th Ave., 40202, ☎ 502/589–5200 or 800/843–4258, FAX 502/585–4266, WEB www.galthouse.com. 600 rooms. Restaurant, pool. AE, D, DC, MC, V.*

$ **Executive Inn.** An English Tudor style characterizes every part of this six-story hotel near the airport. Some rooms have private patios or balconies. *978 Phillips La., off I–64, 40209, 800/626–2706; 800/222–8284 in Kentucky, FAX 502/363–1880, WEB www.executiveinnhotel.com. 465 rooms. Restaurant, 2 pools, gym. AE, D, DC, MC, V.*

$ **Red Roof Inn East.** Basic, inexpensive accommodations are available in this motor inn about 20 minutes east of downtown via I–64 at Hurstbourne Parkway. Rooms are clean and spare. Pets are allowed. *9330 Blairwood Rd., 40222, 502/426–7621, FAX 502/426–7933, WEB www.redroof.com. 108 rooms. AE, D, DC, MC, V.*

$ **Travelodge.** A cinder-block exterior disguises this centrally located, inexpensive motel. Rooms are spacious and clean. *401 S. 2nd St., 40202, 502/583–2841 or 800/255–3050, FAX 502/583–2629, WEB www.travelodge.com. 98 rooms. Restaurant. AE, D, DC, MC, V.*

Nightlife and the Arts

For arts and entertainment events, look for *Louisville* magazine on newsstands and the Friday and Saturday editions of the *Courier-Journal* newspaper. Daily arts updates can be found on the *Courier-Journal*'s entertainment Web page (www.louisvillescene.com).

Nightlife

The **Comedy Caravan Nightclub** (1250 Bardstown Rd., in the Mid-City Mall, 502/459–0022) showcases local and regional stand-up acts. The **Connection** (130 S. Floyd St., 502/585–5752), a giant entertainment complex, has a bar and the biggest dance floor in town. There are talent shows in the bar on Thursday night, and a female impersonator does revues on the weekends in the theater. **Coyote's** (116 W. Jefferson St., 502/589–3866) has live country music, a raucous but friendly clientele, and free two-step and line-dancing instruction. The **Old Seelbach Bar** (500 S. 4th St., in the Seelbach Hilton, 502/585–3200) is a cozy spot for jazz.

The Arts

Actors Theatre of Louisville (316 W. Main St., 502/585–1210, WEB www.actorstheatre.org) is a Tony Award–winning repertory theater in a bank building (circa 1837) designated a National Historic Landmark. Each February, the Actors Theatre sponsors the **Humana Festival of New American Plays,** which has premiered several plays that have gone on to New York and London. The **Broadway Series** (611 W. Main St., 502/584–7469, WEB www.broadwayseries.com/louisville) hosts touring productions of Broadway's best. **Shakespeare in the Park** (Central Park at S. 4th St., 502/634–8237, WEB www.kyshakes.org) transforms Louisville into the Bard's town on summer weekends. **Stage One: The Louisville Children's Theatre** (425 W. Market St., 502/584–7777 or 800/283–7777, WEB www.stageone.org) offers professional productions on weekends from October to May.

The three stages at the **Kentucky Center for the Arts** (5 Riverfront Plaza, 502/562–0100 or 800/283–7777, WEB www.kca.org) are alive with entertainment, from Broadway to Bach and bagpipes to bluegrass. The **Louisville Orchestra** (609 W. Main St., 502/584–7777 or 800/283–7777, WEB www.louisvilleorchestra.org) has received international attention for its recordings of contemporary works. The **Louisville Ballet** and Kentucky Opera (502/584–7777 or 800/283–7777; www.louisvilleballet.org; WEB www.kyopera.org) also perform at the arts center.

Spectator Sports

Baseball: The **Louisville RiverBats,** a farm team of the Cincinnati Reds, play in the Louisville Slugger Stadium near the riverfront (✉ 402 E. Main St., ☎ 502/361–3100 for ticket information).

Horse racing: The **Kentucky Derby** at Churchill Downs is a *very* tough ticket—unless you're willing to join tens of thousands of seatless young revelers in the infield, where you're unlikely to get even a glimpse of a horse. Races occur from late April to mid-July and October to November.

Shopping

Shopping Districts

The **Galleria** (✉ 4th Ave. between Liberty St. and Muhammad Ali Blvd., ☎ 502/584–7170), a glass-enclosed mall with 80 stores and 11 fast-food restaurants, is a city melting pot and the best place to shop downtown. **Bardstown Road,** southeast of downtown, is a 2-mi strip of antiques shops, bookstores, and boutiques. The **Jefferson Mall** (☎ 502/968–4101), 10 mi south of downtown on Outer Loop, is a huge enclosed mall with more than 100 stores. The **Mall St. Matthews** (☎ 502/893–0311) and **Oxmoor Center** (☎ 502/426–3000) are both at the intersection of the Watterson Expressway with Shelbyville Road. Together they house more than 300 stores, including outlets of such retailers as Brooks Brothers, Williams-Sonoma, and Eddie Bauer.

Department Stores

Louisville has several department stores; most are in the suburban shopping malls: **Jacobson's** (✉ Oxmoor Center, ☎ 502/327–0200); **Lazarus** (✉ Jefferson Mall, ☎ 502/966–1800; ✉ Oxmoor Center, ☎ 502/423–3000); and **Lord & Taylor** (✉ The Mall St. Matthews, ☎ 502/895–8887; ✉ Jefferson Mall, ☎ 502/968–6080).

Specialty Stores

The **Kentucky Art & Craft Gallery** (✉ 609 W. Main St., ☎ 502/589–0102) sells top-quality crafts. **Baer Fabrics** (✉ 515 E. Market St., ☎ 502/583–5521) has been building its world-renowned collection of buttons since 1905. **Joe Ley Antiques** (✉ 615 E. Market St., ☎ 502/583–4014) has an outstanding 2-acre litter of hardware, fixtures, and doodads.

Louisville Essentials

AIRPORTS AND TRANSFERS

Louisville International Airport is 15 minutes south of downtown on I–65. It has a comfortable, modern terminal and is served by most major carriers.

➤ AIRPORT INFORMATION: **Louisville International Airport** (✉ 600 Terminal Dr., ☎ 502/367–4636).

AIRPORT TRANSFER

Cab fare from the airport to downtown Louisville runs about $20.

BUS TRAVEL TO AND FROM LOUISVILLE

➤ BUS INFORMATION: **Greyhound** (✉ 720 W. Muhammad Ali Blvd., ☎ 800/231–2222).

CAR TRAVEL

Interstates run all over Louisville: I–64 runs east–west, I–71 northeast, and I–65 north–south. I–264, also known as the Henry Watterson

Expressway, rings the city, as does the outermost ring road, the Gene Snyder Freeway (I–265). These interstates converge downtown in a ramp-ridden tangle known as Spaghetti Junction, where confusion can result in a quick trip to Indiana.

TRANSPORTATION AROUND LOUISVILLE

The downtown area is defined north–south by Broadway and the Ohio River, east–west by Preston and 18th streets. The Transit Authority of River City operates local buses ($1 at peak times, 75¢ other times), as well as a free trolley along 4th Avenue between Broadway and the river. For explorations beyond downtown, a car is a must.

➤ CONTACT: **Transit Authority of River City** (✉ 1000 W. Broadway, ☎ 502/585–1234, WEB www.ridetarc.com).

VISITOR INFORMATION

➤ TOURIST INFORMATION: **Convention & Visitors Bureau** (✉ 400 S. 1st St., 40202, ☎ 502/584–2121 or 800/792–5595, WEB www.louisville-visitors.com). **Greater Louisville, Inc.** (✉ 600 W. Main St., 40202, ☎ 502/625–0060).

LEXINGTON AND THE BLUEGRASS

Lexington, the world capital of racehorse breeding and burley tobacco (a thin-bodied, air-cured variety), was named by patriotic hunters who camped here in 1775 shortly after hearing news of the first battle of the Revolutionary War at Lexington, Massachusetts. A log structure built by a member of that historic hunting party is preserved on the campus of Transylvania University. The Bluegrass is a lush region of rolling hills, meandering streams, and manicured horse farms.

Exploring Lexington and the Bluegrass

Lexington

Lexington Livery Company (☎ 859/259–0000) gives horse-drawn carriage rides ($25 for a 30-minute tour). In the **Gratz Park Historic District,** near 2nd Street and Broadway, are two fine houses from 1814: the lavish, privately owned **Gratz House** (✉ 231 N. Mill St., ☎ no phone), built by a rich hemp manufacturer, and the **John Hunt Morgan House** (✉ 201 N. Mill St., ☎ 859/233–3290; 🎫 $5), which passed from the swashbuckling Confederate general to his great-grandson, Thomas Hunt Morgan, who won a Nobel Prize in 1933 for proving the existence of the gene. The Morgan house is closed December 15–February and Monday the rest of year. A statue of General Morgan stands on the lawn of the **Fayette County Courthouse** (✉ 215 W. Main St.). When it was unveiled in 1911, its portrayal of the Rebel raider astride a stallion caused quite a stir, as his best-known mount was a mare, Black Bess.

The Greek Revival campus of **Transylvania University** (✉ 300 N. Broadway, ☎ 859/233–8120, WEB www.transy.edu), the first college west of the Alleghenies (established in 1780), has left its mark on two U.S. vice presidents, 50 senators, 34 ambassadors, and 36 Kentucky governors. The 1832 **Mary Todd Lincoln House** (✉ 578 W. Main St., ☎ 859/233–9999, WEB www.mtlhouse.org; 🎫 $7) belonged to the parents of Abraham Lincoln's wife and displays Lincoln and Todd family memorabilia. The museum is closed Sunday and Monday and December through mid-March. U.S. senator Henry Clay, the Great Compromiser, was a green 20-year-old lawyer when he came to Lexington in 1797 and opened his **law office** (✉ 176–178 N. Mill St., ☎ no phone).

Two attractions at the **University of Kentucky** (✉ Euclid Ave. and S. Limestone St., ☎ 859/257–3595, WEB www.uky.edu) are an **anthropology museum** (✉ 201 Lafferty Hall, ☎ 859/257–7112, WEB www.uky.edu/as/anthropology/museum/museum.htm; 🎫 free), with exhibits on evolution and Kentucky culture, and an **art museum** (✉ 121 Singletary Center for the Arts, ☎ 859/257–5716, WEB www.uky.edu/artmuseum; 🎫 free), which has a fine permanent collection and frequent special exhibits; both are closed on Monday.

The interactive exhibits at the **Lexington Children's Museum** (✉ 401 W. Main St., ☎ 859/258–3256, WEB www.lexingtonchildrensmuseum.com; 🎫 $3) include an archaeology dig. A Lexington curiosity is the huge **castle** (✉ west of the city on Versailles Rd.), with eight turrets and 70-ft-tall corner towers. A Fayette County developer began, but never finished, construction in 1969 on what was to be his private residence. The **Headley-Whitney Museum** houses an eclectic, personal three-building collection of Asian porcelains, masks, paintings, shells, and jeweled bibelots. ✉ *Old Frankfort Pike,* ☎ *859/255–6653,* WEB *www.headley-whitney.org.* 🎫 *$4. Closed Mon.*

The Bluegrass

Kentucky's **Bluegrass** area has more than 400 horse farms, some with Thoroughbred barns as elegant as French villas. Among the famous breeding farms is **Calumet** (✉ west of the city on Versailles Rd./U.S. 60, ☎ no phone), which has produced a record eight Kentucky Derby winners. The antebellum mansion at **Manchester Farm** (✉ Van Meter Rd., ☎ no phone) is said to have been the inspiration for Tara in *Gone With the Wind.* **Spendthrift** (✉ Ironworks Pike, ☎ 859/299–5271) is one of the few farms that routinely welcome visitors. Famous horses from the **C. V. Whitney Farm,** on Paris Pike, have included Regret, the first filly to win the Kentucky Derby, and the appropriately named Upset, the only horse ever to finish ahead of the legendary Man o' War. **Normandy** (✉ Paris Pike, ☎ no phone) has a famous L-shape barn, built in 1927, with a clock tower and animal-shape roof ornaments.

A number of Lexington-based companies conduct tours that take in several farms and the Keeneland Racecourse. They include **Bluegrass Tours** (✉ Box 1176, 40589, ☎ 859/252–5744; 🎫 $20) and **Historic and Horse Farm Tours** (✉ Box 22593, 40522, ☎ 859/268–2906, FAX 859/266–8603; 🎫 $23). A showcase for Thoroughbreds and other horses, **Kentucky Horse Park** has a museum, an art gallery, and campgrounds. It also offers films, a breeds show, and farm tours. ✉ *4089 Ironworks Pike, off I–75, Lexington,* ☎ *859/233–4303,* WEB *www.state.ky.us/agencies/khp/hp1.htm.* 🎫 *$12. Closed Mon.–Tues.*

The most historic bourbon distillery in Kentucky is **Labrot & Graham,** surrounded on all sides by horse farms. The whiskey is made in copper-pot stills housed in a limestone building dating from the early 1800s. ✉ *7855 McCracken Pike off U.S. 60,* ☎ *859/879–1812,* WEB *www.brown-forman.com.* 🎫 *Free. Closed Sun.–Mon.*

Southward on scenic U.S. 25 is **Fort Boonesborough State Park** (☎ 859/527–3131 or 800/255–7275, WEB www.state.ky.us/agencies/parks/ft.boone; 🎫 $4.50), a reconstruction of one of Daniel Boone's early forts, with a museum and demonstrations of pioneer crafts. The **White Hall State Historic Site** (✉ 500 White Hall Shrine Rd., ☎ 859/623–9178, WEB www.state.ky.us/agencies/parks/whthall.htm; 🎫 $4), in Richmond, home of the abolitionist Cassius Marcellus Clay, a cousin of Henry Clay and an ambassador to Russia. The mansion combines two houses and two styles, Georgian and Italianate.

In Berea, where the Bluegrass meets the mountains, charming, tuition-free **Berea College** (☎ 606/986–9341, WEB www.berea.edu), founded in 1855, has 1,500 students—most from Appalachia—who work for their education. On the campus is the **Appalachian Museum** (✉ Jackson St., ☎ 606/986–9341 or 859/986–6078; free), which charts regional history through arts and crafts.

★ The **Shaker Village of Pleasant Hill** (✉ Hwy. 68, ☎ 859/734–5411, WEB www.shakervillageky.org; $10), 25 mi southwest of Lexington, has 27 restored buildings of frame, brick, or stone erected between 1805 and 1859 by members of a religious sect noted for industry, architecture, and furniture making. In Harrodsburg, the first permanent settlement in Kentucky, **Old Fort Harrod State Park** (☎ 859/734–3314, WEB www.state.ky.us/agencies/ftharrd2.htm; $3.50) has a full-scale reproduction of the old fort, built on its original 1774 site.

About 15 mi south of Lexington the beautiful, deep blue-green **Kentucky River** flows gently but relentlessly through the Bluegrass. The combination of rolling river and rugged rock faces creates dramatic landscapes. Take Jacks Creek Pike from Lexington through one of the most enchanting parts of Kentucky to **Raven Run Nature Sanctuary** (☎ 859/272–6105, WEB www.visitlex.com/media/ravenrun.html), a place of rugged, forested hills and untouched wildlife along the Kentucky River.

In lovely Danville, 30 mi southwest of Lexington, the **McDowell House and Apothecary Shop** (✉ 125 S. 2nd St., ☎ 859/236–2804, WEB www.lexinfo.com/historic/mcdowell.html; free), the residence and shop of Dr. Ephraim McDowell (a noted surgeon of the early 19th century), is refurnished with period pieces. The house is closed November–March. West of Danville on U.S. 150 and north on U.S. 68 is **Perryville Battlefield** (☎ 859/332–8631, WEB www.state.ky.us/agencies/parks/perryvi), the site of Kentucky's most important (and bloodiest) Civil War battle, where 4,241 Union soldiers and 1,822 Confederates were killed or wounded.

Frankfort, between Louisville and Lexington on I–64, was chosen as the state capital in 1792 as a compromise between the cities' rival claims and has been caught in the middle ever since. The **state capitol** (☎ 502/564–3449), overlooking the Kentucky River at the south end of Capitol Avenue, is noted for its Ionic columns, high central dome, and lantern cupola; guided tours are given. Outside the capitol is the famous **Floral Clock,** a working outdoor timepiece whose face—made of thousands of plants—is swept by a 530-pound minute hand and a 420-pound hour hand.

In Frankfort Cemetery, on East Main Street, you can visit **Daniel Boone's grave** (he died in Missouri, but his remains were returned to Kentucky in 1845). The restored Georgian-style **Old Governor's Mansion** (✉ 420 High St., ☎ 502/564–5500; free), built in 1798, served as the residence of 33 governors until a new mansion was built in 1914. The later **governor's mansion** (☎ 502/564–3449; free) is styled after the Petit Trianon, Marie-Antoinette's villa at Versailles. Both mansions are open for tours Tuesday and Thursday.

Dining and Lodging

Although Lexington offers varied dining options, most restaurants outside the city are down-home. Menus tend toward country-fried steak, country ham, and fried chicken. Many of the best places to dine are out of the way and unimpressive looking, at least on the outside.

Restored historic properties, often modestly priced, are short on amenities but long on charm. State park lodges and cottages are bargains, rustic but comfortable. In many rural areas you'll have to settle for bare-bones accommodations. In Lexington **Dial Accommodations** (✉ 430 W. Vine St., ☎ 859/233–7299) can help with reservations.

Berea

$$–$$$ ★ ✕🏨 **Boone Tavern.** Dating from 1909, this grand old Colonial-style hotel is operated by Berea College and outfitted with furniture handmade by students. The restaurant—which requires men to wear a jacket and tie—is famous for its spoon bread, chicken flakes in bird's nest, and Jefferson Davis pie. ✉ *Main and Prospect Sts. (Box 2345, 40403),* ☎ *859/986–9358 or 859/986–9359. 57 rooms. Restaurant. AE, D, DC, MC, V.*

Frankfort

$$–$$$ ✕ **Daniel's.** In a Victorian-era building on the city's main shopping street, this handsome corner bistro serves up grilled steaks and chops and a variety of pasta dishes. A good wine list and weekend bourbon tastings are added attractions. ✉ *243 W. Broadway,* ☎ *502/875–5599. AE, MC, V. Closed Sun.*

Harrodsburg

$–$$ ✕🏨 **Beaumont Inn.** Guest rooms at this exemplar of southern hospitality are scattered among four timeworn (but polished) buildings furnished with antiques. The restaurant specializes in corn pudding and cured Kentucky country ham. ✉ *638 Beaumont Dr., 40330,* ☎ *859/734–3381,* FAX *859/734–6897. 33 rooms. Restaurant, pool, tennis. AE, D, DC, MC, V. Closed mid-Dec.–mid-Mar. CP.*

$ ✕🏨 **Inn at Pleasant Hill.** Rooms in 27 restored buildings (circa 1800)—some with four stories and no elevators—are furnished with Shaker reproductions and handwoven rugs and curtains. The restaurant, Trustees' House at Pleasant Hill, serves hearty family-style meals and specializes in a tangy Shaker lemon pie for which people have been known to drive a hundred miles; reservations are essential. ✉ *3500 Lexington Rd., 40330,* ☎ FAX *859/734–5411,* WEB *www.shakervillageky.org. 80 rooms. Restaurant. MC, V.*

Lexington

$$–$$$ ✕ **A la Lucie.** The tin roof, terrazzo floors, hot colors, green plants, and eclectic art give this chef-owned eatery a Parisian Left Bank ambience. French, German, and American dishes appear on the menu, but the specialty is seasonal seafood. ✉ *150 N. Limestone St.,* ☎ *859/252–5277. AE, DC, MC, V. Closed Sun.*

$$–$$$ ✕ **Dudley's Restaurant.** Huge tulip trees shade the courtyard of this chic, unpretentious restaurant in a 100-year-old schoolhouse. A favorite on the Continental menu is pasta with chicken, sun-dried tomatoes, and vegetables. ✉ *380 S. Mill St.,* ☎ *859/252–1010. AE, MC, V.*

$$–$$$ ✕ **Merrick Inn.** The spacious, comfortable, not-too-formal restaurant is in a sprawling, white-columned building that was once a horse farm (circa 1890). On the extensive menu are steak, lamb, and a variety of pastas, but the specialty is fresh seasonal seafood. ✉ *3380 Tates Creek Rd.,* ☎ *859/269–5417. AE, DC, MC, V. Closed Sun.*

$$–$$$ ✕ **Roy & Nadine's.** An overstuffed sofa, fringed lamp shades, and Erté prints set the tone in this suburban restaurant famous for its list of 25 "shaken, not stirred" martinis. The food is eclectic and might include: pepper-seared carpaccio, a black bean ancho-Caesar salad, cumin-spiced chicken, or grilled rack of lamb. ✉ *3775 Harrodsburg Rd., in the Palomar Center,* ☎ *859/223–0797. AE, MC, V.*

$–$$ ★ ✕ **Alfalfa Restaurant.** Small, woody, and old-fashioned, this restaurant has vegetarian and ethnic dishes. The menu, written on a chalkboard, may include ham-and-apple quiche; the house salad is lavish. Each Wednesday a different cuisine—Greek, Italian, Indian—is served. ✉ *557 S. Limestone St.,* ☎ *859/253–0014. MC, V. No dinner Mon.*

$–$$ ✕ **Atomic Cafe.** The Bluegrass region may not seem like the place for Caribbean cuisine, but the conch fritters taste fresh off the boat. Jerk chicken and pork dishes are fiery. Shrimp lovers should try the coconut-battered variety served here. Decor is tropical, with evocative murals. ✉ *265 N. Limestone St.,* ☎ *859/254–1969. MC, V. Closed Sun.–Mon.*

$–$$ ✕ **Ed and Fred's Desert Moon.** Contemporary southwestern cuisine includes blue corn nachos, lamb with ginger, and linguine with smoked tomato jalapeño sauce. Industrial decor of metal trim and bold desert hues of orange and purple dominates the multilevel dining areas. ✉ *148 Grand Blvd.,* ☎ *859/231–1161. AE, MC, V. Closed Mon.*

$–$$ ★ ✕ **Joe Bologna's.** Feast on pasta and pizza at this college hangout, which occupies a church built in 1890; the original stained-glass windows are still in place. ✉ *120 W. Maxwell St.,* ☎ *859/252–4933. MC, V.*

$$$ **Camberly Club Hotel at Gratz Park.** The guest rooms in this elegantly refurbished three-story medical building from 1887 are furnished with antiques. Continental breakfast, afternoon tea, and evening cordials are available. ✉ *120 2nd St., 40507,* ☎ *859/231–1777 or 800/227–4362,* FAX *859/233–7593,* WEB *www.camberleyhotels.com. 52 rooms. Restaurant. AE, D, DC, MC, V. CP.*

$$ ★ **Marriott's Griffin Gate Resort.** Gleaming and contemporary, this seven-story resort caters to a youngish crowd that likes physical activities and physical comforts. The rooms have private patios or balconies. ✉ *1800 Newtown Pike, 40511,* ☎ *859/231–5100,* FAX *859/255–9944,* WEB *www.marriott.com. 409 rooms. Restaurant, pool, tennis, health club. AE, D, DC, MC, V.*

$ **Campbell House Inn.** The attentive staff gives guests a warm welcome at this three-story motel. Rooms are modern but homey. ✉ *1375 Harrodsburg Rd., 40504,* ☎ *859/255–4281 or 800/354–9235; 800/432–9254 in Kentucky,* FAX *859/254–4368,* WEB *www.campbellhouseinn.com. 370 rooms. Restaurant, pool, tennis. AE, D, DC, MC, V.*

$ **Courtyard by Marriott.** The trademark of this motel is a sunny, gardenlike central courtyard. The green, brown, and mauve rooms are modern, with light woodwork and oversize desks. ✉ *775 Newtown Ct., 40511,* ☎ *859/253–4646,* FAX *859/253–9118,* WEB *www.marriott.com. 146 rooms. Restaurant, pool, gym. AE, D, DC, MC, V.*

Nightlife and the Arts

Nightlife

After-dark events in Lexington are sparse and tame. From Thursday through Sunday check out the **Brewery** (✉ 509 W. Main St., ☎ 859/255–2822), a friendly Texas-roadhouse-style bar with classic rock and country tunes. Or visit **Comedy Off Broadway** (✉ 3199 Nicholasville Rd., ☎ 859/271–5653), where stand-up comics perform.

The Arts

Lexington's performing arts scene is vivacious. Concerts, plays, and lectures are presented at Transylvania University and the University of Kentucky. The **Actors' Guild** is the city's premier dramatic society (☎ 859/233–0663, WEB www.actorsguildoflexington.org). Information about performances of the **Lexington Ballet** can be obtained by calling ☎ 859/233–3925 or trying the Web site www.balletlex.com.The **Lexington Children's Theatre** (☎ 859/254–4546) has performances for young audiences. The **Lexington Philharmonic** (☎ 859/233–4226, WEB www.lexingtonphilharmonic.org) has several concert series. And

Opera of Central Kentucky (☎ 859/231–6994, WEB www.operabase.com) brings vocal masterpieces to the Bluegrass.

Outdoor Activities and Sports

Kentucky's lakes and streams provide great fishing for more than 200 species. You're rarely more than a 30-minute drive from a public golf course. The state parks and national forests are full of hiking trails. Eastern Kentucky has several rivers with mild to moderate white-water rafting. For information contact the **Department of Parks,** tourism offices, or the state **Department of Fish and Wildlife Resources** (✉ 1 Game Farm Rd., Frankfort 40601, ☎ 502/564–4336, WEB www.state.ky.us/agencies/fw/kdwr.htm).

Spectator Sports

College Basketball: Rupp Arena is the home of the **University of Kentucky Wildcats** basketball team (✉ 430 W. Vine St., ☎ 859/233–4567). A warning: Home games are often sold out, as hoards of regular fans buy season tickets to cheer the 1996 and 1998 NCAA champions. **Horse-racing: Keeneland Racecourse** (✉ 4201 Versailles Rd., Lexington, ☎ 859/254–3412 or 800/456–3412, WEB www.keenland.com) holds races in April and in October.

Shopping

In Lexington **Fayette Mall** (✉ 3473 Nicholasville Rd., ☎ 859/272–3493) has more than 100 stores and a dozen places to eat. For something out of the ordinary, try **Dudley Square** (✉ 380 S. Mill St., ☎ no phone), in a restored 1881 school building; its shops sell antiques, prints, quilts, and the like. **Victorian Square** (✉ 401 W. Main St., ☎ 859/252–7575) is an entire downtown block of renovated Victorian buildings that now have retail and dining establishments. Lexington also has many **antiques shops**; the Convention & Visitors Bureau maintains a list.

Lexington and the Bluegrass Essentials

AIRPORTS

Lexington Bluegrass Airport, 4 mi west of downtown Lexington, is served by Delta, US Airways, and regional lines.

➤ AIRPORT INFORMATION: **Lexington Bluegrass Airport** (✉ 4000 Versailles Rd., ☎ 859/254–9336).

CAR TRAVEL

The Lexington area and the Bluegrass are well served by I–64 east–west, I–75 north–south, and the state parkway system, a toll network that bisects the state east–west.

VISITOR INFORMATION

For information on Frankfort and Franklin County, contact the Tourist and Convention Commission in Frankfort.

➤ TOURIST INFORMATION: **Greater Lexington Convention & Visitors Bureau** (✉ 430 W. Vine St., Suite 363, 40507, ☎ 859/233–1221 or 800/845–3959, WEB www.visitlex.com). **Richmond Tourism Commission** (✉ Box 250, City Hall, 40476, ☎ 859/623–1000, WEB www.richmond-ky.com). **Tourist and Convention Commission** (✉ 100 Capital Ave., Frankfort 40601, ☎ 502/875–8687 or 800/960–7200, WEB www.frankfortky.org).

LOUISIANA

Updated by Michaela Morrissey

Capital	Baton Rouge
Population	4,465,430
Motto	Union, Justice, and Confidence
State Bird	Pelican
State Flower	Magnolia
Postal Abbreviation	LA

Statewide Visitor Information

Louisiana Office of Tourism (✉ Box 94291, Baton Rouge 70804-9291, ☎ 800/334–8626, WEB www.crt.state.la.us/crt/tourism.htm).

Scenic Drives

Gators laze along the exotic **Creole Nature Trail,** a circular drive out of Lake Charles designated a National Scenic Byway. **Routes 56 and 57** also form a circular drive south of Houma, where shrimp boats dock along the bayous from May to December. **Route 82** runs through the coastal marshes and wildlife refuges along the Gulf of Mexico. The **Longleaf Trail Scenic Byway,** south of Natchitoches, is a 17-mi highway through the Kisatchie National Forest linking Routes 117 and 119. **Route 182** runs alongside Bayou Teche in southern Louisiana. **Route 93,** between Grand Coteau and Lafayette, passes through farmland and small Cajun towns.

National and State Parks

National Parks

The **Jean Lafitte National Historical Park and Preserve** (✉ 365 Canal St., New Orleans 70130, ☎ 504/589–3882, WEB www.isue.edu/acadgate/lafitte.htm) maintains seven separate parks throughout the state and offers nature trails and canoeing through exotic swampland. The 100,000-acre Kisatchie Ranger District of the **Kisatchie National Forest** (✉ Rte. 6 W [Box 2128, Natchitoches 71457], ☎ 318/352–2568, WEB www.southernregion.fs.fed.us/kisatchie) has hiking and equestrian trails through hardwood and pine forests.

State Parks

A prehistoric Native American site dating between 1800 BC and 500 BC, the 400-acre **Poverty Point State Commemorative Area** (✉ Rte. 577 [Box 276, Epps 71237], ☎ 318/926–5492 or 888/926–5492, WEB www.crt.state.la.us/crt/parks/poverty/pvertypt.htm) is one of the country's most important excavations, with hiking trails and an interpretive center in addition to the ancient Native American mounds. The 600-acre **Louisiana State Arboretum** (✉ Rte. 3042, Ville Platte 70586, ☎ 337/363–6289, WEB www.crt.state.la.us/crt/parks/arbor/Arbor2.htm), lush with trees and plants native to the state, has 2½ mi of nature trails. Fishing, boating, and camping (cabins are available) are all possibilities in the 6,500-acre **Chicot State Park** (✉ Rte. 3042 [Box 494, Ville Platte 70586], ☎ 337/363–2403 or 888/677–2442, WEB www.crt.state.la.us/crt/parks/chicot/chicot.htm). At the wetland retreat of **Bayou Segnette** (✉ 7777 Westbank Expressway, Westwego 70094, ☎ 504/736–7140 or 888/677–2296, WEB www.crt.state.la.us/crt/parks/bayouseg/byusegne.htm), near New Orleans, you can splash in its popular wave pool or skim its waterways in a canoe. Fishing is key at **Lake Bistineau State Park** (✉ Box 589, Doyline 71023, ☎ 318/745–3503 or 888/677–2478, WEB www.crt.state.la.us/crt/parks/lakebist/bistino.htm); **Lake**

Fausse Point State Park (✉ 5400 Levee Rd., along Rte. 3083 [Box 5648, St. Martinville 70582], ☎ 337/229–4764, WEB www.crt.state.la.us/crt/parks/lakefaus/lakefaus.htm) is known for its great fishing. Water sports abound at **North Toledo Bend State Park** (✉ Box 56, Zwolle 71486, ☎ 318/645–4715 or 888/677–6400, WEB www.crt.state.la.us/crt/parks/ntoledo/ntoledo.htm), which includes the Toledo Bend Reservoir, one of the largest man-made reservoirs in the country.

NEW ORLEANS

Tucked beyond miles of marsh, New Orleans sometimes seems closer in spirit to the Caribbean than to Our Town, USA. New Orleanians are often oblivious to national trends and styles, while the European, African, and Caribbean cultures that settled here are intact and even thriving—often, as during Mardi Gras, in exuberant contiguity. Creole cuisine, the continuing legacy of New Orleans jazz, and the unabashed prioritizing of pleasure that define life here are all part of an oh-so-rare mixture of modernity and true individuality, found in the frank indifference of leisure-seeking locals no less than in the raucous revelry of the touristed French Quarter.

Exploring New Orleans

The French Quarter, the CBD, and the Warehouse District

★ The **French Quarter** is the original colony founded in 1718 by French Creoles. A carefully preserved historic district that's also a residential district, the Quarter is home to famous creole restaurants and many a jazz club. An eclectic crowd ambles in and out of small two- and three-story frame, old-brick, and pastel stucco buildings, most of which date from the mid-19th century. Baskets of splashy subtropical plants dangle from the eaves of buildings with filigreed galleries, flourishes of gingerbread, and dormer windows. Secluded courtyards are awash in greenery and brilliant blossoms.

The heart of the Quarter is **Jackson Square,** a formally landscaped park surrounded by a flagstone pedestrian mall and centered by an equestrian statue of Andrew Jackson. The mall is alive with sidewalk artists, food vendors, Dixieland bands, and clowns. The promenade of **Washington Artillery Park,** across Decatur Street from Jackson Square, affords a splendid perspective on the square and Ol' Man River.

St. Louis Cathedral (✉ 615 Père Antoine Alley, ☎ 504/525–9585) is a quiet reminder of the city's spiritual life. The present church dates from 1794 and was restored in 1849. Free tours are conducted daily. **Pirate's Alley** and **Père Antoine's Alley,** two flagstone passageways redolent of bygone days, run alongside St. Louis Cathedral.

The **Louisiana State Museum** (✉ 751 Chartres St., ☎ 504/568–6968, WEB www.lsm.crt.state.la.us) operates three properties on or near Jackson Square, all closed Monday. If you visit two or more state museum properties within a three-day period, you can receive a 20% discount on admission. Transfer papers for the Louisiana Purchase of 1803 were signed on the second floor of the **Cabildo** (🎫 $5), where New Orleans's rich multicultural history is explored through historic documents and artifacts, among them a death mask of Napoléon—one of only three in the world. The **Presbytère** (🎫 $5), originally built as a home for priests, today houses a Mardi Gras museum. You can see what life was like for wealthy 19th-century Creole apartment dwellers in the **1850s House** (✉ 523 St. Ann St.; 🎫 $3), which contains period furnishings, antique dolls, and a quaint kitchen.

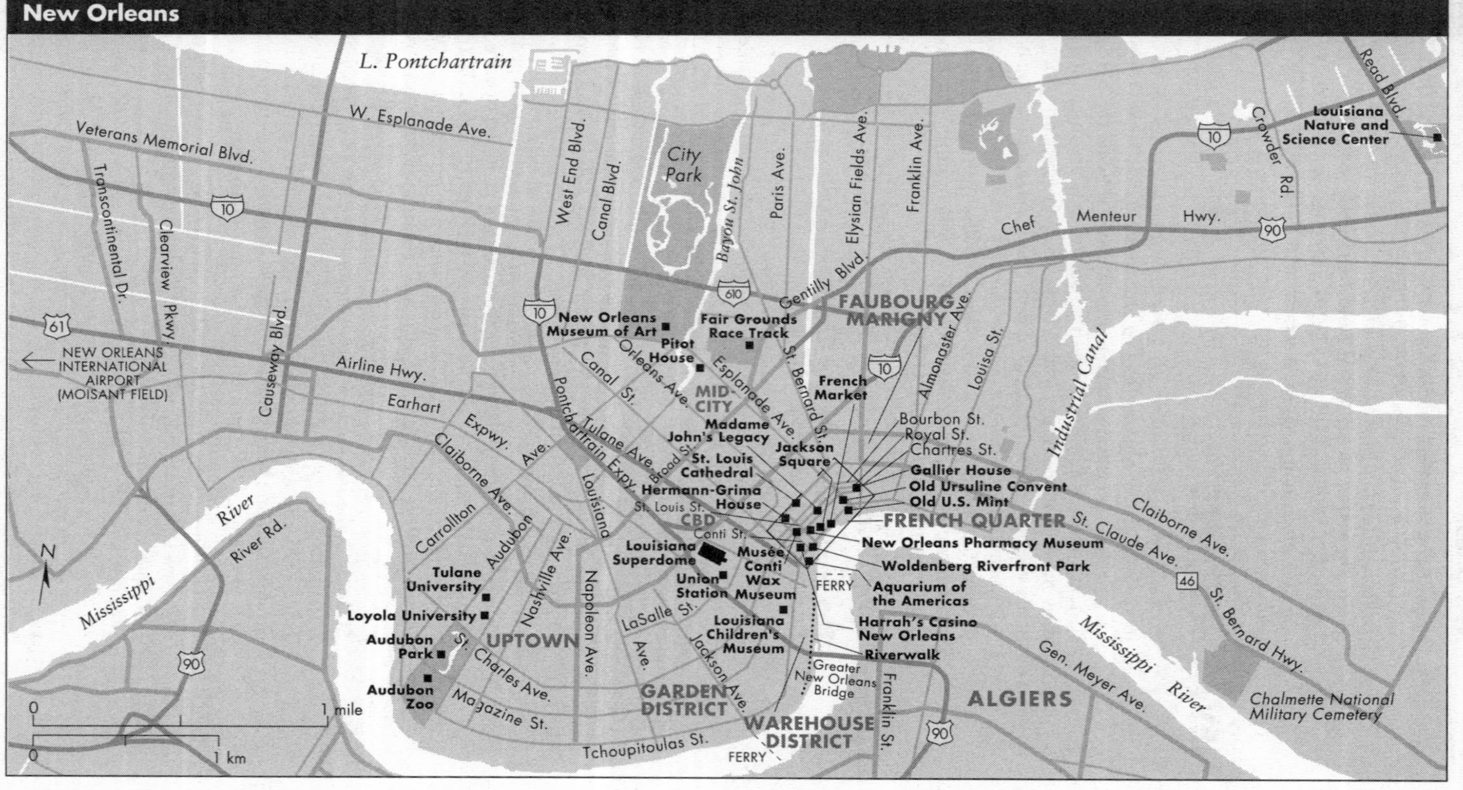

New Orleans
L. Pontchartrain
W. Esplanade Ave.
Veterans Memorial Blvd.
Transcontinental Dr.
Clearview Pkwy.
Causeway Blvd.
NEW ORLEANS INTERNATIONAL AIRPORT (MOISANT FIELD)
Airline Hwy.
Earhart
Expwy.
Ave.
Claiborne Ave.
Carrollton
Audubon
River Rd.
Mississippi River
West End Blvd.
Canal Blvd.
City Park
Bayou St. John
Paris Ave.
Elysian Fields Ave.
Franklin Ave.
Gentilly Blvd.
Chef Menteur Hwy.
Crowder Rd.
Read Blvd.
Louisiana Nature and Science Center
Industrial Canal
Louisa St.
Almonaster Ave.
FAUBOURG MARIGNY
New Orleans Museum of Art
Fair Grounds Race Track
Pitot House
Orleans Ave.
Canal St.
Esplanade Ave.
St. Bernard St.
MID-CITY
French Market
Madame John's Legacy
Jackson Square
Bourbon St.
Royal St.
Chartres St.
Gallier House
Old Ursuline Convent
Old U.S. Mint
FRENCH QUARTER
St. Claude Ave.
Claiborne Ave.
St. Bernard Hwy.
Pontchartrain Expy.
Tulane Ave.
Broad St.
St. Louis Cathedral
Hermann-Grima House
St. Louis St.
CBD
Conti St.
Louisiana Superdome
Musée Conti Wax Museum
New Orleans Pharmacy Museum
Woldenberg Riverfront Park
Aquarium of the Americas
FERRY
Union Station
Louisiana Children's Museum
Harrah's Casino New Orleans
Riverwalk
Greater New Orleans Bridge
Louisiana
Nashville Ave.
Napoleon Ave.
LaSalle St.
Ave.
Jackson Ave.
Tulane University
Loyola University
Audubon Park
Audubon Zoo
UPTOWN
St. Charles Ave.
Magazine St.
GARDEN DISTRICT
Tchoupitoulas St.
WAREHOUSE DISTRICT
Franklin St.
ALGIERS
Gen. Meyer Ave.
Chalmette National Military Cemetery
N
0
1 mile
1 km
10
610
61
90
46

The **Pontalba Buildings,** which line Jackson Square on St. Ann and St. Peter streets, are among the oldest apartment houses in the country. Built between 1849 and 1851, they have some of the city's loveliest ironwork galleries.

The **French Market** (✉ Decatur St. between Jackson Sq. and Esplanade Ave.) is a complex of shops, offices, and eating places in a row of renovated buildings that once housed markets during Spanish and French ★ rule. Here in the French Market, **Café du Monde** (✉ 800 Decatur St., ☎ 504/525–4544) provides a 24-hour haven for café au lait and beignets (squares of fried dough dusted with powdered sugar).

The **Old U.S. Mint** houses exhibits on jazz and Mardi Gras. This was the first branch of the U.S. Mint, in operation from 1838 until 1861. It's now part of the Louisiana State Museum. ✉ *400 Esplanade Ave.,* ☎ *504/568–6968.* *$5. Closed Mon.*

★ The **Old Ursuline Convent,** erected in 1749 by order of Louis XV, is the only building remaining from the original colony. The Sisters of Ursula, who arrived here in 1727, occupied the building from 1749 to 1824. Guided tours of the complex take in the splendid **St. Mary's Church.** ✉ *1112 Chartres St.,* ☎ *504/529–3040.* *Tours $5. Closed Mon.*

The **Gallier House** was built about 1857 by famed architect James Gallier Jr. as his family home. This is one of the best-researched house-museums in the city and an example of how well-heeled Creoles lived. ✉ *1118–32 Royal St.,* ☎ *504/525–5661,* WEB *www.gnofn.org/~hggh.* *$6, combination ticket to Hermann-Grima House $10. Closed Sun.*

The newest branch of the Louisiana State Museum is **Madame John's Legacy** (✉ 632 Dumaine St., ☎ 504/568–8788; $3), a former residence and one of the few structures to survive the great fire of 1794. A recent archaeological excavation yielded a fascinating series of structural foundations, as well as artifacts including pottery and documents. There are also changing exhibits by Louisiana artists.

The **LaBranche House** (✉ 740 Royal St.), a private residence dating from about 1840, wraps around the corner of Royal and St. Peter streets. Its filigreed double galleries are the most photographed in the city.

The **New Orleans Pharmacy Museum** is a musty old place where the nation's first licensed pharmacist lived and worked in the 1820s. It's full of ancient and mysterious medicines. ✉ *514 Chartres St.,* ☎ *504/565–8027,* WEB *www.pharmacymuseum.org.* *$2. Closed Mon.*

★ At the **Hermann-Grima House** guides take you through the Georgian-style town house, built in 1831, and its picturesque outbuildings. On Thursday, October–May, you can watch creole cooking demonstrations—sorry, no tastings! ✉ *820 St. Louis St.,* ☎ *504/525–5661,* WEB *www.gnofn.org/~hggh.* *$6, combination ticket to Gallier House $10. Closed Sun.*

Not to be missed are the tableaux in the **Musée Conti Wax Museum** (✉ 917 Conti St., ☎ 504/525–2605, WEB www.get-waxed.com; $6.25), which immortalizes such Louisiana legends as Andrew Jackson, Jean Lafitte, and Marie Laveau, the 19th-century voodoo queen.

Canal Street forms the upriver border of the French Quarter. Across Canal Street from the French Quarter and the nerve center of the nation's second-largest port, the **Central Business District (CBD)** has the city's newest high-tech convention hotels, along with ritzy shopping malls, fast-food chains, stores, foreign agencies, and the mammoth Superdome.

Harrah's Casino New Orleans (✉ 4 Canal St., ☎ 504/533–6000 or 877/277–4263, WEB www.harrahs.com/our_casinos/nor), the city's first land-based casino, has 100,000 square ft of slots and table games.

★ The **Aquarium of the Americas** (✉ 1 Canal St., ☎ 504/565–3033, WEB www.auduboninstitute.org; aquarium $13, IMAX $7.75, aquarium and IMAX $17.25) offers an IMAX theater and close encounters with aquatic creatures in 60 displays. The 16-acre **Woldenberg Riverfront Park,** which fronts the Aquarium of the Americas, has excellent river views.

The **Riverwalk,** a busy area near the ferry landing, holds Spanish Plaza, a broad, open expanse of mosaic tile with a magnificent fountain; the Riverwalk shopping mall; and riverboat docks.

The **Warehouse District** is home to converted warehouse apartment buildings, art galleries, and a growing number of trendy bars and restaurants. **Julia Street** is the main arts drag; the first Saturday evening of every month is alive with openings and music. The **Contemporary Arts Center** (✉ 900 Camp St., ☎ 504/523–1216, WEB www.cacno.org; $3) presides over the gallery scene with changing exhibits, many by local and regional artists. A café in the center offers free Web access, and two theaters have plays and live music in the evenings.

The **Louisiana Children's Museum** has fun hands-on activities. ✉ *420 Julia St.,* ☎ *504/523–1357,* WEB *www.lcm.org.* *$5. Closed Mon.*

The Garden District and Uptown

Nestled between St. Charles, Louisiana, and Jackson avenues and Magazine Street, the **Garden District** is aptly named. Shunned by the French Creoles when they arrived in the early 19th century, American settlers built palatial estates upriver and surrounded them with lavish lawns. Many of the Garden District houses were built during New Orleans's golden age, from 1830 until the Civil War. Some of these private homes are open to the public during **Spring Fiesta tours** (☎ 504/581–1367), which generally occur in late March.

Uptown is the area upriver of the Garden District. Here, **Tulane** and **Loyola** universities stand side by side on St. Charles Avenue, across from Audubon Park (☞ Parks, Gardens, and Zoos, *below*).

St. Charles Avenue is the beautiful, oak-lined street that strings together the French Quarter, the Garden District, and Uptown. The **St. Charles Streetcar,** the oldest operating streetcar line anywhere, is a wonderful way to trace the development of the city as it spread upriver.

Mid-City

Mid-City is the area between the French Quarter and Lake Pontchartrain. One of Mid-City's major draws is the **Fair Grounds Race Track** (☞ Spectator Sports, *below*), the third-oldest racetrack in the nation. The **New Orleans Museum of Art** (✉ 1 Collins-Diboll Cir., ☎ 504/488–2631, WEB www.noma.org; $6) displays Italian paintings from the 13th to the 18th century, 20th- and 21st-century European and American paintings and sculptures, Chinese jade, and the *Imperial Treasures,* a large collection of Fabergé eggs. It's closed on Monday.

The **Pitot House** is a West Indies–style house built in the late 18th century. Inside are many antiques from 19th-century Louisiana. ✉ *1440 Moss St.,* ☎ *504/482–0312.* *$5. Closed Sun.–Thurs.*

North of town, **Lake Pontchartrain** is a boating and fishing destination with marinas, picnic grounds, and seafood restaurants. The riverboat casino ***Treasure Chest*** (☎ 504/443–8000 or 800/298–0711, WEB www.treasurechest.com) has a Caribbean theme and its own outdoor concert series in the spring. Bally's **Belle of Orleans** (☎ 504/568–9376, WEB www.ballysno.com) has 30,000 square ft of games, slots, and tables.

Parks, Gardens, and Zoos

City Park (✉ City Park Ave., ☎ 504/482–4888), in Mid-City, is a 1,500-acre urban oasis shaded by majestic live oak trees. Its offerings include golf courses, tennis courts, and an ice-skating rink; lagoons for boating, canoeing, and fishing; botanical gardens; and a children's amusement park with a carousel and pony rides.

The lush 400-acre **Audubon Park** (✉ 6500–6800 blocks of St. Charles Ave., WEB www.auduboninstitute.org) has a 2-mi jogging trail with exercise stations, a riding stable, a swimming pool, tennis courts, a golf course, and a zoo.

The **Audubon Zoo** (✉ 6500 Magazine St., ☎ 504/861–2537, WEB www.auduboninstitute.org; $9) covers 58 acres of Audubon Park. Wooden walkways afford an up-close look at more than 1,800 animals in natural-habitat settings, including a Louisiana swamp and an African savanna. There's also a petting zoo; sea lion and elephant feedings are festive events.

Dining

$$$$ ★ ✕ **Grill Room.** New American cuisine with strong Continental overtones is served here in an opulent setting highlighted by original artwork. As the name suggests, there's a grill, over which much good fish is prepared. ✉ *Windsor Court Hotel, 2nd level, 300 Gravier St.,* ☎ *504/522–1992,* WEB *www.windsorcourthotel.com. Reservations essential. Jacket required. AE, D, DC, MC, V.*

$$$–$$$$ ✕ **Arnaud's.** Beveled glass, ceiling fans, and tile floors create an aura of traditional southern dining. The big, ambitious menu includes classic dishes such as rich shrimp bisque and beef Wellington. Cigar aficionados will feel at home in Arnaud's Bar, and the Richelieu Room is open for late-night live music, supping, and dancing. ✉ *813 Bienville St., French Quarter,* ☎ *504/523–5433,* WEB *www.arnauds.com. Reservations essential. Jacket required in main dining room. AE, D, DC, MC, V.*

$$$–$$$$ ★ ✕ **Commander's Palace.** Housed in a renovated Victorian mansion, this elegant restaurant offers the best sampling of old creole cooking. Chef Jamie Shannon's classics include trout with roasted pecans and poached oysters in a seasoned cream sauce with Oregon caviar. ✉ *1403 Washington Ave.,* ☎ *504/899–8221,* WEB *www.commanderspalace.com. Reservations essential. Jacket required. AE, D, DC, MC, V.*

$$$–$$$$ ✕ **Galatoire's.** Operated by the fourth generation of the family owners, Galatoire's is a tradition in New Orleans. Every imaginable creole dish is served in a large, narrow dining room lit with brass chandeliers. ✉ *209 Bourbon St.,* ☎ *504/525–2021,* WEB *www.galatoires.com. Jacket required. AE, DC, MC, V. Closed Mon.*

$$$–$$$$ ★ ✕ **K-Paul's Louisiana Kitchen.** National celebrity chef Paul Prudhomme's restaurant is a shrine to New Orleans Cajun cooking. Inventive gumbos, fried crawfish tails, blackened tuna, and sweet-potato–pecan pie are just a few of the jewels on the menu. Prices are steep at dinner but moderate at lunch. ✉ *416 Chartres St., French Quarter,* ☎ *504/524–7394,* WEB *www.kpauls.com. AE, DC, MC, V. Closed Sun.*

$$–$$$ ★ ✕ **Bayona.** In an early 19th-century creole cottage on a quiet street, chef Susan Spicer skillfully prepares such dishes as turnovers filled with spicy crawfish tails; a bisque of corn, leeks, and chicken; and salmon fillet in white-wine sauce with sauerkraut. In good weather drinks and meals are served on a patio. ✉ *430 Dauphine St.,* ☎ *504/525–4455,*

WEB *www.bayona.com. Reservations essential. AE, DC, MC, V. Closed Sun.*

$$–$$$ ★ ✕ **Nola.** This Emeril Lagasse spin-off serves down-to-earth southern Louisiana dishes in energetic and colorful surroundings. The trout swathed in a horseradish-citrus crust and plank-roasted in a wood oven is unforgettable, as is the coconut cream pie with cinnamon ice cream. ✉ *534 St. Louis St.,* ☎ *504/522–6652,* WEB *www.emerils.com/restaurants/nola. Reservations essential. AE, D, DC, MC, V. No lunch Sun.*

$–$$ ✕ **Praline Connection.** Down-home cooking in the southern creole style is the forte of these laid-back restaurants. The fried or stewed chicken, smothered pork chops, barbecued ribs, and collard greens are definitively done. The Warehouse District location has a weekly Sunday Gospel Brunch. ✉ *542 Frenchmen St.,* ☎ *504/943–3934,* WEB *www.pralineconnection.com;* ✉ *901 S. Peters St.,* ☎ *504/523–3973. Reservations not accepted. AE, D, DC, MC, V.*

$–$$ ✕ **Ralph & Kacoo's.** Getting past the door to the vast dining spaces usually means first taking a ticket and waiting your turn in a crowded bar decorated in a bayou theme. Freshness and consistency are trademarks here. You'll find them in the boiled shrimp, raw oysters, shrimp rémoulade, trout meunière, and fried seafood platter. This restaurant is popular with families. ✉ *519 Toulouse St., French Quarter,* ☎ *504/522–5226. Reservations not accepted. AE, D, MC, V.*

$ ✕ **Camellia Grill.** This classy lunch counter with linen napkins and a maître d' serves the best omelets in town, as well as great hamburgers, pecan pie, cheesecake, and banana cream pie. Expect long lines on weekends for breakfast. ✉ *626 S. Carrollton Ave., Uptown,* ☎ *504/866–9573. No credit cards.*

Lodging

Reserve well in advance, especially during Mardi Gras, the bacchanalian celebration the day before Lent. Hotels frequently offer special packages at reduced rates, but never during Mardi Gras, when rates are much higher and minimum stay requirements are often in effect.

$$$$ ★ **Fairmont Hotel.** The Fairmont is one of the oldest grand hotels in America. Its lobby is decked out in blue-and-gold Victorian splendor. Special touches in every room include down pillows and terry robes. ✉ *123 Baronne St. 70140,* ☎ *504/529–7111 or 800/527–4727,* FAX *504/529–4764,* WEB *www.fairmontneworleans.com. 785 rooms. 3 restaurants, pool, tennis, gym. AE, D, DC, MC, V.*

$$$$ ★ **Windsor Court Hotel.** Exquisite, gracious, eminently civilized—these words try to capture the wonderful quality of this hotel. Four blocks from the French Quarter, the Windsor Court has plush carpeting, canopy and four-poster beds, stocked wet bars, marble vanities, oversize mirrors, and dressing areas. ✉ *300 Gravier St. 70130,* ☎ *504/523–6000 or 800/262–2662,* FAX *504/596–4513,* WEB *www.windsorcourthotel.com. 326 rooms. 2 restaurants, pool, health club. AE, D, DC, MC, V.*

$$$–$$$$ ★ **Royal Orleans Hotel (Omni).** This elegant white-marble hotel is reminiscent of a bygone era. Rooms, though not exceptionally large, are well appointed, with marble baths (telephone in each) and marble-top dressers and tables. ✉ *621 St. Louis St. 70140,* ☎ *504/529–5333,* FAX *504/529–7089,* WEB *www.omnihotels.com. 362 rooms. Restaurant, pool, gym. AE, D, DC, MC, V.*

$$–$$$ **Chateau Le Moyne Holiday Inn.** Old-world atmosphere and decor can be found one block off Bourbon Street. Eight suites are in cottages off a tropical courtyard; all rooms are furnished with antiques and reproductions. ✉ *301 Dauphine St. 70112,* ☎ *504/581–1303,* FAX *504/*

523–5709, WEB *www.holiday-inn.com. 171 rooms. Restaurant, pool. AE, D, DC, MC, V.*

$$ **Pontchartrain Hotel.** Maintaining the grand tradition is the hallmark of this quiet, elegant European-style hotel, which has reigned on St. Charles Avenue since it was built in 1927. Accommodations range from lavish sun-filled suites to small pension-style rooms with shower-baths. ✉ *2031 St. Charles Ave., 70140,* ☎ *504/524–0581 or 800/777–6193,* FAX *504/524–7828,* WEB *www.pontchartrainhotel.com. 122 rooms. 2 restaurants. AE, D, DC, MC, V.*

$–$$ **Josephine Guest House.** European antiques fill the rooms of this restored Italianate mansion built in 1870. The bathrooms are impressive in both size and decor. A complimentary Continental breakfast, served on Wedgwood china from a silver tray, can be brought to your room. ✉ *1450 Josephine St. 70130,* ☎ *504/524–6361 or 800/779–6361,* FAX *504/523–6484,* WEB *www.bbonline.com/la/josephine. 6 rooms. AE, D, DC, MC, V. CP.*

$–$$ ★ **Le Richelieu.** This small, friendly hotel offers many amenities usually found in luxury high-rises. Some rooms have mirrored walls, walk-in closets, and refrigerators. Luxury suites are available. ✉ *1234 Chartres St., 70116,* ☎ *504/529–2492 or 800/535–9653,* FAX *504/524–8179,* WEB *www.lerichelieuhotel.com. 86 rooms. Pool. AE, D, DC, MC, V.*

$–$$ **Rue Royal Inn.** This circa-1850 home has balcony rooms overlooking a courtyard and Royal Street; two suites have Jacuzzis. Each room has a coffeemaker and a small refrigerator. ✉ *1006 Royal St. 70116,* ☎ *504/524–3900 or 800/776–3901,* FAX *504/558–0566,* WEB *www.rueroyalinn.com. 17 rooms. AE, D, DC, MC, V. CP.*

$ **St. Charles Guest House.** Simple and affordable, this European-style pension is in four buildings one block from St. Charles Avenue. Rooms in the A and B buildings are larger. The small "backpacker" rooms share a bath and do not have air-conditioning. ✉ *1748 Prytania St., 70130,* ☎ *504/523–6556,* FAX *504/522–6340,* WEB *www.stcharlesguesthouse.com. 36 rooms, 8 with shared bath. Pool. AE, MC, V. CP.*

Nightlife and the Arts

The Friday edition of the *Times-Picayune* (www.nolalive.com) and the weekly *Gambit* (www.bestofnewlorleans.com) carry comprehensive calendars of arts and entertainment events. *New Orleans* magazine (on newsstands) and *This Week in New Orleans* and *Where: New Orleans* (both available free in hotels) also publish calendars of events. The best dirt on the local music scene comes courtesy of *Offbeat,* a free monthly. Credit-card purchases of tickets for events at the Saenger Performing Arts Center and Kiefer UNO Lakefront Arena can be made through **Ticketmaster** (☎ 504/522–5555 or 800/488–5252, WEB www.ticketmaster.com).

Nightlife

New Orleans is a 24-hour town, meaning there are no legal closing times. Bourbon Street in the French Quarter is lined with clubs; many local hangouts are Uptown.

BARS

The heavily touristed **Pat O'Brien's** (✉ 718 St. Peter St., ☎ 504/525–4823, WEB www.patobriens.com) has three lively bars. At **Lafitte's Blacksmith Shop** (✉ 941 Bourbon St., ☎ 504/523–0066) drinks are served in a rustic 18th-century cottage. According to legend the cottage was once a front for pirate Jean Lafitte's smuggling and slave trade. **Napoleon House** (✉ 500 Chartres St., ☎ 504/524–9752, WEB www.napoleonhouse.com) is a longtime favorite hangout. **Oz** (✉ 800 Bourbon St., ☎ 504/593–9491, WEB www.ozneworleans.com) is a popular dance bar for young gays and lesbians. **Bourbon Pub** (✉ 801 Bourbon St., ☎ 504/529–2107, WEB www.bourbonpub.com) is a popular gay bar for young men. In the Warehouse District, **Ernst Café** (✉ 600 S. Peters St., ☎ 504/525–8544, WEB www.ernstcafe.net) is a friendly, atmospheric old bar.

JAZZ

Buddy Bolden once held court at the **Funky Butt** (✉ 714 N. Rampart St., ☎ 504/558–0872); today this laid-back club presents an impressive roster to a mix of tourists and local jazz aficionados. You'll find real Dixieland jazz at **Pete Fountain's** (✉ 2 Poydras St., in the Hilton hotel, ☎ 504/523–4374); the legendary clarinetist performs at his club when he's in town. The lovably ramshackle **Preservation Hall** (✉ 726 St. Peter St., ☎ 504/522–2841, WEB www.preservationhall.com) always has a line in front for its down-home New Orleans jazz. Restaurant, bar, and intimate performance space in one, **Snug Harbor** (✉ 626 Frenchmen St., across Esplanade Ave. from the French Quarter, ☎ 504/949–0696, WEB www.snugjazz.com) offers a more contemporary twist on the traditional jazz scene, with young hopefuls pushing the envelope nightly. You can catch live traditional jazz at the elegant two-stage **Storyville District** (✉ 125 Bourbon St., ☎ 504/410–1000, WEB www.thestoryvilledistrict.com).

RHYTHM AND BLUES, CAJUN, ROCK, NEW WAVE

An institution, **Tipitina's** (✉ 501 Napoleon Ave., ☎ 504/897–3943, WEB www.tipitinas.com) is a laid-back place with a mixed bag of music. **Jimmy's Music Club** (✉ 8200 Willow St., ☎ 504/861–8200) is popular with the college crowd. You can enjoy a good R&B or blues act at the **Maple Leaf Bar** (✉ 8316 Oak St., ☎ 504/866–9359). Cajun two-stepping can be found at **Mulate's** (✉ 201 Julia St., ☎ 504/522–1492, WEB www.mulates.com). Take bites of fabulous Cajun comfort food in between dance lessons (free with dinner) at **Michaul's** (✉ 840 St. Charles Ave., ☎ 504/522–5517, WEB www.michauls.com). **House of Blues** (✉ 225 Decatur St., ☎ 504/529–2583, WEB www.hob.com) has a contrived atmosphere but nonetheless books top-notch acts.

The Arts

CONCERTS

The esteemed **Louisiana Philharmonic Orchestra** (☎ 504/523–6530) performs classical music in the Orpheum Theater (✉ 129 University Pl., ☎ 504/524–3285, WEB www.lpomusic.com). Nationally known artists perform at **Kiefer UNO Lakefront Arena** (✉ 6801 Franklin Ave., ☎ 504/280–7222).

THEATER

The avant-garde and the satirical are among the offerings at **Contemporary Arts Center** (✉ 900 Camp St., ☎ 504/523–1216, WEB www.cacno.org). **Le Petit Théâtre du Vieux Carré** (✉ 616 St. Peter St., ☎ 504/522–2081) presents more traditional fare as well as children's theater. **Southern Repertory Theater** (✉ Canal Pl. at Canal St., ☎ 504/861–8163) puts on local productions. Touring Broadway shows and top-name talent appear at the **Saenger Performing Arts Center** (✉ 143 N. Rampart St., ☎ 504/524–2490, WEB www.saengertheatre.com).

Outdoor Activities and Sports

Biking

New Orleans is entirely flat, and many distances can be easily covered on two wheels. **Bicycle Michael's** (✉ 622 Frenchmen St., ☎ 504/945–9505, WEB www.bicyclemichaels.com) rents road and mountain bikes and can recommend routes including a popular 25-mi city tour. **French**

Louisiana Bike Tours (✉ 3216 W. Esplanade Ave., PMB 302, ☎ 504/488–9844 or 800/346–7989, WEB www.flbt.com) conducts guided bike tours of the River Road and of Cajun Country. **French Quarter Bicycles** (✉ 522 Dumaine St., ☎ 504/529–3136, WEB www.fqbikes.com) rents wheelchairs and baby joggers along with the standard road and mountain bikes; it has a full repair shop.

Boating

Canoes, rowboats, and pedal boats can be rented for lazing along **City Park's lagoons** (✉ 1 Dreyfous Ave., ☎ 504/483–9371).

Golf

There are four 18-hole courses at **City Park,** as well as a 100-tee double-decker driving range (✉ 1040 Fillmore Ave., ☎ 504/483–9396). **Audubon Park** (✉ 473 Walnut St., ☎ 504/865–8260, WEB www.auduboninstitute.org) has a tightly-packed 18-hole course. At press time, play was disrupted for renovations; construction is ongoing until Fall 2002.

Tennis

Audubon Park (✉ rear of park, 6320 Tchoupitoulas St., ☎ 504/895–1042) has 10 courts. There are 39 courts at **City Park's Wisner Tennis Center** (✉ Victory Ave., ☎ 504/483–9383).

Spectator Sports

Baseball (Minor League): New Orleans Zephyrs (✉ Zephyr Stadium, 6000 Airline Hwy., Metairie, ☎ 504/734–5155, WEB www.zephyrsbaseball.com). **Football: New Orleans Saints** (✉ Superdome, 1 Sugar Bowl Dr., ☎ 504/731–1700, WEB www.neworleanssaints.com). The **Sugar Bowl Classic** (☎ 504/525–8573) is played annually in the Superdome on New Year's Day. **Horse Racing:** There is Thoroughbred racing from Thanksgiving Day to April at the **Fair Grounds** (✉ 1751 Gentilly Blvd., ☎ 504/944–5515). **Hockey: New Orleans Brass** of the East Coast Ice Hockey League (✉ New Orleans Arena, 1501 Girod St., ☎ 504/522–7825, WEB www.brasshockey.com).

Shopping

You will find all types of shopping in New Orleans, but the city is exceptional for antiques and local arts and crafts. Louisiana's **tax-free shopping** program grants shoppers from other countries a sales-tax rebate. Retailers who display the tax-free sign issue vouchers for the 9% sales tax, which can be redeemed on departure. Present the vouchers with your passport and international plane ticket at the tax-rebate office at New Orleans International Airport and receive up to $500 in cash back. If the amount redeemable exceeds $500, a check for the difference will be mailed to you.

Shopping Districts

Most of the **French Quarter**'s ritzy antiques stores, musty bazaars, art galleries, and boutiques are housed in quaint 19th-century structures. The sleek indoor malls of the **CBD** include Riverwalk (✉ 1 Poydras St., ☎ 504/522–1555), with more than 200 specialty shops and restaurants. Canal Place (✉ 365 Canal St., ☎ 504/522–9200) has more than 40 tony shops, a food court, and cinemas. The New Orleans Centre (✉ 1400 Poydras St., ☎ 504/568–0000) is connected by a walkway to the Superdome and a hotel. The **Warehouse District,** especially Julia Street off St. Charles Avenue, is a major center for art galleries. **Magazine Street** has 6 mi of antiques stores and boutiques, many in once-grand Victorian houses, as well as trendy shopping and artisan shops. **Riverbend** has specialty shops and restaurants, many cradled in small creole cottages.

Specialty Stores

ANTIQUES

Royal Street in the Quarter is lined with antiques stores. The three-story **French Antique Shop** (✉ 225 Royal St., ☎ 504/524–9861, WEB www.gofrenchantiques.com) has excellent chandeliers and 18th-century furniture. **Keil's Antiques** (✉ 325 Royal St., ☎ 504/522–4552, WEB www.keilsantiques.com) specializes in jewelry. **Let's Go Antiquing** (✉ 1424 4th St., 70130, ☎ 504/899–3027, WEB www.neworleansantiquing.com) arranges individual shopping sprees. **Mirror, Mirror** (✉ 301 Chartres St., ☎ 504/566–1990, WEB www.mirrorx2.com) sells reflective glass in all shapes and sizes. The Royal Street Guild and the Magazine Street Merchants' Association publish pamphlets that are available free at the **New Orleans Welcome Center** (☞ Visitor Information, *below*).

FLEA MARKET

Locals as well as tourists turn out for the **Community Flea Market,** held daily 7–7 in the French Market (☞ Exploring New Orleans, *above*).

FOOD

Affiliated with the New Orleans School of Cooking, the **Louisiana General Store** (✉ 524 St. Louis St., ☎ 504/525–2665) sells spices, sauces, pralines, and all the cookbooks you'll need to use your new ingredients. **Louisiana Products** (✉ 507 St. Ann St., on Jackson Sq., ☎ 504/524–7331) has packaged Louisiana foods. **Old Town Praline Shop** (✉ 627 Royal St., ☎ 504/525–1413) sells the best pralines in town.

JAZZ RECORDS

The **Louisiana Music Factory** (✉ 210 Decatur St., ☎ 504/586–1094, WEB www.louisianamusicfactory.com) stocks the best supply of local music.

MASKS

Little Shop of Fantasy (✉ 523 Dumaine St., ☎ 504/529–4243, WEB www.littleshopoffantasy.com) specializes in feathered masks, though you can also get papier-mâché, leather, plaster, and cloth designs. **Rumors** (✉ 513 Royal St., ☎ 504/525–0292, WEB www.rumorsno.com) sells masks to fit any personality as well as jewelry and voodoo dolls.

Side Trip to Baton Rouge and Plantation Country

Although the Baton Rouge and Plantation Country area is worth an extended visit, several of these locations can be visited on day trips from New Orleans. For more detailed information on Baton Rouge and Plantation County, contact the Baton Rouge Area Convention and Visitors Bureau (☞ Visitor Information, *below*).

Arriving and Departing

The quickest way to reach plantations along River Road between New Orleans and Baton Rouge by car is to follow I–10 or U.S. 61 to the appropriate exit. From Baton Rouge, U.S. 61 continues on to St. Francisville.

What to See and Do

You can see what went with the wind and hear tales of Yankee invaders and ghosts in some of the fine restored antebellum plantations sprinkled around Baton Rouge, including **Oak Alley** (✉ 3645 Rte. 18, Vacherie, ☎ 225/261–2151 or 800/442–5539, WEB www.oakalleyplantation.com; 🎫 $10), named for the stunning 300-year-old live oaks that stretch out in front of the house. **Houmas House** (✉ Rte. 942, ½ mi off Rte. 44, near Burnside, ☎ 888/323–8314, WEB www.houmashouse.com; 🎫 $10) is a Greek Revival mansion famed for its three-story spiral staircase. **Laura**

Plantation (✉ 2247 Rte. 18, Vacherie, ☎ 225/265–7690 or 888/799–7690, WEB www.lauraplantation.com; 🎫 $10) presents a vivid display of plantation life as the Creoles lived it. **Nottoway Plantation** (✉ Rte. 1, 2 mi north of White Castle, ☎ 225/346–8263, WEB www.nottoway.com; 🎫 $10) is an extravagant Italianate mansion with antiques-filled rooms.

As state capitol, **Baton Rouge** harbors much of Louisiana's history, especially its colorful (some might say scandalous) political history. In the Art Deco **Louisiana State Capitol** (✉ State Capitol Dr., ☎ 225/342–7317; 🎫 free), you can see impressive documents and legislative chambers, as well as the site of Governor Huey P. Long's assassination in 1935. The Gothic Revival **Old State Capitol** (✉ 100 North Blvd. at River Rd., ☎ 225/342–0500 or 800/488–2968; 🎫 $4) was the capitol from 1850 to 1932; it now houses the Center for Political and Governmental History, a museum with some interactive exhibits. The **Enchanted Mansion** (✉ 190 Lee Dr., ☎ 225/769–0005; 🎫 $4.50) has a collection of more than 2,000 dolls. The restored **Old Governor's Mansion** (✉ 502 N. Blvd., ☎ 225/343–3989, WEB www.oldgovernorsmansion.org; 🎫 $4), built in 1930 during Huey Long's administration, is a museum with rooms dedicated to governors who have served since the house was built. Architecturally, the house features some lovely wood paneling and frieze work. Slightly out of the ordinary, the **Rural Life Museum and Windrush Gardens** (✉ Essen La. at I–10, ☎ 225/765–2437, WEB rurallife.lsu.edu; 🎫 $5) is a fascinating combination of buildings and artifacts outlining Louisiana's rural history. There are beautiful landscaped gardens, with European statuary, beyond the buildings. The **Magnolia Mound Plantation** (✉ 2161 Nicholson Dr., ☎ 225/343–4955, WEB asterix.ednet.lsu.edu/~anderson/magnolia/mmp.html; 🎫 $5) and grounds are a lovely example of West Indies influence in southern Louisiana.

North of Baton Rouge, **St. Francisville** is the heart of English Louisiana. A walk down Ferdinand Street takes you by a number of gift and antiques shops. **Grace Episcopal Church** (✉ 11621 Ferdinand St., ☎ 225/635–4065) is splendidly set in a park of old, moss-draped live oaks.

The **West Feliciana Parish Tourist Commission** (✉ 11757 Ferdinand St., ☎ 225/635–6330 or 800/789–4221) has historical exhibits and brochures.

St. Francisville is surrounded by eight plantation homes open for tours. Perhaps the grandest of them is **Rosedown** (✉ 12501 Rte. 10, ☎ 225/635–3110; 🎫 $10), with expansive formal gardens in addition to the stately Greek Revival house itself. James J. Audubon stayed at the West Indies–style **Oakley House** (✉ 11788 Rte. 965, in the Audubon State Commemorative Area, ☎ 225/635–3739; 🎫 $2), where he tutored the owner's daughter for several months. The graceful **Greenwood Plantation** (✉ 6838 Highland Rd., ☎ 225/655–4475, WEB www.butlergreenwood.com; 🎫 $6) still produces pecans, hay, and cattle. Inside, some original antiques and portraits remain.

Near St. Francisville, the **Angola Prison Museum** (✉ Angola, end of Rte. 66, ☎ 225/655–2592; 🎫 free) houses a fascinating, eerie, and often moving collection of photographs documenting the people and events that have been a part of Angola; items such as prisoner weapons and the electric chair used for executions until 1991 are also on display.

New Orleans Essentials

AIRPORTS AND TRANSFERS

New Orleans International Airport (also known as Moisant Field), 15 mi west of New Orleans in Kenner, is served by many carriers.

➤ AIRPORT INFORMATION: **New Orleans International Airport** (✉ 900 Airline Dr., ☎ 504/464–0831).

AIRPORT TRANSFER

Cab fare for the 20- to 30-minute trip from New Orleans International Airport to downtown runs $21–$32, depending on the number of passengers. The 24-hour Airport Shuttle drops passengers off downtown and at French Quarter hotels, St. Charles Avenue, and major universities; the fare is $10 one-way. Buses operated by Louisiana Transit run between the airport and the Central Business District; the fare is $1.50 (exact change in coins).
➤ TAXIS AND SHUTTLES: **Airport Shuttle** (☎ 504/522–3500). **Louisiana Transit** (☎ 504/737–9611).

BOAT AND FERRY TRAVEL

You can arrive from northern ports in grand 19th-century style aboard one of the authentic overnight steamboats that home-port in New Orleans—the *Delta Queen,* the *Mississippi Queen,* or the *American Queen*—all run by the Delta Queen Steamboat Company.

A ferry, the *Crescent City Connection,* crosses the Mississippi from the Canal Street Wharf to Algiers. It's free outgoing and $1 returning per car or person.
➤ BOAT AND FERRY TRAVEL INFORMATION: ***Crescent City Connection*** (☎ 504/364–8100). **Delta Queen Steamboat Company** (✉ 30 Robin St. Wharf, 70130, ☎ 504/586–0631 or 800/543–1949, FAX 504/585–0630, WEB www.deltaqueen.com).

BUS TRAVEL TO AND FROM NEW ORLEANS

Greyhound operates out of Union Passenger Terminal.
➤ BUS INFORMATION: **Greyhound** (☎ 800/231–2222, WEB www.greyhound.com). **Union Passenger Terminal** (✉ 1001 Loyola Ave., ☎ 504/528–1610).

CAR TRAVEL

I–10 is the major east–west artery through the city; I–55, which runs north–south, connects with I–10 west of town. I–59 heads for the northeast. U.S. 61 and U.S. 90 also run through the city.

TRAFFIC

French Quarter streets are often clogged with traffic, and street parking is strictly monitored by meter maids and tow trucks. Elsewhere, traffic is light, though a lack of urgency on the part of local drivers can slow things up.

TAXIS

Cabs cruise the French Quarter, the CBD, and St. Charles Avenue but not beyond. Reliable companies with 24-hour service are United Cabs and Yellow-Checker Cabs. The fare is $2.10 at the flag drop, 20¢ for each additional ¼ mi, and 75¢ for each additional passenger.
➤ TAXI COMPANIES: **United Cabs** (☎ 504/522–9771). **Yellow-Checker Cabs** (☎ 504/943–2411).

TOURS

BUS AND VAN TOURS

Gray Line offers city, plantation, trolley, and combination bus–paddle wheeler tours. Le'Ob's Tours runs a three-hour daily bus tour and a plantation tour, focusing on the contributions of African-Americans. New Orleans Tours has city, swamp, and plantation tours and combination city–paddle wheeler outings. Tours by Isabelle does city, swamp, plantation, and combination swamp-and-plantation tours.

➤ FEES AND SCHEDULES: **Gray Line** (☎ 504/587–0861, WEB www.graylineneworleans.com). **Le'Ob's Tours** (☎ 504/288–3478). **New Orleans Tours** (☎ 504/592–0560, 504/592–1991, or 800/543–6332). **Tours by Isabelle** (☎ 504/391–3544 or 888/223–2093).

BOAT TOURS

Riverboat sightseeing and dinner-jazz cruises are offered by the New Orleans Steamboat Company and New Orleans Paddle Wheels. Bayou tours are given by Honey Island Swamp Tours and Cypress Swamp Tours.

➤ FEES AND SCHEDULES: **Cypress Swamp Tours** (☎ 504/581–4501). **Honey Island Swamp Tours** (☎ 504/641–1769). **New Orleans Paddle Wheels** (☎ 504/524–0814). **New Orleans Steamboat Company** (☎ 504/586–8777).

WALKING TOURS

Gray Line (☞ Bus and Van Tours, *above*) conducts walking tours through the French Quarter and Garden District. Heritage Tours offers literary walking tours of the French Quarter. Le'Ob's Tours (☞ Bus and Van Tours, *above*) has a two-hour French Quarter walking tour focusing on African-American heritage. Pat Bernard's Classic Tours is operated by a native New Orleanian who is in love with the city; her chatty tours cover art, antiques, architecture, and history. Historic New Orleans Walking Tours concentrates on the intriguing history of the French Quarter. Le Monde Creole offers tours that focus on matters creole; tours are conducted in your choice of English or French. Save Our Cemeteries conducts lively guided tours of St. Louis Cemetery No. 1 and Lafayette Cemetery No. 1. Voodoo haunts and such are covered by both Magic Walking Tours and the New Orleans Historic Voodoo Museum.

➤ FEES AND SCHEDULES: **Heritage Tours** (☎ 504/949–9805). **Historic New Orleans Walking Tours** (☎ 504/947–2120). **Le Monde Creole** (☎ 504/528–9426). **Magic Walking Tours** (☎ 504/588–9693). **New Orleans Historic Voodoo Museum** (☎ 504/523–7685, WEB www.voodoomuseum.com). **Pat Bernard's Classic Tours** (☎ 504/899–1862). **Save Our Cemeteries** (☎ 504/525–3377, WEB www.saveourcemeteries.org).

TRAIN TRAVEL

Amtrak serves New Orleans's Union Passenger Terminal (☞ Bus Travel to and from New Orleans, *above*).

➤ TRAIN INFORMATION: **Amtrak** (☎ 800/872–7245, WEB www.amtrak.com).

TRANSPORTATION AROUND NEW ORLEANS

The French Quarter is best savored on leisurely strolls; the Central Business District (CBD) and Warehouse District are also highly walkable. The Regional Transit Authority (RTA) operates the bus and streetcar system and staffs a 24-hour information line. Bus and St. Charles Streetcar fare is $1.25 (exact change); the Riverfront Streetcar ($1.50 exact change) links attractions along the Mississippi. The Vieux Carré Shuttle ($1.25 exact change) runs from Elysian Fields Avenue and Royal Street through the French Quarter, CBD, and Warehouse District to the Convention Center. VisiTour passes, good on all RTA buses and streetcars and the Vieux Carré shuttle, cost $5 (one day) and $12 (three days).

➤ CONTACT: **Regional Transit Authority** (☎ 504/248–3900).

VISITOR INFORMATION

➤ TOURIST INFORMATION: **Baton Rouge Area Convention and Visitors Bureau** (✉ 730 North Blvd., 70802, ☎ 504/383–1825 or 800/527–6843). **New Orleans Metropolitan Convention & Visitors Bureau** (✉

1520 Sugar Bowl Dr., 70112, ☎ 504/566–5011 or 800/672–6124, FAX 504/566–5021, WEB www.neworleanscvb.com). **New Orleans Welcome Center** (✉ 529 St. Ann St., 70116, ☎ 504/568–5661).

CAJUN COUNTRY

Cajun Country, or Acadiana, comprises 22 parishes (counties) of southern Louisiana to the west of New Orleans. Cajuns are descendants of 17th-century French settlers who established a colony they called l'Acadie (*Cajun* is a corruption of *Acadian*) in the present-day Canadian provinces of Nova Scotia and New Brunswick. After the British expelled the Acadians in the mid-18th century (their exile is described in Longfellow's epic poem *Evangeline*), many eventually found a home in southern Louisiana. They have been here since 1762, imbuing the region with a distinctive flavor summed up in the Cajun phrase "Laissez les bons temps rouler!" ("Let the good times roll!")

Exploring Cajun Country

U.S. 90 dips down south of New Orleans into **Terrebonne Parish,** a major center for shrimp and oyster fisheries (the blessing of the shrimp fleets in Chauvin and Dulac is a colorful April event). **Annie Miller's Terrebonne Swamp & Marsh Tours** (☎ 504/879–3934) is one of many outfitters offering swamp tours. **Hammond's Cajun Air Tours** (☎ 504/876–0584) takes passengers up for a gull's-eye view of the alligators and other critters that inhabit the coastal wetlands.

Route 182 west of Morgan City branches off U.S. 90 and ambles northwest toward Lafayette, traveling for much of the way along ★ **Bayou Teche,** the largest of the state's many bayous. (*Teche* is a Native American word meaning "snake." According to an ancient legend, the death throes of a giant snake carved the bayou.) The road runs by rice paddies and canebrakes, and on the bayous you can see Cajun pirogues (canoelike boats) and cypress cabins built on stilts. In the picturesque town of **Franklin,** near the Bayou Teche, old-fashioned street lamps line Main Street, which rolls out beneath an arcade of live oaks. Six antebellum homes are open for tours.

New Iberia, founded in 1779 by Spanish settlers who named it for their homeland, is also known as the Queen City of the Teche. **Shadows-on-the-Teche** (✉ 317 E. Main St., ☎ 337/369–6446, WEB www.nationaltrust.org/national_trust_sites/shadows.html; 🎫 $8), one of the South's best-known plantation homes, was built in 1834 for sugar planter David Weeks. The recent discovery of 40 trunks of documents tracing the various residents' activities provides for a tour filled with lively detail. At the **Konrico Company Store** (✉ 309 Ann St., ☎ 337/367–6163 or 800/551–3245; 🎫 $2.75), you can tour the nation's oldest rice mill.

★ Red-hot Tabasco sauce is a 19th-century Louisiana creation; on **Avery Island** at **McIlhenny's Tabasco Company** (✉ Rte. 329, ☎ 337/373–6129 or 800/634–9599, WEB www.tabasco.com; 🎫 free), you can tour the factory where it's still being manufactured by descendants of its creator. Here also are the 200-acre **Jungle Gardens** and **Bird City,** a sanctuary with flurries of snow-white egrets (☎ 337/369–6243; 🎫 Bird City $5.75).

★ **Rip Van Winkle Gardens** (✉ 5505 Rip Van Winkle Rd., off Rte. 675, ☎ 337/365–3332; 🎫 house and gardens $9), on Jefferson Island, is actually a salt dome, capped by lush vegetation. The 19th-century American actor Joseph Jefferson, who toured the country portraying

Rip Van Winkle, built a winter home here. His three-story house is surrounded by lovely formal and informal gardens.

Along **Route 31,** a pretty country road that hugs the banks of the Teche between New Iberia and Opelousas to the north, you'll find **St. Martinville,** a little town awash with legends. Now a sleepy village, it was known in the 18th century as Petit Paris, a refuge for aristocrats fleeing the French Revolution. It was also a major debarkation point for exiled Acadians. Longfellow's poem *Evangeline* was based on the true story of two young lovers who were separated for years during the Acadian exile. The **Evangeline Oak** (✉ Evangeline Blvd. at Bayou Teche) is said to be the place where the ill-starred lovers met again—albeit briefly. On the town square are **St. Martin de Tours,** mother church of the Acadians, and the **Petit Paris Museum** (✉ 103 S. Main St., ☎ 337/394–7334; 🎫 $1), which showcases the local Mardi Gras traditions. Be sure to visit the small cemetery behind the church, where a bronze statue depicts the real-life Evangeline. The **Longfellow-Evangeline State Commemorative Area** (✉ 1200 N. Main St., ☎ 337/394–3754 or 888/677–2900; 🎫 $2) includes a small museum tracing the history of the Acadians, a creole plantation cottage, and a Cajun cabin. Tours are self-guided, and at the back of the park, picnic tables line the bayou.

Tiny **Breaux Bridge,** north of St. Martinville, calls itself the "crawfish capital of the world." Some decades ago, when crawfish were still viewed as a low-class meat, this town brazenly threw a **Crawfish Festival.** These days the festival, held each May, draws more than 100,000 people. **Café des Amis** is at the forefront of a bubbling artistic and commercial revival in town; the restaurant's walls are lined with the work of regional artists.

Lafayette proudly proclaims itself the capital of French Louisiana. In this part of the state some 40% of the residents can speak Cajun French, a 17th-century dialect. And since many Cajuns also speak standard French as well as English, this is a superb place to test your language skills. **Cajun Mardi Gras** rivals its sister celebration in New Orleans. Lafayette, though it's short on the charm that typifies this region, has a few noteworthy attractions and is a good base for exploring the region.

★ The **Acadian Cultural Center** (✉ 501 Fisher Rd., ☎ 337/232–0789 or 318/232–0961; 🎫 free), a unit of the **Jean Lafitte National Historical Park and Preserve,** traces the history of the Acadians through numerous audiovisual exhibits. The **Children's Museum of Acadiana** has educational hands-on exhibits (✉ 201 E. Congress St., ☎ 337/232–8500; 🎫 $5). The **Alexandre Mouton House** (✉ 1122 Lafayette St., ☎ 337/234–2208; 🎫 $3), formerly the home of wealthy Creoles, is filled with early to mid-19th-century period furniture and documentation of the Mouton family. The main attraction at **St. John the Evangelist Cathedral** (✉ 914 St. John St., at Cathedral St., ☎ 337/261–5500) is the gargantuan, 400-plus-year-old **Cathedral Oak** beside it.

The **Acadian Village** (✉ 200 Greenleaf Dr., ☎ 337/981–2364, WEB www.acadianvillage.org; 🎫 $6) is a re-creation of old-style Acadian digs, featuring authentic houses, shops, and a church. **Vermilionville** (☎ 337/233–4077 or 800/992–2968, WEB www.vermilionville.org; 🎫 $8) is a re-created village with more replicas than authentic structures, but it also showcases local artists, cooks, and craftspeople at work.

South of Lafayette, Route 82 (Hug-the-Coast Highway) whips along the windswept coastal marshes to the **Rockefeller Wildlife Refuge** (☎ 337/538–2165), in **Grand Chenier.** At this 84,000-acre preserve, thousands of ducks, geese, gators, wading birds, and otters while away the winter months.

Dining and Lodging

Breaux Bridge

$$ ★ ✕ **Café des Amis.** Enjoy rich Cajun fare in this open, art-lined restaurant. Owner and chef Dickie Breaux (descended from Breaux Bridge's founders) prides himself on an authentic approach to Cajun cuisine. The saucy house specialty, barbecue shrimp, comes with a bib. A zydeco band entertains for Saturday breakfasts. ✉ *140 E. Bridge St.,* ☎ *337/332–5273,* WEB *www.cafedesamis.com. Reservations essential. AE, D, MC, V. Closed Mon. No dinner Tues.–Wed. or Sun.*

$–$$ ★ ✕ **Mulate's.** This renowned roadhouse with tables covered in checkered plastic has Cajun seafood and dancing to live Cajun music every night. ✉ *325 W. Mills Ave.,* ☎ *337/332–4648 or 800/422–2586. AE, MC, V.*

Lafayette

$$$ ✕ **Café Vermilionville.** Lafayette rivals New Orleans when it comes to fine dining. The restaurant, one of the best bets in town, occupies an antebellum house, formerly an inn. The seasonal menu is essentially Cajun, so expect rich and spicy preparations. Constant favorites include the crawfish beignets and fire-roasted smoked salmon. ✉ *1304 W. Pinhook Rd.,* ☎ *337/237–0100,* WEB *www.cafev.com. Jacket required. AE, D, DC, MC, V. Closed Sun.*

$$–$$$ ★ ✕ **Prejean's.** Housed in a cypress cottage, this local favorite has a cozy oyster bar, red-checked cloths, and live music nightly. Platters of traditional and new Cajun seafood are the specialties. ✉ *3480 U.S. 167 N, next to Evangeline Downs,* ☎ *337/896–3247,* WEB *www.prejeans.com. AE, DC, MC, V.*

$ **Holiday Inn Central–Holidome.** Built around an atrium that's banked with greenery, this modern motel has contemporary rooms and 17 acres with playgrounds, picnic areas, and tennis courts. ✉ *2032 N.E. Evangeline Thruway (Box 91807, 70501),* ☎ *337/233–6815 or 800/942–4868,* FAX *337/235–1954,* WEB *www.holiday-inn.com/lafayettela. 243 rooms. Restaurant, pool, tennis. AE, D, DC, MC, V.*

$ ★ **T'Frere's House.** Hospitality pervades this reputedly haunted old house. The casual rooms, all with private bath, are warmly outfitted with antiques, and breakfast—an excellent, multicourse affair—is always jovial. Hosts Pat and Maugie Pastor serve cocktails when you arrive; cordials are available throughout the day. ✉ *1905 Verot School Rd., 70508,* ☎ *800/984–9347,* ☎ FAX *337/984–9347,* WEB *www.tfreres.com. 6 rooms. D, MC, V. BP.*

New Iberia

$$ ✕ **leRosier.** Across the street from Shadows-on-the-Teche, leRosier is a six-room B&B whose shining star is the restaurant ($$$–$$$$; reservations essential for dinner), presided over by chef Hallman Woods III. Among other accomplishments, Woods has prepared a five-course crawfish degustation for the James Beard Foundation. Expect fresh ingredients and succulent seafood in his small white-cloth dining room. Rooms are sparsely decorated but modern and clean. ✉ *314 E. Main St., 70560,* ☎ *888/804–7673,* ☎ FAX *337/367–5306,* WEB *www.lerosier.com. 6 rooms. Restaurant. AE, MC, V. BP.*

St. Martinville

$ ✕ **La Place d'Evangeline.** Rooms are spacious at this B&B on the banks of the Bayou Teche. The restaurant (closed Sun.–Mon.) serves hearty portions of seafood and Cajun dishes; the homemade bread is superb. ✉ *220 Evangeline Blvd., 70582, ☎ 337/394–4010, FAX 337/394–7983. 7 rooms. Restaurant. AE, D, MC, V. BP.*

Sunset

$$–$$$ **Chretien Point.** This stately home sits in luxurious isolation near a bayou. The rather formal rooms are furnished with period antiques. The Greek Revival layout of the house provides for large, comfortable sitting areas. There was a Civil War battle here, and Jean Lafitte was smuggling in cahoots with the original owner, so stories of hauntings abound. ✉ *665 Chretien Point Rd., across the highway from Grand Coteau, 70584, ☎ 800/880–7050, ☎ FAX 337/662–5876. 5 rooms. Pool, tennis. AE, D, MC, V. BP.*

Nightlife and the Arts

Cajun and Zydeco Music

Try some Cajun two-stepping at the boisterous **Mulate's** in Breaux Bridge. **Prejean's** in Lafayette (☞ Dining and Lodging, *above*) has live music nightly at 7. **Randol's** (✉ 2320 Kaliste Saloom Rd., Lafayette, ☎ 337/981–7080, WEB www.randols.com) regularly features Cajun and zydeco music, with the requisite dancing. **Slim's Y-Ki-Ki** (✉ U.S. 167, Washington Rd., Opelousas, ☎ 337/942–9980), a rural club, is one of the best zydeco dance venues in the state. **Fred's Lounge** (✉ 420 6th St., Mamou, ☎ 337/468–5411), open Saturday morning only (8–1), is a legendary bar with live radio broadcasts and plenty of dancing.

Outdoor Activities and Sports

Pack & Paddle (✉ 601 E. Pinhook Rd., Lafayette, ☎ 337/232–5854 or 800/458–4560, WEB www.packnpaddle.com) is an excellent resource for outdoor gear for almost any sport and for information about outdoor sports in the area.

Biking

French Louisiana Bike Tours (✉ 3216 W. Esplanade Ave., PMB 302, Metairie, LA 70002, ☎ 504/488–9844 or 800/346–7989) offers four- and seven-day tours of Cajun Country that include the rental of a Cannondale hybrid bike (equipped with smooth tires, Avocet computer, backrack, and handlebar pack), van support, lodging, and meals.

Fishing

Salt, Inc. Charter Fishing Service (✉ Rte. 56, Cocodrie, ☎ 504/594–6626 or 800/648–2626), about 20 mi south of Houma, offers fishing trips in the bays and barrier islands of lower Terrebonne Parish as well as into the Gulf of Mexico. **Sportsman's Paradise** (✉ Rte. 56, Cocodrie, ☎ 504/594–2414, WEB www.sportsmansparadisecocodrie.com) offers light tackle and offshore charter service as well as night fishing.

Hiking and Nature Trails

The **Louisiana State Arboretum** (☞ National and State Parks, *above*) in Ville Platte is a 300-acre facility with several miles of nature trails. There are 6 mi of hiking trails in the **Port Hudson State Commemorative Area,** north of Baton Rouge (✉ 756 W. Plains–Port Hudson Rd./U.S. 61, Zachary, ☎ 225/654–3775, WEB www.crt.state.la.us/crt/parks/porthud/pthudson.htm).

Shopping

B. F. Trappey's & Sons (✉ 900 E. Main St., New Iberia, ☎ 337/365–8281) sells "sinus-clearing" hot sauce, pickled peppers, and okra. For Cajun spices and ingredients, try the **Cajun Country Store** (✉ 401 E. Cypress St., Lafayette, ☎ 337/233–7977).

In Lafayette, the **Jefferson Street Market** (✉ 528 Jefferson St., ☎ 337/233–2589) houses many local antiques dealers and craftspeople. You can root fruitfully around **Ruins & Relics** (✉ 900 Evangeline Dr., off University Ave., ☎ 337/233–9163).

In Washington, **O'Connor's Antique School Mall** (✉ 210 Church St., ☎ 337/826–3580), closed Sunday, houses more than 100 dealers in a former school and gym.

Cajun artist Rodrigue has gained international attention with his Blue Dog paintings. The house where Tiffany, Rodrigue's canine inspiration, once lived with the artist's family now has the artist's works and is known as the **Rodrigue Gallery** (✉ 1206 Jefferson St., ☎ 337/232–6398).

What Bayou Trading Company (✉ 153 W. Landry St., ☎ 337/942–2575) is a wonderful small store in Opelousas packed with neat local crafts and artistry, as well as Cajun CDs, cookbooks, and other souvenirs.

Cajun Country Essentials

AIRPORTS

Lafayette Regional Airport is served by American Eagle, Atlantic Southeast (Delta), Continental, and Northwest Airlink.

➤ AIRPORT INFORMATION: **Lafayette Regional Airport** (✉ 200 Terminal Dr., ☎ 318/266–4400).

BUS TRAVEL

Greyhound has frequent daily service to Lafayette and environs.

➤ BUS INFORMATION: **Gray Line** (☎ 504/587–0861 or 800/535–7788). **Greyhound** (☎ 800/231–2222).

CAR TRAVEL

The fastest route from New Orleans through Cajun Country is west on I–10. U.S. 90 is a slower but more scenic drive. If you have time, take the back roads for exploring this area. A ferry across the Mississippi costs $1 per vehicle; most bridges are free.

TOURS

Gray Line offers orientation tours of Cajun country.

➤ FEES AND SCHEDULES: **Gray Line** (☎ 504/587–0861 or 800/535–7788).

TRAIN TRAVEL

Amtrak serves Lafayette and New Iberia.

➤ TRAIN INFORMATION: **Amtrak** (☎ 800/872–7245).

VISITOR INFORMATION

➤ TOURIST INFORMATION: **Lafayette Convention & Visitors Bureau** (✉ 1400 N.W. Evangeline Thruway [Box 52066, Lafayette 70505], ☎ 337/232–3737; 800/346–1958; 800/543–5340 in Canada). **Southwest Louisiana Convention & Visitors Bureau** (✉ 1205 Lakeshore Dr., Lake Charles 70601, ☎ 337/436–9588 or 800/456–7952).

ELSEWHERE IN LOUISIANA

Natchitoches and North-Central Louisiana

What to See and Do

Nestled in the piney hills of north-central Louisiana, **Natchitoches** (pronounced *nak*-a-tish) is the oldest permanent European settlement of the Louisiana Purchase, four years older than New Orleans. The town has a quaint 33-block Historic Landmark District, with brick-paved streets and buildings garbed in lacy ironwork. In the center of the downtown area is pretty Cane River Lake, edged with live oak trees and rolling green lawns. Natchitoches appeared in the film version of *Steel Magnolias*. Tours of the town are conducted in miniature trolleys. Popular events include the **Christmas Festival of Lights,** which draws about 150,000 people annually, and the **October Pilgrimage,** when several historic houses are open for tours. Near Natchitoches, backpackers and hikers explore the 8,700-acre **Kisatchie Hills Wilderness** with its Backbone Trail, part of the Kisatchie National Forest (☞ National and State Parks, *above*).

Famed primitive artist Clementine Hunter lived and worked at **Melrose Plantation** (✉ 3533 Rte. 119, Melrose, ☎ 318/379–0055; 🎫 $6), where nine quaint buildings can be toured. Twenty miles south of
★ Natchitoches, the **Kate Chopin House** (✉ 243 Rte. 495, Cloutierville, ☎ 318/379–2233; 🎫 $6) was home in the 19th century to Kate Chopin, author of *The Awakening*. It now houses the **Bayou Folk Museum** in addition to some memorabilia and documents of the writer.

Hodges Gardens (✉ U.S. 171, ☎ 318/586–3523; 🎫 $5), west of Natchitoches, has 4,700 acres of rolling pine forests with streams, waterfalls, and multilevel formal botanical gardens, where flowers and shrubs bloom year-round. The huge **Toledo Bend Lake** (☎ 800/259–5253), a camping, boating, and bass-fishing delight, lies along the Texas border.

Dining and Lodging

NATCHITOCHES

$$–$$$ ✕ **The Landing.** This popular white-cloth bistro offers pasta, chicken, veal, and seafood dishes; the spicy country-fried steak is a specialty. ✉ *530 Front St.,* ☎ *318/352–1579. AE, MC, V. Closed Mon.*

$$ ✕ **Lasyone's Meat Pie Kitchen.** Natchitoches meat pies are known throughout the state, and this casual little spot does them better than anywhere else. ✉ *622 2nd St.,* ☎ *318/352–3353. No credit cards. Closed Sun.*

$ 🏨 **Fleur-de-lis.** The town's oldest B&B includes two houses: a 1903 rose-color Victorian and, next door, a 1920s Craftsman-style guest house. Proprietors make guests feel right at home, and a full breakfast is served family style. ✉ *336 2nd St., 71457,* ☎ *318/352–6621 or 800/489–6621,* WEB *www.fleurdelisbandb.com. 8 rooms. AE, MC, V. BP.*

$ 🏨 **Ryders Inn.** Comfortable and predictable rooms can be found in this former Holiday Inn. ✉ *Hwy. 1 South Bypass, 71457,* ☎ *318/357–8281 or 888/252–8281,* FAX *318/352–9907. 145 rooms. Restaurant, pool. AE, D, DC, MC, V.*

Natchitoches and North-Central Louisiana Essentials

CAR TRAVEL

I–49 cuts diagonally from southeast to northwest, connecting Lafayette with Natchitoches. Route 1 runs diagonally from the northwest corner all the way to Grand Isle on the Gulf of Mexico. Route 494 follows the Cane River Lake southward from Natchitoches, bordered by arching trees and dotted with handsome plantation houses.

VISITOR INFORMATION

➤ TOURIST INFORMATION: **Natchitoches Parish Tourist Commission** (✉ 781 Front St. [Box 411, 71457], ☎ 318/352–8072 or 800/259–1714).

MAINE

By Hilary M. Nangle

Capital	Augusta
Population	1,275,000
Motto	I Lead
State Bird	Chickadee
State Flower	White pinecone and tassel
Postal Abbreviation	ME

Statewide Visitor Information

Maine Innkeepers Association (✉ 305 Commercial St., Portland 04101, ☎ 207/773–7670). **Maine Office of Tourism** (✉ DECD, 33 Stone St., 59 State House Station, Augusta 04333, ☎ 207/287–5711, FAX 207/287–8070). **Maine Tourism Association** (✉ 325-B Water St. [Box 2300, Hallowell 04347], ☎ 207/623–0363; 800/533–9595 outside Maine; FAX 207/623–0388).

Scenic Drives

See Exploring sections for recommended coastal routes. For a leisurely inland excursion, try **Routes 37** and **35** from Bridgton north through the Waterfords to Bethel, continuing north on **Route 26** past the Sunday River ski resort to Grafton Notch State Park and into northern New Hampshire.

National and State Parks

National Park

★ **Acadia National Park** (✉ Box 177, Bar Harbor 04609, ☎ 207/288–3338; WEB www.nps.gov/acad; 🎫 $10 per vehicle or free, depending on where and when you enter), with fine stretches of shoreline and the highest mountains along the East Coast, offers camping, hiking, biking, and boating.

State Parks

More than two dozen state parks provide outdoor recreation along the coast and in less-traveled interior sections. For information contact the **Bureau of Parks and Lands** (✉ 22 State House Station, Augusta 04333, ☎ 207/287–3821).

THE SOUTHERN COAST

Maine's southern coast has the state's best beaches, seafaring- and boutique-rich towns, fine restaurants, and factory-outlet malls within a day trip of many points in New England. You'll also find museums, lighthouses, walking tours, and boating opportunities.

Exploring the Coast from Kittery to Pemaquid Point

In Kittery, factory outlets line both sides of Route 1. Those who crave the scenic coastline will appreciate the maritime scenery of Routes 103 and 1A, which continues through the Yorks, taking in fashionable **York Harbor** and passing the usually crowded long swaths of sand that compose **York Beach. Ogunquit,** a few miles north of the Yorks, is famed for its long white-sand beach as well as its galleries, shops, restaurants, and homes. The small but worthwhile **Ogunquit Museum of American Art,** dedicated to 20th-century American art, overlooks the ocean from

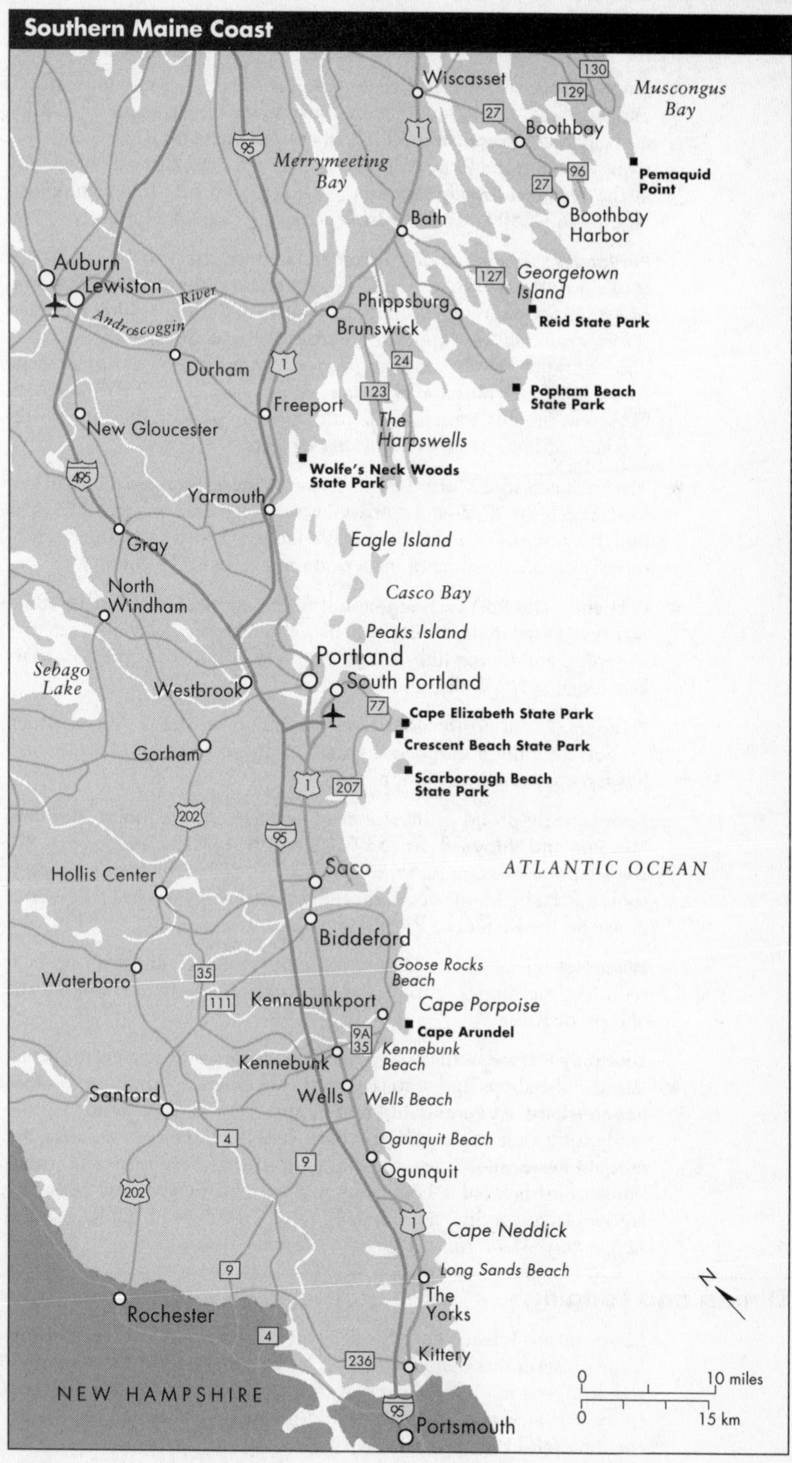
Southern Maine Coast
Wiscasset
Muscongus Bay
Boothbay
Pemaquid Point
Merrymeeting Bay
Boothbay Harbor
Bath
Auburn
Lewiston
Androscoggin River
Georgetown Island
Phippsburg
Brunswick
Reid State Park
Durham
Popham Beach State Park
Freeport
New Gloucester
The Harpswells
Wolfe's Neck Woods State Park
Yarmouth
Gray
Eagle Island
North Windham
Casco Bay
Peaks Island
Sebago Lake
Portland
Westbrook
South Portland
Cape Elizabeth State Park
Crescent Beach State Park
Gorham
Scarborough Beach State Park
ATLANTIC OCEAN
Hollis Center
Saco
Biddeford
Goose Rocks Beach
Waterboro
Kennebunkport
Cape Porpoise
Cape Arundel
Kennebunk
Kennebunk Beach
Sanford
Wells
Wells Beach
Ogunquit Beach
Ogunquit
Cape Neddick
Long Sands Beach
Rochester
The Yorks
Kittery
NEW HAMPSHIRE
Portsmouth
0
10 miles
0
15 km
N

its sculpture garden setting. ✉ *543 Shore Rd.,* ☎ *207/646–4909.* 🎟 *$4. Closed mid-Oct.–June 1.*

★ Summer tourists flock to **Kennebunkport** to soak up salt air, seafood, and sunshine. Dock Square is the busy town center, lined with shops and galleries. **Ocean Avenue** follows the Kennebunk River to the sea, then winds around Cape Arundel. Trolley rides are the order of the day at the **Seashore Trolley Museum** (✉ Log Cabin Rd., Kennebunkport, ☎ 207/967–2800, WEB www.trolleymuseum.org; 🎟 $7.50).

Portland is a thriving seaport whose restaurants, coffeehouses, and shops evoke a romantic mood. On Congress Square, the **Portland Museum of Art** (✉ 7 Congress Sq., ☎ 207/775–6148; 800/639–4067 recorded information, WEB www.portlandmuseum.org; 🎟 $6, free Fri. 5–9) displays works by Winslow Homer, John Marin, Andrew Wyeth, and others. At the **Children's Museum of Maine** (✉ 142 Free St., ☎ 207/828–1234, WEB www.kitetails.com; 🎟 $5), little ones can pretend they are lobster catchers, shopkeepers, or computer experts.

★ The Italianate-style Morse-Libby Mansion **Victoria Mansion** (✉ 109 Danforth St., ☎ 207/772–4841, WEB www.victoriamansion.org; 🎟 $6) was built between 1858 and 1860 and is widely regarded as the most sumptuously ornate dwelling of its period remaining in the country.

★ Portland's **Old Port Exchange,** built following the Great Fire of 1866, was revitalized in the 1960s by artists and artisans. Now it is the city's shopping and dining hub. Allow a couple of hours to stroll on Market, Exchange, Middle, and Fore streets.

Freeport, 17 mi north of Portland, is the home of L. L. Bean, which attracts 3½ million shoppers a year. Nearby, more than 100 other outlets have sprouted (☞ Shopping).

Bath is justly proud of its seafaring heritage. At the **Maine Maritime Museum and Shipyard** (✉ 243 Washington St., ☎ 207/443–1316, WEB www.bathmaine.com; 🎟 $9.50), you can watch boatbuilders wield their tools on classic Maine vessels at the restored shipyard and take a boat cruise on the Kennebec River.

Wiscasset bills itself as "Maine's prettiest village" and lives up to it with historic homes, antiques shops, and museums overlooking the Sheepscot River.

Boothbay Harbor swells in summer with visitors and seasonal residents. ★ Wander the shops and waterfront or ride an excursion boat to **Monhegan Island.** At **Pemaquid Point** be sure your camera stand is at the ready for a shot of a much-photographed lighthouse. At **Colonial Pemaquid Restoration,** view the excavations that have turned up thousands of artifacts of a 17th-century English settlement and of earlier Native American life. ✉ *Rte. 130,* ☎ *207/677–2423.* 🎟 *$2. Closed Labor Day–Memorial Day.*

Dining and Lodging

Maine means lobster, and this delectable crustacean is served at most Maine restaurants. Aficionados prefer to eat them "in the rough" at classic lobster pounds, where you choose your lobster from a pool and enjoy it at a picnic table. B&Bs and inns have joined the family-oriented motels in the coastal towns.

Bath

$$–$$$ ★ ✕ **Robinhood Free Meetinghouse.** Multiethnic cuisine is served in an 1855 Greek Revival meetinghouse. Begin with the artichoke strudel, move on to a classic veal saltimbocca or a confit of duck, and finish

up with Obsession in Three Chocolates. ✉ *Robinhood Rd., Georgetown,* ☎ *207/371–2188. D, MC, V. Call ahead in winter.*

$$ ✕ **Kristina's Restaurant & Bakery.** This frame house turned restaurant bakes some of the finest pies, pastries, and cakes on the coast. Satisfying dinners are mainly new American cuisine. ✉ *160 Centre St.,* ☎ *207/442–8577. D, MC, V. Closed Jan. No dinner Sun. Call ahead in winter.*

$$–$$$ 🏨 **The Inn at Bath.** In Bath's Historic District, this handsome 1810 Greek Revival inn is a convenient and comfortable base for exploring Bath on foot. It is filled with antiques, and five guest rooms have wood-burning fireplaces; two also have two-person whirlpool tubs. ✉ *969 Washington St., 04530,* ☎ *207/443–4294,* FAX *207/443–4295,* WEB *www.innatbath.com. 9 rooms. AE, D, MC, V. BP.*

Boothbay Harbor

$$–$$$ ✕ **Christopher's Boathouse.** You can't beat the view over the harbor or the food at this renovated boathouse. Begin with the award-winning lobster and mango bisque with hot and spicy lobster wontons, then move on to the lobster succotash or Asian-spiced tuna steak with Caribbean salsa, and finish off with the raspberry almond flan. ✉ *25 Union St.,* ☎ *207/633–6565,* FAX *207/633–6178. DC, MC, V. Closed Mar. and Mon.–Wed. Jan.–Feb.*

$–$$ ✕ **Lobstermen's Co-op.** Lobster lovers and landlubbers alike will find something at this dockside lobster pound. Eat indoors or outside while watching the lobstermen at work. ✉ *Atlantic Ave.,* ☎ *207/633–4900. Closed mid-Oct.–mid-May.*

$–$$ 🏨 **Admiral's Quarters Inn.** This renovated 1830 sea captain's house is ideally situated for exploring Boothbay Harbor by foot. All rooms have fireplaces, and some have private decks overlooking the harbor. ✉ *71 Commercial St., 04538,* ☎ *207/633–2474 or 800/644–1878,* FAX *207/633–5904,* WEB *www.admiralsquartersinn.com. 7 rooms. D, MC, V. Closed mid-Dec.–mid-Feb. BP.*

Freeport

$–$$ ✕ **Harraseeket Lunch & Lobster Co.** At this bare-bones lobster pound beside the town landing, fried-seafood baskets and lobster dinners, eaten in the dining room or at picnic tables, are what it's all about. ✉ *On the pier, end of Main St., South Freeport,* ☎ *207/865–4888. Reservations not accepted. No credit cards. Closed mid-Oct.–Apr.*

$$$–$$$$ ✕🏨 **Harraseeket Inn.** Despite modern appointments such as elevators and whirlpool baths, this 1850 Greek Revival home retains an old-fashioned country-inn feel. The formal Maine Dining Room ($$$–$$$$) specializes in contemporary American regional cuisine. The casual Broad Arrow Tavern ($–$$$) serves heartier fare. ✉ *162 Main St., 04032,* ☎ *207/865–9377 or 800/342–6423,* FAX *207/865–1684,* WEB *www.stayfreeport.com. 84 rooms. 2 restaurants, pool. AE, D, DC, MC, V. BP.*

Kennebunkport

$$$$ ★ ✕🏨 **White Barn Inn.** The 19th-century inn has meticulously appointed guest rooms; some have fireplaces and baths with whirlpool tubs. Formally attired waiters and attentive service have earned the restaurant accolades as one of the best in New England. Regional fare is served in the rustic dining room ($$$$; jacket required). ✉ *37 Beach St. (Box 560C, 04046),* ☎ *207/967–2321,* FAX *207/967–1100,* WEB *www.whitebarninn.com. 25 rooms. Restaurant, pool. AE, MC, V. CP.*

$$$–$$$$ ✕🏨 **Cape Arundel Inn.** This shingle-style inn commands a magnificent ocean view that takes in the Bush estate at Walker Point. The rooms are furnished with country-style furniture and antiques, and most have sitting areas with ocean views. In the candlelighted dining room ($$$–

$$$$), every table has a view of the surf. ✉ *108 Ocean Ave., 04046, ☎ 207/967–2125, FAX 207/967–1199, WEB www.capearundelinn.com. 14 rooms. Restaurant. AE, D, MC, V. Closed Jan.–Feb. BP.*

$$$–$$$$ **The Seaside.** The Severance family has owned this handsome seaside property since 1667. The modern motel units, all with sliding-glass doors that open onto private decks or patios (half with ocean views), are appropriate for families; so are the cottages with one to four bedrooms. ✉ *80 Beach Ave., Kennebunk 04046, ☎ 207/967–4461 or 866/300–6750, FAX 207/967–1135, WEB www.kennebunkbeach.com. 22 rooms, 11 cottages. AE, MC, V. Cottages closed Nov.–May. CP.*

Newcastle

$$$–$$$$ ✕ **Newcastle Inn.** This classic country inn overlooks the Damariscotta River. You can spread out in the cozy pub, comfortable living room, or spacious sunporch overlooking the river; some rooms have fireplaces and whirlpools. In the dining room, the four-course, fixed-price menu ($$$$; reservations essential; closed Mon. in summer, Mon.–Wed. in winter) emphasizes Maine seafood. ✉ *60 River Rd., Newcastle 04553, ☎ 207/563–5685 or 800/832–8669, FAX 207/563–6877, WEB www.newcastleinn.com. 15 rooms. Restaurant. AE, MC, V. BP.*

New Harbor

$$–$$$$ ✕ **The Bradley Inn.** Within walking distance of Pemaquid Point Lighthouse, the shingled Bradley Inn charms you with a cozy pub, plentiful antiques, and an excellent dining room ($$$; closed Mon.–Wed. Nov.–Mar.). Guest rooms are comfortable and uncluttered; some have fireplaces. ✉ *3063 Bristol Rd., New Harbor 04554, ☎ 207/677–2105 or 800/942–5560, FAX 207/677–3367, WEB www.bradleyinn.com. 16 rooms. Restaurant. AE, MC, V. BP.*

Ogunquit

$$$–$$$$ ★ ✕ **Hurricane.** Don't let the weather-beaten exterior deter you—this comfortable bar-and-grill dishes up first-rate cooking and spectacular views of the crashing surf. ✉ *Perkins Cove, ☎ 207/646–6348. AE, D, DC, MC, V. Closed late Dec.–mid-Jan.*

$$–$$$ **The Rockmere.** This shingle-style Victorian cottage is an ideal retreat from the hustle and bustle of Perkins Cove. All the rooms are large and airy, and most have ocean views. ✉ *150 Stearns Rd. (Box 278, 03907), ☎ 207/646–2985, FAX 207/646–6947, WEB www.rockmere.com. 8 rooms. AE, D, V. CP.*

Portland

$$–$$$$ ★ ✕ **Street and Co.** At what may be the best seafood restaurant in Maine, you enter through the kitchen, with all its wonderful aromas, and dine at a copper-topped table amid dried herbs and shelves of grocery staples. ✉ *33 Wharf St., ☎ 207/775–0887. AE, MC, V. No lunch.*

$$–$$$ ★ ✕ **Fore Street.** Two of Maine's best chefs opened this restaurant in an old warehouse. Every table in the main dining room has a view of the huge brick oven and hearth and the open kitchen, where entrées such as apple-wood-grilled Atlantic swordfish and roasted lobster are prepared. ✉ *288 Fore St., ☎ 207/775–2717. AE, MC, V. No lunch.*

$$$$ ✕ **Inn by the Sea.** On Greater Portland's most prime real estate, this all-suites inn is set back from the shoreline and has views of the ocean. The architecture is typical New England; the dining room ($$–$$$) serves seafood and other regional cuisine. ✉ *40 Bowery Beach Rd., Cape Elizabeth (7 mi south of Portland) 04107, ☎ 207/799–3134 or 800/888–4287, FAX 207/799–4779, WEB www.innbythesea.com. 43 suites. Restaurant, pool, tennis. AE, D, MC, V.*

$$$–$$$$ **Inn on Carleton.** This elegant brick town house on the city's Western Promenade is a quiet retreat furnished with antiques and decorated with artwork by contemporary Maine artists. A restored faux painting by Charles Schumacher greets you in the entryway. ✉ *46 Carleton St., 04102,* ☎ *207/775–1910 or 800/639–1779,* FAX *207/761–0956,* WEB *www.innoncarleton.com. 6 rooms. D, MC, V. BP.*

$$$ **Pomegranate Inn.** The classic architecture of this handsome inn gives no hint to the surprises that await within. Hand-painted walls, floors, and woodwork combine with contemporary artwork to create a vivid ambience, both challenging and comforting. Rooms are individually decorated; five have fireplaces. ✉ *49 Neal St., 04102,* ☎ *207/772–1006 or 800/356–0408,* FAX *207/773–4426,* WEB *www.pomegranateinn.com. 8 rooms. MC, V. BP.*

Scarborough

$$$$ **Black Point Inn.** At the tip of a peninsula 12 mi south of Portland stands a tastefully updated old-time resort with views up and down the coast. On the grounds are beaches, a bird sanctuary, hiking trails, and sports facilities, including boats and bicycles. Rates include breakfast, afternoon tea, and dinner (jacket required). ✉ *510 Black Point Rd., 04074,* ☎ *207/883–2500 or 800/258–0003,* FAX *207/883–9976,* WEB *www.blackpointinn.com. 85 rooms. Restaurant, pools, golf, tennis court. AE, D, MC, V. MAP.*

The Yorks

$$ ★ **York Harbor Inn.** A mid-17th-century fishing cabin with dark timbers and a fieldstone fireplace forms the heart of this inn, to which various wings and outbuildings have been added. Rooms are furnished with antiques and country pieces; many have decks overlooking the water, and a few have whirlpool tubs or fireplaces. The dining room ($$–$$$) has country charm and great ocean views. ✉ *Rte. 1A (Box 573, York Harbor 03911),* ☎ *207/363–5119 or 800/343–3869,* FAX *207/363–7151,* WEB *www.yorkharborinn.com. 40 rooms. AE, DC, MC, V. No lunch off-season (usually Columbus Day–Memorial Day). CP.*

Nightlife and the Arts

Nightlife

Asylum (✉ 121 Center St., Portland, ☎ 207/772–8274) has live music, dancing on two levels, and a sports bar. For live blues, head to the **Big Easy** (✉ 55 Market St., Portland, ☎ 207/871–8817). The **Pavilion** (✉ 199 Middle St., Portland, ☎ 207/773–6422) is one of Portland's most popular dance clubs. Come to sample its home brew at **Stone Coast Brewery** (✉ 14 York St., Portland, ☎ 207/773–2337).

The Arts

Bowdoin Summer Music Festival (✉ Bowdoin College, Brunswick, ☎ 207/725–3322 information; 207/725–3895 tickets), a six-week concert series, stages performances by students, faculty, and prestigious guest artists. **Chocolate Church Arts Center** (✉ 804 Washington St., Bath, ☎ 207/442–8455) hosts folk, jazz, and classical concerts; theater productions; and performances for children. **Ogunquit Playhouse** (✉ Rte. 1, Ogunquit, ☎ 207/646–5511) mounts plays and musicals from late June to Labor Day. **Portland City Hall's Merrill Auditorium** (✉ 20 Myrtle St., Portland, ☎ 207/874–8200) mounts not only performances by the Portland Symphony Orchestra and Portland Concert Association but numerous theatrical and musical events. **Portland Performing Arts Center** (✉ 25-A Forest Ave., Portland, ☎ 207/744–0465) hosts music, dance, and theater.

Outdoor Activities and Sports

Boat Trips

Balmy Day Cruises (✉ Pier 8, 62 Commercial St., Boothbay Harbor, ☎ 207/633–2284 or 800/298–2284) operates day-boat trips to

Monhegan Island and tours of the harbor. For tours of Portland harbor, Casco Bay, and the scenic nearby islands, try **Bay View Cruises** (✉ Fisherman's Wharf, ☎ 207/761–0496). **Cape Arundel Cruises** (✉ Kennebunkport Marina, ☎ 207/967–5595) runs scenic and theater cruises, deep-sea fishing, and whale-watching trips. **Casco Bay Lines** (✉ Maine State Pier, ☎ 207/774–7871) provides narrated cruises and transportation to Casco Bay Islands. **Eagle Island Tours** (✉ Long Wharf, ☎ 207/774–6498) leads daily cruises to Eagle Island and seal-watching cruises. From Perkins Cove in Ogunquit, **Finestkind** (☎ 207/646–5227) runs boats to Nubble Light and schedules lobstering trips. **First Chance** (✉ 4-A Western Ave., Lower Village, Kennebunk, ☎ 207/967–5507 or 800/967–2628) gives whale-watching cruises and guarantees sightings in season. **Old Port Mariner Fleet** (✉ Long Wharf, ☎ 207/775–0727 or 800/437–3270) leads scenic cruises and whale-watching and fishing trips.

Canoeing

The **Maine Audubon Society** (☎ 207/781–2330Labor Day–mid-June; 207/883–4100 mid-June–Labor Day) leads daily guided canoe trips in Scarborough Marsh (on Route 9 in Scarborough), the largest salt marsh in Maine.

Beaches

Goose Rocks, north of Kennebunkport, is the largest area beach and a favorite of families with small children; the Kennebunkport Town Office (✉ Elm St., ☎ 207/967–4244) sells parking permits. **Kennebunk Beach** is actually three beaches, with cottages and Victorian boardinghouses nearby; for parking permits go to the Kennebunk Town Office (✉ 1 Summer St., ☎ 207/985–2102). **Ogunquit Beach,** a fine stretch at the mouth of the river, is protected from the surf. Families gravitate to the ends, while gay visitors camp at the beach's middle. **Old Orchard Beach,** with an amusement park reminiscent of Coney Island, is only a few miles north of Biddeford on Route 9. **Pemaquid Beach Park** (✉ off Rte. 130, New Harbor, ☎ 207/677–2754) has a sand beach, a snack bar, changing facilities, and picnic tables overlooking John's Bay. **Reid State Park** (☎ 207/371–2303), on Georgetown Island off Route 127, has three beaches, bathhouses, picnic tables, and a snack bar.

Shopping

More than 100 **factory outlets** along U.S. 1 around Kittery sell clothing, shoes, glassware, and other products from top manufacturers and specialty companies. The big names of designer outlets are in **Freeport,** from Coach and Polo Ralph Lauren to Hartmann and Dansk. **L. L. Bean** has a store on Congress Street. Fancy boutiques crowd **Dock Square** in Kennebunkport. **Boothbay Harbor** has a nice selection of galleries and crafts shops. Antiques shops line the main and side streets of **Wiscasset** and overflow across the bridge into Edgecomb. The ***Freeport Visitors Guide*** (☎ 207/865–1212; 800/865–1994 for a copy) lists the more than 100 shops and factory outlet stores that can be found on Main Street, Bow Street, and elsewhere. The **Portland Public Market** (✉ 25 Preble St., ☎ 207/228–2000) has more than 20 locally owned businesses specializing in fresh foods, organic produce, and imported specialty foods.

The Southern Coast Essentials

AIRPORTS

Portland International Airport, 3 mi from Portland, has scheduled daily flights by major U.S. carriers.

➤ Airport Information: **Portland International Airport** (✉ 1001 Westbrook St., ☏ 207/772–0690, WEB www.portlandjetport.org).

BUS TRAVEL

Vermont Transit provides service to Old Orchard Beach, Portland, and Brunswick on the coast as well as inland to Lewiston, Augusta, Waterville, and Bangor. Greyhound Bus Lines serves Portland, Brunswick, Bath, Wiscasset, Damariscotta, and Waldoboro, as well as inland to Augusta, Bangor, and Lewiston. Concord Trailways has daily service between Boston and Bangor (via Portland); a coastal route connects towns between Brunswick and Searsport.

➤ Bus Information: **Concord Trailways** (☏ 800/639–3317, WEB www.concordtrailways.com). **Greyhound** (☏ 207/772–6587 or 800/231–2222, WEB www.greyhound.com). **Vermont Transit** (☏ 207/772–6587 or 800/451–3292, WEB www.vermonttransit.com).

CAR TRAVEL

From Boston take U.S. 1 north to I–95, passing through the short New Hampshire seacoast to Kittery, the first town in Maine. I–95 continues past Portland, which is the quickest way to access southern coastal and inland towns north of Portland. Route 1 follows the coast from Kittery to Calais.

VISITOR INFORMATION

➤ Tourist Information: **Boothbay Harbor Region Chamber of Commerce** (✉ Box 356, Boothbay Harbor 04538, ☏ 207/633–2353, WEB www.boothbayharbor.com). **Chamber of Commerce of the Bath-Brunswick Region** (✉ 45 Front St., Bath 04530, ☏ 207/443–9751; ✉ 59 Pleasant St., Brunswick 04011, ☏ 207/725–8797, WEB www.midcoastmaine.com). **Convention and Visitors Bureau of Greater Portland** (✉ 305 Commercial St., Portland 04101, ☏ 207/772–5800 or 877/833–1374, WEB www.visitportland.com). **Kennebunk-Kennebunkport Chamber of Commerce** (✉ 17 Western Ave., Kennebunk 04043, ☏ 207/967–0857, WEB www.visitthekennebunks.com). The **Yorks Chamber of Commerce** (✉ 571 U.S. 1, York 03903, ☏ 207/363–4422 or 800/639–2442, WEB www.yorkme.org).

PENOBSCOT BAY AND ACADIA

Purists hold that the Maine coast begins at Penobscot Bay, where water vistas are wider and bluer, with the shore a jumble of broken granite boulders, cobblestones, and gravel. East of Penobscot Bay, Acadia is the informal name for Mount Desert (pronounced *dessert*) Island and environs. Mount Desert, Maine's largest island, encompasses most of Acadia National Park, the state's principal tourist attraction.

Exploring Penobscot Bay and Acadia

Tenants Harbor is a quintessential Maine fishing town. Port Clyde, south of Tenants Harbor, is the point of departure for the mail boat that serves tiny, remote **Monhegan Island.** Known to Basque, Portuguese, and Breton fishermen well before Columbus "discovered" America, it was discovered again by some of America's finest painters, including Rockwell Kent, Robert Henri, and Edward Hopper, who sailed out to paint its meadows, cliffs, wild ocean views, and fishermen's shacks. The island's 17 mi of hiking trails provide places to escape crowds as well as mesmerizing views of pounding surf and cathedral pines.

Rockland, home of the Seafood Festival (a.k.a. the Lobster Festival), ranks as the coast's commercial hub, with fishing boats moored alongside a growing flotilla of windjammers. Day trips to Vinalhaven and North Haven islands depart from the harbor, the outer portion of which is bisected by a nearly mile-long granite breakwater. Art galleries line ★ the main and side streets around the **Farnsworth Art Museum,** which specializes in American art, with a focus on Maine-related works. ✉ *356 Main St.,* ☎ *207/596–6457,* WEB *www.farnsworthmuseum.org.* 🎫 *$9; Olson House only, $4. Closed Mon. Oct.–May; Olson House closed mid-Oct.–late May.*

The **Shore Village Museum** displays many lighthouse and Coast Guard artifacts and has exhibits of maritime memorabilia. ✉ *104 Limerock St.,* ☎ *207/594–0311,* WEB *www.lighthouse.cc/shorevillage.* 🎫 *Donation suggested. Mid-Oct.–May.*

★ In **Camden,** mountains tower over the harbor, and the fashionable waterfront is home to a large windjammer fleet; such cruises are a superb way to explore the ports and islands of Penobscot Bay. The 5,500-acre **Camden Hills State Park** (☎ 207/236–3109), 2 mi north of Camden on U.S. 1, contains 20 mi of trails.

Kelmscott Farm is a rare-breed animal farm with a nature trail, children's activities, heirloom gardens, and frequent special events. ✉ *Rte. 52, Lincolnville,* ☎ *207/763–4088,* WEB *www.kelmscott.org.* 🎫 *$5. Closed Mon.*

The houses along **Belfast**'s Church Street are a glossary of 19th-century architectural styles. **Searsport** claims to be the antiques capital of Maine, with shops and a seasonal weekend flea market. Historic **Castine** has two museums and the ruins of a British fort. **Ellsworth** has an array of outlets including an L. L. Bean store. It's also the gateway to Bar Harbor and Acadia and is where you pick up Route 3 to Mount Desert Island.

Although most of **Bar Harbor**'s grand mansions were destroyed in a 1947 fire, this busy resort town on Frenchman Bay has retained its beauty. Shops, restaurants, and hotels are clustered along Main, Mount Desert, ★ and Cottage streets. The **Abbe Museum** contains 50,000 objects spanning 10,000 years of Native American history in Maine; many are on display in both permanent and changing exhibitions. ✉ *26 Mt. Desert St.,* ☎ *207/288–3519,* WEB *www.abbemuseum.org.* 🎫 *$4.50. Closed Mon.–Wed. mid-Oct.–late May.*

Quiet **Southwest Harbor** and elite **Northeast Harbor** both have a smat- ★ tering of shops and restaurants. The Hulls Cove approach to **Acadia National Park** (☞ National and State Parks and Hiking) is northwest of Bar Harbor on Route 3. The Ocean Trail is an easily accessible walk with some of Maine's most spectacular scenery. The 57 mi of gravel carriage roads provide easy access to the park and are ideal for mountain biking or walking. For a mountaintop experience without the hike, drive to the summit of **Cadillac Mountain,** the highest point on the eastern coast, for a spectacular sunset view.

Dining and Lodging

Bar Harbor

$$$ ★ ✕ **George's.** Candles, flowers, and linens grace the tables and art fills the walls of the four small dining rooms in this old house. The menu's Mediterranean influences can be tasted in the phyllo-wrapped lobster. Jazz musicians perform nightly in peak season. ✉ *7 Stephen's La.,* ☎ *207/288–4505. AE, D, DC, MC, V. Closed Nov.–mid-June. No lunch.*

$$–$$$ ★ ✕ **Havana.** Pumpkin-color walls, soft jazz, wood floors, and cloth-covered tables set the tone at this storefront restaurant on the fringe of downtown Bar Harbor. The Latin-influenced menu emphasizes local natural and organic ingredients and changes weekly. ✉ *318 Main St.,* ☎ *207/288–2822. Reservations essential. MC, V. Closed Sun.–Tues. late Oct.–mid-May.*

$$$–$$$$ ✕🏨 **Bar Harbor Inn.** The roots of this genteel inn date from the 1880s. Rooms are spread out over three buildings on nicely landscaped waterfront property, a short walk to town. Most rooms have balconies, hot tubs, fireplaces, and great views. The formal waterfront Reading Room ($$–$$$) serves mostly Continental fare but has some Maine specialties. ✉ *Newport Dr., 04609,* ☎ *207/288–3351 or 800/248–3351,* FAX *207/288–5296,* WEB *www.barharborinn.com. 153 rooms. 2 restaurants, pool, gym. AE, D, DC, MC, V. CP.*

$$–$$$$ ★ 🏨 **Ullikana.** This traditional Tudor cottage juxtaposes traditional antiques with contemporary country pieces, vibrant color with French country wallpapers, and abstract art with folk art. Rooms are large, most have at least a glimpse of the water, many have fireplaces, and some have decks. ✉ *16 The Field, 04609,* ☎ *207/288–9552,* FAX *207/288–3682,* WEB *www.ullikana.com. 16 rooms. MC, V. Closed Nov.–May. BP.*

Camden

$–$$$ ✕ **Waterfront Restaurant.** Come for a ringside seat on Camden Harbor; the best view is from the outdoor deck, open in warm weather. The fare is primarily seafood, but landlubbers will find plenty of beef, chicken, and salads. ✉ *Bay View St.,* ☎ *207/236–3747. Reservations not accepted. MC, V.*

$$ ✕🏨 **Youngtown Inn.** Inside this white Federal-style farmhouse are a French-inspired country retreat and a well-respected French restaurant ($$–$$$). The country location guarantees quiet, and the inn is a short walk to the Fernald Neck Preserve on Lake Megunticook. ✉ *Rte. 52 at Youngtown Rd., Lincolnville 04849,* ☎ *207/763–4290 or 800/291–8438,* FAX *207/763–4078,* WEB *www.youngtowninn.com. 7 rooms. AE, MC, V. BP.*

$$$$ ★ 🏨 **Inn at Ocean's Edge.** Every room in this shingle-style inn has an ocean view as well as a king-size bed, fireplace, and whirlpool for two. The oceanfront setting in Lincolnville is private yet minutes from Camden. ✉ *U.S. 1, Lincolnville (Box 704, Camden 04843),* ☎ *207/236–0945,* FAX *207/236–0609,* WEB *www.innatoceansedge.com. 27 rooms. Gym. MC, V. BP.*

Castine

$–$$ ✕🏨 **Castine Inn.** Upholstered easy chairs and fine prints and paintings are typical appointments in this inn's light, airy guest rooms. The third floor has the best views: overlooking the gardens and the harbor on one side, the village on the other. The creative menu in the dining room ($$$–$$$$; closed Tues.) uses local ingredients. ✉ *Main St. (Box 41, 04421),* ☎ *207/326–4365,* FAX *207/326–4570,* WEB *www.castineinn.com. 19 rooms. Restaurant. MC, V. Closed Nov.–late Apr. BP.*

Hancock

$$$$ ✕🏨 **Le Domaine.** This place is primarily known its haute cuisine ($$$), but its French-country-style guest rooms are also inviting. Ask for a room in the rear, overlooking the lawns and gardens and away from the noise of Route 1. ✉ *Rte. 1 (HC77, Box 496, 04640),* ☎ *207/422–3395 or 800/554–8495,* FAX *207/422–2316,* WEB *www.ledomaine.com. 7 rooms. Restaurant. AE, D, MC, V. Closed late Oct.–mid-May. BP.*

Monhegan Island

$$$–$$$$ **Island Inn.** This three-story inn, which dates from 1807, has a commanding presence on Monhegan's harbor. The waterside rooms are the nicest, with sunset views over the harbor and stark Manana Island. ✉ *1 Ocean Ave. (Box 128, 04852),* ☎ *207/596–0371,* FAX *207/594–5517,* WEB *www.islandinnmonhegan.com. 34 rooms. Restaurant. MC, V. Closed Columbus Day–Memorial Day. BP.*

Rockland

$$ ★ ✕ **Amalfi.** Delicious Mediterranean cuisine, a well-chosen and affordable wine list, and excellent service are the calling cards at this storefront Mediterranean bistro. ✉ *421 Main St.,* ☎ *207/596–0012. D, MC, V. Closed Sun.*

$$ ✕ **Café Miranda.** Expect to wait for a table at this cozy bistro, where the daily-changing menu reflects fresh, seasonal ingredients and the chef's creative renditions of both new American and traditional home-style foods. ✉ *15 Oak St.,* ☎ *207/594–2034. MC, V. Closed Sun.–Mon. No lunch.*

$$ ★ ✕ **Primo.** James Beard award–winning chef Melissa Kelly and baker–pastry chef Price Kushner create cuisine that combines fresh Maine ingredients with Mediterranean influences. The weekly changing menu may include wood-roasted black sea bass or diver scallop and basil ravioli. ✉ *2 S. Main St.,* ☎ *207/594–0770. Reservations essential. AE, D, DC, MC, V. Closed Tues.–Wed. No lunch*

$$$–$$$$ **Samoset Resort.** On the Rockland-Rockport town line next to the breakwater, this sprawling ocean-side resort has spacious rooms, most of which have views of Penobscot Bay over the fairways; all have patios or decks. ✉ *220 Warrenton St., Rockport 04856,* ☎ *207/594–2511; 800/341–1650 outside Maine;* FAX *207/594–0722;* WEB *www.samoset.com. 178 rooms. Restaurant, pools, golf, tennis, health club. AE, D, DC, MC, V.*

Southwest Harbor

$–$$$ ✕ **Beal's Lobster Pier.** You can watch lobstermen bringing in their catch at this working lobster pound. Order lobster at one take-out window, fried foods, burgers, and dessert at another. ✉ *End of Clark Point Rd.,* ☎ *207/244–3202, 207/244–7178, or 800/245–7178. Closed mid-Oct.–mid-May.*

$ **Island House.** This B&B on the island's quiet side has simply decorated bedrooms in the main house and a carriage-house suite, complete with sleeping loft and kitchenette. ✉ *121 Clark Point Rd. (Box 1006, Southwest Harbor 04679),* ☎ *207/244–5180,* WEB *www.acadia.net/islandhouse. 5 rooms. MC, V. BP.*

Tenants Harbor

$$–$$$ ✕ **East Wind Inn & Meeting House.** This comfortably old-fashioned inn has a dreamy view over an island-studded harbor. Rooms in the main inn are plain and unadorned; those in the Meeting House (a converted sea captain's house) and the Wheeler Cottage have more comforts; some have fireplaces. The inn's restaurant ($$) emphasizes local seafood. ✉ *Mechanic St./Rte. 131, 10 mi off Rte. 1 (Box 149, 04860),* ☎ *207/372–6366 or 800/241–8439,* FAX *207/372–6320,* WEB *www.eastwindinn.com. 26 rooms, 4 apartments. 2 restaurants. AE, D, MC, V. Closed Dec.–Apr. No lunch.*

Campgrounds

The two campgrounds in Acadia National Park fill up quickly during summer. You can make reservations four months in advance for a May–October visit to **Blackwoods** (☎ 800/365–2267). Space at **Sea-**

wall (☎ 207/244–3600) is allocated on a first-come, first-served basis, starting at 8 AM. Nearby **Lamoine State Park** (☎ 207/667–4778) has a great location on Frenchman Bay.

The Arts

Arcady Music Festival (☎ 207/288–3151) schedules concerts (primarily classical) at locations around Mount Desert Island and at some off-island sites, year-round. **Bar Harbor Music Festival** (✉ 59 Cottage St., ☎ 207/288–5744) has concerts from early July to early August. **Bay Chamber Concerts** (✉ Rockport Opera House, 6 Central St., Rockport, ☎ 207/236–2823) presents chamber music on Thursday and Friday nights during July and August; concerts are given once a month from September through June.

Outdoor Activities and Sports

Biking

The carriage paths that wind through **Acadia National Park** are ideal for biking; pick up a map from the Hulls Cove visitor center. **Acadia Bike & Canoe** (✉ 48 Cottage St., ☎ 207/288–9605 or 800/526–8615) rents bikes and canoes. **Bar Harbor Bicycle Shop** (✉ 141 Cottage St., ☎ 207/288–3886 or 800/824–2453) rents bikes. In Camden, **Brown Dog Bikes** (✉ 46 Elm St., ☎ 207/236–6664) delivers rental bikes to area lodging. **Maine Sport** (✉ U.S. 1, Rockport, ☎ 207/236–8797 or 800/722–0826) rents bikes, camping and fishing gear, canoes, kayaks, cross-country skis, ice skates, and snowshoes.

Boat Trips

Port Clyde is the point of departure for the ***Laura B.*** (☎ 207/372–8848 schedules), the mail boat that serves Monhegan Island. From Bar Harbor, the ***Acadian Whale Watcher*** (✉ Golden Anchor Pier, 52 West St., ☎ 207/288–9794 or 800/421–3307) runs 3½-hour whale-watching cruises from June to mid-October. **Bar Harbor Whale Watch Co.** (✉ 1 West St., ☎ 207/288–3322 or 800/508–1499) operates the catamaran *Friendship V*, for whale-watching, and the *Katherine*, for lobster fishing and seal watching.

The four-masted schooner ***Margaret Todd*** (✉ Bar Harbor Inn Pier, ☎ 207/288–4585) runs 1½- to 2-hour tours daily between mid-May and October. Camden and Rockland are the East Coast **windjammer** headquarters. For information contact Maine Windjammer Association (✉ Box 1144, Blue Hill 04614, ☎ 800/807–9463). In Southwest Harbor, **Manset Yacht Service** (✉ Shore Rd., Manset, ☎ 207/244–4040) rents powerboats and sailboats.

Hiking

Acadia National Park maintains nearly 200 mi of paths. Among the more rewarding hikes are the Precipice Trail to Champlain Mountain, the Great Head Loop, the Gorham Mountain Trail, and the path around Eagle Lake.

Shopping

In **Camden,** the best shopping streets are Main and Bayview. Antiques shops (abundant in **Searsport**) are scattered around the outskirts of villages. Galleries and boutiques can be found in **Rockland, Blue Hill, Deer Isle,** and **Stonington. Bar Harbor** is a good place to browse for gifts. For bargains head for the outlets along Route 3 in **Ellsworth.**

Penobscot Bay and Acadia Essentials

AIRPORTS

Bangor International Airport, 30 mi north of Penobscot Bay, is served by Business Express, Continental, Delta/Comair, and US Airways. Knox County Regional Airport, 3 mi south of Rockland, is served by Colgan Air/U.S. Air. Hancock County Airport, 8 mi northwest of Bar Harbor, is served by Colgan Air/U.S. Air.

➤ AIRPORT INFORMATION: **Bangor International Airport** (✉ 287 Godfrey Blvd., ☎ 207/947–0384, WEB www.flybangor.com.org). **Hancock County Airport** (✉ Rte. 3, Trenton, ☎ 207/667–7329, WEB www.bhairport.co). **Knox County Regional Airport** (✉ Ash Point Dr., Owls Head, ☎ 207/594–4131, WEB knoxcounty.midcoast.com).

CAR TRAVEL

U.S. 1 follows the west coast of Penobscot Bay, linking Rockland, Camden, and Ellsworth. From Ellsworth, Route 3 will take you onto Mount Desert Island.

VISITOR INFORMATION

➤ TOURIST INFORMATION: **Bar Harbor Chamber of Commerce** (✉ 93 Cottage St. [Box 158, 04609], ☎ 207/288–3393, 207/288–5103, or 800/288–5103, WEB www.barharborinfo.com). **Rockland–Thomaston Area Chamber of Commerce** (✉ Harbor Park [Box 508, Rockland 04841], ☎ 207/596–0376 or 800/562–2529, WEB www.midcoast.com/~rtacc). **Rockport-Camden-Lincolnville Chamber of Commerce** (✉ Public Landing [Box 919, Camden 04843], ☎ 207/236–4404 or 800/223–5459, WEB www.camdenme.org). **Southwest Harbor/Tremont Chamber of Commerce** (✉ Main St. [Box 1143, Southwest Harbor 04679], ☎ 207/244–9264 or 800/423–9264, WEB www.acadiachamber.com).

WESTERN LAKES AND MOUNTAINS

Less than 20 mi northwest of Portland, the lakes and mountains of western Maine stretch along the New Hampshire border to Quebec. The Sebago–Long Lake region has antiques stores and lake cruises on a 42-mi waterway. Kezar Lake, in a fold of the White Mountains, is a hideaway of the wealthy. Bethel is a classic New England town, while the less-developed Rangeley Lakes area is a fishing paradise; both attract skiers and snowmobilers in winter.

Exploring the Western Lakes and Mountains

Sebago Lake State Park (☎ 207/693–6613 mid-June–Sept.; 207/693–6231 Oct.–mid-June) provides swimming, picnicking, camping, boating, and fishing opportunities. To the north is **Naples,** with cruises and boat rentals on Long Lake. **Songo Lock** connects the northern tip of Sebago Lake with Long Lake. The ***Songo River Queen II,*** a 92-ft sternwheeler, runs hour-long cruises on Long Lake and longer voyages down the Songo River and through Songo Lock. ✉ *Rte. 302, Naples Causeway,* ☎ *207/693–6861.* 🎫 *Songo River ride $11, Long Lake cruise $8. Closed Oct.–May; limited schedule June and Sept.*

Bridgton, near Highland Lake, has antiques shops in and around town. U.S. 302 to Route 5 through Lovell or Routes 35 and 37 through Harrison and the Waterfords are scenic routes to **Bethel,** a town with white-clapboard houses, antiques stores, and a mountain vista at the end of every street.

The area from Bethel to **Rangeley Lake** is beautiful, too, particularly in autumn. In **Grafton Notch State Park** (☎ 207/824–2912) you can hike to stunning gorges and waterfalls and into the Baldpate Mountains. For more than a century, **Rangeley** has lured people who fish to its more than 40 lakes and ponds. **Rangeley Lake State Park** (☎ 207/864–3858) has superb scenery, swimming, picnicking, and boating. In the shadow of Sugarloaf Mountain, **Kingfield** is prime ski country—a classic New England town with a general store, historic inns, and a white-clapboard church. **Sandy River & Rangeley Lakes Railroad** has a century-old train that traverses the woods. ✉ *Bridge Hill Rd., Phillips (20 mi southeast of Rangeley),* ☎ *207/639–3352,* WEB *www.srrl-rr.org.* *$3. Closed Nov.–May.*

Dining and Lodging

Bethel has the largest concentration of inns and B&Bs, and its chamber of commerce has a **lodging reservations service** (☎ 207/824–3585).

Bethel

$–$$ **L'Auberge** Built as a barn in the late 1850s, L'Auberge has evolved into a casual inn with a French country accent and one of the area's best restaurants ($$; closed Tues.–Wed.). The inn is on 5 private acres off the Bethel Common. The innkeepers warmly welcome both children and pets. ✉ *24 Mill Hill Rd., 04217,* ☎ *207/824–2774 or 800/760–2774,* WEB *www.laubergecountryinn.com. 6 rooms, 1 apartment. Restaurant. AE, D, MC, V. BP.*

$ **Victoria Inn.** Inside this turreted inn, Victorian details include ceiling rosettes, stained-glass windows, elaborate fireplace mantels, and gleaming oak trim. The restaurant, open to the public for dinner ($$; closed Mon.–Tues.), serves entrées such as lobster ravioli and filet mignon. ✉ *32 Main St. (Box 249, 04217),* ☎ *207/824–8060 or 888/774–1235,* FAX *207/824–3926,* WEB *www.victoria-inn.com. 15 rooms. Restaurant. MC, V. BP.*

Kingfield

$–$$$ **Grand Summit Hotel.** This six-story brick structure dominates Sugarloaf's base village. Ski tuning, lockers, and valet parking are available. ✉ *R.R. 1 (Box 2299, Carrabassett Valley 04947),* ☎ *207/237–2222 or 800/527–9879,* FAX *207/237–2874. 119 rooms. Restaurant, health club. AE, D, DC, MC, V.*

Lovell

$–$$ **Center Lovell Inn.** The eclectic decor at this rambling, old-fashioned country inn mixes pieces from the mid-19th to mid-20th century in a pleasing, homey style. The best tables for dining are on the wraparound porch, which has sunset views over Kezar Lake and the White Mountains. Entrées ($$–$$) may include pan-seared Muscovy duck, fillet of bison, or fresh swordfish. ✉ *Rte. 5 (Box 261, 04016),* ☎ *207/925–1575 or 800/777–2698,* WEB *www.centerlovellinn.com. 7 rooms. Restaurant. MC, V. Closed Nov.–Apr. MAP.*

Rangeley

$$ **Rangeley Inn and Motor Lodge.** Only the three-story, blue inn building (circa 1907) is visible from Main Street; however, its motel wing behind it has views of Haley Pond, a lawn, and a garden. Some of the inn's rooms have iron-and-brass beds, some have claw-foot tubs, and others have whirlpool tubs. The dining room ($$–$$$) prepares Continental-style fare; the tavern serves casual fare such as soups, sandwiches, steaks, and ribs. ✉ *51 Main St. (Box 160, 04970),* ☎ *207/864–3341 or 800/666–3687,* FAX *207/864–3634,* WEB *www.rangeleyinn.com. 51 rooms, 2 cabins. 2 restaurants. AE, D, MC, V. MAP.*

Waterford

$-$$ ★ **Bear Mountain Inn.** After a swim at the private beach on Bear Lake or a hike up Bear Mountain, it's nice to return to this rambling farmhouse inn. Among the activities are badminton, croquet, volleyball, boating, fishing, ice-skating, cross-country skiing, and snowmobiling. ✉ *Rte. 35, South Waterford 04081,* ☎ *207/583–4404,* FAX *207/583–2437,* WEB *www.bearmtninn.com. 9 rooms, 1 cottage. MC, V. BP.*

Outdoor Activities and Sports

Boating

Sebago, Long, Rangeley, and Mooselookmeguntic are the most popular lakes for boating. Contact tourist offices for rentals.

Canoeing

Rangeley and Mooselookmeguntic lakes are good for canoeing, sailing, and motorboating. **Bethel Outdoor Adventures** (✉ 121 Mayville Rd., ☎ 207/824–4224) rents canoes and kayaks. **Dockside Sports Center** (✉ Town Cove, ☎ 207/864–2424) rents a variety of boats, canoes, and other crafts. **River's Edge Sports** (✉ Rte. 4/16, Oquossoc, ☎ 207/864–5582) rents canoes.

Fishing

Fishing licenses (required) can be obtained at many sporting goods and hardware stores and at town halls. The **Department of Inland Fisheries and Wildlife** (✉ 284 State St., Augusta 04333, ☎ 207/287–2871) has further information.

Skiing

Sugarloaf/USA (✉ Kingfield 04947, ☎ 207/237–2000) has both downhill and cross-country trails. **Sunday River** (✉ Box 450, Bethel 04217, ☎ 207/824–3000) has downhill trails. The **Sunday River Cross-Country Ski Center** (✉ 23 Skiway Rd., Newry, ☎ 207/824–2410), based at the Sunday River Inn, has 40 km (25 mi) of trails.

Western Lakes and Mountains Essentials

CAR TRAVEL

U.S. 302 provides access to the region from I–95. U.S. 2, which runs east–west, links Bangor to Bethel.

VISITOR INFORMATION

➤ TOURIST INFORMATION: Bethel Chamber of Commerce (✉ Box 439, Bethel 04217, ☎ 207/824–2282 or 800/442–5526, WEB www.bethelmaine.com). Greater Bridgton–Lakes Region Chamber of Commerce (✉ U.S. 302 [Box 236, Bridgton 04009], ☎ 207/647–3472, WEB www.mainelakeschamber.com). Rangeley Lakes Region Chamber of Commerce (✉ Box 317, Rangeley 04970, ☎ 207/864–5571 or 800/685–2537, WEB www.rangeleymaine.com). Sugarloaf Area Chamber of Commerce (✉ R.R. 1 [Box 2151, Kingfield 04947], ☎ 207/235–2100).

THE NORTH WOODS

What to See and Do

Moosehead Lake, Maine's largest, has rustic camps, restaurants, guides, and outfitters. Its 420 mi of shorefront are virtually uninhabited and in most places accessible only by floatplane or boat. **Greenville** is the locus for canoe rentals, outfitters, and basic lodging. **Moosehead Marine Museum** (✉ Main St. [Box 1151], ☎ 207/695–2716; 🎫 $3; closed early Oct.–late May) has exhibits on the local logging industry and the steamship era on Moosehead Lake.

The Moosehead Marine Museum conducts three- and five-hour trips on Moosehead Lake aboard the ★ ***Katahdin*** (✉ Main St., ☎ 207/695–2716; 🎫 $20–$26; closed Columbus Day–June), a 1914 steamship (now diesel). Dam-controlled flows ensure good white-water rafting from May through September on the Kennebec, Dead, and Penobscot rivers. For information contact **Raft Maine** (☎ 800/723–8633, WEB www.raftmaine.com).

Baxter State Park (✉ 64 Balsam Dr., Millinocket 04462, ☎ 207/723–5140) is a 204,733-acre wooded wilderness with 46 mountains, including **Katahdin**, Maine's highest. They're all accessible from a 150-mi trail network.

Even more remote is the **Allagash Wilderness Waterway,** a 92-mi corridor of lakes and rivers. The **Maine Department of Conservation, Bureau of Parks and Lands** (✉ 22 State House Station 22, Augusta 04333, ☎ 207/287–3821) has information on camping and canoeing.

Dining and Lodging

$$$–$$$$ ★ ✕🏨 **Blair Hill Inn.** Beautiful gardens and a hilltop location overlooking the lake distinguish this 1891 estate. Guest rooms are spacious, and four have fireplaces. The restaurant serves a five-course dinner ($$$$) from late May to mid-October on Friday and Saturday nights. Arrive early to enjoy cocktails on the wraparound porch. ✉ *Lily Bay Rd. (Box 1288, 04441),* ☎ *207/695–0224,* FAX *207/695–4324,* WEB *www.blairhill.com. 10 rooms. Restaurant, gym. D, MC, V. BP.*

$$–$$$ ✕🏨 **Greenville Inn.** This rambling lumber baron's mansion includes ornate cherry and mahogany paneling, Oriental rugs, and leaded glass. Cottages have mountain and lake views, and some have decks. The restaurant ($$; reservations essential; no lunch) has water views and serves Austrian-inspired fare. ✉ *Norris St. (Box 1194, Greenville 04441),* ☎ *207/695–2206 or 888/695–6000,* FAX *207/695–0335,* WEB *www.greenvilleinn.com. 6 rooms, 6 cottages. Restaurant. D, MC, V. BP.*

Outdoor Activities and Sports

Outfitters

Beaver Cove Marina (☎ 207/695–3526) rents boats and snowmobiles. **Big Lake Marina** (☎ 207/695–4487) is a full-service marina with boat rentals. **Moose Country Safaris and Dogsled Trips** (☎ 207/876–4907) leads moose safaris, dogsled trips, and canoe and kayak trips. **Northwoods Outfitters** (☎ 207/695–3288) outfits a variety of sports and offers tours, moose safaris, dogsledding, and trail advice.

The North Woods Essentials

AIR TRAVEL

Bangor International Airport is served by Business Express, Continental, Delta/Comair, and US Airways.

➤ AIRPORT INFORMATION: **Bangor International Airport** (✉ 287 Godfrey Blvd., ☎ 207/947–0384, WEB www.flybangor.com.org).

CAR TRAVEL

Route 6 wends its way from I–95 to Greenville; Route 11 provides access from I–95 to Millinocket.

LODGING

CAMPING

Maine Sporting Camp Association publishes a list of its members, with details on the facilities available at each camp. North Maine Woods maintains 500 primitive campsites on commercial forest land.

➤ CONTACTS: **Maine Sporting Camp Association** (✉ Box 89, Jay 04239, WEB www.mainesportingcamps.com). **North Maine Woods** (✉ 41 Main St. [Box 425, Ashland 04732, ☎ 207/435–6213], WEB www.northmainewoods.org).

VISITOR INFORMATION

➤ TOURIST INFORMATION: **Allagash Wilderness Waterway** (✉ 106 Hogan Rd., Bangor 04401, ☎ 207/941–4014). **Baxter State Park Authority** (✉ 64 Balsam Dr., Millinocket 04462, ☎ 207/723–5140). **Katahdin Area Chamber of Commerce** (✉ 1029 Central St., Millinocket 04462, ☎ 207/723–4443, WEB www.katahdinmaine.com). **Moosehead Lake Region Chamber of Commerce** (✉ Rtes. 6 and 15 [Box 581, Greenville 04441], ☎ 207/695–2702, WEB www.katahdinmaine.com).

MARYLAND

By Francis X. Rocca

Updated by Greg Tasker

Capital	Annapolis
Population	5,296,486
Motto	Manly Deeds, Womanly Words
State Bird	Baltimore Oriole
State Flower	Black-eyed Susan
Postal Abbreviation	MD

Statewide Visitor Information

The **Maryland Office of Tourism Development** (✉ 217 E. Redwood St., 9th floor, Baltimore 21202, ☎ 410/767–3400 or 800/543–1036) provides free publications and operates 13 information centers.

Scenic Drives

Between Frederick and Hagerstown, **Alternate U.S. 40** rolls gently through the picturesque towns of a region steeped in Civil War history. Much of western Maryland is blanketed with colorful foliage in early autumn. In the thin western sliver of the state between Hancock and Cumberland, **I–68** passes through a narrow, 340-ft-deep cut in the rocky crest of a mountain, then opens to sweeping views of the Appalachians. Connecting Annapolis to the Eastern Shore, **U.S. 50/301** traverses the **Chesapeake Bay Bridge,** which provides a view of the fishing boats, pleasure craft, and sailboats on the inlet below.

National and State Parks

National Parks

Antietam National Battlefield (✉ Rte. 65, Sharpsburg, ☎ 301/432–5124; 🎫 $3, $5 per family) marks the site of the bloodiest single day of battle in American history. ★ **Assateague Island National Seashore** (✉ Rte. 611, ☎ 410/641–1441; 🎫 $5 per vehicle, $2 per pedestrian) is famous for its pristine beaches and wild ponies. Thousands of migrating ducks, geese, and swans flock to **Blackwater National Wildlife Refuge** (✉ Rte. 335 at Key Wallace Dr., ☎ 410/228–2677; 🎫 $3 per vehicle, $1 per pedestrian). The presidential retreat of Camp David, mountain vistas, and miles of hiking trails can be found in **Catoctin Mountain Park** (✉ Rte. 77, west of Rte. 15, Thurmont, ☎ 301/663–9330; 🎫 free). The 185-mi-long footpath in **Chesapeake & Ohio Canal National Historical Park** (☎ 301/739–4200; 🎫 free) follows the Potomac River from Washington D.C.'s Georgetown to Cumberland in western Maryland. **Fort McHenry National Monument and Shrine** (✉ Fort Ave. off Key Hwy., Baltimore, ☎ 410/962–4290; 🎫 $5) is where American Patriots saved Baltimore from the British in the War of 1812, inspiring Francis Scott Key to write "The Star-Spangled Banner." Now in the suburbs of Washington, D.C., **Fort Washington Park** (✉ 5 mi southwest of Clinton Hill, ☎ 301/763–4600; 🎫 $5 per vehicle, free weekdays Nov.–Apr.) was the first fort built to protect the nation's capital.

State Parks

Maryland has 47 parks and forests. The Office of Tourism Development has information about each of the parks. The **Department of Natural Resources** (☎ 410/260–8367, WEB www.dnr.state.md.us) organizes guided canoe trips, hiking, backpacking, wildflower walks, forest walks, and mountain-bike trips at many state parks. North of Baltimore, more than 100 mi of hiking and biking trails run through the 13,200-acre **Gunpowder Falls State Park** (✉ 2813 Jerusalem Rd., ☎

410/592–2897; ✉ $2), in the Gunpowder River valley. **Sandy Point State Park** (✉ Rte. 50, 12 mi east of Annapolis, ☎ 410/974–2149; ✉ $3 weekdays, $4 weekends), on the western shore of the Chesapeake Bay, has beaches and park land perfect for picnicking, fishing, and bird-watching. In far western Maryland, McHenry serves as a base for boating and jet skiing at **Deep Creek Lake State Park** (✉ Rte. 219, ☎ 301/387–4111; ✉ $3 per vehicle), which has 65 mi of shoreline. South of Deep Creek Lake State Park, **Swallow Falls State Park** (✉ 222 Herrington La., off Rte. 219, Oakland, ☎ 301/334–9180; ✉ $2 per person Memorial Day–Labor Day; $2 per car Sept.–late May) has paths that wind along the Youghiogheny River past rocky gorges, rapids, towering hemlocks, and the 63-ft Muddy Creek Falls.

BALTIMORE

Baltimore's Inner Harbor serves as the pulse of this vibrant metropolis, a city that traces its roots back to the early 18th century. The waterfront is a veritable urban Disneyland, complete with a promenade, shopping pavilions, restaurants, museums, upscale hotels, and boats. The National Aquarium in Baltimore and Oriole Park at Camden Yards are instantly recognizable landmarks. The redevelopment that transformed this once-moribund waterfront continues on the eastern shore of the Inner Harbor, where a pair of Marriott hotels—the city's first major hotels in a decade—have opened, and restaurants, stores and offices will follow. Though the cityscape is modernizing, no bulldozer could remove the history from a city synonymous with "The Star-Spangled Banner" and local legends Babe Ruth, Edgar Allan Poe, and H. L. Mencken. A small-town feeling still prevails in historic neighborhoods such as Federal Hill, Mount Vernon, and Fells Point, which beckon with an eclectic mix of eateries, shops, pubs, and splendid architecture—from colonial row houses to massive brownstones.

Exploring Baltimore

The city fans out northward from the Inner Harbor, with newer attractions concentrated at the city center, and more historic neighborhoods and sites toward the edges. Baltimore's major northbound artery is Charles Street; cross streets are labeled "East" or "West" relative to it.

Inner Harbor and Environs

★ The acclaimed **American Visionary Art Museum** exhibits thought-provoking paintings, sculpture, and drawings by self-trained artists. ✉ *800 Key Hwy., at Covington St.,* ☎ *410/244–1900,* WEB *www.avam.org.* ✉ *$8. Closed Mon.*

Inside a former oyster cannery, the **Baltimore Museum of Industry** (✉ 1415 Key Hwy., ☎ 410/727–4808, WEB www.thebmi.org; ✉ $6) celebrates the city's industrial heritage. Hands-on exhibits include the Kids' Cannery, where children shuck, pack, and can oyster shells.

The **Maryland Science Center** (✉ 601 Light St., ☎ 410/685–5225, WEB www.mdsci.org; ✉ $16) has hundreds of hands-on exhibits, a planetarium, and a five-story IMAX theater screening 3-D films. For a panoramic view of the harbor and downtown, head for the **Top of the World,** the observation deck on the 27th floor of the World Trade Center (✉ 401 E. Pratt St., ☎ 410/837–8439; ✉ $4).

The World War II submarine USS *Torsk,* the lightship *Chesapeake,* and the Coast Guard cutter *Taney* at the **Baltimore Maritime Museum** give you a good sense of Baltimore's maritime history. ✉ *Piers 3 and 4, Pratt*

St., ☎ 410/396–3453, WEB www.baltomaritimemuseum.org. $6. Closed Mon.–Thurs.

★ The **National Aquarium in Baltimore** (✉ 501 E. Pratt St., ☎ 410/576–3800, WEB www.aqua.org; $16) has more than 10,000 creatures representing 600 species of fish, birds, amphibians, and marine mammals. Simulated habitats include the Amazon River Forest, the South American Rain Forest, and the Atlantic Coral Reef. Dolphins entertain at the Marine Mammal Pavilion. The **Power Plant** (✉ Inner Harbor at Pratt St.), a hulking, turn-of-the-20th-century building, houses chains such as the Hard Rock Cafe, Barnes & Noble, and ESPN Zone, a sports-theme restaurant with virtual sports games.

President Street Station, the oldest surviving big-city depot in the country, has been restored and reopened as the **Baltimore Civil War Museum** (✉ 601 President St., ☎ 410/385–5188, WEB www.civilwarinbaltimore.org; $3). Exhibits focus on Baltimore's role in the Civil War.

Port Discovery—The Baltimore Children's Museum (✉ 35 Market Pl., ☎ 410/727–8120, WEB www.portdiscovery.org; $11), designed by the Walt Disney Co., occupies an old fish market a few blocks north of the Inner Harbor. Activities such as deciphering hieroglyphics to find a tomb, solving a mystery, and creating wind-driven gadgets make learning fun (there's also a futuristic-looking jungle-gym).

East of Inner Harbor is the **Star-Spangled Banner Flag House and 1812 Museum** (✉ 844 E. Pratt St., ☎ 410/837–1793, WEB www.flaghouse.org; $5), where Mary Pickersgill wove the flag that inspired the national anthem. The adjacent museum details the War of 1812.

A 15-minute stroll on the waterfront promenade, or a short taxi ride ★ (water or land) from the Inner Harbor, takes you to **Fells Point,** where antiques shops, galleries, restaurants, and bars line the cobblestone streets of a former shipbuilding center. Farther east is **Canton,** a trendy neighborhood of restaurants and homes within renovated factories. On a nice day, walk the **Baltimore Waterfront Promenade,** a 6-mi stretch a block or so off the water that goes from Canton through Fells Point and the Inner Harbor to South Baltimore.

Though it opened in the early 1990s, **Oriole Park at Camden Yards** (✉ Camden and Howard Sts., ☎ 410/685–9800, WEB www.theorioles.com) looks like the ballparks of the early 1900s but has skyboxes, lounges, and restaurants. Behind-the-scenes **guided ballpark tours** (☎ 410/547–6234; $5) are scheduled year-round.

Charles Street, Mount Vernon Square, and Points North

Charles Street, the main northbound artery dividing East and West Baltimore, has some of the city's most striking architecture. Restaurants and art galleries lend an urbane tone to this neighborhood, with its mix of 19th-century brownstones and modern office buildings.

A block west of Charles Street is Benjamin Latrobe's neoclassic masterpiece, the **Basilica of the National Shrine of the Assumption of the Blessed Virgin Mary** (✉ Mulberry St. at Cathedral St., ☎ 410/539–5741, WEB www.baltimorebasilica.org; free), America's oldest Catholic cathedral, built in 1812.

★ The **Walters Art Museum,** an Italianate palace, has 30,000 pieces from antiquity through the 19th century, including Egyptology exhibits, medieval armor and artifacts, decorative arts, and paintings. The adjacent Hackerman House has a magnificent gallery of Asian art. *✉ 600 N. Charles St., ☎ 410/547–9000, WEB www.thewalters.org. $8. Closed Mon.*

Baltimore
KEY
Rail Lines
0
1500 yards
0
1500 meters
N
Broadway
Madison Square
Eden St.
Chase St.
Eager St.
Madison St.
Monument St.
Aisquith St.
Harford Ave.
147
Mc Elderry St.
Orleans St.
Main Post Office
Johnson Square
Ensor St.
45
Biddle St.
Greenmount Ave.
Front St.
Hillen St.
Low St.
Gay St.
The Fallsway
Gay
83
Holliday
Guilford Ave.
Davis St.
Pleasant St.
Chase St.
Calvert St.
Peabody Library
Read St.
Washington Monument
Saint Paul St.
Saint Paul
TO BALTIMORE MUSEUM OF ART, JOHNS HOPKINS UNIVERSITY, BALTIMORE ZOO
Washington Pl.
Basilica of the Assumption
Charles St.
Eager St.
Mt. Vernon Place
Walters Art Museum
Centre St.
Enoch Pratt Main Library
Cathedral St.
Park Ave.
Saratoga St.
Read St.
Maryland Historical Society
Franklin St.
Mulberry St.
Howard St.
Howard St
Madison St.
Monument St.
Eutaw St.
Biddle St.
40

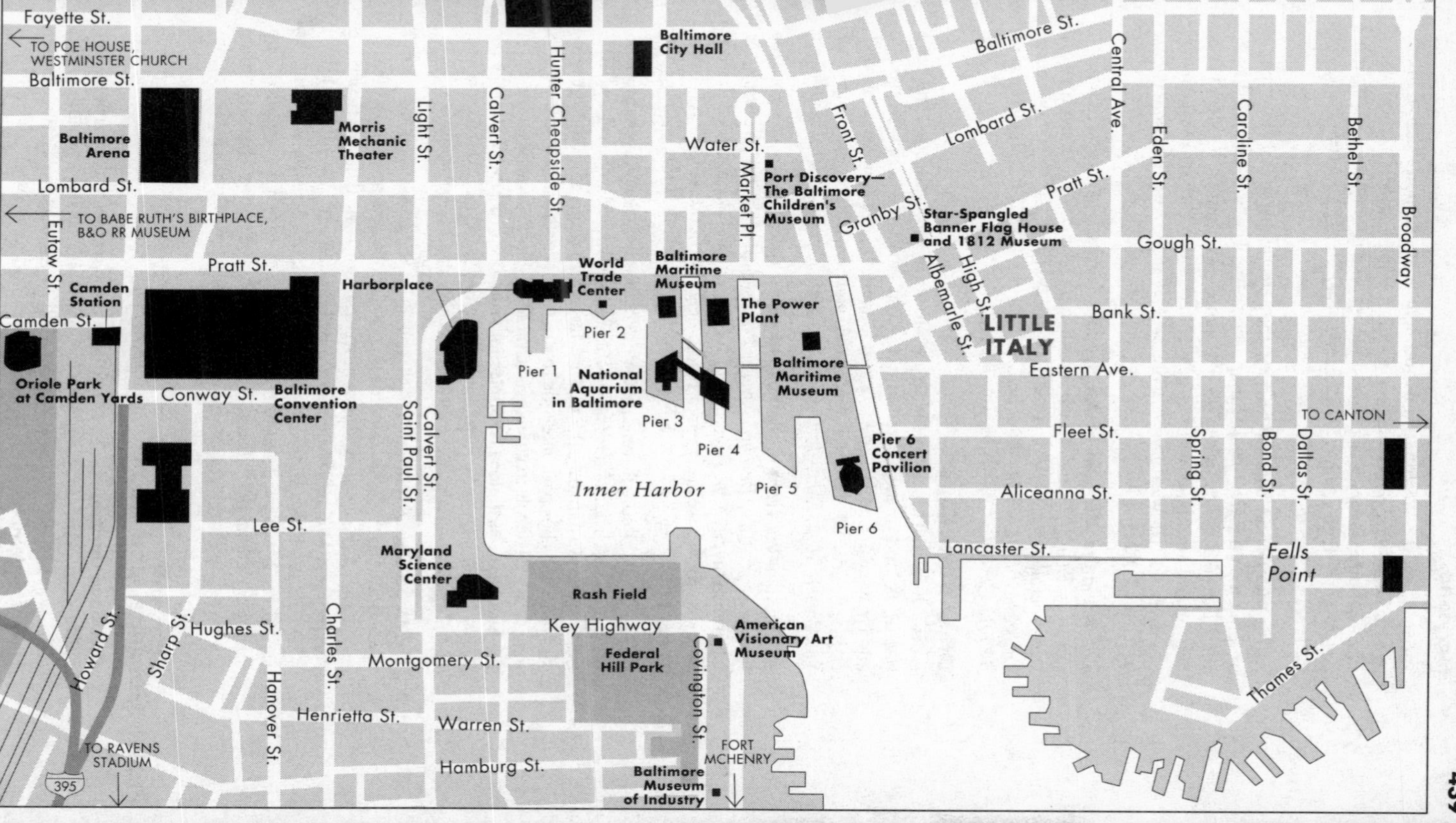

Fayette St.
TO POE HOUSE, WESTMINSTER CHURCH
Baltimore St.
Baltimore Arena
Morris Mechanic Theater
Baltimore City Hall
Light St.
Calvert St.
Hunter Cheapside St.
Baltimore St.
Central Ave.
Eden St.
Caroline St.
Bethel St.
Broadway
Lombard St.
Water St.
Market Pl.
Front St.
Lombard St.
Port Discovery—The Baltimore Children's Museum
Granby St.
Pratt St.
Star-Spangled Banner Flag House and 1812 Museum
Gough St.
TO BABE RUTH'S BIRTHPLACE, B&O RR MUSEUM
Eutaw St.
Pratt St.
Harborplace
World Trade Center
Baltimore Maritime Museum
The Power Plant
Albemarle St.
High St.
LITTLE ITALY
Bank St.
Camden Station
Camden St.
Pier 2
Pier 1
National Aquarium in Baltimore
Baltimore Maritime Museum
Eastern Ave.
Oriole Park at Camden Yards
Conway St.
Baltimore Convention Center
Saint Paul St.
Calvert St.
Pier 3
Pier 4
Pier 6 Concert Pavilion
TO CANTON
Fleet St.
Spring St.
Bond St.
Dallas St.
Inner Harbor
Pier 5
Aliceanna St.
Lee St.
Pier 6
Lancaster St.
Fells Point
Maryland Science Center
Rash Field
Key Highway
American Visionary Art Museum
Sharp St.
Hughes St.
Charles St.
Montgomery St.
Federal Hill Park
Covington St.
Howard St.
Hanover St.
Henrietta St.
Warren St.
Thames St.
TO RAVENS STADIUM
395
Hamburg St.
FORT MCHENRY
Baltimore Museum of Industry

Surrounding the Washington Monument is **Mt. Vernon Place,** flanked by four block-long parks and brownstones along East Mt. Vernon Place. The **Peabody Library** has a handsome reading room with a skylight in its five-story-high ceiling. ✉ *17 E. Mt. Vernon Pl.,* ☎ *410/659–8179.* *Free. Closed weekends.*

At the **Maryland Historical Society,** the eclectic display of state memorabilia includes the original manuscript of "The Star-Spangled Banner." The society has some 200,000 items, including H. L. Mencken's baby grand and the world's largest collection of 19th-century American silver. ✉ *201 W. Monument St.,* ☎ *410/685–3750,* WEB *www.mdhs.org.* *$4. Closed Mon.*

The **Baltimore Museum of Art** displays works by Matisse, Picasso, Cézanne, Renoir, Gauguin, van Gogh, and Monet. A 20th-century art wing includes a gallery devoted to Andy Warhol. ✉ *10 Art Museum Dr.,* ☎ *410/396–7101,* WEB *www.artbma.org.* *$7, free 1st Thurs. of month. Closed Mon.–Tues.*

Other Attractions

North of Inner Harbor is the **Great Blacks in Wax Museum,** the only one of its kind in the United States. Rosa Parks, Frederick Douglass, and Dr. Martin Luther King Jr. are among the figures you'll see. ✉ *1601 E. North Ave.,* ☎ *410/563–6415,* WEB *www.greatblacksinwax.org.* *$6. Closed Mon. Sept.–Jan. and Mar.–June (except federal holidays).*

Edgar Allan Poe lived in the **Poe House** for three years and wrote his first horror story, *Berenice,* here. Poe is buried at the Westminster Church Grave (✉ W. Fayette and Greene Sts.). Take a cab or drive if you visit the house, as it's in a rough neighborhood. ✉ *203 N. Amity St.* ☎ *410/396–7932.* *$3. Closed Sun.–Tues. and Jan.–Mar..*

The NFL's Baltimore Ravens play south of Oriole Park in **Ravens Stadium** (✉ 1101 Russell St., ☎ 410/547–8100, WEB www.ravenszone.net). MARC trains from Washington, the Central Light Rail trains from the suburbs, and numerous bus park-and-ride routes serve the stadium, whose owners may very well decide to change its name. Two blocks west of Oriole Park, the **Babe Ruth Birthplace & Orioles Museum** (✉ 216 Emory St., ☎ 410/727–1539, WEB www.baberuthmuseum.com; $6) has exhibits, photos, and films on the Babe, the Orioles, and Maryland baseball history.

★ The **B&O Railroad Museum** (✉ 901 W. Pratt St., ☎ 410/752–2490, WEB www.borail.org; $8), one of the world's largest train museums, is on the site of the country's first railroad station. The flag that flew over **Fort McHenry National Monument and Shrine** (✉ Fort Ave. off Key Hwy., ☎ 410/962–4290, WEB www.nps.gov/fomc; $5) the morning of September 14, 1814, inspired Francis Scott Key to pen the lyrics to "The Star-Spangled Banner." Tours, exhibits, films, and restored barracks trace the star-shape fort's successful defense against the British attack in the War of 1812.

Parks, Gardens, and Zoos

Sherwood Gardens (✉ Stratford Rd. and Greenway, 3 mi from Inner Harbor east of St. Paul St., ☎ 410/785–0444; free) explodes with color when 80,000 tulips peak in April or early May. South of Inner Harbor, **Federal Hill Park** (✉ Battery St. and Key Hwy.) has an excellent view of the downtown skyline and the remnants of the city's industrial heritage. It's safer during the day.

More than 1,200 animals, including polar bears and penguins, inhabit the 150 acres of the **Baltimore Zoo** (✉ Druid Park Lake Dr., I–83 Exit 7, ☎ 410/366–5466, WEB www.baltimorezoo.org; $10).

Dining

Baltimore is known for its fabulous Chesapeake Bay seafood and great steaks, and there's no shortage of either around the Inner Harbor.

$$–$$$$ ✕ **Hamilton's.** The room is small and intimate in the basement of the historic Admiral Fell Inn. Favorites on the contemporary American menu include grilled beef tenderloins and wild rockfish. Seafood is a menu staple. ✉ *888 S. Broadway,* ☎ *410/522–2195. AE, DC, MC, V.*

$$–$$$$ ✕ **Rusty Scupper.** Contemporary seafood, chicken, and pasta dishes are the specialties in this odd-shape restaurant hugging the Inner Harbor. The dining room has excellent views of the waterfront. ✉ *402 Key Hwy.,* ☎ *410/727–3678. AE, MC, V.*

$$–$$$$ ✕ **Windows.** On the fifth floor of the Renaissance Harborplace Hotel and with great harbor views, Windows is well known for its contemporary preparations of seafood and its wood-fired grill. Dishes include grilled rockfish over a salad of mushrooms and spinach, and mussels pan-roasted with pancetta. ✉ *202 E. Pratt St.,* ☎ *410/547–1200. AE, D, DC, MC, V.*

$$–$$$ ★ ✕ **Charleston Restaurant.** South Carolina meets France in the kitchen of this attractive dining room. Creamy she-crab soup, cornmeal-crusted oysters in a lemon-cayenne sauce, and fiery Cajun fare keep diners coming back. ✉ *1000 Lancaster St.,* ☎ *410/332–7373. AE, MC, V.*

$$–$$$ ✕ **Chiapparelli's.** Family pictures and Baltimore landscapes line the redbrick walls of this homey, cozy restaurant. This is the place to find great spinach ravioli as well as the most famous house salad in Baltimore. ✉ *237 S. High St.,* ☎ *410/837–0309. AE, D, DC, MC, V.*

$$–$$$ ✕ **Joy America Cafe.** With an exuberant menu to match its playful name, Baltimore's most creative kitchen is on the third floor of one of its most interesting museums: the American Visionary Art Museum. The cuisine, as unconventional as some of the artwork on display, is infused with flavors and ingredients from South and Central America and the American Southwest. ✉ *800 Key Hwy.,* ☎ *410/244–6500. AE, DC, MC, V. Closed Mon.*

$$–$$$ ✕ **Obrycki's.** Steamed crabs and seafood are the staples at this no-frills crab house, one of Baltimore's most famous. Pictures of old Baltimore adorn the walls. ✉ *1727 E. Pratt St.,* ☎ *410/732–6399. AE, D, DC, MC, V. Closed mid-Dec.–Mar.*

$$–$$$ ★ ✕ **The Prime Rib.** Black walls, leopard-print carpeting, and a baby grand add to the elegance and romance of this Baltimore fixture. Along with top cuts, including prime rib and New York strip, the traditional menu features superb crab cakes. ✉ *1101 N. Calvert St.,* ☎ *410/539–1804. Reservations essential. Jacket required. AE, DC, MC, V.*

Lodging

$$$$ 🏨 **Baltimore Marriott Waterfront Hotel.** Rising on the eastern shore of the Inner Harbor, this 32-story hotel is the city's newest. It's the closest major hotel to Fells Point, Little Italy, and other attractions on the harbor's east side. Each room, accented in bold, rich colors, has spectacular views. Every evening, guests will find turned-down covers and a Belgian chocolate mint on their pillow. ✉ *700 Aliceanna St., 21202,* ☎ *410/385–3000,* FAX *410/895–1900,* WEB *www.marriott.com. 750 rooms. Restaurant, pool, health club. AE, D, DC, MC, V.*

$$$$ ★ 🏨 **Harbor Court.** This redbrick tower with marble floors, crystal chandeliers, and fine reproduction furniture is Baltimore's most prestigious and luxurious hotel. Its Hampton's Restaurant, with a seasonal menu, ranks among the country's best. ✉ *550 Light St., 21202,* ☎ *410/234–0550 or 800/824–0076,* FAX *410/659–5925,* WEB *www.harborcourt.com. 203 rooms. 2 restaurants, pool, gym. AE, D, DC, MC, V.*

$$$$ 🏨 **Hyatt Regency Baltimore.** A walkway across Light Street links the Hyatt to one of the pavilions of Harborplace and to the Baltimore Convention Center. Rooms facing the water have incomparable harbor views. ✉ *300 Light St., 21202,* ☎ *410/528–1234 or 800/233–1234,* FAX *410/685–3362,* WEB *www.hyatt.com. 486 rooms. 2 restaurants, pool, tennis, gym. AE, D, DC, MC, V.*

$$$$ 🏨 **Renaissance Harborplace Hotel.** Across from the Inner Harbor shopping pavilions and waterfront tourist sights, this is one of the most conveniently located hotels in the city. Don't miss the view from the Window's restaurant. ✉ *202 E. Pratt St. 21202,* ☎ *410/547–1200,* FAX *410/539–5780,* WEB *www.renaissancehotels.com. 622 rooms. Restaurant, pool, gym. AE, D, DC, MC, V.*

$$$–$$$$ 🏨 **Sheraton Inner Harbor.** One block from Harborplace and Oriole Park, the official hotel of the Baltimore Orioles is within walking distance of most downtown attractions. ✉ *300 S. Charles St., 21201,* ☎ *410/962–8300,* FAX *410/962–8211,* WEB *www.sheraton.com. 337 rooms. 2 restaurants, pool, gym. AE, D, DC, MC, V.*

$$$ ★ 🏨 **The Admiral Fell Inn.** Eight adjoining buildings have been transformed into an elegant, European-style inn a block from the water in the heart of Fells Point. Many rooms have canopied beds; some have Jacuzzis and fireplaces. ✉ *888 S. Broadway, 21231,* ☎ *410/522–7377 or 800/292–4667,* FAX *410/522–0707,* WEB *www.AdmiralFell.com. 80 rooms. Restaurant. AE, DC, MC, V. CP.*

$$–$$$ ★ 🏨 **Tremont Plaza Hotel.** This plain, gray 37-story tower has suites with kitchens. Those numbered "06" have the best views. ✉ *222 St. Paul Pl. 21202,* ☎ *410/727–2222 or 800/873–6668,* FAX *410/685–4215. 231 suites. 2 restaurants, pool, gym. AE, D, DC, MC, V.*

Motel

🏨 **Hampton Inn Hunt Valley** (✉ 11200 York Rd., Hunt Valley 21030, ☎ 410/527–1500, FAX 410/771–0819), 125 rooms; AE, D, DC, MC, V; CP; *$$.*

Nightlife and the Arts

Check the *City Paper* (www.citypaper.com), a free weekly, for the most complete events listings. The Thursday *Baltimore Sun* (www.sunspot.net) and the monthly *Baltimore* magazine (www.baltimoremag.com) also have listings.

Nightlife

For blues and rock, head to the hip South Baltimore club the **Eight by Ten** (✉ 8 E. Cross St., ☎ 410/625–2000). Along the streets of the **Fells Point** waterfront you'll find bars and clubs with live performances of everything from Irish folk music to blues. The **Full Moon Saloon** (✉ 1710 Aliceanna St., ☎ 410/276–6388) features live blues seven nights a week in an intimate, neighborhood-style bar. East of the Inner Harbor, **Bohager's** (✉ 701 S. Eden St., ☎ 410/563–7220) attracts top local, regional, and, occasionally, national acts to its indoor and outdoor stages. Just north of the Inner Harbor, the **Havana Club** (✉ 600 Water St., ☎ 410/783–0033) is a busy, upscale cigar lounge; the music varies from swing to disco.

The Arts

The state theater of Maryland, **Center Stage** (✉ 700 N. Calvert St., ☎ 410/332–0033, WEB www.centerstage.org) presents old classics and the works of new playwrights. Opera, concerts, and recitals take place at **Friedberg Hall** (✉ Peabody Conservatory, E. Mt. Vernon Pl. and Charles St., ☎ 410/659–8124). **Lyric Opera House** (✉ 110. W Mount Royal Ave., ☎ 410/685–5086) hosts Broadways musicals and opera productions. **Joseph Meyerhoff Symphony Hall** (✉ 1212 Cathedral St.,

☎ 410/783–8000, WEB www.baltimoresympony.org) is home of the Baltimore Symphony Orchestra. **Morris A. Mechanic Theater** (✉ 25 Hopkins Plaza, ☎ 410/625–4230, WEB www.themechanic.org) is a stop for touring companies and pre-Broadway productions. Top pop, country, and jazz artists frequent the small waterfront venue **Pier Six Concert Pavilion** (✉ Pier 6 at Pratt St., ☎ 410/752–8632).

Spectator Sports

Baseball: Orioles (✉ Oriole Park at Camden Yards, Camden and Howard Sts., ☎ 410/685–9800). **Football: Ravens** (✉ Ravens Stadium, 1101 Russell St., ☎ 410/261–7283).

Shopping

Antique Row, in Mount Vernon on the 700 and 800 blocks of North Howard Street and the 200 block of West Read Street, has more than three dozen first-rate antiques shops. Small and quirky shops, restaurants, and cafés line **Charles Street,** north of the harbor. Old homes in **Fells Point** now house antiques shops, art galleries, and boutiques. The two waterfront pavilions of **Harborplace** (✉ 200 E. Pratt St., ☎ 410/332–4191) are home to many boutiques, souvenir shops, national chain stores, and restaurants. Across Pratt Street, the multilevel **Gallery** (✉ 200 E. Pratt St., ☎ 410/332–4191) has upscale shops and a food court. **Broadway Market** (✉ Broadway and Fleet Sts.) is a good spot to pick up foods for picnicking. **Cross Street Market** (✉ Light and Cross Sts.) has a terrific sushi bar and is convenient to the Inner Harbor and Federal Hill.

Baltimore Essentials

AIRPORTS AND TRANSFERS

Baltimore–Washington International Airport, 10 mi south of town, receives most major domestic and foreign carriers. Washington Dulles International Airport and Ronald Reagan Washington National Airport (☞ Washington, D.C., Essentials *in* Washington, D.C.) are a bit farther from Baltimore but sometimes have cheaper and direct flights.
➤ AIRPORT INFORMATION: **Baltimore–Washington International Airport** (✉ 7062 Friendship Rd., ☎ 410/859–7111, WEB www.bwiairport.com).

AIRPORT TRANSFER

Taxi fare from Baltimore's airport to downtown runs about $20. Amtrak and MARC trains run between the airport station (10 minutes from the terminal via free shuttle bus) and Penn Station, about 20 minutes away. BWI SuperShuttle has van service to downtown hotels for $20 round-trip and to most suburban hotels.
➤ TAXIS AND SHUTTLES: **BWI SuperShuttle** (☎ 410/859–0800). **MARC** (☎ 800/325–7245, WEB www.mtamaryland.com).

BUS TRAVEL TO AND FROM BALTIMORE

➤ BUS INFORMATION: **Greyhound** (✉ 210 W. Fayette St., ☎ 800/231–2222, WEB www.greyhound.com).

CAR TRAVEL

Baltimore is on I–95, the major East Coast artery.

TOURS

BUS TOURS

From spring through fall, Harbor City Tours offers 90-minute narrated minibus tours four times daily; cost of the tour is $12. You can board at Light and Conway streets and can get on and off at attractions.
➤ FEES AND SCHEDULES: **Baltimore Shuttle** (☎ 410/254–8687).

TRAIN TRAVEL

Amtrak serves Baltimore's Penn Station. Central Light Rail Line has service from Hunt Valley, north of the city, through downtown and south to Glen Burnie and BWI Airport. MARC trains travel between Baltimore and Washington, D.C.

➤ TRAIN INFORMATION: **Amtrak** (✉ Charles St. at Mt. Royal Ave., ☎ 800/872–7245, WEB www.amtrak.com). **Central Light Rail Line** (☎ 410/539–5000, WEB www.mtamaryland.com). **MARC** (☎ 800/325–7245, WEB www.mtamaryland.com).

TRANSPORTATION AROUND BALTIMORE

Most attractions are a walk or a short tour-bus ride from the Inner Harbor. Beyond that, a car is useful, as the metro line is limited and riding the bus often means transferring. Call Mass Transit Administration for information. Ed Kane's Water Taxi service stops at 16 sights, including the Inner Harbor, Fells Point, Canton, Fort McHenry, and the Baltimore Museum of Industry; a day pass costs $5.

➤ CONTACTS: **Ed Kane's Water Taxi** (☎ 410/563–3901 or 800/658–8947, WEB www.thewatertaxi.com). **Mass Transit Administration** (☎ 410/539–5000, WEB www.mtamaryland.com).

VISITOR INFORMATION

➤ TOURIST INFORMATION: **Baltimore Area Convention & Visitors Association** (✉ 301 E. Pratt St., 21202, ☎ 410/837–4636 or 800/282–6632, WEB www.baltimore.org).

MARYLAND'S CHESAPEAKE

Nature and nautical pursuits are the lure of the historic Chesapeake Bay region. Annapolis is a world yachting capital with a small-town feel. Across the soaring dual spans of the Bay Bridge is the Eastern Shore of the Delmarva Peninsula, where waterside towns, opulent country inns on former plantations, and seafood shacks make for a perfect getaway. On the Atlantic side of the peninsula is the resort of Ocean City.

Exploring Maryland's Chesapeake

Annapolis

Once briefly the capital of the United States, the state capital of Annapolis is home to the U.S. Naval Academy and has one of the finest collections of 18th- and 19th-century buildings in the country. Begin your visit on the waterfront. Sailboats dock right at the edge of **Market Square,** where there is a visitor information booth. Stop by the Market House for seafood and fresh fruits and vegetables. At **City Dock** look for the sidewalk plaque commemorating the arrival of Kunta Kinte, the African slave immortalized in Alex Haley's *Roots.*

At the **Museum Store and Historic Annapolis Foundation** (✉ 77 Main St., ☎ 410/268–5576, WEB www.annapolis.org; 🎫 free, tape rental $5) you can rent an audiocassette and let narrator Walter Cronkite be your guide on a walking tour of the Historic District.

The three-story redbrick **Hammond-Harwood House** (✉ 19 Maryland Ave., ☎ 410/269–1714; 🎫 $6) is the only verified full-scale example of the work of William Buckland, colonial America's most prominent architect. The grand Georgian **Chase-Lloyd House** (✉ 22 Maryland Ave., ☎ 410/263–2723; 🎫 $2) was built by Samuel Chase, lawyer and signer of the Declaration of Independence. In 1765, another signer of the Declaration of Independence and governor of Maryland built the 37-room redbrick **William Paca House and Garden** (✉ 186 Prince George St., ☎ 410/263–5553, WEB www.annapolis.org; 🎫 $8).

St. John's College (✉ 60 College Ave., ☎ 410/263–2371, WEB www.sjca.edu) is the third-oldest college in the country and alma mater of Francis Scott Key, who wrote America's national anthem.

★ The **Maryland State House** (✉ State Circle, ☎ 410/974–3400; 🎫 free) is the oldest state capitol in continuous legislative use and the only one that has housed the U.S. Congress. Charles Willson Peale's painting *Washington at the Battle of Yorktown* hangs inside. Free 30-minute tours take place daily at 11 and 3.

Begin a visit to the **United States Naval Academy** at the Armel-Leftwich Visitors Center (✉ 52 King George St., Gate 1, ☎ 410/263–6933, WEB www.usnavyonline.com; 🎫 free, tours $6) on the Academy's riverside campus. Towering over the grounds is the bronze-dome U.S. Naval Chapel, burial place of Revolutionary War hero John Paul ("I have not yet begun to fight!") Jones. Outdoors, full-dress parades of midshipmen are a stirring sight.

Southern Maryland

The less-traveled routes through Calvert, St. Mary's, and Queen Anne's counties have bay-side scenery, historic sites, romantic B&Bs, and great restaurants. Scavenge for sharks' teeth and Moicene-era fossils beneath 100-ft cliffs at **Calvert Cliffs State Park** (✉ Rte. 2/4, Lusby, ☎ 301/872–5688; 🎫 $2). The fossil sites are on a beach about a 2-mi walk from the park entrance. For a glimpse of the Eastern Shore on a clear day, try the observation deck at the **Calvert Cliffs Nuclear Power Plant** (✉ Rte. 2/4, Lusby, ☎ 410/495–4600, WEB www.calvertcliffs.com; 🎫 free). The **Battle Creek Cypress Swamp Sanctuary** (✉ Rte. 2/4 to Rte. 506, ☎ 410/535–5327; 🎫 free) is home to the northernmost naturally occurring strand of the ancient bald cypress tree in the United States.

At the tip of the peninsula where the Patuxent River meets the Chesapeake Bay, **Solomons** is popular among boaters and day-trippers for its laid-back feel. The **Calvert Marine Museum** (✉ Rte. 2/4 at Solomons Island Rd., ☎ 410/326–2042, WEB www.calvertmarinemuseum.com; 🎫 $5) exhibits fossils, boats from various eras, and a 19th-century lighthouse. The **Drum Point Lighthouse** (✉ 14200 Solomons Island Rd., ☎ 410/326–2042) is one of the last three 1883 "screwpile" lighthouses left on the Chesapeake Bay.

You'll find vintage aircraft and all sorts of failed flying contraptions like the improbable Goodyear "Inflatoplane" at the **Patuxent River Naval Air Museum** (✉ Rte. 235 and Pegg Rd., Lexington Park, ☎ 301/863–7418, WEB www.paxmuseum.com; 🎫 free).

Maryland's history began at **Historic St. Mary's City.** The first colonists, dispatched by Lord Baltimore, settled here in 1634. Until 1695, St. Mary's served as Maryland's capital. Reconstructions of the first State House and the supply ship that accompanied the settlers, along with a typical tobacco plantation, compose the living-history museum. The complex includes the Godiah Spray Plantation (✉ Rosecroft Rd., St. Mary's City, ☎ 240/895–4990, WEB www.smcm.edu/hsmc), which has demonstrations of planting, cooking, and building from 17th-century plantation life. ✉ *Rte. 5,* ☎ *240/895–4990 or 800/762–1634,* WEB *www.smcm.edu/hsmc.* 🎫 *$7.50. Closed Mon.–Tues. and Dec.–Feb.*

The **Dr. Samuel A. Mudd House** preserves the home of the doctor who had no idea that his patient, John Wilkes Booth, had recently assassinated president Abraham Lincoln. ✉ *Rte. 5 to Rte. 205, then right on Poplar Hill Rd. and right on Dr. Samuel A. Mudd Rd.,* ☎ *301/645–6870.* 🎫 *$3. Closed Dec.–Mar.*

The Eastern Shore

The Chesapeake Bay Bridge links Annapolis to the Eastern Shore, crossing the Chesapeake at **Kent Island,** the bay's largest island. Agents of Virginia's governor set up a trading post here in 1631, making Kent Maryland's first English settlement. Route 50 continues south past historic towns near the bay and then leads east to the Atlantic.

In **Chestertown,** boutiques, cafés, and ornate 18th-century homes line the wide brick sidewalks. In the affluent town of **Easton,** well-preserved buildings from colonial and Victorian times fill the charming downtown; visit the 17th-century Quaker meetinghouse, 18th-century courthouse, and restored Art Deco Avalon Theater.

St. Michaels, once a shipbuilding center, is now a fashionable destination on the Miles River. ★ The **Chesapeake Bay Maritime Museum** (✉ Navy Point, ☎ 410/745–2916, WEB www.cbmm.org; 🎫 $7.50) chronicles the history of the bay and its traditions in boatbuilding, commercial fishing, and navigation.

The **Oxford-Bellevue Ferry** (☎ 410/745–9023; 🎫 $5.50 1-way, $9 round-trip) has been running since 1683. Today it takes cars and pedestrians across the Tred Avon River from a spot 7 mi south of St. Michaels to the 17th-century town of Oxford. Few of the surviving buildings in **Oxford** date before the mid-1800s, but the bigger (and less charming) town of Cambridge, 15 mi to the southeast, has several from the 1700s. Many roads in the area have special bike lanes.

Southwest of Cambridge is the **Blackwater National Wildlife Refuge** (✉ Rte. 335 at Key Wallace Dr., ☎ 410/228–2677; 🎫 $3 per vehicle), with more than 22,000 acres of marsh, woods, waters, and open fields inhabited by Canada geese, ospreys, and bald eagles.

The marshland replicas at the 30,000-square-ft **Ward Museum of Wildfowl Art** (✉ 3416 Schumaker Pond, at Beaglin Park Dr., Salisbury, ☎ 410/742–4988, WEB www.wardmuseum.org; 🎫 $7) give visitors a sense of the wild. A highlight are the artful decoys. From May to October **Smith Island Cruises** (☎ 410/425–2771; 🎫 $20) leave from Crisfield's Somers Cove Marina for the 70-minute trip to Smith Island, which has been sustained by commercial fishing for more than three centuries.

Facing the Atlantic, **Ocean City** has 10 mi of white-sand beach and a flashy 27-block boardwalk. The Coastal Highway, with blocks of high-rise condos, runs down the center of town. Amusement parks dating back to the late 1800s entertain the more than 8 million vacationers who flock here every summer.

Dining and Lodging

The bay area's traditional seafood kitchens and crab houses are now joined by chic bistros and ethnic restaurants. Lodging reservations should be made up to a year in advance for the Annapolis sailboat and powerboat shows in October, the Naval Academy commencement in May, and Easton's Waterfowl Festival in November.

Annapolis

$$–$$$ ✕ **The Corinthian.** With cushioned armchairs, oil-lamp lighting, and a courtyard view, this formal hotel restaurant has the elegant feel of an old Maryland home. The crab cakes have an angel hair–pasta binder, and the New York strip has been aged three weeks. ✉ *Loews Annapolis Hotel, 126 West St.,* ☎ *410/263–7777. AE, D, DC, MC, V.*

$$–$$$ ✕ **Middleton Tavern.** Since 1750 this cozy inn by City Dock has been a popular place to eat and drink; former guests include George Washington, Thomas Jefferson, and Ben Franklin. The seafood is excellent, as are the pasta and southwestern dishes. Fireplaces blaze in all four dining rooms in winter; when it's warm, you can watch the harbor bustle from the tables out front. ✉ *2 Market Space,* ☎ *410/263–3323. AE, D, MC, V.*

$–$$$ ★ ✕ **McGarvey's Saloon and Oyster Bar.** This casual saloon and restaurant is a popular hangout. The kitchen serves standard American fare—burgers, steaks, seafood, and finger foods. ✉ *8 Market Space, at northeast corner of Market House,* ☎ *410/263–5700. AE, MC, V.*

$–$$ ✕ **Cantler's Riverside Inn.** Tucked off back roads outside Annapolis, this former watermen's bar is now a seafood house. Feast on crabs, clams, shrimp, and oysters in season on the screened waterfront deck or inside the casual dining room. ✉ *158 Forest Beach Rd.,* ☎ *410/757–1467. AE, D, DC, MC, V.*

$$$$ **Annapolis Marriott Waterfront.** The city's only waterfront hotel has rooms that face the water, the historic district, or—from private balconies—City Dock. Pusser's Landing is a casual restaurant with a Caribbean flair, Jamaican and English fare, and a waterside setting. ✉ *80 Compromise St., 21401,* ☎ *410/268–7555,* FAX *410/269–5864,* WEB *www.marriott.com. 150 rooms. Restaurant, gym. AE, D, DC, MC, V.*

$$$–$$$$ **Historic Inns of Annapolis.** Rooms at these three 18th-century inns are tastefully furnished in original and reproduction antiques and have the modern pluses of private baths, coffeemakers, and hair dryers. Guests can use a local health club. ✉ *58 State Cir., 21401,* ☎ *410/263–2641,* WEB *www.annapolisinns.com. 124 rooms. Restaurant. AE, D, DC, MC, V.*

$–$$$ **Gibson's Lodgings.** Three detached houses—two of them historic—stand together across the street from the United States Naval Academy. The inn has the character of a bed-and-breakfast; a Continental breakfast is served in a formal dining room. ✉ *110–114 Prince George St., 21401,* ☎ *410/268–5555,* FAX *410/268–2775,* WEB *www.avmcyber.com/gibson. 21 rooms. AE, MC, V. CP.*

Southern Maryland

$$–$$$$ ★ ✕ **Stoney's Seafood House.** This off-the-beaten-path restaurant, popular with sailors, is on Broomes Island overlooking Island Creek, which flows into the Patuxent River. There's ample seating—and a tiki bar—outside. Stoney's is worth the detour for its hefty crab cakes alone, made with plenty of back-fin meat and little filler. Oyster sandwiches and Stoney's Steamer make other good seafood choices. Homemade desserts are not for the faint-hearted. ✉ *Oyster House Rd., Broomes Island,* ☎ *410/586–1888. AE, MC, V. Closed Nov.–Mar.*

$–$$ ✕ **CD Café.** Overlooking the Patuxent River and the main road into Solomons, this cozy café describes itself as a coffeehouse with bistro flair. The limited menu has inventive dishes such as pan-seared chicken breast with pecans, apples, onions, and schnapps. The homemade desserts are spectacular. ✉ *14350 Solomons Island Rd., Solomons,* ☎ *410/326–3877. MC, V.*

$–$$$ **Back Creek Inn.** Rooms in this 19th-century wood-frame house have brass beds with colorful quilts and views of the water, a garden, or a quiet street. Explore the countryside on one of the inn's bicycles. ✉ *Calvert and Alexander Sts., Solomons 20688,* ☎ *410/326–2022,* WEB *www.bbonline.com/md/backcreek. 6 rooms, 1 cottage. MC, V.*

$–$$ ★ **Potomac View Farm Bed & Breakfast.** Construction of this white wood-frame "telescope" house (built in progressively smaller sections) began in 1830. It's emphatically a farmhouse, not a manor, and is furnished accordingly with handsome but simple oak furniture and decorative quilts. But rooms feature some elegant touches, such as 10-ft ceilings with crown moldings. The inn sits by the water on working farmland: 120 acres planted with corn and soybeans. The proprietors also operate the marina, from which guests may arrange charters. ✉ *Rte. 249, Tall Timbers 20690,* ☎ *301/994–2311. 6 rooms, 1 with bath; 1 cottage. Restaurant, pool. AE, MC, V. BP.*

The Eastern Shore

$$$ ★ ✕ **208 Talbot.** An antiques-filled late-19th-century house is the setting for regional cuisine: soft-shell crab in season, Maryland rockfish with wild mushrooms in an oyster-cream sauce, and fresh bay oysters with a champagne-cream sauce, prosciutto, and pistachio nuts. ✉ *208 N. Talbot St., St. Michaels,* ☎ *410/745–3838. D, MC, V.*

$$–$$$ ✕ **Crab Claw.** Bang-them-yourself steamed blue crabs are first rate at this harborside eatery. Spicy deep-fried hard crab is worth a try, too, as is the vegetable crab soup. ✉ *Navy Point, St. Michaels,* ☎ *410/745–2900. No credit cards. Closed Dec.–mid-Mar.*

$$–$$$ ✕ **The Hobbit.** Murals and carved lamps portray J. R. R. Tolkien characters in this Ocean City dining room with a two-angled view of Assawoman Bay. Try the veal with pistachios or the sautéed catch of the day. ✉ *101 81st St., Ocean City,* ☎ *410/524–8100. AE, D, MC, V.*

$$$–$$$$ ★ ✕🏨 **The Inn at Perry Cabin.** A nautical theme prevails throughout this luxurious resort, which underwent a $17 million renovation and expansion in 2002 by new owners Orient-Express Hotels. Frette linens, rich fabrics, and wall coverings accent the new and old rooms. The inn's famous waterfront locale remains the centerpiece of the landscaped 25-acre property. The formal dining room serves excellent seafood and international fare as part of its prix fixe ($70); the wine cellar's selection is stellar. ✉ *308 Watkins La., St. Michaels 21663,* ☎ *410/745–2200 or 800/722–2949,* WEB *www.perrycabin.orient-express.com. 81 rooms. Restaurant, pool, health club. AE, D, DC, MC, V.*

$$–$$$ ✕🏨 **Robert Morris Inn.** Conveniently located near the Oxford-Bellevue Ferry terminal, this friendly inn has efficiencies, river cottages, and simple bedrooms—some with bay windows, others with porches. The inn is known for its excellent food ($$–$$$$), especially the crab cakes. ✉ *314 N. Morris St. (Box 70, Oxford 21654),* ☎ *410/226–5111,* FAX *410/226–5744,* WEB *www.robertmorrisinn.com. 35 rooms. Restaurant. AE, MC, V. Restaurant and inn closed Jan.–Mar.*

$$$–$$$$ 🏨 **Inn on the Ocean.** A wraparound veranda affords sweeping views of the Atlantic, not to mention the crowds along the boardwalk—literally outside the front door. The small Victorian inn has a cozy living room with a working fireplace, to ease the chill in the winter. ✉ *1001 Atlantic Ave., Ocean City 21842,* ☎ *410/289–8894 or 888/226–6223,* WEB *www.innontheocean.com. 6 rooms. AE, D, MC, V. BP.*

$$$ 🏨 **Chesapeake Wood Duck Inn.** Stay at this intimate Victorian on Tilghman Island, a short drive from St. Michaels, and you're likely to avoid the summer crowds. Freshly baked muffins and great omelets make breakfast a treat. ✉ *Gibsontown Rd., Tilghman Island 21671,* ☎ *410/886–2070 or 800/956–2070,* WEB *www.woodduckinn.com. 7 rooms. AE, MC, V. BP*

$$–$$$ 🏨 **Coconut Malorie.** With its blue stone facade and palm trees, the Coconut Malorie is a Caribbean oasis amid the high-rises and condos along the Coastal Highway. Hawaiian art and eclectic pieces from around the globe accent the guest rooms. ✉ *200 59th St., Ocean City,* ☎ *410/723–6100 or 800/767–6060,* FAX *410/524–9327,* WEB *www.coconutmalorie.com. 108 rooms. Restaurant, pool. AE, D, DC, MC, V.*

$$–$$$ 🏨 **White Swan Tavern.** This 18th-century inn, in the heart of Chestertown, has formal guest rooms with canopy beds. The most requested room, the tavern's original kitchen, has a brick floor and a huge fireplace. Afternoon tea is a civilized pleasure. ✉ *231 High St., Chestertown 21620,* ☎ *410/778–2300,* WEB *www.chestertown.com/whiteswan. 6 rooms. MC, V. CP.*

Nightlife and the Arts

Nightlife

Annapolis bars are packed on the weekends; grab a beer at the **Ram's Head Tavern** (✉ 33 West St., Annapolis, ☎ 410/268–4545). Live jazz entertains at **King of France Tavern** (✉ 16 Church Circle, Annapolis, ☎ 410/269–0990). In St. Michaels, the **Town Dock** (✉ 125 Mulberry St., St. Michaels, ☎ 410/745–5577) has a piano lounge. In Solomons, the thatched **Tiki Bar** (✉ 1 Main St., Solomons, ☎ 410/326–4075) overflows with revelers on warm nights. Come sunset, Ocean City is lit with neon and hopping with nightlife, from big band to rock and roll. The **Purple Moose** (✉ 108 S. Boardwalk, Ocean City, ☎ 410/289–6953) plays classic rock for dancing every night, year-round for an over-thirty crowd. The huge **Bonfire Restaurant & Nightclub** (✉ 71st St. and Ocean Hwy., Ocean City, ☎ 410/524–7171) caters to thirties-and-over diners enjoying the live Top 40 music five days a week in summer. It's closed Monday–Thursday, mid-October–mid-March.

The Arts

In summer the **U.S. Naval Academy Band** performs at Annapolis's City Dock on Tuesday evenings. The **Annapolis Summer Garden Theater** (✉ 143 Compromise St., ☎ 410/268–0809, WEB www.summergarden.com) stages musicals and Shakespeare plays across from the City Dock. The city's principal theater group, **Colonial Players** (✉ 108 East St., Annapolis, ☎ 410/268–7373, WEB www.cplayers.com), has been active for more than 50 years. **Ocean City** sponsors free boardwalk concerts; call the Convention and Visitors Bureau (☎ 410/289–2800 or 800/626–2326, WEB www.ocean-city.com) for schedules.

Outdoor Activities and Sports

Southern Maryland beaches are mainly for strolling and fossil-collecting. **Sandy Point State Park** (✉ Rte. 50, 12 mi east of Annapolis) is a good area for fishing, swimming, or launching boats. Six miles south of Ocean City, the northern portion of **Assateague Island National Seashore** (☞ National and State Parks, *above*) is pristine; wild horses roam the beaches.

Biking

Viewtrail 100 is a 100-mi circuit in Worcester County, between Berlin and Pocomoke City on the Eastern Shore. In **Ocean City** the right-hand lanes of Coastal Highway are for buses and bikes. Several boardwalk shops rent bikes.

Fishing

The principal catches are rock fish, black drum, channel bass, flounder, bluefish, white perch, weakfish, croaker, trout, and largemouth bass. One-week licenses are sold at many sporting-goods stores. One-year licenses are available from the **Department of Natural Resources** (✉ Box 1869, Annapolis 21404, ☎ 410/260–8367, WEB www.dnr.state.md.us). Chesapeake Bay charters are available through **Solomons Boat Rental** (✉ Rte. 2 and Alexander St., Solomons, ☎ 410/326–4060, WEB www.somd.com/mp/boatrental), which rents powerboats for fishing, cruising, and waterskiing. The **OC Fishing & Sightseeing Pier** (✉ Wicomico St. at the ocean, Ocean City, ☎ 410/289–3454) offers rod rentals, bait and tackle for ocean pier fishing. **Bahia Marina** (✉ 22nd St. on the bay, Ocean City, ☎ 410/289–7438, WEB www.bahiamarina.com) maintains the largest small-boat rental fleet around; charters are available for bluefish, sharks, tuna, dolphin, and marlin.

Golf

Near several major highways, **Eisenhower Golf Course** (✉ Generals Hwy., Crownsville, northwest of Annapolis, ☎ 410/571–0973) is an 18-hole public golf course. Amid the picturesque woodlands and natural wetlands of the Eastern Shore, the **Bay Club** (✉ 9122 Libertytown Rd., Berlin, ☎ 410/641–4081), west of Ocean City, offers 36 holes in dual 18-hole courses. One of Ocean City's leading golf destinations since 1959, **Ocean City Golf and Yacht Club** (✉ 11401 Country Club Dr., Berlin, ☎ 410/641–1779) has 36 holes, including the 18-hole Newport Bay Course, with marsh and bay vistas.

Sailing

Annapolis Sailing School (✉ 601 6th St., Annapolis, ☎ 410/267–7205 or 800/638–9192) offers outfitting and instruction. **Sailing, Etc.** (✉ 46th St., Bayside, Ocean City, ☎ 410/723–1144) has a wide range of sailboats for rent. **Schooner Woodwind** (✉ 80 Compromise St., Annapolis, ☎ 410/263–7837) runs public and chartered cruises on a 74-ft yacht and rents sailboats and powerboats.

Shopping

Galleries, crafts shops, and stores line the streets of Annapolis, Chestertown, and St. Michaels. On the Eastern Shore, **Prime Outlets at Queenstown** (✉ Rte. 50, 10 mi east of the Bay Bridge) has more than 60 factory outlet stores. **Ocean City Factory Outlets** (✉ Rte. 50 and Golf Course Rd.) has about 40 national retail stores, including Ann Taylor, Bass, and Jones New York.

Maryland's Chesapeake Essentials

BUS TRAVEL

Maryland's Mass Transit Administration has express service on weekdays, and local service on weekends, between Annapolis and Baltimore. Greyhound has service between Baltimore, Annapolis, and some Eastern Shore towns, including Ocean City.

➤ Bus Information: **Greyhound** (✉ 308 Chinquapin Round Rd., Annapolis, ☎ 410/295–2975 or 800/231–2222). **Mass Transit Administration** (☎ 410/539–5000).

CAR TRAVEL

From Baltimore to Annapolis, follow Route 97 to U.S. 50 (Rowe Blvd. exit). From Annapolis to southern Maryland, take Route 2 south, which becomes Route 4 in Calvert County. From Baltimore or Annapolis to the Eastern Shore, cross the Bay Bridge ($2.50 toll eastbound only) northeast of Annapolis and stay on U.S. 50/301.

VISITOR INFORMATION

For information on Queen Anne's County, contact the Department of Business and Tourism in Chester. The Division of Travel and Tourism in Leonardtown has information on St. Mary's County, and the Talbot County Conference and Visitors Bureau has information on St. Michaels.

➤ Tourist Information: **Annapolis & Anne Arundel County Conference and Visitors Bureau** (✉ 26 West St., Annapolis 21401, ☎ 410/280–0445, WEB www.visit-annapolis.org). **Calvert County Department of Economic Development** (✉ 175 Main St., Prince Frederick 20678, ☎ 410/535–4583 or 800/331–9771, WEB www.co.cal.md.us/cced/tourism.htm). **Charles County Office of Tourism** (✉ Box 2150, LaPlata 20646, ☎ 800/766–3386, WEB www.explorecharlescomd.com). **Department of Business and Tourism** (✉ 425 Piney Narrows Rd., Chester 21619, ☎ 410/604–2100, WEB www.qac.org). **Dorchester County Tourism Department** (✉ 2 Rose Hill Pl., Cambridge 21613, ☎ 410/228–1000 or 800/522–8687, WEB www.tourdorchester.org). **Kent County Office of Tourism** (✉ 400 High St., Chestertown 21620, ☎

410/778–0416, WEB www.kentcounty.com). **Ocean City Convention and Visitors Bureau** (✉ 4001 Coastal Hwy., Ocean City 21842, ☎ 800/626–2326, WEB www.ocean-city.com). **St. Mary's County Division of Tourism** (✉ 23115 Leonard Hall Dr., Leonardtown 20650, ☎ 301/475–4411 or 800/327–9023, WEB www.saintmaryscountymd.com/decd). **Talbot County Office of Tourism** (✉ 11 N. Washington St., Easton 21601, ☎ 410/770–8000). **Wicomico County Tourism** (✉ Box 2333, Salisbury 21802, ☎ 410/548–4914, WEB www.wicomicotourism.org). **Worcester County Tourism** (✉ 113 Franklin St., Snow Hill 21863, ☎ 410/632–3110 or 800/852–0335, WEB www.visitworcester.com).

WESTERN MARYLAND

Civil War sights, scenic railroad trips, and the great outdoors are the main attractions of this region, which includes the Allegheny mountains, Appalachian trail, lakes, and rivers. Historic Frederick is Maryland's second-largest city, and Cumberland is a good base for bicycling along the C&O Canal towpath or hiking.

What to See and Do

The **National Museum of Civil War Medicine** (✉ 48 E. Patrick St., Frederick, ☎ 301/695–1864, WEB www.civilwarmed.org; 🎫 $6.50), with more than 3,000 medical artifacts, gives a chilling look at battlefield medical care. According to legend and poetry, an old woman defied Stonewall Jackson by waving the Stars and Stripes from what is now the **Barbara Fritchie House and Museum.** ✉ *154 W. Patrick St., Frederick,* ☎ *301/698–0630.* 🎫 *$2. Closed Dec.–Mar.*

Mount Olivet Cemetery (✉ 515 S. Market St., Frederick, ☎ 301/662–1164; 🎫 free) is the final resting place of some of Maryland's most famous citizens, including Barbara Fritchie and Francis Scott Key, writer of "The Star-Spangled Banner."

★ At **Antietam National Battlefield** (✉ Rte. 65, Sharpsburg, ☎ 301/432–5124, WEB www.nps.gov/anti; 🎫 $3) Union troops repelled Lee's invasion in 1862. At the annual Memorial Illumination, held the first Saturday in December, the glow of 23,100 candles—one for each of the battle's casualties—illuminates the battlefield.

The **Western Maryland Scenic Railroad** takes passengers on a vintage 1916 locomotive through mountains and a mile-long gorge to Frostburg. Train passengers get free entrance to the **Thrasher Carriage Museum** (✉ 19 Depot St., Frostburg, ☎ 301/689–3380, WEB www.cumberland.md.com/thrasher), which displays early 19th- and 20th-century horse-drawn carriages, such as Theodore Roosevelt's inaugural carriage. ✉ *13 Canal St., Cumberland,* ☎ *301/759–4400 or 800/872–4650,* WEB *www.wmsr.com.* 🎫 *Train and museum $19. Railroad and museum closed Jan.–Apr.*

Dining and Lodging

$–$$$ ✕ **Mealey's.** A short drive east of Frederick, this former hotel and stagecoach stop on the National Pike is a busy restaurant in Maryland's self-proclaimed antiques capital—New Market. A stone fireplace dominates a spacious, antiques-filled main dining room. Pasta, steak, and seafood are the specialties. ✉ *8 Main St., New Market,* ☎ *301/865–5488. AE, D, DC, MC, V. No lunch Mon.–Thurs.*

$$$–$$$$ ★ ✕🏨 **Stone Manor.** In the rolling farmland west of Frederick, this centuries-old manor remains a working 114-acre farm. The house has 10 working fireplaces, and antique reproductions fill individually decorated suites. A five-course prix-fixe dinner ($69) is served in the inn's three intimate dining rooms, each decorated with antiques and origi-

nal art. The contemporary American menu reflects the seasons, with greens and herbs from the chef's garden. Dinner favorites include New Zealand venison with sun-dried cherry sauce and braised rabbit on a Guinness Stout reduction. ✉ *5820 Carroll Boyer Rd., Middletown 21769,* ☎ *301/473–5454,* FAX *301/371–5622,* WEB *www.stonemanor.com. 6 suites. Restaurant. AE, MC, V. BP.*

$$–$$$ **Antietam Overlook Farm.** This 19th-century farmhouse overlooks Antietam National Battlefield. Each suite has a fireplace and screened porch with a tub. The inn serves evening cordials and a big breakfast. ✉ *Porterstown Rd., Keedysville 21756,* ☎ *301/432–4200 or 800/878–4241. 6 rooms. AE, D, MC, V. BP.*

$$–$$$ **Rocky Gap Lodge & Golf Resort.** In Rocky Gap State Park, this six-story contemporary lodge is in the center of an 18-hole tournament-grade golf course designed by Jack Nicklaus. ✉ *16701 Lakeview Rd. NE, Flintstone 21530,* ☎ *301/784–8400 or 800/724–0828,* FAX *301/784–8408,* WEB *www.rockygapresort.com. 218 rooms. 2 restaurants, pool, golf. AE, D, DC, MC, V.*

$–$$ **The Inn at Walnut Bottom.** Guest rooms at this cozy 19th-century row-house inn have antiques and reproduction 19th-century furnishings. ✉ *118 Greene St., Cumberland 21502,* ☎ *301/777–0003 or 800/286–9718,* FAX *301/777–8288,* WEB *www.iwbinfo.com. 12 rooms, 8 with bath. AE, D, MC, V. BP.*

Outdoor Activities and Sports

Deep Creek Lake State Park is in Garret County off of Route 219. Year-round recreation on the 3,900-acre lake includes boating, fishing, and waterskiing. The area is also good for bicycling, hiking, and downhill skiing. To ride the mountainous and forested trails in western Maryland, rent bikes at **High Mountain Sports** (✉ 21349 Garrett Hwy., Oakland, ☎ 301/387–4199, WEB www.highmountainsports.com).

Shopping

Head to the small shops of **New Market** and **Frederick** for antiques. **Prime Outlets at Hagerstown** (✉ 495 Prime Outlets Blvd., at I–70 and Rte. 65) has 76 brand-name outlet stores.

Western Maryland Essentials

CAR TRAVEL

From Baltimore I–70 runs westward through Frederick and up to the state's narrowest point, pinched between West Virginia and Pennsylvania. U.S. 40 passes through the Narrows into the Panhandle. From Hancock, I–68—the National Highway—is the quickest route to Cumberland, Deep Creek Lake, and several state parks and forests.

VISITOR INFORMATION

➤ TOURIST INFORMATION: **Allegany County Convention & Visitors Bureau** (✉ Western Maryland Station Center, 13 Canal St., Cumberland 21502, ☎ 301/777–5132, WEB www.mdmountainside.com). **Hagerstown/Washington County Convention and Visitors Bureau** (✉ 16 Public Sq., 21740, ☎ 301/791–3246 or 888/257–2600, WEB www.marylandmemories.org). **Tourism Council of Frederick County** (✉ 19 E. Church St., 21701, ☎ 301/228–2888 or 800/999–3613, WEB www.visitfrederick.org).

MASSACHUSETTS

Updated by Carolyn Heller

Capital	Boston
Population	6,118,000
Motto	By the Sword We Seek Peace, But Peace Only Under Liberty
State Bird	Chickadee
State Flower	Mayflower
Postal Abbreviation	MA

Statewide Visitor Information

Massachusetts Office of Travel and Tourism (✉ 10 Park Plaza, Suite 4510, Boston 02116, ☎ 617/973–8500; 800/227–6277; 800/447–6277 brochures; WEB www.massvacation.com).

Scenic Drives

Much of Cape Cod's **Route 6A,** from Sandwich to Orleans, is a National Historic District preserving traditional New England seacoast towns. **Routes 133 and 1A** on the North Shore, from Gloucester to Newburyport, cover some of the earliest settlements in the United States, dating to the 1630s. In the Berkshires, the **Mohawk Trail,** running 63 mi along Route 2 between Greenfield and North Adams, is famous for its fall foliage, which peaks in late September and early October. In the southwest, **Route 23** from Great Barrington to Westfield travels through wooded hills and rural towns.

National and State Parks

National Park

★ **Cape Cod National Seashore** (☞ Cape Cod and the Islands), a 30-mi stretch of dune-backed beach between Eastham and Provincetown, has excellent swimming, bird-watching, and nature-trail walking.

State Parks

The **Department of Environmental Management** (✉ Division of Forests and Parks, 251 Causeway St., Suite 600, Boston 02114, ☎ 617/626–1250, WEB www.massparks.org) has information on all state parks, including the Heritage state parks, which have exhibits on the state's industrial history.

Mt. Greylock State Reservation (✉ Rockwell Rd. off Rte. 7, Lanesborough, ☎ 413/499–4262 or 413/499–4263, WEB www.state.ma.us/dem/parks/mgry.htm) has the state's highest peak, Mt. Greylock, at 3,491 feet. **Nickerson State Park** (✉ 3488 Main St./Rte. 6A, ☎ 508/896–3491; 877/422–6762 camping reservations; WEB www.state.ma.us/dem/parks/nick.htm), on Cape Cod, has nearly 2,000 acres of forest with walking trails, trout-stocked ponds, and campsites. **Tolland State Forest** (✉ Rte. 8, Otis, ☎ 413/269–6002, WEB www.state.ma.us/dem/parks/toll.htm), in the Berkshires, has camping facilities and hiking trails.

BOSTON

New England's largest and most important city, and the cradle of American independence, Boston is more than 370 years old. Its most famous buildings are not merely civic landmarks but national icons; its greatest citizens—John Hancock, Paul Revere, and the Adamses—live at the crossroads of history and myth.

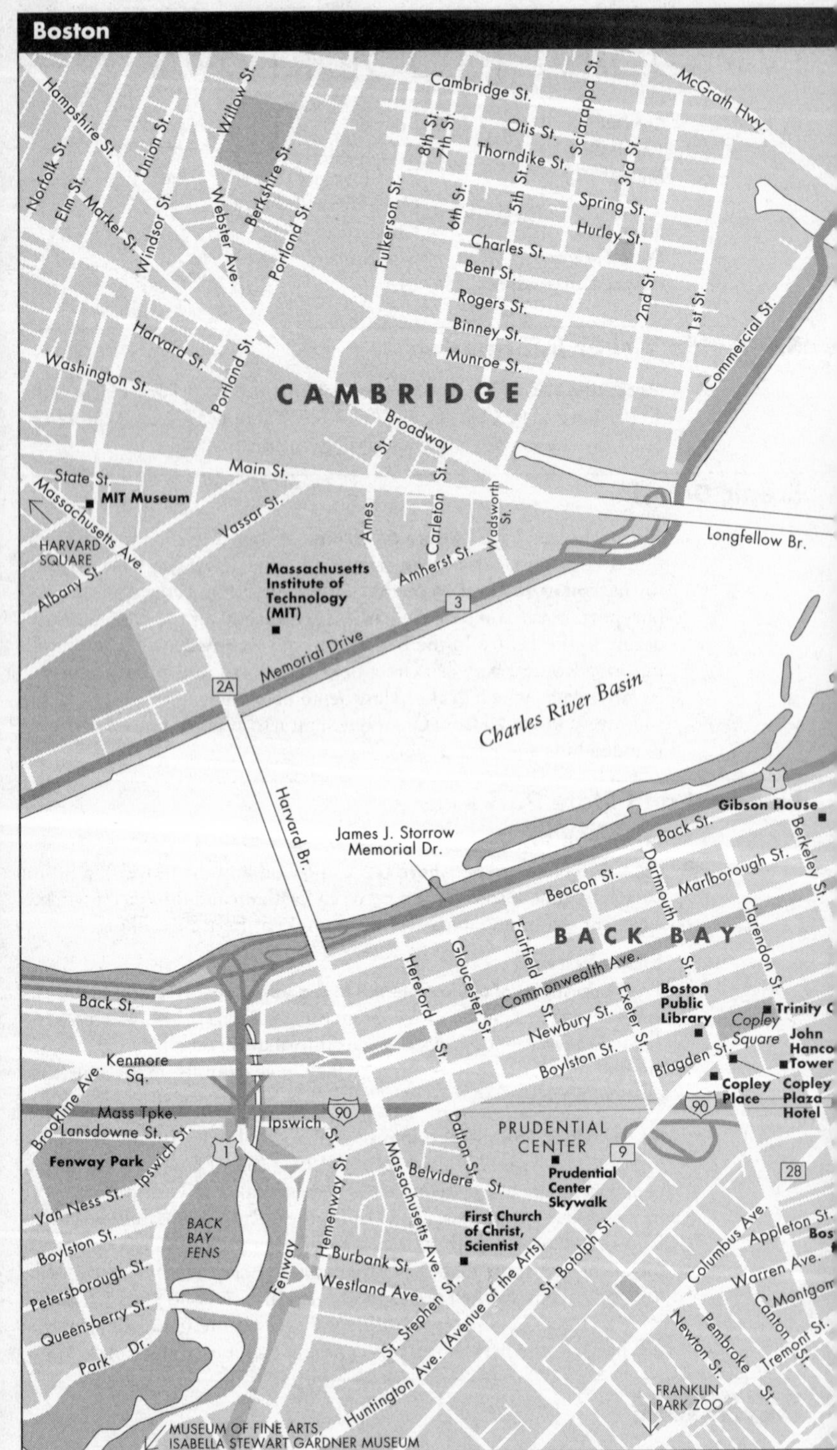
Cambridge St.
McGrath Hwy.
Otis St.
Thorndike St.
Spring St.
Hurley St.
Charles St.
Bent St.
Rogers St.
Binney St.
Munroe St.
Sciarappa St.
3rd St.
2nd St.
1st St.
8th St.
7th St.
6th St.
5th St.
Fulkerson St.
Commercial St.
Hampshire St.
Norfolk St.
Elm St.
Market St.
Union St.
Windsor St.
Willow St.
Webster Ave.
Berkshire St.
Portland St.
Harvard St.
Washington St.
CAMBRIDGE
Broadway
Ames St.
Carleton St.
Wadsworth St.
Main St.
State St.
MIT Museum
Massachusetts Ave.
Vassar St.
HARVARD SQUARE
Albany St.
Massachusetts Institute of Technology (MIT)
Amherst St.
Memorial Drive
Longfellow Br.
3
2A
Charles River Basin
Harvard Br.
1
Gibson House
James J. Storrow Memorial Dr.
Back St.
Berkeley St.
Dartmouth St.
Marlborough St.
Beacon St.
Clarendon St.
Fairfield St.
BACK BAY
Gloucester St.
Hereford St.
Commonwealth Ave.
Exeter St.
Boston Public Library
Trinity C
Copley Square
John Hanco
Tower
Newbury St.
Boylston St.
Blagden St.
Copley Place
Copley Plaza Hotel
Kenmore Sq.
Brookline Ave.
Mass Tpke.
Lansdowne St.
Ipswich St.
Ipswich
90
Dalton St.
PRUDENTIAL CENTER
9
28
Fenway Park
Hemenway St.
Massachusetts Ave.
Belvidere St.
Prudential Center Skywalk
Van Ness St.
BACK BAY FENS
First Church of Christ, Scientist
St. Botolph St.
Columbus Ave.
Appleton St.
Bos
Boylston St.
Burbank St.
Warren Ave.
Petersborough St.
Fenway
Westland Ave.
Montgom
Canton St.
Queensberry St.
St. Stephen St.
Huntington Ave. (Avenue of the Arts)
Pembroke St.
Newton St.
Tremont St.
Park Dr.
FRANKLIN PARK ZOO
MUSEUM OF FINE ARTS, ISABELLA STEWART GARDNER MUSEUM

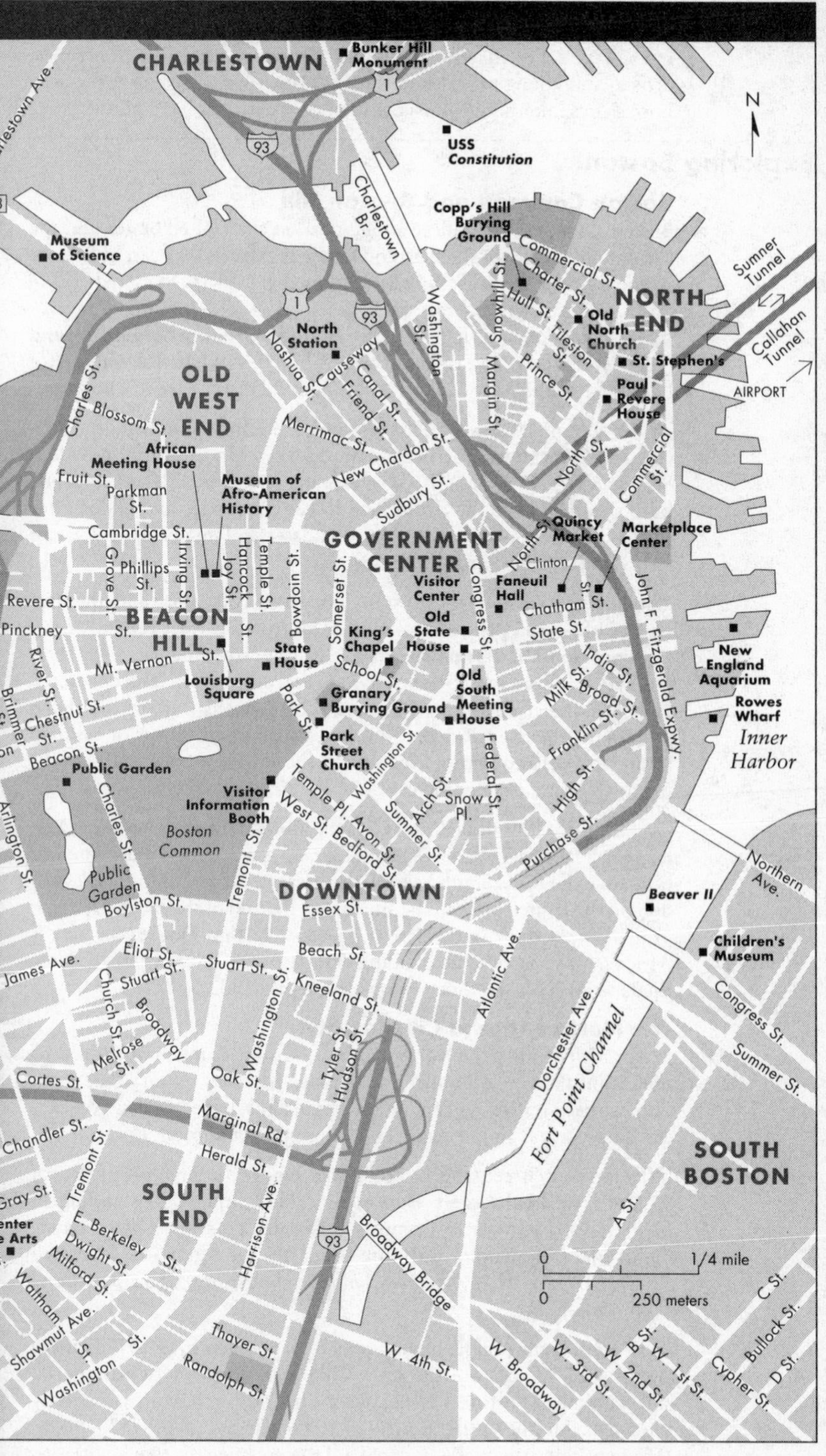
CHARLESTOWN
Bunker Hill Monument
USS Constitution
Museum of Science
Charlestown Br.
Copp's Hill Burying Ground
NORTH END
Old North Church
St. Stephen's
Paul Revere House
Sumner Tunnel
Callahan Tunnel
AIRPORT
North Station
OLD WEST END
African Meeting House
Museum of Afro-American History
GOVERNMENT CENTER
Visitor Center
Faneuil Hall
Quincy Market
Marketplace Center
BEACON HILL
State House
Louisburg Square
King's Chapel
Old State House
Old South Meeting House
Granary Burying Ground
Park Street Church
New England Aquarium
Rowes Wharf
Inner Harbor
Public Garden
Visitor Information Booth
Boston Common
DOWNTOWN
Beaver II
Children's Museum
Fort Point Channel
SOUTH BOSTON
SOUTH END
1/4 mile
250 meters
Charlestown Ave.
Commercial St.
Charter St.
Hull St.
Tileston St.
Prince St.
Snowhill St.
Margin St.
Washington St.
Nashua St.
Causeway
Canal St.
Friend St.
Merrimac St.
New Chardon St.
Sudbury St.
North St.
Charles St.
Blossom St.
Fruit St.
Parkman St.
Cambridge St.
Grove St.
Phillips St.
Irving St.
Hancock St.
Joy St.
Temple St.
Bowdoin St.
Somerset St.
Congress St.
Clinton St.
Chatham St.
State St.
John F. Fitzgerald Expwy.
Revere St.
Pinckney St.
Mt. Vernon St.
River St.
Brimmer St.
Chestnut St.
Beacon St.
School St.
Park St.
India St.
Milk St.
Broad St.
Franklin St.
Federal St.
High St.
Temple Pl.
West St.
Avon St.
Bedford St.
Summer St.
Arch St.
Snow Pl.
Purchase St.
Arlington St.
Tremont St.
Boylston St.
Essex St.
Northern Ave.
Eliot St.
James Ave.
Stuart St.
Church St.
Broadway
Beach St.
Kneeland St.
Atlantic Ave.
Dorchester Ave.
Congress St.
Summer St.
Melrose St.
Tyler St.
Hudson St.
Cortes St.
Oak St.
Marginal Rd.
Chandler St.
Herald St.
Gray St.
E. Berkeley St.
Dwight St.
Milford St.
Waltham St.
Shawmut Ave.
Washington St.
Harrison Ave.
Broadway Bridge
Thayer St.
Randolph St.
W. 4th St.
W. Broadway
W. 3rd St.
W. 2nd St.
B St.
W. 1st St.
A St.
C St.
Bullock St.
Cypher St.
D St.
93
1

Boston is also New England's center of high finance and high technology, a place of granite-and-glass towers rising along what were once rutted village lanes. Its enormous population of students, academics, artists, and young professionals makes the town a haven for the arts, bookstores, alternative music, and unconventional local politics.

Exploring Boston

Boston Common and Beacon Hill

★ **Boston Common,** the oldest public park in the United States and the site of festivals, political rallies, and family outings, is the heart of Boston. At the Congregationalist **Park Street Church** (✉ 1 Park St., ☎ 617/523–3383, WEB www.parkstreet.org.), finished in 1810, Samuel Smith's hymn "America" was first sung in 1831. The **Granary Burying Ground** (✉ Tremont St.), next to Park Street Church, is where Revolutionary heroes Samuel Adams, John Hancock, and Paul Revere are buried.

At the summit of Beacon Hill is Charles Bulfinch's magnificent neo-★ classical **State House** (✉ Beacon St. between Hancock and Bowdoin Sts., ☎ 617/727–3676, WEB www.state.ma.us/sec/trs; 🎫 free), its dome both sheathed in copper from Paul Revere's foundry and gilded after the Civil War. Tours are given on weekdays (call in advance); you can also visit on your own.

With its brick row houses, most built between 1800 and 1850, the clas-★ sic face of **Beacon Hill** is in a style never far from the early Federal norm. **Chestnut and Mt. Vernon streets** are distinguished not only for their individual houses but also for their general atmosphere and character. Henry James lived on Mt. Vernon, which opens out on **Louisburg Square,** the heart of Beacon Hill. Once the home address of William Dean Howells and Louisa May Alcott, the square was an 1840s model for town house development.

On the north slope of Beacon Hill is the **Museum of Afro-American History** (✉ 8 Smith Ct., ☎ 617/725–0022, WEB www.afroammuseum.org), housed in the **Abiel Smith School,** the first public school for black children in the United States. The site marks the end of the Black Heritage Trail®. Next door is the 1806 **African Meeting House,** the oldest African-American church building in the United States, where the New England Anti-Slavery Society was formed in 1832.

The North End and Charlestown

In the 17th century the **North End** *was* Boston, as much of the rest of the peninsula was still under water. Since the 20th century the North End has been Italian Boston, full of restaurants, bakeries, churches, social clubs, cafés, and festivals honoring saints and food.

Off Hanover Street, the North End's main thoroughfare is North Square. The **Paul Revere House,** the oldest home still standing in Boston, was built nearly a century before its illustrious tenant's midnight ride. Colonial-era furniture decorates the rooms. ✉ *19 North Sq.,* ☎ *617/523–2338,* WEB *www.paulreverehouse.org.* 🎫 *$2.50. Closed Mon. Jan.–Mar.*

Past North Square on Hanover Street is **St. Stephen's** (✉ 401 Hanover St., ☎ 617/523–1230), the only Charles Bulfinch–designed church still standing in Boston. The steeple of Christ Church, more commonly ★ known as the **Old North Church** (✉ 193 Salem St., ☎ 617/523–6676, WEB www.oldnorth.com)—where Paul Revere hung the two lanterns to signal Cambridge residents on the night of April 18, 1775—can be seen on Tileston Street. It's the oldest church building in Boston.

Cross the Charlestown Bridge to reach the ***USS Constitution,*** nicknamed "Old Ironsides" for the strength of its oaken hull, which seemed to repel cannon fire. Launched in 1797, it is the oldest commissioned ship in the U.S. Navy and is moored at the Charlestown Navy Yard. During its service against the Barbary pirates and in the War of 1812, the ship never lost an engagement. Nearby is the **Constitution Museum,** which tells the story of the ship with artifacts and hands-on exhibits. ✉ *Charleston Navy Yard, off Water St.,* ☎ *617/242–5670; 617/426–1812 museum;* WEB *www.ussconstitution.navy.mil or www.ussconstitutionmuseum.org.* 🎫 *Constitution free, museum free.*

★ The Battle of Bunker Hill was actually fought on Breed's Hill, and this is where Solomon Willard's **Bunker Hill Monument** (✉ Main St. to Monument St., then straight uphill, ☎ 617/242–5641; 🎫 free)—a 221-ft shaft of Quincy granite—stands. It rises from the spot where on June 17, 1775, a citizens' militia—reputedly commanded not to fire "until you see the whites of their eyes"—inflicted more than 1,100 casualties on British regulars (who eventually did seize the hill). The views from the top are worth the 294-step ascent.

Downtown Boston

Downtown is east of Boston Common. There is little logic to the streets here because they were once village lanes; they are now lined with 40-story office towers. The granite **King's Chapel** (✉ 58 Tremont St., at School St., ☎ 617/227–2155, WEB www.kings-chapel.org), built in 1754, houses Paul Revere's largest and—in his own judgment—sweetest-sounding bell.

The **Old South Meeting House** (✉ 310 Washington St., ☎ 617/482–6439, WEB www.oldsouthmeetinghouse.org; 🎫 $3), built in 1729, is Boston's second-oldest church. Many of the fiery town meetings that led to the Revolution were held here, including the one called by Samuel Adams concerning some dutiable tea that activists wanted returned to England.

A brightly gilded lion and unicorn, symbols of British imperial power, adorn the facade of the **Old State House** (✉ 206 Washington St., ☎ 617/720–3290, WEB www.bostonhistory.org; 🎫 $3). This was the seat of the colonial government from 1713 until the Revolution. The museum within the structure surveys Boston's revolutionary history. The site of the Boston Massacre is marked by a circle of stones in the traffic island in front of the building.

The **Children's Museum** (✉ 300 Congress St., ☎ 617/426–6500; 617/426–8855 recorded information, WEB www.bostonkids.org; 🎫 $7) contains hands-on exhibits, many designed to help children understand science, cultural diversity, and the nature of disabilities.

★ **Faneuil Hall** (✉ Faneuil Hall Sq., ☎ 617/338–2323; 🎫 free), erected in 1742 to serve as both a town meeting hall and a public market, is where in 1772 Samuel Adams first suggested that Massachusetts and the other colonies organize a Committee of Correspondence to maintain semiclandestine lines of communication in the face of hardening British repression. On the top floors are the headquarters and museum of the Ancient and Honorable Artillery Company of Massachusetts, the oldest militia in the nation (1638).

Quincy Market (✉ between Clinton and Chatham Sts., ☎ 617/338–2323, WEB www.faneuilhallmarketplace.com), near Faneuil Hall, has served as a retail and wholesale distribution center for meat and produce for more than 150 years. This pioneer effort at urban recycling now houses retail shops, restaurants, and offices. Some people consider it hopelessly commercial, but the 50,000 visitors who come here daily in the peak summer season seem to enjoy it. **Marketplace Center,** at the waterfront end of Quincy Market, is another complex that houses more shops, eateries, and boutiques.

The most glittering addition to Boston's waterfront can be found on **Rowes Wharf**—a 15-story redbrick Skidmore, Owings & Merrill extravaganza, gaily adorned with white trim and home to chic restaurants, shops, and the Boston Harbor Hotel (☞ Lodging).

Seals, penguins, a variety of sharks, and other sea creatures reside at the **New England Aquarium** (✉ Central Wharf, ☎ 617/973–5200, WEB www.neaq.org; $13), which has a four-story, 187,000-gallon coral reef tank. The glass-and-steel exterior of the West Wing mimics fish scales.

Until an August 2001 lightning strike caused a fire that sent it into storage, the ***Beaver II*** (✉ Congress St. Bridge, ☎ 617/269–7150, WEB www.bostonteapartyship.com), a faithful replica of a Boston Tea Party ship, like the ones forcibly boarded and unloaded on the night Boston Harbor itself became a teapot, bobbed in the Fort Point Channel at the Congress Street Bridge. The ship and museum expect to reopen in 2003.

Back Bay and the South End

Southwest of Boston Common is **Back Bay,** once a tidal flat that formed the south bank of a distended Charles River until it was filled as far as the Fens in the 19th century. Back Bay is a living museum of urban Victorian residential architecture. One of the first Back Bay residences (1859), the **Gibson House** (✉ 137 Beacon St., ☎ 617/267–6338, WEB www.thegibsonhouse.org; $5) has been preserved with all its Victorian fixtures and furniture intact.

Newbury Street, Boston's poshest shopping district, is lined with sidewalk cafés and dozens of upscale specialty shops selling clothing, china, antiques, and art.

Copley Square, where the Boston Marathon runners end their 26-mi race, is dominated by monumental architecture. The 1912 **Fairmont Copley Plaza Hotel** (✉ 138 St. James Ave.) is a stately bowfront structure. **Trinity Church** (✉ 206 Clarendon St., ☎ 617/536–0944, WEB www.trinitychurchboston.org) is Henry Hobson Richardson's Romanesque Revival masterwork of 1877. The **Boston Public Library** (✉ 700 Boylston St., ☎ 617/536–5400, WEB www.bpl.org) confirmed the status of McKim, Mead & White as apostles of Renaissance Revival in 1895. The modern complex **Copley Place** comprises two major hotels (the Westin and the Marriott; ☞ Lodging), dozens of shops and restaurants, and a cinema.

The headquarters of the **First Church of Christ, Scientist** (✉ 175 Huntington Ave., at Massachusetts Ave., ☎ 617/450–3790, WEB www.tfccs.com) is a striking mixture of old and new architecture. Mary Baker Eddy's original church structure (1894) and the domed Renaissance basilica added to the site in 1906 are now surrounded by the offices of the *Christian Science Monitor* and by I. M. Pei's 1973 complex of church administration buildings with its distinctive reflecting pool. Tours of the church are available every day except Saturday. Overlooking the Christian Science Church, the **Prudential Center Skywalk** (✉ 800 Boylston St., ☎ 617/859–0648; $7) is a 50th-floor observatory with great views of the city and suburbs.

The **South End,** eclipsed by the Back Bay more than a century ago, has now been gentrified, with galleries and restaurants catering to young professionals, including a large concentration of Boston's gay population. The houses here continue the pattern established on Beacon Hill (in a uniformly bowfront style) but have more florid decoration.

The South End has a strong Latino and African-American presence, particularly along Columbus Avenue and Massachusetts Avenue, which marks the beginning of the Roxbury neighborhood. The early integration of the South End set the stage for its transformation into a remarkably polyglot population.

On Tremont Street you'll find blocks of trendy restaurants and the **Boston Center for the Arts** (✉ 539 Tremont St., ☎ 617/426–5000, WEB www.bcaonline.org; 🎟 free), which has a gallery, several small theaters, and the "Cyclorama," a large space now devoted to antiques shows, exhibits, and other events.

The Fens

The **Fens,** a park designed by Frederick Law Olmsted, consists of still, irregular, and reed-bound pools surrounded by broad meadows, trees, and flower gardens.

★ The **Museum of Fine Arts** (✉ 465 Huntington Ave., ☎ 617/267–9300, WEB www.mfa.org; 🎟 $14) has holdings of American art surpassing those of all but two or three other U.S. museums; an extensive collection of Asian art; and European artwork from the 11th century through the present. Count on staying a while to have *any* hope of seeing even a smidgen of what is here. The museum has two restaurants, a cafeteria, and a popular gift shop.

★ The **Isabella Stewart Gardner Museum** is a monument to one woman's taste. The emphasis among the 2,000 spectacular paintings, sculptures, furniture, and textiles is on Italian Renaissance and 17th-century Dutch masters. Friend to John Singer Sargent, Edith Wharton, and Henry James, Gardner shocked proper Bostonians with the flamboyance of her Venetian-style palazzo. The highlight of the collection—and according to some scholars, the greatest painting in an American museum—is Titian's *Rape of Europa.* At the center of the building is a soaring courtyard planted with flowers. *✉ 280 The Fenway, ☎ 617/566–1401, WEB www.gardnermuseum.org. 🎟 $10 ($11 weekends). Closed Mon. except for some holidays.*

The Boston shrine known as **Fenway Park** (✉ 4 Yawkey Way, ☎ 617/267–8661; 617/267–1700 for tickets, WEB boston.redsox.mlb.com) is one of the smallest and oldest baseball parks in the major leagues. It was built in 1912 and still has real grass on the field. **Kenmore Square** (✉ Commonwealth Ave., Brookline Ave., and Beacon St. intersection) is home to fast-food parlors, alternative-rock clubs, an abundance of students from nearby Boston University, and the enormous neon CITGO sign, an area landmark.

Cambridge

In 1636 the country's first college was established in Cambridge, across the Charles River from Boston. Three years later it was named in honor of John Harvard, a young Charlestown clergyman who had died, leaving the college his entire library and half his estate. **Harvard** was the only college in the American colonies until 1693. The **Harvard University Events and Information Center** (✉ 1350 Massachusetts Ave., ☎ 617/495–1573), in Holyoke Center, provides area maps and conducts a free one-hour tour of Harvard Yard most days. Near the Cambridge Common is **Radcliffe Institute for Advanced Study** (✉ 10 Garden St., ☎ 617/495–8601, WEB www.radcliffe.edu), founded in 1897 as Radcliffe College; since 1975 Radcliffe students have shared classes and degrees with Harvard students.

Harvard University has three celebrated art museums, each a treasure in itself. A $5 admission price covers all three museums. The **Fogg Art Museum** (✉ 32 Quincy St., ☎ 617/495–9400, WEB www.artmuseums.harvard.edu) is the most famous of the Harvard museums. Founded in 1895, it now owns 80,000 works of art from every major period and from every corner of the world. Its focus is primarily on European and American art from the 14th century to the present. The museum's most significant works are a Van Gogh self-portrait and Edgar Degas's ballet-theme painting *The Rehearsal*. In Werner Otto Hall the **Busch-Reisinger Museum,** which is entered through the Fogg Art Museum, has a collection that specializes in Germanic and Central and Northern European art from the 16th century to the present. Across the street from the Fogg, the **Arthur M. Sackler Museum** (✉ 485 Broadway, ☎ 617/495–9400) concentrates on ancient Greek and Roman, Egyptian, Islamic, Chinese, and other Eastern art.

The **Massachusetts Institute of Technology (MIT),** which borders the Charles River southeast of Harvard Square, has not only distinctive architecture by I. M. Pei and Eero Saarinen but a stellar worldwide academic reputation. The **Information Center** (✉ 77 Massachusetts Ave., Bldg. 7, ☎ 617/253–4795, WEB web.mit.edu) gives free tours of the MIT campus weekdays at 10 and 2. Art and science meet in the **MIT Museum** (✉ 265 Massachusetts Ave., ☎ 617/253–4444, WEB web.mit.edu/museum; 🎟 $5), which showcases scientific instruments and memorabilia. Of special interest are the museum's alluring collection of holograms and stop-motion photography.

Parks, Gardens, and Zoos

★ The **Boston Public Garden,** next to Boston Common, is the oldest botanical garden in the United States. Its pond has been famous since 1877 for its pedal-powered Swan Boats, which you can use for a leisurely cruise during the warm months of the year. The **Franklin Park Zoo** (✉ 1 Franklin Park Rd., ☎ 617/541–5466, WEB www.zoonewengland.com; 🎟 $9.50) includes lions and cheetahs in its roster of exotic animals.

Dining

$$$$ ✕ **L'Espalier.** An elegantly modernized Victorian Back Bay town house is the setting for an intoxicating blend of new French and contemporary New England cuisine. You can simplify the opulent menu by choosing a prix-fixe tasting menu, such as the innovative vegetarian degustation. ✉ *30 Gloucester St.,* ☎ *617/262–3023. Reservations essential. Jacket and tie. AE, D, DC, MC, V. Closed Sun. No lunch.*

$$$–$$$$ ★ ✕ **Biba.** The menu at one of Boston's best restaurants encourages inventive combinations, unusual cuts of meat and produce, haute comfort food, and big desserts. Take your time, and indulge in "classic lobster pizza," or challenge your palate with vanilla chicken with chestnut puree. Try to finagle a seat near the windows for a terrific view of the Public Garden. ✉ *272 Boylston St.,* ☎ *617/426–7878. Reservations essential. AE, D, DC, MC, V.*

$$–$$$$ ★ ✕ **Mamma Maria.** One of the most elegant and romantic restaurants in the North End, Boston's remarkable Little Italy, Mamma Maria sneaks in a lot of serious cuisine, like the smoked-seafood ravioli appetizer, among the homemade pasta entrées you might expect. ✉ *3 North Sq.,* ☎ *617/523–0077. AE, D, DC, MC, V. No lunch.*

$$–$$$ ★ ✕ **Les Zygomates.** This restaurant serves up classic French bistro fare that dares to be simple and simply delicious. Prix-fixe menus are offered for both lunch and dinner. Choices might include oysters by the half dozen or pancetta-wrapped venison with roasted pears. ✉ *129*

South St., ☏ 617/542–5108. Reservations essential. AE, D, DC, MC, V. Closed Sun. No lunch Sat.

$$–$$$ ✕ **Union Oyster House.** At Boston's oldest continuing restaurant (it was established in 1826), it's best to have what Daniel Webster had—oysters on the half shell at the ground-floor raw bar, which is the oldest part of the restaurant and still the best. The rooms at the top of the narrow staircase are very Ye Olde New England. Uncomfortably small tables and chairs tend to undermine the simple, decent, but expensive food. ✉ *41 Union St., ☏ 617/227–2750. AE, D, DC, MC, V.*

$–$$$ ✕ **Legal Sea Foods.** The hallmark here is top-quality seafood, whether you have it wood-grilled or accompanied by an Asia-inspired sauce. The smoked bluefish pâté is a fine appetizer, and don't miss the chowders. ✉ *26 Park Sq., ☏ 617/426–4444;* ✉ *255 State St., ☏ 617/227–3115;* ✉ *Cambridge: 5 Cambridge Center, ☏ 617/864–3400;* ✉ *Logan Airport: Terminal C, ☏ 617/569–4622. Reservations not accepted. AE, D, DC, MC, V.*

$–$$ ✕ **Mr. and Mrs. Bartley's Burger Cottage.** It may be perfect cuisine for the student metabolism: a huge variety of variously garnished thick burgers, french fries, and onion rings—even a competent veggie burger. The nonalcoholic "raspberry lime rickey," made with fresh limes, raspberry juice, sweetener, and soda water, is the must-try drink. Tiny tables in a crowded space make it a convenient place for Phi Beta eavesdropping. ✉ *1246 Massachusetts Ave., Cambridge, ☏ 617/354–6559. Reservations not accepted. No credit cards. Closed Sun.*

Lodging

Many of the city's most costly lodgings have attractively priced weekend packages. Consult the *Boston Travel Planner* (☞ Visitor Information) for current rates. Bed-and-breakfasts can be a less-expensive alternative.

$$$$ ★ **Boston Harbor Hotel at Rowes Wharf.** Everything here is done on a grand scale, starting with the dramatic entrance through an 80-ft archway. Guest rooms—with marble bathrooms, fresh flowers, and custom-made desks—have city or water views. Call ahead for driving directions, as the hotel is near the heart of the Big Dig construction and road closings are common. ✉ *70 Rowes Wharf, 02110, ☏ 617/439–7000 or 800/752–7077, FAX 617/330–9450, WEB www.bhh.com. 230 rooms. 2 restaurants, pool, health club. AE, D, DC, MC, V.*

$$$$ ★ **Eliot Hotel.** The luxurious suites at the Eliot have Italian marble bathrooms, two cable-equipped televisions, and tasteful pastel-hue decor. The airy restaurant, Clio, has been garnering rave reviews for its serene ambience and contemporary French-American cuisine. The Eliot is steps from Newbury Street and a short walk to Kenmore Square. ✉ *370 Commonwealth Ave., 02215, ☏ 617/267–1607 or 800/443–5468, FAX 617/536–9114, WEB www.eliothotel.com. 95 suites. Restaurant. AE, D, DC, MC, V.*

$$$$ ★ **Fairmont Copley Plaza.** The public spaces of this 1912 landmark are grand, with high gilded and painted ceilings, mosaic floors, marble pillars, and crystal chandeliers; guest rooms have antique and repro-antique furniture, elegant marble bathrooms, and fax machines. ✉ *138 St. James Ave., 02116, ☏ 617/267–5300 or 800/441–1414, FAX 617/375–9648, WEB www.fairmont.com. 379 rooms. 2 restaurants. AE, D, DC, MC, V.*

$$$$ ★ **Four Seasons.** The Four Seasons is famed for luxurious personal service of the sort demanded by celebrities and heads of state. It has huge rooms with king-size beds and artwork. The Aujourd'hui restaurant is one of Boston's best, and the Bristol Lounge serves afternoon tea daily. ✉ *200 Boylston St., 02116, ☏ 617/338–4400 or 800/332–*

3442, FAX *617/423–0154,* WEB *www.fourseasons.com. 274 rooms. 2 restaurants, pool, health club. AE, D, DC, MC, V.*

$$$–$$$$ **A Cambridge House Bed and Breakfast.** This Greek Revival B&B is a haven of peace and otherworldliness, with richly carved cherry paneling, a grand cherry fireplace, elegant Victorian antiques, and polished wood floors overlaid with Oriental rugs. Harvard Square is a distant walk, but public transportation is nearby. ✉ *2218 Massachusetts Ave., Cambridge 02140,* ☎ *617/491–6300 or 800/232–9989,* FAX *617/868–2848,* WEB *www.acambridgehouse.com. 15 rooms. AE, D, MC, V. No smoking. BP.*

$$–$$$ **Chandler Inn.** This cozy basic hotel with its friendly staff is one of the best bargains in the city. At the end of one of the South End's prettiest streets, it's an easy walk to the T, the Amtrak station, Newbury Street's boutiques, or any of Tremont Street's trendy restaurants. Rooms are small but comfortable. ✉ *26 Chandler St., 02115,* ☎ *617/482–3450,* FAX *617/542–3428,* WEB *www.chandlerinn.com. 56 rooms. AE, D, DC, MC, V. CP.*

$–$$$ **John Jeffries House.** This turn-of-the-20th-century house has small rooms with triple-glazed windows that block virtually all noise from busy Charles Circle. Most rooms have kitchenettes, and many have views of the Charles River. At the foot of Beacon Hill, the inn is an easy walk from public transportation and most of downtown. ✉ *14 David G. Mugar Way, 02114,* ☎ *617/367–1866,* FAX *617/742–0313. 46 rooms. AE, D, DC, MC, V. CP.*

Motels

Holiday Inn Boston Airport (✉ 225 McClellan Hwy. 02128, ☎ 617/569–5250 or 800/798–5849, FAX 617/569–5159, WEB www.holiday-inn.com), 356 rooms; restaurant, pool, gym; *$$–$$$.*

Cambridge Gateway Inn (✉ 211 Concord Tpke., Cambridge 02140, ☎ 617/661–7800 or 866/427–6660, FAX 617/868–8153), WEB www.cambridgegatewayinn.com; 78 rooms; CP; *$–$$.*

Nightlife and the Arts

The *Boston Globe* calendar and the weekly *Boston Phoenix*, both published on Thursday, provide listings of events for the coming week. Also see the *Globe*'s Sunday "Arts" section and *Boston* magazine's arts listings.

Nightlife

Faneuil Hall Marketplace and **Kenmore Square** in Boston and **Harvard and Central squares** in Cambridge are centers of nightlife.

BARS AND LOUNGES

Bay Tower Room (✉ 60 State St., ☎ 617/723–1666) hosts piano music Wednesday–Saturday and dancing Friday and Saturday; dress up. The **Black Rose** (✉ 160 State St., ☎ 617/742–2286) is a popular Irish pub, complete with live Celtic music. **Boston Beer Works** (✉ 61 Brookline Ave., ☎ 617/536–2337; ✉ 112 Canal St., ☎ 617/896–2337) brews up regular and seasonal brews for a youngish crowd. **Bull & Finch Pub** (✉ 84 Beacon St., at Hampshire House, ☎ 617/227–9605) was the inspiration for the TV series *Cheers*. **John Harvard's Brew House** (✉ 33 Dunster St., ☎ 617/868–3585) serves up ales, lagers, pilsners, and stouts brewed on the premises.

CAFÉS AND COFFEEHOUSES

Caffé Vittoria (✉ 296 Hanover St., ☎ 617/227–7606) is a great after-dinner stop for coffee and desserts such as tiramisu and cannoli. **Tealuxe** (✉ Zero Brattle St., Cambridge, ☎ 617/441–0077) is a tiny "tea bar" with more than 100 different blends. **1369 Coffee House** (✉

757 Massachusetts Ave., Cambridge, ☎ 617/576–4600; ✉ 1369 Cambridge St., Cambridge, ☎ 617/576–1369) is a bohemian coffee house that also serves soups, salads, sandwiches, and pastries.

COMEDY

Comedy Connection (✉ Faneuil Hall Marketplace, ☎ 617/248–9700) books local and nationally known acts. **Dick Doherty's Comedy Vault** (✉ 124 Boylston St., ☎ 617/482–0110) showcases stand-up, improv, and open-mike comedy. **Nick's Comedy Stop** (✉ 100 Warrenton St., ☎ 617/482–0930) presents local comics Thursday–Saturday nights.

DANCE CLUBS

Axis (✉ 13 Lansdowne St., ☎ 617/262–2424) has high-energy dancing for more than 1,000 people; "X Nights" star DJs from alternative radio station WFNX. **Man Ray** (✉ 21 Brookline St., Cambridge, ☎ 617/864–0400) is the home of Boston's goth and alternative scenes, with Friday Fetish nights. **Roxy** (✉ 279 Tremont St., ☎ 617/338–7699), Boston's biggest nightclub, has theme nights ranging from reggae to Latin to swing.

MUSIC

Avalon (✉ 15 Lansdowne St., ☎ 617/262–2424) hosts concerts by alternative, rock, and dance acts, then turns into a dance club. Themes include Euro Night, Top 40, and techno. **Club Passim** (✉ 47 Palmer St., Cambridge, ☎ 617/492–7679) hosts folk music. **House of Blues** (✉ 96 Winthrop St., Cambridge, ☎ 617/491–2583) stages lives blues nightly and a gospel brunch on Sunday. **Middle East Café** (✉ 472 Massachusetts Ave., Cambridge, ☎ 617/497–0576) host live rock and other acts. **Regattabar** (✉ Charles Hotel, One Bennett St., Cambridge, ☎ 617/864–1200; 617/876–7777 tickets) headlines top names in jazz.

The Arts

BosTix (✉ Faneuil Hall Marketplace and Copley Sq., near corner of Boylston and Dartmouth Sts., ☎ 617/482–2849) sells half-price tickets for same-day performances and full-price advance tickets. **NEXT Ticketing** (☎ 617/423–6398, WEB www.nextticketing.com), a Boston-based outlet, handles tickets for many area theaters and nightclubs. With major credit cards, you can charge tickets for many events by phone or online through **Ticketmaster** (☎ 617/931–2000, WEB www.ticketmaster.com).

DANCE

Boston Ballet (✉ 19 Clarendon St., ☎ 617/695–6950), the city's premier dance company, performs at the Wang Center. **Dance Complex** (✉ 536 Massachusetts Ave., Cambridge, ☎ 617/547–9363) presents varied dance styles by local and visiting choreographers in its own studios and other venues. **José Mateo's Ballet Theatre** (✉ 400 Harvard St., Cambridge, ☎ 617/354–7467), a contemporary repertory company, performs primarily in its Harvard Square facility.

MUSIC

Berklee Performance Center (✉ 136 Massachusetts Ave., ☎ 617/266–1400; 617/266–7455 recorded information) is best known for jazz programs. **Jordan Hall at the New England Conservatory** (✉ 30 Gainsborough St., ☎ 617/536–2412) is home to the Boston Philharmonic. **Symphony Hall** (✉ 301 Massachusetts Ave., ☎ 617/266–1492 or 800/274–8499), renowned for its acoustics, is home to the Boston Symphony Orchestra and the Boston Pops.

OPERA

The **Boston Lyric Opera Company** (✉ Shubert Theatre, 265 Tremont St., ☎ 617/542–6772 or 800/447–7400) presents several productions each season.

THEATER

The **Boston Center for the Arts** (✉ 539 Tremont St., ☎ 617/426–7700) houses several quirky, low-budget troupes. **Charles Playhouse** (✉ 74 Warrenton St.) presents two long-running shows: the avant-garde *Blue Man Group* (☎ 617/426–6912) and *Shear Madness* (☎ 617/426–5225), an audience-participation whodunit. The **Colonial Theatre** (✉ 106 Boylston St., ☎ 617/426–9366) hosts major visiting theater productions. **Emerson Majestic Theatre** (✉ 219 Tremont St., ☎ 617/824–8000) hosts everything from dance to drama to classical concerts. The **Huntington Theatre Company** (✉ 264 Huntington Ave., ☎ 617/266–0800), a professional theater company affiliated with Boston University, performs a mix of classic and contemporary plays. **Loeb Drama Center** (✉ 64 Brattle St., Cambridge, ☎ 617/495–2668) is home to the American Repertory Theater, which showcases classic and experimental works. **Wang Center for the Performing Arts** (✉ 270 Tremont St., ☎ 617/482–9393, WEB www.wangcenter.org) stages large-scale productions, such as the Boston Ballet season.

Outdoor Activities and Sports

The **Dr. Paul Dudley White Bikeway,** approximately 18 mi long, follows both banks of the Charles River as it winds from Watertown Square to the Museum of Science.

Baseball: Boston Red Sox (✉ Fenway Park, 4 Yawkey Way, ☎ 617/267–1700, WEB boston.redsox.mlb.com). **Basketball: Boston Celtics** (✉ FleetCenter, Causeway St. at Haverhill St., ☎ 617/624–1000; 617/931–2222 tickets, WEB www.nba.com/celtics). **Football: New England Patriots** (✉ CMGI Field, 45 mins south of Boston, Foxborough, ☎ 800/543–1776, WEB www.patriots.com). **Hockey: Boston Bruins** (✉ FleetCenter, Causeway St. at Haverhill St., ☎ 617/624–1000; 617/931–2222 tickets, WEB www.bostonbruins.com).

Shopping

Most Boston stores are in the area bounded by Quincy Market, the Back Bay, downtown, and Copley Square. Although locals complain about the many chain stores, Boston's strength remains its idiosyncratic boutiques, handicrafts shops, and art and crafts galleries. Boston's two daily newspapers, the *Globe* and the *Herald,* are the best places to learn about sales.

Shopping Districts

Charles Street on Beacon Hill is a mecca for antiques lovers. **Copley Place** (✉ 100 Huntington Ave., ☎ 617/369–5000), an indoor shopping mall connecting two hotels in Back Bay, has stores, restaurants, and cinemas that blend the elegant, the glitzy, and the overpriced. **Downtown Crossing,** between Summer and Washington streets, is a pedestrian mall with outdoor food and merchandise kiosks, street performers, and benches. **Faneuil Hall Marketplace** (☎ 617/338–2323) has crowds, chain stores, kiosks of every description, and one of the area's great food experiences, Quincy Market. **Harvard Square,** in Cambridge, is a book lover's paradise. On **Newbury Street** in the Back Bay, the funky and the trendy give way to the chic and the expensive.The gentrified **South End** has become a retailing force, specializing in offbeat home furnishings and gift shops.

Department Stores

Filene's (✉ 426 Washington St., ☎ 617/357–2100; ✉ CambridgeSide Galleria, ☎ 617/621–3800) carries name-brand men's and women's clothing. **Filene's Basement** (✉ 426 Washington St., ☎ 617/542–

2011) pioneered the idea of discounting; it reduces prices according to the number of days items have been on the rack.

Specialty Stores

Flat of the Hill (✉ 60 Charles St., ☎ 617/619–9977) has something for everyone on your list—with seasonal items, gourmet foods, hard-to-find toiletries, dolls, toys, pillows, and pet products. **Louis Boston** (✉ 234 Berkeley St., ☎ 617/262–6100) carries elegantly tailored designs and subtly updated classics. South American culture is represented by the boldly colored textiles and hand-painted tchotchkes at **Mayan Weavers** (✉ 268 Newbury St., ☎ 617/262–4342). **Shreve, Crump & Low** (✉ 330 Boylston St., ☎ 617/267–9100) is an old, well-respected store that carries the finest in jewelry, china, crystal, and silver.

Side Trip to Lexington and Concord

The events of April 19, 1775—the first military encounters of the American Revolution—are very much a part of present-day Lexington and Concord, two quintessential New England towns. Concord is also rich in literary history: This is the site of Walden Pond, immortalized by Thoreau. Several historic houses can be visited.

Arriving and Departing

To reach Lexington and Concord by car from Boston, take Memorial Drive in Cambridge to the Fresh Pond Parkway, and then follow Route 2 west. Alternatively, follow I–90 (Massachusetts Turnpike) west to I–95/Route 128 north. Exit at Route 2 east for Lexington, Route 2 west for Concord. From Lexington to Concord, follow Route 2A west. Both towns are about a 30- to 45-minute drive from the metropolitan Boston area. The MBTA (☞ Boston Essentials) operates buses to Lexington and commuter trains to Concord.

What to See and Do

Lexington comes alive each Patriot's Day (the Monday nearest April 19), when costume-clad "Minutemen" re-create battle maneuvers and "Paul Revere" reenacts his midnight ride. On April 19, 1775, Minuteman captain John Parker assembled his men on the **Battle Green,** a 2-acre triangular piece of land, to await the arrival of the British, who were marching to Concord to "teach rebels a lesson." Parker's role is commemorated in Henry Hudson Kitson's renowned sculpture, the ***Minuteman* statue.**

Buckman Tavern, built in 1690, is where the Minutemen gathered the morning of April 19, 1775. A tour takes in the tavern's seven rooms. ✉ *1 Bedford St., Lexington,* ☎ *781/862–5598,* WEB *www.lexingtonhistory.org.* 🎟 *$5. Closed Nov.–mid-Mar.*

Though small, the **National Heritage Museum** (✉ 33 Marrett Rd., Rte. 2A at Massachusetts Ave., Lexington, ☎ 781/861–6559, WEB www.monh.org; 🎟 free) does a superb job of displaying items and artifacts from all facets of American life, as well as putting them in a social and political context.

The **Minute Man National Historical Park Visitor Center** (✉ Rte. 2A, ½ mi west of Rte. 128, Lexington, ☎ 978/369–6993 or 781/862–7753, WEB www.nps.gov/mima) is part of the 800-acre Minuteman National Historical Park, which extends into Lexington, Concord, and Lincoln. The center's exhibits and its captivating multimedia presentation focus on the Revolutionary War.

Concord includes sites of historic and literary interest. If you're heading from Lexington to Concord on Route 2A, you may want to stop off at the point where Revere's midnight ride ended with his capture by the British; it's marked with a boulder and plaque. At the **Old North Bridge** off Monument St., ½ mi north of the Concord town center, the tables were turned on the British on April 19, 1775, by the Concord Minutemen. Daniel Chester French's famous statue ***The Minuteman*** (1875) honors the country's first freedom fighters.

Author Nathaniel Hawthorne and essayist-poet Ralph Waldo Emerson both lived at the **Old Manse** at different times. ✉ *269 Monument St., Concord,* ☎ *978/369–3909,* WEB *www.thetrustees.org.* 🎟 *$7. Closed Nov.–mid-Apr.*

From 1835 until his death in 1882, Ralph Waldo Emerson lived in the **Ralph Waldo Emerson House,** where he wrote his *Essays*. The Emerson House furnishings have been preserved as the writer left them, down to his hat resting on the newel post. ✉ *28 Cambridge Tpke., at Lexington Rd., Concord,* ☎ *978/369–2236.* 🎟 *$5. Closed mid-Oct.–mid-Apr.*

The "Why Concord?" exhibit at the **Concord Museum** (✉ 200 Lexington Rd. [entrance on Cambridge Tpke.], Concord, ☎ 978/369–9763, WEB www.concordmuseum.org; 🎟 $7) provides a good overview of the town's history. The museum also has Emerson and Thoreau artifacts and one of the two lanterns hung at the Old North Church the night of April 18, 1775.

Louisa May Alcott's family home, **Orchard House,** is where the author wrote *Little Women*. Many of the original furnishings and the artwork of May Alcott (the model for Amy in *Little Women*) remain. ✉ *399 Lexington Rd., Concord,* ☎ *978/369–4118,* WEB *www.louisamayalcott.org.* 🎟 *$7. Closed 1st 2 wks in Jan.*

The **Wayside,** at different times home to Nathaniel Hawthorne, Louisa May Alcott, and Margaret Sydney, has exhibits on the former literary residents and a tour of Hawthorne's preserved tower-study. ✉ *455 Lexington Rd., Concord,* ☎ *978/369–6975,* WEB *www.nps.gov/mima/wayside.* 🎟 *$4. Closed Nov.–early May.*

Walden Pond (✉ Rte. 126, Concord, ☎ 978/369–3254; 🎟 free; parking mid-Apr.–Labor Day $5 per vehicle, free rest of year) is Henry David Thoreau's most famous residence. Thoreau published *Walden* (1854), a collection of essays on observations he made while living at his cabin here in the woods. You can see an authentically furnished full-size replica of the cabin, and you can swim and hike here.

Visitor Information

Lexington Visitor Center (✉ 1875 Massachusetts Ave., Lexington, 02173, ☎ 781/862–1450, WEB www.lexingtonchamber.org). **Minute Man National Historical Park Visitor Center** (✉ Rte. 2A, ½ mi west of Rte. 128, Lexington, ☎ 978/369–6993 or 781/862–7753, WEB www.nps.gov/mima).

Side Trip to Plymouth

On December 21, 1620, 102 weary pilgrims disembarked from the *Mayflower* to found the first permanent European settlement north of Virginia. Today, Plymouth is characterized by narrow streets, clapboard mansions, quaint shops, and antiques stores.

Arriving and Departing

To get to Plymouth from Boston, take I–93 south to Route 3 (toward Cape Cod); Exits 6 and 4 lead to downtown Plymouth and Plimoth Plantation, respectively; it's about an hour's drive. Plymouth & Brockton Street Railway Buses (☞ Boston Essentials) call at Plymouth en route to Cape Cod. **MBTA** commuter rail service (☞ Boston Essentials) is available to Plymouth; from the station, take the Plymouth Area Link buses to the historic attractions.

What to See and Do

★ The **Plimoth Plantation** living-history museum painstakingly re-creates a 1627 Pilgrim village, complete with thatched roofs, longhorn livestock, and "residents" with quaint accents and mannerisms. ✉ *Warren Ave./Rte. 3A,* ☎ *508/746–1622,* WEB *www.plimoth.org.* *Plantation $20, Plantation and Mayflower II $22. Closed Dec.–Mar.*

At the waterfront is the ***Mayflower II*** (☎ 508/746–1622; $8 or as part of combined Plimoth Plantation fee), a replica of the ship that brought the Pilgrims from England. **Plymouth Rock** is believed to be the very spot on which the Pilgrims first set foot in 1620 after unsuccessfully scouting the Provincetown area as a potential settlement.

Visitor Information

Contact **Destination Plymouth** (✉ 170 Water St., Suite 10C, Plymouth 02360, ☎ 800/872–1620, WEB www.visit-plymouth.com).

Side Trip to the North Shore

The beautiful North Shore extends from the northern suburbs to the Cape Ann region and beyond to the New Hampshire border.

Arriving and Departing

It's about 40 mi from Boston to Gloucester. The primary link between Boston and the North Shore is I–93 north to I–95 north to Route 128, which then follows the line of the coast as far north as Gloucester. A more scenic (but much slower) route is along coastal Route 1A (which leaves Boston via the Callahan Tunnel) to Route 127.

What to See and Do

The narrow, winding streets of **Marblehead** hold ancient clapboard houses and sea captains' mansions. **Salem,** now infamous for the witchcraft hysteria of 1692, includes compelling museums, waterfront stores and restaurants, and a traffic-free shopping area. **Rockport** brims with crafts shops, galleries, and artists' studios. **Gloucester** is the oldest seaport in America. **Newburyport** has a gorgeous redbrick center and rows of clapboard Federal mansions.

Crane Beach (✉ 290 Argilla Rd., Ipswich, ☎ 978/356–4354, WEB www.thetrustees.org), one of the North Shore's most beautiful beaches, is a 4-mi-long stretch of sand and dunes. **Parker River Wildlife Refuge** (✉ Plum Island, Newburyport, ☎ 978/465–5753, WEB www.parkerriver.org) is an undeveloped beach sanctuary. **Cape Ann Whale Watch** (✉ 415 Main St., Gloucester, ☎ 978/283–5110 or 800/877–5110, WEB www.caww.com) takes you to the high seas. **Newburyport Whale Watch** (✉ 54 Merrimac St., Newburyport, ☎ 978/499–0832 or 800/848–1111, www.newburyportwhalewatch.com) operates whale-watching trips. The **Essex River Cruises** (✉ 35 Dodge St., Essex Marina, Essex, ☎ 978/768–6981 or 800/748–3706, WEB www.essexcruises.com) head for the area's salt marshes and rivers.

Visitor Information

For more information on the North Shore area, visit the **North of Boston Visitors and Convention Bureau** (✉ 17 Peabody Sq., Peabody 01960, ☎ 978/977–7760 or 800/742–5306, FAX 978/977–7758, WEB www.northofboston.org).

Boston Essentials

AIRPORTS AND TRANSFERS

Logan International Airport has scheduled flights by most major domestic and foreign carriers.

➤ AIRPORT INFORMATION: **Logan International Airport** (✉ I–93 N, Exit 24, ☎ 800/235–6426, WEB www.massport.com).

AIRPORT TRANSFER

Cab fare to downtown is about $20 including tip. The Massachusetts Bay Transportation Authority Blue Line subway from the Airport station ($1) goes downtown; free shuttle buses connect the station with airline terminals and run every 8–12 minutes from 5:30 AM to 1 AM.

➤ TAXIS AND SHUTTLES: **MBTA** (☎ 617/222–3200 or 800/392–6100).

BUS TRAVEL TO AND FROM BOSTON

Bonanza, Greyhound, Peter Pan, and Plymouth & Brockton serve Massachusetts. South Station is the depot for these companies.

➤ BUS INFORMATION: **Bonanza Bus Lines** (☎ 800/556–3815, WEB www.bonanzabus.com). **Greyhound** (☎ 800/231–2222, WEB www.greyhound.com). **Peter Pan Bus Lines** (☎ 617/426–7838 or 800/237–8747, WEB www.peterpanbus.com). **Plymouth & Brockton Street Railway Buses** (☎ 508/746–0378, WEB www.p-b.com). **South Station** (✉ Atlantic Ave. and Summer St., ☎ 617/345–7451).

CAR TRAVEL

Boston is the traffic hub of New England: I–95 (which is the same as Route 128 in parts) skirts the city, while I–90 (the Massachusetts Turnpike toll road) heads west. I–93 connects Boston to the north and New Hampshire; the highway runs through the city as the Fitzgerald Expressway. This section of I–93 is being turned into an underground highway as part of the massive Central Artery Project (known locally as the Big Dig); expect construction and delays here through 2004.

PARKING

Parking is a tricky business. Some neighborhoods have residents-only rules, with just a handful of two-hour visitor spaces; others have meters (25¢ for 15 minutes, one or two hours maximum). Major public lots are at Government Center and Quincy Market; beneath Boston Common (entrance on Charles Street); beneath Post Office Square; at the Prudential Center; at Copley Place; and off Clarendon Street near the John Hancock Tower. Smaller lots are scattered throughout downtown. Most are expensive; the few city garages are a bargain at about $10 per day.

MEDIA

NEWSPAPERS AND MAGAZINES

Boston magazine (on newsstands) and *Where: Boston* (free in hotels and visitor centers) list arts and entertainment events. The *Boston Travel Planner,* available from the Greater Boston Convention and Visitors Bureau, contains a calendar of events, sports and regional activities, and information on hotel weekend packages.

TAXIS

Cabs are not easily hailed; if you're in a hurry, try a hotel taxi stand or telephone for a cab. Fares run about $2 per mile. Companies providing 24-hour service include Cambridge Checker Cab, Checker, and Independent Taxi Operators Association (ITOA).

➤ TAXI COMPANIES: **Cambridge Checker Cab** (☎ 617/497–1500). **Checker** (☎ 617/536–7000). **Independent Taxi Operators Association** (☎ 617/426–8700).

TOURS

BUS AND TROLLEY TOURS

The red Beantown Trolleys make more than 20 stops; get on and off as many times as you like. The $22 tickets are available from hotel concierges and at many attractions. Brush Hill/Gray Line buses pick up passengers from several suburban and downtown hotels for tours of Boston and neighboring towns like Lexington, Concord, Plymouth, and Salem. Old Town Trolley runs tours from several different locations in Boston every 20 minutes from 9 AM to 3 or 4 PM for $23. Cambridge tours are also available.

➤ FEES AND SCHEDULES: **Beantown Trolleys** (✉ Transportation Bldg., 14 Charles St. S, ☎ 617/236–2148 or 800/343–1328, WEB www.brushhilltours.com). **Brush Hill/Gray Line** (☎ 617/236–2148 or 800/343–1328, WEB www.brushhilltours.com). **Old Town Trolley** (☎ 617/269–7010 or 800/868–7482, WEB www.trolleytours.com).

BOAT TOURS

Boston Harbor Cruises operates several cruises departing from Long Wharf, including a whale-watching cruise from mid-April to October.

➤ FEES AND SCHEDULES: **Boston Harbor Cruises** (✉ 1 Long Wharf, ☎ 617/227–4321, WEB www.bostonharborcruises.com).

WALKING TOURS

The 2½-mi Freedom Trail, marked on the sidewalk by a red line, winds past 16 of Boston's most important historic sites, beginning at the visitor center at Boston Common, where you'll find maps and other brochures. Black Heritage Trail® begins at Boston Common and moves through the Beacon Hill neighborhood. Maps are available at the Museum of Afro-American History on Smith Court, off Joy Street.

➤ FEES AND SCHEDULES: **Black Heritage Trail®** (☎ 617/742–5415 or 617/725–0022, WEB www.afroammuseum.org). **Freedom Trail** (☎ 617/242–5642).

TRAIN TRAVEL

Amtrak serves Boston. All trains stop at South Station; some stop at Back Bay station and the easy-access Route 128 station in Canton, south of the city. Amtrak's pricey, high-speed *Acela* train has cut the travel time between Boston and New York to 3½ hours.

➤ TRAIN INFORMATION: **Amtrak** (☎ 800/872–7245, WEB www.amttrak.com).

TRANSPORTATION AROUND BOSTON

The MBTA, known as the T, operates subways, elevated trains, and trolleys along four connecting lines—Red, Blue, Green, and Orange. Trains run from 5:30 AM to about 12:30 AM daily; adult base fare is $1. Visitor passes, available for $6 for one day, $11 for three days, and $22 for seven days, can be bought at the following MBTA stations: Airport, South Station, North Station, Back Bay, Government Center, and Harvard Square.

Due to a profusion of one-way streets and streets with the same name, Boston is not an easy city to drive in. It's a good idea to look at a map first and keep one with you at all times. The bottom line is that Boston is meant for walking; a majority of its historic and architectural attractions are found in compact areas.

➤ CONTACTS: **MBTA** (☎ 617/722–3200 or 800/392–6100, WEB www.mbta.com).

VISITOR INFORMATION

The Boston Visitor Information Pavilion is open daily 9–5. The Boston Welcome Center is open from Sunday to Thursday between 9 and 5 and on Friday and Saturday between 9 and 6 for most of the year; it's open until 7 except Sunday during the summer. Greater Boston Convention and Visitors Bureau has brochures and information.

➤ TOURIST INFORMATION: **Boston Visitor Information Pavilion** (✉ Boston Common, Tremont St., near beginning of Freedom Trail Boston, ☎ 617/536–4100; 888/733–2678 recorded general information). **Boston Welcome Center** (✉ 140 Tremont St., Boston 02111, ☎ 617/451–2227). **Greater Boston Convention and Visitors Bureau** (✉ 2 Copley Pl., Suite 105, Boston 02116, ☎ 617/536–4100 or 800/888–5515, WEB www.bostonusa.com).

CAPE COD AND THE ISLANDS

Separated from the mainland by the 17½-mi-long Cape Cod Canal, the Cape curves 70 mi from end to end. Every summer crowds are attracted to its charming villages of weathered-shingle houses and white-steepled churches and to its natural beauty of pinewoods, grassy marshes, and beaches backed by rolling dunes. To the south, Martha's Vineyard and Nantucket are resort islands ringed with beautiful sandy beaches; Nantucket preserves a near-pristine whaling-era town.

Exploring Cape Cod and the Islands

U.S. 6 traverses the center of the Cape. Paralleling U.S. 6 but following the north coast is Route 6A, which passes through some of the Cape's old but well-preserved New England towns. The south shore, encompassing Falmouth, Hyannis, and Chatham and traced by Route 28, is heavily populated and is the most commercially developed region of the Cape. The sparse outer portion of the Cape, from Orleans to Provincetown, is edged with white-sand beaches and nature preserves. At the Cape's southwestern corner is **Woods Hole,** an international center for marine research. The **Woods Hole Oceanographic Institute Exhibit Center** (✉ 15 School St., Woods Hole, ☎ 508/289–2663, WEB www.whoi.edu; 🎟 $2 suggested donation) is a good place to learn about oceans and oceanography. The 16 tanks at the modest **National Marine Fisheries Service Aquarium** contain regional fish and shellfish. ✉ *Albatross and Water Sts., Woods Hole,* ☎ *508/495–2267; 508/495–2001 recorded information;* WEB *www.nefsc.nmfs.gov/nefsc/aquarium.* 🎟 *Free. Closed weekends mid-Sept.–late June.*

The village green in **Falmouth** was a military training field in the 18th century and is today flanked by colonial homes, fine inns, and an 1856 Congregational church with a bell made by Paul Revere. The **Falmouth Historical Society** (✉ Village Green, off Palmer Ave., Falmouth, ☎ 508/548–4857, WEB www.falmouthhistoricalsociety.org; 🎟 $4) maintains two museums (open Tuesday–Saturday 10–4 June–August) and conducts free walking tours in season.

Quietly wealthy **Hyannis Port** is the site of the Kennedy family compound. **Hyannis** is the Cape's year-round commercial hub. The **John F. Kennedy Hyannis Museum** (✉ 397 Main St., Hyannis, ☎ 508/790–3077; 🎟 $5) has photographs and videos from the presidential years focusing on John F. Kennedy's ties to the Cape. It's in the Old Town Hall.

At the southeastern tip of Cape Cod, **Chatham** is a seaside town relatively free of the commercialism found elsewhere, though it has a downtown of traditional shops and fine inns. The view from **Chatham Lighthouse** (✉ Main St., near Bridge St., Chatham, ☎ 508/945–0719) is spectacular. Off the coast is **Monomoy National Wildlife Refuge** (Headquarters: ✉ Morris Island, Chatham, ☎ 508/945–0594), a

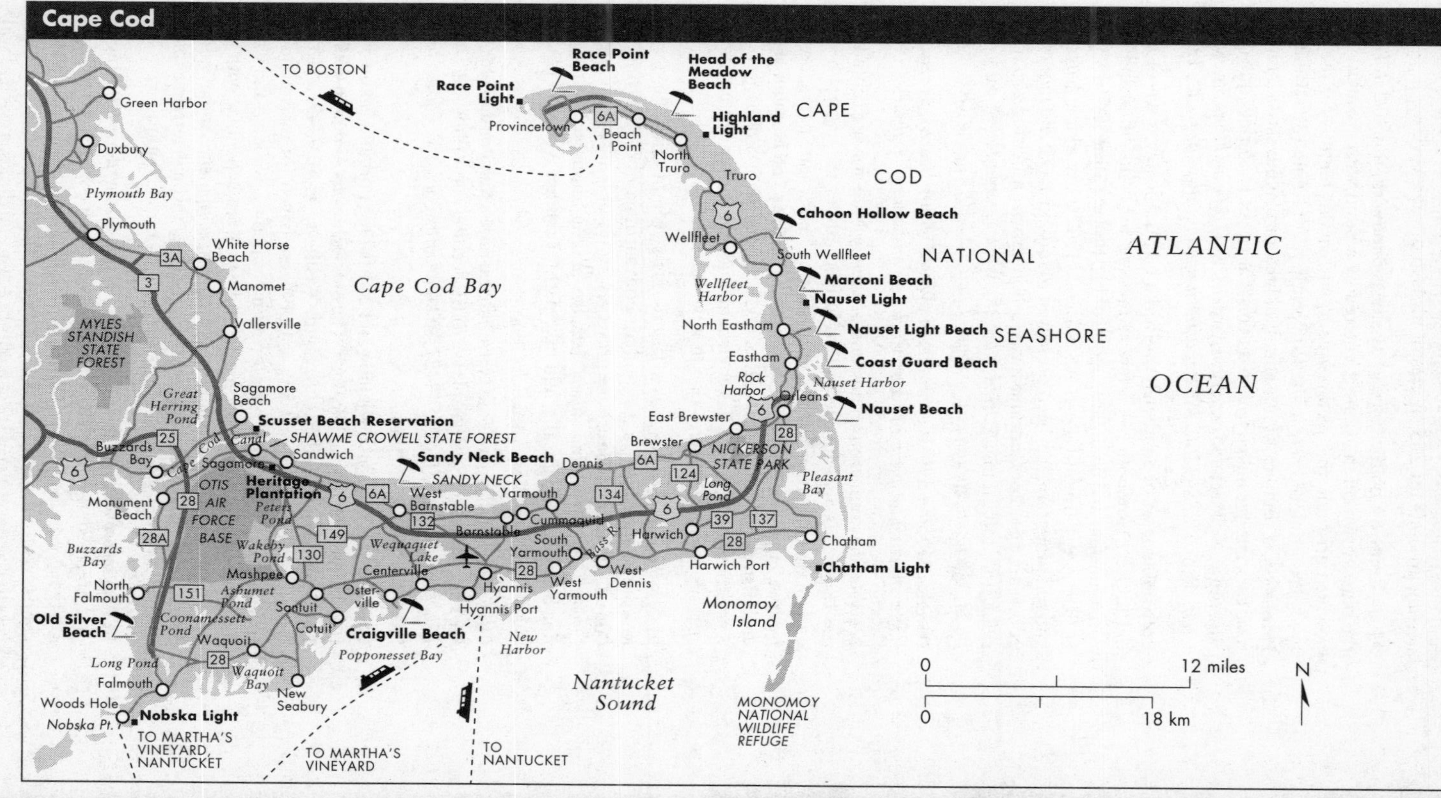

Cape Cod
TO BOSTON
Green Harbor
Duxbury
Plymouth Bay
Plymouth
3A
3
White Horse Beach
Manomet
Vallersville
MYLES STANDISH STATE FOREST
Cape Cod Bay
Race Point Light
Race Point Beach
Provincetown
6A
Beach Point
Head of the Meadow Beach
Highland Light
North Truro
Truro
CAPE
COD
NATIONAL
SEASHORE
ATLANTIC
OCEAN
6
Cahoon Hollow Beach
Wellfleet
South Wellfleet
Wellfleet Harbor
Marconi Beach
Nauset Light
North Eastham
Nauset Light Beach
Eastham
Coast Guard Beach
Rock Harbor
Nauset Harbor
Orleans
Nauset Beach
East Brewster
28
Great Herring Pond
Sagamore Beach
Scusset Beach Reservation
SHAWME CROWELL STATE FOREST
Cape Cod Canal
25
Buzzards Bay
Sagamore
Sandwich
Sandy Neck Beach
SANDY NECK
Heritage Plantation
OTIS AIR FORCE BASE
Peters Pond
Monument Beach
28A
Buzzards Bay
149
130
132
West Barnstable
Barnstable
Yarmouth
Dennis
Cummaquid
134
124
Brewster
NICKERSON STATE PARK
Long Pond
Pleasant Bay
39
137
Harwich
Harwich Port
Chatham
Chatham Light
Wakeby Pond
Wequaquet Lake
Centerville
Mashpee
Ashumet Pond
Santuit
Osterville
Cotuit
Craigville Beach
Hyannis
Hyannis Port
South Yarmouth
West Yarmouth
Bass R.
West Dennis
North Falmouth
151
Coonamessett Pond
Old Silver Beach
Waquoit
Long Pond
Falmouth
Waquoit Bay
New Seabury
Popponesset Bay
New Harbor
Monomoy Island
Woods Hole
Nobska Light
Nobska Pt.
TO MARTHA'S VINEYARD, NANTUCKET
TO MARTHA'S VINEYARD
TO NANTUCKET
Nantucket Sound
MONOMOY NATIONAL WILDLIFE REFUGE
0
12 miles
0
18 km
N

2,500-acre preserve including the Monomoy Islands, which provide nesting grounds for 285 species of birds and waterfowl.

Along Route 6A on the Cape's bay side is **Sandwich,** founded in 1637, the oldest town on the Cape. Centered by a pond with a waterwheel-powered gristmill, this picturesque town remains famous for the colored glass produced here in the 19th century. Off Route 130 is **Heritage Plantation,** a complex of museum buildings displaying classic and historic cars, antique military-related items, Currier & Ives prints, and other Americana—all set amid extensive gardens. ✉ *Grove and Pine Sts., Sandwich,* ☎ *508/888–3300,* WEB *www.heritageplantation.org.* 🎫 *$12.*

Barnstable, east of Sandwich on Route 6A, is a lovely town of large old houses. **Yarmouth** has a few attractions for children, including a zoo-aquarium and a miniature golf course. **Hallet's Store** (✉ 139 Main St./Rte. 6A, Yarmouth Port, ☎ 508/362–3362), a working drugstore and soda fountain, has been preserved to look just as it did more than 100 years ago. **ZooQuarium** has sea-lion shows, a petting zoo, pony rides, and aquariums. ✉ *674 Rte. 28, West Yarmouth,* ☎ *508/775–8883,* WEB *www.zooquariumcapecod.net.* 🎫 *$10. Closed Dec.–Feb.*

***Dennis** is a town with a great beach (West Dennis Beach).* ***Scargo Hill** has a spectacular view of Cape Cod Bay and Scargo Lake.*

Brewster has numerous mansions originally built for sea captains in the 1800s. It's also a perfect place to learn about the natural history of the Cape: the area contains conservation lands, state parks, forests, freshwater ponds, and brackish marshes. The **Cape Cod Museum of Natural History** (✉ 869 Main St./Rte. 6A, Brewster, ☎ 508/896–3867, WEB www.ccmnh.org; 🎫 $5) has environmental and marine exhibits as well as trails through 80 acres rich in wildlife.

In **Orleans,** Nauset Beach is a 10-mi-long sweep of sandy beach with low dunes and large waves good for bodysurfing or boardsurfing. The ★ **Cape Cod National Seashore** preserves 30 mi of landscape along the Lower Cape, including superb beaches and lighthouses. With several fine beaches, hiking trails, and bike paths, **Eastham** is a good place to enjoy the outdoors.

Off Route 6 in Eastham, the National Seashore's **Salt Pond Visitor Center** has a museum with displays, tours, lectures, and films. ✉ *Doane Rd., off U.S. 6,* ☎ *508/255–3421,* WEB *www.nps.gov/caco. Closed weekdays Jan.– Feb.*

Wellfleet was a colonial whaling and cod-fishing port and is now home ★ to fishermen, artists, and artisans. The **Massachusetts Audubon Wellfleet Bay Sanctuary** (✉ off Rte. 6, South Wellfleet, ☎ 508/349–2615, WEB www.wellfleetbay.org; 🎫 $3), a 1,000-acre haven for more than 250 species of birds, is a superb place for bird-watching, walking, and watching the sun set over the salt marsh and bay. **Truro** is popular with writers and artists for its high dunes and lack of development. At the National Seashore's **Pilgrim Heights Area,** trails meander through terrain explored by the *Mayflower* crew before they moved on to Plymouth.

In **Provincetown,** which is filled with shops and galleries, Portuguese and American fishermen mix with painters, poets, whale-watchers, and a large gay and lesbian community. The National Seashore's **Province Lands** (visitor center: ✉ Race Point Rd., ☎ 508/487–1256) allow access to Provincetown's spectacular beaches and dunes, as well as walking, biking, and horse trails; they are closed December–March. The **Pilgrim Monument** (✉ High Pole Hill Rd., ☎ 508/487–1310, WEB www.pilgrim-monument.org; 🎫 $6), on a hill above the town center, commemorates the landing of the Pilgrims in 1620. From atop the 252-ft tower the view of the entire Cape is lovely.

Martha's Vineyard, a hot spot with celebrities, is less developed than Cape Cod yet more cosmopolitan than Nantucket. On the island the lively town of **Oak Bluffs** has a warren of some 300 candy-color Victorian cottages. The historic **Flying Horses Carousel** (✉ Oak Bluffs Ave., Oak Bluffs, ☎ 508/693–9481, WEB www.vineyard.net/org/mvpt/carousel.html; 🎫 $1) delights youngsters. The main port of **Vineyard Haven** has a street of shops and a backstreet preserved to reflect the way it appeared in whaling days. Tidy **Edgartown** has upscale boutiques, elegant sea captains' houses, and beautiful flower gardens. **Chappaquiddick Island,** laced with nature preserves, is accessible by ferry from Edgartown. The dramatically striated red-clay **Aquinnah Cliffs** (formerly Gay Head Cliffs), a major tourist sight, stand in a Wampanoag Indian township on the island's western tip.

The island of **Nantucket** is covered with moors that are scented with bayberry, wild roses, and cranberries; ringing it are miles of clean, white-sand beaches. **Nantucket Town,** an exquisitely preserved National Historic District, encapsulates the island's whaling past in more than a dozen historical museums along its cobblestone streets. The beach community of **Siasconset** provides an unhurried lifestyle amid beautiful surroundings; tiny rose-covered cottages and white-clamshell drives abound.

Dining and Lodging

On Martha's Vineyard only Edgartown and Oak Bluffs allow the sale of liquor. For summer, lodgings should be booked as far in advance as possible. **Martha's Vineyard and Nantucket Reservations** (☎ 508/693–7200, WEB www.mvreservations.com) can help with bookings.

Brewster

$$$$ ★ ✕ **Chillingsworth.** This crown jewel of Cape restaurants is extremely formal, terribly pricey, and completely upscale. The classic French menu and wine cellar win award after award. The seven-course table d'hôte menu includes appetizers, entrées—like super-rich risotto, roast lobster, or grilled venison—and "amusements." At dinner, a more modest bistro menu is served in the Garden Room. ✉ *2449 Main St./Rte. 6A,* ☎ *508/896–3640. Reservations essential. AE, DC, MC, V. Closed late Nov.–early May.*

$$–$$$$ ★ 🏨 **Captain Freeman Inn.** The opulent details at this 1866 Victorian include a marble fireplace, herringbone-inlay flooring, ornate Italian ceiling medallions, and 12-ft ceilings. Guest rooms have hardwood floors, antiques, and eyelet spreads. ✉ *15 Breakwater Rd., 02631,* ☎ *508/896–7481 or 800/843–4664,* FAX *508/896–5618,* WEB *www.captfreemaninn.com. 12 rooms. Pool. MC, V. No smoking. BP.*

Chatham

$$–$$$ ★ ✕ **Vining's Bistro.** The wood grill, where the chef employs zesty spices from all over the globe, is the center of attention here. Spit-roasted Jamaican chicken and the Portobello mushroom sandwich are the restaurant's signature dishes. ✉ *595 Main St.,* ☎ *508/945–5033. Reservations not accepted. AE, D, MC, V. Closed mid-Jan.–Apr.*

$$$–$$$$ ★ 🏨 **Captain's House Inn.** Fine architectural details and a feeling of quiet comfort make this inn one of the Cape's finest. Some rooms in the four buildings are lacy and feminine, others refined and elegant. ✉ *371 Old Harbor Rd., 02633,* ☎ *508/945–0127 or 800/315–0728,* FAX *508/945–0866,* WEB *www.captainshouseinn.com. 19 rooms. AE, D, MC, V. No smoking. BP.*

Falmouth

$$$ ★ **La Maison Cappellari at Mostly Hall.** Set in a landscaped yard, this imposing 1849 house has a wraparound porch and a cupola. Several bedrooms are decorated in an upscale European style, with colorful murals; in the Tuscan Room, the painted walls suggest an intimate Italian garden. Three rooms are more traditional, with canopy beds and other antiques. ✉ *27 Main St., 02540,* ☎ *508/548–3786 or 800/682–0565,* FAX *508/457–1572,* WEB *www.mostlyhall.com. 6 rooms. AE, D, MC, V. Closed mid-Dec.–mid-Apr. BP.*

Hyannis

$$–$$$ ✕ **The Paddock.** The Paddock is synonymous with excellent formal dining. Steak au poivre and Pacific Rim chicken (a grilled breast topped with oranges and mangoes) are among the traditional yet innovative preparations. Manhattans are popular in the lounge, where musicians perform in the evening. ✉ *W. Main St. rotary, next to Melody Tent,* ☎ *508/775–7677. AE, DC, MC, V. Closed mid-Nov.–Mar.*

$–$$ **Sea Breeze Inn.** The rooms at this cedar-shingle seaside B&B have antique or canopy beds. The nicest of the three detached cottages is the three-bedroom Rose Garden, which has two baths, a TV room, a fireplace, and a washer and dryer. ✉ *270 Ocean Ave., at Sea St., 02601,* ☎ *508/771–7213,* FAX *508/862–0663,* WEB *www.seabreezeinn.com. 14 rooms, 3 cottages. AE, D, MC, V. CP.*

Martha's Vineyard

$$–$$$ ✕ **Black Dog Tavern.** This island landmark serves basic chowders, pastas, and fish. Waiting for a table is something of a tradition, although locals have generally adopted Yogi Berra's line: "It's so crowded, no one goes there anymore." ✉ *Beach St. Ext., Vineyard Haven,* ☎ *508/693–9223. Reservations not accepted. AE, D, MC, V. BYOB.*

$$$$ ★ ✕ **Charlotte Inn.** Come to this tasteful inn for an Edwardian fantasy, an escape in one of the luxurious suites, a tranquil winter holiday with the island nearly to yourself, or a sumptuous meal at L'étoile ($$$$; reservations essential), one of the Vineyard's finest traditional restaurants. ✉ *27 S. Summer St., Edgartown 02539,* ☎ *508/627–4751; 508/627–5187 L'étoile;* FAX *508/627–4652;* WEB *www.relaischateaux.com. 23 rooms. Restaurant. AE, MC, V. CP.*

$$$–$$$$ ✕ **Lambert's Cove Country Inn.** Rooms in the 1790 farmhouse of this secluded inn have light floral wallpapers and a sweet country feel. Rooms in outbuildings have screened porches or decks. Enjoy excellent contemporary cooking by soft candlelight in the restaurant ($$$; reservations essential; BYOB). Especially good is the sautéed halibut with seedless grapes, wild mushrooms, shallots, lemon, and Vermouth. ✉ *Off Lambert's Cove Rd., W. Tisbury (R.R. 1, Box 422, Vineyard Haven 02568),* ☎ *508/693–2298,* FAX *508/693–7890,* WEB *www.lambertscoveinn.com. 15 rooms. Restaurant, tennis. AE, MC, V. BP.*

Nantucket

$$$$ ✕ **Chanticleer.** Anne and Jean-Charles Berruet serve superb French food in a formal country setting. This is classicism at its best—the food is unimpeachable and the desserts are profoundly rich. ✉ *9 New St., Siasconset,* ☎ *508/257–6231. Jacket required. AE, MC, V. Closed Mon. and mid-Oct.–early May.*

$$$$ ✕ **Wauwinet.** Eight miles from Nantucket Town, this deluxe establishment has rooms that are lavished with unfussy antiques; some have spectacular views of the ocean. The chic restaurant ($$$$; reservations essential) specializes in fresh seafood. ✉ *120 Wauwinet Rd. (Box 2580, 02584),* ☎ *508/228–0145 or 800/426–8718,* FAX *508/228–7135,* WEB *www.wauwinet.com. 25 rooms, 5 cottages. Restaurant, tennis. AE, DC, MC, V. Closed Nov.–Apr. BP.*

$$$–$$$$ **Pineapple Inn.** Take a handsome 1835 Greek Revival captain's house, add gregarious owners with impeccable taste, and you might approximate this ideal retreat. From the down quilts to the marble-finished baths, no expense was spared in retrofitting this unassuming house on a quiet street. ✉ *10 Hussey St., 02554,* ☎ *508/228–9992,* WEB *www.pineappleinn.com. 12 rooms. AE, D, MC, V. CP.*

Provincetown

$$ ✕ **Bubala's by the Bay.** Personality abounds at this restaurant inside a bright yellow building adorned with campy carved birds. The kitchen serves three meals, with lots of local seafood. The wine list is priced practically at retail. The bar scene picks up in the evening. ✉ *183 Commercial St.,* ☎ *508/487–0773. AE, D, MC, V. Closed late Oct.–Mar.*

$$ ✕ **Café Edwige.** Delicious contemporary cuisine is served in a homey setting at Café Edwige. Appetizers include Maine crab cakes and warm goat cheese on crostini. Among the choices for entrées are lobster and Wellfleet scallops over pasta with a wild mushroom and tomato broth. ✉ *333 Commercial St.,* ☎ *508/487–2008. AE, MC, V. Closed Nov.–May.*

$$$–$$$$ ★ **Bayshore.** This apartment complex on the water, ½ mi from the town center, is great for long stays. Many of the units have decks and large water-view windows; all have full kitchens, modern baths, and phones. Rentals are mostly by the week in season. ✉ *493 Commercial St., 02657–2413,* ☎ *508/487–9133,* FAX *508/487–0520,* WEB *www.provincetown.com/bayshore. 25 apartments. AE, MC, V.*

$–$$$$ **The Masthead.** The Masthead is a charming cluster of shingled houses that overlook a lush lawn, a 450-ft-long boardwalk, and a private beach. Spacious rooms, efficiencies, apartments, and cottages are among the lodging options. ✉ *31–41 Commercial St. (Box 577, 02657),* ☎ *508/487–0523 or 800/395–5095,* FAX *508/487–9251,* WEB *www.capecodtravel.com/masthead. 7 apartments, 3 cottages, 2 efficiencies, 9 rooms. AE, D, DC, MC, V.*

Campgrounds

Nickerson State Park (☞ National and State Parks, *above*). **Shawme–Crowell State Forest** (✉ Rte. 130, Sandwich 02563, ☎ 508/888–0351; 877/422–6762 reservations) has 285 sites and a beach.

Nightlife and the Arts

Nightlife

Hyannis has many nightclubs and bars hosting live rock and jazz (☎ 508/394–5277 Jazz Hot Line). Circuit Avenue in **Oak Bluffs** has rowdy bars and a year-round dance club. Rock clubs and restaurants with sedate piano bars thrive in **Nantucket Town.**

The Arts

Actors Theatre of Nantucket (✉ Methodist Church, 2 Centre St., at Main St., Nantucket Town, ☎ 508/228–6325, WEB www.nantuckettheatre.com) presents several Broadway-style plays each summer. The **Cape Playhouse** (✉ 820 Main St./Rte. 6A, Dennis, ☎ 508/385–3911 or 877/385–3911, WEB www.capeplayhouse.com) is the country's oldest professional summer theater. The **Wellfleet Harbor Actors Theater** (✉ 1 Kendrick St., ☎ 508/349–6835, WEB www.what.org) presents summer stock. The **Vineyard Playhouse** (✉ 24 Church St., Vineyard Haven, ☎ 508/693–6450 winter; 508/696–6300 summer; WEB www.vineyardplayhouse.org) hosts Equity productions and community theater year-round.

Outdoor Activities and Sports

Biking

Cape Cod Rail Trail, a 25-mi paved railroad right-of-way from Dennis to Wellfleet, is the Cape's premier bike path. On either side of the **Cape**

Cod Canal is an easy 7-mi straight trail. The **Cape Cod National Seashore** and **Nickerson State Park** also maintain bicycle trails. On **Martha's Vineyard,** scenic well-paved paths follow the coast from Oak Bluffs to Edgartown and inland from Vineyard Haven to South Beach; some connect with rougher trails that weave through the state forest. **Nantucket** has bike paths extending several miles that meander through the moorland.

Fishing

Tuna, mako and blue sharks, bluefish, and bass are the main ocean catches. The necessary license to fish the Cape's freshwater ponds is available at tackle shops, such as **Eastman's Sport & Tackle** (✉ 150 Main St., Falmouth, ☎ 508/548–6900). **Goose Hummock Shop** (✉ 15 Rte. 6A off the Rte. 6 rotary, Orleans, ☎ 508/255–0455) sells licenses and tackle. **Dick's Bait & Tackle** (✉ 108 New York Ave., Oak Bluffs, ☎ 508/693–7669) on Martha's Vineyard rents gear, sells bait, and has a current list of fishing regulations. **Cross Rip Outfitters** (✉ 24 Easy St., Nantucket, ☎ 508/228–4900, WEB www.crossrip.com) supplies and guides fly-fishers. **Cape Water Sports** (✉ 337 Main St., Harwich Port, ☎ 508/432–7079) rents sailboats, powerboats, and canoes. **Martha's Vineyard Water Sports** (✉ Dockside Marketplace, Oak Bluffs Harbor, ☎ 508/693–8476) rents Boston Whalers, Wave Runners, and kayaks.

You can go for fluke, bluefish, and striped bass from spring to fall with **Cap'n Bill & Cee Jay** (✉ MacMillan Wharf, Provincetown, ☎ 508/487–4330 or 800/675–6723). **Patriot Boats** (✉ 227 Clinton Ave., Falmouth Harbor, ☎ 508/548–2626; 800/734–0088 in Massachusetts) operates deep-sea fishing trips. On Martha's Vineyard the party boat ***Skipper*** (☎ 508/693–1238) leaves for deep-sea fishing trips from Oak Bluffs Harbor. On **Nantucket** charters sail out of Straight Wharf.

Horseback Riding

To ride horseback try **Moby Dick Farm** (✉ 179 Great Fields Rd., Brewster, ☎ 508/896–3544). **Haland Stables** (✉ 878 Rte. 28A, West Falmouth, ☎ 508/540–2552) gives lessons and trail rides by reservation. **Misty Meadows Horse Farm** (✉ Old County Rd., West Tisbury, Martha's Vineyard, ☎ 508/693–1870) conducts trail rides.

Water Sports

Arey's Pond Boat Yard (✉ 43 Arey's La., off Rte. 28, South Orleans, ☎ 508/255–0994, WEB www.by-the-sea.com/areyspondboatyard) has a sailing school. **Wind's Up!** (✉ 199 Beach Rd., Vineyard Haven, ☎ 508/693–4252) on Martha's Vineyard rents catamarans, surfboards, sea kayaks, canoes, Sunfish, and Windsurfers. **Nantucket Community Sailing** (✉ Jetties Beach, ☎ 508/228–5358, WEB www.nantucketsailing.com) has windsurfing, Sunfish and kayak rentals, plus optional instruction.

Whale-Watching

The proximity of the Cape to the whales' feeding grounds at Stellwagen Bank (about 6 mi off the tip of Provincetown) affords the rare opportunity of spotting several species of whales. On **Hyannis Whale Watcher Cruises** (✉ Millway Marina, off Phinney's La., Barnstable, ☎ 508/362–6088 or 800/287–0374, WEB www.whales.net), a naturalist narrates and comments on whale sightings. ***Dolphin Fleet*** (✉ MacMillan Wharf, Provincetown, ☎ 508/349–1900 or 800/826–9300, WEB www.whalewatch.com) tours are accompanied by scientists from the Center for Coastal Studies in Provincetown.

The naturalist-narrated **Cape Cod Whale Watch** trips leave from MacMillan Wharf. ✉ *Ticket office at MacMillan Wharf or 293 Commercial St., Provincetown,* ☎ *508/487–4079 or 877/487–4079.*

Beaches

Beaches fronting on **Cape Cod Bay** generally have cold water and gentle waves. The Cape's south-side beaches, on **Nantucket Sound,** have rolling surf and are warmer. Open-ocean beaches on the ★ **Cape Cod National Seashore** are cold, with serious surf. These beaches, backed by high dunes, have lifeguards and rest rooms. In summer, parking lots can fill up by 10 AM. On **Martha's Vineyard** and **Nantucket,** the beaches facing the sound are warmer than the Atlantic beaches.

Shopping

Provincetown has many fine galleries. **Wellfleet** has emerged as a vibrant center for arts and crafts. There's a giant **flea market** (✉ 51 U.S. 6, South Wellfleet, ☎ 508/349–2520) on weekends and Monday holidays from April to October, plus Wednesday and Thursday in July and August. **Cape Cod Mall** (✉ between Rtes. 132 and 28, Hyannis, ☎ 508/771–0200) holds 120 shops.

The chief shopping town on **Martha's Vineyard** is **Edgartown,** with the best selection of antiques and crafts shops. The **West Tisbury Farmers' Market** (✉ South Rd., West Tisbury, ☎ 508/693–9549), open on Wednesday and Saturday in summer, is the largest of its kind in Massachusetts. **Nantucket**'s specialty is lightship baskets—expensive woven baskets, often decorated with scrimshaw or rosewood.

Cape Cod and the Islands Essentials

AIR TRAVEL

Cape Air/Nantucket Airlines and US Airways Express serve Barnstable Municipal Airport (☞ Airports) on Cape Cod; Cape Air/Nantucket Airlines also flies to Martha's Vineyard Airport, Provincetown Municipal Airport, and Nantucket Memorial Airport.

➤ AIRLINES AND CONTACTS: **Cape Air/Nantucket Airlines** (☎ 508/771–6944 or 800/352–0714, WEB www.flycapeair.com). **US Airways Express** (☎ 800/428–4322, WEB www.usairways.com).

AIRPORTS

Barnstable Municipal Airport is Cape Cod's air gateway. Other regional airports in the area include Martha's Vineyard Airport, Provincetown Municipal Airport, and Nantucket Memorial Airport.

➤ AIRPORT INFORMATION: **Barnstable Municipal Airport** (✉ 480 Barnstable Rd., Rte. 28 rotary, Hyannis, ☎ 508/775–2020).

BOAT AND FERRY TRAVEL

Ferries connect Martha's Vineyard and Nantucket to the mainland from Woods Hole, Hyannis, Falmouth, and New Bedford. The Steamship Authority, Hy-Line Cruises, and the *Island Queen* serve Martha's Vineyard from the Cape. The *Schamonchi* travels between New Bedford and the Vineyard. The Steamship Authority and Hy-Line serve Nantucket.

➤ BOAT AND FERRY INFORMATION: **Hy-Line Cruises** (☎ 508/778–2600, WEB www.hy-linecruises.com). ***Island Queen*** (☎ 508/548–4800. WEB www.islandqueen.com). ***Schamonchi*** (☎ 508/997–1688, WEB www.islandferry.com). **Steamship Authority** (☎ 508/477–8600, WEB www.islandferry.com).

BUS TRAVEL

Bonanza Bus Lines (☞ Bus Travel *in* Boston Essentials) operates direct service to Bourne, Falmouth, and Woods Hole from Boston and Providence. Plymouth & Brockton Street Railway (☞ Bus Travel *in*

Boston Essentials) provides bus service to Provincetown from Boston and Logan Airport, with stops in several Cape towns en route.

CAR TRAVEL

From Boston take I–93 south to Route 3 south to the Sagamore Bridge. From New York take I–95 north to Providence, where you'll pick up I–195 east to Route 25 east to the Bourne Bridge.

VISITOR INFORMATION

➤ TOURIST INFORMATION: **Cape Cod Chamber of Commerce** (✉ Rtes. 6 and 132, Hyannis 02601, ☎ 508/862–0700 or 888/332–2732, WEB www.capecodchamber.org). **Martha's Vineyard Chamber of Commerce** (✉ Beach Rd. [Box 1698, Vineyard Haven 02568], ☎ 508/693–4486, WEB www.mvy.com). **Nantucket Island Chamber of Commerce** (✉ 48 Main St., Nantucket 02554, ☎ 508/228–1700, WEB www.nantucketchamber.org).

THE PIONEER VALLEY

The Pioneer Valley, a string of historic settlements along the Connecticut River from Springfield in the south up to the Vermont border, formed the western frontier of New England from the early 1600s until the late 18th century. The northern regions of the Pioneer Valley remain rural and tranquil; farms and small towns have typical New England architecture. Farther south, the cities of Holyoke and Springfield are more industrial. Educational pioneers came to this region as well—to form major colleges and some well-known prep schools.

What to See and Do

Four museums have set up shop near downtown Springfield at the **Springfield Museums at the Quadrangle** complex. The **Connecticut Valley Historical Museum** surveys the history of the Pioneer Valley. There's also a permanent Dr. Seuss exhibit in honor of Theodore Geisel, the children's-books writer who grew up in the area. The **George Walter Vincent Smith Art Museum** contains Japanese armor, ceramics, and textiles and a gallery of American paintings. The **Museum of Fine Arts** has paintings by Gauguin, Renoir, Degas, and Monet, as well as 18th-century American paintings and contemporary works. The **Springfield Science Museum** has an "Exploration Center" of touchable displays, a planetarium, and dinosaur exhibits. ✉ *220 State St., at Chestnut St.,* ☎ *413/263–2800,* WEB *www.quadrangle.org.* *Pass valid for all museums $6. Closed Mon.–Tues.*

★ **Six Flags New England,** outside Springfield, is New England's largest theme park and water park, with more than 160 rides and shows, including the tallest and fastest steel coaster on the East Coast. ✉ *1623 Main St./Rte. 159, south from Rte. 57 west of Springfield, Agawam,* ☎ *877/474–9352,* WEB *www.sixflags.com.* *$39.99 ($26.99 after 4 PM), $10 parking. Closed Nov.–late Apr.*

Deerfield, in the north, has many historic buildings and is the site of the ★ prestigious Deerfield Academy. The village of **Historic Deerfield** includes the **Street** (✉ Rte. 5, ☎ 413/774–5581, WEB www.historic-deerfield.org; pass for all houses $12, single house $6), a tree-lined avenue of 18th- and 19th-century houses, with 14 of the preserved buildings open to the public year-round. In **Amherst** are three of the valley's five major colleges—the University of Massachusetts, Amherst College, and Hampshire College. The **Emily Dickinson Homestead,** which can be viewed by tour only, is the house in which the poet spent her entire life. Reservations are recommended. ✉ *280 Main St.,* ☎ *413/542–8161,* WEB *www.dickinsonhomestead.org.* 🎫 *$5. Closed Sun.–Tues. and Dec.–Feb.*

Northampton, once home to the 30th U.S. president, Calvin Coolidge, is now the site of Smith College, a lively arts scene, and good bookstores. The village of **South Hadley** is best known for Mount Holyoke, founded in 1837 as the country's first women's college.

★ East of the southern end of the valley is **Old Sturbridge Village** (✉ 1 Old Sturbridge Village Rd., Sturbridge, ☎ 800/733–1830, WEB www.osv.org; 🎫 $20, good for 2 consecutive days), a living, working model of an early 1800s New England town, with more than 40 buildings on a 200-acre site.

Dining and Lodging

Amherst

$$ ✕🏨 **Lord Jeffery Inn.** Many bedrooms at this gabled brick inn have a floral decor; others have stencils and pastel woodwork. The formal dining room, where traditional dishes are served, has old wood panels and a large fireplace. Burgers, salads, and the like are served at Boltwood's Tavern ($$–$$$), which has a small bar and a wraparound porch. ✉ *30 Boltwood Ave., 01002,* ☎ *413/253–2576 or 800/742–0358,* FAX *413/256–6152,* WEB *www.lordjefferyinn.com. 48 rooms. 2 restaurants. AE, DC, MC, V.*

$$–$$$ ★ 🏨 **Allen House Victorian and Amherst Inns.** These nearby late-19th-century inns have been meticulously restored to the Victorian era. Busy, colorful wall coverings reach to the high ceilings of this restored inn. Antiques include wicker "steamship" chairs, screens, and carved golden-oak beds. Lace curtains grace the windows in the rooms, whose comfortable beds have goose-down comforters. It's a short walk from the center of Amherst. ✉ *599 Main St., 01002,* ☎ *413/253–5000,* WEB *www.allenhouse.com. 14 rooms. No credit cards. BP.*

Deerfield

$$ ★ ✕ **Sienna.** The atmosphere at Sienna is soothing, but the food is what really shines. Choices from the ever-changing menu might include a wild-mushroom crepe on a cantaloupe melon, followed by pan-seared sea bass on Swiss chard, with fingerling potatoes and a sweet corn flan. ✉ *6 Elm St., South Deerfield,* ☎ *413/665–0215. MC, V. Closed Mon.–Tues. No lunch.*

$$$$ ★ ✕🏨 **Deerfield Inn.** Period wallpapers decorate the rooms in the main inn, which was built in 1884; the rooms in an outbuilding have identical papers but are newer (1981) and closer to the parking lot. All rooms have antiques and replicas; some have four-poster or canopy beds. The restaurant ($$–$$$) showcases such creative American fare as pan-seared pheasant with crushed peppercorns. ✉ *81 Old Main St., 01342,* ☎ *413/774–5587 or 800/926–3865,* FAX *413/773–8712,* WEB *www.deerfieldinn.com. 23 rooms. Restaurant. AE, MC, V. No smoking. BP.*

Northampton

$$$–$$$$ ✕ **Del Raye.** This upscale eatery is housed in a sexy, dimly lighted space with closely spaced tables and a swanky lounge. Among the otherworldly creations are banana-encrusted sea scallops with dates, sweet tomatoes, and a cactus-fruit beurre rouge; and tangerine-glazed duck. ✉ *1 Bridge St.,* ☎ *413/586–2664. AE, MC, V. No lunch.*

$$ 🏨 **Clark Tavern Inn.** Early customers at this 1742 inn not far from Northampton included Minutemen on their way to fight in Concord and Lexington. More than two centuries later, braided rugs, canopy beds, and stencils create a colonial atmosphere. Fires warm two common rooms; in summer, you can nap in the garden hammock or take

a dip in the pool. ✉ *98 Bay Rd., Hadley 01035,* ☎ *413/586–1900,* WEB *www.clarktaverninn.com. 3 rooms. Pool. AE, D, DC, MC, V. BP.*

The Pioneer Valley Essentials

AIRPORTS

The most convenient airport for flying into the Pioneer Valley is Bradley International Airport.

BUS TRAVEL

Peter Pan Bus Lines links Boston, Springfield, Northampton, Amherst, and South Hadley.

CAR TRAVEL

I–91 runs north–south the entire length of the Pioneer Valley, from Greenfield to Springfield; I–90 (the Mass Pike) links Springfield to Boston; Route 2 connects Boston with Greenfield in the north.

TRAIN TRAVEL

Amtrak (☞ Train Travel *in* Boston Essentials) stops in Springfield on routes from Boston and New York.

VISITOR INFORMATION

➤ TOURIST INFORMATION: **Greater Springfield Convention and Visitors Bureau** (✉ 1441 Main St., Southfield 01103, ☎ 413/787–1548 or 800/723–1548, WEB www.valleyvisitor.com).

THE BERKSHIRES

Though only about a 2½-hour drive west from Boston or north from New York City, the Berkshires live up to storybook images of rural New England, with wooded hills; narrow, winding roads; and compact, charming villages. Summer provides a variety of cultural events, including the renowned Tanglewood festival of classical music, in Lenox. Fall brings a blaze of brilliant foliage. In winter the Berkshires are a popular ski area. Springtime visitors can enjoy maple-sugaring. The region can be crowded any weekend.

Exploring the Berkshires

Williamstown is the northernmost Berkshires town, at the junction of Route 2 and U.S. 7. **Williams College** opened in 1793, and the town still revolves around it. Gracious campus buildings lining the wide main street are open to visitors.

The **Sterling and Francine Clark Art Institute** is an outstanding small museum, with paintings by Renoir, Monet, and Degas. ✉ *225 South St., Williamstown,* ☎ *413/458–9545,* WEB *www.clarkart.edu.* 🎫 *$10 July–Oct., free Nov.–June. Closed Mon. Sept.–June.*

The **Mohawk Trail,** a scenic 63-mi stretch along Route 2 from Orange to Williamstown, follows a former Native American path. **Mt. Greylock,** south of Williamstown off Route 7, is, at 3,491 ft, the highest point in the state.

Mass MoCA (✉ 87 Marshall St., North Adams, ☎ 413/664–4481, WEB www.massmoca.org; 🎫 $7) is the nation's largest center for contemporary performing and visual arts, with more than 250,000 square ft of galleries, studios, performance venues, cafés, and shops. Its size enables the museum to display monumentally scaled works such as Robert Rauschenberg's *¼ Mile or 2 Furlong Piece.*

Pittsfield, county seat and geographic center of the Berkshires, has a lively small-town atmosphere. **Hancock Shaker Village** (☎ 413/443–0188 or 800/817–1137, WEB www.hancockshakervillage.org; 🎫 $15, $10 in winter), 5 mi west of Pittsfield on Route 20, was founded in the 1790s as the third Shaker community in America. The religious community closed in 1960, and the site, complete with living quarters, round stone barn, and working crafts shops, is now a museum.

The village of **Lenox,** 5 mi south of Pittsfield on Route 7, epitomizes the Berkshires for many visitors. In the thick of the summer-cottage region, it's rich with old inns and majestic mansions. Novelist Edith Wharton designed the house and grounds for her summer home, **The Mount,** a turn-of-the-20th-century classical American mansion. ✉ *2 Plunkett St.,* ☎ *413/637–1899 or 888/637–1902,* WEB *www.edithwharton.org.* 🎫 *$7.50. Closed Nov.–late May.*

★ **Tanglewood** (☞ The Arts *in* Nightlife and the Arts) is summer headquarters of the Boston Symphony. Thousands flock to the 200-acre estate every summer weekend to picnic on the lawns as musicians perform on the open-air stage.

The touristy, archetypal New England small town of **Stockbridge** has a history of literary and artistic inhabitants, including painter Norman Rockwell and writers Norman Mailer and Robert Sherwood. The **Norman Rockwell Museum** (✉ Rte. 183, ☎ 413/298–4100, WEB www.nrm.org; 🎫 $10) holds the world's largest collection of the artist's original paintings.

Chesterwood was for 33 years the summer home of the sculptor Daniel Chester French, who created *The Minuteman* in Concord and the Lincoln Memorial in Washington, D.C. Tours are given of the house and of the studio, where you can see the casts and models French used to create the Lincoln Memorial. ✉ *Williamsville Rd. off Rte. 183,* ☎ *413/298–3579,* WEB *www.chesterwood.net. Tour* 🎫 *$8.50; grounds only, $6.50. Closed Nov.–Apr.*

Great Barrington is the largest town in the southern Berkshires and a mecca for antiques hunters. **Bartholomew's Cobble** (✉ Rte. 7A, ☎ 413/229–8600; 🎫 $4), south of Great Barrington, is a natural rock garden beside the Housatonic River (the Native American name means "river beyond the mountains"). The 277-acre site is filled with trees, ferns, wildflowers, and hiking trails. The visitor center has a museum.

Dining and Lodging

Lenox

$$$$ ✕🏨 **Blantyre.** Modeled after a castle in Scotland, Blantyre is awe-inspiring, with massive public rooms and nearly 100 acres of beautiful grounds. Huge and lavishly decorated, the rooms in the main house have hand-carved four-poster beds, overstuffed chaise longues, and Victorian bathrooms. The rooms in the carriage house are well appointed but can't compete with the grandeur of the main house. The restaurant ($$$$) serves upscale country-house fare; a typical entrée might be roasted arctic char with fennel confit, crispy potatoes, mussels, and saffron. ✉ *16 Blantyre Rd., off Rte. 20, 01240,* ☎ *413/637–3556,* FAX *413/637–4282,* WEB *www.blantyre.com. 23 rooms. Restaurant, pool, tennis. AE, DC, MC, V. Closed early Nov.–early May. CP.*

North Adams

$$ ✕ **Gramercy Bistro.** Occupying the space of an old downtown diner, this casual, upbeat eatery, with a wood-beam ceiling and walls lined with black-and-white photos of the town, serves eclectic grills, burg-

ers, and salads, plus a memorable weekend brunch. ✉ *24 Marshall St.,* ☎ *413/663–5300. AE, MC, V.*

$$$–$$$$ 🏨 **Porches Inn.** This former row of once-dilapidated 1890s millworkers' houses, across from Mass MoCA, has emerged as one of New England's most delightful and quirky small hotels. The design balances high-tech and historic—rooms have a mix of retro '40s and '50s lamps and Arts and Crafts furnishings along with such contemporary touches as marble-accented bathrooms with whirlpool tubs. ✉ *231 River St., 01247,* ☎ *413/664–0400,* WEB *www.porches.com. 52 rooms. Pool. AE, MC, V. CP.*

South Egremont

$$–$$$ ✕🏨 **Egremont Inn.** The public rooms in this 1780 inn are enormous, and each has a fireplace. The bedrooms are on the small side but have four-poster beds and unpretentious furnishings (some have claw-foot baths, too). Windows sweep around two sides of the stylish restaurant ($$–$$$; reservations essential summer and fall weekends). The menu changes frequently but always includes fresh fish, a homemade pasta, and a hearty meat dish. ✉ *Old Sheffield Rd. (Box 418, 01258),* ☎ *413/528–2111 or 800/859–1780,* FAX *413/528–3284,* WEB *www.egremontinn.com. 20 rooms. Restaurant, pool, tennis. AE, D, MC, V. CP.*

Stockbridge Area

$$–$$$ ✕🏨 **Red Lion Inn.** An inn since 1773, the Red Lion has a large main building and seven annexes. The rooms in the annex houses tend to be nicer. All the rooms are furnished with antiques and reproductions. The main dining room ($$–$$$) has a somewhat formal ambience and serves such creative American fare as baked bluefish with almond-mustard crust and watercress-citrus salad. The tavern serves heartier dishes, including venison stew and grilled sausage. ✉ *30 Main St., 02162,* ☎ *413/298–5545 or 413/298–1690,* FAX *413/298–5130,* WEB *www.redlioninn.com. 110 rooms, 14 with shared bath. 3 restaurants, pool, gym. AE, D, DC, MC, V. CP.*

Williamstown

$$–$$$ ✕ **Main Street Cafe.** This dark, romantic restaurant specializes in northern Italian fare, such as pan-seared jumbo shrimp with prosciutto, sage, and fresh seasonal melon, and grilled filet mignon over spinach and roasted potatoes. You can always try the pizza of the day. ✉ *16 Water St.,* ☎ *413/458–3210. AE, DC, MC, V. Closed Mon.*

$$$ ★ 🏨 **Field Farm Guest House.** Built in 1948 on 296 acres, this house, which resembles a modern museum, is now run as a B&B by a nonprofit organization. Three rooms have private decks; two have working fireplaces with tiles depicting animals, birds, and butterflies. ✉ *554 Sloan Rd. off Rte. 43, 01267,* ☎ *413/458–3135,* WEB *www.thetrustees.org. 5 rooms. Pool, tennis. D, MC, V. BP.*

Nightlife and the Arts

Listings appear daily in the *Berkshire Eagle* from June to Columbus Day. *Berkshires Week* is the summer bible for events listings. Weekly listings appear in the *Williamstown Advocate.* Major concerts are listed in the Thursday *Boston Globe.*

Nightlife

A popular local nightspot is the **Lion's Den** (☎ 413/298–5545), at the Red Lion Inn in Stockbridge (☞ Dining and Lodging), which presents live jazz, folk, or blues nightly.

The Arts

DANCE

Jacob's Pillow Dance Festival (✉ 358 George Carter Rd., at Rte. 20, Becket, ☎ 413/637–1322; 413/243–0745 box office mid-May–Aug.;

WEB www.jacobspillow.org) happens over nine weeks each summer. The participants range from well-known classical ballet companies to Native American dance groups.

MUSIC

The season at **Tanglewood** (✉ West St., off Rte. 183, ☎ 413/637–5165; 617/266–1492 information; 617/266–1200 tickets only; WEB www.bso.org), where the Boston Symphony Orchestra performs, runs from mid-June to Labor Day.

THEATER

The **Berkshire Theatre Festival** (✉ Main St., Stockbridge 01262, ☎ 413/298–5536; 413/298–5576 box office; WEB www.berkshiretheatre.org) stages nightly performances in summer at a century-old theater. The **Williamstown Theatre Festival** (✉ Williams College, Adams Memorial Theatre, 1000 Main St. [Box 517, Williamstown 01267], ☎ 413/597–3400 tickets; 413/597–3399 information; WEB www.wtfestival.org) presents classics and contemporary works each summer.

Outdoor Activities and Sports

Biking

The back roads of Berkshire County can be hilly, but the views and the countryside are incomparable. **Mountain Goat Bicycle Shop** (✉ 130 Water St., Williamstown, ☎ 413/458–8445) rents mountain bikes and can provide information on routes in the Mt. Greylock area.

Boating

The **Housatonic River** flows south from Pittsfield between the Berkshire Hills and the Taconic Range toward Connecticut. **Onota Boat Livery** (✉ 463 Pecks Rd., Pittsfield, ☎ 413/442–1724) rents canoes, rowboats, and other small craft; provides dock space on Onota Lake; and sells fishing tackle and bait.

Golf

Waubeeka Golf Links (✉ Rte. 7 and Rte. 43, Williamstown, ☎ 413/458–5869) has an 18-hole course that's open to the public. The 18-hole course at the **Cranwell Resort, Spa, and Golf Club** (✉ 55 Lee Rd., Lenox 02140, ☎ 413/637–1364 or 800/272–6935, WEB www.cranwell.com) is open to the public; there's also a golf school.

Hiking

The **Appalachian Trail** goes through Berkshire County. Hiking is particularly rewarding in the higher elevations of **Mt. Greylock State Reservation** (☞ National and State Parks). **Tolland State Forest** (☞ National and State Parks) has camping facilities and hiking trails.

Ski Areas

Cross-Country

Brodie (✉ Rte. 7, New Ashford 01237, ☎ 413/443–4752, WEB www.skibrodie.com). **Butternut Basin** (✉ Rte. 23, Great Barrington 01230, ☎ 413/528–2000, WEB www.skibutternut.com).

Downhill

Berkshire East (✉ S. River Rd. [Box 727, Charlemont 01339], ☎ 413/339–6617, WEB www.berkshireeast.com). **Bousquet Ski Area** (✉ 101 Dan Fox Dr., Pittsfield 01201, ☎ 413/442–8316, 413/442–2436 snow conditions, WEB www.bousquets.com). **Brodie** (☞ Cross-Country). **Butternut Basin** (☞ Cross-Country). **Jiminy Peak** (✉ Corey Rd., Hancock 01237, ☎ 413/738–5500; 413/738–7325 snow conditions, WEB www.jiminypeak.com). **Otis Ridge Ski Area** (✉ Rte. 23, Otis 01253, ☎ 413/269–4444, WEB www.otisridge.com).

Shopping

Antiques

The greatest concentration of antiques stores is around Great Barrington, South Egremont, and Sheffield. For a list of storekeepers who belong to the **Berkshire County Antiques Dealers Association** and guarantee the authenticity of their merchandise, send a self-addressed, stamped envelope to Box 95, Sheffield 01257 or check the Web site at www.berkshireantiquesandart.com.

Outlet Stores

Along Route 7 north of Lenox are two factory-outlet malls, **Lenox House Country Shops** and **Brushwood Farms.**

The Berkshires Essentials

AIRPORTS

The closest airports are in Boston (☞ Airports *in* Boston Essentials), Albany and New York City (☞ New York), and Hartford (☞ Connecticut).

BUS TRAVEL

Peter Pan Bus Lines serves Lee and Pittsfield from Boston and Albany. Bonanza Bus Lines (☞ Bus Travel to and from Boston *in* Boston Essentials) connects the Berkshires with Albany, New York City, and Providence.

➤ Bus Information: **Peter Pan Bus Lines** (☎ 413/426–7838 or 800/237–8747, WEB www.peterpanbus.com).

CAR TRAVEL

The Massachusetts Turnpike (I–90) connects Boston with Lee and Stockbridge. The scenic Mohawk Trail (Route 2) parallels the northern border of Massachusetts. To reach the Berkshires from New York City, take the New York Thruway (I–87) or the Taconic State Parkway. Within the Berkshires the main north–south road is Route 7.

VISITOR INFORMATION

➤ Tourist Information: **Berkshire Visitors Bureau** (✉ Berkshire Common Plaza, Pittsfield 01201, ☎ 413/443–9186 or 800/237–5747, WEB www.berkshires.org). **Lenox Chamber of Commerce** (✉ at the Curtis on Walker Street, Lenox 01240, ☎ 413/637–3646, WEB www.lenox.org). **Mohawk Trail Association** (✉ Box 1044, North Adams 01247, ☎ 413/743–8127, WEB www.mohawktrail.com).

MICHIGAN

Updated by Khristi Zimmeth

Capital	Lansing
Population	9,938,444
Motto	If You Seek a Pleasant Peninsula, Look About You
State Bird	Robin
State Flower	Apple blossom
Postal Abbreviation	MI

Statewide Visitor Information

Travel Michigan (✉ Box 30226, Lansing 48909, ☎ 800/543–2937, WEB www.michigan.org). **Information centers:** I–94 at New Buffalo and Port Huron; I–69 at Coldwater; U.S. 23 at Dundee; U.S. 2 at Ironwood and Iron Mountain; U.S. 41 at Marquette and Menominee; I–75 at St. Ignace, Sault Sainte Marie, and Monroe; U.S. 27 in a rest area 1 mi north of Clare; and Route 108 in Mackinaw City.

Scenic Drives

Route BR–15 between Pentwater and Montague follows the Lake Michigan shoreline for about 25 mi. **Route M–23** between Tawas City and Mackinaw City follows the Lake Huron shoreline for more than 160 mi. In the Upper Peninsula **Route M–28** follows the Lake Superior shoreline between Marquette and Munising.

National and State Parks

National Parks

Isle Royale National Park (✉ 800 E. Lakeshore Dr., Houghton 49940, ☎ 906/482–0984, WEB www.nps.gov/isro), 48 mi off the Michigan coast in Lake Superior, is a wilderness park, accessible by ferry from ★ Houghton or Copper Harbor or by seaplane from Houghton. **Pictured Rocks National Lakeshore** (✉ Box 40, Munising 49862, ☎ 906/387–2607, WEB www.nps.gov/piro), in the Upper Peninsula, extends 40 mi along Lake Superior between Munising and Grand Marais. **Sleeping Bear Dunes National Lakeshore** (✉ 9922 Front St., Empire 49630, ☎ 231/326–5134, WEB www.nps.gov/slbe) encompasses 35 mi of lower Michigan's Lake Michigan shore and includes the Manitou Islands; the 71,000-acre preserve has the highest sand dunes outside the Sahara.

State Parks

Michigan has 96 state parks, including 21 in the Upper Peninsula, many with spectacular waterfalls. Admission to all state parks is $4 per car, per day or $20 for an unlimited, annual pass. Most parks allow camping. A motor-vehicle permit, available at each park entrance, is required for admission. The *Michigan Travel Ideas and State Park Guide,* available from Travel Michigan, details park facilities.

Brimley State Park (✉ 9200 W. 6 Mile Rd., Brimley 49715, ☎ 906/248–3422, WEB www.dnr.state/mi/us), overlooking Lake Superior's Whitefish Bay, is one of 14 parks where you can rent a tent that's already set up and equipped with two cots and two sleeping pads. **Porcupine Mountains Wilderness State Park** (✉ 412 S. Boundary Rd., Ontanagon 49953, ☎ 906/885–5275, WEB www.dnr.state.mi.us), on the rugged western edge of the Upper Peninsula, is one of 13 parks with cabins for rent. At **J. W. Wells State Park** (✉ N7670 Hwy. M–35, Cedar River 49813, ☎

906/863–9747, WEB www.dnr.state.mi.us), some cabins are a mere few yards from the softly lapping Lake Michigan shoreline.

DETROIT

Founded seven decades before the American Revolution, the oldest city in the Midwest is a busy industrial center, producing roughly a quarter of the nation's autos, trucks, and tractors. The riverfront harbor is one of the busiest ports on the Great Lakes. Downtown, a constant flow of traffic moves in and out of the Detroit–Windsor Tunnel and across the Ambassador Bridge, both of which connect Detroit with Windsor, Ontario, directly across the Detroit River.

Though Detroit nicknamed itself the Renaissance City in the 1970s, it did little to deserve the title until recently. The new millennium brought new sports stadiums, a trio of controversial casinos, and a number of revitalized downtown areas, including the glitzy theater district—now second only to New York's Great White Way in number of seats.

Exploring Detroit

Starting from the riverside Renaissance Center, downtown, you can move outward to east Detroit and then on to the northwest side, the cultural heart of the city.

Downtown

Detroit's most prominent landmark, the big, brassy **Renaissance Center,** known as the Ren Cen, dominates the city's skyline with six office towers and the spectacular 73-story Marriott Hotel, one of the tallest hotels in the world. A city within a city, the waterfront complex has retail stores, services, and popular restaurants. It was purchased in 1997 by General Motors, which then moved in and established its new world headquarters here. There's a People Mover stop right out front.

Old Mariners' Church (☒ 170 E. Jefferson Ave., ☎ 313/259–2206) was made famous in Gordon Lightfoot's song "The Wreck of the *Edmund Fitzgerald.*" The 75-acre **Civic Center,** next to Old Mariners' Church, is a riverfront center for entertainment, festivals, and sports. At the heart of the Civic Center is **Philip A. Hart Plaza,** designed by Isamu Noguchi. In warm weather lunchtime crowds come here to enjoy the open spaces, sculptures, and computer-controlled **Dodge Fountain.**

Randolph Rogers, who created the bronze doors of the U.S. Capitol, also designed **Cadillac Square,** site of many presidential speeches and the 1872 Civil War Soldiers' and Sailors' Monument. The blinking red light atop the 47-story **Penobscot Building** (☒ 645 Griswold, ☎ 313/961–8800), the state's tallest office tower, has been part of the skyline since 1928. A statue of Steven T. Mason, Michigan's first governor, stands over his grave in **Capitol Park,** site of the state's first capitol.

Grand Circus Park was envisioned as a full circus (as open circular spaces were then known) when Detroit was rebuilt after a disastrous fire in 1805; only half the park was completed. A fountain in the west park honors Thomas A. Edison. Nearby is the opulent **Fox Theatre** (☒ 2211 Woodward Ave., ☎ 313/596–3200), which opened in 1928 as America's largest movie palace. Today it's an Art Deco showcase for top musical acts and large-screen movies.

The **Detroit Opera House** (☒ 1526 Broadway, ☎ 313/327–3279, WEB www.motopera.com) is the newly restored home of the acclaimed Michigan Opera Theatre; it also hosts visiting ballet and musical troupes from around the country.

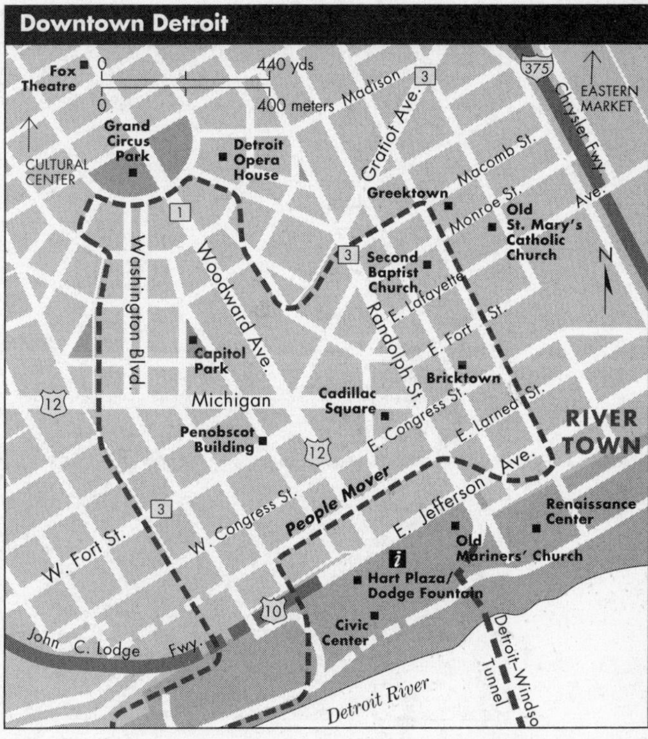

Greektown, one of Detroit's most popular entertainment districts, is centered on Monroe Street. It percolates day and night with markets, bars, coffeehouses, shops, and restaurants serving authentic Greek fare with an American flair. Greektown has become home to one of the city's three "temporary" casinos; the Greektown Casino, owned and operated by one of the state's indigenous Native American tribes, has a Mediterranean theme and is a local favorite.

Second Baptist Church (✉ 441 Monroe St., ☎ 313/961–0920), organized in 1836, is Detroit's oldest black congregation and was an important stop on the Underground Railroad. African-Americans gathered here to celebrate the Emancipation Proclamation. **Old St. Mary's Catholic Church** (✉ 646 Monroe Ave., ☎ 313/961–8711), built in 1885, began as a parish of German and Irish immigrants in 1833.

Bricktown, characterized by its brick facades, is a refurbished industrial corner of downtown filled with restaurants and bars; it's a good place for a leisurely lunch, a shopping spree, or cocktails.

Detroit East

In the 1880s the section east of the Renaissance Center, between the river and Jefferson Avenue, exploded with lumberyards, shipyards, and railroads. Known as **Rivertown,** the area is seeing new life today, with parks, shops, restaurants, and nightspots set in rejuvenated warehouses and carriage houses. **Stroh River Place,** opened in 1988, has attracted businesses, restaurants, and an Omni Hotel to a 21-acre site that stood empty for years.

Rivertown is the home of **Pewabic Pottery** (✉ 10125 E. Jefferson Ave., ☎ 313/822–0954, WEB www.pewabic.com; 🎫 free), founded in 1907, which produced the brilliantly glazed ceramic Pewabic tiles

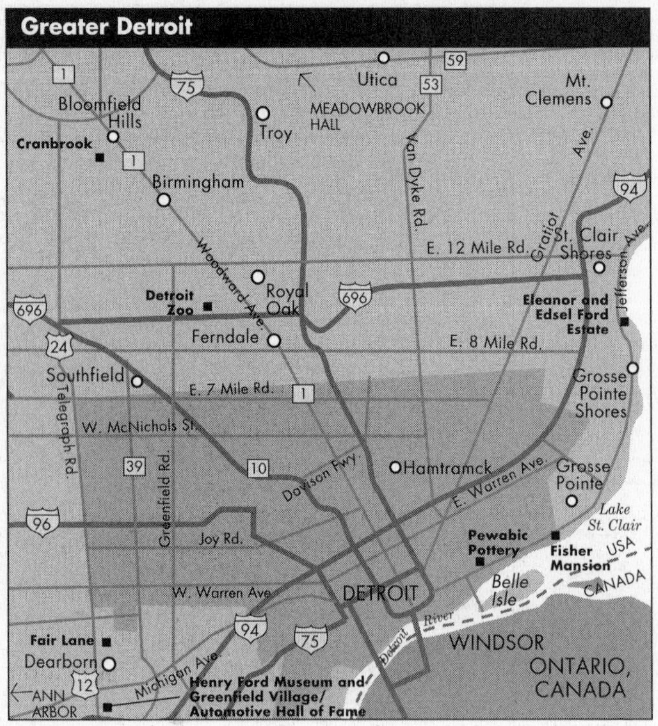

found in buildings throughout the nation, including the Detroit Public Library and Washington National Cathedral. The pottery now houses a ceramics museum, a workshop, and a learning center.

Near Northwest Detroit

Two and a half miles from downtown via Woodward Avenue is the **University Cultural Center,** a collection of art, history, and science museums and institutions clustered throughout some 40 city blocks near Wayne State University.

The main exhibit at the **Detroit Historical Museum** (✉ 5401 Woodward Ave., ☎ 313/833–1805, WEB www.detroithistorical.org; 🎫 $4.50, free Wed.) explores the city's ties to the automobile. Other worthwhile exhibits are the Lawrence Scripps Wilkinson toy collection and the Streets of Old Detroit—a walk through the city's long history.

With more than 100 galleries, the **Detroit Institute of Arts** (✉ 5200 Woodward Ave., ☎ 313/833–7900, WEB www.dia.org; 🎫 $4) displays 5,000 years of art treasures, including works by van Gogh, Rembrandt, and Renoir. Diego Rivera's *Detroit Industry,* four immense frescoes, is a must-see. The institute is open Wednesday–Sunday.

With 1.3 million books, the Cultural Center branch of the **Detroit Public Library** (✉ 5201 Woodward Ave., ☎ 313/833–1000; 313/833–1722 for recorded information, WEB www.detroit.lib.mi.us) is the system's largest. Its Burton Historical Collection is the state's most comprehensive on Great Lakes lore and genealogy. The library is open Tuesday–Saturday.

The **International Institute of Metropolitan Detroit** (✉ 111 E. Kirby St., ☎ 313/871–8600; 🎫 free) is a museum, a working resource center for foreigners, and a lunchtime café. Its Gallery of Nations displays the arts and crafts of 43 countries. The **Charles H. Wright Museum of African-American History** (✉ 315 E. Warren Ave., ☎ 313/494–5800, WEB www.

maah-detroit.org; 🎫 $5), the largest museum of its kind in the world, tells the story of the black experience in America through exhibits and audiovisual presentations.

Other Attractions

Scattered around Detroit are the lavish homes of four of the city's famed auto barons. Henry Ford's **Fair Lane** (✉ 4901 Evergreen Rd., Dearborn, ☎ 313/593–5590, WEB www.umd.umich.edu/fairlane; 🎫 $8) blends a Scottish Baronial style with a simple Arts and Crafts design. Here, you'll get a look at the bowling alley where Ford used to shoot pins with his friends Thomas Edison and naturalist John Burroughs. Ford's son Edsel built the **Eleanor and Edsel Ford Estate** (✉ 1100 Lakeshore Rd., Grosse Pointe Shores, ☎ 313/884–4222, WEB www.fordhouse.org; 🎫 $8), a 1929 Cotswold-style residence with beautiful artwork and gardens. The largest of the auto baron's homes, the opulent **Meadowbrook Hall** (✉ Oakland University, Rochester, ☎ 248/370–3140, WEB www.meadowbrookhall.org; 🎫 $8) was built in the late 1920s for Matilda Dodge, widow of auto pioneer John Dodge. Among its more than 100 rooms is a two-story ballroom; there are also formal gardens. The most lavish residence in its day, **Fisher Mansion** (✉ 383 Lenox Ave., ☎ 313/331–6740, WEB www.fishermansion.com; 🎫 $6) is the only auto baron's mansion within city limits. With 24-karat gold-leaf ceilings, it was modeled after William Randolph Hearst's San Simeon and is now a vegetarian restaurant and cultural center.

Dearborn's **Henry Ford Museum and Greenfield Village** (✉ 20900 Oakwood Blvd., ☎ 313/271–1620, WEB www.hfmgv.org; 🎫 museum and village $22, each $12.50) is America's largest indoor-outdoor museum. It charts the country's evolution from a rural to an industrial society through exhibits covering communications, transportation, domestic life, agriculture, and industry. Greenfield Village preserves 80 famous historic structures, including the bicycle shop where the Wright brothers built their first airplane; Thomas Edison's laboratory; an Illinois courthouse where Abraham Lincoln practiced law; and the Dearborn farm where Ford himself was born. The Automobile in American Life, inside the museum, is a lavish collection of chrome and neon that traces the country's love affair with cars. W. Buckminster Fuller's futuristic Dymaxion House is a recent addition well worth checking out. The adjacent **Automotive Hall of Fame** (✉ 21400 Oakwood Blvd., ☎ 888/298–4748, WEB www.automotivehalloffame.org; 🎫 $6) has profiles of the men behind the machines, a mural of automotive history, and a full-size replica of the world's first gas-powered car.

Cranbrook, in Bloomfield Hills, is a cultural and educational center with a graduate art academy and college-preparatory schools. **Historic Cranbrook House and Gardens** (✉ 380 Lone Pine Rd., ☎ 248/645–3149 or 800/462–7262, WEB www.cranbrook.edu; 🎫 $6), a mansion built for newspaper publisher George Booth, has lead-glass windows, art objects, and formal gardens with fountains and sculpture. The **Cranbrook Art Museum** (✉ 39221 N. Woodward Ave., ☎ 248/645–3323 or 800/462–7262, WEB www.cranbrook.edu; 🎫 $5) has major exhibitions of contemporary art and a permanent collection that includes works by Eliel and Eero Saarinen and Charles Eames. **Cranbrook Institute of Science** (✉ 1221 N. Woodward Ave., ☎ 248/645–3200 or 800/462–7262, WEB www.cranbrook.edu; 🎫 $7) has intriguing hands-on physics experiments, geology displays, and dinosaur-excavation findings.

Parks, Gardens, and Zoos

More than 1,200 animals from 300 species live uncaged in natural habitats at the **Detroit Zoo** (✉ 8450 W. Ten Mile Rd., Royal Oak, ☎ 248/

398–0900, WEB www.detroitzoo.org; 🎫 $8). Highlights include the world's largest "penguinarium," a walk-through aviary with tropical birds and plants, and a wildlife interpretive gallery with a butterfly house. Don't miss the Arctic Ring of Life exhibit, with polar bears and other cold-weather animals in a simulated habitat; an underwater tunnel gives you the chance to see polar bears and seals swim overhead.

Belle Isle (☎ 313/852–4075), 3 mi southeast of the city center on a 1,000-acre island in the Detroit River, is reached by way of East Jefferson Avenue and East Grand Boulevard. Here you'll find woods, walking trails, sports facilities, a 9-hole golf course, and a ½-mi-long beach. Like many other urban parks, Belle Isle is best visited during the day. Friends of Belle Isle (WEB www.fobi.org) is a good source of information.

Among Belle Isle's other attractions is the **Anna Scripps Whitcomb Conservatory** (☎ 313/852–4065; 🎫 $2), with one of the largest orchid collections in the country. **Belle Isle Aquarium** (☎ 313/852–4141; 🎫 $2), the nation's oldest freshwater aquarium, exhibits more than 200 species of fish, reptiles, and amphibians, including a popular electric eel. The **Belle Isle Nature Center** (☎ 313/852–4075; 🎫 donations accepted) has changing exhibits and presentations on local natural history. The **Belle Isle Zoo** (☎ 313/852–4083; 🎫 $3), closed November–April, has an elevated walkway that gives you a bird's-eye view of animals roaming in natural settings.

Also on Belle Isle, the **Dossin Great Lakes Museum** (✉ 100 Strand Dr., ☎ 313/852–4051, WEB www.detroithistorical.org/html/information/dossin; 🎫 $2) has displays on Great Lakes shipping and the Prohibition era in Detroit. The ongoing exhibit, "The Storm of 1913," recounts the Great Lakes' worst storm ever. You can also listen to ship-to-shore radio messages and view the river and city through a periscope. The museum is open Wednesday–Sunday.

Dining

Each wave of immigrants to Detroit has made its culinary mark: You'll find soul food in the inner city, a vibrant Mexican community on the west side, and Greek restaurants in Greektown. Detroiters often dine across the river in Windsor, Ontario, where a favorable rate of exchange makes for excellent values.

$$–$$$$ ✕ **Rattlesnake Club.** There are innovative pickerel, salmon, and veal dishes, but the signature dish is rack of lamb. The dining room is all marble and rosewood, with terrific views of the Detroit River and Windsor skyline. ✉ *300 River Pl.,* ☎ *313/567–4400. AE, D, DC, MC, V.*

$$–$$$$ ★ ✕ **The Whitney.** Once the mansion of lumber baron David Whitney, this posh restaurant turns out creative American dishes, snappy pastas, and very fresh seafood. Brunch is served on Sunday. ✉ *4421 Woodward Ave.,* ☎ *313/832–5700. Reservations essential. Jacket and tie. AE, D, MC, V.*

$$–$$$ ✕ **The Summit.** On the top floor of the Marriott Renaissance Center, this revolving restaurant has a superb view of Detroit. Steaks and seafood are staples. ✉ *400 Jefferson Court, Renaissance Center,* ☎ *313/568–8600. Jacket and tie. AE, D, DC, MC, V.*

$–$$$ ✕ **Beans & Cornbread.** In suburban Southfield, this upscale eatery pays homage to its southern roots with vintage *Life* magazine posters of famous African-Americans and mounds of solidly prepared soul food. ✉ *29508 Northwestern Hwy.,* ☎ *248/208–1680. AE, DC, MC, V.*

$–$$$ ★ ✕ **Fishbone's Rhythm Kitchen Cafe.** In the heart of Greektown, this authentic New Orleans–style restaurant is loud, brash, funky, and fun. The spicy Creole fare on the seasonal menu includes gator, gumbo, crawfish, and Gulf oysters on the half shell. The whiskey ribs are tops year-round. If you're staying in the suburbs, check out the branches in St. Clair Shores and West Bloomfield. ✉ *400 Monroe Ave.,* ☎ *313/965–4600. AE, D, DC, MC, V.*

$–$$$ ✕ **Pegasus Taverna.** Specialties such as *pastitsio* (Greek-style lasagna) and *avgolemono* (chicken-lemon soup) are prepared in a huge open kitchen at this Greek tavern. You'll also find American classics like Caesar salad and sandwiches. ✉ *558 Monroe Ave.,* ☎ *313/964–6800. AE, D, DC, MC, V.*

$$ ✕ **Caucus Club.** A venerable Detroit institution, this spot recalls a time when elegant restaurants had boardroom decor, lots of oil paintings, and wood. The menu is of similar vintage: corned-beef hash, steaks, chops, Dover sole, and the club's famous baby back ribs. ✉ *150 W. Congress St.,* ☎ *313/965–4970. AE, D, DC, MC, V. Closed weekends.*

$–$$ ★ ✕ **Blue Nile.** Detroit's only Ethiopian restaurant is, oddly enough, in the heart of Greektown. Richly seasoned meats and vegetables are served on communal platters with *injera,* a crepelike flat bread used to scoop up the foods. ✉ *Trappers Alley, 508 Monroe Ave.,* ☎ *313/964–6699. AE, D, DC, MC, V.*

$–$$ ✕ **Traffic Jam & Snug.** The menu changes often, but you can count on wheatberry and other interesting breads, inventive salads, and daily specials like spinach lasagna and Caesar salad. Dessert is key: opt for a sweet Death by Chocolate sundae. ✉ *511 W. Canfield St.,* ☎ *313/831–9470. Reservations not accepted. D, DC, MC, V. No dinner Mon., no lunch weekends.*

$–$$ ✕ **Under the Eagle.** The Eagle's food is first-rate, with generous portions of stick-to-your-ribs roast duckling and kielbasa. For the adventuresome there's *czarnina* (duck-blood soup). ✉ *9000 Joseph Campau St., Hamtramck,* ☎ *313/875–5905. No credit cards. Closed Wed.*

$ ✕ **Lafayette Coney Island.** Try the Coney Island, loose beef in a hot-dog bun, smothered with cheese, onions, and chili. At 3 AM, suburbanites and visiting celebrities in stretch limos share counter stools with workers getting off the night shift. ✉ *115 Lafayette St.,* ☎ *313/964–8198. Reservations not accepted. No credit cards.*

Lodging

In addition to those in downtown Detroit, accommodations are available in suburban Troy, with its high concentration of corporate headquarters, and in Dearborn, where the Ford Motor Company is based. Most hotels, motels, and inns offer reduced-price weekend packages.

$$$–$$$$ **Atheneum Suite Hotel.** Business travelers and visiting celebrities favor this downtown property. The spacious, individually decorated suites have Greek overtones, and the lobby bar bustles with activity. ✉ *1000 Brush St., 48226,* ☎ *313/962–2323 or 800/772–2323,* FAX *313/962–2424,* WEB *www.atheneumsuites.com. 174 suites. Restaurant, pool, health club. AE, DC, MC, V.*

$$$–$$$$ ★ **Ritz-Carlton, Dearborn.** Like Ritz-Carlton hotels around the world, Dearborn's is known for impeccable taste and service. Its mahogany-paneled walls, overstuffed settees, and antique art suggest a clubby, British elegance. Reinforcing that image is a traditional afternoon tea and hors d'oeuvres served in the lobby lounge. ✉ *300 Town Center Dr., Dearborn 48126,* ☎ *313/441–2000 or 800/241–3333,* FAX *313/441–2051,* WEB *www.ritzcarlton.com. 308 rooms. Restaurant, pool, gym. AE, D, DC, MC, V.*

$$$ **Hyatt Regency Dearborn.** Opposite Ford's world headquarters, this large, modern, and recently renovated hotel with a trademark Hyatt atrium is five minutes from the Henry Ford Museum and Greenfield

Village. ✉ *Fairlane Town Center, Dearborn 48126,* ☎ *313/593–1234 or 800/233–1234,* FAX *313/593–3366,* WEB *www.hyatt.com. 771 rooms. 2 restaurants, pool. AE, D, DC, MC, V.*

$$–$$$ ★ **Courtyard by Marriott Downtown.** One of Detroit's most modern hotels, the Courtyard (formerly a Doubletree and an Omni) is connected by skywalk to the Renaissance Center, and by the People Mover to the rest of downtown. Rooms are bright and large. ✉ *333 E. Jefferson Ave., 48226,* ☎ *313/222–7700 or 800/222–8733,* FAX *313/222–8517,* WEB *www.courtyard.com. 254 rooms. Restaurant, pool, tennis, health club. AE, D, DC, MC, V.*

$$–$$$ **Dearborn Inn–A Marriott Hotel.** Henry Ford built this hotel in 1931 to house foreign dignitaries and such inventors as Thomas Edison and Charles Lindbergh. The colonial-inspired property is across from the Henry Ford Museum and Greenfield Village; adjacent to the main building are five historic homes associated with such famous Americans as Patrick Henry, Edgar Allan Poe, and Walt Whitman. ✉ *20301 Oakwood Blvd., Dearborn 48124,* ☎ *313/271–2700 or 800/228–9290,* FAX *313/271–7464,* WEB *www.marriott.com. 220 rooms, 5 cottages. 2 restaurants, pool, tennis, gym. AE, D, DC, MC, V.*

$$–$$$ **Embassy Suites.** A feast for the eyes, this all-suites hotel has an eight-story atrium full of trees, flowers, and ivy. It's centrally located for Troy business and the nearby Somerset Mall. ✉ *850 Tower Dr., Troy 48098,* ☎ *248/879–7500 or 800/424–2900,* FAX *248/879–9139,* WEB *www.embassysuites.com. 251 suites. Restaurant, pool, health club. AE, D, DC, MC, V. BP.*

$$–$$$ ★ **Marriott Renaissance.** At 73 stories and 1,342 rooms, this hotel is known for its size more than anything else. Guest rooms are neither large nor special, but each commands a waterfront view of the city and of neighboring Windsor, Ontario. ✉ *Renaissance Center, Jefferson Ave. at Randolph St., 48243,* ☎ *313/568–8000 or 800/228–9290,* FAX *313/568–8146,* WEB *www.marriott.com. 1,342 rooms. Restaurant, pool, health club. AE, D, DC, MC, V.*

$$–$$$ **Somerset Inn.** In the heart of Troy's corporate district, 25 mi north of Detroit, the Somerset is a favorite of the business set. Guest rooms are small and standard, but the entry level is lovely, with several small sitting rooms tucked around the perimeter. ✉ *2601 W. Big Beaver Rd., Troy 48084,* ☎ *248/643–7800 or 800/228–8769,* FAX *248/643–2296,* WEB *www.somersetinn.com. 250 rooms. Restaurant, pool, health club. AE, D, DC, MC, V.*

$$ **Crowne Plaza Hotel Pontchartrain.** The Pontch, as it is familiarly known, has light, airy rooms done in neutral shades accented by green-and-rose fabrics. Most rooms have wonderful views of the city and the river; do not, however, accept a room at the back of the hotel—which is across the street from a fire station—unless you are a heavy sleeper. ✉ *2 Washington Blvd., 48226,* ☎ *313/965–0200,* FAX *313/965–9464,* WEB *www.crowneplaza.com. 413 rooms. Restaurant, pool, health club. AE, DC, MC, V.*

$–$$ **Shorecrest Motor Inn.** Two blocks east of the Renaissance Center and within walking distance of downtown attractions is this pleasant, no-frills two-story hotel. ✉ *1316 E. Jefferson Ave., 48207,* ☎ *313/568–3000 or 800/992–9616,* FAX *313/568–3002,* WEB *www.shorecrestmi.com. 54 rooms. Restaurant. AE, D, DC, MC, V.*

Nightlife and the Arts

Nightlife

Much of Detroit's nightlife is centered downtown and in suburban Royal Oak, home to cutting-edge restaurants and smoky coffeehouses. In Greektown, tourists crowd the **Bouzouki Lounge** (✉ 432 E. Lafayette

St., ☏ 313/964–5744) for traditional Greek music, folk singers, and belly dancers. On the west side of the city is **Baker's Keyboard Lounge** (✉ 20510 Livernois Ave., ☏ 313/345–6300), a dimly lighted, smoke-filled club with nightly jazz and great soul food.

Poetry readings, art exhibitions, and no-nonsense live acts give **Alvin's** (✉ 5756 Cass St., ☏ 313/832–2355) a bohemian appeal, especially among students at nearby Wayne State University. Alternative music can be had at **St. Andrews Hall** (✉ 431 E. Congress St., ☏ 313/961–8137)

The Arts

Metro Times, a free weekly available throughout the metropolitan area, has a comprehensive calendar of events. Also check the arts sections of the *Detroit News* and *Detroit Free Press,* and the calendar section of *Hour Detroit,* the award-winning city magazine.

The **Detroit Repertory Theater** (✉ 13103 Woodrow Wilson Ave., ☏ 313/868–1347) is one of the city's oldest resident theater companies. Touring Broadway shows and nationally known entertainers appear at the **Fisher Theater** (✉ 3011 W. Grand Blvd., ☏ 313/872–1000, WEB www.nederlanderdetroit/com/fisher) and the **Masonic Temple** (✉ 500 Temple St., ☏ 313/832–7100). **Detroit Symphony Orchestra Hall** (✉ 3663 Woodward Ave., ☏ 313/576–5100, WEB www.detroitsymphony.com) hosts the Chamber Music Society of Detroit and the Detroit Symphony. The **Detroit Opera House** (✉ 1526 Broadway, ☏ 313/327–3279, WEB www.motopera.com) is home to the acclaimed Michigan Opera Theatre. Across the street is the relocated **Gem Theatre** (✉ 333 Madison Ave., ☏ 313/963–9800, WEB www.gemtheatre.com), which used to stand across from the Fox but was moved to a new site near the Opera House to make way for the new Detroit Tigers ball park.

Spectator Sports

Baseball: Glitzy Comerica Park has all the bells and whistles of a modern stadium, but purists still reminisce about classic Tiger Stadium, closed in 1999. **Detroit Tigers** (✉ 2121 Trumbull at Michigan Ave., ☏ 313/962–4000, WEB www.detroittigers.com). **Basketball: Detroit Pistons** (✉ The Palace of Auburn Hills, 2 Championship Dr., 30 mi north of Detroit, Auburn Hills, ☏ 248/377–0100, WEB www.nba.com/pistons). **Football: Detroit Lions** (✉ Pontiac Silverdome, 30 mi north of Detroit, Pontiac, ☏ 248/335–4131, WEB www.detroitlions.com). **Hockey: Detroit Red Wings** (✉ Joe Louis Arena, downtown on the riverfront, ☏ 313/983–6606, WEB www.detroitredwings.com).

Shopping

Thanks to the bustle at the Renaissance Center, shopping is not as scarce as it once was downtown. These days, however, you can get the best bang for your buck in nearby suburbs, particularly Birmingham, home to some of the Midwest's finest art galleries and exclusive boutiques, and Royal Oak, with small stores stocking everything from leather clothing and paraphernalia to fine antiques.

Markets

Farmers and city-slickers alike have gathered in the historic open-air **Eastern Market** (✉ 2934 Russell St., Detroit, ☏ 313/833–1560) since 1892 to bargain and barter over fresh produce, meats, fish, and plants. Public shopping hours start Saturday at 5 AM. Stores stay open until 5 PM; open-air markets shut down around 2 PM, when the stock runs out.

Shopping Centers and Malls

New Center One (✉ 3031 W. Grand Blvd.), 2½ mi northwest of downtown, near University Cultural Center, attracts office workers during lunchtime.

The five glass towers of the **Renaissance Center** (✉ Jefferson Ave. at Beaubien St., ☎ 313/568–5600) contain retail shops, a Westin hotel, offices, restaurants, and theaters.

The **Somerset Collection** (✉ 2800 W. Big Beaver Rd., Troy) has boutiques and upscale chains such as Neiman Marcus, Saks Fifth Avenue, and Nordstrom. The mall is 2 mi west of the I–75's Exit 69.

The five-story **Trapper's Alley** (✉ 508 Monroe St.) was once one of the largest fur-processing centers in the world. Today the complex, inspired by Faneuil Hall in Boston, houses restaurants, shops, and entertainment venues.

Detroit Essentials

AIRPORTS AND TRANSFERS

Detroit Metropolitan Wayne County Airport is in Romulus, about 26 mi west of downtown Detroit. It's served by most major airlines, with nearly 1,000 arrivals and departures daily.

➤ AIRPORT INFORMATION: **Detroit Metropolitan Wayne County Airport** (✉ 1 Rogell Dr., ☎ 734/247–7265, WEB www.waynecounty.com/airport).

BUS TRAVEL TO AND FROM DETROIT

➤ BUS INFORMATION: **Greyhound** (✉ 1001 Howard St., ☎ 800/231–2222, WEB www.greyhound.com).

BUS TRAVEL AROUND DETROIT

The Department of Transportation operates bus service throughout Detroit; the fare is $1.50. Suburban Mobility Authority Regional Transportation (SMART) provides suburban bus service.

➤ BUS INFORMATION: **Department of Transportation** (☎ 313/933–1300). **Suburban Mobility Authority Regional Transportation** (☎ 313/962–5515).

CAR TRAVEL

I–75 enters Detroit from the north and south, U.S. 10 from the north. Approaching from the west and northeast is I–94; from the west, I–96 and I–696. From the east, Canadian Route 401 becomes Route 3 upon entering Detroit from Windsor via the Ambassador Bridge and Route 3B upon entering via the Detroit–Windsor Tunnel.

RULES OF THE ROAD

Detroit is the Motor City, and everyone does drive. Many downtown streets are one-way; a detailed map is a necessity. The main streets into downtown are Woodward Avenue (north–south) and Jefferson Avenue (east–west). Rush hours should be avoided.

TAXIS

The taxi fare is $2.50 upon entry, $1.60 for each mile. Taxis can be ordered by phone or hired at stands at most major hotels. The two largest companies are Checker Cab and City Cab.

➤ TAXI COMPANIES: **Checker Cab** (☎ 313/963–7000). **City Cab** (☎ 313/833–7060).

TRAIN TRAVEL

➤ TRAIN INFORMATION: **Amtrak** (✉ 16121 Michigan Ave., Dearborn, ☎ 800/872–7245).

TRANSPORTATION AROUND DETROIT

The People Mover is an elevated, automated monorail that makes a 14-minute, 3-mi circuit of 13 downtown stations. Trains run about every three minutes; the fare is 50¢ (tokens are sold at each station).

➤ CONTACT: **People Mover** (☎ 313/224–2160).

VISITOR INFORMATION

➤ TOURIST INFORMATION: **Detroit Metropolitan Convention and Visitors Bureau** (✉ 211 W. Fort St., Suite 1000, 48226, ☎ 313/202–1800, WEB www.visitdetroit.com).

ELSEWHERE IN MICHIGAN

Ann Arbor

What to See and Do

Leafy, liberal, and young (thanks to the student population of the University of Michigan), Ann Arbor is consistently rated among the country's most desirable communities. The downtown shopping district, which extends along **Main Street,** is known for its funky specialty stores, run by knowledgeable, independent owners. The State Street area, closer to campus, has one of the finest concentrations of book and music stores in the country. Among them is the original **Borders Books and Music** (✉ 612 E. Liberty, ☎ 734/668–7100), started in 1971 by two University of Michigan graduates. On campus are three exceptional free museums. The **University of Michigan Museum of Art** (✉ 525 S. State St., ☎ 734/764–0395, WEB www.umich.edu/umma) has a permanent collection of 13,000 pieces, including works by Rodin, Picasso, and Monet. Exhibits at the **University of Michigan Exhibit Museum of Natural History** (✉ 1109 Geddes Ave., ☎ 734/763–6085, WEB www.exhibits.lsa.umich.edu) range from miniature dioramas to towering dinosaur skeletons. The **Kelsey Museum of Archaeology** (✉ 434 S. State St., ☎ 734/764–9304, WEB www.umich.edu/kelsey) has ancient Greek, Egyptian, Roman, and Near Eastern artifacts. Try your hands at the 250 working-science exhibits at the newly expanded **Ann Arbor Hands-On Museum** (✉ 220 E. Ann St., ☎ 734/995–5439, WEB www.aahom.org; 🎟 $5), in an 1882 firehouse downtown.

Dining and Lodging

$$–$$$ ✕ **Gandy Dancer.** In a 19th-century railroad depot on the edge of town, this flagship of the Muer family's popular seafood chain specializes in fresh seafood and tasty pastas. The Sunday brunch is a lavish, diet-busting spread. ✉ *401 Depot St.,* ☎ *734/769–0592. AE, DC, MC, V.*

$$–$$$ ✕ **Zanzibar.** Amid tropical decor and a lively atmosphere, this hip, centrally located eatery serves entrées from tropical countries around the equator. ✉ *216 S. State St.,* ☎ *734/994–7777. AE, DC, MC, V.*

$$$ ✕🏨 **Bell Tower.** The only hotel in the heart of campus has a traditional, intimate European style. The elegant restaurant, Escoffier, serves such French dishes as baked rainbow trout stuffed with scallop mousse and sautéed sweetbreads with grapes and Madeira. ✉ *300 S. Thayer St., 48104,* ☎ *734/769–3010 or 800/562–3559,* FAX *734/769–4339,* WEB *www.belltowerhotel.com. 66 rooms. Restaurant. D, DC, MC, V.*

Ann Arbor Essentials

CAR TRAVEL

Ann Arbor, 50 mi west of downtown Detroit, is intersected by U.S. 23 and I–94.

VISITOR INFORMATION

➤ TOURIST INFORMATION: Ann Arbor Convention and Visitors Bureau (✉ 120 W. Huron St., 48104, ☎ 800/888–9487, WEB www.annarbor.org).

Mackinac Island

What to See and Do

No autos are allowed on **Mackinac Island** (island, town, and straits are all pronounced *mack*-i-naw), but the quaint Victorian village begs to be explored on foot. A small park at the eastern end of the village, along the boardwalk, affords terrific views of the Mackinac Bridge and ships passing through the straits. Farther afield, 8 mi of paved roads circle the island; bicycles rent by the hour or day at concessions near the ferry docks on Huron Street. **Mackinac Island Carriage Tours** (✉ Main St., ☎ 906/847–3573) conducts horse-drawn tours covering historic points of interest, including Fort Mackinac, Arch Rock, Skull Cave, Surrey Hill, and the Grand Hotel.

On a bluff above the harbor, **Fort Mackinac** (☎ 906/847–3328, WEB www.mackinacparks.com/fortmackinac) was a British stronghold during the American Revolution and the War of 1812. Fourteen original buildings are preserved as a museum; costumed guides conduct tours and reenactments. **Marquette Park,** directly below the fort along Main Street, commemorates the work of French missionary Jacques Marquette with a bark chapel patterned after those built on the island in the 1600s. The venerable **Grand Hotel** (☎ 906/847–3331, WEB www.grandhotel.com), now more than a century old, charges visitors $10 just to look, but the Victorian opulence of the public rooms and the view from the world's longest porch are worth it.

Dining and Lodging

$$–$$$ ✕🏨 **Island House.** The island's oldest hotel and a registered historic site is also the home of Governor's Dining Room, one of the area's most acclaimed restaurants. Fish and steak are served in a formal dining room with views of the lake and nearby islands. *✉ 1 Lakeshore Dr., 49757, ☎ 906/847–3347, FAX 906/847–3819, WEB www.theislandhouse.com. 97 rooms. Restaurant, pool. MC, V.*

Mackinac Island Essentials

BOAT AND FERRY TRAVEL

Island ferries depart from Mackinaw City and St. Ignace, at the northern end of the Mackinac Bridge.

CAR TRAVEL

By car, take I–75 N from Detroit to Mackinaw City.

VISITOR INFORMATION

➤ TOURIST INFORMATION: Mackinac Island Chamber of Commerce (✉ Box 451, Mackinac Island 49757, ☎ 906/847–3783, WEB www.mackinacisland.com).

Keweenaw Peninsula

What to See and Do

Curving into Lake Superior like a crooked finger, the Keweenaw (*key*-wa-naw) was the site of extensive copper mining from the 1840s to the 1960s. In Hancock, you can take a guided tour of now-defunct mine workings, **Quincy Mine Hoist** (☎ 906/482–5569, WEB www.quincymine.com; 🎟 $10). Houghton is home to Michigan Technical University, whose **Seaman Mineral Museum** (☎ 906/487–2572, WEB www.geo.mtu.

edu/museum; 🎫 $4) has displays of minerals native to the Upper Peninsula.

North on U.S. 41, the Victorian stone architecture in **Calumet** gives a hint of the wealth in the copper towns during the boom days. Stars such as Sarah Bernhardt and Douglas Fairbanks Sr. once performed at the circa-1900 **Calumet Theater** (☎ 906/337–2610, WEB www.calumettheatre.com). At **Coppertown, U.S.A.** (☎ 906/337–4579, WEB www.uppermichigan.com/coppertown; 🎫 $4), a visitor center and museum tell the story of the mines, towns, and hearty people of the Keweenaw. Michigan's northernmost community, **Copper Harbor,** at the tip of the Keweenaw peninsula, is a crowd-free biking and camping destination. **Fort Wilkins State Historic Park** (☎ 906/289–4215) contains the restored buildings of an army post established in 1844 and abandoned in 1870; the complex also has copper-mine shafts, hiking trails, and campgrounds. **Brockway Mountain Drive** climbs 900 ft above Copper Harbor for magnificent views of the peninsula and Lake Superior.

Keweenaw Peninsula Essentials

CAR TRAVEL

The Keweenaw, in the northwestern section of the Upper Peninsula, is reached by U.S. 41.

VISITOR INFORMATION

➤ TOURIST INFORMATION: **Keweenaw Tourism Council** (✉ 326 Shelden Ave., Houghton 49931, ☎ 906/482–2388 or 800/338–7982, WEB www.keweenaw.org).

Lake Michigan Shore

What to See and Do

The Lake Michigan shoreline, which extends from the southwestern corner of the state up to the Mackinac Bridge, is one of Michigan's greatest natural resources. Its placid waters, cool breezes, and sugary beaches (including some of the largest sand dunes in the world) have attracted generations of tourists, including such regulars as Al Capone, Ernest Hemingway, and L. Frank Baum (who wrote many of his books about Oz over the course of several summer vacations here). The southern stretch is especially popular with Chicago residents and expatriates.

Resort towns, some of which triple in population between Memorial Day and Labor Day, dot the shoreline. **St. Joseph** is a picturesque community whose turn-of-the-20th-century downtown and two 1,000-ft-long piers make it ideal for walkers. The artists' colony of **Saugatuck** has many fine restaurants and shops, an active gay and lesbian community, and enough B&Bs to make it the bed-and-breakfast capital of the state. **Saugatuck Dune Rides** (☎ 616/857–2253) offers freewheeling dune-buggy rides along Lake Michigan. In **Douglas,** the ***S. S. Keewatin*** (☎ 616/857–2701), one of the Great Lakes' last passenger steamboats, is permanently docked as a maritime museum.

Near Douglas is **Holland,** home of the **Tulip Time Festival** in May. The **De Klomp Wooden Shoe and Delftware Factory** (✉ 12755 Quincy St., ☎ 616/399–1900, WEB www.veldheertulip.com; 🎫 free) is the only place outside the Netherlands where earthenware is hand-painted and fired using Delft blue glaze.

North of Holland is the eastern shore's largest city, **Muskegon,** an industrial town known mainly as the home of the **Muskegon Winter Sports Complex** (☎ 231/744–9629), with the only luge run in the Midwest. The Art Deco **Frauenthal Center for the Performing Arts** (✉ 425 W.

Western St., ☎ 231/722–4538, WEB www.frauenthalcenter.org) hosts traveling Broadway-quality plays, silent films, and the West Shore Symphony Orchestra. Eight miles north of Muskegon is **Michigan's Adventure Amusement Park** (✉ 4750 Whitehall Rd., ☎ 231/766–3377, WEB www.miadventure.com; 🎫 $22), with more than 20 rides, 10 water slides, a wave pool, shows, games, food, and the only two roller coasters in Michigan.

A two-hour drive north of Muskegon is **Traverse City,** Michigan's premier sports-vacation destination. Much to the chagrin of longtime residents, the area south of Grand Traverse Bay was "discovered" by sportsmen—and developers—about 25 years ago. Unfortunately, the roads have not kept pace with the boom in sailors, golfers, and skiers: The two-lane highways can resemble parking lots, particularly during the popular **National Cherry Festival.** For a pleasant diversion follow Route 37 around the **Old Mission Peninsula,** filled with the cherry orchards and vineyards that are the area's main industry next to tourism. A good time to visit is in the spring, when crowds are small.

Savor some of the finest views of Lake Michigan from the **Leelanau Peninsula,** the finger that juts into Little Traverse Bay. Follow Route 119 to **Harbor Springs,** a resort village overlooking Little Traverse Bay.

Lake Michigan Shore Essentials

CAR TRAVEL

U.S. 31 edges Lake Michigan from St. Joseph to Mackinaw City.

VISITOR INFORMATION

The West Michigan Tourist Association provides information on the Lake Michigan Shore area.

➤ TOURIST INFORMATION: **West Michigan Tourist Association** (✉ 1253 Front St., Grand Rapids 49504, ☎ 616/456–8557, WEB www.wmta.org).

MINNESOTA

By Don Davenport and Karin Winegar

Updated by Jim Umhoefer

Capital	St. Paul
Population	4,919,479
Motto	Star of the North
State Bird	Common loon
State Flower	Pink lady's slipper
Postal Abbreviation	MN

Statewide Visitor Information

Minnesota Office of Tourism (✉ 100 Metro Sq., 121 7th Pl. E, St. Paul 55101, ☎ 651/296–5029 or 800/657–3700, WEB www.exploreminnesota.com). There are 12 visitor centers around the state.

Scenic Drives

U.S. 61, along the Mississippi River between Red Wing and Winona, is often compared with the Rhine Valley in beauty; between Duluth and the Canadian border, it hugs the edge of Lake Superior for 160 mi, providing spectacular views of the lake and its rocky shoreline. **Route 59,** between Fergus Falls and Detroit Lakes, traverses some of central Minnesota's prime lake country.

National and State Parks

National Parks

Voyageurs National Park, in far northern Minnesota, has 30 major lakes and is part of the watery highway that makes up the state's northern border with Canada.

Pipestone National Monument, in southwestern Minnesota, protects the red stone quarry mined for centuries by Native Americans for material to carve their ceremonial pipes. The quarry is still in use, and traditional stone craft is practiced at the **cultural center** in the Monument Headquarters (✉ 36 Reservation Ave., Pipestone 56164, ☎ 507/825–5464).

State Parks

Minnesota has 68 state parks, 62 with camping facilities. For information contact the **Department of Natural Resources** (✉ DNR Information Center, 500 Lafayette Rd. [Box 40, St. Paul 55155–4040], ☎ 651/296–6157, WEB www.dnr.state.mn.us).

Fort Snelling State Park, south of downtown St. Paul (✉ 1 Post Rd., St. Paul 55111, ☎ 612/725–2389), preserves the historic fort built at the junction of the Mississippi and Minnesota rivers in 1819. **Itasca State Park** (✉ HC05, Box 4, Lake Itasca 56460, ☎ 218/266–2100) is Minnesota's oldest state park, established in 1891 to protect the headwaters of the Mississippi River, which rises from Lake Itasca. **Soudan Underground Mine State Park** (✉ 1379 Stuntz Bay Rd., Soudan 55782, ☎ 218/753–2245) has hiking trails and tours of the Soudan Mine, Minnesota's oldest and largest iron mine, which operated until 1962. **Gooseberry Falls State Park** (✉ 3206 Hwy. 61, Two Harbors 55616, ☎ 218/834–3855) and **Temperance River State Park** (✉ Hwy. 61, Schroeder [Box 33, 55613], ☎ 218/663–7476), with their roaring waterfalls and scenic views, are typical of the parks along Lake Superior's shore.

MINNEAPOLIS AND ST. PAUL

Though both Minneapolis and St. Paul straddle the Mississippi River, the two cities have completely different personalities. St. Paul feels slightly reserved and antique, as it has preserved much of its architectural heritage; downtown Minneapolis is newer, hipper, noisier, and busier. Both cities have tall, gleaming glass skylines; St. Paul's blends with its Art Deco and Victorian architecture, and Minneapolis's skyline is eclectic. Riverboat traffic calls at the Twin Cities from as far away as New Orleans.

To bear the harsh winter climate, the cities have constructed several-mile-long skyway systems. Using the skyway, you can drive downtown, park, walk to work, go to lunch, shop, see a show, and return to your car without once setting foot outdoors—a blessing in the blustery Minnesota winters.

Exploring Minneapolis and St. Paul

Minneapolis

Downtown Minneapolis is easily walkable in any season. The climate-controlled skyway system connects hundreds of shops and restaurants. In general, skyways remain open during the business hours of the buildings they connect.

The Mississippi River's **Falls of St. Anthony,** discovered by Father Louis Hennepin, drop 16 ft at the eastern edge of downtown. Harnessed by dams and diminished in grandeur, the historic falls are today bypassed by the **Upper St. Anthony Lock** (✉ foot of Portland Ave.), which allows river traffic to reach industrial sections of Minneapolis. An observation deck provides views of lock operations.

The **Stone Arch Bridge,** a railroad bridge over the Mississippi River near the Upper St. Anthony Lock, was built in the late 19th century by railroad baron James J. Hill and later restored and opened to foot and bicycle traffic. Guided walking tours of the **St. Anthony Falls Historic District** (☎ 612/627–5433) are available April–October.

With an enrollment of close to 60,000, the **University of Minnesota** is one of the largest campuses in the country. **Dinkytown,** on the east bank, and **Seven Corners,** on the west bank, are good places to find campus bars, nightspots, university shops, record emporiums, and bookstores.

The University of Minnesota's **James Ford Bell Museum of Natural History** (✉ University Ave. SE at 17th Ave., ☎ 612/624–7083, WEB www.umn.eduþbellmuse; $3) has dioramas of Minnesota wildlife, an art gallery of wildlife paintings, and a touch-and-see room for kids. The most talked-about building on campus is the **Weisman Art Museum** (✉ 333 E. River Rd., ☎ 612/625–9494, WEB www.weisman.umn.edu; free), a wild-looking metallic structure designed by famed avant-garde architect Frank Gehry. The permanent collection includes works and installations by American pop artists and modernists like Andy Warhol, Roy Lichtenstein, and Georgia O'Keeffe.

Much of Minneapolis's towering downtown was built in the past 25 years, several blocks west of the university. Two of the downtown's landmarks are the 57-story **Norwest Center** (✉ 77 S. 7th St.), designed by Cesar Pelli, and its smaller companion, **Gaviidae Common** (✉ 651 Nicollet Mall), a major downtown shopping hub. The mirrored, 51-story **IDS Building** (✉ 80 S. 8th St.) contains **Crystal Court,** a focal point of the skyway system, with shops, restaurants, and offices. The 42-story **Piper Jaffray Tower** (✉ 222 S. 9th St.), sheathed in aqua-color glass,

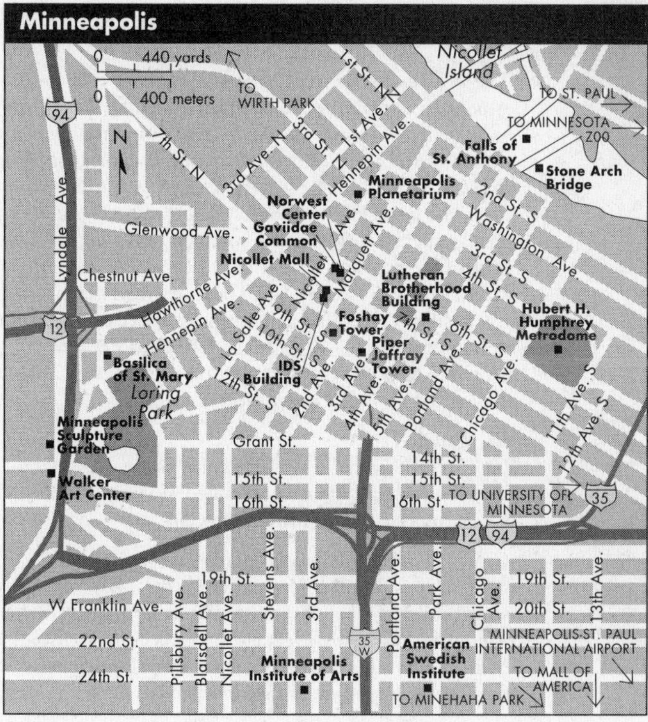

and the 17-story **Lutheran Brotherhood Building** (⊠ 625 4th Ave. SE), in copper-color glass, are sparkling members of the skyline. At the **Foshay Tower** (⊠ 821 Marquette Ave.)—Minneapolis's first skyscraper, constructed in 1929—the 31st-floor observation deck has spectacular views of the city.

Nicollet Mall, a mile-long pedestrian mall, runs from Washington Avenue S to Grant Street E, with an extensive system of skyways connecting its many shops and the public library. Inside the library, the **Minneapolis Planetarium** (⊠ 300 Nicollet Mall, ☎ 612/630–6150, WEB www.mplanetarium.org; 🎫 $2.50–$4.50) gives shows that tour the night sky and investigate the latest discoveries in space science.

Another downtown landmark, the **Hubert H. Humphrey Metrodome** (⊠ 900 S. 5th St., ☎ 612/332–0386, WEB www.msfc.com), is home to the Minnesota Twins baseball team and the Minnesota Vikings and University of Minnesota football teams. Tours of the locker rooms, playing field, and press box are available.

The **Minneapolis Institute of Arts** (⊠ 2400 3rd Ave. S, ☎ 612/870–3131, WEB www.artsMIA.org; 🎫 free, except during special exhibits), 1 mi south of downtown and west of I–35 W, displays more than 80,000 works of art from every age and culture, including works by the French Impressionists, rare Chinese jade, and a photography collection from 1863 to the present. The building also houses the **Children's Theatre Company,** which puts on adventurous plays for all ages. The institute and theater company are both closed on Monday.

The **American Swedish Institute** (⊠ 2600 Park Ave., ☎ 612/871–4907, WEB www.americanswedishinst.org; 🎫 $5) is in a 33-room Romanesque château filled with decorative woodwork. The museum, five blocks east of the Minneapolis Institute of Arts, displays art, pioneer items, Swedish glass, ceramics, and furniture relating to the area's Swedish heritage.

★ The **Walker Art Center** has an outstanding collection of 20th-century American and European sculpture, prints, and photography, as well as traveling exhibits. The center also brings national and international acts to Minneapolis. Adjacent to the museum is the **Minneapolis Sculpture Garden** (free), the nation's largest outdoor urban sculpture garden. The **Irene Hixon Whitney Footbridge,** designed by sculptor Siah Armajani, connects the arts complex to Loring Park, across I–94. The footbridge provides a clear view of the 250-ft dome of the **Basilica of St. Mary** (✉ 88 N. 17th St.). The exterior was completed in 1914, when the basilica celebrated its first mass. It became the United States' first designated basilica in 1926. ✉ *Vineland Pl., adjoining Guthrie Theater,* ☎ *612/375–7600,* WEB *www.walkerart.org.* *$6, free Thurs. and 1st Sat. of month. Closed Mon.*

St. Paul

Like its twin, downtown St. Paul is easily explored on foot thanks to its all-weather, climate-controlled skyway system. The Mississippi River runs east–west through the city.

City Hall and the **Ramsey County Courthouse** (✉ 15 W. Kellogg Blvd., ☎ 651/266–8000) look out across the Mississippi River from a 20-story building of a design known as American Perpendicular. Here, Memorial Hall (4th Street entrance) is home to Swedish sculptor Carl Milles's towering *Vision of Peace* statue, which at 36 ft and 60 tons is the largest carved-onyx figure in the world.

Rice Park, at the corner of West 5th and Washington streets, is St. Paul's oldest urban park, dating from 1849. It's a favorite with downtowners. Facing Rice Park on the north is the **Landmark Center** (✉ 75 W. 5th St., ☎ 651/292–3225, WEB www.landmarkcenter.org), which is the restored Federal Courthouse, constructed in 1902. This towering Romanesque Revival structure has a six-story indoor courtyard, stained-glass skylights, and a marble-tile foyer. Of particular interest inside the Landmark Center are a branch of the **Minnesota Museum of American Art** (☎ 651/292–4355; donation requested), which has strong holdings in Asian and 19th- and 20th-century American art, as well as changing exhibits of contemporary sculpture, paintings, and photography; and the **Schubert Club Musical Instrument Museum** (☎ 651/292–3267), with an outstanding collection of keyboard instruments dating from the 1700s.

On the south side of Rice Park is the **St. Paul Public Library** (✉ 90 W. Fourth St., ☎ 651/266–7000). On the west side of Rice Park is the **Ordway Music Theater** (✉ 345 Washington St., ☎ 651/224–4222) a state-of-the-art auditorium with faceted-glass walls set in a facade of brick and copper.

West of Rice Park is the **Alexander Ramsey House** (✉ 265 S. Exchange St., ☎ 651/296–8760, WEB www.mnhs.org; $6), home to the first governor of the Minnesota Territory. Built in 1872, the restored French Second Empire mansion has 15 rooms, elegantly appointed with period furnishings. The house contains ornate marble fireplaces and fine collections of silver and china. It's open May–December.

The **Minnesota Children's Museum** (✉ 10 W. 7th St., ☎ 651/225–6000, WEB www.mcm.org; $6.95), has educational, hands-on exhibits, plus story times and sing-alongs. It's closed Monday from Labor Day to Memorial Day.

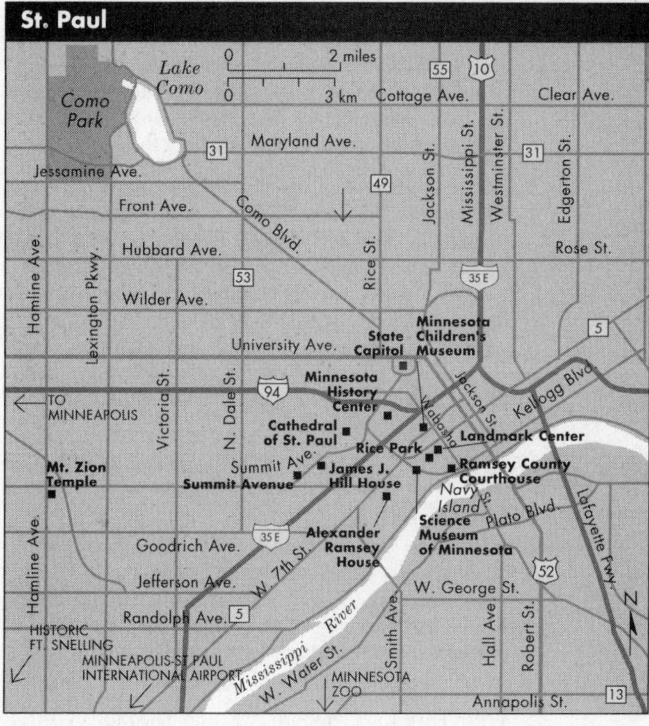

The **Science Museum of Minnesota** (✉ 120 W. Kellogg Blvd., ☎ 651/221–9488, WEB www.smm.org; 🎫 $7, films extra) has exhibits on archaeology, technology, and biology and many hands-on exhibits for kids. In the McKnight Omnitheater 70mm films are projected overhead on a massive tilted screen. Between Labor Day and late December the theater and museum are closed Monday.

Constructed of more than 25 varieties of marble, sandstone, and granite, the **Minnesota State Capitol** (✉ Aurora and Cedar Sts., ☎ 651/296–2881) is northwest of downtown St. Paul. Its 223-ft-high marble dome is the world's largest.

The **Cathedral of St. Paul** (✉ 239 Selby Ave., ☎ 651/228–1766), a classic Renaissance-style domed church in the style of St. Peter's in Rome, lies ½ mi southwest of the capitol. Inside are beautiful stained-glass windows, statues, paintings, and other works of art, as well as a small historical museum on the lower level.

The **Minnesota History Center,** established in 1849, is a modern discovery center that preserves and shares Minnesota's history. Kids can climb aboard a full-size railroad boxcar and through a replica grain elevator. Interactive exhibits show the story of the state from the perspectives of Native Americans, explorers, settlers, and more recent Minnesota personalities such as aviator Charles Lindbergh and explorer Will Steger. A research library and museum store are on site. *✉ 345 Kellogg Blvd. W., ☎ 651/296–6126 or 800/657–3773, WEB www.mnhs.org. 🎫 Free. Closed Mon. Sept.–June*

★ **Summit Avenue,** which runs 4½ mi from the cathedral to the Mississippi River, has the nation's longest stretch of intact residential Victorian architecture. F. Scott Fitzgerald was living at 599 Summit in 1918 when he wrote *This Side of Paradise*. The **James J. Hill House** (✉ 240

Summit Ave. ☎ 651/297–2555, WEB www.mnhs.org; 🎫 $6), once the home of the builder of the Great Northern Railroad, is a Richardsonian Romanesque mansion, with carved woodwork, tiled fireplaces, and a skylighted art gallery with changing exhibits. **Mt. Zion Temple** (✉ 1300 Summit Ave., ☎ 651/698–3881) is the home of the oldest (1856) Jewish congregation in Minnesota.

At the confluence of the Mississippi and Minnesota rivers is **Historic Fort Snelling** (✉ Rtes. 5 and 55, near the International Airport south of St. Paul, ☎ 612/726–1171, WEB www.mnhs.org; 🎫 $5 per vehicle). As the northernmost outpost in the old Northwest Territories, it remained an active military post until after World War II. Seventeen buildings have been restored, and costumed guides portray 1820s fort life with demonstrations of blacksmithing, carpentry, and military ceremonies. Exhibits and short films on the fort are shown in the **History Center,** which is closed weekends November–April. (The fort is closed daily November–April.)

Parks, Gardens, and Zoos

Minneapolis

Minnehaha Park, on the Mississippi near the airport, is the site of Minnehaha Falls, which was made famous by Longfellow's *Song of Hiawatha.* Above the waterfall is a statue of Hiawatha and Minnehaha. Minnehaha Parkway follows Minnehaha Creek, providing miles of jogging, biking, and in-line-skating trails that run west to Lake Harriet, one of the many lakes in Minneapolis.

Wirth Park (✉ Plymouth Ave. and Theodore Wirth Pkwy.) has bicycling and walking paths through wooded areas and the **Eloise Butler Wildflower Garden**—a little Eden of local forest and prairie flora. Wirth also has a moderately challenging 18-hole public golf course, which doubles as a cross-country ski area in winter.

In Minneapolis's Apple Valley suburb, the **Minnesota Zoo** (✉ 13000 Zoo Blvd., Apple Valley, ☎ 952/431–9500, WEB www.mnzoo.org; 🎫 $10) houses some 1,700 animals in natural settings along six year-round trails. There's also a monorail, the Zoo Lab, a seasonal children's zoo, bird and animal shows, and daily films and slide shows.

St. Paul

Como Park (✉ N. Lexington Ave. at Como Ave.) has picnic areas, walking trails, playgrounds, and tennis and swimming facilities. **Como Park Zoo** (☎ 651/487–8201, WEB www.comozooconservatory.org) is home to large cats, land and water birds, primates, and aquatic animals. The adjacent **Como Park Conservatory,** in a domed greenhouse, has sunken gardens, a fern room, biblical plantings, and seasonal flower shows.

Dining

Although Minnesotans are known for the culinary traditions of their Scandinavian and German ancestors, the growing immigrant population is introducing ethnic food to the Twin Cities' cuisine.

Minneapolis

$$$–$$$$ ✕ **D'Amico Cucina.** From the gleaming white linens to the marble floors and leather chairs, this is a haute place. The seasonal menu has a modern Italian accent and includes artistically presented pastas. ✉ *Butler Sq., 100 N. 6th St.,* ☎ *612/338–2401. AE, D, DC, MC, V.*

$$$–$$$$ ✕ **Goodfellow's.** The changing menu at this plush restaurant includes regional game such as venison, pheasant, and trout in season, as well as excellent presentations of lamb, veal, and pork. ✉ *City Center, 40 S. 7th St.,* ☎ *612/332–4800. AE, D, MC, V. Closed Sun.*

$$–$$$$ ✕ **Ichiban Japanese Steakhouse.** At this gardenlike restaurant, experience Japanese teppan yaki–style cooking, where chefs prepare lobster, scallops, shrimp, chicken, and filet mignon at your table. ✉ *1333 Nicollet Mall,* ☎ *612/339–0540. AE, D, DC, MC, V.*

$$–$$$$ ✕ **Murray's.** Since 1946, this local institution has been serving up steak. Silver Butter Knife steaks, hickory-smoked shrimp, and Murray's signature garlic toast are served in a plush room with piano and violin accompaniment. ✉ *26 S. 6th St.,* ☎ *612/339–0909. AE, D, DC, MC, V.*

$$$ ✕ **Aquavit.** In an unornamented but sleek atmosphere on the ground floor of the IDS Tower downtown, try herring tacos or miso-grilled bass. The restaurant even serves its own aquavits—clear liquors flavored with cloudberries and other delicacies. ✉ *80 S. 8th St.,* ☎ *612/343–3333. AE, D, DC, MC, V.*

$$–$$$ ✕ **Kincaid's Fish, Chop and Steak House.** Kincaid's imposing interior of marble, brass, glass, and wood sets the mood for all-American standards such as filet mignon, mesquite-grilled salmon, grilled rosemary lamb, and roasted chicken Dijon. ✉ *8400 Normandale Lake Blvd., Bloomington,* ☎ *952/921–2255. AE, D, DC, MC, V.*

$$–$$$ ✕ **Whitney Grille.** In the lavish Whitney Hotel, the Grille has a flower-filled garden plaza and a hushed main room with rich woods and muted floral fabrics. The regional American specialties change seasonally and might include beef tenderloin with goose-liver pâté and port wine demiglace, and crisp whole red snapper. ✉ *150 Portland Ave.,* ☎ *612/372–6405. AE, D, DC, MC, V.*

$–$$$ ✕ **Loring Cafe.** There's a terrific view of Loring Park from this bohemian-chic café. The menu changes nightly and includes pasta, vegetarian, and meat dishes. The artichoke ramekin appetizer stands out. ✉ *1624 Harmon Pl.,* ☎ *612/332–1617. AE, MC, V.*

$–$$ ✕ **Bryant-Lake Bowl.** One of the Twin Cities' hippest restaurants is nestled in this 1930s-era eight-lane bowling alley. Impressive wine and beer lists complement such specials as soft-shell tacos and fresh ravioli with four cheeses. After your meal, bowl a few frames or catch a live performance in the attached 99-seat theater. Breakfast is a bargain. ✉ *810 W. Lake St.,* ☎ *612/825–3737. AE, D, DC, MC, V.*

St. Paul

$$$–$$$$ ✕ **St. Paul Grill.** The Saint Paul Hotel's stylish, contemporary bistro has a view of Rice Park. The menu is American with dry-aged steaks, fresh fish, pastas, chicken potpie, homemade roast beef hash, and weekly specials. ✉ *350 Market St.,* ☎ *651/224–7455. AE, D, DC, MC, V.*

$$–$$$ ✕ **Dakota Bar and Grill.** The Twin Cities' best jazz club also serves creative midwestern fare, including grilled rainbow trout and salmon-walleye croquettes. ✉ *1021 E. Bandana Blvd.,* ☎ *651/642–1442. AE, D, DC, MC, V. No lunch.*

$–$$$ ✕ **Pazza Luna.** A floor-to-ceiling mural of the face of Botticelli's Venus overlooks this artfully designed trattoria, which manages to be busy and tranquil at once. Pazza Luna stakes its reputation on innovative dishes such as the fritto misto calamari but brings panache to standards like handmade fettuccine in a Bolognese meat sauce. ✉ *360 St. Peter St.,* ☎ *651/223–7000. AE, D, DC, MC, V.*

$–$$$ ✕ **Ristorante Luci.** Intimate and popular, this family-run neighborhood trattoria serves such carefully crafted regional Italian dishes as *vitello saltimbocca,* pounded veal medallions with prosciutto and fontina cheese. Reservations are recommended. ✉ *470 Cleveland Ave. S,* ☎ *651/699–8258. MC, V.*

$–$$ ✕ **Khyber Pass Cafe.** An unassuming storefront across from a coin laundry encloses a small slice of Afghani culture and cuisine. Tangy spice combinations enliven such dishes as baba ghanouj (eggplant dip) and *shola* (mung beans) with chunks of tender stewed lamb. ✉ *1399 St. Clair Ave.,* ☎ *651/698–5403. No credit cards.*

$ ✕ **Mickey's Diner.** On the National Register of Historic Places, this quintessential 1930s diner is accented with lots of chrome and vinyl. Sit at the lunch counter or in one of the few tiny booths to enjoy stick-to-your-ribs fare; stop by for a great breakfast. ✉ *36 W. 7th St., at St. Peter St.,* ☎ *651/222–5633. D, MC, V.*

Lodging

Accommodations are plentiful in each city's downtown, along I–494 in the suburbs, in the industrial parks of Bloomington and Richfield (known as the Strip), and near the Minneapolis/St. Paul International Airport and the Mall of America. Some hotels in downtown Minneapolis and St. Paul are connected to the skyway system, making it possible to avoid—at least part of the time—Minnesota's fierce winter cold.

Minneapolis

$$$$ **Hyatt Regency Hotel.** In the heart of downtown Minneapolis, this hotel is connected by skyways to restaurants and shopping areas. The building's design centers on a sweeping lobby with a fountain and trees. Many rooms have a view of the city skyline. ✉ *1300 Nicollet Mall, 55403,* ☎ *612/370–1234,* FAX *612/370–1463,* WEB *www.hyatt.com. 533 rooms. 2 restaurants, pool, health club. AE, D, DC, MC, V.*

$$$–$$$$ ★ **Hyatt Whitney Hotel.** The 1880s flour mill converted into a small European-style hotel has suites only; half of them overlook the Mississippi. The lobby is warm with rich woods, brass, and marble. ✉ *150 Portland Ave., 55401,* ☎ *612/375–1234 or 800/233–1234,* FAX *612/339–1333,* WEB *www.hyatt.com. 96 suites. Restaurant. AE, D, DC, MC, V.*

$$$ **Millennium Hotel Minneapolis.** Many of the contemporary rooms in this 14-story hotel, in the middle of Minneapolis's downtown, have sweeping views of the city. ✉ *1313 Nicollet Mall, 55403,* ☎ *612/332–6000 or 866/866–8086,* FAX *612/359–2160,* WEB *www.millennium-hotels.com. 325 rooms. Restaurant, pool, gym. AE, DC, MC, V.*

$$–$$$ **Marriott City Center Hotel.** Within the City Center shopping mall and close to all downtown attractions is this sleek 31-story hotel. ✉ *30 S. 7th St., 55402,* ☎ *612/349–4000,* FAX *612/332–7165,* WEB *www.marriotthotels.com. 583 rooms. Restaurant, health club. AE, D, DC, MC, V.*

$$–$$$ **Nicollet Island Inn.** The charming 1893 limestone inn is on Nicollet Island in the middle of the Mississippi River, with downtown Minneapolis on one shore and the Riverplace and St. Anthony Main on the other. There's early American reproduction furniture in the rooms, some of which have river views. ✉ *95 Merriam St., 55401,* ☎ *612/331–1800,* FAX *612/331–5667,* WEB *www.nicolletislandinn.com. 24 rooms. Restaurant. AE, D, DC, MC, V.*

$–$$$ **Holiday Inn Metrodome.** A 10-minute bus ride from downtown, this hotel is in the heart of the theater and entertainment district and is close to both the Metrodome and the University of Minnesota. ✉ *1500 Washington Ave. S, 55454,* ☎ *612/333–4646 or 800/448–3663,* FAX *612/333–7910,* WEB *www.metrodome.com. 265 rooms. Restaurant, pool, health club. AE, D, DC, MC, V.*

St. Paul

$$$$ **Saint Paul Hotel.** Built in 1910, this stately stone hotel overlooks Rice Park and is within walking distance of St. Paul's shopping and entertainment

district. Rooms are elegant, with such furnishings as grand, comfortable chairs and four-poster beds. ✉ *350 Market St., 55102,* ☎ *651/292–9292 or 800/292–9292,* FAX *651/228–9506,* WEB *www.stpaulhotel.com. 255 rooms. 2 restaurants, gym. AE, D, DC, MC, V.*

$$$–$$$$ **The Covington Inn.** Relax on the spacious decks of the historic towboat *Covington,* moored on the Mississippi River across from downtown St. Paul. Rooms have private baths and fireplaces. ✉ *Pier One, Harriet Island, 55107,* ☎ *651/292–1411,* WEB *www.covingtoninn.com. 4 rooms. MC, V. BP.*

$$$ **Embassy Suites–St. Paul.** With terra-cotta, brickwork, tropical plants, and a courtyard fountain, this hotel has a neo–New Orleans Garden District style. It is close to I–35 E and within walking distance of major downtown businesses. ✉ *175 E. 10th St., 55101,* ☎ *651/224–5400,* FAX *651/224–0957,* WEB *embassysuites.com. 210 suites. Restaurant, pool, gym. AE, D, DC, MC, V. BP.*

$$$ **Radisson Riverfront Hotel.** The 22-story riverside tower has a lobby with Asian touches and traditional American-style rooms, many with river views. ✉ *11 E. Kellogg Blvd., 55101,* ☎ *651/292–1900,* FAX *651/224–8999,* WEB *www.radisson.com. 474 rooms. Restaurant, pool, gym. AE, D, DC, MC, V.*

$$ **Best Western Kelly Inn.** Visiting legislators have frequented this clean, efficient hotel for several decades, as it's within walking distance of the state capitol. ✉ *161 St. Anthony St., 55103,* ☎ *651/227–8711,* FAX *651/227–1698,* WEB *www.bestwestern.compkellyinnstpaul. 126 rooms. Restaurant, pool. AE, DC, MC, V.*

$$ **Holiday Inn Express.** In what was once a paint shop for the Pacific Northern Railroad, this hotel is connected by skyway to the Bandana Square shopping center. Rooms are contemporary. ✉ *1010 W. Bandana Blvd., 55108,* ☎ *651/647–1637,* FAX *651/647–0244,* WEB *www.holidayinn.com. 109 rooms. Pool. AE, D, DC, MC, V. CP.*

Nightlife and the Arts

Nightlife

With closing time at 1 AM, "the wee small hours" does not apply to the Twin Cities. Most bars and clubs attract a youngish crowd. Plenty of nightspots serve the Twin Cities' sizable gay and lesbian community.

MINNEAPOLIS

Clubs and bars are generally clustered in three areas—downtown Minneapolis, Uptown, and Seven Corners. Downtown, the intimate **Fine Line Music Café** (✉ 318 1st Ave. N, ☎ 612/338–8100) presents locally and nationally known rock musicians. In a former bus station, **First Avenue** (✉ 29 N. 7th St., ☎ 612/332–1775) attracts top rock groups and is a great place for dancing; the club was featured in the movie *Purple Rain.* Blues, rock, and alternative bands take the stage six nights a week at the **Cabooze** (✉ 917 Cedar Ave. S, ☎ 612/338–6425). The best gay bar in downtown Minneapolis is the **Gay Nineties** (✉ 408 S. Hennepin Ave., ☎ 612/333–7755).

ST. PAUL

St. Paul is said to close down with the end of the business day, but there are several good nightspots downtown and on Grand Avenue. The **Dakota Bar and Grill** (✉ Bandana Sq., 1021 E. Bandana Blvd., ☎ 651/642–1442) is one of the best jazz bars in the Midwest, with some of the Twin Cities' finest performers. The **Artist's Quarter** (✉ St. Peter St. and 7th Pl., ☎ 651/292–1359) hosts local and national jazz performers in a dark, jazz-minimalist space. For blues check out **Lucy's** (✉ 601 Western Ave. N, ☎ 651/228–9959).

The Arts

The "About Town" section of the monthly *Minneapolis St. Paul* magazine has extensive listings of events. Check out the *St. Paul Pioneer Press,* the Minneapolis-based *Star Tribune,* and the free newsweekly *City Pages* for events. **Ticketmaster** (☎ 651/989–5151) sells tickets for sporting events, concerts, theater, attractions, and special events.

MINNEAPOLIS

The Hennepin Avenue Theatre District, between 8th and 10th streets in downtown Minneapolis, is home to the city's hottest entertainment. The Twin Cities Broadway Theatre season brings national touring productions to the historic **State Theater** (✉ 805 Hennepin Ave., ☎ 612/339–7007) and **Orpheum Theater** (✉ 910 Hennepin Ave., ☎ 612/339–7007). The **Hey City Theater,** with two stages under one roof, produces live musical and comedy theater (✉ 824 Hennepin Ave., ☎ 612/333–9202).

The **Guthrie Theater** (✉ 725 Vineland Pl., ☎ 877/447–8243, WEB www.guthrietheater.org) has a repertory company praised for its balance of classic and avant-garde productions. High-caliber national acts come to the **Walker Art Center** (✉ Vineland Pl., ☎ 612/375–7622). The **Brave New Workshop** (✉ 2605 Hennepin Ave. S, ☎ 612/377–8445) will keep you laughing with original-sketch comedy. The acclaimed Minnesota Orchestra performs in **Orchestra Hall** (✉ 1111 Nicollet Mall, ☎ 612/371–5656).

ST. PAUL

The **Great American History Theater** (✉ 30 E. 10th St., ☎ 651/292–4323) presents plays about Minnesota and midwestern history. The **Penumbra Theater Company** (✉ 270 N. Kent St., ☎ 651/224–3180) is Minnesota's only African-American professional theater company. The **Ordway Music Theater** (✉ 345 Washington St., ☎ 651/224–4222, WEB www.ordway.org) is home to the St. Paul Chamber Orchestra, the Minnesota Opera, and other performing-arts groups.

Outdoor Activities and Sports

Beaches

Quite a few of Minnesota's 10,000 lakes are in or near the Twin Cities' metro area. For the best of the urban beaches, try sunbathing on the shores of Cedar Lake, Lake Harriet, or Lake Calhoun. More information about the city's famous chain of lakes is available from the **Minneapolis Parks and Recreation Board** (☎ 612/661–4800).

Spectator Sports

Baseball: Minnesota Twins (✉ Hubert H. Humphrey Metrodome, 501 Chicago Ave. S, Minneapolis, ☎ 612/335–3370). **Basketball: Minnesota Timberwolves** (✉ Target Center, 600 1st Ave. N, Minneapolis, ☎ 612/337–3865). **Football: Minnesota Vikings** (✉ Hubert H. Humphrey Metrodome, 501 Chicago Ave. S, Minneapolis, ☎ 612/335–3370).

Shopping

The skyway systems in each of the Twin Cities connect hundreds of stores, shops, and enclosed shopping malls.

Minneapolis

Among the many shops along **Nicollet Mall** are **Marshall Fields** (✉ 700 Nicollet Mall), the city's largest department store, and **Gaviidae Common** (✉ 651 Nicollet Mall), with three levels of upscale shops, including branches of Saks Fifth Avenue and Neiman Marcus. **City Center** (✉ 7th St. and Nicollet Mall) has three floors of shopping and the largest food court downtown. There are more than 40 mostly one-of-a-kind, hip urban shops and several restaurants at **Uptown** (✉ Lake and Hennepin Aves.), a smaller shopping center on Calhoun Square.

St. Paul

The **World Trade Center** (✉ 30 E. 7th St.) has more than 100 specialty shops and restaurants, including Marshall Fields. **Victoria Crossing** (✉ 850 Grand Ave.) is a collection of small shops and specialty stores anchoring the 100-plus other stores along Grand Avenue's 26 blocks. **Bibelot** (✉ 1082 Grand Ave.; 2276 Como Ave.) combines an extensive array of truly unusual and tasteful gift items with locally designed and made women's fashions.

Bloomington

Bloomington, south of Minneapolis, is Minnesota's third-largest city and home to the **Mall of America** (✉ 24th Ave. S and Killebrew Dr., ☎ 952/883–8800), the nation's largest enclosed mall. Appropriately nicknamed the Megamall, it has more than 500 stores and shops, including Macy's, Bloomingdale's, Sears, and Nordstrom. Beneath its central dome is Camp Snoopy, a large amusement park.

Minneapolis and St. Paul Essentials

AIRPORTS AND TRANSFERS

Minneapolis/St. Paul International Airport lies between the cities on I–494, 8 mi south of downtown St. Paul and 10 mi south of downtown Minneapolis. It is served by most major domestic airlines and several foreign carriers.

➤ AIRPORT INFORMATION: **Minneapolis/St. Paul International Airport** (✉ 4300 Glumack Dr., St. Paul 55111, ☎ 612/726–5555).

AIRPORT TRANSFER

From the airport to either city, Metropolitan Transit Commission buses cost $1.25 ($2 during rush hour); taxis take about 30 minutes and charge $17–$25 to both downtown Minneapolis and St. Paul.

➤ TAXI AND SHUTTLE: **Metropolitan Transit Commission** (☎ 612/349–7000).

BUS TRAVEL TO AND FROM MINNEAPOLIS AND ST. PAUL

Greyhound has stations in St. Paul and in Minneapolis.

➤ BUS INFORMATION: **Greyhound** (✉ 1100 Hawthorne Ave., Minneapolis, ☎ 612/371–3325; ✉ 166 W. University Ave., St. Paul, ☎ 651/222–0509).

BUS TRAVEL WITHIN MINNEAPOLIS AND ST. PAUL

Express fare on Metropolitan Transit Commission buses between Minneapolis and St. Paul during rush hour is $2.25. Within each city's central business district the fare is 50¢. Outside the downtown area the fare is $1.25, $1.75 during peak hours (6–9 AM and 3:30–6:30 PM).

➤ BUS INFORMATION: **Metropolitan Transit Commission** (☎ 612/349–7000).

CAR TRAVEL

The major north–south route through the area is I–35, which divides into I–35 W bisecting Minneapolis and I–35 E through St. Paul. I–94 goes east–west through both cities. A beltway circles the Twin Cities, with I–494 looping through the southern suburbs and I–694 cutting through the north.

RULES OF THE ROAD

Both cities are laid out on a grid, with streets running north–south and east–west. However, many downtown streets parallel the Mississippi

River and run on a diagonal, and not all streets cross the river. Many St. Paul attractions can be reached on foot, but most of those in Minneapolis require wheels.

TAXIS

Taxi fare is $3.40 for the first mile and $1.60 for each additional mile. Minimum fares apply. The largest taxi firms in St. Paul are Yellow and City Wide, and in Minneapolis, Blue and White, and Yellow. Town Taxi serves all suburbs.

➤ TAXI COMPANIES: **Blue and White** (☎ 612/333–3333). **City Wide** (☎ 651/489–1111). **Town Taxi** (☎ 612/331–8294). **Yellow** (☎ 612/824–4444 in Minneapolis; 651/222–4433 in St. Paul).

TRAIN TRAVEL

St. Paul's Amtrak station serves both cities.

➤ TRAIN INFORMATION: **Amtrak** (✉ 730 Transfer Rd., St. Paul, ☎ 800/872–7245).

TRANSPORTATION AROUND MINNEAPOLIS AND ST. PAUL

Both downtowns have extensive skyway systems.

VISITOR INFORMATION

➤ TOURIST INFORMATION: **Minneapolis Convention and Visitors Association** (✉ 33 S. 6th St., 55402, ☎ 612/661–4700 or 888/676–6757, WEB www.minneapolis.org). **St. Paul Convention and Visitors Bureau** (✉ 175 W. Kellogg Blvd., 55102, ☎ 651/265–4900 or 800/627–6101, WEB www.stpaulcvb.org).

ELSEWHERE IN MINNESOTA

Southeastern Minnesota

What to See and Do

High, wooded bluffs provide vast panoramas of the Mississippi River in this picturesque corner of the state. The river towns and villages are noted for their charming 19th-century architecture. **Red Wing** is famous for boots and pottery bearing its name. Levee Park, Bay Point Park, and Covill Park have stunning views of the Mississippi, which widens into Lake Pepin here. The Victorian **St. James Hotel,** built in 1875, has boutiques, shops, and an art gallery as well as grand public spaces recalling the heyday of riverboats.

Frontenac State Park (☎ 651/345–3401), 10 mi south of Red Wing on U.S. 61, has a picnic area with a 400-ft-high bluff and great views of Lake Pepin, as well as a bird sanctuary. Just outside the park is Old Frontenac, a Civil War–era village with a charming 1865 Craftsman-style bed-and-breakfast inn.

Winona is an early lumbering town settled by New Englanders and Germans. Here **Garvin Heights Scenic Lookout** (✉ Huff St. past U.S. 14 and U.S. 61) has picnic facilities, hiking trails, and scenic views from atop a 575-ft bluff. The **Julius C. Wilkie Steamboat Center** (✉ foot of Main St. in Levee Park, ☎ 507/454–1254; 🎟 $3), open Memorial Day–Labor Day, is a steamboat replica with exhibits on steamboating and river life. Exhibits of the local Polish heritage found at the **Polish Cultural Institute** (✉ 102 Liberty St., ☎ 507/454–3431; 🎟 free) include family heirlooms and many religious artifacts. The museum is open May–November.

About a half hour east of St. Paul via MN-36 is the city of Stillwater, tucked into the bluffs of the St. Croix River. The former logging town has such historical attractions as the state's first court house and remnants of Minnesota's first territorial prison. The city is also the only North America location of Christmas-ornament purveyor **Käthe Wohlfahrt** (✉ 129 S. Main St., Stillwater, ☎ 651/275–1072). The store has sold traditional handcrafted Christmas items in Germany for nearly 40 years.

Dining and Lodging

$$–$$$ ✕ **Staghead Restaurant.** At this casual eatery with pressed-tin ceilings, oak tables, and brick walls, the menu usually includes pork, chicken, and pasta, as well as scones and muffins for breakfast. ✉ *219 Bush St., Red Wing,* ☎ *651/388–6581. MC, V. Closed Sun. No dinner Mon.*

$$$ ✕🏨 **St. James Hotel.** The 1875 hotel is the area's most stately lodging. The elegant, lower-level Port of Red Wing restaurant serves such sophisticated meals as smoked, roasted duckling and lobster-stuffed chicken. ✉ *406 Main St., Red Wing 55066,* ☎ *651/388–2846,* FAX *651/388–5226,* WEB *www.st-james-hotel.com. 61 rooms. 3 restaurants. AE, D, DC, MC, V.*

Southeastern Minnesota Essentials

CAR TRAVEL

From the Twin Cities follow U.S. 61 southeast along the Mississippi River.

VISITOR INFORMATION

➤ TOURIST INFORMATION: Red Wing Chamber of Commerce (✉ 418 Levee St., 55066, ☎ 651/385–5934 or 800/498–3444, WEB www.redwing.org). Winona Convention and Visitor's Bureau (✉ 67 Main St., 55987, ☎ 507/452–2272 or 800/657–4972, WEB www.visitwinona.com).

Duluth and the North Shore

What to See and Do

Set at the edge of the north-woods wilderness and the western end of Lake Superior is **Duluth,** a city of gracious old homes with one of the largest ports on the Great Lakes. **Skyline Parkway,** a 16-mi scenic boulevard above the city, has views of Lake Superior and the Duluth-Superior Harbor, with its 50 mi of dock line. Vista Fleet Excursions (✉ 5th Ave. W and the waterfront, ☎ 218/722–6218) operates narrated boat tours of the harbor. The **Aerial Lift Bridge** (✉ Canal Dr.), an unusual 386-ft elevator bridge, spans the canal entrance to the harbor. Not far from the harbor, the **Depot** (✉ 506 W. Michigan St., ☎ 218/727–8025, WEB www.duluthdepot.org), an 1892 landmark train station, houses the Lake Superior Museum of Transportation (🎟 $8.50), with an extensive collection of locomotives and rolling stock. **Lake Superior Zoological Gardens** (✉ 7210 Fremont St., ☎ 218/723–3748, WEB www.szoo.org; 🎟 $6) has a children's zoo and animals from all over the world.

Lake Superior's rugged **North Shore** is best viewed from Hwy. 61 north of Duluth. **Gooseberry Falls State Park** (✉ 3206 Hwy. 61, Two Harbors, ☎ 218/834–3855) and **Temperance River State Park** (✉ Hwy. 61 [Box 33, Schroeder, 55613] ☎ 218/663–7476) are typical of parks found along Lake Superior's shore, with roaring waterfalls and scenic vistas.

North of Grand Marais, the **Gunflint Trail** attracts cross-country skiers with about 100 mi of groomed trails leading deep into Superior National Forest. **Gunflint Lake** was once a busy route traveled by voyagers and modern pioneers such as Justine Kerfoot, author of *Woman of the*

Boundary Waters. Kerfoot's son and his wife now run the famous **Gunflint Lodge** (✉ 143 S. Gunflint Lake, Grand Marais 55604, ☎ 218/388–2294 or 800/328–3325, WEB www.gunflint.com) and its restaurant.

Dining and Lodging

$–$$ ✕ **Grandma's Saloon & Grill.** Duluth's famous Grandma's Marathon is sponsored by this lively restaurant on the waterfront. The hands-down favorite dish is chicken tetrazzini, fettuccine and sautéed chicken in a mozzarella-Mornay sauce. *✉ 522 S. Lake Ave., ☎ 218/727–4192. AE, D, DC, MC, V.*

$$–$$$$ **Fitger's Inn.** All the rooms in this cozy inn have lake views; some also have fireplaces and skylights. All rooms have high-speed Internet access. Newer suites have double whirlpools. The building—the old Fitger's Brewery—dates to the 1850s and is part of the Fitger's Brewery Complex, a cluster of nightclubs and retail shops four blocks from downtown. *✉ 600 E. Superior St., 55802, ☎ 218/722–8826 or 888/348–4377, FAX 218/722–8826, WEB www.fitgers.com. 62 rooms. 4 restaurants, health club. AE, D, DC, MC, V. CP.*

Duluth and the North Shore Essentials

CAR TRAVEL

From the Twin Cities head north on I–35.

VISITOR INFORMATION

➤ TOURIST INFORMATION: **Duluth Convention and Visitors Bureau** (✉ 100 Lake Place Dr., 55802, ☎ 218/722–4011 or 800/438–5884, WEB www.visitduluth.com).

The Iron Range and Boundary Waters

What to See and Do

The discovery of iron ore in the north woods brought an influx of immigrants who wove a rich and varied cultural heritage. Known as the Range because it encompasses the huge Mesabi and Vermilion iron ranges, the region is ringed by deep forests and many lakes.

Eveleth, which produces taconite, a form of processed iron ore, is home to the **United States Hockey Hall of Fame** (✉ 801 Hat Trick Ave., ☎ 218/744–5167, WEB www.ushockeyhall.com; 🎟 $6), where pictures, films, and artifacts tell the story of hockey in America. In Virginia, 2 mi north of Eveleth, rimmed with open-pit mines and reserves of iron ore, the **Mine View in the Sky observation platform,** at the southern edge of town, overlooks part of the vast Rochleau Mine works. Chisholm is home to the **Ironworld Discovery Center** (✉ W. Hwy. 169 [Box 392, 55719], ☎ 800/372–6437, WEB www.ironworld.com; 🎟 $8), depicting the saga of the region's settlers through entertainment and interpretation.

West of Virginia on U.S. 169 is **Hibbing** (211 E. Howard St.in US Bank Bldg., ☎ 800/444–2246, WEB www.hibbing.org), the largest town in the Mesabi Range and the place where the Greyhound bus system began in 1914. The **Greyhound Origin Center** (✉ 1201 Greyhound Blvd., ☎ 218/263–5814; 🎟 $3) has displays and artifacts on the history of the company. Tours of the **Hull-Rust Mahoning Mine** (✉ 211 E. Howard St. [Box 727, 55746], ☎ 800/444–2246; 🎟 free), the world's largest open-pit iron-ore mine, may be arranged during the summer at the Hibbing Area Chamber of Commerce. The **Paulucci Space Theater** (✉ U.S. 169 and 23rd St., ☎ 218/262–6720, WEB www.spacetheater.mnscu.edu; 🎟 $4.50) has programs on astronomy and space exploration.

Ely, east of Virginia on U.S. 169, lies in the heart of the Superior National Forest. It is the gateway to the western portion of the **Boundary**

Waters Canoe Area Wilderness (✉ 118 S. 4th Ave. E, ☎ 218/365–7600 for Kawishiwi Ranger Station, WEB www.bwcaw.org), a federally protected area of more than 1,000 pristine lakes surrounded by dense forests. Area outfitters rent canoes and camping equipment and provide assistance in planning canoe trips. The **Vermilion Interpretive Center** (✉ 1900 E. Camp St., ☎ 218/365–3226; 🎫 $3), closed in winter, has exhibits on the Vermilion iron range, the fur trade, and Native Americans. The **International Wolf Center** (✉ 1396 Hwy. 169, ☎ 218/365–4695 or 800/359–9653, WEB www.wolf.org; 🎫 $6.50), celebrates and studies the wolf, which still thrives in northern Minnesota; more than 2,000 live in the state's wilderness. The center has exhibits, programs, and a few live examples of *canis lupus*.

International Falls, at the northern terminus of U.S. 53 on the Canadian border, is known as the "icebox of the nation" because of its severe winters. The town lies at the western edge of **Voyageurs National Park,** where the Rainy Lake Visitor Center has a slide show, exhibits, maps, and information, as well as guided boat tours of the lake and other points in the park. In town is the **Koochiching County Historical Museum** (✉ 214 6th Ave., ☎ 218/283–4316), with exhibits on early settlement, gold mining, and Native Americans. The **International Falls Chamber of Commerce** (✉ 301 2nd Ave., 56649, ☎ 218/283–9400 or 800/325–5766, WEB www.intlfalls.org) has brochures and information on area outfitters, camping, and attractions.

Dining and Lodging

$–$$ ✕🏨 **Hibbing Park Hotel.** The best hotel in the Range has a lovely lobby with a marble fireplace, and an excellent restaurant, Grandma's in the Park. ✉ *1402 Howard St., Hibbing 55746,* ☎ *218/262–3481 or 800/262–3481,* FAX *218/262–1906,* WEB *www.hibbingparkhotel.com. 121 rooms. Restaurant, pool. AE, D, DC, MC, V.*

The Iron Range and Boundary Waters Essentials

CAR TRAVEL

From Duluth take U.S. 53 N.

VISITOR INFORMATION

The Ely Chamber of Commerce provides information on canoe outfitters and trips. The Rainy Lake Visitor Center is at Voyageurs National Park.

➤ Tourist Information: **Ely Chamber of Commerce** (✉ 1600 Sheridan St., 55731, ☎ 218/365–6123 or 800/777–7281, WEB www.ely.org). **Rainy Lake Visitor Center** (✉ 11 mi east of International Falls on Rte. 11, ☎ 218/286–5258, WEB www.nps.gov/voya).

MISSISSIPPI

Updated by Linda Peal Herbst

Capital	Jackson
Population	2,814,658
Motto	By Virtue and Arms
State Bird	Mockingbird
State Flower	Magnolia
Postal Abbreviation	MS

Statewide Visitor Information

Mississippi Division of Tourism Development (✉ 501 N. West St., Jackson 39201, ☎ 601/359–3297 or 800/927–6378).

Scenic Drives

The **Natchez Trace Parkway** cuts a 313-mi swath across Mississippi from northeast of Tupelo to Natchez in the southwest, passing through Jackson at the center of the state. **U.S. 90** runs along the Mississippi Sound from Alabama to Louisiana, offering views of Gulf Coast beaches, ancient live oaks, and historic homes. Along the Mississippi River, **U.S. 61**—also known as Blues Alley and the birthplace of that musical form—runs through flat Delta cotton land to the hills of Vicksburg, then through Natchez to Louisiana.

National and State Parks

National Parks

Gulf Islands National Seashore (☞ The Gulf Coast *in* Elsewhere in Mississippi, *below*) includes Ship, Horn, and Petit Bois islands; there are nature trails and expeditions into the marsh. Vicksburg's **National Military Park** (☞ Vicksburg *in* Elsewhere in Mississippi, *below*) rivals Gettysburg in historic appeal and scenic beauty.

State Parks

Just north of Port Gibson is **Grand Gulf Military Monument Park** (☞ Exploring the Natchez Trace, *below*). **J. P. Coleman State Park** (✉ 13 mi north of Iuka off Hwy. 25, 613 CR 321, Iuka 38852, ☎ 662/423–6515) includes scenic Pickwick Lake, which has a lodge, cabins, camping, and swimming. **Tishomingo State Park** (✉ 105 CR 90, 15 mi south of Iuka and 3 mi north of Dennis off Hwy. 25 [Box 880, Tishomingo 38873], ☎ 601/438–6914), which vies with J. P. Coleman for the title of most spectacular Mississippi park, lies in the Appalachian foothills, making its terrain unique in Mississippi. Bring your own provisions to enjoy hiking and water sports. Canoe trips can be arranged at the park, and there's fishing in Haynes Lake.

THE NATCHEZ TRACE

The Natchez Trace Parkway, a long, thin park running for almost 450 mi from Nashville to Natchez, crosses early paths worn by the Choctaw and Chickasaw, flatboatmen, outlaws, itinerant preachers, post riders, soldiers, and settlers. The parkway extends for more than 300 mi in Mississippi, with other sections in Alabama and Tennessee. Meticulously manicured by the National Park Service, it is unmarred by billboards, and commercial traffic is prohibited.

The Natchez Trace

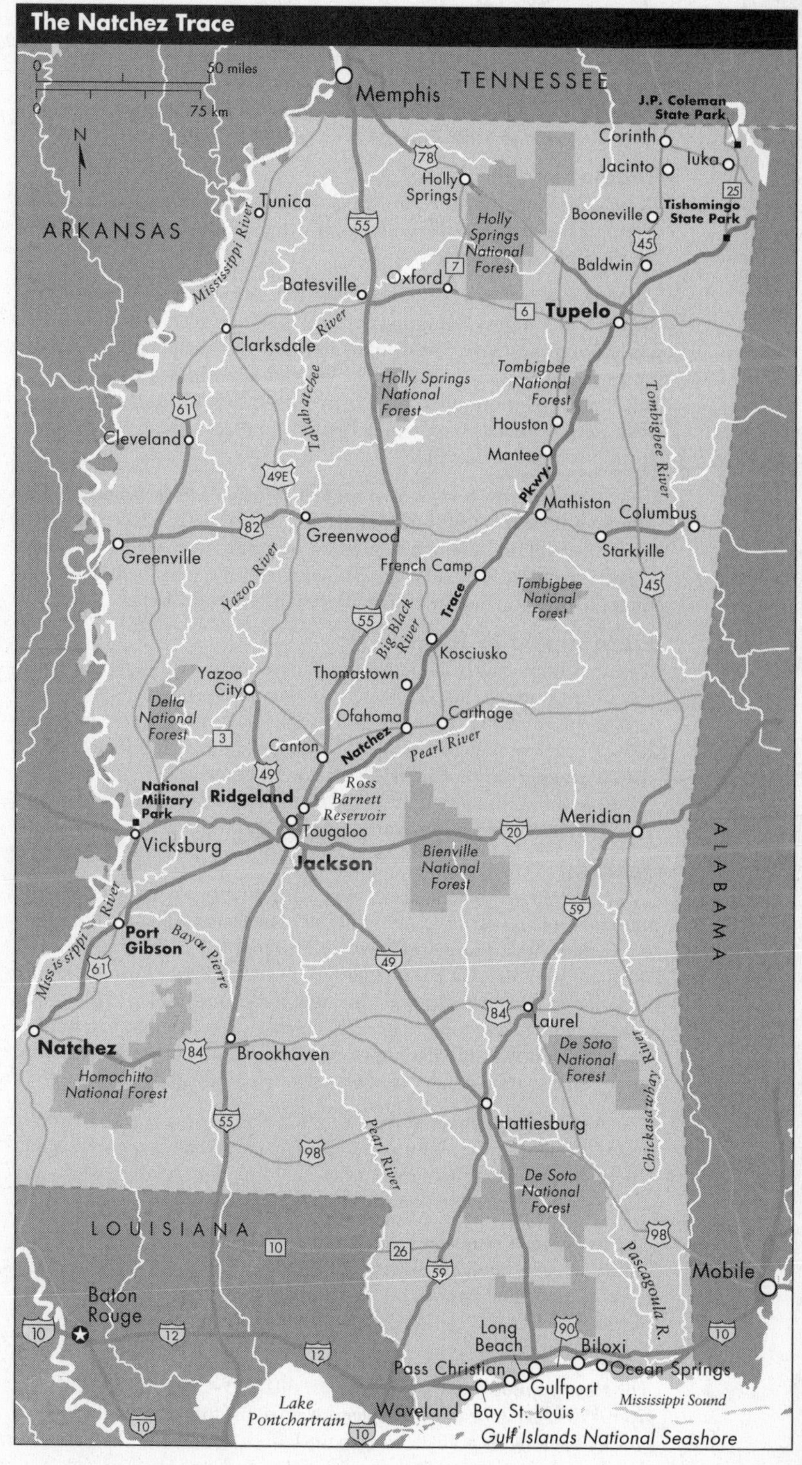

Exploring the Natchez Trace

The Mississippi segment of the Natchez Trace begins near Tupelo, in the northeast corner of the state, in a hilly area of dense forests and sparkling streams. Enjoy this natural beauty at **J. P. Coleman State Park** or at **Tishomingo State Park** (☞ National and State Parks, *above*).

Tupelo

Tupelo (named after the gum tree), the largest city in northern Mississippi, sits in scenic hill country. It's the site of the 1864 Civil War battle of the same name.

At Milepost 266 in Tupelo is the **Natchez Trace Parkway Visitor Center** that has exhibits pertaining to the history of the Trace and the area's agricultural business. On display are early surveying equipment, old maps of the area, examples of the indigenous wildlife, a few pioneering tools, and more. Pick up a copy of the *Official Map and Guide,* with detailed mile-by-mile information on places along the parkway from Nashville to Natchez.

Tupelo is probably best known for **Elvis Presley's Park & Museum** (✉ 306 Elvis Presley Dr., ☎ 662/841–1245; 🎫 birthplace $2, museum $5). Here you will find the tiny two-room shotgun house where the singer was born on January 8, 1935. The surrounding park includes a museum, a gift shop, and the **Elvis Presley Memorial Chapel.**

From Tupelo to Jackson

The four-hour trip from Tupelo to Jackson can easily take an entire day if you stop to read the brown wooden markers describing historic sites, explore nature trails, and admire the neat fields, trees, and wildflower meadows along the way. At Ridgeland, housed in a dogtrot cabin, the **Mississippi Crafts Center** (✉ Trace Milepost 102.4, ☎ 601/856–7546) sells high-quality crafts created by members of the Craftsman's Guild of Mississippi. There are rest rooms and picnic tables.

Jackson

Jackson, the state capital, has an interesting downtown, with many small museums and most of the city's notable architecture. The **Jim Buck Ross Mississippi Agriculture and Forestry Museum** (✉ 1150 Lakeland Dr., ☎ 601/713–3365; 🎫 $4) includes 10 old Mississippi farm buildings, as well as a farm (operational during harvesttime) and a 1920s crossroads town. The general store sells snacks and souvenirs. Just outside the gates a shop sells Mississippi crafts, and a down-home restaurant serves blue-plate lunches (veggies, crisp-fried catfish).

The **Mississippi Museum of Art** (✉ 201 E. Pascagoula St., ☎ 601/960–1515, WEB www.msmuseumart.org; 🎫 $5) has changing exhibits and a permanent collection of more than 3,600 works, including 19th- and 20th-century American, southern, and Mississippi art.

The **Governor's Mansion** has been the official home of the state's first family since its completion in 1842. Reservations are required to view the antiques-filled interior on free tours that leave on the half hour between 9:30 and 11 AM. ✉ *300 E. Capitol St.,* ☎ *601/359–6421.* 🎫 *Free. Closed Sat.–Mon.*

The **New Capitol** (✉ 400 High St., ☎ 601/359–3114; 🎫 free), dating from 1903, sits in Beaux Arts splendor, its dome topped by a gold-plated copper eagle with a 15-ft wingspan. Elaborate interior architectural details include two stained-glass skylights and a painted ceiling.

The **Manship House,** built in 1857, is a restored Gothic Revival home built by the mayor who surrendered the city to General Sherman during the Civil War. ✉ *420 E. Fortification St. (enter parking area from Congress St.),* ☎ *601/961–4724.* 🎫 *Free. Closed Sun.–Mon.*

Jackson's **Zoological Park** (✉ 2918 W. Capitol St., ☎ 601/352–2585; 🎫 $4) has animals, including endangered species, in natural settings.

Port Gibson

Port Gibson, about 60 mi southwest of Jackson, is one of the oldest surviving towns along the Trace. Along **Church Street** many houses and churches have been restored; here, too, is the much-photographed **First Presbyterian Church** (1859), its spire topped by a 10-ft hand pointing heavenward. Information on the town's historic sites is available from the **Port Gibson Chamber of Commerce** (✉ 1601 Church St., ☎ 601/437–4351).

Grand Gulf Military Monument Park (✉ 12006 Grand Gulf Rd., 7 mi west of U.S. 61, ☎ 601/437–5911; 🎫 $2), north of Port Gibson, was built on the site of the town of Grand Gulf, once the most thriving river port between New Orleans and St. Louis. Grand Gulf was partially destroyed in the 1850s when capricious currents caused the Mississippi to change its course and flood much of the town. Already in decline, Grand Gulf was completely destroyed by Union gunners during the Civil War. Children especially love the steep trail, the observation tower, the waterwheel, and the bloodstained Civil War uniforms on display.

Natchez

Because Natchez had little military significance, it survived the Civil War almost untouched. Today it is famous for the opulent plantation homes and stylish town houses built between 1819 and 1860, when cotton plantations and the bustling river port poured riches into the city. A number of these houses are open year-round, but others are open only during Natchez Pilgrimage weeks, when crowds flock to see them. The pilgrimages—started in 1932 by the women of Natchez as a way to raise money for preservation—are held twice a year: three weeks in October and four weeks in March and April. Tickets are available at **Pilgrimage Tour Headquarters** (✉ 200 State St., 39121, ☎ 601/446–6631 or 800/647–6742; 🎫 4-house pass $24, pageants $12), where all tours originate. **Carriage tours** (🎫 $10) of downtown Natchez begin at Pilgrimage Tour Headquarters.

★ **Rosalie** (✉ 100 Orleans St., ☎ 601/445–4555; 🎫 $6), built in 1823, established the ideal form of the southern mansion, with its white columns, hipped roof, and red bricks. Furnishings purchased for the house in 1858 include a rare parlor set. A trip down south is not complete without a visit to the grand and gracious **Stanton Hall** (✉ 401 High St., ☎ 601/442–6282; 🎫 $6), one of the most photographed houses in the country. Built around 1857 for cotton broker Frederick Stanton, the palatial former residence is now run as a house-museum by the Pilgrimage Garden Club.

Longwood (✉ 140 Lower Woodville Rd., ☎ 601/442–5193; 🎫 $6) is the largest octagonal house in North America. Construction began in 1860, but the outbreak of the Civil War prevented its completion; unfinished and mysterious, it will interest both adults and children.

Dining and Lodging

Jackson

$$–$$$ ★ ✕ **BRAVO!** This cheery, bustling restaurant in a shopping mall serves traditional regional Italian cuisine: pastas, wood-fired pizzas, antipasti, and grilled meats with inventive sauces, chutneys, and herb rubs.

✉ *244 Highland Village, South Plaza,* ☎ *601/982–8111. AE, D, DC, MC, V. Closed Mon.*

$$–$$$ ✕ **Nick's.** This elegant restaurant serves nouvelle versions of regional dishes. Lunch specialties are pasta salad and fish; for dinner another choice is beef tenderloin. ✉ *1501 Lakeland Dr.,* ☎ *601/981–8017. Jacket and tie. AE, MC, V.*

$–$$$ ★ ✕ **Schimmel's.** Schimmel's specializes in prime meat and fresh Gulf seafood. Signature dishes include the veal chop, breadless crab cake, fried lobster tails, and the Asiago-crusted flounder, which nestles under a layer of Italian cheese. ✉ *2615 N. State St.,* ☎ *601/981–7077. AE, MC, V.*

$–$$$ ✕ **Broad Street Baking Co. & Café.** You can enjoy breakfast, lunch, or dinner here, where some dozen different breads are baked fresh daily using European and old family recipes. Specialties include pizzas, sandwiches, pastries, and croissants. ✉ *101 Banner Hall, I–55 at Northside Dr.,* ☎ *601/362–2900. AE, D, DC, MC, V. No dinner Sun.*

$ ★ ✕ **Char.** Fashioned after a 1940s Chicago steak house, Char serves everything from sandwiches to salads to seafood. Steaks of all cuts are the specialty here. ✉ *4500 I–55 N, Highland Village Shopping Center,* ☎ *601/956–9562. AE, DC, D, MC, V.*

$$–$$$ ★ 🏨 **Millsaps-Buie House.** This 1888 Queen Anne Victorian, restored as a bed-and-breakfast in 1987, is listed on the National Register of Historic Places. Guest rooms are decorated with antiques, and the staff is attentive. A full southern breakfast is served. ✉ *628 N. State St., 39202,* ☎ *800/784–0221,* WEB *www.millsapsbuiehouse.com. 11 rooms. AE, DC, MC, V. BP.*

$$–$$$ 🏨 **The Old Capitol Inn.** A charming renovation of the old YWCA building in the heart of downtown Jackson, this bed-and-breakfast offers designer-showcase suites, each reflecting a Mississippi personality, including the Eudora Welty Room, the Elvis Room, and the Delta Blues Room. There is a charming rooftop garden, secure off-street parking, wine and cheese every evening, and a full southern breakfast. ✉ *226 N. State St., 39201,* ☎ *601/359–9000,* FAX *601/355–5587,* WEB *www.oldcapitolinn.com. 24 suites. AE, MC, V.*

$$ 🏨 **Edison Walthall Hotel.** The cornerstone and huge brass mailbox are about all that remain of the original 1920s Walthall Hotel, but the marble floors and paneled library–cum–writing room almost fool you into thinking this is a restoration. Guest rooms are plushly decorated, and many have refrigerators and microwaves. ✉ *225 E. Capitol St., 39201,* ☎ *601/948–6161 or 800/932–6161,* FAX *601/948–0088,* WEB *www.edisonwalthallhotel.com. 208 rooms. Restaurant, pool. AE, DC, MC, V.*

$$ 🏨 **Jackson Hilton and Convention Center.** This high-rise convention hotel in the north end of town is sleekly contemporary. ✉ *1001 County Line Rd., 39211,* ☎ *601/957–2800,* FAX *601/957–3191,* WEB *www.hilton.com. 273 rooms. 2 restaurants, pool. AE, DC, MC, V.*

Natchez

$–$$ ✕ **Cock of the Walk.** The famous original of a regional franchise, this restaurant, in an old train depot overlooking the Mississippi River, specializes in fried catfish fillets, fried dill pickles, hush puppies, mustard greens, and coleslaw. ✉ *200 N. Broadway, on the Bluff,* ☎ *601/446–8920. AE, D, DC, MC, V.*

$–$$ ✕ **Pearl Street Pasta.** The fresh pasta dishes at this intimate restaurant, including pasta primavera and breast of chicken with *tasso* (spiced ham), onions, and mushrooms are a taste of Italy in the Mississippi heartland. ✉ *105 S. Pearl St.,* ☎ *601/442–9284. AE, D, DC, MC, V.*

$$–$$$$ 🏨 **Monmouth.** This plantation mansion (circa 1818) was owned by Mississippi governor John A. Quitman from 1826 until his death in 1858. Guest rooms are in the main house as well as in a courtyard building, garden cottages, and other outbuildings. ✉ *36 Melrose Ave., 39120,* ☎ *601/442–5852 or 800/828–4531,* FAX *601/446–7762,* WEB *www.monmouthplantation.com. 30 rooms. AE, D, MC, V. BP.*

$$–$$$ **Dunleith.** At stately, colonnaded Dunleith a wing for overnight guests has rooms with antiques, fireplaces, and wonderful views of the landscaped grounds. ✉ *84 Homochitto St., 39120,* ☎ *601/446–8500 or 800/433–2445,* WEB *www.natchez-dunleith.com. 26 rooms. AE, D, MC, V. BP.*

$ **Ramada Hilltop Motel.** This motel sits on a bluff overlooking the Mississippi River to the north and Louisiana to the west. ✉ *130 John R. Junkin Dr., 39120,* ☎ *601/446–6311,* FAX *601/446–6321,* WEB *www.ramada.com. 162 rooms. Restaurant, pool. AE, DC, MC, V.*

Tupelo

$–$$ ✕ **The Cottage Shop.** In a charming alleyway in the downtown historic district, this sandwich shop/ smoke shop serves Texas barbecue, smoked turkey, beef brisket, and hand-rolled chicken and beef tamales. There is a good selection of cigars. ✉ *208 N. Spring St.,* ☎ *662/842–9191. No credit cards. Closed weekends. No dinner.*

$–$$ ✕ **Harvey's.** A local favorite, Harvey's serves consistently good chow. Specialties are prime rib, steaks, seafood, and pasta. ✉ *424 N. Gloster St.,* ☎ *662/842–6763. AE, D, MC, V. Closed Sun.*

$–$$ ✕ **Jefferson Place.** This rambling late-Victorian house is lively inside, with red-checked tablecloths and bric-a-brac. It's popular with the college crowd and specializes in short orders and steaks. ✉ *823 Jefferson St.,* ☎ *662/844–8696. AE, D, MC, V. Closed Sun.*

$–$$ ✕ **Vanelli's.** Family pictures and scenes of Greece decorate this comfortably nondescript restaurant. Specialties include pizza with a choice of 10 toppings, lasagna, and Greek salad. ✉ *1302 N. Gloster St.,* ☎ *601/844–4410. AE, D, DC, MC, V.*

$ **Ramada Inn.** This modern hotel caters to business travelers and conventioneers, as well as families. Breakfast and lunch buffets are served. ✉ *854 N. Gloster St., 38804,* ☎ *662/844–4111,* FAX *662/840–7960,* WEB *www.ramada.com. 246 rooms. Restaurant, pools. AE, DC, MC, V.*

$ **Trace Inn.** This old, rustic inn on 15 acres near the Natchez Trace has neat rooms and friendly service. ✉ *3400 W. Main St., 38801,* ☎ *662/842–5555,* FAX *662/844–3105. 95 rooms. Restaurant, pool. AE, D, MC, V.*

Nightlife

Jackson

For live entertainment, from bluegrass to Celtic, try **Hal and Mal's** (✉ 200 S. Commerce St., ☎ 601/948–0888) Tuesday–Saturday nights. At the **Dock** (✉ Main Harbor Marina at Ross Barnett Reservoir, ☎ 601/856–7765), the mood is set by people who step off their boats to dine, drink, and listen to rock or rhythm and blues. **Rodeo's** (✉ 6107 Ridgewood Rd., ☎ 601/957–9300) is a spot where patrons line up outside to line-dance inside.

Natchez

Under-the-Hill is a busy strip of restaurants, gift shops, and bars on the river. There is gambling at the permanently docked riverboat casino, the ***Isle of Capri*** (☎ 601/445–0605). **Under-the-Hill Saloon** (✉ 25 Silver St., ☎ 601/446–8023) has live music on weekends.

Shopping

In Jackson, **Everyday Gourmet and Everyday Gardener** (✉ 2905 Old Canton Rd., ☎ 601/981–0273; ✉ 1625 E. County Line Rd., ☎ 601/977–9258) stocks state products including pecan pie, muscadine jelly, jams, cookbooks, fine ceramic tableware, and bread and biscuit mixes. You'll also find gardening equipment and locally made pottery.

The Natchez Trace Essentials

AIRPORTS

Jackson International Airport, east of the city off I–20, 10 minutes from downtown, is served by American, Continental Express, Delta, Northwest Airlink, Southwest Airlines, and US Airways.

➤ AIRPORT INFORMATION: **Jackson International Airport** (✉ 100 International Dr., ☎ 601/939–5631, WEB www.jmaa.com).

CAR TRAVEL

The Natchez Trace is interrupted at Jackson; I–55, I–220, and I–20, which run through the city, connect the two segments. Natchez, at the southwestern end of the Natchez Trace Parkway, is also bisected by U.S. 61.

TRAIN TRAVEL

Amtrak stops in Jackson on its way south from Memphis to New Orleans.

➤ TRAIN INFORMATION: **Amtrak** (☎ 800/872–7245, WEB www.amtrak.com).

VISITOR INFORMATION

➤ TOURIST INFORMATION: **Metro Jackson Convention and Visitors Bureau** (✉ Box 1450, 39215, ☎ 601/960–1891 or 800/354–7695, WEB www.visitjackson.com). **Natchez–Adams County Convention & Visitors Bureau** (✉ 640 S. Canal St., Box C, Natchez 39120, ☎ 601/446–6345 or 800/647–6724). **Natchez Trace Parkway Visitor Center** (✉ 2680 Natchez Trace Pkwy., Tupelo 38801, ☎ 601/680–4025 or 800/305–7417). **Tupelo Convention and Visitors Bureau** (☎ 662/841–6521 or 800/533–0611).

OXFORD AND HOLLY SPRINGS

Holly Springs and Oxford, in northern Mississippi, are sophisticated versions of the Mississippi small town. In these courthouse towns incorporated in 1837, you'll find historic architecture, arts and crafts, literary associations, and those unhurried pleasures of southern life that remain constant from generation to generation: entertaining conversation, good food, and nostalgic walks at twilight. Oxford and Lafayette counties were immortalized as "Jefferson" and "Yoknapatawpha County" in the novels of Oxford native William Faulkner.

Exploring Oxford and Holly Springs

Oxford

Even if you're not a Faulkner fan, this is a great place to experience small-town living. You won't be bored; the kinds of characters who fascinated Faulkner still live here, and the University of Mississippi keeps things lively. Oxford's **Courthouse Square** is a National Historic Landmark. At its center is the white-sandstone **Lafayette** (pronounced luh-*fay*-it) **County Courthouse,** rebuilt in 1873 after Union troops burned it; the courtroom on the second floor is original. There's an information center at the nearby city hall.

University Avenue, from South Lamar Boulevard to the university, is one of the state's most beautiful sights when the trees flame orange and gold in the fall or when the dogwoods blossom in spring. The **University of Mississippi,** the state's beloved "Ole Miss," opened in 1848. Its tree-shaded campus centers on the **Grove,** surrounded by historic buildings.

Facing it is the beautifully restored antebellum **Barnard Observatory** (☎ 662/232–5993; 🎟 free), which houses the **Center for the Study of Southern Culture,** with exhibits on southern music, folklore, and literature and the world's largest blues archive (40,000 records). The **Mississippi Room** (☎ 662/915–7408), in the John Davis Williams Library, contains a permanent exhibit on Faulkner, including the Nobel Prize for literature he won in 1949, as well as first editions of works by other Mississippi authors. The room is closed on weekends.

★ **Rowan Oak,** built in 1848, was William Faulkner's home from 1930 until his death in 1962. The two-story white-frame house is now a National Historic Landmark owned by the university. The writer's typewriter, desk, and other personal items evoke his presence. ✉ *Old Taylor Rd.,* ☎ *662/234–3284.* 🎟 *Free. Closed Mon.*

Faulkner's funeral was held at Rowan Oak, and he was buried in the family plot in **St. Peter's Cemetery** (✉ Jefferson and N. 16th Sts.; 🎟 free). The **College Hill Presbyterian Church** (✉ 8 mi northwest of Oxford on College Hill Rd., ☎ 662/234–5020; 🎟 free), is where Faulkner and Estelle Oldham Franklin were married on June 20, 1929.

Holly Springs

Holly Springs, 29 mi north of Oxford on Route 7, contains more than 200 structures (61 of which are antebellum homes) listed on the National Register of Historic Places. On Salem Avenue, **Cedarhurst** and **Airliewood** are two privately owned mansions. The 1858 mansion **Montrose** (✉ 307 E. Salem Ave., ☎ 662/252–2943; 🎟 $5) is open by appointment only.

Dining and Lodging

Holly Springs

$ ✕ **City Cafe.** Breakfast and lunch specials pack them in at this "meat-and-three" (meat with three side orders) eatery, serving homemade soups, roast beef, and fried chicken livers. ✉ *135-E Van Dorn Ave.,* ☎ *662/252–9895. No credit cards.*

$ ✕ **Phillips Grocery.** The building was constructed in 1882 as a saloon for railroad workers. Decorated with antiques and crafts, the grocery serves big, old-fashioned hamburgers. ✉ *541-A Van Dorn Ave.,* ☎ *662/252–4671. No credit cards. Closed Sun. No dinner.*

$ 🏨 **Heritage Inn.** Rooms are comfortable if nondescript, with either a king-size bed or two doubles, and the restaurant's lunch buffet has home-style southern cooking. The motel is on U.S. 78, where it meets Routes 7 and 4. ✉ *U.S. 78 (Box 476, 38635),* ☎ FAX *662/252–1120. 48 rooms. Restaurant, pool. AE, DC, MC, V.*

Oxford

$$–$$$ ★ ✕ **City Grocery.** The menu at this trendy bistro in a former grocery store on Oxford's historic Courthouse Square is more suggestive of New Orleans than north Mississippi. A signature dish is the shrimp and grits, and there's a great wine list. ✉ *152 Courthouse Sq.,* ☎ *662/232–8080. AE, D, DC, MC, V. Closed Sun.*

$$–$$$ ✕ **Downtown Grill.** The Grill could be a club in Oxford, England, but the balcony overlooking the square is pure Oxford, Mississippi. Specialties include creole filet mignon, corn crab bisque, and Cajun-style spicy catfish Lafitte. ✉ *110 Courthouse Sq.,* ☎ *662/234–2659. AE, D, DC, MC, V. Closed Sun.*

$–$$ ✕ **Ajax Diner.** Upscale down-home cooking is what you'll get at this lively southern version of a diner. Specialties include chicken and dumplings, sweet potato casserole, po'boys, and Cajun dishes. ✉ *118 Courthouse Sq.,* ☎ *662/232–8880 AE, D, MC, V. Closed Sun.*

$ ✕ **The Bottletree Bakery.** European-style crusty bread and croissants, as well as bagels and muffins, are served with excellent coffee every weekday morning from 7 AM (later on weekends). Later in the day you can choose from homemade focaccia sandwiches and soups. ✉ *923 Van Buren Ave.,* ☎ *662/236–5000. MC, V. Closed Mon.*

$ **Downtown Inn.** The guest rooms are functional and comfortable, but don't expect high style. The restaurant prepares breakfast and a noon buffet. ✉ *400 N. Lamar Blvd., 38655,* ☎ *662/234–3031,* FAX *662/234–2834. 123 rooms. Restaurant, pool. AE, D, DC, MC, V.*

$ **Oliver-Britt House.** In a restored circa-1900 house, this conveniently located B&B has pleasant rooms. ✉ *512 Van Buren Ave., 38655,* ☎ *662/234–8043. 5 rooms. AE, D, MC, V. BP weekends.*

Nightlife

In Oxford, **Proud Larry's** (✉ 211 S. Lamar Blvd., ☎ 662/232–5993) schedules regional bands playing blues, folk, funk, jazz, and rock.

Shopping

At Oxford's well-stocked **Square Books** (✉ 160 Courthouse Sq., ☎ 662/236–2262), you can chat with the knowledgeable staff about local writers and savor cappuccino or dessert.

Oxford and Holly Springs Essentials

BUS TRAVEL

Greyhound has a station in Holly Springs.

➤ BUS INFORMATION: **Greyhound** (✉ 490 Craft St., Holly Springs, ☎ 800/231–2222, WEB www.greyhound.com).

CAR TRAVEL

Oxford is accessible from I–55; it is 23 mi east of Batesville on Route 6. Holly Springs, 29 mi north of Oxford on Route 7, near the Tennessee state line, is reached via U.S. 78 and Routes 4, 7, and 311.

TRAIN TRAVEL

Amtrak stops in Batesville, 23 mi west of Oxford.

➤ TRAIN INFORMATION: **Amtrak** (☎ 800/872–7245, WEB www.amtrak.com).

VISITOR INFORMATION

➤ TOURIST INFORMATION: **Holly Springs Chamber of Commerce** (✉ 154 S. Memphis St., 38365, ☎ 662/252–2943). **Oxford Chamber of Commerce** (✉ Jackson Ave., across from the fire station [Box 147, 38655], ☎ 662/234–4651).

ELSEWHERE IN MISSISSIPPI

The Delta

What to See and Do

Between Memphis and Vicksburg is the **Delta,** a vast agricultural plain created by the Mississippi River. Drive through the Delta on U.S. 61, which will take you past **Tunica**'s gambling halls and their towering new hotels, or down Route 1 (the Great River Road) or Route 8 for good views of the Mississippi.

Stop for lunch in **Clarksdale,** where a renovated train depot houses the **Delta Blues Museum.** The exhibits and programs at the museum trace the history of the blues and its influence on other music. ✉ *1 Blues Alley,* ☎ *662/627–6820.* 🎫 *$6. Closed Sun.*

The historic port city of **Greenville** has produced an extraordinary number of writers, including William Alexander Percy, Ellen Douglas, Hodding Carter, and Shelby Foote. The area was also home to the late Jim Henson, creator of Kermit the Frog. It's also noted as the home of Doe's (☞ Dining, *below*).

Dining

CLARKSDALE

$-$$ ✕ **Rest Haven.** The Delta's large Lebanese community influences the food, making Middle Eastern cuisine a regional specialty. Among the favorites are *kibbeh* (seasoned lean ground steak with cracked wheat), spinach and meat pies, and cabbage rolls. Daily plate-lunch specials include chicken and dumplings, salmon croquettes, and catfish. Patrons choose from three meats and seven vegetables. Breakfast is also served. ☒ *419 State St./U.S. 61,* ☎ *662/624–8601. No credit cards. Closed Sun.*

CLEVELAND

$$–$$$$ ✕ **KC's Restaurant.** The eclectic, sophisticated menu at this funky but fabulous restaurant changes seasonally, but it always has French, Italian, Asian, and southwestern influences. Count on sampling wild game, fresh fish, free-range meats, and organic vegetables. ☒ *U.S. 61 N at 1st St.,* ☎ *662/843–5301. AE, MC, V. Closed Sun. No lunch Sat.*

GREENVILLE

$$–$$$$ ★ ✕ **Doe's.** This tumbledown building is visually uninspiring, but when you see that huge steak hanging off your plate, you'll know why this place is famous. Aside from the porterhouse steaks, the hot tamales (a popular takeout item) are a specialty. ☒ *502 Nelson St.,* ☎ *662/334–3315. AE, D, DC, MC, V. No lunch.*

The Delta Essentials

CAR TRAVEL

U.S. 61 runs from Memphis through the Delta to Vicksburg, Natchez, and Baton Rouge, Louisiana.

VISITOR INFORMATION

➤ Tourist Information: **Greenville/Washington County Convention and Visitors Bureau** (☒ 410 Washington Ave., Greenville 38701, ☎ 662/334–2711 or 800/467–3582, WEB www.thedelta.org). **Mississippi Welcome Center** (☒ 4210 Washington St., Vicksburg 39180, ☎ 601/638–4269).

The Gulf Coast

What to See and Do

Oak-shaded **Ocean Springs** originated in 1699 as a French fort. It is now known as the former home of artist Walter Anderson. The **Walter Anderson Museum of Art** (☒ 510 Washington Ave., ☎ 228/872–3164; 🎫 $5) displays Anderson's work, including his cottage studio with intricately painted walls. The artist (1903–65) revealed his ecstatic communion with nature in thousands of drawings and watercolors, most kept secret until his death.

★ Ocean Springs is the headquarters of the **Gulf Islands National Seashore** (☒ 3500 Park Rd., Ocean Springs 39564, ☎ 228/875–9057). On the mainland there are nature trails and ranger programs. Out in the Gulf, pristine Ship, Horn, and Petit Bois islands have beaches as white and soft as sugar. Excursion boats to Ship, rimmed by about 7 mi of this remarkable sand, leave from Biloxi in summer and from Gulfport from May through October. Charter operators regularly take wilderness lovers to Horn and Petit Bois, both nationally designated wilderness areas, where camping is permitted.

A string of casino openings has turned **Biloxi** and its quiet beach into a mini–Las Vegas. Along with the neon lights and traffic jams have come big-name entertainment and more dining choices. In **Gulfport,** two casinos share the waterfront with the shrimp boats and banana warehouses vital to the area's economy.

Dining and Lodging

BILOXI

$$–$$$ ★ ✕ **La Cucina.** Located inside the Beau Rivage casino, La Cucina takes advantage of fresh seafood to put a Gulf Coast twist on Italian cuisine. The food is tasty, the service attentive. ✉ *875 Beach Blvd.,* ☎ *228/386–7111. AE, D, DC, MC, V.*

$$–$$$ ✕ **Mary Mahoney's Old French House.** This longtime favorite of locals prepares fresh seafood dishes, steaks, lamb, and veal. Among its most tantalizing fare is the lobster Georgio, the snapper stuffed with shrimp and crab au gratin, and the veal Antonio, topped with three cheeses and sautéed crabmeat. ✉ *116 Rue Magnolia,* ☎ *228/374–0163. AE, D, DC, MC, V. Closed Sun.*

$–$$$$ **Beau Rivage.** This hotel has all the elegance that its owner, Steve Wynn of Mirage Resorts, is famous for—plus a casino. In keeping with its southern theme, the lobby is graced by huge live magnolias, the state's flower, and other fragrant flowers that are changed regularly. ✉ *875 Beach Blvd., 39530,* ☎ *228/386–7111 or 888/567–6667,* WEB *www.beaurivage.com. 1,800 rooms. 6 restaurants, pools. AE, D, DC, MC, V.*

GULFPORT

$$–$$$ ✕ **Vrazel's.** Dining nooks with windows facing the beach add charm here. Special attractions include the red snapper, Gulf trout, flounder, and shrimp prepared every which way. ✉ *3206 W. Beach Blvd./U.S. 90,* ☎ *228/863–2229. AE, D, DC, MC, V. Closed Sun. No lunch Sat.*

$–$$$ **Grand Casino Gulfport Oasis Resort & Spa.** The Oasis has an Olympic-size swimming pool, surrounded by a grotto with waterfall and a "lazy river" that takes guests on a 15-minute inner-tube float ride. There are also outside Jacuzzis and a cabana bar. ✉ *3215 W. Beach Blvd., 39501,* ☎ *228/769–7777 or 800/946–7777. 600 rooms. Restaurant, pools, golf, tennis, gym. AE, D, DC, MC, V.*

The Gulf Coast Essentials

CAR TRAVEL

U.S. 90 runs through the heart of Ocean Springs, Biloxi, and Gulfport.

VISITOR INFORMATION

➤ TOURIST INFORMATION: **Mississippi Beach Convention and Visitors Bureau** (✉ Box 6128, Gulfport 38506, ☎ 228/896–6699 or 800/237–9493). **Ocean Springs Chamber of Commerce** (✉ Box 187, 39566, ☎ 228/875–4424).

Vicksburg

What to See and Do

During the Civil War the Confederacy and the Union vied for control of this strategic location on the Mississippi Delta across the river from Louisiana. After a 47-day siege the city surrendered to Ulysses S. Grant on July 4, 1863, giving the Union control of the river and sounding the death knell for the Confederacy. Vicksburg's **National Military Park** (✉ Visitor Center, 3201 Clay St., I–20, Exit 4B onto U.S. 80, Vicksburg 39180, ☎ 601/636–0583) details the events of these turbulent times. Battle positions are marked, and monuments line the 16-mi drive through the park. Tours of grand antebellum homes and 24-hour riverfront gambling are other draws.

Dining and Lodging

$$–$$$ ✕ **Rusty's Riverfront Grill.** Chef Rusty creates incredible salads, sandwiches, and entrées with fresh fish flown in daily. Fresh pasta comes with simple but inventive sauces. ✉ *615 Crawford St.,* ☎ *601/638–2030. MC, V. Closed Sun. No dinner Tues.*

$ ✕ **Walnut Hills.** If you're yearning for authentic regional cooking, this restaurant is a must. Diners eat round-table style, sampling two or three meats, seven vegetables, and desserts such as blackberry cobbler. Don't pass up the outstanding fried chicken, fresh snap beans, or purple-hull peas. ✉ *1214 Adams St.,* ☎ *601/638–4910. AE, DC, MC, V. Closed Sat. No dinner Sun.*

$$–$$$ ★ **Cedar Grove.** This 1840s mansion and its grounds cover a full city block. The entire house is furnished with period antiques. You can hear nearby river traffic from the quiet, gaslit grounds or survey the scene from the rooftop veranda. A house tour and hearty breakfast are included. Croquet and bicycles are available. ✉ *2200 Oak St., 39180,* ☎ *601/636–1000 or 800/862–1300,* FAX *601/634–6126. 29 rooms. Restaurant, pool, tennis. AE, D, MC, V. BP.*

$$–$$$ ★ **Duff Green Mansion.** This 1856 mansion was used as a hospital during the Civil War. Each guest room is decorated with antiques, including half-tester beds. A large southern breakfast and a tour of the home are included. ✉ *1114 1st East St., 39180,* ☎ *601/636–6968 or 800/992–0037,* WEB *www.duffgreenmansion.com. 4 rooms. Pool. AE, MC, V. BP.*

Vicksburg Essentials

CAR TRAVEL

I–20 runs east–west and U.S. 61 north–south through Vicksburg.

VISITOR INFORMATION

➤ TOURIST INFORMATION: **Vicksburg Convention and Visitors Bureau** (✉ Box 110, Vicksburg 39181, ☎ 601/636–9421 or 800/221–3536).

MISSOURI

Updated by Diana Lambdin Meyer

Capital	Jefferson City
Population	5,595,000
Motto	Let the Welfare of the People Be the Supreme Law
State Bird	Eastern bluebird
State Flower	Hawthorn
Postal Abbreviation	MO

Statewide Visitor Information

The **Missouri Division of Tourism** (✉ Truman State Office Bldg. [Box 1055, Jefferson City 65102], ☎ 573/751–4133; 800/877–1234 in Missouri; WEB www.missouritourism.org) operates six visitor centers: Kansas City (✉ 4010 Blue Ridge Cutoff at I–70, ☎ 816/889–3330); St. Louis (✉ I–270 at Riverview exit, ☎ 314/869–7100); Ozarks (✉ I–44 at Joplin exit, ☎ 417/629–3030); Bootheel (✉ I–55 at New Madrid exit, ☎ 573/643–2654); Northwest Missouri (✉ I–29 at Rockport exit,, ☎ 660/744–6300); Northeast Missouri (✉ Hwy. 61, Hannibal, ☎ 573/248–2420). The Heart of Missouri Tourism Center (✉ I–70 Exit 148 at Kingdom City, ☎ 573/642–7692), in the center of the state, has Missouri-made products, free coffee, and Internet access.

Scenic Drives

Route 21 from St. Louis to Doniphan, in extreme southern Missouri, passes through national forests and rugged hill country. Scenic routes in southwestern Missouri's Ozark Mountains include **Route 76, Route 248,** and **U.S. 65** south of Springfield.

National and State Parks

National Parks

The **Ozark National Scenic Riverways** (✉ National Park Service, Box 490, Van Buren 63965, ☎ 573/323–4236, WEB www.nps.gov/ozar) includes the Current and Jacks Fork rivers, two south-central Missouri rivers that were the first to be federally protected. Both offer good canoeing. The **Mark Twain National Forest** (✉ 401 Fairgrounds Rd., Rolla 65401, ☎ 573/364–4621, WEB www.fs.fed.us/r9/marktwain) is in southern Missouri.

State Parks

Lake of the Ozarks State Park (✉ U.S. 54, ☎ 573/348–2694) is the largest state park in Missouri. The popular **Katy Trail State Park** (☎ 660/882–8196) is a 225-mi walking-and-cycling path, much of it along the Missouri River between Clinton and St. Charles. Other significant parks include **Elephant Rocks** (✉ Box 509, Pilot Knob 63663, ☎ 573/546–3454), **Johnson's Shut-Ins** (✉ Middle Brook 63656, ☎ 573/546–2450), **Mastodon State Historic Site** (✉ Imperial 63052, ☎ 636/464–3079), and **Onondaga Cave State Park** (✉ Leasburg 65535, ☎ 573/245–6576). For information on any of Missouri's 81 state parks, contact the **Missouri Department of Natural Resources** (Division of State Parks, ✉ Box 176, Jefferson City 65101, ☎ 573/751–2479 or 800/334–6946, WEB www.dnr.state.mo.us).

ST. LOUIS

Founded by the French in 1764 as a fur-trading settlement on the west bank of the Mississippi River, St. Louis is best known for the soaring silver arch that so impresses travelers entering the city from the east. In its early days the city thrived as a river port, then as a rail hub, and today it's the world headquarters for such mega-corporations as Anheuser-Busch and Boeing. The construction of the Gateway Arch in 1965 did more than commemorate the city's role in westward expansion—it helped spark the rebirth of a downtown that had been abandoned in the rush for the suburbs.

Exploring St. Louis

Downtown

A ride to the top of the 630-ft **Gateway Arch** is a must. The centerpiece of the 91-acre **Jefferson National Expansion Memorial Park,** the arch was built in 1965 to commemorate the city where thousands of 19th-century pioneers stopped for provisions before traveling west. For $8, a tram takes you up through one of the arch's legs to an observation room with a terrific view of the city and the Mississippi. Beneath the arch is the underground visitor center and the **Museum of Westward Expansion.** ✉ *On the riverfront at Market St.,* ☎ *314/655–1700,* WEB *www.nps.gov/jeff.*

Just down the steps from the Gateway Arch is the Mississippi riverfront and its cobblestone levee, where permanently moored **riverboats** house a handful of mostly fast-food restaurants. The ***Tom Sawyer*** and ***Becky Thatcher*** (☎ 314/621–4040 or 800/878–7411, WEB www.gatewayarchriverboats.com), replicas of 19th-century steamboats, offer one-hour sightseeing trips and two-hour dinner cruises. Northwest of the Gateway Arch is **Laclede's Landing** (✉ bordered by I–70, Martin Luther King Bridge, and Eads Bridge, ☎ 314/241–5875, WEB www.lacledeslanding.org), nine square blocks of cobblestone streets and restored 19th-century warehouses now filled with shops, galleries, restaurants, and nightspots. Along the river downtown is the **President Casino on the *Admiral*** (☎ 314/622–1111 or 800/772–3647, www.presidentcasino.com; 🎫 $2), a noncruising riverboat that offers casino gambling. Other riverboat casinos in the St. Louis area include the **AmeriStar Casino St. Charles** (✉ S. 5th St., ☎ 636/949–7777 or 800/325–7777, www.ameristarcasinos.com) and, upriver, the **Argosy *Alton Belle* Riverboat Casino** (✉ 219 Piasa St., Alton, IL 62002, ☎ 618/223–7568 or 800/336–7568, WEB www.argosycasinos.com).

West of the Gateway Arch is St. Louis's oldest church, the **Old Cathedral Basilica of St. Louis, the King** (✉ 209 Walnut St., ☎ 314/231–3250), a simple Greek Revival structure built in 1834 that still holds daily masses. On Market Street, the **Old Courthouse** (✉ 11 N. 4th St., ☎ 314/655–1700) has displays and photographs of early St. Louis.

South of the Old Courthouse is **Busch Stadium** (✉ off I–40 [exit at 9th St.], ☎ 314/421–3060), home of the St. Louis Cardinals. Just across the street from the stadium is the **International Bowling Hall of Fame,** where you can bowl in a 1930s alley and learn more about the history of the sport. The Bowling Hall of Fame shares a building with the **St. Louis Cardinals Hall of Fame,** with sports memorabilia and audio and video highlights of the history of St. Louis baseball. ✉ *111 Stadium Plaza,* ☎ *314/231–6340,* WEB *www.bowlingmuseum.com.* 🎫 *$6. Closed weekends Jan.–Mar.*

Downtown St. Louis

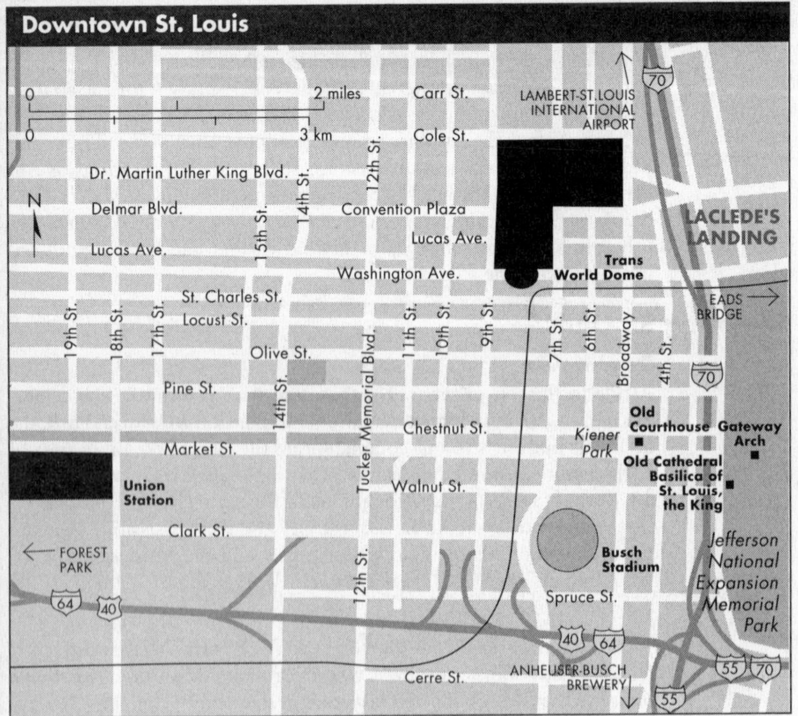

Other Attractions

St. Louis is home to the world's largest brewer, **Anheuser-Busch,** maker of Budweiser beer. Tours of the company's world headquarters, in south St. Louis, include the stables where the famous Clydesdale horses are kept. ✉ *12th and Lynch Sts.,* ☎ *314/577–2626,* WEB *www.budweisertours.com.* 🎫 *Free. Closed Sun.*

On the western edge of town is **Forest Park** (✉ north of U.S. 40 between Kingshighway and Skinker Blvds.), whose grounds include the city zoo, the art museum, and the science museum. The **St. Louis Zoo** (✉ 1 Government Dr., ☎ 314/781–0900, WEB www.stlzoo.org; 🎫 free) has a high-tech education center. The **St. Louis Art Museum** (✉ 1 Fine Arts Dr., ☎ 314/721–0072, WEB www.slam.org; 🎫 free) has outstanding pre-Columbian and German expressionist collections. The **St. Louis Science Center** (✉ 5050 Oakland Ave., ☎ 314/289–4444; 🎫 free), in the southeast part of Forest Park, contains more than 600 hands-on exhibits on ecology, space, and humanity.

The Magic House (✉ 516 S. Kirkwood Rd., ☎ 314/822–8900, WEB www.magichouse.org; 🎫 $6) is a children's museum with interactive learning experiences in a restored Victorian house in Kirkwood.

A mind-boggling collection of mosaics covers the walls, ceilings, and three domes of the **Cathedral of St. Louis** (✉ Lindell Blvd. and Newstead Ave., ☎ 314/533–2824 or 314/533–0544, WEB www.cathedralstl.org), also known as the New Cathedral.

The **Missouri Botanical Garden** (✉ 4344 Shaw Ave., ☎ 314/577–5100, WEB www.mobot.org; 🎫 $7), known locally as Shaw's Garden for founder Henry Shaw, is a 15-minute drive southwest of downtown. Highlights include a Japanese garden and a tropical rain forest.

The **City Museum** (✉ 701 N. 15th St., ☎ 314/231–2489, WEB www.citymuseum.org, 🎟 $7.50) is unlike any museum you've been to before. You can crawl through fish-head trees, participate in a real circus, and escape from an enchanted castle via a slide and tunnel system.

Six Flags St. Louis (✉ I–44 and Allenton Rd., Eureka, ☎ 314/938–4800, WEB www.sixflags.com/stlouis; 🎟 $38.99), about 30 mi southwest of St. Louis, has rides, shows, and a water park. **Grant's Farm** (✉ 10501 Gravois, ☎ 314/843–1700, WEB www.grantsfarm.com), open April–October, is a favorite with St. Louis children for its 160-acre petting zoo, animal preserve, and train ride to visit the Clydesdales.

Dining

St. Louis's Hill neighborhood has an Italian restaurant on nearly every corner; even the abundant steak houses carry an Italian dish or two. Other ethnic restaurants are scattered throughout the city. The Central West End and Laclede's Landing have a number of restaurants, as does Clayton, the St. Louis County seat, about 7 mi west of downtown.

$$$–$$$$ ✕ **Mike Shannon's Steaks & Seafoods.** The name Mike Shannon is synonymous with the glory days of Cardinal baseball thanks to his extensive career as an announcer on KMOX Radio. People flock to this downtown steak house as much for Shannon's impressive sports-memorabilia collection as for the fine steaks and gourmet desserts. ✉ *100 N. 7th St.,* ☎ *314/421–1540. AE, DC, MC, V.*

$$$–$$$$ ✕ **Tony's.** This four-star, family-owned restaurant has been a St. Louis favorite since the 1950s. Superb Italian dishes, prime steaks, and superior service make it well worth the price. ✉ *410 Market St.,* ☎ *314/231–7007. Reservations essential. Jacket and tie. AE, D, DC, MC, V. Closed Sun. No lunch.*

$$$ ✕ **Cardwell's.** At this sophisticated establishment, you can eat in either the airy café, with marble-top tables and French doors, or in the more formal, elegant dining room. The changing menu may include duck breast or roasted rack of lamb, among other specialties. ✉ *8100 Maryland St.,* ☎ *314/726–5055. AE, DC, MC, V. No lunch weekends.*

$$ ✕ **Big Sky Café.** Owned and operated by the same family as the Blue Water Grill, this casual café is popular with the business-lunch crowd. Try the garlic mashed potatoes or the corn-bread-stuffed chicken breast. ✉ *47 S. Old Orchard,* ☎ *314/962–5757. AE, D, DC, MC, V.*

$$ ✕ **Blue Water Grill.** Grilled seafood with a southwestern flair is the specialty at this small, festive Kirkwood restaurant. On Monday night diners can mix and match "Flying Saucers," miniature entrées. ✉ *343 S. Kirkwood,* ☎ *314/821–5757. AE, D, DC, MC, V. Closed Sun.*

$–$$ ★ ✕ **Cunetto's House of Pasta.** There's usually a wait at this popular Hill restaurant, but relaxing in the cocktail lounge is part of the experience. Once seated, you'll find plenty of veal and beef dishes as well as more than 30 different pastas. ✉ *5453 Magnolia Ave.,* ☎ *314/781–1135. AE, D, DC, MC, V. Closed Sun.*

$ ✕ **Blueberry Hill.** Dart competitions and local bands draw crowds to this trendy gathering spot. A burger, a locally brewed Rock 'n' Roll beer, and a quarter in the famous 2,000-tune jukebox get the good times going. ✉ *6504 Delmar Blvd.,* ☎ *314/727–0880. AE, D, DC, MC, V.*

$ ✕ **Rigazzi's.** Generous, inexpensive servings of homemade pasta keep locals coming back to this no-frills, family-style restaurant. ✉ *4945 Daggett St.,* ☎ *314/772–4900. AE, DC, MC, V. Closed Sun.*

Lodging

Most of St. Louis's big hotels are downtown or in Clayton, about 7 mi west. For bed-and-breakfasts in town, call or write **Bed and Break-**

fast Inns of Missouri (✉ 204 E. High St., Jefferson City 65101–3207, ☎ 800/213–5642, WEB www.bbim.org).

$$$$ **Ritz-Carlton, St. Louis.** Chandeliers and museum-quality oil paintings fill this luxury hotel. Some rooms on the top floors have views of the downtown St. Louis skyline. ✉ *100 Carondelet Plaza, Clayton 63105,* ☎ *314/863–6300 or 800/241–3333,* FAX *314/863–3525,* WEB *www.ritzcarlton.com. 301 rooms. 2 restaurants, pool, gym. AE, D, DC, MC, V.*

$$$–$$$$ **Hyatt Regency St. Louis at Union Station.** Most of these rooms are in a contemporary garden setting beneath the arched trusses of Union Station's original train station. Deluxe rooms and suites are available in the Regency Club. ✉ *1 St. Louis Union Station, 63103,* ☎ *314/231–1234 or 800/233–1234,* FAX *314/436–6827,* WEB *www.hyatt.com. 536 rooms. 2 restaurants, pool, gym. AE, D, DC, MC, V.*

$$–$$$ **Omni Majestic.** This small, European-style hotel downtown is a frequent choice of visiting celebrities. It was built in 1913 and is filled with reproduction antiques. ✉ *1019 Pine St., 63101,* ☎ *314/436–2355 or 800/843–6664,* FAX *314/436–0223,* WEB *www.omnihotels.com. 91 rooms. Restaurant, gym. AE, D, DC, MC, V.*

$$ ★ **Drury Inn–Union Station.** Lead-glass windows and marble columns give historic charm to this former YMCA. Among its assets are free parking and an excellent location, next to Union Station. ✉ *201 S. 20th St., 63103,* ☎ *314/231–3900,* FAX *314/231–3900,* WEB *www.druryinn.com. 176 rooms. Restaurant, pool, gym. AE, D, DC, MC, V. CP.*

Motels

Red Roof Inn (✉ 5823 Wilson Ave., 63110, ☎ 314/645–0101, FAX 314/645–0119), 110 rooms; *$.* **Baymont Inn & Suites** (✉ 12330 Dorsett Rd., 63043, ☎ 314/878–1212, FAX 314/878–3409), 145 rooms; *$.* **Fairfield Inn by Marriott** (✉ 9079 Dunn Rd., 63042, ☎ 314/731–7700, FAX 314/731–1898), 135 rooms; pool; *$.*

Nightlife and the Arts

Nightlife

Much of St. Louis's nightlife can be found in the jazz and blues clubs in the redeveloped areas of **Laclede's Landing,** on the riverfront, and in **Soulard,** on the southern edge of downtown. To find out who's playing where, consult the Thursday calendar section in the *St. Louis Post-Dispatch* or the free, weekly *Riverfront Times.* Dinner theater is popular throughout the city; the **Royal Dumpe** (✉ 711 1st St., ☎ 314/621–5800, WEB www.royaldumpe.com) is the oldest dinner theater in the country. The **Bissell Mansion Restaurant and Dinner Theatre** (✉ 4426 Randall Pl., ☎ 314/533–9830 or 800/690–9838, WEB www.bissellhouse.com) has luncheon and matinee performances, and a participatory show weekend nights. St. Louis is home to the country's oldest and largest outdoor theater, the **Muny** (☎ 314/361–1900, WEB www.muny.com), in Forest Park, with Broadway shows from June to August. Those who like ballroom and swing dancing will enjoy the 5,000-square-ft **Casa Loma Ballroom** (✉ 3354 Iowa Ave., ☎ 314/664–8000).

The Arts

The **Fabulous Fox Theatre** (✉ 527 N. Grand Blvd., ☎ 314/534–1678) hosts major shows and concerts. The **Riverport Amphitheatre** (✉ 14141 Riverport Dr., ☎ 314/298–9944) stages big-name concerts. The St. Louis Symphony Orchestra performs at **Powell Symphony Hall** (✉ 718 N. Grand Blvd., ☎ 314/534–1700). For tickets to major events call **Ticketmaster** (☎ 314/241–1888). For arts events call **MetroTix** (☎ 314/534–1111).

Spectator Sports

Baseball: St. Louis Cardinals (✉ Busch Stadium, 250 Stadium Plaza, ☎ 314/421–3060, WEB www.stlcardinals.com). **Football: St. Louis Rams** (✉ The Edward Jones Dome, 801 Convention Plaza, ☎ 314/425–8830, WEB www.stlouisrams.com). **Ice hockey: St. Louis Blues** (✉ Savvis Center, 1401 Clark Ave., ☎ 314/622–2500, WEB www.stlouisblues.com). **Missouri River Otters** (✉ St. Charles Family Arena, ☎ 636/946–0003, WEB www.riverotters.com). **Indoor soccer: St. Louis Steamers** (✉ St. Charles Family Arena, ☎ 314/216–2000, WEB www.stlsteamers.com).

Shopping

For browsing in boutiques and specialty shops, try **Union Station** (✉ 1820 Market St.), an impressive former train station with more than 100 shops and restaurants. **Laclede's Landing** (✉ bordered by I–70, Martin Luther King Bridge, and Eads Bridge) has some eclectic shops and restaurants. The **Central West End** (✉ Euclid Ave. east of Forest Park) is an area of hip boutiques and restaurants. The city's most sophisticated shoppers head for **Plaza Frontenac** (✉ Clayton Rd. and Lindbergh Blvd., ☎ 314/432–0604), home to nearly 50 upscale stores, including Neiman Marcus and Saks Fifth Avenue. Antiques and crafts lovers should visit historic downtown **St. Charles** (✉ I–70 and First Capital Dr.), seven cobblestone blocks of shops and restaurants on the banks of the Missouri River. For contemporary crafts, try the **Apropos Gallery** (✉ 7750 Forsyth Blvd., ☎ 314/212–5500).

St. Louis Essentials

AIRPORTS AND TRANSFERS

Lambert–St. Louis International Airport, 10 mi northwest of downtown on I–70, has scheduled flights on most major domestic and foreign carriers.

➤ AIRPORT INFORMATION: **Lambert–St. Louis International Airport** (✉ 10701 Lambert International Blvd., ☎ 314/426–8000).

AIRPORT TRANSFER

It's about a 20-minute drive from the airport to downtown St. Louis; taxis cost about $30. Transportation is also provided to downtown stops by the Bi-State bus and MetroLink and to downtown hotels by Trans Express and St. Louis Express Transportation shuttle vans. Exit Express is a major taxi-cab company that will take you directly to any location. MetroBus will get you primarily to tourist destinations but not to hotels.

➤ TAXIS AND SHUTTLES: **Exit Express** (☎ 314/646–1166). **MetroBus** (☎ 314/231–2345). **MetroLink** (☎ 314/231–2345). **St. Louis Express Transportation** (☎ 314/277–7070). **Trans Express** (☎ 314/427–3311).

BUS TRAVEL TO AND FROM ST. LOUIS

➤ BUS INFORMATION: **Greyhound** (✉ 1450 N. 13th St., ☎ 800/231–2222).

CAR TRAVEL

From I–70, I–55, and I–44 follow the exits for downtown St. Louis. From U.S. 40 (I–64), exit at Broadway. I–270 makes a loop around the city from the airport.

TRAIN TRAVEL

➤ TRAIN INFORMATION: **Amtrak** (☎ 800/872–7245; downtown: ✉ 550 S. 16th St., ☎ 314/331–3300; Kirkwood: ✉ 110 W Argonne Dr., ☎ 314/966–6475).

TRANSPORTATION AROUND ST. LOUIS

Explore the downtown sights on foot; elsewhere you'll need a car. MetroLink, the city's light-rail system, stops near major attractions downtown. A one-way ticket costs $1.25. Rides are free between Laclede's Landing and Union Station weekdays 10–3.

➤ CONTACTS: **MetroLink** (☎ 314/231–2345).

VISITOR INFORMATION

The Convention and Visitors Commission operates four walk-up visitor centers, on Keiner Plaza, across from the Old Courthouse downtown; at the America's Center Convention Center, 7th and Washington, downtown; and at the Main and East terminals at Lambert International Airport. The St. Louis Visitor Center is operated independently by volunteers.

➤ TOURIST INFORMATION: **Convention and Visitors Commission** (✉ One Metropolitan Sq., Suite 1100, 63102, ☎ 314/421–1023 or 800/916–0040, WEB www.explorestlouis.com). **St. Louis Visitor Center** (✉ 308 Washington Ave., ☎ 314/241–1764).

KANSAS CITY

With upward of 200 fountains—more than any city except Rome—and more miles of boulevards (155) than Paris, Kansas City is attractive and cosmopolitan. The sprawling metropolitan area straddling the Missouri-Kansas line has a rich history as a frontier river port and trade center, where wagon trains were outfitted before heading west on the Santa Fe and Oregon trails. Through the years it has gained note as home to the nation's second-largest stockyards, to saxophone player Charlie "Bird" Parker and his Kansas City–style bebop, and to some of the best barbecue in the world. It's also a base of operations for leading pharmaceutical companies, telecommunications giants, and Hallmark, the preeminent name in greeting cards.

Exploring Kansas City

Plaza, Midtown, Downtown

Kansas City's **Country Club Plaza** (✉ 47th and Main Sts., ☎ 816/753–0100) is known for its more than 180 fine shops and restaurants, its Spanish-style architecture, and its annual display of holiday lights from Thanksgiving to January. Here you'll also find many of Kansas ★ City's fountains and statues. Two blocks east of the Plaza is the **Nelson-Atkins Museum of Art** (✉ 4525 Oak St., ☎ 816/561–4000, WEB www.nelson-atkins.org; 🎫 free, charge for some special exhibits), known for its outstanding Asian-art collection and the Henry Moore Sculpture Garden on the south grounds.

The **Kemper Museum of Contemporary Art and Design** (✉ 4420 Warwick Blvd., ☎ 816/753–5784, WEB www.kemperart.org; 🎫 free) has a permanent collection of 700 works in a broad range of media.

Before there was a Kansas City, there was a **Westport** (✉ Broadway and Westport Rd., ☎ 816/756–2789), built along the Santa Fe Trail as an outfitting center for wagon trains heading west. Today the area is filled with renovated and new buildings housing trendy shops, restaurants, and nightspots.

On the crest of a hill at the northern edge of Penn Valley Park, north of Westport, is the **Liberty Memorial** (✉ 100 W. 26th St., ☎ 816/221–1918), dedicated to those who served in World War I. Extensive structural renovation, completed in 2002, has stabilized the tower's 217-ft observation deck and improved the underground museum.

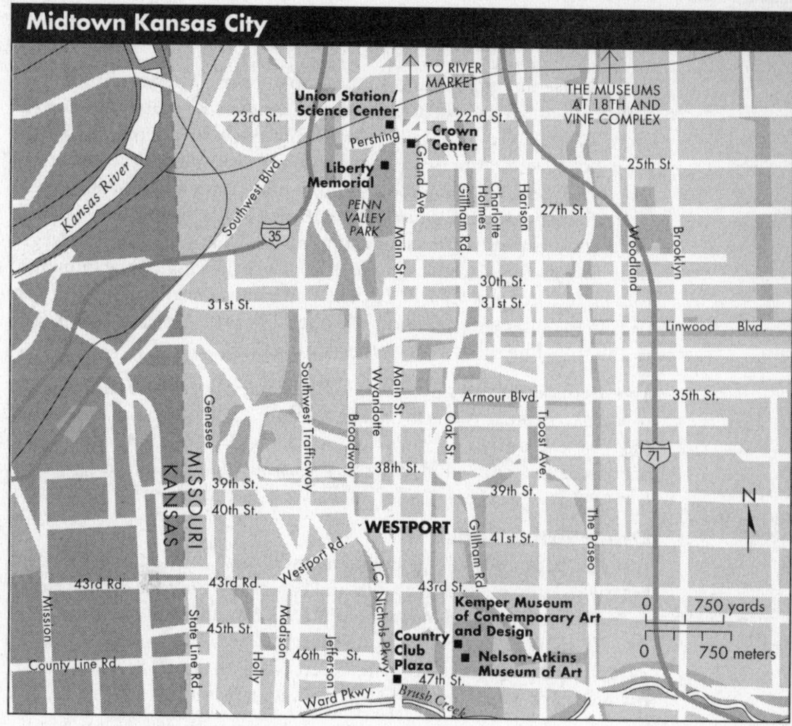

Across Pershing Road from the Liberty Memorial is the jewel in Kansas City's attractions, **Union Station/Science City** (✉ 30 W. Pershing Rd., ☎ 816/460–2020, WEB www.sciencecity.com; 🎟 $12.50), a 55,000-square-ft science museum in the restored train station, which was once the second largest in the country. The old station now contains 50 hands-on learning environments, including a space center and media lab, as well as restaurants, shops, and theaters.

Just across Main Street from the Liberty Memorial and Union Station, joined by an enclosed walkway called the Link, is **Crown Center** (✉ 2450 Grand Ave., ☎ 816/274–8444, WEB www.crowncenter.com), an 85-acre shopping mall and entertainment, office, and hotel complex. In summer, free concerts are held on the terrace on Friday nights; in winter, there's a covered outdoor ice-skating rink. Hallmark Cards, the largest maker of greeting cards in the world, built Crown Center and has its headquarters here. From Monday through Saturday you can stop by the **Hallmark Visitors Center** (✉ 2501 McGee St., ☎ 816/274–3613), which has a display on the history of the greeting-card industry and a machine that makes those big round bows (you can keep the bow). **Kaleidoscope** (✉ 2501 McGee St., ☎ 816/274–8300, WEB www.hallmarkkaleidoscope.com; 🎟 free, reservations required) is a hands-on creative-arts center for children staffed as a public service by Hallmark employees.

North of downtown, the **River Market** (✉ Grand Blvd. and 5th St.) has some of the city's most distinctive ethnic restaurants and markets. In the summer months, a Saturday-morning farmers' market draws thousands, and the Sunday-morning artists' market is growing in popularity. ★ Year-round, tourists and locals enjoy the ***Arabia* Steamboat Museum** (✉ 400 Grand Ave., ☎ 816/471–1856, WEB www.1856.com; 🎟 $8.50), which houses goods—from French perfume to buttons to coffeepots—

salvaged from the *Arabia*'s muddy grave 132 years after it sank in the Missouri River in 1856.

In the Museums at 18th and Vine complex, the cornerstone of the historic 18th and Vine district, the **Negro Leagues Baseball Museum** (✉ 1616 E. 18th St., ☎ 816/221–1920, WEB www.nlbm.com; 🎫 $6, $8 joint ticket with American Jazz Museum) documents the history of African-Americans in baseball through films and a multimedia gallery. The **American Jazz Museum** (✉ 1616 E. 18th St., ☎ 816/474–8463, WEB www.americanjazzmuseum.com; 🎫 $6, $8 joint ticket with Negro Leagues Baseball Museum) honors Louis Armstrong, Duke Ellington, Ella Fitzgerald, and Charlie Parker. You can listen to hundreds of jazz CDs in the interactive studio and sound library. Numerous shops and restaurants line the streets of this historic area.

Riverboat gambling is popular along the banks of this Missouri River town. Two noncruising casinos in the Kansas City area are the **Argosy** (✉ Hwy. 9 and I–635, Riverside, ☎ 816/746–3100, WEB www.argosycasinos.com) and **Harrah's Casino** (✉ Armour Rd., North Kansas City, ☎ 816/472–7777, WEB www.harrahs.com).

Other Attractions

Just east of Kansas City is **Independence,** once the home of President Harry S. Truman. Truman's life and career are the focus at the **Harry S. Truman Library and Museum** (✉ U.S. 24 and Delaware St., ☎ 816/833–1225, WEB www.trumanlibrary.org; 🎫 $5). The **Truman Home** (✉ 219 N. Delaware St.; ticket center: 223 N. Main St., ☎ 816/254–9929, WEB www.nps.gov/hstr; 🎫 $3) was the Trumans' summer White House.

Fleming Park (✉ 22807 Woods Chapel Rd., ☎ 816/795–8200), in Blue Springs, south of Independence, contains the 970-acre **Lake Jacomo,** which hosts sailing regattas each weekend from April through October. Also in Fleming Park is **Missouri Town 1855** (🎫 $3), a reproduction 1800s town created from more than 30 transplanted period houses, barns, stores, and outbuildings. The staff and volunteers wear period clothing. It's closed on weekdays in fall and winter, and Monday and Tuesday in spring and summer.

★ **Worlds of Fun/Oceans of Fun** are two adjoining theme parks with roller coasters, shows, water shenanigans, and attractions for people of all ages. *✉ East loop of I–435 at Exit 54, ☎ 816/454–4545, WEB www.worldsoffun.com. 🎫 Worlds of Fun $35.00, Oceans of Fun $22.95, combination ticket $41.95. Closed mid-Oct.–mid-Apr.*

The **Kansas City Zoo** (✉ I–435 and 63rd St., ☎ 816/513–5800, WEB www.kansascityzoo.org; 🎫 $6) includes a 5,000-acre African-plains exhibit as well as an **IMAX theater** (☎ 816/513–4629; 🎫 $6).

Just north of downtown Kansas City is the historic riverboat community of **Weston** (☎ 816/640–2909). Every building in the five-block downtown shopping district is on the National Register of Historic Places, and the surrounding area is filled with fruit orchards open for tours.

Dining

Kansas City is best known for its steaks and barbecue. Both the Country Club Plaza and Westport have a variety of good restaurants.

$$$$ ★ ✕ **Plaza III—The Steakhouse.** This handsome, nationally known restaurant serves excellent steaks, prime rib, and seafood. The steak soup is legendary. *✉ 4749 Pennsylvania Ave., ☎ 816/753–0000. AE, D, DC, MC, V. No lunch Sun.*

$$$ ✕ **Golden Ox.** Down the street from Kemper Arena, this popular steak house serves prime rib in a comfortable western atmosphere. ✉ *1600 Gennessee St.,* ☎ *816/842–2866. AE, D, DC, MC, V. No lunch Sun.*

$$$ ✕ **Savoy Grill.** Locals often choose this historic, turn-of-the-20th-century beauty when celebrating a special occasion. Maine lobster and a T-bone steak from the restaurant's own herd are good choices. ✉ *219 W. 9th St.,* ☎ *816/842–3890. AE, D, DC, MC, V. No lunch Sun.*

$$ ★ ✕ **Stroud's.** This sprawling building on Kansas City's north side was once the first stagecoach stop for travelers on their way to St. Joseph. After feasting on fried chicken and homemade pies, take a stroll around the grounds, complete with ponds, geese, and swans. ✉ *5410 N.E. Oak Ridge Dr.,* ☎ *816/454–9600. AE, D, DC, MC, V.*

$$ ✕ **Lidia's.** Northern Italian cuisine, such as veal with spinach tagliatelle, is the house specialty in classic restaurant operated by New York chef and TV star Lidia Bastianich. ✉ *101 W. 22nd St.,* ☎ *816/221–3722. AE, DC, MC, V.*

$ ★ ✕ **Arthur Bryant's.** Although there are scores of barbecue joints in Kansas City, Bryant's—low on decor but high on taste—tops the list for locals, who don't mind standing in long lines to order at the counter. ✉ *1727 Brooklyn Ave.,* ☎ *816/231–1123. AE, MC, V.*

Lodging

Kansas City has a core of major hotels within walking distance of Country Club Plaza and Westport and in the Crown Center complex. For a listing of B&Bs contact **Bed & Breakfast Kansas City** (✉ 7955 Colony La., Lenexa, KS 66215, ☎ 913/888–3636).

$$$ 🏨 **Fairmont.** Crystal chandeliers, imported marble, and fine art fill this luxury hotel. Some rooms have balconies and views of the Plaza. ✉ *401 Ward Pkwy., 64112,* ☎ *816/756–1500,* FAX *816/756–1635,* WEB *www.fairmont.com. 366 rooms. Restaurant, pool, health club. AE, D, DC, MC, V.*

$$$ 🏨 **The Raphael.** Built in 1927 as an apartment house, the Raphael today is an intimate, European-style hotel, yet many of the rooms are large, with excellent views of the Plaza. ✉ *325 Ward Pkwy., 64112,* ☎ *816/756–3800 or 800/821–5343,* FAX *816/802–2131,* WEB *www.raphaelkc.com. 123 rooms. Restaurant. AE, D, DC, MC, V.*

$$$ 🏨 **Westin Crown Center.** Part of the Crown Center complex, the Westin has a bustling lobby complete with a five-story waterfall and a natural limestone cliff. All rooms have views; the best ones face Crown Center Square to the east. ✉ *1 Pershing Rd., 64108,* ☎ *816/474–4400 or 800/228–3000,* FAX *816/391–4438,* WEB *www.westin.com. 729 rooms. 2 restaurants, pool, health club. AE, D, DC, MC, V.*

$$–$$$ 🏨 **Southmoreland on the Plaza.** Within walking distance of the Country Club Plaza and the Nelson-Atkins Museum, this urban inn has rooms named for and decorated in honor of some of the big names of local history, such as William Rockhill Nelson and Satchel Paige. ✉ *116 E. 46th St., 64112,* ☎ *816/531–7979,* FAX *816/531–2407,* WEB *www.southmoreland.com. 13 rooms. AE, MC, V. BP.*

$–$$ 🏨 **Quarterage Hotel.** This intimate brick hotel is central to many activities in the metropolitan area. ✉ *560 Westport Rd., 64111,* ☎ *816/931–0001 or 800/942–4233,* FAX *816/931–8891,* WEB *www.quarteragehotel.com. 123 rooms. Health club. AE, D, DC, MC, V. BP.*

$ 🏨 **Drury Inn–Stadium.** Across from the sports complex, this chain hotel offers clean, comfortable rooms. Make reservations well ahead of time during sporting events. ✉ *3830 Blue Ridge Cutoff, 64133,* ☎ FAX *816/923–3000,* WEB *www.druryinn.com. 133 rooms. Pool. AE, D, DC, MC, V. CP.*

Nightlife and the Arts

Nightlife

Much of Kansas City's nightlife happens in the Westport and Plaza areas. The 18th and Vine Historic District has an increasing number of offerings. The **Grand Emporium** (✉ 3832 Main St., ☎ 816/531–1504, WEB www.grandemporium.com) has twice been honored as the best blues club in the nation by the Blues Foundation of America. The city is justly proud of its jazz heritage. Several venues host live performances; for information call the **Jazz Hotline** (☎ 816/763–1052). The **Blue Room** (✉ 1616 E. 18th St., ☎ 816/474–2929, WEB www.americanjazzmuseum.com), in the American Jazz Museum, has live performances Monday, Thursday, Friday, and Saturday nights.

Standford's Comedy House (✉ 504 Westport Rd., ☎ 816/756–1450; 🎟 $8 weeknights, $17 weekends) features local and nationally known comedians. **Comedy City** (✉ 300 Charlotte, ☎ 816/842–2744) has family-oriented comedy along with food and drinks. The **American Heartland Theatre** (☎ 816/842–9999) in Crown Center offers strong local theater productions and seasonal events.

The Arts

The **Folly Theater** (✉ 12th and Central Sts., ☎ 816/842–5500) stages comedy acts, ballet, operas, and theater. The **Midland Center for the Performing Arts** (✉ 1228 Main St., ☎ 816/471–8600), listed on the National Registry of Historic Places, is Kansas City's only surviving 1920s movie palace and hosts top shows and concerts. The Lyric Opera of Kansas City and the Kansas City Symphony perform at the **Lyric Theatre** (✉ 11th and Central Sts., ☎ 816/471–7344). For information on upcoming events check the Friday and Sunday editions of the *Kansas City Star.* Call **Ticketmaster** (☎ 816/931–3330) for tickets to major events.

Spectator Sports

Baseball: Kansas City Royals (✉ Kauffman Stadium, Truman Sports Complex, I–70 and Blue Ridge Cutoff, ☎ 816/504–4040 or 800/676–9257, WEB www.kcroyals.com). **Football: Kansas City Chiefs** (✉ Arrowhead Stadium, Truman Sports Complex, ☎ 816/920–9300, WEB www.kcchiefs.com). **Indoor Soccer: Kansas City Comets** (✉ Kemper Arena, 1800 Gennessee, ☎ 816/474–2255, WEB www.kccomets.com). **Outdoor soccer: Kansas City Wizards** (✉ Arrowhead Stadium, Truman Sports Complex, ☎ 816/920–9300, WEB www.kcwizards.com). **Basketball: Kansas City Knights** (✉ Kemper Arena, 1800 Gennessee, ☎ 816/471–4222, WEB www.kansascityknights.com).

Shopping

Kansas City's finest shopping is on the **Country Club Plaza,** and a number of specialty shops and boutiques are clustered in **Westport, Crown Center,** and the **River Market. Parkville,** a historic river town 10 minutes north of downtown Kansas City, has antiques, crafts, and one of the finest quilt shops in the country.

Kansas City Essentials

AIRPORTS AND TRANSFERS

Kansas City International Airport, 20 minutes northwest of downtown on I–29, is served by major domestic airlines.

➤ AIRPORT INFORMATION: Kansas City International Airport (✉ 601 Brasilia, ☎ 816/243–5237, WEB www.iflykansascity.com).

AIRPORT TRANSFER

Taxi service is zoned; the maximum fare from the airport to downtown Kansas City is $35. KCI Shuttle buses will take you to major hotels for $13.

➤ TAXIS AND SHUTTLES: **KCI Shuttle** (☎ 816/243–5000).

BUS TRAVEL TO AND FROM KANSAS CITY

➤ BUS INFORMATION: **Greyhound** (✉ 11th St. and Troost Ave., ☎ 800/231–2222).

CAR TRAVEL

From I–70 or I–35 exit at Broadway for downtown. From the airport, I–29 from the north merges with I–35 north of the city. I–435 makes a 360-degree loop around the city.

TRAIN TRAVEL

➤ TRAIN INFORMATION: **Amtrak** (✉ 2200 Main St., ☎ 816/421–3622 or 800/872–7245).

TRANSPORTATION AROUND KANSAS CITY

Attractions are scattered throughout the metropolitan region, making a car important for travelers. However, Kansas City Trolley Co. runs replica trolleys between the sites downtown and the River Market area, as well as Crown Center, Westport, and the Country Club Plaza. The drivers are usually entertaining and well versed in local history. The fare is $9, exact change required.

➤ CONTACTS: **Kansas City Trolley Co.** (☎ 816/221–3399).

VISITOR INFORMATION

Greater Kansas City Convention and Visitors Bureau is in City Center Square in downtown Kansas City. Its recorded visitor information provides a weekly list of activities.

➤ TOURIST INFORMATION: **Greater Kansas City Convention and Visitors Bureau** (✉ 1100 Main St., Suite 2550, 64105, ☎ 816/221–5242 or 800/767–7700; 816/691–3800 recorded visitor information; WEB www.visitkc.com).

THE OZARKS

The Ozark hill region of central and southern Missouri is famed for its wooded mountaintops; clear, spring-fed streams; and water playgrounds, the Lake of the Ozarks and Table Rock Lake. Branson, the nation's second country-music capital after Nashville, attracts 7 million visitors a year to its star-studded theaters.

Exploring the Ozarks

Central Missouri's **Lake of the Ozarks,** formed by the damming of the Osage River in 1931, is the state's largest lake, with 1,300 mi of shoreline sprawling over 58,000 acres. In summer crowds of vacationing families descend on the numerous resorts, motels, and tourist attractions; better times to visit may be spring, when the dogwoods are in bloom, and fall, when the wooded hills come alive with color.

Lake of the Ozarks State Park (✉ U.S. 54, ☎ 573/348–2694), just south of Osage Beach, encompasses 90 mi of shoreline and offers hiking trails, boating, fishing, and other diversions, plus tours of **Ozark Caverns** (☎ 573/346–2500; 🎫 $6); it's open April–October.

You're deep in the Bible Belt when you reach **Springfield** (✉ off I–44), home to two Bible colleges, a theological seminary, the world headquarters of the Assemblies of God Church, and several other sights and cultural events with religious themes. For many people, the first stop in Springfield is the enormous **Bass Pro Shops Outdoor World** (✉ 1935 S. Campbell Ave., ☎ 417/887–7334, WEB www.bassproshops.com), dubbed the Sportsman's Disney World. It has cascading waterfalls, a wildlife-trophy collection, a boat showroom, sporting-goods shops, and three restaurants serving wild game.

The **American National Fish and Wildlife Museum** (✉ 500 W. Sunshine Blvd., 65807, ☎ 417/890–9453 or 877/245–9453, WEB www.wondersofwildlife.org), features live fish, birds and mammals, as well as natural history exhibits and hands-on interactive activities that mirror the interconnectedness of the outside world.

The visitor center at **Wilson's Creek National Battlefield** (✉ 6424 W. Farm Rd. 182, Republic 65738, ☎ 417/732–2662; 🎟 $3), southwest of Springfield, documents the first major Civil War battle fought west of the Mississippi. In Mansfield, roughly 40 mi east of Springfield on U.S. 60, is the **Laura Ingalls Wilder Home** (✉ 3068 Hwy. A, ☎ 417/924–3626; 🎟 $6), a National Historic Landmark, where the much-loved children's author wrote her *Little House* books; it's open March–October. About 70 mi west of Springfield near the town of Diamond ★ is the **George Washington Carver National Monument** (✉ 5646 Carver Rd., ☎ 417/325–4151; 🎟 free), honoring the birthplace of the famous black botanist and agronomist. North of the Carver Monument, in Carthage, you can tour the **Precious Moments Chapel** (✉ 4321 Chapel Rd., ☎ 800/543–7975; 🎟 donations accepted), which features 30 stained-glass windows and 52 colorful murals designed by Sam Butcher, creator of the Precious Moments dolls and figurines. A gift shop on the premises sells these popular items.

About 40 mi south of Springfield on U.S. 65 is **Lake Taneycomo,** the first of Missouri's man-made lakes. **Table Rock State Park** (✉ Branson, ☎ 417/334–4704), larger and more developed than neighboring Lake Taneycomo, offers boating, picnicking, and plenty of motels, resorts, and commercial campgrounds. Kimberling City is the main resort town serving Lake Taneycomo and Table Rock. Just north of Springfield is **Truman Lake,** which provides some of the best lake fishing in the United States.

With more than a dozen glittering music halls, **Branson** rivals Nashville as a country-music mecca. Most growth has occurred along Route 76, already crowded with miniature-golf courses, bumper-car concessions, souvenir and hillbilly-crafts shops, motels, and resorts.

White Water (✉ 3505 W. Hwy. 76, Branson, ☎ 417/334–7488; 🎟 $27) is the place for water-soaked rides and activities.

★ At **Silver Dollar City** (✉ Rte. 76, ☎ 800/952–6626, WEB www.silverdollarcity.com; 🎟 $35), just west of Branson, Ozark artisans demonstrate traditional crafts, and rides and music shows keep all amused. Also west of Branson is the **Shepherd of the Hills Homestead and Outdoor Theatre,** a working pioneer homestead, with a gristmill, a sawmill, and smith and wheelwright shops. The drama *Shepherd of the Hills* is performed here. ✉ *Rte. 76,* ☎ *417/334–4191.* 🎟 *$32. Closed Jan.–Apr.*

Dining and Lodging

For information on B&Bs, contact the **Ozark Mountain Country Bed and Breakfast** reservation service (✉ Box 295, Branson 65615, ☎ 417/334–4720 or 800/695–1546, WEB www.ozarkbedandbreakfast.com).

Branson Area

$$$ ★ ✕ **Candlestick Inn.** Fresh seafood and prime rib rubbed in garlic and seared on the grill are the specialties at this elegant restaurant overlooking Lake Taneycomo. ✉ *Rte. 76 E, Branson,* ☎ *417/334–3633. AE, D, MC, V.*

$ **Dogwood Inn.** This modern hotel is not right on Lake Taneycomo, but you can see the lake from some rooms. Service is friendly, and the location is convenient to area attractions. ✉ *1420 Rte. 76 W (Box 6288, Branson 65616),* ☎ *417/334–5101,* FAX *417/334–0789. 220 rooms. Restaurant, pool. AE, D, DC, MC, V.*

$ **Kimberling Inn Resort and Conference Center.** This small resort motel on Table Rock Lake is walking distance from Kimberling City Shopping Village's crafts shops and restaurants. ✉ *Box 159, Kimberling City 65686,* ☎ *417/739–4311 or 800/833–5551,* FAX *417/739–5174,* WEB *www.kimberling.com. 120 rooms, 120 condos. 4 restaurants, pools, tennis. AE, D, DC, MC, V.*

Lake of the Ozarks

$$$$ ✕ **Blue Heron.** Enjoy cocktails poolside before moving to the lake-view dining room at this award-winning seasonal restaurant. Steak and seafood are the mainstays. ✉ *Business Rte. 54 and Rte. HH, Osage Beach,* ☎ *573/365–4646. Reservations not accepted. AE, D, MC, V. Closed Dec.–Mar. and Sun.–Mon. No lunch.*

$$$–$$$$ ★ ✕ **Lodge of the Four Seasons.** Golf is the draw here (45 holes). There's also fine dining in the Toledo Room. Rates drop dramatically in winter, but you'll still get the pampering of a first-class resort. ✉ *State Rd. HH; Box 215, Lake Ozark 65049,* ☎ *573/365–3000 or 800/843–5253,* FAX *573/365–8525,* WEB *www.4seasonsresort.com. 311 rooms. 3 restaurants, pools, tennis. AE, D, DC, MC, V.*

$$$–$$$$ ★ ✕ **Marriott's Tan-Tar-A Resort and Golf Club.** One of the top choices in the region for both vacations and business meetings, the Tan-Tar-A offers two golf courses and fine dining in the Windrose Restaurant. ✉ *Rte. KK, Osage Beach 65065,* ☎ *573/348–3131 or 800/826–8272,* FAX *573/348–3206,* WEB *www.tan-tar-a.com. 938 rooms. 5 restaurants, pools, golf, tennis, gym. AE, D, DC, MC, V.*

$$ **Holiday Inn Sunspree Resort.** You don't have lake access, but for a slightly higher rate you can have a lake view. ✉ *Business Rte. 54 (Box 1930, Lake Ozark 65049),* ☎ *573/365–2334 or 800/532–3575,* FAX *573/365–6887,* WEB *www.lakeozarkmo.sunspreeresorts.com. 211 rooms. Restaurant, pools, gym. AE, D, DC, MC, V. BP.*

Springfield

$$–$$$ ✕ **Hemingway's Blue Water Cafe.** Part of the Bass Pro Shops Outdoor World, this restaurant serves seafood, steak, pasta, and poultry. ✉ *1935 S. Campbell Ave.,* ☎ *417/891–5100. AE, D, MC, V.*

$$ **University Plaza Holiday Inn.** Here the guest rooms are arranged around a nine-story atrium. ✉ *333 John Q. Hammons Pkwy., 65806,* ☎ *417/864–7333,* FAX *417/831–5893,* WEB *www.lakeozarkmo.sunspreeresorts.com. 271 rooms. 2 restaurants, pools, tennis, gym. AE, D, DC, MC, V.*

$ **Clarion Inn.** Rooms at this hotel in the southern end of town are clean and comfortable. ✉ *3333 S. Glenstone Ave., 65804,* ☎ *417/883–6550,* FAX *417/883–5720,* WEB *www.choicehotels.com. 200 rooms. Restaurant, pool. AE, D, DC, MC, V.*

Motels

EconoLodge (✉ 2808 N. Kansas Expressway, Springfield 65803, ☎ 417/869–5600), 83 rooms; *$.* **Red Roof Inn** (✉ 2655 N. Glenstone Ave., Springfield 65803, ☎ 417/831–2100), 112 rooms; *$.*

Campgrounds

Missouri Association of RV Parks and Campgrounds (✉ 3020 S. National Ave., No. D149, Springfield 65804). In the Lake of the Ozarks area: ⛺ **Deer Valley Park and Campground** (✉ Sunrise Beach, ☎ 573/374–5277; closed mid-Oct.–mid-Apr.). ⛺ **Lake of the Ozarks State Park** (✉ U.S. 54, ☎ 573/348–2694). In the Branson area: ⛺ **Blue Mountain Campground** (✉ Branson, ☎ 800/779–2114). ⛺ **Port of Kimberling Marina and Campground** (✉ Kimberling City, ☎ 417/739–5377). ⛺ **Silver Dollar City Campground** (✉ Branson, ☎ 417/338–8189 or 800/477–5164; closed Oct.–Apr.).

Nightlife and the Arts

Music theaters in Branson include the **Andy Williams Moon River Theater** (✉ 2500 W. Hwy. 76, ☎ 417/334–4500 or 800/666–6094); **Baldknobbers Hillbilly Jamboree Show** (✉ 2635 W. Hwy. 76, ☎ 417/334–4528); **Grand Palace** (✉ 2700 W. Hwy. 76, ☎ 417/336–1220); **Jim Stafford Theater** (✉ 1340 W. Hwy. 76, ☎ 417/335–8080); **Mel Tillis Theater** (✉ 2527 State Hwy. 248, ☎ 417/335–6635); **Mickey Gilley's Family Theater** (✉ 3455 W. Hwy. 76, ☎ 417/334–3210); **Presley's Country Music Jubilee** (✉ 2920 76 Country Blvd., ☎ 417/334–4874); **Hughes Brothers Celebrity Theater** (✉ 3425 W. Hwy. 76, ☎ 417/334–0076); **Shoji Tabuchi Show** (✉ 3260 Shepherd of the Hills Expressway, ☎ 417/334–7469); and **Lawrence Welk Champagne Theatre** (✉ 1984 U.S. 165, ☎ 800/505–9355). Contact the **Branson Lakes Area Chamber of Commerce** (✉ Box 1897, 65616, ☎ 417/334–4136 or 800/214–3661, WEB www.explorebranson.com) for a complete list of venues.

Outdoor Activities and Sports

Canoeing

The Ozarks have some of the finest streams in the country, including the Current and Jacks Fork rivers, two waterways protected as the **Ozark National Scenic Riverways** (✉ National Park Service, Box 490, Van Buren 63965, ☎ 573/323–4236, WEB www.nps.gov/ozar). For a list of canoeing outfitters contact the **Missouri Division of Tourism** (✉ Truman State Office Bldg., [Box 1055, Jefferson City 65102], ☎ 573/751–4133; 800/877–1234 in Missouri).

Fishing

Bull Shoals Lake, Lake Taneycomo, and **Table Rock Lake** all offer excellent fishing for bass, catfish, trout, and other fish. Other good spots include **Lake of the Ozarks** and **Truman Lake.** Contact the **Missouri Department of Natural Resources** (✉ Box 180, Jefferson City 65102, ☎ 573/751–4115, WEB www.dnr.state.mo.us) for information on permits, costs, and seasons.

Hiking and Backpacking

The partially completed **Ozark Trail** passes through national and state forest and parkland as well as private property. For information and maps contact the **Missouri Department of Natural Resources** (✉ Division of State Parks, 101 Adams St., Jefferson City 65101, ☎ 573/751–2479 or 800/334–6946, WEB www.dnr.state.mo.us).

Shopping

Osage Village (✉ U.S. 54, Osage Beach, ☎ 573/348–2065) is a major factory-outlet mall with about 115 stores, restaurants, and theaters. For clothing, crafts, and homemade candies in Osage Beach, try the **Main Street Shopping Village** (✉ U.S. 54, ☎ 573/348–5101). Crafts and souvenir shops dominate Highway 76 in Branson, but for more consolidated shopping, try the 90 stores at the **Factory Merchants Outlet Mall** (☎ 417/335–6686).

Ozarks Essentials

CAR TRAVEL

Many of the towns and attractions in this vast region can be reached from I–44, which cuts diagonally across the state from St. Louis to Springfield, or south out of Kansas City on U.S. 71. Branson lies about 40 mi south of Springfield on U.S. 65. The Lake of the Ozarks is centrally located between St. Louis and Kansas City.

VISITOR INFORMATION

➤ TOURIST INFORMATION: **Branson Lakes Area Chamber of Commerce** (✉ Box 1897, 65616, ☎ 417/334–4136 or 800/214–3661, WEB www.explorebranson.com). **Greater Lake of the Ozarks Convention and Visitors Bureau** (✉ Box 1498, Osage Beach 65065, ☎ 573/348–1599 or 800/386–5253, WEB www.funlake.com). **Springfield Convention and Visitors Bureau and Tourist Information Center** (✉ 3315 E. Battlefield Rd., 65804-4048, ☎ 417/881–5300 or 800/678–8767, WEB www.springfieldmo.org). **Table Rock Lake/Kimberling City Area Chamber of Commerce** (✉ Box 495, Kimberling City 65686, ☎ 417/739–2564 or 800/595–0393, WEB www.tablerocklake.org).

ELSEWHERE IN MISSOURI

Hannibal

What to See and Do

Hannibal is Mark Twain country. The author's boyhood home is preserved at the **Mark Twain Home and Museum** (✉ 208 Hill St., ☎ 573/221–9010, WEB www.marktwainmuseum.org; $6). The **Mark Twain Cave** (✉ Rte. 79, ☎ 573/221–1656, WEB www.marktwaincave.com; $12) is where Tom Sawyer and Becky Thatcher got lost in Twain's classic *Adventures of Tom Sawyer.* An adjacent campground offers 100 shaded campsites and kids' activities.

Dining and Lodging

$$ ✕ **Lula Belle's Cafe and Bed & Breakfast.** Listed on the National Register of Historic Places, this former bordello attracts a more family-minded clientele today for a wide selection of soups and salads for lunch, shrimp and prime rib for dinner. Above the restaurant are three guest rooms, each designed with a distinctive theme: safari, Renaissance, and local arts and crafts. ✉ *111 Bird St.,* ☎ *573/221–6662 or 800/882–4890,* WEB *www.lulabelles.com. AE, D, DC, MC, V. Café closed Sun.*

Hannibal Essentials

CAR TRAVEL

Hannibal is about two hours north of St. Louis on U.S. 61.

VISITOR INFORMATION

➤ TOURIST INFORMATION: **Hannibal Convention and Visitors Bureau** (✉ 505 N. 3rd St., 63401, ☎ 573/221–2477 or 866/263–4825, WEB www.visithannibal.com).

Ste. Genevieve

What to See and Do

Numerous historic homes in this small river town south of St. Louis—the oldest permanent settlement in Missouri—include examples of 18th-century French-Creole architecture, characterized by vertical log construction. The **Great River Road Interpretive Center** (✉ 66 S. Main St., 63670, ☎ 573/883–7097 or 800/373–7007, WEB www.saintegenevieve.org) houses the visitor center, includes informative exhibits on the ecosystem of the Mississippi River, and sells tickets for the ferryboat ride across the river into Illinois.

Lodging

$$ **The Southern Hotel.** Housed in a 1790 Federal-style brick building, this inn invites you to relax in historic gardens or shoot a game of pool on the 1870 pool table. Some guest rooms have fireplaces. *✉ 146 S. 3rd St., 63670, ☎ 573/883–3493 or 800/275–1412, WEB www.southernhotelbb.com. 8 rooms. D, MC, V.*

$–$$ **Main Street Inn.** One of the many inns and restaurants in the National Historic District, this 1883 home is fully furnished with period antiques and offers a pleasant view of the Mississippi River. Complimentary wine is served in the evening. *✉ 221 N. Main St., 63670, ☎ 573/883–9199 or 800/918–9199, WEB www.mainstreetinnbb.com. 8 rooms. AE, D, MC, V. BP.*

St. Genevieve Essentials

CAR TRAVEL

Ste. Genevieve is about one hour south of St. Louis on I–55.

St. Joseph

What to See and Do

During the short experiment called the Pony Express, riders set out on the 2,000-mi trip to Sacramento, California, from what is now St. ★ Joseph's **Pony Express Museum** (✉ 914 Penn St., ☎ 816/279–5059, WEB www.ponyexpress.org; 🎫 $4). The **Jesse James Home and Patee House Museum** (✉ 12th and Penn Sts., ☎ 816/232–8206; 🎫 $4) is where a member of James's own gang shot and killed the notorious outlaw. You can still see a bullet hole in the wall.

Dining

$$ ✕ **Hoof and Horn.** In business since 1898, this is the oldest restaurant in St. Joseph and serves some of the best prime rib and steak in the Midwest. The decor in the rustic building recalls the days when cattle drivers would walk in fresh from the trail. *✉ 429 Illinois Ave., ☎ 816/238–0742. AE, DC, MC, V. Closed Sun.*

$$ ✕ **Jerre Anne's Cafeteria and Bakery.** Although this restaurant is small and often crowded, locals return for the heaping portions of meat loaf, mashed potatoes, and homemade pie. *✉ 2640 Mitchell St., ☎ 816/232–6585. MC, V. Closed Sun.–Mon.*

St. Joseph

CAR TRAVEL

St. Joseph is about one hour north of Kansas City on I–29.

VISITOR INFORMATION

➤ TOURIST INFORMATION: **St. Joseph Convention and Visitors Bureau** (✉ 109 S. 4th St. [Box 445, 64502], ☎ 816/233–6688 or 800/785–0360, WEB www.stjomo.com).

MONTANA

Updated by
Tom Griffith

Capital	Helena
Population	902,195
Motto	Oro y Plata (Gold and Silver)
State Bird	Western meadowlark
State Flower	Bitterroot
Postal Abbreviation	MT

Statewide Visitor Information

Travel Montana (✉ Dept. of Commerce, 1424 9th Ave., Helena 59620, ☎ 406/444–2654 or 800/847–4868, WEB www.visitmt.com).

Scenic Drives

Beartooth Highway, the stretch of U.S. 212 from Red Lodge to Yellowstone National Park, is a slow but spectacular 68-mi route over a 10,947-ft mountain pass; it's generally open mid-June–mid-October. For 187 mi between Helena and East Glacier, **I–15, U.S. 287,** and **U.S. 89** parallel the Rocky Mountain Front as it rises from the eastern plains. The 50-mi-long **Going-to-the-Sun Road** runs through Glacier National Park.

National and State Parks

Millions of acres of Big Sky Country—Montana's nickname for its vast wide-open spaces—are public reserves, including national parks, monuments, and recreation areas. There are eight national wildlife refuges, 10 national forests, and 15 wilderness areas. Yellowstone National Park is also a logical part of a Montana itinerary.

National Parks

Glacier National Park crowns the Continental Divide on the Montana-Canada border. **Little Bighorn Battlefield National Monument** preserves the battle site in southeastern Montana.

State Parks

The **Montana Department of Fish, Wildlife and Parks** (✉ 1420 E. 6th Ave., Helena 59620, ☎ 406/444–2535, WEB www.fwp.state.mt.us) manages 42 state parks, including **Bannack State Park,** west of Dillon, a ghost town of homes, saloons, and a gallows; **Missouri Headwaters State Park,** near Three Forks, where Lewis and Clark came upon the confluence of the three rivers that form the Missouri; and **Makoshika State Park,** northeast of Billings near Glendive, which features dramatic badlands formations and dinosaur fossils.

THE FLATHEAD AND WESTERN MONTANA

The northwestern, or Flathead, region is a destination resort area, with such attractions as Flathead Lake and Glacier National Park. In western Montana south of the Flathead, you'll find forests, lakes, and meadows among ranch country and small valley towns.

Exploring the Flathead and Western Montana

The Flathead

The relatively close proximity of Flathead's towns is atypical of Montana. Bigfork, Kalispell, and Whitefish make good touring bases.

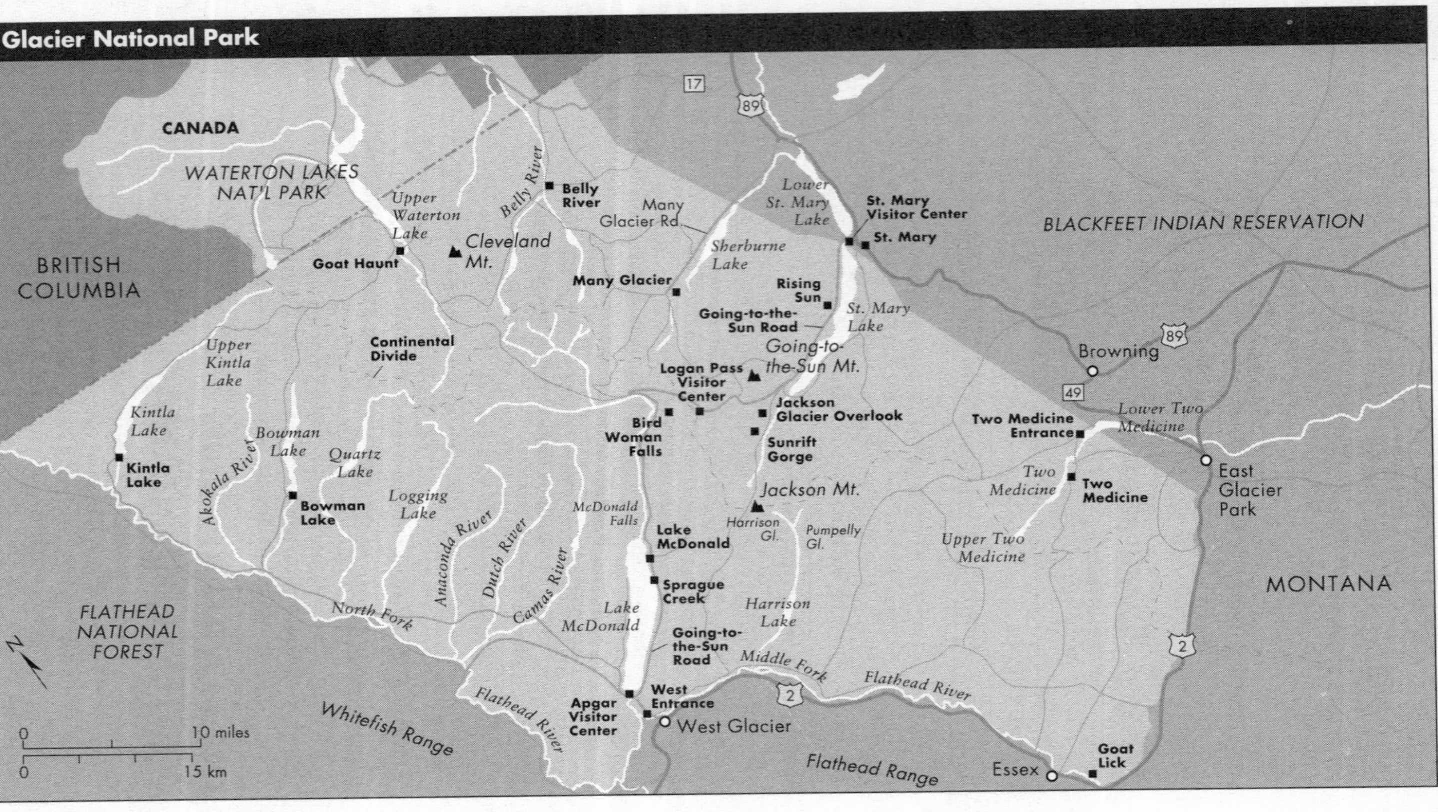
Glacier National Park
CANADA
WATERTON LAKES NAT'L PARK
BRITISH COLUMBIA
Upper Waterton Lake
Goat Haunt
Cleveland Mt.
Belly River
Belly River
Many Glacier Rd.
Many Glacier
Sherburne Lake
Lower St. Mary Lake
St. Mary Visitor Center
St. Mary
BLACKFEET INDIAN RESERVATION
Rising Sun
Going-to-the-Sun Road
St. Mary Lake
Going-to-the-Sun Mt.
Continental Divide
Upper Kintla Lake
Kintla Lake
Kintla Lake
Bowman Lake
Bowman Lake
Quartz Lake
Akokala River
Logging Lake
Anaconda River
Dutch River
Camas River
North Fork
Logan Pass Visitor Center
Bird Woman Falls
Jackson Glacier Overlook
Sunrift Gorge
Jackson Mt.
Harrison Gl.
Pumpelly Gl.
McDonald Falls
Lake McDonald
Sprague Creek
Lake McDonald
Harrison Lake
Going-to-the-Sun Road
Middle Fork
Flathead River
West Entrance
Apgar Visitor Center
West Glacier
Flathead River
Whitefish Range
Flathead Range
FLATHEAD NATIONAL FOREST
Browning
Two Medicine Entrance
Lower Two Medicine
Two Medicine
Two Medicine
Upper Two Medicine
East Glacier Park
MONTANA
Essex
Goat Lick
17
89
89
49
2
2
N
0 10 miles
0 15 km

★ **Glacier National Park** (✉ West Glacier 59936, ☎ 406/888–7800; 🎫 $10 per vehicle for 7 days) preserves more than a million spectacular acres of peaks, waterfalls, lakes, and wildlife best seen from a hiking trail or on horseback. Mountain goats and bighorn sheep often can be seen ambling along the 52-mi **Going-to-the-Sun Road,** the park's only through road. The narrow, winding roadway is a cliff-hanger and unsuitable for oversize vehicles. A **shuttle service** and guided **bus tours** (☎ 406/892–2525) leave from either end. **Sun Tours** (☎ 800/786–9220) runs trips highlighting Blackfoot Indian culture from East Glacier. Most of the park, including this road, is closed to vehicles in winter.

South of Kalispell is **Flathead Lake,** the largest freshwater lake west of the Mississippi. An 85-mi loop drive around it takes in cherry orchards, parks, sweeping views of the Mission and Swan ranges, and the arts community of **Bigfork,** which has a summer repertory theater company and rows of galleries and shops along Electric Avenue.

Pointer Scenic Cruises (✉ 452 Grand Dr., Bigfork, ☎ 406/837–5617) operates custom charter tours on Flathead Lake. Options range from dinner cruises and wildlife viewing to Wild Horse Island excursions.

Western Montana

Scenic, outdoorsy **Missoula,** 60 mi south of Kalispell via U.S. 93, is home to the **University of Montana** (☎ 406/243–4399 to arrange a free guided tour) and to a thriving community of writers and artists. The Clark Fork, Bitterroot, and Blackfoot rivers converge here—it's not unusual to see anglers casting downstream of the movie theater. The **Art Museum of Missoula** (✉ 335 N. Pattee St., ☎ 406/728–0447; 🎫 free) exhibits contemporary works. Hand-carved steeds circle 'round **A Carousel for Missoula** (☎ 406/549–8382; 🎫 $1) in downtown Caras Park, along the Clark Fork River.

The **Rocky Mountain Elk Foundation Wildlife Visitor Center** (✉ 2291 W. Broadway, ☎ 406/523–4545 or 800/225–5355, WEB www.elklink.org; 🎫 donations accepted) offers engaging natural history, art, and wildlife displays. At **Smokejumper Visitor Center** (✉ 5765 W. Broadway, ☎ 406/329–4934, WEB www.missoulasmokejumpers.com; 🎫 donations accepted), firefighter-guides conduct summer tours peppered with firsthand accounts of forest fires and smoke jumping. View bison, elk, deer, antelope, and bighorn sheep through your car window at the ★ **National Bison Range** (☎ 406/644–2211; 🎫 $4 per vehicle) at Moiese, north of Missoula en route to the Flathead. A visitor center explains the history, habits, and habitat of bison.

East of Missoula, Route 200 leads to **Seeley-Swan Valley,** densely forested and dotted with easily accessed lakes. View loons and other waterfowl from turnouts along the scenic 18-mi **Clearwater Chain-of-Lakes** (✉ Rte. 83, from Salmon Lake to Rainy Lake).

South of Missoula on U.S. 93, **Bitterroot Valley** stretches between the Sapphire Mountains and the Bitterroots, one of the northern Rockies' most rugged ranges. Jesuit missionaries founded **St. Mary's Mission** (☎ 406/777–5734; 🎫 $3) in 1841 at Stevensville. Guided tours are offered April–October.

Dining and Lodging

Reserve well in advance for the summer and ski seasons.

Bigfork

$$ ✕ **Swan River Cafe.** This relaxed yet elegant eatery serves prime rib and seafood inside or on the terrace overlooking Bigfork Bay. The Sun-

day brunch and dinner buffets attract throngs of hungry locals. ✉ *360 Grand Ave., Bigfork,* ☎ *406/837–2220. AE, D, MC, V.*

$$ ★ **O'Duachain Country Inn.** In a quiet lodgepole-pine forest near Flathead Lake and the Swan River, this log house and neighboring cabin are filled with Old West antiques and Navajo rugs; two stone fireplaces warm the main house. Hiking opportunities abound. Multicourse breakfast options include maple nut cereal and stuffed Irish toast. ✉ *675 N. Ferndale Dr., 59911,* ☎ *406/837–6851 or 800/837–7460,* FAX *406/837–0778,* WEB *www.montanainn.com. 5 rooms. AE, MC, V. BP.*

Glacier National Park

Glacier Park, Inc. runs Glacier's **grand lodges,** which were built by the Great Northern Railroad at the turn of the 20th century. All three offer horseback riding, hiking, and fishing. Rooms are rustic—no TVs—but comfortable. The hotels are open in summer only; make reservations long in advance. ✉ *774 Railroad St. (Box 2025, Columbia Falls 59912),* ☎ *406/892–2525,* WEB *www.glacierparkinc.com.*

$$$ **Glacier Park Lodge.** On the east side of the park across from the Amtrak station, this beautiful 1913 hotel is constructed of giant timbers. For dining ($$), a Western theme dominates: hearty options include steak, barbecued ribs, chicken, and fish. *154 rooms. Restaurant, pool, golf. D, MC, V. Closed mid-Sept.–mid-May.*

$$ **Lake McDonald Lodge.** This former hunting refuge near West Glacier has four-person cabins, plus motel units and a lodge on the lake. Boating, fishing, and horseback riding are prime activities. The lodge dining room evokes an outdoor charm, with its rough-hewn beams and hunting trophies. The theme is echoed in the menu, which is strictly American. Full buffet breakfast and an à la carte lunch are also served. *100 rooms. Restaurant. AE, D, MC, V. Closed mid-Sept.–mid-May.*

$$ **Many Glacier Hotel.** On the east side of the park, 12 mi west of Babb, the park's largest lodge has commanding views of Swiftcurrent Lake and the mountains. The area is known as the "Switzerland of North America." The main dining room serves a breakfast buffet, as well as Continental and Swiss à la carte options for dinner. *213 rooms. Restaurant. AE, D, MC, V. Closed mid-Sept.–mid-June.*

Hot Springs

$$ **Fairmont Hot Springs.** This family-friendly resort offers naturally heated indoor and outdoor pools, a water slide, massage, a ski area, a petting zoo, and 18 holes of golf in a beautiful setting. For dinner, try the stuffed rainbow trout. ✉ *1500 Fairmont Rd., Fairmont 59711,* ☎ *406/797–3241 or 800/332–3272,* FAX *406/797–3337,* WEB *www.fairmontmontana.com. 140 rooms. Restaurant. AE, D, MC, V.*

$ **Lost Trail Hot Springs Resort.** Hot springs feed the swimming pool and a hot tub at this resort 90 mi south of Missoula in the Bitterroot National Forest. RV spaces are available. Locals love the prime rib. ✉ *8321 Hwy. 93 S, Sula 59871,* ☎ *406/821–3574,* FAX *406/821–4012 or 800/825–3574,* WEB *www.losttrailhotsprings.com. 8 rooms, 9 cabins. Restaurant, pool. AE, D, MC, V.*

Missoula

$–$$$ ★ **Guy's Lolo Creek Steak House.** This quintessentially Montana restaurant resides in a massive log structure 8 mi south of Missoula that resembles a hunting lodge (stuffed wildlife on the walls). Guy's signature sirloins are cooked over an open-pit barbecue and come in three sizes. Portions are hearty and the fare is fresh and well prepared. ✉ *6600 U.S. 12 W, Lolo 59847,* ☎ *406/273–2622. AE, D, MC, V.*

$–$$ ★ **The Shack.** Innovative omelets and hash browns with herb-scented gravy draw a crowd of locals to this attractive eatery for breakfast.

You'll also find creative lunch and dinner specials. ✉ *222 W. Main St.,* ☎ *406/549–9903. AE, MC, V.*

$$ **Goldsmith's Inn.** Built in 1911 as the residence of the University of Montana's first president, this prairie-style redbrick B&B has big white eaves and a huge porch. It's on the shore of the Clark Fork River, near the university campus. Rooms are beautiful: hardwood floors, period furniture, and hand-painted tiles in the private bath; four rooms have balconies with lovely views. ✉ *809 E. Front St., 59802,* ☎ *406/728–1585,* WEB *www.goldsmithsinn.com. 7 rooms. D, MC, V. BP.*

Ranches

Montana's guest ranches range from working ranches to deluxe spreads with nary a cow in sight; check Travel Montana's directory (☞ Statewide Visitor Information, *above*). Those listed throughout this chapter are categorized as either $$ (less than $1,000 per person per week), $$$ ($1,000–$1,900 per person per week), or $$$$ (more than $1,900 per person based on double occupancy). Meals and recreation are included unless otherwise noted.

$$$$ ✕ **Averill's Flathead Lake Lodge.** Reserve a year in advance (one-week minimum) for this deluxe 2,000-acre dude ranch on the shores of Flathead Lake. Each of the rustic western lodges has a big stone fireplace. Horseback riding, boating, tennis, basketball, volleyball, waterskiing, and fishing are among the activities. ✉ *Box 248, Bigfork 59911,* ☎ *406/837–4391,* FAX *406/837–6977,* WEB *www.averills.com. 18 rooms, 20 cottages. Restaurant, pool. AE, MC, V. Closed Oct.–May. FAP.*

Motels

Doubletree Hotel Edgewater (✉ 100 Madison St., Missoula 59802, ☎ 406/728–3100 or 800/222–8733, FAX 406/728–2530), 172 rooms; 2 restaurants, pool; *$$–$$$.*

Aero Inn (✉ 1830 Hwy. 93 S, Kalispell 59901, ☎ 406/755–3798, FAX 406/752–1304), 62 rooms; CP; *$.*

Campgrounds

Most of Glacier National Park's 13 campgrounds are available on a first-come, first-served basis; they often fill up before noon. Only Fish Creek and St. Mary Lake may be reserved in advance. Other public campgrounds are in national forests and state parks. Look for private campgrounds with RV services near towns or check Travel Montana's directory.

Outdoor Activities and Sports

Biking

Glacier's Going-to-the-Sun Road is a challenging ride. **Austin-Lehman Adventures** (✉ Box 81025, Billings 59108, ☎ 406/655–4591 or 800/575–1540) organizes five- to seven-day trips in Glacier National Park as well as the rest of the state.

Fishing

In the Flathead Valley, fish for cutthroat and bull trout in the Flathead River or perch, whitefish, and lake trout in Flathead Lake. For western Montana waterways, fish the Clark Fork, Bitterroot, and Blackfoot rivers; Rock Creek, a blue-ribbon trout stream; or Seeley Lake. Local stores sell two-day licenses for $10, or $45 for the season.

Golf

Eagle Bend Golf Club (✉ Box 1257, Bigfork 59911, ☎ 406/837–7300 or 800/255–5641, WEB www.golfmt.com) is a 27-hole championship course with splendid views.

Hiking and Backpacking

Glacier National Park has 730 mi of trails. **Glacier Wilderness Guides** (✉ Box 330, West Glacier 59936, ☎ 406/387–5555 or 800/521–7238, WEB www.glacierguides.com) leads backcountry trips. The **Great Bear, Bob Marshall,** and **Scapegoat wilderness areas** (✉ Flathead National Forest, 1935 3rd Ave. E, Kalispell 59901, ☎ 406/758–5208) constitute a million-acre refuge along the Continental Divide. The **Jewel Basin Hiking Area,** 13 mi east of Bigfork off Route 83, is a short, minimal-ascent trail to high-country lakes and superb views. For information on hiking, contact the **U.S. Forest Service Northern Region Office** (✉ 200 E. Broadway Ave., Missoula 59807, ☎ 406/329–3511).

Rafting and Canoeing

Rafting outfitters include **Glacier Raft Co.** (✉ Box 210M, West Glacier 59936, ☎ 406/888–5454 or 800/235–6781, WEB www.glacierraftco.com). Canoes take the calmer waters of Glacier Park's Lake McDonald. For canoe rentals try **Glacier Park Boat Company** (✉ Box 5262, Kalispell 59903, ☎ 406/257–2426 May–Sept.; 406/752–5488 Oct.–Apr.).

Most stretches of the Clark Fork and Bitterroot can be run by raft or canoe; the Blackfoot is more difficult. A good outfitter is **Western Waters** (✉ 1093 Mullan Rd. E, Superior 59872, ☎ 406/822–9900 or 866/703–0301, WEB www.westernwaters.com). Northeast of Missoula near Seeley Lake, the **Clearwater River Canoe Trail** follows an easy 4-mi stretch.

Water Sports

Flathead Lake supports a large sailing community, countless water-skiers and windsurfers, and cruises on the ***Port Polson Princess*** (✉ Polson, ☎ 800/882–6363).

Ski Areas

For **ski reports** call ☎ 406/444–2654 or 800/847–4868.

Cross-Country

You'll find trails in Glacier National Park, the Flathead National Forest, and Lolo National Forest near Missoula. On Glacier's southern border, the **Izaak Walton Inn** (✉ U.S. 2, Essex 59916, ☎ 406/888–5700, FAX 406/888–5200) has 23 mi of groomed trails and food and lodging.

Downhill

Big Mountain (✉ Box 1400, Whitefish 59937, ☎ 406/862–1900 or 800/858–5439, WEB www.skiwhitefish.com) has 81 runs, 9 lifts, and a 2,500-ft vertical drop.

The Flathead and Western Montana Essentials

AIRPORTS

Glacier Park International Airport, northeast of Kalispell, and Missoula International Airport are served by major domestic airlines, including Delta, Northwest, and United.

➤ Airport Information: **Glacier Park International Airport** (☎ 406/257–5994). **Missoula International Airport** (☎ 406/728–4381).

BUS TRAVEL

Greyhound serves Missoula. Rimrock Trailways stops in Kalispell.

➤ Bus Information: **Greyhound** (☎ 800/231–2222). **Rimrock Trailways** (☎ 406/755–4011).

CAR TRAVEL

I–90 and U.S. 93 pass through Missoula. U.S. 93 and Route 35 lead off I–90 to Kalispell, in the Flathead; from there U.S. 2 leads to Glacier

National Park. From Great Falls take I–15 and then U.S. 89 to St. Mary, at the east entrance to Glacier's Going-to-the-Sun Road, open mid-June–September, depending on snowfall. In winter, skirt along the southern edge of the park by taking U.S. 2 west from U.S. 89 at Browning.

TRAIN TRAVEL

Amtrak's *Empire Builder* stops in Essex, Whitefish, West Glacier, and East Glacier.

➤ TRAIN INFORMATION: **Amtrak** (☎ 800/872–7245).

VISITOR INFORMATION

➤ TOURIST INFORMATION: **Glacier Country Regional Tourism Commission** (✉ Box 1035, Bigfork 59911, ☎ 406/837–6211 or 800/338–5072, WEB www.glacier.visitmt.com).

SOUTHWESTERN MONTANA

Montana's pioneer history began here, and evidence of the early mining frontier—from rough-and-tumble camps to the mansions of the magnates—is inescapable. In the high country north and west of Yellowstone National Park you'll find world-class fishing and some of the state's best ski terrain.

Exploring Southwestern Montana

The humble mining origins of **Helena,** Montana's capital, are visible in its earliest commercial district, **Reeder's Alley.** By 1888, the "Queen City of the Rockies" had 50 resident millionaires and a legacy of major gold rushes. The mansions on the **West Side** and commercial buildings on the main street, **Last Chance Gulch,** preserve the era's opulence.

Helena's vibrant arts scene includes dramatic performances and movies in the two auditoriums within the **Myrna Loy Center** (✉ 15 N. Ewing St. 59601, ☎ 406/443–0287, WEB www.myrnaloycenter.com). Free tours are conducted at the **Archie Bray Foundation** (✉ 2915 Country Club Ave., 59602, ☎ 406/443–3502, WEB www.archiebray.org), a nationally known center for ceramic arts. The **Montana Historical Society Museum** (✉ 225 N. Roberts St., ☎ 406/444–1799, WEB www.montanahistoricalsociety.org; 🎫 $3) showcases valuable collections of western paintings and historic memorabilia across from the state capitol. In front of the museum, the **Last Chance** automotive tour train through Helena (☎ 406/442–1023, WEB www.lctours.com; 🎫 $5.50) departs on the hour in summer.

The millionaires may have resided in Helena, but the miners lived in **Butte,** a tough, wily town with a rich ethnic mix.

The **Berkeley Pit,** a mile-wide open-pit copper mine, sits at the edge of the **Butte National Historic District,** a downtown area of ornate buildings with an Old West feel. Self-guided tour brochures are available at the Chamber of Commerce (✉ 1000 George St., 59701, ☎ 406/723–3177 or 800/735–6814, WEB www.butteinfo.org). On the northern edge of Deer Lodge, 24 mi north of Butte, the **Grant-Kohrs Ranch National Historic Site** (✉ 316 Main St., ☎ 406/846–2070; 🎫 free) preserves the home and outbuildings of a 19th-century ranch, still worked by cowboys and draft horses.

★ Montana's oldest state park, **Lewis and Clark Caverns** (✉ Rte. 2, off I–90, ☎ 406/287–3541; 🎫 $4 entry, $8 tour) lies near Whitehall, 40 mi east of Butte. Two-hour tours lead through narrow passages and vaulted chambers past colorful, intriguingly varied limestone formations. The park is closed mid-October–April.

Bozeman, 50 mi east of Butte on I–90, is a cowboy town, a regional trade center, and a place crazy for food, art, and the outdoors.

★ At Montana State University, the **Museum of the Rockies** (✉ 600 W. Kagy Blvd., ☎ 406/994–3466; $7) presents paleontology exhibits, a hands-on dinosaur playroom, planetarium shows, and western art and history exhibits.

South of town, U.S. 191 follows the Gallatin River to West Yellowstone, the gateway to **Yellowstone National Park.** On the U.S. 89 approach to Yellowstone, **Livingston**—former home of Calamity Jane and now a haven for hiking, fishing, and other outdoor activities—sits at the head of Paradise Valley, which is bisected by the Yellowstone River. U.S. 212, the most spectacular route to Yellowstone, passes through **Red Lodge.** The coal mines here attracted immigrants from Great Britain, Italy, Finland, Yugoslavia, and other nations at the turn of the 20th century. The town celebrates its diverse heritage each August with a weeklong celebration.

Dining and Lodging

Big Sky

$$–$$$ ✕ **Big Sky Resort.** After enjoying a stint of golfing, fishing, horseback riding, or skiing, come back to large, bright rooms in the ski lodge or condominiums of this resort in gorgeous Gallatin Canyon, 43 mi south of Bozeman and 18 mi from Yellowstone National Park. The resort has 36 restaurants, with every kind of food available, at every price range. ✉ *Box 160001, 1 Lone Mountain Trail, Big Sky, 59716,* ☎ *406/995–5000 or 800/548–4486,* FAX *406/995–5001,* WEB *www.bigskyresort.com. 660 rooms. 36 restaurants, pool, health club. AE, D, DC, MC, V. Closed mid-Apr.–late May and early Oct.–late Nov.*

Bozeman

$–$$ ✕ **Mackenzie River Pizza Co.** In addition to zesty gourmet pizzas baked in a brick oven, expect tasty salads, sandwiches, and bread sticks. ✉ *232 E. Main St.,* ☎ *406/587–0055. Reservations not accepted. AE, MC, V.*

$$ ★ **Voss Inn.** Afternoon tea is served in the parlor of this antiques-filled, 1883 Victorian B&B in Bozeman's historic district. The lovely English garden is perfect for an afternoon stroll. ✉ *319 S. Willson Ave., 59715,* ☎ *406/587–0982,* FAX *406/585–2964,* WEB *www.bozeman-vossinn.com. 6 rooms. AE, D, MC, V. BP.*

Butte

$–$$$ ✕ **Uptown Café.** Choose from fresh seafood, steaks, and pasta at this informal café. ✉ *47 E. Broadway,* ☎ *406/723–4735. AE, MC, V.*

Helena

$$ ✕ **The Windbag Saloon and Grill.** The cherrywood-paneled saloon, once a sporting house called Big Dorothy's, was named in honor of the hot political debates you're likely to overhear while dining on burgers, quiche, salads, and sandwiches. ✉ *19 S. Last Chance Gulch,* ☎ *406/443–9669. AE, D, MC, V.*

$–$$ ★ **The Sanders.** Wilbur Fisk Sanders, frontier politician and vigilante, once lived in this 1875 Queen Anne mansion, now a centrally located B&B on the National Register of Historic Places. Most furnishings are original. Breakfasts have innovative entrées; complimentary sherry, fruit, and cookies are offered each afternoon. ✉ *328 N. Ewing St., 59601,* ☎ *406/442–3309,* FAX *406/443–2361,* WEB *www.sandersbb.com. 7 rooms. AE, D, MC, V. BP.*

Motels

🏨 **Bozeman Inn** (✉ 1235 N. 7th Ave., Bozeman 59715, ☎ 406/587–3176 or 800/648–7515, FAX 406/585–3591), 49 rooms; restaurant, pool; $.

🏨 **Jorgenson's Holiday Motel** (✉ 1714 11th Ave., Helena 59601, ☎ 406/442–1770; 800/272–1770 in Montana; FAX 406/449–0155), 117 rooms; restaurant, pool; $.

🏨 **Red Lion Hotel** (✉ 2100 Cornell Ave., Butte 59701, ☎ 406/494–7800, WEB www.redlion.com), 131 rooms; restaurant, pool, gym; $.

Ranch

$$$$ ✕🏨 **Rainbow Ranch Lodge.** Nestled in the breathtaking Gallatin River Canyon 15 minutes from Yellowstone National Park, this ranch offers blue-ribbon trout fishing, trail rides, and some fine food. The 16 guest rooms have river views and lodgepole-pine beds with thick down comforters. Meals are not included in the lodging price. After working the stream into a lather with your new fly rod, sit down to a dinner of cardamom- and peppercorn-crusted veal rib chop with almond and crawfish potato gratin or go for the rack of lamb roasted with Japanese black mustard, smoked chèvre gnocchi, beet puree, and roasted chestnuts. You'll find lots of Montana game, as well as other options. *✉ Box 160336, Big Sky 59716, ☎ 406/995–4132 or 800/937–4132, FAX 406/995–2861, WEB www.rainbowranch.com. 16 rooms. Restaurant. AE, D, MC, V.*

Campgrounds

Public campgrounds are in national forests and state parks; private ones with RV services are near towns. Check Travel Montana's directory. In peak season, campgrounds near Yellowstone fill early in the day.

The Arts

The String Orchestra of the Rockies performs at the **Big Sky Arts Festival** at the Big Sky Resort in July. In August be part of the **Montana Cowboy Poetry Gathering** (☞ Statewide Visitor Information, *above*).

Outdoor Activities and Sports

Fishing

Few trout streams rival the Missouri, Beaverhead, and Big Hole rivers; the **Complete Fly Fisher** (✉ Box 127, Wise River 59762, ☎ 406/832–3175 or 866/832–3175) provides lodging.

Livingston, Ennis, and West Yellowstone are base towns for the superb fly-fishing on the Yellowstone, Madison, and other local rivers; **Dan Bailey's Fly Shop** (✉ 209 W. Park St., Livingston, ☎ 406/222–1673 or 800/356–4052) is a Montana legend. Licenses are sold at local stores (residents: full-season $17; nonresidents: full-season $50, or $15 for the first two days and $10 for every other two days).

Golf

Big Sky Golf Course (✉ Rte. 64, Big Sky 59716, ☎ 406/995–4706) has 18 holes.

Hiking and Backpacking

Wilderness areas include the **Gates of the Mountains** (☎ 406/449–5201), near Helena; the **Anaconda-Pintler Wilderness** (☎ 406/683–3900), near Anaconda; the **Lee Metcalf Wilderness** (☎ 406/522–2520), near Bozeman; and **Absarokee-Beartooth Wilderness** (☎ 406/587–6743), near Livingston.

Rafting and Canoeing

The Missouri River north of Helena is easy for rafts and canoes. Bear Trap Canyon, on the Madison River near Ennis, and Yankee Jim, on the Yellowstone near Gardiner, require white-water experience or an outfitter, such as the **Yellowstone Raft Co.** (✉ Box 46, Gardiner 59030, ☎ 406/848–7777 or 800/858–7781, WEB www.yellowstoneraft.com).

Ski Areas

For **ski reports** call ☎ 800/847–4868.

Cross-Country

In winter many national forest roads and trails become backcountry ski trails. **Lone Mountain Ranch** (✉ Box 160069, Big Sky 59716, ☎ 406/995–4644 or 800/514–4644, FAX 406/995–4670) has 45 mi of groomed and tracked trails, food, lodging, and even guided cross-country ski tours of nearby Yellowstone National Park.

Downhill

Big Sky Resort has 150 runs, 18 lifts, and a 4,350-ft vertical drop.

Southwestern Montana Essentials

AIRPORTS

Helena Regional Airport, Bozeman's Gallatin Field Airport, and Butte's Bert Mooney Airport are served by major domestic airlines.

➤ AIRPORT INFORMATION: **Bert Mooney Airport** (☎ 406/494–3771). **Gallatin Field Airport** (☎ 406/388–6632). **Helena Regional Airport** (☎ 406/442–2821).

BUS TRAVEL

Rimrock Trailways stops in Helena and Butte. Greyhound serves Bozeman. In summer Karst Stages runs between Bozeman, Livingston, and Yellowstone.

➤ BUS INFORMATION: **Greyhound** (☎ 800/231–2222). **Karst Stages** (☎ 800/287–4759). **Rimrock Trailways** (☎ 406/442–5860 or 406/723–3287).

CAR TRAVEL

I–15 passes through Helena. Use I–90 for Butte and Bozeman. U.S. 191, 89, 287, and 212 link the region with Yellowstone.

VISITOR INFORMATION

➤ TOURIST INFORMATION: **Gold West Country Regional Tourism Office** (✉ 1155 Main St., Deer Lodge 59722, ☎ 406/846–1943 or 800/879–1159, WEB www.goldwest.visitmt.com). **Yellowstone Country Regional Tourism Office** (✉ 1822 W. Lincoln, Bozeman 59715, ☎ 406/556–8680 or 800/736–5276, WEB www.yellowstone.visitmt.com).

BIGHORN COUNTRY

Despite the heavy influence of cowboy culture, southeastern Montana is Native American land. The Northern Cheyenne and the Crow inhabit this stunning country of rimrock, badlands, wide-open grasslands, and rugged mountains. Billings is a convenient base for touring.

Exploring Bighorn Country

Booms in coal, oil, and gas made **Billings** Montana's largest town. Sprawled between steep-face rimrocks and the Yellowstone River, it has big-city services and a stockman's heart. Rodeos are held on weekend nights throughout the summer. The **Moss Mansion** (✉ 914 Division St. 59101, ☎ 406/256–5100, WEB www.mossmansion.com; $6) is an elegantly restored 1903 red-sandstone dwelling. Tours run hourly. A broader view of the social history of the Yellowstone Valley becomes clear in the varied exhibits of the **Western Heritage Center** (✉ 2822 Montana Ave., ☎ 406/256–6809; donations accepted). The **Yellowstone Art Museum** (✉ 401 N. 27th St., 59101, ☎ 406/256–6804; $5) showcases regional art in the original county jail.

Southeast of Billings on I–94 lie the Crow and Northern Cheyenne Indian reservations. **Crow Fair** (☎ 406/638–3784), held in Crow Agency for five days in August, draws visitors from all over the West for parades, rodeos, traditional dancing, and horse races.

★ Sixty miles southeast of Billings on I–90, **Little Bighorn Battlefield National Monument** (✉ National Park Service, Crow Agency 59022, ☎ 406/638–2621; $10 per vehicle) preserves the site where in 1876 the Cheyenne and Sioux defended their homeland in a bloody battle with Lieutenant Colonel George Armstrong Custer. You can explore the windswept prairie on your own or with a guided tour. An interpretive display includes items from recent archaeological digs, which help explain what might have happened in the battle.

Dining and Lodging

Billings

$–$$$ ✕ **CJ's Restaurant.** Mesquite-grilled ribs, steaks, chicken, and seafood dominate the fare, with barbecue sauces ranging from mild to three-alarm. ✉ *2456 Central Ave.,* ☎ *406/656–1400. AE, D, DC, MC, V.*

$$ ✕ **Northern Hotel.** This hotel has an American West theme, with woven rugs, bedspreads, and a gaming table. A massive fireplace dominates the lobby. The Golden Belle restaurant serves fine Continental cuisine. ✉ *Broadway at 1st Ave. N (Box 1296, 59101),* ☎ *406/245–5121 or 800/542–5121,* FAX *406/259–9862,* WEB *www.northernhotel.net. 160 rooms. Restaurant. AE, D, DC, MC, V.*

Motel

Best Western Ponderosa Inn (✉ 2511 1st Ave. N, Billings 59101, ☎ 406/259–5511 or 800/628–9081, FAX 406/245–8004, WEB www.ponderosainn.com), 133 rooms; restaurant, pool; CP; $.

Campgrounds

Public campgrounds are in **Custer National Forest** and **Bighorn Canyon National Recreation Area**; for private campgrounds check Travel Montana's listing (☞ Statewide Visitor Information, *above*).

Outdoor Activities and Sports

Fishing

Trout anglers fish the Yellowstone River above Columbus. Walleye, bass, and warmer-water fish are found downriver. The Bighorn River below Yellowtail Dam near Pryor is trout heaven; lake species inhabit the reservoir above the dam.

Hiking and Backpacking

The northern region of the arid Pryor Mountains, south of Billings, is on the Crow Reservation; permits for backcountry travel are issued by the **Crow Tribal Council** (✉ Crow Agency 59022, ☎ 406/638–3784). The southern Pryors are in **Custer National Forest** (✉ 2602 1st Ave. N, Billings 59103, ☎ 406/657–6200).

Rafting and Canoeing

Canoes, rafts, and drift boats ply the Yellowstone River and the Bighorn River below Yellowtail Dam. **Elk River Outfitters** (✉ 1809 Darlene,

Billings 59102, ☎ 406/252–5859) has float trips, fishing excursions, and trail rides.

Ski Area

Red Lodge Mountain (✉ Box 750, Red Lodge 59068, ☎ 406/446–2610 or 800/444–8977), an hour southwest of Billings, has 69 runs, eight lifts, and a 2,400-ft vertical drop.

Bighorn Country Essentials

AIRPORTS

Major domestic airlines, including Delta, Northwest, and United, fly to Logan International Airport in Billings.

➤ AIRPORT INFORMATION: **Logan International Airport** (☎ 406/238–3420).

BUS TRAVEL

Greyhound and Rimrock Trailways serve Billings.

➤ BUS INFORMATION: **Greyhound** (☎ 800/231–2222). **Rimrock Trailways** (☎ 406/245–5392 or 800/255–7655).

CAR TRAVEL

The main routes between Yellowstone and Broadus, in the southeastern corner of the state, are I–94, I–90, U.S. 212, and Route 59.

VISITOR INFORMATION

➤ TOURIST INFORMATION: **Custer Country Regional Tourism Office** (✉ Box 160, Laurel 59044, ☎ 406/628–1432 or 800/346–1876, WEB www.custer.visitmt.com).

ELSEWHERE IN MONTANA

Central and Eastern Montana

What to See and Do

Montana's heartland is open grasslands and, rising abruptly from the plains, the sheer escarpment of the Rocky Mountain Front.

★ In Great Falls, the **C. M. Russell Museum** (✉ 400 13th St. N, 59401, ☎ 406/727–8787, WEB www.cmrussell.org; 💵 $6) has a large collection of works by the cowboy artist, along with his original log-cabin studio. Cowboy life thrives 146 mi northeast of Billings in **Miles City**, which in May hosts the **Miles City Bucking Horse Sale** (☎ 406/234–2890), three days of horse trading, rodeo, and street dances.

Dining

$$–$$$ ✕ **Jaker's.** Arrive hungry for heaping plates of ribs, steaks, and seafood. *✉ 1500 10th Ave. S, Great Falls, ☎ 406/727–1033. AE, D, MC, V.*

Central and Eastern Montana Essentials

CAR TRAVEL

I–15 and U.S. 89 traverse the region north–south; U.S. 2 and I–94 run east–west.

VISITOR INFORMATION

➤ TOURIST INFORMATION: **Russell Country Regional Tourism Commission** (✉ Box 3166, Great Falls 59403, ☎ 406/761–5036 or 800/527–5348, WEB www.russell.visitmt.com).

NEBRASKA

Updated by Diana Lambdin Meyer

Capital	Lincoln
Population	1,711,263
Motto	Equality Before the Law
State Bird	Western meadowlark
State Flower	Goldenrod
Postal Abbreviation	NE

Statewide Visitor Information

The **Nebraska Department of Economic Development, Division of Travel and Tourism** (✉ Box 98907, Lincoln 68509-8907, ☎ 402/471–3796 or 800/228–4307, WEB www.visitnebraska.org) staffs 24 rest and information areas along I–80.

Scenic Drives

Route 2, from Grand Island west to Crawford, is a long, lonesome road through the Sandhills, traversing 332 mi of delicate wildflowers, tranquil rivers, and grazing cattle. The 130-mi drive north on **U.S. 83** from North Platte to Valentine affords views of the Sandhills' native shortgrass prairie. **U.S. 26** from Ogallala to Scottsbluff is a 128-mi historic segment of the Oregon Trail, passing such natural landmarks as Ash Hollow; Courthouse, Jail, and Chimney rocks; and Scotts Bluff National Monument.

National and State Parks

National Parks

Homestead National Monument (✉ 8523 W. State Hwy. 4, 68310, ☎ 402/223–3514, WEB www.nps.gov/home; 🎫 free), near Beatrice, includes walking trails and a museum that commemorate the Homestead Act of 1862 and the pioneers who settled the prairies between 1863 and 1936. **Nebraska National Forest** (✉ Box 39, 69142, ☎ 308/533–2257, WEB www.fs.fed.us/grasslands; 🎫 free), at Halsey, is the largest planted forest in the country, with more than 20,000 acres of conifers.

State Parks

The **Nebraska Game and Parks Commission** (✉ Box 30370, Lincoln 68503, ☎ 402/471–0641 or 800/826–7275, WEB www.ngpc.state.ne.us) manages and provides information on all eight state parks. You can buy a day pass ($2.50) or an annual pass ($14) at any state park; they're good for admission to all of them. ⛺ **Chadron State Park** (✉ 9 mi south of Chadron, ☎ 308/432–6167) has camping, fishing, and swimming. **Eugene T. Mahoney State Park**(✉ 3 mi east of Ashland, ☎ 402/944–2523) has excellent tent and RV camping. **Fort Robinson State Park** (✉ 3 mi west of Crawford, ☎ 308/665–2900) has campsites and boating. **Indian Cave State Park** (✉ 4 mi east of Barada, ☎ 402/883–2575) has a variety of trails. **Niobrara State Park** (✉ 1 mi south and 5 mi west of Niobrara, ☎ 402/857–3373) offers guided float trips on the Upper Missouri, among other activities. **Platte River State Park** (✉ 2.5 mi south of Louisville, ☎ 402/234–2217) has fishing, swimming, and buffalo-stew cookouts on Friday and Saturday nights in summer. **Ponca State Park** (✉ 2 mi north of Ponca, ☎ 402/755–2284) has an archery range and boating. See the state's largest waterfall at **Smith Falls State Park** (✉ 12 mi east of Valentine, ☎ 402/376–1306).

SOUTHEAST NEBRASKA

The southeast region of the state is a land of both city sophistication and country charm. Here you can tour museums and historic buildings, shop in restored warehouses, and ride riverboats.

Exploring Southeast Nebraska

Nebraska's state capitol dominates the Lincoln skyline; the river city of Omaha is the region's center of commerce and industry. Minutes away from both downtowns are expansive prairies, state parks, and attractions that chronicle the opening of the West to settlement. **Omaha** is a quintessentially friendly midwestern city with a refurbished 12-block market area by the river, known as **Old Market,** where shoppers may choose from more than 100 shops and boutiques.The **Henry Doorly Zoo** (✉ 3701 S. 10th St., ☎ 402/733–8401, WEB www.omahazoo.org; $8) has the world's largest indoor rain forest—the Lied Jungle—and a saltwater aquarium with one of the country's largest penguin exhibits. The zoo also has the world's largest nocturnal desert exhibit below ground. "Ride the rails" at the **Durham Western Heritage Museum** (✉ 801 S. 10th St., ☎ 402/444–5071, WEB www.dwhm.org; $5), where you can climb aboard at Nebraska's largest restored Art Deco railroad station. Formerly Omaha's Union Station, the museum highlights the history of the Omaha and Union Pacific railroads through interactive exhibits. Lifelike sculptures of soldiers, salesmen, and other rail travelers of the 1930s and '40s sit in restored train cars and "talk" about the politics, music, and the society of the time.

In 1917 Father Edward J. Flanagan founded Father Flanagan's Boys' Home as a refuge for boys. Today, it's known as **Girls and Boys Town** (✉ 13628 Flanagan Blvd., 68010, ☎ 402/498–1140, WEB www.boysandgirlstown.org; free). On its large campus just outside Omaha, about 2 mi west of I–680, you can tour Father Flanagan's House, gardens, a chapel, and other facilities. On display is the Academy Award won by Spencer Tracy for his portrayal of Flanagan in the 1938 movie *Boys' Town.*

In Fremont, about 50 mi northwest of Bellevue, board the historic **Fremont and Elkhorn Valley Railroad** (✉ 1835 N. Somers Ave., ☎ 402/727–0615; $11) for a tour through the lush Elkhorn River valley. Hop the **Fremont Dinner Train** (✉ 650 N. H St., ☎ 800/942–7245; $44.95) for a dining experience that recalls rail travel in the 1940s. The scenic, 30-mi round-trip takes about three hours and includes a five-course meal.At the **Strategic Air and Space Museum** (✉ I–80, Exit 426, Ashland, ☎ 402/944–3100 or 800/358–5029, WEB www.strategicairandspace.com; $7), displays include real aircraft that have changed the course of history, missiles, rare film footage, and military artifacts.

Lincoln, home of the University of Nebraska and the state government, rises to meet you as you drive along I–80 W.You can scan the city's skyline from atop the **Nebraska State Capitol Building** (✉ 1445 K St., ☎ 402/471–0448), with its 400-ft spire that towers over the surrounding plains. Free tours are given daily 9–4.

A five-minute drive north from the capitol will take you to the **University of Nebraska,** at 14th and U streets. There you'll find the State Museum of Natural History (☎ 402/472–2642, WEB www.museum.unl.edu; $2), nicknamed Elephant Hall for its exhibit of elephant fossils, collected from animals that once roamed the Great Plains. Within the State Museum is the Ralph Mueller Planetarium (☎ 402/472–2641, WEB www.spacelaser.com), with regularly scheduled laser and astronomy shows. Call for ticket information. At **Nine-Mile Prairie** (✉ 1 mi west of N.W. 48th St. and Fletcher Ave.; 🎫 free) you can park your car and hop out to hike the natural prairies.

From Lincoln you can take Route 2 southeast to U.S. 75, then U.S. 136 southeast to Brownville. At the **Brownville State Recreation Area,** the *Spirit of Brownville* riverboat (☎ 402/825–6441) makes various sightseeing, dining, and dancing cruises on the mighty Missouri River.U.S. 75 N brings you to **Nebraska City,** a tidy town rimmed with historic sites and apple orchards, including the **Arbor Day Farm** (✉ 100 Arbor Ave., ☎ 402/873–8710, WEB www.arborday.org), where you can buy apples in season and apple cider year-round. Lip-smacking desserts are served in the Pie Garden from May through October.While
★ at the Arbor Day Farm, peek into the past at the **Arbor Lodge State Historical Park and Arboretum** (✉ 2nd and Centennial Aves., ☎ 402/ 873–7222, WEB www.ngpc.state.ne.us/parks; 🎫 $3). On these grounds are the 52-room mansion and carriage house of J. Sterling Morton, the 19th-century politician and lover of trees who inaugurated the first Arbor Day. The mansion was later inhabited by his son, Morton Salt baron Joy Morton.Hop the **Nebraska City Trolley** (☎ 402/873–3393; 🎫 $5) throughout town. It links historic sites to 11 downtown factory outlets clustered around 8th and 1st Corso streets and to the **Factory Stores of America Mall** (✉ 1001 Rte. 2, ☎ 402/873–7727). The trolley also stops at **John Brown's Cave and Historical Village** (✉ 1908 4th Corso St., ☎ 402/873–3115; 🎫 $5), where you can visit a cave and a passageway once part of the Underground Railroad. It's open May–November.

Dining and Lodging

For information on B&Bs contact the **Nebraska Association of Bed and Breakfasts** (✉ 11 Lakeview Acres, Johnson Lake 68937, ☎ 877/223–6222, WEB www.nabb1.com).

Lincoln

$–$$ ★ ✕ **Billy's.** A fascinating collection of political memorabilia and antiques decorates this upscale restaurant. The menu covers all the classics—steak, lamb, veal, duck—and has nightly fresh-fish specials. ✉ *1301 H St.,* ☎ *402/474–0084. AE, D, DC, MC, V.*

$–$$ ✕ **Misty's Restaurant.** Adorned with Cornhusker football paraphernalia, this is, by locals' accounts, the prime-rib palace of the Plains. ✉ *6235 Havelock Ave.,* ☎ *402/466–8424. AE, D, MC, V.*

$ ✕ **Arturo's Restaurant & Cantina.** Lincoln's first Mexican restaurant serves a wide variety of traditional dishes, all made with fresh ingredients, plus "tasha," a family recipe made with refried beans and cheese in a corn tortilla. ✉ *803 Q St.,* ☎ *402/475–8226. D, MC, V.*

$ ✕ **Rock 'n' Roll Runza.** Waitresses on roller skates serve Runzas—hamburger-cabbage sandwiches—at this 1950s-style restaurant, part of a Nebraska chain. ✉ *210 N. 14th St.,* ☎ *402/474–2030. AE, D, MC, V.*

$ ★ ✕ **Valentino's Restaurant.** Besides pizza with original or home-style crust, this restaurant also serves Italian specials and "dessert pizzas" with such toppings as cherries and cream cheese. ✉ *3457 Holdrege St.,* ☎ *402/ 467–3611. AE, D, MC, V.*

$$–$$$ 🏨 **The Cornhusker.** The lobby of this elegant hotel has a grand curving staircase, hand-painted murals, and an Italian-marble floor. Rooms in the east and south wings have good views of downtown Lincoln. ✉ *333 S. 13th St., 68508,* ☎ *402/474–7474 or 800/793–7474,* FAX *402/ 474–1847,* WEB *www.thecornhusker.com. 290 rooms. Restaurant, pool, gym. AE, D, DC, MC, V.*

$–$$ ★ 🏨 **Rogers House Bed and Breakfast.** Built in 1914, this ivy-covered brick mansion was converted into a B&B by the current owners in 1984. The antiques-filled public areas, with oak floors, include a living room with a fireplace and a sunroom where guests eat breakfast. ✉ *2145 B St., 68502,* ☎ *402/476–6961,* FAX *402/476–6473,* WEB *www.rogershouseinn.com. 12 rooms. AE, D, MC, V. BP.*

Nebraska City

$ ★ ✕ **Sunrise Cafe.** Booths line the walls of this country kitchen, where old-fashioned fare like meat loaf and homemade lemon pie is served at yesterday's prices. ✉ *812 Central Ave.,* ☎ *402/873–9100. MC, V.*

$–$$ 🏨 **Arbor Day Farm Lied Conference Center.** In a 260-acre complex devoted to environmental programs, the farm is surrounded by arboretums and interpretive nature trails. ✉ *2700 Sylvan Rd., 68410,* ☎ *402/873–8733 or 800/546–5433,* FAX *402/873–4999,* WEB *www.adflcc.com. 144 rooms. Restaurant, pool, health club. AE, D, MC, V.*

$ 🏨 **Whispering Pines.** Nestled among pines on 6½ quiet acres, this 1886 two-story brick house has been restored as a B&B. Take a dip in the six-person hot tub before you turn in for the night. ✉ *21st St. and 6th Ave., 68410,* ☎ *402/873–5850 or 877/558–7014,* WEB *www.bbonline.com/ne/whispering. 5 rooms. AE, MC, V. BP.*

Omaha

$–$$ ✕ **Johnny's Café.** Johnny's has been *the* place in Omaha for mouth-watering steaks, seafood, and midwestern dishes since 1922. ✉ *4702 S. 27th St.,* ☎ *402/731–4774. AE, D, DC, MC, V.*

$–$$ ✕ **McFoster's Natural Kind Cafe.** Seafood and free-range chicken are offered at this cozy spot, but the main attractions, whether grilled, roasted, or fried, are the vegetables. Libations are available from two full bars—one juice, the other alcohol. There's live acoustic entertainment nightly. ✉ *302 S. 38th St.,* ☎ *402/345–7477. AE, D, MC, V.*

$ ✕ **Austins.** Feel free to throw your peanut shells on the floor at this casual eatery, where the atmosphere is western and the food pure country. Chicken-fried steak, prime rib, and barbecued ribs are house specialties. ✉ *12020 Anne St.,* ☎ *402/896–5373. AE, MC, V.*

$ ✕ **Bohemian Cafe.** Gaily painted Czech plates hang on the walls of this family-style restaurant, where you can try such Eastern European favorites as goulash. ✉ *1406 S. 13th St.,* ☎ *402/342–9838. D, MC, V.*

$ ✕ **Garden Café.** In the historic Old Market, this café is known for its home-style cooking, with everything made from scratch. Highlights are the potato casseroles, soups, salads, and desserts. ✉ *12th and Harney Sts.,* ☎ *402/422–1574. AE, D, DC, MC, V.*

$ ★ ✕ **Mr. C's.** Christmas lights surround you at this Italian steak house, where specialties include the sirloin, lasagna, and manicotti. ✉ *5319 N. 30th St.,* ☎ *402/451–1998. AE, MC, V.*

$$–$$$ ★ 🏨 **Double Tree Hotel.** In the heart of the downtown business and entertainment district, the Double Tree is close to the Old Market and Henry Doorly Zoo and only 10 minutes from Eppley Airfield. Rooms on all of its 19 stories are spacious. ✉ *1616 Dodge St., 68102,* ☎ *402/346–7600,* FAX *402/346–5722,* WEB *www.doubletreehotels.com. 413 rooms. Restaurant, pool, gym. AE, D, DC, MC, V.*

$$–$$$ 🏨 **Marriott Hotel.** The six-story hotel in suburban Omaha is near the upscale Regency Fashion Court shopping area. ✉ *10220 Regency Cir., 68114,* ☎ *402/399–9000,* FAX *402/399–0223,* WEB *www.marriott.com. 299 rooms. Restaurant, 2 pools, gym. AE, D, DC, MC, V.*

Motel

🏨 **Quality Inn Central** (✉ 2808 S. 72nd St., Omaha 68124, ☎ 402/397–7137, FAX 402/397–3492), 102 rooms; pool, gym; *$.*

Outdoor Activities and Sports

Fishing

The 13 Salt Valley lakes surrounding Lincoln, especially **Branched Oak** (✉ N.W. 140th St. and W. Raymond Rd.) and **Pawnee** (✉ N.W. 98th and W. Adams Sts.), contain a variety of fish, including largemouth bass, northern pike, walleye, and channel catfish. For more information about fishing in Nebraska, contact the **Game and Parks Commission** (☎ 402/471–0641).

Spectator Sports

Football: University of Nebraska Cornhuskers (✉ 117 S. Stadium St., ☎ 402/472–3111, WEB www.huskers.com).

Shopping

The **Nebraska Furniture Mart** (✉ 700 S. 72nd St., Omaha, ☎ 402/397–6100 or 800/359–1200, WEB www.nfm.com) is said to be the largest furniture store west of the Mississippi. Omaha's **Old Market** (✉ Between 10th and 13th Sts., ☎ 402/346–4445) is a collection of boutiques, galleries, and restaurants. Lincoln's charming, restored warehouse shopping district, **Historic Haymarket** (✉ between 7th and 9th Sts. and between O and S Sts., ☎ 402/435–7496), has quaint antiques stores, novelty gift shops, and some fine restaurants.

Southeast Nebraska Essentials

AIR TRAVEL

United Express serves Omaha.

➤ AIRLINES AND CONTACTS: **United Express** (☎ 800/554–5111).

AIRPORTS

Eppley Airfield, about 3 mi from downtown Omaha, is served by most domestic carriers. Cab fare from the airport to downtown is about $9.50. Lincoln Municipal Airport, about 3 mi from downtown Lincoln, is served by several major airlines; taxis to downtown cost about $10. Eppley Express runs an airport van from Lincoln Municipal Airport to Eppley Airfield ($19).

➤ AIRPORT INFORMATION: **Eppley Airfield** (✉ 4501 Abbott Dr., ☎ 402/422–6800, WEB www.eppleyairfield.com). **Eppley Express** (☎ 800/888–9793). **Lincoln Municipal Airport** (✉ 2400 W. Adams St., ☎ 402/458–2400, WEB www.lincolnairport.com).

BUS TRAVEL

Omaha and Lincoln are served by Greyhound. Local bus service is provided in Lincoln by StarTran and in Omaha by Metro Area Transit.

➤ BUS INFORMATION: **Greyhound** (☎ 800/231–2222). **Metro Area Transit** (☎ 402/341–0800). **StarTran** (☎ 402/476–1234).

CAR TRAVEL

I-80 links Des Moines with Omaha (I–480 serves downtown Omaha) and Lincoln. U.S. 75 S from Omaha leads to Nebraska City. From Lincoln, Route 2 goes to Nebraska City. To get to Beatrice, take U.S. 77 S from Lincoln.

TRAIN TRAVEL

Amtrak's *Desert Wind, Pioneer,* and *California Zephyr* stop in Lincoln and Omaha.

➤ TRAIN INFORMATION: **Amtrak** (☎ 800/872–7245).

VISITOR INFORMATION

➤ TOURIST INFORMATION: **Beatrice/Gage County Convention and Visitors Bureau** (✉ 226 S. 6th St., 68310, ☎ 402/223–2338 or 800/755–

7745, WEB www.beatrice-ne.com). **Greater Omaha Convention and Visitors Bureau** (✉ 6800 Mercy Rd., Suite 202, 68106, ☎ 402/444–4662 or 866/937–6624, WEB www.visitomaha.com). **Lincoln Convention and Visitors Bureau** (✉ 1135 M St., Suite 300, 68508, ☎ 402/434–5335 or 800/423–8212, WEB www.lincoln.org). **Nebraska City Tourism** (✉ 806 1st Ave., 68410, ☎ 402/873–3000 or 800/514–9113, WEB www.nebraskacity.com).

NORTHWEST NEBRASKA

Rugged and beautiful, this is true Old West territory, with dramatic buttes and bluffs, ponderosa pines, craggy ridges, and canyons.

Exploring Northwest Nebraska

You can retrace the route of the wagon trains by exiting I–80 near Ogallala and heading west on U.S. 26. Four miles south of Bridgeport on Route 88, you can see **Courthouse** and **Jail rocks,** sandstone outcroppings that pioneers used as landmarks on the trail west. One mile south of the junction of U.S. 26 and Route 92 and 4 mi south of Bayard, the **Chimney Rock National Historic Site** (☎ 308/586–2581, WEB www.nebraskahistory.org; 🎫 $3) is an outcrop that pioneers described as "towering to the heavens." The visitor center, open year-round, commemorates those who traveled the Oregon Trail. Oregon Trail wagon traces are still visible at the **Scotts Bluff National Monument** (✉ 3 mi west of Gering on Rte. 92, ☎ 308/436–4340, WEB www.nps.gov/scbl; 🎫 $5), an enormous bluff that rises out of the rocky plains. Once described as the "lighthouse of the Plains," it now has a museum at its base.

About 35 mi north of Mitchell on Route 29, the **Agate Fossil Beds National Monument** has fossil deposits dating back 20 million years. A museum (☎ 308/668–2211, WEB www.nps.gov/agfo; 🎫 $3) preserves and displays fossils and Native American artifacts.North on Route 29 to Harrison, then east on U.S. 20 is **Fort Robinson State Park** (☎ 308/665–2900, WEB www.outdoornebraska.com; 🎫 $2.50), where activities include trail rides, historic tours, cookouts, swimming, trout fishing, hiking, and stagecoach rides. From late May to late August there's also a summer-theater program. Tent sites, electrical hookups, and lodge rooms are available, as well as horse corrals.

Dining and Lodging

Travelers to northwest Nebraska eat at casual, out-of-the-way restaurants, wagon train–style cookouts, and ranches. Inexpensive cattle ranches and B&Bs (contact the **Nebraska Association of Bed and Breakfasts;** ✉ 11 Lakeview Acres, Johnson Lake 68937, ☎ 877/223–6222, WEB www.nabb1.com) are charming alternatives to chain motels.

Bayard

$–$$ ★ ✕🏨 **Oregon Trail Wagon Train.** On covered-wagon tours through some of Nebraska's remaining short-grass prairies, sleep under the stars and dine on cookouts of rib eyes, stew, spoon bread, and vinegar pudding. One- to four-day treks are available. ✉ *Rte. 2 [Box 502, 69334], ☎ 308/586–1850, FAX 308/586–1848, WEB www.oregontrailwagontrain.com. 3 six-person cabins. Reservations essential. MC, V.*

Crawford

$ 🏨 **Fort Robinson State Park Lodge.** Dating from the 1800s, this fort in Fort Robinson State Park has a two-story lodge with large verandas and tall columns. Built in 1909 as an enlisted men's barracks, the lodge now has 22 modern rooms with private baths (but no telephones

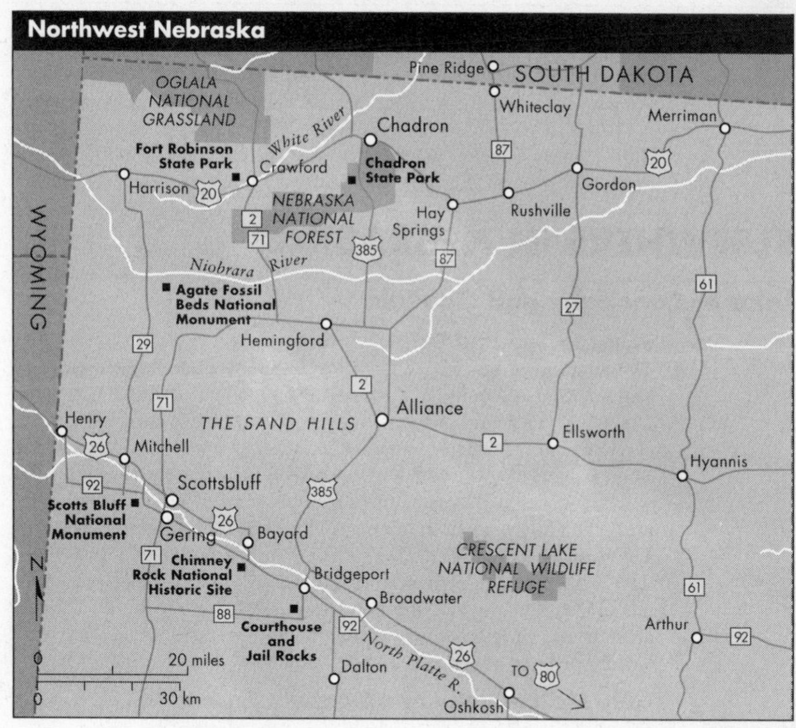

or TVs). Cabins, which sleep up to 20 people, are also available, and there are the officers' quarters, a group facility that can sleep up to 60. ✉ *3 mi west of Crawford, Box 392, Crawford 69339,* ☎ *308/665–2900,* FAX *308/665–2906,* WEB *www.outdoornebraska.com. 22 rooms, 31 cabins. Restaurant. MC, V.*

Motels

Days Inn (✉ 1901 21st Ave., Scottsbluff 69361, ☎ 308/635–3111; 800/597–3111 for reservations only; FAX 308/635–7646), 138 rooms; restaurant, pool, gym; $; **Landmark Inn** (✉ 246 Main St., Bayard 69334, ☎ 308/586–1375 or 800/658–4424), 10 rooms; $; **Town Line Motel** (✉ 3591 Hwy. 20, Crawford [Box 423, 69339], ☎ 308/665–1450 or 800/903–1450), 24 rooms; $.

Ranches

$$–$$$ **Meadow View Ranch Bed and Breakfast Bunkhouse.** Guests stay in the converted bunkhouse of this 5,000-acre working ranch 18 mi from the South Dakota border. Accommodations include a kitchenette, a living room, and two bedrooms. Complimentary breakfast is served in the ranch kitchen, and picnic lunches are packed on request. Activities include horseback riding, fishing, hiking in the nearby Sandhills, and going on wagon rides and cattle drives. ✉ *HC 91, Box 29, Gordon 69343,* ☎ *308/282–0679,* FAX *308/282–1078. Bunkhouse sleeps 8. No credit cards. Closed Nov.–Apr.*

Northwest Nebraska Essentials

CAR TRAVEL

From Omaha and Lincoln take I–80 W about 275 mi to U.S. 26, which closely follows the Oregon and Mormon trails as it takes you to Scottsbluff. To bypass Kearney and North Platte, take I–80 to Grand Island, then scenic Route 2 to the north, which runs parallel to I–80 through Nebraska's Sandhills.

VISITOR INFORMATION

➤ TOURIST INFORMATION: Box Butte Visitors Committee (✉ Alliance Chamber of Commerce, Box 571, Alliance 69301, ☎ 308/762–1520, WEB www.chamberpremaonline.com). Chadron Chamber of Commerce (✉ Box 646, 69337, ☎ 308/432–4401, WEB www.chadron.com). Scotts Bluff County Tourism (✉ 1517 Broadway, 69361, ☎ 308/632–2133 or 800/788–9475, WEB www.westnebraska.com).

ELSEWHERE IN NEBRASKA

Lake McConaughy and Ogallala

What to See and Do

★ The white-sand beaches of **Lake McConaughy State Recreation Area and the Kingsley Dam** (✉ 9 mi north of Ogallala on Rte. 61, ☎ 308/284–8800, WEB www.outdoornebraska.com; 🎫 $2.50) attract thousands every year. In Ogallala, **Front Street** (☎ 308/284–6000) depicts an 1880s Main Street, complete with a wooden boardwalk, jail, barbershop, and cowboy museum. The restaurant proudly serves Nebraska steaks and puts on nightly western shows from Memorial Day through Labor Day. The **Mansion on the Hill** (✉ W. 10th and Spruce Sts., ☎ 308/284–4066; 🎫 $2) is a museum with exhibits on 19th-century cattle drives. Ogallala is also home to the infamous **Boot Hill Cemetery** (✉ W. 10th St. and Parkhill Dr.), so named because the outlaws first buried there were left in graves so shallow that their boots stuck out.

Lake McConaughy and Ogallala Essentials

CAR TRAVEL

From Lincoln and Omaha take I–80 W to Ogallala.

VISITOR INFORMATION

➤ TOURIST INFORMATION: Ogallala/Keith County Tourism Center (✉ 204 E. A St., 69153, ☎ 308/284–4066 or 800/658–4390, WEB www.visitogallala.com).

Red Cloud

What to See and Do

Red Cloud was the home of Pulitzer Prize–winning author Willa Cather. The **Willa Cather Foundation** (✉ 326 N. Webster St., ☎ 402/746–2653, WEB www.willacather.org; 🎫 $5) is dedicated to the writer, who loved the Plains; 610 acres are preserved as the **Cather Memorial Prairie** (✉ 5 mi south of Red Cloud).

On the National Register of Historic Places is the **Starke Round Barn,** 4 mi east of Red Cloud on Highway 136. Built in 1902 by four brothers from Milwaukee named Starke, this three-story barn is held together by balanced tension and stress rather than nails or pegs.

Red Cloud Essentials

CAR TRAVEL

From Lincoln and Omaha take I–80 W to Grand Island, then U.S. 34 S to U.S. 281, and continue south.

The Great Platte River Road

What to See and Do

Westward-bound pioneers on the Mormon and Oregon trails once hugged the shores of the Platte River, a verdant natural pathway. Today I–80 follows the same route, cutting through the state's heartland and affording glimpses of the pioneer past. **Sculpture gardens** dot the landscape along the highway for 500 mi across the Nebraska plains. At nine rest areas, large stone-and-metal artworks constitute what some have called a "museum without walls."The **Stuhr Museum of the Prairie Pioneer** (✉ junction of U.S. 34 and U.S. 281, ☎ 308/385–5316, WEB www.stuhrmuseum.org; 🎫 $7.25), in Grand Island, has Native American and Old West artifacts and the 60-building Railroad Town, which includes the birthplace of actor Henry Fonda, antique farm machinery, a restored 19th-century farmhouse, and folks in period costumes. It's open May–mid-October.From early March to mid-April, people flock to an area near Grand Island and Kearney to witness the migration of thousands of Sandhill cranes as they pause here before resuming their flight north. The **Crane Meadows Nature Center** (✉ ½ mi south of I–80 at the Alda exit, ☎ 308/382–1820, WEB www.cranemeadows.org; 🎫 tours $15) and the **Lillian Annette Rowe Sanctuary** (☎ 308/468–5282, WEB www.rowesanctuary.org; 🎫 tours $15) offer tours. The Crane Meadows Nature Center also has a **visitor center** (🎫 $3) with wildlife displays.

Fort Kearney State Historical Park (✉ 2 mi south of I–80 on Rte. 44 and then 4 mi east on L–50A, ☎ 308/865–5305; 🎫 $2.50) has a recreated stockade and interpretive exhibits detailing the role of the outpost on the frontier. **Great Platte River Road Archway Monument** (✉ One Archway Pkwy., Kearney, ☎ 308/237–1000 or 877/511–2724, WEB www.archway.org; 🎫 $9.25). As travelers approach Exit 272 on I–80 near Kearney, they will see what appears to be a huge log fort spanning the interstate. Reaching eight stories and modeled after nearby Fort Kearney, this interactive museum honors those who traveled this route throughout history, including Native Americans, Mormons, and railroad workers.

★ **Harold Warp's Pioneer Village** (✉ junction of U.S. 6, U.S. 34, and Hwy. 10 in Minden, ☎ 308/832–1181, WEB www.pioneervillage.org; 🎫 $8) has pioneer memorabilia, horse-drawn covered-wagon rides, and craftwork demonstrations.Tour Buffalo Bill Cody's ranch house, enjoy trail rides, or chow down on buffalo stew in the **Buffalo Bill Ranch State Historical Park** (☎ 308/535–8035; 🎫 $2.50), 6 mi northwest of I–80. In Hastings, which lies near the junction of U.S. 34 and Highway 281, you'll find the **Hastings Museum of Natural and Cultural History** (✉ 1330 N. Burlington Ave., ☎ 402/461–4629 or 800/508–4629, WEB www.hastingsmuseum.org; 🎫 $5), which includes a planetarium and exhibits on natural history and frontier days. Another exhibit explores the history of Kool-Aid, which was created in Hastings. Modern and education-related films are shown in its Lied Superscreen Theatre. Ninety-minute tours of the **Dancing Leaf Earth Lodge Cultural Learning Center** (✉ 6100 E. Opal Springs Rd., Wellfleet, ☎ 308/963–4233; 🎫 $7) allow you to experience Native American life as it was about 1,000 years ago. An earth lodge, museum, a natural trail, and archaeological sites are among the attractions. Guests may also canoe on a spring-fed lake or spend the night in the earthen lodge.

Sandhills/Valentine Region

What to See and Do

Fort Hartsuff State Historical Park (✉ 3 mi north of Elyria off Hwy. 11, ☎ 308/346–4715; 🎫 $2.50), open May–October, is a restored 1870s infantry post with guides in period uniforms and costumes.For a view of the Great Plains as it once was, you can take a drive through hundreds of miles of mixed-grass prairie, where numerous outdoor attractions beckon. The **Niobrara River** draws canoeists from throughout the state; outfitters include Dryland Aquatics (✉ Box 33C, Sparks 69220,

☎ 800/337–3119), **A&C Canoe Rentals** (✉ 518 N. Ray St., Valentine 69201, ☎ 402/376–2839), **Brewers Canoers** (✉ 433 E. U.S. 20, Valentine 69201, ☎ 402/376–2046), **Graham Canoe Outfitters** (✉ HC 13, Box 16A, Valentine 69201, ☎ 402/376–3708), and **Little Outlaw Canoe & Tube Rentals** (✉ Box 15, Valentine 69201, ☎ 402/376–1822). Native wildlife is abundant at the **Valentine National Wildlife Refuge** (✉ HC 14, Box 67, Valentine 69201, ☎ 402/376–1889), south of Valentine on U.S. 83. Its 70,000 acres of prairie and wetlands shelter ducks, geese, hawks, eagles, deer, coyotes, beavers, and other species. Trails encourage both driving and hiking through this open country; there are information kiosks at entrances to the refuge.

The **Fort Niobrara National Wildlife Refuge** (✉ HC 14, Box 67, Valentine 69201, ☎ 402/376–3789), 5 mi east of Valentine on Route 12, has forested terrain and sizable species, such as bison, elk, and longhorn cattle. A visitor center and picnic facilities are available.Two sites on Main Street in Valentine are worth a visit. **Backporch Friends Factory** (✉ 227 N. Main St., ☎ 402/376–3369) makes soft-filled hand-sewn dolls sold around the world. Also, the front of the **First National Bank** (✉ 253 N. Main St., ☎ 402/376–2470) includes the largest brick mural in the country created by sculptor Jack Curran, which celebrates the spirit of discovery of early pioneers to the region.

Dining

$$ ✕ **The Peppermill.** Known for steaks and seafood, this local favorite has mirrored walls, linen tablecloths, and mixed drinks, in addition to an outdoor beer garden open in appropriate weather. ✉ *112 N. Main St.,* ☎ *402/376–1440. AE, D, MC, V.*

Sandhills/Valentine Region Essentials

CAR TRAVEL

From Lincoln and Omaha take I–80 W to Grand Island. Go north on U.S. 281 to Route 22; then follow it west 9 mi and go north on Route 11. At Burwell follow Route 91 W, U.S. 183 N, and U.S. 20 W to Valentine.

VISITOR INFORMATION

➤ Tourist Information: **Valentine Visitor Center** (✉ Box 201, Valentine 69201, ☎ 402/376–2969 or 800/658–4024, WEB www.heartcity.com).

NEVADA

Updated by Deke Castleman

Capital	Carson City
Population	2,063,000
Motto	Battle Born
State Bird	Mountain bluebird
State Flower	Sagebrush
Postal Abbreviation	NV

Statewide Visitor Information

Nevada Commission on Tourism (✉ Capitol Complex, Carson City 89710, ☎ 702/687–4322 or 800/638–2328; WEB www.travelnevada.com).

Scenic Drives

The **"Loneliest Road in America"** is U.S. 50 in Nevada, which winds across the central part of the state from Lake Tahoe to Great Basin National Park. **U.S. 93** runs from north of Las Vegas through more than 500 mi of long desert valleys and passes 13,061-ft **Wheeler Peak,** the second-highest point in the state. For a good look at some southwestern desert, particularly in the spring, take **U.S. 93/95** southeast from Las Vegas, turning east onto Route 147 in Henderson, which takes you through Lake Mead National Recreation Area to Valley of Fire State Park (☞ Las Vegas, *below*).

National and State Parks

National Park

Great Basin National Park (✉ off U.S. 50 at the Nevada-Utah border, Baker 89311, ☎ 702/234–7331, WEB www.nps.gov/grba; 🎫 free) consists of 77,092 acres of dramatic mountains, lush meadows, alpine lakes, limestone caves, and a stand of bristlecone pines (the oldest living beings in the world), with many camping, hiking, and picnicking areas.

State Parks

For information on Nevada's 23 state parks, contact the state tourism office (☞ Statewide Visitor Information, *above*). **Washoe Lake State Recreation Area** (✉ off U.S. 395; 4855 E. Lake Blvd., Carson City 89704, ☎ 702/687–4319, WEB www.state.nv.us/stparks), with views of the majestic Sierra Nevada, is popular for fishing and horseback riding.

LAS VEGAS

Las Vegas is known worldwide as a fantasyland for adults. It was given its name, which means "The Meadows," by a Spanish scouting party who found a spring in the area in the 1820s. Mormons settled the valley briefly in 1855, but until the turn of the 20th century it was little more than a handful of ranches and homesteads. The San Pedro, Los Angeles, and Salt Lake Railroad founded the town of Las Vegas in 1905 as a watering stop for its steam trains. The construction of Hoover Dam in the 1930s brought a large wave of settlers seeking jobs.

Las Vegas as we know it was born in the 1940s, when four motel-casinos were built on the incipient Las Vegas Strip; in the 1950s, eight more gambling resorts opened, including the 1,000-room Stardust, at the time the largest hotel in the world. The city is now home to 19 of the 21 largest hotels in the world.

Exploring Las Vegas

Las Vegas is a relatively small city; downtown and small sections of the Strip are easy to explore on foot. Just beware the extremely hot months of June, July, and August, when walking outdoors for an extended length of time is not recommended. The massive casino-hotels along the Strip make distances deceptive; a stroll "next door" may take 10 minutes, because properties are so large. Take taxis or buses for longer distances along the Strip or between the Strip and downtown.

The downtown casino center occupies the most brightly lit four blocks in the world, thanks to the **Fremont Street Experience,** a four-block pedestrian mall covered by an arched, 100-ft-high awning illuminated by 2 *million* lightbulbs. After dark, a kaleidoscopic light-and-sound show is presented here every hour on the hour until midnight. A focal point of downtown is **Jackie Gaughan's Plaza** (✉ 1 N. Main St., ☎ 702/386–2110, WEB www.plazahotelcasino.com), built on the site of the old Union Pacific train station. Freight trains still rumble past the back door at all hours.

Among the downtown casino-hotels, the **Golden Nugget** (✉ 129 E. Fremont St., ☎ 702/385–7111, WEB www.goldennugget.com) has a particularly attractive lobby, where you can gawk at a 61-pound gold nugget. **Binion's Horseshoe** (✉ 128 E. Fremont St., ☎ 702/382–1600, WEB www.binions.com) is an old-fashioned gambling joint with a huge crap pit and a display of custom guns nearby.

Lied Discovery Children's Museum (✉ 833 Las Vegas Blvd. N, ☎ 702/382–5473, WEB www.ldcm.org; 🎟 $6) has hands-on science exhibits. **Southern Nevada Zoological Park** (✉ 1775 N. Rancho Dr., ☎ 702/648–5955, WEB www.lvrj.com/communitylink/zoo; 🎟 $6.50) is a small but enjoyable zoo.

At 1,149 ft, the **Stratosphere Tower** (✉ 2000 Las Vegas Blvd. S, ☎ 702/380–7777, WEB www.stratlv.com; 🎟 $6) is the tallest building west of the Mississippi. High-speed elevators whisk you to a 12-story pod with a revolving restaurant, bar, and meeting rooms. The tower's most unusual features, however, are its roller coaster (which runs 900 ft above ground!) and the Big Shot thrill ride, which thrusts up and free-falls down the needle. Only in Las Vegas.

The famous **Strip** is a 3½-mi stretch of Las Vegas Boulevard South. It begins at the **Sahara** (✉ 2535 Las Vegas Blvd. S, ☎ 702/737–2111, WEB www.saharavegas.com), whose newest addition is Speed, the fastest of five roller coasters on the Strip. **Wet n' Wild** (✉ 2600 Las Vegas Blvd. S, ☎ 702/737–3819, WEB www.lasvegashost.com/lvh_wnw.htm; 🎟 $27.95) is a 26-acre amusement park with every water ride imaginable. **Circus Circus** (✉ 2880 Las Vegas Blvd. S, ☎ 702/734–0410, WEB www.circuscircus.com) was the first Las Vegas hotel to cater to families with children. It has a midway with carnival games, free circus acts, and a 5-acre indoor amusement park called **Adventuredome** (☎ 702/794–3939; 🎟 free), which has the world's largest indoor roller coaster. The **Candlelight Wedding Chapel** (✉ 2855 Las Vegas Blvd. S, ☎ 702/735–4179, WEB www.candlelightchapel.com) is the busiest chapel in town.

The **Riviera** (✉ 2901 Las Vegas Blvd. S, ☎ 702/734–5110, WEB www.theriviera.com) is noted for its four showrooms. The venerable Desert Inn was imploded in late 2001 (seventh Las Vegas implosion in eight years) to make way for master-developer Steve Wynn's new megaresort **Le Reve,** scheduled to open in 2004. The MGM-Mirage–owned **Treasure Island** resort (✉ 3300 Las Vegas Blvd. S, ☎ 702/894–7111,

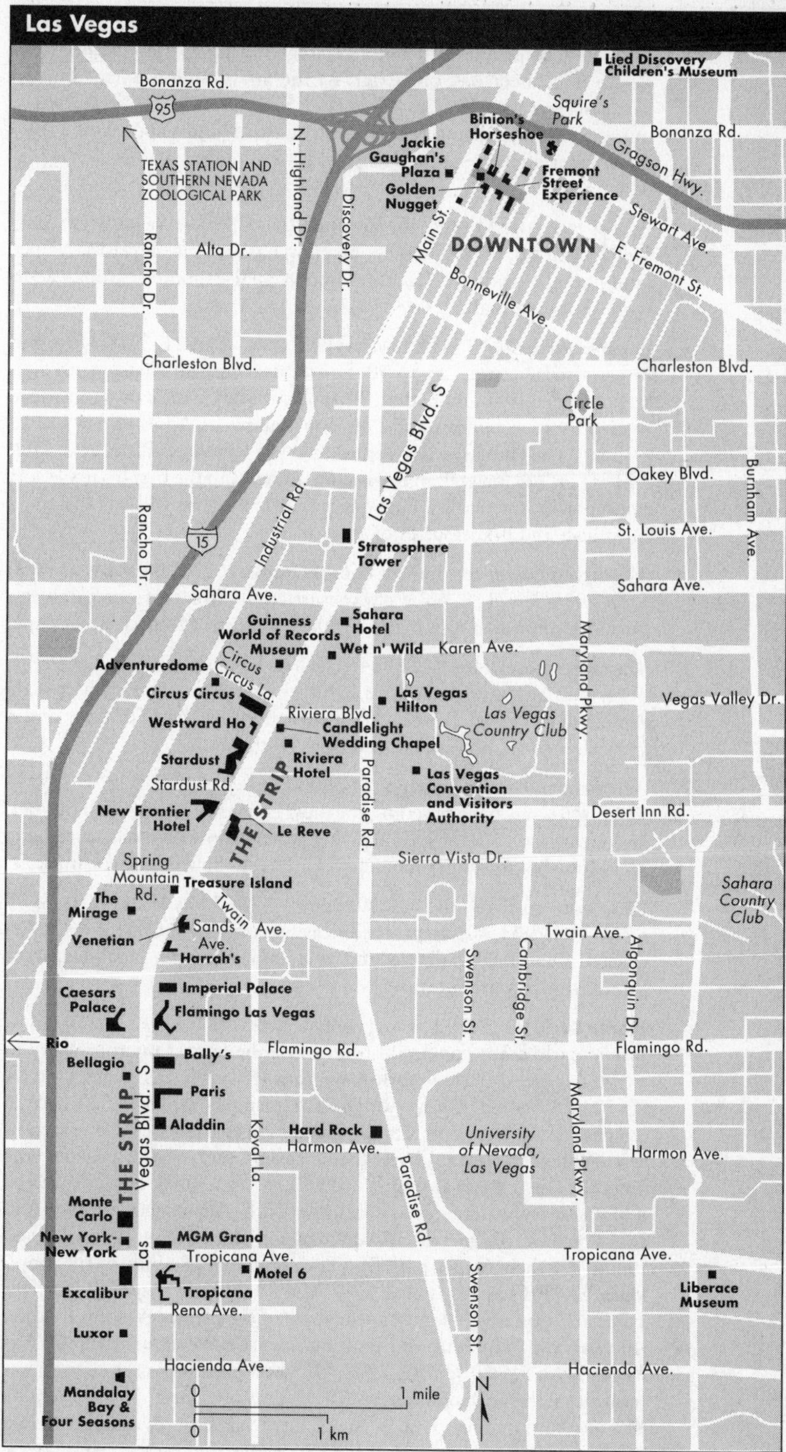
Las Vegas
Bonanza Rd.
95
TEXAS STATION AND SOUTHERN NEVADA ZOOLOGICAL PARK
N. Highland Dr.
Discovery Dr.
Lied Discovery Children's Museum
Squire's Park
Binion's Horseshoe
Bonanza Rd.
Jackie Gaughan's Plaza
Golden Nugget
Fremont Street Experience
Gragson Hwy.
Stewart Ave.
Main St.
DOWNTOWN
E. Fremont St.
Bonneville Ave.
Alta Dr.
Rancho Dr.
Charleston Blvd.
Charleston Blvd.
Las Vegas Blvd. S
Circle Park
Oakey Blvd.
Burnham Ave.
Industrial Rd.
St. Louis Ave.
15
Stratosphere Tower
Sahara Ave.
Sahara Ave.
Guinness World of Records Museum
Sahara Hotel
Wet n' Wild
Karen Ave.
Maryland Pkwy.
Adventuredome
Circus Circus La.
Circus Circus
Las Vegas Hilton
Vegas Valley Dr.
Riviera Blvd.
Westward Ho
Candlelight Wedding Chapel
Las Vegas Country Club
Stardust
Riviera Hotel
Paradise Rd.
Las Vegas Convention and Visitors Authority
Stardust Rd.
New Frontier Hotel
THE STRIP
Le Reve
Desert Inn Rd.
Spring Mountain Rd.
Sierra Vista Dr.
Treasure Island
The Mirage
Twain Ave.
Sahara Country Club
Venetian
Sands Ave.
Twain Ave.
Harrah's
Swenson St.
Cambridge St.
Algonquin Dr.
Imperial Palace
Caesars Palace
Flamingo Las Vegas
Rio
Flamingo Rd.
Flamingo Rd.
Bellagio
Bally's
Paris
Aladdin
Koval La.
Hard Rock
Harmon Ave.
University of Nevada, Las Vegas
Maryland Pkwy.
Harmon Ave.
Paradise Rd.
THE STRIP
Las Vegas Blvd. S
Monte Carlo
New York-New York
MGM Grand
Tropicana Ave.
Tropicana Ave.
Motel 6
Excalibur
Tropicana
Swenson St.
Liberace Museum
Reno Ave.
Luxor
Hacienda Ave.
Hacienda Ave.
Mandalay Bay & Four Seasons
0
1 mile
0
1 km
N

WEB www.treasureisland.com) is loosely based on Robert Louis Stevenson's novel—pirates and sailors engage in ship-to-ship cannon battles in Buccaneer Bay out front. At the $670 million palace known as the **Mirage** (✉ 3400 Las Vegas Blvd. S, ☎ 702/791–7111, WEB www.mirage.com), a volcano erupts in a front yard landscaped with a towering waterfall, lagoons, and tropical plants; inside is a glassed-in tigers' den.

Across from the Mirage, the **Venetian** (✉ 3335 Las Vegas Blvd. S, ☎ 702/733–5000, WEB www.venetian.com) has replicas of historic Venice landmarks, including a 1,200-ft Grand Canal—running through a 90-store shopping mall.

Imperial Palace (✉ 3535 Las Vegas Blvd. S, ☎ 702/731–3311, WEB www.imperialpalace.com ; $6.50) houses the Imperial Palace Auto Collection, a display of more than 300 antique and classic cars, many once owned by such famous and notorious figures as Adolf Hitler and Al Capone. The **Flamingo Las Vegas** (✉ 3555 Las Vegas Blvd. S, ☎ 702/733–3111, WEB www.flamingolv.com) grew from the first luxury resort on the Strip, opened by Bugsy Siegel in 1946, and still has the city's most lush and luxurious pool area.

The high stakes at the opulent **Caesars Palace** (✉ 3570 Las Vegas Blvd. S, ☎ 702/731–7110, WEB www.caesars.com) attract serious gamblers; the indoor Forum Shops mall resembles an ancient Roman streetscape.

The centerpiece of **Paris** (✉ 3645 Las Vegas Blvd. S, ☎ 702/739–4612, WEB www.parislasvegas.com), a 2,900-room megaresort, is a half-scale replica of the Eiffel Tower, with a restaurant on the 17th floor and a glass elevator to an observation deck on the 44th.

Across from Paris is **Bellagio** (✉ 3600 Las Vegas Blvd. S, ☎ 702/693–7111, WEB www.bellagio.com), the most expensive hotel ever built. Bellagio features a $30 million dancing-waters show on an 11-acre lake; an indoor botanical garden; and a Cirque du Soleil extravaganza.

Next door to Paris, the new **Aladdin** (✉ 3667 Las Vegas Blvd. S, ☎ 877/333–WISH, WEB www.aladdincasino.com) has 2,600 rooms, a distinct Arabian Nights theme, and an 85-store shopping mall featuring grand Moorish architecture.

Monte Carlo (✉ 3770 Las Vegas Blvd. S, ☎ 702/730–7777, WEB www.monte-carlo.com) has 3,000 rooms and the largest microbrewery in town. Megaresort **New York–New York** (✉ 3790 Las Vegas Blvd. S, ☎ 702/740–6969, WEB www.nynyhotelcasino.com) has 2,035 rooms, a replica of the New York City skyline, a food court modeled after Greenwich Village, a Central Park–theme casino, and a roller coaster. The emerald-green **MGM Grand** (✉ 3799 Las Vegas Blvd. S, ☎ 702/891–1111, WEB www.mgmgrand.com) houses the second-largest casino in the world, so large that it's divided into four parts, distinguished mainly by their carpet patterns. The sprawling grounds of the **Tropicana** (✉ 3801 Las Vegas Blvd. S, ☎ 702/739–2222, WEB www.tropicanalv.com) are attractively landscaped; some of the plantings are more than 40 years old. The blue-and-pink quasi-castle **Excalibur** (✉ 3850 Las Vegas Blvd. S, ☎ 702/597–7777, WEB www.excalibur-casino.com) has a medieval theme. **Luxor** (✉ 3900 Las Vegas Blvd. S, ☎ 702/262–4000, WEB www.luxor.com) is a 30-story Egyptian-style pyramid with an ultra-high-tech arcade, a 3-D IMAX theater, and motion simulators. **Mandalay Bay** (✉ 3950 Las Vegas Blvd. S, ☎ 702/632–7777, WEB www.mandalaybay.com) resembles a South Seas beach resort, with the scent of coconut oil drifting through the casino. The **Liberace Museum** (✉ 1775 E. Tropicana Ave., ☎ 702/798–5595, WEB www.liberace.org/

museum.html; 🎫 $6.95), 2 mi east of the Strip, has three buildings: one for the entertainer's pianos and cars, one for his costumes, and the third for general memorabilia.

Outside Vegas

The awe-inspiring **Hoover Dam** (✉ Rte. 93, east of Boulder City, ☎ 702/293–8321, WEB www.hooverdam.usbr.gov; 🎫 Discovery Tour $10), about 35 mi east of Las Vegas, was built in the 1930s to tame the destructive waters of the Colorado River and produce electricity. Explore the 727-ft-high, 660-ft-thick dam at your own pace on the Discovery Tour.

The construction of Hoover Dam created **Lake Mead** (✉ Alan Bible Visitor Center, U.S. 93 and Lakeshore Dr., ☎ 702/293–8906, WEB www.nps.gov/lame), the largest man-made lake in the western hemisphere, with more than 500 mi of shoreline. It's popular for boating, fishing, and swimming. For water tours of the lake and Hoover Dam, contact **Lake Mead Cruises** (☎ 702/293–6180, WEB www.lakemeadcruises.com).

Dramatic **Valley of Fire State Park** (✉ Rte. 169, Overton, ☎ 702/397–2088, WEB www.state.nv.us/stparks/vf.htm), 55 mi northeast of Lake Mead, contains distinctive polychrome sandstone formations and mysterious, ancestral Puebloan petroglyphs.

Red Rock Canyon (✉ Rte. 159, ☎ 702/363–1921, WEB www.redrockcanyon.blm.gov; 🎫 $5) is closer to Las Vegas (only 20 mi west) than Valley of Fire, but slightly less spectacular. Still, its sheer sandstone cliffs and twisting canyons are an internationally known rock-climbing destination. A 13-mi loop drive begins at the Red Rock visitor center.

For a respite from the bustle of Las Vegas and the heat of the desert, travel 35 mi northwest of the city on U.S. 95 and Route 157 to **Mt. Charleston,** with a forest, canyons, and a 12,000-ft peak. There's excellent skiing, both cross-country and downhill, in winter (at Lee Canyon) and hiking, camping, and picnicking the rest of the year.

Though it isn't exactly in the vicinity of the Grand Canyon (five hours by car; one hour by small plane; 40 minutes by jet), Las Vegas considers itself a gateway to the awesome, vastly silent **Grand Canyon National Park** (✉ Box 129, Grand Canyon, AZ 86023, ☎ 520/638–7888, WEB www.nps.gov/grca/index.htm; ☞ Arizona). **South Rim Travel** (☎ 520/638–2748 or 800/682–4393), a full-service travel agency, can arrange rooms, cars, and Colorado River trips. **Eagle Canyon Airlines** (☎ 702/736–3333), based in Las Vegas, is one of several Grand Canyon flightseeing companies.

Casino Gambling

Most major hotels in Las Vegas (as well as in Reno and Lake Tahoe) are centered on large casinos. The largest casinos in town are at the MGM Grand, Bellagio, and Riviera. The games are slot machines, blackjack, baccarat, craps, roulette, keno, video poker, live poker, Let It Ride, Caribbean Stud, wheel of fortune, as well as race and sports betting. Admission to the casinos is free—until you start playing, of course. Most larger casinos give free gaming lessons, usually during the slower, weekday-morning hours. Slot machines are by far the favorite game; thanks to progressive computer-linked slot jackpots—such as Megabucks and Quartermania—wins have gone into the millions.

With more than 65 major casino-hotels competing for your dollars in Vegas, most try to separate themselves from the pack with some distinguishing characteristic. Listed below are those with the most imaginative themes or attractive particulars.

Bellagio (✉ 3600 Las Vegas Blvd. S, ☎ 702/693–7111, WEB www.bellagio.com) is the second-largest casino in Las Vegas: sprawling, luxurious, and a bit overdecorated. The race and sports book has arena seating and massive electronic reader boards; each station is equipped with its own TV monitor. Club Bellagio is one of Las Vegas's most user-friendly slot clubs.

Binion's Horseshoe (✉ 128 E. Fremont St., ☎ 702/382–1600, WEB www.binions.com) hosts the world's highest-paying gambling tournament, the World Series of Poker, and sees some of the largest wagers in the world thanks to its no-limit policy.

Caesars Palace (✉ 3570 Las Vegas Blvd. S, ☎ 702/731–7110, WEB www.caesars.com), a sprawling ersatz temple for serious gamblers with money to burn, lays on the antiquity, complete with toga-clad cocktail waitresses and a lounge called (and styled after) Cleopatra's Barge.

Circus Circus (✉ 2880 Las Vegas Blvd. S, ☎ 702/734–0410, WEB www.circuscircus.com), arranged under a pink-and-white big top, takes on the hurly-burly atmosphere of a three-ring circus. For such a huge hotel, it has surprisingly low minimums.

Flamingo Las Vegas (✉ 3555 Las Vegas Blvd. S, ☎ 702/733–3111, WEB www.flamingolv.com) bears no resemblance to the "classy little joint" built by Bugsy Siegel in 1946. The splendiferous pink-flamingo theme is rampant in the huge casino, which is typical of a center-Strip megaresort: sprawling and raucous, with all the $5-minimum tables jammed with players.

Golden Nugget (✉ 129 E. Fremont St., ☎ 702/385–7111, WEB www.goldennugget.com) is more Hollywood than Vegas, with white marble, gold leaf, and brass-plated elevators. The casino combines high Strip class with low downtown minimums.

Hard Rock (✉ 4455 Paradise Rd., ☎ 702/693–5000, WEB www.hardrockhotel.com) is widely considered the hippest casino anywhere, packed with rock and pop memorabilia, the best-looking staff, and celebrities galore.

Jackie Gaughan's Plaza (✉ 1 N. Main St., ☎ 702/386–2110, WEB www.plazahotelcasino.com) is low-roller heaven, with penny slots, full-pay nickel video poker, 25¢ craps, and $3 blackjack galore.

Las Vegas Hilton (✉ 3000 W. Paradise Rd., ☎ 702/732–5111, WEB www.lv-hilton.com) has a NASA-esque sports book, with 46 video screens, and the imaginative Space Quest casino, which fronts the Star Trek attraction.

Luxor (✉ 3900 Las Vegas Blvd. S, ☎ 702/262–4000, WEB www.luxor.com) recalls ancient Egypt with its 29-million-cubic-ft atrium, the largest in the world. The casino is roomy, regal, and round, with surprisingly fresh air throughout.

MGM Grand (✉ 3805 Las Vegas Blvd. S, ☎ 702/891–1111, WEB www.mgmgrand.com) is the world's second-largest casino (Foxwoods in Ledyard, Connecticut, is the largest), with 3,500 slot machines, more than 100 gaming tables, and a Hollywood-entertainment theme.

The **Mirage** (✉ 3400 Las Vegas Blvd. S, ☎ 702/791–7111, WEB www.mirage.com) transports you to the South Seas, with thatch-roof gaming areas and tropical plants and flowers flanking an indoor stream and pond. Some of the machines in the high-roller slot area take $500 tokens.

Tropicana (✉ 3801 Las Vegas Blvd. S, ☎ 702/739–2222, WEB www.tropicanalv.com) is lush and tropical, with a stunning pool area complete with swim-up blackjack in summer.

Getting Married in Las Vegas

Nevada is one of the easiest—and least-expensive—states in which to get married. There is no blood test or waiting period; all you need is a license ($50) from the **Marriage License Bureau** (✉ 200 S. 3rd St., ☎ 702/455–4415), and you're ready to go. In Las Vegas there are about 25 chapels along the Strip, not including the numerous chapels in the casino-hotels (☞ Exploring Las Vegas, *above*). Services start at around $50.

Dining

Las Vegas has become the hottest restaurant market in the United States. Most hotels have multiple restaurants, including a buffet for which the city is justly famous: breakfast, on average, is $5–$9, lunch $7–$12, and dinner $10–$22. One of the cheapest buffets is at Circus Circus; two of the best are at Bellagio and Paris. Bally's has the best (and most expensive) Sunday champagne brunch, the Sterling, in town.

$$$$ ★ ✕ **Picasso.** By almost all accounts, the best restaurant in town is this Mediterranean-French eatery, operated by celebrity-chef Julian Serrano. Choose between the tasting and prix fixe menus—and marvel over the original Picasso artwork surrounding you. ✉ *Bellagio Hotel, 3600 Las Vegas Blvd. S,* ☎ *702/693–7111. AE, D, DC, MC, V.*

$$–$$$$ ✕ **Top of the World.** Floor-to-ceiling windows provide 360-degree views of the valley as this airy eatery rotates near the top of the 1,149-ft-tall Stratosphere Tower. Continental fare is spiced with a few twists: tequila-and-lime shrimp, spinach-and-wild-mushroom salad, and the like. ✉ *Stratosphere Tower, 2000 Las Vegas Blvd. S,* ☎ *702/380–7731. AE, D, DC, MC, V. No lunch.*

$$–$$$ ✕ **Battista's Hole in the Wall.** Battista Locatelli, a former opera singer, roams his domain here, a short walk from the Strip. Decorated with wine bottles, garlic, and celebrity photos, this Italian restaurant offers lots of specials and all the free wine you can drink. ✉ *4041 Audrie St.,* ☎ *702/732–1424. AE, D, DC, MC, V. No lunch.*

$$–$$$ ★ ✕ **Mayflower Cuisinier.** Head to this off-Strip restaurant for creative Chinese dishes with eclectic accents such as pan-seared ostrich with brandy sauce and an Asian Portobello mushroom burrito. ✉ *4750 W. Sahara Ave.,* ☎ *702/870–8432. AE, D, DC, MC, V.*

$$–$$$ ✕ **Pamplemousse.** The loving creation of Georges LaForges, a former Las Vegas maître d', this restaurant looks like a little French country inn. Classic French food is served *sans* menu; the waiter recites the daily specials. ✉ *400 E. Sahara Ave.,* ☎ *702/733–2066. Jacket required. AE, D, DC, MC, V. No lunch.*

$–$$$ ✕ **Bertolini's.** This sidewalk café inside the Forum Shops at Caesars can be noisy, but the northern Italian fare is first-rate. Order individual pizzas, soups, salads, and luscious gelato and sorbet. ✉ *3570 Las Vegas Blvd. S,* ☎ *702/735–4663. AE, DC, MC, V.*

$–$$$ ✕ **The Broiler.** A good, popular, and fairly inexpensive steak house, the Broiler has an excellent salad bar (including soups and desserts) as well as mesquite-grilled steaks, veal, and chicken. ✉ *Boulder Station, 4111 Boulder Hwy.,* ☎ *702/432–7777. AE, D, DC, MC, V. No lunch.*

$–$$$ ✕ **Second Street Grill.** Although you'll find steaks, lamb chops, and veal on the menu, seafood—flown in fresh daily from around the Pacific Rim—is the specialty. This place has been around for years, but it's fairly unknown in the Las Vegas fine-dining firmament, so you can almost always get a reservation. ✉ *Fremont Hotel, 200 E. Fremont St., ☎ 702/385–3232. AE, D, DC, MC, V. No lunch.*

$–$$ ✕ **Roberta's.** Las Vegas's most venerable "bargain gourmet" room is at the historic El Cortez downtown. You won't believe the prices, especially for a 16-ounce prime rib or a pound of king-crab legs. ✉ *El Cortez, 600 E. Fremont St., ☎ 702/386–0692. AE, MC, V. No lunch.*

$–$$ ✕ **Thai Spice.** Another fine eatery tucked away in one of Las Vegas's thousand strip shopping centers, Thai Spice wins locals polls year after year. Try the *tom kha kai* soup, Siamese duck, and blackjack noodles. ✉ *4433 W. Flamingo Ave., ☎ 702/362–5308. AE, D, MC, V.*

$–$$ ✕ **Viva Mercado's.** Don't let the shopping-center location fool you: this is one of the most popular Mexican restaurants in town. The room is cozy, and the food is low-fat and creative. ✉ *6182 W. Flamingo Rd., ☎ 702/871–8826. Reservations not accepted. AE, MC, V.*

Lodging

Las Vegas lodging ranges from virtual palaces to simple motels. The hotels are better for cleanliness and location; the motels, while a little frayed around the edges, can be great bargains. In general, lodging in Vegas is far less expensive than lodging in other major U.S. resort areas, though rates fluctuate widely according to supply and demand. The largest and most lavish hotels are on the Strip; downtown hotels are often less expensive. The cost structure we're quoting is for a standard room on a regular weekday; expect that room rates might be twice the weekday rate on a regular weekend (other than a holiday or special event).

$$$–$$$$ ★ 🏨 **Bellagio.** Las Vegas's greatest mousetrap is also one of its most expensive and exquisite. It caters only to adults (families are actively discouraged from staying here), and preferably high rollers, though the standard rooms are fairly ordinary. ✉ *3600 Las Vegas Blvd. S, 89109, ☎ 702/693–7111 or 888/987–6667, FAX 702/697–7111, WEB www.bellagio.com. 3,025 rooms. 10 restaurants, pools. AE, D, DC, MC, V.*

$$$–$$$$ ★ 🏨 **Venetian.** All 3,036 standard guest rooms at the Venetian, the world's largest convention center–hotel, are 700-square-ft suites, nearly twice the size of the average Las Vegas hotel room. Each has a sunken living room, two 27-inch TVs, a 130-square-ft-bathroom with separate tub and shower and telephone, a minibar, a fax machine–copier–printer, three dual-line telephones, and a queen-size hide-a-bed. ✉ *3355 Las Vegas Blvd. S, 89109, ☎ 702/693–7111 or 888/283–6423, FAX 702/733–5000, WEB www.venetian.com. 3,036 rooms. 14 restaurants, pools. AE, D, DC, MC, V.*

$$–$$$$ ★ 🏨 **Caesars Palace.** Caesars caters to an upscale clientele, with world-class service, lavish restaurants, and headliners such as David Copperfield. Most guest rooms are opulent, even by Las Vegas standards, and many have Roman-style bathtubs. ✉ *3570 Las Vegas Blvd. S, 89109, ☎ 702/731–7110 or 800/634–6661, FAX 702/731–6636, WEB www.caesars.com. 2,512 rooms. 19 restaurants, pools. AE, D, DC, MC, V.*

$$–$$$$ 🏨 **Hard Rock.** A couple of miles off the beaten Strip, the Hard Rock is still the choice for the wild, the young, and the free (as well as rock-and-roll geezers). The rooms are understated in the European fashion, especially by Las Vegas's over-the-top standards. The best view is from rooms overlooking the lush pool area, but take what you can get: with only 660 of them, rooms are always booked months in advance. ✉ *4455 Paradise Rd., 89109, ☎ 702/693–5000 or 800/473–7625, FAX 702/693–5010, WEB www.hardrockhotel.com. 660 rooms. 5 restaurants, pools, health club. AE, D, DC, MC, V.*

$$–$$$$ 🏨 **The Mirage.** When this extravagant hotel opened in 1989, it launched the current Las Vegas building boom. It's still the centerpiece of the

Strip, with its lush tropical landscaping, minimal neon, efficient use of recycled water, rain-forest dome, and exemplary service. ✉ *3400 Las Vegas Blvd. S, 89109,* ☎ *702/791–7111 or 800/627–6667,* FAX *702/791–7446,* WEB *www.mirage.com. 3,049 rooms. 8 restaurants, pool, gym. AE, D, DC, MC, V.*

$–$$$$ **Flamingo Las Vegas.** The first luxury hotel in Las Vegas—it was surrounded only by desert in 1946, when it was built—the Flamingo has been completely reconstructed over the years and is now the fifth-largest hotel in Las Vegas. With a time-share tower; a lush, 15-acre pool area and wildlife park (yes, it has flamingos); and very reasonable rates, it would still make founder Bugsy Siegel proud. ✉ *3555 Las Vegas Blvd. S, 89109,* ☎ *702/733–3111 or 800/732–2111,* FAX *702/733–3528,* WEB *www.flamingolv.com. 3,530 rooms. 8 restaurants, pools. AE, D, DC, MC, V.*

$–$$$$ **Golden Nugget.** The largest and classiest joint in Glitter Gulch, the Nugget runs the gamut from traditional downtown bargain (dollar draft beer) to Strip-style exclusivity (a segregated baccarat pit for high rollers). The lobby is all marble and etched glass; guest rooms reflect the same elegance. ✉ *129 E. Fremont St., 89101,* ☎ *702/385–7111 or 800/634–3454,* FAX *702/386–8362,* WEB *www.goldennugget.com. 1,909 rooms. 5 restaurants, pool, health club. AE, D, DC, MC, V.*

$–$$$$ **Las Vegas Hilton.** With 29 floors and three wings, this megasize hotel seems even larger next to the low-rise convention center; it's one of the most recognizable hotels in town. The rooms are spacious, and those on the higher floors have great views. The high-tech Star Trek virtual-reality show draws crowds. ✉ *3000 Paradise Rd., 89109,* ☎ *702/732–5111 or 800/732–7117,* FAX *702/794–3611,* WEB *www.lv-hilton.com. 3,174 rooms. 9 restaurants, pool. AE, D, DC, MC, V.*

$–$$$$ **MGM Grand.** This movie-theme megaresort is the largest in the world. Four emerald-green hotel towers bring to mind the *Wizard of Oz*; a 33-acre theme park re-creates Hollywood back lots with rides and performances. ✉ *3799 Las Vegas Blvd. S, 89119,* ☎ *702/891–1111 or 800/929–1111,* FAX *702/891–1030,* WEB *www.mgmgrand.com. 5,035 rooms. 11 restaurants, pool, health club. AE, D, DC, MC, V.*

$–$$$$ ★ **Rio Suite.** These four red-and-blue towers contain only suites. Ask for a unit on the east side of one of the top floors, facing the Strip. The 41-story tower has the most festive casino in town: singers, dancers, and jugglers in Mardi Gras costumes perform in a Masquerade Show wherein parade floats inch along a 950-ft track suspended from the high ceiling. ✉ *3700 W. Flamingo Rd., at Valley View, 89109,* ☎ *702/252–7777 or 800/888–1808,* FAX *702/253–6090,* WEB *www.playrio.com. 2,569 suites. 14 restaurants, pool, health club. AE, D, DC, MC, V.*

$–$$$ **Harrah's Las Vegas.** In 1997 Harrah's replaced its signature riverboat facade with a more tasteful design, but it's still the flagship of Harrah's extensive national gambling fleet. The rooms are modest by Strip standards. ✉ *3475 Las Vegas Blvd. S, 89109,* ☎ *702/369–5000 or 800/634–6765,* FAX *702/369–5008,* WEB *www.harrahsvegas.com. 2,700 rooms. 6 restaurants, pool, health club. AE, D, DC, MC, V.*

$–$$$ **Luxor.** This bronze-color pyramid recalls its ancient Egyptian namesake with a sphinx out front and a replica of King Tut's tomb inside. "Inclinators" rise to the top floor at a 39-degree angle; the Egyptian theme continues in the large guest rooms. ✉ *3900 Las Vegas Blvd. S, 89119,* ☎ *702/262–4000 or 800/288–1000,* FAX *702/262–4454,* WEB *www.luxor.com. 4,476 rooms. 7 restaurants, pool. AE, D, DC, MC, V.*

$–$$$ **Stardust.** From its first incarnation as a motor hotel to its more recent 32-story tower, the Stardust has been one of the best-known hotels on the Strip. The rooms are large, attractive, and usually available when the rest of the Strip is sold out. ✉ *3000 Las Vegas Blvd. S, 89109,* ☎ *702/732–6111 or 800/634–6757,* FAX *702/732–6296,* WEB *www.*

stardustlv.com. 2,500 rooms. 5 restaurants, pool, health club. AE, D, DC, MC, V.

$–$$$ **Treasure Island.** This hotel's theme is loosely based on Robert Louis Stevenson's novel, and the landscaping and decor are ersatz South Seas. There's a monorail to the Mirage. Rooms are smallish, but they were remodeled in 1999. ✉ *3300 Las Vegas Blvd. S, 89109,* ☎ *702/894–7111 or 800/944–7444,* FAX *702/894–7446,* WEB *www.treasureisland.com. 2,912 rooms. 6 restaurants, pool, health club. AE, D, DC, MC, V.*

$–$$$ **Tropicana.** Two high-rise towers loom above beautiful grounds, complete with waterfalls and swans. Rooms have a tropical theme, with bamboo and pastels. The courtyard rooms are the only ones left on the Strip from the old days—and they have patios. ✉ *3801 Las Vegas Blvd. S, 89109,* ☎ *702/739–2222 or 800/634–4000,* FAX *702/739–2469,* WEB *www.tropicanalv.com. 1,912 rooms. 6 restaurants, pools, health club. AE, D, DC, MC, V.*

$–$$ **Excalibur.** This pastel, turreted castle is the third-largest resort hotel in Las Vegas. Families come for the medieval theme, complete with a King Arthur jousting tournament, old-world midway, and strolling minstrels, mimes, and musicians. The rooms are smallish, but comfortable and affordable, especially for the great location. ✉ *3850 Las Vegas Blvd. S, 89109,* ☎ *702/597–7777 or 800/937–7777,* FAX *702/597–7009,* WEB *www.excalibur-casino.com. 4,032 rooms. 7 restaurants, pool. AE, D, DC, MC, V.*

$–$$ **Sahara.** Like many of its neighbors, the Sahara began as a small motor hotel and built itself up by adding towers. It has a casino and serves as a business hotel for the convention center down the street. Tower rooms are large, and those that face south overlook the Strip. ✉ *2535 Las Vegas Blvd. S, 89109,* ☎ *702/737–2111 or 800/634–6666,* FAX *702/791–2027,* WEB *www.saharavegas.com. 1,710 rooms. 5 restaurants, health club. AE, D, DC, MC, V.*

$–$$ **Sam's Town.** This hotel caters mostly to local residents and their families. Some rooms have views of the desert and mountains; those facing inside overlook an 18-story courtyard with trees, creeks, and a waterfall. ✉ *5111 Boulder Hwy., 89122,* ☎ *702/456–7777 or 800/634–6371,* FAX *702/454–8014,* WEB *www.samstownlv.com. 650 rooms. 7 restaurants, pool. AE, D, DC, MC, V.*

$ **Circus Circus.** Catering primarily to families with children, the hotel has painted circus tents in the hallways and is generally chaotic. The brightly colored rooms (red carpets and chairs; red-, pink-, and blue-striped wallpaper) are small but clean. ✉ *2880 Las Vegas Blvd. S, 89109,* ☎ *702/734–0410 or 800/634–3450,* FAX *702/734–2268,* WEB *www.circuscircus.com. 3,774 rooms. 7 restaurants, pools. AE, D, DC, MC, V.*

$ **Jackie Gaughan's Plaza.** This casino-hotel was built on the original site of the Union Pacific train station; the rooms facing front look down at Glitter Gulch, and those in back face the railroad yards. Rooms are almost always available at bargain rates. ✉ *1 Main St., 89101,* ☎ *702/386–2110 or 800/634–6575,* FAX *702/382–8281,* WEB *www.plazahotelcasino.com. 1,037 rooms. 3 restaurants, pool. AE, D, DC, MC, V.*

Motels

Days Inn–Town Hall (✉ 4155 Koval La., 89109, ☎ 702/731–2111 or 800/634–6541, FAX 702/731–1113, WEB www.daysinntownhall.com), 360 rooms; restaurant, pool; $.

Motel 6 (✉ 195 E. Tropicana Ave., 89109, ☎ 702/798–0728, FAX 702/798–5657, WEB www.motel6.com), 877 rooms; pools; $.

Westward Ho (✉ 2900 Las Vegas Blvd. S, 89109, ☎ 702/731–2900 or 800/634–6651, FAX 702/731–6154, WEB www.westwardho.com), 1,000 rooms; restaurant, pools; $.

Nightlife and the Arts

Nightlife

SHOWS

Hotel showrooms seat from several hundred to 2,000. Most are luxurious and intimate, with few, if any, bad seats. The old-style seating system involves arriving early and tipping the maître d' or captain. The new trend is reserved seating, which eliminates the waiting and "survival of the tippest." When a show is expected to sell out, hotel guests are given preference.

Showrooms present seven main types of entertainment: headliner shows, such as David Copperfield, Tom Jones, and Debbie Reynolds; big production shows, such as Bally's *Jubilee!* or the Tropicana's *Folies Bergères,* which include elaborate song-and-dance numbers, smaller specialty acts, and topless showgirls; large-scale illusion shows, such as the Mirage's *Siegfried & Roy* and Monte Carlo's *Lance Burton*; small production shows, with song and dance on a smaller scale, such as *Storm* at Mandalay Bay; low-budget afternoon shows, such as Harrah's *Mac King Magic and Comedy Show,* perhaps Las Vegas's best-value entertainment; the ubiquitous lounge shows, where pop bands play dance music and the only admission charge is the purchase of a drink or two; and two productions of Cirque du Soleil, a new-age circus with an international cast.

COMEDY CLUBS

MGM Grand: **Catch a Rising Star.** Harrah's: **The Improv.** Tropicana: **The Comedy Stop.** Riviera: **The Comedy Club.**

The Arts

Most arts events in Las Vegas are associated with the **University of Nevada, Las Vegas** (☎ 702/895–3011). For additional information call the **Allied Arts Council** (☎ 702/731–5419).

Outdoor Activities and Sports

Spectator Sports

Boxing: Caesars Palace and **MGM Grand. Golf: PGA Las Vegas Invitational** (✉ TPC at the Canyons, ☎ 702/256–2500), October. **Rodeo: National Finals Rodeo** (✉ Thomas & Mack Center, University of Nevada, ☎ 702/731–2115), early December.

Shopping

The chichi retail area at the hotel **Bellagio** (✉ 3600 Las Vegas Blvd. S, ☎ 702/693–7111) is now the most upscale shopping in Las Vegas with Gucci, Prada, Tiffany's, and restaurants such as Le Cirque. Some of Las Vegas's best shopping is on the Strip at the **Fashion Show Mall** (✉ 3200 Las Vegas Blvd. S, ☎ 702/369–8382), a collection of more than 200 shops and department stores, including Saks Fifth Avenue, Nordstrom's, and Neiman Marcus. The **Forum Shops at Caesars** (✉ 3570 Las Vegas Blvd. S, ☎ 702/893–4800), a complex of 135 specialty stores adjoining Caesars Palace, dazzles shoppers with two replicated Roman markets, complete with fountains, a simulated sky above, and two shows with animatronic-statues, enormous figures that talk and move. You'll find the likes of Gucci, Ann Taylor, the Museum Company, and F.A.O. Schwarz, along with half a dozen popular restaurants. Inspired by the ancient trade routes through Spain, North Africa, and India, the **Desert Passage at the Aladdin** (✉ 3663 Las Vegas Blvd. S, ☎ 702/866–070) has more than 130 retail stores and 14 restaurants. Storm clouds gather hourly at the Merchant's Harbor; a gentle desert thunderstorm washes in and then passes quickly through the port. **Gam-**

blers General Store (✉ 800 S. Main St., ☎ 702/382–9903) carries all manner of gambling paraphernalia.

Las Vegas Essentials

AIRPORTS AND TRANSFERS

McCarran International Airport (LAS), about 2 mi from the southern end of the Strip, is served by major airlines.

➤ AIRPORT INFORMATION: **McCarran International Airport** (✉ 1 Wayne Newton Dr., ☎ 702/261–5743, WEB www.mccarran.com).

AIRPORT TRANSFER

Taxi fare from the airport to Strip hotels is about $11–$18; to the downtown hotels, about $20–$25. The least expensive way to reach your hotel ($5–$8 per person) is by Gray Line Airport Transportation; follow the signs for "Shuttles" on the baggage level.

➤ TAXIS AND SHUTTLES: **Checker, Star,** and **Yellow Cab** (☎ 702/873–2000). **Gray Line Airport Transportation** (☎ 702/739–5770).

BUS TRAVEL TO AND FROM LAS VEGAS

➤ BUS INFORMATION: **Greyhound** (✉ 200 S. Main St., ☎ 800/231–2222, WEB www.greyhound.com).

CAR TRAVEL

Major highways leading into Las Vegas are I–15 from Los Angeles and Salt Lake City, U.S. 95 from Reno, and U.S. 93 from Arizona.

TRANSPORTATION AROUND LAS VEGAS

Taxis, in ready supply at every hotel, are the most convenient way to get around. The Strip bus (Citizens Area Transit, or CAT) costs $2 and links the Strip and the downtown with stops near major hotels. You can rent a car to drive out of town or explore the desert, but be sure to fuel up before you go; you won't find many stations out there.

➤ CONTACTS: **Checker, Star,** and **Yellow Cab** (☎ 702/873–2000). **CAT** (☎ 702/228–7433).

VISITOR INFORMATION

➤ TOURIST INFORMATION: **Las Vegas Chamber of Commerce** (✉ 711 E. Desert Inn Rd., 89109, ☎ 702/735–1616, WEB www.lvchamber.com). **Las Vegas Convention and Visitors Authority** (✉ 3150 Paradise Rd., 89109, ☎ 702/892–0711, WEB www.lasvegas24hours.com).

RENO

Reno, once the gambling and divorce capital of the country, is smaller, less crowded, friendlier, and prettier than Las Vegas. Established in 1859 as a trading station at a bridge over the Truckee River, Reno grew along with the silver mines of nearby Virginia City (starting in 1860), the railroad (railroad officials named the town in 1868), and gambling (legalized in 1931). Today Reno is getting a boost from the National Bowling Stadium—the only one of its kind in the country—as well as the 1,700-room Silver Legacy downtown.

Exploring Reno

One advantage Reno has over Las Vegas is weather: its summer temperatures are much more temperate, making strolling a pleasure. The city's focal point is the famous Reno Arch, a sign over the upper end of Virginia Street proclaiming it "The Biggest Little City in the World." As in Las Vegas, gambling is a favorite pastime here. Although not as garish as their Vegas counterparts, Reno's casinos still offer plenty of glitz.

Circus Circus (✉ 500 N. Sierra St., ☎ 775/329–0711 or 800/648–5010, WEB www.circusreno.com), marked by a neon clown sucking a lollipop, is the best stop for families with children. Complete with clowns, games, fun-house mirrors, and circus acts, the midway on the mezzanine above the casino floor is open from 10 AM to midnight.

Club Cal-Neva (✉ 38 E. 2nd St., ☎ 775/323–1046 or 877/777–7303, WEB www.clubcalneva.com) is the best place in town to gamble, with low limits and optimal rules.

Eldorado (✉ 345 N. Virginia St., ☎ 775/786–5700 or 800/648–5966, WEB www.eldoradoreno.com) is action-packed, with tons of slots, good bar-top video poker, and great coffee-shop and food-court fare.

Harrah's (✉ 219 N. Center St., Sparks, ☎ 775/786–3232 or 800/648–3773, WEB www.harrahsreno.com) debuted in 1937 as the Tango Club and now occupies two city blocks, with a sprawling casino, a race and sports book, and an outdoor promenade; it also has a 29-story Hampton Inn annex. Minimums are low, and service is friendly.

Silver Legacy (✉ 407 N. Virginia St., ☎ 775/329–4777 or 800/687–7833, WEB www.silverlegacyresort.com) is a classy, Victorian-theme casino with a 120-ft-tall mining rig that mints silver-dollar tokens.

Five casinos lie outside the downtown area. The **Reno Hilton** (✉ 2500 E. 2nd St., ☎ 775/789–2000 or 800/648–5080, WEB www.renohilton.com) is the largest casino in Reno, with 100,000 square ft. The **Peppermill** (✉ 2707 S. Virginia St., ☎ 775/826–2121 or 800/648–6992, WEB www.peppermillcasinos.com) is the gaudiest, glitziest, and noisiest. The **Atlantis** (✉ 3800 S. Virginia St., ☎ 775/825–4700 or 800/723–6500, WEB www.atlantiscasino.com) has a lush Polynesian theme. Orozko, the newest restaurant at **John Ascuaga's Nugget** (✉ 1100 Nugget Ave., Sparks, ☎ 775/356–3300 or 800/648–1177, WEB www.janugget.com), gives the small casino a new flair with its Pyrenees village-square design. **Silver Club** (✉ 1040 Victorian Ave., Sparks, ☎ 775/358–4771 or 800/905–7774, WEB www.silverclubreno.com) is a popular little locals casino in downtown Sparks, directly across from the Nugget. At night, a rockin' lounge band entertains the players at the low-limit table games and high-return slot and video poker machines.

Besides the casino-hotels, Reno has a number of cultural and family-friendly attractions. On the University of Nevada campus, the sleekly designed **Fleischmann Planetarium** (✉ 1600 N. Virginia St., ☎ 775/784–4811, WEB www.planetarium.unr.nevada.edu; 🎟 free) has films and astronomy shows. The **Nevada Museum of Art** (✉ 160 W. Liberty St., ☎ 775/329–3333, WEB www.nevadaart.org; 🎟 $3), the state's largest art museum, has changing exhibits. More than 220 antique and classic automobiles, including an Elvis Presley Cadillac, are on display at the **National Automobile Museum** (✉ Mill and Lake Sts., ☎ 775/333–9300, WEB www.automuseum.org; 🎟 $7.50).

Wilbur D. May Great Basin Adventure (✉ 1502 Washington St., ☎ 775/785–4153; 🎟 $3; open Memorial Day–Labor Day) in Rancho San Rafael Park has a petting zoo, a flume ride, and a mining exhibit that traces the evolution of the Great Basin. In the town of Sparks, the family amusement park **Wild Island** (✉ 250 Wild Island Ct., ☎ 775/331–9453; 🎟 call for prices) includes a water park; a 36-hole minigolf course; Indy, sprint, and bumper cars; and a state-of-the-art video arcade.

The always-festive **Downtown River Walk** (✉ S. Virginia St. and the river, ☎ 775/334–2077) often hosts special events featuring street performers, musicians, dancers, food, art exhibits, and games. **Victorian Square** (✉ Victorian Ave. between Rock and Pyramid) is fringed by restored turn-of-the-20th-century houses and Victorian-dressed casinos and storefronts; its bandstand is the focal point for the many festivals held here.

Outside Reno

Virginia City, only 25 mi from Reno (U.S. 395 south to Rte. 341), was once the largest population center in Nevada, with more than 20,000 residents, 110 saloons, and—ahem—one church. The Comstock Lode, one of the largest gold and silver deposits ever discovered, was responsible for the city's boom (1860–80), and Virginia City is still one of the liveliest historic mining towns in the West. Contact the **Virginia City Chamber of Commerce** (⊠ C St. across from the post office [Box 464, 89440], ☎ 775/847–0311, WEB www.virginiacitychamber.com) for more information.

You can still belly up to the grand mahogany bar and hear honky-tonk piano music at the **Bucket of Blood** (☎ 775/847–0322) saloon on C Street. The lavish interiors of **Mackay Mansion** (⊠ 129 D St., ☎ 775/847–0173, WEB www.mackaymansion.com; 🎫 $3) and the **Castle** (⊠ B St. south of Taylor, ☎ 775/847–0275, WEB www.thecastlemansion.com; 🎫 $3) offer a glimpse of the past with such adornments as Oriental rugs, Italian marble, and Brussels lace, as well as table settings made from the silver mined beneath their floors. The **Virginia & Truckee Railroad** (⊠ Washington and F Sts., ☎ 775/847–0380; 🎫 $5.50) can take you through the Comstock mining region on a historic, steam-powered locomotive. Virginia City's most famous resident was Mark Twain, who lived here from 1861 to 1864 while working as a reporter for the *Territorial Enterprise*; the **Mark Twain Museum** (⊠ 47 S. C St., ☎ 775/847–0525; 🎫 $1) occupies the newspaper's pressroom and displays 19th-century printing equipment.

South of Virginia City is **Carson City,** the state capital.The **Carson City Chamber of Commerce** (⊠ 1900 S. Carson St., ☎ 775/882–1565, WEB www.carsoncitychamber.com) has information on the town's attractions.

The **Nevada State Museum** (⊠ 600 N. Carson St., ☎ 775/687–4811; 🎫 $3), once a U.S. mint, is packed with exhibits on Nevada's natural history, the early mining days, CC-minted silver and gold coins, and willow baskets woven by Washoe artists. The **Nevada State Railroad Museum** (⊠ 2180 S. Carson St., ☎ 775/687–6953, WEB www.nsrm-friends.org; 🎫 $2) has an extensive collection of historical passenger and freight cars and two restored Virginia & Truckee trains; be sure to take the tour of the restoration shop.

Genoa (pronounced juh-*no*-uh), the oldest settlement in Nevada, is a quaint Victorian town about 20 mi south of Carson City, west of U.S. 395. **Mormon Station State Historic Park** (⊠ Foothill Rd. and Genoa La., ☎ 775/687–4379, WEB www.state.nv.us/stparks/ms.htm; 🎫 free) contains an early log cabin and Mormon artifacts. **Walley's Hot Springs Resort** (⊠ 2001 Foothill Rd., ☎ 775/782–8155, WEB www.nvohwy.com/w/wlhotspr.htm) has lodging and dining, along with hot mineral pools dating from 1862.

Dining

As in Las Vegas, your most economical meals are the casino-hotel breakfast, lunch, and dinner buffets. Favorites are those at the **Atlantis, John Ascuaga's Nugget,** and the **Peppermill** (☞ Exploring Reno, *above*).

$$$–$$$$ ★ ✕ **White Orchid.** The fanciest and some say best restaurant in northern Nevada, this cozy room at the Peppermill hosts a menu of contemporary cuisine that changes regularly according to what's fresh. The selection of wine by the glass is extensive. ✉ *2707 S. Virginia St.,* ☎ *775/689–7300. D, MC, V. No lunch.*

$$–$$$ ★ ✕ **Harrah's Steak House.** This casino-hotel's dark and romantic restaurant has been serving prime beef and fresh seafood since 1967. ✉ *219 N. Center St.,* ☎ *775/786–3232. AE, D, DC, MC, V.*

$$–$$$ ✕ **Monte Vigna.** The newest fine-dining addition to the Atlantis, Monte Vigna offers a Tuscan-style menu, including homemade pastas, wood-fired meats, fresh seafood, and classic Italian desserts, all prepared in an exhibition-style kitchen. The wine cellar has 4,000 bottles. ✉ *3800 S. Virginia St.,* ☎ *775/825–4700. AE, D, DC, MC, V. No lunch.*

$$ ✕ **La Strada.** The excellent northern Italian cuisine is served upstairs from the Eldorado Casino. The pastas and sauces are homemade, and the gourmet pizzas bake in a wood-fired oven. ✉ *345 N. Virginia St.,* ☎ *775/786–5700. AE, D, DC, MC, V. No lunch.*

$–$$ ✕ **Café de Thai.** The soups, salads, stir-fries, and curries are expertly prepared by a Thai national trained at the Culinary Institute. ✉ *7499 Longley La.,* ☎ *775/829–8424. MC, V.*

$–$$ ✕ **John A's Oyster Bar.** Entirely nautical in theme, John A's restaurant and bar serves the best steamers, pan roasts, cioppino, chowder, shrimp Louie, and cocktails this side of Fisherman's Wharf. ✉ *1100 Nugget Ave., Sparks,* ☎ *775/356–3300. AE, D, DC, MC, V.*

$–$$ ★ ✕ **Louis' Basque Corner.** Basque shepherds once populated northern Nevada; sample their heritage at this family-style restaurant, which specializes in oxtail, lamb, and tongue. ✉ *301 E. 4th St.,* ☎ *775/323–7203. AE, DC, MC, V.*

$ ✕ **Bertha Miranda's Mexican Restaurant.** Begun as a hole-in-the-wall, this has grown into a highly successful establishment. The food is made fresh by Bertha's family, and the salsa is the best in town. ✉ *336 Mill St.,* ☎ *775/786–9697. MC, V.*

$ ✕ **Nugget Diner.** Think classic Americana diner: seating is on stools at front and back counters. The "Awful Awful Burger" is renowned, as is the prime rib. ✉ *Nugget Casino, 233 N. Virginia St.,* ☎ *775/323–0716. MC, V.*

Lodging

$–$$$$ 🏨 **Eldorado.** Owned by fourth-generation locals, the Eldorado is known for its fine food and attention to detail. Rooms, including an all-suite tower, overlook the mountains or downtown. ✉ *345 N. Virginia St., 89501,* ☎ *775/786–5700 or 800/648–5966,* FAX *702/322–7124,* WEB *www.eldoradoreno.com. 836 rooms. 8 restaurants, pool. AE, D, DC, MC, V.*

$–$$$$ 🏨 **Silver Legacy.** This two-tower megaresort centers on a 120-ft-tall mining machine that coins dollar tokens. Skywalks connect it to Circus Circus (☞ *below*) and the Eldorado (☞ *above*). The rooms are still the newest in Reno. ✉ *407 N. Virginia St., 89501,* ☎ *775/329–4777 or 800/687–8733,* WEB *www.silverlegacy.com. 1,700 rooms. 5 restaurants. AE, D, DC, MC, V.*

$–$$$ 🏨 **Harrah's.** This is one of the most luxurious hotels in downtown Reno. Large guest rooms decorated in blues and mauves overlook downtown and the entire mountain-ringed valley. ✉ *219 N. Center St., 89501,* ☎ *775/786–3232 or 800/648–3773,* WEB *www.harrahsreno.com. 565 rooms. 6 restaurants, pool, health club. AE, D, MC, V.*

$–$$$ 🏨 **John Ascuaga's Nugget.** This casino-hotel in neighboring Sparks offers some of the largest and most luxurious rooms around—as well as the only indoor pool in town. ✉ *1100 Nugget Ave., Sparks 89431,*

☎ *775/356–3300 or 800/648–1177,* FAX *775/356–3434,* WEB *www janugget.com. 1,983 rooms. 7 restaurants, pool. AE, D, DC, MC, V.*

$–$$$ **Reno Hilton.** This 27-story hotel near the airport is Nevada's largest hotel north of Las Vegas. In fact, almost everything here is the area's largest: the buffet, race and sports books, showroom, convention facilities, bowling alley, arcade, wedding chapel, driving range, and RV park. ✉ *2500 E. 2nd St., 89595,* ☎ *775/789–2000 or 800/648–5080,* FAX *775/789–2418,* WEB *www.renohilton.com. 6 restaurants, pool, health club. AE, D, DC, MC, V.*

$–$$ **Boomtown.** Ten miles west of Reno on I–80, this is the first hotel-casino on the way in from California. It has comfortable newer rooms and suites, a large RV park, a good bargain buffet, and the largest family fun center in northern Nevada. ✉ *I–80 Exit 4, Verdi 89431,* ☎ *775/345–6000 or 877/726–6686,* FAX *775/345–8550,* WEB *www.boomtowncasinos.com. 347 rooms. 3 restaurants, pool. AE, D, DC, MC, V.*

$ **Circus Circus.** This smaller version of the giant Las Vegas hotel has the same family-oriented atmosphere. The rooms, though small and garish, are good values—when you can get one. ✉ *500 N. Sierra St., 89503,* ☎ *775/329–0711 or 800/648–5010,* FAX *775/329–0599,* WEB *www.circusreno.com. 1,625 rooms. 3 restaurants. AE, DC, MC, V.*

Nightlife and the Arts

Nightlife

As in Las Vegas, Reno-area nightlife breaks down into several categories: headliners, big production shows, small production shows, and lounge acts. Here are the options at the major Reno hotels (for addresses and phone numbers, *see* Lodging, *above*). **Circus Circus** has continual circus acts. **Eldorado** has a small production show. **Harrah's Reno** has headliners and small production shows. Mostly country-and-western headliners play **John Ascuaga's Nugget. Reno Hilton** has headliners, a large production show, and a comedy club.

The Arts

Most of the arts in Reno—such as the **Nevada Festival Ballet** (☎ 775/785–7915), the **Nevada Opera Association** (☎ 775/786–4046), the **Reno Philharmonic** (☎ 775/323–6393), and the **Performing Arts Series** (☎ 775/348–9413)—center on the **University of Nevada, Reno** (☎ 775/784–1110).

Shopping

Arlington Gardens (✉ 600 W. Plumb La., ☎ 775/828–1911) is a trendy mall with a cookbook store, a bath-and-body shop, clothiers, and a café. The **Meadowood Mall** (✉ Virginia St. at McCarran Blvd., ☎ 775/827–8450) is the Reno area's big mall, with 90 stores and a food court. **AAA Slots of Fun** (✉ 2800 Dickerson Rd., ☎ 775/324–7711) sells a large selection of new and used slot and video-poker machines.

Reno Essentials

AIRPORTS AND TRANSFERS

Reno-Tahoe International Airport (RNO), served by national and regional airlines, is on the east side of the city, minutes from downtown.

➤ AIRPORT INFORMATION: Reno-Tahoe International Airport (✉ 2001 E. Plumb La., ☎ 775/328–6400, WEB www.renoairport.com).

AIRPORT TRANSFER

Many large hotels run courtesy buses around town and to and from the airport. There are rental-car agencies at the airport.

BUS TRAVEL TO AND FROM RENO

➤ Bus Information: **Greyhound** (✉ 155 Stevenson St., ☎ 775/322–2970 or 800/231–2222, WEB www.greyhound.com).

BUS TRAVEL WITHIN RENO

Reno Citifare provides local bus service.

➤ Bus Information: **Reno Citifare** (☎ 702/348–7433).

CAR TRAVEL

The major highways leading to Reno are I–80 (east–west) and U.S. 395 (north–south).

TAXIS

Reno is such a small city that it's easy to get around on foot or by cab. Taxis are easily hired at the airport and in front of the major hotels; the main taxi firms are Reno-Sparks Cab Co., Whittlesea Taxi, and Star Taxi.

➤ Taxi Companies: **Reno-Sparks Cab Co.** (☎ 775/333–3333). **Star Taxi** (☎ 775/355–5555). **Whittlesea Taxi** (☎ 775/322–2222).

TRAIN TRAVEL

➤ Train Information: **Amtrak** (✉ 135 E. Commercial Row, ☎ 775/329–8638 or 800/872–7245, WEB www.amtrak.com).

VISITOR INFORMATION

➤ Tourist Information: **Reno-Sparks Convention and Visitors Authority** (✉ 4590 S. Virginia St., Reno 89502, ☎ 775/827–7600 or 800/367–7366, WEB www.renolaketahoe.com).

LAKE TAHOE

Southwest of Reno, Lake Tahoe's vast expanse of crystal-blue water surrounded by rugged peaks is a playground for both locals and visitors. Half in Nevada and half in California, it's the largest alpine lake in North America, 22 mi long and 12 mi wide. The region is known for outstanding skiing in winter; boating, fishing, and mountain sports in summer; and casino entertainment year-round.

Exploring Lake Tahoe

The scenic drive encircling Lake Tahoe (Routes 28 and 89) affords stunning lake, forest, and mountain vistas. You can also explore the lake from on board the ***MS Dixie II*** (✉ Zephyr Cove, ☎ 775/588–3508, WEB www.tahoedixie2.com; 🎟 $24–$49). **Crystal Bay,** the northernmost community on the Nevada side, has a small-town, outdoorsy feel and several casinos. Affluent **Incline Village,** 2 mi east of Crystal Bay, has lakeshore residences, weekend condos, and inviting shopping areas. South of Incline Village, the **Ponderosa Ranch** (✉ Rte. 28, ☎ 775/831–0691, WEB www.ponderosaranch.com; 🎟 $9.50–$13.50) is a Hollywood-style western "town" based on the TV series *Bonanza,* open early May–October.

At the south end of the lake are the neon lights of **Stateline,** where four towering and two low-rise casinos cluster in two long blocks. Across the border in California is **South Lake Tahoe,** the most populous town on the lake. At the **Heavenly Ski Area** (☎ 775/586–7000, WEB www.skiheavenly.com; 🎟 $12), the gondola lifts you to fantastic skiing in winter and unbeatable views over the water year-round.

Dining and Lodging

Incline Village

$–$$$ ★ ✕ **Lone Eagle Grille.** This restaurant adjacent to the Hyatt Regency Hotel has a fantastic view of the lake. Specialties include duck, fish, and lamb. ✉ *Country Club Dr. at Lakeshore,* ☎ *775/831–1111. AE, D, DC, MC, V.*

$–$$ ✕ **Azzara's.** This typical trattoria serves excellent food—a dozen different pasta dishes, along with pizza, chicken, lamb, veal, and shrimp—with understated elegance. ✉ *930 Tahoe Blvd.,* ☎ *775/831–0346. AE, MC, V. No lunch.*

$$–$$$$ 🏨 **Hyatt Regency Lake Tahoe.** Rooms are large and attractive, with warm color schemes and lake views. Amenities include a private beach, water sports, Camp Hyatt for kids, and a casino with a forest theme. ✉ *Country Club Dr. at Lakeshore, Incline Village 89450,* ☎ *775/832–1234 or 800/233–1234,* FAX *775/831–7508,* WEB *www.hyatt.com. 460 rooms. 3 restaurants, pool, health club. AE, DC, MC, V.*

Stateline

$$$– $$$$ ✕ **The Summit.** The view from this 16th-floor restaurant is spectacular. The creative menu includes artfully presented salads, seafood entrées, and decadent desserts. ✉ *Harrah's Casino/Hotel Lake Tahoe, U.S. 50,* ☎ *775/588–6611. AE, D, DC, MC, V.*

$$–$$$$ ✕ **Sage Room Steak House.** This romantic restaurant is descended from the Wagon Wheel Saloon and Gambling Hall—the origins of Harvey's Resort. The sautéed prawns are excellent. ✉ *Harvey's Resort Hotel/Casino, U.S. 50,* ☎ *775/588–2411. AE, D, DC, MC, V.*

$–$$ ✕ **El Vaquero.** Wrought iron, a fountain, and tiles give this restaurant a touch of Old Mexico. The fare is traditional Mexican. ✉ *Harvey's Resort Hotel/Casino, U.S. 50,* ☎ *775/588–2411. AE, D, DC, MC, V.*

$–$$ ✕ **Empress Court.** Plush velvet booths and etched-glass partitions are the backdrop for traditional Chinese cuisine. The grilled-squab salad is a standout. ✉ *Caesars Tahoe, U.S. 50,* ☎ *775/588–3515. AE, DC, MC, V. No lunch.*

$–$$ ✕ **The Forest Buffet.** On the 18th floor of Harrah's, the Forest has the best view of any buffet in Nevada. ✉ *Harrah's Casino/Hotel Lake Tahoe, U.S. 50,* ☎ *775/588–6611. Reservations not accepted. AE, DC, MC, V.*

$$$–$$$$ ★ 🏨 **Harrah's Casino/Hotel Lake Tahoe.** Rooms are large and comfortable, and each has two full bathrooms, complete with telephone and TV. Most rooms also have excellent views. ✉ *U.S. 50 (Box 8, 89449),* ☎ *775/588–6606 or 800/648–3773,* FAX *775/586–6607,* WEB *www.harrahs.com. 533 rooms. 7 restaurants, pool, health club. AE, DC, MC, V.*

$$–$$$$ 🏨 **Caesars Tahoe.** Once you negotiate the lobby staircase and casino areas, you'll find hallways with faux Corinthian columns and plush rooms in fantastical color schemes, such as hot pink with mint green. The indoor pool has a waterfall and a swim tunnel. ✉ *U.S. 50 (Box 5800, 89449),* ☎ *775/588–3515 or 800/648–3353,* FAX *775/586–2050,* WEB *www.caesars.com/tahoe. 440 rooms. 5 restaurants, pool, health club. AE, D, DC, MC, V.*

$$–$$$$ 🏨 **Harvey's Resort Hotel/Casino.** Harvey's is Lake Tahoe's oldest and largest resort. Rooms have a conventional style; most look out on the lake and the mountains. ✉ *U.S. 50 (Box 128, 89449),* ☎ *775/588–2411 or 800/648–3361,* FAX *775/588–6643,* WEB *www.harveys.com. 740 rooms. 8 restaurants. AE, D, DC, MC, V.*

Nightlife

Lake Tahoe nightlife centers on the top-name entertainment and production shows at the casino-hotels. **Caesars Tahoe** and **Harrah's** (☞

Dining and Lodging, *above*) both present headliners; **Harrah's** presents small production shows.

Outdoor Activities and Sports

Fishing

The lake is renowned for mighty Macinkaw and rainbow trout. Nonresident fishing permits are available at most sporting goods stores. For more information call the **Department of Wildlife** (☎ 775/688–1500).

Golf

Edgewood at Tahoe (✉ Stateline, ☎ 775/588–3566) has 18 holes. **Glenbrook Golf Course** (✉ Glenbrook, ☎ 775/749–5201) has 9 holes. **Incline Village Championship Golf Course** (✉ 955 Fairway Blvd., ☎ 775/832–1144) has 18 holes. **Incline Village Executive Course** (✉ 690 Wilson Way, ☎ 775/832–1150) has 18 holes.

Hiking

More than 250 mi of hiking trails traverse this area, many through high mountain passes or along streams and meadows with sweeping views. Twenty years in the making, the 150-mi **Tahoe Rim Trail,** which completely circles the lake, is now complete. Contact the **U.S. Forest Service** (☎ 530/573–2600) for information.

Ski Areas

Lake Tahoe has more than 15 world-class downhill resorts and nearly a dozen cross-country ski centers, all within an hour of one another. Elevations range from 6,000 to 10,000 ft, with vertical drops up to nearly 4,000 ft. More than 150 lifts operate during the season, which usually lasts from November through May.

Cross-Country

Diamond Peak (✉ 1210 Ski Way, Incline Village 89450, ☎ 775/832–1177, WEB www.diamondpeak.com) has 22 mi of groomed high-elevation track, including skating lanes.

Downhill

Diamond Peak (☞ *above*) has 7 lifts, 30 runs, and a 1,840-ft vertical drop. **Heavenly Ski Area** (✉ Box 2180, Stateline 89449, ☎ 775/586–7000 or 800/243–2836, WEB www.skiheavenly.com), straddling the Nevada-California border, has 26 lifts, 72 trails (including the longest run in Tahoe), and a 3,600-ft drop. **Mt. Rose** (✉ 22222 Mt. Rose Hwy., Reno 89511, ☎ 775/849–0704, WEB www.mtrose.com) has one of the highest base elevations in the area, with unequaled powder skiing, 5 lifts, 41 runs, and a 1,440-ft drop.

Lake Tahoe Essentials

AIRPORTS

The closest major airport to Lake Tahoe is Reno-Tahoe International Airport (☞ Reno Essentials, *above*). No scheduled commercial flights serve the Lake Tahoe Airport, near Stateline.

➤ AIRPORT INFORMATION: **Lake Tahoe Airport** (✉ 1901 Airport Rd., ☎ 530/542–6180, WEB www.laketahoeairport.com).

CAR TRAVEL

From Reno take U.S. 395 south through Carson City to U.S. 50, which leads to South Lake Tahoe; U.S. 395 south to Route 431 leads to North Lake Tahoe.

VISITOR INFORMATION

➤ TOURIST INFORMATION: **Incline Village/Crystal Bay Visitors and Convention Bureau** (✉ 969 Tahoe Blvd., Incline Village 89451-9508, ☎ 775/832–1606 or 800/468–2463, WEB www.gotahoe.com). **Tahoe-Douglas Chamber of Commerce** (✉ U.S. 50 at the Round Hill Shopping Center [Box 7139, Stateline 89449], ☎ 775/588–4591, WEB www.tahoechamber.org).

NEW HAMPSHIRE

By Ed and Roon Frost

Updated by Andrew Collins

Capital	Concord
Population	1,235,786
Motto	Live Free or Die
State Bird	Purple finch
State Flower	Purple lilac
Postal Abbreviation	NH

Statewide Visitor Information

New Hampshire Office of Travel and Tourism Development (✉ 172 Pembroke Rd. [Box 1856, Concord 03302], ☏ 603/271–2343 or 800/386–4664 for free vacation packet, WEB www.visitnh.gov). **Alpine ski and foliage hot line** (☏ 800/258–3608).

Scenic Drives

The **Kancamagus Highway** (Route 112) rolls through 36 mi of the White Mountains between Lincoln and Conway. The 32-mi stretch of **Route 113** between Holderness and South Tamworth is full of hills and curves and winds between mountains and lakes. **Routes 12A and 12** parallel the Connecticut River along the Vermont border between Lebanon and Keene, with views of the river and picturesque towns.

National and State Parks

National Forest

The **White Mountain National Forest** (✉ U.S. Forest Service, 719 N. Main St., Laconia 03246, ☏ 603/528–8721 or 877/444–6777; 🎟 $5 day-use fee, good for 7 consecutive days) occupies 770,000 acres of northern New Hampshire. There are hiking trails and 20 campgrounds.

State Parks

The **Division of Parks and Recreation** (☏ 603/271–3556) maintains about 70 state parks, beaches, and historic sites.

THE SEACOAST

The southern end of New Hampshire's 18-mi coastline is dominated by Hampton Beach—5 mi of sand, sunbathers, motels, arcades, and a boardwalk. At the northern end is Portsmouth, with its beautifully restored historical downtown, hip restaurants, and the state's only working port. In between are dunes, beaches, salt marshes, and state parks where you can picnic, hike, swim, boat, and fish.

Exploring the Seacoast

The Atlantic is rarely out of sight on Route 1A, and there are spots to pull over. In summer, stop to see the 2,000 rosebushes at **Fuller Gardens** (✉ 10 Willow Ave., North Hampton, ☏ 603/964–5414; 🎟 $6).

Rye has great beaches, and **Wallis Sands State Beach** (✉ Rte. 1A, ☏ 603/436–9404; 🎟 parking $8 weekends, $5 weekdays) is one of the nicest. There's no beach, but **Odiorne Point State Park** (✉ 570 Ocean Blvd. [Rte. 1A], ☏ 603/436–1552; 🎟 $3) has more than 330 acres of tidal pools and footpaths. The Seacoast Science Center (☏ 603/436–8043, WEB www.seacentr.org; 🎟 $1), in the park, has exhibits and an aquarium. At Rye Harbor State Marina, **New Hampshire Seacoast Cruises** (☏ 603/

964–5545 or 800/964–5545) conducts whale-watching excursions and trips to the Isles of Shoals, a colonial fishing settlement.

★ Walkable **Portsmouth** is an easy day trip from Boston. The **John Paul Jones House** (✉ 43 Middle St., ☎ 603/436–8420, WEB www.seacoastnh.com/touring/jpjhouse.html; 🎫 $4), the home of the Portsmouth Historical Society, is one stop on a self-guided walking tour of six historical houses open to the public in summer.

Showcasing Portsmouth's architectural diversity is **Strawbery Banke Museum,** a 10-acre village-museum whose 46 buildings date from 1695 to 1820. The gardens are splendid. ✉ *Marcy St.,* ☎ *603/433–1100,* WEB *www.strawberybanke.org.* 🎫 *$12. Closed Jan.*

Prescott Park has a formal garden and fountains. Kids will want to start at the hands-on **Children's Museum of Portsmouth** (✉ 280 Marcy St., ☎ 603/436–3853, WEB www.childrens-museum.org; 🎫 $5). The **Port of Portsmouth Maritime Museum** (✉ 600 Market St., ☎ 603/436–3680; 🎫 $5) is home to the USS *Albacore,* a vintage sub.

Dining and Lodging

Hampton

$–$$ **Victoria Inn.** Built as a carriage house in 1875, this B&B is filled with things that the Victorians loved best: wicker, chandeliers, and lace. The Honeymoon Suite has a sunroom. ✉ *430 High St., 03842,* ☎ *603/929–1437 or 800/291–2672,* FAX *603/929–0747,* WEB *www.thevictoriainn.com. 5 rooms. AE, MC, V. BP.*

Hampton Beach

$$–$$$ ✕ **Ron's Landing at Rocky Bend.** This casually elegant restaurant serves seafood and pasta. Check out the ocean views from the second-floor porch. ✉ *379 Ocean Blvd.,* ☎ *603/929–2122. AE, D, DC, MC, V.*

$$–$$$ ✕ **Ashworth by the Sea.** Generations of beachgoers have stayed here. Most rooms have decks; some have four-poster beds and cherrywood furnishings. The Ashworth Dining Room ($$–$$$) serves steaks, poultry, and seafood. ✉ *295 Ocean Blvd., 03842,* ☎ *603/926–6762 or 800/345–6736,* FAX *603/926–2002,* WEB *www.ashworthhotel.com. 105 rooms. 3 restaurants, pool. AE, D, DC, MC, V.*

$$–$$$ ★ **D. W.'s Oceanside Inn.** Rooms with carefully selected antiques and such touches as reading lights and comfortable love seats give the Oceanside the feel of a turn-of-the-20th-century home. ✉ *365 Ocean Blvd., 03842,* ☎ FAX *603/926–3542,* WEB *www.oceansideinn.com. 9 rooms, 1 cottage. AE, D, MC, V. Closed mid-Oct.–mid-May. BP.*

Portsmouth

$$–$$$ ✕ **Dunfey's Aboard the *John Wanamaker.*** Portsmouth's only floating restaurant, aboard a restored 1920s tugboat, offers such delicacies as tandoori game hen with a turmeric-pomodoro sauce, sautéed spinach, and polenta. The upper-level deck is a favorite on starry summer nights. ✉ *1 Harbour Pl.,* ☎ *603/433–3111. AE, MC, V.*

$$ ✕ **Blue Mermaid World Grill.** The stately exterior of this 1810 house belies the globally influenced fare prepared on its wood-burning grill. Specialties include lobster-and-shrimp pad thai and pan-seared cod with a coconut cream sauce and plantain chips. ✉ *409 Hanover St.,* ☎ *603/427–2583. AE, D, DC, MC, V.*

$$$ **Sise Inn.** This Queen Anne town house, full of chintz and gleaming armoires, is convenient for waterfront strolls. No two rooms are alike; some have whirlpool baths. ✉ *40 Court St., 03801,* ☎ *877/747–3466,* ☎ FAX *603/433–1200,* WEB *www.someplacesdifferent.com/sise.htm. 34 rooms. AE, DC, MC, V. CP.*

$$–$$$ **Sheraton Harborside Portsmouth Hotel.** Portsmouth's only luxury hotel, this five-story redbrick building is within easy walking distance of shops and attractions. Suites have full kitchens and living rooms. ✉ *250 Market St., 03801,* ☎ *603/431–2300 or 800/325–3535,* FAX *603/431–7805,* WEB *www.sheratonportsmouth.com. 203 rooms. 2 restaurants, pool, health club. AE, D, DC, MC, V.*

Nightlife and the Arts

Summer concerts draw crowds to the **Hampton Beach Casino Ballroom** (✉ 169 Ocean Blvd., ☎ 603/929–4100). The 1878 **Music Hall** (✉ 28 Chestnut St., Portsmouth, ☎ 603/436–2400 or 603/436–9900 for film line) hosts touring events and an ongoing film series. Catch jazz, folk, or blues at the **Press Room** (✉ 77 Daniel St., Portsmouth, ☎ 603/431–5186). The **Prescott Park Arts Festival** (✉ 105 Marcy St., ☎ 603/436–2848) presents theater, dance, and music outdoors June–August.

Outdoor Activities and Sports

Boating and Fishing

Al Gauron Deep Sea Fishing (☎ 603/926–2469) maintains a fleet for whale-watching cruises and fishing charters. Boat rentals and fishing charters are available from **Atlantic Fishing Fleet** (☎ 603/964–5220 or 800/942–5364) in Rye Harbor. **Smith & Gilmore** (☎ 603/926–3503) conducts deep-sea fishing expeditions and whale-watching trips.

Shopping

The streets off Market Square in Portsmouth are filled with crafts shops and clothing boutiques. For regional crafts, try **Kumminz Gallery** (✉ 65 Daniel St., ☎ 603/433–6488). **N. W. Barrett** (✉ 53 Market St., ☎ 603/431–4262) specializes in jewelry, pottery, and other arts and crafts. Antiques stores, including **Antiques at Hampton Falls** (☎ 603/926–1971), line U.S. 1 in Hampton and Hampton Falls.

The Seacoast Essentials

BUS TRAVEL

➤ BUS INFORMATION: C&J (☎ 603/430–1100 or 800/258–7111). Concord Trailways (☎ 603/228–3300 or 800/639–3317). Vermont Transit (☎ 800/552–8737).

CAR TRAVEL

I–95 connects to the region from Main and Massachusetts. Route 1A follows the coast. U.S. 4 links Portsmouth with Concord.

VISITOR INFORMATION

➤ TOURIST INFORMATION: Greater Portsmouth Chamber of Commerce (✉ 500 Market St., Portsmouth 03802, ☎ 603/436–1118, WEB www.portcity.org). Hampton Beach Area Chamber of Commerce (✉ 409 Lafayette Rd., Hampton 03842, ☎ 603/926–8718, WEB www.hamptonbeaches.com). Seacoast Area (WEB www.seacoastnh.com).

THE LAKES REGION

The eastern half of central New Hampshire is scattered with beautifully preserved 18th- and 19th-century villages nestled among sparkling lakes—Winnipesaukee ("smile of the great spirit") is the largest—that echo with squeals and splashes all summer long.

Exploring the Lakes Region

Alton Bay, at Winnipesaukee's southernmost tip, has cruise-boat docks and a Victorian bandstand. In Colonial Gilford you'll find **Ellacoya State Beach** (✉ Rte. 11, ☎ 603/293–7821). **Gunstock USA** (✉ Rte. 11A, ☎ 603/293–4341 or 800/486–7862, WEB www.gunstock.com) is a ski area where you can also swim, hike, mountain bike, camp, and go horseback riding. At **Canterbury Shaker Village** (✉ 288 Shaker Rd., Canterbury, ☎ 603/783–9511 or 866/783–9511; 🎟 $10 for 2 consecutive days), southwest of Winnipesaukee via Route 106, crafts demonstrations and tours illuminate 19th-century Shaker life.

In honky-tonk **Weirs Beach,** fireworks light up summer nights. The ***M/S Mount Washington*** (☎ 603/366–5531 or 888/843–6686) departs from Weirs Beach for Lake Winnipesaukee cruises. **Amusement centers** like Funspot (☎ 603/366–4377), Surf Coaster (☎ 603/366–4991), and Water Slide (☎ 603/366–5161) line U.S. 3. Commercial **Meredith,** on Lake Winnipesaukee's north shore, has restaurants and shops. The **Winnipesaukee Scenic Railroad** (✉ U.S. 3, Meredith, ☎ 603/279–5253 or 603/745–2135, WEB www.hoborr.com; 🎟 $9.95 and up) carries passengers alongside the lake.

Moultonborough has a country store and several miles of lakeside shoreline. The 5,000-acre **Castle in the Clouds** (✉ Rte. 171, ☎ 603/476–2352 or 800/729–2468, WEB www.castlesprings.com; 🎟 $12 with tour, $6 without) estate is anchored by an odd, stone mansion built by an eccentric millionaire. Tours include the mansion and the on-site Castle Springs Microbrewery. At the **Loon Center** (✉ Lees Mills Rd., ☎ 603/476–5666, WEB www.loon.org; 🎟 free) you'll learn about the popular black-and-white birds whose calls haunt New Hampshire's lakes. **Holderness** is the gateway to pristine Squam Lake. The **Squam Lakes Natural Science Center** (✉ Rtes. 113 and 25, ☎ 603/968–7194, WEB www.nhnature.org; 🎟 $9) has hands-on activities and nature trails.

President Grover Cleveland summered in tiny **Tamworth.** His son, Francis, returned to stay and founded the Barnstormers Theatre. The **Remick Country Doctor Museum and Farm** (✉ 58 Cleveland Hill Rd., ☎ 603/323–7591, WEB www.remickmuseum.org; 🎟 free) illustrates the life of a country doctor and the activities of a working farm.Lake-hugging Route 109 leads from Moultonborough to **Wolfeboro,** an old-line resort. Uniforms, vehicles, and other artifacts at the **Wright Museum** (✉ 77 Center St., ☎ 603/569–1212, WEB www.wrightmuseum.org; 🎟 $6) show the contributions of those on the home front to America's World War II effort.

Dining and Lodging

Holderness

$$$–$$$$ ★ ✕🏨 **Manor on Golden Pond.** This dignified inn has a dock on Squam Lake, the setting for the movie *On Golden Pond*, so boating and swimming are part of the fun. You can stay in the main inn, carriage-house suites, or cottages. The five-course prix-fixe dinner ($$$$) may include rack of lamb, filet mignon, and nonpareil apple pie. ✉ *U.S. 3 and Shepard Hill Rd., 03245,* ☎ *603/968–3348 or 800/545–2141,* FAX *603/968–2116,* WEB *www.manorongoldenpond.com. 24 units. Restaurant, pool, tennis. AE, MC, V. BP.*

Meredith

$$–$$$$ ★ ✕🏨 **The Inns at Mill Falls.** Overlooking Lake Winnipesaukee and incorporating sections of the 19th-century Meredith Linen Mills, the luxurious Inns at Mill Falls offer the amenities of a full resort but with great warmth and personality. The upscale Boathouse Grill ($–$$)

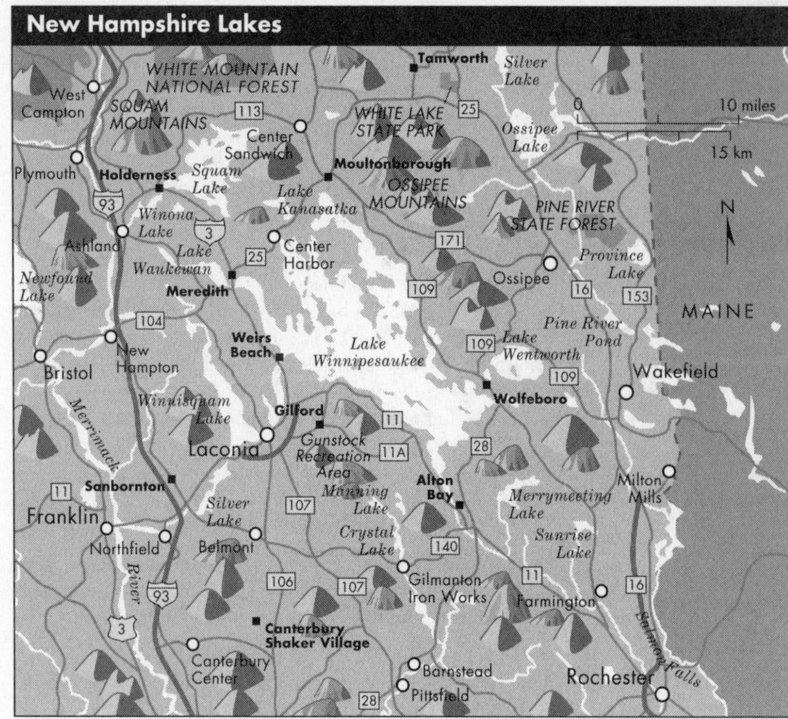

serves stellar contemporary fare. ✉ *U.S. 3 at Rte. 25, 03253,* ☎ *603/279–7006 or 800/622–6455,* FAX *603/279–6797,* WEB *www.millsfalls.com. 101 rooms. 4 restaurants, pool. AE, D, DC, MC, V.*

Moultonborough

$$–$$$ ✕ **The Woodshed.** Farm tools and antiques decorate this former barn, built in 1860. Feast at the raw bar or try the New England clam chowder, the sea scallops, and Indian pudding for dessert. ✉ *128 Lee Rd.,* ☎ *603/476–2311. AE, D, DC, MC, V. Closed Mon.*

Sanbornton

$–$$ 🏨 **Ferry Point House.** Built in the 1800s as a summer retreat for the Pillsbury family, this red farmhouse B&B has superb views of Lake Winnisquam and a gazebo by the water's edge. There's a beach, boating, and fishing. Rooms have Oriental-style rugs and antique Victorian furniture. ✉ *100 Lower Bay Rd., 03269,* ☎ *603/524–0087,* WEB *www.new-hampshire-inn.com. 6 rooms. No credit cards. Closed Nov.–Mar. BP.*

Tamworth

$$$ 🏨 **Tamworth Inn.** This renovated Victorian inn has a cozy beamed-ceiling pub and a formal dining room with such seasonal specialties as lobster-stuffed black ravioli. Guest rooms have brass or antique beds. Beautiful grounds border the Swift River. ✉ *Main St., 03886,* ☎ *603/323–7721 or 800/642–7352,* FAX *603/323–2026,* WEB *www.tamworth.com. 16 rooms. Restaurant, pool. AE, MC, V. Closed Apr. and 2 wks in Nov. BP, MAP.*

Wolfeboro

$$$ ✕🏨 **Wolfeboro Inn.** Partly dating from the 19th century, this landmark waterfront resort has polished cherry and pine pieces, stenciled borders, and country quilts. There's a bar, beach, and boating. The 1812 Steakhouse ($–$$) serves a popular slow-roasted prime rib. ✉ *90 N.*

Main St. (Box 1270, 03894), ☎ 603/569–3016 or 800/451–2389, FAX 603/569–5375. 45 rooms. 2 restaurants. AE, D, MC, V. CP.

Campgrounds

⛺ **Clearwater Campground** (✉ Meredith, ☎ 603/279–7761). ⛺ **Gunstock Campground** (✉ Gilford, ☎ 603/293–4341 or 800/486–7862). ⛺ **White Lake State Park** (✉ Tamworth, ☎ 603/323–7350). ⛺ **Yogi Bear's Jellystone Park** (✉ Ashland, ☎ 603/968–9000).

Nightlife and the Arts

The early 19th-century brick **Belknap Mill** (✉ Mill Plaza, 25 Beacon St., Laconia, ☎ 603/524–8813) has year-round concerts. **Barnstormers** (✉ Main St., Tamworth, ☎ 603/323–8500), New Hampshire's oldest professional theater company, performs in July and August. The ***M/S Mount Washington*** (✉ Weirs Beach, ☎ 603/366–5531 or 888/843–6686) has moonlight cruises with dinner and dancing; it docks in Weirs Beach, Alton Bay, and Wolfeboro.

Outdoor Activities and Sports

Beaches

Most beaches are private, so it's good to know about **Ellacoya State Beach,** in Gilford, a 600-ft beach that's the area's major public strand. **Wentworth State Beach** is in Wolfeboro.

Biking

Lakeside roads make for pleasant pedaling—though summer's traffic can be heavy. **Gunstock USA** (✉ Rte. 11A, Gilford, ☎ 603/293–4341) has trails for mountain biking and rentals.

Boating

Meredith Marina and Boating Center (✉ Bayshore Dr., ☎ 603/279–7921) rents powerboats. **Thurston's Marina** (✉ U.S. 3 at the bridge, ☎ 603/366–4811 or 800/834–4812) rents pontoon and power boats. **Wetwolfe Boat Rentals** (✉ 17 Bay St., ☎ 603/569–1503) rents motorboats. **Wild Meadow Canoes & Kayaks** (✉ Rte. 25 between Center Harbor and Meredith, ☎ 603/253–7536 or 800/427–7536) has canoes and kayaks for rent. **Winnipesaukee Kayak Company** (✉ 17 Bay St., ☎ 603/569–9926) gives kayak lessons and leads excursions.

Fishing

Local waters yield trout; Winnipesaukee also has salmon. The **New Hampshire Fish and Game Department** (603/271–3211) has information about permits and on where the action is.

Shopping

About 170 dealers operate out of the three-floor **Burlwood Antique Center** (✉ U.S. 3, Meredith, ☎ 603/279–6387), open May–October. The **Meredith League of New Hampshire Craftsmen** (✉ 279 U.S. 3, ½ mi north of Rte. 104, ☎ 603/279–7920) sells works by area artisans. **Mill Falls Marketplace,** part of the Inns at Mills Falls, contains shops with clothing, gifts, and books. The 53 shops at the **Lakes Region Factory Stores** center (✉ 120 Laconia Rd., I–93 Exit 20, Tilton, ☎ 888/746–7333) include Brooks Brothers, Eddie Bauer, and Black & Decker.

The Lakes Region Essentials

BUS TRAVEL

Concord Trailways serves Laconia, Meredith, Center Harbor, and Moultonborough.

➤ BUS INFORMATION: **Concord Trailways** (☎ 603/228–3300 or 800/639–3317).

CAR TRAVEL

I–93 is the principal north–south artery. From the coast, Route 11 goes to southern Lake Winnipesaukee; en route to the White Mountains, north–south Route 16 accesses spurs to the lakes.

VISITOR INFORMATION

➤ TOURIST INFORMATION: **Lakes Region Association** (✉ Box 430, Rte. 104, off 93 Exit 23, New Hampton 03256, ☎ 603/744–8664 or 800/605–2537, WEB www.lakesregion.org). **Squam Lakes Area Chamber of Commerce** (✉ Box 665, Ashland 03217, ☎ 603/968–4494, WEB www.squamlakeschamber.com). **Wolfeboro Chamber of Commerce** (✉ Box 547, 32 Central Ave., Wolfeboro 03894, ☎ 603/569–2200 or 800/516–5324, WEB www.wolfeborooonline.com/chamber).

THE WHITE MOUNTAINS

Northern New Hampshire is the home of New England's highest mountains and the 770,000-acre White Mountain National Forest. Rivers start here, gorges slash the forests, and summer brings hikers, climbers, and Sunday drivers. In winter, skiers and snowboarders flock to the region's peaks. Year-round, shoppers hunt bargains in North Conway's outlets. But it's the short foliage season that draws the biggest crowds.

Exploring the White Mountains

One-street **North Conway** overflows with outlet stores, restaurants, and inns. Trails from **Echo Lake State Park** (✉ off U.S. 302, ☎ 603/356–2672; 🎫 $3), in North Conway, lead up to the 1,000-ft White Horse and Cathedral ledges. Youngsters love the antique steam- and diesel-powered **Conway Scenic Railroad** (✉ Rte. 16/U.S. 302, North Conway, ☎ 603/356–5251 or 800/232–5251, WEB www.conwayscenic.com; 🎫 $9.50 and up). **Hartmann Model Railway Museum** (✉ Rte. 16/U.S. 302 and Town Hall Rd., Intervale, ☎ 603/356–9922, WEB www.hartmannrr.com; 🎫 $6) houses 14 operating layouts.

Glen is home to a couple of family-oriented attractions. **Story Land** (✉ Rte. 16, ☎ 603/383–4186, WEB www.storylandnh.com; 🎫 $19) has life-size nursery-rhyme characters and theme rides. At **Heritage New Hampshire** (✉ Rte. 16, ☎ 603/383–4186, WEB www.heritagenh.com; 🎫 $10) theatrical sets, sound effects, and animation are used to immerse you in New England history.

Mountain-rimmed **Jackson** has retained its storybook New England character and is nationally known as a destination for cross-country skiers. Dramatic Pinkham Notch, in the **White Mountain National Forest** (☎ 603/528–8721 for U.S. Forest Service), is the departure point for hikes to the top of the Northeast's highest mountain, 6,288-ft Mt. Washington (be sure to carry warm clothing year-round in case of sudden storms). Weather permitting, you can corkscrew up via the **Mt. Washington Auto Road** (✉ Glen House, Rte. 16, Pinkham Notch, ☎ 603/466–3988, WEB www.mt-washington.com; 🎫 $16 per car and driver, $6 per passenger, or $22 van fare), either in your own car or by guided van tour. In winter, the tour goes to above the tree line, and you can cross-country ski or snowshoe down.

In summer, **Attitash Bear Peak** (✉ U.S. 302, Bartlett, ☎ 603/374–2368, WEB www.attitash.com) ski resort has two dry alpine slides, water slides, a children's play pool, horseback riding, mountain biking, and a driving range. The steam-powered **Mt. Washington Cog Railway** (✉ off U.S. 302, Bretton Woods, ☎ 603/278–5404 or 800/922–8825 outside New Hampshire; $49) has been carrying passengers to and from the top of Mt. Washington since 1869.

In Franconia, you can visit poet Robert Frost's home **Frost Place** (✉ Ridge Rd., off Rte. 116, ☎ 603/823–5510; $3). **Franconia Notch State Park** (✉ Franconia Notch Pkwy., Exit 2, ☎ 603/745–8391, WEB www.nhparks.state.nh.us/parkops/parks/franconia.html; $8 for Flume) has the Old Man of the Mountains, a granite formation that looks like a profile, and the 800-ft-long chasm known as the Flume.

Lincoln is home to the **Whale's Tale** (✉ U.S. 3, Exit 3 off I–93, ☎ 603/745–8810, WEB www.whalestalewaterpark.com; $20), site of water-sliding fun from mid-June through Labor Day. In summer and fall at the **Loon Mountain** (✉ Kancamagus Hwy. [Rte. 112], Lincoln, ☎ 603/745–8111, WEB www.loonmtn.com; gondola $9.50) ski resort, you can ride New Hampshire's longest gondola to the summit, where daily activities include lumberjack shows and nature tours. At the base, there's horseback riding, skateboarding, and in-line skating as well as lift-service mountain biking.

Dining and Lodging

Bretton Woods

$$–$$$$ ★ **Mount Washington Hotel.** The 1902 construction of this resort was one of the most ambitious projects of its day. Noted for its 900-ft-long veranda, which affords full mountain views, this leviathan retains a turn-of-the-20th-century formality; jacket and tie are required in the dining room ($$–$$$). Although the menu changes daily, you'll find such entrées as lemon lobster ravioli with shrimp and scallops. In winter, you can ski. ✉ *U.S. 302, 03575,* ☎ *603/278–1000 or 800/258–0330,* FAX *603/278–8838,* WEB *www.mtwashington.com. 200 rooms. 2 restaurants, pools, golf, tennis. AE, D, MC, V. MAP.*

Dixville Notch

$$$$ ★ **Balsams Wilderness.** This resort on 15,000 acres is a real Victorian, built in 1866. Rooms are homey, and the activities—including downhill and cross-country skiing—gives you no reason to leave the grounds. In the restaurant ($–$$$, reservations essential, jacket and tie), the summer buffet lunch is heaped upon a 100-ft-long table. ✉ *Rte. 26, 03576,* ☎ *603/255–3400 or 800/255–0600; 800/255–0800 in New Hampshire,* FAX *603/255–4221,* WEB *www.thebalsams.com. 204 rooms. 3 restaurants, pool, golf, tennis. AE, D, MC, V. Closed Apr.–mid-May and late Oct.–mid-Dec. MAP winter, FAP spring–fall.*

Franconia

$$ **Franconia Inn.** Play tennis, ride horses, cross-country ski, swim, hike, or soak in the hot tub at this family resort. Rooms have canopy beds and country furnishings; some have whirlpool baths or fireplaces. At the restaurant ($$–$$$), savor grilled black Angus beef with sweet onion confit, Yukon gold mashed potatoes, and a bourbon-peppercorn demiglace. ✉ *1300 Easton Rd., 03580,* ☎ *603/823–5542 or 800/473–5299,* WEB *www.franconiainn.com. 32 rooms. Restaurant, pool, tennis. AE, MC, V. Closed Apr.–mid-May.*

Jackson

$$$–$$$$ ★ **Inn at Thorn Hill.** Architect Stanford White designed this 1895 Victorian house, just a few steps from cross-country trails and Jackson

village. Many of the antiques-filled rooms have spa tubs and gas fireplaces. The restaurant ($$$) serves fine contemporary fare such as cider-and-chipotle-glazed shrimp with toasted barley and herbed-sausage risotto. ✉ *Thorn Hill Rd. (Box A, 03846),* ☎ *603/383–4242 or 800/289–8990,* FAX *603/383–8062,* WEB *www.innatthornhill.com. 19 rooms. Restaurant, pool. AE, MC, V. BP, MAP.*

Lincoln

$$–$$$$ **Mountain Club on Loon.** This first-rate slope-side resort hotel has an assortment of accommodations: suites that sleep as many as eight, studios with Murphy beds, and 117 units with kitchens. Entertainers perform in the lounge on most winter weekends. ✉ *Kancamagus Hwy. (Rte. 112), 03251,* ☎ *603/745–2244 or 800/229–7829,* FAX *603/745–2317,* WEB *www.mtnclubonloon.com. 234 units. Restaurant, pool, health club. AE, D, MC, V.*

North Conway

$$–$$$$ **Snowvillage Inn.** Journalist Frank Simonds built the main gambrel-roof house in 1916. To complement the inn's tome-jammed bookshelves, guest rooms are named for famous authors. Two additional buildings—the carriage house and the chimney house—also have libraries. Menu highlights in the candlelit dining room ($$–$$$) include grilled hanger steak with a roasted onion and Stilton sauce. ✉ *Stuart Rd., 5 mi southeast of Conway (Box 68, Snowville 03849),* ☎ *603/447–2818 or 800/447–4345,* FAX *603/447–5268,* WEB *www.snowvillageinn.com. 18 rooms. Restaurant. AE, D, DC, MC, V. BP, MAP.*

Sugar Hill

$$–$$$ ★ **Sunset Hill House.** Since it opened in 1882, this sprawling compound has been famous for having perhaps the best sunset views of any resort in New England. Some of the meticulously kept rooms have antiques dating from the inn's first years. The acclaimed restaurant ($–$$$) serves such regional American fare as roasted seasoned game hen with a lemon-spinach cream. ✉ *Sunset Hill Rd., 03585,* ☎ *603/823–5522 or 800/786–4455,* FAX *603/823–5738,* WEB *www.sunsethillhouse.com. 28 rooms. 2 restaurants, bar. AE, D, MC, V. BP, MAP.*

Nightlife and the Arts

Horsefeather's (✉ Main St., North Conway, ☎ 603/356–6862), a restaurant and bar, often has music on weekends. The **Mt. Washington Valley Theater Company** (✉ Eastern Slope Playhouse, Main St., North Conway, ☎ 603/356–5425) stages productions from mid-June to Labor Day. Catch music or theater at the **North Country Center for the Arts** (✉ Papermill Theatre, Kancamagus Hwy. [Rte. 112], Lincoln, ☎ 603/745–6032; 603/745–2141 for box office). The **Red Parka Pub** (✉ U.S. 302, Glen, ☎ 603/383–4344) is favored by under-thirties.

Outdoor Activities and Sports

Biking

Great Glen Trails Outdoor Center (✉ Rte. 16, Pinkham Notch, ☎ 603/466–2333) rents mountain bikes for use on its network of trails at the base of Mt. Washington.

Fishing

Clear White Mountain streams and lakes yield trout, salmon, and bass. You can take lessons in fly-fishing at **Great Glen Trails** (✉ Rte. 16, Pinkham Notch, ☎ 603/466–2333). The **New Hampshire Fish and Game Department** (☎ 603/271–3211) has the latest information.

Hiking

The Maine-to-Georgia Appalachian Trail crosses the state. The **Appalachian Mountain Club** (✉ Box 298, Gorham 03851, ☎ 603/466–2721; 603/466–2727 for reservations) suggests routes, operates hikers' huts and the Joe Dodge Lodge in Pinkham Notch, and runs year-round outdoor-skills workshops. **New England Hiking Holidays–White Mountains** (☎ 603/356–9696 or 800/869–0949, WEB www.nehikingholidays.com) conducts guided hikes with lodging at country inns. The **White Mountains National Forest** (☎ 603/528–8721 for U.S. Forest Service) is a good source of hiking information and the place to obtain the recreation permit needed to park in national forest areas.

Ski Areas

New Hampshire's best skiing is in the White Mountains. For the latest conditions statewide, contact **Ski New Hampshire** (☎ 800/887–5464, WEB www.skinh.com).

Cross-Country

In Jackson nearly 100 mi of trails maintained by the **Jackson Ski Touring Foundation** (✉ Main St., ☎ 603/383–9355) string together inns, restaurants, and woodlands and connect to another 40 mi of trails maintained by the Appalachian Mountain Club. There are many other well-maintained areas with reasonable selections of terrain, both groomed and backcountry trails, and rental equipment. **Balsams Wilderness** (✉ Rte. 26, ☎ 603/255–3400 or 800/255–0600; 800/255–0800 in New Hampshire). **Bear Notch Ski Touring Center** (✉ U.S. 302, Bartlett, ☎ 603/374–2277). **Bretton Woods** (✉ U.S. 302, ☎ 603/278–3320 or 800/232–2972). **Franconia Village Cross-Country Center** (✉ 1300 Easton Rd., Franconia, ☎ 603/823–5542 or 800/473–5299). **Great Glen Trails** (✉ Rte. 16, Pinkham Notch, ☎ 603/466–2333). **Waterville Valley** (✉ 1 Ski Area Rd. [Rte. 49], Waterville Valley, ☎ 603/236–8311).

Downhill

For New Hampshire's largest ski areas, the 1990s were a decade of growth. But plenty of smaller, low-key areas still offer a pleasant counterpoint, including these: **Attitash Bear Peak** (✉ U.S. 302, Bartlett, ☎ 603/374–2368), **Balsams Wilderness** (✉ Rte. 26, ☎ 603/255–3400 or 800/255–0600; 800/255–0800 in New Hampshire), **Black Mountain** (✉ Rte. 16B, Jackson, ☎ 603/383–4490), **Bretton Woods** (✉ U.S. 302, ☎ 603/278–3320 or 800/232–2972), **Cannon Mountain** (✉ Franconia Notch State Park, I–93 Exit 3, Franconia, ☎ 603/823–8800), **Cranmore Mountain Resort** (✉ Skimobile Rd., North Conway, ☎ 603/356–5543), **Loon Mountain** (✉ Kancamagus Hwy. [Rte. 112], Lincoln, ☎ 603/745–8111), **Waterville Valley** (✉ 1 Ski Area Rd. [Rte. 49], Waterville Valley, ☎ 603/236–8311), **Wildcat** (✉ Rte. 16, Pinkham Notch, Jackson, ☎ 603/466–3326).

Shopping

Route 16 through Conway and North Conway is the region's major shopping area. More than 150 outlets and shops line this busy route, including crafts stores, boutiques, and antiques shops. You can pick up a guide to the shopping opportunities at visitor centers in either town and at most stores.

The White Mountains Essentials

BUS TRAVEL

Concord Trailways serves Littleton, Jackson, Berlin, Conway, Plymouth, and other towns.

➤ BUS INFORMATION: **Concord Trailways** (☎ 603/228–3300 or 800/639–3317).

CAR TRAVEL

North–south routes include I–93 and U.S. 3 in the west and Route 16 in the east. The Kancamagus Highway (Route 112) and U.S. 302 are the main east–west thoroughfares.

VISITOR INFORMATION

➤ TOURIST INFORMATION: **Mt. Washington Valley Chamber of Commerce** (✉ Box 2300, North Conway 03860, ☎ 603/356–5701, WEB www.4seasonresort.com). **White Mountains Visitors Bureau** (✉ Box 10, Kancamagus Hwy. [Rte. 112] at I–93, North Woodstock 03262, ☎ 603/745–8720 or 800/346–3687, WEB www.whitemtn.org).

WESTERN AND CENTRAL NEW HAMPSHIRE

The countryside bordered by the Connecticut River to the west, I–93 to the east, Massachusetts to the south, and the White Mountains to the north is a land of covered bridges, calendar-page villages, hardwood forests, jewel-like lakes, and lonely mountains. New Hampshire's largest cities, such as Manchester and Nashua, are clustered along the central I–93 corridor, as is the capital, Concord.

Exploring Western and Central New Hampshire

Concord, New Hampshire's capital, is undergoing an awakening. The "Concord on Foot" walking trail covers the historic district and includes the **Pierce Manse,** once home to Franklin Pierce, the nation's 14th president. ✉ *14 Penacook St.,* ☎ *603/225–2068 or 603/224–5954.* *$3. Closed early Sept.–mid-June.*

Reserve seats for shows at **Christa McAuliffe Planetarium** (✉ 2 Institute Dr., ☎ 603/271–7831, WEB www.starhop.com; $8). It was named for the Concord teacher—and first civilian in space—who was killed in the space shuttle *Challenger* explosion in 1986.

Visit the **Museum of New Hampshire History** to see exhibits spanning from the days of the Abenaki Indians to the present. ✉ *6 Eagle Sq.,* ☎ *603/226–3189,* WEB *www.nhhistory.org/museum.html.* *$5. Closed Mon. Nov.–June.*

Three governors were born in Warner. Now the quiet town is home to the **Mt. Kearsarge Indian Museum, Education and Cultural Center** (✉ Kearsarge Mountain Rd., ☎ 603/456–2600, WEB www.indianmuseum.org; $6.50), where you'll find exhibits on Native American crafts. Mountains and parks set off bright, clear **Lake Sunapee.** You can cruise the water on the **M/V *Mt. Sunapee II*** (✉ Main St., Sunapee, ☎ 603/763–4030). Folks often picnic by the side at quiet, woodsy **Sunapee State Beach** (✉ Rte. 103, Newbury, ☎ 603/763–5561; $3). At **Mount Sunapee** (✉ Rte. 103, Newbury, ☎ 603/763–2356), the region's largest ski area, you can take the express quad to the summit and hike to Lake Solitude, try lift-service mountain biking, or enjoy the in-line skate park at the base. **The Fells** (✉ Rte. 103A, Newbury, ☎ 603/763–4789, WEB www.thefells.org; $4) is the former summer estate of John M. Hay, who served as private secretary to Abraham Lincoln and as Secretary of State for Presidents Mckinley and Theodore Roosevelt.

Tiny Enfield is home to the **Enfield Shaker Museum,** which displays and explains Shaker artifacts and crafts. ✉ *24 Caleb Dyer La.,* ☎ *603/*

632–4346, WEB *www.shakermuseum.org.* *$7. Closed weekdays late Oct.–May.*

★ **Dartmouth College,** in Hanover, is an Ivy League archetype of redbrick and white clapboard around a village green. Its **Hood Museum of Art** (✉ Wheelock St., ☎ 603/646–2808, WEB www.dartmouth.edu/~hood; free) houses works from Africa, Asia, Europe, and America. In modest **Cornish,** to the south of Hanover via Route 12A, you can cross four covered bridges.The **Saint-Gaudens National Historic Site** (✉ off Rte. 12A, Cornish, ☎ 603/675–2175; $4) displays some of the sculptor's heroic, sensitive work.

Charlestown's **Fort at No. 4** was a frontier outpost in colonial times. Today costumed interpreters demonstrate crafts and reenact the lives of the settlers. ✉ *Rte. 11,* ☎ *603/826–5700 or 888/367–8284,* WEB *www.fortat4.com.* *$8. Closed Nov.–mid-May.*

In **Monadnock State Park** (✉ off Rte. 124, Jaffrey, ☎ 603/532–8862; $3) 20 trails ascend to the bald summit of 3,165-ft Mt. Monadnock, one of the world's most-climbed mountains. Beautifully preserved **Fitzwilliam,** spreading from the edges of an oval common, warrants a detour.Acres of wild rhododendrons burst into bloom in mid-July at **Rhododendron State Park** (✉ off Rte. 12, 2½ mi northwest of the common, Fitzwilliam, ☎ 603/239–8153; $3).

The four villages that make up **Hillsborough** include Hillsborough Center, where 18th-century houses surround a picture-perfect town green. The Hillsborough Historical Society operates the **Pierce Homestead** where 14th president Franklin Pierce was reared. ✉ *Rte. 31, north of Rte. 9,* ☎ *603/478–3165,* WEB *www.conknet.com/~hillsboro/pierce.* *$3. Closed mid-Oct.–May.*

Keene, the largest city in the state's southwest corner, is rapidly gentrifying its main street. Each October, the city's Pumpkin Festival attempts to break its own record for assembling the most lighted jack-o'-lanterns—nearly 24,000 some years. **Keene State College,** hub of the local arts community, fringes downtown.

Manchester is the state's largest city and home to some of its prime cultural attractions. The **Currier Gallery of Art** (✉ 201 Myrtle Way, Manchester, ☎ 603/669–6144; $5, $9 for Zimmerman House), in a 1929 Beaux Arts Italianate building, has European and American paintings, sculpture, and decorative arts from the 13th to the 20th century. The museum also owns and arranges tours of the Frank Lloyd Wright–designed Zimmerman House.

The **Amoskeag Mills** houses restaurants and museums. Here the **SEE Science Center** (☎ 603/669–0400; $4) is a hands-on science lab and children's museum. The **Millyard Museum** (☎ 603/625–2821; $5) contains exhibits depicting the region's history, from when Native Americans lived alongside and fished the Merrimack River to the heyday of Amoskeag Mills. ✉ *Mill No. 3, 200 Bedford St. (entrance at 255 Commercial St.),* ☎ *603/625–2821,* WEB *www.mv.com/org/mha.*

Dining and Lodging

Charlestown

$–$$ **MapleHedge.** Guest rooms in the 1820 Federal-style section are decorated with flair. The Cobalt Room, for example, features a collection of cobalt glass and mahogany furnishings. Freshly ironed linens and a three-course breakfast are among the amenities. ✉ *355 Main St. (Box 638, 03603),* ☎ *800/962–7539,* ☎ FAX *603/826–5237,* WEB *www.maplehedge.com. 5 rooms. MC, V. Closed Jan.–Mar. BP.*

Chesterfield

$$–$$$ ★ ✕ 🏨 **Chesterfield Inn.** Rooms in this B&B, which is surrounded by gardens, are spacious and tastefully decorated with antiques and colonial-style fabrics. Favorites from the dining room ($$–$$$) include leg of venison with cranberry-port sauce. ✉ Rte. 9 (Box 155, 03443), ☎ 603/256–3211 or 800/365–5515, FAX 603/256–6131, WEB www.chesterfieldinn.com. 15 rooms. Restaurant. AE, D, MC, V. BP.

Concord

$$–$$$ ✕ 🏨 **Centennial Inn.** Each room in this charming brick-and-stone structure, built for widows of Civil War veterans in 1896, is individually decorated with antiques and reproductions. In the Franklin Pierce dining room ($$–$$$), the menu changes seasonally. ✉ *96 Pleasant St., 03301,* ☎ *603/225–7102 or 800/360–4839,* FAX *603/225–5031,* WEB *www.someplacesdifferent.com/centennialinn.htm. 32 rooms. Restaurant. AE, D, DC, MC, V.*

Enfield

$$–$$$ ✕ 🏨 **The Shaker Inn.** Built between 1837 and 1841, the Great Stone Dwelling on Lake Mascoma is the largest main dwelling ever built by a Shaker community. It's now an inn adjacent to the Enfield Shaker Museum. Guest rooms in the original sleeping chambers have reproduction Shaker furniture and are decorated with simplicity and style. The dining room ($–$$) serves Shaker-inspired cuisine. ✉ *447 Rte. 4A, 03748,* ☎ *603/632–7810 or 888/707–4257,* WEB *www.theshakerinn.com. 24 rooms. Restaurant. AE, D, MC, V. BP.*

Fitzwilliam

$ ★ 🏨 **Hannah Davis House.** The original beehive oven still sits in the kitchen of this 1820 Federal B&B, and one suite has two Count Rumford fireplaces. Your host has the scoop on area antiquing. ✉ *106 Rte. 119, 03447,* ☎ *603/585–3344. 6 rooms. MC, V. BP.*

Hanover

$$$$ ✕ 🏨 **Hanover Inn.** Three stories of white-trimmed brick, this embodiment of American traditional architecture is owned by Dartmouth College and handsomely furnished with 19th-century antiques and reproductions. You can get innovative cuisine, such as grilled monkfish with tempura lobster tail and soba noodles, in the Daniel Webster Room ($–$$$) and lighter bites in Zins Wine Bistro. ✉ *The Green (Box 151, 03755),* ☎ *603/643–4300 or 800/443–7024,* FAX *603/646–3744. 92 rooms. 2 restaurants. AE, D, DC, MC, V.*

Manchester

$–$$ ★ ✕ **Cotton.** Mod lighting and furnishings and an arbored patio set a swanky tone at this restaurant inside one of the old Amoskeag Mill buildings. The kitchen churns out updated comfort food such as a casserole with yellowfin tuna, julienne vegetables, and pappardelle tossed with wild-mushroom cream and toasted lemony crumbs. ✉ *75 Arms Park,* ☎ *603/622–5488. AE, D, DC, MC, V.*

$$$ ★ ✕ 🏨 **Bedford Village Inn.** This 1810 Federal-style inn, a few miles southwest of Manchester, was once a farmstead. Its old hayloft and milking rooms now contain suites with king-size four-poster beds and whirlpool baths. The restaurant ($$–$$$$) and tavern ($$–$$$) present creative regional American fare. ✉ *2 Village Inn La., Bedford 03110,* ☎ *603/472–2001 or 800/852–1166,* FAX *603/472–2379,* WEB *www.bedfordvillageinn.com. 14 rooms. 2 restaurants. AE, DC, MC, V.*

Peterborough

$–$$ ★ ✕ **Acqua Bistro.** People like to congregate at the long bar of this smart bistro. You might join them before dining on a thin-crust pizza or an entrée of wild Arctic char with roasted vegetable-dill couscous and basil-walnut pesto. Save room for the bittersweet chocolate soufflé. ✉ *9 School St.,* ☎ *603/924–9905. MC, V.*

Nightlife and the Arts

Nashua is home to the state's largest professional theater, the **American Stage Festival** (✉ 14 Court St., ☎ 603/886–7000 winter; 603/673–7515 summer). The arts flourish at the **Capitol Center for the Arts** (✉ 44 S. Main St., Concord, ☎ 603/225–1111). The **Colonial Theatre** (✉ 95 Main St., Keene, ☎ 603/352–2033) hosts concerts and movies. The lounge at **Hermanos Cocina Mexicana** (✉ 11 Hills Ave., Concord, ☎ 603/224–5669) has live jazz Sunday–Thursday nights. **Monadnock Music** (☎ 603/924–7610 or 800/868–9613) has concerts in July and August at various venues. Revelers come from all over to drink and mingle at the **Yard** (✉ 1211 S. Mammoth Rd., Manchester, ☎ 603/623–3545), which is also a steak house and seafood restaurant.

Outdoor Activities and Sports

Biking

Try **Route 10** from south of Keene and through the Sunapee region into Hanover. You can rent bikes or get yours serviced at **Spokes and Slopes** (✉ 30 Grove St., ☎ 603/924–9961) in Peterborough.

Boating

The Connecticut River, while usually safe after June 15, isn't for beginners. Rent gear at **Northstar Canoe Livery** (✉ Rte. 12A, Balloch's Crossing, ☎ 603/542–5802), near Cornish.

Fishing

To find out where the action is on the area's 200 lakes and ponds, call the **New Hampshire Fish and Game Department** (☎ 603/271–3211).

Hiking

Networks of trails can be found in many state parks and forests. **Fox State Forest** (✉ Center Rd., ☎ 603/464–3453), near Hillsborough, has 20 mi of hiking trails and an observation tower.

Shopping

Look for artisans' studios marked by blue-and-white New Hampshire state signs. Antiques dealers sell "by chance or by appointment"; keep an eye peeled along Route 119 west of Fitzwilliam and along Route 101 east of Marlborough.

Keene has malls and the **Colony Mill Marketplace** (✉ 222 West St., Keene, ☎ 603/357–1240), which counts an antiques emporium among its offerings. Goldsmith Paul Gross of **Designer Gold** (✉ 3 Lebanon St., Hanover, ☎ 603/643–3864) designs settings for gemstones—all one-of-a-kind or limited-edition. The corporate headquarters and retail outlet of **Eastern Mountain Sports** (✉ 1 Vose Farm Rd., Peterborough, ☎ 603/924–7231) sells everything from tents to skis to hiking boots. The wares of some 40 dealers are for sale at **Fitzwilliam Antiques Centre** (✉ Rtes. 12 and 119, ☎ 603/585–9092).

At **Gibson Pewter** (✉ 18 E. Washington Rd., Hillsborough, ☎ 603/464–3410), Raymond Gibson and his son Jonathan create and sell museum-quality pewter pieces. In Concord, visit the **League of New Hampshire Craftsmen** (✉ 36 N. Main St., ☎ 603/228–8171) for a wide variety of juried crafts. **Sharon Arts Downtown** (✉ Depot Sq., Peterborough, ☎ 603/924–2787) has a gallery that exhibits locally made pottery, fabric, and woodwork and other crafts.

Western and Central New Hampshire Essentials

AIRPORTS

Manchester Airport is served by most major airlines. Lebanon Municipal Airport, near Dartmouth College, is served by Colgan Air (an affiliate of US Airways) from Boston and by US Airways Express from Philadelphia and New York.

➤ AIRPORT INFORMATION: **Lebanon Municipal Airport** (✉ 5 Airpark Rd., West Lebanon, ☎ 603/298–8878). **Manchester Airport** (✉ 1 Airport Rd., Manchester 03103, ☎ 603/624–6539).

BUS TRAVEL

Concord Trailways, Dartmouth Coach, and Vermont Transit serve the region.

➤ BUS INFORMATION: **Concord Trailways** (☎ 603/228–3300 or 800/639–3317). **Dartmouth Coach** (☎ 603/448–2800 or 800/637–0123). **Vermont Transit** (☎ 800/552–8737).

CAR TRAVEL

I–89 cuts southeast–northwest into Vermont. North–south, I–93 provides scenic travel while I–91 follows the Connecticut River on its Vermont shore; in New Hampshire, Routes 12 and 12A are slow but beautiful.

VISITOR INFORMATION

➤ TOURIST INFORMATION: **Concord Chamber of Commerce** (✉ 40 Commercial St., Concord 03301, ☎ 603/224–2508, WEB www.concordnhchamber.com). **Lake Sunapee Region Chamber of Commerce** (✉ Box 532, Sunapee 03782, ☎ 603/526–6575 or 877/526–6575, WEB sunapeevacations.com). **Monadnock Travel Council** (✉ 58 Central Sq. [Box 358, Keene 03431], ☎ 800/432–7864, WEB www.monadnocktravel.com).

NEW JERSEY

Updated by Robert DiGiacomo

Capital	Trenton
Population	8,484,431
Motto	Liberty and Prosperity
State Bird	Eastern goldfinch
State Flower	Common meadow violet
Postal Abbreviation	NJ

Statewide Visitor Information

New Jersey Department of Commerce and Economic Development (✉ Division of Travel and Tourism, Box 820, Trenton 08625-0820, ☎ 609/292–2470 or 800/537–7397, FAX 609/633–7418, WEB www.state.nj.us/travel).

For information on state parks contact the **Department of Environmental Protection, Division of Parks and Forestry** (✉ Box 404, Trenton 08625, ☎ 609/984–0370 or 800/843–6420, WEB www.state.nj.us/dep/forestry).

Scenic Drives

For Hudson River views take the **Palisades Interstate Parkway** north from the George Washington Bridge to the state line or take **River Road** from Weehawken north to Fort Lee. Both **Route 23,** northwest from Newfoundland through High Point State Park, and **Route 15,** northwest from I–80, give you glimpses of lakes, rural estates, and higher-elevation vistas. The back roads off **Routes 202** and **206** in central New Jersey pass by horse farms, antiques shops, and historic sites. Along the southern shore, **Ocean Drive** is a causeway that links barrier islands.

National and State Parks

National Parks

On the Delaware River boundary between New Jersey and Pennsylvania is the **Delaware Water Gap National Recreation Area** (✉ Visitor Center, Kittatinny Point, off I–80, Bushkill, PA 18324, ☎ 908/496–4458 or 570/588–2451, WEB www.nps.gov/dewa), the largest national recreation area in the Northeast. The 40,000-acre **Edwin B. Forsythe National Wildlife Refuge's Brigantine Division** (✉ Great Creek Rd., Box 72, Oceanville 08231, ☎ 609/652–1665, WEB forsythe.fws.gov) has an 8-mi wildlife drive, mainly through diverse coastal habitat, and two short, circular nature trails that are especially worthwhile during spring and fall bird migrations. **Sandy Hook Unit of Gateway National Recreation Area** (✉ Box 530, Fort Hancock 07732, ☎ 732/872–0115, WEB www.nps.gov/gate) preserves sandbar ecology and fortifications built to protect New York Harbor.

State Parks

New Jersey has the third-largest state park system in the nation, with 36 parks, 11 forests, 4 recreation areas, 42 natural areas, 23 historic sites, 4 marinas, and 1 golf course. Many of New Jersey's 19 lighthouses are preserved in state parks, including Barnegat Lighthouse, Cape May Point Lighthouse, and Sandy Hook Lighthouse.

High Point State Park (✉ 1480 Rte. 23, Sussex 07461, ☎ 973/875–4800, WEB www.state.nj.us/dep/forestry/parks/high.htm) is named after the state's tallest peak and has swimming and water sports on Lake Marcia in summer and cross-country skiing in winter. The Appalachian Trail comes through here. **Wharton State Forest** (✉ Rte. 542,

Hammonton 08037, ☏ 609/561–3262, WEB www.state.nj.us/dep/forestry/parks/wharton.htm), New Jersey's largest, contains the **Batsto State Historic Site** (✉ Rte. 542, ☏ 609/561–7310), a restored late-18th- and 19th-century Pinelands ironworking village.

THE JERSEY SHORE

The Jersey Shore is 127 mi of public beachfront stretching like a pointing finger along the Atlantic Ocean from the Sandy Hook Peninsula in the north to Cape May at the southern tip. There is no one description of what it's like "down the shore." Things change town by town and sometimes season by season—winter storms have a habit of rearranging beaches and boardwalks. Activities along the shore include saltwater fishing from pier, bridge, dock, or boat (licenses not required); all kinds of water sports; bird-, whale-, and dolphin-watching; and bicycling or strolling on the ubiquitous wood-plank or concrete boardwalks. In Atlantic City are the famed gambling casinos; in Cape May, Victorian bed-and-breakfasts; and in between—in Seaside Heights, Point Pleasant, and Wildwood—quintessential seaside amusements.

Exploring the Jersey Shore

The **New Jersey Coastal Heritage Trail** (☏ 856/447–0103) connects significant natural and cultural resources along the Atlantic coast and Delaware Bay. A network of routes (primarily vehicular) stretches more than 275 mi, from Perth Amboy south along the Atlantic coast to Cape May, then north along the Delaware Bay coast to the Delaware Memorial Bridge in Deepwater. The project area has been divided into five regions: Sandy Hook, Barnegat Bay, Absecon, Cape May, and the Delsea region on the western shore. Each area will have its own regional welcome center to provide interpretive information; two centers have opened, one at Fort Mott State Park in Salem County and another at Milepost 18.3 of the Garden State Parkway near Cape May Oceanview Service Area. Five theme routes—wildlife migration, maritime history, historic settlements, relaxation and inspiration, and coastal habitats—highlight the heritage of this region.

At the shore's north end the **Sandy Hook Lighthouse,** the oldest continuously operating lighthouse in the country (built in 1764), stands in the **Sandy Hook Unit of Gateway National Recreation Area,** 4 mi east of Atlantic Highlands on Route 36. On this peninsula of barrier beach you can splash in the usually gentle, shallow surf; explore sleepy **Fort Hancock,** established in 1895; and glimpse the New York City skyline, 19 mi across the harbor from North Beach.

Just south on Route 36, **Long Branch** was founded in the 18th century as one of America's first resorts; over the years it has hosted seven presidents, from Grant to Wilson.

A century ago **Asbury Park** was the shore's toniest resort, but efforts to revive that glory have so far been disappointing. It is still known for its place in rock history, as the young Bruce Springsteen performed here in the 1960s; but the club where he played, the Stone Pony, was torn down in 1998. By contrast, neighboring **Ocean Grove** was established in 1859 by Methodists as a camp-meeting area and still serves that purpose. The town's dignified tone echoes in its Victorian hotels and inns; relatively quiet beaches; a short, gameless boardwalk; and shops and cafés. Ocean Grove is also one of two shore towns that do not sell alcohol—the other is Ocean City, a Methodist town patterned after it. The imposing **Great Auditorium** (✉ Pilgrim Pathway,

The Jersey Shore

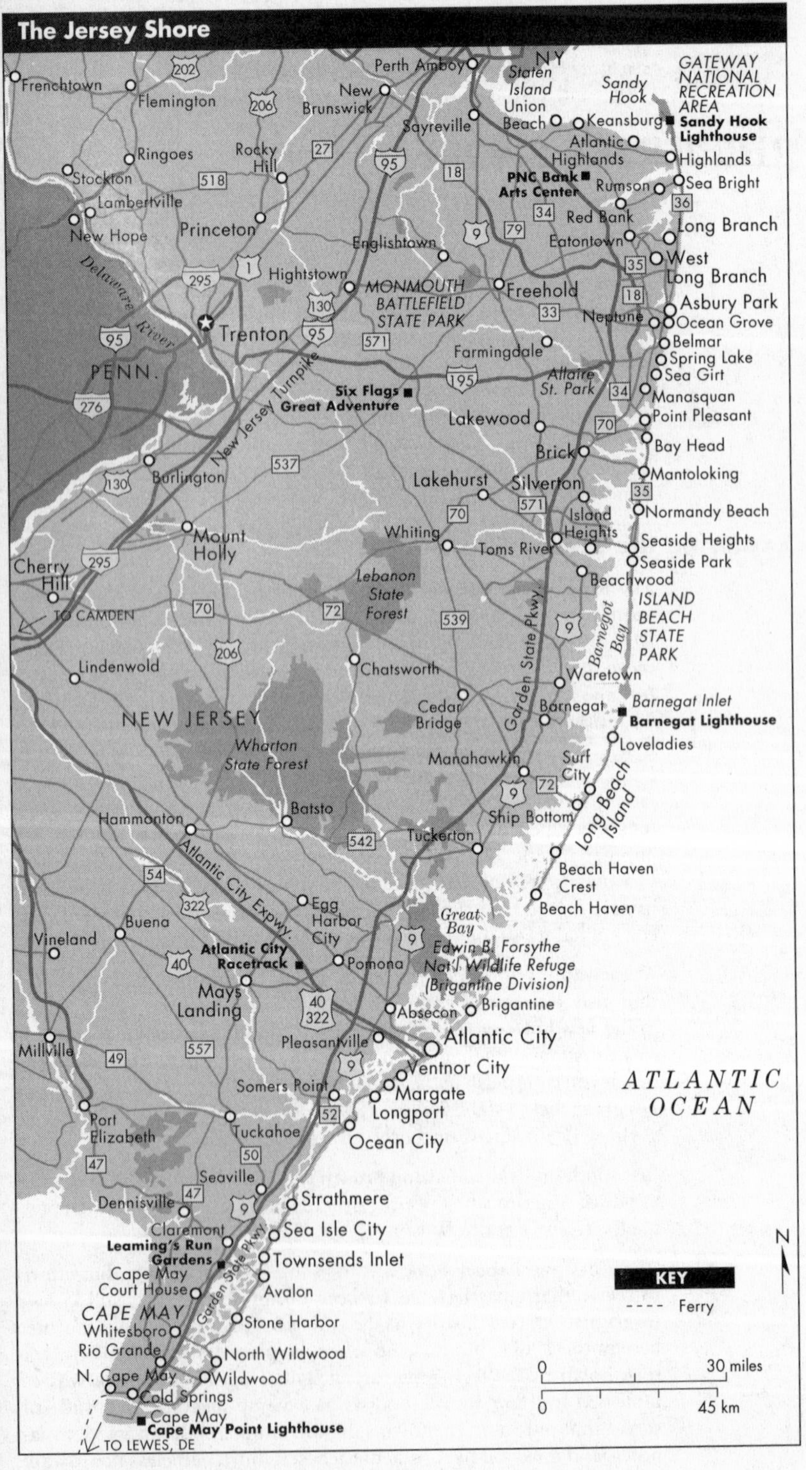

☎ 732/775–0035, WEB www.oceangrovenj.com/auditorium.htm) presents a summer schedule of concerts on Saturday nights.

In **Belmar** the **Municipal Marina** (✉ Rte. 35, ☎ 732/681–2266), on the Shark River, has party and charter boats that head for the ocean daily in search of blackfish, blues, fluke, tuna, and shark. Neighboring **Spring Lake** has an uncommercialized boardwalk, three spring-fed lakes with swans, a small town center, and numerous romantic B&Bs. At the family-oriented **Point Pleasant Beach, Jenkinson's Aquarium** (✉ Ocean Ave., ☎ 732/899–1659, WEB www.jenkinsons.com; $7), on the boardwalk at the Broadway Beach area, is a nice rainy-day diversion.

★ **Six Flags Great Adventure,** inland from Spring Lake, comprises both an amusement park with a multitude of the newest rides and a drive-through safari park. ✉ *Rte. 537, I–195 Exit 16, Jackson,* ☎ *732/928–2000,* WEB *www.sixflags.com. Theme park and safari $45.99, safari only $17.99. Closed late Oct.–mid-Apr.*

On Barnegat Peninsula, the side-by-side resorts of **Seaside Heights** and **Seaside Park** have two major amusement piers plus water rides. Don't miss a turn on the antique Dentzel-Looff carousel. Just south, but seemingly a world away, is narrow ★ **Island Beach State Park** (☎ 732/793–0506, WEB www.state.nj.us/dep/forestry/parks/island.htm; Labor Day–Memorial Day $4; Memorial Day–Labor Day $6 weekdays, $7 weekends), 10 mi of ocean and bay beaches with almost no evidence of human habitation.

Return inland over Barnegat Bay to **Toms River,** once a pirate and privateering port, and today the center of a booming region of retirement communities. The **Ocean County Historical Museum** (✉ 26 Hadley Ave., ☎ 732/341–1880, WEB www.oceancountyhistory.org/museum.html; donations accepted) has Victorian artifacts, a research library for tracing genealogy, and exhibits on the dirigibles that flew from the Lakehurst Naval Air Station, site of the 1937 *Hindenburg* tragedy.

Head south on U.S. 9 and east on Route 72 over Barnegat Bay to **Long Beach Island. Barnegat Lighthouse** (☎ 609/494–2016, WEB www.state.nj.us/dep/forestry/parks/barnlig.htm), known locally as Old Barney, completed in 1858, is at the northern tip of the island. **Beach Haven,** the island's commercial center, has Victorian houses set around a town square, a family atmosphere, and beautiful beaches. The **Long Beach Island Museum** (✉ Engleside and Beach Aves., ☎ 609/492–0700, WEB www.lbinet.com/nonprof/lbimuseum.thml) conducts walking tours of the historic district from late June to early September.

Back on the mainland, the Garden State Parkway and U.S. 9 lead to **Atlantic City,** the gambling capital of the East Coast (bettors drop about $10 million daily). A visitor welcome center (☎ 888/228–4748) is off the Atlantic City Expressway. Read the street signs and you'll find the roads that made the board game Monopoly famous, including the **Boardwalk,** the nation's first elevated wood walkway (1870), where saltwater taffy is still sold. The resort's earlier 19th-century stone hotels have been replaced by 12 **casino-hotels**—outrageous in design and entertainment, from the Mardi Gras festivity of the Showboat to the onion domes of the Taj Mahal. Although there are still pockets of down-at-the-heels buildings and pawnshops in Atlantic City, renovations, increased security, and infusions of capital have decreased the incidence of crime and given the entire city a more optimistic tone. Atlantic City even has its own **Hard Rock Cafe** (☎ 609/441–0007, www.hardrock.com) and **Ripley's Believe It or Not Museum** (✉ New

York Ave. and the Boardwalk, ☎ 609/347–2001, WEB www.ripleys.com/atlanticcity2.htm).

You can still see some of Atlantic City's famous ocean amusement piers, but only the **Central Pier** (✉ St. James Pl. and Tennessee Ave.), on the boardwalk, retains its original 1884 appearance. The **Garden Pier** (✉ New Jersey Ave. and the Boardwalk) has been converted to an art center; don't miss the terrific little **Atlantic City Historical Museum and Cultural Center** (☎ 609/347–5839; free), with an evocative collection of memorabilia and a thorough video on the history of the seaside resort. **Steel Pier,** at Virginia Avenue, is now an amusement pier and arcade. A link to the city's Victorian history, the **Historic Absecon Lighthouse** (✉ Pacific and Rhode Island Aves., ☎ 609/449–1360; free) is once again open the public. **The Ocean Life Center** (☎ 609/345–7571 or 609/348–2880, WEB www.oceanlifecenter.com; $7) on the bay at Historic Gardner's Basin offers 10 themed exhibits and eight aquariums filled with area fish and sea animals.

In Margate **Lucy the Elephant** (✉ Atlantic and Decatur Aves., ☎ 609/823–6473, WEB www.lucytheelephant.org; $4), an elephant-shape building six stories high and a National Historic Landmark, has been drawing the curious of all ages since 1881. It is open April–October.

Ocean City, across Great Egg Harbor, has a **boardwalk** and boardwalk parades that are family-oriented. Summer-evening concerts at the **Music Pier** (✉ Moorlyn Terr., ☎ 609/525–9248, WEB www.oceancitypops.org) are a tradition.

Strathmere Beach is a great place for a quiet walk. Take time out to explore the **Wetlands Institute** (☎ 609/368–1211, WEB www.wetlandsinstitute.org; $5), in Stone Harbor, a research and education center on coastal ecology; the institute is open daily from May 15 to October 15 and Tuesday–Saturday from October 16 to May 14. The Wings 'n Water Festival is held here and in neighboring towns the third weekend of September.

Ocean Drive leads to the little boroughs known as the Wildwoods. The best known, loudest, kitschiest, and wildest is **Wildwood** itself. Its 2-mi **boardwalk** has the greatest concentration of outdoor amusement rides on the shore, including seven amusement piers. In the last few years, the town's funky, original 1950s architecture has become a launching pad for a renewed interest in this seashore resort.

★ At the southern tip of the shore, the meticulously restored Victorian town of **Cape May** offers a dramatic change of pace and scenery. The state's oldest ocean resort, it was named for the Dutch captain Cornelius Mey, who sighted it in 1620. Cape May today has plenty of bed-and-breakfasts, many in elaborate gingerbread-style Victorian houses. **Victorian Week** (☎ 609/884–4600 or 800/275–4278) combines madcap frivolity with house tours, dinners, and lectures (make reservations well in advance). The July 4 celebration is vintage Americana, while Christmastime has Dickensian flair, with trolley, candlelight, and walking tours of houses.

Cape May, at the southern tip of New Jersey, is one of the strategic stops along the Atlantic Flyway, so it attracts flocks of birds and bird-watchers, especially during the spring and fall migrations.

A favorite birding locale is **Cape May Point State Park** (✉ Lighthouse Ave., ☎ 609/884–2159, WEB www.state.nj.us/dep/forestry/parks/capemay.htm), site of the **Cape May Point Lighthouse** (☎ 609/884–5404 or 800/275–4278, WEB www.capemaymac.org), built in 1859, which marks the end of the Jersey Shore. Not far from Cape May Point Lighthouse, **Sunset Beach** (✉ Sunset Blvd., Cape May Point) is the place to collect "Cape May diamonds," pebbles of pure quartz that wash up on the beach, and to watch the sun set over Delaware Bay.

Dining and Lodging

Seafood is the Jersey Shore's strongest suit, with local catches on most menus. Ocean City and Ocean Grove don't sell alcohol.

Lodgings should be booked far in advance in summer. Beachfront rooms are more expensive. Rooms in Atlantic City casino-hotels are the most popular, the most costly, and the most difficult to reserve, especially on weekends from mid-June to Labor Day.

The **Bed & Breakfast Innkeepers Association of New Jersey** (☎ 732/449–3535, WEB www.njinns.com) offers a free guidebook featuring 85 inns statewide.

Atlantic City

$$$$ ★ ✕ **Peregrines'.** Named for the peregrine falcons that nest on the penthouse ledge, this small, elegant, yet friendly restaurant has both à la carte and prix-fixe menus. Among the specialties are Belon oysters from France, truffles from Belgium, and quinoa from the Indies. ✉ *Atlantic City Hilton Casino Resort, Boston Ave. and Boardwalk,* ☎ *609/347–7111,* WEB *www.hiltonac.com. AE, D, DC, MC, V. Closed Mon.–Wed. No lunch.*

$$$ ★ ✕ **Le Grand Fromage.** This charming French bistro serves updates on classic dishes like steak frites and veal Oscar (asparagus, crab, and hollandaise sauce) in a building dating to the early 20th century. ✉ *25 Gordon's Alley,* ☎ *609/347–2743. AE, MC, V. Closed Sun.–Mon.*

$$–$$$ ✕ **Dock's Oyster House.** Owned and operated by the Dougherty family since 1897, the city's oldest restaurant serves seafood in a setting of wood and stained glass engraved with nautical scenes. ✉ *2405 Atlantic Ave.,* ☎ *609/345–0092. AE, DC, MC, V. Closed Dec.–Feb.*

$–$$$ ★ ✕ **Angelo's Fairmount Tavern.** Locals flock here for lots of good Italian fare, dished out by the Mancuso family, owners since 1935. ✉ *2300 Fairmount Ave.,* ☎ *609/344–2439,* WEB *www.angelosfairmounttavern.com. AE, MC, V.*

$–$$ ✕ **Los Amigos.** South-of-the-border specialties such as Mexican pizza, burritos, and margaritas, served in the dimly lit back room, are good bets at this small bar and restaurant two blocks from the boardwalk casinos. ✉ *1926 Atlantic Ave.,* ☎ *609/344–2293. AE, DC, MC, V.*

$ ✕ **White House Sub Shop.** The White House claims to have sold more than 17 million overstuffed sandwiches since 1946. Celebrities seem to love it; check out the photos on the walls. ✉ *Mississippi and Arctic Aves.,* ☎ *609/345–1564 or 609/345–8599. Reservations not accepted. No credit cards.*

$$$–$$$$ 🏨 **Trump Marina Hotel Casino.** Blandly modern on the outside, this bayside marina is removed from some of the boardwalk glitz. Service is first-rate. ✉ *Huron Ave. and Brigantine Blvd., 08401,* ☎ *609/441–2000 or 800/777–8477,* FAX *609/345–7604,* WEB *www.trumpmarina.com. 728 rooms. 8 restaurants, pool, tennis, health club. AE, D, DC, MC, V.*

$$–$$$$ ★ 🏨 **Bally's Park Place Casino Hotel & Tower.** Guests can stay in the Art Deco rooms of the historic Dennis Hotel, built in 1860, or in the newer 37-story tower, whose spacious, angular rooms have picture windows even in the marble-tile bathrooms. The spa facilities are exceptional. ✉ *Park Pl. at Boardwalk, 08401,* ☎ *609/340–2000 or 800/225–5977,* FAX *609/340–4713,* WEB *www.ballysac.com. 1,268 rooms. 8 restaurants, pool, gym. AE, D, DC, MC, V.*

$$$ 🏨 **Sheraton Atlantic City Convention Center Hotel.** The 16-story Art Deco hotel, connected to the convention center by an enclosed walkway, showcases Miss America Pageant memorabilia in display windows.

Inside, a grand circular staircase leads to the Miss America–theme Shoe Bar, restaurant, and meeting rooms. Every room has a coffeemaker and a stash of Ellis coffee. ✉ *2 Ocean Way, 08401,* ☎ *609/344–3535 or 800/325–3535,* FAX *609/348–4336,* WEB *www.starwood.com/sheraton. 502 rooms. 2 restaurants, tennis, health club. AE, D, MC, V.*

$$–$$$ **Flagship Resort.** This pleasant, modern, salmon-color condo hotel is across from the boardwalk (facing Brigantine and the Absecon Inlet), away from the casino action. Every suite has a private terrace with a view, as well as a microwave, refrigerator, and wet bar. ✉ *60 N. Main Ave., 08401,* ☎ *609/343–7447 or 800/647–7890,* FAX *609/343–1608,* WEB *www.flagshipresort.com. 300 suites. Restaurant, pool, health club. AE, D, MC, V.*

$$–$$$ ★ **Quality Inn Atlantic City.** Half a block from the boardwalk, one of Atlantic City's best values has a 17-story modern guest wing above a Federal-style base. Rooms are outfitted with handsome colonial reproductions. Resorts Atlantic City is next door. ✉ *S. Carolina and Pacific Aves., 08401,* ☎ *609/345–7070 or 800/356–6044,* FAX *609/345–0633,* WEB *www.qualityinnatlanticcity.com. 203 rooms. Restaurant. AE, D, DC, MC, V.*

Cape May

$$–$$$$ ✕ **Mad Batter.** Eclectic contemporary cuisine is served in the skylighted Victorian dining room or outside on the porch or the garden terrace. Breakfasts are imaginative, albeit pricey; Belgian waffles and eggs Benedict are favorites. For lunch try the crab-cake sandwich; for dinner, crab *mappatello* (crabmeat, spinach, and ricotta in a puff pastry). Upstairs is Carroll Villa, a 21-room B&B. ✉ *19 Jackson St.,* ☎ *609/884–5970,* WEB *www.madbatter.com. AE, MC, V. Closed Jan.*

$$$ **Angel of the Sea.** A stunning, sprawling Victorian presence in Cape May, this 1850s inn consistently winds up on "best-of" lists nationwide; it also won the Restoration of the Year Award from the National Trust for Historic Preservation. Complimentary afternoon tea as well as wine and cheese are served daily. ✉ *5–7 Trenton Ave., 08204,* ☎ *609/884–3369 or 800/848–3369,* WEB *www.angelofthesea.com. 27 rooms. AE, MC, V. BP.*

$$$ **Captain Mey's Inn.** A wraparound veranda and a small, walled courtyard and tulip garden bring charm to this 1890 house close to the Washington Mall and the beach. The Victorian antiques include a collection of Delft china. Two guest rooms have whirlpool tubs. ✉ *202 Ocean St., 08204,* ☎ *609/884–7793 or 800/981–3702,* WEB *www.captainmeys.com. 8 rooms. AE, MC, V. BP.*

$$$ **Chalfonte.** With its simple original furnishings, this authentic Victorian summer hotel attracts a mix of longtime guests, families, and new clientele. Special programs include evening entertainment; volunteer work weekends during which students and other volunteers pay a small registration fee but basically stay free at the hotel in return for help with its upkeep; and a supervised children's dining room, where youngsters eat from a special menu while parents dine on the inn's famous, mostly southern home-style cooking. ✉ *301 Howard St., 08204,* ☎ *609/884–8409 or 888/411–1998,* FAX *609/884–4588,* WEB *www.chalfonte.com. 78 rooms, 2 cottages. Restaurant. AE, D, MC, V. Closed Columbus Day–Memorial Day weekend. MAP.*

$$$ ★ **The Mainstay Inn.** This 1872 men's gambling club reincarnated as a B&B captures the feel of another era with 14-ft ceilings, stenciling, historic wallpapers, and harmoniously arranged antiques. Across the street is the Officers' Quarters, a suites-only sister property in another restored building. ✉ *635 Columbia Ave., 08204,* ☎ *609/884–8690,* WEB *www.mainstayinn.com. 16 rooms. No credit cards. CP or BP, depending on season and building.*

$$$ **Queen Victoria B&B and the Queen's Hotel.** In the center of the historic district, four restored Victorian houses (two devoted to the B&B, two to the hotel) pay homage to the queen and the period named for her. Rooms, though full of antiques, also have modern touches, including refrigerators, whirlpool baths in some rooms, and TVs in the suites. ✉ *B&B: 102 Ocean St., 08204,* ☎ *609/884–8702, www.queenvictoria.com;* ✉ *hotel: 601 Columbia Ave., 08204,* ☎ *609/884–1613,* WEB *www.queenshotel.com. 21 rooms. AE, MC, V. CP (B&B only).*

$$$ **The Virginia Hotel.** With turndown and room service, a morning newspaper, and privileges at local golf clubs, the Virginia is a full-service hotel on an intimate scale. Rooms have cherry and poplar furnishings with Victorian lines. Grilled seafood and meats and rich desserts are served at the Ebbitt Room Restaurant. ✉ *25 Jackson St., 08204,* ☎ *609/884–5700 or 800/732–4236,* FAX *609/884–1236,* WEB *www.virginiahotel.com. 24 rooms. Restaurant. AE, D, DC, MC, V. CP.*

$$ **Manor House.** On a quiet, tree-lined street two blocks from the beach, this 1905 guest house mixes antiques, stained glass, art, and eclectic touches, such as an old-fashioned player piano. Innkeepers Tom and Nancy McDonald prepare the four-course breakfasts from scratch. ✉ *612 Hughes St., 08204,* ☎ *609/884–4710,* WEB *www.manorhouse.net. 10 rooms. D, MC, V. Closed Jan. BP.*

Ocean City

$–$$ **Serendipity Bed & Breakfast.** At this beautifully restored inn a half block from the beach, owners Clara and Bill Plowfield place an emphasis on natural-foods cooking, serving breakfast throughout the year and dinner from October to May. ✉ *712 9th St., 08226,* ☎ *609/399–1554 or 800/842–8544,* WEB *www.serendipitynj.com. 6 rooms. AE, D, MC, V. BP.*

Spring Lake

$$$ **Normandy Inn.** This huge 1888 Italianate mansion, filled with museum-quality American Victorian antiques, has been a guest house since 1909. The Tower Room, with windows on four sides, has views of the ocean, which is a two-minute walk away. ✉ *21 Tuttle Ave., 07762,* ☎ *732/449–7172 or 800/449–1888,* FAX *732/449–1070,* WEB *www.normandyinn.com. 18 rooms. AE, D, DC, MC, V. BP.*

$$$ **Sea Crest by the Sea.** This 1885 Queen Anne Victorian is one of many in town. Eight rooms have gas-log fireplaces, seven have ocean views, and six have whirlpool tubs; all have feather beds and luxurious fabrics. Buttermilk scones are a breakfast standard; there's also daily afternoon tea. ✉ *19 Tuttle Ave., 07762,* ☎ *732/449–9031 or 800/803–9031,* FAX *732/974–0403,* WEB *www.seacrestbythesea.com. 11 rooms. AE, MC, V. BP.*

$$–$$$ **Hollycroft.** Overlooking Lake Como at the northern edge of town, Hollycroft is a mountain-style lodge without the mountains. A 16-ft ironstone fireplace and walls of knotty pine in the living room make it a charming getaway. ✉ *North Blvd. (Box 448, 07762),* ☎ *732/681–2254 or 800/679–2254,* WEB *www.hollycroft.com. 7 rooms. AE, D, MC, V. BP.*

Toms River

$–$$ ✕ **Old Time Tavern.** Italian dishes, steaks, seafood, and sandwiches are the lures at this restaurant and taproom. Early birds can get soup-to-dessert meals at bargain prices. ✉ *N. Main St., Rte. 166 off Rte. 37,* ☎ *732/349–8778. AE, DC, MC, V.*

Motels

Ascot Motel (✉ Iowa and Pacific Aves. [Box 1824, Atlantic City 08404], ☎ 609/344–5163 or 800/225–1476), 80 rooms; pool; *$–$$.*
Clarion Bayside Resort at Golf & Tennis World (✉ 8029 Black Horse

Pike, W. Atlantic City 08232, ☎ 609/641–3546 or 800/999–9466, FAX 609/641–4329, WEB www.clarionac.com), 110 rooms; restaurant, pool, tennis, health club; $–$$. **Sandpiper** (✉ Long Beach Blvd. at 10th St., Ship Bottom 08008, ☎ 609/494–6909), 20 rooms; pool; closed Nov.–Apr.; $–$$.

Nightlife and the Arts

Outside of Atlantic City the Jersey Shore doesn't have much in the way of nightlife. Families and couples hit the boardwalk's arcades, or stroll into town for ice cream and a movie. The younger crowds are usually content to get a couple of six-packs at the local liquor store and hunker down on the beach or in their rentals, though the boardwalk at Point Pleasant and Seaside Heights has quite a few bars and dance clubs that draw an 18–25 crowd. Local papers will give you the lowdown on what bars have live entertainment, the quality of which can range from surprisingly competent to uproariously cheesy.

PNC Bank Arts Center (✉ Garden State Pkwy. Exit 116, Holmdel, ☎ 732/335–0400, WEB www.artscenter.com) has a summer roster of performing-arts groups, big-name pop acts, and ethnic festivals.

Outdoor Activities and Sports

Biking

Boardwalks are grand for biking if you don't mind dodging weekend walkers and joggers. Many towns restrict riding to the early morning hours, before the crowds gather. The road around Cape May Point takes you past Cape May Point State Park and its lighthouse.

Canoeing

Try the many freshwater creeks, and streams in the 1.1-million-acre **Pinelands National Reserve** (☎ 609/894–7300, WEB www.state.nj.us/pinelands/pnrpc.htm), the country's first national reserve.

Fishing

Monmouth County has more charter and party boats than any other area along the shore; most popular is the Belmar Marina. In Ocean County numerous party and charter boats sail from Point Pleasant and Long Beach Island.

Fishing boats sail from **state marinas** in Leonardo and Atlantic City (☎ 732/291–1333 Leonardo; 609/441–8482 Atlantic City, WEB www.state.nj.us/dep/forestry/parks/marinas.htm).

Gardens

Leaming's Run Gardens (✉ 1845 Rte. 9 N, Swainton, ☎ 609/465–5871, WEB www.leamingsrun.com; $7), with 25 designed and planted gardens, is the largest annuals garden in the country.

Spectator Sports

Baseball: The national pastime, begun in Hoboken more than a century ago, has come to New Jersey in a big way: In 1998 Atlantic City opened a 5,900-seat minor-league stadium for its own pro team, the **Atlantic City Surf.** Catch a game at the stadium, the **Sandcastle** (✉ 545 N. Albany Ave., Atlantic City, ☎ 609/344–8873, www.acsurf.com), from mid-May to mid-September. The 6,500-seat **Campbell Field** (☎ 856/963–2600, WEB www.riversharks.com), on the Camden waterfront across the Delaware River from Philadelphia's historic district, houses the minor-league **Camden Riversharks** from early May to mid-September. **Horse Racing: Monmouth Park Racetrack** (✉ Rte. 36 and Oceanport Ave., Oceanport, ☎ 732/222–5100, WEB www.monmouthpark.com) is the area's best-known track, with Thoroughbred races from Memorial Day–Labor Day. The **Atlantic City Racetrack** (✉ 4501 Black Horse Pike, Mays Landing, ☏ 609/641–2190) has Thoroughbred racing for one day (call for date) and simulcasting year-round. There's harness racing at **Freehold Raceway** (✉ U.S. 9 and Rte. 33, Freehold, ☏ 732/462–3800, WEB www.freeholdraceway.com) from mid-August through May.

Beaches

From Memorial Day to Labor Day the **Beach Information Hotline** (☏ 800/648–7263) supplies reports on the shore's water quality and beach conditions. Beaches usually charge a fee from Memorial Day or mid-June to Labor Day. Windsurfing is especially good in the calm waters of the open bays. Sailing, rowing, and powerboating are superb on sheltered Barnegat Bay in Ocean County. ★ **Island Beach State Park** is the most scenic natural beach on the Jersey Shore.

Shopping

The **Shore Antique Center** (✉ Point Pleasant Beach, ☏ 732/295–5771) is a warren of high-quality merchandise, including folk art, lawn ornaments, and fine art, from more than 40 dealers. Nearby are several other treasure chests, including the **Antique Emporium** (✉ Bay and Trenton Aves., ☏ 732/892–2222). In Red Bank, where you'll find more than a dozen antiques markets; the largest of these is the three-building **Red Bank Antique Center** (✉ 195, 195-B, and 226 W. Front St., ☏ 732/842–3393, WEB wwsw.redbankartsantique.com) with pieces from more than 150 dealers.

The Jersey Shore Essentials

AIRPORTS

Philadelphia International (☞ Pennsylvania), Newark International Airport, and the New York City airports (☞ New York) are closest to Atlantic City and shore points. Atlantic City International Airport serves the southern shore.

➤ AIRPORT INFORMATION: **Atlantic City International Airport** (☏ 609/645–7895 or 888/235–9229, WEB www.acairport.com). **Newark International Airport** (✉ Tower Rd., ☏ 973/961–6000, WEB www.panynj.gov/aviation/ewrframe.htm).

BOAT AND FERRY TRAVEL

The Cape May–Lewes Ferry is a year-round 70-minute car ferry (1,000 passengers, 100 cars per ferry) across the Delaware Bay.

➤ BOAT AND FERRY INFORMATION: **Cape May–Lewes Ferry** (☏ 609/886–1725; 800/643–3779 for reservations, WEB www.capemaylewesferry.com).

BUS TRAVEL

New Jersey Transit provides bus service to most Jersey Shore towns. Academy Lines also runs buses between New York City and shore points. Greyhound serves Atlantic City. Ask Atlantic City casino-hotels about direct service to their properties.

➤ BUS INFORMATION: **Academy Lines** (☏ 732/291–1300 or 800/442–7272, WEB www.academybus.com). **Greyhound** (☏ 609/345–6617 or 800/231–2222, WEB www.greyhound.com).

CAR TRAVEL

The main road serving the Jersey Shore is the Garden State Parkway, a north–south toll road that ends in Cape May. From New York City, I–80 and the New Jersey Turnpike (toll) connect with the Garden State. From Philadelphia and southern New Jersey suburbs, take the

Atlantic City Expressway (toll). From the south take the Delaware Memorial Bridge and continue north on the New Jersey Turnpike. Toms River, Barnegat, and Tuckerton are linked by U.S. 9.

TRAIN TRAVEL

Amtrak serves Atlantic City. New Jersey Transit operates local commuter service to Atlantic City from Philadelphia and to the shore towns in Monmouth and Ocean counties from New York City.

➤ TRAIN INFORMATION: **Amtrak** (✉ 1 Atlantic City Expressway, near Kirkman Blvd., ☎ 800/872–7245 or 973/762–5100, WEB www.amtrak.com). **New Jersey Transit** (☎ 800/772–2222 from northern New Jersey; 800/582–5946 from southern New Jersey, WEB www.njtransit.com).

VISITOR INFORMATION

The Mid-Atlantic Center for the Arts has information on Cape May, and the Department of Tourism and Economic Development in the Cape May Court House has information on Cape May County. Contact the Department of Promotion and Tourism in Freehold for information on Monmouth County.

➤ TOURIST INFORMATION: **Atlantic City Convention & Visitors Authority** (✉ 2314 Pacific Ave., 08401, ☎ 609/348–7100 or 888/248–4748, FAX 609/348–3426, WEB www.atlanticcitynj.com). **Cape May County Chamber of Commerce** (✉ Box 74, Cape May Court House 08210, ☎ 609/465–7181, FAX 609/465–5017, WEB www.capemaycountychamber.com). **Cape May County Department of Tourism and Economic Development** (✉ Cape May Court House, Box 365, Cape May 08210, ☎ 609/463–6415 or 800/227–2297, WEB www.thejerseycape.com). **Chamber of Commerce of Greater Cape May** (✉ 609 Lafayette St. [Box 556, 08204], ☎ 609/884–5508, WEB www.capemaychamber.com). **Mid-Atlantic Center for the Arts** (✉ Box 340, 08204, ☎ 609/884–5404, WEB www.capemaymac.org). **Monmouth County Department of Promotion and Tourism** (✉ 31 E. Main St., Freehold 07728, ☎ 732/431–7476 or 800/523–2587, FAX 732/294–5930, WEB www.visitmonmouth.com/tourism). **Ocean County Tourism Advisory Council** (✉ Box 2191, Toms River 08754, ☎ 732/929–2138 or 800/365–6933, FAX 732/506–5000, WEB www.oceancountygov.com). **Wildwoods Information Center** (✉ Box 609, Wildwood 08260, ☎ 609/522–1407 or 800/992–9732, WEB www.wildwoodsnj.com).

ELSEWHERE IN NEW JERSEY

The Northwest Corner

What to See and Do

This sparsely developed region of small lakes and low mountains attracts skiers in winter; the rest of the year brings outdoorsy types who come to enjoy water sports on the Delaware River and Lake Hopatcong, scenic roads, hikes on the Appalachian Trail, and historical sites from the 18th and 19th centuries.

The state's highest elevation (1,803 ft) is in **High Point State Park** (☞ State Parks, *above*), 7 mi northwest of Sussex. Hugging the river from ★ I–80 to the northern tip of the state is the **Delaware Water Gap National Recreation Area** (☞ National Parks, *above*). **Waterloo Village** (✉ Waterloo Rd., Stanhope, ☎ 973/347–0900, WEB www.waterloovillage.org) is a restored early 19th-century canal town. The summer concert series attracts renowned jazz, classical, rock, and country performers. **Skylands Park** (✉ Rte. 565 E, Augusta, ☎ 973/579–7500 or 888/652–2737, WEB www.njcards.com), home to the minor-league New Jersey Cardinals, is a great place to see a ball game for under $10 or catch the park's occasional fireworks show. There is also a baseball museum and batting cages.

Campgaw Mountain Ski Area (✉ 200 Campgaw Rd., Mahwah, ☎ 201/327–7800, www.skicampgaw.com) is very compact (two chairlifts, two handle-tows, one T-bar, eight trails) and good for learning how to ski or snowboard. **Hidden Valley** (✉ Rte. 515, Vernon, ☎ 973/764–4200, WEB www.hiddenvalleynj.com) is a lively alternative, with three chairlifts and 12 trails. **Mountain Creek** (✉ Rte. 94, Vernon, ☎ 973/827–2000, WEB www.mountaincreek.com) is the biggest ski resort in New Jersey, with 52 trails on three mountains and state-of-the-art equipment.

Dining and Lodging

MILFORD

$$ ✕ **Ship Inn.** New Jersey's first brewpub serves home brews and more than a dozen British draught ales. The fare includes burgers and British specialties such as shepherd's pie. ✉ *61 Bridge St.,* ☎ *908/995–7007 or 800/651–2537,* WEB *www.shipinn.com. AE, MC, V.*

$$ **Chestnut Hill on the Delaware.** The rocker-lined veranda of this 1860-vintage B&B has some beautiful views. There's also a country cottage with carousel horses, modern conveniences, and absolute privacy. ✉ 63 Church St. (Box N, 08848), ☎ 908/995–9761, FAX 908/995–0608, WEB www.chestnuthillnj.com. 6 rooms, 1 cottage. No credit cards. No smoking.

STANHOPE

$$ **Whistling Swan Inn.** Tiger-oak woodwork and an octagonal tower room with a conical ceiling are among the features of this 1904 house, now a lovely Victorian B&B. In a tiny village in New Jersey's highlands, the inn is close to winter skiing and ice-skating, summer water sports on the lakes, and cultural activities in Waterloo Village; the Delaware River is a 25-minute drive away. ✉ *110 Main St., 07874,* ☎ *973/347–6369,* FAX *973/347–3391,* WEB *www.whistlingswanninn.com. 10 rooms. AE, D, MC, V. BP.*

WALPACK CENTER

$–$$$ ✕ **Walpack Inn.** The only restaurant within the boundaries of the Delaware Water Gap National Recreation Area has been here since 1949. Lobster comes solo (two tails) or with steak. The Swedish brown bread is so popular it's sold by the loaf. Deer usually prance by in the field beyond the skylit greenhouse dining room. The rustic piano bar, with a fieldstone fireplace and mounted moose, bear, and deer heads, is worth the trip in itself. ✉ *Rte. 615, 4 mi due south of Walpack Center Historic District,* ☎ *973/948–9849 or 973/948–6505. MC, V. Closed Mon.–Thurs. No lunch.*

The Northwest Corner Essentials

CAR TRAVEL

There's easy access from northwestern New Jersey to Manhattan via I–80 and Routes 23 and 15.

Along the Delaware

What to See and Do

Forming New Jersey's "other shore" (its border with Pennsylvania), the Delaware slowly changes from a relatively small, often rock-studded river in the north to a mighty, navigable river as it flows past Philadelphia and empties into Delaware Bay. The towns that line it change as well. Part of the way down the state, quaint towns like **Milford, Frenchtown, Stockton,** and, the largest of these, **Lambertville** hug the river below ridges and rolling hills beyond. Gracing the pastoral scenery are 18th-century buildings, galleries, antiques and crafts stores, excellent restaurants, and B&Bs and inns. Across the bridge from Lambertville is the artsy town of **New Hope,** in Bucks County (☞ Pennsylvania). Inland a bit, **Flemington** also has some antiques stores but is best known for its outlets. Flemington's **Liberty Village** (✉ 1 Church St., ☎ 908/782–8550) has more than 60 factory and designer outlets.

★ **Washington Crossing State Park** (✉ Rte. 546, Titusville, ☎ 609/737–0623, WEB www.state.nj.us/dep/forestry/parks/washcros.htm) is the site of Washington's Christmas-night 1776 crossing (reenacted each Christmas Day). Follow Washington's trail south to the state capital, **Trenton,** previously a colonial pottery and manufacturing center, today a small city struggling with a quiet rebirth. One of Trenton's gems is **Chambersburg,** also known as the Burg, a residential neighborhood with dozens of superb Italian restaurants. Washington surprised the sleeping Hessians in the **Old Barracks** (✉ Barrack St., Trenton, ☎ 609/396–1776, WEB www.barracks.org; 🎫 $6), now a museum. The two-centuries-old **New Jersey State Museum** (✉ 205 W. State St., Trenton, ☎ 609/292–6464, WEB www.state.nj.us/state/museum; 🎫 free) has exhibits in archaeology and ethnology, cultural history, fine arts, and natural history, along with a planetarium, which offers nighttime laser rock shows on the weekend. Washington followed his victory in Trenton with one in **Princeton,** to the north. The two battles were the first major victories for the Continental Army. Princeton is now a pretty university town, with upscale shops and the governor's mansion, **Drumthwacket** (✉ 354 Stockton St., ☎ 609/683–0057; 🎫 free), which is open March–July and September–December, Wednesday noon–2 PM.

South of Trenton, the gritty industrial town of **Camden** is enjoying some degree of revitalization along its waterfront. The **Thomas H. Kean New Jersey State Aquarium** (✉ 1 Riverside Dr., ☎ 856/365–3300, WEB www.njaquarium.org; 🎫 $12.95) has added **C.O.O.L.** (Conservation Outreach and Observation Lab), a highly interactive area focusing on South and Central America, the Caribbean and the Indo-Pacific, to its award-winning **Ocean Base Atlantic exhibit,** which features interactive displays and an artful underwater effect that makes you feel like you're entering the marine home of more than 4,000 fish. The **Camden Children's Garden,** a 4-acre interactive horticultural playground (✉ 3 Riverside Dr., ☎ 856/365–8733, WEB www.camdenchildrensgarden.org; 🎫 $5, aquarium and Children's Garden $12.95) has such exhibits as a giant tree house, dinosaur fossil area, and a carousel ride.

Within walking distance along Camden's waterfront is the $56 million **Tweeter Center** (✉ 1 Harbour Blvd., ☎ 856/365–1300, WEB www.tweetercenter.com/philadelphia). The state-of-the-art amphitheater accommodates 25,000 people, including 18,000 on the lawn. The **USS *New Jersey* Battleship Museum** (✉ 62 Battleship Pl., Camden, ☎ 856/966–1652, WEB www.battleshipnewjersey.org; 🎫 $10) is one of the most decorated battleships in the history of the U.S. navy, now a floating museum. Camden's unlikely literary heritage includes **Walt Whitman's house** (✉ 328–330 Mickle Blvd., ☎ 856/964–5383, WEB www.ci.camden.nj.us/walt.html; 🎫 free) and his **tomb** in the Harleigh Cemetery (✉ Vesper and Haddon Aves.); the house is open Wednesday–Sunday.

Dining and Lodging

FRENCHTOWN

$$$ ✕ **Frenchtown Inn.** This 1805 former tavern and boardinghouse is one of the state's most romantic restaurants. Top-notch, modern, French-influenced cuisine is served in three beautiful dining rooms, including the less-formal Grill Room, which serves wonderful salads, meat, pasta dishes, and fish entrées, such as grilled salmon with hollandaise

sauce and red wine au jus. ✉ *5 Bridge St.,* ☎ *908/996–3300,* WEB *www.frenchtowninn.com. AE, MC, V.*

$$ **Widow McCrea House.** Built in the 1870s, this grand Victorian is a short walk from the center of Frenchtown. Those wishing to venture farther away can borrow bikes and on return can enjoy afternoon tea and evening cordials. All rooms are furnished in period antiques and outfitted with feather beds; some have whirlpool tubs and fireplaces. ✉ *53 Kingwood Ave., 08825,* ☎ *908/996–4999,* WEB *www.widowmccrea.com. 4 rooms, 1 cottage. AE, MC, V. CP.*

LAMBERTVILLE

$$$ **Chimney Hill Bed & Breakfast.** This circa-1820 stone manor house sits on 8 acres above the town of Lambertville. Rooms have canopy beds and fireplaces; there are four with kitchens and studies. The candlelight breakfast includes homemade pastries, Belgian waffles, and French toast. Afternoon port, sherry, and tea are served. ✉ *207 Goat Hill Rd., 08530,* ☎ *609/397–1516 or 800/211–4667,* WEB *www.chimneyhillnj.com. 12 rooms. AE, MC, V. CP.*

$$–$$$ **Inn at Lambertville Station.** This well-run small hotel overlooks the Delaware River. ✉ *11 Bridge St., 08530,* ☎ *609/397–8300 or 800/524–1091,* FAX *609/397–9744,* WEB *www.lambertvillestation.com. 45 rooms. Restaurant. AE, MC, V.*

STOCKTON

$$–$$$ **The Woolverton Inn.** This pretty inn in a 1792 stone manor house is situated on a 10-acre, tree-lined property. ✉ *6 Woolverton Rd., 08559,* ☎ *609/397–0802 or 888/264–6648,* WEB *www.woolvertoninn.com. 8 rooms, 1 cottage. AE, MC, V. CP.*

$–$$$ **The Stockton Inn.** In 1934 Richard Rodgers and Lorenz Hart escaped from Manhattan to this inn, which inspired their musical *On Your Toes* and its song "There's a Small Hotel with a Wishing Well." The wishing well still stands in the terraced garden. Built as a private home in 1710, the inn became a stagecoach stop in 1796 and a hotel in 1832 (it now comprises five houses). Historic touches remain—eight bedrooms and the five dining rooms have working fireplaces. The restaurant serves contemporary American and Continental fare Memorial Day to Labor Day. ✉ *1 Main St. (Box C, 08559),* ☎ *609/397–1250,* WEB *www.stocktoninn.com. 11 rooms. Restaurant. AE, DC, MC, V. CP.*

Along the Delaware Essentials

CAR TRAVEL

From Manhattan the New Jersey Turnpike skirts the area, and U.S. 1 and I–195 are key access roads. From Philadelphia I–95 runs up the Pennsylvania side of the river, crossing north of Trenton, while I–295 and the New Jersey Turnpike parallel it on the Jersey side.

VISITOR INFORMATION

➤ TOURIST INFORMATION: **Camden Waterfront Marketing Bureau** (✉ One Port Center, 2 Riverside Dr., Suite 102, Camden 08103, ☎ 856/757–9400, WEB www.camdenwaterfront.com). **Trenton Convention and Visitors Bureau** (✉ Lafayette and Barrack Sts., Trenton 08608, ☎ 609/292–2470 or 609/777–1770, WEB www.trentonnj.com/travel.tcvb.html).

North Jersey

What to See and Do

Although Newark International Airport is all some travelers experience of this part of the state, a wealth of activities are available to those who care to linger. Among the suburban bedroom communities of Manhattan-bound commuters are parks, performing-arts venues, museums, great shopping, and some of the state's finest restaurants and lodgings.

Jersey City, at first glance merely gritty and urban, is nonetheless worth a visit—most obviously for its superb views of the broad Hudson River and the Manhattan skyline. **Liberty State Park** (✉ New Jersey Turnpike Exit 14B, ☎ 201/915–3400, WEB www.state.nj.us/dep/forestry/parks/liberty.thm) is the departure point for ferries to the Statue of Liberty and the Ellis Island Immigration Museum. Within the park is the restored, open-sided 1889 **Central Railroad of New Jersey Terminal,** now used for special events and exhibits. You can also stroll along **Liberty Walkway,** a waterfront promenade. The **Liberty Science Center** (✉ 251 Phillip St., ☎ 201/200–1000, WEB www.lsc.org; 🎟 $10) has three floors of hands-on and interactive exhibits and a Kodak Omni Theater (a domed screen 88 ft across and 125 ft high).

The "mile-square" city of **Hoboken** has several claims to fame. It was the setting for the movie *On the Waterfront*; the birthplace of baseball, first played on Elysian Fields (at the site of the now-defunct Maxwell House plant) in 1846; and the hometown of Frank Sinatra. Though its relationship with Old Blue Eyes was a love-hate one—Sinatra spurned his hometown after being pelted with fruit at a concert there in 1952—hard feelings seem to have been put aside since his death in 1998. Today Hoboken feels like it could be another borough of New York City: many Manhattanites have settled here, bringing the city's active nightlife, soaring rents, and parking problems with them. Yuppified **Washington Street** is the main drag.

Hoboken has always been a big artist community, and many artists open their studios for an annual tour in October. A plaque marks **Sinatra's birthplace** (✉ 415 Monroe St.), destroyed by fire in 1967. **Frank Sinatra Way,** hugging the bank of the Hudson River, commands some of the best views in town. A new waterfront park was named in Sinatra's honor shortly after his death, and many of the town's long-standing businesses display faded photos of the singer. **Maxwell's** (✉ 1039 Washington St., ☎ 201/798–0406, WEB www.nj.com/maxwell's) is the granddaddy of Hoboken music clubs, with a solid reputation (Manhattanites will actually cross the river to come here) for presenting eclectic—and sometimes well-known—alternative-music acts.

Newark, the state's largest city, is making a remarkable comeback from many years of economic stagnation and urban decay. The **New Jersey Performing Arts Center** (✉ 1 Newark Center, between Military Park and waterfront, ☎ 888/466–5722, WEB www.njpac.org) is one of the major factors in Newark's renewal. It attracts internationally recognized performers, such as Itzhak Perlman and the Alvin Ailey dance troupe as well as sellout crowds to its intimate 514-seat Victoria Theater and 2,750-seat Prudential Hall. The $180 million facility has two restaurants, parking facilities, and a landscaped plaza and is the home of the New Jersey Symphony Orchestra. The **Newark Museum** (✉ 49 Washington St., ☎ 973/596–6550 or 800/768–7386, WEB www.newarkmuseum.org; 🎟 free) has outstanding fine-arts, science, and industry collections; its restored Ballantine House, a National Historic Landmark, has two floors of Victorian period rooms and decorative arts. It's open Wednesday–Sunday. Newark's **Ironbound District,** east of Newark Penn Station, is a Portuguese neighborhood popular for its ethnic restaurants. Ferry Street is the main drag.

★ The **Edison National Historic Site** (✉ Main and Lakeside Ave., West Orange, ☎ 973/736–0550, WEB www.nps.gov/edis/home.htm; 🎟 $2), on the site of Thomas Alva Edison's former home, includes the inventor's main laboratory, machine shop, and library and replicas of many of his creations. The site was scheduled to close in August 2002 for several years of renovations.

In Millburn, the **Paper Mill Playhouse** (✉ Brookside Dr., ☎ 973/376–4343, WEB www.papermill.org) has long been regarded as one of the finest off-Broadway theaters, with a constantly changing slate of plays and musicals.

To the west, outside suburban Morristown, is the **Morristown National Historical Park/Jockey Hollow** (✉ Washington Pl., ☎ 973/539–2085, WEB www.nps.gov/morr; 🎫 $4), where George Washington and his Continental Army camped during the winter of 1779–80. The park includes the elegant Ford Mansion, once Washington's quarters, and replicas of the soldiers' log huts.

From Morristown U.S. 202 leads south past antiques shops and farm stands. This is horse country, with estates and meadows edged with wood fencing, especially around **Bedminster.** Many horse farms are off U.S. 202 on Route 523. At the headquarters of the **U.S. Equestrian Team** (✉ Rtes. 512 and 206, Gladstone, ☎ 908/234–1251, WEB www.uset.com; 🎫 free), you can visit the stables and the trophy room, which displays the team's Olympic medals, photos, and other mementos. Competitions, including a major festival in June, are held throughout the year. The complex is open on weekdays.

The U.S. Golf Association keeps its museum, **Golf House** (✉ Rte. 512, ☎ 908/234–2300, WEB www.usga.org; 🎫 free), in Far Hills.

The **Great Swamp National Wildlife Refuge** (✉ Basking Ridge, ☎ 973/425–1222; 🎫 free) encompasses 7,300 acres of wildlife sanctuary, crossed with 8½ mi of trails, blinds, and boardwalks.

For wildlife of a different sort, the **Meadowlands Racetrack,** at the Meadowlands Sports Complex (✉ Rte. 3 and New Jersey Turnpike, East Rutherford, ☎ 201/935–8500, WEB www.thebigm.com), has Thoroughbred racing in the fall, with harness racing and simulcasts from other tracks the rest of the year. Check local newspapers for gate times. Pegasus (✉ 600 Meadowlands Pkwy., Secaucus, ☎ 201/935–8500) is the most upscale of the four restaurants on site.

The **Secaucus Outlet Center** (☎ 201/392–9756, WEB www.secaucusoutlets.com) has acres and acres of outlet shops that put this city on the map.

Dining and Lodging

BERGENFIELD

$$$ ✕ **Chez Dominique.** Tables at this romantic French restaurant are small and candlelit, and the mood is elegantly cozy. The menu changes often but has included bouillabaisse, coq au vin, and roasted duck à la orange. Bring your own wine. ✉ *Bedford Ave.,* ☎ *201/384–7637,* WEB *www.chezdominique.com. Reservations essential. DC, MC, V. Closed Sun.–Mon.*

EAST RUTHERFORD

$$–$$$ ✕ **Park & Orchard.** Vegetarians appreciate the many meatless dishes, including meat- and dairy-free lasagna and vegetarian shepherd's pie, at this cavernous, noisy, and always busy spot. Non–red meat entrées such as boneless chicken breast and shrimp stir-fry are also available. The 1,900-bottle wine list has won many awards; the house wines are usually terrific choices. Save room for the peanut-butter pie. ✉ *240 Hackensack St.,* ☎ *201/939–9292,* WEB *www.parkandorchard.com. AE, D, DC, MC, V.*

SHORT HILLS

$$$–$$$$ ★ ✕🏨 **Hilton Short Hills Hotel and Spa.** This is one of New Jersey's finest hotels. Its gourmet restaurant, the Dining Room, receives raves for its French-influenced contemporary American cuisine, which is served as a multicourse tasting menu only, and the hotel's beautiful spa is reason enough for a visit. The Mall at Short Hills, across the road, is great for tony shopping, including a Neiman Marcus—and, unlike its sister store in the town of Paramus, it's open on Sunday. ✉ *41 JFK Pkwy., 07078,* ☎ *973/379–0100 or 800/445–8667,* FAX *973/379–6870,* WEB *www.spaatshorthills.com. 304 rooms. 2 restaurants, pool, health club. AE, D, MC, V.*

TENAFLY

$$$ 🏨 **Clinton Inn Hotel.** Tucked into a pretty suburban neighborhood, the Clinton Inn is especially popular for weddings and other special occasions. Good food and personalized service are the hallmarks. ✉ *145 Dean Dr., 07670,* ☎ *201/871–3200 or 800/275–4411,* FAX *201/871–3435,* WEB *www.clinton-inn.com. 119 rooms. Restaurant, gym. AE, D, DC, MC, V.*

WEST ORANGE

$$–$$$ ✕ **The Manor.** Countless romantic evenings have been lived out at this local institution, which serves American and Continental cuisine. The menu changes seasonally but may include pan-seared foie gras; caramelized day-boat scallops with mushroom crepes; and, for dessert, Tahitian vanilla crème brûlée or a Sacher torte. There's live piano music in the Terrace Lounge and dancing weekends in Le Dome nightclub, which has a cigar bar, too. ✉ *111 Prospect Ave.,* ☎ *973/731–2360,* WEB *www.themanorrestaurant.com. Jacket required. AE, D, DC, MC, V. Closed Mon.*

North Jersey Essentials

CAR TRAVEL

From Manhattan take either the Lincoln Tunnel or the George Washington Bridge, and you're in North Jersey. I–80, to the north, and I–78, through Jersey City and Newark, connect with the New Jersey Turnpike, the Garden State Parkway, and I–287, which all run northeast–southwest through the region.

VISITOR INFORMATION

There is no main tourist information center for North Jersey, but the web site www.hobokeni.com has background information and entertainment listings for the city of Hoboken.

NEW MEXICO

Updated by Jeanie Puleston Fleming

Capital	Santa Fe
Population	1,819,046
Motto	It Grows as It Goes
State Bird	Roadrunner
State Flower	Yucca
Postal Abbreviation	NM

Statewide Visitor Information

New Mexico Department of Tourism (✉ Lamy Bldg., 491 Old Santa Fe Trail, Santa Fe 87503, ☎ 505/827–7400 or 800/733–6396, FAX 505/827–8594, WEB www.newmexico.org). For outdoor activity information, contact the **USDA Forest Service, Southwestern Region** (✉ Public Affairs Office, 517 Gold Ave. SW, Albuquerque 87102, ☎ 505/842–3292, WEB www.fs.fed.us/r3). For information about New Mexico's Native American reservations, contact the **Indian Pueblo Cultural Center** (✉ 2401 12th St. NW, Albuquerque 87102, ☎ 505/843–7270,WEB www.indianpueblo.org).

Scenic Drives

The old **High Road** is not the most direct route from Santa Fe to Taos, but it takes you through hills studded with orchards and tiny picturesque villages set against a rugged mountain backdrop. No visit to northern New Mexico is complete without the 100-mi trip along the **Enchanted Circle,** a breathtaking panorama of deep canyons, passes, alpine valleys, and towering mountains of the verdant Carson National Forest. **Route 66,** America's most nostalgic highway, includes a colorful stretch that now constitutes Albuquerque's Central Avenue. A scenic route between Albuquerque and Santa Fe, the **Turquoise Trail** (Route 14) snakes up through a portion of Cibola National Forest and several mining semi-ghost towns.

National and State Parks

National Parks

Carlsbad Caverns National Park is a spectacular system of caves and rock formations; **White Sands National Monument** is a white wonderland of gypsum sand dunes (☞ *both* Elsewhere in New Mexico, *below*).

State Parks

New Mexico's 33 state parks range from the high mountain lakes and pine forests of the north to the Chihuahuan Desert lowlands in the south. Pristine and unspoiled, they have every conceivable outdoor recreational facility. For maps and brochures contact the **State Parks and Recreation Division** (✉ Energy, Minerals, and Natural Resources Dept., 2040 S. Pacheco St. [Box 1147, Santa Fe 87504-1147], ☎ 505/827–7173 or 888/667–2757, FAX 505/827–1376,WEB www.emnrd.state.nm.us/nmparks).

Native American Reservations

Pueblo Indians established an agricultural civilization here many centuries ago. Nomadic tribes—the Navajo, Mescalero Apache, and Jicarilla Apache—came into the area much later. The settlements of various Pueblo peoples are described in the Albuquerque and Santa Fe sections. Note: When visiting Indian lands, it's important to respect all rules and requests regarding photography, videotaping, recording, and sketching. Some pueblos charge a fee for these activities; others ban them outright. The pueblos generally welcome visitors, but they expect their sovereignty to be respected.

The **Jicarilla Apache Tribe** (✉ Box 507, Dulce 87528, ☎ 505/759–3242, FAX 505/759–3005, WEB www.jicarillaonline.com) lives on a 750,000-acre reservation in north-central New Mexico. The tribe allows tourists to fish and camp on a 15,000-acre preserve.

A reservation of a half-million acres of timbered mountains and green valleys in southeastern New Mexico is home to the **Mescalero Apache Tribe** (✉ Tribal Office, 101 Central [Box 227, Mescalero 88340], ☎ 505/671–4494,WEB www.newmexico.org/culture/res_mescalero.html). The tribe owns and operates one of the most elegant luxury resorts in the state, Inn of the Mountain Gods, as well as Ski Apache, 16 mi from Ruidoso.

The Navajo Reservation, where the largest Native American group in the United States lives, covers 17.6 million acres in New Mexico, Arizona, and Utah. There are a few towns on the reservation, but for the most part it is a vast area of stark pinnacles, colorful rock formations, high desert, and mountains. The tribe encourages tourism; write or call the **Navajo Nation Tourism Office** (✉ Box 663, Window Rock, AZ 86515, ☎ 520/871–6436 or 520/871–7371, FAX 520/871–7381, WEB www.navajoland.com).

ALBUQUERQUE

A large city (metro area population is about 670,000), Albuquerque spreads out in all directions. As in the rest of New Mexico, Albuquerque's Native American, Spanish, and Anglo cultures are well blended. The city began as an important trade and transportation station on the Camino Real–Chihuahua Trail, which wound down into Mexico. Albuquerque remains a travel crossroads today. The original four-block core, known as Old Town, is the city's tourist hub, with unique shops, galleries, museums, and restaurants.

Exploring Albuquerque

Historic and colorful Route 66 is Albuquerque's Central Avenue, unifying as nothing else can the diverse areas of the city: Old Town, to the west, cradled at the bend of the Rio Grande; the downtown business and government centers; the University of New Mexico to the east; and, farther east, Nob Hill, a lively strip of restaurants, boutiques, galleries, and shops. The railroad tracks, running north and south, and east–west Central Avenue divide the city into quadrants: southwest (SW), northwest (NW), southeast (SE), and northeast (NE).

The city began in 1706 in what is now Old Town, and tree-shaded **Old Town Plaza** remains the heart of Albuquerque's heritage. Most of the old adobe houses surrounding the plaza have been converted into charming shops, galleries, and restaurants. The massive adobe walls of **San Felipe de Neri Church** (✉ 2005 Plaza NW, ☎ 505/243–4628) date from 1793; the church still serves an active congregation.

The **Albuquerque Museum of Art and History** (✉ 2000 Mountain Rd. NW, ☎ 505/243–7255, WEB www.cabq.gov/museum; 🎟 $2) showcases traditional and contemporary art of New Mexico and has an outstanding collection of Spanish colonial art. The striking glass-and-sandstone **New Mexico Museum of Natural History and Science** (✉ 1801 Mountain Rd. NW, ☎ 505/841–2800, WEB museums.state.nm.us/nmmnh; 🎟 $5) presents a simulated volcano, a frigid Ice Age cave, dinosaurs, and a six-minute high-tech ride through 35 million years of New Mexico's geologic history. The spectacular two-story **Indian Pueblo Cultural Center** (✉ 2401 12th St. NW, ☎ 505/843–7270, WEB www.indianpueblo.org; 🎟 free, museum $4) has a museum that holds one of the largest collections of Native American arts and crafts in the Southwest. The 19 Pueblo tribes of New Mexico each operate separate alcoves where they display and sell their arts and crafts. Free performances of ceremonial dances are given on most weekends and on special holidays. On Albuquerque's western fringe lies **Petroglyph National Monument** (✉ 4735 Unser Blvd. NW, ☎ 505/899–0205, WEB www.nps.gov/petr; 🎟 weekdays $1 per car, weekends $2 per car), which contains more than 15,000 ancient rock drawings inscribed as early as AD 1300 in the volcanic rocks and cliffs.

Sandia Peak Aerial Tramway (✉ 10 Tramway Loop NE, ☎ 505/856–7325, WEB www.sandiapeak.com; 🎟 $15), among the world's longest, makes an awesome 2¾-mi climb from the edge of the city to a point near 10,678-ft Sandia Crest for a panorama of Albuquerque—and half of New Mexico. At sunset the sky is a kaleidoscope of colors over the desert. At the **Explora Science Center and Children's Museum of Albuquerque** (✉ Winrock Shopping Center, I–25 and Louisiana NE, ☎ 505/842–1537, www.esccma.org/information; 🎟 $4), arts and cultural exhibits, a computer lab, and the Make-It-Take-It Art Room keep youngsters entertained for hours. Leave time for the hands-on science center, where changing exhibits allow kids to conduct their own experiments.

Spend an afternoon at **Albuquerque Biological Park** (✉ 903 10th St. SW, ☎ 505/764–6200, WEB www.cabq.gov/biopark; 🎟 $5), an environmental museum that includes the **Albuquerque Aquarium, Rio Grande Zoo,** and **Rio Grande Botanic Garden.** The eel cave and shark tank are real kid pleasers, and the zoo houses more than 1,000 animals, including elephants, bison, koalas, and endangered Mexican wolves, known as *lobos*. Wander through the beautiful gardens, which showcase plants from the Southwest and other climates.

Outside Albuquerque

Coronado State Monument and Park (✉ off I–25 on Rte. 44 [Box 95, Bernalillo 87004], ☎ 505/867–5351, WEB www.museumofnewmexico.org/CoronadoStateMonument), a prehistoric Native American pueblo once known as Kuaua, sits on a bluff overlooking the Rio Grande near Bernalillo, 20 mi north of Albuquerque; it is believed to have been the headquarters of Coronado's army of 1,200, who came seeking the legendary Seven Cities of Gold in 1540.

The beautiful **San Jose de los Jemez Mission** (☎ 505/829–3530; 🎟 $2), a stone structure built in 1622, is at the Jemez State Monument, 60 mi north of Albuquerque in Jemez Springs.

Pueblos near Albuquerque

Made up of a series of terraced adobe structures and dominated by the massive mission church of San Estevan del Rey, **Acoma Pueblo** (☎ 505/470–4966 or 800/747–0181, WEB www.puebloofacoma.org; 🎟 $10, including guided tour) sits atop a 367-ft mesa that rises abruptly from the valley floor 64 mi west of Albuquerque. Most of its people now live on the valley floor but retain traditional residences on the mesa. Also known as Sky City, the pueblo may be visited only on paid, guided tours. Pueblo artists sell their prized thin-walled pottery.

Jemez Pueblo (☎ 505/834–7359, WEB www.newmexico.org/culture/pueblo_jemez.html; 🎟 free), 51 mi northwest of Albuquerque, is the state's sole Towa-speaking pueblo. It is noted for its polychrome pottery and fine yucca-frond baskets. **Santo Domingo Pueblo** (☎ 505/465–2214, WEB www.newmexico.org/culture/pueblo_santodomingo.html; free), off I–25 at the Santo Domingo exit between Albuquerque and Santa Fe, operates a Tribal Cultural Center, where its outstanding *heishi* (shell) jewelry is sold. The August Four Corn Dance is one of the most colorful and dramatic of all the Pueblo ceremonial dances. The sun symbol appearing on New Mexico's flag was adopted from the **Zia Pueblo** (✉ off I–25, northwest from the Bernalillo exit between Albuquerque and Santa Fe, ☎ 505/867–3304, WEB www.newmexico.org/culture/pueblo_zia.html; free), which has been at its present site since the early 1300s. Skillful Zia potters make polychrome wares, and painters produce highly prized watercolors.

Dining

$$–$$$$ ★ ✕ **Artichoke Café.** Grilled duck, pumpkin ravioli with fresh spinach and butternut squash, and rack of lamb with rosemary-merlot sauce are a few specialties served in this turn-of-the-20th-century brick building east of downtown. The large, modern, bi-level dining room spills onto a small courtyard. ✉ *424 Central Ave. SE,* ☎ *505/243–0200. AE, D, DC, MC, V. Closed Sun. No lunch Sat.*

$$–$$$$ ✕ **High Finance Restaurant and Tavern.** To get to this restaurant in the center of Cibola National Park, you must either take the Sandia Peak Tram, hike 3 mi into the park, or ski through the Sandia Ski Area. On the edge of Sandia Peak, more than 10,000 ft above sea level, it's a sublime place to watch a New Mexico sunset; every seat in the house has a view that spans 11,000 square mi. Entrées run along the steak, seafood, and pasta lines. ✉ *40 Tramway Rd. NE,* ☎ *505/243–9742. Reservations essential. AE, D, DC, MC, V. Closed Apr. and Nov.*

$$–$$$ ✕ **Maria Teresa.** This nationally preserved landmark, next to the Sheraton, is a restored 1840s adobe with 32-inch-thick brick adobe walls, fireplaces, early Spanish-American furnishings, and gardens. Aged beef, seafood, chicken, and New Mexican specialties, such as *carne adovada* (cubed pork marinated and baked in red chili), are served. ✉ *618 Rio Grande Blvd. NW,* ☎ *505/242–3900. AE, DC, MC, V.*

$$–$$$ ✕ **Monte Vista Fire Station.** Now a national historic landmark, this spacious, airy restaurant was once a working firehouse. The American menu includes seafood, beef, and pasta dishes; highlights are crab ravioli and duck with raspberry coulis. ✉ *3201 Central Ave. NE,* ☎ *505/255–2424. AE, D, DC, MC, V. No lunch weekends.*

$–$$ ★ ✕ **Scalo Northern Italian Grill.** Bankers and bikers gather at this lively, informal restaurant with an open kitchen and full-service bar. In addition to excellent pizza, Scalo serves such dishes as spinach-and-ricotta-stuffed pasta in a light cream sauce and grilled salmon with a balsamic-citrus glaze. ✉ *3500 Central Ave. SE, in the Nob Hill Business Center,* ☎ *505/255–8781. AE, D, MC, V. No lunch Sun.*

Lodging

$$–$$$ **Brittania & W. E. Mauger Estate B&B.** Popular with professionals because of its location and updated business services, this fine B&B is situated in an 1897 Queen Anne Victorian with an Old West front veranda and hardwood floors. ✉ *701 Roma Ave. NW, 87102,* ☎ *505/242–8755 or 800/719–9189,* FAX *505/842–8835,* WEB *www.maugerbb.com. 8 rooms. AE, D, DC, MC, V. BP.*

$–$$ **Barcelona Suites.** Filled with tiles and wrought iron, the public spaces of this colorful hotel off I–40 evoke Old Mexico, whereas the rooms have a southwestern aesthetic. Complimentary breakfast and evening cocktails are served around the atrium fountain. Each two-room suite has a galley kitchen with a wet bar and microwave oven. ✉ *900 Louisiana Blvd. NE, 87110,* ☎ *505/255–5566 or 877/227–7848,* FAX *505/266–6644,* WEB *www.barcelonasuiteshotel.com. 164 suites. Pools. AE, D, MC, V. CP.*

$–$$ **Best Western Rio Grande Inn.** Rooms in this Best Western have handcrafted wood furniture, tin sconces, and artwork from local artisans. The hotel is conveniently off I–40 and within an easy walk of Old Town. ✉ *1015 Rio Grande Blvd. NW, 87104,* ☎ *505/843–9500 or 800/959–4726,* FAX *505/843–9238,* WEB *www.riograndeinn.com. 173 rooms. Restaurant, pool.*

$–$$ **La Posada de Albuquerque.** A tiled lobby fountain, an encircling balcony, massive vigas, and Native American war-dance murals are a few of the atmospheric touches that set this historic hotel apart—thanks to New Mexico native Conrad Hilton, who opened the hotel in 1939. Hopi pottery and R. C. Gorman prints lend character to the rooms. ✉ *125 2nd St. NW, 87102,* ☎ *505/242–9090 or 800/777–5732,* FAX *505/242–8664,* WEB *www.laposada-abq.com. 112 rooms. Restaurant. AE, D, DC, MC, V.*

Campgrounds

Within Albuquerque, there are tent sites and RV facilities at the **Albuquerque KOA Central** (✉ 12400 Skyline Rd. NE, 87123, ☎ 505/296–2729). North of town is the **Albuquerque North Bernalillo KOA** (✉ 555 S. Hill Rd. [Box 758, Bernalillo 87004], ☎ 505/867–5227). Fifteen minutes south of Albuquerque on I–25, the **Isleta Lakes and Recreation Area** (✉ Box 383, Isleta 87022, ☎ 505/877–0370) has complete campground facilities with tent sites and RV hookups.

Nightlife and the Arts

To find out what's going on in town, check the *Albuquerque Journal* on Friday and Sunday or the *Albuquerque Tribune* on Thursday.

The Arts

Founded in 1932, the **New Mexico Symphony Orchestra** (✉ 3301 Menaul Blvd. NE, Suite 4, ☎ 505/881–8999, WEB www.nmso.org) performs classical and contemporary music and has a children's program.

Outdoor Activities and Sports

The **Kodak Albuquerque International Balloon Fiesta** (☎ 888/422–7277 or 505/821–1000, WEB www.balloonfiesta.com) is the world's largest gathering of balloonists. For a week each October, ballooning competitions and exhibitions fill the skies over the city. You can hire a pilot and balloon from **Rainbow Ryders** (✉ 11520 San Bernadino NE, ☎ 505/823–1111). **World Balloon Corporation** (✉ 4800 Eubank NE, ☎ 505/293–6800) can safely take you up and away.

Shopping

To find dozens of one-of-a-kind shops, meander down the tiny lanes and small plazas of **Old Town.** With several major retailers and more than 160 specialty shops, **Coronado Center** (✉ Louisiana and Menaul Blvds., ☎ 505/881–4600) is the largest mall in the state. Albuquerque's newest shopping venue, **Cottonwood Mall** (✉ Coors Blvd. at Coors Bypass, ☎ 505/899–7467), has 147 shops. **Winrock Center** (✉ Louisiana Blvd. exit off I–40, ☎ 505/888–3038) has 90 shops and restaurants, including New Mexico's largest Dillard's. **Nob Hill,** a seven-block strip of shops stretching along Central Avenue from Girard to Washington Street, is the city's newest and trendiest shopping district. Neon-lighted boutiques, restaurants, galleries, and performing-arts spaces encourage strolling and people-watching.

Albuquerque Essentials

AIRPORTS AND TRANSFERS

Albuquerque International Sunport is 5 mi south of downtown; the trip takes 10–15 minutes.

➤ AIRPORT INFORMATION: **Albuquerque International Sunport** (☎ 505/842–4366).

AIRPORT TRANSFERS

Taxis charge $15–$20 plus tip between the airport and downtown. In Albuquerque, Sun Tran buses pick up on the baggage claim level about every 20 minutes; the fee is 75¢.

➤ TAXIS AND SHUTTLES: **Sun Tran** (☎ 505/843–9200).

BUS TRAVEL

Albuquerque is served by Greyhound and TNMO Coaches Transportation Center.

➤ BUS INFORMATION: **Greyhound** (✉ 300 2nd St. SW, ☎ 800/231–2222). **TNMO Coaches Transportation Center** (✉ 300 2nd St. SW, ☎ 505/243–4435 or 800/231–2222).

CAR TRAVEL

I–25 enters Albuquerque from points north and south; I–40, from points east and west.

TRAIN TRAVEL

Amtrak serves the Albuquerque station.

➤ TRAIN INFORMATION: **Amtrak** (✉ 214 1st St. SW, ☎ 505/842–9650 or 800/872–7245).

VISITOR INFORMATION

➤ TOURIST INFORMATION: **Convention and Visitors Bureau** (✉ 20 First Plaza NW [Box 26866, 87125], ☎ 505/842–9918 or 800/284–2282, WEB www.abqcvb.org).

SANTA FE

With its crisp, clear air and bright, sunny weather, New Mexico's capital couldn't be more welcoming. Perched on a 7,000-ft plateau at the base of the Sangre de Cristo Mountains, Santa Fe is surrounded by the remnants of a 2,000-year-old Pueblo civilization and filled with evidence of the Spanish, who founded the city as early as 1607. Rows of chic art galleries, smart restaurants, and shops selling southwestern furnishings and apparel combine to give the city an unusual cosmopolitan flair. Its population, an estimated 65,000, swells to nearly double that during the peak summer season and to a lesser degree in the winter, with the arrival of skiers.

Exploring Santa Fe

Before setting out on your exploration of Santa Fe, consider purchasing the four-day **museum pass** (🎫 $10), which will admit you to Santa Fe's four state museums (Museum of Fine Arts, Museum of Indian Arts and Culture, Museum of International Folk Art, and Palace of the Governors). The pass is available at any of the museums. Admission to the museums is free on Friday 5–8.

★ The heart of Santa Fe is its historic **Plaza.** Emerging as early as 1607 as the city's social and political hub, it was later the terminus of the

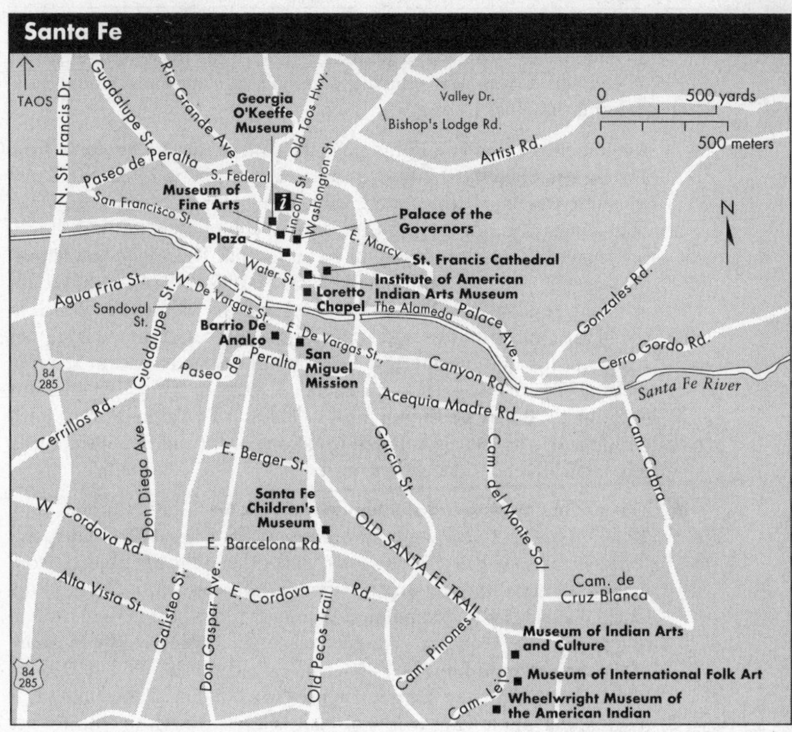

Santa Fe Trail, where freight wagons unloaded after completing their arduous journeys. Today the Plaza is lined with shops, art galleries, and restaurants. Fronting the Plaza is the oldest public building in the ★ United States: the Pueblo-style **Palace of the Governors** (✉ N. Plaza, ☎ 505/476–5100, WEB www.palaceofthegovernors.org. 🎫 $5. Closed Mon.) built by the Spanish as the seat of their colonial government. The Palace houses the **State History Museum.** Under the palace's portal, Native American artisans display and sell their wares.

Built in Pueblo Revival style, the **Museum of Fine Arts** (✉ 107 W. Palace Ave., ☎ 505/476–5072, WEB www.museumofnewmexico.org. 🎫 $5. Closed Mon. Jan.–June) displays the works of regional artists, as well as those of early Modernist painters who migrated to Santa Fe and Taos in the early 20th century, putting Taos and Santa Fe on the national map as vibrant arts communities. The **Georgia O'Keeffe Museum** (✉ 217 Johnson St., ☎ 505/995–0785, WEB www.okeeffemuseum.org. 🎫 $8. Closed Wed. Nov.–June) houses the world's largest collection of art by O'Keeffe. One of the many artists who have drawn their inspiration from the unique beauty of the New Mexico landscape, O'Keeffe is one of the few whose work has achieved worldwide fame.

The magnificent French Romanesque–style **St. Francis Cathedral** (✉ 231 Cathedral Pl., ☎ 505/982–5619) contains the crypt of Jean Baptiste Lamy, Santa Fe's first archbishop, and the statue *La Conquistadora* (Our Lady of the Conquest), carried to Santa Fe in 1692 by Don Diego de Vargas. If you walk to the southern edge of the cathedral grounds, you will come to the **Archives of the Archdiocese,** a museum of historic church artifacts. In a renovated former post office, the **Institute of American Indian Arts Museum** (✉ 108 Cathedral Pl., ☎ 505/983–8900, WEB www.iaiancad.org/museum.htm; 🎫 $4) holds the more than 8,000-object **National Collection of Contemporary Indian Art.**

Its paintings, photography, and traditional crafts showcase the work of students and teachers, past and present, of the prestigious **Institute of American Indian Arts,** which was founded as a one-room studio classroom in the early 1930s.

A number of Santa Fe's sights trace the path of the **Old Santa Fe Trail.** The **Loretto Chapel** (✉ 207 Old Santa Fe Trail, ☎ 505/982–0092, WEB www.lorettochapel.com; 🎫 $2.50) is known for its Miraculous Staircase—an engineering marvel leading to the choir loft; many of the faithful believe the staircase was built by St. Joseph. The adobe **San Miguel Mission** (✉ 401 Old Santa Fe Trail, ☎ 505/983–3974; 🎫 $1), built in about 1625 by the Tlaxcala Indians and the oldest church still in use in the continental United States, has a number of priceless statues and paintings and the San Jose Bell, said to have been cast in Spain in 1356. This site has been known to close early in winter, so schedule accordingly. **Barrio De Analco** (now called East De Vargas Street), lined with historic houses, is believed to be one of the oldest continuously inhabited streets in the United States.

★ The fascinating **Museum of International Folk Art** (✉ 706 Camino Lejo, ☎ 505/476–1200, WEB www.moifa.org. 🎫 $5. Closed Mon.) displays textiles, dolls, jewelry, ornaments, and other folk art objects from many countries. It is among the premier museums of its kind in the world. Rearing up from a piñon-and-juniper forest behind the Museum of International Folk Art is the privately owned **Wheelwright Museum of the American Indian** (✉ 704 Camino Lejo, ☎ 505/982–4636, WEB www.wheelwright.org; 🎫 free), housed in a building shaped like a traditional Navajo hogan; works of many Native American cultures are on exhibit. The **Museum of Indian Arts and Culture** (✉ 710 Camino Lejo, ☎ 505/476–1250, WEB www.miaclab.org; 🎫 $5) interweaves the history and contemporary culture of New Mexico's Pueblo, Navajo, and Apache tribes.

Outside Santa Fe

Forty-five minutes (about 40 mi) northwest of Santa Fe, **Los Alamos,** birthplace of the atomic bomb, spreads over fingerlike mesas at an altitude of 7,300 ft. You can drop in on the interesting **Bradbury Science Museum** (✉ 15th St. at Central Ave., ☎ 505/667–4444, WEB www.lanl.gov/worldview/museum/visiting.shtml; 🎫 free). The Los Alamos area abounds with archaeological sites, including **Bandelier National Monument** (✉ HCR1, off Rte. 4 about 12 mi from Los Alamos, ☎ 505/672–3861, WEB www.nps.gov/band; 🎫 $10 per car for 7 days), which contains the remains of one of the largest Anasazi population centers.

A kind of Williamsburg of the Southwest, **El Rancho de las Golondrinas** (✉ 334 Los Pinos Rd., in the village of La Cienega, ☎ 505/471–2261, WEB www.golondrinas.org; 🎫 $5, $7 during festivals. Closed Nov.–Mar.), 15 mi south of Santa Fe off I–25, is a reconstruction of a small, traditional 19th-century New Mexico farming village, complete with grinding mills, a blacksmith shop, animals, working fields, homes, and a *morada* (meeting place) of the Penitente order.

About 25 mi southeast of Santa Fe via I–25 north, **Pecos National Historical Park** (✉ Rte. 63 [Box 418, Pecos 87552], ☎ 505/757–6032, WEB www.nps.gov/peco; 🎫 $3 per person for 7 days) is the site of a once-flourishing Native American pueblo. An early trading center, Pecos was the largest and easternmost pueblo reached by the Spanish conquistadors in 1541. Franciscan priests built a mission church here in the 1620s, but the pueblo was abandoned in 1838 because of disease and raiding nomadic tribes.

Pueblos near Santa Fe

The Native American pueblos near Santa Fe vary in their crafts specialties and in the recreational facilities they offer tourists. On feast days, most have ceremonial dances that are open to the public, but call ahead for regulations. To find out when pueblo events are held, call the **Eight Northern Pueblos** office (☎ 505/852–4265).

About 20 mi north of Santa Fe on U.S. 84/U.S. 285 is **Pojoaque Pueblo** (✉ Rte. 11, Santa Fe, ☎ 505/455–2278, WEB www.newmexico.org/culture/pueblo_pojoaque.html). The pueblo operates an official **state tourist center** on U.S. 285/U.S. 84, with an extensive selection of northern New Mexican arts and crafts. Pojoaque Pueblo's **Poeh Museum** (☎ 505/455–2489, WEB www.poehcenter.com; free) is a cultural center focusing on the Tewa-speaking Native Americans. **San Ildefonso Pueblo** (✉ Rte. 5, Santa Fe, ☎ 505/455–3549; $3 per car), north of Route 502, about 15 mi east of Los Alamos, was the home of the most famous of all pueblo potters, Maria Martinez, whose exquisite polished black-on-black pottery is revered among collectors. A number of highly acclaimed potters, as well as other artists and craftspeople, are still at work here.

San Juan Pueblo (✉ U.S. 74 [take Rte. 68 1 mi north of Espanola, turn left onto U.S. 74 at sign, entrance is 1 mi farther], ☎ 505/852–4400, WEB www.newmexico.org/culture/pueblo_sanjuan.html) is headquarters of the Eight Northern Indian Pueblos Council. In its beautiful arts center, the **Oke Oweenge Crafts Cooperative,** the pueblo's distinctive redware and micaceous clay pottery can be purchased. Two handsome kivas and a New England–style church are other attractions. **Santa Clara Pueblo** (✉ Rte. 30, 4 mi south from Espanola, crossing the Rio Grande, Espanola, ☎ 505/753–7326, WEB www.newmexico.org/culture/pueblo_santaclara.html) is famous for its shiny red-and-black engraved pottery and for its many painters and sculptors. Tours are conducted on weekdays. The beautiful 740-room **Puyé Cliff Dwellings** ($5) is a national landmark believed to have been built between the 13th and 14th centuries.

Dining

$$$–$$$$ ✕ **Coyote Cafe.** Try the "Cowboy"—a 22-ounce rib-eye steak served with barbecued black beans and red chili–dusted onion rings. Other favorites are the squash-blossom and corn-cake appetizers. From April through October, the restaurant opens its less-expensive Rooftop Cantina, which serves Mexican fare. ✉ *132 W. Water St.,* ☎ *505/983–1615. AE, D, DC, MC, V.*

$$–$$$$ ★ ✕ **Café Pasqual's.** A block southwest of the Plaza, this cheerful, informal café decked out with chile ristras is known for fabulous brunches of huevos rancheros and quesadillas with apple-smoked bacon, as well as chicken mole and grilled Chimayo chili–rubbed New York steak with serrano mayonnaise. Expect a line. ✉ *121 Don Gaspar Ave.,* ☎ *505/983–9340. AE, MC, V.*

$$–$$$$ ★ ✕ **The Compound.** This restaurant changed ownership in 2000 but retained designer Alexander Girard's spacious and elegant interiors. The seasonal menu includes year-round favorites such as tuna tartar with caviar, a mouth-watering beef tenderloin with foie gras hollandaise, and liquid chocolate cake. There's patio dining in warm weather. ✉ *653 Canyon Rd.,* ☎ *505/982–4353. Dinner reservations essential. AE, MC, V. No lunch Mon.–Thurs.*

$$–$$$ ✕ **El Nido.** Since 1920 this former dance hall and trading post has been known for its cozy, firelit rooms and menu of choice aged beef and seafood. ✉ *U.S. 285, 6 mi north of Santa Fe to Tesuque exit, then 1½* *mi to restaurant, ☎ 505/988–4340. AE, D, DC, MC, V. Closed Mon. No lunch.*

$–$$$ ✕ **Pink Adobe.** The old adobe walls add a magical touch to the dining experience at this cozy restaurant, which has been operating for more than 50 years. Perennial specials on the menu are steak Dunnigan, smothered in green chili and mushrooms; and savory shrimp Louisianne—fat and crispy deep-fried shrimp. ✉ *406 Old Santa Fe Trail, ☎ 505/983–7712. AE, D, DC, MC, V. No lunch weekends.*

$–$$ ✕ **Guadalupe Café.** A local favorite, this informal café serves up New Mexican dishes, including sizable *sopapillas* (fluffy fried bread). The seasonal raspberry pancakes are one of many breakfast favorites that keep the place crowded every morning. Generous salads, homemade bread, and guacamole enchiladas are all popular. ✉ *422 Old Santa Fe Trail, ☎ 505/982–9762. Reservations not accepted. D, DC, MC, V.*

$–$$ ✕ **The Shed.** It's in the rambling adobe hacienda that once belonged to the Sena family, dating from 1692. Try the red-chili enchiladas or *posole* (hominy stew). Expect a line at lunchtime. ✉ *113½ E. Palace Ave., ☎ 505/982–9030. Reservations not accepted for lunch. AE, DC, MC, V. Closed Sun.*

Lodging

$$$$ **Bishop's Lodge.** Three miles north of downtown Santa Fe, in the foothills of the Sangre de Cristo Mountains, this 45-acre resort has rooms in 15 one- and three-story lodges. Organized outdoor activities such as horseback riding abound, and there's a summer children's program. ✉ *Bishop's Lodge Rd., Santa Fe 87504, ☎ 505/983–6377 or 800/732–2240, FAX 505/989–8739, WEB www.bishopslodge.com. 111 rooms. Restaurant, pool, tennis, health club. AE, D, MC, V.*

$$$$ **Eldorado Hotel.** One of the city's most luxurious hotels, in the heart of downtown, has southwestern-style rooms in desert colors; many have fireplaces and balconies with mountain views. The Old House restaurant is outstanding. Evenings, there's live music in the lounge. ✉ *309 W. San Francisco St., 87501, ☎ 505/988–4455 or 800/955–4455, FAX 505/995–4455, WEB www.eldoradohotel.com. 219 rooms, 55 casitas. 2 restaurants, pool, health club. AE, D, DC, MC, V.*

$$$$ ★ **Inn of the Anasazi.** One of Santa Fe's finer hotels, the inn has rooms with beamed ceilings, kiva fireplaces, and handcrafted furnishings. The excellent restaurant serves a mix of American and cowboy cuisines. ✉ *113 Washington Ave., 87501, ☎ 505/988–3030 or 800/688–8100, FAX 505/988–3277, WEB www.innoftheanasazi.com. 59 rooms. Restaurant. AE, D, DC, MC, V.*

$$$$ **La Posada de Santa Fe Resort & Spa.** Most rooms have fireplaces, beamed ceilings, Native American rugs, and Spanish flair; the five rooms in the main building are drenched in Victoriana. The spa has a full-time staff for body treatments at additional charge. ✉ *330 E. Palace Ave., 87501, ☎ 505/986–0000 or 800/727–5276, FAX 505/982–6850, WEB www.laposadasantafe.com. 159 rooms. Restaurant, pool, health club. AE, DC, MC, V.*

$$$–$$$$ **Hotel Santa Fe.** This posh Native American–owned hotel has rooms with locally handmade furniture and Pueblo paintings. Its gift shop sells works by Picurís and other Pueblo Indian artists. Native American dances are performed during peak season (May–October). The Corn Dance Cafe serves Native American cuisine with a nouvelle twist. ✉ *1501 Paseo de Peralta, 87505, ☎ 505/982–1200 or 800/825–9876, FAX 505/984–2211, WEB www.hotelsantafe.com. 162 rooms. Restaurant. AE, D, DC, MC, V.*

$$$–$$$$ **Inn of the Governors.** This unpretentious inn, one of the nicest in town, is two blocks from the Plaza. Rooms have a Mexican theme, with bright colors, hand-painted folk art, southwestern fabrics, and handmade furnishings. Price includes breakfast buffet. ✉ *101 W. Alameda St., 87501,* ☎ *505/982–4333 or 800/234–4534,* FAX *505/989–9149,* WEB *www.innofthegovernors.com. 100 rooms. Restaurant, pool. AE, DC, MC, V.*

$$$–$$$$ **La Fonda.** The oldest hotel in Santa Fe may be the only one that has hosted both Kit Carson and John F. Kennedy. Each room is unique, with hand-crafted Spanish colonial–style furniture and motifs painted by local artists. ✉ *100 E. San Francisco St., 87501,* ☎ *505/982–5511 or 800/523–5002,* FAX *505/988–2952,* WEB *www.lafondasantafe.com. 167 rooms. Restaurant, pool. AE, D, DC, MC, V.*

$$–$$$ **Inn of the Turquoise Bear.** This rambling inn on the edge of downtown was fashioned out of the 30-room estate of the late poet Witter Bynner, who hosted Willa Cather, W. H. Auden, Thornton Wilder, and Errol Flynn, among other notables. Rooms, in many shapes and sizes, are tastefully furnished; though not lavish, they exude character. Most have fireplaces, and some open onto private courtyards. ✉ *342 E. Buena Vista St., 87501,* ☎ *505/983–0798 or 800/396–4104,* FAX *505/988–4225,* WEB *www.turquoisebear.com. 11 rooms. AE, D, MC, V.*

$$–$$$ **Territorial Inn.** This 100-year-old Victorian home is two blocks from the Plaza. Some rooms have their own fireplaces. Fifteen of the guest rooms and a light-filled breakfast room are in a new annex off the back patio. ✉ *215 Washington Ave., 87501,* ☎ *505/989–7737 or 800/745–9910,* FAX *505/984–8482,* WEB *www.territorialinn.com. 25 rooms, 2 with shared bath. AE, D, MC, V.*

Campgrounds

Los Camposde Santa Fe RV Resort (✉ 3574 Cerrillos Rd., 87505, ☎ 505/473–1949 or 900/852–8160) is a full-service RV park. Children and pets are welcome. The **Santa Fe National Forest** (✉ 1220 S. St. Francis Dr. [Box 1689, 87504], ☎ 505/438–7840, WEB www.fs.fed.us/r3/sfe), right in Santa Fe's backyard, has public sites open May–October. **La Bajada Welcome Center** (✉ La Bajada Hill, 13 mi southwest of Santa Fe on I–25, ☎ 505/424–0823) provides information on private campgrounds near Santa Fe.

Nightlife and the Arts

Check the entertainment listings in Santa Fe's daily newspaper, the *New Mexican,* for performances and events. On Friday, the paper includes the arts and entertainment supplement, the *Pasatiempo,* which covers the gamut of gallery openings, movies, and community happenings, among other events. Or, check the free weekly *Santa Fe Reporter,* published on Wednesday, for its listing of current events.

Nightlife

At **Paramount** (✉ 331 Sandoval St., ☎ 505/982–8999) you can dance to live music and DJs. It hosts theme evenings, which include swing, salsa, and disco. **El Farol** (✉ 808 Canyon Rd., ☎ 505/983–9912) presents live blues, jazz, folk, and flamenco music in a rustic centuries-old adobe that's the oldest restaurant and cantina in Santa Fe. **Rodeo Nites** (✉ 2911 Cerrillos Rd., ☎ 505/473–4138) attracts a country-and-western crowd.

The Arts

The city's cultural crown jewel, the famed **Santa Fe Opera** (✉ U.S. 285, WEB www.santafeopera.org, ☎ 505/986–5900) performs every summer in a modern open-air amphitheater carved into a hillside 7 mi north of the city. In 2001 the old Lensic theater reopened as the totally renovated **Lensic Performing Arts Center** (✉ 211 W. San Francisco St., ☎

505/988–1234, WEB www.lensic.com), where many performances take place year-round. **Santa Fe Pro Musica** (☎ 505/988–4640) and the **Santa Fe Symphony** (☎ 505/983–1414, WEB www.sf-symphony.org) play here September–May. The **Santa Fe Chamber Music Festival** (☎ 505/983–2075) brings internationally known musicians to the Lensic and to St. Francis Auditorium at the Museum of Fine Arts from July to August.

Outdoor Activities and Sports

Bishop's Lodge (✉ Bishop's Lodge Rd., ☎ 505/983–6377) conducts trail rides from April through November. **Broken Saddle Riding Co.** (✉ High Desert Ranch in Cerrillos, ☎ 505/470–0074) leads excursions into the historic and scenic canyons of the Cerrillos hills, 23 mi southeast of Santa Fe.

Shopping

For an all-inclusive Santa Fe shopping experience with a global twist, drive north of town near the village of Tesuque for the weekend **Tesuque Pueblo Flea Market** (✉ U.S. 84/285, 7 mi north of Santa Fe). May–October it's open Friday as well. The market closes altogether January–mid-February.

Santa Fe Essentials

AIRPORTS AND TRANSFERS

Albuquerque International Sunport serves Santa Fe, too. For charter flights between Albuquerque and Santa Fe, contact the Albuquerque airport or the Santa Fe Municipal Airport, which is 20 minutes southwest of downtown.

➤ AIRPORT INFORMATION: **Albuquerque International Sunport** (☎ 505/842–4366). **Santa Fe Municipal Airport** (☎ 505/473–7243).

AIRPORT TRANSFER

Shuttle bus service from the Albuquerque International Sunport to Santa Fe is available through Sandia Shuttle; the trip takes 70 minutes and runs 10 times per day. The cost is $20 one-way.

➤ TAXIS AND SHUTTLES: **Sandia Shuttle** (☎ 505/474–5696).

BUS TRAVEL

Santa Fe can be reached via Greyhound.

➤ BUS INFORMATION: **Greyhound** (✉ 858 St. Michael's Dr., ☎ 505/471–0008 or 800/231–2222).

CAR TRAVEL

Santa Fe is accessible from points north and south on I–25 or U.S. 84/285. It is 60 mi north of Alburquerque on I–25.

TAXIS

➤ TAXI COMPANIES: **Capital City Cab Company** (☎ 505/438–0000).

TRAIN TRAVEL

The Amtrak station nearest to Santa Fe is in Lamy; Amtrak runs a shuttle bus service from Lamy 17 mi to Santa Fe.

➤ TRAIN INFORMATION: **Amtrak** (☎ 800/872–7245 reservations and national schedules). **Amtrak Lamy Shuttle Service** (☎ 505/982–8829 in Santa Fe). **Lamy Station** (☎ 505/466–451 local station information only).

TRANSPORTATION AROUND SANTA FE

Santa Fe's downtown core is easily maneuvered on foot. The city's public bus system is limited, so you'll need a car to visit attractions in the outer reaches.

VISITOR INFORMATION

➤ TOURIST INFORMATION: **Convention and Visitors Bureau** (✉ 201 W. Marcy St. [Box 909, 87504], ☎ 505/955–6200 or 800/777–2489, FAX 505/955–6222, WEB www.santafe.org).

TAOS

At the base of the rugged Sangre de Cristo Mountains about 60 mi northeast of Santa Fe, Taos is a small town steeped in the history of New Mexico. Stately elms and cottonwood trees, narrow streets, and a profusion of adobe all cast a lingering spell; the charming old Plaza, surrounded by art galleries and boutiques, adds to the allure. Georgia O'Keeffe, Ansel Adams, and D. H. Lawrence are among Taos's former residents; so are such Wild West figures as Kit Carson and New Mexico's first governor, Charles Bent. Taos Ski Valley is a famed ski resort in winter and a hiking and mountain-biking venue in the summer.

Exploring Taos

At the base of 12,282-ft Taos Mountain, 2 mi north of the town plaza, **Taos Pueblo** (☎ *505/758–9593,* WEB www.indianpueblo.org/ipcc/taospage.htm; 🎫 $10) is the home of the Taos Tiwa-speaking Indians, whose apartment house–style pueblo dwelling is one of the oldest continuously inhabited communities in the United States. Life here predates Marco Polo's 13th-century travels in China and the arrival of the Spanish in America in 1540. Unlike many nomadic Native American tribes forced to relocate to government-designated reservations, these people have resided at the base of the Taos Mountain for centuries; this continuity has made possible the link between pre-Columbian inhabitants who originally lived in the Taos Valley and their descendants who reside there now. Special feast days are the Corn Dance held May 3 and San Geronimo Day, September 30. The pueblo is closed to outsiders for several weeks annually, often in March and April.

Four miles south of Taos in the farming and ranching community of Ranchos de Taos is the beautiful **San Francisco de Asís Church** (✉ NM 68 south of NM 518, ☎ *505/758–2754*). Its massive, buttressed adobe walls and graceful towers are a prime example of early Mission architecture. Generations of painters and photographers, including Georgia O'Keeffe and Ansel Adams, have been inspired by the earthy, clean lines of the exterior walls and supporting bulwarks, which cast eerie shapes and shadows.

Dining and Lodging

$$–$$$ ✕ **Doc Martin's.** This pleasant, casual restaurant in the Historic Taos Inn has imaginative specials such as piñon-crusted salmon with anchovy pesto sauce and Southwest lacquered duck. Don't skip the superb desserts: Aztec chocolate mousse with roasted-banana sauce or coconut-milk crème brûlée. ✉ *125 Paseo del Pueblo Norte,* ☎ *505/758–1977. AE, D, MC, V.*

$–$$$ ✕ **Trading Post Cafe.** Perfectly marinated salmon gravlax; first-rate paella; excellent pasta, fowl, and fresh fish; a great wine list; and homemade raspberry sorbet are some of the reasons this chic yet comfortable restaurant attracts a crowd. ✉ *4179 Rte. 68, at Rte. 518, Ranchos de Taos,* ☎ *505/758–5089. MC, V. Closed Sun.–Mon.*

$$ ✕ **Apple Tree.** Named for the large tree in the umbrella-shaded courtyard, this is a great lunch and early dinner spot in a historic adobe one block from the Plaza. The food is fresh—among the well-crafted dishes are grilled lamb and chicken fajitas. The restaurant has received regular awards for its wine selection. Sunday brunch is served. ✉ *123 Bent St.,* ☎ *505/758–1900. AE, D, DC, MC, V.*

$$ ✕ **Bravo!** Casual but not tacky, this restaurant and full bar inside an upscale grocery store and beer-and-wine shop is a great stop for gourmet picnic fixings or an on-site meal. The fare runs the gamut from hearty sandwiches to escargots–and there's a children's menu as well. ✉ *1353-A Paseo del Pueblo Sur,* ☎ *505/758–8100. Reservations not accepted. MC, V. Closed Sun.*

$ ★ ✕ **Taos Cow's Casa Vaca Deli & Cafe.** Taos Cow has expanded its original world headquarters for tasty ice cream (made from growth-hormone-free milk) into the former Casa Fresen Bakery building in Arroyo Seco. It's a magnet for locals in need of a sandwich, coffee, tea, chai, pastries, cookies, and fresh-baked bread from the kitchen inside. Favorites among the three-dozen ice cream flavors are Cherry Ristra, Piñon Caramel, and—the true test—Vanilla. ✉ *482 Hwy. 150,* ☎ *505/776–5640.*

$$$$ ★ **Inn at Snakedance.** The Taos Ski Valley forms a stunning backdrop to this spotlessly clean resort hotel right on the ski slopes. The dining room, part of an older building, has a soaring ceiling with 100-year old beams and a polished wood bar frequented by off-duty ski instructors. Generously sized rooms, many with fireplaces, have a southwestern theme. Come in summer to score bargain rates here (a double for $75 per night, or three nights for $140); the hotel also has summer courses in cooking and outdoor fitness. ✉ *Off Taos Ski Valley Rd. (CR 150, Box 89, Taos Ski Valley 87525),* ☎ *505/776–2277 or 800/322–9815,* FAX *505/776–1410,* WEB *www.innsnakedance.com. 60 rooms. AE, DC, MC, V.*

$$–$$$$ **Touchstone Inn.** Nestled against the Taos Pueblo land, this B&B enjoys magnificent views of the mountains. Each luxury guest room has a kiva fireplace, a whirlpool bath, and antiques. The owner, Bren Price, is an artist, and her work is displayed throughout the inn. ✉ *110 Mabel Dodge La., 87571,* ☎ *800/758–0192,* FAX *505/758–3498,* WEB *www.touchstoneinn.com. 8 rooms. MC, V.*

$$–$$$ **Casa Europa.** Pastures and mountains surround this spacious 17th-century pueblo-style adobe B&B outside town. The delightful rooms have kiva fireplaces and marble bathrooms; there's also a five-room suite with a hot tub. Gourmet breakfasts are served every morning and European-style homemade pastries every afternoon—except during ski season, when there are fireside hors d'oeuvres in the evenings instead. A hot tub and sauna soothe ski-weary muscles. ✉ *840 Upper Ranchitos Rd. (HC 68, Box 3F, 87571),* ☎ FAX *505/758–9798,* ☎ *888/758–9798,* WEB *www.casaeuropanm.com. 7 rooms. AE, MC, V. BP.*

$$–$$$ **Historic Taos Inn.** Steps from Taos Plaza, this local landmark is listed on the National Register of Historic Places. The lobby, with its popular Adobe Bar, is built around an old town well, from which a fountain now bubbles forth. Rooms have Native American–style wood-burning fireplaces and furniture built by local artists. ✉ *125 Paseo del Pueblo Norte, 87571,* ☎ *505/758–2233 or 800/826–7466,* FAX *505/758–5776,* WEB *www.taosinn.com. 36 rooms. Restaurant. AE, D, MC, V.*

$$ **San Geronimo Lodge.** Set on 2½ acres outside of Carson National Forest, this lodge was originally constructed in 1925 by an Oklahoma socialite wanting to accommodate her friends. Rooms have handcrafted furniture, and most have kiva fireplaces. A hot tub and massage services are added bonuses. ✉ *1101 Witt Rd., 87571,* ☎ *505/751–3776 or 800/894–4119,* FAX *505/751–1493,* WEB *www.SanGernonimoLodge.com. 18 rooms. Pool. AE, MC, V. BP.*

$–$$$ ★ **Mabel Dodge Luhan House.** D. H. and Frieda Lawrence, Georgia O'Keeffe, and Willa Cather stayed at this National Historic Landmark hotel, once the home of Taos socialite Mabel Dodge Luhan. The guest rooms in the main house are simple but tasteful; there's also a two-bedroom gatehouse cottage. Two of the rooms do not have private baths. ✉ *240 Morada La., 87571,* ☎ *505/751–9686 or 800/846–2235,* FAX *505/737–0365,* WEB *www.mabeldodgeluhan.com. 17 rooms, 2 with shared bath; 1 cottage. AE, MC, V.*

Campgrounds

Carson National Forest Service (✉ 208 Cruz Alta Rd., Taos 87571, ☎ 505/758–6200, WEB www.fs.fed.us/r3/carson) provides information about the many camping sites in the forest. **Taos RV Park** (✉ Rte. 68 [Box 729TCVG, Ranchos de Taos 87557], ☎ 505/758–1667 or 800/323–6009), with 29 spaces, is open year-round.

Outdoor Activities and Sports

Cross-Country Skiing

Carson National Forest (✉ 208 Cruz Alta Rd., Taos 87571, ☎ 505/758–6200, WEB www.fs.fed.us/r3/carson) has 440 mi of trails. **Enchanted Forest/Miller's Crossing Cross-Country Ski Area** (✉ Box 219, Red River 87558, ☎ 505/754–2374 or 800/966–9381, WEB www.enchantedforestxc.com), about 40 mi NE of Taos, has 24 mi of trails.

Downhill Skiing

Angel Fire Resort (✉ Drawer B, Angel Fire 87710, ☎ 505/377–6401 or 800/633–7463, WEB www.angelfireresort.com) has a 2,077-ft drop, 67 trails, and 5 lifts. **Red River Ski Area** (✉ Box 900, Red River 87558, ☎ 505/754–2223, FAX 505/754–6184, WEB www.redriverskiarea.com) has a 1,600-ft drop, 58 trails, and 6 lifts. **Sipapu Lodge and Ski Area** (✉ Box 29, Vadito 87579, ☎ 505/587–2240, WEB www.sipapunm.com) has an 865-ft drop, 19 trails, and 3 lifts. **Taos Ski Valley** (✉ Box 90, Taos Ski Valley 87525, ☎ 505/776–2291, FAX 505/776–8596, WEB www.skitaos.org) has a whopping 2,612-ft drop, 72 trails, and 11 lifts.

Taos Essentials

AIRPORTS AND TRANSFERS

The Taos Municipal Airport, 12 mi west of the city, services only private planes and a commuter service to Albuquerque, Rio Grande Air.
➤ AIRPORT INFORMATION: **Rio Grande Air** (☎ 877/435–9742 or 505/737–0505, WEB www.riograndeair.com). **Taos Municipal Airport** (✉ U.S. 64, ☎ 505/758–4995).

AIRPORT TRANSFERS

Twin Hearts Express runs daily shuttle service from Taos to the Albuquerque airport ($40 one-way, $75 round-trip); reserve in advance. Faust's Transportation (☞ Taxis, *below*), in nearby El Prado, provides taxi service between the Taos airport and town (about $20) and a shuttle between the Albuquerque airport and Taos ($35 each way).
➤ SHUTTLE: **Twin Hearts Express** (☎ 505/751–1201 or 800/654–9456).

BUS TRAVEL

Texas, New Mexico & Oklahoma Coaches, a subsidiary of Greyhound/Trailways, runs buses once a day from Albuquerque to the Taos Bus Station. The trip is about three hours. Twin Hearts Express (☞ Airport Transfer, *above*) runs daily shuttle service between Taos and Santa Fe ($25 each way); reserve in advance.

➤ Bus Information: **Texas, New Mexico & Oklahoma Coaches** (✉ 1006 Paseo del Pueblo Sur, ☎ 505/758–1144).

CAR TRAVEL

The main route from Santa Fe to Taos is via U.S. 84/U.S. 285 to Route 68—a 70-mi drive with stunning river and canyon views. For spectacular mountain scenery, the High Road to Taos (☞ Scenic Drives, *above*) is tops and well worth the slightly longer drive (about two hours). From points north, take Route 522; from points east or west, take U.S. 64.

TAXIS

Faust's Transportation, in nearby El Prado, has a fleet of radio-dispatched cabs.

➤ Taxi Companies: **Faust's Transportation** (☎ 505/758–3410 or 800/830–3410).

TOURS

Taos Historical Trolley Tours provides three-hour narrated tours ($33 per person) of Taos Pueblo and of Taos cultural and historic sites. Tours depart twice a day from the Taos County Chamber of Commerce (☞ Visitor Information, *below*) and the Plaza.

➤ Fees and Schedules: **Historic Taos Trolley Tours** (☎ 505/751–0366, WEB www.taostrolleytours.com).

TRAIN TRAVEL

Amtrak provides service into Lamy Station, a half hour outside Santa Fe, in the opposite direction of Taos, but still the closest train station to Taos. Faust's Transportation (☞ Taxis, *above*) dispatches taxis to the train station.

➤ Train Information: **Amtrak** (☎ 800/872–7245). **Lamy Station** (✉ Rte. 41, Lamy 87500).

TRANSPORTATION AROUND TAOS

Taos radiates around a central plaza. The main street through town is Paseo del Pueblo Norte, coming down from Colorado; the route then becomes Paseo del Pueblo Sur and heads out toward Santa Fe. A car is a big help for exploring Taos, unless you choose lodging right downtown and don't plan on venturing out to Taos Pueblo or Ranchos de Taos.

VISITOR INFORMATION

➤ Tourist Information: **Taos County Chamber of Commerce** (✉ 1139 Paseo del Pueblo Sur [Drawer 1, Taos 87571], ☎ 505/758–3873 or 800/732–8267, WEB www.taoschamber.com).

ELSEWHERE IN NEW MEXICO

Carlsbad Caverns National Park

What to See and Do

★ **Carlsbad Caverns National Park** (✉ 3225 National Parks Hwy., Carlsbad 88220, ☎ 505/785–2232; 800/967–2283 ranger tours; WEB www.carlsbad.caverns.national-park.com; 🎫 $6) contains one of the world's largest and most spectacular cave systems: 83 caves, with huge subterranean chambers, fantastic rock formations, and delicate mineral sculptures. Only two caves, Carlsbad and Slaughter Canyon, are open to the public for regular tours, but some off-trail viewing options are available during special trips. At **Carlsbad Cavern** the descent to the 750-ft level is made by foot or elevator; either way, you will see the Big Room, large enough to hold 14 football fields. Reservations are essential a day in advance for tours of the relatively undeveloped **Slaughter Canyon Cave,** 25 mi from Carlsbad Cavern. The last few miles of the road are gravel, and there's a ½-mi trek up a 500-ft rise to reach the cave's entrance.

Carlsbad Caverns National Park is the area's main lure, but the town of **Carlsbad** is an interesting place to see as well. **Living Desert State Park** (✉ 1504 Miehls Dr., Carlsbad 88220, ☎ 505/887–5516, WEB www.emnrd.state.nm.us/nmparks; 🎟 $4) is worth a visit while you're in the area.

Dining and Lodging

$ ✕ **Lucy's Mexicali Restaurant & Entertainment Club.** All the standards are prepared at this family-owned oasis of great Mexican food, along with some not-so-standard items such as chicken fajita burritos, and Tucson-style chimichangas. Low-fat and fat-free Mexican dishes and microbrewery beers are served. Live entertainment is offered on weekends. ✉ *701 S. Canal St.,* ☎ *505/887–7714. AE, D, DC, MC, V.*

$ ★ 🏨 **Best Western Stevens Inn.** Classy accommodations and reliable service make this reasonably priced inn a steal. Some of the spacious rooms have kitchenettes. Prime rib and steaks are served in the evening at the motel's Flume Room, and Mexican food and sandwiches are served throughout the day at the Green Tree Room. ✉ *1829 S. Canal St. (Box 580, 88220),* ☎ *505/887–2851 or 800/730–2851,* FAX *505/887–6338,* WEB *www.bestwestern.com. 220 rooms. 2 restaurants. AE, D, DC, MC, V.*

Carlsbad Caverns National Park Essentials

AIR TRAVEL

Mesa Airlines provides air-shuttle service between Albuquerque International Sunport and Cavern City Air Terminal in Carlsbad.

➤ AIRLINES AND CONTACTS: **Mesa Airlines** (☎ 800/637–2247; 505/885–0245 in Carlsbad; WEB www.mesa-air.com/airlines.html).

CAR TRAVEL

The park is in the southeastern part of the state, 320 mi from Albuquerque via I–25, U.S. 380, and U.S. 285 and 167 mi west of El Paso, Texas, via U.S. 180.

VISITOR INFORMATION

➤ TOURIST INFORMATION: **Carlsbad Chamber of Commerce** (✉ 302 S. Canal St., 88220, ☎ 505/887–6516).

White Sands National Monument

What to See and Do

With shifting sand dunes 60 ft high, **White Sands National Monument** (✉ off U.S. 70/82, 15 mi southwest of Alamogordo or 52 mi east of Las Cruces, ☎ 505/679–2599, WEB www.nps.gov/whsa, 🎟 $3) encompasses 145,344 acres and the largest deposit of gypsum sand in the world. The monument, one of the few landforms recognizable from space, has displays in its visitor center that describe how the dunes were formed. A 17-minute introductory video that's very helpful if you intend to hike among the dunes is screened at the visitor center, where there's a gift shop, a snack bar, and a bookstore. A walk on the 1-mi **Big Dune Trail** will give you a good overview of the site. Backpackers' campsites are available by permit, obtainable at the visitor center, but there aren't any facilities.

Dining and Lodging

$ ✕ **Margo's.** *Chalupas* (beans, meat, and cheese served on crisp tortillas) are the specialty Mexican dish at family-owned Margo's in Alamogordo. In winter, *menudo,* made of hominy and tripe, is served hot and steaming. The southwestern dining room includes colorful blankets. ✉ *504 1st St.,* ☎ *505/434–0689. AE, D, MC, V.*

$ 🏨 **Days Inn.** Contemporary rooms with standard chain-motel quality have extra nice touches such as hair dryers and microwaves in every room. ✉ *907 S. White Sands Blvd., 88310,* ☎ *505/437–5090,* FAX *505/434–5667,* WEB *www.the.daysinn.com. 40 rooms. Pool, gym. AE, D, DC, MC, V. CP.*

White Sands National Monument Essentials

CAR TRAVEL

The park is in the south-central part of the state, 220 mi south of Albuquerque via I–25 and U.S. 70/82, and 95 mi north of El Paso, Texas, via U.S. 54 and U.S. 70/82.

VISITOR INFORMATION

➤ TOURIST INFORMATION: **White Sands National Monument** (✉ Box 1086, Holloman AFB, 88330, ☎ 505/679–2599, WEB www.nps.gov/whsa).

NEW YORK

Updated by J. Paull, D. Kirdahy, and J. Zarem

Capital	Albany
Population	18,138,000
Motto	Excelsior
State Bird	Bluebird
State Flower	Rose
Postal Abbreviation	NY

Statewide Visitor Information

New York State Division of Tourism (✉ 1 Commerce Plaza, Albany 12245, ☎ 518/474–4116 or 800/225–5697).

Scenic Drives

The **Taconic Parkway,** particularly the stretch from Hopewell Junction to East Chatham, passes through rolling hills, orchards, woods, and pastures reminiscent of England's Yorkshire countryside. To make a dramatic loop around the Adirondacks' **High Peaks** region, pick up Route 73 off the Northway (I–87) at Exit 30, drive northwest through Lake Placid, proceed on Route 86 through Saranac Lake, and then head southwest on Route 3 to Tupper Lake, due south on Route 30 to Long Lake, and east on Route 28N to North Creek. For information on the dozen officially designated scenic drives, call **New York State Travel Information Center** (☎ 800/225–5697).

National and State Parks

National Parks

The **Gateway National Recreation Area** (✉ Floyd Bennett Field, Bldg. 69, Brooklyn 11234, ☎ 718/338–3338) extends through Brooklyn, Queens, Staten Island, and into New Jersey. It includes the **Jamaica Bay Wildlife Refuge,** a good spot to see migrating birds; **Jacob Riis Park,** where a boardwalk stretches along the surfy Atlantic; plus various beaches, parklands, and facilities for outdoor and indoor festivals. **Fire Island National Seashore** (✉ 120 Laurel St., Patchogue 11772, ☎ 516/289–4810) offers Atlantic surf and beaches on a barrier island.

State Parks

New York has 150 state parks. The **Empire State Passport,** permitting unlimited entrance to the parks for a year (April–March), is available for $49 at most parks; you can also contact the **State Office of Parks and Recreation** (☎ 518/474–0456) or write for an application (✉ Passport, State Parks, Albany 12238).

NEW YORK CITY

Whatever you're looking for in a big-city vacation, you'll find it in New York. The city has a rich history, from the arrival of early Dutch settlers and the swearing in of George Washington as the first U.S. president to the influx of millions of immigrants in the late 19th and early 20th centuries. Today's New York City is known around the world for its distinctive skyline—even post–September 11, 2001—its first-rate museums and performing arts companies, and its status as the capital of finance, fashion, art, publishing, broadcasting, theater, and advertising. And, of course, New Yorkers themselves are world famous—if not always for their charm, at least for their panache, ethnic diversity, and street smarts.

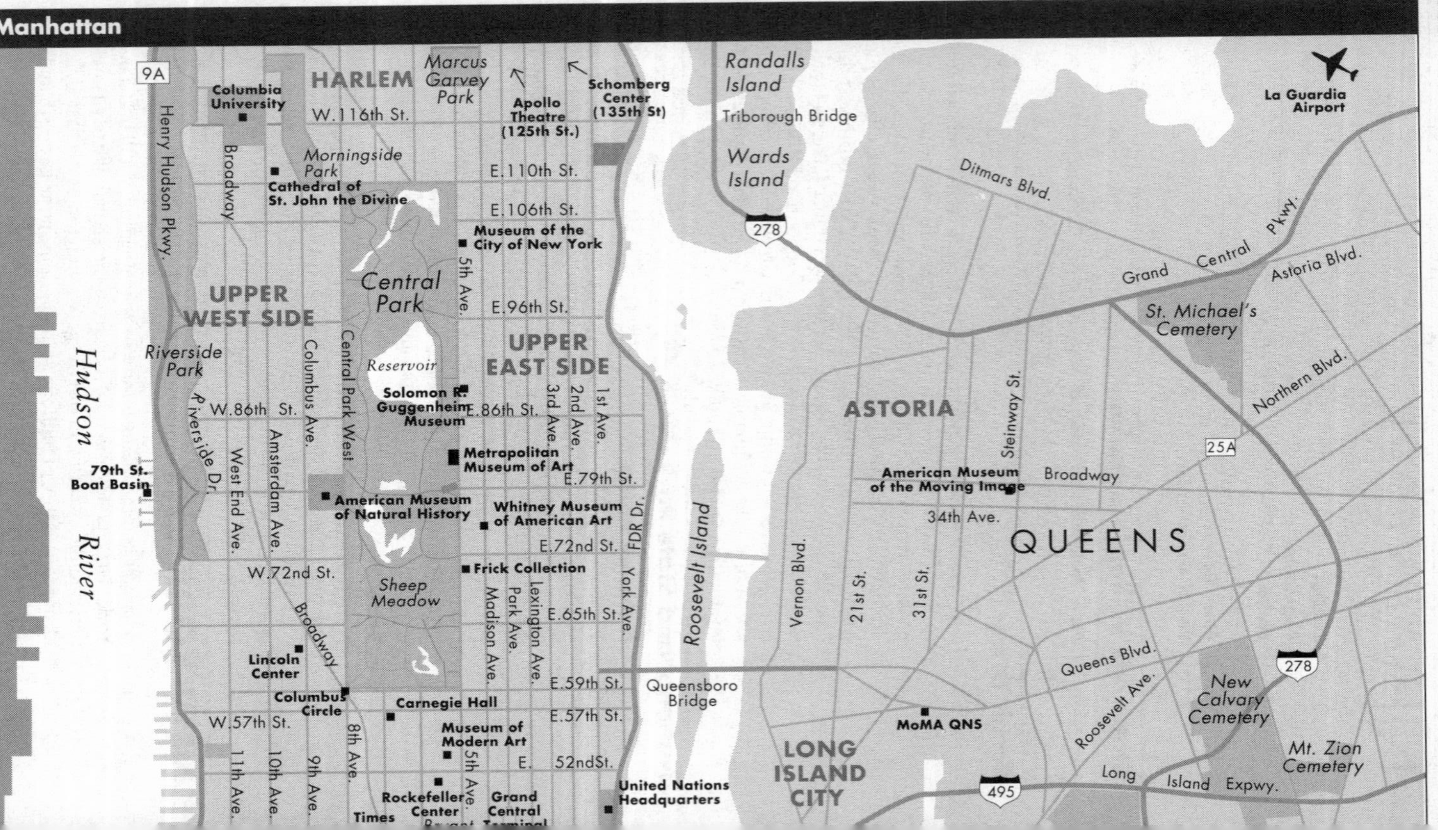

Manhattan
9A
Columbia University
HARLEM
Marcus Garvey Park
W. 116th St.
Apollo Theatre (125th St.)
Schomberg Center (135th St)
Randalls Island
Triborough Bridge
Wards Island
278
La Guardia Airport
Henry Hudson Pkwy.
Broadway
Morningside Park
Cathedral of St. John the Divine
E. 110th St.
E. 106th St.
Museum of the City of New York
Ditmars Blvd.
Grand Central Pkwy.
Astoria Blvd.
St. Michael's Cemetery
UPPER WEST SIDE
Central Park
5th Ave.
E. 96th St.
UPPER EAST SIDE
Riverside Park
Reservoir
Hudson River
Solomon R. Guggenheim Museum
E. 86th St.
3rd Ave.
2nd Ave.
1st Ave.
W. 86th St.
Riverside Dr.
Columbus Ave.
Central Park West
Amsterdam Ave.
West End Ave.
ASTORIA
Steinway St.
Northern Blvd.
25A
Metropolitan Museum of Art
E. 79th St.
79th St. Boat Basin
American Museum of Natural History
Whitney Museum of American Art
American Museum of the Moving Image
Broadway
34th Ave.
E. 72nd St.
FDR Dr.
QUEENS
W. 72nd St.
Frick Collection
Sheep Meadow
Madison Ave.
Park Ave.
Lexington Ave.
E. 65th St.
York Ave.
Roosevelt Island
Vernon Blvd.
21st St.
31st St.
Lincoln Center
Queens Blvd.
E. 59th St.
Queensboro Bridge
Roosevelt Ave.
New Calvary Cemetery
Columbus Circle
Carnegie Hall
E. 57th St.
W. 57th St.
8th Ave.
Museum of Modern Art
MoMA QNS
LONG ISLAND CITY
Mt. Zion Cemetery
E. 52ndSt.
11th Ave.
10th Ave.
9th Ave.
Rockefeller Center
Grand Central
Times
United Nations Headquarters
495
Long Island Expwy.

Lincoln Tunnel
Port Authority Bus Terminal
New York Public Library
Midtown Tunnel
Newtown Creek
Calvary Cemetery
Javits Convention Center
W. 34th St.
MIDTOWN
Morgan Library
Madison Square Garden/ Pennsylvania Station
Empire State Building
7th Ave.
Ave. of the Americas
Broadway
3rd Ave.
2nd Ave.
1st Ave.
East River
Flatiron Building
W. 23rd St.
E. 23rd St.
Gramercy Park
CHELSEA
GRAMERCY
Union Square
W. 14th St.
E. 14th St.
Tompkins Square Park
GREENWICH VILLAGE
Grace Church
EAST VILLAGE
Washington Square
Sheridan Square
E. 4th St.
West Side Hwy.
Hudson St.
New York University
NOLITA
LOWER EAST SIDE
FDR Dr.
W. Houston St.
E. Houston St.
Williamsburg Bridge
Holland Tunnel
SOHO
LITTLE ITALY
Orchard St.
Delancy St.
Canal St.
Lafayette St.
Broadway
Bowery
E. Broadway
TRIBECA
CHINA-TOWN
West St.
W. Broadway
Manhattan Bridge
Chambers St.
City Hall
Brooklyn Bridge
Hudson River
NEW JERSEY
N
World Trade Center Site
Fulton St.
South Street Seaport
Trinity Church
Wall St.
NY Stock Exchange
LOWER MANHATTAN
Brooklyn Heights Promenade
BROOKLYN HEIGHTS
BROOKLYN
0
880 yards
0
800 meters
National Museum of the American Indian
Battery Park
Staten Island Ferry Terminal
Statue of Liberty, Ellis Island
Brooklyn-Battery Tunnel
Montague St.
Flatbush Ave.
Humboldt Ave.
Expwy.
Brooklyn-Queens
Grand Ave.
Flushing Ave.
Bushwick Ave.
Myrtle Ave.
Broadway
Lafayette Ave.
Bedford Ave.
Fulton St.
Atlantic Ave.

Beyond the allure of must-see sights, from the Statue of Liberty to Times Square, from Central Park to the Metropolitan Museum of Art, New York has an indefinable aura all its own. It's a special intensity that comes from being in the big leagues, where everybody's chasing a dream and still keeping score. To paraphrase a slogan originally coined for the Plaza Hotel, you get the feeling that "nothing unimportant ever happens in New York."

Exploring Manhattan

Midtown is the heart of New York City, so it makes sense to start your exploration here. Then move on to the museum-rich Upper West and Upper East sides, downtown to Chelsea, Greenwich Village, SoHo, Little Italy, and Chinatown, and finally to Lower Manhattan, the city's financial center.

Midtown

★ At the center of midtown is **Rockefeller Center,** a complex of 19 buildings occupying nearly 22 acres of prime real estate between 5th and 7th avenues and 47th and 52nd streets. A gilded statue of Prometheus hovers above an outdoor ice rink on the Lower Plaza between 49th and 50th streets. The rink becomes an open-air café in warm weather. In December the plaza is decorated with a huge Christmas tree. The center's 6,000-seat Art Deco Radio City Music Hall (✉ 1260 6th Ave. at 50th St., ☎ 212/247–4777, WEB www.radiocity.com; 🎟 tour $16), is America's largest indoor theater. It produces major concerts, Christmas and Easter extravaganzas, awards presentations, and other special events and is home of the Rockettes chorus line.

The stretch of **5th Avenue** between Rockefeller Center and 59th Street glitters with world-famous shops, including Saks Fifth Avenue, F.A.O. Schwarz, Prada, and Tiffany & Co.Gothic-style **St. Patrick's** (✉ 5th Ave. at 50th St., ☎ 212/753–2261), the Roman Catholic cathedral of New York, is dedicated to the patron saint of the Irish. The stone structure was begun in 1859, consecrated in 1879, and completed in 1906.

The **Museum of Modern Art** (MoMA; ✉ 11 W. 53rd St., ☎ 212/708–9480, WEB www.moma.org), which has an astounding collection of 20th-century art, is in the throes of a major overhaul. Japanese architect Yoshio Taniguchi leads the redesign of the 53rd Street site; the space is expected to re-open in 2005. In the meantime, selections from the collection are being exhibited in MoMA QNS (☞ *See* Queens *in* Side Trips to Outer Boroughs, *below*).

Times Square, one of New York's principal energy centers, is perhaps best known as the core of the Broadway Theater District. Most Broadway theaters are actually on streets west of Broadway. Redevelopment on and around 42nd Street has dramatically transformed and tidied the area, especially 42nd Street between 7th and 8th avenues. Construction will continue well into the year 2003.

At the historic **New Amsterdam Theater** (✉ 214 W. 42nd St., ☎ 212/282–2900), the acclaimed stage version of *The Lion King* draws crowds nightly. Across from the New Amsterdam another renovated theatrical landmark, the **New Victory Theater** (✉ 209 W. 42nd St., 212/382–4000), stages productions mostly by and for children. The **Ford Center for the Performing Arts** (✉ 213 43rd St. between 7th and 8th Aves., ☎ 212/307–4100) combines elements from two landmark early 20th-century theaters, the Lyric and the Apollo.

Two crouching marble lions guard the 5th Avenue entrance to the **New York Public Library (NYPL) Humanities and Social Sciences Library.** This

1911 Beaux Arts masterpiece has frequent exhibits and a majestic **main reading room. Bryant Park,** Midtown's most distinctive green space, is just behind the library; on sunny days office workers jockey for a chair on the central lawn. ✉ *5th Ave., at 42nd St.,* ☎ *212/930–0800.* WEB *www.nypl.org.* 🎟 *Free.* ⏲ *Closed Sun.–Mon.*

United Nations headquarters is on a lushly landscaped riverside tract along 1st Avenue between 42nd and 48th streets. The flags of member nations fly when the General Assembly is in session inside the striking 505-ft-high slab of the Secretariat Building. Tours depart from the General Assembly lobby. ✉ *Visitor entrance: 1st Ave. and E. 46th St.,* ☎ *212/963–7713,* WEB *www.un.org,* 🎟 *tour $7.50.*

The **Morgan Library,** at the southern end of midtown, is a small, patrician museum centered on the famous banker's red-damask-lined study and his majestic personal library, with tiers of handsomely bound rare books, letters, and illuminated manuscripts; both rooms were completed in 1906. Rotating exhibitions from the permanent collection also showcase drawings and prints. ✉ *29 E. 36th St.,* ☎ *212/685–0008,* WEB *www.morganlibrary.org.* 🎟 *Donation suggested. Closed Mon.*

★ The 1931 Art Deco **Empire State Building** (✉ 5th Ave. and 34th St., ☎ 212/736–3100, WEB www.esbnyc.com; observatory 🎟 $9), two blocks southwest of the Morgan Library, is no longer the world's tallest building, but post–September 11, 2001, it is New York City's. Go to the concourse level to buy a ticket for the 86th- and 102nd-floor observation decks.

Upper East Side

The **Upper East Side,** east of Central Park between 59th and 96th streets, is the focus of the wealthy, high-society New York glamorized in literature and film. The neighborhood includes singles bars and high-rise apartment buildings on 1st Avenue, sedate town houses in the East 60s, and an outstanding concentration of art museums and galleries along 5th and Madison avenues. Along **Madison Avenue** between 59th and 79th streets are patrician art galleries, unique specialty stores, and the boutiques of many of the world's major fashion designers. **Museum Mile** is a strip of cultural institutions devoted to a broad spectrum of subjects and artistic styles, on or near 5th Avenue between 70th and 104th streets.

★ The **Frick Collection,** housed in a Beaux Arts–style palace built by Pittsburgh Coke-and-steel baron Henry Clay Frick, is the city's finest small art museum. Specializing in European works from the late 13th to the late 19th century, it has masterpieces by Rembrandt, Fragonard, Bellini, Turner, and Vermeer, among others. ✉ *1 E. 70th St., at 5th Ave.,* ☎ *212/288–0700,* WEB *www.frick.org.* 🎟 *$10. Closed Mon.*

The **Whitney Museum of American Art,** a gray granite Bauhaus vault, has an intelligent survey of 20th-century American works, from naturalism and impressionism to pop art, abstract expressionism, postmodernism, and whatever comes next. ✉ *945 Madison Ave., at 75th St.,* ☎ *212/570–3676,* WEB *www.whitney.org.* 🎟 *$10. Closed Mon.*

★ The **Metropolitan Museum of Art,** on the edge of Central Park, is the largest art museum in the western hemisphere. Galleries display prehistoric to postindustrial works from around the world, including impressive Greek and Egyptian collections and an entire wing devoted to tribal arts. The museum has the world's most comprehensive collection of American art, and its holdings of European art are unequaled outside Europe. Also here are the Temple of Dendur, an entire

Egyptian temple (circa 15 BC), and galleries devoted to musical instruments, Asian art, and arms and armor. Walking tours and lectures are free with admission. The museum's separate **Cloisters** (☎ 212/923–3700), an amalgam of monastery buildings transported stone by stone from Europe, overlooks the Hudson River in Fort Tryon Park at the top of Manhattan. It houses the museum's medieval collection. ✉ *5th Ave. at 82nd St.,* ☎ *212/535–7710,* WEB *www.metmuseum.org.* 🎫 *Donations suggested. Closed Mon.*

★ The **Solomon R. Guggenheim Museum,** designed by Frank Lloyd Wright, is visited as much for its famous architecture as it is for its art collection. The exhibits, which fill the six-story spiral and adjoining galleries, alternate between new artists and modern masters. ✉ *1071 5th Ave., at 89th St.,* ☎ *212/423–3500,* WEB *www.guggenheim.org.* 🎫 *$15. Closed Thurs.*

The **Museum of the City of New York** brings the history of the Big Apple to life, from its seafaring beginnings to yesterday's headlines, in period rooms, videos, clever displays of memorabilia, and a dollhouse collection. ✉ *1220 5th Ave., at 103rd St.,* ☎ *212/534–1672,* WEB *www.mcny.org.* 🎫 *Donations suggested. Closed Mon.–Tues.*

Upper West Side

The **Upper West Side** is a perennially lively and attractive neighborhood, with boutiques and cafés lining the avenues, renovated brownstones on the side streets, and a park on each flank (Central to the east, Riverside to the west). **Lincoln Center** (✉ W. 62nd to 66th St. between Broadway and Amsterdam Ave., ☎ 212/546–2656 general information; 212/875–5350 tour schedule and reservations; WEB www.lincolncenter.org; 🎫 tour $9.50) is the area's cultural anchor. Flanking the central fountain are three major concert halls: **Avery Fisher Hall,** where the New York Philharmonic Orchestra performs; the glass-fronted **Metropolitan Opera House,** home of the Metropolitan Opera and the American Ballet Theatre; and the **New York State Theater,** home of the New York City Ballet and the New York City Opera.

★ 🦢 The **American Museum of Natural History,** with more than 36 million artifacts and specimens, is the world's largest and most important museum of natural history. Forty-two exhibition halls display an awe-inspiring collection of items, including dinosaur skeletons, a 94-ft replica of a blue whale, the 563-carat Star of India sapphire, and the 4 ½-billion-year-old *Ahnighito,* the largest meteorite ever recovered on the earth's surface. An **IMAX Theater** screens films about nature. The spectacular **Hayden Planetarium,** an aluminum-clad sphere that appears to float inside the enormous glass cube of the Rose Center for Earth and Space, features high-tech space shows. ✉ *Central Park West at W. 79th St.,* ☎ *212/769–5200 museum tickets and programs; 212/769–5100 museum information; 212/769–5034 IMAX Theater show times;* WEB *www.amnh.org.* 🎫 *Museum donations suggested; IMAX theater $14; combination tickets available. Closed Mon.*

Founded in 1754, **Columbia University** (☎ 212/854–4900, WEB www.columbia.edu) is New York City's only Ivy League school. The main campus is bounded by 114th and 120th streets, Broadway, and Amsterdam Avenue; College Walk, at 116th Street, leads across the expansive main quadrangle. Close to Columbia University is the **Cathedral Church of St. John the Divine** (✉ 1047 Amsterdam Ave., at 112th St., ☎ 212/316–7540; WEB www.stjohndivine.org), an immense limestone-and-granite church that, although unfinished, is the largest Gothic structure in the world. In December 2001, a fire seriously damaged the cathedral.

Harlem

Harlem has been a center of African-American culture for nearly a century. In the 1920s, during the Harlem Renaissance, black novelists, playwrights, musicians, and artists gathered here. By the 1960s crowded housing, poverty, and crime had turned the neighborhood into a simmering ghetto. Today Harlem is restoring itself. Mixed in with some seedy remains of the past are old jewels like the refurbished **Apollo Theatre** (✉ 253 W. 125th St., ☎ 212/749–5838; 212/531–5337 to arrange tours), where such music greats as Ella Fitzgerald and Duke Ellington brought black musicians into the limelight. **Schomburg Center for Research in Black Culture** (✉ 515 Malcolm X Blvd., at 135th St., ☎ 212/491–2200; WEB www.schomburgcenter.org; 🎫 free) has more than 5 million items in its collection, including rare manuscripts, art and artifacts, records, and videotapes. It hosts regular exhibits, performing arts programs, and lectures.

Chelsea and the Flatiron District

In the late 1990s **Chelsea** replaced SoHo as New York's art gallery headquarters, as high-profile galleries gravitated to the larger spaces and cheaper rents in the former warehouse center west of 10th Avenue. The diverse neighborhood stretches from 5th Avenue west to the Hudson River and from 14th to 29th Street, encompassing the literary landmark **Chelsea Hotel,** lots of quiet side streets lined with restored town houses, and the ultramodern **Chelsea Piers Sports and Entertainment Complex.** An active gay community frequents the lively stores and restaurants on 8th and 7th avenues. Several blocks north along 9th Avenue, **Hell's Kitchen** is home to great ethnic eateries.

Eastern Chelsea merges with the **Flatiron District,** which lies between 14th and 34th streets and spreads east to Park Avenue South. The neighborhood, centered on the revolutionary **Flatiron Building** (✉ 175 5th Ave., at Broadway), owes its identity and flavor to the scores of photographic studios and design firms that have set up shop in former manufacturing and warehouse lofts. A bit farther south lies **Union Square** (✉ E. 14th to E. 17th St., between Broadway and Park Ave. S), a statue-studded park surrounded by stores and restaurants.

Greenwich Village and the East Village

With its narrow tree-lined streets, brick town houses, and hidden ★ courtyards, **Greenwich Village** is like a small town in Manhattan. The Village is ideal for strolling, window-shopping, and café-hopping; it extends from 14th Street south to Houston Street (pronounced *How*-stun) and from the Hudson River to 5th Avenue. For generations the haunt of writers, artists, and musicians, the Village is synonymous with many of the avant-garde artists of this century, including abstract expressionist painters like Franz Kline and Mark Rothko, Beat writers and poets such as Jack Kerouac and Allen Ginsberg, and folk musicians, notably Bob Dylan and Peter, Paul, and Mary.

Washington Square, at the foot of 5th Avenue, is a good place to begin a walking tour of the Village. At the top of the square is the Washington Memorial Arch, designed by Stanford White and built in 1889 to commemorate the 100th anniversary of George Washington's inauguration. The surrounding area attracts New York University students to its shops, bars, jazz clubs, Off-Broadway theaters, cabarets, coffeehouses, and cafés.

Tiny **Sheridan Square** anchors Christopher Street, a hub of New York's gay community and a busy shopping strip. West of 7th Avenue South, the Village turns into a picture-book warren of twisting streets filled with **historical buildings,** quaint houses, and tiny restaurants. At different times Edna St. Vincent Millay and John Barrymore each lived at 75½ Bedford Street—at 9½ ft wide, New York's narrowest house. Theodore Dreiser wrote *An American Tragedy* at 16 St. Luke's Place. The stretch of West 4th Street is particularly pleasant.

As far west as the Hudson, on 14th Street and just below, is the **Meatpacking District,** which was once just that but now shares its sidewalks with shoppers and gallery hunters, gourmands, and club kids.

The **East Village,** east of 4th Avenue (Lafayette Street) and south of East 14th Street, has housed Jewish, Ukrainian, and Puerto Rican immigrants; beatniks; hippies; punks; students, artists; and, most recently, affluent young professionals. Soak up the eclectic atmosphere along St. Marks Place and 9th Street east of 3rd Avenue, and along Avenues A and B between East Houston and 12th streets. You'll find restaurants and bars both chic and cheap, vintage and cutting-edge clothing boutiques, cafés, and offbeat shops. To the south, bounded by the Bowery and East Houston, Pitt and Delancey streets, the **Lower East Side,** once a neighborhood of Jewish immigrants, offers more of the same; on Orchard Street, for example, the traditional bargain clothing hawkers rub shoulders with avant-garde boutiques.

SoHo, NoLita, and TriBeCa

SoHo (so named because it is the district *So*uth of *Ho*uston Street, bounded by Broadway, Canal Street, and 6th Avenue) defines urban elegance—a mix of artists, young Wall Streeters, pricey boutiques, art spaces, and restaurants with a modernist approach to both food and design. West Broadway, paralleling Broadway four blocks to the west, and Prince and Spring streets, running east–west, are the area's main arteries. On Saturday, the big day for shopping and gallery hopping, it can be crowded but still great for people-watching. At 28–30 and 72–76 Greene Street you'll find two fine examples of the abundant **cast-iron architecture** for which SoHo is world-famous.

South of SoHo is its offspring **TriBeCa** (from *Tri*angle *be*low *Ca*nal Street). Its glamorous loft apartments, converted from prewar industrial spaces, are among the city's most coveted and expensive. Correspondingly excellent and expensive restaurants occupy the stunning storefronts. SoHo's stylish character has also spread east into **NoLita,** as in *No*rth of *Li*ttle I*ta*ly. Mulberry, Mott, and Elizabeth streets between Houston and Spring streets have sprouted trendy clothing, design, and secondhand boutiques as well as restaurants and cafés worth exploring.

Chinatown and Little Italy

In booming **Chinatown,** Canal and Grand streets abound with food shops and outdoor markets bursting with fresh seafood, Chinese vegetables, almond cookies, and roasted ducks. The main drag is narrow and twisting **Mott Street,** crammed with souvenir shops in pagoda-style buildings, and crowded with pedestrians at all hours. Within a few dense blocks, hundreds of restaurants serve every type of Chinese cuisine, from simple noodles and dumplings to sumptuous Hunan, Szechuan, Cantonese, Mandarin, and Shanghai feasts.

Squeezed between Chinatown and East Houston Street, **Little Italy** is a shrinking enclave of Italian life. **Mulberry Street,** lined with tenement buildings, long the heart of Little Italy, is now virtually the entire body. Between Broome and Canal streets, Mulberry consists of restaurants, cafés, bakeries, food shops, and souvenir stores. Each September the Feast of San Gennaro turns the streets into a bright and bustling Italian kitchen.

Lower Manhattan

New York City remained packed into Manhattan's southernmost area until the middle of the 19th century; no matter how much the city and its population have grown, much of what New York is known for remains at its old starting point in **Lower Manhattan.** Wall Street dominates the area; the thoroughfare is both an actual street and a shorthand name for the vast, powerful financial community that clusters around the New York and American stock exchanges. But this setting of New York's feverish capitalism looks out onto symbols relevant to all of America: the Statue of Liberty and Ellis Island, port of entry for countless immigrants to a new land. Lower Manhattan continues to recover from the terrorist attacks of September 11, 2001; plenty of construction work attests to the considerable number of businesses and residents determined to stay in their neighborhood.

Outside the **Staten Island Ferry Terminal,** at the southernmost tip of Manhattan, is a good place to start your exploration. For great harbor views of the Statue of Liberty, Ellis Island, and the Lower Manhattan skyline, consider the free ferry ride to Staten Island. **Battery Park,** a verdant landfill loaded with monuments and sculpture, and the point of embarkation for visits to the Statue of Liberty and Ellis Island, is a short walk up the Battery Park waterfront from the ferry terminal. Buy your ticket for the boat to the Statue of Liberty or Ellis Island at **Castle Clinton National Monument** (☎ 212/269–5755; 🎫 ferry $8 round-trip), inside the park; arrive early and be prepared to wait.

★ 🖐 The **Statue of Liberty** (☎ 212/363–3200, WEB www.nps.gov/stli; 🎫 free) is one of America's greatest symbols of freedom. Lady Liberty stands a proud 152 ft tall atop an 89-ft pedestal; Emma Lazarus's sonnet *The New Colossus* ("Give me your tired, your poor, your huddled masses . . .") is inscribed on a bronze plaque at the statue's base. Once on Liberty Island you may have to wait as many as four hours to take the elevator 10 stories to the top of the pedestal. The strong of heart and limb can climb another 12 stories to the crown.

★ **Ellis Island** (☎ 212/363–3200, WEB www.ellisisland.org; 🎫 free) was once the main East Coast federal immigration facility. Between 1892 and 1954, millions of men, women, and children—the ancestors of 40% of the Americans living today—were processed here. More than 30 galleries chronicle the immigrant experience with artifacts, photographs, and taped oral histories; the American Immigrant Wall of Honor inscribes the names of more than 500,000 immigrants.

The **National Museum of the American Indian** (✉ 1 Bowling Green, ☎ 212/668–6624, WEB www.si.edu/nmai; 🎫 free), in a stunning Beaux Arts–style building, is the first national museum dedicated solely to Native American culture, and its exhibits of fascinating objects from around the Americas are accompanied with good documentation.

Fraunces Tavern is best remembered as the site of George Washington's 1783 farewell address to his officers celebrating the British evacuation of New York. The Colonial house, built in 1719, contains two fully furnished period rooms and other displays on 18th- and 19th-century American history. ✉ *Broad and Pearl Sts.,* ☎ *212/425–1778.* 🎫 *$3. Closed Sun.–Mon.*

The **New York Stock Exchange** has its august Corinthian main entrance around the corner from Wall Street, on Broad Street. Tours and multimedia presentations, which help interpret the chaos that seems to reign on the trading floor, have been closed since September 11. Call for possible reopenings. Free tour tickets are distributed beginning at

8:45 AM; come before 1 PM to assure entrance. ✉ *20 Broad St.,* ☎ *212/656–5165.*

The twin World Trade Center towers, once the tallest skyscrapers in New York and an unforgettable part of the city's skyline, were destroyed in the terrorist attacks of September 11, 2001. Plans are under debate for a memorial and other buildings where the towers and five other buildings once stood, at the site now called **Ground Zero.** Most of the surrounding streets are open to pedestrians, and visitors continue to make pilgrimages here to remember those who died or simply try to grasp the enormity of the disaster. A viewing area of the site is on Liberty Street at the corner of Church Street. ⏲ *Daily 9–9.* 🎫 *Free.* WEB *www.nyc.gov.*

The **South Street Seaport Historic District** is an 11-block stretch on the East River that encompasses a museum, shopping, historic ships, cruise boats, a TKTS booth, and innumerable places to eat and drink. You can view the historic ships from Pier 16, which is the departure point for the one-hour Seaport Liberty Cruise (☎ 212/630–8888).

★ The **Brooklyn Bridge,** New York's oldest and best known, is north of the South Street Seaport. The bridge, designed by John Augustus Roebling, has been called a "drive-through cathedral." When completed in 1883, it was the world's longest suspension bridge and the tallest structure in the city. Walking across the Brooklyn Bridge is a peak New York experience.

Parks, Gardens, and Zoos

★ For many residents, **Central Park** is the greatest part of New York City. Bounded by 59th and 110th streets, 5th Avenue, and Central Park West, the park contains grassy meadows, wooded groves, and formal gardens; numerous fountains, sculptures, and bodies of water; paths for jogging, strolling, horseback riding, and biking; playing fields; a small zoo; two ice-skating rinks; a carousel; and an outdoor theater. But no matter how close to nature New Yorkers feel when reveling in it, Central Park was in fact the United States' first artificially landscaped park. Frederick Law Olmsted and Calvert Vaux conceived the design in 1857.

★ The **Bronx Zoo** (✉ Bronx River Pkwy. and Fordham Rd., ☎ 718/367–1010, WEB www.wcs.org/zoos/bronxzoo. 🎫 Apr.–Oct., Thurs.–Tues. $9; Nov.–Dec., Thurs.–Tues. $7; Jan.–Mar., Thurs.–Tues. $5; free Wed.; Children's Zoo $4) is the nation's largest urban zoo, with more than 46,500 animals on 265 acres of woods, ponds, streams, and parkland.

The **New York Botanical Garden,** a 250-acre botanical treasury around the dramatic gorge of the Bronx River, is within Bronx Park. Its 40-acre forest, conservatory, museum, and outdoor gardens draw nature enthusiasts from around the world. ✉ *200th St. and Kazimiroff Blvd.,* ☎ *718/817–8700,* WEB *www.nybg.org.* 🎫 *$3, free Sat. 10–noon and Wed.; Enid A. Haupt Conservatory $5. Closed Mon.*

Dining

By Mitchell Davis and Josh Greenwald

New York is the restaurant capital of the country, maybe even the world. Dining options run the gamut, from small, out-of-the-way ethnic eateries to formal French temples of gastronomy. You can spend $5 on dinner or $500, and some of the better restaurants offer real deals at lunch. When they are accepted, reservations are essential (make them well in advance); when they aren't you may have to wait. Don't fret. In general—though not always—a long line augurs a good experience.

$$$$ ★ ✕ **Daniel.** Open the lengthy, predominantly French, prix-fixe only menu to begin one of the most memorable meals available in Manhattan today. Choose from modern classics such as chestnut crusted venison with braised red cabbage and sweet potato puree. The service is fittingly excellent. The neo-Renaissance dining room provides an extremely formal setting; dinner in the lounge is a more relaxed experience. ✉ *60 E. 65th St., between Park and Madison Aves.,* ☏ *212/288–0033. Reservations essential. Jacket required. AE, DC, MC, V. Closed Sun. No lunch Mon.*

$$$$ ★ ✕ **Gramercy Tavern.** This urbanely rustic restaurant is divided into two rooms—the first-come, first-served tavern in front offers a light menu. Some choices are prepared in the wood-burning oven while you watch. The more formal but still unintimidating dining room in the back features a carefully conceived American table d'hôte menu. Friendly service and a dessert menu that rivals any in the city complete the experience. ✉ *42 E. 20th St., between Broadway and Park Ave. S,* ☏ *212/477–0777. Reservations essential. AE, DC, MC, V.*

$$$$ ✕ **Jean Georges.** The main dining room here, with dramatic picture windows overlooking Central Park, pairs luxury with understatedness in both its decor and its menu. Chef Jean-Georges Vongerichten presents unusual combinations that intrigue the palate without overwhelming it: sea scallops in caper-raisin emulsion with caramelized cauliflower is an outstanding example. ✉ *1 Central Park W, at 59th St.,* ☏ *212/299–3900. Reservations essential. Jacket and tie. AE, DC, MC, V. Closed Sun.*

$$$$ ★ ✕ **Le Bernardin.** Chef-partner Eric Ripert works magic with anything that swims—preferring at times not to cook it at all. Deceptively simple dishes on the prix-fixe menu such as Spanish mackerel tartare with osetra caviar and steamed halibut on a pea puree are typical of his style. Such luscious French cooking is happily coupled with equally memorable desserts. ✉ *155 W. 51st St., between 6th and 7th Aves.,* ☏ *212/489–1515. Reservations essential. Jacket required. AE, DC, MC, V. Closed Sun. No lunch Sat.*

$$$$ ✕ **Le Cirque 2000.** Sirio Maccioni has fed the world's elite for more than 25 years; in the landmark Villard House, he contrasts the original ornate decor with a whimsical, futuristic circus chic. The French-leaning menu includes a few homages to Sirio's Italian roots, although the famed lobster salad is still served at lunch. Over-the-top desserts come in Venetian glass goblets and sugar domes. ✉ *455 Madison Ave., between 50th and 51st Sts.,* ☏ *212/794–9292. Reservations essential. Jacket and tie. AE, DC, MC, V. No lunch Sun.*

$$$$ ✕ **"21" Club.** This four-story brownstone landmark, a former speakeasy, first opened on December 31, 1929. Here is one of the world's great wine cellars, with some 50,000 bottles. The Grill Room is *the* place to be, with its banquettes, red-checked tablecloths, and a ceiling hung with toys; it serves such standbys as the signature "21" burger and a host of more exciting dishes, such as venison carpaccio with truffle dressing. ✉ *21 W. 52nd St., between 5th and 6th Aves.,* ☏ *212/582–7200. Reservations essential. Jacket and tie. AE, DC, MC, V. Closed Sun. No lunch Sat.*

$$$–$$$$ ★ ✕ **Café Boulud.** At this "casual bistro," only the atmosphere is relaxed; the food and service are as serious and as disciplined as can be. The changing four-part menu features dishes from the classic French repertoire, others based on seasonal ingredients, still others adapted from cuisines of the world, and a number of vegetarian options. ✉ *Surrey Hotel, 20 E. 76th St., at Madison Ave.,* ☏ *212/772–2600. Reservations essential. AE, DC, MC, V. No lunch Sun.–Mon.*

$$$–$$$$ ✕ **Firebird.** These two antiques-filled brownstones may be just the place to indulge in an elegant caviar presentation—steaming hot blini drenched in butter, slathered with sour cream, and filled with beluga, sevruga, or osetra by waiters in white gloves. Other staples of the Russian regional cuisine range from *zakuska* (assorted Russian hors d'oeuvres) to tea with cherry preserves. Don't fail to sample the extraordinary vodka selection. ✉ *365 W. 46th St., between 8th and 9th Aves.,* ☎ *212/586–0244. Reservations essential. AE, DC, MC, V. No lunch Sun.*

$$$–$$$$ ★ ✕ **Nobu.** A curved wall of river-worn black pebbles, bare wood tables, birch trees, and a hand-painted beech floor serve as the dramatic setting for the Japanese-inspired food. You can sample classic Japanese sushi and sashimi, among the best in town, or contemporary dishes such as the defyingly delicious seared black cod with sweet miso or Peruvian-style sashimi. If you can't get a reservation, try the new Next Door Nobu, where you can get highlights of the Nobu menu on a first-come, first-served basis. ✉ *105 Hudson St., off Franklin St.,* ☎ *212/219–0500; 212/219–8095 same-day reservations. Reservations essential. AE, DC, MC, V. No lunch weekends.*

$$$–$$$$ ✕ **Picholine.** Named for a small green Mediterranean olive, this mellow restaurant is designed to look like a Provençal farmhouse. The French food with Mediterranean accents is among the finest in Manhattan. Top dishes include wild mushroom and duck risotto and tournedos of salmon with horseradish crust, cucumbers, and salmon caviar. The cheese selection holds a justifiably sterling reputation. ✉ *35 W. 64th St., off Broadway,* ☎ *212/724–8585. Reservations essential. AE, DC, MC, V. No lunch Sun.–Mon.*

$$$–$$$$ ✕ **Tabla.** From the time the waiter sets down the bread—freshly baked roti and nan served with an apple and onion puree—you know you're about to embark on a delicious culinary journey. Dishes like lamb and turmeric ravioli with tomato *kasundi* (sauce) and mint oil and tandoori rabbit with *Goan bacalao* (salt-cod) set the tone. A downstairs "bread bar" affords a more casual, less expensive experience. ✉ *11 Madison Ave., at 25th St.,* ☎ *212/889–0667. Reservations essential. AE, DC, MC, V. No lunch weekends.*

$$–$$$$ ✕ **Kuruma Zushi.** Only a sign in Japanese indicates the location of this extraordinary restaurant, which devotes itself to sushi and sashimi. The best way to enjoy the exotic delicacies available here is to sit at the sushi bar and put yourself in the hands of the talented chef, who imports hard-to-find fish from Japan, as well as other traditional choices. ✉ *7 E. 47th St., 2nd floor, between 5th and Madison Aves.,* ☎ *212/317–2802. AE, MC, V. Closed Sun.*

$$–$$$$ ✕ **The Mercer Kitchen.** The sleek, modern, industrial space is surprisingly comfortable, and the room sizzles with the palpable energy of the New York downtown elite. Dinner might include black sea bass carpaccio or Alsatian tart flambée with fromage blanc, onions, and bacon. ✉ *The Mercer Hotel, 99 Prince St., at Mercer St.,* ☎ *212/966–5454. Reservations essential. AE, DC, MC, V. No dinner Sun.*

$$$ ★ ✕ **Babbo.** After your first bite of the kitchen's ethereal homemade pasta or the tender suckling pig, you'll know that this is Italian food as it was meant to be, combining the finest ingredients with impeccable technique and a passion for adventure. A five-course pasta tasting menu is the best way to get your fill of fresh noodles. Babbo's owners opened **Lupa** (✉ 170 Thompson St., between Bleecker and Houston Sts., ☎ 212/982–5089), a casual trattoria, with excellent food and friendly service. ✉ *110 Waverly Pl., between MacDougal St. and 6th Ave.,* ☎ *212/777–0303. Reservations essential. AE, MC, V. No lunch.*

$$$ ✕ **Balthazar.** Restauranteur Keith McNally went to extraordinary lengths to re-create the look and feel of a Parisian brasserie. Nightly specials are based on classic French dishes, and the breads are superb.

For a first-come, first-served alternative, try Balthazar's baby cousin **Pastis** (✉ 9 9th Ave., at Little W. 12th St., ☎ 212/929–4844) in the meatpacking district. ✉ *80 Spring St., between Broadway and Lafayette St.,* ☎ *212/965–1414. Reservations essential. AE, MC, V.*

$$$ ✕ **Churrascaria Plataforma.** This sprawling, boisterous shrine to meat, best experienced with a group, is a popular Brazilian prix-fixe spot. Order a full pitcher of *caipirinhas* and head for the center of the room, where a vast salad bar beckons. But exercise restraint—the real show begins with the parade of lamb, beef, chicken, ham, sausage, and innards, brought to the table on skewers. ✉ *316 W. 49th St., between 8th and 9th Aves.,* ☎ *212/245–0505. AE, DC, MC, V.*

$$$ ★ ✕ **Peter Luger Steak House.** You cannot find a better porterhouse steak anywhere. Period. Sure, you can find better lighting, a more sophisticated atmosphere, a more comfortable chair. But if prime aged beef is what you want (and maybe a shrimp cocktail, home fries, and creamed spinach), and if you don't want to dress up, then this is well worth the trip to Brooklyn. ✉ *178 Broadway, at Driggs Ave., Brooklyn,* ☎ *718/387–7400. Reservations essential. No credit cards.*

$$–$$$ ✕ **I Trulli.** Rough-hewn gold walls, a fireplace, a garden for summer dining, and a whitewashed open grill distinguish this Italian winner. Start with a glass of wine from a little-known producer and one of the enticing appetizers. Almost all of the pasta is made by hand, and the special preparations of the day shouldn't be overlooked. A lovely casual wine bar next door (**Enoteca**) offers a simple menu of the same exquisite food and an impressive selection of wines. ✉ *122 E. 27th St., between Lexington and Park Ave. S,* ☎ *212/481–7372. Reservations essential. AE, DC, MC, V. Closed Sun. No lunch Sat.*

$$–$$$ ✕ **Rosa Mexicano.** When the staff slips open the parchment package that contains a lamb shank braised in a three-chili sauce, the room fills with the fragrance of Oaxaca. A better guacamole, prepared table-side and served with warm corn tortillas, cannot be found—not even in Mexico. The lively, jam-packed barroom in the front makes you feel as though you've happened upon a Mexican fiesta. ✉ *1063 1st Ave., at 58th St.,* ☎ *212/753–7407. Reservations essential. AE, DC, MC, V. No lunch.*

$$–$$$ ★ ✕ **Second Avenue Deli.** A face-lift may have removed the wrinkles of time, but the strictly kosher, dairy-free food here is as good as ever. The deli's bevy of classics includes chicken in the pot, matzo ball soup, chopped liver, pastrami sandwiches, and *cholent* (a Sabbath dish of meat, beans, and grain). A welcome bowl of pickles, sour green tomatoes, and coleslaw satisfies from the start, but at the finish, don't order dessert. ✉ *156 2nd Ave., at 10th St.,* ☎ *212/677–0606. AE, DC, MC, V.*

$–$$$ ★ ✕ **Blue Ribbon.** Open for dinner from 4 PM until 4 AM, this small American bistro is a popular hangout for off-duty chefs and other night crawlers. At the raw bar, a shucker turns out terrifically fresh oysters and other seasonal shellfish delicacies. The something-for-everyone menu offers a mix of dishes from around the world—a towering pupu platter, a duck club sandwich, and matzo ball soup. ✉ *97 Sullivan St., between Prince and Spring Sts.,* ☎ *212/274–0404. Reservations essential. AE, DC, MC, V. Closed Mon. No lunch.*

$$ ✕ **Virgil's Real BBQ.** This massive roadhouse in the Theater District looks just the way a barbecue place should. Start with stuffed jalapeños or buttermilk onion rings with blue-cheese dip. Then go for "The Pig Out": a rack of pork ribs, Texas hot links, pulled pork, rack of lamb, chicken, and more. ✉ *152 W. 44th St., between 6th Ave. and Broadway,* ☎ *212/921–9494. Reservations essential. AE, MC, V.*

$–$$ ✕ **Barney Greengrass.** This place hasn't changed much since it opened in 1908. Order anything with smoked salmon or sturgeon in it: scrambled eggs with onions; bagels or bialys with cream cheese, tomato, and red onion; or the austere platters of fish. End with an individual chocolate babka "muffin" and you will have forgotten the long wait to get in. ✉ *541 Amsterdam Ave., between 86th and 87th Sts.,* ☎ *212/724–4707. Reservations not accepted. No credit cards. Closed Mon.*

$–$$ ✕ **Holy Basil.** It's not often you get to enjoy authentic Thai food within a clubby setting of brick walls and gilt-framed mirrors. Dishes are beautifully presented: spicy *som tum* (green papaya salad) and rich *tom kah gai* (chicken and coconut milk soup), not to mention anything in *kaw praw* (a traditional curried preparation). Vegetarian selections abound, and a large and informative wine list is an added bonus. ✉ *149 2nd Ave., between 9th and 10th Sts.,* ☎ *212/460–5557. AE, DC, MC, V. No lunch.*

$–$$ ★ ✕ **Lombardi's.** The aroma of thin-crust pies emerging from the coal oven sets the mood for some of the best pizza in Manhattan. The mozzarella is always fresh, resulting in an almost greaseless slice, and the toppings, such as homemade meatballs, pancetta, or imported anchovies, are also top quality. ✉ *32 Spring St., between Mott and Mulberry Sts.,* ☎ *212/941–7994. No credit cards.*

$–$$ ★ ✕ **Moustache.** No New York spot serves Middle Eastern food as fresh, flavorful, or appealingly presented as Moustache. The focal point is the pita, steam-filled pillows of dough baked in a searingly hot oven. Use it to scoop up the tasty salads—lemony chickpea and spinach, creamy hummus, and hearty lentil and bulghur among them. For entrées, try the leg of lamb or merguez sausage sandwiches or the ouzi, a large phyllo package stuffed with chicken and fragrant rice. ✉ *90 Bedford St., between Barrow and Grove Sts.,* ☎ *212/229–2220;* ✉ *265 E. 10th St., between Ave. A and 1st Ave.,* ☎ *212/228–2022. Reservations not accepted. No credit cards.*

$–$$ ★ ✕ **Sweet 'n' Tart Cafe & Restaurant.** There are several menus at this clean, multilevel restaurant: one lists an extensive selection of dim sum prepared to order, another is organized according to principles of Chinese medicine, a third features more familiar Chinese dishes, and a fourth lists drinks and curative "teas," which are actually more like soups: little white bowls composed of such exotica as almond milk, black sesame paste, and chestnuts. Don't miss the yam noodle soup with assorted dumplings or the Chinese broccoli in oyster sauce. The original café, with a more limited menu, is up the street (✉ 76 Mott St., at Canal St., ☎ 212/334–8088), and some think it has better food. ✉ *20 Mott St., between Chatham Sq. and Pell St.,* ☎ *212/964–0380. No credit cards.*

$ ✕ **Cafe Habana.** The simple Cuban-Mexican menu at this small neighborhood hangout reflects the friendly, casual atmosphere: Cubano sandwiches, grilled corn with cojito cheese, and *camarones al ajillo* (shrimp in garlic sauce), all at budget prices. ✉ *17 Prince St., at Elizabeth St.,* ☎ *212/625–2001. AE, DC, MC, V.*

$ ★ ✕ **Le Pain Quotidien.** This international Belgian chain brings its homeland ingredients with it, treating New Yorkers to crusty breads and delicious Belgian chocolate sweetening the café mochas and hot chocolate. For a more substantial meal, take a seat at the long wooden communal table and sample hearty sandwiches like roast beef with caper mayonnaise. ✉ *1131 Madison Ave., between E. 84th and E. 85th Sts.,* ☎ *212/327–4900;* ✉ *833 Lexington Ave., between E. 63rd and E. 64th Sts.,* ☎ *212/744–5810;* ✉ *1336 1st Ave., at E. 72nd St.,* ☎ *212/717–4800. No credit cards.*

$ ✕ **Pongal.** Service may be a bit slow, but the gentle prices and marvelous dishes more than compensate at this pretty vegetarian Indian restaurant, which happens to be kosher. Magnificent *dosas* (thin pancakes) made with lentils and rice flour are wrapped around potatoes and a fiery chutney. The Gujarati thali offers a taste of many dishes. ✉ *110 Lexington Ave., between 27th and 28th Sts.,* ☎ *212/696–*

9458; ✉ 81 Lexington Ave., at E. 26th St., ☎ 212/696–5130. No credit cards.

$ ✕ **Viet-Nam.** It may be difficult to find the little elbow of a street where this rathskeller dive is located, but after one bite of the fresh, flavorful, and cheap Vietnamese food you'll remember how to get back. Among the highlights are the green papaya salad with beef jerky, sweet-and-sour shrimp soup, and anything in black bean sauce. ✉ *11–13 Doyers St., between Bowery and Pell St.,* ☎ *212/693–0725. AE, MC, V.*

Lodging

A constant demand for hotel rooms here means hoteliers can command a nightly rate of $300. Don't be put off, though, many offer deals through their front desks, Web sites, or on-line discounters that cut rates significantly. Don't be afraid to ask.

$$$$ ★ **The Carlyle.** European tradition and Manhattan swank shake hands at this elegant baby grand on Madison Avenue, just steps from Central Park. Everything here suggests refinement, from the Mark Hampton–designed rooms, with their fine antique furniture and artfully framed Audubons and botanicals, to the first-rate service. ✉ *35 E. 76th St., 10021,* ☎ *212/744–1600 or 800/227–5737,* FAX *212/717–4682,* WEB *www.dir-dd.com/the-carlyle.html. 190 rooms. Restaurant, health club. AE, DC, MC, V.*

$$$$ **Essex House.** The lobby of this stately Central Park South property is an Art Deco masterpiece fit for Fred and Ginger. Guest rooms, all with large, marble bathrooms, are outfitted with British Chippendale or French Louis XIV antiques. Views from parkside rooms—which range from tiny queens to suites you could get lost in—are stunning year-round. ✉ *160 Central Park S, 10019,* ☎ *212/247–0300 or 800/937–8461,* FAX *212/315–1839,* WEB *www.starwood.com. 597 rooms. 2 restaurants, health club. AE, D, DC, MC, V.*

$$$$ ★ **The Inn at Irving Place.** The city's most charming small inn occupies two grand 1830s town houses just steps from Gramercy Park. Rooms have ornamental fireplaces, four-poster beds with embroidered linens, wood shutters, and glossy cherrywood floors. In the morning, steaming pots of tea and coffee are served in the tea salon, along with a free Continental breakfast. ✉ *56 Irving Pl., 10003,* ☎ *212/533–4600 or 800/685–1447,* FAX *212/533–4611,* WEB *www.innatirving.com. 11 rooms. AE, D, DC, MC, V.*

$$$$ ★ **Library Hotel.** This handsome landmark building gets its intellectual inspiration from the nearby New York Public Library. Each of its 10 floors is dedicated to one of the 10 categories of the Dewey Decimal System, with modern rooms stocked with art and books relevant to a subtopic (such as medicine or poetry). ✉ *299 Madison Ave., 10017,* ☎ *212/983–4500 or 877/793–7323,* FAX *212/499–9099,* WEB *www.libraryhotel.com. 60 rooms. Restaurant. AE, DC, MC, V. CP.*

$$$$ **Mercer Hotel.** Guest rooms at this minimalist masterpiece are enormous, with long entryways, high ceilings, and walk-in closets; dark African woods and high-tech light fixtures make a subtle statement. Bathrooms steal the show with their decadent two-person tubs, some of them surrounded by mirrors. ✉ *147 Mercer St., 10012,* ☎ *212/966–6060 or 888/918–6060,* FAX *212/965–3838. 75 rooms. Restaurant. AE, DC, MC, V.*

$$$$ **The Plaza.** Towering like a giant wedding cake on 5th Avenue opposite Central Park, this is one of New York's most beloved hotels. Suites are magnificent, but even the smallest guest rooms have crystal chandeliers and 14-ft ceilings. Though service could be much more efficient, the hotel still reigns as stately as a queen, if somewhat past her prime. ✉ *5th Ave. at W. 59th St., 10019,* ☎ *212/759–3000 or 800/*

759–3000, FAX *212/546–5324,* WEB *www.fairmont.com. 805 rooms. 4 restaurants, health club. AE, D, DC, MC, V.*

$$$$ ★ **The St. Regis.** A one-of-a-kind New York classic, this 5th Avenue Beaux Arts landmark is a hive of activity in its unparalleled public spaces. The King Cole Bar is an institution in itself. Guest rooms, all with butler service, are the last word in classic luxury, with crystal chandeliers, Louis XV antiques, Tiffany silver services, and outstanding marble bathrooms. ✉ *2 E. 55th St., 10022,* ☎ *212/753–4500 800/325–3589,* FAX *212/787–3447,* WEB *www.starwoodhotels.com. 314 rooms. 2 restaurants, health club. AE, D, DC, MC, V.*

$$$$ **Waldorf-Astoria.** This Art Deco masterpiece built in 1931 is a hub of city life; the lobby, with its original murals and mosaics, is a meeting place for the rich and powerful. Guest rooms, each individually decorated, are all traditional and elegant. ✉ *301 Park Ave., 10022,* ☎ *212/355–3000 or 800/925–3673,* FAX *212/872–7272,* WEB *www.waldorf.com. 1,452 rooms. 4 restaurants, health club. AE, D, DC, MC, V.*

$$$$ ★ **The Warwick.** Built by William Randolph Hearst in 1927, the Warwick remains a midtown favorite, well placed for theater and points west. Its handsome, Regency-style rooms have soft pastel color schemes, mahogany armoires, and nice marble bathrooms. ✉ *65 W. 54th St., 10019,* ☎ *212/247–2700 or 800/223–4099,* FAX *212/489–3926,* WEB *www.warwickhotels.com. 426 rooms. Restaurant. AE, DC, MC, V.*

$$$–$$$$ **Holiday Inn Wall Street.** You know the future has arrived when a Holiday Inn offers T-1 Internet access in every room (a New York first). Half the rooms have desktop PCs, and on the "smart floor" wireless laptops and printers are at the ready. The comfortable rooms are surprisingly spacious; thoughtful touches include ergonomically designed work spaces and oversize shower heads that simulate falling rain. ✉ *15 Gold St., 10038,* ☎ *212/232–7700 or 800/465–4329,* FAX *212/425–0330,* WEB *www.holidayinnwsd.com. 137 rooms. Restaurant. AE, D, DC, MC, V.*

$$$ **Hotel Beacon.** The Upper West Side's best buy is a short walk from both Central Park and Lincoln Center. All rooms and suites have kitchenettes with coffeemakers, full-size refrigerators, and stoves; some even have microwaves. What's more, the closets are huge, and the bathrooms come complete with Hollywood dressing room–style mirrors. ✉ *2130 Broadway, 10023,* ☎ *212/787–1100 or 800/572–4969,* FAX *212/787–8119,* WEB *www.beaconhotel.com. 239 rooms. AE, D, DC, MC, V.*

$$–$$$ ★ **Broadway Inn.** This comfortable, inexpensive theater district gem is one of the best deals in town. Impeccably clean neo-deco rooms with black-lacquer beds are basic but cheerful. Single travelers can get their own room for as little as $89, and the kitchenette suites are perfect for small families on a New York getaway. ✉ *264 W. 46th St., 10036,* ☎ *212/997–9200 or 800/826–6300,* FAX *212/768–2807,* WEB *www.broadwayinn.com. 41 rooms. Restaurant. AE, D, DC, MC, V. CP.*

$$ **The Gershwin.** Young travelers flock to this hip budget hotel-cum-hostel, housed in a 13-story Greek Revival. Enter, and be visually assaulted by a giant primary-color cartoony sculpture, one of many works by house artist Brad Howe. Dormitories have four or eight beds and a remarkable $22 rate. ✉ *7 E. 27th St., 10016,* ☎ *212/545–8000,* FAX *212/684–5546,* WEB *www.gershwinhotel.com. 120 rooms, 15 dorm rooms. Restaurant. AE, MC, V.*

$$ **Herald Square Hotel.** Vintage magazine covers adorning the hallways inside lend character to this historic hotel, housed in the former *Life* magazine building. Rooms are basic and clean; this is a no-frills option, but it's a rare thing to find a single room for the downright suburban sum of $60. ✉ *19 W. 31st St., 10001,* ☎ *212/279–4017 or*

800/727–1888, FAX 212/643–9208, WEB www.heraldsquarehotel.com. 120 rooms. AE, D, MC, V.

$$ **Howard Johnson.** This new hotel at the nexus of East Village and Lower East Side nightlife is perfect for those wanting to check out the downtown scene. The tidy rooms each have enough room for a desk, and with amenities such as in-room hair dryers and voice-mail, plus free local calls, you're getting more than your money's worth in New York's hotel market. Just next door is a century-old knish bakery. ✉ *135 E. Houston St., 10002,* ☎ *212/358–8844 or 800/446–4656,* FAX *212/473–3500,* WEB *www.hojo.com. 46 rooms. AE, D, DC, MC, V.*

$$ ★ **Larchmont Hotel.** You might miss the entrance to this Beaux Arts brownstone, whose geranium boxes and lanterns blend right in with the old New York feel of West 11th Street. If you don't mind shared bathrooms and no room service or concierge, the residential-style accommodations are all anyone could ask for at this price. ✉ *27 W. 11th St., 10011,* ☎ *212/989–9333,* FAX *212/989–9496,* WEB *www.larchmonthotel.com. 60 rooms without bath. AE, D, DC, MC, V. CP.*

$$ **Malibu Studios Hotel.** This hip, young, budget crash pad could very well pass for a college dorm, especially given its proximity to the Columbia University campus. Though it's farther north than some would care to venture, the neighborhood is lively and safe. Clean, modern double-occupancy rooms with private bath start at $99, and those with shared bath start at $55. ✉ *2688 Broadway, at 103rd St., 10025,* ☎ *212/222–2954 or 800/647–2227,* FAX *212/678–6842,* WEB *www.malibuhotelnyc.com. 150 rooms, 100 with bath. MC, V.*

Nightlife and the Arts

Full listings of entertainment and cultural events appear in the weekly magazines *New York* and *Time Out New York*; they include capsule summaries of plays, concerts, and exhibitions, as well as performance times and ticket prices. The *New York Times* has excellent event listings on Friday, and the "Arts & Leisure" section on Sunday also lists and describes events. The Theater Directory in the daily *New York Times* advertises ticket information for Broadway and Off-Broadway shows. Listings of events also appear weekly in *The New Yorker* and the *Village Voice,* a free weekly newspaper that probably has more nightclub ads than any other rag in the world. For the tattooed and pierced, *Paper* magazine's "P.M. 'Til Dawn" and bar sections have as good a listing as exists of the roving clubs and the best of the fashionable crowd's hangouts. The best place to get gay nightlife info is either from *HX* or *Next Magazine*; for lesbians, it's *GO NYC.* All are free and available at almost any gay bar in town.

Nightlife

BAR-LOUNGES

The **Campbell Apartment** (✉ 15 Vanderbilt Ave., ☎ 212/953–0409), a restored space inside Grand Central Terminal, dates to the '30s, when it was the private office of an executive who obviously knew the good life. Martinis are the rule at the cellar-like, stylish, Russian-theme **Pravda** (✉ 281 Lafayette St., ☎ 212/226–4944). The **Screening Room** (✉ 54 Varick St., ☎ 212/334–2100) offers good food, drinks, and movies all in one congenial space.

CABARET

The **Oak Room** at the Algonquin Hotel (✉ 59 W. 44th St., ☎ 212/840–6800) still offers yesteryear's charms. Just head straight for the long, narrow club–cum–watering hole; you might find the hopelessly romantic singer Andrea Marcovicci.

COMEDY CLUBS

Caroline's Comedy Club (✉ 1626 Broadway, ☎ 212/757–4100), a high-gloss venue, features established names as well as comedians on the edge of stardom. The **Gotham Comedy Club** (✉ 34 W. 22nd St., between 5th and 6th Aves., ☎ 212/367–9000) is housed in a landmark building and showcases popular headliners such as Chris Rock and David Brenner.

DANCE CLUBS

Irving Plaza (✉ 17 Irving Pl., ☎ 212/777–6800) has ballroom dancing Sunday nights to live orchestras, organized by the Swing Dance Society. For information on the society, call 212/696–9737. Perhaps the no-alcohol policy at **Vinyl** (✉ 6 Hubert St., ☎ 212/343–1379) draws a more determined gang, but whatever the reason, the crowd is friendly, the vibe is good, and the dancing is among the city's hottest. **Webster Hall** (✉ 125 E. 11th St., ☎ 212/353–1600), a fave among NYU students and similar species, has four floors and five eras of music.

JAZZ CLUBS

Many consider the **Blue Note** (✉ 131 W. 3rd St., ☎ 212/475–8592) the jazz capital of the world. The laid-back, three-level **Knitting Factory** (✉ 74 Leonard St., ☎ 212/219–3055) hosts avant-garde jazz in a variety of settings. The **Village Vanguard** (✉ 178 7th Ave. S, ☎ 212/255–4037) is a basement joint that has ridden the crest of every new wave in jazz.

POP, ROCK, BLUES, AND COUNTRY

The **Bitter End** (✉ 147 Bleecker St., ☎ 212/673–7030) has been giving a break to folk, rock, jazz, and country acts for more than 25 years. A granddaddy among clubs, the **Bottom Line** (✉ 15 W. 4th St., ☎ 212/228–6300), an intimate sit-down space, features folk and rock headliners. American punk rock and New Wave (the Ramones, Blondie, the Talking Heads) were born in the long, black tunnel of **CBGB & OMFUG** (✉ 315 Bowery, at Bleecker St., ☎ 212/982–4052). **Rodeo Bar** (✉ 375 3rd Ave., ☎ 212/683–6500), a full-scale Texas roadhouse, never charges a cover for its country, rock, rockabilly, and blues bands.

FOR SINGLES (UNDER 30)

Traipse through an alley to find **Lansky Lounge and Grill** (✉ 104 Norfolk St., between Delancey and Rivington Sts., ☎ 212/677–9489), a former haunt of gangster Myer Lansky, now a cocktail venue. At **Max Fish** (✉ 178 Ludlow St., ☎ 212/529–3959), a kitschy palace with a pool table and a twisted image of a grimacing Julio Iglesias over the bar, a young, grungy crowd gathers around midnight. **McSorley's Old Ale House** (✉ 15 E. 7th St., ☎ 212/473–9148), one of New York's oldest saloons, is a must-see for beer-loving first-timers to Gotham, even if only two kinds of brew are served: McSorley's light and McSorley's dark. Put on something black and make your way to **MercBar** (✉ 151 Mercer St., ☎ 212/966–2727) for a terrific martini.

FOR SINGLES (OVER 30)

Café des Artistes (✉ 1 W. 67th St., ☎ 212/877–3500) has a small, warm bar where interesting strangers tell their life stories and the house drink is pear champagne. **Monkey Bar** (✉ 60 E. 54th St., ☎ 212/838–2600) is a posh '90s creation that draws mannered banker types who shoot back Scotch.

GAY AND LESBIAN BARS AND CLUBS

The comfy couches in back are the big draw at **Barracuda** (✉ 275 W. 22nd St., ☎ 212/645–8613). **g** (✉ 223 W. 19th St., ☎ 212/929–1085), an up-to-the-minute favorite, draws an upscale, mostly male crowd to its huge circular bar and two airy rooms lined with leather settees. The lesbian club **Henrietta Hudson** (✉ 438 Hudson St., ☎ 212/924–3347) has two large rooms, a DJ, and a pool table. **Meow Mix** (✉ 269 E. Houston St., ☎ 212/254–0688) puts out live music and cheap drinks and pulls in some of the city's cutest girls.

The Arts

CLASSICAL MUSIC

Lincoln Center (☞ Upper West Side *in* Exploring Manhattan, *above*) has magnificent concert halls and theaters showcasing much of New York's serious music scene. Its **Avery Fisher Hall** (☎ 212/875–5030) is home to the New York Philharmonic Orchestra, the Mostly Mozart Festival, and visiting orchestras and soloists. **Carnegie Hall** (✉ 154 W. 57th St., at 7th Ave., ☎ 212/247–7800), the city's most famous classical-music palace, is more than 100 years old. This is where Leonard Bernstein made his conducting debut in 1943; where Jack Benny and Isaac Stern fiddled together; and where the Beatles played one of their first U.S. concerts.

DANCE

The **American Ballet Theatre** (☎ 212/477–3030) in Lincoln Center is the resident dance company of the Metropolitan Opera House. **City Center** (✉ 131 W. 55th St., ☎ 212/581–1212) hosts innovative performance groups and dance companies, such as the Alvin Ailey and the Paul Taylor dance companies. The **Joyce Theater** (✉ 175 8th Ave., at 19th St., ☎ 212/242–0800) schedules a potpourri of international dance troupes. The **New York City Ballet** (☎ 212/870–5570) performs at Lincoln Center's New York State Theater. It reached world-class prominence under the direction of the late George Balanchine; Peter Martins is now ballet master-in-chief.

FILM

On any day of the year film buffs find all the major new releases, plus renowned classics, unusual foreign offerings, and experimental works. For information on schedules and theaters dial 212/777–FILM (MovieFone), or check the local newspapers. *New York, The New Yorker,* and *Time Out New York* magazines publish programs and reviews. The vast majority of Manhattan theaters are first-run houses. Among the art film and revival houses are the **Angelika Film Center** (✉ W. Houston and Mercer Sts., ☎ 212/995–2000), **Film Forum** (✉ 209 W. Houston St., ☎ 212/727–8110), **Landmark's Sunshine Cinema** (✉ 143 E. Houston St., ☎ 212/358–7709), and the **Walter Reade Theater** (✉ 165 W. 65th St., ☎ 212/875–5600).

OPERA

The **Metropolitan Opera House** (☎ 212/362–6000), at Lincoln Center, is a sublime setting for mostly classic operas performed by world-class stars. The diverse repertoire of the **New York City Opera** (☎ 212/870–5570), at Lincoln Center's State Theater, consists of adventurous and rarely seen works as well as classic opera favorites.

THEATER

Nearly 40 Broadway theaters, three dozen Off-Broadway theaters, and 200 Off-Off-Broadway houses make New York a theater lover's paradise. Most Broadway theaters are in the Theater District, between Broadway and 8th Avenue, from 40th to 53rd Street. Off- and Off-Off-Broadway theaters are scattered all over town.

The **TKTS booth** (✉ Duffy Square, W. 47th St. and Broadway; South Street Seaport, corner of Front and John Sts. ☎ 212/221–0013) is New York's best-known source of discount tickets. TKTS sells day-of-performance tickets for Broadway and some Off-Broadway plays at discounts of 25% or 50% (plus $2.50 per ticket), depending on a show's popularity. For evening performances Monday–Sunday, the Duffy Square booth is open 3–8; for Wednesday and Sunday matinee shows, 10–2; for Sunday matinee and evening performances, 11–8. TKTS accepts only cash or traveler's checks. Downtown hours are Monday–Saturday 11–6 and Sunday 11–3:30.

Spectator Sports

Baseball: New York Mets (✉ Shea Stadium, Roosevelt Ave. off Grand Central Pkwy., ☎ 718/507–8499). **New York Yankees** (✉ Yankee Stadium, 161st St. and River Ave., ☎ 718/293–6000). **Basketball: New York Knicks** (✉ Madison Square Garden, 7th Ave. between 31st and 33rd Sts., ☎ 212/465–6741; 212/465–5867 Knicks hot line). **New Jersey Nets** (✉ Continental Airlines Arena, Rte. 3, East Rutherford, NJ, ☎ 201/935–3900). **New York Liberty** (✉ Madison Square Garden, 7th Ave. between 31st and 33rd Sts., ☎ 877/962–2849). **Football: New York Giants** (✉ Giants Stadium, Rte. 3, East Rutherford, NJ, ☎ 201/935–8111). **New York Jets** (✉ Giants Stadium, Rte. 3, East Rutherford, NJ, ☎ 516/560–8200). **Hockey: New York Rangers** (✉ Madison Square Garden, 7th Ave. between 31st and 33rd Sts., ☎ 212/465–6741). **Running: New York Marathon** (✉ New York Road Runners Club, 9 E. 89th St., at 5th Ave., ☎ 212/860–4455). **Tennis: U.S. Open,** late August and early September at the USTA National Tennis Center in Flushing Meadows–Corona Park, Queens (☎ 718/760–6200).

Shopping

You can buy almost anything you might want or need at almost any time of day or night somewhere in New York City, but in general, stores are open every day and keep late hours on Thursday. Many of the high-end shops along upper 5th and Madison avenues close on Sunday. The bargain shops along Orchard Street on the Lower East Side are closed on Saturday, mobbed on Sunday. For specialty stores with several branches in the city we have listed the locations in the busier shopping neighborhoods.

Shopping Neighborhoods

Fifth Avenue from 50th to 58th Street contains many of the world's most famous—and expensive—stores, including several excellent jewelers and department stores. **Fifty-seventh Street** between Park and 5th Avenues is an audacious mix of couture flagships and more accessible retail blockbusters. **Madison Avenue** between 59th and 79th streets has scads of ultraexclusive stores from the best-known American and international designers. **SoHo** is packed with trendy and top-designer clothing boutiques, makeup stores, and housewares shops. A few blocks east, the streets of **NoLita** (North of Little Italy), are lined with carefully arranged pocket-size boutiques offering precious housewares and fashions. NoLita's parallel spines are Elizabeth, Mott, and Mulberry streets, between Houston and Broome. **Chinatown,** which abuts NoLita and Little Italy, is a maze of teeming streets where everything from dried shrimp to silk cheongsams to porcelain tea sets. Check Canal Street for fake Rolexes and Prada (and be sure to bargain). The **Lower East Side** offers bargains of all kinds, from luggage to lingerie, plus the city's most avant-garde shops, which often double as performance spaces or galleries. Directly north, the **East Village** has eclectic boutiques and inexpensive vintage clothing shops. **Chelsea** is scattered with art galleries and funky shops, many catering to the neighborhood's gay community.

Department Stores

Barneys (✉ 660 Madison Ave., at 60th St., ☎ 212/826–8900) is monied, modern New York to the hilt: floor after floor of cutting-edge designer clothes, cosmetics, and accessories for women and men, plus a tiny boutique for tots. **Bergdorf Goodman** (✉ 754 5th Ave., ☎ 212/753–7300) is where devastating elegance reigns in a *vieux riches* setting; the men's store, with its vaulted marble lobby, is across the street. **Bloomingdale's** (✉ 59th St. and Lexington Ave., ☎ 212/355–5900) is a New York institution, with a stupefying maze of cosmetics counters on the main floor and a good, dependable selection of merchandise for women, men, kids, and the home. **Century 21** (✉ 22 Cortlandt St., between Broadway and Church St., ☎ 212/227–9092) is the mother lode of discount shopping; four large floors are crammed with everything from designer suits to high-quality bedding. **Macy's** (✉ 34th St. and Broadway, ☎ 212/695–4400) has huge housewares and gourmet-foods departments, as well as not-too-fancy designer clothes for all ages. Chinatown's **Pearl River Mart** (✉ 277 Canal St., at Broadway, ☎ 212/431–4770; ✉ 200 Grand St., at Mott St., ☎ 212/966–1010) sells imported wares, bamboo steamers, silk pajamas, and, of course, perennially popular Chinese slippers at very low prices. **Saks Fifth Avenue** (✉ 611 5th Ave., at 49th St., ☎ 212/753–4000) is a fashion-only department store, with rack after rack of voguish designer goods for women, men, and children.

Specialty Stores

ANTIQUES

At **Florian Papp** (✉ 962 Madison Ave., ☎ 212/288–6770) the shine of gilt lures knowledgeable collectors. **Israel Sack, Inc.** (✉ 730 5th Ave., ☎ 212/399–6562) is widely considered one of the very best places in the country for 18th-century American furniture. The twins behind **Leigh Keno American Antiques** (✉ 127 E. 69th St., ☎ 212/734–2381) have a good eye and an interesting inventory. At **Manhattan Art & Antiques Center** (✉ 1050 2nd Ave., ☎ 212/355–4400) more than 100 dealers stock three floors with antiques from around the world.

BOOKS

All the big national **chain bookstores** are here, with branches all over town—Barnes & Noble, Borders, and Waldenbooks—but New York is the perfect place to rediscover the intimate touch of the independent bookseller. **Crawford Doyle Booksellers** (✉ 1082 Madison Ave., ☎ 212/288–6300) has a thoughtful selection of fiction, nonfiction, biographies, and so on, plus some rare books on the narrow upstairs balcony. **Gotham Book Mart** (✉ 41 W. 47th St., at 5th Ave., ☎ 212/719–4448) is now legendary among bibliophiles; it's due to move in late 2002. **Rizzoli Bookstore** (✉ 31 W. 57th St., ☎ 212/759–2424) is a hushed environment with a rich book selection. **St. Mark's Bookshop** (✉ 31 3rd Ave., ☎ 212/260–7853) extends far beyond the *New York Times* bestseller list; this store's New Titles section might have a study of postmodernism next to the latest Nick Hornby. Student-filled **Shakespeare & Co. Booksellers** (✉ 939 Lexington Ave., ☎ 212/570–0201; ✉ 716 Broadway, ☎ 212/529–1330) stocks the latest in just about every field. The scruffy **Strand** (✉ 828 Broadway, ☎ 212/473–1452; ✉ 95 Fulton St., ☎ 212/732–6070), North America's largest used-book store, offers more than 2 million volumes; rare books are located next door at 826 Broadway. The Fulton Street branch is less overwhelming than the Broadway behemoth.

JEWELRY

Bulgari (✉ 730 5th Ave., ☎ 212/315–9000; ✉ 783 Madison Ave., ☎ 212/717–2300; 2 E. 61st St., in the Hotel Pierre, ☎ 212/486–0326) has beautiful, weighty pieces. **Cartier** (✉ 653 5th Ave., ☎ 212/753–0111) still dazzles with extravagant gems; favorite items include the three-band trinity ring and the gold "love bracelet." Virtually every store is a jewelry shop in the **Diamond District** (✉ 47th St. between 5th and 6th Aves.); be ready to haggle. **Harry Winston** (✉ 718 5th Ave., ☎ 212/245–2000) is a long-standing source for outsize stones. **Me & Ro Jewelry** (✉ 239 Elizabeth St., ☎ 917/237–9215) creates ethnic-inspired designs that are both earthy and delicate. At legendary **Tiffany & Co.** (✉ 727 5th Ave., ☎ 212/755–8000) prices can be extravagant, but there's always a selection of lower-price gift items, not to mention some of the most creative display windows on 5th Avenue.

MEN'S AND WOMEN'S WEAR

Brooks Brothers (✉ 666 5th Ave., ☎ 212/276–9440) defines traditional American style. It's still the place that suits up most of Wall Street, not to mention the Ivy League. **Calvin Klein** (✉ 654 Madison Ave., ☎ 212/292–9000) has a stark store right next to Barneys that showcases the luxe end of the designer's clothing line, plus housewares, accessories, and yes, underwear. **Canal Jean** (✉ 504 Broadway, ☎ 212/226–1130) is a sort of clothing jumble shop—stacks of Levi's, vintage Hawaiian shirts, discounted name brands, and Army-Navy surplus. Hometown designer Donna Karan shows her **DKNY** lines (✉ 655 Madison Ave., ☎ 212/223–3569; ✉ 420 W. Broadway, ☎ 646/613–1100) in spaces rapidly adapted to the latest trends. **Giorgio Armani** (✉ 760 Madison Ave., ☎ 212/988–9191) displays stunning clothes in a museumlike space, or check **A/X: Armani Exchange** (✉ 568 Broadway, ☎ 212/431–6000; ✉ 645 5th Ave., ☎ 212/980–3037) for Armani style at lower prices. Sophisticated from its sunglasses to its shoes, **Gucci** (✉ 685 5th Ave., ☎ 212/826–2600) epitomizes desirability. Crowds swarm over the racks at **H&M** (✉ 640 5th Ave., ☎ 212/489–8777; ✉ 1328 Broadway, ☎ 646/473–1165; ✉ 558 Broadway, ☎ 212/343–2722) in search of up-to-the-minute trends at unbelievably low prices. For a perfectly edited selection of women's clothing that looks like it jumped right out of a fashion magazine, check out **Intermix** (✉ 1033 Madison Ave., ☎ 212/249–7858). **J. Crew** (✉ 99 Prince St., ☎ 212/966–2739; ✉ 203 Front St., ☎ 212/385–3500; ✉ 30 Rockefeller Plaza, ☎ 212/767–4227) lines up fresh-scrubbed essentials: wool sweaters, button-downs, easy-cut suits, jeans, and some of the best-fitting swimsuits around. The first retail powerhouse to set up shop in the newly chic meatpacking district, **Jeffrey** (✉ 449 W. 14th St., ☎ 212/206–3928) resembles the closet of your wildest dreams: piles of fancy shoes and racks of ultraluxe garments from top designers. Superboutique **Kirna Zabête** (✉ 96 Greene St., ☎ 212/941–9656) carries a truly eclectic mix of high-price designers. The gossamer silks, slick black technofabric, and ultraluxe shoes and leather goods at **Prada** (✉ 841 Madison Ave., ☎ 212/327–4200; 724 5th Ave., ☎ 212/664–0010; ✉ 575 Broadway, ☎ 212/334–8888) embody one of the great fashion coups of the last millennium. It's hard to top the **Polo/Ralph Lauren** (✉ 867 Madison Ave., ☎ 212/606–2100) location in its turn-of-the-20th-century mansion; the velvet evening gowns and pinstripe suits look right at home. **Polo Sport** is right across the street.

MUSIC STORES

Bleecker Bob's Golden Oldies Record Shop (✉ 118 W. 3rd St., ☎ 212/475–9677) is a spot with good rock on vinyl. Eclectic **Kim's Video & Music** (✉ 6 St. Marks Pl., at 2nd Ave., ☎ 212/598–9985; ✉ 144 Bleecker St., between Thompson St. and La Guardia Pl., ☎ 212/260–1010; ✉ 350 Bleecker St., at W. 10th St., ☎ 212/675–8996) crystallizes the downtown music scene. For gigantic spaces where you can browse for books, laser discs, DVDs, and videos—besides thousands of CDs—there are several monoliths. **HMV** (✉ 234 W. 42nd St., ☎ 212/302–1451; ✉ 565 5th Ave., ☎ 212/681–6700; ✉ 1280 Lexington Ave., ☎ 212/348–0800) is a formidable store with a good selection. A veteran of the behemoth record emporiums is **Tower Records** (✉ 1961 Broadway, ☎ 212/799–2500; ✉ 725 5th Ave., ☎ 212/838–8110; ✉ 692 Broadway, ☎ 212/505–1500).Find CDs and other merchandise at **Virgin Megastore** (✉ 1540 Broadway, ☎ 212/921–1020; ✉ 52 E. 14th St., ☎ 212/598–4666).

Side Trips to Other Boroughs

The Bronx

The 250-acre **New York Botanical Garden,** built around the dramatic gorge of the Bronx River, is considered one of the leading botany centers of the world.Less than a mile from the botanical garden is the world-class **Bronx Zoo** (for both, ☞ Parks, Gardens, and Zoos, *above*).

ARRIVING AND DEPARTING

For the botanical garden, take Metro-North to the New York Botanical Garden stop, or take Subway D to Bedford Park Boulevard. For the zoo, take Subway 2 to Pelham Parkway and walk three blocks west, or take the **Liberty Line** BxM-11 express bus from Manhattan to the Bronx Zoo (☎ 718/652–8400 for bus schedules, locations of stops, and fares).

Brooklyn

★ **Brooklyn Heights** was New York's first suburb, linked to the city first by ferry and later by the Brooklyn Bridge. In the 1940s and 1950s the Heights was an alternative to the bohemian haven of Greenwich Village—home to writers including Carson McCullers, W. H. Auden, and Norman Mailer. In the late 1960s the neighborhood was designated New York's first historic district. The **Plymouth Church of the Pilgrims** (✉ Orange St., between Henry and Hicks Sts., ☎ 718/624–4743) was a center of abolitionist sentiment in the years before the Civil War, thanks to the oratory of the eminent theologian Henry Ward Beecher. **Willow Street,** between Clark and Pierrepont streets, is one of Brooklyn Heights' prettiest and most architecturally varied blocks. Pierrepont Street ends at the **Brooklyn Heights Promenade,** a quiet sliver of park lined with benches offering a dramatic vista of the Manhattan skyline. Just off the promenade's south end, **Montague Street,** the commercial spine of the Heights, offers a flurry of shops, cafés, and restaurants.

ARRIVING AND DEPARTING

Walk across the Brooklyn Bridge from lower Manhattan near city hall and return on Subway 2 or 3 from the Clark Street station, a few blocks southwest of the walkway terminus.

Queens

Astoria, in Queens, is one of New York's most vital ethnic neighborhoods; once German, then Italian, it is now heavily Greek and is filled with shops and restaurants reflecting the community. Astoria is the site of the **American Museum of the Moving Image,** where a theater shows clips from the works of leading Hollywood cinematographers and galleries display interactive exhibits on filmmaking techniques. ✉ *35th Ave. at 36th St.,* ☎ *718/784–0077,* WEB *www.ammi.org.* *$8.50. Closed Mon.*

While the Museum of Modern Art (MoMA) undergoes a $650 million reconstruction of its famous 53rd Street building (to be completed ★ in 2005), its peerless collection of 20th-century art resides at **MoMA QNS,** a former factory in Long Island City, Queens. Look for highlights from the permanent collection as well as changing exhibitions. ✉ *45–*

20 33rd St., ☎ 718/389–4729, WEB www.moma.org. ✉ $10. Closed Wed.

ARRIVING AND DEPARTING

Take the N train from Manhattan to the Broadway stop. For the Museum of the Moving Image, walk five blocks along Broadway to 36th Street; turn right and walk two blocks to 35th Avenue. To visit MoMA QNS, take the 7 train to 33rd Street.

New York City Essentials

AIRPORTS AND TRANSFERS

Virtually every major U.S. and foreign airline serves one or more of New York's three airports. La Guardia and John F. Kennedy International airports are in Queens. Newark International Airport is in New Jersey.

➤ AIRPORT INFORMATION: **John F. Kennedy International** (☎ 718/244–4444, WEB www.jfkairport.com). **La Guardia** (☎ 718/533–3400, WEB www.laguardiaairport.com). **Newark International Airport** (☎ 973/961–6000, WEB www.newarkairport.com).

AIRPORT TRANSFER

Cab fare to midtown Manhattan runs $20–$30 plus tolls and tip from La Guardia, $35 plus tolls and tip from JFK, and $35–$55 plus tolls and tip from Newark. SuperShuttle connects all three airports to various locations in Manhattan. By public transportation, the A train (subway) to Howard Beach connects with a free airport shuttle bus to JFK.

➤ TAXIS AND SHUTTLES: **SuperShuttle** (☎ 800/258–3826, or 800/451–0455, WEB www.supershuttle.com).

BUS TRAVEL TO AND FROM NEW YORK CITY

The Port Authority Terminal handles all long-haul and commuter bus lines. Among the bus lines serving New York are Greyhound, Bonanza for travel from New England, Peter Pan Trailways in the Northeast, Martz Trailways from northeastern Pennsylvania, and New Jersey Transit from New Jersey.

➤ BUS INFORMATION: **Bonanza** (☎ 800/556–3815, WEB www.bonanzabus.com). **Greyhound** (☎ 800/231–2222, WEB www.greyhound.com). **Martz Trailways** (☎ 800/233–8604, WEB www.martztrailways.com). **New Jersey Transit** (☎ 973/762–5100, WEB www.njtransit.state.nj.us). **Peter Pan Trailways** (☎ 800/237–8747, WEB www.peterpanbus.com). **Port Authority Terminal** (✉ 40th to 42nd St., between 8th and 9th Aves., ☎ 212/564–8484, WEB www.panynj.gov).

BUS TRAVEL WITHIN NEW YORK CITY

Most buses follow easy-to-understand routes along the Manhattan grid, and some run 24 hours. Routes go up or down the north–south avenues, east and west on the major two-way crosstown streets: 96th, 86th, 79th, 72nd, 57th, 42nd, 34th, 23rd, and 14th. To find a bus stop, look for a light blue sign (or green for an express bus) on a green pole. Bus fare is $1.50 in exact coins (no pennies or bills) or a subway token; a MetroCard can also be used on all city buses. If you need to transfer to a connecting bus line and you are not using a MetroCard, request a free transfer coupon when paying the fare. Transfers between the bus and the subway are also free if you use a MetroCard. For 24-hour bus and subway information call the number listed below.

➤ BUS INFORMATION: **Metropolitan Transit Authority (MTA) Travel Information Center** (☎ 718/330–1234, WEB www.mta.nyc.ny.us).

CAR TRAVEL

A complex network of bridges and tunnels provides access to Manhattan. I–95 enters via the George Washington Bridge. I–495 enters from Long Island via the Midtown Tunnel. From upstate the city is accessible via the New York (Dewey) Thruway (I–87), which is known as the Major Deegan Expressway within New York City.

PARKING

Free parking is almost nonexistent in midtown, and parking lots everywhere are exorbitant ($10 for half an hour is not unusual in midtown).

RULES OF THE ROAD

If you're traveling by car, don't plan to use it much in Manhattan. Driving in the city can be a nightmare of gridlocked streets and aggressive fellow motorists. On city streets the speed limit is 30 mph, unless otherwise posted. In the front and back seats, the law requires that seat belts should be worn at all times. There's no right turn on red allowed within the city limits. It is illegal to use a hand-held cell phone while driving in New York State.

SUBWAY TRAVEL

The 714-mi subway system, the fastest and cheapest way to get around the city, serves Manhattan, Brooklyn, Queens, and the Bronx and operates 24 hours a day.

FARES AND SCHEDULES

Tokens cost $1.50 each—an unlimited daily use Fun Pass is $4—and are sold in subway stations. Pay-Per-Ride MetroCards, purchased for any amount between $3 and $80, are also available at all subway stations; to use one, swipe it through a reader at the turnstile; the fare is automatically deducted from the card's value. When you purchase a MetroCard for $15 or more you get an additional 10% credit. For $17 you can purchase an unlimited-ride MetroCard offering as many rides as you desire within a seven-day period—a good deal if you plan to take more than 12 rides. Transfers among subway lines are free at designated interchanges. For subway or bus maps ask at token booths.

➤ SUBWAY INFORMATION: **Metropolitan Transit Authority (MTA) Travel Information Center** (☎ 718/330–1234, WEB www.mta.nyc.ny.us).

TAXIS

Taxis (official, licensed ones are yellow) are usually easy to hail on the street, in front of major hotels, and by bus and train stations. The fare is $2 for the first ⅕ mi, 30¢ for each ⅕ mi thereafter, and 20¢ for each 90 seconds not in motion. A 50¢ surcharge is added to rides begun between 8 PM and 6 AM. Bridge and tunnel tolls are extra, and drivers expect a 15% tip. Barring performance above and beyond the call of duty, don't feel obliged to give more.

TOURS

BUS TOURS

Gray Line New York Tours offers a number of standard city and double-decker bus tours in several languages, plus trolley tours and day trips to Atlantic City. New York Doubledecker Tours covers the major attractions. Both tour lines allow you to hop on and off.

➤ FEES AND SCHEDULES: **Gray Line New York Tours** (✉ Port Authority Bus Terminal, 625 8th Ave., at 42nd St., ☎ 212/397–2600, WEB www.graylinenewyork.com). **New York Doubledecker Tours** (☎ 718/361–5788, WEB www.nydecker.com).

BOAT TOURS

From March to mid-December Circle Line Cruises offers a three-hour circumnavigation of Manhattan. Semi-Circle tours run from mid-December through March.
➤ FEES AND SCHEDULES: **Circle Line Cruises** (✉ Pier 83, at 42nd St. and 12th Ave., ☎ 212/563–3200, WEB www.circleline.com).

WALKING TOURS

Big Onion Walking Tours has year-round special-interest tours on weekdays and weekends. New York City Cultural Walking Tours focuses on the city's landmarks, memorials, and outdoor art. The Municipal Art Society offers walking tours covering history and architecture.
➤ FEES AND SCHEDULES: **Big Onion Walking Tours** (☎ 212/439–1090, WEB www.bigonion.com). **Municipal Art Society** (☎ 212/935–3960, WEB www.mas.org). **New York City Cultural Walking Tours** (☎ 212/979–2388, WEB www.nycwalk.com).

TRAIN TRAVEL

All train lines servicing Manhattan arrive or depart from either Pennsylvania Station or Grand Central Terminal, including Amtrak, MTA Metro-North Railroad, and New Jersey Transit.
➤ TRAIN INFORMATION: **Amtrak** (☎ 800/872–7245, WEB www.amtrak.com). **MTA Metro-North Railroad** (☎ 212/532–4900 or 800/638–7646, WEB www.mta.nyc.ny.us/mnr). **New Jersey Transit** (☎ 973/762–5100, WEB www.panynj.gov).

TRANSPORTATION AROUND NEW YORK CITY

New York is a city of neighborhoods best explored at a leisurely pace, up close, and on foot. Extensive public transportation easily bridges gaps between areas of interest.

VISITOR INFORMATION

➤ TOURIST INFORMATION: **NYC & Company–Convention & Visitors Bureau** (✉ 810 7th Ave., at 53rd St., 10019, ☎ 212/484–1222, FAX 212/246–6310, WEB www.nycvisit.com).

LONG ISLAND

Long Island is the largest island on America's East Coast—1,682 square mi—and the most varied. From west to east, it encompasses two New York City boroughs (Brooklyn and Queens), congested commuter towns, the farmland of the North Fork, and the world-famous summer resorts of the Hamptons and Montauk on the South Fork. It has arguably the nation's finest stretch of white-sand beach, as well as the notoriously clogged Long Island Expressway (LIE).

Exploring Long Island

Avoid the traffic-choked LIE and take the more leisurely roads that parallel the coasts. On the North Shore your best bet is Route 25A and, on the North Fork, Route 25; on the South Shore, Route 27 (Sunrise Highway) and Route 27A (Montauk Highway).

The string of wealthy suburbs on the **North Shore** that stretches east from Great Neck, about 40 mi outside New York City, to Huntington is known as the Gold Coast. The Vanderbilts, Whitneys, Roosevelts, and other such families built mansions here in the late 19th and early 20th centuries, making this area on Long Island Sound a fashionable playground for the rich; several of the mansions still standing (www.ligoldcoast.com) are open to the public.

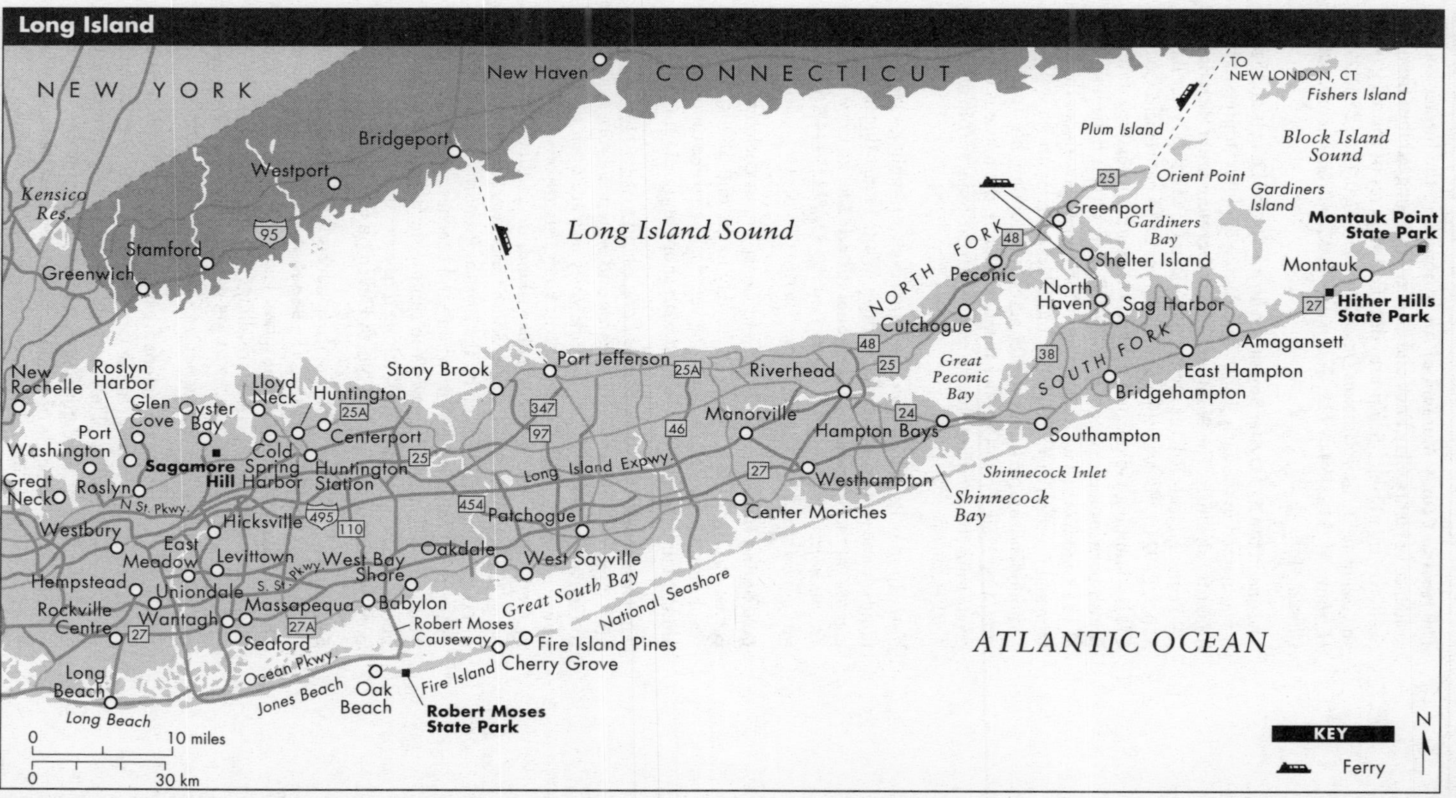
Long Island
NEW YORK
CONNECTICUT
New Haven
TO NEW LONDON, CT
Fishers Island
Plum Island
Block Island Sound
Orient Point
Gardiners Island
Kensico Res.
Bridgeport
Westport
Long Island Sound
Greenport
Gardiners Bay
Montauk Point State Park
Stamford
Greenwich
NORTH FORK
Shelter Island
Peconic
Montauk
North Haven
Sag Harbor
Hither Hills State Park
Cutchogue
Amagansett
SOUTH FORK
New Rochelle
Roslyn Harbor
Stony Brook
Port Jefferson
Riverhead
Great Peconic Bay
East Hampton
Bridgehampton
Glen Cove
Oyster Bay
Lloyd Neck
Huntington
Manorville
Hampton Bays
Southampton
Port Washington
Centerport
Cold Spring Harbor
Huntington Station
Sagamore Hill
Long Island Expwy.
Westhampton
Shinnecock Inlet
Shinnecock Bay
Great Neck
Roslyn
N St. Pkwy.
Center Moriches
Patchogue
Westbury
Hicksville
East Meadow
Levittown
West Bay Shore
Oakdale
West Sayville
Hempstead
Uniondale
S. St. Pkwy.
Great South Bay
National Seashore
Rockville Centre
Wantagh
Massapequa
Babylon
Robert Moses Causeway
Seaford
Fire Island Pines
ATLANTIC OCEAN
Long Beach
Ocean Pkwy.
Fire Island
Cherry Grove
Jones Beach
Oak Beach
Robert Moses State Park
0
10 miles
0
30 km
KEY
Ferry
N
95
25
48
27
38
25A
347
97
46
24
454
495
110
27A

The **Nassau County Museum of Art** is housed in the former country residence of Henry Clay Frick and displays changing exhibits from Botticelli to Frida Kahlo. Sculptures dot the 145 acres of formal gardens and rolling fields. ✉ *1 Museum Dr., at Northern Blvd. (Rte. 25A), Roslyn Harbor,* ☎ *516/484–9338,* WEB *www.nassaumuseum.com.* 🎫 *$6. Closed Mon.*

The quaint town of **Oyster Bay** sits on an inlet of the Long Island Sound. It was named in the early 1600s by a Dutch explorer impressed by its bountiful shellfish. The **Planting Fields Arboretum State Historic Park** (✉ Planting Fields Rd. off Oyster Bay–Glen Cove Rd., Oyster Bay, ☎ 516/922–9210, WEB www.plantingfields.org; 🎫 $5 per vehicle, Coe Hall $5) is a stunning Gold Coast property with an impressive estate. The British-born insurance magnate William Robertson Coe bought the place in 1913 and worked with landscape artist James Dawson, of the famed Olmsted Brothers' firm, to plan grand allées of trees, azalea walks, and a rhododendron park on the 409 acres surrounding his Tudor mansion, Coe Hall. From October through March, the house is open for group tours, by appointment; the rest of the year, tours are offered noon–3:30.

You can tour President Theodore Roosevelt's rambling Queen Anne family home—often called the Summer White House during his presidency—at the **Sagamore Hill National Historic Site.** ✉ *Cove Neck Rd. 1.7 mi north of Rte. 25A, Oyster Bay,* ☎ *516/922–4447,* WEB *www.nps.gov/sahi.* 🎫 *$5. Closed Mon.–Tues.*

Cold Spring Harbor, one of the Gold Coast's most enchanting towns, is east of Oyster Bay. During its heyday in the mid-1800s, this town was home port to a fleet of whaling vessels. Take some time to browse along Main Street, which is lined with shops and restaurants.

The **North Fork,** the upper part of Long Island's eastern tail, is bucolic farm country with thriving vineyards and wineries. From Aquebogue to Greenport, some 20 North Fork vineyards are open to the public (www.northfork.org/wineries). Most vineyards are on or off Route 25 or 48. Beautiful and historic **Shelter Island,** in Gardiners Bay, nestled between Long Island's North and South forks, was among the first parts of Long Island to be settled by the British. Primarily a summer resort today, it has quiet inns, some white-sand beaches, and the 2,000-acre Mashomack Nature Preserve. You can use the island as a scenic stepping-stone between the forks, taking the ferries that leave from Greenport on the North Fork and North Haven on the South Fork.

Sag Harbor, on the north shore of the South Fork, was an important whaling center from 1775 to 1871. The **Sag Harbor Whaling Museum**—an 1845 Greek Revival house—displays logbooks, scrimshaw, and harpoons, as well as some period furnishings and oil paintings. ✉ *200 Main St., Sag Harbor,* ☎ *631/725–0770,* WEB *www.sagharborwhalingmuseum.org.* 🎫 *$3. Closed weekdays in Oct., and Nov.–mid-May.*

On the South Fork, the **Hamptons** are seaside villages that the East Coast upper crust "discovered" in the late 1800s and transformed into elegant summer resorts. They include (west to east) Westhampton, Southampton, Bridgehampton, Sagaponack, Wainscott, and Amagansett. At the pinnacle of fashion and fame is **East Hampton**; despite hordes of tourists and celebrities who descend each summer, it retains its colonial heritage. Main Street has a classic white-frame Presbyterian church and stately old homes and inns, which mingle with trendy shops and galleries.

At the eastern tip of the South Fork is **Montauk,** with its seaside motels and condos, thriving fishing and boating community, and surfer-studded beaches. The village doesn't put on any airs, which makes it suitable for families. **Hither Hills State Park** (✉ Rte. 27, 12 mi west of Montauk village, ☎ 631/668–2554, WEB nysparks.state.ny.us; 🎫 free) preserves miles of rolling moors and dunes and forests.

You can climb the 137 steps that lead to the top of the **Montauk Point Lighthouse,** a Long Island landmark that was completed in 1796. ✉ *Rte. 27, 6 mi east of Montauk village,* ☎ *631/668–2544,* WEB *www.montauklighthouse.com.* 🎫 *$6. Closed early Dec.–mid.-Jan. and weekdays mid-Jan.–mid-May and Nov.–early Dec.*

Fire Island, a 32-mi-long barrier island on Long Island's south shore, encompasses a national wilderness area. Its six tiny communities include two longtime lesbian and gay enclaves, Cherry Grove and the Pines. To reach the west end of the island, take the Robert Moses Causeway to Robert Moses State Park—you can leave your car here for a small fee. You can reach the island's central and eastern communities by ferry.

Dining and Lodging

The major motel chains are represented on the island, though resort hotels and small inns predominate in the Hamptons. Lodging prices tend to double, if not triple, from Memorial Day through Labor Day.

Amagansett

$–$$ ✕ **Lobster Roll.** The crowds streaming through this simple shanty—a local landmark often referred to as Lunch—come for the lobster roll, burgers, and grilled tuna. ✉ *1980 Montauk Hwy.,* ☎ *631/267–3740. MC, V. Closed Nov.–Apr. and weekdays Apr. and Oct.*

Bridgehampton

$$–$$$$ ✕ **Bobby Van's.** The steaks are fabulous, but the menu is fairly diversified. There's a definite see-and-be-seen attitude here. ✉ *2393 Main St.,* ☎ *631/537–0590. Reservations essential. AE, D, DC, MC, V.*

East Hampton

$–$$$ ✕ **Babette's.** The emphasis at this funky indoor-outdoor café is on organic ingredients—there's even a juice bar—and the menu offers innovative choices for vegetarians and carnivores alike. ✉ *66 Newtown La.,* ☎ *631/329–5377. AE, MC, V. Closed Mon.–Thurs. Jan.–Mar.*

$$$–$$$$ ★ ✕🏨 **Maidstone Arms.** Dating to 1740, this Greek Revival inn is the coziest and most comfortable in town. It also has one of the best locations—across from a pond and a pristine park, surrounded by East Hampton's oldest streets and most beautiful houses. The always-busy restaurant serves French-inspired American cuisine, such as potato-wrapped striped bass on smothered red beans and crab butter. ✉ *207 Main St., 11937,* ☎ *631/324–5494 restaurant; 631/324–5006 inn;* FAX *631/324–5037;* WEB *www.maidstonearms.com. 16 rooms, 3 cottages. Restaurant. AE, DC, MC, V. BP.*

$$$$ 🏨 **J. Harper Poor Cottage.** At the *definitive* East Hampton retreat, you are coddled as you should be in the Hamptons. More mansion than cottage, the house dates back to the mid-1600s. Exquisite William Morris papers cover the walls, and overstuffed furniture graces the sitting rooms, which are filled with flowers and books. ✉ *181 Main St., 11937,* ☎ *631/324–4081,* FAX *631/329–5931,* WEB *www.jharperpoor.com. 5 rooms. AE, DC, MC, V. BP.*

Greenport

$$–$$$ ✕ **Claudio's.** The same family has run this classic seafood restaurant since its opening in 1870. Forget fancy culinary creations: go for the baked clams, fresh mussels, or fried calamari for starters and the shrimp scampi or grilled swordfish as a main dish. ✉ *111 Main St.,* ☎ *631/477–0627. MC, V. Closed Dec.–mid-Apr.*

Montauk

$$$$ 🏨 **Gurney's Inn Resort and Spa.** The fabulous location, on a bluff overlooking 1,000 ft of private ocean beach, and the European-style spa are the main attractions at this Montauk mainstay. The large, luxurious rooms and suites all have ocean views. ✉ *290 Old Montauk Hwy., 11954,* ☎ *631/668–2345,* FAX *631/668–3576,* WEB *www.gurneys-inn.com. 104 rooms, 5 cottages. 3 restaurants, pool, health club. AE, D, DC, MC, V. MAP.*

Sag Harbor

$$$–$$$$ ★ ✕🏨 **The American Hotel.** This small hotel includes a well-known restaurant that serves such fine dishes as crab cakes with chanterelles and truffles and a porterhouse steak Florentine. The bar is inviting and the rooms upstairs are big, with nice modern bathrooms. ✉ *25 Main St., 11963,* ☎ *631/725–3535,* FAX *631/725–3573,* WEB *www.theamericanhotel.com. 8 rooms. Restaurant. AE, D, DC, MC, V. No lunch weekdays. CP.*

Shelter Island

$$–$$$$ ★ ✕🏨 **Ram's Head Inn.** The 1929 center-hall colonial-style island retreat makes for the perfect romantic getaway—far from the Hamptons crowds. The inn overlooks 800 ft of beachfront. The dining room ($$$–$$$$), one of the best on eastern Long Island, serves contemporary fare. Look for Long Island duck and other local game, seafood, and produce. ✉ *108 Ram Island Dr., 11965,* ☎ *631/749–0811,* FAX *631/749–0059,* WEB *www.shelterislandinns.com. 17 rooms. Restaurant, tennis. AE, MC, V. CP.*

Motels

🏨 **Drake Motor Inn** (✉ 16 Penny La., Hampton Bays 11946, ☎ 631/728–1592, FAX 631/728–8770), 15 rooms; pool; *$$–$$$.*

🏨 **Best Western** (✉ 1830 Rte. 25, Riverhead 11901, ☎ 631/369–2200, FAX 631/369–1202), 100 rooms; restaurant, pool, health club; *$$$–$$$$.*

Campground

⛺ **Hither Hills State Park** (✉ Rte. 27, 12 mi west of Montauk village, ☎ 631/668–2554 or 800/456–2267, WEB nysparks.state.ny.us or www.licamping.com/camps/hither.htm) offers tent and RV sites from April through November, but you must reserve nearly 11 months ahead.

Nightlife and the Arts

Check the Friday edition of *Newsday,* the Long Island newspaper, which has a weekend supplement containing information about Long Island arts and entertainment, as well as the magazine *Long Island Monthly.*

Nightlife

The Long Island scene is lively, especially in the Hamptons. You can hear live acts every summer night at the **Stephen Talkhouse** (✉ 161 Main St., Amagansett, ☎ 631/267–3117). In Southampton, serious nightclubbers head to **Jet East** (✉ 1811 North Sea Rd., Southampton, ☎ 631/283–0808), but beware: lots of hype has made this place a scene. The **Tavern** (✉ 125 Tuckahoe La., Southampton, ☎ 631/287–2125) has a bar, dancing, and lots of fabulous people.

The Arts

Major pop and rock musicians play **Jones Beach Theater** (✉ Jones Beach State Park, Wantagh, ☎ 516/221–1000), off Zach's Bay at the end of Wantagh Parkway, May–September. **Nassau Veterans Memorial Coliseum** (✉ 1255 Hempstead Tpke., Uniondale, ☎ 516/794–9300) hosts everything from the county fair to big-name pop acts. **Westbury Music Fair** (✉ 590 Brush Hollow Rd., Westbury, ☎ 516/334–0800) presents live concerts, shows, and theater.

Outdoor Activities and Sports

Participant Sports

BOATING

Oyster Bay Sailing School (☎ 516/922–7245) offers classes April through October as well as off-season vacation packages; charter sailboats are also available.

Spectator Sports

Hockey: New York Islanders (✉ Nassau Veterans Memorial Coliseum, 1255 Hempstead Tpke., Uniondale, ☎ 516/794–9300). **Horse Racing: Belmont Park Race Track** (✉ 2150 Hempstead Tpke., Exit 26D off Cross Island Pkwy., Elmont, ☎ 718/641–4700) is home to the third jewel in horse racing's triple crown, the Belmont Stakes, held in early June.

Beaches

★ **Jones Beach State Park** (✉ Wantagh Pkwy. S, Wantagh, ☎ 516/785–1600), a wide, sandy 6½-mi stretch of ocean beach, is the most crowded but also the biggest and most fully equipped of Long Island's beaches. **Robert Moses State Park** (✉ Robert Moses Causeway S, Exit 40 off Southern State Pkwy., Babylon, ☎ 516/631–0449), on the west end of Fire Island, is an uncrowded, beautiful, sandy ocean beach. In the Hamptons, you need a town permit to park at many of the beaches, but some of them do sell day passes. Ditch Plains, in Montauk (east of town off Ditch Plains Road), is where the surfers head.

Shopping

Long Island is known for its shopping malls. With Fendi, Prada, Burberry, and the like, **Americana Manhasset** (✉ 2110 Northern Blvd., Manhasset, ☎ 516/627–2277 or 800/818–6767) is about as high-end as a mall can get. **Roosevelt Field** (✉ Meadowbrook Pkwy., Garden City, ☎ 516/742–8000) has more than 220 stores, including anchors Bloomingdale's, Macy's, and Nordstrom. Coach, Nike, and Pottery Barn are some of the names at **Tanger Outlet** (✉ 1770 W. Main St./Rte. 25, Riverhead, ☎ 800/407–4894 or 631/369–2732).

Long Island Essentials

AIRPORTS

In addition to John F. Kennedy and La Guardia airports, in Queens (☞ New York City Essentials, *above*), Long Island is served by Long Island MacArthur Airport.

➤ AIRPORT INFORMATION: **Long Island MacArthur Airport** (ISP; ✉ 100 Arrivals Ave., Ronkonkoma, ☎ 631/467–3210, WEB www.macarthurairport.com).

BOAT AND FERRY INFORMATION

A few ferries service Fire Island: The Sayville Ferry Service shuttles from Sayville to Cherry Grove, Fire Island Pines, and Sailor's Haven. Fire Island Ferries, Inc. runs from Bayshore to several Fire Island communities. North Ferry Co. shuttles between Shelter Island and Greenport; South Ferry Inc. leaves for the island from North Haven.

➤ BOAT AND FERRY INFORMATION: **Fire Island Ferries, Inc.** (☎ 631/665–3600). **North Ferry Co.** (☎ 631/749–0139, WEB www.northferry.com). **Sayville Ferry Service** (☎ 631/589–0810). **South Ferry Inc.** (☎ 631/749–1200, WEB www.southferry.com).

BUS TRAVEL

The Hampton Jitney and the Hampton Luxury Liner link Manhattan with towns on the southeastern end of Long Island.

➤ BUS INFORMATION: **Hampton Jitney** (☎ 631/283–4600, 800/936–0440 in metropolitan New York area, WEB www.hamptonjitney.com). **Hampton Luxury Liner** (☎ 631/537–5800, WEB www.hamptonluxuryliner.com).

CAR TRAVEL

The Queens Midtown Tunnel (I–495), Queensborough Bridge (Northern Boulevard, Route 25A), and the Triborough Bridge (I–278) connect Long Island with Manhattan. The Throgs Neck Bridge (I–295) and the Whitestone Bridge (I–678) provide access from the Bronx and New England. Although mass transit makes Long Island very accessible, a car is necessary to explore the island's nooks and crannies.

TRAIN TRAVEL

The Long Island Railroad has frequent service from Penn Station in Manhattan to major towns on Long Island.

➤ TRAIN INFORMATION: **Long Island Railroad** (☎ 718/330–1234).

VISITOR INFORMATION

The center in Riverhead is open year-round.

➤ TOURIST INFORMATION: **Fire Island Tourism Bureau** (✉ 49 N. Main St., Sayville 11782, ☎ 631/563–8448, WEB www.asapnet.com/fireislandtourism). **Long Island Convention and Visitors Bureau** (✉ 350 Vanderbilt Motor Pkwy., Suite 103, Hauppauge 11788, ☎ 631/951–3440 or 800/441–4601, WEB www.licvb.com). **Visitor Information Centers** (✉ Southern State Pkwy. between Exits 13 and 14, Valley Stream; ✉ LIE between Exits 52 and 53, Dix Hills–Deer Park; ✉ Tanger Outlet, 1770 W. Main St./Rte. 25, Riverhead).

THE HUDSON VALLEY AND THE CATSKILLS

The landscape along the Hudson River for the 140 mi from Westchester County to Albany, the state capital, is among the loveliest in America. This natural beauty—dramatic palisades, pine forests, cool mountain lakes and streams—inspired an entire art movement: the Hudson River School, which originated in the 19th century. Still a rich agricultural region, the valley has scores of orchards, vineyards, and farm markets. The upper west valley is fringed by the Catskill Mountains, where fly-fishing, hiking, rock climbing, and skiing are a few of the activities available. Proximity to Manhattan makes this a viable destination for day trips, but the numerous country inns, B&Bs, and resorts make more-leisurely journeys especially enjoyable.

Exploring the Hudson Valley and the Catskills

U.S. 9 hugs the east bank of the Hudson, passing through many picturesque towns, including Tarrytown, Hyde Park, and Rhinebeck. U.S. 9 West travels the west bank from Nyack to Catskill, through Newburgh and

Hudson Valley and the Catskills

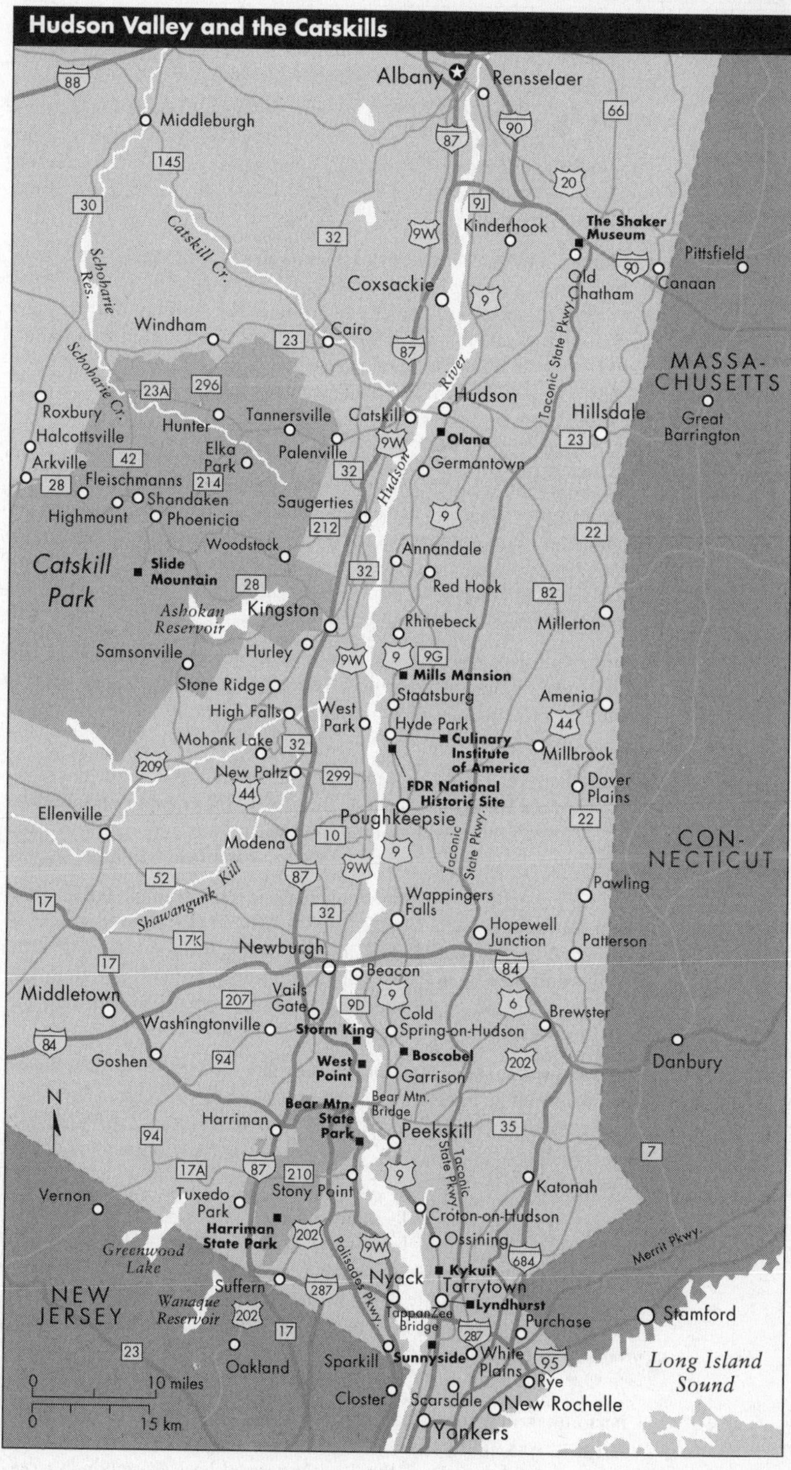

Kingston. To reach the heart of the Catskills from Kingston, head west on Route 28.

East Bank

Sunnyside was the estate of Washington Irving, author of *The Legend of Sleepy Hollow.* Guides in Victorian dress give tours regularly; the 10 rooms include Irving's library. ✉ *W. Sunnyside La., off U.S. 9, Tarrytown,* ☎ *914/591–8200.* 🎫 *$8. Closed Jan.–Feb., weekdays in Mar., and Tues. Apr.–Dec.*

Lyndhurst, one of America's finest examples of Gothic Revival architecture, overlooks the Hudson River in Tarrytown. Three noteworthy New Yorkers and their families had occupied the mansion: former New York City mayor William Paulding, merchant George Merritt, and railroad tycoon Jay Gould. ✉ *635 S. Broadway, off U.S. 9, Tarrytown,* ☎ *914/631–4481,* WEB *www.lyndhurst.org.* 🎫 *$9. Closed Mon. mid-Apr.–Oct. and weekdays Nov.–mid-Apr.*

You can glimpse the private life of one of America's most famous families at ★ **Kykuit,** the country house of the great American philanthropist John D. Rockefeller and his son John D. Rockefeller, Jr. Antiques, ceramics, and famous artworks fill the Beaux Arts house; sculptures by Calder, Brancusi, Nevelson, and Picasso adorn the grounds. ✉ *200 Lake Rd., Pocantico Hills,* ☎ *914/631–9491.* 🎫 *$20. Closed Jan.–Mar. and Tues. late Apr.–early Nov.*

The Hudson River views from **Boscobel Restoration,** a restored early 19th-century mansion filled with Federal-style furniture, are breathtaking. ✉ *1601 Rte. 9D, 8 mi north of Bear Mountain Bridge,* ☎ *845/265–3638,* WEB *www.boscobel.org.* 🎫 *$8. Closed Tues. and Jan.–Mar.*

Across the river from the military academy at West Point, the small village of **Cold Spring-on-Hudson,** once one of the largest iron foundries in the United States, was founded in the 19th century. Antiques and crafts shops, boutiques, and charming restaurants line its quiet streets.

On the Hudson River north of Poughkeepsie is the **Franklin Delano Roosevelt National Historic Site** (✉ 4097 Albany Post Rd., Hyde Park, ☎ 845/229–9115 or 800/967–2283, WEB www.nps.gov/hofr; 🎫 $10). **Springwood,** the large Roosevelt family home, contains original furnishings and a museum displaying personal items. The former president's grave site is also here.

The **Eleanor Roosevelt National Historic Site** is near the Roosevelt family home in Hyde Park. **Val-Kill,** the cottage where Eleanor Roosevelt lived from 1945 to 1962, is set on 188 wooded acres. ✉ *4097 Albany Post Rd., Hyde Park,* ☎ *845/229–9115,* WEB *www.nps.gov/elro.* 🎫 *$5. Closed weekdays Nov.–Apr.*

The grand Beaux Arts **Mills Mansion,** in Staatsburg, is the result of a major late-1890s remodeling by the McKim, Mead and White architectural firm. You can see the interior by guided tour only. The estate is on two connecting state parks where you can golf, cross-country ski, sled, fish, picnic, hike, and bike. ✉ *Old Post Rd. (off U.S. 9 about 5 mi north of Hyde Park), Staatsburg,* ☎ *845/889–8851.* 🎫 *$3. Closed late Oct.–mid-Apr. and Mon.–Tues. mid-Apr.–late Oct.*

Charming storefronts, fine restaurants and inns, and several galleries line the streets in **Rhinebeck.** An affluent village off U.S. 9, across the Hudson from Kingston, Rhinebeck is a good base from which to explore the Hudson River mansions. In summer, weekenders pack the place and traffic crawls through town.

The riverfront town of **Hudson** is known for its antiques stores, many of them very high-end. Four miles south of town, Frederic Church, the ★ foremost artist of the Hudson River School, built **Olana,** a 37-room Moorish-style castle, on a hilltop with panoramic valley and river vistas. The interior is an extravaganza of tile and stone, carved screens, Persian rugs, and paintings, including some by Church. The house is open for guided tours (reservations recommended); the grounds are open year-round. ✉ *Olana State Historic Site, Rte. 9G, Hudson,* ☎ *518/828–0135,* WEB *www.olana.org.* 🎫 *Tours $3; grounds free. House closed Nov.–Mar. and Mon.–Tues. Apr.–Oct.*

As you drive north from Hudson toward the villages of Chatham and Old Chatham, the landscape becomes more open and rolling. The **Shaker Museum and Library** houses the largest collection of Shaker artifacts in the United States. ✉ *88 Shaker Museum Rd., off Rte. 13, Old Chatham,* ☎ *518/794–9100,* WEB *www.shakermuseumandlibrary.org.* 🎫 *$8. Closed Tues.–Wed. and Dec.–late May.*

West Bank

Bear Mountain State Park (☎ 845/786–2701; 🎫 parking $5 weekends) is accessible from the Palisades Parkway, I–87, and U.S. 6 and 9 W. Biking, boating and swimming, cross-country skiing, hiking, and ice-skating are among your options here, and there's a small zoo. **Harriman State Park** (☎ 845/786–2701), off the Palisades Parkway and adjacent to Bear Mountain State Park, encompasses dozens of lakes and streams; cross-country skiing, hiking, and bridle trails; and camping and fishing areas.

The 16,000 acres of the **United States Military Academy at West Point** (✉ U.S. 9 W, 5 mi north of Bear Mountain State Park, Highland Falls, ☎ 845/938–2638, WEB www.usma.edu; 🎫 $7) overlook the Hudson River. Visits are by tour only (bring photo ID).

★ Sculptures dot the 500 acres of fields and rolling hills at **Storm King Art Center.** The collection includes pieces by Alexander Calder, David Smith, and Isamu Noguchi. ✉ *Old Pleasant Hill Rd., Mountainville,* ☎ *845/534–3115,* WEB *www.stormking.org.* 🎫 *$9. Closed mid-Nov.–Mar.*

Kingston, a former commercial port city, served as the state's first capital. Its Stockade District has houses that date back to the 1600s, when the Dutch settled here, as well as small shops and pleasant restaurants. **Woodstock,** northwest of Kingston via Route 28, has been an artists' colony since the early 1900s. Don't expect to see the site of the famous 1969 concert here; while Woodstock got the notoriety, it was actually held in Bethel, about 60 mi away.

The village of **Catskill,** in the northeast Catskills, has its share of museums and quaint buildings. The **Catskill Game Farm** is home to 2,000 birds and animals, including a large collection of rare hoofed species, and has a petting zoo and a playground. ✉ *400 Game Farm Rd. (off Rte. 32), Catskill,* ☎ *518/678–9595,* WEB *www.catskillgamefarm.com.* 🎫 *$15.95. Closed Nov.–late Apr.*

Tubing down the Esopus River is a popular warm-weather activity in **Phoenicia,** a small village west of Woodstock. In the **High Peaks** area, which stretches north from Phoenicia to the ski resort town of Hunter, Route 214 winds through **Stoney Clove,** a spectacular mountain cleft. Another scenic route from Phoenicia heads south, across the Esopus and through lovely Woodland Valley, to the well-marked trail to **Slide Mountain,** the highest peak in the Catskills.

Delaware County has gentler terrain than the High Peaks region to its east. Fishermen prize the east and west branches of the Delaware River, and the county's more than 500 farms offer honey, eggs, cider, and maple syrup at roadside stands. **Roxbury,** on Route 30, has the kind of Main Street Norman Rockwell might have painted.

Albany

A visit to Albany should start at the **Albany Heritage Area Visitors Center** (✉ 25 Quackenbush Sq., corner of Broadway and Clinton Ave., ☎ 518/434–0405, WEB www.albany.org), which has exhibits depicting the state capital's past and present and informative brochures. The Henry Hudson Planetarium (🎫 $4.50), part of the Albany Visitors Center, presents star shows and an orientation film about the city.

Empire State Plaza (✉ between Madison and Washington Aves., ☎ 518/474–2418) is a ¼-mi-long concourse that includes modern art and sculpture and a mix of government, business, and cultural buildings. The Corning Tower has a free observation deck on the 42nd floor. At the **New York State Museum** (✉ Cultural Education Center, Empire State Plaza, Madison Ave., ☎ 518/474–5877, WEB www.nysm.nysed.gov; 🎫 $2 donation), one of the oldest state museums in the country, life-size exhibits depicting the state's natural and cultural history include a reproduction of an Iroquois village. The **New York State Capitol** (✉ Empire State Plaza, Madison Ave., ☎ 518/474–2718), which took more than 30 years (1867–99) to complete, incorporates many interesting architectural elements and eclectic styles. Free tours are conducted; call for times.

Dining and Lodging

In addition to the mammoth resort hotels for which the Catskills are best known, the area includes plenty of B&Bs and country inns, as well as ski-center condos.

Albany

$$ ★ ✕ **Ogden's.** On the ground floor of a 1903 brick-and-limestone building, this dining room has two-story arched windows built into 30-ft-high ceilings. The menu focuses on Continental and new American cuisine and includes such dishes as pan-roasted sea bass with a mustard-coriander rub. ✉ *42 Howard St.,* ☎ *518/463–6605. AE, MC, V. Closed Sun. No lunch Sat.*

$$$ ✕🏨 **Mansion Hill Inn and Restaurant.** The intimate, dozen-table restaurant with imaginative, new American cuisine is the real draw at this downtown B&B. Dinner entrées could include sesame-crusted salmon with a sweet soy sauce or grilled duck breast. The guest rooms are large and spare. ✉ *115 Philip St., at Park Ave., 12202,* ☎ *518/465–2038 or 888/299–0455,* FAX *518/434–2313,* WEB *www.mansionhill.com. 8 rooms. Restaurant. AE, D, DC, MC, V. BP.*

$$–$$$$ ★ 🏨 **The Morgan State House.** At this late-19th-century town house on Washington Park, mahogany architectural accents complement the interior's hand-glazed walls, high ceilings, and fireplaces. ✉ *393 State St., 12210,* ☎ *518/427–6063 or 888/427–6063,* FAX *518/463–1316,* WEB *www.statehouse.com. 12 rooms. AE, D, DC, MC, V. BP.*

Bear Mountain

$ 🏨 **Bear Mountain Inn.** Since 1915, this chalet-style resort has been known for both its warm hospitality and its bucolic location, on the shores of Hessian Lake in Bear Mountain State Park. Rooms are in the classic Stone Lodge, the hotel-style Overlook Lodge, or in rustic lakeside lodges. ✉ *U.S. 9 W, 10911,* ☎ *845/786–2731,* FAX *845/786–2543. 60 rooms. Restaurant, pool. AE, D, MC, V.*

Catskill

$–$$$ ✕ **La Conca D'Oro.** In addition to the usual Italian offerings, the menu here includes elk, boar, and pheasant prepared with a northern Italian accent. ✉ *440 Main St.,* ☎ *518/943–3549. MC, V. Closed Tues. No lunch weekends.*

Cold Spring

$$–$$$ ✕ **Hudson House.** Clean and simple, this 1832 clapboard inn is within walking distance of many antiques shops and nearly sits on the Hudson River. The feeling here is homey, with French country furnishings and wide-plank floorboards. Tasty American fare is served in the dining room. ✉ *2 Main St., 10516,* ☎ *845/265–9355,* WEB *www.hudsonhouseinn.com. 13 rooms. Restaurant. AE, DC, MC, V. BP.*

Dover Plains

$$$–$$$$ ★ ✕ **Old Drovers Inn.** The 1750s inn has four rooms, but guests are pampered as if it were a luxury hotel. Fireplaces and claw-foot tubs contribute to the romantic atmosphere of this Relais & Châteaux member. The dining room serves contemporary fare; dinner entrées may include edamame-crusted salmon, but such classic staples as cheddar-cheese soup and rack of lamb haven't been cast aside. ✉ *Old Rte. 22, 12522,* ☎ *845/832–9311,* FAX *845/832–6356,* WEB *www.olddroversinn.com. 4 rooms. Restaurant. MC, V. Restaurant closed Tues.–Wed.; no lunch Mon.–Thurs. MAP weekends, CP weekdays.*

Elka Park

$–$$$ ✕ **The Redcoat's Country Inn & Restaurant.** Antiques fill the 1860 house, a piece of New England that sits on 15 acres within the Catskill Game Reserve, about a 20-minute drive to Windham Mountain. The dining room offers hearty Continental dishes, which might include filet mignon with Portobello–and–red wine ragout and sun-dried tomato ravioli with basil cream sauce. ✉ *50 Dale La., 12427,* ☎ FAX *518/589–9858,* WEB *www.redcoatsonline.com. 14 rooms. Restaurant. AE, D, MC, V. Restaurant closed Mon.–Wed. BP.*

Hyde Park

$–$$$ ✕ **Culinary Institute of America.** The institute has five public eateries: **Escoffier** ($$$) serves classic French cuisine; **American Bounty** ($$–$$$) offers regional American fare; **Caterina de Medici** ($$) focuses on nouvelle Italian cooking; **St. Andrew's Café** ($–$$) serves contemporary cuisine; and **Apple Pie Bakery Café** ($) has light lunches and pastries. Only Apple Pie Bakery doesn't require reservations. ✉ *1946 Campus Dr.,* ☎ *845/471–6608,* WEB *www.ciachef.edu. Reservations essential. AE, DC, MC, V. Closed Sun.–Mon. and 3 wks in July.*

Kingston

$–$$$ ✕ **Le Canard Enchainé.** This relaxed bistro offers a slice of France in uptown Kingston. For lunch, you can choose from the prix-fixe three-course lunch menus ($11.95 or $14.95); a $16.95 prix-fixe dinner is offered 5–7 nightly. Friday and Saturday nights you can hear live jazz. ✉ *276 Fair St.,* ☎ *845/339–2003. AE, D, DC, MC, V.*

Lew Beach

$$$$ **Beaverkill Valley Inn.** Built in 1893 and developed by Laurance Rockefeller, this inn caters to those who cherish privacy. Its surrounding forests and nearby fields are protected from development. Fly-fishing is the big draw here. Those not hooked on angling can head for the croquet court, indoor basketball court, game room, or the wide front porch lined with rockers. In winter, there's ice-skating and cross-country skiing. ✉ *Barnhart Rd., off Beaverkill Rd., off Rte. 151/Rte. 152 (Box 136, 12753),* ☎ *845/439–4844,* FAX *845/439–3884,* WEB *www.*

beaverkillvalley.com. 20 rooms, 5 with shared bath. Pool, tennis. AE, MC, V. FAP.

New Paltz

$$$$ **Mohonk Mountain House.** The rambling Victorian-era hotel sits at the edge of a lake amid a 20,000-acre preserve. The property is veined with 85 mi of hiking trails; golf, tennis, croquet, boccie ball, swimming, boating, horseback riding, cross-country skiing, and ice-skating are also available. The spa offers everything from manicures and facials to salt rubs and reflexology. Room rates include three hearty meals and afternoon tea. ✉ *1000 Mountain Rest Rd., Exit 18 off I–87, 12561,* ☎ *845/255–1000 or 800/772–6646,* FAX *845/256–2180.* WEB *www.mohonk.com 251 rooms. Restaurant, golf, tennis, gym. AE, DC, MC, V. FAP.*

Rhinebeck

$–$$$ **Beekman Arms and Delamater Inn.** In all, 10 buildings make up this lodging complex in the village center. The original 1766 building has smallish though cheery and comfortable colonial-style rooms (with modern baths); a contemporary building has motel-style rooms; and, a block away, the mid-19th-century Delamater House has primarily Victorian-style rooms. Six smaller buildings also have rooms. The restaurant, Traphagen, serves regional American fare, including applewood-grilled salmon and turkey potpie. ✉ *6387 Mill St./U.S. 9, 12572,* ☎ *845/871–1766 restaurant,* ☎ FAX *845/876–7077 inn,* WEB *www.beekmanarms.com. 63 rooms. Restaurant. AE, D, DC, MC, V.*

Tannersville

$–$$ **Deer Mountain Inn.** Moose and boar heads, bearskin rugs, paintings of European mountain villages, and heavy overstuffed furniture fill this circa-1900 house on a 15-acre wooded enclave. The dining room ($$–$$$), bracketed by two huge stone fireplaces, serves American fare—trout, veal, and seafood—with a European accent. ✉ *Rte. 25 (Box 443, 12485),* ☎ FAX *518/589–6268,* WEB *www.deermountaininn.com. 7 rooms. Restaurant. AE, MC, V. BP. Restaurant closed Tues. No lunch.*

Windham

$$–$$$ **Albergo Allegria.** The slopes of Windham Mountain are 1 mi from this Victorian B&B, in the northern Catskills. Stained-glass windows, fireplaces, cathedral ceilings, and chestnut moldings distinguish the rooms. An annex has five private-entrance suites. ✉ *Rte. 296, less than 1 mi south of Rte. 23, 12496,* ☎ *518/734–5560,* FAX *518/734–5570,* WEB *www.albergoUSA.com. 21 rooms. MC, V. BP.*

Woodstock

$$ **Gypsy Wolf Cantina.** Multicolored geckos march across the ceiling, wolf masks eye a coop of ceramic chickens, and red chili-pepper lights enhance the playful vibe of this restaurant. But the Mexican food here, from the hearty taco–enchilada combo plates to the chilies rellenos, is seriously delicious. ✉ *261 Tinker Ave.,* ☎ *845/679–9563. MC, V. Closed Mon. No lunch.*

$$–$$$ **Woodstock Country Inn.** Two miles west of Woodstock center, hidden several hundred yards from the quiet main road through Bearsville, this B&B sits in a beautiful meadow. Rooms have no fussy prints or ruffles, just simple luxuries like 300-thread-count cotton sateen sheets. Don't pass up the lavish, home-cooked breakfast. ✉ *Cooper Lake Rd., 12498,* ☎ *845/679–9380,* WEB *www.woodstockcountryinn.com. 4 rooms. Pool. D, MC, V. BP.*

Motels

Holiday Inn (✉ 503 Washington Ave., Kingston 12401, ☎ 845/338–0400 or 800/465–4329, WEB www.holidayinnkingston.com), 212 rooms; restaurant, pool; *$–$$.*

Hunter Inn (✉ Rte. 23A, Hunter 12442, ☎ 518/263–3777, FAX 518/263–3981, WEB www.hunterinn.com), 40 rooms; restaurant, gym; *$–$$$*.

Nightlife and the Arts

Contact the regional visitor centers for schedules of the area's performing-arts events. The **Egg** (✉ Empire State Plaza, Albany, ☎ 518/473–1061, WEB www.theegg.org) presents music, dance, and theater performances in two theaters. The **Palace Theater** (✉ 19 Clinton Ave., Albany, ☎ 518/465–4663) is home to the Albany Symphony Orchestra (www.albanysymphony.com). Hunter, New Paltz, and Poughkeepsie have some lively nightspots.

Outdoor Activities and Sports

Canoeing

The 73-mi Upper Delaware Scenic and Recreational River is one of the finest and most picturesque areas in the region for paddling. **Indian Head Canoe & Campground** (✉ Rte. 97 N, Barryville 12719, ☎ 845/557–8777 or 800/874–2628, WEB www.indianheadcanoes.com) rents canoes and operates guided trips from mid-April to mid-October. For a list of canoe outfitters, contact the **Sullivan County Visitors Association** (☎ 845/794–3000 ext. 5010 or 800/882–2287, WEB www.scva.net).

Fishing

The Hudson River estuary contains a remarkable variety of fish, most notably American shad, black bass, smallmouth and largemouth bass, and sturgeon. Trout is abundant in Catskill streams; smallmouth bass, walleye, and pickerel can be found in many lakes and in six reservoirs. For information on licenses (required in fresh waters) and restrictions, as well as fishing hot spots and charts, contact the **New York State Department of Environmental Conservation** (✉ 21 S. Putt Corners Rd., New Paltz 12561, ☎ 845/256–3000; ✉ 625 Broadway, Albany 12233, ☎ 518/402–9945; WEB www.dec.state.ny.us). The **Catskills/Greene County Tourism Office** (✉ Rte. 23B, Catskill [Box 527, 12414], ☎ 518/943–3223 or 800/355–2287, WEB www.greene-ny.com) has a "Catskill Fishing" brochure and map.

Golf

East Bank: Beekman Country Club (✉ 11 Country Club Rd., Hopewell Junction, ☎ 845/226–7391) has a 27-hole championship course. The 18-hole **Dinsmore Golf Course** (✉ Old Post Rd., U.S. 9, Staatsburg, ☎ 845/889–3126), in Mills-Norrie State Park, has been in use since 1890. **James Baird State Park Golf Course** (✉ 122D Freedom Rd., Pleasant Valley, ☎ 845/452–1489) has an 18-hole course designed by Robert Trent Jones.

West Bank: Apple Greens Golf Course (✉ 11 Country Club Rd., Highland, ☎ 845/883–5500) is an 18-hole course with mountain views. **Catskill Golf Club** (✉ 27 Brooks La., Catskill, ☎ 518/943–0302) is an 18-hole Scottish-design course. You don't have to stay at **Christman's Windham House** (✉ 5742 Rte. 23, Windham, ☎ 518/734–4230 or 888/294–4053) to play its 18-hole course. The 18-hole **Concord Monster Golf Course** (✉ 42 Winarick Dr., Kiamesha Lake, ☎ 845/794–4000, WEB www.concordresort.com) is at the Concord Resort & Golf Club. The 27-hole championship golf facility at the **Nevele Grande Resort & Country Club** (✉ One Nevele Rd., off U.S. 209, Ellenville, ☎ 845/647–6000 or 800/647–6000, WEB www.nevele.com) has 9 Robert Trent Jones–designed holes and 18 holes that were redesigned by Tom Fazio. The 18-hole course at **Windham Country Club** (✉ South St., Windham,

☎ 518/734–9910, WEB www.windhamcountryclub.com) has been a regional favorite since 1927.

Hiking

About 300 mi of trails are accessible to hikers in the Catskill Game Preserve. Slide Mountain is the region's highest peak. The **New York State Department of Environmental Conservation** (✉ 215 S. Putt Corners Rd., New Paltz 12561, ☎ 845/256–3000, WEB www.dec.state.ny.us) has several brochures about Catskill Forest Preserve hiking trails.

Skiing

Ski the Catskills (✉ 71 Barnes St., Arkville [Box 135, 12406], ☎ 845/586–1944) can provide information about area slopes and trails.

Cross-Country

East Bank: Fahnestock Winter Park (✉ 12 Dennytown Rd., Cold Spring, ☎ 845/225–3998) has 10 mi of groomed trails. The 6 mi of trails at **Mills-Norrie State Park** (✉ Old Post Rd., Staatsburg 12580, ☎ 845/889–4646) have Hudson River views. **Olana State Historic Site** (✉ Rte. 9G, Hudson, ☎ 518/828–0135, WEB www.olana.org) has 5 mi of trails. About 20 mi of trails lace **Rockefeller State Park Preserve** (✉ Rte. 117, North Tarrytown, ☎ 914/631–1470).

West Bank: Bear Mountain State Park (☎ 845/786–2701), accessible from the Palisades Parkway, I–87, and U.S. 6 and 9 W, has 5 mi of trails. **Belleayre Mountain Ski Center** (✉ off Rte. 28, Highmount, ☎ 845/254–5600 or 800/942–6904, WEB www.belleayre.com) has 5 mi of trails. The **Mountain Trails Cross-Country Ski Center** (✉ Rte. 23A, Tannersville, ☎ 518/589–5361, WEB www.mtntrails.com) offers 21 mi of groomed trails.

Downhill

Downhill ski areas in the Catskills have snowmaking capabilities. **Belleayre Mountain Ski Center** (✉ off Rte. 28, Highmount, ☎ 845/254–5600 or 800/942–6904, WEB www.belleayre.com), with 35 runs, 7 lifts, and a 1,404-ft vertical drop, is the only state-run ski facility in the Catskills. **Hunter Mountain** (✉ Rte. 23A, Hunter, ☎ 518/263–4223 or 888/486–8376, WEB www.huntermtn.com) has 53 runs, 11 lifts, and a 1,600-ft drop. **Windham Mountain** (✉ C. D. Lane Rd., Windham, ☎ 518/734–4300 or 800/754–9463, WEB www.skiwindham.com) has 34 runs, 7 lifts, and a 1,600-ft drop.

Tubing

The **Town Tinker** (✉ Bridge St., Phoenicia, ☎ 845/688–5553) rents tubes for beginner and advanced routes on the Esopus Creek between Shandaken and Mount Pleasant.

Shopping

The area is scattered with shopping villages, auction houses, flea markets, farm stands, crafts fairs, antiques shops, and galleries. **Woodbury Common Premium Outlets** (✉ Rte. 32, Exit 16 off I–87, Harriman, ☎ 845/928–6840) has more than 200 stores, including Coach, J. Crew, and Donna Karan.

Hudson Valley and the Catskills Essentials

AIRPORTS

The New York metro area's La Guardia, John F. Kennedy, and Newark airports (☞ New York City Essentials, *above*) are manageable distances from the Hudson Valley. Most major airlines or their shuttles fly into Albany International Airport. Stewart International Airport, in New

Windsor (near Newburgh), and Westchester County Airport, in White Plains, are served by some major airlines.

➤ AIRPORT INFORMATION: **Albany International Airport** (☎ 518/242–2200, WEB www.albanyairport.com). **Stewart International Airport** (☎ 845/564–2100, WEB www.stewartair.com). **Westchester County Airport** (☎ 914/285–4860, WEB www.co.westchester.ny.us/airport).

BOAT AND FERRY INFORMATION

New York Waterways offers boat tours up the Hudson River from Manhattan; one includes a stop at Kykuit.

➤ BOAT AND FERRY INFORMATION: **New York Waterways** (☎ 800/533–3779).

BUS TRAVEL

Adirondack Trailways and Shortline service the area.

➤ BUS INFORMATION: **Adirondack Trailways** (☎ 800/225–6815, WEB www.trailways.com). **Shortline** (☎ 800/631–8405, WEB www.shortlinebus.com).

CAR TRAVEL

The New York State Thruway (I–87) parallels the west bank of the Hudson River from Rockland County, about 10 mi north of New York City, to Albany; the northern Catskills can be reached from the Kingston (Route 28), Saugerties (Route 212), and Catskill (Routes 23 and 23A) exits. The western edge of the Catskills is accessible via Route 17, which links with 1–87 near Harriman. The scenic Taconic Parkway parallels the east bank from the Tarrytown area to Chatham. I–84 provides access to the region from Connecticut and northeastern Pennsylvania.

TRAIN TRAVEL

Amtrak provides service to Hudson, Rhinecliff, Rensselaer (Albany), and points west and north of Poughkeepsie. In summer, Metro North, which connects much of the lower Hudson Valley and New York City, offers sightseeing packages that include admission to historic sites.

➤ TRAIN INFORMATION: **Amtrak** (☎ 800/872–7245, WEB www.amtrak.com). **Metro North** (☎ 212/532–4900 or 800/638–7646, WEB www.mnr.org).

VISITOR INFORMATION

➤ TOURIST INFORMATION: **Albany Convention and Visitors Bureau** (✉ 25 Quackenbush Sq., Albany 12207, ☎ 518/434–1217 or 800/258–3582, WEB www.albany.org). **Catskills/Greene County Tourism Office** (✉ Rte. 23B, Catskill [Box 527, 12414], ☎ 518/943–3223 or 800/355–2287, WEB www.greene-ny.com). **Columbia County Tourism Dept.** (✉ 401 State St., Hudson 12534, ☎ 518/828–3375 or 800/724–1846, WEB www.columbiacountyny.org). **Delaware County Chamber of Commerce** (✉ 114 Main St., Delhi 13753, ☎ 607/746–2281 or 800/642–4443 WEB www.delawarecounty.org). **Dutchess County Tourism Promotion Agency** (✉ 3 Neptune Rd., Suite M, No. 17, Poughkeepsie 12601, ☎ 845/463–4000 or 800/445–3131, WEB www.dutchesstourism.com). **Hudson Valley Tourism Development Council** (✉ 308 Clinton Ave., Kingston 12401, ☎ 845/339–8399 or 800/232–4782, WEB www.travelhudsonvalley.org). **Orange County Tourism** (✉ 30 Matthews St., Suite 111, Goshen 10924, ☎ 845/291–2136 or 800/762–8687, WEB www.orangetourism.org). **Putnam Visitors Bureau** (✉ 100 Old Rte. 6, Bldg. 3, Carmel 10512, ☎ 845/225–0381 or 800/470–4854, WEB www.visitputnam.org). **Rockland County Dept. of Tourism** (✉ 10 Piermont Ave., Nyack 10960, ☎ 845/353–5533 or 800/295–5723, WEB www.rockland.org). **Sullivan County Visitors Association** (✉ 100 North St., Monticello [Box 5012, 12701], ☎ 845/794–3000 ext.

5010 or 800/882–2287, WEB www.scva.net). **Westchester County Office of Tourism** (✉ 222 Mamaroneck Ave., Suite 100, White Plains 10605, ☎ 914/995–8500 or 800/833–9282, WEB www.westchestertourism.com).

SARATOGA SPRINGS AND THE NORTH COUNTRY

Saratoga Springs, about 30 mi north of Albany, is one of American high society's oldest summer playgrounds. The six-week Thoroughbred-racing season, starting in late July, is the high point of the year. Northwest of Saratoga are the rugged mountains, immense forests, and abundant lakes and streams of Adirondack Park, the largest state park in the United States outside of Alaska. The North Country—anchored by the resort towns of Lake Placid and Lake George—hums year-round. Hikers and canoeists descend in the spring and summer, autumn brings leaf peepers, and with the snow come many winter-sports enthusiasts.

Exploring Saratoga Springs and the North Country

People have been frequenting **Saratoga Springs** for its medicinal properties since the late 18th century. In the late 19th century, Saratoga emerged as one of North America's principal resorts, both for its spa waters and its gambling casino. It also became a horse-racing center in the 1890s; crowds still come for the mid-summer Thoroughbred races and yearling sale.

You can still see mineral-water springs bubbling from the ground at **Saratoga Spa State Park** (✉ 19 Roosevelt Dr., between U.S. 9 and Rte. 50, Saratoga Springs, ☎ 518/584–2535, WEB www.nysparks.com; 🎫 $5 parking May–Sept.). Listed on the National Register of Historic Places, this 2,000-acre park has walking paths to the springs. Mineral baths and massages are available at the Roosevelt and Lincoln Park bathhouses. Tennis courts, swimming pools, two golf courses, and 12 mi of cross-country skiing trails are available as well.

Across from the Saratoga Race Course is the **National Museum of Racing** (✉ 191 Union Ave., Saratoga Springs, ☎ 518/584–0400, WEB www.racingmuseum.org; 🎫 $7). Its centerpiece is the Hall of Fame, which has video clips of races featuring the horses and jockeys enshrined here.

The **National Museum of Dance** has rotating exhibits on the history and development of the art form. Its Hall of Fame honors dance luminaries. The studios allow visitors to watch or participate in a dance class. ✉ *99 S. Broadway, Saratoga Springs,* ☎ *518/584–2225.* 🎫 *$3.50. Closed Mon.*

The **Historical Society Museum of Saratoga Springs** is housed in the Canfield Casino, an 1870s Italianate building that was a casino. A museum devoted to the town's colorful gambling history occupies three floors. ✉ *Congress Park, Broadway and Circular St., Saratoga Springs,* ☎ *518/584–6920.* 🎫 *$3. Closed Mon.–Tues. Oct.–Apr.*

In the Adirondack Mountain range, the 6-million-acre **Adirondack Park** encompasses 1,000 mi of rivers and more than 2,500 lakes and ponds. The southern sections are more developed, while the High Peaks region, in the north-central sector, offers the greatest variety of wilderness activities. Adirondack Park differs in several important ways from most public lands. Only about 47% of the park is public property; the rest is owned by individuals, corporations, clubs, and municipalities. You can't set foot in these sections without the owner's approval. There are no user fees and no "entrances," other than occasional road signs marking boundaries. Park services are relatively limited. In the middle of the park there are two **Visitor Interpretive Centers** (✉ Rte. 30, 1 mi north of Paul Smiths College, Paul Smiths, ☎ 518/327–3000; ✉ Rte. 28 N, Newcomb, ☎ 518/582–2000).

Lake George, 40 mi north of Saratoga, has amusement parks, souvenir shops, miniature golf, and other family-oriented activities. South of Lake George is **Six Flags Great Escape and Splashwater Kingdom,** the North Country's largest theme park. ✉ *U.S. 9, Lake George,* ☎ *518/792–3500,* WEB *www.thegreatescape.com.* *$33. Closed weekdays in Sept. and Mon.–Thurs. Oct.–late May.*

Kids love the caves and gorge at **Natural Stone Bridge and Caves.** A self-guided tour takes you past unusual rock formations and a cascading brook and into several fascinating caves. ✉ *Stone Bridge Rd., Exit 26 off I–87, Pottersville,* ☎ *518/494–2283,* WEB *www.stonebridgeandcaves.com.* *$9. Closed Oct.–May.*

Those not big on hiking can sample the beauty of the Adirondack region at **Ausable Chasm,** north of Keeseville. The massive stone formations at the 150-ft gorge are spectacular. Visitors amble around the rim, into the inner canyon, and over an awesome footbridge. For an extra fee you can raft down the river. ✉ *U.S. 9, Ausable Chasm,* ☎ *518/834–7454,* WEB *www.ausablechasm.com.* *Trail $15.95, trail and rafting $23.95. Closed Oct.–mid-May.*

High Falls Gorge has three dramatic waterfalls and a self-guided tour on steel bridges and paths along 700 ft of the Ausable River. In winter, you can clamp on ice-cleats and trek through the frozen gorge. ✉ *Rte. 86, Wilmington,* ☎ *518/946–2278,* WEB *www.highfallsgorge.com.* *$7; waterfall train in winter $8.95; $19.95 with snowshoes. Closed Apr. and Nov.*

Lake Placid is the hub of the northern Adirondacks. The mountain town is probably best known for hosting the 1932 and 1980 winter Olympics. You can tour many of the Olympic sites and even take a bobsled or luge ride. The Ice Arena and speed-skating oval are in the center of town; the ski jump is 2 mi out; **Whiteface Mountain** (scene of the downhill competitions) is a 10-minute drive away, on Route 86; and the bobsled run at Mt. Van Hoevenberg, on Route 73, is 15 minutes away. The **Lake Placid Winter Olympic Museum** has athletes' uniforms and historic memorabilia. ✉ *Olympic Center, 218 Main St., Lake Placid,* ☎ *518/523–1655 or 800/462–6236,* WEB *www.orda.org.* *$4.*

The **John Brown Farm State Historic Site** includes the home and burial place of the famed abolitionist. ✉ *John Brown Rd. off Rte. 73, by the Olympic ski jumps, Lake Placid,* ☎ *518/523–3900,* WEB *www.nysparks.com.* *$2. Closed Mon.–Tues.*

The serenity and mountain air of **Saranac Lake** (elevation: 1,600 ft) made it a health resort for the tubercular in the late 19th century. Ten miles west of Lake Placid, it's the embarkation point for canoe trips.

★ Overlooking Blue Mountain Lake, the open-air **Adirondack Museum** has a day's worth of exhibits on the history, culture, and crafts of the region. ✉ *Rtes. 28 N and 30, Blue Mountain Lake,* ☎ *518/352–7311,* WEB *www.adkmuseum.org.* *$10. Closed mid-Oct.–mid-June.*

Dining and Lodging

Saratoga is indisputably the North Country's culinary champion in quality and variety, with Lake Placid a distant second. Elsewhere expect large portions, home cooking, and a rustic atmosphere. Lodging runs the gamut from roadside motels to grand resorts.

Bolton Landing

$$$–$$$$ ✕🏨 **The Sagamore.** The large public rooms and gracious style of this grand resort, built in 1883 on its own 72-acre island on Lake George, take you back to another era. The rooms are spread among the main hotel and contemporary lakeside lodges. Each of the six dining rooms ($$–$$$$) has its own atmosphere and cuisine—from the formal, slightly nouvelle touches of Trillium (reservations essential, jacket required, no lunch) to the hearty burgers and steaks of Mr. Brown's Pub. Activities include boating, tennis, swimming, golf, and skiing. ✉ *110 Sagamore Rd., Bolton Lake 12814,* ☎ *518/644–9400 or 800/358–3585,* FAX *518/644–2626,* WEB *www.thesagamore.com. 350 rooms. 6 restaurants, pool, golf, tennis, health club. AE, D, DC, MC, V.*

Chestertown

$$$$ ★ ✕🏨 **Friends Lake Inn.** Most of this inn's cozy guest rooms have mountain or lake views. There's plenty to do in the area—cross-country skiing, hiking, swimming, or just relaxing in an Adirondack-style chair on the inn's spacious lawn. The regionally acclaimed restaurant serves new American cuisine. ✉ *963 Friends Lake Rd., 12817,* ☎ *518/494–4751,* FAX *518/494–4616,* WEB *www.friendslake.com. 17 rooms. Restaurant, pool. MC, V. MAP.*

Keene Valley

$ ✕ **Noon Mark Diner.** The classic small-town diner is the perfect spot for lunch; if you've already eaten, at least stop in for some homemade pie. The food is better than at your average greasy spoon. *Rte. 73,* ☎ *518/576–4499. D, MC, V.*

Lake Placid

$–$$ ✕ **Cottage Cafe.** This always-crowded café overlooks Mirror Lake. When the weather's good, the open-air deck is the perfect place for cocktails. Lunch and dinner fare includes salads, sandwiches, and pub-style favorites. ✉ *Mirror Lake Dr.,* ☎ *518/523–9845. AE, D, MC, V.*

$ ★ ✕ **Tail o' the Pup.** Halfway between Lake Placid and Saranac Lake, this classic roadside restaurant specializes in savory barbecued items, including chicken and ribs. You can dine inside, at the outdoor picnic tables, or in your car—honk twice for service. ✉ *Rte. 86, Ray Brook,* ☎ *518/891–5092. MC, V. Closed Oct.–May.*

$$$$ ★ ✕🏨 **Lake Placid Lodge.** Originally a rustic lodge built before the turn of the 20th century, this small hotel embodies the spirit of Lake Placid's past and cossets guests with the comforts of luxurious amenities. Rooms are furnished with twig and birch-bark furniture and Adirondack antiques; all have granite fireplaces. Amenities include featherbeds, terry robes, and soaking tubs. The dining room's new-American menu ($$$–$$$$) changes seasonally but might include grilled salmon with lime and ginger, sun-dried-tomato couscous, and baby vegetables. ✉ *Whiteface Inn Rd., (Box 550, 12946),* ☎ *518/523–2700,* FAX *518/523–1124,* WEB *www.lakeplacidlodge.com. 17 rooms, 17 cabins. Restaurant. AE, MC, V. BP.*

$$$–$$$$ 🏨 **Mirror Lake Inn Resort & Spa.** On the shores of Mirror Lake, this stately Adirondack inn is within walking distance of downtown Lake Placid. The elegant interior includes an antiques-filled library and a living room with stone fireplaces and walnut floors. The rooms are spread among several buildings; those on the lake have private balconies. Guests take advantage of the outdoor sports, spa, and meeting rooms. ✉ *5 Mirror Lake Dr., 12946,* ☎ *518/523–2544,* FAX *518/523–2871,* WEB *www.mirrorlakeinn.com. 128 rooms. 2 restaurants, pools, tennis. AE, D, DC, MC, V.*

$-$$$ **Lake Placid Resort Holiday Inn.** This friendly hotel and golf club high on a hill above Lake Placid's Main Street is by no means your typical Holiday Inn: the service is personal, original art decorates public spaces, and amenities include 45 holes of golf on a Scottish-style links course. The lobby's floor-to-ceiling windows overlook Mirror Lake and the mountains beyond. ✉ *1 Olympic Dr., 12946,* ☎ *518/523–2556 or 800/874–1980,* FAX *518/523–9410,* WEB *www.lpresort.com. 199 rooms. 4 restaurants, pool, golf, tennis, health club. AE, D, DC, MC, V.*

Saratoga Springs

$$$-$$$$ ✕ **43 Phila Bistro.** The innovative offerings at this Saratoga hot spot, in the heart of town, may include pan-seared duck breast with lingonberry sauce, shellfish risotto, or grilled tournedos of beef. ✉ *43 Phila St.,* ☎ *518/584–2720. MC, V. Closed Sun. Sept.–May.*

$$$-$$$$ ★ ✕ **Eartha's Restaurant.** This small bistro is a local favorite, especially for the mesquite-grilled seafood and meat dishes that come from the wood-fired grill. ✉ *60 Court St.,* ☎ *518/583–0602. Reservations essential. DC, MC, V. Closed Mon.–Tues. Sept.–May. No lunch.*

$$-$$$$ **Adelphi Hotel.** The opulent lobby of this downtown Saratoga showpiece is done in a style so reminiscent of La Belle Epoque that one could picture Sarah Bernhardt holding court amid its splendor. Furnishings are eclectic—and recherché. ✉ *365 Broadway, 12866,* ☎ *518/587–4688,* FAX *518/587–0851,* WEB *www.adelphihotel.com. 39 rooms. Pool. AE, MC, V. BP. Closed Nov.–Apr.*

Motels

Lake George–Days Inn Queensbury (✉ 1454 U.S. 9, Lake George 12845, ☎ 518/793–3196 or 800/329–7466, FAX 518/783–6028, WEB www.daysinnlakegeorge.com), 104 rooms; restaurant, pool; *$–$$.*

Wildwood on the Lake (✉ 88 Saranac Ave., Lake Placid 12946, ☎ 518/523–2624, FAX 518/523–3248, WEB www.wildwoodmotel.com), 35 rooms; pools; *$–$$.*

Campgrounds

The New York State Department of Environmental Conservation operates public campgrounds in Adirondack Park. State campgrounds outside the forest preserve are operated by the New York State Office of Parks, Recreation, and Historic Preservation. **Adirondack Loj Wilderness Campground** (✉ off Rte. 73, Lake Placid [Box 867, 12946], ☎ 518/523–3441, WEB www.adk.org), on Heart Lake, has tent sites, lean-tos, and cabins, as well as water, picnic tables, seasonal showers, and toilets—but no gas or electricity. It's run by the Adirondack Mountain Club.

The Arts

Adirondack Lakes Center for the Arts (✉ Rte. 28, Blue Mountain Lake, ☎ 518/352–7715) is a multipurpose arts center that presents art exhibits and concerts and has coffeehouses and workshops. The **Saratoga County Arts Council** (✉ 320 Broadway, Saratoga Springs, ☎ 518/584–4132, WEB www.saratoga-arts.org) is home to a 2,000-square-ft art gallery and a theater-performance space. The **Saratoga Performing Arts Center** (✉ Saratoga Spa State Park, 19 Roosevelt Dr., between U.S. 9 and Rte. 50, Saratoga Springs, ☎ 518/587–3330, WEB www.spac.org) hosts the New York City Opera, the New York City Ballet, the Philadelphia Orchestra, and the Newport Jazz Festival–Saratoga, as well as big-name pop stars, from May to September.

Outdoor Activities and Sports

Biking

Roadside signs mark several bike routes, most quite hilly, that wind through the North Country. **Bike Adirondacks** (✉ Box 295, Saranac Lake 12983, ☎ 518/891–3139, WEB www.bikeadirondacks.org) has information on bicycling opportunities in the Adirondacks, including bike shops, touring routes, and trails. **High Peaks Mountain Adventures** (✉ 331 Main St., Lake Placid, ☎ 518/523–9572, WEB www.highpeakscyclery.com) guides adventure-bike trips.

Canoeing

Shoot the rapids at Hudson River Gorge or simply paddle around the 3,000 lakes and ponds and 6,000 mi of rivers in the Adirondacks. The 170-mi **Raquette River** and the **St. Regis Canoe Area,** east of Saranac Lake, are among the best and most popular canoe routes in the North Country. The Web site of the **Adirondack Regional Tourism Council** (✉ Box 2149, Plattsburgh 12901, ☎ 518/846–8016, WEB www.adirondacks.org) has a Waterway Guide outlining canoe and rafting routes. **High Peaks Adventures** (✉ 331 Main St., Lake Placid, ☎ 518/523–9572, WEB www.highpeakscyclery.com) offers guided canoe adventures. **Jones Outfitters Ltd.** (✉ 37 Main St., Lake Placid, ☎ 518/523–3468), on Mirror Lake, rents canoes and kayaks. **Middle Earth Expeditions** (✉ Rte. 73, Lake Placid, ☎ 518/523–9572, WEB www.adirondackrafting.com) leads canoe tours.

Fishing

The thousands of lakes and streams of the North Country contain all species of freshwater fish, including Atlantic salmon, small- and large-mouthed bass, pike, and trout. Licenses can be obtained at town- or county-clerk offices, sporting-goods stores, and outfitters. The **Fishing Hotline** (☎ 518/891–5413) has recorded fishing info. The **New York State Department of Environmental Conservation** (☎ 518/457–8862, WEB www.dec.state.ny.us) has information about licenses.

Golf

The 45 holes at the **Lake Placid Resort Golf Course** (✉ 1 Olympic Dr., Lake Placid, ☎ 518/523–2566, WEB www.lpresort.com) are designed in a Scottish-links style with bunker-laden fairways. The **Sagamore** (✉ 110 Sagamore Rd., Bolton Landing, ☎ 518/644–9400, WEB www.thesagamore.com) has an 18-hole course. On the shore of upper Saranac Lake, the **Saranac Inn Golf & Country Club** (✉ Saranac Lake, ☎ 518/891–1402. WEB www.saranacinn.com) has a challenging 18-hole course. At the **Whiteface Golf Club** (✉ Whiteface Inn Rd., Lake Placid, ☎ 518/523–2551, WEB www.whiteface.club.com), the 18-hole course is perched dramatically on the edge of Lake Placid.

Hiking

The Adirondacks have 2,000 mi of marked hiking trails. The most popular area for hiking is the High Peaks region, accessible from the Lake Placid area in the north, Keene and Keene Valley in the east, and Newcomb in the south. The **Adirondack Mountain Club** (✉ Box 867, Lake Placid 12946, ☎ 518/523–3441, WEB www.adk.org) has information about hiking in the region. For guided hikes, contact **High Peaks Adventures** (✉ 331 Main St., Lake Placid, ☎ 518/523–9572, WEB www.highpeakscyclery.com).

Rafting

Hudson River Rafting Company (✉ 1 Main St., North Creek, ☎ 800/888–7238, WEB www.hudsonriverrafting.com) offers rafting day trips on the Hudson River Gorge, the Sacandaga River in Lake Luzerne, and the Black River from April to October.

Spectator Sports

The **Olympic Authority** (☏ 518/523–1655 or 800/462–6236) can provide information about Lake Placid summer and winter athletic competitions. Events include concerts, ski jumping, and figure-skating shows. The six-week Thoroughbred-racing season starts in late July at the **Saratoga Race Course** (✉ Union Ave., Saratoga Springs, ☏ 518/584–6200, WEB www.nyra.com/saratoga).

Ski Areas

Cross-Country

Mt. Van Hoevenberg, on Route 73, has 30 mi of groomed tracks, which connect with the **Jackrabbit Trail,** a 33-mi network of public ski trails through the High Peaks region that links Lake Placid, Saranac Lake, and Paul Smiths. For $12 a day, the Interconnect Pass permits access to four ski centers (Cascade, Lake Placid Club, Mt. Van Hoevenberg, and the Whiteface Club). For information and conditions contact **Adirondack Ski Touring Council** (✉ Box 843, Lake Placid 12946, ☏ 518/523–1365 or 800/447–5224).

Downhill

Whiteface Mountain Ski Center (✉ 8 mi northeast of Lake Placid, Wilmington, ☏ 518/946–2223) has 65 runs, 10 lifts, a 3,351-ft vertical drop, and snowmaking capabilities.

Shopping

The region's maple syrup and sharp cheddar cheese make great gifts. **Blue Mountain Lake** and **Lake Placid** are good bets for crafts hunting. Look for birch-bark baskets, pottery, and an array of jewelry, leather work, and quilting. Adirondack-style furniture also makes a superb souvenir. More than 300 local artisans show their wares at the **Adirondack Crafts Center** (✉ Lake Placid Center for the Arts, 93 Saranac Ave., Lake Placid, ☏ 518/523–2062), a year-round facility.

Saratoga Springs and the North Country Essentials

AIRPORTS

The principal airports are in Albany, New York City (207 mi south of Lake George), and Montréal (177 mi north of Lake George). The Syracuse airport is another option.

➤ AIRPORT INFORMATION: **Syracuse Hancock International Airport** (✉ 1000 Col. Eileen Collins Blvd., Syracuse, ☏ 315/454–3263, WEB www.syrairport.org).

BUS TRAVEL

Adirondack Trailways provides bus service to Saratoga Springs, Lake Placid, Lake George, Chestertown, Bolton Landing (summer only), and many other area towns.

➤ BUS INFORMATION: **Adirondack Trailways** (☏ 800/225–6815).

CAR TRAVEL

The primary route through the region is the Northway (I–87), which links Albany and Montréal.

TRAIN TRAVEL

Amtrak operates the *Adirondack,* a daily train between New York and Montréal, with many North Country stops.

➤ TRAIN INFORMATION: **Amtrak** (☏ 800/872–7245).

VISITOR INFORMATION

➤ TOURIST INFORMATION: **Adirondack Regional Tourism Council** (✉ Box 2149, Plattsburgh 12901, ☎ 518/846–8016, WEB www.adirondacks.org). **Lake Placid/Essex County Convention & Visitors Bureau** (✉ 216 Main St., Olympic Center 12946, ☎ 518/523–2999 or 800/447–5224, WEB www.lakeplacid.com). **Saratoga Chamber of Commerce** (✉ 28 Clinton St., Saratoga Springs 12866, ☎ 518/584–3255 or 800/526–8970, WEB www.saratoga.org). **Warren County (Lake George) Dept. of Tourism** (✉ Municipal Center, 1340 U.S. 9, Lake George 12845, ☎ 518/761–6366 or 800/958–4748, WEB www.visitlakegeorge.com).

LEATHERSTOCKING COUNTRY AND THE FINGER LAKES

Exploring Leatherstocking Country and the Finger Lakes

The early Yankees in their leather leggings gave the region its nickname; it is quintessential rural America, with gently rolling countryside and tree-shaded small towns. Rich in both Native American and early American history, this part of the country is also known for its sports-related sights, including the baseball and soccer halls of fame.

★ Charming Cooperstown is home to the **National Baseball Hall of Fame and Museum** (✉ 25 Main St., Cooperstown, ☎ 607/547–7200 or 888/425–5633, WEB www.baseballhalloffame.org; $9.50), where displays and paintings honor the heroes, recall great moments, and trace the history of the game. The first baseball game is said to have taken place at **Doubleday Field,** down the street from the National Baseball Hall of Fame.

The **Fenimore Art Museum** has an outstanding collection of Native American and American art and is beautifully set on the banks of Otsego Lake. *✉ Lake Rd., Rte. 80, Cooperstown, ☎ 607/547–1400 or 888/547–1450, WEB www.nysha.org. $9. Closed Jan. and Mon. Apr.–May and Oct.–Dec.*

The **National Soccer Hall of Fame** (✉ 18 Stadium Cir., Oneonta, ☎ 607/432–3351, WEB www.soccerhall.org; $8), which opened on a 61-acre campus in 1999, includes video and interactive exhibits.

The **Roberson Museum and Science Center** (✉ 30 Front St., Binghamton, ☎ 607/772–0660, WEB www.roberson.org; $5) comprises a restored 1910 historic house, a complex of museums, and a planetarium. Kids are especially fond of the wooded **Ross Park Zoo** (✉ 60 Morgan Rd., Binghamton, ☎ 607/724–5461, WEB www.rossparkzoo.com; $4), where more than 150 exotic animals (including tigers and a timber wolf pack) reside.

The 11 parallel **Finger Lakes,** from Conesus Lake (south of Rochester) to Otisco Lake (southwest of Syracuse), stretch north to south like long, narrow fingers through western New York. The region's diverse terrain—waterfalls, gorges, rocky hillsides, lush forests—is the perfect backdrop for the area's many vineyards and wineries. The two largest lakes, Seneca and Cayuga, have wine trails; the visitor center has brochures that map them out.

In Seneca Falls, about 5 mi west of Cayuga Lake's north end, 300 people attended America's first women's rights convention, which was held at the Wesleyan Methodist Chapel in July 1848. The **Women's Rights National Historical Park** (Visitor Center: ✉ 136 Falls St., Seneca Falls, ☎ 315/568–2991, WEB www.nps.gov.wori/home.htm; park $3, house tour $1) encompasses the chapel as well as the former home of Elizabeth Cady Stanton, a pioneer of the women's rights movement.

The design studios and factory of the **MacKenzie-Childs, Ltd.** empire are housed in an old country house and barn on the eastern shore of Cayuga Lake. You can see artisans creating the company's signature majolica pottery, glassware, and trimmings on weekdays at 9:30 AM. Tour reservations are recommended. ✉ *3260 Rte. 90, Aurora,* ☎ *315/364–7123,* WEB *www.mackenzie-childs.com.* 🎫 *$10. Closed Sun.*

Ithaca, at the tip of Cayuga Lake, is the home of both Cornell University and Ithaca College. The town is more spectacular than most others in the Finger Lakes because of the deep gorges and more than 100 waterfalls that lace it. **Geneva,** at the northern tip of Seneca Lake, seems preserved in time. Its South Main Street, overlooking the lake, is lined with 19th-century houses and century-old trees. The picturesque campuses of Hobart and William Smith colleges are here, too.

The village of **Watkins Glen** is at the southern end of Seneca Lake, adjoining the 1,000-acre **Watkins Glen State Park** (✉ off Rtes. 14 and 414, Watkins Glen, ☎ 607/535–4511 or 800/456–2267, WEB www.nysparks.state.ny.us). The 1½-mi gorge here is highlighted by 200-ft cliffs, rock formations, and 19 waterfalls. It's a great spot for hiking and camping. **Watkins Glen International Raceway** (✉ 2790 Rte. 16, Watkins Glen, ☎ 607/535–2481, WEB www.theglen.com) is a world-renowned auto-racing circuit that hosts top events.

Rochester is the headquarters of the Eastman Kodak Company. The **George Eastman House,** the mansion and gardens belonging at one time to the company founder and photographic innovator, now houses the **International Museum of Photography,** the world's largest museum devoted to photographic art and technology. ✉ *900 East Ave., Rochester,* ☎ *585/271–3361,* WEB *www.eastman.org.* 🎫 *$6.50. Closed Mon.*

It was in Rochester that the 19th-century civil and women's rights advocate Susan B. Anthony was arrested for voting in 1872 and wrote *The History of Woman Suffrage.* The **Susan B. Anthony House,** a National Historic Site, is furnished in the style of the mid-1800s. ✉ *17 Madison St., Rochester,* ☎ *585/235–6124,* WEB *www.susanbanthonyhouse.org.* 🎫 *$5. Closed Mon.–Tues.*

The **Corning Museum of Glass** (✉ 1 Museum Way, off Rte. 17, Corning, ☎ 607/937–5371 or 800/732–6845, WEB www.cmog.com; 🎫 $12) contains the world's most comprehensive collection of glass and a library with pretty much everything ever written about the subject. You can take a self-guided tour of the Steuben glass factory and even test your glassblowing skills.

Dining and Lodging

Cooperstown

$$$$ 🏨 **The Otesaga Resort Hotel.** This grand hotel, built circa 1909, is still considered the fanciest place in town. The resort's 18-hole Leatherstocking Golf Course is a main draw, but so the Lake Otsego setting. ✉ *Lake St., Rte. 80, Cooperstown 13326,* ☎ *607/547–9931 or 800/348–6222,* FAX *607/547–9675,* WEB *www.otesaga.com. 136 rooms. 2 restaurants, pool, golf, tennis, gym. AE, D, MC, V. Closed mid-Nov.–mid-Apr. MAP.*

$–$$ 🏨 **Fieldstone Farm.** A great place for families, this informal former farm has 178 acres of fields, ponds, and woods. There's plenty to keep kids busy, too—from tennis and volleyball to fishing, Ping-Pong, and an 80-ft rec room. The eclectically furnished accommodations, with two levels and kitchenettes, are more like town houses than rooms; cabins are available, too. ✉ *201 Rose's Hill Rd., Richfield Springs 13439,* ☎ *315/858–0295 or 888/353–3276,* WEB *www.fieldstonefarmresort.com. 7 apartments, 13 cabins. Pool, tennis. D, DC, MC, V.*

Geneva

$$$$ **Geneva on the Lake.** Built in 1910, this impressive Renaissance-style palazzo was modeled after the Villa Lancelotti in Frascati, Italy. Originally a private residence, it has served as a monastery and an apartment complex. Rooms are spacious; some have fireplaces, and almost all have a view of the lake and formal gardens. ✉ *1001 Lochland Rd./Rte. 14 S, 14456,* ☎ *315/789–7190 or 800/343–6382,* FAX *315/789–0322,* WEB *www.genevaonthelake.com. 30 suites. Restaurant, pool. AE, D, MC, V. CP.*

Ithaca

$$ ✕ **Moosewood Restaurant.** A natural-foods mecca famous for its cookbooks, Moosewood has been creating appealing eclectic fare since 1973. Savor dishes such as creamy sweet-potato soup with ginger, *tortino di verdure* (layered roasted eggplant, potatoes, and zucchini with tomatoes, basil, and mozzarella), and creole beans and rice. ✉ *215 N. Cayuga St.,* ☎ *607/273–9610,* WEB *www.mooseheadrestaurant.com. Reservations not accepted. MC, V. No lunch Sun.*

Leatherstocking Country and the Finger Lakes Essentials

CAR TRAVEL

The Leatherstocking region is 200 mi to 300 mi from New York City via the New York State Thruway (I–87) and, from Kingston, Route 28. I–90, at this point also called the New York State Thruway, runs east–west through both Leatherstocking Country and the Finger Lakes, connecting Albany with Buffalo. I–88 runs northeast–southwest, leading from Binghamton to northwest of Albany.

VISITOR INFORMATION

➤ TOURIST INFORMATION: **Cooperstown Chamber of Commerce** (✉ 31 Chestnut St., 13326, ☎ 607/547–9983 or 877/867–4737, WEB www.cooperstownchamber.org). **Finger Lakes Association** (✉ 309 Lake St., Penn Yan 14527, ☎ 315/536–7488 or 800/548–4386, WEB www.fingerlakes.org). **Ithaca/Tompkins County Convention & Visitors Bureau** (✉ 904 E. Shore Dr., Ithaca 14850, ☎ 607/272–1313 or 800/284–8422, WEB www.visitithaca.com). **Leatherstocking Country** (✉ 800 Mohawk St., Herkimer 13350, ☎ 315/724–7221 or 800/233–8778, WEB www.leatherstockingny.com).

BUFFALO AND NIAGARA FALLS

Exploring Buffalo and Niagara Falls

Buffalo is a city of Victorian elegance, with many churches and strongly ethnic neighborhoods. Elmwood Street, downtown, offers a taste of the city's eclectic mix of shops and restaurants; Chippewa Street (or the Chippewa District), known for its nightclubs and jazz bars, is another lively area in the heart of the city.

The **Albright-Knox Art Gallery,** north of the city, has a superb collection of modern and contemporary art, including works by Mondrian, Miró, and van Gogh. ✉ *1285 Elmwood Ave., Buffalo,* ☎ *716/882–8700,* WEB *www.albrightknox.org.* *$5. Closed Mon.*

The Albright-Knox Art Gallery sits on the western side of the 350-acre **Delaware Park** (✉ Parkside and Elmwood Ave., Buffalo, ☎ 716/851–5806), which was designed by Frederick Law Olmsted. More than 23 acres of Delaware Park are dedicated to one of the oldest zoos in the country, the **Buffalo Zoological Gardens** (✉ 300 Parkside Ave., Buffalo, ☎ 716/837–3900, WEB www.buffalozoo.org; $7).

Niagara Falls, the most accessible and famous waterfall in the world, is actually three cataracts: the **American** and **Bridal Veil falls,** in New York, and **Horseshoe Falls,** in Ontario, Canada. The Niagara Visitor Center in the **Niagara Falls State Park** (✉ Prospect Park, Niagara Falls, ☎ 716/278–1701, WEB www.niagarafallsstatepark.com), the oldest state park in the nation, provides a good orientation to the falls. **Goat Island** offers the closest view of the American Falls; cross to the Canadian side for the best view of Horseshoe Falls. The famous ***Maid of the Mist*** boat ride (✉ 151 Buffalo Ave., Niagara Falls, ☎ 716/284–8897, WEB www.maidofthemist.com) lets you view the falls from the water.

Dining and Lodging

Buffalo

$$$–$$$$ ★ ✕ **The Hourglass.** Open for business for more than 50 years, this spot continues to maintain its reputation as one of greater Buffalo's best restaurants. All the Continental classics are available here, but with such contemporary touches as balsamic vinegar. *✉ 981 Kenmore Ave., ☎ 716/877–8788. AE, MC, V. Closed Sun.–Mon. No lunch.*

$–$$ ✕ **Just Pasta.** Spinach-and-egg spaghetti with prosciutto, peas, and cream, and Gorgonzola ravioli with ricotta and tomato sauce are among the choices at this popular casual Italian. *✉ 307 Bryant St., ☎ 716/881–1888. AE, DC, MC, V. Closed Sun.*

$–$$$ **Hyatt Regency Buffalo.** The 16-floor hotel is housed in a historic office building, erected in 1923; the building was converted to a hotel in 1983. *✉ 2 Fountain Plaza, 14202, ☎ 716/856–1234 or 800/233–1234, FAX 716/852–6157, WEB www.buffalo.hyatt.com. 395 rooms. 3 restaurants. AE, D, MC, V.*

Niagara Falls

$$–$$$$ ✕ **Red Coach Inn.** The 1923 inn with mostly suites has an Old England atmosphere. One- and two-bedroom suites are luxurious, with gas-burning fireplaces and kitchenettes; all but two of the rooms have a spectacular view of the upper rapids. The restaurant ($$–$$$) serves such classics as charbroiled filet mignon and apricot-glazed roast duck; the patio is splendid for summer dining. *✉ 2 Buffalo Ave., 14303, ☎ 716/282–1459 or 800/282–1459, FAX 716/282–2650, WEB www.redcoach.com. 14 rooms. Restaurant. AE, D, DC, MC, V.*

$–$$$ **Holiday Inn Select.** The largest hotel in Niagara Falls, this Holiday Inn is 1,600 ft from the falls and it's loaded with amenities, including a whirlpool, saunas, and convention and business services. *✉ 300 3rd St., 14303, ☎ 716/285–3361 or 800/953–2557, FAX 716/285–3900, WEB www.holiday-inn.com. 397 rooms. Restaurant, pool, health club. AE, D, DC, MC, V.*

Nightlife and the Arts

Stroll along Buffalo's Elmwood Avenue, near Buffalo State College, or on Main Street, near the University of Buffalo, to sample the college scene.

Shea's Performing Arts Center (✉ 646 Main St., Buffalo, ☎ 716/847–0850) presents concerts, opera, dance, and touring theater performances in an historic facility reminiscent of a European opera house.

Contact the **Buffalo Philharmonic Orchestra** for performance schedules (✉ Kleinhans Music Hall, 71 Symphony Cir., Buffalo, ☎ 716/885–5000 or 800/699–3168, WEB www.bpo.org).

Outdoor Activities and Sports

Spectator Sports

The National Football League's **Buffalo Bills** (✉ Ralph Wilson Stadium, 1 Bills Dr., Orchard Park, ☎ 716/648–1800 or 877/228–4257, WEB www.buffalobills.com) have a strong following. Home games of the **Buffalo Sabres** National Hockey League team (✉ HSBC Arena, 1 Seymour H. Knox III Plaza, Buffalo, ☎ 716/855–4444 ext. 82 or 888/223–6000, WEB www.sabres.com) are played at HSBC Arena. The **Buffalo Bisons** (✉ Dunn Tire Park, 275 Washington St., Buffalo, ☎ 716/846–2003 or 888/223–6000, WEB www.bisons.com) play minor-league baseball.

Buffalo and Niagara Falls Essentials

AIRPORTS

Buffalo International Airport serves the Buffalo-Niagara area. Flying time from New York City to Buffalo is one hour.

➤ AIRPORT INFORMATION: **Buffalo International Airport** (✉ 4200 Genessee St., Buffalo, ☎ 716/630–6000, WEB www.buffaloairport.com).

BUS TRAVEL

Service to and from Buffalo is via Greyhound and New York Trailways, which arrive at the Metropolitan Transportation Center.

➤ BUS INFORMATION: **Metropolitan Transportation Center** (✉ 181 Ellicott St., Buffalo, ☎ 716/855—7531). **Greyhound** (☎ 800/229–9494, WEB www.greyhound.com). **New York Trailways** (☎ 800/225–6515 or 800/858–8555, WEB www.trailways.com).

CAR TRAVEL

Access to Buffalo and Chautauqua County is primarily via I–90, the New York State Thruway. From Buffalo, I–190 leads to Niagara Falls.

VISITOR INFORMATION

➤ TOURIST INFORMATION: **Buffalo Niagara Convention and Visitors Bureau** (✉ 617 Main St., Suite 400, Buffalo, ☎ 716/852–0511 or 888/228–3369, WEB www.buffalocvb.org). **Niagara Falls Convention and Visitors Bureau** (✉ 310 4th St., Niagara Falls, ☎ 716/285–2400 or 800/421–5223, WEB www.nfcvb.com).

NORTH CAROLINA

Updated by Rob Fleming

Capital	Raleigh
Population	7,846,220
Motto	To Be Rather Than to Seem
State Bird	Cardinal
State Flower	Dogwood
Postal Abbreviation	NC

Statewide Visitor Information

North Carolina Division of Tourism, Film and Sports Development (✉ 301 N. Wilmington St., Raleigh 27601, ☎ 919/733–8372 or 800/847–4862, WEB www.visitnc.com). **Welcome centers:** I–77 south near Charlotte, I–77 north near Dobson, I–85 south near Kings Mountain, I–85 north near Norlina, I–95 south near Rowland, I–95 north near Roanoke Rapids, I–26 west near Columbus, and I–40 west near Waynesville.

Scenic Drives

The **Blue Ridge Parkway** runs from the Virginia state line to the Great Smoky Mountains National Park entrance near Cherokee. In North Carolina the recreation-oriented byway extends more than 250 mi and offers stunning mountain views, nature exhibits, historic sites, parks, picnic areas, and hiking trails. **U.S. 441** from Cherokee to Gatlinburg, Tennessee, cuts through the middle of the national park for about 35 mi, climbing to a crest of 6,643 ft at Clingman's Dome, a short distance from Newfound Gap. Portions of **U.S. 64** travel through the Hickory Nut Gorge between Lake Lure and Chimney Rock and the Cullasaja Gorge between Lake Toxaway and Franklin, affording spectacular views of mountain peaks and cascading waterfalls. **Route 12,** which connects the Outer Banks, offers great views of the ocean and landscapes dotted with lighthouses and weathered beach cottages.

National and State Parks

The state tourism division's travel guide includes a complete listing of state and national parks and recreation areas as well as state forests.

National Parks

Cape Hatteras National Seashore (✉ Rte. 1 [Box 675, Manteo 27954], ☎ 252/473–2111, WEB www.nps.gov/caha; 🎫 free), a natural habitat for hundreds of species of birds, wild animals, and aquatic life, stretches 75 mi from Nags Head to Ocracoke and encompasses 30,318 acres of marshland and sandy beaches. **Cape Lookout National Seashore** (✉ 131 Charles St., Harkers Island 28531, ☎ 252/728–2250, WEB www.nps.gov/calo; 🎫 free) extends 56 mi from Portsmouth Island to Beaufort Inlet and includes 28,400 acres of uninhabited land and marsh, accessible only by boat or ferry. Portsmouth, a deserted village that was inhabited from 1753 until 1971, has been restored and is open to the public from April through November. **Great Smoky Mountains National Park** (✉ 107 Park Headquarters Rd., Gatlinburg, TN 37738, ☎ 423/436–1200, WEB www.nps.gov/grsm; 🎫 free), with 9 million visitors a year, is the most visited national park in the country. Its 521,000 acres straddle the North Carolina–Tennessee border and have camping, hiking, fishing, historic sites, and nature lore. To enter the park from North Carolina, take U.S. 441 north from Cherokee.

State Parks

Many of North Carolina's 43 state parks and recreation areas preserve unique geological and biological resources. Home to extremely rare plants and animals is **Lake Waccamaw State Park** (✉ 1866 State Park Dr., Lake Waccamaw 28450, ☎ 910/646–4748), which has boating, camping, fishing, and picnicking. **Jockey's Ridge State Park** (✉ Box 592, Nags Head 27959, ☎ 252/441–7132) offers hang-gliding instruction and flights from the tallest sand dune in the East. **Eno River State Park** (✉ 6101 Cole Mill Rd., Durham 27705, ☎ 919/383–1686) is a green, wild, and watery buffer in an urban area. It includes a swinging bridge, white-water rapids, hiking, fishing, and primitive camping. **Mt. Mitchell State Park** (✉ Rte. 5 [Box 700, Burnsville 28714], ☎ 828/675–4611) has camping and a picnic area and organizes guided nature walks on the highest mountain in the East (6,684 ft).

THE PIEDMONT

The Piedmont is the heartland of North Carolina, a vast area of rolling hills that extends from the coastal plain, which is east of the Triangle area (Raleigh, Durham, and Chapel Hill), to the foothills of the Blue Ridge Mountains, which are west of Charlotte and the Triad area (Greensboro, Winston-Salem, and High Point). Scattered along I–40, I–77, and I–85, the major arteries of the region, are the state's biggest towns, cities, and industries. Here also are large rivers and woodlands; historic villages dating from the mid-1700s; crafts, antiques, and outlet shops; world-renowned colleges and universities; and one of the largest concentrations of golf courses in the world.

Exploring the Piedmont

Charlotte, the region's largest city, is known as a financial center and prides itself on its cosmopolitan flair. At **Discovery Place** (✉ 301 N. Tryon St., ☎ 704/372–6261 or 800/935–0553, WEB www.discoveryplace.org; 🎫 $7.50), an award-winning hands-on science museum, there's a touch tank, aquariums, an indoor rain forest, an Omnimax theater, a planetarium, and special exhibits.

The **Charlotte Museum of History and Hezekiah Alexander Homesite,** built in 1774, is the city's oldest dwelling. The site, which was named for the settler who built it, includes a log kitchen. Costumed docents give guided tours. ✉ *3500 Shamrock Dr.,* ☎ *704/568–1774,* WEB *www.charlottemuseum.org.* 🎫 *Museum and homesite $6, free Sun. Closed Mon.*

Though it has displayed art since 1936, the **Mint Museum of Art** was built in 1837 as a U.S. mint. Its permanent collection includes American and European decorative and fine art, as well as pre-Columbian and Spanish colonial objects. It also hosts internationally acclaimed exhibits. ✉ *2730 Randolph Rd.,* ☎ *704/337–2000,* WEB *www.mintmuseum.org.* 🎫 *$6. Closed Mon.*

The **Mint Museum of Craft & Design** in Charlotte's center city houses collections of ceramics, glass, fiber, metal, and wood. ✉ *220 N. Tryon St.,* ☎ *704/337–2000,* WEB *www.mintmuseum.org.* 🎫 *$6. Closed Mon.*

Straddling the North Carolina–South Carolina border near Charlotte is **Paramount's Carowinds,** a 100-acre amusement park with water rides and movie-theme rides and shows. ✉ *14523 Carowinds Blvd., off I–77,* ☎ *704/588–2600 or 800/888–4386,* WEB *www.carowinds.com.* 🎫 *$40. Closed mid-Dec.–mid-Mar.*

Greensboro, an hour and a half north of Charlotte on I–85, is the largest city in the Triad. **Guilford Courthouse National Military Park** (✉ 2332 New Garden Rd., ☎ 336/288–1776, WEB www.nps.gov/guco; 🎫 free) has more than 200 acres of wooded hiking trails, monuments, and military memorabilia dating back to the Revolutionary War.

You'll find a dinosaur gallery, dozens of gems and minerals, and lemurs, snakes, and amphibians at the **Natural Science Center of Greensboro** (✉ 4301 Lawndale Dr., ☎ 336/288–3769, WEB www.greensboro.com; 🎫 $6). Young children will enjoy the petting zoo.

Forty minutes south of Greensboro on U.S. 220, the **North Carolina Zoological Park** (✉ 4401 Zoo Pkwy., ☎ 336/879–7000 or 800/488–0444, WEB www.nczoo.org; 🎫 $10) in Asheboro has more than 1,100 animals and 60,000 exotic and tropical plants. The African Plains exhibit alone is larger than most zoos.

A half hour west of Greensboro on I–40 is **Winston-Salem,** whose residents are known for their support of the arts and the city's museums. ★ **Old Salem** (✉ 600 S. Main St., ☎ 336/721–7350, WEB www.oldsalem.org; 🎫 Old Salem $15, Old Salem and Museum of Early Southern Decorative Arts $20), a restored 18th-century village, re-creates the life of the Moravians, a Protestant sect that settled in the area in 1766. The **Museum of Early Southern Decorative Arts,** also in the village, displays period furnishings.

An hour's drive east from Greensboro on I–85 will bring you to **Durham,** a city once known for its tobacco production but known today as the home of Duke University and an eclectic arts scene.

Duke University Chapel (✉ Chapel Dr., West Campus, ☎ 919/681–1704, WEB www.chapel.duke.edu; 🎫 free), an ornate neo-Gothic cathedral, is open for tours and free organ demonstrations. The 55-acre **Sarah P. Duke Gardens** (✉ main entrance at Anderson St., Duke University's West Campus, ☎ 919/668–5100; 🎫 free) has landscaped and woodland gardens, a wisteria-draped gazebo, and a Japanese garden with a lily pond filled with goldfish.

The **North Carolina Museum of Life and Science** (✉ 433 Murray Ave., ☎ 919/220–5429, WEB www.ncmls.org; 🎫 $8) has exhibits ranging from life-size dinosaur models and NASA artifacts to Carolina wildlife. The Magic Wings House has tropical plants and 1,000 exotic butterflies in open flight.

In Chapel Hill, 15 minutes south of Durham on U.S. 15/501, you can star-gaze, take classes, and attend narrated presentations, including laser and children's shows, at the University of North Carolina's **Morehead Planetarium** (✉ 250 E. Franklin St., ☎ 919/962–1236, WEB www.morehead.unc.edu; 🎫 $4.50), one of the largest planetariums in the country.

Raleigh, the state's capital, is a 30-minute drive from Chapel Hill on I–40. Its downtown is easily explored on foot. The Greek Revival–style **state capitol** (✉ Capitol Square, ☎ 919/733–4994; 🎫 free), completed in 1840, commands the highest point in Capitol Square. The **North Carolina Museum of History** (✉ 5 E. Edenton St., ☎ 919/715–0200; 🎫 free) uses artifacts, audiovisual programs, and interactive exhibits to bring the state's history to life. The **Executive Mansion** (✉ 200 N. Blount St., ☎ 919/733–3456; 🎫 free), a turn-of-the-20th-century Queen Anne–style structure in brick, is the governor's home.

The **North Carolina Museum of Natural Sciences** (✉ 11 W. Jones St., ☎ 919/733–7450, WEB www.naturalsciences.org; 🎫 free) has an elegant building. The skeleton of Acrocanthosaurus, a giant carnivore that lived in the South 110 million years ago and preyed on dinosaurs larger than itself, is featured in a multistory glass-enclosed tower.

In addition to being an architectural showplace, **Exploris** is a children's museum and science center focusing on language, culture, geography, global trade, and communications. Films about natural wonders and adventures are screened regularly at the IMAX theater. ✉ *201 E. Hargett St.,* ☎ *919/834–4040,* WEB *www.exploris.org.* *Exhibits $7.95, exhibits and IMAX movie $12.95. Closed Mon.*

The **North Carolina Museum of Art,** on a 140-acre tract near Raleigh's western edge, has exhibits representing 5,000 years of artistic heritage. The Museum Café is a favorite for lunch or Friday-night entertainment. ✉ *2110 Blue Ridge Rd.,* ☎ *919/715–5923,* WEB *www.ncartmuseum.org.* *Free. Closed Mon.*

Dining and Lodging

The Piedmont has a growing number of upscale restaurants and ethnic eateries, as well as restaurants that specialize in the more traditional—barbecue, fresh seafood, fried chicken, and country ham. Many city hotels have weekend packages with discounted rates.

Chapel Hill

$$$–$$$$ ★ ✕ **Fearrington House.** On a 200-year-old farm, this French-style country inn anchors a bustling village center and is a member of Relais & Châteaux. Rooms are decorated with chintz, antiques, and original art. The restaurant's prix-fixe menu ($$$$) is a blend of regional and French cuisines. ✉ *Fearrington Village Center, Pittsboro 27312,* ☎ *919/542–2121,* FAX *919/542–4202,* WEB *www.fearringtonhouse.com. 31 rooms. 2 restaurants. AE, MC, V.*

Charlotte

$$–$$$ ✕ **Atlantic Beer & Ice Co.** This uptown eatery has a cigar and Scotch bar with billiards on the top floor, a restaurant and bar on the main floor, and a jazz club on the lower level. The seasonal menu is varied—from knockwurst and pastrami sandwiches to tenderloin tips. Beef is always a good bet. ✉ *330 N. Tryon St.,* ☎ *704/339–0566,* FAX *704/339–0261. AE, DC, MC, V.*

$$–$$$ ✕ **Campania.** The walls are golden and textured, the room is full of rich wood and candlelight, and the music is genuinely Italian, from opera to contemporary. The *gamberoni Mergellina,* shrimp sautéed in garlic butter and herbs, and linguine Posillipo, clams paired with red or white sauce, are characteristic dishes here. ✉ *6414 Rea Rd.,* ☎ *704/541–8505. AE, D, MC, V.*

$–$$ ✕ **Hyatt Charlotte at Southpark.** Rooms surround a four-story atrium lobby at this modern hotel, popular with business travelers. The restaurant serves northern Italian cuisine. ✉ *5501 Carnegie Blvd., 28209-3462,* ☎ *704/554–1234 or 800/233–1234,* FAX *704/554–8319,* WEB *www.hyatt.com. 262 rooms. Restaurant, pool, health club. AE, D, DC, MC, V.*

$$ **Homeplace.** This turn-of-the-20th-century Victorian gem in a residential neighborhood is now a B&B filled with antiques and memorabilia. Rooms have four-poster beds and antique reproductions. The no-smoking inn is best for adults and older children. ✉ *5901 Sardis Rd., 28270,* ☎ *704/365–1936,* FAX *704/366–2729. 3 rooms. AE, MC, V. BP.*

$ **Comfort Inn–Lake Norman.** North of Charlotte on I–77 near Lake Norman and Davidson College, this motel offers rooms with refrigerators and coffeemakers. Some have VCRs, microwaves, and whirlpool baths. Jogging trails are nearby. ✉ *20740 Torrence Chapel Rd., Cor-*

nelius 28031, ☎ *704/892–3500 or 800/848–9751,* FAX *704/892–6473,* WEB *www.comfortinn.com. 90 rooms. Pool. AE, D, DC, MC, V. CP.*

Durham

$$$–$$$$ ★ ✕ **Magnolia Grill.** This award-winning bistro is one of the finest, most innovative places to dine in the state. It is especially known for its desserts—co-owner Karen Barker has won best pastry chef in America in *Bon Appétit.* ✉ *1002 9th St.,* ☎ *919/286–3609,* WEB *www.magnoliagrillcookbook.com. MC, V. Closed Sun. No lunch.*

$$$–$$$$ ★ ✕🏨 **Washington Duke Inn & Golf Club.** Part of the Duke University campus, this luxurious inn overlooks a Robert Trent Jones golf course. Among the entrées at the Fairview restaurant ($$$$) are Muscovy duck with mashed white beans, roasted garlic, and cranberry sauce; and homemade fettuccine tossed with mussels. There is also a lounge-bar. ✉ *3001 Cameron Blvd., 27706,* ☎ *919/490–0999 or 800/443–3853,* FAX *919/688–0105,* WEB *www.washingtondukeinn.com. 171 rooms. Restaurant, pool. AE, DC, MC, V.*

Greensboro

$$$–$$$$ ✕ **Paisley Pineapple.** The dining is formal in this romantic Old Greensborough restaurant in a restored 1920s building. The menu, heavy on hearty fare, such as rack of lamb, and sautéed beef tenderloin, is tempered by light soups. Upstairs there's a sofa bar with live jazz. ✉ *345 S. Elm St.,* ☎ *336/279–8488. AE, MC, V. Closed Sun.–Mon.*

$$–$$$ 🏨 **Sheraton Greensboro Hotel at Four Seasons.** The accommodations here are standard. But if it's convenience you want, they've got it—it's near major thoroughfares and shopping areas. The facility hosts large conventions. ✉ *3121 High Point Rd., 27407,* ☎ *336/292–9161 or 800/242–6556,* FAX *336/294–3516,* WEB *www.sheratongreensboro.com. 1,016 rooms. 5 restaurants, pools, gym. AE, D, DC, MC, V.*

Raleigh

$$$–$$$$ ★ ✕ **Angus Barn, Ltd.** Housed in a huge rustic barn, this Raleigh fixture is known for its steaks, seafood, prime rib, homemade desserts, and extensive wine list. Its Wild Turkey lounge is a favorite gathering spot among locals. ✉ *U.S. 70 W at Aviation Pkwy.,* ☎ *919/781–2444,* WEB *www.angusbarn.com. AE, D, DC, MC, V.*

$–$$ ✕ **TÍR NA NÓG.** The interior is styled in the manner of a traditional Irish pub with lots of stone and even a thatched roof. The name means "land of eternal youth." Choices range from pub grub to fancy, and the popular Sunday brunch has southern specialties (sausage and biscuits) as well as a Bloody Mary bar. There's live entertainment many evenings. ✉ *218 S. Blount St.,* ☎ *919/833–7795. AE, DC, MC, V.*

$$$ 🏨 **Raleigh Marriott Crabtree Valley.** Standard guest rooms have Asian floral prints and dark cherrywood furnishings. You can dine at Crabtree Grill or Quinn's, which serves light fare. An airport shuttle is available. ✉ *4500 Marriott Dr., 27612,* ☎ *919/781–7000 or 800/228–9290,* FAX *919/781–3059,* WEB *www.marriotthotels.com. 379 rooms. Restaurant, pool, gym. AE, D, DC, MC, V.*

$$–$$$ 🏨 **William Thomas House.** A stately Victorian home is now a B&B on the edge of downtown Raleigh. Rooms are traditional: elegantly decorated, with oversize windows, 12-ft ceilings, modem lines, and inconspicuous refrigerators. ✉ *530 N. Blount St., 27604,* ☎ *919/755–9400 or 800/653–3466,* FAX *919/755–3966,* WEB *www.williamthomashouse.com. 4 rooms. AE, D, DC, MC, V. BP.*

Winston-Salem

$$ ✕ **Old Salem Tavern Dining Room.** Dine on Moravian dishes, such as chicken potpie and beef ragout, in a Moravian setting with costumed servers. In warm months drinks are served under the arbor on the patio. ✉ *736 S. Main St.,* ☎ *336/748–8585. AE, D, MC, V.*

$–$$ ★ **Henry F. Shaffner House.** At the majestic Queen Anne, built around 1907 with tiger-oak paneling and the finest materials, you'll get luxurious accommodations and lots of personal attention. Another plus is its wonderfully convenient setting near Old Salem and many downtown attractions. ✉ *150 S. Marshall St., 27101,* ☎ *336/777–0052 or 800/952–2256,* FAX *336/777–1188. 9 rooms. AE, MC, V. BP.*

Nightlife and the Arts

In Winston-Salem, the **Stevens Center at the North Carolina School of the Arts** (✉ 405 W. 4th St., ☎ 336/721–1945) stages events and performances. The **Eastern Music Festival** (✉ 200 N. Davie St., ☎ 877/833–6753) presents six weeks of classical music concerts each summer in Greensboro. High Point's **North Carolina Shakespeare Festival** (✉ 220 E. Commerce Ave., ☎ 800/627–3849) puts on several productions in late summer and early autumn and *A Christmas Carol* in December. In Charlotte, the **North Carolina Blumenthal Performing Arts Center** (✉ 130 N. Tryon St., ☎ 704/372–1000) hosts operas, concerts, plays, and other cultural events.

Raleigh's **BTI Center for the Performing Arts** (✉ 2 E. South St.) is home to seasonal musical, dramatic and dance productions presented by the **North Carolina Symphony Orchestra** (☎ 919/733–2750), **North Carolina Theatre** (☎ 919/831–6941), and the **Carolina Ballet** (☎ 919/856–0083).

Outdoor Activities and Sports

Golf

The Sandhills area, in the southern part of the Piedmont, has more than three dozen courses, including Pinehurst's famous Number 2. For details contact the **Pinehurst Area Convention and Visitors Bureau** (✉ Box 2270, Southern Pines 28388, ☎ 910/692–3330 or 800/346–5362, WEB www.homeofgolf.com).

Spectator Sports

Basketball: Charlotte Hornets (✉ Charlotte Coliseum, 100 Hive Dr., Tyvola Rd. off Billy Graham Pkwy., ☎ 704/357–0252) is the state's NBA team. From November through March, the Piedmont is a college basketball fan's dream, with Atlantic Coast Conference rivals **Duke University** (☎ 919/681–2583 or 800/672–2583) in Durham, **North Carolina State** (☎ 919/515–2106 or 800/310–7225) in Raleigh, the **University of North Carolina** (☎ 919/962–2296 or 800/722–4335) in Chapel Hill, and **Wake Forest University** (☎ 336/758–3322 or 888/758–3322) in Winston-Salem. **Football: Carolina Panthers** (✉ Ericsson Stadium, 800–1 S. Mint St., Charlotte, ☎ 704/358–7800), one of the National Football League's youngest franchises, plays in a 72,000-seat stadium in uptown Charlotte. **Ice Hockey:** The National Hockey League's **Carolina Hurricanes** (✉ 1400 Edwards Mill Rd., ☎ 919/467–7825 or 888/645–8491) play in Raleigh at the high-tech, 21,000-seat Entertainment & Sports Arena. **NASCAR Racing:** The Coca-Cola 600 and UAW-GM 500 races draw huge crowds to the **Lowe's Motor Speedway** (✉ 5555 Concord Pkwy. S, ☎ 704/455–3200), off I–85 near Concord.

Shopping

The Piedmont is ideal for lovers of **antiques and crafts**; towns such as Waxhaw, Cameron, Pineville, and Matthews are devoted almost entirely to antiques. For more information, call Charlotte's visitor center. Burlington, between Greensboro and Durham, is a hub for **outlet**

stores. Charlotte and Raleigh are retail centers; the latter i[s] one of the largest **farmers' markets** in the Southeast.

Concord Mills (✉ 15 mi north of Charlotte, intersection of I–8[5 and] Concord Mills Blvd., Concord, ☎ 704/979–3000 or 877/626–4[...]) offers the latest in "shoppertainment," with more than 200 stores[,] theme restaurants, a 24-screen movie theater, arcades, even a wat[er]fall and trout pond, arranged around a 1-mi oval walking lane.

High Point, 20 minutes southwest of Greensboro, is known as the furniture capital of the world.

One of the country's largest antiques centers is **Metrolina Expo** (✉ 7100 N. Statesville Rd., ☎ 704/596–4643 or 800/824–3770), near Charlotte.

The **N. C. Pottery Center** (✉ 250 East Ave., ☎ 336/873–8430) in Seagrove, between Greensboro and Pinehurst, has information about and samples of work by potters from the state Tuesday–Saturday.

Replacements, Ltd. (✉ 1089 Knox Rd., at Exit 132 off I–85/40, between Burlington and Greensboro, ☎ 800/737–5223) is the world's largest retailer of discontinued and active china, crystal, flatware, and collectibles. There are more than 6 million pieces of inventory and 125,000 patterns represented. Tours are offered daily 8:30 AM–8 PM.

The Piedmont Essentials

AIRPORTS

Major carriers serve Charlotte-Douglas International Airport, Raleigh-Durham International Airport, and Piedmont Triad International Airport. Taxi and limousine services are available at all airports.

➤ AIRPORT INFORMATION: **Charlotte-Douglas International Airport** (✉ 5501 Josh Birmingham Blvd., Charlotte, ☎ 704/359–4013, WEB www.charlotteairport.com). **Piedmont Triad International Airport** (✉ 6451 Bryan Blvd., Greensboro, ☎ 336/665–5666, WEB www.ptia.org). **Raleigh-Durham International Airport** (✉ 1600 Terminal Blvd., Morrisville, ☎ 919/840–2123, WEB www.rdu.com).

BUS TRAVEL

Greyhound/Carolina Trailways provides service to Charlotte, Raleigh, Durham, Chapel Hill, Greensboro, and Winston-Salem.

➤ BUS INFORMATION: **Greyhound** (☎ 800/231–2222, WEB www.greyhound.com).

CAR TRAVEL

I–40, U.S. 64, and U.S. 74 run east–west through the Piedmont; I–77 runs north from Charlotte; I–85 runs from Charlotte northeast through Greensboro and the Triangle area.

TRAIN TRAVEL

Amtrak's *Carolinian* provides daily service to stations in 12 Piedmont cities, while the *Piedmont* connects nine cities daily. The *Crescent* services five cities, and the *Silver Service* trains make local stops.

➤ TRAIN INFORMATION: **Amtrak** (☎ 800/872–7245, WEB www.amtrak.com).

VISITOR INFORMATION

➤ TOURIST INFORMATION: **Capital Area Visitor Center** (✉ 301 N. Blount St., Raleigh 27611, ☎ 919/733–3456). **Durham Convention & Visitors Bureau** (✉ 101 E. Morgan St., 27701, ☎ 919/687–0288 or 800/446–8604, WEB www.durham-nc.com). **Greensboro Convention and Visitors Bureau** (✉ 317 S. Greene St., 27401, ☎ 336/274–2282

-2282, WEB www.greensboronc.org). **INFO! Charlotte** (✉ ...yon St., 28202, ☎ 704/331–2700 or 800/231–4636). **Raleigh ...ention and Visitors Bureau** (✉ 421 Fayetteville St. Mall, Suite 1505, ...601, ☎ 919/834–5900 or 800/849–8499, WEB www.raleighcvb.org). **Winston-Salem Convention & Visitors Bureau** (✉ 601 N. Cherry St., Suite 100, 27102, ☎ 336/777–3796 or 800/331–7018, WEB www.visitwinstonsalem.com).

THE COAST

English settlers came to the shores of the North Carolina coast more than 400 years ago to establish a colony on Roanoke Island and mysteriously disappeared. They were not alone: the Outer Banks came to be called the Graveyard of the Atlantic as its seas swallowed hundreds of ships and provided refuge to marauding pirates in the 1700s. For years the region remained isolated, home only to a few fishermen and their families. But now, linked by bridges and ferries, the islands are a popular vacation spot. The chain of barrier islands that flanks the coast has three main regions. The Outer Banks stretch some 130 mi from the Virginia state line south to Cape Lookout; the Crystal Coast includes the stretch from Cape Lookout to the Bogue Banks; the southern coast, to the South Carolina line, includes the Cape Fear River region and Wilmington, the state's primary port. Nearby, the Albemarle region comprises charming towns full of early architecture. Hundreds of films and television programs have been shot in Wilmington, which has a restored historic district and waterfront. On the surrounding coast visitors can tour old plantation houses and azalea gardens, study sea life, and bask in the sun at nearby beaches.

Exploring the Coast

Start your tour of the Outer Banks at Nags Head and Kill Devil Hills, where the Cape Hatteras National Seashore begins (☞ National and State Parks, *above*). You can drive from Nags Head to Ocracoke in a day, but allow plenty of time in summer, when ferries are crowded. During major storms and hurricanes, follow the evacuation signs to safety.

Kill Devil Hills is the site of the first manned flight in history. The **Wright Brothers National Memorial** (✉ U.S. 158 Bypass, ☎ 252/441–7430; 🎫 $2 per adult, $4 per car) is a tribute to Wilbur and Orville's feat of December 17, 1903. A replica of the *Flyer* is displayed in the visitor center. You can fly a kite from the tallest sand dune in the East (about 110 ft) in **Jockey's Ridge State Park,** a few miles south of the Wright Brothers National Memorial.

Roanoke Island, accessible from U.S. 158 Bypass via U.S. 64/264, was the site of several ill-fated attempts at English colonization of the New World. Today, four sites alone focus on Sir Walter Raleigh's Lost Colonists. During the summer months the place is a beehive of tourist-related activity. Yet, the island hasn't succumbed to full-scale commercialization; it remains a place of quiet neighborhoods and forests as wild as the days when Native Americans were the only inhabitants.

From mid-June to late August, the outdoor drama ***Lost Colony*** (✉ Hwy. 64, Waterford Theatre, ☎ 252/473–3414 or 800/488–5012, WEB www.thelostcolony.org; 🎫 $16) reenacts the story of the first colonists, who settled on Roanoke Island in 1587 and then disappeared. The **Elizabethan Gardens** (✉ 1411 U.S. 64, Manteo, ☎ 252/473–3234; 🎫 $5) are a lush re-creation of a 16th-century English garden. The gardens, with their antique statuary, are closed on weekends in December, January, and sometimes February. **Fort Raleigh National Historic Site** (✉

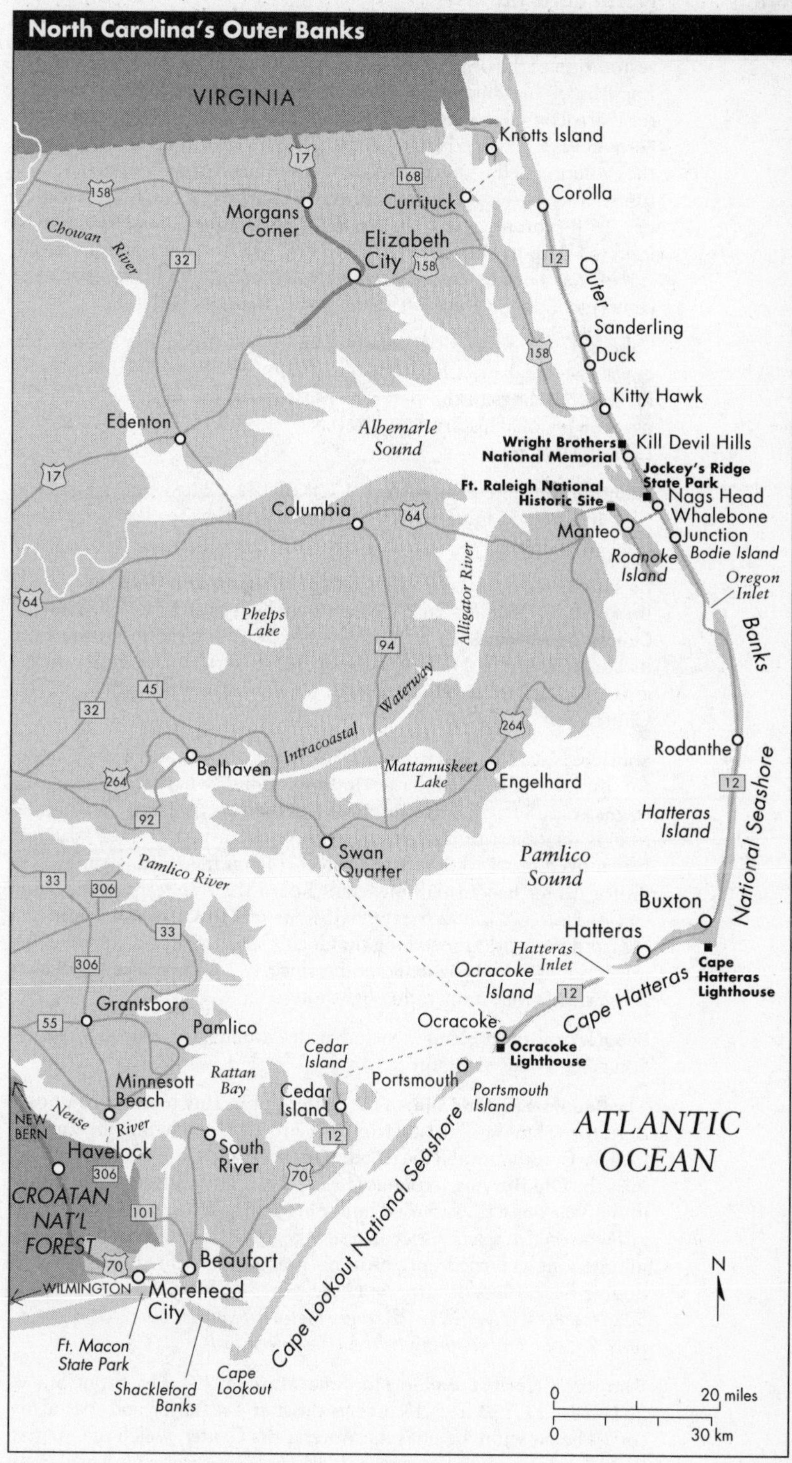
North Carolina's Outer Banks
VIRGINIA
Knotts Island
Corolla
Currituck
Morgans Corner
Elizabeth City
Chowan River
Outer Banks National Seashore
Sanderling
Duck
Kitty Hawk
Edenton
Albemarle Sound
Wright Brothers National Memorial
Kill Devil Hills
Jockey's Ridge State Park
Ft. Raleigh National Historic Site
Nags Head
Whalebone Junction
Columbia
Manteo
Roanoke Island
Bodie Island
Oregon Inlet
Alligator River
Phelps Lake
Intracoastal Waterway
Rodanthe
Belhaven
Mattamuskeet Lake
Engelhard
Hatteras Island
Swan Quarter
Pamlico Sound
Pamlico River
Buxton
Hatteras
Hatteras Inlet
Cape Hatteras Lighthouse
Ocracoke Island
Cape Hatteras
Grantsboro
Pamlico
Ocracoke
Ocracoke Lighthouse
Cedar Island
Portsmouth
Portsmouth Island
Minnesott Beach
Rattan Bay
Neuse River
NEW BERN
Havelock
South River
ATLANTIC OCEAN
CROATAN NAT'L FOREST
Cape Lookout National Seashore
Beaufort
WILMINGTON
Morehead City
Ft. Macon State Park
Shackleford Banks
Cape Lookout
N
0
20 miles
0
30 km

off U.S. 64/264 north of Manteo, ☎ 252/473–5772; free) is a restoration of the original 1585 earthworks that mark the beginning of English colonial history in America. The history, education, and cultural arts complex opposite the waterfront in Manteo, **Roanoke Island Festival Park** (✉ One Festival Park, ☎ 252/475–1506; $8) explores the evolution of the Outer Banks from the 16th century to the 21st. Costumed interpreters conduct tours of the *Elizabeth II,* a 69-ft re-creation of a 16th-century vessel. The **North Carolina Aquarium at Roanoke Island** (✉ Airport Rd., ☎ 252/473–3494, WEB www.ncaquariums.com; $4) has been extensively renovated to double its former size. The centerpiece tank is the *Graveyard of the Atlantic* exhibit.

Take a day trip to visit **Elizabeth City,** on the Albemarle Sound. The city's historic district has the largest number of pre–Civil War commercial buildings in the state.The **Museum of the Albemarle** has displays on regional history. ✉ *1116 U.S. 17 S,* ☎ *252/335–1453.* *Free. Closed Mon.*

Edenton, the state capital from 1728 to 1743, lies west of Elizabeth City. In 1774, 51 local women staged the Edenton Tea Party to protest English taxation.

Be sure to see the Jacobean-style **Cupola House and Gardens** (✉ 408 Broad St., ☎ 252/482–2637), which were built circa 1758. The **Chowan County Courthouse** (✉ E. King St.) has been in continuous use since its construction in 1767. Three colonial governors are buried in the graveyard behind **St. Paul's Church** (✉ corner of S. Broad St. and W. Church St.).

South of Nags Head on Route 12, the Herbert C. Bonner Bridge arches for 3 mi over Oregon Inlet to **Hatteras Island,** where the blue marlin reigns.At 208 ft, the **Cape Hatteras Lighthouse** (☎ 252/473–2111; free) is the tallest brick lighthouse in America. In 1999, the structure was moved nearly 3,000 ft to protect it from the shifting sands. The visitor center has a small museum. Board the free ferry at the south end of Hatteras Island for the half-hour trip to **Ocracoke Island,** cut off from the world for so long that locals speak with a distinctive, but now endangered, brogue. Standing since 1823, **Ocracoke Lighthouse** is the state's oldest operating lighthouse.

Beaufort, the third-oldest town in North Carolina, was named for Henry Somerset, Duke of Beaufort.

The **Beaufort Historic Site,** in the center of this tiny town, is composed of restored buildings dating from 1767 to 1859, including the Carteret County Courthouse and the Apothecary Shop and Doctor's Office. Don't miss the Old Burying Grounds (1731). Here Otway Burns, a privateer in the War of 1812, is buried under his ship's cannon; a nine-year-old girl who died at sea is buried in a rum keg; and an English soldier saluting the king is buried upright in his grave. Tours on an English-style double-decker bus depart from here. ✉ *130 Turner St.,* ☎ *252/728–5225 or 800/575–7483,* WEB *www.historicbeaufort.com.* *Bus tour only $6, bus and walking tour $10. Closed Sun.*

Beaufort's **North Carolina Maritime Museum** (✉ 315 Front St., ☎ 252/728–7317; free) documents the state's seafaring and coastal history. The museum includes the Watercrafts Center, which offers boatbuilding classes. Its education staff also provides year-round programs, including trips to the marsh and barrier islands.

Morehead City is a fishing and boating center across Bogue Sound from Bogue Banks. Atlantic Beach and Emerald Isle are popular family beaches.

Exhibits at the **North Carolina Aquarium at Pine Knoll Shores** (✉ Salter Path Rd., Milepost 7, Atlantic Beach, ☎ 252/247–4004, WEB www.ncaquariums.com; 🎫 $3), in a maritime forest on Bogue Banks, include a 2,000-gallon salt marsh tank with live alligators and a loggerhead turtle nursery.

New Bern, northwest of Morehead City, was the state capital during English rule until immediately after the Revolution.

The reconstructed **Tryon Palace** (✉ 610 Pollock St., ☎ 252/514–4900 or 800/767–1560, WEB www.tyronpalace.com; 🎫 $15), an elegant Georgian building, was the colonial capitol and the home of Royal Governor William Tryon in the 1770s. An audiovisual orientation is given, costumed interpreters conduct tours of the house and gardens, and (in summer) actors deliver monologues describing a day in the life of local citizens. Tours of the garden are self-guided. The stately **John Wright Stanly House** (circa 1783), the **Dixon-Stevenson House** (circa 1826), and **New Bern Academy** (circa 1809) are within or very near the 13-acre Tryon Palace complex.

U.S. 17 south leads to **Wilmington,** a bustling harbor town and film-making center. Wilmington's restored waterfront and historic district, with its 18th-century churches, can be explored with the aid of a self-guided walking-tour map from the Cape Fear Coast Convention and Visitors Bureau.

The **USS *North Carolina* Battleship Memorial** (☎ 910/251–5797, WEB www.battleshipnc.com; 🎫 $8) is permanently docked off U.S. 421. You can park next to the site or take the river taxi from Riverfront Park (in summer only) for a self-guided tour that can last up to 2½ hours.

The 1770 **Burgwin-Wright House** (✉ 224 Market St., ☎ 910/762–0570) is built on the foundation of a jail. Downtown's Italianate **Zebulon Latimer House** was built in 1852 and can be seen from 3rd Street.

The **St. John's Museum of Art** is composed of three distinctive buildings. One houses a permanent collection of etchings by Mary Cassatt. *✉ 114 Orange St., ☎ 910/763–0281. 🎫 $2. Closed Mon.*

The **Cape Fear Museum,** the state's oldest history museum, traces the natural and cultural history of Cape Fear River country, and the Michael Jordan Discovery Exhibit. *✉ 814 Market St., ☎ 910/341–7413. 🎫 $5. Closed Mon.*

U.S. 421 leads south from Wilmington to the **Fort Fisher State Historic Site,** the largest Confederate earthwork fortification of the Civil War. War relics and artifacts from sunken Confederate blockade runners are on display. *✉ Kure Beach, ☎ 910/458–5538. 🎫 Free. Closed Mon.*

Not far from Kure Beach is the **North Carolina Aquarium at Fort Fisher** (✉ 2201 Fort Fisher Blvd., ☎ 910/458–8257; 🎫 $3).

On the west side of the Cape Fear River, south of Wilmington on Route 133, a passenger ferry links Southport and **Bald Head Island** (☎ 910/457–5003). On a day trip to the car-free island you can take a historic tour (reservations required) to see the 109-ft Old Baldy Lighthouse, dating from 1817. Have a picnic or lunch at one of the restaurants, or play golf, swim, or fish.

Dining and Lodging

Fresh seafood is plentiful here, prepared in all sorts of ways. Hearty southern cooking, with chicken, ham, and fresh vegetables, is also widespread. Cottages, condominiums, motels, resorts, B&Bs, and country inns abound all along the coast. Most places offer lower rates from September through May. Condos and beach cottages can be rented through local realtors by the week or month.

Beaufort

$$–$$$ ✕ **Clawson's 1905 Restaurant and Pub.** Housed in what was a general store in the early 1900s, Clawson's serves hearty food: ribs, steaks, pasta, and local seafood. It gets crowded in summer, so arrive early, regardless of whether you're coming for lunch or dinner. The coffee bar opens at 7 AM. ✉ *425 Front St.,* ☎ *252/728–2133,* WEB *www.clawsonsrestaurant.com. D, MC, V. Closed Sun. mid-Sept.–mid-May.*

$–$$ ★ **Langdon House.** You'll sleep surrounded by antiques at this three-story B&B built in 1733. The host provides everything from sightseeing suggestions to sumptuous southern breakfasts and full beach baskets for picnics. ✉ *135 Craven St., 28516,* ☎ *252/728–5499,* WEB *www.langdonhouse.com. 4 rooms. No credit cards. BP.*

Duck

$$$–$$$$ ★ ✕ **Sanderling Inn Resort & Conference Center.** This remote beachside resort actually encompasses three inns. Ceiling fans, wicker, and neutral tones give rooms a cool and casual feel. The Sanderling Restaurant, in a restored lifesaving station, has such delicacies as crab cakes, roast Carolina duckling with black-cherry sauce, and fricassee of shrimp. ✉ *1461 Duck Rd., 27949,* ☎ *252/261–4111 or 800/701–4111,* FAX *252/261–1638,* WEB *www.sanderlinginn.com. 88 rooms, 29 efficiencies. 2 restaurants, pool, tennis, health club. AE, D, MC, V.*

$$$ **Advice 5¢.** This modern B&B in Duck's North Beach is a short walk from downtown and offers the use of Sea Pines tennis courts and swimming pool. All rooms have crisp and colorful linens, ceiling fans, and decks. ✉ *111 Scarborough La., 27949,* ☎ *252/255–1050 or 800/238–4235,* WEB *www.advice5.com. 5 rooms. MC, V. Closed Dec.–Feb. CP.*

Kill Devil Hills

$–$$ ✕ **Flying Fish Cafe.** Brightly colored and casual are the bywords for this downtown café, but the food and wine are taken very seriously. A perennial favorite entrée is the shrimp on spinach fettuccine with feta cheese. ✉ *2003 Croatan Hwy.,* ☎ *252/441–6894. AE, D, MC, V. No lunch weekends.*

$$–$$$ **Ramada Inn Outer Banks Resort.** Guest rooms in this convention-style hotel have private balconies, some with ocean views. All rooms are equipped with refrigerators, microwave ovens, and coffeemakers. The restaurant, Peppercorns, serves breakfast and dinner; lunch is available on the sundeck next to the pool. ✉ *1701 S. Virginia Dare Trail, off U.S. 158, Milepost 9.5 (Box 2716, 27948),* ☎ *252/441–2151 or 800/635–1824,* FAX *252/441–1830,* WEB *www.outerbanksresort.com. 172 rooms. Restaurant, pool. AE, D, DC, MC, V.*

Manteo

$–$$$ ✕ **Weeping Radish Brewery and Restaurant.** This Bavarian-style restaurant and microbrewery is known for its German cuisine and annual Octoberfest weekend featuring German and blues bands. Free tours of the brewery are given on request. ✉ *U.S. 64,* ☎ *252/473–1157. D, MC, V.*

$$–$$$ ✕ **Tranquil House Inn.** This waterfront B&B is only a few steps from shops and restaurants; bikes are provided for adventures beyond. The restaurant, named 1587, serves inventive entrées, such as sesame-crusted tuna with wasabi vinaigrette, and encourages vegetarian requests; hundreds of wines are available. ✉ *405 Queen Elizabeth Ave., 27954,* ☎ *252/473–1404 or 800/458–7069,* FAX *252/473–1526,* WEB *www.1587.com. 25 rooms. Restaurant. AE, D, MC, V. CP.*

Morehead City

$-$$ ✕ **Sanitary Fish Market & Restaurant.** Sixty-one years ago, when the Sanitary was founded, many fish houses were ill-kept. The owners wanted to signal their difference. Hush puppies are a specialty at this simple waterfront eatery. It can get noisy (the restaurant seats 600), but guests from around the world gush about the food. ✉ *501 Evans St.,* ☎ *252/247–3111. D, MC, V. Closed Dec.–Jan.*

Nags Head

$$$ ✕ **Windmill Point.** The menu changes often, but you can always count on the signature seafood trio. Dinner promises stunning views of the sound at sunset. ✉ *U.S. 158 Bypass, Milepost 16.5,* ☎ *252/441–1535. AE, D, DC, MC, V.*

$$$–$$$$ ★ **First Colony Inn.** Verandas encircle this 1932 B&B. Some rooms have Jacuzzis or ocean views; others have four-poster or canopy beds and armoires. The entire property is smoke-free. ✉ *6720 S. Virginia Dare Trail, 27959,* ☎ *252/441–2343 or 800/368–9390,* FAX *252/441–9234,* WEB *www.firstcolonyinn.com. 27 rooms. Pool. AE, D, MC, V. BP.*

New Bern

$-$$ ✕ **The Chelsea.** Caleb Bradham invented Pepsi in this 1912 building (it was once a drugstore). You can get French, southwestern, and Asian fusion entrées and, appropriately, a diverse wine list. ✉ *335 Middle St.,* ☎ *252/637–5469. AE, D, DC, MC, V.*

$-$$ ★ **Harmony House Inn.** At this historic B&B convenient to all the attractions, guests sleep in spacious rooms where Yankee soldiers stayed during the Civil War. Today the rooms are furnished with a mix of antiques and reproductions. The inn serves a hot breakfast buffet and complimentary white and dessert wines in the evening. ✉ *215 Pollock St., 28560,* ☎ *800/636–3113,* FAX *252/636–3810,* WEB *www.harmonyhouseinn.com. 10 rooms. AE, D, DC, MC, V. BP.*

Ocracoke

$ ✕ **Island Inn.** This well-worn turn-of-the-20th-century inn has third-floor rooms with cathedral ceilings and lovely views. Families will be more comfortable in the newer, roomier addition across the street. The dining room is known for its oyster omelets, crab cakes, and hush puppies. ✉ *Rte. 12 (Box 9, 27960),* ☎ *252/928–4351 or 877/456–3466,* FAX *252/928–4352,* WEB *www.ocracokeislandinn.com. 35 rooms. Restaurant, pool. AE, D, MC, V.*

Southport

$$ ✕ **Bald Head Island Resort.** Reached by ferry from Southport, this self-contained, carless community has its own grocery and general stores, restaurants, and golf course. The bleached-wood villas and shingled cottages have won architectural design awards. Guests travel the island on foot, on bicycles, or in golf carts. Historic day tours are $36; this includes parking and ferry fees, lunch, and a guided tour. The five restaurants on the resort serve everything from steaks and steamed seafood to hot dogs and pizza. ✉ *5079 Southport-Supply Rd., Bald Head Island 28461,* ☎ *910/457–5000 or 800/234–1666,* FAX *910/457–9232,* WEB *www.bald-head-island.com. 195 homes/condos/villas, 2 B&Bs. 5 restaurants, pool, golf, tennis. AE, DC, MC, V.*

Wilmington

$$–$$$$ ★ ✕ **Pilot House.** This Chandler's Wharf restaurant is known for its Sunday brunch, Carolina bisque, and shrimp and grits—a lunch favorite. You can dine indoors or on a riverside deck. ✉ *2 Ann St.,* ☎ *910/343–0200. AE, D, MC, V.*

\$\$–\$\$\$ ✕ **Circa 1922.** The city's only tapas restaurant serves everything from sushi and salads to cioppino, Italian seafood stew. You can order several of the small dishes to sample a bit of everything, and choose from more than 180 vintages, served by the glass, at the opulent 1920s-style wine bar. ✉ *8 N. Front St.,* ☎ *910/762–1922. AE, D, DC, MC, V.*

\$–\$\$ ✕ **Front Street Brewery.** It's one of the most popular restaurants in town. Three huge kilns at the entrance welcome you to this working microbrewery, where you can sample 10 distinct house brews to complement the pub fries, roast pork tenderloin, or a juicy rib-eye steak. ✉ *9 N. Front St.,* ☎ *910/251–1935. AE, MC, V.*

\$\$–\$\$\$\$ ★ **The Wilmingtonian.** In the heart of the historic district, five former commercial buildings and a convent have been transformed into luxurious suites, each decorated in a different theme. ✉ *101 S. 2nd St., 28401,* ☎ *910/343–1800 or 800/525–0909,* FAX *910/251–1149,* WEB *www.thewilmingtonian.com. 40 suites. Restaurant. AE, D, DC, MC, V. CP.*

\$\$–\$\$\$ **Hilton-Riverside.** Overlooking the Cape Fear River on one side and the historic section of the city on the other, the Hilton is one of the most convenient places to stay in town. Guest rooms are traditional, with dark woods and autumnal colors. ✉ *301 N. Water St., 28401,* ☎ *910/763–5900 or 800/445–8667,* FAX *910/763–0038,* WEB *www.wilmingtonhilton.com. 274 rooms. Restaurant, pool. AE, D, DC, MC, V.*

Campgrounds

Camping is permitted in designated areas of the **Cape Hatteras** and **Cape Lookout national seashores** from mid-April through mid-October and at most state parks. Private campgrounds are scattered all along the coast. For more information contact the state's division of tourism.

Nightlife and the Arts

A favorite haunt on the Wilmington waterfront is the **Water Street Café** (✉ 5 S. Water St., ☎ 910/343–0042), an indoor-outdoor bar with live rhythm and blues. In Wrightsville Beach at the **Blockade Runner Resort Hotel** (✉ 275 Waynick Blvd., ☎ 910/256–2251) there's a lounge and entertainment for both adults and children during the summer. In Wilmington, the **Thalian Hall Center for the Performing Arts** (✉ 310 Chestnut St., ☎ 910/343–3664 or 800/523–2820), built between 1855 and 1858 and restored to its former grandeur, hosts more than 250 theater, dance, and musical performances each year.

Outdoor Activities and Sports

Boating

You can travel hundreds of miles over the sounds and inlets of this vast region along the Intracoastal Waterway. For marina and docking information, pick up a copy of the ***North Carolina Coastal Boating Guide*** or contact the appropriate county chamber of commerce.

Fishing

The region teems with bass, billfish, flounder, mullet, spot, trout, and other fish. Fishing is permitted from piers all along the coast and from certain bridges and causeways. Charter boats for deep-sea fishing are available at the **Oregon Inlet Fishing Center** (☎ 252/441–6301 or 800/272–5199) on the Outer Banks; **Flapjack & Gung Ho Charters** (☎ 910/458–4362 or 800/288–3474) at Carolina Beach Municipal Marina; and the ***Carolina Princess*** (☎ 252/726–5479 or 800/682–3456) in Morehead City. Fishing licenses are available from the **North Carolina Wildlife Resources Commission** (☎ 919/773–2881).

Golf

Among the public and semiprivate courses in the Greater Wilmington area is the breathtaking **Bald Head Island Golf Course** (☎ 910/457–7310), designed by George Cobb. Ocean Isle, near the South Carolina state line, also has a number of outstanding courses. Contact the **Cape Fear Coast Convention and Visitors Bureau** or the **South Brunswick Islands Chamber of Commerce** (✉ Box 1380, Shallotte 28459, ☎ 910/754–6644 or 800/426–6644) for additional golf information.

Scuba Diving

With more than 1,500 known shipwrecks off the coast of the Outer Banks, diving opportunities are legion. Dive shops include **Outer Banks Dive Center** (✉ 3917 S. Croatan Hwy., Nags Head, ☎ 252/449–8349), **Aquatic Safaris** (✉ 5751-4 Oleander Dr., Wilmington, ☎ 910/392–4386), and **Olympus Dive Center** (✉ 713 Shepard St., Morehead City, ☎ 252/726–9432 or 800/992–1258).

Surfing and Windsurfing

Kitty Hawk Kites (☞ Shopping, *below*), the oldest hang-gliding school on the East Coast, provides gear and instruction. Rentals are also available at shops in Wilmington, Wrightsville Beach, and Carolina Beach.

Beaches

Cape Hatteras and **Cape Lookout national seashores** offer more than 100 mi of beaches. **Atlantic Beach** and **Emerald Isle,** on Bogue Banks near Morehead City; **Wrightsville, Carolina,** and **Kure beaches,** near Wilmington; and **Ocean Isle,** farther south, are other top spots.

Shopping

You can find **nautical items** at antiques shops and **hand-carved wooden ducks and birds** at local crafts shops in Duck, a few miles north of Nags Head, and in Wanchese, at the south end of Roanoke Island. New Bern and Wilmington are centers for **antiques**; in Wilmington many shops are at Chandler's Wharf, the Cotton Exchange, and the Water Street Market on the waterfront. Nags Head is the main retail outlet for **Kitty Hawk Kites** (☎ 252/441–4124 or 800/334–4777). The largest kite store on the East Coast, it offers every type of kite and wind sock known to man, as well as toys and outdoor clothing.

The Coast Essentials

AIR TRAVEL

SouthEast Air and Outer Banks Airways provide charter service to the area from Dare County Regional Airport (☞ Airports, *below).*

➤ AIRLINES AND CONTACTS: **Outer Banks Airways** (☎ 252/473–2227). **SouthEast Air** (☎ 252/473–3222 or 800/289–8202).

AIRPORTS

The closest airports are Raleigh-Durham International; Wilmington International; and Virginia's Norfolk International Airport.

➤ AIRPORT INFORMATION: **Dare County Regional Airport** (✉ 410 Airport Rd., Manteo, ☎ 252/473–2600). **Norfolk International Airport** (✉ 2200 Norview Ave., Norfolk, VA, ☎ 757/857–3351). **Wilmington International** (✉ 1740 Airport Blvd., Wilmington, ☎ 910/341–4333).

BOAT AND FERRY TRAVEL

Toll ferries connect Ocracoke with Cedar Island, to the south, and with Swan Quarter on the mainland; a free ferry travels between Hatteras Island and Ocracoke Island.

There are nearly 150 marinas along the Intracoastal Waterway, including Manteo Waterfront Docks and the National Park Service's Silver Lake Marina in Ocracoke. Beaufort is a popular stopover. The Wilmington area has public marinas at Carolina Beach State Park and Wrightsville Beach. The *North Carolina Coastal Boating Guide,* compiled by the North Carolina Department of Transportation, lists marinas and other facilities for boaters.

➤ BOAT AND FERRY INFORMATION: **Carolina Beach State Park** (☎ 910/458–7770). **Manteo Waterfront Docks** (☎ 252/473–3320). **North Carolina Department of Transportation** (☎ 919/733–7600). **Silver Lake Marina** (☎ 252/928–5111). **Toll Ferries** (☎ 800/293–3779). **Wrightsville Beach** (☎ 910/256–6666).

BUS TRAVEL

Greyhound/Carolina Trailways serves Elizabeth City, on the Albemarle Sound; Wilmington; and Norfolk, Virginia.

➤ BUS INFORMATION: **Greyhound** (☎ 800/231–2222, WEB www.greyhound.com).

CAR TRAVEL

Roads link the mainland to the Outer Banks at their northern end: U.S. 158 enters from the north, near Kill Devil Hills, and U.S. 64/264 enters Manteo on Roanoke Island, from the west. These connect with Route 12, the main route in the region, running south from Corolla to Ocracoke Island. From I–95 near Raleigh, U.S. 70 leads to Cedar Island via New Bern and Morehead City, and I–40 serves Wilmington.

VISITOR INFORMATION

For information on Carteret County, contact the Crystal Coast Visitors Center in Morehead City.

➤ TOURIST INFORMATION: **Cape Fear Coast Convention and Visitors Bureau** (✉ 24 N. 3rd St., Wilmington 28401, ☎ 910/341–4030 or 800/222–4757, WEB www.cape-fear.nc.us). **Craven County Convention and Visitors Bureau** (✉ 314 S. Front St., New Bern 28563, ☎ 252/637–9400 or 800/437–5767, WEB www.visitnewbern.com). **Crystal Coast Visitors Center** (✉ 3409 Arendell St., Morehead City 28557, ☎ 252/726–8148 or 800/786–6962, WEB www.crystalcoast.com). **Dare County Tourist Bureau** (✉ U.S. 64/264, Manteo 27954, ☎ 252/473–2138 or 800/466–6262). **Historic Albemarle Tour, Inc.** (✉ 1 Harding Sq., Washington 27858, ☎ 252/974–2950, WEB www.albemarle-nc.com). **Ocracoke Visitor Center** (✉ Cape Hatteras National Seashore, NC Hwy. 12, Ocracoke 27960-0340, ☎ 252/928–4531, WEB www.ocracoke-nc.com).

THE MOUNTAINS

The majestic peaks, meadows, and valleys of the Appalachian, Blue Ridge, and Smoky mountains characterize the west end of the state. There are three distinct mountain regions: the southern mountains (home to the Eastern Band of the Cherokee Nation); the northern mountains, known as the High Country (Boone, Blowing Rock, Banner Elk); and the central mountains, anchored by Asheville, for decades a retreat for the wealthy and famous. National parks, national forests, centers for handmade crafts, and the Blue Ridge Parkway are the area's main attractions, providing prime opportunities for shopping, skiing, hiking, bicycling, camping, fishing, canoeing, or taking in the breathtaking views.

Exploring the Mountains

The town of **Cherokee** is the capital of Qualla Boundary, a 56,000-acre Cherokee Indian Reservation.

The **Museum of the Cherokee Indian** (✉ U.S. 441 at Drama Rd., ☎ 828/497–3481, WEB www.cherokeemuseum.org; 🎫 $8) covers 10,000 years of Cherokee history with high-tech exhibits and an extensive artifact collection. There's also an art gallery and an outdoor living exhibit of Cherokee life as it was in the 15th century.

The **Qualla Arts and Crafts Mutual** (✉ U.S. 441 at Drama Rd., ☎ 828/497–3103; 🎫 free), across the street from the Museum of the Cherokee Indian, is a cooperative that displays and sells baskets, masks, pottery, and wood carvings handcrafted by 300 Cherokee artisans. At **Oconaluftee Indian Village** (✉ U.S. 441 at Drama Rd., ☎ 828/497–2315; 🎫 $10), guides in Native American costumes will lead you through the re-created village of the 1750s, while others demonstrate skills such as weaving, pottery, canoe construction, and hunting techniques. With 2,300 gaming machines, video poker, video blackjack, and video craps. **Harrah's Cherokee Casino** (✉ Hwy. 19 off U.S. 441 N, ☎ 828/497–7777) is the largest casino in a 500-mi radius. The complex also has a 1,500-seat concert hall, three restaurants, and a child-care area. You're guaranteed a find at **Smoky Mountain Gold and Ruby Mine,** on the Qualla Boundary, where gems such as aquamarines, rubies, and sapphires are plentiful. You can purchase the treasures you dig up and pan for. Gold ore costs $5 per bag. ✉ *U.S. 441 N,* ☎ *828/497–6574.* 🎫 *Free. Closed Dec.–Feb.* The second-highest point in the Great Smoky Mountains, **Clingman's Dome,** is across the Tennessee border. Views from the 54-ft observation tower atop the 6,643-ft summit can extend to more than 100 mi and seven states. Don't worry if you can't climb a mountain; you can drive to the top. ✉ *U.S. 441 N, 10 mi north of Cherokee.* 🎫 *Free. Closed Dec.–Mar.*

The largest and most cosmopolitan city in the mountains, **Asheville** has been rated America's favorite place to live of cities its size. The city's downtown is a pedestrian-friendly place, with upscale shopping, art galleries, museums, restaurants, and nightlife.

The 92,000-square-ft **Pack Place Education, Arts & Science Center,** in downtown Asheville, houses the Asheville Art Museum, Colburn Gem & Mineral Museum, Health Adventure, and Diana Wortham Theatre. The YMI Cultural Center, also maintained by Pack Place, is directly across the street. ✉ *2 S. Pack Sq.,* ☎ *828/257–4500,* WEB *www.packplace.org.* 🎫 *$6. Closed Mon. June–Oct. and Sun.–Mon. Nov.–May.*

East of Asheville is America's largest private residence, the astonishing ★ **Biltmore Estate** (✉ Exit 50 off I–40 E, ☎ 828/255–1700 or 800/624–1575, WEB www.biltmoreestate.com; 🎫 $34), built in the 1890s as the home of George Vanderbilt. The 250-room French Renaissance–style château is filled with priceless antiques and art treasures. The grounds, landscaped by Frederick Law Olmsted, include 75 acres of elaborate gardens, 72 acres of vineyards, and a state-of-the-art winery.

The **North Carolina Arboretum** (✉ 100 Frederick Law Olmsted Way, ☎ 828/665–2492, WEB www.ncarboretum.org; 🎫 free), 426 acres that were part of the original Biltmore Estate, completes Frederick Law Olmsted's dream of creating a world-class arboretum in the western part of the state. It features southern Appalachian flora in a stunning number of settings.

A 45-minute drive from Asheville is Madison County, home of the picturesque village of Hot Springs, a way station for hikers on the Appalachian Trail, and the **Hot Springs Spa** (✉ 1 Bridge St., ☎ 828/622–7676 or 800/462–0933, WEB www.hotspringsspa-nc.com; 🎫 $12–$30 per hr, depending on time of day and number of guests). These mineral springs maintain a natural 100°F temperature year-round, and since the turn of the 20th century, they have provided relief for visitors suffering a variety of ailments.

The **Great Smoky Mountains Railway,** 45 minutes west of Asheville, is one of the most popular attractions in western North Carolina. Choose from five excursions on diesel-electric and steam locomotives (fares vary). Open-sided cars or cabooses are ideal for picture taking as the spectacular scenery glides by. ✉ *119 Front St., Dillsboro 28725,* ☎ *828/586–8811 or 800/872–4681,* WEB *www.gsmr.com.* 🎫 *$20–$50; some rides include a meal. Closed Jan.–Mar.*

The most scenic route from Asheville to the Boone–Blowing Rock area is via the **Blue Ridge Parkway** (☎ 828/271–4779), a stunningly beautiful 469-mi road that gently winds through mountains and meadows and crosses mountain streams on its way from Waynesboro, Virginia, to Cherokee, North Carolina. The parkway is generally open year-round but often closes during heavy snows and icy conditions. Maps and information are available at visitor centers along the highway.

At Milepost 316.3 on the Blue Ridge Parkway is the **Linville Falls Visitor Center** (✉ Rte. 1 [Box 789, Spruce Pine 28777], ☎ 828/765–1045; 🎫 free), a part of the Linville Falls Recreation Area. It's an easy ½-mi hike from here to one of North Carolina's most photographed waterfalls.

Just off the parkway, on U.S. 221 at Milepost 305, is **Grandfather Mountain,** which soars 6,000 ft and is famous for its mile-high swinging bridge. Sweaty-palmed visitors cross the 228-ft bridge, which sways over a 1,600-ft drop into Linville Valley. The United Nations has designated Grandfather Mountain a Biosphere Reserve. The **Nature Museum** has exhibits on native minerals, flora and fauna, and pioneer life. ☎ *828/733–2013 or 800/468–7325,* WEB *www.grandfather.com.* 🎫 *$12. Closed in inclement weather.*

Blowing Rock refers to both a quiet mountain village and the nearby 4,000-ft rock for which it was named. The **observation tower** offers a 180-degree view of mountaintops, valleys, and gorges. ☎ *828/295–7111.* WEB *www.blowingrock.org.* 🎫 *$4. Closed weekdays Jan.–Feb.*

The **Tweetsie Railroad** is a popular Wild West theme park where you can pan for gold, ride a train beset by robbers, and catch a musical with cancan girls. ✉ *U.S. 321/221, Blowing Rock 28605,* ☎ *828/264–9061 or 800/526–5740,* WEB *www.tweetsie-railroad.com.* 🎫 *$23. Closed Nov.–mid-May.*

Blue Ridge Gemstone Mine, midway between Asheville and Boone on the Blue Ridge Parkway, is in a region with one of the richest mineral deposits in the country. Though you can't enter the mine, you can purchase a gem bucket for anywhere from $5 to $100, take it to the flume line, and sort through it for rubies, emeralds, and more. ✉ *Box 327, Little Switzerland 28749,* ☎ *828/765–5264.* 🎫 *Free. Closed Jan.–Mar.*

Boone, named for frontiersman Daniel Boone, is at the convergence of three major highways—U.S. 321, U.S. 421, and Route 105.

Horn in the West (✉ Amphitheater off U.S. 321, ☎ 828/264–2120; 💵 $12), a project of the Southern Appalachian Historical Association, is an outdoor drama that traces the story of Daniel Boone. The show runs Tuesday–Sunday from mid-June to mid-August. Boone's **Appalachian Cultural Museum** is dedicated to the history and culture of the region, including the geographic origins of the mountains, the beginnings of stock car racing, and antiques and quilt traditions. ✉ *University Hill Dr., near Greene's Motel, U.S. 321,* ☎ *828/262–3117.* 💵 *$4. Closed Mon.*

Dining and Lodging

The spirit of the pioneers who settled the mountains has always been present in the area's food and shelter—basic, hardy, and family-oriented. Be sure to make reservations early for visits in the fall, when every nook and cranny is crammed with leaf peepers.

Asheville

$$–$$$ ✕ **Café on the Square.** The menu for this street-side bistro, which faces historic Pack Square downtown, is heavy on fresh seafood and pastas cooked with various salsas, chutneys, and marinades. The local business crowd frequents the restaurant during lunch, but theatergoers come for dinner. ✉ *One Biltmore Ave.,* ☎ *828/251–5565. AE, D, MC, V.*

$–$$ ✕ **Mountain Smoke House.** Local musicians entertain here, making dinner much more than just a meal. Yet, the mountain barbecue and pig-pickin' buffets may make you want to be a regular at this family-style restaurant. Vegetarians can be accommodated, too. ✉ *802 Fairview Rd.,* ☎ *828/298–8121. AE, D, DC, MC, V. Closed Sun.–Mon. No lunch Tues.–Fri.*

$$$–$$$$ ★ ✕🏨 **Grove Park Inn.** Supervised children's activities, racquetball and tennis courts, views of the Blue Ridge Mountains, and a new spa complex make this Asheville's premier resort. Since its opening in 1913, the inn's guest list has included Thomas Edison, F. Scott Fitzgerald, and Michael Jordan. The two newer wings are in line with the original design—oak antiques in the Arts and Crafts style. The restaurants offer plenty of choices. Horizons gets creative with game dishes from ostrich to boar. ✉ *290 Macon Ave., 28804,* ☎ *828/252–2711 or 800/438–5800,* FAX *828/253–7053 guests; 828/252–6102 reservations;* WEB *www.groveparkinn.com. 510 rooms. 6 restaurants, pools, golf, tennis, health club. AE, D, DC, MC, V.*

$$$–$$$$ ★ ✕🏨 **Richmond Hill Inn.** This Victorian mansion, once a private residence, is on the National Register of Historic Places. Many of the 12 rooms in the mansion are furnished with canopy beds, Victorian sofas, and other antiques, while the more modern guest rooms have contemporary pine poster beds. The restaurant, Gabrielle's, known for its innovative cuisine, is open to the public only for dinner and Sunday brunch; jacket and tie are required. ✉ *87 Richmond Hill Dr., 28806,* ☎ *828/252–7313 or 888/742–4565,* FAX *828/252–8726,* WEB *www.richmondhillinn.com. 27 rooms, 9 cottages. 2 restaurants. AE, MC, V. BP.*

$ 🏨 **Comfort Inn.** This hotel, off I–240 near the River Ridge Outlet Mall, has a walking trail and standard but comfortable guest rooms and suites with garden-tub Jacuzzis, private balconies, and dinette areas. ✉ *800 Fairview Rd., 28803,* ☎ *828/298–9141,* FAX *828/298–6629,* WEB *www.comfortinn.com. 177 rooms. Pool. AE, D, DC, MC, V. CP.*

$ 🏨 **Mountaineer Inn.** A fixture along Tunnel Road, this motel is popular with families and others who care less about fanciness than about affordable, comfortable surroundings. Refrigerators and coffeemakers are in each uniquely styled room. ✉ *155 Tunnel Rd., 28805,* ☎ *800/255–4080. 79 rooms. AE, D, MC, V. CP.*

Blowing Rock

$ **Alpine Village Inn.** In the heart of Blowing Rock, this motel harks back to a simpler time. Its rooms are neat as a pin and are decorated with antiques, quilts, and even flowers on holidays. ✉ *297 Sunset Dr., 28605,* ☎ *828/295–7206,* WEB *www.alpine-village-inn.com. 15 rooms. AE, D, MC, V.*

Boone

$ ✕ **High Country Inn.** A popular honeymoon choice that also draws skiers, golfers, and other groups interested in the discount packages, the inn, made of native stone and surrounded by ponds, has rooms that range from luxurious to comfortable. The dining choices include Geno's Sports Lounge and Geno's Restaurant. ✉ *1785 Hwy. 105, 28607,* ☎ *828/264–1000 or 800/334–5605,* FAX *828/262–0073,* WEB *www.highcountryinn.com. 120 rooms, 2 log cabins. Restaurant, pool, gym. AE, D, MC, V.*

Cherokee

$–$$ ✕ **Nantahala Village Restaurant.** Located about 10 mi southwest of Cherokee, this restaurant is a favorite of folks in Swain County. The dining area features a locally crafted fireplace. The menu is eclectic—trout, chicken, country ham, and Wild Forest Pasta. ✉ *9400 U.S. 19 W, Bryson City,* ☎ *828/488–9616 or 800/438–1507. D, MC, V. Closed late Nov.–early Mar.*

$ **Holiday Inn Cherokee.** Guest rooms are standard at this friendly, well-equipped motel. The Chestnut Tree restaurant has dinner buffets that are veritable groaning boards, and the on-site native crafts shop, the Hunting Ground, has works by local artists. ✉ *U.S. 19 S, 28719,* ☎ *828/497–9181 or 800/465–4329,* FAX *828/497–5973,* WEB *www.hicherokee.com. 154 rooms. Restaurant, pools, gym. AE, D, DC, MC, V.*

Hot Springs

$ ✕ **Bridge Street Cafe & Inn.** This renovated storefront, circa 1922, is right on the Appalachian Trail and overlooks Spring Creek. Upstairs are brightly decorated rooms filled with antiques. Two rooms share baths. The café downstairs has a hand-built wood-fired oven and grill for gourmet pizzas. ✉ *Bridge St. (Box 502, 28743),* ☎ *828/622–0002,* FAX *828/622–7282,* WEB *www.main.nc.us/bridgecafe. 4 rooms. Restaurant. AE, D, MC, V. Closed Nov.–Mar.*

Nightlife

An intimate, smoke-free listening room, **Be Here Now** (✉ 5 Biltmore Ave., Asheville, ☎ 828/258–2071) offers dancing and concerts. The **Manor House Restaurant** (✉ N. Main St., off NC 321 Bypass, Blowing Rock, ☎ 828/295–5500) at Chetola Resort is just the number for those in a mellow mood. Entertainment—usually jazz—is live and seasonal.

Outdoor Activities and Sports

Canoeing and White-Water Rafting

Near Boone and Blowing Rock, the New River, a federally designated Wild and Scenic River (Classes I and II), provides hours of excitement for canoeists, as do the Watauga River, Wilson Creek, and the Toe River. The Toe becomes the Nolichucky River as it goes into Tennessee. As the Nolichucky traverses the deepest, most spectacular canyon east of the Grand Canyon, its rapids offer heart-pounding excitement for the adrenaline-deprived. **Nantahala Outdoor Center** (✉ 13007 Hwy. 19, ☎ 888/662–1662), **Edge of the World Outfitters** (✉ Hwy. 184, ☎ 828/

898–9550 or 800/789–3343), and **High Mountain Expeditions** (☎ 828/295–4200 or 800/262–9036) run trips down the Nolichucky via raft.

Ski Areas

North Carolina's first ski resort opened 37 years ago, but it wasn't until snowmaking technology was perfected that the sport really took off here. Today there are eight ski areas, and, generally, the season runs from mid-November through March. All offer ski schools, programs for children, night skiing, and snowboarding. Downhill skiing is available at **Appalachian Ski Mountain** (☎ 828/295–7828 or 800/322–2373), at Blowing Rock; **Hawksnest Golf & Ski Resort** (☎ 828/963–6561 or 888/429–5763), at Banner Elk; **Ski Beech** (☎ 828/387–2011 or 800/438–2093), at Beech Mountain, the highest resort in eastern North America; and **Sugar Mountain** (☎ 828/898–4521 or 800/784–2768), at Banner Elk.

Shopping

The **Folk Art Center** (☎ 828/298–7928), at Milepost 382 on the Blue Ridge Parkway, sells mountain arts and crafts made by the 700 artisans of the Southern Highland Handicraft Guild. **Biltmore Village,** on the Biltmore Estate, has specialty shops, restaurants, and galleries along its cobbled sidewalks. There's a turn-of-the-20th-century English hamlet feel and a shop for everything from children's books to music, antiques, and wearable art. **Malaprops** (⊠ 55 Haywood St., ☎ 828/254–6734 or 800/441–9829) bookstore and café is a mainstay in Asheville. Its two stories are filled with books about the region. The original **Mast General Store** is in Valle Crucis. There are now five of these nostalgic country stores, including ones in Asheville (⊠ 15 Biltmore Ave., ☎ 828/232–1883) and Boone (⊠ 630 W. King St., ☎ 828/262–0000). They sell everything from jellies to shoes, cradles to caskets.

The Mountains Essentials

AIRPORTS

Asheville Regional Airport is 15 mi south of Asheville.

➤ AIRPORT INFORMATION: **Asheville Regional Airport** (⊠ Rte. 280, Fletcher, ☎ 828/684–2226, WEB www.ashevilleregionalairport.com).

BUS TRAVEL

Greyhound/Carolina Trailways serves Asheville.

➤ BUS INFORMATION: **Greyhound** (☎ 800/231–2222, WEB www.greyhound.com).

CAR TRAVEL

You can reach Asheville from the east or the west via I–40. I–26 begins in Asheville and heads south, connecting with I–240, which circles the city. U.S. 23/19A also runs through Asheville.

The High Country is reached off I–40 via U.S. 321 at Hickory, Route 181 at Morganton, and U.S. 221 at Marion. U.S. 421 is a major east–west artery. The Blue Ridge Parkway bisects the region, traveling over mountain crests in the High Country.

VISITOR INFORMATION

➤ TOURIST INFORMATION: **Appalachian Trail Conference** (⊠ 160–A Zillicoa St. [Box 2750, Asheville 28802], ☎ 828/254–3708, WEB www.atconf.org). **Asheville Convention and Visitors Bureau** (⊠ 151 Haywood St.

[Box 1010, 28802], ☎ 828/258–6101 or 800/257–1300). **Blowing Rock Chamber of Commerce** (✉ Box 406, 28605, ☎ 828/295–7851, WEB www.blowingrock.com). **Blue Ridge Parkway Superintendent** (✉ 400 BB&T Bldg., 1 Pack Sq., Asheville 28801, ☎ 828/298–0398, WEB www.blueridgeparkway.org). **Boone Chamber of Commerce** (✉ 208 W. Howard St., 28607, ☎ 828/262–3516 or 800/852–9506, WEB www.boonechamber.com). **Cherokee Visitor Center** (✉ U.S. 441 Business, ☎ 828/497–9195 or 800/438–1601, WEB www.cherokee-nc.com). **Fall Foliage Forecast** (☎ 800/847–4862). **NC High Country Host** (✉ 1700 Blowing Rock Rd., Boone 28607, ☎ 828/264–1299 or 800/438–7500, WEB www.highcountryhost.com). **Smoky Mountain Host of NC** (✉ 4437 Georgia Rd., Franklin 28734, ☎ 828/369–9606 or 800/432–4678).

NORTH DAKOTA

Updated by Tom Griffith

Capital	Bismarck
Population	642,200
Motto	Liberty and Union, Now and Forever, One and Inseparable
State Bird	Western meadowlark
State Flower	Wild prairie rose
Postal Abbreviation	ND

Statewide Visitor Information

North Dakota Tourism Department (✉ Liberty Memorial Bldg., 604 E. Blvd., Bismarck 58505, ☎ 701/328–2525 or 800/435–5663, WEB www.ndtourism.com). **Welcome centers:** along I–94 east, 1 mi west of Beach; off I–94 at the Oriska Rest Area, 12 mi east of Valley City; off I–29 north at the Lake Agassiz Rest Area, 8 mi south of Hankinson interchange; along I–29 south, 1 mi north of the Pembina interchange; 1 block west of the junction of U.S. 2 and U.S. 85 in Williston; at the junction of U.S. 12 and U.S. 85 in Bowman; and at the 45th Street interchange off I–94 west in Fargo.

Scenic Drives

The **Pembina Gorge,** in northeastern North Dakota, is a beautiful forested valley created by glaciers and the winding Pembina River. From I–29 at the Joliette exit near the northern border, drive west on Route 5, then north on Route 32 to Walhalla. The **South Unit Loop Road** in **Theodore Roosevelt National Park** begins near park headquarters in Medora and winds 36 mi through an eerie world of lonesome pinnacles and spires, steep gorges, and ravaged buttes. The 14-mi **North Unit** Road begins at the park entrance along U.S. 85, 15 mi south of Watford City; the high ground above the Little Missouri River has dramatic overlooks, and a lower area near the visitor center features a series of slump rocks, huge sections of bluff that gradually slid intact to the valley floor.

National and State Parks

National Park

Theodore Roosevelt National Park (✉ 315 2nd Ave. [Box 7, Medora 58645], ☎ 701/623–4466, WEB www.nps.gov/thro).

State Parks

Of the 16 state parks in North Dakota, all open year-round, these are some of the best; all have camping facilities. **Cross Ranch State Park** (✉ 1403 River Rd., Center 58530, ☎ 701/794–3731) is 40 mi north of Mandan off Highway 25. Two parks on U.S. 2 and Highway 19 are part of **Devils Lake State Parks** (✉ 152 S. Duncan Rd., Devils Lake 58301, ☎ 701/766–4015): **Fort Abraham Lincoln State Park** (✉ Hwy. 1806, Mandan 58554, 701/663–9571), and **Icelandic State Park** (✉ 13571 Hwy. 5, Cavalier 58220, 5 mi west of town, ☎ 701/265–4561). **Lake Sakakawea State Park** (✉ Rte. 200 [Box 732, Riverdale 58565], 1 mi north of Pick City, ☎ 701/487–3315) has many water-based activities. For summer camping reservations at state parks, contact the **North Dakota Parks and Recreation Department** (✉ 1835 E. Bismarck Expressway, Bismarck 58504, ☎ 701/328–5357 or 800/807–4723).

MISSOURI RIVER CORRIDOR

The Missouri River is a geographic and symbolic barrier between the two North Dakotas, the east and the west. The state capital, Bismarck, on the east bank of the Missouri, is a busy political hub, while at sprawling Lake Sakakawea, a short drive to the northwest, urban life seems a world away. Meriwether Lewis and William Clark followed the Missouri River through North Dakota during their famous exploration of the Louisiana Purchase; on their way west, Lewis and Clark spent the winter of 1804–05 near present-day Washburn, where they were joined by the guide Sakakawea, her husband, and her infant son. Lewis and Clark returned through North Dakota in 1806. Today's Routes 1804 and 1806 mark parts of the Lewis and Clark Trail in North Dakota.

Many attractions don't have firm closing dates or opening dates, primarily because of the vagaries of the weather in the Dakotas. Many rely simply on the level of tourist traffic to dictate when they close or open for the season. Some attractions are open in summer (often Memorial Day–Labor Day); be sure to call ahead before your visit.

Exploring the Missouri River Corridor

The 19-story **State Capitol** (✉ 600 E. Boulevard Ave., ☎ 701/328–2480), in north Bismarck, is visible for miles across the Dakota prairie. Free tours of the limestone-and-marble art-deco structure, built in the 1930s, are offered weekdays year-round and weekends Memorial Day to Labor Day. The **North Dakota Heritage Center** (✉ 612 E. Boulevard Ave., Bismarck, ☎ 701/328–2666; 🎫 donations welcome) is the state's largest museum and archive. Exhibits include Native American and pioneer artifacts and natural-history displays. The **Former Governors' Mansion State Historic Site** (✉ 4th St. and Ave. B, Bismarck, ☎ 701/328–2666; 🎫 free) is an elegant Victorian building containing political memorabilia and period furnishings. The ***Lewis and Clark* Riverboat** (✉ Port of Bismarck, 1700 N. River Rd., ☎ 701/255–4233; 🎫 $15) has summer cruises on the Missouri River, plying the route taken by the traders, trappers, and settlers of the late 19th century.

General George Armstrong Custer buffs often visit **Fort Abraham Lincoln State Park** (✉ Hwy. 1806, Mandan, ☎ 701/663–9571; 🎫 $4). It was from this fort that Custer and his Seventh Calvary rode out on their ill-fated expedition against the Sioux at Little Bighorn. You can reach the park from Bismarck by crossing the river on I–94 to Mandan, then either traveling 8 mi south on Route 1806 or taking the **Fort Lincoln Trolley** (✉ 29 Captain Leach Dr., ☎ 701/663–9018) from south Mandan. Trolley tickets are $5. Among the reconstructed buildings at the fort are the **barracks** and the **Custer House,** a replica of the 1870s house where General George Custer lived with his wife, Libby, before his fateful expedition to Little Bighorn. Nearby is the reconstructed **On-A-Slant Indian Village,** once home to the Mandan tribe.

Forty-four miles south of Mandan is the **Prairie Knights Casino and Resort** (✉ 7932 Hwy. 1806 Fort Yates, ☎ 701/854–7777 or 800/425–8277, WEB www.prairieknights.com) on Standing Rock Sioux Reservation. The fanciest of North Dakota's five reservation casinos, Prairie Knights has murals by Native American artists and first-class dining. A new events center, the Pavilion, opened in 2001. Games, two bars, and two restaurants are open 24 hours. The resort ($) has 102 rooms.

The **Lewis & Clark Interpretive Center** (✉ ¼ mi west off U.S. 83, Washburn, ☎ 701/462–8535; 🎫 $5) is slated as the hub of bicentennial celebrations in 2004. The center is one of four in the world with a complete set of reproduction prints by Karl Bodmer, the artist-explorer who followed Lewis and Clark's trail some 25 years later. From Bismarck, take U.S. 83 north 40 mi.

The **Fort Clark State Historical Site** (✉ Rte. 200A, Center, 16 mi west of Washburn, ☎ 701/328–2666; 🎟 free) was a fur-trade post along the Missouri River where a steamboat full of passengers with smallpox docked, infecting and wiping out most of the nearby Mandan Indian population.

Knife River Indian Villages National Historic Site (✉ Rte. 200, Stanton, ¼ mi north of town, ☎ 701/745–3309; 🎟 donations welcome) preserves depressions formed by the Hidatsa and Mandan tribes' circular earth-and-timber lodges. The museum and interpretive center display pottery shards, other artifacts, and a full-scale furnished replica of an earth lodge.

Countless recreational opportunities at the 600-square-mi **Lake Sakakawea** (✉ Rte. 200, Stanton, 20 mi north of town, ☎ 701/328–2525 or 800/435–5663) include swimming and boating. State parks and small resort communities are sprinkled along its shores. A good portion of Lake Sakakawea is surrounded by **Fort Berthold Indian Reservation,** home of the Mandan, Hidatsa, and Arikara. They're organized as the Three Affiliated Tribes, with headquarters in New Town.

Popular **Roosevelt Park and Zoo,** with more than 200 animals, is about 40 mi north of Lake Sakakawea on U.S. 83. Take a park tour on the miniature train. ✉ *1219 Burdick Expressway E, Minot,* ☎ *701/857–4166,* WEB *www.rpzoo.com.* 🎟 *$4.50. Closed Oct.–Apr.*

Dining and Lodging

For a listing of area bed-and-breakfasts, contact the North Dakota Tourism Department (☞ Statewide Visitor Information, *above*).

Bismarck

$$ ★ ✕ **Peacock Alley Bar and Grill.** Once the historic Patterson Hotel, this restaurant was the scene of countless political deals, captured in period photographs. Regional dishes include pan-blackened prime rib. ✉ *422 E. Main St.,* ☎ *701/255–7917. AE, D, DC, MC, V.*

$–$$ ✕ **Fiesta Villa.** This family-run Mexican restaurant is suitably housed in a Mission-style building. Beef or chicken fajitas are a good choice, and they go well with the excellent margaritas. ✉ *411 E. Main St.,* ☎ *701/222–8075. AE, D, MC, V.*

$ 🏨 **Radisson Inn.** Rooms are spacious and comfortable at this hotel across from Kirkwood Mall. ✉ *800 S. 3rd St., 58504,* ☎ *701/258–7700 or 800/333–3333,* FAX *701/224–8212,* WEB *www.radisson.com. 306 rooms. Restaurant, pool, health club. AE, D, DC, MC, V.*

Mandan

$ ★ ✕ **Mandan Drug.** For a fun lunch, order a sandwich or homemade soup with an old-fashioned cherry soda or a brown cow—a root-beer float with chocolate syrup. The homemade candy is hard to resist. ✉ *316 W. Main St., 58554,* ☎ *701/663–5900. D, MC, V. Closed Sun.*

$ 🏨 **Best Western Seven Seas Inn and Conference Center.** Nautical decor is the unlikely theme in the public areas, from 200-year-old anchors to carpeting in the pattern of ship's planking. Rooms are adorned with maritime art. ✉ *2611 Old Red Trail, 58554, off I–94 Exit 152,* ☎ *701/663–7401 or 800/597–7327,* FAX *701/663–0025,* WEB *www.bestwestern.com. 103 rooms. Restaurant, pool. AE, D, DC, MC, V.*

Minot

$ ★ **International Inn.** The larger-than-average rooms have contemporary furnishings at this five-story hotel on a hill above downtown. ✉ *1505 N. Broadway, 58703, ☎ 701/852–3161 or 800/735–4493, FAX 701/838–5538. 270 rooms. Restaurant, pool. AE, D, DC, MC, V.*

Motel

Expressway Inn (✉ 200 E. Bismarck Expressway, Bismarck 58504, ☎ FAX 701/222–2900, ☎ 800/456–6388), 162 rooms; pool; AE, D, DC, MC, V; CP; $.

Campgrounds

Fort Abraham Lincoln State Park (✉ Hwy. 1806, Mandan, ☎ 701/663–9571; $4). **Lake Sakakawea State Park** (✉ Rte. 200, Riverdale, 1 mi north of Pick City, ☎ 701/487–3315).

Outdoor Activities and Sports

Biking

The 403-mi **CANDISC (Cycling Around North Dakota in Sakakawea Country)** is a bike tour along Lake Sakakawea, Fort Berthold Indian Reservation, the Badlands, and coal country, following some of the route traveled by Lewis and Clark. Contact the North Dakota Tourism Department (☎ 701/328–2525 or 800/435–5663) for details. **Dakota Cyclery** (✉ 1606 E. Main Ave., Bismarck, ☎ 701/222–1218) rents bicycles and can provide information about area biking.

Fishing

Walleye, salmon, and northern pike are the big catches on Lake Sakakawea. The **North Dakota Game and Fish Department** (✉ 100 N. Bismarck Expressway, Bismarck 58501, ☎ 701/328–6300, WEB www.state.nd.us/gnf) lists local fishing guides and publishes the *North Dakota Hunting and Fishing Guide,* which outlines seasons and regulations.

Hiking

Bismarck–Mandan maintains 30-plus mi of paved paths, including a 12-mi trail that follows the Missouri River from north Bismarck to Fort Abraham Lincoln State Park south of Mandan. Contact **Bismarck Parks and Recreation Department** (✉ 420 E. Front Ave., 58504, ☎ 701/222–6455) for details.

Shopping

Kirkwood Mall (✉ between S. 3rd and S. 7th Sts., Bismarck, ☎ 701/223–3500) has four major department stores and 100 specialty shops. Locally owned **Maxwell's** (☎ 701/222–4332) is a cozy bookstore with a special section on regional interests.

Across the river in Mandan, the **Five Nations Arts** (✉ 401 W. Main St., ☎ 701/663–4663) sells handmade Native American star quilts, beadwork, sculptures, and more.

Missouri River Corridor Essentials

AIRPORTS

Bismarck Municipal Airport and Minot International Airport are both about 5 mi from downtown; cab fare is about $6. Northwest serves Minot and Bismarck. United Express serves Bismarck.

➤ AIRPORT INFORMATION: **Bismarck Municipal Airport** (✉ 2301 University Dr., ☎ 701/222–6502). **Minot International Airport** (✉ 25 Airport Rd., ☎ 701/857–4724).

BUS TRAVEL

Greyhound and Minot-Bismark Bus serve Bismarck and Minot.

➤ Bus Information: **Greyhound** (☏ 800/231–2222). **Minot-Bismarck Bus Service** (✉ 300 18th Ave. SW, Minot, ☏ 701/852–2477; ✉ 3750 E. Rosser Ave., Bismarck, ☏ 701/223–6576).

CAR TRAVEL

I–94, the state's major east–west thoroughfare, runs through the Bismarck–Mandan area. U.S. 83 runs north–south from Bismarck to Minot, the state's second- and fourth-largest cities, respectively. U.S. 2 runs east–west along the top half of the state, including Minot.

TRAIN TRAVEL

Amtrak stops in Minot and Williston.

➤ Train Information: **Amtrak** (☏ 800/872–7245).

VISITOR INFORMATION

➤ Tourist Information: **Bismarck-Mandan Convention and Visitors Bureau** (✉ 1600 Burnt Boat Dr., Bismarck, ☏ 701/222–4308 or 800/767–3555). **Minot Convention and Visitors Bureau** (✉ Box 2066, Minot 58702, ☏ 701/857–8206 or 800/264–2626).

THE BADLANDS

Theodore Roosevelt, who ranched in western North Dakota in the late 1800s, once said, "I would never have been president if it had not been for my experiences in North Dakota." He was referring to the **Badlands,** where a national park that bears his name is now the heart of this wide-open country, largely unchanged since the president's time.

Exploring the Badlands

★ **Theodore Roosevelt National Park** (✉ 315 2nd Ave., Medora, ☏ 701/623–4466, WEB www.nps.gov/thro; 🎫 $5 per person on foot or bike or $10 per vehicle) is divided into three units, separated by about 50 mi of Badlands and the **Little Missouri National Grasslands.** Scenic loops through the **South Unit** are marked with low speed limits to protect the bison, wild horses, mule deer, pronghorn antelope, and bighorn sheep that roam here. You can get a panoramic view of the Badlands from the park's **Painted Canyon Overlook and Visitors Center** (✉ I–94, Medora, 7 mi east of town, ☏ 701/623–4466), a good place to start a tour. The center has picnic tables and trail maps for hikers. The park has 80 mi of marked horse trails; if you're up for a 90-minute horseback ride in the South Unit, contact **Peaceful Valley Ranch** (✉ 7 mi north of the park entrance, ☏ 701/623–4568; 🎫 $20). The **North Unit** (✉ off U.S. 85, south of Watford City) has the same scenic driving, wildlife-viewing, and hiking opportunities as the South Unit, but it tends to be less crowded.

Historic **Medora** is a walkable small town with tiny shops, museums, and other attractions. The **Château de Mores State Historic Site** (✉ Hwy. 10, Medora, ¼ mi southwest of town, ☏ 701/623–4355; 🎫 $5), a rustic but aristocratic 26-room home on a bluff overlooking the town, was built in 1883 by the Marquis de Mores, the French nobleman who founded Medora.

You can see antique dolls in the **Medora Doll House** (✉ 485 Broadway, Medora, ☏ 701/623–4444; 🎫 $4). The **Museum of the Badlands** (✉ 195 3rd Ave., Medora, ☏ 701/623–4444; 🎫 $4) has Native American artifacts, wildlife exhibits, and wax figures depicting frontier days. The **Harold Schafer Heritage Center** (✉ 335 4th St., Medora, ☏

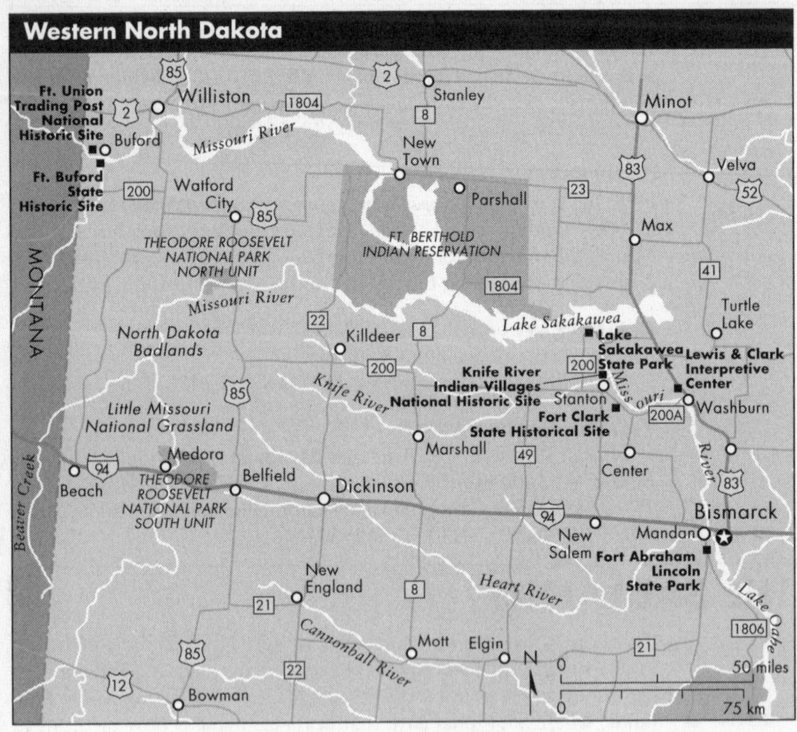

701/623–4444; free) is an art gallery with an exhibit on Harold Schafer, the inventor of Mr. Bubble, the bubble soap for kids. Schafer has been using his fortune to rebuild Medora since the early 1960s.

Dickinson, an oil-boom-and-bust community on I–94, is now renowned for its dinosaur deposits. The **Dakota Dinosaur Museum** has 10 full-scale dinosaurs and other fossil, mineral, and animal collections. ✉ *200 Museum Dr., off I–94 Exit 61, Dickinson,* ☎ *701/225–3466,* WEB *www.dakotadino.com.* *$6. Closed Nov.–Apr.*

Fort Buford State Historic Site is built around the 1866 fort that once imprisoned famous Native American leaders, including Sioux leader Sitting Bull and Nez Perce chief Joseph. ✉ *Hwys. 58 and 1804, Buford, 22 mi southwest of Williston via Rte. 1804,* ☎ *701/572–9034.* *$4. Closed mid-Sept.–mid-May.*

Three miles west of Fort Buford is the **Fort Union Trading Post National Historic Site.** A reconstructed fur-trading post used by John Jacob Astor's American Fur Company, Fort Union dominated the fur trade along the upper Missouri River from 1828 to 1867. ✉ *15550 Hwy. 1804, Dickinson,* ☎ *701/572–9083.* *Free. Closed Sept.–May.*

Dining and Lodging

Dickinson

$–$$ ✕ **Rattlesnake Creek Brewery and Grill.** If the remarkable beer doesn't bite you, the Killdeer Mountain potatoes might. The scalloped potatoes in cream have secret spices for fiery flavor. The chili is a close second behind the inventive meat-and-potatoes options. ✉ *2 W. Villard* ☎ *701/483–9518. AE, D, DC, MC, V. Closed Sun.*

Medora

$–$$ ★ ✕ **Rough Rider Hotel Dining Room.** In a two-story wood-frame building, this rustic restaurant serves barbecued buffalo ribs, prime rib, and other beef specialties. The B&B operates October–April. ✉ *Main St.,* ☎ *701/623–4444. AE, D, MC, V.*

Williston

$–$$ ✕ **Gramma Sharon's Cafe.** Come here for home-cooked, inexpensive meals, not for the atmosphere (it's attached to a gas station). Gramma's is known for its omelets. ✉ *Hwys. 2 and 85 N,* ☎ *701/572–1412. No credit cards.*

$ ✕ **Dakota Farms Family Restaurant.** Breakfast is served all day at Dakota Farms, which has a reputation for fair prices and good service. Friday is all-you-can-eat-fish night. There's a kids' menu. Alcohol is not served. ✉ *1906 2nd Ave. W, 58801,* ☎ *701/572–4480. D, MC, V.*

Motels

Airport International Inn (✉ Hwys. 2 and 85 N, Williston 58801, ☎ 701/774–0241 or 888/304–4855, FAX 701/774–0318), 144 rooms; restaurant, pool; AE, D, DC, MC, V; $.

AmericInn Motel & Suites (✉ 75 E. River Rd. S, Medora 58645, ☎ 701/623–4800 or 800/634–3444, FAX 701/623–4890), 56 rooms; pool; AE, D, DC, MC, V; CP; $$.

Badlands Motel (✉ Pacific Ave. [Box 198, Medora 58645], ☎ 701/623–4444 or 800/633–6721, FAX 701/623–4494), 116 rooms; pool; AE, D, MC, V; closed Oct.–Apr.; $.

Travelodge Hotel (✉ I–94 and Rte. 22, Dickinson 58601, ☎ 701/483–5600 or 800/422–0949, FAX 701/483–0090), 149 rooms; restaurant, pool; AE, D, MC, V; $.

Campgrounds

Cottonwood Campground (✉ 5 mi inside Theodore Roosevelt National Park, 315 2nd Ave., Medora, ☎ 701/623–4466). **Medora Campground** (✉ Off Hwy. 10, Medora, west side of Little Missouri River, on town's western fringe, ☎ 701/623–4444 or 800/633–6721). **Red Trail Campground** (✉ E. River Rd. [Box 367, Medora], south of town, across railroad tracks, ☎ 701/623–4317 or 800/621–4317).

Nightlife

The ***Medora Musical*** (✉ Burning Hills Amphitheater, Chateau Dr., Medora, 1 mi west of town, ☎ 701/623–4444; $22) is an outdoor theater tribute to western Americana, with everything from singing to history to fireworks. Before the show, you can dine at the **Pitchfork Fondue** (✉ on prairie bluff outside Burning Hills Amphitheater, Chateau Dr., Medora, 1 mi west of town; $19.50 prix fixe), a cowboy name for a steak-dinner picnic.

Outdoor Activities and Sports

Biking

The roads in the north and south units of **Theodore Roosevelt National Park** (✉ 315 2nd Ave., Medora 58645, ☎ 701/623–4466, WEB www.nps.gov/thro; $5 per person on foot or bike or $10 per vehicle) are challenging and scenic.

Hiking and Backpacking

All units of **Theodore Roosevelt National Park** (✉ 315 2nd Ave., Medora 58645, ☎ 701/623–4466) offer spectacular hiking and backpacking. The **Little Missouri National Grasslands,** which stretches between the main park units, is a popular spot.

The challenging **Maah Daah Hey Trail** (✉ trailhead at Sully Creek State Park, 5 mi south of Medora) crosses 96 mi of rugged western North Dakota, mostly in Badlands territory. The nonmotorized trail is open for hiking, horseback riding, and some biking. Contact the National Park Service (☎ 701/623–4466) for information.

Shopping

Chateau Nuts (✉ 370 Main St., Medora, ☎ 701/623–4825), one of the many specialty stores along Main Street, stocks every nut imaginable in quantities large enough to make a squirrel's heart race.

The Badlands Essentials

AIRPORTS

Bismarck Municipal Airport (☞ Missouri River Corridor Essentials) is the nearest large airport. Commuter airline United Express serves Williston Airport and Dickinson Airport.

➤ AIRPORT INFORMATION: **Dickinson Airport** (✉ 11168 42nd R St. SW, ☎ 701/483–1062 or 701/225–3822). **Williston Airport** (✉ Hwy. 2 and 85 N, Williston, ☎ 701/774–8594).

BUS TRAVEL

Greyhound stops in Dickinson and Medora.

➤ BUS INFORMATION: **Greyhound** (☎ 800/231–2222).

CAR TRAVEL

I–94 crosses the Badlands, with an exit at Medora for the South Unit of Theodore Roosevelt National Park. U.S. 85 links the park's North and South units.

VISITOR INFORMATION

For information on Medora, contact the Theodore Roosevelt Medora Foundation.

➤ TOURIST INFORMATION: **Dickinson Convention and Visitors Bureau** (✉ 72 Museum Dr., Dickinson 58601, ☎ 701/483–4988 or 800/279–7391, WEB www.dickinsoncvb.com). **Theodore Roosevelt Medora Foundation** (✉ 301 5th St. [Box 198, Medora 58645], ☎ 701/623–4444 or 800/633–6721, WEB www.medora.com). **Williston Convention and Visitors Bureau** (✉ 10 Main St., Williston 58801, ☎ 701/774–9041 or 800/615–9041, WEB www.willistonndtourism.com).

ELSEWHERE IN NORTH DAKOTA

The Lakes Region

What to See and Do

Jamestown, at U.S. 281 and I–94, marks the southern end of this region. The world's largest buffalo sculpture and a live bison herd are both clearly visible from I–94. **Devils Lake,** the heart of the lakes region, is surrounded by hundreds of smaller lakes and prairie potholes filled with marsh water. A major breeding ground for North America's migratory waterfowl, Devils Lake has fine birding and excellent jumbo-perch and walleye fishing. Check ahead before you make fishing or camping plans: rising lake levels have eroded rural roadways. Call the **North Dakota Department of Transportation** (☎ 701/665–5123) for road reports. For more information on fishing in the Jamestown area, contact the Game and Fish Department (✉ 100 N. Bismarck Expressway, Bismarck 58501, ☎ 701/328–6300, WEB www.state.nd.us/gnf).

Within the Spirit Lake Sioux Indian Reservation is the **Fort Totten State Historic Site,** among the best-preserved military forts west of the Mississippi River. Built in 1867, it later served as one of the nation's largest government-run schools for Native Americans. ✉ *Rte. 57, Fort Totten,* ☎ *701/766–4441.* 🎫 *$4. Closed mid-Sept.–mid-May.*

Rugby, west of Devils Lake on U.S. 2, is the geographical center of North America. Marked by a stone monument, the landmark at North America's axis includes a spacious **Geographical Center Pioneer Village and Museum** containing thousands of objects, such as 19th-century farming equipment and antique cars. ✉ *102 Hwy. 2 E, Rugby,* ☎ *701/776–6414.* 🎫 *$5. Closed mid-Sept.–mid-May.*

★ The **International Peace Garden** (✉ U.S. 281, Dunseith, 13 mi north of town, ☎ 701/263–4390 or 888/432–6733; 🎫 $5 per person, $10 per vehicle, free in winter), a 2,300-acre garden straddling the border between Canada and the United States, is a symbol of peace between the two nations and recognizes the longest undefended border in the history of the civilized world. South of the International Peace Garden is the **Turtle Mountain Band of Chippewa Reservation** (✉ Hwy. 5 [Box 900, Belcourt 58316], ☎ 701/477–0470), whose Heritage Center has museum exhibits and crafts for sale.

Dining and Lodging

$ ✕ **Birchwood Steakhouse and Northern Lights Lounge.** Delicious prime rib is a staple at this beautiful lakeside restaurant bordering Canada. ✉ *North of Rte. 43, Lake Metígoshe,* ☎ *701/263–4283. MC, V.*

$ ✕ **Mr. & Mrs. J's.** The Pig-out Omelette is the specialty here. A huge salad bar complements traditional fare. ✉ *U.S. 2 E, Devils Lake,* ☎ *701/662–8815. D, MC, V.*

MOTELS

Comfort Inn (✉ 811 20th St. SW, Jamestown 58401, ☎ 701/252–7125 or 800/228–5150, FAX 701/252–7125), 52 rooms; restaurant, pool; AE, D, DC, MC, V; $.

Great American Inn & Suites (✉ 1116 Hwy. 2 E, Devils Lake 58301, ☎ 701/662–4001 or 888/688–3230, FAX 701/665–2999), 80 rooms; restaurant, pool; AE, D, MC, V; CP; $.

CAMPGROUND

Grahams Island State Park (✉ 152 S. Duncan Rd., off Rte. 19, Devils Lake 58301, 15 mi southwest of town, ☎ 701/766–4015). Call ahead for updates on lake flooding.

The Lakes Region Essentials

AIRPORTS

Devils Lake Airport is served by United Express.

➤ AIRPORT INFORMATION: **Devils Lake Airport** (✉ Hwy. 19, Devils Lake, ☎ 701/662–5833).

CAR TRAVEL

U.S. 2 is the principal east–west route through the region, connecting with I–29 at Grand Forks. U.S. 281 runs north–south, with secondary roads leading to lakes and area attractions.

TRAIN TRAVEL

Amtrak stops in Devils Lake and Rugby.

➤ TRAIN INFORMATION: **Amtrak** (☎ 800/872–7245).

VISITOR INFORMATION

➤ TOURIST INFORMATION: **Devils Lake Tourism & Promotion** (✉ Box 879, Devils Lake 58301, ☎ 701/662–4903 or 800/233–8048). **Jamestown Promotion & Tourism Center** (✉ Box 389, Jamestown 58402, ☎ 800/222–4766).

The Red River Valley

What to See and Do

The **Red River of the North** forms the eastern boundary of North Dakota with Minnesota. The fertile valley formed by the river attracted northern European immigrants in the late 19th century and still contains more than a third of the state's population. The region is an enormous shopping hub, drawing bargain hunters from Minnesota, Canada, and the rest of North Dakota.

In the southeast corner of North Dakota, off I–29, is **Wahpeton.** The **Roger Ehnstrom Learning Center and Chahinkapa Park Zoo** has such native species as eagles, bison, and elk. While you're at the zoo, take a ride on the restored 1926 **Prairie Rose Carousel** (🎟 $1). ✉ *N. 2nd St., Wahpeton,* ☎ *701/642–8709.* 🎟 *$5. Closed Nov.–Apr.*

The ***Bagg Bonanza Farm*** is a national historic site that re-creates the Bonanza-like farm life of the late 1800s and early 1900s. Sixteen of the 21 buildings have been restored. ✉ *Hwy. 13, Mooreton, 1 mi west of I–29,* ☎ *701/274–8989.* 🎟 *$3.50. Closed Oct.–May and Mon.–Thurs.*

Head north 50 mi on I–29 to **Fargo,** the state's largest city and the setting for the Coen brothers' acclaimed 1996 film of the same name. **Bonanzaville USA** is a pioneer village and museum with 40 original and re-created buildings illustrating life in 1880s Dakota Territory. ✉ *Off I–94 Exit 343, West Fargo,* ☎ *701/282–2822 or 800/700–5317.* 🎟 *$6. Closed Nov.–May.*

The **Roger Maris Baseball Museum** (✉ West Acres Shopping Center, I–29 and 13th Ave. S, Fargo, ☎ 701/282–2222; 🎟 free) honors the baseball hero who for 37 years held the single-season home-run record, at 61 runs, until Mark McGuire hit 70 in 1998.

Hands-on learning is the theme at the **Children's Museum at Yunker Farm** (✉ 1201 28th Ave. N, Fargo, ☎ 701/232–6102; 🎟 $3). The **Plains Art Museum** has one of the largest fine arts collections between Minneapolis and Seattle, with traditional Native American and African examples, regional art, and contemporary pieces. ✉ *704 1st Ave. N, Fargo 58102,* ☎ *701/232–3821 or 800/333–0903.* 🎟 *$3. Closed Mon.*

Seventy-five miles north of Fargo on I–29 is **Grand Forks,** North Dakota's cultural and technological center. The **North Dakota Museum of Art** (✉ University of North Dakota, Centennial Dr., ☎ 701/777–4195; 🎟 free) has permanent and traveling contemporary art exhibits in a building that was formerly the campus gym. At the **Odegard School of Aerospace Sciences** (✉ University of North Dakota, University Ave. and Tulane Dr., ☎ 701/777–2791; 🎟 free by appointment) aviation, meteorology, and space studies are taught in futuristic buildings. On a tour you can see an altitude chamber, flight simulators, and an air traffic control center.

The **Pembina State Museum** (✉ 805 Hwy. 59, Pembina, 70 mi north of Grand Forks via I–29, ☎ 701/825–6840; 🎟 free, elevator to top of tower $2) has an observation tower and exhibits on North Dakota's 100-million-year history. The **Pioneer Heritage Interpretive Center** uses artifacts and exhibits to showcase the region's ethnic diversity. ✉ *Icelandic State Park, 13571 Hwy. 5, Cavalier,* ☎ *701/265–4561.* 🎟 *$4 per vehicle. Closed Sat. Sept.–mid-May.*

Dining and Lodging

$–$$ ✕ **Santa Lucia.** Chicken and pork souvlaki reign supreme at this Greek restaurant; seafood specials and gyros are also popular. The indoor fountain is a focal point. ✉ *505 40th St. SW, Fargo,* ☎ *701/281–8656. D, MC, V.*

MOTELS

Best Western Doublewood Inn & Conference Center (✉ 3333 13th Ave. S, Fargo 58103, ☎ 701/235–3333 or 800/528–1234, FAX 701/280–9482, WEB www.bestwestern.com), 170 rooms; restaurant, pool; AE, D, DC, MC, V; *$*.

Road King Inn Columbia Mall (✉ 3300 30th Ave. S, Grand Forks 58201, ☎ 701/746–1391 or 800/707–1391, FAX 701/746–8586), 85 rooms; pool; AE, D, MC, V; CP; *$*.

The Red River Valley Essentials

AIRPORTS

Hector International Airport is served by Northwest and United. Grand Forks International Airport is served by Northwest and Mesaba.

➤ AIRPORT INFORMATION: **Grand Forks International Airport** (✉ 2787 Airport Dr., ☎ 701/795–6981). **Hector International Airport** (✉ 2800 32nd Ave. NW, Fargo, 1 mi east of I–28 Exit 67, ☎ 701/241–1501).

BUS TRAVEL

➤ BUS INFORMATION: **Greyhound Fargo** (✉ 402 Northern Pacific Ave., Fargo, ☎ 701/293–1222). **Greyhound Grand Forks** (✉ 1724 Gateway Dr., Grand Forks, ☎ 701/775–4781). **Greyhound Lines** (☎ 800/231–2222).

CAR TRAVEL

I–94 links Fargo with Minneapolis–St. Paul to the east and with Billings, Montana, to the west. I–29 connects Fargo with Grand Forks, 75 mi north, and with Sioux Falls, South Dakota, to the south.

TRAIN TRAVEL

➤ TRAIN INFORMATION: **Amtrak** (☎ 800/872–7245). **Fargo Amtrak Station** (✉ 420 N. 4th St. N, Fargo, ☎ 701/232–2197). **Grand Forks Amtrak Station** (✉ 5555 Demers Ave., Grand Forks, ☎ 701/775–0484).

VISITOR INFORMATION

➤ TOURIST INFORMATION: **Fargo/Moorhead Convention and Visitors Bureau** (✉ 2001 44th St. SW, Fargo 58103, ☎ 701/282–3653 or 800/235–7654). **Grand Forks Convention and Visitors Bureau** (✉ 4251 Gateway Dr., Grand Forks 58203, ☎ 701/746–0444 or 800/866–4566). **Wahpeton Visitors Center** (✉ 118 N. 6th St., Wahpeton 58075, ☎ 701/642–8744 or 800/892–6673).

Updated by Nicki Chodnoff

Capital	Columbus
Population	11,353,140
Motto	With God, All Things Are Possible
State Bird	Cardinal
State Flower	Scarlet carnation
Postal Abbreviation	OH

Statewide Visitor Information

Ohio Division of Travel and Tourism (⊠ Box 1001, Columbus 43216, ☎ 800/282–5393, WEB www.ohiotourism.com). **Ohio Historical Society** (⊠ 1982 Velma Ave., Columbus 43211, ☎ 614/297–2300, WEB www.ohiohistory.org).

Scenic Drives

The **Lake Erie Circle Tour** (☎ 800/255–3743, WEB www.circle-erie.com) consists of nearly 200 mi of state routes and U.S. highways along the Lake Erie shoreline from Toledo to Conneaut. The **Ohio River Scenic Route, a National Scenic Byway, Route 7** (☎ 513/553–1500 for information, WEB www.byways.org) runs parallel to the Ohio River on the state's southeastern border and cuts through the French-settled village of Gallipolis. The byway also passes the site of Ohio's only significant Civil War battle, near Pomeroy, and brings you past Marietta, the historic first city of the Northwest Territory.

National and State Parks

National Parks

National monuments include the **Hopewell Culture National Historic Park** (⊠ 16062 State Rte. 104, Chillicothe, ☎ 740/774–1125, WEB www.nps.gov/hocu), with its earthen wall enclosures built in geometric patterns and mounds of various shapes. **Perry's Victory and International Peace Memorial,** in Put-in-Bay (☎ 419/285–2184, WEB www.nps.gov/pevi), was built to commemorate the American naval victory and dedicated to peace. **William Howard Taft National Historic Site** (⊠ 2038 Auburn Ave., Cincinnati, ☎ 513/684–3262, WEB www.nps.gov/wiho) honors the only man to serve as both president and chief justice of the United States. The **Cuyahoga Valley National Park Recreation Area** (⊠ 15610 Vaughn Rd., Brecksville 44141, ☎ 216/524–1497 or 440/526–5256, WEB www.nps.gov/cuva) is on 33,000 acres of forested valley between Cleveland and Akron along the Cuyahoga River and follows the path of the historic Ohio and Erie Canal. **Dayton Aviation Heritage National Historical Park** (⊠ 22 S. Williams St., Dayton, ☎ 937/225–7705, WEB www.nps.gov/daav) honors Wilbur Wright, Orville Wright, and Paul Laurence Dunbar and their innovations. **James A. Garfield National Historic Site** (⊠ 8095 Mentor Ave., Mentor 44060, ☎ 440/255–8722, WEB www.nps.gov/ja) was acquired by the 20th president in 1876 to accommodate his large family.

State Parks

Of Ohio's 73 state parks, 8 are classified as **Ohio State Park Resorts** (☎ 800/282–7275), which have rooms for rent and facilities for swimming, boating, golf, tennis, and dining. For more information contact the **Ohio Department of Natural Resources** (⊠ Ohio State Parks Information Center, Fountain Sq., Bldg. C–1, Columbus 43224, ☎ 614/265–7000 or 800/282–5393, WEB www.dnr.state.oh.us).

COLUMBUS

Columbus, Ohio's state capital and largest city, is known for its entrepreneurial spirit and economic vitality. The city has embraced the country's first stadium built specifically for soccer, introduced a new Arena district, and doubled the size of its favorite science attraction, COSI (Center of Science and Industry). The state's largest university, Ohio State, is here, as are the headquarters of a number of Fortune 500 companies, many of whose executives claim they would not leave the city—even if they were promoted.

Exploring Columbus

On the grounds of the Ohio Expo Center is the **Crew Stadium,** home of Major League Soccer's Columbus Crew. It's the first stadium in the country built specifically for a professional soccer team and can hold 22,500 fans. The NHL's Columbus Blue Jackets face off at the **Nationwide Arena,** in the downtown Arena district.At the heart of downtown is the domeless Greek Revival **state capitol** (✉ corner of High and Broad Sts., ☎ 614/752–9777), with its distinguished skylights, stained glass, and period details. The Veterans Memorial on the east side of the building is an addition to this historic structure. The lively **Riffe Gallery** (✉ 77 S. High St., ☎ 614/644–9624, WEB www.oac.state.oh.us.riffegallery), in the Vern Riffe Center for Government and the Arts, has works by Ohio artists. COSI (pronounced co-*sigh*), the **Center of Science and Industry** (✉ 333 W. Broad St., ☎ 614/228–2674, WEB www.cosi.org; $12), has interactive science exhibits that encourage you to touch, feel, and create.The **Short North** (☎ 614/228–8050), a strip of trendy shops, clubs, vintage clothing and antiques stores, restaurants, and art galleries north of downtown, holds a Gallery Hop the first Saturday of every month. ★ The **Wexner Center for the Arts** (✉ N. High St. at 15th Ave., ☎ 614/292–0330 or 614/292–3535, WEB www.wexarts.org) shows contemporary art in a dramatic building designed by Peter Eisenmann.

★ **German Village** (☎ 614/221–8888, WEB www.germanvillage.com), a neighborhood of tightly packed brick homes built by immigrants in the 19th century, is south of downtown. In the **Brewery District,** next to German Village, old breweries are now restaurants and bars.It looks like the plains of Africa at **The Wilds** (✉ 14000 International Rd., ☎ 740/638–5030; $10), in Cumberland, about 80 mi southeast of Columbus. Camels, giraffes, and bison roam 10,000 square acres of surface-mined land that has been reclaimed as an endangered species center. Buses take you within feet of the animals. The park is closed November–April.At the **Columbus Zoo and Aquarium** (✉ 9990 Riverside Dr., about 18 mi northwest of downtown off I–270, ☎ 614/645–355, WEB www.colszoo.org; $8) three generations of gorillas, monkeys, and other animals call the new African Forest exhibit home. This is one of four manatee preserves outside of Florida and has a new pachyderm area.

Dining

Though dubbed the Fast Food Capital of the World by the *New York Times* and *Wall Street Journal,* Columbus has a lively restaurant scene. Eateries tucked into the Short North, German Village, the Arena district, and surrounding suburbs offer everything from down-home barbecue to haute cuisine.

$$$–$$$$ ✕ **Mitchell's Steakhouse.** Mitchell's, in the heart of downtown near the State House, is called by some the city's most beautiful restaurant. The renovated former bank building retains its ornate 20-ft-high ceilings. This nirvana for carnivores specializes in aged steaks and chops. ✉ *45 N. 3rd St., at Gay St.,* ☎ *614/621–2333. AE, D, DC, MC, V.*

$$$–$$$$ ✕ **Plaza Restaurant.** In the Hyatt on Capitol Square, the Plaza is one of the city's most beautiful and romantic dining spots. It's the only downtown restaurant with a spectacular view of the state capitol building and an outdoor fountain courtyard, but the views are eclipsed by the food. Imaginative appetizers complement fine game that might include osso buco, Weiner schnitzel, or a New York strip steak. ✉ *75 E. State St., at High St.,* ☎ *614/365–4550. AE, DC, MC, V.*

$$–$$$$ ✕ **G. Michael's Italian American Bistro and Bar.** Inside a historic town house in quaint German Village, this spot is fancy without feeling stuffy. Don't expect all red sauces and spaghetti and meatballs in these renditions of contemporary Italian-American cuisine. Check out the intimate outdoor patio, which seats 24 in the summer. ✉ *595 S. 3rd St.,* ☎ *614/464–0575. AE, D, DC, MC, V.*

$ ✕ **City Barbecue.** Go for the food, not the surroundings at this no-frills restaurant about 15 minutes northwest of downtown, which now has a branch in the northeast suburb of Gahanna. The tables are crammed together, there's no table service, and the smoker sits in the parking lot. You'll be rewarded with big portions of North Carolina–style barbecue or ribs dressed with corn, baked beans, and other traditional fixings. ✉ *2111 W. Henderson Rd.,* ☎ *614/538–8890;* ✉ *207 W. Johnstown Rd.,* ☎ *614/416–8890. AE, D, MC, V.*

$ ✕ **Haiku.** The sushi bar is the center of activity at this stylish Pan-Asian restaurant in the trendy Short North. Hot entrées include creative Asian dishes like the house specialty, noodles served in sauce or broth. There's a full sake menu to wash down the food. ✉ *800 N. High St.,* ☎ *614/294–8168. AE, D, DC, MC, V.*

Lodging

Columbus lodging is mostly in downtown, nearby German Village, and the surrounding outer belt.

$$$$ **Hyatt on Capitol Square.** Service puts this hotel ahead of the pack. The modern exterior counters a traditional interior done in marble floors, gilt mirrors, and Chinese vases. ✉ *75 E. State St., 43215,* ☎ *614/228–1234,* FAX *614/469–9664,* WEB *www.hyatt.com/usa/columbus/hotels/hotel_capit.html. 400 rooms. Restaurant, pool, health club. AE, D, DC, MC, V.*

$$$–$$$$ ★ **The Westin Columbus.** High ceilings, marble floors, and stone columns give this turn-of-the-20th-century hotel a grand air. Rooms are done in a Queen Anne style, with marble baths. ✉ *310 S. High St., 43215,* ☎ *614/228–3800,* FAX *614/228–7666,* WEB *www.starwood.com/westin. 197 rooms. Restaurant. AE, D, DC, MC, V.*

$$$ **Adam's Mark Columbus.** An elegant player in the downtown hotel scene, this modern and ample property caters to a business clientele. ✉ *50 N. 3rd St., 43215,* ☎ *614/228–5050 or 800/444–2326,* FAX *614/228–2525,* WEB *www.adamsmark.com/columbus/index.asp. 415 rooms. Restaurant, pool, health club. AE, D, DC, MC, V.*

$$$ **Hyatt Regency, Columbus.** Adjacent to the convention center, this ultramodern high-rise caters mainly to business travelers. ✉ *350 N. High St., 43215,* ☎ *614/463–1234,* FAX *614/280–3034,* WEB *www.hyatt.com/usa/columbus/hotels/hotel_cmhrc.html. 632 rooms. Restaurant, pool, gym. AE, D, DC, MC, V.*

$$–$$$ ★ **Lofts Hotel, Columbus.** Italian furniture and exposed brick walls make the 44 rooms feel like New York lofts; the Lofts' midwestern charms remind you where you are. ✉ *55 Nationwide Blvd., 43215,* ☎ *614/461–2663 or 800/735–6387,* FAX *614/461–5828,* WEB *www.55lofts.com. 44 rooms. Restaurant, pool. AE, D, DC, MC, V.*

$$ **Courtyard by Marriott.** Formerly a warehouse, this unusual hotel has a bi-level, contemporary lobby and luxurious suites with kitchens. The location is convenient to most area attractions. ✉ *35 W. Spring St., 43215,* ☎ *614/228–3200,* FAX *614/228–6752,* WEB *www.55lofts.com. 149 rooms. Restaurant. AE, D, DC, MC, V.*

$ **German Village Inn.** Friendly service and low rates are the selling points of this no-frills German Village hotel near downtown. ✉ *920 S. High St., 43206,* ☎ *614/443–6506,* FAX *614/443–5663. 43 rooms. AE, D, DC, MC, V.*

Nightlife and the Arts

Two free weekly newspapers—the *Other Paper,* and *Columbus Alive!*—have complete listings of goings-on in the city.

Nightlife

Most of Columbus's hot spots are scattered near the Ohio State University campus (expect crowds when the OSU Buckeye football and basketball teams play) and the downtown neighborhoods around German Village, the Short North, and the Brewery District. Live bands play on the weekends and monthly art exhibits are presented at the **Short North Tavern** (✉ 674 N. High St., ☎ 614/221–3432), which reverts to a neighborhood bar during the week. Live out a musical fantasy at **Howl at the Moon** (✉ 450 S. Front St., ☎ 614/224–4695), where you can sing along with dueling pianos at this 21-and-older club in the Brewery District. **Shadowbox Cabaret** (✉ 164 Easton Town Center, ☎ 614/416–7625 or 888/887–4236) showcases raucous and original live comedy and rock-and-roll music; performers play characters while they take your drink and food orders. Jazz up your evening with live jazz seven nights a week at **Barrister Hall** (✉ 560 S. High St., ☎ 614/621–1213), an upscale cigar bar in the Brewery District with fine scotch and bourbons. From alternative and country to blues and rock, **Little Brother's** (✉ 1100 N. High St., ☎ 614/421–2025) presents the music of local and nationally known singer-songwriters and bands.

The Arts

The **Southern Theater** (✉ 21 E. Main St., ☎ 614/340–9698) hosts performances of the **Columbus Jazz Orchestra** (☎ 614/294–5200) and productions of the **Columbus Light Opera** (614/236–6237). The **Columbus Association for the Performing Arts** (☎ 614/469–0939), known as CAPA, operates the **Capitol Theatre,** in the **Riffe Center** (✉ 77 S. High St., ☎ 614/460–7214), where **Ballet Met** (☎ 614/229–4860; 614/229–4848 for tickets) performs part of its schedule. Touring Broadway shows are among the fare at the stately **Ohio Theater** (✉ 55 E. State St., ☎ 614/469–1045; 614/469–0939 for tickets). The Ohio is also home to the **Columbus Symphony Orchestra** (☎ 614/228–8600) and some performances of Ballet Met. **Opera Columbus** (☎ 614/461–8101) and touring Broadway shows take the stage at the **Palace Theatre** (✉ 34 W. Broad St., ☎ 614/469–9850; 614/431–3600 for tickets).

Shopping

Columbus is the world headquarters of Leslie Wexner's empire of clothing stores, which include the Limited, Express, Structure, Victoria's Secret, and Abercrombie & Fitch, all of which are in **Columbus City Center** (✉ 111 S. 3rd St., ☎ 614/221–4900). You can't miss **Lazarus** (✉ 141 S. High St., ☎ 614/463–2121), the granddaddy of Columbus department stores; its old-fashioned water tower sticks up out of the skyline like a Tootsie Roll Pop. **Prime Outlets at Jefferson-**

ville I and II (✉ at I–71 Exits 65 and 69, Jeffersonville, ☎ 800/746–7644), 35 minutes south of Columbus, has more than 150 outlets. Browse through more than 130 stores at the **Mall at Tuttle Crossing** (✉ 5043 Tuttle Crossing Blvd., ☎ 614/717–9300). The **Easton Town Center** (✉ I–270 and Easton Way, ☎ 614/337–2200), 16 minutes from downtown in the northeast part of the city, offers shopping and entertainment and is home to Nordstrom. **Polaris Fashion Place** (✉ 1500 Polaris Pkwy., ☎ 614/846–1550), 20 minutes north of downtown at I–71, is a shopping complex with such upscale stores as Saks Fifth Avenue.

Columbus Essentials

AIR TRAVEL

Air Ontario and Midwest Express are among more than 20 airlines that serve Columbus.

➤ AIRLINES AND CONTACTS: **Air Ontario** (☎ 800/776–3000). **Midwest Express** (☎ 800/452–2022).

AIRPORTS AND TRANSFERS

Port Columbus International Airport is 10 mi east of downtown Columbus.

➤ AIRPORT INFORMATION: **Port Columbus International Airport** (☎ 614/239–4000).

AIRPORT TRANSFERS

A cab from the airport to downtown costs about $18; Urban Express airport shuttle from downtown costs $12. The Capital City Flyer, operated by the Central Ohio Transit Authority (COTA), connects the airport with downtown hotels and attractions for $5 each way.

➤ TAXIS AND SHUTTLES: **Urban Express** (☎ 877/840–0411).

BUS TRAVEL TO AND FROM COLUMBUS

Greyhound serves Columbus.

➤ BUS INFORMATION: **Greyhound** (✉ E. Town St. at 3rd St., ☎ 800/231–2222).

CAR TRAVEL

Columbus is in the center of the state, at the intersection of I–70 and I–71.

TRANSPORTATION AROUND COLUMBUS

Downtown is fairly compact and easily walkable. Some government buildings are connected to each other and to nearby buildings through underground walkways. COTA operates buses within Columbus.

➤ CONTACTS: **Central Ohio Transit Authority** (☎ 614/228–1776, WEB www.cota.com).

VISITOR INFORMATION

➤ TOURIST INFORMATION: **Greater Columbus Convention and Visitors Bureau** (✉ 90 N. High St., 43215, ☎ 614/221–6623 or 800/345–4386, WEB www.columbuscvb.org).

CINCINNATI

Cincinnati has a proud history, an active riverfront, and a busy downtown. A river's width from the South, in many respects it resembles a southern city: Its summers are hot and humid, a result of being in a basin along the Ohio River, and its politics lean toward the conservative.

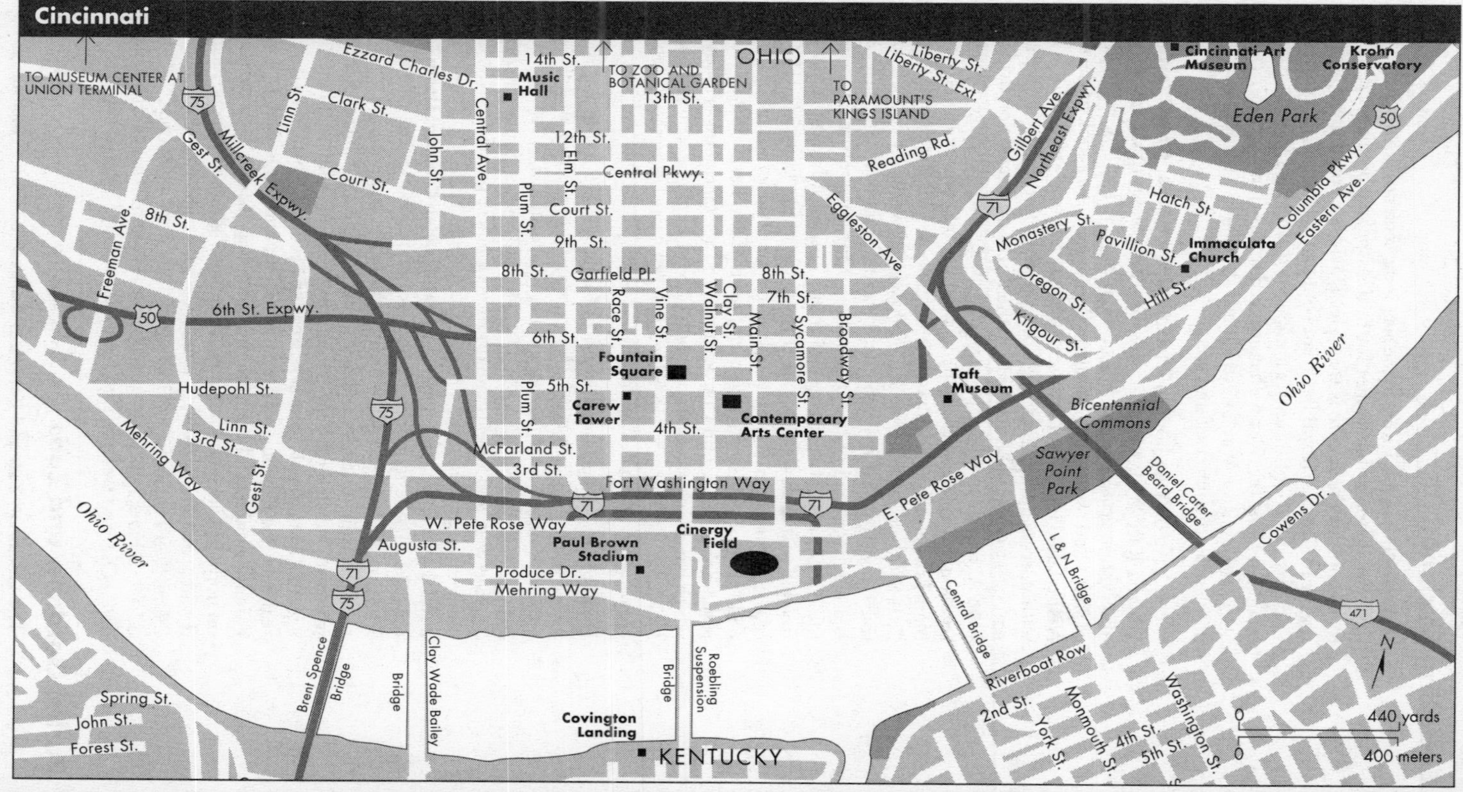

Cincinnati
TO MUSEUM CENTER AT UNION TERMINAL
14th St.
Music Hall
TO ZOO AND BOTANICAL GARDEN
13th St.
OHIO
TO PARAMOUNT'S KINGS ISLAND
Liberty St.
Liberty St. Ext.
Cincinnati Art Museum
Krohn Conservatory
Eden Park
Ezzard Charles Dr.
Clark St.
Linn St.
Gest St.
Millcreek Expwy.
John St.
Central Ave.
12th St.
Central Pkwy.
Reading Rd.
Gilbert Ave.
Northeast Expwy.
Columbia Pkwy.
Eastern Ave.
Court St.
Elm St.
Plum St.
Court St.
Hatch St.
Monastery St.
Pavillion St.
Immaculata Church
8th St.
Freeman Ave.
9th St.
Eggleston Ave.
8th St.
Garfield Pl.
8th St.
7th St.
Oregon St.
Hill St.
6th St. Expwy.
Race St.
Vine St.
Walnut St.
Clay St.
Main St.
Sycamore St.
Broadway St.
Kilgour St.
6th St.
Fountain Square
Ohio River
Hudepohl St.
5th St.
Carew Tower
Taft Museum
Contemporary Arts Center
Bicentennial Commons
Linn St.
3rd St.
Mehring Way
4th St.
McFarland St.
3rd St.
Sawyer Point Park
E. Pete Rose Way
Daniel Carter Beard Bridge
Gest St.
Fort Washington Way
Ohio River
W. Pete Rose Way
Cinergy Field
Paul Brown Stadium
Cowens Dr.
Augusta St.
Produce Dr.
Mehring Way
L & N Bridge
Central Bridge
Riverboat Row
Brent Spence Bridge
Clay Wade Bailey Bridge
Roebling Suspension Bridge
2nd St.
York St.
Monmouth St.
4th St.
5th St.
Washington St.
Spring St.
John St.
Forest St.
Covington Landing
KENTUCKY
N
0 440 yards
0 400 meters

Exploring Cincinnati

Fountain Square (✉ 5th and Vine Sts.) is the center of downtown Cincinnati and a popular lunch spot for businesspeople in fair weather. The focal point of the square is the **Tyler Davidson Fountain,** which was cast in 1867 at the Royal Bavarian Foundry in Munich, Germany. The square is the site of the city's annual Oktoberfest ceremony. The city is laid out along the river, with numbered streets running east–west (2nd Street is Pete Rose Way); north–south streets have names. Vine Street divides the city into east and west.

If you have only an hour in Cincinnati, spend it at **Carew Tower** (✉ 5th and Race Sts.), which affords sweeping views of the city from its observation deck. The building dates from 1930 and is home to dozens of shops and restaurants. While in the tower, have a look at the **Omni Netherland Plaza Hotel,** whose marble-and-rosewood interior is filled with mirrors and murals.You can cross the Ohio River from Cincinnati into Covington, Kentucky, on the **Roebling Suspension Bridge,** by John A. Roebling, who later designed the Brooklyn Bridge. **Covington Landing,** a floating entertainment complex and a wharf, is west of Roebling Bridge. At the Covington Landing dock is **BB Riverboats** (☎ 859/261–8500 or 800/261–8586, WEB www.bbriverboats.com), running tours year-round. **Covington** itself straddles the Roebling Bridge and is a neighborhood of fine antebellum mansions.On the Ohio side of the river, the narrow streets and funky houses of **Mount Adams,** the first hill east of downtown, are reminiscent of San Francisco. The yard of the **Immaculata Church** (✉ Pavilion and Guido Sts., ☎ 513/721–6544) provides a sterling view of the city.**Eden Park,** on Mt. Adams, is the site of the **Krohn Conservatory** and the **Cincinnati Art Museum,** which has an outstanding collection of Near Eastern and ancient art. ✉ *953 Eden Park Dr.,* ☎ *513/721–5204,* WEB *www.cincinnatiartmuseum.com.* 🎟 *$5, free Sat. Closed Mon.*

Downtown, the **Contemporary Arts Center** (✉ 115 E. 5th St., ☎ 513/345–8400 or 513/721–0390, WEB www.spiral.org; 🎟 $3.50, free Mon.) presents some of today's most cutting-edge artists. The **Taft Museum of Art** (✉ 316 Pike St., ☎ 513/241–0343, WEB www.taftmuseum.org; 🎟 $4, free Wed. and Sun.) is famous for its Chinese porcelains. Closed for renovations at press time, it is slated to reopen in 2003.You could spend a full day in the magnificently restored **Museum Center at Union Terminal** (✉ 1301 Western Ave., off I–75 at Ezzard Charles Dr., ☎ 513/287–7000 or 800/733–2077), which looks like a huge Art Deco cabinet radio. This historic former train station houses the **Cinergy Children's Museum,** a delightfully inventive, hands-on museum for children of all ages; the **Museum of Natural History and Science,** which has a cave with real bats; the **Cincinnati History Museum;** and the **Robert D. Lindner Family Omnimax Theater.** **Paramount's Kings Island,** a theme park 24 mi north of Cincinnati in Kings Mills, has eight theme areas, including a water park and the world's longest wooden roller coaster. ✉ *I–71 Exit 24 north or Exit 25 S,* ☎ *800/288–0808,* WEB *www.pki.com.* 🎟 *$41.99; $20.99 seniors, children. Closed Labor Day–mid-Apr., except weekends Sept.–Oct. and weekdays mid-Apr.–Memorial Day.*

Parks, Gardens, and Zoos

The **Cincinnati Zoo and Botanical Garden** (✉ 3400 Vine St., ☎ 513/281–4700, WEB www.cincyzoo.org; 🎟 $11.50), famous for its white Bengal tigers, is the second-oldest zoo in the country. Follow the paw-print signs off I–75 Exit 6 or I–71 Exit 5, the Dana Avenue exit.

Bicentennial Commons, an outdoor recreation center at Sawyer Point on the Ohio River, uses monuments to tell the story of Cincinnati's origins. Note the famous flying pigs, a playful reminder of the city's prominence as a meatpacking center. **Krohn Conservatory** (☏ 513/421–4086, WEB www.cinci-parks.org; 🎫 free), in Eden Park, has a greenhouse and gardens with more than 5,000 species of plants.

Dining and Lodging

Famous for its chili, Cincinnati has more good restaurants than the most ravenous traveler could sample in one visit, including riverboat restaurants and rathskellers. Downtown Cincinnati has several choice hotels. Many offer weekend packages including tickets to Reds or Bengals games. Staying in the suburbs is less expensive.

$$$–$$$$ ★ ✕ **The Celestial.** The views from the top of Mt. Adams are as much of a draw as the French and American cuisine. ✉ *1071 Celestial St.,* ☏ *513/241–4455. Jacket required. AE, DC, MC, V. Closed Sun.*

$$$–$$$$ ✕ **The Maisonette.** Since 1964 the Maisonette has been ranked among the foremost restaurants in the United States. The food is fresh and French, the atmosphere formal. ✉ *114 E. 6th St.,* ☏ *513/721–2260. Reservations essential. Jacket required. AE, D, DC, MC, V. Closed Sun.*

$$–$$$$ ✕ **Jump Café & Bar.** The first-floor of this hip and sleek spot has a generous bar and a scattering of tables for wine service and a tasting menu. Upstairs is a white-tablecloth restaurant with chef Allen Stickell's modern fare with American, French, and Asian accents. Entrées might include citrus-infused halibut with a sweet corn cake, Moroccan barbecue-spiced lamb loin, or pepper-encrusted ahi tuna and beef fillet. The bar gets jumping Wednesday through Saturday nights with a DJ in the house. ✉ *1203 Main St.,* ☏ *513/665–4677. Reservations essential. AE, D, DC, MC, V. Closed Sun.–Tues. No lunch.*

$–$$$ ✕ **Montgomery Inn at the Boathouse.** The barbecued ribs are famous, and you can't get any closer to the river without jumping in for a swim. Lunchtime and happy hour both draw crowds. ✉ *925 Eastern Ave.,* ☏ *513/721–7427. AE, D, DC, MC, V. No lunch weekends.*

$–$$ ✕ **Rookwood Pottery Bistro.** The wood-and-brick dining rooms contain what were once the kilns of the famous Mt. Adams pottery. Families come here for giant burgers and other simple fare. ✉ *1077 Celestial St.,* ☏ *513/721–5456. AE, DC, MC, V.*

$ ✕ **Christy's & Lenhardt's.** Schnitzel, Viennese and Hungarian goulash, sauerbraten, and potato pancakes are served at this casual place. The outdoor beer garden is a great summer escape. ✉ *151 W. McMillan St.,* ☏ *513/281–3600. AE, D, MC, V. Closed Sun.–Mon., 1st 2 wks in Aug., 2 wks at Christmas.*

$$$–$$$$ ★ ✕🏨 **Cincinnatian Hotel.** A sedate French Second Empire–style hotel, the Cincinnatian offers haute-contemporary elegance along with gracious personal service. This showplace has a wedding suite and a luxury whirlpool room. Reservations are essential at the **Palace** (☏ 513/381–6006), where the chef delights with his Continental cuisine—and his crème brûlée. ✉ *601 Vine St., 45202,* ☏ *513/381–3000; 800/942–9000 in Ohio,* FAX *513/651–0256,* WEB *www.cincinnatianhotel.com. 146 rooms. 2 restaurants, health club. AE, D, DC, MC, V.*

$$$ ★ ✕🏨 **Hilton Cincinnati Netherland Plaza.** Downtown's grand Art Deco hotel is in the Carew Tower. The two-story lobby has bas-relief sculptures and dramatic fountains and light fixtures; guest rooms have 10-ft ceilings and soft pastel colors. The formal Palm Court restaurant serves buffet lunches and fine American cuisine. ✉ *35 W. 5th St., 45202,* ☏ *513/421–9100,* FAX *513/421–4291,* WEB *www.hilton.com. 621 rooms. 2 restaurants, health club. AE, D, DC, MC, V.*

$–$$$ **Amos Shinkle Townhouse B&B.** The master bedroom in this antebellum mansion, once home to the man who hired John A. Roebling to build the Roebling Suspension Bridge, has a whirlpool and a crystal chandelier in the bathroom. Covington is a short ride from Cincinnati, on the other side of the bridge. ✉ *215 Garrard St., Covington, KY 41011,* ☎ *859/431–2118 or 800/972–7012,* FAX *859/491–4551,* WEB *www.amosshinkle.net. 7 rooms. AE, D, DC, MC, V.*

$ **Best Western Mariemont Inn.** Even the cash machine is in Tudor style at this inn on the National Register of Historic Places. Amenities include a pub and free parking. ✉ *6880 Wooster Pike/U.S. 50, Mariemont 45227,* ☎ *513/271–2100 or 800/528–1234,* FAX *513/271–5710,* WEB *www.bestwestern.com. 60 rooms. Restaurant. AE, D, DC, MC, V.*

Nightlife and the Arts

Nightlife

The **Blind Lemon** (✉ 936 Hatch St., ☎ 513/241–3885), on Mt. Adams, has a courtyard, a funky old interior, and a cozy fireplace. **Bogarts** (✉ 2621 Vine St., ☎ 513/281–8400, WEB www.bogarts.com), in Clifton, hosts local garage bands, college bands, and such national acts as the Mighty Mighty Bosstones, G. Love and Special Sauce, and the Psychedelic Furs. The downtown **Japps Cigar and Martini Bar** (✉ 1134 Main St., ☎ 513/684–0007) is in an 1800s building once home to a wig maker. The new, sleek incarnation attracts businesspeople and those in touch with the good life. The downtown **Rhythm & Blues Cafe** (✉ 1142 Main St., ☎ 513/684–0080; closed Sun.–Tues.) has live funk, soul, reggae, and blues bands.

The Arts

The **Music Hall** (✉ 1243 Elm St., ☎ 513/721–8222), built in the 18th century in a style since dubbed "sauerbraten Gothic," is home to the Cincinnati Symphony Orchestra as well as the **Cincinnati Pops Orchestra** (☎ 513/381–3300), which performs from September through May at the Music Hall and June and July at Riverbend; and the **Cincinnati Opera** (☎ 513/241–2742), with performances in June and July. The **Cincinnati Ballet** performs from October through May at the Aronoff Center for the Arts (✉ 650 Walnut St., ☎ 513/621–2787) and holds special shows at the Music Hall.

Spectator Sports

Baseball: The **Cincinnati Reds** (✉ 100 Cinergy Field, Pete Rose Way, ☎ 513/421–4510, WEB www.cincinnatireds.com), baseball's oldest team and the 1990 World Champions, play at **Cinergy Field** from April through October. The **Great American Ball Park** is being built next door. The new park should be ready in 2003. **Football:** The **Cincinnati Bengals** (✉ 1 Paul Brown Stadium, ☎ 513/621–3550, WEB www.bengals.com) play in the state-of-the-art **Paul Brown Stadium** on the riverfront.

Shopping

Tower Place at the Carew Tower (✉ 28 W. 4th St., ☎ 513/381–8849) is a downtown atrium shopping mall with skywalks, enclosed parking, three levels of retailers, and a food court. Skywalks connect Tower Place with **Saks Fifth Avenue** (✉ 101 W. 5th St., at Race St., ☎ 513/421–6800), where you can browse through the designer clothing collections and fancy perfumes and cosmetics. There are upscale stores in the downtown **Fountain Place** (✉ 5th and Race Sts.) shopping area, with Tiffany & Co. and Brooks Brothers setting the tone. At **Tiffany & Co.** (✉ Fountain Place, 505 Vine St., ☎ 513/721–2022), installed on a prominent corner in the downtown Fountain Place shopping center, you can pick up signature jewelry, housewares, and giftware. **Rookwood Commons** (✉ Edwards Rd. and Madison Rd., Norwood) shopping center, in Norwood, near Hyde Park, has a Wild Oats health food emporium, P. F. Chang's China Bistro, and many other stores.

Cincinnati Essentials

AIR TRAVEL

ComAir is one of many airlines serving the Cincinnati area.

➤ AIRLINES AND CONTACTS: **ComAir** (☎ 800/354–9822).

AIRPORTS AND TRANSFERS

Cincinnati/Northern Kentucky International Airport (☎ 859/767–3151) is 12 mi south of downtown, off I–275, in Kentucky. It is served by major airlines.

AIRPORT TRANSFER

Jetport Express makes regular trips from the airport to downtown hotels ($12 one-way, $16 round-trip). Taxis downtown cost about $25 plus tip.

➤ TAXIS AND SHUTTLES: **Airport Taxi Service** (☎ 859/767–3260). **Jetport Express** (☎ 859/767–3702).

BUS TRAVEL TO AND FROM CINCINNATI

➤ BUS INFORMATION: **Greyhound** (✉ 1005 Gilbert Ave., ☎ 800/231–2222 or 513/352–6012, WEB www.greyhound.com).

CAR TRAVEL

I–71, I–75, and I–74 all converge on downtown Cincinnati.

TRAIN TRAVEL

➤ TRAIN INFORMATION: **Amtrak** (✉ Union Terminal, 1301 Western Ave., ☎ 800/872–7245).

TRANSPORTATION AROUND CINCINNATI

Downtown Cincinnati is entirely walkable. Skywalks connect hotels, convention centers, stores, and garages. Metro runs buses out of Government Square. There is also a downtown loop bus (Bus 79).

➤ CONTACTS: **Government Square** (✉ 5th St. between Walnut and Main Sts.). **Metro** (☎ 513/621–4455).

VISITOR INFORMATION

➤ TOURIST INFORMATION: **Greater Cincinnati Convention and Visitors Bureau** (✉ 300 W. 6th St. 45202, ☎ 513/621–6994 or 800/344–3445, WEB www.cincyusa.com).

NORTHWEST OHIO AND THE LAKE ERIE ISLANDS

Between Toledo and Cleveland lie a stretch of the Lake Erie shore and a group of islands that constitute the Riviera and Madeira of Ohio. Families rent cottages at Catawba Point or Put-in-Bay (the port village on South Bass Island) and swim, fish, and boat, topping the week off with a trip to Cedar Point Amusement Park in Sandusky.

Exploring Northwest Ohio and the Lake Erie Islands

A true lakefront town, **Toledo** combines natural beauty with local artistry such as glassblowing. Its multicultural mix supports great ethnic eats, interesting architecture, and a host of unusual storefront shops. Just down the coastline the shores of Lake Erie teem with wildlife. The Toledo Mud Hens, a Detroit Tigers farm team, play in the new downtown stadium, **5/3rd Field** (✉ 406 Washington St. ☎ 419/725–4367, WEB www.mudhens.com).The **Toledo Museum of Art** (✉ 2445 Monroe St., at Scottwood Ave., off I–75, ☎ 419/255–8000, WEB www.toledomuseum.org) has a fine collection of European and American paintings, ancient Greek and Egyptian statues, and regionally produced and internationally recognized blown glass.

Vacationland begins at **Port Clinton,** a center for fishing excursions, at the northern base of the Marblehead Peninsula, some 30 mi east of Toledo on Route 2. Port Clinton is also the base for a ferry to South Bass Island's **Put-in-Bay,** a port village with a marina, a grassy lakefront park dotted with small cannons, and a strip of shops, bars, and restaurants, with a vintage wooden merry-go-round. Now a town of wild parties, Put-in-Bay was the site of Commodore Oliver Hazard Perry's naval victory over the British in the War of 1812. From the top of **Perry's Victory and International Peace Memorial,** a single massive Doric column east of downtown, you can see all the way to Canada. From May through September you can hop on a ferry to **Middle Bass Island.** The undeveloped shoreline, glacial grooves (waves in the rock), wetlands, and grasslands—home to several endangered species of plants and animals—are open for exploration.Back on the mainland, at the eastern tip of the peninsula, is **Marblehead,** site of the oldest continuously working lighthouse on Lake Erie. From Marblehead it's a short ferry ride to **Kelleys Island**: Glacial grooves carved during the Ice Age are visible on the north shore, and the south shore has prehistoric Native American pictographs. **Sandusky,** a small port city with lush gardens enlivening its town square, makes a good touring base. It's near the highways and ferries, has many motel rooms, and a few romantic Victorian hideaways. **Cedar Point Amusement Park** (✉ off U.S. 250 N, ☎ 419/627–2350; 🎫 $38) is in the *Guinness Book of Records* for having the most roller coasters in the world (14, and counting), including the new Millennium Force, the tallest and fastest roller coaster in the world. It also has Snake River Falls, the tallest, deepest, and quickest water ride in the world; a water park; and a mile-long sandy beach. The park is open daily in summer and on weekends in September.

Dining and Lodging

The chambers of commerce in Put-in-Bay and on Kelleys Island give advice on lodging, which should be arranged well in advance.

Grand Rapids

$–$$ 🏨 **Mill House.** On the Maumee River and 40 minutes from downtown Toledo, this country-Victorian house was built in 1900 as a working gristmill. One of the four French country–style guest rooms has its own private entrance and whirlpool tub. *✉ 24070 Front St., 43522, ☎ 419/832–6455. 4 rooms. AE, D, MC, V. CP.*

Marblehead

$–$$ 🏨 **Old Stone House Bed & Breakfast.** Victorian antiques fill this Federal-style mansion. *✉ 133 Clemons St., 43440, ☎ 419/798–5922 or 877/798–5922. 13 rooms. D, MC, V. CP.*

Port Clinton

$$–$$$ ★ ✕ **Mon Ami.** Pasta and fish are the specialties at this well-established winery and restaurant, which has a chalet-style dining room with 4-ft-thick stone walls and a patio surrounded by wooden casks. Enjoy live jazz during the summer. ✉ *3845 E. Wine Cellar Rd., off N.E. Catawba Rd./Rte. 53,* ☎ *419/797–4445 or 800/777–4266. AE, MC, V.*

$$ ✕ **Garden at the Lighthouse.** American cuisine is served with casual elegance in the terraced garden of this Victorian house originally built for the lighthouse keeper. ✉ *226 E. Perry St.,* ☎ *419/732–2151. AE, D, DC, MC, V. Closed Sun.–Mon. Sept.–May.*

$–$$$ ✕🏨 **Island House Inn.** The casual dining room of the 110-year-old red-brick hotel has tall windows and serves fresh fish. ✉ *102 Madison St., 43452,* ☎ *419/734–2166 or 800/233–7307. 39 rooms. Restaurant. AE, D, DC, MC, V.*

$ 🏨 **Beach Cliff Lodge.** Unpretentious and handy, the lodge, near the ferry and the Catawba State Park boat ramp, has fish-cleaning services and freezers. ✉ *4189 N.W. Catawba Rd., 43452,* ☎ *419/797–4553,* WEB *www.beach-cliff.com. 8 rooms, 19 cottages. No credit cards.*

Put-in-Bay

$$–$$$ ✕ **Crescent Tavern.** If you're only going to eat one meal in Put-in-Bay, come to this gracious Victorian house for seafood, steak, or pasta. ✉ *198 Delaware Ave.,* ☎ *419/285–4211. D, MC, V. Closed Oct.–Mar.*

$–$$ ✕ **Frosty's.** With a bar and a pool table on one side, and Formica tables on the other, this noisy hangout caters both to singles and families. ✉ *Delaware Ave.,* ☎ *419/285–4741. D, MC, V. Closed Oct.–Mar.*

$–$$ 🏨 **Park Hotel.** Dating from the 1870s, this white-frame hotel has etched glass and a Victorian lobby. It's also smack in the middle of the island revelry, so bring earplugs. ✉ *234 Delaware Ave. (Box 60, 43456),* ☎ *419/285–3581. 26 rooms. AE, MC, V. Closed Oct.–Mar. CP.*

Sandusky

$$–$$$$ 🏨 **Radisson Harbor Inn.** What appears to be a rambling, weathered beach house is actually a big hotel. It's on the property of Cedar Point Amusement Park, connected via a walkway to many restaurants and shops. ✉ *2001 Cleveland Rd., at Cedar Point Causeway, 44870,* ☎ *419/627–2500,* FAX *419/627–0745. 237 rooms. Restaurant, pool, gym. AE, D, DC, MC, V.*

$–$$$$ ★ 🏨 **Hotel Breakers.** Built in 1905 to resemble a French château, with a five-story rotunda, stained glass, and vintage wicker furniture, this is *the* place to stay on the beach at Cedar Point, especially if you can get a turret room. ✉ *Cedar Point Amusement Park (Box 5006, 44871),* ☎ *419/627–2106. 400 rooms. 4 restaurants, pool. D, MC, V.*

$–$$ 🏨 **Wagner's 1844 Inn.** Each of the three guest rooms at this inn a block from downtown has a private bath, canopy beds, and globe lamps. Guests can use the pool table, TV, and travel library. ✉ *230 E. Washington St., 44870,* ☎ *419/626–1726. 3 rooms. D, MC, V. CP.*

Toledo

$–$$ ✕ **Tony Packo's Cafe.** Before Max Klinger ever mentioned it on *M*A*S*H*, Tony Packo's was famous for its Tiffany lamps and Hungarian hot dogs. (The buns are imprinted with the restaurant's logo, lest you forget where you are.) ✉ *1902 Front St.,* ☎ *419/691–6054. AE, D, MC, V.*

$–$$$ 🏨 **Wyndham Hotel.** The only downtown hotel right on the Maumee River, the Wyndham is also convenient for business travelers: it's connected by indoor walkways to several office buildings and is two blocks from the SeaGate Convention Centre. ✉ *2 SeaGate/Summit St., 43604,* ☎ *419/241–1411,* FAX *419/241–8161,* WEB *www.wyndham.com/Toledo. 241 rooms. Restaurant, pool, gym. AE, D, DC, MC, V.*

Motels

The majority of area motels are in and around Sandusky, on the roads to Cedar Point.

🏨 **Best Western Resort Inn** (✉ 1530 Cleveland Rd., Sandusky 44870, ☎ 419/625–9234, 800/528–1234), 106 rooms; restaurant, pool; *$$–$$$*. 🏨 **Comfort Inn** (✉ 11020 U.S. 250, Milan Rd., Milan 44846, ☎ 419/499–4681), 103 rooms; pool; *$$–$$$*.

Outdoor Activities and Sports

Beaches and Water Sports

The best Lake Erie beach is at **East Harbor State Park,** off Route 163 on Marblehead Peninsula. **Cedar Point Amusement Park** also has good swimming. You can rent sailboats and take sailing lessons from **Adventure Plus Yacht Charters and Sailing** (1027 Columbus Ave., at the Sandusky Harbor Marina, ☎ 419/625–5000).

Fishing

The western Lake Erie Basin is known as the Walleye Capital of the World. The Division of Wildlife provides a recorded message, updated weekly, about the latest fishing conditions at ☎ 888/466–5347. In addition to providing information on walleye, the hot line reports on smallmouth bass and Lake Erie perch. Nonresident fishing licenses are sold at bait shops, or contact the **Division of Wildlife** (☎ 419/625–8062).The breakwater in Port Clinton and the pier at Catawba Point are both good fishing areas. Charter and walk-on fishing boats leave from **Fisherman's Wharf** in Port Clinton (☎ 419/734–0488). You don't need a boat to satisfy your fishing urge. Drop a fishing line from the public fishing pier at the **Battery Park Marina** at Sandusky Water and Meigs streets (☎ 419/625–6142).

Northwest Ohio and the Lake Erie Islands Essentials

AIR TRAVEL

Griffing Island Airlines out of Port Clinton Airport and Griffing Flying Service, out of Griffing–Sandusky Airport, fly to the Lake Erie Islands.

➤ AIRLINES AND CONTACTS: **Griffing Flying Service** (☎ 419/626–5161). **Griffing Island Airlines** (☎ 419/734–3149).

AIRPORTS

Toledo Express Airport is served by six airlines, Cleveland Hopkins Airport by major airlines and several commuter lines. Port Clinton Airport and Griffing–Sandusky Airport service the Lake Erie Islands.

➤ AIRPORT INFORMATION: **Griffing–Sandusky Airport** (✉ 3115 Cleveland Rd., east of Sandusky,, ☎ 419/626–5161). **Port Clinton Airport** (✉ 3255 E. State Rand Dr., ☎ 419/734–3149). **Toledo Express Airport** (✉ State Rte. 2 W, ☎ 419/865–2351).

BOAT AND FERRY TRAVEL

Ferries serve the Lake Erie islands from May through October. Put-in-Bay Jet Express, from Port Clinton to Put-in-Bay, takes passengers and bicycles only and has late-night service. Starting in March, Miller Boat Line takes passengers and cars (reservations required) from Catawba to Lime Kiln Dock (on the opposite side of South Bass Island from Put-in-Bay) and to Middle Bass Island. Neuman's Kelleys Island Ferry takes passengers from Marblehead to Kelleys Island.

➤ BOAT AND FERRY TRAVEL INFORMATION: **Miller Boat Line** (☎ 419/285–2421, 800/500–2421, WEB www.millerferry.com). **Neuman's Kelleys Island Ferry** (☎ 419/798–5800 or 800/876–1907, WEB www.neumanferry.com). **Put-in-Bay Jet Express** (☎ 800/245–1538, WEB www.jet-express.com).

BUS TRAVEL

Greyhound has national service from Toledo. Toledo Area Regional Transit Authority covers Toledo and its suburbs.

➤ Bus Information: **Greyhound** (✉ 811 Jefferson Ave., ☎ 800/231–2222). **Toledo Area Regional Transit Authority** (TARTA; ☎ 419/243–1241).

CAR TRAVEL

The Ohio Turnpike (I–80/90) runs between 5 and 10 mi south of the Lake Erie shoreline. For Toledo take Exit 4 (I–75) or Exit 5 (U.S. 280); for Port Clinton, Exit 6 (Route 53); for Sandusky, Exit 7 (U.S. 250). Toledo is on I–75. Route 2 hugs the lake between Toledo and Sandusky; Route 269 loops out to Marblehead.

TRAIN TRAVEL

Amtrak stops in Toledo and Sandusky.

➤ Train Information: **Amtrak** (☎ 800/872–7245).

VISITOR INFORMATION

For information on Erie County, which covers Cedar Point, Kelleys Island, and Sandusky, contact the Erie County Visitors Bureau in Sandusky. The Ottawa County Visitors Bureau in Port Clinton covers Catawba, Lakeside, Marblehead, Port Clinton, Oak Harbor, and Put-in-Bay.

➤ Tourist Information: **Erie County Visitors Bureau** (✉ 4424 Milan Rd., Suite A, Sandusky 44870, ☎ 419/625–2984 or 800/255–3743, WEB www.buckeyenorth.com). **Greater Toledo Convention and Visitors Bureau** (✉ SeaGate Convention Center, 401 Jefferson Ave., 2nd floor, 43604, ☎ 419/321–6404 or 800/243–4667, WEB www.toledoohionow.com). **Kelleys Island Chamber of Commerce** (✉ Box 783, 43438, ☎ 419/746–2360). **Ottawa County Visitors Bureau** (✉ 109 Madison St., Port Clinton 43452, ☎ 419/734–4386 or 800/441–1271, WEB www.lake-erie.com). **Put-in-Bay Chamber of Commerce** (✉ Box 250, 43456, ☎ 419/285–2832, WEB www.put-in-bay.com).

CLEVELAND

In recent years Cleveland has emerged with a new cultural identity. Major attractions such as the Rock and Roll Hall of Fame and Museum, the Great Lakes Science Center, and the Gateway sports venues have been the main catalysts, along with the world-class orchestra, stunning art museum, fully restored downtown Theater district, and blooming gardens on the east side of town. Neighborhoods such as the Flats, the Warehouse District, the Gateway district, and Northcoast Harbor buzz with restaurants, shops, and nightclubs.

Exploring Cleveland

Begin your tour at **Terminal Tower,** the city's central landmark. **Tower City Center,** an office and shopping complex, includes the shops of the Avenue. Pick up a copy of "Walks," a brochure outlining some popular Cleveland walking tours, at the **visitor information center** inside the entrance to Tower City Center. The **Old Arcade,** now home to the Hyatt Regency, is filled with specialty shops on the first two floors and runs between Superior and Euclid avenues, a short block east of Public Square. Built in 1890, this is still downtown's most architecturally significant building. Like a nave without a cathedral, it rises five stories, with brass railings, ironwork, walkways, and a skylight.

South of Public Square on Ontario Street is **Gund Arena** (✉ 1 Center Court, ☎ 216/420–2000), a sports venue that hosts basketball, hockey,

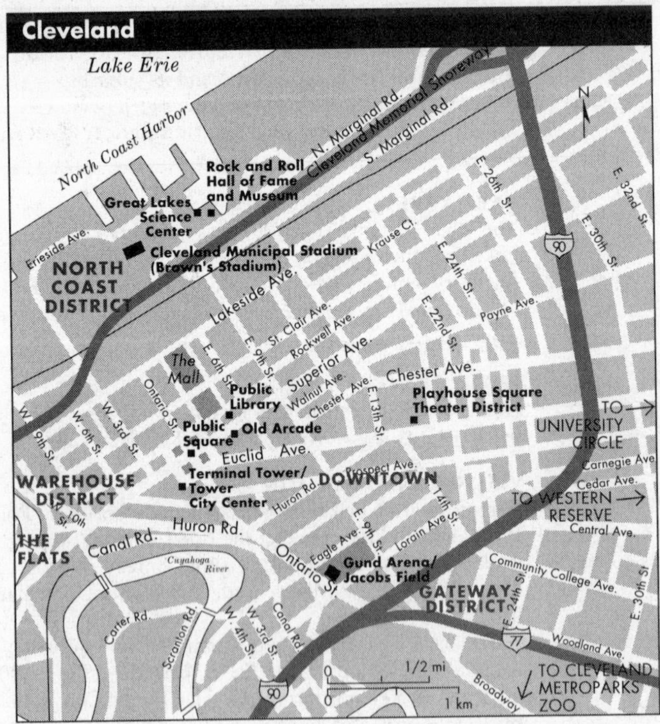

indoor football, concerts, and other events. Next to the arena is **Jacobs Field** (✉ 2401 Ontario St., ☎ 216/420–4200), a trapezoid-shape baseball park that looks at once old-fashioned and brand new.

For a fabulous view of the lake, take East 9th Street to North Coast Harbor, formerly the East 9th Street Pier. The **Rock and Roll Hall of Fame and Museum** (✉ 1 Key Plaza, ☎ 216/781–7625, WEB www.rockhall.com; 🎫 $15) has more than 55 high- and low-tech exhibits including interactive kiosks that provide a video and sound exploration of performers' contributions to the rock genre, and the Sun recording studio, where Elvis Presley, Carl Perkins, and Roy Orbison made their first records. Stage costumes that once belonged to Chuck Berry and Iggy Pop, handwritten lyrics by Jimi Hendrix, Janis Joplin's Porsche, and a number of thought-provoking films are among the museum's holdings. **The Great Lakes Science Center** (✉ 601 Erieside, ☎ 216/694–2000, WEB www.glsc.org; 🎫 $7.95) focuses on the environment and technology. The 165,000-square-ft museum has hands-on exhibits and a 324-seat Omnimax Theater. From June through September, the *Goodtime III* (☎ 216/861–5110) gives sightseeing tours on the Cuyahoga River and short lake cruises.

University Circle, reached by rapid transit or a 15-minute drive from downtown, has more than 50 cultural institutions. The centerpiece of University Circle is the **Cleveland Museum of Art** (✉ 11150 E. Blvd., ☎ 216/421–7340, WEB www.cma-oh.org; 🎫 free), a white-marble temple among spring-flowering trees and reflected in a lagoon. The museum (closed Monday) is renowned for its medieval European collection, Egyptian art, and European and American paintings. The **Museum of Natural History** (✉ 1 Wade Oval Dr., ☎ 216/231–4600, WEB www.cmnh.org; 🎫 $6.50) has an observatory and planetarium. The **Children's Museum** (✉ 10730 Euclid Ave., ☎ 216/791–7114, WEB www.museum4kids.com; 🎫 $5) has interactive exhibits on topics such as geography, bridge-building, climate, and weather. Juno, the see-through woman, and a remodeled 18-ft-high tooth are among the favorite permanent exhibits at the **Health Museum** (✉ 8911 Euclid Ave., ☎ 216/231–5010, WEB www.healthmuseum.org; 🎟 $5); traveling exhibits focus on current health issues and are designed to be fun for kids. The **Western Reserve Historical Society** (✉ 10825 East Blvd., ☎ 216/721–5722, WEB www.wrhs.org; 🎟 $7.50), closed Monday, has an extensive Napoleonic collection, and just about every old car you'd want to see is in the **Crawford Auto-Aviation Museum.** Also in University Circle is **Severance Hall,** home of the Cleveland Orchestra, with the city's most beautiful Art Deco interior.

Parks, Gardens, and Zoos

Cleveland Metroparks Zoo and Rainforest (✉ Brookside Park Dr. off W. 25th St., ☎ 216/661–6500, WEB www.clemetzoo.com; 🎟 $8) has tropical plants and animals in a simulated rain-forest environment, as well as an excellent outdoor zoo. At **Edgewater Park,** west of downtown, you can swim while enjoying a startlingly close-up view of downtown. The park also has a fishing pier, bait shop, fitness course, playgrounds, and picnic facilities. The stiff wind off the lake attracts kite flyers, boomerang enthusiasts, windsurfers, and the occasional hang glider. Drive through the **Cleveland Cultural Gardens** (✉ Martin Luther King Blvd., University Circle, north of Chester Ave. and south of I–90, ☎ 216/664–2220) to see gardens representing more than 20 nationalities. The **Rockefeller Park Greenhouse** (✉ 750 E. 88th St., ☎ 216/664–3103), the oldest civic horticultural center in the country, has seasonal flower and plant exhibits indoors; outside you'll find a Japanese garden, a formal English garden, and a talking garden for people with vision impairments. In Aurora, 30 mi southeast of Cleveland, **Six Flags World of Adventure** (✉ 1060 N. Aurora Rd., Aurora, ☎ 330/562–8303, WEB www.sixflags.com; 🎟 $39.99 adults, $19.99 children) is a 750-acre family-friendly park with wild rides, a water park, and sea-life park; it is closed weekdays in September and October and closed all week November–May.

Dining

Ethnic food reigns in Cleveland, whether it's a spicy burrito or Polish kielbasa smothered with Cleveland's famous Stadium Mustard. There are restaurant rows in the Flats, the Warehouse District, the area around Gund Arena and Jacobs Field, Little Italy, and on Coventry Road in Cleveland Heights.

$$$–$$$$ ✕ **Lola Bistro & Wine Bar.** Chef-owner Michael Simon has received national attention from food and wine critics for the creations he describes as "urban comfort food." Best-sellers on the winter menu are seafood pierogi, and macaroni-and-cheese with fresh rosemary, goat cheese, and roasted chicken. Fish and game are first-rate; desserts are out of this world. ✉ *900 Literary Rd., Tremont,* ☎ *216/771–5652. Reservations essential. AE, D, DC, MC, V.*

$$$–$$$$ ✕ **Sans Souci.** Sophisticated seafood dishes and hearty French Provençal fare are served in a comfortably elegant dining room overlooking Public Square. ✉ *24 Public Sq.,* ☎ *216/696–5600. Reservations essential. AE, D, DC, MC, V.*

$$$ ★ ✕ **Moxie.** In the upscale town of Beachwood, 20 minutes southeast of downtown Cleveland by car, this trendy eatery is a must. It's unassuming from the outside, but once you step into the large, bright room and taste the creatively prepared American fare with a nouvelle twist, you'll understand why they named it Moxie. ✉ *3355 Richmond Rd., off I–271, Beachwood,* ☎ *216/831–5599. AE, D, MC, V.*

$$–$$$ ✕ **La Dolce Vita.** In addition to offering trendy Italian food, this neighborhood restaurant has an eclectic schedule of musicians that includes strolling mariachis and live opera performers. On Monday night there's an eight-course meal; on other days, specials include veal, seafood, and risotto dishes. ✉ *12112 Mayfield Rd.,* ☎ *216/721–8155. Reservations essential Mon. MC, V.*

$$–$$$ ✕ **Watermark.** In a converted warehouse on the banks of the busy Cuyahoga River in Cleveland's Flats district, try seafood specialties and local products like Ohio Italian chicken sausage. ✉ *1250 Old River Rd.,* ☎ *216/241–1600. AE, D, DC, MC, V.*

$$ ✕ **The Palazzo.** The third generation of the original owners prepare northern Italian cuisine in this romantic hideaway. Whether turning out updated versions of her recipes or new dishes inspired by annual trips back to Italy, they do their grandma proud. ✉ *10031 Detroit Ave.,* ☎ *216/651–3900. AE, D, MC, V. Closed Sun.–Mon.*

$–$$ ✕ **Luchita's.** With great authentic Mexican food, generous portions, good margaritas, and friendly service, it's no wonder this restaurant with two locations is jammed on the weekends. The menu changes every three months. ✉ *3456 W. 117th St.,* ☎ *216/252–1169;* ✉ *13112 Shaker Sq.,* ☎ *216/561–8537. AE, MC, V. Closed Mon.*

$–$$ ✕ **Nate's Deli and Restaurant.** Deli fare, as well as Middle Eastern and vegetarian specialties, is served at this breakfast and lunch spot on the West Side. The creamy hummus may be the best in town. ✉ *1923 W. 25th St.,* ☎ *216/696–7529. No credit cards. Closed Sun. No dinner.*

$–$$ ✕ **Tommy's.** A vegetarian institution on Coventry Road, Tommy's serves hefty salads and sandwiches and embarrassingly large but delicious milk shakes made with Cleveland's own Pierre's ice cream. ✉ *1824 Coventry Rd., Cleveland Heights,* ☎ *216/321–7757. D, MC, V.*

Lodging

Many downtown hotels have weekend packages; those in the suburbs have lower weekday rates.

$$$$ ★ **Ritz-Carlton.** The city's only four-star hotel is filled with antiques and original 18th-century art. The Century restaurant has a railroad theme and serves American fare with a flair. ✉ *1515 W. 3rd St., 44113,* ☎ *216/623–1300,* FAX *216/623–0515,* WEB *www.ritzcarlton.com. 208 rooms. Restaurant, pool, gym. AE, D, DC, MC, V.*

$$$–$$$$ **Walden Country Inn and Stables.** The all-suites bed-and-breakfast inn, surrounded by 1,000 acres of country club and meadows, provides convenient access to Six Flags Worlds of Adventure. ✉ *1119 Aurora Hudson Rd., at I–271, Aurora 44146,* ☎ *330/562–5508 or 888/808–5003,* FAX *330/562–8001,* WEB *www.waldenco.com/thecountryinn.html. 25 suites. Restaurant, pool, golf. AE, D, DC, MC, V.*

$$–$$$$ **Embassy Suites Hotel Cleveland–Downtown.** The lobby of this all-suites hotel feels like an old-style ocean liner. Some rooms have kitchens. ✉ *1701 E. 12th St., 44114,* ☎ *216/523–8000,* FAX *216/523–1698. 283 suites. Restaurant, pool, health club. AE, D, DC, MC, V.*

$$–$$$$ **Renaissance Cleveland Hotel.** The city's original grand hotel has a lobby with an ornate Carrara marble fountain. Guest rooms have period furniture and spacious marble bathrooms. ✉ *24 Public Sq., 44113,* ☎ *216/696–5600,* FAX *216/696–0432. 491 rooms. 2 restaurants, pool, health club. AE, D, DC, MC, V.*

$–$$$$ **Mario's International Spa and Hotel Aurora.** A charming country getaway, Mario's is full of antiques. The restaurant, open to the public, has a private area for robe-clad spa diners. Meals are wholesome and tasty, ranging from Roman pizza to six-course northern Italian dinners. ✉ *35 E. Garfield Rd. (Rtes. 82 and 306), Aurora 44202,* ☎ *330/*

562–9171, FAX *330/562–2386,* WEB *www.marios-spa.com/aurora.htm. 15 rooms. Restaurant, health club. AE, D, DC, MC, V.*

$$$ ☐ **Cleveland Marriott Key Center.** Attached to Key Tower, the tallest building in Cleveland, this hotel faces the historic Mall "C" and abuts Public Square. Plush accommodations have fantastic views of Lake Erie and the downtown skyline. ✉ *127 Public Sq., 44114,* ☎ *216/696–9200,* FAX *216/696–0966,. 400 rooms. Restaurant, gym. AE, D, DC, MC, V.*

$$$ ☐ **Wyndham Cleveland at Playhouse Square.** The 14 stories of the Wyndham overlook the bright lights of the vibrant theater district. The hotel's airy, modern lobby is flanked by Winsor's, an exceptional restaurant and bar. ✉ *1260 Euclid Ave., 44106,* ☎ *216/615–7500,* FAX *216/231–3329,* WEB *www.wyndham.com/PlayhouseSquare. 205 rooms. 3 restaurants, pool, gym. AE, D, DC, MC, V.*

$–$$$ ☐ **Holiday Inn–Lakeshore.** Across from Burke Lakefront Airport and convenient to the train station, the Rock and Roll Hall of Fame and Museum, and the Great Lakes Science Center, this hotel has lake views and an unbeatable location. ✉ *1111 Lakeside, 44114,* ☎ *216/241–5100,* FAX *216/241–5437. 380 rooms. Restaurant, pool, gym. AE, D, DC, MC, V.*

$$ ☐ **Baricelli Inn.** This simple European-style brownstone mansion turned bed-and-breakfast is convenient to University Circle. The dining room (closed Sunday) serves contemporary European and American dinners. ✉ *2203 Cornell Rd., 44106,* ☎ *216/791–6500,* FAX *216/791–9131. 7 rooms. Restaurant. AE, DC, MC, V. CP.*

$$ ☐ **Sheraton Cleveland City Centre Hotel.** Geared toward business travelers, this hotel has 15 meeting rooms and ample work space in all guest rooms. ✉ *777 St. Clair Ave., 44114,* ☎ *216/771–7600; 800/321–1090 in Ohio,* FAX *216/566–0736. 470 rooms. Restaurant, health club. AE, D, DC, MC, V.*

$ ☐ **Brooklyn Family YMCA.** While the Y itself is family oriented, the bare-bones single rooms are for men only and are available on a first-come, first-served basis. ✉ *3881 Pearl Rd., 44109,* ☎ *216/749–2355. 69 rooms. Pool, gym. D, MC, V.*

Motels

Motels are concentrated around the Berea–Middleburg Heights exit off I–71 (near the airport), the Rockside Road/Brecksville exit off I–77, and the Chagrin Boulevard/Beachwood exit off I–271. At those closer to Aurora, rates are higher in summer.

☐ **Six Flag Woodlands Hotel** (✉ 800 N. Aurora Rd., Aurora 44202, ☎ 330/562–9151 or 800/877–7849), 144 rooms; restaurant, pool, gym; *$$$–$$$$.* ☐ **Radisson Inn Beachwood** (✉ 26300 Chagrin Blvd., Beachwood 44122, ☎ 330/831–5150 or 800/221–2222), 196 rooms; restaurant, pool, gym; *$$$.* ☐ **Day's Inn Airport** (✉ 16161 Brook Park Rd., 44142, ☎ 216/267–5100, 800/446–4656, FAX 216/267–2428), 158 rooms; restaurant, 2 pools; *$.* ☐ **La Siesta Motel** (✉ 8300 Pearl Rd., Strongsville 44136, ☎ 440/234–4488), 38 rooms; *$.*

Nightlife and the Arts

Nightlife

Nightlife is concentrated on both banks of the Flats—where the crowd is young and into everything from bar-hopping to live music—as well as in the more mature Warehouse District.At the south end of the Flats, the **Powerhouse** is a beautifully restored building that was originally a power station for Cleveland's trolley cars; today it houses the Improv Comedy Club (☎ 216/696–4677) and other shops and restaurants. For a look at the Flats the way it used to be—a blue-collar haven—stop in at the **Harbor Inn** bar (✉ 1219 Main Ave., ☎ 216/241–

3232). At **Liquid Café & Bar** (✉ 1212 W. 6th St., ☎ 216/479–7717) patrons sit in comfy chairs playing Scrabble and other board games. The rest of the Warehouse district is lined with dance clubs and restaurants. Across the river in Ohio City, Market Avenue bustles with sidewalk cafés in the summer. In the center of the action is the **Great Lakes Brewing Company** (✉ 2516 Market Ave., ☎ 216/771–4404). **Market Avenue Wine Bar** (✉ 2524 Main Ave., ☎ 216/696–9463) has a brilliant wine list and simple appetizers.

The Arts

Playhouse Square Center (✉ 1501 Euclid Ave., at E. 17th St., ☎ 216/771–4444, WEB www.playhousesquare.com) is home to the Cleveland Ballet, Cleveland Opera, and the Great Lakes Theater Festival.The **Cleveland Play House** (✉ 8500 Euclid Ave., ☎ 216/795–7000, WEB www.clevelandplayhouse.com) is America's first permanently established professional theatre company. **Karamu House** (✉ 2355 E. 89th St., at Quincy Ave., ☎ 216/795–7070, WEB www.karamu.com) is the nation's oldest African-American cultural institution. **Severance Hall** (✉ 11001 Euclid Ave., ☎ 216/231–1111 or 800/686–1141, WEB www.clevelandorch.com) is home to the Cleveland Orchestra, except in summer, when the orchestra performs in a pastoral outdoor shed, Blossom Music Center (☎ 330/920–8040), between Cleveland and Akron. Tickets to many events are sold through **TicketMaster** (☎ 216/241–5555). **Advantix** (☎ 216/241–6000) is an alternate source for event tickets.

Spectator Sports

Baseball: For a dose of Major League baseball catch the **Cleveland Indians** (✉ Jacobs Field, 2401 Ontario St., at Carnegie Ave., ☎ 216/420–4200). **Basketball:** Cleveland's NBA franchise is the **Cavaliers** (✉ Gund Arena, Ontario St. at Huron Rd., ☎ 216/420–2000). **Football:** Suit up in your brown, orange, and white and see the **Cleveland Browns** (✉ Municipal Stadium, 1085 W. 3rd St., ☎ 216/891–5000).

Shopping

The **Galleria** (✉ 1301 E. 9th St., ☎ 216/621–9999) is one of Cleveland's two glitzy downtown malls; the **Avenue** (✉ Tower City Center, ☎ 216/623–4750), with views of the river, is the other. The **West Side Market** (✉ corner of W. 25th St. and Lorain Rd., ☎ 216/664–3386), the world's largest indoor-outdoor farmers' market, sells freshly baked breads, fruit picked that morning, and perhaps the sharpest cheddar cheese you've ever eaten.

Cleveland Essentials

AIRPORTS AND TRANSFERS

Cleveland Hopkins International Airport, 10 mi southwest of downtown, is served by major airlines and several commuter lines.

➤ AIRPORT INFORMATION: Cleveland Hopkins International Airport (☎ 216/265–6030).

AIRPORT TRANSFER

From the airport, the Rapid Transit Authority rail system takes 20 minutes to Public Square and costs $1.50. A taxi takes twice as long and costs about $20.

➤ TAXIS AND SHUTTLES: Rapid Transit Authority (☎ 216/566–5100).

BUS TRAVEL

➤ BUS INFORMATION: Greyhound (✉ E. 15th St. and Chester Ave., ☎ 800/231–2222).

CAR TRAVEL

I–90 runs east–west through downtown Cleveland. I–71 and I–77 come up from the south. Driving from the east on the Ohio Turnpike (I–80), take Exit 10 to I–71 N.

TRAIN TRAVEL

➤ TRAIN INFORMATION: **Amtrak** (✉ 200 Memorial Shoreway NE, ☎ 800/872–7245).

TRANSPORTATION AROUND CLEVELAND

The RTA rapid-transit system efficiently bridges east and west, with Tower City as its hub. RTA buses travel from Public Square on five downtown loop routes. A light-rail system, the Waterfront Line, links Tower City with the Flats entertainment district, Municipal Stadium, the Rock and Roll Hall of Fame and Museum, the Great Lakes Science Center, downtown shopping, and municipal parking lots.

VISITOR INFORMATION

➤ TOURIST INFORMATION: **Cleveland Convention and Visitors Bureau, Visitor Information Center** (✉ 50 Public Sq., Suite 3100, ☎ 216/621–4110 or 800/321–1004).

ELSEWHERE IN OHIO

Akron

What to See and Do

Akron is about 25 mi south of Cleveland, off I–77. The **Akron/Summit Convention and Visitors Bureau** (✉ 77 E. Mill St., ☎ 330/374–7560 or 800/245–4254, WEB www.visitakron-summit.org) has information on attractions and events around the Rubber City, which began as one of the first canal towns on the Ohio & Erie Canal and still is home to nearly 1,500 of the country's most important manufacturers. **National Inventors Hall of Fame** (✉ 221 S. Broadway, at University Ave., ☎ 330/762–4463 or 800/968–4332, WEB www.invent.org; 🎫 $7.50) honors famous inventors and inventions in a striking museum in downtown Akron. In the spirit of encouraging future inventors, the museum has one room full of computers, which you're invited to play with and even disassemble.

Dining and Lodging

$$$–$$$$ ✕ **Inn at Turner's Mill.** Just outside of Akron, this country cove is cozy and inviting, with a fireplace and a straightforward menu of midwestern game and fresh vegetables. There's live jazz on weekends. ✉ *36 E. Streetsborough Rd., Hudson,* ☎ *330/656–2949. AE, D, MC, V.*

$–$$ ✕ **Luigi's.** Come here for crisp-crust pizza, piping-hot pasta, and red wine served in carafes. A miniature big band plays above the entranceway when you put a nickel in the jukebox. ✉ *105 N. Main St.,* ☎ *330/253–2999,* FAX *330/762–9140. No credit cards.*

$$–$$$$ ★ 🏨 **Akron Crowne Plaza at Quaker Square.** Connected to the Quaker Square retail complex and across the street from the convention center, this hotel on the National Register of Historic Places is actually built from mills and 19th-century grain silos. Each round room takes the shape of the silo and retains the coarse texture of the original walls. ✉ *135 S. Broadway, Akron 44308,* ☎ *330/253–5970,* FAX *330/253–7021,* WEB *www.quakersquare.com/sleep1.htm. 173 rooms. 2 restaurants, pool. AE, D, DC, MC, V.*

$ 🏨 **Comfort Inn–Akron West.** Some rooms in this standard hotel have whirlpool tubs. ✉ *130 Montrose West Ave. 44321,* ☎ *330/666–5050,*

FAX *330/668–2550,* WEB *www.comfortinnakron.com. 132 rooms. Pool. AE, D, DC, MC, V.*

Canton

What to See and Do

Canton is about 50 mi south of Cleveland, off I–77. The **Canton/Stark County Convention & Visitors Bureau** (✉ 229 Wells Ave. NW, Canton 44703, ☎ 330/454–1439 or 800/533–4302, WEB www.visitcantonohio.com) maintains an information center along the approach road to the Pro Football Hall of Fame. The **Pro Football Hall of Fame** (✉ 2121 George Halas Dr. NW, Fulton Rd. exit off I–77 and U.S. 62, ☎ 330/456–8207, WEB www.profootballhof.com; 🎫 $12) has a dome shaped like a football in kickoff position. Two enshrinement halls are the serious attraction, but displays include a chronology of the game, mementos of the great players, and video replays showing great moments in football.

Dining and Lodging

$$$–$$$$ ✕ **Bender's Tavern.** Jerry Jacob has fresh ingredients flown in for his top-quality American-cuisine preparations. The turn-of-the-20th-century barn and livery has been in the Jacob family for more than 60 years and is still going strong. ✉ *137 Court Ave. SW, Canton,* ☎ *330/453–8424. MC, V.*

$$–$$$ ✕ **Cité Grille.** The friendly, trendy waitstaff sets a brisk pace for fun and smart contemporary American food. ✉ *6041 Whipple Ave. NW, North Canton,* ☎ *330/494–6758,* FAX *330/494–6761. AE, MC, V.*

$–$$$$ 🏨 **Four Points by Sheraton at Belden Village.** You can try your hand at a golf simulator at this hotel in Canton's shopping district. A free shuttle takes guests to the Hall of Fame. ✉ *4375 Metro Circle NW, Canton 44720,* ☎ *330/494–6494,* FAX *330/494–7129. 152 rooms. Restaurant, pool. AE, D, DC, MC, V.*

$–$$ 🏨 **Canton Hilton.** Rooms are bright and sunny at this hotel near the Pro Football Hall of Fame and shopping centers. ✉ *320 Market Ave. S, 44702,* ☎ *330/454–5000,* FAX *330/454–5090. 170 rooms. Restaurant, pool. AE, D, DC, MC, V.*

Dayton

What to See and Do

Aviation is central to the history of Dayton. The **Dayton/Montgomery County Convention and Visitors Bureau** (✉ 1 Chamber Plaza, Suite A, 5th and Main Sts., 45409, ☎ 937/226–8212 or 800/221–8235, WEB www.daytoncvb.com) publishes a helpful visitors' guide and operates an information center at the United States Air Force Museum.The **Dayton Aviation Heritage National Historical Park** (☎ 937/225–7705, WEB www.nps.gov/daav) includes the field where Dayton natives Orville and Wilbur Wright first practiced flying, as well as the **Wright Cycle Shop** (✉ 22 S. Williams St.), the **John W. Berry Sr. Wright Brothers Aviation Center** (✉ Carillon Historical Park), and the **Dunbar House State Memorial** (✉ 219 N. Paul Laurence Dunbar St.), home of a Wright Brothers associate, noted African-American poet Paul Laurence Dunbar. The **United States Air Force Museum** (✉ Wright-Patterson Air Force Base, Gate 28-B, Springfield Pike, ☎ 937/255–3286, WEB www.wpafb.af.mil/museum; 🎫 free), an internationally known attraction, explains the story of flight, from Icarus to the space age and features more than 300 aircraft including *Air Force One* and *Apollo 15*. The **IMAX Theater** shows flight-related films several times daily (☎ 937/253–4629; 🎫 $6). Also here are museum shops, a café, and picnic tables. Take I–75 to the Route 4/Harshman Road exit.Southeast of Dayton, the **National Afro-American Museum**

and Cultural Center is one of the largest African-American museums in the United States—and the only such museum chartered by Congress. Among its exhibits exploring history and art is the permanent "From Victory to Freedom," which examines black politics from the 1940s through the '60s. To get here, take U.S. 35 to Route 42. The museum is 1 mi west of State Route 42 N, adjacent to Central State University. ✉ *1350 Brush Row Rd., Wilberforce 45384,* ☎ *937/376–4944 or 800/255–4478,* WEB *www.ohiohistory.org/places/afroam.* 🎫 *$4. Closed Mon.*

Dining and Lodging

$$–$$$ ✕ **Jay's Seafood.** In the historic Oregon District, house specialties include all manner of seafood. A glimpse of the 1882 Honduras mahogany bar, carved from 5,400 pounds of wood, is as rewarding as the food. Jay's is only open for dinner. ✉ *225 E. 6th St., Dayton,* ☎ *937/222–2892. AE, MC, V. No lunch.*

$–$$ ✕ **Pine Club.** Fresh panfried trout, extra-thick lamb chops, and stewed tomatoes are the house specialties in this aptly named restaurant with pine-paneled walls and a large bar in the center. ✉ *1926 Brown St.,* ☎ *937/228–7463. No credit cards. Closed Sun. No lunch.*

$$–$$$ ✕🏨 **Crowne Plaza.** The big plush chairs in the rooms will make you feel right at home. From the rooftop restaurant you can often see military jets cruising to the nearby air force base. ✉ *5th and Jefferson Sts., 45402,* ☎ *937/224–0800,* FAX *937/224–1231. 293 rooms. Restaurant, pool. AE, D, DC, MC, V.*

$ 🏨 **Signature Inn.** Guests receive discounts at local eateries, shops, and fitness centers. Some rooms are equipped with Jacuzzis. ✉ *250 Byers Rd., Miamisburg 45342,* ☎ *937/865–0077,* FAX *937/865–0077. 125 rooms. Pool. AE, D, DC, MC, V. CP.*

Dayton Essentials

AIRPORTS

➤ DAYTON INTERNATIONAL AIRPORT: (☎ 937/454–8200 or 877/359–3291) is served by several major carriers and commuter lines.

CAR TRAVEL

Dayton is 54 mi north of Cincinnati on I–75, below the interchange with I–70.

Wapakoneta

What to See and Do

★ Ohio is a leading producer of astronauts. At the **Neil Armstrong Air and Space Museum** (✉ I–75 Exit 111, ☎ 419/738–8811 or 800/860–0142, WEB www.ohiohistory.org/places/armstron; 🎫 $5), you can begin to identify with these explorers. The museum is off I–75, halfway between Cincinnati and Toledo (about an hour from either), in Wapakoneta, Neil Armstrong's hometown.

OKLAHOMA

Updated by Karen Gibson

Capital	Oklahoma City
Population	3,450,654
Motto	Labor Conquers All Things
State Bird	Scissor-tailed flycatcher
State Flower	Mistletoe
Postal Abbreviation	OK

Statewide Visitor Information

Oklahoma Tourism and Recreation Department (✉ 15 N. Robinson Ave. [Box 60789, Oklahoma City 73146-0789], ☎ 405/521–2409 or 800/652–6552, WEB www.travelok.com). **State Historical Society** (✉ 2100 N. Lincoln Blvd., Oklahoma City 73105, ☎ 405/521–2491).

Scenic Drives

State Highway 49 traverses the prairies and granite peaks of the Wichita Mountains National Wildlife Refuge. **Route 66,** the road of nostalgia, cruises through Oklahoma, treating travelers to unique historical roadside attractions such as Arcadia's Round Barn and the Giant Blue Whale in Catoosa while surrounded by a backdrop of unblemished scenery. **State Highway 1,** also called the Talimena Scenic Byway, was built for the breathtaking view winding through the Winding Stair Mountains in the Ouachita National Forest. It is known as a prime location for colorful fall foliage yet provides scenic vistas during any season.

National and State Parks

National Park

Mineral and freshwater springs are the main attraction at the **Chickasaw National Recreation Area** (✉ off I–35, Sulphur [Box 201, 73086], ☎ 580/622–3165), in southern Oklahoma. In southeastern Oklahoma, **Ouachita National Forest** (✉ east of State Hwy. 271 [HC 63, Box 5184, Heavener 74939], ☎ 918/653–2991, WEB www.fs.fed.us/oonf/ouachita) is a scenic region of small mountain ranges and dense forests.

State Parks

Oklahoma has 51 state parks, and all but 2 have camping facilities. Information on all the state's parks, resorts, and golf courses can be found at the Web site for **Oklahoma Parks, Lakes & Golf** (WEB www.touroklahoma.com). **Alabaster Caverns State Park** (✉ State Hwy. 50 [Rte. 1, Box 32, Freedom 73842], ☎ 580/621–3381), 6 mi south of Freedom, is one of the largest gypsum caves in the world. Smaller caves attract spelunkers. Rangers hold bat tours to study the flying mammals that frequent the area. **Black Mesa State Park** (✉ Kenton [HCR1, Box 8, 73946], ☎ 580/426–2222), 27 mi northwest of Boise City on State Highway 325, is the highest point in Oklahoma, at 4,973 ft, and is located deep in the panhandle. A hike to the top awards climbers views into neighboring states Colorado, Kansas, and Texas.

Robbers Cave State Park (✉ State Hwy. 2 [Box 9, Wilburton 74578], ☎ 918/465–2565), 5 mi north of town, is famous for hiding notorious outlaws like Jesse James and Belle Starr from federal marshals during the latter 19th century. Today, Robbers Cave is a popular place for hiking and horseback riding. **Lake Murray Resort Park** (✉ 3310 S. Lake Murray Dr., No. 12A, Ardmore 73401, ☎ 405/223–4044), Oklahoma's first and largest state park, is midway between Oklahoma City and Dallas, Texas. The crystal-blue lake is well suited for swimming, fishing, boating, and scuba diving. **Roman Nose Resort** (✉ State Hwy. 8 [Rte. 1, Watonga 73772], ☎ 580/623–4215), 7 mi north of town, is an oasis in the midst of the western Oklahoma prairie. Once a winter campground of the Cheyenne tribe, the canyon is still filled with majestic mesas, cedar, and the Springs of Everlasting Water.

CENTRAL OKLAHOMA

Oklahoma's image as a western state was largely forged in central Oklahoma, where pickup trucks, cowboy boots, and oil wells were the original status symbols. The Chisholm Trail, the most famous of the cattle trails that moved Texas cattle north through Oklahoma Territory after the end of the Civil War, came through here 130 years ago, and the country's largest live cattle auction still gets under way in Oklahoma City's Stockyards City every Monday and Tuesday morning. Many towns in central Oklahoma, including Guthrie, Oklahoma City, and Norman, share a common heritage: They were born in a single day. The land run of April 22, 1889, opened parcels of land in central Oklahoma to non-Indian settlement. Would-be homesteaders lined up on the borders and literally raced to stake their claims.

Exploring Central Oklahoma

Visiting **Guthrie,** Oklahoma's first capitol, is like taking a trip back in time. A delightful mix of Victorian architecture and Old West atmosphere, Guthrie has more than 100 historical buildings. As the largest urban area on the National Register of Historic Places, Guthrie is home to turn-of-the-20th-century buildings adorned with stained-glass windows and stamped-tin ceilings. The Guthrie Chamber of Commerce conducts guided walking tours. **First Capitol Trolley** (✉ 2nd St. and Harrison Ave., ☎ 405/282–6000; 🎫 $2) makes regular tours of downtown Guthrie. Stroll over to the **International Scottish Rite Temple** for a look at one of the world's largest Masonic lodges. Talented artisans built this impressive structure with 396 stained-glass windows during Oklahoma's oil boom. ✉ *900 E. Oklahoma Ave.,* ☎ *405/282–1281.* 🎫 *$5. Closed Sun.*

Experience Guthrie's western heritage at the **Lazy E Arena** (✉ I–35 south, 4 mi east of Seward Rd., ☎ 405/282–3004 or 800/595–7433, WEB www.lazye.com), 5 mi east of Guthrie. This completely modern arena hosts a variety of western entertainment, including world-class rodeo events and championships.

Oklahoma City, 20 mi south of Guthrie, has benefited from an extensive downtown renewal project, particularly in the east area known as Bricktown.An industrial area largely abandoned by the 1950s, **Bricktown** has emerged as Oklahoma City's new entertainment district with the presence of trendy restaurants and clubs, one-of-a-kind shops, and the Bricktown Ballpark. **Bricktown Water Taxi** narrated tours are available for the mile-long canal winding through historic Bricktown. ✉ *Corner of Mickey Mantle Dr. and E. Reno,* ☎ *405/234–8294,* WEB *www.watertaxi.com.* 🎫 *$5. Closed Dec.–Feb.*

The **Oklahoma Spirit Trolley** (☎ 405/235–7433, WEB www.gometro.org; 🎫 50¢) traverses downtown and outer areas, including the Stockyards and Meridian hotel district.The **Oklahoma City National Memorial and Memorial Center** (✉ 620 N. Harvey Ave., ☎ 405/235–3313, WEB www.oklahomacitynationalmemorial.org; 🎫 museum $7) contains a reflecting pool bordering 168 bronze, glass, and granite chairs in remembrance of the victims who lost their lives in the 1995 bombing. Adjacent to the outdoor memorial is a museum and the Institute for the Prevention of Terrorism. Visiting is an emotional experience for many.

Many Oklahoma City attractions are found east and north of downtown, including the limestone-and-granite **Oklahoma State Capitol** (✉ N.E. 23rd St. and Lincoln Blvd., ☎ 405/521–3356; 🎫 free). Oil derricks mark the sites of seven wells that once surrounded the Capitol. The Oklahoma Capitol is also the only capitol in the world with an oil well underneath the building—Petunia #1. While the capitol is open daily, tours are available on weekdays only; reservations are recommended. A new dome was put on the capitol in 2002.

An extensive collection of western artifacts and fine art is on display at the **National Cowboy and Western Heritage Museum** (✉ 1700 N.E. 63rd St., ☎ 405/478–2250, WEB www.nationalcowboymuseum.org; 🎫 $8.50), north of the capitol off I–44, which celebrates the heritage of the American West. World-famous fine art decorates several galleries, plus a life-size western town shows what life was like in times past. Find out more about rodeos or your favorite western performers.

Twenty miles south of Oklahoma City is **Norman,** home to the **University of Oklahoma** and an interesting blend of cultural opportunities. Free walking tours are available of the lovely landscaped university grounds and historical buildings from the OU Visitor Center. ✉ *Jacobson Hall, 550 Parrington Oval,* ☎ *405/325–1188 or 800/234–6868,* WEB *www.ou.edu/visitorcenter. Closed Sun.*

★ The **Sam Noble Oklahoma Museum of Natural History** (✉ 2401 Chautauqua Ave., ☎ 405/325–4712, WEB www.snomnh.ou.edu; 🎫 $4) is the largest natural history museum in the world connected to a university. The paleontology exhibit contains the world's largest apatosaurus specimen. Other exhibits highlight extensive Native American artifacts, the Hall of Natural Wonders, and a hands-on Discovery Room.

Parks, Gardens, and Zoos

An interactive experience awaits you at the **Little River Zoo** (✉ 3405 120th Ave. SE, Norman, ☎ 405/366–7229, WEB www.littleriverzoo.com; 🎫 $4). Rescued residents, including monkeys, kangaroos, black bears, and wild cats, live on 55 wooded acres. Guided tours allow you to know the animals by name and background.

A walk through the Crystal Bridge Tropical Conservatory, a glass botanical tube at the 17-acre **Myriad Botanical Gardens** (✉ 301 W. Reno Ave., Oklahoma City, ☎ 405/297–3995; 🎫 $4), takes visitors through habitats ranging from desert to rain forest, complete with a 35-ft waterfall.

One of the Great Plains' oldest, the **Oklahoma City Zoological Park** (✉ 2101 N.E. 50th St., Oklahoma City, ☎ 405/424–3344, WEB www.okczoo.com; 🎫 $6) makes the most of natural habitats for primates, wildcats, and other species. A 4.2-acre Cat Forest is home to lions, snow leopards, and other wild cats. Swing by Great EscApe, a lush, tropical rain forest, and watch the gorillas, chimpanzees, and orangutans frolic.

Cruise 68 mi south of Norman for one of Oklahoma's scenic wonders, **Turner Falls Park** (✉ I–35, east of Exit 51, Davis, ☎ 580/369–2917; 🎫 $6 in summer, $2.50 in winter). Surrounded by the ancient cliffs of the Arbuckle Mountains is the state's largest waterfall, at 77 ft. Trails and caves are enjoyable, but on a hot summer day, people are drawn to the deliciously cool waters below the waterfall.

Dining and Lodging

Ames

$$ 🏨 **Island Guest Ranch.** At this 3,000-acre working ranch 90 mi north of Oklahoma City, guests help herd cattle, ride horses, fish, hike, and attend staged powwows and team roping and penning in the ranch's own rodeo arena. Rooms, each with a private bath, are in two rustic bunkhouses; meals are served in the main log lodge. Rates include all meals and activities; reservations should be made at least several weeks in advance. ✉ *Ames 73718,* ☎ *580/753–4574 or 800/928–4574,* FAX *580/753–4574. 10 rooms. MC, V. Closed Oct.–Mar. FAP.*

Guthrie

$–$$ ✕ **Blue Bell Saloon.** Famed cowboy star Tom Mix tended bar here in the early 20th century. Oklahoma's oldest saloon serves up steaks, seafood, and burgers along with a healthy dose of atmosphere. ✉ *224 W. Harrison St.,* ☎ *405/260–2355. AE, D, DC, MC, V.*

$ ✕ **Granny Had One.** This old-fashioned eatery in the middle of the historic district offers up homemade soups and breads, plus filling sandwiches for heartier appetites. ✉ *113 W. Harrison St.,* ☎ *405/282–4482. AE, D, DC, MC, V.*

$–$$ ★ 🏨 **Harrison House Inn.** Each room in this 1893 inn's four historical buildings is named after a famous historical figure. The Teddy Roosevelt Room is a guest favorite, and all rooms are in high Victorian style. ✉ *124 W. Harrison St., 73044,* ☎ *405/282–1000 or 800/375–1001,* FAX *405/282–1000. 34 rooms. AE, D, MC, V. BP.*

Norman

$–$$ ✕ **Coach's Restaurant & Brewery.** Norman's historic downtown is busy with activity these days. One of the reasons is the friendly atmosphere at Coach's Restaurant and Brewery. Hand-tossed pizza, barbecue, and microbrewed beer top the menu with a particular favorite being the barbecue chicken pizza. A billiards room adds to the fun. ✉ *102 W. Main St.,* ☎ *405/360–5726. AE, D, MC, V.*

$–$$$ ★ 🏨 **Montford Inn Bed & Breakfast.** Native American collectibles and football memorabilia celebrating nearby University of Oklahoma blend seamlessly with antiques in this supremely comfortable inn. Rooms have fireplaces, whirlpool tubs, and writing desks. ✉ *322 W. Tonhawa St., 73069,* ☎ *405/321–2200 or 800/321–8969,* FAX *405/321–8347,* WEB *www.montfordinn.com. 10 rooms, 6 cottages. AE, D, MC, V. BP.*

Oklahoma City

Two-centuries-old brick warehouses in downtown Oklahoma City have turned Bricktown into a favorite dining district for locals. Western Avenue north of 50th Street is known as Restaurant Row.

$$ ★ ✕ **Bricktown Restaurant & Brewery.** Even the shrimp are steamed in beer in this airy brewpub, where historical photographs are displayed against exposed brick. Land Run Lager and Copperhead Ale complement the chicken potpie, fish-and-chips, and hot links (spicy smoked sausages). ✉ *1 N. Oklahoma Ave.,* ☎ *405/232–2739. AE, D, DC, MC, V.*

$$ ★ ✕ **Cattlemen's Steakhouse.** Beef is the star attraction at this classic steak house in the heart of Stockyards City, although you shouldn't miss the opportunity to order some authentic lamb fries. Cowboys clad in spurs look right at home among the western murals, cattle-branding irons, and other western paraphernalia. ✉ *1309 S. Agnew Ave.,* ☎ *405/236–0416. AE, D, MC, V.*

$–$$ ✕ **Abuelo Mexican Embassy.** While you'll find many Mexican restaurants in Oklahoma City, Abuelo's is an original. Serving mostly central Mexican cuisine, Abuelo's offers 10 varieties of enchiladas that can be ordered in any combination. One house specialty is the enchiladas de Cozumel—avocado enchiladas with a seafood and mushroom white sauce. ✉ *17 E. Sheridan Ave.,* ☎ *405/235–1422. AE, D, MC, V.*

$ ✕ **Ann's Chicken Fry.** Home-style cooking joins nostalgic 1950s and 1960s decor at this Route 66 establishment. The chicken-fried steak is a special treat. ✉ *4106 N.W. 39th St.,* ☎ *405/943–8915. No credit cards. Closed Sun.*

$–$$ **The Biltmore.** Just minutes from the airport, the Biltmore offers a casual elegance that appeals to adults. Meeting facilities within the hotel are available for meetings and conventions. ✉ *401 S. Meridian Ave., 73108,* ☎ *405/947–7681 or 800/522–6620,* FAX *405/947–4253,* WEB *www.biltmoreokc.com. 509 rooms. 2 restaurants, pools, gym. AE, D, DC, MC, V.*

$–$$ **Courtyard by Marriott.** The hotel's location on NW Expressway makes getting anywhere relatively quick and easy. ✉ *1515 NW Expressway, 73118,* ☎ *405/848–0808 or 800/321–2211,* FAX *405/848–3113,* WEB *www.courtyard.com. 122 rooms. Restaurant, pool, gym. AE, D, DC, MC, V.*

Motels

Governors Suites (✉ 2308 S. Meridian St., 73108, ☎ 405/682–5299 or 888/819–7575, FAX 405/682–3047, WEB www.governorssuites-okc.com), 50 rooms; restaurant, pool; *$.* **Quality Inn North** (✉ 12001 N. I–35 Service Rd., 73131, ☎ 405/478–0400 or 800/228–5151, FAX 405/478–2774), 213 rooms; pool; *$.*

Shopping

Malls are abundant and do include locally owned shops amid the familiar chains. The downtown areas of Guthrie, Oklahoma City, and Norman are all thriving and provide a variety of merchandise. A fun place to shop is the eclectic Campus Corner area north of the University of Oklahoma in Norman. **Penn Square Mall** (✉ Pennsylvania Ave. and NW Expressway, Oklahoma City, WEB www.pennsquaremall.com) has a good selection of locally owned shops. **Quail Springs** (✉ Memorial Rd. and May Ave., Oklahoma City, WEB www.quailspringsmall.com) has 160 stores and a large multiplex theater. The **Route 66 Traders Market** (✉ 3201 N. Richland Rd., Yukon, ☎ 405/350–3366, WEB rt66traders.com), an upscale flea market off Route 66 west of Oklahoma City, has acres of shopping and entertainment. If you're in the market for western duds like the real cowboys wear, visit **Langston's** (✉ 2224 Exchange Ave., Oklahoma City, ☎ 405/235–9536, WEB langstons.com), south of downtown in Stockyard's City. You'll see plenty of tourists, but you also see quite a bit of the real thing.

Central Oklahoma Essentials

AIRPORTS

The Will Rogers World Airport in southwestern Oklahoma City is served by major domestic airlines.

➤ AIRPORT INFORMATION: **Will Rogers World Airport** (✉ Airport Rd., Oklahoma City, ☎ 405/680–3200, WEB www.flyokc.com).

BUS TRAVEL

➤ BUS INFORMATION: **Greyhound** (✉ 427 W. Sheridan St., Oklahoma City, ☎ 405/235–6425 or 800/231–2222).

CAR TRAVEL

The sometimes congested I–35 is in the middle of a massive reconstruction project. It is open and takes travelers north and south through central Oklahoma; I–40 crosses east and west. I–44, which runs diagonally from the northeast to the southwest, intersects both I–35 and I–40 in Oklahoma City. A car is a necessity.

TRAIN TRAVEL

Amtrak's *Heartland Flyer* offers daily service from Oklahoma City south to Ft. Worth with stops also in Norman, Purcell, Pauls Valley, and Ardmore.

➤ TRAIN INFORMATION: **Amtrak** (☎ 800/872–7245, WEB www.amtrak.com).

VISITOR INFORMATION

➤ TOURIST INFORMATION: **Guthrie Chamber of Commerce** (✉ 212 W. Oklahoma St. [Box 995, Guthrie 73044], ☎ 405/282–1947 or 800/299–1889, WEB www.guthrieok.com). **Norman Convention & Visitors Bureau** (✉ 224 W. Gray St., Suite 104, Norman 73069, ☎ 405/366–8095 or 800/664–5960, WEB www.visitnorman.com). **Oklahoma City Convention & Visitors Bureau** (✉ 189 W. Sheridan St., Oklahoma City 73102, ☎ 405/297–8912 or 800/225–5652, WEB www.visitokc.com). **Oklahoma City Welcome Center** (✉ State Capitol rotunda, N.E. 23rd St. and Lincoln Blvd., Oklahoma City; I–35 and N.E. 122nd St.; I–40 at the Air Depot exit).

NORTHEASTERN OKLAHOMA

More than half of Oklahoma's state parks can be found in northeastern Oklahoma, where the western boundaries of the Ozark and Ouachita mountains lie. Beautiful, unspoiled scenery is kept a vibrant green by the many lakes, rivers, and creeks. The eastern half of Oklahoma was once Indian Territory, the place where Native Americans of the southeastern United States were relocated after the tragic journey known as the Trail of Tears. One of the largest tribes in the United States, the Cherokee, have their tribal headquarters here.

Exploring Northeastern Oklahoma

Tulsa, Oklahoma's second-largest city and also known as T-town, was created by the oil barons of days gone by. The skyline speaks to that origin—sleek, modern skyscrapers erupting from the prairie and stretching to the heavens. The oil barons also left a legacy of culture, art, and widespread Art Deco architecture second only to those of New York and Miami. Stop by the chamber of commerce for a walking-tour map that includes more than a dozen downtown buildings. For a bit of nature, head west to Riverside Drive. Join others in walking, jogging, and biking along winding paths that follow the Arkansas River. Playgrounds, piers, a floating amphitheater, and a ¼-mi pedestrian bridge are all part of the extensive 26-mi network.

The **Greenwood Cultural Center** (✉ 322 N. Greenwood, ☎ 918/596–1020, WEB www.greenwoodculturalcenter.com; 🎫 free) celebrates the area once known as the "black Wall Street," which continues to be a thriving neighborhood for business and culture. The Oklahoma Jazz Hall of Fame and summer jazz festivals are just a few of the enjoyable surprises found in the Greenwood District.

About 3 mi from the downtown area is the **Gilcrease Museum** (✉ 1400 Gilcrease Museum Rd., ☎ 918/596–2700 or 888/655–2278, WEB www.gilcrease.org; 🎫 $5). Its collection, dedicated to western art and Americana, includes paintings by such artists as Frederic Remington and Charles Russell, as well as Native American art and artifacts. A few miles southeast of downtown, a wide-ranging collection from Italian Renaissance paintings to Native American art resides at the **Philbrook**

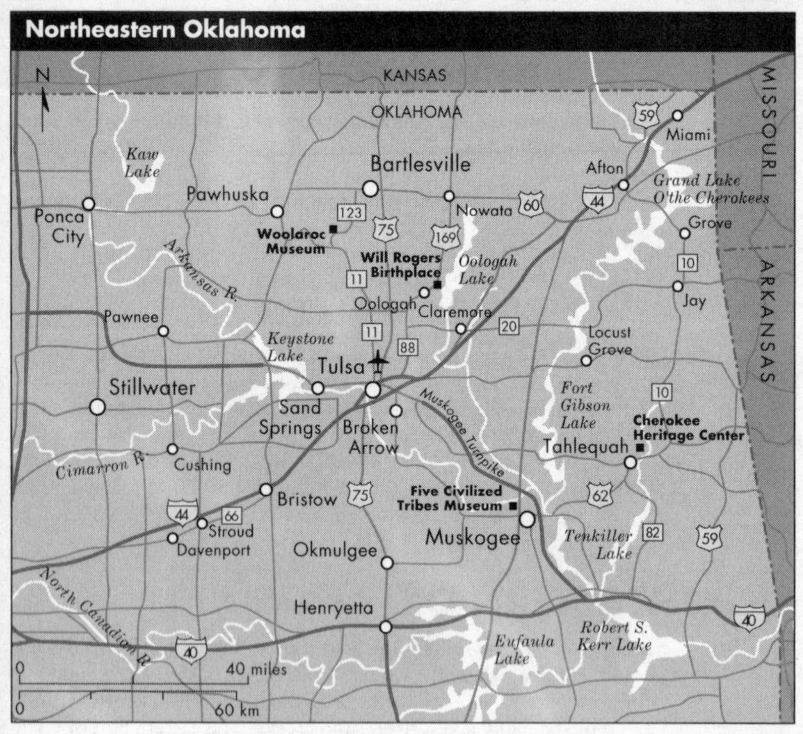

Museum of Art, occupying former oil baron Waite Phillips's historic Italian villa, located on 23 artistically landscaped acres. ✉ *2727 S. Rockford Rd.,* ☎ *918/749–7941 or 800/324–7941,* WEB *www.philbrook.org.* 🎟 *$5. Closed Mon.*

Not only is the title song of the famous Rodgers and Hammerstein musical Oklahoma's state song, but *Oklahoma!* has been a summertime tradition since 1975 at **Discoveryland,** where nightly performances can be seen in an outdoor amphitheater. Get in the true spirit of being an Oklahoman by joining the barbecue held before each performance. ✉ *19501 W. 41st St., 5 mi west of 41st and State Hwy. 97,* ☎ *918/245–6552.* 🎟 *$15. Closed Sept.–May. and Sun.*

★ North of Tulsa is **Woolaroc** (✉ State Hwy 123, 12 mi southwest of Bartlesville, ☎ 918/336–0307 or 888/966–5276, WEB www.woolaroc.org; 🎟 $5), once the ranch of oilman Frank Phillips. Today, it's a drive-through wildlife preserve that's home to bison and 40 other species (visitors must remain in their vehicles). The preserve surrounds a museum packed with memorabilia of art and artifacts of the Southwest.

Southeast of Woolaroc by way of Nowata lies the Dog Iron Ranch and **Will Rogers Birthplace** (✉ 2 mi east of Oologah, ☎ 918/341–0719 or 800/324–9455; 🎟 free). The great humorist's childhood home, built in 1875, is a two-story clapboard structure containing period furnishings; you'll also find longhorn cattle and barnyard animals on the grounds of the working ranch. On Route 88 in Claremore is the sandstone **Will Rogers Memorial Museum** (✉ 1720 W. Will Rogers Blvd., Claremore, ☎ 918/341–0719 or 800/324–9455, WEB www.willrogers.com; 🎟 free), where Oklahoma's favorite son and members of his family are buried; the museum contains memorabilia, theaters that show Rogers's movies and newsreels, and a hands-on children's museum.

Take I–44 and U.S. 59 to Grove and the **Grand Lake O' the Cherokees.** Numerous recreational options here include a dinner cruise or sightseeing tour aboard the *Cherokee Queen* paddle wheel boat (✉ 11350 U.S. Hwy. 59 N at Sailboat Bridge, Grove, ☎ 918/786–4272; 🎟 2-hr sightseeing tour $8.50, 3-hr dinner cruise $19.50).

About 50 mi south of Grove on State Highway 10 is **Tahlequah,** capital of the Cherokee Nation. The **Cherokee Heritage Center,** 3 mi south of Tahlequah off U.S. 62, chronicles the history of the Cherokee Nation from the time of the Trail of Tears to the present. Within the Heritage Center are the **Cherokee National Museum,** where an exhibit focuses on the oral tradition of the elders; the **Ancient Village at Tsa-La-Gi,** where costumed tribal members demonstrate basket weaving, pottery, stickball games, and other Cherokee traditions; and **Adams Corner Rural Village,** a re-created pioneer village from the 1800s. A moving Trail of Tears drama is also featured in an outdoor amphitheater each summer. ✉ *Willis Rd., Tahlequah,* ☎ *918/456–6007 or 888/999–6007,* WEB *www.cherokeeheritage.com.* 🎟 *$8.50. Closed Jan. and Sun.*

The nearby **Illinois River** is a popular site for float trips. Canoes and kayaks can be rented along State Highway 10.

South from Tulsa on the Muskogee Turnpike is the quintessential Oklahoma town of **Muskogee.** Known for its azaleas, Muskogee is also home to Bacone College, which started as an Indian Art School. To learn about Oklahoma's Native American Heritage, visit the **Five Civilized Tribes Museum** (✉ Honor Heights Dr., ☎ 918/683–1701, WEB fivetribes.com; 🎟 $2).

Dining and Lodging

$ ✕ **Nelson's Buffeteria.** For more than 70 years, this Tulsa institution has been providing southern home-cooked breakfasts and lunches. Mouthwatering biscuits and gravy are popular with the locals. The walls share a history of Oklahoma sports legends. ✉ *514 S. Boston Ave., Tulsa,* ☎ *918/584–9969. AE, D, DC, MC, V.*

$$–$$$ 🏨 **Hotel Ambassador.** This Italianate building, which was built in 1929, is listed on the National Register of Historic Places. Finished in 2000, a restoration of the rooms and public spaces has created a boutique hotel with a great deal of attention to personal service. ✉ *1324 S. Main St., Tulsa 74119,* ☎ *918/587–8200 or 888/408–8282,* FAX *918/587–8208,* WEB *www.hotelambassador-tulsa.com. 55 rooms. Restaurant. AE, MC, V.*

$$–$$$ 🏨 **McBirney Mansion.** The historic McBirney Mansion is now a luxury bed-and-breakfast overlooking the Arkansas River. The surroundings are so peaceful that it's hard to believe you're minutes from downtown Tulsa. ✉ *1414 S. Galveston, 74127,* ☎ *918/585–3234,* FAX *918/585–9377,* WEB *www.mcbirneymansion.com. 8 rooms. AE, D, MC, V. BP.*

$$ 🏨 **Western Hills Guest Ranch.** Sitting on a scenic peninsula on Fort Gibson Lake, this ranch provides a taste of the cowboy life with horseback riding and chuck-wagon cookouts. For more gentrified sensibilities, there's also golf and tennis. ✉ *12 mi east of State Hwy. 51, Wagoner 74467,* ☎ *918/772–2545 or 800/368–1486,* FAX *918/587–1642. 101 rooms, 54 cottages. Restaurants, golf, tennis. AE, MC, V.*

Motels

🏨 **Best Western Trade Winds East** (✉ 3337 E. Skelly Dr., Tulsa 74135, ☎ 918/743–7931, FAX 918/749–6312, WEB www.bestwestern.com), 152 rooms; pool, gym; *$.* 🏨 **LaQuinta South** (✉ 12525 S.E. 52nd St., Tulsa

74146, ☎ 918/254–1626 or 800/531–5940, FAX 918/252–3408, WEB www.laquinta.com), 117 rooms; pool; *$*.

Campgrounds

⛺ **Greenleaf State Park** (✉ State Hwy. 10-A, north of Gore, ☎ 918/487–5196) is one of the loveliest state parks, with a sparkling blue 900-acre lake and wooded hiking and biking trails. The cabins and shelters at ⛺ **Osage Hills State Park** (✉ 13 mi northeast of Pawhuska on U.S. 60 [HC73, Box 84, Pawhuska 74056], ☎ 918/336–4141) were built in the 1930s by the Civilian Conservation Corps on rolling hills covered with blackjack oak. It's 11 mi west of Bartlesville.

The Arts

Tulsa's **Performing Arts Center** (✉ 110 E. 2nd St., ☎ 918/596–7122; 918/596–2525 24-hr event line for schedules and info, WEB www.tulsapac.org) encompasses half a city block in Tulsa's downtown historic area. This mega-complex, designed by architect Minoru Yamasaki, includes five theaters and hosts groups such as the **Tulsa Philharmonic,** the lovely music of the **Tulsa Opera,** and the nationally acclaimed **Tulsa Ballet Theatre.**

Outdoor Activities and Sports

Fishing

The sports section of the city's daily newspaper, *Tulsa World*, has up-to-date fishing information. Fishing licenses can be purchased in most tackle shops. The **Oklahoma Department of Wildlife and Conservation** (☎ 405/521–3851, WEB www.wildlifedepartment.com) has detailed information on its Web site.

Hiking

Every park in the area has hiking trails. For general information call the **Tourism and Recreation Department.**

Shopping

Tulsa's **Brookside** and **Cherry Street** districts are home to charming boutiques, antiques shops, and a variety of dining establishments. **Utica Square,** at Utica Avenue and 21st Street, is an outdoor mall with upscale chain stores, including Saks Fifth Avenue, and such specialty shops as Petty's Fine Foods, and Miss Jackson's, one of Oklahoma's best-known designer fashion stores. **Lyon's Indian Store** (✉ 401 E. 11th St., Tulsa, ☎ 918/582–6372) has been marketing Native American clothing and crafts since 1916. Local art, Frankoma pottery, and Pendleton blankets are some of the treasures you'll find.

Northeastern Oklahoma Essentials

AIRPORTS

Tulsa International Airport, 10 mi northeast of downtown Tulsa, is served by major domestic airlines. Average cab fare to the downtown area is about $17.

➤ AIRPORT INFORMATION: **Tulsa International Airport** (✉ U.S. 169 and 36th St. N, Tulsa, ☎ 918/838–5000, WEB www.tulsaairports.com).

BUS TRAVEL

Greyhound serves Tulsa.

➤ BUS INFORMATION: **Greyhound** (✉ 317 S. Detroit St., Tulsa, ☎ 800/231–2222, WEB www.greyhound.com).

CAR TRAVEL

In Tulsa I–44 and I–244 form a downtown loop. The Keystone, Cherokee, and Broken Arrow expressways also lead downtown. From Tulsa U.S. 75 leads north to the Bartlesville area. I–44 is the main route northeast from Tulsa and connects with many smaller, more scenic highways. I–44 is also a toll road ($3.50 toll) linking Tulsa and Oklahoma City.

VISITOR INFORMATION

➤ TOURIST INFORMATION: **Tahlequah Chamber of Commerce** (✉ 123 E. Delaware St., Tahlequah 74464, ☎ 918/456–3742 or 800/456–4860, WEB tourtahlequah.com). **Tulsa Convention & Visitor Bureau** (✉ 616 S. Boston St., Tulsa 74119, ☎ 918/585–1201 or 800/558–3311, WEB www.visittulsa.com).

SOUTHWESTERN OKLAHOMA

The frontier isn't far away from this rugged, sparsely populated region; oceans of grass are broken by blue-granite mountains, and almost every small town has a saddle shop. During the 19th century this was the domain of the buffalo and the Kiowa and Comanche tribes; travelers may still spot Native American tepees and brush arbors in rural areas during the summer.

Exploring Southwestern Oklahoma

At the foot of the Wichita Mountains, **Lawton** makes a good base for exploring the region. It's the largest of the Wichita Mountain communities and the business center for southwestern Oklahoma. The **Museum of the Great Plains** (✉ 601 N.W. Ferris Ave., ☎ 580/581–3460, WEB museumgreatplains.org; 🎟 $3) has a reproduction trading post and an outdoor fort recalling the pre–Louisiana Purchase days.

A short drive north of Lawton on I–44 brings you to the **Fort Sill Military Museum** (✉ Key Gate, off Sheridan Rd., 437 Quanah Rd., ☎ 580/442–5123 or 580/442–5123; 🎟 free), built in 1869 as the old post building. The guardhouse where Geronimo, Fort Sill's most famous prisoner, was held is one of several buildings open to the public. Chief's Knoll, located east of the base, features Apache and Comanche cemeteries.

North of Lawton I–44 crosses State Highway 49, which runs along the ★ northern border of Fort Sill and westward to the **Wichita Mountains National Wildlife Refuge** (✉ Indiahoma, ☎ 580/429–3222), one of the most beautiful areas in the state. Here the wildlife is thick and the scenery—boulder-topped mountains overlooking clear, still lakes—often breathtaking. The refuge is home to bison, longhorn cattle, and other wildlife. It's also the best place in the state for rock climbing. Hiking trails are abundant and camping is allowed, but backcountry camping and biking are by permit only. The visitor center has some of the best educational displays in the state.

From the western end of the Wichita Mountains Wildlife Refuge, State Highway 54 and U.S. 62 lead southwest to Altus. From here travel north on U.S. 283/Route 44 to **Quartz Mountain State Park** (✉ Lone Wolf, ☎ 580/563–2238). The scenery is worth the trip—bare rock outcroppings reflected in pristine Lake Altus-Lugert and abundant wildflowers in spring. You can also enjoy the lake's sandy beaches, visit the park's nature center, or take advantage of guided tours and special programs.

In **Anadarko**, north of Lawton on Routes 281 and 8, learn how the Southern Plains Indian tribes once lived and enjoy the art and culture of today's Native Americans. **Indian City USA** (✉ State Hwy. 8, 2½ mi southeast of Anadarko, ☎ 405/247–5661 or 800/433–5661, WEB www.indiancityusa.com; 🎫 $7.50) is an outdoor museum showing how different Plains tribes once lived. View fine art and authentic crafts at the **Southern Plains Indian Museum** ✉ *715 E. Central Blvd. at U.S. 62E, Anadarko,* ☎ *405/247–6221.* 🎫 *$3. Closed Mon. Oct.–May.*

Next door to the Southern Plains Indian Museum is the **National Hall of Fame for Famous American Indians** (✉ 851 E. Central Blvd., ☎ 405/247–5555; 🎫 free).

Drive north on U.S. 183 to reach Clinton, where you can relive travel
★ on the Mother Road at the **Oklahoma Route 66 Museum.** Exhibits are organized by decade, beginning with the road's construction in the 1920s, continuing through the Dust Bowl in the '30s, the military highway days of the '40s, and the vacation-oriented '50s (complete with a re-created diner and drive-in movie theater). ✉ *2229 W. Gary Blvd., off I–40, Clinton,* ☎ *580/323–7866,* WEB *www.route66.org.* 🎫 *$3. Closed Mon.*

West on I–40 will bring you to Elk City, where the **National Route 66 Museum** (✉ 2717 W. Rte. 66, Elk City, ☎ 580/225–6266; 🎫 $5) opened in 1998. Thousands made their way to California during the Dust Bowl era. The national museum explores the history of transportation and the significance of the road during those days in the Depression.

Dining and Lodging

When possible, pack lunches for park picnics; at night you'll probably have to content yourself with chain restaurants, although there are a few gems mainly specializing in southern cuisine. Unless you plan to camp, your hotel will probably be little more than a convenient base for exploring.

Altus

$–$$ 🏨 **Quartz Mountain Resort Park Lodge.** Overlooking the 4,500-acre state park, this lodge reopened in the summer of 2000 after reconstruction. Once the sacred grounds of the Kiowa and Comanche, Quartz Mountain is now a popular location for artists and for retreats. ✉ *State Hwy. 44A, 17 mi north of Altus (Rte. 1, Box 37, Lone Wolf 73655),* ☎ *580/563–2424 or 877/999–5567,* WEB *quartzmountainresort.com. 120 rooms, 8 cottages. Restaurant, golf. AE, MC, V.*

Lawton

$ ★ ✕ **Woody's BBQ.** Seated under a ceiling fan in one of two rustic dining rooms, you'll be treated to pork ribs or beef brisket with side dishes such as okra, fried mushrooms, and "wood chips" (fried potatoes with melted cheese and bacon). ✉ *1107 W. Lee Blvd.,* ☎ *580/355–4950. AE, D, MC, V.*

$ 🏨 **Howard Johnson Hotel and Convention Center.** The public areas of this low-rise stucco hotel off I–44 are a hodgepodge of decorative themes, from Victorian-style frosted glass to a rustic chandelier of antlers. ✉ *1125 E. Gore Blvd., 73501,* ☎ *580/353–0200,* FAX *580/353–6801,* WEB *www.hojo.com. 145 rooms. Restaurant, pool, gym. AE, D, DC, MC, V.*

Meers

$ ✕ **Meers Store.** All that's left of a boomtown that grew up during a brief gold rush in 1901 are this eatery and a seismographic station by the cash register. The restaurant's claim to fame is the Meersburger—a 7-inch burger made of 100% longhorn beef. ✉ *Rte. 115, 4 mi east* *of the Wichita Mountains Wildlife Refuge,* ☎ *580/429–8051. No credit cards.*

Motels

Best Western Tradewinds Courtyard Inn (✉ 2128 Gary Blvd., Clinton 73601, ☎ 580/323–2610 or 800/528–1234, FAX 580/353–6162), 76 rooms; restaurant; $.

Campgrounds

Doris Campgrounds is a fully developed camping area surrounded by the wild beauty of the Wichita Mountains Wildlife Refuge. Nearby lakes offer fishing for largemouth bass, sunfish, crappie, and channel catfish.

Outdoor Activities and Sports

Fishing

Lake Altus-Lugert or any of the lakes at the Wichita Mountains Wildlife Refuge offer peaceful, unspoiled fishing. The sports section in the *Daily Oklahoman* has fishing reports for the lakes in the area. The **Oklahoma Department of Wildlife and Conservation** (☎ 405/521–3851, WEB www.wildlifedepartment.com) has detailed information on its Web site.

Hiking

The best hiking is found at Wichita Mountains National Wildlife Refuge and at state parks including **Quartz Mountain Resort Park** and the rugged cliffs of **Red Rock Canyon,** located between Clinton and Oklahoma City south of I–40, and also a popular rappelling spot.

Southwestern Oklahoma Essentials

AIRPORTS

The Will Rogers World Airport in Oklahoma City gives the best access to the region.

BUS TRAVEL

➤ BUS INFORMATION: **Jefferson Lines** (✉ 15 N.E. 20th St., Lawton, ☎ 580/353–1010).

CAR TRAVEL

As with most of the state, you'll need a car to tour this region. I–44 is a toll road from Oklahoma City to Lawton ($2.75). I–40 joins Route 66 through western Oklahoma. State highways and county roads connect with these interstates.

VISITOR INFORMATION

➤ TOURIST INFORMATION: **Lawton/Fort Sill Chamber of Commerce** (✉ 629 S.W. C St., Lawton 73501, ☎ 580/355–3541 or 800/872–4540, WEB www.lcci.org).

SOUTHEASTERN OKLAHOMA

The green and hilly southeastern corner of the state seems a world apart from the rest of Oklahoma. Here pine and hardwood forests traversed by fast-running mountain streams are populated by plentiful wildlife. Outdoor enthusiasts favor this part of the state, where food, lodging, and entertainment tend toward the rustic. Much of southeastern Oklahoma belonged to the Choctaw Indians during Indian Territory days. The Choctaw Tribe is still a powerful presence with a tribal headquarters in Durant. The original Choctaw Capitol and council grounds in

Tushka Homma (Tuskahoma) continue to be the site of cultural festivities. The word "Oklahoma" actually comes from the Choctaw language and means "red people."

Exploring Southeastern Oklahoma

Robbers Cave State Park (✉ State Hwy. 2, Wilburton, ☎ 918/465–2562), 5 mi north of town, enjoys a colorful history. Outlaws once found Indian Territory a good place to hide from federal marshals, as the Native Americans in the area didn't much care for the federal lawmen either. One place in particular was deep in the San Bois Mountains, where caves camouflaged by the forests provided the perfect cover. Outlaws like the James and Dalton gangs occasionally used Robbers Cave to hide themselves or the profits from their heists. Today, people can explore the caves independently or take a tour with a park ranger.

A place with even more history is **Spiro Mounds Archaeological Park.** Spiro Mounds is believed to be one of the most significant prehistoric Indian sites east of the Rocky Mountains. Twelve mounds and a center with artifacts explain how these ancient people may have once lived. The site is 6 mi east of town. ✉ *South of I–40 near Arkansas border, Spiro,* ☎ *918/962–2062.* 🎫 *Free. Closed Mon.–Tues.*

Hugo has a secret identity as Circus City, U.S.A. The southern Oklahoma town is the winter home for Carson & Barnes as well as the Mill Brothers Circuses. **Showman's Rest** (✉ Trice and S. 8th Sts., ☎ 580/326–7511 or 580/326–9263; 🎫 free) at Mt. Olivet Cemetery is the final resting place for many big-top performers—the two-legged and four-legged variety. If you're interested in seeing the countryside in comfort and style (and in town on a summer or fall Saturday), you'll want to take State Highway 70 to Hugo and ride the vintage train at **Hugo Historic Railroad.** Reservations are required. While you're waiting, take a look at the train museum or stop by the restored Harvey House Restaurant. ✉ *309 W. Jackson St., Hugo,* ☎ *580/326–6630 or 888/773–3768.* 🎫 *$17 and up, depending on the route. Closed Dec.–Mar. and Sun.–Fri.*

Spectacular views can be seen from the **Talimena Scenic Byway,** marked State Highway 1 and running east–west through the heart of the Ouachita National Forest. The highway extends west into the Sans Bois Mountain area and intersects with U.S. 259, which continues into the Kiamichi Mountains.

The scenic byway intersects with U.S. 259, which takes travelers south about 40 mi to **Beavers Bend Resort Park** (✉ State Hwy. 259A [Box 10, Broken Bow 74728], ☎ 580/494–6300 or 800/654–8240, WEB www.beaversbend.com), 7 mi north of town. Built on the Mountain Fork River at the edge of the Ouachita National Forest, the park is so secluded that wild turkeys have been spotted strolling on the resort's golf fairways. Black bears have even been sighted in the north part of the park. The history and culture of the forest from prehistoric times to the present are interpreted at the park's Forest Heritage Center (☎ 580/494–6497; 🎫 free).

Dining and Lodging

Lodging tends to be rustic in southeast Oklahoma, and many restaurants close by 9 PM.

Broken Bow

$ ✕ **Stevens Gap Restaurant.** Enjoy catfish fillets served with hush puppies or southern-fried chicken. You can also get breakfast (biscuits, gravy, and the works) all day long. It's about 2½ mi north from Hochatown State Park's main entrance via U.S. 259. ✉ *U.S. 259 and Stevens Gap Rd.,* ☎ *580/494–6350. D, MC, V.*

$$–$$$ ★ **Lakeview Lodge.** Every room at this state-operated lodge has a balcony view of Broken Bow Lake. Breakfast is served in the lodge's Great Room, where a fire roars in a native stone fireplace when weather warrants. ✉ *U.S. 259 (Box 10, Broken Bow 74728),* ☎ *580/494–6179 or 800/435–5514,* WEB *www.beaversbend.com. 40 rooms. Restaurant, golf. AE, D, DC, MC, V. CP.*

Krebs

$$ ★ **Pete's Place.** Pete Prichard started selling sandwiches and illicit beer out of his house in 1925; now his grandchildren operate a sprawling restaurant with a (legal) microbrewery and 25 private dining rooms clustered around three main dining areas. Krebs, an old mining community nicknamed Little Italy, is about 30 mi west of Wilburton via U.S. 270. ✉ *120 S.W. 8th St.,* ☎ *918/423–2042. No lunch Mon.–Sat. AE, D, DC, MC, V.*

Smithville

$$ **Eagle Creek Guest Cottages.** Twelve secluded log cottages are spread out over 40 acres on the back side of a mountain; some are on the banks of Big Eagle Creek or on a private lake. The luxury log cabins have kitchens, stone fireplaces, whirlpools, and big back porches. Smithville is 6 mi south of Octavia via U.S. 270. ✉ *U.S. 259 (HC 15, Box 250, Smithville 74957),* ☎ *580/244–7597,* FAX *580/244–7255,* WEB *www.guestcottages.com. 12 cottages. AE, MC, V.*

Wilburton

$ **Belle Starr View Lodge.** Overlooking a valley in Robbers Cave State Park, the lodge has comfortable rooms with color TVs but no phones. Breakfast (not included in the rates) requires a bit of a hike to the park restaurant. ✉ *Rte. 2 (Box 9, Wilburton 74578),* ☎ *918/465–2562 or 800/654–8240,* FAX *918/465–5763. 20 rooms. AE, D, DC, MC, V.*

Outdoor Activities and Sports

You can camp, hike, and fish in 10 areas in **Ouachita National Forest.**

Boating and Fishing

Mountain Fork River is stocked with rainbow trout; there are brown trout in the Lower Mountain Fork. The required trout-fishing stamp is obtainable at park offices and bait shops. The white-water Mountain Fork River is also popular with canoeists. Broken Bow Lake is surrounded by the Kiamichi Mountains and offers numerous secluded inlets to drop anchor and swim or fish. **Beavers Bend River Floats** (✉ Beavers Bend Resort Park, OK 259A, Broken Bow, ☎ 580/494–6070) rents canoes from March to October. **WW Trading Post and Canoes** (✉ Mountain Fork Park Rd., Broken Bow, ☎ 580/584–6856) rents fly-fishing equipment and supplies, along with canoes from March to October. The **Beavers Bend Marina** (✉ off State Hwy. 259, Broken Bow, ☎ 580/494–6455, WEB brokenbowlake.com) also rents Jet Skis, boats, and barges.

Hiking

The **Ouachita Trail,** a 192-mi frontier trail through the Ouachita mountains, was pieced together from bison paths, military roads, and centuries-old footpaths. Forty miles of trails through the Ouachita National Forest can be hiked in Oklahoma. Backcountry camping is allowed all along the trail; numerous campgrounds have also been established. For more information, contact the **Choctaw Ranger District** (✉ HC 64, Box 3467, Heavener 74937, ☎ 918/653–2991).

Southeastern Oklahoma Essentials

AIRPORTS

Either the Will Rogers World Airport in Oklahoma City or the Tulsa International Airport provides the best access to the northern Ouachita National Forest area. Extreme southeastern Oklahoma is closer to Dallas and the Dallas–Fort Worth International Airport.

➤ AIRPORT INFORMATION: **Dallas–Fort Worth International Airport** (☎ 972/574–6701).

BUS TRAVEL

Greyhound provides bus service to Wilburton.

➤ BUS INFORMATION: **Greyhound** (☎ 800/231–2222, WEB www.greyhound.com).

CAR TRAVEL

Much of southeastern Oklahoma is accessible only by two-lane roads. From I–40 near Sallisaw, U.S. 259 leads south. From I–35 take U.S. 70 E. The Indian Nations Turnpike starts near Tulsa and heads south, intersecting I–40 and U.S. 70 until it ends at the Oklahoma-Texas border. This sprawling, mountainous region requires a car. Highways are generally well marked, but navigating along winding mountain roads can require patience and a little extra time. Be especially careful along county and rural roads—some are not paved and can be treacherous after rain or sleet.

VISITOR INFORMATION

➤ TOURIST INFORMATION: **Kiamichi Country Regional Tourism Association** (✉ Rte. 2 N [Box 638, Wilburton 74578], ☎ 918/465–2367 or 800/722–8180).

OREGON

By Donald S. Olson

Updated by Jeffrey Boswell

Capital	Salem
Population	3,472,000
Motto	She Flies with Her Own Wings
State Bird	Western meadowlark
State Flower	Oregon grape
Postal Abbreviation	OR

Statewide Visitor Information

Oregon Tourism Commission (✉ 775 Summer St. NE, Salem 97310, ☎ 800/547–7842, WEB www.traveloregon.com).

Scenic Drives

The **Columbia Gorge Scenic Highway** (Route 30) twists and turns its way above I–84 through the heavily wooded, waterfall-laced Columbia Gorge east of Portland. **U.S. 101** hugs the pristine Oregon coastline. **Route 138** from Roseburg to Crater Lake is a national scenic byway through rugged canyons and past waterfalls, mountain lakes, and camping areas.

National and State Parks

National Parks

Crater Lake National Park (✉ Box 7, Crater Lake 97604, ☎ 541/594–2211, WEB www.nps.gov/crla; 🎫 $10 per vehicle) has guided boat trips of the lake, and many nature trails. In the high-desert country of eastern Oregon, **John Day Fossil Beds National Monument** (✉ HCR 82, Box 126, Kimberly 97848–9701, ☎ 541/987–2333, WEB www.nps.gov/joda; 🎫 free) contains the richest concentration of prehistoric plant and animal fossils in the world. **Newberry Volcanic National Monument,** on U.S. 97, 10 mi south of Bend, is administered by the Deschutes National Forest Service (✉ 1645 U.S. 20 E, Bend 97701, ☎ 541/383–5300; 🎫 $5 per vehicle) and provides recreation for campers, cross-country skiers, snowmobilers, fishers, and hikers. **Oregon Caves National Monument** (✉ 19000 Caves Hwy., off U.S. 199, Cave Junction 97523, ☎ 541/592–3400, WEB www.nps.gov/orca; 🎫 $7 per vehicle) conducts guided tours of the Marble Halls of Oregon. **Oregon Dunes National Recreation Area** (✉ 855 Highway Ave., Reedsport 97467, ☎ 541/271–3611; 🎫 $5 per vehicle) covers 40 mi of undulating camel-color sand and freshwater lakes.

State Parks

Oregon's 225 state parks run the gamut from sage-scented desert to mountains to beaches. **Oregon State Parks and Recreation Department** (✉ 1115 Commercial St. NE, Salem 97310, ☎ 800/551–6949, WEB www.oregonstateparks.org) has information on the parks, campsites, and facilities. Many parks charge day-use fees of $3 per vehicle.

PORTLAND

Portland, one of America's most important gateways to the Pacific Rim, has a reputation as a well-planned, charming city. With 2,265,000 people, Portland ranks as the 23rd-largest metropolitan area in the nation, and, straddling the banks of the wide Willamette River, it's one of the largest inland ports on the West Coast. It also has flower-filled parks, efficient mass transit, excellent hotels and restaurants, and restored his-

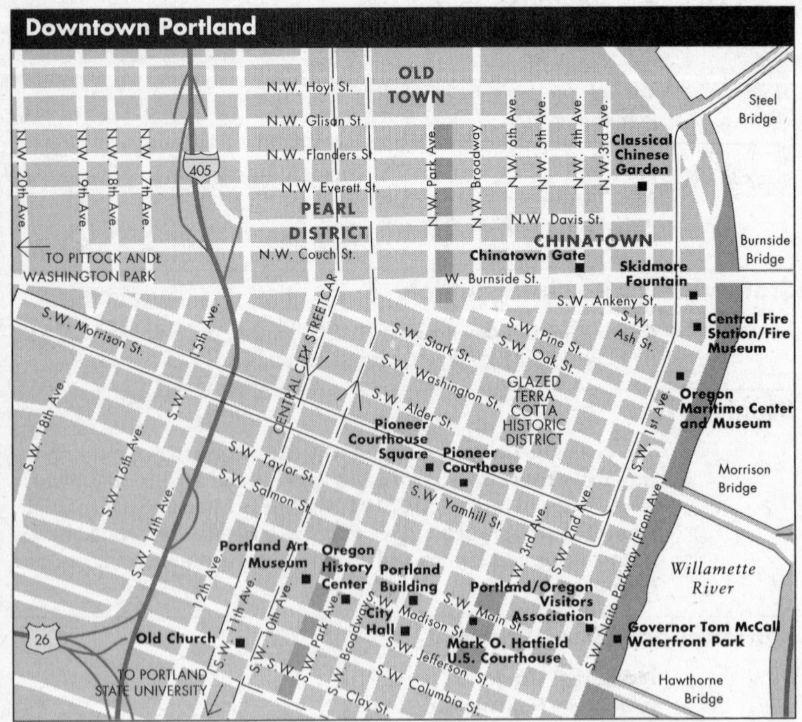

toric buildings. The **Rose Festival** (✉ 202 N.W. 2nd Ave., 97209, ☎ 503/227–2681, WEB www.rosefestival.org), held in early June, is a monthlong series of parades and events drawing more than 2 million people each year from around the world.

Exploring Portland

Downtown

Four **Vintage Trolleys** run from Lloyd Center to Pioneer Courthouse Square on the MAX light-rail line. They operate daily from May to December and weekends only in March and April. ✉ *Board at Lloyd Center or Pioneer Courthouse Square.* 🎟 *Free.*

★ The 1930s-era **Portland Art Museum** is one of several interesting buildings that line the South Park Blocks, a tree-lined boulevard of parks with statues and fountains. The museum contains 35 centuries of Asian, European, and Native American art and is a regional venue for large traveling exhibitions. ✉ *1219 S.W. Park Ave.,* ☎ *503/226–2811,* WEB *www.pam.org.* 🎟 *$7.50. Closed Mon.*

Across from the art museum, towering murals of Lewis and Clark and the Oregon Trail frame the entrance to the **Oregon History Center,** where the state's history from prehistoric times to the present is documented in dramatic galleries and hands-on exhibits. ✉ *1200 S.W. Park Ave.,* ☎ *503/222–1741.* 🎟 *$6. Closed Mon.*

The **Old Church,** built in 1882, is a prime example of Carpenter Gothic architecture, complete with rough-cut lumber, tall spires, and the original stained-glass windows. Free concerts are held on Wednesday at noon. ✉ *1422 S.W. 11th Ave.,* ☎ *503/222–2031,* WEB *www.oldchurch.org.* 🎟 *Free. Closed Sun.*

Architect Michael Graves's **Portland Building** (✉ 1120 S.W. 5th Ave.) was one of the country's first postmodern designs. **Portlandia,** the second-largest hammered-copper sculpture in the world (after the Statue of Liberty), kneels on the second-story balcony.

Across Naito Parkway along the Willamette River you'll find **Governor Tom McCall Waterfront Park,** a grassy 2-mi expanse (a former expressway) used as a venue for festivals and concerts as well as picnicking, jogging, and biking. From the park you can see some of the many distinctive bridges that have earned Portland the name Bridgetown.

Many fine examples of 19th-century cast-iron architecture are preserved in the **Yamhill and Skidmore National Historic districts,** which begin on Naito Parkway across from the waterfront park. The former commercial waterfront of Portland is now a district of galleries, fountains, and shops that is particularly lively on weekends.

The main mast of the battleship ***Oregon,*** which served in three wars, stands at the foot of Oak Street. The exterior of the **Oregon Maritime Center and Museum** incorporates fine street-level examples of cast-iron architecture. Inside are models of ships that once plied the Columbia River. The admission fee allows you to board the last operating sternwheeler tug in the United States, docked across the street. ✉ *113 S.W. Naito Pkwy.,* ☎ *503/224–7724.* *$4. Closed Mon.–Tues.*

The official entrance to Portland's **Chinatown** is the ornate Chinatown Gate (✉ N.W. 4th Ave. and W. Burnside St.). The area covers several blocks and has many Chinese restaurants, shops, and grocery stores. The adjacent **Old Town** area, home to the Classical Chinese Garden, has several good restaurants and a few gay bars.

★ Step back 400 years to China's Ming era in the peaceful **Classical Chinese Garden** (✉ N.W. 3rd Ave. and Everett St., ☎ 503/228–8131, WEB www.chinesegarden.org; $6). It's the largest Suzhou-style garden outside China, with a large lake, bridged and covered walkways, statues, waterfalls, courtyards, and plenty of bamboo. Have a look through the gift shop, and stop in at the two-story **teahouse** (☎ 503/224–8455) overlooking the lake and garden to taste any of 25 exotic teas served by the Tao of Tea.

Pittock Mansion (✉ 3229 N.W. Pittock Dr., ☎ 503/823–3624, WEB www.pittockmansion.com; $5), 1,000 ft above the city about 2 mi west of downtown, yields superb views of the skyline, rivers, and Cascade Mountains. Set in its own scenic park, the opulent manor is filled with art and antiques of the 1880s.

★ The **Oregon Museum of Science and Industry (OMSI)** is housed in a restored steam plant on the Willamette's east bank. It has touring exhibits, permanent displays, a planetarium, a submarine, laser shows, and an OMNIMAX theater. ✉ *1945 S.E. Water Ave.,* ☎ *503/797–4000,* WEB *www.omsi.edu.* *$7–$16. Closed Mon.*

Other Neighborhoods

Many of the storefronts and warehouses in the formerly industrial **Pearl District,** bordered by Burnside and Marshall streets and Northwest 8th and Northwest 15th avenues, have been converted during the past 10 years into lofts, art galleries, furniture and design stores, and restaurants. A few blocks west of the Pearl District, grand old Portland houses, some dating back 100 years, line the streets of **Nob Hill.** At the heart of Nob Hill are the fashion-conscious blocks of **Northwest 23rd Avenue between Burnside and Vaughn streets**—now a citywide destination for dining and café hopping. Several of the avenue's old homes have been turned into upscale boutiques, with everything from women's clothing to antique linens. **Northwest 21st Avenue between Everett and Vaughn streets** also has trendy restaurants and watering holes. Finding parking in this neighborhood has become such a challenge that the city put in an electric streetcar line. The Central City Streetcar runs from Legacy Good Samaritan Hospital through the Pearl District, links up with MAX light-rail near Pioneer Courthouse Square downtown, and then continues up 10th Avenue to Portland State University. Across the Willamette River, **Southeast Hawthorne Boulevard between 30th and 39th avenues** has become the east side's most popular stomping ground. More down-to-earth than Northwest 23rd and still countercultural around the edges, Southeast Hawthorne is lined with bookstores, coffeehouses, taverns, restaurants, antiques stores, and unusual boutiques. **Northeast Alberta Street between Martin Luther King Jr. Boulevard and 30th Avenue** is developing as an art center, with more than two dozen art galleries and studios and a growing number of coffeehouses, restaurants, barbecues, and specialty shops. Galleries and businesses host the "Art on Alberta" sidewalk event on the last Thursday evening of each month. A street fair in September enlivens the neighborhood with arts and crafts booths, music, and food vendors.

Parks, Gardens, and Zoos

Washington Park (✉ 611 S.W. Kingston Ave., ☎ 503/823–7529), on 322 acres in the West Hills, is the site of the renowned **International Rose Test Garden** (☎ 503/823–3636; free); the serene **Japanese Garden** (☎ 503/223–1321, WEB www.japanesegarden.com; $6) is considered one of the most authentic outside Japan.

★ The **Oregon Zoo** (✉ 4001 S.W. Canyon Rd., ☎ 503/226–7627, WEB www.oregonzoo.org; $7.50) has Asian elephants, an African section, and animals indigenous to the Pacific Northwest. Steller Cove, with Steller sea lions and sea otters, is not to be missed. The Washington Park MAX station is adjacent to the zoo entrance.

Dining

Bounteous local produce from land and sea receives star billing at many Portland dining establishments, and Pacific Rim immigrants have added variation and spice to the restaurant scene.

$$$$ ★ ✕ **Genoa.** Widely regarded as the finest restaurant in Portland, Genoa serves a seven-course, prix-fixe menu on Friday and Saturday evenings; weekdays there are four courses. The menu, which changes every two weeks, might include roasted chicken stuffed with homemade ricotta cheese. Seating is limited to a few dozen diners, so service is excellent. *✉ 2822 S.E. Belmont St., ☎ 503/238–1464. Reservations essential. AE, D, DC, MC, V. Closed Sun. No lunch.*

$$$–$$$$ ✕ **El Gaucho.** Three dimly lit dining rooms with blue walls and striped upholstery invite those with healthy pocketbooks. The specialty here is 28-day dry-aged Angus beef cooked in an open kitchen. Service is impeccable at this Seattle transplant. *✉ 319 S.W. Broadway, ☎ 503/227–8794. AE, D, DC, MC, V. No lunch.*

$$–$$$$ ✕ **Jake's Famous Crawfish.** White-coated waiters serve up fresh seafood, selected from a lengthy sheet of daily specials, in a warren of old-fashioned wood-paneled dining rooms. Alder-smoked salmon and crab-crawfish-salmon cakes are consistent standouts. *✉ 401 S.W. 12th Ave., ☎ 503/226–1419. Reservations essential. AE, D, DC, MC, V. No lunch weekends.*

$$–$$$ ✕ **Caprial's.** PBS cooking-show star Caprial Pence prepares Mediterranean-inspired surf-and-turf creations at her bustling bistro with an open kitchen and full bar. The dinner menu changes monthly. *✉ 7015 S.E. Milwaukie Ave., ☎ 503/236–6457. MC, V. Closed Sun.–Mon.*

$$–$$$ ✕ **Heathman Restaurant.** In the Heathman Hotel, master chef Philippe Boulot assembles Pacific Northwest ingredients and presents them to you with a French flair. Duck, lamb, salmon, specialty seafood dishes, and local free-range game—venison, veal, rabbit—appear on the seasonally changing menu. ✉ *1001 S.W. Broadway,* ☎ *503/790–7752. Reservations essential. AE, D, DC, MC, V.*

$$–$$$ ★ ✕ **Higgins.** Higgins uses organic herbs and produce in its fusion cooking, which draws influence from French and Pacific Northwest cuisine. Fresh seafood dishes are excellent and might include a French seafood chowder served with new potatoes and braised greens. The elegant, three-level dining area has an open kitchen, wood floors, mahogany paneling, and tapestry upholstery. ✉ *1239 S.W. Broadway,* ☎ *503/222–9070. AE, MC, V. No lunch weekends.*

$$–$$$ ✕ **Paley's Place.** This charming bistro serves Pacific Northwest–style French cuisine. Weather permitting, seating is available on the front porch and back patio. Among the entrées are dishes featuring duck, New York steak, chicken, and halibut. Paley's has a fine selection of Willamette Valley and French wines. ✉ *1204 N.W. 21st Ave.,* ☎ *503/243–2403. AE, MC, V. No lunch.*

$$–$$$ ✕ **Typhoon!** This trendy restaurant serves excellent Thai food at reasonable prices in a cozy but lively environment. Curry dishes, spicy chicken or shrimp with crispy basil, and vegetarian spring rolls are standouts. It's packed for lunch. ✉ *400 S.W. Broadway,* ☎ *503/224–8285. AE, D, DC, MC, V. No lunch weekends.*

$$ ✕ **Southpark.** The specialty here is wood-fired Mediterranean seafood. There's a wide selection of fresh Pacific Northwest oysters and fine regional wines. The interior is contemporary, with art deco touches and warm, reddish lighting. Southpark is near the Arlene Schnitzer Concert Hall and the Portland Art Museum. ✉ *901 S.W. Salmon St.,* ☎ *503/326–1300. AE, MC, V. No lunch Sun.*

Brewpubs

Portland has one of the largest microbrewery scenes in North America. The **Bridgeport Brew Pub** (✉ 1313 N.W. Marshall St., ☎ 503/241–7179) serves thick hand-thrown pizzas; wash them down with creamy pints of Bridgeport real ale. **McMenamins Edgefield** (✉ 2126 S.W. Halsey St., Troutdale, ☎ 503/669–8610) is the showpiece of the vast microbrewing empire of the McMenamin brothers; the 12-acre estate has its own pub, restaurant, movie theater, 105-room inn, winery, and brewery. The McMenamin brothers' newest venture, **Ringlers** restaurant (✉ 1332 W. Burnside St., ☎ 503/225–0543), occupies the first floor of a historic (1914) Portland building that also houses the Crystal Ballroom, a dance club and concert venue.

Lodging

You'll find many national and regional chains near the airport. The city center and waterfront support both elegant new and historic hotels. Bed-and-breakfasts cluster in the West Hills and across the river in the Lloyd Center/Convention Center area.

Northwest Bed & Breakfast (☎ 503/243–7616) is a good source for information and reservations in Portland and the entire coastal region.

$$$–$$$$ **The Benson.** Portland's grandest hotel, built in 1912, has maintained its turn-of-the-20th-century splendor, with Russian walnut–paneled walls in the rooms and a piano in the lobby. ✉ *309 S.W. Broadway, 97205,* ☎ *503/228–2000 or 800/426–0670,* FAX *503/226–4603,* WEB *www.bensonhotel.com. 287 rooms. 2 restaurants. AE, D, DC, MC, V.*

$$$–$$$$ **The Governor.** This distinctive hotel has a clubby lobby with mahogany walls and a mural of Northwest Indians fishing in Celilo Falls. Guest rooms, painted in soothing earth tones, are elegant with large windows and fireplaces. Suites have whirlpool tubs and and balconies. ✉ *611 S.W. 10th Ave., 97205,* ☎ *503/224–3400 or 800/554–3456,* FAX *503/241–2122,* WEB *www.govhotel.com. 100 rooms. Restaurant, pool, health club. AE, D, DC, MC, V.*

$$$–$$$$ ★ **The Heathman.** Superior service, a top-notch restaurant, an elegant tea court, and a library of signed first editions by authors who have been guests here have earned the Heathman a reputation for quality. ✉ *1001 S.W. Broadway, 97205,* ☎ *503/241–4100 or 800/551–0011,* FAX *503/790–7110,* WEB *www.heathmanhotel.com. 150 rooms. Restaurant, gym. AE, D, DC, MC, V.*

$$$ ★ **Embassy Suites Portland Downtown.** There is no lack of space in this all-suites hotel in the historic Multnomah Hotel building. Each suite's two rooms are well appointed—you'll find two televisions, a microwave, a refrigerator, and a dining table that doubles as a work area. A full breakfast and happy-hour cocktails are included in the room rate. ✉ *319 S.W. Pine St., 97204,* ☎ *503/279–9000 or 800/362–2779,* FAX *503/497–9051,* WEB *www.embassy-suites.com. 276 suites. Restaurant, pool, gym. AE, D, DC, MC, V. BP.*

$$$ **Hilton Portland.** Upper-floor rooms in this high-rise yield outstanding views of the Willamette Valley and surrounding mountains. The Hilton Portland is Oregon's largest hotel. The Performing Arts Center, the Portland Art Museum, and MAX light-rail are all nearby. ✉ *921 S.W. 6th Ave., 97204,* ☎ *503/226–1611 or 800/445–8667,* FAX *503/220–2565,* WEB *www.hilton.com. 455 rooms. 2 restaurants, pool, health club. AE, D, DC, MC, V.*

$$–$$$ **Doubletree Hotel Portland–Lloyd Center.** At Portland's second-largest hotel, service runs like a well-oiled machine. Many of the rooms have views of the mountains or the city center. Lloyd Center shopping and MAX light-rail are across the street. ✉ *1000 N.E. Multnomah St. 97232,* ☎ *503/281–6111,* FAX *503/284–8553,* WEB *www.doubletree.com. 476 rooms. 3 restaurants, pool, gym. AE, D, DC, MC, V.*

$$–$$$ **Portland's White House.** Fountains, antiques, and hardwood floors with Oriental rugs create a warm, romantic mood at this elegant inn in a Greek Revival mansion. ✉ *1914 N.E. 22nd Ave., 97212,* ☎ *503/287–7131 or 800/272–7131,* FAX *503/249–1641,* WEB *www.portlandswhitehouse.com. 9 rooms. AE, D, MC, V.*

$$ **Doubletree Hotel–Jantzen Beach.** The four-story Doubletree, on the Columbia River, has larger-than-average guest rooms, many with balconies and good views of the river and Vancouver, Washington. Public areas glitter with brass and bright lights. ✉ *909 N. Hayden Island Dr. (east of I–5's Jantzen Beach exit), 97217,* ☎ *503/283–4466 or 800/222–8733,* FAX *503/283–4743,* WEB *www.doubletree.com. 320 rooms. Restaurant, pool, gym. AE, D, DC, MC, V.*

$–$$ **MacMaster House.** This 17-room colonial revival mansion, built in 1886, is near fashionable Washington Park. Each room or suite, though small, is uniquely decorated: The Miller Room has a mahogany sleigh bed and antique chairs; the Writer's Retreat has an iron bed, a desk, and bookshelf. Some rooms have shared bath; most have fireplaces. The Victorian-style living and dining rooms are very inviting. ✉ *1041 S.W. Vista Ave., 97205,* ☎ *503/223–7362 or 800/774–9523,* WEB *www.macmaster.com. 9 rooms, 5 with bath. AE, D, DC, MC, V. BP.*

$–$$ **Mallory Hotel.** The rooms are on the small side, but this Portland stalwart, five blocks from the city center, is clean and friendly. It's on the MAX light-rail line. ✉ *729 S.W. 15th Ave., 97205,* ☎ *503/223–6311 or 800/228–8657,* FAX *503/223–0522,* WEB *www.malloryhotel.com. 136 rooms. Restaurant. AE, D, DC, MC, V.*

Nightlife and the Arts

The *Oregonian,* Portland's daily newspaper; *Willamette Week*; the biweekly *Portland Tribune*; and *Just Out,* the city's gay paper, list arts and entertainment events. The latter three are free in the metro area.

Nightlife

The **Crystal Ballroom** (✉ 1332 W. Burnside St., ☎ 503/225–0047), dating from 1914 and completely restored, hosts dancing to live bands on its huge "elastic" floor, built on ball bearings. **Brasserie Montmartre** (✉ 626 S.W. Park Ave., ☎ 503/224–5552) offers live jazz and fine cuisine. Dine on prime rib at **Jazz De Opus** (✉ 33 N.W. 2nd Ave., ☎ 503/222–6077), which attracts area jazz musicians and aficionados. **Polly Esther's Culture Club** (✉ 424 S.W. 4th Ave., ☎ 503/221–1970) is a dance bar with several levels and a DJ playing a '70s and '80s nostalgia mix. Young hipsters pack **Muu-Muus** (✉ 612 N.W. 21st Ave., ☎ 503/223–8169) nightly. The upscale, martini set chill at **Wildwood** (✉ 1221 N.W. 21st Ave., ☎ 503/248–9663). For laughs try **Harvey's Comedy Club** (✉ 436 N.W. 6th Ave., ☎ 503/241–0338), which presents headliners with a national reputation.

C. C. Slaughters (✉ 200 N.W. 3rd Ave., ☎ 503/248–9135) is a popular gay bar with a restaurant and a dance floor that's crowded on weekend nights; weeknights bring karaoke and country dancing. There are several other gay bars on Southwest Stark Street. **Scandals** (✉ 1038 S.W. Stark St., ☎ 503/227–5887) is a neighborhood bar with a pool table. **Boxxes/Panorama/Fish Grotto** (✉ 1035 S.W. Stark St., ☎ 503/221–7262) has a video bar, a patio bar, a disco, and a restaurant.

Performing Arts

The **Portland Center for the Performing Arts** (✉ 1111 S.W. Broadway, ☎ 503/248–4335), which includes the Arlene Schnitzer Concert Hall and (across the street) the Performing Arts Building, presents symphony orchestra and rock concerts, theater, dance, lectures, and touring Broadway musicals. **Portland Center Stage** (☎ 503/274–6588, WEB www.pcs.org) performs plays from November to April at the Newmark Theater in the Performing Arts Building. The **Oregon Symphony** (☎ 503/228–1353, WEB www.orsymphony.org) performs more than 40 concerts each season at the Arlene Schnitzer Concert Hall. **The Oregon Ballet Theater** (☎ 503/222–5538, WEB www.obt.org) performs at the **Civic Auditorium** (✉ 222 S.W. Clay St., ☎ 503/796–9293).

Spectator Sports

Baseball: Remodeled in 2001, PGE Park (✉ 1844 S.W. Morrison St., ☎ 503/553–5400, WEB www.pgepark.com) hosts the **Portland Beavers (AAA).** No parking is available at the 20,000-seat park; MAX lightrail is the most convenient option. Your event ticket entitles you to a free round-trip. **Basketball:** The NBA's **Portland Trail Blazers** play at the 20,000-seat Rose Garden arena (✉ 1 Center Ct., at east end of Broadway Bridge, ☎ 503/231–8000). **Horse Racing:** Thoroughbred and quarter horses race, rain or shine, at **Portland Meadows** (✉ 1001 N. Schmeer Rd., ☎ 503/285–9144) from October to April. **Ice Hockey:** The **Portland Winter Hawks** (☎ 503/236–4295) of the Western Hockey League play home games from September through March at Memorial Coliseum (✉ 300 N. Winning Way, ☎ 503/238–6366) and at the Rose Garden arena (✉ 1 Center Ct., ☎ 503/231–8000). **Soccer:** The **Portland Timbers** play at PGE Park (✉ 1844 S.W. Morrison St., ☎ 503/553–5400, WEB www.pgepark.com).

Shopping

For local products try the **Made In Oregon** shops, with locations at Portland International Airport, Lloyd Center, the Galleria, Old Town, Washington Square, and Clackamas Town Center. Merchandise ranges from books to smoked salmon, hazelnuts, honey, dried fruits, local wines, and Pendleton woolen products.

Pioneer Place (✉ 700 S.W. 5th Ave., ☎ 503/228–5800) is the jewel in the city's shopping crown with more than 80 specialty shops. **Saks Fifth Avenue** (✉ 850 S.W. 5th Ave., ☎ 503/226–3200) is Pioneer Place's anchor store. The original **Meier & Frank** (✉ 621 S.W. 5th Ave.) department store, a Portland landmark since 1857, is across the street from Pioneer Place. **Nordstrom** (✉ 701 S.W. Broadway, ☎ 503/224–6666), across from Pioneer Courthouse Square, has high-quality apparel and accessories and a large shoe department. High-tech **Niketown** (✉ 930 S.W. 6th Ave., ☎ 503/221–6453), the original branch of a now-national chain, is part sports shrine, part sales outlet. With more than a million new and used volumes, **Powell's City of Books** (✉ 1005 W. Burnside St., ☎ 503/228–4651) is one of the largest bookstores in the world. The **Portland Pendleton Shop** (✉ 900 S.W. 5th Ave., ☎ 503/242–0037) carries men's and women's wear, including the Oregon mill's famous Pendleton shirts and blankets.

Across the Willamette River on Portland's east side, **Lloyd Center** (✉ N.E. Multnomah St. at N.E. 9th Ave., ☎ 503/282–2511), which is on the MAX light-rail line, contains more than 170 shops, including Nordstrom, Sears, and Meier & Frank; a large food court; a multi-screen cinema; and an ice-skating pavilion.

The **Hawthorne District,** along Southeast Hawthorne Boulevard from Southeast 17th Avenue to Southeast 43rd Avenue, has attracted bohemian and artsy types with its coffeehouses, music clubs, funky shops, and galleries. **Sellwood,** in the city's southeast corner between Southeast Tacoma Street and Southeast 13th Avenue, is a modest neighborhood known for its antiques stores and restaurants.

Portland Essentials

AIRPORTS AND TRANSFERS

Portland International Airport is about 10 mi northeast of the city.

➤ AIRPORT INFORMATION: **Portland International Airport (PDX;** (✉ 7000 N.E. Airport Way, ☎ 503/460–4234).

AIRPORT TRANSFER

Transportation to and from the airport is available through Broadway Cab, as well as hotel shuttles. A taxi ride downtown costs about $25. The most convenient and least expensive way to get to the airport is via MAX light-rail's Red Line trains, which run directly to the terminal from downtown. Tickets are less than $2 each way.

➤ TAXIS AND SHUTTLES: **Broadway Cab** (☎ 503/227–1234). **Tri-Met** (☎ 503/238–7433).

BUS TRAVEL TO AND FROM PORTLAND

➤ BUS INFORMATION: **Greyhound** (✉ 550 N.W. 6th Ave., ☎ 800/231–2222, WEB www.greyhound.com).

CAR TRAVEL

I–84 (Banfield Freeway) and U.S. 26 (the Sunset) run east–west; I–5, I–205, and I–405 run north–south. I–405 runs west of the downtown district. I–205 bypasses downtown on the city's east side.

TRAIN TRAVEL

➤ TRAIN INFORMATION: **Amtrak** (✉ Union Station, 800 N.W. 6th Ave., ☎ 503/273–4865 or 800/872–7245, WEB www.amtrak.com).

TRANSPORTATION AROUND PORTLAND

The metropolitan area is laid out in a grid system, with numbered avenues running north–south and named streets running east–west. Locations with northwest or southwest addresses are on the west side of the Willamette River, northeast and southeast on the east side. Burnside Street separates north from south addresses. The MAX light-rail line links eastern and western Portland suburbs to the downtown core, the Portland International Airport, the Lloyd Center District, the Convention Center, and the Rose Quarter, which includes Memorial Coliseum and the Rose Garden sports arena. The Westside MAX line includes an underground stop at the Oregon Zoo in Washington Park. At 260 ft below the surface, the transit station is the deepest in the nation. The Tri-Met bus system covers the metro area extensively. The Central City Streetcar line runs from Legacy Good Samaritan hospital in Northwest Portland, through the Pearl District and downtown, to Portland State University. Streetcars stop every few blocks.

➤ CONTACT: **Tri-Met** (☎ 503/238–7433).

VISITOR INFORMATION

Portland Guides in green jackets walk the sidewalks downtown; they can assist with directions and answer questions about the city.

➤ TOURIST INFORMATION: **Portland/Oregon Visitors Association** (✉ 2 World Trade Center, 26 S.W. Salmon St., 97204, ☎ 503/222–2223 or 800/962–3700, WEB www.pova.com).

THE OREGON COAST

Oregon has 400 mi of white-sand beaches, not a grain of which is privately owned. U.S. 101 parallels the coast from Astoria south to California, past monoliths of sea-tortured rock, brooding headlands, hidden beaches, historic lighthouses, tiny ports, and, of course, the tumultuous Pacific. Many knowledgeable coastal travelers consider the 63-mi stretch of U.S. 101 between Port Orford and Gold Beach, where the highway soars up green headlands some hundreds of feet high, Oregon's most beautiful. Take time to admire the views by making use of the many turnouts along the way.

Exploring the Oregon Coast

Astoria, founded in 1811 at the site where the mighty Columbia River meets the Pacific Ocean, is believed to be the first official settlement established by the United States on the West Coast. Here Lewis and Clark wept with joy when they first saw the Pacific. The Victorian houses once owned by fur, timber, and fishing magnates still dot the flanks of Coxcomb Hill; some are now inviting B&Bs. Patterned after Trajan's Column in Rome, the 125-ft **Astor Column** atop Coxcomb Hill rewards a climb up 164 spiral stairs with breathtaking views over Astoria, the Columbia, the Coast Range, and the ocean.

The **Columbia River Maritime Museum** (✉ 1792 Marine Dr., ☎ 503/325–2323, WEB www.crmm.org; $5) has exhibits ranging from the fully operational lightship *Columbia* to poignant personal belongings from some of the 2,000 ships that have been wrecked at the mouth of the river since 1811.

★ Five and a half miles southeast of Astoria is the **Fort Clatsop National Memorial** (✉ Fort Clatsop Loop Rd., ☎ 503/861–2471, WEB www.nps.

Western Oregon

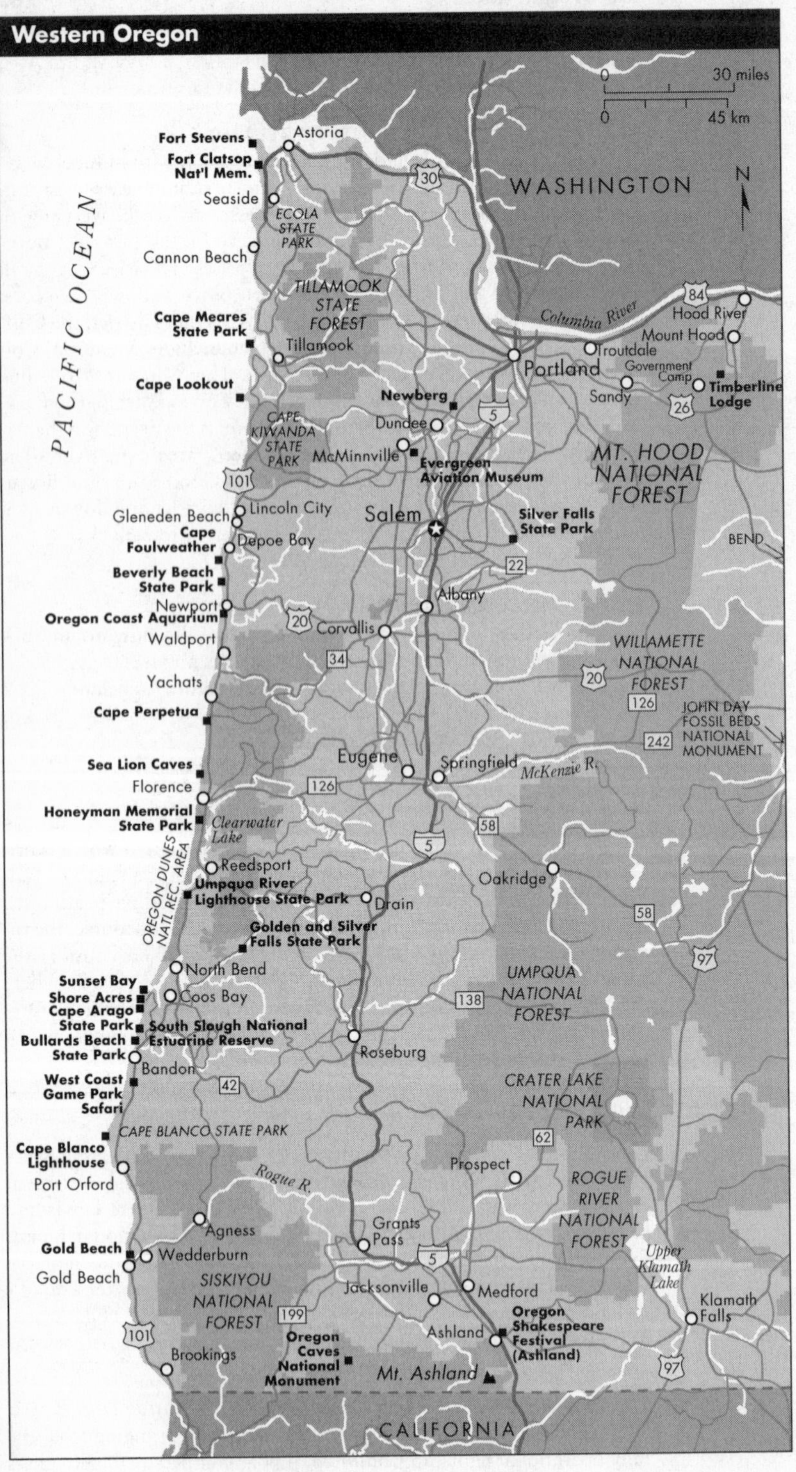

gov/focl; 🎫 $4 per vehicle), a replica of the log stockade depicted in William Clark's journal, commemorating the achievement of Lewis and Clark.

★ Thirty miles south of Astoria and close enough to Portland to make it a popular weekend getaway, **Cannon Beach** draws vacationers to its long and sandy beach, restaurants, and weathered-cedar shopping district. It's especially popular in June, when the **Cannon Beach Sandcastle Contest** (☎ 503/436–2623) takes place. **Haystack Rock**, a 235-ft offshore sea stack with tidal pools at its base, is one of the most photographed sites on the coast.

At the north end of Cannon Beach, **Ecola State Park** (☎ 800/551–6949; 🎫 $3 per vehicle) is a playground of sea-sculpted rock, sandy beach, tidal pools, green headlands, and panoramic views.

South of Tillamook Bay, on the lush coastal plain that is Oregon's dairy country, **Tillamook** is known for its cheese and ice cream. Taste the famous cheddar, or head for the 40-flavor ice cream counter, at the **Tillamook County Creamery** (✉ 4175 U.S. 101 N, ☎ 503/842–4481). The **Three Capes Scenic Loop,** west of Tillamook, takes you by magnificent coastal scenery, a lighthouse, offshore wildlife refuges, sand dunes, camping areas, and hiking trails.

Bustling **Lincoln City,** 43 mi south of Tillamook on U.S. 101, is known for its good seafood restaurants, ocean-view motels, casino, and proximity to some of the Oregon coast's most scenic landscapes. **Chinook Winds Casino and Convention Center** (✉ 1777 N.W. 44th St., 97367, ☎ 800/244–6665, WEB www.chinookwindscasino.com), on the beach in Lincoln City, has slot machines, gaming tables, a buffet, big-name entertainers, and oceanfront dining.

Twenty-five miles south of Lincoln City, **Newport,** with its fishing fleet, art galleries, famous aquarium, and seafood markets along a charming old bay front, is a fine place for an afternoon stroll or an overnight getaway.

★ Across Yaquina Bay, the **Oregon Coast Aquarium** has more than 4 acres of outdoor pools, cliffs, and caves for frolicking sea otters and sea lions. It was once the temporary home of Keiko, the orca featured in the *Free Willy* movies. Keiko's former digs have been transformed into a deep-sea exhibit complete with a wrecked ship. You'll pass through underwater tunnels, coming face to face with sharks, sunfish, and sea turtles swimming above and below. Indoor galleries are devoted to Oregon's coastal habitats and native marine life. ✉ *2820 S.E. Ferry Slip Rd.,* ☎ *541/867–3474,* WEB *www.aquarium.org.* 🎫 *$10.25.*

★ South of Newport, the coast takes on a very different character—slower paced, less touristy, far less crowded, but just as rich in scenery and outdoor sporting activities. **Cape Perpetua** (✉ 9 mi south of Yachats, off U.S. 101, ☎ 541/547–3289; 🎫 interpretive center $3), the highest lookout point on the Oregon coast, towers 800 ft above the rocky shoreline and has hiking trails and an informative visitor center. The **Sea Lion Caves** (✉ 91560 U.S. 101, 1 mi south of Heceta Head, ☎ 541/547–3111, WEB www.sealioncaves.com; 🎫 $7) include a huge vaulted chamber where kids can get a close view of hundreds of sea lions, the largest of which weigh a ton or more.

★ The peaceful village of Florence is the northern gateway to the **Oregon Dunes National Recreation Area** (✉ 855 Highway Ave., Reedsport 97467, ☎ 541/271–3611; 🎫 $5 per vehicle), a remarkable 40-mi swath of tawny sand. The dunes, some more than 500 ft high, are popular with campers, hikers, mountain bikers, dune-buggy enthusiasts, and even dogsledders. Children particularly enjoy the sandy slopes surrounding cool Cleawox Lake. **Umpqua River Lighthouse State Park** (✉ 6 mi south of Reedsport on U.S. 101, ☎ 800/551–6949) adjoins an operating lighthouse and encompasses a small freshwater lake and campground. Also in the park are a whale-watching station and 500-ft-high sand dunes.

Coos Bay is the Oregon coast's largest metropolitan area. There are several attractions, state parks, and wildlife areas nearby.

★ You can see more than 75 exotic animal species, including lions, tigers, bears, camels, and zebras—and you can pet some of the babies—at **West Coast Game Park Safari** (✉ U.S. 101, 7 mi south of Bandon, ☎ 541/347–3106, WEB www.gameparksafari.com; $7.95).

At the end of a gravel road in **Golden and Silver Falls State Park** (✉ 24 mi northeast of Coos Bay off U.S. 101, ☎ 800/541–6949; free), Glenn Creek pours over a high rock ledge deep in the old-growth forest. West of Coos Bay, the **Cape Arago Highway** presents spectacular scenery at three state parks: Sunset Bay (✉ 2 mi south of Charleston off Cape Arago Hwy.; free) has a white-sand beach, picnicking, and campgrounds. Shore Acres (✉ 10965 Cape Arago Hwy., 1 mi south of Sunset Bay State Park; $3 per vehicle), once the estate of a timber baron, has a 7½-acre formal garden and a glass-enclosed stormwatch viewpoint.Cape Arago (✉ end of Cape Arago Hwy., 1 mi south of Shore Acres State Park; free), overlooking the Oregon Islands National Wildlife Refuge, is a prime site for viewing sea lions and seabirds. Four miles south of the small fishing village of Charleston, the rich tidal estuaries of **South Slough National Estuarine Reserve** (✉ Seven Devils Rd., 4 mi south of Charleston, ☎ 541/888–5558; free) support life ranging from algae to bald eagles and black bears.

Bullards Beach State Park (✉ U.S. 101, 2 mi north of Bandon, ☎ 800/551–6949; free) spreads over miles of shoreline and sand dunes. It has a campground as well as the restored Coquille River Lighthouse. Take a tour to the top of **Cape Blanco Lighthouse** (✉ Cape Blanco Hwy., 10 mi west of U.S. 101, 9 mi north of Port Orford, ☎ 541/756–0100), built in 1870 and still operating. It is the most westerly lighthouse in the contiguous 48 states. You can visit it Thursday–Monday 10–3:30. Adjacent Cape Blanco State Park (☎ 541/332–6774; free) has sweeping views of rocks and beaches plus a campground.

Gold Beach, about 30 mi north of the California border, is where the wild Rogue River meets the ocean. Daily jet-boat excursions roar up the scenic, rapids-filled Rogue from Wedderburn, Gold Beach's sister city across the bay, from late spring to late fall. Gold Beach also marks the entrance to Oregon's banana belt, where milder temperatures encourage a blossoming trade in lilies and daffodils. You'll even see a few palm trees here.

Dining and Lodging

Astoria

$–$$$ ✕ **Cannery Café.** Housed in a 100-year-old renovated cannery on a pier, this bright, contemporary restaurant has windows that look onto the Columbia River. Fresh salads, large sandwiches, clam chowder, and crab cakes are lunch staples. ✉ *1 6th St.,* ☎ *503/325–8642. MC, V. Closed Mon. No dinner Sun.*

$–$$ **Franklin Street Station Bed & Breakfast.** The ticking of a grandfather clock and the mellow marine light shining through lead-glass windows set a relaxed tone at this B&B, built in 1900. Breakfasts are huge, hot, and satisfying. ✉ *1140 Franklin St., 97103,* ☎ *503/325–4314 or 800/ 448–1098,* WEB *www.franklin-st-station-bb.com. 6 rooms. MC, V. BP.*

Brookings

$$ ★ 🏨 **Chetco River Inn.** Acres of private forest surround this modern fishing lodge 17½ mi up the Chetco River from Brookings. Fishing guides are available on request, as are eclectic dinners cooked by the B&B's owner, Sandra Burgger; she's also a font of information on the many hiking trails in the area. Quilts and fishing gear decorate the comfortable bedrooms. ✉ *21202 High Prairie Rd., 97415,* ☎ *541/670–1645 or 800/327–2688,* WEB *www.chetcoriverinn.com. 4 rooms. MC, V. BP.*

Cannon Beach

$$$ ✕ **The Bistro.** Cannon Beach's most romantic restaurant is candlelit and intimate. The three-course prix-fixe menu treats you to imaginatively prepared fresh seafood. ✉ *263 N. Hemlock St.,* ☎ *503/436–2661. Reservations essential. MC, V. Closed Tues.–Wed. Nov.–Jan. No lunch.*

$–$$ ✕ **Dooger's.** This family-style eatery's fresh and well-prepared seafood, exquisite clam chowder, and low prices keep 'em coming back for more. ✉ *1371 S. Hemlock St.,* ☎ *503/436–2225. AE, D, MC, V.*

$$$–$$$$ ★ ✕🏨 **Stephanie Inn.** Country-style furnishings, fireplaces, large bathrooms with Jacuzzi tubs, and balconies overlooking outstanding views of Haystack Rock make this oceanfront hotel a treat. The inn also serves four-course prix-fixe dinners of Pacific Northwest cuisine; reservations are essential. Room rates include generous country breakfasts and evening wine and hors d'oeuvres. ✉ *2740 S. Pacific St., 97110,* ☎ *503/ 436–2221 or 800/633–3466,* FAX *503/436–9711,* WEB *www.stephanie-inn.com. 50 rooms. Restaurant. AE, D, DC, MC, V. BP.*

Coos Bay

$–$$ ✕ **Portside Restaurant.** At this unpretentious spot with picture windows overlooking the busy Charleston boat basin, you'll be treated to seafood straight off the fishing boats. Try the steamed Dungeness crab with drawn butter, a local specialty, or the all-you-can-eat seafood buffet on Friday night. ✉ *8001 Kingfisher Rd. (follow Cape Arago Hwy. from Coos Bay),* ☎ *541/888–5544. AE, DC, MC, V.*

$ 🏨 **Coos Bay Manor.** This 15-room colonial revival manor was built in 1912 on a quiet residential street and now is listed on the National Register of Historic Places. An unusual open balcony on the second floor leads to the five large, comfortable guest rooms. Breakfast is served in the wainscoted dining room or, weather permitting, outside on the second-floor porch. ✉ *955 S. 5th St., 97420,* ☎ *541/269–1224 or 800/ 269–1224,* FAX *541/269–1224. 5 rooms, 3 with bath. D, MC, V. FP.*

Depoe Bay

$–$$ ★ ✕ **Gracie's Sea Hag.** Across the street from the beach, Gracie's has been specializing in fresh seafood for more than 30 years. There's a seafood buffet on Friday night; prime rib with Yorkshire pudding is the focus on Saturday. ✉ *53 U.S. 101,* ☎ *541/765–2734. AE, D, DC, MC, V.*

Florence

$$ ✕ **Bridgewater Seafood Restaurant.** The salty air of Florence's photogenic Old Town permeates this spacious, creaky-floored fish house. Steaks, salads, and plenty of fresh seafood are the mainstays. ✉ *1297 Bay St.,* ☎ *541/997–9405. MC, V.*

$–$$ 🏨 **Driftwood Shores Surfside Resort Inn.** The chief amenity of this resort is its location directly above Heceta Beach, one of the longest sand beaches on the south coast. The simple rooms have ocean views and kitchens; the three-bedroom suites have fireplaces and balconies. ✉ *88416 1st Ave., 97439 (from U.S. 101 take Heceta Beach Rd. west about 3 mi north of Florence),* ☎ *541/997–8263 or 800/422–5091,*

FAX 541/997–5857, WEB *www.driftwoodshores.com. 153 rooms. Restaurant, pool. AE, D, DC, MC, V.*

Gleneden Beach

$$$–$$$$ ✕🏨 **Westin Salishan Lodge and Golf Resort.** Nestled in a 350-acre forest preserve, Salishan embodies northwest elegance and tranquillity, with soothing silver cedar, fireplaces, balconies, and a collection of original art. The dining room is famous for its seasonal Northwest cuisine and wine list. ✉ *7760 U.S. 101 N, 97388,* ☎ *541/764–3605 or 800/452–2300,* FAX *541/764–3681,* WEB *www.salishan.com. 205 rooms. 3 restaurants, pool, golf, tennis, gym. AE, D, DC, MC, V.*

Gold Beach

$$–$$$$ ★ ✕🏨 **Tu Tu Tun Lodge.** Private decks at this luxurious fishing resort overlook the clear blue Rogue River. All units have an upscale rustic charm. Four-course prix-fixe dinners are served at one sitting each night. ✉ *96550 N. Bank Rogue, 97444,* ☎ *541/247–6664 or 800/864–6357,* FAX *541/247–0672,* WEB *www.tututun.com. 18 rooms, one 3-bedroom house. Restaurant, golf. D, MC, V. Dining room closed Nov.–Apr.*

$ 🏨 **Ireland's Rustic Lodges.** Original one- and two-bedroom cabins filled with rough-and-tumble charm plus newer motel rooms and three houses are set amid landscaped grounds. Most units have a fireplace and a deck overlooking the sea. ✉ *29330 Ellensburg Ave./U.S. 101, 97444,* ☎ *541/247–7718,* FAX *541/247–0225,* WEB *www.irelandsrusticlodges.com. 33 rooms, 7 cabins. MC, V.*

Lincoln City

$$ ★ ✕ **Bay House.** This restaurant serves meals to linger over while you enjoy views across sunset-gilded Siletz Bay. The seasonal Northwest cuisine includes shellfish linguine, fresh halibut with Parmesan, and roast duckling with dried cherries and pinot noir sauce. The wine list is extensive, the service impeccable. ✉ *5911 S.W. U.S. 101,* ☎ *541/996–3222. AE, D, MC, V. Closed Mon.–Tues. Nov.–Apr. No lunch.*

$–$$ ✕ **Kyllo's.** Perched on stilts beside the world's shortest river (the D) and bestowing views of Pacific surf and sand, Kyllo's is a spacious, light-filled aerie. It's also one of the best places in Lincoln City to enjoy simple but satisfying seafood, meat, and pasta dishes. ✉ *1110 N.W. 1st Ct.,* ☎ *541/994–3179. AE, D, MC, V.*

$–$$ ✕ **Mo's.** Come here for clear bay-front views and a creamy bowl of clam chowder. This coastal institution has been around for more than 40 years, consistently providing fresh seafood and down-home service. ✉ *860 S.W. 51st St.,* ☎ *541/996–2535. D, MC, V.*

$–$$ 🏨 **Shilo Inn Oceanfront Resort.** This four-building motel is popular because it's on the beach next to Chinook Winds Casino and within walking distance of shopping. Suites have kitchenettes, fireplaces, and balconies. ✉ *1501 N.W. 40th Pl., 97367,* ☎ *541/994–3655 or 800/222–2244,* FAX *503/994–2199,* WEB *www.shiloinn.com. 248 rooms. Restaurant, pool, gym. AE, D, DC, MC, V.*

Newport

$–$$ ✕ **Canyon Way Restaurant and Bookstore.** The best dining (and bookstore) in Newport is just up the hill from the center of the Bay Front. Cod, Dungeness crab cakes, bouillabaisse, and Umpqua Bay oysters are among the specialties served inside or on the outdoor patio. There's also a deli counter for takeout. ✉ *S.W. Canyon Way, off Bay Front Blvd.,* ☎ *541/265–8319. AE, MC, V. No dinner Mon.*

$–$$ ✕ **Whale's Tale.** Fresh local seafood, thick clam chowder, burgers, and hearty sandwiches are all on the menu of this casual, family-oriented bay-front eatery; the breakfasts are fabulous. ✉ *452 S.W. Bay Blvd.,* ☎ *541/265–8660. AE, D, DC, MC, V. Closed Wed. Nov.–Apr.*

$-$$$ ★ **Sylvia Beach Hotel.** Each of the phoneless, TV-less, antiques-filled guest rooms at this restored 1912 B&B is named for a famous writer and decorated accordingly. (A pendulum swings over the bed in the Poe Room.) Upstairs is a well-stocked library with a fireplace, a slumbering cat, and too-comfortable chairs. Tables of Content, the hotel's restaurant, serves a prix-fixe dinner; reserve early. ✉ *267 N.W. Cliff St., 97365,* ☎ *541/265–5428 or 888/795–8422,* WEB *www.sylviabeachhotel.com. 20 rooms. Restaurant. AE, MC, V. No lunch. BP.*

Yachats

$$-$$$ ★ **La Serre.** Perhaps the best restaurant on the Oregon coast, La Serre serves fresh seafood dishes, including razor clams lightly breaded and flash-fried in lemon-garlic butter, fishermen's stew, and a famous seafood extravaganza with grilled salmon, blackened cod, and Dungeness crab cakes. ✉ *2nd and Beach Sts.,* ☎ *541/547–3420. AE, MC, V. Closed Tues. and Jan. No lunch.*

$-$$$ **The Adobe Resort.** The knotty-pine rooms in this unassuming motel are on the smallish side, but they're warm and inviting. High-beam ceilings and picture windows frame beautiful ocean views. Many rooms have wood-burning fireplaces. ✉ *1555 U.S. 101, 97498,* ☎ *541/547–3141 or 800/522–3623,* FAX *541/547–4234,* WEB *www.adoberesort.com. 101 units. Restaurant. AE, D, DC, MC, V.*

Campgrounds

Seventeen state parks along the coast have campgrounds, most with trailer hookups and tent sites. Many are near the shore, and some have group facilities and hiker/biker or horse camps. The **Oregon State Parks and Recreation Department** (✉ 1115 Commercial St. NE, Salem 97310, ☎ 800/551–6949, WEB www.oregonstateparks.org) has details.

Honeyman State Park (✉ Oregon Dunes National Recreation Area, Florence 97439, ☎ 800/551–6949, WEB www.oregonstateparks.org; $5 per vehicle) adjoins the Oregon Dunes National Recreation Area. Reserve well ahead.

Outdoor Activities and Sports

Biking

The **Oregon Coast Bike Route** parallels U.S. 101 and the coast from Astoria south to Brookings.

Fishing

Salmon, delectable Dungeness crab, and dozens of species of bottom fish are the quarry here, accessible from jetties, docks, and riverbanks from Astoria to Brookings. Charter boats and guides are plentiful; contact local chambers of commerce (☞ Visitor Information, *below*) for information on fishing permits, seasons, rates, and schedules.

Golf

The Oregon coast has about 20 public and private courses. **Salishan Golf Links** (✉ 7760 U.S. 101, Gleneden Beach, ☎ 541/764–3632) is the coast's most challenging course, with 18 holes. Newport has the 9-hole **Agate Beach Golf Course** (✉ 4100 N. Coast Hwy., ☎ 541/265–7331). Gold Beach's **Cedar Bend Golf Course** (✉ 34391 Squaw Valley Rd., ☎ 541/247–6911) has 9 holes.

Beaches

Virtually the entire 400-mi coastline of Oregon consists of clean white-sand beaches, accessible to all. Thanks to its sea-sculpted stone, **Face Rock Wayside,** in Bandon, is thought by many to have the most beautiful walking beach in the state. The placid, semicircular lagoon at **Sunset Bay State Park,** on Cape Arago, is Oregon's safest swimming beach. Fossils, clams, mussels, and other eons-old marine creatures embedded in soft sandstone cliffs make **Beverly Beach State Park,** 5 mi north of Newport, a favorite with young beachcombers.

Shopping

Hemlock Street, the main drag of Cannon Beach, is the best place on the coast to browse for unusual clothing, souvenirs, picnic supplies, books, and gifts. Newport's **Bay Boulevard** is a good place to find local artwork, gifts, and fresh seafood. There are bargains galore at the **Factory Stores at Lincoln City** (✉ 1500 S.E. Devils Lake Rd., ☎ 541/996–5000). Particularly good deals on vintage items can be found in the antiques malls in Astoria, Seaside, and Lincoln City.

The Oregon Coast Essentials

BUS TRAVEL

Greyhound serves Coos Bay, Florence, Newport, and Lincoln City.

➤ BUS INFORMATION: **Greyhound** (☎ 800/231–2222, WEB www.greyhound.com).

CAR TRAVEL

The best way to see the coast is by car, but all travel is by two-lane highways. U.S. 26 connects Portland to U.S. 101 at Seaside. The direct route to Lincoln City is I–5 south to Route 99 W to McMinnville, where it connects with Route 18.

VISITOR INFORMATION

➤ TOURIST INFORMATION: **Astoria-Warrenton Chamber of Commerce** (✉ 111 W. Marine Dr., Astoria 97103, ☎ 503/861–1031 or 800/875–6807). **Bay Area Chamber of Commerce** (✉ 50 E. Central Ave., Coos Bay 97420, ☎ 541/269–0215 or 800/824–8486, WEB www.oregonsbayareachamber.com). **Cannon Beach Chamber of Commerce** (✉ 2nd and Spruce Sts., 97110, ☎ 503/436–2623, WEB www.cannonbeach.org). **Florence Area Chamber of Commerce** (✉ 270 U.S. 101, 97439, ☎ 541/997–3128 or 800/524–4864, WEB www.florencechamber.com). **Greater Newport Chamber of Commerce** (✉ 555 S.W. Coast Hwy., 97365, ☎ 503/265–8801 or 800/262–7844, WEB www.newportchamber.org). **Lincoln City Visitors Center** (✉ 801 S.W. U.S. 101, Suite 1, 97367, ☎ 541/994–8378 or 800/452–2151, WEB www.oregoncoast.org). **Seaside Visitors Bureau** (✉ 7 N. Roosevelt Ave., 97138, ☎ 503/738–6391 or 800/444–6740, WEB www.seasideor.com).

ELSEWHERE IN OREGON

Mt. Hood and Bend

What to See and Do

★ Mt. Hood, 11,235 ft high and surrounded by the 1.1-million-acre **Mt. Hood National Forest** (information center: ✉ 3 mi west of town of Zigzag on north side of U.S. 26, ☎ 503/622–7674, WEB www.mthood.org), is an all-season playground that attracts more than 7 million visitors annually for skiing, camping, hiking, and fishing.

The skiing is excellent near **Bend,** which occupies a tawny high-desert plateau in the very center of Oregon, framed on the west by three 10,000-ft Cascade peaks. With its plentiful dining and lodging options, Bend makes a fine base camp for skiing at nearby **Mt. Bachelor,** whitewater rafting on the **Deschutes River,** world-class rock climbing at **Smith Rocks State Park,** and other outdoor activities.

Don't miss the archaeological and wildlife displays at the **High Desert Museum** (✉ 59800 U.S. 97, 3½ mi south of Bend, ☎ 541/382–4754, WEB www.highdesert.org; 💳 $8.50). **Newberry National Volcanic Monument** (25 mi southeast of Bend, ☎ 541/383–5300; 💳 $5 per vehicle) contains more than 50,000 acres of lakes, lava flows, and geological features.

$–$$$ ★ **Timberline Lodge.** Everything at this National Historic Landmark (off U.S. 26 a few miles east of Government Camp) has a handcrafted, rustic feel, from the wrought-iron chairs with rawhide seats to the massive hand-hewn beams. The expert cuisine at the Cascade Dining Room incorporates the freshest Oregon ingredients. ✉ *Timberline Rd., Timberline 97028,* ☎ *503/231–5400 or 800/547–1406,* FAX *503/727–3710,* WEB *www.timberlinelodge.com. 60 rooms. Restaurant, pool. AE, D, MC, V.*

$$–$$$$ **Sunriver Resort.** One of Oregon's premier outdoor resort destinations, Sunriver provides a slew of facilities and is convenient to skiing at Mt. Bachelor; Class IV white-water rafting on the Deschutes River (which flows right through the complex); and high-desert hiking and mountain biking. A former army base, the self-contained community has stores, restaurants, contemporary homes, condominiums, and even a private airstrip—all in a pine-scented desert landscape. ✉ *West of U.S. 97, 15 mi south of Bend (Box 3609, Sunriver 97707),* ☎ *800/801–8765,* FAX *541/593–5458,* WEB *www.sunriver-resort.com. 510 units. 4 restaurants, 2 pools, golf, tennis. AE, D, DC, MC, V.*

Mt. Hood and Bend Essentials

AIR TRAVEL

➤ AIRLINES INFORMATION: **Bend–Redmond Municipal Airport** (☎ 541/548–6059).

CAR TRAVEL

Mt. Hood lies about an hour east of Portland on U.S. 26; the only way to get there is by car. Continue east on U.S. 26, then south on U.S. 97 for the resort town of Bend, two hours beyond Mt. Hood.

Columbia River Gorge

What To See and Do

Multnomah Falls, a 620-ft-high double-decker torrent, is the fifth-highest waterfall in the nation. From the parking lot, a paved path winds to a bridge over the lower falls. A much steeper trail climbs to a view point overlooking the upper falls.

The 1937 **Bonneville Dam** (✉ from I–84 take Exit 40, head northeast, and follow signs 1 mi to visitor center, ☎ 541/374–8820; 💳 free), is Oregon's most impressive man-made attraction. Its generators have a capacity of nearly a million kilowatts, enough to supply power to more than 200,000 single-family homes. There is a modern visitor center on Bradford Island, complete with underwater windows for viewing migrating salmon as they struggle up fish ladders.

Hood River, a town 60 mi east of Portland on I–84 in the spectacular Columbia Gorge, is the self-proclaimed sailboarding capital of the world.

Columbia Gorge Sailpark (✉ I–84 Exit 64, Port Marina, ☎ 541/386–1645), on the river downtown, has a boat basin, a swimming beach, jogging trails, and picnic tables.

Dining

$$–$$$ ✕ **Multnomah Falls Lodge.** The lodge, built in 1925 and listed on the National Register of Historic Places, has vaulted ceilings and classic stone fireplaces. Freshwater trout, salmon, and a platter of prawns, halibut, and scallops are the specialties. The restaurant is famous for its wild-huckleberry daiquiris and desserts. ✉ *Historic Columbia River Hwy. (or Exit 31 off I–84),* ☎ *503/695–2376. AE, D, MC, V.*

Columbia River Gorge Essentials

CAR TRAVEL

The Columbia River Gorge is a short drive northeast of Portland on I–84. Multnomah Falls is 20 mi east of Troutdale; Bonneville Dam is another 10 mi east; Hood River is 30 mi farther.

Willamette Valley/Wine Country

What to See and Do

Oregon's **wine country** occupies the wet, temperate trough between the Coast Range to the west and the Cascades to the east. More than 60 wineries dot the hills west of Portland and Salem, and dozens more are scattered from Newport to as far south as Ashland, on the California border. Although tiny in comparison with California's, Oregon's wine industry is booming. Cool-climate varietals such as pinot noir, chardonnay, and Johannesberg Riesling have gained the esteem of international connoisseurs.

The best way to tour is by car. *Discover Oregon Wineries,* an indispensable map and guide to the wine country, is available free at wine shops and wineries or by calling the **Oregon Winegrowers Association** (☎ 800/242–2363).

McMinnville, 14 mi south of Newberg on U.S. 99 W, is where to find the **Evergreen Aviation Museum,** where the famed *Spruce Goose* is on permanent display. Also known as the Hughes Flying Boat, the plane belonged to eccentric millionaire Howard Hughes, though he flew it only once. It was moved here in 1992 from Long Beach, California. Also on display are about a dozen military planes. ✉ *3850 Three Mile La., McMinnville 97128,* ☎ *503/472–9361,* WEB *www.sprucegoose.org.* 🎫 *$9.50.* ⏲ *Daily 9–5.*

Salem, the state capital, is a lovely spot to overnight. In addition to its hotels, B&Bs, and restaurants, there are some fine gardens and museums.

A gilded 23-ft-high bronze statue of the Oregon Pioneer atop the 106-ft capitol dome is the centerpiece of the **Capitol** (✉ 900 Court St., ☎ 503/986–1388, WEB www.oregon.gov), where Oregon's legislators convene every two years. **Deepwood Estate** (✉ 1116 Mission St. SE, ☎ 503/363–1825; 🎫 $4), on the National Register of Historic Places, encompasses 5½ acres of lawns, formal English gardens, and a fanciful 1894 Queen Anne mansion with splendid interior woodwork and original stained glass. **Mission Mill Village** (✉ 1313 Mill St. SE, ☎ 503/585–7012, WEB www.missionmill.org; 🎫 $5) offers tours of its circa 1889 woolen mill and pioneer homes. ★ **Silver Falls State Park** (✉ Rte. 214, 26 mi east of Salem, ☎ 800/551–6949; 🎫 $3 per vehicle) covers 8,700 acres and includes 10 waterfalls accessible to hikers.

Liberal-minded **Eugene** is Oregon's second-largest city. The **University of Oregon**'s green campus spreads over the southeast portion of the city. Eugene's two best museums are affiliated with the university. The collection of Asian art at the **University of Oregon Museum of Art** (✉ 1430 Johnson La., ☎ 541/346–3027, WEB www.uoma.uoregon.edu), next to the library, includes examples of Chinese imperial tomb figures, textiles, and furniture. Relics of a more localized nature are on display at the **University of Oregon Museum of Natural History** (✉ 1680 E. 15th Ave., ☎ 541/346–3024, WEB www.natural-history.uoregon.edu). The **University of Oregon Ducks** play their home football games at Autzen Stadium (✉ 2700 Centennial Blvd., ☎ 800/932–3668).

Wistec, Eugene's imaginative, hands-on Willamette Science and Technology Center, assembles rotating exhibits designed for curious young minds. The adjacent **planetarium,** one of the largest in the Pacific Northwest, presents star shows and entertainment events. ✉ *2300 Leo Harris Pkwy.,* ☎ *541/682–7888,* WEB *www.wistec.org.* *$4. Closed Mon.–Tues.*

South of Eugene, the sleepy farming community of **Roseburg,** on the Umpqua River, is famous among anglers. West of town are a dozen of the region's wineries. The **Douglas County Museum** (✉ Douglas County Fairgrounds, I–5 Exit 123, ☎ 541/957–7007; $3.50) has an exceptional fossil collection.

Dining and Lodging

Northwest Bed & Breakfast (☎ 503/243–7616 or 503/370–9033) can help you with reservations in the Willamette Valley.

$$–$$$ ✕ **DaVinci.** Salem politicos flock to this two-story downtown restaurant for Italian-inspired dishes cooked in a wood-burning oven. No shortcuts are taken in the preparation, so don't come if you're in a rush. But if you're in the mood to linger over seafood and fresh pasta that's made on the premises, you'll be more than content. The wine list is one of the longest in the Northwest; the staff is courteous and extremely professional. ✉ *180 High St., Salem,* ☎ *503/399–1413. AE, DC, MC, V. No lunch Sun.*

$$–$$$$ ★ ✕ **Valley River Inn.** Most of the plushly furnished rooms at this hotel on the picturesque banks of the Willamette River have outdoor patios or balconies with river or pool views. Its restaurant, Sweetwaters, has good Pacific Northwest cuisine. ✉ *1000 Valley River Way, Eugene 97401,* ☎ *503/629–9465 or 800/543–8266,* FAX *541/682–0289,* WEB *www.valleyriverinn.com. 257 rooms. Restaurant, pool, gym. AE, D, DC, MC, V.*

$$–$$$ ★ ✕ **Excelsior Inn.** This small, stylish hotel across from the University of Oregon campus is quietly sophisticated, with cherrywood doors and moldings, marble-and-tile baths, and in-room VCRs and modem lines. A full breakfast is served in the appealing Excelsior Café, which also has a seasonal menu for lunch and dinner. ✉ *754 E. 13th St., Eugene 97401,* ☎ *541/342–6963 or 800/321–6963,* FAX *541/342–1417,* WEB *www.excelsiorinn.com. 14 rooms. Restaurant. AE, D, DC, MC. BP.*

Willamette Valley/Wine Country Essentials

AIRPORTS

➤ AIRPORT INFORMATION: **Eugene Airport** (✉ 28855 Lockheed Dr., ☎ 541/687–5430).

CAR TRAVEL

I–5, the state's main north–south freeway, runs through the center of the Willamette Valley from Portland to California.

Ashland/The Rogue Valley

What to See and Do

★ Ashland hosts the Tony Award–winning **Oregon Shakespeare Festival** (✉ 15 S. Pioneer St., 97520, ☎ 541/482–4331, WEB www.osfashland.org), which annually attracts more than 100,000 theatergoers to this relaxing Rogue Valley town. A few miles south of Ashland you'll find excellent downhill and Nordic skiing atop 7,523-ft **Mt. Ashland.** West of Ashland, the famous Rogue River boils and churns through the rugged, remote Kalmiopsis Wilderness in **Siskiyou National Forest** (☎ 541/471–6500). The local wineries are also worth a visit.

Jacksonville, west of Ashland, preserves the look and feel of an Old West pioneer settlement; the entire town is a National Historic Landmark.Each summer Jacksonville hosts the **Britt Festivals** (☎ 541/773–6077 or 800/882–7488), a concert series with some of the world's best jazz and classical musicians performing in an outdoor amphitheater.

★ The main attraction at **Crater Lake National Park** (✉ Box 7, Crater Lake 97604, ☎ 541/594–2211, WEB www.nps.gov/crla; 🎟 $10 per vehicle) was created 6,800 years ago, when Mt. Mazama decapitated itself in a huge explosion. Rain and snowmelt eventually filled the caldera, creating a sapphire-blue lake so clear that sunlight penetrates to a depth of 400 ft. You can drive or hike the park's 25-mi **Rim Drive,** explore nature trails, and (in summer) take boat trips on the lake. The park is about 80 mi northeast of Jacksonville along Route 62.

★ **Wildlife Safari** lets you come face to face with free-roaming animals from the comfort of your car. There's also a petting zoo, a miniature train, and elephant rides at this 600-acre, drive-through wildlife park. The admission price includes two drive-throughs in the same day. ✉ *Box 1600, Winston 97496,* ☎ *800/355–4848,* WEB *www.wildlifesafari.org.* 🎟 *$14.50. AE, D, MC, V.*

Lodging

$$–$$$ **Crater Lake Lodge.** The historic 1915 lodge on the rim of the caldera will charm you with lodgepole pine columns, gleaming wood floors, and stone fireplaces that grace the common areas. There are no electronic diversions of any kind. ✉ *1211 Ave. C, White City 97503,* ☎ *541/830–8700,* FAX *541/830–8514,* WEB *www.craterlakelodge.com. 71 rooms. Restaurant. MC, V. Closed mid-Oct.–mid-May.*

$$–$$$ **Mt. Ashland Inn.** Built from hand-hewn cedar logs close to the summit ski area on Mt. Ashland, this modern, 5,500-square-ft lodge provides magnificent views of Mt. Shasta and the Siskiyou range. Antiques and hand-stitched quilts lend character to the guest rooms; a sauna and outdoor hot tub overlook the alpine splendor. ✉ *550 Mt. Ashland Rd., 97520,* ☎ *541/482–8707 or 800/830–8707,* FAX *541/482–8707,* WEB *www.mtashlandinn.com. 5 rooms. D, MC, V. BP.*

Ashland/The Rogue Valley Essentials

AIRPORTS

➤ AIRPORT INFORMATION: **Rogue Valley International Airport** (✉ 3650 Biddle Rd., ☎ 541/772–8068).

CAR TRAVEL

Ashland is midway between Portland and San Francisco on I–5, about 15 mi north of the California state line.

PENNSYLVANIA

Updated by Robert DiGiacomo and Clark Henderson

Capital	Harrisburg
Population	12,281,000
Motto	Virtue, Liberty, and Independence
State Bird	Ruffed grouse
State Flower	Mountain laurel
Postal Abbreviation	PA

Statewide Visitor Information

Pennsylvania Department of Commerce, Office of Travel and Tourism (✉ 480 North St., 4th floor, Harrisburg 17120, ☎ 717/787–5453 or 800/847–4872, WEB www.experiencepa.com). **Welcome centers** are on major highways.

Scenic Drives

In Bucks County, **River Road** (Route 32) wends 40 mi along the Delaware River, past 18th- and 19th-century stone farmhouses, tucked-away villages, and wooded hills. In the Poconos, **Route 209,** from Stroudsburg to Milford, passes forests and waterfalls. The Lancaster County countryside, with its Amish farms and roadside stands, can best be seen along the side roads between **Routes 23 and 340.**

National and State Parks

National Parks

Pennsylvania has 17 national parks, historic sites, and monuments overseen by the **National Park Service** (✉ 200 Chestnut St., Philadelphia 19106, ☎ 215/597–7013, WEB www.nps.gov), a few of which have camping. The 500,000-acre **Allegheny National Forest** (✉ 222 Liberty St., Warren 16365, ☎ 814/723–5150, WEB www.fs.fed.us/r9/allegheny), in the northwestern part of the state, has hiking and cross-country skiing trails, three rivers suitable for canoeing, and stream fishing. The **Delaware Water Gap National Recreation Area** (✉ River Rd., Bushkill 18324, ☎ 570/588–2451, WEB www.nps.gov/dewa), a 40-mi-long preserve in the northeast corner of the state and across the Delaware River in New Jersey, has camping, fishing, river rafting, and tubing.

State Parks

Pennsylvania's 116 state parks have more than 7,000 campsites. The **Bureau of State Parks** (✉ Rachel Carson State Bldg., Box 8551, Harrisburg 17105, ☎ 717/772–0239 or 888/727–2757, WEB www.dcnr.state.pa.us) provides information and campsite reservations. In the Poconos the wooded, 15,480-acre **Hickory Run State Park** (✉ R.D. 1, Box 81, White Haven 18661, ☎ 570/443–0400, WEB www.dcnr.state.pa.us) offers fishing, camping, and Boulder Field, an area of rock formations dating to the Ice Age. **Presque Isle State Park** (✉ Rte. 832, Erie 16505, ☎ 814/833–7424, WEB www.dcnr.state.pa.us), a 3,200-acre peninsula that extends 7 mi into Lake Erie, is popular for fishing, swimming, and boating.

PHILADELPHIA

Almost a century after English Quaker William Penn founded Philadelphia in 1682, the city became the birthplace of the nation and the home of its first government. Today, Philadelphia is synonymous with Independence Hall, the Liberty Bell, cheese steaks and hoagies, ethnic

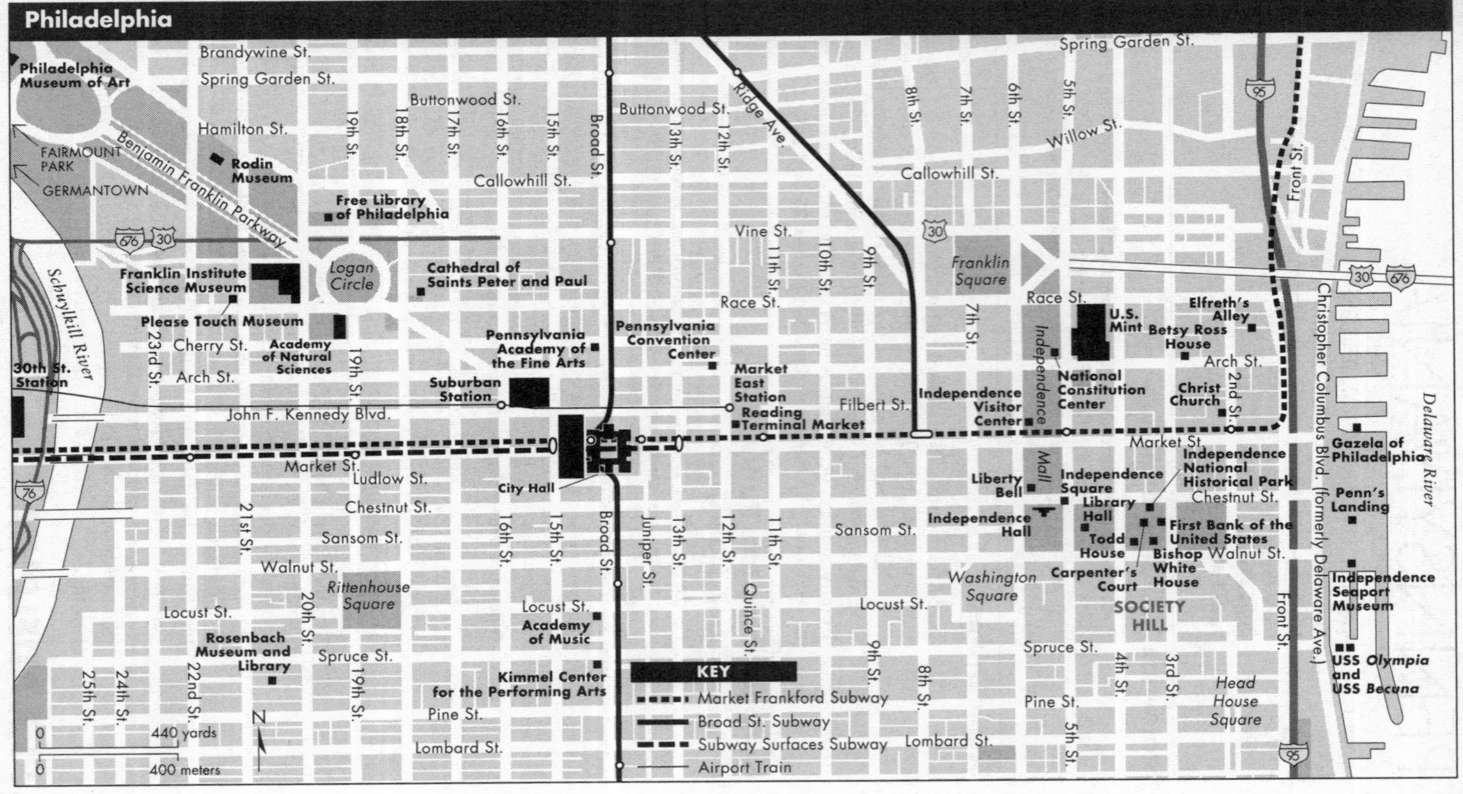
Philadelphia
Philadelphia Museum of Art
Brandywine St.
Spring Garden St.
Buttonwood St.
Hamilton St.
FAIRMOUNT PARK
GERMANTOWN
Benjamin Franklin Parkway
Rodin Museum
Free Library of Philadelphia
Callowhill St.
19th St.
18th St.
17th St.
16th St.
15th St.
Broad St.
13th St.
12th St.
Ridge Ave.
Vine St.
11th St.
10th St.
9th St.
8th St.
7th St.
6th St.
5th St.
Willow St.
Front St.
Schuylkill River
Franklin Institute Science Museum
Logan Circle
Cathedral of Saints Peter and Paul
Please Touch Museum
Cherry St.
Academy of Natural Sciences
23rd St.
Arch St.
30th St. Station
Pennsylvania Academy of the Fine Arts
Suburban Station
Pennsylvania Convention Center
Race St.
Market East Station
Reading Terminal Market
John F. Kennedy Blvd.
Filbert St.
Franklin Square
Independence Visitor Center
Independence Mall
National Constitution Center
U.S. Mint
Betsy Ross House
Elfreth's Alley
Christ Church
2nd St.
Christopher Columbus Blvd. (formerly Delaware Ave.)
Delaware River
Gazela of Philadelphia
Penn's Landing
Independence Seaport Museum
USS Olympia and USS Becuna
Market St.
Ludlow St.
City Hall
Chestnut St.
21st St.
Sansom St.
Walnut St.
Rittenhouse Square
20th St.
Locust St.
Rosenbach Museum and Library
Spruce St.
Academy of Music
Kimmel Center for the Performing Arts
Pine St.
Lombard St.
Juniper St.
Quince St.
25th St.
24th St.
22nd St.
N
0
440 yards
400 meters
KEY
Market Frankford Subway
Broad St. Subway
Subway Surfaces Subway
Airport Train
Liberty Bell
Independence Hall
Independence Square
Library Hall
Todd House
Carpenter's Court
Independence National Historical Park
First Bank of the United States
Bishop White House
Washington Square
SOCIETY HILL
4th St.
3rd St.
Head House Square
30
676
95
76

neighborhoods, theaters—and city streets teeming with life. Penn's "City of Brotherly Love" is the fifth-largest city in the country, yet it maintains the feel of a friendly small town.

Exploring Philadelphia

The *Calendar of Events* at the visitor center (☞ Visitor Information *in* Philadelphia Essentials, *below*) lists free events and attractions.

Historic District

★ Even if you're not a history buff, it's hard not to get excited by the "most historic square mile in America"—**Independence National Historical Park** (✉ 313 Walnut St., 19106, ☎ 215/597–8974, WEB www.nps.gov/inde; 🎫 free).

The **Independence Visitor Center** (✉ 6th St., between Market and Arch Sts., ☎ 215/965–7676 or 800/537–7676, WEB www.independencevisitorcenter.com) has park rangers staffing the information desk. The **National Constitution Center** (✉ 525 Arch St., ☎ 215/923–0004, WEB www.constitutioncenter.org; 🎫 call for price), an interactive museum opening in July 2003, celebrates the U.S. Constitution. The **Liberty Bell Pavilion** (✉ 6th and Market Sts., ☎ 215/597–8974, WEB www.nps.gov/inde; 🎫 free), an angled glass building with sightlines of Independence Hall, is scheduled to open in March 2003. The 2,080-pound bell, Philadelphia's best-known symbol, contains the biblical inscription PROCLAIM LIBERTY THROUGHOUT ALL THE LAND UNTO ALL THE INHABITANTS THEREOF.

★ Stately **Independence Hall** (✉ Chestnut St. between 5th and 6th Sts., ☎ 215/597–8974, WEB www.nps.gov/inde; 🎫 free), opened in 1732 as the state house for the colony of Pennsylvania, was the site of many historic events: the Second Continental Congress, convened on May 10, 1775; the adoption of the Declaration of Independence a year later; the signing of the Articles of Confederation in 1778; and the formal signing of the Constitution by its framers on September 17, 1787. When you stand on the spot where the Declaration of Independence was first read to the public, you can almost hear "When in the course of human events . . . ." It's easy to imagine the impact those words and this setting had on the colonists on July 8, 1776. Tours of Independence Hall are given year-round; though a timed-ticket system has just about eliminated the long lines here, expect crowds from early May to Labor Day.

In **Carpenter's Court** (✉ Chestnut St. between 3rd and 4th Sts.) you'll find **Carpenter's Hall,** where the first Continental Congress convened in 1774, and the **New Hall Military Museum.**

Steepled **Christ Church** (✉ 2nd St. north of Market St., ☎ 215/922–1695, WEB www.christchurchphila.org; 🎫 free) is where noted colonists, including 15 signers of the Declaration of Independence, worshiped. **Elfreth's Alley** (✉ off Front and 2nd Sts. between Arch and Race Sts.) is the oldest continuously occupied residential street in America, dating from 1702. **Two houses** (✉ 124–126 Elfreth's Alley, ☎ 215/574–0560, WEB www.elfrethsalley.org; 🎫 $2) have been restored—one as the home of a colonial-era Windsor chair maker, the other of a seamstress.

The **Betsy Ross House** (✉ 239 Arch St., ☎ 215/686–1252, WEB www.ushistory.org/betsy; 🎫 donation) is a splendid example of a colonial Philadelphia home, although the story that Ross sewed the first American flag in this house hangs by only a few threads of evidence.

The Waterfront and Society Hill

★ **Society Hill** was—and still is—Philadelphia's showplace, the city's most charming and photogenic neighborhood. Federal brick row houses and narrow streets stretch from the Delaware River to 7th Street. (The "Society" in the neighborhood's moniker refers not to the wealthy Anglicans who first settled here but to the Free Society of Traders, business investors who moved to the area on William Penn's advice.)

At Society Hill's eastern edge, the spot where William Penn stepped ashore in 1682 is today a 37-acre park known as **Penn's Landing** (✉ Delaware Riverfront from Lombard St. to Market St., ☎ 215/922–2386, WEB www.pennslandingcorp.com), with festivals and concerts from spring to fall. Construction of an entertainment complex here may cause concerts to move to Festival Pier at Columbus Boulevard and Spring Garden Street.

The **Independence Seaport Museum** (✉ 211 S. Columbus Blvd., ☎ 215/925–5439, WEB seaport.philly.com; $8 includes admission to the Olympia and Becuna) has nautical artifacts, ship displays, and interactive exhibits. The **USS *Olympia*** (✉ Penn's Landing at Spruce St., ☎ 215/922–1898; $8 includes admission to Becuna and Independence Seaport Museum) was Commodore George Dewey's flagship in the Spanish-American War. The **USS *Becuna*** (✉ Penn's Landing at Spruce St., ☎ 215/922–1898; $8 includes admission to Olympia and Independence Seaport Museum) is a World War II submarine.

The ***Gazela of Philadelphia,*** built in 1883, is the last of a Portuguese fleet of cod-fishing ships, known as "The White Fleet," and the oldest wooden square-rigger still sailing. ✉ *Penn's Landing at Market St.,* ☎ *215/218–0110,* WEB *www.gazela.org.* *Free. Closed Oct.–May.*

You can take a 10-minute ride on the **Riverlink Ferry** across the Delaware River to Camden (☞ New Jersey) and the New Jersey State Aquarium. ✉ *Penn's Landing at Walnut St.,* ☎ *215/925–5465,* WEB *www.riverlinkferry.org.* *$5 round-trip. Closed Jan.–Mar.*

The **Bishop White House** (✉ 309 Walnut St., ☎ 215/597–8974, WEB www.nps.gov/inde; $3 tour includes Todd House), built in 1786 as the home of the rector of Christ Church, has been restored to its colonial elegance. The simply furnished **Todd House** (✉ 4th and Walnut Sts., ☎ 215/597–8974, WEB www.nps.gov/inde; $3 tour includes Bishop White House) has been restored to its 1790s appearance, when Dolley Payne Todd (later Mrs. James Madison) lived here.

Head House Square (✉ 2nd and Pine Sts., ☎ 215/790–0782), an open-air colonial marketplace, is the site of crafts fairs and other activities on weekends from Memorial Day through September.

City Hall and Environs

★ At the geographic center of Penn's original city stands **City Hall**—the largest city hall in the country (it has 642 rooms). For a tour of the interior and a 360-degree view of the city from the William Penn statue, go to Room 121 via the northeast corner of the courtyard and ride the elevator to the top of the 548-ft tower. ✉ *Broad and Market Sts.,* ☎ *215/686–1776; 215/686–2840 tour information;* WEB *www.geocities.com/athens/delphi/2115.* *Free. Closed weekends.*

★ The **Pennsylvania Academy of the Fine Arts,** in a stunning Victorian building by Philadelphia architects Frank Furness and George Hewitt, is the oldest art institution in the United States (founded 1804). Its museum holds works by artists ranging from Winslow Homer and Benjamin West to Red Grooms. ✉ *118 N Broad St., at Cherry St.,* ☎ *215/972–7600,* WEB *www.pafa.org.* *$8, free Sun. 3–5. Closed Mon.*

The glass-roofed **Kimmel Center for the Performing Arts** (✉ Broad and Spruce Sts., ☎ 215/893–1999 tickets; 215/790–5800 tour information; WEB www.kimmelcenter.org), the home of the Philadelphia Orchestra, Philly Pops, Philadelphia Dance Company, and other arts groups, offers regular, free performances at its indoor plaza.

The sprawling **Reading Terminal Market** (✉ 12th and Arch Sts.; ☞ Dining, *below*), one floor beneath the former Reading Railroad's 1891 train shed, holds 80 food stalls and other shops.

★ The city's most elegant small park, **Rittenhouse Square** (✉ Walnut St. between 18th and 19th Sts.) resembles a Parisian park and frequently hosts arts festivals. The **Rosenbach Museum and Library** (✉ 2010 Delancey Pl., ☎ 215/732–1600, WEB www.rosenbach.org; 🎫 $5) offers a 75-minute tour of its sumptuous paintings, rare books (including the original manuscript of James Joyce's *Ulysses*), and objets d'art. The museum is closed until April 2003 because of construction.

Museum District

The **Benjamin Franklin Parkway** angles across the grid of city streets from city hall to Fairmount Park. Lined with distinguished museums, hotels, and apartment buildings, this 250-ft-wide boulevard inspired by the Champs-Elysées was built in the 1920s. The Italian Renaissance–style **Cathedral of Sts. Peter and Paul** (✉ 18th and Race Sts., ☎ 215/561–1313), built between 1846 and 1864, is the basilica of the Roman Catholic archdiocese of Philadelphia.

The **Free Library of Philadelphia** (✉ north side of Benjamin Franklin Pkwy. at 19th St., ☎ 215/686–5322, WEB www.library.phila.gov) has more than 1 million volumes. The **Academy of Natural Sciences** (✉ south side of Benjamin Franklin Pkwy. at 19th St., ☎ 215/299–1000, WEB www.acnatsci.org; 🎫 $9) includes "Dinosaur Hall," a permanent exhibit with six fossil skeletons, an interactive paleontology lab, and a "rain forest" with live butterflies. The **Please Touch Museum** (✉ 210 N. 21st St., ☎ 215/963–0667, WEB www.pleasetouchmuseum.org; 🎫 $8.95), designed for children ages seven and younger, encourages hands-on participation. The **Rodin Museum** (✉ 22nd St., ☎ 215/763–8100, WEB www.rodinmuseum.org; 🎫 free) has the largest collection outside France of sculptor Auguste Rodin's works, including masterworks like *The Kiss, The Thinker,* and *The Burghers of Calais.* The ★ **Franklin Institute Science Museum** (✉ 20th St. and Benjamin Franklin Pkwy., ☎ 215/448–1200, WEB www.fi.edu; 🎫 $12) is as clever as its namesake and contains a wealth of hands-on and high-tech exhibits. The museum has a planetarium and an IMAX theater.

★ Modeled on ancient Greek temples, the **Philadelphia Museum of Art** is the city's premier cultural attraction and one of the country's finest art museums. The 200 galleries house more than 300,000 works, with paintings by Renoir, Picasso, Matisse, Marcel Duchamp, and Thomas Eakins; Early American furniture; Amish and Shaker crafts; and reconstructions of a 12th-century French cloister and a 16th-century Indian temple. ✉ *26th St. and Benjamin Franklin Pkwy.,* ☎ *215/763–8100,* WEB *www.philamuseum.org.* 🎫 *$10. Closed Mon.*

Lloyd Hall (✉ 1 Boathouse Row, ☎ 215/685–3936, WEB www.parkalacarte.com), behind the Philadelphia Museum of Art in Fairmount Park, has bike and skate rentals in season, a café, and rest rooms.

Germantown

In 1683 Francis Pastorius led 13 Mennonite families out of Germany to seek religious freedom in the New World; they settled 6 mi northwest of Philadelphia in what is now the city neighborhood of Germantown, and many became Quakers. The **Germantown Historical Society** (✉ 5501 Germantown Ave., ☎ 215/844–0514, WEB www.libertynet.org/ghs) has information about the area.

Cliveden, an elaborate country house built in 1763, was occupied by the British during the Revolution. On October 4, 1777, George Washington's attempt to dislodge them resulted in the Yankees' defeat in the Battle of Germantown. ✉ *6401 Germantown Ave.,* ☎ *215/848–1777,* WEB *www.cliveden.org.* *$6. Closed Jan.–Mar.*

During the yellow fever epidemic of 1793–94, Washington lived in the **Deshler-Morris House** to avoid the unhealthy air of sea-level Philadelphia. ✉ *5442 Germantown Ave.,* ☎ *215/596–1748,* WEB *www.nps.gov/inde.* *$1. Closed Dec.–Mar.*

Other Attractions

The **University of Pennsylvania Museum** (✉ 33rd and Spruce Sts., ☎ 215/898–4000, WEB www.upenn.edu/museum; $5), one of the finest archaeology-anthropology museums in the world, has galleries devoted to ancient Egypt, Greece, the world of Islam, Native Alaska, Mesoamerica, Africa, China, and other areas.

★ One of the world's great collections of Impressionist and post-Impressionist art—175 Renoirs, 66 Cézannes, 65 Matisses, plus masterpieces by van Gogh, Degas, Picasso, and others—is at the **Barnes Foundation,** 8 mi west of Center City. Reservations are required (make these several months in advance), as the number of visitors per day is limited. ✉ *300 Latches La., Merion,* ☎ *610/667–0290,* WEB *www.barnesfoundation.org.* *$5, by reservation only. Closed Mon.–Thurs. Jan.–June and Sept.–Dec., Sat.–Tues. July–Aug.*

★ **Sesame Place,** a 45-minute drive northeast of downtown, is an amusement park for children ages 3–13, based on the television show *Sesame Street.* ✉ *100 Sesame Rd., Langhorne,* ☎ *215/757–1100,* WEB *www.sesameplace.com.* *$36.95. Closed Oct.–Apr.*

Parks, Gardens, and Zoos

Along both banks of the Schuylkill River is **Fairmount Park** (✉ accesses from Kelly Dr., West River Dr., and Belmont Ave., ☎ 215/685–0000, WEB www.phila.gov/fairpark), with woodlands, meadows, and hills. Within its 8,500 acres you'll find tennis courts, playgrounds, trails, the Ellen Phillips Samuel Memorial Sculpture Garden, and some early American country houses (Laurel Hill, Strawberry Mansion, and others). Boathouse Row, 11 19th-century buildings on the banks of the Schuylkill that house 13 rowing clubs, is best viewed from the West River Drive. In the northwest section of the park is the Wissahickon, a 5½-mi-long forested gorge. The University of Pennsylvania's **Morris Arboretum** (✉ Hillcrest Ave. between Germantown and Stenton Aves., ☎ 215/247–5777, WEB www.upenn.edu/arboretum; $8) is 92 acres of romantically landscaped seclusion. Opened in 1874 as the country's first zoo, the **Philadelphia Zoo** (✉ 34th St. and Girard Ave., ☎ 215/243–1100, WEB www.phillyzoo.org; $10.95) has 2,000 animals on 42 acres; the Primate Reserve is a state-of-the-art habitat.

Dining

$$$$ ★ ✕ **The Fountain.** Nestled in the lavish yet dignified lobby of the Four Seasons, with windows overlooking Logan Circle's Swann Fountain, this oasis serves sophisticated American fare such as roasted duck breast with Asian barbecue glaze and hazelnut-crusted softshell crab.

A six-course tasting menu is available. ✉ *1 Logan Sq.*, ☎ *215/963–1500. Reservations essential. Jacket and tie. AE, D, DC, MC, V.*

$$$$ ★ ✕ **Le Bec-Fin.** The Fine Beak (more loosely, the Fine Palate) is arguably the best restaurant in Philadelphia. Louis XV furniture, apricot silk walls, and crystal chandeliers create a luxurious mise-en-scène. Owner-chef Georges Perrier oversees every detail of the excellent haute French six-course prix-fixe menu ($120). The $38 three-course lunch is a relative bargain. ✉ *1523 Walnut St.*, ☎ *215/567–1000. Reservations essential. Jacket and tie. AE, D, DC, MC, V. Closed Sun.*

$$$–$$$$ ★ ✕ **Striped Bass Restaurant and Bar.** A visually stunning room with 28-ft ceilings is the background for such seafood specialties as prosciutto-wrapped halibut served with fig-rosemary polenta. Oysters from the raw bar are superb. ✉ *1500 Walnut St.*, ☎ *215/732–4444. Reservations essential. AE, MC, V.*

$$–$$$$ ★ ✕ **Susanna Foo.** Contemporary Chinese artwork in a handsome dining room sets the tone for chef-owner Susanna Foo's nationally acclaimed cuisine, which combines French technique and Western ingredients with pure, essentially Chinese dishes. Favorites include Hundred-Corner Crab Cakes, tea-smoked duck breast with grilled Asian pears, and rack of lamb with coconut sweet-rice compote. ✉ *1512 Walnut St.*, ☎ *215/545–2666. Reservations essential. Jacket and tie. AE, DC, MC, V.*

$$–$$$ ✕ **Buddakan.** In a sleek yet theatrical setting, Philadelphia restaurateur Stephen Starr presents a pan-Asian menu as stylish as the bustling main dining area, with its white draped walls, cherrywood floors, and giant, gold Buddha statue. Dishes include crispy calamari salad, wasabi-crusted filet mignon, and Japanese black cod with miso glaze. ✉ *325 Chestnut St.*, ☎ *215/574–9440. AE, DC, MC, V.*

$$–$$$ ✕ **Fork.** This intimate American bistro—with an open kitchen, 7-ft-high padded banquettes, and custom light fixtures with hand-painted shades—manages to be both comfortable and sophisticated. Choices might include house-cured salmon with onion confit, braised short ribs with fontina polenta, or sautéed monkfish in creamy roasted garlic sauce. ✉ *306 Market St.*, ☎ *215/625–9425. AE, DC, MC, V.*

$$ ✕ **Azafran.** No question that there's an artist at work here, as indicated by the colorful paintings and the creative fare. Pan-Latin best describes the food that keeps patrons lined up outside this tiny place on weekends. Empanadas, looking vaguely like eggrolls, are tops. Bring your own bottle. ✉ *617 S. 3rd St.*, ☎ *215/928–4019. Reservations not accepted. AE, DC, MC, V. Closed Mon. No lunch.*

$$ ✕ **Los Catrines Restaurant, Tequila's Bar.** Chef Carlos Molina makes this a prime choice for Mexican food, with authentic dishes such as *chilies rellenos* (poblano peppers stuffed with cheese or ground meat and baked in tomato sauce or fried in light batter) or *pozole* (pork and hominy stew). ✉ *1602 Locust St.*, ☎ *215/546–0181. AE, DC, MC, V. Closed Sun. No lunch Sat.*

$–$$ ✕ **Monk's Cafe.** Mussels are practically the national dish of Belgium. Whether cooked in classic style with wine and shallots or with cream, they are a high point at this casual, lively bar and restaurant, as are the fries that accompany them. Burgers and Belgian beers are other menu favorites. ✉ *264 S. 16th St.*, ☎ *215/545–7005. Reservations not accepted. MC, V. Closed Sun.*

$ ✕ **Jim's Steaks.** A Philadelphia phenomenon, a cheese steak is shaved slices of beef, fried onions, and melted cheese loaded onto an untoasted roll, all dripping with oil and juices. Add some greasy fries topped with more melted cheese and a Tastykake for dessert, and you have a unique Philadelphia dining experience. ✉ *400 South St.*, ☎ *215/928–1911. No credit cards.*

$ ★ ✕ **Reading Terminal Market.** This local treasure, with 80 stalls, shops, and lunch counters, offers a smorgasbord of cuisines, including Chinese, Greek, Mexican, Japanese, soul food, Middle Eastern, and Pennsylvania Dutch. Arrive early to beat the daily lunch rush. ✉ *12th and Arch Sts.,* ☎ *215/922–2317. Closed Sun. No dinner.*

Lodging

Most bed-and-breakfasts operate under the auspices of booking agencies, such as **Bed and Breakfast Connections** (✉ Box 21, Devon 19333, ☎ 610/687–3565 or 800/448–3619, WEB www.bnbphiladelphia.com).

$$$$ ★ **Four Seasons.** With its exemplary service, impeccable maintenance, and high-quality food, this luxurious member of the worldwide chain ranks consistently among the best hotels in the United States. Rooms in the square, eight-story hotel are furnished in a classic style with contemporary touches, and the best have views overlooking the fountains in Logan Circle. ✉ *1 Logan Sq., 19103,* ☎ *215/963–1500,* FAX *215/963–9506,* WEB *www.fourseasons.com. 364 rooms. 2 restaurants, pool, gym. AE, D, DC, MC, V.*

$$$–$$$$ **Philadelphia Marriott.** This modern, 23-story full-service convention hotel—the biggest in Pennsylvania—takes up an entire city block. The spacious guest rooms have large windows and traditional cherry furniture. ✉ *1201 Market St., 19107,* ☎ *215/625–2900,* FAX *215/625–6000,* WEB *www.philadelphiamarriott.com. 1,484 rooms. 4 restaurants, pool, health club. AE, D, DC, MC, V.*

$$$–$$$$ **Radisson Plaza–Warwick Hotel.** The spacious guest rooms in this centrally located, freshly renovated landmark hotel come in three distinct categories—standard, deluxe, and large Towers rooms. The Prime Rib is an upscale steak house; Capriccio, a European-style café, offers desserts and espresso until late at night. ✉ *1701 Locust St., 19103,* ☎ *215/735–6000 or 800/523–4210,* FAX *215/790–7766,* WEB *www.radisson.com. 545 rooms. 2 restaurants. AE, DC, MC, V.*

$$$–$$$$ ★ **The Rittenhouse.** This small luxury hotel, which contains condominium residences on other floors of the building, takes full advantage of its elegant Rittenhouse Square location. Many of the rooms and both restaurants overlook the city's classiest park. ✉ *210 W. Rittenhouse Sq., 19103,* ☎ *215/546–9000 or 800/635–1042,* FAX *215/732–3364,* WEB *www.rittenhousehotel.com. 98 rooms. 2 restaurants, pool, health club. AE, D, DC, MC, V.*

$$–$$$$ **Sheraton Rittenhouse Square Hotel.** This 193-room hotel promises eco-friendly features such as fresh, filtered air; organic cotton linens; and a bamboo garden designed to oxygenate air in the lobby. In keeping with the organic theme, the color scheme is a soothing beige and peach. ✉ *227 S. 18th St., 19103,* ☎ *215/546–9400 or 800/854–8002,* WEB *www.sheratonphiladelphia.com. 193 rooms. 4 restaurants, health club. AE, D, DC, MC, V.*

$$$ ★ **Penn's View Inn.** A refurbished 19th-century commercial building holds this cosmopolitan boutique hotel on the fringe of the city's oldest warehouse district. Deluxe rooms, in somber tapestry, have windows overlooking the Delaware River. Accommodations are rather European, if not strictly stylish, though street noise can be a concern. The hotel's Ristorante Panorama has a great wine bar. ✉ *14 N. Front St., 19106,* ☎ *215/922–7600 or 800/331–7634,* FAX *215/922–7642,* WEB *www.pennsviewhotel.com. 28 rooms. Restaurant. AE, DC, MC, V. CP.*

$$–$$$ **Doubletree Philadelphia.** The hotel's sawtooth design gives each room a bay window with a whopping 180-degree view. East-side rooms get a panoramic view of the city and New Jersey. You can also sit in the four-story atrium lobby lounge and observe one of the busiest corners of Philly's theater district. Rooms are decorated in earth tones and have modern furnishings. ✉ *Broad St. at Locust St., 19107,* ☎ *215/893–*

1600 or 800/222–8733, FAX *215/893–1664,* WEB *www.doubletree.com. 427 rooms. 2 restaurants, pool, health club. AE, D, DC, MC, V.*

$$–$$$ **Latham.** At this small, elegant boutique hotel with a European accent and an emphasis on personal service, guest rooms have marble-top bureaus and French writing desks; most have minibars. ✉ *135 S. 17th St., 19103,* ☎ *215/563–7474,* FAX *215/568–0110,* WEB *www.lathamhotel.com. 139 rooms. Restaurant, gym. AE, D, DC, MC, V.*

$–$$ ★ **Thomas Bond House.** Spend the night in the heart of the historic city, the way Philadelphians did more than two centuries ago. Built in 1769, this four-story house has rooms with marble fireplaces and four-poster Thomasville beds—and whirlpool baths. ✉ *129 S. 2nd St., 19106,* ☎ *215/923–8523 or 800/845–2663,* FAX *215/923–8504,* WEB *www.winston-salem-inn.com/philadelphia. 12 rooms. AE, D, DC, MC, V. CP.*

$ **Bank Street Hostel.** This clean, well-run establishment offers a dormitory arrangement that is a downtown-Philly lodging bargain. ✉ *32 S. Bank St., 19106,* ☎ *215/922–0222 or 800/392–4678,* FAX *215/922–4082,* WEB *www.bankstreethostel.com. 70 beds. No credit cards.*

Nightlife and the Arts

Philadelphia magazine (at newsstands), *Calendar of Events* (free at the Independence Visitor Center), the *Philadelphia Weekly* and the *City Paper* (weeklies available free from news boxes in Center City), and the *Inquirer* and the *Daily News* (the city's daily papers) list arts and entertainment events. Tickets, often at a discount, for more than 75 performing and cultural organizations can be obtained at **UpStages** (✉ 1412 Chestnut St., ☎ 215/569–9700).

Nightlife

South Street from Front to 7th Street and the Delaware Waterfront still attract nighttime crowds. But the big noise is in Old City, particularly on Market Street, from 2nd to 4th streets, and 2nd Street, from Market to Chestnut, the site of several dozen trendy bars and restaurants. Germantown Avenue in Chestnut Hill is an upscale area in which to dine, shop, and stroll. On Wednesday night downtown shops and some museums stay open late; outside, street bands entertain the crowds. About two dozen art galleries in Old City stay open late for First Friday each month. **Clear Channel Entertainment** (☎ 215/568–3222) has information about pop and rock concerts.

BARS, LOUNGES, AND CABARETS

The **Continental Restaurant & Martini Bar** (✉ 138 Market St., ☎ 215/923–6069) draws a hip crowd for cocktails and dinner. **Copa Too** (✉ 263 S. 15th St., ☎ 215/735–0848) serves up superb margaritas and is an informal gathering spot for burgers and beer. **Shampoo** (✉ 417 N. 8th St., ☎ 215/922–7500) is one of Philly's hottest clubs. **Woody's Bar and Restaurant** (✉ 202 S. 13th St., ☎ 215/545–1893) is the city's most popular gay bar. **Zanzibar Blue** (✉ 200 S. Broad St., ☎ 215/732–5200) presents top local and national names in jazz.

The Arts

CONCERTS

The **Philadelphia Orchestra** performs at the Kimmel Center for the Performing Arts (✉ Broad and Spruce Sts., ☎ 215/893–1999) in winter and at the Mann Music Center in Fairmount Park in summer. The **Philly Pops** (☎ 215/546–6400), conducted by Peter Nero, performs at the Kimmel Center.

DANCE

The **Pennsylvania Ballet** (☎ 215/551–7000) dances at the Academy of Music (✉ Broad and Locust Sts.) from October to June. The **Philadel-**

phia Dance Company (☎ 215/387–8200) performs modern and jazz dance and ballet at the Kimmel Center for the Performing Arts (✉ Broad and Spruce Sts.).

OPERA

The **Opera Company of Philadelphia** (☎ 215/928–2100) performs at the Academy of Music (✉ Broad and Locust Sts.) from October to May.

PERFORMANCE VENUE

By day **Painted Bride Art Center** (✉ 230 Vine St., ☎ 215/925–9914) is an art gallery, by night a stage featuring performance art, readings, dance, and theater.

THEATER

The **Arden Theatre Company** (✉ 40 N. 2nd St., ☎ 215/922–8900) presents new works and classics. The **Forrest Theater** (✉ 1114 Walnut St., ☎ 215/923–1515) stages Broadway blockbusters. The **Merriam Theater** (✉ 250 S. Broad St., ☎ 215/732–5446) stages performances by touring companies and pre-Broadway productions. The **Walnut Street Theater** (✉ 9th and Walnut Sts., ☎ 215/574–3550) presents musicals, comedies, and the occasional drama. The **Wilma Theater** (✉ Broad and Spruce Sts., ☎ 215/546–7824) focuses on innovative work with American and European drama and musicals.

Outdoor Activities and Sports

Golf

Of the six 18-hole courses in Philadelphia open to the public, **Cobbs Creek and Karakung** (✉ 7200 Lansdowne Ave., ☎ 215/877–8707) are the most challenging.

Jogging and Running

Philly runners' favorite is the **river loop**—an 8.2-mi circuit starting at the Art Museum and heading up Kelly Drive along the Schuylkill River, then across Falls Bridge and down West River Drive.

Spectator Sports

Baseball: Philadelphia Phillies (✉ Veterans Stadium, Broad St. and Pattison Ave., ☎ 215/463–1000). **Basketball: Philadelphia 76ers** (✉ First Union Center, Broad St. and Pattison Ave., ☎ 215/339–7676). **Football: Philadelphia Eagles** (✉ Veterans Stadium, Broad St. and Pattison Ave., ☎ 215/463–5500). **Hockey: Philadelphia Flyers** (✉ First Union Center, Broad St. and Pattison Ave., ☎ 215/755–9700). **Horse Racing: Philadelphia Park** (✉ Street Rd., Bensalem, ☎ 215/639–9000) has Thoroughbred racing year-round. For off-track betting, try the **Turf Club Center City** (✉ 1635 Market St., ☎ 215/246–1556).

Shopping

There is no sales tax on clothing, medicine, or food bought in stores. Otherwise, Pennsylvania has a 6% sales tax, 7% in Philadelphia.

Shopping Districts

Pine Street from 9th to 12th Street is **Antiques Row.** For local color visit the outdoor stalls and indoor stores of the **Italian Market,** on 9th Street between Christian Street and Washington Avenue in South Philadelphia. **Jewelers' Row,** centered on Sansom Street between 7th and 8th streets, is one of the world's oldest and largest markets of precious stones. At 16th and Chestnut streets, the **Shops at Liberty Place** offer more than 70 stores and restaurants under a 90-ft glass-roof atrium. Along **South Street** more than 300 stores sell everything from New Age books to avant-garde art. **Walnut Street** between Broad Street and Rittenhouse Square (a.k.a. Rittenhouse Row) and the intersecting streets are filled with upscale boutiques and galleries.

Department Stores

Philadelphians still rendezvous at the eagle statue in the grand court of the former John Wanamaker department store, now **Lord & Taylor** (✉ 13th and Market Sts., ☎ 215/241–9000). **Strawbridge's** (✉ 8th and Market Sts., ☎ 215/829–0346) is the anchor store for the Gallery at Market East, a four-level indoor mall.

Specialty Stores

AIA Bookstore (✉ 117 S. 17th St., ☎ 215/569–3188) specializes in books on architecture and interior design and carries posters and unusual gifts. **American Pie** (✉ 327 South St., ☎ 215/922–2226; ✉ 4303 Main St., ☎ 215/487–0226) displays handcrafted jewelry, blown glass, and wood pieces. **Architectural Antiques Exchange** (✉ 715 N. 2nd St., ☎ 215/922–3669) handles everything from embellishments of Victorian saloons to stained and beveled glass. **Boyd's** (✉ 1818 Chestnut St., ☎ 215/564–9000), the largest single-store men's clothier in the country, also has a small women's department. The family-owned **Fante's Cookware** (✉ 1006 S. 9th St., ☎ 215/922–5557), in the heart of the Italian Market, is a good source for fine cookware, cookbooks, French copper, cutlery, coffee, and tea. **J. E. Caldwell** (✉ 1339 Chestnut St., ☎ 215/864–7800), since 1839 a local landmark for jewelry, is adorned with antique crystal chandeliers by Baccarat.

Side Trip to the Brandywine Valley

Arriving and Departing

The Brandywine Valley is about 25 mi west of downtown Philadelphia by U.S. 1S.

What to See and Do

The Brandywine River valley has inspired generations of Wyeths and du Ponts—the Wyeths to capture its peaceful harmony on canvas, the du Ponts to recontour the landscape with grand gardens, mansions, and mills. Antiques shops and inns dot the region, making it a popular escape from the city. Some of its major sights are in Delaware, near Wilmington. The **Brandywine River Museum** (✉ U.S. 1 and Rte. 100, Chadds Ford, ☎ 610/388–7601, WEB www.brandywinemuseum.org; 🎫 $6), in a preserved 19th-century gristmill, celebrates the Brandywine school of artists, including Andrew Wyeth, illustrator N. C. Wyeth, and ★ Jamie Wyeth. **Longwood Gardens** (✉ U.S. 1, Kennett Square, ☎ 610/388–6741, WEB www.longwoodgardens.org; 🎫 $12), Pierre-Samuel du Pont's 350 acres of ultimate estate gardens and conservatories, has an international reputation. The **Brandywine Battlefield State Park** (✉ U.S. 1, Chadds Ford, ☎ 610/459–3342, WEB www.ushistory.org/brandywine; 🎫 buildings $3.50, park free) is near the site of the British defeat of Washington and his troops on September 11, 1777. The **Brandywine Conference and Visitors Bureau** (✉ 1 Beaver Valley Rd., Chadds Ford 19137, ☎ 610/565–3679 or 800/343–3983, WEB www.brandywinecvb.org) provides information about Delaware County.The **Brandywine Valley Tourist Information Center** (✉ 300 Greenwood Rd., Kennett Square 19348, ☎ 610/388–2900 or 800/228–9933, WEB www.brandywinevalley.com) has information about visiting Chester County.

Side Trip to Bucks County

Arriving and Departing

From Philadelphia follow I–95 north to the Yardley exit, and then go north on Route 32 toward New Hope. The trip takes one hour.

What to See and Do

Bucks County is known for antiques, covered bridges, and country inns. A number of pretty towns are close to the Delaware River. **New Hope** is a hodgepodge of art galleries, old stone houses, and shops along crooked little streets by the Delaware River. **Washington Crossing Historic Park** (✉ Rtes. 532 and 32, ☎ 215/493–4076; 🎫 historic houses $4, park free) is where George Washington and his troops crossed the river on Christmas night 1776.

William Penn's reconstructed Georgian-style mansion, **Pennsbury Manor,** off U.S. 13, presents living-history demonstrations of 17th-century life. ✉ *400 Pennsbury Memorial Rd., Morrisville,* ☎ *215/946–0400,* WEB *www.pennsburymanor.org.* 🎫 *$5. Closed Mon.*

The **Bucks County Conference and Visitors Bureau** (✉ 152 Swamp Rd., Doylestown 18901, ☎ 215/345–4552 or 800/836–2825, WEB www.buckscountycvb.org) has regional information. The **New Hope Information Center** (✉ 1 W. Mechanic St., at Main St., 18938, ☎ 215/862–5880 or 215/862–5030, WEB www.newhopepa.com) provides information about the town and several others nearby.

Side Trip to Valley Forge

Arriving and Departing

By car take the Schuylkill Expressway (I–76) west from Philadelphia to Exit 25; then take Route 363 to North Gulph Road and follow the signs to Valley Forge National Historical Park, 18 mi from the city. By bus take SEPTA Route 125 from 16th Street and John F. Kennedy Boulevard.

What to See and Do

The monuments, huts, and headquarters on the 3,500 acres of gentle ★ hills in the **Valley Forge National Historical Park** (✉ Rte. 23 and N. Gulph Rd., Valley Forge, ☎ 610/783–1077, WEB www.nps.gov/vafo; 🎫 $2 Washington's Headquarters, Apr.–Nov.; free rest of year) preserve the moment in American history when General George Washington and the Continental Army endured the bitter winter of 1777–78. The first U.S. home of artist and naturalist John James Audubon, **Mill Grove** is now a museum displaying Audubon's work. The house is on the grounds of the 175-acre **Audubon Wildlife Sanctuary,** which has 5 mi of hiking trails. ✉ *Audubon and Pauling Rds., Audubon,* ☎ *610/666–5593,* WEB *www.montcopa.org.* 🎫 *Free. Closed Mon.*

For information, contact the **Valley Forge Convention and Visitors Bureau** (✉ 600 W. Germantown Pike, Suite 130, Plymouth Meeting 19462, ☎ 610/834–1550 or 800/441–3549, WEB www.valleyforge.org).

Philadelphia Essentials

AIRPORTS AND TRANSFERS

Philadelphia International Airport, 8 mi southwest of downtown, has scheduled flights on most major domestic and foreign carriers.

➤ AIRPORT INFORMATION: **Philadelphia International Airport** (✉ 8800 Essington Ave., ☎ 215/937–6937, WEB www.phl.org).

AIRPORT TRANSFER

A SEPTA (☞ Transportation Around Philadelphia, *below*) rail line connects the airport with Center City stations; the trip takes 20 minutes and costs $5.50. Airport shuttle services, such as U.S.A. Limousine and Lady Liberty, charge about $10 per person. Taxis cost $20, plus tip.

➤ TAXIS AND SHUTTLES: **Lady Liberty** (☎ 215/724–8888). **U.S.A. Limousine** (☎ 610/522–8360).

BUS TRAVEL TO AND FROM PHILADELPHIA

Greyhound has service to and from New York, Washington, and points beyond out of the terminal at 10th and Filbert streets.

➤ BUS INFORMATION: **Greyhound** (✉ 10th and Filbert Sts., ☎ 800/231–2222, WEB www.greyhound.com).

BUS TRAVEL AROUND PHILADELPHIA

SEPTA's Bus Route 76 connects the zoo in western Fairmount Park with Penn's Landing at the Delaware River. The purple PHLASH buses, designed for visitors, make 33 stops in the downtown loop; an all-day pass is $4. For further information, *see* Transportation Around Philadelphia, *below.*

CAR TRAVEL

The main north–south highway through Philadelphia is I–95; to reach Center City, as the downtown area is called, take the Vine Street (I–676) exit off I–95 south or I–95 north. From the west the Schuylkill Expressway (I–76) has several exits to Center City. From the east the New Jersey Turnpike and I–295 provide access to either U.S. 30/I–676, which enters the city via the Benjamin Franklin Bridge, or New Jersey Route 42 and the Walt Whitman Bridge.

PARKING

On-street parking is often forbidden during rush hours (parking facilities include those at 41 North 6th Street; 16th and Arch streets; and 10th and Locust streets).

RULES OF THE ROAD

Many of the city's narrow streets were designed for colonial traffic of the four-legged kind, and driving can be difficult. During rush hours avoid the major arteries leading into and out of the city, particularly I–95, U.S. 1, and the Schuylkill Expressway.

TAXIS

Cabs are plentiful during the day—especially along Broad Street and near hotels and train stations. At night and outside Center City, taxis can be scarce, and you may have to call for service. Fares start at $1.80 and increase by 30¢ for every subsequent mile. Some of the main companies are Olde City Taxi, Quaker City Cab, and Liberty Cab.

➤ TAXI COMPANIES: **Liberty Cab** (☎ 215/389–8000). **Olde City Taxi** (☎ 215/338–0838). **Quaker City Cab** (☎ 215/728–8000).

TOURS

The Independence Visitor Center (☞ Visitor Information, *below*) has information about special-interest tours on subjects such as the Italian Market and African-American history.

BUS TOURS

American Trolley Tours ($14) and Philadelphia Trolley Works ($18) provide narrated tours on buses designed to resemble Victorian trolleys; the fare is an all-day pass, allowing unlimited stops, but you can ask about shorter tours.

➤ FEES AND SCHEDULES: **American Trolley Works** (☎ 215/333–2119). **Philadelphia Trolley Works** (☎ 215/925–8687, WEB www.phillytour.com).

BOAT TOURS

The *Spirit of Philadelphia* and the *Liberty Belle* run cruises along the Delaware River. Both dock at Penn's Landing at the foot of Lombard Street. To combine a meal with a cruise on the Delaware River, climb aboard the *Spirit of Philadelphia*.

➤ FEES AND SCHEDULES: ***Liberty Belle*** (☎ 215/629–1131, WEB www.libertybelle.com). ***Spirit of Philadelphia*** (☎ 215/923–1419, WEB www.spiritcruises.com).

CARRIAGE TOURS

Philadelphia Carriage Co. and '76 Carriage Co. run tours of the historic area in antique horse-drawn carriages.

➤ FEES AND SCHEDULES: **Philadelphia Carriage Co.** (☎ 215/922–6840, WEB philanet.com/carriage). **'76 Carriage Co.** (☎ 215/923–8516, WEB www.phillytour.com).

WALKING TOURS

Each night (April–November) starting at dusk Lights of Liberty gives out head phones, turns on surround-sound narration, and leads tours through Independence National Historical Park. Five 3-D presentations about the events leading to the American Revolution are digitally projected onto the historic buildings; cost is $17.76. Centipede Tours organizes candlelight strolls through Old Philadelphia; cost is $5.

➤ FEES AND SCHEDULES: **Centipede Tours** (☎ 215/735–3123, WEB www.centipedeinc.com). **Lights of Liberty** (☎ 877/462–1776, WEB www.lightsofliberty.org).

TRAIN TRAVEL

Amtrak serves 30th Street Station. New Jersey Transit trains connect with SEPTA (☞ Transportation Around Philadelphia, *below*) trains at Trenton.

➤ TRAIN INFORMATION: **Amtrak** (✉ 30th and Market Sts., ☎ 800/872–7245, WEB www.amtrak.com). **New Jersey Transit** (✉ 10th and Filbert Sts., ☎ 215/569–3752, WEB www.njtransit.com).

TRANSPORTATION AROUND PHILADELPHIA

The traditional heart of the city is the intersection of Broad and Market streets, where City Hall now stands. Market Street divides the city north and south. North–south streets are numbered, starting at the Delaware River with Front (1st) Street and increasing to the west. Most historical and cultural attractions are easy walks from the midtown area, which is safe during the day. After dark ask hotel personnel about the safety of places you're interested in visiting, but in general, taking a cab is safer than walking.

SEPTA operates an extensive network of buses, trolleys, subways, and commuter trains that make it easy to get around the city; the base fare is $2, transfers 60¢, and exact change is required. Tokens can be purchased from machines at stations for the discounted price of $1.30 each. Certain lines run 24 hours a day. SEPTA's Day Pass, good for a day's unlimited riding, can be purchased at the visitor center (☞ Visitor Information, *below*) for $5.50.

VISITOR INFORMATION

Greater Philadelphia Tourism Marketing Corporation offers a Web site with information on events, sites, lodging, and restaurants. The Independence Visitor Center, the official visitor center for Independence National Historical Park, the city of Philadelphia, and the region, has brochures, maps, and discount coupons for tourist sites.

A CityPass ($28.50) allows you to take in five popular attractions—the Franklin Institute Science Museum, the Philadelphia Zoo, the Academy of Natural Sciences, Independence Seaport Museum, and the Philadelphia Trolley Tour—for half the amount of the sights' combined admission. The pass can be purchased at any of the facilities.

➤ TOURIST INFORMATION: **City Pass** (☎ 707/256–0490, WEB www.citypass.net). **Greater Philadelphia Tourism Marketing Corporation** (✉ 30 S.

17th St., Suite 1710, 19103, ☎ 215/599–0776, WEB www.gophila.com). Independence Visitor Center (✉ 6th St., between Market and Arch Sts., 19106, ☎ 215/965–7676 or 800/537–7676 outside the Philadelphia area, WEB www.independencevisitorcenter.com).

PENNSYLVANIA DUTCH COUNTRY

The Pennsylvania Dutch aren't Dutch; the name comes from *Deutsch* (German). In the 18th century this rolling farmland 65 mi west of Philadelphia became the home of the Amish, the Mennonites, and other German and Swiss immigrants escaping religious persecution. Today their descendants continue to turn their backs on the modern world—and in doing so attract the world's attention. In summer, buses jam Route 30, the main thoroughfare. But there is still charm on the back roads, where you will discover Amish farms, hand-painted signs advertising quilts, fields worked with mules, and horse-drawn buggies.

Exploring Pennsylvania Dutch Country

Lancaster, an attractive colonial city, is the heart of Pennsylvania Dutch Country. Guides impart anecdotes about local architecture and history during the **Historic Lancaster Walking Tour** (☎ 717/392–1776; 🎫 $7), a two-hour stroll through the city. **Central Market** (✉ Penn Sq., ☎ 717/291–4723), which began with open-air stalls in 1742 and now occupies an 1889 Romanesque structure, is where the locals shop for produce, meats, and baked goods. The old city hall, reborn as the **Heritage Center of Lancaster County,** shows the work of Lancaster County artisans and craftspeople from the past. ✉ *13 W. King St.,* ☎ *717/299–6440,* WEB *www.lancasterheritage.com.* 🎫 *Free. Closed Jan.–mid-Mar.*

★ 🐥 The **People's Place** (✉ 3513 Rte. 340, Intercourse, ☎ 717/768–7171 or 800/390–8436, WEB www.thepeoplesplace.com; $8) provides an excellent introduction to the Amish, Mennonite, and Hutterite communities in a multiscreen slide show and interactive family museum. Several furnished farmhouses offer simulated up-close looks at how the Amish live, including the **Amish Farm and House** (✉ 2395 Lincoln Hwy. E, Smoketown, ☎ 717/394–6185, WEB www.amishfarmandhouse.com; 🎫 $6.50). **Aaron & Jessica's Buggy Rides** (✉ Rte. 340, Bird-in-Hand, ☎ 717/768–8828, WEB www.amishbuggyrides.com; 🎫 $10) let you see the countryside from an Amish carriage. Rides depart from Plain & Fancy Farm restaurant.

Wheatland, an 1828 Federal-style mansion, was the home of the only president from Pennsylvania, James Buchanan. It is 1½ mi west of Lancaster on Route 23. ✉ *1120 Marietta Ave.,* ☎ *717/392–8721,* WEB *www.wheatland.org.* 🎫 *$5.50. Closed Dec.–Mar. and weekdays in Nov.*

Strasburg has a half dozen museums and sights devoted to trains. 🐥 The **Strasburg Railroad** (✉ Rte. 741 E, ☎ 717/687–7522, WEB www.strasburgrailroad.com; 🎫 $8.75) is a scenic 9-mi round-trip excursion 🐥 on a wooden coach pulled by a steam locomotive. The **Railroad Museum of Pennsylvania** (✉ Rte. 741, ☎ 717/687–8628, WEB www.rrmuseumpa.org; 🎫 $6) displays colossal engines, railcars, and memorabilia.

Ephrata, a classic American town with an old-fashioned Main Street, began life as a religious commune. The 18th-century Protestants of the **Ephrata Cloister** (✉ Rtes. 272 and 322, Ephrata, ☎ 717/733–6600, WEB www.cob-net.org/cloister.htm; 🎫 $6) led an ascetic life, following William Penn's "holy experiment." Guides now give tours of the restored medieval-style German buildings. The 30-acre **Green Dragon Farmers Market and Auction** (✉ 955 N. State St., ☎ 717/738–1117,

WEB www.greendragonmarket.com) draws crowds on Friday, when local Amish and Mennonite farmers sell their goods.

Lititz, founded by Moravians who settled in Pennsylvania to do missionary work among Native Americans, is a lovely town with a tree-shaded main street of 18th-century cottages and shops. At the **General Sutter Inn** (✉ 14 E. Main St., ☎ 717/626–2115) pick up a Historical Foundation brochure that details a town walking tour.

Dining and Lodging

Like the German cuisine from which it derives, Pennsylvania Dutch cooking is hearty. To sample such regional fare as ham, buttered noodles, chowchow, and shoofly pie, eat at one of the bustling family-style restaurants where diners share tables and the food is passed around.

Bird-in-Hand

$–$$ ✕ **Bird-in-Hand Family Restaurant.** This family-owned spot specializes in hearty Pennsylvania Dutch home cooking, served buffet-style or à la carte. ✉ *Rte. 340 west of N. Ronks Rd.,* ☎ *717/768–8266. MC, V. Closed Sun.*

Ephrata

$$$ ★ ✕ **The Restaurant at Doneckers.** Classic and country-French cuisine is served downstairs amid colonial antiques and upstairs in a country garden. The menu from chef Greg Gable, who worked at Philadelphia's noted Le Bec-Fin, lists dishes such as grilled Dover sole in a citrus beurre blanc. A lower-priced tavern menu is also available. ✉ *333 N. State St.,* ☎ *717/738–9501. AE, D, DC, MC, V. Closed Wed. and Sun.*

Lancaster

$$–$$$ ✕ **Carr's.** The cuisine is contemporary American, and steaks, seafood, and veal are served in a cozy dining room with upholstered armchairs and 19th-century paintings, drawings, and photographs. Homemade soups and breads highlight the diverse menu. ✉ *Market and Grant Sts.,* ☎ *717/299–7090. AE, D, DC, MC, V. Closed Mon.*

$$–$$$ 🏨 **Best Western Eden Resort and Conference Center.** Spacious modern rooms and attractive grounds make a stay here pleasant. Suites have kitchens and fireplaces. ✉ *222 Eden Rd. (U.S. 30 and Rte. 272), 17601,* ☎ *717/569–6444,* FAX *717/569–4208,* WEB *www.edenresort.com. 315 rooms. 2 restaurants, 2 pools, tennis, gym. AE, D, DC, MC, V.*

Lititz

$–$$ ★ ✕🏨 **General Sutter Inn.** Built in 1764, the state's oldest continuously run inn is a Victorian delight. Furnishings range from Pennsylvania folk art to Louis XIV sofas. The 1764 Restaurant serves sophisticated fare such as Pennsylania trout (different style each day) and pan-seared veal with a shallot and woodland mushroom sauce; the café is less expensive. The inn is within walking distance of the historic district. ✉ *14 E. Main St., 17543,* ☎ *717/626–2115,* FAX *717/626–0992,* WEB *www.generalsutterinn.com. 16 rooms, 2 restaurants. AE, D, MC, V.*

Strasburg

$$$ ★ ✕🏨 **Historic Strasburg Inn.** This colonial-style inn is set on 58 peaceful acres overlooking farmland. Rooms have crown moldings, rocking chairs, and dried floral arrangements. Updated American specialties, including steaks, jumbo lump crab cakes, and wild game, fill the dinner menu. ✉ *1 Historic Dr., 17579,* ☎ *717/687–7691 or 800/872–0201,* FAX *717/687–6098,* WEB *www.historicstrasburginn.com. 101 rooms. 2 restaurants, pool, gym. AE, D, DC, MC, V. BP.*

Campgrounds

⛺ **Historic Mill Bridge Village and Campresort** (✉ S. Ronks Rd., ½ mi south of U.S. 30 [Box 7, Paradise 17562], ☎ 717/687–8181 or 800/645–2744, WEB www.millbridge.com). ⛺ **Spring Gulch Resort Campground** (✉ 475 Lynch Rd., New Holland 17557, ☎ 717/354–3100, WEB www.springgulch.com).

Nightlife and the Arts

The **American Music Theatre** (✉ 2425 Lincoln Hwy. E, Lancaster, ☎ 717/397–7700; 800/648–4102; WEB www.americanmusictheatre.com), a 1,600-seat facility, presents shows that celebrate American music. The **Fulton Opera House** (✉ 12 N. Prince St., Lancaster, ☎ 717/394–7425, WEB www.fultontheatre.org) has plays, concerts, and performances by the Lancaster Symphony Orchestra and the Lancaster Opera.

Shopping

Antiques

Dozens of antiques shops and antiques malls are on Route 272 between Adamstown and Denver, 2 mi east of Pennsylvania Turnpike Exit 21. The 400 stalls at **Renninger's Antique and Collector's Market** (✉ Rte. 272, Adamstown, ☎ 717/336–2177), ½ mi north of Pennsylvania Turnpike Exit 21, overflow with every kind of antique on Sundays year-round. **Shupp's Grove** (✉ off Rte. 897, Adamstown, ☎ 717/484–4115) has acres of dealers selling antiques and art; it's open weekends April–October. **Stoudt's Black Angus Antiques Mall** (✉ Rte. 272, Adamstown, ☎ 717/484–4385) hosts more than 500 dealers with everything from books to furniture; the mall is open Sunday, and there's a restaurant.

Crafts

Ten Thousand Villages (✉ 240 N. Reading Rd., Ephrata, ☎ 717/721–8400), operated by the Mennonite Central Committee, sells crafts made by artisans in low-income countries. The 32-shop **Kitchen Kettle Village** (✉ Rte. 340, Intercourse, ☎ 717/768–8261 or 800/732–3538) showcases local crafts including decoy carving and tin punching. The **Weathervane Shop** (✉ 2451 Kissel Hill Rd., Lancaster, ☎ 717/569–9312) at the Landis Valley Museum sells crafts made on-site.

Outlet Malls

Gift shops and outlet malls line U.S. 30 and Rte. 340; some have appealing discounts, but it's best to know prices before you shop. The **Rockvale Square Outlet** (✉ U.S. 30 and Rte. 896, Lancaster, ☎ 717/293–9595) has more than 120 stores, from Sony to Gap to Nike.

Side Trip to Gettysburg

Arriving and Departing

From Lancaster take U.S. 30 west to Gettysburg (53 mi, or about 1¼ hours).

What to See and Do

The Battle of Gettysburg, fought in July 1863, was, along with Ulysses S. Grant's successful Vicksburg campaign, the turning point of the Civil ★ War. At the **Gettysburg National Military Park** (✉ Visitor Center, 97 Taneytown Rd., ☎ 717/334–1124, WEB www.nps.gov/gett; 🎫 free, $3 for electric map) you can follow the course of the fighting on a 750-square-ft electric map or obtain brochures that will guide you along 18 mi of roads or various walking tails around the battleground. A new visitor center will open sometime between 2004 and 2006.The **Gettysburg Convention and Visitors Travel Bureau** (✉ 35 Carlisle St.,

17325, ☎ 717/334–6274, WEB www.gettysburg.com) provides information on the area, including Civil War reenactments; Gettysbury has more than 20 museums.

Side Trip to Hershey

Arriving and Departing

Take I–76 to Exit 20 and follow the signs—it's about 30 mi, or 45 minutes, northwest of Lancaster.

What to See and Do

The streets have names like Cocoa Avenue, and the streetlights look like Hershey's Kisses at **Hersheypark** (✉ U.S. 422, ☎ 717/534–3900, WEB www.hersheypark.com; 🎫 $33.95), an amusement park. At **Chocolate World** (✉ Park Blvd., ☎ 717/534–4900; 🎫 free) you can take a 10-minute ride through the process of chocolate making. There's also a visitor center and shop. The **Hershey Information Center** (☎ 800/437–7439, WEB www.hersheypa.com) can help you plan a trip.

Pennsylvania Dutch Country Essentials

BUS TRAVEL

Greyhound has three runs daily from Philadelphia to Lancaster; travel time is 2½ hours.

➤ BUS INFORMATION: **Greyhound** (☎ 800/231–2222, WEB www.greyhound.com).

CAR TRAVEL

From Philadelphia (65 mi away) take the Schuylkill Expressway (I–76) west to the Pennsylvania Turnpike, exiting at Exit 20, 21, or 22.

TRAIN TRAVEL

Amtrak has service from Philadelphia to Lancaster; travel time is 80 minutes.

➤ TRAIN INFORMATION: **Amtrak** (☎ 800/872–7245, WEB www.amtrak.com).

VISITOR INFORMATION

➤ TOURIST INFORMATION: **Mennonite Information Center** (✉ 2209 Millstream Rd., Lancaster 17602, ☎ 717/299–0954 or 800/858–8320, WEB www.mennoniteinfoctr.com). **Pennsylvania Dutch Convention and Visitors Bureau** (✉ 501 Greenfield Rd., Lancaster 17601, ☎ 717/299–8901 or 800/723–8824, WEB www.padutchcountry.com).

PITTSBURGH

Pittsburgh lies where the Allegheny and Monongahela rivers meet to form the Ohio River, in the hills of southwestern Pennsylvania. From its beginnings as an 18th-century French fortress and trading post, Fort Duquesne, and then as the British Fort Pitt, the city emerged as an industrial powerhouse in the 1800s, largely due to iron and steel production. Today, the days of steel manufacturing are mostly gone, and with them the industrial pollution that earned the city the nickname "Smoky City." Pittsburgh has been recast into a pleasing blend of 19th- and 20th-century architectural masterpieces and modern skyscrapers and ranks among the nation's most livable cities.

Exploring Pittsburgh

Downtown, an area framed by the three rivers and called the Golden Triangle, contains Point State Park and major hotels, restaurants, and

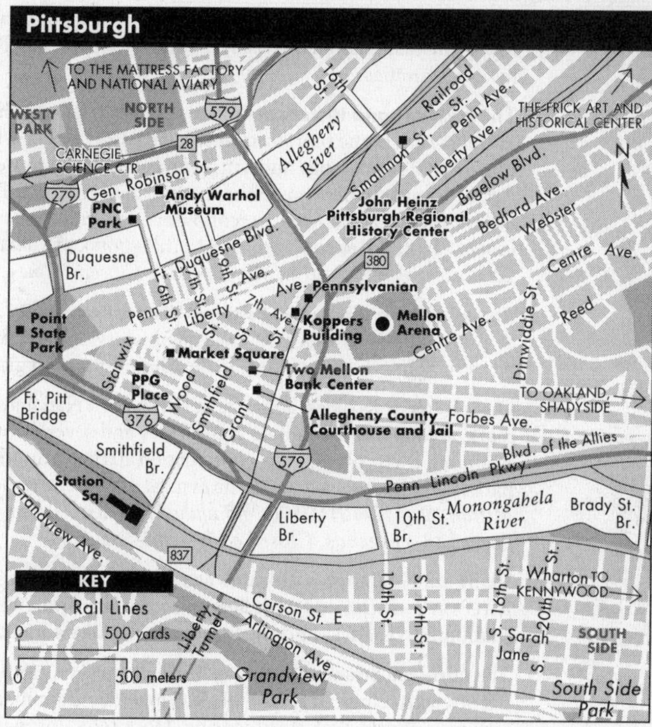

theaters. Philip Johnson's 1984 postmodern **PPG Place** (✉ Stanwix St. and 4th Ave., ☎ 412/434–3131), whose glass spires and towers were modeled after London's Houses of Parliament, exemplifies the Pittsburgh renaissance; it includes an ice-skating rink. Among the beautifully maintained buildings from Pittsburgh's early boom days is the Flemish-Gothic **Two Mellon Bank Center** (✉ 5th Ave. and Grant St., ☎ 412/234–5000), originally the Union Trust Building, with a stained-glass dome above the central lobby. Daniel Burnham's Union Station (built 1898–1903) is now an apartment building, the **Pennsylvanian** (✉ Grant St. and Liberty Ave., ☎ 412/391–6730). The **Allegheny County Courthouse and Jail** (✉ 5th Ave. and Grant St., ☎ 412/350–5313), designed by the influential architect Henry Hobson Richardson and completed in 1888, is one of the country's outstanding Romanesque buildings. The **Koppers Building** (✉ 7th Ave. and Grant St., ☎ 412/227–2919), one of Pittsburgh's first skyscrapers, has a beautiful Art Deco lobby dating to 1929. **Station Square** (✉ Station Square Dr., ☎ 412/261–2811, WEB www.stationsquare.com), on the Monongahela across the historic Smithfield Bridge, is a converted turn-of-the-20th-century rail station with more than 40 shops and restaurants.

★ East of downtown, **Oakland** has many of the city's cultural, educational, and medical institutions. The **Carnegie** is an opulent cultural center, with the **Museum of Art,** the **Museum of Natural History,** the **Music Hall,** and the **Carnegie Library** all under one Beaux-Arts roof. Don't miss the 19th-century French and 20th-century American paintings, the Hall of Architecture, the dinosaur and Egyptian collections, and the extravagant Music Hall lobby. ✉ *4400 Forbes Ave.,* ☎ *412/622–3131; 412/622–3289 group tours;* WEB *www.carnegiemuseum.org.* 🎟 *$8. Closed Mon.*

★ Towering over Oakland is the University of Pittsburgh's Gothic skyscraper, the **Cathedral of Learning** (✉ 4200 5th Ave., ☎ 412/624–6000,

WEB www.pitt.edu; free, taped tours $3), with 26 **Nationality Classrooms,** meticulously and lavishly executed to represent Pittsburgh's ethnic communities.

The **Frick Art and Historical Center** includes **Clayton,** the turn-of-the-20th-century home of industrialist Henry Clay Frick, which preserves the original furnishings and art; a **car and carriage museum;** the **Frick Art Museum,** which possesses a small but choice collection of old master works; a Victorian greenhouse; and a café serving an excellent lunch. ✉ *7227 Reynolds St.,* ☎ *412/371–0606,* WEB *www.frickart.org.* *Museums free, tour of Clayton $10. Closed Mon.*

The **John Heinz Pittsburgh Regional History Center** (✉ 1212 Smallman St., ☎ 412/454–6000, WEB www.pghhistory.org; $6) focuses on western Pennsylvania history from ethnic culture to glassmaking.

One of America's oldest amusement parks and a National Historic Landmark, **Kennywood** contains water rides and several roller coasters—including three of wooden construction dating from the 1920s. The park is 10 mi southeast of downtown. ✉ *4800 Kennywood Blvd., West Mifflin,* ☎ *412/461–0500,* WEB *www.kennywood.com.* *$23 weekdays, $28 weekends. Closed early Sept.–late Apr.*

Many of Pittsburgh's cultural attractions are across the Allegheny River on the historic **North Side,** also the site of the Pirates' baseball stadium, PNC Park, and the Steelers' football stadium, Heinz Field.

The **Carnegie Science Center** (✉ 1 Allegheny Ave., ☎ 412/237–3300, WEB www.csc.clpgh.org; $14; $18 includes Omnimax) has a planetarium, a World War II submarine, more than 250 hands-on science exhibits, and a four-story Omnimax theater.

The **Andy Warhol Museum** devotes seven floors to the work of the native Pittsburgher and pop art icon. ✉ *117 Sandusky St.,* ☎ *412/237–8300,* WEB *www.warhol.org.* *$8. Closed Mon.*

The **Mattress Factory,** in the North Side's historic Mexican War Streets district, is devoted to contemporary installation art. ✉ *505 Jacksonia St.,* ☎ *412/231–3169,* WEB *www.mattress.org.* *$6. Closed Mon.*

The **National Aviary** (✉ Allegheny Commons W, ☎ 412/323–7234, WEB www.aviary.org; $5) has more than 200 species of birds, including parrots, bald eagles, and a condor.

Outside Pittsburgh

Northeast of Pittsburgh, the **Laurel Highlands** region has Revolutionary War–era forts and battlefields, restored inns and taverns, and lush mountain scenery. The region is noted for white-water rafting, hiking, and skiing. Contact **Laurel Highlands Visitors Bureau** (✉ Ligonier Town Hall, 120 E. Main St., Ligonier, ☎ 724/238–5661 or 800/925–7669, WEB www.ligonier.org) for a visitor's guide. ★ **Fallingwater** is Frank Lloyd Wright's residential masterwork—a stone, concrete, and glass house dramatically cantilevered over a waterfall. ✉ *Rte. 381, Mill Run,* ☎ *724/329–8501,* WEB *www.wpconline.org/fallingwaterhome.* *$10 weekdays, $15 weekends; detailed tour $40 weekdays, $50 weekends; reservations essential. Closed Jan.–Feb., Mon. mid-Mar.–mid-Nov., and weekdays mid-Nov.–mid-Dec. and early Mar.–mid-Mar.*

Parks and Gardens

In the 36-acre **Point State Park** (✉ 101 Commonwealth Plaza, WEB www.dcnr.state.pa.us, ☎ 412/471–0235) are the **Ft. Pitt Blockhouse** (☎ 412/471–1764) and **Ft. Pitt Museum** (☎ 412/281–9284). **Schenley Park** (✉ Overlook Dr., ☎ 412/422–6523, WEB www.pittsburghparks.org) has a lake, trails, golf, tennis courts, ice skating, and cross-country skiing. The park includes the beautiful iron-and-glass **Phipps Conservatory** (✉ 1 Schenley Park, ☎ 412/622–6914, WEB www.phipps.conservatory.org; 🎫 $5), which contains 13 gardens with everything from tropical and desert plants to a bonsai collection.

Dining

$$$ ✕ **Monterey Bay Fish Grotto.** This restaurant on top of Mt. Washington offers more than 20 kinds of fish—sautéed, char-grilled, blackened, and other preparations—and an unrivaled view of the downtown skyline. Pastas and meat dishes round out the menu. ✉ *1411 Grandview Ave.,* ☎ *412/481–4414. AE, D, DC, MC, V.*

$$–$$$ ★ ✕ **Casbah.** An eclectic menu influenced by the cuisines of southern France, Italy, Greece, Turkey, and Tunisia includes dishes from grilled quail with red-grape relish and saffron basmati rice to salmon steamed in grape leaves with a lemon–pine nut vinaigrette. The extensive wine list includes more than 40 labels available by the glass. ✉ *229 S. Highland Ave.,* ☎ *412/661–5656. AE, D, DC, MC, V.*

$–$$ ★ ✕ **Cafe Zinho.** A converted garage full of odds-and-ends furniture holds this lively bistro-style restaurant in Shadyside. It serves first-rate sandwiches and salads all day, and the seasonal dinner menu lists vegetarian rice bowls and dishes with mussels, tuna, lamb, and game, often prepared with Mediterranean touches. Bring your own bottle of wine. ✉ *238 Spahr St.,* ☎ *412/363–1500. No credit cards.*

$ ✕ **Primanti Brothers.** What started out in 1933 as a working-class bar is now a Pittsburgh favorite with eight locations. The cheese steak comes with fries, coleslaw, and tomato—all *in* the sandwich. ✉ *46 18th St.,* ☎ *412/263–2142;* ✉ *11 Cherry Way,* ☎ *412/566–8051;* ✉ *Market Sq.,* ☎ *412/261–1599. No credit cards.*

$ ✕ **Road to Karakesh.** The exotic North African–style interior of this Oakland restaurant beautifully matches an eclectic menu that includes African, Middle Eastern, and Southeast Asian dishes. Chairless pillow seating is an option for the limber. ✉ *320 Atwood St.,* ☎ *412/687–0533. AE, D, DC, MC, V.*

Lodging

$$$ ★ 🏨 **Omni William Penn.** Pittsburgh's grand hotel has a sumptuous lobby with a coffered ceiling and crystal chandeliers where people relax over drinks. The guest rooms are filled with light, and many are large enough for a couch and a wing chair. ✉ *530 William Penn Pl., Mellon Sq., 15219,* ☎ *412/281–7100,* FAX *412/553–5252,* WEB *www.omnihotels.com. 596 rooms. 2 restaurants, gym. AE, D, DC, MC, V.*

$$$ 🏨 **Ramada Plaza Suites and Conference Center.** In the Golden Triangle, across from the Mellon Arena and adjacent to the Steel Plaza subway station, the Ramada is a convenient hotel with modern rooms. ✉ *1 Bigelow Sq., 15219,* ☎ *412/281–5800 or 800/225–5858,* FAX *412/642–2231,* WEB *www.ramada.com. 311 suites. Restaurant, pool, health club. AE, D, DC, MC, V.*

$$$ 🏨 **Westin Convention Center.** The dramatically designed lobby leads to a 26-story tower with rooms in contemporary style. ✉ *1000 Penn Ave., 15222,* ☎ *412/281–3700,* FAX *412/227–4501,* WEB *www.westin.com. 618 rooms. 3 restaurants, pool, gym. AE, D, DC, MC, V.*

$$ 🏨 **Holiday Inn Select–University Center.** This modern nine-story hotel in the heart of Oakland is within easy walking distance of the universities and the Carnegie museums. ✉ *100 Lytton Ave., 15213,* ☎ *412/682–6200 or 800/465–4329,* FAX *412/682–5745,* WEB *www.sixcontinentshotels.com/holiday-inn. 251 rooms. Restaurant, pool, gym. AE, D, DC, MC, V.*

$$ ★ **The Priory.** Antiques and reproduction pieces furnish this European-style hotel. It's on the North Side but provides complimentary shuttle service to the downtown area. ✉ *614 Pressley St., 15212,* ☎ *412/231–3338,* FAX *412/231–4838,* WEB *www.thepriory.com. 24 rooms. AE, D, DC, MC, V. CP.*

$–$$ ★ **Country Inns and Suites.** At this garden-style hotel 7 mi from the airport, the pleasant country-style guest rooms overlook a courtyard. ✉ *5311 Campbells Run Rd., 15205,* ☎ *412/788–8400,* FAX *412/788–2577,* WEB *www.countryinns.com. 152 rooms. Pool, club. AE, D, DC, MC, V. BP.*

Nightlife and the Arts

Nightlife

The **Strip District** (✉ between Liberty Ave. and Smallman St., and 16th and 22nd Sts.) has become Pittsburgh's nightlife center, with many bars and nightclubs. At **Metropol** (✉ 1600 Smallman St., ☎ 412/261–4512), DJs spin dance music. For live music try **Rosebud** (✉ 1650 Smallman St., ☎ 412/261–2221). **Valhalla** (✉ 1150 Smallman St., ☎ 412/434–1440), a microbrewery bar–restaurant, often has live music.

A nightlife district thrives along **East Carson Street,** across the Monongahela on the revitalized South Side. **Club Cafe** (✉ 56 S. 12th St., ☎ 412/431–4950), sleek but cozy, showcases music from jazz and blues to country and rock. **Dowe's** (✉ 121 9th St., ☎ 412/281–9225), the city's premier jazz spot, is a lush, spacious club downtown.

The Arts

The **Pittsburgh Ballet** (☎ 412/281–0360) appears at the Benedum Center for the Performing Arts (✉ 719 Liberty Ave., ☎ 412/456–6666), which also hosts many Broadway shows. The **Pittsburgh Opera** (☎ 412/281–0912) performs at the Benedum Center for the Performing Arts (✉ 719 Liberty Ave., ☎ 412/456–6666). The world-class **Pittsburgh Symphony Orchestra,** conducted by Mariss Jansons, appears at the Heinz Hall for the Performing Arts (✉ 600 Penn Ave., ☎ 412/392–4800).

The **Pittsburgh Public Theater** (✉ O'Reilly Theater, 621 Penn Ave., ☎ 412/316–1600), in a downtown facility designed by Michael Graves, consistently stages quality productions.

Outdoor Activities and Sports

Golf

The **North Park Golf Course** (✉ Kummer Rd., North Park, ☎ 724/935–1967) is one of the more than 50 public courses within a 30-minute drive of downtown.

Jogging

Point State Park (✉ 101 Commonwealth Plaza, ☎ 412/471–0235) has an upper and a lower path, each forming a circuit of about 1 mi in length, with views of the skyline and the city's three rivers.

Spectator Sports

Baseball: Pittsburgh Pirates (✉ PNC Park, 115 Federal St., ☎ 412/321–2827). **Football: Pittsburgh Steelers** (✉ Heinz Park, 100 Art Rooney Ave., ☎ 412/323–1200). **Hockey: Pittsburgh Penguins** (✉ Mellon Arena, 300 Auditorium Pl., ☎ 412/642–7367).

Shopping

East of Oakland in **Shadyside,** one of Pittsburgh's most desirable neighborhoods, is Walnut Street, which has upscale clothing boutiques, housewares stores, restaurants, and cafés. The artsy Ellsworth Avenue, along Shadyside's northern edge, has galleries and vintage-clothing stores. Explore the unique clothing stores, antiques shops, used-book stores, and art galleries along East Carson Street on the **South Side. Station Square** (✉ Station Square Dr.) has numerous shops and restaurants. In the **Strip District** (✉ between Liberty Ave. and Smallman St., and 16th and 22nd Sts.) are streets lined with market stalls and sellers of imported food and dry goods.

Kaufmann's (✉ 400 5th Ave., at Smithfield St., ☎ 412/232–2000) is one of downtown's better department stores. **Lord & Taylor** (✉ 514 Smithfield St., ☎ 412/261–3000) sells classic American clothing. **Saks Fifth Avenue** (✉ 513 Smithfield St., ☎ 412/263–4800) carries upscale clothing in its downtown store.

Fifth Avenue Place (✉ Penn and 5th Aves.) has about a dozen specialty shops and a food court downtown. **PPG Place** (✉ Stanwix St. and 4th Ave) includes specialty shops.

Pittsburgh Essentials

AIRPORTS AND TRANSFERS

Greater Pittsburgh International Airport, served by most major airlines, is 14 mi west of downtown.

➤ Airport Information: **Greater Pittsburgh International Airport** (✉ 1000 Airport Blvd., ☎ 412/472–3525, WEB www.pitairport.com).

AIRPORT TRANSFER

A cab ride from the airport to downtown is about $30. Express Shuttle USA provides motor-coach or van service to the major downtown hotels for $16 one-way and $30 round-trip. Port Authority Transit operates daily bus service (No. 28X) from around 5:30 AM to midnight between the airport and downtown and Oakland ($2).

➤ Taxis and Shuttles: **Express Shuttle USA** (☎ 412/321–4990). **Port Authority Transit** (☎ 412/442–2000, WEB www.porthauthority.org).

BUS TRAVEL TO AND FROM PITTSBURGH

➤ Bus Information: **Greyhound** (✉ 11th St. and Liberty Ave., ☎ 800/231–2222, WEB www.greyhound.com).

CAR TRAVEL

From the north or south, take I–79 to I–279, which leads into downtown. From the east take the Pennsylvania Turnpike (I–76), then I–376 to the Grant Street exit. From the west take I–76 to I–79 south, and then follow I–279 to downtown.

TRAIN TRAVEL

Amtrak has daily service to Pittsburgh from Chicago and Philadelphia.

➤ Train Information: **Amtrak** (✉ 1100 Liberty St., ☎ 800/872–7245, WEB www.amtrak.com).

TRANSPORTATION AROUND PITTSBURGH

Port Authority Transit (☞ Airport Transfer, *above*) operates daily bus and trolley service. Within the central business district, the subway, called the T, is always free, and buses are free during the day. Two cable cars—the *Duquesne Incline,* from West Carson Street on the Ohio River to the restaurant area of Grandview Avenue, and the *Monongahela Incline,* from Station Square on the Monongahela to Grandview Avenue—carry passengers from river level to the top of Mt. Washington, which has a magnificent view of the city.

VISITOR INFORMATION

Information can be accessed via the Convention and Visitors Bureau's phone number 24 hours a day. The same phone number connects to all Visitor Information Centers throughout the city.

➤ TOURIST INFORMATION: **Greater Pittsburgh Convention and Visitors Bureau** (✉ Regional Enterprise Tower, 425 6th Ave., 15219, ☎ 800/366–0093, WEB www.pittsburgh-cvb.org). **Visitor Information Centers** (✉ Downtown: Liberty Ave., adjacent to Gateway Center; ✉ Oakland: Forbes Ave., next to the Cathedral of Learning; ✉ Mount Washington: 315 Grandview Ave.; ✉ Airport: 1000 Airport Blvd., lower level near baggage claim).

ELSEWHERE IN PENNSYLVANIA

The Poconos

What to See and Do

The Poconos, in the northeastern corner of the state, encompass 2,400 square mi of wilderness bordering the Delaware River, with lakes, streams, waterfalls, resorts, and country inns. Bushkill, Milford, Mount Pocono, Stroudsburg, and Tannersville are some of the towns in the area. A back-roads drive will turn up quaint villages such as **Jim Thorpe** (✉ Rte. 209), a late-Victorian mountain-resort town that has first-rate antiques shops and galleries. Winter brings downhill and cross-country skiing, skating, and snowmobiling; summer offers golfing, boating, horseback riding, and hiking. The **Pocono Mountains Vacation Bureau** (✉ 1004 Main St., Stroudsburg 18360, ☎ 570/421–5791 or 800/762–6667, WEB www.poconos.org) provides information.

Dining and Lodging

$$–$$$ ✕🏨 **French Manor.** Forget the heart-shape bathtubs and other honeymoon hokeyness this area is known for—the French Manor is *the* most romantic spot in the Poconos. The chateau-style mansion, secluded on the top of a mountain, offers panoramic views, luxurious amenities, and excellent French cuisine. ✉ *Huckleberry Rd., South Sterling 18460,* ☎ *570/676–3244 or 800/523–8200,* FAX *570/676–9786,* WEB *www.thefrenchmanor.com. 15 rooms. Restaurant. AE, D, DC, MC, V. BP.*

$ 🏨 **Sterling Inn.** Built in 1857, the clapboard main house and cluster of cottages, including 10 suites with fireplaces and whirlpool baths, have a bright country style. ✉ *Rte. 191, South Sterling 18460,* ☎ *570/676–3311 or 800/523–8200,* FAX *570/676–9786,* WEB *www.thesterlinginn.com. 65 rooms. Restaurant, pool. AE, D, DC, MC, V. BP.*

The Poconos Essentials

CAR TRAVEL

I–80 leads to the Delaware Water Gap, I–84 to Milford. From the south U.S. 611 skirts the Delaware River and takes you into Stroudsburg, which is 98 mi from Philadelphia, 135 mi from Harrisburg, and 318 mi from Pittsburgh.

RHODE ISLAND

Updated by Paula M. Bodah

Capital	Providence
Population	1,048,000
Motto	Hope
State Bird	Rhode Island red hen
State Flower	Violet
Postal Abbreviation	RI

Statewide Visitor Information

Rhode Island Tourism Division (✉ 1 W. Exchange St., Providence 02903, ☎ 401/222–2601; 800/556–2484 literature).

Scenic Drives

From Wickford to Point Judith, travel **Route 1A** and **Ocean Road** to see 19th-century mansions, a lighthouse, and various historic sights. Two bridges on **Route 138** link Newport to Narragansett; this drive affords unbeatable views of Narragansett Bay. **Route 77** runs through the idyllic towns of Tiverton and Little Compton. And nothing compares with the grand mansions along **Newport's Bellevue and Ocean Avenues.**

State Parks

Rhode Island's 37 state parks and recreational grounds encompass beaches, tidal marshes, swamp lands, woodlands, and bay shores. **Burlingame State Park, Charlestown Breachway, Fishermen's Memorial State Park, George Washington Camping Area,** and the **Ninigret Conservation Area** allow camping. For state parks information contact **Rhode Island Division of Parks and Recreation** (☎ 401/884–2010) or the Rhode Island Tourism Division (☞ Statewide Visitor Information).

THE SOUTH COAST

Exploring the South Coast

Beautiful beaches line the southern coast of Rhode Island. **Misquamicut State Beach** in Westerly, **Charlestown Beach** in Charlestown, and **Scarborough State Beach** in Narragansett are three of the best.

Watch Hill is a Victorian-era resort village with miles of beautiful beaches and a lighthouse. **Napatree Point** is one of the best long beach walks in Rhode Island. A walk to the end of Bay Street and a left onto Fort Road will lead you to the beach. The **Flying Horse Carousel** (✉ Bay St.; 🎟 50¢), which operates from mid-June to Labor Day, is the oldest merry-go-round in America, built in 1861.

Within the 15 villages of **South Kingstown** you can visit historic sights, crafts shops, galleries, and Matunuck Beach. At the **Washington County Jail,** built in 1792, you can tour jail cells, colonial-period rooms, and a colonial garden. ✉ *1348 Kingstown Rd.,* ☎ *401/783–1328.* 🎟 *Free. Closed Mon., Wed., Fri., Sun., and Nov.–Apr.*

Built in 1751, the **Gilbert Stuart Birthplace** was the home of America's foremost portraitist of George Washington. It lies on a pretty country road and is adjacent to the first snuff mill in America. ✉ *815 Gilbert Stuart Rd.,* ☎ *401/294–3001.* 🎟 *$3. Closed Tues.–Wed. and Nov.–May.*

Theatre-by-the-Sea (✉ Cards Pond Rd., ☎ 401/782–8587) presents summer-stock musicals and plays in a playhouse listed on the National Register of Historic Places.

Narragansett, which includes the maritime village of Galilee and the Point Judith Lighthouse, is a top summer destination for its beaches, bay vistas, and restaurants. The **Towers** (✉ Ocean Rd., Narragansett Pier) are all that remains of the casino that was once the centerpiece of the beachside village known as Narragansett Pier.

South County Museum houses 20,000 artifacts dating from 1800. ✉ *Anne Hoxie La., off Rte. 1A,* ☎ *401/783–5400.* *$3.50. Closed Mon.–Tues. and Nov.–Apr.*

The fishing port of **Galilee** is a departure point for ferries to Block Island and charter-fishing trips. The **Frances Fleet** (✉ 2 State St., ☎ 401/783–4988 or 800/662–2824) conducts whale-watching excursions between June and September. On Ocean Road are public beaches and, at land's end, the **Point Judith Lighthouse** (☎ 401/789–0444).

Dining and Lodging

If you're interested in local fare, try the stuffies—large native clams called quahogs (pronounced *ko*-hog) that are stuffed and baked. "Shore dinners" consist of clam chowder, steamers, clam cakes, sausage, corn-on-the-cob, lobster, watermelon, and Indian pudding (a steamed pudding made with cornmeal and molasses). And just so you're not surprised, Rhode Island clam chowder is made with a clear broth. Along the south shore and in North Kingstown are many small motels and B&Bs.

Narragansett

$$ ✕ **Coast Guard House.** This restaurant, which dates from 1888 and was a lifesaving station for 50 years, displays interesting photos of Narragansett Pier and the Casino. The menu is American—seafood, pasta, veal, steak, and lamb. ✉ *40 Ocean Rd.,* ☎ *401/789–0700. AE, D, DC, MC, V.*

$$ ★ ✕ **Spain Restaurant.** The cuisine and service in this spacious eatery near the Point Judith Lighthouse are the work of well-trained professionals. Generously portioned main courses include lobster and steak dishes, as well as a variety of paellas. Even basic fare, like chicken with rice, is unforgettable. ✉ *1144 Ocean Rd.,* ☎ *401/783–9770. AE, D, DC, MC, V.*

$$–$$$ **The Richards.** Imposing and magnificent, this English manor–style mansion has a broodingly Gothic mystique. Some rooms have 19th-century English antiques, floral-upholstered furniture, and fireplaces. Two of the rooms share a bath. ✉ *144 Gibson Ave., 02882,* ☎ *401/789–7746. 5 rooms. No credit cards. BP.*

Shopping

The **Fantastic Umbrella Factory** (✉ 4920 Old Post Rd., off Rte. 1, ☎ 401/364–6616) comprises four rustic shops and a barn built around a wild garden where peacocks, pheasants, and chickens parade. For sale in the backyard bazaar are kites, crafts, tapestries, incense, and blown-glass jewelry.

The colonial village of **Wickford,** 10 mi north of Narragansett Pier along Route 1A, has a little harbor, dozens of 18th- and 19th-century homes, and numerous antiques and curiosity shops.

The South Coast Essentials

BUS TRAVEL

RIPTA (Rhode Island Public Transportation Authority) provides service from Providence and Warwick to Kingston, Wakefield, Narragansett, and Galilee.

➤ Bus Information: **RIPTA** (☎ 401/847–0209; 800/244–0444 in Rhode Island).

CAR TRAVEL

I–95 passes 10 mi north of Westerly before heading inland toward Providence. Routes 1 and 1A follow the coastline along Narragansett Bay and are the primary routes through the South County (Washington County) resort towns.

TRAIN TRAVEL

Amtrak stops at Westerly and Kingston.

➤ Train Information: **Amtrak** (☎ 800/872–7245).

VISITOR INFORMATION

South County is the common name for Washington County.

➤ Tourist Information: **South County Tourism Council** (✉ 4808 Tower Hill Rd., Wakefield 02879, ☎ 401/789–4422 or 800/548–4662).

NEWPORT

Newport is one of the great sailing cities of the world and the host to world-class jazz, blues, folk, and classical music festivals. More than 200 colonial homes and shops still stand from the city's first period of prosperity, the 18th-century golden age. In the 19th century, during what became known as the gilded age, Newport was a summer playground for America's wealthiest families.

Exploring Newport

★ The French admiral de Ternay used the 1748 **Hunter House** as his Revolutionary War headquarters. The elliptical arch in the central hall is a typical Newport detail. ✉ *54 Washington St.,* ☎ *401/847–7516,* WEB *www.newportmansions.org.* 🎫 *$8. Closed Nov.–Apr. and weekdays Oct.*

Museum of Newport History at the Brick Market. This restored 1760 building houses a city museum with multimedia exhibits that explore Newport's social and economic influences. The museum and the Gateway Information Center are departure points for walking tours of Newport; call for times. ✉ *127 Thames St.,* ☎ *401/841–0813.* 🎫 *$5.*

Colony House faces the Brick Market on Washington Square. Built in 1739, it was the government's headquarters—from its balcony the Declaration of Independence was read to Newporters.

The **Friends Meeting House** (✉ 29 Farewell St., ☎ 401/846–0813; 🎫 $5) was built in 1699 and is the oldest Quaker meetinghouse in America; tours are by appointment. Austere from the outside but elaborate within, the **Touro Synagogue** (✉ 85 Touro St., ☎ 401/847–4794, WEB www.tourosynagogue.org), dedicated in 1763, is the oldest synagogue in the country.

Walking tours of Newport depart from the **Newport Historical Society.** ✉ *82 Touro St.,* ☎ *401/846–0813.* 🎫 *Free. Closed Sun.–Mon.*

Trinity Church (✉ Queen Anne Sq., ☎ 401/846–0660), built in 1724, has a three-tier wineglass pulpit. The 1748 **Redwood Library** (✉ 50 Belle-

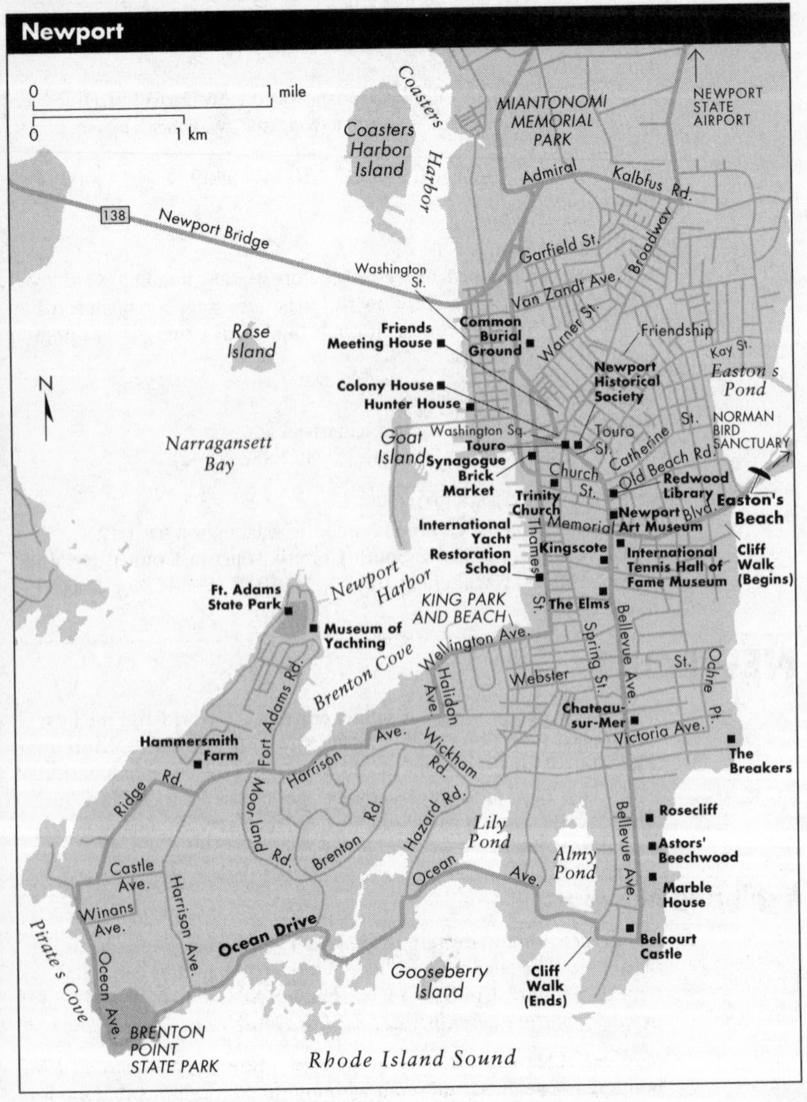

vue Ave., ☎ 401/847–0292, WEB www.redwood1747.org), the country's oldest continually operating library, houses paintings by early American artists. The **Newport Art Museum and Art Association** (✉ 76 Bellevue Ave., ☎ 401/848–8200, WEB www.newportartmuseum.com; 🎟 $6) exhibits contemporary works by New England artists.

Easton's Beach (✉ Memorial Blvd.), also known as First Beach, is popular for its expansive beach, children's aquarium, and other amusements. A small, sheltered beach at **Fort Adams State Park** (✉ Ocean Dr.) has a picnic area, lifeguards, and views of Newport Harbor.

The **Preservation Society of Newport County** (☎ 401/847–1000, WEB www.newportmansions.org) maintains 12 mansions, some of which are described below. Guided tours are given of each; you can purchase a combination ticket at any of the properties for a substantial discount. The hours and days the houses are open during the off-season are subject to change, so it's wise to call ahead.

Kingscote was built in 1839 for a plantation owner from Savannah, Georgia. It's decorated with antique furniture, glass, Asian art, and Tiffany windows. ✉ *Bowery St. off Bellevue Ave.,* ☎ *401/847–1000.* 🎫 *$8. Closed Nov.–Mar. and weekdays Apr. and Oct.*

Isaac Bell House. Considered one of the finest examples of American shingle-style architecture, this Bellevue Avenue home currently being restored is open to the public as a work in progress. ✉ *Bellevue Ave. at Perry St.,* ☎ *401/847–1000.* 🎫 *$9. Closed Nov.–Apr.*

The **Elms,** a graceful 48-room French neoclassical mansion, was designed by architect Horace Trumbauer, who paid homage to the style, broad lawn, fountains, and formal gardens of the Château d'Asnières near Paris. ✉ *Bellevue Ave.,* ☎ *401/842–0546.* 🎫 *$9. Closed mid-Nov.–Thanksgiving Day and weekdays Jan.–Mar.*

Chateau-sur-Mer, the first of Bellevue Avenue's stone mansions, was built in the Victorian Gothic style in 1852. Some rooms were created by leading 19th-century designers. ✉ *Bellevue Ave.,* ☎ *401/847–1000.* 🎫 *$8. Closed weekdays Oct.–mid-Nov. and weekdays Jan.–Mar.*

★ The **Breakers,** a four-story Italian Renaissance palace built in 1893 for railroad heir Cornelius Vanderbilt II, contains such marvels as a gold-ceiling music room and a blue-marble fireplace. To build the Breakers today would cost about $400 million. ✉ *Ochre Point Ave.,* ☎ *401/847–6544.* 🎫 *$10. Closed Dec. (most yrs), Jan.–Mar., weekends in Apr., and weekdays in Nov.*

Rosecliff, Newport's most romantic mansion (complete with heart-shape staircase), was modeled after the Grand Trianon palace at Versailles. ✉ *Bellevue Ave.,* ☎ *401/847–5793.* 🎫 *$8. Closed Nov.–Mar.*

The **Marble House,** perhaps the most opulent Newport mansion, was the gift of William Vanderbilt to his wife in 1892. ✉ *Bellevue Ave.,* ☎ *401/847–1000.* 🎫 *$9. Closed Nov., Dec. (most yrs), and weekdays Jan.–Mar.*

At **Astors' Beechwood,** which was built for the wealthy Astor family, actors in period costume play the parts of family members, servants, and household guests. ✉ *580 Bellevue Ave.,* ☎ *401/846–3772.* 🎫 *$9. Closed Jan. and weekdays Feb.–Apr.*

Belcourt Castle is so filled with European and Asian treasures that locals have dubbed it the Metropolitan Museum of Newport. ✉ *Bellevue Ave.,* ☎ *401/846–0669 or 401/849–1566.* 🎫 *$8. Closed Jan.*

★ **Hammersmith Farm** was the childhood summer home of Jacqueline Bouvier Kennedy Onassis, and a summer White House during the Kennedy Administration. The home is no longer open to the pubic. ✉ *Ocean Dr. near Fort Adams.*

The **International Tennis Hall of Fame Museum** (✉ 194 Bellevue Ave., ☎ 401/849–3990, WEB www.tennisfame.com; 🎫 $8) is in the magnificent Newport Casino. The **Museum of Yachting** (✉ Fort Adams Park, Ocean Dr., ☎ 401/847–1018; 🎫 $3; closed Nov.–Apr.) has four galleries of sailing exhibits.

The **National Museum of American Illustration** (✉ 492 Bellevue Ave., ☎ 401/851–8949, WEB www.americanillustration.org; 🎫 $25), open by appointment, showcases original drawings and paintings created for books, advertisements, art prints, and periodicals.

Shipwrights overhaul historic oceangoing vessels, and the public is welcome to watch, at the **International Yacht Restoration School** (✉ 449 Thames St., ☎ 401/848–5577, WEB www.iyrs.org).

Old Colony & Newport Railway (✉ 19 America's Cup Ave., ☎ 401/624–6951; $6), a vintage diesel train, follows an 8-mi route along Narragansett Bay from Newport to the Green Animals Topiary Gardens in Portsmouth.

North of Second Beach, the **Norman Bird Sanctuary** (✉ 583 3rd Rd., Middletown, ☎ 401/846–2577; $4) is a 450-acre nature preserve with hiking trails, guided tours, and a small natural history museum.

Dining and Lodging

Entering Newport from the direction of Providence, you will find a number of motels whose room rates are considerably lower than those downtown.

$$$–$$$$ ✕ **Scales & Shells.** This busy restaurant serves as many as 15 types of superbly fresh wood-grilled fish. The dining is more formal upstairs at Upscales. ✉ *527 Thames St.,* ☎ *401/848–9378. No credit cards.*

$$–$$$ ★ ✕ **Asterix & Obelix.** Fine dining here is as fun and colorful as the madcap French cartoon strip after which this eatery was named. Occasional Asian twists enliven the French and Mediterranean fare. "Crispy duck" is roasted with honey and ginger and served with stir fry; sole meunière is topped with a spinach anglaise. ✉ *599 Thames St.,* ☎ *401/841–8833. AE, D, DC, MC, V.*

$$–$$$ ✕ **Black Pearl.** Tourists and yachters flock to this dignified converted dock shanty, where award-winning clam chowder is sold by the quart. Dining is in the casual tavern or the formal Commodore's Room (reservations essential; jacket required), where the French and American entrées include swordfish with Dutch pepper butter. ✉ *Bannister's Wharf,* ☎ *401/846–5264. AE, MC, V.*

$–$$ ✕ **Flo's Clam Shack.** Fried seafood, steamed clams, cold beer, and the best raw bar in town keep the lines long here in summer. The upstairs bar serves baked, chilled lobster, and outside seating is available. It's located across the street from First Beach. ✉ *4 Wave Ave.,* ☎ *401/847–8141. Reservations not accepted. MC, V.*

$–$$ ✕ **Puerini's.** The aroma of garlic and basil greets you as soon as you enter this laid-back neighborhood restaurant. The intriguing menu includes green noodles with chicken in marsala wine sauce and tortellini with seafood. ✉ *24 Memorial Blvd.,* ☎ *401/847–5506. Reservations not accepted. MC, V. Closed Mon. in winter. No lunch.*

$$$–$$$$ ✕🏨 **Vanderbilt Hall.** The city's most sophisticated inn and restaurant is downtown in a building formerly owned by the Vanderbilt family. All the rooms are individually decorated with antiques. A fire crackles in the somber dining room ($$–$$$), where a veteran and meticulous waitstaff tends to your needs. The inn has a whirlpool, sauna, and steam room. ✉ *41 Mary St., 02840,* ☎ *401/846–6200,* FAX *401/846–0701,* WEB *www.vanderbilthall.com. 50 rooms. Restaurant, pool. AE, DC, MC, V.*

$$$–$$$$ ★ 🏨 **Francis Malbone House.** This 1760 structure was tastefully doubled in size in the mid-1990s; the nine newer rooms have whirlpool tubs and fireplaces. The rooms in the main house are all in corners (with two windows) and look out over the courtyard, which has a fountain, or across the street to the harbor. Six of these rooms have fireplaces. ✉ *392 Thames St., 02840,* ☎ *401/846–0392 or 800/846–0392,* WEB *www.malbone.com. 18 rooms. AE, MC, V. BP.*

$$$–$$$$ 🏨 **Hotel Viking.** Listed on the National Register of Historical Places, this redbrick hotel has a prestigious address that makes it easy to walk to the waterfront, the historic district, and many nearby shops. The wood paneling and original chandeliers, among other details, evoke the hotel's sophisticated history. ✉ *One Bellevue Ave., 02840,* ☎ *401/847–3300* or 800/556–7126, FAX 401/848–4864, WEB www.hotelviking.com. 227 rooms. Restaurant, pool. AE, D, DC, MC, V.

$$–$$$$ **Castle Hill Inn and Resort.** Much of the furniture at this inn is original to the structure, a summer home built in 1874 on a cliff at the mouth of the Narragansett Bay. The inn, 3 mi from the center of Newport, is famous for its Sunday brunches. Three of the rooms share a bath. ✉ *Ocean Dr., 02840,* ☎ *401/849–3800,* WEB *www.castlehillinn.com. 35 with bath. Restaurant. AE, D, MC, V. Restaurant closed Nov.–Mar. BP.*

$$–$$$ ★ **Ivy Lodge.** This grand (though small by Newport's standards) Victorian B&B with large and lovely rooms has gables and a turret. The defining feature is a Gothic-style 33-ft-high oak entryway with a three-story turned baluster staircase and a dangling wrought-iron chandelier. ✉ *12 Clay St., 02840,* ☎ *401/849–6865,* WEB *www.ivylodge.com. 8 rooms. AE, MC, V. BP.*

$ **Harbor Base Pineapple Inn.** All the rooms at this basic motel, a five-minute drive from downtown, contain two double beds; some also have kitchenettes. ✉ *372 Coddington Hwy., 02840,* ☎ *401/847–2600. 48 rooms. AE, D, DC, MC, V.*

Nightlife

Thames Street is the nexus of Newport's lively nightlife. **Newport Blues Café** (✉ 286 Thames St., ☎ 401/841–5510) hosts great blues performers. **One Pelham East** (✉ 270 Thames St., ☎ 401/847–9460) draws a young crowd for progressive rock, reggae, and R&B.

Outdoor Activities and Sports

Adventure Sports (✉ The Inn at Long Wharf, America's Cup Ave., ☎ 401/849–4820) rents wave runners, sailboats, kayaks, and canoes. **Old Port Marine Services** (✉ Sayer's Wharf, ☎ 401/847–9109) operates harbor tours and crewed yacht charters. **Sail Newport** (✉ Fort Adams State Park, ☎ 401/846–1983) rents sailboats by the hour.

Ten Speed Spokes (✉ 18 Elm St., ☎ 401/847–5609) rents bikes.

Tennis Indoor Club (✉ Memorial Blvd., one block east of Bellevue, ☎ 401/846–4777) rents indoor courts for $25 per hour.

Shopping

Many of Newport's arts and antiques shops are on Thames Street; others are on Spring Street, Franklin Street, and at Bowen's and Bannister's wharves. The **Brick Market** area—between Thames Street and America's Cup Avenue—has more than 40 shops that carry crafts, clothing, antiques, and toys. Stores at **Bannister's Wharf** stock clothing and gifts with a nautical theme. **Arnold Art Store and Gallery** (✉ 210 Thames St., ☎ 401/847–2273) has a large collection of marine-inspired paintings and prints. The delicate and dramatic blown-glass gifts at **Thames Glass** (✉ 688 Thames St., ☎ 401/846–0576) are designed by Matthew Buechner and created in the adjacent studio.

Side Trip to Block Island

Arriving and Departing

BOAT AND FERRY TRAVEL

Interstate Navigation Co. (☞ Newport Essentials) has ferry service from Galilee to Block Island; fare is $8.40 from Galilee. Nelesco Navigation Co. (☞ Newport Essentials) operates car and passenger ferry service from New London to Block Island daily from June to September. The trip costs around $15. Viking Ferry Lines (☞ Newport Essentials) operates passenger and bicycle service from Montauk, Long Island, from mid-May to mid-October; fare is $16. None of these ferries take passenger reservations.

AIRPORTS

Block Island State Airport (☞ Newport Essentials) is served by New England Airlines from Westerly.

What to See and Do

Approaching 10-square-mi Block Island by sea from New London or Point Judith, you'll see the **Old Harbor** area. Here in the island's only village are most of the inns, shops, and restaurants. Three docks, two hotels, and four restaurants huddled in the southeast corner of the Great Salt Pond make up the **New Harbor** commercial area, where two ferries dock. ★ Hiking paths at **Rodman's Hollow,** a fine example of a glacial outwash basin, lead to pristine beaches. The **Southeast Lighthouse** (✉ Mohegan Trail, ☎ 401/466–5009) is a National Historic Landmark that was built in 1875. **Block Island Chamber of Commerce** (✉ Drawer D, Water St., 02807, ☎ 401/466–2982) provides information on available lodgings.

Newport Essentials

AIRPORTS AND TRANSFERS

Newport State Airport is 3 mi northeast of Newport. Charter companies fly from here to T. F. Green State Airport in Warwick. You can also fly into T. F. Green State Airport, 10 mi south of Providence, and drive a rental car to Newport. Take I–95 south to Route 4, then Route 138 to Newport; it's a 25-minute drive. Block Island is served by Block Island State Airport.

➤ AIRPORT INFORMATION: **Block Island State Airport** (☎ 401/466–5511). **New England Airlines** (☎ 401/596–2460 or 800/243–2460). **Newport State Airport** (✉ 500 Airport Rd., ☎ 401/846–9400). **T. F. Green State Airport** (✉ Rte. 1, Warwick, ☎ 401/737–4000).

AIRPORT TRANSFER

By reservation, Cozy Cab runs a shuttle service ($15) between the Newport State Airport and Newport's visitor's bureau.

➤ TAXI: **Cozy Cab** (☎ 401/846–2500).

BOAT AND FERRY TRAVEL

Jamestown and Newport Ferry Company runs frequently from Jamestown. Interstate Navigation Co., Nelesco Navigation Co., and Viking Ferry Lines all serve Block Island.

➤ BOAT AND FERRY INFORMATION: **Interstate Navigation Co.** (✉ Galilee State Pier, Narragansett, ☎ 401/783–4613). **Jamestown and Newport Ferry Company** (☎ 401/423–9900). **Nelesco Navigation Co.** (✉ 2 Ferry St., New London, CT, ☎ 860/442–7891). **Viking Ferry Lines** (✉ West Lake Dr., Montauk, NY, ☎ 516/668–5709).

BUS TRAVEL TO AND FROM NEWPORT

Bonanza runs from Boston. RIPTA serves Newport from Providence and elsewhere in Rhode Island.

➤ BUS INFORMATION: **Bonanza** (☎ 401/751–8800 or 800/556–3815). **RIPTA** (☎ 401/847–0209; 800/244–0444 in Rhode Island).

CAR TRAVEL

From Providence take I–95 east into Massachusetts and head south on Route 24. From South County take Route 1 north to Route 138 east. From Boston take I–93 south to Route 24 south.

VISITOR INFORMATION

Gateway Information Center provides long-term parking and a wide array of visitors' resources.

➤ TOURIST INFORMATION: **Gateway Information Center** (✉ 23 America's Cup Ave., Newport 02840, ☎ 401/849–8048 or 800/326–6030).

PROVIDENCE

New England's third-largest city (behind Boston and Worcester) is a prime example of how U.S. cities can be redesigned and culturally revived. In the past decade, Providence rivers have been rerouted and unsightly railroad tracks have been placed underground. In downtown Providence, a convention center, an outdoor ice rink, a riverfront park, and an upscale shopping mall now draw tourists and visitors from outlying towns. In addition, many travelers now prefer revamped T. F. Green Airport over Boston's Logan Airport.

Exploring Providence

The **Providence Athenaeum** (✉ 251 Benefit St., ☎ 401/421–6970, WEB www.providenceathenaeum.org; 🎫 free), established in 1753 and one of the oldest lending libraries in the world, displays Rhode Island art and artifacts, as well as an original set of the folio *Birds of America* prints by John J. Audubon.

The small but comprehensive **Museum of Art, Rhode Island School of Design** contains textiles, Japanese prints, Paul Revere silver, 18th-century porcelain, French Impressionist paintings, and a mummy dating from circa 300 BC. *✉ 224 Benefit St., ☎ 401/454–6500, WEB www.risd.edu. 🎫 $5. Closed Mon.*

On **Benefit Street**—known as the Mile of History—a row of colonial and Revolutionary War–era houses are crammed shoulder to shoulder on a steep hill overlooking downtown Providence. The **Providence Preservation Society** (✉ 21 Meeting St., at Benefit St., ☎ 401/831–7440) provides maps and pamphlets with self-guided tours.

The **Arcade** (✉ 65 Weybosset St., ☎ 401/598–1199; closed Sun.), America's first shopping mall, was built in 1828. A National Historic Landmark, this graceful Greek Revival building has three tiers of shops and restaurants.

The **First Unitarian Church of Providence** (✉ 1 Benevolent St., ☎ 401/421–7970; 🎫 free), built in 1816, houses the largest bell ever cast in Paul Revere's foundry—a 2,500 pounder.

The awe-inspiring **Rhode Island State House** was built in 1900. Its dome, one of the world's largest, was modeled after St. Peter's Basilica in Rome. On display is the original parchment charter granted by King Charles to the colony of Rhode Island in 1663. Booklets for self-guided tours are available in Room 220. *✉ 82 Smith St., ☎ 401/222–2357. Closed weekends.*

Roger Williams contributed so significantly to the concepts leading to the Declaration of Independence and the Constitution that the National Park Service dedicated the 4½-acre **Roger Williams National Memorial** (✉ 282 N. Main St., ☎ 401/521–7266; 🎫 free) to his memory. Displays document the life and times of Rhode Island's extraordinary founder.

Waterplace Park and Riverwalk (✉ Boat House Clock Tower, 2 American Express Way, ☎ 401/751–1177)—a 4-acre tract with Venetian-style footbridges, cobblestone walkways, and an amphitheater encircling a tidal pond on the Providence River—is a critical component of the ongoing revitalization of the downtown.

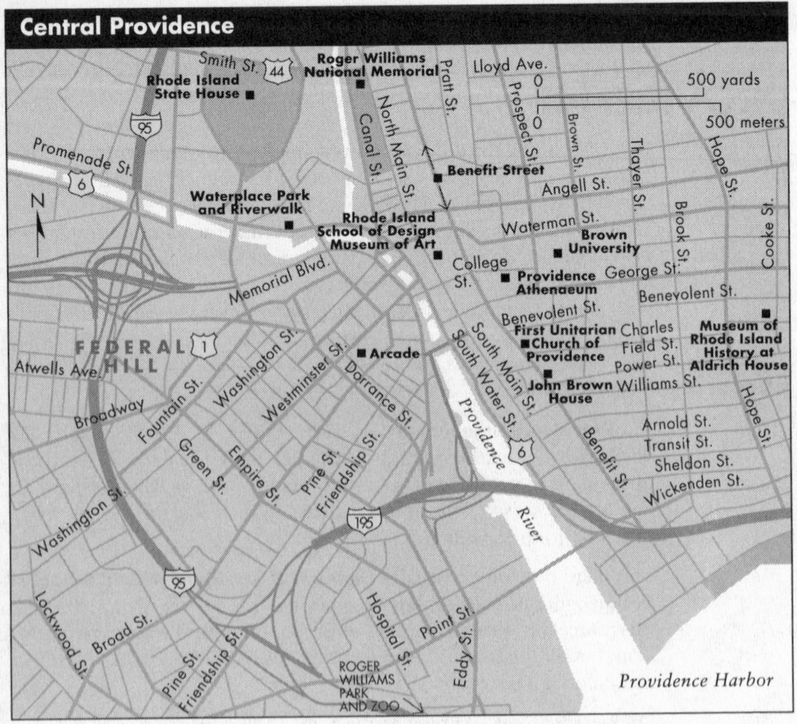

★ The 1786 **John Brown House,** one of America's first mansions, is named for a China trader famous for his Revolutionary-era role in the burning of the British customs ship *Gaspee.* The three-story Georgian mansion has elaborate woodwork and furniture, silver, linens, Chinese porcelain, and an antique doll collection. ✉ *52 Power St.,* ☎ *401/331–8575,* WEB *www.rihs.org.* 🎫 *$6. Closed weekdays Jan.–Feb.*

Roger Williams Park and Zoo (✉ Elmwood Ave., ☎ 401/785–3510; 🎫 $6) is a beautiful 430-acre Victorian park. The zoo is home to more than 900 animals and 150 different species. In the park you can have a picnic, feed the ducks in the lakes, ride a pony, or rent a paddleboat.

Dining and Lodging

$$–$$$ ★ ✕ **Al Forno.** Roasted clams and spicy sausage served in a tomato broth as well as charcoal-seared tournedos of beef with mashed potatoes are among the entrées at this regionally renowned contemporary eatery. Made-to-order desserts include crepes with apricot puree and crème anglaise. ✉ *577 S. Main St.,* ☎ *401/273–9760. Reservations not accepted. AE, DC, MC, V. Closed Sun.–Mon. No lunch.*

$$–$$$ ★ ✕ **The Gatehouse.** Views of the Seekonk River and fine modern art by local artists complement the internationally influenced American cuisine, which spans the globe, from Asian duck spring rolls to New Orleans–style barbecue shrimp to blackened yellowfin tuna to a simple American meat loaf. Reservations are essential on weekends. ✉ *4 Richmond Sq.,* ☎ *401/521–9229. AE, DC, MC, V. No lunch.*

$$–$$$ ★ ✕ **Pot au Feu.** For a quarter century Pot au Feu has worked to perfect basics such as pâté du foie gras, beef bourguignonne, and potatoes au gratin. The dining experience is more casual at the downstairs Bistro than at the upstairs Salon (closed Sunday–Monday) ✉ *44 Custom House St.,* ☎ *401/273–8953. AE, DC, MC, V.*

$$ ✕ **L'Epicureo.** Formerly a Federal Hill butcher shop, this refined Italian bistro has won high marks for its wood-grilled steaks, veal chops, and pasta dishes, such as fettuccine tossed with arugula, garlic, and lemon. ✉ *238 Atwells Ave.,* ☎ *401/454–8430. AE, D, DC, MC, V. Closed Sun.–Mon. No lunch.*

$ ✕ **Angelo's Civita Farnese.** On Federal Hill in the heart of Little Italy, lively (even boisterous) Angelo's is a family-run place with old-world charm. Locals come here for good-size portions of fresh and simply prepared pasta. ✉ *141 Atwells Ave.,* ☎ *401/621–8171. Reservations not accepted. No credit cards.*

$$–$$$ ★ ✕🏨 **Westin Providence.** The multiturreted 25-story Westin towers over Providence's compact downtown, connected by skywalks to the city's gleaming convention center and the Providence Place mall. Its rooms have reproduction period furniture, and half have king-size beds; many have views of the city. The redbrick hotel's Agora restaurant ($$$$) has a superb wine cellar. ✉ *1 W. Exchange St., 02903,* ☎ *401/598–8000 or 800/937–8461,* FAX *401/598–8200,* WEB *www.westin.com. 386 rooms. 2 restaurants, pool, health club. AE, D, DC, MC, V.*

$$–$$$ 🏨 **Courtyard by Marriott Providence.** The newest of Providence's hotels is housed in a seven-story redbrick building, carefully designed to match the other buildings in its historic Union Station Plaza location. Nearly every room has views of Waterplace Park. The hotel is steps away from the Providence Place mall. ✉ *32 Exchange Terr., 02903,* ☎ *401/272–1191 or 800/321–2211,* FAX *401/272–1416,* WEB *www.marriott.com. 216 rooms. Restaurant, pool, gym. AE, D, DC, MC, V.*

$$ ★ 🏨 **Providence Biltmore.** The Biltmore, completed in 1922, has a sleek Art Deco exterior, an external glass elevator with delightful views of Providence, a grand ballroom, and an interesting history. The attentiveness of its staff, the downtown location, and modern amenities make this hotel one of the city's best. ✉ *Kennedy Plaza, Dorrance and Washington Sts., 02903,* ☎ *401/421–0700 or 800/294–7209,* FAX *401/421–0210,* WEB *www.grandheritage.com. 238 rooms. Restaurant, gym. AE, DC, MC, V.*

$–$$ 🏨 **C. C. Ledbetter's.** The unmarked somber green exterior of innkeeper C. C. Ledbetter's mansard-roof 1770 home gives few hints of the vibrancy within—lively art, photographs, quilts, and a shrewd blend of contemporary furnishings and antiques fill the place. Two rooms share a bath. ✉ *326 Benefit St., 02903,* ☎ FAX *401/351–4699. 4 rooms. D, MC, V. CP.*

Nightlife and the Arts

The **Custom House Tavern** (✉ 36 Weybosset St., ☎ 401/751–3630) is a friendly downtown gathering place. The **Hot Club** (✉ 575 S. Water St., ☎ 401/861–9007) is a waterside bar where scenes from *Something About Mary* were filmed. **Lupo's Heartbreak Hotel** (✉ 239 Westminster St., ☎ 401/272–5876), a nightclub, books local and international musical talents. The **Providence Performing Arts Center** (✉ 220 Weybosset St., ☎ 401/421–2787) hosts touring Broadway shows, concerts, and other events. **Snookers** (✉ 145 Clifford St., ☎ 401/351–7665) is a stylish billiard hall in the Jewelry District. **Trinity Square Repertory Company** (✉ 201 Washington St., ☎ 401/351–4242), one of New England's best theater companies, presents plays in the renovated Majestic movie house.

Outdoor Activities and Sports

Biking

For trail information call **Rhode Island Tourism Division** (☎ 800/556–2484). The **East Bay Bicycle Path** is a 14½-mi paved trail linking Providence's India Point Park to Bristol.

Tennis

Roger Williams Park (✉ off Elmwood Ave., ☎ 401/785–9450) has eight public courts.

Shopping

The upscale **Providence Place Mall** (✉ 1 Providence Pl., Francis and Hayes Sts., ☎ 401/270–1000) is anchored by Filene's, Lord & Taylor, and Nordstrom; 150 other shops and restaurants complete the mix. Antiques stores and art galleries line **Wickenden Street. Tilden-Thurber** (✉ 292 Westminster St., ☎ 401/272–3200) carries high-end colonial- and Victorian-era furniture, antiques, and estate jewelry.

Providence Essentials

AIRPORTS AND TRANSFERS

T. F. Green State Airport, 10 mi south of Providence, is served by major U.S. airlines and regional carriers.

➤ AIRPORT INFORMATION: **T. F. Green State Airport** (✉ 2000 Post Rd. [also Rte. 1], Warwick, ☎ 401/737–4000).

AIRPORT TRANSFER

Airport Van Shuttle provides service to downtown Providence and elsewhere.

➤ SHUTTLE: **Airport Van Shuttle** (☎ 888/736–1900).

BUS TRAVEL TO AND FROM NEWPORT

Both Bonanza and Greyhound service Providence. RIPTA provides local transportation in Providence and service to other parts of the state.

➤ BUS INFORMATION: **Bonanza** (☎ 800/556–3815). **Greyhound** (☎ 800/231–2222). **RIPTA** (☎ 401/781–9400; 800/224–0444 in Rhode Island).

CAR TRAVEL

I–95 cuts diagonally across the state and is the fastest route to Providence from Boston, coastal Connecticut, and New York City. I–195 links Providence with New Bedford and Cape Cod. U.S. 1 follows the coast east from Connecticut before turning north to Providence.

TRAIN TRAVEL

Amtrak trains stop at Providence Station. MBTA Commuter Rail runs between Boston and Providence weekday mornings and evenings.

➤ TRAIN INFORMATION: **Amtrak** (☎ 800/872–7245). **MBTA** (☎ 617/722–3200). **Providence Station** (✉ 100 Gaspee St., ☎ 401/727–7379).

VISITOR INFORMATION

➤ TOURIST INFORMATION: **Greater Providence Convention and Visitors Bureau** (✉ 1 W. Exchange St., 02903, ☎ 401/274–1636).

SOUTH CAROLINA

Updated by Mary Sue Lawrence

Capital	Columbia
Population	3,684,000
Mottoes	While I Breathe, I Hope; Prepared in Mind and Resources
State Bird	Carolina wren
State Flower	Yellow jessamine
Postal Abbreviation	SC

Statewide Visitor Information

South Carolina Department of Parks, Recreation and Tourism (✉ 1205 Pendleton St. [Box 71, Columbia 29202], ☎ 803/734–0235 or 800/872–3505, WEB www.travelsc.com). **Welcome centers:** U.S. 17 near Little River; I–95 near Dillon, Santee, Lake Marion, and Hardeeville; I–77 near Fort Mill; I–85 near Blacksburg and Fair Play; I–26 near Landrum; I–20 at North Augusta, Georgia; and U.S. 301 near Allendale.

Scenic Drives

The **Cherokee Foothills Scenic Highway** (Route 11) passes small towns, peach orchards, and historical sites as it traverses 130 mi of Blue Ridge foothills in the northwest corner of the state. The **Ashley River Road** (Route 61), which runs parallel to the river for about 11 mi north of Charleston, leads to famous plantations and gardens. The **Savannah River Scenic Highway** (follow signs from Route 28 near North Augusta to Route 24 near Westminster) traces the Savannah River for 100 mi along the Georgia border, winding past three lakes.

National and State Parks

National Parks

At **Cowpens National Battlefield** (✉ Rte. 11 [Box 308, Chesnee 29323], ☎ 864/461–2828; 🎫 free) the American patriots defeated the British in 1781; exhibits in the visitor center explain the battle. **Kings Mountain National Military Park** (✉ I–85 near Blacksburg [Box 40, Kings Mountain, NC 28086], ☎ 864/936–7921, WEB www.nps.gov/kimo; 🎫 free), where patriot forces whipped the redcoats in 1780, has exhibits depicting the famous battle and a self-guided trail. For whitewater enthusiasts, the **Chattooga National Wild and Scenic River** (✉ U.S. Forest Service, 4931 Broad River Rd., Columbia 29210-4021, ☎ 803/561–4000; 🎫 free) forms the border between South Carolina and Georgia for 40 mi. **Congaree Swamp National Monument** (✉ Old Bluff Rd., Hopkins 29061, ☎ 803/776–4396, WEB www.nps.gov/cosw; 🎫 free) contains the oldest and largest trees east of the Mississippi River.

State Parks

Several of South Carolina's 48 state parks operate like resort communities, with everything from deluxe accommodations to golf. **Hickory Knob State Resort Park** (✉ Rte. 1 [Box 199-B, McCormick 29835], ☎ 864/391–2450 or 800/491–1764), on Strom Thurmond Lake in the western part of South Carolina, has facilities for fishing, golfing, and skeet shooting. **Devil's Fork State Park** (✉ 161 Holcombe Cir., Salem 29676, ☎ 864/944–2639), in Sumter National Forest in the northwest corner of the state, has luxurious accommodations overlooking beautiful Lake Jocassee. **Calhoun Falls State Outdoor Recreation Area** (✉ 46 Maintenance Shop Rd., off Rte. 81, Calhoun Falls 29628, ☎

864/447–9367), on the western edge of the state, has a full-service marina, a campground, nature trails, and a picnic area.

The state's **coastal parks**—known for broad beaches, camping facilities, and nature preserves—draw the most visitors and are often booked months in advance. **Huntington Beach State Park** (✉ Murrells Inlet 29576, ☎ 843/237–4440) has a splendid beach, surf fishing, and a salt-marsh boardwalk, as well as Atalaya, a Moorish-style mansion. **Myrtle Beach State Park** (✉ U.S. 17, Myrtle Beach 29577, ☎ 843/238–5325) has cabins and year-round nature programs. **Hunting Island State Park** (✉ St. Helena Island 29920, ☎ 843/838–2011), a secluded beach domain, has beachfront cottages, nature trails, and varied fishing. **Edisto Beach State Park** (✉ Rte. 174, Edisto Island 29438, ☎ 843/869–2156) has cabins by the marsh and campsites by the ocean. For more information contact the **South Carolina Division of State Parks** (✉ 1205 Pendleton St., Columbia 29201, ☎ 803/734–0159, WEB www.southcarolinaparks.com).

CHARLESTON

The port city of Charleston has withstood three centuries of epidemics, earthquakes, fires, and hurricanes to become one of the South's best-preserved and most beloved cities. Residents have lovingly restored old downtown homes and commercial buildings, as well as more than 180 historic churches—so many that Charlestonians call their home the Holy City. Each spring the city—festooned with dogwood and azaleas—celebrates its heritage with symphony galas, plantation oyster roasts, candlelight tours of historic homes and churches, and the renowned Spoleto Festival USA, a celebration of the arts staged in streets and performance halls throughout the city.

Exploring Charleston

You can get a quick orientation to the city by viewing ***Forever Charleston,*** a 24-minute multimedia presentation shown by the Charleston Area Convention and Visitors Bureau.

★ The **Charleston Museum** (✉ 360 Meeting St., ☎ 843/722–2996, WEB www.charlestonmuseum.com; 🎟 museum $8, museum and houses $18, for any 2 of the 3 sites $12), founded in 1773, has 500,000 items in its collection, including Charleston silver, fashions, toys, and snuffboxes, as well as exhibits on natural history, archaeology, and ornithology. Also part of the museum are two historic homes. The **Joseph Manigault House** (✉ 350 Meeting St., 843/723–2926) was designed in 1803 and is noted for its carved-wood mantels and elaborate plasterwork. It is furnished with British, French, and American antiques, including rare Wedgwood pieces. The **Heyward-Washington House** (✉ 87 Church St., 843/722–0354) was the residence of President George Washington during his 1791 visit and the setting for DuBose Heyward's novel *Porgy.* It has period furnishings by local craftspeople, and includes a restored 18th-century kitchen.

The stately 1819 mansion, **Aiken-Rhett House** (✉ 48 Elizabeth St., ☎ 843/723–1159, WEB www.historiccharleston.org. 🎟 $7; with Nathaniel Russell House $12; with Nathaniel Russell House and the Old Powder Magazine $14), was the headquarters of Confederate general P. G. T. Beauregard during his 1864 Civil War defense of Charleston. The house, kitchen, slave quarters, and work yard are much as they were when the original occupants lived here, making this one of the most complete examples of African-American urban life of the period.

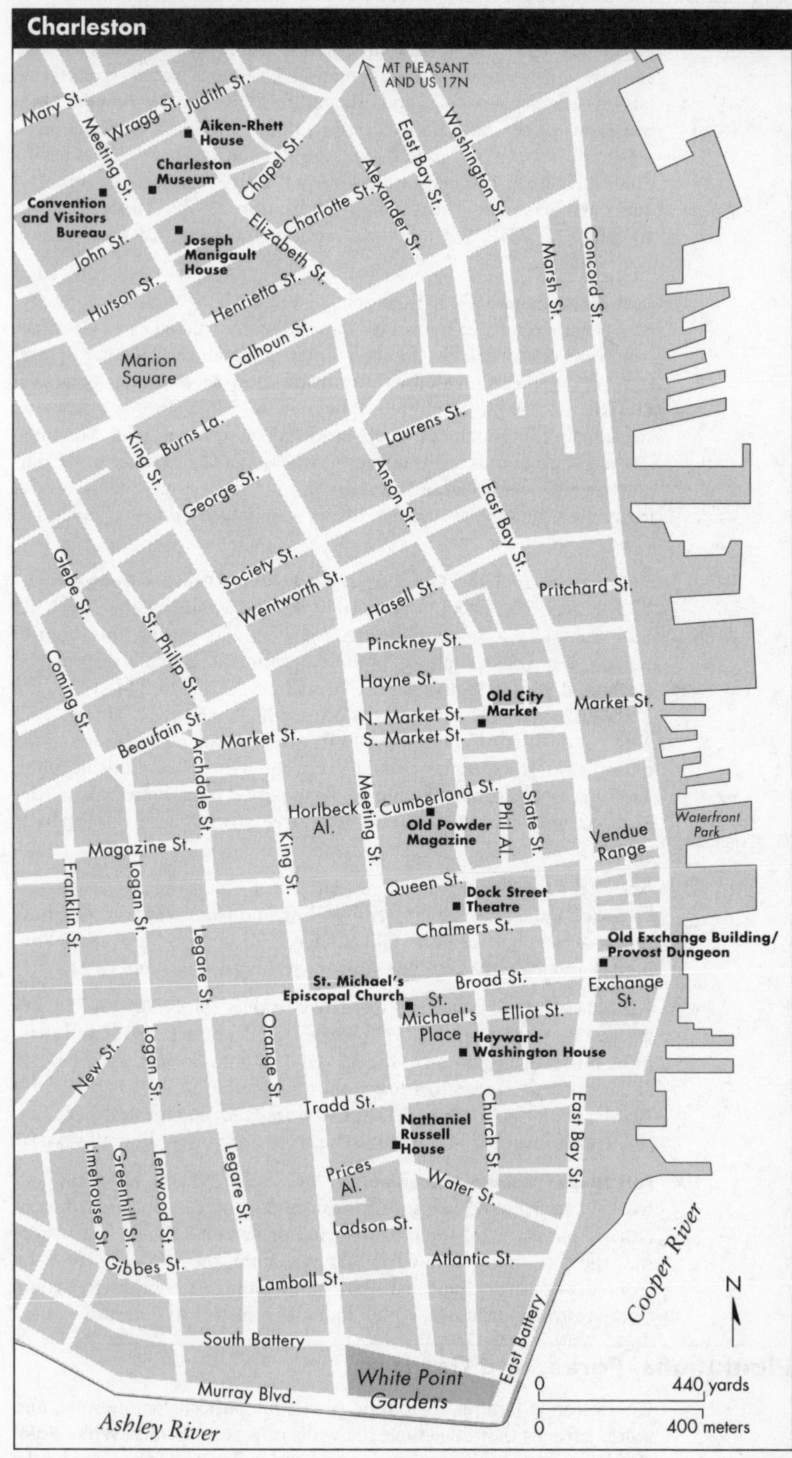
Charleston
MT PLEASANT AND US 17N
Mary St.
Judith St.
Wragg St.
Meeting St.
Aiken-Rhett House
Charleston Museum
Convention and Visitors Bureau
Chapel St.
Elizabeth St.
Charlotte St.
Alexander St.
East Bay St.
Washington St.
John St.
Joseph Manigault House
Hutson St.
Henrietta St.
Marsh St.
Concord St.
Calhoun St.
Marion Square
Laurens St.
Burns La.
King St.
George St.
Anson St.
East Bay St.
Society St.
Wentworth St.
Glebe St.
Hasell St.
Pritchard St.
St. Philip St.
Pinckney St.
Coming St.
Hayne St.
Old City Market
Market St.
N. Market St.
S. Market St.
Beaufain St.
Market St.
Archdale St.
Horlbeck Al.
Cumberland St.
Meeting St.
Old Powder Magazine
Phil Al.
State St.
Vendue Range
Waterfront Park
Magazine St.
Franklin St.
Logan St.
King St.
Queen St.
Dock Street Theatre
Chalmers St.
Legare St.
Old Exchange Building/ Provost Dungeon
Broad St.
St. Michael's Episcopal Church
Exchange St.
St. Michael's Place
Elliot St.
Orange St.
Heyward-Washington House
New St.
Logan St.
Tradd St.
Church St.
East Bay St.
Nathaniel Russell House
Limehouse St.
Greenhill St.
Lenwood St.
Legare St.
Prices Al.
Water St.
Ladson St.
Atlantic St.
Gibbes St.
Lamboll St.
Cooper River
East Battery
South Battery
N
White Point Gardens
Murray Blvd.
0
440 yards
0
400 meters
Ashley River

The heart of Charleston is the **Old City Market,** between Meeting and East Bay streets, with restaurants, shops, and vendor stands. Here you can buy various knickknacks, benne-seed (sesame) wafers, sweet-grass baskets, jewelry, seashells, and other crafts items.The **Old Powder Magazine,** on one of Charleston's few remaining cobblestone thoroughfares, was built in 1713 and used during the Revolutionary War. It is now a museum with a fascinating audiovisual tour, costumes, armor, and other artifacts from 18th-century Charleston. ✉ *79 Cumberland St.,* ☎ *843/805–6730,* WEB *www.historiccharleston.org.* 🎫 *Free. Closed Nov.–Mar.*

Dock Street Theatre (✉ 135 Church St., ☎ 843/720–3968, WEB www.cityofcharleston.com; 🎫 free) combines the reconstructed early Georgian playhouse that originally stood on the site with the 1809 Planter's Hotel to form one theater; call for tour information. **St. Michael's Episcopal Church** (✉ 14 St. Michael's Alley, ☎ 843/723–0603, WEB www.stmichaelschurch.net; 🎫 free), modeled on London's St. Martin's-in-the-Fields, stands at the corner of Meeting and Broad streets. Completed in 1761, this beautiful structure is Charleston's oldest surviving church. Its steeple clock and bells were imported from England in 1764.

The British used the **Old Exchange Building/Provost Dungeon** (✉ 122 E. Bay St., ☎ 843/727–2165, WEB www.oldexchange.com; 🎫 $6), originally a customs house, for prisoners during the Revolutionary War. Today a tableau of lifelike mannequins recalls this era.The ★ **Nathaniel Russell House** (✉ 51 Meeting St., ☎ 843/724–8481, WEB www.historiccharleston.org; 🎫 $8; with Aiken–Rhett House $12; with Aiken-Rhett House and Old Powder Magazine $14), one of the nation's finest examples of Federal architecture, was built in 1808. The interior has ornate detailing, lavish period furnishings, and a "flying" circular staircase that spirals three stories with no apparent support.

Across the Cooper River bridges, via U.S. 17 N, is the town of **Mount Pleasant,** named for a plantation in England from which some of the area's settlers hailed. In its Old Village neighborhood are antebellum homes and a sleepy, old-time town center with shops and cafés.

Patriot's Point (✉ foot of Cooper River bridges, ☎ 843/884–2727, WEB www.state.sc.us/patpt; 🎫 $11) is the world's largest naval and maritime museum and home to the Medal of Honor Society. Berthed here are the aircraft carrier *Yorktown,* the nuclear ship *Savannah,* the World War II submarine *Clamagore,* the cutter *Ingham,* and the destroyer *Laffey.* Tours, included in the admission price, are offered on all vessels.

★ **Fort Sumter National Monument** (☎ 843/722–1691, WEB www.nps.gov/fosu; 🎫 tour boat $11), in Charleston Harbor, can be reached from either Charleston's Municipal Marina or Patriot's Point. It was here that the first shot of the Civil War was fired, on April 12, 1861, by Confederate forces. National Park Service rangers conduct free tours of the restored structure, which includes a historical museum.

Plantations, Parks, and Gardens

Charleston is famous for public parks, magnificent plantations, and secret gardens that lie behind the walls of private homes. **White Point Gardens,** on the point of the narrow Battery Peninsula bounded by the Ashley and Cooper rivers, is a popular gathering spot. **Waterfront Park,** along Concord Street on the Cooper River, has a fishing pier, unique interactive fountains, a picnic area, and landscaped gardens.

★ **Drayton Hall** (✉ 3390 Ashley River Rd./Rte. 61, ☎ 843/766–0188, WEB www.draytonhall.org; 🎟 $8), built between 1738 and 1742, is the only plantation on the Ashley River that survived the Civil War. It is unfurnished, which serves to highlight the original plaster moldings and opulent hand-carved woodwork. This is considered one of the finest examples of Georgian Palladian architecture. ★ **Magnolia Plantation and Gardens** (✉ Ashley River Rd./Rte. 61, 2 mi beyond Drayton Hall, ☎ 843/571–1266 or 800/367–3517, WEB www.magnoliaplantation.com; 🎟 $12, house tour $7 extra, tram tour $6 extra, swamp tour $6 extra) dates from 1865. The gardens hold one of the largest collections of azaleas and camellias in North America. Nature lovers can canoe through the 125-acre Waterfowl Refuge, see the 60-acre Audubon Swamp Garden along boardwalks and bridges, explore 500 acres of wildlife trails, and visit the petting zoo.

Middleton Place (✉ Ashley River Rd./Rte. 61, 4 mi north of Magnolia Plantation, ☎ 843/556–6020 or 800/782–3608, WEB www.middletonplace.org; 🎟 $15, house tour $8 extra) has the nation's oldest landscaped gardens, dating from 1741. Much of the mansion was destroyed during the Civil War, but a restored wing houses impressive silver, furniture, paintings, and historical documents. Children will enjoy the lively stableyards. An avenue of oaks leads to **Boone Hall Plantation** (✉ 1253 Long Point Rd., Mt. Pleasant, ☎ 843/884–4371, WEB www.boonehallplantation.com; 🎟 $12.50), which is said to have been the inspiration for Tara in the film *Gone With the Wind*. You can explore the gardens, the first floor of the mansion, and the original slave quarters. Lunch is served in the old cotton-gin building.

Charles Towne Landing State Park (✉ Rte. 171, ☎ 843/852–4200, WEB www.southcarolinaparks.com; 🎟 $5), across the Ashley River Bridge, is built on the site of a 1670 settlement. It includes a reconstructed village and fortifications, a replica of a 17th-century sailing vessel, gardens with bike trails and walking paths, and an animal park. **Cypress Gardens** (✉ 24 mi north of Charleston in Moncks Corner, via U.S. 52, ☎ 843/553–0515, WEB www.cypressgardens-sc.org; 🎟 $7) was created from a swamp that was once the freshwater reserve of a vast rice plantation. You can explore the inky waters by boat or walk along paths lined with moss-draped cypress trees and flowering bushes. The Butterfly House has hundreds of butterflies and birds.

Dining

Best known for Low Country specialties like she-crab soup, sautéed shrimp, grits, and pecan pie, Charleston is also famous for contemporary cookery blending down-home cooking with haute cuisine.

$$$$ ★ ✕ **Woodlands Inn.** Residents regularly make the 30-mi drive from Charleston for superb, prix-fixe meals at this luxury inn's restaurant. Try entrées such as Angus beef with celery-root home fries and Barolo-wine reduction. ✉ *125 Parsons Rd., Summerville,* ☎ *843/875–2600 or 800/774–9999. AE, D, DC, MC, V.*

$$–$$$ ★ ✕ **Magnolias.** Housed in an 1823 warehouse and decorated in a magnolia theme, this self-designated "uptown/down South" restaurant is prized for its Low Country fare, including shrimp and sausage over creamy grits, and Down South egg roll with collard greens and tasso. ✉ *185 E. Bay St.,* ☎ *843/577–7771. AE, D, MC, V.*

$$–$$$ ✕ **McCrady's.** With its sleek bar area and dining room, this restaurant in a 1778 tavern has locals raving over its potato gnocchi, honey glazed moulard duck, and molten chocolate cake. ✉ *2 Unity Alley,* ☎ *843/577–0025. AE, MC, V.*

$$–$$$ ★ ✕ **Peninsula Grill.** Surrounded by olive-green wall coverings, black iron chandeliers, and 18th-century-style portraits, diners at this sophisticated restaurant in the Planters Inn feast on such delights as lobster martini and wild mushroom grits with oysters. For dessert, try the lemon tart with lemon sorbet. ✉ *112 N. Market St.,* ☎ *843/723–0700. AE, D, DC, MC, V.*

$$–$$$ ✕ **Slightly North of Broad.** This whimsical eatery has several seats that overlook the action-packed kitchen. Low Country cuisine is given trendy treatment here: try the shiitake mushroom filled with foie gras mousse or the grilled, barbecued tuna. ✉ *192 E. Bay St.,* ☎ *843/723–3424. AE, D, DC, MC, V.*

$–$$$ ✕ **Carolina's.** Bustling Carolina's is a black-and-white bistro with terra-cotta tiles and 1920s French posters. Fans return for the pasta with crawfish and *tasso* (spiced ham) in a spicy cream sauce, and pecan brittle with fruit and ice cream. ✉ *10 Exchange St.,* ☎ *843/724–3800. AE, MC, V. No lunch.*

$$ ✕ **The Wreck.** Full of wacky character, this dockside spot serves up traditional dishes like boiled peanuts, fried shrimp, shrimp pilaf, deviled crab, and oyster platters in a shabby, candlelit, screened-in porch and small dining area. ✉ *106 Haddrell St., Mount Pleasant,* ☎ *843/884–0052. Reservations not accepted. No credit cards. No lunch.*

$–$$ ★ ✕ **Gaulart and Maliclet French Café.** Chic and upbeat, this bar-stools-only café serves ethnic and French-bistro food. The menu of soups, salads, and sandwiches is enlivened by such evening specials as seafood Normandy and chicken sesame. ✉ *98 Broad St.,* ☎ *843/577–9797. AE, D, DC, MC, V. Closed Sun. No dinner Sat.*

$–$$ ✕ **Sermet's Corner.** Chef Sermet Aslan is also an artist whose colorful and bold work decorates the walls of this hip eatery. The Mediterranean menu includes panini sandwiches at lunchtime, seafood, and a lovely lavender-scented pork tenderloin. Upstairs, the jazz bar Mezzane is popular with a young beatnik crowd. ✉ *276 King St.,* ☎ *843/853–7775. AE, MC, V.*

$ ★ ✕ **Alice's Fine Foods.** The food Southerners crave is here in its original form: baked or fried chicken, ribs, fried fish, or other entrées come with a choice of three vegetables, including green beans, collard greens, okra and tomatoes, lima beans, yams, and squash. ✉ *468–470 King St.,* ☎ *843/853–9366. MC, V.*

Lodging

Hotels and inns on the peninsula are generally more expensive than those in outlying areas of the city. Rates tend to increase during festivals, when reservations are essential, and on weekends. From December through February some rates drop by as much as 50%. Nearby world-class accommodations include the Kiawah Island, Wild Dunes, and Seabrook Island resorts. Bed-and-breakfast reservation services include **Historic Charleston B&B** (✉ 60 Broad St., 29401, ☎ 843/722–6606 or 800/743–3583), **Southern Hospitality B&B Reservations** (✉ 110 Amelia Dr., Lexington 29464, ☎ 843/356–6238 or 800/374–7422) , and **RSVP Reservation Service** (✉ 9489 Whitefield Ave. [Box 49, Savannah, GA 31406], ☎ 800/729–7787).

$$$$ ★ 🏨 **Charleston Place.** This graceful, luxurious hotel, an Orient-Express property, has rooms with period reproductions, French bed linens, and fax machines. It's near upscale shops in the historic district. The Charleston Grill, with its mahogany-paneled walls, provides an elegant dining experience. ✉ *130 Market St., 29401,* ☎ *843/722–4900 or 800/611–5545,* FAX *843/724–7215,* WEB *www.charleston-place.com. 440 rooms. 2 restaurants, pool, gym. AE, D, DC, MC, V.*

$$$$ ★ **John Rutledge House Inn.** An ornate main house, built in 1763 by a signatory of the U.S. Constitution, and two carriage houses, make up this luxury B&B. Rooms have plaster molding, wood floors, antiques, and four-poster beds. ✉ *116 Broad St., 29401,* ☎ *843/723–7999 or 800/476–9741,* FAX *843/720–2615,* WEB *www.charminginns.com. 19 rooms. AE, D, DC, MC, V. CP.*

$$$–$$$$ **Governor's House Inn.** This mid-18th century inn has opulent parlors, hardwood floors, 12-ft ceilings, nine fireplaces, and 19th-century antiques. Some of the palatial guest rooms have private piazzas; the third-floor "Roofscape" rooms are cozy, with outstanding city views. Guests are served afternoon tea (on the veranda in cooler months). ✉ *117 Broad St., 29401,* ☎ *843/720–2070 or 800/720–9812,* WEB *www.governorshouse.com. 11 rooms. No credit cards. CP.*

$$$–$$$$ **Hayne House Bed and Breakfast.** Trees shade the brick courtyard of the Hayne House, built in 1755, in the now-prestigious South of Broad neighborhood. Rooms are filled with family heirlooms and watercolors by local artists. Four rooms are in the kitchen house, with its narrow stairway, colonial brickwork, and chimney. ✉ *30 King St., 29401,* ☎ *843/577–2633,* FAX *843/577–5906,* WEB *www.haynehouse.com. 6 rooms. MC, V. BP.*

$$–$$$$ **Doubletree Guest Suites Hotel Historic Charleston.** This all-suite hotel at the Old City Market has a restored entrance portico from an 1874 bank. The spacious suites have canopy beds and full kitchens or wet bars; some open up onto a courtyard. ✉ *181 Church St., 29401,* ☎ *843/577–2644 or 800/527–1133,* FAX *843/577–2697,* WEB *www.www.doubletree.com. 182 rooms. Gym. AE, D, DC, MC, V.*

$$–$$$$ **Meeting Street Inn.** Originally built as a tavern in 1874, this inn in the historic district overlooks a lovely courtyard with fountains and gardens. Spacious rooms have hardwood floors, high ceilings, and four-poster beds. Afternoon refreshments are complimentary. ✉ *173 Meeting St., 29401,* ☎ *843/723–1882 or 800/842–8022,* FAX *843/577–0851,* WEB *www.meetingstreetinn.com. 56 rooms. AE, D, DC, MC, V. CP.*

$$$ ★ **Francis Marion Hotel.** The largest hotel in the Carolinas when it was built in 1924, this property retains big-band and tea-dance glamour with its windowed ballrooms, wrought-iron railings, columns, high ceilings, and scenic views of Marion Square and the harbor. Spaces are original, so rooms and baths are small. On the street level, Elliott's ($$–$$$) serves good southern fare. ✉ *387 King St., 29403,* ☎ *843/722–0600,* FAX *843/723–4633,* WEB *www.westin.com. 226 rooms. Restaurant, health club. AE, D, DC, MC, V.*

$$$ **Kiawah Island Resort.** Choose from inn rooms and one- to five-bedroom villas and private homes in two luxurious resort villages on 10,000 mostly undeveloped acres. Most rooms have an ocean or wooded view. There are fine broad beaches and an array of recreational opportunities. ✉ *12 Kiawah Beach Dr., 21 mi south of Charleston via U.S. 17, Kiawah Island 29455,* ☎ *843/768–2121 or 800/654–2924,* FAX *843/768–6099,* WEB *www.kiawahresort.com. 150 rooms, 580 villas and homes. 8 restaurants, golf, tennis. AE, D, DC, MC, V.*

$–$$$ **1837 Bed and Breakfast and Tea Room.** This inn is long on hospitality, and you'll get a sense of what it's really like to live in one of Charleston's beloved homes. Rooms are filled with antiques, including romantic canopy beds. A breakfast of homemade breads and sausage pie or ham frittata is included, as is afternoon tea. ✉ *126 Wentworth St., 29401,* ☎ *843/723–7166 or 877/723–1837,* WEB *www.1837bb.com. 8 rooms. AE, MC, V. BP.*

Motel

Red Roof Inn (✉ 301 Johnnie Dodds Blvd., 29464, ☎ 843/884–1411 or 800/843–7663, FAX 843/971–0726), 126 rooms; pool; *$–$$.*

Nightlife and the Arts

Nightlife

Charlie's Little Bar, above Saracen's Restaurant (✉ 141 E. Bay St., ☎ 843/723–6242), is a popular cocktail spot. Favored by an elegant, older crowd, the **Mills House Hotel** (✉ 115 Meeting St., ☎ 843/577–2400) has a hopping bar and live big band swing music on Tuesday. The **Music Farm** (✉ 32 Ann St., ☎ 843/853–3276) hosts national and local alternative bands. **Mitchell's** (✉ 102 N. Market St., ☎ 843/722–7032) has live music and great dancing. **Southend Brewery** (✉ 161 E. Bay St., ☎ 843/853–4677) has a lively bar with beer brewed on the premises. You can dine and dance on the yacht ***Spirit of Carolina*** (☎ 843/722–2628; board at Patriot's Point). Try **Trio Lounge** (✉ 139 Calhoun St., ☎ 843/965–5333) for dance music Wednesday–Saturday. **Vickery's Bar & Grill** (✉ 15 Beaufain St., ☎ 843/577–5300) is a festive nightspot with a spacious outdoor patio. **Windjammer** (✉ 1000 Ocean Blvd., ☎ 843/886–8596), on the Isle of Palms, is an oceanfront spot with live rock music.

The Arts

Spoleto Festival USA, a world-class annual celebration, showcases opera, dance, theater, symphonic and chamber music, jazz, and the visual arts in late spring. **Piccolo Spoleto Festival** (☎ 843/724–7305) is the spirited companion festival of Spoleto Festival USA, with the best in local and regional talent from every artistic discipline. Most performances are free. The **Charleston Symphony Orchestra** (☎ 843/723–7528) presents a variety of series at Gaillard Municipal Auditorium (✉ 77 Calhoun St., ☎ 843/577–4500) and chamber and pops series elsewhere.

Outdoor Activities and Sports

Golf

For a listing of area golf packages, contact the Charleston Area Convention and Visitors Bureau. Nonguests may play on a space-availability basis at **private island resorts** such as Kiawah Island (☎ 843/768–2121), Seabrook Island (☎ 843/768–2529), and Wild Dunes (☎ 843/886–2180) on the Isle of Palms. The prestigious Pete Dye–designed Ocean Course at Kiawah Island (☎ 843/768–7272) was the site of the 1991 Ryder Cup.

Top public courses in the area include **Charleston Municipal** (✉ 2110 Maybank Hwy., ☎ 843/795–6517), **Charleston National Country Club** (✉ 1360 National Dr., Mount Pleasant, ☎ 843/884–7799), the **Dunes West Golf Club** (✉ 3535 Wando Plantation Way, Mount Pleasant, ☎ 843/856–9000), **Links at Stono Ferry** (✉ 5365 Forest Oaks Dr., Hollywood, ☎ 843/763–1817), **Oak Point Golf Course** (✉ 4255 Bohicket Rd., Johns Island, ☎ 843/768–7431), **Patriot's Point Links** (✉ 1 Patriots Point Rd., Mount Pleasant, ☎ 843/881–0042), and **Shadowmoss Golf Club** (✉ 20 Dunvegan Dr., Charleston, ☎ 843/556–8251).

Beaches

South Carolina's climate allows swimming from April through October. There are **public beaches** at Beachwalker Park on Kiawah Island; Folly Beach County Park and Folly Beach on Folly Island; the Isle of Palms; and Sullivan's Island. Resorts with private beaches include Fairfield Ocean Ridge on Edisto Island; Kiawah Island Resort (☞ Lodging, *above*); Seabrook Island; and Wild Dunes Resort on the Isle of Palms. For more information contact the Charleston Area Convention and Visitors Bureau (☞ Visitor Information, *below*).

Shopping

The three-block **Old City Market** yields varied knickknacks, clothing, T-shirts and gifts, including the sweet-grass baskets unique to this area. The craft, originally introduced by West Africans brought here as slaves, is now practiced by only a handful of their descendants. The **Shops at Charleston Place** (✉ 130 Market St., ☎ 843/722–4900), in the historic district, includes Gucci, Brookstone, and Crabtree & Evelyn. **King Street** is lined with both small boutiques and popular national stores including Banana Republic, Gap, Ann Taylor, and Abercrombie & Fitch. There is a small but pleasant **Saks Fifth Avenue** (✉ 211 King St., ☎ 843/853–9888). The **Rainbow Market** (✉ 40 N. Market St., ☎ 843/577–0380) is in two interconnected 150-year-old buildings. **The Sugar Plantation** (✉ 48 N. Market St., ☎ 843/853–3924) sells Charleston's famed benne-seed wafers, pralines, fudge, and Charleston chews.

Elegant antiques shops line the lower part of King Street. **Geo. C. Birlant & Co.** (✉ 191 King St., ☎ 843/722–3842) has 18th- and 19th-century English selections and the famous Charleston Battery bench. **Livingston Antiques** (✉ 163 King St., ☎ 843/723–9697; ✉ 2137 Savannah Hwy., ☎ 843/556–6162) specializes in European antiques. At **Historic Charleston Reproductions** (✉ 105 Broad St., ☎ 843/723–8292), you can find superb replicas of Charleston furniture and accessories approved by the Historic Charleston Foundation.

Among the town's chic art galleries is the **Marty Whaley Adams Gallery** (✉ 2 Queen St., ☎ 843/853–8512), which carries original watercolors and monotypes plus prints and posters by this Charleston artist. **Charleston Crafts** (✉ 87 Hasell St., ☎ 843/723–2938) has a fine selection of pottery, weavings, sculptures, and jewelry by local artists. **Charleston Gardens** (✉ 61 Queen St., ☎ 843/723–0252) has lovely garden ornamentations and home accessories, including Charleston-style iron gates. The **Elizabeth O'Neill Verner Studio & Gallery** (✉ 79 Church St., ☎ 843/722–4246), in a 17th-century house, is open to the public, with prints of Elizabeth O'Neill Verner's pastels and etchings for sale. **Blink** (✉ 62-B Queen St., ☎ 843/577–5688) has regionally and locally produced paintings, photos, pottery, jewelry, and garden art.

Charleston Essentials

AIRPORTS AND TRANSFERS

Charleston International Airport, 12 mi west of downtown Charleston along I–26, is served by Continental, Comair, Delta, Midway Express, United Express, Northwest, TWA, and US Airways.

➤ AIRPORT INFORMATION: **Charleston International Airport** (✉ 5500 International Blvd., ☎ 843/767–1100).

AIRPORT TRANSFER

Several shuttle and cab companies service the airport, including Thurman's Limo, Absolute Charleston, Harvie's Taxi Limo Service and Lee's Limousine. It costs about $18–$22 to travel downtown by taxi; to Mt. Pleasant, $23–$35. Airport Ground Transportation arranges shuttles, which cost $10 per person to the downtown area.

➤ TAXIS AND SHUTTLES: **Absolute Charleston** (☎ 843/817–4044). **Airport Ground Transportation** (☎ 843/767–1100). **Harvie's Taxi Limo Service** (☎ 843/709–4276). **Lee's Limousine** (☎ 843/797–0041). **Thurman's Limo** (☎ 843/607–2912).

BOAT AND FERRY TRAVEL

Boaters arriving at Charleston Harbor via the Intracoastal Waterway may dock at City Marina, Ashley Marina, and at the Isle of Palms' Wild Dunes Yacht Harbor.

➤ BOAT AND FERRY INFORMATION: **Ashley Marina** (✉ Lockwood Blvd., ☎ 843/722–1996). **City Marina** (✉ Lockwood Blvd., ☎ 843/723–5098). **Wild Dunes Yacht Harbor** (✉ Palm Blvd., ☎ 843/886–5100).

BUS TRAVEL TO AND FROM CHARLESTON

➤ BUS INFORMATION: **Greyhound** (✉ 3610 Dorchester Rd., North Charleston, ☎ 800/231–2222).

CAR TRAVEL

I–26 crosses the state from northwest to southeast and ends at Charleston. U.S. 17, a north–south coastal route, passes through the city. I–526, also called the Mark Clark Expressway, runs primarily east–west, connecting the West Ashley area to Mt. Pleasant.

TAXIS

➤ TAXI COMPANIES: **Checker Taxi** (☎ 843/747–9200). **Yellow Cab** (☎ 843/577–6565).

TOURS

Guided tours are a popular option for seeing Charleston.

BUS TOURS

Gullah Tours, a bus-tour company, focuses on African-American influences on Charleston architecture, history, and culture.

➤ FEES AND SCHEDULES: **Gullah Tours** (☎ 843/763–7551, WEB www.gullahtours.com).

CARRIAGE TOURS

Old South Carriage Co., the city's oldest horse-drawn-carriage tour company, conducts one-hour tours of the historic district.

➤ FEES AND SCHEDULES: **Old South Carriage Co.** (☎ 843/577–0042, WEB www.oldsouthcarriagetours.com).

WALKING TOURS

Charleston Tea Party Walking Tour offers city walking tours.

➤ FEES AND SCHEDULES: **Charleston Tea Party Walking Tour** (☎ 843/577–5896 or 843/722–1779).

TRAIN TRAVEL

➤ TRAIN INFORMATION: **Amtrak** (✉ 4565 Gaynor Ave., North Charleston, ☎ 843/744–8264 or 800/872–7245).

TRANSPORTATION AROUND CHARLESTON

You can park your car and walk in the city's historic district, but you'll need a car to see attractions in outlying areas. Charleston Transit provides bus service ($1 each way) within the city and to James Island, Isle of Palms, Sullivan's Island, Mount Pleasant, and North Charleston. It also operates the trolley-style Downtown Area Shuttle buses, called DASH. Fare for either is $1, or $3 for a one-day DASH pass, which can be bought on the bus.

➤ CONTACTS: **Charleston Transit** (☎ 843/747–0922).

VISITOR INFORMATION

➤ TOURIST INFORMATION: **Charleston Area Convention and Visitors Bureau** (✉ 375 Meeting St. [Box 975, 29402], ☎ 843/853–8000 or 800/868–8118, WEB www.charlestoncvb.com).

THE COAST

The South Carolina coast is a land of extremes, from glitzy to gracious. The Grand Strand, from the state's northeastern border to historic Georgetown, is one of the East Coast's family-vacation megacenters and the state's top tourist area. Here you'll find 60 mi of white-sand beaches, championship golf courses, campgrounds, seafood restaurants, malls and factory outlets, and, at last count, nearly a dozen live-entertainment theaters with everything from country-and-western music to magic acts. The Low Country is the area between Georgetown and the state's southeastern boundary, including Beaufort, as well as the barrier islands of Hilton Head, Edisto, and Fripp. Beaufort is a charming antebellum town with a compact historic district of lavish 18th- and 19th-century homes. Hilton Head's exclusive resorts and genteel good life make it one of the coast's most popular vacation getaways.

Exploring the Coast

With its high-rise beachfront hotels, nightlife, and amusement parks, **Myrtle Beach** is the hub of the Grand Strand. Downtown Myrtle Beach has a festive look, with its T-shirt shops, ice cream parlors, and amusement venues, including the classic **Myrtle Beach Pavilion and Amusement Park** (✉ 9th Ave. N and Ocean Blvd., ☎ 843/448–6456, WEB www.mbpavilion.com; fees for individual attractions; one-day pass for unlimited access to most rides $23.60). At the **Butterfly Pavilion** (✉ 1185 Celebrity Cir., Broadway at the Beach, ☎ 843/839–4446 or 877/280–2751; $12.95) you can walk amid thousands of North American butterflies, visit the Lorikeet Aviary, and walk through a working beehive. **Ripley's Aquarium** (✉ 9th Ave. N and U.S. 17 N Bypass, ☎ 843/916–0888 or 800/734–8888, WEB www.ripleysaquarium.com; $14.95) has touch tanks, an underwater tunnel exhibit longer than a football field, and exotic marine creatures from poisonous lionfish to moray eels and an octopus.

Myrtle Beach is the minigolf capital of the world, with courses that mimic Jurassic Park and Never-Never Land, and **Hawaiian Rumble** (✉ 3210 U.S. 17 S, ☎ 843/272–7812, WEB www.prominigolf.com; $8 9–5, $6 per round after 5 PM) is the crown jewel. The best part of the course is the volcano that erupts fire and rumbles at timed intervals. A fun course, featuring a fire-breathing dragon, is **Dragon's Lair** (✉ Hwy. 17 at Broadway at the Beach, ☎ 843/444–3215; $8.50 all day 10–6, $6.50 per round after 6 PM).

South of Myrtle Beach, **Wild Water** (✉ 910 U.S. 17 S, Surfside, ☎ 843/238–9453, WEB www.wild-water.com; $17, $12 after 3 PM) provides splashy family fun for all ages.

Murrells Inlet, south of Myrtle Beach via U.S. 17, is a picturesque fishing village where you'll find fishing charters and some of the most popular seafood restaurants on the Strand. From a 1,400-ft-long wooden and oyster-shell marsh walk, you can bird-watch, crab, or just watch the boats pass by.

★ **Brookgreen Gardens** (☎ 843/237–4218 or 800/849–1931, WEB www.brookgreen.com; $12 for a seven-day pass), a few miles south of Murrells Inlet off U.S. 17, has more than 2,000 plant species as well as more than 500 sculptures, including works by Frederic Remington. Several miles down U.S. 17 from Brookgreen Gardens, **Pawleys Island** has weathered old summer cottages nestled in groves of oleander and oak. The famed Pawleys Island hammocks have been made by hand here since 1880.

Georgetown, on the shores of Winyah Bay at the end of the Grand Strand, was founded in 1729 and soon became the center of America's colonial rice empire. It has a quaint waterfront and historic homes and churches. The **Rice Museum** (✉ Front and Screven Sts., ☎ 843/546–7423, WEB www.ricemuseum.com; 🎫 $5) traces the history of rice cultivation through maps, tools, and dioramas. It is housed in a graceful structure topped by an 1842 clock and tower.

Beaufort, about 18 mi east of U.S. 17 on U.S. 21 (about 70 mi southeast of Charleston), is a handsome waterfront town. Established in 1710, it achieved prosperity at the end of the 18th century, when Sea Island cotton became a major cash crop. A few lavish houses built by landowners and merchants have been converted into B&Bs or museums; others are open for tours part of the year. The **Beaufort Museum** has exhibits on prehistoric relics, Native American pottery, the Revolutionary and Civil wars, and decorative arts. ✉ *713 Craven St.,* ☎ *843/525–7077,* WEB *www.beaufortcitysc.com.* 🎫 *$2. Closed Sun.*

St. Helena Island, 9 mi southeast of Beaufort via U.S. 21, is the site of the **Penn Center Historic District** and **York W. Bailey Museum.** Penn Center (✉ Martin Luther King Jr. Dr., ☎ 843/838–8563), established in the middle of the Civil War as the South's first school for freed slaves, is now an educational and cultural resource center. The **York W. Bailey Museum** (✉ Land's End Rd., ☎ 843/838–2432; 🎫 donation suggested) has photos and artifacts reflecting the heritage and lifestyles of sea-island African-Americans. These islands are where Gullah, a musical language that combines English and African, developed.

Hilton Head Island, a 42-square-mi semitropical barrier island settled by cotton planters in the 1700s, has developed as a resort destination. Oak and pine woods, lagoons, and a temperate climate provide an incomparable environment for tennis, water sports, and golf. Choice stretches of the island are occupied by resorts, many of which have shops, restaurants, marinas, and several recreational facilities.

Hilton Head is blessed with vast nature preserves, including the **Sea Pines Forest Preserve** (✉ at southwest tip of island, via U.S. 278, ☎ 843/363–1872; 🎫 $5 per car for nonguests), a 605-acre wilderness tract within the Sea Pines Plantation resort. On 4,000 acres of salt marsh and small islands, **Pinckney Island Wildlife Refuge** (✉ Coastal Discovery Museum, 100 William Hilton Pkwy., ☎ 843/785–3673; 🎫 free) is laced with walking and biking trails.

Dining and Lodging

Freshwater and ocean fish and shellfish reign supreme throughout the region, from family-style restaurants to elegant resorts and upscale restaurants featuring haute cuisine. You can have your choice of hotels, cottages, villas, or high-rise condominiums. Attractive package plans are available between Labor Day and spring break.

Beaufort

$$–$$$ ✕ **11th Street Dockside Restaurant.** Succulent fried oysters, shrimp and fish, plus other local specialties such as a steamed seafood pot, are available at this classic wharfside spot with water views from nearly every table. ✉ *11th St. W,* ☎ *843/524–7433. AE, D, DC, MC, V. No lunch.*

$$–$$$ ✕🏨 **Beaufort Inn.** Guest rooms in this 1897 Victorian have pine floors, tasteful floral and plaid fabrics, and comfortable chairs. The inn's superb restaurant serves sumptuous complimentary breakfasts and afternoon tea (reservations required); it's open to the public for unique Low Country fare like Parmesan grits and she-crab soup. ✉ *809 Port*

Republic St., 29902, ☎ 843/521–9000, FAX 843/521–9500, WEB www.beaufortinn.com. 11 rooms. Restaurant. AE, MC, V. BP.

$$$–$$$$ ★ **Rhett House Inn.** This stately 1820 Greek Revival mansion in the center of town is filled with antiques, original artwork, and Oriental rugs. A house across the street expands the inn by seven more rooms, each with gas fireplace, whirlpool tub, private entrance, and porch. ✉ *1009 Craven St., 29902, ☎ 843/524–9030, FAX 843/524–1310, WEB www.rhetthouseinn.com. 17 rooms. AE, MC, V. CP.*

$$$ **Cuthbert House Inn.** This pillared 1790 home overlooks the bay and has original Federal fireplaces. The owners have filled it with 18th- and 19th-century heirlooms; rooms are elegant but cozy, with Oriental rugs on pine floors and handmade quilts on the beds. ✉ *1203 Bay St., 29902, ☎ 843/521–1315 or 800/327–9275, FAX 843/521–1314, WEB www.cuthberthouseinn.com. 8 rooms. AE, D, MC, V. BP.*

$ **Howard Johnson.** This hotel sits on the edge of the marsh a few miles from the historic district. Rooms are spacious and have desks; many have views of the river and marsh. ✉ *3651 Trask Pkwy./U.S. 21, 29902, ☎ 843/524–6020 or 800/528–1234, FAX 843/524–2027. 43 rooms. Pool. AE, D, DC, MC, V. CP.*

Georgetown

$–$$ ✕ **Kudzu Bakery.** Here you'll find the greatest deep-dish pecan pie anywhere and other delectables; you can grab them to go or eat them at the small counter. There are also sandwiches on homemade breads, and some cheeses. ✉ *714 Front St., ☎ 843/546–1847. MC, V. Closed Wed. and Sun. No dinner.*

$$ **1790 House.** Built in the center of town after the Revolution, at the peak of Georgetown's rice culture, this restored white Georgian house with a wraparound porch is filled with 18th- and 19th-century Asian and European antiques. Amenities include whirlpools, robes, and TVs. ✉ *630 Highmarket St., 29440, ☎ 843/546–4821 or 800/890–7432, WEB www.1790house.com. 6 rooms. AE, D, MC, V. BP.*

Hilton Head Island

$$–$$$$ ✕ **Old Fort Pub.** Tucked away on a quiet site overlooking the marshlands and beside the Civil War ruins of Fort Mitchell, this pub-like restaurant specializes in oyster stew, corn-crusted pork chops, and mesquite-smoked filet mignon with mushroom cabernet sauce. ✉ *65 Skull Creek Dr., ☎ 843/681–2386. AE, D, DC, MC, V. No lunch.*

$$–$$$ ✕ **Juleps.** In this dimly lit, terrace-style restaurant, southern ingredients such as grits, cured ham, fresh fish, and peach preserves add sparkle to the Continental-style menu. Try the quail stuffed with andouille and greens. ✉ *14 Greenwood Dr., The Galley of Shops, ☎ 843/842–5857. AE, DC, MC, V. Closed Sun.*

$–$$ ✕ **Baja Tacos.** At this simple taco stand (easy to miss, in a rather rundown strip mall), freshness is key. Counter service, café tables, fluorescent lights, and a condiments bar with fresh salsas and relishes lend an authentic flavor. ✉ *160 Fairfield Sq., ☎ 843/342–3409. MC, V.*

$$$–$$$$ ★ **Disney's Hilton Head Island Resort.** This resort has Adirondack lodge–country themes carried out in fun detail. More than 100 villas (from studios to units with three bedrooms and four baths, which sleep up to 12) have fully furnished kitchen, dining, living, sleeping, and porch areas; all have marsh or marina views. About a mile away, the resort's 13,000-square-ft beach house has a fireplace in the living room, a heated pool, and an arcade. ✉ *22 Harbourside La., 29928, ☎ 843/341–4100 or 800/453–4911, FAX 843/341–4130, WEB www.disneyworld.com. 102 units. Restaurant, pools. AE, MC, V.*

$$$–$$$$ **Hilton Oceanfront Resort.** The grounds at this five-story hotel are beautifully landscaped; the spacious oceanfront rooms have kitchenettes, warm colors, and contemporary furnishings. ✉ *23 Ocean*

La., 29928, ☎ *843/842–8000 or 800/845–8001,* FAX *843/842–4988,* WEB *www.hiltonheadhilton.com. 323 rooms. Two restaurants, pools, health club. AE, D, DC, MC, V.*

$$$–$$$$ **Main Street Inn.** Outside it resembles an Italianate villa; inside, rooms have velvet and silk brocade linens, feather duvets, and porcelain and brass sinks. Included in the rate is a European breakfast of cheeses, quiche, and pastries. ✉ *2200 Main St., 29926,* ☎ *843/681–3001 or 800/471–3001,* FAX *843/681–5541,* WEB *www.mainstreetinn.com. 33 rooms. Pool. AE, MC, V. CP.*

$$$–$$$$ ★ **Westin Resort, Hilton Head Island.** One of the island's most luxurious properties, this sprawling hotel has a lushly landscaped oceanfront setting. Rooms have down pillows, warm colors, and comfortable wicker and contemporary furniture. For dinner, try the resort's Barony Grill Restaurant. ✉ *2 Grass Lawn Ave., 29928,* ☎ *843/681–4000 or 800/228–3000,* FAX *843/681–1087,* WEB *www.westin.com. 450 rooms. 3 restaurants, pools, health club. AE, D, DC, MC, V.*

Motel

Red Roof Inn (✉ 5 Regency Pkwy., 29928, ☎ 843/686–6808 or 800/843–7663, FAX 843/842–3352), 112 rooms; pool; *$–$$.*

Myrtle Beach

$$–$$$ ★ ✕ **Collectors Cafe.** A restaurant, art gallery, and coffeehouse rolled into one, this unpretentiously arty spot has bright, funky paintings and tile work covering its walls and tabletops. Try the black bean cakes and veal-stuffed ravioli. ✉ *7726 N. Kings Hwy.,* ☎ *843/449–9370. AE, D, DC, MC, V. Closed Sun. No lunch.*

$$ ✕ **Sea Captain's House.** This picturesque restaurant with a nautical theme and a fireplace has sweeping ocean views. Home-baked breads and desserts accompany Low Country fare. ✉ *3002 N. Ocean Blvd.,* ☎ *843/448–8082. AE, D, MC, V.*

$–$$ ✕ **Villa Katrina's Underground Cantina.** Head downstairs into a fun, tavernlike space for Mexican fare of the elegant variety, including flaming coffees and desserts. Lunch is festive, too. ✉ *821 Main St.,* ☎ *843/946–6216. No credit cards. Closed Sun.*

$ ✕ **Croissants Bakery & Cafe.** The lunch crowd loves this spot, which has an on-site bakery. Try the chicken or broccoli salad, the Monte Cristo sandwich, and the peanut butter cheesecake. ✉ *504 A 27th Ave. N,* ☎ *843/448–2253. D, MC, V. Closed Sun. No dinner.*

$$$–$$$$ **Kingston Plantation—Embassy Suites.** Set amid 145 acres of oceanside woodlands, this resort—the nicest in town—includes a 20-story hotel, restaurants, and one- to four-bedroom condos. Guest rooms in the oceanfront inn have VCRs, Nintendo Game Boys, and kitchenettes. ✉ *9800 Lake Dr., 29572,* ☎ *843/449–0006 or 800/876–0010,* FAX *843/497–1110,* WEB *www.embassy-suites.com. 255 suites, 510 condos. 2 restaurants, pools, tennis, gym. AE, D, DC, MC, V.*

$$ **Breakers Resort Hotel.** The oceanfront Breakers is one of the better values along the Grand Strand. There are 24 types of rooms—the suites with kitchenettes are ideal for families. The Pavilion and Broadway at the Beach are within walking distance. ✉ *2006 N. Ocean Blvd. (Box 485, 29578-0485),* ☎ *843/444–4444 or 800/845–0688,* FAX *843/626–5001,* WEB *www.breakers.com. 557 rooms. 2 restaurants, pools, gym. AE, D, DC, MC, V.*

MOTELS

Red Roof Inn (✉ 2801 S. Kings Hwy., 29577, ☎ 843/626–4444 or 800/843–7663, FAX 843/626–0753), 166 rooms; pool; *$$.*

Days Inn at Waccamaw (✉ 3650 U.S. 501, 29577, ☎ 843/236–1950 or 800/325–2525, FAX 843/236–9415), 160 rooms; restaurant, pool; *$–$$.*

Pawleys Island

$$–$$$ ✕ **Frank's.** Seasonal ingredients make this a local favorite. In a former 1930s grocery store, diners indulge in large portions of fish, seafood, beef, and lamb cooked over an oak-burning grill. Behind Frank's is the casual (but still pricey) Outback at Frank's, specializing in rotisserie chicken, salads, and lighter fare. ✉ *10434 Ocean Hwy./U.S. 17,* ☎ *843/237–3030. Reservations essential. D, MC, V. Closed Sun.*

$$ ✕ **Pawleys Island Tavern.** This little restaurant has terrific crab cakes plus hickory-smoked barbecue, roast chicken, and pizza (and they deliver). Summer nights, the tiki torches blaze outside and live music rocks the place. ✉ *The Island Shops, 10625 Ocean Hwy./U.S. 17,* ☎ *843/237–8465. AE, MC, V.*

$ ✕ **Landolphi's.** This fourth-generation owned Italian pastry shop and deli has excellent coffee, delicious pastries including cannoli and *pastacciotti,* homemade sorbet, hearty hoagies, and incredible panini. ✉ *9305 Ocean Hwy./U.S. 17,* ☎ *843/237–7900. AE, MC, V. Closed Sun. No dinner Mon.–Thurs.*

$$–$$$ 🏨 **Litchfield Beach and Golf Resort.** This 4,500-acre resort along both sides of U.S. 17 has almost 2 mi of oceanfront accommodations. These range from condos to the 160-room Litchfield Inn; other units line the fairways or overlook pools (most are within a 10-minute walk to the beach). ✉ *U.S. 17, 2 mi north of Pawleys Island (Drawer 320, Litchfield 29585),* ☎ *843/237–3000 or 800/845–1897,* FAX *843/237–4282,* WEB *www.litchfieldbeach.com. 356 rooms; 200 condominiums, cottages, and villas. 2 restaurants, pools, golf, tennis, health club. AE, D, DC, MC, V.*

$$–$$$ 🏨 **Sea View Inn.** Sea View is a no-frills beachside boardinghouse with long porches. Rooms have half baths; showers are down the hall and outside. Three meals, served family style—with grits, gumbo, crab salad, pecan pie, and oyster pie—make this an unbeatable deal. ✉ *Myrtle Ave., 29585,* ☎ *843/237–4253,* FAX *843/237–7909,* WEB *www.seaviewinn.net. 20 rooms. Dining room. 2-night minimum May and Sept.; 1-wk minimum June–Aug. No credit cards. Closed Nov.–Mar. FAP.*

Nightlife and the Arts

Nightlife

Country-and-western shows are popular along the Grand Strand, which is fast emerging as the eastern focus of country-music culture. Music lovers have several venues to choose from, including the 2,250-seat **Alabama Theater** (✉ at Barefoot Landing, 4750 U.S. 17, North Myrtle Beach, ☎ 843/272–1111 or 800/342–2262); **Carolina Opry** (✉ 82nd Ave. N, Myrtle Beach, ☎ 843/238–8888 or 800/843–6779); **Dolly Parton's Dixie Stampede** (✉ 8901-B U.S. 17 Business, next door to Carolina Opry, Myrtle Beach, ☎ 843/497–9700 or 800/433–4401); and **Legends in Concert** (✉ 301 U.S. 17 Business, Surfside Beach, ☎ 843/238–7827 or 800/843–6779). The **House of Blues** (✉ 4640 U.S. 17S, N. Myrtle Beach, ☎ 843/272–3000), adjacent to Barefoot Landing, presents blues, rock, jazz, and country on stages in its restaurant and in its concert hall; there's a gospel brunch on Sunday.

Shagging (the state dance) is popular at **Duck's** (✉ 229 Main St., North Myrtle Beach, ☎ 843/249–3858). You can also try the shag at **Studebaker's** (✉ U.S. 17 at 21st Ave. N, Myrtle Beach, ☎ 843/626–3855 or 843/448–9747). At **Broadway at the Beach** (✉ U.S. 17 Bypass between 21st and 24th Sts., North Myrtle Beach, ☎ 843/444–3200) you'll find an assortment of bars and nightclubs, including Hard Rock Cafe, Planet Hollywood, and the NASCAR Cafe. Locals looking for great blues music along with a great wine list hit **Gypsy's** (✉ 501 8th Ave. N, Myrtle Beach, ☎ 843/916–2244).

Hilton Head's hotels and resorts stage a variety of musical entertainment. **Monkey Business** (✉ Park Plaza, ☎ 843/686–3545) is a dance nightclub in Hilton Head. Try the **Blue Nite** (✉ 4 Target Rd., ☎ 843/842–6683) for live music. The **Hilton Head Brewing Co.** (✉ Hilton Head Plaza, ☎ 843/785–2739) has late-night discoing every Wednesday.

The Arts

Festivals in Myrtle Beach include the Canadian/American Days Festival in March, the Sun Fun Festival in early June, and the Atalaya Arts Festival in fall. At Art in the Park, held in Myrtle Beach's Chapin Park three times each summer, you can buy handmade crafts and original works by local artists. The annual Beaufort Water Festival draws residents from all over the Low Country each summer; the Gullah Festival has great demonstrations and food in the fall.

Hilton Head's **Self Family Arts Center** (✉ Shelter Cove La., ☎ 843/842–2787) has an art gallery, a theater, and a theater program for kids. During the warmer months there are free **outdoor concerts** at Harbour Town and Shelter Cove in Hilton Head.

Outdoor Activities and Sports

Biking

Pedaling is popular along the beaches and pathways of **Hilton Head Island.** Rentals are available at most hotels and resorts and at such shops as **Harbour Town Bicycles** (✉ Heritage Plaza, ☎ 843/785–3546) and **South Beach Cycles** (✉ Sea Pines Plantation, ☎ 843/671–2453).

Fishing

Fishing is usually good from early spring through December. Licenses, required for fresh- and saltwater fishing from a private boat, can be purchased at local tackle shops. The **Grand Strand** has several piers and jetties, and fishing and sightseeing excursions depart from Murrells Inlet, North Myrtle Beach, Little River, and the Intracoastal Waterway at Route 544. Fishing tournaments are popular. On **Hilton Head** you can fish, pick oysters, dig for clams, or cast for shrimp.

Golf

The **Grand Strand** has 100 golf courses, most of them public and many of championship quality. **Myrtle Beach Golf Holiday** (☎ 843/477–8833 or 800/845–4653) offers package plans throughout the year; most area hotels have golf packages, too. **Tee Times Central** (☎ 800/344–5590) books for several area courses in Myrtle Beach. Some of **Hilton Head's** 29 courses are among the world's best; several are open to the public, including Palmetto Dunes (✉ 7 Trent Jones La., ☎ 843/785–1138), Sea Pines (☎ 843/842–8484), and Port Royal (✉ 10-A Grasslawn Ave., ☎ 843/689–5600). Sea Pines' Harbour Town Golf Links hosts the annual MCI Classic in April (☎ 843/671–2448).

Horseback Riding

On Hilton Head trails wind through woods; horses can be rented at Sea Pines' **Lawton Stables** (☎ 843/671–2586), which also offers lessons and pony rides.

Tennis

There are more than 200 courts throughout the **Grand Strand,** including free municipal courts in Myrtle Beach, North Myrtle Beach, and Surfside Beach. **Hilton Head** has more than 300 courts; four resorts on the island—Sea Pines, Shipyard Plantation, Palmetto Dunes, and Port Royal—are rated among the top 50 tennis destinations in the United States.

Water Sports

In Myrtle Beach surfboards, Hobie Cats, Jet Skis, Windsurfers, and sailboats are for rent at **Downwind Sails** (✉ Ocean Blvd. at 29th Ave. S, ☎ 843/448–7245). On Hilton Head you can take windsurfing or kayaking lessons and rent equipment from **Outside Hilton Head** at either **Sea Pines Resort's South Beach Marina** (☎ 843/671–2643) or **Shelter Cove Plaza** (☎ 843/686–6996 or 800/686–6996).

Beaches

Almost all **Grand Strand** beaches are open to the public. The widest expanses are in North Myrtle Beach. The ocean side of **Hilton Head Island** is a 12-mi stretch of gently sloping white sand. Although resort beaches on Hilton Head are reserved for guests and residents, there are about 35 public-beach entrances, from Folly Field to South Forest Beach near Sea Pines.

Shopping

The **Grand Strand** is a great place to find bargains. **Waccamaw Pottery and Factory Shoppes** (✉ U.S. 501 at the Waterway, Myrtle Beach, ☎ 843/236–6152) is a large outlet center including Gap, Nike, and Off 5th Saks Fifth Avenue stores. In North Myrtle Beach shoppers head for the **Myrtle Beach Factory Stores** (✉ Hwy. 501 and Waccamaw Pines Dr., ☎ 843/903–1614) for Brooks Brothers, Donna Karan, and Eddie Bauer stores. The **Hammock Shops at Pawleys Island** (✉ U.S. 17, ☎ 843/237–8448) sell the famous handmade hammocks; there are about a dozen boutiques and restaurants, too. Hilton Head specialty shops include **Red Piano Art Gallery** (✉ 220 Cordillo Pkwy., ☎ 843/785–2318) and, for shell and sand-dollar jewelry, the **Bird's Nest** (✉ Coligny Plaza, off Coligny Cir., ☎ 843/785–3737). **Hilton Head Factory Stores I and II** (✉ U.S. 278 at the island gateway, ☎ 843/837–4339) have more than 80 outlets, including London Fog, J. Crew, and Gap. On St. Helena Island near Beaufort, the **Red Piano Too Art Gallery** (✉ 853 Sea Island Pkwy., ☎ 843/838–2241) is filled with quirky folk and southern art, beads, and pottery.

The Coast Essentials

AIRPORTS

The Myrtle Beach International Airport is served by Air Canada, Air Tran, ASA/Delta/Comair, Continental, Midway/Corporate, Spirit, US Airways, and Vanguard. Hilton Head Island Airport is served by US Air Express and Continental.

➤ AIRPORT INFORMATION: **Hilton Head Island Airport** (✉ 120 Beach City Rd., ☎ 843/689–5400). **Myrtle Beach International Airport** (✉ 1100 Jetport Blvd., ☎ 843/448–1589).

BOAT AND FERRY TRAVEL

The South Carolina coast is accessible by boat via the Intracoastal Waterway. At Myrtle Beach you may dock at Hague Marina, HarbourGate, and Marlin Quay. Hilton Head marinas include Shelter Cove Marina, Harbour Town Yacht Basin, and Schilling Boathouse.

➤ BOAT AND FERRY INFORMATION: **Hague Marina** (✉ 1 Hague Dr., ☎ 843/293–2141). **HarbourGate** (✉ 1 Harper Pl., ☎ 843/249–8888). **Harbour Town Yacht Basin** (✉ 149 Lighthouse Rd., ☎ 843/671–2704). **Marlin Quay** (✉ 1398 S. Waccamaw Dr., ☎ 843/651–4444). **Schilling Boathouse** (✉ 405 Squire Pope Rd., ☎ 843/681–2628). **Shelter Cove Marina** (✉ 1 Shelter Cove La., ☎ 843/842–7002).

BUS TRAVEL

➤ BUS INFORMATION: **Greyhound** (☎ 800/231–2222).

CAR TRAVEL

Major interstates connect with U.S. 17, the principal north–south coastal route. Hilton Head Island has a 6-mi-long bridge (toll $1), the Cross Island Parkway, that leads to the south end of the island, where most of the resorts and attractions are located.

TRAIN TRAVEL

Amtrak does not make stops in this area, although several of its stops are within driving distance: Florence is about 70 mi northwest of the Grand Strand; Yemassee, about 22 mi northwest of Beaufort; and Savannah, about 40 mi southwest of Hilton Head.

➤ TRAIN INFORMATION: **Amtrak** (☎ 800/872–7245).

VISITOR INFORMATION

➤ TOURIST INFORMATION: **Greater Beaufort Chamber of Commerce and Visitor Center** (✉ 1106 Carteret St., 29901-0910, ☎ 843/524–3163 or 800/638–3525). **Georgetown County Chamber of Commerce and Info Center** (✉ 101 Front St. [Box 1776, Georgetown 29442], ☎ 843/546–8436 or 800/777–7705). **Hilton Head Island Chamber of Commerce and Visitor & Convention Center** (✉ Box 5647, 29938, ☎ 843/785–3673 or 800/523–3373). **Myrtle Beach Area Chamber of Commerce and Visitor Center** (✉ 1200 N. Oak St. [Box 2115, 29578-2115], ☎ 843/626–7444; 800/356–3016 ext. 136 for brochures). **Pawleys Island Chamber of Commerce** (✉ U.S. 17 [Box 569, 29577], ☎ 843/237–1921).

ELSEWHERE IN SOUTH CAROLINA

Columbia

What to See and Do

Columbia, founded in 1786 as the capital city, was a center of political, commercial, cultural, and social activity. However, in early 1865, General Sherman invaded South Carolina and incinerated two-thirds of Columbia; only a few homes and public buildings were spared. Today the city is a sprawling blend of modern office blocks, suburban neighborhoods, and the occasional antebellum home. The **State House** (✉ Main and Gervais Sts., ☎ 803/734–2430; 🎫 free), built in 1855 from local granite, contains marble and mahogany accents and a replica of Houdon's statue of George Washington. You can still see where Sherman shelled the State House—each hit is marked with a bronze star.

The **South Carolina State Museum** (✉ 301 Gervais St., ☎ 803/898–4921, WEB www.museum.state.sc.us; 🎫 $5), set in a refurbished textile mill, interprets state history through exhibits on archaeology, fine arts, and scientific and technological accomplishments.

★ Two miles from the capitol area is **Riverbanks Zoological Park and Botanical Garden** (✉ I–26 at Greystone Blvd., ☎ 803/779–8717; 🎫 $7.25), with more than 2,000 animals and birds, some endangered, in natural habitats. There are sea lions, polar bears, Siberian tigers, and black rhinos, as well as a 70-acre botanical garden.

Dining and Lodging

$$–$$$ ✕ **Motor Supply Co. Bistro.** Dine on cuisine from around the world at this restaurant in the heart of town. Fresh seafood and homemade desserts are among the many offerings. There is brunch on Sunday. ✉ *920 Gervais St.,* ☎ *803/256–6687. AE, DC, MC, V. Closed Mon.*

$–$$ ★ ✕ **Mangia! Mangia!** Hammered copper and mosaic tiles transform this turn-of-the-20th-century building; a lively outdoor patio has heaters for chilly nights. Try the wild mushroom pizza baked in the wood-burning oven or lamb shank roasted in red wine with herbs. ✉ *100 State St., West Columbia,* ☎ *803/791–3443. AE, D, DC, MC, V. Closed Sun.*

$ ★ ✕ **Maurice Gourmet Barbecue–Piggie Park.** One of the South's best-known barbecue chefs, Maurice Bessinger has a fervent national following for his mustard sauce–based, pit-cooked ham barbecue. ✉ *1600 Charleston Hwy.,* ☎ *803/796–0220. D, MC, V.*

$$–$$$ 🏨 **Adam's Mark.** Public areas of this downtown hotel have leather armchairs, suspended lights, and brass accents. Guest rooms have period reproduction armoires and desks. Finlay's Restaurant, in a spectacular atrium, serves American fare. ✉ *1200 Hampton St., 29201,* ☎ *803/771–7000 or 800/444–2326,* FAX *803/254–2911. 300 rooms. Restaurant, pool, health club. AE, D, DC, MC, V.*

$$–$$$ ★ 🏨 **Richland Street B&B.** Relax on the front porch or in the spacious common area of this inn in the heart of Columbia's historic district. Each antiques-furnished room has its own personality. There are afternoon refreshments. ✉ *1425 Richland St., 29201,* ☎ *803/779–7001 or 800/779–7011,* FAX *803/765–0370,* WEB *www.inns.com. 8 rooms. AE, MC, V. BP.*

$–$$ 🏨 **Claussen's Inn.** This small hotel, in a converted bakery warehouse in the attractive Five Points neighborhood, is near nightlife and specialty shops. It has an airy lobby with a Mexican tile floor; the rooms, some two stories, are arranged around it. ✉ *2003 Greene St., 29205,* ☎ *803/765–0440 or 800/622–3382,* FAX *803/799–7924,* WEB *www.columbiasc.com/claussensinn. 29 rooms. AE, D, DC, MC, V. CP*

$ 🏨 **La Quinta Motor Inn.** At this three-story inn on a quiet street near the zoo, the rooms are spacious and well lit, with large working areas. ✉ *1335 Garner La., 29210,* ☎ *803/798–9590 or 800/531–5900,* FAX *803/731–5574. 122 rooms. Pool. AE, D, DC, MC, V.*

Columbia Essentials

AIRPORTS

The Columbia Metropolitan Airport is served by Delta, US Airways, Continental, United Express, and Comair.

➤ AIRPORT INFORMATION: **Columbia Metropolitan Airport** (✉ 120 Beach City Rd., ☎ 803/822–5000 or 888/562–5002, WEB www.columbiaairport.com).

CAR TRAVEL

I–20 leads northeast from Georgia to Columbia. I–77 runs south to Columbia, where it terminates. I–26 runs north–south through town.

VISITOR INFORMATION

➤ TOURIST INFORMATION: **Columbia Metropolitan Convention & Visitors Bureau** (✉ 1276 Assembly St. [Box 15, 29202], ☎ 803/254–0479 or 800/264–4884, WEB www.columbiasc.net). **Capital City/Lake Murray Country Visitor Center** (✉ 2184 N. Lake Dr. [Box 1783, Irmo 29063], ☎ 803/781–5940 or 866/725–3935, WEB www.lakemurraycountry.com).

SOUTH DAKOTA

Updated by Tom Griffith

Capital	Pierre
Population	756,000
Motto	Under God the People Rule
State Bird	Chinese ring-necked pheasant
State Flower	Pasqueflower
Postal Abbreviation	SD

Statewide Visitor Information

The **South Dakota Department of Tourism** (✉ 711 E. Wells Ave., Pierre 57501, ☎ 800/732–5682, WEB www.travelsd.com) dispenses state highway maps and the annual *South Dakota Vacation Guide* free of charge. Call the **Department of Transportation** (☎ 605/773–3571 or 605/773–7515) for maps of road construction in summer and reports on road conditions in winter.

Scenic Drives

Beautiful **Needles Highway** (Route 87) passes some spectacular, needle-sharp granite spires. **Iron Mountain Road** (U.S. 16A) has views of Mt. Rushmore over pigtail bridges and through tunnels. Both highways run through Custer State Park. U.S. 14A follows scenic **Spearfish Canyon,** a National Scenic Byway.

National and State Parks

National Parks

Visitors to 244,000-acre **Badlands National Park** (✉ Rte. 240 S, Off I–90 Exit 110 or Exit 131, 80 mi east of Rapid City [Box 6, Interior 57750], ☎ 605/433–5361; 💵 $10 per car), a moonscape of rugged ridgelines, deep ravines, and towering pinnacles, are often captivated by an expansive terrain that has changed but little since man first came here yet, due to constant weathering, changes every day. **Jewel Cave National Monument** (✉ R.R. 1 [Box 60AA, Custer 57730], 53 mi southwest of Rapid City on U.S. 16, ☎ 605/673–2288) gets its name from the calcite crystals lining the walls of one of the world's longest caves. Scenic tours are offered year-round; historic and spelunking tours are offered June–August. **Wind Cave National Park** (✉ R.R. 1 [Box 190, Hot Springs 57747], 50 mi south of Rapid City on U.S. 385, ☎ 605/745–4600) is 28,000 acres of prairie and forest above one of the world's longest caves with perhaps the world's best collection of box work—a honeycomb-like calcite formation. Five different guided tours are offered daily June–August; the walking tour is offered year-round.

State Parks

★ The crown jewel of South Dakota's 13-park system is **Custer State Park** (✉ East entrance: Rte. 36, off Rte. 79 south of Rapid City; West entrance: Rte. Hwy. 16A, 3 mi east of Custer [HC 83, Box 70, Custer 57730], ☎ 605/255–4515; 800/710–2267 campground reservations), which has 73,000 spectacular acres of grasslands and pine-covered hills that are home to bison, deer, bighorn sheep, prairie dogs, and pronghorn.

THE BLACK HILLS, DEADWOOD, AND THE BADLANDS

Unlike the agricultural eastern half of the state, western South Dakota is a land of mountain meadows, pine forests, and desolate, rocky landscapes. It's also where most tourists go, to visit such places as Deadwood, the 19th-century mining town turned gambling mecca; the mountain carving in progress known as Crazy Horse; and Mt. Rushmore, whose giant stone carvings of four U.S. presidents have retained their stern grandeur for more than 60 years.

Exploring the Black Hills, Deadwood, and the Badlands

The Black Hills

As with the rest of the state, many of this region's attractions don't have firm closing dates or opening dates, primarily because of the vagaries of the weather in the Dakotas, and rely simply on the level of tourist traffic to dictate when they close or open for the season. Some attractions are open in summer (often Memorial Day–Labor Day); be sure to call ahead before your visit.

To locals, **Rapid City** is West River, meaning west of the Missouri. South Dakota's second-largest city, a cross between western town and progressive community, is a good base from which to explore the Black Hills. Cowboy boots are common here, and business leaders often travel by pickup truck or four-wheel-drive vehicle. Still, the city supports a convention center, museum, and a modern, acoustically advanced performance hall as well as numerous book, gift, and specialty shops downtown and a modern shopping mall on the outskirts. The **Journey** (⊠ 222 New York St., Rapid City, near the Rushmore Plaza Civic Center, ☎ 605/394–6923; 🎫 $6) combines the collections of the **Sioux Indian Museum**, the **Minnilusa Pioneer Museum**, the **Museum of Geology**, the **State Archaeological Research Center**, and a private collection of Native American artifacts into a sweeping pageant of the history and evolution of the Black Hills. The **South Dakota Air & Space Museum** (⊠ 2890 Davis Dr., Box Elder, ¾ mi north of I–90, Exit 66, outside Rapid City and the Ellsworth Air Force Base, ☎ 605/385–5188; 🎫 free, tour $4.50) has a model of a Stealth bomber that's 60% actual size. Also here are General Dwight D. Eisenhower's Mitchell B-25 bomber and more than two dozen other planes, as well as a once-operational missile silo. There are no tours in winter.

The films *Dances with Wolves* (winner of the 1990 Academy Award for best picture) and *Thunderheart* have generated new interest and new businesses in the Black Hills. The **Ft. Hays *Dances with Wolves* Movie Set** (⊠ Ft. Hays Dr. and U.S. 16, Rapid City, ☎ 605/394–9653; 🎫 free) displays photos and shows a video taken during the making of the film. A chuck-wagon dinner show ($15) is offered Memorial Day–Labor Day. **Storybook Island** (⊠ 1301 Sheridan Lake Rd., Rapid City, ☎ 605/342–6357, WEB www.storybookisland.org; 🎫 free) lets children romp through scenes from fairy tales and nursery rhymes.

Reptile Gardens has the world's largest reptile collection, 50,000 flowers, and a variety of staged animal shows. ⊠ *8955 S. U.S. 16, Rapid City, 5 mi south of town,* ☎ *605/342–5873,* WEB *www.reptilegardens.com.* 🎫 *$10. Closed Nov.–Mar.*

At the drive-through wildlife park **Bear Country U.S.A.,** you encounter black bears, wolves, and other North American wildlife, as well as a walk-through wildlife center with bear cubs, wolf pups, and other offspring. ⊠ *13820 S. U.S. 16, Rapid City, 8 mi south of town,* ☎ *605/*

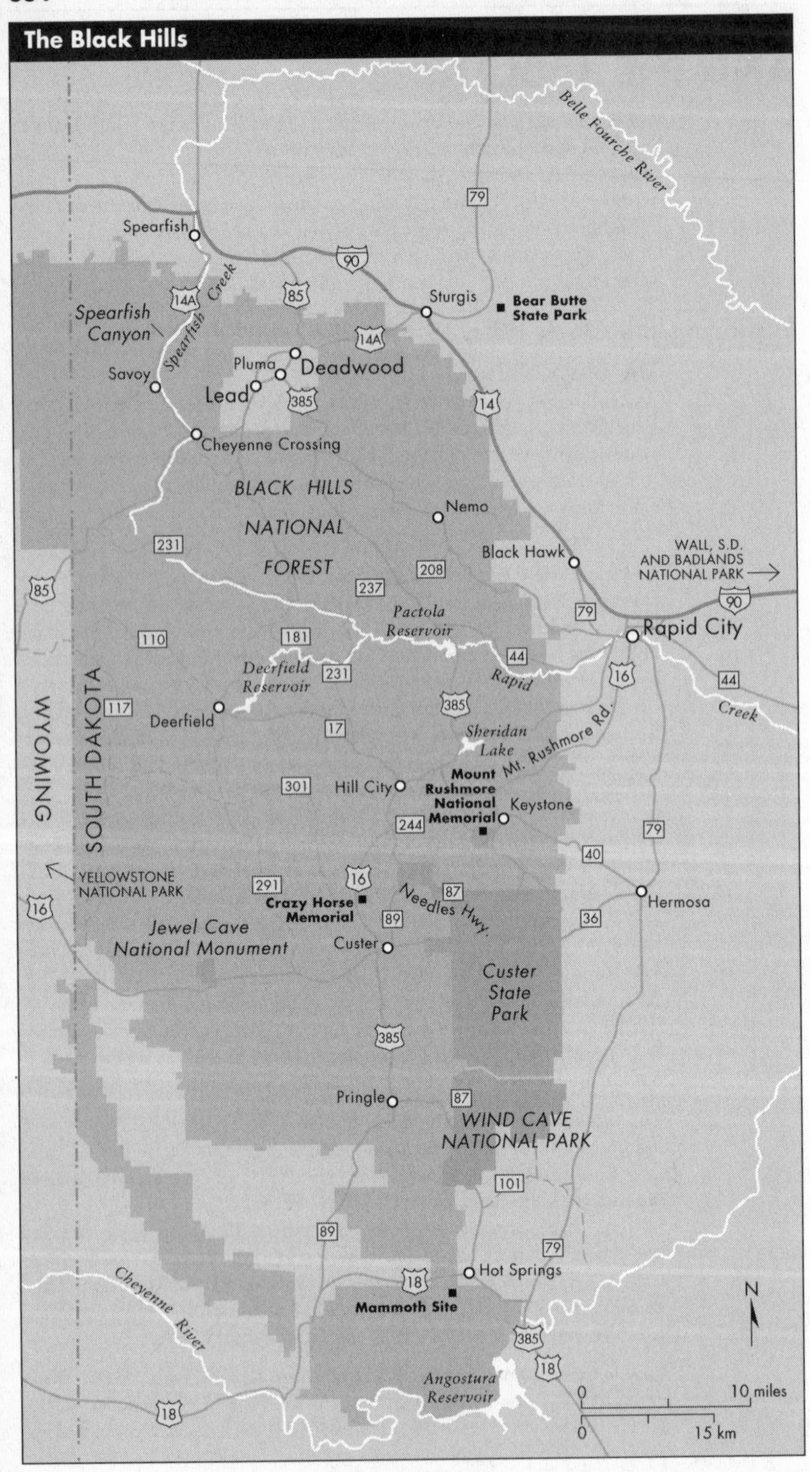
The Black Hills
Belle Fourche River
Spearfish
Sturgis
Bear Butte State Park
Spearfish Canyon
Spearfish Creek
Savoy
Pluma
Deadwood
Lead
Cheyenne Crossing
BLACK HILLS NATIONAL FOREST
Nemo
Black Hawk
WALL, S.D. AND BADLANDS NATIONAL PARK
Pactola Reservoir
Rapid City
Deerfield Reservoir
Rapid Creek
Deerfield
Sheridan Lake
Mt. Rushmore Rd.
Hill City
Mount Rushmore National Memorial
Keystone
WYOMING
SOUTH DAKOTA
YELLOWSTONE NATIONAL PARK
Crazy Horse Memorial
Needles Hwy.
Hermosa
Jewel Cave National Monument
Custer
Custer State Park
Pringle
WIND CAVE NATIONAL PARK
Hot Springs
Mammoth Site
Cheyenne River
Angostura Reservoir
N
0 10 miles
0 15 km

343–2290, WEB *www.bearcountryusa.com.* 🎟 *$9.50. Closed Nov.–Apr.*

★ The vast **Black Hills National Forest** (✉ R.R. 2, Custer, ☎ 605/673–9200; 🎟 free) covers 1.3 million acres on the state's western edge. **Mt. Rushmore National Memorial** (✉ U.S. 16, Keystone, 21 mi southwest of Rapid City, ☎ 605/574–2523; 🎟 free), the granite cliff where the faces of Presidents Washington, Jefferson, Lincoln, and Theodore Roosevelt are carved is the most famous attraction in Black Hills National Forest. Sculptor Gutzon Borglum labored at this monumental task for more than 14 years; his son, Lincoln, provided the finishing touches following the sculptor's death in 1941. The memorial is spectacular in the morning light and at night, when a special lighting ceremony (June to mid-September) dramatically illuminates the carving.

The **Rushmore-Borglum Story Museum** contains newsreel footage of the original blasting of the rock face, as well as exhibits, artwork, paintings, and drawings of Mt. Rushmore sculptor Gutzon Borglum. ✉ *342 Winter St., Keystone,* ☎ *605/666–4448.* 🎟 *$7. Closed Oct.–Apr.*

★ When finished, the **Crazy Horse Memorial** (✉ U.S. 16/385, Custer, 5 mi north of town, ☎ 605/673–4681, WEB www.crazyhorse.org; 🎟 $9 per person, $20 per vehicle) will be the world's largest sculpture and will depict the legendary Lakota warrior who defeated General Custer at Little Bighorn. The project's completion date is unknown, as the work is limited by weather and funding. Open at the site are an impressive orientation and communications center, the **Indian Museum of North America, Native American Educational & Cultural Center,** the sculptor's studio home and workshop, indoor and outdoor sculpture galleries, and the Laughing Water Restaurant. Expect frequent blasting at this work-in-progress.

Flintstones, Bedrock City (✉ U.S. 16 at U.S. 385, Custer, ☎ 605/673–4079, WEB www.flintstonesbedrockcity.com; 🎟 $6) is a full-scale tribute to the enduring cartoon characters, with a curio shop, a train ride, a drive-in restaurant serving Brontoburgers, and a campground. Southeast of Custer is **Wind Cave National Park** (✉ R.R. 1, Hot Springs, 50 mi south of Rapid City on U.S. 385, ☎ 605/745–4600). Lakota tradition holds that it was at Wind Cave that the first Lakota people were tricked by Iktomi (spider person) into leaving their ancestral home.

★ The fossilized remains of ancient mammoths at the **Mammoth Site** (✉ 1 block north of the U.S. 18 Bypass, Hot Springs, ☎ 605/745–6017, WEB www.mammothsite.com; 🎟 $6) prove fascinating to children and adults alike. Discovered in 1974, the site is believed to contain up to 100 mammoths (52 have been unearthed so far) and 35 other species in the sinkhole where the mammoths came to drink some 26,000 years ago. A visitor center is built over the area; excavation is in progress.

Sturgis, 29 mi northwest of Rapid City via I–90, is a sleepy town of about 5,600, whose population swells to more than a quarter-million during the first full week of August. The **Sturgis Motorcycle Rally** has drawn bike buffs from around the world since 1938. During the week-long event, many businesses turn their buildings over to sellers of leather goods, raly T-shirts, and other bike-related paraphernalia. For specific dates and events information, contact the **Sturgis Motorcycle Rally and Champion Rally Productions** (✉ Box 507, Sturgis 57785, ☎ 605/347–9190, WEB www.sturgismotorcyclerally.com).

About 45 mi northwest of Rapid City via I–90, the ***Black Hills Passion Play*** (✉ Spearfish Amphitheatre, 100 St. Joe St., Spearfish, ☎ 605/642–2646, WEB www.blackhills.com/bhpp; 🎟 $12–$18) has, since 1939, been recounting the final seven days in the life of Jesus. Performances are Tuesday, Thursday, and Sunday at 8 PM from June through August.

Deadwood

More than a decade after the legalization of gaming in South Dakota, the town of Deadwood stands as a testament to an unlikely benefactor. In 1989, South Dakota voters approved limited-stakes gaming for Deadwood—the nation's third-largest gambling venue, behind Nevada and Atlantic City—on the condition that a portion of revenues be devoted to historic preservation. Since then, $170 million has gone into restoring and preserving this once infamous gold-mining boomtown, earning Deadwood a designation as a National Historic Landmark. Streets have been repaved with bricks, and guests are greeted by old-time trolleys, period lighting, and original Victorian architecture. Small gaming halls, good restaurants, and hotels occupy virtually every storefront on Main Street. Walk in the same footsteps as legendary lawman Wild Bill Hickok, cigar-smoking Poker Alice Tubbs, and the fabled Calamity Jane, who swore she could out-drink, out-spit, and out-swear any man—and usually did.

Mt. Moriah Cemetery (⊠ top of Lincoln St., ☎ 605/578–2600; 🎟 $1) is the final resting place of Hickok, Calamity Jane, and other notable Deadwood residents. Currently in the midst of a major restoration project, this classic "Boot Hill" has the best panoramic view of the town and the gold-filled gulch.

The **Adams Museum** (⊠ 54 Sherman St., ☎ 605/578–1714; 🎟 donations accepted) has three floors of displays, including the first locomotive used in the area, photos of the town's early days, and the largest gold nugget ever discovered in the Black Hills.

The **Adams House Museum** (⊠ 22 Van Buren St., ☎ 605/578–3724; 🎟 $4) recounts the tragedies and triumphs of two of the community's founding families. Restored and preserved, the house was opened to the public in July 2000, revealing an incredible time capsule.

Lead (pronounced *leed*), about 5 mi north of Deadwood and 50 mi north of Rapid City via I–90 and Alternate Route 14A, is a mining community born in the Black Hills gold-rush frenzy of the late 19th century. **Homestake Visitor Center** (⊠ 160 W. Main St., Lead, ☎ 605/584–3110; 🎟 free) offers a glimpse at the oldest underground gold mine in the western hemisphere; it closed in 2001 after more than 125 years of exploration. The visitor center includes an area for viewing the mine's massive open cut. Free ore samples are available. The town has a number of historic houses, many once home to immigrant miners. **Black Hills Mining Museum** (⊠ 323 W. Main St., Lead, ☎ 605/584–1605; 🎟 $4.50) shows the history of mining through life-size models, videos, gold-panning, and guided tours through a simulated mine.

The Badlands

Badlands National Park (⊠ Hwy. 240 [Box 6, Interior 57750], 9 mi off I–90 Exit 110, 80 mi east of Rapid City, ☎ 605/433–5361; 🎟 $10 per vehicle) can seem like another planet. Millions of years of erosion have left these 244,000 acres with desolate gorges and ridges in rust, pink, and gold. The **Ben Reifel Visitor Center,** 2 mi north of Interior via Route 377 or from I–90 off Exit 131 or 110, has maps and information. South of Badlands National Park is the **Wounded Knee Massacre Monument** (⊠ Pine Ridge Indian Reservation, Hwy. 18, Pine Ridge, 12 mi northwest of town), a small obelisk that commemorates the site where more than 300 Sioux, mostly women and children, were killed when soldiers opened fire after a brief skirmish in 1890.

Wall, a quiet community on the edge of the Badlands, has several motels and restaurants. If you're traveling on I–90, you'll see the signs every few miles for **Wall Drug** (✉ 510 Main St., Wall, ☎ 605/279–2175, WEB www.walldrug.com), the pharmacy turned tourist mecca that enticed Depression-era travelers with offers of free ice water. The store has nearly every tourist trinket imaginable plus a restaurant that seats more than 500, a bookstore with an excellent selection of western literature, a chapel, a selection of knives and boots, and Western art.

Dining and Lodging

In summer, reservations are often required to ensure lodging; calling two or three days ahead is usually adequate.

Deadwood

$$–$$$ ✕ **Jakes.** This elegant restaurant takes up the fourth floor of the Midnight Star Casino, owned by actor Kevin Costner. The rest of the building contains a bar-and-grill and a gaming hall. Costumes worn by Costner in his numerous feature films are displayed throughout the facility. ✉ *677 Main St.,* ☎ *605/578–1555. AE, D, DC, MC, V.*

$–$$ ★ ✕ **Deadwood Social Club.** On the second floor of historic Saloon No. 10, this warm restaurant wraps you in wood and old-time photos of Deadwood's past. The menu stretches from wild-mushroom pasta-and-seafood nest with basil cream to chicken piccata and melt-in-your-mouth rib eyes. ✉ *657 Main St.,* ☎ *605/578–3346. AE, MC, V.*

$$ ★ 🏨 **Bullock Hotel.** In this 1895 hotel, guest rooms are furnished with Victorian reproductions and have large windows. The first floor, which contains the gaming hall, has high ceilings and brass-and-crystal chandeliers. ✉ *633 Main St., 57732,* ☎ *605/578–1745 or 800/336–1876,* FAX *605/578–1382,* WEB *www.bullockhotel.com. 36 rooms. Restaurant, gym. AE, D, MC, V.*

$$ 🏨 **The Days Inn at Deadwood Gulch Resort.** The Black Hills' most complete resort includes a hotel, casinos, a creek-side restaurant, lounges, a convention center, and immediate access to the vast Black Hills trail system. An amusement park, arcade and campground are across the road. ✉ *Hwy. 85 S (Box 643, 57732),* ☎ *605/578–1294 or 800/695–1876,* FAX *605/578–2505,* WEB *www.deadwoodgulch.com. 98 rooms. Restaurant, pool. AE, D, MC, V.*

Interior

$ ★ ✕🏨 **Cedar Pass Lodge.** The wood-frame cabins in this Badlands lodge have knotty-pine interiors and a vintage-1950s look. The restaurant ($) specializes in Native American tacos (fried bread covered with traditional taco fixings) and serves meat-and-potatoes fare, plus trout and fresh-baked desserts. ✉ *1 Cedar St. (Box 5, Interior 57750),* ☎ *605/433–5460,* FAX *605/433–5560. 24 cabins. Restaurant. AE, D, MC, V. Closed Nov.–mid-Mar.*

Rapid City

$$–$$$ ✕ **Landmark Restaurant and Lounge.** This hotel restaurant is popular for its lunch buffet and for dinner specialties like prime rib, beef Wellington, Cajun dishes, and wild game. ✉ *Alex Johnson Hotel, 523 6th St.,* ☎ *605/342–1210. AE, D, DC, MC, V.*

$$ ✕ **Fireside Inn Restaurant & Lounge.** One of the two dining rooms has tables around a slate fireplace. Guests also may dine on an outdoor deck, weather permitting. The large menu has 54 entrées and includes prime rib, seafood, and Italian dishes. ✉ *Rte. 44, Rapid City, 6½ mi west of town,* ☎ *605/342–3900. AE, D, DC, MC, V.*

$$ ✕ **Flying T Chuckwagon.** Ranch-style meals of barbecued beef, grilled chicken, potatoes, and baked beans are served on tin plates in this converted barn. At 6:30 PM, dinner is followed by a western show with music and cowboy comedy. The prix fixe includes dinner and the show. ✉ *U.S. 16, Rapid City, 6 mi south of town,* ☎ *605/342–1905 or 888/256–1905. MC, V. Closed mid-Sept.–mid-May. No lunch.*

$–$$ ✕ **Botticelli Ristorante Italiano.** With a wide selection of delectable veal and chicken dishes as well as creamy pastas, this Italian eatery offers a welcome respite from traditional midwestern meat and potatoes. ✉ *523 Main St., Rapid City,* ☎ *605/348–0089. AE, MC, V.*

$–$$ ✕ **Minerva's.** A pub and pool room complement this spacious restaurant next to hotels and the city's largest shopping mall. Specialties include linguine Minerva, rotisserie chicken, and the scrumptious Hunter's Ribeye. ✉ *Best Western Ramkota Hotel, 2111 N. LaCrosse St.,* ☎ *605/394–9505. AE, D, DC, MC, V.*

$$–$$$ 🏨 **Audrie's Bed & Breakfast.** Victorian antiques and an air of romance greet you at this out-of-the-way B&B. Suites, cottages, and creek-side cabins sleeping two come with old-world furnishings, fireplaces, private baths, hot tubs, and big-screen TVs. Children are not allowed. ✉ *23029 Thunderhead Falls Rd., Rapid City, off U.S. 44, 7 mi west of town,* ☎ *605/342–7788,* WEB *www.audriesbb.com. 2 suites, 7 cottages and cabins. No credit cards. BP.*

$$ 🏨 **Holiday Inn Rushmore Plaza.** This eight-story hotel has a central lobby with an atrium, glass elevators, and a 60-ft waterfall. ✉ *505 N. 5th St., 57701,* ☎ *605/348–4000,* FAX *605/348–9777,* WEB *www.holidayinnrapidcity.com. 205 rooms. Restaurant, gym. AE, D, DC, MC, V.*

$–$$ ★ 🏨 **Alex Johnson Hotel.** Native American patterns and artwork predominate at this landmark hotel officially dedicated to the Lakota peoples. Rooms have replicas of their original furniture (the hotel opened in 1928). The lobby has a torch chandelier made of Lakota war lances. ✉ *523 6th St., 57701,* ☎ *605/342–1210 or 800/888–2539,* WEB *www.alexjohnson.com. 143 rooms. Restaurant. AE, D, DC, MC, V.*

Sturgis

$–$$ ✕ **World Famous Roadkill Cafe.** Started by two bike-rally enthusiasts, the café promises to bring food "from your grill to ours!" including the Chicken That Didn't Quite Cross the Road and the daily special, Guess That Mess! Clever monikers attempt to disguise fairly standard stuff—breakfast, tuna melts, and buffalo and beef burgers. ✉ *1333 Main St., Sturgis,* ☎ *605/347–4502. Reservations not accepted. MC, V. Closed Sept.–May.*

Wall

$–$$ ✕ **Cactus Family Restaurant and Lounge.** This downtown restaurant is open for breakfast, lunch, and dinner and specializes in delicious hotcakes and pies. A giant roast-beef buffet is offered in summer. ✉ *519 Main St.,* ☎ *605/279–2561. D, MC, V.*

$–$$ ★ ✕ **Elkton House Restaurant.** This comfortable restaurant with wood paneling and a sunroom has fast service and a terrific hot roast-beef sandwich, served on white bread with gravy and mashed potatoes. ✉ *203 South Blvd.,* ☎ *605/279–2152. D, MC, V.*

Motel

🏨 **Super 8 Motel** (✉ 1–90, Exit 110 [Box 426, Wall 57790], ☎ 605/279–2688), 29 rooms; AE, D, DC, MC, V; $.

Campgrounds

For information on state campgrounds contact the **Department of Game, Fish, and Parks** (✉ 412 W. Missouri, Pierre 57501, ☎ 605/773–3485; 800/710–2267 camping reservations).

Around Deadwood: ⛺ **Custer Crossing Campground and Store** (✉ HCR 73, Deadwood, 15 mi south of town, ☎ 605/584–1009). ⛺ **Deadwood KOA** (✉ Hwy. 14A, Deadwood, 1 mi west of town, ☎ 605/578–

3830). ⚠ **Whistler Gulch RV Park & Campground** (✉ 235 Cliff St., Deadwood, on southern edge of town, ☎ 605/578–2092 or 800/704–7139). ⚠ **Wild Bill's Campground** (✉ 21372 U.S. 385, Deadwood, ☎ 605/578–2800).

Around the Badlands: ⚠ **Circle 10 Campground** (✉ HCR 1, Philip 57567, ☎ 605/433–5451).

Outdoor Activities and Sports

Biking

The **George S. Mickelson Trail** (WEB www.mickelsontrail.com) is South Dakota's longest, skinniest state park and one of the newest outdoor attractions in the Black Hills. Spanning 110 mi, from sagebrush-flat to ponderosa-pine forest, the trail is ideal for hiking, biking, horseback riding, and skiing. For more information contact the South Dakota Department of Tourism (☎ 800/732–5682) or the Department of Game, Fish, and Parks ☎ (605/773–3485).

Fishing

Some of the best fishing in the state lies east of the Badlands in the large reservoirs of the Missouri River, but mountain streams throughout the **Black Hills** offer good trout fishing. **Custer State Park, Pactola Lake,** and **Sheridan Lake** have excellent trout fishing. For information on fishing, contact the **South Dakota Department of Tourism** (☎ 800/732–5682).

Hiking

The 111-mi **Centennial Trail** runs through the Black Hills National Forest, from the Plains Indians' sacred site at Bear Butte in the north to Wind Cave National Park, passing from grasslands into the hills in the high country. For more information contact the South Dakota Department of Tourism (☎ 800/732–5682).

Snowmobiling

With 335 mi of marked and groomed trails, the **Black Hills** are a premier spot in the country for snowmobiling. A map of the trail network is available from the South Dakota Department of Tourism (✉ 711 E. Wells Ave., Pierre 57501, ☎ 800/732–5682, WEB www.travelsd.com). For winter trail conditions, updated three times weekly, call the **South Dakota Winter Snow Report hot line** (☎ 800/445–3474).

Ski Areas

The Black Hills' winter-sports magazine, *Romancing the Snow,* has information on cross-country and downhill skiing; it's available from the **Black Hills, Badlands and Lakes Association** (✉ 1851 Discovery Cir., Rapid City 57701, ☎ 605/355–3600, WEB www.blackhillsbadlands.com). For ski reports call the **South Dakota Winter Snow Report hot line** (☎ 800/445–3474).

Cross-Country Skiing

The Black Hills offer skiing on 600 mi of abandoned logging roads, railroad beds, and fire trails, as well as several trail networks, including the **Big Hill** (✉ Forest Service Rd. 134, Spearfish, 8 mi southwest of town), which is 16 mi of trails on the rim of Spearfish Canyon. Contact Ski Cross Country (✉ 701 3rd St., Spearfish, ☎ 605/722–3851), a ski-equipment sales and rental shop, for information.

Downhill Skiing

Deer Mountain Ski Area (✉ 1000 Deer Mountain Rd., ☎ 605/584–3230, WEB www.skideermountain.com) has 45 trails, an 850-ft vertical drop, one double lift, one triple chair, one Poma lift (akin to a T-bar), snowmaking equipment, and 10 mi of cross-country trails. The base lodge offers rentals and lessons and a full-service restaurant and lounge. **Terry Peak Ski Area** (✉ Hwy. 85, 3 mi west of town, ☎ 605/584–2165; 800/456–0524 ski conditions) has a 1,100-ft vertical drop, five chairlifts, and state-of-the-art snowmaking. Each of the two lodges has a restaurant, lounge, and gift shop, and one rents equipment.

Shopping

Rapid City stores carry western souvenirs, crafts, and clothing. Nearly every gift shop carries the locally famous "Black Hills Gold," a combination of metals that produce distinctive green and red tints. Watch jewelry being made at **Landstrom's Original Black Hills Gold Creations** (✉ 405 Canal St., Rapid City, ☎ 800/770–5000). You must make reservations for the tour. **Prairie Edge Trading Co. & Galleries** (✉ 606 Main St., Rapid City, ☎ 605/342–3086) displays fine arts and crafts of the Plains Indians, as well as works by various other Great Plains artists, in a restored 1886 three-story building. A turn-of-the-20th-century-style trading company in the same building has books, regional crafts, and a world-class collection of Italian glass beads. **Prince & Pauper Village and Bookshop** (✉ 902 Mt. Rushmore Rd., Rapid City, ☎ 605/342–7964 or 800/354–0988) has a large selection of books by regional and Native American authors, rare and out-of-print local-history books, plus an espresso bar, café, Internet access, and gifts. **Alex Johnson's Mercantile** (✉ 608 St. Joseph St., Rapid City, ☎ 605/343–2383) sells books, wood carvings, jewelry, and unique gifts.

Rushmore Mall (✉ off I–90 north of Rapid City, ☎ 605/348–3378) contains department stores, specialty shops, and western-wear stores. Among the latter is RCC-Western Stores (☎ 605/341–6633), which has one of the area's largest selections of boots and can outfit you from head to toe in the latest fashions in the West. For Native American art, jewelry, baskets, and other goods, visit the gift shop of the **Indian Museum of North America** (✉ Crazy Horse Memorial, U.S. 16/385, Custer, 5 mi north of town, 19 mi southwest of Keystone, ☎ 605/673–4681).

The Black Hills, Deadwood, and the Badlands Essentials

AIRPORTS

Rapid City Regional Airport is served by Northwest Airlines, Skywest (a Delta connection), and United Express.

➤ AIRPORT INFORMATION: **Rapid City Regional Airport** (✉ 4550 Terminal Rd., Rapid City, 10 mi southeast of downtown via Rte. 44, ☎ 605/393–9924, WEB www.rapairport.org).

BUS TRAVEL

Gray Line of the Black Hills offers bus tours of the region, including trips to Mt. Rushmore and Black Hills National Forest. Jack Rabbit Lines serves Wall, Rapid City, Mitchell, and Pierre, the capital.

➤ BUS INFORMATION: **Gray Line of the Black Hills** (☎ 605/342–4461). **Jack Rabbit Lines** (☎ 800/444–6287).

CAR TRAVEL

Unless you're traveling with a package tour, a car is essential here. Make rental reservations early; Rapid City has many business travelers, and rental agencies are often booked. I–90 bisects the state slightly south of its center; it leads to Wall and Rapid City. From Rapid City, U.S. 14 leads to towns and attractions in the northern part of the Black Hills, while U.S. 16 winds through its southern half. Route 44 is an alternate route between the Black Hills and the Badlands. The Black Hills has seven tunnels with limited clearance; they are marked on state maps and in the state's tourism booklet.

TOURS

Affordable Adventures specializes in individual and group tours to many of western South Dakota's most scenic and historic locations, including Rapid City, Mt. Rushmore, Custer State Park, Crazy Horse Memorial, Badlands National Park, Wounded Knee, Pine Ridge, Lead/Deadwood, Hot Springs, and Devils Tower.

➤ FEES AND SCHEDULES: **Affordable Adventures** (✉ Box 546, Rapid City 57709, ☎ 605/342–7691, FAX 605/341–6301).

VISITOR INFORMATION

USDA Forest Service Buffalo Gap National Grasslands Visitor Center has 24 exhibits informing travelers on local history, flora and fauna, and activities in the national grasslands.

➤ TOURIST INFORMATION: **Black Hills, Badlands and Lakes Association** (✉ 1851 Discovery Cir., Rapid City 57701, ☎ 605/355–3600, FAX 605/355–3601, WEB www.blackhillsbadlands.com). **Deadwood Area Chamber of Commerce & Visitor Bureau** (✉ 735 Main St., Deadwood 57732, ☎ 605/578–1876 or 800/999–1876, FAX 605/578–2429, WEB www.deadwood.org). **Rapid City Chamber of Commerce and Convention & Visitors Bureau** (✉ Civic Center, 444 N. Mt. Rushmore Rd. [Box 747, Rapid City 57709], ☎ 605/343–1744 or 800/487–3223, FAX 605/348–9217, WEB www.rapidcitycvb.com). **USDA Forest Service Buffalo Gap National Grasslands Visitor Center** (✉ 708 Main St. [Box 425, Wall 57790], ☎ 605/279–2125).

ELSEWHERE IN SOUTH DAKOTA

Sioux Falls

What to See and Do

South Dakota's largest city is an ideal starting point for most attractions in the eastern part of the state. Restaurants, hotels, and shops are numerous in this commercial hub.

Besides live animals, the **Great Plains Zoo and Delbridge Museum of Natural History** (✉ 805 S. Kiwanis Ave., ☎ 605/367–7059, WEB www.gpzoo.org; 🎫 $6.75) has one of the world's largest collections of mounted animals. The **Old Courthouse Museum** (✉ 200 W. 6th St., ☎ 605/367–4210; 🎫 free) is a massive Romanesque structure made of a native red stone called Sioux quartzite. It has exhibits on the history of this area, including Native American artifacts. Built in 1889, the **Pettigrew Home and Museum** (✉ 131 N. Duluth Ave., ☎ 605/367–7097; 🎫 free) was later the home of South Dakota's first full-term U.S. senator, Richard F. Pettigrew. The Queen Anne–style home contains period furnishings and Native American and natural-history exhibits.

Dining

$$–$$$$ ✕ **Minerva's.** Wooden floors, a salad bar, and a strong wine list complement a menu of pasta, fresh seafood, and aged steak. ✉ *301 S. Phillips Ave.,* ☎ *605/334–0386. AE, D, DC, MC, V. Closed Sun.*

$–$$ ✕ **Champps Sports Cafe.** This spot is reliable in its lively atmosphere and great pub fare, including pastas, sandwiches, hamburgers, fries, onion rings. ✉ *Western Mall, 2101 W. 41st St.,* ☎ *605/331–4386. AE, D, DC, MC, V.*

Sioux Falls Essentials

AIRPORTS

Sioux Falls Regional Airport is served by American, Northwest, and United.

➤ AIRPORT INFORMATION: **Sioux Falls Regional Airport** (✉ 2801 Jaycee La., ☎ 605/336–0762).

CAR TRAVEL

Sioux Falls is in the southeastern corner of the state, at the intersection of I–90 and I–29.

VISITOR INFORMATION

➤ TOURIST INFORMATION: **Sioux Falls Convention and Visitors Bureau** (✉ Box 1425, 57101-1425, ☎ 605/336–1620 or 800/333–2072, FAX 605/336–6499, WEB www.siouxfalls.com).

Mitchell

What to See and Do

The city of Mitchell trumpets the "world's only" **Corn Palace** (✉ 604 N. Main St., ☎ 605/996–5031 or 866/273–2676; free). This fanciful structure, built in 1892, is topped by gaily painted Moorish domes and covered with multicolored corn, grain, and grass murals. Inside is an exhibition hall built to showcase the state's agricultural production. The exterior designs are changed annually. Across the street from the Corn Palace is the **Enchanted World Doll Museum** (✉ 615 N. Main St., ☎ 605/996–9896; $3.50), with 4,800 antique and modern dolls displayed in 435 scenes.

Dining

$–$$$$ ✕ **Chef Louie's Steakhouse.** Steaks, barbecued ribs, and seafood are served in a casual setting. Pheasant is served in summer and fall. ✉ *601 E. Havens St., ☎ 605/996–7565. AE, D, DC, MC, V. Closed Sun.*

Mitchell Essentials

CAR TRAVEL

Mitchell is 70 mi west of Sioux Falls on I–90.

VISITOR INFORMATION

➤ TOURIST INFORMATION: **Mitchell Convention and Visitors Bureau** (✉ 601 N. Main St. [Box 1026, Mitchell 57301], ☎ 605/996–6223 or 866/273–2676, FAX 605/996–8273).

DeSmet

What to See and Do

Fans of the ***Little House on the Prairie*** children's books can visit the town where author Laura Ingalls Wilder lived for 15 years. The Ingalls family moved to DeSmet in 1879, when Laura was 12, and lived first in a surveyor's house, next in a shanty, then in a farmhouse, and finally in town. The **Surveyors' House** (✉ 103 Olivet Ave., DeSmet, ☎ 605/854–3383), is open to the public and has period furnishings and memorabilia. The **Ingalls Town Home** (✉ 210 3rd St. SW, DeSmet, ☎ 605/854–3383) was built by Pa Ingalls in 1887. A one-time admission fee of $6 covers both sites.

The last weekend in June and first two weekends in July, the community hosts the annual **Laura Ingalls Wilder Pageant** (✉ Laura Ingalls Wilder Memorial Society, Box 426, 57231, ☎ 605/854–3383, WEB www.liwms.com), where food, period costumes, and crafts demonstrations are topped off by dramatizations of the *Little House* books themselves.

Dining and Lodging

$ ✕ **The Oxbow.** There's a little of everything—burgers, steaks, fish—on the menu at this homey restaurant, run by the Myers family. ✉ *Hwy. 14, ☎ 605/854–9988. No credit cards.*

$ **Cottage Inn Motel.** Across the street from the Oxbow restaurant, and also run by the Myers family, this motel has clean, spacious rooms. ✉ *Hwy. 14, 57231,* ☎ *605/854–3396 or 800/848–0215. 37 rooms. AE, D, DC, MC, V.*

DeSmet Essentials

CAR TRAVEL

From Sioux Falls follow I–29 north for 49 mi, then U.S. 14 west for about 37 mi.

VISITOR INFORMATION

➤ Tourist Information: **Glacial Lakes and Prairies Association** (✉ Box 244, Watertown 57201, ☎ 605/886–7305 or 800/244–8860, FAX 605/886–7935).

Pierre

The city's name is pronounced *peer.*

What to See and Do

The **State Capitol** (✉ 500 E. Capitol Ave., ☎ 605/773–3765; free), a magnificent Greek Revival building completed in 1910, is richly decorated with mosaic floors, stained-glass skylights, allegorical murals, and an impressive columned staircase. The state historical society has a museum and archives at the **Cultural Heritage Center** (✉ 900 Governors Dr., ☎ 605/773–3458, WEB www.sdhistory.org; $3). Exhibits focus on the history of South Dakota. The third and final phase of the permanent exhibit *South Dakota Experience* is scheduled for completion in 2004. The first phase offers a taste of the state from 1743, the year European trappers first arrived, through the beginning of the 20th century. The second phase focuses on the culture of the Sioux Indians. The third phase will cover the 20th century.

Dining and Lodging

$$ ✕ **Best Western Ramkota Inn.** The largest hotel in Pierre is also one of the capital's social hubs. Hearty breakfasts and buffets are hallmarks at the hotel restaurant ($–$$) with views of the Missouri River. Steak, prime rib, and walleye are the dinner favorites. ✉ *920 W. Sioux Ave., 57501,* ☎ *605/224–6877,* FAX *605/224–1042,* WEB *www.ramkota.com. 151 rooms. Restaurant, pool, gym. AE, D, DC, MC, V.*

$–$$ ✕ **Comfort Inn Pierre.** This capitol-city hotel is clean, friendly, and reasonably priced and offers guests a nightly cookie reception. It's within walking distance of all of Pierre's attractions. ✉ *410 W. Sioux Ave., 57501,* ☎ FAX *605/224–0377. 58 rooms. Pool. AE, D, DC, MC, V. CP.*

Pierre Essentials

CAR TRAVEL

Pierre is on U.S. 83, about 225 mi west of Sioux Falls.

VISITOR INFORMATION

➤ Tourist Information: **Pierre Convention and Visitors Bureau** (✉ Box 548, 57501-0548, ☎ 605/224–7361 or 800/962–2034, FAX 605/224–6485, WEB www.pierrechamber.com).

TENNESSEE

Updated by Martha L. Rodríguez Rivera

Capital	Nashville
Population	5,368,283
Motto	Agriculture and Commerce
State Bird	Mockingbird
State Flower	Iris
Postal Abbreviation	TN

Statewide Visitor Information

Tennessee Department of Tourist Development (✉ 320 6th Ave. N, Nashville 37243, ☎ 615/741–2159 or 800/462–8366, WEB www.state.tn.us).

Scenic Drives

U.S. 421 from Bristol to Trade passes through the Cherokee National Forest and crosses the Appalachian Trail. **Route 73** south from Townsend leads through a high valley ringed by the Great Smoky Mountains to the pioneer village of Cades Cove in Great Smoky Mountains National Park. **Route 25** from Gallatin to Springfield travels through an area of Thoroughbred farms and antebellum houses. Between Monteagle and Chattanooga **I-24** winds through the Cumberland Mountains.

National and State Parks

National Parks

Great Smoky Mountains National Park (✉ Gatlinburg 37738, ☎ 865/436–1200, WEB www.greatsmoky.com) encompasses tall peaks and lush valleys, with camping and fishing sites and more than 900 mi of horse and hiking trails.

State Parks

The State Parks Division of the **Tennessee Department of Environment and Conservation** (✉ 401 Church St., L&C Tower, 7th floor, Nashville 37243, ☎ 615/532–0001 or 800/421–6683, WEB www.tnstateparks.com) provides information on Tennessee's 50-plus state parks. The 21,000-acre **Fall Creek Falls State Resort Park** (✉ Rte. 3, Pikeville 37367, ☎ 865/881–5241 or 423/881–3297) has the highest waterfall east of the Rockies. Thick stands of cypress trees make **Reelfoot Lake State Resort Park** (✉ Rte. 1 [Box 2345, Tiptonville 38079], ☎ 731/253–7756, WEB www.state.tn.us), in northwestern Tennessee, a favorite wintering ground for the American bald eagle. **Roan Mountain State Resort Park** (✉ 527 Hwy. 143, Roan Mountain 37687, ☎ 423/772–3303, WEB www.state.tn.us), in northeastern Tennessee, has a 600-acre natural rhododendron garden that blooms in late June.

MEMPHIS

On the bluffs overlooking the Mississippi River, Memphis is Tennessee's largest city and the commercial and cultural center of the western part of the state. It is a blend of southern tradition and modern efficiency, where aging cotton warehouses stand near sleek new office buildings, and old-fashioned paddle wheelers steam upriver past the city's unusual landmark, the gleaming stainless-steel Pyramid Arena. Memphis is perhaps best known for its music and for the two extraordinary men who introduced that music to the world: W. C. Handy, the Father of the Blues, and Elvis Presley, the King of Rock and Roll.

Exploring Memphis

Downtown

Memphis begins at the Mississippi River, which is celebrated in a 52-acre river park (☎ 901/576–6595 or 800/507–6507, WEB www.mudisland.com) on **Mud Island.** A footbridge and monorail at 125 North Front Street get you to the island, where a five-block **River Walk** replicates the Mississippi's every twist, turn, and sandbar from Cairo, Illinois, to New Orleans, Louisiana. Also in the park are the **Mississippi River Museum** (🎫 $8), the famed World War II B-17 bomber ***Memphis Belle,*** an amphitheater, shops, and a pool.

The 32-story, 22,000-seat stainless-steel **Pyramid Arena** (✉ 1 Auction Ave., ☎ 901/521–9675, WEB www.mudisland.com), opposite the south end of Mud Island, hosts concerts, athletic games, and conventions. **Magevney House,** built in the 1830s by a pioneer schoolteacher, is Memphis's oldest dwelling. It's a 20-minute walk from the Pyramid Arena. *✉ 198 Adams Ave., ☎ 901/526–4464. 🎫 Free. Closed Sun.–Mon. Jan.–Feb.*

Mallory-Neely House was built in 1852. The Victorian mansion belonged to an affluent Memphis family of cotton factors. It is one of the few historic houses in Memphis that still have most of their original furnishings. *✉ 652 Adams Ave., ☎ 901/523–1484, WEB www.memphismuseums.org. 🎫 $5. Closed Tues.–Sun. Jan.–Mar.* The beautifully restored **Peabody Hotel** stands on Union Avenue between 2nd and 3rd streets. **Beale Street,** where W. C. Handy played the blues in the early decades of the 20th century, is once again thriving with clubs and restaurants. The **W. C. Handy Memphis Home and Museum** recalls the influential blues musician through a variety of memorabilia. *✉ 352 Beale St., ☎ 901/522–1556. 🎫 $2. Closed Sun.–Mon.*

The **Hunt-Phelan Home** (✉ 533 Beale St., ☎ 800/350–9009, WEB www.hunt-phelan.com; 🎫 $10), with costumed docents, transports visitors to the mid-1800s. Ulysses S. Grant and Jefferson Davis were among the home's historic visitors (at different times, of course). **Sun Studio** (✉ 706 Union Ave., ☎ 901/521–0664 and 800/441–6249, WEB www.sunstudio.com; 🎫 $8.50), the birthplace of rock and roll, is where Elvis Presley, Jerry Lee Lewis, B. B. King, and Roy Orbison launched their careers. Tours are given daily; the studio is seven blocks east of downtown.

South of downtown, the motel where Dr. Martin Luther King Jr. was assassinated in 1968 has been transformed into the **National Civil Rights Museum,** an outstanding facility that documents the movement through exhibits and clever audiovisual displays. *✉ 450 Mulberry St., ☎ 901/521–9699, WEB www.civilrightsmuseum.org. 🎫 $8.50, free Mon. 3–5. Closed Tues.*

Other Attractions

★ **Graceland,** the estate once owned by Elvis Presley, is 12 mi south of downtown. A guided tour of the mansion, automobile museum, and burial site reveals the spoils of stardom. Graceland might be the only colonial suburban home on record to have a jungle room, a pink Cadillac, and more than 700,000 guests annually. Reservations are recommended especially in August during "Elvis Week." *✉ 3717 Elvis Presley Blvd., ☎ 901/332–3322 or 800/238–2000, WEB www.elvis.com. 🎫 Mansion only, $16; all attractions $25. Closed Tues. Nov.–Mar.*

The **Memphis Brooks Museum of Art,** east of downtown in Overton Park, houses a collection of fine and decorative arts from antiquity to the present, including Renaissance and Baroque works, English por-

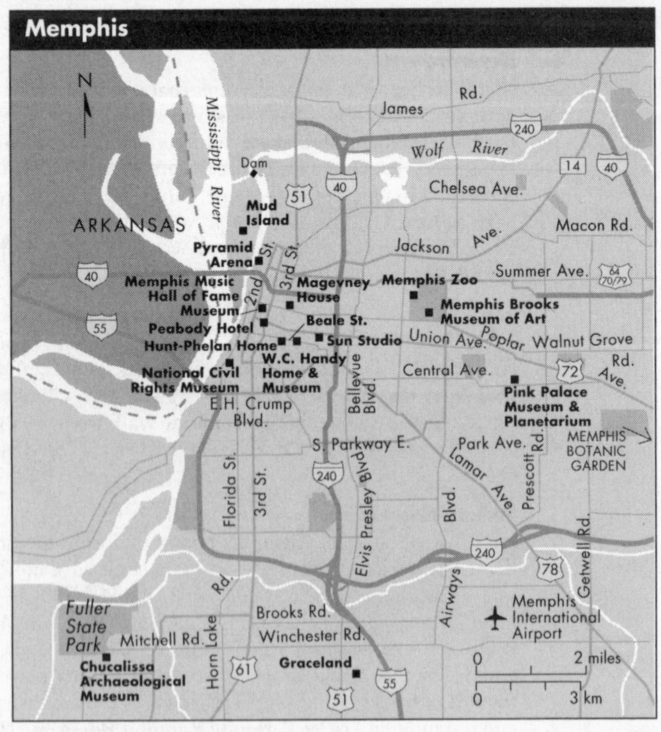

traiture, Hellenistic and classical Roman art, as well as contemporary local artists. ✉ *1934 Poplar Ave.,* ☎ *901/722–3500,* WEB *www.brooksmuseum.org.* 🎟 *$6, free Wed. Closed Mon.*

At the **Children's Museum of Memphis** youngsters can touch, climb, and explore their way through a child-size city, and explore the many interactive exhibitions. ✉ *2525 Central Ave.,* ☎ *901/458–2678 and 901/320–3170,* WEB *www.cmom.com.* 🎟 *$7. Closed Mon.*

The **Memphis Pink Palace Museum and Planetarium** (✉ 3050 Central Ave., ☎ 901/320–6320, WEB www.memphismuseums.org; 🎟 museum $6, planetarium $3.50) has a mix of natural history and cultural history exhibits, planetarium laser shows, and an IMAX theater.

Chucalissa Archaeological Museum is a reconstruction of a Native American village that existed from AD 1000 to AD 1500. Skilled Choctaw craftspeople fashion jewelry, weapons, and pottery outside the **C. H. Nash Museum,** which houses historic originals of the same articles. ✉ *1987 Indian Village Dr.,* ☎ *901/785–3160,* WEB *www.cas.memphis.edu.* 🎟 *$5. Closed Sun.–Mon. Nov.–Mar.*

Parks, Gardens, and Zoos

Overton Park (☎ 901/274–6046, WEB www.overtonparkshell.org), a few miles east of downtown at 1928 Poplar Avenue, has picnic areas, sports fields, hiking and biking trails, a nine-hole golf course, an art museum, and outdoor concerts. Overton Park houses the popular 70-acre **Memphis Zoo** (✉ 2000 Prentiss Pl., ☎ 901/725–3400, WEB www.memphis-zoo.org; 🎟 $9.50), which includes a 9-acre Cat Country and Primate Canyon. In East Memphis the 96-acre **Memphis Botanic Garden** (✉ 750 Cherry Rd., ☎ 901/685–1566, WEB www.memphisbotanicgarden.com; 🎟 $4) has scores of species, from camellias to cacti.

Dining

Although Memphis has a satisfying variety of restaurants, the local passion is barbecue; the city has 70-odd barbecue places. The popular meat-and-threes (diners serving meat with three vegetable side dishes), such as "The Cupboard," specialize in turnip greens, fried chicken, corn bread, and other southern specialties.

$$$$ ★ ✕ **Chez Philippe.** Chef José Gutierrez serves sophisticated dishes in an ornately decorated dining room. Nightly creations may include beef tenderloin, or Chilean snapper with Portobello mushrooms on a horseradish reduction. ✉ *Peabody Hotel, 149 Union Ave.,* ☎ *901/529–4188. Jacket required. AE, DC, MC, V. Closed Sun.–Mon. No lunch.*

$$$–$$$$ ✕ **Erling Jensen.** Jensen first earned a loyal following as the chef at La Tourelle. He's Danish, but the cuisine here is French; most noteworthy is the rack of lamb. ✉ *1044 S. Yates Rd.,* ☎ *901/763–3700. Reservations essential. AE, DC, MC, V. No lunch.*

$$$–$$$$ ✕ **Landry's Seafood House.** A converted riverfront warehouse, this place packs 'em in for such seafood dishes as fried shrimp and stuffed flounder. ✉ *263 Wagner Pl.,* ☎ *901/526–1966. AE, D, DC, MC, V.*

$$$–$$$$ ✕ **La Tourelle.** This turn-of-the-20th-century bungalow in Overton Square has the romance of a French country inn. Five-course prix-fixe meals with an emphasis on French cuisine supplement the à la carte menu. Men will feel most comfortable in a jacket and tie. ✉ *2146 Monroe Ave.,* ☎ *901/726–5771. MC, V.*

$$–$$$ ✕ **McEwen's on Monroe.** Upscale regional food described as "contemporary southern" is served at this popular downtown restaurant, with the menu changing every two months. ✉ *122 Monroe St.,* ☎ *901/527–7085,* WEB *www.mcewensonmonroe.com. AE, D, DC, MC, V.*

$$–$$$ ★ ✕ **Paulette's.** This Overton Square classic serves delicious crepes (try the hot chocolate dessert crepe) and salads and excellent grilled chicken, salmon, and swordfish. ✉ *2110 Madison Ave.,* ☎ *901/726–5128. AE, D, DC, MC, V.*

$–$$ ✕ **Cafe Olé.** This popular midtown hangout offers a healthy version of Mexican cuisine (no animal fats are used), including spinach enchiladas and chile rellenos (cheese-stuffed fried green chilies). ✉ *959 S. Cooper St.,* ☎ *901/274–1504. AE, D, DC, MC, V.*

$–$$ ✕ **Charlie Vergos' Rendezvous.** Tourists and locals alike flock to this downtown basement restaurant to savor Vergos's "dry" barbecued pork ribs and other barbecue specialties. ✉ *52 S. 2nd St.,* ☎ *901/523–2746,* WEB *www.hogsfly.com. AE, D, DC, MC, V. Closed Sun.–Mon. No lunch Tues.–Thurs.*

$–$$ ★ ✕ **Corky's.** There's always a line at this no-frills barbecue restaurant. Once you taste the ribs (or sandwiches, or beef or pork platters), you'll understand why. ✉ *5259 Poplar Ave.,* ☎ *901/685–9744,* WEB *www.corkysbbq.com. AE, D, DC, MC, V.*

$ ✕ **The Cupboard.** Owner Charles Cavallo knows fresh produce, and his cooks turn out masterful "meat-and-three" plates. Lucky is the soul who visits when both macaroni and cheese and fried green tomatoes are offered. ✉ *1400 Union Ave.,* ☎ *901/276–8015. AE, D, MC, V.*

Lodging

Memphis hotels are especially busy during the monthlong Memphis-in-May International Festival, and in mid-August during Elvis Tribute Week; book well ahead at these times. For bed-and-breakfasts contact the **Tennessee Bed & Breakfast Innkeepers Association** (✉ 5341 Mt. View Rd., Suite 15, Antioch 37013, ☎ 800/820–8144, FAX 281/403–9335, WEB www.tennessee-inns.com).

$$$$ ★ **Peabody Hotel.** Even if you're not staying here, it's worth a stop to see this 12-story downtown landmark, built in 1925. The lobby has the original stained-glass skylights and the travertine-marble fountain that is home to the hotel's resident ducks. The rooms are decorated in a variety of period styles. ✉ *149 Union Ave., 38103,* ☎ *901/529–4000 or 800/732–2639,* FAX *901/529–3600. 468 rooms. 4 restaurants, pool, health club. AE, D, DC, MC, V.* WEB *www.peabodymemphis.com.*

$$$ **Radisson Hotel.** Across the street from the Peabody is this downtown hotel with its own lobby fountain and waterfall. Glass-walled elevators whisk guests to rooms around a 10-story atrium. ✉ *185 Union Ave., 38103,* ☎ *901/528–1800,* FAX *901/526–3226,* WEB *www.radisson.com. 280 rooms. Restaurant, pool. AE, D, DC, MC, V*

$$ ★ **Adam's Mark Memphis.** Set in the flourishing eastern suburbs near I–240, this 27-story glass tower has views of the sprawling metropolis and its outskirts. ✉ *939 Ridge Lake Blvd., 38120,* ☎ *901/684–6664 or 800/444–2326,* FAX *901/762–7411,* WEB *www.adamsmark.com. 408 rooms. Restaurant, pool, health club. AE, D, DC, MC, V.*

$$ **French Quarter Suites.** This pleasant Overton Square hotel is reminiscent of a New Orleans–style inn. All suites have oversize whirlpool tubs, and some have balconies. ✉ *2144 Madison Ave., 38104,* ☎ *901/728–4000 or 800/843–0353,* FAX *901/278–1262,* WEB *www.memphisfrenchquarter.com. 105 suites. Restaurant, pool, health club. AE, D, DC, MC, V.*

$$ **Holiday Inn SelectEast.** Close to I–240 and the bustling Poplar/Ridgeway office complex, this sleek 10-story hotel is popular with business travelers. ✉ *5795 Poplar Ave., 38119,* ☎ *901/682–7881,* FAX *901/685–2407,* WEB *www.holiday-inn.com. 243 rooms. Restaurant, indoor pool, health club. AE, D, DC, MC, V.*

$ **Best Value Inn.** This four-story motor lodge near Graceland has spacious, well-appointed rooms. They also have meeting facilities for business travelers. ✉ *3222 Airways Blvd., 38116,* ☎ *901/332–3800 or 888/315–2378,* FAX *901/345–8118,* WEB *www.bestvalueinn.com. 118 rooms. Pool, gym. DC, MC, V.*

$ **La Quinta Inn–Medical Center.** This two-story inn is convenient to midtown and has spacious rooms. ✉ *42 S. Camilla St., 38104,* ☎ *901/526–1050,* FAX *901/525–3219,* WEB *www.laquinta.com. 130 rooms. Pool. AE, D, DC, MC, V. CP.*

$ **Quality Inn.** All units have private patios or balconies; many have refrigerators and microwave ovens, and four have kitchens. ✉ *1541 Sycamore View, 38134,* ☎ *901/388–1300,* WEB *www.qualityinn.com. 96 rooms. Pool, laundry facilities. AE, D, DC, MC, V. CP.*

Nightlife and the Arts

Nightlife

To hear the blues as they were meant to be played, head for Beale Street. Among the most popular clubs is **B. B. King's Blues Club** (✉ 143 Beale St., ☎ 901/524–5464, WEB www.bbkingsclub.com), where B. B. himself occasionally performs. **Rum Boogie Cafe** (✉ 182 Beale St., ☎ 901/528–0150, WEB www.rumboogie.com) is a good spot for the blues.

The Arts

The **Orpheum Theatre** (✉ 203 S. Main St., ☎ 901/525–3000, WEB www.orpheum-memphis.com) hosts touring Broadway shows as well as performances by Opera Memphis and Ballet Memphis. The **Memphis Symphony Orchestra** (☎ 901/324–3627) performs at various locations from September through May.

Spectator Sports

Baseball: The **Memphis Redbirds,** the St. Louis Cardinals AAA farm team, play at AutoZone Park (✉ 8 S. 3rd St., ☎ 901/721–6050, WEB www.memphisredbirds.com), the downtown stadium that opened in April 2000. **Golf:** Southwind Tournament Players Club (✉ 3325 Club Rd., at Southwind, ☎ 901/748–0330) hosts the **FedEx St. Jude Classic Golf Tournament** each summer, drawing the PGA tour's top pros. **Tennis:** The **Kroger St. Jude International Indoor Tennis Tournament** (☎ 901/765–4400) is played in February at the Racquet Club (✉ 5111 Sanderlin Ave.).

Shopping

The **Mid America Mall,** on Main Street between Beale and Poplar, is one of the nation's longest pedestrian malls—known for its trolley rides and people-watching as well as for shopping. It has maintained the architecture of an older, more neighborly Memphis. Antique shops, art galleries, and cafés bracket Mid America Mall and **South Main,** on Main Street between Beale and Calhoun. The **Pinch District,** just north of downtown between Front and 3rd streets, is known for its bars and restaurants. For more local color, midtown's **Cooper Young District,** at the intersection of Cooper Street and Young Avenue, offers a handful of funky shops, vintage clothing stores, and cafés. **Overton Square** (✉ Madison and Cooper Sts., ☎ 901/278–6300), a three-block shopping, restaurant, and entertainment complex, has upscale boutiques, a movie theater, and specialty shops. **Oak Court Mall** (✉ 4465 Poplar Ave., ☎ 901/682–8928), in the busy Poplar/Perkins area of East Memphis, has 85 specialty stores and two department stores. At **Wolfchase Galleria** (✉ 2760 N. Germantown Pkwy., at U.S. 64, about 18 mi east of downtown Memphis, ☎ 901/381–2769), the four anchor stores are Goldsmith's, Dillard's, Sears, and JCPenney. A large carousel attracts scores of children, and there is also a multiplex cinema. **Belz Factory Outlet Mall** (✉ 3536 Canada Rd., Exit 20 off I–40, 20 mi east of downtown Memphis, Lakeland, ☎ 901/386–3180) has 50 stores.

Memphis Essentials

AIRPORTS AND TRANSFERS

Memphis International Airport, 9 mi southeast of downtown, is served by most major airlines and is a hub for Northwest Airlines.

➤ AIRPORT INFORMATION: **Memphis International Airport** (✉ 2491 Winchester Rd., ☎ 901/922–8000, WEB www.mscaa.com).

AIRPORT TRANSFER

Cab fare between the airport and downtown runs about $20 plus tip; Yellow Cab is one of the companies that make the trip. Driving time to downtown is about 15 minutes on I–240.

➤ TAXIS AND SHUTTLES: **Yellow Cab** (☎ 901/577–7777).

BOAT AND FERRY TRAVEL

Memphis is one stop on the paddle-wheeler cruises of the Delta Queen Steamboat Company. The *Delta Queen*, the *Mississippi Queen*, and the *American Queen* travel between St. Louis and New Orleans.

➤ BOAT AND FERRY INFORMATION: **Delta Queen Steamboat Company** (✉ Robin Street Wharf, New Orleans, LA 70130, ☎ 800/543–1949, WEB www.deltaqueen.com).

BUS TRAVEL

➤ BUS INFORMATION: **Greyhound** (✉ 203 Union Ave., ☎ 800/231–2222 and 901/523–9253, WEB www.greyhound.com).

CAR TRAVEL

You can access Memphis via the north–south I–55 or the east–west I–40. I–240 loops around the city.

TRAIN TRAVEL

Amtrak provides limited service.

➤ TRAIN INFORMATION: **Amtrak** (✉ 545 S. Main St., ☎ 800/872–7245 or 901/526–0052, WEB www.amtrak.com).

TRANSPORTATION AROUND MEMPHIS

Memphis's streets are well marked, and there's plenty of parking, so the city is best explored by car. The Memphis Area Transit Authority operates buses ($1.10) throughout downtown and the suburbs (additional fare for zones outside the city limits); a trolley (50¢) runs a 5-mi route linking the north and south ends of downtown via a riverfront loop.

➤ CONTACTS: **Memphis Area Transit Authority** (☎ 901/274–6282).

VISITOR INFORMATION

➤ TOURIST INFORMATION: **Memphis Convention & Visitors Bureau** (✉ 47 Union Ave., 38103, ☎ 901/543–5300 or 800/873–6282, WEB www.memphistravel.com). **Memphis Visitors Information Center** (✉ 119 N. Riverside Dr., ☎ 901/543–5333, WEB www.memphisguide.com).

NASHVILLE

Hailed as Music City, U.S.A. (country music, that is), and the birthplace of the Nashville Sound, Tennessee's capital city is also a leading center of higher education, appropriately known as the Athens of the South. The city has spawned such dissimilar institutions as the Grand Ole Opry and Vanderbilt University and has prospered from them both, becoming one of the mid-South's most vibrant communities.

Exploring Nashville

Downtown

Downtown attractions can be covered easily on foot. Overlooking the river is **Fort Nashborough** (✉ 170 1st Ave. N; 🎫 free), a replica of the crude log fort built in 1779 by Nashville's first settlers. In the **District,** the historic 2nd Avenue area south of Church Street, 19th-century buildings have been handsomely restored to house restaurants, clubs, boutiques, offices, and residences. The **Downtown Presbyterian Church** (✉ 5th Ave. and Church St., ☎ 615/254–7584; 🎫 free), an Egyptian Revival tabernacle (circa 1851), was designed by noted Philadelphia architect William Strickland.

A ticket to the **Country Music Hall of Fame and Museum** (✉ 222 5th Avenue S, ☎ 615/416–2001, WEB www.countrymusichalloffame.com; 🎫 $14.95) gives you access to its impressive two-story permanent display, as well as its numerous interactive features and daily music performances. **Ryman Auditorium and Museum** (✉ 116 5th Ave. N, ☎ 615/871–6500; 615/889–3060 tickets to events; WEB www.ryman.com; 🎫 tours $8), the home of the Grand Ole Opry from 1943 to 1974, is a shrine for die-hard fans. The renovated Ryman once again hosts performances. From November 2002 through February 2003, the Opry will return to the Ryman for its weekly shows.

The James K. Polk Office Building houses the **Tennessee State Museum,** where more than 6,000 artifacts trace the history of life in Tennessee. ✉ *505 Deaderick St.,* ☎ *615/741–2692,* WEB *www.tnmuseum.org.* 🎫 *Free. Closed Mon.* In a park along Charlotte Avenue is the Greek Re-

Downtown Nashville

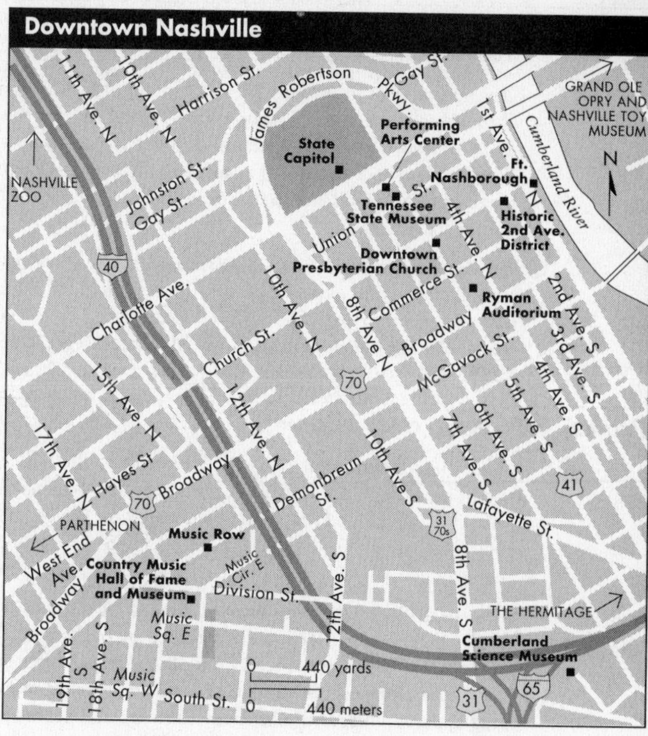

vival **state capitol,** designed by William Strickland, who is interred here, as are the 11th U.S. president, James Polk, and his wife. ☎ *615/741–1621; 615/741–0830 tour reservations.* *Free. Closed weekends.*

The **First Center for the Visual Arts** (✉ 919 Broadway, ☎ 615/244–3340, WEB www.fristcenter.org; $6.50) opened in April 2002 in the former Nashville Post Office. Come here to see national and international traveling exhibitions; recent shows have ranged from medieval Europe to contemporary art.

Other Attractions

Music Row (✉ Demonbreun St. exit off I–40) is the heart of Nashville's recording industry, where Sony, MCA, and BMI are located. Watch out for passing stretch limousines carrying your favorite country stars to and from work.

★ Since 1974, the **Grand Ole Opry** (✉ 2804 Opryland Dr., ☎ 615/889–3060, WEB www.opry.com; $27.50 for shows) has been staged at the complex that housed the Opryland U.S.A. theme park, which closed in 1997. Each weekend top stars perform at the Opry, which is the nation's oldest continuous radio show, first airing in 1925. The Opry is broadcast from the world's largest broadcast studio (it seats 4,424); advance ticket purchase is advised. The musical lineup for the Friday- and Saturday-night shows is announced on Wednesday evenings. The Opry survives and thrives, even as the former theme park's grounds have been converted into Opry Mills, a 200-store shopping, dining, and entertainment complex.

The **Hermitage,** 12 mi east of downtown (Exit 221 off I–40), was built by Andrew Jackson, the seventh U.S. president, for his wife, Rachel. Their lives and times are reflected with great care in the mansion, visitor center, and grounds. Both Jackson and his wife are entombed here. ✉ *4580 Rachel's La., Hermitage,* ☎ *615/889–2941.* 🎫 *$9.50. Closed 3rd wk of Jan.*

Two miles west of downtown in Centennial Park—built for the 1897 Tennessee Centennial Exposition—stands the **Parthenon,** an exact copy of the Athenian original and now used as an art gallery. *Athena Parthenos* is a 42-ft copy of a statue in the original Parthenon. ✉ *West End and 25th Aves.,* ☎ *615/862–8431.* 🎫 *$3.50. Closed Mon., and Sun. Oct.–Mar.*

At the **Cumberland Science Museum** children are invited to touch, smell, climb, and explore. ✉ *800 Ridley Blvd.,* ☎ *615/862–5160.* WEB *www.csmisfun.com.* 🎫 *$7.95. Closed Mon.* The toy collection at the **Nashville Toy Museum** (✉ 2613-B McGavock Pike, ☎ 615/391–3516; 🎫 $3.50) spans more than 150 years.

Parks, Gardens, and Zoos

The 50-acre **Nashville Zoo** (✉ 3777 Nolensville Rd., Nashville [from I–65: Harding Place Exit East, then north on Nolensville Rd.; from I–24: Harding Place Exit West, then north on Nolensville Rd.; from I–440: Nolensville Rd. Exit South], ☎ 615/833–1534, WEB www.nashville-zoo.org; 🎫 $6) includes an African savanna and a reptile house.

The 14,200-acre **J. Percy Priest Lake** (✉ 11 mi east of downtown off I–40, ☎ 615/889–1975) is surrounded by parks where you can swim, fish, camp, hike, bike, picnic, paddle, or ride. Thirty acres of gardens ★ at the **Cheekwood Botanical Garden and Museum of Art** showcase annuals, perennials, and seasonal wildflowers. The museum is in a carefully restored neo-Georgian mansion. The permanent exhibition shows American art to 1945, while the "Temporary Contemporary" gallery presents local and national artists. ✉ *1200 Forrest Park Dr.,* ☎ *615/356–8000,* WEB *www.cheekwood.org.* 🎫 *$10. Closed Mon.*

Dining

Nashville dining is not all corn bread, turnip greens, and grits. Here you will find some of Tennessee's most sophisticated restaurants alongside the classic "meat-and-threes" (diners serving meat with three vegetable side dishes).

$$$–$$$$ ★ ✕ **Mario's.** Country music stars, visiting celebrities, and local socialites come here to see and be seen—and to savor the memorable osso buco and saltimbocca from chef Giovanni Giosa. ✉ *2005 Broadway,* ☎ *615/327–3232. Reservations essential. Jacket and tie. AE, D, DC, MC, V. Closed Sun. No lunch.*

$$$–$$$$ ✕ **Wild Boar.** This restaurant serves excellent contemporary French cuisine, such as game, trout, duck, and beef; it also has an outstanding wine cellar. ✉ *2014 Broadway,* ☎ *615/329–1313. AE, D, DC, MC, V. Closed Sun. No lunch.*

$$–$$$$ ✕ **Sunset Grill.** Don't be surprised to see your favorite country stars at this hip hangout. Sample the traditional Beggar's Purse, a phyllo pastry with crab and shrimp. In summer, the outdoor courtyard is the place to be seen. ✉ *2001-A Belcourt Ave.,* ☎ *615/386–3663,* WEB *www.sunsetgrill.com. AE, D, DC, MC, V. No lunch Sat.–Mon.*

$$–$$$ ★ ✕ **F. Scott's.** This elegant café and wine bar has one of the largest wine selections in town. The cuisine is American bistro with global influences, varying with the season, but always including fresh fish, beef, pork, and lamb. There's live jazz nightly. ✉ *2210 Crestmoor,* ☎ *615/269–5861. AE, D, DC, MC, V. No lunch*

$$–$$$ ✕ **The Merchants.** An outdoor patio is an added attraction at this opulent three-level restaurant. Specialties include fresh seafood, grilled meats, and key lime pie. ✉ *401 Broadway,* ☎ *615/254–1892,* WEB *www.cardenco.com. AE, D, DC, MC, V.*

$ ✕ **Elliston Place Soda Shop.** Come to this old-fashioned soda shop for great burgers and frothy ice cream sodas. The chocolate shake is Nashville's best. ✉ *2111 Elliston Pl.,* ☎ *615/327–1090. MC, V. Closed Sun.*

$ ✕ **Hermitage House Smorgasbord.** No need to be shy about helping yourself to the bountiful spread of salads, meats, vegetables, and desserts here. Don't miss the apple fritters. ✉ *3131 Lebanon Rd.,* ☎ *615/883–9525. No dinner Sun. MC, V.*

$ ✕ **Loveless Cafe.** Down-home southern cooking is the draw: fried chicken, country ham and red-eye gravy, and featherlight homemade biscuits and preserves. ✉ *8400 Rte. 100,* ☎ *615/646–9700.* WEB *www.lovelesscafe.com. AE, MC, V.*

$ ✕ **Old Spaghetti Factory.** This 2nd Avenue District spot offers pasta dishes in a lively setting that's great for families. ✉ *160 2nd Ave. N,* ☎ *615/254–9010. AE, D, MC, V.*

$ ✕ **Sylvan Park Restaurant.** The original location is a beacon for "meat-and-three" fans; purists say the three spin-off eateries aren't quite as good. ✉ *4502 Murphy Rd.,* ☎ *615/292–9275. No credit cards.*

Lodging

Nashville hotels are especially busy during the second week of June, when the International Country Music Fan Fair takes over the city. Many tour companies offer packages, but plan ahead; this is country music's premier event and it sells out months in advance.

For information on B&Bs in the area, contact **Tennessee Bed & Breakfast Innkeepers Association** (✉ 5341 Mt. View Rd., Suite 150, Antioch 37013, ☎ 800/820–8144, FAX 281/403–9335, WEB www.tennessee-inns.com).

$$$$ 🏨 **Loews Vanderbilt Plaza.** This beautiful hotel near Vanderbilt University has a well-deserved reputation for attentive service. ✉ *2100 West End Ave., 37203,* ☎ *615/320–1700 or 800/336–3335,* FAX *615/320–5019,* WEB *www.loewshotels.com. 340 rooms. 2 restaurants. AE, D, MC, V.*

$$$$ ★ 🏨 **Opryland Hotel.** This massive plantation-style hotel adjacent to Opryland has a 2-acre glass-walled conservatory filled with 10,000 tropical plants and a skylighted indoor area with water cascades and a half-acre lake. The 18-hole golf course was designed by Larry Nelson. ✉ *2800 Opryland Dr., 37214,* ☎ *615/889–1000,* FAX *615/871–7741,* WEB *www.opryhotel.com. 2,883 rooms. 7 restaurants, pools, gym. AE, D, MC, V.*

$$$ 🏨 **Renaissance Nashville Hotel.** This ultracontemporary high-rise adjoins the Nashville Convention Center. The spacious rooms have period reproduction furnishings. ✉ *611 Commerce St., 37203,* ☎ *615/255–8400 or 800/468–3571,* FAX *615/255–8202,* WEB *www.renaissancehotels.com. 673 rooms. 2 restaurants, pool, health club. AE, D, DC, MC, V.*

$$ ★ 🏨 **Courtyard by Marriott–Airport.** This handsome low-rise motor inn offers some amenities found in higher-price hotels: spacious rooms, king-size beds, and oversize desks. ✉ *2508 Elm Hill Pike, 37214,* ☎ *615/883–9500 or 800/321–2211,* FAX *615/883–0172,* WEB *www.courtyard.com. 145 rooms. Restaurant, pool, exercise room. AE, D, DC, MC, V.*

$$ **Hampton Inn Vanderbilt.** The rooms at this contemporary inn near Vanderbilt University are colorful and spacious. There's a hospitality suite for social or business use. ✉ *1919 West End Ave., 37203,* ☎ *615/329–1144 or 800/426–7866,* FAX *615/320–7112,* WEB *www.hamptoninn.com. 171 rooms. Pool. AE, D, DC, MC, V. CP.*

$ **Comfort Inn Hermitage.** Near the Hermitage is this inn offering comfortable accommodations, some with water beds or whirlpool baths. ✉ *5768 Old Hickory Blvd., 37076,* ☎ *615/889–5060,* FAX *615/871–4137,* WEB *www.comfortinn.com. 106 rooms. Pool. AE, D, DC, MC, V. CP.*

$ **Wilson Inn.** Three miles from the Grand Ole Opry, this five-story hotel is also conveniently near Nashville's airport. Many rooms have kitchens. ✉ *600 Ermac Dr. (Elm Hill Pike exit from Briley Pkwy.), 37214,* ☎ *615/889–4466 or 800/333–9457,* FAX *615/889–0484,* WEB *www.wilsonhotels.com. 110 rooms. AE, D, DC, MC, V. CP.*

Nightlife and the Arts

Nightlife

The **Grand Ole Opry** (☞ Exploring, *above*) has packed in the crowds on Friday and Saturday nights since 1925. At the famous **Bluebird Cafe** (✉ 4104 Hillsboro Rd., ☎ 615/383–1461), country singers try out their latest material. **Exit/In** (✉ 2208 Elliston Pl., ☎ 615/321–4400) showcases the most cutting-edge blues and rock bands from the United States and beyond. Groove to the music in an unpretentious atmosphere. In the District, check out the **Wild Horse Saloon** (✉ 120 2nd Ave. N, ☎ 615/251–1000, WEB www.wildhorsesaloon.com), which offers daily two-step lessons in the early evening. Bring the family to learn on weekend afternoons. The local branch of the **Hard Rock Cafe** (✉ 100 Broadway, ☎ 615/742–9900, WEB www.hardrock.com) is packed with rock memorabilia from around Nashville and the world.

The Arts

The **Tennessee Performing Arts Center** (✉ 505 Deaderick St., ☎ 615/782–4000) is the venue for performances by the **Nashville Ballet** (☎ 615/297–2966, WEB www.tpac.org), **Nashville Opera** (☎ 615/832–5242), **Nashville Symphony Orchestra** (☎ 615/783–1200), and **Tennessee Repertory Theatre** (☎ 615/244–4878, WEB www.tnrep.org). The center's Andrew Jackson Hall also hosts touring Broadway shows. Call **Ticketmaster** (☎ 615/255–2787) for tickets and information about arts events. In the second week of June, the **International Country Music Fan Fair** brings country music stars and their fans face to face at the Tennessee State Fairgrounds.

Spectator Sports

Football: Nashville's new **Adelphia Coliseum** (✉ 1 Titans Way, ☎ 615/565–4200, WEB www.titansonline.com) is home to the NFL's **Tennessee Titans.** The 67,000-seat, natural-grass stadium, which opened in 1999, sits on the banks of the Cumberland River. **Hockey: Nashville Arena** (✉ 501 Broadway, ☎ 615/770–7825, WEB www.arenafootball.com) hosts the NHL's **Nashville Predators,** an expansion team that first played here in 1998. **Baseball:** The **Nashville Sounds,** a AAA farm team of the Pittsburgh Pirates, play at Herschel Greer Stadium (✉ 534 Chestnut St., ☎ 615/242–4371, WEB www.nashvillesounds.com) just south of downtown, off I–65.

Shopping

New **Opry Mills** (✉ 433 Opry Mills Dr.) offers more than a million square feet of stores, restaurants, and entertainment spots. In addition to mall perennials such as Bass, Barnes & Noble, and multiple movie screens, this supercomplex also houses a bluegrass showcase, a simulated race-car speedway, and an IMAX theater. The huge **Bellevue Center** mall, in southwest Nashville (✉ Bellevue exit from I–40, ☎ 615/646–8690, WEB www.bellevuecenter.com), has more than 120 stores. Twenty-five miles east of Nashville, the **Prime Outlets of Lebanon** (✉ Exit 238 off I–40 East, Lebanon, ☎ 615/444–0433) are a favorite of locals looking for deals on Brooks Brothers, Ralph Lauren, Nike, and more. The shops along **8th Avenue South** make a good browsing ground for antiques lovers. For the latest look in country-and-western wear, two-step over to the **District** (☞ Exploring Nashville, *above*).

Nashville Essentials

AIRPORTS AND TRANSFERS

Nashville International Airport, about 8 mi east of downtown, is served by most major airlines.

➤ AIRPORT INFORMATION: **Nashville International Airport** (✉ 1 Terminal Dr., ☎ 615/275–1600, WEB www.nashintl.com).

AIRPORT TRANSFER

To reach downtown by car, take I–40 west. Cab fare runs about $20 plus tip. Downtown Airport Express has service to downtown hotels at $11 to $17 for a round-trip.

➤ TAXIS AND SHUTTLES: **Downtown Airport Express** (☎ 615/275–1180.)

BUS TRAVEL TO AND FROM NASHVILLE

➤ BUS INFORMATION: **Greyhound** (✉ 200 8th Ave. S, ☎ 615/255–3556 and 800/231–2222).

BUS TRAVEL WITHIN NASHVILLE

Metropolitan Transit Authority (MTA) buses serve the county; fare is $1.45 in exact change.

➤ BUS INFORMATION: **Metropolitan Transit Authority** (☎ 615/862–5950, WEB www.rta-ride.org).

CAR TRAVEL

I–65 leads into Nashville from the north and south; I–24, from the northwest and southeast; I–40, from the east and west. I–440 loops around the city.

TRANSPORTATION AROUND NASHVILLE

The central city is bisected by the Cumberland River; numbered avenues are west of and parallel to it, numbered streets east of and parallel to it. Nashville Trolley Company trolleys cover downtown and Music Row in summer months; the fare is lower than the MTA buses.

➤ CONTACTS: **Nashville Trolley Company** (☎ 615/862–5950).

VISITOR INFORMATION

➤ TOURIST INFORMATION: **Nashville Convention & Visitors Bureau** (✉ 161 4th Ave. N, 37219, ☎ 615/259–4700, WEB www.browncounty.com). **Visitor information center** (✉ 501 Broadway, 37219, ☎ 615/259–4747, WEB www.nashvillecvb.com).

EAST TENNESSEE

From the Great Smoky Mountains to the rippling waters of the Holston, French Broad, Nolichucky, and Tennessee rivers, East Tennessee offers a cornucopia of scenic grandeur and recreational opportunities.

Mountain folkways may persist in certain smaller communities, but cities such as Knoxville and Chattanooga are modern and quite diverse.

Exploring East Tennessee

Founded in 1786, **Knoxville** became the first state capital when Tennessee was admitted to the Union in 1796. This scenic city at the foothills of the Great Smoky Mountains continues to grow with **Volunteer Landing,** a development along the Tennessee River with shops, restaurants, and residential space. Knoxville is home to the main campus of the **University of Tennessee,** as well as the headquarters of the **Tennessee Valley Authority** (TVA), with its vast complex of hydroelectric dams and recreational lakes. The TVA was a massive work project initiated by Franklin Delano Roosevelt in 1933 as part of the New Deal.

Among the historic sites in Knoxville is the 1792 **Governor William Blount Mansion,** where the governor and his associates planned the admission of Tennessee as the 16th state in the Union. ✉ *200 W. Hill Ave.,* ☎ *865/525–2375,* WEB *www.blountmansion.org.* 🎟 *$4.95. Closed Sun. and weekends Dec.–Mar.*

The **Armstrong-Lockett House,** an 1834 farm mansion, is a showcase of American 19th-century and English furniture and silver. ✉ *2728 Kingston Pike,* ☎ *865/637–3163* WEB *www.korrnet.org.* 🎟 *$5. Closed Mon. and Jan.–Feb.*

Housed in the 1874 U.S. Customs House, the **East Tennessee Historical Center** displays books and artifacts relating to the history of the state. ✉ *600 Market St.,* ☎ *865/215–8830,* WEB *www.east-tennessee-history.org.* 🎟 *Free.*

The **Knoxville Museum of Art** has four exhibition galleries with contemporary prints, drawings, and paintings. Shows feature local, national, and international artists and have included Indian art, landscapes, photography, and late 1980s art. ✉ *1050 World's Fair Park Dr.,* ☎ *865/525–6101,* WEB *www.knoxart.org.* 🎟 *$3. Closed Mon.*

The **Knoxville Zoological Gardens** is famous for its reptile complex and for its breeding of large cats and African elephants. ✉ *Rutledge Pike S, Exit 392 off I–40,* ☎ *865/637–5331,* WEB *www.knoxville-zoo.org.* 🎟 *$8. Closed Sun.*

Kids like the hands-on displays and audiovisual exhibits at the **East Tennessee Discovery Center and Akima Planetarium.** ✉ *516 N. Beaman St.,* ☎ *865/594–1480,* WEB *www.korrnet.org.* 🎟 *$3. Closed Sun.*

Gatlinburg, the busy, tourist-oriented northern gateway to **Great Smoky Mountains National Park** is southeast of Knoxville via U.S. 441/321.Set in the narrow valley of the Little Pigeon River (actually a turbulent mountain stream), Gatlinburg has an abundance of family attractions, including the **Gatlinburg Sky Lift** (✉ 765 Parkway, Gatlinburg 37738, ☎ 865/436–4307, WEB www.gatlinburg-attractions.com; 🎟 $9) to the top of Crockett Mountain.

Pigeon Forge, about 6 mi north of Gatlinburg on U.S. 441, has factory outlet malls and family attractions.One Pigeon Forge highlight is **Dollywood,** Dolly Parton's popular theme park, with rides, live music, a re-created mountain village, and a water park. Dolly performs annually, usually in December. Other concerts between May and October are apt to include such stars as the Oak Ridge Boys or Lorrie Morgan. ✉ *1020 Dollywood La.,* ☎ *865/428–9488 or 800/365–5996,* WEB *www.dollywood.com.* 🎟 *$38.15. Closed Jan.–Apr.*

The **Gatlinburg/Pigeon Forge area** has many amusement parks and offbeat museums, such as Gatlinburg's **Guinness World Records Museum** (631 Parkway, Gatlinburg 37738, ☎ 865/436–9100, WEB www.gatlinburg.com; $8.95). **Newfound Gap,** south from Gatlinburg on scenic U.S. 441, provides a haunting view of the Tennessee–North Carolina border. From here a 7-mi spur road leads to **Clingmans Dome**—at 6,643 ft the highest point in Tennessee.

Chattanooga, a city of Civil War battlefields, museums of all kinds (art, antiques, history, even knives and tow trucks), and a famous choo-choo, is southwest of Knoxville off I–75. Begin your meandering here with a stop at the **Chattanooga Area Convention and Visitors Center Bureau** (✉ 2 Broad St., Chattanooga 37402, ☎ 423/266–711 or 800/322–3344, WEB www.chattanoogafun.com). Dominating Chattanooga's skyline is 2,215-ft **Lookout Mountain,** 6 mi away, with panoramic views and the world's steepest **Incline Railway** (✉ 827 E. Brow Rd., ☎ 423/821–4224, WEB www.lookoutmtnattractions.com; $9). From Lookout Mountain Scenic Highway, tours depart every 15 minutes to the 145-ft **Ruby Falls** (✉ 1720 S. Scenic Hwy., ☎ 423/821–2544, WEB www.rubyfalls.com; $11.50), 1,120 ft underground and reached by elevator.

★ The **Tennessee Aquarium** (✉ 1 Broad St., ☎ 423/265–0698 and 800/262–0695, WEB www.tnaqua.org; aquarium $12.95, IMAX theater $7.25) is the world's largest freshwater aquarium, with 350 species of fish, mammals, birds, reptiles, and amphibians; an IMAX theater is nearby. Surrounding the aquarium is **Ross's Landing Park and Plaza,** commemorating Chattanooga's Civil War history as well as its role as a major railroad town.

A restored Classical Revival mansion houses the **Hunter Museum of American Art** (✉ 10 Bluff View, ☎ 423/267–0968, WEB www.huntermuseum.org; $5), whose collection spans American art from the colonial period to the present day. The paintings, sculpture, furniture, and other art represent diverse artists such as Winslow Homer, Mary Cassatt, Thomas Hart Benton, George Segal, Duane Hanson, and Robert Rauschenberg.

The **Creative Discovery Children's Museum** (✉ 321 Chestnut St., ☎ 423/756–2738, WEB www.cdmfun.org; $7.95) has exhibits in four areas: invention, art, music, and science.

Oak Ridge, about 100 mi northeast of Chattanooga (take U.S. 27 to I–40 E or I–75 to I–40 W), is where atomic energy was secretly developed during World War II. The **American Museum of Science and Energy** focuses on the uses of nuclear, solar, and geothermal energy. *✉ 300 S. Tulane Ave., ☎ 865/576–3200, WEB www.amse.org. $3. Closed Mon.*

Dining and Lodging

Expect hearty food in the mountains: barbecued ribs, thick pork chops, and country ham with red-eye gravy.

For reservations in hotels, motels, chalets, and condominiums in Gatlinburg, contact **Smoky Mountain Accommodations Reservation Service** (✉ 103 Silverbell La., Gatlinburg 37738, ☎ 865/436–9700 or 800/231–2230; closed Sun.).

Chattanooga

$$–$$$$ ✕ **The Loft.** Locals and visitors alike flock to this cozy, candlelit restaurant for the extensive wine list and hearty specialties. The varied entrées include king crab legs, seafood fettuccine, and steak—all served with soup, salad, home-baked bread, fresh vegetables, and a baked potato or wild rice pilaf. ✉ *328 Cherokee Blvd.,* ☎ *423/266–3601. AE, D, DC, MC, V.*

$–$$$ ★ ✕ **212 Market.** Creative American cuisine is served at this hip spot directly across from the Tennessee Aquarium. The fish entrées are especially good, the homemade breads scrumptious, and the wine list impressive. ✉ *212 Market St.,* ☎ *423/265–1212,* WEB *www.212market.com. AE, D, DC, MC, V.*

$–$$ ✕ **Big River Grille Brewing & Works.** This restored trolley-warehouse has high ceilings, exposed-brick walls, and hardwood floors. You can watch the inner workings of the microbrewery through a soaring glass wall by the bar. The sandwiches and salads are large; wash them down with the sampler of six brews. ✉ *222 Broad St.,* ☎ *423/267–2739. AE, D, DC, MC, V.*

$–$$ ✕ **Town & Country.** Even though this classic "meat-and-three" across the bridge from the Tennessee Aquarium seats more than 425, expect to wait for the mouthwatering southern cuisine, from vegetable plates to steaks. ✉ *110 N. Market St.,* ☎ *423/267–8544. AE, D, DC, MC, V.*

$$–$$$$ **Bluff View Inn.** Chattanooga's best B&B comprises three turn-of-the-20th-century Mansions hugging a bluff high above the Tennessee River as part of the Bluff View Art District. The complex includes two more houses, three restaurants, and a sculpture garden. Tastefully decorated bedrooms have whirlpool baths and fireplaces. ✉ *412 E. 2nd St., 37403,* ☎ *423/265–5033 or 800/725–8338,* FAX *423/757–0120,* WEB *www.tennessee-inns.com. 16 rooms. 3 restaurants. AE, DC, MC, V. BP.*

$$ **Chattanooga Choo-Choo Holiday Inn.** The hotel adjoins the 1905 Southern Railway Terminal, now a 30-acre complex with restaurants, shops, gardens, tennis courts, and an operating trolley. Rooms are comfortably furnished, and you can also stay in one of the 48 parlor cars. ✉ *1400 Market St., 37402,* ☎ *423/266–5000 or 800/465–4329,* FAX *423/265–4635,* WEB *www.choochoo.com. 361 rooms. 5 restaurants, pools. AE, D, DC, MC, V.*

$$ **Chattanooga Marriott.** One of the city's largest hotels, it's convenient to town attractions. Rooms compare to those at any Marriott, offering corporate comfort a couple of notches above Holiday Inn. ✉ *2 Carter Plaza, 37402,* ☎ *423/756–0002 or 800/841–1674,* FAX *423/266–2254,* WEB *www.marriott.com. 342 rooms. Restaurant, pool, health club. AE, D, DC, MC, V.*

$ ★ **Read House.** The Georgian-style Read House, on the National Register of Historic Places, dates from the 1920s and has been restored to its original grandeur. Guest rooms in the main hotel continue the Georgian motif; rooms in the annex are contemporary. ✉ *827 Broad St., 37402,* ☎ *423/266–4121,* FAX *423/267–6447,* WEB *www.readhouse.com. 238 rooms. 2 restaurants, pool. AE, D, DC, MC, V.*

Gatlinburg

$$–$$$ ✕ **Burning Bush Restaurant.** Reproduction furnishings evoke the colonial era, but the menu leans toward Continental. Specialties include broiled Tennessee quail. ✉ *1151 Parkway,* ☎ *865/436–4669,* WEB *burningbushrestaurant.com. AE, D, DC, MC, V.*

$$–$$$ ✕ **Smoky Mountain Trout House.** Trout is prepared 15 ways; otherwise, choose prime rib, country ham, or fried chicken. This restaurant is a truly rustic mountain cottage. ✉ *410 N. Parkway,* ☎ *865/436–5416. AE, DC, MC, V. Closed Dec.–Mar.*

$$$ ★ **Buckhorn Inn.** This country inn about 6 mi outside town has welcomed guests to its rustic rooms and one-bedroom cottages since 1938. The mountain views are spectacular. Breakfast and dinner are available for an extra charge. ✉ *2140 Tudor Mountain Rd., 37738,* ☎ *865/436–4668,* WEB *www.buckhorninn.com. 9 rooms, 7 cottages, two guest houses. Restaurant. D, MC, V.*

$$ ★ 🏨 **Holiday Inn SunSpree Resort.** Near the Convention Center and the Ober Gatlinburg aerial tramway, this hotel offers the Holidome Indoor Recreation Center, with a general store, whirlpool, sauna, and game area. ✉ *520 Airport Rd., 37738,* ☎ *865/436–9201 or 800/435–9201,* FAX *865/436–7974,* WEB *www.holiday-inn.com. 402 rooms. 2 restaurants, pools, gym. AE, D, DC, MC, V.*

$ 🏨 **Best Western Twin Islands Motel.** Even though it's in busy downtown Gatlinburg, this motel has a peaceful air, thanks to the Little Pigeon River, which flows past each room. ✉ *539 Parkway, 37738,* ☎ *865/436–5121,* FAX *865/436–6208,* WEB *www.bestwestern.com. 97 rooms, 10 suites. Restaurant, pool. AE, D, DC, MC, V.*

Knoxville

$$$–$$$$ ★ ✕ **Regas Restaurant.** This cozy Knoxville classic, with fireplaces and original art, has been around since 1919. The specialty, prime rib, is sliced to order and served with horseradish sauce. ✉ *318 Gay St.,* ☎ *865/637–9805. AE, D, DC, MC, V. Closed Sun. No lunch Sat.*

$$$ ✕ **Copper Cellar/Cumberland Grill.** A favorite of the college crowd and young professionals, the original downstairs Copper Cellar is cozy and intimate. Upstairs, the Cumberland Grill serves salads and sandwiches. Both serve outstanding desserts. ✉ *1807 Cumberland Ave.,* ☎ *865/673–3411,* WEB *www.coppercellar.com. AE, DC, MC, V.*

$–$$$ ★ 🏨 **Hyatt Regency Knoxville.** This handsome, contemporary adaptation of an Aztec pyramid sits atop a hill overlooking the city. An impressive eight-story atrium greets guests as they enter the hotel. ✉ *500 Hill Ave. SE, 37915,* ☎ *865/637–1234,* FAX *865/637–1193,* WEB *www.hyatt.com. 384 rooms. Restaurant, pool, gym. AE, D, DC, MC, V.*

$ 🏨 **Best Western Cedar Bluff Inn.** Between downtown Knoxville and Oak Ridge, this affordable hotel has rooms with spacious work areas. ✉ *420 Peters Rd. N, 37922,* ☎ *865/539–0058 or 800/348–2562,* FAX *865/539–4887,* WEB *www.bestwestern.com. 96 rooms. Pool. AE, D, DC, MC, V. CP.*

Nightlife and the Arts

Chattanooga

The **Memorial Auditorium** (✉ 399 McCaulley Ave., ☎ 423/757–5050) has been part of Chattanooga's cultural life for decades. The **Tivoli Theater** (✉ 709 Broad St., ☎ 423/757–5050) presents concerts and operas. The **Chattanooga Theatre Center** (✉ 400 River St., ☎ 423/267–8534, WEB www.theatrecentre.com) stages productions year-round.

Gatlinburg

Sweet Fanny Adams Theatre and Music Hall (✉ 461 Parkway, ☎ 865/436–4039 or 877/388–5484, WEB www.sweetfannyadamstheatre.com) stages original musical comedies and Gay '90s revues. At Ober Gatlinburg, the **Heidelberg Restaurant** (✉ 756 Parkway, ☎ 865/430–9256, WEB www.oldheidelbergcastle.com) has dancing and a show starring international entertainers, mostly German, from 5:30 to 11.

Knoxville

The **Bijou Theater** (✉ 803 S. Gay St., ☎ 865/522–0832, WEB www.bijoutheatre.com) offers seasonal ballet, concerts, and plays. **Clarence Brown/Carousel Theatre,** on the University of Tennessee campus (☎ 865/974–5161, WEB www.web.utk.edu), is a theater-in-the-round with student and professional actors. **Old City,** on the north side of downtown, has lively restaurants, clubs, and shops. Try **Lucille's** (✉ 106 N. Central St., ☎ 865/546–3742), in Old City, for jazz. For dancing, there's the **Underground** (✉ 214 W. Jackson Ave., ☎ 865/525–3675), in Old City. **Patrick Sullivan's** (✉ 100 N. Central St., ☎ 865/637–4255) has saloon-style food and live rock and roll on weekends.

Outdoor Activities and Sports

Fishing

East Tennessee's lakes offer seasonal angling for striped bass, walleye, white bass, and muskie. **Gatlinburg**'s streams and rivers are stocked with trout from April to November. There are boat-launch ramps at **Norris Dam State Park** (☎ 865/494–8138), on Lake Norris (with 700 mi of shoreline), located north of Knoxville. **Booker T. Washington State Park** (☎ 423/894–4955, WEB www.state.tn.us/environment/parks), along Lake Chickamauga near Chattanooga, has boat-launch ramps and a fishing pier.

Golf

East Tennessee courses open to the public include 18-hole, par-72 **Brainerd Golf Course** (✉ 5203 Old Mission Rd., ☎ 423/855–2692), in Chattanooga; 18-hole, par-70 **Whittle Springs Public Golf Course** (✉ 3113 Valley View Dr., ☎ 865/525–1022), in Knoxville; and 18-hole, par-72 **Sunterra's Bent Creek Golf Resort** (✉ 3919 East Parkway, ☎ 865/436–2875), in Gatlinburg.

Hiking

A scenic portion of the **Appalachian Trail** runs along high ridges in the Great Smoky Mountains National Park (✉ Gatlinburg, ☎ 865/436–1200). The trail can be reached at Newfound Gap, off U.S. 441.

Horseback Riding

McCarter's Riding Stables (✉ U.S. 441 south of Gatlinburg, ☎ 865/436–5354) is open mid-March–October.

Rafting and Canoeing

East Tennessee has five white-water rivers: Ocoee, Hiwassee, French Broad, Tellico, and Nolichucky. The rafting season runs from April to early November. **Outdoor Adventures** (✉ 629 Welcome Valley Rd., Ocoee, ☎ 800/627–7636, WEB www.raft.com) offers ropes courses as well as rafting and tubing on the Ocoee. **Wildwater, Ltd.** (✉ Ducktown, ☎ 800/451–9972, WEB www.wildwaterrafting.com) organizes rafting, canoeing, and kayaking on the Ocoee and Pigeon rivers. **Rafting in the Smokies** (✉ 2470 East Parkway, Gatlinburg, ☎ 865/436–5008 or 800/776–7238, WEB www.raftinginthesmokes.com) has rafting and tubing trips for all levels of adventure seekers.

Shopping

At the **Great Smoky Arts and Crafts Community** (✉ Glades and Buckhorn Rds. off U.S. 321, 3 mi east of Gatlinburg, ☎ 865/671–3600 ext. 3504 or 800/568–4748, WEB www.smokymtnarts-crafts.com), a collection of 80 shops and crafts studios along 8 mi of country road, you can watch crafters at work and buy their wood carvings, dulcimers, quilts, and other Appalachian folk crafts. Pigeon Forge is famous for its **factory outlet malls** on U.S. 441. **Warehouse Row** (✉ 12th and Market Sts., ☎ 423/267–1111) in Chattanooga contains factory outlets for such top brands as Ellen Tracy, Ralph Lauren, Tommy Hilfiger, and Perry Ellis. Chattanooga's **Bluff View Art District,** around East 2nd Street and Bluff View, on the cliffs overlooking the Tennessee River, is a pleasant destination for art lovers. It offers a handful of restaurants, galleries, and bakeries along narrow, cobblestone streets next to the Hunter Museum of American Art.

East Tennessee Essentials

AIRPORTS

Knoxville Airport, served by Airtran, American Eagle, Continental Express, Delta, Northwest, TWA, United, and US Airways, is about 12 mi from town. The Chattanooga Airport, served by ASA, ComAir, Delta, Northwest Airlink, United Express, and US Airways, is about 8 mi from town.

➤ AIRPORT INFORMATION: **Chattanooga Airport** (✉ 1001 Airport Rd., ☎ 423/855–2200, WEB www.chattairport.com). **Knoxville Airport** (✉ 2055 Alcoa Hwy., ☎ 865/342–2900 or 865/342–3333, WEB www.tys.org).

BUS TRAVEL

Greyhound has stops in Chattanooga and in Knoxville.

➤ BUS INFORMATION: **Greyhound** (☎ 423/892–1277 or 800/231–2222 in Chattanooga; 865/522–5144 or 800/231–2222 in Knoxville; WEB www.greyhound.com).

CAR TRAVEL

I–75 runs north–south from Kentucky through Knoxville, then to Chattanooga. I–81 heads southwest from the Virginia border at Bristol, ending at I–40 northeast of Knoxville. I–40 enters from North Carolina and continues west to Knoxville, Nashville, and Memphis.

VISITOR INFORMATION

➤ TOURIST INFORMATION: **Chattanooga Area Convention and Visitors Bureau** (✉ 2 Broad St., 37402, ☎ 423/756–8687 or 800/322–3344, WEB www.chattanoogafun.com). **Knoxville Area Convention and Visitors Bureau: Gateway Visitors Center** (✉ 900 Volunteer Landing La., Suite 200-B, Knoxville 37915, ☎ 865/523–7263 or 800/727–8045, WEB www.knoxville.org).

TEXAS

Updated by Kim Harwell, Elizabeth McGuire, and Robin Sussman

Capital	Austin
Population	20,851,820
Motto	Friendship
State Bird	Mockingbird
State Flower	Bluebonnet
Postal Abbreviation	TX

Statewide Visitor Information

Texas Department of Tourism (✉ Box 12728, Austin 78711, ☏ 800/888–8839, WEB www.traveltex.com).

Scenic Drives

In far southwest Texas, **Route 170** from Lajitas through Presidio and into the Chinati Mountains is one of the most spectacular drives in the state, plunging over mountains and through canyons along the Rio Grande. **U.S. 83** from Leakey to Uvalde is a roller coaster of a ride through the lush western edges of Hill Country, in central Texas. In the northern panhandle, **I–27** from Lubbock to Amarillo carries you through the buffalo grass and high, flat lands of the Llano Estacado, or Staked Plains. It's thought that they were named for the stakes settlers drove into the treeless, featureless ground as landmarks. From Center, a small town near the Louisiana border, south into the Sabine National Forest, **Route 87** takes you over several dramatic lakes and through one of the huge pine forests for which east Texas is famous.

National and State Parks

National Parks

★ **Big Bend National Park** (✉ U.S. 385 from Marathon [Box 129, 79834], ☏ 915/477–2251, WEB www.nps.gov/bibe), the state's premier natural attraction, is an 801,163-acre landscape laid bare by millions of years of erosion, with spectacular canyons, a junglelike floodplain, the sprawling Chihuahuan Desert, and the cool woodlands of the Chisos Mountains. Though the park has hundreds of campsites, the only hotel is the **Chisos Mountain Lodge** (☏ 915/477–2291, WEB www.chisosmountainslodge.com), which is often booked months in advance.

Canoeing and camping are top draws to **Davy Crockett National Forest** (✉ Rte. 1 [Box 55 FS, Kennard 75847], ☏ 936/655–2299), a 161,842-acre park in the "piney woods" of east Texas, about 20 mi east of the historic town of Crockett on Route 7.

Aransas National Wildlife Refuge (✉ Rte. 2040 [Box 100, Austwell 77950], ☏ 512/286–3559), on a peninsula jutting 12 mi into the Gulf of Mexico near Rockport, is the principal wintering ground of the endangered whooping crane; the best time to spot them and some 300 other species of birds is between November and April.

State Parks

You can call a **central reservations number** (☏ 512/389–8900) to book any campsite in the Texas state park system.

In East Texas, **Caddo Lake State Park** (✉ Rte. 43, Karnack 75661, ☏ 903/679–3351, WEB www.tpwd.state.tx.us/park/caddo) occupies 484 acres on the southern shore of the lake, including campgrounds, cabins, and facilities for fishing, swimming, and boating.

Named after the local term for "high plains," **Caprock Canyons State Park** (✉ Rte. 1065, Quitaque 79255, ☎ 806/455–1492, WEB www.tpwd.state.tx.us/park/caprock), in the panhandle, is marked by canyons, striking geologic formations, and an abundance of wildlife, including African aoudad, buffalo, antelope, and golden eagles.

Enchanted Rock State Natural Area (✉ 16710 Ranch Rd. 965, Fredericksburg 78624, ☎ 915/247–3903, WEB www.tpwd.state.tx.us/park/enchantd), 18 mi north of Fredericksburg in the Hill Country, is so named partly because of the strange noises emitted by the underground heating and cooling of its massive, 425-ft-high dome of solid pink granite. The rock is the reputed site of ancient human sacrifices and is the second-largest batholith (underground rock formation uncovered by erosion) in the United States. The park closes when parking capacity is reached, which can be as early as 11 AM on weekends.

Fishing is the draw at **Inks Lake State Park** (✉ 3630 Park Rd. 4 W, Burnet 78611, ☎ 512/793–2223, WEB www.tpwd.state.tx.us/park/inks), northwest of Austin at the edge of the Hill Country.

★ On the high plains 12 mi east of the panhandle town of Canyon is **Palo Duro Canyon State Park** (✉ 11450 Park Rd. 5, Canyon 79015, ☎ 806/488–2227, WEB www.tpwd.state.tx.us/park/paloduro), site of the last great battle with the Comanche. Among its rock spires and precipitous cliffs is an outdoor amphitheater where the historical drama *Texas* is presented each summer.

HOUSTON AND GALVESTON

Unbridled energy has always been **Houston**'s trademark. Once a swamp near the junction of the Buffalo and White Oak bayous, Houston is now the nation's fourth-largest city and a world energy center, where exploration is pushed as far as outer space—indeed, the first words spoken from the moon were "Houston, Tranquility Base here. The Eagle has landed."

Houston is an international business hub and the energy capital of the United States. Additionally, medical institutions spawned from the discoveries of the famous heart transplant team of Cooley and DeBakey and research conducted at M.D. Anderson Cancer Center have earned Houston its reputation as a top-notch healing center. Excellent museums, galleries, and performance halls affirm the city's commitment to the arts, and its many ethnic restaurants add to the cosmopolitan flavor.

One of Texas's most popular year-round coastal destinations, **Galveston** is an island in the Gulf of Mexico 50 mi southeast of Houston, connected to the mainland by a causeway and bridge. The restored Victorian Strand district, resort hotels, and beachfront businesses are on the busy north end of the island, while miles of sandy beaches, and private and rental residences, are on the southern end.

Once one of the world's great port cities, Galveston was nearly devastated by a hurricane in 1900. In the 1950s, preservationists launched Galveston's renaissance by restoring stately homes and building commercial districts. The result is a resort city with a southern flair—a petite and blended version of New Orleans and Charleston.

Exploring Houston and Galveston

Houston

Houston can be divided neatly into three major areas. One is its very modern downtown (including the theater district), which spurred one architecture critic to declare the city "America's future." Another is the area a couple of miles south of downtown, where some of the Southwest's leading museums are found along with Rice University and the internationally renowned Texas Medical Center. Finally, there is the thriving shopping and business center west of downtown, known as both the Galleria and Uptown.

DOWNTOWN

Start by taking in the entire urban panorama from the observation deck (weekdays only) of I. M. Pei's 75-story **Chase Tower** (✉ 600 Travis St.), built in 1981. **Texas Avenue,** visible from the tower, is 100 ft wide, precisely the width needed to accommodate 14 Texas longhorns tip to tip in the days when cattle were driven to market along this route. **Tranquility Park** (✉ between Walker and Rusk Sts. east of Smith St.), a cool oasis of fountains and walkways, was built to commemorate the first landing on the moon by the *Apollo 11* mission.

The major buildings of the theater district (www.houstontheaterdistrict.org) are a few steps from Tranquility Park. The **Jesse H. Jones Hall for the Performing Arts** (✉ 615 Louisiana St., ☎ 713/227–1910 or 800/828–2787), home to the Houston Symphony Orchestra and the Society for the Performing Arts, appears almost encased by a second, colonnaded building; its teak auditorium is more attractive than the exterior. The **Alley Theatre** (✉ 615 Texas Ave., ☎ 713/228–8421 or 800/259–2553, WEB www.alleytheatre.org), a fortresslike low-lying structure, is the venue of the city's resident professional theater company. At the **Gus S. Wortham Theater Center** (✉ 500 Texas Ave., ☎ 713/237–1439 or 800/828–2787, WEB www.wortham.org), the Houston Grand Opera and the Houston Ballet perform in two side-by-side theaters. **Bayou Place** (✉ 520 Texas Ave., ☎ 713/693–1600) is a huge dining and entertainment complex including an art-house cinema and theater. The **Verizon Wireless Theater** (☎ 713/225–8551, WEB www.verizonwireless.com), formerly the Aerial, hosts live performance from jazz to comedy. **City Hall** (✉ 901 Bagby St., ☎ 713/247–1000), which has a visitor center on the ground floor, is northwest of Tranquility Park, in a 1939 modernist structure of Texas limestone designed by Joseph Finger, Houston's premier architect of the time.

Architectural additions to the skyline have spread out from the **Smith-Louisiana corridor,** a daunting canyon formed by towers of glass and steel, running south from Tranquility Park on the west side of downtown. A walk down these streets may be the truest measure of the city's modernism, intensified by the **outdoor sculptures** of Joan Miró, Claes Oldenburg, Louise Nevelson, and Jean Dubuffet. (Dubuffet's *Monument au Fantôme,* on Louisiana Street between Lamar and Dallas streets, is a particular delight to children.) The downtown area is experiencing a vigorous revival with residential and entertainment space being reclaimed in famous old commercial buildings such as the stately **Rice Hotel** (1913) and the **Albert Thomas Convention Center** (1963). **Minute Maid Field** (formerly Enron Field) is a state-of-the-art baseball stadium with a retractable roof to defy Houston's frequently changing weather. The stadium incorporates the 1911 **Union Station** (designed by Warren and Wetmore of New York's Grand Central Station fame), which houses the ball club offices, retail stores, and **Ruggles Café** (☎ 713/259–8070).More than 70 of the major business and government buildings downtown are connected by a 6¾-mi labyrinth of **underground tunnels and skywalks,** used by those in the know as a welcome escape from the heat and humidity for which Houston is justly infamous. Walking tours of Houston's remarkable downtown art and architecture, and its fascinating tunnel system, are available through **Greater Houston**

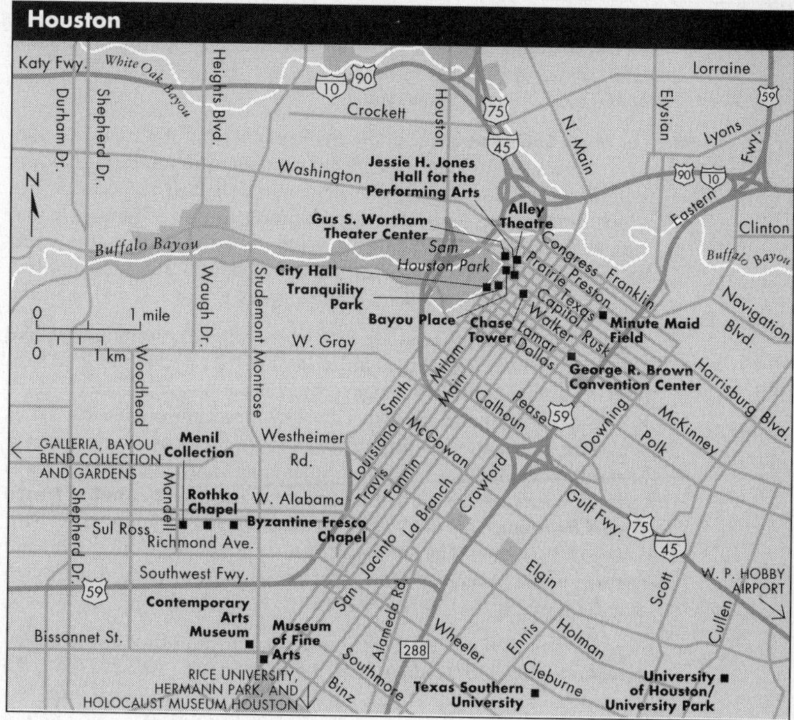

Preservation Alliance (☎ 713/216–5000), **Discover Houston Tours** (☎ 713/222–9255), and the **Houston Chapter of the American Institute of Architects** (☎ 713/520–0155).

THE MUSEUM DISTRICT

Most museums are clustered within an area bordering the verdant campus of **Rice University,** one of Texas's finest educational institutions, and **Hermann Park,** the city's playground. Walking from one institution to the other is possible, but the expanse can be taxing; it's best to segment your visit.

The **Museum of Fine Arts** is remarkable for the completeness of its enormous collection, housed in a complicated series of wings and galleries, many designed by Ludwig Mies van der Rohe. The Audrey Jones Beck Building, the work of famed Spanish architect Rafael Maneo, opened in 2000, doubling the museum's size. Renaissance and 18th-century art is particularly well represented, and there's a nice selection of Impressionist and Post-Impressionist works. ✉ *1001 Bissonnet St., north of Rice University, between Montrose Blvd. and Main St.,* ☎ *713/639–7300,* WEB *www.mfah.org.* 🎟 *$5, free Thurs. Closed Mon.*

The **Lillie and Hugh Roy Cullen Sculpture Garden** (✉ 1001 Bissonnet St., at Montrose Ave.; 🎟 free), across the street from the Museum of Fine Arts, displays 19th- and 20th-century sculptures by Rodin, Matisse, Giacometti, and Stella in an outdoor space designed by Isamu Noguchi.

In a stark, cylindrical edifice, the **Holocaust Museum Houston** (✉ 5401 Caroline St., ☎ 713/942–8000; 🎟 free) is a memorial and education center. The main exhibit, "Bearing Witness: A Community Remembers," can be viewed individually or by tour. The 30-minute film *Voices* is an oral history by local survivors.

The **Contemporary Arts Museum,** housed in an aluminum-sheathed trapezoid, is the home of avant-garde art in Houston, with many traveling exhibitions. ✉ *5216 Montrose Blvd.,* ☎ *713/284–8250,* WEB *www.camh.org.* 🎫 *Free. Closed Mon.*

★ The **Menil Collection** is one of the city's premier cultural treasures. Italian architect Renzo Piano designed the spacious building, with its airy galleries. John and Dominique de Menil collected the eclectic art, which ranges from tribal African sculptures to Andy Warhol's paintings of Campbell's soup cans. A separate gallery across the street houses the paintings of American artist Cy Twombly. ✉ *1515 Sul Ross St.,* ☎ *713/525–9400,* WEB *www.menil.org.* 🎫 *Free. Closed Mon.–Tues.*

Adjacent to the lawns surrounding the Menil complex, the moody **Rothko Chapel** (✉ 3900 Yupon St., at Sul Ross St., ☎ 713/524–9839; 🎫 free) is an octagonal sanctuary designed by Philip Johnson. Fourteen Mark Rothko paintings panel the chapel's walls. Outside the ecumenical chapel is Barnett Newman's sculpture *Broken Obelisk,* which symbolizes the life and assassination of Martin Luther King Jr.Frescoes from a 13th-century votive chapel have been preserved in the **Byzantine Fresco Chapel Museum,** a block from the Rothko (✉ 4011 Yupon St., ☎ 713/521–3990; 🎫 free). The dome and apse were rescued from thieves and restored under a unique arrangement with the Greek Orthodox Church and the Republic of Cyprus.

Across town in the River Oaks residential neighborhood, the **Bayou Bend Collection and Gardens** (✉ 1 Westcott St., ☎ 713/639–7750, WEB www.mfah.org; 🎫 home $10, gardens $3 or $7 for guided tour) lets you step back in time to witness the elegant lifestyle of the first half of the 20th century. Noted Houston philanthropist and collector Ima Hogg donated the 28-room mansion, complete with period pieces dating back to the 1600s, to the Fine Arts Museum. Guided and self-guided tours must be scheduled in advance.

THE GALLERIA, OR UPTOWN, AREA

The **Galleria** is one of the country's most upscale commercial zones. On the west side of Houston, near the intersection of Westheimer Road and I–610, it started out as a single mall. Shopping complexes, office towers, hotels, and other businesses have sprung up around that mall, making the area one of the most important business districts in the city. Many of Houston's best restaurants are here; and the River Oaks neighborhood, with its multimillion-dollar mansions and garden parkways, is nearby.

OTHER NEIGHBORHOODS

Kids and adults can learn about space exploration at **Space Center Houston** (✉ 1601 NASA Rd. 1, off I–45, ☎ 281/244–2100, WEB www.spacecenter.org; 🎫 $12.95). Life on the deck of a space shuttle is simulated in the **Space Center Plaza.** In the **Kids Space Place,** children can ride on the lunar rover and try out tasks in the *Apollo* command module. The adjacent **Johnson Space Center** tour includes a visit to Mission Control and laboratories that simulate weightlessness and other space-related concepts. Allow several hours for your visit.

Perennial favorites, **Six Flags AstroWorld** and **WaterWorld** are enormous amusement and water parks adjacent to each other within the city perimeter (✉ 9001 Kirby Dr. at I–610, ☎ 713/799–1234; 🎫 AstroWorld $31.95, WaterWorld $16.95).

Detour off I–45 between Houston and Galveston to the **Kemah Boardwalk** (✉ Bradford and 2nd St., Kemah, ☎ 877/285–3624), a cluster of restaurants, amusement rides, game arcades, and inns on the bustling ship channel. It's a family-oriented destination where you can catch a Gulf breeze, eat seafood, and watch personal and commercial marine craft motor by.

Galveston

History and the waterfront are the main draws to Galveston, once the largest city in Texas. Its wealthy classes built the Victorian homes that give the island its elegant, turn-of-the-20th-century appearance. These homes as well as some beautifully restored iron-front commercial buildings are concentrated on the northern, or bay, side of the island and on Broadway. Also hugging the north rim of the island, from 9th to 51st Street, is the harbor, port to small fishing boats and shrimp trawlers and to the *Elissa,* the tall ship that is Galveston's pride and joy. The southern, or ocean, side of the island is lined with beaches, hotels, parks, and restaurants. The laid-back, easy-chair town explodes twice yearly for a Mardi Gras celebration (12 days in late February, early March) and Dickens on the Strand (first weekend of December).

THE STRAND AND BROADWAY

The **Strand,** especially the five blocks from 20th to 25th Street, is defined by the architecture of its 19th- and early 20th century buildings, many of which survived the storm of 1900 and are on the National Register of Historic Places. When Galveston was still a powerful port city—before the Houston Ship Channel was dug, diverting most boat traffic inland—this stretch, formerly the site of stores, offices, and warehouses, was known as the Wall Street of the South. As you stroll up the Strand, you'll pass dozens of shops, stores, and restaurants.

The **Center for Transportation and Commerce** (✉ 2500 Strand, ☎ 409/765–5700), which also houses the **Railroad Museum,** is an Art Deco building that was once the Santa Fe Railroad terminal. The **Tremont House,** a block from the Center for Transportation and Commerce, is an 1879 dry-goods warehouse converted into a hotel; full of Victorian elegance, it's considered the top hotel on the island. Two blocks south of the Strand, on Postoffice Street, is the revitalized arts area **Gallery Row,** where you'll find art galleries, antiques stores, and the **Grand 1894 Opera House** (☞ Nightlife and the Arts, *below*).

Broadway, a major thoroughfare 5 minutes by car (or 20 minutes by foot) south of the Tremont House, is where to find the "Broadway Beauties," three of the finest examples of historic restoration in Texas. The Victorian **Bishop's Palace** (✉ 1402 Broadway, ☎ 409/762–2475; 🎫 $6), a limestone-and-granite castle built in 1886 for Colonel Walter Gresham, has 11 rare stone and wood mantels—a testament to the colonel's fondness for fireplaces—and a wooden staircase that took 61 craftsmen seven years to carve.

Ashton Villa (✉ 2328 Broadway, ☎ 409/762–3933; 🎫 $5), a formal Italianate villa, was built in 1859 of brick—appropriately so, as owner James Moreau Brown started out as a humble mason. A freethinking man, Brown had to install curtains to shield modest guests from the naked Cupids painted on one wall. **Moody Mansion** (✉ 2618 Broadway, ☎ 409/762–7668; 🎫 $6), the residence of generations of one of Texas's most powerful families, was completed in 1895. Designed by English architect William Tyndall, the brick Richardsonian Romanesque manse withstood the great storm of 1900. Its interiors of exotic woods and gilded trim are filled with family heirlooms and personal effects.

THE ELISSA

In 1961 a marine archaeologist and naval historian named Peter Throckmorton spotted a rotting iron hulk in the shipyards outside Athens, Greece, and realized the 150-ft wreck was what remained of a beautiful square-rigger constructed in 1877. The Scottish-built **Elissa**—the oldest ship on the Lloyd's Register—has been restored by the Galveston Historical Foundation and hundreds of volunteers. The ship, which carried cargoes to ports around the world for 90 years, may be toured above and below decks and is the centerpiece of the **Texas Seaport Museum** (✉ Pier 21, ☎ 409/763–1877; $6). From the seawall you'll see dozens of offshore oil rigs. Climb aboard the **Ocean Star** (✉ Pier 19, ☎ 409/766–7827; $5) for a first-hand view of how the rigs operate and what life is like out on the huge platforms.

★ **Moody Gardens** (✉ 1 Hope Blvd., ☎ 409/741–8484 or 800/582–4673, WEB www.moodygardens.com; $7–$10 per venue, discount combination tickets available) is a multifaceted complex that teaches, entertains, and fascinates. Attractions include the 13-story **Aquarium Pyramid,** showcasing marine life from four oceans in tanks and touch pools; **Rainforest Pyramid,** a 40,000-square-ft tropical habitat for exotic flora and fauna; **Discovery Pyramid,** a joint venture with NASA featuring more than 40 interactive exhibits; and two **IMAX theaters,** one of which has a space adventure ride. Also, don't miss the **botanical garden** or **Hope Therapy Program,** an internationally recognized hippotherapy (rehabilitation through horseback riding) treatment center.

Another family favorite is the free, 15-minute ride on the **Port Bolivar Ferry** (✉ north of Stewart Beach on Ferry Rd.; parking available adjacent to ferry landing), which crosses Galveston Bay.

Parks, Gardens, and Zoos

Houston

Hermann Park, with its 545 acres of trees, lawns, duck-filled reflecting pools, picnic areas, and 18-hole golf course, is only a short drive south of downtown on Main Street. The **Houston Zoological Gardens** (✉ 1513 N. MacGregor St., ☎ 713/523–5888, WEB www.houstonzoo.org; $2.50) include a primate rain forest, petting zoo, and aquarium. The excellent **Museum of Natural Science** (✉ 1 Hermann Circle Dr., ☎ 713/639–4600, WEB www.hmns.org; $4 entry, plus additional charges for each venue; combination discount tickets available) includes the **Baker Planetarium, Cockrell Butterfly Center,** and **Wortham IMAX Theatre.**

Memorial Park, several miles west of downtown between the 610 Loop and South Shepherd Drive, has 1,500 acres of mostly virgin woodland—prime territory for walking, jogging, and biking. An **Arboretum and Nature Center** creates a sanctuary for native species. The small downtown **Sam Houston Park,** bounded by Bagby, McKinney, and Dallas streets, is a green space where several of the city's 19th-century buildings have been moved. Tickets for guided tours are available at the Heritage Society (☎ 713/655–1912; $4), on the Bagby side.

Galveston

Stewart Beach Park has a bathhouse, amusement park, bumper boats, miniature-golf course, and water coaster. ✉ *6th St. and Seawall Blvd.,* ☎ *409/765–5023.* *$5 parking. Closed mid-Oct.–mid-Mar.* **Galveston Island State Park,** toward the western, unpopulated end of the island (✉ 3 Mile Rd., ☎ 409/737–1222; $3), is a 2,000-acre natural habitat ideal for birding, walking, and camping.

Dining

Houston

$$$$ ✕ **Morton's of Chicago.** For a fine steak dinner with a cosmopolitan flair, head to the Galleria. Morton's pampers you with choice cuts of aged beef, plus seafood, chicken, and exceptional wines. Save room for the sumptuous Godiva hot chocolate cake, the house specialty. ✉ *5000 Westheimer Rd.,* ☎ *713/629–1946. Reservations essential. AE, D, DC, MC, V.*

$$$–$$$$ ★ ✕ **Cafe Annie.** Chef Robert Del Grande, one of the founders of southwestern cuisine, serves up the best of his innovative, fiery cooking at this acclaimed restaurant. Start any meal with the layered Gulf crabmeat tostada, and then move on to the beef fillet roasted with coffee beans or the wood-grilled salmon served with a green chili mole. End with a *tres leches* (three-milk) cake. ✉ *1728 Post Oak Blvd.,* ☎ *713/840–1111. Reservations essential. AE, DC, MC, V.*

$$$–$$$$ ✕ **Pesce.** For a glamorous (and noisy) scene in River Oaks, head for this posh seafood newcomer brought to you by iconic Houston restaurateurs Damian Mandola and Johnny Carrabba (of Damian's Cucina Italiana and Carrabba's). The kitchen prepares catches from all over the world, from Gulf Coast shellfish to New Zealand barramundi. Anchor at the raw bar for Gulf oysters. ✉ *3029 Kirby Dr.,* ☎ *713/522–4858. Reservations essential. AE, D, DC, MC, V. Closed Sun.*

$$$–$$$$ ★ ✕ **Tony's.** Houston's culinary icon, Tony Vallone introduced European cuisine to the city when he opened his restaurant. An exceptional wine list complements artfully prepared dishes such as Sweetwater Hen Nancy (roasted hen served atop a wild-mushroom risotto with a morel-and-sherry sauce) and pan-seared halibut Strauss (lump crabmeat, caviar, and smoked salmon). ✉ *1801 Post Oak Blvd.,* ☎ *713/622–6778. Reservations essential. AE, D, DC, MC, V. Closed Sun. No lunch.*

$$–$$$$ ✕ **Brennan's.** A cousin of New Orleans's Commander's Palace, Brennan's puts a Texas spin on creole cuisine. The landmark building's interiors are as charming as the hospitality is southern-gracious. Chef Carl Walker's specialties, like turtle soup with sherry and pecan-crusted fish, repeatedly impress. Brunch in the peaceful courtyard is a memorable experience. ✉ *3300 Smith St.,* ☎ *713/522–9711. Reservations essential. AE, D, DC, MC, V.*

$$–$$$ ✕ **Ouisie's Table.** Here American cuisine is prepared with eclectic, southern accents. Dine in the main room, or request a table on adjoining Lucy's Porch for a view of the herb plantings snipped daily by the kitchen staff. Enjoy such favorites as chicken-fried steak salad with Roquefort dressing or a grilled lime redfish *chalupa* (a fried corn tortilla). There's a fabulous weekend brunch and an afternoon "little bites" menu. ✉ *3939 San Felipe Rd.,* ☎ *713/528–2264. AE, D, DC, MC, V.*

$–$$$ ✕ **Carrabba's.** After all these years, the original location of Carrabba's still packs them in. The bustling, trendy restaurant is the quintessential, inner-loop destination for reliable, Americanized Italian cooking. From steaming vessels of robust pasta dishes (heavy on the garlic) to crusty pizzas and hefty grilled meats, the kitchen fires on all cylinders to keep the customers happy. Service is fast and ultra-chummy. ✉ *3115 Kirby Dr.,* ☎ *713/522–3131. AE, D, DC, MC, V.*

$–$$ ✕ **Solero.** Professionals and arts patrons pack this chic downtown restaurant for Spanish and South American tapas—assorted hot and cold small plates. Exceptional paella and bouillabaisse showcase fresh Gulf Coast seafood. For dessert, try the Caribbean banana. Solero is an excellent choice for vegetarians. The Czar bar upstairs serves 71 types of vodka. ✉ *910 Prairie Ave.,* ☎ *713/227–2665. AE, D, MC, V. Closed Sun.–Mon.*

$ ✕ **Goode Company.** Down-home Texas barbecue is prepared ranch-style—smoked and served with tasty red sauce. Patrons line up on the sidewalk to eat at picnic tables on the covered patio. A standard order is the chopped-beef brisket sandwich on jalapeño-cheese bread. Don't miss the celebrated pecan pie for dessert. ✉ *5109 Kirby Dr.,* ☎ *713/522–2530. AE, D, DC, MC, V.*

$ ✕ **Irma's.** Irma and her family dish out home-style Mexican specialties to a wait-in-line breakfast and lunch crowd. There's no menu: your server will tell you what is available. Opt for the chicken and spinach enchiladas with green chili sauce. ✉ *22 N. Chenevert St.,* ☎ *713/222–0767. AE, DC, MC, V. Closed weekends.*

Galveston

$$–$$$ ✕ **Gaido's and Casey's.** Dine on linen at the venerable Gaido's or kick back casually at the adjacent Casey's. These family-owned restaurants have the same lineage, dating back to 1911, when Grandfather Gaido opened an eatery atop Murdoch's bathhouse. Adamant that the seafood be fresh, the kitchen here peels, shucks, and fillets by hand, just as in the early days. Gulf views are blocks wide at this landmark. ✉ *37th to 39th St. and Seawall Blvd.,* ☎ *409/762–9625. AE, DC, MC, V.*

$$–$$$ ✕ **Luigi's Ristorante Italiano.** Northern Italian cuisine is served trattoria-style in this converted 1895 bank building with muted sienna walls, a fruitwood-paneled bar, and mural-size replicas of Italian art. One taste of the chicken Parmesan or veal piccata and you will think you walked in off a piazza in Florence instead of the Strand on Galveston Bay. ✉ *2318 The Strand,* ☎ *409/763–6500. AE, D, DC, MC, V.*

$–$$$ ✕ **Fisherman's Wharf.** New restaurants have joined this harborside institution, but locals keep coming here for the fresh seafood and reasonable prices. Dine indoors or out, keeping an eye on traffic in the ship channel. Start off with a cold combo—boiled shrimp and grilled rare tuna. The fresh fish, shrimp, and oysters from the grill or fryer are hard to beat. ✉ *3901 Ave. O,* ☎ *409/765–5708. AE, D, DC, MC, V.*

$–$$$ ✕ **Saltwater Grill.** This restaurant is just what Galveston needed: a hip downtown spot with splendid seafood. Inventive dishes include a fried-asparagus and crab appetizer, yellowfin tuna over soba Thai noodles, and warm chocolate truffle cake. High-tech steam kettles stock fresh gumbo, and a lively bar makes any cocktail you like. ✉ *2017 Post Office St.,* ☎ *409/726–3474. AE, D, DC, MC, V.*

$–$$ ✕ **Mosquito Café.** This chichi eatery in Galveston's historic district serves fresh, contemporary food in a casual, high-ceilinged dining room or outdoor patio. Wake up to a fluffy egg frittata or a homemade scone topped with whipped cream. For lunch, there's big West Coast–inspired salads and the best BLT on the island; for dinner, grilled snapper or peppercorn steak with Parmesan grits. ✉ *628 14th St.,* ☎ *409/763–1010. AE, D, DC, MC, V.*

$ ✕ **The Phoenix.** Every community needs a gathering place for breakfast, and this bakery is it. The Phoenix brews a flavorful cup of java and espresso. Selections range from New Orleans beignets to country-style bacon and eggs. The pastry case is impossible to resist. Dining hours extend through lunch, with freshly prepared soups and sandwiches. ✉ *221 Tremont St.,* ☎ *409/763–4611. AE, D, DC, MC, V.*

Lodging

Houston

$$$$ 🏨 **Four Seasons Hotel.** This city-center hotel is convenient to the convention center, downtown businesses, and the ballpark. The Four Seasons offers deluxe amenities and top-notch service, making it a discriminating traveler's first choice. ✉ *1300 Lamar St., 77010,* ☎

713/650–1300 or 800/332–3442, FAX 713/650–8169, WEB *www.fourseasons.com. 399 rooms. 2 restaurants, pool, health club. AE, D, DC, MC, V.*

$$$$ **Houstonian Hotel, Club and Spa.** Spread over 18 acres in a wooded area near Memorial Park, the Houstonian has luxurious rooms and sports facilities galore—golf, tennis, a climbing wall, and indoor racket games. ✉ *111 N. Post Oak La., 77024,* ☎ *713/680–2626 or 800/231–2759,* FAX *713/680–2992,* WEB *www.houstonian.com. 286 rooms. 3 restaurants, pools, health club. AE, D, DC, MC, V.*

$$$$ **Lancaster.** In the heart of the theater district, this small luxury hotel has the feel of a European manor house. The Chippendale furniture, plaid upholstered chairs, oil landscapes and portraits, and brass cachepots contrast with the steel-and-glass surroundings. ✉ *701 Texas Ave., 77002,* ☎ *713/228–9500,* FAX *713/223–4528,* WEB *www.lancaster.com. 93 rooms. Restaurant, gym. AE, D, DC, MC, V.*

$$–$$$$ **Hotel Derek.** This is the perfect choice for the cosmopolitan traveler. Mod furnishings grace the glossy-floored lobby and the sleek, contemporary rooms. The hotel restaurant, Ling & Javier, serves fusion Chinese and Cuban cooking and also sustains a sizzling bar scene. ✉ *2525 W. Loop S, 77027,* ☎ *713/961–3000,* FAX *713/297–4392,* WEB *www.hotelderek.com. 314 rooms. Restaurant, pool, gym. AE, D, DC, MC, V.*

$$–$$$$ **Warwick Park Plaza.** The best location for museum hopping or having medical center appointments, the restored Warwick is noted for its spectacular views of Hermann Park and the downtown skyline. The richly paneled Hunt Room restaurant is perfect for special occasions. ✉ *5701 Main St., 77005,* ☎ *713/526–1991 or 800/670–7275,* FAX *713/526–0359,* WEB *www.srs-worldhotels.com. 308 rooms. 3 restaurants, pool, gym. AE, D, DC, MC, V.*

$$–$$$ **J. W. Marriott.** Across from the Galleria, this hotel is a shopper's haven. Business travelers enjoy easy access to Fortune 500 companies headquartered in the I–610/Uptown corridor. You can play basketball and racquetball. ✉ *5150 Westheimer Rd., 77056,* ☎ *713/961–1500 or 800/228–9290,* FAX *713/961–5045,* WEB *www.mariotthotels.com. 513 rooms. Restaurant, pool, health club. AE, D, DC, MC, V.*

Galveston

$$$–$$$$ **Moody Gardens Hotel.** This is one of the latest additions to the popular Moody Gardens complex, which includes a series of natural habitats housed in huge pyramids, parks, theaters, and water attractions. The contemporary, tropical-style, high-rise hotel has the best views of the Gulf, bay, gardens, and pyramids. The Texas-size outdoor pool surrounded by lush gardens and waterfalls is a playground for all ages. ✉ *1 Hope Blvd., 77554,* ☎ *409/744–1745 or 888/388–8484,* FAX *409/744–1631,* WEB *www.moodygardens.com. 303 rooms. 2 restaurants, pools, gym. AE, D, DC, MC, V.*

$$$–$$$$ **Tremont House.** Just steps off the Strand, this hotel recalls the grandeur of Victorian days. Once a busy dry-goods warehouse, Tremont House has rooms with soaring ceilings and 11-ft windows, as well as period furnishings. The four-story atrium lobby, with ironwork balconies and full-size palm trees, showcases an 1872 hand-carved rosewood bar. ✉ *2300 Ship's Mechanic Row, 77550,* ☎ *409/763–0300 or 800/996–3426,* FAX *409/763–1539,* WEB *www.wyndham.com. 127 rooms. Restaurant, pool. AE, DC, MC, V.*

$$$–$$$$ **The Victorian.** This condominium complex at the beach has ocean views from many of its balconies. One- and two-bedroom units have fully equipped kitchens. ✉ *6300 Seawall Blvd., 77551,* ☎ *409/740–3555 or 800/231–6363,* FAX *409/744–3801. 254 suites. Restaurant, pool, tennis, gym. AE, D, DC, MC, V.*

$$$ **Hotel Galvez.** This seaside grande dame was once called "Queen of the Gulf." The six-story Spanish colonial hotel, built in 1911, has been restored to its original splendor. The lobby, music hall, parlors, loggia, and veranda evoke memories of a bygone era. A pool, swim-up bar, and outdoor grill have been added to the tropical garden facing the sea. ✉ *2024 Seawall Blvd., 77550,* ☎ *409/765–7721 or 800/996–3426,* FAX *409/765–5780,* WEB *www.wyndham.com. 231 rooms. Restaurant, pool. AE, DC, MC, V.*

$$–$$$ **Stacia Leigh.** Step aboard a 120-ft vintage schooner for a harborside stay at a unique floating bed-and-breakfast berthed alongside the historic *Elissa.* Commissioned in the early 1900s by the founder of Renault automobile works, the yacht changed many hands and was once owned by Fascist Italian dictator Benito Mussolini. Completely restored from the hull out, the 11 staterooms and elegant salon use wicker furniture and multicolor quilts to create a coastal Americana feel. ✉ *Pier 22, Harborside Dr., 77550,* ☎ *409/750–8858,* WEB *www.stacia-leigh.com. 11 rooms. AE, D, DC, MC, V. BP.*

Nightlife and the Arts

Nightlife

There are other hot spots around Houston, but downtown is the main magnet for after-hours activity, with new clubs and restaurants springing up all the time in renovated storefronts and warehouses. **Bayou Place** (✉ 500 Texas Ave.), Houston's largest entertainment complex, is a 130,000-square-ft, two-story center of evening activity, with restaurants, clubs, a theater, and cinema. The Bayou's **Angelika Film Center** (☎ 713/255–1470), a spin-off of the famous NYC cinema, screens independent and foreign films, plus it offers timely before- or after-theater dinners. For jazz, head to **Sambuca** (✉ 909 Texas Ave., ☎ 713/224–5299). For blues, **Silky's** (✉ 4219 Washington Ave., ☎ 713/880–2990) is hard to beat. For fancy cocktails and late-night dancing (often swing), head for the **Mercury Room** (✉ 1008 Prairie Ave., ☎ 713/225–6372). A sister of the legendary Austin location (open since the 1950s), the **Continental Club** (✉ 3700 Main St., ☎ 713/529–9666) in Houston brings more loud, live music to an even bigger dance floor.

The Arts

HOUSTON

Houston is one of the few cities in the United States with four resident performance companies, which stage shows at **Jones Hall, Alley Theatre,** and **Gus S. Wortham Theater Center** (☞ Downtown *in* Exploring Houston and Galveston, *above*). Ticket information on the city's **symphony orchestra, opera, ballet,** and **theater** may be obtained by calling a **central ticketing facility** (☎ 713/227–2787 or 800/828–2787).

The largest professional African-American theater company, the **Ensemble Theater** (✉ 3535 Main St., ☎ 713/520–0055) appears in gripping performances on its own stage in the theater district.

Complete listings of events are carried in the *Houston Chronicle's* "Friday Weekend Preview," the *Houston Press,* and *Where* magazine.

GALVESTON

The **Grand 1894 Opera House** (✉ 2020 Postoffice St., ☎ 409/765–1894 or 800/821–1894), where performances of various kinds are held year-round, is worth visiting for the architecture alone. Sarah Bernhardt and Anna Pavlova both performed on this storied stage. The **Strand Street Theater** (✉ 2317 Ship's Mechanic Row, ☎ 409/763–4591) is another venue for variety theater.

Spectator Sports

Baseball: Houston Astros (✉ Astros Field, 1920 Preston Ave., ☎ 713/799–9500). **Basketball: Houston Rockets** (✉ Compaq Center, 10 Greenway Plaza, ☎ 713/627–3865). **Houston Comets (WNBA)** (✉ Compaq Center, 10 Greenway Plaza, ☎ 713/627–9622). **Football: Houston Texans** (✉ Reliant Stadium, 8400 Kirby Dr., ☎ 713/336–7700). **Hockey: Houston Aeros** (✉ Compaq Center, 10 Greenway Plaza, ☎ 713/627–2376). **Racing: TEXACO/Havoline Grand Prix** (☎ 713/739–7223) roars through downtown the last weekend of September as part of CART's (Championship Auto Racing Team) street circuit. **Rodeo:** The **Houston Livestock Show and Rodeo** takes place mid-February to early March in Reliant Stadium (✉ Reliant Stadium, 8400 Kirby Dr., ☎ 713/336–7700).

Beaches

Galveston's ocean beaches are all open to the public. The eastern end of the island, especially around Stewart Beach Park, has amenities of all kinds, including rentals of surfboards, Windsurfers, sailboats, chairs, and umbrellas. To the west are quieter, less crowded beaches. The seawall along the waterfront attracts runners, cyclists, and rollerbladers.

Shopping

Houston

The city's premier shopping area is the **Galleria,** or Uptown. Here, the **Galleria mall** (✉ Post Oak Blvd. and Westheimer Rd.) is famous for high-quality stores like Neiman Marcus, Saks Fifth Avenue, and Tiffany & Co. The **Pavilion on Post Oak** is a mall north of the Galleria mall. **Westheimer Road,** on the east side of I–610, expands the shopping area further with specialty retailers, superstores, and galleries. The headquarters for boots and other western gear is **Stelzig's Western Wear** (✉ 3123 Post Oak Blvd., ☎ 713/629–7779). Gift packs of sauces, cooking equipment, and stylish western wear are found at **Goode Company BBQ Hall of Flame** (✉ 5015 Kirby Dr., ☎ 713/643–5263). The **Village** (✉ University Blvd. and Kirby Dr.), next to Rice University, was Houston's first mall; it still has many small shops as well as some national names. For antiques, vintage clothing, and folk art, try the stores in the **Heights,** a re-gentrified neighborhood north of I–10 (19th Street between Heights Boulevard and Yale Street). You will find everything from treasures to junk at **Trader's Village Flea Market and RV Park** (✉ 7979 Eldridge Rd.), a 60-acre sprawl of merchants and peddlers open on Saturday and Sunday only. Admission is $2.

Gremillion & Co. (✉ 2501 Sunset Blvd., ☎ 713/522–2701) showcases contemporary art. **Nolan-Rankin** (✉ 4621 Montrose Blvd., ☎ 713/528–0664) focuses on the European masters.

Galveston

The historic stretches along the Strand and Gallery Row (Postoffice Street) are the best places to shop in Galveston. The **Old Strand Emporium** (✉ 2112 Strand, ☎ 409/763–9445) is a charming deli and grocery that is reminiscent of an old-fashioned ice cream parlor and sandwich shop, with candy bins, packaged nuts, and more. The shops at the Tremont House, **Gatherings and Sean Miles** (✉ 2300 Strand, ☎ 409/763–1770 or 409/763–7177), offer a fine selection of upscale women's apparel, accessories, and gifts. More than 50 antiques dealers are represented at **Eiband's Gallery** (✉ 2001 Postoffice St., ☎ 409/763–5495), an upscale showroom filled with furniture, books, art, and jewelry.

Houston and Galveston Essentials

AIRPORTS AND TRANSFERS

Houston's two major airports are served by about 22 airlines between them. The airport more convenient to downtown is W. P. Hobby Airport, 9 mi to the southeast. George Bush Intercontinental Airport, 15 mi north of downtown, is the city's international airport.

➤ AIRPORT INFORMATION: **George Bush Intercontinental Airport** (✉ 2800 North Terminal Rd., 77032, ☎ 281/230–3100, WEB www.houstonairportsystem.org). **W. P. Hobby Airport** (✉ 7800 Airport Blvd., 77061, ☎ 713/640–3000, WEB www.houstonairportsystem.org).

AIRPORT TRANSFER

During rush hour, the trip into the city from W. P. Hobby Airport takes about 45 minutes; taxi fare is about $20. The trip downtown from George Bush Intercontinental Airport during peak hours takes up to an hour; cab fare is about $32 (confirm the fee with your driver before setting out). Metro city express bus service to the George Bush costs $1.50. Airport Express van service connects several Houston hotels to both Hobby ($12) and the George Bush ($17).

Galveston Limousine Service has regularly scheduled service to island locations from both Houston airports for $21–$26.

➤ TAXIS AND SHUTTLES: **Airport Express** (☎ 713/523–8888, WEB www.airportexpress.com). **Galveston Limousine Service** (☎ 409/744–5466 in Galveston; 800/640–4826 elsewhere in Texas). **Metro city express bus** (☎ 713/635–4000, WEB www.metrobus.com).

BUS TRAVEL TO AND FROM HOUSTON AND GALVESTON

➤ BUS INFORMATION: **Greyhound** (✉ 2121 Main St., Houston, ☎ 800/231–2222, WEB www.greyhound.com). **Kerrville Bus Company** (✉ 714 25th St., Galveston, ☎ 409/765–7731).

CAR TRAVEL

Houston is ringed by I–610 and Beltway 8. A tighter loop, comprising several expressways, circles the downtown and provides remarkable views of the city, especially at dawn and dusk. Radiating out from these rings like spokes of a wheel are I–10, heading east to Louisiana and west to San Antonio; U.S. 59, northeast to Longview or southwest to Victoria; and I–45, southeast to Galveston (about an hour away) or north to Dallas. High Occupancy Vehicle (HOV) lanes, tollways, and crosstown connectors have reduced traffic congestion, but all these highways can be extremely crowded during rush hours.

TOURS

The Treasure Island Tour Train in Galveston departs regularly for a 1½-hour narrated excursion ($5.50) from outside the convention center called "Beach Central" at 21st Street and Seawall Boulevard.

➤ FEES AND SCHEDULES: **Treasure Island Tour Train** (✉ 2106 Seawall Blvd., Galveston, ☎ 409/765–9564).

TRAIN TRAVEL

In Houston, Amtrak trains arrive at the old Southern Pacific Station.

➤ INFORMATION: **Amtrak** (☎ 713/224–1577 or 800/872–7245, WEB www.amtrak.com). **Southern Pacific Station** (✉ 902 Washington Ave.).

TRANSPORTATION AROUND HOUSTON AND GALVESTON

Both Houston and Galveston demand cars, as attractions are spread out. Public transportation, though available, is not easy to figure out and may require multiple transfers. Houston's city bus system is most useful for straight-line routes. A free Downtown Trolley provides shuttle service between the George R. Brown Convention Center and the theater district. Colorful trolleys run throughout the day and late at night stopping at hotels, restaurants, and entertainment centers.

Galveston has island bus service, but of far more interest is the Galveston Island Trolley (60¢).

➤ CONTACTS: **Downtown Trolley** (☎ 713/635–4000). **Galveston Island Trolley** (✉ 2100 Seawall Blvd.; ✉ 2016 Strand; ☎ 409/797–3900). **Metro** (☎ 713/635–4000, WEB www.metrobus.com).

VISITOR INFORMATION

➤ TOURIST INFORMATION: **Galveston Historical Foundation Heritage Visitors Center** (✉ 2328 Broadway, ☎ 409/762–3933). **Galveston Island Convention & Visitors Bureau** (✉ 2428 Seawall Blvd., 77550, ☎ 409/763–4311 or 888/425–4753, WEB www.galvestontourism.com). **Greater Houston Convention & Visitors Bureau** (✉ 901 Bagby St., 77002, ☎ 713/437–5200 or 800/446–8786, WEB www.houston-guide.com).

SAN ANTONIO AND THE HILL COUNTRY

The Alamo—symbol either of Texan heroism or Anglo arrogance—is by no means the only reason to visit **San Antonio.** A mélange of easily mingling ethnic groups, it is in many ways Texas's most beautiful and atmospheric city. Northwest of San Antonio is the **Hill Country,** an anomaly in generally flat Texas, rich with pretty landscapes, early American history, and echoes of the linen-to-silk story of Lyndon Baines Johnson, the nation's 36th president.

Exploring San Antonio and the Hill Country

San Antonio

At the heart of San Antonio, the **Alamo** (✉ Alamo Plaza, ☎ 210/225–1391, WEB www.thealamo.org; 🎟 free), originally a Franciscan mission, stands as a repository of Texas history, a monument to the 189 volunteers who died there in 1836 during a 13-day siege by the Mexican dictator, General Antonio López de Santa Anna. Today the historic chapel and barracks contain the guns and other paraphernalia used by William Travis, Davy Crockett, James Bowie, and other Texas heroes. Outside in the peaceful courtyard, a history wall elucidates the story of the Alamo and the mission it once was. In the Rivercenter mall, the **San Antonio IMAX Theatre** (✉ 849 E. Commerce St., ☎ 210/225–4629 or 800/354–4629, WEB www.imax-sa.com; 🎟 $8.95) shows a 45-minute film, *Alamo . . . The Price of Freedom,* on a giant screen five times a day.

On Alamo Plaza is the 1859 **Menger Hotel,** San Antonio's most historic lodging. As legend has it, William Menger built the hotel to accommodate the many carousers who frequented his brewery, which stood on the same site. Step inside the hotel to see its moody, mahogany bar, a precise replica of the pub in London's House of Lords. Here cattlemen closed deals with a handshake over three fingers of rye, and Teddy Roosevelt supposedly recruited his Rough Riders—hard-living cowboys fresh from the Chisholm Trail. The **Texas Star Trail,** which begins and ends at the Alamo, is a 2½-mi walking tour marked by blue disks in the sidewalks. Information on the trail, which takes you past 80 historic sites and landmarks, is available at the Alamo Visitor Center.

★ **River Walk** (WEB www.thesanantonioriverwalk.com), or Paseo del Rio, is the city's leading tourist attraction. Built a full story below street level, it comprises about 3 mi of scenic stone pathways lining both banks of

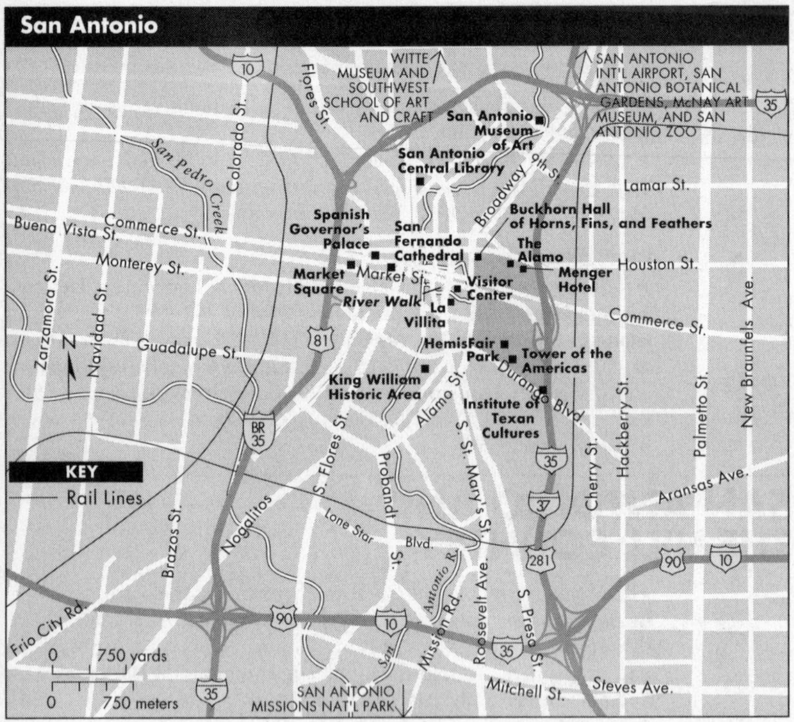

the San Antonio River as it flows through downtown. In some places the walk is peaceful and quiet; in others it is a mad conglomeration of restaurants, bars, hotels, and strolling mariachi bands, all of which can also be seen from river taxis and charter boats.To book a narrated boat tour contact **Yanaguana Riverboat Rides** (☎ 210/244–5700 or 800/417–4139). Near La Mansion del Rio hotel, at the Navarro Street Bridge, is the huge retail-and-entertainment complex known as **South Bank.** Each January parts of the river are drained to clear the bottom of debris, and locals revel in the **River Walk Mud Festival and Mud Parade.** During the annual **Mardi Gras Parade** in February, colorfully festooned floats create a spectacle. If you miss an event, don't worry—there are at least two a month, each with food, music, and lots of entertainment.

HemisFair Park, downtown near the convention center, was once the site of a World's Fair. Now the 15 acres are landscaped with waterfalls and a playground; a few historic buildings remain as well. The 750-ft **Tower of the Americas** (✉ 600 HemisFair Way, ☎ 210/207–8615, WEB www.toweroftheamericas.com; 🎫 observation deck $3) is popular for its observation deck and rotating restaurant, affording bird's-eye views of the city.

The University of Texas's **Institute of Texan Cultures** (✉ 801 S. Bowie St., ☎ 210/458–2300, WEB www.texancultures.utsa.edu; 🎫 $5), beyond the Tower of the Americas, is an interactive museum focusing on the 30 ethnic groups who made Texas what it is today. Here you can walk through a re-created sharecropper's house; listen to an animated, recorded conversation that might have taken place between a Spanish governor and a Comanche chief in the 1790s; or learn how and when your ancestors settled in Texas. It's closed Monday.

Leading German merchants settled the **King William Historic Area** in the late 19th century. The Victorian mansions, set in a quiet, leafy neighborhood, are a pleasure to behold; Madison, Guenther, and King William streets are particularly pretty for a stroll or drive. For a walking tour of the area, visit www.saconservation.org/kwwtmap.html. Stop in for a guided visit of the 1876 Victorian **Steves Homestead** (✉ 509 King William St., ☎ 210/225–5924; 🎫 $3). The 1860 **Guenther House** (✉ 205 E. Guenther St., ☎ 210/227–1061, WEB www.guentherhouse.com; 🎫 free), home of the family that founded the adjacent Pioneer Flour Mills, welcomes self-guided tours. At the latter you'll find a small museum of mill memorabilia, a gift shop, and a cheerful restaurant serving fine German pastries and full breakfasts and lunches.

Except for the Alamo, all of San Antonio's historic missions constitute **San Antonio Missions National Park** (✉ 2202 Roosevelt Ave., ☎ 210/932–1001, WEB www.nps.gov/saan; 🎫 free). Established along the San Antonio River in the 18th century, the missions stand as reminders of Spain's most successful attempt to extend its New World dominion northward from Mexico. All of the missions are active parish churches, and all are beautiful, in their way. Start your tour at the stunning **Mission San José** (✉ 6701 San Jose Dr., ☎ 210/922–0543), the "Queen of Missions," where a National Park Service visitor center illuminates the history of the missions. San José's outer wall, Native American dwellings, granary, water mill, and workshops have been restored. Here you can pick up a map of the **Mission Trail** that connects San José with the other missions. **Mission Concepción** (✉ 807 Mission Rd., at Felisa St., ☎ 210/534–1540) is known for its frescoes. **Mission San Juan** (✉ 9101 Graf Rd., ☎ 210/534–0749), with its Romanesque arches, has a serene chapel. **Espada** (✉ 10040 Espada Rd., ☎ 210/627–2021), the southernmost mission, includes an Arab-inspired aqueduct that was part of the missions' famous *acequia* water management system.

Now in the Buckhorn Saloon, the **Buckhorn Hall of Horns, Fins, and Feathers** (✉ 318 E. Houston St., ☎ 210/247–4000, WEB www.buckhornmuseum.com; 🎫 $8.99) is said to contain the world's largest collection of animal horns. The **San Fernando Cathedral** (✉ 115 Main Plaza, ☎ 210/227–1297, WEB www.sfcathedral.org; 🎫 free) west of the river, is where Santa Anna raised his flag—an ominous message of no mercy—to intimidate the Alamo defenders. The seat of a bishopric, it was visited by Pope John Paul II in 1987. The beautiful 18th-century **Spanish Governor's Palace** (✉ 105 Plaza de Armas, ☎ 210/224–0601; 🎫 $1.50), seat of Spanish power in Texas, is an ideal picnic site.

San Antonio has a thriving arts scene. The **San Antonio Museum of Art** (✉ 200 W. Jones Ave., ☎ 210/978–8100, WEB www.sa-museum.org; 🎫 $6) houses choice collections of pre-Columbian, Native American, and Spanish colonial art, as well as the Nelson A. Rockefeller Center for Latin American Art, the nation's largest such facility, with more than 2,500 folk art objects. It's closed Monday. The **Southwest School of Art and Craft** (✉ 300 Augusta St., ☎ 210/224–1848, WEB www.swschool.org; 🎫 free), once an Ursuline school for girls, has a gallery filled with local crafts made by artists-in-residence.

You can't miss the 240,000-square-ft **San Antonio Central Library** (✉ 600 Soledad St., ☎ 210/207–2500). Its burnt-orange color, locally known as enchilada-red, and its modern design by the Mexican architect Ricardo Legoretta have been a source of contention among traditionalists. At the **Witte Museum** (✉ 3801 Broadway, Brackenridge Park, ☎ 210/357–1900, WEB www.wittemuseum.org; 🎫 $5.95), a four-level "science tree house" is filled with interactive exhibits that let kids lift themselves with pulleys and ropes, play music with laser beams, and launch tennis balls 30 ft in the air.

The **San Antonio Zoo** (✉ 3903 N. St. Mary's St., ☎ 210/734–7183, WEB www.sazoo-aq.org; 🎫 $7) has the nation's third-largest animal collection, most in outdoor habitats.On the outskirts of the city, in a private mansion with a Moorish-style courtyard, the **McNay Art Museum** (✉ 6000 N. New Braunfels Ave., ☎ 210/824–5368, WEB www.mcnayart.org) has a collection of post-Impressionist and modern paintings and sculpture, along with an arts library. It's free except for special exhibits. Not far from the McNay Art Museum are the **San Antonio Botanical Gardens** (✉ 555 Funston Pl., ☎ 210/207–3250, WEB www.sabot.org; 🎫 $4), 33 acres containing formal gardens, wildflower-spangled meadows, native Texas vegetation, and a "touch and smell" garden specially designed for blind people.

The Hill Country

A drive through the Hill Country from San Antonio makes a pleasant excursion. Starting toward the northwest, it's less than an hour's trip on I–10 to the Kerrville area. However, you may want to take the far prettier Route 16, a hilly road that leads to **Bandera** (population: 900), one of the nation's oldest Polish communities (dating from 1855) and site of an 1854 Mormon colony.

Boerne (population: 6,200), on I–10, was founded by Germans and named after a German writer. One of its fine early buildings is the **Kuhlmann-King House** (✉ 402 E. Blanco St., ☎ 830/249–2030; 🎫 donations accepted), which can be toured by appointment with the local historical society. About 4 mi from Boerne, **Cascade Caverns** (✉ 226 Cascade Caverns Rd., Exit 543 off I–10, ☎ 830/755–8080; 🎫 $8.50) has a 90-ft underground waterfall and visitor facilities, including RV campsites and a pool.

Kerrville, a town made for taking it easy, is said to have the best climate in the nation. This has led to a proliferation of hotels, children's summer camps, guest ranches, and religious centers, along with an annual 18-day folk music festival that draws national talents to its stage. **Kerrville State Park** (☎ 830/257–5392; 🎫 $3), 500 acres along the cypress-edged Guadalupe River, is a good place to spot the area's abundant white-tail deer.

Fredericksburg, Hill Country's prettiest town and the heart of its predominantly German-American population, is 24 mi north of Kerrville, on Route 16. Its main street (bilingually signposted as HAUPTSTRASSE) is a sort of German version of a classic western movie scene except that it's lined with chic stores, antiques shops, and small German eateries. One of Fredericksburg's famous sons was Chester W. Nimitz, commander in chief of the U.S. Pacific fleet in World War II.The restored Nimitz Steamboat Hotel now forms part of the **Admiral Nimitz National Museum of the Pacific War** (✉ 340 E. Main St., ☎ 830/997–4379, WEB www.nimitz-museum.org; 🎫 $5), which displays restored hotel rooms, exhibits on the war in the Pacific, and the Garden of Peace, donated by the Japanese government. Eighteen miles north of Fredericksburg, eons of uplift and erosion have exposed a sleeping giant at **Enchanted Rock State Natural Area** (✉ 16710 Ranch Rd. 965, ☎ 915/247–3903; 🎫 $5), where an enormous pink granite rock swells 425 ft aboveground and covers 640 acres. The views atop the behemoth make the short but steep hike worthwhile.

The **Lyndon Baines Johnson National Historical Park** (✉ 100 Lady Bird La., ☎ 830/868–7128, WEB www.nps.gov/lyjo) is separated into two districts: one in Johnson City and the other near Stonewall, 14 mi away. At the center of **Johnson City** (U.S. 281, 60 mi north of San Antonio; U.S. 290, 50 mi west of Austin)—the poor, dusty town where our 36th president was born and raised—is the **visitor center**, with books, films, and exhibits on the area. Nearby are LBJ's small, white-frame **boyhood home**, where rangers give free guided tours daily, and the **Johnson Settlement** (free), a ranch complex once owned by LBJ's family. On certain weekends, costumed interpreters demonstrate the skills and trades of frontier Texas; call for a schedule. A worthwhile **bus tour** ($3) departs daily from the **LBJ Ranch District** (⊠ east of Stonewall on U.S. 290, ☎ 830/644–2420), with stops at Johnson's birthplace, the one-room school he attended, and his grave; along the way you'll also pass the **White House**, where Lady Bird Johnson still lives.

Blanco (south of Johnson City on U.S. 281), the onetime county seat, is ornamented by a fine bit of classic Texas: the Second Empire–style **Old Blanco County Courthouse.**The drive back to San Antonio on U.S. 281 is pleasant, but if you have time, go by way of **San Marcos** on Route 32. This road, which skips along parts of a ridge called the **Devil's Backbone**, leads through classic Hill Country landscapes.If time permits, make a short detour to **Natural Bridge Caverns** (⊠ 26495 Natural Bridge Caverns Rd., Exit 175 from I–35, 78266, ☎ 210/651–6101, WEB www.naturalbridgecaverns.com; $12), a mile-long series of multicolored subterranean rooms and corridors. The caverns are between San Antonio and New Braunfels; follow signs from Route 1863. "Thunder lizard" tracks dating from 100 million years ago can be found at **Dinosaur Flats** (⊠ Rte. 306, 2 mi southwest of Sattler), along the trail on the south edge of Canyon Lake.

Dining and Lodging

The Bandera and Kerrville visitor centers have information on guest ranches. The Hill Country is chock-full of bed-and-breakfasts, particularly in popular towns like Fredericksburg. Ask for listings at local convention and visitor centers or try a reservations service. **Be My Guest** (⊠ 110 N. Milam St., Fredericksburg 78624, ☎ 830/997–7227) provides information about bed-and-breakfasts and other lodging in and around Fredericksburg. **Gastehaus Schmidt** (⊠ 231 W. Main St., Fredericksburg 78624, ☎ 830/997–5612 or 866/427–8374, WEB www.fbglodging.com) provides a 24-hour reservation service via its Web site.

San Antonio

$$$–$$$$ ✕ **Polo's.** Inside the Fairmount hotel is the equally classic Polo's, serving artfully blended contemporary southwestern and Asian cuisine. Try the scallops in a spicy, roasted coconut sauce; the tempura oysters on Hijaki salad; or the black pasta stuffed with lobster and crab. The adjacent lounge hosts live jazz on Friday and Saturday nights. ⊠ *401 S. Alamo St.,* ☎ *210/224–8800. AE, DC, MC, V. Closed Sun.*

$$–$$$$ ★ ✕ **Biga.** Chef-owner Bruce Auden's contemporary restaurant on the River Walk has a patio, a full bar, and a menu that will amaze you. Appetizers include Hudson Valley fois gras served with a maple waffle, and fried sweetbreads with bacon, spinach, sherry vinegar, goat cheese, and candied pecans. Entrées include phyllo-wrapped sea bass with creamy mustard leeks. ⊠ *203 S. St. Mary's St.,* ☎ *210/225–0722. AE, D, DC, MC, V.*

$$–$$$ ✕ **Boudro's.** Among the better River Walk options, this cavelike southwestern original serves seafood, steak, and awesome ribs in a turn-of-the-20th-century limestone building. For an appetizer, try the guacamole prepared table-side. You may have a hard time choosing between the excellent wines and the attractive cocktails. ⊠ *421 E. Commerce St.,* ☎ *210/224–8484. AE, D, DC, MC, V.*

$$–$$$ ★ ✕ **Zuni Grill.** Given the choice between the warehouse-style interior and the patio with big shade umbrellas and a view of the river, pick the patio. The restaurant is known for its breakfast tacos, fajitas, and the Zuni Burger (served with white cheddar and onion bread). Try a cactus margarita—it's made with real prickly pear cactus juice. ✉ *511 River Walk St.,* ☎ *210/227–0864. AE, D, DC, MC, V.*

$–$$ ✕ **Liberty Bar.** Built in 1890 and leaning conspicuously on its foundation (attributed to a 1921 flood), Liberty Bar is a hip, funky restaurant with a definite "scene." The menu lists basic, old-time favorites like pot roast, peppered steak, and pasta. Dessert may be what they do best—try the chocolate cake or a slice of homemade pie. Guinness is on tap. ✉ *328 E. Josephine St.,* ☎ *210/227–1187. AE, MC, V.*

$$$$ **La Mansion del Rio.** Gorgeous, even inspirational, Spanish-style luxury rooms and suites set this enormous hotel apart from the rest of the River Walk. Inside and out it's replete with Mediterranean tiles, archways, and soft wood tones. Rooms are equipped with data ports, and most have balconies or verandas. ✉ *112 College St., 78205,* ☎ *210/225–2581 or 800/292–7300,* FAX *210/226–0389,* WEB *www.lamansion.com. 337 rooms. 2 restaurants, pool. AE, D, DC, MC, V.*

$$$$ ★ **Menger Hotel.** Since its 1859 opening, the Menger has lodged, among others, Robert E. Lee, Ulysses S. Grant, Theodore Roosevelt, Oscar Wilde, Sarah Bernhardt, and Roy Rogers and Dale Evans. Guests appreciate the charming three-story Victorian lobby, sunny dining room, flowered courtyard, and four-poster beds (in the oldest part of the hotel only). ✉ *204 Alamo Plaza, 78205,* ☎ *210/223–4361 or 800/345–9285,* FAX *210/228–0022,* WEB *www.mengerhotel.com. 316 rooms. Restaurant, pool, health club. AE, D, DC, MC, V.*

$$$–$$$$ **The Fairmount.** This historic luxury hotel made the *Guinness Book of Records* when its 3.2-million-pound brick bulk was moved six blocks in 1985 to its present location. Rooms have canopy beds, overstuffed chairs, and marble baths. ✉ *401 S. Alamo St., 78205,* ☎ *210/224–8800 or 800/996–3426,* FAX *210/475–0082,* WEB *www.wyndham.com/fairmount. 37 rooms. Restaurant. AE, D, DC, MC, V.*

$$$–$$$$ **The Gunter.** Since 1909 this downtown hotel has been a favorite of cattlemen and business travelers. The marble lobby has a beautiful coffered ceiling supported by massive columns. Rooms have antique reproduction furniture and modern conveniences such as large desks with data ports. ✉ *205 E. Houston St., 78205,* ☎ *210/227–3241 or 800/325–3535,* FAX *210/227–3299,* WEB *www.gunterhotel.com. 322 rooms. Restaurant, pool, gym. AE, D, DC, MC, V.*

$$$–$$$$ ★ **Havana Riverwalk Inn.** San Antonio's most bohemian boutique hotel occupies a Mediterranean Revival structure built in 1914. You'll find teak and wicker chairs from India, beds fashioned from the grillwork of old buildings, and vintage chairs from French hotels and bistros. Don't miss Club Cohiba, the martini bar in the basement, and Siboney restaurant. ✉ *1015 Navarro St., 78205,* ☎ *210/222–2008 or 888/224–2008,* FAX *210/222–2717. 27 rooms. Restaurant. AE, D, DC, MC, V.*

$$$–$$$$ **Hyatt Regency Hill Country Resort.** On the western edge of the city, near Sea World, this sophisticated country resort occupies 200 acres on former ranch land. On the grounds is a 4-acre water park with a man-made river where you can go tubing. *9800 Hyatt Dr., 78251,* ☎ *210/647–1234,* FAX *210/681–9681,* WEB *www.sanantonio.hyatt.com/sanhc. 500 rooms. 2 restaurants, pools, tennis, health club. AE, D, DC, MC, V.*

$ **Bullis House.** Rooms in this big, white, historic mansion are spacious and well restored; they're a good deal in a town where lodging is surprisingly expensive. Next door in a separate building is a modern youth hostel. ✉ *621 Pierce St., 78208,* ☎ *210/223–9426 or 877/477–4100. 10 rooms, 42 hostel beds. Pool. AE, D, MC, V. CP.*

The Hill Country

$$ ✕ **Friedhelm's.** This Bavarian restaurant is known as the best in town, no small feat in an area full of such eateries. Try the Bavarian schnitzel, a breaded cutlet topped with Emmentaler cheese and jalapeño sauce. ✉ *905 W. Main St., Fredericksburg 78624,* ☎ *830/997–6300. AE, D, MC, V. Closed Mon.*

$$$$ **Holiday Inn Y. O. Ranch.** This sprawling hotel is named after a well-known 50,000-acre dude ranch to which regular excursions are arranged. The large rooms—sporting cattle horns and the like—carry out the western theme. ✉ *2033 Sidney Baker St., Kerrville 78028,* ☎ *830/257–4440 or 877/967–3767,* FAX *830/896–8189,* WEB *www.yoresort.com. 200 rooms. Restaurant, pool, tennis. AE, D, DC, MC, V.*

Nightlife and the Arts

Nightlife

Around the 3000 block of San Antonio's **North St. Mary's Street,** you'll find a colorful assortment of bars and restaurants in converted commercial buildings, many with live entertainment. River Walk favorites include **Durty Nellie's Pub** (✉ Hilton Palacio del Rio, 200 S. Alamo St., ☎ 210/222–1400), where sing-alongs are popular. World-class Jim Cullum's Jazz Band plays superb Dixieland at the **Landing** (✉ Hyatt Regency, 123 Losoya St., ☎ 210/223–7266). Don't miss the **Menger Hotel bar** (☞ Dining and Lodging, *above*).

The Arts

At San Antonio's **Mexican Cultural Institute** (✉ 600 HemisFair Plaza, ☎ 210/227–0123; free), Mexican culture is depicted in film, dance, art, and other media. It's closed weekends. A 1929 movie-vaudeville theater has been restored to its Baroque splendor as the **Majestic Performing Arts Center** (✉ 224 E. Houston St., ☎ 210/226–5700), a venue for touring Broadway shows and the San Antonio Symphony Orchestra. **Kerrville** annually hosts one of the country's largest folk music festivals, usually beginning the Thursday before Memorial Day and running for 24 hours a day for 18 days. Contact the **Convention & Visitors Bureau** (☎ 830/792–3535 or 800/221–7958).

Outdoor Activities and Sports

Water Sports

Rafting, tubing, and canoeing are popular on the **Guadalupe River** between Canyon Lake, north of San Antonio, and New Braunfels. **Jerry's Rentals** (✉ 4970 River Rd., north of New Braunfels, ☎ 830/625–2036) offers rentals and guided trips. **Rockin' R River Rides** (✉ 1405 Gruene Rd., ☎ 830/629–9999 or 800/553–5628) hosts rafting trips along the Guadalupe River and the Comal. Raft trips with **Gruene River Co.** (✉ 1404 Gruene Rd., ☎ 830/625–2800 or 888/705–2800) begin near Canyon Lake and end in Gruene, traveling through some exciting water, including Huaco Falls, the largest rapids on the Guadalupe River. With the steep evergreen hills surrounding it, **Canyon Lake** is one of the most scenic lakes in Texas. It has two yacht clubs, two marinas, a waterskiing club, and excellent fishing (an 86-pound flathead catfish is one local record). Within 20 minutes of San Antonio are two Texas-size amusement parks. **Six Flags Fiesta Texas** (✉ 17000 I–10 W, at La Cantera Pkwy., ☎ 800/473–4378) combines the thrill of roller-coasters and the joy of water rides into one giant park. Occupying 250 acres, **Sea World San Antonio** (✉ 10500 Sea World Dr., ☎ 210/523–3611) is the world's largest marine life park, with spectacular animal shows and exhilarating water rides.

Spectator Sports

Baseball: San Antonio Missions (✉ 5757 U.S. 90 W and Callahan Rd., ☎ 210/675–7275). **Basketball: San Antonio Spurs** (✉ Alamodome, 100 Montana St., ☎ 210/554–7787 or 800/884–3663). **Horse Racing: Retama Park** (✉ I–35, Exit 174A, San Antonio, ☎ 210/651–7000); April–October, Friday–Sunday, but some Wednesdays and Thursday in the fall; simulcasts daily, year-round.

Shopping

San Antonio

With its rich ethnic heritage, this city is a wonderful place to buy Mexican imports, most of them inexpensive and many of high quality. **El Mercado** is the Mexican market building that is part of **Market Square** (✉ 514 W. Commerce St., ☎ 210/207–8600). The building contains about 35 shops, including stores selling blankets, Mexican dresses, men's guayabera shirts, and strings of brightly painted papier-mâché vegetables. The lively **Farmer's Market** is another area of Market Square worth visiting. **La Villita** (✉ 418 Villita St., ☎ 210/207–8610), a block of restored buildings on the southern edge of downtown, includes crafts shops and small restaurants, some in adobe buildings dating from the 1820s. It's noteworthy for its Latin American importers and demonstrations by its resident glassblower. **Rivercenter** (✉ 849 E. Commerce St., ☎ 210/225–0000) is a fairly standard, if very ritzy, shopping mall right on the river. **Paris Hatters** (✉ 119 Broadway, ☎ 210/223–3453) is an atmospheric place to buy western hats.

San Antonio and the Hill Country Essentials

AIRPORTS AND TRANSFERS

➤ AIRPORT INFORMATION: **San Antonio International Airport** (✉ 9800 Airport Blvd., 78216, ☎ 210/207–3411). **Shuttle Services** (☎ 210/281–9900 or 210/824–3000).

BUS TRAVEL

➤ BUS INFORMATION: **San Antonio Greyhound station** (✉ 500 N. St. Mary's St., ☎ 210/270–5824 or 800/231–2222).

CAR TRAVEL

While much of San Antonio can be explored on foot, a car is a must for Hill Country; you can visit several towns in a day, catching some of the landscapes in between as you drive. The area is served by good highways, including I–35 from Dallas and Austin and I–10 from Houston. I–410 rings the city, and several highways take you downtown.

TRAIN TRAVEL

Amtrak serves San Antonio's station with thrice-weekly trains north to Fort Worth, Dallas, east Texas, and Chicago and east to New Orleans and beyond; on Monday, Thursday, and Saturday there is service west to Los Angeles.

➤ TRAIN INFORMATION: **Amtrak** (☎ 210/223–3226 or 800/872–7245). **San Antonio Station** (✉ 350 Hoefgen St.).

VISITOR INFORMATION

➤ TOURIST INFORMATION: **Alamo Visitor Center** (✉ 216 Alamo Plaza, San Antonio 78202, ☎ 210/225–8587). **Bandera Convention & Visitors Bureau** (✉ 606 Rte. 16 S [Box 171, 78003], ☎ 830/796–3045 or 800/364–3833). **Fredericksburg Convention & Visitors Bureau** (✉ 106 N. Adams St., 78624, ☎ 830/997–6523 or 800/997–3600; WEB www.fredericksburg-texas.com). **Kerrville Convention & Visitors Bu-**

reau (✉ 2108 Sidney Baker St., 78028, ☎ 830/792–3535 or 800/221–7958, WEB www.ktc.net/kerrcvb). **San Antonio Convention & Visitors Bureau** (✉ 203 S. St. Mary's St., 78205, ✉ 317 Alamo Plaza, near the Alamo; ☎ 210/207–6700 or 800/447–3372, WEB www.sanantoniocvb.com).

AUSTIN

Created as the capital of the then-new Republic of Texas in 1839, **Austin** is a liberal enclave in a generally conservative state and a heavily treed, hilly town in a land commonly known for its monotonous flatness. For many years a quiet university town, Austin has grown rapidly within the past two decades, developing into another Silicon Valley. The growth of high-tech industry, combined with the state government and the university, has made for a vital and culturally diverse community; indeed, Austin now has one of the country's fastest-growing job markets.

With numerous clubs and music venues, Austin draws many top musicians. Billing itself as the "live music capital of the world," the city puts on the annual music industry conference South by Southwest in March, which also draws film notables from around the world.

Exploring Austin

Downtown Austin is dominated by the impressive **capitol** (✉ 1100 Congress Ave., ☎ 512/463–0063), constructed in 1888 of Texas pink granite. Free historical tours run 8:30–4:30. If you wish to see the nearby **Governor's Mansion** (✉ 1010 Colorado St., ☎ 512/463–5518, WEB www.governor.state.tx.us/Mansion), arrive early for the free, first-come, first-served tours held Monday–Thursday 10 AM–noon. The **Capitol Complex Visitors Center** (✉ 112 E. 11th St., 78701, ☎ 512/305–8400) can help you plan your visit to the capitol. There are temporary exhibits, videos, and a gift shop.

The **University of Texas** campus flanks the capitol's north end. On the campus is the **Lyndon Baines Johnson Presidential Library and Museum** (✉ 2313 Red River St., ☎ 512/916–5136, WEB www.lbjlib.utexas.edu; 🎫 free). Also of interest on the UT campus is the **Jack S. Blanton Museum of Art,** formerly the Huntington Art Gallery (✉ 23rd and San Jacinto Sts., ☎ 512/471–7324, WEB www.blantonmuseum.org; 🎫 free), which is the permanent home of one of the largest and most important private collections of old master paintings and drawings; it comprises 700 works by Poussin, Veronese, Rubens, Tiepolo, Boucher, Corregio, and other Italian, French, and German artists of the 14th to the 18th century. **Austin Lyric Opera** (✉ 901 Barton Springs Rd., ☎ 512/472–5992, WEB www.austinlyricopera.org) produces four major operas in a season that runs November–May. Austin's oldest performing arts group, the **Austin Symphony** (✉ 1101 Red River St., ☎ 512/476–6064, WEB www.austinsymphony.org) presents exceptional classical music through a series of eight concerts running September–April. **Ballet Austin** (✉ 3002 Guadalupe St., ☎ 512/476–9051, WEB www.balletaustin.org) performs at the Bass Concert Hall during a season that generally runs October–May. **Guadalupe Street,** also known as "the Drag," borders the west side of the UT campus and is lined with trendy boutiques and restaurants. The stately capitol is seated at the north end of **Congress Avenue,** while at the south end—specifically, under the bridge—is a colony of hundreds of thousands of Mexican bats. Attracted to the small space between the arches of the bridge and the road above, the nocturnal critters swarm into town every evening at dusk from May until October, creating a creepy but memorable cocktail-hour spectacle for hundreds of onlookers. The grass areas on the bridge's northeastern or southeastern ends are good vantage points.

Parks and Gardens

Many people and companies have moved to Austin for a quality of life enhanced by pristine waterways and extensive greenbelts for hiking, biking, and running. **Zilker Park** (✉ 2100 Barton Springs Rd., ☎ 512/974–6700), the city's largest public park, connects to **Town Lake's hike and bike trail. Barton Springs Pool** (☎ 512/867–3080; 🎫 $2.50), a huge natural-spring pool, is Zilker Park's main attraction. Built in the early 1900s when the city dammed Barton Creek, the pool is more than ¼ mi long, and it's a constant 68°F. It is considered one of the nation's premier swimming holes, and Austinites cherish it as the jewel of their city. It's closed Thursday. Little ones enjoy free rides on the **miniature Amtrak train** that circles the park April–October.

The **Zilker Botanical Gardens** (✉ 2220 Barton Springs Rd., ☎ 512/477–8672; 🎫 free), across from Zilker Park, has more than 26 acres of horticultural delights, including butterfly trails and Xeriscape gardens with native plants that thrive in an arid southwestern climate. The **Austin Nature and Science Center** (✉ 301 Nature Center Dr., ☎ 512/327–8180; 🎫 donations requested), adjacent to the botanical gardens, has 80 acres of trails, interactive exhibits teaching about the environment, and animal exhibits.

The **Lady Bird Johnson Wildflower Center** (✉ 4801 LaCrosse Ave., ☎ 512/292–4100; 🎫 $5) includes a 43-acre complex sponsored by Lady Bird Johnson and has educational programs and extensive plantings of wildflowers that bloom all year-round. It's closed Monday.Off the western thoroughfare of Austin sits 227-acre **Wild Basin Wilderness Preserve** (✉ 805 N. Capital of Texas Hwy., ☎ 512/327–7622; 🎫 donation requested), where even in the midst of a growing city unobstructed views of the verdant hill country are readily available. Call for guided tour information.

Dining

$$$$ ✕ **Hudson's on the Bend.** A bit outside town, overlooking a bend in beautiful Lake Austin (a portion of the Colorado River northwest of Austin), Hudson's serves exotic dishes such as Jamaican jerked Australian kangaroo with chipotle cream sauce. ✉ *3509 Ranch Rd. 620,* ☎ *512/266–1369. Reservations essential. AE, DC, MC, V. No lunch.*

$$–$$$ ✕ **Bitter End.** A slightly industrial interior sets the scene for the see-and-be-seen crowd at this sleek brewpub. Duck liver pâté, wood-fired pizzas, and an ever-updated Italian-tinged menu are all enhanced by outstanding home-brewed ales. The service is fast and friendly, and there's a patio for outdoor dining. ✉ *311 Colorado St.,* ☎ *512/478–2337. AE, D, DC, MC, V.*

$$ ✕ **Castle Hill Café.** Here you'll find great tortilla soup, imaginative salads, and eclectic entrées such as grilled Indian lamb loin with Makhani cream and cauliflower-ginger relish. The menu changes weekly. ✉ *1101 W. 5th St.,* ☎ *512/476–7218. AE, D, MC, V. Closed Sun.*

$ ✕ **Güeros.** The ceiling is high, the floorboards worn, and the windows long and tall in this former feed store, now a favorite Mexican restaurant with a spacious, rustic bar and adored salsas. ✉ *1412 S. Congress Ave.,* ☎ *512/447–7688. AE, D, DC, MC, V.*

$ ✕ **Threadgill's.** Southern food and friendly service make Threadgill's a local legend, having drawn the likes of Janis Joplin to sample its fare. Go for the massive chicken-fried steak; then enjoy some homemade cobbler and live music. ✉ *6416 N. Lamar Blvd.,* ☎ *512/451–5440;* ✉ *301 W. Riverside Dr.,* ☎ *512/472–9304. D, MC, V.*

Lodging

$$$$ **Driskill Hotel.** This historic Renaissance Revival edifice, fronting Congress Avenue, was built in 1886 by cattle baron Jesse Driskill. Inside, its lobby is highlighted by vaulted ceilings, beautiful columns, and chandeliers. Each room is decorated with original art and rich fabrics. ✉ *604 Brazos St., 78701,* ☎ *512/474–5911 or 800/252–9367,* FAX *512/474–2214,* WEB *www.driskillhotel.com. 188 rooms. Restaurant. AE, D, DC, MC, V.*

$$$$ **Four Seasons.** Built along the banks of Town Lake in downtown Austin, this luxury hotel has beautiful views of sunsets over the water and the loveliest lakeside Sunday brunch in town. It is also a prime location in summer for watching the bat exodus from under the Congress Avenue Bridge. Rooms are spacious with classic furnishings. ✉ *98 San Jacinto Blvd., 78701,* ☎ *512/478–4500 or 800/332–3442,* FAX *512/478–3117,* WEB *www.fourseasons.com. 291 rooms. Restaurant, pool. AE, DC, MC, V.*

Nightlife

Numerous traveling and homegrown bands play nightly in the city's many music venues, most of which are clustered around downtown's **6th Street,** between Red River Street and Congress Avenue. To find out who's playing where, pick up a free *Austin Chronicle* or Thursday's *Austin American Statesman.* Some of the town's most distinctive clubs are removed from the 6th Street scene: if live country music and dancing are your thing, two-step down to the venerable **Broken Spoke** (✉ 3201 S. Lamar Blvd., ☎ 512/442–6189). Rustic, quirky, and no bigger than your parents' basement, the smoky, no-frills **Continental Club** (✉ 1315 S. Congress Ave., ☎ 512/441–2444) plays country-tinged rock. **Antone's** (✉ 213 W. 5th St., ☎ 512/474–5315) is another local musical institution, booking legendary blues and funk acts. A restored downtown movie palace, the **Paramount Theatre** (✉ 713 Congress Ave., ☎ 512/472–5470) now presents musicals and plays by touring theater companies. Local theater thrives at the **Zachary Scott Theatre** (✉ 1510 Toomey Rd., ☎ 512/476–0541), named for an Austin native who was successful in 1930s Hollywood.

Austin Essentials

AIRPORTS AND TRANSFERS

➤ AIRPORT INFORMATION: **Austin Bergstrom International Airport** (✉ 3600 Presidential Blvd., 78719, ☎ 512/530–2242).

BUS TRAVEL TO AND FROM AUSTIN

➤ BUS INFORMATION: **Greyhound** (✉ 916 E. Koenig La., ☎ 512/458–4463 or 800/229–9424).

CAR TRAVEL

Between Dallas–Fort Worth and San Antonio on I–35, Austin is accessible from Houston via U.S. 290.

TRAIN TRAVEL

Amtrak serves the city with three trains weekly west to Los Angeles and the same number north to Chicago.

➤ TRAIN INFORMATION: **Amtrak** (✉ 250 N. Lamar Blvd., ☎ 512/476–5684 or 800/872–7245).

VISITOR INFORMATION

➤ TOURIST INFORMATION: **Austin Convention and Visitors Bureau** (✉ 201 E. 2nd St., 78701, ☎ 512/474–5171 or 800/926–2282, WEB www.austin360.com/partners/acvb). **Chamber of Commerce** (✉ 111 Congress Ave., 78701, ☎ 512/478–9383, WEB www.austin-chamber.org).

DALLAS AND FORT WORTH

These twin cities, separated by 30 mi of suburbs, are an odd couple. **Dallas** has come a long way since being known primarily as the assassination site of President John F. Kennedy. The "Big D" is a swelling, modernistic business metropolis with a sophisticated dining scene and one of the largest urban arts districts in the country. **Fort Worth,** also known as "Cowtown," lives in the shadow of its wild history as a rip-roaring cowboy town, a place of gunfights and cattle drives. In Fort Worth, that fellow in the faded jeans and cowboy hat could well be the president of the bank. In Dallas, people tend to be a bit more formal, but you'll still find that down-home Texas friendliness and, in Deep Ellum east of downtown, a nightlife that buzzes until the wee hours.

Exploring Dallas and Fort Worth

Dallas

Many thousands visit Dallas, in spite of—or in some cases because of—the city's unhappy legacy as the assassination site of President John F. Kennedy, which occurred downtown. Also downtown is one of the most remarkable flowerings of skyscraping architecture anywhere—that same skyline familiar to the world from the television show *Dallas*—and a multitude of restaurants and shops in the **West End,** a former warehouse district. Near the West End are several major cultural institutions, and only a little farther away is **Deep Ellum,** the lively center of the city's alternative arts and music scene. A short car trip from downtown are several historic areas that give a sense of the old Dallas. To the north, where the city's establishment has long been entrenched, there's shopping galore.

DOWNTOWN

On November 22, 1963, shots rang out on Dealey Plaza, at the west end of downtown, as the presidential motorcade rounded the corner from Houston Street onto the Elm Street approach to the Triple Underpass. Eventually the Warren Commission would conclude—to the continuing disbelief of many Americans—that President Kennedy was gunned down by Lee Harvey Oswald, acting alone and firing from the sixth floor of the Texas School Book Depository. The building is now ★ known as the **Sixth Floor Museum at Dealey Plaza** (✉ 411 Elm St., ☎ 214/747–6660, WEB www.jfk.org; 🎟 $10, $13 with audio tour), where exhibits explore the life and legacy of JFK.

The grassy knoll from which many believe a second gunman fired is to the right of the Sixth Floor Museum, on the Elm Street side. **Dealey Plaza,** where visitors inevitably congregate to look up at the so-called sniper's perch, is directly across the street. The stark, square **John F. Kennedy Memorial,** a cenotaph (empty tomb) designed by architect Philip Johnson, is a short walk from Dealey Plaza, at Main and Market streets.

Those with more of an *X-Files* view of life can check out the **Conspiracy Museum** (✉ 110 S. Market St., ☎ 214/741–3040, WEB www.conspiracymuseum.com; 🎟 $7), where the history of presidential assassinations and government cover-ups is meticulously examined.

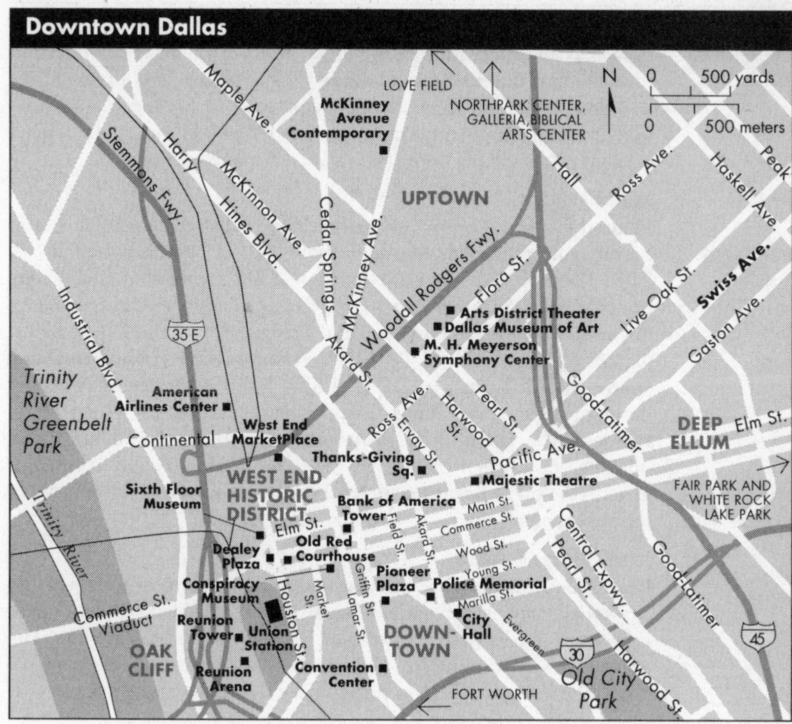

The **West End Historic District** (WEB www.dallaswestend.org) is an area of brick warehouses built between 1900 and 1930 and brought back to life in 1976. Now filled with restaurants and shops, it is one of the city's most tourist-friendly spots. Within the historic district is the **West End MarketPlace** (✉ 603 Munger Ave., ☎ 214/748–4801), once a candy-and-cracker factory and now a lively, five-story shopping-and-eating center built around an atrium.

The **Old Red Courthouse** (✉ 100 S. Houston St., WEB www.oldred.org) faces the John F. Kennedy Memorial. This 1892 Romanesque building of red sandstone is one of the city's oldest surviving structures; it now houses a fully staffed visitor information center. The **John Neely Bryan Cabin,** a restored log cabin similar to one erected in 1841 by city founder Bryan, is adjacent to the courthouse on the Dallas County Historical Plaza.

Renowned architect I. M. Pei is responsible for the striking inverted-pyramid design of **Dallas City Hall** (✉ 1500 Marilla St., ☎ 214/670–5111). The building is set on a 7-acre plaza complete with reflecting pools and a stunning bronze Henry Moore sculpture. Next to City Hall in **Pioneer Plaza,** on the site of the historic Shawnee Cattle Trail, is a herd of larger-than-life bronze longhorns accompanied by a trio of cowboys. Robert Summers's work is said to be the largest bronze sculpture in the world. The **Dallas Police Memorial** (✉ Marilla, Akard, and Young Sts.) opened in 2001. The tribute to officers slain in the line of duty includes badge numbers cut into a stainless-steel canopy, as well as names engraved on the rear of the edifice.

Dallas's tallest building, the 920-ft **Bank of America Tower** (✉ 901 Main St.), is visible for miles at night, thanks to the green argon tubing—2 mi of it—that outlines its 72 stories. Lending a peculiar, science-fiction twist to the skyline is 50-story **Reunion Tower** (✉ 300 Reunion

Blvd., ☏ 214/651–1234), topped by a dome 118 ft in diameter. The dome has an **observation deck** (🎫 $2) and a revolving rooftop restaurant and bar. **Thanks-Giving Square** (✉ Pacific Ave. and Ervay St., ☏ 214/969–1977, WEB www.thanksgiving.org; 🎫 $5 suggested donation), a small triangular plaza designed by Philip Johnson, contains quiet gardens and a chapel with stained glass by Gabriel Loire.

ARTS DISTRICT

Housed in a series of low, white limestone galleries built off a central barrel vault, the **Dallas Museum of Art** (✉ 1717 N. Harwood St., ☏ 214/922–1200, WEB www.dm-art.org; 🎫 $6) is on the northern edge of downtown. Standout works are Claes Oldenburg's *Stake Hitch,* a huge stake and rope sculpture, and Frederic Church's chilling painting *The Icebergs.*The I. M. Pei–designed **Morton H. Meyerson Symphony Center** (✉ 2301 Flora St., ☏ 214/670–3600) is a place of sweeping dramatic curves, ever-changing vanishing points, and surprising views. Inside is the **Herman W. Lay Family Organ,** a hand-built and -installed Fisk organ with 4,535 pipes. **De Musica,** a solid iron sculpture by the great Basque sculptor Eduardo Chillida, rests in front of the Symphony Center.

OTHER ATTRACTIONS

Deep Ellum, a 20-minute walk east from downtown, was born as the city's first black neighborhood. Today it is the throbbing center of Dallas's avant-garde, with art galleries, bars, clubs, and restaurants. The area centers on Commerce, Main, and Elm streets; its name is a phonetic rendering of *deep elm* pronounced with a southern drawl.

★ **Fair Park** (✉ 1300 Robert B. Cullum Blvd., ☏ 214/421–9600), southeast of Deep Ellum, is a 277-acre National Historic Landmark with the largest collection of 1930s Art Deco architecture in the United States. In the **Hall of State** (✉ 3939 Grand Ave., ☏ 214/421–4500, WEB www.hallofstate.com; 🎫 free) murals tell the story of Texas in heroic terms. Fair Park also contains seven major exhibit spaces (most of which are closed Monday or Tuesday): the **African American Museum** (✉ 3536 Grand Ave., ☏ 214/565–9026; 🎫 free); the **Age of Steam Railroad Museum** (✉ 1105 N. Washington Ave., ☏ 214/428–0101; 🎫 $5); the **Dallas Aquarium** (✉ 1462 1st Ave., ☏ 214/670–8443; 🎫 $3); the **Texas Discovery Gardens** (✉ 3601 Martin Luther King Blvd., ☏ 214/428–7476; 🎫 free); the **Dallas Museum of Natural History** (✉ 3535 Grand Ave., ☏ 214/421–3466, WEB www.dallasdino.org; 🎫 $6.50); the **Women's Museum** (✉ 3800 Parry Ave., ☏ 214/915–0860, WEB www.thewomensmuseum.org; 🎫 $5); and the **Science Place** (✉ 1318 2nd Ave., ☏ 214/428–5555, WEB www.scienceplace.org; 🎫 $7.50), which also houses one of Dallas's **IMAX theaters** (🎫 $6.50).

In east Dallas, **Swiss Avenue** has the city's best representations of two distinct periods. On lower Swiss Avenue (2900 block), nearer to downtown, the **Wilson Block Historic District** is an unaltered block of turn-of-the-20th-century frame houses restored as offices for nonprofit groups. Set-back Prairie-style and other mansions are common in the **Swiss Avenue Historic District** (particularly the 5000–5500 blocks).

McKinney Avenue, in the city's burgeoning Uptown neighborhood, is lined with bustling bars and trendy restaurants. Authentic, restored **trolleys** (☏ 214/855–0006, WEB www.mata.org; 🎫 $1.50 round-trip) run up McKinney from outside the Dallas Museum of Art. The **McKinney Avenue Contemporary** (✉ 3120 McKinney Ave., ☏ 214/953–1622, WEB www.the-mac.org; 🎫 free), locally known as "the MAC," consists of a theater, gallery space, and video installation space.In the **Biblical Arts Center** (✉ 7500 Park La., ☏ 214/691–4661, WEB www.biblicalarts.org;

$7), a bit north of McKinney Avenue, sound and light bring a 124-ft by 20-ft biblical mural to life. Here you'll also find a replica of Christ's tomb at Calvary.

Though not as in demand as it was in its late-1980s heyday, the **Studios at Las Colinas** (✉ 6301 N. O'Connor Rd., Irving, ☎ 972/869–3456, WEB www.studiosatlascolinas.com; $12.95) is the largest soundstage complex between Florida and California. Tours include a visit to the soundstage facilities used in the filming of such movies as *JFK*, *Silkwood*, and *Robocop*.Minutes north of Dallas lies one of the city's most enduring landmarks, **Southfork Ranch** (✉ 3700 Hogge Dr., Parker, ☎ 972/442–7800, WEB www.southforkranch.com; $7.95). Built in 1970, the ranch became one of the city's best-known symbols when the TV show *Dallas* premiered in 1978. You can still tour the mansion, have lunch at Miss Ellie's Deli, and try to remember who shot J. R.

Fort Worth

Downtown is where you'll find the city's financial core, most of its historic buildings, and Sundance Square, the restored turn-of-the-20th-century neighborhood that is one of the city's main attractions. The Stockyards and adjacent western-theme stores, restaurants, and hotels are clustered around Main Street and Exchange Avenue, north of downtown. The cultural district, west of downtown on Lancaster Avenue, is known for four museums, a coliseum complex, and several parks.

DOWNTOWN

In Fort Worth's underrated downtown, modern glass-and-steel towers stand face-to-face with human-scale century-old Victorian buildings. The billionaire Bass brothers of Fort Worth are to be thanked for what may be the most eye-pleasing juxtaposition of scale: rather than tear down several blocks of brick buildings to accommodate the twin towers of their giant City Center development, they created **Sundance Square** (WEB www.sundancesquare.com), bounded by Houston, Commerce, 2nd, and 3rd streets, by restoring the area as a center of tall-windowed restaurants, shops, nightclubs, and offices.Sundance Square's name recalls the Sundance Kid (Harry Longabaugh), who with Butch Cassidy (Robert Leroy Parker) hid out around 1898 in the nearby neighborhood, south and east of the present square, known as Hell's Half-Acre. This was a violent quarter of dank saloons, drunken cowboys, and dirty brothels. The **Sid Richardson Collection of Western Art** (✉ 309 Main St., ☎ 817/332–6554, WEB www.sidrmuseum.org; free) conjures up parts of this dark world in the idealized oils of Frederic Remington and Charles Russell. **Fire Station No. 1** (✉ 215 Commerce St., ☎ 817/732–1631, WEB www.fwmuseum.org/firesta.html; free) houses an exhibit on 150 years of city history. The 1907 building—site of the city's first fire station and first city hall—is on the street where cattle headed for the Chisholm Trail used to pass.

THE STOCKYARDS

The **Stockyards National Historic District** recalls the prosperity brought to the city in 1902 when two major Chicago meat packers, Armour and Swift, set up plants here to ship meat across the country in refrigerator cars. In the **Livestock Exchange Building** (✉ 131 E. Exchange Ave.), where cattle agents kept their offices, you'll find the Stockyards Collection Museum (☎ 817/625–5082; free); the city's only daily cattle drive runs down East Exchange Avenue in front of this building. Across the street from the Livestock Exchange Building, **Stockyards Station** (✉ 130 E. Exchange Ave., ☎ 817/625–9715, WEB www.stockyardsstation.com) is a marketplace of shops and restaurants in what used to be sheep and hog pens. **Cowtown Coliseum** (✉ 121 E. Exchange Ave., ☎ 817/625–1025 or 888/269–8696, WEB www.

cowtowncoliseum.com) was constructed in 1908 to house what became the Southwestern Exposition and Fat Stock Show; today it is the site of Friday- and Saturday-night rodeos. A restored 1896 steam locomotive is one of the highlights of the **Tarantula Train** (✉ 140 E. Exchange Ave., ☎ 817/625–7245, WEB www.tarantulatrain.com; 🎫 $10 round-trip), which takes passengers on a 10-mi journey along the Chisholm Trail. You can take the Tarantula Train to **Grapevine** (🎫 $20 round-trip), where four of Texas's numerous wineries have tasting rooms. Information on the Stockyards area is available at the **Stockyards Visitors Center** (✉ 130 E. Exchange Ave., ☎ 817/624–4741).

THE CULTURAL DISTRICT

★ Architect Louis Kahn's last and finest building was the **Kimbell Art Museum,** made up of six long concrete vaults with skylights running the length of each. Here are top-notch collections of both early 20th-century European art and old masters, including Munch's *Girls on a Bridge* and Goya's *The Matador Pedro Romero,* depicting the great bullfighter who allegedly killed more than 6,000 of the animals without sustaining an injury. *✉ 3333 Camp Bowie Blvd., ☎ 817/332–8451, WEB www.kimbellart.org. 🎫 Free. Closed Mon.*

The **Amon Carter Museum,** along with the city's two other major museums, is a short walk from the Kimbell. Designed by Philip Johnson, the Amon Carter has a collection of American art centered on Remingtons and Russells. The museum reopened in 2001 after a two-year, $39 million renovation that tripled the amount of exhibition space. *✉ 3501 Camp Bowie Blvd., ☎ 817/738–1933, WEB www.cartermuseum.org. 🎫 Free. Closed Mon.*

The **Modern Art Museum of Fort Worth,** Texas's oldest, is slated to open its new space across from the Kimbell Art Museum in December 2002. With 53,000 square ft, the museum is second only to New York's Museum of Modern Art in gallery space devoted to contemporary art. *✉ 1309 Montgomery St., ☎ 817/738–9215, WEB www.mamfw.org. 🎫 Free. Closed Mon.*

Biology, geology, computer science, and astronomy are the order of the day at the **Fort Worth Museum of Science and History** (✉ 1501 Montgomery St., ☎ 817/255–9300, WEB www.fwmuseum.org; 🎫 $7), which also incorporates the Noble Planetarium (🎫 $3.50) and the Omni Theater (🎫 $7).The **Will Rogers Memorial Center** (✉ 3300 W. Lancaster Ave., ☎ 817/871–8150), near Fort Worth's museums, is a partially restored coliseum–and–stock pen complex named after the humorist and Fort Worth booster, who described the city as "where the West begins" (and Dallas as "where the East peters out"). The center includes an equestrian arena that's used for horse and livestock shows.

Parks, Gardens, and Zoos

Dallas

Fair Park, with its many museums and formal gardens, is one of the city's most visited parks; every fall it hosts Texas's largest State Fair (☎ 214/565–9931, WEB www.texfair.com). At **White Rock Lake Park** (✉ 8300 Garland Rd., ☎ 214/670–8283), a 9⅓-mi jogging and bicycling path circles the sailboat-dotted lake. The **Dallas Arboretum and Botanical Garden** (✉ 8525 Garland Rd., ☎ 214/327–8263, WEB www.dallasarboretum.org; 🎫 $6) is composed of 66 acres of gardens and lawns in White Rock Lake Park. **Old City Park** (✉ 1717 Gano St., ☎ 214/421–5141; 🎫 $7) is an outdoor museum consisting of 38 historic buildings, including log cabins, antebellum mansions, and a Victorian bandstand. At the **Dallas Zoo** (✉ 621 E. Clarendon Dr., ☎ 214/670–

5656, WEB www.dallas-zoo.org; $7), a monorail brings you past the most noted exhibit: lowland gorillas in a natural habitat.

Fort Worth

★ **Water Gardens Park** (✉ 15th and Commerce Sts.), a free, outdoor public sculpture garden, holds a dramatic blend of modern sculpture and cascading fountains designed by Philip Johnson and John Burgee. In one area, you can stand 38 ft below street level and view 1,000 gallons of water tumbling down a 710-ft wall. South of the cultural district, the **Fort Worth Botanic Garden** (✉ 3220 Botanic Garden Blvd., at University Dr., ☎ 817/871–7686; $1, Japanese garden $2.50) has a 10,000-square-ft conservatory. ★ The **Fort Worth Zoo** (✉ 1989 Colonial Pkwy., ☎ 817/759–7555, WEB www.fortworthzoo.com; $8.50) is the oldest continuous zoo site in Texas and houses more than 6,000 exotic and native animals, including Komodo dragons, koala bears, and a rare white tiger.

Dining

Dallas

$$$–$$$$ ✕ **Abacus.** This high-profile restaurant fits the Texas "everything's bigger" image. The interior—warm cherry woods, metal and glass sculpture, soft lighting—cost a reported $6 million. The food melds southwestern and Asian cuisine, resulting in creations like lobster "shooters" flavored with red chili and sake. People come back for the sushi. ✉ *4511 McKinney Ave.,* ☎ *214/559–3111. Reservations essential. AE, D, DC, MC, V. Closed Sun. No lunch.*

$$$–$$$$ ★ ✕ **York Street.** Meals begin with a complimentary tot of dry sherry and salted almonds; where you venture from there is up to you, but offerings like organic Jamison lamb ensure the journey will be memorable. The wine list gives poetic descriptions, while sleek pewter chairs and black-and-white photography lend the small dining room an urban feel. ✉ *6047 Lewis St.,* ☎ *214/826–0968. Reservations essential. AE, MC, V. Closed Sun.–Mon. No lunch.*

$$–$$$ ✕ **Ciudad.** A crowded dining room and lively bar scene are de rigueur at Monica Greene's tribute to Mexico City. Be prepared: this isn't Tex-Mex. Duck flautas and cumin-crusted lamb chops exemplify the sophisticated menu. Stucco walls colored in rich eggplant and maize, and flickering candles on wrought-iron pedestals, put polish on a rustic Mexican vibe. ✉ *3888 Oak Lawn Ave.,* ☎ *214/219–3141. AE, D, DC, MC, V. Closed Mon. No lunch Sat., no dinner Sun.*

$$–$$$ ★ ✕ **Jeroboam.** This urban brasserie in a restored 1913 building infuses French classics with a new American style. Soups are one highlight of the seasonal menu—think curried cauliflower or chilled lemon asparagus. And even traditional favorites like braised lamb shanks seem new when cooked with dried figs. A raw bar offers Jonah crab claws, pickled rock shrimp, and oysters. The all-French wine list may seem daunting with its 56-page addendum of maps, regional descriptions, and tasting notes, but servers are ready and willing to help. ✉ *1501 Main St.,* ☎ *214/748–7226. AE, D, MC, V. No lunch weekends.*

$$–$$$ ✕ **Nick & Sam's.** Cattle is king in Dallas, and you'd be hard pressed to find a better slab of beef than Nick & Sam's 22-ounce, prime aged Cowboy Cut. Lighter appetites can opt for grilled swordfish with orange butter sauce—make sure to save room for a side of the Damn Good fries. The raw bar in the open kitchen and the grand piano, not to mention the complimentary caviar and "negotiable" wine prices, make this upscale steak house more than a cut above. ✉ *3008 Maple Ave.,* ☎ *214/871–7444. AE, D, DC, MC, V. No lunch.*

$–$$ ✕ **Matt's Rancho Martinez.** Tex-Mex is served up for the masses in this Dallas institution. Specialties include chicken-fried steak, chiles rellenos, frogs' legs, and the signature Bob Armstrong dip, a decadent *chile con queso* dip loaded with beef, guacamole, and sour cream. The tree-covered patio is a pleasant spot for margarita sipping. ✉ *6332 La Vista Dr.,* ☎ *214/823–5517. AE, D, DC, MC, V. Closed Sun.*

$ ✕ **Sonny Bryan's Smokehouse.** The original location has been dishing up smoky brisket and fall-off-the-bone pork ribs from the same ramshackle digs since 1958, attracting fans ranging from President George W. Bush to director Steven Spielberg. Locals know to get there early; when Sonny's is out of barbecue, you're out of luck. ✉ *2202 Inwood Rd.,* ☎ *214/357–7120. AE, D, MC, V. No dinner.*

Fort Worth

$$$ ★ ✕ **Saint-Emilion.** Though it doesn't look like much from the outside, this is one of Tarrant County's best restaurants, with a legendary crispy-roast duck, excellent daily specials, and a long wine list. The prix-fixe option makes dinner an affordable taste of French country cuisine. ✉ *3617 W. 7th St.,* ☎ *817/737–2781. Reservations essential. AE, D, DC, MC, V. Closed Sun.–Mon. No lunch.*

$$–$$$ ✕ **Angeluna.** A yuppie and sometimes-raucous crowd fills this hot spot on weekends. The restaurant's mixed-cuisine menu may include ahi tuna grilled over hickory or rolled in sesame seeds and lightly seared. The dining room's tall windows look out on the majestic angel sculptures of Bass Performance Hall; the ceiling, painted blue with fluffy clouds, adds to the heavenly motif. ✉ *215 E. 4th St.,* ☎ *817/334–0080. AE, MC, V.*

$$–$$$ ✕ **Bistro Louise.** People drive 30 mi from Dallas to dine on smoked duck, potato-crusted salmon, and the like. High ceilings and bright colors add to the sunny Mediterranean vibe. ✉ *2900 S. Hulen St.,* ☎ *817/922–9244,* WEB *www.bistrolouisetexas.com. AE, D, DC, MC, V. Closed Sun.*

$$–$$$ ✕ **Randall's.** The cheesecake at this wine bar and café deserves to be mentioned first. You can start with a savory blend of smoked salmon and black lumpfish caviar, a fine prelude to an entrée of tuna Wellington or the Paris enchilada (a crepe stuffed with escargots, mushrooms, and goat cheese), but try to save room for the cheesecake. There are more than 60 varieties. ✉ *907 Houston St.,* ☎ *817/336–2253. Reservations essential. AE, D, MC, V. Closed Sun.–Mon. No lunch.*

$ ✕ **Angelo's Barbecue.** A Fort Worth institution since 1958, Angelo's is famous for succulent smoked ribs, so tender that the meat falls off the bone, and for the stuffed bear that guards the front door. Arrive early, as they've been known to run out of ribs well before closing. ✉ *2533 White Settlement Rd.,* ☎ *817/332–0357. Reservations not accepted. No credit cards. Closed Sun.*

$ ★ ✕ **Joe T. Garcia's.** This is the ultimate Tex-Mex joint, where cowboy boot–clad customers drink Mexican beer and the bartenders mix potent margaritas. There's usually a wait for tables, but with seating for more than 1,000 in the maze of dining rooms and patio areas, the line moves quickly. Dinner is limited to two choices: an enchilada-and-taco combo plate or fajitas. Lunch offers a more traditional menu, and on weekends there are Mexican breakfast specialties, including purported hangover-cure *menudo* (stew made with tripe, hominy, onions, and chili). ✉ *2201 N. Commerce St.,* ☎ *817/626–4356. Reservations not accepted. No credit cards.*

Dining and Lodging

$$$$ ★ ✕🏨 **Hotel St. Germain.** Built as a private residence in 1906, this tiny boutique hotel with white-glove service is one of the most romantic in the city. The beautiful rooms are filled with antiques and collectibles; each has a working fireplace. The dining room ($$$$; closed Sun.–Mon.)

is known for its $85-per-person prix-fixe dinner. ✉ *2516 Maple Ave., 75201,* ☎ *214/871–2516,* FAX *214/871–0740,* WEB *www.hotelstgermain.com. 7 suites. Restaurant. AE, D, DC, MC, V. CP.*

$$$$ ★ ✕🏨 **Mansion on Turtle Creek.** Opulent rooms are appointed with antiques and original artwork. The service is legendary, as is the hotel restaurant (*$$$$*). Chef Dean Fearing helped pioneer southwestern cuisine, and he continues to impress with amazing renditions of tortilla soup, warm lobster tacos, and even halibut with cashews in basil sauce. Count on finding Dallas–Fort Worth's most beautiful, celebrated, and powerful inside. ✉ *2821 Turtle Creek Blvd., 75219,* ☎ *214/559–2100,* FAX *214/528–4187,* WEB *www.mansiononturtlecreek.com. 143 rooms. 2 restaurants, pool, health club. AE, D, DC, MC, V.*

Lodging

Dallas

$$$$ 🏨 **Adolphus.** Beer baron Adolphus Busch created this Beaux Arts building, Dallas's finest old hotel, in 1912, sparing nothing in the way of rich ornamentation. The romantic European-style rooms have modern amenities. The celebrated French Room restaurant ($$$$; closed Sun.–Mon.) serves classics such as roast duck in port sauce. ✉ *1321 Commerce St., 75202,* ☎ *214/742–8200 or 800/221–9083,* FAX *214/651–3561,* WEB *www.hoteladolphus.com. 428 rooms. 3 restaurants, gym. AE, D, DC, MC, V.*

$$$$ ★ 🏨 **Four Seasons Resort and Club.** Looking like a Frank Lloyd Wright–designed country club, this hotel is quite possibly the city's best. Rooms have balconies that overlook the Tournament Players Course golf course, site of the PGA's GTE Byron Nelson Classic. ✉ *4150 N. MacArthur Blvd., Irving, 75038,* ☎ *972/717–0700 or 800/332–3442,* FAX *972/717–2550,* WEB *www.fourseasons.com. 357 rooms. 3 restaurants, pools, golf, tennis, health club. AE, D, DC, MC, V.*

$$$–$$$$ 🏨 **Wyndham Anatole.** Politicians, including George W. Bush and Colin Powell, have made this huge glass-and-chrome complex their home away from home. The rooms are standard, but the Anatole has seven bars, a nightclub, and a piano bar to keep you entertained. ✉ *2201 Stemmons Fwy., 75207,* ☎ *214/748–1200 or 800/996–3426,* FAX *214/761–7242,* WEB *www.wyndham.com. 1,620 rooms. 6 restaurants, pool, tennis, health club. AE, D, MC, V.*

$$–$$$$ 🏨 **Hotel Inter-Continental.** This north Dallas hotel, formerly the Grand Kempinski, is one of the best bargains in town. Downtown Dallas is a 10-minute jaunt down the Tollway, and nearby Belt Line Road offers plenty of dining and nightlife options. Standard rooms may not be particularly posh, but the many hotel amenities make up for any shortcomings. ✉ *15201 Dallas Pkwy., 75001,* ☎ *972/386–6000 or 800/327–0200,* FAX *972/991–6937,* WEB *www.interconti.com. 498 rooms. Restaurant, pools, tennis, health club. AE, D, DC, MC, V.*

$–$$$ 🏨 **Magnolia.** When it opened in 1922, the 29-story Magnolia building was the tallest structure south of Washington, D.C. Today it is best known as the home of the neon red Pegasus sign, installed atop the structure in 1934. It opened as a hotel in 1999, with tailored rooms that have an urban-loft feel. ✉ *1401 Commerce St., 75201 ,* ☎ *214/915–6500 or 888/915–1110,* FAX *214/253–0053,* WEB *www.themagnoliahotel.com. 200 rooms. Health club. AE, D, MC, V. CP.*

Fort Worth

$$$ ★ 🏨 **Renaissance Worthington.** This 12-story, white-concrete structure stretches along two city blocks, connected by a sky bridge to the Fort Worth Outlet Square mall. ✉ *200 Main St., 76102,* ☎ *817/870–1000 or 800/468–3571,* FAX *817/338–9176,* WEB *www.renaissancehotels.com. 504 rooms. Restaurant, pool, gym. AE, D, DC, MC, V.*

$$–$$$ **Miss Molly's.** Once a prim little inn, then a raucous bordello, this place above the Star Café has reincarnated as an attractive B&B. Each room is different, but all are furnished with Old West antiques. Only one has a private bath. ✉ *109½ W. Exchange Ave., 76106,* ☎ *817/626–1522 or 800/996–6559,* FAX *817/625–2723,* WEB *www.missmollys.com. 8 rooms, 1 with bath. AE, D, DC, MC, V. CP.*

$$ **Stockyards Hotel.** A storybook place that's seen more than its share of cowboys, rustlers, gangsters, and oil barons, this hotel has been used in many a movie. There are four styles of rooms to choose from: Victorian, Native American, Mountain Man, and Old West. In the Booger Red Saloon, the bar stools are saddles. ✉ *109 E. Exchange Ave., 76106,* ☎ *817/625–6427 or 800/423–8471,* FAX *817/624–2571,* WEB *www.stockyardshotel.com. 52 rooms. Restaurant. AE, D, DC, MC, V.*

$–$$ **Green Oaks Hotel.** From the outside, the Green Oaks is certainly unimpressive, but the interior is clean, the staff is efficient, and it's one of the few places in the Metroplex where you can get a decent room for under $100. ✉ *6901 West Fwy., 76116,* ☎ *817/738–7311 or 800/772–2341,* FAX *817/737–4486,* WEB *www.greenoakshotel.com. 284 rooms. Restaurant, pools, golf, tennis, health club. AE, D, MC, V.*

Nightlife and the Arts

Nightlife

DALLAS

Bars and Nightclubs. Much of Dallas bar life swirls around lower and upper **Greenville Avenue,** north of downtown. **Mick's** (✉ 2825 Greenville Ave., ☎ 214/827–0039) is a sophisticated place to swill martinis. Next door to Mick's, the **Greenville Bar & Grill** (✉ 2821 Greenville Ave., ☎ 469/334–0001) has operated under various owners since 1933. In its current incarnation, the tavern is notable for unusual food. Try the cheeseburger soup. The **Dubliner** (✉ 2818 Greenville Ave., ☎ 214/818–0911) is a rowdy Irish pub in which to hoist pints or throw darts. **Ozona Grill and Bar** (✉ 4615 Greenville Ave., ☎ 214/265–9105) has a large, tree-shaded patio where SMU students kick back after class.

Live Music. Open since 1977, **Poor David's Pub** (✉ 1924 Greenville Ave., ☎ 214/821–9891, WEB www.poordavidspub.com) is one of Dallas's longest-running live-music venues. The warehouselike **Trees** (✉ 2707 Elm St., ☎ 214/748–5009, WEB www.trees.com) has played host to such notable alternative bands as Pearl Jam and the Wallflowers. **Gypsy Tea Room** (✉ 2548 Elm St., ☎ 214/744–9779, WEB www.gypsytearoom.com) is actually two rooms: a 10,000-square-ft ballroom and a connecting, more intimate performance spot. Local and touring cutting-edge country and rock acts play here. For country music and two-stepping, try **Cowboys Red River** (✉ 10310 Technology Blvd., ☎ 214/352–1796, WEB www.cowboysdancehall.com).

Dance Clubs. At **Red Jacket** (✉ 3606 Greenville Ave., ☎ 214/823–8333, WEB www.thejacket.com) you can dance to everything from lounge to swing to 1980s retro. The **Club Clearview** complex (✉ 2806 Elm St., ☎ 214/939–0077, WEB www.clubclearview.com) houses four distinct yet connected clubs. **Village Station** (✉ 3911 Cedar Springs Rd., ☎ 214/559–0650, WEB www.caven.com/village.htm) caters to a predominately gay and lesbian crowd and has after-hours dancing till 4 AM on weekends.

FORT WORTH

Cowtown's best western-style watering hole may be the **White Elephant Saloon** (✉ 106 E. Exchange Ave., ☎ 817/624–1887, WEB www.whiteelephantsaloon.com), a legendary Wild West bar with live country music seven nights a week. **Billy Bob's Texas** (✉ 2520 Rodeo Plaza,

☎ 817/624–7117 or 817/589–1711, WEB www.billybobstexas.com), built in an old cattle-pen building, bills itself as the world's largest honky-tonk and plays host to big-name country music performers. **City Streets** (✉ 425 Commerce St., ☎ 817/335–5400) rolls four clubs into one, including a karaoke room and a dueling-piano lounge.

The Arts

DALLAS

The top performing-arts attraction in Dallas is whatever's on at the Morton H. Meyerson Symphony Center, where the **Dallas Symphony Orchestra** (☎ 214/692–0203, WEB www.dallassymphony.com) plays. The highest-profile theater performances are from the **Dallas Theater Center** (☎ 214/522–8499, WEB www.dallastheatercenter.org), which has two locations: the Kalita Humphreys Theatre (✉ 3636 Turtle Creek Blvd.), the only theater ever designed by Frank Lloyd Wright, and the Arts District Theater (✉ 2401 Flora). The **Majestic Theatre** (✉ 1925 Elm St., ☎ 214/880–0137), a beautifully restored 1920s vaudeville house and movie palace, hosts various performance groups. The Music Hall at Fair Park (✉ 909 1st Ave., ☎ 214/565–1116) gets a workout when the **Dallas Summer Musicals** (☎ 214/691–7200, WEB www.dallassummermusicals.org) comes to town.

The biggest touring musical acts set up stage at **American Airlines Center** (✉ 2500 Victory Ave., ☎ 214/222–3687, WEB www.americanairlinescenter.com), the David M. Schwarz–designed arena that opened to great fanfare in 2001. **Smirnoff Music Center** (✉ 1818 1st Ave., ☎ 214/421–1111), formerly the Starplex, is the outdoor site of most of the big summer tours. The **Bronco Bowl** (✉ 2600 Fort Worth Ave., ☎ 214/943–1777, WEB www.broncobowldallas.com) hosts small shows in a 3,000-seat arena. There's also an arcade and a bowling alley.

FORT WORTH

Casa Mañana Theater (✉ 3101 W. Lancaster Ave., ☎ 817/332–2272, WEB www.casamanana.org), a theater-in-the-round under one of Buckminster Fuller's first geodesic domes, is the site of the performing arts organization's main-stage productions, as well as its popular Children's Playhouse series. Public tours are available of the majestic **Nancy Lee and Perry R. Bass Performance Hall** (✉ 555 Commerce St., ☎ 817/212–4325, WEB www.basshall.com). Five resident companies call the world-class venue home: the Fort Worth Symphony Orchestra (☎ 817/665–6000, WEB www.fwsymphony.org), Fort Worth Dallas Ballet (☎ 817/212–4280, WEB www.fwdballet.com), Fort Worth Opera (☎ 817/731–0833, WEB www.fwopera.org), the Van Cliburn Foundation (☎ 817/335–9000, WEB www.cliburn.org), and the Casa Mañana Broadway at the Bass series (☎ 817/332–2272).

Spectator Sports

Auto racing: Texas Motor Speedway (✉ 3601 Rte. 114, Justin, ☎ 817/215–8500, WEB www.texasmotorspeedway.com). **Texas Motorplex** (✉ 7500 W. Rte. 287, Ennis, ☎ 972/878–2641, WEB www.texasmotorplex.com). **Baseball: Texas Rangers** (✉ The Ballpark at Arlington, 1000 Ballpark Way, Arlington, ☎ 817/273–5100, WEB www.texasrangers.com). **Basketball: Dallas Mavericks** (✉ American Airlines Center, 2500 Victory Ave. Dallas, ☎ 214/747–6287, WEB www.nba.com/mavericks). **Football: Dallas Cowboys** (✉ Texas Stadium, 2401 E. Airport Fwy., Irving, ☎ 972/785–5000, WEB www.dallascowboys.com). **Hockey: Dallas Stars** (✉ American Airlines Center, 2500 Victory Ave. Dallas, ☎ 214/467–8277, WEB www.dallasstars.com). **Fort Worth Brahmas** (✉ Fort Worth Convention Center, 1111 Houston St., Fort Worth, ☎ 817/336–4423).

Horse racing: Lone Star Park (✉ 1000 Lone Star Pkwy., Grand Prairie, ☎ 972/263–7223, WEB www.lonestarpark.com). **Soccer: Dallas Sidekicks** (✉ Reunion Arena, 777 Sports St. Dallas, ☎ 214/653–0200, WEB www.dallassidekicks.com). **Dallas Burn** (✉ Cotton Bowl, 3750 Midway Plaza Blvd., Dallas, ☎ 214/979–0303, WEB www.dallasburn.com).

Shopping

Dallas

Ever since 1873, when Dallas ensured its future by successfully finagling to become the site of the intersection of two intercontinental rail lines, the city has been the southwestern hub of American commerce. The **Galleria** (✉ 13355 Noel Rd., ☎ 972/702–7100, WEB www.dallasgalleria.com), with more than 200 retailers and anchor stores Macy's, Nordstrom, and Saks Fifth Avenue, is one of Dallas's best-known malls. Well known high-end retailers like Prada and Hermès, **Highland Park Village** (✉ Mockingbird La. at Preston Rd., ☎ 214/559–2740, WEB www.hpvillage.com) is touted as one of the first planned shopping centers in America. **NorthPark Center** (✉ Central Expressway at Northwest Hwy., ☎ 214/363–7441), developed as the nation's first indoor mall by art collector Ray Nasher, has rotating exhibits of world-class art on its walls. The original **Neiman Marcus** (✉ 1618 Main St., ☎ 214/741–6911) is a huge draw.

If you're in the mood for the fresh fruit and vegetables that have made the Rio Grande valley famous, stop by the **Dallas Farmers Market** (✉ 1010 S. Pearl St., ☎ 214/939–2808, WEB www.dallasfarmersmarket.org). Shop-a-holics shouldn't miss **Grapevine Mills Mall** (✉ 3000 Grapevine Mills Pkwy., Grapevine, ☎ 972/724–4900, WEB www.grapevinemills.com), with more than 1.5 million square ft of discount shopping; it's 20 mi northwest of Dallas.

Fort Worth

Both Fort Worth's attitude and its economy have always pointed west, and that's reflected in the shopping here. You can head right to the **Stockyards,** where there are several good western-wear outlets. Check out **Fincher's** (✉ 115 E. Exchange Ave., ☎ 817/624–7302, WEB www.fincherswhitefront.com), a western store since 1902 in a building that began life as a bank; you can still walk into the old vaults. A great place for boots is **M. L. Leddy's Boot and Saddlery** (✉ 2455 N. Main St., ☎ 817/624–3149). Downtown's **Sundance Square** is a perennial draw, with several small stores. **Fort Worth Outlet Square** (✉ 150 Throckmorton St., ☎ 817/390–3720 or 800/414–2817) is a large, modern indoor mall with its own privately operated subway. **Barber's Book Store** (✉ 215 W. 8th St., ☎ 817/335–5469), specializing in Texana and rare and fine books, is the oldest bookstore in Texas.

Dallas and Fort Worth Essentials

AIRPORTS AND TRANSFERS

Dallas–Fort Worth International Airport is the main airport for both cities and is currently the second-largest airport in the United States and the third largest in the world.

➤ AIRPORT INFORMATION: **Dallas–Fort Worth International Airport** (DFW; ✉ 3200 E. Airfield Dr., between Dallas and Fort Worth 75261, ☎ 972/574–8888, WEB www.dfwairport.com). **Love Field** (DAL; ✉ 8008 Cedar Springs Rd., at Mockingbird La., 75235, ☎ 214/670–6073).

AIRPORT TRANSFER

Taxi service to either downtown Dallas or downtown Fort Worth generally runs around $40. Love Field is about a $15 taxi ride from downtown Dallas. Cheaper van service is provided by the 24-hour

SuperShuttle. The Fort Worth Transportation Authority runs a $10 shuttle between the airport and downtown Fort Worth. Ritzier service is provided by Aadvantage Limousine.

➤ TAXIS AND SHUTTLES: **Aadvantage Limousine** (☎ 972/618–7313). **Fort Worth Transportation Authority** (☎ 817/215–8600, WEB www.the-t.com). **SuperShuttle** (☎ 800/258–3826, WEB www.supershuttle.com).

BUS TRAVEL TO AND FROM DALLAS AND FORT WORTH

➤ BUS INFORMATION: **Greyhound** (✉ 205 S. Lamar St. Dallas; ✉ 901 Commerce St., Fort Worth; ☎ 800/229–9424; WEB www.greyhound.com).

CAR TRAVEL

The Metroplex, as the Greater Dallas–Fort Worth area is known, is well served by interstates. The main approaches include I–35 from Oklahoma to the north and Waco to the south (this interstate splits near Denton, with I–35 E heading to Dallas and I–35 W branching off to Fort Worth); I–30 from Arkansas; I–20 from Louisiana and New Mexico; and I–45 from Houston. The twin cities are linked by I–20, which is the southern route, and I–30, generally the more useful road for visitors because many tourist destinations are in the northern part of town. There are three tollways in the Dallas area: the Dallas North Tollway, running from I–35 E north of downtown into Collin County to the north; George Bush Turnpike (Route 190), an east–west route in the area's northern suburbs; and Mountain Creek Bridge, in southwestern Dallas County. Three major expressways, I–30, I–35, and I–635, have High Occupancy Vehicle (HOV) lanes for vehicles with two or more occupants. Though the highway number designations are easy to find on a map, many of these thoroughfares are also known and referred to locally by name, which can make getting directions somewhat confusing. For example, Route 183, which leads to the south entrance of DFW Airport, is often referred to as Airport Freeway, and U.S. 75 is known to locals as Central Expressway. Dallas is circled by the I–635 ring road, known as LBJ Freeway; Fort Worth is looped by I–820.

TRAIN TRAVEL

➤ TRAIN INFORMATION: **Amtrak** (☎ 214/653–1101 or 800/872–7245, WEB www.amtrak.com). **Santa Fe Depot** (✉ 1501 Jones St., ☎ 817/332–2931). **Union Station** (✉ 400 Houston St., ☎ 214/653–1101).

TRANSPORTATION AROUND DALLAS AND FORT WORTH

A car is the best way to see Dallas and Forth Worth, though both cities have bus systems. Public transportation in Dallas is run by Dallas Area Rapid Transit (DART) and consists of buses that service Dallas and 12 suburban cities along with a light-rail system with a limited route. The Fort Worth Transportation Authority provides regular bus service on "The T" buses and trolleys. Commuter rail service between Dallas and Fort Worth is provided by Trinity Railway Express.

➤ CONTACTS: **Dallas Area Rapid Transit** (☎ 214/979–1111, WEB www.dart.org). **Fort Worth Transportation Authority** (☎ 817/215–8600, WEB www.the-t.com). **Trinity Railway Express** (☎ 877/657–0146, WEB www.trinityrailwayexpress.org).

VISITOR INFORMATION

➤ TOURIST INFORMATION: **Dallas Convention & Visitors Bureau** (✉ Old Red Courthouse, Main and Houston Sts.; information booths: ✉ NorthPark Center, Northwest Hwy. at Central Expressway; ✉ West End MarketPlace, 603 Munger Ave., Suite 124, West End; ☎ 214/746–6677; 800/232–5527; 214/746–6679 recorded schedule of events; WEB www.dallascvb.com). **Dallas–Fort Worth International Airport** (✉ 3200 E.

Airfield Dr., 75261, ☎ 972/574–3694, WEB www.dfwairport.com). **Fort Worth Convention & Visitors Bureau** (✉ 415 Throckmorton St., 76102; information centers: ✉ Downtown, 4th St. at Throckmorton St.; ✉ Cultural District, Will Rogers Center, Lancaster Ave. at University Dr.; ✉ The Stockyards, 130 E. Exchange Ave.; ☎ 817/336–8791 or 800/433–5747; WEB www.fortworth.com).

ELSEWHERE IN TEXAS

East Texas

What to See and Do

Heading into east Texas from the Dallas–Fort Worth area, you'll pass two great boundaries: a natural line, marking the start of a piney, hilly region totally unlike the Great Plains; and a man-made one, the beginning of what was the slaveholding part of the United States. In every way, east Texas—a region once dependent on cotton—feels more southern than western. After Texas seceded from the union in 1861, **Marshall** became the seat of civil authority west of the Mississippi and the wartime capital of Missouri; five Confederate generals are buried in its cemetery. Marshall is full of historic homes, some of which—like the **Starr Family Home** (✉ 407 W. Travis St., ☎ 903/935–3044; 🎫 $3)—can be toured; others are small hostelries. On beautiful **Stagecoach Road** (take Poplar Street, which heads east from U.S. 59, and follow markers) you can see wheel ruts from stages, some cutting 2 ft into the ground. Off U.S. 59 signs lead to **Marshall Pottery** (✉ 4901 Elysian Fields Rd., ☎ 903/927–5400, 888/768–8721, WEB www.marshallpottery.com; 🎫 free), a huge working pottery factory.

Jefferson, a 20-minute drive north of Marshall, is one of Texas's most historic towns, a charming place on Big Cypress Bayou that once served hundreds of steamboats coming up from New Orleans. When his offer to run track through the town was rebuffed, railroad baron Jay Gould is said to have angrily scrawled in the hotel register of the Excelsior House the prophetic words "The End of Jefferson." Today the superb **Excelsior House** (✉ 211 W. Austin St., ☎ 903/665–2513, WEB www.theexcelsiorhouse.com), built in the 1850s, is a tribute to the restorer's art (reservations are required months in advance). **Gould's private railroad car** is across the street from the Excelsior House.

Caddo Lake, overhung with Spanish moss and edged with bald cypresses, is a major fishing destination straddling the Texas-Louisiana border. At various times it has been home to the beleaguered Caddo Indians, to bootleggers hiding out in its dense shore growth, to the great singer of spirituals Leadbelly (reared at Swanson's Landing), to thriving steamboat traffic from New Orleans, and to all manner of other legends. **Caddo Lake State Park** (✉ Rte. 43, Karnack 75661, ☎ 903/679–3351, WEB www.tpwd.state.tx.us/park/caddo) is on the south shore.

Lodging

$–$$$ 🏨 **Pride House.** Ornate woodwork and original stained glass distinguish this old Victorian mansion. ✉ *409 E. Broadway, Jefferson 75657,* ☎ *903/665–2675 or 800/894–3526. 11 rooms. MC, V. BP.*

$$ 🏨 **Cypress Moon Cottage.** This secluded lakeside cabin includes two bedrooms, a full bath, large living area, and fully equipped kitchen. A canoe and boat ramp are available for guest use. ✉ *Rte. 2 (Box 100, Uncertain 75661),* ☎ *903/679–3154,* FAX *903/679–3087,* WEB *www.cypressmooncottage.com. 1 cottage. No credit cards. CP.*

East Texas Essentials

TRAIN TRAVEL

Amtrak trains serve Marshall twice a day. The station is on Washington Street, but there is no Amtrak staff there.

➤ TRAIN INFORMATION: **Amtrak** (☎ 800/872–7245, WEB www.amtrak.com).

CAR TRAVEL

Between Dallas and Shreveport, Louisiana, lies east Texas, whose main east–west artery is I–20. Marshall, the heart of the region, is about a three-hour drive from Dallas or a half hour from the Louisiana line.

El Paso

What to See and Do

Dramatically situated a few miles between the southern end of the Rockies and the northern terminus of Mexico's Sierra Madre range, **El Paso** (population: 563,662), established by the Spanish in 1598, was a major stopping point on the way west during the California gold rush. Outside the city, in El Paso's lower valley, are several important historic ★ sites, including the famed **Mission Trail** (WEB www.missiontrail.com). **Mission Ysleta** (✉ 131 S. Zaragoza Rd., ☎ 915/859–9848), the oldest Spanish mission in the Southwest, has a distinctive silver domed bell tower. **Mission Socorro** (✉ 328 S. Nevarez, ☎ 915/859–7718) is known for its fine vigas (the carved ceiling beams that mark local architecture). **Presidio Chapel San Elceario** (✉ 1556 San Elizario Rd., ☎ 915/851–2333) was first established as a military garrison to protect the missions. Adjacent to Mission Ysleta is the **Tigua Indian Reservation** (✉ 122 S. Old Pueblo Rd., ☎ 915/859–7913), home of the oldest ethnic group in Texas, where Tigua pottery, jewelry, art, and replicas of ancient Native American homes are for sale.

The history of the U.S. Border Patrol from the Old West to the present is portrayed at the **Border Patrol Museum,** with displays of aircraft and vehicles, surveillance equipment, and confiscated items. ✉ *4315 Transmountain Rd.,* ☎ *915/759–6060.* 🎫 *Free. Closed Mon.*

Across the Rio Grande from El Paso is the Mexican city of **Juárez,** where the shopping is often sensational. The **El Paso–Juárez Trolley** (✉ Santa Fe and San Francisco Sts., ☎ 915/544–0061 or 800/259–6284; 🎫 $12 round-trip) is really a bus, but the so-called Border Jumper runs every hour—and if your stay is less than 72 hours, you won't even need proof of citizenship. Panoramic views of El Paso can be seen from **Scenic Drive,** which you'll find by driving north on Mesa Street and then right on Rim Road. **Transmountain Road,** off I–10 west of downtown, takes you through Smuggler's Gap, a dramatic cut across the Franklin Mountains.

Lodging

$$–$$$ 🏨 **Hilton Camino Real.** This brick hotel is listed on the National Register of Historic Places. The jewel of the lobby is the dark-wood circular Dome Bar, which sits under a superb 1912 Tiffany skylight. The adjoining Dome restaurant is one of the city's best. ✉ *101 S. El Paso St., 79901,* ☎ *915/534–3000 or 800/722–6466,* FAX *915/534–3024,* WEB *www.hilton.com. 359 rooms. 4 restaurants, pool, health club. AE, D, DC, MC, V.*

El Paso Essentials

AIRPORTS

➤ AIRPORT INFORMATION: **El Paso International Airport** (✉ 6701 Convair Dr., ☎ 915/780–4749 or 800/435–9792, WEB www.elpasointernationalairport.com).

CAR TRAVEL

At Texas's far southwestern corner, El Paso is an 11-hour drive from San Antonio; about 12 hours from Dallas–Fort Worth; 6 from Santa Fe, New Mexico; and 5 from Phoenix, Arizona.

TRAIN TRAVEL

➤ TRAIN INFORMATION: **Amtrak** (☎ 800/872–7245, WEB www.amtrak.com).

VISITOR INFORMATION

➤ TOURIST INFORMATION: **El Paso Convention & Visitors Bureau** (✉ 1 Civic Center Plaza, 79901, ☎ 915/534–0600 or 800/351–6024, WEB www.elpasocvb.com).

South Padre Island

What to See and Do

At the southern tip of one of the largest barrier islands in the world—113-mi-long Padre Island—the resort town and white-sand beaches of **South Padre Island** (population: 2,149) attract college students at spring break but delight nature seekers, beach and sun lovers, and fishermen the rest of the year. North of South Padre Island, the 80½-mi ★ **Padre Island National Seashore** (✉ 9405 South Padre Island Dr., Corpus Christi 78418, ☎ 361/949–8173) is essentially unchanged from the days when scavenging Karankawa Indians roamed among its sand dunes, sea oats, and morning glories.

South Padre Island Essentials

CAR TRAVEL

South Padre Island is in the southeastern corner of the state, near the Mexican border town of Matamoros. The island is reached by a bridge across the Intracoastal Waterway from Port Isabel, which, in turn, is accessible from Routes 48 and 100.

VISITOR INFORMATION

➤ TOURIST INFORMATION: **South Padre Island Convention & Visitors Bureau** (✉ 600 Padre Island Blvd. [Box 3500, 78597], ☎ 956/761–6433 or 800/767–2373, WEB www.sopadre.com).

UTAH

Updated by Kate Boyes

Capital	Salt Lake City
Population	2,233,169
Motto	Industry
State Bird	California gull
State Flower	Sego lily
Postal Abbreviation	UT

Statewide Visitor Information

Utah Travel Council (✉ Council Hall, 300 N. State St., Salt Lake City 84114, ☎ 800/200–1160, WEB www.utah.com) has many free directories, including those for campgrounds and rafting outfitters. Ten **regional visitor information centers** supply brochures and travel advice, and **welcome centers** are near all major entrances to the state.

Scenic Drives

Utah has 27 designated scenic byways. At the northern tip of the state, **U.S. 89** runs north from Logan through a limestone canyon with steep, striated walls, cresting above Bear Lake on the Utah-Idaho border. In the corner that borders Colorado and Wyoming, **U.S. 191** jogs north out of Vernal, passing geologic formations that are up to a billion years old before meeting **Route 44,** which yields an elongated view of Flaming Gorge National Recreation Area. **Route 12,** in southern Utah, turns east from U.S. 89, skirting through Bryce Canyon National Park and Grand Staircase–Escalante National Monument, and then runs north over aspen-covered Boulder Mountain to Capitol Reef National Park.

National and State Parks

National Parks

Utah's five national parks are all in the southern part of the state. Geologic formations shaped like spires and turrets fill the orange-colored amphitheaters of **Bryce Canyon** (✉ Hwy. 63 [Box 170001, Bryce Canyon 84717], ☎ 435/834–5322). **Capitol Reef** (✉ Hwy. 24 [HCR 70, Box 15, Torrey 84775], ☎ 435/425–3791) is distinguished by colorfully striped rock walls, ancient petroglyphs, and orchards where you can pick fruit. Towering cliffs and hanging gardens can be found throughout **Zion** (✉ Rte. 9, Springdale 84767, ☎ 435/772–3256). Three geologically distinct districts make up **Canyonlands** (✉ 2282 S.W. Resource Blvd., Moab 84532, ☎ 435/259–7164). The red sandstone formations of **Arches** (✉ U.S. 191 [Box 907, Moab 84532], ☎ 435/259–8161) have become a symbol for the state of Utah.

Join the fossil excavations at **Dinosaur National Monument** (✉ Quarry Visitor Center [Box 128, Jensen 84035], ☎ 435/781–7700). Water sports abound at **Flaming Gorge National Recreation Area** (✉ Box 279, Manila 84046, ☎ 435/784–3445). Fish or boat on Lake Powell within the **Glen Canyon National Recreation Area** (☎ 928/608–6404). Hike through **Grand Staircase–Escalante National Monument** (Bureau of Land Management, ✉ 318 North 100 East, Kanab 84741, ☎ 435/644–4600; 🎫 free), which has few amenities and services but stunning river canyons and giant steplike cliffs. Along a remote stretch of the Utah-Colorado border southeast of Blanding (28 mi east of U.S. 191 on Rte. 262), discover the buildings and lifeways of ancient peoples at **Hovenweep National Monument** (✉ McElmo Rte., Cortez, CO 81321, ☎ 435/459–4344). Hike under the giant, stream-formed spans of **Natu-**

ral Bridges National Monument (✉ Box 1, Lake Powell 84533, ☎ 435/692–1234). Utah will probably have a new national monument by 2003, tentatively named the **San Rafael Swell National Monument,** which has miles of trails that wind through unusual geological formations. The limestone caverns of **Timpanogos Cave National Monument** (✉ R.R. 3 [Box 200, American Fork 84003], ☎ 801/756–5238 visitor center; 801/756–5239 headquarters; WEB www.nps.gov/tica; $6) are 36 mi from Salt Lake City.

State Parks

The **Division of State Parks** (✉ 1594 W. North Temple St., Salt Lake City 84114, ☎ 801/538–7220 or 800/322–3770 for camping reservations, WEB www.stateparks.ut.gov) publishes a directory of Utah's 45 state parks. **Goblin Valley State Park** (✉ Box 637, Green River 84525, ☎ 435/564–3633, WEB www.parks.state.ut.us/parks/goblin; $5), off I–70 on Route 24 in eastern Utah, has acres of wind-eroded sandstone "goblins" around a desert campground. **This Is the Place Heritage Park** (✉ 2601 Sunnyside Ave., Salt Lake City 84108, ☎ 801/582–1847, WEB www.parks.state.ut.us/parks/heritage; $6) details the trek of Mormon pioneers and re-creates an 1850s township, complete with cooking, crafts making, and blacksmithing demonstrations.

SALT LAKE CITY

A growing, dynamic metropolis, Salt Lake City is a high-tech hub of the Rocky Mountains. The Salt Lake area has evolved into a world-class destination for winter sports, which made it the perfect host for the 2002 Olympic Winter Games. The city's roots date to July 24, 1847, when Mormon leader Brigham Young looked out over the Salt Lake Valley and announced to the ragged party behind him, "This is the right place." So began the religious settlement that nurtured the Church of Jesus Christ of Latter-Day Saints, as the Mormon Church is officially known. Although the population of Salt Lake City is now religiously and ethnically diverse, the influence of the Mormon Church is strong.

Exploring Salt Lake City

City attractions fan out from Temple Square. To the north is the Capitol Hill District; to the south are shopping and arts locations; to the west is the Great Salt Lake; and to the east lie the ski resorts of the Wasatch Mountains.

Historic **Temple Square** (✉ North Visitors' Center, 50 W. North Temple St., ☎ 801/240–2534) is the 10-acre center of sites important to Mormonism. The six-spire granite **Salt Lake Temple** is open to church members, but the public may enter the other buildings and monuments on the beautifully landscaped grounds, including two visitor centers with exhibits and art with religious themes. The famous Mormon Tabernacle Choir rehearses at 8 PM on Thursday and performs at 9:30 AM Sunday in the squat, domed Salt Lake **Tabernacle.**

East of Temple Square, the **Joseph Smith Memorial Building** offers programs, films, and exhibits about the history of the LDS Church and the emigration of Mormons to the Salt Lake Valley. At the computerized genealogical research center, visitors can trace their family heritage. The center, housed in the elegant building that was once the Hotel Utah, also has two restaurants. ✉ *South Temple and Main Sts.,* ☎ *801/240–1266 or 800/537–9703.* *Free. Closed Sun.*

Directly west of Temple Square is the **Museum of Church History and Art** (✉ 45 N. West Temple St., ☎ 801/240–3310; free), displaying

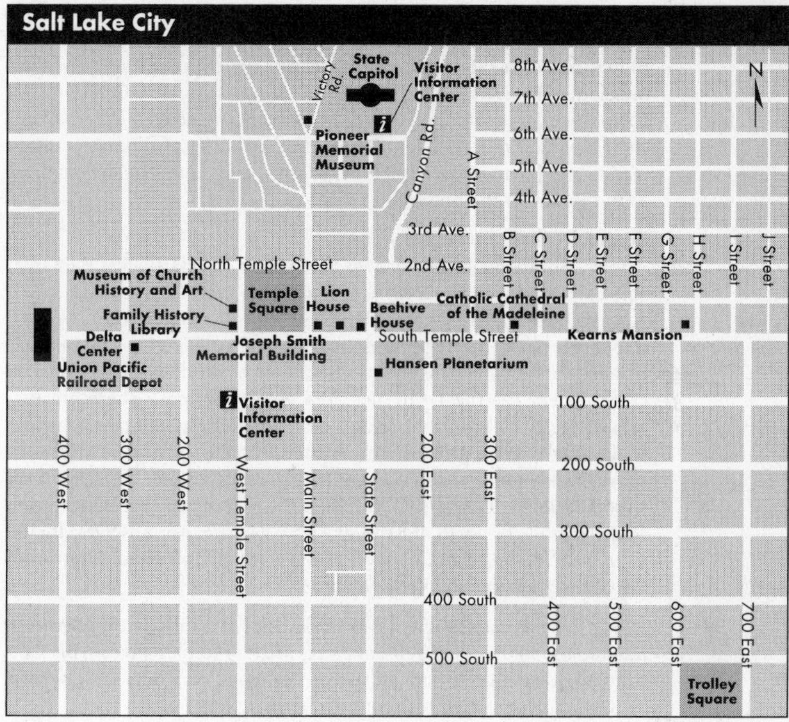

Mormon artifacts, paintings, fabric art, and sculptures. The **Family History Library** provides free public access to the Mormons' huge collection of genealogical records. ✉ *35 N. West Temple St.,* ☎ *801/240–2331,* WEB *www.familysearch.org.* 🎫 *Free. Closed Sun.*

Brigham Young lived in the 1854 **Beehive House** (✉ 67 E. South Temple St., ☎ 801/240–2671; 🎫 free) when he served as territorial governor. Young built the Lion House next door to house his 27 wives and 56 children. It's now a social center and restaurant.

A moon-rock display is among the exhibits at the **Hansen Planetarium** (✉ 15 S. State St., ☎ 801/538–2104, WEB www.hansenplanetarium.org; 🎫 free, shows $3.50–$7.50). A domed theater hosts star shows and laser shows set to music. The planetarium will move to a new building in 2003.

The Renaissance Revival–style **Utah State Capitol** (✉ 300 N. State St., ☎ 801/538–1563 or 801/538–3000) was completed in 1915. There are free hourly tours of meeting rooms and chambers, and in the rotunda are Depression-era murals that depict events from Utah's past. The **Pioneer Memorial Museum,** directly west of the state capitol grounds, holds thousands of artifacts, including tools and carriages from the late 1800s and a doll and toy collection. ✉ *300 N. Main St.,* ☎ *801/538–1050.* 🎫 *Free; donations accepted. Closed Sun. Sept.–June.*

Historic houses line South Temple Street east of Temple Square. The early 20th-century **Catholic Cathedral of the Madeleine** (✉ 331 E. South Temple St., ☎ 801/328–8941) is Gothic in style. Among the finest houses on South Temple Street is the governor's residence, **Kearns Mansion,** accessible by guided tours. Tours are daily during the first week of December. ✉ *603 E. South Temple St.,* ☎ *801/538–1005.* 🎫 *Free. Closed Mon., Wed., Fri.–Sun., and mid-Dec.–late Mar.*

The **Utah Museum of Natural History** (✉ President's Circle, ☎ 801/581–4303, WEB www.umnh.utah.edu; 🎫 $4) has Native American artifacts, dinosaur skeletons, and hands-on science adventures. The **Utah Museum of Fine Art** (✉ 1530 E. South Campus Dr., ☎ 801/581–7332, WEB www.utah.edu/umfa; 🎫 free) houses a permanent collection of ancient Egyptian relics, Italian Renaissance paintings, Chinese ceramics, traditional Japanese screens, Navajo rugs, and American art from the 17th century to the present.

Outside Salt Lake City

About 16 mi west of downtown Salt Lake City via I–80 is the Great Salt Lake, accessed by **Great Salt Lake State Park** (✉ Frontage Rd., 2 mi east of I–80 Exit 104, ☎ 801/250–1898; 🎫 free). Water flows into it, but there is no outlet other than evaporation. Minerals and salts are trapped in the lake, causing it to be the most saline body of water on earth except for the Dead Sea. Yes, you will float. There are two beaches here, each with showers. The south and west shores and neighboring wetlands are prime nesting grounds for many species of migratory, shore, and wading birds. Wide, sandy beaches ring much of **Antelope Island State Park** (☎ 801/773–2941; 🎫 $7 per vehicle), which is accessed from I–15 north of Salt Lake City via a 7½-mi causeway. Inland trails provide breathtaking views of Great Salt Lake and glimpses of the island's bison and antelope herds.

Rising to more than 11,000 ft east of the Salt Lake Valley are the **Wasatch Mountains.** Southeast of Salt Lake City are two scenic canyons, Big Cottonwood on Route 190 and Little Cottonwood on Route 210. Resorts in these canyons offer year-round activities.

Over the ridge line of the Wasatch Mountains, but 29 mi east of Salt Lake City via I–80, is **Park City,** Utah's premier ski destination. Park City's three ski areas and the Utah Winter Sports Park hosted many events during the 2002 Olympic Winter Games. Main Street has a museum, galleries, shops, and restaurants. The town also offers fine bed-and-breakfast accommodations, three golf courses, and an outlet mall.

Parks, Gardens, and Zoos

Tracy Aviary (✉ 600 E. 900 South St., ☎ 801/596–8500, WEB www.tracyaviary.org; 🎫 $3) covers more than 7 acres of a park 1 mi south of downtown and features 133 species of birds from around the globe. During the summer, there are two free-flight bird shows each day.

Red Butte Gardens and Arboretum (✉ enter on Wakara Way, east of Foothill Dr., ☎ 801/585–0556, WEB www.redbutte.utah.edu; 🎫 $5), east of the University of Utah campus and Research Park, consists of 25 acres of gardens and 125 undeveloped acres. There are also nature trails and stream-fed pools tucked into a private canyon in the Wasatch foothills. A concert series is held each summer.

In the city's eastern foothills, **Utah's Hogle Zoo** (✉ 2600 E. Sunnyside Ave., ☎ 801/582–1631, WEB www.hoglezoo.org; 🎫 $7) has more than 1,400 animals, including a new primate forest that features spider, colobus, and capuchin monkeys. Bring walking shoes and a hat—exhibits are spread out, and shade is at a premium.

Dining

Although liquor laws have some peculiarities, mixed drinks, wine, and beer are available at most restaurants. When in doubt, call ahead.

$$$$ ★ ✕ **La Caille.** Norwegian silver salmon baked in parchment, Chateaubriand with béarnaise sauce, escargots à la bourguignonne: every

dish served here is excellent. The location—an 18th-century French-château replica surrounded by a nature preserve—adds immeasurable charm to the dining experience. ✉ *9565 Wasatch Blvd.,* ☎ *801/942–1751. Reservations essential. AE, D, DC, MC, V.*

$$$–$$$$ ★ ✕ **Grappa.** Heavy floor tiles, bricks, and timbers lend a warm, farmhouse feel to this Italian restaurant. Innovative entrées include crisp, pan-fried game hen with spinach tortellini and roasted garlic velouté, as well as pancetta-wrapped chicken fricassee filled with spinach and mushroom risotto. The menu changes with the seasons. ✉ *151 Main St., Park City,* ☎ *435/645–0636. AE, D, MC, V.*

$$$–$$$$ ★ ✕ **Metropolitan.** The setting is comfortably urban, and the staff has the time and knowledge necessary to make your meal memorable. Specialties include wild game, European delicacies, and absolutely fresh seafood, and an extensive tasting menu provides a chance to sample out-of-the-ordinary dishes. Jazz musicians perform on Saturday night. ✉ *173 W. Broadway,* ☎ *801/364–3472. AE, D, MC, V.*

$$–$$$$ ★ ✕ **Log Haven Restaurant.** South of Salt Lake City, this 80-year-old retreat in the pines has lured the likes of Margaret Thatcher and pampered members of the International Olympics Committee for dinner. The eclectic menu has entrées such as coriander-rubbed ahi tuna, pepper-seared filet mignon, and Cajun-spiced duck confit. ✉ *4 mi up Millcreek Canyon, Salt Lake City,* ☎ *801/272–8255,* WEB *www.log-haven.com. AE, D, MC, V.*

$$–$$$$ ★ ✕ **Market Street Grill.** The stylish black-and-white decor is catchy, and the atmosphere is lively, but the fresh, well-prepared seafood is the real draw. Be sure to check the daily fish specials, and do try the New England clam chowder. ✉ *48 Market St.,* ☎ *801/322–4668,* WEB *www.gastronomyinc.com. AE, D, DC, MC, V.*

$$–$$$ ✕ **Zoom.** This "western chic" eatery, owned by Robert Redford, specializes in comfort food kicked up a notch. Locals favor the tri-tip steak served with garlic and Asiago cheese grits. ✉ *660 Main St.,Park City,* ☎ *435/649–9108. AE, D, DC, MC, V.*

$$ ✕ **Santa Fe Restaurant.** Inside a streamside lodge in scenic Emigration Canyon, 15 minutes east of downtown, Santa Fe Restaurant earns acclaim for its creative regional dishes, such as Utah rainbow trout, and its appetizers, which combine meat and seafood with chiles and fresh salsas. The warm bread served with all meals is outstanding. ✉ *2100 Emigration Canyon Rd.,* ☎ *801/582–5888. AE, D, MC, V.*

$–$$ ✕ **Bangkok Thai.** Curry, rice and noodle, vegetarian, and vegan dishes are mainstays here, and the entrées featuring fresh fish and seafood are a real treat. The heat level of this carefully prepared Asian food ranges from mild to wild. ✉ *1400 S. Foothill Dr.,* ☎ *801/582–8424 or 888/852–8424. AE, D, DC, MC, V.*

$–$$ ✕ **Lamb's Grill Café.** Lamb's is reminiscent of a classy 1930s diner, though it opened back in 1919. Most of Salt Lake City's movers and shakers convene here for breakfast. The lunch and dinner menus feature beef, chicken, and seafood dishes, plus a selection of sandwiches. ✉ *169 S. Main St.,* ☎ *801/364–7166. AE, D, DC, MC, V. Closed Sun.*

$–$$ ✕ **Tucci's.** Don't let the reasonable prices fool you: the food, service, and ambience here are far above the ordinary. Try the chicken breasts topped with shrimp and artichokes, and save room for dessert—the gratino custard and the chocolate mousse are both excellent. A variety of seating areas make the restaurant suitable for any occasion. ✉ *515 S. 700 East St.,* ☎ *801/533–9111. AE, D, DC, MC, V.*

Lodging

Prices vary widely with the seasons. The ski resorts listed below are no more than 30 mi away from Salt Lake City.

$$$$ ★ **Cliff Lodge.** The large guest rooms in this resort hotel are decorated in mountain colors and desert pastels, and they have wide glass walls with spectacular views. The lobby, draped with a private collection of Persian rugs, is sumptuous. On the grounds is a full-service day spa. ✉ *Snowbird Ski and Summer Resort, 9900 E. Little Cottonwood Canyon Rd., 84092,* ☎ *801/742–2222 or 800/453–3000,* FAX *801/947–8227,* WEB *www.snowbird.com. 511 rooms. 4 restaurants, pools, gym. AE, D, DC, MC, V.*

$$$$ ★ **Grand America.** The gardens, pools, shops, ballrooms, and meeting rooms on this hotel's 20-acre site in downtown Salt Lake City make it more a destination than a place to spend the night. The European flavor is thanks to English wool carpets, French furniture and tapestries, and Italian marble. Original art from around the world hangs everywhere, even in the spacious guest rooms, which include high-speed T1 data ports. ✉ *555 S. Main St. 84111,* ☎ *801/258–6000 or 800/621–45005,* FAX *801/258–6911,* WEB *www.grandamerica.com. 810 rooms. 2 restaurants, pools, health club. AE, D, DC, MC, V.*

$$$$ ★ **Stein Eriksen Lodge.** With imported fabrics, chandeliers, hot tubs, and fireplaces in most guest rooms, and stunning views throughout the lodge, this world-class resort combines a gracious atmosphere with the convenience of ski-out access to some of the finest runs in the Park City area. ✉ *7700 Stein Way, Deer Valley 84060,* ☎ *435/649–3700 or 800/453–1302,* FAX *435/649–5825,* WEB *www.steinlodge.com. 81 rooms. 4 restaurants, pool, golf, tennis, gym. AE, D, DC, MC, V.*

$$$–$$$$ **Shadow Ridge Resort.** You can ski straight into Park City Mountain Resort's lift lines from most of the rooms here, which range from a single hotel room to a two-bedroom condominium suite with full kitchen. ✉ *50 Shadow Ridge St. (Box 1820, Park City 84060),* ☎ *435/655–3315 or 800/451–3031,* FAX *435/649–5951. 150 rooms. Pool, gym. AE, D, DC, MC, V.*

$$–$$$$ **Little America Hotel.** Elegant rooms with textured fabrics, plush seating, and variable lighting and enormous brick fireplaces in the lobby and mezzanine make this one of the most pleasant places to stay in Salt Lake City. ✉ *500 S. Main St., 84101,* ☎ *801/363–6781 or 800/453–9450,* FAX *801/596–5910,* WEB *www.littleamerica.com. 850 rooms. 2 restaurants, pool, health club. AE, D, DC, MC, V.*

$–$$$ ★ **Saltair Bed & Breakfast.** This 1903 Victorian home is listed on the state and national registers of historic places. Fine oak woodwork and period antiques lend elegance to the rooms. Sitting in the formal parlor with a book before a roaring fire is the perfect way to end a day. ✉ *164 S. 900 East St., 84102,* ☎ *801/533–8184 or 800/733–8184,* FAX *801/595–0332,* WEB *www.saltlakebandb.com. 16 rooms. AE, D, DC, MC, V. BP.*

$–$$ **Anton Boxrud Bed & Breakfast.** This antiques-filled Victorian manor near the governor's mansion is a pleasant 15-minute walk from the city center. The complimentary evening snacks and beverages served near the parlor's bay window are as delicious as the bountiful breakfasts. ✉ *57 S. 600 East St., 84102,* ☎ *801/363–8035 or 800/524–5511,* FAX *801/596–1316,* WEB *www.netoriginals.com/antonboxrud. 7 rooms. AE, D, DC, MC, V. BP.*

Motels

Holiday Inn Express (✉ 2080 W. North Temple St., 84116, ☎ 801/355–0088 or 800/465–4329, FAX 801/355–0099), 92 rooms; restaurant, pool; *$–$$.*

Ramada Inn—Downtown (✉ 230 W. 600 South St. 84103, ☎ 801/364–5200, FAX 801/364–0974, WEB www.ramadainnslc.com), 120 rooms; restaurant, pool, gym; *$.*

Travelodge (✉ 524 S. West Temple St., 84101, ☎ 801/531–7100 or 800/578–7878, FAX 801/359–3814), 60 rooms; pool; $.

Nightlife and the Arts

A calendar of events is available at the Salt Lake Convention and Visitors Bureau. The free *City Weekly* newspaper is widely available throughout the city. Both the *Salt Lake Tribune* and the *Deseret News* carry daily arts-and-entertainment listings.

Nightlife

Many nightspots are private clubs due to Utah's unusual liquor laws, meaning that membership is required (temporary memberships cost about $5). Weekends are wild at the **Dead Goat Saloon** (✉ 165 S. West Temple St., ☎ 801/328–4628), a subterranean hangout with live music and a busy dance floor. A good place to spot Utah Jazz basketball players is **Port O' Call** (✉ 78 W. 400 South St., ☎ 801/521–0589), a sports bar with 14 satellite dishes and 26 TVs. The art deco–style **Zephyr Club** (✉ 301 S. West Temple St., ☎ 801/355–5646) hosts nationally known touring acts that get people dancing to blues, rock, and reggae. The **Bay** (✉ 404 S. West Temple St., ☎ 801/363–2623) is a smoke- and alcohol-free club with three dance floors. Burgers and rock-and-roll memorabilia are the hallmarks of the **Hard Rock Cafe** (✉ 505 S. 600 East St., ☎ 801/532–7625).

The Arts

Salt Lake City takes pride in its wide range of performing arts companies and venues. **Ballet West** (✉ 50 W. 200 South St., ☎ 801/355–2787) is considered one of the nation's top ballet companies. Rock and pop concerts are presented regularly at the **Delta Center** (✉ 301 W. South Temple St., ☎ 801/325–7328). In addition to sports events, the **"E" Center** (✉ 3200 S. Decker Lake Dr., ☎ 801/988–8888) also hosts concerts and other performing arts events. The **Pioneer Theater Company** (✉ 300 S. 1400 East St., ☎ 801/581–6961) stages classic and contemporary musicals and plays. **Salt Lake Acting Company** (✉ 168 W. 500 North St., ☎ 801/363–7522) is nationally recognized for its development of new plays. The **Utah Opera Company** (✉ 50 W. 200 South St., ☎ 801/355–2787) produces four operas each year. The **Utah Symphony** orchestra (✉ Abravanel Hall, 123 W. South Temple St., ☎ 801/533–6683) performs 260 concerts annually.

Spectator Sports

Baseball: The Pacific Coast League **Salt Lake Buzz** (✉ 77 W. 1300 South St., ☎ 801/485–3800) play at Franklin Covey Field. **Basketball:** The NBA's **Utah Jazz** (✉ 301 W. South Temple St., ☎ 801/355–3865) play home games at the Delta Center. **Utah Starzz** (✉ 300 W. South Temple St., ☎ 801/358–7328) of the WNBA share the Delta Center with the Utah Jazz. **Hockey:** The International Hockey League **Utah Grizzlies** (✉ 3200 S. Decker La., West Valley City, ☎ 801/988–8000) use the "E" Center as their home base.

Ski Areas

Cross-Country

Solitude (✉ 12000 Big Cottonwood Canyon Rd., ☎ 801/534–1400 or 800/748–4754, WEB www.skisolitude.com) has 12 mi of groomed trails. Between Park City and the Canyons, the golf course used by **White Pine Ski Touring Center** (✉ Park City, ☎ 801/649–8710 or 801/649–8701) is flat and has 12 mi of trails. The **Sundance Nordic Center** (✉ off Rte. 52, Sundance, ☎ 801/225–4107 or 800/892–1600, WEB www.

sundanceresort.com) features 15 km of skiing and offers night skiing lit by lanterns.

Downhill

Alta (✉ Rte. 210, ☎ 801/359–1078, WEB www.alta.com or www.altaskiarea.com) has more than 40 runs and bowls, 8 lifts, and a 2,020-ft vertical drop. **Brighton** (✉ Rte. 190, ☎ 801/532–4731 or 800/873–5512, WEB www.skibrighton.com) has more than 65 runs, 7 lifts, and a 1,745-ft vertical drop. The **Canyons** (✉ The Canyons Resort Dr., off Rte. 224, Park City, ☎ 435/649–5400 or 888/226–9667, WEB www.thecanyons.com) has 132 runs, 12 lifts, a gondola, and a 3,190-ft vertical drop. **Deer Valley** (✉ Rte. 224, Park City, ☎ 435/649–1000 or 800/424–3337, WEB www.deervalley.com), has 88 runs, 19 lifts, and a 3,000-ft vertical drop. **Park City Mountain Resort** (✉ Rte. 224 off I–80, Park City, ☎ 435/647–5449 or 800/222–7275, WEB www.parkcitymountain.com) has 100 runs, 14 lifts, and a 3,100-ft vertical drop. **Solitude** (✉ 12000 Big Cottonwood Canyon Rd., ☎ 801/534–1400 or 800/748–4754, WEB www.skisolitude.com) has 63 runs and bowls, 7 lifts, a 2,047-ft vertical drop, and 12 mi of groomed cross-country track. **Snowbird** (✉ Rte. 210, ☎ 800/385–2002, WEB www.snowbird.com) has 89 runs and bowls, 9 lifts and a high-speed tram, and a 3,240-ft vertical drop.

Shopping

Directly south of Temple Square, **Crossroads Plaza** (✉ 50 S. Main St., ☎ 801/531–1799) has four floors of stores. Scores of stores fill the **ZCMI Center Mall** (✉ South Temple and Main Sts., ☎ 801/321–8745). **Trolley Square** (✉ 600 S. 700 East St., ☎ 801/521–9877) once housed electric trolleys; today it has the city's most varied shopping under one roof. Clustered around a flour mill built in 1877 are the shops of **Gardner Village** (✉ 1100 W. 7800 South St., ☎ 801/566–8903, WEB www.gardnervillage.com). East of I–15 in the south end of the city, the **Factory Stores of America Mall** (✉ 12101 S. Factory Outlet Dr., ☎ 801/571–2933) has three dozen discount outlets.

Salt Lake City Essentials

AIRPORTS AND TRANSFERS

➤ AIRPORT INFORMATION: **Salt Lake International Airport** (✉ 776 North Terminal Dr., 7 mi west of downtown, ☎ 801/575–2400).

AIRPORT TRANSFER

Major hotels provide shuttles, and Utah Transit Authority buses link the airport to regular city routes for $1. Taxi fare to downtown averages $13–$15, including tip.

➤ SHUTTLES: **Utah Transit Authority** (☎ 801/743–3882 or 888/743–3882, WEB www.rideuta.com).

BUS TRAVEL TO AND FROM SALT LAKE CITY

➤ BUS INFORMATION: **Greyhound** (✉ 160 W. South Temple St., ☎ 801/355–9579 or 800/231–2222).

CAR TRAVEL

I–15 runs north–south through Salt Lake, I–80 east–west. I–215 circles the valley.

TRAIN TRAVEL

➤ TRAIN INFORMATION: **Amtrak Passenger Station** (✉ 340 S. 600 West St., ☎ 801/322–3510).

TRANSPORTATION AROUND SALT LAKE CITY

Salt Lake City streets are laid out geometrically and numbered in increments of 100 in each direction, with Temple Square as their root. Parking is inexpensive. Utah Transit Authority buses and trolleys serve the valley. The fare is $1, with a free-fare zone in downtown shopping areas. A light-rail train system, known as TRAX, runs north and south through Salt Lake City, with a spur line that runs from the downtown area to the University of Utah in the city's Foothills district.

➤ CONTACT: **Utah Transit Authority** (☎ 801/743–3882 or 888/743–3882, WEB www.rideuta.com).

VISITOR INFORMATION

➤ TOURIST INFORMATION: **Salt Lake Convention and Visitors Bureau** (✉ Salt Palace Convention Center, 90 S. West Temple St., 84101, ☎ 801/521–2822, WEB www.visitsaltlake.com).

SOUTHWESTERN UTAH

Southwestern Utah is a panoply of natural wonders. Heading the list are Zion, Capitol Reef, and Bryce Canyon national parks, where clear air and high elevations create spectacular 100-mi vistas. The picturesque towns of St. George, Cedar City, Springdale, and Torrey are full of historic sites. The weather here is mild year-round in the lower elevations, although summers can be hot.

Exploring Southwestern Utah

At **Bryce Canyon National Park** millions of years of geologic mayhem have created gigantic bowls filled with strange pinnacles and quilted drapes of stone. An 18-mi scenic drive skirts the western rim. Relatively short hikes begin off of the various viewpoints. ✉ *Hwy. 63,* ☎ *435/834–5322,* WEB *www.nps.gov/brca.* 🎫 *$20 per vehicle. Some roads closed Nov.–Mar.*

Once called "Land of the Sleeping Rainbow" because of its colorfully striped cliffs, **Capitol Reef National Park** is dominated by the Waterpocket Fold, a 100-mi-long stone uplift created when the earth's crust folded over on itself. At the base of this soaring "reef" are riverside orchards planted by early settlers; you may pick fruit, in season, June–October. Hikes lead to petroglyphs and hidden formations. The park also has an impressive backcountry scenic route ($5 per vehicle). ✉ *Hwy. 24,* ☎ *435/425–3791,* WEB *www.nps.gov/care.*

The Virgin River carved the towering cliffs of Zion Canyon and still flows along its floor. Spring-fed hanging gardens sprout lush greens along the walls. Tram tours, and horseback and hiking trails of **Zion National Park** provide access to the beauties of this vividly hued canyon and its tributaries. The park can be very crowded in summer and early fall. ✉ *Rte. 9, Springdale,* ☎ *435/772–3256,* WEB *www.nps.gov/zion,* 🎫 *$20 per vehicle.*

Southwest of Zion National Park in St. George, you can tour the historic district and **Brigham Young's winter home** (✉ 67 W. 200 North St., St. George, ☎ 435/673–2517; 🎫 free).

Dining and Lodging

Travel Utah Reservations (☎ 800/259–3343) provides area-wide lodging recommendations.

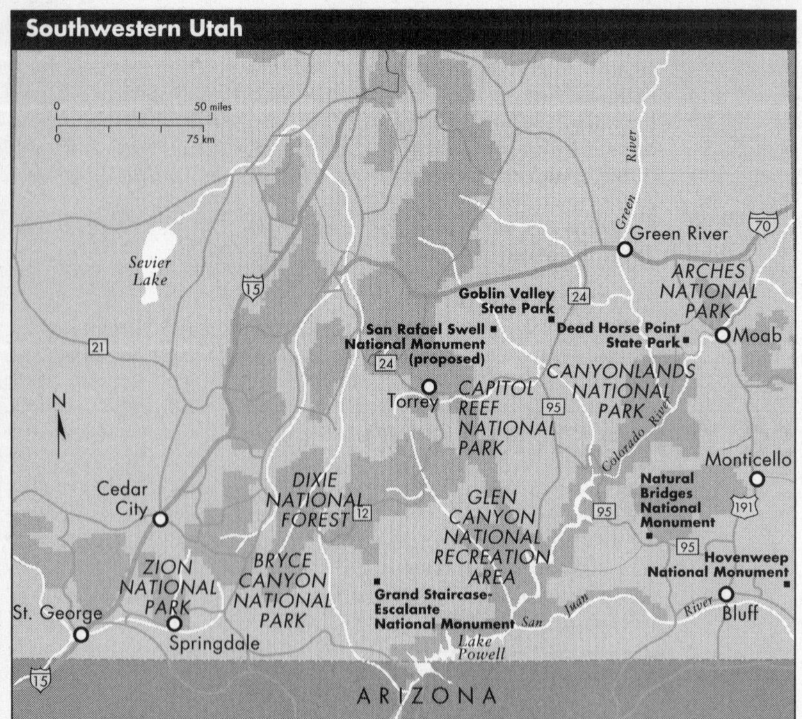

Bryce Canyon

$–$$ ✕🏨 **Best Western Ruby's Inn.** Just north of the park entrance, this is Grand Central Station for visitors to Bryce. A nightly rodeo takes place nearby during the summer. Sprawling wings make up most of the property. ✉ *Rte. 63 (Box 1, 84764),* ☎ *435/834–5341 or 800/468–8660,* FAX *435/834–5265,* WEB *www.rubysinn.com. 369 rooms. Restaurant, pool. AE, D, DC, MC, V.*

$–$$ ✕🏨 **Bryce Canyon Lodge.** A huge limestone fireplace dominates the lobby of this National Historic Landmark building inside the park. Guests have their choice of motel-style rooms with porches, or cozy lodgepole-pine cabins, some with fireplaces. Reserve far in advance, or call the day before your arrival—cancellations occasionally make last-minute reservations possible. ✉ *1 Bryce Canyon Lodge, Bryce Canyon 84717,* ☎ *303/297–2757 advance reservations; 435/834–5361 same-day availability;* FAX *435/586–3157;* WEB *www.amfac.com. 74 rooms, 40 cabins. Restaurant. AE, D, DC, MC, V. Closed Nov.–Apr.*

Cedar City

$–$$$$ ★ ✕ **Milt's Stage Stop.** Locals swear by the 12-ounce rib-eye steak, prime rib, and seafood at this restaurant in scenic Cedar Canyon. In winter, deer feed in front of the restaurant as a fireplace blazes inside. The mountain views are splendid year-round. ✉ *Rte. 14, 5 mi east of Cedar City,* ☎ *435/586–9344. AE, D, DC, MC, V.*

St. George

$$–$$$ ✕ **Painted Pony.** Patio dining and local art are good accompaniment to the creative southwestern meals served in this downtown restaurant. A margarita can round out your lunch or dinner, if you're so inclined. Be sure to try the Chilean sea bass or, if you're not a fish eater, the tamales, which are the best for miles around. ✉ *2 W. St. George Blvd., Suite 22,* ☎ *435/634–1700. AE, D, MC, V. Closed Sun.*

$-$$$ ✕ **Scaldoni's Grill.** Voted best dining in Dixie by *Salt Lake City Magazine,* best Italian restaurant in St. George by the local paper, and winner of a people's-choice award for favorite restaurant, this charming eatery is a sure bet for fine dining. They also serve a wide variety of steaks and seafood. ✉ *929 Sunset Blvd.,* ☎ *435/674–1300. AE, D, MC, V.*

$–$$ **Ramada Inn.** On St. George's major thoroughfare and close to restaurants, shopping, and the historic district, this is one of the city's most convenient and best-appointed properties. ✉ *1440 E. St. George Blvd., 84790,* ☎ *435/628–2828 or 800/713–9435,* FAX *435/628–0505. 136 rooms. Pool. AE, D, DC, MC, V.*

Springdale

$–$$ ★ ✕ **Bit and Spur Restaurant and Saloon.** This low-slung eatery serves healthful southwestern-style Mexican food. Works by local artists fill the pine-paneled interior, and the patio is scented by the restaurant's herb garden. ✉ *1212 Zion Park Blvd.,* ☎ *435/772–3498. D, MC, V.*

$–$$$ ✕ **Flannigan's.** Rooms in this cozy lodge are decorated with the work of local artists, and each has a deck or patio where guests can sit back and enjoy spectacular views of canyons and cliffs. Pastas, chicken, fish, and steaks, some prepared with southwestern zest, compose the menu of the intimate restaurant ($$–$$$), and an extensive selection of fine wines complements meals. ✉ *428 Zion Park Blvd., 84767,* ☎ *435/772–3244 or 800/765–7787,* FAX *435/772–3396,* WEB *www.flannigans.com. 35 rooms. Restaurant, pool. AE, D, MC, V.*

$$ **Cliffrose Lodge and Gardens.** Acres of lawn, trees, and gardens surround this hotel on the banks of the Virgin River, ¼ mi from Zion. Rooms are warm with desert hues, and a spa and conference center were added in 2002. ✉ *281 Zion Park Blvd., 84767,* ☎ *435/772–3234 or 800/243–8824,* FAX *435/772–3900,* WEB *www.cliffroselodge.com. 36 rooms. Pool. AE, D, MC, V.*

$–$$ ★ **Desert Pearl Inn.** Every room is a suite here, and you get spa-like facilities at standard room prices. Rooms have vaulted ceilings and thickly padded carpets. Large balconies or patios off each room overlook either the Virgin River or the pool. Near the pool are a double-size hot tub and waterfall. ✉ *707 Zion Park Blvd., Springdale 84767,* ☎ *435/772–8888 or 888/828–0898,* FAX *435/772–8889,* WEB *www.desertpearl.com. 60 suites. Pool. AE, D, MC, V.*

Torrey

$$–$$$ ✕ **Café Diablo.** Come here for innovative southwestern cuisine such as hearty chipotle-baked ribs, local trout crusted with pumpkin seeds, pork tenderloin with mango salsa, and vegetarian dishes. ✉ *599 W. Main St.,* ☎ *435/425–3070. MC, V. Closed Nov.–Apr.*

$$–$$$ ★ **SkyRidge Bed & Breakfast.** This three-story inn has comfortable guest rooms, two with private outdoor hot tubs. There are 75 windows in the building, and all have exceptional views of the desert and mountains surrounding Capitol Reef National Park. Evening hors d'oeuvres are served by the fireplace. The full breakfast might include a casserole or pecan griddle cakes with sausage. ✉ *950 E. Hwy. 24 (Box 750220, 84775),* ☎ FAX *435/425–3222,* WEB *www.bbiu.org/skyridge. 6 rooms. MC, V. BP.*

Outdoor Activities and Sports

Biking

A spin along Route 9 through Zion, Route 18 through Snow Canyon, along the lift-served trails at the Brian Head Resort, or the Bryce Canyon Scenic Loop yields classic southwestern scenery. Route 24 through Capitol Reef accesses historic sites and off-road riding. **Utah Travel Council** provides a free directory of biking routes.

Golf

St. George attracts golfers year-round to more than a dozen courses, including **Dixie Red Hills** (✉ 645 W. 1250 North St., ☎ 435/634–5852), with 9 holes. **Entrada at Snow Canyon** (✉ 2511 W. Entrada Trail, ☎ 435/674–7500) has 18 holes surrounded by red sandstone cliffs and the cinder cone of an extinct volcano. **South Gate** (✉ 1975 Tonaquint Dr., ☎ 435/628–0000) offers 18 holes in a quiet valley setting. The **St. George Area Convention and Visitor Bureau** (☎ 435/628–7003 or 800/869–6635, WEB www.utahsdixie.com) has more golfing information.

Southwestern Utah Essentials

AIR TRAVEL

St. George and Cedar City airports are served by SkyWest. Las Vegas is a major airport to consider, as it's about a three-hour drive from Zion National Park.

➤ CONTACT: SkyWest (☎ 800/453–9417).

BUS TRAVEL

Greyhound stops in St. George and Cedar City.

VISITOR INFORMATION

➤ TOURIST INFORMATION: Capitol Reef Country Visitor Information (✉ Rte. 2 [Box 7, Teasdale 84773], ☎ 800/858–7951). St. George Area Convention and Visitor Bureau (✉ 1835 Convention Center Dr., St. George 84790, ☎ 800/869–6635, WEB www.utahsdixie.com).

SOUTHEASTERN UTAH

For years the canyon country of southeastern Utah has captured the imagination of filmmakers, serving as the site of such western and adventure films as *Stagecoach, Indiana Jones and the Last Crusade,* and *Thelma and Louise.* Rugged Arches and Canyonlands national parks invite exploration via scenic drives, four-wheeling, hiking, rock climbing, river running, and cycling.

Exploring Southeastern Utah

The town of **Green River,** at the junction of I–70 and U.S. 6/191, is named for the river running through it and is the major "put-in" for raft trips on the Green River to its confluence with the Colorado. **Moab,** below I–70 on U.S. 191, has become a base for those exploring the national and state parks of the area, as well as a major destination for mountain bikers. Bike shops, T-shirt stores, restaurants, and motels anchor virtually every corner.

Arches National Park (✉ U.S. 191 [Box 907, Moab 84532], ☎ 435/259–8161, WEB www.nps.gov/arch; $10 per vehicle), north of Moab, contains sandstone formations carved by wind and water. Trails and two scenic roads lead past towering pillars and arches. Delicate Arch is perhaps the most dramatic formation.

The landscape of **Canyonlands National Park** (✉ 2282 South West Resource Blvd., Moab 84532, ☎ 435/259–7164, WEB www.nps.gov/cany; $10 per vehicle), southwest of Moab, is divided into three geologically distinct districts; the Island in the Sky and Needles districts have visitor centers. Scenic loops, trails, and four-wheel-drive roads lead to views of massive canyons or uplifts crowded with stone spires.

A sweeping view of the Canyonlands' multicolored upside-down geography is found at **Dead Horse Point State Park** (✉ Rte. 313, 18 mi off U.S. 191 [Box 609, Moab 84532], ☎ 435/259–2614, WEB parks.state.ut.us; 🎫 $7 per vehicle), an isolated peninsula.

The city of **Monticello** is 53 mi south of Moab on U.S. 191, but at a 7,000-ft elevation compared to Moab's 4,000, it has much cooler temperatures. South and west of Monticello, north of Route 95, a 9-mi scenic drive takes in views of three river-carved bridges at **Natural Bridges National Monument** (✉ Box 1, Lake Powell 84533, ☎ 435/692–1234, WEB www.nps.gov/nabr; 🎫 $6 per vehicle).

Lake Powell, part of the **Glen Canyon National Recreation Area** (☎ 928/608–6404, WEB www.nps.gov/glca; 🎫 $10 per vehicle), is a stark meeting of water and stone, with nearly 2,000 mi of meandering shoreline resulting from the construction of Glen Canyon Dam on the Colorado River. Side canyons and coves hold Indian ruins, rock art, and natural wonders such as the **Rainbow Bridge National Monument.** To get here from Monticello, take U.S. 191 south and U.S. 95 west. From U.S. 95 you could also branch south on Route 276 west. Spring and fall are the best times to visit—summer temperatures are often over 100°F.

The town of Bluff, 48 mi south of Monticello on U.S. 191, rests on the bank of the San Juan River at the border of the vast Navajo Nation. Houses built in the 1880s of sandstone and red adobe are clustered at the town's center. East of Bluff, **Hovenweep National Monument** (✉ McElmo Rte., Cortez, CO 81321, ☎ 435/459–4344, WEB www.nps.gov/hove; 🎫 $6 per vehicle) has several tower structures built by the ancestral Puebloan peoples about 800 years ago. A visitor center exhibits the work of local artists.

Dining and Lodging

Bluff

$–$$ ★ ✕ **Cow Canyon Trading Post.** Southwestern, Greek, Italian—you never know what might appear on the menu at this small restaurant. Choices could range from chicken-and-vegetable shish kebabs on a bed of wild rice or a phyllo pie stuffed with spinach and ham. The adjacent trading post carries a wide selection of authentic Navajo and Zuni baskets, pottery, rugs, and jewelry. ✉ *Hwy. 163 Mission Rd.,* ☎ *435/672–2208. AE, MC, V. Closed Nov.–Mar. No lunch.*

$ 🏨 **Pioneer House Inn.** The cozy rooms in this historic home are decorated with the work of local artists, and each has an outdoor sitting area from which to enjoy views. The hearty breakfasts might include a southwestern omelet or a stack of apple-blueberry pancakes. The owners are happy to help plan trips by boat, car, skis, or foot to nearby archaeological sites, wilderness areas, and cultural locations. ✉ *Corner of Mulberry St. and 300 East St. (Box 219, 84512),* ☎ *435/672–2446 or 888/637–2582,* WEB *www.pioneerhouseinn.com. 5 rooms. MC, V. BP.*

$ 🏨 **Recapture Lodge.** This locally owned property is unassuming, clean, and comfortable. Evening slide shows highlight local geology, art, and history. ✉ *U.S. 191 (Box 309, 84512),* ☎ *435/672–2281,* FAX *435/672–2284. 28 rooms. Pool. AE, D, MC, V.*

Green River

$–$$ ✕ **Ray's Tavern.** Half-pound hamburgers served on a heap of hearty fries share the menu with steaks, chops, and seafood at this watering hole revered by river runners, tourists, and locals looking for lunch and a game of pool. ✉ *25 S. Broadway,* ☎ *435/564–3511. AE, D, MC, V.*

Moab

$$–$$$$ ★ ✕ **Center Café.** The "globally inspired" menu at this side-street café might feature grilled prawns with basil-crab flan and spicy gazpacho sauce, or lamb with chanterelle mushrooms, among other culinary delights. ✉ *92 E. Center St.,* ☎ *435/259–4295. D, MC, V.*

$–$$$ ✕ **Buck's Grill House.** For a real taste of the American West, try the buffalo meat loaf or venison stew. The meats are thick and tender and the gravies are finger-licking good. Southwestern entrées include duck tamales and buffalo chorizo tacos. You'll definitely find something on the wine list to complement your meal. ✉ *1393 N. Hwy. 191,* ☎ *435/259–5201. AE, D, MC, V. No lunch.*

$–$$ ✕ **Eddie McStiff's.** This casual restaurant and microbrewery serves up pizzas and zesty Italian specialties to go with 13 freshly brewed concoctions. ✉ *57 S. Main St.,* ☎ *435/259–2337. MC, V.*

$ ✕ **Eklecticafe.** Breakfast and lunch items at this tiny restaurant include burritos and wraps, scrambled tofu, Polish sausage, Indonesian satay kebabs, and organic salads. On nice days, you can eat on the covered patio. A wood-burning stove heats the room on winter days. ✉ *352 N. Main St.,* ☎ *435/259–6896. MC, V. No dinner.*

$$–$$$$ 🏨 **Pack Creek Ranch.** This bed-and-breakfast on a forested mountain loop has rustic log cabins and activities ranging from horseback riding to swimming and biking. Breakfasts are included in the rates, although guests can cook for themselves in each cabin's full kitchen. ✉ *La Sal Mt. Loop Rd. (Box 1270, Moab 84532),* ☎ *435/259–5505,* FAX *435/259–8879,* WEB *www.packcreekranch.com. 9 cabins, one 4-bedroom ranch house that sleeps 12. Pool. AE, D, MC, V. BP.*

$$–$$$ ★ 🏨 **Sunflower Hill Bed and Breakfast.** Moab's best bed-and-breakfast consists of two separate buildings, the Garden Cottage and the Farmhouse, connected by perennial gardens. For breakfast, a hot entrée is served with yogurt and homemade bread or huge fruit muffins. ✉ *185 N. 300 East St., 84532,* ☎ *435/259–2974 or 800/662–2786,* FAX *435/259–3065,* WEB *www.sunflowerhill.com. 11 rooms. AE, D, MC, V. BP.*

Outdoor Activities and Sports

Biking

Southeastern Utah has hundreds of charted mountain-biking trails, and several Moab bike outfitters lead multiday trips into Canyonlands National Park. The **Moab Slickrock Trail,** 4 mi east of Moab, is a 10-mi roller-coaster route marked by dashes of paint on raw rock. Bikes are ideal for exploring the landscape and roads of **Hovenweep National Monument.** The **Abajo Mountain Loop,** west of Monticello, winds through cool pine and aspen forests. For area-wide rentals and advice, try **Moab Cyclery and Kaibab Outfitters** (✉ 391 S. Main St., Moab, ☎ 435/259–7423 or 800/451–1133).

Hiking and Backpacking

Call the travel councils of Grand County or San Juan for advice on trails. Remember to bring water along on any hike in this region.

Rafting

Outfitters operate float trips and white-water treks on the Colorado River through black-granite-walled Westwater Canyon and the rapids of Cataract Canyon and also on the Green River through Desolation and Gray canyons, both of which shelter Anasazi Indian ruins. Float trips on the San Juan River wind through petroglyph-etched cliffs.

Southeastern Utah Essentials

VISITOR INFORMATION

➤ TOURIST INFORMATION: **Grand County Travel Council and Visitor Center** (✉ Main and Center Sts. [Box 550, Moab 84532], ☎ 800/635–6622, WEB www.canyonlands-utah.com). **San Juan County Multi-Agency Visitors Center** (✉ 117 S. Main St. [Box 490, Monticello 84535], ☎ 435/587–3235 or 800/574–4386, WEB www.southeastutah.com).

ELSEWHERE IN UTAH

Northeastern Utah

Dinosaurs left their remains in these mountains, and Butch Cassidy and other outlaws stashed caches of "loot" as they fled through the canyons. Sheep- and cattle-ranching and oil and gas development are the predominant industries today. Some working ranches arrange horseback riding adventures and even full-fledged cattle drives.

What to See and Do

The excavations at **Dinosaur National Monument** (✉ Quarry Visitor Center, ☎ 435/781–7700, WEB www.nps.gov/dino; 🎫 $10 per vehicle) showcase the largest collection of Jurassic-period fossils ever unearthed. Some 2,000 dinosaur bones—discoveries began in 1909—lie exposed in a sandstone face inside the visitor center, 20 mi east of Vernal.

Flaming Gorge National Recreation Area (✉ U.S. 191, ☎ 435/784–3445, WEB www.nps.gov/flgo; 🎫 $5 per vehicle) is north of Dinosaur National Monument via U.S. 191. Behind 500-ft-high Flaming Gorge Dam, Flaming Gorge Lake stretches north for 91 mi between twisting red-rock canyon walls. The lake is good for boating, camping, and trophy trout fishing. South of the dam, the Green River is known for excellent fishing and calm-water rafting.

Dining and Lodging

$–$$$ ★ ✕ **The Curry Manor.** The diverse menu includes entrées such as pesto chicken, baked salmon stuffed with crab, and pork tenderloin with wildberry sauce. ✉ *189 S. Vernal Ave., Vernal,* ☎ *435/789–2289. AE, D, MC, V.*

$$$ ★ 🏨 **Falcon's Ledge Lodge.** The draws here are the multiday luxury sporting packages—focusing on falconry and fly-fishing in season, or wilderness excursions. The packages include five- to seven-course dinners with entrées such as filet mignon and bacon-wrapped halibut. Fresh home-baked bread is served with every meal. ✉ *Stillwater Canyon (Box 67, Altamont 84001),* ☎ *435/454–3737,* FAX *435/454–3392,* WEB *www.falconsledge.com. 9 rooms. AE, MC, V. BP.*

$–$$$ 🏨 **Landmark Inn Bed & Breakfast.** Housed in a former Baptist church building, this lovely inn has a homey feel. Rooms are individually decorated with quilts and western Americana, and some have four-poster beds, gas fireplaces, and jetted tubs. ✉ *288 E. 100 South St., Vernal 84078,* ☎ *435/781–1800 or 888/738–1800,* WEB *www.landmark-inn.com. 10 rooms. AE, D, DC, MC, V. CP*

$–$$ 🏨 **Flaming Gorge Lodge.** With a good restaurant, a store, raft rentals, and guided fishing service, this is the best lodging choice near Flaming Gorge. ✉ *155 Greendale/U.S. 191, Dutch John 84023,* ☎ *435/889–3773,* FAX *435/889–3788,* WEB *www.fglodge.com. 21 motel rooms, 24 condos. Restaurant. AE, D, MC, V.*

$ 🏨 **Best Western Antlers Motel.** Locals favor this clean, comfortable motel with a pool, hot tub, gym, and playground. Rooms are equipped for computer modems. ✉ *423 W. Main St., Vernal 84078,* ☎ *435/789–1202 or 888/791–2929,* FAX *435/789–4979. 44 rooms. Restaurant, pool, gym. AE, D, DC, MC, V.*

Northeastern Utah Essentials

VISITOR INFORMATION

➤ TOURIST INFORMATION: **Dinosaurland Travel Board** (✉ 25 E. Main St., Vernal 84078, ☎ 800/477–5558, WEB www.dinoland.com).

VERMONT

Updated by Bill and Kay Scheller

Capital	Montpelier
Population	593,000
Motto	Freedom and Unity
State Bird	Hermit thrush
State Flower	Red clover
Postal Abbreviation	VT

Statewide Visitor Information

Vermont Chamber of Commerce (✉ Box 37, Montpelier 05601, ☎ 802/223–3443, WEB www.vtchamber.com). **Vermont Department of Tourism and Marketing** (✉ 134 State St., Montpelier 05602, ☎ 802/828–3237 or 800/837–6668, WEB www.1-800-VERMONT.com).

Scenic Drives

Route 100 passes through the eastern edge of Green Mountain National Forest, the Mad River valley, and the town of Stowe, then continues on to Canada.

National and State Parks

National Park

The 355,000-acre **Green Mountain National Forest** (✉ 231 N. Main St., Rutland 05701, ☎ 802/747–6700) runs through the center of the state, from Bristol south to the Massachusetts border. **Marsh-Billings-Rockefeller National Historical Park** (✉ Rte. 12, Woodstock 05091, ☎ 802/457–3368, WEB www.nps.marshbillings.com) is a 500-acre park dedicated to the land-management legacy of Vermont conservationist George Perkins Marsh.

State Parks

Within the 50 parks maintained by the **Department of Forests, Parks, and Recreation** (✉ 103 S. Main St., 10 South, Waterbury 05671, ☎ 802/241–3655 or 800/833–6668, WEB www.vtstateparks.com) you'll find nature and hiking trails, campsites, swimming, boating facilities, and fishing. Especially popular are the **Champlain Islands** sites: Burton Island, Kill Kare, North Hero, Grand Isle, Knight Point, and Sand Bar.

SOUTHERN VERMONT

Many of the southern Vermont towns with village greens and white-spired churches were founded in the early 18th century as frontier outposts and later became trading centers. In the 19th century, as many towns turned to manufacturing, the farmers here retreated to hillier regions; as the modern ski and summer-home booms got under way, they retreated even further. The influx of new residents in the past 20 years means the quaintness often comes with a patina of sophistication or funk; shoppers can find not only antiques but New Age crystals, Vermont-made salsa, and the highest-tech ski gear.

Exploring Southern Vermont

It was at **Bennington** that Ethan Allen formed the Green Mountain Boys, who helped capture Fort Ticonderoga in 1775. The **Bennington Battle Monument** (✉ 15 Monument Ave., ☎ 802/447–0550; 🎫 $1.50), a 306-ft stone obelisk, commemorates General John Stark's defeat of

Vermont

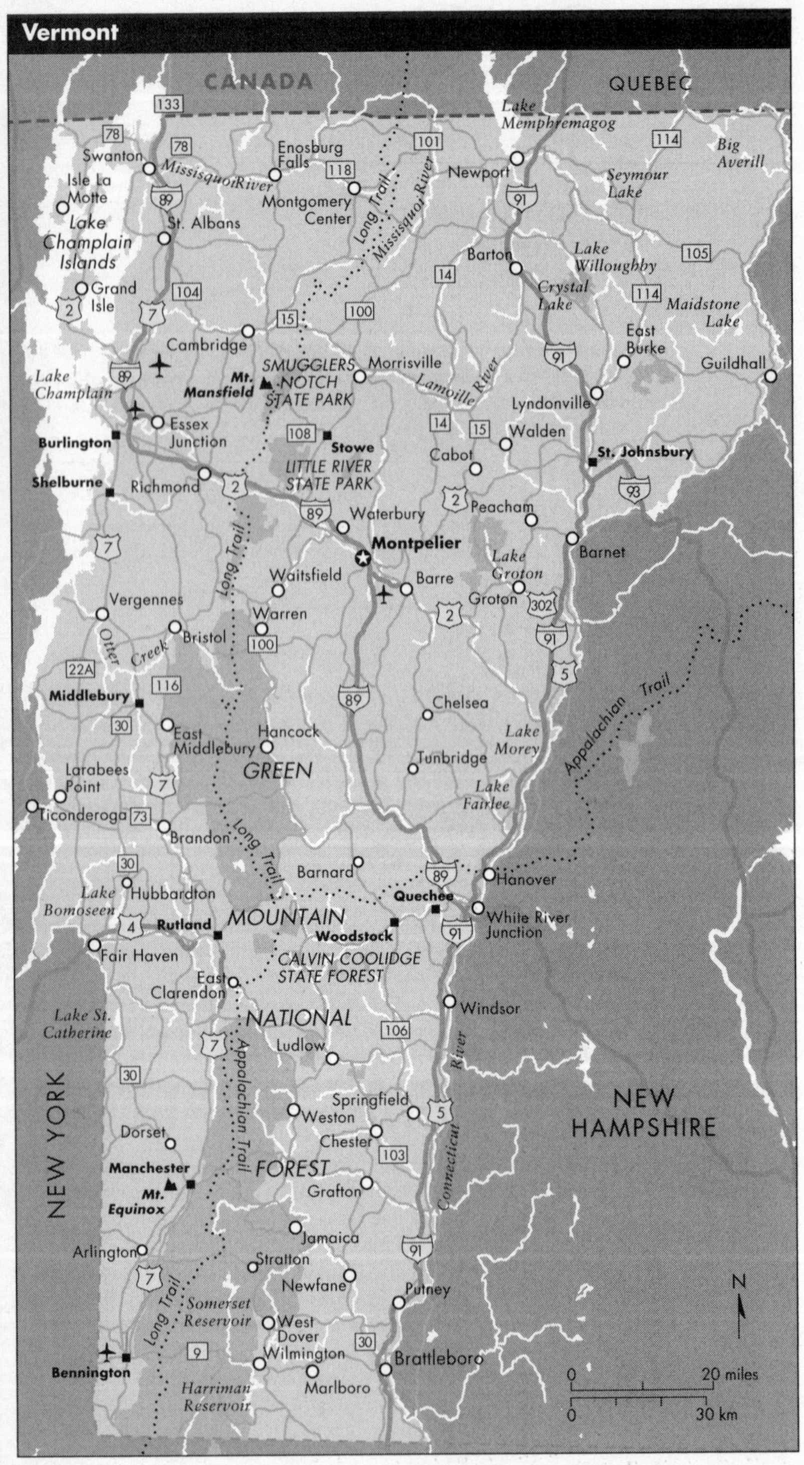

CANADA
QUEBEC
Lake Memphremagog
Big Averill
Seymour Lake
Swanton
Missisquoi River
Enosburg Falls
Montgomery Center
Newport
Isle La Motte
Lake Champlain Islands
St. Albans
Long Trail
Missisquoi River
Barton
Lake Willoughby
Crystal Lake
Maidstone Lake
Grand Isle
Cambridge
East Burke
Guildhall
Lake Champlain
Mt. Mansfield
SMUGGLERS NOTCH STATE PARK
Morrisville
Lamoille River
Lyndonville
Burlington
Essex Junction
Stowe
Walden
St. Johnsbury
Shelburne
Richmond
LITTLE RIVER STATE PARK
Cabot
Waterbury
Peacham
Montpelier
Barnet
Lake Groton
Waitsfield
Barre
Groton
Vergennes
Warren
Bristol
Otter Creek
Middlebury
Chelsea
East Middlebury
Hancock
Lake Morey
Appalachian Trail
GREEN
Tunbridge
Larabees Point
Lake Fairlee
Ticonderoga
Brandon
Barnard
Hanover
Lake Bomoseen
Hubbardton
Quechee
Rutland
MOUNTAIN
Woodstock
White River Junction
Fair Haven
CALVIN COOLIDGE STATE FOREST
East Clarendon
Windsor
Lake St. Catherine
NATIONAL
Ludlow
NEW YORK
Springfield
Weston
NEW HAMPSHIRE
Dorset
Chester
Connecticut River
Manchester
Mt. Equinox
FOREST
Grafton
Jamaica
Arlington
Stratton
Newfane
Putney
Somerset Reservoir
West Dover
N
Wilmington
Brattleboro
Bennington
Harriman Reservoir
Marlboro
0
20 miles
0
30 km
133
78
78
101
118
114
89
91
105
14
114
104
7
2
15
100
91
89
108
14
15
2
89
93
2
7
302
2
91
100
5
22A
116
89
30
7
73
30
89
4
91
106
7
30
5
103
91
7
30
9

the British in their attempt to capture Bennington's stockpile of supplies. It is closed from late October to mid-April. The artifacts at the **Bennington Museum** (✉ W. Main St./Rte. 9, ☎ 802/447–1571, WEB www.benningtonmuseum.com; 🎟 $6) include the largest public collection of the work of Grandma Moses, who lived and painted in the area; the only surviving automobile of Bennington's Martin Company; and one of the oldest Stars and Stripes in existence.

The tree-shaded marble sidewalks and stately houses of **Manchester** reflect the luxurious summer-resort lifestyle of two centuries ago, while upscale factory-outlet stores appeal to the ski crowd. **Hildene** (✉ Rte. 7A, 2 mi south of intersection with Rtes. 11 and 30, ☎ 802/362–1788, WEB www.hildene.org; 🎟 $8; closed Nov.–mid-May) was the summer home of Abraham Lincoln's son Robert. Noteworthy features in the 24-room mansion include its Georgian Revival symmetry, formal gardens, grand curved staircase, and 1,000-pipe organ.

The **American Museum of Fly Fishing** (✉ Rte. 7A, ☎ 802/362–3300, WEB www.amff.org; 🎟 $3) displays the tackle of such noted anglers as Jimmy Carter, Winslow Homer, and Bing Crosby.

The steep 5-mi drive to the top of **Mt. Equinox** brings you to the summit via the **Saddle**, where the views are outstanding. ✉ *Rte. 7A,* ☎ *802/362–1114.* 🎟 *Car and driver $6, each additional adult $2. Closed Nov.–Apr.*

In **Rutland** strips of shopping centers augment a seemingly endless row of traffic lights. The **Chaffee Center for the Visual Arts** (✉ 16 S. Main St., ☎ 802/775–0356), closed Tuesday, houses the work of more than 200 Vermont artists. At the **Vermont Marble Exhibit,** northwest of Rutland, you can watch the transformation of rough stone into slabs, blocks, and gift items. ✉ *62 S. Main St., off Rte. 3, Proctor,* ☎ *802/459–2300 or 800/427–1396.* 🎟 *$6. Closed Sun. and Nov.–mid-May.*

Woodstock is the quintessential New England town, on the eastern side of Vermont on U.S. 4. Exquisitely preserved Federal-style houses surround the tree-lined village green. The **Vermont Institute of Natural Science's Raptor Center** has nature trails and 23 living species of birds of prey. ✉ *Church Hill Rd.,* ☎ *802/457–2779,* WEB *www.vinsweb.org.* 🎟 *$7. Closed Sun.*

A half mile north of the center of Woodstock, the reconstructed farmhouse and barns at the **Billings Farm and Museum** demonstrate the daily activities of early Vermonters and house draft horses, sheep, and prize dairy cattle. ✉ *Rte. 12,* ☎ *802/457–2355,* WEB *www.billingsfarm.org.* 🎟 *$8. Closed Jan.–May and weekdays Nov.–Dec.*

The mile-long **Quechee Gorge** is visible from U.S. 4, but you can also scramble down one of several descents. The town of **Quechee** is perched astride the Ottauquechee River. At **Simon Pearce** (✉ Main St., ☎ 802/295–2711 or 800/774–5277; 🎟 free) you can watch potters and glassblowers and purchase their creations.

Dining and Lodging

Bennington

$ ✕ **Blue Benn Diner.** Breakfast is available all day in this authentic diner, which serves some twists to standard fare, such as turkey hash and burritos with scrambled eggs, sausage, and chili. The menu includes all kinds of pancakes as well as many vegetarian selections. You may have to wait for a seat on weekends. ✉ *Rte. 7 N,* ☎ *802/442–5140. No credit cards. No dinner Sat.–Tues.*

$$–$$$ **South Shire Inn.** Canopy beds in plushly carpeted rooms, ornate plaster molding on the ceilings, and the mahogany fireplace in the library add up to turn-of-the-20th-century grandeur in a quiet residential neighborhood. Most rooms have fireplaces; some have whirlpool baths. ✉ *124 Elm St., 05201,* ☎ *802/447–3839,* FAX *802/442–3547,* WEB *www.southshire.com. 9 rooms. AE, MC, V. BP.*

$–$$ ★ **Molly Stark Inn.** This gem of a B&B makes you feel as if you were staying with old friends. Blue-plaid wallpaper, hardwood floors, antique furnishings, and a woodstove in the brick alcove of the sitting room give a country charm to this 1860 Queen Anne Victorian. ✉ *1067 E. Main St./Rte. 9, 05201,* ☎ *802/442–9631 or 800/356–3076,* FAX *802/442–5224,* WEB *www.mollystarkinn.com. 7 rooms. AE, D, MC, V. BP.*

Manchester

$$$–$$$$ ✕ **Chantecleer.** Intimate dining rooms have been created in a dairy barn that has a large fieldstone fireplace. Appetizers include *Bundnerfleisch* (air dried Swiss beef) and frogs' legs in garlic butter; among the entrées are rack of lamb, whole Dover sole filleted table-side, and veal chops. The restaurant is 5 mi north of Manchester. ✉ *Rte. 7A, East Dorset,* ☎ *802/362–1616. Reservations essential. AE, DC, MC, V. Closed late Oct.–Thanksgiving; mid-Apr.–mid-May; Mon.–Tues. in winter; and Tues. in summer. No lunch.*

$$–$$$ ✕ **Bistro Henry's.** Just outside town, this spacious restaurant attracts a devoted clientele for its authentic French bistro fare, extensive wine list, and attention to detail. Popular items are merlot-braised lamb shank with balsamic glazed onions and rare tuna with wasabi and soy. ✉ *Rte. 11/30, Manchester,* ☎ *802/362–4982. AE, DC, MC, V. Closed Mon. No lunch.*

$$$–$$$$ **The Equinox.** This grand white-columned resort was a landmark on Vermont's tourism scene even before Abraham Lincoln's family began summering here. Rooms have pine furnishings, and the front porch is perfect for watching the passing parade. There's a medically supervised spa program and a falconry school. ✉ *Rte. 7A, Manchester Village 05254,* ☎ *802/362–4700 or 800/362–4747,* FAX *802/362–1595,* WEB *www.equinoxresort.com. 155 rooms, 10 town houses. 2 restaurants, pools, golf, tennis. AE, D, DC, MC, V.*

$$–$$$$ ★ **1811 House.** Staying here is like staying at an elegant English country house. Six rooms have fireplaces; the Robinson room has a marble-enclosed tub. The pub-style bar serves 58 single-malt scotches. ✉ *Rte. 7A (Box 39, 05254),* ☎ *802/362–1811 or 800/432–1811,* FAX *802/362–2443,* WEB *www.1811house.com. 14 rooms. No smoking. AE, D, MC, V. BP.*

$$–$$$ **Barnstead Inn.** This 1830s barn was transformed in 1968 into a handful of rooms that combine exposed beams and barn-board walls with modern plumbing and cheerful wallpaper. ✉ *Rte. 30, 05255,* ☎ *802/362–1619 or 800/331–1619,* FAX *802/362–0688,* WEB *www.barnsteadinn.com. 14 rooms. Pool. AE, MC, V.*

Rutland

$–$$ ✕ **The Palms.** This Rutland landmark, opened in 1933, was the first restaurant in the state to serve pizza. It's still owned by the same family. The menu is primarily southern Italian, with specialties such as fried mozzarella; antipasto Neapolitan; and the chef's personal creation, veal à la Palms—veal scallops topped with mushrooms. ✉ *36 Strongs St.,* ☎ *802/773–2367. AE, MC, V. Closed Sun. No lunch.*

$–$$$ **Comfort Inn.** Rooms at this chain hotel are a cut above the standard, with upholstered wing chairs and blond-wood furnishings. ✉ *19 Allen St., 05701,* ☎ *802/775–2200 or 800/432–6788,* FAX *802/775–2694,* WEB *www.comfortinns.com. 104 rooms. Restaurant, pool. AE, D, DC, MC, V. CP.*

$-$$$ **Inn at Rutland.** In this Victorian mansion an ornate oak staircase leads to rooms with such turn-of-the-20th-century touches as botanical prints, elaborate ceiling moldings, and frosted glass. Relax for a soak in the inn's hot tub. ✉ *70 N. Main St., 05701,* ☎ *802/773–0575 or 800/808–0575,* FAX *802/775–3506,* WEB *www.innatrutland.com. 12 rooms. AE, D, DC, MC, V. BP fall and winter, CP spring and summer.*

Woodstock

$$-$$$ ★ ✕ **Prince and the Pauper.** Nouvelle French dishes with a Vermont accent are served in a romantically candlelit Colonial setting. Standouts include grilled duck breast with an Asian five-spice sauce. ✉ *24 Elm St.,* ☎ *802/457–1818. AE, D, MC, V. No lunch.*

$$ ✕ **Pane & Salute.** Regional Italian breads are a specialty, but this restaurant also serves Tuscan pizzas and pasta entrées such as penne with spinach, pine nuts, raisins, and garlic. Add a glass of Chianti and *mangia bene.* Desserts include meringues with whipped cream and raspberry sauce. ✉ *61 Central St.,* ☎ *802/457–4882. D, MC, V. Closed Tues.–Wed.*

$$$-$$$$ ✕ **Kedron Valley Inn.** Family quilts and antiques adorn the rooms at this inn, one of the state's oldest hotels. Many units have a fireplace or Franklin stove. The dining room ($$–$$$) prepares dishes using classic French technique and Vermont ingredients. Try the salmon fillet stuffed with seafood mousse and wrapped in puff pastry or the pasta with basil pesto. ✉ *Rte. 106, 05071,* ☎ *802/457–1473 or 800/836–1193,* FAX *802/457–4469,* WEB *www.kedronvalleyinn.com. 28 rooms. Restaurant. AE, D, MC, V. Closed Apr. and 10 days before Thanksgiving. MAP.*

$$$-$$$$ ✕ **Woodstock Inn and Resort.** Patchwork quilts and landscape paintings enliven the standard modern ash furnishings at this inn owned by the Rockefeller family. The dining room ($$–$$$; jacket and tie) serves nouvelle New England fare. Among the many activities are croquet and cross-country and downhill skiing. ✉ *14 The Green, 05091,* ☎ *802/457–1100 or 800/448–7900,* FAX *802/457–6699,* WEB *www.woodstockinn.com. 151 rooms. 2 restaurants, pool, golf, tennis, health club. AE, MC, V.*

$$ ★ **Winslow House.** An unpretentious place with great cross-country skiing and golf nearby, this 200-year-old farmhouse has a small common area; two spacious upstairs quarters have separate sitting rooms. ✉ *38 Rte. 4, 05091,* ☎ *802/457–1820,* FAX *802/457–1820,* WEB *www.thewinslowhousevt.com. 5 rooms. D, DC, MC, V. BP.*

Motels

Aspen Motel (✉ Box 548, Manchester Center 05255, ☎ 802/362–2450, FAX 802/362–1348), 24 rooms; pool; *$–$$.* **Harwood Hill Motel** (✉ Rte. 7A, Bennington 05201, ☎ 802/442–6278, FAX 802/442–6278), 16 rooms, 3 cottages; *$.* **Pond Ridge Motel** (✉ U.S. 4, Woodstock 05091, ☎ 802/457–1667, FAX 802/457–1667), 21 rooms; *$.*

Campgrounds

The state park system runs more than 40 campgrounds with more than 2,000 campsites. Contact the **Department of Forests, Parks, and Recreation** (✉ 103 S. Main St., 10 South, Waterbury 05671, ☎ 802/241–3655 or 800/837–6668, WEB www.vtstateparks.com) for a copy of the Vermont Campground Guide. The official state map lists private campgrounds.

At **Green Mountain National Forest** (✉ 231 N. Main St., Rutland 05701, ☎ 802/747–6700), one camping area can be reserved in advance; the remaining areas are first-come, first-served.

Nightlife and the Arts

Most nightlife is concentrated at and around the ski resorts or in the larger towns and cities. The **Marlboro Music Festival** (✉ Marlboro Music Center, ☎ 802/254–2394 July–Aug.; 215/569–4690 Sept.–June; WEB www.marlboromusic.org) presents chamber music in weekend concerts during July and August. The popular **New England Bach Festival** (✉ Marlboro College, ☎ 802/257–4523), held in October, stages classical music.

Outdoor Activities and Sports

Biking

Bike Vermont (✉ 52 Pleasant St. [Box 207, Woodstock 05091], ☎ 802/457–3553 or 800/257–2226, FAX 802/457–1236, WEB www.bikevt.com) focuses on inn-to-inn tours along the Connecticut River valley and in other scenic corners of Vermont. **Vermont Bicycle Tours** (✉ Box 711, Bristol 05443, ☎ 802/453–4811 or 800/245–3868, WEB www.vbt.com) conducts guided tours throughout Vermont.

Canoeing

The **Connecticut River** and the **Battenkill** provide easygoing canoe outings. Rentals are available from **Battenkill Canoe** (✉ Rte. 7A, Arlington, ☎ 802/362–2800 or 800/421–5268, WEB www.battenkill.com). **Wilderness Trails** (✉ Quechee Inn, Clubhouse Rd., Quechee, ☎ 802/295–7620) has canoe rentals, put-in and take-out service, and maps for touring the White, Ottauquechee, and Connecticut rivers.

Fishing

The **Battenkill River** is famous for trout. **Orvis** (✉ Rte. 7A, Manchester, ☎ 802/362–3900 or 800/235–9763, WEB www.orvis.com) runs a fly-fishing school. The necessary fishing license is available through tackle shops or call **Department of Fish and Wildlife** (☎ 802/241–3700).

Hiking and Backpacking

The **Green Mountain Club** (✉ Rte. 100, Waterbury Center 05677, ☎ 802/244–7037, WEB www.greenmountainclub.org) maintains the southern half of the **Long Trail,** which is part of the **Appalachian Trail.** The club staffs huts in summer and provides maps for hiking elsewhere in Vermont.

Ski Areas

For up-to-date **snow conditions** in the state, call ☎ 802/828–3239. All listed downhill ski areas have snowmaking equipment.

Cross-Country

Mt. Snow/Haystack (✉ 400 Mountain Rd., Mt. Snow 05356, ☎ 802/464–3333, WEB www.mtsnow.com) maintains 62 mi of trails. **Stratton** (✉ Stratton Mountain 05155, ☎ 802/297–2200, WEB www.stratton.com) has 20 mi of trails.

Downhill

Bromley (✉ Box 1130, Manchester Center 05255, ☎ 802/824–5522 or 800/865–4786, WEB www.bromley.com) has 41 runs, 9 lifts, 1,334-ft vertical drop. **Killington/Pico** (✉ 4763 Killington Rd., Killington 05751, ☎ 802/422–6200 or 800/621–6867, WEB www.killington.com) maintains 212 runs, 3 gondolas, 34 lifts, and a 3,150-ft drop. **Mt. Snow/Haystack** (✉ 400 Mountain Rd., Mt. Snow 05356, ☎ 802/464–3333 or 800/245–7669, WEB www.mtsnow.com) provides 135 trails, 26 lifts, and a 1,700-ft drop. **Stratton** (✉ Stratton Mountain 05155, ☎ 802/297–2200, WEB www.stratton.com) has 90 trails, gondola, 12 lifts, and a 2,000-ft drop.

Shopping

Antiques and traditional and contemporary crafts are everywhere. Particularly good is **U.S. 7** north of Manchester to Danby and Route 30 around Newfane. The **Bennington Potters Yard** (✉ 324 County St., ☎ 802/447–7531 or 800/205–8033) carries firsts and seconds. **Manchester** has many designer and factory outlets. **Quechee Gorge Village** (✉ Rte. 4, Quechee, east of Woodstock, ☎ 802/295–1550) houses more than 350 antiques and crafts dealers in an immense reconstructed barn. The **Vermont Country Store** (✉ Rte. 100, Weston, ☎ 802/824–3184) carries such forgotten items as Monkey Brand black tooth powder, Flexible Flyer sleds, and pickles in a barrel.

Southern Vermont Essentials

BUS TRAVEL

Vermont Transit links Bennington, Manchester, and Brattleboro.

➤ Bus Information: **Vermont Transit** (a subsidiary of Greyhound; ☎ 800/552–8737; 800/642–3133 in Vermont).

CAR TRAVEL

I–91 runs north–south along the eastern edge of Vermont. U.S. 7 goes north–south through western Vermont, and Route 9 runs east–west across the state through Bennington and Brattleboro.

TRAIN TRAVEL

Amtrak stops at Brattleboro, Bellows Falls, Rutland, and White River Junction.

➤ Train Information: **Amtrak** (☎ 800/872–7245).

VISITOR INFORMATION

➤ Tourist Information: **Bennington Chamber of Commerce** (✉ Veterans Memorial Dr., 05201, ☎ 802/447–3311, WEB www.bennington.com). **Brattleboro Chamber of Commerce** (✉ 180 Main St., 05301, ☎ 802/254–4565, WEB www.brattleboro.com). **Manchester Chamber of Commerce** (✉ 5046 Main St., 05255, ☎ 802/362–2100, WEB www.manchestervermont.com). **Rutland Chamber of Commerce, Convention and Visitors Division** (✉ 256 N. Main St., 05701, ☎ 802/773–2747 or 800/756–8880, WEB www.rutlandvermont.com). **Woodstock Chamber of Commerce** (✉ 18 Central St. [Box 486, 05091], ☎ 802/457–3555 or 888/496–6378, WEB www.woodstockvt.com).

NORTHERN VERMONT

Northwestern Vermont is more mountainous than the southern part of the state and includes the closest thing Vermont has to a seacoast, Lake Champlain; the nation's smallest state capital, Montpelier; and Burlington, Vermont's largest and most cosmopolitan city. The region's recorded history dates from 1609, when Samuel de Champlain explored the lake now named for him. Northeastern Vermont, known as the Northeast Kingdom, is the least populated part of the state. A great pleasure here is driving through pastoral scenery and discovering charming small towns such as Peacham, Greensboro, and Craftsbury Common.

Exploring Northern Vermont

Middlebury is Robert Frost country; Vermont's late poet laureate spent 23 summers at a farm near here. The **Robert Frost Wayside Trail,** east of Middlebury on Route 125, winds through quiet woodland and has Frost quotations posted along the way.

The University of Vermont's **Morgan Horse Farm** conducts tours of its stables and paddocks. ✉ *Follow signs off Rte. 23, 2½ mi from Middlebury,* ☎ *802/388–2011.* *$4. Closed Nov.–Apr.*

Shelburne, a town on the banks of Lake Champlain, is known for two ★ attractions. The 37 buildings of the **Shelburne Museum** (✉ U.S. 7, 5 mi south of Burlington, ☎ 802/985–3346, WEB www.shelburnemuseum.org; $17.50 for 2 consecutive days) contain one of the largest Americana collections in the nation. Exhibits include 18th- and 19th-century houses and furniture, fine and folk art, farm tools, carriages and sleighs, and an old side-wheel steamship. At the 1,400-acre **Shelburne Farms** (✉ east of U.S. 7, 6 mi south of Burlington, ☎ 802/985–8686, WEB www.shelburnefarms.org; day pass $6, tour additional $5) you can see a working dairy farm, attend nature lectures, visit farm animals at the Children's Farmyard, and stroll along a stretch of Lake Champlain's waterfront. The landscaping, designed by Frederick Law Olmsted, creator of New York's Central Park, gently channels the eye to expansive vistas.

Burlington is home to the University of Vermont and three smaller colleges. **Church Street Marketplace**—with its down-to-earth shops, chic boutiques, and appealing menagerie of sidewalk cafés, food and crafts vendors, and street performers—is an animated downtown focal point. Narrated tours are conducted during the day—and **evening dinner-and-dance cruises**—on the *Spirit of Ethan Allen,* a 500-passenger, triple-deck cruise vessel. ✉ *Burlington Boat House, College St. at Battery St.,* ☎ *802/862–8300.* *Narrated day cruises $9.95. Closed mid-Oct.–May.*

Smugglers' Notch is the scenic pass beneath the brow of Mt. Mansfield said to have been a route of 18th-century outlaws. There are roadside picnic tables and a spectacular waterfall. Take Route 15 to Jeffersonville; then go south on narrow, twisting Route 108.

Stowe Mountain Resort (✉ entrance on Mountain Rd., 8 mi from Rte. 100 at Stowe Village, ☎ 802/253–3000) is a venerable ski center. From June to late October you can take the 4½-mi toll road ($14 per car) from the resort to the top of Vermont's highest peak, **Mt. Mansfield.** At the road's end is a short and beautiful walk. Another way to ascend Mt. Mansfield is in the **gondola** ($14) that shuttles from the base of the ski area up 4,393 ft to the section known as the Chin, where there are scenic views and a restaurant.

Nine miles south of Stowe village is the mecca, the nirvana, the veritable Valhalla for ice cream lovers: **Ben & Jerry's Ice Cream Factory** (✉ Rte. 100, 1 mi north of I–89, ☎ 802/882–1260, WEB www.benjerry.com; $2).

Montpelier, which has fewer than 9,000 residents, is the nation's least-populous state capital. The impressive **Vermont State House** has a gleaming gold dome and columns 6 ft in diameter fashioned from granite from neighboring Barre. ✉ *State St.,* ☎ *802/828–2228.* *Free. Closed Sun. and mid-Oct.–June.*

The chief city of the Northeast Kingdom is **St. Johnsbury.** The **Fairbanks Museum and Planetarium** (✉ Main and Prospect Sts., ☎ 802/748–2372; $5) engrosses visitors with its eclectic ethnographic, natural history, and Vermontiana collections and a 50-seat planetarium ($3). The **St. Johnsbury Athenaeum** is an architectural gem, with dark paneling, polished Victorian woodwork, and a gallery displaying 19th-century artworks, most notably Albert Bierstadt's *Domes of Yosemite.* ✉ *1171 Main St.,* ☎ *802/748–8291.* *Free. Closed Sun.*

Dining and Lodging

Burlington

$$ ✕ **Trattoria Delia.** Didn't manage to rent that villa in Umbria this year? The next best thing is this superb Italian country eatery around the corner from City Hall Park. Local game and produce are the stars, as in roast rabbit marinated in herbs, wine, and olive oil. The chef's passion for the truly homemade extends to wild boar sausage, salami, and fresh mozzarella. Wood-grilled items are a specialty. ✉ *152 St. Paul St.,* ☎ *802/864–5253. AE, D, DC, MC, V. No lunch.*

$–$$ ✕ **Parima Thai Restaurant.** Chef's specials such as crispy roasted duck in tamarind sauce and seafood *phuket* (shrimp, mussels, cod, and squid sautéed in basil sauce) join a menu of traditional Thai including curries and *pad thai* (stir-fried noodles with shrimp or chicken). This handsomely appointed restaurant has one of the most elegant bars in town and a seasonal patio. ✉ *185 Pearl St.,* ☎ *802/864–7917. AE, D, DC, MC, V.*

$$–$$$$ ★ ✕🏨 **Inn at Shelburne Farms.** Built at the turn of the 20th century, this Tudor-style inn overlooks Lake Champlain, the distant Adirondacks, and the sea of pastures on this 1,400-acre working farm. Each guest room is different, from the wallpaper to the period antiques. The seasonal contemporary menu ($$–$$$) makes clever use of local ingredients. Try the rack of lamb with sun-dried tomato crust. ✉ *Harbor Rd., Shelburne 05482,* ☎ *802/985–8498,* FAX *802/985–8123,* WEB *www.shelburnefarms.org. 24 rooms, 17 with bath. Restaurant, tennis. AE, D, DC, MC, V. Closed mid-Oct.–mid-May.*

$$–$$$$ 🏨 **Willard Street Inn.** Perched high in the historic hill section is this grand house, which incorporates elements of Queen Anne and Colonial–Georgian Revival styles and has an exterior marble staircase and English gardens. Rooms are individually decorated; some have lake views and canopy beds. ✉ *349 S. Willard St., 05401,* ☎ *802/651–8710 or 800/577–8712,* FAX *802/651–8714,* WEB *www.willardstreetinn.com. 14 rooms. AE, D, DC, MC, V. BP.*

Middlebury

$$–$$$ ✕ **Fire & Ice.** A 55-item salad bar (with peel-and-eat shrimp), prime rib, steak, fish, and a house specialty—homemade mashed potatoes—are all choices at this family-friendly spot. Although large, the space is divided into several rooms (each with a different theme) and has numerous intimate nooks and crannies for diners who seek privacy. ✉ *26 Seymour St.,* ☎ *802/388–7166 or 800/367–7166. AE, D, DC, MC, V. No lunch Mon.*

$$–$$$ 🏨 **Swift House Inn.** The main building at Swift House, the Georgian home of a 19th-century governor, contains white-panel wainscoting, elaborately carved mahogany and marble fireplaces, and cherry paneling in the dining room. The rooms—each with Oriental rugs and nine with fireplaces—have canopy beds, curtains with swags, and claw-foot tubs. Rooms in the gatehouse suffer from street noise but are charming; a carriage house holds six luxury rooms. ✉ *25 Stewart La., 05753,* ☎ *802/388–9925,* FAX *802/388–9927,* WEB *www.swifthouseinn.com. 22 rooms. AE, D, DC, MC, V. CP.*

Montpelier

$$ ✕ **Chef's Table.** The staff at the Chef's Table and its sister restaurant, Main Street Bar and Grill, are New England Culinary Institute students. Upstairs at the Chef's Table, the menu changes daily but always serves well-prepared, inventive dishes, such as swordfish with spinach and cherry tomatoes. Downstairs at the Grill, the atmosphere is more casual but the food no less delicious. ✉ *118 Main St.,* ☎ *802/229–9202; 802/223–3188 the Grill. AE, D, MC, V. Chef's Table closed Sun. No lunch Sat.*

$–$$ ✕ **Sarducci's.** Legislative lunches have been a lot more leisurely ever since Sarducci's came along to fill the trattoria void in Vermont's capital. These bright, cheerful rooms alongside the Winooksi River are a great spot for pizza fresh from wood-fired ovens, homemade Italian breads, and imaginative pasta dishes. ✉ *3 Main St.,* ☎ *802/223–0229. Reservations not accepted. AE, MC, V. No lunch Sun.*

$$–$$$ 🏨 **Inn at Montpelier.** This spacious early 1800s house has antique four-posters, tapestry-upholstered wing chairs, and classical guitar on the stereo. The sitting room has a Federal feel to it, and the wide wraparound Colonial Revival porch is perfect for reading or watching the townsfolk stroll by. ✉ *147 Main St., 05602,* ☎ *802/223–2727,* FAX *802/223–0722,* WEB *www.innatmontpelier.com. 19 rooms. AE, D, DC, MC, V. CP.*

St. Johnsbury

$$$$ ✕🏨 **Rabbit Hill Inn.** Some rooms have canopy beds, whirlpool baths, mountain views, and fireplaces. A fixed-price menu ($$$$) of eclectic, regional cuisine is served in the low-ceiling dining room. Meat and fish are smoked on the premises, and the herbs and vegetables often come from gardens out back. You can indulge in canoeing, cross-country skiing, or sipping cocktails in the pub. ✉ *Rte. 18, Lower Waterford 05848,* ☎ *802/748–5168 or 800/762–8669,* FAX *802/748–8342,* WEB *www.rabbithillinn.com. 19 rooms. Restaurant. AE, MC, V. Closed 1st 3 wks in Apr. and 1st 2 wks in Nov. MAP.*

$$–$$$$ ★ ✕🏨 **Wildflower Inn.** Guest rooms in the restored Federal-style main house, as well as in the carriage houses, are decorated simply with reproductions and contemporary furnishings; nearly all have incredible views of the property's 500 acres. Meals ($$–$$) comprise hearty country-style food, with freshly made breads and vegetables from the garden. The many activities available include fishing, ice-skating, cross-country skiing, and sleigh riding. There's a hot tub and sauna as well as a recreation room, and afternoon snacks are served. ✉ *2059 Darling Hill Rd., north of St. Johnsbury, Lyndonville 05851,* ☎ *802/626–8310 or 800/627–8310,* FAX *802/626–3039,* WEB *www.wildflowerinn.com. 21 rooms. Restaurant, pool, tennis. MC, V. Closed Apr. and Nov. BP.*

Stowe

$$ ★ ✕ **Mes Amis.** Chef Carole Fisher has the locals queueing up for house specialties such as fresh oysters, lobster bisque, braised lamb shanks, roast duck (secret recipe), and bananas Foster. Opt for the patio on a warm summer's night. ✉ *311 Mountain Rd.,* ☎ *802/253–8669. D, MC, V. Closed Mon.*

$$$–$$$$ ★ ✕🏨 **Edson Hill Manor.** At this French-Canadian–style manor atop 225 acres of rolling hills Oriental rugs accent the dark wide-board floors. Guest rooms have fireplaces, canopy beds, and down comforters. The dining room ($$–$$$; closed Sun.–Thurs. Apr.–May; no lunch) has walls of windows, wildflower paintings, and vines climbing to the ceiling. The contemporary cuisine might include rack of lamb or pan-seared salmon. ✉ *1500 Edson Hill Rd., 05672,* ☎ *802/253–7371 or 800/621–0284,* FAX *802/253–4036,* WEB *www.stowevt.com. 25 rooms. Restaurant, pool. D, MC, V. BP, MAP.*

$$$$ 🏨 **Topnotch at Stowe Resort and Spa.** The lobby of this resort, one of the state's poshest, has floor-to-ceiling windows, a freestanding circular stone fireplace, and cathedral ceilings. Rooms have thick carpeting and accents such as painted barn-board walls or Italian prints. Aerobics, horseback riding, cross-country skiing, and sleigh rides are among the many available activities. ✉ *Mountain Rd., Stowe 05672,* ☎ *802/253–8585 or 800/451–8686,* FAX *802/253–9263,* WEB *www.topnotch-resort.com. 90 rooms, 20 town houses. Restaurant, pool, golf, tennis, health club. AE, D, DC, MC, V. BP.*

Motels

🏨 **Econo Lodge** (✉ 101 Northfield St., Montpelier 05602, ☎ 802/223–5258 or 800/330–5258, FAX 802/223–0716), 54 rooms; restaurant; CP; *$*. 🏨 **Greystone Motel** (✉ U.S. 7, Middlebury 05753, ☎ 802/388–4935), 10 rooms; *$*.

Nightlife and the Arts

Nightlife

Burlington's nightlife caters to its college-age population, with pubs and a few dance spots. Touring and local musicians come to **Higher Ground** (✉ 1 Main St., Winooski, ☎ 802/654–8888). **Comedy Zone** (✉ Radisson Hotel, 60 Battery St., Burlington, ☎ 802/658–6500) provides the laughs in town on weekends. The **Metronome** (✉ 188 Main St., Burlington, ☎ 802/865–4563) entertains with an eclectic mix of live music almost every night. **Nectar's** (✉ 188 Main St., Burlington, ☎ 802/658–4771) is always jumping to the sounds of local bands and never charges a cover. The **Vermont Pub and Brewery** (✉ College and St. Paul Sts., Burlington, ☎ 802/865–0500) frequently hosts folk performers.

The Arts

Burlington and environs host the summer-long **Vermont Mozart Festival** (☎ 802/862–7352 or 800/639–9097, WEB www.vtmozart.com). The **Flynn Theater for the Performing Arts** (✉ 153 Main St., Burlington, ☎ 802/652–4500, WEB www.flynncenter.org) presents theater, dance, and lectures. Stowe has a summer **performing arts festival** (☎ 802/253–7792).

Outdoor Activities and Sports

Biking

In addition to the numerous back roads in the Champlain Valley, Stowe has a recreational path, and Burlington has a 9-mi path along its waterfront. **Vermont Bicycle Tours** (✉ 614 Monkton Rd. [Box 711, Bristol 05443], ☎ 802/453–4811 or 800/245–3868, WEB www.vbt.com) conducts tours throughout the state. **P.O.M.G. Bike Tours of Vermont** (✉ Box 1080, Richmond 05477, ☎ 802/434–2270 or 888/635–2453, WEB www.pomgbike.com) leads weekend and midweek tours and rents bikes.

Boating

Lake Champlain has marinas with rentals and charters in or near Vergennes and Burlington. The **North Beaches** border the northern edge of Burlington and are popular for swimming and sailboarding. **Burlington Community Boathouse** (✉ foot of College St., Burlington Harbor, ☎ 802/865–3377) rents sailboards and boats. **True North Kayak Tours** (✉ 53 Nash Pl., Burlington, ☎ 802/860–1910) gives guided tours of Lake Champlain.

Fishing

Lake Champlain contains salmon, lake trout, bass, pike, and more. **Malletts Bay Marina** (✉ 288 Lakeshore Dr., Colchester, ☎ 802/862–4072) provides marina services. **Point Bay Marina** (✉ 1401 Thompson's Point Rd., Charlotte, ☎ 802/425–2431) can handle your boating needs.

Golf

The Ralph Myhre Golf Course, run by Middlebury College (✉ Rte. 30, Middlebury, ☎ 802/443–5125), has 18 holes. The Jack Nicklaus–designed **Vermont National Country Club** (✉ 1227 Dorset St., South Burlington, ☎ 802/864–7770) is an 18-hole course.

Hiking and Backpacking

Day hikes in northern Vermont include the Little River area in Mt. Mansfield State Forest, near Stowe, and trails leading to the Mt. Mansfield summit from Smugglers' Notch State Park, Route 108, Jeffersonville, and Underhill State Park, off Route 15.

Ski Areas

For statewide snow conditions call ☎ 802/828–3239. All downhill areas listed except Mad River Glen have snowmaking. All except Mad River Glen allow snowboarding.

Cross-Country

Alpine resorts that have cross-country trails include Burke Mountain, 57 mi; Jay Peak, 20 mi; Smugglers' Notch, 23 mi; Stowe, 22 mi of groomed trails, 24 mi of backcountry trails; and Sugarbush, 15 mi.

Downhill

Burke Mountain (✉ Box 247, East Burke 05832, ☎ 802/626–3322, WEB www.skiburke.com) has 43 trails, 4 lifts, and a 2,000-ft vertical drop. **Jay Peak** (✉ Rte. 242, Jay 05859, ☎ 802/988–2611 or 800/451–4449, WEB www.jaypeakresort.com) maintains 66 trails, 8 lifts, and a 2,153-ft vertical drop. **Mad River Glen** (✉ Rte. 17, Waitsfield 05673, ☎ 802/496–3551, WEB www.madriverglen.com) provides 45 runs, 5 lifts, and a 2,037-ft drop. **Smugglers' Notch** (✉ Smugglers' Notch 05464, ☎ 802/644–8851 or 800/451–8752, WEB www.smuggs.com) has 67 runs, 9 lifts, and a 2,610-ft drop. **Stowe** (✉ 5781 Mountain Rd., Stowe 05672, ☎ 802/253–3000; 800/253–4754 lodging; WEB www.stowe.com) has 48 trails, 11 lifts, and a 2,360-ft drop. **Sugarbush** (✉ R.R. 1 [Box 350, Warren 05674], ☎ 802/583–2381; 800/537–8427 lodging; WEB www.sugarbush.com) manages 115 trails, 18 lifts, and 2,400- and 2,600-ft drops.

Shopping

Burlington's **Church Street Marketplace** is a pedestrian thoroughfare lined with boutiques. The **Vermont State Craft Center** (✉ Church St., ☎ 802/863–6458) is a display of the work of more than 200 Vermont artisans.

Northern Vermont Essentials

AIRPORTS

Burlington Airport, in South Burlington, is 4½ mi east of town off Route 2 and is served by major airlines. Private planes are accommodated at several state airports; call the Vermont State Transportation Agency, Aeronautics Operations, Aeronautics Division for information.

➤ AIRPORT INFORMATION: **Burlington Airport** (☎ 802/863–2874). **Vermont State Transportation Agency, Aeronautics Operations** (☎ 802/828–2093).

BUS TRAVEL

Vermont Transit links Burlington, Waterbury, Montpelier, St. Johnsbury, and Newport.

➤ BUS INFORMATION: **Vermont Transit** (☎ 800/552–8737; 800/642–3133 in Vermont).

CAR TRAVEL

I–89 runs from White River Junction to Vermont's northwestern corner at the Canadian border. To get to the eastern part of the state, drive up I–91.

TRAIN TRAVEL

Amtrak stops at Montpelier, Waterbury, Essex Junction, and St. Albans.
➤ TRAIN INFORMATION: **Amtrak** (☎ 800/872–7245).

VISITOR INFORMATION

For information on the Barre-Montpelier area, contact the Central Vermont Chamber of Commerce. Information on the Greater Burlington area is available from the Lake Champlain Regional Chamber of Commerce. St. Johnsbury and environs are covered by the Northeast Kingdom Chamber of Commerce.

➤ TOURIST INFORMATION: **Central Vermont Chamber of Commerce** (✉ Box 336, Barre 05641, ☎ 802/229–5711, WEB www.central-vt.com). **Lake Champlain Regional Chamber of Commerce** (✉ 60 Main St., Suite 100, Burlington 05401, ☎ 802/863–3489 or 877/686–5253, WEB www.vermont.org). **Northeast Kingdom Chamber of Commerce** (✉ 357 Western Ave., St. Johnsbury 05819, ☎ 802/748–3678 or 800/639–6379, WEB www.vermontnekchamber). **Smugglers' Notch Chamber of Commerce** (✉ Box 364, Jeffersonville 05464, ☎ 802/644–2239, WEB www.smugnotch.com). **Stowe Area Association** (✉ Main St. [Box 1320, Stowe 05672], ☎ 802/253–7321 or 877/603–8693, WEB www.stoweinfo.com).

VIRGINIA

By Francis X. Rocca

Updated by Kevin Myatt, Deanna Wrenn, and CiCi Williamson

Capital	Richmond
Population	7,078,515
Motto	Thus Always to Tyrants
State Bird	Cardinal
State Flower	Dogwood
Postal Abbreviation	VA

Statewide Visitor Information

Virginia Tourism Corporation (✉ 901 E. Byrd St., Richmond 23219, ☎ 804/786–2051 or 800/932–5827, WEB www.virginia.org) will mail travel brochures and travel information to you. Call **Visit Virginia** (☎ 800/786–4484) for visitor information and a free state map. **Welcome centers** are in Bracey (on I–85), Bristol (I–81), Clearbrook (I–81), Covington (I–64), Fredericksburg (I–95), King George (Rte. 301), Lambsburg (I–77), Manassas (I–66), New Church (U.S. 13), Rocky Gap (I–77), and Skippers (I–95).

Scenic Drives

Skyline Drive, the **Blue Ridge Parkway,** and **Goshen Pass** wind through spectacular mountain scenery. A 25-mi drive north along **Route 20** from Charlottesville to Orange takes you through gently rolling countryside, past stately horse farms and vineyards. For a stirring panorama of the famous buildings and monuments of Washington, D.C., drive north from Alexandria on the **George Washington Memorial Parkway.** Between Virginia Beach and the Eastern Shore stretches the 17½-mi **Chesapeake Bay Bridge-Tunnel,** an engineering wonder that has you surrounded by sea without leaving your car; a fishing and observation pier and a restaurant are along the way.

National and State Parks

National Parks

At **Shenandoah National Park** (✉ 3655 U.S. 211 E, Luray 22835, ☎ 540/999–3500), 196,500 acres with a vertical change in elevation of 3,500 ft, you can hike, ride horses, and fish. The 1.8-million-acre **George Washington and Jefferson National Forests** (✉ 5162 Valleypointe Pkwy., Roanoke 24019, ☎ 540/265–5100 or 888/265–0019) have places to camp, boat, hike, fish, swim, and ride horses. **Mt. Rogers National Recreation Area** (✉ 3714 Hwy. 16, Marion 24354, ☎ 540/783–5196) is a 116,000-acre expanse that contains the state's highest point—5,729 ft above sea level.

State Parks

The **Department of Conservation and Recreation** (✉ 203 Governor St., Richmond 23219, ☎ 804/786–1712) has information on Virginia's 28 state parks, which range in size from 500 to 4,500 acres. The **Douthat State Park** (✉ Rte. 629 [Box 212, Millboro 24460], ☎ 540/862–8100), built in 1936, has a 50-acre lake for boating, swimming, and fishing. Virginia Beach's **First Landing/Seashore State Park** (✉ 2500 Shore Dr., 23451, ☎ 757/481–2131) has oceanfront campsites.

CHARLOTTESVILLE AND THE SHENANDOAH VALLEY

Residents of Charlottesville, in the Piedmont region, call it "Mr. Jefferson's Country." They speak of the Sage of Monticello as if he were still writing, building, and governing. With a top-ranked state university and a fashionable retreat for tycoons, movie stars, and a smattering of celebrity writers, it is one of America's most sophisticated small cities. On the other side of the Blue Ridge on Charlottesville's western horizon is the Shenandoah Valley. From the Civil War crossroads at Winchester to the crisscrossing railroads at Roanoke, as well as the many former frontier outposts that lie between the two cities, the region is rich in history, culture, and recreation.

Exploring Charlottesville and the Shenandoah Valley

Charlottesville

★ Jefferson built his beloved **Monticello** (✉ Rte. 53, ☎ 434/984–9800, WEB www.monticello.org; 🎟 $11) on a "little mountain" over a period of 40 years, from 1769 to 1809. Monticello was a revolutionary structure, a neoclassical repudiation of the colonial style with all its political connotations. Throughout the house are Jefferson's inventions, including a seven-day clock and a "polygraph," a clever two-pen contraption that allowed him to copy letters as he wrote them.

The cozy rooms of **Ash Lawn–Highland** (✉ Rte. 795, southwest of Rte. 53, ☎ 434/293–9539, WEB monticello.avenue.org/ashlawn; 🎟 $8), James Monroe's modest farmhouse retreat, evoke the fifth president—the first to spring from the middle class. Outside, sheep and peacocks roam the grounds of this 550-acre working plantation (at its height it covered 3,500 acres).

In downtown Charlottesville, a six-block-long pedestrian shopping mall along Main Street contains boutiques, art galleries, bookshops, restaurants, movie theaters, and even a skating rink. At the eastern end of the pedestrian mall is the **Virginia Discovery Museum** (✉ 524 E. Main St., ☎ 434/977–1025; 🎟 $4; closed Mon.), where children can step inside a giant kaleidoscope and observe a working beehive in action. At the west end of town is the **University of Virginia** (✉ Emmet St., ☎ 434/924–3239, WEB www.virginia.edu; 🎟 free), founded and designed by Thomas Jefferson. The centerpiece of his revered "academical village" is the Rotunda, a half-scale replica of Rome's Pantheon, which is flanked by pavilions and a terraced expanse known as the Lawn.

The Shenandoah Valley

At the top of the valley near the state's northern tip is **Winchester.** A young Colonel George Washington spent more than a year here during the French and Indian Wars; the log cabin in which he worked is now **George Washington's Office Museum** (✉ 32 W. Cork St., ☎ 540/662–4412; 🎟 $5; closed Nov.–Mar.). As the gateway to the strategically important Shenandoah Valley and a crossroads close to the boundary between North and South, Winchester changed hands 72 times during the Civil War. In an effort to keep the Shenandoah in Southern hands, **Stonewall Jackson's headquarters** (✉ 415 N. Braddock St., Winchester, ☎ 540/667–3242; 🎟 $5; closed Nov.–Mar.) were set up here during the Valley Campaign of 1861–62. The headquarters are furnished as they were when the Confederate general used it, down to his prayer book and camp table.

Belle Grove (✉ U.S. 11, ☎ 540/869–2028, WEB www.bellegrove.org; 🎟 $7; closed Dec.–Mar.), south of Middletown, is a grand 1794 limestone mansion designed with advice from Thomas Jefferson. It served as headquarters for victorious Union forces during the Battle of Cedar Creek (1864) and is today a working farm. Group tours can still be arranged when it closes in winter.

Shenandoah National Park (✉ 3655 U.S. 211 E, Luray 22835, ☎ 540/999–3500, WEB www.shenandoah.national-park.com; 🎫 park and Skyline Drive $10 for cars, $5 for motorcycles, bicycles, and pedestrians), encompassing some 60 peaks, runs more than 80 mi along the Blue Ridge, between Front Royal and Waynesboro. Heavily forested, the park is the habitat of deer, bear, bobcat, and roughly 200 species of birds. **Skyline Drive** winds 105 mi along the spine of the Blue Ridge, affording panoramas of the valley to the west and the Piedmont to the east. On holidays and weekends from spring through fall, expect at least some degree of congestion.

Luray Caverns (✉ U.S. 211, Luray, ☎ 540/743–6551, WEB www.luraycaverns.com; 🎫 $16), the largest caves in the eastern United States, are west of Skyline Drive. Water seepage over millions of years has created towering rock and mineral formations, a section of which has been transformed into the world's only "stalacpipe organ." Tours begin every 20 minutes.

At **New Market,** the site of a costly Confederate victory late in the Civil War, the **New Market State Battlefield Historical Park** (✉ 8895 Collins Dr.; I–81, Exit 264, ☎ 540/740–3102; 🎫 $5) has exhibits on the battle and maps for self-guided walking tours.

★ The **Frontier Culture Museum** (✉ 1290 Richmond Rd., ☎ 540/332–7850, WEB www.frontiermuseum.org; 🎫 $8), outside Staunton (pronounced *Stan*-ton), re-creates early agrarian life in the Shenandoah Valley through four authentic farmsteads: Scots-Irish, German, English, and American.

The 470-mi **Blue Ridge Parkway** begins where Skyline Drive ends at Waynesboro, extending south to Great Smoky Mountains National Park in North Carolina. Reaching as high as 4,000 ft in Virginia, the drive offers numerous "overlooks," where you can turn off the main road and park for a commanding view. At the **Peaks of Otter Recreation Area** (Milepost 86, northeast of Roanoke), you can hike or ride to the rocky crown of Sharp Top mountain, where there's a 360-degree view. **Explore Park** (Milepost 115, near Roanoke) offers historic exhibits on Native American and colonial Virginian culture, trails for hiking and biking, and a parkway visitor center.

In Lexington, **Washington and Lee University,** founded in 1749, is named for the first U.S. president (an early benefactor) and the Confederate commander Robert E. Lee, who served as college president after the Civil War. Among the campus's white-columned neoclassical buildings is the tiny **Lee Memorial Chapel and Museum** (☎ 540/463–8768; 🎫 free), where a recumbent statue of the general marks his tomb. The lower level preserves Lee's office as he left it on September 28, 1870.

Adjacent to Washington and Lee University are the imposing neo-Gothic buildings of the **Virginia Military Institute.** An all-male institution since its founding in 1839, it became coeducational in 1997. On display at the **Institute Museum** (☎ 540/464–7232; 🎫 free) are some 15,000 military artifacts, including antique firearms and Civil War–era cadet equipment and uniforms. Near the Virginia Military Institute, the **Stonewall Jackson House** (✉ 8 E. Washington St., ☎ 540/463–2552, WEB www.stonewalljackson.org; 🎫 $5) offers a glimpse of the Confederate general's private life.

About 20 mi from Lexington is **Bath County,** where thermal springs with supposed medicinal powers have made it a popular resort area since the 1700s. Between Lexington and Bath County runs **Goshen Pass,** a stunning 3-mi stretch of Route 39 that follows the Maury River as it winds its way through the Alleghenies.

★ **Natural Bridge** (✉ I–81, Exit 175 or 180, ☎ 540/291–2121 or 800/533–1410, WEB www.naturalbridgeva.com; 🎫 $10), south of Lexington, is a 215-ft-high, 90-ft-long arch that was created as the creek below gradually carved out the limestone. Called the Bridge of God by the Monocan Indians who discovered it, the formation today really *is* a bridge, supporting U.S. 11.

Sandwiched between the Blue Ridge Parkway and the Appalachian Trail is **Roanoke,** known as the "Star City of the South" for the 100-ft lighted star atop **Mill Mountain.** Also on the mountain are two overlooks that are 1,000 ft above the city and the Roanoke Valley. The **Mill Mountain Zoo** (✉ Mill Mountain Spur, ☎ 540/343–3241, WEB www.mmzoo.org; 🎫 $6), houses North American and Asian animals, including bald eagles and snow leopards.

A restored downtown Roanoke warehouse, **Center in the Square** (✉ Market Sq., ☎ 540/342–5700, WEB www.centerinthesquare.org) contains a theater, art gallery, shops, a planetarium, and museums. The **Science Museum of Western Virginia** (✉ ☎ 540/342–5710; 🎫 $7; closed Mon.), inside Center in the Square, has interactive exhibits and computer games. Roanoke's history as a railroad hub is celebrated at the **Virginia Museum of Transportation** (✉ 303 Norfolk Ave., ☎ 540/342–5670, WEB www.vmt.org; 🎫 $6.30; closed Mon.–Tues. Jan.–Feb.), which has the nation's largest collection of locomotives. A restored 19th-century tobacco farm southeast of Roanoke, **Booker T. Washington National Monument** (✉ Rte. 122, ☎ 540/721–2094; 🎫 free) is the birthplace of the great black educator and a museum of slave life.

The **National D-Day Memorial** (✉ U.S. 460, Bedford, ☎ 800/351–3329, WEB www.dday.org; 🎫 $10), a half-hour drive east of Roanoke, is made up of a granite arch and realistic sculptures of soldiers high on a hill. The town it overlooks lost almost an entire generation of its young men in the 1944 invasion of Normandy.

About two hours east of Roanoke and less than two hours south of Charlottesville is **Appomattox Courthouse National Historical Park** (✉ Rte. 24, Appomattox, ☎ 434/352–8987; 🎫 $4), a village of 27 buildings restored to what they looked like on April 9, 1865, when Lee surrendered to Grant in the parlor of the McLean House.

Dining and Lodging

Bed-and-breakfast reservations in the region can be made through **Blue Ridge Bed & Breakfast** (✉ 2458 Castleman Rd., Berryville 22611, ☎ 540/955–1246 or 800/296–1246, FAX 540/955–4240, WEB www.blueridgebb.com) and **Guesthouses** (✉ Box 5737, Charlottesville 22905, ☎ 434/979–7264, FAX 434/293–7791, WEB www.va-guesthouses.com).

Bath County

$$$$ ★ ✕🏨 **The Homestead.** This resort ranks as one of the country's most luxurious. Rooms have Georgian-style furnishings; some have fireplaces. The 15,000-acre property has 100 mi of riding trails, nine ski slopes, and 4 mi of streams stocked with rainbow trout. The resort has a full-service spa, and an orchestra performs nightly in the formal dining room, which serves up Continental and traditional Virginia cuisine as part

of the prix-fixe ($$$$), the only option. ✉ *U.S. 220, Hot Springs 24445,* ☎ *540/839–1766 or 800/838–1766,* FAX *540/839–7670,* WEB *www.thehomestead.com. 506 rooms. 6 restaurants, pools, golf, tennis, gym. AE, D, DC, MC, V. MAP.*

$–$$ ✕ **Inn at Gristmill Square.** Most of the rustic, colonial-style rooms in this state landmark have fireplaces, and all are spacious. The rooms are scattered throughout a 19th-century miller's house, blacksmith's shop, hardware store, gristmill, and cottage. The Waterwheel Restaurant ($$–$$$), also in the gristmill, has entrées that include breast of chicken stuffed with wild rice, sausage, apple, and pecans. ✉ *Rte. 645 (Box 359, Warm Springs 24484),* ☎ *540/839–2231,* FAX *540/839–5770,* WEB *www.gristmillsquare.com. 18 rooms, 1 apartment. Restaurant, pool, tennis. D, MC, V. CP.*

Blue Ridge Parkway

$$–$$$$ **Wintergreen.** From December through March those staying at this 11,000-acre mountain resort are sometimes able to ski and golf on the same day. There are plenty of additional sports options all year long: tennis, hiking, horseback riding, boating, and bicycling, as well as a spa. Accommodations range from studio mountain condos to seven-bedroom houses. All the exteriors are made of wood painted in earth tones that blend in with the resort's natural surroundings. ✉ *Rte. 664, Wintergreen 22958,* ☎ *434/325–2200 or 800/325–2200,* FAX *434/325–8003,* WEB *www.wintergreenresort.com. 300 units. 6 restaurants, pools, gym. AE, D, MC, V.*

Charlottesville

$$–$$$ ✕ **C&O Restaurant.** A dingy-looking storefront hung with an old, illuminated Pepsi sign conceals one of the most venerated restaurants in town. The formal dining room upstairs (seating begins at 6:30), the bistro below, and the cozy mezzanine in between share a menu that is French influenced, with Pacific Rim and American Southwest touches. Try the flank steak pan-fried with tamari (similar to soy sauce) and fresh ginger cream. ✉ *515 E. Water St.,* ☎ *434/971–7044. AE, MC, V. No lunch.*

$$–$$$ ✕ **Duner's.** Locals flock to this eatery 5 mi west of Charlottesville, because its fanciful menu, which changes daily, never disappoints. Fresh, seasonal fare, including seafood and pasta dishes, predominates. Try the grilled shrimp with flying-fish roe and sesame seaweed salad or the rack of lamb with pecan barbecue sauce. ✉ *Rte. 250 W, Ivy,* ☎ *434/293–8352. Reservations not accepted. MC, V. No lunch.*

$$$$ ★ ✕ **Keswick Hall at Monticello.** This sprawling 1912 Tuscan villa is set on 600 lush acres. All guest rooms and common areas are furnished with English and American antiques, and some rooms have whirlpool baths and balconies. The facilities of the private Keswick Club are open to those staying overnight. There's an 18-hole golf course, tennis, croquet, fishing, and bicycling. In the formal restaurant ($$$–$$$$), the finely prepared dishes emphasize local products: try the lamb loin with eggplant-spinach strudel or the grilled filet of beef with Maytag blue cheese cake and wild mushrooms. ✉ *701 Club Dr., 5 mi east of Charlottesville, Keswick 22947,* ☎ *434/979–3440 or 800/274–5391,* FAX *434/977–4171,* WEB *www.keswick.com. 48 rooms. 2 restaurants, pools, health club. AE, D, DC, MC, V.*

$$–$$$ ★ ✕ **Silver Thatch Inn.** This 1780 white-clapboard farmhouse has been transformed into an intimate inn, with four-poster beds and antiques accenting the rooms, some of which have fireplaces. In the restaurant ($$–$$$), supplied by organic farms, the fish is always fresh and the rabbits and chickens are often locally raised. The chef's grilled beef tenderloin is renowned, and the wine cellar wins national awards. Restaurant reservations are essential. ✉ *3001 Hollymead Dr., 22911,* ☎ *434/*

978–4686 or 800/261–0720, FAX 434/973–6156, WEB www.silverthatch.com. 7 rooms. Restaurant, pool. AE, DC, MC, V. BP.

Lexington

$–$$$ ✕🏨 **Maple Hall.** At this former 1850 plantation house you can hike and fish on its 56-acre plot. Rooms have period antiques and modern amenities. A notable entrée on the seasonal menu ($–$$) is chicken Chesapeake (a chicken breast stuffed with spinach and crabmeat). ✉ *Rte. 11 (6 mi north of Lexington), 24450,* ☎ *540/463–6693 or 877/463–2044,* FAX *540/463–7262,* WEB *www.lexingtonhistoricinns.com/maplehall.htm. 21 rooms. Restaurant, pool, tennis. D, MC, V. BP.*

Roanoke

$$$ ✕🏨 **Hotel Roanoke and Conference Center.** This elegant Tudor Revival building has a richly paneled lobby and Florentine marble floors. The rooms are furnished with reproduction antiques. The Regency Dining Room ($$–$$$), which has a rotating menu of classic European dishes, pays heed to regional southern cuisine through such dishes as peanut soup, spoon bread, and steak Diane. ✉ *110 Shenandoah Ave., 24016,* ☎ *540/985–5900 or 800/222–8733,* FAX *540/853–8264,* WEB *www.hotelroanoke.com. 332 rooms. 2 restaurants, pool, gym. AE, D, DC, MC, V.*

Staunton

$$–$$$$ ✕🏨 **Belle Grae Inn.** Canopy beds, antiques, and rocking chairs in this restored Victorian mansion give the guest rooms a turn-of-the-20th-century mood. In the restaurant's formal dining room, the prix-fixe menu ($30–$35), which changes weekly, emphasizes Continental cuisine with a regional flair. ✉ *515 W. Frederick St., 24401,* ☎ *540/886–5151 or 888/541–5151,* FAX *540/886–6641,* WEB *www.bellegrae.com. 17 rooms. Restaurant. AE, MC, V. MAP.*

$–$$ 🏨 **Sampson Eagon Inn.** In the historic Gospel Hill section of town, this circa-1840 Greek Revival home has been restored to its period charm. The spacious guest rooms have antique canopy beds, cozy sitting areas, and modern amenities. Don't miss the Kahlúa Belgian waffles for breakfast. ✉ *238 E. Beverley St., 24401,* ☎ *540/886–8200 or 800/597–9722,* WEB *www.eagoninn.com. 5 rooms. AE, MC, V. BP.*

Washington

$$$$ ✕ **The Inn at Little Washington.** The town, 60 mi north of Lexington, was the first to be named after the "father of our country." Although the inn does have 14 guest rooms, most people visiting it know the Inn at Little Washington for dining comparable to any in its bigger namesake to the northeast. The seven-course dinner ranges from $98 per person on weekdays to $128 on weekends. Despite the fixed price, the menu is abundant with choices, prepared almost exclusively with local products. Main-course selections include various dishes of seafood, veal, beef, chicken and, of course, Virginia ham. ✉ *Middle and Main Sts.,* ☎ *540/675–3800,* FAX *540/675–3100. MC, V. Closed Tues.*

Winchester

$$$–$$$$ ★ ✕🏨 **L'Auberge Provençale.** The owners, originally from Avignon, bring the warm elegance of the south of France to this 1750s country inn. Rooms are eclectically decorated with French art and fabrics and Victorian wicker and antiques, and some have fireplaces. The elegant breakfast includes fresh homemade croissants and apple crepes with maple syrup. At the Provençale restaurant, memorable entrées include fois gras in a spicy lentil sauce on country bread. Restaurant reservations are essential on weekends. ✉ *Rte. 340, 10 mi east of Winchester (Box 190, White Post 22663),* ☎ *540/837–1375 or 800/638–1702,* FAX *540/837–2004,* WEB *www.laubergeprovencale.com. 14 rooms.*

Restaurant, pool. AE, D, MC, V. Closed Jan. Restaurant closed Mon.–Tues. No lunch. BP.

Motels

Most major chains and many locally operated motels can be found on I–64 and I–81 exits, with the heaviest concentration in the Charlottesville and Roanoke areas.

Best Western Inn at Valley View Mall (✉ 5050 Valley View Blvd., Roanoke 24012, ☎ 800/362–2410, FAX 540/362–2400), 85 rooms; pool; $.

Holiday Inn University Area (✉ 1901 Emmett St., Charlottesville 22901, ☎ 434/977–7700 or 800/242–5973), 131 rooms; pool, restaurant; $.

Campgrounds

Shenandoah National Park's **Big Meadows Campground** (☎ 540/999–3500 or 800/365–2267) requires reservations for stays between May and November. Other campsites in the park are available on a first-come, first-serve basis; for information contact the park. **Roanoke Mountain Campground** (✉ Milepost 121, 5 mi southeast of downtown, ☎ 540/982–9242 or 540/767–2490; closed Nov.–Mar.) has 74 campsites and 30 RV sites. Hiking trails and a scenic drive to the top of Roanoke Mountain are nearby.

Nightlife and the Arts

Nightlife

In Charlottesville the large and comfortable **Miller's** (✉ 109 W. Main St., Downtown Mall, ☎ 434/971–8511), where rock star Dave Matthews got his start, hosts blues and jazz musicians. At the **Homestead** in Hot Springs (✉ U.S. 220, ☎ 540/839–1766 or 800/838–1766) there's nightly dancing to live music. At Roanoke's **Corned Beef & Co. Bar and Grill** (✉ 107 S. Jefferson St., ☎ 540/342–3354), one block from the lively Market Square, live jazz, funk, and rock music drift out the doors on Friday and Saturday nights.

The Arts

CHARLOTTESVILLE

For details on performances at the University of Virginia, check the free *C'ville Weekly* (c-ville.com) or *Cavalier Daily* (www.cavalierdaily.com). **McGuffey Art Center** (✉ 201 2nd St. NW, ☎ 434/295–7973, WEB www.avenue.org/mcguffey; ⏲ Tues.–Sat. 10–5, Sun. 1–5) contains the Second Street Gallery and the studios of painters, metal workers, and sculptors, all of which are open to the public.

SHENANDOAH VALLEY

Blackfriars Playhouse (✉ 10 S. Market St., Staunton, ☎ 540/885–5588, WEB www.shenandoahshakespeare.com) brings the plays of Shakespeare alive in an authentic reproduction of an Elizabethan theater. **Garth Newel Music Center** (✉ U.S. 220 N, 3 mi north of Hot Springs, Hot Springs, ☎ 540/839–5018, WEB www.garthnewel.org) hosts chamber music concerts throughout the year. Roanoke's **Jefferson Center** (✉ 541 Luck Ave. SW, ☎ 540/343–2624, WEB www.jeffcenter.org) mounts ballet, opera, and symphony performances as well as art exhibits and lectures.

Mill Mountain Theatre (✉ 1 Market Sq. SE, ☎ 540/342–5740, WEB www.millmountain.org) in Roanoke offers year-round professional theater. The **Theater at Lime Kiln** (✉ Borden Rd., off U.S. 60 W; turn left ¼ mi west of Washington & Lee University bridge, Lexington, ☎ 540/463–3074, WEB www.theateratlimekiln.com) is an outdoor rockwall pit (the ruins of a lime kiln) where musicals and concerts—folk, bluegrass, classical, and more—take place in the summer.

Outdoor Activities and Sports

Canoeing

Downriver Canoe (✉ Rte. 613, ☎ 540/635–5526, WEB www.downriver.com) and **Front Royal Canoe** (✉ U.S. 340, ☎ 540/635–5440, WEB www.frontroyalcanoe.com) are both near Front Royal. **James River Runners Inc.** (✉ 10082 Hatton Ferry Rd., Scottsville, ☎ 434/286–2338, WEB www.jamesriver.com) is about 25 mi south of Charlottesville. **Shenandoah River Outfitters** (✉ Rte. 684, ☎ 540/743–4159, WEB www.shenandoahriver.com) is near Luray.

Fishing

To take advantage of the abundance of trout in some 50 streams of **Shenandoah National Park,** get a five-day Virginia fishing license at concession stands along Skyline Drive.

Golf

Caverns Country Club Resort (✉ U.S. 211, Luray, ☎ 540/743–6551). **Hanging Rock Golf Club** (✉ 1500 Red La. [I-81, Exit 140], Salem, ☎ 540/389–7275). The **Homestead** (✉ U.S. 220, Hot Springs, ☎ 540/839–1766 or 800/838–1766).

Hiking

The **Appalachian Trail** extends across the region, weaving through Shenandoah National Park, the George Washington and Jefferson National Forests, the Roanoke and New River valleys to Mount Rogers National Recreation Area. Its proximity to Skyline Drive and the Blue Ridge Parkway in the north allows for easy access and variable hiking lengths. Two of the most often-photographed formations along the entire 2,000-mi trail, McAfee Knob and Dragon's Tooth, are near Roanoke. Other trails can be found along the Blue Ridge Parkway and elsewhere in the national forests.

Ski Areas

The **Homestead** (✉ U.S. 220, Hot Springs, ☎ 540/839–1766 or 800/838–1766) has cross-country, downhill, and night skiing. **Massanutten Resort** (✉ Rte. 644 off U.S. 33, McGaheysville, ☎ 540/289–9441) has 15 slopes, a snow-tubing park, and equipment rental. **Wintergreen** (✉ Rte. 664, Wintergreen, ☎ 434/325–2200 or 800/325–2200) maintains 17 slopes and trails.

Spectator Sports

Equestrian events: The **Virginia Horse Center** (✉ Rte. 39, Lexington, ☎ 540/463–2194) stages show jumping, hunter trials, and multibreed shows year-round.

Football, soccer, basketball, softball, golf, tennis, lacrosse, and field hockey: The **University of Virginia** (☎ 434/924–8821) is nationally ranked in several varsity sports. The *Cavalier Daily* has listings.

Tennis

Caverns Country Club Resort (✉ U.S. 211, Luray, ☎ 540/743–6551).

Shopping

Lewis Glaser Quill Pens (✉ 1700 Sourwood Pl., Charlottesville, ☎ 434/973–7783 or 800/446–6732) sells handcrafted feather pens and pewter inkwells of the kind it has made for the U.S. Supreme Court and the British royal family. The Downtown Mall in Charlottesville has a concentration of used and antiquarian bookstores with rare and hard-to-find tomes. **Blue Whale Books** (✉ 115 W. Main St., ☎ 434/296–4646) stocks art prints and maps as well as about 25,000 books. **Daedalus Bookshop** (✉ 123 4th St. NE, ☎ 434/293–7595) has roughly 90,000 titles on hand.

Charlottesville and the Shenandoah Valley Essentials

AIRPORTS

Charlottesville-Albemarle Airport is 8 mi north of town at the intersection of Routes 606 and 649, off U.S. 29. Roanoke Regional Airport is northwest of downtown, off I–581.

➤ AIRPORT INFORMATION: **Charlottesville-Albemarle Airport** (☎ 434/973–8341, WEB www.gocho.com). **Roanoke Regional Airport** (☎ 540/362–1999, WEB www.roanokeregionalairport.com).

BUS TRAVEL

Greyhound serves Charlottesville, Lexington (via the station in Buena Vista), Roanoke, and Staunton.

➤ BUS INFORMATION: **Greyhound** (✉ 211 W. 21st St., Buena Vista; ✉ 310 W. Main St., Charlottesville; ✉ 26 Salem Ave., Roanoke; ✉ 211 Lee Hwy., Staunton; ☎ 800/231–2222; WEB www.greyhound.com).

CAR TRAVEL

Charlottesville is where U.S. 29 (north–south) meets I–64. I–81 and U.S. 11 run north–south the length of the Shenandoah Valley and continue south into Tennessee. I–66 meets I–81 and U.S. 11 at the northern end of the valley; I–64 connects I–81 and U.S. 11 with Charlottesville. Route 39 runs through Bath County and connects with I–81/I–64, north of Lexington. U.S. 220 (north–south) and U.S. 460 (east–west) connect with I–81 at Roanoke.

TRAIN TRAVEL

Amtrak has service to Charlottesville's Union Station, to Clifton Forge—for the Homestead resort in Bath County—and to Staunton.

➤ TRAIN INFORMATION: **Amtrak** (☎ 800/872–7245, WEB www.amtrak.com). **Charlottesville Union Station** (✉ 810 W. Main St.). **Clifton Forge** (✉ 400 Ridgeway St.). **Staunton** (✉ 1 Middlebrook Ave.).

VISITOR INFORMATION

➤ TOURIST INFORMATION: **Bath County Chamber of Commerce** (✉ U.S. 220 [Box 718, Hot Springs 24445], ☎ 540/839–5409 or 800/628–8092, WEB www.bathcountyva.org). **Charlottesville-Albemarle Convention and Visitors Bureau** (✉ Rte. 20 S [Box 178, 22902], ☎ 434/977–1783 or 877/386–1102, WEB www.charlottesvilletourism.org). **Lexington Visitor Center** (✉ 106 E. Washington St., 24450, ☎ 540/463–3777 or 877/453–9822, WEB www.lexingtonvirginia.com). **Roanoke Valley Convention and Visitors Bureau** (✉ 114 Market St., Roanoke 24011, ☎ 540/342–6025 or 800/635–5535, WEB www.visitroanokeva.com). **Shenandoah Valley Travel Association** (✉ Box 1040, New Market 22844, ☎ 540/740–3132 or 877/847–4878, WEB www.shenandoah.org). **Winchester Chamber of Commerce** (✉ 1360 S. Pleasant Valley Rd., 22601, ☎ 540/662–4135 or 800/662–1360, WEB www.winchesterva.org).

NORTHERN VIRGINIA

The affluent and cosmopolitan residents of this region have closer ties to neighboring Washington, D.C., than to the rest of the state, yet they take pride in being Virginians and in protecting the historic treasures they hold in trust for the rest of the nation. Here is some of America's most precious acreage, including Arlington National Cemetery, Mount Vernon, and the Civil War battlefield of Manassas (Bull Run). In the rural Hunt Country, around Leesburg and Middleburg, the gracious Old South lives on in fox hunting and steeplechases.

Exploring Northern Virginia

★ George Washington's **Mount Vernon** (✉ southern end of George Washington Pkwy., ☎ 703/780–2000, WEB www.mountvernon.org; 🎫 $9) is the nation's best-known country house. Washington inherited the land in 1761 and farmed what was then an 8,000-acre plantation before taking command of the Continental Army. Throughout the house are small symbols of Washington's eminence, including his presidential chair.

Woodlawn (✉ Rte. 1, via Rte. 235, ☎ 703/780–4000, WEB www.nationaltrust.org; 🎫 $7.50 for either or $13 for both Woodlawn and the Pope-Leighey House), designed by the amateur architect of the Capitol, William Thornton, and completed in 1805, was built for Washington's step-granddaughter, Nelly Custis, who married his favorite nephew, Lawrence Lewis. The small, contemporary-style **Pope-Leighey House,** was built in 1940 by Frank Lloyd Wright. It was moved here from Falls Church in 1964 and is one of few homes of the great architect that are open to the public.

South of Mount Vernon is the lesser-known **Gunston Hall** (✉ 10709 Gunston Rd., Mason Neck, ☎ 703/550–9220 or 800/811–6966, WEB www.gunstonhall.org; 🎫 $7), the 1755 Georgian plantation home of George Mason, one of the framers of the Constitution and author of the Virginia Declaration of Rights, the basis of our Bill of Rights.

North of Mount Vernon is **Alexandria,** a couple of miles from and much older than Washington, D.C. It enjoys a colorful past, linked to the most significant events and personages of the colonial, Revolutionary, and Civil War periods. **Old Town** is a picturesque neighborhood of mostly redbrick 18th- and 19th-century town houses with a few cobblestone streets. Its major sights can be seen on foot within 20 blocks or so, and the area has scores of import and specialty shops, galleries, and restaurants, including some with exotic cuisine. Parking is usually scarce, but the **Convention and Visitors Association** provides a free 24-hour pass that allows out-of-town visitors free parking at two-hour meters.

Alexandria's visitor center—the best place to start a tour—is in the town's oldest structure, **Ramsay House** (✉ 221 King St., ☎ 703/838–4200 or 800/388–9119), believed to have been built around 1724 in Dumfries (25 mi south) and moved here in 1749. The 1753 **Carlyle House** (✉ 121 N. Fairfax St., ☎ 703/549–2997, WEB www.nvrpa.org; 🎫 $4), built by Scottish merchant John Carlyle, is still the grandest house in town. The **Old Presbyterian Meeting House** (✉ 321 S. Fairfax St., ☎ 703/549–6670; 🎫 free) was both a church and a gathering place for Scottish patriots during the Revolution. John Carlyle and other Alexandria notables are buried here.

Since George Washington lived in Alexandria, he frequented many of the historic buildings in what's now known as "Old Town," including the **Stabler-Leadbeater Apothecary Museum** ((✉ 105– 107 S. Fairfax St., ☎ 703/836–3713; 🎫 $2.50). The second oldest apothecary in the country, the museum has a fine collection of more than 800 bottles.

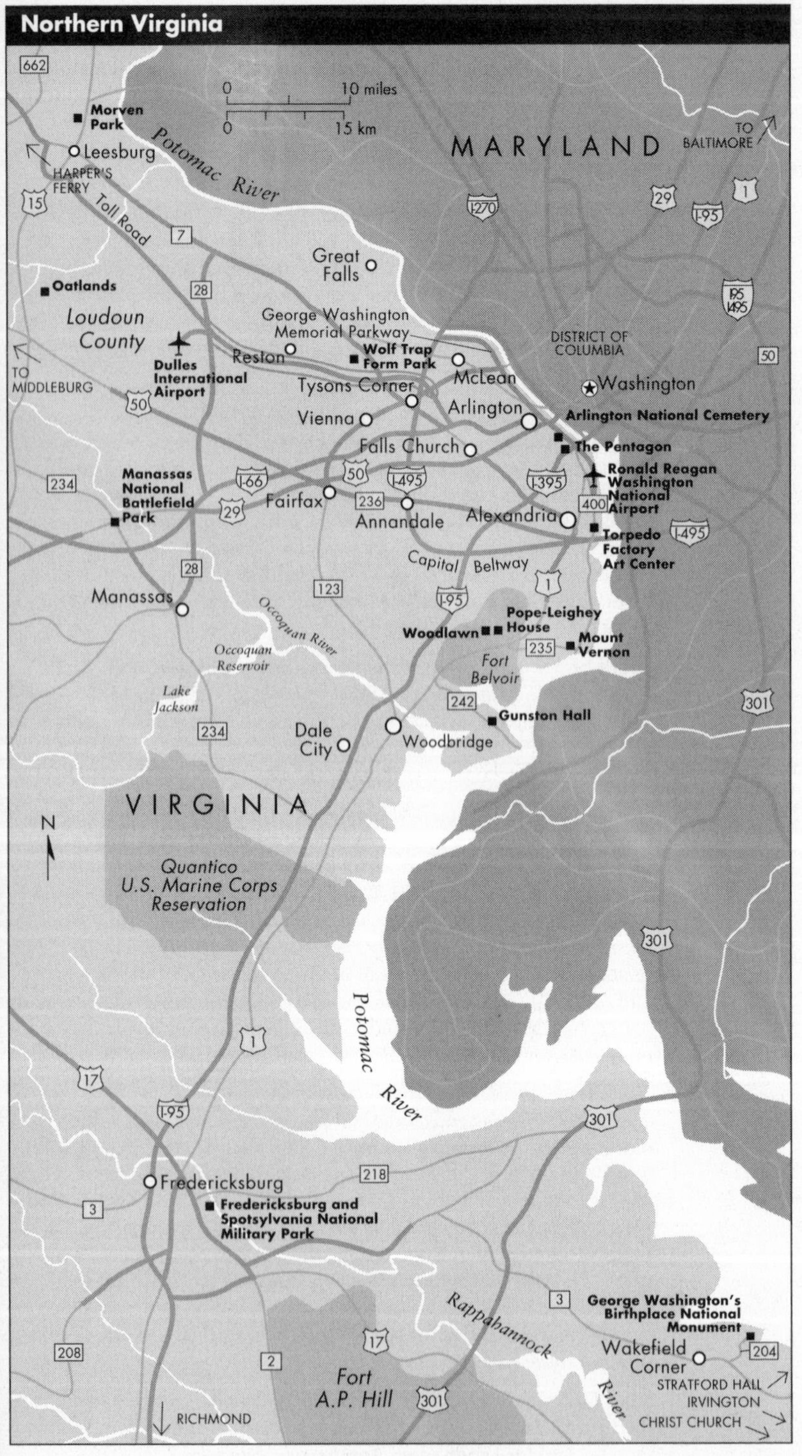

Northern Virginia
0
10 miles
0
15 km
MARYLAND
TO BALTIMORE
Morven Park
Leesburg
HARPER'S FERRY
Potomac River
Toll Road
Great Falls
Oatlands
Loudoun County
George Washington Memorial Parkway
Reston
Wolf Trap Farm Park
McLean
DISTRICT OF COLUMBIA
Washington
TO MIDDLEBURG
Dulles International Airport
Tysons Corner
Vienna
Arlington
Arlington National Cemetery
Falls Church
The Pentagon
Manassas National Battlefield Park
Fairfax
Annandale
Alexandria
Ronald Reagan Washington National Airport
Torpedo Factory Art Center
Capital Beltway
Manassas
Occoquan River
Occoquan Reservoir
Pope-Leighey House
Woodlawn
Mount Vernon
Fort Belvoir
Lake Jackson
Gunston Hall
Dale City
Woodbridge
VIRGINIA
N
Quantico U.S. Marine Corps Reservation
Potomac River
Fredericksburg
Fredericksburg and Spotsylvania National Military Park
Rappahannock River
George Washington's Birthplace National Monument
Wakefield Corner
STRATFORD HALL
IRVINGTON
CHRIST CHURCH
Fort A.P. Hill
RICHMOND

Gadsby's Tavern Museum (✉ 134 N. Royal St., ☎ 703/838–4242, WEB www.gadsbys.com; 🎫 $4) was once a tavern and hotel. Its ballroom hosted two birthday celebrations for our first president; the buildings have been restored to the way they looked then. Washington was a member (or "pewholder") of **Christ Church** (✉ 118 N. Washington St., ☎ 703/549–1450; 🎫 free), a fine original English Georgian country–style edifice.

Alexandria's cultural heritage is honored at the **Lyceum** (✉ 201 S. Washington St., ☎ 703/838–4994; 🎫 free), with displays of decorative arts ★ and exhibits on local history. The **Torpedo Factory Art Center** (✉ 105 N. Union St., ☎ 703/838–4565, WEB www.torpedofactory.org; 🎫 free) is a former munitions plant that now houses the workshops and galleries of about 160 professional artists.

Across from the King Street Metro and Alexandria Amtrak Station is the 333-ft-high **George Washington Masonic National Memorial** (✉ 101 Callahan Dr., ☎ 703/683–2007, WEB www.gwmemorial.org; 🎫 free). Here you'll see relics of the first president and exhibits on the Masonic Order. At the top, there's a spectacular view of Alexandria and—6 mi away—Washington, D.C.

For information on **Arlington National Cemetery** and the **Pentagon,** *see* Washington, D.C.

Fredericksburg, about an hour south of Washington, D.C., has numerous sites worth checking out. The town's 40-block National Historic District contains more than 350 original 18th- and 19th-century buildings. Fredericksburg rivals Alexandria and Mount Vernon for associations with the Washington family. From ages 6 to 20 the future first president lived at Ferry Farm, across the Rappahannock River from Fredericksburg. For information about Washington family sites as well as the other venues in and around the town, head to the **Fredericksburg Visitor Center.** (The center building itself was constructed in 1824 as a residence and confectionery; during the Civil War it was used as a prison.) ✉ *706 Caroline St.,* ☎ *540/373–1776 or 800/678–4748,* WEB *www.fredericksburgvirginia.net.*

Washington's sister Betty and her husband lived at **Kenmore** (✉ 1201 Washington Ave., ☎ 540/373–3381, WEB www.kenmore.org; 🎫 $7), a house whose simple, brick facade and slate roof belie a lavish interior. The home of Charles Washington, George's brother, later became the **Rising Sun Tavern** (✉ 1306 Caroline St., ☎ 540/371–1494; 🎫 $4), a watering hole for such revolutionaries as Patrick Henry and Thomas Jefferson. The **Mary Washington House** (✉ 1200 Charles St., ☎ 540/373–1569; 🎫 $4) is a modest house George bought for his mother during her last years.

At the **Hugh Mercer Apothecary Shop** (✉ 1020 Caroline St., ☎ 540/373–3362; 🎫 $4), the guide's explicit descriptions of amputations, cataract operations, and tooth extractions may make you wince.

★ **Fredericksburg Area Museum and Cultural Center.** The museum's six permanent exhibits tell the story of the area from prehistoric times through the Revolutionary and Civil wars to the present. Displays include dinosaur footprints from a nearby quarry, Native American artifacts, and Confederate memorabilia. The museum is in an 1816 building once used as a market and town hall. ✉ *907 Princess Anne St.,* ☎ *540/371–3037,* WEB *www.famcc.org.* 🎫 *$5.*

★ **Fredericksburg/Spotsylvania National Military Park.** The park incorporates four battlefields and three historic buildings, all accessible for a single admission price. In season, park rangers lead walking tours.

The centers offer tour cassettes and maps that show how to reach hiking trails at the Wilderness, Chancellorsville, and Spotsylvania Court House battlefields (all within 15 mi of Fredericksburg). ✉ *Fredericksburg Battlefield Visitor Center, Lafayette Blvd. and Sunken Rd.,* ☎ *540/373–6122,* WEB *www.nps.gov/frsp;* ✉ *Chancellorsville Battlefield Visitor Center, Plank Rd./Rte. 3 W,* ☎ *540/786–2880.* 🎫 *$4 includes all 4 battlefields, Chatham Manor, and other historic buildings; valid for 1 wk; children 16 and under free.*

Twenty-six miles west of Washington is **Manassas National Battlefield Park,** or Bull Run (✉ 12521 Lee Hwy., north of I–66, Exit 47, ☎ 703/361–1339, WEB www.nps.gov/mana; 🎫 $2), where the Confederacy won two major victories and Stonewall Jackson earned his nickname.

About an hour west of Washington lies **Loudoun County,** which is horse country. In the fashionable towns of **Leesburg** and **Middleburg,** well-heeled residents (many of them Yankee transplants) keep up the local traditions of fox hunts and steeplechases. The Loudoun Convention and Visitors Association in Leesburg can suggest scenic drives.

The mansion at 1,200-acre **Morven Park** (✉ 17263 Southern Planter La., take Morven Park Rd. 1 mi north of Leesburg, ☎ 703/771–6034, WEB www.morvenpark.org; 🎫 $7) resembles the White House. The last home of Governor Westmoreland Davis, it contains two museums: one of horse-drawn carriages, the other of hounds and hunting.

Dining and Lodging

Alexandria's restaurants are varied and, on weekend nights, crowded. Arlington has several Latin American restaurants throughout the county. Little Saigon, on and around Wilson Boulevard, has several low-priced Vietnamese restaurants.

Bed-and-breakfasts tend to cost about the same as hotels in Virginia: many are housed in historic homes and serve as romantic weekend hideaways for regular customers from Washington.

The **Virginia Bed & Breakfast Service** (800/934–9184), run by the state, provides information about bed-and-breakfasts and is also a reservation service. The **Virginia Country Inns and Bed & Breakfasts** (800/262–1293) mails free booklets and also offers a reservation service.

Alexandria

$$$ ★ ✕ **La Bergerie.** This Old Town restaurant serves food of the French Basques. Offerings include duck confit and parillade of seafood (assorted seafood in light garlic tomato sauce), cod and clams in a Basque sauce, and pear clafouti (fruit covered with a cakey topping). ✉ *218 Lee St.,* ☎ *703/683–1007. AE, DC, MC, V. Closed Sun.*

★ ✕🏨 **Morrison House.** Though established in 1985, this small hotel was built in a traditional Federal style. Inside, the tasteful ruse continues with reproductions of antiques and fireplaces of the period. Amenities, though, are fully modern. The Elysium restaurant serves Mediterranean cuisine. ✉ *116 S. Alfred St., 22314,* ☎ *703/838–8000 or 800/367–0800,* FAX *703/684–6283,* WEB *www.morrisonhouse.com. 45 rooms. 2 restaurants. AE, DC, MC, V.*

Arlington

$–$$ ★ ✕ **Aegean Taverna.** This white stucco eatery near Wilson Boulevard serves excellent, authentic Greek food, including favorites like pastitsio, moussaka, and spinach pie. There's dining outside in good weather. Greek musicians perform Friday and Saturday nights, and parking is free and easy. ✉ *2950 Clarendon Blvd.,* ☎ *703/841–9494. AE, D, DC, MC, V.*

$-$$ ★ ✕ **Queen Bee.** Arlington's Little Saigon area has several good Vietnamese restaurants; this is one of the best. Saigon pancakes—with a mix of crab, pork, and shrimp—and the moist and delicately flavored spring rolls are two reasons that diners are willing to wait for a table. ✉ *3181 Wilson Blvd.,* ☎ *703/527–3444. AE, MC, V.*

$$$-$$$$ ★ **Ritz-Carlton Pentagon City.** This 18-story Ritz-Carlton at the Pentagon City Metro stop is more convenient to downtown Washington than many D.C. hotels. Public spaces are full of 18th- and 19th-century art and antiques, and many rooms have views of the monuments across the river. ✉ *1250 S. Hayes St., 22202,* ☎ *703/415–5000 or 800/241–3333,* FAX *703/415–5060,* WEB *www.ritzcarlton.com. 366 rooms. Restaurant, bar, pool, health club. AE, DC, MC, V.*

Great Falls

$$$$ ★ ✕ **L'Auberge Chez François.** White stucco, dark exposed beams, and a garden make this restaurant, 20 minutes from Tysons Corner, seem like a country inn. Among the Alsatian cuisine on hand are game, a salmon soufflé with salmon-and-scallop mousse and lobster sauce, and a plum tart. ✉ *332 Springvale Rd./Rte. 674,* ☎ *703/759–3800. Jacket and required. AE, D, DC, MC, V. Closed Mon. No lunch Tues.–Sat.*

Middleburg

$$$ ✕ **Red Fox Inn.** This handsome fieldstone tavern in Middleburg's center has been in operation since 1728. Its cozy rooms are furnished in an 18th-century manner, with antique four-poster beds and period wallpaper; some have fireplaces. The restaurant ($$$–$$$$), in seven cozy dining rooms, serves Continental cuisine, from crab and artichoke casserole to filet mignon. ✉ *2 E. Washington St., 22117,* ☎ *540/687–6301 or 800/223–1728,* FAX *540/687–6187,* WEB *www.redfox.com. 23 rooms. Restaurant. AE, MC, V.*

Nightlife and the Arts

Nightlife

The **Birchmere** (✉ 3701 Mount Vernon Ave., Alexandria, ☎ 703/549–7500) hosts nationally known bluegrass, acoustic, and folk music acts. **Two Nineteen** (✉ 219 King St., Alexandria, ☎ 703/549–1141) is a restaurant with jazz nightly Tuesday through Saturday.

The Arts

Wolf Trap Farm Park (✉ 1551 Trap Rd., Vienna, ☎ 703/255–1860, WEB www.wolf-trap.org) presents top musical and dance performers in a grand outdoor pavilion during the warmer months and in the **Barns** (✉ 1635 Trap Rd., ☎ 703/938–2404), 18th-century farm buildings, the rest of the year. The facility also hosts many children's activities, including mime, puppet, and animal shows.

Outdoor Activities and Sports

Biking

The 19-mi **Mount Vernon Bicycle Trail** runs along the Potomac, from Theodore Roosevelt Island near Rosslyn through Alexandria to Mount Vernon. The Arlington Parks and Recreation Bureau (☎ 703/228–4747) will mail a free map of the county **Bikeway System.**

Golf

There are many public golf courses in northern Virginia. **Burke Lake Park** (✉ 7315 Ox Rd., Fairfax Station, ☎ 703/323–6600), which shares the property with a 218-acre lake stocked with largemouth bass, is a notable example. **Penderbrook** (✉ 3700 Golf Trail La., Fairfax, ☎ 703/385–3700) has water in play and is managed by Arnold Palmer Golf.

Water Sports

Belle Haven Marina (✉ George Washington Pkwy., south of Old Town Alexandria, ☎ 703/768–0018, WEB www.saildc.com) rents canoes, board sailers, and three different types of sailboats. It also provides lessons on the Potomac River.

Shopping

Potomac Mills Mall (✉ 2700 Potomac Mills Cir., at I–95, Dale City, ☎ 703/643–1770 or 800/826–4557, WEB www.millscorp.com) is the state's most-visited attraction; Swedish furniture giant IKEA is one of 220 outlets. The old towns of Alexandria and Fredericksburg are dense with **antiques shops,** many quite expensive. The stores are particularly strong on the Federal and Victorian periods: the towns' visitor centers have maps and lists of the stores.

Northern Virginia Essentials

AIRPORTS

Two major airports serve both northern Virginia and the Washington, D.C., area. The busy Ronald Reagan Washington National Airport, in Arlington, has scheduled daily flights by all major U.S. carriers. Dulles International Airport, 26 mi west of Washington, is a modern facility served by major U.S. airlines and many international carriers. Baltimore–Washington International Airport, 10 mi south of Baltimore, also serves the metropolitan Washington area and has its own train station for Amtrak and Maryland trains.

➤ AIRPORT INFORMATION: **Baltimore–Washington International Airport** (☎ 410/859–7100, WEB www.bwiairport.com). **Dulles International Airport** (☎ 703/572–2700, WEB www.metwashairports.com/Dulles). **Ronald Reagan Washington National Airport** (☎ 703/417–8000, WEB www.metwashairports.com/National).

BUS TRAVEL

Greyhound serves Fairfax, Arlington, Fredericksburg, and Springfield.

➤ BUS INFORMATION: **Greyhound** (✉ 3860 S. Four Mile Run Dr., Arlington, ☎ 703/998–6312; ✉ 4103 Rust St., Fairfax; ✉ 1400 Jefferson Davis Hwy., Fredericksburg; ✉ 6770 Frontier Dr., Springfield, ☎ 703/971–7598; ☎ 800/231–2222; WEB www.greyhound.com).

CAR TRAVEL

I–95 runs north–south along the eastern side of the region. I–66 runs east–west. Fredericksburg is 50 mi south of Washington, D.C., on I–95.

TRAIN TRAVEL

Amtrak stops in Alexandria and Fredericksburg; some travelers find it easiest to arrive at the capital's Union Station instead. The Virginia Rail Express (VRE) provides more frequent workday commuter service between Alexandria, Fredericksburg, Manassas, and Washington, with additional stops near hotels in Crystal City, L'Enfant Plaza, and elsewhere. Ticket prices are about a third those of Amtrak.

➤ TRAIN INFORMATION: **Amtrak** (☎ 800/872–7245). **Alexandria Station** (✉ 110 Callahan Dr.). **Fredericksburg Station** (✉ 200 Lafayette Blvd.). **Virginia Rail Express** (☎ 800/743–3873).

VISITOR INFORMATION

➤ TOURIST INFORMATION: **Alexandria Convention and Visitors Association** (✉ 221 King St., 22314, ☎ 703/838–4200 or 800/388–9119, WEB www.funside.com). **Fairfax County Convention and Visitors Bureau** (✉ 8180 Silverbrook Rd., off I–95 S at Exit 163, Lorton, ☎ 703/790–3329 or 800/732–4732; WEB www.visitfairfax.org). **Fredericksburg**

Visitor Center (✉ 706 Caroline St., 22401, ☎ 540/373–1776 or 800/678–4748, WEB www.fredericksburgvirginia.org). **Loudoun Convention and Visitors Association** (✉ 108D South St. SE, Leesburg 20175, ☎ 703/771–2170 or 800/752–6118, WEB www.visitloudoun.com).

RICHMOND AND TIDEWATER

Tidewater Virginia is the eastern region of that area whose water flows into the Atlantic and the Chesapeake Bay. But "Tidewater" has broader connotations, summoning images of the genteel Old South. Although Richmond is about 70 mi up the James River from the Chesapeake Bay, it is the heart of Tidewater gentility. Richmond lies at the fall line—the point on the James River beyond which further ship traffic upriver is not possible. Bridging the flat, swampy Tidewater and hilly Piedmont regions, it also bridges Virginia's past and present, with remnants of the Confederacy preserved in the midst of the urgent commercial bustle of a modern state capital.

An hour southeast are two former capitals: Colonial Williamsburg, a restored 18th-century town, and Jamestown, Virginia's original capital, long deserted and all the more stirring for it. With Yorktown, where the Colonies won their independence, these prerevolutionary towns form the Historic Triangle. On the nearby Northern Neck—which contains the birthplaces of George Washington and Robert E. Lee—you can combine historic sightseeing with fishing, water sports, and excursions to interesting residential islands in the Chesapeake Bay.

Exploring Richmond and Tidewater

Richmond

Most of Richmond's historic attractions lie north of the James River, which bisects the city in a sweeping curve. West of downtown is the **Fan District,** so named because the streets fan out from downtown Richmond. The neighborhood has been restored; architecturally diverse turn-of-the-20th-century town houses abound. Its grandest street, Monument Avenue, is a wide and leafy boulevard of stately homes. On Monument you'll also find equally imposing statues of Civil War notables and others.

The heart of old Richmond is the **Court End District,** which contains seven National Historic Landmarks, three museums, and 11 more buildings on the National Register of Historic Places—all within eight blocks. At either of the following museums you will receive a self-guided walking tour with the purchase of a discount block ticket ($15), good for all admission fees in this district. The 1790 **John Marshall House** (✉ 818 Marshall St., at 8th St., ☎ 804/648–7998; 🎫 $3), one of the Court End museums, was the home of the early U.S. chief justice. The ★ **Museum and White House of the Confederacy** (✉ 1201 E. Clay St., ☎ 804/649–1861, WEB www.moc.org; 🎫 $9.50) was the official residence of Confederate president Jefferson Davis. Adjacent to this 1818 house is the museum, which claims to have the world's largest collection of Confederate memorabilia.

★ The **Virginia State Capitol** (✉ Capitol Sq., ☎ 804/698–1788; 🎫 free), designed by Thomas Jefferson in 1785, contains a life-size statue of George Washington by Jean-Antoine Houdon, the only existing work for which he posed.

In the Church Hill Historic District, east of downtown, is **St. John's Episcopal Church** (✉ 2401 E. Broad St., ☎ 804/648–5015; 🎫 free). It was here on March 23, 1775, that Patrick Henry demanded of the Second Virginia Convention: "Give me liberty or give me death!"

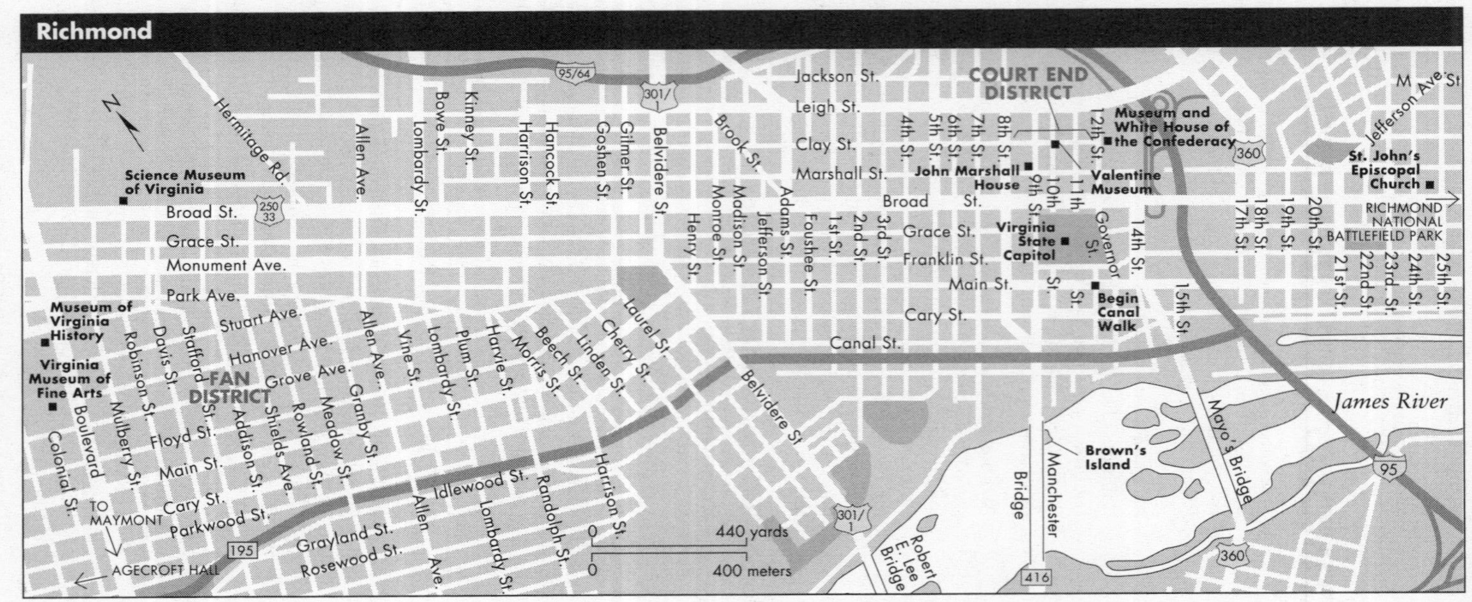
Richmond
COURT END DISTRICT
FAN DISTRICT
James River
Brown's Island
Museum and White House of the Confederacy
Valentine Museum
John Marshall House
Virginia State Capitol
Begin Canal Walk
St. John's Episcopal Church
RICHMOND NATIONAL BATTLEFIELD PARK
Science Museum of Virginia
Museum of Virginia History
Virginia Museum of Fine Arts
Mayo's Bridge
Manchester Bridge
Robert E. Lee Bridge
Jefferson Ave.
M St.
Jackson St.
Leigh St.
Clay St.
Marshall St.
Broad St.
Grace St.
Franklin St.
Main St.
Cary St.
Canal St.
Governor St.
25th St.
24th St.
23rd. St.
22nd St.
21st St.
20th St.
19th St.
18th St.
17th St.
15th St.
14th St.
12th St.
11th St.
10th St.
9th St.
8th St.
7th St.
6th St.
5th St.
4th St.
3rd St.
2nd St.
1st St.
Foushee St.
Adams St.
Jefferson St.
Madison St.
Monroe St.
Henry St.
Brook St.
Belvidere St.
Gilmer St.
Goshen St.
Hancock St.
Harrison St.
Kinney St.
Bowe St.
Lombardy St.
Allen Ave.
Hermitage Rd.
Monument Ave.
Park Ave.
Laurel St.
Cherry St.
Linden St.
Beech St.
Morris St.
Harvie St.
Plum St.
Vine St.
Stuart Ave.
Hanover Ave.
Grove Ave.
Granby St.
Meadow St.
Rowland St.
Shields Ave.
Addison St.
Stafford St.
Davis St.
Robinson St.
Floyd St.
Mulberry St.
Boulevard
Colonial St.
Parkwood St.
Idlewood St.
Randolph St.
Grayland St.
Rosewood St.
TO MAYMONT
AGECROFT HALL
440 yards
400 meters
0
N
95
360
301/1
95/64
250/33
195
416

The visitor center for **Richmond National Battlefield Park** (✉ 3215 E. Broad St., ☎ 804/226–1981, WEB www.nps.gov/rich; 🎫 free) provides a movie and a slide show about the three campaigns fought here, as well as maps for a self-guided tour.

West of downtown is the **Science Museum of Virginia,** once the Broad Street train station. People of all ages have fun with the hands-on exhibits, which cover everything from life sciences and biological timing to aerospace and undersea exploration. The Ethyl IMAXDOME and Planetarium has planetarium shows and shows films on a giant screen. *✉ 2500 W. Broad St., ☎ 804/367–1080 or 800/659–1727, WEB www.smv.org. 🎫 Exhibits $6, exhibits and film $10–$12.*

★ In the heart of the artsy Fan District is the **Virginia Museum of Fine Arts,** where the diverse collections include art nouveau, art deco, Indian, Roman, Asian, contemporary, impressionist, British sporting art, and five Fabergé eggs. *✉ 2800 Grove Ave., at the Boulevard, ☎ 804/367–0844, WEB www.vmfa.state.va.us. 🎫 Free; $5 suggested donation. Closed Mon.*

Just southwest of the Fan District stands **Agecroft Hall** (✉ 4305 Sulgrave Rd., ☎ 804/353–4241; 🎫 $5), a 15th-century house rescued from destruction in England and reassembled here in 1926. Formal gardens surround the manor, which is extensively furnished with Tudor and early Stuart art and furniture.

Petersburg

Twenty miles south of Richmond on I–95 lies **Petersburg,** the so-called last ditch of the Confederacy: its siege in 1865 led to the fall of Richmond and the surrender at Appomattox. ★ At **Petersburg National Battlefield** (✉ Washington St., off Rte. 36, ☎ 804/732–3531; 🎫 $4 for cars, $2 for bicycles and pedestrians) you can tread the ground where 70,000 soldiers died. The 1,500-acre park, laced with miles of earthworks, includes two forts. The **Pamplin Historical Park** (✉ 6125 Boydton Plank Rd., off U.S. 1, Petersburg, ☎ 804/861–2408; 🎫 $10), where Union troops successfully penetrated General Robert E. Lee's defense line, includes an interpretive center and the **Museum of the Civil War Soldier,** as well as a 2-mi-long battle trail, reconstructed soldier huts, and an 1812 plantation home.

In Old Town Petersburg the Civil War is examined from a local perspective at the **Siege Museum** (✉ 15 W. Bank St., ☎ 804/733–2404; 🎫 $3). The prerevolutionary **Blanford Church** (✉ 319 S. Crater Rd., ☎ 804/733–2396; 🎫 $3) is today a Confederate shrine. Behind the church through an archway is the memorial area where 30,000 Southern dead are buried. The church's 15 stained-glass Tiffany windows are memorials donated by Confederate states.

Northern Neck

Route 3 east of Fredericksburg takes you into the **Northern Neck,** a narrow peninsula bounded by the Potomac and Rappahannock rivers. At the top of the Neck is Westmoreland County.

George Washington's Birthplace National Monument (✉ 1732 Popes Creek Rd., Oak Grove, ☎ 804/224–1732, WEB www.nps.gov/gewa; 🎫 $3) preserves the memory of the first president with a working farm and a reproduction of the early 18th-century plantation house (the original burned down on Christmas Day 1779). Some of Washington's family, including his father and grandfather, are buried on the property.

Robert E. Lee was born at **Stratford Hall** (✉ Rte. 214, off Rte. 3, Stratford, ☎ 804/493–8038, WEB www.stratfordhall.org; 🎟 $8), a massive Georgian built in the 1730s by Lee's grandfather, Colonel Thomas Lee. Farmers still cultivate 1,600 of the original acres, and their yield, including corn and wheat, is milled and available for sale at the Hall's Gift Shop. Lunch is served in a log cabin year-round except December 23–January 4.

At the far southeast end of the Northern Neck is Irvington's **Christ Church** (✉ junction of Rtes. 646 and 709, ☎ 804/438–6855, WEB www.christchurch1735.org; 🎟 free), a redbrick sanctuary of cruciform design, was built in 1735 in the Georgian style.

WATER SPORTS

The Northern Neck gives sailors, water-skiers, and windsurfers access to two rivers and the Chesapeake Bay. For information contact the **Northern Neck Tourism Council** (☎ 804/333–1919 or 800/393–6180, WEB www.northernneck.org).

The James River Plantations

Southeast of Richmond on Route 5, along the north bank of the James River, lie historic plantations. **Shirley** (✉ 501 Shirley Plantation Rd., ☎ 804/232–1613, WEB www.shirleyplantation.com; 🎟 $10), the oldest plantation in Virginia, has belonged to the same family, the Carters, for 10 generations. The plantation was founded in 1613, six years after the English landed at Jamestown. The 1723 Georgian manor is filled with family silver, ancestral portraits, and rare books. The grounds and house are open daily 9–5.

Berkeley plantation (✉ Rte. 5, ☎ 804/829–6018, WEB www.berkeleyplantation.com; 🎟 $10.50) is the birthplace of Benjamin Harrison, a signer of the Declaration of Independence. His son was the short-termed ninth president, William Henry Harrison. The 1726 Georgian brick house has been restored and furnished with period antiques, and the boxwood gardens are well tended. In addition to a restaurant, there are outdoor tables for picnickers. Berkeley is open daily 8–5.

At 300 ft, **Sherwood Forest** (✉ Rte. 5, ☎ 804/829–5377, WEB www.sherwoodforest.org; 🎟 house $10.50, grounds $4) may be the longest frame house in the country. The circa-1730 house was the retirement home of John Tyler, the 10th U.S. president, and remains in his family. The house, furnished with heirloom antiques, and the five outbuildings are open daily 9–5.

The Historic Triangle

★ **Colonial Williamsburg** (✉ I-64, Exits 238 and 242, ☎ 757/220–7645 or 800/447–8679, WEB www.history.org; all-day pass 🎟 $33 allows admission to multiple sights) is a marvel: a tidy, sanitized, but otherwise convincing re-creation of the city that was the capital of Virginia from 1699 until 1780. The restoration project, financed by John D. Rockefeller Jr., began in 1926; the work of archaeologists and historians of the Colonial Williamsburg Foundation continues to this day.

On Colonial Williamsburg's 173 acres, 88 original 18th- and early 19th-century structures, such as the **Courthouse**, have been painstakingly restored; another 50, including the **Capitol** and the **Governor's Palace**, were reconstructed on their original sites.

All year hundreds of costumed interpreters, wearing bonnets or three-cornered hats, rove and ride through the cobblestone streets. Dozens of craftspeople (also in character), such as the shoemaker and gunsmith, demonstrate and explain their trades inside their workshops; their wares are for sale nearby. The restored area must be toured on foot, as all vehicles are banned between 8 AM and 6 PM. Free shuttle buses (available to ticket holders only) run continually to and from the visitor center and around the edge of the restored area. Vehicles for visitors with disabilities are permitted by prior arrangement.

Add another dimension to the colonial experience by visiting the **DeWitt Wallace Decorative Arts Museum** (✉ Francis St., ☎ 757/220–7724, WEB www.history.org; 🎫 $8 or free with Williamsburg day pass). Inside is an 8,000-piece collection of English and American decorative arts from 1600 to 1830. Prized among this varied collection is the full-length portrait of George Washington by Charles Willson Peale. Enter through the Public Hospital.

East of Williamsburg is **Busch Gardens Williamsburg.** Rides include an especially fast and steep roller coaster as well as other traditional rides. Nine re-creations of European and French Canadian hamlets present the cuisine and entertainment of different countries. *✉ U.S. 60, ☎ 757/253–3350, WEB www.buschgardens.com. 🎫 $42.99. Closed Dec.–Mar.*

Jamestown Island (✉ Colonial Pkwy., ☎ 757/229–1733, WEB www.nps.gov/jame; 🎫 $6), separated from the mainland by a narrow isthmus, was the site of the first permanent English settlement in North America (1607) and the capital of Virginia until 1699. The island is now uninhabited. Foundation walls show the layout of the settlement, and audio stations narrate the local history. A 5-mi nature drive ringing the island is posted with historical markers.

Near Jamestown Island, and not to be confused with it, is **Jamestown Settlement** (✉ Rte. 31 off Colonial Pkwy., ☎ 757/229–1607, WEB www.jamestown2007.org; 🎫 $10.75; $16 combination ticket with Yorktown Victory Center), a living-history museum with a reconstructed fort and a Powhatan Indian village, both staffed by interpreters in costume. At the pier are full-scale replicas of the *Godspeed,* the *Discovery,* and the *Susan Constant,* the ships that carried the settlers to the New World.

In 1781, American and French forces surrounded British troops and forced an end to the American War of Independence at **Yorktown Battlefield** (✉ Colonial Pkwy., ☎ 757/898–3400, WEB www.nps.gov/yonb; 🎫 $5). Today the museum here displays George Washington's original field tent; dioramas, illuminated maps, and a short movie tell the story. You can rent the taped audio tour and explore the battlefield by car or join a ranger-led walking tour.

The **Yorktown Victory Center** (✉ Rte. 238 off Colonial Pkwy., ☎ 757/253–4838 or 888/593–4682, WEB www.historyisfun.org; 🎫 $8.25, $16 combination ticket with Jamestown Settlement), next door to the Yorktown Battlefield, consists of a Continental Army encampment, with tents, a covered wagon, and interpreters—costumed as soldiers or female auxiliaries—who speak in the regional dialects of the time. Also on -site are a small working tobacco farm and a museum focusing on the experience of ordinary people during the Revolutionary War.

Unlike Jamestown, **Yorktown** remains a living community, albeit a tiny one. Its Main Street is lined with preserved 18th-century buildings on a bluff overlooking the York River. The elegant **Nelson House** was the residence of a Virginia governor and signer of the Declaration of Independence. Along the Battlefield Tour Road is Moore House, where the British Army's terms of surrender were negotiated. The houses are open for tours daily in summer and weekends in spring and fall. *Nelson and Moore houses: ☎ 757/898–3400. 🎫 $5 for both.*

Dining and Lodging

The established upmarket dining rooms of Richmond compare favorably with those in cities renowned for their restaurants. The luxurious trappings and innovative menus here are pricey but not nearly so much as in larger cities. Additionally, favorite local haunts offer delicious meals at moderate prices—especially in the Fan District west of the downtown area and in Shockoe, an in-vogue renovated warehouse area east of the Capitol and near the James River. Richmond's hotel rates are slightly below those of big eastern cities. Accommodations vary from pre–Civil War historic properties to ultramodern glass towers.

In Williamsburg, dining rooms within walking distance of the restored area are often crowded, and reservations are advised—the historic taverns often fill up some months in advance. The Colonial capital of Virginia has a greater variety of lodging options for the money, but there will be fewer choices at the height of the summer tourist season.

Richmond

$$–$$$$ ✕ **Amici Ristorante.** Homemade pasta, breads, and desserts as well as seafood and game specialties appear regularly on a menu emphasizing authentic northern Italian dishes. Flowered tapestries and oil paintings of Italy keep things cozy, as does the alfresco dining that's available at this Carytown eatery. ✉ *3343 W. Cary St.,* ☎ *804/353–4700. AE, MC, V. Closed Mon. No lunch Sun. or Tues.*

$$–$$$ ★ ✕ **The Tobacco Company.** Housed in a refurbished tobacco warehouse built in the 1860s, this multi-storied, popular restaurant centers on an atrium where live music plays every night but Sunday. On the versatile menu are veal Marsala, chicken Chesapeake (with crabmeat), and prime rib (seconds on the house). The Company serves brunch on Sunday. ✉ *1201 E. Cary St.,* ☎ *804/782–9431. AE, D, MC, V.*

$–$$ ✕ **Siné Irish Pub and Restaurant.** This Irish pub and restaurant in Richmond's trendy Shockoe Slip serves lunch and dinner daily indoors and on the back deck and patio. An old-fashioned bar surrounds booths and pub tables, where you can enjoy traditional Irish dishes and other bar food, such as fish-and-chips. ✉ *1327 E. Cary St.,* ☎ *804/649–7767. AE, DC, MC, V.*

$$$–$$$$ ★ 🏨 **Jefferson Hotel.** A 1895 National Historic Landmark, this hotel retains an opulence matched by no other in Richmond. The guest rooms have poster headboards and are decorated in English country style. Complimentary transportation to downtown and a daily newspaper are included in rates. ✉ *Franklin and Adams Sts., 23220,* ☎ *804/788–8000 or 800/424–8014,* FAX *804/225–0334,* WEB *www.jefferson-hotel.com. 275 rooms. 2 restaurants, pool, health club. AE, D, DC, MC, V.*

$–$$$ ★ 🏨 **Commonwealth Park Suites Hotel.** The original hostelry on this site burned down during the Civil War battle for Richmond and was rebuilt around 1896 as a 10-story hotel. The refurbished, suites-only building, across the street from the capitol and its magnolia-filled park, resembles a small European hotel. Still, its reproduction 18th-century mahogany furniture, museum prints, and brass chandeliers confirm that you are in a southern state. ✉ *901 Bank St., 23219,* ☎ *804/343–7300 or 888/343–7301,* FAX *804/343–1025,* WEB *www.commonwealthparksuites.com. 51 suites. Restaurant. AE, D, DC, MC, V. CP.*

$$ ★ 🏨 **Linden Row Inn.** This handsome inn, on the National Register of Historic Places, is composed of a row of restored 1840s Greek Revival town houses. Guest rooms have high ceilings, tall windows, and 19th-century furnishings throughout. ✉ *100 E. Franklin St., 23219,* ☎ *804/783–7000 or 800/348–7424,* FAX *804/648–7504,* WEB *www.lindenrowinn.com. 71 rooms. Restaurant. AE, D, DC, MC, V. CP.*

Williamsburg

$$–$$$ ★ ✕ **The Trellis.** Hardwood floors, ceramic tiles, and green plants evoke Napa Valley, setting the mood for world-class American cuisine that changes with the seasons. Save room for "Death by Chocolate": layers of chocolate topped with cream sauce. ✉ *Merchants Sq., Duke of Gloucester St.,* ☏ *757/229–8610. AE, MC, V.*

$$$$ ★ ✕ **Williamsburg Inn.** This is the grandest local hotel, built in 1937 and decorated in English Regency style. At the hotel's esteemed Regency Room restaurant, crystal chandeliers, Asian silk-screen prints, and full silver service set the tone. Chateaubriand is carved tableside; other specialties are lobster bisque and rich ice cream desserts. Reservations for the restaurant ($$–$$$) are essential; jacket and tie are required for dinner and Sunday brunch. Croquet, hiking, golf, tennis, and lawn bowling are all available on the premises, as are children's programs. ✉ *136 E. Francis St. (Box 1776, 23185),* ☏ *757/229–1000,* FAX *757/220–7096,* WEB *www.history.org/Visit/accommodations. 102 rooms. Restaurant, pool, gym. AE, D, DC, MC, V.*

$$$–$$$$ **Liberty Rose B&B Inn.** At this 1920s hilltop estate 1 mi from the historic area, rooms are individually appointed with European antiques and rich silk and damask; each has windows on three sides. ✉ *1022 Jamestown Rd., 23185,* ☏ *757/253–1260 or 800/545–1825,* WEB *www.libertyrose.com. 4 rooms. AE, MC, V. BP.*

$$ **Williamsburg Sampler.** Walking into this B&B is like stepping back in time. Antiques from the 18th and 19th centuries adorn the Colonial-style house, which exudes an unmistakable warmth and has a wonderful overlook of Colonial Williamsburg. The rooms are of good size. ✉ *922 Jamestown Rd., 23185,* ☏ *757/253–0398 or 800/722–1169,* WEB *www.williamsburgsampler.com. 6 rooms. AE, D, DC, MC, V. BP.*

Motels

Woodlands Hotel and Suites (✉ 102 Visitor Center Dr., Williamsburg 23185, ☏ 757/229–1000 or 800/447–8679, FAX 757/565–8942, WEB www.colonialwilliamsburg.com), 300 rooms; restaurant, pool; *$$.*

Duke of York Motel (✉ 508 Water St., Yorktown 23690, ☏ 757/898–3232, FAX 757/898–5922, WEB www.dukeofyorkmotel.com), 57 rooms; restaurant, pool; *$.*

Nightlife and the Arts

Nightlife

Bogart's (✉ 203 N. Lombardy St., Richmond, ☏ 804/353–9280) has late-night entertainment, but never on Sunday. **Chowning's Tavern** (✉ Duke of Gloucester St., Williamsburg, ☏ 757/229–1000 or 800/447–8679, WEB www.colonialwilliamsburg.com/visit/dining) has lively "gambols," or colonial-style games, with music and other entertainment, daily 9 PM–1 AM; during the summer, a family version is offered 7 PM–9 PM.

The Arts

Barksdale Theatre (✉ 1601 Willow Lawn Dr., Richmond, ☏ 804/282–2620), founded in 1953, is the area's oldest theater company. Comedies, dramas, and musicals are presented year-round. The **Richmond Ballet** (✉ 407 E. Canal St., ☏ 804/359–0906) is the city's classical ballet company. The **Richmond Symphony** (✉ 300 W. Franklin St., ☏ 804/788–1212) often features internationally known soloists. The **Company of Colonial Players** (✉ Box 1776, Williamsburg 23187-1776, ☏ 757/229–1000) presents rollicking 18th-century plays.

Outdoor Activities and Sports

Open to the public in Richmond—for free or at a nominal charge—are more than 150 tennis courts, 11 swimming pools, a golf driving range, and about 7 mi of fitness trails. The **Department of Parks, Recreation, and Community Facilities** (☎ 804/646–5733) has listings.

Biking

In Colonial Williamsburg ticket holders can rent bicycles at the **Williamsburg Lodge** (✉ South England St., ☎ 757/229–1000 or 800/447–8679, WEB www.colonialwilliamsburg.com). Also try **Bikesmith** (✉ 515 York St., ☎ 757/229–9858).

Golf

Colonial Williamsburg (☎ 757/220–7696 or 800/648–6653, WEB www.colonialwilliamsburg.com) operates three courses. **Crossings Golf Club** (✉ I–95 and I–295, Glen Allen, ☎ 804/266–2254), north of Richmond, has an 18-hole course open to the public. **Kingsmill Resort** (☎ 757/253–3906 or 800/832–5665, WEB www.kingsmill.com), east of Williamsburg near Busch Gardens, has one 9-hole and three 18-hole courses.

Water Sports

From March through November **Richmond Raft** (☎ 804/222–7238 or 800/540–7238) organizes guided white-water rafting on the James River (Class III and IV rapids) and float trips. It costs $60 per person Sunday–Friday and $65 on Saturday. Price includes a light meal on the river. Minimum age requirement for a trip is 12. **Adventure Challenge** (☎ 804/276–7600, WEB www.adventurechallenge.com) offers trips, lessons, and tours in white-water kayaking, coastal kayaking, river tubing, and white-water rafting.

Tennis

There are 10 tennis courts around the **Colonial Williamsburg** historic area (☎ 757/220–7794 or 800/447–8679). **Kingsmill** (☎ 757/253–3945) has 15 courts open to the public. For additional public courts, contact the **Williamsburg Convention and Visitors Bureau** (☎ 757/253–0192 or 800/368–6511).

Shopping

Fresh produce is for sale outdoors at Richmond's **Farmers' Market** (✉ 17th and Main Sts.), held beside the Main Street Station (at which trains no longer stop). Myriad art galleries, boutiques, and antiques shops are at the Farmers' Market and in **Shockoe Slip,** on East Cary Street between 12th and 15th streets. The **Williamsburg Pottery Factory** (✉ U.S. 60 W, Lightfoot, ☎ 757/564–3326, WEB www.williamsburgpottery.com) is an enormous outlet store that sells clothing, furniture, tools, china, pottery, food, and wine. All along the same stretch of U.S. 60 are dozens of other outlet malls.

Richmond and Tidewater Essentials

AIRPORTS

Richmond International Airport is served by several major airlines. Newport News–Williamsburg International Airport, in Newport News, and Norfolk International Airport also serve the region.

➤ AIRPORT INFORMATION: Newport News–Williamsburg International Airport (☎ 757/877–0924, WEB www.nnwairport.com). Norfolk International Airport (☎ 757/857–3351, WEB www.norfolkairport.com). Richmond International Airport (☎ 804/226–3000, WEB www.flyrichmond.com).

BUS TRAVEL

Greyhound serves Richmond, Petersburg, and Williamsburg. There is no bus service to the Northern Neck.

➤ BUS INFORMATION: **Greyhound** (✉ 108 E. Washington St., Petersburg; ✉ 2910 N. Boulevard, Richmond; ✉ 468 N. Boundary St., Williamsburg; ☎ 800/231–2222; WEB www.greyhound.com).

CAR TRAVEL

Richmond is at the intersection of I–95 and I–64; U.S. 1 runs north–south by the city. Petersburg is 20 mi south of Richmond on I–95. Route 3 runs the length of the Northern Neck. Williamsburg is 51 mi east of Richmond via I–64; the Colonial Parkway joins it with Jamestown and Yorktown.

TRAIN TRAVEL

Amtrak serves Richmond, Petersburg, and Williamsburg.

➤ TRAIN INFORMATION: **Amtrak** (☎ 800/872–7245, WEB www.amtrak.com). **Petersburg** (✉ 3516 South St.). **Richmond** (✉ 7519 Staples Mill Rd.). **Williamsburg** (✉ 468 N. Boundary St.).

VISITOR INFORMATION

➤ TOURIST INFORMATION: **Colonial Williamsburg** (✉ Box 1776, 23187-1776, ☎ 757/220–7645 or 800/447–8679, WEB www.colonialwilliamsburg.com). **Hanover Visitor Center** (✉ 112 N. Railroad Ave., off I–95, Exit 92B, Ashland 23005, ☎ 804/752–6766 or 800/897–1479, WEB www.town.ashland.va.us). North of Richmond, the **Jamestown–Yorktown Foundation** (✉ Dept. BC, Box 1607, Williamsburg 23187, ☎ 757/253–4838 or 888/593–4682, WEB www.nps.gov/colo). **Metro Richmond Visitors Center** (✉ 405 N. 3rd St., 23210, ☎ 804/783–7450 or 888/742–4663, FAX 804/780–2577, WEB www.richmondva.org). **Northern Neck Tourism Council** (✉ Box 312, Reedville 22539, ☎ 800/453–6167, WEB www.northernneck.org). **Petersburg Visitors Center** (✉ 425 Cockade Alley, 23803, ☎ 804/733–2400 or 800/368–3595, WEB www.petersburg-va.org). **Virginia Tourism Corporation Visitor Center** (✉ Bell Tower at Capitol Sq., 9th and Franklin Sts., 23219, ☎ 804/648–3146, WEB www.virginia.org). **Williamsburg Convention and Visitors Bureau** (✉ 421 N. Boundary St., 23185, ☎ 757/253–0192 or 800/368–6511, FAX 757/229–2047, WEB www.visitwilliamsburg.com).

ELSEWHERE IN VIRGINIA

Hampton Roads, Virginia Beach, and the Eastern Shore

What to See and Do

The cities of Newport News and Hampton on the north and Norfolk on the south flank the enormous port of **Hampton Roads,** where the ★ James empties into the Chesapeake Bay. In Newport News the **Mariner's Museum** (✉ I–64 Exit 258A, ☎ 757/595–0368 or 800/581–7245, WEB www.mariner.org; 🎫 $6) displays tiny hand-carved models of ancient vessels and full-size specimens of more recent ones, including a gondola and a Chinese sampan.

The history of flight and space exploration can be viewed in Hampton at the futuristic **Virginia Air and Space Center** (✉ 600 Settlers Landing Rd., ☎ 757/727–0800, WEB www.vasc.org; 🎫 $9.50); exhibits include a 3-billion-year-old lunar rock and an *Apollo* lunar modular simulator.

At Hampton's **Fort Monroe** (✉ off I–64, Exit 268, ☎ 757/788–3391; 🎫 free), the **Casemate Museum** (☎ 757/788–3391; 🎫 free) tells the

Civil War history of this moat-enclosed Union stronghold, which was the object of the battle between the *Monitor* and the *Merrimac*. After the Confederacy's defeat, President Jefferson Davis was imprisoned here.

Norfolk is best known for its **U.S. Naval Base** (✉ Hampton Blvd., ☎ 757/444–7955 or 757/444–1577, WEB www.navstanorva.navy.mil; 🎟 $5), the world's largest naval installation. Kept on site are about 115 ships of the Atlantic and Mediterranean fleets, including the nuclear-powered USS *Theodore Roosevelt*—the world's second-largest warship. Norfolk shows off its naval heritage at **Nauticus** (✉ Waterside Dr., ☎ 757/664–1000, WEB www.nauticus.org; 🎟 $9.50), where there are more than 150 exhibits on the commercial, military, and biological aspects of the ocean.

At the **Norfolk Botanical Gardens** (✉ I–64, airport Exit 279, ☎ 757/441–5831, WEB www.virginiagarden.org; 🎟 $6), 155 acres are planted with azaleas, camellias, and roses—plus a fragrance garden for the blind. ★ The collections at the **Chrysler Museum of Art** (✉ 245 W. Olney Rd., ☎ 757/664–6200, WEB www.chrysler.org; 🎟 $7), one of America's major art museums, range from Gainsborough to Roy Lichtenstein. The **General Douglas MacArthur Memorial** (✉ Bank St. and City Hall Ave., ☎ 757/441–2965, WEB sites.communitylink.org/mac; 🎟 donation suggested), in the restored former city hall, is the burial place of the controversial war hero.

The heart of **Virginia Beach,** 6 mi of crowded public beach and a raucous 40-block boardwalk, has been a popular summer gathering place for many years. One advantage of the commercialism: easy access to sailing, surfing, and scuba rentals. Be mindful, however, that the beach gets extremely crowded mid-summer. Almost 2 mi inland, at the southern end of Virginia Beach, is one of the state's most-visited museums, the **Virginia Marine Science Museum** (✉ 717 General Booth Blvd., ☎ 757/425–3474, WEB www.vmsm.com; 🎟 $9.95), where you can bird-watch in a salt marsh and use computers to predict the weather. On the Eastern Shore U.S. 13 takes you past historic 17th- to 19th-century towns such as **Eastville,** which has a courthouse from 1730. **Onancock** has a working general store established in 1842 and a wharf where you just might be able to witness a sunset over the bay.

Assateague Island is a 37-mi-long wildlife refuge and recreational area that extends north into Maryland. Despite invasive tourism and ★ overdevelopment, **Chincoteague Island** has had at least one tradition survive from a simpler time: every July wild ponies from Assateague are driven across the channel and placed at auction here; those unsold swim back home.

On nearby Wallops Island is NASA's **Wallops Flight Facility** (✉ Rte. 175, ☎ 757/824–2298, WEB www.wff.nasa.gov/vc; 🎟 free), where a museum tells the story of the space program on the site of early rocket launchings.

Dining and Lodging

$$–$$$$ ★ ✕ **La Galleria.** Large urns imported from Italy, Corinthian columns, and a softly playing pianist make this a warm and sophisticated space. Known for its excellent pastas, the restaurant has other good choices that include a salmon sautéed in herbs, garlic, and white wine. ✉ *120 College Pl., Norfolk,* ☎ *757/623–3939. AE, MC, V.*

$–$$ ★ ✕ **The Wild Monkey Gourmet Diner.** The eclectic menu, which includes zesty pork and ginger dumplings, jambalaya, and Angus beef meat loaf, is set off by a fantastic wine list. A small restaurant in the heart of Norfolk's Ghent neighborhood, it might be a bit off the beaten path, but it's worth it. ✉ *1603 Colley Ave., Norfolk,* ☎ *757/627–6462. AE, D, DC, MC, V.*

$$$–$$$$ ★ **The Cavalier.** This Jazz Age hotel (1927) has a marvelous view of the ocean, exceptional service, and a well-manicured 18-hole golf course. Genteelly furnished, it's one of the state's premier hotels. ✉ *42nd and Atlantic Aves., Virginia Beach,* ☎ *757/425–8555 or 800/446–8199,* WEB *www.cavalierhotel.com. 394 rooms. Restaurant, golf, health club. AE, D, DC, MC, V.*

$$$–$$$$ **Ramada Plaza Resort Oceanfront.** With its 17-story tower, the Ramada is the city's tallest hotel. Rooms either face or have a partial view of the ocean, or overlook the swimming pool. Rooms come with a microwave, refrigerator, coffee maker, iron, and ironing board. ✉ *57th St. and Oceanfront, Virginia Beach 23451,* ☎ *757/428–7025 or 800/365–3032,* FAX *757/428–2921,* WEB *www.ramada.com. 245 rooms. 2 restaurants, pool, gym. AE, D, DC, MC, V.*

Hampton Roads, Virginia Beach, and the Eastern Shore Essentials

AIRPORTS

Norfolk International and Newport News–Williamsburg International airports are served by most major airlines.

➤ AIRPORT INFORMATION: **Newport News–Williamsburg International Airport** (☎ 757/877–0924, WEB www.nnwairport.com). **Norfolk International Airport** (☎ 757/857–3351, WEB www.norfolkairport.com).

BUS TRAVEL

Greyhound serves Hampton, Norfolk, Virginia Beach, and various locations along U.S. 13 on the Eastern Shore.

➤ BUS INFORMATION: **Greyhound** (✉ 2 W. Pembrook Ave., Hampton, ☎ 757/722–9861; ✉ 701 Monticello Ave., Norfolk, ☎ 757/625–7500; ✉ 1017 Laskin Rd., Virginia Beach, ☎ 757/422–2998 or ☎ 800/231–2222).

CAR TRAVEL

I–64 connects Richmond with Hampton Roads. U.S. 58 and Route 44 connect I–64 with Virginia Beach. U.S. 13 runs between Virginia Beach and the Eastern Shore via the Chesapeake Bay Bridge-Tunnel.

VISITOR INFORMATION

➤ TOURIST INFORMATION: **Chincoteague Chamber of Commerce** (✉ 6733 Maddox Blvd., 23336, ☎ 757/336–6161, WEB www.chincoteaguechamber.com). **Eastern Shore of Virginia Chamber of Commerce** (✉ Box 460, Melfa 23410, ☎ 757/787–2460, WEB esvachamber.org). **Norfolk Convention and Visitors Bureau** (✉ 232 E. Main St., 23510, ☎ 757/664–6620 or 800/368–3097, WEB www.norfolkcvb.com). **Virginia Beach Visitor Information Center** (✉ 2100 Parks Ave., 23451, ☎ 757/437–4888 or 800/446–8038, WEB www.va-beach.com/tourist.htm).

WASHINGTON

By Tom Gauntt

Updated by Eric Lucas

Capital	Olympia
Population	5,894,121
Motto	By-and-by
State Bird	American goldfinch
State Flower	Rhododendron
Postal Abbreviation	WA

Statewide Visitor Information

Washington Tourism Development Division (✉ Box 42500, Olympia 98504-2500, ☎ 360/586–2088 or 800/544–1800, WEB www.experiencewashington.com).

Scenic Drives

About 80 mi north of Seattle, starting from south of Bellingham on I–5, **Route 11** winds 25 mi along Chuckanut Bay between steep, heavily wooded cliffs and sweeping views of Puget Sound and the San Juan Islands. Near the Oregon border, **Route 14** winds east from Vancouver into the Columbia River National Scenic Area. The road clings to the steep slopes of the gorge and traverses several tunnels and picturesque towns such as Carson, known for its hot springs, white salmon, and incredible windsurfing. **U.S. 195** winds 105 mi south from Spokane to Lewiston, Idaho, traversing the heart of eastern Washington's wheat-covered Palouse region and plunging the final 3 mi down the Lewiston Grade into Snake River Canyon.

National and State Parks

National Parks

Mt. Rainier National Park (✉ Tahoma Woods, Star Rte., Ashford 98304, ☎ 360/569–2211, WEB www.nps.gov/mora), about 85 mi southeast of Seattle, was named for 14,411-ft Mt. Rainier—the fifth-highest mountain in the lower 48 states. The Jackson Memorial Visitor Center at Paradise has exhibits, films, and a 360-degree view of the summit and surrounding peaks. Call for off-season hours. For a vision of the apocalypse, head for the **Mount St. Helens National Volcanic Monument** (✉ 42218 N.E. Yale Bridge Rd., Amboy 98601). The visitor center (☎ 360/247–3900) is on Route 504, 5 mi east of the Castle Rock exit off I–5, and the monument is 45 mi east of Castle Rock. **Olympic National Park** (✉ 600 E. Park Ave., Port Angeles 98362, ☎ 360/452–4501, WEB www.nps.gov/olym) is one of the most outstanding places of natural beauty in the United States, with its jagged wilderness coastline; a lush, temperate rain forest; 60-odd active glaciers; and the alpine contours of Hurricane Ridge. **North Cascades National Park** (✉ 2105 Rte. 20, Sedro-Woolley 98284, ☎ 360/856–5700, WEB www.nps.gov/noca), a beautiful and remote park about 120 mi northeast of Seattle, holds some of the state's most rugged mountains, craggy peaks, and jewel-like lakes. Heavy snows close Route 20 through the park most winters from October through April.

State Parks

Two beautiful state parks are perched on either end of the narrow Long Beach Peninsula. **Leadbetter Point State Park** (✉ Stackpole Rd., 3 mi north of Oysterville, 98624, ☎ 360/642–3078), on the northern tip, is a wildlife refuge that's good for bird-watching. The dunes at the very tip are closed from April to August to protect the nesting snowy plover.

Black brant, sandpipers, turnstones, yellowlegs, sanderlings, knots, and plovers are among the 100 species known to inhabit the point. **Fort Canby State Park** (✉ Robert Gray Dr., 3 mi southwest of Ilwaco off U.S 101, ☎ 360/642–3078, WEB www.parks.wa.gov) attracts beachcombers, hikers, fishermen, and military history enthusiasts.

SEATTLE

Although Seattle's extravagant growth of the late 1990s has slowed, evidence of the city's building boom, high profile, and growth pains remains. Many new and renovated buildings exemplify the prosperity that internationally prominent businesses, such as Boeing, Microsoft, and Starbucks, brought to the region. Alternately, the constant traffic on the main highways is the first indication that city planning was not sufficient to meet the needs of the expanding Pacific Rim metropolis. Traffic problems notwithstanding, Seattle's countless innovative restaurants, full-service hotels, and entertainment venues delight both residents and visitors. Add that to the natural beauty of Puget Sound, Lake Washington, and the surrounding mountains, and you'll probably be too enthralled to notice the gray skies.

Exploring Seattle

Downtown

Downtown Seattle is bounded by Safeco Field to the south, the Seattle Center to the north, I–5 to the east, and the waterfront to the west. You can reach most points of interest by foot, bus, or monorail. Seattle is a city of hills, so wear your walking shoes.

★ The five-story **Seattle Art Museum** (✉ 100 University St., ☎ 206/654–3100, WEB www.seattleartmuseum.org; 🎫 $7), by postmodern theorist Robert Venturi, is a work of art in itself, with a limestone exterior and vertical fluting accented by terra-cotta, cut granite, and marble. Inside are extensive collections of Asian, Native American, African, Oceanic, and pre-Columbian art; a café; and a gift shop. The famous *Hammering Man* statue out front, honoring Seattle's industrial past.

Pike Place Market (✉ 1st Ave. at Pike St., ☎ 206/682–7453, WEB www.pikeplacemarket.org) got its start in 1907, when the city issued permits allowing farmers to sell produce from their wagons parked at Pike Place; a public vote saved it from "urban renewal" demolition in 1971. Sold here are fresh seafood (which can be packed in dry ice for your flight home), produce, cheese, Northwest wines, bulk spices, teas, coffees, and arts and crafts. The Market's **Starbucks** (✉ 1912 Pike Pl., ☎ 206/448–8762), opened in 1971, is the original outlet of this now global chain.

At the base of the Pike Street Hillclimb at Pier 59 is the **Seattle Aquarium** (✉ 1483 Alaskan Way, ☎ 206/386–4320, WEB www.seattleaquarium.org; 🎫 $9), showcasing Northwest marine life. Sea otters and seals swim and dive in their pools, and the "State of the Sound" exhibit shows aquatic life and the ecology of Puget Sound.

An 1889 fire destroyed many of the wood-frame buildings in the area ★ now known as **Pioneer Square** (WEB www.pioneersquare.org), bounded by Columbia Street, Alaskan Way, King Street, and 2nd Avenue, but the residents rebuilt them with fire-resistant brick and mortar. The area was in a state of decline from the Depression until the 1970s, when buildings were restored and stores and cafés moved in. Some older saloons remain, giving the district a gritty, historical flavor. College kids party hearty here at night; during the day you can browse through the

Seattle
Green Lake
N.W. 65th St.
N.E. 65th St.
BALLARD LOCKS
Phinney Ave. N
Woodland Park Zoo
Roosevelt Way NE
15th Ave. NE
20th Ave. NE
25th Ave. NE
35th Ave. NE
N.E. 55th St.
N.W. Market St.
3rd Ave. N
Meridian Ave. N
Eastern Ave. N
NE 50th St.
UNIVERSITY DISTRICT
Leary Way N.W.
Fremont Ave. N
Stone Way N
NE 45th St.
Thomas Burke Memorial Washington State Museum
WALLINGFORD
University of Washington
Lake Washington Ship Canal
FREMONT
Union Bay
W. Commodore Way
Portage Bay
Museum of History and Industry
520
On the Boards
QUEEN ANNE HILL
Lake Union
Eastlake Ave. N.
Boyer Ave
Queen Ann Ave.
Aurora Ave. N.
Westlake Ave. N.
10th Ave.
Washington Park Arboretum
Volunteer Park
Seattle Asian Art Museum
E. Valley St.
Lake Washington Blvd. E
99
Seattle Repertory Theater
W. Mercer St.
Seattle Children's Theater
Key Arena
Seattle Center
Children's Museum
EMP
Space Needle
12th Ave.
E. Mercer St.
E. Thomas St.
MADISON VALLEY
DOWNTOWN
Denny Way
Broadway Ave. E.
CAPITOL HILL
Annex Theater
Western Ave.
Virginia St.
Westlake Center
Olive Way
Pacific Place
E. Pike St.
E. Union St.
Benaroya Hall
Pike St.
Madison St.
Pike Place Market
Convention Center
Seattle Art Museum
15th Ave. E.
19th Ave.
23rd Ave.
E. Cherry St.
Aquarium
1st Ave.
2nd Ave.
4th Ave.
Boren Ave.
Martin Luther King Jr. Way
Elliott Bay
E. Yesler Way
Colman Dock
Pioneer Square
Nippon Kan Theater
INTERNATIONAL DISTRICT
Rainier Ave. S.
Jackson St.
S. Dearborn St.
0
500 yards
0
500 meters
Safeco Field
S. Lake Way
90
Lake Washington
S. Holgate St.
900
17th Ave. S
Harbor Island
E. Marginal Way S
1st Ave. S
4th Ave.
S. McClellan St.
TO BOEING FIELD
5

art galleries and eclectic, folksy shops. Pioneer Square's most popular destination is **Elliott Bay Book Co.** (✉ 101 S. Main St., ☎ 206/624–6600), where thousands of volumes line the old brick walls and the basement café offers coffee, quiet, and rest-room chalkboards for literate graffiti. On the **Underground Tour** (✉ 608 1st Ave., ☎ 206/682–4646, WEB www.undergroundtour.com; 🎫 $9) beneath the streets of Pioneer Square, guides explain the often humorous cultural and architectural history of the district.

Gallery Walk (☎ 206/587–0260) is a free open house hosted the first Thursday of every month by Seattle's art galleries, most of them in Pioneer Square.

Southeast of Pioneer Square is the **International District.** The ID began as a haven for Chinese workers who had finished work on the transcontinental railroad. Today the district is full of Chinese, Japanese, and Korean residents and restaurants, as well as herbalists, massage parlors, and acupuncturists. The area is bordered by Yesler Way to the north, 4th Avenue to the west, Dearborn on the south, and I–5 on the east. The **Nippon Kan Theater** (✉ 628 S. Washington St., ☎ 206/224–0181) was historically the focal point for Japanese-American activities. It includes the Kabuki theater, now a national historic site, which hosts many Asian-oriented productions.

North of Downtown

From Westlake Center (☞ Shopping, *below*), you can catch the monorail to **Seattle Center** (WEB www.seattlecenter.com), a 74-acre complex built for the 1962 Seattle World's Fair. It includes an amusement park, theaters, a renovated coliseum, exhibition halls, museums, and shops. Look for the **Pacific Science Center** (☎ 206/443–2001, WEB www.pacsci.org; 🎫 $7.50) with its planetarium and six-story Boeing IMAX Theater. Inside the **Tropical Butterfly House and Insect Village**, hundreds of rare and beautiful butterflies flutter amid thick jungle vegetation. The **Children's Museum** (☎ 206/441–1768; 🎫 $5.50) has hands-on exhibits replicating home life around the globe, as well as intergenerational programs, special exhibits, and workshops. The museum is on the first level of the Center House. The **Space Needle** (☎ 206/443–2111, WEB www.spaceneedle.com; 🎫 $12), rising above Seattle Center, looks like something from the *Jetsons*. Take the glass elevator to the observation deck for a sweeping view of the city. Microsoft billionaire Paul Allen's **Experience Music Project** (EMP; ✉ 325 5th Ave. N, ☎ 206/367–5483, WEB www.emplive.com; 🎫 $19) aroused much controversy as architect Frank Gehry's radical design of folded, curving metal rose from what used to be a 2-acre lawn. Exhibits inside trace the history of rock music, focusing on Seattle native Jimi Hendrix and other guitar greats. Interactive programs allow you to try music-making.

On the northwest corner of the **University of Washington** campus is the **Burke Museum of Natural History and Culture** (✉ 17th Ave. NE and N.E. 45th St., ☎ 206/543–5590, WEB www.burkemuseum.org; 🎫 $5.50), Washington's natural history and anthropological museum. South of the university's Husky Stadium, across the Montlake Cut, is the **Museum of History and Industry** (✉ 2700 24th Ave. E, ☎ 206/324–1125, WEB www.seattlehistory.org; 🎫 $5.50).

Parks, Gardens, and Zoos

Near the university at the **Washington Park Arboretum** (✉ 2300 Arboretum Dr. E, ☎ 206/543–8800), Rhododendron Glen and Azalea Way are in bloom from March to June. The Hiram M. Chittenden Locks, better known as the **Ballard Locks** (✉ 3015 N.W. 54th St., west of the Ballard Bridge, ☎ 206/783–7059), control the 8-mi-long Lake Washington Ship Canal, which connects freshwater Lake Washington to Puget Sound. You can watch ships traverse the locks as salmon jump up the glassed-in fish ladder. Animals at the 92-acre **Woodland Park Zoo** (✉ N. 50th St. and Fremont Ave., ☎ 206/684–4800, WEB www.zoo.org; $9.50) roam freely within "bioclimatic" zones that re-create their native habitats. From downtown or the Seattle Center head north on Route 99 (Aurora Avenue N), across the Aurora Bridge to the 45th Street exit.

Dining

$$–$$$$ ★ ✕ **Canlis.** The sensational view over Lake Union used to be the main draw at Seattle's oldest fine-dining restaurant, but since executive chef Greg Atkinson reinvigorated the steak-and-salad menu, the view has taken second place. Contemporary selections range from Kobe-style beef to Portobello lasagna. ✉ *2526 Aurora Ave. N,* ☎ *206/283–3313. Reservations essential. AE, DC, MC, V. Closed Sun. No lunch.*

$$–$$$$ ★ ✕ **Rover's.** Specialties of particular note at this intimate Madison Valley restaurant are the diver's sea scallops with foie gras, served over chestnut puree, and the duck breast with wild mushrooms and huckleberry sauce, all available as part of the five- and eight-course prix-fixe menus. ✉ *2808 E. Madison St.,* ☎ *206/325–7442. Reservations essential. AE, DC, MC, V. Closed Sun.–Mon. No lunch.*

$$–$$$ ✕ **Campagne.** Overlooking Pike Place Market and Elliott Bay, Campagne is intimate and urbane, with white walls, picture windows, and colorful modern prints. The flavors of Provence pervade the menu in dishes such as striped bass fillet grilled with fennel and served with lemon-thyme sabayon. Downstairs is a more casual café. ✉ *Inn at the Market, 86 Pine St.,* ☎ *206/728–2800. Reservations essential. AE, MC, V.*

$$–$$$ ✕ **Flying Fish.** Fish don't fly at Christine Keff's glittering Belltown restaurant, but wondrous seafood platters do. Most popular are the tapas-style servings of crab, fried fish, oysters, and clams. Her version of fish tacos truly elevates them to a new epicurean category. ✉ *2234 1st Ave.,* ☎ *206/728–8595. Reservations essential. AE, D, DC, MC, V. No lunch.*

$–$$$ ★ ✕ **Wild Ginger.** Rick and Anne Yoder's restaurant across from Benaroya Hall is bigger, more conspicuous, and more glamorous than the original Western Avenue location, but they haven't changed the Pan-Asian creations that first brought them fame. Try the laksa, a Malaysian bouillabaisse, or any of numerous flavorful satays. ✉ *1401 3rd Ave.,* ☎ *206/623–4450. AE, D, DC, MC, V. No lunch Sun.*

$–$$ ✕ **Anthony's Bell Street Diner and Pier 66.** In addition to having one of the best views of Elliott Bay, this waterfront diner has become known for its Manila clam chili, mahimahi tacos, and wild blackberry cobbler. It's also convenient to the market and the waterfront. ✉ *2201 Alaskan Way,* ☎ *206/448–6688. AE, D, DC, MC, V.*

Lodging

Seattle has an abundance of lodgings, from deluxe downtown hotels to less expensive digs in the University District. For information on bed-and-breakfasts, contact the **Pacific Bed & Breakfast Agency** (✉ Box 46894, Seattle 98146, ☎ 206/439–7677, FAX 206/431–0932).

$$$$ ★ **Four Seasons Olympic Hotel.** Restored to its 1920s grandeur, the Olympic is Seattle's most elegant hotel. Public rooms are furnished with marble, thick rugs, wood paneling, and potted plants. The less luxurious guest rooms are homey, with comfortable reading chairs and floral-print fabrics. ✉ *411 University St., 98101,* ☎ *206/621–1700 or 800/332–3442,* FAX *206/682–9633,* WEB *www.fourseasons.com. 450 rooms. 3 restaurants, pool, health club. AE, D, DC, MC, V.*

$$$–$$$$ ★ **Alexis.** This intimate hotel is in a restored 1901 building near the waterfront. Guest rooms are vividly decorated with colorful fabrics and original art. Some suites have whirlpool baths; others have wood-burning fireplaces. Pets are welcome. ✉ *1007 1st Ave., 98104,* ☎ *206/624–4844 or 800/426–7033,* FAX *206/621–9009,* WEB *www.alexishotel.com. 109 rooms. Restaurant, gym. AE, D, DC, MC, V.*

$$$–$$$$ **Edgewater.** The only hotel on Elliott Bay has comfortably rustic rooms with wood furnishings and plaid fabrics in red, green, and blue. ✉ *Pier 67, 2411 Alaskan Way, 98121,* ☎ *206/728–7000 or 800/624–0670,* FAX *206/441–4119. 236 rooms. Restaurant. AE, D, DC, MC, V.*

$$$ **Claremont.** In a restored 1920s apartment building, the Claremont is closer to Seattle Center than other business-class downtown hotels. Rooms are remarkably spacious. ✉ *2000 4th Ave., 98121,* ☎ *206/448–8600 or 800/448–8601,* FAX *206/441–7140,* WEB *www.claremonthotel.com. 120 rooms. Restaurant. AE, D, DC, MC, V.*

$$$ **Hotel Monaco.** Goldfish in your room (upon request) are just one of the eclectic touches you'll find at this luxury hotel in Seattle's financial district. Spacious rooms with bold colors come with CD players, data ports, and fax machines. Join other guests around the fireplace in the lobby for complimentary evening wine. ✉ *1101 4th Ave., 98101,* ☎ *206/621–1770 or 800/945–2240,* FAX *206/621–7779,* WEB *www.monaco-seattle.com. 189 rooms. Restaurant, gym. AE, D, DC, MC, V.*

$$$ ★ **Inn at the Market.** Adjacent to Pike Place Market, this hotel combines the best aspects of a small, deluxe hotel with the informality of the Pacific Northwest. Rooms are large, with contemporary furnishings, ceramic sculptures, and views of either the city, Elliott Bay, or the hotel courtyard. ✉ *86 Pine St., 98101,* ☎ *206/443–3600,* FAX *206/448–0631,* WEB *www.innatthemarket.com. 65 rooms. AE, D, DC, MC, V.*

$$–$$$ **Edmond Meany Tower Hotel.** At this art deco–style hotel a few blocks from the University of Washington campus, nearly all the rooms have views of the Cascades or the Olympic mountains, the University of Washington, or Lake Union. ✉ *4507 Brooklyn Ave. NE, 98105,* ☎ *206/634–2000,* FAX *206/547–6029,* WEB *www.meany.com. 155 rooms. 2 restaurants. AE, DC, MC, V.*

$ **Seattle YMCA.** This member of the American Youth Hostels Association has single and double rooms that are clean and plainly furnished with bed, phone, desk, and lamp. Ten dollars extra gets you a room with a private bath; for another $3 or $4 you'll have a view of Elliott Bay. ✉ *909 4th Ave., 98104,* ☎ *206/382–5000. 120 beds, 3 rooms with bath. Pool, health club. D, MC, V.*

Motels

Seattle Airport Hilton (✉ International Blvd. at S. 176th St., ☎ 206/244–4800, FAX 206/248–4495), 178 rooms; restaurant, pool, gym; *$$–$$$*. **University Plaza Hotel** (✉ 400 N.E. 45th St., 98105, ☎ 206/634–0100, FAX 206/633–2743), 135 rooms; restaurant, pool, gym; *$$–$$$*.

Nightlife and the Arts

Nightlife

Seattle has a strong and diverse music scene. The most famous development to come out of the city so far has been grunge rock, a movement of the early 1990s, exemplified by Nirvana and still practiced by Pearl Jam.

BARS AND NIGHTCLUBS

The **Bookstore** (✉ 1007 1st Ave., ☎ 206/382–1506) is a quiet haunt with window tables are great for people-watching. **Comet Tavern** (✉ 922 E. Pike St., ☎ 206/323–9853) is Seattle's oldest post-Prohibition tavern turned hippie hangout turned upscale singles watering hole. **Entros** (✉ 823 Yale Ave. N, ☎ 206/624–0057) bills itself as an "intelligent amusement park," where patrons play socially interactive games such as "interface, the high-tech trust walk." **Meridian** (✉ 1900 N. Northlake Way, ☎ 206/547–3242) has a lounge with giant windows overlooking Gas Works Park and Lake Union. **Palace Kitchen** (✉ 2030 5th Ave., ☎ 206/448–2001) is a happening bar with great food. A Seattle favorite, **Ray's Boathouse** (✉ 6049 Seaview Ave. NW, ☎ 206/789–3770) is on the shore of Shilshole Bay, a perfect spot for watching the sun set behind the Olympic Mountains.

BREWPUBS

The **Elysian Brewing Company** (✉ 1221 E. Pike St., ☎ 206/860–1920) serves lunch and dinner in a remodeled furniture warehouse on Capitol Hill. Near Safeco Field and the waterfront is the bigger, more mainstream **Pyramid Alehouse** (✉ 1201 1st Ave., ☎ 206/682–3377), serving great pub food at lunch and dinner. It's packed before Mariners games. The **Trolleyman Pub** (✉ 3400 Phinney Ave. N, ☎ 206/548–8000), in the eclectic Fremont neighborhood, is the smaller of the two Red Hook breweries; the other is in Woodinville. The emphasis is on beer rather than food, but some sandwiches are available.

BLUES/R&B CLUBS

The **Ballard Firehouse** (✉ 5429 Russell St. NW, ☎ 206/784–3516) sticks to blues. The **Central Tavern** (✉ 207 1st Ave. S, ☎ 206/622–0209), often crowded, presents local and national blues and reggae acts. The **Tractor Tavern** (✉ 5213 Ballard Ave. NW, ☎ 206/789–3599) is Seattle's leading venue for alternative country, bluegrass, folk, and blues.

COMEDY CLUB

Comedy Underground (✉ 222 Main St., ☎ 206/628–0303), beneath Swannie's restaurant, presents stand-up comedy and open-mike nights.

DANCE CLUBS

Swing, country, tango, salsa—anything goes at **Century Ballroom** (✉ 915 E. Pine St., ☎ 206/324–7263). **Neighbors** (✉ 1509 Broadway E, ☎ 206/324–5358) attracts a good mix of gay men and everyone else.

JAZZ CLUB

Dimitriou's Jazz Alley (✉ 2037 6th Ave., ☎ 206/441–9729) books nationally known performers every night except Monday, when local talent is showcased. Dinner is served before the first show.

ROCK CLUBS

The **Alibi Room** (✉ 85 Pike St., ☎ 206/623–3180), in the Pike Place Market, is a restaurant and bar with live music, disco dancing, and independent film screenings in conjunction with the Seattle Film Festival. **Crocodile Cafe** (✉ 2200 2nd Ave., ☎ 206/448–2114) rocks with live local groups from Tuesday through Saturday. At the **OK Hotel** (✉ 212 Alaskan Way S, ☎ 206/621–7903), closed Monday, you'll find grunge, acoustic, and jazz, plus occasional poetry readings. **Showbox** (✉ 1426 1st Ave., ☎ 206/628–3151) brings in major regional as well as national alternative rock and pop acts.

The Arts

Seattle's free weekly papers, the *Seattle Weekly* (Wednesday) and the *Stranger* (Thursday), produce the city's most comprehensive arts and entertainment coverage. Thursday's editions of the *Seattle Times* and the Friday calendar insert of the *Post-Intelligencer* also list events. To charge tickets, call **Ticketmaster** (☎ 206/628–0888). **Ticket/Ticket,** with two locations (✉ 401 Broadway E.; ✉ 1st Ave. at Pike St.; ☎ 206/324–2744), sells half-price same-day tickets for cash only.

DANCE

The **Pacific Northwest Ballet** (✉ Opera House, 1020 John St., 98109, ☎ 206/441–2424, WEB www.pnb.org) is a resident company and school that presents 60–70 performances annually. **On the Boards** (✉ 100 W. Roy, ☎ 206/217–9886) is the foremost center in the region for contemporary dance, theater, music, and multimedia presentation.

MUSIC

Northwest Chamber Orchestra (☎ 206/343–0445), the Northwest's only professional chamber orchestra, presents a full spectrum of music, from Baroque to modern, at various venues. The **Seattle Symphony** (✉ Benaroya Hall, 2nd Ave. and University St., ☎ 206/215–4747, WEB www.seattlesymphony.org) presents some 160 concerts a year in and around town. Its symphony hall opened in late 1998.

OPERA

The **Seattle Opera** (✉ Opera House, 1020 John St., 98109, ☎ 206/389–7600, WEB www.seattleopera.org), considered one of the top companies in America, presents five productions during its August–May season. Its biennial summer presentations of Wagner's Ring cycle draw fans from around the world.

THEATER

The **Seattle Repertory Theater** (✉ Bagley Wright Theater, 155 Mercer St., ☎ 206/443–2222) presents high-quality programming in nine productions during its October–May season. The **Seattle Children's Theater** (✉ 2nd Ave. N and Thomas St., ☎ 206/441–3322) has a strong reputation. **Annex Theatre** (✉ 1916 4th Ave., ☎ 206/728–0933) is Seattle fringe theater at its best, with six main productions throughout the year. **Theater Schmeater** (✉ 1500 Summit Ave., ☎ 206/324–5801) also offers exceptional drama as well as its long-running, late-night spoofs of the *Twilight Zone*. **A Contemporary Theatre** (ACT; ✉ 7th Ave. and Union St., ☎ 206/292–7676) develops works by new playwrights.

Spectator Sports

Baseball: The **Seattle Mariners** play in Safeco Field (✉ 83 S. King St., Suite 300, ☎ 206/622–4487), which has exquisite views of Elliott Bay from the third level. **Basketball: Seattle SuperSonics** play in KeyArena (✉ 1st Ave. N, ☎ 206/281–5850) at Seattle Center. **Football:** The **Seattle Seahawks** opened their new stadium (✉ 421 1st Ave. S, ☎ 206/682–2800) on the site of the old Kingdome in fall 2002.

Shopping

Shopping Centers

City Centre (✉ 1420 5th Ave., ☎ 206/624–8800), a gleaming marble tower, houses upscale shops such as Ann Taylor and Barneys of New York. **Pacific Place** (✉ 600 Pine St., ☎ 206/405–2655) is Seattle's newest upscale shopping center, with 50 shops, including Tiffany & Co. and J. Crew. **Westlake Center** (✉ 400 Pine St., at 4th Ave., ☎ 206/467–1600) is a three-story steel-and-glass building with 80 shops and covered walkways that connect it to branches of Seattle's major department stores, Nordstrom and the Bon Marché. The nearby plaza hosts everything from protests to Christmas carousels.

Food Market

Vendors at the partially open-air **Pike Place Market** sell fresh meat, seafood, produce, flowers, and crafts. Lunch at one of the Market's many cafés is a Seattle tradition.

Specialty Stores

CLOTHING

Boutique Europa (✉ 1420 5th Ave., ☎ 206/587–6292) carries sophisticated European clothing. On the edge of the Pike Place Market, **Local Brilliance** (✉ 1535 1st Ave., ☎ 206/343–5864) showcases fashions by local designers. **Mario's** (✉ 1513 6th Ave., ☎ 206/223–1461) has trendy and designer fashions for men. **Nubia's** (✉ 1507 6th Ave., ☎ 206/622–0297) sells unconstructed knits for women's business and casual wear as well as belts, beads, and other accessories.

GIFTS

Simply Seattle (✉ 1600 1st Ave., ☎ 206/448–2207) stocks an excellent selection of locally made products and souvenirs.

OUTDOOR WEAR AND EQUIPMENT

Eddie Bauer (✉ 5th Ave. and Union St., ☎ 206/622–2766) specializes in classic sports and outdoor apparel. With its 65-ft climbing wall, the 8,000-square-ft flagship branch of **REI** (✉ 222 Yale Ave. N, ☎ 206/223–1944) is one of Seattle's most-visited landmarks.

TOYS

Children will love **Magic Mouse Toys** (✉ 603 1st Ave., ☎ 206/682–8097), with its two floors of toys, from small windups to giant plush animals.

Side Trip to Whidbey Island

On a nice day there's no better short excursion from Seattle than a ferry trip across Puget Sound to Whidbey Island. It's a great way to watch seagulls, sailboats, and massive container vessels in the sound—not to mention the scenery, including the Kitsap Peninsula and Olympic Mountains, Mt. Rainier, the Cascade Range, and the Seattle skyline.

Arriving and Departing

BY CAR

Whidbey Island can be reached by ferry via I–5 from Mukilteo (follow signs), or you can drive from Seattle north on I–5, then head west on Route 20 and cross the dramatic Deception Pass bridge.

BY FERRY

Drive or walk onto the ferry at Mukilteo, 30 mi north of Seattle. It lets you off in Clinton on Whidbey Island.

➤ CONTACT: **Washington State Ferries** (☎ 206/464–6400 or 800/843–3779, WEB www.wsdot.wa.gov/ferries).

BY PLANE

From Seattle-Tacoma International Airport, **Harbour Airlines** (☎ 800/359–3220) flies to Oak Harbor. **Kenmore Air** (☎ 425/486–1257 or 800/543–9595), on Lake Union, provides seaplane charter service.

What to See and Do

Whidbey Island (☎ 888/747–7777, WEB www.islandweb.org) is mostly rural, with undulating hills, gentle beaches, and little coves. **Langley,** a quaint town with inviting inns and a handful of good restaurants, shops, and galleries, sits atop a 50-ft bluff overlooking the southeastern shore. A little more than halfway up 50-mi-long Whidbey Island is **Coupeville,** site of many restored Victorian houses and one of the largest National Historic Districts in the state. The town was founded in 1852 by Captain Thomas Coupe, whose house, built the next year, is one of the state's oldest.

Ebey's Landing National Historic Reserve (☎ 360/678–4636, WEB www.nps.gov/ebla) is a 17,000-acre area including Keystone, Coupeville, and Penn Cove. Established by Congress in 1978, the reserve is the first and largest of its kind, dotted with 91 nationally registered historic structures along with farmland, parks, and trails. At **Deception Pass State Park** (☎ 360/675–2417), at the north end of Whidbey Island, you can take in the spectacular view while strolling among the madrona trees, with their peeling reddish-brown bark.

Dining

$$$$ ✕ **Country Kitchen.** Tables for two line the walls of this intimate restaurant. The prix-fixe, five-course menu might include locally gathered mussels in a black bean sauce, breast of duck in a loganberry sauce, or Columbia River salmon. ✉ *Inn at Langley, 400 1st St., Langley,* ☎ *360/221–3033. Reservations essential. MC, V.*

$$–$$$ ✕ **The Captain Whidbey Inn Dining Room.** The small, rustic dining room at the Captain Whidbey Inn has great views of the shore and the tranquil waters of Penn Cove. For more than 20 years, the inn has served delectable, locally raised mussels and oysters, and seasonal Whidbey Island produce. ✉ *3072 Captain Whidbey Inn Rd., Coupeville,* ☎ *360/678–4110. Reservations essential. AE, D, MC, V. No lunch.*

$$ ✕ **Garibyan Brothers Café Langley.** Mediterranean fare is served at this casual café. ✉ *113 1st St., Langley,* ☎ *360/221–3090. AE, MC, V. Closed Tues. in winter.*

Side Trip to Tacoma

Seattleite skepticism notwithstanding, Tacoma has a strong cultural scene, restored residential neighborhoods and historic theaters, fine bay views, and a world-class zoo.

Arriving and Departing

Tacoma is about 35 mi south of Seattle via I–5. Sea-Tac Airport is a 40-minute drive away.

What to See and Do

Union Station (✉ 1717 Pacific Ave., ☎ 253/593–6313) is an heirloom from the golden age of railroads, when Tacoma was the western terminus for the transcontinental Northern Pacific Railroad. Built by Reed and Stem, the architects of New York City's Grand Central Station, the massive copper-domed Beaux Arts depot was opened in 1911. It now houses federal district courts, but the rotunda—which houses an outstanding display of glass art by Tacoma native Dale Chihulyand—is open to the public. Across the street is the **University of Washington, Tacoma** campus, housed in beautifully restored 19th-century warehouses. The **Washington State Historical Society Museum** (✉ 1911 Pacific Ave., ☎ 253/272–3500, WEB www.wshs.org; 🎟 $7) near Union Station houses exhibits on the natural, Native American, pioneer, maritime, and industrial history of the state. It's closed Monday.

A new contemporary art museum, the **Museum of Glass** (✉ 1801 Dock St., ☎ 253/396–1768, WEB www.museumofglass.org; 🎟 $6), was slated at press time to open in July 2002. The museum is the first U.S. project for famed Canadian architect Arthur Erickson, who chose a cone as the building's centerpiece to reflect the hog fuel burners once common in Northwest timber mills. Inside the cone, you can watch glass artists at work. Rotating exhibits focus on glass and ceramic sculptures, as well as paintings.

Downtown on Broadway is **Antique Row,** with antiques shops, two restored theaters, and funky boutiques. The **Tacoma Art Museum** (✉ 1123 Pacific Ave., ☎ 253/272–4258, WEB www.tacomaartmuseum.org; 🎟 $5) contains a rich collection of American and French paintings, as well as Chinese jades and imperial robes. **Wright Park** (✉ 6th and Division

Sts., I and G Sts.) is a 30-acre park north of downtown. Within the park is the **W. W. Seymour Botanical Conservatory** (✉ 316 S. G St., ☎ 253/591–5330; free), a Victorian-style greenhouse.

Northeast of Tacoma, the 700-acre **Point Defiance Park** is one of the largest urban parks in the country. The **Point Defiance Zoo and Aquarium,** founded in 1888, is one of the top small-city zoos in America. ✉ *5400 N. Pearl St.,* ☎ *253/591–5337,* WEB *www.pdza.org.* *$7.*

Dining

$–$$$ ✕ **Primo Grill.** Mediterranean cuisine is the foundation of Primo's menu, probably the best in Tacoma. Risotto with prawns, scallops, mushrooms, and artichoke hearts is a specialty, as is the fresh fish. ✉ *601 S. Pine St.,* ☎ *253/383–7000. AE, MC, V.*

$–$$ ✕ **Swiss.** You'll find good pub fare and Northwest microbrews at this restaurant in a distinctive 1913 building that was once Tacoma's Swiss Hall. ✉ *1904 S. Jefferson Ave.,* ☎ *253/572–2821. No credit cards.*

$ ✕ **Grassi's.** Good, hearty, uncomplicated soups, salads, and sandwiches make this café a good spot for lunch. It's across the street from the Washington State Historical Museum. ✉ *1702 Pacific Ave.,* ☎ *253/572–1744. MC, V.*

Side Trip to Olympia

Arriving and Departing

Olympia is on I–5, about 60 mi southwest of Seattle and 25 mi southwest of Tacoma.

What to See and Do

Olympia, Washington's state capital, is fairly quiet except when the legislature is in session. You can tour the **Legislative Building** (✉ Capitol Way between 10th and 14th Aves.), a handsome Romanesque structure with a 287-ft dome that closely resembles the Capitol in that *other* Washington.

Dining

$$–$$$ ✕ **Louisa.** Ten minutes south of downtown Olympia is Louisa, an elegant dining room for sophisticated Northwest cuisine. House-made butternut-squash ravioli with sage pesto and goat cheese is the perfect treat on a rainy day on the Sound. ✉ *211 Cleveland Ave., Tumwater,* ☎ *360/352–3732. MC, V. Closed Sun.–Mon. No lunch Sat.*

Seattle Essentials

AIRPORTS AND TRANSFERS

Seattle-Tacoma International Airport (Sea-Tac) is 20 mi south of downtown and is served by major American and some foreign airlines.

➤ AIRPORT INFORMATION: **Seattle-Tacoma International Airport** (✉ 17801 Pacific Hwy. S, 98168-0727, ☎ 206/433–4444).

AIRPORT TRANSFER

A cab ride between the airport and downtown takes 30–45 minutes and costs about $25. Gray Line Airport Express runs to and from major downtown hotels; fare is $8.50 one-way, $14 round-trip.

➤ TAXIS AND SHUTTLES: **Gray Line Airport Express** (☎ 206/626–6088).

BUS TRAVEL TO AND FROM SEATTLE

➤ BUS INFORMATION: **Greyhound** (✉ 8th Ave. and Stewart St., ☎ 800/231–2222).

CAR TRAVEL

I–5 enters Seattle from the north and south, I–90 from the east.

RULES OF THE ROAD

Hills, tunnels, reversible express lanes, and rush hours can make driving a chore. Main thoroughfares into downtown are Aurora Avenue (Route 99 is called the Alaskan Way Viaduct along the waterfront) and I–5.

➤ CONTACT: **Traffic and pass information** (☎ 800/695–7623).

TAXIS

Pick up a cab at any hotel taxi stand or call the cab company directly—standing on a street to flag a passing cab is not always successful in Seattle. Fare is $1.80 at the flag drop and then $1.80 per mile. Major companies are Farwest and Yellow Cab.

➤ TAXI COMPANIES: **Farwest** (☎ 206/622–1717 or 425/454–5055). **Yellow Cab** (☎ 206/622–6500 or 425/455–4999).

TOURS

BOAT TOURS

Argosy Cruises operates one-hour tours of Elliott Bay, the Port of Seattle, Lake Union, Hiram M. Chittenden Locks, and Lake Washington; admission is $15–$28. The company's wonderful dinner-cruise ship, the *Royal Argosy,* is designed to reflect the Mosquito Fleet boats that sailed Puget Sound a century ago. Cruises cost $70–$79.

➤ FEES AND SCHEDULES: **Argosy Cruises** (✉ Pier 55, ☎ 206/623–1445, WEB www.argosycruises.com).

BUS TOURS

Gray Line provides guided bus tours of the city and environs. Tour prices are $29–$60.

➤ FEES AND SCHEDULES: **Gray Line Tour** (✉ Washington State Convention and Trade Center, 800 Convention Pl., ☎ 206/626–5208, WEB www.graylineofseattle.com).

TRAIN TOURS

Spirit of Washington Dinner Train involves seven vintage railcars that transport diners on a four-hour round-trip excursion from Renton to Woodinville, along the eastern shore of Lake Washington, passing through Mercer Island, Bellevue, Kirkland, and the Sammamish River valley. During the 45-minute stop in Woodinville, you are invited to tour the Columbia Winery and visit the tasting room.

➤ FEES AND SCHEDULES: **Spirit of Washington Dinner Train** (✉ 625 S. 4th St., Renton, ☎ 425/227–7245 or 800/876–7245, WEB www.spiritofwashingtondinnertrain.com; 💳 $50–$70).

TRAIN TRAVEL

➤ TRAIN INFORMATION: **Amtrak** (✉ 303 S. Jackson St., ☎ 800/872–7245).

TRANSPORTATION AROUND SEATTLE

A car is the handiest way to get around metropolitan Seattle, but bus service is convenient and efficient, too. Despite occasional steep hills, downtown is great for walking. Metropolitan Transit provides free rides in the downtown-waterfront area until 7 PM; fares to other destinations range from $1.25 to $1.90, depending on the zone and time of day. The elevated monorail runs the 2 mi from Seattle Center to Westlake Center every 15 minutes; the fare is $1.25.

➤ CONTACTS: **Metropolitan Transit** (☎ 206/553–3000). **Monorail** (☎ 206/441–6038).

VISITOR INFORMATION

➤ TOURIST INFORMATION: **Seattle Convention and Visitors Bureau** (✉ 520 Pike St., Suite 1300, 98101, ☎ 206/461–5800, WEB www.

seeseattle.org). Tacoma–Pierce County Visitors and Convention Bureau (✉ 906 Broadway, Tacoma 98402, ☎ 253/627–2836 or 800/272–2662, WEB www.tpctourism.org).

THE OLYMPIC PENINSULA

The rugged Olympic Peninsula forms the northwest corner of the continental United States. Much of it is wilderness, with the Olympic National Park and National Forest at its heart. The peninsula has tremendous variety: the wild Pacific shore, the sheltered waters along the Hood Canal and the Strait of Juan de Fuca, the rivers of the Olympic's rain forests, and the towering Olympic Mountains.

Exploring the Olympic Peninsula

From Olympia go west along U.S. 101 and Routes 8 and 12 to **Gray's Harbor** and the twin seaports of **Hoquiam** and **Aberdeen.** From Hoquiam you can drive north on **Route 109,** which sticks to the coast and passes through resorts and ample beach areas such as Copalis Beach, Pacific Beach, and Moclips. Route 109 eventually leads to the Quinault Indian Reservation and the tribal center of **Taholah,** whose main draw is pristine, expansive scenery.

Route 109 dead-ends at Taholah, and you must backtrack to return to U.S. 101. About 20 mi north of Aberdeen on U.S. 101, 1½ mi north of the Hoh River Bridge, is Hoh River Rainforest Road, which goes ★ east to the **Hoh Rain Forest** (☎ 360/452–4501), part of the Olympic National Park. This complex ecosystem of conifers, hardwoods, grasses, mosses, and other flora shelters such wildlife as elks, otters, beavers, salmon, and flying squirrels. The average annual rainfall here is 145 inches. The Hoh Visitor Center (often unstaffed September–May) at the campground and the ranger station at road's end (18 mi east of U.S. 101) have interpretative displays and information on nature trails.

On U.S. 101 north of Hoh River Rainforest Road is the small logging town of **Forks,** a former lumber town that is changing into a hot spot for rain-forest explorers and back-country hikers. From Forks, La Push Road leads west about 15 mi to **La Push,** a coastal village and the tribal center of the Quileute Indians. Several points along this road have short trails with access to the ocean and fabulous views of nearby islands.

Returning to U.S. 101, which swings to the east as you go north from Forks, you go through the **Sol Duc River valley,** famous for its salmon fishing. The Soleduck Fish Hatchery (☎ 360/327–3246) has interpretive displays on fish breeding. A few miles past the tiny town of Sappho are the deep azure waters of **Lake Crescent.** The area has abundant campsites, resorts, trails, canoeing, and fishing. Twelve miles south of Lake Crescent on Soleduck Road (which meets U.S. 101 1 mi west of the western tip of Lake Crescent) is an entrance to Olympic National Park and to **Sol Duc Hot Springs** (☎ 360/327–3583), closed October–April, where you can dip into three hot sulfur pools ranging from 98°F to 104°F.

On the northern tip of the Olympic Peninsula, on U.S. 101 E, is **Port Angeles,** once a bustling fishing port and mill town and now the gateway to Olympic National Park (✉ 600 E. Park Ave., Port Angeles 98362, ☎ 360/452–4501, WEB www.nps.gov/olym). A bus will take you or you can drive up the road to **Hurricane Ridge,** 17 mi south of Port Angeles, which rises nearly a mile above sea level yielding spectacular views of the Olympics, the Strait of Juan de Fuca, and Vancouver Island.

Western Washington

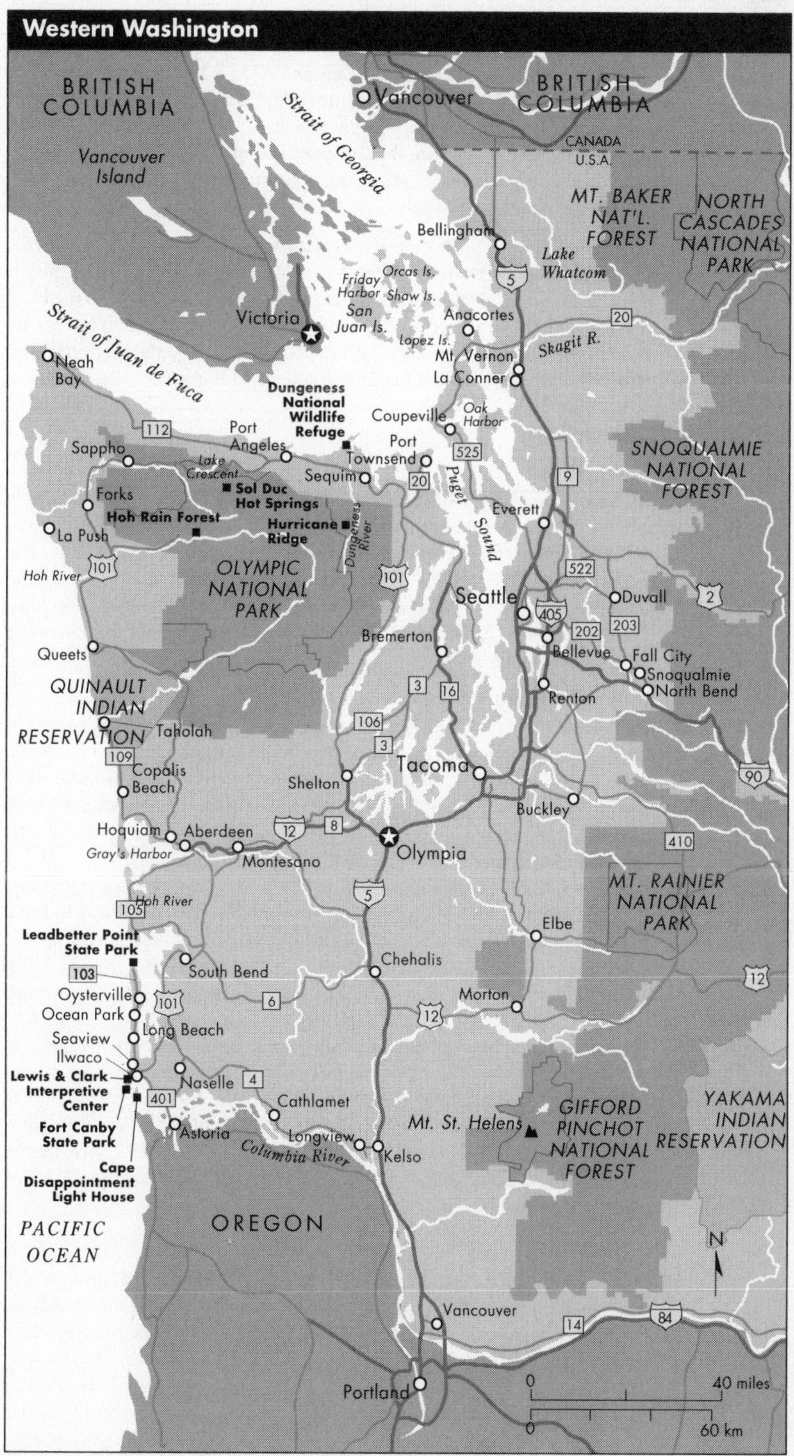

Seventeen miles east of Port Angeles on U.S. 101 is the charming town of **Sequim** (pronounced *squim*). Animal life present and past can be found at the **Museum and Arts Center** (✉ 175 W. Cedar St., ☎ 360/683–8110, WEB www.sequimmuseum.org; free) in the Sequim-Dungeness Valley. In the fertile plain at the mouth of the Dungeness River, 4 mi northwest of Sequim, the **Dungeness National Wildlife Refuge** (☎ 360/457–8451) is home to thousands of migratory waterfowl, as well as clams, oysters, and seals.

About 10 mi east of Sequim, Route 20 turns northward 12 mi to **Port Townsend.** Its waterfront is lined with carefully restored brick buildings from the 1870s that house shops and restaurants. High on the bluff are large gingerbread-trim Victorian homes, many of which have been turned into B&Bs. Driving south on U.S. 101 through the oyster and mill town of **Shelton** will bring you back to Olympia.

Dining and Lodging

Hoquiam

$–$$ ★ **Sandpiper Beach Resort.** Within the four-story Sandpiper complex are 31 suites, most with a sitting room, dining area, fireplace, small kitchen, and porch. With no in-room phones, no pool, no TVs, and no restaurant, this is the place to get away from it all. ✉ *4159 Rte. 109, 1½ mi south of Pacific Beach (Box A, 98571),* ☎ *360/276–4580 or 800/567–4737,* FAX *360/276–4464,* WEB *www.sandpiperbeachresort.com. 31 suites. MC, V.*

Port Angeles

$$–$$$ ✕ **C'est Si Bon.** This locally famous spot run by a French couple is probably the most elegant restaurant on the informal Olympic Peninsula. Fine art on the walls competes with views of the flower-laden terrace and the Olympic Mountains beyond. The cuisine, of course, is French. ✉ *23 Cedar Park Dr. (4 mi east of town),* ☎ *360/452–8888. Reservations essential. AE, D, MC, V. Closed Mon. No lunch.*

$$ **Lake Crescent Lodge.** A big main lodge and small cabins overlooks Lake Crescent. Units in the lodge are minimal—some are dimly lighted, with bathrooms down the hall—but the setting makes up for sparse amenities. ✉ *416 Lake Crescent Rd., 98363,* ☎ *360/928–3211,* WEB *www.lakecrescentlodge.com. 52 rooms, 47 with bath. Restaurant. AE, DC, MC, V. Closed late Oct.–Apr.*

$–$$ **Sol Duc Hot Springs Resort.** This casual resort dates from the turn of the 20th century. Some of the minimally outfitted cabins are rustic; others are more modern. There are three hot springs and plenty of hiking trails nearby. ✉ *12 mi south of U.S. 101 on Soleduck Rd. (Box 2169, 98362),* ☎ *360/327–3398,* FAX *360/327–3593,* WEB *www.northolympic.com/solduc. 32 units, camping and RV facilities. Restaurant, pool. AE, D, MC, V. Closed Nov.–Mar.*

Port Townsend

$$ ★ ✕ **Fountain Café.** This small café off the main tourist drag is one of the best restaurants in town. Count on seafood and pasta specialties with imaginative twists, such as oysters in anchovy-wine sauce. ✉ *920 Washington St.,* ☎ *360/385–1364. MC, V. Closed Tues. No lunch.*

$–$$ ✕ **Salal Café.** Home-style cooking with an emphasis on daily specials is what you'll find at this cooperatively run restaurant. The ample breakfasts stand out—try one of many variations on the potato-egg scramble. Seafood inspires the specials, such as mussels in miso broth and oyster-mushroom risotto. ✉ *634 Water St.,* ☎ *360/385–6532. Reservations not accepted. MC, V. No dinner Tues.–Wed.*

$$ **James House.** Commanding a spot on the bluff overlooking downtown and the waterfront, this antiques-filled Victorian B&B is a great

place to see how the well-heeled lived in the late 1800s. ✉ *1238 Washington St., 98368,* ☎ *360/385–1238 or 800/385–1238,* WEB *www.jameshouse.com. 12 rooms. AE, MC, V. BP.*

$ **Palace Hotel.** This friendly hotel in the historic section of downtown is decorated to reflect its 1889 construction date and its past as a bordello. Rooms have no phones, but they do have cable TV. ✉ *1004 Water St., 98368,* ☎ *360/385–0773 or 800/962–0741,* FAX *360/385–0780,* WEB *www.olympus.net/palace. 15 units. AE, D, MC, V.*

Quinault

$–$$ **Lake Quinault Lodge.** This historic lodge, built of cedar and fir in 1926, is set on a broad glacial lake in the midst of the Olympic rain forest. The lobby has antique reproductions and a fireplace. ✉ *345 S. Shore Rd. (Box 7, 98575),* ☎ *360/288–2900,* FAX *360/288–2901,* WEB *www.visitlakequinault.com. 92 rooms. Restaurant, pool. AE, MC, V.*

Campgrounds

Some of the best campgrounds in **Olympic National Park** (✉ 600 E. Park Ave., Port Angeles 98362, ☎ 360/452–4501) are **Hoh River** (☎ 360/374–6925), **Mora** (☎ 360/374–5460), and **Fairholm** (☎ 360/928–3380). **Bogachiel State Park** (✉ 6 mi south of Forks on U.S. 101, ☎ 360/374–6356) is another beautiful spot, though it's closed after dusk in winter. **Fort Flagler State Park** (✉ 8 mi northeast of Port Hadlock on Rte. 116, ☎ 360/385–1259) is closed for overnight camping November–February. **Ocean City State Park** (✉ 148 Rte. 115, Hoquiam 98550, ☎ 360/289–3553), with direct access to the beach, is very popular and has one of the largest campgrounds in the state. **Pacific Beach State Park** (✉ 1 mi south of Pacific Beach on Rte. 109, ☎ 360/276–4297) has a small, relatively quiet campground next to the beach. There is also camping at **Sol Duc Hot Springs Resort** (✉ 12 mi south of U.S. 101 on Soleduck Rd. [Box 2169, Port Angeles 98362], ☎ 360/327–3398).

Outdoor Activities and Sports

Biking

Biking is popular in the flatter areas around Port Townsend and within Olympic National Park. There are bike-rental shops in Port Townsend and other resort areas on the peninsula.

Fishing

Trout, salmon, and steelhead are abundant in rivers throughout the peninsula. The best time to fish is in the fall and winter. Contact the North Olympic Peninsula Visitor & Convention Bureau (✉ Box 670, Port Angeles 98362, ☎ 360/452–8552 or 800/942–4042, WEB www.olympicpeninsula.org) for information about the best places to fish.

Hiking

Washington is well known for excellent hiking, both in the mountains and on the coast. Although **Olympic National Forest** (☎ 360/288–2525) has large clear-cut areas, the parts of it adjacent to the national park offer untouched rain forest to wander through. For information about hiking through protected coastal rain forests, contact the **Olympic National Park Visitor Center** (✉ 3002 Mt. Angeles Rd., Port Angeles 98362, ☎ 360/452–0330).

Skiing

Hurricane Ridge, 12 mi south of Port Angeles on Hurricane Ridge Road, has 25 mi of cross-country ski trails in addition to its incredible views. It's open weekends in winter and spring.

Beaches

A long, sandy beach stretches from Ocean Shores north to Taholah, but north of there and along Juan de Fuca Strait, there are mostly small pocket beaches (many of them rocky and surf-swept). Keep in mind that the beaches on tribal or private lands are not generally accessible. Also, remember that the North Pacific is not for swimming—unless you wear a wet suit and are a very strong and experienced swimmer. Be alert at all times for rogue waves, which can and have swept unwary visitors into the ocean. For walking and exploring, the main beaches are Copalis and Pacific, north of Hoquiam; a series of scenic, unnamed beaches north of Kalaloch; and Rialto Beach, near La Push.

Shopping

Confirmed shoppers head for the waterfront boutiques and stores of **Port Townsend,** all of which showcase Northwest arts and crafts.

The Olympic Peninsula Essentials

AIR TRAVEL

Horizon Air (800/547–9308) flies into Port Angeles from the Seattle-Tacoma airport. Private charter airlines fly into Port Angeles, Forks, and Hoquiam.

BOAT AND FERRY TRAVEL

The Washington State Ferry System provides car and passenger service from downtown Seattle to Bremerton. The Black Ball Ferry Line operates between Port Angeles, on the Olympic Peninsula, and Victoria, British Columbia.

➤ BOAT AND FERRY INFORMATION: **Black Ball Ferry Line** (☎ 360/457–4491, WEB www.northolympic.com/coho). **Washington State Ferry System** (☎ 206/464–6400 or 800/843–3779, WEB www.wsdot.wa.gov/ferries).

BUS TRAVEL

➤ BUS INFORMATION: **Olympic Van Tours and Bus Lines** (☎ 360/452–3858).

CAR TRAVEL

U.S. 101 loops around the Olympic Peninsula, which can be reached from Olympia via Routes 8 and 101 and from Tacoma, 50 mi away, via Route 16.

VISITOR INFORMATION

➤ TOURIST INFORMATION: **North Olympic Peninsula Visitor & Convention Bureau** (✉ Box 670, Port Angeles 98362, ☎ 360/452–8552 or 800/942–4042, WEB www.olympicpeninsula.org). **Port Angeles Visitor Center** (✉ 121 E. Railroad Ave., 98362, ☎ 360/452–2363, WEB www.portangeles.net).

LONG BEACH PENINSULA

Where the turbulent waters of the Pacific and the Columbia River clash, ever-shifting sandbanks present a threat to boats and ships of all sizes. Upriver from Astoria, the low, densely vegetated islands are inhabited by only a few fishermen, but a hundred years ago, during the heyday of salmon fishing, the northern bank of the river was lined with canneries and boat docks. Only a 3½-hour drive southwest of Seattle and 2 hours northwest of Portland, the small beach towns of the Long Beach Peninsula have been among the regions's favorite weekend getaways for more than a century. There's still a lot of open space, and there's no development directly on the beach. The peninsula separates the Pacific Ocean and Willapa Bay and is known for excellent bird-watching, beachcombing, hiking, and dining.

Exploring Long Beach Peninsula

U.S. 101 crosses the broad Columbia River between Astoria, Oregon, and Megler, Washington, on a long bridge, which starts out as a high, graceful span and soon drops down to a low-level elevated roadway that barely skims the surface of the river. Signs will tell you that the bridge runs to "Megler, WA," but don't look for that former cannery town. It vanished decades ago. A few miles downriver, on Route 103, is **Ilwaco,** a small fishing community of about 1,000.The **Ilwaco Heritage Museum** (✉ 115 S.E. Lake St., ☎ 360/642–3446; 🎫 $2) uses dioramas to present the history of southwestern Washington.

A couple of miles south of Ilwaco is the **Cape Disappointment Lighthouse,** first used in 1856 and one of the oldest lighthouses on the West Coast. The cape was named by John Meares, an English trader in 1788 in honor of his unsuccessful attempt to find the mouth of the Columbia River (and a rich, new source of furs).

Fort Canby State Park (✉ Robert Gray Dr., ☎ 360/642–3078, WEB www.fortcanby.org), 3 mi west of Ilwaco, off U.S. 101, was an active military installation until 1957, when it was turned over to the Washington State Parks and Recreation Commission. Now it is best known for great views of the Columbia River Bar during winter storms. The **Lewis & Clark Interpretive Center** (✉ Robert Gray Dr., ☎ 360/642–3029; 🎫 free) documents the 8,000-mi round-trip journey of the famous pair, from Wood River, Illinois, to the mouth of the Columbia.

The town of **Long Beach** has beach activities and an old-fashioned amusement park with go-carts and bumper cars. About halfway up the peninsula is **Ocean Park,** the region's commercial center.A few miles north of Ocean Park is **Oysterville,** established as an oystering town in 1854. When the native shellfish were fished to extinction, a Japanese oyster was introduced. The town never made a comeback as a commercial center, but the village's old homes, schoolhouse, and church have been beautifully preserved. Maps inside the vestibule of the restored **Oysterville Church** direct you through town, which is now on the National Register of Historic Places.At the northern tip of the peninsula is **Leadbetter Point State Park** (✉ Robert Gray Dr., 2 mi south of Ilwaco, 98624, ☎ 360/642–3078), an excellent spot to view coastal birds.

Dining and Lodging

Ilwaco

$ 🏨 **The Inn at Ilwaco.** This B&B is set in a renovated New England–style church. The cozy guest accommodations—most of them upstairs in the old Sunday-school rooms—have eyelet or printed chintz curtains and coverlets. ✉ *120 Williams Ave. NE, 98624,* ☎ *360/642–8686 or 888/244–2523,* WEB *www.longbeachlodging.com. 9 rooms. MC, V.*

Nahcotta

$–$$ 🏨 **Moby Dick Hotel and Oyster Farm.** This small, historic 1930s inn sits on spacious grounds above the Willapa Bay shoreline at the "quiet and peaceful" end of the peninsula. The Moby Dick has eight guest rooms, wildflower and organic gardens, and a separate bayside sauna pavilion. A restaurant serves dinner by reservation. ✉ *25814 Sandridge Rd. (Box 82, 98627),* ☎ *360/665–4543,* FAX *360/665–6887,* WEB *www.nwplace.com/mobydick.html. 8 rooms. Restaurant. AE, D, MC, V.*

Seaview

$$–$$$ ✕ **Shoalwater Restaurant.** The dining room at the Shelburne Inn serves seafood brought in straight from the fishing boats, as well as mushrooms and salad greens gathered from the peninsula's woods and gardens. ✉ *Pacific Hwy. and N. 45th St.,* ☎ *360/642–4142. AE, D, MC, V.*

$$ ★ ✕ **42nd Street Cafe.** Chef Cheri Walker spent more than a decade honing her skills at the Shoalwater Restaurant before opening her own place, which is now by far the best restaurant on the peninsula. Her fare, focusing on seafood, is inspired, original, and reasonably priced. In 1999, Walker was nominated for a James Beard Award. ✉ *Rte. 103 and 42nd St.,* ☎ *360/642–2323. MC, V.*

$ ✕ **My Mom's Pie Kitchen.** Fresh blackberry, banana-cream, chocolate-almond, and sour cream–raisin are among the pie varieties you'll find in this cozy restaurant inside a Victorian house. Also on the menu are clam chowder and quiche. Hours vary, so call ahead. ✉ *4316 S. Pacific Hwy.,* ☎ *360/642–2342. MC, V. No dinner.*

$$ **Shelburne Inn.** This bright and cheerful antiques-filled inn built in 1896, complete with a pub, is on the National Register of Historic Places. It is also right on the highway; the quietest rooms are on the west side. ✉ *4415 Pacific Way (Box 250, Seaview 98644),* ☎ *360/642–2442 or 800/466–1896,* FAX *360/642–8904,* WEB *www.theshelburneinn.com. 18 rooms. Restaurant. AE, MC, V.*

$ **Sou'wester.** Choose from rooms and apartments in a historic lodge, in cabins, or in classic mobile-home units. The lodge was built in 1892 as the summer retreat of a wealthy businessman and politician from Portland. ✉ *Beach Access Rd., 38th Pl. (Box 102, 98644),* ☎ *360/642–2542,* WEB *www.souwesterlodge.com. 9 rooms, 6 with bath; 4 cabins; 10 trailers. D, MC, V.*

Campgrounds

You can camp at △ **Fort Canby State Park** (✉ 3 mi west of Ilwaco, off U.S. 101, ☎ 360/642–3078, WEB www.fortcanby.org).

Outdoor Activities and Sports

Fishing

Salmon, rock cod, lingcod, flounder, perch, sea bass, and sturgeon are plentiful. There are tackle shops all over Long Beach Peninsula, and most sell fishing licenses for about $7. The **Department of Fisheries and Wildlife** (☎ 360/902–2200) can provide information about the very complex regulations governing salmon, steelhead, and saltwater fishing in the region.

Pacific Salmon Charters (✉ Box 519, 98624, ☎ 800/831–2695, WEB www.pacificsalmoncharters.com) can accommodate up to 120 people on guided trips six to eight hours long. The clamming season varies depending on the supply; for details call the **Shellfish Lab: Nahcotta Field Station** (☎ 360/665–4166).

Golf

Peninsula Golf Course (✉ 9604 Pacific Hwy., ☎ 360/642–2828) has 9 holes at the north end of Long Beach. **Surfside Golf Course** (✉ 31508 Jay Pl., ☎ 360/665–4148), 2 mi north of Ocean Park, has 9 holes.

Hiking

There are hiking trails at **Fort Canby** and **Leadbetter Point** state parks.

Shopping

The **Bookvendor** (✉ 101 Pacific Ave., Long Beach, ☎ 360/642–2702) stocks children's books, classics, travel books, and an excellent selection of local history titles. **North Head Gallery** (✉ 600 S. Pacific Ave.,

Long Beach, ☏ 360/642–8884) has a large selection of Elton Bennett originals and Bennett, plus works from other Northwest artists.

Long Beach Peninsula

CAR TRAVEL

Long Beach is accessible from the east via Route 4, which connects with I–5 near Longview, and from the north and south via U.S. 101.

VISITOR INFORMATION

➤ Tourist Information: **Visitors Bureau** (✉ intersection of U.S 101 and Rte. 103, Seaview 98631, ☏ 360/642–2400 or 800/451–2542, WEB www.funbeach.com).

ELSEWHERE IN WASHINGTON

The San Juan Islands

The wooded knobs, rocky cliffs, and pebble beaches of the San Juan Islands provide a sunny reprieve to rain-weary mainlanders. While many rocky islets barely rise above high tide, the lofty hills of the larger islands rise to a height of more than 2,000 ft. Hike the backcountry trails, paddle among the tidal rocks in a seaworthy kayak, go on a whale-watching cruise, or just sit quietly on a grassy outcropping and watch the eagles circle overhead. Lopez, Orcas, and San Juan all have many excellent bed-and-breakfasts.

What to See and Do

Lopez Island, with its old orchards, weathered barns, and sheep and cow pastures, inspires peaceful walks through woods and over beaches. Tiny **Shaw Island,** where Franciscan nuns in traditional habits run the ferry dock, is a good place to fish. **Orcas,** a large, mountainous horseshoe-shape island with marvelous hilltop views, is home to accomplished artists and several good restaurants. **San Juan Island**'s active waterfront town of Friday Harbor attracts the most visitors. Friday Harbor's **Whale Museum** (✉ 62 1st St. N, ☏ 360/378–4710, WEB www.whalemuseum.com; 🎫 $4) is the world's leading orca research institution. Exhibits depict the challenges facing Puget Sound's three killer whale pods.

Dining and Lodging

$$–$$$ ★ ✕ **Christina's.** Some of the best salmon entrées in Washington compete with romantic water views for your attention at this Orcas Island favorite. *✉ N. Beach Rd. and Horseshoe Hwy., Eastsound, ☏ 360/376–4904. AE, D, DC, MC, V. Closed Tues.–Wed. Oct.–Apr.*

$$–$$$ ✕ **Springtree Café.** Chef James Boyle plans a daily menu around fresh seafood and organic Waldron Island produce. Try the Caesar salad made with tofu instead of eggs, followed by king salmon in pesto sauce or ginger shrimp with mango and rum. *✉ 310 Spring St., Friday Harbor, ☏ 360/378–4848. AE, MC, V. Closed Tues.–Thurs.*

$$$–$$$$ ✕🏨 **Friday Harbor House.** Perched on a bluff overlooking the town's harbor, this sleek modern inn has elegant rooms with light wood trim, Jacuzzi tubs, fireplaces, and splendid views. The restaurant is a leading practitioner of Northwest contemporary cuisine. *✉ 130 West St., Friday Harbor 98250, ☏ 360/378–8455, FAX 360/378–8453, WEB www.fridayharborhouse.com. 18 rooms. AE, MC, V. CP.*

$$$ ✕🏨 **Roche Harbor Village.** San Juan Island's biggest and snazziest resort has its own harbor marina, a condominium complex, hiking and biking trails, and a historic 1888 hotel, which has hosted Teddy Roosevelt, John Wayne, and other luminaries. *✉ 248 Reuben Memorial*

Dr., Roche Harbor 98250, ☎ 360/378–2155 or 800/451–8910, FAX 360/378–6809, WEB www.rocheharbor.com. 57 rooms. Restaurant, tennis. AE, MC, V. BP.

$–$$ **Turtleback Farm.** Looking out over a pastoral valley, this restored 19th-century farmhouse, with its clear-fir floors and Victorian furnishings, is the essence of tranquillity. Breakfast is made from farm-raised produce such as local eggs, sausage, and fruit. ✉ *1981 Crow Valley Rd., Eastsound 98245, ☎ 360/376–4914 or 800/376–4914, WEB www.turtlebackinn.com. 12 rooms. AE, MC, V. BP..*

$–$$ **Edenwild.** This large, gray Victorian-style farmhouse is surrounded by gardens and framed by Fisherman's Bay. The boldly painted rooms are airy; some have fireplaces. ✉ *Eades La. at Lopez Village Rd., Lopez Island 98261, ☎ 360/468–3238, FAX 360/468–4080, WEB www.edenwildinn.com. 8 rooms. D, MC. BP.*

The San Juan Islands Essentials

AIR TRAVEL

From Seattle-Tacoma International Airport, Harbor Airlines flies to San Juan Island. Kenmore Air flies sea planes from Lake Union in Seattle to the San Juan Islands. West Isle Air flies to San Juan Island from Anacortes, Bellingham, and Seattle.

➤ AIRLINES AND CONTACTS: **Harbour Airlines** (☎ 800/359–3220, WEB www.harbour-air.com). **Kenmore Air** (☎ 425/486–1257 or 800/543–9595, WEB www.kenmoreair.com). **West Isle Air** (☎ 360/293–4691 or 800/874–4434, WEB www.westisleair.com).

BOAT AND FERRY TRAVEL

The Washington State Ferry System provides car and passenger service from Anacortes, about 90 mi north of Seattle, to the San Juan Islands. The San Juan Islands Shuttle Express provides daily passenger service from Bellingham to Orcas Island and San Juan Island's Friday Harbor along with a lecture on the wildlife and natural history of the area. You can also take a three-hour whale-watching trip out of Friday Harbor.

The San Juan Island Commuter provides daily passenger service during the summer season from Bellingham to Orcas Island and San Juan Island's Friday Harbor and makes special drop-off and pick-up trips, on request, to *all* of the San Juan Islands, as far north as remote Sucia.

➤ BOAT AND FERRY INFORMATION: **San Juan Island Commuter** (✉ Alaska Ferry Terminal, 355 Harris Ave, Bellingham 98225, ☎ 360/734–8180 or 888/734–8180). **San Juan Islands Shuttle Express** (✉ Alaska Ferry Terminal, 355 Harris Ave., No. 105, Bellingham 98225, ☎ 888/373–8522 or 360/671–1137).**Washington State Ferry System** (☎ 206/464–6400 or 800/843–3779).

CAR TRAVEL

By car from Seattle, drive north on I–5 to La Conner; go west on Route 534 to Route 20 and follow signs to Anacortes; then pick up the ferry for the San Juan Islands.

VISITOR INFORMATION

➤ TOURIST INFORMATION: **San Juan Islands Visitor Information Service** (✉ Box 65, Lopez Island 98261, ☎ 360/468–3663 or 888/468–3701, WEB www.guidetosanjuans.com).

Yakima Valley

What to See and Do

Aside from the views of 12,688-ft Mt. Adams to the south and 14,411-ft Mt. Rainier to the west, the main attractions are the dozens of small wineries. Some of the best known are **Hogue Cellars, Château Ste.**

Michelle, and Covey Run Winery. The **Yakima Valley Wine Growers Association** (☎ 509/786–1304) publishes maps of the region and a brochure that lists wineries with tasting-rooms and tours.

Dining and Lodging

$ ✕ **Grant's Brewery Pub.** North America's oldest brewpub is a Yakima institution. Burgers, salads, and sandwiches complement the suds daily, and there's live jazz on weekends. ✉ *32 N. Front St., Yakima,* ☎ *509/575–2922. AE, MC, V.*

$$ ★ **Birchfield Manor.** The only true luxury accommodation in the valley sits on a perfectly flat plateau, surrounded by fields and grazing cattle. The Old Manor House has four rooms upstairs and a contemporary Pacific Northwest restaurant downstairs; naturally, the Yakima Valley wine list is extensive. A cottage next door has a country flavor and modern conveniences such as TVs, whirlpool tubs, steam-sauna showers, and gas fireplaces. ✉ *2018 Birchfield Rd., Moxee City 98901,* ☎ *509/452–2334 or 800/375–3420,* FAX *509/452–2334,* WEB *www.birchfieldmanor.com. 11 rooms. AE, DC, MC, V. CP or BP..*

Yakima Valley Essentials

AIRPORTS

Yakima has a small airport with limited service from Seattle, Spokane, and Portland on Horizon Air.

➤ CONTACT: **Yakima Airport Travel Services** (☎ 509/575–0292).

BUS TRAVEL

Greyhound buses stop in Yakima, Toppenish, Sunnyside, Wapato, and Prosser.

CAR TRAVEL

The Yakima valley encompasses the lower course of the Yakima River, from Union Gap to its junction with the Columbia River at Richland/Kennewick. It is traversed by I–82, which branches off I–90 at Ellensburg and runs south from Kennewick to the Columbia River (it merges into I–84 in Oregon). The drive from Seattle to Yakima via I–90 and I–82 is about 150 mi and takes about 1½ hours (Snoqualmie Pass slows things down).

VISITOR INFORMATION

➤ TOURIST INFORMATION: **Yakima Valley Visitor and Convention Bureau** (✉ 10 N. 8th St., Yakima 98901–2515, ☎ 509/575–3010 or 800/221–0751, WEB www.visityakima.com).

Spokane

Spokane (pronounced spo-*can*) takes its name from a local Indian tribe, the "Children of the Sun." Indeed, Spokane is aptly named, for the city has more than its share of sunny days. The "Capital of the Inland Empire," a city of about 500,000, radiates outward from the falls of the Spokane River. It is a city of parks and beautiful mansions, educational institutions, and performing arts.

What to See and Do

In town the main attraction is **Riverfront Park** (✉ 507 N. Howard St., ☎ 509/625–4386), 100 acres covering several islands in the Spokane River, including a spectacular waterfall. The U.S. Pavilion houses an IMAX theater, a skating rink (winters only), and exhibition space. At the southern edge of the park, the 1909 carousel hand-carved by master builder Charles Looff is a local landmark. In sharp architectural contrast to Riverfront Park's Expo '74 building is the tall stone clock tower of the (demolished) 1902 **Great Northern Railroad Station,** close to the center of the park near Washington Street.

Two miles south on Grand Boulevard at 18th Avenue, **Manito Park** has a formal English garden, a conservatory, rose and perennial gardens, a Japanese garden complete with ponds stocked with koi, and a duck pond. It's a pleasant place to stroll in summer; in winter bring ice skates for a turn or two on the frozen duck pond.

Dining and Lodging

$$–$$$ ✕ **Clinkerdagger's.** In a building that housed a flour mill in Spokane's early days, Clinks, as it's known locally, has a fine view of the Spokane River and Riverfront Park to the south. There might be four or five specials when fresh seafood is available. ✉ *621 W. Mallon Ave.,* ☎ *509/328–5965. AE, D, DC, MC, V.*

$$–$$$ ✕ **Luna.** Luna's seasonal cuisine has strong southwestern and Californian influences. The focus on fruits and vegetables makes sense—the building was once a produce market. ✉ *5620 S. Perry St.,* ☎ *509/448–2383. AE, D, MC, V.*

$$–$$$ ★ ✕ **Patsy Clark's.** One of Spokane's finest mansions—complete with Italian marble, wood carvings and clocks, and a Tiffany stained-glass window—is a suitably elegant place to dine on Continental cuisine. Entrées might include veal medallions stuffed with wild mushrooms, prosciutto, and spinach, then doused with blackberry port demiglace. ✉ *2208 W. 2nd Ave.,* ☎ *509/838–8300. AE, D, DC, MC, V.*

$$ 🏨 **West Coast Grand Hotel at the Park.** This hotel's greatest asset is its location, adjacent to Riverfront Park and two blocks from the downtown shopping district. All five floors in the main building open onto the spacious atrium lobby; more guest rooms are in two newer wings. ✉ *303 W. North River Dr., 99201,* ☎ *509/326–8000 or 800/325–4000,* FAX *509/325–7329,* WEB *www.westcoasthotels.com. 402 rooms. 2 restaurants, pool, gym. AE, D, DC, MC, V.*

The Arts

Interplayers Ensemble (✉ 174 S. Howard St., ☎ 509/455–7529) is a professional theater company with productions from October through June. Call ☎ 509/747–2787 for more listings. The **Spokane Symphony,** under the direction of Brazilian-born conductor Fabio Mechetti, plays a season of classical and pops concerts from September to April in the Opera House (✉ 601 W. Riverside Dr., ☎ 509/624–1200).

Outdoor Activities and Sports

Just 30 mi east of Spokane on I–90 is Idaho's **Lake Coeur d'Alene** (☎ 208/664–3194, WEB www.coeurdalene.org), which has fishing, camping, hiking, water sports, and resort accommodations. A walking path named the Centennial Trail flanks the Spokane River continuously from west of downtown Spokane to east of Coeur d'Alene.

GOLF

The most challenging Spokane golf course is the 18-hole **Creek at Qualchan** (✉ 301 E. Meadow La., ☎ 509/448–9317).

SKIING

Skiers flock to **Mt. Spokane** (✉ Rte. 206, 31 mi north of Spokane, ☎ 509/238–6281; 509/238–6845 for cross-country ski area), which holds the modest **49 Degrees North** (✉ U.S. 395, 58 mi north of Spokane near Chewelah, ☎ 509/935–6649) downhill resort and 11 mi of groomed cross-country ski trails. A state Sno-Park pass, available at the resort and numerous outlets throughout the state, is required at the cross-country ski areas.

SPECTATOR SPORTS

Baseball: Spokane Indians (✉ Seafirst Stadium, Broadway and Havana St., ☎ 509/535–2922). **Hockey: Spokane Chiefs** (✉ Spokane Arena, 701 Mallon Ave., at N. Howard St., ☎ 509/328–0450).

Spokane Essentials

AIRPORTS

Spokane International Airport is served by Horizon, Northwest, Alaska, Delta, and United airlines.

➤ CONTACT: **Spokane International Airport** (✉ 9000 W. Airport Dr., ☎ 509/455–6455).

BUS AND TRAIN TRAVEL

Greyhound and Amtrak both serve Spokane.

CAR TRAVEL

By car Spokane can be reached by I–90 (east–west), by U.S. 195 from the south, by U.S. 395 from the south and the north, and by U.S. 2 from the west and the east.

VISITOR INFORMATION

➤ TOURIST INFORMATION: **Spokane Area Convention & Visitors Bureau** (✉ 801 W. Riverside, Suite 301, 99201, ☎ 509/624–1341 or 888/776–5263, WEB www.visitspokane.com).

The Palouse

What to See and Do

The Palouse is rich in Northwest history. The Lewis and Clark expedition passed through in 1805, and in 1836 missionary Marcus Whitman built a medical mission 7 mi west of present-day Walla Walla. A band of Cayuse Indians massacred Whitman and more than a dozen other settlers in 1847; the **Whitman Mission National Historic Site** (✉ off U.S. 12, 7 mi west of Walla Walla, ☎ 509/529–2761, WEB www.nps.gov/whmi) marks the spot. Nearby **Fort Walla Walla Park** (✉ 755 Myra Rd., ☎ 509/525–7703) has 14 historic buildings and a pioneer museum.

The U.S. Calvary lost an important battle to Nez Percé Indians on the site of the **Steptoe Battlefield,** north of Pullman on U.S. 195 near Rosalia. On U.S. 12 between Colfax and Walla Walla, **Dayton** is worth a stop just to see the impressive 88 Victorian buildings listed on the National Register of Historic Places. A brochure with two self-guided walking tours of Dayton is available from the **Dayton Chamber of Commerce** (✉ 166 E. Main St., ☎ 509/382–4825, WEB www.daytonwa.com).

History buffs can take a walking or bicycle tour of **Walla Walla,** one of the earliest settlements in the Inland Northwest. Maps are available from the Chamber of Commerce (✉ 29 E. Sumach St., 99362, ☎ 509/525–0850 or 877/998–4748, WEB www.wwchamber.com). **Pioneer Park** (✉ E. Alder St.), which has a fine aviary, was landscaped by the sons of Frederick Law Olmsted, who designed New York City's Central Park.

In winter, skiers head southeast of Walla Walla to the Blue Mountains, to **Ski Bluewood** (✉ Touchet River Rd., 21 mi south of Dayton, ☎ 509/382–4725), for downhill and snowboarding. Just north of the confluence with the Snake River, the **Palouse River** gushes over a basalt cliff higher than Niagara Falls and drops 198 ft into a steep-walled basin. Surefooted hikers venture to the overlook above the falls, which are at their fastest during spring runoff in March.

Dining and Lodging

$$$ ✕ **Paisano's.** This Italian mainstay has the largest wine inventory in Walla Walla, with local vineyards well represented. Breads and desserts are baked fresh daily. ✉ *26 E. Main St., Suite 1, Walla Walla,* ☎ *509/527–3511. MC, V. Closed Sun.*

$$ **Green Gables Inn.** A 1909 Craftsman-style mansion houses this lovely B&B. Rooms are have terrycloth robes and cable TV. A full breakfast is served by candlelight on antique china. ✉ *922 Bonsella St., Walla Walla, 99362,* ☎ *509/525–5501 or 888/525–5501,* WEB *www.greengablesinn.com. 5 rooms. AE, D, MC, V. BP.*

The Palouse Essentials

AIRPORTS

Pullman has a small airport that it shares with Moscow, Idaho, 8 mi to the east, with limited service from Lewiston, Idaho.

➤ CONTACT: **Pullman-Moscow Regional Airport** (✉ 3200 Airport Complex North, Pullman, ☎ 509/334–4555).

BUS TRAVEL

Greyhound buses stop in Pullman and Walla Walla.

➤ BUS INFORMATION: **Greyhound** (800/231–2222, www.greyhound.com).

CAR TRAVEL

From Spokane drive south on U.S. 195 to Pullman, or at Colfax take Route 26, Route 127, and then U.S. 12 to Walla Walla.

VISITOR INFORMATION

➤ TOURIST INFORMATION: **Pullman Chamber of Commerce** (✉ 415 N. Grande Ave., 99163, ☎ 509/334–3565, WEB www.pullman-wa.com). **Walla Walla Chamber of Commerce** (✉ 29 E. Sumach St., 99362, ☎ 509/525–0850 or 877/998–4748, WEB www.wwchamber.com).

WASHINGTON, D.C.

By John F. Kelly

Updated by Kathy McCabe

Population	598,000
Motto	Justice to All
Official Bird	Wood thrush
Official Flower	American Beauty rose

Washington, the District of Columbia, was founded in 1791 as the world's first planned national capital. It's a city of architectural splendors and unforgettable memorials, where the striking image of the Washington Monument is never far from sight and the stirring memories of a young democratic republic are never far from mind. Of course, the capital's attractions are more than monumental and governmental. Washington's world-class museums, shady parks, and vibrant arts scene make it an American showcase.

Exploring Washington, D.C.

The major museums that make up the Smithsonian Institution surround the vast lawn known as the Mall. The U.S. Capitol stands watch at the eastern end, while the Washington Monument is to the west. The White House is just a stone's throw away, as are the Jefferson Memorial and the Lincoln Memorial. Unless noted, museums and monuments in the city are free. Since virtually every major sight is appropriate to visit with kids, child-friendly attractions are not specifically noted.

The Mall

The first museum built by the Smithsonian was architect James Renwick's Norman-style **Castle** (☒ 1000 Jefferson Dr. SW, ☎ 202/357–2700 all Smithsonian museums, WEB www.si.edu). Today the impressive red-stone structure houses the Smithsonian Information Center. It's a great place to start your visit, as you can watch a film on the various Smithsonian offerings and read about the day's special events.

A clutch of Smithsonian museums surrounds the Castle. The **Freer Gallery of Art** (☒ 12th St. and Jefferson Dr. SW) is a repository of Asian works. It's also known for the Peacock Room, a stunning dining room decorated by painter James McNeill Whistler. The **Arthur M. Sackler Gallery** (☒ 1050 Independence Ave. SW) houses a collection of works from China, India, Thailand, and Indonesia. An underground tunnel connects it to the Freer Gallery. The **National Museum of African Art** (☒ 950 Independence Ave. SW) is dedicated to the traditional arts of sub-Saharan Africa. The beautiful **Arts and Industries Building** (☒ 900 Jefferson Dr. SW), east of the Castle, is decorated in High Victorian style. Inside are rotating exhibits of photography.

Walking counterclockwise around the Mall, you'll come first to the cylindrical **Hirshhorn Museum and Sculpture Garden** (☒ 7th St. and Independence Ave. SW, WEB www.hirshhorn.si.edu), which exhibits modern art indoors and sculpture in its outdoor garden.

★ Attracting more than 9 million visitors each year, the **National Air and Space Museum** (☒ Jefferson Dr. at 6th St. SW, WEB www.nasm.si.edu) holds 23 galleries that tell the story of aviation, from the earliest attempts at flight to travels beyond the solar system. Sensational IMAX films are shown on the five-story screen of the museum's Langley Theater, while images of celestial bodies are projected on a domed ceiling in the Albert Einstein Planetarium.

Washington, D.C.
WASHINGTON NAT'L. CATHEDRAL
NATIONAL ZOOLOGICAL PARK
ADAMS-MORGAN
DUMBARTON OAKS
Phillips Collection
DUPONT CIRCLE
Dupont Circle
Sheridan Circle
Rock Creek
Scott Circle
Thomas Circle
National Geographic Society's Explorer Hall
GEORGE-TOWN
C&O CANAL
Washington Circle
FOGGY BOTTOM
FARRAGUT NORTH
FARRAGUT WEST
Hay-Adams Hotel
St. John's Episcopal Church
McPHERSON SQUARE
National Museum of Women in the Arts
Decatur House
Lafayette Square
Renwick Gallery
Blair House
Old Executive Office Building
Treasury Building
Octagon House
The White House
Corcoran Gallery of Art
Hotel Washington
Willard Hotel
Commerce Dept Bldg.
National Aquarium
Memorial Continental Hall (DAR Museum)
The Ellipse
FEDERAL TRIANGLE
Vietnam Veterans Memorial
Vietnam Women's Memorial
National Museum of American History
Washington Monument
ARLINGTON NATIONAL CEMETERY
Lincoln Memorial
Reflecting Pool
Korean War Veterans Memorial
U.S. Holocaust Memorial Museum
SMITHSONIAN
Memorial Bridge
Independence Ave.
Kutz Bridge
West Potomac Park
Ohio Dr.
W. Basin Dr.
Tidal Basin
Potomac River
FDR Memorial
Outlet Bridge
Jefferson Memorial
Columbia Island
NW
SW
N
California St.
Massachusetts Ave.
Florida Ave.
New Hampshire Ave.
Connecticut Ave.
Rhode Island Ave.
Pennsylvania Ave.
New York Ave.
Virginia Ave.
Constitution Ave.
T St.
S St.
R St.
Decatur Pl.
Corcoran St.
Q St.
Church St.
P St.
O St.
N St.
M St.
L St.
K St.
I St.
H St.
G St.
F St.
E St.
D St.
C St.
29th St.
28th St.
27th St.
26th St.
25th St.
24th St.
23rd St.
22nd St.
21st St.
20th St.
19th St.
18th St.
17th St.
16th St.
15th St.
14th St.
29
50
66
1
395

SHAW/HOWARD U.
NW
NE
T St.
S St.
R St.
Q St.
P St.
O St.
N St.
M St.
L St.
Vermont Ave.
Rhode Island Ave.
Florida Ave.
New Jersey Ave.
Lincoln Rd.
NATIONAL ARBORETUM
9th St.
3rd St.
1st St.
12th St.
11th St.
10th St.
8th St.
7th St.
6th St.
5th St.
4th St.
New York Ave.
North Capitol St.
Massachusetts Ave.
Mt. Vernon Square
MT. VERNON
I St.
H St.
G St.
E St.
D St.
C St.
National Portrait Gallery
GALLERY PLACE
Nat'l Building Museum
International Spy Museum
CHINA-TOWN
JUDICIARY SQUARE
UNION STATION
Ford's Theatre
J. Edgar Hoover FBI Building
2nd St.
Columbus Memorial Fountain
Navy Memorial
ARCHIVES / NAVY MEMORIAL
Louisiana Ave.
Pennsylvania Ave.
National Archives
Supreme Court
National Museum of Natural History
National Gallery of Art
U.S. Capitol
Smithsonian Castle/ Information Center
THE MALL
E. Capitol St.
Jefferson Dr.
National Air and Space Museum
Maryland Ave.
U.S. Botanic Garden
Library of Congress (Jefferson Bldg)
Independence Ave.
Arts and Industries Bldg.
Hirshhorn Museum
Arthur M. Sackler Gallery
National Museum of African Art
Freer Gallery of Art
Canal St.
L'ENFANT PLAZA
Folger Shakespeare Library
FEDERAL CENTER S.W.
CAPITOL SOUTH
Dep't of Trans.
Southwest Fwy.
G St.
Virginia Ave.
FRED. DOUGLASS NAT'L. HIST. SITE
0
500 yards
500 meters
Washington Navy Yard
PENTAGON
SW
SE

★ Standing on the north side of the Mall, the two buildings of the **National Gallery of Art** (✉ Madison Dr. and 4th St. NW, ☎ 202/737–4215, WEB www.nga.gov) hold more than 100 galleries. Architect John Russell Pope's elegant **West Building,** punctuated by a dramatic dome, presents masterworks of Western art from the 13th to the 20th century, including pieces by Rembrandt, Rubens, Dalí, and Degas. I. M. Pei's angular **East Building,** with its stunning interior spaces, shows modern works by artists like Rothko and Warhol.

A favorite with kids, the **National Museum of Natural History** (✉ Madison Dr. between 9th and 12th Sts. NW, WEB www.mnh.si.edu) is filled with bones and fossils—more than 124 million specimens. Especially popular are the fearsome creatures in Dinosaur Hall, the Hope Diamond, and a sea-life display with a living coral reef.

The mammoth **National Museum of American History** (✉ Madison Ave. between 12th and 14th Sts. NW, WEB www.americanhistory.si.edu) traces the social, political, and technological history of the United States. Here you'll find a 280-ton steam locomotive, a collection of first ladies' inaugural gowns, and Julia Child's kitchen.

★ The **United States Holocaust Memorial Museum** (✉ 15th St. and Independence Ave. SW, ☎ 202/488–0400, WEB www.ushmm.org) tells the story of the 11 million Jews, Gypsies, homosexuals, political prisoners, and others killed by the Nazis between 1933 and 1945. There are documentary films, taped oral histories, and a collection that includes a freight car used to transport prisoners to a concentration camp. Arrive early (by 9 AM to be safe) to get free tickets for the same day. Advance tickets are available through **Protix** (☎ 703/218–6500 or 800/400–9373, WEB www.tickets.com) for a small service charge.

The **Bureau of Engraving and Printing** is the birthplace of all paper currency in the United States. Although there are no free samples, the 40-minute guided tour—which takes you past presses that turn out $696 million worth of currency a day—is one of the city's most popular. ✉ *14th and C Sts. SW,* ☎ *202/874–3019,* WEB *www.bep.treas.gov. Closed weekends.*

The Monuments

The tallest of the city's structures is the **Washington Monument** (✉ Constitution Ave. at 15th St. NW, ☎ 202/426–6840, WEB www.nps.gov/wamo/home.htm), a 555-ft obelisk started in 1848. Because the Civil War and other events caused delays, there's a slight change in color about a third of the way up. Pick up free tickets at the kiosk on 15th Street for the elevator ride to the unrivaled view at the top.

★ The exquisite **Jefferson Memorial** (✉ south side of Tidal Basin, ☎ 202/426–6821, WEB www.nps.gov/thje), honoring America's third president, is set amid the cherry trees that line the Tidal Basin. One of the best views of the White House is from the top steps of the memorial, John Russell Pope's classical reinterpretation of the Pantheon in Rome.

★ Cherry trees, covered in pink and white blossoms each April, surround the approach to the **Lincoln Memorial** (✉ west end of the Mall, ☎ 202/426–6895, WEB www.nps.gov/linc). Henry Bacon's monument is considered one of the most moving spots in the city, its mood set by Daniel Chester French's statue of the seated president gazing over the adjacent reflecting pool. The memorial served as a backdrop for Martin Luther King Jr.'s "I Have a Dream" speech in 1963.

Adjacent to the Lincoln Memorial is the **Korean War Veterans Memorial** (✉ west end of the Mall, ☎ 202/426–6895, WEB www.nps.gov/kwvm), with its 19 statues of soldiers reflected in a black granite wall bearing the inscription "Freedom Is Not Free."

★ The **Vietnam Veterans Memorial** (✉ 23rd St. and Constitution Ave. NW, ☎ 202/634–1568, WEB www.nps.gov/vive), a V-shape slab of black granite designed by Maya Lin, is another landmark that encourages introspection. The names of more than 58,000 Americans who died in Vietnam are etched in stone. The adjacent **Vietnam Women's Memorial** was dedicated on Veterans' Day 1993 and sits southeast of the Vietnam Veterans Memorial.

The **Franklin Delano Roosevelt Memorial** (✉ west side of Tidal Basin, ☎ 202/619–7222, WEB www.nps.gov/fdrm), dedicated in 1997, is a 7½-acre tribute to the 32nd president. Four outdoor galleries—each symbolizing one of his four terms as president—are set among waterfalls and reflecting pools.

The President's Neighborhood

★ The **White House,** one of the world's most famous residences, governs Pennsylvania Avenue. The building was designed by Irishman James Hoban, who drew upon the Georgian design of Leinster Hall, in Dublin, and other Irish country houses. After the terrorist attacks of September 2001, public tours of the White House were suspended. Phone ahead for up-to-date information. ✉ *1600 Pennsylvania Ave. NW,* ☎ *202/619–7222; 202/456–7041 recorded information;* WEB *www.whitehouse.gov. Closed Sun.–Mon.*

Next door to the White House, the French Empire–style **Old Executive Office Building** (✉ 17th St. and Pennsylvania Ave. NW) houses the vice president's ceremonial office (he also has one in the west wing of the White House) and those of others in the executive branch.

Lafayette Square is an intimate oasis in the midst of downtown Washington. This quiet park served as a campsite for soldiers of both the War of 1812 and the Civil War—in full view of presidents Madison and Lincoln across the way in the White House. At the top of the square, golden-domed **St. John's Episcopal Church** (✉ 16th and H Sts. NW, ☎ 202/347–8766) is also known as the Church of the Presidents.

The first floor of the Federal-style **Decatur House** (✉ 748 Jackson Pl. NW, ☎ 202/842–0920, WEB www.decaturhouse.org; 🎫 $4) is decorated as it was when occupied by naval hero Stephen Decatur in 1819. A green canopy marks the entrance to **Blair House** (✉ 1651 Pennsylvania Ave.), the residence used by visiting heads of state. Flags from their respective countries fly from the outside lampposts when these dignitaries are in town.

While most of the Smithsonian museums are on the Mall, the **Renwick Gallery** (✉ Pennsylvania Ave. and 17th St. NW, ☎ 202/357–2531, WEB americanart.si.edu) is near the White House. Dedicated to the decorative arts, it holds exquisite glass and porcelain pieces. Upstairs is the Grand Salon, restored to its original 1870s splendor.

Washington's largest nonfederal art museum is the impressive **Corcoran Gallery of Art.** Its collection ranges from works by early American artists to late-19th- and early 20th-century paintings from Europe. A highlight is the 18th-century Grand Salon from the Hôtel d'Orsay in Paris. ✉ *17th St. and New York Ave. NW,* ☎ *202/639–1700,* WEB *www.corcoran.org.* 🎫 *Donation requested. Closed Tues.*

Despite its name, the **Octagon** actually has six sides. The Treaty of Ghent, ending the War of 1812, was signed in an upstairs study. The building now houses the museum of the American Architectural Foundation, with exhibits relating to architecture, decorative arts, and Washington history. ✉ *1799 New York Ave. NW,* ☎ *202/638–3105.* 🎫 *$3. Closed Mon.*

The **Treasury Building** (✉ 15th St. and Pennsylvania Ave. NW, ☎ 202/622–0896, WEB www.ustreas.gov/curator/tours.htm), once used as a repository for currency, is the largest Greek Revival edifice in Washington. Inside are the Andrew Johnson suite, which he used as the executive office while Mrs. Lincoln moved out of the White House, and the two-story marble cash room. At this writing, tours are suspended.

The well-known magazine comes to life at the **National Geographic Society's Explorers Hall** (✉ 17th and M Sts. NW, ☎ 202/857–7588, WEB www.nationalgeographic.com). Interactive exhibits teach about geography, weather, and the planets. The centerpiece is a hand-painted globe, 11 ft in diameter, that floats and spins on a cushion of air.

Capitol Hill

Pierre L'Enfant, the French designer of Washington, called Capitol Hill (then known as Jenkins Hill) "a pedestal waiting for a monument." ★ That monument is the **U.S. Capitol,** the gleaming white-dome building in which elected officials toil. George Washington laid the cornerstone on September 18, 1793, and in November 1800 Congress moved here from Philadelphia. It contains some of the city's most inspiring art, from Constantino Brumidi's *Apotheosis of Washington,* the fresco at the center of the dome, to the splendid Statuary Hall. There are also live attractions: senators and representatives speechifying in their respective chambers. Timed-entry tickets, needed for Monday–Saturday 9:30–3:30 tours, are distributed at 8:15 [am]. ✉ *East end of the Mall,* ☎ *202/224–3121,* WEB *www.aoc.gov.*

After being shunted around several locations, including a spell in a tavern, the **Supreme Court** got its own building in 1935. The impressive white-marble temple, with twin rows of Corinthian columns, was designed by Cass Gilbert. ✉ *1st and E. Capitol Sts. NE,* ☎ *202/479–3000,* WEB *www.supremecourtus.gov. Closed weekends.*

East of the Capitol are the three buildings that make up the **Library of Congress** (✉ 1st St. and Independence Ave. SE, ☎ 202/707–8000, WEB www.loc.gov), which contains 115 million books and other documents. There are also manuscripts, prints, films, photographs, sheet music, and the largest collection of maps in the world. The opulent Jefferson Building, with its octagonal reading room and mahogany study tables, stands across from the Capitol.

Union Station (✉ 50 Massachusetts Ave. NE, WEB www.dcnrhs.org/union.htm) is now a sprawling shopping center as well as a train and subway station. The lovely Beaux Arts building's vast waiting room is the setting for the inaugural ball that's held here every four years.

The **Folger Shakespeare Library** holds a world-class collection of Shakespeareana. A gallery—resembling an Elizabethan great hall—hosts exhibits from the library's collection of works by and about the Bard. Plays by Shakespeare and others are often performed in a theater that calls to mind the Old Globe. ✉ *201 E. Capitol St. SE,* ☎ *202/544–4600,* WEB *www.folger.edu. Closed Sun.*

The **United States Botanic Garden** (✉ 1st St. and Maryland Ave. SW, ☎ 202/225–8333, WEB www.aoc.gov/pages/usbgpage.htm), south of the Capitol, is a peaceful plant-filled conservatory that includes a cactus house, a fern house, and a subtropical house filled with orchids.

Old Downtown and Federal Triangle

Before the glass office blocks around 16th and K streets NW became the business center of town, Washington's mercantile hub was farther east. The open-air markets are gone, but some of the 19th-century character of Washington's east end remains. In the 1930s the huge Federal

Triangle complex was built to accommodate the expanding federal bureaucracy.

The massive redbrick structure on F Street was constructed in the 1880s to house workers who processed the pension claims of veterans and their survivors. It currently holds the **National Building Museum** (✉ F St. between 4th and 5th Sts. NW, ☎ 202/272–2448, WEB www.nbm.org), devoted to architecture.

The **National Portrait Gallery** (✉ 8th and G Sts. NW, ☎ 202/357–2700) has a wonderful collection of paintings and photographs of presidents and other notable Americans. It is housed in the Old Patent Office Building. Currently closed for renovation, it is scheduled to reopen in 2004.

Ford's Theatre (✉ 511 10th St. NW, ☎ 202/426–6924, WEB www.fordstheatre.org), where Abraham Lincoln was assassinated by John Wilkes Booth in 1865, now includes a museum that displays items connected with Lincoln's life and untimely death.

The Declaration of Independence, the Constitution, and the Bill of Rights are on display in the rotunda of the **National Archives** (✉ Constitution Ave. between 7th and 9th Sts. NW, ☎ 202/501–5000, WEB www.nara.gov). Other objects in the vast collection include Richard Nixon's resignation letter and the rifle Lee Harvey Oswald used to assassinate John F. Kennedy.

When it was completed in 1899, the Romanesque **Old Post Office Pavilion** (✉ Pennsylvania Ave. and 12th St. NW, ☎ 202/289–4224) was the largest government building in the city, the first with a clock tower, and the first with an electric power plant. Today it holds an assortment of shops and restaurants inside the airy central courtyard.

The **International Spy Museum** (✉ 800 F St. NW, ☎ 202/393–7798, WEB www.spymuseum.org; 🎫 $10) has the largest collection of espionage artifacts ever put on public display. See Enigma, the legendary WWII German cipher machine, and a shoe transmitter used by Soviet spies.

The **National Museum of Women in the Arts** (✉ 1250 New York Ave. NW, ☎ 202/783–5000, WEB www.nmwa.org) displays the works of prominent female artists from the Renaissance to the present, including Georgia O'Keeffe, Mary Cassatt, and Judy Chicago.

Georgetown

At one time a tobacco port, this poshest of Washington neighborhoods is where you'll find the homes of some of its wealthiest citizens. It's also the nucleus of the district's nightlife scene, with dozens of hot spots near the crossroads at Wisconsin Avenue and M Street.

Downhill from the main bustle of Georgetown, the **Chesapeake & Ohio Canal** (✉ 1057 Thomas Jefferson St. NW, ☎ 202/653–5190) allows for a scenic getaway from the streets. Dug in the 19th century as an alternative to the rough, rocky Potomac, it transported lumber, coal, iron, and flour into northwest Maryland. Runners now tread its scenic towpath, and in summer mule-drawn barges ply its placid waters.

Georgetown University (✉ 37th and O St., ☎ 202/687–0100), the oldest Jesuit school in the country, has its campus at the western edge of the neighborhood. When seen from the Potomac or from Washington's high ground, the Gothic spires of the university's older buildings look like a town from the Middle Ages.

Dumbarton Oaks, an estate where you'll find two museums—one of Byzantine works, the other of pre-Columbian art—is surrounded by

10 acres of stunning formal gardens. *Museums:* ✉ *1703 32nd St. NW,* ☎ *202/339–6401.* 🎫 *$1. Closed Mon. Gardens:* ✉ *31st and R Sts. NW,* WEB *www.doaks.org.* 🎫 *$4*

Other Attractions

At **Arlington National Cemetery** (✉ west end of Memorial Bridge, Arlington, ☎ 703/607–8052, WEB www.arlingtoncemetery.org) you can trace America's history through the aftermath of its battles. Dominating the cemetery is the Greek Revival Arlington House, onetime home of Robert E. Lee, which offers a breathtaking view across the Potomac to the Lincoln Memorial and the Mall. On a hillside below, John F. Kennedy is buried under an eternal flame. The Tomb of the Unknowns is also in the cemetery.

North of Arlington Cemetery is the **United States Marine Corps War Memorial,** honoring marines who have given their lives. The memorial statue, sculpted by Felix W. de Weldon, is based on Joe Rosenthal's Pulitzer Prize–winning photograph of six soldiers raising a flag atop Iwo Jima's Mt. Suribachi on February 19, 1945.

The **Pentagon** (✉ off I–395, Arlington, ☎ 703/695–1776, WEB www.defenselink.mil/pubs/pentagon), headquarters of the Department of Defense, is an exercise in immensity: 23,000 military and civilian employees work here. It's as wide as three Washington Monuments laid end to end; and inside it contains 685 drinking fountains, 7,748 windows, and 17½ mi of corridors. Tours have been suspended indefinitely.

Thanks to the events that took place on the night of June 17, 1972, the **Watergate** (✉ 2600 Virginia Ave.) is possibly the world's most notorious apartment complex. Within its curving lines and behind its "toothpick" balusters have lived some of Washington's most famous—and infamous—citizens, including Alan Cranston, Bob and Elizabeth Dole, and, more recently, Monica Lewinsky.

★ The **Frederick Douglass National Historic Site** (✉ 1411 W St. SE, ☎ 202/426–5961; 🎫 $3) is at Cedar Hill, the Washington home of the noted abolitionist. The house displays mementos from Douglass's life and has a wonderful view across the Anacostia River.

The **Phillips Collection** was the first permanent museum of modern art in the country. Holdings include works by Braque, Cézanne, Klee, and Matisse. Don't miss Renoir's *Luncheon of the Boating Party.* ✉ *1600 21st St. NW,* ☎ *202/387–2151,* WEB *www.phillipscollection.org.* 🎫 *$6.50. Closed Mon.*

It took 83 years to complete the Gothic Revival **Washington National Cathedral** (✉ Wisconsin and Massachusetts Aves. NW, ☎ 202/537–6200, WEB www.cathedral.org), the sixth-largest cathedral in the world. Besides flying buttresses, a nave, transepts, and rib vaults that were built stone by stone, it is adorned with fanciful gargoyles.

Parks, Gardens, and Zoos

The 444-acre **National Arboretum** (✉ 3501 New York Ave. NE, ☎ 202/245–2726) blooms with all manner of plants; clematis, peonies, rhododendrons, and azaleas are among its showier inhabitants. The National Bonsai Collection, National Herb Garden, and an odd and striking hilltop construction of old marble columns from the U.S. Capitol are also well worth seeing.

The 160-acre **National Zoological Park** (✉ 3001 Connecticut Ave. NW, ☎ 202/673–4800, WEB www.natzoo.si.edu) is one of the top zoos in the world. Innovative compounds show animals in naturalistic settings, and the ambitious Amazonia re-creates the ecosystem of a South American rain forest. Its most famous residents are a pair of giant pandas, Mei Xiang and Tian Tian, who arrived from China in 2001.

Rock Creek Park (✉ park starts at P St. on edge of Georgetown and runs along both sides of creek all the way to the Maryland border; ☎ 202/426–6829) is a cool sliver of green jutting down into the center of the city. Its 1,800 acres include picnic sites and trails that wend through groves of dogwood, beech, oak, and cedar.

Dining

As the nation's capital, Washington hosts visitors from around the world. This infusion of cultures means that D.C. restaurants are getting better and better (and, sometimes, cheaper and cheaper, as more of the top spots now offer reasonably priced fare). Good ethnic meals can be found in Adams-Morgan (lots of Ethiopian), Georgetown (Afghan to Indonesian), and Chinatown.

$$$$ ★ ✕ **Citronelle.** The essence of California chic, Citronelle's glass-front kitchen lets you see all the action as chefs scurry to and fro. Try the loin of venison, served with an endive tart and garnished with dried apples. ✉ *3000 M St. NW,* ☎ *202/625–2150. AE, DC, MC, V.*

$$$$ ★ ✕ **Galileo.** The Piedmontese-style cooking here is deceptively simple: the veal chop might be served with mushroom-and-rosemary sauce, the beef with black-olive sauce and polenta. Several nights a week, watch owner Roberto Donna work magic in his restaurant-within-a-restaurant, Laboratorio da Galileo. ✉ *1110 21st St. NW,* ☎ *202/293–7191. AE, D, DC, MC, V. No lunch weekends.*

$$$$ ★ ✕ **Vidalia.** The namesake onions are a specialty at this elegant eatery, but there's also new American cuisine that revolves around the best seasonal fruits, vegetables, and seafood. Don't miss the roasted onion soup with spoon bread or the shrimp on yellow grits. ✉ *1990 M St. NW,* ☎ *202/659–1990. AE, D, DC, MC, V. No lunch weekends.*

$$–$$$$ ✕ **Occidental Grill.** In the stately Willard Hotel, this popular restaurant serves up innovative dishes amid photos of politicians and other power brokers past and present. The menu changes frequently, but you can count on grilled poultry, fish, and steak, as well as salads and sandwiches. ✉ *1475 Pennsylvania Ave. NW,* ☎ *202/783–1475. AE, MC, V.*

$$–$$$ ✕ **Bistro Bis.** Housed in the slick George Hotel, this modern bistro prepares French classics with American flair. For entrées, try roasted chicken, veal stew, or Moroccan lamb. The desserts, including traditional tarts, are good. ✉ *15 E St. NW,* ☎ *202/661–2700. AE, D, DC, MC, V.*

$$–$$$ ★ ✕ **City Lights of China.** Always on the critics' lists, this Chinese restaurant serves excellent traditional dishes. Less common specialties, such as lamb in a tangy peppery sauce, are also deftly prepared. Jumbo shrimp with spicy salt are baked in their shells, then stir-fried with ginger and spices. ✉ *1731 Connecticut Ave. NW,* ☎ *202/265–6688. AE, D, DC, MC, V.*

$$–$$$ ✕ **Georgia Brown's.** This "new South" eatery catering to local politicians serves shrimp Carolina-style (with the head on and steaming grits on the side) and beef tenderloin medallions with a bourbon-pecan sauce. Fried green tomatoes get the gourmet treatment. ✉ *950 15th St. NW,* ☎ *202/393–4499. AE, DC, MC, V. No lunch Sat.*

$$–$$$ ✕ **Lauriol Plaza.** This longtime favorite serves Latin American, Cuban, and Spanish dishes—ceviche, paella, fajitas, and so on—to enthusiastic crowds. Rustic entrées such as *lomo saltado* (Peruvian-style strip steak with onions, tomatoes, and fiery jalapeño peppers) are specialties. The dining room can get noisy, but the roof terrace offers an airy alternative in good weather. ✉ *1835 18th St. NW,* ☎ *202/387–0035. AE, D, DC, MC, V.*

$$–$$$ ✕ **Pizzeria Paradiso.** This petite pizzeria sticks to crowd-pleasing basics like *panini* (small sandwiches with fillings such as Italian cured ham and sun-dried tomatoes and basil). Although the standard pizza is satisfying, you can enliven things by ordering unusual toppings like potatoes, capers, and mussels. ✉ *2029 P St. NW,* ☎ *202/223–1245. DC, MC, V.*

$$–$$$ ✕ **Two Quail.** One of the city's most romantic settings, this quaint dining room serves hearty fare—Muscovy duck, pork loin, chicken stuffed with corn bread and pecans, and filet mignon. ✉ *320 Massachusetts Ave. NE,* ☎ *202/543–8030. AE, D, DC, MC, V. No lunch weekends.*

$–$$$ ✕ **Peacock Café.** This sleek, modern Georgetown eatery draws a crowd because it has something for most everyone, including a full-service bar and a juice bar. Try the famous vegetarian chili or one of the sandwiches named after a movie star (the Shirley Temple, for instance, contains mozzarella and provolone cheeses, with tomato, alfalfa sprouts and olive oil on your choice of bread). ✉ *3251 Prospect St. NW,* ☎ *202/625–2740. AE, MC, V.*

$$ ★ ✕ **Bombay Club.** A block from the White House, this Indian restaurant tries to re-create a private club like those established by 19th-century Brits. The menu includes unusual seafood specialties and a large number of vegetarian dishes, but the real standouts are the breads and the seafood appetizers. ✉ *815 Connecticut Ave. NW,* ☎ *202/659–3727. AE, DC, MC, V. No lunch Sat.*

$–$$ ★ ✕ **Meskerem.** Head straight for the balcony where you can eat Ethiopian style: seated on leather floor cushions with large woven baskets for tables. Stews are served on *injera,* a spongy sourdough bread. Diners use extra bread to scoop up the tangy offerings. ✉ *2434 18th St. NW,* ☎ *202/462–4100. AE, DC, MC, V.*

$ ✕ **Ben's Chili Bowl.** Long before U Street became hip, Ben's was offering chili on hot dogs, chili on half-smoked sausages, chili on burgers, and just plain chili. With its faux-marble bar and shiny red vinyl stools, it doesn't look like much has changed since the '50s. ✉ *1213 U St. NW,* ☎ *202/667–0909. No credit cards.*

$ ✕ **Burma.** Batter-fried eggplant and squash are deliciously paired with peppery sauces at this exquisite Chinatown restaurant. Such entrées as mango pork, tamarind fish, and Kokang chicken are equally satisfying. ✉ *740 6th St. NW,* ☎ *202/638–1280. AE, D, DC, MC, V. No lunch weekends.*

$ ✕ **Teaism.** A novel counterpoint to all the area's coffee bars, Teaism offers not only an impressive selection of more than 50 teas but also delicious Japanese, Indian, and Thai finger food. ✉ *2009 R St. NW,* ☎ *202/667–3827. AE, MC, V.*

Lodging

Many hotels, particularly those downtown, offer special reduced rates and package deals on weekends, so be sure to ask before you book. **Capitol Reservations** (☎ 202/452–1270 or 800/847–4832, WEB www.capitolreservations.com) and **Washington D.C. Accommodations** (☎ 202/289–2220 or 800/554–2220, WEB www.wdcahotels.com) book rooms discounts of 20%–40% off listed rates at many hotels.

To find reasonably priced accommodations in small guest houses and private homes, contact **Bed & Breakfast Accommodations** (✉ Box 12011, 20005, ☎ 202/328–3510, FAX 202/332–3885, WEB www.bedandbreaskfastdc.com). Another company booking rooms at small inns is the **Bed & Breakfast League** (✉ Box 9490, 20016-9490, ☎ 202/363–7767, FAX 202/363–8396).

$$$$ ★ **Four Seasons Hotel.** With impeccable service and a wealth of wonderful amenities, this contemporary hotel is a perennial favorite among celebrities. The quieter rooms face the courtyard; others have a view of the C&O Canal. ✉ *2800 Pennsylvania Ave. NW, 20007,* ☎ *202/342–0444,* FAX *202/944–2076,* WEB *www.fourseasons.com/washington. 262 rooms. 2 restaurants, pool, health club. AE, D, DC, MC, V.*

$$$$ ★ **Hay-Adams Hotel.** Across from the White House, this Italian Renaissance–style landmark is a common choice for important policy-making meetings. Its elegance extends to guest rooms, where you'll find European and Asian antiques. ✉ *1 Lafayette Sq., 20006,* ☎ *202/638–6600 or 800/424–5054,* FAX *202/638–2716,* WEB *www.hay-adams.com. 143 rooms. Restaurant. AE, D, DC, MC, V.*

$$$–$$$$ ★ **St. Regis.** Gilded ornamental ceilings and Louis XVI furnishings make the St. Regis resemble an Italian mansion. A few blocks from the White House, this landmark offers cordial, dignified service, including day and night butler service. ✉ *923 16th St. NW, 20006,* ☎ *202/638–2626 or 800/325–3535,* FAX *202/638–4231. 193 rooms. Restaurant, gym. AE, D, DC, MC, V.*

$$$–$$$$ **Topaz Hotel.** With a promise to "transcend the everyday," this trendy hotel has rooms decorated in vibrant colors and exotic textures. There are offbeat extras, such as morning power drinks. The Topaz Bar is one of the hipper, louder establishments in Dupont Circle. ✉ *1733 N St. NW, 20036,* ☎ *202/393–3000,* FAX *202/785–9851,* WEB *www.topazhotel.com. 99 rooms. Restaurant. AE, D, DC, MC, V.*

$$$–$$$$ ★ **Westin Fairfax.** Once an apartment building, this intimate hotel in the heart of Dupont Circle may be best known as former vice president Al Gore's childhood home. Rooms in the stately building have views of Embassy Row. ✉ *2100 Massachusetts Ave. NW, 20008,* ☎ *202/293–2100 or 800/325–3589,* FAX *202/835–0641,* WEB *www.westin.com. 209 rooms. Restaurant, gym. AE, DC, MC, V.*

$$$–$$$$ ★ **Willard Inter-Continental.** Popular with travelers who expect nothing less than perfection, the Willard has long been a favorite of presidents and visiting dignitaries. This opulent Beaux Arts building is a feast for the eyes, especially the great columns, huge chandeliers, and elaborately carved ceilings in the main lobby. The service is superb. ✉ *1401 Pennsylvania Ave. NW, 20004,* ☎ *202/628–9100,* FAX *202/637–7326,* WEB *www.washington.interconti.com. 340 rooms. 2 restaurants, health club. AE, D, DC, MC, V.*

$$–$$$$ **Latham Hotel.** In one of the city's liveliest neighborhoods, this neo-colonial hotel is popular with diplomats. Rooms are sleek and contemporary. Some are underground, while others have views of the tranquil C&O Canal or busy M Street. The polished brass and glass lobby leads to Citronelle, one of Washington's best restaurants. ✉ *3000 M St. NW, 20007,* ☎ *202/726–5000,* FAX *202/337–4250,* WEB *www.thelatham.com. 143 rooms. Restaurant, pool. AE, D, DC, MC, V. CP.*

$$–$$$ **Holiday Inn on the Hill.** You can expect clean, comfortable rooms in this hotel near Union Station. The hotel offers the same magnificent vistas of the Capitol as the pricier Hyatt Regency. Children under 18 stay free. ✉ *415 New Jersey Ave. NW, 20001,* ☎ *202/638–1616 or 800/638–1116,* FAX *202/638–0707,* WEB *www.holiday-inn.com. 342 rooms. Restaurant, pool. AE, D, DC, MC, V. CP.*

$$–$$$ **Washington Courtyard by Marriott.** One of the city's best values, this hotel is a good choice for international tourists and business travelers. Many of the rooms have excellent views of the skyline because of the hotel's location on upper Connecticut Avenue. ✉ *1900 Connecticut Ave. NW, 20009,* ☎ *202/332–9300 or 800/842–4211,* FAX *202/328–7039,* WEB *www.courtyard.com. 147 rooms. Restaurant, pool, health club. AE, D, DC, MC, V.*

$–$$$ **Tabard Inn.** Three Victorian town houses near Dupont Circle were linked in the 1920s to form this quirky little inn. Furnishings are broken-in Victorian and American Empire antiques; a Victorian-inspired carpet cushions the labyrinthine hallways. ✉ *1739 N St. NW, 20036,* ☎ *202/785–1277,* FAX *202/785–6173,* WEB *www.tabardinn.com. 40 rooms, 25 with bath. Restaurant. AE, DC, MC, V. CP.*

$–$$ ★ **Jurys Normandy Inn.** This European-style hotel on a quiet street is near restaurants, shops, and many stately embassies. Rooms are neat and comfortable. ✉ *2118 Wyoming Ave. NW, 20008,* ☎ *202/483–1350 or 800/424–3729,* FAX *202/387–8241,* WEB *www.jurys.com/usa/normandy.htm. 75 rooms. AE, D, DC, MC, V. CP.*

Nightlife and the Arts

Area arts and entertainment events are listed in the "Weekend" section of Friday's *Washington Post,* in the free weeklies *City Paper* and the gay-oriented *Washington Blade,* and in the monthly magazine *Washingtonian.*

Nightlife

No matter where you're staying, there's probably a bar or club nearby. Georgetown, Adams-Morgan, Dupont Circle, and Capitol Hill are the main nightlife centers in D.C.

BARS

The **Brickskeller** (✉ 1523 22nd St. NW, ☎ 202/293–1885) sells more than 700 brands of beer—from Central American lagers to U.S.-microbrewed ales. Hipsters relax on sofas and sip sangria at **Chi Cha Lounge** (✉ 1624 U St. NW, ☎ 202/234–8400).

The **Dubliner** (✉ Phoenix Park Hotel, 520 N. Capitol St. NW, ☎ 202/737–3773) serves up thick and tasty Guinness as Irish musicians perform. **JR.'s Bar & Grill** (✉ 1519 17th St. NW, ☎ 202/328–0090) is where gay men come for cocktails and conversation.

JAZZ

Blues Alley (✉ Rear, 1073 Wisconsin Ave. NW, ☎ 202/337–4141, WEB www.bluesalley.com) books some of the biggest names in jazz.

ROCK

The **Black Cat** (✉ 1831 14th St. NW, ☎ 202/667–7960, WEB www.blackcatdc.com) rocks almost every night. The **9:30 Club** (✉ 815 V St. NW, ☎ 202/393–0930, WEB www.930.com) books an eclectic mix of artists, mostly playing alternative rock.

The Arts

All manner of cultural events, from ballet to classical music, are offered at the **John F. Kennedy Center for the Performing Arts** (✉ New Hampshire Ave. and Rock Creek Pkwy. NW, ☎ 202/467–4600 or 800/444–1324, WEB www.kennedycenter.org). **TicketPlace** (✉ Old Post Office Pavilion, 1100 Pennsylvania Ave. NW, ☎ 202/842–5387) sells half-price day-of-performance tickets; it's closed Sunday and Monday. **Ticketmaster** (☎ 202/432–7328 or 800/551–7328, WEB www.ticketmaster.com) takes phone charges for events around the city.

DANCE

Dance Place (✉ 3225 8th St. NE, ☎ 202/269–1600) brings the most eclectic dance troupes to town. The **Washington Ballet** (☎ 202/362–3606) performs at the Kennedy Center and other venues.

MUSIC

The **National Symphony Orchestra** (☎ 202/416–8100, WEB www.nationalsymphony.org) performs at the Kennedy Center's Concert

Hall from September to June. The **Washington Opera** (☎ 202/295–2420, WEB www.dc-opera.org) presents eight lavish operas each season in the Kennedy Center's Opera House. The legendary Placido Domingo is the opera's artistic director and headlines at least one of the offerings each season.

THEATER

With three theaters, **Arena Stage** (✉ 6th St. and Maine Ave. SW, ☎ 202/488–3300, WEB www.arenastage.org) is the city's most respected resident company. The historic **Ford's Theatre** (✉ 511 10th St. NW, ☎ 202/347–4833 box office, WEB www.fordstheatre.org) hosts mainly musicals. The **National Theatre** (✉ 1321 Pennsylvania Ave. NW, ☎ 202/628–6161, WEB www.nationaltheatre.org) presents tryouts and national touring companies of Broadway shows. The **Shakespeare Theatre** (✉ 450 7th St. NW, ☎ 202/547–1122, WEB www.shakespearedc.org) presents classics. The **Warner Theater** (✉ 1299 Pennsylvania Ave. NW, ☎ 202/783–4000, WEB www.warnertheater.com), a restored 1920s movie house, hosts everything from stand-up comedy to theatrical dramas.

Spectator Sports

Basketball

The **Wizards** (☎ 202/432–7328 or 202/628–3200) play downtown at the MCI Center. Since Michael Jordan came out of retirement to play for the team, tickets have been hard to come by. The **Mystics** (☎ 202/628–3200 or 202/432–7328) are a women's team that plays from late May to August. The games are also at the MCI Center.

Football

The NFL **Redskins** (☎ 301/276–6050) are now based at Jack Kent Cooke Stadium in nearby Landover, Maryland. There are about 20,000 more seats than at the team's old home at RFK Stadium, but all tickets are held by season-ticket holders. If you're willing to pay dearly, you can get tickets from brokers who advertise in the *Washington Post.*

Hockey

If you like your sports on ice, the **Capitals** (☎ 202/432–7328 or 202/628–3200) play at the MCI Center.

Shopping

Shopping Districts

Georgetown (around Wisconsin Ave. and M St. NW) is probably Washington's densest shopping area, with boutiques selling everything from antiques to designer fashions. In bohemian **Adams-Morgan** (around 18th St. and Columbia Rd. NW) you'll find used-book stores and vintage-clothing shops. **Dupont Circle** (around Connecticut Ave. and Q St. NW) is a great place for books and records.

Shopping Malls

The **Shops at Georgetown Park** (✉ 3222 M St. NW, ☎ 202/298–5577) is where you'll find such high-ticket stores as J. Crew and Ralph Lauren. The **Shops at National Place** (✉ 13th and F Sts. NW, ☎ 202/662–1250) is a glittering collection of stores, including B. Dalton, Filene's Basement, and Casual Corner. **Union Station** (✉ 50 Massachusetts Ave. NE, ☎ 202/371–9441) has clothing boutiques and special-interest shops. **Mazza Gallerie** (✉ 5300 Wisconsin Ave. NW, ☎ 202/966–6114) is an upscale mall anchored by a ritzy Neiman Marcus store. Across the street from Mazza Gallerie is **Chevy Chase Pavilion** (✉ 5335 Wisconsin Ave. NW, ☎ 202/686–5335), with a selection of equally elegant stores.

Washington, D.C., Essentials

AIRPORTS AND TRANSFERS

Ronald Reagan Washington National Airport, 4 mi south of downtown Washington, has scheduled flights by most major domestic carriers. Many transcontinental and international flights arrive at Dulles International Airport, a modern facility 26 mi west of Washington. Baltimore–Washington International Airport is about 25 mi northeast of D.C.

➤ AIRPORT INFORMATION: **Baltimore–Washington International Airport** (☎ 410/859–7100, WEB www.bwiairport.com). **Dulles International Airport** (☎ 703/572–2700, WEB www.metwashairports.com/dulles). **Ronald Reagan Washington National Airport** (☎ 703/417–8000, WEB www.metwashairports.com/national).

AIRPORT TRANSFER

Ronald Reagan Washington National Airport is a convenient 20-minute Metro ride from the city center ($1.10 or $1.40, depending on the time of day). Cab fare to downtown averages $13, including tip.

Bus service is provided to Reagan National by Metrobus and to Dulles by the Washington Flyer. SuperShuttle offers service to National, Dulles, and BWI.

➤ TAXIS AND SHUTTLES: **Metrobus** (☎ 202/637–7000, WEB www.wmata.com). **SuperShuttle** (☎ 800/258–3826, WEB www.supershuttle.com). **Washington Flyer** (☎ 703/685–1400, WEB ww.washfly.com).

BUS TRAVEL TO AND FROM WASHINGTON, D.C.

Greyhound and Peter Pan Trailways have adjoining terminals on Capitol Hill, north of Union Station.

➤ BUS INFORMATION: **Greyhound** (✉ 1005 1st St. NE, ☎ 800/231–2222, WEB www.greyhound.com). **Peter Pan Trailways** (✉ 1000 1st St. NE, ☎ 800/343–9999, WEB www.peterpanbus.com).

CAR TRAVEL

I–95 approaches Washington from the north and south, skirting east of the city as part of the Capital Beltway. I–495 is the western loop of the Beltway. I–395 connects D.C. with the Beltway to the south. Connecticut Avenue is the best approach from the north, dropping down from the Beltway in Maryland.

PARKING

Parking in Washington is an adventure. There's free, three-hour parking around the Mall on Jefferson Drive and Madison Drive, but good luck grabbing a spot! You can also park free—in some spots all day—in areas south of the Lincoln Memorial, on Ohio and West Basin drives in West Potomac Park. Private lots charge up to $4 an hour.

TRAFFIC

A car can be a drawback in D.C. Traffic is horrendous, especially at rush hours (6:30 AM–9:30 AM and 3:30 PM–7 PM), and one-way and diagonal streets can make the city seem like a maze.

TAXIS

Taxis in D.C. operate on a zone system, with a one-zone fare of $5. There are charges for extra passengers as well as rush-hour surcharges, so ask the driver for the total fare before you depart. Two major companies are Capitol Cab and Diamond Cab. Maryland and Virginia taxis are metered and cannot take you between points within D.C.

➤ TAXI COMPANIES: **Capitol Cab** (☎ 202/546–2400). **Diamond Cab** (☎ 202/387–6200).

TOURS

BUS TOURS

Gray Line Tours offers a four-hour tour of Washington and Arlington National Cemetery; four-hour tours of Mount Vernon and Alexandria; and a combination of both. Buses from Old Town Trolley Tours and Tourmobile take routes around the city's major attractions, allowing you to get on and off as often as you like.

➤ FEES AND SCHEDULES: **Gray Line Tours** (☎ 301/386–8300, WEB www.graylinedc.com). **Old Town Trolley Tours** (☎ 301/985–3021, WEB www.trolleytours.com). **Tourmobile** (☎ 202/554–7950 or 202/554–5100, WEB www.tourmobile.com).

WALKING TOURS

Not a specific walking route but groups of sites within historic neighborhoods, the Black History National Recreation Trail illustrates aspects of African-American history in Washington, from slavery days to the New Deal. A brochure is available from National Park Service.

➤ FEES AND SCHEDULES: **National Park Service** (✉ 1100 Ohio Dr. SW, 20242, ☎ 202/619–7222).

TRAIN TRAVEL

Amtrak trains pull into Union Station, on Massachusetts Avenue near the Capitol.

➤ TRAIN INFORMATION: **Amtrak** (☎ 800/872–7245, WEB www.amtrak.com).

TRANSPORTATION AROUND WASHINGTON, D.C.

Washington's best-known sights are a short walk—or a short Metro ride—from one another. The Washington Metropolitan Area Transit Authority provides Metrorail and Metrobus service in D.C. and the Maryland and Virginia suburbs. The base rail fare is $1.10. The final fare depends on the time of day and the distance you travel. All bus rides within D.C. are $1.10; a $5 Metro Tourist Pass entitles you to one day of unlimited subway travel weekdays from 9:30 AM to midnight or all day any weekend or holiday.

➤ CONTACT: **Washington Metropolitan Area Transit Authority** (☎ 202/637–7000, WEB www.wmata.com).

VISITOR INFORMATION

Dial-A-Park is a daily recording of events at National Park Service attractions.

➤ TOURIST INFORMATION: **Dial-A-Park** (☎ 202/619–7275). **Washington Convention and Tourism Corporation** (✉ 1212 New York Ave. NW, 6th floor, 20005, ☎ 202/789–7000, FAX 202/789–7037, WEB www.washington.org).

WEST VIRGINIA

Updated by Deanna Wrenn

Capital	Charleston
Population	1,808,000
Motto	Mountaineers Are Always Free
State Bird	Cardinal
State Flower	Rhododendron maximum
Postal Abbreviation	WV

Statewide Visitor Information

West Virginia Division of Tourism (✉ 90 MacCorkle Ave. SW, Charleston 25305, ☎ 304/558–2200 or 800/225–5982, FAX 304/558–0108, WEB www.callwva.com).

Scenic Drives

In the eastern mountains a **National Scenic Byway** (W. Va. 39/55 and connecting W. Va. 150) roams between Richwood and U.S. 219/W. Va. 55 north of Edray, in the Monongahela National Forest. The **Midland Trail** follows historic U.S. 60, running east–west for 120 mi between White Sulphur Springs and Charleston, tracing the 200-year-old path through the Appalachians first used by Native Americans. The **Coal Heritage Trail** begins at Chimney Corner and continues through Beckley, Sophia, Mullens, and into Bluefield.

National and State Parks

National Parks

Harpers Ferry National Historical Park (✉ Box 50, Harpers Ferry 25425, ☎ 304/535–6298, WEB www.nps.gov/hfc; 💵 $2 per day, 7-day pass $5) is at the picturesque confluence of the Potomac and Shenandoah rivers. The **New River Gorge National River** (✉ Box 246, Glen Jean 25846, ☎ 304/465–0508, WEB www.nps.gov/neri), a 53-mi section of the New River, contains some of America's best white-water recreation. The **Monongahela National Forest** (✉ 200 Sycamore St., Elkins 26241, ☎ 304/636–1800, WEB www.fs.fed.us/r9/mnf) draws 3 million people annually to explore 909,000 acres of backwoods trails among more than 50 rare or endangered species. The **George Washington National Forest** (✉ 109 Molineu Rd., Edinburg, VA 22824, ☎ 540/984–4101, WEB www.southernregion.fs.fed.us/gwj) encompasses 190,000 acres first surveyed by its namesake.

State Parks

Eight of West Virginia's 46 state parks, forests, and wildlife management facilities have fine lodges with restaurants and resort amenities, such as downhill skiing or championship golf courses. Most have cottages, cabins, and campsites with full hookups. **Cacapon Resort State Park** (✉ 818 Cacapon Lodge Dr., Berkeley Springs 25411, ☎ 304/258–1022 or 800/225–5982, WEB www.cacaponresort.com) is noted for its Robert Trent Jones golf course; amenities include 30 cottages and a 49-room lodge with restaurant. At **Canaan Valley Resort State Park** (✉ HC 70, Box 330, Davis 26260, ☎ 304/866–4121 or 800/622–4121, WEB www.canaanresort.com), the 250-room lodge, 23 deluxe cabins, restaurant, and lounge are bustling year-round; the park has an alpine-skiing area, ice-skating, an 18-hole golf course, and outdoor and indoor pools and a fitness center. **Pipestem Resort State Park** (✉ Box 150, Pipestem 25979, ☎ 304/466–1800 or 800/225–5982, WEB www.pipestemresort.com), southeast of Beckley, has two lodges (142 rooms) with restaurants, 26 deluxe cottages, and 82 campsites as well as golf, tennis, horseback riding, indoor and outdoor pools, an aerial tramway, cross-country skiing, and tobogganing.

EASTERN WEST VIRGINIA

West Virginia's easternmost counties are replete with captivating, yet largely unsung, evidence of colonial and Civil War history. The towns of Harpers Ferry, Berkeley Springs, Charles Town, Martinsburg, and Shepherdstown predate the Revolutionary War, bear the scars of the Civil War, and have remained largely untouched, architecturally, since the 1950s.

To the west the scene changes to one of rugged splendor. This swath of mountain land is blessed with Canadian weather patterns—and the ski industry to prove it. In spring the focus shifts to white-water rafting on some of the nation's most exciting rivers.

Exploring Eastern West Virginia

Old and new mingle here in surprising harmony. In one day in the eastern panhandle you can explore pre-Revolutionary buildings, shop for the latest fashions, and relax in a Roman bath. To the west and south, the mountain roads are scenic but sometimes narrow and limited to 40 mph. Do your driving by day to enjoy the many scenic overlooks and small towns.

★ At the panhandle's southeastern tip is **Harpers Ferry National Historical Park,** where the Shenandoah and Potomac rivers join. Hand-carved stone steps lead to the overlook where Thomas Jefferson proclaimed the view "worth a trip across the Atlantic." The township of Harpers Ferry grew around a U.S. armory built between 1798 and 1802, and many of its original buildings have been preserved. Lining the cobblestone streets are shops and museums, where park employees in period costume demonstrate Early American skills and interpret the evolution of American firearms. Each year on the second Saturday in October the park service stages Election Day 1860. Near the park, the **John Brown Wax Museum** (☎ 304/535–2792; 🎫 $2.50) depicts the abolitionist's raid on the town.

Charles Town, named for George Washington's brother, an early resident, is irrevocably linked with Harpers Ferry, for it is where John Brown (1800–59) was hanged for treason. The Jefferson County Courthouse here houses a museum that includes among its artifacts the wagon that delivered Brown to his fate on the courthouse square.

In **Martinsburg** two pre–Civil War roundhouses (circular buildings for housing and repairing locomotives) at the foot of Martin Street attract railroad buffs, though they're in poor condition. Downtown, there are antebellum structures in the Federal and Greek Revival styles on John, Race, and North Spring streets.

Shepherdstown, on the Potomac River northwest of Harpers Ferry, is one of the region's oldest towns, established in 1730 as Mechlenberg. Today its old-fashioned wooden storefronts and tree-lined brick streets are the framework for a collection of specialty shops, small inns, and restaurants that lure city folk from the Washington-Baltimore area.

Berkeley Springs was officially chartered in 1776 as the Town of Bath by George Washington and speculating friends, who envisioned the site of these ancient healing springs as a spa. The buoyant warm waters still flow freely, attracting a thriving community of massage therapists, homeopathic specialists, and artists. The small inns, antiques shops, spa retreats, and similar businesses make this a year-round haven for relaxation. **Berkeley Springs State Park** (✉ 121 S. Washington St., Berkeley Springs 26222, ☎ 304/258–2711 or 800/225–5982, WEB www.berkeleyspringssp.com) offers heated Roman baths and massages.

Potomac Eagle Scenic Rail Excursions (✉ 1 mi north of Romney on W.Va. 28, ☎ 800/223–2453, WEB www.wvweb.com/www/potomac_eagle; 🎟 $22–$49, depending on type of railcar and time of year) takes passengers in vintage railcars into the wilderness of the South Branch of the Potomac River, where bald-eagle sightings are common.

A southwesterly route leads through the Potomac Highlands—rich in ★ outdoor recreation—to the **National Radio Astronomy Observatory** (✉ Rte. 28/92, ☎ 304/456–2011, WEB www.gb.nrao.edu; 🎟 free), in Green Bank, where huge radio telescopes listen for life in outer space. Bus tours and a slide presentation are available, though tours must be arranged in advance from November through May.

Cass Scenic Railroad State Park encompasses an authentic early 1900s lumber town. Here you can take a tow up to Bald Knob, the second-highest peak in West Virginia. The open railcars were once used for hauling logs off the mountain. Trains are drawn by geared Shay steam locomotives, built at the turn of the 20th century to negotiate steep terrain. ✉ *Rte. 66, Cass,* ☎ *304/456–4300 or 800/225–5982,* WEB *www.cassrailroad.com.* 🎟 *$13–$17 weekdays, $15–$19 weekends. Closed Nov.–mid-May.*

The **Youth Museum of Southern West Virginia** (✉ New River Park [Box 1815, Beckley 25802], ☎ 304/252–3730; 🎟 $2) has a permanent village of reconstructed or relocated log structures that depict agricultural life in the area before the advent of mining.

The **Beckley Exhibition Coal Mine** (✉ New River Park [Box 2514, Beckley, 25802], ☎ 304/256–1747; 🎟 $10) has 1,500 ft of restored passages accessible by guided tours and is open April–October, with some additional holiday tours in December.

The **Lewisburg National Historic District** (✉ U.S. 219, ☎ 304/645–1000 or 800/833–2068, WEB www.greenbrierwv.com/lewisburg/lewisburg.html) encompasses 236 acres and more than 60 18th-century buildings, many of native limestone or brick. At night, gas lamps flicker on storefronts and signs—no overhead power lines spoil the image of a bygone era. Carnegie Hill's visitor center on Church Street can supply you with a map for a walking tour.

The mammoth **West Virginia State Fair** (✉ 3 mi south of I–64 on Rte. 219, Lewisburg, ☎ 304/645–1090, WEB www.wvstatefair.com; 🎟 $7) fills two weeks in August with livestock shows, harness racing, crafts, and entertainment. Master artists offer more than 200 classes in traditional music, dance, crafts, and folklore at the **Augusta Heritage Workshops** (✉ 100 Campus Dr., Elkins 26241, ☎ 304/637–1209), held at Davis & Elkins College. The engineering marvel of the **New River Gorge Bridge,** the world's longest steel arch span, is celebrated annually near Fayetteville on the third Saturday in October; more than 200 food and crafts vendors sell their wares while crowds watch parachutists leap hundreds of feet into the New River Gorge.

Dining and Lodging

Real West Virginia cooking is hearty, simple, and usually made from local ingredients—buckwheat cakes for breakfast, beef stew for lunch, brook trout or game for dinner—but more urbane fare is available. Local bed-

and-breakfasts (☎ 800/225–5982 for B&B listings and booklet) afford the best access to the state's greatest treasure: its hospitable people.

Berkeley Springs

$$$ ✕ **Country Inn.** As the name hints, you'll find an interior that makes use of lots of natural wood and old prints. The best entrée is the crab cakes. ✉ *207 S. Washington St.,* ☎ *304/258–2210 or 800/822–6630. AE, D, DC, MC, V.*

$–$$ ★ ✕🏨 **Coolfont Resort & Spectrum Spa.** Accommodations are in chalets, rustic cabins, or lodge rooms, and the spa offers programs to learn about nutrition, exercise, and stress reduction. In the restaurant ($$), the soup-salad-bread bar is exceptional, as is the daily buffet. ✉ *3621 Cold Run Valley Rd., 25411,* ☎ *304/258–4500 or 800/888–8768,* FAX *304/258–6314,* WEB *www.coolfont.com. 82 units. Restaurant, pool, tennis, health club. AE, D, DC, MC, V. MAP.*

$ ★ 🏨 **Cacapon Resort State Park.** Locally crafted heavy oak pieces furnish the guest rooms and woodsy dining room in the main lodge, which overlooks the golf course and Cacapon Ridge. Rustic cabins are tucked into the surrounding woods. ✉ *818 Cacapon Lodge Dr., off 522 (Box 230, 25411),* ☎ *304/258–1022,* FAX *304/258–5323,* WEB *www.cacaponresort.com. 48 rooms, 31 cabins. Restaurant, tennis. AE, MC, V.*

Davis

$–$$$ ✕ **Blackwater Falls State Park.** The park's stone-pillar dining room, furnished in handmade red oak, perches on the rim of the Blackwater Canyon. Favorites are the breakfast bar, charbroiled chicken breast, and locally caught rainbow trout. ✉ *Rte. 32 to Blackwater Falls State Park Rd.,* ☎ *304/259–5216,* FAX *304/259–5881,* WEB *www.blackwaterfalls.com. AE, MC, V.*

$–$$$ 🏨 **Canaan Valley Resort State Park.** The rooms here are motel style but spacious, and the location (surrounded by woods) is superb. Golf, downhill skiing, snowboarding, and ice-skating are popular activities. ✉ *HC 70, Box 330, 26260,* ☎ *304/866–4121 or 800/622–4121,* FAX *304/866–2172,* WEB *www.canaanresort.com. 250 rooms, 23 cabins. Restaurant, pools. D, DC, MC, V.*

Durbin

$$$–$$$$ ★ 🏨 **Cheat Mountain Club.** This 1887 spruce log cabin that once attracted notable outdoorsmen like Thomas Edison and Henry Ford now draws families and friends on retreats. Part of the 901,000-acre Monongahela National Forest surrounds the property, which is close to skiing, hiking, and mountain biking. The pine-panel guest rooms on the lodge's second floor are immaculately kept, and room rates include meals. The restaurant's three daily menus have hearty, homemade dishes; prime rib, local trout, and Cornish hens are typical dinner entrées. Vegetarian meals are also available. ✉ *Rte. 250 (Box 28, Durbin 26264),* ☎ *304/456–4627,* FAX *304/456–3192,* WEB *www.cheatmountainclub.com. 9 rooms, 5-bed dormitory. MC, V. FAP.*

Lewisburg

$–$$ ★ ✕🏨 **The General Lewis.** Dating from 1834, this inn is one of 60 historic structures in the Lewisburg National Historic District. After touring the town, you can relax in a rocking chair on the veranda; browse through the collection of antique tools, guns, household utensils, and musical instruments in Memory Hall; or head to the restaurant ($$) to feast on such local specialties as country ham and fried chicken. ✉ *301 E. Washington St., 24901,* ☎ *304/645–2600,* FAX *304/645–2601,* WEB *www.generallewisinn.com. 25 rooms. Restaurant. AE, D, MC, V.*

Shepherdstown

$–$$ ✕ **Bavarian Inn and Lodge.** In various alpine chalets overlooking the Potomac River and the gardens, the Bavarian has luxurious rooms with canopy beds, fireplaces, and whirlpool tubs. The dining areas are decorated with antiques and fine china. The German and American cuisine ($$–$$$) includes wild pheasant, venison, and elk. ✉ *Rte. 3 (Box 30, 25443),* ☎ *304/876–2551,* FAX *304/876–9355. 73 units. Restaurant, pool, tennis. AE, D, DC, MC, V.*

Snowshoe/Slatyfork

$$$ ★ ✕ **Red Fox Restaurant.** A cozy tavern room, plush seating, and greenhouse windows set this restaurant apart, as do its extensive menu and exceptional service. The chefs use local meats, fish, herbs, and cheeses in such specialties as wild game pâtés and roast quail cooked with apples, country ham, sausages, and applejack brandy. ✉ *No. 1 Whistlepunk, Snowshoe,* ☎ *304/572–1111,* FAX *304/572–2222. AE, D, MC, V.*

$$–$$$$ ★ **Snowshoe/Silver Creek Mountain Resort.** This gargantuan resort can accommodate up to 9,000. Lodging varies from motel-style rooms to luxury condos. Snowshoe has an assortment of natural-wood structures in the forest fringing the ski slopes; Silver Creek has rooms in a high-rise. ✉ *10 Snowshoe Dr., off U.S. 219, 26209,* ☎ *304/572–1000,* WEB *www.snowshoemtn.com. 1,250 houses and condos, 302 rooms. 9 restaurants, pools, tennis, gym. AE, MC, V.*

White Sulphur Springs

$$$$ ★ **The Greenbrier.** This 6,500-acre spa is decorated in grand turn-of-the-20th-century style. Massive white columns rise six stories against a white facade, and nine lobbies provide vast, chandeliered common areas. Every guest room is different, but all are decorated in Dorothy Draper pastel prints. The restaurants serve such dishes as farm-raised striped bass and rack of lamb. Horseback riding and golf are among the many activities available. ✉ *300 W. Main St., White Sulphur Springs 24986,* ☎ *304/536–1110 or 800/624–6070,* FAX *304/536–7854,* WEB *www.greenbrier.com. 739 units. 4 restaurants, pool, tennis, health club. AE, DC, MC, V.*

Motel

Holiday Inn (✉ 301 Foxcroft Ave., Martinsburg 25401, ☎ 304/267–5500 or 800/862–6282), 120 rooms; restaurant, pools, health club; *$$$.*

Campgrounds

State-park camping facilities and more than 100 commercial campgrounds are listed in a booklet available from the West Virginia Division of Tourism.

Nightlife and the Arts

At Grandview State Park's **Theatre West Virginia** (☎ 304/256–6800 or 800/666–9142, WEB www.wvweb.com/www/twv), you'll find the state's premier outdoor theatrical productions: *Honey in the Rock,* a Civil War story; *Hatfields and McCoys,* depicting the famous feud; and a different musical each season, which runs June–August.

Outdoor Activities and Sports

Biking

Rentals, instruction, and tours are available from **Blackwater Bikes** (✉ Rte. 32, Davis, ☎ 304/259–5286, WEB www.blackwaterbikes.com). The **Elk River Touring Center** (✉ Hwy. 219, Slatyfork, ☎ 304/572–3771) rents bikes and organizes mountain-bike tours; it also runs a fly-fishing school. **Snowshoe Mountain Biking Centers** (✉ Hwy. 219, Snowshoe, ☎ 304/572–1000, WEB www.snowshoemtn.com) organizes tours as well as America's largest 24-hour mountain-bike relay race.

Canoeing

The **Greenbrier River** is one of the best paddling rivers in the country. Area outfitters can put you on this and other waterways; for a list of operators contact the West Virginia Division of Tourism.

Fishing

Trout are abundant in faster streams, while bass, crappie, and walleye lurk in big rivers and lakes. Licenses, which are required, are available at sporting and convenience stores. Most rafting companies organize fishing trips. **Elk Mountain Outfitters** (✉ corner of Rte. 66 and Rte. 219 [Box 8, Slatyfork 26291], ☎ 304/572–3000) runs fly-fishing schools and trout expeditions.

Golf

Cacapon (☎ 304/258–1022) and **Canaan Valley Resort** (☎ 304/866–4121) state parks have 18 holes each; the **Greenbrier** (☎ 304/536–1110), in White Sulphur Springs, 54 holes; **Locust Hill** (☎ 304/728–7300), in Charles Town, 18 holes; **Pipestem Resort State Park** (☎ 304/466–1800 or 800/225–5982, WEB www.pipestemresort.com), in Pipestem, 27 holes; **Stonebridge** (☎ 304/263–4653), in Martinsburg, 18 holes; the **Woods** (☎ 304/754–7977 or 800/248–2222), in Hedgesville, 27 holes.

Hiking

State and national parks have extensive trail systems. The **Appalachian Trail Conference** (✉ 799 Washington St., Harpers Ferry 25425, ☎ 304/535–6331, WEB www.atconf.org) is a volunteer organization that helps manage the trail, which stretches 2,168 mi from Maine to Georgia. Harpers Ferry is considered a sort of psychological halfway point for those hikers attempting to do the whole thing. The **Big Blue Trail** (✉ Potomac Appalachian Trail Club, 118 Park St. SE, Vienna, VA 22180, ☎ 703/242–0693) runs along the border with Virginia.

Horseback Riding

You can horseback-ride on trails in most state parks. Stables at **Glade Springs Resort & Conference Center** (✉ 3000 Lake Dr., Daniels 25832, ☎ 800/634–5233) have short rides as well as more elaborate overnight expeditions and wagon rides. The horse farm **Swift Level** (✉ Rte. 2 [Box 269, Lewisburg 24901], ☎ 304/645–1155 or 888/645–1155) gives experienced equestrians the chance to take multiday long-distance treks.

Rafting

The **New, Gauley,** and **Shenandoah** are West Virginia's most heavily traveled rivers, followed by the **Tygart** and **Cheat.** First-timers can tackle all but the Gauley. For information on more than 30 commercial outfitters that run white-water excursions, contact the West Virginia Division of Tourism.

Ski Areas

Cross-Country

Elk River Touring Center (✉ Slatyfork, ☎ 304/572–3771) and the **White Grass Ski Touring Center** (✉ Rte. 1 [Box 299, Davis 26260], ☎ 304/866–4114) offer rentals, instruction, and tours.

Downhill

Call ☎ 800/225–5982 for snow conditions at these ski areas: **Canaan Valley Resort State Park** (✉ Davis), 34 slopes and trails, 3 chairlifts, vertical drop 850 ft, 1¼-mi run; **Snowshoe/Silver Creek** (✉ Snowshoe), 56 trails, 11 chairlifts, vertical drop 1,500 ft, 1½-mi run; **Timberline**

(✉ Davis), 35 trails, 3 chairlifts, vertical drop 1,000 ft, 2-mi run, terrain park (for snowboarding, tubing, and sledding), 200-ft half-pipe for snowboarders; and **Winterplace** (✉ Flat Top), 27 trails, 7 chairlifts, vertical drop 603 ft, 1¼-mi run.

Shopping

West Virginia's many **fairs and festivals** are perfect places to shop for mountain handicrafts; check with the state Division of Tourism for a calendar of events. The works of 1,500 artists and craftspeople whose works have passed muster with a state jury are sold at **Tamarack** (✉ 1 Tamarack Park, Beckley, ☎ 304/256–6843 or 800/263–7115, WEB www.tamarackwv.com), a sprawling center off I–77/64. **Berkeley Springs** has two large antiques consortiums and several independent dealers in glass, collectibles, and political memorabilia. **Harpers Ferry's Bolivar District** houses wall-to-wall antiques and specialty shops. Martinsburg offers antiques stores and several outlet malls, including the **Blue Ridge Outlet Center** (✉ 315 W. Stephen St., ☎ 304/263–7467 or 800/445–3993), which houses 50 select manufacturers and designers of quality goods.

Eastern West Virginia Essentials

AIRPORTS

The region is served by Beckley's Raleigh County Memorial Airport, Chantilly's Dulles International Airport, Hagerstown's Washington County Regional Airport, Lewisburg's Greenbrier Valley Airport, and Winchester Regional Airport.

➤ AIRLINES AND CONTACTS: **Dulles International Airport** (☎ 703/572–2700). **Greenbrier Valley Airport** (☎ 304/645–3961). **Raleigh County Memorial Airport** (☎ 304/255–0476). **Washington County Regional Airport** (☎ 301/791–3333). **Winchester Regional Airport** (☎ 540/662–5786).

BUS TRAVEL

Greyhound serves major towns, including Lewisburg.

➤ BUS INFORMATION: **Greyhound** (☎ 800/231–2222).

CAR TRAVEL

Three interstates traverse the region: I–64, between White Sulphur Springs and Beckley; I–77, Princeton to Charleston; and I–81, in the eastern panhandle. U.S. 340 enters Harpers Ferry from the east. U.S. 50, I–79, and I–64 provide the best access from the west.

TRAIN TRAVEL

Amtrak has stations in Harpers Ferry, Martinsburg, and White Sulphur Springs.

➤ TRAIN INFORMATION: **Amtrak** (☎ 800/872–7245, WEB www.amtrak.com).

VISITOR INFORMATION

For information on the Potomac Highlands, contact Jefferson County Visitors and Convention Bureau or the Martinsburg/Berkeley County Convention and Visitors Bureau. The Convention and Visitors Bureau in Beckley and Travel Berkeley Springs have information on southern West Virginia.

➤ TOURIST INFORMATION: **Convention and Visitors Bureau** (✉ 511 Ewart Ave., Beckley 25802, ☎ 304/252–2244, FAX 304/252–2252, WEB www.visitwv.com). **Jefferson County Visitors and Convention Bureau** (✉ Box A, Harpers Ferry 25425, ☎ 304/535–2627 or 800/848–8687, FAX 304/535–2131, WEB www.jeffersoncountycvb.com). **Martinsburg/Berkeley**

County Convention and Visitors Bureau (✉ 208 S. Queen St., Martinsburg 25401, ☎ 304/264–8801 or 800/498–2386, WEB www.travelwv.com). **Travel Berkeley Springs** (✉ 304 Fairfax St., Berkeley Springs 25411, ☎ 304/258–9147 or 800/447–8797, WEB www.berkeleysprings.com).

WESTERN WEST VIRGINIA

The Charleston-Huntington area is a center of commerce and culture, quite different from the mountain wilderness to the east and the farmland to the north. Skilled craftspeople, such as those who supplied the Kennedy White House with glassware, make their homes in this area in the central Ohio River valley. Its northern panhandle suffers from steel-industry troubles, but its fine old mansions and Victorian architecture are reminders of better times. Wheeling's Oglebay Resort and Conference Center is a cultural jewel and one of the finest municipal parks in the nation.

Exploring Western West Virginia

This area is heavily influenced by the early history and commerce of the Ohio River. Charleston, Huntington, and Parkersburg set an urban tone with museums, shopping malls, and cultural and entertainment centers, but the activity is balanced by lazy days on the river. Moving north through valley farmland, you can watch glassblowers and other craftspeople at work. The boom of the 1890s is reflected throughout the area in grand mansions and nicely preserved Victorian architecture.

Charleston, first settled in 1794, has been the state capital since 1885 and is the hub of the Great Kanawha Valley. The Italian Renaissance **state capitol,** designed by Cass Gilbert (1859–1934) in 1932, is considered one of America's most beautiful. From the massive gilt dome, which rises 300 ft above the street, hangs a 2-ton chandelier of hand-cut crystal. ✉ *1900 Kanawha Blvd. E,* ☎ *304/558–3456.* 🎫 *Free. Closed Sun.*

Within the capitol complex is the **Cultural Center** (✉ Greenbrier and Washington Sts., ☎ 304/558–0162; 800/723–4687 for information; 304/342–5757 for tickets, WEB www.wvculture.org; 🎫 free), with its marble **Great Hall** and the **State Museum,** which traces West Virginia history. **Mountain Stage** (☎ 800/723–4687 for information; 304/342–5757 for tickets; 🎫 prices vary), a live contemporary-music radio show, is taped here before an audience from 6 to 8 most Sunday evenings; each show has a different emphasis, from world beat to jazz, blues, folk, and rock.

Overlooking the capitol from atop a hill is the **Sunrise Museum,** two historic mansions that house art galleries, a hands-on science center, and a planetarium. Outside are 16 acres of wooded grounds with gardens and trails. ✉ *746 Myrtle Rd.,* ☎ *304/344–8035,* WEB *www.sunrisemuseum.org.* 🎫 *$4. Closed Mon.–Tues.*

Downtown are a large civic center and the pleasant **Charleston Town Center** shopping area. Eight styles of 19th-century architecture are represented in the **East End Historic District,** bordered by Bradford, Quarrier, and Michigan streets and Kanawha Boulevard.

Charleston takes pride in downtown **Haddad Riverfront Park,** which bustles during the annual Sternwheel Regatta (WEB www.sternwheelregatta.com), before Labor Day.

It takes an hour by I–64 to reach metropolitan **Huntington,** the state's second-largest city, a river and rail town whose meticulously laid out streets are lined with stately turn-of-the-20th-century houses. In the

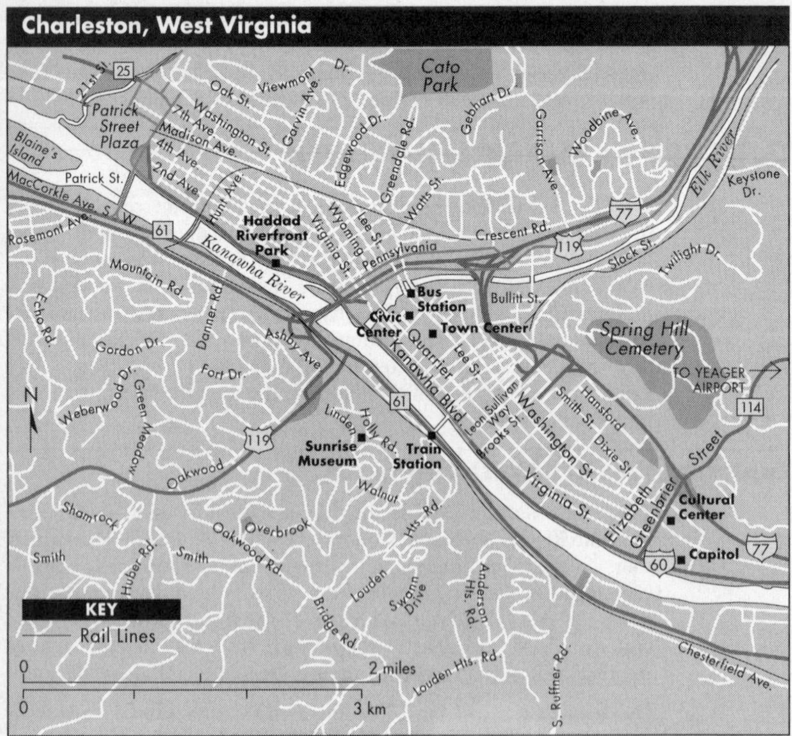

9th Street West Historic District the streets are brick, the houses Victorian frame bordered with wrought-iron fences. The **Huntington Museum of Art,** the state's largest museum, covers 52 acres and houses the Junior Art Museum, a celestial observatory, and an amphitheater. ✉ *2033 McCoy Rd.,* ☎ *304/529–2701,* WEB *www.hmoa.org.* 🎫 *Donations accepted. Closed Mon.*

Near Huntington, at Milton, is the **Blenko Glass Visitor Center and Factory Outlet,** one of several handblown-glass factories between Huntington and Parkersburg. ✉ *Exit 28 off I–64 to U.S. 60,* ☎ *304/743–9081,* WEB *www.blenkoglass.com. Factory closed 1st 2 wks in July, last 2 wks in Dec.*

Parkersburg, another thriving Ohio River town, has many restored turn-of-the-20th-century houses, but its main attraction is **Blennerhassett Island Historical State Park.** In 1800 Harman Blennerhassett's magnificent island estate was the talk of the Northwest Territory, but he was later arrested with Aaron Burr for treason. Besides the Palladian mansion, you can visit a crafts village and tour the island by horse-drawn wagon. For $7, you ride to the island itself aboard a stern-wheeler. ✉ *Blennerhassett Museum of Regional History, 2nd and Juliana Sts.,* ☎ *304/420–4800 or 800/225–5982,* WEB *www.blennerhassettislandstatepark.com. Island closed Nov.–Apr.*

In the heart of the state is the Mountain Lakes region, dotted with prime fishing areas and a number of Civil War landmarks, such as **Carnifex Ferry Battlefield State Park.** The battle here dashed the South's hopes of controlling the Kanawha Valley. Within the park, the **Patterson House,** which marked the line between Union and Confederate forces, has been restored as a museum. ✉ *Rte. 2, Summersville at Carnifex Ferry Battlefield,* ☎ *304/872–0825.* 🎫 *Free. Museum closed Labor Day–Memorial Day.*

North of Clarksburg is **Morgantown,** an industrial and educational center known internationally for its glass. It is the home of **West Virginia University,** where the world's first fully automated transportation system has carried students between campuses since the 1970s. There's all the bustle of a college town here, plus the 1,700-acre **Cheat Lake,** a perfect place to wind down for a bit.

In the northern panhandle, **Wheeling** was once the gateway to the West. Parks, museums, riverboat rides, and a wealth of restored Victorian houses are reminders of the old days.The **Victorian House Tours** (☎ 304/233–1600, WEB www.victorianwheeling.com; 💳 $10 for 4-house tour or $3 for 1) allow you to visit four homes built in the lates 1800s.

★ **Oglebay Resort and Conference Center** (☎ 304/243–4000 or 800/624–6988, WEB www.oglebay-resort.com) is a 1,500-acre municipal park–resort with a hotel, a 65-acre petting zoo, a planetarium, a museum, indoor and outdoor swimming pools, naturalist programs for all ages, and two championship golf courses. From early November through mid-January both the park and downtown Wheeling explode into gigantic thematic displays for the immense **Winter Festival of Lights**—touted as the largest festival of its kind in the nation.

Dining and Lodging

Charleston

$$$ ✕ **The Chop House.** This elegant but cozy downtown steak house serves seafood flown in from Boston as well as U.S.D.A. prime cuts of beef. Impeccable service, valet parking, and innovative side dishes like garlic spinach add to the restaurant's high-class appeal. Reservations are recommended. ✉ *1003 Charleston Town Center,* ☎ *888/456–3463. AE, D, MC, V.*

$$–$$$$ ✕🏨 **Embassy Suites.** In the heart of downtown, this comfortable all-suites hotel is two blocks from the Civic Center and across from the Town Center Mall. Rooms have standard but well-kept furnishings. The Athletic Club Sports Bar & Grill ($–$$) serves hearty soups, salads, sandwiches, and pasta dishes for lunch and dinner. ✉ *300 Court St., 25301,* ☎ *304/347–8700 or 800/362–2779,* FAX *304/347–8737,* WEB *www.embassysuites.com. 253 suites. Restaurant, pool, health club. AE, D, DC, MC, V. BP.*

$$ ✕🏨 **Charleston Marriott Town Center.** Within walking distance of the Civic Center and the Charleston Town Center Mall, this hotel has clean and spacious rooms decorated with dark wood and greens, blues, and burgundies. The Tarragon Room ($$$), open only for dinner, has a contemporary American menu. Allie's American Grill ($) is popular with families, especially for its ample Sunday brunch offerings. ✉ *200 Lee St. E, 25301,* ☎ *304/345–6500 or 800/228–9290,* FAX *304/353–3722,* WEB *www.marriotthotels.com. 352 rooms. Pool, health club. AE, D, DC, MC, V.*

Morgantown

$$$ ★ ✕🏨 **Lakeview Scanticon Resort and Conference Center.** This country club turned resort sits on a dramatic cliff overlooking Cheat Lake. A warren of halls and stairways leads to comfortable motel-style rooms. Two golf courses and a $2 million fitness center serve the convention trade. Prime rib and poached salmon are the main attractions in the Reflections on the Lake restaurant ($$–$$$$). The Grill Restaurant serves light, healthy fare. ✉ *One Lakeview Dr., 26508,* ☎ *304/594–1111 or 800/624–8300,* FAX *304/594–9472,* WEB *www.lakeviewresort.com. 187 rooms. 2 restaurants, pools, tennis, health club. AE, D, DC, MC, V.*

Wheeling

$–$$ ★ **Stratford Springs.** This inn, composed of two turn-of-the-20th-century houses, stands on 30 wooded, secluded acres. The rooms are colonial style, with cherry furniture. Among the restaurants, which cater mainly to nonguests, the formal Stratford Room ($$–$$$$), for which a jacket and tie are required, serves such dishes as stuffed strip steak and baby coho salmon. ✉ *355 Oglebay Dr., 26003,* ☎ *304/233–5100 or 800/521–8435,* FAX *304/232–6447. 3 rooms. Restaurant, pool, health club. AE, MC, V.*

$$–$$$ **Oglebay Resort and Conference Center.** Connected to the rustic lodge, which has a huge stone-floor lobby and a stone fireplace, are motel-style rooms and once-detached chalets. The nearby cabins, sleeping 12 to 20, are rustic outside and ultramodern inside. ✉ *Rte. 88 N, 4 mi off I–70 at Exit 2A, 26003,* ☎ *304/243–4000 or 800/624–6988,* FAX *304/243–4070,* WEB *www.oglebay-resort.com. 220 rooms, 50 cabins. Restaurant, pools, tennis. AE, D, DC, MC, V.*

Motel

Elk River Town Center Inn (✉ 2 Kanawha Blvd. E, Charleston 25301, ☎ 304/343–4521), 259 rooms; restaurant, pool; $.

Campgrounds

The West Virginia Division of Tourism has listings of commercial campgrounds as well as facilities in more than a dozen state parks.

Nightlife and the Arts

WWVA radio's *Jamboree USA* puts on live performances by country-music greats and throws two big-name jamborees in July and August at **Capitol Music Hall** (✉ 1015 Main St., Wheeling, ☎ 800/624–5456, WEB www.jamboreeusa.com).

Outdoor Activities and Sports

Canoeing

The area's many lakes are ideal for canoeing; contact the **Army Corps of Engineers** (☎ 304/529–5211).

Fishing

Native trout are abundant in the faster streams and rivers, while bass, crappie, and walleye lurk in the lakes. Licenses are available at sporting and convenience stores. Rafting companies organize fishing trips. **Sutton Lake** (✉ Sutton, ☎ 304/765–2705) is considered a good fishing area. Some fishermen consider **Stonewall Jackson Lake** (✉ Weston, ☎ 304/269–0523) a prime fishing site.

Golf

Coonskin Golf Course (✉ 2000 Coonskin Dr., Charleston, ☎ 304/341–8013), 18 holes. **Lakeview Scanticon Resort's Lakeview and Mountainview courses** (✉ One Lakeview Dr., Morgantown, ☎ 304/594–1111 or 800/624–8300), 36 holes. **Oglebay Park's Crispin and Speidel courses** (✉ Oglebay, Rte. 88 N, Wheeling, ☎ 304/243–4000 or 800/624–6988), 36 holes. **Twin Falls Resort State Park Golf Course** (✉ Rte. 97, Mullens, ☎ 304/294–4000 or 800/225–5982), 18 holes. **Worthington Golf Club** (✉ 3414 Roseland Ave., Parkersburg, ☎ 304/428–4297), 18 holes.

Hiking and Backpacking

The **Allegheny Trail** (✉ 633 West Virginia Ave., Morgantown 26505, ☎ 304/296–5158) and the **Kanawha Trace** (✉ 733 7th Ave., Huntington 25701, ☎ 304/523–3408) pass through state and national forests and wilderness areas with rocky overlooks and thickets of rhododendron and mountain laurel.

Rafting

The white waters of the **Cheat** and **Tygart** rivers flow through this region. Call ☎ 800/225–5982 for brochures on guided trips and a list of more than 50 licensed outfitters.

Shopping

Antiques and local crafts, particularly handblown glass, are abundant here; vendors vary from roadside shops to outdoor fairs to sprawling glass-factory outlets. The largest showcase of West Virginia wares is the **Mountain State Art & Craft Fair** (☎ 800/225–5982; 🎫 $5), held in Ripley the week of July 4. In downtown Charleston, the **Charleston Town Center** (✉ Quarrier and Lee Sts., ☎ 304/345–9525, WEB www.charlestontowncenter.com) has more than 130 shops.

Western West Virginia Essentials

AIRPORTS

The region is served by Charleston's Yeager Airport, Huntington's Tri-State Airport, Parkersburg's Wood County Airport, Clarksburg/Fairmont's Benedum Airport, and the Morgantown Municipal Airport/Hart Field.

➤ AIRLINES AND CONTACTS: **Benedum Airport** (☎ 304/842–3400). **Morgantown Municipal Airport/Hart Field** (☎ 304/291–7461). **Tri-State Airport** (☎ 304/453–6165). **Wood County Airport** (☎ 304/464–5113). **Yeager Airport** (☎ 304/344–8033 or 800/241–6522).

CAR TRAVEL

Major routes covering the region are I–64 west; I–77 north–south; I–79 north–south; U.S. 50 between Clarksburg and Parkersburg; and I–70, crossing the northern panhandle at Wheeling.

TRAIN TRAVEL

Amtrak provides service from White Sulphur Springs through Charleston to Huntington.

➤ TRAIN INFORMATION: **Amtrak** (☎ 800/872–7245, WEB www.amtrak.com).

VISITOR INFORMATION

For information on northern West Virginia, contact the Convention and Visitors Bureau in Morgantown.

➤ TOURIST INFORMATION: **Cabell-Huntington Convention and Visitors Bureau** (✉ Box 347, 25708, ☎ 304/525–7333 or 800/635–6329, WEB www.wvvisit.org). **Charleston Convention and Visitors Bureau** (✉ 200 Civic Center Dr., 25301, ☎ 304/344–5075 or 800/733–5469, FAX 304/344–1241, WEB www.charlestonwv.com). **Morgantown Convention and Visitors Bureau** (✉ 709 Beechurst Ave., Morgantown 26505, ☎ 304/292–5081 or 800/458–7373, FAX 304/291–1354, WEB www.mgtn.com). **Wheeling Convention and Visitors Bureau** (✉ 1401 Main St., Heritage Square, 26003, ☎ 304/233–7709 or 800/828–3097, FAX 304/233–1320, WEB www.wheelingcvb.com).

WISCONSIN

By Don Davenport

Updated by Jim Umhoefer

Capital	Madison
Population	5,169,700
Motto	Forward
State Bird	Robin
State Flower	Wood violet
Postal Abbreviation	WI

Statewide Visitor Information

Wisconsin Department of Tourism (☒ Box 7976, Madison 53707, ☎ 608/266–2161 or 800/432–8747, WEB www.travelwisconsin.com). **Information centers:** I–90 north at Rest Area 22, near Beloit; I–94 east at Rest Area 25, near Hudson; I–94 north at Rest Area 26, near Kenosha; I–90 east at Rest Area 31, near La Crosse; Route 12 north at Rest Area 24, near Genoa City; Prairie du Chien, at the Route 18 bridge; 201 W. Washington Ave., Madison; Highways 2 and 53 in Superior; Highways 151 and 61 near Dickeyville; Highways 51 and 2 in Hurley; 1680 Bridge St. in Marinette; and at 52 W. Adams St., in Chicago, Illinois.

Scenic Drives

Part of the **Great River Road,** scenic Route 35 follows the Mississippi River between Prairie du Chien and Prescott. Route 107, between Merrill and Tomahawk, travels along the 400-mi-long **Wisconsin River valley.** In northeastern Wisconsin, routes 57 and 42 circle the **Door County Peninsula,** providing 250 mi of Lake Michigan scenery.

National and State Parks

National Park

Apostle Islands National Lakeshore (☒ accessible by ferry from Bayfield city dock, ☎ 715/779–3397) includes 21 of Lake Superior's 22 Apostle Islands and a segment of mainland near Bayfield.

State Parks

Wisconsin's state park system includes 48 parks and recreation areas, nine forests, and numerous trails. Camping is allowed in 36 state parks and seven state forests. The **Wisconsin Department of Natural Resources** (☒ Bureau of Parks and Recreation, Box 7921, Madison 53707, ☎ 608/266–2181, WEB www.wiparks.net) provides information.

Devil's Lake State Park (☒ S5975 Park Rd., Baraboo 53913, ☎ 608/356–8301) is one of the state's most popular parks, with hiking trails, campsites, and 500-ft bluffs overlooking Devil's Lake. **Pattison State Park** (☒ 6294 S. State Rd. 35, Superior 54880, ☎ 715/399–3111) is distinguished by its 165-ft Big Manitou Falls, Wisconsin's highest waterfall and the fourth highest east of the Rockies. **Peninsula State Park** (☒ 9462 Shore Rd., Fish Creek 54212, ☎ 920/868–3258) covers nearly 4,000 acres on the shores of Green Bay. With golf, hiking, bicycling, and lakeshore campsites, it is one of the most heavily used parks in the state. **Wyalusing State Park** (☒ 13081 State Park La., Bagley 53801, ☎ 608/996–2261), at the confluence of the Wisconsin and Mississippi rivers, provides sweeping views of the river valleys.

MILWAUKEE

Wisconsin's largest city feels more like a small town as it's not so much a city as a collection of neighborhoods on the shores of Lake Michigan. This international seaport is the state's primary commercial and manufacturing center. Modern steel-and-glass high-rises share the skyline with restored and well-kept 19th-century buildings from the city's early heritage. First settled by Potawatomi and later by French fur traders in the late 18th century, Milwaukee boomed in the 1840s with the arrival of German brewers, whose influence is still present. Milwaukee is known as a city of festivals, the biggest being Summerfest and the Great Circus Parade.

Exploring Milwaukee

Downtown

Milwaukee's central business district is 1 mi long, a few blocks wide, and is divided by the Milwaukee River. As you cross the river from the east to the west side, notice that the east-side streets are not directly opposite the west-side streets and that the bridges across the river are built at an angle. This layout dates from the 1840s, when the area east of the river was called Juneautown and the region to the west was known as Kilbourntown. The rival communities had a fierce argument over which would pay for the bridges that connected them; the antagonism was so intense that citizens venturing into rival territory carried white flags. The Great Bridge War was finally settled by the state legislature in 1845, but the streets on either side of the river were never aligned.

On the east side of the city, the **Iron Block Building** (✉ N. Water St. and E. Wisconsin Ave.) is one of the few remaining ironclad buildings in the United States. It was designed by George H. Johnson and built between 1860 and 1861. The metal facade was brought in by ship from an eastern foundry and installed during the Civil War. In the 1860s Milwaukee exported more wheat than any other port in the world. The mass exportation gave impetus to the building of the **Grain Exchange Room** in the Mackie Building (✉ 225 E. Michigan St.). The 10,000-square-ft trading room has three-story-high columns and painted ceiling panels depicting Wisconsin wildflowers. The building was designed by Edward Townsend Mix and built between 1879 and 1880. The **City of Milwaukee Public Library** (✉ 814 W. Wisconsin Ave., ☎ 414/286–3000, WEB www.mpl.org), near the business district, is an impressive example of the Classical Revival style; it was built between 1893 and 1897 by the architectural firm Ferry & Clas.

★ The **Milwaukee Art Museum,** on the lakefront, houses notable collections of paintings, drawings, sculpture, photography, and decorative arts. Its permanent collection is strong in European and American art of the 19th and 20th centuries. ✉ *700 N. Art Museum Dr.,* ☎ *414/224–3200,* WEB *www.mam.org;* 🎫 *$6. Closed Mon.*

En route from the lakefront to the river, **Cathedral Square** (✉ E. Kilbourn Ave. and Jefferson St.) is a quiet park on the site of Milwaukee's first courthouse. Across from Cathedral Square, **St. John's Cathedral** (✉ 802 N. Jackson St., ☎ 414/276–9814), dedicated in 1853, was the first Roman Catholic cathedral built in Wisconsin.

The **Milwaukee County Historical Society** (✉ 910 N. Old World 3rd St., ☎ 414/273–8288; 🎫 free), a museum in a former bank building, displays early fire-fighting equipment, military artifacts, toys, and women's fashions. It also has a research library with naturalization records and genealogical resources.

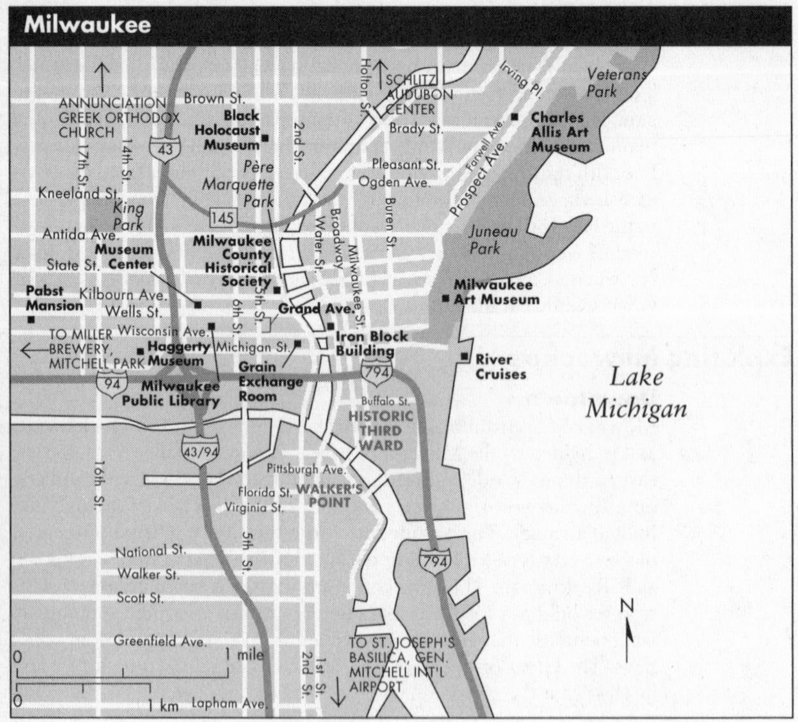

The banks of the Milwaukee River, especially along the striking downtown riverwalk, are busy in summer when downtown workers lunch in the nearby parks and public areas such as **Père Marquette Park** (⊠ Old World 3rd St. and W. Kilbourn Ave.), on the river. There are **river cruises** of Milwaukee's harbor and lakefront during warm weather. Call the Convention and Visitors Bureau (☎ 608/255–2537 or 800/373–6376) for details on cruise companies.

★ Considered among the best natural history museums in the country, the **Milwaukee Public Museum** (⊠ 800 W. Wells St., ☎ 414/278–2700, WEB www.mpm.edu; museum \$6.50, museum and IMAX \$10.50) is known for its collection of more than 6 million specimens and artifacts. Its walk-through exhibits include "Streets of Old Milwaukee," depicting the city in the 1890s; a two-story rain forest; and "Third Planet" (complete with full-size dinosaurs), where visitors walk into the interior of Earth to learn about its history. Within the museum, the Humphrey IMAX Dome Theater (☎ 414/278–2700; \$6.75) is run in cooperation with Discovery World.

Called Discovery World, the **James Lovell Museum of Science, Economics, and Technology** (⊠ Milwaukee Public Museum, 815 N. James Lovell St., ☎ 414/765–9966, WEB www.discoveryworld.org; \$5.50) has more than 140 interactive exhibits on magnets, motors, electricity, health, and computers. It also puts on the "Great Electric Show" and the "Light Wave–Laser Beam Show" on weekends and some weekdays. **America's Black Holocaust Museum** (⊠ 2233 N. 4th St., ☎ 414/264–2500, WEB www.blackholocaustmuseum.com; \$5; closed Wed.), near Old World 3rd Street, educates visitors about race, racism, and the era of slavery and lynchings in America.

St. Joan of Arc Chapel (⊠ Marquette University, 1415 W. Wisconsin Ave., central mall, behind Memorial Library, ☎ 414/288–6873, WEB www.mu.edu; 🎫 free), a small, stone 15th-century chapel, was moved from its original site near Lyon, France, in 1964 and reconstructed here. One of the stones was reputedly kissed by Joan before she was sent to her death and is discernibly colder than the others. The **Patrick and Beatrice Haggerty Museum of Art** (✉ 13th and Clybourn Sts., ☎ 414/288–1669, WEB www.mu.edu; 🎫 free) houses Marquette University's collection of more than 6,000 works of art, including Renaissance, Baroque, and modern paintings as well as sculpture, prints, photography, and decorative arts. It also has changing exhibitions.

Completed in 1892 for the beer baron Captain Frederick Pabst, the ★ **Pabst Mansion** (✉ 2000 W. Wisconsin Ave., ☎ 414/931–0808, WEB www.pabstmansion.com; 🎫 $7; closed Mon.) is one of Milwaukee's treasured landmarks. The 37-room Flemish Renaissance–style mansion, designed by the architectural firm Ferry & Clas, has a tan pressed-brick exterior with carved-stone and terra-cotta ornamentation. Inside are woodwork, ironwork, marble, tile, and stained glass. The ★ **Mitchell Park Conservatory** (✉ 524 S. Layton Blvd., ☎ 414/649–9800, WEB www.countyparks.com/horticulture; 🎫 $4.50) consists of three 85-ft-high glass domes housing tropical, arid, and seasonal plants and flowers. Its lilies and poinsettias are spectacular at Easter and Christmas.

Elsewhere in Milwaukee

The **Allen-Bradley Co. Clock** (✉ 1201 S. 2nd St.) is a Milwaukee landmark and, according to the *Guinness Book of Records,* "the largest four-faced clock in the world." Great Lakes ships often use the clock as a navigational reference point. The **American Geographical Society Collection** (✉ 2311 E. Hartford Ave., ☎ 414/229–6282, WEB www.uwm.edu/library; 🎫 free; closed weekends), in the Golda Meir Library on the University of Wisconsin–Milwaukee campus, has an exceptional assemblage of maps, old globes, atlases, and charts, plus about 200,000 books and journals.

Worthwhile **University of Wisconsin–Milwaukee art galleries** (☎ 414/229–5070, WEB www.uwm.edu; 🎫 free; closed Mon.–Tues.) include the **Institute of Visual Arts** (✉ 3253 N. Downer Ave.), **Gallery Three** (✉ 2400 E. Kenwood Blvd.), and **Gallery Two** (✉ 3203 N. Downer Ave.). These venues show avant-garde exhibits by regional, national, and international artists.

The **Charles Allis Art Museum** (✉ 1801 N. Prospect Ave., ☎ 414/278–8295, WEB www.charlesallismuseum.org; 🎫 $5; closed Mon.–Tues.) occupies an Tudor-style house built in 1911. The home has stained-glass windows by Louis Comfort Tiffany and a stunning worldwide collection of paintings and objets d'art, including works by major 19th- and 20th-century French and American painters.

The **Lowell Damon House** (✉ 2107 N. Wauwatosa Ave., Wauwatosa, ☎ 414/273–8288, WEB www.milwaukeecountyhistsoc.org; 🎫 free; closed Mon.–Tues. and Thurs.–Sat., except by appointment), completed in 1847, is a classic example of colonial-style architecture. The **Annunciation Greek Orthodox Church** (✉ 9400 W. Congress St., ☎ 414/461–9400; 🎫 $2; closed except by prearranged group tours Tues. and Fri.) was Frank Lloyd Wright's last major work; the famed Wisconsin architect called it his "little jewel." Since it opened in 1961, the blue-domed Byzantine-style church has drawn visitors from all over the world.

Built by immigrant parishioners and local craftsmen at the turn of the 20th century, **St. Josephat's Basilica** (✉ 601 W. Lincoln Ave., ☎ 414/645–5623; 🎫 $3; closed except for group tours Sun. or by appointment) has a copper dome modeled after the one atop St. Peter's in Rome. Inside is a remarkable collection of relics.

The **Pettit National Ice Center** (✉ 500 S. 84th St., ☎ 414/266–0100, WEB www.thepettit.com; 🎫 $6) has an Olympic-size skating rink, two hockey rinks, and plenty of space for jogging. Visitors can spend time on the ice or watch local Olympic speed skaters practice. **Betty Brinn Children's Museum** (✉ 929 E. Wisconsin Ave., ☎ 414/291–0888, WEB www.bbcmkids.org; 🎫 $4; closed Mon.) is a hands-on museum for children ages 10 and under.

Outside Milwaukee

The State Historical Society's living-history museum near Eagle, ★ **Old World Wisconsin,** celebrates the state's ethnic heritage in architecture, with more than 65 historic buildings on 576 acres in the Southern Kettle Moraine State Forest. The restored farm and village buildings gathered from across the state depict 19th- and 20th-century rural Wisconsin. All were originally built and inhabited by European immigrants; they are grouped in German, Norwegian, Danish, and Finnish farmsteads. Costumed interpreters representing each ethnic group relate the story of immigration to Wisconsin and perform chores, such as making soap, that were intrinsic to rural life two centuries ago. From January through March, the forest is open for cross-country skiing ($4). ✉ *S103 W37890 Rte. 67,* ☎ *262/594–6300,* WEB *www.shsw.wisc.edu/sites/oww.* 🎫 *$11, museum closed Nov.–May, except Christmas holiday.*

Kohler is a planned, landscaped village surrounding the factories of the plumbing-fixtures manufacturer Kohler Company. The **Kohler Design Center** (✉ 101 Upper Rd., ☎ 920/457–3699, WEB www.kohler.com; 🎫 free) houses the company's ceramic art collection, archives, artifacts from an earlier factory and village, and an elaborate showroom of model bathrooms. There are daily guided tours of **Waelderhaus** (✉ W. Riverside Dr., ☎ 920/452–4079; 🎫 free), a reproduction of founder John M. Kohler's ancestral home in Austria. The **Woodlake Kohler Complex** (✉ Woodlake Rd.) comprises more than 25 shops, galleries, and restaurants. The **American Club** (✉ Highland Dr., ☎ 920/457–8000 or 800/344–2838), built in 1918 as a company-owned hotel for workers, is now a posh resort hotel on the National Register of Historic Places. The compound has two 18-hole golf courses, an indoor sports complex, a 500-acre wilderness preserve, and several restaurants.

Parks, Gardens, and Zoos

★ The 660-acre **Whitnall Park** (✉ 5879 S. 92nd St., in suburban Hales Corners, WEB www.countyparks.com), one of the largest municipal parks in the nation, has an 18-hole golf course, recreational facilities, picnic areas, and nature and cross-country skiing trails. Within the park are the internationally famous **Alfred L. Boerner Botanical Gardens** (☎ 414/425–1130; 🎫 free), with trees, shrubs, and flowers in formal and informal gardens. The park's **Wehr Nature Center** (☎ 414/425–8550; 🎫 free) has wildlife exhibits, woodlands and wetlands, a lake, nature trails, and wild gardens.

Forests, ponds, marshland, and nature trails attract nature lovers to the **Schlitz Audubon Center** (✉ 1111 E. Brown Deer Rd., ☎ 414/352–2880, WEB www.sanc.org; 🎫 $4; closed Mon.), a 225-acre wildlife area with an environmental research and education center. ★ The **Milwaukee County Zoo** (✉ 10001 W. Bluemound Rd., ☎ 414/771–3040, WEB www.milwaukeezoo.org; 🎫 $9) has more than 3,000 wild animals and birds—including endangered species—plus educational programs, a petting zoo, narrated tram tours, miniature-train rides, and cross-country skiing trails.

Dining

Milwaukee is known for its wide variety of good ethnic restaurants, especially those that serve German cuisine. Despite its small-town atmosphere, many of the city's restaurants could hold their own with those in New York and Chicago.

$$$$ ★ ✕ **Sanford.** Nationally acclaimed chef Sanford D'Amato serves contemporary American cuisine in this restaurant, which occupies a remodeled grocery store on Milwaukee's east side. ✉ *1547 N. Jackson St.,* ☎ *414/276–9608. AE, D, DC, MC, V. Closed Sun. No lunch.*

$$$–$$$$ ★ ✕ **Grenadier's.** Imaginative dishes such as tenderloin of veal with raspberry sauce that combine French classics with Asian or Indian flavors are served in the dining room and in the handsome, darkly furnished piano bar. ✉ *747 N. Broadway St.,* ☎ *414/276–0747. AE, D, DC, MC, V. Closed Sun. No lunch Sat.*

$$$–$$$$ ★ ✕ **Steven Wade's Cafe.** Creative dishes distinguish this eatery: Try marinated duck breasts pan-roasted with cranberry-pecan Chambord sauce, or seared steer tenderloin with coffee-cognac demiglace. The café, once a residence, has a casual, intimate atmosphere and a small bar. ✉ *17001 W. Greenfield Ave., New Berlin,* ☎ *262/784–0774. AE, D, DC, MC, V. Closed Sun. No lunch Sat. or Mon.*

$$–$$$$ ✕ **Boulevard Inn.** This restaurant overlooking Lake Michigan serves Continental cuisine. Enjoy Caesar salad or honey duck while listening to contemporary piano music. A sit-down brunch is served on Sunday. Reservations are recommended. ✉ *925 E. Wells St.,* ☎ *414/765–1166. AE, D, DC, MC, V.*

$$–$$$$ ✕ **Giovanni's.** This bright Sicilian eatery serves large portions of rich Italian food. Veal steak Giovanni is excellent, and pasta is a sure bet. ✉ *1683 N. Van Buren St.,* ☎ *414/291–5600. AE, D, DC, MC, V. No lunch weekends.*

$$–$$$ ✕ **Bartolotta.** On a quaint street in the village of Wauwatosa, this place is known for its rustic Italian cuisine, especially fresh fish. ✉ *7616 W. State St.,* ☎ *414/771–7910. AE, D, DC, MC, V. No lunch weekends.*

$$–$$$ ★ ✕ **Celia.** Milwaukee's premier hotel restaurant has a formal atmosphere and a modern decor. Recommended dishes are rack of lamb, seared crab cakes, and lobster-and-shrimp bisque. ✉ *Pfister Hotel, 424 E. Wisconsin Ave.,* ☎ *414/390–3832. AE, D, DC, MC, V.*

$$–$$$ ✕ **Jake's.** This longtime Milwaukee favorite earned its reputation with perfectly prepared steaks and heaps of french-fried onion rings. Not to be missed are the fresh fish selections, escargots, roast duckling, and Bailey's chocolate-chip cheesecake. ✉ *21445 W. Capitol Dr., Brookfield,* ☎ *262/781–7995. AE, DC, MC, V. No lunch.*

$$–$$$ ★ ✕ **Karl Ratzsch's Old World Restaurant.** In German tradition dirndl-skirted waitresses serve schnitzel, roast duckling, and sauerbraten at this family-owned restaurant that's decked out with murals, chandeliers made from antlers, and antique beer steins. Piano music on Friday and Saturday nights adds to the fun. ✉ *320 E. Mason St.,* ☎ *414/276–2720. AE, D, DC, MC, V. Closed Sun. No lunch.*

$$ ✕ **Chip and Py's.** In the northern suburbs, this stylish restaurant has light gray dual-level dining rooms, a huge fireplace, and contemporary art. There's an eclectic menu and live jazz on weekends and Wednesday evenings. ✉ *1340 W. Town Square Rd., Mequon,* ☎ *262/241–9589. AE, D, DC, MC, V. Closed Mon. No lunch weekends.*

$–$$ ✕ **Coquette Cafe.** Fine food is served in a casual atmosphere at this French café in a large, renovated warehouse in Milwaukee's trendy Third Ward district. ✉ *316 N. Milwaukee St.,* ☎ *414/291–2655. AE, D, DC, MC, V. Closed Sun.*

$–$$ ★ ✕ **De Marinis.** This popular Italian-American restaurant has excellent pizza and pasta. The pesto-and-artichoke Garden Pizza is one of the best. ✉ *N88 W15229 Main St., Menomonee Falls,* ☎ *262/253–1568;* ✉ *1211 E. Conway St.,* ☎ *414/481–2348. D, MC, V.*

$–$$ ✕ **Three Brothers.** In an 1887 tavern, this revered Eastern European restaurant serves chicken *paprikash* (stewed with paprika), roast goose and duck, boneless leg of lamb stuffed with spinach and cheese, and homemade desserts at family-style kitchen tables. It's about 10 minutes from downtown, on the near south side. ✉ *2414 S. St. Clair St.,* ☎ *414/481–7530. No credit cards. Closed Mon. No lunch.*

$–$$ ✕ **Watts Tea Shop.** A genteel spot for breakfast, lunch, or tea with scones, this eatery is above George Watts & Sons, Milwaukee's premier store for china, crystal, and silver. Indulge in fresh-squeezed juice and a custard-filled sunshine cake. ✉ *761 N. Jefferson St.,* ☎ *414/290–5720. AE, D, MC, V. Closed Sun. No dinner.*

$ ✕ **Elsa's on the Park.** Across from Cathedral Square Park, this chic but casual restaurant has frequently changing art exhibits and serves big, juicy hamburgers and pork-chop sandwiches. ✉ *833 N. Jefferson St.,* ☎ *414/765–0615. AE, MC, V. No lunch weekends.*

Lodging

$$$–$$$$ **Hilton Milwaukee City Center.** Adjacent to Milwaukee's convention center, and minutes from the Grand Avenue Shopping Center, this sophisticated hotel underwent a major renovation in 2001. ✉ *509 W. Wisconsin Ave., 53203,* ☎ *414/271–7250 or 800/445–8667,* FAX *414/271–1039,* WEB *www.hilton.com. 730 rooms. 3 restaurants, gym. AE, D, DC, MC, V.*

$$$–$$$$ ★ **Pfister Hotel.** Milwaukee's grandest old hotel dates from 1893. Rooms in the tower, which was added in 1975, are bright and contemporary with a Victorian accent in keeping with the original style. A collection of 19th-century art hangs in the lobby. ✉ *424 E. Wisconsin Ave., 53202,* ☎ *414/273–8222 or 800/558–8222,* FAX *414/273–5025,* WEB *www.thepfisterhotel.com. 307 rooms. 3 restaurants, pool. AE, D, DC, MC, V.*

$$$ ★ **Embassy Suites–Milwaukee West.** The sweeping atrium lobby, with fountains, potted plants, and glass elevators, is the focal point of this hotel in the western suburbs. The hotel, which has two-bedroom suites, is within walking distance of a large shopping center. ✉ *1200 S. Moorland Rd., Brookfield 53005,* ☎ *262/782–2900 or 800/362–2779,* FAX *262/796–9159,* WEB *www.embassysuites.com. 203 suites. Restaurant, pool, gym. AE, D, DC, MC, V. CP.*

$$$ **Hyatt Regency.** This high-rise hotel has an 18-story open atrium, a revolving rooftop restaurant, and an enclosed walkway to the Grand Avenue Shopping Center. ✉ *333 W. Kilbourn Ave., 53203,* ☎ *414/276–1234 or 800/233–1234,* FAX *414/276–6338,* WEB *www.hyatt.com. 484 rooms. 2 restaurants, gym. AE, D, DC, MC, V.*

$$ **Four Points Sheraton Hotel Milwaukee Airport.** The Four Points, across from the airport, has a nightclub and extensive sports and recreation facilities. The marble-walled lobby is illuminated with chandeliers. ✉ *4747 S. Howell Ave., 53207,* ☎ *414/481–8000 or 800/558–3862,* FAX *414/615–8065,* WEB *www.fourpoints.com/milwaukeeairport. 510 rooms. 2 restaurants, pool, gym. AE, D, DC, MC, V.*

$$ ★ **Wyndham Milwaukee Center.** In the center of the city's growing theater district by the river and near the Grand Avenue Shopping Center, the Wyndham has an opulent lobby tiled with Italian marble. Guest rooms are contemporary, with mahogany furnishings. The hotel has an excellent pasta bar. ✉ *139 E. Kilbourn Ave., 53202,* ☎ *414/276–*

8686 or 800/996–3426, FAX 414/276–8007, WEB www.wyndham.com. 221 rooms. Restaurant, health club. AE, D, DC, MC, V.

Motels

Holiday Inn Express (✉ 11111 W. North Ave., Wauwatosa 53226, ☎ 414/778–0333 or 800/465–4329, FAX 414/778–0331, WEB www.sixcontinentshotels.com/hiexpress), 122 rooms; CP; *$$–$$$*.

Radisson Hotel Milwaukee Airport (✉ 6331 S. 13th St., 53221, ☎ 414/764–1500 or 800/303–8002, FAX 414/764–6531, WEB www.radisson.com), 159 rooms; restaurant, pool, gym; *$$–$$$*.

Best Western Midway Hotel–Airport (✉ 5105 S. Howell Ave., 53207, ☎ 414/769–2100 or 800/528–1234, FAX 414/769–0064, WEB www.bestwestern.com), 139 rooms; restaurant, pool; CP; *$$*.

Nightlife and the Arts

Milwaukee Magazine (on newsstands) lists arts and entertainment events. Also check the daily entertainment sections of the *Milwaukee Journal Sentinel.* Nightlife here comprises clubs, bars, and a slew of friendly saloons. Milwaukee's theater district is in a two-block downtown area bounded by the Milwaukee River, East Wells Street, North Water Street, and East State Street. Most tickets are sold at box offices.

Nightlife

The **Safe House** (✉ 779 N. Front St., ☎ 414/271–2007), with a James Bond spy-hideout decor, is a favorite hangout for young people and out-of-towners who want to eat, drink, dance, or watch a magician. **Major Goolsby's** (✉ 340 W. Kilbourn Ave., ☎ 414/271–3414) is regarded as one of the country's top-10 sports bars. It's also known for its great brats and burgers. Jazz fans go to the **Estate** (✉ 2423 N. Murray Ave., ☎ 414/964–9923).

The Arts

The **Riverside Theater** (✉ 116 W. Wisconsin Ave., ☎ 414/224–3000) hosts touring theater companies, Broadway shows, and other entertainment. The **Pabst Theater** (✉ 144 E. Wells St., ☎ 414/286–3663) presents live entertainment. The **Milwaukee Center** (✉ 108 E. Wells St., ☎ 414/224–9490) is home to the Milwaukee Repertory Theater. The **Marcus Center for the Performing Arts** (✉ 929 N. Water St., ☎ 414/273–7206) comprises the Milwaukee Symphony Orchestra, Milwaukee Ballet Company, Florentine Opera Company, and First Stage Milwaukee.

Spectator Sports

Baseball: Milwaukee Brewers (✉ Miller Park, 1 Brewers Way, ☎ 414/902–4000, WEB www.milwaukeebrewers.com). **Basketball: Milwaukee Bucks** (✉ Bradley Center, 1001 N. 4th St., ☎ 414/227–0500, WEB www.bucks.com). **Football: Green Bay Packers** (✉ Lambeau Field, 1265 Lombardi Ave., Green Bay, ☎ 920/496–5700, WEB www.packers.com). Green Bay is about a two-hour drive from Milwaukee. **Hockey: Milwaukee Admirals** (✉ Bradley Center, 1001 N. 4th St., ☎ 414/227–0550, WEB www.milwaukeeadmirals.com).

Beaches

Lake Michigan is the place to swim, but be prepared: mid-summer water temperatures linger in the 50s and 60s. The following narrow, sandy beaches are among the most popular: **Bradford Beach** (✉ 2400 N. Lincoln Memorial Dr.); **Doctors Beach** (✉ 1870 E. Fox La., Fox Point); **Grant Beach** (✉ 100 Hawthorne Ave., South Milwaukee); and **McKinley Beach** (✉ 1750 N. Lincoln Memorial Dr.). The **Milwaukee County**

Parks Swimming Pools and Beaches Office (☎ 414/645–4806) has information about beaches.

Shopping

Using the downtown skywalk system, it's possible to browse in hundreds of stores over several blocks without once setting foot outside. Downtown Milwaukee's major shopping area is Wisconsin Avenue west of the Milwaukee River. The major downtown retail center, the **Grand Avenue Mall** (✉ 275 W. Wisconsin Ave.), spans four city blocks and has 130 specialty shops and kiosks and 17 eateries. **Historic Third Ward,** a turn-of-the-20th-century wholesale and manufacturing district listed on the National Register of Historic Places, borders the harbor, the river, and downtown. Two Milwaukee landmarks, Usinger's Sausage and Mader's Restaurant, are on Old World 3rd Street, along with several interesting stores and markets. **Jefferson Street,** stretching four blocks from Wisconsin to Kilbourn, is lined with upscale stores and shops. **George Watts and Son, Inc.** (✉ 761 N. Jefferson St., ☎ 414/291–5120) has more than a thousand patterns of china, silver, and crystal.

In the metropolitan area, near the Milwaukee County Zoo, **Mayfair Mall** (✉ 2500 N. Mayfair Rd., Wauwatosa) has more than 160 shops that surround a multistory atrium complete with swaying bamboo. Some 145 stores at **Northridge Shopping Center** (✉ 7700 W. Brown Deer Rd.) include a Younkers department store, Boston Store, and Sears. Wisconsin's largest shopping center, **Southridge Mall** (✉ 5300 S. 76th St., Greendale), has more than 145 specialty stores and five major department stores. **Brookfield Square** (✉ 95 N. Moorland Rd., Brookfield) is a sprawling suburban complex with about 100 stores. **Bayshore** (✉ 5900 N. Port Washington Rd., Glendale) has about 70 stores, including Sears and the Boston Store.

About 40 minutes south of downtown Milwaukee, on I–94 east, are two large discount shopping malls. The **Factory Outlet Centre,** off Highway 50, has more than 100 stores with brand-name merchandise. Two miles south of the Factory Outlet Centre, off Highway 165, is **Lakeside Market Place,** with more than 75 designer outlet stores.

Side Trip to Cedarburg

Arriving and Departing

To get to Cedarburg from Milwaukee, take I–94 west to I–43 north; then get off at the Cedarburg Exit (County C). Drive west to Washington Avenue, Cedarburg's main street. For more information, contact the **Cedarburg Chamber of Commerce and Visitors Center** (☎ 262/377–9620 or 800/237–2874, WEB www.cedarburg.org).

What to See and Do

The entire downtown district of Cedarburg, most of it built of Niagara limestone by 19th-century pioneers, is on the National Register of Historic Places. Victorian "Painted Ladies" with beautifully landscaped yards abound. Throughout a nine-block area are antiques shops, crafts shops, candy stores, and restaurants. Weekend flea markets take place in May, July, September, and October. Within the Wittenberg Woolen Mill, built in 1864, **Cedar Creek Settlement** (✉ N70 W6340 Bridge Rd., Cedarburg, ☎ 800/827–8020) is a collection of specialty and antiques shops. Also within the mill is a winery ($2). Wisconsin's last remaining **covered bridge** (✉ Covered Bridge Rd., Cedarburg) crosses Cedar Creek 3 mi north of town. The 120-ft white-pine bridge was built in 1876 and retired in 1962. The small park beside the bridge invites picnicking.

Milwaukee Essentials

AIRPORTS AND TRANSFERS

General Mitchell International Airport, 6 mi south of downtown via I–94, is served by several domestic and international carriers.

➤ AIRPORT INFORMATION: **General Mitchell International Airport** (✉ 5300 S. Howell Ave., ☎ 414/747–5300).

AIRPORT TRANSFER

Milwaukee County Transit operates buses to and from the airport. Fare is $1.50; exact change is required. Taxis between the airport and downtown take about 20 minutes; fares are $22–$25.

➤ TAXIS AND SHUTTLES: **Milwaukee County Transit System** (☎ 414/344–6711).

BUS TRAVEL TO AND FROM MILWAUKEE

➤ BUS INFORMATION: **Greyhound Lines** (☎ 800/231–2222). **Greyhound Milwaukee** (✉ 606 N. James Lovell St., ☎ 414/272–6688).

CAR TRAVEL

From the north, I–43 provides access into downtown Milwaukee. I–94 leads to downtown from Chicago and other points south and west. If you are traveling to sites in the wider metropolitan area, from I–94 you can connect to I–894, which bypasses central Milwaukee.

RULES OF THE ROAD

Lake Michigan is the city's eastern boundary; Wisconsin Avenue is the main east–west thoroughfare. The Milwaukee River divides the downtown area east and west. The East–West Expressway (I–94/I–794) is the dividing line between north and south. Streets are numbered in ascending order from the Milwaukee River west well into the suburbs.

TAXIS

Taxis can be ordered by phone; try Yellow Cab or American United.

➤ TAXI COMPANIES: **American United** (☎ 414/220–5000). **Yellow Cab** (☎ 414/271–1800).

TRAIN TRAVEL

➤ TRAIN INFORMATION: **Amtrak** (✉ 433 W. St. Paul Ave., ☎ 800/872–7245).

TRANSPORTATION AROUND MILWAUKEE

Many downtown attractions are near the Milwaukee River and can be reached on foot. Milwaukee County Transit provides bus service.

➤ CONTACT: **Milwaukee County Transit System** (☎ 414/344–6711).

VISITOR INFORMATION

➤ TOURIST INFORMATION: **Cedarburg Chamber of Commerce and Visitors Center** (✉ W61 N480 Washington Ave. [Box 104, Cedarburg 53012], ☎ 262/377–9620 or 800/237–2874, WEB www.cedarburg.org). **Greater Milwaukee Convention and Visitors Bureau** (✉ 101 W. Wisconsin Ave., 53203, ☎ 414/273–7222 or 800/554–1448, WEB www.milwaukee.org).

ELSEWHERE IN WISCONSIN

Madison and Southern Wisconsin

What to See and Do

Madison, named after President James Madison, is the state capital. The center of the city lies on an eight-block-wide isthmus between Lakes

Mendota and Monona.The Roman Renaissance–style **Wisconsin State Capitol** (✉ 1 E. Main St., Madison, ☎ 608/266–0382; 🎟 free), built between 1906 and 1917, dominates the downtown skyline; there are tours daily. A **farmers' market** is held on Capitol Square every Saturday from May through October.

The **State Historical Society Museum** has permanent and changing exhibits on Wisconsin history, from prehistoric Native American cultures to contemporary social issues. ✉ *Capitol Sq., 30 N. Carroll St., Madison,* ☎ *608/264–6555,* WEB *www.shsw.wisc.edu.* 🎟 *Free for Wisconsin residents, $2 for nonresidents. Closed Mon.*

Capitol Square, at the center of downtown with 12 streets radiating outward, is connected to the university's campus by State Street, a mile-long tree-lined shopping district of imports shops, ethnic restaurants, and artisans' galleries.

The **Madison Art Center** has a large permanent collection and frequent temporary exhibits. ✉ *Civic Center lobby, 211 State St., Madison,* ☎ *608/257–0158,* WEB *www.madisonartcenter.org.* 🎟 *Free. Closed Mon.*

The **University of Wisconsin–Madison** (✉ 750 University Ave., Madison), which opened in 1849 with 20 students, now has an enrollment of more than 40,000. The university's **Elvehjem Museum of Art** (✉ 800 University Ave., Madison, ☎ 608/263–2246, WEB www.lvm.wisc.edu; 🎟 free) is one of the state's best, with a permanent collection of paintings, sculpture, and decorative arts dating from 2300 BC to the present. Away from downtown, the **University Arboretum** (✉ 1207 Seminole Hwy., Madison, ☎ 608/263–7888; 🎟 free) has more than 1,200 acres of natural plant and animal communities, such as prairie and forest landscapes, and horticultural collections of upper Midwest specimens.

The newest downtown showpiece is **Monona Terrace Community and Convention Center** (✉ 1 John Nolen Dr., Madison, ☎ 608/261–4000, WEB www.mononaterrace.com; 🎟 free, tour $3) on the shore of Lake Monona. It includes a rooftop garden, café, and a memorial to singer Otis Redding, who died in a plane crash nearby. Designed by Frank Lloyd Wright in 1937 but not completed until 1997, the 250,000-square-ft structure is open to the public for guided tours daily.

The **Henry Vilas Zoo** (✉ 702 S. Randall Ave., Madison, ☎ 608/266–4732, WEB www.vilaszoo.org; 🎟 free) has exhibits of nearly 200 animal species, plus a petting zoo. On Madison's east side, **Olbrich Botanical Gardens** (✉ 3330 Atwood Ave., Madison, ☎ 608/246–4550, WEB www.olbrich.org; 🎟 gardens free, conservatory $1) has 14 acres of outdoor rose, herb, and rock gardens and a glass-pyramid conservatory with tropical plants and flowers.

At the eastern edge of Wisconsin's lead-mining region, **Blue Mound State Park** (✉ State Park Rd., Blue Mounds, 2 mi northwest of town, off County ID, ☎ 608/437–5711), provides glorious vistas from towers on one of the hill's summits—the highest point in southern WIsconsin.

Cave of the Mounds is small but filled with diverse and colorful mineral formations. ✉ *2975 Cave of the Mounds Rd., Blue Mounds, north off Hwy. 18/151,* ☎ *608/437–3038,* WEB *www.caveofthemounds.com.* 🎟 *$12.50. Closed weekdays mid-Nov.–mid-Mar.*

Nestled in a verdant valley, **Little Norway** is a restored 1856 Norwegian homestead with its original log buildings and an outstanding collection of Norwegian antiques and pioneer arts and crafts. ✉ *3576 Hwy. JG N, Blue Mounds,* ☎ *608/437–8211,* WEB *www.littlenorway.com.* 🎟 *$8. Closed Nov.–May.*

Founded in 1845 by Swiss settlers from the canton of Glarus, **New Glarus** retains its Swiss character in language, food, architecture, and festivities. The **Swiss Historical Village** contains original buildings and reconstructions from early New Glarus. Displays trace Swiss immigration to America. ✉ *612 7th Ave. New Glarus,* ☎ *608/527–2317,* WEB *www.swisshistoricalvillage.com.* 🎫 *$6. Closed Nov.–May.*

Frank Lloyd Wright chose the farming community of **Spring Green,** on the Wisconsin River, for his home Taliesin and for his architectural school. Wright's influence is evident in a number of buildings in the village; notice the use of geometric shapes, low flat-roofed profiles, cantilevered projections, and steeplelike spires. There are summertime walking tours of the Wright-designed buildings at **Taliesin** (✉ Hwy. 23, Spring Green, 3 mi south of town, ☎ 608/588–7900, WEB www.taliesinpreservation.org; 🎫 tours $10–$65), including his home and office for nearly 50 years, the 1903 Hillside Home School, galleries, a drafting studio, and a theater. More expensive tours include admission to buildings. In November and April, tours are by shuttle bus ($20).

The extraordinary multilevel stone **House on the Rock** stands atop a 60-ft chimney of rock overlooking the Wyoming Valley. Begun by artist Alex Jordan in the early 1940s and opened to the public in 1961, the complex now contains re-creations of historic village streets complete with shops, as well as extensive collections of dolls, cannons, and musical machines. Here you'll also find the world's largest carousel. ✉ *5754 Hwy. 23, Spring Green,* ☎ *608/935–3639,* WEB *www.houseontherock.com.* 🎫 *$19.50. Closed Jan.–mid-Mar.*

The renowned **American Players Theater** presents evening performances of Shakespeare and other classics in a beautiful, wooded outdoor amphitheater near the Wisconsin River. ✉ *5950 Golf Course Rd., Spring Green,* ☎ *608/588–7401,* WEB *www.americanplayers.org.* 🎫 *$26–$44. Closed mid-Oct.–mid-June and Mon.*

On the western edge of the state, **Prairie du Chien** dates from 1673, when explorers Marquette and Joliet reached the confluence of the Wisconsin and Mississippi rivers 6 mi to the south. It became a flourishing fur market in the late 17th century. Now a bustling river community, it's a summertime destination of the steamers *Delta Queen* and *Mississippi Queen.*

The family of the fur trader Hercules Dousman (Wisconsin's first millionaire) built the **Villa Louis Mansion** in 1870. It contains one of the finest collections of Victorian decorative arts in the country. The **Fur Trade Museum** on the villa grounds has exhibits on the fur trade of the upper Mississippi. Wyalusing State Park is near the fur warehouse. ✉ *521 Villa Louis Rd., Prairie du Chien,* ☎ *608/326–2721,* WEB *www.shsw.wisc.edu.* 🎫 *$8.50. Closed Nov.–May.*

Dining

$$–$$$ ★ ✕ **White Horse Inn.** This local favorite serves a dynamite chicken Mafalda (grilled chicken, sausage, leeks, and pasta in cream sauce). Sunday brunch draws a crowd. ✉ *202 N. Henry St., Madison, behind the Civic Center,* ☎ *608/255–9933. AE, DC, MC, V. No lunch.*

$–$$ ★ ✕ **Pasta Per Tutti.** Fresh pasta and seafood and homemade breads and desserts make this contemporary Italian restaurant near the theater district a local favorite. ✉ *2009 Atwood Ave., Madison,* ☎ *608/242–1800. MC, V. No lunch.*

Lodging

$$–$$$$ 🏨 **Sheraton Madison.** Across from the Dane County Expo Center and minutes from the State Capitol and campus is this Sheraton with mod-

ern, comfortable rooms. Make reservations well in advance. ✉ *706 John Nolen Dr., Madison 53713,* ☎ *608/251–2300 or 800/325–3535,* FAX *608/251–1189,* WEB *www.sheraton.com. 237 rooms. 2 restaurants, pool, gym. AE, D, DC, MC, V.*

$$ **Madison Concourse Hotel and Governor's Club.** The marble lobby welcomes visitors into this hotel near Manona Terrace and State Street shops. Reserve early. ✉ *1 W. Dayton St., Madison 53703,* ☎ *608/257–6000 or 800/356–8293,* FAX *608/257–5280,* WEB *www.concoursehotel.com. 360 rooms. Restaurant, pool, gym. AE, D, DC, MC, V.*

Madison and Southern Wisconsin Essentials

CAR TRAVEL

Take I–94 west from Milwaukee to Madison or I–90 west from Chicago.

VISITOR INFORMATION

➤ Tourist Information: **Greater Madison Convention and Visitors Bureau** (✉ 615 E. Washington Ave., Madison 53703, ☎ 608/255–2537 or 800/373–6376, FAX 608/258–4950, WEB www.visitmadison.com).

Wisconsin Dells and Baraboo

What to See and Do

One of the state's foremost natural attractions is the **Wisconsin Dells,** nearly 15 mi of soaring, eroded rock formations created over thousands of years as the Wisconsin River cut into soft sandstone. The two small communities encompassed by the Dells—Wisconsin Dells and Lake Delton, with a combined population of fewer than 4,000—draw nearly 3 million visitors annually to frolic in the water parks, play miniature golf, and enjoy the rides, shows, and other planned attractions that today nearly overshadow the area's scenic wonders.

During the summer and fall tourist seasons you can view the river and its spectacular rock formations on cruise boats or aboard World War II amphibious vehicles. Several water parks have slides, wave pools, and inner-tube and raft rides. The notorious Confederate spy Belle Boyd, who died here while on a speaking tour in 1910, is buried in **Spring Grove Cemetery** (✉ 1680 Broadway Rd., Wisconsin Dells, east of town off Hwy. 23, next to the Public Works Garage).

Scenic **Mirror Lake State Park** (✉ U.S. 12, Lake Delton, south of Wisconsin Dells, ☎ 608/254–2333) has campgrounds, hiking trails, and 20 mi of cross-country ski trails. **Rocky Arbor State Park** (✉ U.S. 12, Wisconsin Dells, ☎ 608/254–8001 summer; 608/254–2333 off-season) has camping, hiking, and great scenery.

South of Wisconsin Dells is **Baraboo,** former site of an early 19th-century fur-trading post run by a Frenchman named Baribault. It is best known as the place where the five Ringling brothers began their circus careers in 1882, and as the winter headquarters of their Ringling Brothers Circus from 1884 to 1918. The **Circus World Museum** (✉ 550 Water St., ☎ 608/356–8341, WEB www.circusworldmuseum.com; 🎫 $15), a State Historical Society site, preserves the history of the more than 100 circuses that began in Wisconsin. Along with an outstanding collection of antique circus wagons, the museum presents big-top performances from mid-May through early September.

Dining and Lodging

$–$$$$ ✕ **Dell-Bar Steak House.** More than 60 years old, this restaurant built in the Frank Lloyd Wright style serves seafood and meat dishes. Expect a crackling fire in winter, and piano music year-round. ✉ *800 Wisconsin Dells Pkwy., Lake Delton,* ☎ *608/253–1861. AE, D, DC, MC, V.*

$$$$ **Great Wolf Lodge.** This hotel and recr door and outdoor water activity centers incl indoor and outdoor pools. Some rooms h places, big-screen televisions, and/or patio *Wisconsin Dells 53965,* ☎ *800/559–965 www.greatwolflodge.com. 309 rooms. Res D, DC, MC, V.*

Wisconsin Dells and Baraboo Essentials

CAR TRAVEL

Take I–90 west from Milwaukee to Madison, then I–90/94 northwest to the Dells. Baraboo is off U.S. 12 south of I–90/94.

VISITOR INFORMATION

➤ TOURIST INFORMATION: **Baraboo Chamber of Commerce** (✉ 600 Chestnut St., 53913, ☎ 608/356–8333 or 800/227–2266, WEB www.baraboo.com/chamber). **Wisconsin Dells Visitor and Convention Bureau** (✉ 701 Superior St., Wisconsin Dells 53965, ☎ 608/254–8088 or 800/223–3557, WEB www.dells.com).

Door County

What to See and Do

Jutting out from the Wisconsin mainland like the thumb on a mitten, 70-mi-long Door County Peninsula is bordered by Lake Michigan and Green Bay. It was named for the Porte des Morts (Door of Death), a treacherous strait separating the peninsula from nearby islands. Scores of ships have come to grief in these waters, but today large freighters often slip through the Door to seek shelter in the lee of the islands during Lake Michigan's autumn storms. Soil conditions and climate make the peninsula ideal for cherry and apple production, and its orchards produce more than 20 million pounds of fruit each year. The peninsula is carpeted in blossoms when the trees bloom in late May.

Each of the half-dozen quaint lakeshore towns on the peninsula is filled with charming restaurants, shops, and inns. First-time visitors often make a circle tour via routes 57 and 42. The Lake Michigan side of the peninsula is somewhat less settled and the landscape rougher. The peninsula's rugged beauty attracts artists, whose works are shown in studios, galleries, and shops in the villages.

Just north of Jacksonport (on the Lake Michigan side of Door County) you cross the 45th parallel, halfway between the equator and the north pole. Villages on the Green Bay side of the peninsula evoke New England in atmosphere and charm and provide exceptional views of Green Bay, where sunsets can be breathtaking.

Your visit to Door County is not complete unless you sample the region's famed fish boil, which originated more than 100 years ago. It's a simple but delicious meal that has reached legendary status in the region. A huge caldron of water is brought to a boil over a wood fire. A basket of red potatoes is cooked in the caldron, followed by a basket of fresh local whitefish steaks. At the moment the fish is cooked to perfection, kerosene is dumped on the fire, and the flames shoot high in the air, causing the caldron to boil over, expelling most of the fish oils and fat. The steaming whitefish is then served with melted butter, potatoes, coleslaw, and another favorite, Door County cherry pie.

Sturgeon Bay, the peninsula's chief community and a busy shipbuilding port, sits on a partially man-made ship canal connecting the waters of Lake Michigan and Green Bay. The **Door County Maritime Museum** (✉ 120 N. Madison Ave., Sturgeon Bay, at foot of bridge leadng into town, ☎ 920/743–5958, WEB www.dcmm.org; 🎫 $6) has displays on local shipbuilding and commercial fishing.

Beside Route 57, along the peninsula's Lake Michigan side, you can see the rocky shoreline and sea caves at **Cave Point County Park** (✉ Clarks Lake Rd., Sturgeon Bay, between Valmy and Jacksonport, off County Rd. WD).

Northport, at the tip of the Door County Peninsula, is the port of departure for the daily car ferries to **Washington Island** (✉ ferries leave from Gills Rock; follow ferry signs as you enter the village), 6 mi offshore. Narrated tram tours aboard the Washington Island *Cherry Train* (☎ 920/847–2039; 🎫 $9) or the *Viking Tour Train* (☎ 920/854–2972; 🎫 $9, $16 for tour-and-ferry package) leave from the ferry dock between late May and mid-October. The island's 600 inhabitants celebrate their heritage with an annual **Scandinavian Festival** in August.The island has nearly 100 mi of roads that are great for cycling. You may take your own bicycle on the ferry or rent one on the island.

To get away from it all, take the ferry to remote **Rock Island State Park** (✉ ferries leave from Jackson Harbor on the northeast tip of Washington Island, ☎ 920/847–2235), an island-wide wilderness area permitting only hiking and backpack camping.

The **Peninsula Players Theater** (✉ W4351 Peninsula Players Rd., Fish Creek, ☎ 920/868–3287, WEB www.peninsulaplayers.com), America's oldest professional resident summer theater, presents drama, comedy, and musical productions from late June through mid-October. Beautiful **Peninsula State Park** (✉ 9462 Shore Rd., Fish Creek, ☎ 920/868–3258) has an abundance of hiking and bicycling trails.

Dining and Lodging

$$–$$$ ✕ **Kortes English Inn.** Continental cuisine is served in a formal yet cozy setting. The inn, which is surrounded by trees, has stained glass, polished wood, and fireplaces. There is an extensive wine list and specialty coffees. ✉ *3713 Hwy. 42, Fish Creek,* ☎ *920/868–3076. DC, MC, V. Closed Nov.–Apr.*

$–$$ ✕ **Al Johnsons Swedish Restaurant and Butik.** Goats graze on the grass roof of this locally famous restaurant, a breakfast hot spot. Specialties include Swedish limpa bread, fruit soups, and wafer-thin pancakes topped with fresh fruit and whipped cream. ✉ *702 N. Bay Shore Dr., Sister Bay,* ☎ *920/854–2626. AE, D, MC, V.*

$–$$ ✕ **The Cookery.** Door County products—mostly cherries—are used in many of the dishes on this restaurant's breakfast, lunch, and dinner menus. Don't miss the cherry muffins and cherry-chocolate-chip coffee cake. The pantry offers goodies to go. ✉ *Main St. and Hwy. 42, Fish Creek,* ☎ *920/868–3634. Closed Mar., first 2 wks in Apr., first 3 wks in Dec., and weekdays Nov. and Jan.–Feb.*

$–$$ ✕ **Sister Bay Café.** This quaint café on Sister Bay's main street serves Scandinavian-American dishes such as Norwegian farmer's stew, heart-shape waffles topped with strawberries and whipped cream, and *risegrot* (a hot, creamy rice pudding–like dish), a breakfast favorite. ✉ *611 Bay Shore Dr., Sister Bay,* ☎ *920/854–2429. DC, MC, V. Closed Jan.–Mar. and some weekends off-season.*

$$–$$$$ ★ ✕🏨 **White Gull Inn.** Since 1896, the White Gull has provided intimate lodging and excellent food. Cottages and rooms are rustic with hardwood floors, canopy beds, and porches. Lamb, beef, and seafood dishes with unusual sauces are served in the candlelit, antiques-filled restaurant. ✉ *4225 Main St., Fish Creek 54212,* ☎ *920/868–3517,* FAX *920/868–2367,* WEB *www.whitegullinn.com. 13 rooms, 4 cottages. Restaurant. AE, D, DC, MC, V.*

$$–$$$ ★ **Inn at Cedar Crossing.** At this inn in Sturgeon Bay's historic district sample some of the area's best cuisine before retiring to your room with a four-poster bed, fireplace, whirlpool, and sitting area. Restaurant specialties include shrimp and scallops over risotto, ostrich tenderloin, and pan-seared duck breast. ✉ *336 Louisiana St., Sturgeon Bay 54235,* ☎ *920/743–4200,* FAX *920/743–4422,* WEB *www.innatcedarcrossing.com. 9 rooms. D, MC, V. CP.*

$$$–$$$$ **High Point Inn.** This modern facility overlooks the town of Ephraim. Clean and comfortable one-, two-, and three-bedroom condominium suites are available. ✉ *10386 Water St., Ephraim 54211,* ☎ *920/854–9773 or 800/595–6894,* FAX *920/854–9738,* WEB *www.highpointinn.com. 42 rooms. 2 pools, gym. D, MC, V.*

$$$–$$$$ **White Lace Inn.** Guest rooms at this inn have plenty of white lace, as well as antiques, fireplaces, and whirlpools. Gardens surround the four houses, which are connected by a gazebo. The cozy lobby has Victorian furniture and original hardwood floors, walls, and ceilings. ✉ *16 N. 5th Ave., Sturgeon Bay 54235,* ☎ *920/743–1105,* WEB *www.whitelaceinn.com. 18 rooms. AE, D, MC, V. BP.*

$$–$$$ ★ **Baileys Harbor Yacht Club Resort.** A 1,000-acre wildlife sanctuary and nature preserve near the waterfront provide the backdrop for the rooms, suites, villas, and cottages of this resort. Some suites have gas fireplaces and large whirlpool baths. ✉ *8151 Ridges Rd., Baileys Harbor 54202,* ☎ *920/839–2336 or 800/927–2492,* FAX *920/839–2093,* WEB *www.bhycr.com. 67 rooms. Pool, tennis. AE, D, MC, V.*

$–$$$ **Landmark Resort and Conference Center.** The largest resort in Door County is in a wooded area overlooking a golf course and rolling farmland. Many of its suites have spectacular views. ✉ *7643 Hillside Rd., Egg Harbor 54209,* ☎ *920/868–3205 or 800/273–7877,* FAX *920/868–2569,* WEB *www.thelandmarkresort.com. 293 suites. Restaurant, 4 pools, tennis, gym. AE, D, DC, MC, V.*

Door County Essentials

CAR TRAVEL

Take I–43 north from Milwaukee to Green Bay, then Route 57 north.

VISITOR INFORMATION

➤ TOURIST INFORMATION: **Door County Chamber of Commerce** (✉ Box 406, Sturgeon Bay 54235, ☎ 920/743–4456 or 800/527–3529, WEB www.doorcountyvacations.com). **Washington Island Chamber of Commerce** (✉ Rte. 1 [Box 222, Washington Island 54246], ☎ 920/847–2179, WEB www.washingtonislandwi.org).

Apostle Islands National Lakeshore

Accessible from Bayfield, the Apostle Islands National Lakeshore comprises 21 of Lake Superior's 22 Apostle Islands and a segment of mainland near Bayfield. Named by French missionaries who mistakenly thought the islands numbered 12, the Apostles encompass 42,000 acres spread over 600 square mi of Lake Superior. Primitive camping and hiking are allowed on most of the islands. Sailing is a favorite pastime here, as is charter-boat fishing for lake trout or whitefish.

What to See and Do

At **Lakeshore Headquarters** (✉ Washington Ave. and 4th St. [Box 4, Bayfield 54814], ☎ 715/779–3397, WEB www.nps.gov/apis) you can find publications, exhibits, and a movie about the Apostle Islands. Call the headquarters for more information about Apostle Islands sights. The **Apostle Islands Cruise Service** (✉ City Dock at the base of Rittenhouse Ave., Bayfield, ☎ 715/779–3925, WEB www.apostleisland.com; $17–$30) schedules Apostle Island cruises, including stops at Stockton, Raspberry, and Manitou islands.

In summer, the **Little Sand Bay Visitor Center** has free exhibits and daily guided tours of a former commercial fishing operation. ✉ *Hwy. 13, Bayfield, 13 mi north of town. Closed early Sept.–mid-May.*

Stockton Island, the largest island in the national lakeshore, has a visitor center with history exhibits and a park naturalist on duty. There are free guided tours of the **Raspberry Island Lighthouse** buildings and gardens. Historic **Manitou Island Fish Camp** has free guided tours. The fish camp is closed from early September to mid-May.

Madeline Island is the largest of the Apostle Islands and the only one to have private homes and resorts. Here the village of **La Pointe** was established in the early 17th century as a French trading post. **Big Bay State Park** (✉ Hagen Rd., Bayfield, ☎ 715/747–6425) has camping, a long sandy beach, picnic areas, and hiking and nature trails. Sea kayaking and biking are especially popular. To get to the park, take a right at end of ferry dock for one block, then a left onto Middle Road for about 4 mi to Hagen Road.

The **Madeline Island Historical Museum,** on the site of a former fur-trading post, houses exhibits on island history. ✉ *Ferry Dock, La Pointe,* ☎ *715/747–2415,* WEB *www.shsw.wisc.edu.* *$5.50. Closed Oct.–June.*

From April to December the car- and passenger-carrying Madeline Island Ferry (E Washington Ave., Bayfield, P 715/747–2051) connects Bayfield to Madeline Island. Narrated island tours are given by Madeline Island Bus Tours (E Ferry Dock, La Pointe, P 715/747–2051; A $9) from mid-June through early September.

The commercial fishing village of **Bayfield** (population 700) is known as the gateway to the Apostle Islands National Lakeshore. The **Maritime Museum** depicts the story of the Bayfield area, highlighting its fishing and logging heritage. ✉ *Wilson and 1st St., Bayfield,* ☎ *800/323–7619,* WEB *www.apostleisland.com.* *$5. Closed mid-Oct.–mid-May.*

Lake Superior Big Top Chautauqua hosts concerts, plays, lectures, and original historical musicals under canvas in the spirit of old-time summer tent shows. ✉ *Ski Hill Rd., Bayfield, 2 mi west off Hwy. 13, 3 mi south of town,* ☎ *715/373–5552 or 888/244–8368,* WEB *www.bigtop.org.* *$12–$40. Closed early Sept.–mid-June.*

Dining and Lodging

$–$$ ✕ **Maggie's Restaurant.** Flamingo memorabilia is ubiquitous at this eatery. Great burgers share the menu with more sophisticated fare. ✉ *257 Manypenny Ave., Bayfield,* ☎ *715/779–5641. MC, V.*

$–$$ **Winfield Inn.** Flower gardens and a large deck overlooking the bay and Madeline Island set this inn apart. Apartments have kitchens. ✉ *225 E. Lynde Ave., Bayfield 54814,* ☎ *715/779–3252,* FAX *715/779–5180,* WEB *www.winfieldinn.com. 31 rooms. AE, D, MC, V.*

Apostle Islands National Lakeshore Essentials

CAR TRAVEL

Take I–94 west from Milwaukee to Portage, U.S. 51 north to Hurley, U.S. 2 west to Ashland, and then Hwy. 13 north to Bayfield.

VISITOR INFORMATION

➤ TOURIST INFORMATION: **Bayfield Chamber of Commerce** (✉ Box 138, 54814, ☎ 715/779–3335 or 800/447–4094, FAX 715/779–5080, WEB www.bayfield.org). **Madeline Island Chamber of Commerce** (✉ Box 274, La Pointe 54850, ☎ 715/747–2801 or 888/475–3386, FAX 715/747–2800, WEB www.madelineisland.com).

WYOMING

By Geoffrey O'Gara

Updated by Candy Moulton

Capital	Cheyen
Population	493,7
Motto	Equa
State Bird	Mea
State Flower	Indian pa
Postal Abbreviation	WY

Statewide Visitor Information

Wyoming Division of Tourism (✉ I–25 at College Dr., Cheyenne 82002, ☎ 307/777–7777 or 800/225–5996, WEB www.wyomingtourism.org). Information centers in Cheyenne, Evanston, Jackson, and Sheridan are open year-round. Those in Pine Bluffs, Chugwater, and near Laramie close in winter.

Scenic Drives

North of Cody and east of Yellowstone is the 60-mi **Beartooth Highway,** U.S. 212. Switchbacking across Beartooth Pass at 10,947 ft, it's the state's highest highway and open only in summer. Add a few miles to your drive and take the **Chief Joseph Scenic Highway** (Route 296, south from Beartooth Highway toward Cody) to see the gorge carved by the Clarks Fork of the Yellowstone River. There is more scenery than service on these roads, so gas up in Cody or at the northeastern end of the route, in Red Lodge or in Cooke City, Montana.

National and State Parks

National Parks

Yellowstone National Park (✉ Box 168, Mammoth 82190-0168, ☎ 307/344–7381, WEB www.nps.gov/yell) is widely considered the crown jewel of the national park system. **Grand Teton National Park** (✉ Moose 83012, ☎ 307/739–3300 or 307/739–3399, WEB www.nps.gov/grte) encompasses the jagged Teton Range, the Snake River, and, in between, a string of pristine lakes. **Devils Tower National Monument** (✉ Rte. 24, 6 mi off U.S. 14, ☎ 307/467–5283, WEB www.nps.gov/deto) is a site sacred to Native Americans.

State Parks

The state has dozens of historic sites and museums. State parks are listed on the Division of Tourism's state road map. **South Pass City** (✉ 125 South Pass Main, ☎ 307/332–3684, WEB www.spacr.state.wy.us/sphs/south.htm) is a history-rich gold camp near the Oregon Trail in central Wyoming. **Fort Bridger State Historic Site** (✉ Fort Bridger, ☎ 307/782–3842, WEB www.spacr.state.wy.us/sphs/bridger1.htm), is the pioneer trading post started by Jim Bridger and later used by the military. **Hot Springs State Park** (✉ Thermopolis on U.S. 20, ☎ 307/864–2176, WEB www.spacr.state.wy.us/sphs/hot1.htm) has the world's largest hot spring.

YELLOWSTONE, GRAND TETON, JACKSON, AND CODY

When John Colter's descriptions of Yellowstone were reported in St. Louis newspapers in 1810, most readers dismissed them as tall tales. Colter had left the Lewis and Clark expedition to trap and explore in a region virtually unknown to whites, and his reports of giant elk roam-

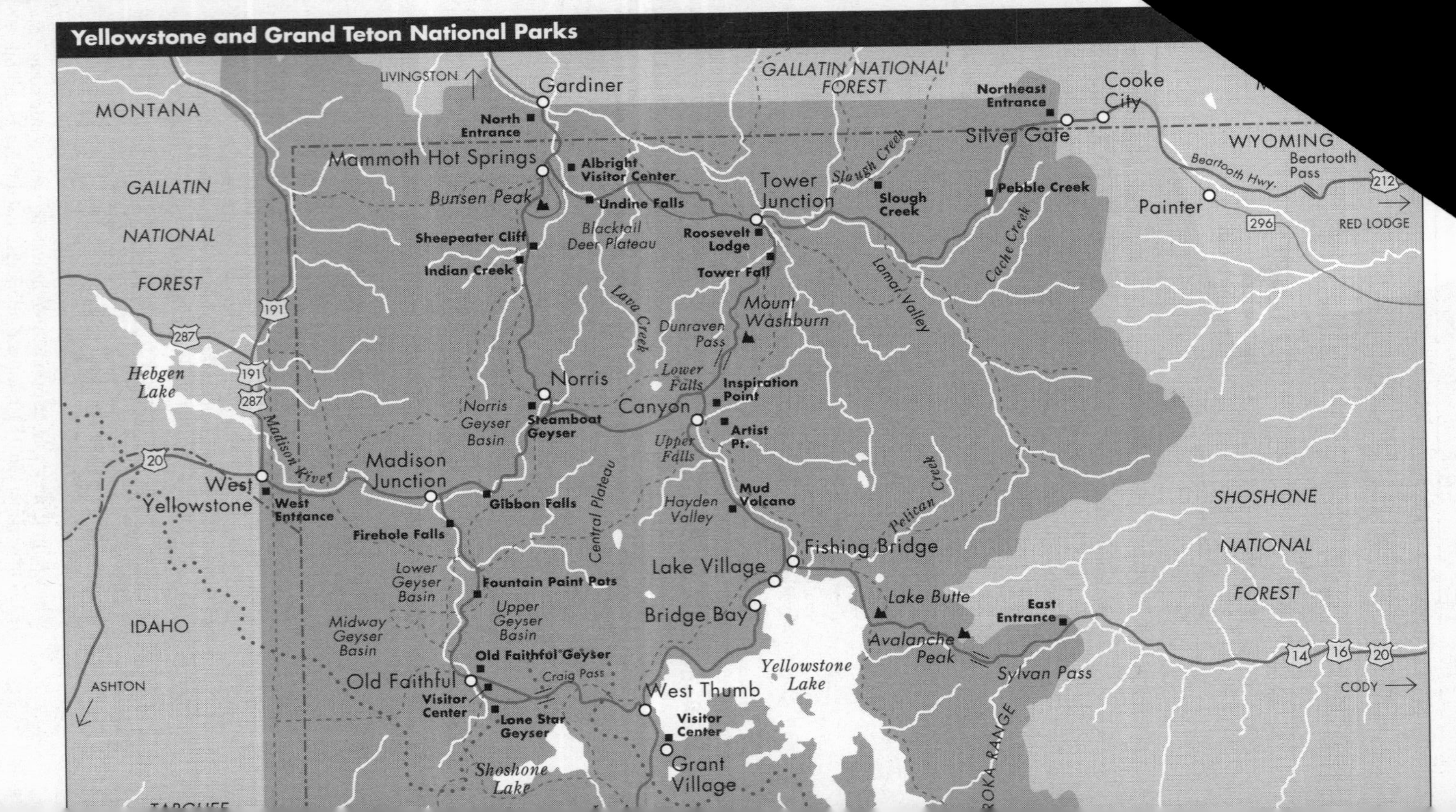

Yellowstone and Grand Teton National Parks
MONTANA
GALLATIN NATIONAL FOREST
LIVINGSTON
Gardiner
North Entrance
Mammoth Hot Springs
Albright Visitor Center
Bunsen Peak
Undine Falls
Blacktail Deer Plateau
Sheepeater Cliff
Indian Creek
GALLATIN NATIONAL FOREST
Tower Junction
Roosevelt Lodge
Tower Fall
Slough Creek
Lamar Valley
Northeast Entrance
Cooke City
Silver Gate
Pebble Creek
Cache Creek
WYOMING
Beartooth Hwy.
Beartooth Pass
Painter
212
296
RED LODGE
191
287
Hebgen Lake
Madison River
Lava Creek
Dunraven Pass
Mount Washburn
Lower Falls
Inspiration Point
Norris
Norris Geyser Basin
Steamboat Geyser
Canyon
Upper Falls
Artist Pt.
20
West Yellowstone
West Entrance
Madison Junction
Gibbon Falls
Central Plateau
Hayden Valley
Mud Volcano
Pelican Creek
Firehole Falls
Fishing Bridge
Lake Village
SHOSHONE NATIONAL FOREST
Lower Geyser Basin
Fountain Paint Pots
Upper Geyser Basin
Bridge Bay
Lake Butte
East Entrance
IDAHO
Midway Geyser Basin
Old Faithful Geyser
Avalanche Peak
Yellowstone Lake
14
16
Sylvan Pass
ASHTON
Old Faithful
Visitor Center
Craig Pass
West Thumb
CODY
Lone Star Geyser
Visitor Center
Shoshone Lake
Grant Village

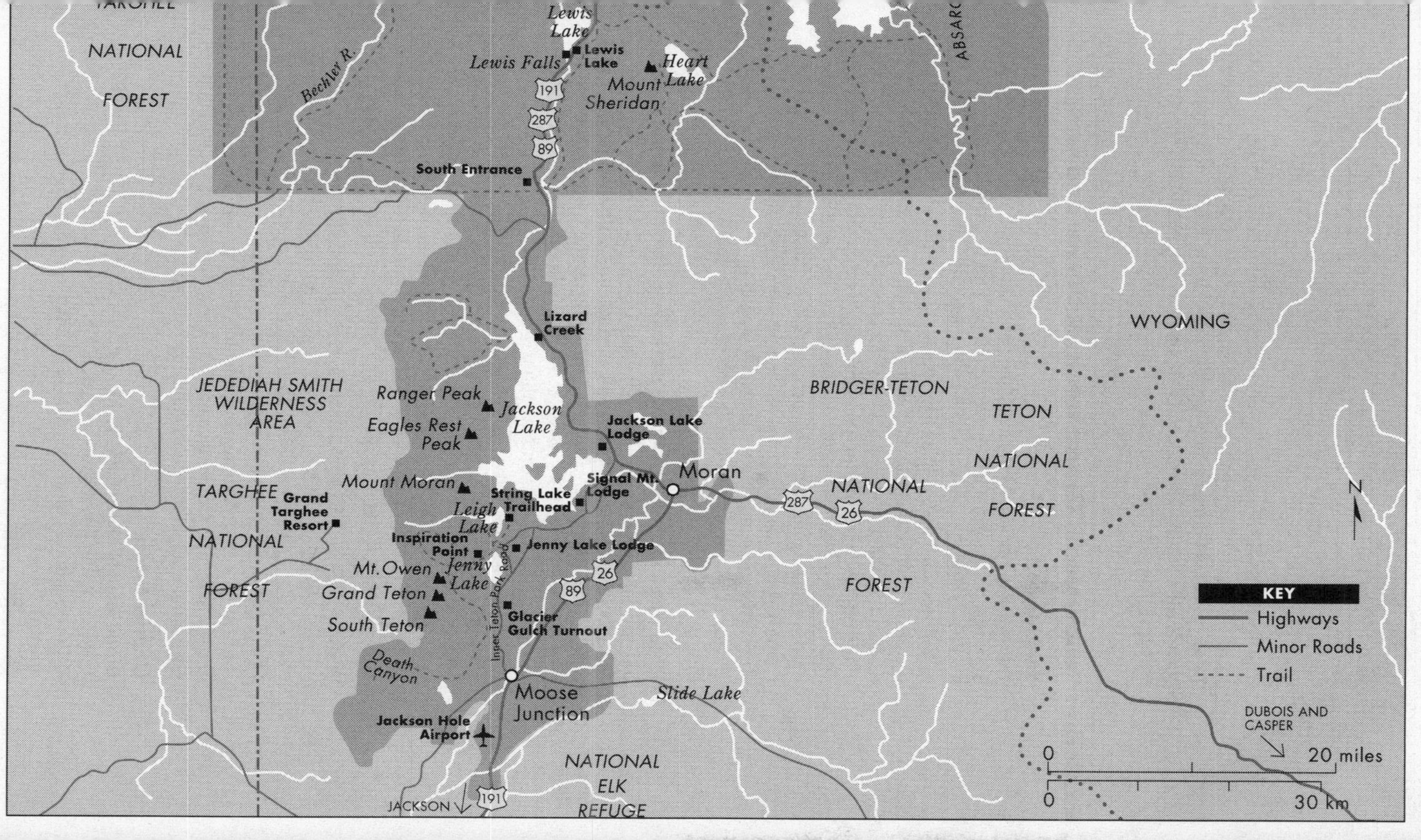

NATIONAL
FOREST
Bechler R.
Lewis Lake
Lewis Falls
Lewis Lake
Heart Lake
Mount Sheridan
191
287
89
South Entrance
Lizard Creek
WYOMING
JEDEDIAH SMITH WILDERNESS AREA
Ranger Peak
Jackson Lake
Eagles Rest Peak
Jackson Lake Lodge
BRIDGER-TETON
TETON
NATIONAL
Mount Moran
Moran
Signal Mt. Lodge
String Lake Trailhead
TARGHEE
Grand Targhee Resort
Leigh Lake
NATIONAL
287
26
NATIONAL
FOREST
N
Inspiration Point
Jenny Lake Lodge
Mt. Owen
Jenny Lake
Inner Teton Park Road
26
89
FOREST
Grand Teton
South Teton
Glacier Gulch Turnout
FOREST
KEY
Highways
Minor Roads
Trail
Death Canyon
Moose Junction
Slide Lake
DUBOIS AND CASPER
Jackson Hole Airport
NATIONAL ELK REFUGE
0
20 miles
0
30 km
JACKSON
191

ing among fuming mud pots, waterfalls, and geysers in a wilderness of evergreens and towering peaks were just too far-fetched to be taken seriously. Sixty years and several expeditions later, however, the nation was convinced, and in 1872 Yellowstone became the country's first national park.

The **Snake River** runs through Jackson Hole Valley, making its way south and west along the foot of the Grand Tetons and through **Grand Teton National Park,** which is nestled between the Tetons and the Gros Ventre Mountains. The town of **Jackson** was first a rendezvous for fur trappers, then the gateway to the nearby parks and dude ranches, and later the center of a booming ski industry.

Exploring Yellowstone, Grand Teton, Jackson, and Cody

Yellowstone

Yellowstone National Park (✉ Box 168, Mammoth 82190-0168, ☎ 307/344–7381, WEB www.nps.gov/yell; 🎫 $20 per vehicle, also good for Grand Teton) preserves and provides access to natural treasures such as **Yellowstone Lake,** with its 110-mi shoreline and lake cruises, wildlife, waterfowl, and trout fishing; **Grand Canyon of the Yellowstone,** a 24 mi-long, 1,200-ft deep expanse of red and ocher surrounded by emerald-green forest; the multicolor, steaming **Mammoth Hot Springs;** and 900 mi of horse trails, 1,000 mi of hiking trails, and 370 mi of public roads. Visitor centers throughout the park are the departure points for guided hikes and are the sites of evening talks and campfire programs (check the park newsletter *Discover Yellowstone* for details). Park-service literature and warnings about interaction with the wildlife—grizzly bears and bison, especially—should be taken seriously.

Roads from all five Yellowstone entrances eventually join the figure-8 that is **Grand Loop Road,** which makes many areas accessible by vehicle. If you enter from the south, start in the Old Faithful area. The best-known geyser is, of course, **Old Faithful,** the crowd pleaser that erupts every 80 minutes or so. Earthquakes have affected the geyser schedule, but it still spouts to about 140 ft, approximately the same height that it always has. Wooden walkways wind by other geysers, mud pots, and colorful springs and along nearby Firehole River. Stay on the walkways—geysers can be dangerous. Elk and bison frequent this area. Near the west park entrance is **Norris Geyser Basin.** Among its hundreds of springs and geysers is the unpredictable Steamboat Geyser, which shoots water more than 300 ft into the air.

A short hike from **Canyon,** at the intersection of the loops, are Inspiration, Grandview, and Lookout points, where the vistas confirm Colter's accounts. The **North Rim Trail** leads to views of the 308-ft Upper Falls and 109-ft Lower Falls. In the northeast corner of the park is beautiful **Lamar Valley,** which attracts bison in the summer. Winter activities include snow-coach touring, snowmobiling, and cross-country skiing, particularly in the Old Faithful area.

Grand Teton

Grand Teton National Park (✉ Moose 83012, ☎ 307/739–3300 or 307/739–3399, WEB www.nps.gov/grte; 🎫 $20 per vehicle, also good for Yellowstone) was established in 1929 and expanded to its present size when the Rockefeller family donated land it owned in Jackson Hole. The park is south of Yellowstone and linked to it by the John D. Rockefeller Memorial Parkway (U.S. 89).

Technical climbers rope up and drag themselves to the 13,770-ft summit of the **Grand,** but day hikers find many rewards, too—from a journey up Cascade Canyon to a lakeshore ramble. Jenny, Leigh, and

Jackson lakes, strung along the base of the Tetons, attract anglers and canoeists; windsurfers and sailors favor Jackson Lake. The **Snake River** is great for rafting, with smooth and fast-moving water and occasional moose or bison sightings on the shore. Willow Flats and Oxbow Bend are excellent places to see waterfowl, and Signal Mountain Road affords a top-of-the-park view of the Tetons.

Jackson

The raised wooden sidewalks and old-fashioned storefronts of **Jackson** may make it look like a western-movie set, but it's the real thing. The town remains compact and folksy, a place where a few genuine cowboys rub shoulders with the store-bought variety and where the antler-arched town square, whoop-it-up nightlife, and surrounding wilderness are pretty much intact.

Jackson is walk-around size and easy to relax in after white-water rafting, hiking, or skiing. Whether your idea of relaxation is enjoying an epicurean meal, lolling in a hot tub, or two-stepping at the **Cowboy Bar** (✉ 25 N. Cache Dr., ☎ 307/733–2207), Jackson fills the bill.

Granite Hot Springs, south of Jackson to Granite Creek off U.S. 191 and 10 mi into Bridger–Teton National Forest along a gravel road, has a creekside campground, a hot-springs pool, hiking trails, and scenery, plus dogsledding in the winter. The **National Elk Refuge** (✉ Elk Refuge Visitor's Center, 2820 Rungius Rd., Jackson, ☎ 307/733–3534), 3 mi north of Jackson, operates horse-drawn sleigh trips through the herd of more than 7,000 elk in their winter preserve. Trips run from December 15 to March; the cost is $8 per person.

Cody

Most people use Cody as a way station en route to or from Yellowstone's east entrance, though it's a great destination on its own. The town's historical center is world class and a must-see for anyone interested in the history of the American West. The **Buffalo Bill Historical Center** (✉ 720 Sheridan Ave., ☎ 307/587–4771, WEB www.bbhc.org; 🎫 $10) has a **Plains Indian Museum,** the **Cody Firearms Museum,** the **Buffalo Bill Museum,** the **Whitney Gallery of Western Art** and, new in 2002, the **Draper Wildlife Museum.** Annual events such as Cowboy Songs and Range Ballads in April, the Plains Indian Powwow in June, and an Old West art show in September add to the cultural experience. For more information about these events, call the **Chamber of Commerce** (☎ 307/587–2297, WEB www.codychamber.org).

Dining and Lodging

You can make reservations for a stay in Jackson or Jackson Hole Ski Resort through **Central Reservations** (☎ 800/443–6931). Make reservations at one of the area's bed-and-breakfasts by contacting **Jackson Hole B & B Association** (☎ 307/739–1411). For information about the many guest ranches between Cody and Yellowstone, contact the **Wapati Valley Association** (✉ 1170 Yellowstone Hwy., Cody 82414, ☎ 307/587–9595).

Cody

$–$$ ✕ **Proud Cut Saloon.** Looking straight out of the Old West, with game mounts and vintage photos, this popular downtown eatery serves what it bills as "kick-ass cowboy cuisine": steak, prime rib, fish, and chicken. ✉ *1227 Sheridan Ave.,* ☎ *307/527–6905. D, MC, V.*

$–$$ 🏨 **Pahaska Teepee Resort.** Buffalo Bill's original getaway in the high country is 2 mi east of Yellowstone's East Entrance. Guided fishing, horseback and snowmobile treks, as well as cross-country skiing are available on the grounds. Cabins have two, four, or six rooms. ✉ *183*

Yellowstone Hwy., 82414, ☎ 307/527–7701 or 800/628–7791, FAX 307/527–4019, WEB www.pahaska.com. 52 cabins. Restaurant. D, MC, V.

$ **Irma Hotel.** This hotel retains some frontier charm, with brass beds and period furniture in many rooms, a large restaurant, and an elaborate cherrywood bar. If you want true history be sure to stay in the hotel (which has 15 rooms) and not in the annex, which are standard contemporary rooms. During the summer, locals stage a gunfight on the porch Tuesday–Saturday at 7 PM. ✉ *1192 Sheridan Ave., 82414, ☎ FAX 307/587–4221, WEB www.irmahotel.com. 40 rooms. Restaurant, bar. AE, D, DC, MC, V.*

Grand Teton

Grand Teton Lodge Company operates three of the park's lodges—Jackson Lake, Jenny Lake, and Colter Bay Village; all reservations go through the company. ✉ *Box 240, Moran 83013, ☎ 307/543–3100 or 800/628–9988, FAX 307/543–3143, WEB www.gtlc.com. AE, D, DC, MC, V.*

$$$$ ★ ✗ **Jenny Lake Lodge.** Set amid pines, some of which were burned in a fire in 2001, and a wildflower meadow, this lodge has cabins and rooms that are rustic yet luxurious. Handmade quilts and electric blankets cover the sturdy pine beds. In the restaurant you can sample Rocky Mountain cuisine such as roast prime rib of buffalo or breast of pheasant. ✉ *Jenny Lake Rd. 37 cabins. Restaurant. AE, D, MC, V. Closed mid-Oct.–May.*

$$–$$$ ✗ **Jackson Lake Lodge.** This brownstone edifice has huge windows overlooking Willow Flats. Guest rooms in the adjacent buildings are larger and more attractive than those in the main lodge. The Mural Room's menu sometimes features local game such as venison or antelope. The lodge has the park's only swimming pool. ✉ *Off U.S. 89 north of Jackson Lake Junction. 385 rooms. 2 restaurants, pool. AE, D, MC, V. Closed late Oct.–mid-May.*

$–$$$ ✗ **Colter Bay Village.** There are log cabins and less expensive tent cabins (canvas-covered wood frames) at this resort near the shore of Jackson Lake. The restaurant serves lasagna, trout, and barbecued spareribs. ✉ *Off U.S. 89. 166 cabins, 66 tent cabins, 112 RV spaces. 2 restaurants. AE, D, MC, V. Closed early Oct.–late May.*

$–$$ ★ ✗ **Signal Mountain Lodge.** On the shore of Jackson Lake, the lodge's main building is made of volcanic stone and pine shingle; inside is a cozy lounge with a fireplace, a piano, and Adirondack furniture. Guest rooms are in a separate cluster of cabinlike units, some with kitchenettes. Peaks restaurant serves such dishes as shrimp linguine and medallions of elk, but the real emphasis is on fish such as Rocky Mountain trout. ✉ *Inner Teton Park Rd., Moran 83013, ☎ 307/543–2831, FAX 307/543–2569, WEB www.signalmtnlodge.com. 79 rooms. Restaurant. AE, DC, MC, V. Closed mid-Oct.–mid-May.*

Jackson

$$ ★ ✗ **Nani's Genuine Pasta House.** The ever-changing menu at this cozy Italian restaurant may include braised veal shanks with saffron risotto and other regional dishes. ✉ *242 N. Glenwood St., ☎ 307/733–3888. MC, V.*

$$ ★ ✗ **Sweetwater Restaurant.** Mediterranean meals are served in a log-cabin atmosphere. Start with smoked buffalo carpaccio or roasted red pepper hummus; then go on to roast duckling, venison tenderloin, or yellowfin tuna. ✉ *85 S. King St., ☎ 307/733–3553. AE, D, MC, V.*

$–$$ ✗ **The Bunnery.** This pine-paneled whole-grain bakery and restaurant serves irresistible breakfasts, from omelets with Swiss cheese and sautéed spinach to home-baked pastries. Sandwiches, burgers, and Mexican dishes are served for lunch and dinner. ✉ *130 N. Cache St., ☎ 307/733–5474. Reservations not accepted. MC, V.*

$$–$$$$ ★ ✕🏨 **Spring Creek Ranch.** You can spend all day gazing at the Tetons from this luxury resort atop Gros Ventre Butte, near Jackson. Other activities include tennis, horseback riding, cross-country skiing, and sleigh rides. There are 36 hotel rooms, plus a mix of studios, suites, and condos with lofts and kitchenettes, and executive homes. Native American art decorates the fine Granary restaurant, where reservations are essential. ✉ *1800 Spirit Dance Rd., 83001,* ☎ *307/733–8833 or 800/443–6139,* FAX *307/733–1524,* WEB *www.springcreekranch.com. 117 units. Restaurant, pool, 2 tennis courts. AE, D, DC, MC, V.*

$$$ 🏨 **Parkway Inn.** Each room has a distinctive look, with oak or wicker, and all are filled with antiques, from 19th-century pieces onward. The homey effect is especially appealing if you plan to stay several days or longer. ✉ *125 N. Jackson St., 83001,* ☎ *307/733–3143 or 800/247–8390,* FAX *307/733–0955,* WEB *www.parkwayinn.com. 49 rooms. Pool, gym. AE, D, DC, MC, V. CP.*

$$ 🏨 **Cowboy Village Resort.** Each of the pine-log cabins in this quiet complex has bunk beds and a kitchenette, making it a good choice for families who don't mind close quarters. Both the START bus and Targhee Express buses that service the ski areas stop at the property. ✉ *120 S. Flat Creek Dr., 83001,* ☎ *307/733–3121 or 800/962–4988,* FAX *307/739–1955,* WEB *www.townsquareinns.com. 82 cabins. AE, D, MC, V.*

MOTELS

🏨 **Days Inn** (✉ 350 S. Hwy. 89, Jackson 83001, ☎ 307/733–0033 or 800/329–7466, FAX 307/733–0044, WEB www.daysinnjacksonhole.com), 191 rooms; CP; *$$$*. 🏨 **Trapper Inn** (✉ 235 N. Cache Dr., Jackson 83001, ☎ 307/733–2648 or 800/341–8000, FAX 307/739–9351, WEB www.trapperinn.com), 54 rooms; *$$*. 🏨 **Antler Inn** (✉ 43 W. Pearl St., Jackson 83001, ☎ 307/733–2535 or 800/483–8667, FAX 307/733–4158, WEB www.townsquareinns.com), 110 rooms; *$–$$*. 🏨 **Motel 6** (✉ 600 S. Hwy. 89, Jackson 83001, ☎ 307/733–1620, FAX 307/734–9175), 155 rooms; pool; *$–$$*.

Teton Village

$–$$ ★ ✕ **Mangy Moose.** Folks pour in off the ski slopes for food and talk at this noisy two-level restaurant with a bar and outdoor deck. This place is full of antiques and oddities, including a caribou and sleigh suspended from the ceiling. ✉ *South end of Teton Village,* ☎ *307/733–4913. AE, MC, V.*

$$$–$$$$ ★ ✕🏨 **The Alpenhof.** This Austrian-style hotel is close to Jackson Hole's ski lifts. All rooms have hand-carved Bavarian furniture; some have fireplaces and hot tubs. The restaurant, which serves veal, wild game, and seafood, is small, quiet, and comfortable. The upstairs Alpenhof Bistro has a more limited menu of wild game, pork, and beef at reasonable prices. ✉ *3255 W. McCollister Dr., Teton Village, 83025,* ☎ *307/733–3242,* FAX *307/739–1516,* WEB *www.alpenhoflodge.com. 42 rooms. 2 restaurants, pool. AE, D, DC, MC, V. Closed Oct.–Nov. and mid-Apr.–May.*

Yellowstone

The lodgings, campgrounds and restaurants, and activities within Yellowstone are operated by **AmFac Parks and Resorts.** There are gas stations, snack bars, and other services throughout the park. ✉ *Yellowstone National Park, 82190,* ☎ *307/344–7311 or 307/344–7901 to contact a guest,* FAX *307/344–7456,* WEB *www.travelyellowstone.com. AE, D, DC, MC, V.*

$$–$$$ ★ ✕🏨 **Lake Yellowstone Hotel.** The park's oldest (late 1800s) and most elegant resort, at the north end of the lake, has a pale-yellow neoclassical facade. The lobby's tall windows overlook the water, and some rooms have brass beds and vintage fixtures. The restaurant ($$–$$$;

☎ 307/242–3701) serves fettuccine with smoked salmon and other eclectic fare; reservations are essential. ✉ *Lake Village Rd., Lake Village. 186 rooms, 110 cabins. Restaurant. Closed early Oct.–mid-May.*

$–$$$ ★ ✕🏨 **Old Faithful Inn.** You can loll in front of the lobby's immense stone fireplace and look up six stories at wood balconies that seem to disappear into the night sky. Guest rooms are a mixed bag: In some you might find brass beds and Victorian cherrywood furnishings; others have inexpensive motel-style furniture. The dining room ($–$$$; ☎ 307/344–7901 ext. 4999), a huge hall centered on a fireplace of volcanic stone, serves grilled chicken breast, shrimp scampi, and other delights; dinner reservations are essential. ✉ *First left turn off Old Faithful Bypass Rd., Old Faithful. 327 rooms. Restaurant. Closed late Oct.–early May.*

$$ ★ ✕🏨 **Old Faithful Snow Lodge.** Built in 1998, this establishment brings back the grand tradition of classic western park lodges with large beams, western furnishings, unique lighting, a fireplace in the spacious lobby, and another centered between the bar and restaurant. In the long sitting room there are Molesworth-style writing desks and overstuffed chairs in which to relax. The small second-floor mezzanine has wicker chairs and a view of the lobby. ✉ *Off Old Faithful Bypass Rd., next to visitor center, Old Faithful. 100 rooms. Restaurant. Closed mid-Oct.–mid-Dec. and mid-Mar.–early May.*

$ ✕🏨 **Mammoth Hot Springs Hotel.** The hotel rooms have fluffy comforters, while the smallish cabins here are arranged around "auto courts"; four have hot tubs. The art deco–style dining room (☎ 307/344–7901) serves regional American fare. The cafeteria-style Terrace Grill, across from the lodge, has large windows that take in the scenic outdoors. Horseback riding can be arranged. ✉ *North entrance to park, Mammoth. 97 rooms, 115 cabins. 2 restaurants. Closed mid-Oct.–mid-Dec., early Mar.–late May.*

$ ★ ✕🏨 **Roosevelt Lodge.** Near the Lamar Valley in the park's northeast corner, this simple, homey log lodge is more ranch house than resort. The dining room serves barbecued ribs, Roosevelt beans, and other western fare, or you can take a horseback rode or stagecoach to a chuckwagon cookout. ✉ *Tower–Roosevelt Junction on Grand Loop Rd., Tower-Roosevelt. 80 cabins. Restaurant. Closed early Sept.–early June.*

Campgrounds

A $15 nonrefundable fee is charged for advanced reservations at backcountry campsites in both the national parks, otherwise the sites are free. You will need a permit from park rangers in either case.In Grand Teton the **Grand Teton National Park** (✉ Drawer 170, Moose 83012, ☎ 307/739–3300) has five campgrounds, none with RV hookups, but all with fire grates and rest rooms. The privately run **Colter Bay Trailer Village** (✉ Grand Teton Lodge Co., Box 240, Moran 83013, ☎ 307/543–3100) has 112 full RV hookups and 198 tent sites.

Among the 11 **Yellowstone National Park** (☎ 307/344–7381, WEB www.travelyellowstone.com) campsite areas and one RV park, **Bridge Bay** (40 sites and a marina) is the largest, and **Slough Creek** (29 tent-trailer sites) is the smallest. There are also 300 backcountry campsites.

Outdoor Activities and Sports

The **Jackson Hole Chamber of Commerce** has lists of outfitters and news about activities. For sports in the parks—including skiing, horseback riding, hiking, and climbing—contact the visitor centers.

Boating

You can rent boats on Jackson Lake through **Colter Bay Marina** (☎ 307/543–3100, WEB www.gtlc.com) and **Signal Mountain Marina** (☎ 307/543–2831, WEB www.signalmountain.com).

Climbing

Jackson Hole has excellent climbing opportunities. For instruction contact **Jackson Hole Mountain Guides** (☏ 307/733–4979, WEB www.jhmg.com) or **Exum Mountain Guides** (☏ 307/733–2297, WEB www.exumguides.com).

Fishing

Blue-ribbon trout streams thread through northwestern Wyoming, and Jackson Lake has set records for mackinaw trout. The license for fishing in Yellowstone costs $10 for seven days or $20 for the season. In Grand Teton a license is $6 per day, plus you must have a Wyoming state day license ($10) or a season permit ($65) along with a state conservation stamp ($10). You can buy licenses at entrance gates or park offices. For fishing elsewhere, buy licenses at sporting goods or general merchandise stores, or contact **Wyoming Game and Fish** (✉ 5400 Bishop Blvd., Cheyenne 82002, ☏ 307/777–4600). Gear from poles to flies and waders is sold at **Jack Dennis Sporting Goods** (✉ 50 E. Broadway, Jackson, ☏ 307/733–3270). **High Country Flies** (✉ 165 N. Center St., Jackson, ☏ 307/733–7210) sells fishing flies and other tackle.

Golf

Jackson Hole Golf and Tennis Club (✉ 5000 Spring Gulch Rd., ☏ 307/733–3111, WEB www.gtlc.com) is a championship 18-hole course near the Jackson Hole Airport, with tennis, fly-fishing, horseback riding, and swimming facilities. The 18-hole **Teton Pines Golf Club** (✉ 3450 N. Clubhouse St., ☏ 307/733–1733, WEB www.tetonpines.com) is south of the Jackson Hole Ski Resort.

Rafting and Canoeing

Floats on the Upper Snake include the beautiful Oxbow, which you can navigate by canoe or kayak. **Barker-Ewing Scenic Float Trips** (✉ Moose, ☏ 307/733–1800 or 800/365–1800, WEB www.barkerewingscenic.com) takes guided rafting trips on the Upper Snake. **Snake River Kayak & Canoe School** (✉ Jackson, ☏ 307/733–3127 or 800/529–2501, WEB www.snakeriverkayak.com) has rentals and provides instruction and guides for kayakers and canoeists. **Triangle X** (✉ Moose, ☏ 307/733–5500, WEB www.trianglex.com) runs guided rafting trips through Grand Teton Park. For guided white-water trips in Snake River Canyon, try **Mad River Boat Trips** (✉ Jackson, ☏ 307/733–6203 or 800/458–7238, WEB www.mad-river.com). **Lewis & Clark Expeditions** (✉ 145 W. Gill St., Jackson, ☏ 307/733–4022 or 800/824–5375, WEB www.lewisandclarkexpeds.com) runs white water on the Snake River and in Hoback Canyon.

Ski Areas

Cross-Country

Cross-country skiing and snowshoeing are permitted in parts of both Yellowstone and Grand Teton national parks and surrounding forests. In **Yellowstone** you can ski on trails around Old Faithful, Canyon, or Mammoth. Rentals are available from AmFac at Mammoth Ski Shop at the Hot Springs Hotel or the Old Faithful Snow Lodge. **Cowboy Village Resort at Togwotee** (✉ Box 91, Moran 83013, ☏ 307/543–2847, WEB www.cowboyvillage.com), at Togwotee Pass within Bridger–Teton and Shoshone national forests (U.S. 26/287), operates 13½ mi of trails. **Spring Creek Ranch** (✉ 1800 Spirit Dance Rd. [Box 3154, 83001], ☏ 307/733–8833 or 800/443–6139) has 8 mi of trails. **Jackson Hole Nordic Center** (✉ Box 290, Teton Village 83025, ☏ 307/733–2292, WEB www.jacksonhole.com) has 12 mi of trails.

Downhill

Grand Targhee (✉ Box SKI, Alta 83422, ☎ 307/353–2300 or 800/827–4433) has 2,000 acres of skiing with at least 64 runs, 5 lifts, 1 rope tow, and a 2,400-ft vertical drop. **Jackson Hole Mountain Resort** (✉ Box 290, Teton Village 83025, ☎ 307/733–2292 or 800/443–6931, WEB www.jacksonhole.com) has 76 runs, 9 lifts including 3 high-speed quads, a 4,139-ft drop (the longest of any U.S. ski area), an ice-skating rink, a children's center with day care and a playground, and a snowboard demo center. **Snow King** (✉ Box SKI, Jackson 83001, ☎ 307/733–5200 or 800/522–5464) has 400 acres of slopes, 3 lifts, and a 1,571-ft drop.

Shopping

Shopping in Jackson is centered on the town square. Western wear and outdoor clothing, some of it locally made, along with artwork dominate in stores around the boardwalk. **Jackson Hole Clothiers** (✉ 45 E. Deloney St., Jackson, ☎ 307/733–7211) sells fleece garments and other outdoor clothing. **Hide Out Leather** (✉ 40 Center St., Jackson, ☎ 307/733–2422) has a wide selection of shearling and leather coats, vests, and slippers. Specialists in the latest outdoor equipment include **Teton Mountaineering** (✉ 170 N. Cache Dr., Jackson, ☎ 307/733–3595). **Trailside Gallery** (✉ 105 N. Center St., Jackson, ☎ 307/733–3186) features western jewelry, paintings, and sculpture. For photographic art including area wildlife, try **Tom Mangelsen Images of Nature Gallery** (✉ 170 N. Cache St., Jackson, ☎ 307/733–9752).

Yellowstone, Grand Teton, Jackson, and Cody Essentials

AIRPORTS

American, Delta/Sky West, and United have daily service from Denver and Salt Lake City into Jackson Hole Airport, 9 mi north of town and about 40 mi south of Yellowstone National Park. East of Yellowstone, at Cody, Yellowstone Regional Airport is served by airlines out of Denver. For information on additional services, *see* Montana.

➤ AIRLINES AND CONTACTS: **Jackson Hole Airport** (☎ 307/733–7682). **Yellowstone Regional Airport** (☎ 307/587–5096).

BUS TRAVEL

Jackson Hole Express operates a shuttle service from Salt Lake City, Utah, to Jackson, with pickups at the Salt Lake City International Airport, Amtrak station, and Greyhound bus station. Buses run daily during ski season, four times each week in summer, and fewer days in spring and fall; the cost is $45 each way. During ski season START buses operate between town and the Jackson Hole Ski Resort; the fare is $4 one-way. The Targhee Express crosses Teton Pass on its way to the Grand Targhee Ski Resort. AmFac Parks and Resorts has bus tours of Yellowstone in summer and snow-coach tours in winter.

➤ BUS INFORMATION: **AmFac Parks and Resorts** (☎ 307/344–7901). **Jackson Hole Express** (☎ 307/733–1719 or 800/652–9510). **START** (☎ 307/733–4521). **Targhee Express** (☎ 307/734–9754).

CAR TRAVEL

To reach Yellowstone through the Teton Valley and Jackson Hole, turn north off I–80 at Rock Springs and take U.S. 191 the 177 mi to Jackson; Yellowstone is 60 mi farther north on U.S. 191/89. You can also approach Yellowstone from the east through Cody, 52 mi from Yellowstone on U.S. 14/16/20; or through central Wyoming via U.S. 287 and U.S. 26 through Dubois. Grand Teton National Park is 10 mi north of Jackson on U.S. 191/89.

VISITOR INFORMATION

➤ TOURIST INFORMATION: **Cody Chamber of Commerce** (✉ 836 Sheridan Ave., 82414, ☎ 307/587–2297, WEB www.codychamber.org). **Jackson Hole Chamber of Commerce** (✉ Box E, 83001, ☎ 307/733–3316, WEB www.jacksonholeinfo.com).

ELSEWHERE IN WYOMING

Cheyenne

What to See and Do

The **Frontier Days** rodeo (☎ 307/778–7222 or 800/227–6336, WEB www.cfdrodeo.com), held the last week of July, is a reminder that the state's capital city was once nicknamed Hell on Wheels. Outside the gold-domed **State Capitol** (✉ Capitol Ave.) is a statue of Esther Hobart Morris, who helped gain equal rights for Wyoming women; she got the vote in 1869, 51 years before the rest of the nation. Morris was the first woman to hold U.S. public office and was appointed a justice of the peace in 1870.

The **Cheyenne Frontier Days Old West Museum** has 125 carriages among its vast collection of westernabilia. During Frontier Days, top western wildlife and landscape artists from around the country exhibit their work here. Guided tours are tailored for children. *✉ Frontier Park, 4501 N. Carey Ave., ☎ 307/778–7290 or 800/778–7290, WEB www.oldwestmuseum.com. $5. Closed Sun. Labor Day–Memorial Day.*

Dining and Lodging

$–$$$ **Best Western Hitching Post Inn.** The Hitch, as locals call it, books country-western performers in its lounge, and there is a miniature golf course on the premises with an ice-skating rink nearby. *✉ 1700 W. Lincolnway, 82001, ☎ 307/638–3301, FAX 307/778–7914, WEB www.hitchingpostinn.com. 175 rooms. 3 restaurants, 2 pools, health club. AE, D, DC, MC, V.*

$–$$ **Little America Hotel and Resort.** This resort at the intersection of I–80 and I–25 has a 9-hole golf course. The large rooms have double vanities and comfy beds with plenty of pillows. *✉ 2800 W. Lincolnway, 82001, ☎ 307/775–8400 or 800/445–6945, FAX 307/775–8425, WEB www.littleamerica.com. 188 rooms. 2 restaurants, pool, golf. AE, D, DC, MC, V.*

$$–$$$$ **Nagle Warren Mansion.** This historic mansion, built in 1888, has gorgeous woodwork, ornate staircases, period furniture and wallpaper, and lavish rooms with antiques. It's close to downtown, within walking distance of area stores and adjacent to two restaurants. Some rooms have gas fireplaces, and a full breakfast is included. High tea is served on Friday. *✉ 222 E. 17th St., 82001, ☎ 307/637–3333 or 800/811–2610, FAX 307/638–6879, WEB www.naglewarrenmansion.com. 12 rooms. Gym. AE, MC, V. BP.*

$ **Rainsford Inn.** The inn is on historic Cattleman's Row, in the heart of downtown Cheyenne; its masculine "Cattle Baron Corner" room overlooks 17th Street, where Cheyenne's cattle barons lived in the late 1800s. All rooms have whirlpool tubs, and one has a gas fireplace. *✉ 219 E. 18th St., 82001, ☎ 307/638–2337, FAX 307/634–4506, WEB www.rainsfordinnbedandbreakfast.com. 7 rooms. AE, MC, V. BP.*

Cheyenne Essentials

AIRPORTS

Commuter flights from Denver serve Cheyenne Municipal Airport.

➤ AIRLINES AND CONTACTS: **Cheyenne Municipal Airport** (☎ 307/634–7071).

VISITOR INFORMATION

➤ TOURIST INFORMATION: Cheyenne Area Convention and Visitors Bureau (✉ 309 W. 16th St., ☎ 307/778–3133, FAX 307/778–1450, WEB www.cheyenne.com). Cheyenne Chamber of Commerce (✉ Box 1147, 82003, ☎ 307/638–3388, FAX 307/778–1450).

Devils Tower Area

What to See and Do

Native American legend has it that the corrugated **Devils Tower National Monument** (✉ Rte. 24, 6 mi off U.S. 14, ☎ 307/467–5283, WEB www.nps.gov/deto; 🎫 $4) was formed when a tree stump turned into granite and grew taller to protect some stranded children from a clawing bear. Geologists say that the rock tower, rising 1,280 ft above the Belle Fourche River, is the core of a defunct volcano. It was a tourist magnet long before a spaceship landed on top of it in the movie *Close Encounters of the Third Kind,* and the tower is still a sacred site for Native Americans. It's the country's first national monument.

Dining and Lodging

$ ✕ **Country Cottage.** This one-stop shop sells gifts, flowers, and simple daytime meals such as submarine sandwiches. ✉ *423 Cleveland St., Sundance,* ☎ *307/283–2450. MC, V. No dinner.*

$ ✕ **Log Cabin Café.** Locals crowd this small log-cabin restaurant full of country crafts for burgers, steaks, and seafood. ✉ *E. Hwy. 14,* ☎ *307/283–3393. MC, V.*

$ 🏨 **Bear Lodge Motel.** This downtown motel has a cozy lobby with a stone fireplace and wildlife mounts on the walls. There's also a hot tub to warm you up. ✉ *218 Cleveland St., Sundance 82729,* ☎ *307/283–1611,* FAX *307/283–2537,* WEB *www.bestvalueinn.com/Lodges/W143.htm. 33 rooms. AE, D, DC, MC, V.*

$ 🏨 **Best Western Inn at Sundance.** Located at the edge of town, rooms here are spacious with dark-green carpet and plum-color drapes. You might see deer feeding outside. ✉ *2719 E. Cleveland St. (Box 927, Sundance 82729),* ☎ *307/283–2800 or 800/238–0965,* FAX *307/283–2727,* WEB *www.bestwestern.com. 44 rooms. Pool. AE, D, DC, MC, V. CP.*

Devils Tower Area Essentials

➤ TOURIST INFORMATION: Sundance Chamber of Commerce (✉ Box 1004, 82729, ☎ 307/283–1000 or 800/477–9340, FAX 500/437–6689, WEB www.sundancewyoming.com/chamber.htm).

Saratoga

What to See and Do

Tucked away in a valley formed by the Snowy Range and Sierra Madre mountains, with the North Platte River bisecting the region, Saratoga is a rarely visited treasure. Fine shopping and dining combine with elegant lodging facilities and outstanding opportunities such as river floating and fishing, and cross-country skiing and snowmobiling.Recreational opportunities abound in the **Medicine Bow National Forest** (☎ 307/326–5258). The **Hobo Pool Hot Springs** (✉ 201 S. River St., ☎ 307/326–5417; 🎫 free) and swimming pool are main attractions in Saratoga. The **Grand Encampment Museum** has a complete historic town and a modern interpretive center. ✉ *18 mi south of Saratoga on Hwy. 230, Encampment,* ☎ *307/327–5308.* 🎫 *Free. Closed Labor Day–Memorial Day.*

Dining and Lodging

For information on dude-ranch opportunities, contact the Saratoga Platte Valley Chamber of Commerce.

$$–$$$$ ✕ **Saratoga Inn.** Pole-frame furniture gives a western flair to southern Wyoming's most elegant inn. The North Platte River runs through the inn's property, so fishing is literally right out the back door. The inn brews all its own beers, which guests can sample during the daily social hour. ✉ *E. Pic-Pike Rd. (Box 869, 82331),* ☎ *307/326–5261,* FAX *307/326–5109,* WEB *www.saratogainn.com. 50 rooms. Restaurant, pool, golf, tennis. AE, DC, MC, V.*

$ ✕ **Hotel Wolf.** This Victorian downtown hotel on the National Register of Historic Places has suites and rooms on the second and third floors (there are no elevators). The restaurant, with antique oak tables, crystal chandeliers, and lacy drapes, serves the best prime rib and steak in town, and the Wolf Burger is hard to beat. ✉ *101 E. Bridge St., 82331,* ☎ *307/326–5525. 9 rooms. Restaurant. AE, DC, MC, V.*

Saratoga Essentials

CAR TRAVEL

Saratoga is in south-central Wyoming, 20 mi south of I–80. It's also accessible via Wyoming 130 (the Snowy Range Road) in summer only, or via Wyoming 230 year-round.

VISITOR INFORMATION

➤ TOURIST INFORMATION: **Saratoga Platte Valley Chamber of Commerce** (✉ Box 1095, 82331, ☎ 307/326–8855, FAX 307/326–8850, WEB spvcc.1wyo.net/).

Casper

What to See and Do

Nearly in the center of Wyoming, Casper is the state's largest city. Five major emigrant trails passed near or through Casper between 1843 and 1870, including the Oregon, California, and Mormon trails, which crossed the nearby North Platte River. You can learn about central Wyoming's military history during the 1860s era at **Fort Caspar Historic Site** (✉ 4001 Fort Caspar Rd., ☎ 307/235–8462, WEB www.fortcasparwyoming.com; 🎟 free). The early history of the emigrant and Pony Express trails is interpreted at the **National Historical Trails Interpretive Center** (✉ 1501 N. Poplar St., ☎ 307/265–8030; 🎟 $6). **Werner Wildlife Museum** displays birds and animals indigenous to Wyoming. ✉ *405 E. 15th St.,* ☎ *307/235–2108.* 🎟 *Free. Closed Sun.*

Dining and Lodging

$–$$ ✕ **Sanfords Grub & Pub.** Street signs, stoplights, and memorabilia make this a lively setting. Pasta, pizza, burgers, chicken, and steaks go down easy with the homemade brews. Children are welcome. ✉ *241 S. Center St.,* ☎ *307/234–4555. AE, D, DC, MC, V.*

$ ✕ **Parkway Plaza.** Furnishings are contemporary in the large and quiet guest rooms but western in the public areas. Poor Boys Steakhouse ($–$$$) is one of Casper's best, with blue-and-white checked tablecloths and hearty portions of steak, seafood, and chicken. ✉ *123 W. E St., 82601,* ☎ *307/235–1777,* FAX *307/235–8068,* WEB *www.parkwayplaza.net. 295 rooms. Restaurant, pool. AE, D, MC, V.*

$ **Radisson.** The large rooms are contemporary and comfortable. There's an indoor pool and a hot tub. ✉ *800 N. Poplar St., 82601,* ☎ *307/266–6000,* FAX *307/473–1010,* WEB *www.radisson.com. 229 rooms. Restaurant, pool. AE, D, DC, MC, V.*

Casper Essentials

AIR TRAVEL

Commuter airlines, including United Express from Denver and Delta/Skywest from Salt Lake City, fly to Natrona County airport in Casper.

➤ AIRLINES AND CONTACTS: **Natrona County International Airport** (☎ 307/472–6688).

BUS TRAVEL

➤ BUS INFORMATION: **Powder River Transportation** (✉ ☎ 307/682–0960).

VISITOR INFORMATION

➤ TOURIST INFORMATION: **Casper Chamber of Commerce** (✉ 500 N. Center St., 82601, ☎ 307/234–5311 or 800/852–1889, WEB www.casperwyoming.org).

Sheridan

What to See and Do

This is authentic cowboy country, with a touch of dudish sophistication. The **Trail End State Historic Site** (✉ 400 Clarendon Ave., ☎ 307/674–4589, WEB www.trailend.org) includes authentic furnishings in a Flemish Revival home completed for cattleman John B. Kendrick in 1913. Mosey into **King's Saddlery, Ropes and Museum** (✉ 184 N. Main St., ☎ 307/672–2702 or 800/443–8919) to view hundreds of lariats, as well as hand-tooled leather saddles. Or see western collectibles, saddles, and tack in the store's museum.

Dining and Lodging

$–$$$$ ★ ✕ **Ciao Bistro.** This is truly one of the best restaurants in Wyoming. Nine tables are squeezed into the European-style café's cramped quarters, but the menu is full of choices such as lamb shanks, Chilean sea bass, and halibut. ✉ *120 N. Main St.,* ☎ *307/672–2838. MC, V.*

$–$$ ✕🏨 **Sheridan Holiday Inn.** This five-floor lodging with a four-story atrium is five minutes from downtown. Facilities include a sauna, hot tub, putting green, and racquetball court. ✉ *1809 Sugarland Dr., 82801,* ☎ *307/672–8931,* FAX *307/672–6388,* WEB *www.basshotels.com/holiday-inn. 212 rooms. Restaurant, pool, gym. AE, D, DC, MC, V.*

$$$$ 🏨 **Eaton's Guest Ranch.** Credited with creating the dude ranch, Eaton's is still going strong after nearly a century as a working cattle ranch that takes guests. The price includes all meals and activities such as horseback riding, fishing, cookouts, and pack trips. The ranch is west of Sheridan on the edge of the Bighorn National Forest. Make summer reservations by March. ✉ *270 Eaton Ranch Rd., Wolf 82844,* ☎ *307/655–9285 or 307/655–9552,* FAX *307/655–9269. 51 cabins. Pool. D, MC, V. Closed Oct.–May. FAP.*

Sheridan Essentials

AIRPORTS

Commuter airlines fly from Denver to Sheridan County Airport.

➤ AIRPORT INFORMATION: **Sheridan County Airport** (☎ 307/674–4222).

BUS TRAVEL

➤ BUS INFORMATION: **Powder River Transportation** (☎ 307/674–6188).

CAR TRAVEL

Sheridan is 130 mi south of Billings, Montana, via I–90 and 140 mi north of Casper via I–25.

VISITOR INFORMATION

➤ TOURIST INFORMATION: **Sheridan Chamber of Commerce** (✉ Box 707, 82801, ☎ 307/672–2485 or 800/453–3650, FAX 307/672–7321, WEB www.sheridanwyo.com).

INDEX

Icons and Symbols

★ Our special recommendations
✕ Restaurant
🏨 Lodging establishment
✕🏨 Lodging establishment whose restaurant warrants a special trip
⛺ Campgrounds
🐤 Good for kids (rubber duck)
☞ Sends you to another section of the guide for more information
✉ Address
☎ Telephone number
⏲ Opening and closing times
🎟 Admission prices

Numbers in white and black circles ③ ❸ that appear on the maps, in the margins, and within the tours correspond to one another.

A

C

D

E

G

M

O

P

S

Y

Z